BARRON'S

PROFILES OF AMERICAN COLLEGES

12TH EDITION

NORTHEAST

Regional Edition

Compiled and Edited by the College Division
of Barron's Educational Series

Barron's Educational Series, Inc.

All inquiries should be addressed to:
Barron's Educational Series, Inc.
250 Wireless Boulevard
Hauppauge, New York 11788

Library of Congress Catalog Card No. 87-640102

International Standard Book No. 0-8120-9305-4

International Standard Serial No. 1075-8275

PRINTED IN THE UNITED STATES OF AMERICA
98765432

CONTENTS

PREFACE

The first edition of *Profiles of American Colleges*, published in 1964, was included in *Outstanding Reference Books, 1964*, compiled by the Reference Services Division of the American Library Association. Revised editions have appeared regularly since then; each not only has updated facts contained in earlier editions but also has included new kinds of information. *Profiles* has become the standard college directory used by students, parents, and guidance counselors.

The newly revised Northeast edition anticipates the needs and concerns of college-bound students in the 1990s. This is a time when career choice is increasingly dictated by the demands of the job market, and students are selecting colleges with occupational goals in mind. The occupation-oriented categories of programs of study, including listings of the best and most popular, will help students find colleges with a program in their desired major. Students will also be able to gauge the success of each school's recent graduates by comparing percentages of graduates who found jobs or went on to graduate school within six months of graduation.

In addition, the profiles in this edition cover numerous other areas of importance. A detailed admissions section lists requirements and other factors colleges use in arriving at admissions decisions. The financial-aid information in the profiles and the article on financial aid will be especially important to many because of ever-increasing tuition costs at many schools. Statistics on financial aid awards and debt will be especially relevant.

As in the past, Barron's *Profiles of American Colleges Northeast Edition* is the most comprehensive, easy-to-use regional guide available. All four-year institutions that offer bachelor's degrees are described if they are fully accredited or are recognized candidates for accreditation. The comprehensive, readable capsule and detailed essay on each school give an easy-to-absorb, complete picture of the colleges that interest the reader. College-locator maps help pinpoint geographic area of school in each state.

The capsule of each profile lists important information for quick reference: address and phone and fax numbers; enrollment; calendar; fall application deadline; size and salary level of the faculty; percentage of faculty members who hold doctorates; student/faculty ratio; tuition and fees; room and board costs; the number of students who applied to the freshman class, were accepted, and enrolled; the median SAT I* and/or ACT scores for 1995–96; and finally, the College Admissions Selector Rating for the school. The essay portion of each profile summarizes 171 questions Barron's asked of the colleges. There are 21 categories of information under eight main headings: Student Life, Programs of Study, Admissions, Financial Aid, International Students, Computers, Graduates, and Admissions Contact. The Admissions Contact section also gives E-mail address and video availability.

Several other features in this edition will be especially helpful to parents and students alike: two self-help questionnaires aimed at helping students set priorities and an article giving advice on surviving the freshman year. There is more information on tutoring and remedial math, reading, and writing programs. Information about faculty, size of classes and whether graduate students teach any introductory courses are also part of this edition. The College Admissions Selector, Barron's rating of colleges and universities by degree of admissions competitiveness, will help students assess their chances of being accepted by various schools.

We are confident that all of these features make this new Northeast edition of *Profiles* the best guide available to the college-bound student.

A Word of Thanks

To all of the college admissions officers, to participating high school advisers, to the students, parents, and other supporters of Barron's *Profiles of American Colleges*, we offer our sincere thanks.

Grateful acknowledgment is made to the late Gloria M. Barron, who inspired the editors and production personnel to create a book that would offer every possible assistance in selecting the best college.

We acknowledge, with thanks, the demanding editing task performed by Max Reed and Sally Strauss, along with our database designers, our editorial assistants, and our staff of diligent writers, copy editors, and data entry personnel.

---

*SAT, Advanced Placement, and AP are registered trademarks owned by the College Entrance Examination Board. No endorsement of this product is implied or given.

You have in your hands a book that will give you answers to your questions about the qualities and features of more than 465 colleges. But before you start reading the descriptions and getting the answers, you need to know what questions to ask about finding the college that is right for you. Although you need to ask questions about "getting in" i.e., exploring colleges in terms of ease of admission for you, most of your questions should focus on the more significant issue of "fitting in." Fitting in means finding a college where you will be comfortable; where you are compatible with your peers, and where the overall atmosphere encourages your growth as a student and as a person.

This article is designed to help you assess some values and attitudes that will help you determine where you will fit in. It will enable you to ask the right questions. Not all colleges are for everyone; careful thinking about your interests, ideals, and values will lead you to find the college that is right for you. Colleges are not "good" or "bad" in a generic sense; they are either good or bad matches for you.

The two tests that follow will be helpful in thinking about yourself as a future college student; they should help you make the right college choice.

THE COLLEGE PLANNING VALUES ASSESSMENT

Students have different reasons for going to college. Ten reasons or values are found to be most important to students as they think about college. Knowing about your values is important as the first step in identifying the colleges where you will fit in and be happy.

To complete the assessment, read through the list of ten values—A–J. Think about the outcomes you hope college will produce for you. Each student will rank them differently; hence, there are no "right" answers. Whereas several, or even most, of these values may be significant for you in one way or another, the goal is to decide the relative importance of each. With 10 being highest and 1 being lowest, *rank* them on the basis of:

What do you want college to do for you?
—— A. To provide me with an academic challenge.
—— B. To provide me with opportunities to exchange intellectual ideas with teachers and students.
—— C. To provide me with lots of fun experiences.
—— D. To prepare me to make a lot of money.
—— E. To provide me with recognition for accomplishments.
—— F To provide me with opportunities to contribute to others' welfare.
—— G. To help me prepare for a career.
—— H. To give me independence.
—— I. To provide opportunities for me to grow religiously or spiritually.
—— J. To provide me with a variety of new experiences.

Now go back and circle the values that you have marked with either a 10, 9, or 8. What do your college planning values say about you?

If **A** was among the top three priorities on your list, you will want to explore the academic character of the colleges you are considering. Although all colleges are, by definition, intellectual centers, some put more priority on challenging students and pushing them to their limits. Reading about the academic features of the colleges you are considering will be important. (In the college profiles, pay attention to the *special* section to learn about these features.) Your high ranking of this value says that you will be able to take advantage of intellectual opportunities at college. You may want to select a college where your SAT I scores are similar to or slightly above the ranges of other admitted students: at those colleges you will be able to shine academically. You may desire to take an active part in classroom discussions and will want a college where the student faculty ratio is low. A word of caution here:

some students select this value because they see the prestige of the college as all-important in their choice. Although it is appropriate to look for a strong faculty and a highly regarded college, you want a college that will give you the greatest chance of academic success. It is success in college, not just academic reputation or prestige, that will lead to admission into graduate school or a broad selection of jobs.

If **B** was among your top three priorities, you feel challenged and stimulated by academics and classroom learning. You will want to find a college where your mind will be stretched. You will want to choose a college where you can explore a range of new academic subjects. A liberal arts and sciences college may give you an enriching breadth of academic offerings. You will want to look for a college where academic clubs are popular and where you have a good chance of knowing professors and sharing ideas with them. Access to faculty is important to you and you will want to look at the student faculty ratio in colleges you consider. Also note the ratio of undergraduate students to graduate students. Primarily undergraduate institutions will be the colleges that may best be able to meet your needs, because you will be the focus of teachers' attention. Teachers at such colleges place their priority on teaching and are not distracted by the needs of graduate students or by pressure to balance teaching and student time with research and writing.

If **C** was circled, you derive satisfaction from social opportunities. You will want a college where the academic demands will not diminish your ability to socialize. You likely will want a good balance between the social and academic sides of campus life. You will want to explore the percentage of students who get involved in intramural sports, clubs, or fraternities and sororities. (This information is listed in each college profile.) Look at your college choices on the basis of school spirit and sporting events offered. The profiles list popular campus events: see if they sound exciting to you. Also look at the percentage of students who stay on campus over the weekend. You will also want a college where it is easy to make friends. Both small and larger colleges would be appropriate for you. Although a larger college would expose you to more students and a larger quantity of potential friends, studies show that students at smaller colleges become more involved in activities and build deep friendships more quickly. Look for supportiveness and camaraderie in the student body.

If **D** is circled, you will want to consider earning potential, advancement opportunities, and the future market for the careers you consider. You will want to consider this value in your career planning. Remember, however, that there is no sure road to riches! You not only must pick a career direction carefully, but must choose a college where the potential for academic success—good grades—is high. The name of a particular college is less important than good grades or contributions to campus life when securing a good job or being admitted to graduate school. Even if you find that a particular career has tremendous earning potential, those earnings may come to only those who are most successful in the profession. Look at average salaries, but also consider your interests, values, and personality before making your final career choice.

If **E** is high on your list, you take pleasure in being known for your success in an area of interest. For instance, you might feel good about being recognized or known in school as a good student, a top athlete, or a leader in a club. No doubt this type of recognition contributes to your confidence. You might look for colleges where you will be able to acquire or continue to receive this recognition. Often, recognition is easier to achieve at smaller colleges where you would not be competing against large numbers of students hoping to achieve the same recognition. You will also want to choose colleges where it is easy to get involved and where the activities offered are appealing to you. You may want to consider the benefits of being a "big fish in a small pond."

If **F** is important, that value will no doubt guide your vocational or avocational pursuits. You may find yourself choosing a career in which this value can be fulfilled, or you may seek opportunities on a college campus where you can be of service. You will want to choose a college where community service is valued. Look at the *activities* section and note whether community service-related involvements are available.

If **G** was circled, you may know what career you want to pursue or you may be concerned but uncertain about your career decision. If you have tentatively selected a career, you will want to choose a college where you can take courses leading to the attainment of a degree in your chosen field. Explore the *programs of study* section in the profiles to determine whether a college you are considering offers the course work you desire. You will want to make a note of the most popular majors and the strongest majors as they are listed. If you don't yet know what career would suit you, remember, that for most careers, a broad, solid liberal arts foundation is considered good preparation. You will want to look at opportunities for internships and take advantage of the career planning and placement office at your chosen college. Finding a career that will be fulfilling is one of the most important choices you will make in your life. Your selection of a college will be your first step toward achieving your career goal.

If **H** is circled, it suggests that personal autonomy is important to you. College is, in general, a time for independence, and students are often anxious to make their own decisions without parental involvement. If you feel you can handle lots of independence, you will want to look for colleges where there is some freedom in choosing courses and where students are given responsibility for their own lives. Colleges vary in terms of these factors. Note particularly the *required* section under *programs of study*, which tells you the courses that must be fulfilled by all students. Be certain that you will not be stifled by too many rules and regulations. You may also want to look for colleges where the personal development of students receives high priority. A priority on independence also suggests that you will be comfortable being away from home and on your own.

If **I** is one of your top three choices, you will want to look first at the religious affiliation of each of your college options. You may want a college that has a relationship with your particular religious group. Or you may desire a large number of students who belong to the same denomination as you do. The profiles will also give you the percentage of students who are members of the major religious denominations. As you explore colleges, you will also want to see if the college has a commitment to the values and ideals held by you or your family.

If **J** is appealing, you like newness and will likely be stimulated by new experiences and new activities. You may see college-going as an adventure and will want to pick colleges where you can meet your need for stimulation and excitement. Because you value newness, you should not hesitate to attend college in a different part of the country or to experience an environment or a climate that is quite different from your high school. You will also want to look for evidence of diversity in the student body. As you read the descriptions, look for colleges with lots of new opportunities for growth and for personal expansion.

Now that you've read about your top three values, answer the following question on a separate sheet of paper: In your own words, what do your top three values say about what you are looking for in a college? Then, share that information with your college adviser as he or she assists you in finding colleges that are right for you.

SELF-KNOWLEDGE QUESTIONNAIRE

The following seven items—A–G—will help you in thinking about yourself as a college student and the ease with which you will likely proceed through the college selection process. Read each statement and determine whether it is true or not true of you. After each question, you will see numbers ranging from 1

to 5. Circle 1 if the statement is very true of you. Circle 5 if the statement is not true of you. Use 2, 3, or 4 to reflect varying levels of preference. Be realistic and honest.

A. I am confident about my academic abilities for college (such as reading, writing, and note taking).
Very true of me 1 2 3 4 5 Not true of me
Academic abilities such as reading speed and comprehension, writing, note taking, calculating, speaking, and listening are important for college students. You will be called upon to use such skills in your college classes. If you are confident about your academic skills, you can approach picking a college with the ease of knowing that you will be able to master the academic rigors of college life. If you circled 3, 4, or 5 you will want to work on these skills in your remaining days in high school. You will want to choose colleges where you can work to strengthen these skills. Some colleges provide a learning skills center in which you are able to get help if you are having difficulty writing a paper or understanding the content of a class. If you are less than confident, you might look to colleges where you will not be intimidated by the skills of the other students.

B. My study skills and time management are good.
Very true of me 1 2 3 4 5 Not true of me
Study skills and time management are two of the most important qualities for an efficient and productive college student. Successful college students are average or above in organizing themselves for studying, scheduling, and using study time productively, and differentiating important content of a lecture or a book from supplementary information. In addition, they complete assignments on time and don't get flustered if they have several papers or a couple of tests due on the same day. If you circled 3, 4, or 5, it is important to work on improving these skills during your remaining high school days. You might consider the following:

- Seek help from your parents, a teacher, a counselor, or a learning specialist in becoming more organized.
- Try keeping a calendar. Anticipate each step necessary in preparing for every test and every paper.
- Be responsible for your own appointments.
- Check to see if a study skills course is offered at a local community college or university. Or consider reading a book on study skills.

C. I am motivated to succeed in college.
Very true of me 1 2 3 4 5 Not true of me
Motivation is definitely the most important skill you bring to college. Those students who want to succeed do succeed! Studies show that it is motivation, not your SAT scores, that determines academic success in college. And motivation means knowing not only that you want to go to college, but that you also want to be a student. Some students want to go to college for the fun aspects, but forget that college is primarily an academic experience. So if you circled 1 or 2, great, you're off to a good start. If you circled 3, 4, or 5, it may be an appropriate time to consider your wants and needs in a college. What sort of college would help motivate you? Would a college with a balance between academics and social life be appealing? Would you be more motivated if you were near a large and interesting city? Would nice weather be a distraction rather than an energizer? Is a trade or technical school best for you? Have you considered taking some time off between high school and college? Considering such questions is important, and the time to do that exploration is now.

D. I am a good decision maker.
Very true of me 1 2 3 4 5 Not true of me
Decisions, decisions, decisions. The college selection process is full of decisions! What colleges will I initially consider? To which colleges will I apply for admission? What college will I eventually attend? You will be facing these decisions in the upcoming months. If you circled 1 or 2, you are on your way. If you circled 3, 4, or 5, think about an important decision you made recently. Why didn't it go well? If you can analyze your decision-making weakness in that situation, it may help to avoid any potential pitfalls in your college decision making. The following suggestions will help you improve your ability to make the right college choice:

- Clearly articulate what you're looking for in a college. Write down those features that will make a college right for you.

- List and compare pros and cons of alternative colleges. Every college has both.
- Evaluate each college on the basis of the criteria you set for yourself. Remember, you're looking for a college where you will get in and fit in.

E. I'm a good information gatherer; for example, I am usually able to find books, articles, and so on to help me do a history research paper.

Very true of me   1   2   3   4   5   Not true of me

Finding a college requires you to be a good researcher. There is so much information about colleges to sort through and analyze. If you feel you can do good research, fine, you're on your way. If you circled 3, 4, or 5, the following ideas may be helpful:

- Start with this book and look for colleges that are consistent with what you want. Remember that your primary concern is where you will fit in. Use your college-going values and your responses in this questionnaire to guide your thinking about colleges that will match you.
- Work closely with your college counselor, and seek impressions from students and others with reliable and up-to-date information about colleges of interest. You will make a better decision with credible and extensive input.
- Look for differences in features that are important to you. Is ease of making friends important to you? What about balance between academics and social life? Do you want teachers to know you?

F. I feel I adapt to new situations easily.

Very true of me   1   2   3   4   5   Not true of me

Everyone goes through changes in life. Some move through transition periods with great ease, others find them more difficult. You may have experienced the changes that come after a change of schools (even from middle school to high school), the illness or death of a relative, or the divorce of your parents. If you circled 1 or 2, you are not likely to be intimidated by a college in another part of the country or a college very different from your high school. If you circled 3, 4, or 5, you may want to carefully look at colleges that are a bit closer to home or colleges where the same values, perceptions and attitudes exist as were true in your high school. Almost everyone has fear and apprehension about leaving for college. But if that fear is significant, you will want to choose a college where you will feel comfortable. Visits to college campuses may be particularly significant in feeling good about potential choices.

G. It is easy for me to meet people and establish friendships.

Very true of me   1   2   3   4   5   Not true of me

Identifying and nurturing friendships is an important skill for college adjustment. If you circled 3, 4, or 5, you will want to look carefully at colleges where there are few cliques, where there is an atmosphere of sharing, and where students report that it is relatively easy to integrate into the campus environment. Your choice of a college is a quest for a good social fit. Your thorough review of the profiles and even visits to college campuses will be helpful in assuring your ability to fit in and be comfortable.

FINAL THOUGHTS

If you took time to carefully consider the issues raised in both the Values Assessment and the Self-Knowledge Questionnaire, you should have gained new insights and perspectives about yourself. You will want to share these results with your parents and with your guidance counselor. Elicit their help in getting more insight as to how they see you as a prospective college student. Finally, two suggestions:

- As you research colleges, consider what you have learned about yourself. You want a college that is a good match with your values and interests.
- Spend time on your college search. It will take many hours of organized planning and investigation. But the time spent will result in a better choice and a greater likelihood that you will spend four productive and exciting years in college.

Good luck. There are lots of colleges out there that want you. Let your knowledge of yourself and your objective analysis of potential college options guide you to college environments where you will be able to shine. Success in college is in your hands. Make the most of the opportunity.

Steven R. Antonoff, Ph.D.
Educational Consultant
Antonoff Associates, Inc.
Denver, Colorado

Americans today have more access to college education than any previous generation, anywhere in the world. This is true no matter what your age or what you want to study. Most readers of these profiles are high school seniors or recent high school graduates planning to enroll full-time in four-year colleges or universities. For such students, the choice is especially wide. That makes the task of choosing complicated, but it also gives you the opportunity to get the best possible education for which you are qualified. The choice is yours.

THE BUYERS' MARKET

When your parents graduated from high school in the 60's and 70's, colleges were crowded with the "baby boom" generation. It was not easy to gain admission. Within the last 15 years or so, this situation has changed considerably. Teenaged population has been decreasing, whereas the number and variety of colleges has continued to expand. The law of supply and demand is now on your side.

Since 1960, the number of American four-year colleges and universities has grown from about 1400 to about 2000, of which approximately 600 are specialized institutions, such as music and art conservatories or theological seminaries. Most existing institutions grew larger, and many expanded their programs, offering master's and doctoral degrees as well as bachelor's. The number of two-year colleges expanded dramatically, more than doubling since 1960 from about 600 to about 1400 today.

The total number of graduate and undergraduate students has also grown, from under 4 million in 1960 to more than 14 million today. Almost half are part-time students, including many working adults who started attending in large numbers during the 1960s and 1970s. Part-time enrollments are mostly concentrated in the two-year colleges, which enroll about a third of all students.

You Are In Demand

Four-year colleges and universities doubled their enrollments in the 1960s and 1970s, and they still need to fill their classrooms and dormitories with full-time students between 18 and 22 years of age. Such students are getting harder to find. The number of high school seniors hit an all-time high of 3.1 million in 1977. Based on current projections, graduating classes will fall to 2.3 million by the late 1990s. That's why institutions are recruiting so vigorously, sending you mailings, visiting your high schools, and setting up displays at college fairs. They need you as much as you need them.

MAKING A SHORT LIST

You have probably already started a list of colleges you know about from friends or relatives who have attended them, from recommendations by teachers, or by their academic or athletic reputations. This list will grow as you read the profiles, receive college mailings, and attend college fairs. If you are interested in preparing for a very specific career, such as engineering, agriculture, health care, or architecture, you should add only institutions that offer that program. If you want to study business, teacher education, or the arts and sciences, almost every college can provide a suitable major. Either way, your list will soon include dozens of institutions. Most students apply to between two and five colleges. In order to narrow your list, you should follow a three-step process:

- **Check your realistic options,** eliminating colleges at which you would not qualify for admission and those that are beyond your family's financial means.
- **Screen the list** according to your preferences, such as institutional size, type, and location.

- **Evaluate the institutions,** using published information and campus visits to make judgments about which colleges can give you the best quality and value.

The following sections will guide you through each of these steps.

REALISTIC OPTIONS

Admissions Competitiveness

The first question most students ask about a college is, "How hard is it to get in?" It should certainly not be the last question. Admissions competitiveness is not the only, or even the most important, measurement of institutional quality. It makes sense to avoid wasting time, money, and useless disappointment applying to institutions for which you clearly are not qualified. Nevertheless, there are many colleges for which you are qualified, and you can make a good choice from among them. The buyer's market has not necessarily forced admission standards down everywhere. The most prestigious institutions are rarely affected by market conditions. Some of the better known public colleges and universities have raised their admission standards in recent years, as their lower prices have attracted larger numbers of applicants. But there remain hundreds of fine public and private colleges, with good local reputations, that will welcome your application.

Use the College Admissions Selector to compare your qualifications to the admissions competitiveness of the institutions of your list. Make sure you read the descriptions of standards very carefully. Even if you meet the stated qualifications for *Most Competitive* or *Highly Competitive* institutions, you cannot assume that you will be offered admission. These colleges receive applications from many more students than they can enroll and reject far more than they accept. When considering colleges rated *Very Competitive* or *Competitive*, remember that the median test scores identify the middle of the most recent freshman class; half of the admitted students had scores lower than the median, and half were above. If your high school grades and class rank are within the stated range, and your SAT I and ACT scores are even a little below the stated median, your chances of acceptance are very good. Students in the top quarter of their high school classes who score above 1000 on SAT I or 25 on the ACT are likely to be accepted at several of the *Very Competitive* colleges and universities.

Students of average ability are admissible to most of the colleges and universities rated as *Competitive* and to virtually all of those rated as *Less Competitive*. They would need high school grades of C+ or better and SAT I total scores of about 900 or ACT composite scores of about 21.

Cost

The most expensive colleges and universities now cost more than $20,000 a year. This is widely publicized and very frightening, especially to your parents. But you don't have to spend that much for a good education. Most private colleges charge between $13,000 and $18,000 a year for tuition and room and board. Public institutions generally cost between $6000 and $8000 a year for in-state residents. Because many states have been cutting budgets in recent years, tuition at public institutions is now rising faster than at private ones. If you can commute to school from home, you can save about $3500 to $4500 in room and board, but should add the cost of transportation. The least expensive option is to attend a local community college for two years, at about $1000 a year, and then transfer to a four-year institution to complete your bachelor's degree. Depending on what you may qualify for in financial aid, and what your family is willing to sacrifice, you may have more choices than you think.

SCREEN BY PREFERENCE

The self-knowledge tests should indicate whether you are more likely to be comfortable far from or near to home, at an urban or rural campus, in a college that is secular or religious, coed or single sex. It is best, however, not to eliminate any options without at least visiting a few campuses of different types to judge their feeling and style at first hand. Choosing the proper institutional size and whether to live on campus or commute from home are more complicated questions.

Large Universities and Small Colleges

Only one-fifth of American colleges and universities have enrollments of 5000 or more, but they account for more than half the 7 million plus students who are pursuing bachelor's degrees. The rest are spread out among more than 1000 smaller schools. There are advantages and disadvantages that go with size.

At a college of 5000 or fewer students, you will get to know the campus quickly. You will not have to compete with many other students for the use of the library or when registering for courses. You can get to know your professors personally and become familiar with most of your fellow students. On the other hand, you may have little privacy and a limited choice of activities. Students at small schools often feel pressure to conform to prevailing customs.

As colleges and universities enroll more students, they offer a greater variety of courses, professors, facilities, and activities. Within a large campus community, you can probably find others who share your special interests and form a circle of good friends. But you may also find the libraries more crowded, many classes closed out, and competition very stiff for athletic teams or musical groups.

Many of the largest institutions are universities offering Ph.Ds., medicine, law, or other doctoral programs as well as bachelor's and master's degrees. Many colleges that do not offer these programs call themselves universities; and a few universities, Dartmouth among them, continue to call themselves colleges. Within the last decade, state colleges in Connecticut, Pennsylvania, and South Carolina have been named universities without a real change in their programs. Don't go by the name, but by the academic program. Universities emphasize research. University faculty need specialized laboratory equipment, computers, library material, and technical assistance for their research.

Because this is very expensive, universities usually charge higher tuition than colleges, even to their undergraduate students. Tuition at public universities can run 25 to 100 percent more than at public colleges in the same state. Private universities generally charge about 50 percent more than similarly located private colleges. In effect, undergraduates at universities subsidize the high cost of graduate programs. Freshmen and sophomores usually receive some instruction from graduate student assistants and fellows, who are paid to be apprentice faculty members.

However, most private universities and many public ones have extensive reputations. They have larger and more up-to-date libraries, laboratories, computers, and other special resources than colleges. They attract students from many states and countries and provide a rich social and cultural environment.

Living On and Off Campus

Deciding whether you will stay in a dormitory or at home is more than a matter of finances or how close to the college you live. You should be aware that students who live on campus, especially during the freshman year, are more likely to pass their courses and graduate than students who commute from home. Campus residents spend more time with faculty members, have more opportunity to use the library and laboratories, and are linked to other students who help one another with their studies. Residence hall life usually helps students mature faster as they participate in social and organizational activities.

About 25 percent of college freshmen live with their parents. If you commute to school, you can get maximum benefits from your college experience by spending time on campus between and after classes. If you need a part-time job, get employment in the college library, offices, or dining halls. Use the library to do homework in an environment that may be less distracting than at home. If possible, have some dinners on campus, to make friends with other students and participate in evening social and cultural events. Get involved in campus activities, participating in athletics, working on the newspaper, attending a meeting, or rehearsing a play.

If you will be living on campus, you may be able to choose among different types of residence buildings. Small dormitories are two to four stories high and house 250 or fewer students. They foster more quiet and privacy than larger buildings. High-rise units can house 1000 or more. They usually offer dining halls, snack bars, game rooms, and laundries all under one roof. Most older halls provide single or double rooms, with shared bathrooms on each floor. Newer halls frequently offer suites, in which a common living/study area and bathroom are shared by eight to twelve students occupying single or double bedrooms. Some students enjoy a larger "family" group; others prefer having only one roommate.

Campus food is usually wholesome, bland, and laden with carbohydrates to meet the high energy demands of active young people. You may have a choice of food plans between 10 and 21 meals a week. Other plans allow you to prepay a fixed dollar amount and purchase food by the item rather than by the meal. Food services make most of their profits on meals that are paid for but never eaten. Choose a meal plan that fits your own eating habits. Meal plans can usually be supplemented or increased, but they rarely can be reduced or refunded.

Many students live off campus after their freshman or sophomore year, either by choice or because the school does not have room for them on campus. Schools try to provide listings of available off-campus rooms and apartments that meet good standards for safety and cleanliness. Many colleges also offer health care and food services to students who live off campus.

It is usually more expensive to live in an apartment than in a dormitory, especially if you plan to prepare your own meals. Great care must be taken in choosing apartment mates. In addition to the usual problems that may arise through personality conflicts, others may develop because apartment mates share payments for rent and utilities and responsibilities for cleaning, shopping, and cooking. It is much harder to find new people to share an apartment in mid-lease than it is to change roommates on campus.

MAKING QUALITY JUDGMENTS

Once you have narrowed your list, you should decide where to apply on the basis of quality. It is not as difficult as you may think to make such judgments. You have to be willing to read the information in this book and the literature that the schools send out, to visit a few campuses, and to ask plenty of questions. You can usually ask questions of the admissions office, by mail or in person during a campus visit. Sometimes, as indicated in the following sections, it is better to ask questions at the offices most directly involved. Because colleges sincerely are interested in helping you make the right choice, they generally will welcome your questions and answer them politely and honestly.

The Faculty

The most important resources of any college or university are its professors. Admissions brochures usually point out the strengths of the faculty, but provide little detail. You should direct your questions about the faculty and other academic matters to the office of academic affairs. Find out what percentage of the faculty have the Ph.D. or other doctoral degrees. Although there is no fixed right number, it should be at least the majority. Schools start bragging in their brochures when 70 percent or more of the faculty have the Ph.D., so that seems to be a common benchmark of quality.

Recruiting brochures also emphasize faculty research, because the prestige of professors depends largely on the books and articles they have published. Good researchers may or may not make good teachers. Ask how often the best researchers teach undergraduate courses, and whether they instruct small as well as large classes. For example, a Nobel prize chemist may lecture to 500 students at a time but never show up in the laboratories where graduate assistants actually teach individual students.

Also ask about class size, because this determines the amount of individual attention students get from professors. Student/faculty ratios, which usually range from 10 to 20 students per professor, don't really tell you much. Every school offers a mixture of large and small classes. Here are some general standards:

- Science and technology courses should enroll only 25 to 30 students in each laboratory session, but may combine a number of laboratory classes for large weekly lectures.
- Skill development courses such as speech, foreign language, English composition, and fine and performing arts should have classes of 25 or fewer. Mathematics and computing require considerable graded homework, and classes should be no larger than 35.
- Clinical courses in nursing and other health fields are partly based in hospitals or other health care facilities. In such courses, each 10 students should be supervised by a professor. Similarly, each student teacher should be placed with an experienced elementary or secondary school teacher and visited periodically by a member of the college faculty.
- Most other courses in humanities, social sciences, and professional areas are taught by classroom lectures and discussion. Classes should average 35 to 45 in introductory courses such as general psychology or American government. They should be smaller in advanced or specialized courses, such as Shakespeare or tax accounting.
- Many introductory courses, especially at universities, are taught in lecture classes of 100 or more. This is acceptable, if those courses also include small weekly discussion groups for individual instruction. Sometimes these discussion groups are taught by graduate student assistants rather than regular professors. Although graduate assistants lack teaching experience, they are very often highly capable. You should ask whether the teaching done by graduate assistants is closely supervised by regular faculty members.

Academic Programs

Even colleges and universities that boast fine and well qualified faculties can be short of professors in certain programs, particularly in business, computing, and engineering. These continue to be popular majors although business, the most popular, has declined slightly since 1990. Some schools depend on instruction by part-time faculty members or fill in with available teachers from other specializations. Many international students are enrolled in technical doctoral programs, so you may find yourself being taught mathematics or engineering by a teaching assistant whose English you cannot understand. If you are interested in these subjects, check to see whether full-time faculty members teach at least 80 percent of the courses.

Other programs may have sufficient faculty but too few student majors. Physics, foreign languages, and philosophy usually have many students in required introductory courses but few taking the major. Because of small enrollments, these departments may not be able to offer their advanced and specialized courses on a regular basis. You should review the college catalog to see whether all of the courses required for majoring in the program are offered at least once every two years.

The academic department gives strength to the program by bringing together faculty members who share a common area of study and make sure their students get the instruction they need. Even at a small college, a department should have at least three full-time professors to offer a major program. Some programs, usually called interdisciplinary, are taught by groups of faculty members from several departments. These programs generally have the word *studies* in their titles; for example, Middle-Eastern Studies, Communication Studies, Women's Studies, or Ethnic Studies. Interdisciplinary committees are usually effective for a few years, after

which the faculty members tend to pay more attention to their own departments. If you enroll in one of these programs, you may not have a regular faculty adviser or a good choice of courses for enrollment.

Sometimes highly specialized programs are offered within more general departments. Examples are semantics or linguistics (within the English department), social work or anthropology (within sociology), or broadcasting (within speech). Such a program may be taught by one faculty specialist, and you could be left stranded if that person leaves. On the other hand, that faculty member may hold tenure and teach the subject successfully for many years.

Accreditation

General standards of academic quality are established by associations of colleges and universities through a process called voluntary accreditation. The criteria include: standards for admission of students; faculty qualifications; content of courses; grading standards; professional success of alumni; adequacy of libraries, laboratories, computers, and other support facilities; administrative systems and policy decision making; and financial support.

Six regional associations (New England, Middle States, Southern, North Central, Northwest, and Western) evaluate and accredit colleges as total institutions. Bible colleges have their own accrediting association. Other organizations evaluate and accredit specific programs, primarily in technical fields, like engineering and architecture; or those that require licensing, such as teaching and health care.

Accreditation must be periodically renewed, usually every five to ten years. Any school that is more than five years old and is not accredited probably has serious quality problems. One that was previously granted accreditation and then lost it is in deep trouble. On the other hand, accreditation means only that the school meets minimum standards. It is not a rating of school quality or a comparison to other schools.

Libraries

Most people judge libraries by the size of the collection, the bigger the better. Collection size is important, but only in relation to the variety and level of programs offered. A small liberal arts college can support its baccalaureate programs with a collection of 200,000 to 300,000 volumes. A university with many professional schools and doctoral programs may require over 2 million. Many books and journals are now available on microfilm or microfiche, so even a small college has money and space to enlarge its collection.

You may often find that the book or journal you need is owned by the library but unavailable. Frequently used material may be misplaced, lost, or out on loan. Many libraries are better at purchasing books than at getting them into the hands of their readers. You can look for some indications of the quality of a library's services.

The main stacks should be open to students, with the possible exception of rare books, bound journals, and other special items. Open stacks encourage browsing and save students from waiting on line while a library assistant fetches a few books at a time. Instead, assistants constantly should be picking up unused materials from reading desks or carts and putting them back on the shelves.

Good circulation policies encourage students to check materials out for short periods and to return them promptly. One week or less loans are appropriate for books regularly used in courses, and four week loans should be the maximum for other materials. A recall system should be available to get back borrowed material when it is needed. Journals, reference material, or books placed on reserve for assigned reading should be used within the library while it is open, and circulated overnight only at closing time.

Much of your reading and research will require work within the library. The library should be open at night and on weekends, at least at those times when it is most likely to be used. Friday and Saturday nights and Sunday mornings are the times when libraries can usually be closed without serious loss of access to students. Professional librarians should be available to assist you whenever the library is open.

A modern academic library also should offer the following services, free or at a nominal charge:

- Interlibrary loans to get materials from other libraries.
- Online computerized searching of bibliographic databases. These databases automatically provide listings and summaries of books and articles by subject, author, and date.
- Tours and workshops to guide students in using the library.
- Reading lists for various subjects and courses.

Computing

Whatever your courses of study, you should expect to use computers. You will learn to do mathematical and scientific problem solving; to classify, sort, and retrieve information; and to write, revise, and type manuscripts. A few institutions require students to buy personal computers to use as microcomputers or as time-sharing terminals.

Many colleges are still scrambling to catch up with the changing technology and to equip enough classrooms and laboratories for courses that require computing. At a minimum, you should have access to both microcomputers for routine work and terminals connected to a mainframe or minicomputer for more complex instructional and research programs. There should be a number of campus locations where you can do computing, including during evenings and weekends.

During the busy times of the term, particularly around midterms and finals, computer laboratories are likely to be crowded. If you have to wait more than a second or two for a response on a time-sharing terminal, the college is probably trying to serve more students at one time than its computer capacity can handle.

GETTING THE MOST FROM YOUR CAMPUS VISIT

To learn everything important about a college, you need more than the standard presentation and tour given to visiting students and parents. Plan your visit for a weekday during the school term. This will let you see how classes are taught and how students live. It also is the best time to meet faculty and staff members, or to go to a dean's office for information. If the college does not schedule group presentations or tours at the time you want, call the office of admissions to arrange for an individual tour and interview. At the same time, ask the admissions office to make appointments with people you want to meet.

To find out about a specific academic program, ask to meet the department chairperson. If you are interested in athletics, religion, or music, meet the coach, the chaplain, or the conductor of the orchestra. Your parents will also want to talk to a financial aid counselor about scholarships, grants, and loans. The office of academic affairs can help with your questions about courses or the faculty. The office of student affairs is in charge of residence halls, health services, and extracurricular activities. Each of these areas has a dean or vice president and a number of assistants, so you should be able to get your questions answered even if you go in without an appointment.

Take advantage of a group presentation and tour if one is scheduled on the day of your visit. Much of what you learn may be familiar, but other students and parents will ask about some of the same things you want to know. Student tour guides are also good sources of information. They love to talk about their own courses, professors, and campus experiences.

Finally, explore the campus on your own. Visit the library and computing laboratories, to see whether they are adequate for all the students using them. Check the condition of the buildings and the grounds. If they appear well maintained, the college probably has good overall management. If they look run down, the college may have financial problems that also make it scrimp on the book budget or laboratory supplies. Visit a service office, such as the registrar, career planning, or academic advising. Observe whether they treat students courteously and seem genuinely interested in helping them.

Talk to some of the students who are already enrolled at the college. They will usually speak frankly about weekend activities, whether they find it easy to talk to professors out of class, and how much drinking or drug abuse there is on campus. Most importantly, meeting other students will help you discover how friendly the campus is and whether the college will suit you socially and intellectually.

More than buildings and courses of study, a college is a community of people. Only during a campus visit can you experience the human environment in which you will live and work during four critical years.

CHECKLIST QUESTIONS

The following questions form a checklist to evaluate each college or university you are considering. Use profiles, literature from the colleges, and your own inquiries and observations to get the answers.

I. Identify good possibilities. Only colleges for which all five answers are "Yes" should go on your final list.
1. Is the college accredited by its regional association?
2. Does the college offer the program I want to study?
3. Do I have a good chance to be admitted?
4. Can my family manage the costs? (Read Finding the Money, page 14, before answering this question.)
5. Is the location at an acceptable distance from home?

II. Compare colleges for quality and value. The more questions you answer "Yes," the better that college is for you.
A. Academics
1. Does a majority of the faculty have doctoral degrees?
2. Do the best research professors teach undergraduate courses?
3. Do class sizes meet the standards described in this article?
4. Do regular faculty members teach at least 80 percent of courses?
5. Does the major program have enough full-time faculty members?
6. Does the major program offer its courses on a regular schedule?
B. Support Services
1. Is the library collection adequate for the college programs?
2. Does the library offer good services and accessible hours?
3. Are student computing facilities readily available?
4. Do the people in the admissions, financial aid, and other service offices seem attentive and genuinely interested in helping students?
C. Campus Environment
1. Will I be comfortable with the size and setting of the campus?
2. Will I find activities that meet my interests?
3. Will I find the other students compatible?
4. Will I find the housing and food services suitable?
5. Does the campus seem well maintained and managed?

Sheldon Halpern
Dean of Enrollment Management
Caldwell College

WHY COLLEGE ENTRANCE TESTS?

Testing is the only standardized device that may be used to compare candidates from many varied high schools. It is only too well known that marking standards vary from school to school. It is also well known that a student in the top fifth of his class at X high school might very well have fallen into the bottom fifth if he had attended Y school.

Many parents and students are very critical of these standardized tests. It must be noted, however, that they afford equal opportunity to each college-bound student. From the point of view of the college, students who can perform well on this examination will, in all probability, continue to do well in their college studies.

Because college entrance examinations play such an important role in deciding who is admitted and who is rejected, it is necessary to clarify some of their surrounding mystery. These objective tests are scientifically constructed and aim to predict how well a student will perform in college. Their predictive capacity has been excellent. Poor results on these examinations, therefore, may make it difficult for a student to gain acceptance to college, in spite of a relatively good high school record. College admissions officers place a considerable amount of reliance on applicants' scores.

KINDS OF COLLEGE ENTRANCE TESTS

College-bound students must cope with one or more of the following:
- PSAT/NMSQT or the Preliminary SAT/National Merit Scholarship Qualifying Test.
- SAT I: Reasoning Tests.
- SAT II: Subject Tests.
- Advanced Placement (AP) Examinations.
- The ACT Assessment.

The PSAT/NMSQT

The PSAT/NMSQT measures verbal and mathematical ability necessary for success in college. It is a standardized test taken by students in high schools throughout the country, usually in their junior year. The test consists of two parts: four 30-minute verbal sections and two 30-minute math sections. The reading passages with comprehension questions are used to measure critical reading skills and knowledge of vocabulary.

Students taking this preliminary college board examination will find that this is also the qualifying test for the scholarship competition conducted by the National Merit Scholarship Corporation, an independent, nonprofit organization supported by grants from over 600 corporations, private foundations, colleges and universities. Top-scoring PSAT/NMSQT participants in every state are named semifinalists. Those who advance to finalist standing by meeting additional requirements compete for onetime National Merit $2000 Scholarships and renewable four-year Merit Scholarships, which may be worth as much as $8000 a year for four years.

In addition, this test is used by the National Achievement Scholarship Program for outstanding African American students. Top-scoring black students in each of the regional selection units established for the competition continue in the competition for nonrenewable National Achievement $2000 Scholarships and for four-year Achievement Scholarships sponsored by over 175 organizations.

Test-Taking Strategies for the PSAT/NMSQT

1. Know what to expect. In the verbal section of the PSAT you will have sentence completions and analogies but no antonym questions. The math section will have quantitative comparison questions, some multiple-choice questions, as well as questions that will ask you to produce your own responses. For these you will be asked to enter your answers on a grid. Calculators on the math test will be permitted but not required.

2. Don't be guilty of wild guessing. Wild guessing will lower your score because a fraction of your wrong answers is subtracted from the number of correct answers. Because wrong answers count against you on the test, you may think that you should never guess if you aren't sure of the right answer to a question. But even if you guessed wrong four times for every time you guessed right, you would still come out even. A wrong answer costs you only 1/4 of a point (1/3 on the quantitative comparison questions). The best advice is to guess if you can eliminate one or two of the answers. You have a better chance of hitting the right answer when you make this sort of educated guess.

3. Expect easy questions at the beginning of each set of the same question type. Within each set (except for the reading comprehension questions), the questions progress from easy to difficult. In other words, the first antonym question in a set will be easier than the last antonym question in that set; the first quantitative comparison question will be easier than the last one.

4. Take advantage of the easy questions to boost your score. Remember: each question is worth the same number of points. Whether it was easy or difficult, whether it took you ten seconds or two minutes to answer, you get the same number of points for each question you answer correctly. Your job is to answer as many questions as you possibly can without rushing ahead so fast that you make careless errors or lose points for failing to give some questions enough thought. Take enough time to get those easy questions right!

5. For the multiple-choice questions, eliminate as many wrong answers as you can. Deciding between two choices is easier than deciding among five. Even if you have to guess, every answer you eliminate improves your chances of guessing correctly.

SAT I

The SAT I is a reasoning test consisting of two parts—Verbal Reasoning and Mathematical Reasoning. It is designed to measure your ability to do college work. Part of the test deals with verbal skills with an emphasis on critical reading including a double passage with different points of view. The verbal sections measure the extent of your vocabulary, your ability to interpret and create ideas, and your ability to reason logically and draw conclusions correctly. The mathematics part measures your ability to use and reason with numbers or mathematical concepts. It tests your ability to handle general number concepts rather than specific achievement in mathematics. Some questions require students to produce their own responses in contrast to multiple-choice questions. Calculators are permitted in the test room. For the 60 questions, 70–75 minutes are allowed.

The Verbal Reasoning sections are 30, 30, and 15 minutes in length and include 19 Sentence Completion, 19 Analogy, and 40 Reading Comprehension questions. The Mathematics Reasoning sections are 25, 25, and 15 minutes in length and include 35 Multiple Choice, 15 Quantitative Comparison, and 10 Student-Produced Response questions.

SAT I is usually given in January, March, May, June, October (in some states), November, and December. Applicants may request, for religious reasons, to take the test on the Sunday following the regularly scheduled date.

If a registration form is not available at your school, request one by mail. You can obtain a form from the College Entrance Examination Board, Box 6200, Princeton, New Jersey 08451.

The test is scored on a scale that ranges from 800 (highest) to 200 (lowest). You will get separate grades for the mathematics and verbal sections of the test.

Your score is based on the number of questions you answered correctly, minus points for those you answered incorrectly. Wrong answers on five-choice questions subtract 1/4 of a point from your raw score. Wrong answers on the four-choice quantitative comparison questions subtract 1/3 of a point from your score. The raw score is then scaled. The scale varies slightly from year to year and all scores were "recentered" by ETS in 1995. This change is discussed in more detail on page 28.

Test-Taking Strategies for SAT I

1. Know what to expect. For the critical reading part of the verbal section, be prepared to find 4 passages with content as follows: one in social science, one in natural science, and two in fiction or nonfiction. In the mathematical reasoning section be prepared to find 15 questions on quantitative comparison, 35 multiple-choice questions, and 10 questions for which you will be required to produce a response.

2. Pace yourself. Most school tests don't put a premium on speed. They test achievement, not scholastic aptitude. The test sets a time limit. Therefore, work rapidly but don't give up accuracy. Don't spend too much time on one particular question. Remember, all questions carry the same point value.

3. Read carefully. Make sure you are answering the question asked, not the one that is similar to one you once encountered. Underline key words (i.e., NOT and EXCEPT) to make sure you do not answer the opposite of the question asked. Sometimes data are given for one of two possibilities and you will find that the question deals with a third possibility.

4. Keep calm. Don't get flustered over a single question. Just remind yourself that few people, if any, answer all questions correctly.

5. Know the rules. Learn the directions for the various types of questions. If you know the directions ahead of time you will save time in the examination room.

6. Guessing or not? SAT I penalizes for guessing. Therefore, leave the question blank if you have no idea of the correct answer. Remember, on SAT I and the PSAT your test score is based on the number of correct answers minus a fraction of the number of wrong answers. For the ACT, you should give some answer for all questions. The score on the ACT is based on the number of questions answered correctly, with no deductions for wrong answers.

7. Take advantage of the format of the multiple-choice questions which is the format of most of the math questions. One of the answers given has to be the correct one. Always look at all the answers before doing any computations. The correct answer may, by inspection, prove to be the only possible correct answer. Also, you should know that each of the four incorrect responses has been carefully chosen to look plausible or to be the result of a common error. You can make a mistake and still find one of the answers listed. If, after working the problem, you don't find your answer among the choices, you have made an uncommon error. You do, however, have an opportunity to try another method (with the penalty of consuming test time). This is why you should set a time limit in the tests, for the person who gets the correct answer quickly deserves more credit than the one who had to make several trials. Finally, with the multiple-choice format, it is often possible to work back from the answers, eliminating those choices that are contrary to fact.

SAT II: Subject Tests (formerly known as the Achievement Tests)

These tests are one-hour, multiple-choice question tests. The registration form is the same as the SAT I. The additional fee entitles you to take one, two, or three tests on any one test date. Unlike SAT I these tests measure knowledge and application of knowledge. Some colleges require specific subject tests whereas others allow applicants to choose the ones they wish to present with the admission application. Those colleges that do require these tests may use them to determine acceptance or placement in college courses. The tests in foreign language not only are used for placement but also for possible exemption from a foreign language requirement. Although many colleges do not require these tests, some not only specify which ones they require but also specify that they would like applicants to take them no later than December or January of their senior year. If the college of your choice does not require these tests and you would like to demonstrate proficiency in a particular field, take the test. The admissions committee will see your scores, along with your SAT I scores.

Tests are given in writing, literature, history, mathematics, sciences, and foreign languages, including Japanese. In the near future, tests will be given in other Asian languages, along with a proficiency test in English-as-a-Second Language.

Advanced Placement (AP) Examinations

The College Board also conducts Advanced Placement tests, given to high school students who have completed advanced or honors courses and wish to get college credit. Many secondary schools offer college level courses in mathematics, European history, American history, Latin, Spanish, French, German, biology, chemistry, and physics. As a result of scores obtained on these tests, colleges grant credit or use the results for placement in advanced college courses.

The ACT Assessment

The registration form for the ACT includes a detailed questionnaire that takes about one hour to complete. As a result of the answers to those questions about your high school courses, personal interests, and career plans, plus the scores on your ACT, an ACT Assessment Student Report is produced. This is made available to you, your high school, and to any college or scholarship source that you request. Decisions regarding college acceptance and award of scholarships are the result. This information is kept confidential and is released only according to your written instructions. To obtain an ACT application form, write or call ACT Registration, P.O. Box 414, Iowa City, Iowa 52243, telephone (319) 337-1270.

The ACT measures knowledge, understanding, and skills acquired in the educational process. The test is made up of four distinct sections: English, mathematics, reading, and science reasoning.

A distinct difference between the ACT and SAT I is that on SAT I, a raw score is obtained by counting the number of correct answers and deducting a fraction of the incorrect answers. The raw score is then converted into a scale in the range of 200 to 800. On the ACT, you are advised to answer all questions because the score is based on the number of questions answered correctly. There is no penalty for guessing. The ACT score is obtained by counting the number of correct answers with no deduction for wrong answers. For each of the four tests the total number of correct responses yields a *raw score*. A table is used to convert the raw scores to *scale scores*. The highest possible scale score for each test is 36. The average of the four scale scores yields the *composite score*.

The ACT English Test is a 75-item, 45-minute test that measures punctuation, grammar, usage, sentence structure, spelling, and vocabulary. The test consists of five passages, each accompanied by multiple-choice test items. A total score is reported as well as a subscore for the 40 usage questions and a subscore for the 35 questions dealing with the rhetorical skills.

Test-Taking Strategies for the ACT English Test

1. Pace yourself. You have 45 minutes to complete 75 questions.
2. Skim through the whole passage quickly to get the author's view
3. Read the sentences immediately before and after the one containing an underlined portion.

The ACT Mathematics Test is a 60-question in 60-minute test that emphasizes quantitative reasoning rather than memorized formulas. Five content areas are included in the mathematics test. About 12 questions deal with pre-algebra topics, such as operations with whole numbers, decimals, fractions, and integers. About the same number of questions deal with elementary algebra. Usually 18 questions are based on intermediate algebra and coordinate geometry. About 14 questions are based on plane geometry and usually four items are based on right triangle trigonometry and basic trigonometric identities.

Test-Taking Strategies for the ACT Mathematics Test

1. Spend about one minute on each question.
2. Make sure you answer the question. Incorrect answer choices may be based on incomplete solutions.
3. Make sure your answer is reasonable.

The ACT Reading Test is a 40-item, 35-minute test that measures reading comprehension. Three scores are reported for this test: a total score, a subscore based on the 20 items in the social studies and natural sciences sections, and a subscore on the 20 items in the prose fiction and humanities sections.

Test-Taking Strategies for the ACT Reading Test

1. Read the passage carefully. Underline important ideas in the passage.
2. Pace yourself. You have 40 questions to answer in 35 minutes.
3. Refer to the passage and in particular to your underlined sections when answering the questions.

The ACT Science Reasoning Test presents seven sets of scientific information in three different formats: graphs, tables, and other schematic forms (38%); description of experiments (45%); and expression of conflicting viewpoints (17%). The 40 items are to be answered in 35 minutes. The content of the test is drawn from biology, chemistry, physics, geology, astronomy, and meteorology. Background knowledge at the level of a high school general science course is all that is needed to answer these questions. The test emphasizes scientific reasoning skills rather than recall of scientific content, skill in mathematics, or reading ability.

Test-Taking Strategies for the ACT Science Reasoning Test

1. Read the scientific material before you begin answering a question. Read tables and text carefully, underlining important ideas.
2. Look for flaws in the experiments and devise ways of improving the experiments.
3. When you are asked to compare viewpoints, make notes in the margin of the printed material summarizing each viewpoint.

A FINAL WORD

Don't walk into the examinations without preparation, even though you will find descriptions of these tests that say they test skills developed over years of study both in and out of school. Don't walk in cold, even though you believe that you meet all the qualities colleges are looking for.

Although the College Board suggests no special preparation, It does distribute to applicants the booklet, "Taking the SAT I Reasoning Test." It also makes available other publications containing former test questions along with advice on how to cope with the questions. Evidently, all candidates need some form of preparation.

The American College Testing Program furnishes, without cost, a booklet, "Preparing for the ACT Assessment." This gives specific information about the test, test questions, and strategies for taking each of the four parts. It also describes what to expect on the test day and gives practice with typical questions.

College entrance exams are one of the necessities of life for the college-bound student. Whereas they may not be the brightest spot of your high school career, neither should they be approached with anxiety or dread. By knowing what to expect and how to approach the tests, you will stay calm and do your very best in this precollege experience.

Samuel C. Brownstein
Co-author of Barron's *How to Prepare for SAT I*,
Barron's *How to Prepare for the Graduate Record Exam*,
and many other test preparation books.

The college admission process—getting in—begins the minute you start making your first choices in course selection and in cocurricular activities in junior high school, middle school, and high school. These initial and ongoing decisions are crucial to your future well-being. They lay the groundwork for the curriculum you will follow throughout your high school career; they are not easily reversed. These are the decisions that will allow you to market yourself to the colleges of your choice.

STUDENTS TAKE NOTE!

There is a myth prevalent among college-bound students throughout the country that the best way to gain entrance to the selective colleges is to be well rounded. This term usually refers to students who have earned good grades in high school (B+ or better) and participated in a wide range of cocurricular activities.

However, most admission officers at the selective colleges prefer applications from candidates they term angular—students who have demonstrated solid academic achievement in and out of school AND who have developed one or two particularly strong cocurricular skills, interests, and activities. These angular students are very different in character from the well-rounded students who are very good at everything, yet excel at little, if anything.

Bill Fitzsimmons, dean of admission at Harvard, says that Harvard is looking for a well-rounded class, which means Harvard is most interested in admitting angular students—students who have excelled at something. He cautions though that ... *It is a mistake to denigrate or underestimate that persuasive power of high grades, rank, double 700s on SAT I, 33 and above on the ACT, and equally impressive SAT II scores. The selective colleges take many of these academically high profile applicants. But the numbers game alone often won't get you in! It would be fairly simple for Harvard to enroll an entire freshman class with a superior academic profile and little depth of quality in areas that make up the personality of the class. We just would not do that!*

Dean Fitzsimmons is saying that the majority of the successful applicants to selective colleges must have some major commitment(s) combined with excellent academic qualities. A strong impact results from quality involvements rather than a proliferation of *joinings* and transient interests. Essentially the angular applicant is a committed individual, whereas the well-rounded candidate is merely involved.

STUDENTS AND PARENTS TAKE AN EARLY, ACTIVE ROLE

Students and parents must make time to ensure an early, active role in the college admissions process. Each year, starting in the seventh grade, students and parents should take the time to sit down with the student's guidance counselor and talk meaningfully about:

- Selection and level of courses; projecting through the senior year of high school;
- Cocurricular activities available, i.e., drama, music, athletics, academic clubs, community activities, student government and other special interest groups; and
- Summer study, work, or recreation.

Why is this important to getting in? As sure as death and taxes there is going to come a time in your senior year when you, the college-bound student, will be asked to choose colleges, complete the college application, write your college essay(s), and have an interview, either on the college campus or in your hometown.

You must create the personal marketing process that will take place during the application process in your senior year long before your senior year starts. By the time you reach that long-awaited dream of being a senior, you and you alone have created the person you must market to the colleges of your choice. You must understand that the person you have created is the only person you have to market. There is no Madison Avenue glitz involved in this marketing process! You don't create a pseudo marketing campaign that shows you jumping off a bridge with a bungie cord tied to your sneakers. Admission counselors can tell the difference between a real marketing effort and a pseudo marketing campaign.

THE APPLICATION FORM

Each printed or computer disk application form differs with the exception of those colleges that use the common application. When you start to work, be sure to note all deadlines, follow all directions, be complete, be neat, fill out the geographical data with accurate facts, and type all unless you print exceptionally well. Always review the entire application before you start to fill it out, and complete the entire application before you start the next one. Remember the application is you to the admissions committee member reading it. Even though "a book should not be judged by its cover," appearances do influence opinions. It is best to work through a rough draft of the application before you actually work on the application copy to be submitted. Remember to make a copy of all parts of the finished application in the event that yours gets lost and a replacement must be sent.

Your high school guidance counselor will fill out the school record data: grades, rank in class, and academic profile. You must fill out the forms from ETS and/or ACT for your SAT I and SAT II: Subject tests and/or ACT scores to be sent directly from each governing body directly to each college to which you have applied, even if your scores are on your high school transcript. Your college file will not be considered complete, and will not go to the admissions committee for a decision, without the official scores sent directly from the governing body to each college. Also, many colleges want recommendations from one or two teachers. Choose wisely and allow each teacher plenty of time. Request letters from teachers who know you best. If English is your interest, be sure to choose an English teacher. If you are fluent in Spanish and have future interest in Spanish at college, ask the Spanish teacher. Remember, though you have many interests and have participated in many activities, you are developing an admissions package as part of your marketing of yourself. Emphasize your strengths and show how they are integrated into your activities and achievements.

Cocurricular activities usually are athletic or nonathletic. If you have won athletic awards, note them. If you have had the starring role in the spring musical for the last two years, say so. If you are an editor on the school paper, specify this. Admissions people view your activities with special interest. They realize how very time-consuming these activities can be and sometimes with very few accolades. Put these activities in the order of importance to you. Be honest!

Some applications have mini essays. When space is provided, be sure you are concise, clear, and grammatically correct. Here less is more. Your ability to organize your thoughts and present them concisely is being tested. Some colleges have as many as six essays, whereas some large state institutions require none.

Some colleges encourage you to support your application with additional materials. If you are given this option, consider what will strengthen your application. Musical tapes, art or photography portfolios, published writings, an exceptional graded term paper; all are additional opportunities for the college to get to know you better and for you to increase your image as an *angular* candidate. Such additions help the admissions committee to get a better handle on you.

Proofread all parts of the application. Be sure you, the student, place your signature where it is required. Then place everything, including the registration fee check, in a large manila envelope and give it to your college guidance counselor. After adding the completed school's record section to the application itself, your guidance counselor will mail it. Your job is now done and the waiting begins!

PC- and Mac-Based Computer Disk Applications

Many colleges now have a PC- or Mac-based computer disk application. Make sure that each college for which you have a computer disk application has authorized the disk; there are a number of organizations selling computer disk applications without the consent of the college. Additionally, make sure you send a hard copy of the application along with the disk and keep a copy for yourself—it is very easy to lose information on a disk if it is scanned by the post office.

The Common Application

More than 150 colleges in the United States agreed that students may apply to their colleges by completing one common application instead of individual applications for each college. Many students will face a choice as to whether they will complete the college's individual application or the common application, which substantially reduces the time spent composing different essay answers and neatly typing different application forms. All the colleges participating in the common application agreement sign a statement that they do NOT discriminate among the students who submit the common application instead of the individual application. However, there are those counselors who believe that the individual application may often give the student more of a chance to convey personal information because frequently the individual application requests more essays, long ones and short ones, than does the common application.

THE INTERVIEW

The interview is a contrived situation that few people enjoy, of which many people misunderstand the value, and about which everyone is apprehensive. However, no information from a college catalog, no friend's friend, no high school guidance counselor's comments, and no parental remembrances from bygone days can surpass the value of your college campus visit and interview. This firsthand opportunity to assess your future alma mater will confirm or contradict other impressions and help you make a sound college acceptance.

Many colleges will recommend or request a personal interview. It is best to travel to the campus to meet with a member of the admissions staff if you can; however, if you can't, many colleges will arrange to have one of their representatives, usually an alumnus, interview you in your hometown.

Even though the thought of an interview might give you enough butterflies to lift you to the top of your high school's flagpole, here are some tips that might make it a little easier.

1. **Go prepared.** Read the college's catalog ahead of time so you won't ask "How many books are in your library?" or "How many students do you have?" Ask intelligent questions that introduce a topic of conversation that you want the interviewer to know about you. The key is to distinguish yourself in a positive way from thousands of other applicants. Forge the final steps in the marketing process you have built up since your first choices in the college admission process were taken back in junior high school. The interview is your chance to enhance those decisions.

2. **Nervousness...**is absolutely and entirely normal. The best way to handle it is to admit it, out loud, to the inter-

viewer. Miles Uhrig, past Director of Admission at Tufts University, sometimes relates this true story to his apprehensive applicants: One extremely agitated young applicant sat opposite him for her interview with her legs crossed, wearing loafers on her feet. She swung her top leg back and forth to some inaudible rhythm. The loafer on her top foot flew off her foot, hit him in the head, ricocheted to the desk lamp and broke it. She looked at him in terror, but when their glances met, they both dissolved in laughter. The moral of the story—the person on the other side of the desk is also a human being and wants to put you at ease. So admit to your anxiety, and don't swing your foot if you're wearing loafers! (By the way, she was admitted.)

3. **Be yourself.** Nobody's perfect, and everyone knows nobody's perfect, so admit to a flaw or two before the interviewer goes hunting for them. The truly impressive candidate will convey a thorough knowledge of self.

4. **Interview the interviewer.** Don't passively sit there and allow the interviewer to ask all the questions and direct the conversation. Participate in this responsibility by assuming an active role. A thoughtful questioner will accomplish three important tasks in a successful interview:

   a. **demonstrate interest,** initiative, and maturity for taking partial responsibility for the content of the conversation;
   b. **guide the conversation** to areas where he/she feels most secure and accomplished; and
   c. **obtain answers.**
      Use your genuine feelings to react to the answers you hear. If you are delighted to learn of a certain program or activity, show it. If you are curious, ask more questions. If you are disappointed by something you learn, try to find a path to a positive answer or...consider yourself lucky that you discovered this particular inadequacy in time.

5. **Parents do belong** in your college decision process as your advisers! Often it is they who spend the megabucks for your next four years, and they can provide psychological support and a stabilizing influence for sensible, rational decisions. In essence, the sage senior will find constructive ways to include parents in the decision-making process as catalysts, without letting them take over (as many are apt to do). You may want your parents to meet and speak briefly to your interviewer. That's fine to do before or after, but not during your interview time.

6. **Practice makes perfect.** Begin your interviews at colleges that are low on your list of preferred choices, and leave your first-choice colleges until last. If you are shy, you will have a chance to practice vocalizing what your usually silent inner voice tells you. Others will have the opportunity to commit their inevitable first blunders where it won't count as much.

7. **Departing impressions.** There is a remarkable tendency for the student to base final college preferences on the quality of the interview only, or on the personal reaction to the interviewer as the personification of the entire institution. Do not do yourself the disservice of letting it influence an otherwise rational selection, one based on institutional programs, students, services, and environment. After the last good-bye and thank you has been smiled, and you exhale deeply on your way out the door, go ahead and congratulate yourself. If you used the interview properly, you will know whether or not you wish to attend that college and why.

8. **Send a thank-you note** to your interviewer A short and simple handwritten or typed note will do; and if you forgot to mention something important about yourself at the interview, here's your chance.

WRITING THE COLLEGE ESSAY

Do the colleges read the essays you write on their applications? You bet your diploma they do. Here is your chance to "strut your stuff," stand up and be counted, and stylize your way into the hearts of the decision makers.

Write it, edit it, review it, rewrite it. Try to show why you are unique and how the college will benefit having you in its student body. This is not a routine homework assignment, but a college level essay that will be carefully examined for spelling, content and style *of a high school senior.* As strenuous an effort as it may be, by completing the college essays you give the admissions committee a chance to know the real you, a three-dimensional human being with passions and preferences, strengths, weaknesses, imagination, energy, and ambition. Your ability to market yourself will help the deans and directors of admission remember your application from among the sea of thousands that flood their offices each year.

First, maximize your strengths—use your essays to say what you want to say. The answer to a specific question on the college's part still provides an opening for you to furnish background information about yourself, your interests, ambitions, and insights. For example, the essay that asks you to name your favorite book and the reason for your selection could be answered with the title of a Dr. Seuss book because you are considering a career as an elementary school teacher. If you are interested in business, read about a famous businessman you admire and then discuss your interest in business.

Whatever the essay questions are, autobiographical or otherwise, select the person or issue that puts you in the position to discuss the subject in which you are the most well versed. In essence, all of your essay responses are auto-biographical in the sense that they will illustrate something important about yourself, your values, and the kind of person you are or hope to become. If personal values are important to you, and they should be, then here is your opportunity to stress their importance.

Because many colleges will ask for more than one essay, make sure that the SUM of the essays in any one college application covers your best points. Do not repeat your ansers, even if the questions sound alike. Cover the most important academic and extracurricular activities (most important meaning the ones in which you excelled and/or spent most the time.)

If you are lucky enough to have a cooperative English teacher, you might request a critique of your first draft, but be sure to allow enough time for a careful evaluation and your revision.

Write the essays yourself—no substitutes or stand-ins. College admission professionals can discern mature adult prose from student prose.

PARTING WORDS

Finding and applying to the best colleges for you isn't supposed to be easy, but it can be fun. Parents, guidance counselors, and teachers are there to help you, so don't struggle alone. Keep your sense of humor and a smile on your face as you go about researching, exploring, and discovering your "ideal college."

Anthony F. Capraro, III, Ph.D.
President, Teach...Inc.
College Counseling
Larchmont, New York

Postsecondary education is a major American industry. A greater proportion of students pursue postsecondary education in the United States than in any other industrialized country. Annually, more than 13 million students study at over 8000 institutions of higher learning. The diversity of our system of higher education is admired by educators and students throughout the world. There is no reason to believe that this system will change in the future. However, college costs and the resources available to parents and students to meet those costs have changed.

Unfortunately, many high school students and their parents believe either that there is no financial aid available or that they will not qualify for any type of financial assistance from any source. Neither assumption is correct. College costs have increased and will continue to increase. Federal allocations, for some financial aid programs, have decreased. But this decline has been met with generous increases in financial aid from state and school sources.

American students and their parents should realize that they must assume the primary role in planning to meet their future college costs and that the family financial planning process must begin much earlier than has been the case.

COLLEGE COSTS

- Eighty-two percent of all parents believe college costs are too expensive.
- In 1995–96, tuition and fees at a public school were approximately $2860 and about $12,432 at private colleges.
- While college costs will increase each year, it is important to remember that currently about 4% of all college students attend schools with tuition costs exceeding $10,000 and only 50% pay the full cost of attendance at these colleges and universities.

STUDENT FINANCIAL AID

- In 1995–96, the total amount of financial aid available from federal, state, and institutional sources to postsecondary students exceeded $30 billion.
- Approximately 60% of all students enrolled in higher education receive some type of financial assistance.
- Federal student aid remains the largest source of funding at 75% of total aid.
- Financial aid from sources other than parents pays for about 60% of the bills of financial aid recipients.
- Ten years ago the majority of federal financial assistance was grants. Today, an equal amount of grant and loan money is awarded from federal sources.

TIMETABLE FOR APPLYING FOR FINANCIAL AID

Sophomore Year of High School

Most families wait until a child has been accepted into a college or university to begin planning on how the family will meet those college costs. However, a family's college financial planning should begin much earlier.

Students, as early as the sophomore year of high school, should begin a systematic search for colleges that offer courses of study that are of interest. There are many computer programs that can be helpful in this process. These programs can match a student's interest with colleges fitting the profile. Considering that half of all students who enter college either drop out or transfer to another school, this type of early selection analysis can be invaluable.

After selecting certain schools for further consideration, you should write to the school and request a viewbook, catalog, and financial aid brochure. After receiving this information, you and your family should compare the schools. Your comparison should include academic considerations as well as financial. Don't rule out a school because you think you can't afford it. Remember the financial aid programs at that school may be more generous than at a lower-priced school. If possible, visit the college and speak with both an admission and financial aid counselor. If it is not possible to visit all the schools, call the schools and obtain answers to your questions about admission, financial aid, and placement after graduation.

Junior Year of High School

The comparative analysis of colleges and universities that you began in your sophomore year should continue in your junior year. By the completion of your junior year, you and your parents should have some idea of what it will cost to attend and the financial aid policies of each of the schools you are considering.

Some colleges and universities offer prospective applicants an early estimate of their financial aid award. This estimate is based upon information supplied by the family and can provide assistance in planning a family's budget. Remember that for most families, financial aid from federal, state, and school sources will probably not meet the total cost of attendance.

Families should remember that college costs can be met over the course of the academic year. It is not necessary to have all of the money needed to attend school available at the beginning of the academic year. Student and family savings, as well as student employment throughout the year, can be used to meet college costs.

Senior Year of High School

January

By January of your senior year of high school you should know which colleges and universities you want to receive your financial aid application forms. Be certain that you have completed not only the federal financial aid application form, but also any necessary state or school forms. Read carefully all of the instructions. Application methods and deadline dates may differ from one college to another. Submit an application clean of erasures or notations in the margins, and sign all of the application forms.

February

Approximately six weeks after you submit your application for financial aid, you will receive a report from the service agency you selected containing information on your family's expected contribution and your eligibility for financial aid. You and your parents should discuss the results of the financial aid application with regard to family contribution, educational costs, and how those costs can be met.

March

Beginning in March, most colleges begin to make financial aid decisions. If your application is complete, your chances of receiving an award letter early are greater than if additional information is required.

The financial aid award letter you receive from your school serves as your official document indicating the amount of financial aid you will receive for the year. You must sign and return a copy of the award letter to your school if you agree to accept their offer of financial aid.

If your family's financial circumstances change and you need additional funding, you should make an appointment to speak with your school's financial aid director or counselor. College financial aid personnel are permitted to exercise professional judgment and make adjustments to a student's financial need. Your letter of appeal should state explicitly how much money you need and why you need it.

TIPS ON APPLYING FOR FINANCIAL AID

1. Families can no longer wait until a child is accepted into college before deciding how they will finance that education. Earlier college financial planning is necessary.

2. Families should assume a much more active role in locating the resources necessary to fund future college costs.

3. Families should assume that college costs will continue to increase.

4. Families should assume that in the future the federal government will not substantially increase financial aid allocations.

5. Families should obtain information on a wide range of colleges including the many excellent low-cost schools.

6. Families should seek information about all of the funding sources available at each school they are considering.

7. Families should seek the advice and expertise of financial experts for college financing strategies. College financial planning should specify the amount of money a family should invest or save each month in order to meet future college bills.

8. Families should investigate all of the legitimate ways of reducing their income and assets before filing for financial aid.

9. Families should know how financial aid is awarded and the financial aid policies and programs of each school they are considering.

10. Families should realize that although the job of financing a college education rests primarily with them, they probably will not be able to save the entire cost of their child's college education. They probably will be eligible to receive some type of financial aid from some source and they will have to borrow a portion of their child's college education costs.

11. Families should be advised that the federal government frequently changes the rules and regulations governing financial aid eligibility. Check with your high school guidance counselor or college financial aid administrator for the latest program qualifications.

Marguerite J. Dennis
Vice President for Development and Enrollment
Suffolk University
Boston, Massachusetts
and author of Barron's *Complete College Financing Guide*, Barron's *Guide to Financing a Medical School Education*, and *Keys to Financing a College Education*

COLLEGE: IT'S DIFFERENT

In college you are likely to hear fellow students say, "I don't know what that prof *wants*, and she won't *tell* me." "I wrote about three papers in high school, and now they want one every week." Though these students may be exaggerating a bit, college *is* different, both in the quality and the amount of work expected. Sometimes in high school the basic concepts of a course are reduced to a set of facts on a study sheet, handed to students to be reviewed and learned for a test.

In college, it is the concepts and ideas that are most important. These can only be grasped through a real understanding of the facts as they interrelate and form larger patterns. Writing papers and answering essay questions on tests can demonstrate a genuine understanding of the concepts, and this is why they are so important to college instructors. Learning to deal with ideas in this way can be a long-term asset, developing your independence, intellectual interests, and self-awareness.

Don't be discouraged; you are not alone. Most of your fellow students are having equally difficult times adjusting to a new learning method. Persist, and you will improve, leading to a lifetime habit of critical thinking and problem solving that can benefit you in many important ways.

College is also different outside of classes. Now that you have the freedom to choose how to spend time and what types of relationships to make, you have a bewildering number of possibilities.

MAKING A GOOD IMPRESSION

Here you are, plopped down in a strange place, feeling a bit like Dorothy transported to Oz. Your first goal is to make a good impression, showing your best self to those who will be important in your life for the next four years and even longer.

Impressing Faculty Members Favorably

Faculty members come in all ranks, from the graduate assistant, who teaches part-time while pursuing a degree, to a lofty full professor, who teaches primarily graduate students. Though different in rank and seniority, they respond to their students in roughly the same ways. They are, after all, people, with families and relationships much like your own. To have a good working relationship with them, try the following suggestions:

- **Make up your own mind about your instructors.** Listening to other students talk about teachers can be confusing. If you listen long enough, you will hear arguments for and against each of them. Don't allow hearsay to affect your own personal opinion.
- **Get to know your instructors firsthand.** Set up a meeting during regular office hours. Don't try to settle important issues in the few moments before and after class.
- **Approach a discussion of grades carefully.** If you honestly believe that you have been graded too low, schedule a conference. Do not attack your instructor's integrity or judgment. Instead, say that you had expected your work to result in a better grade and would like to know ways to improve. Be serious about overcoming faults.
- **Don't make excuses.** Instructors have heard them all and can rarely be fooled. Accept responsibility for your mistakes, and learn from them.
- **Pay attention in class.** Conversing and daydreaming can insult your instructor and inhibit the learning process.
- **Arrive ahead of time for class.** You will be more relaxed, and you can use these moments to review notes or talk with classmates. You also demonstrate to your instructor a commitment to the class.
- **Participate in class discussions.** Ask questions and give answers to the instructor's questions. Nothing pleases an instructor more than an intelligent question that proves you are interested and prepared.
- **Learn from criticism.** It is an instructor's job to correct your errors in thinking. Don't take in-class criticism personally.

Impressing Fellow Students Favorably

Relationships with other students can be complex, but there are some basic suggestions that may make life easier in the dorms and classrooms:

- **Don't get into the habit of bragging.** Frequent references to your wealth, your outstanding friends, your social status, or your family's successes are offensive to others.
- **Don't pry.** When your fellow students share their feelings and problems, listen carefully and avoid any tendency to intrude or ask embarrassing questions.
- **Don't borrow.** Borrowing a book, a basketball, or a few bucks may seem like a small thing to you, but some people who have trouble saying no may resent your request.
- **Divide chores.** Do your part; agree on a fair division of work in a lab project or a household task.
- **Support others.** Respect your friends' study time and the "Do not disturb" signs on their doors. Helping them to reach their goals will help you as well.
- **Allow others to be upset.** Sometimes, turning someone's anger into a joke, minimizing their difficulties, or belittling their frustration is your worst response. Support them by letting them release their emotions.
- **Don't preach.** Share your opinions when asked for, but don't try to reform the world around you.
- **Tell the truth.** Your reputation is your most important asset. When you make an agreement, keep it.

MANAGING YOUR TIME

Everyone, no matter how prominent or how insignificant, has 168 hours a week to spend. In this one asset we are all equal. There are students on every college campus, however, who seem to accomplish all their goals and still find time for play and socializing. There are others who seem to be alternating between frantic dashes and dull idleness, accomplishing very little. To the first group, college is a happy, fulfilling experience; to the latter, it is maddeningly frustrating. The first group has gained control of time, the second is controlled by that elusive and precious commodity.

- **Know where your time goes.** Unfortunately, we cannot store up time as we do money, to be used when the need is greatest. We use it as it comes, and it is amazing how it sometimes comes slowly (as in the last five minutes of a Friday afternoon class) or quickly (as in the last hour before a final exam). The first step in controlling time is to determine exactly how you use it. For a while, at least, you should carefully record how much time you spend in class, going to and from class, studying, sleeping, eating, listening to music, watching television, and running errands. You need to know what happens to your 168 hours. Only then can you make sensible decisions about managing them.

- **Make a weekly schedule.** You can schedule your routine for the week, using the time plan forms available at most college bookstores or by making your own forms.
- **First schedule the inflexible blocks of time.** Your class periods, transportation time, sleeping, and eating will form relatively routine patterns throughout the week. Trying to shave minutes off these important activities is often a mistake.
- **Plan your study time.** It is preferable, though not always possible, to set your study hours at the same time every weekday. Try to make your study time *prime time,* when your body and mind are ready for a peak performance.
- **Plan time for fun.** No one should plan to spend four years of college as a working robot. Fun and recreation are important, but they can be enjoyed in short periods just as well as long. For example, jogging with friends for thirty minutes can clear the mind, tone up the muscles, and give you those all-important social contacts. Parties and group activities can be scheduled for weekends.
- **Be reasonable in your time allotments.** As you progress through your freshman year, you will learn more precisely how much time is required to write a paper or complete a book report. Until then, schedule some extra minutes for these tasks. You are being unfair to yourself by planning one hour for a job that requires two.
- **Allow flexibility.** The unexpected is to be expected. There will be interruptions to your routine and errands that must be run at certain times. Allow for these unforeseen circumstances.

3. **Seven categories of information are commonly found in textbooks.** Be particularly alert when you see the following; get your marking pen ready.
   Definitions of terms.
   Types or *categories* of items.
   Methods of accomplishing certain tasks.
   Sequences of events or stages in a process.
   Reasons or *causes.*
   Results or *effects.*
   Contrasts or *comparisons* between items.
4. **Repeat information you need to learn.** When the object is to learn information, nothing is so effective as reciting the material, either silently or aloud.
5. **Don't read all material the same way.** Decide what you need to learn from the material and read accordingly. You read a work of fiction to learn the characters and the narrative; a poem, to learn an idea, an emotion, or a theme; a work of history, to learn the interrelationships of events. Do not read every sentence with the same speed and concentration; learn when to skim rapidly along. Remember, your study time is limited and the trick is to discriminate between the most important and the least important. No one can learn *everything* equally well.
6. **The five-minute golden secret.** As soon as possible after class is over—preferably at your desk in the classroom—skim through the chapter that has just been covered, marking the points primarily discussed. Copy what was written on the board. Now you know what the professor thinks is important!

STUDYING EFFECTIVELY

Your most important activity in college is studying. Efficient study skills separate the inept student (who may spend just as many hours studying as an "A" student) from the excellent student, who thinks while studying and who uses common sense strategies to discover the important core of courses. The following suggested game plan for good study has worked in the past; it can work for you.

- **Make a commitment.** It is universally recommended that you spend two hours studying for every hour in class. At the beginning of your college career, be determined to do just that. It doesn't get easy until you make up your mind to do it.
- **Do the tough jobs first.** If certain courses are boring or particularly difficult, study them first. Don't read the interesting, enjoyable materials first, saving the toughies for the last sleepy twinges of your weary brain.
- **Study in short sessions.** Three two-hour sessions, separated from each other by a different activity, are much better than a long six-hour session.
- **Use your bits of time.** Use those minutes when you're waiting for a bus, a return call, laundry to wash, or a friend to arrive. Some of the best students I know carry 3 x 5 cards filled with definitions, formulas, or equations and learn during brief waiting periods. Most chief executives form the habit early of using bits of time wisely.

Digesting a textbook

1. **Preview chapters.** Before you read a chapter in your textbook, preview it. Quickly examine the introductory paragraphs, headings, tables, illustrations, and other features of the chapter. The purpose is to discover the major topics. Then you can read with increased comprehension because you know where the author is leading.
2. **Underline the important points as you read.** Underlining should never be overdone; it can leave your textbook almost completely marked and less legible to read. Only the major ideas and concepts should be highlighted.

TAKING TESTS SKILLFULLY

Try to predict the test questions. At some college libraries, copies of old examinations are made available to students. If you can legally find out your professor's previous test methods do so.

Ask your professor to describe the format of the upcoming test: multiple-choice? true-false? essay questions? problems? Adjust your study to the format described.

Listen for clues in the professor's lecture. Sometimes the questions posed in class have a way of reappearing on tests. If a statement is repeated several times or recurs in a subsequent lecture, note it as important.

As you review for the test, devise questions based on the material, and answer them. If you are part of a study group, have members ask questions of the others.

Common Sense Tactics

Arrive on the scene early; relax by breathing deeply. If the instructor gives instructions while distributing the test, listen very carefully.

- **Scan the whole test first.** Notice the point value for each section and budget your time accordingly.
- **Read the directions carefully** and then reread them. Don't lose points because you misread the directions.
- **Answer the short, easy questions first.** A bit of early success stimulates the mind and builds your confidence.
- **Leave space between answers.** You may think of a brilliant comment to add later.
- **Your first instinct is often the best** in answering true-false and multiple-choice questions. Look for qualifiers such as *never, all, often,* or *seldom* in true-false statements. Usually a qualifier that is absolute (*never, all,* or *none*) will indicate a false statement. Work fast on short-answer questions: they seldom count many points.
- **Open-book tests are no picnic.** Don't think that less study is required for an open-book test. They are often the most difficult of all examinations. If the material is unfamiliar,

you won't have time to locate it and learn it during the test period.

Important Essay Strategies

- **Read the question carefully** and find out exactly what is asked for. If you are asked to contrast the French Revolution with the American Revolution and you spend your time describing each, without any contrasting references, your grade will be lowered.
- **Know the definitions of key words** used in essay questions:
  analyze: discuss the component parts.
  compare: examine for similarities.
  criticize: give a judgment or evaluation.
  define: state precise meaning of terms.
  describe: give a detailed picture of qualities and characteristics.
  discuss: give the pros and cons: debate them, and come to a conclusion.
  enumerate: briefly mention a number of ideas, things, or events.
  evaluate: give an opinion, with supporting evidence.
  illustrate: give examples (illustrations) relating to a general statement.
  interpret: usually means to state in other words, to explain, make clear.
  outline: another way of asking for brief listings of principal ideas or characteristics. Normally the sentence or topic outline format is not required.
  prove: give evidence and facts to support the premise stated in the test.
  summarize: give an abbreviated account, with your conclusions.
- **Write a short outline** before you begin your essay. This organizes your thinking, making you less likely to leave out major topics.
- **Get to the point immediately.** Don't get bogged down in a lengthy introduction.
- **Read your essay over** before you hand it in. Words can be left out or misspelled. Remember that essay answers are graded somewhat subjectively, and papers that are correctly and neatly written make a better impression.
- **Learn from your test paper** when it is returned. Students who look at a test grade and discard the paper are throwing away a valuable tool. Analyze your mistakes honestly; look for clues for improvement in the professor's comments.

WRITING A TERM PAPER

Doing convincing library research and writing a term paper with correct footnotes and bibliography is a complicated procedure. Most first-year English composition courses include this process. Good students will work hard to master this skill because they know that research papers are integral parts of undergraduate and graduate courses.

Many students make the mistake of waiting until near the deadline to begin a term paper. At the busy end of the term, with final exams approaching, they embark on the uncertain time span of research and writing. Begin your term paper early, when the library staff is unhurried and ready to help and when you are under less pressure. It will pay dividends.

REGULATING YOUR RELATIONSHIPS

Find your special friends who believe in your definition of success. In a fast-paced environment like college, it is important to spend most of your time with people who share your ideas toward learning, where you can be yourself, without defensiveness. To find your kind of friends, first ask yourself: What is success? Is it a secure position and a comfortable home? A life of serving others? A position of power with a commodious executive suite? A challenging job that allows you to be creative? When you have answered honestly, you will have a set of long-range personal goals, and you can begin looking for kindred souls to walk with you on the road to success.

There will be, of course, some persons around you who are determined not to succeed, who for some reason program their lives for failure. Many college freshmen never receive a college degree; some may start college with no intention of passing courses. Their goal is to spend one hectic term as a party animal. If you intend to succeed at college, spending time among this type will be a considerable handicap. Consider making friends who will be around longer than the first year.

If possible, steer clear of highly emotional relationships during your first year of college. You don't have time for a broken heart, and relationships that begin with a rush often end that way.

MAINTAINING YOUR HEALTH

Poor health can threaten your success in the first year of college as nothing else can. No matter how busy you are, you must not forget your body and its needs: proper food, sufficient sleep, and healthy exercise. Many students, faced with the stress of college life, find themselves overmunching junk foods and gaining weight. Guard against this. Drugs and alcohol threaten the health and the success of many college students.

A FINAL WORD

So there it is. If you have read this far, you probably have a serious interest in succeeding in your first year of college. You probably have also realized that these suggestions, even if they sound a bit preachy, are practical and workable. They are based on many years of observing college students.

Benjamin W. Griffith
Former Dean of the Graduate School
West Georgia College
Carrollton, Georgia

Author of Barron's *Study Keys to English Literature* and Barron's *Pocket Guide to Literature and Language Terms*

Coauthor of Barron's *Essentials of English, Essentials of Writing,* and *Pocket Guide to Correct Grammar*

COLLEGE ADMISSIONS SELECTOR

This index groups all the colleges listed in this book according to degree of admissions competitiveness. The *Selector* is not a rating of colleges by academic standards or quality of education; it is rather an attempt to describe, in general terms, the situation a prospective student will meet when applying for admission.

THE CRITERIA USED

The factors used in determining the category for each college were: median entrance examination scores for the 1995–96 freshman class (the SAT I score used was derived by averaging the median verbal reasoning and the median mathematics reasoning nonrecentered scores; the ACT score used was the median composite score); percentages of 1995–96 freshmen scoring 500 and above and 600 and above on both the verbal reasoning and mathematics reasoning sections of SAT I (nonrecentered); percentages of 1995–96 freshmen scoring 21 and above and 27 and above on the ACT; percentage of 1995–96 freshmen who ranked in the upper fifth and the upper two fifths of their high school graduating classes; minimum class rank and grade point average required for admission (if any); and percentage of applicants to the 1995–96 freshman class who were accepted. The *Selector* cannot, and does not, take into account all the other factors that each college considers when making admissions decisions. Colleges place varying degrees of emphasis on the factors that comprise each of the categories.

USING THE SELECTOR

To use the *Selector* effectively, the prospective student's records should be compared realistically with the freshmen enrolled by the colleges in each category, as shown by the SAT I or ACT scores, the quality of high school record emphasized by the colleges in each category, and the kinds of risks that the applicant wishes to take. Use the SAT I chart on page 28 to convert nonrecentered scores to your own recentered scores, for comparison purposes.

The student should also be aware of what importance a particular school places on various non-academic factors; when available, this information is presented in the profile of the school. If a student has unusual qualifications that may compensate for exam scores or high school record, the student should examine the admissions policies of the colleges in the next higher category than the one that encompasses his or her score and consider those colleges that give major consideration to factors other than exam scores and high school grades. The "safety" college should usually be chosen from the next lower category, where the student can be reasonably sure that his or her scores and high school record will fall above the median scores and records of the freshmen enrolled in the college.

The listing within each category is alphabetical and not in any qualitative order. State-supported institutions have been classified according to the requirements for state residents, but standards for admission of out-of-state students are usually higher. Colleges that are experimenting with the admission of students of high potential but lower achievement may appear in a less competitive category because of this fact.

A WORD OF CAUTION

The *Selector* is intended primarily for preliminary screening, to eliminate the majority of colleges that are not suitable for a particular student. Be sure to examine the admissions policies spelled out in the *Admissions* section of each profile. And remember that many colleges have to reject *qualified* students; the *Selector* will tell you what your chances are, not which college will accept you.

MOST COMPETITIVE

Even superior students will encounter a great deal of competition for admission to the colleges in this category. In general, these colleges require high school rank in the top 10% to 20% and grade averages of A to B+. Median freshman test scores at these colleges are generally between 625 and 800 (nonrecentered) on SAT I and 29 and above on the ACT. In addition, many of these colleges admit only a small percentage of those who apply—usually fewer than one third.

Amherst College, MA
Bates College, ME
Boston College, MA
Bowdoin College, ME
Brown University, RI
Bryn Mawr College, PA
Colby College, ME
Colgate University, NY
Columbia University/Barnard College, NY
Columbia University/Columbia College, NY
Columbia University/School of Engineering and Applied Science, NY
Cooper Union for the Advancement of Science and Art, NY
Cornell University, NY
Dartmouth College, NH
Georgetown University, DC
Harvard University/Harvard and Radcliffe Colleges, MA

Haverford College, PA
Johns Hopkins University, MD
Massachusetts Institute of Technology, MA
Middlebury College, VT
Princeton University, NJ
Smith College, MA
Swarthmore College, PA
Tufts University, MA
United States Coast Guard Academy, CT
United States Military Academy, NY
United States Naval Academy, MD
University of Pennsylvania, PA
Webb Institute, NY
Wellesley College, MA
Wesleyan University, CT
Williams College, MA
Yale University, CT

HIGHLY COMPETITIVE

Colleges in this group look for students with grade averages of B+ to B and accept most of their students from the top 20% to 35% of the high school class. Median freshman test scores at these colleges range from 575 to 625 (nonrecentered) on SAT I and 27 or 28 on the ACT. These schools generally accept between one third and one half of their applicants.

To provide for finer distinctions within this admissions category, a plus (+) symbol has been placed before some entries. These are colleges with median freshman scores of 615 (nonrecentered) or more on SAT I or 28 or more on the ACT (depending on which test the college prefers), and colleges that accept fewer than one quarter of their applicants.

Allegheny College, PA
Boston University, MA
Bucknell University, PA
+Carnegie Mellon University, PA
College of the Holy Cross, MA
Connecticut College, CT
Franklin and Marshall College, PA
George Washington University, DC
Gettysburg College, PA
Grove City College, PA
Hamilton College, NY
Jewish Theological Seminary/List College of Jewish Studies, NY
Lehigh University, PA
Mount Holyoke College, MA
Rensselaer Polytechnic Institute, NY
Rutgers, The State University of New Jersey/College of Engineering, NJ

Rutgers, The State University of New Jersey/College of Pharmacy, NJ
Rutgers, The State University of New Jersey/Rutgers College, NJ
Saint Mary's College of Maryland, MD
Sarah Lawrence College, NY
State University of New York at Binghamton, NY
+State University of New York College of Environmental Science and Forestry, NY
State University of New York/College at Geneseo, NY
Syracuse University, NY
+Trenton State College, NJ
Trinity College, CT
Union College, NY
United States Merchant Marine Academy, NY
University of Rochester, NY
Vassar College, NY
Villanova University, PA
Worcester Polytechnic Institute, MA

VERY COMPETITIVE

The colleges in this category admit students whose averages are no less than B- and who rank in the top 35% to 50% of their graduating class. They report median freshman test scores in the 525 to 575 (nonrecentered) range on SAT I and from 24 to 26 on the ACT. The schools in this category generally accept between one half and three quarters of their applicants.

The plus (+) has been placed before colleges with median freshman scores of 565 (nonrecentered) or above on SAT I or 26 or better on the ACT (depending on which test the college prefers), and colleges that accept fewer than one third of their applicants.

American University, DC
Babson College, MA
Bard College, NY
+Bennington College, VT
Bentley College, MA
Brandeis University, MA
Catholic University of America, DC
City University of New York/Baruch College, NY
City University of New York/City College, NY
City University of New York/Hunter College, NY
Clark University, MA
+Clarkson University, NY
College of Insurance, NY
+College of the Atlantic, ME
Columbia University/School of General Studies, NY
+Drew University/College of Liberal Arts, NJ
Duquesne University, PA
Elizabethtown College, PA
Emerson College, MA
Fairfield University, CT
Fashion Institute of Technology/State University of New York, NY
Fordham University/College of Business Administration, NY
Fordham University/Fordham College at Lincoln Center, NY
Fordham University/Fordham College at Rose Hill, NY
+Hampshire College, MA
Hobart and William Smith Colleges, NY
Houghton College, NY
+Juniata College, PA
Lafayette College, PA
Loyola College, MD
Marlboro College, VT
Massachusetts College of Pharmacy and Allied Health Sciences, MA
Messiah College, PA
Moravian College, PA
Muhlenberg College, PA
New Jersey Institute of Technology, NJ

New York University, NY
Penn State University at Erie/Behrend College, PA
Penn State University/University Park Campus, PA
Philadelphia College of Pharmacy and Science, PA
Polytechnic University/Brooklyn, NY
Polytechnic University/Farmingdale, NY
Providence College, RI
Richard Stockton College of New Jersey, NJ
Rochester Institute of Technology, NY
Rutgers, The State University of New Jersey/Camden College of Arts and Sciences, NJ
Rutgers, The State University of New Jersey/Cook College, NJ
Rutgers, The State University of New Jersey/Douglass College, NJ
+Saint John's College, MD
Saint Joseph's University, PA
+Saint Lawrence University, NY
Salisbury State University, MD
Siena College, NY
+Simon's Rock College of Bard, MA
Skidmore College, NY
State University of New York at Albany, NY
State University of New York at Buffalo, NY
State University of New York at Stony Brook, NY
State University of New York/College at New Paltz, NY
+Stevens Institute of Technology, NJ
Stonehill College, MA
Susquehanna University, PA
University of Connecticut, CT
University of Delaware, DE
University of Maryland/Baltimore County, MD
University of Maryland/College Park, MD
University of Pittsburgh, PA
Ursinus College, PA
Washington and Jefferson College, PA
Western Maryland College, MD
+Wheaton College, MA
York College of Pennsylvania, PA

COMPETITIVE

This category is a very broad one, covering colleges that generally have median freshman test scores between 450 and 525 (nonrecentered) on SAT I and between 21 and 23 on the ACT. Some of these colleges require that students have high school averages of B- or better, although others state a minimum of C+ or C. Generally, these colleges prefer students in the top 50% to 65% of the graduating class and accept between 75% and 85% of their applicants.

Colleges with a plus (+) are those with median freshman SAT I scores of 515 (nonrecentered) or more or median freshman ACT scores of 24 or more (depending on which test the colleges prefers), and those that admit fewer than half of their applicants.

Albertus Magnus College, CT
Albright College, PA
+Alfred University, NY
Allentown College of Saint Francis de Sales, PA
American International College, MA
Assumption College, MA
Beaver College, PA
+Bloomsburg University of Pennsylvania, PA
Bradford College, MA
Bridgewater State College, MA
Brooklyn Campus of Long Island University, NY
Bryant College, RI
Cabrini College, PA
Caldwell College, NJ
Canisius College, NY
Cedar Crest College, PA
Central Connecticut State University, CT
Chatham College, PA
Chestnut Hill College, PA
Cheyney University of Pennsylvania, PA
City University of New York/Brooklyn College, NY
City University of New York/Queens College, NY
Clarion University of Pennsylvania, PA
Colby-Sawyer College, NH
College Misericordia, PA
College of Mount Saint Vincent, NY
College of New Rochelle, NY
College of Notre Dame of Maryland, MD
College of Our Lady of The Elms, MA
College of Saint Elizabeth, NJ
College of Saint Joseph, VT
College of Saint Rose, NY
Columbia Union College, MD
Coppin State College, MD
Curry College, MA
D'Youville College, NY
Daemen College, NY
Daniel Webster College, NH
Delaware State University, DE
Delaware Valley College, PA
Drexel University, PA
East Stroudsburg University of Pennsylvania, PA
Eastern College, PA
Eastern Nazarene College, MA
Elmira College, NY
Endicott College, MA
+Eugene Lang College of the New School for Social
    Research, NY
Fairleigh Dickinson University, NJ
Felician College, NJ
Framingham State College, MA
Frostburg State University, MD
Gannon University, PA
Geneva College, PA
Georgian Court College, NJ
Goddard College, VT
Gordon College, MA
Goucher College, MD
Green Mountain College, VT
Gwynedd-Mercy College, PA
Hartwick College, NY
Hellenic College/Holy Cross Greek Orthodox School of
    Theology, MA
Hofstra University, NY
Hood College, MD
Husson College, ME
Indiana University of Pennsylvania, PA
Iona College, NY
Ithaca College, NY
+Jersey City State College, NJ
Kean College of New Jersey, NJ

Keene State College, NH
Keuka College, NY
King's College, PA
Kutztown University, PA
La Salle University, PA
Le Moyne College, NY
Lebanon Valley College of Pennsylvania, PA
+Lock Haven University of Pennsylvania, PA
+Long Island University/
    Southampton College, NY
Lycoming College, PA
Maine Maritime Academy, ME
Manhattan College, NY
Manhattanville College, NY
Mansfield University, PA
Marist College, NY
Marymount College/Tarrytown, NY
Marywood College, PA
Mercyhurst College, PA
Merrimack College, MA
Millersville University of Pennsylvania, PA
Monmouth University, NJ
+Montclair State University, NJ
Mount Saint Mary College, NY
Mount Saint Mary's College, MD
Mount Vernon College, DC
Nazareth College of Rochester, NY
Neumann College, PA
New England College, NH
Niagara University, NY
North Adams State College, MA
Northeastern University, MA
Norwich University, VT
Nyack College, NY
Pace University, NY
Philadelphia College of Bible, PA
Philadelphia College of Textiles and Science, PA
Plymouth State College, NH
Pratt Institute, NY
Quinnipiac College, CT
+Ramapo College of New Jersey, NJ
Regis College, MA
Rider University, NJ
Roberts Wesleyan College, NY
Roger Williams University, RI
Rosemont College, PA
+Rowan College of New Jersey, NJ
Russell Sage College, NY
+Rutgers, The State University of New Jersey/Livingston
    College, NJ
Rutgers, The State University of New Jersey/Newark College
    of Arts and Sciences, NJ
Sacred Heart University, CT
Saint Anselm College, NH
Saint Bonaventure University, NY
Saint Francis College, PA
Saint John Fisher College, NY
Saint John's University, NY
Saint Joseph College, CT
Saint Joseph's College, ME
Saint Joseph's College, New York, NY
Saint Michael's College, VT
Saint Peter's College, NJ
Saint Thomas Aquinas College, NY
Saint Vincent College, PA
Seton Hall University, NJ
Seton Hill College, PA
Shippensburg University of Pennsylvania, PA
Simmons College, MA
Slippery Rock University, PA
Southern Connecticut State University, CT

State University of New York College of Technology at Farmingdale, NY
State University of New York/College at Brockport, NY
State University of New York/College at Buffalo, NY
+State University of New York/College at Cortland, NY
State University of New York/College at Fredonia, NY
State University of New York/College at Old Westbury, NY
State University of New York/College at Oneonta, NY
State University of New York/College at Oswego, NY
State University of New York/College at Plattsburgh, NY
State University of New York/College at Potsdam, NY
State University of New York/College at Purchase, NY
State University of New York/Maritime College, NY
Suffolk University, MA
Temple University, PA
Towson State University, MD
+Trinity College, DC
University of Bridgeport, CT
University of Hartford, CT
University of Maine, ME
University of Maine at Farmington, ME
University of Maine at Machias, ME
University of Massachusetts Amherst, MA
University of Massachusetts Boston, MA
University of Massachusetts Dartmouth, MA

University of Massachusetts Lowell, MA
University of New England, ME
University of New Hampshire, NH
University of New Haven, CT
University of Pittsburgh at Bradford, PA
University of Pittsburgh at Johnstown, PA
University of Rhode Island, RI
University of Scranton, PA
+University of Southern Maine, ME
University of Vermont, VT
Utica College of Syracuse University, NY
Wagner College, NY
+Washington College, MD
Waynesburg College, PA
+Wells College, NY
West Chester University of Pennsylvania, PA
Westbrook College, ME
Western Connecticut State University, CT
Westfield State College, MA
Westminster College, PA
Widener University, PA
+William Paterson College, NJ
Wilson College, PA
Worcester State College, MA
Yeshiva University, NY

LESS COMPETITIVE

Included in this category are colleges with median freshman test scores below 450 (nonrecentered) on SAT I and below 21 on the ACT; some colleges that require entrance examinations but do not report median scores; and colleges that admit students with averages below C who rank in the top 65% of the graduating class. These colleges usually admit 85% or more of their applicants.

Adelphi University, NY
Alvernia College, PA
Anna Maria College, MA
Atlantic Union College, MA
Audrey Cohen College, NY
Bloomfield College, NJ
Boricua College, NY
Bowie State University, MD
California University of Pennsylvania, PA
Capitol College, MD
Carlow College, PA
Castleton State College, VT
Cazenovia College, NY
Centenary College, NJ
Champlain College, VT
City University of New York/Herbert H. Lehman College, NY
City University of New York/John Jay College of Criminal Justice, NY
Concordia College, NY
Dominican College, NY
Dowling College, NY
Eastern Connecticut State University, CT
Edinboro University of Pennsylvania, PA
Emmanuel College, MA
Fitchburg State College, MA
Franklin Pierce College, NH
Friends World Program, NY
Goldey-Beacom College, DE
Hebrew College, MA
Holy Family College, PA
Howard University, DC
Immaculata College, PA
Johnson and Wales University, RI
Johnson State College, VT
La Roche College, PA
Lesley College, MA
Lincoln University, PA
Long Island University/C.W. Post Campus, NY
Lyndon State College, VT
Marymount Manhattan College, NY
Massachusetts Maritime Academy, MA
Medaille College, NY
Mercy College, NY

Molloy College, NY
Morgan State University, MD
Mount Ida College, MA
New Hampshire College, NH
New York Institute of Technology/Old Westbury, NY
Nichols College, MA
Notre Dame College, NH
Pennsylvania College of Technology, PA
Pine Manor College, MA
Point Park College, PA
Rhode Island College, RI
Rivier College, NH
Robert Morris College, PA
Rutgers, The State University of New Jersey/University College—Newark, NJ
Saint Francis College, NY
Salem State College, MA
Salve Regina University, RI
Sojourner-Douglass College, MD
Southeastern University, DC
Southern Vermont College, VT
Springfield College, MA
State University of New York/College of Agriculture and Technology at Cobleskill, NY
Strayer College, DC
Teikyo Post University, CT
Thiel College, PA
Thomas College, ME
Thomas More College of Liberal Arts, NH
Touro College, NY
Trinity College of Vermont, VT
Unity College, ME
University of Maine at Fort Kent, ME
University of Maine at Presque Isle, ME
University of Maryland/Eastern Shore, MD
University of Pittsburgh at Greensburg, PA
Villa Julie College, MD
Wentworth Institute of Technology, MA
Wesley College, DE
Western New England College, MA
Wheelock College, MA
Wilkes University, PA

NONCOMPETITIVE

The colleges in this category generally only require evidence of graduation from an accredited high school (although they may also require completion of a certain number of high school units). Some require that entrance examinations be taken for placement purposes only, or only by graduates of unaccredited high schools or only by out-of-state students. In some cases, insufficient capacity may compel a college in this category to limit the number of students that are accepted; generally, however, if a college accepts 98% or more of its applicants, it automatically falls in this category. Colleges are also rated Noncompetitive if they admit all state residents, but have some requirements for nonresidents.

Academy of the New Church College, PA
Burlington College, VT
City University of New York/College of Staten Island, NY
City University of New York/Medgar Evers College, NY
City University of New York/New York City Technical College, NY
City University of New York/York College, NY

College of Aeronautics, NY
Gratz College, PA
University of Maine at Augusta, ME
University of Maryland/University College, MD
University of the District of Columbia, DC
Wilmington College, DE

SPECIAL

Listed here are colleges whose programs of study are specialized; professional schools of art, music, or theater arts. In general, the admissions requirements are not based primarily on academic criteria, but on evidence of talent or special interest in the field. Many other colleges and universities offer special-interest programs in addition to regular academic curricula, but such institutions have been given a regular competitive rating based on academic criteria. Other schools with this rating may be oriented toward working adults.

Albany College of Pharmacy, NY
Baltimore Hebrew University, MD
Berklee College of Music, MA
Boston Architectural Center, MA
Boston Conservatory, MA
Charter Oak State College, CT
College for Lifelong Learning, NH
College of New Rochelle - School of New Resources, NY
Corcoran School of Art, DC
Curtis Institute of Music, PA
Eastman School of Music, NY
Five Towns College, NY
Gallaudet University, DC
Juilliard School, NY
Laboratory Institute of Merchandising, NY
Maine College of Art, ME
Manhattan School of Music, NY
Mannes College of Music, NY
Maryland Institute, College of Art, MD
Massachusetts College of Art, MA

Montserrat College of Art, MA
Moore College of Art and Design, PA
New England Conservatory of Music, MA
Parsons School of Design, NY
Rhode Island School of Design, RI
Rutgers, The State University of New Jersey/College of Nursing, NJ
Rutgers, The State University of New Jersey/Mason Gross School of the Arts, NJ
Rutgers, The State University of New Jersey/University College—Camden, NJ
Rutgers, The State University of New Jersey/University College—New Brunswick, NJ
School of Visual Arts, NY
State University of New York Empire State College, NY
The University of the State of New York Regents College Degrees, NY
Thomas A. Edison State College, NJ
University of the Arts, PA
Westminster Choir College of Rider University, NJ

THE BASICS

More than 465 colleges in 11 states and the District of Columbia are described in the profiles that follow.

The Choice of Schools

Colleges and universities in this country may achieve recognition from a number of professional organizations, but we have based our choice of U.S. colleges on accreditation from two of the six U.S. regional accrediting associations.

Accreditation amounts to a stamp of approval given to a college. The accreditation process evaluates institutions and programs to determine whether they meet established standards of educational quality. The regional associations listed below supervise an aspect of the accrediting procedure—the study of a detailed report submitted by the institution applying for accreditation, and then an inspection visit by members of the accrediting agency. The six agencies are associated with the Commission on Recognition of Postsecondary Accreditation (CORPA). They include:

Middle States Association of Colleges and Schools
New England Association of Schools and Colleges
North Central Association of Colleges and Schools
Northwest Association of Schools and Colleges
Southern Association of Colleges and Schools
Western Association of Schools and Colleges

Getting accreditation for the first time can take a school several years. To acknowledge that schools have begun this process, the agencies accord them candidate status. Most candidates eventually are awarded full accreditation.

The schools included in this book are fully accredited by the Middle States Association or the New England Association, or are candidates for that status. If the latter is the case, it is indicated below the address of the school.

Four-Year Colleges Only

This book presents profiles for all accredited four-year colleges that grant bachelor's degrees and admit freshmen with no previous college experience. Most of these colleges also accept transfer students. Profiles of upper division schools, which offer only the junior or senior year of undergraduate study, are not included.

Consistent Entries

Every profile is organized in the same way. Each one begins with a capsule and is followed by separate sections covering the campus environment, student life, programs of study, admissions, financial aid, information for international students, computers, graduates, and the admissions contact. These categories are always introduced in the same sequence, so you can find data and compare specific points easily. The following commentary will help you evaluate and interpret the information given for each college.

Data Collection

Barron's *Profiles of American Colleges*, from which the information in this book was extracted, was first published in 1964. Since then, it has been revised almost every year; comprehensive revisions are undertaken every two years. Such frequent updating is necessary because so much information about colleges—particularly enrollment figures, costs, programs of study, and admissions standards—changes rapidly.

The facts included in this edition were gathered in the fall of 1995 and apply to the 1995–96 academic year. You should expect all the entries in this edition to become somewhat dated, but some facts will change faster than others. Figures on tuition and room-and-board costs generally change soon after the book is published. For the most up-to-date information on such items, you should always check with the colleges. Other information—such as the basic nature of the school, its campus, and the educational goals of its students—changes less rapidly. A few new programs of study might be added or new services made available, but the basic educational offerings generally will remain constant.

THE CAPSULE

The capsule of each profile provides basic information about the college at a glance. An explanation of the standard capsule is shown in the accompanying box.

All 800 phone numbers are presumed to be out-of-state or both in-state and out-of-state, unless otherwise noted.

A former name is given only if the name has been changed since the previous edition of *Profiles*. To use the map code to the right of the college name, turn to the appropriate college-locator map at the beginning of each chapter. Wherever "n/av" is used in the capsule, it means the information was not available. The abbreviation "n/app" means not applicable.

Full-time, Part-time, Graduate

Enrollment figures are the clearest indication of the size of a college, and show whether or not it is coeducational and what the male-female ratio is. Graduate enrollment is presented to give a better idea of the size of the entire student body; some schools have far more graduate students enrolled than undergraduates.

Year

Some of the more innovative college calendars include the 4-1-4, 3-2-3, 3-3-1, and 1-3-1-4-3 terms. College administrators

---

COMPLETE NAME OF SCHOOL
(Former Name, if any)
City, State, Zip Code
(Accreditation Status, if a candidate)

MAP CODE

Fax and Phone Numbers

Full-time: Full-time undergraduate enrollment
Part-time: Part-time undergraduate enrollment
Graduate: Graduate enrollment
Year: Type of calendar, whether there is a summer session
Application Deadline: fall admission deadline
Freshman Class: Number of students who applied, number accepted, number enrolled
SAT I: Median Verbal, Median Math

Faculty: Number of full-time faculty; AAUP category of school, salary-level symbol
Ph.Ds: Percentage of faculty holding Ph.D. or highest terminal degree
Student/Faculty: Full-time student/full-time faculty ratio
Tuition: Yearly tuition and fees (out-of-state tuition and fees if different)
Room & Board: Yearly room and board costs
ACT: Median composite of ACT

ADMISSIONS SELECTOR RATING

sometimes utilize various intersessions or interims—special short terms—for projects, independent study, short courses, or travel programs. The early semester calendar, which allows students to finish spring semesters earlier than those of the traditional semester calendar, gives students a head start on finding summer jobs. A modified semester (4-1-4) system provides a January or winter term, approximately four weeks long, for special projects that usually earn the same credit as one semester-long course. The trimester calendar divides the year into three equal parts; students may attend college during all three but generally take a vacation during any one. The quarter calendar divides the year into four equal parts; students usually attend for three quarters each year. The term calendar is essentially the same as the quarter calendar without the summer quarter; it has three sessions between September and June. The capsule also indicates schools that offer a summer session.

Application Deadline

Indicated here is the deadline for applications for admission to the fall semester. If there are no specific deadlines, it will say "open." Application deadlines for admission to other semesters are, where available, given in the admissions section of the profile.

Faculty

The first number given refers to the number of full-time faculty members at the college or university.

The Roman numeral and symbol that follow represent the salary level of faculty at the school as compared with faculty salaries nationally. This information is based on the salary report* published by the American Association of University Professors (AAUP). The Roman numeral refers to the AAUP category to which the particular college or university is assigned (this allows for comparison of faculty salaries at the same types of schools). Category I includes "institutions that offer the doctorate degree, and that conferred in the most recent three years an annual average of fifteen or more earned doctorates covering a minimum of three nonrelated disciplines." Category IIA includes "institutions awarding degrees above the baccalaureate, but not included in Category I." Category IIB includes "institutions awarding only the baccalaureate or equivalent degree." Category III includes "institutions with academic ranks, mostly two-year institutions." Category IV includes "institutions without academic ranks (with the exception of a few liberal arts colleges, this category includes mostly two-year institutions)."

The symbol that follows the Roman numeral indicates into which percentile range the average salary of professors, associate professors, assistant professors, and instructors at the school falls, as compared with other schools in the same AAUP category. The symbols used in this book represent the following:

++$	80th percentile
+$	60th percentile
av$	40th percentile
–$	20th percentile
––$	lower than 20th percentile

If the school is not a member of AAUP, nothing will appear.

Ph.D.s

The figure here indicates the percentage of full-time faculty who have Ph.D.s or the highest terminal degree in their field.

Student/Faculty

Student/faculty ratios may be deceptive because the faculties of many large universities include scholars and scientists who do little or no teaching. Nearly every college has some large lecture classes, usually in required or popular subjects, and many small classes in advanced or specialized fields. Here, the ratio reflects full-time students and faculty, and some colleges utilize the services of a large part-time faculty. In general, a student/faculty ratio of 10 to 1 is very good.

If the faculty and student body are both mostly part-time, the entry will say "n/app."

Tuition

It is important to remember that tuition costs change continually and that in many cases, these changes are substantial. Particularly heavy increases have occurred recently and will continue to occur. On the other hand, some smaller colleges are being encouraged to lower tuitions, in order to make higher education more affordable. Students are therefore urged to contact individual colleges for the most current tuition figures.

The figure given here includes tuition and student fees for the school's standard academic year. If costs differ for state residents and out-of-state residents, the figure for nonresidents is given in parenthesis. Where tuition costs are listed per credit hour (p/c), per course (p/course), or per unit (p/unit), student fees are not included. In some university systems, tuition is the same for all schools. However, student fees, and therefore the total tuition figure, may vary from school to school.

Room and Board

It is suggested that students check with individual schools for the most current room-and-board figures because, like tuition figures, they increase continually. The room-and-board figures given here represent the annual cost of a double room and all meals. The word "none" indicates that the college does not charge for room and board; "n/app" indicates that room and board are not provided.

Freshman Class

The numbers apply to the number of students who applied, were accepted, and enrolled in the 1995–96 freshman class or in a recent class.

SAT I, ACT

Whenever available, the median SAT I scores—both Verbal and Mathematics—and the median ACT composite score for the 1995–96 freshman class are given. If the school has not reported median SAT I or ACT scores, the capsule indicates whether the SAT I or ACT is required. Note: Nonrecentered SAT I scores are reported here; see explanation on page 28.

Admissions Selector Rating

The College Admissions Selector Rating indicates degree of competitiveness of admission to the college.

THE GENERAL DESCRIPTION

The Introductory Paragraph

This paragraph indicates, in general, what types of programs the college offers, when it was founded, whether it is public or private, and its religious affiliation. Baccalaureate program accreditation and information on the size of the school's library collection are also provided.

In evaluating the size of the collection, keep in mind the difference between college and university libraries: A university's graduate and professional schools require many specialized books that would be of no value to an undergraduate. For a university, a ratio of one undergraduate to 500 books generally means an outstanding library, one to 200 an adequate library, one to 100 an inferior library. For a college, a ratio of one to 400 is outstanding, one to 300 superior, one to 200 adequate, one to 50 inferior.

These figures are somewhat arbitrary, because a large university with many professional schools or campuses requires more books than a smaller university. Furthermore, a recently founded college would be expected to have fewer books than an older school, since it has not inherited from the past what might be a great quantity of outdated and useless books. Most libraries can make up for deficiencies through interlibrary loans.

*Source: Annual Report on the Economic Status of the Profession published in the March-April 1995 issue of *Academe*, Bulletin of the AAUP 1012 Fourteenth St., N.W., Suite 500, Washington, D.C. 20005. Prepared by Maryse Eymonerie, special consultant to AAUP.

The ratio of students to the number of subscriptions to periodicals is less meaningful, and again, a university requires more periodicals than a college. But for a university, subscription to more than 15,000 periodicals is outstanding, and 5000 is more than adequate. For a college, 1500 subscriptions are exceptional, 700 very good, and 400 adequate. Subscription to fewer than 200 periodicals generally implies an inferior library with a very tight budget. Microform items are assuming greater importance within a library's holdings, and this information is included when available. Services of a Learning Resource Center and special facilities, such as a museum, and radio or TV station are also described in this paragraph.

This paragraph also provides information on the campus: its size, the type of area in which it is located, and its proximity to a large city.

At most institutions, the existence of classrooms, administrative offices, and dining facilities may be taken for granted, and they generally are not mentioned in the entries unless they have been recently constructed or are considered exceptional.

Student Life

This section, with subdivisions that detail housing, campus activities, sports, facilities for handicapped students, and services offered to students, concentrates on the everyday life of students.

The introductory paragraph, which includes various characteristics of the student body, gives an idea of the mix of attitudes and backgrounds. It includes, where available, percentages of students from out-of-state and from private or public high schools. It also indicates what percentage of the students belong to minority groups and what percentages are Protestant, Catholic, and Jewish. Finally, it tells the average age of all enrolled freshmen and of all undergraduates, and gives data on the freshman dropout rate and the percentage of freshmen who remain to graduate.

Housing. Availability of on-campus housing is described here. If you plan to live on campus, note the type, quantity, and capacity of the dormitory accommodations. Some colleges provide dormitory rooms for freshmen, but require upperclass students to make their own arrangements to live in fraternity or sorority houses, off-campus apartments, or rented rooms in private houses. Many small colleges require all students who do not live with parents or other relatives to live on campus. Some colleges have no residence halls.

This paragraph tells whether special housing is available and whether campus housing is single-sex or coed. It gives the percentage of those who live on campus and those who remain on campus on weekends. Finally, it states if alcohol is not permitted on campus and whether students may keep cars on campus.

Activities. Campus organizations play a vital part in students' social lives. This subsection lists types of activities, including student government, special interest or academic clubs, fraternities and sororities, and cultural and popular campus events sponsored at the college.

Sports. Sports are important on campus, so we indicate the extent of the athletic program by giving the number of intercollegiate and intramural sports offered for men and for women. We have also included the athletic and recreation facilities and campus stadium seating capacity.

Disabled Students. The colleges' own estimates of how accessible their campuses are to the physically disabled are provided. This information should be considered along with the specific kinds of special facilities available. If a profile does not include a subsection on the disabled, the college did not provide the information.

Services. Services that may be available to students—free or for a fee—include health care, birth control information, day-care services, psychological, vocational, personal, and military students counseling, tutoring, remedial instruction, and reader service for the blind.

Programs of Study

Listed here are the bachelor's degrees granted, strongest and most popular majors, and whether associate, masters,

and doctoral degrees are awarded. Major areas of study have been included under broader general areas (shown in capital letters in the profiles) for quicker reference; however, the general areas do not necessarily correspond to the academic divisions of the college or university but are more career-oriented.

Required. Wherever possible, information on specific required courses and distribution requirements is supplied, in addition to the number of credits or hours required for graduation. If the college requires students to maintain a certain grade point average (GPA) or pass comprehensive exams to graduate, that also is given. Whether a computer course or physical education is required is mentioned here.

Special. Special programs are described here. Students at almost every college now have the opportunity to study abroad, either through their college or through other institutions. Internships with businesses, schools, hospitals, and public agencies permit students to gain work experience as they learn. The pass/fail grading option, now quite prevalent, allows students to take courses in unfamiliar areas without threatening their academic average. Many schools offer students the opportunity to earn a combined B.A.-B.S. degree, pursue a general studies (no major) degree, or design their own major. Frequently students may take advantage of a cooperative program offered by two or more universities. Such a program might be referred to, for instance, as a 3-2 engineering program; a student in this program would spend three years at one institution and two at another. The number of national honor societies represented on campus is included. Schools also may conduct honors programs for qualified students, either university-wide or in specific major fields, and these also are listed.

Faculty/Classroom. The percentage of male and female faculty are mentioned here if provided by the college. Also, the percentage of introductory courses taught by graduate students, if any. The average class size in an introductory lecture, laboratory, and regular class offering may also be indicated.

Admissions

The admissions section gives detailed information on standards so you can evaluate your chances for acceptance. Where the SAT I or ACT scores of the 1995–96 freshman class are broken down, you may compare your own scores. SAT I score ranges here reflect nonrecentered scores, unless otherwise noted (see explantion on page 28). Because the role of standardized tests in the admissions process has been subject to criticism, more colleges are considering other factors such as recommendations from high school officials, leadership record, special talents, extracurricular activities, and advanced placement or honors courses completed. A few schools may consider education of parents, ability to pay for college, and relationship to alumni. Some give preference to state residents; others seek a geographically diverse student body.

If a college indicates that it follows an open admissions policy, it is noncompetitive and generally accepts all applicants who meet certain basic requirements, such as graduation from an accredited high school. If a college has rolling admissions, it decides on each application as soon as possible if the applicant's file is complete and does not specify a notification deadline. As a general rule, it is best to submit applications as early as possible.

Some colleges offer special admissions programs for nontraditional applicants. Early admissions programs allow students to begin college either during the summer before their freshman year or during what would have been their last year of high school; in the latter case, a high school diploma is not required. These programs are designed for students who are emotionally and educationally prepared for college at an earlier age than usual.

Deferred admissions plans permit students to spend a year at another activity, such as working or traveling, before beginning college. Students who take advantage of this option can relax during the year off, because they already have been accepted at a college and have a space reserved. During the year off from study, many students become clearer about their educational goals, and they perform better when they do begin study.

Early decision plans allow students to be notified by their first-choice school during the first term of the senior year. This plan may eliminate the anxiety of deciding whether or not to send a deposit to a second-choice college that offers admission before the first-choice college responds.

The Ivy League institutions, along with the Massachusetts Institute of Technology, have adopted an early evaluation procedure under which applicants receive, between November 1 and February 15, an evaluation of their chances for admission. They are told that acceptance is likely, possible, or unlikely, or that the colleges have received insufficient evidence for evaluation. This information helps applicants decide whether to concentrate on another school. Final notification is made on a common date in April.

Requirements. This subsection specifies the minimum high school class rank and GPA, if any, required by the college for freshman applicants. It indicates what standardized tests (if any) are required, whether an essay, interview, or audition is necessary, and if AP/CLEP credit is given. If a college accepts applications on computer disk or on-line, those facts are so noted and described. Other factors used by the school in the admissions decision are also listed.

Procedure. This subsection indicates when you should take entrance exams, the application deadlines for various sessions, the application fee, and when students are notified of the admissions decision. Some schools note that their application deadlines are open; this can mean either that they will consider applications until a class is filled, or that applications are considered right up until registration for the term in which the student wishes to enroll. If a waiting list is an active part of the admissions procedure, the college may indicate what percentage of applicants are placed on that list.

Transfer. Nearly every college admits some transfer students. These students may have earned associate degrees at two-year colleges and want to continue their education at a four-year college or wish to attend a different school. One important thing to consider when transferring is how many credits earned at one school will be accepted at another, so entire semesters won't be spent making up lost work. Because most schools require students to spend a specified number of hours in residence to earn a degree, it is best not to wait too long to transfer if you decide to do so.

Visiting. Some colleges hold special orientation programs for prospective students to give them a better idea of what the school is like. Many also will provide guides for informal visits, often allowing students to spend a night in the residence halls. You should make arrangements with the college before visiting.

Financial Aid

This paragraph in each profile describes the availability of financial aid. It includes the percentage of freshmen and continuing students who receive aid, the average scholarship, loan, and work contract aid to freshmen, the average amount of need-based scholarships from all sources and the types and sources of aid available, such as scholarships, grants, loans, and work-study. It indicates if there is a formal appeal process for obtaining more money for the second semester. Aid application deadlines and required forms are also indicated.

International Students

This section begins by telling how many of the school's students come from outside the United States. It tells which English proficiency exam, if any, applicants must take and the minimum score required, if there is one. Any necessary college entrance exams, including SAT II: Subject tests, are listed, as are any minimum scores required on those exams.

Computers

This section details the make and model of the mainframe and the scope of computerized facilities that are available for academic use. Limitations (if any) on student use of computer facilities are outlined. It also gives information on the required or recommended ownership of a personal computer.

Graduates

This section gives the number of graduates in the 1994–95 class, the most popular majors and percentage of graduates earning degrees in those fields, and the percentages of men and women in the 1993–94 class who enrolled in graduate school or found employment within 6 months of graduation.

Admissions Contact

This is the name or title of the person to whom all correspondence regarding your application should be sent. E-mail addresses are included here, along with the availability of a video of the campus.

RECENTERED SAT I SCORES

In the spring of 1995, the results of SAT I: Reasoning tests administered by the Educational Testing Service (ETS) began being reported on a "recentered" basis. Thus, for example, a verbal score of 580 before the recentering would translate to a score of 650 after recentering.

This was done, according to ETS, to "make them easier to understand and to improve the technical characteristics of the test." The average SAT I score is now near the center of the scale—500—and the verbal and math average scores are aligned, so they can be compared directly to each other.

Generally speaking, members of the freshman class entering college in the fall of 1995 took their SAT I: Reasoning tests *before* the recentering took place—that is,

prior to April 1995. Thus, we have chosen to report nonrecentered SAT I scores in this edition of *Profiles of American Colleges Northeast*.

The users of this book, however, will in nearly all cases have taken the examinations *after* the recentering was instituted. Those scores, therefore, should not be compared to the scores reported here. The following conversion chart allows users either to adjust the reported scores to compare with their own, or to adjust their scores to compare with those reported in the capsule.

Similarly, the range of SAT I scores appearing in the "Admissions" paragraph of some profiles is based on the test-takers' nonrecentered scores, unless otherwise noted.

SAT I Conversion Table

VERBAL						MATH					
OLD	NEW	OLD	NEW	OLD	NEW	OLD	NEW	OLD	NEW	OLD	NEW
790	800	590	660	390	470	790	800	590	600	390	430
780	800	580	650	380	460	780	800	580	590	380	430
770	800	570	640	370	450	770	790	570	580	370	420
760	800	560	630	360	440	760	770	560	570	360	410
750	800	550	620	350	430	750	760	550	560	350	400
740	800	540	610	340	420	740	740	540	560	340	390
730	800	530	600	330	410	730	730	530	550	330	380
720	790	520	600	320	400	720	720	520	540	320	370
710	780	510	590	310	390	710	700	510	530	310	350
700	760	500	580	300	380	700	690	500	520	300	340
690	750	490	570	290	370	690	680	490	520	290	330
680	740	480	560	280	360	680	670	480	510	280	310
670	730	470	550	270	350	670	660	470	500	270	300
660	720	460	540	260	340	660	650	460	490	260	280
650	710	450	530	250	330	650	650	450	480	250	260
640	700	440	520	240	310	640	640	440	480	240	240
630	690	430	510	230	300	630	630	430	470	230	220
620	680	420	500	220	290	620	620	420	460	220	200
610	670	410	490	210	270	610	610	410	450	210	200
600	670	400	480	200	230	600	600	400	440	200	200

Source: *The New York Times*

DEGREES

A.A.—Associate of Arts
A.A.S.—Associate of Applied Science
A.B. or B.A.—Bachelor of Arts
A.B.J.—Bachelor of Arts in Journalism
A.S.—Associate of Science

B.A.A.—Bachelor of Applied Arts
B.A.A.S. or B.Applied A.S.—Bachelor of Applied Arts and Sciences
B.Ac. or B.Acc.—Bachelor of Accountancy
B.A.C.—Bachelor of Science in Air Commerce
B.A.C.V.I.—Bachelor of Arts in Computer and Video Imaging
B.A.E. or B.A.Ed.—Bachelor of Arts in Education
B.A.G.E.—Bachelor of Arts in General Education
B.Agri.—Bachelor of Agriculture
B.A.G.S.—Bachelor of Arts in General Studies
B.A.J.S.—Bachelor of Arts in Judaic Studies
B.A.M.—Bachelor of Arts in Music
B.Applied Sc.—Bachelor of Applied Science
B.A.R.—Bachelor of Religion
B.Arch.—Bachelor of Architecture
B.Arch.Hist.—Bachelor of Architectural History
B.Arch.Tech.—Bachelor of Architectural Technology
B.Ar.Sc.—Baccalaurium Artium et Scientiae (honors college degree) (Bachelor of Arts & Sciences)
B.Art.Ed.—Bachelor of Art Education
B.A.S.—Bachelor of Arts and Sciences
B.A.Sec.Ed.—Bachelor of Arts in Secondary Ed.
B.A.S.W.—B.A. in Social Work
B.A.T.—Bachelor of Arts in Teaching
B.B. or B.Bus.—Bachelor of Business
B.B.A.—Bachelor of Business Administration
B.B.E.—Bachelor of Business Education
B.C. or B.Com. or B.Comm.—Bachelor of Commerce
B.C.A.—Bachelor of Creative Arts
B.C.E.—Bachelor of Civil Engineering
B.C.E.—Bachelor of Computer Engineering
B.Ch. or B.Chem.—Bachelor of Chemistry
B.Ch.E.—Bachelor of Chemical Engineering
B.C.J.—Bachelor of Criminal Justice
B.C.M.—Bachelor of Christian Ministries
B.Church Mus.—Bachelor of Church Music
B.C.S.—Bachelor of College Studies
B.E.—Bachelor of English
B.E. or B.Ed.—Bachelor of Education
B.E.—Bachelor of Engineering
B.E.D.—Bachelor of Environmental Design
B.E.E.—Bachelor of Electrical Engineering
B.En. or B.Eng.—Bachelor of Engineering
B.E.S. or B.Eng.Sc.—Bachelor of Engineering Science
B.E.T.—Bachelor of Engineering Technology
B.F.A.—Bachelor of Fine Arts
B.G.S.—Bachelor of General Studies
B.G.S.—Bachelor of Geological Sciences
B.H.E.—Bachelor of Health Education
B.H.S.—Bachelor of Health Science
B.H.P.E.—Bachelor of Health and Physical Education
B.I.D.—Bachelor of Industrial Design
B.I.M.—Bachelor of Industrial Management
B.Ind.Tech.—Bachelor of Industrial Technology
B.Int.Arch.—Bachelor of Interior Architecture
B.Int.Design—Bachelor of Interior Design
B.I.S.—Bachelor of Industrial Safety
B.I.S.—Bachelor of Interdisciplinary Studies
B.J.—Bachelor of Journalism
B.J.S.—Bachelor of Judaic Studies
B.L.A. or B.Lib.Arts—Bachelor of Liberal Arts
B.L.A. or B.Land.Arch.—Bachelor in Landscape Architecture
B.L.I.—Bachelor of Literary Interpretation
B.L.S.—Bachelor of Liberal Studies
B.M. or B.Mus. or Mus.Bac.—Bachelor of Music
B.M.E.—Bachelor of Mechanical Engineering
B.M.E. or B.M.Ed. or B.Mus.Ed.—Bachelor of Music Education

B.Med.Lab.Sc.—Bachelor of Medical Laboratory Science
B.Min—Bachelor of Ministry
B.M.P. or B.Mu.—Bachelor of Music in Performance
B.Mus.A.—Bachelor of Applied Music
B.M.T.—Bachelor of Music Therapy
B.O.T.—Bachelor of Occupational Therapy
B.P.A.—Bachelor of Public Administration
B.P.E.—Bachelor of Physical Education
B.Perf.Arts—Bachelor of Performing Arts
B.Ph.—Bachelor of Philosophy
B.Pharm.—Bachelor of Pharmacy
B.Phys.Hlth.Ed.—Bachelor of Physical Health Education
B.P.S.—Bachelor of Professional Studies
B.P.T.—Bachelor of Physical Therapy
B.R.E.—Bachelor of Religious Education
B.R.T.—Bachelor of Respiratory Therapy
B.S. or B.Sc. or S.B.—Bachelor of Science
B.S.A. or B.S.Ag. or B.S.Agr.—Bachelor of Science in Agriculture
B.Sacred Mus.—Bachelor of Sacred Music
B.Sacred Theol.—Bachelor of Sacred Theology
B.S.A.E.—Bachelor of Science in Agricultural Engineering
B.S.A.E. or B.S.Art Ed.—Bachelor of Science in Art Education
B.S.Ag.E.—Bachelor of Science in Agricultural Engineering
B.S.A.S.—Bachelor of Science in Administrative Sciences
B.S.B.—Bachelor of Science (business)
B.S.B.A. or B.S.Bus. Adm.—Bachelor of Science in Business Administration
B.S.Bus.—Bachelor of Science in Business
B.S.Bus.Ed.—Bachelor of Science in Business Education
B.S.C.—Bachelor of Science in Commerce
B.S.C.E. or B.S.C.I.E.—Bachelor of Science in Civil Engineering
B.S.C.E.T—B.S. in Computer Engineering Technology
B.S.Ch. or B.S.Chem. or B.S. in Ch.—Bachelor of Science in Chemistry
B.S.C.H.—Bachelor of Science in Community Health
B.S.Ch.E.—Bachelor of Science in Chemical Engineering
B.S.C.I.S.—Bachelor of Science in Computer Information Sciences
B.S.C.J.—Bachelor of Science in Criminal Justice
B.S.Comp.Eng.—Bachelor of Science in Computer Engineering
B.S.Comp.Sci. or B.S.C.S.—Bachelor of Science in Computer Science
B.S.Comp.Soft—Bachelor of Science in Computer Software
B.S.Comp.Tech.—Bachelor of Science in Computer Technology
B.Sc.(P.T.)—Bachelor of Science in Physical Therapy
B.S.C.S.T.—Bachelor of Science in Computer Science Technology
B.S.D.H.—Bachelor of Science in Dental Hygiene
B.S.Die—Bachelor of Science in Dietetics
B.S.E. or B.S.Ed. or B.S.Educ.—Bachelor of Science in Education
B.S.E. or B.S in E. or B.S. in Eng.—Bachelor of Science in Engineering
B.S.E.E.—Bachelor of Science in Electrical Engineering
B.S.E.E.T.—Bachelor of Science in Electrical Engineering Technology
B.S.E.H.—Bachelor of Science in Environmental Health
B.S.Elect.T.—Bachelor of Science in Electronics Technology
B.S.El.Ed. or B.S. in Elem. Ed.—Bachelor of Science in Elementary Education
B.S.E.P.H.—Bachelor of Science in Environmental and Public Health
B.S.E.S.—Bachelor of Science in Engineering Science
B.S.E.S.—Bachelor of Science in Environmental Studies
B.S.E.T.—Bachelor of Science in Engineering Technology
B.S.F.—Bachelor of Science in Forestry
B.S.F.R.—Bachelor of Science in Forestry Resources
B.S.F.W.—Bachelor of Science in Fisheries and Wildlife
B.S.G.—Bachelor of Science in Geology
B.S.G.—Bachelor of Science in Gerontology
B.S.G.E.—Bachelor of Science in Geological Engineering
B.S.G.S.—Bachelor of Science in General Studies

B.S.H.C.A.—Bachelor of Science in Health Care Administration
B.S.H.E.—Bachelor of Science in Home Economics
B.S.H.S.—Bachelor of Science in Health Sciences
B.S.H.S.—Bachelor of Science in Human Services
B.S.I.A.—Bachelor of Science in Industrial Arts
B.S.I.E.—Bachelor of Science in Industrial Engineering
B.S.I.M.—Bachelor of Science in Industrial Management
B.S. in Biomed.Eng.—Bachelor of Science in Biomedical Engineering
B.S. in C.D.—Bachelor of Science in Communication Disorders
B.S.Ind.Ed.—Bachelor of Science in Industrial Education
B.S.Ind.Tech.—Bachelor of Science in Industrial Technology
B.S. in Sec.Ed.—Bachelor of Science in Secondary Education
B.S.I.S.—Bachelor of Science in Interdisciplinary Studies
B.S.I.T.—Bachelor of Science in Industrial Technology
B.S.J.—Bachelor of Science in Journalism
B.S.L.E.—Bachelor of Science in Law Enforcement
B.S.M.—Bachelor of Science in Management
B.S.M.—Bachelor of Science in Music
B.S.M.E.—Bachelor of Science in Mechanical Engineering
B.S.Med.Tech. or B.S.M.T.—Bachelor of Science in Medical Technology
B.S.Met.E.—Bachelor of Science in Metallurgical Engineering
B.S.M.R.A.—Bachelor of Science in Medical Records Administration
B.S.Mt.E.—Bachelor of Science in Materials Engineering
B.S.Mus.Ed.—Bachelor of Science in Music Education
B.S.N.—Bachelor of Science in Nursing
B.S.Nuc.T.—Bachelor of Science in Nuclear Technology
B.S.O.A.—Bachelor of Science in Office Administration
B.S.O.E.—Bachelor of Science in Occupational Education
B.S.O.T.—Bachelor of Science in Occupational Therapy
B.S.P. or B.S.Pharm—Bachelor of Science in Pharmacy
B.S.P.A.—Bachelor of Science in Public Administration
B.S.Pcs.—Bachelor of Science in Physics
B.S.P.E.—Bachelor of Science in Physical Education
B.S.P.T.—Bachelor of Science in Physical Therapy
B.S.Rad.Tech.—Bachelor of Science in Radiation Technology
B.S.S.—Bachelor of Science in Surveying
B.S.S.—Bachelor of Special Studies
B.S.S.A.—Bachelor of Science in Systems Analysis
B.S.Soc. Work or B.S.S.W.—Bachelor of Science in Social Work
B.S.Sp.—Bachelor of Science in Speech
B.S.S.T.—Bachelor of Science in Surveying and Topography
B.S.T. or B.S.Tech.—Bachelor of Science in Technology
B.S.S.W.E.—Bachelor of Science in Software Engineering
B.S.V.T.E.—Bachelor of Science in Vocational Technical Education
B.S.W.—Bachelor of Social Work
B.T. or B.Tech.—Bachelor of Technology
B.Th.—Bachelor of Theology
B.T.S.—Bachelor of Technical Studies
B.U.S.—Bachelor of Urban Studies
B.V.M.—Bachelor of Veterinarian Medicine
B.Voc.Arts or B.V.A.—Bachelor of Vocational Arts
B.V.E.D. or B.Voc.Ed.—Bachelor of Vocational Education

S.B. or B.S. or B.Sc.—Bachelor of Science

OTHER ABBREVIATIONS

AACSB—American Assembly of Collegiate Schools of Business
ABET—Accreditation Board for Engineering and Technology
ABFSE—American Board of Funeral Service Education
ABHES—Accrediting Bureau of Health Education Schools
ACBSP—Association of Collegiate Business Schools and Programs
ACE JMC—American Council on Education in Journalism and Mass Communication
ACPE—Association for Clinical Pastoral Education, Inc.

ACPE—American Council on Pharmaceutical Education
ACT—American College Testing Program
ADA—American Dietetic Association
ADA—American Dental Association

BEOG—Basic Educational Opportunity Grant (now Pell Grant)

CAS—Certificate of Advanced Study
CEEB—College Entrance Examination Board
CELT—Comprehensive English Language Test
CEPH—Council on Education for Public Health
CLAST—College Level Academic Skills Test
CLEP—College-Level Examination Program
CRDA—Candidates Reply Date Agreement
CRE—Council on Rehabilitation Education
CSAB—Computing Science Accreditation Board
CSS—College Scholarship Service
CSWE—Council on Social Work Education
CWS—College Work-Study

EESL—Examination of English as a Second Language
ELS/ALA—English Language Services/American Language Academy
EMH—Educable Mentally Handicapped
EOP—Equal Opportunity Program
ESL—English as a Second Language
ETS—Educational Testing Service

FAF—Financial Aid Form
FAFSA—Free Application for Federal Student Aid
FFS—Family Financial Statement
FIDER—Foundation for Interior Design Education Research
FISL—Federally Insured Student Loan

GED—General Educational Development (high school equivalency examination)
GPA—Grade Point Average
GRE—Graduate Record Examination
GSLP—Guaranteed Student Loan Program

HEOP—Higher Equal Opportunity Program
HPER—Health, Physical Education, and Recreation

MELAB—Michigan English Language Assessment Battery

NAAB—National Architectural Accrediting Board
NASAD—National Association of Schools of Art and Design
NASDTEC—National Association of State Development Teacher Education
NASM—National Association of Schools of Music
NCATE—National Council for Accreditation of Teacher Education
NLN—National League for Nursing
NRPA—National Recreation and Park Association

PCS—Parents' Confidential Statement
PAIR—PHEAA Aid Information Request
PHEAA—Pennsylvania Higher Education Assistance Agency
PSAT/NMSQT—Preliminary SAT/National Merit Scholarship Qualifying Test

SAF—Society of American Foresters
SAM—Single Application Method
SAR—Student Aid Report
SAT—Scholastic Assessment Testing (formerly ATP—Admissions Testing Program)
SCAT—Scholastic College Aptitude Test
SCS—Students' Confidential Statement
SEOG—Supplementary Educational Opportunity Grant

TAP—Tuition Assistance Program (New York State)
TDD—Telecommunication Device for the Deaf
TOEFL—Test of English as a Foreign Language

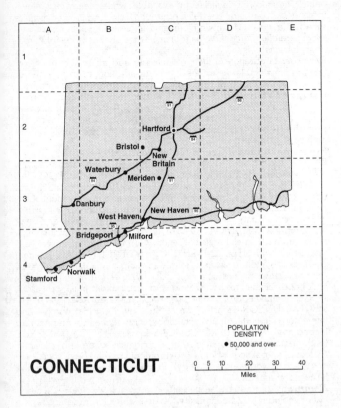

CONNECTICUT

POPULATION DENSITY

● 50,000 and over

0 5 10 20 30 40

Miles

ALBERTUS MAGNUS COLLEGE   C-3
New Haven, CT 06511-1189

(203) 773-8501
(800) 578-9160; FAX: (203) 773-9539

Full-time: 241 men, 433 women	Faculty: 36; IIB, -$
Part-time: 54 men, 187 women	Ph.D.s: 90%
Graduate: 4 men, 16 women	Student/Faculty: 19 to 1
Year: trimesters, summer session	Tuition: $12,520
Application Deadline: open	Room & Board: $5664
Freshman Class: 530 applied, 251 accepted, 91 enrolled	
SAT I Verbal/Math: 406/411	**COMPETITIVE**

Albertus Magnus College, founded in 1925, is affiliated with the Roman Catholic Church and operated by the Dominican Sisters of St. Mary of the Springs. The college offers undergraduate and graduate degrees in the liberal arts and sciences and in business. The library contains 115,000 volumes, 6000 microform items, and 984 audiovisual forms, and subscribes to 501 periodicals. Computerized library sources and services include the card catalog, interlibrary loans, and database searching. Special learning facilities include a learning resource center and a theater. The 55-acre campus is in a suburban area 80 miles from New York City. Including residence halls, there are 17 buildings on campus.

Student Life: 60% of undergraduates are from Connecticut. Students come from 15 states and 8 foreign countries. 50% are from public schools; 50% from private. 81% are white. Most are Catholic. The average age of freshmen is 19; all undergraduates, 22. 10% do not continue beyond their first year; 70% remain to graduate.

Housing: 500 students can be accommodated in college housing. College-sponsored living facilities include single-sex and coed dormitories. Residence halls are old mansions that have been converted into student housing. Each building houses 15 to 65 students. On-campus housing is guaranteed for all 4 years. 60% of students live on campus; of those, 60% remain on campus on weekends. All students may keep cars on campus.

Activities: There are no fraternities or sororities. There are 20 groups on campus, including art, choir, chorale, chorus, computers, dance, drama, ethnic, honors, international, literary magazine, musical theater, newspaper, orchestra, photography, political, professional, religious, social, social service, student government, and yearbook. Popular campus events include Fall Candlelight Ceremony, Christmas events, and Laurel Day.

Sports: There are 7 intercollegiate sports for men and 7 for women, and 10 intramural sports for men and 10 for women. Athletic and recreation facilities include an Olympic-size pool, a gymnasium, indoor and outdoor tracks, racquetball and volleyball courts, weight and dance rooms, soccer and softball fields, 4 tennis courts, and a game room.

Disabled Students: The entire campus is accessible to disabled students. The following facilities are available: wheelchair ramps, elevators, special parking, specially equipped rest rooms, special class scheduling, lowered drinking fountains, and lowered telephones.

Services: In addition to many counseling and information services, tutoring is available in every subject. There is remedial math, reading, and writing.

Campus Safety and Security: Campus safety and security measures include 24-hour foot and vehicle patrol, shuttle buses, informal discussions, and pamphlets/posters/films. In addition, there are lighted pathways/sidewalks.

Programs of Study: Albertus Magnus confers B.A. and B.F.A. degrees. Associate and master's degrees are also awarded. Bachelor's degrees are awarded in BIOLOGICAL SCIENCE (biology/biological science), BUSINESS (accounting and business economics), COMMUNICATIONS AND THE ARTS (classics, communications, dramatic arts, English, fine arts, French, Italian, romance languages, and Spanish), COMPUTER AND PHYSICAL SCIENCE (mathematics and physical sciences), HEALTH PROFESSIONS (health care administration, predentistry, premedicine, and preveterinary science), SOCIAL SCIENCE (criminology, economics, history, human services, humanities, industrial and organizational psychology, liberal arts/general studies, philosophy, political science/government, prelaw, psychology, religion, sociology, and urban studies). Liberal arts is the strongest academically. Business/economics, English, and psychology have the largest enrollments.

Required: To graduate, all students must complete at least 120 credit hours, including 60 outside the major and 30 in the major. General education requirements, including 6 credits each in English, humanities, and foreign language and 3 each of fine arts, mathematics, and science must be fulfilled. A minimum 2.0 GPA is required.

Special: The college offers cross-registration with Quinnipiac College and the University of New Haven, junior- and senior-year internships allowing up to 15 credits, study abroad, a Washington semester, work-study programs, and accelerated degree programs in business and economics, communications, English, humanities, and general studies. Also available are dual and student-designed majors, nondegree study, pass/fail options, independent study, and preprofessional programs. Students may take accelerated degree programs in the evening or take weekend courses. A summer theater workshop is offered. There is a freshman honors program on campus, as well as 10 national honor societies. 12 departments have honors programs.

Faculty/Classroom: 46% of faculty are male; 54%, female. All teach undergraduates, 60% do research. No introductory courses are taught by graduate students. The average class size in an introductory lecture is 20; in a laboratory, 10; and in a regular course offering, 15.

Admissions: 47% of the 1995–96 applicants were accepted. The SAT I Verbal scores for the 1995–96 freshman class were as follows: 75% below 500, 20% between 500 and 599, and 5% between 600 and 700. 22% of the current freshmen were in the top fifth of their class; 42% were in the top two fifths.

Requirements: The SAT I is required, with a minimum recommended composite score of 800. Albertus Magnus requires applicants to be in the upper 50% of their class. A minimum GPA of 2.5 is required. Applicants must be graduates of an accredited secondary school or have a GED certificate and have completed 16 academic credits, including 4 years of English, 2 or 3 years each of foreign language, mathematics, and science, 2 years of history, and 1 year of social studies. High school transcripts, rank, and 2 letters of recommendation are required. The SAT II: Writing test and an interview are recommended. AP and CLEP credits are accepted. Important factors in the admissions decision are advanced placement or honor courses, recommendations by school officials, and leadership record.

Procedure: Freshmen are admitted fall, winter, and spring. Entrance exams should be taken between April of the junior year and November of the senior year. There are early decision and deferred admissions plans. Application deadlines are open. Application fee is $30. Notification of early decision is sent November 15; regular decision, on a rolling basis.

Transfer: 29 transfer students enrolled in 1995–96. Transfer students must present a minimum 2.0 overall GPA, and a 2.0 GPA for all transferable, compatible course work. 45 credits of 120 must be completed at Albertus Magnus.

Visiting: There are regularly scheduled orientations for prospective students, consisting of registration, a general introduction, a financial aid/major introduction, lunch, a campus tour, and an interview. Visitors may sit in on classes and stay overnight at the school. To schedule a visit, contact the Admissions Office.

Financial Aid: In a recent year, 75% of all freshmen and 70% of continuing students received some form of financial aid. 75% of freshmen and 70% of continuing students received need-based aid. The average freshman award was $5568. Of that total, scholarships or need-based grants averaged $1027; loans averaged $2504; work contracts averaged $600; and non-need-based aid averaged $2037. 3% of undergraduate students work part-time. Average earnings from campus work for the school year are $600. Albertus Magnus is a member of CSS. The FAF and the college's own financial statement are required. The application deadline for fall entry is February 15.

International Students: There were 33 international students enrolled in a recent year. They must take the TOEFL and achieve a minimum score of 500. The student must also take the SAT I or the ACT.

Computers: The college provides computer facilities for student use. The mainframe is a Prime 2450. There are also 25 terminals and 10 personal computers available for student use in the computer center and the library. All students may access the system 9 A.M. to 5 P.M. There are no time limits and no fees.

Graduates: In 1994–95, 199 bachelor's degrees were awarded. The most popular majors among graduates were business/economics (35%), English (17%), and communications (17%). Within an average freshman class, 50% graduate in 3 years, 25% in 4 years, and 25% in 5 years. 12 companies recruited on campus in 1994–95.

Admissions Contact: Richard Lolatte, Dean of Admissions and Enrollment Management.

BRIDGEPORT ENGINEERING INSTITUTE
(See Fairfield University)

CENTRAL CONNECTICUT STATE UNIVERSITY C-2
New Britain, CT 06050 (860) 832-2278

Full-time: 2903 men, 2961 women	Faculty: 367; IIA, +$
Part-time: 1686 men, 1886 women	Ph.D.s: 70%
Graduate: 758 men, 1558 women	Student/Faculty: 16 to 1
Year: semesters, summer session	Tuition: $3266 ($8358)
Application Deadline: May 1	Room & Board: $4380
Freshman Class: 3801 applied, 2588 accepted, 1070 enrolled	
SAT I Verbal/Math: 480/470	COMPETITIVE

Central Connecticut State University, founded in 1849, offers degree programs in liberal arts, engineering technology, business, and education. It is part of the Connecticut State University system. There are 4 undergraduate schools and one graduate school. In addition to regional accreditation, Central Connecticut has baccalaureate program accreditation with ABET, NCATE, and NLN. The library contains 545,463 volumes, 453,555 microform items, and 805 audiovisual forms, and subscribes to 3108 periodicals. Computerized library sources and services include the card catalog, interlibrary loans, and database searching. Special learning facilities include a learning resource center, art gallery, planetarium, radio station, a writing center, and a mathematics center. The 152-acre campus is in a suburban area 10 miles west of Hartford. Including residence halls, there are 30 buildings on campus.

Student Life: 94% of undergraduates are from Connecticut. Students come from 25 states, 30 foreign countries, and Canada. 85% are white. 41% are Catholic; 43% claim no religious affiliation. The average age of freshmen is 18; all undergraduates, 21. 27% do not continue beyond their first year; 45% remain to graduate.

Housing: 1700 students can be accommodated in college housing. College-sponsored living facilities include single-sex and coed dormitories. In addition there are honors houses and special interest houses. On-campus housing is guaranteed for all 4 years. 75% of students commute. All students may keep cars on campus.

Activities: 1% of men and about 1% of women belong to 1 national fraternity; 1% of women belong to 1 local sorority and 1 national sorority. There are 100 groups on campus, including art, band, cheerleading, choir, chorale, chorus, computers, dance, drama, ethnic, gay, honors, international, literary magazine, marching band, newspaper, orchestra, pep band, photography, political, professional, radio and TV, religious, social, social service, student government, and yearbook. Popular campus events include Winter and Spring weekends, First Week, International Festival, and planetarium shows.

Sports: There are 11 intercollegiate sports for men and 9 for women, and 11 intramural sports for men and 11 for women. Athletic and recreation facilities include a 4500-seat gymnasium, 8 tennis courts, a 6000-seat football stadium, a softball field, a baseball field, a soccer field, and a 3700-square-foot air-supported recreation facility.

Disabled Students: 90% of the campus is accessible to disabled students. The following facilities are available: wheelchair ramps, elevators, special parking, specially equipped rest rooms, special class scheduling, lowered drinking fountains, and lowered telephones. Personal care attendants serve as roommates for physically disabled resident students.

Services: In addition to many counseling and information services, tutoring is available in some subjects. In addition, there is a reader service for the blind, and remedial math, reading, and writing.

Campus Safety and Security: Campus safety and security measures include 24-hour foot and vehicle patrol, self-defense education, escort service, and informal discussions. In addition, there are pamphlets/posters/films, emergency telephones, and lighted pathways/sidewalks.

Programs of Study: Central Connecticut confers B.A., B.S., B.F.A., B.S.E.D., B.S.E.T., B.S.I.T., and B.S.N. degrees. Master's degrees are also awarded. Bachelor's degrees are awarded in BIOLOGICAL SCIENCE (biology/biological science), BUSINESS (accounting, banking and finance, business administration and management, international business management, management information systems, marketing/retailing/merchandising, and office supervision and management), COMMUNICATIONS AND THE ARTS (art, communications, dramatic arts, English, French, German, Italian, music, and Spanish), COMPUTER AND PHYSICAL SCIENCE (actuarial science, chemistry, computer science, earth science, mathematics, physical sciences, physics, and science), EDUCATION (art, business, early childhood, elementary, marketing and distribution, music, physical, special, technical, and vocational), ENGINEERING AND ENVIRONMENTAL DESIGN (construction technology, industrial engineering technology, manufacturing technology, and mechanical engineering technology), HEALTH PROFESSIONS (nursing), SOCIAL SCIENCE (anthropology, East Asian studies, economics, geography, history, philosophy, political science/government, psychology, social science, social work, and sociology). Business and education have the largest enrollments.

Required: To graduate, all students must complete at least 122 credit hours, including 62 hours in the general education program, with a minimum GPA of 2.0.

Special: The university offers co-op programs and cross-registration with several other Connecticut educational institutions, study abroad in more than 35 countries, internships in most departments, work-study programs, dual majors, and student-designed majors. There is a freshman honors program on campus, as well as 7 national honor societies. One department has an honors program.

Faculty/Classroom: 65% of faculty are male; 35%, female. All teach undergraduates. No introductory courses are taught by graduate students. The average class size in an introductory lecture is 35; in a laboratory, 20; and in a regular course offering, 25.

Admissions: 68% of the 1995–96 applicants were accepted. The SAT I scores for the 1995–96 freshman class were as follows: Verbal—60% below 500, 32% between 500 and 599, 7% between 600 and 700, and 1% above 700; Math—65% below 500, 29% between 500 and 599, and 6% between 600 and 700. 14% of the current freshmen were in the top fifth of their class; 42% were in the top two fifths.

Requirements: The SAT I is required, with recommended minimum scores of 480 verbal and 440 mathematics. A minimum GPA of 2.0 is reuqired. An interview is also recommended. Central Connecticut recommends that applicants have 13 academic credits: 4 in English, 3 in mathematics, and 2 each in foreign language, science, and social studies. The GED is accepted. AP and CLEP credits are accepted. Important factors in the admissions decision are extracurricular activities record, recommendations by school officials, and advanced placement or honor courses.

Procedure: Freshmen are admitted fall and spring. Entrance exams should be taken in May of the junior year and November of the senior year. There are early admissions and deferred admissions plans. Applications should be filed by May 1 for fall entry and November 1 for spring entry, along with an application fee of $20. Notification is sent on a rolling basis.

Transfer: 624 transfer students enrolled in 1995–96. Transfer applicants must have a minimum of 12 transferrable credits and a GPA of 2.0. 45 credits of 122 must be completed at Central Connecticut.

Visiting: There are regularly scheduled orientations for prospective students, including a fall open house in October and daily and select Saturday visits throughout fall and spring. There are guides for informal visits and visitors may sit in on classes. To schedule a visit, contact the Admissions Office.

Financial Aid: In 1995–96, 37% of all freshmen and 27% of continuing students received some form of financial aid. 25% of freshmen and 17% of continuing students received need-based aid. The average freshman award was $4500. Of that total, scholarships or need-based grants averaged $1000 ($8000 maximum); loans averaged

$1850 ($8500 maximum); and work contracts averaged $600 ($1000 maximum). 35% of undergraduate students work part-time. Average earnings from campus work for the school year are $1000. The average financial indebtedness of the 1994–95 graduate was $6000. Central Connecticut is a member of CSS. The FAFSA is required. The application deadline for fall entry is April 22.

International Students: 131 international students were enrolled in a recent year. They must take the TOEFL and achieve a minimum score of 500.

Computers: The college provides computer facilities for student use. The mainframe is a DEC VAX 7000/640. The microcomputer laboratory provides numerous networked microcomputers as well as terminals connected to the mainframe. Additional terminals are located in other buildings. Another laboratory provides a variety of Apple and Macintosh microcomputers for general student use. All students may access the system 8:30 A.M. to 12 P.M., Monday to Thursday; 8:30 A.M. to 6 P.M., Friday; 9 A.M. to 6 P.M., Saturday; and 1 P.M. to 10 P.M., Sunday. There are no time limits and no fees.

Graduates: In a recent year, 1404 bachelor's degrees were awarded. The most popular majors among graduates were education (13%), accounting (9%), and psychology (8%). Within an average freshman class, 15% graduate in 4 years, 40% in 5 years, and 45% in 6 years. 63 companies recruited on campus in 1994–95. Of the 1994 graduating class, 20% were enrolled in graduate school within 6 months of graduation and 70% had found employment.

Admissions Contact: Admissions Office.

CHARTER OAK STATE COLLEGE C-2
Newington, CT 06111-2646

(860) 666-4595 ext. 23
FAX: (860) 666-4852

Full-time: none	Faculty: 63 part-time
Part-time: 590 men, 608 women	Ph.D.s: 76%
Graduate: none	Student/Faculty: n/app
Year: n/app	Tuition: $360 ($540)
Application Deadline: open	Room & Board: n/app
Freshman Class: n/av	
SAT I or ACT: not required	SPECIAL

Charter Oak State College, founded in 1973, is a public, coeducational liberal arts institution offering an external degree program for adult students who cannot complete a college degree by conventional means because of family, job, or financial considerations. Credits may be earned by transfer, testing, portfolio review, and contract learning. The offices are in a suburban area 7 miles south of Hartford.

Student Life: 81% of undergraduates are from Connecticut. Students come from 42 states and 3 foreign countries. 89% are white.

Housing: There are no residence halls.

Disabled Students: The entire college is accessible to disabled students. The following facilities are available: wheelchair ramps, elevators, special parking, specially equipped rest rooms, and lowered drinking fountains.

Programs of Study: Charter Oak confers B.A. and B.S. degrees. Associate degrees are also awarded. Bachelor's degrees are awarded with concentrations in BIOLOGICAL SCIENCE (biology/biological science), BUSINESS (business administration and management), COMMUNICATIONS AND THE ARTS (applied art, art history and appreciation, communications, languages, literature, and music), COMPUTER AND PHYSICAL SCIENCE (chemistry, computer science, geology, mathematics, natural sciences, physics, and science technology), ENGINEERING AND ENVIRONMENTAL DESIGN (technological management), SOCIAL SCIENCE (economics, fire control and safety technology, geography, history, human services, humanities, interdisciplinary studies, philosophy, political science/government, psychology, social science, and sociology). Business, human services, and interdisciplinary studies have the largest enrollments.

Required: All students must complete 120 total credits, 60 of which should be in liberal arts and 36 in the field of concentration. Distribution should include 12 credits in humanities, 9 in social science, 4 to 6 in sciences, and 3 in mathematics. Students also need to maintain a minimum GPA of 2.0 and earn credits in English composition and history or political science.

Special: Accelerated degree programs, student-designed majors, and B.A.-B.S. degrees are available in all fields of concentration.

Faculty/Classroom: 59% of faculty are male; 41%, female.

Requirements: Charter Oak State College requires applicants to have either a high school diploma or an equivalency certificate and to have earned at least 9 credits from an accredited college or university. AP and CLEP credits are accepted.

Procedure: Application deadlines are open. Application fee is $30. Notification is sent on a rolling basis.

Transfer: 485 transfer students enrolled in a recent year. Most students who enroll in Charter Oak State College have attended college previously.

Financial Aid: Some college fees may be waived for students who demonstrate financial need and show academic promise.

Graduates: In 1994–95, 249 bachelor's degrees were awarded. The most popular majors among graduates were business (25%), human services (10%), and interdisciplinary studies (10%). Of the 1994 graduating class, 40% were enrolled in graduate school within 12 months of graduation.

Admissions Contact: Ruth Budlong, Dean of Program Services and Public Information. E-mail: rbudlong@commnet.edu.

CONNECTICUT COLLEGE E-3
New London, CT 06320-4195

(860) 439-2200
FAX: (860) 439-4301

Full-time: 706 men, 909 women	Faculty: 163; IIB, +$
Part-time: 101 men, 142 women	Ph.D.s: 97%
Graduate: 14 men, 41 women	Student/Faculty: 10 to 1
Year: semesters	Tuition: $26,325
Application Deadline: January 15	Room & Board: see profile
Freshman Class: 3151 applied, 1571 accepted, 453 enrolled	
SAT I Verbal/Math: 590/620	ACT: 25 HIGHLY COMPETITIVE

Connecticut College, founded in 1911, is a private coeducational institution offering degree programs in the liberal arts and sciences. Tuition, room and board are combined in a comprehensive fee. The library contains 456,706 volumes, 259,101 microform items, and 17,446 audiovisual forms, and subscribes to 2161 periodicals. Computerized library sources and services include the card catalog, interlibrary loans, and database searching. Special learning facilities include a radio station and an arboretum. The 702-acre campus is in a small town midway between Boston and New York City. Including residence halls, there are 51 buildings on campus.

Student Life: 76% of undergraduates are from out-of-state, mostly the Northeast. Students come from 47 states, 51 foreign countries, and Canada. 51% are from public schools. 82% are white. 30% are Protestant; 26% Catholic; 14% claim no religious affiliation; 10% Jewish. The average age of freshmen is 18; all undergraduates, 19.4. 9% do not continue beyond their first year; 87% remain to graduate.

Housing: 1625 students can be accommodated in college housing. College-sponsored living facilities include coed dormitories. In addition there are language houses and special interest houses. On-campus housing is guaranteed for all 4 years. 98% of students live on campus; of those, 85% remain on campus on weekends. All students may keep cars on campus.

Activities: There are no fraternities or sororities. There are 75 groups on campus, including art, chess, choir, chorale, computers, dance, drama, ethnic, film, gay, honors, international, jazz band, literary magazine, musical theater, newspaper, orchestra, photography, political, radio and TV, religious, social, social service, student government, symphony, and yearbook. Popular campus events include Eclipse Weekend, Harvestfest, and Floralia.

Sports: There are 11 intercollegiate sports for men and 12 for women, and 4 intramural sports for men, 2 for women, and 10 coed. Athletic and recreation facilities include an 800-seat gymnasium, playing fields, an ice rink, a boat house, a weight training room, an indoor pool, a dance studio, 12 tennis courts, and courts for squash, racquetball, badminton, basketball, and volleyball.

Disabled Students: 25% of the campus is accessible to disabled students. The following facilities are available: wheelchair ramps, elevators, special parking, specially equipped rest rooms, special class scheduling, lowered drinking fountains, and lowered telephones.

Services: In addition to many counseling and information services, tutoring is available in most subjects.

Campus Safety and Security: Campus safety and security measures include 24-hour foot and vehicle patrol, escort service, informal discussions, and pamphlets/posters/films. In addition, there are emergency telephones, lighted pathways/sidewalks, and an electronic access system in student residences.

Programs of Study: Connecticut College confers the B.A. degree. Master's degrees are also awarded. Bachelor's degrees are awarded in BIOLOGICAL SCIENCE (biochemistry, biology/biological science, botany, and zoology), COMMUNICATIONS AND THE ARTS (art history and appreciation, Chinese, classics, dance, dramatic arts, English, French, German, Japanese, languages, music, and studio art), COMPUTER AND PHYSICAL SCIENCE (chemistry, mathematics, and physics), SOCIAL SCIENCE (anthropology, Asian/Oriental studies, child psychology/development, economics, Hispanic American studies, history, international relations, philosophy, political science/government, psychology, religion, sociology, and urban studies). Government, history, and economics have the largest enrollments.

Required: To graduate, students must complete at least 128 credit hours with a minimum GPA of 2.0. Distribution requirements cover 7 courses from 7 academic areas, plus a foreign language.

Special: Cross-registration with area colleges, internships in government, human services, and other fields, a Washington semester at American University, dual majors, student-designed majors, a 3–2 engineering degree with Washington University in St. Louis, nondegree study, and pass/fail options are available. One third of the junior class studies abroad. An international studies certificate program is available, which combines competency in a foreign language and an internship and study abroad. There are 2 national honor societies on campus, including Phi Beta Kappa.

Faculty/Classroom: 58% of faculty are male; 42%, female. All teach undergraduates. No introductory courses are taught by graduate students. The average class size in an introductory lecture is 27; in a laboratory, 17; and in a regular course offering, 20.

Admissions: 50% of the 1995–96 applicants were accepted. The SAT I scores for the 1995–96 freshman class were as follows: Verbal—11% below 500, 41% between 500 and 599, 41% between 600 and 700, and 7% above 700; Math—8% below 500, 27% between 500 and 599, 56% between 600 and 700, and 9% above 700. 71% of the current freshmen were in the top fifth of their class; 94% were in the top two fifths. There were 2 National Merit finalists and 9 semifinalists. 5 freshmen graduated first in their class.

Requirements: The SAT II: Subject tests or the ACT is required. In addition, applicants must be graduates of an accredited secondary school. An essay is required and an interview is recommended. AP credits are accepted. Important factors in the admissions decision are advanced placement or honor courses, leadership record, and evidence of special talent.

Procedure: Freshmen are admitted fall and spring. There are early decision and deferred admissions plans. Early decision applications should be filed by November 15; regular applications, by January 15 for fall entry and December 1 for spring entry, along with an application fee of $45. Notification of early decision is sent December 15; regular decision, March 30. 113 early decision candidates were accepted for the 1995–96 class. A waiting list is an active part of the admissions procedure, with about 11% of all applicants on the list.

Transfer: 44 transfer students enrolled in 1995–96. Transfer applicants must have a minimum college GPA of 3.0 and should submit SAT I or ACT scores. An interview is recommended. 64 credits of 128 must be completed at Connecticut College.

Visiting: There are regularly scheduled orientations for prospective students, including an introduction to the college, student perspectives, academic programs, a luncheon for parents and students, tours, and a reception. There are guides for informal visits and visitors may sit in on classes and stay overnight at the school. To schedule a visit, contact the Admissions Office.

Financial Aid: In 1995–96, 50% of all freshmen and 52% of continuing students received some form of financial aid. 50% of freshmen and 52% of continuing students received need-based aid. The average freshman award was $15,862. Of that total, scholarships or need-based grants averaged $14,025 ($27,000 maximum); loans averaged $2426 ($2625 maximum); and work contracts averaged $963 ($1000 maximum). 43% of undergraduate students work part-time. Average earnings from campus work for the school year are $700. The average financial indebtedness of the 1994–95 graduate was $8294. The FAFSA, the college's own financial statement, and parent and student tax forms are required. The application deadline for fall entry is February 1.

International Students: There are currently 113 international students enrolled. The school actively recruits these students. They must take the TOEFL and achieve a minimum score of 590. The student must also take the SAT II: Subject tests or the ACT. Students may take SAT II: Subject tests in any 3 subjects.

Computers: The college provides computer facilities for student use. The mainframes are a DEC MicroVAX 3900 and a DEC System 5500. There are 3 public terminal rooms for the mainframe system. Apple Macintoshes and IBM PCs are available for student use in computer laboratories and individual departments. Laser printers, plotters, and scanners are also available. A campuswide network links computer clusters, classrooms, laboratories, dormitory rooms, and the library with voice data and video transmission capabilities. Bitnet and Internet are also available. All students may access the system 8 A.M. to midnight. There are no time limits and no fees.

Graduates: In 1994–95, 448 bachelor's degrees were awarded. The most popular majors among graduates were psychology (14%), government (13%), and English (8%). Within an average freshman class, 1% graduate in 3 years, 84% in 4 years, and 87% in 5 years. 70 companies recruited on campus in 1994–95. Of the 1994 graduating class, 27% were enrolled in graduate school within 6 months of graduation and 69% had found employment.

Admissions Contact: Lee A. Coffin, Dean of Admissions. E-mail: admit@conncoll.edu.

CONNECTICUT STATE UNIVERSITY SYSTEM

The Connecticut State University system is the largest public university system in the state. CSU consists of 4 comprehensive universities and a system office, serving nearly 34,000 students. The CSU universities are located in urban areas: Central Connecticut State University in New Britain, Eastern Connecticut State University in Willimantic, Southern Connecticut State University in New Haven, and Western Connecticut State University in Danbury. The system is governed by a 16-member Board of Trustees. CSU offers 130 academic programs at the bachelor's, master's, and 6th-year levels. Courses are taught by approximately 2100 faculty members. Students may enroll on a full- or part-time basis in fall, spring, and summer terms. The primary goal of the system is teaching. The main priorities are access with emphasis on a multicultural experience, quality within a context of curriculum diversity and a range of delivery systems, and public service including linkages with schools, state government, and private enterprise.

EASTERN CONNECTICUT STATE UNIVERSITY D-2
Willimantic, CT 06226
(860) 465-4373

Full-time: 1270 men, 1500 women	**Faculty:** 127; IIA, +$
Part-time: 520 men, 1000 women	**Ph.D.s:** n/av
Graduate: 50 men, 235 women	**Student/Faculty:** 22 to 1
Year: semesters, summer session	**Tuition:** $3180 ($8270)
Application Deadline: see profile	**Room & Board:** $4490
Freshman Class: n/av	
SAT I: required	**LESS COMPETITIVE**

Eastern Connecticut State University, founded in 1889, is a public coeducational institution offering undergraduate programs in liberal arts and sciences, business, and education. Figures given in the above capsule are approximate. There are 3 undergraduate schools and 1 graduate school. The library contains 212,500 volumes and 350,000 microform items, and subscribes to 1850 periodicals. Computerized library sources and services include the card catalog, interlibrary loans, and database searching. Special learning facilities include a learning resource center, art gallery, planetarium, radio station, and TV station. The 174-acre campus is in a suburban area 29 miles east of Hartford and 90 miles southwest of Boston. Including residence halls, there are 29 buildings on campus.

Student Life: 90% of undergraduates are from Connecticut. Students come from 16 states, 31 foreign countries, and Canada. 88% are from public schools; 12% from private. 83% are white. The average age of freshmen is 18; all undergraduates, 23. 12% do not continue beyond their first year; 50% remain to graduate.

Housing: 1520 students can be accommodated in college housing. College-sponsored living facilities include single-sex and coed dormitories and on-campus apartments. On-campus housing is guaranteed for all 4 years. 60% of students live on campus. Alcohol is not permitted. Upperclassmen may keep cars on campus.

Activities: There are no fraternities or sororities. There are 48 groups on campus, including art, band, cheerleading, choir, chorus, computers, dance, drama, ethnic, gay, honors, international, jazz band, literary magazine, musical theater, newspaper, orchestra, photography, political, professional, radio and TV, religious, social, social service, student government, and yearbook. Popular campus events include Homecoming, Spring Weekend, and Parents Day.

Sports: There are 5 intercollegiate sports for men and 6 for women, and 17 intramural sports for men and 14 for women. Athletic and recreation facilities include a 2800-seat field house, a 6-lane swimming pool, a soccer field, baseball and softball stadiums, and tennis, basketball, racquetball, and squash courts.

Disabled Students: 75% of the campus is accessible to disabled students. The following facilities are available: wheelchair ramps, elevators, special parking, specially equipped rest rooms, special class scheduling, lowered drinking fountains, and lowered telephones.

Services: In addition to many counseling and information services, tutoring is available in most subjects. There is a reader service for the blind, and remedial math, reading, and writing.

Campus Safety and Security: Campus safety and security measures include 24-hour foot and vehicle patrol, self-defense education, escort service, and shuttle buses. There are informal discussions, pamphlets/posters/films, emergency telephones, and lighted pathways/sidewalks.

Programs of Study: ECSU confers B.A., B.S., and B.G.S. degrees. Associate and master's degrees are also awarded. Bachelor's degrees are awarded in BIOLOGICAL SCIENCE (biology/biological science), BUSINESS (accounting, business administration and management, and recreation and leisure services), COMMUNICATIONS AND THE ARTS (communications, English, fine arts, and Spanish), COMPUTER AND PHYSICAL SCIENCE (computer science and mathematics), EDUCATION (early childhood, elementary, and physical), ENGINEERING AND ENVIRONMENTAL DESIGN (environmental science), SOCIAL SCIENCE (economics, history, political science/government, prelaw, psychology, and sociology). Liberal arts and sciences, business, and education are the strongest academically. Business administration, education, and psychology have the largest enrollments.

Required: To graduate, students must complete 120 credit hours, including 30 to 48 hours in the major, with a GPA of 2.0. General education requirements include 12 credits in interdisciplinary studies, 9 in social sciences, 7 in natural sciences, and 3 each in mathematics, fine arts, literature, writing, health and physical education, and computer literacy. Students must also fulfill a foreign language requirement.

Special: ECSU offers co-op programs in all majors, cross-registration with the University of Connecticut, internships, study abroad, a Washington semester, work-study programs, accelerated degree programs, dual majors, a general studies degree, nondegree study, pass/fail options, and credit for military experience. In addition to the B.S./certification programs for early childhood and elementary education, teacher certification is available for middle school and secondary education studies. There is a freshman honors program on campus, as well as 5 national honor societies. 4 departments have honors programs.

Faculty/Classroom: All teach undergraduates. No introductory courses are taught by graduate students. The average class size in an introductory lecture is 35; in a laboratory, 18; and in a regular course offering, 35.

Admissions: The SAT I scores for the a recent freshman class were as follows: Verbal—80% below 500, 16% between 500 and 599, 3% between 600 and 700, and 1% above 700; Math—67% below 500, 27% between 500 and 599, 5% between 600 and 700, and 1% above 700. 27% of recent freshmen were in the top fifth of their class; 82% were in the top two fifths.

Requirements: The SAT I is required. ECSU requires applicants to be in the upper 50% of their class with a 2.5 GPA. Applicants must be graduates of an accredited secondary school or have a GED. They should have completed 13 high school academic credits, including 4 years of English, 3 of mathematics, and 2 each of foreign language, social studies, and science (including 1 of laboratory science). An interview is recommended. AP and CLEP credits are accepted. Important factors in the admissions decision are recommendations by school officials, advanced placement or honor courses, and leadership record.

Procedure: Freshmen are admitted fall and spring. Entrance exams should be taken in November or December of the senior year. There are early admissions and deferred admissions plans. Check with the school for current application deadlines and fee. Notification is sent on a rolling basis. A waiting list is an active part of the admissions procedure, with about 10% of all applicants on the list in a recent year.

Transfer: 534 transfer students were enrolled in a recent year. Applicants should have completed a minimum of 12 credit hours with a GPA of 2.5. Official college and high school transcripts are required, and an associate degree and an interview are recommended. 30 credits of 120 must be completed at ECSU.

Visiting: There are regularly scheduled orientations for prospective students, including small group discussions, a tour of the campus, and a personal interview. There are guides for informal visits and visitors may sit in on classes. To schedule a visit, contact the Admissions Office.

Financial Aid: In a recent year, 60% of all students received some form of financial aid. 60% of all students received need-based aid. The average freshman award was $5700. Of that total, scholarships or need-based grants averaged $4000 ($9900 maximum); loans averaged $850 ($2100 maximum); and work contracts averaged $850 ($2100 maximum). 50% of undergraduate students work part-time. Average earnings from campus work for the school year are $1300. ECSU is a member of CSS. The FAFSA is required. Check with the school for current deadlines.

International Students: In a recent year there were 103 international students enrolled. The school actively recruits these students. They must score 550 on the TOEFL.

Computers: The college provides computer facilities for student use. The mainframe is a DEC VAX 7620 minicomputer. The main laboratory houses approximately 100 microcomputer stations, comprised of IBM, Apple, and Zenith equipment. Other computer laboratories are located in the Media Center Building and in the Learning Center. All systems are connected to the campus Ethernet network. All students may access the system. There are no time limits and no fees.

Graduates: In a recent year, 733 bachelor's degrees were awarded. The most popular majors among graduates were business administration (32%), education (16%), and psychology (10%). Within an average freshman class, 40% graduate in 4 years and 50% in 5 years. 200 companies recruited on campus in a recent year.

Admissions Contact: Director of Admissions and Enrollment Planning.

FAIRFIELD UNIVERSITY   B-4

Fairfield, CT 06430-5195   (203) 254-4100; FAX: (203) 254-4199

Full-time: 1354 men, 1673 women	**Faculty:** 184; IIA, +$
Part-time: 597 men, 589 women	**Ph.Ds:** 93%
Graduate: 213 men, 554 women	**Student/Faculty:** 16 to 1
Year: semesters, summer session	**Tuition:** $16,340
Application Deadline: March 1	**Room & Board:** $6600
Freshman Class: 4841 applied, 3425 accepted, 784 enrolled	
SAT I Verbal/Math: 501/567	**VERY COMPETITIVE**

Fairfield University, founded by the Jesuits in 1942, is an independent, Roman Catholic Jesuit coeducational institution. There are 3 undergraduate and 2 graduate schools. In addition to regional accreditation, Fairfield has baccalaureate program accreditation with ABET and NLN. The library contains 300,000 volumes, 466,287 microform items, and 8093 audiovisual forms, and subscribes to 1842 periodicals. Computerized library sources and services include interlibrary loans and database searching. Special learning facilities include an art gallery, radio station, TV station, a media center, a 750-seat concert hall/theater, and a rehearsal and improvisation theater. The 200-acre campus is in a suburban area 60 miles northeast of New York City. Including residence halls, there are 30 buildings on campus.

Student Life: 69% of undergraduates are from out-of-state, mostly the Northeast. Students come from 34 states, 27 foreign countries, and Canada. 50% are from public schools; 50% from private. 88% are white. Most are Catholic. The average age of freshmen is 18; all undergraduates, 21. 11% do not continue beyond their first year; 84% remain to graduate.

Housing: 2230 students can be accommodated in college housing. College-sponsored living facilities include coed dormitories and on-campus apartments. In addition there are special interest houses, a wellness floor, and a service floor. On-campus housing is guaranteed for all 4 years. 80% of students live on campus; of those, 80% remain on campus on weekends. Upperclassmen may keep cars on campus.

Activities: There are no fraternities or sororities. There are 100 groups on campus, including art, band, cheerleading, chorale, computers, dance, drama, ethnic, film, honors, international, jazz band, literary magazine, musical theater, newspaper, orchestra, pep band, photography, political, professional, radio and TV, religious, social, social service, student government, and yearbook. Popular campus events include the Dogwood Festival, Martin Luther King Week, Luck of the Roommate Dance, and May Day.

Sports: There are 10 intercollegiate sports for men and 8 for women, and 20 intramural sports for men and 20 for women. Athletic and recreation facilities include a gymnasium, a 25-meter swimming pool, weight rooms, indoor and outdoor tennis courts, racquetball and volleyball courts, indoor and outdoor tracks, a sauna, and whirlpool.

Disabled Students: The entire campus is accessible to disabled students. The following facilities are available: wheelchair ramps, elevators, special parking, specially equipped rest rooms, special class scheduling, lowered drinking fountains, and lowered telephones. Single rooms are available for disabled students, seeing-eye dogs can be accommodated, and there is a library computer station for physically challenged students.

Services: In addition to many counseling and information services, tutoring is available in every subject. There is a reader service for the blind.

Campus Safety and Security: Campus safety and security measures include 24-hour foot and vehicle patrol, self-defense education, escort service, and shuttle buses. In addition, there are informal discussions, pamphlets/posters/films, emergency telephones, lighted pathways/sidewalks, EMT security officers, and bike patrol.

Programs of Study: Fairfield confers B.S. and B.A. degrees. Master's degrees are also awarded. Bachelor's degrees are awarded in BIOLOGICAL SCIENCE (biology/biological science and neurosciences), BUSINESS (accounting, banking and finance, business administration and management, international business management, and marketing/retailing/merchandising), COMMUNICATIONS AND THE ARTS (communications, English, fine arts, French, German, Italian, and Spanish), COMPUTER AND PHYSICAL SCIENCE (chemistry, computer science, information sciences and systems, mathematics, and physics), HEALTH PROFESSIONS (nursing), SOCIAL SCIENCE (economics, history, philosophy, political science/government, psychology, religion, and sociology). Economics, politics, prelaw and premedicine are the strongest academically. English, biology, and accounting have the largest enrollments.

Required: In order to graduate, students must complete 120 credits, 60 of them in general education core requirements, with a minimum GPA of 2.0. Distribution requirements include 12 credits in mathematics and natural sciences, 12 credits in history and social sciences, 15 credits in philosophy, religious studies, and ethics, 15 credits in English and fine arts, and 6 credits in foreign languages. First-year students are required to take a course in multiculturalism.

Special: Fairfield offers study abroad in 6 countries, a Washington semester, federal work-study program, B.A.-B.S. degrees in economics, international studies, and psychology, and dual majors. A 3-2 engineering degree is offered with the University of Connecticut, Rensselaer Polytechnic Institute, and Columbia University. A general studies degree and credit for life, military, and work experience are available through the School of Continuing Education. Internships, both credit and noncredit, are offered at area corporations, publications, banks, and other businesses. New minors include women's studies, marine science, black studies, environmental studies, jazz, classical studies, and Russian and Eastern studies. There is a freshman honors program on campus. There is an interdisciplinary honors program, as well as 14 national honor societies, including Phi Beta Kappa.

Faculty/Classroom: 63% of faculty are male; 37%, female. All both teach undergraduates and do research. No introductory courses are taught by graduate students. The average class size in an introductory lecture is 35; in a laboratory, 20; and in a regular course offering, 24.

Admissions: 71% of the 1995–96 applicants were accepted. The SAT I scores for the 1995–96 freshman class were as follows: Verbal—47% below 500, 41% between 500 and 599, 11% between 600 and 700, and 1% above 700; Math—19% below 500, 43% between 500 and 599, 33% between 600 and 700, and 5% above 700. 52% of the current freshmen were in the top fifth of their class; 91% were in the top two fifths. There were 15 National Merit semifinalists. 11 freshmen graduated first in their class.

Requirements: The SAT I is required. Fairfield requires applicants to be in the upper 40% of their class. A minimum GPA of 3.0 is required. Applicants must be graduates of an accredited secondary school. The GED is accepted. A B average is required. Students should have completed 16 academic credits, including 4 credits of English, 3 credits each of history and mathematics, and 2 credits each of a foreign language, science, and social studies. The school recommends SAT II: Subject tests in writing, literature, and mathematics, and, for nursing and science majors, in the sciences. An interview is recommended. Applications are accepted on-line via ExPAN, CollegeLink, and Mac Apply. AP and CLEP credits are accepted. Important factors in the admissions decision are advanced placement or honor courses, leadership record, and evidence of special talent.

Procedure: Freshmen are admitted in the fall. Entrance exams should be taken in spring of the junior year or fall of the senior year. There are early decision and deferred admissions plans. Early decision applications should be filed by December 1; regular applications, by March 1 for fall entry, along with an application fee of $35. Notification of early decision is sent January 1; regular decision, May 1. 111 early decision candidates were accepted for the 1995–96 class. A waiting list is an active part of the admissions procedure, with about 4% of all applicants on the list.

Transfer: 48 transfer students enrolled in 1995–96. The SAT I and a college GPA of 2.5 are required. 60 credits of 120 must be completed at Fairfield.

Visiting: There are regularly scheduled orientations for prospective students, consisting of a summer orientation the third week in June and a fall program 2 days before classes begin. There are guides for informal visits and visitors may sit in on classes and stay overnight at the school. To schedule a visit, contact the Admission Office.

Financial Aid: In 1995–96, 75% of all freshmen and 68% of continuing students received some form of financial aid. 54% of freshmen and 50% of continuing students received need-based aid. The average freshman award was $9222. Of that total, scholarships or need-based grants averaged $8500 ($23,100 maximum); loans averaged $2750 ($6000 maximum); and work contracts averaged $1500 (maximum). 10% of undergraduate students work part-time. Average earnings from campus work for the school year are $950. Fairfield is a member of CSS. The FAF, parent and student tax returns, and a verification statement are required. The application deadline for fall entry is February 15.

International Students: There are currently 42 international students enrolled. The school actively recruits these students. They must take the TOEFL and achieve a minimum score of 550.

Computers: The college provides computer facilities for student use. The mainframe is a VAX 6430. Staffed computer laboratories are maintained in all academic buildings. Macintosh, IBM PS/2, and Apple II microcomputers are available. The mainframe is accessible through 20 terminals. All students may access the system daily until midnight. There are no time limits. The fees are $45.

Graduates: In 1994–95, 771 bachelor's degrees were awarded. The most popular majors among graduates were English (14%), nursing (10%), and biology (8%). Within an average freshman class, 84% graduate in 4 years, 1% in 5 years, and 1% in 6 years. 99 companies recruited on campus in 1994–95. Of the 1994 graduating class, 20% were enrolled in graduate school within 6 months of graduation and 44% had found employment.

Admissions Contact: Dave Flynn, Dean of Admission. A campus video is available. E-mail: admis@fair1.fairfield.edu.

QUINNIPIAC COLLEGE   C-3
Hamden, CT 06518   (203) 281-8600
(800) 462-1944; FAX: (203) 281-8906

Full-time: 1260 men, 1890 women	Faculty: 208; IIA, ++$
Part-time: 254 men, 382 women	Ph.D.s: 70%
Graduate: 681 men, 622 women	Student/Faculty: 15 to 1
Year: semesters, summer session	Tuition: $13,430
Application Deadline: February 15	Room & Board: $6450
Freshman Class: 5280 applied, 3144 accepted, 974 enrolled	
SAT I or ACT: required	**COMPETITIVE**

Quinnipiac College, founded in 1929, is a private, coeducational institution offering undergraduate and graduate degrees in allied health and natural sciences, business, communications, and liberal arts. There are 3 undergraduate and 2 graduate schools. In addition to regional accreditation, Quinnipiac has baccalaureate program accreditation with APTA, CAHEA, and NLN. The 2 libraries contain 304,875 volumes, 9100 microform items, and 1890 audiovisual forms, and subscribe to 3900 periodicals. Computerized library sources and services include interlibrary loans and database searching. Special learning facilities include a learning resource center, radio station, TV station, and critical care nursing laboratory. The 185-acre campus is in a suburban area 10 miles north of New Haven and 35 miles south of Hartford. Including residence halls, there are 35 buildings on campus.

Student Life: 63% of undergraduates are from out-of-state, mostly the Northeast. Students come from 29 states, 18 foreign countries, and Canada. 75% are from public schools; 25% from private. 88% are white. 65% are Catholic; 20% Protestant; 12% Jewish. The average age of freshmen is 19; all undergraduates, 21. 12% do not continue beyond their first year; 78% remain to graduate.

Housing: 2300 students can be accommodated in college housing. College-sponsored living facilities include single-sex and coed dormitories and on-campus apartments. In addition, there are quiet houses and wellness houses. On-campus housing is guaranteed for all 4 years. 75% of students live on campus; of those, 70% remain on campus on weekends. All students may keep cars on campus.

Activities: 3% of men belong to 1 local and 3 national fraternities; 3% of women belong to 1 local and 2 national sororities. There are 65 groups on campus, including cheerleading, dance, drama, ethnic, film, honors, international, literary magazine, musical theater, newspaper, photography, political, professional, radio and TV, religious, social, social service, student government, and yearbook. Popular campus events include May Weekend, Lip Sync Contest, Holiday Dinner, NICHE Conference, Thursdays at Quinnipiac, and jazz concerts.

Sports: There are 8 intercollegiate sports for men and 7 for women, and 9 intramural sports for men and 9 for women. Athletic and recreation facilities include more than 20 acres of playing fields, a 1500-seat gymnasium, 2 basketball courts, a weight training room, a steam room, aerobic rooms with sauna, and a fitness facility with a large multipurpose room for indoor tennis, basketball, volleyball, and track.

Disabled Students: The entire campus is accessible to disabled students. The following facilities are available: wheelchair ramps, elevators, special parking, specially equipped rest rooms, special class scheduling, lowered drinking fountains, lowered telephones, and residence rooms designed for students with wheelchairs.

Services: In addition to many counseling and information services, tutoring is available in most subjects, including all freshman-level courses and others by request. Special workshops on study skills, time management, and note taking are available also. There is a reader service for the blind, and remedial math, reading, and writing.

Campus Safety and Security: Campus safety and security measures include 24-hour foot and vehicle patrol, self-defense education, escort service, and informal discussions. In addition, there are pamphlets/posters/films, lighted pathways/sidewalks, perimeter security in the form of contract security officers at all entrances, and vehicle and pedestrian check-in identification.

Programs of Study: Quinnipiac confers B.A., B.S., and B.H.S. degrees. Master's degrees are also awarded. Bachelor's degrees are awarded in BIOLOGICAL SCIENCE (biochemistry, biology/biological science, biotechnology, and microbiology), BUSINESS (accounting, banking and finance, business administration and management, business economics, international business management, management science, and marketing/retailing/merchandising), COMMUNICATIONS AND THE ARTS (communications, English, and Spanish), COMPUTER AND PHYSICAL SCIENCE (chemistry, computer science, and mathematics), HEALTH PROFESSIONS (health care administration, health science, medical laboratory science, medical laboratory technology, nursing, occupational therapy, physical therapy, predentistry, premedicine, radiological science, respiratory therapy, and veterinary science), SOCIAL SCIENCE (economics, gerontology, history, liberal arts/general studies, paralegal studies, political science/government, prelaw, psychobiology, psychology, social science, and sociology). Psychology, mass communications, and physical therapy are the strongest academically. Physical therapy, mass communications, and accounting have the largest enrollments.

Required: All students must complete 50 semester hours of the core curriculum, which includes competency in English, mathematics, foreign languages, oral communications, and computer information systems. Courses in arts, behavioral and social sciences, humanities, physical and biological sciences, economics, and management are also part of the core. One hour of physical education and completion of a computer skills workshop are required. To graduate, students must maintain a minimum GPA of 2.0 over 120 total semester hours.

Special: Quinnipiac offers cross-registration with the University of New Haven and Albertus Magnus College, internships in most majors, study abroad in more than 25 countries, a Washington semester with American University, work-study programs, dual and student-designed majors, B.A.-B.S. degrees, credit for life experience, and nondegree study. There is a freshman honors program on campus, as well as 8 national honor societies. 9 departments have honors programs.

Faculty/Classroom: 68% of faculty are male; 32%, female. 85% teach undergraduates and 35% both teach and do research. No introductory courses are taught by graduate students. The average class size in an introductory lecture is 23; in a laboratory, 15; and in a regular course offering, 20.

Admissions: 60% of the 1995–96 applicants were accepted. The SAT I scores for a recent freshman class were as follows: Verbal—48% below 500, 34% between 500 and 599, 14% between 600 and 700, and 4% above 700; Math—35% below 500, 45% between 500 and 599, 14% between 600 and 700, and 6% above 700. 40% of the current freshmen were in the top fifth of their class; 75% were in the top two fifths. 12 freshmen graduated first in their class.

Requirements: The SAT I or ACT is required, with a minimum composite score of 950 on the SAT I or 20 on the ACT recommended. Quinnipiac requires applicants to be in the upper 50% of their class. A minimum GPA of 2.5 is required. All students must have completed 16 academic credits, including 4 in English, 3 in mathematics, 2 each in science and social studies, and 5 in electives. The GED is accepted. An interview is recommended, and an essay is required. Quinnipiac accepts applications on-line through ExPAN. AP and CLEP credits are accepted. Important factors in the admissions decision are advanced placement or honor courses, extracurricular activities record, and leadership record.

Procedure: Freshmen are admitted fall and spring. Entrance exams should be taken in the junior year and early in the senior year. There are early admissions and deferred admissions plans. Applications should be filed by February 15 for fall entry and December 15 for spring entry, along with an application fee of $40. Notification is sent on a rolling basis. A waiting list is an active part of the admissions procedure for the physical therapy and occupational therapy programs, with about 3% of applicants on the list.

Transfer: 170 transfer students enrolled in 1995–96. Students must have a minimum college GPA of 2.0 and must submit SAT I scores and high school or college transcripts. An interview is recommended. 45 credits of 120 must be completed at Quinnipiac.

Visiting: There are regularly scheduled orientations for prospective students, consisting of interviews, a group information session, student-guided tours, financial aid sessions, an opportunity to speak with faculty, and open houses. There are guides for informal visits and visitors may sit in on classes and stay overnight at the school. To schedule a visit, contact the Admissions Office.

Financial Aid: In 1995–96, 70% of all freshmen and 65% of continuing students received some form of financial aid. 66% of freshmen and 60% of continuing students received need-based aid. The average freshman award was $8821. Of that total, scholarships or need-based grants averaged $4696 ($12,800 maximum); loans averaged $2625; and work contracts averaged $1500 ($2000 maximum). 17% of undergraduate students work part-time. Average earnings from campus work for the school year are $1000. The average financial indebtedness of the 1994–95 graduate was $8250. Quinnipiac is a member of CSS. The FAFSA and the college's own financial statement are required. The application deadline for fall entry is March 1.

International Students: There are currently 60 international students enrolled. The school actively recruits these students. They must take the TOEFL and achieve a minimum score of 550. Quinnipiac recommends that the student also take the SAT I or the ACT.

Computers: The college provides computer facilities for student use. The mainframe is a DEC 5500. Every freshman is required to take a 5-week workshop on word processing and spreadsheets in the computer center's 22-station teaching laboratory. The center has 45 IBM PCs and compatibles connected to an HP 3000/Series 68 minicomputer. The instructional classroom consists of 20 IBM PS/2 Model 55s operating on an IBM 05/2 LAN Server Network. All students may access the system 8 A.M. to midnight, 7 days a week. There are no time limits and no fees.

Graduates: In 1994–95, 566 bachelor's degrees were awarded. The most popular majors among graduates were marketing (12%), physical therapy (11%), and occupational therapy (11%). Within an average freshman class, 76% graduate in 4 years, 78% in 5 years, and 79% in 6 years. 75 companies recruited on campus in 1994–95. Of the 1994 graduating class, 13% were enrolled in graduate school within 6 months of graduation and 85% had found employment.

Admissions Contact: Joan Isaac Mohr, Dean of Admissions. E-mail: admissions@quinnipiac.edu.

SACRED HEART UNIVERSITY B-4
Fairfield, CT 06432–1000　　(203) 371-7880; FAX: (203) 371-7889

Full-time: 945 men, 1177 women	Faculty: 111; IIB, +$
Part-time: 537 men, 1267 women	Ph.D.s: 81%
Graduate: 522 men, 970 women	Student/Faculty: 19 to 1
Year: semesters, summer session	Tuition: $12,100
Application Deadline: rolling	Room & Board: $6080
Freshman Class: 2721 applied, 2324 accepted, 632 enrolled	
SAT I: required	COMPETITIVE

Sacred Heart University, founded in 1963, is a private Catholic institution that offers majors with health sciences, liberal arts and sciences, and business. There is 1 graduate school. In addition to regional accreditation, SHU has baccalaureate program accreditation with CSWE and NLN. The library contains 153,000 volumes, 52,400 microform items, and 10,900 audiovisual forms, and subscribes to 717 periodicals. Computerized library sources and services include interlibrary loans and database searching. Special learning facilities include a learning resource center, art gallery, radio station, TV station, and theater. The 56-acre campus is in a suburban area in southwestern Connecticut, 55 miles northeast of New York City. Including residence halls, there are 10 buildings on campus.

Student Life: 52% of undergraduates are from Connecticut. Students come from 18 states, 55 foreign countries, and Canada. 60% are from public schools; 40% from private. 81% are white. The average age of freshmen is 18; all undergraduates, 20. 15% do not continue beyond their first year; 75% remain to graduate.

Housing: 1250 students can be accommodated in college housing. College-sponsored living facilities include coed dormitories, on-campus apartments, and off-campus apartments. On-campus housing is guaranteed for all 4 years. 60% of students live on campus; of those, 75% remain on campus on weekends. Upperclassmen may keep cars on campus.

Activities: 5% of men belong to 4 local fraternities; 5% of women belong to 5 local sororities. There are 70 groups on campus, including art, band, cheerleading, choir, chorale, chorus, computers, dance, debate, drama, ethnic, film, honors, international, jazz band, literary magazine, marching band, musical theater, newspaper, orchestra, pep band, photography, political, professional, radio and TV, religious, social, social service, student government, and yearbook. Popular campus events include Harvest and Pioneer weekends, International Festival, and Springfest.

Sports: There are 14 intercollegiate sports for men and 15 for women, and 6 intramural sports for men and 3 for women. Athletic and recreation facilities include 6 championship tennis courts, an artificial turf field and track, an 1100-seat gymnasium, and soccer, softball, and baseball fields.

Disabled Students: All of the campus is accessible to disabled students. The following facilities are available: wheelchair ramps, elevators, special parking, specially equipped rest rooms, special class scheduling, lowered drinking fountains, and room nameplates.

Services: In addition to many counseling and information services, tutoring is available in most subjects. There is remedial math, reading, and writing.

Campus Safety and Security: Campus safety and security measures include 24-hour foot and vehicle patrol, self-defense education, escort service, and shuttle buses. In addition, there are informal discussions, pamphlets/posters/films, emergency telephones, and lighted pathways/sidewalks.

Programs of Study: SHU confers B.A. and B.S. degrees. Associate and master's degrees are also awarded. Bachelor's degrees are awarded in BIOLOGICAL SCIENCE (biology/biological science), BUSINESS (accounting, banking and finance, business administration and management, and international business management), COMMUNICATIONS AND THE ARTS (art, English, media arts, and Spanish), COMPUTER AND PHYSICAL SCIENCE (chemistry, computer science, and mathematics), HEALTH PROFESSIONS (medical technology and nursing), SOCIAL SCIENCE (criminal justice, economics, history, international studies, liberal arts/general studies, philosophy, political science/government, psychology, religion, social work, and sociology). Business, biology, and psychology are the strongest academically. Business, accounting, and psychology have the largest enrollments.

Required: All students must complete 120 credit hours, including 30 to 58 in the major, while maintaining a minimum 2.0 GPA. Distribution requirements include an 18 credit required core consisting of freshman writing, oral communication, college mathematics, and literature and civilization; and a 30 to 32 credit elective core consisting of 9 credits of social science, 9 of philosophy and religious studies, 6 of arts and humanities, and 6 of science and mathematics. B.S. candidates need an additional course each of mathematics and science; B.A. candidates, an additional 6 credits of foreign language.

Special: SHU offers co-op programs in all majors, paid and unpaid internships at area corporations, including Fortune 500 companies, hospitals, newspapers, and social service agencies, study abroad worldwide, a Washington semester, and on-campus work-study. There is a freshman honors program on campus, as well as 7 national honor societies, including Phi Beta Kappa.

Faculty/Classroom: 58% of faculty are male; 42%, female. All teach undergraduates. No introductory courses are taught by graduate students. The average class size in an introductory lecture is 30; in a laboratory, 10; and in a regular course offering, 19.

Admissions: 85% of the 1995–96 applicants were accepted. 33% of the current freshmen were in the top fifth of their class; 63% were in the top two fifths. There were 3 National Merit semifinalists. 2 freshmen graduated first in their class.

Requirements: The SAT I is required, with a recommended score ranging from 530 to 710 for verbal and 480 to 650 for math; SAT II: Subject tests in writing, mathematics, and language are advised. SHU requires applicants to be in the upper 40% of their class, with a 3.0 GPA. In addition, applicants must have 16 academic credits and 16 Carnegie units, including 4 years in English, 3 each in mathematics and science, 2 each in foreign language and social studies, and 1 in history. An essay is required and an interview recommended. Applications may be submitted on computer disk using CollegeLink or Apply. AP and CLEP credits are accepted. Important factors in the admissions decision are advanced placement or honor courses, leadership record, and recommendations by school officials.

Procedure: Freshmen are admitted in the fall and spring. Entrance exams should be taken in May of the junior year or November of the senior year. There are early decision, early admissions, and deferred admissions plans. Early decision applications should be filed by December 7, along with an application fee of $30. Notification of early decision is sent December 21; regular decision, on a rolling basis. 129 early decision candidates were accepted for the 1995–96 class.

Transfer: 160 transfer students enrolled in 1995–96. Applicants must submit 2 letters of recommendation and high school and college transcripts. 30 credits of 120 must be completed at SHU.

Visiting: There are regularly scheduled orientations for prospective students, including open houses on weekends and daily tours. There are guides for informal visits and visitors may sit in on classes and stay overnight at the school. To schedule a visit, contact the Admissions Office.

Financial Aid: In 1995–96, 89% of all freshmen and 73% of continuing students received some form of financial aid. 76% of freshmen and 70% of continuing students received need-based aid. The average freshman award was $8305. Of that total, scholarships or need-based grants averaged $4855 ($8800 maximum); loans averaged $2594 ($2625 maximum); and work contracts averaged $570 ($1500 maximum). 26% of undergraduate students work part-time. Average earnings from campus work for the school year are $1100. The average financial indebtedness of the 1994–95 graduate was $13,250. SHU is a member of CSS. The FAF or FAFSA is required. The application deadline for fall entry is March 1.

International Students: There are currently 86 international students enrolled. The school actively recruits these students. They must take the TOEFL, the MELAB, the Comprehensive English Language Test, or the college's own test. The student must also take the SAT I or the ACT.

Computers: The college provides computer facilities for student use. The mainframes are a DEC VAX 11/750 and an MIPS M120. There are nearly 150 computer terminals and microcomputers, including DEC, IBM-compatible, and Apple models. The campuswide DEC fiber-optic network and academic computing technology serves the entire university, with every residence hall room wired to a port for the network. All students may access the system 7 days per week. There are no time limits and no fees.

Graduates: In 1994–95, 333 bachelor's degrees were awarded. The most popular majors among graduates were business (36%), accounting (13%), and psychology (9%). Within an average freshman class, 70% graduate in 4 years, 73% in 5 years, and 75% in 6 years. 50 companies recruited on campus in 1994–95.

Admissions Contact: Karen N. Pagliuco, Dean of Freshman Admissions. E-mail: enroll@sacredheart.edu.

SAINT JOSEPH COLLEGE

West Hartford, CT 06117

C-2

(203) 232–4571, ext. 216
(800) 285–6565; FAX: (860) 233–5695

Full-time: 2 men, 575 women	Faculty: 68; IIA, –$
Part-time: 50 men, 580 women	Ph.D.s: 68%
Graduate: 78 men, 631 women	Student/Faculty: 8 to 1
Year: semesters, summer session	Tuition: $13,020
Application Deadline: May 1	Room & Board: $4810
Freshman Class: 410 applied, 288 accepted, 166 enrolled	
SAT I Verbal/Math: 450/500	COMPETITIVE

Saint Joseph College, founded in 1932 and affiliated with the Roman Catholic Church, is a private, primarily women's college offering a liberal arts education with preprofessional programs in nursing, education, and business at the undergraduate level. The Weekend College and graduate school offer coeducational studies. There are 2 undergraduate schools and one graduate school. In addition to regional accreditation, the college has baccalaureate program accreditation with ADA, CSWE, and NLN. The library contains 129,000 volumes, 6661 microform items, and 2983 audiovisual forms, and subscribes to 641 periodicals. Computerized library sources and services include the card catalog, interlibrary loans, and database searching. Special learning facilities include a learning resource center, art gallery, academic resources center, and 2 laboratory schools: the Gengras Center for Exceptional Children and the School for Young Children. The 84-acre campus is in a suburban area 3 miles west of Hartford. Including residence halls, there are 13 buildings on campus.

Student Life: 97% of undergraduates are from Connecticut. Students come from 10 states and 3 foreign countries. 79% are from public schools; 21% from private. 90% are white. 74% are Catholic; 15% Protestant. The average age of freshmen is 18; all undergraduates, 23. 21% do not continue beyond their first year; 67% remain to graduate.

Housing: 333 students can be accommodated in college housing. College-sponsored living facilities include single-sex dormitories. On-campus housing is guaranteed for all 4 years. 51% of students commute. All students may keep cars on campus.

Activities: There are no fraternities or sororities. There are 20 groups on campus, including choir, chorale, chorus, dance, drama, ethnic, honors, international, literary magazine, musical theater, political, professional, religious, social, social service, student government, and yearbook. Popular campus events include Halloween Hayride, Winter Weekend, Festival of Lights, Ring Ceremony, and Spring Weekend.

Sports: There are 7 intercollegiate sports for women and 7 intramural sports for women. Athletic and recreation facilities include an all-weather track, a gymnasium, an exercise room, tennis and platform tennis courts, a dance studio, and a pool.

Disabled Students: 70% of the campus is accessible to disabled students. The following facilities are available: wheelchair ramps, elevators, special parking, specially equipped rest rooms, special class scheduling, lowered drinking fountains, and lowered telephones. Other needs are met on a case-by-case basis.

Services: In addition to many counseling and information services, tutoring is available in most subjects, including ESL. There is remedial math, reading, and writing. Other services are arranged as needed through the Academic Resource Center.

Campus Safety and Security: Campus safety and security measures include 24-hour foot and vehicle patrol, self-defense education, shuttle buses, and informal discussions. In addition, there are pamphlets/posters/films, emergency telephones, lighted pathways/sidewalks, and an escort service by request.

Programs of Study: The college confers B.A., B.S., and B.S.N. degrees. Master's degrees are also awarded. Bachelor's degrees are awarded in BIOLOGICAL SCIENCE (biochemistry and biology/biological science), BUSINESS (accounting, business economics, and management science), COMMUNICATIONS AND THE ARTS (art history and appreciation, English, French, and Spanish), COMPUTER AND PHYSICAL SCIENCE (chemistry, computer mathematics, mathematics, and natural sciences), EDUCATION (early childhood, home economics, and special), ENGINEERING AND ENVIRONMENTAL DESIGN (environmental science), HEALTH PROFESSIONS (nursing), SOCIAL SCIENCE (American studies, dietetics, family/consumer studies, history, humanities, philosophy, political science/government, psychology, religion, social science, social work, and sociology). Nursing, sciences, and education are the strongest academically. Nursing, education, and business have the largest enrollments.

Required: All students must maintain a minimum GPA of 2.0, pass a written or oral comprehensive examination, and take 120 total credit hours including a minimum of 30 in the major and liberal arts requirements of 12 credits in 4 core areas, plus 6 credits in religion, 9 in humanities, 9 in social studies, 7 to 8 in natural science/mathematics, and 1 in physical education.

Special: The college offers cross-registration through the Hartford and Wesleyan consortiums, numerous internships, study abroad in Great Britain, Europe, Japan, and Spain, accelerated degree programs in business administration, interdisciplinary majors, student-designed majors, a 3–2 engineering degree with George Washington University, and a dual major in biology-chemistry. Credit for life experience, nondegree study, and pass/fail options is available. There is a freshman honors program on campus, 1 national honor society, and interdepartmental honors programs.

Faculty/Classroom: 35% of faculty are male; 65%, female. The average class size in an introductory lecture is 30; in a laboratory, 20; and in a regular course offering, 20.

Admissions: 70% of the 1995–96 applicants were accepted. The SAT I scores for the 1995–96 freshman class were as follows: Verbal—66% below 500, 29% between 500 and 599, 3% between 600 and 700, and 2% above 700; Math—66% below 500, 24% between 500 and 599, and 10% between 600 and 700. 38% of the current freshmen were in the top fifth of their class; 67% were in the top two fifths.

Requirements: The SAT I is required. A minimum GPA of 3.0 is required. Applicants need 16 academic credits distributed among English, foreign language, history, mathematics, science, and social studies. The GED is accepted, and an interview is recommended. Applications are accepted on-line through the Internet. AP and CLEP credits are accepted. Important factors in the admissions decision are advanced placement or honor courses, recommendations by school officials, and evidence of special talent.

Procedure: Freshmen are admitted fall and spring. There is a deferred admissions plan. Early decision applications should be filed by December 1; regular applications, by May 1 for fall entry and December 1 for spring entry, along with an application fee of $25. Notification is sent on a rolling basis.

Transfer: Saint Joseph accepts transfers up to the beginning of the junior year. Applicants need a minimum college GPA of 2.7 in addition to an interview. Nursing applicants are required to take the SAT I. 60 credits of 120 must be completed at the college.

Visiting: There are regularly scheduled orientations for prospective students. There are guides for informal visits and visitors may sit in on classes and stay overnight at the school. To schedule a visit, contact Mary C. Demo, Director of Admissions.

Financial Aid: In 1995–96, 92% of all freshmen and 73% of continuing students received some form of financial aid. 84% of freshmen and 64% of continuing students received need-based aid. The average freshman award was $10,305. Of that total, scholarships or need-based grants averaged $6414 ($17,800 maximum); loans averaged $3672; and work contracts averaged $1200 (maximum). 27% of undergraduate students work part-time. Average earnings from campus work for the school year are $1200. The average financial indebtedness of the 1994–95 graduate was $6098. the college is a member of CSS. The FAFSA, the college's own financial statement, and parent tax returns and W-2 statements are required. The application deadline for fall entry is February 1.

International Students: There are currently 7 international students enrolled. They must take the TOEFL and achieve a minimum score of 530. The student must also take the SAT I or the ACT.

Computers: The college provides computer facilities for student use. The mainframe is a DEC VAX 3400. The VAX laboratory is open to all students daily until 9 P.M. The IBM token ring laboratory (LAN) is used by many classes both formally and informally. The IBM and Macintosh microcomputer laboratory is open during library hours for general student use. All students may access the system during scheduled laboratory hours. There are no time limits and no fees.

Graduates: In 1994–95, 196 bachelor's degrees were awarded. The most popular majors among graduates were nursing (28%), social work (11%), and child study (9%). Within an average freshman class, 1% graduate in 3 years, 57% in 4 years, 4% in 5 years, and 5% in 6 years. 10 companies recruited on campus in 1994–95. Of the 1994 graduating class, 15% were enrolled in graduate school within 6 months of graduation and 94% had found employment.

Admissions Contact: Mary C. Demo, Director of Admissions. A campus video is available. E-mail: admissions@mercy.syc.edu.

SOUTHERN CONNECTICUT STATE UNIVERSITY

C-3

New Haven, CT 06515   (203) 392–5644; FAX: (203) 392–5863

Full-time: 2353 men, 3108 women	Faculty: 368
Part-time: 1014 men, 1230 women	Ph.D.s: 72%
Graduate: 959 men, 2927 women	Student/Faculty: 15 to 1
Year: semesters, summer session	Tuition: $3425 ($8517)
Application Deadline: May 1	Room & Board: $5061
Freshman Class: 3675 applied, 2467 accepted, 957 enrolled	
SAT I Verbal/Math: 380/410	COMPETITIVE

Southern Connecticut State University, founded in 1893, provides undergraduate and graduate liberal arts programs emphasizing business and education. It is part of the Connecticut State University system. There are 5 undergraduate and 6 graduate schools. In addition to regional accreditation, SCSU has baccalaureate program accreditation with CSWE and NLN. The library contains 369,838 volumes, 671,485 microform items, and 3549 audiovisual forms, and subscribes to 3146 periodicals. Special learning facilities include a learning resource center, art gallery, planetarium, radio station, and TV station. The 168-acre campus is in an urban area 35 miles south of Hartford and 90 miles from New York City. Including residence halls, there are 28 buildings on campus.

Student Life: 90% of undergraduates are from Connecticut. Students come from 43 states and 26 foreign countries. 81% are white. 64% are Catholic; 18% Protestant. The average age of freshmen is 19; all undergraduates, 21. 11% do not continue beyond their first year.

Housing: 2400 students can be accommodated in college housing. College-sponsored living facilities include single-sex dormitories and on-campus apartments. On-campus housing is guaranteed for all 4 years. 65% of students commute. Upperclassmen may keep cars on campus.

Activities: 1% of men belong to 3 local and 3 national fraternities; 1% of women belong to 1 local and 2 national sororities. There are 70 groups on campus, including art, band, cheerleading, choir, chorale, chorus, computers, dance, drama, drill team, ethnic, gay, honors, international, jazz band, literary magazine, marching band, musical theater, newspaper, pep band, photography, political, professional, radio and TV, religious, social, social service, student government, and yearbook. Popular campus events include Springfest, Parents Day, and Octoberfest.

Sports: Athletic and recreation facilities include a 6000-seat artificial-surface playing complex for football, soccer, field hockey, and track; field house and gymnasium facilities for basketball, gymnastics, badminton, tennis, track and field, volleyball, and indoor baseball; and an 8-lane swimming pool.

Disabled Students: 80% of the campus is accessible to disabled students. The following facilities are available: wheelchair ramps, elevators, special parking, specially equipped rest rooms, special class scheduling, lowered drinking fountains, lowered telephones, and special computer facilities.

Services: In addition to many counseling and information services, tutoring is available in every subject. There is a reader service for the blind, and remedial math, reading, and writing.

Campus Safety and Security: Campus safety and security measures include 24-hour foot and vehicle patrol, self-defense education, escort service, and shuttle buses. There are informal discussions, pamphlets/posters/films, emergency telephones, lighted pathways/sidewalks. Campus security is provided by the State Police of Connecticut.

Programs of Study: SCSU confers B.A. and B.S. degrees. Associate and master's degrees are also awarded. Bachelor's degrees are awarded in BIOLOGICAL SCIENCE (biochemistry and biology/biological science), BUSINESS (accounting, banking and finance, business administration and management, business economics, marketing/retailing/merchandising, and recreation and leisure services), COMMUNICATIONS AND THE ARTS (art history and appreciation, communications, dramatic arts, English, fine arts, French, German, Italian, journalism, Spanish, and studio art), COMPUTER AND PHYSICAL SCIENCE (chemistry, computer science, earth science, mathematics, and physics), EDUCATION (art, early childhood, elementary, foreign languages, health, library science, physical, science, secondary, and special), HEALTH PROFESSIONS (nursing and public health), SOCIAL SCIENCE (economics, geography, history, philosophy, political science/government, psychology, social work, and sociology). Business and economics, education, and communication have the largest enrollments.

Required: All students must complete distribution requirements that include 3 credits each in American politics, fine arts, foreign languages, mathematics, literature, philosophy, and Western civilization, 6 credits each in English composition and speech, natural sciences, and social sciences, and 1 credit each in physical education and health. Students must take 122 total credits, with a minimum of 30 hours in the major field, and maintain a minimum overall GPA of 2.0.

Special: SCSU offer co-op programs in all academic majors, internships in many departments, study abroad in a variety of countries, a combined B.A.-B.S. degree, dual majors, a general studies degree, student-designed majors in liberal studies, and pass/fail options. There is a freshman honors program on campus, as well as 2 national honor societies. One department has an honors program.

Faculty/Classroom: No introductory courses are taught by graduate students. The average class size in an introductory lecture is 35; in a laboratory, 21; and in a regular course offering, 40.

Admissions: 67% of the 1995–96 applicants were accepted.

Requirements: The SAT I is required, with a minimum composite score of 800 on the SAT I, with at least 400 each in verbal and math, or a score of 15 on the ACT. Applicants must be in the upper 50% of their class, with a 2.5 GPA. In addition, applicants should graduate with 4 years in English, 3 in mathematics, and 2 each in natural sciences and social sciences, including American history. The GED is accepted. 2 years of foreign language are recommended. An essay also is needed. AP and CLEP credits are accepted. Important factors in the admissions decision are advanced placement or honor courses, recommendations by school officials, and leadership record.

Procedure: Freshmen are admitted fall and spring. Applications should be filed by May 1 for fall entry and December 1 for spring entry, along with an application fee of $20. Notification is sent on a rolling basis.

Transfer: 778 transfer students were enrolled in a recent year. Transfer applicants must have a minimum of 6 college credits with a grade of C or better and an overall GPA of 2.0. The SAT I is required for applicants with fewer than 24 college credits. 30 credits of 122 must be completed at SCSU.

Visiting: There are regularly scheduled orientations for prospective students. Visitors may sit in on classes. To schedule a visit, contact the Student Affairs Office at (203) 397–4281.

Financial Aid: SCSU is a member of CSS. The FAFSA and the college's own financial statement are required. The application deadline for fall entry is March 16.

International Students: In a recent year, there were 90 international students enrolled. They must score 525 on the TOEFL and also take SAT I or the ACT.

Computers: The college provides computer facilities for student use. The mainframe is a DEC VAX 8650. More than 200 microcomputers are available for student use in various campus locations. All students may access the system 24 hours a day. There are no time limits and no fees.

Graduates: In a recent year, 1506 bachelor's degrees were awarded. 150 companies recruited on campus in 1994–95.

Admissions Contact: Michael Swaby-Rowe, Assistant Director of Admissions.

TEIKYO POST UNIVERSITY
B-3
Waterbury, CT 06723–2540

(203) 596–4520
(800) 345–2562; FAX: (203) 756–5810

Full-time: 700 men and women	Faculty: 30; IIB, av$
Part-time: none	Ph.D.s: n/av
Graduate: none	Student/Faculty: 23 to 1
Year: semesters, summer session	Tuition: $11,960
Application Deadline: open	Room & Board: $5600
Freshman Class: 473 applied, 363 accepted, 145 enrolled	
SAT I or ACT: required	LESS COMPETITIVE

Teikyo Post University, founded in 1890, is a private coeducational institution offering liberal arts and business programs with an international focus. There are 2 undergraduate schools. The library contains 45,000 volumes, 4200 microform items, and 700 audiovisual forms, and subscribes to 525 periodicals. Computerized library sources and services include the card catalog, interlibrary loans, and database searching. Special learning facilities include a learning resource center and a tutorial center. The 70-acre campus is in a suburban area 1 mile west of Waterbury. Including residence halls, there are 12 buildings on campus.

Student Life: 82% of undergraduates are from Connecticut. Students come from 17 states, 32 foreign countries, and Canada. 70% are from public schools; 30% from private. 82% are white. The average age of freshmen is 20; all undergraduates, 24.

Housing: 330 students can be accommodated in college housing. College-sponsored living facilities include single-sex and coed dormitories and off-campus apartments. In addition there are honors houses. On-campus housing is guaranteed for all 4 years. 57% of students live on campus; of those, 40% remain on campus on weekends. All students may keep cars on campus.

Activities: There are no fraternities or sororities. There are 26 groups on campus, including cheerleading, chorale, chorus, drama, ethnic, honors, international, social, social service, student government, and

yearbook. Popular campus events include Peer Guide Program, Spring Week, Career Fair, and Karaoke Nights.

Sports: There are 2 intercollegiate sports for men and 2 for women, and 15 intramural sports for men and 15 for women. Athletic and recreation facilities include a gymnasium, a soccer/football field, a fitness center, a health club, a swimming pool, and handball and tennis courts.

Disabled Students: 70% of the campus is accessible to disabled students. The following facilities are available: wheelchair ramps, elevators, special parking, and specially equipped rest rooms.

Services: In addition to many counseling and information services, tutoring is available in some subjects, including English and mathematics. There is a reader service for the blind, and remedial math, reading, and writing.

Campus Safety and Security: Campus safety and security measures include 24-hour foot and vehicle patrol, self-defense education, escort service, and informal discussions. There are pamphlets/posters/films and lighted pathways/sidewalks.

Programs of Study: Teikyo Post confers B.A. and B.S. degrees. Associate degrees are also awarded. Bachelor's degrees are awarded in BUSINESS (accounting, banking and finance, business administration and management, management science, and marketing/retailing/merchandising), COMMUNICATIONS AND THE ARTS (English), SOCIAL SCIENCE (history, liberal arts/general studies, psychology, and sociology). Business and general studies are the strongest academically. Management and general studies have the largest enrollments.

Required: To graduate, all students must maintain a minimum GPA of 2.0 and earn a total of 120 credits for a B.S degree or 122 for a B.A. degree.

Special: Co-op programs in all majors with the universities of Hartford and Bridgeport, cross-registration with Mattatuck Community College, study abroad in England, the Netherlands, Poland, and Japan, internships with area businesses, B.A.-B.S. degrees, general studies degrees, student-designed majors, and credit for life experience are available. There are 2 national honor societies on campus. One department has an honors program.

Faculty/Classroom: 53% of faculty are male; 47%, female. All teach undergraduates. The average class size in an introductory lecture is 30; in a laboratory, 16; and in a regular course offering, 21.

Admissions: 77% of the 1995–96 applicants were accepted. There were 3 National Merit semifinalists in a recent year. One freshman graduated first in her class.

Requirements: The SAT I or ACT is required. Applicants must be in the upper 50% of their class with a 2.0 GPA. They must be graduates of an accredited secondary school, with 4 years of English and at least 16 total academic credits. The GED is accepted. AP and CLEP credits are accepted. Important factors in the admissions decision are advanced placement or honor courses, recommendations by school officials, and personality, intangible qualities.

Procedure: Freshmen are admitted to all sessions. Entrance exams should be taken as early as possible. There are early decision, early admissions, and deferred admissions plans. Application deadlines are open. The application fee is $40. Notification is sent on a rolling basis.

Transfer: Transfer applicants must have a minimum college GPA of 2.0. The SAT I is recommended. 30 credits of 120 must be completed at Teikyo Post.

Visiting: There are regularly scheduled orientations for prospective students, including tours, interviews with admissions counselors, and meetings with faculty and students. There are guides for informal visits and visitors may sit in on classes and stay overnight at the school. To schedule a visit, contact the Admissions Office.

Financial Aid: In a recent year, 85% of all freshmen and 70% of continuing students received some form of financial aid. The average freshman award was $6629. Of that total, scholarships or need-based grants averaged $5838 ($10,219 maximum); loans averaged $2625 ($4000 maximum); and work contracts averaged $1400 (maximum). 15% of undergraduate students work part-time. The average financial indebtedness of a recent graduate was $11,250. Teikyo Post is a member of CSS. The FAF, the college's own financial statement, and parent and student federal tax returns are required. The application deadline for fall entry is March 15.

International Students: In a recent year, there were 45 international students enrolled. The school actively recruits these students. They must score 550 on the TOEFL and also take SAT I or the college's own entrance exam.

Computers: The college provides computer facilities for student use. The mainframe is a DEC. IBM and Apple Macintosh microcomputers are available for student use in the computer laboratory, the library, and the tutorial center. All students may access the system. There are no time limits and no fees.

Admissions Contact: Jane LaRocco, Acting Director of Admissions.

TRINITY COLLEGE
C-2

Hartford, CT 06106   (860) 297-2180; FAX: (860) 297-2287

Full-time: 914 men, 873 women	Faculty: 163; IIB, + +$
Part-time: 68 men, 108 women	Ph.D.s: 98%
Graduate: 82 men, 75 women	Student/Faculty: 11 to 1
Year: semesters	Tuition: $20,450
Application Deadline: January 15	Room & Board: $6130
Freshman Class: 3054 applied, 1751 accepted, 509 enrolled	
SAT I Verbal/Math: 550/620	ACT: 26 HIGHLY COMPETITIVE

Trinity College, founded in 1823, is an independent, nonsectarian liberal arts college emphasizing interdisciplinary study and interaction with Hartford. There is 1 graduate school. In addition to regional accreditation, Trinity has baccalaureate program accreditation with ABET. The library contains 893,858 volumes, 302,116 microform items, and 20,446 audiovisual forms, and subscribes to 2273 periodicals. Computerized library sources and services include the card catalog, interlibrary loans, and database searching. Special learning facilities include an art gallery and radio station. The 96-acre campus is in an urban area southwest of downtown Hartford. Including residence halls, there are 50 buildings on campus.

Student Life: 72% of undergraduates are from out-of-state, mostly the Northeast. Students come from 44 states and 23 foreign countries. 52% are from public schools; 48% from private. 82% are white. The average age of freshmen is 18; all undergraduates, 20. 4% do not continue beyond their first year; 87% remain to graduate.

Housing: 1600 students can be accommodated in college housing. College-sponsored living facilities include coed dormitories, on-campus apartments, fraternity houses, and sorority houses. In addition there are special interest houses. On-campus housing is guaranteed for all 4 years and is available on a lottery system for upperclassmen. 96% of students live on campus; of those, 70% remain on campus on weekends. Upperclassmen may keep cars on campus.

Activities: 30% of men and 10% of women belong to 6 local coed fraternities. There are no sororities. There are 70 groups on campus, including art, band, cheerleading, chess, choir, chorale, dance, drama, ethnic, film, gay, international, jazz band, literary magazine, musical theater, newspaper, pep band, photography, political, radio and TV, religious, social, social service, student government, and yearbook.

Sports: There are 15 intercollegiate sports for men and 13 for women, and 7 intramural sports for men and 3 for women. Athletic and recreation facilities include a pool, outdoor and indoor tracks, tennis, squash, and basketball courts, playing fields, a weight room, and a fitness center.

Disabled Students: 60% of the campus is accessible to disabled students. The following facilities are available: wheelchair ramps, elevators, special parking, specially equipped rest rooms, special class scheduling, lowered drinking fountains, and lowered telephones.

Services: In addition to many counseling and information services, tutoring is available in every subject. There is a reader service for the blind.

Campus Safety and Security: Campus safety and security measures include 24-hour foot and vehicle patrol, self-defense education, escort service, and shuttle buses. In addition, there are informal discussions, pamphlets/posters/films, emergency telephones, and lighted pathways/sidewalks.

Programs of Study: Trinity confers B.A. and B.S. degrees. Master's degrees are also awarded. Bachelor's degrees are awarded in BIOLOGICAL SCIENCE (biochemistry, biology/biological science, and neurosciences), COMMUNICATIONS AND THE ARTS (classics, dance, dramatic arts, English, fine arts, French, German, Italian, modern language, music, Russian, and Spanish), COMPUTER AND PHYSICAL SCIENCE (chemistry, computer science, mathematics, and physics), ENGINEERING AND ENVIRONMENTAL DESIGN (engineering), SOCIAL SCIENCE (American studies, area studies, economics, history, international studies, philosophy, political science/government, psychology, public affairs, religion, sociology, and women's studies). English, history, and psychology have the largest enrollments.

Required: All students must complete 36 course credits, including 10 to 15 in the major and 1 from each of 5 distribution areas: arts, humanities, natural sciences, numerical and symbolic reasoning, and social sciences. There is also an integration of knowledge requirement (usually 5 to 6 courses). Students must maintain at least a C average overall.

Special: Trinity offers special freshman programs for exceptional students, including interdisciplinary programs in the sciences and the humanities. There is an intensive study program under which students can devote a semester to 1 subject. Cross-registration through such programs as the Hartford Consortium and the Twelve-College Exchange Program, hundreds of internships, study abroad virtually worldwide, a Washington semester, dual and student-designed majors, nondegree study, and pass/fail options also are offered. A 5-

year advanced degree in engineering with Rensselaer Polytechnic Institute also is available. There are 4 national honor societies on campus, including Phi Beta Kappa.

Faculty/Classroom: 58% of faculty are male; 42%, female. All both teach and do research. No introductory courses are taught by graduate students. The average class size in an introductory lecture is 35; in a laboratory, 20; and in a regular course offering, 19.

Admissions: 57% of the 1995–96 applicants were accepted. The SAT I scores for the 1995–96 freshman class were as follows: Verbal—19% below 500, 53% between 500 and 599, 25% between 600 and 700, and 3% above 700; Math—5% below 500, 31% between 500 and 599, 53% between 600 and 700, and 11% above 700. The ACT scores were 2% below 21, 19% between 21 and 23, 35% between 24 and 26, 19% between 27 and 28, and 25% above 28. 72% of the current freshmen were in the top fifth of their class; 94% were in the top two fifths.

Requirements: The SAT I or ACT is required, along with the SAT II: Subject test in writing. Trinity strongly emphasizes individual character and personal qualities in admission. Consequently, an interview and essay are recommended. The college requires 4 years of English, 2 years each in foreign language and algebra, and 1 year each in geometry, history, and laboratory science. AP credits are accepted. Important factors in the admissions decision are advanced placement or honor courses, extracurricular activities record, and evidence of special talent.

Procedure: Freshmen are admitted in the fall. Entrance exams should be taken in the fall of the senior year. There are early decision, early admissions, and deferred admissions plans. Early decision applications should be filed by November 15; regular applications, by January 15 for fall entry, along with an application fee of $50. Notification of early decision is sent December 31; regular decision, in early April. 104 early decision candidates were accepted for the 1995–96 class. A waiting list is an active part of the admissions procedure, with about 10% of all applicants on the list.

Transfer: 35 transfer students enrolled in 1995–96. Applicants must take the SAT I or ACT. A minimum college GPA of 3.0 is recommended. 18 course credits of 36 must be completed at Trinity.

Visiting: There are regularly scheduled orientations for prospective students. There are guides for informal visits and visitors may sit in on classes and stay overnight at the school. To schedule a visit, contact the Admissions Office.

Financial Aid: In 1995–96, 50% of all freshmen and 45% of continuing students received some form of financial aid, including need-based aid. The average freshman award was $17,990. Of that total, scholarships or need-based grants averaged $13,000 ($22,700 maximum); loans averaged $3625 (maximum); and work contracts averaged $1350 (maximum). 65% of undergraduate students work part-time. Average earnings from campus work for the school year are $1450. The average financial indebtedness of the 1994–95 graduate was $18,125. Trinity is a member of CSS. The FAF or FAFSA and the college's own financial statement are required. The application deadline for fall entry is February 1.

International Students: There are currently 31 international students enrolled. The school actively recruits these students. They must take the TOEFL and achieve a minimum score of 550. The student must also take the SAT I or the ACT.

Computers: The college provides computer facilities for student use. The mainframe is a Sun SPARC network. More than 100 Apple Macintosh and other microcomputers are networked and available for student use. Each can access the Sun or other Internet hosts. A wide variety of applications are available. Student-owned Apple Macintoshes in the residence halls are directly connected to the campus network. All students may access the system 24 hours daily. There are no time limits and no fees.

Graduates: In 1994–95, 477 bachelor's degrees were awarded. The most popular majors among graduates were history (13%), English (10%), and psychology (10%). Within an average freshman class, 81% graduate in 4 years, 87% in 5 years, and 87% in 6 years.

Admissions Contact: David M. Borus, Dean of Admissions. E-mail: admissions.office@mail.trincoll.edu.

UNITED STATES COAST GUARD ACADEMY
E-3

New London, CT 06320-4195   (203) 444-8500

(800) 883-8724; FAX: (203) 437-6700

Full-time: 659 men, 204 women	Faculty: 112
Part-time: none	Ph.D.s: 30%
Graduate: none	Student/Faculty: 8 to 1
Year: semesters, summer session	Tuition: see profile
Application Deadline: December 15	Room & Board: see profile
Freshman Class: 2231 applied, 433 accepted, 243 enrolled	
SAT I Verbal/Math: 552/639	ACT: 26 MOST COMPETITIVE

The U.S. Coast Guard Academy, founded in 1876, is an Armed Forces Service Academy for men and women. Appointments are made solely on the basis of an annual nationwide competition. Except for an entrance fee of $3,000, the federal government covers all cadet expenses by providing a monthly allowance of $550 plus a daily food allowance. In addition to regional accreditation, the academy has baccalaureate program accreditation with ABET. The library contains 150,000 volumes, 60,000 microform items, and 1500 audiovisual forms, and subscribes to 850 periodicals. Computerized library sources and services include the card catalog and database searching. Special learning facilities include the Coast Guard Museum and a $5-million bridge simulator. The 110-acre campus is in a suburban area 45 miles southeast of Hartford. Including residence halls, there are 25 buildings on campus.

Student Life: 93% of undergraduates are from out-of-state, mostly the Northeast. Students come from 48 states and 13 foreign countries. 79% are white. 33% are Catholic; 30% claim no religious affiliation; 29% Protestant. The average age of freshmen is 18; all undergraduates, 21. 21% do not continue beyond their first year; 67% remain to graduate.

Housing: 900 students can be accommodated in college housing. College-sponsored living facilities include coed dormitories. On-campus housing is guaranteed for all 4 years. All students live on campus and remain on campus on weekends. Alcohol is not permitted. Upperclassmen may keep cars on campus.

Activities: There are no fraternities or sororities. There are many groups and organizations on campus, including band, choir, chorale, chorus, drill team, drum and bugle corps, ethnic, jazz band, literary magazine, marching band, musical theater, newspaper, pep band, political, professional, religious, social service, student government, and yearbook. Popular campus events include Homecoming, Parents Weekend, Graduation, Coast Guard Day, and Hispanic Heritage and Black History months.

Sports: There are 13 intercollegiate sports for men and 9 for women, and 13 intramural sports for men and 10 for women. Athletic and recreation facilities include a field house with 3 basketball courts, a 6-lane swimming pool, 5 racquetball courts, and facilities for track meets, tennis matches, and baseball and softball games; an additional athletic facility with wrestling and weight rooms, basketball courts, gymnastics areas, a swimming pool, and saunas; a 4500-seat stadium; and practice and playing fields, outdoor tennis courts, and rowing and seamanship-sailing centers.

Disabled Students: 24% of the campus is accessible to disabled students. The following facilities are available: wheelchair ramps, elevators, special parking, and specially equipped rest rooms.

Services: In addition to many counseling and information services, tutoring is available in every subject.

Campus Safety and Security: Campus safety and security measures include 24-hour foot and vehicle patrol, self-defense education, and lighted pathways/sidewalks.

Programs of Study: The academy confers the B.S. degree. Bachelor's degrees are awarded in BIOLOGICAL SCIENCE (marine science), BUSINESS (management science and operations research), ENGINEERING AND ENVIRONMENTAL DESIGN (civil engineering, electrical/electronics engineering, mechanical engineering, and naval architecture and marine engineering), SOCIAL SCIENCE (political science/government). Political science/government has the largest enrollment.

Required: To graduate, cadets must pass at least 37 courses, of which 25 are core; accumulate a minimum of 126 credit hours, with at least 90 credits of C or better, exclusive of physical education; complete the academic requirements for one of the approved majors and attain a minimum GPA of 2.0 in all required upper-division courses in the major; successfully complete all professional development and physical education requirements; and maintain a high sense of integrity.

Special: Cross-registration with Connecticut College, summer cruises to foreign ports, 6-week internships with various government agencies, and a 1-semester exchange program with the 3 other military academies are available. All graduates are commissioned in the U.S. Coast Guard. There is a freshman honors program on campus, as well as 2 national honor societies. 3 departments have honors programs.

Faculty/Classroom: 90% of faculty are male; 10%, female. The average class size in an introductory lecture is 28; in a laboratory, 18; and in a regular course offering, 20.

Admissions: 19% of the 1995–96 applicants were accepted. The SAT I scores for the 1995–96 freshman class were as follows: Verbal—22% below 500, 44% between 500 and 599, 28% between 600 and 700, and 3% above 700; Math—1% below 500, 22% between 500 and 599, 58% between 600 and 700, and 19% above 700. 94% of the current freshmen were in the top fifth of their class; 100% were in the top two fifths.

Requirements: The SAT I or ACT is required. Applicants must have reached the age of 17 but not the age of 22 by July 1 of the year of admission, be citizens of the United States, and be single at the time of appointment and remain single while attending the academy. Required secondary school courses include 3 years each of English and

mathematics. AP credits are accepted. Important factors in the admissions decision are leadership record, extracurricular activities record, and advanced placement or honor courses.

Procedure: Freshmen are admitted in the summer. Entrance exams should be taken by December 15. Applications should be filed by December 15 for fall entry. Notification is sent on a rolling basis. A waiting list is an active part of the admissions procedure, with about 5% of all applicants on the list.

Transfer: All transfer students must meet the same standards as incoming freshmen and must begin as freshmen no matter how many semesters or years of college they have completed. 126 credits of 126 must be completed at the academy.

Visiting: There are regularly scheduled orientations for prospective students, including an admissions briefing and tour of the academy every Friday. To schedule a visit, contact the Director of Admissions at (203) 444-8501.

International Students: There are currently 18 international students enrolled. They must take the TOEFL and achieve a minimum score of 550. The student must also take the SAT I or the ACT and achieve a minimum score of 550 on the mathematics portion of the SAT I or 24 on the mathematics portion of the ACT.

Computers: The college provides computer facilities for student use. Students may use computer rooms in the dormitories and academic building. Access to the Sun Model 10 main server is also available. All students may access the system 24 hours a day. There are no time limits and no fees. It is recommended that students in all programs have personal computers. The Apple Macintosh is recommended.

Graduates: In 1994–95, 173 bachelor's degrees were awarded. The most popular majors among graduates were management (21%), marine science (19%), and government (17%). Within an average freshman class, 66% graduate in 4 years and 1% in 5 years.

Admissions Contact: Robert W. Thorne, Director of Admissions. E-mail: uscgatr@dcseq.uscga.edu. A campus video is available.

UNIVERSITY OF BRIDGEPORT
Bridgeport, CT 06602

B-4

(203) 576-4552
(800) 243-9496; FAX: (203) 576-4941

Full-time: 326 men, 385 women	**Faculty:** 83; IIA, -$
Part-time: 102 men, 128 women	**Ph.D.s:** 88%
Graduate: 475 men, 499 women	**Student/Faculty:** 9 to 1
Year: semesters, summer session	**Tuition:** $13,124
Application Deadline: April 1	**Room & Board:** $6810
Freshman Class: 1009 applied, 666 accepted, 140 enrolled	
SAT I Verbal/Math: 410/495	**COMPETITIVE**

The University of Bridgeport, founded in 1927, is a private, independent coeducational university offering programs in the arts, humanities, social sciences, business, engineering, human services, dental hygiene, chiropractic, and teacher preparation. There are 8 undergraduate and 6 graduate schools. In addition to regional accreditation, UB has baccalaureate program accreditation with ABET, ADA, and NASAD. The library contains 264,000 volumes, 980,000 microform items, and 5000 audiovisual forms, and subscribes to 1700 periodicals. Computerized library sources and services include interlibrary loans and database searching. Special learning facilities include a learning resource center and art gallery. The 86-acre campus is in an urban area 60 miles northeast of New York City. Including residence halls, there are 30 buildings on campus.

Student Life: 60% of undergraduates are from out-of-state, mostly the Middle Atlantic. Students come from 29 states and 60 foreign countries. 88% are from public schools; 12% from private. 38% are foreign nationals; 32% white; 17% African American. 16% are Catholic. The average age of freshmen is 19; all undergraduates, 25. 33% do not continue beyond their first year; 50% remain to graduate.

Housing: 500 students can be accommodated in college housing. College-sponsored living facilities include coed dormitories. In addition, there are alcohol- and tobacco-free floors. On-campus housing is guaranteed for all 4 years. 52% of students commute. All students may keep cars on campus.

Activities: 1% of men belong to 2 local fraternities; 2% of women belong to 3 local and 1 national sororities. There are 32 groups on campus, including art, band, cheerleading, choir, chorale, chorus, computers, drama, ethnic, gay, honors, international, jazz band, literary magazine, musical theater, newspaper, photography, political, professional, radio, religious, social, social service, student government, symphony, and yearbook. Popular campus events include Spring Week, International Festival, Winter Prelude, Halloween Ball, and Wisteria Ball.

Sports: There are 4 intercollegiate sports for men and 5 for women, and 8 intramural sports for men and 8 for women. Athletic and recreation facilities include a gymnasium, athletic fields, tennis and racquetball courts, and a recreation center with an indoor pool.

Disabled Students: 60% of the campus is accessible to disabled students. The following facilities are available: wheelchair ramps, elevators, special parking, specially equipped rest rooms, and special class scheduling.

Services: In addition to many counseling and information services, tutoring is available in every subject. There is a reader service for the blind, and remedial math, reading, and writing.

Campus Safety and Security: Campus safety and security measures include 24-hour foot and vehicle patrol, escort service, informal discussions, and pamphlets/posters/films. In addition, there are emergency telephones, lighted pathways/sidewalks, and campus security systems.

Programs of Study: UB confers B.A., B.S., B.E.S., B.F.A., and B.M. degrees. Associate, master's, and doctoral degrees are also awarded. Bachelor's degrees are awarded in BIOLOGICAL SCIENCE (biology/biological science), BUSINESS (accounting, banking and finance, business administration and management, fashion merchandising, international business management, management information systems, management science, and marketing/retailing/merchandising), COMMUNICATIONS AND THE ARTS (communications, English, fine arts, graphic design, illustration, industrial design, journalism, literature, and music), COMPUTER AND PHYSICAL SCIENCE (computer science and mathematics), ENGINEERING AND ENVIRONMENTAL DESIGN (computer engineering and interior design), HEALTH PROFESSIONS (chiropractic, dental hygiene, medical laboratory technology, predentistry, premedicine, and respiratory therapy), SOCIAL SCIENCE (economics, human services, prelaw, and social science). Computer science/engineering, business, and dental hygiene are the strongest academically. Dental hygiene, business administration, and computer science/engineering have the largest enrollments.

Required: All students are required to complete at least 120 credit hours including at least 30 in the major field. A minimum GPA of 2.0 is necessary. Distribution requirements cover 33 core credits and are comprised of skills, heritage, and capstone sections, including 3 hours each in English composition and quantitative skills, and 24 semester hours consisting of 6 hours each in humanities, natural science, and social science and 3 each in integrated studies and fine arts.

Special: UB offers co-op programs with several local institutions, cross-registration with Sacred Heart and Fairfield universities, internships in many degree programs, study abroad in England, Switzerland, or Spain, a Washington semester, and work-study programs. In addition, an elective studies accelerated degree program, dual majors, student-designed majors, and B.A.-B.S. degrees are available. Credit for life experience, nondegree study, and pass/fail options are offered. There are 14 national honor societies on campus. One department has an honors program.

Faculty/Classroom: 81% of faculty are male; 19%, female. All both teach and do research. No introductory courses are taught by graduate students. The average class size in an introductory lecture is 15; in a laboratory, 10; and in a regular course offering, 14.

Admissions: 66% of the 1995–96 applicants were accepted. The SAT I scores for the 1995–96 freshman class were as follows: Verbal—83% below 500, 14% between 500 and 599, 1% between 600 and 700, and 2% above 700; Math—50% below 500, 21% between 500 and 599, 22% between 600 and 700, and 7% above 700. 31% of the current freshmen were in the top fifth of their class; 52% were in the top two fifths.

Requirements: The SAT I or ACT is required. UB requires applicants to be in the upper 50% of their class. A minimum GPA of 2.0 is required. In addition, applicants are required to have 16 academic credits or Carnegie units, including 4 units of English, 3 of mathematics, 2 of history, and 1 each of social studies and a laboratory science. A portfolio is required for B.F.A. students and an audition for B.M. candidates. AP and CLEP credits are accepted. Important factors in the admissions decision are advanced placement or honor courses, extracurricular activities record, and recommendations by school officials.

Procedure: Freshmen are admitted fall and spring. Entrance exams should be taken during the senior year. There are early decision, early admissions, and deferred admissions plans. Applications should be filed by April 1 for fall entry and December 1 for spring entry, along with an application fee of $35. Notification is sent on a rolling basis.

Transfer: 76 transfer students enrolled in 1995–96. Applicants need a minimum GPA of 2.5 and at least 12 earned credit hours. The SAT I or ACT and an interview are recommended. 30 credits of 120 must be completed at UB.

Visiting: There are regularly scheduled orientations for prospective students. There are guides for informal visits and visitors may sit in on classes and stay overnight at the school. To schedule a visit, contact the Admissions Office.

Financial Aid: In 1995–96, 87% of all freshmen and 96% of continuing students received some form of financial aid. 52% of freshmen and 69% of continuing students received need-based aid. The average freshman award was $17,700. Of that total, scholarships or need-based grants averaged $13,875 ($21,274 maximum); loans averaged $4025 ($8025 maximum); and work contracts averaged $1400 ($2000 maximum). 47% of undergraduate students work part-time. Average earnings from campus work for the school year are $1000. The average financial indebtedness of the 1994–95 graduate was $17,800. UB is a member of CSS. The FAFSA and the college's own financial statement are required. The application deadline for fall entry is April 15.

International Students: There are currently 356 international students enrolled. The school actively recruits these students. They must take the TOEFL and achieve a minimum score of 500.

Computers: The college provides computer facilities for student use. The mainframe is a Prime 6350. Computer systems available throughout campus include Sun Microsystems workstations, Apollo workstations, a DEC VAX ll/785, 7 all-purpose PC laboratories, and a specialized microprocessor laboratory. All students may access the system 8 A.M. to 11 P.M. daily. There are no time limits and no fees.

Graduates: In 1994–95, 108 bachelor's degrees were awarded. The most popular majors among graduates were business (30%), elective studies (22%), and engineering (10%). Within an average freshman class, 40% graduate in 4 years, 45% in 5 years, and 50% in 6 years. 50 companies recruited on campus in 1994–95.

Admissions Contact: Dr. Suzanne D. Wilcox, Dean of Admissions and Financial Aid. A campus video is available.

UNIVERSITY OF CONNECTICUT
D-2

Storrs, CT 06269   (860) 486-3137; FAX: (860) 486-1476

Full-time: 5066 men, 5205 women	**Faculty:** 1143; I, +$
Part-time: 621 men, 438 women	**Ph.D.s:** 93%
Graduate: 2112 men, 2293 women	**Student/Faculty:** 9 to 1
Year: semesters, summer session	**Tuition:** $4810 ($12,800)
Application Deadline: April 1	**Room & Board:** $5124
Freshman Class: 9886 applied, 6884 accepted, 2021 enrolled	
SAT I Verbal/Math: 479/549	**VERY COMPETITIVE**

The University of Connecticut, founded in 1881, is a public, land-grant, sea-grant, multicampus, coeducational research institution offering degree programs in liberal arts and sciences and professional studies. There are 10 undergraduate and 5 graduate schools. In addition to regional accreditation, UConn has baccalaureate program accreditation with AACSB, ABET, ACPE, APTA, ASLA, NASAD, NASM, NCATE, and NLN. The library contains 2,012,767 volumes, 2,890,142 microform items, and 25,637 audiovisual forms, and subscribes to 8476 periodicals. Computerized library sources and services include the card catalog and database searching. Special learning facilities include a learning resource center, art gallery, natural history museum, planetarium, radio station, and TV station. The 5000-acre campus is in a rural area 25 miles east of Hartford. Including residence halls, there are 150 buildings on campus.

Student Life: 85% of undergraduates are from Connecticut. Students come from more than 90 foreign countries. 82% are white. The average age of freshmen is 19; all undergraduates, 21. 14% do not continue beyond their first year; 70% remain to graduate.

Housing: 8633 students can be accommodated in college housing. College-sponsored living facilities include single-sex and coed dormitories and married-student housing. In addition there are language houses, special interest houses, a floor for older students, and a living/learning center. On-campus housing is guaranteed for all 4 years. 65% of students live on campus; of those, 70% remain on campus on weekends. Upperclassmen may keep cars on campus.

Activities: 13% of men belong to 17 national fraternities; 7% of women belong to 9 national sororities. There are 285 groups on campus, including art, band, cheerleading, chess, choir, chorale, chorus, computers, dance, drama, ethnic, gay, honors, international, jazz band, literary magazine, marching band, musical theater, newspaper, opera, orchestra, pep band, photography, political, professional, radio and TV, religious, social, social service, student government, symphony, and yearbook. Popular campus events include Homecoming, Spring Weekend, 'UConn Do It' campus clean-up day, Winter Weekend, and Black History Month.

Sports: There are 11 intercollegiate sports for men and 10 for women, and 20 intramural sports for men and 20 for women. Athletic and recreation facilities include a sports center, a field house, and a 16000-seat stadium.

Disabled Students: 75% of the campus is accessible to disabled students. The following facilities are available: wheelchair ramps, elevators, special parking, specially equipped rest rooms, special class scheduling, lowered drinking fountains, lowered telephones, a tactile map, and 2 specially equipped transportation vans.

Services: In addition to many counseling and information services, tutoring is available in most subjects. There is a reader service for the blind. Also available are a Braille printer, a Kurzweil reading machine, and Apple computer with voice synthesizer, a machine to enlarge printed material, a talking calculator, and a TDD.

Campus Safety and Security: Campus safety and security measures include 24-hour foot and vehicle patrol, self-defense education, escort service, and shuttle buses. In addition, there are informal discussions, pamphlets/posters/films, emergency telephones, and lighted pathways/sidewalks.

Programs of Study: UConn confers B.A., B.S., B.F.A., B.Mus., B.Pharm., B.S.E., and B.G.S. degrees. Associate, master's, and doctoral degrees are also awarded. Bachelor's degrees are awarded in AGRICULTURE (agricultural economics, agriculture, animal science, horticulture, and natural resource management), BIOLOGICAL SCIENCE (biology/biological science, biophysics, molecular biology, nutrition, and physiology), BUSINESS (accounting, banking and finance, business administration and management, insurance and risk management, management information systems, marketing/retailing/merchandising, and real estate), COMMUNICATIONS AND THE ARTS (art, art history and appreciation, classics, communications, design, dramatic arts, English, fine arts, French, German, graphic design, Italian, journalism, linguistics, music, Portuguese, Spanish, and theater design), COMPUTER AND PHYSICAL SCIENCE (chemistry, geology, mathematics, physics, and statistics), EDUCATION (agricultural, elementary, English, foreign languages, mathematics, music, physical, recreation, and special), ENGINEERING AND ENVIRONMENTAL DESIGN (chemical engineering, civil engineering, computer engineering, electrical/electronics engineering, landscape architecture/design, and mechanical engineering), HEALTH PROFESSIONS (cytotechnology, medical laboratory technology, nursing, pharmacy, and physical therapy), SOCIAL SCIENCE (anthropology, dietetics, Eastern European studies, economics, geography, history, human development, Latin American studies, Middle Eastern studies, philosophy, political science/government, psychology, Russian and Slavic studies, sociology, urban studies, and women's studies). Psychology, education, and biological sciences have the largest enrollments.

Required: To graduate, students must complete 120 credits with a GPA of 2.0. There are general education requirements in foreign language, expository writing, mathematics, literature and the arts, culture and modern society, philosophical and ethical analysis, social scientific and comparative analysis, and science and technology.

Special: UConn offers co-op programs in most majors, internships, study abroad in 28 countries, dual majors, general studies degrees, student-designed majors, work-study programs, nondegree study, and pass/fail options. There is a freshman honors program on campus, as well as 24 national honor societies, including Phi Beta Kappa. 83 departments have honors programs.

Faculty/Classroom: 76% of faculty are male; 24%, female. 95% both teach and do research. The average class size in an introductory lecture is 33 and in a regular course offering, 30.

Admissions: 70% of the 1995–96 applicants were accepted. The SAT I scores for the 1995–96 freshman class were as follows: Verbal—60% below 500, 30% between 500 and 599, 9% between 600 and 700, and 1% above 700; Math—29% below 500, 38% between 500 and 599, 26% between 600 and 700, and 7% above 700. 48% of the current freshmen were in the top fifth of their class; 86% were in the top two fifths. There were 16 National Merit semifinalists. 20 freshmen graduated first in their class.

Requirements: The SAT I or ACT is required. The SAT I is preferred. Applicants must be graduates of an accredited secondary school and rank in the upper 50% of their class. The GED is accepted. Students should have completed 15 high school academic units, including 4 years of English, 3 years of mathematics, and 2 years each of foreign language, science, social studies, and electives. An essay is recommended. An audition is required for music students and a portfolio for art students. Applications are accepted on computer disk through CollegeLink. AP credits are accepted. Important factors in the admissions decision are evidence of special talent, advanced placement or honor courses, and leadership record.

Procedure: Freshmen are admitted fall and spring. Entrance exams should be taken in the spring of the junior year or fall of the senior year. There are early admissions and deferred admissions plans. Applications should be filed by April 1 for fall entry and October 1 for spring entry, along with an application fee of $40. Notification is sent on a rolling basis.

Transfer: 640 transfer students enrolled in 1995–96. Applicants for transfer should have a minimum GPA of 2.5. An associate degree or a minimum of 54 credit hours is recommended. 30 credits of 120 must be completed at UConn.

Visiting: There are regularly scheduled orientations for prospective students, including daily tours and information sessions. There are guides for informal visits and visitors may sit in on classes and stay overnight at the school. To schedule a visit, contact Barry Wilson at (203) 486-3137 for overnight reservation or (203) 486-4866 for tour reservation.

Financial Aid: In a recent year, 35% of all freshmen and 65% of continuing students received some form of financial aid. Scholarships or need-based grants averaged $985; loans averaged $2400 ($3800

maximum); and work contracts averaged $1300 ($1500 maximum). Average earnings from campus work for the school year are $1500. The average financial indebtedness of the 1994–95 graduate was $6900. UConn is a member of CSS. The FAFSA and the college's own financial statement are required. The application deadline for fall entry is February 15.

International Students: There are currently 105 international students enrolled. The school actively recruits these students. They must take the TOEFL or the college's own test and achieve a minimum score on the TOEFL of 550. The student must also take the SAT I or the ACT.

Computers: The college provides computer facilities for student use. The mainframes are an IBM 3090, Models 150E and 180E. There are more than 1800 terminals on campus, located in the computer center, the library, the various schools and colleges, and some residence halls. All students may access the system 24 hours weekdays; 8 A.M. to 12 P.M. weekends. There are no time limits and no fees.

Graduates: In 1994–95, 3470 bachelor's degrees were awarded. The most popular majors among graduates were psychology (7%), general studies (7%), and English (6%). Within an average freshman class, 40% graduate in 4 years, 64% in 5 years, and 68% in 6 years. 206 companies recruited on campus in 1994–95.

Admissions Contact: Dr. Ann Huckenbeck, Director of Admissions.

UNIVERSITY OF HARTFORD
West Hartford, CT 06117

C-2

(860) 243-4296
(800) 947-4303; FAX: (860) 768-4961

Full-time: 2051 men, 1931 women	Faculty: 314; IIA, -$
Part-time: 549 men, 698 women	Ph.D.s: 78%
Graduate: 740 men, 1053 women	Student/Faculty: 13 to 1
Year: semesters, summer session	Tuition: $15,636
Application Deadline: March 1	Room & Board: $6266
Freshman Class: 5445 applied, 4226 accepted, 1198 enrolled	
SAT I Verbal/Math: 450/500	ACT: 21 COMPETITIVE

The University of Hartford, founded in 1877, is an independent, nonsectarian, coeducational institution offering extensive undergraduate and graduate programs ranging from liberal arts to business. There are 9 undergraduate and 7 graduate schools. In addition to regional accreditation, the university has baccalaureate program accreditation with ABET, CAHEA, NASAD, NASM, and NCATE. The 3 libraries contain 366,610 volumes, 243,891 microform items, and 26,945 audiovisual forms, and subscribe to 3601 periodicals. Computerized library sources and services include the card catalog, interlibrary loans, and database searching. Special learning facilities include a learning resource center, art gallery, radio station, TV station, and the Museum of American Political Life. The 320-acre campus is in a suburban area 4 miles northwest of Hartford. Including residence halls, there are 35 buildings on campus.

Student Life: 68% of undergraduates are from out-of-state, mostly the Northeast. Students come from 41 states, 61 foreign countries, and Canada. 74% are from public schools; 26% from private. 80% are white. 50% claim no religious affiliation; 26% Catholic; 11% Protestant; 11% Jewish. The average age of freshmen is 18; all undergraduates, 23. 26% do not continue beyond their first year; 58% remain to graduate.

Housing: 3495 students can be accommodated in college housing. College-sponsored living facilities include coed dormitories and on-campus apartments. In addition there are honors houses, special interest houses, and the Residential College for the Arts and the International Residential College. On-campus housing is guaranteed for all 4 years. 72% of students live on campus; of those, 85% remain on campus on weekends. All students may keep cars on campus.

Activities: 12% of men belong to 8 national fraternities; 12% of women belong to 5 national sororities. There are more than 100 groups and organizations on campus, including art, band, cheerleading, choir, chorale, chorus, computers, drama, ethnic, gay, honors, international, jazz band, literary magazine, musical theater, newspaper, opera, orchestra, pep band, political, professional, radio and TV, religious, social, social service, student government, symphony, and yearbook. Popular campus events include Welcome Weekend, Spring Weekend, Winter Carnival, University Players Productions, Hartt School performances, and Homecoming.

Sports: There are 9 intercollegiate sports for men and 9 for women, and 16 intramural sports for men and 16 for women. Athletic and recreation facilities include playing fields, a 25-meter outdoor pool, tennis courts, golf practice cages, a fitness trail, and a sports center with a 4600-seat multipurpose court, an 8-lane swimming pool, a weight room, racquetball courts, a squash court, and saunas.

Disabled Students: The entire campus is accessible to disabled students. The following facilities are available: wheelchair ramps, elevators, special parking, specially equipped rest rooms, lowered drinking fountains, and lowered telephones.

Services: In addition to many counseling and information services, tutoring is available in most subjects. There is a reader service for the blind, and remedial math, reading, and writing. The health education office offers peer counseling and workshops on health-related topics. Professional counseling is available.

Campus Safety and Security: Campus safety and security measures include 24-hour foot and vehicle patrol, self-defense education, escort service, and shuttle buses. In addition, there are informal discussions, pamphlets/posters/films, emergency telephones, lighted pathways/sidewalks, and bicycle patrol.

Programs of Study: The university confers B.A., B.F.A., B.Mus., B.S.A.E.T., B.S.B.A., B.S.C.E., B.S.Comp.E., B.S.Ed., B.S.E.E., B.S.E.E.T., B.S.M.E., and B.S.N. degrees. Associate, master's, and doctoral degrees are also awarded. Bachelor's degrees are awarded in BIOLOGICAL SCIENCE (biology/biological science), BUSINESS (accounting, entrepreneurial studies, insurance, management information systems, management science, and marketing/retailing/merchandising), COMMUNICATIONS AND THE ARTS (art history and appreciation, audio technology, communications, dance, design, dramatic arts, drawing, English, film arts, fine arts, illustration, languages, music, painting, performing arts, photography, printmaking, sculpture, technical and business writing, theater management, and video), COMPUTER AND PHYSICAL SCIENCE (actuarial science, chemistry, computer science, mathematics, physics, and radiological technology), EDUCATION (early childhood, elementary, music, secondary, and special), ENGINEERING AND ENVIRONMENTAL DESIGN (architectural technology, ceramic science, chemical engineering technology, civil engineering, computer engineering, computer technology, electrical/electronics engineering, electrical/electronics engineering technology, engineering, environmental engineering, manufacturing engineering, mechanical engineering, and mechanical engineering technology), HEALTH PROFESSIONS (chiropractic, medical laboratory technology, nursing, occupational therapy, physical therapy, predentistry, preoptometry, and respiratory therapy), SOCIAL SCIENCE (criminal justice, economics, history, human services, Judaic studies, philosophy, political science/government, psychology, sociology, and women's studies). Computer science, engineering, and actuarial science are the strongest academically. Communication, psychology, and marketing have the largest enrollments.

Required: To graduate, students must complete at least 120 credit hours, fulfill the university's core curriculum requirements, and maintain an overall GPA of 2.0. Specific core and course requirements vary with the major.

Special: Cross-registration with the Greater Hartford Consortium, internships in all majors, study abroad, a Washington semester, work-study programs, credit for life experience, nondegree study, and pass/fail options are available. In addition, students may pursue accelerated degrees, B.A.-B.S. degrees, dual majors, or their own individually designed majors. There are interdisciplinary majors in acoustics and music and in experimental studio combining performing, literary, and visual arts. Also available are preprofessional programs in biology/preoptometry with the New England College of Optometry, predentistry with the New York University School of Dentistry, and prechiropractic with the New York Chiropractic College. There is a freshman honors program on campus, as well as 7 national honor societies. 9 departments have honors programs.

Faculty/Classroom: 70% of faculty are male; 30%, female. 96% teach undergraduates, and all do research. No introductory courses are taught by graduate students. The average class size in an introductory lecture is 40; in a laboratory, 20; and in a regular course offering, 30.

Admissions: 78% of the 1995–96 applicants were accepted. The SAT I scores for the 1995–96 freshman class were as follows: Verbal—72% below 500, 22% between 500 and 599, and 6% between 600 and 700; Math—49% below 500, 33% between 500 and 599, 16% between 600 and 700, and 2% above 700. The ACT scores were 44% below 21, 30% between 21 and 23, 14% between 24 and 26, 8% between 27 and 28, and 4% above 28. 55% of the current freshmen were in the top fifth of their class; 84% were in the top two fifths.

Requirements: The SAT I is required. Applicants should have 16 academic high school credits and 16 Carnegie units, including 4 units in English, 3 in mathematics (3.5 for B.S. candidates), and 2 each in foreign language, science, and social studies. A portfolio and an audition are required for B.F.A. and B.Mus. candidates, respectively. A personal statement is required and an interview is recommended for all students. AP and CLEP credits are accepted. Important factors in the admissions decision are advanced placement or honor courses, recommendations by school officials, and leadership record.

Procedure: Freshmen are admitted fall and spring. Entrance exams should be taken in the spring of the junior year or the fall of the senior year. There are early admissions and deferred admissions plans. Applications should be filed by March 1 for fall entry and December 1

for spring entry, along with an application fee of $35. Notification is sent on a rolling basis.

Transfer: 327 transfer students enrolled in 1995–96. Transfer students must have a minimum college GPA of 2.0, with 2.5 recommended, and must submit SAT I or ACT scores if they have fewer than 30 transferable college-level credits. An interview is also recommended. 30 credits of 120 must be completed at the university.

Visiting: There are regularly scheduled orientations for prospective students. There are guides for informal visits and visitors may sit in on classes and stay overnight at the school. To schedule a visit, contact the Office of Admissions at (860) 768-4296.

Financial Aid: In 1995–96, 88% of all freshmen and 80% of continuing students received some form of financial aid. 70% of freshmen and 75% of continuing students received need-based aid. The average freshman award was $12,600. Of that total, scholarships or need-based grants averaged $7980 ($15,900 maximum); loans averaged $3640 ($4000 maximum); and work contracts averaged $980 ($1200 maximum). 25% of undergraduate students work part-time. Average earnings from campus work for the school year are $1000. The average financial indebtedness of the 1994–95 graduate was $11,000. The university is a member of CSS. The FAFSA is required. The application deadline for fall entry is February 1.

International Students: There are currently 440 international students enrolled. The school actively recruits these students. They must take the TOEFL and achieve a minimum score of 550.

Computers: The college provides computer facilities for student use. The mainframe is a DEC VAX 6610. Approximately 400 personal computers, terminals, and workstations are available for student use in a variety of university locations, some of which are open 8 A.M. to midnight. All students may access the system. There are no time limits and no fees.

Graduates: In 1994–95, 792 bachelor's degrees were awarded. The most popular majors among graduates were communication (12%), marketing (6%), and mechanical engineering (5%). Within an average freshman class, 47% graduate in 4 years, 56% in 5 years, and 57% in 6 years. 63 companies recruited on campus in 1994–95.

Admissions Contact: Richard A. Zeiser, Director of Admissions. E-mail: admission@uhavax.hartford.edu. A campus video is available.

UNIVERSITY OF NEW HAVEN   C-3
West Haven, CT 06516   (203) 932-7319; (800) DIAL-UNH

Full-time: 961 men, 560 women	Faculty: 150; IIA, av$
Part-time: 1250 men, 567 women	Ph.D.s: 95%
Graduate: 1318 men, 1116 women	Student/Faculty: 10 to 1
Year: 4-1-4, summer session	Tuition: $11,400
Application Deadline: open	Room & Board: $4665
Freshman Class: n/av	
SAT I or ACT: required	COMPETITIVE

The University of New Haven, founded in 1920, is an independent, coeducational institution offering undergraduate programs in arts and sciences, business, engineering, public safety and professional studies, and hotel, restaurant, and tourism administration. There are 5 undergraduate schools and one graduate school. In addition to regional accreditation, UNH has baccalaureate program accreditation with ABET. The library contains 370,000 volumes, 49,000 microform items, and 10,000 audiovisual forms, and subscribes to 1700 periodicals. Computerized library sources and services include interlibrary loans and database searching. Special learning facilities include a learning resource center, art gallery, and radio station. The 73-acre campus is in a suburban area 5 miles west of New Haven. Including residence halls, there are 22 buildings on campus.

Student Life: 65% of undergraduates are from Connecticut. Students come from 25 states, 51 foreign countries, and Canada. 79% are from public schools; 21% from private. 75% are white; 12% African American. The average age of all undergraduates is 20. 25% do not continue beyond their first year; 40% remain to graduate.

Housing: 733 students can be accommodated in college housing. College-sponsored living facilities include coed dormitories and on-campus apartments. On-campus housing is guaranteed for the freshman year only, is available on a first-come, first-served basis, and is available on a lottery system for upperclassmen. 68% of students commute. All students may keep cars on campus.

Activities: 8% of men belong to 4 local fraternities and 1 national fraternity; 8% of women belong to 3 local sororities. There are 40 groups on campus, including cheerleading, chorus, drama, ethnic, honors, international, jazz band, literary magazine, newspaper, photography, political, professional, radio and TV, religious, social, social service, student government, and yearbook. Popular campus events include Homecoming, Parents Weekend, AIDS Awareness Week, Alcohol Awareness Week, May Day, and International Festival.

Sports: There are 8 intercollegiate sports for men and 5 for women, and 10 intramural sports for men and 6 for women. Athletic and recreation facilities include playing fields, tennis courts, a gymnasium with a basketball court, weight training room, racquetball court, and gymnastics area.

Disabled Students: 60% of the campus is accessible to disabled students. The following facilities are available: wheelchair ramps, elevators, special parking, specially equipped rest rooms, special class scheduling, lowered drinking fountains, lowered telephones, and special door handles.

Services: In addition to many counseling and information services, tutoring is available in most subjects. There is remedial math, reading, and writing.

Campus Safety and Security: Campus safety and security measures include 24-hour foot and vehicle patrol, informal discussions, pamphlets/posters/films, and required programs during orientation for new students.

Programs of Study: UNH confers B.A. and B.S. degrees. Associate, master's, and doctoral degrees are also awarded. Bachelor's degrees are awarded in BIOLOGICAL SCIENCE (biology/biological science), BUSINESS (accounting, banking and finance, business administration and management, business economics, hotel/motel and restaurant management, human resources, international business management, management information systems, marketing/retailing/merchandising, sports management, and tourism), COMMUNICATIONS AND THE ARTS (art, audio technology, communications, creative writing, English, fine arts, graphic design, music, and public relations), COMPUTER AND PHYSICAL SCIENCE (applied mathematics, chemistry, computer science, mathematics, natural sciences, and statistics), ENGINEERING AND ENVIRONMENTAL DESIGN (aviation administration/management, chemical engineering, civil engineering, electrical/electronics engineering, environmental science, fire protection engineering, industrial engineering, interior design, mechanical engineering, and occupational safety and health), HEALTH PROFESSIONS (health care administration, medical technology, predentistry, premedicine, and preveterinary science), SOCIAL SCIENCE (clinical psychology, community psychology, criminal justice, criminology, dietetics, economics, fire science, forensic studies, history, industrial and organizational psychology, liberal arts/general studies, political science/government, psychology, and public administration). Engineering, criminal justice, and forensic science are the strongest academically. Business, engineering, and arts and sciences have the largest enrollments.

Required: All students must maintain a GPA of 2.0 and complete a total of 121 to 134 credits, depending on the major. Students must take 34 credits from the university core curriculum, which includes English composition, literature, mathematics or computer science, the scientific method, laboratory science, history, social science, and fine arts or theater.

Special: Co-op programs in most majors, internships, work-study programs, student-designed majors in the school of professional studies, interdisciplinary majors including biomedical computing, and nondegree study are possible. There is a freshman honors program on campus, as well as 5 national honor societies.

Faculty/Classroom: 88% of faculty are male; 12%, female. All teach undergraduates. No introductory courses are taught by graduate students. The average class size in a regular course offering is 19.

Admissions: The SAT I scores for a recent freshman class were as follows: Verbal—91% below 500, 6% between 500 and 599, and 3% between 600 and 700; Math—48% below 500, 50% between 500 and 599, and 2% between 600 and 700.

Requirements: The SAT I or ACT is required, with the SAT I preferred. UNH requires applicants to be in the upper 60% of their class. A minimum GPA of 2.0 is required. In addition, applicants should be graduates of an accredited secondary school and have 16 academic credits or Carnegie units, including 4 in English, 3 each in mathematics and electives, and 2 each in science and history, with an additional 2 credits in foreign language advised. An interview is recommended. The GED is accepted. AP and CLEP credits are accepted. Important factors in the admissions decision are advanced placement or honor courses, evidence of special talent, and extracurricular activities record.

Procedure: Freshmen are admitted fall and spring. Entrance exams should be taken in the fall or winter of the senior year. There is a deferred admissions plan. Application deadlines are open. Application fee is $25. Notification is sent on a rolling basis.

Transfer: 248 transfer students enrolled in a recent year. Transfer applicants should have a minimum college GPA of 2.0 and should submit all official transcripts. An interview is recommended, and the SAT I is required for students with fewer than 30 college credits. 30 credits of 121 to 134 must be completed at UNH.

Visiting: There are regularly scheduled orientations for prospective students, including 2 open houses in the fall, and in March each undergraduate school of the university hosts a special day for accepted students. There are guides for informal visits and visitors may sit in on classes and stay overnight at the school. To schedule a visit, contact the Admissions Office.

Financial Aid: In a recent year, 70% of all students received some form of financial aid. 70% of all students received need-based aid. The average freshman award was $9699. Of that total, scholarships or need-based grants averaged $5067 ($15,250 maximum); loans averaged $3340 ($4425 maximum); and work contracts averaged $4292. 55% of undergraduate students work part-time. Average earnings from campus work for the school year are $882. UNH is a member of CSS. The FAFSA, the college's own financial statement, and the 1040 tax form are required. Check with the school for application deadlines.

International Students: There were 500 international students enrolled in a recent year. The school actively recruits these students. They must take the TOEFL and achieve a minimum score of 500. English-speaking students must also take the SAT I.

Computers: The college provides computer facilities for student use. The mainframes are a DEC VAX 6220, a Prime 9955, and a Data General MV/800. There are 140 microcomputers located in the computer center, the library, and academic and administrative buildings. All students may access the system 24 hours a day. There are no time limits and no fees.

Admissions Contact: Steven T. Briggs, Dean of Undergraduate Admissions and Financial Aid.

WESLEYAN UNIVERSITY

C-3

Middletown, CT 06457   (860) 685-3000; FAX: (860) 685-3001

Full-time: 1294 men, 1399 women	**Faculty:** 279; IIA, + +$
Part-time: 8 men, 15 women	**Ph.D.s:** 95%
Graduate: 207 men, 321 women	**Student/Faculty:** 10 to 1
Year: semesters	**Tuition:** $20,820
Application Deadline: January 1	**Room & Board:** $5810
Freshman Class: 5500 applied, 1956 accepted, 711 enrolled	
SAT I Verbal/Math: 620/670	**ACT:** 29 **MOST COMPETITIVE**

Wesleyan University, founded in 1831, is an independent, coeducational liberal arts institution. There is 1 graduate school. The 5 libraries contain 1 million volumes and 190,000 microform items, and subscribe to 3358 periodicals. Computerized library sources and services include the card catalog, interlibrary loans, and database searching. Special learning facilities include a learning resource center, art gallery, radio station, and observatory. The 120-acre campus is in a suburban area 15 miles south of Hartford. Including residence halls, there are 90 buildings on campus.

Student Life: 90% of undergraduates are from out-of-state, mostly the Northeast. Students come from 48 states, 21 foreign countries, and Canada. 63% are from public schools; 31% from private. 67% are white; 12% Asian American; 11% African American. 25% are Jewish; 22% Protestant; 16% Catholic. The average age of freshmen is 18; all undergraduates, 20. 2% do not continue beyond their first year; 91% remain to graduate.

Housing: 2400 students can be accommodated in college housing. College-sponsored living facilities include single-sex and coed dormitories, on-campus apartments, off-campus apartments, married-student housing, fraternity houses, and sorority houses. In addition, there are language houses and special interest houses. On-campus housing is guaranteed for all 4 years. 90% of students live on campus; of those, 95% remain on campus on weekends. All students may keep cars on campus.

Activities: 10% of men and about 3% of women belong to 2 local and 5 national fraternities; 5% of women belong to 2 local sororities. There are 150 groups on campus, including art, bagpipe band, band, cheerleading, chess, choir, chorale, chorus, computers, dance, drama, ethnic, film, gay, honors, international, jazz band, literary magazine, musical theater, newspaper, opera, orchestra, pep band, photography, political, professional, radio and TV, religious, social, social service, student government, symphony, and yearbook. Popular campus events include the Fall Ball and Spring Fling.

Sports: There are 15 intercollegiate sports for men and 14 for women, and 10 intramural sports for men and 10 for women. Athletic and recreation facilities include a 5000-seat stadium, a 3000-seat gymnasium, a 50-meter Olympic pool, a 400-meter outdoor track, a 200-meter indoor track, a hockey arena, a strength and fitness center, 16 tennis courts, 14 squash courts, 4 soccer fields, 2 football practice fields, 2 rugby pitches, field hockey, ultimate frisbee, baseball, and softball fields, and a boathouse.

Disabled Students: 25% of the campus is accessible to disabled students. The following facilities are available: wheelchair ramps, elevators, special parking, specially equipped rest rooms, special class scheduling, lowered drinking fountains, and lowered telephones.

Services: In addition to many counseling and information services, tutoring is available in most subjects. There is remedial math, reading, and writing.

Campus Safety and Security: Campus safety and security measures include 24-hour foot and vehicle patrol, self-defense education, escort service, and shuttle buses. There are informal discussions, pamphlets/posters/films, emergency telephones, and lighted pathways/sidewalks.

Programs of Study: Wesleyan confers the B.A. degree. Master's and doctoral degrees are also awarded. Bachelor's degrees are awarded in BIOLOGICAL SCIENCE (biochemistry, biology/ biological science, molecular biology, and neurosciences), COMMUNICATIONS AND THE ARTS (art, Chinese, dance, dramatic arts, English, film arts, fine arts, French, German, Greek, Hebrew, Italian, Japanese, Latin, music, photography, romance languages, Russian, and Spanish), COMPUTER AND PHYSICAL SCIENCE (astronomy, chemistry, computer science, earth science, geology, mathematics, and physics), EDUCATION (physical), ENGINEERING AND ENVIRONMENTAL DESIGN (environmental science), SOCIAL SCIENCE (African American studies, African studies, American studies, anthropology, Asian/Oriental studies, classical/ancient civilization, economics, history, humanities, international relations, Latin American studies, medieval studies, philosophy, political science/government, psychology, public administration, religion, social science, sociology, urban studies, and women's studies). Sciences, economics, and history are the strongest academically. English, history, and biology have the largest enrollments.

Required: To graduate, all students must complete 119 credit hours, including 35 in the major. Distribution requirements include 3 courses in humanities and arts, 3 in social and behavioral sciences, and 3 in natural science and mathematics. A minimum academic average of 70 must be maintained.

Special: Wesleyan offers cross-registration with 11 area colleges, internships, study abroad in 10 countries, a Washington semester, work-study programs, and pass/fail options. Accelerated degree programs in all majors, dual and student-designed majors, and 3–2 engineering programs with Caltech and Columbia University are also available. There are 2 national honor societies on campus, including Phi Beta Kappa. 40 departments have honors programs.

Faculty/Classroom: 69% of faculty are male; 31%, female. 98% teach undergraduates, and all do research. No introductory courses are taught by graduate students. The average class size in an introductory lecture is 50; in a laboratory, 15; and in a regular course offering, 23.

Admissions: 36% of the 1995–96 applicants were accepted. The SAT I scores for the 1995–96 freshman class were as follows: Verbal—9% below 500, 25% between 500 and 599, 52% between 600 and 699, and 14% 700 and above; Math—5% below 500, 13% between 500 and 599, 45% between 600 and 699, and 37% 700 and above. The ACT scores were 5% below 21, 4% between 21 and 23, 17% between 24 and 26, 19% between 27 and 28, and 56% above 28. 88% of the current freshmen were in the top fifth of their class; 97% were in the top two fifths.

Requirements: The SAT I or ACT is required, as are SAT II: Subject tests in writing and 2 other subjects. In addition, applicants should have 20 academic credits, including 4 years each of English, foreign language, mathematics, science, and social studies. An essay is necessary. AP credits are accepted. Important factors in the admissions decision are advanced placement or honor courses, recommendations by school officials, and leadership record.

Procedure: Freshmen are admitted in the fall. Entrance exams should be taken in the spring of the junior year or the fall of the senior year. There are early decision and deferred admissions plans. Early decision applications should be filed by November 15; regular applications, by January 1 for fall entry, along with an application fee of $55. Notification of early decision is sent December 15; regular decision, April 7. 195 early decision candidates were accepted for the 1995–96 class. A waiting list is an active part of the admissions procedure, with about 10% of all applicants on the list.

Transfer: Transfer applicants need an exceptional academic record and SAT I or ACT scores. An interview is recommended.

Visiting: There are regularly scheduled orientations for prospective students. There are guides for informal visits and visitors may sit in on classes and stay overnight at the school. To schedule a visit, contact the Admissions Office.

Financial Aid: In a recent year, 48% of all freshmen and 47% of continuing students received some form of financial and need-based aid. Scholarships or need-based grants averaged $12,000 ($16,100 maximum); loans averaged $2000 ($2450 maximum); and work contracts averaged $1200 ($1250 maximum). 75% of undergraduate students work part-time. Wesleyan is a member of CSS. The FAF and the college's own financial statement are required. The application deadline for fall entry is February 1.

International Students: There were 58 international students enrolled in a recent year. The school actively recruits these students. They must score 600 on the TOEFL and also take the SAT I or the ACT, as well as SAT II: Subject tests: writing.

Computers: The college provides computer facilities for student use. The mainframe is a DEC VAX 8550. There are more than 200 terminals connected to the mainframe at various campus locations. Software for word processing and statistical analysis is also available. All

students may access the system. There are no time limits and no fees.

Admissions Contact: Barbara-Jan Wilson, Dean of Admissions. E-mail: admissions@wesleyan.edu.

WESTERN CONNECTICUT STATE UNIVERSITY A-3

Danbury, CT 06810–9972   (203) 837-9000; FAX: (203) 837-8320

Full-time: 1378 men, 1428 women	Faculty: 183
Part-time: 749 men, 1079 women	Ph.Ds: 70%
Graduate: 279 men, 694 women	Student/Faculty: 15 to 1
Year: semesters, summer session	Tuition: $3168 ($8260)
Application Deadline: open	Room & Board: $4108
Freshman Class: 2252 applied, 1386 accepted, 465 enrolled	
SAT I or ACT: recommended	COMPETITIVE

Western Connecticut State University, founded in 1903, is a public, coeducational institution offering programs in business, arts and sciences, and professional studies. It is part of the Connecticut State University system. There are 3 undergraduate schools and one graduate school. In addition to regional accreditation, WestConn has baccalaureate program accreditation with CSWE and NLN. The 2 libraries contain 154,503 volumes, 50,268 microform items, and 4080 audiovisual forms, and subscribe to 1669 periodicals. Special learning facilities include an art gallery, radio station, observatory, electron microscope, and photography studio. The 346-acre campus is in a suburban area 65 miles north of New York City. Including residence halls, there are 14 buildings on campus.

Student Life: 87% of undergraduates are from Connecticut. 98% are from public schools. 90% are white. The average age of all undergraduates is 20. 33% do not continue beyond their first year; 32% remain to graduate.

Housing: 896 students can be accommodated in college housing. College-sponsored living facilities include single-sex and coed dormitories and on-campus apartments. On-campus housing is guaranteed for all 4 years. 66% of students commute. Alcohol is not permitted. All students may keep cars on campus.

Activities: 7% of men belong to 5 national fraternities; 6% of women belong to 1 local and 3 national sororities. There are 42 groups on campus, including art, band, cheerleading, chess, chorale, computers, dance, drama, ethnic, film, gay, honors, international, jazz band, literary magazine, marching band, musical theater, newspaper, orchestra, photography, political, professional, radio and TV, religious, social, social service, student government, and yearbook.

Sports: There are 6 intercollegiate sports for men and 5 for women, and 7 intramural sports for men and 7 for women. Athletic and recreation facilities include a gymnasium, a weight training area, 4 tennis courts, and 2 playing fields.

Disabled Students: 95% of the campus is accessible to disabled students. The following facilities are available: wheelchair ramps, elevators, special parking, specially equipped rest rooms, special class scheduling, lowered drinking fountains, and lowered telephones.

Services: In addition to many counseling and information services, tutoring is available in some subjects. There is also a reader service for the blind, and remedial math, reading, and writing.

Campus Safety and Security: Campus safety and security measures include 24-hour foot and vehicle patrol, escort service, shuttle buses, and informal discussions. In addition, there are pamphlets/posters/films, emergency telephones, and lighted pathways/sidewalks.

Programs of Study: WestConn confers B.A., B.S., B.B.A., and B.Mus. degrees. Associate and master's degrees are also awarded. Bachelor's degrees are awarded in BIOLOGICAL SCIENCE (biology/biological science), BUSINESS (accounting, banking and finance, business administration and management, management information systems, and marketing/retailing/merchandising), COMMUNICATIONS AND THE ARTS (art, communications, dramatic arts, English, fine arts, graphic design, illustration, music, music performance, photography, Spanish, and studio art), COMPUTER AND PHYSICAL SCIENCE (atmospheric sciences and meteorology, chemistry, computer mathematics, computer science, earth science, and mathematics), EDUCATION (elementary, health, music, and secondary), ENGINEERING AND ENVIRONMENTAL DESIGN (environmental science), HEALTH PROFESSIONS (medical laboratory technology and nursing), SOCIAL SCIENCE (American studies, economics, history, law enforcement and corrections, political science/government, psychology, social science, social work, and sociology). Social science is the strongest academically. Business has the largest enrollment.

Required: To graduate, students must complete 122 credit hours with a minimum GPA of 2.0. A common core of courses is required, along with physical education. All students must also fulfill the foreign language requirement.

Special: The university offers co-op programs with local corporations and cross-registration with the New England Regional Student Program. A B.A.-B.S. degree, dual and student-developed majors, and pass/fail options are available. Credit for military service is accepted.

Nondegree study is offered at the Center for Lifelong Learning. There is a freshman honors program on campus

Faculty/Classroom: 65% of faculty are male; 35%, female. All teach undergraduates; 25% also do research.

Admissions: 62% of the 1995–96 applicants were accepted. The SAT I scores for the 1995–96 freshman class were as follows: Verbal—51% below 500, 37% between 500 and 599, and 11% between 600 and 700; Math—58% below 500, 33% between 500 and 599, and 8% between 600 and 700. 16% of the current freshmen were in the top fifth of their class; 43% were in the top two fifths.

Requirements: The SAT I or ACT is recommended. Applicants must be graduates of an accredited secondary school with a 2.5 GPA. The GED is accepted. Students should have completed 16 high school academic credits, including 4 in English, 3 in mathematics, 2 to 3 in foreign language, 2 in science, and 1 each in history and social studies. Additional credits in art, music, and computer science are highly recommended. An essay and an interview are recommended. AP and CLEP credits are accepted. Important factors in the admissions decision are advanced placement or honor courses, evidence of special talent, and recommendations by school officials.

Procedure: Freshmen are admitted fall and spring. Entrance exams should be taken by December of the senior year. There are early admissions and deferred admissions plans. Application deadlines are open. Application fee is $20. Notification is sent on a rolling basis. A waiting list is an active part of the admissions procedure, with about 1% of all applicants on the list.

Transfer: Transfers must have a minimum of 7 college credits. Applicants must have a minimum GPA of 2.5 for all college course work. 30 credits of 122 must be completed at WestConn.

Visiting: There are regularly scheduled orientations for prospective students. There are guides for informal visits and visitors may sit in on classes. To schedule a visit, contact the Office of Admissions.

Financial Aid: 90% of undergraduate students work part-time. Average earnings from campus work for the school year are $800. WestConn is a member of CSS. The FAFSA and the college's own financial statement are required. The application deadline for fall entry is March 15.

International Students: International students must take the TOEFL and achieve a minimum score of 550.

Computers: The college provides computer facilities for student use. IBM and Apple microcomputers are available for student use in various campus locations. All students may access the system at any time. There are no time limits and no fees.

Admissions Contact: Delmore Kinney, Director of Admissions.

YALE UNIVERSITY
New Haven, CT 06520-8234

C-3

(203) 432-9300

Full-time: 2721 men, 2445 women	Faculty: 646; I, +$
Part-time: 35 men, 58 women	Ph.D.s: 96%
Graduate: 3117 men, 2586 women	Student/Faculty: 8 to 1
Year: semesters, summer session	Tuition: $21,000
Application Deadline: December 31	Room & Board: $6630
Freshman Class: 12,620 applied, 2522 accepted, 1369 enrolled	
SAT I or ACT: required	MOST COMPETITIVE

Yale University, founded in 1701, is a private liberal arts institution. There is 1 undergraduate and 11 graduate schools. In addition to regional accreditation, Yale has baccalaureate program accreditation with ABET, CAHEA, NAAB, NASM, NLN, and SAF. The 43 libraries contain 10.2 million volumes, 4 million microform items, and 168,000 audiovisual forms, and subscribe to 54,601 periodicals. Computerized library sources and services include the card catalog, interlibrary loans, and database searching. Special learning facilities include an art gallery, natural history museum, planetarium, radio station, the Beinecke Rare Books and Manuscript Library, the Marsh Botanical Gardens and Yale Natural Preserves, and several research centers. The 170-acre campus is in an urban area 75 miles northeast of New York City. Including residence halls, there are 200 buildings on campus.

Student Life: 92% of undergraduates are from out-of-state, mostly the Middle Atlantic. Students come from 50 states, 51 foreign countries, and Canada. 60% are from public schools; 40% from private. 67% are white; 16% Asian American. The average age of freshmen is 18; all undergraduates, 20. 2% do not continue beyond their first year; 98% remain to graduate.

Housing: 4628 students can be accommodated in college housing. College-sponsored living facilities include coed dormitories and on-campus apartments. On-campus housing is guaranteed for the freshman year only and is available on a lottery system for upperclassmen. 90% of students live on campus. All students may keep cars on campus.

Activities: There are 33 groups on campus, including art, band, cheerleading, chess, choir, chorale, chorus, computers, dance, drama, ethnic, film, gay, honors, international, jazz band, literary magazine, marching band, musical theater, newspaper, opera, orchestra, pep band, photography, political, professional, radio and TV, reli-

gious, social, social service, student government, symphony, and yearbook. Popular campus events include Communiversity Day, fall and spring concerts, and the East/West Film Festival.

Sports: There are 18 intercollegiate sports for men and 16 for women, and 25 intramural sports for men and 21 for women. Athletic and recreation facilities include the 71000-seat Yale Bowl, a sports complex, a gymnasium, a swimming pool, a skating rink, a sailing center, an equestrian center, and golf courses.

Disabled Students: The following facilities are available: wheelchair ramps, elevators, special parking, specially equipped rest rooms, special class scheduling, lowered drinking fountains, lowered telephones, and door to door lift-van service.

Services: In addition to many counseling and information services, tutoring is available in every subject. There is a reader service for the blind.

Campus Safety and Security: Campus safety and security measures include 24-hour foot and vehicle patrol, self-defense education, escort service, and shuttle buses. In addition, there are informal discussions, pamphlets/posters/films, emergency telephones, and lighted pathways/sidewalks.

Programs of Study: Yale confers B.A., B.S., and B.L.S. degrees. Master's and doctoral degrees are also awarded. Bachelor's degrees are awarded in BIOLOGICAL SCIENCE (biology/biological science), COMMUNICATIONS AND THE ARTS (art, Chinese, classics, comparative literature, dramatic arts, English, film arts, French, German, Italian, Japanese, linguistics, literature, music, Russian, and Spanish), COMPUTER AND PHYSICAL SCIENCE (applied mathematics, astronomy, chemistry, computer science, mathematics, and physics), ENGINEERING AND ENVIRONMENTAL DESIGN (architecture, chemical engineering, electrical/electronics engineering, engineering, and mechanical engineering), SOCIAL SCIENCE (African American studies, American studies, anthropology, archeology, classical/ancient civilization, East Asian studies, Eastern European studies, economics, history, history of science, humanities, Judaic studies, Latin American studies, Near Eastern studies, philosophy, political science/government, psychology, religion, sociology, and women's studies). History, biology, and English have the largest enrollments.

Required: To graduate, students must complete 36 semester courses, including at least 3 courses in each of 4 distributional groups, and at least 12 courses from outside the distributional group that includes their major. Foreign language proficiency must be demonstrated.

Special: The university offers study abroad in England, Russia, Germany, and Japan, an accelerated degree program, B.A.-B.S. degrees, dual majors, and student-designed majors. Directed Studies, a special freshman program in the humanities, offers outstanding students the opportunity to survey the Western cultural tradition. Programs in the residential colleges allow students with special interests to pursue them in a more informal atmosphere. There is a chapter of Phi Beta Kappa on campus.

Faculty/Classroom: 71% of faculty are male; 29%, female.

Admissions: 20% of the 1995–96 applicants were accepted. The SAT I scores for the 1995–96 freshman class were as follows: Verbal—2% below 500, 14% between 500 and 599, 48% between 600 and 700, and 36% above 700; Math—1% below 500, 4% between 500 and 599, 27% between 600 and 700, and 68% above 700. 98% of the current freshmen were in the top fifth of their class.

Requirements: The SAT I or ACT is required. Only those applicants submitting SAT I scores must also take any 3 SAT II: Subject tests. Most successful applicants rank in the top 10% of their high school class. All students must have completed a rigorous high school program encompassing all academic disciplines. An essay is required and an interview is recommended. Applications are accepted on-line through ExPAN. AP credits are accepted. Important factors in the admissions decision are advanced placement or honor courses, leadership record, and extracurricular activities record.

Procedure: Freshmen are admitted in the fall. Entrance exams should be taken anytime up to and including the January test date in the year of application. There are early decision, early admissions, and deferred admissions plans. Early decision applications should be filed by November 1; regular applications, by December 31 for fall entry, along with an application fee of $65. Notification of early decision is sent mid-December; regular decision, mid-April. A waiting list is an active part of the admissions procedure.

Transfer: 35 transfer students enrolled in 1995–96. Applicants must take either the SAT I or ACT and have 1 full year of credit. An essay and 3 letters of recommendation are required. 18 semester courses of 36 must be completed at Yale.

Visiting: There are regularly scheduled orientations for prospective students. There are guides for informal visits and visitors may sit in on classes and stay overnight at the school. To schedule a visit, contact the Admissions Office.

Financial Aid: In 1995–96, 68% of all freshmen and 57% of continuing students received some form of financial aid. 41% of all students received need-based aid. The average freshman award was

$19,900. Of that total, scholarships or need-based grants averaged $15,710; loans averaged $3275; and work contracts averaged $2000. 52% of undergraduate students work part-time. Average earnings from campus work for the school year are $1400. The average financial indebtedness of the 1994–95 graduate was $12,600. Yale is a member of CSS. The FAFSA, the college's own financial statement, student and parent tax returns, the CSS Divorced/ Separated Parents Statement and Business/Farm Supplement, if applicable, the CSS Profile Application, and Yale's own financial aid form are required. The application deadline for fall entry is February 1.

International Students: There are currently 228 international students enrolled. The school actively recruits these students. They must take the TOEFL and achieve a minimum score of 600. The student must also take the SAT I and 3 SAT II: Subject tests, or the ACT.

Computers: The college provides computer facilities for student use. The mainframes are a 2 IBM 4341s, 5 DEC 11/750s, and a DEC VAX 8600. There are also IBM and Apple Macintosh microcomputers available in dormitories, libraries, classrooms, and the computer center. All students may access the system 24 hours a day. There are no time limits and no fees.

Graduates: In 1994–95, 1260 bachelor's degrees were awarded. The most popular majors among graduates were history (15%), English (9%), and biology (8%). Within an average freshman class, 87% graduate in 4 years, 93% in 5 years, and 95% in 6 years. 300 companies recruited on campus in 1994–95. Of the 1994 graduating class, 35% were enrolled in graduate school within 6 months of graduation and 60% had found employment.

Admissions Contact: Dean of Undergraduate Admissions. E-mail: admissions.receptionist@am.yale.edu. A campus video is available.

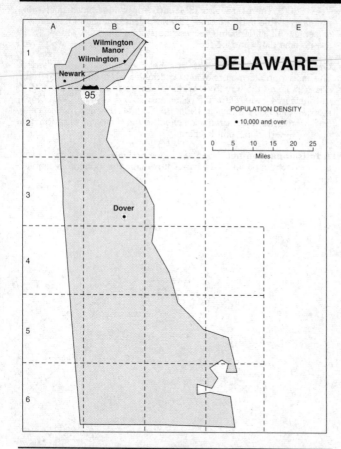

DELAWARE

POPULATION DENSITY

• 10,000 and over

0   5   10   15   20   25
Miles

DELAWARE STATE COLLEGE

B-3

Dover, DE 19901

Full-time: 969 men, 1299 women	(302) 739–4917; (302) 739–2856
Part-time: 247 men, 387 women	Faculty: 168; IIA, --$
Graduate: 84 men, 189 women	Ph.D.s: 67%
Year: semesters, summer session	Student/Faculty: 14 to 1
Application Deadline: June 1	Tuition: $2390 ($5872)
Freshman Class: 1765 applied, 1389 accepted, 624 enrolled	Room & Board: $4310
SAT I or ACT: required	COMPETITIVE

Delaware State College, founded in 1891, is a public institution offering programs in agricultural and technical fields, business, engineering, liberal and fine arts, health science, professional training, and teacher preparation. There are 2 undergraduate schools and 1 graduate school. The 2 libraries contain 156,605 volumes, 353,222 microform items, and 5369 audiovisual forms, and subscribe to 1111 periodicals. Computerized library sources and services include the card catalog, interlibrary loans, and database searching. Special learning facilities include a learning resource center, art gallery, planetarium, and radio station. The 400-acre campus is in a suburban area 45 miles south of Wilmington. Including residence halls, there are 21 buildings on campus.

Student Life: 64% of undergraduates are from Delaware. Students come from 26 foreign countries. 90% are from public schools; 10% from private. 64% are African American; 32% white. The average age of freshmen is 19; all undergraduates, 19.

Housing: 1002 students can be accommodated in college housing. College-sponsored living facilities include single-sex dormitories. On-campus housing is available on a first-come, first-served basis. 66% of students commute. Alcohol is not permitted. All students may keep cars on campus.

Activities: 50% of men and about 50% of women belong to 4 national fraternities; 50% of women belong to 4 national sororities. There are 53 groups on campus, including cheerleading, choir, drama, ethnic, honors, international, jazz band, marching band, newspaper, pep band, radio and TV, religious, social service, student government, and yearbook. Popular campus events include Parents Day, Homecoming, and Annual Career Fair.

Sports: There are 7 intercollegiate sports for men and 6 for women, and 20 intramural sports for men and 20 for women. Athletic and recreation facilities include an indoor swimming pool, a gymnasium, a dance studio, and racquetball and handball courts.

Disabled Students: The following facilities are available: wheelchair ramps, elevators, special parking, and specially equipped rest rooms.

Services: In addition to many counseling and information services, tutoring is available in every subject. There is remedial reading and writing.

Campus Safety and Security: Campus safety and security measures include 24-hour foot and vehicle patrol, shuttle buses, informal discussions, and pamphlets/posters/films. In addition, there are lighted pathways/sidewalks.

Programs of Study: Delstate confers B.A., B.S., and B.Tech. degrees. Master's degrees are also awarded. Bachelor's degrees are awarded in AGRICULTURE (agricultural business management, fish and game management, and natural resource management), BIOLOGICAL SCIENCE (biology/biological science and botany), BUSINESS (accounting, business administration and management, fashion merchandising, hotel/motel and restaurant management, and marketing/retailing/merchandising), COMMUNICATIONS AND THE ARTS (English, French, journalism, music, and Spanish), COMPUTER AND PHYSICAL SCIENCE (chemistry, computer science, mathematics, and physics), EDUCATION (agricultural, art, business, early childhood, elementary, health, home economics, music, physical, science, and special), ENGINEERING AND ENVIRONMENTAL DESIGN (chemical engineering, civil engineering, electrical/electronics engineering, and mechanical engineering), HEALTH PROFESSIONS (community health work, environmental health science, and nursing), SOCIAL SCIENCE (economics, history, parks and recreation management, political science/government, psychology, social work, and sociology). Education is the strongest academically. Marketing and business administration have the largest enrollments.

Required: 42 credits of general education requirements include 12 hours of humanities, 11 of basic intellectual skills, 7 of social science, and 6 each of mathematics and natural science. 2 semesters of physical education are also required. A total of 121 credit hours and a minimum GPA of 2.0 is required.

Special: The college offers accelerated degrees, combined B.A.-B.S. degrees, student-designed majors, and a 3–2 engineering program with the University of Delaware. Work-study is available on campus. There are assisted internships in airway science and nursing, and co-op programs in business, education, home economics, social work, and agriculture. There is a freshman honors program on campus, as well as 6 national honor societies, including Phi Beta Kappa.

Faculty/Classroom: 62% of faculty are male; 38%, female. No introductory courses are taught by graduate students.

Admissions: In a recent year, 74% of applicants were accepted.

Requirements: 75% of the 1995–96 applicants were accepted. The SAT I or ACT is required. Candidates should graduate from an accredited secondary school with a 2.0 GPA or have a GED. 15 academic credits are required, including 4 units of English and 2 each of mathematics, science, and social studies. CLEP credit is accepted. Important factors in the admissions decision are extracurricular activities record, advanced placement or honor courses, and recommendations by school officials.

Procedure: Freshmen are admitted fall and spring. Entrance exams should be taken in December or January of the senior year. There is an early admissions plan. Check with the school for current application deadlines and fee. Notification is sent on a rolling basis.

Transfer: Transfer applicants must submit a statement of honorable withdrawal and high school and college transcripts. 30 credits of 121 must be completed at Delstate.

Visiting: There are regularly scheduled orientations for prospective students, including a High School Day Program. There are guides for informal visits. To schedule a visit, contact Jethro Williams at (302) 739-3559.

Financial Aid: Delstate is a member of CSS. The FAF or FFS is required. Check with the school for current deadlines.

International Students: Students must score 500 on the TOEFL and also take the SAT I or the ACT.

Computers: The college provides computer facilities for student use. The mainframe is an IBM. There is a computer laboratory specifically for students. Students may also use terminals in the library. All students may access the system 8:30 A.M. to 4:30 A.M. There are no fees.

Admissions Contact: Jethro C. Williams, Admissions Director.

GOLDEY-BEACOM COLLEGE
B-1

Wilmington, DE 19808 | (302) 998-8814; (800) 833-4877

Full-time: 250 men, 423 women	Faculty: 24; IIB, av$
Part-time: 226 men, 517 women	Ph.D.s: 25%
Graduate: 102 men and women	Student/Faculty: 28 to 1
Year: semesters, summer session	Tuition: $6780
Application Deadline: open	Room & Board: $3134
Freshman Class: 487 applied, 436 accepted, 213 enrolled	
SAT I Verbal/Math: 436/499	**LESS COMPETITIVE**

Goldey-Beacom College, founded in 1886, is a private, coeducational business college that provides undergraduate training and education for careers in business, industry, and government. There are 2 undergraduate schools and 1 graduate school. The library contains 27,900 volumes, 27,283 microform items, and 693 audiovisual forms, and subscribes to 394 periodicals. Computerized library sources and services include interlibrary loans and database searching. Special learning facilities include a learning resource center. The 28-acre campus is in a suburban area 10 miles west of Wilmington. Including residence halls, there are 6 buildings on campus.

Student Life: 60% of undergraduates are from Delaware. Students come from 10 states and 26 foreign countries. 75% are from public schools; 25% from private. 81% are white; 10% African American. The average age of freshmen is 19; all undergraduates, 21. 30% do not continue beyond their first year; 70% remain to graduate.

Housing: 300 students can be accommodated in college housing. College-sponsored living facilities include coed on-campus apartments. In addition, there are special interest houses. On-campus housing is available on a first-come, first-served basis. 84% of students commute. All students may keep cars on campus.

Activities: 10% of men belong to 2 national fraternities; 10% of women belong to 2 national sororities. There are 15 groups on campus, including chorus, computers, ethnic, honors, international, literary magazine, newspaper, professional, religious, social service, and student government. Popular campus events include the Goldey-Beacom Follies.

Sports: There is 1 intercollegiate sport for men and 1 for women, and 7 intramural sports for men and 5 for women. Athletic and recreation facilities include soccer and softball fields, and tennis, basketball, and handball courts.

Disabled Students: All of the campus is accessible to disabled students. The following facilities are available: wheelchair ramps, elevators, special parking, specially equipped rest rooms, lowered drinking fountains, and lowered telephones.

Services: In addition to many counseling and information services, tutoring is available in most subjects. There is a reader service for the blind, remedial math, reading, and writing, and computer-based tutorials.

Campus Safety and Security: Campus safety and security measures include 24-hour foot and vehicle patrol, self-defense education, informal discussions, and pamphlets/posters/films. There are lighted pathways/sidewalks and security from 6 P.M. to 6 A.M. on the small campus.

Programs of Study: Goldey-Beacom College confers the B.S. degree. Associate and master's degrees are also awarded. Bachelor's degrees are awarded in BUSINESS (accounting, banking and finance, international business management, marketing/retailing/merchandising, and office supervision and management), COMMUNICATIONS AND THE ARTS (communications), COMPUTER AND PHYSICAL SCIENCE (computer programming). Accounting and computer science are the strongest academically. Accounting and management have the largest enrollments.

Required: To graduate, students must complete a minimum of 126 credit hours with an overall GPA of 2.0. Students must also fulfill the college's core requirements in English and mathematics.

Special: Co-op programs in all majors, an accelerated degree program, a 5-year advanced business degree, dual majors, internships, study abroad, and work-study programs are available. There is a freshman honors program on campus, as well as 1 national honor society. 3 departments have honors programs.

Faculty/Classroom: 66% of faculty are male; 34%, female. All teach undergraduates. No introductory courses are taught by graduate students. The average class size in an introductory lecture is 35 and in a regular course offering, 25.

Admissions: 90% of the 1995-96 applicants were accepted. 20% of the current freshmen were in the top fifth of their class; 45% were in the top two fifths.

Requirements: The SAT I is required. Applicants must be high school graduates with a 2.0 GPA or have a GED. AP and CLEP credits are accepted. Important factors in the admissions decision are evidence of special talent, advanced placement or honor courses, and parents or siblings attending the school.

Procedure: Freshmen are admitted to all sessions. There are early admissions and deferred admissions plans. Application deadlines are open. Application fee is $30. Notification is sent on a rolling basis.

Transfer: 75 transfer students enrolled in a recent year. Applicants must submit high school and college transcripts. 50 credits of 126 must be completed at Goldey-Beacom College.

Visiting: There are regularly scheduled orientations for prospective students, including an open house. There are guides for informal visits and visitors may sit in on classes and stay overnight at the school. To schedule a visit, contact the Admissions Office.

Financial Aid: In a recent year, 89% of all freshmen and 57% of continuing students received some form of financial aid. Scholarships or need-based grants averaged $1171 ($2300 maximum); loans averaged $2850 ($5500 maximum); and work contracts averaged $1200 ($6700 maximum). Average earnings from campus work for the school year are $1200. The average financial indebtedness of the recent graduate was $6012. Goldey-Beacom College is a member of CSS. The FAFSA is required. The application deadline for fall entry is February 15.

International Students: There are currently 130 international students enrolled. The school actively recruits these students. They must score 500 on the TOEFL.

Computers: The college provides computer facilities for student use. The mainframes are an IBM Series 4361 and a VM/SP Release 5. The college's 4 computer labs contain more than 160 IBM PS/2 Model 50 terminals. Modems may access the mainframe from off campus 24 hours a day. There are no fees.

Graduates: In a recent year, 174 bachelor's degrees were awarded. The most popular majors among graduates were management (33%), office technology (26%), and accounting (17%). Within an average freshman class, 30% graduate in 3 years, 40% in 4 years, 20% in 5 years, and 10% in 6 years.

Admissions Contact: Kevin M. McIntyre, Director of Admissions. E-mail: mcintyrk@goldey.gbc.edu. A campus video is available.

UNIVERSITY OF DELAWARE
A-1

Newark, DE 19716 | (302) 831-8123; FAX: (302) 831-6905

Full-time: 5765 men, 7525 women	Faculty: 969; I, av$
Part-time: 574 men, 804 women	Ph.D.s: 88%
Graduate: 1724 men, 1500 women	Student/Faculty: 14 to 1
Year: 4-1-4, summer session	Tuition: $4286 ($11,156)
Application Deadline: March 1	Room & Board: $4420
Freshman Class: 13,860 applied, 10,062 accepted, 3179 enrolled	
SAT I or ACT: required	**VERY COMPETITIVE**

The University of Delaware, founded in 1743 and chartered in 1833, is a public, land-grant, coeducational institution offering programs in agricultural sciences, arts and science, business and economics, education, engineering, human resources, nursing, and physical education. There are 8 undergraduate and 2 graduate schools. In addition to regional accreditation, the university has baccalaureate program accreditation with AACSB, ABET, ADA, APTA, CAHEA, NASDTEC, NASM, and NLN. The 4 libraries contain more than 2.1 million volumes, 2.6 million microform items, and 5000 audiovisual forms, and subscribe to more than 19,000 periodicals. Computerized library sources and services include the card catalog, interlibrary loans, and database searching. Special learning facilities include a learning resource center, an art gallery, radio and TV stations, a preschool laboratory, ice skating, a science center, a computer-controlled greenhouse, simulated hospital rooms for nursing, a physical therapy clinic, a 400-acre agricultural research complex, and an exercise physiology laboratory. The 1000-acre campus is in a small town 12 miles southwest of Wilmington. Including residence halls, there are 400 buildings on campus.

Student Life: 58% of undergraduates are from out-of-state, mostly the Middle Atlantic. Students come from 46 states, 85 foreign countries, and Canada. 77% are from public schools; 23% from private. 88% are white. 42% are Catholic; 30% Protestant; 14% claim no religious affiliation; 11% Jewish. The average age of freshmen is 18; all undergraduates, 20.5. 14% do not continue beyond their first year; 71% remain to graduate.

Housing: More than 7300 students can be accommodated in college housing. College-sponsored living facilities include single-sex and coed dormitories, on-campus apartments, and married-student housing. In addition there are honors houses, language houses, special interest houses, alcohol/smoke-free residence halls, and suites. On-campus housing is guaranteed for all 4 years. 53% of students live on campus; of those, 75% remain on campus on weekends. Alcohol is not permitted. All students may keep cars on campus.

Activities: 18% of men belong to 25 national fraternities; 18% of women belong to 15 national sororities. There are 150 groups on campus, including art, band, cheerleading, chess, choir, chorale, chorus, dance, drama, ethnic, gay, honors, international, jazz band, literary magazine, marching band, musical theater, newspaper, orchestra, political, professional, radio and TV, religious, social, social service, student government, symphony, and yearbook. Popular campus events include Homecoming, Delaware Day, Greek Week, Convocation, Graduation, and Parents Day.

Sports: There are 11 intercollegiate sports for men and 11 for women, and 19 intramural sports for men and 18 for women. Athletic and recreation facilities include a 23,000-seat football stadium, 3 multipurpose gymnasiums, 6 outdoor multipurpose fields, 8 outdoor basketball courts, 2 squash courts, 15 racquetball courts, 22 outdoor tennis courts, indoor and outdoor pools, a universal weight room, a 6000-seat basketball arena, a rock climbing wall, a high-ropes challenge course, 3 student fitness centers, a strength and conditioning room with free weights, outdoor and indoor tracks, softball, baseball, lacrosse, and soccer fields, and 2 ice arenas.

Disabled Students: 95% of the campus is accessible to disabled students. The following facilities are available: wheelchair ramps, elevators, special parking, specially equipped rest rooms, special class scheduling, lowered drinking fountains, lowered telephones, and specially designed residence hall rooms.

Services: In addition to many counseling and information services, tutoring is available in every subject. There is a reader service for the blind, and remedial math, reading, and writing. There is also a writing center, a mathematics center, and an academic services center for assistance with academic self-management development, critical thinking, and problem solving and for individual assistance for learning-disabled students.

Campus Safety and Security: Campus safety and security measures include 24-hour foot and vehicle patrol, self-defense education, escort service, and shuttle buses. In addition, there are informal discussions, pamphlets/posters/films, emergency telephones, lighted pathways/sidewalks, and ongoing student-awareness programs conducted within the residence halls.

Programs of Study: The university confers B.A., B.S., B.A.Lib.Arts, B.C.E., B.Ch.E., B.E.E., B.F.A., B.M.E., B.Mus., B.S.Acc., B.S.Ag., B.S.B.A., B.S.Ed., B.S.N., and B.S.P.E. degrees. Associate, master's, and doctoral degrees are also awarded. Bachelor's degrees are awarded in AGRICULTURE (agricultural business management, agricultural economics, agriculture, animal science, plant science, and soil science), BIOLOGICAL SCIENCE (biochemistry, biology/biological science, biotechnology, entomology, nutrition, and plant pathology), BUSINESS (accounting, banking and finance, business administration and management, hotel/motel and restaurant management, management science, marketing/retailing/merchandising, and recreation and leisure services), COMMUNICATIONS AND THE ARTS (art, art history and appreciation, classics, communications, comparative literature, English, fine arts, historic preservation, Italian, journalism, languages, music, music theory and composition, and theater management), COMPUTER AND PHYSICAL SCIENCE (astronomy, chemistry, computer science, geology, geophysics and seismology, information sciences and systems, mathematics, physics, and statistics), EDUCATION (agricultural, early childhood, education, elementary, English, foreign languages, home economics, mathematics, music, physical, psychology, science, secondary, and special), ENGINEERING AND ENVIRONMENTAL DESIGN (agricultural engineering technology, chemical engineering, civil engineering, electrical/electronics engineering, engineering technology, environmental engineering, environmental science, mechanical engineering, and textile engineering), HEALTH PROFESSIONS (medical laboratory technology and nursing), SOCIAL SCIENCE (anthropology, community services, consumer services, criminal justice, dietetics, economics, family and community services, fashion design and technology, food science, geography, history, human development, interdisciplinary studies, international relations, Latin American studies, parks and recreation management, philosophy, physical fitness/movement, political science/government, psychology, sociology, textiles and clothing, and women's studies). Engineering, all sciences, and accounting are the strongest academically. Biological sciences, elementary teacher education, and psychology have the largest enrollments.

Required: For graduation, students must complete at least 124 credits with a minimum GPA of 2.0. All students must take freshman English and 3 credits of course work with multicultural or multiethnic content. Some majors require more than 124 credits. Most degree programs require that half of the courses be in the major field of study.

Special: Students may participate in cooperative programs, internships, study abroad in 14 countries, a Washington semester, and work-study programs. The university offers accelerated degree programs, B.A.-B.S. degrees, dual majors, student-designed majors (Bachelor of Arts in Liberal Studies), and pass/fail options. Nondegree study is available through the Division of Continuing Education. There is an extensive undergraduate research program. Students may earn an enriched degree through the University Honors Program. There is a freshman honors program on campus, as well as 39 national honor societies, including Phi Beta Kappa. All departments have honors programs.

Faculty/Classroom: 68% of faculty are male; 32%, female. All teach undergraduates. Graduate students teach fewer than 5% of introductory courses. The average class size in a laboratory is 18 and in a regular course offering, 35.

Admissions: 73% of the 1995–96 applicants were accepted. 49% of the current freshmen were in the top fifth of their class; 84% were in the top two fifths. There were 50 National Merit finalists. 42 freshmen graduated first in their class.

Requirements: The SAT I or ACT is required. Applicants should be graduates of an accredited secondary school. The GED is accepted. Students should have completed 16 high school academic credits, including 4 years of English, 2 years each of mathematics, science, foreign language, and history, 1 year of social studies, and 3 years of academic course electives. SAT II: Subject tests are recommended, especially for honors consideration. A writing sample is required for honors consideration. Applicants may apply through the World Wide Web to http((NULL))((NULL))www.udel.edu. AP credits are accepted. Important factors in the admissions decision are advanced placement or honor courses, parents or siblings attending the school, and recommendations by school officials.

Procedure: Freshmen are admitted fall and spring. Entrance exams should be taken at the end of the junior year or the beginning of the senior year. There are early decision, early admissions, and deferred admissions plans. Early decision applications should be filed by November 15; regular applications, by March 1 for fall entry and November 15 for spring entry, along with an application fee of $40. Notification of early decision is sent December 15; regular decision, on a rolling basis from January 1 to April 15. 400 early decision candidates were accepted for the 1995–96 class.

Transfer: 632 transfer students enrolled in 1995–96. Applicants for transfer should have completed at least 24 credits with a minimum GPA of 2.5 for most majors; some majors require a GPA of 3.0 or better. 30 credits of 124 must be completed at the university.

Visiting: There are regularly scheduled orientations for prospective students. There are guides for informal visits and visitors may sit in on classes. To schedule a visit, contact the Admissions Office.

Financial Aid: In 1995–96, 75% of all freshmen and 55% of continuing students received some form of financial aid. 66% of freshmen and 43% of continuing students received need-based aid. The average freshman award was $6100. Of that total, scholarships or need-based grants averaged $3700 ($15,576 maximum); loans averaged $2600 ($4000 maximum); and work contracts averaged $1000 ($2000 maximum). 50% of undergraduate students work part-time. Average earnings from campus work for the school year are $1000. The average financial indebtedness of the 1994–95 graduate was $8700. The university is a member of CSS. The application deadline for fall entry is May 1.

International Students: There are currently 141 international students enrolled. The school actively recruits these students. They must take the TOEFL and achieve a minimum score of 550.

Computers: The college provides computer facilities for student use. The mainframes are an IBM 3090–400E/2VF, 2 IBM RS/6000–98E systems, a Sun Microsystems SPARCenter 2000, and 3 SPARCserver 690MP-41 systems. 28 computing sites are available to students, offering more than 700 terminals, IBMs, IBM-compatibles, and Apple Macintosh PCs. All residence hall rooms are equipped with data outlets for PCs. Those registered in computer courses or doing research that requires it may access the system 24 hours a day. There are no time limits and no fees.

Graduates: In 1994–95, 3248 bachelor's degrees were awarded. The most popular majors among graduates were psychology (7%), English (7%), and elementary teacher education (6%). Within an average freshman class, 48% graduate in 4 years, 68% in 5 years, and 71% in 6 years. 219 companies recruited on campus in 1994–95. Of the 1994 graduating class, 20% were enrolled in graduate school within 6 months of graduation and 75% had found employment.

Admissions Contact: Bruce Walker, Associate Provost, Admissions and Student Financial Aid. E-mail: ask.admissions@mvs.udel.edu.

WESLEY COLLEGE
Dover, DE 19901   B-3
(302) 736-2400
(800) WESLEYU; FAX: (302) 736-2301

Full-time: 415 men, 392 women	Faculty: 55; IIB, -$
Part-time: 214 men, 295 women	Ph.D.s: 58%
Graduate: none	Student/Faculty: 15 to 1
Year: semesters, summer session	Tuition: $10,295
Application Deadline: open	Room & Board: $4674
Freshman Class: 1032 applied, 932 accepted, 305 enrolled	
SAT I Verbal/Math: 380/412	LESS COMPETITIVE

Wesley College, founded in 1873, is a private, coeducational, liberal arts institution affiliated with the United Methodist Church. In addition to regional accreditation, Wesley has baccalaureate program accreditation with NLN. The library contains 72,000 volumes, 2118 microform items, and 1594 audiovisual forms, and subscribes to 471 periodicals. Computerized library sources and services include interlibrary loans and database searching. Special learning facilities include a learning resource center, radio station, and TV station. The 20-acre campus is in a small town 75 miles south of Philadelphia. Including residence halls, there are 20 buildings on campus.

Student Life: 58% of undergraduates are from Delaware. Students come from 15 states and 9 foreign countries. 85% are from public schools; 15% from private. 86% are white; 11% African American. 53% are Protestant; 41% Catholic. The average age of freshmen is 18; all undergraduates, 20. 25% do not continue beyond their first year; 58% remain to graduate.

Housing: 630 students can be accommodated in college housing. College-sponsored living facilities include single-sex and coed dormitories. On-campus housing is guaranteed for all 4 years. 55% of students live on campus; of those, 75% remain on campus on weekends. Alcohol is not permitted. All students may keep cars on campus.

Activities: 15% of men belong to 2 national fraternities; 15% of women belong to 2 local sororities. There are 25 groups on campus, including band, cheerleading, choir, chorus, computers, drama, ethnic, film, honors, international, jazz band, literary magazine, newspaper, photography, political, professional, radio and TV, religious, social, social service, student government, and yearbook. Popular campus events include Family Day, Homecoming, International Fair, and Spring Fling.

Sports: There are 8 intercollegiate sports for men and 4 for women, and 4 intramural sports for men and 4 for women. Athletic and recreation facilities include a swimming pool, tennis courts, a football stadium, athletic fields, a gymnasium, a game room, and an exercise room.

Disabled Students: All of the campus is accessible to disabled students. The following facilities are available: wheelchair ramps, elevators, special parking, specially equipped rest rooms, special class scheduling, lowered drinking fountains, and lowered telephones.

Services: In addition to many counseling and information services, tutoring is available in every subject. There is remedial math, reading, and writing.

Campus Safety and Security: Campus safety and security measures include 24-hour foot and vehicle patrol, escort service, informal discussions, and pamphlets/posters/films. In addition, there are emergency telephones and lighted pathways/sidewalks.

Programs of Study: Wesley confers B.A. and B.S. degrees. Associate and master's degrees are also awarded. Bachelor's degrees are awarded in BIOLOGICAL SCIENCE (biology/biological science), BUSINESS (accounting, business administration and management, management science, and marketing/retailing/merchandising), COMMUNICATIONS AND THE ARTS (communications and English), EDUCATION (elementary, English, physical, secondary, and social studies), ENGINEERING AND ENVIRONMENTAL DESIGN (environmental science), HEALTH PROFESSIONS (medical laboratory technology), SOCIAL SCIENCE (history, liberal arts/general studies, paralegal studies, political science/government, and psychology). Biological science is the strongest academically. Management science and education have the largest enrollments.

Required: For graduation, students must complete 128 credit hours, with at least 30 hours in the major and a minimum GPA of 2.0. Fifty hours of core courses, including English, orientation, religion, science, American culture, non-American culture, and physical education, are required.

Special: The college offers internships in business and industry, nursing, environmental science, and medical technology; study abroad in 5 countries; work-study programs; pass/fail options; and credit for life, military, and work experience. There is a freshman honors program on campus, as well as 2 national honor societies. One department has an honors program.

Faculty/Classroom: 58% of faculty are male; 42%, female. The average class size in an introductory lecture is 30; in a laboratory, 20; and in a regular course offering, 19.

Admissions: 90% of the 1995–96 applicants were accepted. The SAT I scores for the 1995–96 freshman class were as follows: Verbal—96% below 500 and 1% between 600 and 700; Math—85% below 500, 12% between 500 and 599, and 3% between 600 and 700. 9% of the current freshmen were in the top fifth of their class; 26% were in the top two fifths. 5 freshmen graduated first in their class.

Requirements: The SAT I is required. Wesley requires applicants to be in the upper 80% of their class. A minimum GPA of 2.0 is required. Applicants must be graduates of an accredited secondary school; the GED is accepted. Students should have completed 12 academic credits or 16 Carnegie units, including 4 units of English and 2 units each of mathematics, history, science, and social studies. An interview is recommended. AP and CLEP credits are accepted. Important factors in the admissions decision are recommendations by school officials, extracurricular activities record, and leadership record.

Procedure: Freshmen are admitted fall and winter. Entrance exams should be taken in the junior year. There are early decision, early admissions, and deferred admissions plans. Early decision applications

should be filed by November 1; regular application deadlines are open. Application fee is $20. Notification of early decision is sent November 30; regular decision, on a rolling basis. 20 early decision candidates were accepted for a recent class. A waiting list is an active part of the admissions procedure, with about 10% of all applicants on the list.

Transfer: 55 transfer students enrolled in 1995–96. Applicants must have a minimum GPA of 2.0 and a minimum composite SAT I score of 800. 32 credits of 128 must be completed at Wesley.

Visiting: There are regularly scheduled orientations for prospective students. There are guides for informal visits and visitors may sit in on classes and stay overnight at the school. To schedule a visit, contact the Office of Admissions.

Financial Aid: In a recent year, 72% of all freshmen and 77% of continuing students received some form of financial aid. 68% of freshmen and 73% of continuing students received need-based aid. The average freshman award was $6695. Of that total, scholarships or need-based grants averaged $3070 ($4000 maximum); loans averaged $2625 ($3125 maximum); and work contracts averaged $1000 (maximum). 24% of undergraduate students work part-time. Average earnings from campus work for the school year are $1000. The average financial indebtedness of a recent graduate was $10,000. Wesley is a member of CSS. The FAFSA or the SFS and the college's own financial statement are required. The application deadline for fall entry is April 15.

International Students: There are currently 18 international students enrolled. The school actively recruits these students. They must take the TOEFL and achieve a minimum score of 500.

Computers: The college provides computer facilities for student use. The mainframe is a DEC MicroVAX 3400. It may be accessed from 16 terminals across campus for use in word processing, programming, accounting, and statistics. Microcomputers are available for student use in the writing center, computer center, and accounting laboratory. All students may access the system 24 hours a day, 7 days a week. There are no time limits. The fees are $30 per course. It is strongly recommended that all students have a personal computer.

Graduates: In 1994–95, 104 bachelor's degrees were awarded. The most popular majors among graduates were management (18%), elementary education (13%), and nursing (9%). Within an average freshman class, 14% graduate in 3 years, 38% in 4 years, 43% in 5 years, and 48% in 6 years.

Admissions Contact: Vice President for Enrollment Management. A campus video is available.

WILMINGTON COLLEGE B-1

New Castle, DE 19720	(302) 328-9407; FAX: (302) 328-5902
Full-time: 324 men, 485 women	Faculty: 30
Part-time: 407 men, 988 women	Ph.D.s: 45%
Graduate: 377 men, 681 women	Student/Faculty: 27 to 1
Year: semesters, summer session	Tuition: $5515
Application Deadline: open	Room & Board: n/app
Freshman Class: 280 applied, 280 accepted, 171 enrolled	
SAT I or ACT: not required	NONCOMPETITIVE

Wilmington College, founded in 1967, is a private, coeducational liberal arts commuter college. In addition to regional accreditation, Wilmington has baccalaureate program accreditation with NLN. The library contains 110,500 volumes, 27,000 microform items, and 6547 audiovisual forms, and subscribes to 337 periodicals. Computerized library sources and services include the card catalog, interlibrary loans, and database searching. Special learning facilities include a radio station and TV station. The 15-acre campus is in an urban area 7 miles south of Wilmington. There are 17 buildings on campus.

Student Life: 85% of undergraduates are from Delaware. Students come from 7 states. 95% are from public schools; 5% from private. 80% are white; 16% African American. The average age of freshmen is 21; all undergraduates, 27. 6% do not continue beyond their first year; 88% remain to graduate.

Housing: There are no residence halls. The college provides a list of housing accommodations in the community. All students commute. Alcohol is not permitted. All students may keep cars on campus.

Activities: There is 1 national fraternity. There are no sororities. There are 11 groups on campus, including aviation, Business Professionals of America, cheerleading, film, honors, newspaper, photography, psychology, radio and TV, student government, and yearbook. Popular campus events include the Honors Convocation and cultural and social affairs.

Sports: There are 2 intercollegiate sports for men and 3 for women, and 2 intramural sports for men and 3 for women. Athletic and recreation facilities include a 1000-seat gymnasium and a recreation room.

Disabled Students: The entire campus is accessible to disabled students. The following facilities are available: wheelchair ramps, elevators, special parking, specially equipped rest rooms, lowered drinking fountains, and lowered telephones.

Services: In addition to many counseling and information services, tutoring is available in most subjects. There is remedial math, reading, and writing. Staff members also are available to assist students with study skills such as test taking, reading, concentration development, and time management.

Campus Safety and Security: Campus safety and security measures include 24-hour foot and vehicle patrol, escort service, informal discussions, and pamphlets/posters/films. In addition, there are emergency telephones and lighted pathways/sidewalks.

Programs of Study: Wilmington confers B.A., B.S., and B.S.N. degrees. Associate, master's, and doctoral degrees are also awarded. Bachelor's degrees are awarded in BUSINESS (accounting, banking and finance, business administration and management, personnel management, and sports management), COMMUNICATIONS AND THE ARTS (communications and dramatic arts), EDUCATION (early childhood and elementary), ENGINEERING AND ENVIRONMENTAL DESIGN (aviation administration/management), HEALTH PROFESSIONS (nursing), SOCIAL SCIENCE (behavioral science and criminal justice). Nursing and elementary education are the strongest academically. Business, nursing, and elementary education have the largest enrollments.

Required: To graduate, students must complete a total of 120 hours with a minimum GPA of 2.0. 54 hours are required in the major. The 36-hour general studies core requirement includes 12 hours of social science, 9 each of English and humanities, and 3 each of mathematics and science. At least 45 credit hours of upper-division course work are required, as is demonstrated competence in verbal and written communication and in computational skills. At least 3 credits must be taken in computer operations. Nursing students must also submit official transcripts verifying graduation from a diploma or associate degree nursing program. Candidates for the B.S.N. degree must possess an R.N. license.

Special: The school offers practicums for education students, co-op programs, work-study programs with area employers, internships, a general studies degree, an accelerated degree program, dual majors, pass/fail options, credit for life experience, and by-challenge exam. 2 departments have honors programs.

Faculty/Classroom: 70% of faculty are male; 30%, female. 75% teach undergraduates. No introductory courses are taught by graduate students. The average class size in an introductory lecture is 25; in a laboratory, 10; and in a regular course offering, 17.

Admissions: All of the 1995–96 applicants were accepted.

Requirements: Graduation from an accredited secondary school or satisfactory scores on the GED are required for admission. An interview may be required of some students and an essay is recommended. AP and CLEP credits are accepted. Important factors in the admissions decision are recommendations by school officials, advanced placement or honor courses, and ability to finance college education.

Procedure: Freshmen are admitted to all sessions. There are early admissions and deferred admissions plans. The application deadlines are open. The application fee is $25. The college accepts all applicants. Notification is sent on a rolling basis.

Transfer: 450 transfer students enrolled in 1995–96. Applicants must have a 2.0 GPA; those with a lower GPA must have an interview. Some applicants may be required to submit SAT I or ACT scores. Those with fewer than 15 semester credits must submit high school transcripts. No more than 75 semester credits will be accepted for transfer credit. 45 credits of 120 must be completed at Wilmington.

Visiting: There are guides for informal visits and visitors may sit in on classes. To schedule a visit, contact the Dean of Admissions, Financial Aid, and Marketing.

Financial Aid: 2% of undergraduate students work part-time. Average earnings from campus work for the school year are $1100. Wilmington is a member of CSS. The FAF or FFS is required.

International Students: They must take the TOEFL and achieve a minimum score of 500, or they may submit a transcript of successful completion of at least 12 credit hours from an American institution of higher education.

Computers: The college provides computer facilities for student use. The mainframe is a DEC MicroVAX 3300. IBM models 25, PC, XT, and AT are available in the library and in the faculty study. There are no time limits and no fees.

Graduates: In 1994–95, 513 bachelor's degrees were awarded. The most popular majors among graduates were nursing (22%), business management (17%), and human resources management (17%). 13 companies recruited on campus in a recent year.

Admissions Contact: Ms. JoAnn Ciuffetelli, Admissions Associate.

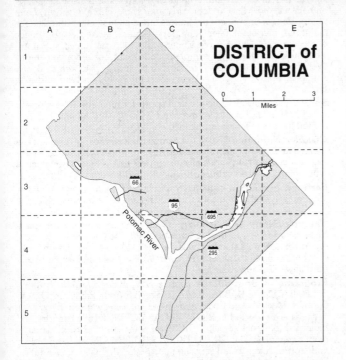

DISTRICT of COLUMBIA

0   1   2   3
Miles

AMERICAN UNIVERSITY
Washington, DC 20016–8001

A-2

(202) 885–6000
FAX: (202) 885–6014

Full-time: 1786 men, 2712 women
Part-time: 205 men, 279 women
Graduate: 2024 men, 2624 women
Year: semesters, summer session
Application Deadline: February 15
Freshman Class: 5646 applied, 4381 accepted, 1276 enrolled
SAT I Verbal/Math: 542/577

Faculty: 452; I, av$
Ph.Ds: 92%
Student/Faculty: 10 to 1
Tuition: $17,110
Room & Board: $6698

VERY COMPETITIVE

American University, founded in 1893, is an independent liberal arts institution affiliated with the Methodist Church. There are 5 undergraduate and 6 graduate schools. In addition to regional accreditation, AU has baccalaureate program accreditation with AACSB, ACE-JMC, and NCATE. The 2 libraries contain 618,000 volumes, 790,000 microform items, and 10,880 audiovisual forms, and subscribe to 3500 periodicals. Computerized library sources and services include the card catalog, interlibrary loans, and database searching. Special learning facilities include a learning resource center, an art gallery, radio and TV stations, a langauage resource center, a media center, a computing center, and a national center for health fitness. The 78-acre campus is in a suburban area 5 miles northwest of downtown Washington, D.C. Including residence halls, there are 37 buildings on campus.

Student Life: 87% of undergraduates are from out-of-state, mostly the Middle Atlantic. Students come from 50 states, 130 foreign countries, and Canada. 78% are from public schools; 22% from private. 73% are white. The average age of freshmen is 18; all undergraduates, 21. 15% do not continue beyond their first year; 66% remain to graduate.

Housing: 3500 students can be accommodated in college housing. College-sponsored living facilities include single-sex and coed dormitories and off-campus apartments. In addition there are honors floors and special interest floors. On-campus housing is guaranteed for the freshman year only, is available on a first-come, first-served basis, and is available on a lottery system for upperclassmen. 65% of students live on campus; of those, 80% remain on campus on weekends. Alcohol is not permitted. Upperclassmen may keep cars on campus.

Activities: 20% of men belong to 7 national fraternities; 20% of women belong to 8 national sororities. There are 85 groups on campus, including art, band, cheerleading, chess, chorale, computers, dance, drama, ethnic, film, forensics/debate, gay, honors, international, jazz band, literary magazine, musical theater, newspaper, orchestra, pep band, photography, political, professional, radio and TV, religious, social, social service, student government, symphony, and yearbook. Popular campus events include International Week, Spring Concert, Heritage Festival, Family Weekend, and Artemus Ward Weekend.

Sports: There are 7 intercollegiate sports for men and 8 for women, and 11 intramural sports for men and 8 for women. Athletic and recreation facilities include a 6000-seat gymnasium, 2 swimming pools, hockey and soccer fields, a softball diamond, an all-purpose field, weight rooms, and courts for tennis, racquetball, squash, badminton, basketball, and volleyball.

Disabled Students: 60% of the campus is accessible to disabled students. The following facilities are available: wheelchair ramps, elevators, special parking, specially equipped rest rooms, special class scheduling, lowered drinking fountains, and lowered telephones. A university shuttle is equipped to accommodate students in wheelchairs.

Services: In addition to many counseling and information services, tutoring is available in every subject. There is a reader service for the blind, and remedial math, reading, and writing.

Campus Safety and Security: Campus safety and security measures include 24-hour foot and vehicle patrol, self-defense education, escort service, and shuttle buses. In addition, there are informal discussions, pamphlets/posters/films, emergency telephones, lighted pathways/sidewalks, and safety orientation programs.

Programs of Study: AU confers B.A., B.S., B.F.A., and B.S.B.A. degrees. Master's and doctoral degrees are also awarded. Bachelor's degrees are awarded in BIOLOGICAL SCIENCE (biology/biological science), BUSINESS (accounting, banking and finance, business administration and management, international business management, management information systems, and marketing/retailing/merchandising), COMMUNICATIONS AND THE ARTS (art history and appreciation, audio technology, communications, design, dramatic arts, English, film arts, fine arts, French, German, journalism, languages, music, Russian, Spanish, and studio art), COMPUTER AND PHYSICAL SCIENCE (chemistry, computer science, information sciences and systems, mathematics, physics, and statistics), EDUCATION (elementary), SOCIAL SCIENCE (American studies, anthropology, criminal justice, economics, history, international studies, Judaic studies, philosophy, political science/government, psychology, religion, and sociology). Political science, international studies, and communications are the strongest academically. International studies and political science have the largest enrollments.

Required: To graduate, students must complete 120 credit hours with a minimum GPA of 2.0. In addition, students must complete 30 credit hours of general education requirements in 5 curricular areas and fulfill the school's competency requirements in English composition and mathematics by either passing an examination or taking a course in each area.

Special: AU offers co-op programs and internships in all majors, study abroad in 12 countries, and a Washington semester program. Work-study is available on campus and with local community service agencies. Dual majors, a liberal studies degree, an interdisciplinary program in environmental studies, student-designed majors, and B.A.-B.S. degrees are also available. Cross-registration may be arranged through the Consortium of Universities of the Washington Metropolitan Area. Credit for life experience, nondegree study, and pass/fail options are available. There is a freshman honors program on campus, as well as 20 national honor societies, including Phi Beta Kappa.

Faculty/Classroom: 75% of faculty are male; 25%, female. 94% teach undergraduates. No introductory courses are taught by graduate students. The average class size in an introductory lecture is 26 and in a regular course offering, 22.

Admissions: 78% of the 1995–96 applicants were accepted. The SAT I scores for the 1995–96 freshman class were as follows: Verbal—30% below 500, 43% between 500 and 599, 24% between 600 and 700, and 3% above 700; Math—19% below 500, 38% between 500 and 599, 34% between 600 and 700, and 9% above 700. The ACT scores were 5% below 21, 20% between 21 and 23, 30% between 24 and 26, 20% between 27 and 28, and 25% above 28. 58% of the current freshmen were in the top fifth of their class; 86% were in the top two fifths. There were 29 National Merit finalists and 14 semifinalists.

Requirements: The SAT I or ACT is required. A minimum GPA of 2.5 is required. Students must have graduated from an accredited secondary school or have satisfactory scores on the GED. Sixteen Carnegie units are required, and high school courses must include 4 years of English, 3 years each of mathematics, science, and academic electives, 2 years each of history and foreign language, and 1 year of social studies. Students must submit an essay. On-line applications are accepted through ExPAN, CollegeLink, and Apply. AP and CLEP credits are accepted. Important factors in the admissions decision are advanced placement or honor courses, leadership record, and recommendations by school officials.

Procedure: Freshmen are admitted to all sessions. Entrance exams should be taken in the spring of the junior year or the fall of the senior year. There are early decision, early admissions, and deferred admissions plans. Early decision applications should be filed by November 15; regular applications, by February 15 for fall entry, December 1 for spring entry, and April 15 for summer entry, along with an application fee of $45. Notification of early decision is sent December 15; regular decision, March 30. 290 early decision candidates were accepted for the 1995–96 class. A waiting list is an active part of the admissions procedure, with about 2% of all applicants on the list.

Transfer: 350 transfer students were enrolled in a recent year. Transfer applicants must have 24 semester credits with a minimum GPA of 2.5. 45 credits of 120 must be completed at AU.

Visiting: There are regularly scheduled orientations for prospective students, including daily tours and information sessions, open houses, and overnight programs. There are guides for informal visits and visitors may sit in on classes and stay overnight at the school. To schedule a visit, contact the Assistant Director for On-Campus Programs.

Financial Aid: In a recent year, 60% of all students received some form of financial aid. 40% of freshmen and 38% of continuing students received need-based aid. The average freshman award was $13,200. Of that total, scholarships or need-based grants averaged $8000; loans averaged $3700; and work contracts averaged $1500. 60% of undergraduate students work part-time. Average earnings from campus work for the school year are $1500. The average financial indebtedness of a recent graduate was $10,500. The FAF or FAFSA and the college's own financial statement are required. The application deadline for fall entry is March 1.

International Students: There were 500 international students enrolled in a recent year. The school actively recruits these students. They must take the TOEFL or the college's own test. The student must also take the SAT I or ACT if the applicant attends a school with a U.S.-patterned system.

Computers: The college provides computer facilities for student use. The mainframe is an IBM 3090. More than 200 IBM, Apple Macintosh, and other microcomputers are available for student use in various campus locations. All students may access the system. There are no time limits and no fees.

Graduates: In 1994–95, 1098 bachelor's degrees were awarded. The most popular majors among graduates were international studies (23%), communications (13%), and government (12%). Within an average freshman class, 2% graduate in 3 years, 60% in 4 years, 66% in 5 years, and 67% in 6 years.

Admissions Contact: Director of Admissions. E-mail: afa@american.edu. A campus video is available.

CATHOLIC UNIVERSITY OF AMERICA C-2
Washington, DC 20064   (202) 319-5305
                                    (800) 673-2772; FAX: (202) 319-6533

Full-time: 981 men, 1201 women	Faculty: 291; I, --$
Part-time: 94 men, 141 women	Ph.D.s: 97%
Graduate: 1807 men, 1884 women	Student/Faculty: 7 to 1
Year: semesters, summer session	Tuition: $15,062
Application Deadline: February 15	Room & Board: $6614
Freshman Class: 2527 applied, 1529 accepted, 570 enrolled	
SAT I: required	**VERY COMPETITIVE**

Catholic University of America, founded in 1887 and affiliated with the Roman Catholic Church, offers undergraduate programs through the schools of arts and sciences, engineering, architecture, nursing, philosophy, the Benjamin T. Rome School of Music, and the Metropolitan College. There are 7 undergraduate and 10 graduate schools. In addition to regional accreditation, CUA has baccalaureate program accreditation with ABET, ACPE, CSWE, NAAB, NASDTEC, NASM, NCATE, and NLN. The 8 libraries contain 1,342,339 volumes, 1,125,635 microform items, and 37,951 audiovisual forms, and subscribe to 9310 periodicals. Computerized library sources and services include the card catalog, interlibrary loans, and database searching. Special learning facilities include an art gallery, radio station, archeology laboratory, and rare book collection. The 155-acre campus is in an urban area in Washington, D.C. Including residence halls, there are 50 buildings on campus.

Student Life: 94% of undergraduates are from out-of-state, mostly the Middle Atlantic. Students come from 50 states, 109 foreign countries, and Canada. 37% are from public schools; 62% from private. 84% are white; 12% foreign nationals. Most are Catholic. The average age of freshmen is 18; all undergraduates, 21. 15% do not continue beyond their first year; 74% remain to graduate.

Housing: 1582 students can be accommodated in college housing. College-sponsored living facilities include single-sex and coed dormitories. In addition there are special interest houses, senior housing, and a freshman residential college. On-campus housing is guaranteed for all 4 years. 76% of students live on campus; of those, 90% remain on campus on weekends. Upperclassmen may keep cars on campus.

Activities: 1% of men belong to 1 local fraternity; 1% of women belong to 1 local sorority and 1 national sorority. There are 122 groups on campus, including art, cheerleading, choir, chorale, chorus, computers, dance, drama, ethnic, honors, international, jazz band, literary magazine, musical theater, newspaper, opera, orchestra, pep band, photography, political, professional, radio, religious, social, social service, student government, symphony, and yearbook. Popular campus events include Parents Weekend, Homecoming, Oktoberfest, Beaux Arts Ball, Spring Fling Week, Intercultural Week, and the Mistletoe Ball.

Sports: There are 8 intercollegiate sports for men and 9 for women, and 11 intramural sports for men and 9 for women. Athletic and recreation facilities include an athletic center.

Disabled Students: 65% of the campus is accessible to disabled students. The following facilities are available: wheelchair ramps, elevators, special parking, specially equipped rest rooms, special class scheduling, lowered drinking fountains, and lowered telephones.

Services: In addition to many counseling and information services, tutoring is available in most subjects. There is a reader service for the blind.

Campus Safety and Security: Campus safety and security measures include 24-hour foot and vehicle patrol, self-defense education, escort service, and shuttle buses. In addition, there are informal discussions, pamphlets/posters/films, emergency telephones, and lighted pathways/sidewalks.

Programs of Study: CUA confers B.A., B.S., B.A.G.S., B.Arch., B.B.E., B.C.E., B.E.E., B.M., B.M.E., B.Ph., B.S.Arch, B.S.E., and B.S.N. degrees. Master's and doctoral degrees are also awarded. Bachelor's degrees are awarded in BIOLOGICAL SCIENCE (biochemistry and biology/biological science), BUSINESS (accounting and management science), COMMUNICATIONS AND THE ARTS (art, art history and appreciation, classics, communications, dramatic arts, English, French, German, Latin, music, musical theater, piano/organ, Spanish, and voice), COMPUTER AND PHYSICAL SCIENCE (chemistry, computer science, mathematics, and physics), EDUCATION (art, drama, early childhood, elementary, English, mathematics, music, and secondary), ENGINEERING AND ENVIRONMENTAL DESIGN (architecture, biomedical engineering, civil engineering, electrical/electronics engineering, engineering, and mechanical engineering), HEALTH PROFESSIONS (medical laboratory technology and nursing), SOCIAL SCIENCE (anthropology, economics, history, medieval studies, philosophy, political science/government, psychology, religion, social work, and sociology). Politics is the strongest academically. Nursing has the largest enrollment.

Required: To graduate, students must complete 120 credit hours, including 42 hours in the major, with a minimum GPA of 2.0. Courses must meet distribution requirements in English composition, philosophy, religion and religious study, language and literature, humanities, mathematics and natural sciences, and social and behavioral sciences. A comprehensive examination is required in most majors.

Special: Cross-registration is available with the Consortium of Universities of the Washington Metropolitan Area. Opportunities are also provided for internships, accelerated degree programs, dual majors, B.A.-B.S. degrees, student-designed majors, pass/fail options, and study abroad in 10 countries. There is a freshman honors program on campus, as well as 14 national honor societies, including Phi Beta Kappa. All departments have honors programs.

Faculty/Classroom: 64% of faculty are male; 36%, female. All do research and 80% also teach undergraduates. Graduate students teach 20% of introductory courses. The average class size in an introductory lecture is 21; in a laboratory, 20; and in a regular course offering, 19.

Admissions: 61% of the 1995–96 applicants were accepted. The SAT I scores for the 1995–96 freshman class were as follows: Verbal—11% below 500, 42% between 500 and 599, 40% between 600 and 700, and 8% above 700; Math—17% below 500, 39% between 500 and 599, 41% between 600 and 700, and 3% above 700. The ACT scores were 18% below 21, 16% between 21 and 23, 30% between 24 and 26, 15% between 27 and 28, and 21% above 28. 47% of the current freshmen were in the top fifth of their class; 78% were in the top two fifths. 4 freshmen graduated first in their class.

Requirements: The SAT I is required. The SAT II: Writing test is required for placement, and 2 additional SAT II: Subject tests are recommended. An SAT I minimum composite score of 1000 (500 verbal and 500 mathematics) is recommended. Applicants must be graduates of an accredited secondary school. The GED is accepted. Students should present 16 academic credits, including 4 in English, 3 each in mathematics and science, and 2 each in social studies, history, and foreign languages. An essay is required. An audition is required for music applicants, and a portfolio for architecture applicants is recommended. AP and CLEP credits are accepted. Important factors in the admissions decision are advanced placement or honor courses, recommendations by school officials, and leadership record.

Procedure: Freshmen are admitted fall and spring. Entrance exams should be taken by February of the senior year of high school. There are early decision, early admissions, and deferred admissions plans. Early decision applications should be filed by November 15; regular applications, by February 15 for fall entry and December 1 for spring entry, along with an application fee of $30. Notification of early decision is sent December 15; regular decision, April 1. 249 early decision candidates were accepted for the 1995–96 class. A waiting list is an active part of the admissions procedure.

Transfer: 155 transfer students enrolled in 1995–96. Applicants must submit a high school transcript showing a B average and a college transcript showing at least 12 credit hours earned with a minimum GPA of 2.7. A minimum composite SAT I score of 1000 is recommended. A letter of recommendation and an essay are required, and an interview is recommended. 30 credits of 120 must be completed at CUA.

Visiting: There are regularly scheduled orientations for prospective students. There are guides for informal visits and visitors may sit in on classes. To schedule a visit, contact the Admissions Office.

Financial Aid: In 1995–96, 77% of all freshmen and 72% of continuing students received some form of financial aid. 56% of all students received need-based aid. The average freshman award was $13,526. Of that total, scholarships or need-based grants averaged $8738 ($14,612 maximum); loans averaged $6318 ($23,000 maximum); and work contracts averaged $988 ($1000 maximum). 35% of undergraduate students work part-time. Average earnings from campus work for the school year are $1400. The average financial indebtedness of the 1994–95 graduate was $18,325. CUA is a member of CSS. The FAF is required. The application priority date for fall entry is January 15.

International Students: There are currently 698 international students enrolled. The school actively recruits these students. They must take the TOEFL and achieve a minimum score of 550. The student must also take the SAT I or the ACT.

Computers: The college provides computer facilities for student use. The mainframe is a DEC VAX 4000. There are 200 terminals and 150 Macintosh, IBM, and IBM-compatible microcomputers available for student use in the computer center and in residence halls. All students may access the system weekdays 9 A.M. to midnight, Saturdays 11 A.M. to 6 P.M., and Sundays 11 A.M. to 11 P.M. There is also dial-up access 24 hours a day. Computers may be used freely, but students are limited to 1 to 2 hours of use when demand is high. There are no fees.

Graduates: In 1994–95, 505 bachelor's degrees were awarded. The most popular majors among graduates were architecture (14%), nursing (12%), and politics (11%). Within an average freshman class, 4% graduate in 3 years, 67% in 4 years, 75% in 5 years, and 75% in 6 years. 50 companies recruited on campus in 1994–95. Of the 1994 graduating class, 37% were enrolled in graduate school within 6 months of graduation and 82% had found employment.

Admissions Contact: David R. Gibson, Dean of Admissions and Financial Aid. E-mail: cua-admissions@cua.edu.

CORCORAN SCHOOL OF ART
C-3
Washington, DC 20006   (202) 628-9484

Full-time: 140 men, 160 women	Faculty: 45
Part-time: none	Ph.D.s: 90%
Graduate: none	Student/Faculty: 7 to 1
Year: semesters	Tuition: $10,500
Application Deadline: open	Room & Board: $4000
Freshman Class: n/av	
SAT I or ACT: required	SPECIAL

Established in 1890, the Corcoran School of Art is a private professional art college offering undergraduate programs in fine art and design, and photography. Figures given in the above capsule are approximate. In addition to regional accreditation, Corcoran has baccalaureate program accreditation with NASAD. The library contains 13,300 volumes, and subscribes to 111 periodicals. Computerized library sources and services include the card catalog. Special learning facilities include a learning resource center and art gallery. The 7-acre campus is in an urban area. Including residence halls, there are 3 buildings on campus.

Student Life: 64% of undergraduates are from the District of Columbia. Students come from 28 states and 9 foreign countries. 75% are from public schools; 25% from private. 70% are white; 10% foreign nationals. The average age of freshmen is 19; all undergraduates, 23. 7% do not continue beyond their first year; 60% remain to graduate.

Housing: 23 students can be accommodated in college housing. College-sponsored living facilities include coed dormitories. On-campus housing is guaranteed for the freshman year only and is available on a first-come, first-served basis. Priority is given to out-of-town students. 92% of students commute. Alcohol is not permitted.

Activities: There are no fraternities or sororities. There are some groups and organizations on campus, including art, literary magazine, and newspaper. Popular campus events include student art openings, museum and gallery openings, and visiting artists lectures.

Sports: There is no sports program at Corcoran.

Disabled Students: 70% of the campus is accessible to disabled students. The following facilities are available: wheelchair ramps, elevators, specially equipped rest rooms, and lowered telephones.

Campus Safety and Security: Campus safety and security measures include 24-hour foot and vehicle patrol.

Programs of Study: Corcoran confers the B.F.A. degree. Bachelor's degrees are awarded in COMMUNICATIONS AND THE ARTS (fine arts, graphic design, and photography). Fine arts has the largest enrollment.

Required: Students must complete 126 credits, with 65 to 70 of these in the major and 23 in the core curriculum, and must maintain a minimum GPA of 2.0. Course distribution must involve the disciplines of art history, humanities, liberal arts, and writing. Curricula will include courses in drawing, design, idea resources, and media.

Special: Cooperative programs are permitted with the ACE and AICA art college consortiums. Opportunities are provided for internships in graphic design and photography, credit by examination, work-study programs with the Corcoran Gallery of Art, and nondegree study.

Faculty/Classroom: 50% of faculty are male; 50%, female. All teach undergraduates. The average class size in an introductory lecture is 23; in a laboratory, 10; and in a regular course offering, 10.

Admissions: In a recent year, 82% of applicants were accepted. The SAT I scores for a recent freshman class were as follows: Verbal—60% below 500, 29% between 500 and 599, 10% between 600 and 700, and 1% above 700

Requirements: A minimum GPA of 2.0 is required. The SAT I or ACT is required. Applicants must have graduated from an approved secondary school; a GED will be accepted. A portfolio is required, and an interview is recommended. AP credits are accepted. Important factors in the admissions decision are evidence of special talent, personality/intangible qualities, and recommendations by alumni.

Procedure: Freshmen are admitted fall and spring. There is a deferred admissions plan. Application deadlines are open. Check with the school for current fee. Notification is sent on a rolling basis. A waiting list is an active part of the admissions procedure, with about 5% of all applicants on the list.

Transfer: A review of studio art transcripts will be considered for the level of entry of transfer students. A portfolio review will be the final determining factor. 63 credits of 126 must be completed at Corcoran.

Visiting: There are regularly scheduled orientations for prospective students. There are guides for informal visits and visitors may sit in on classes. To schedule a visit, contact the Admissions Department.

Financial Aid: Corcoran is a member of CSS. The FAF and the college's own financial statement are required. Check with the school for current deadlines.

International Students: In a recent year, there were 18 international students enrolled. The school actively recruits these students. They must take the TOEFL and achieve a minimum score of 525. The student must also take the SAT I.

Computers: The college provides computer facilities for student use. There are 17 Apple Macintosh Plus SE microcomputers available in the Graphic Design Department and the computer laboratory. All students may access the system. There are no fees.

Admissions Contact: Mark Sistek, Director of Admissions.

GALLAUDET UNIVERSITY
C-3
Washington, DC 20002-3695   (202) 651-5750
(800) 995-0550; FAX: (202) 651-5744

Full-time: 659 men, 746 women	Faculty: 346; IIA, av$
Part-time: 34 men, 47 women	Ph.D.s: 58%
Graduate: 80 men, 309 women	Student/Faculty: 7 to 1
Year: semesters, summer session	Tuition: $5280
Application Deadline: open	Room & Board: $5690
Freshman Class: n/av	
SAT I or ACT: not required	SPECIAL

Gallaudet University, founded in 1864 as a university designed exclusively for deaf and hard-of-hearing students, offers programs in liberal and fine arts, teacher preparation, and professional training. There are 4 undergraduate and 4 graduate schools. In addition to regional accreditation, Gallaudet has baccalaureate program accreditation with CSWE and NCATE. The library contains 215,500 volumes, 371,000 microform items, and 4530 audiovisual forms, and subscribes to 1415 periodicals. Computerized library sources and services include the card catalog, interlibrary loans, and database searching. Special learning facilities include a learning resource center, TV station, child development center, national and international centers on deafness, and a research institute on deafness. The 99-

acre campus is in an urban area in Washington, D.C. Including residence halls, there are 30 buildings on campus.

Student Life: 95% of undergraduates are from out-of-state, mostly the Northeast. Students come from 50 states and Canada. 74% are white; 14% foreign nationals.

Housing: College-sponsored living facilities include single-sex and coed dormitories. On-campus housing is guaranteed for the freshman year only and is available on a first-come, first-served basis. 51% of students live on campus; of those, 51% remain on campus on weekends. Alcohol is not permitted. All students may keep cars on campus.

Activities: 15% of men belong to 1 local and 3 national fraternities; 20% of women belong to 2 local and 3 national sororities. There are 32 groups on campus, including art, cheerleading, computers, dance, drama, ethnic, gay, honors, international, literary magazine, newspaper, political, religious, social, social service, student government, and yearbook. Popular campus events include a rock festival, drama productions, and a lecture series.

Sports: There are 9 intercollegiate sports for men and 8 for women, and 12 intramural sports for men and 12 for women. Athletic and recreation facilities include a field house, a gymnasium, a swimming pool, tennis and racquetball courts, weight training rooms, playing fields, and bowling alleys.

Disabled Students: The following facilities are available: wheelchair ramps, elevators, special parking, specially equipped rest rooms, special class scheduling, lowered drinking fountains, lowered telephones, and phones with HY. Sign language skills are required of all faculty and professional staff.

Services: In addition to many counseling and information services, tutoring is available in every subject through the tutorial, English, and writing centers. There is remedial math, reading, and writing. An information-on-deafness center is also available.

Campus Safety and Security: Campus safety and security measures include 24-hour foot and vehicle patrol, escort service, shuttle buses, and informal discussions. There are pamphlets/posters/films and lighted pathways/sidewalks.

Programs of Study: Gallaudet confers B.A. and B.S. degrees. Associate, master's, and doctoral degrees are also awarded. Bachelor's degrees are awarded in BIOLOGICAL SCIENCE (biology/biological science), BUSINESS (accounting, business administration and management, entrepreneurial studies, management science, and recreation and leisure services), COMMUNICATIONS AND THE ARTS (apparel design, art history and appreciation, communications, dramatic arts, English, French, German, graphic design, media arts, Russian, Spanish, and studio art), COMPUTER AND PHYSICAL SCIENCE (chemical technology, chemistry, computer science, mathematics, and physics), EDUCATION (art, early childhood, elementary, home economics, physical, and secondary), ENGINEERING AND ENVIRONMENTAL DESIGN (engineering technology), HEALTH PROFESSIONS (recreation therapy), SOCIAL SCIENCE (child care/child and family studies, economics, family/consumer studies, history, interpreter for the deaf, parks and recreation management, philosophy, political science/government, psychology, religion, and social work).

Required: The core curriculum requires 12 hours each of social science and English, 9 of literature and humanities, 8 of laboratory science, 5 of communication arts, 4 of physical education, and 3 of philosophy, plus demonstrated proficiency in a foreign language. A total of 124 credits, with 30 to 60 in the major, and a minimum 2.0 GPA are required for graduation.

Special: Gallaudet offers co-op programs with Oberlin College in Ohio and Western Maryland College, cross-registration with the Consortium of Universities of the Washington Metropolitan Area, and a 3–2 engineering degree with George Washington University. Internships, study abroad, dual majors, work-study programs, and B.A.-B.S. degrees are available. There is a freshman honors program on campus

Faculty/Classroom: No introductory courses are taught by graduate students.

Requirements: Applicants must submit a recent audiogram and results of the most recent edition of the Stanford Achievement Test. SAT I or ACT scores may be submitted, but are not required. High school transcripts, letters of recommendation, and writing samples are also required. The GED is accepted. AP and CLEP credits are accepted. Important factors in the admissions decision are advanced placement or honor courses, recommendations by school officials, and leadership record.

Procedure: Freshmen are admitted fall and spring. Entrance exams should be taken in October or November of the senior year. There is a deferred admissions plan. Application deadlines are open. Application fee is $35. Notification is sent on a rolling basis.

Transfer: 98 transfer students were enrolled in a recent year. Deaf and hard-of-hearing transfer applicants must submit a recent audiogram, official college transcripts from all schools attended, and at least 2 letters of recommendation. Students should have completed 12 or more credit hours with at least a 2.0 GPA; those who do not

meet these requirements must submit recent SAT I or ACT scores and a final high school transcript. Half of the credits for the major must be completed at Gallaudet.

Visiting: There are regularly scheduled orientations for prospective students, including a tour of campus, classroom observations, and interviews with selected offices and programs. There are guides for informal visits and visitors may sit in on classes. To schedule a visit, contact the Gallaudet University Visitor's Center at (202) 651-5050.

Financial Aid: In a recent year, 69% of all freshmen and 54% of continuing students received some form of financial aid. 59% of freshmen and 46% of continuing students received need-based aid. The average freshman award was $6841. Of that total, scholarships or need-based grants averaged $2244 ($5000 maximum); state support for disabled students averaged $4285 ($6147 maximum); loans averaged $302 ($2625 maximum); and work contracts averaged $10 ($1400 maximum). The average financial indebtedness of a recent graduate was $4143. The FAFSA and the college's own financial statement are required. Check with the school for current deadlines.

International Students: In a recent year, there were 254 international students enrolled. They must take the TOEFL, the MELAB, the Comprehensive English Language Test, the college's own test, or the most recent edition of the Stanford Achievement Test. SAT I or ACT scores may also be submitted.

Computers: The college provides computer facilities for student use. The mainframes are 2 DEC VAX 6250s and 2 DEC VAX 8650s. There are about 1100 microcomputers, including 145 in public user areas. All residence halls have VT terminals, with Benson Hall housing a computer laboratory. There is national network access via Bitnet, NSFnet, and the Internet. All students may access the system 24 hours a day. There are no fees.

Graduates: 30 companies recruited on campus in a recent year.

Admissions Contact: Deborah DeStefano, Director of Admissions.

GEORGE WASHINGTON UNIVERSITY
Washington, DC 20052

B-3

(202) 994-6040
(800) 447-3765; FAX: (202) 994-0325

Full-time: 2661 men, 3147 women	Faculty: 468; I, +$
Part-time: 307 men, 263 women	Ph.D.s: 89%
Graduate: 4846 men, 4508 women	Student/Faculty: 12 to 1
Year: semesters, summer session	Tuition: $19,032
Application Deadline: December 1	Room & Board: $6590
Freshman Class: 10,469 applied, 5738 accepted, 1395 enrolled	
SAT I Verbal/Math: 550/610	ACT: 27 HIGHLY COMPETITIVE

George Washington University, founded in 1821, is a private coeducational institution providing degree programs in arts and sciences, business, engineering, international affairs, and health sciences. There are 5 undergraduate and 7 graduate schools. In addition to regional accreditation, GW has baccalaureate program accreditation with AACSB, ABET, NASAD, and NASM. The 3 libraries contain 1,730,274 volumes, 1,982,995 microform items, and 7025 audiovisual forms, and subscribe to 14,210 periodicals. Computerized library sources and services include the card catalog, interlibrary loans, and database searching. Special learning facilities include a learning resource center, art gallery, radio station, and TV station. The 37-acre campus is in an urban area 3 blocks west of the White House. Including residence halls, there are 93 buildings on campus.

Student Life: 80% of undergraduates are from out-of-state, mostly the Middle Atlantic. Students come from 50 states, 127 foreign countries, and Canada. 70% are from public schools; 30% from private. 65% are white; 12% Asian American; 11% foreign nationals. The average age of freshmen is 18; all undergraduates, 21. 9% do not continue beyond their first year; 71% remain to graduate.

Housing: 3189 students can be accommodated in college housing. College-sponsored living facilities include single-sex and coed dormitories, on-campus apartments, and fraternity houses. In addition there are special interest houses and sorority floors. On-campus housing is available on a lottery system for upperclassmen. 59% of students live on campus. All students may keep cars on campus.

Activities: 19% of men belong to 12 national fraternities; 12% of women belong to 7 national sororities. There are 208 groups on campus, including art, band, cheerleading, chess, choir, chorale, chorus, computers, dance, drama, ethnic, film, folklore, gay, geology, honors, international, jazz band, literary magazine, marching band, musical theater, newspaper, opera, orchestra, pep band, photography, political, professional, radio and TV, religious, social, social service, student government, symphony, and yearbook. Popular campus events include a yearly benefit auction, Spring Fling, Fall Fest, and Honors Convocation.

Sports: There are 9 intercollegiate sports for men and 8 for women, and 16 intramural sports for men and 16 for women. Athletic and recreation facilities include a 5000-seat gymnasium with 2 auxiliary gymnasiums, an AAU swimming pool, weight rooms, a jogging track, squash and racquetball courts, and soccer and baseball fields.

Disabled Students: 90% of the campus is accessible to disabled students. The following facilities are available: wheelchair ramps, elevators, special parking, specially equipped rest rooms, special class scheduling, lowered drinking fountains, and lowered telephones.

Services: In addition to many counseling and information services, tutoring is available in every subject. There is a reader service for the blind.

Campus Safety and Security: Campus safety and security measures include 24-hour foot and vehicle patrol, self-defense education, escort service, and informal discussions. In addition, there are pamphlets/posters/films, emergency telephones, lighted pathways/sidewalks, and a bike patrol.

Programs of Study: GW confers B.A., B.S., B.Accy., B.B.A., B.Mus., B.S.C.E., B.S.C.Eng., B.S.C.S., B.S.E.E., B.S.M.E., and B.S.S.A. and E. degrees. Associate, master's, and doctoral degrees are also awarded. Bachelor's degrees are awarded in BIOLOGICAL SCIENCE (biology/biological science), BUSINESS (accounting, banking and finance, business administration and management, business economics, international business management, marketing management, and tourism), COMMUNICATIONS AND THE ARTS (art history and appreciation, broadcasting, Chinese, classics, communications, dance, dramatic arts, English, fine arts, French, German, journalism, literature, music, music performance, Russian, and Spanish), COMPUTER AND PHYSICAL SCIENCE (applied mathematics, chemistry, computer science, geology, information sciences and systems, mathematics, physics, statistics, and systems analysis), ENGINEERING AND ENVIRONMENTAL DESIGN (civil engineering, computer engineering, electrical/electronics engineering, engineering, environmental science, and mechanical engineering), HEALTH PROFESSIONS (clinical science, emergency medical technologies, medical laboratory technology, nuclear medical technology, physician's assistant, premedicine, radiological science, speech pathology/audiology, and ultrasound technology), SOCIAL SCIENCE (American studies, anthropology, archeology, classical/ancient civilization, criminal justice, East Asian studies, economics, European studies, geography, history, human services, humanities, interdisciplinary studies, international relations, Judaic studies, liberal arts/general studies, Middle Eastern studies, philosophy, physical fitness/movement, political science/government, psychology, religion, and sociology). Political communication, international affairs, and psychology are the strongest academically. Psychology, political science, and international affairs have the largest enrollments.

Required: Students must complete 120 semester hours with a minimum GPA of 2.0 for most majors. Arts and sciences majors must meet general curriculum requirements that include literacy, quantitative and logical reasoning, natural sciences, social and behavioral sciences, creative and performing arts, literature, Western civilization, and foreign languages or culture. Other specific course requirements vary with the different divisions of the university.

Special: Cross-registration is available through the Consortium of Colleges and Universities. There are co-op programs in education, business, engineering, arts and sciences, and international affairs, and internships throughout the Washington metropolitan area. Study abroad in locations throughout the world, work-study programs, dual majors, student-designed majors, and a 3–2 engineering degree program with 8 colleges are also available. Nondegree study, a general studies degree, credit by examination, and pass/fail options are possible. There is a freshman honors program on campus, as well as 12 national honor societies, including Phi Beta Kappa. 21 departments have honors programs.

Faculty/Classroom: 73% of faculty are male; 27%, female. Graduate students teach 7% of introductory courses. The average class size in a laboratory is 22 and in a regular course offering, 21.

Admissions: 55% of the 1995–96 applicants were accepted. The SAT I scores for the 1995–96 freshman class were as follows: Verbal—22% below 500, 48% between 500 and 599, 27% between 600 and 700, and 3% above 700; Math—7% below 500, 34% between 500 and 599, 43% between 600 and 700, and 15% above 700. The ACT scores were 3% below 21, 15% between 21 and 23, 26% between 24 and 26, 24% between 27 and 28, and 31% above 28. 72% of the current freshmen were in the top fifth of their class; 95% were in the top two fifths. There were 50 National Merit finalists. 49 freshmen graduated first in their class.

Requirements: The SAT I or ACT is required. Students must have successfully completed a strong academic program in high school. SAT II: Subject tests are strongly recommended. An essay, 1 teacher recommendation, and 1 counselor recommendation are required. An interview is encouraged. Common App applications are accepted on disk, and applications may also be submitted via the College Link. AP and CLEP credits are accepted. Important factors in the admissions decision are advanced placement or honor courses, recommendations by school officials, and leadership record.

Procedure: Freshmen are admitted to all sessions. Entrance exams should be taken in the junior year and the fall semester of the senior year. There are early decision, early admissions, and deferred admissions plans. Early decision applications should be filed by November 1 or December 1; regular applications, by December 1 or February 1 for fall entry, along with an application fee of $50. Notification of early decision is sent December 15; regular decision, March 15. 220 early decision candidates were accepted for the 1995–96 class. A waiting list is an active part of the admissions procedure, with about 1% of all applicants on the list.

Transfer: 338 transfer students enrolled in 1995–96. In addition to a record of high marks and examination scores, applicants must submit official transcripts of all postsecondary work. Minimum GPA requirements vary from 2.5 to 3.0, depending on the major. The SAT I or ACT is required, and an interview is encouraged. 45 credits of 120 must be completed at GW.

Visiting: There are regularly scheduled orientations for prospective students, including group information sessions and campus tours. Class visitation, lunch with current students, and other activities can be arranged, if requested in advance. There are guides for informal visits and visitors may sit in on classes and stay overnight at the school. To schedule a visit, contact the University Visitor Center at (202) 994-6602.

Financial Aid: In 1995–96, 67% of all freshmen and 70% of continuing students received some form of financial aid. 50% of freshmen and 48% of continuing students received need-based aid. The average freshman award was $14,304. Of that total, scholarships or need-based grants averaged $9982 ($25,772 maximum); loans averaged $3689; and work contracts averaged $1888. 20% of undergraduate students work part-time. Average earnings from campus work for the school year are $1600. GW is a member of CSS. The FAFSA, the college's own financial statement, and the CSS Profile Application are required. The application deadline for fall entry is February 1.

International Students: There are currently 529 international students enrolled. The school actively recruits these students. They must take the TOEFL or the college's own test and achieve a minimum score on the TOEFL of 550. The student must also take the SAT I or the ACT.

Computers: The college provides computer facilities for student use. The mainframes are an IBM 4381/R14 and a Sun SPARC Station 2000. All residence halls have computer rooms, and the campus computer center is open 24 hours a day. In addition, 7 computer classrooms are available as walk-in laboratories when classes are not scheduled. Modems are available on the campus network. All students may access the system. There are no time limits and no fees.

Graduates: In 1994–95, 1313 bachelor's degrees were awarded. The most popular majors among graduates were international affairs (12%), international business (8%), and biology (7%). Within an average freshman class, 2% graduate in 3 years, 64% in 4 years, 69% in 5 years, and 71% in 6 years. 127 companies recruited on campus in 1994–95.

Admissions Contact: Frederic A. Siegel, Executive Director of Enrollment Management and Admissions. E-mail: gwadm@gwis2.circ.gwu.edu. A campus video is available.

GEORGETOWN UNIVERSITY   B-3
Washington, DC 20057   (202) 687-3600

Full-time: 2937 men, 3111 women	Faculty: 525; I, +$
Part-time: 105 men, 221 women	Ph.D.s: 92%
Graduate: 3373 men, 2871 women	Student/Faculty: 12 to 1
Year: semesters, summer session	Tuition: $19,402
Application Deadline: January 10	Room & Board: $7466
Freshman Class: 12,813 applied, 2860 accepted, 1410 enrolled	
SAT I or ACT: required	MOST COMPETITIVE

Georgetown University, founded in 1789, is a private coeducational institution affiliated with the Roman Catholic Church and offers programs in arts and sciences, business administration, foreign service, languages and linguistics, and nursing. There are 4 undergraduate and 3 graduate schools. In addition to regional accreditation, Georgetown has baccalaureate program accreditation with AACSB and NLN. The 2 libraries contain 2,017,927 volumes, 2,605,469 microform items, and 56,572 audiovisual forms, and subscribe to 26,036 periodicals. Computerized library sources and services include the card catalog, interlibrary loans, and database searching. Special learning facilities include a learning resource center, art gallery, planetarium, and radio station. The 110-acre campus is in an urban area 1.5 miles northwest of downtown Washington, D.C. Including residence halls, there are 60 buildings on campus.

Student Life: 97% of undergraduates are from out-of-state, mostly the Middle Atlantic. Students come from 50 states, 128 foreign countries, and Canada. 42% are from public schools; 58% from private. 67% are white; 10% foreign nationals. 54% are Catholic; 24% Protestant; 14% claim no religious affiliation. The average age of freshmen is 18; all undergraduates, 20. 4% do not continue beyond their first year; 91% remain to graduate.

Housing: 3768 students can be accommodated in college housing. College-sponsored living facilities include coed dormitories, on-campus apartments, and off-campus apartments. In addition there are language houses, special interest houses, and handicapped housing. On-campus housing is available on a lottery system for upperclassmen. 64% of students live on campus. Alcohol is not permitted. Upperclassmen may keep cars on campus.

Activities: There are no fraternities or sororities. There are 100 groups on campus, including art, band, cheerleading, chess, choir, chorale, chorus, computers, dance, drama, ethnic, gay, honors, international, literary magazine, musical theater, newspaper, orchestra, pep band, political, professional, religious, social, social service, student government, symphony, and yearbook. Popular campus events include Founders Day, Spring Fest, and new student orientation.

Sports: There are 12 intercollegiate sports for men and 10 for women, and 13 intramural sports for men and 13 for women. Athletic and recreation facilities include a field house, a 150,000-square-foot underground facility with a swimming pool, handball/racquetball/squash courts, a jogging track, and weight training equipment, and multipurpose courts for basketball, volleyball, and tennis.

Disabled Students: 90% of the campus is accessible to disabled students. The following facilities are available: wheelchair ramps, elevators, special parking, specially equipped rest rooms, special class scheduling, lowered drinking fountains, lowered telephones, a special map of the campus with accessibility routes, a tactile map of the campus for visually disabled students, and a paratransit vehicle for mobility on the main campus.

Services: In addition to many counseling and information services, tutoring is available in every subject. There is a reader service for the blind.

Campus Safety and Security: Campus safety and security measures include escort service, shuttle buses, informal discussions, and pamphlets/posters/films. In addition, there are emergency telephones and lighted pathways/sidewalks.

Programs of Study: Georgetown confers B.A., B.S., B.S.B.A., and B.S.N. degrees. Master's and doctoral degrees are also awarded. Bachelor's degrees are awarded in BIOLOGICAL SCIENCE (biology/biological science), BUSINESS (accounting, banking and finance, business administration and management, international business management, and marketing/retailing/merchandising), COMMUNICATIONS AND THE ARTS (Arabic, Chinese, English, fine arts, French, German, Italian, Japanese, languages, linguistics, Portuguese, Russian, and Spanish), COMPUTER AND PHYSICAL SCIENCE (chemistry, computer science, mathematics, and physics), EDUCATION (foreign languages), HEALTH PROFESSIONS (nursing), SOCIAL SCIENCE (economics, history, international public service, international relations, philosophy, political science/government, psychology, religion, and sociology). Biology, economics, and English are the strongest academically. Government, finance, and international affairs have the largest enrollments.

Required: Students must complete 120 credits and maintain a minimum GPA of 2.0. A core of liberal arts courses is required, consisting of 2 courses each in literature, philosophy, theology, history, social science, and mathematics/science. Computer science is required of students majoring in business, mathematics, science, and computer science.

Special: Cross-registration is available with a consortium of universities in the Washington metropolitian area, and a 3–2 engineering degree is available with Catholic University of America. Opportunities are provided for internships, study abroad in 24 countries, work-study programs, student-designed majors, and dual majors. A general studies degree, B.A.-B.S. degrees, nondegree study, credit by examination, and pass/fail options are also offered. There is a freshman honors program on campus, as well as 13 national honor societies, including Phi Beta Kappa. 4 departments have honors programs.

Faculty/Classroom: 69% of faculty are male; 31%, female. 94% teach undergraduates and all do research. No introductory courses are taught by graduate students. The average class size in an introductory lecture is 34 and in a regular course offering, 23.

Admissions: 22% of the 1995–96 applicants were accepted. The SAT I scores for the 1995–96 freshman class were as follows: Verbal—12% below 500, 29% between 500 and 599, 48% between 600 and 700, and 11% above 700; Math—3% below 500, 15% between 500 and 599, 50% between 600 and 700, and 32% above 700. The ACT scores were 3% below 21, 7% between 21 and 23, 17% between 24 and 26, 17% between 27 and 28, and 56% above 28. 90% of the current freshmen were in the top fifth of their class; 98% were in the top two fifths. There were 40 National Merit finalists and 122 semifinalists. 242 freshmen graduated first in their class.

Requirements: The SAT I or ACT is required. In addition, graduation from an accredited secondary school is required, including 4 years of English, a minimum of 2 each of a foreign language, mathematics, and social studies, and 1 of natural science. An additional 2 years each of mathematics and science is required for students intending to major in mathematics, science, nursing, or business. SAT

II: Subject tests are strongly recommended. Applicants to the Walsh School of Foreign Service and the Faculty of Languages and Linguistics are required to submit results of an SAT II: Subject test in a modern foreign language. A disk application is available from the Office of Undergraduate Admissions. Mac Apply may also be used. AP credits are accepted. Important factors in the admissions decision are advanced placement or honor courses, personality/intangible qualities, and evidence of special talent.

Procedure: Freshmen are admitted in the fall. Entrance exams should be taken in the junior year and again at the beginning of the senior year. There are early action and deferred admissions plans. Early action applications should be filed by November 1; regular applications, by January 10 for fall entry, along with an application fee of $50. Notification of early action is sent December 15; regular decision, April 1. 619 early action candidates were accepted for the 1995–96 class. A waiting list is an active part of the admissions procedure, with about 10% of all applicants on the list.

Transfer: 293 transfer students enrolled in 1995–96. Applicant must have successfully completed a minimum of 12 credit hours with a minimum GPA of 3.0. Either the SAT I or the ACT is required. An interview is recommended. Transfers must complete their last 2 years at Georgetown. 60 credits of 120 must be completed at Georgetown.

Visiting: There are regularly scheduled orientations for prospective students. There are guides for informal visits and visitors may sit in on classes. To schedule a visit, contact the Office of Undergraduate Admissions.

Financial Aid: In 1995–96, 55% of all freshmen and 52% of continuing students received some form of financial aid. 47% of freshmen and 45% of continuing students received need-based aid. The average freshman award was $17,695. Of that total, scholarships or need-based grants averaged $13,462 ($22,495 maximum); loans averaged $2625 (maximum); and work contracts averaged $2200 (maximum). 55% of undergraduate students work part-time. Average earnings from campus work for the school year are $2500. The average financial indebtedness of the 1994–95 graduate was $16,250. Georgetown is a member of CSS. The FAF and FAFSA are required. The application deadline for fall entry is February 1.

International Students: There are currently 1375 international students enrolled. The school actively recruits these students. They must take the TOEFL and achieve a minimum score of 550. The student must also take the SAT I or the ACT.

Computers: The college provides computer facilities for student use. The mainframes are an IBM ES/9000–320 and a DEC VAX 4000–200, 4000–300, and 8700. In addition, there are more than 200 terminals and PCs in the library, computer laboratories, and the School of Business Administration. All students may access the system. There are no time limits and no fees.

Graduates: In 1994–95, 1563 bachelor's degrees were awarded. The most popular majors among graduates were international affairs (15%), English (9%), and finance (9%). Within an average freshman class, 1% graduate in 3 years, 85% in 4 years, 3% in 5 years, and 1% in 6 years. 140 companies recruited on campus in 1994–95.

Admissions Contact: Charles A. Deacon, Dean of Admissions.

HOWARD UNIVERSITY
Washington, DC 20059

	C-3
Full-time: 2570 men, 4140 women	(202) 806-2700; (800) 822-6363
Part-time: 370 men, 500 women	Faculty: 1195; I, --$
Graduate: 1290 men, 1670 women	Ph.D.s: 82%
Year: semesters, summer session	Student/Faculty: 6 to 1
Application Deadline: see profile	Tuition: $8100
Freshman Class: n/av	Room & Board: $4150
SAT I or ACT: required	**LESS COMPETITIVE**

Howard University, founded in 1867, is a private, nonsectarian, coeducational institution and the largest predominantly black university in the United States. Figures given in the above capsule are approximate. There are 10 undergraduate and 13 graduate schools. In addition to regional accreditation, Howard has baccalaureate program accreditation with AACSB, ABET, ACEJMC, ACPE, ADA, AHEA, APTA, ASLA, CSWE, NAAB, NASAD, NASDTEC, NASM, NCATE, and NLN. The 7 libraries contain 1.8 million volumes and 3,335,282 microform items, and subscribe to 26,280 periodicals. Computerized library sources and services include the card catalog, interlibrary loans, and database searching. Special learning facilities include a learning resource center, art gallery, radio station, TV station, and history and culture research center. The 260-acre campus is in an urban area in Washington, D.C. Including residence halls, there are 65 buildings on campus.

Student Life: 88% of undergraduates are from out-of-state, mostly the Middle Atlantic. Students come from 48 states, 90 foreign countries, and Canada. 75% are from public schools; 25% from private. 80% are African American; 15% Native American/Eskimo. The average age of freshmen is 18; all undergraduates, 21. 20% do not continue beyond their first year; 45% remain to graduate.

Housing: 5000 students can be accommodated in college housing. College-sponsored living facilities include single-sex and coed dormitories, on-campus apartments, off-campus apartments, and married-student housing. On-campus housing is guaranteed for the freshman year only, is available on a first-come, first-served basis, and is available on a lottery system for upperclassmen. Priority is given to out-of-town students. 57% of students commute. All students may keep cars on campus.

Activities: 3% of men and about 1% of women belong to 4 national fraternities; 3% of women belong to 4 national sororities. There are 150 groups on campus, including bagpipe band, band, cheerleading, chess, choir, chorale, chorus, computers, dance, drama, drill team, drum and bugle corps, honors, international, jazz band, literary magazine, marching band, newspaper, orchestra, political, professional, radio and TV, religious, social, social service, student government, and yearbook. Popular campus events include Spring Festival, Opening Convocation, and Charter Day.

Sports: There are 15 intercollegiate sports for men and 15 for women, and 5 intramural sports for men and 5 for women. Athletic and recreation facilities include a sports center, a gymnasium, and practice fields.

Disabled Students: 98% of the campus is accessible to disabled students. The following facilities are available: wheelchair ramps, elevators, special parking, specially equipped rest rooms, special class scheduling, lowered drinking fountains, and lowered telephones.

Services: In addition to many counseling and information services, tutoring is available in most subjects. There is a reader service for the blind, and remedial math, reading, and writing.

Campus Safety and Security: Campus safety and security measures include 24-hour foot and vehicle patrol, escort service, shuttle buses, and informal discussions. There are lighted pathways/sidewalks.

Programs of Study: Howard confers B.A., B.S., B.Arch., B.B.A., B.F.A., and B.S.W. degrees. Master's and doctoral degrees are also awarded. Bachelor's degrees are awarded in BIOLOGICAL SCIENCE (biology/biological science, botany, microbiology, and zoology), BUSINESS (accounting, banking and finance, business administration and management, hotel/motel and restaurant management, insurance, international business management, and marketing/retailing/merchandising), COMMUNICATIONS AND THE ARTS (Arabic, broadcasting, classics, communications, dance, design, dramatic arts, English, film arts, fine arts, French, German, Greek, journalism, Latin, music, photography, Russian, and Spanish), COMPUTER AND PHYSICAL SCIENCE (actuarial science, chemistry, computer programming, computer science, information sciences and systems, mathematics, and physics), EDUCATION (art, early childhood, elementary, music, and physical), ENGINEERING AND ENVIRONMENTAL DESIGN (architecture, chemical engineering, civil engineering, computer engineering, electrical/electronics engineering, and mechanical engineering), HEALTH PROFESSIONS (medical laboratory technology, nursing, occupational therapy, pharmacy, physical therapy, physician's assistant, predentistry, premedicine, radiograph medical technology, and speech pathology/audiology), SOCIAL SCIENCE (African American studies, African studies, anthropology, criminal justice, dietetics, economics, history, international relations, philosophy, political science/government, psychology, and sociology). Business and engineering are the strongest academically. Accounting, finance, and electrical engineering have the largest enrollments.

Required: To graduate, students must complete 124 to 171 credit hours, including 21 to 78 in a major and 12 to 39 in a minor, with a minimum GPA of 2.0. General requirements include 4 units of physical education, along with at least 1 year of precalculus mathematics in most majors and at least 1 course in Afro-American studies.

Special: Cross-registration is available with the Consortium of Universities in the Washington Metropolitan Area. Opportunities are also provided for internships, work-study and co-op programs, study abroad in Europe and Africa, B.A.-B.S. degrees in engineering and business, pass/fail options, and accelerated degree programs in medicine and dentistry. There is a freshman honors program on campus. One department has an honors program.

Faculty/Classroom: 71% of faculty are male; 29%, female. The average class size in an introductory lecture is 40; in a laboratory, 20; and in a regular course offering, 20.

Requirements: The SAT I or ACT is required, with a score of 800 on the SAT I (400 verbal, 400 math) or 21 on the ACT. Graduation in the upper 50% from an accredited secondary school with a 2.0 GPA is required. The GED is accepted. Students must have a minimum of 16 academic credits, including 4 in English, 2 each in foreign language, mathematics, science, and either history or social studies, and 4 in electives. Other requirements vary by college. Engineering majors must take the SAT II: Subject test in mathematics I. Art majors must submit a portfolio, and music and theater majors must audition. AP credits are accepted. Important factors in the admissions decision

are recommendations by school officials and advanced placement or honor courses.

Procedure: Freshmen are admitted to all sessions. Entrance exams should be taken in the fall of the senior year. There are early admissions and deferred admissions plans. Check with the school for current application deadlines and fees. Notification is sent on a rolling basis.

Transfer: All applicants must submit 2 official transcripts from each college or university attended. Students transferring to the School of Business must have successfully completed 18 semester hours or 23 quarter hours of courses, with a minimum GPA of 2.5. For many other majors, the requirement is 12 semester hours or 18 quarter hours, with a minimum GPA of 2.0. Applicants to the College of Arts and Sciences need 3 credits each in English composition and college-level algebra. 30 credits of 124 to 171 must be completed at Howard.

Visiting: There are regularly scheduled orientations for prospective students, including an admissions interview, classroom visits, and conversations with faculty and students. There are guides for informal visits and visitors may sit in on classes and stay overnight at the school. To schedule a visit, contact the Office of Student Recruitment at (202) 806-2900.

Financial Aid: 9% of undergraduate students work part-time. Average earnings from campus work for the school year are $3500. Howard is a member of CSS. The FAFSA is required. Check with the school for current deadlines.

International Students: In a recent year there were 1200 international students enrolled. They must score 500 on the TOEFL and also take SAT II: Subject tests in mathematics I, SAT I or the ACT.

Computers: The college provides computer facilities for student use. The mainframe is an IBM 3033. Microcomputer laboratories are available across campus for academic use. Computer science and research students may access the system 8 a.m to 12 P.M. Monday through Thursday and 8 A.M. to 5 P.M. Friday and Saturday. There are no time limits and no fees.

Admissions Contact: Emmett R. Griffin, Jr., Director of Admissions.

MOUNT VERNON COLLEGE

MOUNT VERNON COLLEGE　　　　　　　　　　**B-3**
Washington, DC 20007　　　(202) 625-4682; (800) 682-4636

Full-time: 365 women	**Faculty:** 33
Part-time: 145 women	**Ph.Ds:** 50%
Graduate: 131 men and women	**Student/Faculty:** 11 to 1
Year: semesters, summer session	**Tuition:** $14,850
Application Deadline: open	**Room & Board:** $7200
Freshman Class: n/av	
SAT I or ACT: required	**COMPETITIVE**

Mount Vernon College, founded in 1875, is an independent liberal arts college for women offering undergraduate and graduate programs. In addition to regional accreditation, Mount Vernon has baccalaureate program accreditation with FIDER. The library contains 59,151 volumes, 10,471 microform items, and 136 audiovisual forms, and subscribes to 192 periodicals. Computerized library sources and services include interlibrary loans and database searching. Special learning facilities include a learning resource center and art gallery. The 26-acre campus is in a suburban area, the northwest residential area of Georgetown. Including residence halls, there are 17 buildings on campus.

Student Life: 75% of undergraduates are from out-of-state, mostly the Middle Atlantic. Students come from 36 states, 48 foreign countries, and Canada. 70% are from public schools; 30% from private. 44% are white; 29% African American; 19% foreign nationals.

Housing: 300 students can be accommodated in college housing. College-sponsored living facilities include dormitories. On-campus housing is available on a first-come, first-served basis and is available on a lottery system for upperclassmen. 60% of students commute. Alcohol is not permitted. Upperclassmen may keep cars on campus.

Activities: There are no sororities. There are 6 groups on campus, including chorus, honors, newspaper, political, student government, and yearbook. Popular campus events include Founders Day, Winter and Spring Weekends, Winter and Spring Follies, the Performing Arts Series at Mount Vernon, Family Weekend, and International Day festivals.

Sports: Athletic and recreation facilities include a pool, tennis courts, weight room, gymnasium, basketball, badminton, and volleyball courts, lacrosse and field hockey fields, and a dance studio.

Disabled Students: The following facilities are available: wheelchair ramps, special parking, specially equipped rest rooms, special class scheduling, and accessible dining room and residence facilities.

Services: In addition to many counseling and information services, tutoring is available in every subject. There is remedial math and writing.

Campus Safety and Security: Campus safety and security measures include shuttle buses, informal discussions, and emergency telephones.

Programs of Study: Mount Vernon confers the B.A. degree. Associate and master's degrees are also awarded. Bachelor's degrees are awarded in BUSINESS (business administration and management), COMMUNICATIONS AND THE ARTS (communications), COMPUTER AND PHYSICAL SCIENCE (information sciences and systems), EDUCATION (early childhood), ENGINEERING AND ENVIRONMENTAL DESIGN (interior design), HEALTH PROFESSIONS (health science), SOCIAL SCIENCE (human development, humanities, interdisciplinary studies, international studies, political science/government, and urban studies).

Required: Students must complete 120 credit hours, with at least 24 in upper-level courses in the student's major, and must maintain a minimum GPA of 2.0. All students must meet a 48-credit liberal arts core requirement, which includes courses in social science, humanities, fine arts, and natural sciences.

Special: Cross-registration is permitted with 11 other schools in the Consortium of Universities of the Washington Metropolitan Area. Opportunities are also provided for internships, work-study programs, study abroad in London, Paris, and Madrid, student-designed majors, credit by examination, nondegree study, and credit for life and work experience. There is a freshman honors program on campus, as well as 1 national honor society.

Faculty/Classroom: 32% of faculty are male; 68%, female. All both teach and do research. No introductory courses are taught by graduate students. The average class size in an introductory lecture is 20; in a laboratory, 15; and in a regular course offering, 10.

Requirements: The SAT I or ACT is required. A minimum GPA of 2.0 is required. Graduation from an accredited secondary school is required; a GED will be accepted. Applicants should submit 16 academic credits, including 4 units in English, 2 in mathematics, 2 in a foreign language, 1 each in a laboratory science and in social science, and 6 in other academic electives. An essay and a recommendation from a high school counselor or teacher are required. AP and CLEP credits are accepted. Important factors in the admissions decision are advanced placement or honor courses, evidence of special talent, and parents or siblings attending the school.

Procedure: Freshmen are admitted fall and spring. Entrance exams should be taken at least one month prior to the semester of enrollment. There is an early admissions plan. Application deadlines are open. The application fee is $35. Notification is sent on a rolling basis. A waiting list is an active part of the admissions procedure.

Transfer: 80 transfer students enrolled in 1995–96. Students applying for transfer should submit an essay, an official transcript from each college previously attended, showing a minimum GPA of 2.0, and a recommendation from an academic adviser or teacher. If the student has not completed more than one year of college, an official high school transcript and SAT I or ACT scores are required. 30 credits of 120 must be completed at Mount Vernon.

Visiting: There are regularly scheduled orientations for prospective students, consisting of meetings with administrators, faculty, and students, visits to classes, and participation in campus social life. There are guides for informal visits and visitors may sit in on classes and stay overnight at the school. To schedule a visit, contact the Admissions Office.

Financial Aid: In 1995–96, 92% of all freshmen and 69% of continuing students received some form of financial aid. 67% of freshmen and 56% of continuing students received need-based aid. The average freshman award was $13,925. Of that total, scholarships or need-based grants averaged $6850 ($13,500 maximum); loans averaged $2625; work contracts averaged $1800 ($2000 maximum); and Pell grants, SEOG, and SSIG averaged $2650 ($7240 maximum). 20% of undergraduate students work part-time. Average earnings from campus work for the school year are $1000. The average financial indebtedness of the 1994–95 graduate was $14,125. Mount Vernon is a member of CSS. The FAFSA is required. The application deadline for fall entry is March 1.

International Students: In a recent year, 57 international students were enrolled. The school actively recruits these students. They must take the TOEFL or the Comprehensive English Language Test and achieve a minimum score on the TOEFL of 500. The student must also take the SAT I or the ACT.

Computers: The college provides computer facilities for student use. The mainframe is a Prime. There is a Compaq laboratory providing IBM-compatible hardware for students, and a word processing center in the library. All students may access the system Monday through Friday until midnight, and daytime hours on weekends. There are no time limits and no fees.

Graduates: In 1994–95, 49 bachelor's degrees were awarded. The most popular majors among graduates were business management (47%) and interior design (33%).

Admissions Contact: Dreama Skorupski, Director of Admissions.

SOUTHEASTERN UNIVERSITY   D-4

Washington, DC 20024   (202) 488–8162; FAX: (202) 488–8093

Full-time: 210 men, 100 women	**Faculty:** 24
Part-time: 140 men, 200 women	**Ph.D.s:** n/av
Graduate: 180 men, 170 women	**Student/Faculty:** 13 to 1
Year: four 12-week terms, summer session	**Tuition:** $7000
	Room & Board: n/app
Application Deadline: open	
Freshman Class: n/av	
SAT I or ACT: recommended	**LESS COMPETITIVE**

Southeastern University, founded as Washington School for Accountancy in 1879, is a private, coeducational commuter institution offering programs in business administration, accounting, computer information systems, finance, banking, and marketing to a student body comprised primarily of working adults. There are 4 graduate schools. Figures given in the above capsule are approximate. The library contains 40,000 volumes and subscribes to 1200 periodicals. Special learning facilities include a learning resource center. The campus is in an urban residential part of southwest Washington, D.C. There is 1 building on campus.

Student Life: 90% of undergraduates are from District of Columbia. Students come from 2 states and 65 foreign countries. The average age of freshmen is 26; all undergraduates, 32. 10% do not continue beyond their first year; 40% remain to graduate.

Housing: There are no residence halls. Referral listings of long- and short-term housing are available. Alcohol is not permitted.

Activities: There is 1 local fraternity. There are no sororities. There are some groups and organizations on campus, including chess, computers, newspaper, and student government. Popular campus events include Halloween, Christmas, and graduation dances, and the Annual Awards Ceremony.

Sports: There is no sports program at Southeastern.

Disabled Students: All of the campus is accessible to disabled students. The following facilities are available: wheelchair ramps, special parking, specially equipped rest rooms, special class scheduling, and lowered telephones.

Services: In addition to many counseling and information services, tutoring is available in most subjects. There is remedial math, reading, and writing. There are also individualized learning programs for students in upper-level courses.

Campus Safety and Security: Campus safety and security measures include 24-hour foot and vehicle patrol and lighted pathways/sidewalks.

Programs of Study: Southeastern confers the B.S. degree. Associate and master's degrees are also awarded. Bachelor's degrees are awarded in BUSINESS (accounting, banking and finance, business administration and management, and marketing/retailing/merchandising), COMPUTER AND PHYSICAL SCIENCE (information sciences and systems), SOCIAL SCIENCE (law and public administration). Business is the strongest academically and has the largest enrollment.

Required: To graduate, students must complete 120 credit hours, including the general studies core curriculum, which consists of 30 hours in the fields of English, information systems, mathematics, humanities, and social science. Also required are 27 hours each of major and professional core courses, 24 of general studies electives, and 6 each of professional and general electives. All students must take an orientation course and a computer course.

Special: Southeastern offers extensive co-op programs, internships, dual majors, and credit by exam and for life/military/work experience. The Add-a-Degree program allows any student with a bachelor's degree to add a second area of expertise, add professional qualifications, or prepare for graduate study by completing necessary foundation courses. There is 1 national honor society on campus.

Requirements: The SAT I or ACT is recommended. Students must be graduates of an accredited secondary school with a 2.0 GPA or have a GED, and they must pass Southeastern's placement test for regular admission. CLEP credit is accepted.

Procedure: Application deadlines are open. Check with the school for current application fee.

Transfer: Applicants must submit transcripts. 60 credits of 120 must be completed at Southeastern.

Financial Aid: The FAF or FAFSA and the college's own financial statement are required. Check with the school for current deadlines.

International Students: They must score 500 on the TOEFL. Applicants scoring below 550 are required to take 2 English courses and enroll in the university's Language Institute.

Computers: The college provides computer facilities for student use. Southeastern's computer center has a mainframe and microcomputers. Those students required to use computing in their major may access the system. There are no time limits and no fees.

Admissions Contact: Shazad Ahmad, Marketing Department.

STRAYER COLLEGE

Washington, DC 20005 C-3

(202) 408-2400 or (703) 892-5100
FAX: (202) 289-1831 or (703) 769-2677

Full-time: 1078 men, 1221 women	Faculty: 68
Part-time: 1679 men, 2409 women	Ph.D.s: 90%
Graduate: 586 men, 446 women	Student/Faculty: 34 to 1
Year: quarters, summer session	Tuition: $6750
Application Deadline: open	Room & Board: n/app
Freshman Class: 1388 enrolled	
SAT I or ACT: recommended	**LESS COMPETITIVE**

Strayer College, founded in 1892, is an independent coeducational business college with 8 campuses in the Washington, D.C. metropolitan area. All programs are computer- or business-related. There are 4 undergraduate and 3 graduate schools. The library contains 20,000 volumes and 350 audiovisual forms, and subscribes to 420 periodicals. Computerized library sources and services include the card catalog and database searching. Special learning facilities include a learning resource center. 2 of the campuses are located in Washington D.C., and 6 are in suburban Virginia. There is 1 building on each campus.

Student Life: All undergraduates are from District of Columbia, Virginia, and Maryland, although 80 foreign countries are represented. 43% are white; 35% African American. The average age of all undergraduates is 31.

Housing: There are no residence halls. All students commute. Alcohol is not permitted. All students may keep cars on campus.

Activities: There is 1 national sorority. There are no fraternities. There are 9 groups on campus, including arts and music, computers, honors, international, and professional. Popular campus events include International Day.

Sports: There is no sports program at Strayer.

Disabled Students: The entire campus is accessible to physically disabled persons. The following facilities are available: wheelchair ramps, elevators, special parking, specially equipped rest rooms, lowered drinking fountains, and lowered telephones.

Services: In addition to many counseling and information services, tutoring is available in some subjects, including accounting, computer information systems, English, and mathematics. There is remedial reading and writing.

Campus Safety and Security: Campus safety and security measures include informal discussions, pamphlets/posters/films. There are security guards at all the urban campuses. Crime seminars are held each fall and spring quarter at various campuses. A campus crime awareness booklet is published annually.

Programs of Study: Strayer confers the B.S. degree. Associate and master's degrees are also awarded. Bachelor's degrees are awarded in BUSINESS (accounting and business administration and management), COMPUTER AND PHYSICAL SCIENCE (information sciences and systems), SOCIAL SCIENCE (economics). Computer information systems, business administration, and accounting are the strongest academically. Computer information systems and business administration have the largest enrollments.

Required: For the bachelor's degree, students must complete 180 quarter hours, with 54 in the major and a minimum GPA of 2.0. There is a core general studies component to each undergraduate degree, as well as a general business curriculum.

Special: The college offers cooperative programs, dual majors, internships with area businesses, and an accelerated diploma program in computer information systems, and gives credit for military and work experience. There is 1 national honor society on campus.

Faculty/Classroom: 79% of faculty are male; 21%, female. All teach undergraduates. No introductory courses are taught by graduate students. The average class size in an introductory lecture is 28 and in a regular course offering, 21.

Requirements: The SAT I or ACT is recommended. A GED is accepted. AP and CLEP credits are accepted.

Procedure: Freshmen are admitted to all sessions. Placement examinations should be taken prior to the beginning of first quarter of attendance. There are early admissions and deferred admissions plans. Application deadlines are open. Application fee is $25. Notification is sent on a rolling basis.

Transfer: 373 transfer students enrolled in 1995–96. Requirements are the same as for freshmen. 54 credits of 180 must be completed at Strayer.

Visiting: There are guides for informal visits. To schedule a visit, contact Michael Williams, Washington Campus Coordinator.

Financial Aid: In a recent year, 45% of all freshmen and 35% of continuing students received some form of financial aid. 40% of freshmen and 30% of continuing students received need-based aid. The average freshman award was $5325. Of that total, scholarships or need-based grants averaged $1700 ($2700 maximum); and loans averaged $2625 ($3312 maximum). The average financial indebtedness of the 1994–95 graduate was $19,000. The FAFSA is required. The application deadline for fall entry is May 1.

International Students: There are currently 439 international students enrolled. The school actively recruits these students. They must take the TOEFL and achieve a minimum score of 450.

Computers: The college provides computer facilities for student use. The mainframe is a Sun SPARC 1000. There are 550 microcomputers available for student use, some located in the library and 7 learning resource centers. Students have access to the Internet and other on-line services through these terminals. Additionally, each campus has at least 1 microcomputer laboratory and 1 networking UNIX laboratory. All students may access the system. There are no time limits and no fees.

Graduates: In 1994–95, 787 bachelor's degrees were awarded. The most popular majors among graduates were computer information systems (44%), business administration (41%), and accounting (14%).

Admissions Contact: Michael Williams, DC Campus Coordinator.

TRINITY COLLEGE

Washington, DC 20017 C-2

(202) 939-5040
(800) 492-6882; FAX: (202) 939-5134

Full-time: 406 women	Faculty: 49; IIB, -$
Part-time: 629 women	Ph.D.s: 95%
Graduate: 451 women	Student/Faculty: 8 to 1
Year: see profile	Tuition: $11,900
Application Deadline: March 1	Room & Board: $6490
Freshman Class: 242 applied, 188 accepted, 100 enrolled	
SAT I Verbal/Math: 544/508	**COMPETITIVE**

Trinity College, founded in 1897, is a private, women's liberal arts college affiliated with the Roman Catholic Church. The school year consists of traditional semesters plus 1-week courses during January and May. There are 2 graduate schools. In addition to regional accreditation, Trinity has baccalaureate program accreditation with NASDTEC and NCATE. The library contains 178,232 volumes, 5392 microform items, and 2922 audiovisual forms, and subscribes to 620 periodicals. Computerized library sources and services include the card catalog, interlibrary loans, and database searching. Special learning facilities include a learning resource center, art gallery, and writing center. The 26-acre campus is in an urban area 2 1/2 miles north of the U.S. Capitol. Including residence halls, there are 7 buildings on campus.

Student Life: Students come from 35 states, 15 foreign countries, and Canada. 40% are from public schools; 60% from private. 48% are white; 38% African American; 10% Hispanic. 60% are Catholic; 37% Protestant. The average age of freshmen is 18; all undergraduates, 20. 11% do not continue beyond their first year; 87% remain to graduate.

Housing: 500 students can be accommodated in college housing. College-sponsored living facilities include dormitories. On-campus housing is guaranteed for all 4 years. 95% of students live on campus; of those, 95% remain on campus on weekends. All students may keep cars on campus.

Activities: There are no sororities. There are 28 groups on campus, including chorale, computers, dance, drama, ethnic, gay, honors, international, jazz band, literary magazine, newspaper, orchestra, photography, political, professional, religious, social, social service, student government, and yearbook. Popular campus events include Founders Day, Junior Ring Day, Christmas and spring formals, and Pub Night.

Sports: There are 6 intercollegiate sports. Athletic and recreation facilities include 2 athletic fields for soccer and field hockey, a fitness center, 6 tennis courts, and an outdoor sand volleyball court.

Disabled Students: The entire campus is accessible to disabled students. The following facilities are available: wheelchair ramps, elevators, special parking, specially equipped rest rooms, and lowered telephones.

Services: In addition to many counseling and information services, tutoring is available in every subject. There is a reader service for the blind and signing for hearing-impaired students.

Campus Safety and Security: Campus safety and security measures include 24-hour foot and vehicle patrol, self-defense education, escort service, and shuttle buses. In addition, there are informal discussions, pamphlets/posters/films, emergency telephones, and lighted pathways/sidewalks.

Programs of Study: Trinity confers B.A. and B.S. degrees. Master's degrees are also awarded. Bachelor's degrees are awarded in BIOLOGICAL SCIENCE (biochemistry and biology/biological science), BUSINESS (business administration and management), COMMUNICATIONS AND THE ARTS (communications, English, French, and Spanish), COMPUTER AND PHYSICAL SCIENCE (chemistry), EDUCATION (early childhood and elementary), ENGINEERING AND ENVIRONMENTAL DESIGN (environmental science), HEALTH PROFESSIONS (premedicine), SOCIAL SCIENCE (American studies, economics, history, international studies, political science/

government, prelaw, and psychology). English, history, and political science are the strongest academically. Business administration, political science, and psychology have the largest enrollments.

Required: To graduate, students must complete a total of 128 credit hours with a minimum GPA of 2.0. Between 42 and 50 hours are required in the major. All students must take the courses required in the Foundation for Leadership curriculum and must complete a senior seminar.

Special: Cross-registration and the Mentor Program are offered through the Consortium of Universities of the Washington Area. Trinity offers internships in all majors and minors, as well as work-study programs. Students may study in France, Italy, and various other countries by arrangement with their faculty adviser. B.A.-B.S. degrees, a 5-year accelerated degree in teaching, a 3–2 engineering degree with George Washington University, dual and student-designed majors, a general studies degree, credit for life experience, nondegree study, and pass/fail options are also available. There is a freshman honors program on campus, as well as 2 national honor societies, including Phi Beta Kappa.

Faculty/Classroom: 25% of faculty are male; 75%, female. All both teach and do research. The average class size in an introductory lecture is 20; in a laboratory, 10; and in a regular course offering, 17.

Admissions: 78% of the 1995–96 applicants were accepted. 42% of the current freshmen were in the top fifth of their class; 70% were in the top two fifths.

Requirements: The SAT I or ACT is required. Trinity requires applicants to be in the upper 50% of their class. A minimum GPA of 2.5 is required. In addition, graduation from an accredited secondary school or satisfactory scores on the GED are required for admission. A total of 16 academic credits is required, including 4 years of English and 3 to 4 each of a foreign language, history, mathematics, and science. AP examinations and SAT II: Subject tests are recommended. An interview and an essay or graded writing sample are required. Trinity accepts applications on computer disk. Instructions will be sent to students upon request. AP and CLEP credits are accepted. Important factors in the admissions decision are leadership record, extracurricular activities record, and recommendations by school officials.

Procedure: Freshmen are admitted fall, spring, and summer. Entrance exams should be taken in the junior year. There are early decision, early admissions, and deferred admissions plans. Early decision applications should be filed by November 15; regular applications, by March 1 for fall entry and December 1 for spring entry, along with an application fee of $35. Notification of early decision is sent January 15; regular decision, within 2 weeks after the completed application is received. 12 early decision candidates were accepted for the 1995–96 class.

Transfer: 45 transfer students enrolled in 1995–96. Applicants must have a GPA of 2.0. An interview is required. 32 credits of 128 must be completed at Trinity.

Visiting: There are regularly scheduled orientations for prospective students, consisting of a full-day program on the third Friday of each month: an overview of the college, the curriculum, financing, and student life, and a trolley tour of Washington, D.C. There are guides for informal visits and visitors may sit in on classes and stay overnight at the school. To schedule a visit, contact the Office of Admissions.

Financial Aid: In 1995–96, 80% of all freshmen and 75% of continuing students received some form of financial aid. 82% of continuing students received need-based aid. Scholarships or need-based grants averaged $6000 ($8500 maximum); loans averaged $5130; and work contracts averaged $1000 (maximum). 55% of undergraduate students work part-time. Average earnings from campus work for the school year are $1000. The average financial indebtedness of the 1994–95 graduate was $8000. Trinity is a member of CSS. The FAF is required. The application deadline for fall entry is March 15.

International Students: In a recent year, there were 15 international students enrolled. The school actively recruits these students. They must take the TOEFL and achieve a minimum score of 550. The student must also take the SAT I or the ACT.

Computers: The college provides computer facilities for student use. Students may use the 31 IBM and 9 Apple microcomputers located in the computer center and in residence halls. All have printer access. There are no fees. It is recommended that all students have a 486 IBM PC or Apple Macintosh LC III.

Graduates: The most popular majors among graduates were biology (10%), psychology (10%), and political science (10%). Within an average freshman class, 75% graduate in 4 years and 9% in 5 years. 150 companies recruited on campus in 1994–95.

Admissions Contact: Susan Grogan Ikerd, Dean of Enrollment Management. E-mail: http://:www.consortium.com.

UNIVERSITY OF THE DISTRICT OF COLUMBIA   C-2
Washington, DC 20008
(202) 282-2300

Full-time: 1660 men, 1990 women	Faculty: 343; IIA, av$
Part-time: 2640 men, 3690 women	Ph.D.s: 52%
Graduate: 270 men, 350 women	Student/Faculty: 11 to 1
Year: semesters, summer session	Tuition: $1130 ($4150)
Application Deadline: see profile	Room & Board: n/app
Freshman Class: n/av	
ACT: required	NONCOMPETITIVE

The University of the District of Columbia, founded in 1977, is a publicly funded, land-grant, coeducational commuter institution offering programs in liberal arts, business, education, and technical fields. Figures given in the above capsule are approximate. There are 5 undergraduate schools and 1 graduate school. In addition to regional accreditation, UDC has baccalaureate program accreditation with ABET, CAHEA, CSWE, NASDTEC, NASM, and NLN. The 4 libraries contain 470,330 volumes, 623,991 microform items, and 21,207 audiovisual forms, and subscribe to 2787 periodicals. Computerized library sources and services include database searching. Special learning facilities include a learning resource center, art gallery, radio station, TV station, and early childhood learning center. The 22-acre campus is in a suburban area in northwest Washington, D.C. There are 26 buildings on campus.

Student Life: 87% of undergraduates are from the District of Columbia. Students come from 50 states and 55 foreign countries. 85% are from public schools; 2% from private. 72% are African American. The average age of freshmen is 18; all undergraduates, 27. 35% do not continue beyond their first year; 65% remain to graduate.

Housing: There are no residence halls. All students commute. Alcohol is not permitted.

Activities: 2% of men belong to 7 national fraternities; 2% of women belong to 5 national sororities. There are 139 groups on campus, including art, band, cheerleading, chess, choir, chorale, computers, dance, drama, drum and bugle corps, ethnic, film, honors, international, jazz band, marching band, newspaper, orchestra, pep band, photography, political, professional, radio and TV, religious, social, social service, student government, and yearbook. Popular campus events include the Cross-Cultural Extended Family Program, International Multicultural Recognition Day, Homecoming, and International Day.

Sports: There are 6 intercollegiate sports each for men and women, and 8 intramural sports for men and 6 for women. Athletic and recreation facilities include a 3000-seat gymnasium, a swimming pool, a weight room, and racquetball and tennis courts.

Disabled Students: All of the campus is accessible to disabled students. The following facilities are available: wheelchair ramps, elevators, special parking, specially equipped rest rooms, lowered drinking fountains, and lowered telephones.

Services: In addition to many counseling and information services, tutoring is available in every subject. There is a reader service for the blind and remedial math and reading.

Campus Safety and Security: Campus safety and security measures include 24-hour foot and vehicle patrol, emergency telephones, and lighted pathways/sidewalks.

Programs of Study: UDC confers B.A., and B.S. degrees. Associate and master's degrees are also awarded. Bachelor's degrees are awarded in BIOLOGICAL SCIENCE (biology/biological science), BUSINESS (accounting, banking and finance, business administration and management, marketing/retailing/merchandising, and office supervision and management), COMMUNICATIONS AND THE ARTS (dramatic arts, English, fine arts, French, media arts, music, and Spanish), COMPUTER AND PHYSICAL SCIENCE (chemistry, computer science, mathematics, and physics), EDUCATION (early childhood, elementary, health, and physical), ENGINEERING AND ENVIRONMENTAL DESIGN (architecture, aviation administration/management, civil engineering, construction engineering, electrical/electronics engineering, electromechanical technology, environmental science, and mechanical engineering), HEALTH PROFESSIONS (nursing and speech pathology/audiology), SOCIAL SCIENCE (criminal justice, economics, fire science, food science, geography, history, philosophy, political science/government, psychology, public administration, social work, sociology, and urban studies). Business is the strongest academically. Fine arts has the largest enrollment.

Required: To graduate, students must complete 120 to 130 semester hours with a minimum GPA of 2.0. All students must take 6 hours each of English composition, literature and advanced writing, foreign language, social science, mathematics, and natural sciences, 4 of personal and community health, and 3 each of philosophy and fine arts.

Special: Cross-registration may be arranged through the Consortium of Universities of the Washington Metropolitan Area. Co-op programs with the federal government, internships, study abroad in 4 countries, work-study programs, and B.A.-B.S. degrees in administration of justice, chemistry, and physics are offered. Nondegree study and credit for life experience are also available. There is a freshman honors program on campus, as well as 4 national honor societies.

Faculty/Classroom: 66% of faculty are male; 34%, female. 89% teach undergraduates, 3% do research, and 20% do both. No introductory courses are taught by graduate students. The average class size in an introductory lecture is 23; in a laboratory, 23; and in a regular course offering, 23.

Requirements: The ACT is required. A high school diploma or GED is required for admission, along with an interview. High school courses must include 4 years of English and 2 each of foreign language, social science, laboratory science, and mathematics (algebra and geometry). AP and CLEP credits are accepted. Important factors in the admissions decision are ability to finance college education, advanced placement or honor courses, and recommendations by school officials.

Procedure: Freshmen are admitted to all sessions. The college accepts all applicants. Check with the school for current application deadlines and fee.

Transfer: 428 transfer students enrolled in a recent year. Applicants must have a minimum GPA of 2.0. Those with fewer than 30 hours of college credit must submit a high school transcript along with college records. 30 credits of 120 to 130 must be completed at UDC.

Visiting: There are guides for informal visits and visitors may sit in on classes. To schedule a visit, contact the Office of Student Recruitment at (202) 282–3350.

Financial Aid: 1% of undergraduate students work part-time. UDC is a member of CSS. The FAF or FFS is required. Check with the school for current deadlines.

International Students: In a recent year, 950 international students were enrolled. They must take the TOEFL and achieve a minimum score of 550. The student must also take the college's own English, mathematics, or reading tests.

Computers: The college provides computer facilities for student use. The mainframes are an IBM 4381 and a DEC VAX 8650. Microcomputers are also available. All students may access the system 24 hours a day. There are no time limits and no fees.

Graduates: In a recent year, 521 bachelor's degrees were awarded. 25 companies recruited on campus in a recent year.

Admissions Contact: Director of Recruitment and Admissions.

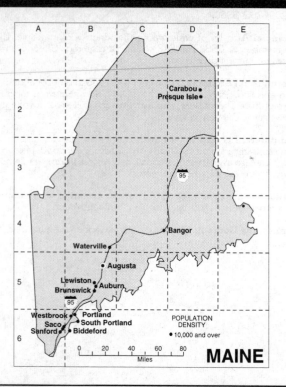

POPULATION DENSITY
● 10,000 and over

0 20 40 60 80
Miles

MAINE

BATES COLLEGE
Lewiston, ME 04240

B-5

(207) 786-6000; FAX: (207) 786-6025

Full-time: 799 men, 837 women
Part-time: none
Graduate: none
Year: 4-4-1 (5-week spring short term)
Application Deadline: January 15
Freshman Class: 3550 applied, 1287 accepted, 450 enrolled
SAT I Verbal/Math: 590/650

Faculty: 146; IIB, + +$
Ph.D.s: 93%
Student/Faculty: 11 to 1
Tuition: see profile
Room & Board: see profile

MOST COMPETITIVE

Bates College, founded in 1855, is a private, coeducational liberal arts institution. A comprehensive fee of $26,300 includes tuition and room and board. The library contains 605,656 volumes, 290,587 microform items, and 20,669 audiovisual forms, and subscribes to 1919 periodicals. Computerized library sources and services include the card catalog. Special learning facilities include an art gallery, planetarium, radio station, TV station, a 574-acre mountain conservation area, the Muskie archives, and an observatory. The 109-acre campus is in a suburban area 140 miles north of Boston. Including residence halls, there are 70 buildings on campus.

Student Life: 88% of undergraduates are from out-of-state, mostly the Northeast. Students come from 48 states, 26 foreign countries, and Canada. 65% are from public schools; 35% from private. 87% are white. The average age of freshmen is 18; all undergraduates, 20. 4% do not continue beyond their first year; 87% remain to graduate.

Housing: 1523 students can be accommodated in college housing. College-sponsored living facilities include single-sex and coed dormitories. In addition, there is an alcohol-free house. On-campus housing is guaranteed for all 4 years. 91% of students live on campus; of those, 75% remain on campus on weekends. All students may keep cars on campus.

Activities: There are no fraternities or sororities. There are 67 groups on campus, including art, chess, choir, chorale, chorus, computers, dance, drama, ethnic, film, gay, honors, international, jazz band, literary magazine, musical theater, newspaper, orchestra, photography, political, professional, radio and TV, religious, social, social service, student government, and yearbook. Popular campus events include Winter Carnival, international dinners, periodic semiformal dances, and ocean clambakes.

Sports: There are 13 intercollegiate sports for men and 13 for women, and 4 intramural sports for men and 4 for women. Athletic and recreation facilities include a pool, a field house, indoor and outdoor tracks, indoor and outdoor tennis courts, 3 basketball courts, 3 volleyball courts, football, soccer, baseball, softball and lacrosse fields, dance and fencing space, squash and racquetball courts, training rooms, a rock climbing wall, a boat house, a winter sports arena, and a weight room.

Disabled Students: 60% of the campus is accessible to disabled students. The following facilities are available: wheelchair ramps, elevators, special parking, specially equipped rest rooms, special class scheduling, and lowered telephones.

Services: In addition to many counseling and information services, tutoring is available in every subject. In addition, there is a reader service for the blind and remedial math and writing.

Campus Safety and Security: Campus safety and security measures include 24-hour foot and vehicle patrol, self-defense education, escort service, and informal discussions. In addition, there are pamphlets/posters/films, emergency telephones, and lighted pathways/sidewalks.

Programs of Study: Bates confers B.A. and B.S. degrees. Bachelor's degrees are awarded in BIOLOGICAL SCIENCE (biochemistry and biology/biological science), COMMUNICATIONS AND THE ARTS (art, dramatic arts, East Asian languages and literature, English, French, German, music, Russian, Spanish, and speech/debate/rhetoric), COMPUTER AND PHYSICAL SCIENCE (chemistry, geology, mathematics, and physics), ENGINEERING AND ENVIRONMENTAL DESIGN (environmental science), SOCIAL SCIENCE (African American studies, American studies, anthropology, classical/ancient civilization, economics, history, philosophy, political science/government, psychology, religion, sociology, and women's studies). Political science, psychology, and English have the largest enrollments.

Required: Requirements for graduation include 5 courses in humanities, 3 each in natural science and social science, and 1 in physical education. The total number of hours in the major varies by department, but students should take at least 32 courses, plus 2 short terms, and maintain a minimum GPA of 2.0. A senior thesis is required.

Special: Internships, research apprenticeships, study abroad, and a Washington semester are possible. Dual, student-designed, and interdisciplinary majors, including classical and medieval studies, and a 3-2 engineering degree with Columbia University, Dartmouth College, Case Western Reserve University, Rensselaer Polytechnic Institute, and Washington University in St. Louis are available. Students in any major may graduate in 3 years and a B.A.-B.S. is possible in all majors. Students may also participate in the Williams-Mystic Seaport program in marine biology and maritime history. There are 2 national honor societies on campus, including Phi Beta Kappa. 29 departments have honors programs.

Faculty/Classroom: 64% of faculty are male; 36%, female. All both teach and do research. The average class size in an introductory lecture is 21; in a laboratory, 16; and in a regular course offering, 17.

Admissions: 36% of the 1995–96 applicants were accepted. The SAT I scores for the 1995–96 freshman class were as follows: Verbal—6% below 500, 47% between 500 and 599, 43% between 600 and 700, and 3% above 700; Math—2% below 500, 18% between 500 and 599, 61% between 600 and 700, and 19% above 700. 85% of the current freshmen were in the top fifth of their class; 100% were in the top two fifths.

Requirements: Candidates for admission should have completed 4 years of English, 3 each of mathematics, history or social studies, and 2 each of science and foreign language. Essays are required and an interview on or off campus is strongly recommended. The submission of test scores is optional. Bates accepts applications on computer disk, but a printed copy is also required. AP credits are accepted. Important factors in the admissions decision are top courses offered at the high school, evidence of special talent, and recommendations by school officials.

Procedure: Freshmen are admitted in the fall and winter. There are early decision, early admissions, and deferred admissions plans. Early decision applications should be filed by January 1; regular applications, by January 15 for fall entry and November 1 for winter entry, along with an application fee of $50. Notification of early decision is sent January 24; regular decision, by April 3. 150 early decision candidates were accepted for the 1995–96 class. A waiting list is an active part of the admissions procedure, with about 7% of all applicants on the list.

Transfer: 13 transfer students enrolled in 1995–96. More weight is given to the student's college record than to high school credentials. 16 courses of 32 must be completed at Bates.

Visiting: There are guides for informal visits and visitors may sit in on classes and stay overnight at the school. To schedule a visit, contact the Admissions Office.

Financial Aid: In 1995–96, 55% of all freshmen and 54% of continuing students received some form of financial aid. 42% of freshmen and 43% of continuing students received need-based aid. The average freshman award was $17,850. Of that total, scholarships or need-based grants averaged $12,241 ($22,000 maximum); loans averaged $4209 ($4300 maximum); and work contracts averaged

$1400. 50% of undergraduate students work part-time. Average earnings from campus work for the school year are $1400. Bates is a member of CSS. The CSS Profile Application, along with parent and student tax returns and W-2 forms, are required. The application deadline for fall entry is January 15.

International Students: There were 52 international students enrolled in a recent year. The school actively recruits these students. They must take the TOEFL.

Computers: The college provides computer facilities for student use. The mainframes are a DEC 5000/260 and a Prime 7330 (RISC). There are 130 public microcomputers with access to the mainframe and Internet. An additional 150 microcomputers are in departmental laboratories and 75% can access the mainframe and Internet. All students may access the system. There are no time limits and no fees.

Graduates: In 1994–95, 360 bachelor's degrees were awarded. The most popular majors among graduates were biology (15%), psychology (13%), and English (11%). Within an average freshman class, 1% graduate in 3 years, 82% in 4 years, and 6% in 5 years. 70 companies recruited on campus in 1994–95.

Admissions Contact: Wylie L. Mitchell, Dean of Admissions. A campus video is available.

BOWDOIN COLLEGE
Brunswick, ME 04011

B-5
(207) 725-3100

Full-time: 745 men, 776 women	Faculty: 118; IIB, + +$
Part-time: 2 men, 7 women	Ph.D.s: 95%
Graduate: none	Student/Faculty: 13 to 1
Year: semesters	Tuition: $20,555
Application Deadline: January 15	Room & Board: $5945
Freshman Class: 4122 applied, 1255 accepted, 449 enrolled	
SAT I Verbal/Math: 610/680	MOST COMPETITIVE

Bowdoin College, established in 1794, is a private, coeducational, liberal arts institution. The 2 libraries contain 842,629 volumes, 249,200 microform items, and 12,733 audiovisual forms, and subscribe to 2110 periodicals. Computerized library sources and services include the card catalog, interlibrary loans, and database searching. Special learning facilities include an art gallery, radio station, museum of art, arctic museum, language media center, women's resource center, and electronic classroom. The 110-acre campus is in a small town 25 miles northeast of Portland. Including residence halls, there are 75 buildings on campus.

Student Life: 86% of undergraduates are from out-of-state, mostly the Northeast. Students come from 50 states, 28 foreign countries, and Canada. 51% are from public schools; 49% from private. 81% are white. The average age of freshmen is 18; all undergraduates, 20. 7% do not continue beyond their first year; 92% remain to graduate.

Housing: 1152 students can be accommodated in college housing. College-sponsored living facilities include single-sex and coed dormitories, on-campus apartments, and off-campus apartments. In addition, there are special interest houses, the Wellness House, with a focus on healthful living, an Afro-American House, and a World Interest House. On-campus housing is guaranteed for the freshman year only and is available on a lottery system for upperclassmen. 75% of students live on campus; of those, 99% remain on campus on weekends. All students may keep cars on campus.

Activities: There are no sororities. 28% of students belong to 8 coed fraternities. There are 50 groups on campus, including a cappella singing, art, choir, chorale, chorus, computers, dance, drama, ethnic, film, gay, improvisational comedy, international, jazz band, literary magazine, musical theater, newspaper, orchestra, outing, photography, political, professional, radio and TV, religious, social, social service, student government, and yearbook. Popular campus events include James Bowdoin Day, Parents Weekend, Ivies Weekend, Winter Weekend, Homecoming, and a pop concert series.

Sports: There are 12 intercollegiate sports for men, 13 for women and coed, and 8 coed intramural sports. Athletic and recreation facilities include an arena, a field house, a swimming pool, 2 gymnasiums, indoor and outdoor track facilities, tennis and squash courts, and cross-country ski trails. There are also Nautilus, weight, and aerobics rooms, and 35 acres of playing fields for baseball, softball, lacrosse, field hockey, and soccer.

Disabled Students: 20% of the campus is accessible to disabled students. The following facilities are available: wheelchair ramps, elevators, special parking, specially equipped rest rooms, lowered drinking fountains, and lowered telephones. All new buildings are built to ADA compliance standards.

Services: In addition to many counseling and information services, tutoring is available in most subjects. A counselor is available to assist students with accommodations as needed.

Campus Safety and Security: Campus safety and security measures include 24-hour foot and vehicle patrol, self-defense education, escort service, and shuttle buses. In addition, there are informal discussions, pamphlets/posters/films, emergency telephones, lighted pathways/sidewalks, and emergency warning whistles. Residences

are locked at night, and a staffed communications center is available round the clock.

Programs of Study: Bowdoin confers A.B. and B.A. degrees. Bachelor's degrees are awarded in BIOLOGICAL SCIENCE (biochemistry, biology/biological science, and neurosciences), COMMUNICATIONS AND THE ARTS (art history and appreciation, classics, English, French, German, music, romance languages, Russian, Spanish, and studio art), COMPUTER AND PHYSICAL SCIENCE (chemistry, computer science, geology, mathematics, and physics), ENGINEERING AND ENVIRONMENTAL DESIGN (environmental science), SOCIAL SCIENCE (African studies, anthropology, Asian/Oriental studies, classical/ancient civilization, economics, history, philosophy, political science/government, psychology, religion, sociology, and women's studies). Anthropology, biology, chemistry, and economics are the strongest academically. Biology, government and legal studies, English, and economics have the largest enrollments.

Required: Degree requirements include 32 courses, with at least 2 semesters in natural science and mathematics, social and behavioral sciences, humanities and fine arts, and non-Eurocentric studies, and completion of major requirements.

Special: Students may take advantage of approved programs with Boston University (city semester), Williams College (Mystic Seaport), the National Theater Institute, and American University (Washington semester), among several other schools. Dual majors in any combination, study abroad in virtually any country, interdisciplinary majors, student-designed majors, pass/fail options, limited nondegree study, and credit for life, military, or work experience are also available. The college offers a 3–2 engineering degree with Stanford University, California Institute of Technology, and Columbia University, and 3–2 engineering and 3–3 legal studies degrees with Columbia University Law School. There is a chapter of Phi Beta Kappa on campus.

Faculty/Classroom: 62% of faculty are male; 38%, female. All both teach and do research.

Admissions: 30% of the 1995–96 applicants were accepted. The SAT I scores for the 1995–96 freshman class were as follows: Verbal—6% below 500, 34% between 500 and 599, 54% between 600 and 700, and 6% above 700; Math—2% below 500, 8% between 500 and 599, 64% between 600 and 700, and 26% above 700. 91% of the current freshmen were in the top fifth of their class; 100% were in the top two fifths. There was 1 National Merit finalist.

Requirements: There are no specific academic requirements, but typical applicants for admission will have 4 years each of English, social studies, foreign language, and mathematics, 3 1/2 years of science, and 1 course each in art, music, and history. A high school record, 2 teacher recommendations, and an essay are required. AP credits are accepted. Important factors in the admissions decision are advanced placement or honor courses, recommendations by school officials, and extracurricular activities record.

Procedure: Freshmen are admitted in the fall. Entrance exams are required for counseling and placement only and should be submitted by the late summer before the freshman year. There are early decision and deferred admissions plans. Early decision I applications should be filed by November 15; early decision II by January 15. Regular applications should be filed by January 15 for fall entry, along with an application fee of $50. Notification of early decision I is sent December 15; early decision II, February 15; regular decision, April 15. 174 early decision candidates were accepted for the 1995–96 class. A waiting list is an active part of the admissions procedure, with about 1% of all applicants on the list.

Transfer: 13 transfer students enrolled in 1995–96. College grades of B or better are required to transfer. Applicants should submit high school and college transcripts, a dean's or adviser's statement from the most recent college attended, and 2 recommendations from recent professors. A total of 2 years in residence, and typically, 16 courses out of 32, must be completed at Bowdoin.

Visiting: There are regularly scheduled orientations for prospective students, in which students should be prepared to talk informally about their academic record, interests, talents, and goals. There are guides for informal visits and visitors may sit in on classes and stay overnight at the school. To schedule a visit, contact the Admissions Office at (207) 725-3100.

Financial Aid: In 1995–96, 49% of all freshmen and 36% of continuing students received some form of financial aid. 45% of freshmen and 41% of continuing students received need-based aid. The average freshman award was $17,727. Of that total, scholarships or need-based grants averaged $14,260 ($26,300 maximum); loans averaged $3194 ($3300 maximum); and work contracts averaged $850 (maximum). 87% of undergraduate students work part-time. Average earnings from campus work for the school year are $956. The average financial indebtedness of the 1994–95 graduate was $13,640. Bowdoin is a member of CSS. The FAFSA and the college's own financial statement, and the CSS Profile Application are required. The application deadline for fall entry is March 1.

International Students: There were 43 international students enrolled in a recent year. The school actively recruits these students. They must take the TOEFL and achieve a minimum score of 600. SAT I scores must be submitted at matriculation for counseling and placement.

Computers: The college provides computer facilities for student use. The mainframes are 2 DEC ALPHA 1000 servers. Students access servers from 90 public microcomputers and terminals. Network access is available from all dormitory rooms. All students may access the system 24 hours a day by modem; from 8 A.M. to midnight on public terminals. There are no time limits and no fees.

Graduates: In 1994–95, 387 bachelor's degrees were awarded. The most popular majors among graduates were government and legal studies (21%), English (13%), and economics (13%). Within an average freshman class, 1% graduate in 3 years, 82% in 4 years, 90% in 5 years, and 92% in 6 years. 64 companies recruited on campus in 1994–95. Of the 1994 graduating class, 17% were enrolled in graduate school within 6 months of graduation and 76% had found employment.

Admissions Contact: Richard E. Steele, Dean of Admissions.

COLBY COLLEGE
Waterville, ME 04901

B-4

(207) 872-3168
(800) 723-3032; FAX: (207) 872-3474

Full-time: 810 men, 975 women	Faculty: 139; IIB, ++$
Part-time: none	Ph.D.s: 98%
Graduate: none	Student/Faculty: 13 to 1
Year: 4-1-4	Tuition: $20,990
Application Deadline: January 15	Room & Board: $5650
Freshman Class: 4217 applied, 1605 accepted, 544 enrolled	
SAT I Verbal/Math: 580/640	ACT: 27 MOST COMPETITIVE

Colby College, founded in 1813, is a private coeducational liberal arts college. The 3 libraries contain 504,825 volumes, 275,620 microform items, and 15,445 audiovisual forms, and subscribe to 2825 periodicals. Computerized library sources and services include the card catalog, interlibrary loans, and database searching. Special learning facilities include a learning resource center, art gallery, radio station, TV station, an observatory, satellite dish, arboretum, and state wildlife management area. The 714-acre campus is in a small town 75 miles north of Portland. Including residence halls, there are 46 buildings on campus.

Student Life: 89% of undergraduates are from out-of-state, mostly the Northeast. Students come from 46 states, 45 foreign countries, and Canada. 62% are from public schools; 38% from private. 85% are white. The average age of freshmen is 18; all undergraduates, 20. 4% do not continue beyond their first year; 93% remain to graduate.

Housing: 1586 students can be accommodated in college housing. College-sponsored living facilities include coed dormitories. In addition, there are substance-free and quiet residence halls. On-campus housing is guaranteed for all 4 years. 90% of students live on campus. All students may keep cars on campus.

Activities: There are no fraternities or sororities. There are 90 groups on campus, including art, band, choir, chorale, chorus, computers, dance, drama, ethnic, film, gay, honors, international, jazz band, literary magazine, musical theater, newspaper, orchestra, photography, political, professional, radio and TV, religious, social, social service, student government, symphony, and yearbook. Popular campus events include Asian Festival, Bisexual, Gay, and Lesbian Days, Family Weekend, Feminist Fortnight, Hispanic Awareness Month, Homecoming, Martin Luther King Day Celebration, and Spring Charity Ball.

Sports: There are 15 intercollegiate sports for men and 16 for women, and 12 intramural sports for men and 12 for women. Athletic and recreation facilities include an athletic center with fitness, weight training, and exercise areas; a gymnasium with badminton, volleyball, and basketball courts; a hockey and skating rink; a field house for track, baseball, softball, tennis, lacrosse, and golf; a swimming pool and saunas; and squash and handball courts. There are also outdoor playing fields, tennis courts, an all-weather track, and cross-country trails.

Disabled Students: 90% of the campus is accessible to disabled students. The following facilities are available: wheelchair ramps, elevators, special parking, specially equipped rest rooms, special class scheduling, and lowered telephones.

Services: In addition to many counseling and information services, tutoring is available in every subject. There is a reader service for the blind, a writing center, and a support program for learning-disabled students.

Campus Safety and Security: Campus safety and security measures include 24-hour foot and vehicle patrol, self-defense education, escort service, and shuttle buses. In addition, there are informal discussions, pamphlets/posters/films, emergency telephones, lighted pathways/sidewalks, a women's safety program, a property identification program, party monitors (security officers), and a student emergency response team.

Programs of Study: Colby confers the A.B. degree. Bachelor's degrees are awarded in BIOLOGICAL SCIENCE (biochemistry, biology/biological science, and cell biology), BUSINESS (management science), COMMUNICATIONS AND THE ARTS (art, art history and appreciation, classics, English, German, music, performing arts, Russian, Spanish, and studio art), COMPUTER AND PHYSICAL SCIENCE (chemistry, computer science, earth science, geology, mathematics, and physics), ENGINEERING AND ENVIRONMENTAL DESIGN (environmental science), SOCIAL SCIENCE (African American studies, American studies, anthropology, classical/ancient civilization, East Asian studies, economics, French studies, history, international studies, Latin American studies, philosophy, political science/government, psychology, religion, sociology, and women's studies). American studies, biology, and biochemistry are the strongest academically. Biology, English, and government have the largest enrollments.

Required: To graduate, all students must take English composition and fulfill a foreign language requirement. They must also take 2 courses in the natural sciences and 1 course each in the arts, historical studies, literature, the social sciences, and human or cultural diversity, and earn 4 credits in wellness through seminars, classes, or participation in athletics. Students must complete a total of 120 credit hours, including 3 January term courses, and maintain a GPA of 2.0.

Special: Colby offers study abroad through various programs in numerous countries, Washington semester programs through American University and the Washington Center, on-campus work-study, exchange programs with various colleges and universities, a 3–2 engineering degree with Dartmouth College, the University of Rochester, and Case Western Reserve University, and maritime and oceanographic studies programs. Dual and student-designed majors are possible. There are 9 national honor societies on campus, including Phi Beta Kappa. 16 departments have honors programs.

Faculty/Classroom: 60% of faculty are male; 40%, female. All both teach and do research. The average class size in a regular course offering is 17.

Admissions: 38% of the 1995–96 applicants were accepted. The SAT I scores for the 1995–96 freshman class were as follows: Verbal—10% below 500, 50% between 500 and 599, 37% between 600 and 700, and 3% above 700; Math—3% below 500, 24% between 500 and 599, 55% between 600 and 700, and 18% above 700. The ACT scores were 2% below 21, 10% between 21 and 23, 25% between 24 and 26, 22% between 27 and 28, and 42% above 28. 92% of the current freshmen were in the top fifth of their class; 99% were in the top two fifths. 16 freshmen graduated first in their class.

Requirements: The SAT I or ACT is required. Candidates should be high school graduates with a recommended academic program of 4 years of English, 3 each of foreign language and mathematics, and 2 each of science (including laboratory work), social studies/history, and other college-preparatory courses. To obain Colby's application on disk, write or call the Admissions Office, or download from http://www.colby.edu/. AP credits are accepted. Important factors in the admissions decision are advanced placement or honor courses, leadership record, and personality/intangible qualities.

Procedure: Freshmen are admitted in the fall and winter. Entrance exams should be taken by January of the senior year. There are early decision, early admissions, and deferred admissions plans. Early decision applications should be filed by November 15 and January 1; regular applications, by January 15 for fall entry, along with an application fee of $45. Notification of early decision is sent December 15 and January 31; regular decision, April 1. 213 early decision candidates were accepted for the 1995–96 class. A waiting list is an active part of the admissions procedure, with about 9% of all applicants on the list.

Transfer: 9 transfer students enrolled in 1995–96. Candidates must have a minimum GPA of 3.0 and, as a rule, have earned enough credit hours to qualify for at least sophomore standing. They must be in good academic and social standing and should submit references from a faculty member and a dean of their current school. If the SAT I or ACT has been taken, the results must be submitted as well. 60 credits of 120 must be completed at Colby.

Visiting: There are guides for informal visits and visitors may sit in on classes and stay overnight at the school. To schedule a visit, contact the Admissions Office.

Financial Aid: In 1995–96, 44% of all freshmen and 38% of continuing students received some form of financial aid. 42% of freshmen and 36% of continuing students received need-based aid. The average freshman award was $15,320. Of that total, scholarships or need-based grants averaged $12,040 ($27,000 maximum); loans averaged $2280 ($2950 maximum); and work contracts averaged $1000 ($1500 maximum). 66% of undergraduate students work part-time. Average earnings from campus work for the school year are $700. The average financial indebtedness of the 1994–95 graduate was

$11,650. Colby is a member of CSS. The FAFSA and the college's own financial statement are required. The application deadline for fall entry is January 15.

International Students: There are currently 99 international students enrolled. The school actively recruits these students. They must take the TOEFL and achieve a minimum score of 550. The student must also take the SAT I or the ACT.

Computers: The college provides computer facilities for student use. The mainframes are an HP 827S, an HP G40, and an HP G25. Access to the campus network and its services is available from all classrooms, laboratories, and offices, as well as from the residence halls, including most dormitory rooms. The Apple Macintosh is the standard microcomputer on campus, 135 of which are available for student use in student clusters and laboratories. Laserwriters are also available for student use. There is access to the Internet, and all students are assigned an E-mail address. All students may access the system 24 hours a day. There are no time limits and no fees.

Graduates: In 1994–95, 461 bachelor's degrees were awarded. The most popular majors among graduates were English (15%), biology (13%), and economics (11%). Within an average freshman class, 84% graduate in 4 years, 89% in 5 years, and 93% in 6 years. 48 companies recruited on campus in 1994–95. Of the 1994 graduating class, 13% were enrolled in graduate school within 6 months of graduation and 80% had found employment.

Admissions Contact: Parker J. Beverage, Dean of Admissions and Financial Aid. E-mail: admissions@colby.edu.

COLLEGE OF THE ATLANTIC   D-5
Bar Harbor, ME 04609

(207) 288-5015
(800) 528-0025; FAX: (207) 288-4126

Full-time: 206 men and women	Faculty: 24
Part-time: 28 men and women	Ph.D.s: 82%
Graduate: 2 men, 2 women	Student/Faculty: 9 to 1
Year: terms	Tuition: $15,321
Application Deadline: March 1	Room & Board: $4500
Freshman Class: 278 applied, 216 accepted, 87 enrolled	
SAT I Verbal/Math: 560/600	ACT: 28 VERY COMPETITIVE +

College of the Atlantic, founded in 1969, is a private, coeducational institution primarily concerned with the study of human ecology. There is 1 graduate school. The library contains 32,000 volumes, 65 microform items, and 400 audiovisual forms, and subscribes to 347 periodicals. Computerized library sources and services include the card catalog, interlibrary loans, and database searching. Special learning facilities include an art gallery, natural history museum, writing center, taxidermy laboratory, and photography laboratory. The 25-acre campus is in a small town 45 miles southeast of Bangor, along the Atlantic Ocean shoreline. Including residence halls, there are 12 buildings on campus.

Student Life: 81% of undergraduates are from out-of-state, mostly the Northeast. Students come from 34 states, 11 foreign countries, and Canada. 70% are from public schools; 30% from private. 94% are white. The average age of freshmen is 19; all undergraduates, 22. 10% do not continue beyond their first year; 65% remain to graduate.

Housing: 100 students can be accommodated in college housing. College-sponsored living facilities include coed dormitories. In addition, there is a substance-free house. On-campus housing is guaranteed for the freshman year only, is available on a first-come, first-served basis, and is available on a lottery system for upperclassmen. Priority is given to out-of-town students. 60% of students commute. Alcohol is not permitted. All students may keep cars on campus.

Activities: There are no fraternities or sororities. There are 25 groups on campus, including art, chess, choir, chorus, computers, dance, drama, environmental, gay, international, jazz band, literary magazine, musical theater, newspaper, photography, political, social, social service, and student government. Popular campus events include the annual horseshoe tournaments, annual Bar Island Swim, Contra Dances, Halloween Party, and weekly film series.

Sports: There are 4 intramural sports for men and 3 for women. All students are members of the local YMCA and may use its pool, Nautilus equipment, and volleyball and basketball facilities, as well as nearby tennis courts. Acadia National Park offers seasonal outdoor activities. The college has canoes, sea kayaks, and sailboats for student use, and offers a sailing class.

Disabled Students: 80% of the campus is accessible to disabled students. The following facilities are available: wheelchair ramps, elevators, special parking, specially equipped rest rooms, lowered drinking fountains, and lowered telephones.

Services: There is remedial math and writing.

Campus Safety and Security: Campus safety and security measures include 24-hour foot and vehicle patrol, escort service, shuttle buses, and informal discussions. In addition, there are pamphlets/posters/films, emergency telephones, and lighted pathways/sidewalks.

Programs of Study: COA confers the B.A. degree. Master's degrees are also awarded. Bachelor's degrees are awarded in SOCIAL SCIENCE (human ecology).

Required: Students design their own program. They must complete a total of 36 COA credits, including 2 interdisciplinary core courses and 2 courses each in environmental science, human studies, and arts and design. Also required are group study, a 3-credit internship, a human ecology essay, participation in a 3-credit senior project, and community service.

Special: Teacher certification is offered in elementary, secondary, and science education. Students may cross-register with the University of Maine. Study abroad is available in Uruguay, Belgium, and the Czech Republic. Students may arrange a work-study program with Acadia National Park or Kids Corner day care. Pass/fail grading options are available.

Faculty/Classroom: 66% of faculty are male; 33%, female. All teach undergraduates and 60% both teach and do research. No introductory courses are taught by graduate students. The average class size in an introductory lecture is 20; in a laboratory, 14; and in a regular course offering, 14.

Admissions: 78% of the 1995–96 applicants were accepted. The SAT I scores for the 1995–96 freshman class were as follows: Verbal—17% below 500, 51% between 500 and 599, 26% between 600 and 700, and 6% above 700; Math—12% below 500, 29% between 500 and 599, 47% between 600 and 700, and 12% above 700. The ACT scores were 50% between 24 and 26, 25% between 27 and 28, and 25% above 28. 46% of the current freshmen were in the top fifth of their class; 94% were in the top two fifths. There was 1 National Merit finalist and 3 semifinalists. 5 freshmen graduated first in their class.

Requirements: The SAT I is recommended. Candidates for admission must be high school graduates who have completed 4 years of English, 3 to 4 of mathematics, 2 to 3 of science, 2 of a foreign language, and 1 of history. AP and CLEP credits are accepted. Important factors in the admissions decision are advanced placement or honor courses, leadership record, and personality/intangible qualities.

Procedure: Freshmen are admitted to all sessions. Entrance exams should be taken in the junior or senior year. There are early decision, early admissions, and deferred admissions plans. Early decision applications should be filed by December 1 or January 1; regular applications, by March 1 for fall entry, November 15 for winter entry, and February 15 for spring entry, along with an application fee of $40. Notification of early decision is sent December 15 or January 15; regular decision, April 1. 30 early decision candidates were accepted for the 1995–96 class. A waiting list is an active part of the admissions procedure, with about 3% of all applicants on the list.

Transfer: 18 credits of 36 must be completed at COA.

Visiting: There are regularly scheduled orientations for prospective students. There are guides for informal visits and visitors may sit in on classes and stay overnight at the school. To schedule a visit, contact Donna McFarland.

Financial Aid: In 1995–96, 63% of all freshmen and 51% of continuing students received need-based aid. The average freshman award was $12,355. Of that total, scholarships or need-based grants averaged $8125 ($14,000 maximum); loans averaged $2756 ($5000 maximum); and work contracts averaged $1450 ($1800 maximum). 86% of undergraduate students work part-time. Average earnings from campus work for the school year are $1600. The average financial indebtedness of the 1994–95 graduate was $17,125. COA is a member of CSS. The FAFSA and the college's own financial statement are required. The application deadline for fall entry is March 1.

International Students: There were 13 international students enrolled in a recent year. They must take the TOEFL and achieve a minimum score of 550.

Computers: The college provides computer facilities for student use. More than 40 microcomputers, including Dell System 220/325, IBM XT and AT compatibles, and Apple Macintosh, are available in 2 computer centers and a science laboratory. The graphics laboratory contains 7 workstations and peripherals. There is Internet access in each dormitory room, with worldwide E-mail capability. All students may access the system 24 hours a day. There are no time limits and no fees. It is strongly recommended that students have personal computers.

Graduates: In 1994–95, 65 bachelor's degrees were awarded. Within an average freshman class, 55% graduate in 4 years, 65% in 5 years, and 70% in 6 years.

Admissions Contact: Steve Thomas, Director of Admission and Student Services. E-mail: inq@ecology.coa.edu. A campus video is available.

HUSSON COLLEGE
C-4
Bangor, ME 04401-2999 (207) 941-7100
(800) 4-HUSSON; FAX: (207) 941-7988

Full-time: 355 men, 585 women	Faculty: 45; IIB, --$
Part-time: 212 men, 627 women	Ph.D.s: 42%
Graduate: 133 men, 124 women	Student/Faculty: 21 to 1
Year: semesters, summer session	Tuition: $8140
Application Deadline: open	Room & Board: $4300
Freshman Class: 873 applied, 732 accepted, 326 enrolled	
SAT I Verbal/Math: 421/449	COMPETITIVE

Husson College, founded in 1898, is a private coeducational institution offering business, nursing, teaching, and other professional training. There is 1 graduate school. In addition to regional accreditation, Husson has baccalaureate program accreditation with NLN. The library contains 38,321 volumes and 409 audiovisual forms, and subscribes to 355 periodicals. Computerized library sources and services include interlibrary loans and database searching. Special learning facilities include a learning resource center, art gallery, and radio station. The 200-acre campus is in an urban area in Bangor. Including residence halls, there are 6 buildings on campus.

Student Life: 76% of undergraduates are from Maine. Students come from 29 states, 21 foreign countries, and Canada. 93% are from public schools; 7% from private. 92% are white. The average age of freshmen is 20.9; all undergraduates, 23. 23% do not continue beyond their first year.

Housing: 800 students can be accommodated in college housing. College-sponsored living facilities include coed dormitories. In addition, there are honors houses. On-campus housing is guaranteed for all 4 years. 50% of students live on campus; of those, 40% remain on campus on weekends. All students may keep cars on campus.

Activities: 7% of men belong to 2 local and 2 national fraternities; 6% of women belong to 3 local sororities. There are 25 groups on campus, including cheerleading, computers, drama, ethnic, international, newspaper, pep band, professional, radio and TV, social, social service, student government, and yearbook. Popular campus events include Spring Fling, Winter Carnival, Greek Alumni Weekend, and Chief Week.

Sports: There are 6 intercollegiate sports for men and 7 for women, and 8 intramural sports for men and 8 for women. Athletic and recreation facilities include a gymnasium, an Olympic-size swimming pool, weight training and mat rooms, a health and fitness center, and basketball, racquetball, and tennis courts.

Disabled Students: 90% of the campus is accessible to disabled students. The following facilities are available: wheelchair ramps, elevators, special parking, specially equipped rest rooms, lowered drinking fountains, and lowered telephones.

Services: In addition to many counseling and information services, tutoring is available in most subjects. There is remedial math and writing.

Campus Safety and Security: Campus safety and security measures include informal discussions, pamphlets/posters/films, and lighted pathways/sidewalks.

Programs of Study: Husson confers the B.S. degree. Associate and master's degrees are also awarded. Bachelor's degrees are awarded in BUSINESS (accounting, banking and finance, business administration and management, marketing/retailing/merchandising, personnel management, secretarial studies/office management, and sports management), COMPUTER AND PHYSICAL SCIENCE (computer programming), EDUCATION (business), HEALTH PROFESSIONS (nursing and physical therapy). Accounting, nursing, and physical therapy are the strongest academically. Business administration has the largest enrollment.

Required: Requirements for graduation vary by program, but a total of 120 credit hours with a minimum GPA of 2.0 is necessary. A course in computer information systems is required in the first year for most programs.

Special: Husson offers sports management and accounting internships as well as co-op programs in most majors. The 5-year physical therapy major leads to an accelerated graduate degree. Study abroad, credit for life, military, and work experience, and nondegree study are also available.

Faculty/Classroom: 42% of faculty are male; 58%, female. All teach undergraduates. No introductory courses are taught by graduate students. The average class size in an introductory lecture is 30; in a laboratory, 22; and in a regular course offering, 30.

Admissions: 84% of the 1995–96 applicants were accepted. The SAT I scores for the 1995–96 freshman class were as follows: Verbal—85% below 500, 13% between 500 and 599, and 2% between 600 and 700; Math—59% below 500, 36% between 500 and 599, 4% between 600 and 700, and 1% above 700. 27% of the current freshmen were in the top fifth of their class; 52% were in the top two fifths. 2 freshmen graduated first in their class.

Requirements: The SAT I is required. Husson requires applicants to be in the upper 60% of their class. A minimum GPA of 2.0 is required. Applicants must be graduates of an accredited secondary school or have earned a GED. A recommendation from a high school counselor is required. AP and CLEP credits are accepted. Important factors in the admissions decision are advanced placement or honor courses, recommendations by school officials, and leadership record.

Procedure: Freshmen are admitted to all sessions. Entrance exams should be taken prior to enrollment. There are early decision, early admissions, and deferred admissions plans. Application deadlines are open for regular admission, December 15 for early admission. Application fee is $25. Notification is sent on a rolling basis. 8 early decision candidates were accepted for the 1995–96 class.

Transfer: 90 transfer students enrolled in 1995–96. Applicants must have a 2.0 GPA. Courses with a C grade or better transfer to Husson. 30 credits of 120 must be completed at Husson.

Visiting: There are regularly scheduled orientations for prospective students, including an interview and campus tour. There are guides for informal visits and visitors may sit in on classes and stay overnight at the school. To schedule a visit, contact the Admissions Office.

Financial Aid: In 1995–96, 88% of all freshmen and 80% of continuing students received some form of financial aid. 86% of freshmen and 80% of continuing students received need-based aid. The average freshman award was $6996. Of that total, scholarships or need-based grants averaged $3363 ($13,412 maximum); loans averaged $2825 ($5625 maximum); and work contracts averaged $1160 ($1775 maximum). 90% of undergraduate students work part-time. Average earnings from campus work for the school year are $1302. The average financial indebtedness of the 1994–95 graduate was $17,125. Husson is a member of CSS. The FAFSA is required. The application deadline for fall entry is open.

International Students: There are currently 28 international students enrolled. The school actively recruits these students. They must take the TOEFL and achieve a minimum score of 500; students who score less than 500 may be accepted conditionally and must enroll in a full-time intensive English program at Husson.

Computers: The college provides computer facilities for student use. The mainframe is an IBM AS/400. Computer laboratories with a total of 76 microcomputer workstations are available exclusively for student use. All students may access the system 24 hours a day. There are no time limits. The fees are $40.

Graduates: In 1994–95, 287 bachelor's degrees were awarded. The most popular majors among graduates were business administration (37%), accounting (20%), and nursing (16%). 52 companies recruited on campus in 1994–95. Of the 1994 graduating class, 1% were enrolled in graduate school within 6 months of graduation and 93% had found employment.

Admissions Contact: Jane Goodwin, Director of Admissions. E-mail: jgoodwin@husson.husson.edu. A campus video is available.

MAINE COLLEGE OF ART
B-6
Portland, ME 04101 (207) 775-3052
(800) 639-4808; FAX: (207) 772-5069

Full-time: 100 men, 200 women	Faculty: 23
Part-time: 10 men, 20 women	Ph.D.s: 2%
Graduate: none	Student/Faculty: 13 to 1
Year: semesters	Tuition: $12,355
Application Deadline: open	Room & Board: $5600
Freshman Class: 292 applied, 275 accepted, 112 enrolled	
SAT I Verbal/Math: 500/430	ACT: 22	SPECIAL

Maine College of Art, established in 1882, is a private, independent fine arts college. In addition to regional accreditation, MECA has baccalaureate program accreditation with NASAD. The library contains 18,000 volumes and 40 audiovisual forms, and subscribes to 114 periodicals. Computerized library sources and services include the card catalog, interlibrary loans, and database searching. Special learning facilities include an art gallery. The campus is in an urban area 200 miles north of Boston in downtown Portland. Including residence halls, there are 8 buildings on campus.

Student Life: 55% of undergraduates are from out-of-state, mostly the Northeast. Students come from 28 states and 7 foreign countries. 93% are white. The average age of freshmen is 22; all undergraduates, 23. 33% do not continue beyond their first year; 42% remain to graduate.

Housing: 59 students can be accommodated in college housing. College-sponsored living facilities include coed dormitories. On-campus housing is available on a first-come, first-served basis. 80% of students commute. Alcohol is not permitted. All students may keep cars on campus.

Activities: There are no fraternities or sororities. There are 5 groups on campus, including art, film, newspaper, and student government. Popular campus events include Halloween dance, Christmas art sale, student show, senior show, and art auction.

Sports: There is no sports program at MECA.

Disabled Students: The following facilities are available: specially equipped rest rooms.

Services: In addition to many counseling and information services, tutoring is available in most subjects. There is remedial math, reading, and writing. Academic support for writing papers, study skills, and time management is available. Recorded books may be obtained through the Portland Public Library.

Campus Safety and Security: Campus safety and security measures include self-defense education, informal discussions, and pamphlets/posters/films.

Programs of Study: MECA confers the B.F.A. degree. Master's degrees are also awarded. Bachelor's degrees are awarded in COMMUNICATIONS AND THE ARTS (graphic design, metal/jewelry, painting, photography, printmaking, and sculpture), ENGINEERING AND ENVIRONMENTAL DESIGN (ceramic science).

Required: All students must take 2 years in studio foundation courses (drawing and design), 1 year of English composition, 3 semesters of an art history survey and humanities/social science, and 2 semesters of natural science. Total credit hours necessary are 134, with 36 class credits in the major. Students must maintain a minimum GPA of 2.0. A senior thesis is required.

Special: Cross-registration with Bowdoin College and the Greater Portland Alliance of Colleges and Universities is available, as are internships utilizing professional artists and design and photography studios. The continuing studies program provides for nondegree study. A minor in art history is also offered.

Faculty/Classroom: 56% of faculty are male; 44%, female. All teach undergraduates. The average class size in an introductory lecture is 18 and in a regular course offering, 17.

Admissions: 94% of the 1995–96 applicants were accepted. The SAT I scores for the 1995–96 freshman class were as follows: Verbal—64% below 500, 31% between 500 and 599, and 6% between 600 and 700. 12% of the current freshmen were in the top fifth of their class; 33% were in the top two fifths.

Requirements: The SAT I or ACT is required. It is recommended that candidates for admission complete 4 years of English, 3 years each of art, mathematics, and 2 years each of foreign language, science, and social studies. AP credits are accepted. Important factors in the admissions decision are evidence of special talent, recommendations by school officials, and advanced placement or honor courses.

Procedure: Freshmen are admitted in the fall. Entrance exams should be taken in the fall of the senior year. There are early admissions and deferred admissions plans. Application deadlines are open. Application fee is $30. Notification is sent on a rolling basis.

Transfer: 30 transfer students enrolled in 1995–96. 64 credits of 134 must be completed at MECA.

Visiting: There are regularly scheduled orientations for prospective students. There are guides for informal visits and visitors may sit in on classes and stay overnight at the school. To schedule a visit, contact Admissions.

Financial Aid: In 1995–96, 87% of all freshmen and 86% of continuing students received some form of financial aid. 82% of freshmen and 84% of continuing students received need-based aid. The average freshman award was $7730. Of that total, scholarships or need-based grants averaged $4904 ($9650 maximum); loans averaged $1916 ($4125 maximum); and work contracts averaged $1015 ($2093 maximum). 73% of undergraduate students work part-time. Average earnings from campus work for the school year are $1025. The average financial indebtedness of the 1994–95 graduate was $18,882. MECA is a member of CSS. The FAFSA, FAF, and the college's own financial statement are required. The application deadline for fall entry is March 1.

International Students: There are currently 12 international students enrolled. The school actively recruits these students. They must take the TOEFL and achieve a minimum score of 500.

Computers: The college provides computer facilities for student use. 2 computers for general student use are located in the student service area. 4 computers are used in graphic design classes. Only graphic design majors have full access. There are no time limits and no fees.

Graduates: In 1994–95, 55 bachelor's degrees were awarded. The most popular majors among graduates were graphic design (39%), jewelry and painting (26%), and photography (15%).

Admissions Contact: Elizabeth Shea, Director of Admissions. A campus video is available.

MAINE MARITIME ACADEMY
C-5

Castine, ME 04420   (207) 326-4311; (800) 227-8465

Full-time: 580 men, 65 women	**Faculty:** 45; IIB, --$
Part-time: none	**Ph.D.s:** 16%
Graduate: 60 men	**Student/Faculty:** 14 to 1
Year: see profile	**Tuition:** $4190 ($7330)
Application Deadline: July 1	**Room & Board:** $4750
Freshman Class: 485 applied, 349 accepted, 177 enrolled	
SAT I or ACT: required	**COMPETITIVE**

Maine Maritime Academy, founded in 1941, is a public, coeducational institution offering degree programs in ocean and marine-oriented studies with emphasis on engineering, transportation, management, and ocean sciences, as well as preparing graduates for merchant marine and other uniformed services of the United States. The academic calendar consists of 2 semesters plus a 2- to 3-month annual training cruise. There is 1 graduate school. In addition to regional accreditation, MMA has baccalaureate program accreditation with ABET. The library contains 75,381 volumes, and subscribes to 950 periodicals. Computerized library sources and services include the card catalog, interlibrary loans, and database searching. Special learning facilities include a planetarium and bridge, radar, power plant, and cargo system simulators. The 50-acre campus is in a small town 38 miles south of Bangor on the east coast of Penobscot Bay. Including residence halls, there are 14 buildings on campus.

Student Life: 63% of undergraduates are from Maine. Students come from 33 states, 7 foreign countries, and Canada. 98% are white. The average age of freshmen is 18; all undergraduates, 22. 20% do not continue beyond their first year; 75% remain to graduate.

Housing: 600 students can be accommodated in college housing. College-sponsored living facilities include coed dormitories and on-campus apartments. On-campus housing is guaranteed for all 4 years. 80% of students live on campus; of those, 25% remain on campus on weekends. Alcohol is not permitted. Upperclassmen may keep cars on campus.

Activities: 6% of men and about 25% of women belong to 1 national fraternity. There are no sororities. There are more than 30 groups and organizations on campus, including amateur radio, band, cheerleading, drama, drill team, engineering, ethnic, international, marching band, newspaper, outing, pep band, photography, professional, social, social service, student government, and yearbook. Popular campus events include Daisy Day and Klondike Derby.

Sports: There are 6 intercollegiate sports for men and 3 for women, and 5 intramural sports for men and 5 for women. Athletic and recreation facilities include a weight room, an Olympic pool, a field house, a gymnasium, racquetball and squash courts, an aerobics room, and a multisports athletic field.

Disabled Students: The entire campus is accessible to disabled students. The following facilities are available: wheelchair ramps, elevators, special parking, and specially equipped rest rooms.

Services: In addition to many counseling and information services, tutoring is available in most subjects. There is remedial math, reading, and writing.

Campus Safety and Security: Campus safety and security measures include 24-hour foot and vehicle patrol, informal discussions, lighted pathways/sidewalks, and medical and counseling services.

Programs of Study: MMA confers the B.S. degree. Associate and master's degrees are also awarded. Bachelor's degrees are awarded in COMPUTER AND PHYSICAL SCIENCE (oceanography), ENGINEERING AND ENVIRONMENTAL DESIGN (engineering, engineering technology, marine engineering, maritime science, and transportation technology). Marine systems engineering is the strongest academically. Marine engineering technology has the largest enrollment.

Required: A minimum GPA of 2.0 in an average of 140 total credit hours is required for graduation.

Special: The annual training cruise gives students practical experience aboard the academy's 500-foot ship or on assigned merchant ships. Co-op programs are possible in every major.

Faculty/Classroom: 85% of faculty are male; 15%, female. All teach undergraduates; 5% also do research. No introductory courses are taught by graduate students. The average class size in an introductory lecture is 30; in a laboratory, 15; and in a regular course offering, 25.

Admissions: 72% of the 1995–96 applicants were accepted.

Requirements: The SAT I or ACT is required. MMA requires applicants to be in the upper 50% of their class. A minimum GPA of 2.0 is required. Candidates for admission must have completed 4 years of English, 3 years of mathematics, and 2 years of science. In addition, the academy recommends 1 year of a foreign language. Applications are accepted on-line via CollegeLink. AP and CLEP credits are accepted.

Procedure: Freshmen are admitted in the fall and spring. Entrance exams should be taken as early as possible in the senior year. There are early decision and deferred admissions plans. Early decision applications should be filed by December 20; regular applications, by July 1 for fall entry and November 1 for spring entry, along with an application fee of $15. Notification is sent on a rolling basis. 15 early decision candidates were accepted for the 1995–96 class.

Transfer: 25 transfer students enrolled in a recent year. Applicants must have a minimum 2.0 GPA in previous college work and meet the same prerequisites as entering freshmen.

Visiting: There are regularly scheduled orientations for prospective students. There are guides for informal visits and visitors may sit in on classes and stay overnight at the school. To schedule a visit, contact the Admissions Office.

Financial Aid: In a recent year, more than 70% of all students received need-based aid. MMA is a member of CSS. The FAFSA is required. The application deadline for fall entry is March 1.

International Students: There were 14 international students enrolled in year a recent year. They must take the TOEFL and achieve a minimum score of 550.

Computers: The college provides computer facilities for student use. PCs are available. All students may access the system. There are no time limits and no fees.

Graduates: The most popular majors among graduates in a recent year were marine engineering (70%), nautical science (20%), and power engineering (10%). Within an average freshman class, 70% graduate in 4 years and 5% in 5 years. 60 companies recruited on campus in a recent year. Of the 1994 graduating class, 1% were enrolled in graduate school within 6 months of graduation and 95% had found employment.

Admissions Contact: Jeff Wright, Director of Admissions. A campus video is available.

SAINT JOSEPH'S COLLEGE

A-6

Standish, ME 04084-5203   (207) 893-7746

(800) 338-7057; FAX: (207) 893-7861

Full-time: 298 men, 448 women	Faculty: 48; IIB, --$
Part-time: 136 men, 205 women	Ph.D.s: 86%
Graduate: none	Student/Faculty: 16 to 1
Year: semesters, summer session	Tuition: $10,925
Application Deadline: open	Room & Board: $5380
Freshman Class: 852 applied, 596 accepted, 254 enrolled	
SAT I Verbal/Math: 430/470	**COMPETITIVE**

Saint Joseph's College, founded in 1912, is a private, coeducational, Roman Catholic institution offering liberal arts and preprofessional programs. In addition to regional accreditation, Saint Joe's has baccalaureate program accreditation with NLN. The library contains 75,000 volumes, 3287 microform items, and 3350 audiovisual forms, and subscribes to 447 periodicals. Computerized library sources and services include interlibrary loans and database searching. Special learning facilities include a learning resource center, radio station, and TV station. The 328-acre campus is in a rural area 16 miles west of Portland. Including residence halls, there are 18 buildings on campus.

Student Life: 55% of undergraduates are from Maine. Students come from 14 states, 6 foreign countries, and Canada. 84% are from public schools; 16% from private. 95% are white. Most are Catholic. The average age of freshmen is 18; all undergraduates, 20. 15% do not continue beyond their first year; 77% remain to graduate.

Housing: 600 students can be accommodated in college housing. College-sponsored living facilities include single-sex and coed dormitories. On-campus housing is guaranteed for all 4 years. 75% of students live on campus; of those, 70% remain on campus on weekends. All students may keep cars on campus.

Activities: There are no fraternities or sororities. There are 30 groups on campus, including art, cheerleading, chess, chorale, computers, drama, ethnic, film, honors, international, literary magazine, musical theater, newspaper, photography, political, professional, radio and TV, religious, social, social service, student government, and yearbook. Popular campus events include Wellness Week, Siblings Weekend, Christmas Benefit Concert, Parents Weekend, Pentathlon, Campus Life Awards Banquet, Casino Night, Earth Day, and lip syncs.

Sports: There are 5 intercollegiate sports for men and 6 for women, and 12 intramural sports for men and 12 for women. Athletic and recreation facilities include a multipurpose gymnasium with weight and dance aerobics rooms, a private beach on a lake, a lighted athletic field for baseball, softball, and intramurals, and wooded cross-country running and ski trails.

Disabled Students: 25% of the campus is accessible to disabled students. The following facilities are available: wheelchair ramps, elevators, special parking, specially equipped rest rooms, and lowered drinking fountains.

Services: In addition to many counseling and information services, tutoring is available in some subjects, including English, mathematics, chemistry, biology, and physics. There is remedial math, reading, and writing.

Campus Safety and Security: Campus safety and security measures include 24-hour foot and vehicle patrol, informal discussions, pamphlets/posters/films, and lighted pathways/sidewalks. In addition, there are round-the-clock security guards.

Programs of Study: Saint Joe's confers B.A., B.S., B.S.B.A., and B.S.N. degrees. Associate degrees are also awarded. Bachelor's degrees are awarded in BIOLOGICAL SCIENCE (biology/biological science), BUSINESS (accounting, banking and finance, business administration and management, international business management, management science, and marketing/retailing/merchandising), COMMUNICATIONS AND THE ARTS (communications and English), COMPUTER AND PHYSICAL SCIENCE (mathematics, natural sciences, and radiological technology), EDUCATION (elementary, physical, and secondary), ENGINEERING AND ENVIRONMENTAL DESIGN (environmental science), HEALTH PROFESSIONS (nursing, predentistry, premedicine, and prepharmacy), SOCIAL SCIENCE (criminal justice, history, philosophy, prelaw, psychology, religion, social work, and sociology). Business, nursing, and communications are the strongest academically. Nursing, business, and elementary education have the largest enrollments.

Required: To graduate, all students must complete 12 hours of English, 9 of philosophy, 6 each of religious studies and history, 6 to 8 of science, and 3 each of mathematics, fine arts, and seminar studies. B.A. candidates must also have 6 hours of intermediate-level language. Students must complete 128 to 134 credit hours with a minimum GPA of 2.0, including at least 30 in the major, with a minimum GPA of 2.5.

Special: Saint Joe's offers internships, cross-registration with 6 southern Maine colleges, study in Nova Scotia, a semester at sea, dual majors in most programs, and limited nondegree study. Students may participate in work-study programs either on or off campus. The college has an external degree program providing directed home study in several fields. There is a 2–3 pharmacy program with the Massachusetts College of Pharmacy and Allied Health Sciences in Boston. There is a freshman honors program on campus, as well as 2 national honor societies. 6 departments have honors programs.

Faculty/Classroom: 36% of faculty are male; 64%, female. All teach undergraduates. The average class size in an introductory lecture is 35; in a laboratory, 16; and in a regular course offering, 22.

Admissions: 70% of the 1995–96 applicants were accepted. The SAT I scores for the 1995–96 freshman class were as follows: Verbal—85% below 500, 13% between 500 and 599, and 2% between 600 and 700; Math—67% below 500, 27% between 500 and 599, and 6% between 600 and 700. 24% of the current freshmen were in the top fifth of their class; 55% were in the top two fifths. 3 freshmen graduated first in their class.

Requirements: The SAT I is required. A minimum high school average of 70% is required. Candidates for admission must be high school graduates who have completed 4 units in English, 3 to 4 in mathematics, 2 in foreign language, and 1 to 3 each in history, science, and social studies. AP and CLEP credits are accepted. Important factors in the admissions decision are advanced placement or honor courses, leadership record, and evidence of special talent.

Procedure: Freshmen are admitted in the fall and spring. Entrance exams should be taken by January of the senior year. There are early admissions and deferred admissions plans. Application deadlines are open. Application fee is $25. Notification is sent on a rolling basis.

Transfer: 48 transfer students enrolled in 1995–96. Transfer students should have a minimum GPA of 2.0. 32 credits of 128 to 134 must be completed at Saint Joe's.

Visiting: There are regularly scheduled orientations for prospective students, including an open house in October and 5 group Saturday programs in the fall. There are guides for informal visits and visitors may sit in on classes and stay overnight at the school. To schedule a visit, contact the Admissions Office.

Financial Aid: In 1995–96, 95% of all freshmen and 85% of continuing students received some form of financial aid. 88% of freshmen and 77% of continuing students received need-based aid. The average freshman award was $9900. Of that total, scholarships or need-based grants averaged $5500 ($12,000 maximum); loans averaged $3800 ($8625 maximum); and work contracts averaged $600 ($1000 maximum). 51% of undergraduate students work part-time. Average earnings from campus work for the school year are $670. The average financial indebtedness of the 1994–95 graduate was $12,420. Saint Joe's is a member of CSS. The FAFSA and CSS Profile Application are required.

International Students: There are currently 6 international students enrolled. The school actively recruits these students. They must take the TOEFL and achieve a minimum score of 500. The student must also take the SAT I.

Computers: The college provides computer facilities for student use. The mainframes are an AT&T 3430 server and a Pyramid Mis-Z. There are 71 microcomputer terminals available to students in the computer room, the library, the resource center, and most academic departments. All students may access the system 24 hours a day in all laboratories and until 10 P.M. in the library. There are no time limits and no fees. It is strongly recommended that students have personal computers.

Graduates: In 1994–95, 136 bachelor's degrees were awarded. The most popular majors among graduates were education (23%), nursing (22%), and business (13%). Within an average freshman class, 70% graduate in 4 years and 10% in 5 years. 23 companies recruited on campus in 1994–95. Of the 1994 graduating class, 16% were enrolled in graduate school within 6 months of graduation and 100% had found employment.

Admissions Contact: Fredric V. Stone, Director of Admissions.

THOMAS COLLEGE
B-4

Waterville, ME 04901   (207) 877–0101; (800) 339–7001

Full-time: 173 men, 221 women	Faculty: 16; IIB, --$
Part-time: 78 men, 216 women	Ph.D.s: 50%
Graduate: 79 men, 68 women	Student/Faculty: 25 to 1
Year: semesters	Tuition: $10,050
Application Deadline: open	Room & Board: $4825
Freshman Class: 274 applied, 266 accepted, 125 enrolled	
SAT I Verbal/Math: 370/440	LESS COMPETITIVE

Thomas College, founded in 1894, is a private, coeducational college offering a business and professional education with a foundation in liberal arts. There is 1 graduate school. The library contains 28,000 volumes, 2 microform items, and 100 audiovisual forms, and subscribes to 230 periodicals. Computerized library sources and services include the card catalog, interlibrary loans, and database searching. Special learning facilities include a learning resource center and art gallery. The 70-acre campus is in a rural area 75 miles north of Portland. Including residence halls, there are 5 buildings on campus.

Student Life: 96% of undergraduates are from Maine. Students come from 9 states and 3 foreign countries. 85% are from public schools; 15% from private. 96% are white. The average age of freshmen is 23; all undergraduates, 25.

Housing: 275 students can be accommodated in college housing. College-sponsored living facilities include coed dormitories and off-campus apartments. On-campus housing is guaranteed for the freshman year only, is available on a first-come, first-served basis, and is available on a lottery system for upperclassmen. 56% of students live on campus; of those, 80% remain on campus on weekends. All students may keep cars on campus.

Activities: 20% of men belong to 2 local fraternities and 1 national fraternity; 25% of women belong to 2 local sororities and 1 national sorority. There are 19 groups on campus, including cheerleading, chorus, computers, drama, honors, newspaper, professional, religious, social, social service, student government, and yearbook. Popular campus events include Winter Carnival, Spring Fling, and Olympic Day.

Sports: There are 5 intercollegiate sports for men and 6 for women, and 10 intramural sports for men and 8 for women. Athletic and recreation facilities include a gymnasium, a basketball court, a weight and fitness room, soccer and softball fields, a training area, an intramural field, a skating facility, and cross-country skiing and snowshoe trails. Facilities for swimming, indoor tennis, racquetball, and hockey are available locally.

Disabled Students: 80% of the campus is accessible to disabled students. The following facilities are available: special parking, specially equipped rest rooms, and special class scheduling.

Services: In addition to many counseling and information services, tutoring is available in most subjects. There is remedial math, reading, and writing.

Campus Safety and Security: Campus safety and security measures include 24-hour foot and vehicle patrol, informal discussions, pamphlets/posters/films, and lighted pathways/sidewalks.

Programs of Study: Thomas confers the B.S. degree. Associate and master's degrees are also awarded. Bachelor's degrees are awarded in BUSINESS (accounting, business administration and management, business economics, management information systems, management science, marketing management, marketing/retailing/merchandising, retailing, and sports management), COMPUTER AND PHYSICAL SCIENCE (information sciences and systems), EDUCATION (business), SOCIAL SCIENCE (international studies). Accounting and management information systems are the strongest academically. Accounting, management, marketing, and sports management have the largest enrollments.

Required: To graduate, students must maintain a minimum GPA of 2.0, fulfill the liberal arts core requirements, and complete 120 total credit hours of study, including 30 hours in the major.

Special: Students may cross-register with Colby College and Kennebec Valley Technical College. There are co-op programs and internships available in most majors. The college also offers study in Canada through the New England-Quebec Exchange and in France. A 5-year degree in business is offered. There are 2 national honor societies on campus.

Faculty/Classroom: 70% of faculty are male; 30%, female. All teach undergraduates. The average class size in an introductory lecture is 25 and in a regular course offering, 15.

Admissions: 97% of the 1995–96 applicants were accepted. The SAT I scores for the 1995–96 freshman class were as follows: Verbal—87% below 500 and 13% between 500 and 599; Math—71% below 500, 22% between 500 and 599, and 7% between 600 and 700. 18% of the current freshmen were in the top fifth of their class; 43% were in the top two fifths. One freshman graduated first in the class.

Requirements: The SAT I is required. Applicants must be in the upper 50% of their class with a 2.3 GPA. High school academic program should include 4 years of English and 3 of mathematics. A letter of recommendation from a secondary school counselor is required. An interview is highly recommended. Applications are accepted online. AP and CLEP credits are accepted. Important factors in the admissions decision are advanced placement or honor courses, personality/intangible qualities, and leadership record.

Procedure: Freshmen are admitted fall and spring. Entrance exams should be taken by the fall of the senior year. There are early decision, early admissions, and deferred admissions plans. Application deadlines are open. Application fee is $25. Notification is sent on a rolling basis.

Transfer: 44 transfer students enrolled in 1995–96. Applicants should have a minimum college GPA of 2.0. The school recommends the SAT I (with a minimum score of 400 on each section) as well as an interview. Official transcripts from all previously attended postsecondary institutions are required. 30 credits of 120 must be completed at Thomas.

Visiting: There are guides for informal visits and visitors may sit in on classes. To schedule a visit, contact the Admissions Office.

Financial Aid: In 1995–96, 93% of all freshmen and 89% of continuing students received some form of financial aid. 90% of freshmen and 87% of continuing students received need-based aid. The average freshman award was $9800. Of that total, scholarships or need-based grants averaged $5100 (maximum); the Maine High School Teachers Scholarship Program awards up to 10 full-time scholarships each year averaging $9720 (maximum); loans averaged $3400 ($5000 maximum); and work contracts averaged $1300 ($1700 maximum). 25% of undergraduate students work part-time. Average earnings from campus work for the school year were $1300. The average financial indebtedness of the 1994–95 graduate was $19,000. Thomas is a member of CSS. The FAFSA is required. The application deadline for fall entry is open.

International Students: In a recent year, 6 international students were enrolled. The school actively recruits these students. They must score 500 on take the TOEFL and also take SAT I.

Computers: The college provides computer facilities for student use. The mainframes are a DEC MicroVAX 3400 and a MicroVAX II. Microcomputer facilities are available to students at various locations. All terminals are networked to the mainframes, one running VMS, the other, UNIX. 6 PCs are also networked (virtual disk, printers); the remaining PCs are stand-alone. Desktop publishing, spreadsheet, database, word processing, graphics, presentation, and expert systems software is available. All students may access the system 8 A.M. to 11 P.M. There are no time limits.

Graduates: In a recent year, 79 bachelor's degrees were awarded. 58 companies recently recruited on campus.

Admissions Contact: Susan Potter, Director of Admission.

UNITY COLLEGE
C-4

Unity, ME 04988   (207) 948–3131

Full-time: 336 men, 167 women	Faculty: 34; IIB, --$
Part-time: none	Ph.D.s: 56%
Graduate: none	Student/Faculty: 15 to 1
Year: 4–1–4, summer session	Tuition: n/av
Application Deadline: open	Room & Board: n/app
Freshman Class: n/av	
SAT I or ACT: not required	LESS COMPETITIVE

Unity College, founded in 1965, is a private, independent, coeducational institution offering undergraduate programs in environmental science, natural resource management, and wilderness-based outdoor recreation. In addition to regional accreditation, Unity has baccalaureate program accreditation with SAF. The library contains 40,000 volumes, and subscribes to 651 periodicals. Computerized library sources and services include the card catalog, interlibrary loans, and database searching. Special learning facilities include a learning resource center and art gallery. The 205-acre campus is in a rural area 18 miles east of Waterville. Including residence halls, there are 17 buildings on campus.

Student Life: 72% of undergraduates are from out-of-state, mostly the Northeast. Students come from 18 states and 3 foreign countries. 97% are from public schools; 3% from private. 99% are white. 57% are Catholic; 30% Protestant. The average age of freshmen is 18; all undergraduates, 20. 18% do not continue beyond their first year; 82% remain to graduate.

Housing: 291 students can be accommodated in college housing. College-sponsored living facilities include single-sex and coed dormitories and off-campus apartments. On-campus housing is guaranteed for all 4 years. 80% of students live on campus; of those, 80% remain on campus on weekends. All students may keep cars on campus.

Activities: There are no fraternities or sororities. There are 22 groups on campus, including art, drama, literary magazine, newspaper, photography, student government, and yearbook. Popular campus events include Regional Woodsman's Meet in October.

Sports: There are 3 intercollegiate sports for men and 2 for women, and 10 intramural sports for men and 8 for women. Athletic and recreation facilities include a gymnasium, a weight training room, playing fields, a nature trail, and game rooms.

Disabled Students: 80% of the campus is accessible to disabled students. The following facilities are available: wheelchair ramps, special parking, and special class scheduling.

Services: In addition to many counseling and information services, tutoring is available in every subject. There is remedial math, reading, and writing. A full-time learning disability specialist is on staff.

Campus Safety and Security: Campus safety and security measures include 24-hour foot and vehicle patrol, informal discussions, and emergency telephones.

Programs of Study: Unity confers B.A. and B.S. degrees. Associate degrees are also awarded. Bachelor's degrees are awarded in AGRICULTURE (conservation and regulation and fishing and fisheries), BIOLOGICAL SCIENCE (ecology and wildlife biology), EDUCATION (environmental), ENGINEERING AND ENVIRONMENTAL DESIGN (environmental science), SOCIAL SCIENCE (interdisciplinary studies and parks and recreation management). Aquaculture, fisheries, and ecology are the strongest academically. Conservation law enforcement, wilderness-based recreation, and wildlife have the largest enrollments.

Required: General education requirements include 38 credits in English composition, oral communication, mathematics, computer science, life science, physical science, and electives, as well as 9 credits in a specialization outside the major field. Students must complete at least 120 credit hours with a minimum GPA of 2.0. An internship, thesis, or seminar is required in all bachelor degree programs.

Special: The college offers co-op programs, credit-bearing internships, study abroad, a Washington semester, work-study programs, accelerated degree programs, dual and student-designed majors, and credit for life experience. A mentor program, in which a faculty member assists a student with research, is available to those students who earn a minimum GPA of 3.33 in their first 30 credit hours. There is a freshman honors program on campus, as well as 1 national honor society.

Faculty/Classroom: All teach undergraduates.

Requirements: Applicants must be graduates of an accredited secondary school with a GPA of 2.0. The GED is accepted. SAT I or ACT scores, though not required, should be submitted if available for placement purposes. An essay is required and an interview is recommended. AP and CLEP credits are accepted. Important factors in the admissions decision are advanced placement or honor courses, evidence of special talent, and leadership record.

Procedure: Freshmen are admitted fall and spring. Entrance exams should be taken in the junior or senior year. There are early admissions and deferred admissions plans. Application deadlines are open. Application fee is $25. Notification is sent on a rolling basis. A waiting list is an active part of the admissions procedure.

Transfer: 51 transfer students enrolled in 1995–96. Applicants must present a minimum college GPA of 2.0 and are encouraged to submit SAT I scores. 60 credits of 120 must be completed at Unity.

Visiting: There are regularly scheduled orientations for prospective students. There are guides for informal visits and visitors may sit in on classes and stay overnight at the school. To schedule a visit, contact the Admissions Office.

Financial Aid: In 1995–96, 81% of all freshmen and 79% of continuing students received some form of financial aid. 78% of freshmen and 72% of continuing students received need-based aid. The average freshman award was $7705. Of that total, scholarships or need-based grants averaged $2925 ($10,000 maximum); loans averaged $3304 ($10,500 maximum); and work contracts averaged $1475 ($2448 maximum). 57% of undergraduate students work part-time. Average earnings from campus work for the school year are $1322. Unity is a member of CSS. The FAF or FAFSA and the college's own financial statement are required. The application deadline for fall entry is April 15.

International Students: There were 8 international students enrolled in a recent year. The school actively recruits these students. They must score 500 on the TOEFL.

Computers: The college provides computer facilities for student use. A network of IBM-compatible personal computers is available in the environmental science building. Apple microcomputers are available in a number of locations on campus. Macintosh computers are also available. All students may access the system. There are no time limits and no fees.

Graduates: In a recent year, 88 bachelor's degrees were awarded. 81 companies recruited on campus in a recent year.

Admissions Contact: Dr. John M. B. Craig, Vice President and Dean. A campus video is available.

UNIVERSITY OF MAINE SYSTEM

The University of Maine system, established in 1968, is a public system. It is governed by a board of trustees, whose chief administrator is the chancellor. The primary goals of the system are teaching, research, and public service. The main priorities are to strengthen human services through programs in education, health, and social services; to provide international exchange and foreign language programs; and to conduct science and technology education and basic and applied research. The total enrollment of all 7 campuses is about 30,000, with nearly 1500 faculty members. There are 208 baccalaureate, 75 master's, and 23 doctoral programs offered within the system. Profiles of the 4-year campuses, located at Augusta, Farmington, Fort Kent, Machias, and Presque Isle are included in this chapter.

UNIVERSITY OF MAINE

C-4

Orono, ME 04469

(207) 581-1561

Full-time: 3123 men, 2716 women	Faculty: 511; I, --$
Part-time: 468 men, 536 women	Ph.D.s: 82%
Graduate: 853 men, 1413 women	Student/Faculty: 11 to 1
Year: semesters, summer session	Tuition: $3860 ($10,010)
Application Deadline: February 1	Room & Board: $4680
Freshman Class: 4320 applied, 1573 enrolled	
SAT I Verbal/Math: 470/530	COMPETITIVE

The University of Maine, established in 1865, is a publicly funded, land-grant institution in the University of Maine System. The school has 7 undergraduate colleges: College of Arts and Humanities, College of Business Administration, College of Engineering, College of Education, College of Sciences, College of Social and Behavioral Sciences, and College of Natural Resources, Forestry, and Agriculture. There is 1 graduate school. In addition to regional accreditation, UMaine has baccalaureate program accreditation with AACSB, ABET, AHEA, CAHEA, CSWE, NASAD, NASM, NCATE, and SAF. The library contains 875,000 volumes, and subscribes to 5400 periodicals. Computerized library sources and services include the card catalog, interlibrary loans, and database searching. Special learning facilities include an art gallery, natural history museum, planetarium, radio station, TV station, music facilities, and 2 theaters. The Maine Center for the Arts houses a concert hall, art gallery, and natural history museum. The 3300-acre campus is in a small town 8 miles north of Bangor. Including residence halls, there are 158 buildings on campus.

Student Life: 82% of undergraduates are from Maine. Students come from 45 states, 69 foreign countries, and Canada. 80% are from public schools; 20% from private. 95% are white. The average age of freshmen is 18; all undergraduates, 21. 25% do not continue beyond their first year; 75% remain to graduate.

Housing: 4400 students can be accommodated in college housing. College-sponsored living facilities include single-sex and coed dormitories, on-campus apartments, off-campus apartments, and married-student housing. In addition there are honors houses, language houses, special interest houses, and lifestyle and academic housing wings. On-campus housing is guaranteed for the freshman year only and is available on a first-come, first-served basis. 52% of students live on campus. Alcohol is not permitted. All students may keep cars on campus.

Activities: 6% of men belong to 14 national fraternities; 4% of women belong to 7 national sororities. There are 130 groups on campus, including band, cheerleading, chess, choir, chorale, chorus, computers, dance, drama, drill team, ethnic, film, gay, honors, international, jazz band, literary magazine, marching band, musical theater, newspaper, opera, orchestra, pep band, political, professional, radio and TV, religious, social, social service, student government, symphony, and yearbook. Popular campus events include Maine Day, Homecoming, and Family and Friends Weekend.

Sports: There are 10 intercollegiate sports for men and 9 for women, and 22 intramural sports for men and 21 for women. Athletic and recreation facilities include a sports arena for hockey and basketball, a fitness center, baseball, soccer, field hockey, and football fields, basketball and tennis courts, a swimming pool, a weight room, an indoor track, a dance studio, an archery range, and volleyball, badminton, squash, and racquetball courts.

Disabled Students: 75% of the campus is accessible to disabled students. The following facilities are available: wheelchair ramps, elevators, special parking, specially equipped rest rooms, special class scheduling, and lowered drinking fountains.

Services: In addition to many counseling and information services, tutoring is available in some subjects, including 100 and 200 level courses. There is a reader service for the blind. Developmental courses are offered in remedial mathematics, remedial reading, and remedial writing.

Campus Safety and Security: Campus safety and security measures include 24-hour foot and vehicle patrol, self-defense education, escort service, and informal discussions. In addition, there are pamphlets/posters/films, emergency telephones, and lighted pathways/sidewalks.

Programs of Study: UMaine confers B.A. and B.S. degrees. Associate, master's, and doctoral degrees are also awarded. Bachelor's degrees are awarded in AGRICULTURE (agricultural business management, agriculture, animal science, fishing and fisheries, forest engineering, forestry and related sciences, horticulture, natural resource management, wildlife management, and wood science), BIOLOGICAL SCIENCE (biochemistry, biology/biological science, botany, microbiology, molecular biology, nutrition, and zoology), BUSINESS (business administration and management), COMMUNICATIONS AND THE ARTS (art, communications, dramatic arts, English, French, German, journalism, Latin, modern language, music, music performance, romance languages, Spanish, and speech/debate/rhetoric), COMPUTER AND PHYSICAL SCIENCE (chemistry, computer science, geology, mathematics, and physics), EDUCATION (early childhood, elementary, health, music, physical, recreation, and secondary), ENGINEERING AND ENVIRONMENTAL DESIGN (bioengineering, chemical engineering, civil engineering, computer engineering, construction technology, electrical/electronics engineering, electrical/electronics engineering technology, engineering physics, mechanical engineering, paper and pulp science, and surveying engineering), HEALTH PROFESSIONS (medical laboratory technology and nursing), SOCIAL SCIENCE (anthropology, child psychology/development, economics, food science, history, international studies, parks and recreation management, philosophy, political science/government, psychology, public administration, social work, and sociology). Engineering and technology, business administration, and forest resources are the strongest academically. Business administration, education, and mechanical engineering have the largest enrollments.

Required: A minimum of 120 credit hours with a minimum GPA of 2.0 is required for graduation. 72 hours must be completed in the student's major. The distribution and curricula requirements vary with each undergraduate college. All students are required to take English 101.

Special: A Professional Preparation Team program is offered by the College of Education. Cross-registration through the National Student Exchange, internships at the upper level, a Washington semester, work-study programs both on and off campus, a B.A.-B.S. degree, dual majors, a general studies degree, and pass/fail options are available. Students may study abroad in more than 40 countries. Cooperative programs are available in most majors, and accelerated degree programs may be arranged. There is a freshman honors program on campus, as well as 9 national honor societies, including Phi Beta Kappa. 7 departments have honors programs.

Faculty/Classroom: 68% of faculty are male; 32%, female. The average class size in an introductory lecture is 22; in a laboratory, 15; and in a regular course offering, 22.

Admissions: The SAT I scores for the 1995–96 freshman class were as follows: Verbal—69% below 500, 25% between 500 and 599, 5% between 600 and 700, and 1% above 700; Math—38% below 500, 40% between 500 and 599, 18% between 600 and 700, and 4% above 700. 49% of the current freshmen were in the top fifth of their class; 81% were in the top two fifths. There were 7 National Merit finalists. 11 freshmen graduated first in their class.

Requirements: The SAT I or ACT is required. In addition, applicants must be graduates of an accredited secondary school or a school approved by the state of Maine. The GED is accepted. The number of academic or Carnegie credits and courses required vary according to the program, but should include 4 credits of English, 3 of mathematics, 2 each of science, social studies, and a foreign language, and 3 electives. The school recommends that students submit an essay. An audition is required for music majors. AP and CLEP credits are accepted. Important factors in the admissions decision are advanced placement or honor courses, recommendations by school officials, and evidence of special talent.

Procedure: Freshmen are admitted fall and spring. Entrance exams should be taken by January of the senior year. There are early admissions and deferred admissions plans. Early decision applications should be filed by November 30; regular applications, by February 1 for fall entry and November 1 for spring entry, along with an application fee of $25. Notification is sent on a rolling basis.

Transfer: 417 transfer students enrolled in 1995–96. Transfer students must submit transcripts of all college and high school records. A minimum GPA of 2.0 is required. 30 credits of 120 must be completed at UMaine.

Visiting: There are regularly scheduled orientations for prospective students, including an opening welcome, classroom visits, campus tours, advisor sessions, and registration. There are guides for informal visits and visitors may sit in on classes and stay overnight at the school. To schedule a visit, contact the Admissions Office at (207) 581–1572.

Financial Aid: In 1995–96, 50% of all freshmen and 72% of continuing students received some form of financial aid. 50% of freshmen and 72% of continuing students received need-based aid. The average freshman award was $5763. Of that total, scholarships or need-based grants averaged $3004 ($4900 maximum); loans averaged $2791 ($5125 maximum); and work contracts averaged $1050 ($1200 maximum). 36% of undergraduate students work part-time. Average earnings from campus work for the school year are $1127. The average financial indebtedness of the 1994–95 graduate was $10,004. UMaine is a member of CSS. The FAFSA is required. The application deadline for fall entry is March 1.

International Students: There are currently 381 international students enrolled. The school actively recruits these students. They must take the TOEFL and achieve a minimum score of 500. The student must also take the SAT I or the ACT.

Computers: The college provides computer facilities for student use. The mainframe is an IBM 3090 UM/CMS. There are 3 computer clusters on campus, and microcomputers are available in the residence halls. All students may access the system 24 hours per day. There are no time limits and no fees. It is recommended that all students have personal computers.

Graduates: The most popular majors among graduates were elementary education (9%), business administration (9%), and nursing (6%). Within an average freshman class, 28% graduate in 4 years, 48% in 5 years, and 53% in 6 years.

Admissions Contact: Joyce D. Henckler, Assistant Vice President for Enrollment Management. E-mail: um__admit@maine.maine.edu.

UNIVERSITY OF MAINE AT FARMINGTON   B-4
Farmington, ME 04938–1990
(207) 778-7050
FAX: (207) 778-8182

Full-time: 587 men, 1305 women	**Faculty:** 110; IIB, -$
Part-time: 89 men, 187 women	**Ph.D.s:** 78%
Graduate: none	**Student/Faculty:** 17 to 1
Year: semesters, summer session	**Tuition:** $3220 ($7450)
Application Deadline: April 15	**Room & Board:** $4050
Freshman Class: 1203 applied, 893 accepted, 481 enrolled	
SAT I Verbal/Math: 436/466 (mean)	**COMPETITIVE**

The University of Maine at Farmington is a public institution offering programs in arts and sciences, teacher education and human services. There are 2 undergraduate schools. In addition to regional accreditation, UMF has baccalaureate program accreditation with NCATE. The library contains 114,059 volumes, 49,512 microform items, and 2985 audiovisual forms, and subscribes to 713 periodicals. Computerized library sources and services include the card catalog, interlibrary loans, and database searching. Special learning facilities include a learning resource center, art gallery, radio station, instructional media center, and archaeology research center. The 50-acre campus is in a small town 38 miles northwest of Augusta. Including residence halls, there are 35 buildings on campus.

Student Life: 89% of undergraduates are from Maine. Students come from 18 states and 16 foreign countries. 88% are from public schools; 12% from private. 97% are white. The average age of freshmen is 18; all undergraduates, 23.9. 29% do not continue beyond their first year; 68% remain to graduate.

Housing: 834 students can be accommodated in college housing. College-sponsored living facilities include single-sex and coed dormitories and on-campus apartments. In addition, there are an international guest house, a language floor, and a hall for the French immersion program. On-campus housing is guaranteed for all 4 years. 63% of students commute. All students may keep cars on campus.

Activities: There are no fraternities or sororities. There are 45 groups on campus, including band, cheerleading, choir, chorus, dance, drama, film, gay, honors, international, literary magazine, musical theater, newspaper, orchestra, pep band, photography, political, professional, radio and TV, religious, social, social service, student government, and yearbook. Popular campus events include Winter Carnival Weekend.

Sports: There are 4 intercollegiate sports for men and 5 for women, and 11 intramural sports each for men and women. Athletic and recreation facilities include a 500-seat gymnasium, baseball, softball, and soccer fields, a field house with an indoor jogging track, 4 multipurpose courts, a swimming pool, a weight-training center, a ski area, and mountain climbing, canoeing, and white water rafting opportunities nearby.

Disabled Students: 50% of the campus is accessible to disabled students. The following facilities are available: wheelchair ramps, elevators, special parking, specially equipped rest rooms, special class scheduling, lowered drinking fountains, lowered telephones, accessible van, a swimming pool, and TDD.

Services: In addition to many counseling and information services, tutoring is available in every subject. There is a reader service for the blind, and remedial math, reading, and writing.

Campus Safety and Security: Campus safety and security measures include 24-hour foot and vehicle patrol, self-defense education, escort service, and informal discussions. There are pamphlets/posters/films, emergency telephones, and lighted pathways/sidewalks.

Programs of Study: UMF confers B.A., B.S., B.F.A., and B.G.S. degrees. Bachelor's degrees are awarded in BIOLOGICAL SCIENCE (biology/biological science), BUSINESS (business economics), COMMUNICATIONS AND THE ARTS (creative writing, dramatic arts, English, music, and visual and performing arts), COMPUTER AND PHYSICAL SCIENCE (computer mathematics, geochemistry, and mathematics), EDUCATION (early childhood, education of the emotionally handicapped, education of the mentally handicapped, elementary, English, health, mathematics, science, secondary, social science, and special), ENGINEERING AND ENVIRONMENTAL DESIGN (environmental science), HEALTH PROFESSIONS (rehabilitation therapy and speech pathology/audiology), SOCIAL SCIENCE (geography, history, international studies, liberal arts/general studies, political science/government, psychology, and sociology). Elementary education, secondary education, and interdisciplinary have the largest enrollments.

Required: All students must maintain a minimum GPA of 2.0 while earning 120 semester hours, including 30 in their major. Core requirements include a foreign language, 8 hours in science, 9 each in social and behavioral sciences and the humanities, 3 each in mathematics and health and physical education, 4 in English composition, and 1 in computer science.

Special: Study abroad in 4 countries, as well as numerous opportunities through the National Student Exchange program, work-study with UMF, and student-designed majors are available. Internships are required in rehabilitation and health and are available in many disciplines. Also possible are a 3-2 engineering program, a program of interdisciplinary field study in physical sciences, a ski industry certificate, a French immersion program, nondegree study, and pass/fail options. There is a freshman honors program on campus, as well as 6 national honor societies. 10 departments have honors programs.

Faculty/Classroom: 69% of faculty are male; 31%, female. All teach undergraduates. The average class size in an introductory lecture is 50; in a laboratory, 18; and in a regular course offering, 25.

Admissions: 74% of the 1995-96 applicants were accepted. 35% of the current freshmen were in the top quarter of their class; 78% were in the top half.

Requirements: UMF requires applicants to be in the upper 50% of their class with a 2.0 GPA. Applicants are required to have 16 to 19 college preparatory courses including 4 in English, 2 each in social science and foreign language, 3 to 4 in mathematics, 2 to 3 in laboratory science and 3 electives. An essay is required, and an interview recommended. A counselor recommendation is required. The GED is accepted for older, highly motivated students. AP and CLEP credits are accepted. Important factors in the admissions decision are advanced placement or honor courses, recommendations by school officials, and leadership record.

Procedure: Freshmen are admitted fall and spring. There are early action and deferred admissions plans. Early action applications should be filed by December 15; regular applications, by April 15 for fall entry and January 1 for spring entry, along with an application fee of $25. Notification of early action is sent January 7; regular decision, on a rolling basis.

Transfer: 121 transfer students enrolled in a recent year. Transfer applicants must have a minimum GPA of 2.0 (2.5 for some majors). 30 credits of 120 must be completed at UMF.

Visiting: There are regularly scheduled orientations for prospective students, including sessions on financial aid, majors, and the admissions process. There are guides for informal visits and visitors may sit in on classes. To schedule a visit, contact the Admissions Office.

Financial Aid: In a recent year, 65% of all freshmen and 57% of continuing students received some form of financial aid. 70% of freshmen received need-based aid. The average freshman award was $4600. 27% of undergraduate students work part-time. Average earnings from campus work for the school year are $1100. The average financial indebtedness of a recent graduate was $9012. UMF is a member of CSS. The FAFSA is required. The application deadline for fall entry is March 1.

International Students: In a recent year, 34 international students were enrolled. The school actively recruits these students. They must score 520 on the TOEFL.

Computers: The college provides computer facilities for student use. The mainframes are an IBM 3090, IBM PC-RT, and SUN SPARC station 1 +. There are 110 microcomputers, 76 of which are networked. Workstations are DOS-based. There are 4 dumb terminals. Nearly all are located in the Academic Computing Center. The rest are located in departmental student laboratories. Students may access Internet and Bitnet. All students may access the system 24 hours, 7 days, for most stations. There are no time limits. There is a $90 per year instruction-related technology fee.

Graduates: In a recent year, 360 bachelor's degrees were awarded. The most popular majors among graduates were elementary education (27%), interdisciplinary (13%), and rehabilitation services (9%). Within an average freshman class, 40% graduate in 4 years and 68% in 5 years. 52 companies recruited on campus in a recent year.

Admissions Contact: James Collins, Associate Director of Admissions. E-mail: umfadmit@maine.maine.edu.

UNIVERSITY OF MAINE AT FORT KENT D-1
Fort Kent, ME 04743-1292

(207) 834-7600
FAX: (207) 834-7556

Full-time: 190 men, 200 women	Faculty: 32; IIB, --$
Part-time: 81 men, 260 women	Ph.D.s: 52%
Graduate: none	Student/Faculty: 12 to 1
Year: semesters, summer session	Tuition: $2835 ($6795)
Application Deadline: open	Room & Board: $3600
Freshman Class: 121 applied	
SAT I Verbal/Math: 384/415	LESS COMPETITIVE

The University of Maine at Fort Kent, founded in 1878, is a publicly funded liberal arts institution within the University of Maine system. In addition to regional accreditation, UMFK has baccalaureate program accreditation with NLN. The library contains 56,078 volumes, 5296 microform items, and 1914 audiovisual forms, and subscribes to 367 periodicals. Computerized library sources and services include the card catalog, interlibrary loans, and database searching. Special learning facilities include a learning resource center, radio station, greenhouse, and biological park. The 52-acre campus is in a small town 200 miles north of Bangor. Including residence halls, there are 14 buildings on campus.

Student Life: 92% of undergraduates are from Maine. Students come from 6 states, 19 foreign countries, and Canada. 97% are white. The average age of freshmen is 23; all undergraduates, 26. 40% do not continue beyond their first year; 35% remain to graduate.

Housing: 175 students can be accommodated in college housing. College-sponsored living facilities include coed dormitories. On-campus housing is guaranteed for all 4 years. 77% of students commute. Alcohol is not permitted. All students may keep cars on campus.

Activities: 3% of men belong to 1 national fraternity; 3% of women belong to 2 national sororities. There are 25 groups on campus, including cheerleading, chorale, chorus, computers, dance, drama, environmental, international, literary magazine, literature, musical theater, newspaper, outing, professional, radio and TV, religious, and student government. Popular campus events include French Heritage Festival, Spring Meltdown, Winter Carnival, and Homecoming.

Sports: There are 2 intercollegiate sports for men and 2 for women, and 9 intramural sports for men and 9 for women. Athletic and recreation facilities include a gymnasium, a multipurpose room, racquetball courts, a soccer field, and game rooms in the residence halls.

Disabled Students: 75% of the campus is accessible to disabled students. The following facilities are available: wheelchair ramps, elevators, special parking, specially equipped rest rooms, and special class scheduling.

Services: In addition to many counseling and information services, tutoring is available in every subject. There is a reader service for the blind, and remedial math, reading, and writing.

Campus Safety and Security: Campus safety and security measures include informal discussions, pamphlets/posters/films, and lighted pathways/sidewalks.

Programs of Study: UMFK confers B.A., B.S., B.S.E.S, B.S.N., and B.U.S. degrees. Associate degrees are also awarded. Bachelor's degrees are awarded in BIOLOGICAL SCIENCE (biology/biological science), BUSINESS (business administration and management), COMMUNICATIONS AND THE ARTS (English and French), COMPUTER AND PHYSICAL SCIENCE (computer science and mathematics), EDUCATION (elementary and middle school), ENGINEERING AND ENVIRONMENTAL DESIGN (environmental science), HEALTH PROFESSIONS (nursing), SOCIAL SCIENCE (behavioral science, crosscultural studies, history, liberal arts/general studies, and social science). Environmental studies, nursing, and biology are the strongest academically. Education, nursing, and behavioral science have the largest enrollments.

Required: A minimum GPA of 2.0 and a total of 120 credit hours (2.5 GPA and 127 credit hours for nursing) are required for graduation. Curricula and distribution requirements vary by major.

Special: Internships required for business majors, a general studies degree, a B.A.-B.S. degree in bilingual-bicultural studies, credit for life experience, and nondegree study are available. Students may cross-register with the College Universitaire St. Louis Maillet in New Brunswick. Study abroad may be arranged in Canada, France, and Mexico through the University of Maine at Farmington. Interactive television courses broadcasted from other universities are available on campus. There is 1 national honor society on campus.

Faculty/Classroom: 61% of faculty are male; 39%, female. All teach undergraduates.

Admissions: The SAT I scores for the 1995–96 freshman class were as follows: Verbal—94% below 500, 4% between 500 and 599, and 2% between 600 and 700; Math—81% below 500, 14% between 500 and 599, 3% between 600 and 700, and 2% above 700. 9% of the current freshmen were in the top fifth of their class; 18% were in the top two fifths.

Requirements: The SAT I is required. Applicants should be graduates of an accredited secondary school. The GED is accepted. Required secondary school courses include 4 years of English and 2 each of social studies, mathematics, and science with laboratory. A foreign language is suggested. An essay and an interview are recommended. AP and CLEP credits are accepted. Important factors in the admissions decision are recommendations by school officials, advanced placement or honor courses, and evidence of special talent.

Procedure: Freshmen are admitted in the fall and spring. Entrance exams should be taken before March of the senior year. There are early decision, early admissions, and deferred admissions plans. Application deadlines are open. Application fee is $25. Notification is sent on a rolling basis.

Transfer: 107 transfer students enrolled in 1995–96. Applicants must submit transcripts from each college and secondary school attended. The SAT I and an interview are recommended. 30 credits of 120 must be completed at UMFK.

Visiting: There are regularly scheduled orientations for prospective students, including placement testing, meetings with advisers, campus tours, and get-acquainted activities. There are guides for informal visits and visitors may sit in on classes and stay overnight at the school. To schedule a visit, contact the Admissions Office.

Financial Aid: In 1995–96, 80% of all students received need-based aid. The average freshman award was $5083. Of that total, scholarships or need-based grants averaged $2287; loans averaged $1795; and work contracts averaged $1000. 25% of undergraduate students work part-time. Average earnings from campus work for the school year are $1000. The average financial indebtedness of the 1994–95 graduate was $2520. UMFK is a member of CSS. The FAFSA and income tax forms are required. The application deadline for fall entry is April 1.

International Students: There are currently 138 international students enrolled. The school actively recruits these students. They must take the TOEFL or the college's own test and achieve a minimum score on the TOEFL of 500. SAT I scores may be submitted in place of the TOEFL.

Computers: The college provides computer facilities for student use. The mainframes are a Novell 311 and Novell 3.12. PCs are available in the dormitories, the library, and 2 computer centers. All students may access the system from 8 A.M. to 11 P.M. in the library and computer centers, and 24 hours a day in the dormitories. There are no time limits. The fees are $5.

Graduates: In 1994–95, 157 bachelor's degrees were awarded. The most popular majors among graduates were education (43%), nursing (8%), and English (6%). Within an average freshman class, 30% graduate in 4 years and 33% in 5 years. Of the 1994 graduating class, 10% were enrolled in graduate school within 6 months of graduation and 27% had found employment.

Admissions Contact: Jerald R. Nadeau, Director of Admissions.

UNIVERSITY OF MAINE AT MACHIAS E-4
Machias, ME 04654

(207) 255-3313, ext. 318
FAX: (207) 255-4864

Full-time: 244 men, 359 women	Faculty: 40; IIB, --$
Part-time: 99 men, 227 women	Ph.D.s: 52%
Graduate: none	Student/Faculty: 15 to 1
Year: semesters, summer session	Tuition: $2935 ($4315–6895)
Application Deadline: open	Room & Board: $3835
Freshman Class: 442 applied, 372 accepted, 159 enrolled	
SAT I Verbal/Math: 440/482	COMPETITIVE

The University of Maine at Machias, founded in 1909, is a publicly funded liberal arts institution in the University of Maine system. In addition to regional accreditation, UMM has baccalaureate program accreditation with NRPA. The library contains 82,089 volumes, 3501 microform items, and 1562 audiovisual forms, and subscribes to 524 periodicals. Computerized library sources and services include the card catalog and database searching. Special learning facilities include a learning resource center, art gallery, and aquariums for marine and aquaculture studies. The 47-acre campus is in a rural area 85 miles east of Bangor. Including residence halls, there are 8 buildings on campus.

Student Life: 80% of undergraduates are from Maine. Students come from 21 states, 16 foreign countries, and Canada. 98% are from public schools; 2% from private. 96% are white. The average age of freshmen is 20; all undergraduates, 26.5.

Housing: 310 students can be accommodated in college housing. College-sponsored living facilities include single-sex and coed dormitories. On-campus housing is guaranteed for all 4 years. 67% of students commute. All students may keep cars on campus.

Activities: 3% of men belong to 1 local and 1 national fraternity; 2% of women belong to 2 local sororities and 1 national sorority. There are 25 groups on campus, including art, cheerleading, chorus, computers, dance, drama, honors, international, literary magazine, newspaper, pep band, photography, professional, religious, social service, student government, and yearbook. Popular campus events include Winter Carnival, Family Christmas Party, Spring Weekend, and Coffee House Events.

Sports: There are 2 intercollegiate sports for men and 2 for women, and 15 intramural sports for men and 12 for women. Athletic and recreation facilities include a gymnasium, a weight room, and a 64-acre recreational center with a lodge and cabins on the lake.

Disabled Students: 85% of the campus is accessible to disabled students. The following facilities are available: wheelchair ramps, elevators, special parking, specially equipped rest rooms, and lowered drinking fountains.

Services: In addition to many counseling and information services, tutoring is available in every subject. There is remedial math, reading, and writing.

Campus Safety and Security: Campus safety and security measures include informal discussions, pamphlets/posters/films, lighted pathways/sidewalks, a keyless entry system for residence halls, and a security patrol from 5 P.M. to 1 P.M. Sunday to Wednesday and from 5 P.M. to 5 A.M. Thursday to Saturday.

Programs of Study: UMM confers B.A. and B.S. degrees. Associate degrees are also awarded. Bachelor's degrees are awarded in BIOLOGICAL SCIENCE (biology/biological science and marine biology), BUSINESS (accounting, business administration and management, marketing/retailing/merchandising, and recreation and leisure services), COMMUNICATIONS AND THE ARTS (English), EDUCATION (business, elementary, health, middle school, and secondary), ENGINEERING AND ENVIRONMENTAL DESIGN (environmental science), SOCIAL SCIENCE (behavioral science, history, human services, psychology, social science, and social work). Elementary education, marine biology, and environmental studies are the strongest academically and have the largest enrollments.

Required: A minimum of 120 credit hours and a GPA of 2.0 are required for graduation. All students must complete the core requirements of 9 credits in English, 6 in history, 4 each in arts and laboratory science, 3 each in interdisciplinary studies, computer science, and mathematics beyond algebra II, and 2 in physical education.

Special: Co-op programs, cross-registration, internships, work-study programs, an accelerated degree program, a B.A.-B.S. degree, and a general studies degree are available. UMM also offers student-designed majors, credit for life experience, nondegree study, and a pass/fail option in certain courses. There is a transfer program in community health education with the University of Maine at Farmington. There is a freshman honors program on campus.

Faculty/Classroom: 62% of faculty are male; 38%, female. All teach undergraduates. The average class size in an introductory lecture is 25; in a laboratory, 18; and in a regular course offering, 14.

Admissions: 84% of the 1995–96 applicants were accepted. 2 freshmen graduated first in their class.

Requirements: The SAT I is required, with a minimum composite score of 1000. UMM requires applicants to be in the upper 50% of their class. A minimum GPA of 2.6 is required. All candidates must be graduates of an accredited secondary school. The GED is accepted. Required secondary school courses include 4 years of English, 3 each of social science and mathematics, and 2 of laboratory science. 2 years of foreign language, an essay, and an interview are strongly recommended. AP and CLEP credits are accepted. Important factors in the admissions decision are advanced placement or honor courses, evidence of special talent, and leadership record.

Procedure: Freshmen are admitted fall and spring. There are early admissions and deferred admissions plans. Application deadlines are open. Application fee is $25. Notification is sent on a rolling basis.

Transfer: 73 transfer students enrolled in 1995–96. A minimum college GPA of 2.0 and evidence of good standing are required of transfer applicants. 30 credits of 120 must be completed at UMM.

Visiting: There are regularly scheduled orientations for prospective students, consisting of programs just prior to fall and spring semester. There are guides for informal visits and visitors may sit in on classes and stay overnight at the school. To schedule a visit, contact the Assistant Director of Admissions.

Financial Aid: In 1995–96, 80% of all students received some form of financial aid and 75% of all students received need-based aid. The average freshman award was $2500. Of that total, scholarships or need-based grants averaged $1500 ($4000 maximum); loans averaged $2500 ($6000 maximum); and work contracts averaged $700 ($1000 maximum). 85% of undergraduate students work part-time. Average earnings from campus work for the school year are $800. The average financial indebtedness of the 1994–95 graduate was $6000. The FAFSA is required. The application deadline for fall entry is March 1.

International Students: There are currently 43 international students enrolled. The school actively recruits these students. They must take the TOEFL or the college's own test and achieve a minimum score on the TOEFL of 500.

Computers: The college provides computer facilities for student use. The mainframes are an IBM 3090–180E/VF and an IBM 4341, linked to an AT&T 3132/400 and 500 microcomputer network. Students have access to 2 major laboratories and 2 clusters of MS-DOS microcomputers as well as 1 laboratory of Macintosh microcomputers. Machines are all on interconnected lines for file servers and mail servers. All students have access to the mainframe as well as to Internet resources. All students may access the system from 8 a.m to 10 P.M. and by request. There are no time limits and no fees.

Graduates: In 1994–95, 117 bachelor's degrees were awarded. The most popular majors among graduates were business (24%), environmental science (18%), and behavioral science (15%). Within an average freshman class, 1% graduate in 3 years, 30% in 4 years, 15% in 5 years, and 5% in 6 years. 10 companies recruited on campus in 1994–95.

Admissions Contact: David P. Baldwin, Director of Admissions. A campus video is available.

UNIVERSITY OF MAINE AT PRESQUE ISLE   D-2

Presque Isle, ME 04769   (207) 768-9532; FAX: (207) 768-9608

Full-time: 995	Faculty: 66; IIB, --$
Part-time: 295	Ph.D.s: 64%
Graduate: none	Student/Faculty: 15 to 1
Year: semesters, summer session	Tuition: $3260 ($7220)
Application Deadline: August 15	Room & Board: $3704
Freshman Class: 404 applied, 333 accepted, 211 enrolled	
SAT I Verbal/Math: 378/421	LESS COMPETITIVE

The University of Maine at Presque Isle, founded in 1903, is a public, coeducational, 2-campus institution within the University of Maine system. Interactive television connects the 2 campuses. There is one graduate school. In addition to regional accreditation, UM-Presque Isle has baccalaureate program accreditation with NRPA. The library contains 116,700 volumes, and subscribes to 930 periodicals. Computerized library sources and services include the card catalog, interlibrary loans, and database searching. Special learning facilities include a learning resource center, art gallery, radio station, TV station, and theater. The 150-acre campus is in a rural area 150 miles north of Bangor. Including residence halls, there are 10 buildings on campus.

Student Life: 92% of undergraduates are from Maine. Students come from 10 states, 8 foreign countries, and Canada. 90% are from public schools; 10% from private. 89% are white. 55% are Catholic; 27% Protestant; 10% claim no religious affiliation. The average age of freshmen is 20. 45% do not continue beyond their first year; 28% remain to graduate.

Housing: 400 students can be accommodated in college housing. College-sponsored living facilities include dormitories and on-campus apartments. On-campus housing is guaranteed for all 4 years. 79% of students commute. Alcohol is not permitted. All students may keep cars on campus.

Activities: There are 3 national fraternities and 3 national sororities. There are 17 groups on campus, including art, cheerleading, chess, choir, computers, drama, honors, international, literary magazine, musical theater, newspaper, pep band, political, professional, radio and TV, religious, social service, student government, and yearbook.

Sports: There are 4 intercollegiate sports each for men and women, and 10 intramural sports each for men and women. Athletic and recreation facilities include a multifunctional structure that houses a gymnasium, a weight room, physical education laboratories, a sports medicine facility, a student lounge, and an auditorium. A large playing field contains baseball, soccer, and tennis courts. There are also hiking trails and a bike path.

Disabled Students: 10% of the campus is accessible to disabled students. The following facilities are available: wheelchair ramps, elevators, special parking, specially equipped rest rooms, and special class scheduling.

Services: In addition to many counseling and information services, tutoring is available in most subjects. There is a reader service for the blind, and remedial math, reading, and writing.

Campus Safety and Security: Campus safety and security measures include 24-hour foot and vehicle patrol, escort service, pamphlets/posters/films, and emergency telephones. In addition, there are lighted pathways/sidewalks.

Programs of Study: UM-Presque Isle confers B.A., B.S., B.F.A., B.L.S., and B.S.W. degrees. Associate degrees are also awarded. Bachelor's degrees are awarded in BIOLOGICAL SCIENCE (biology/biological science), BUSINESS (accounting, business administration and management, and recreation and leisure services), COMMUNICATIONS AND THE ARTS (English, French, and speech/debate/rhetoric), COMPUTER AND PHYSICAL SCIENCE (mathematics), EDUCATION (art, elementary, English, foreign languages, health, mathematics, physical, science, secondary, and social science), ENGINEERING AND ENVIRONMENTAL DESIGN (environmental science), SOCIAL SCIENCE (behavioral science, criminal justice, history, humanities, political science/government, social science, social work, and sociology). Education has the largest enrollment.

Required: Core requirements for the B.A. degree include 18 credits in humanities, 12 in social science, 10 in mathematics/science, and 3 in physical education/health. The student must complete a minimum of 60 credits in the major, with a cumulative GPA of 2.0 in 120 credit hours. Requirements for the B.S. and other degrees vary considerably with each major.

Special: The university participates in transfer programs in agriculture, physical science, and engineering with the University of Maine at Orono. There is also cross-registration with Northern Maine Technical College, study abroad in France, Ireland, and Canada, and internships in many majors. UM-Presque Isle offers work-study programs, dual and student-designed majors, and nondegree study. Students can apply for credit by examination and credit for life, military, and work experience. A credit/no credit option is available. There is a freshman honors program on campus.

Faculty/Classroom: 64% of faculty are male; 36%, female. All teach undergraduates. The average class size in an introductory lecture is 22.

Admissions: 82% of the 1995–96 applicants were accepted. There were 2 National Merit semifinalists.

Requirements: The SAT I is required. Applicants should have completed 16 academic credits at an accredited secondary school, including 4 in English, 2 each in mathematics, science, and social studies, and the rest in electives. A GED certificate may be substituted. The university recommends an essay and an interview for all candidates. Art majors must submit a portfolio. AP and CLEP credits are accepted. Important factors in the admissions decision are advanced placement or honor courses, evidence of special talent, and recommendations by school officials.

Procedure: Freshmen are admitted to all sessions. Entrance exams should be taken by January 1. There are early decision, early admissions, and deferred admissions plans. Applications should be filed by August 15 for fall entry and January 1 for spring entry, along with an application fee of $25. Notification is sent on a rolling basis.

Transfer: 88 transfer students enrolled in 1995–96. A GPA of 2.0 from an accredited college or university is required. It is recommended that applicants submit SAT I scores and arrange an interview. 30 credits of 120 must be completed at UM-Presque Isle.

Visiting: There are regularly scheduled orientations for prospective students. There are guides for informal visits and visitors may sit in on classes. To schedule a visit, contact Bev McAvaddy.

Financial Aid: In a recent year, 85% of all freshmen and 75% of continuing students received some form of financial aid or need-based aid. The average freshman award was $4064. UM-Presque Isle is a member of CSS. The FAF is required. The application deadline for fall entry is June 1.

International Students: In a recent year, 70 international students were enrolled. The school actively recruits these students. They must take the TOEFL and achieve a minimum score of 500.

Computers: The college provides computer facilities for student use. Apple and IBM microcomputers are available in the computer laboratory. Those students taking computer courses may access the system. There are no time limits and no fees.

Graduates: In a recent year, 170 bachelor's degrees were awarded. 10 companies recruited on campus in 1994–95.

Admissions Contact: Dr. Gerald Wuori, Director of Admission. E-mail: infoumpi@polaris.umpi.maine.edu.

UNIVERSITY OF NEW ENGLAND
A-6
Biddeford, ME 04005

(207) 283-0171

(800) 477-4UNE; FAX: (207) 286-3678

Full-time: 242 men, 589 women	Faculty: 72; IIA, --$
Part-time: 36 men, 74 women	Ph.D.s: 56%
Graduate: 284 men, 345 women	Student/Faculty: 12 to 1
Year: semesters, summer session	Tuition: $12,810
Application Deadline: see profile	Room & Board: $5225
Freshman Class: 1355 applied, 902 accepted, 265 enrolled	
SAT I Verbal/Math: 430/480	**COMPETITIVE**

The University of New England, founded in 1953, is a small, private, coeducational institution offering undergraduate and graduate programs in liberal arts and sciences, education, and health professions. In addition to regional accreditation, UNE has baccalaureate program accreditation with APTA, CSWE, and NLN. The library contains 90,000 volumes, 1220 microform items, and 960 audiovisual forms, and subscribes to 800 periodicals. Computerized library sources and services include the card catalog, interlibrary loans, and database searching. Special learning facilities include a learning resource center and a video studio. The 410-acre campus is in a rural area 16 miles south of Portland. Including residence halls, there are 27 buildings on campus.

Student Life: 56% of undergraduates are from Maine. Students come from 27 states, 3 foreign countries, and Canada. 98% are white. The average age of freshmen is 19; all undergraduates, 22. 15% do not continue beyond their first year.

Housing: 380 students can be accommodated in college housing. College-sponsored living facilities include single-sex and coed dormitories, on-campus apartments, off-campus apartments, and married-student housing. In addition, there are special interest houses and a wellness house. On-campus housing is guaranteed for the freshman and sophomore years. 65% of students commute. Upperclassmen and second-semester freshmen may keep cars on campus.

Activities: There are no fraternities or sororities. There are 16 groups on campus, including cheerleading, chorale, drama, environment, gay, honors, international, musical theater, newspaper, professional, religious, sailing, social, social service, student government, and yearbook. Popular campus events include Spring Fling, fall and spring semiformal dances, and a student-faculty variety show.

Sports: There are 4 intercollegiate sports for men and 5 for women, and 4 intramural sports for men and 4 for women. Athletic and recreation facilities include a 1500-seat gymnasium, a fitness center, a pool, racquetball courts, soccer and softball fields, and outdoor volleyball facilities.

Disabled Students: 85% of the campus is accessible to disabled students. The following facilities are available: wheelchair ramps, elevators, special parking, specially equipped rest rooms, special class scheduling, lowered drinking fountains, lowered telephones, and stair climbers.

Services: In addition to many counseling and information services, tutoring is available in every subject. There is a reader service for the blind, remedial math, reading, and writing, as well as a complete learning assistance center and a special program for the learning disabled.

Campus Safety and Security: Campus safety and security measures include 24-hour foot and vehicle patrol, escort service, shuttle buses, and informal discussions. In addition, there are pamphlets/posters/films, and lighted pathways/sidewalks. A safe-ride program provides drivers for students.

Programs of Study: UNE confers B.A., B.S., and B.S.N. degrees. Associate, master's, and doctoral degrees are also awarded. Bachelor's degrees are awarded in BIOLOGICAL SCIENCE (biology/biological science and marine biology), BUSINESS (business administration and management and sports management), EDUCATION (elementary, science, and secondary), ENGINEERING AND ENVIRONMENTAL DESIGN (environmental science), HEALTH PROFESSIONS (biomedical science, health care administration, medical laboratory technology, nursing, occupational therapy, physical therapy, predentistry, premedicine, and prepharmacy), SOCIAL SCIENCE (prelaw and psychology). Health professions and life sciences are the strongest programs academically and have the largest enrollments, particularly physical therapy, occupational therapy, marine biology, and medical biology.

Required: A total of 120 credits with a minimum GPA of 2.0 is required for graduation. Students must take 41 credits in a liberal arts core curriculum of humanities, sciences, and social sciences. Most majors require 1-semester internships. Courses in English composition, computer science, and Western traditions are required.

Special: UNE offers cross-registration with the Greater Portland Alliance of Colleges and Universities, internships in all majors, work-study programs, study abroad, student-designed and dual majors in all departments, and a 3-4 medical program. The Freshmen Biology Learning Community provides combined studies in English and life sciences. There is 1 national honor society on campus.

Faculty/Classroom: 49% of faculty are male; 51%, female. All teach undergraduates. No introductory courses are taught by graduate students. The average class size in an introductory lecture is 35; in a laboratory, 20; and in a regular course offering, 20.

Admissions: 67% of the 1995-96 applicants were accepted. The SAT I scores for the 1995-96 freshman class were as follows: Verbal—79% below 500, 18% between 500 and 599, and 3% between 600 and 700; Math—54% below 500, 31% between 500 and 599, and 15% between 600 and 700. 35% of the current freshmen were in the top fifth of their class; 68% were in the top two fifths.

Requirements: The SAT I or ACT is required. Applicants should be high school graduates with 4 years of English, 3 years each of mathematics and science, and 2 years each of history and social studies. The GED is accepted. A personal interview is recommended. AP and CLEP credits are accepted. Important factors in the admissions decision are advanced placement or honor courses, recommendations by school officials, and geographic diversity.

Procedure: Freshmen are admitted in the fall and spring. Entrance exams should be taken in the spring of the junior year or the fall of the senior year. Regular application deadlines are open, except for the physical therapy applicant deadline of February 15. There are early decision, early admissions, and deferred admissions plans. Early decision applications should be filed by November 15, along with an application fee of $40. Notification of early decision is sent December 15; regular decision, on a rolling basis. 84 early decision candidates were accepted for the 1995-96 class. A waiting list is an active part of the admissions procedure, with about 9% of all applicants on the list.

Transfer: 59 transfer students enrolled in 1995-96. Transfer applicants should present a GPA of at least 2.5 in college work. An interview is recommended. 30 credits of 120 must be completed at UNE.

Visiting: There are regularly scheduled orientations for prospective students, including a tour and information session, and an interview if the student has formally applied. There are guides for informal visits and visitors may sit in on classes and stay overnight at the school. To schedule a visit, contact the Admissions Office at (207) 283-0171, ext. 297.

Financial Aid: 85% of all students received some form of financial aid. 82% of all students received need-based aid. The average freshman award was $8000. Of that total, scholarships or need-based grants averaged $1300 ($7500 maximum); loans averaged $4400 ($5625 maximum); and work contracts averaged $500 ($1000 maximum). 50% of undergraduate students work part-time. Average earnings from campus work for the school year are $900. The average financial indebtedness of the 1994-95 graduate was $2200. UNE is a member of CSS. The FAFSA is required.

International Students: There are currently 4 international students enrolled. They must take the TOEFL and achieve a minimum score of 550.

Computers: The college provides computer facilities for student use. The mainframe is a Data General C/7800. There are 32 microcomputers available in the main academic building and the library. There are no time limits and no fees.

Graduates: In 1994-95, 129 bachelor's degrees were awarded. The most popular majors among graduates were occupational therapy (26%), physical therapy (26%), and biology (17%). Within an average freshman class, 60% graduate in 4 years and 2% in 5 years. 80 companies recruited on campus in 1994-95.

Admissions Contact: Patricia T. Cribby, Dean of Admissions.

UNIVERSITY OF SOUTHERN MAINE
B-6
Gorham, ME 04038

(207) 780-5670

(800) 800-4876; FAX: (207) 780-5640

Full-time: 1506 men, 1941 women	Faculty: 321; IIA, -$
Part-time: 1690 men, 2771 women	Ph.D.s: 73%
Graduate: 602 men, 1211 women	Student/Faculty: 11 to 1
Year: semesters, summer session	Tuition: $3500 ($9320)
Application Deadline: February 15	Room & Board: $4494
Freshman Class: 2235 applied, 1737 accepted, 798 enrolled	
SAT I Verbal/Math: 520/510	**COMPETITIVE +**

The University of Southern Maine, founded in 1878, is a publicly funded multicampus liberal arts institution serving the University of Maine system. There are 6 undergraduate and 7 graduate schools. In addition to regional accreditation, USM has baccalaureate program accreditation with ABET, CSWE, NCATE, and NLN. The 2 libraries contain 366,708 volumes, 1,043,985 microform items, and 4751 audiovisual forms, and subscribe to 3610 periodicals. Computerized library sources and services include interlibrary loans and database searching. Special learning facilities include a learning resource center, art gallery, planetarium, radio station, TV station, and cartography collections. The 126-acre campus is in a small town 110 miles north of Boston, Massachusetts, and 10 miles west of the urban Portland campus. Including residence halls, there are 60 buildings on campus.

Student Life: 94% of undergraduates are from Maine. Students come from 23 states, 31 foreign countries, and Canada. 97% are white. The average age of all undergraduates is 28.

Housing: 1332 students can be accommodated in college housing. College-sponsored living facilities include coed dormitories, on-campus apartments, married-student housing, and fraternity houses. In addition, there is a fine arts house and the Plus Program, in which students live together, take 2 classes together, and have study groups and workshops. On-campus housing is guaranteed for all 4 years. 86% of students commute. All students may keep cars on campus.

Activities: There are 4 national fraternities and 2 local and 2 national sororities. There are more than 75 groups and organizations on campus, including art, band, cheerleading, chess, choir, chorale, chorus, commuter, computers, dance, drama, environmental, ethnic, film, gay, honors, international, jazz band, literary magazine, musical theater, newspaper, opera, orchestra, outing, photography, political, professional, radio and TV, religious, social, social service, student government, and yearbook. Popular campus events include Children's Holiday Party, Winter Carnival, and New Student Welcome.

Sports: There are 8 intercollegiate sports for men and 8 for women, and 13 intramural sports for men and 13 for women. Athletic and recreation facilities include gymnasiums, tennis courts, athletic fields, racquetball and squash courts, cross-country ski trails, and weight training and exercise facilities.

Disabled Students: All of the campus is accessible to disabled students. The following facilities are available: wheelchair ramps, elevators, special parking, specially equipped rest rooms, special class scheduling, lowered drinking fountains, and lowered telephones.

Services: In addition to many counseling and information services, tutoring is available in some subjects, including English, mathematics, and introductory-level courses. In addition, there is a reader service for the blind, and remedial math, reading, and writing.

Campus Safety and Security: Campus safety and security measures include 24-hour foot and vehicle patrol, escort service, shuttle buses, and informal discussions. In addition, there are pamphlets/posters/films, emergency telephones, and lighted pathways/sidewalks.

Programs of Study: USM confers B.A., B.S., B.F.A., and B.Mus. degrees. Associate and master's degrees are also awarded. Bachelor's degrees are awarded in BIOLOGICAL SCIENCE (biology/biological science), BUSINESS (accounting and business administration and management), COMMUNICATIONS AND THE ARTS (communications, dramatic arts, English, fine arts, French, music, and music performance), COMPUTER AND PHYSICAL SCIENCE (chemistry, computer science, geology, mathematics, and physics), EDUCATION (music and technical), ENGINEERING AND ENVIRONMENTAL DESIGN (electrical/electronics engineering, environmental science, and industrial engineering technology), HEALTH PROFESSIONS (nursing and recreation therapy), SOCIAL SCIENCE (anthropology, economics, geography, history, philosophy, political science/government, psychology, social work, and sociology). Electrical engineering, computer science, and nursing are the strongest academically. Business administration, nursing, and English have the largest enrollments.

Required: A total of 120 hours, with 36 to 94 in the major and a minimum GPA of 2.0, is required for graduation. All students must fulfill the distribution requirements of the 3-part core curriculum: basic competence, methods of inquiry and ways of knowing, and interdisciplinary studies.

Special: Cross-registration within the University of Maine system and 5 Greater Portland colleges, a Washington semester, and study abroad in more than 12 countries are offered. Internships, co-op and work-study programs, a B.A.-B.S. degree, dual and student-designed majors, credit for life experience, nondegree study, and pass/fail options are also available. There is a January intersession. There is a freshman honors program on campus, as well as 11 national honor societies, including Phi Beta Kappa. 9 departments have honors programs.

Faculty/Classroom: 58% of faculty are male; 42%, female. 80% teach undergraduates and all do research. Graduate students teach 1% of introductory courses. The average class size in an introductory lecture is 50; in a laboratory, 20; and in a regular course offering, 30.

Admissions: 78% of the 1995–96 applicants were accepted. The SAT I scores for the 1995–96 freshman class were as follows: Verbal—80% below 500, 13% between 500 and 599, 6% between 600 and 700, and 1% above 700; Math—42% below 500, 43% between 500 and 599, 14% between 600 and 700, and 1% above 700. 23% of the current freshmen were in the top fifth of their class; 65% were in the top two fifths.

Requirements: The SAT I or ACT is required. USM requires applicants to be in the upper 50% of their class. In addition, applicants must be graduates of an accredited secondary school. The GED is accepted. Either 41 academic credits or 20 1/2 Carnegie units are re-

quired. Secondary school courses should include 4 years of English, 3 of mathematics, 2 each of a foreign language and laboratory science, and 1 each of history and social studies. An essay is required, as are auditions for music applicants and interviews for applicants to the School of Applied Science. USM uses ExPAN software to accept applications on-line. AP and CLEP credits are accepted. Important factors in the admissions decision are advanced placement or honor courses, leadership record, and recommendations by school officials.

Procedure: Freshmen are admitted fall and spring. Entrance exams should be taken between May of the junior year and January of the senior year. There is an early admissions plan. Applications should be filed by February 15 for priority consideration for fall entry and December 1 for spring entry, along with an application fee of $25. Notification is sent on a rolling basis.

Transfer: 741 transfer students enrolled in 1995–96. Applicants must have a minimum GPA of 2.0; 2.75 for those from nonregionally accredited institutions. Students who have fewer than 30 college credits or who have been out of high school for less than 3 years must submit SAT I scores. 30 credits of 120 must be completed at USM.

Visiting: There are regularly scheduled orientations for prospective students, including group information sessions and tours by appointment. There are guides for informal visits and visitors may sit in on classes and stay overnight at the school. To schedule a visit, contact the Admissions Office.

Financial Aid: In 1995–96, 81% of all freshmen and 74% of continuing students received some form of financial aid. 32% of freshmen and 57% of continuing students received need-based aid. The average freshman award was $5500. Of that total, scholarships or need-based grants averaged $1450 ($4000 maximum); loans averaged $700 ($2250 maximum); work contracts averaged $725 ($2000 maximum); and Stafford loans average $2625. 80% of undergraduate students work part-time. Average earnings from campus work for the school year are $1200. The average financial indebtedness of the 1994–95 graduate was $10,200. USM is a member of CSS. The FAFSA is required; the FAT is required for students transferring from another college or vocational school. The application deadline for fall entry is March 1.

International Students: There are currently 64 international students enrolled. They must take the TOEFL and achieve a minimum score of 500. The student must also take the SAT I or the ACT.

Computers: The college provides computer facilities for student use. The mainframe is an IBM 4341. The mainframe is linked to the Bitnet, Internet, and Gopher networks. There are about 1000 terminals and microcomputers, 250 available for student use. Most residence rooms have computer hookups. All students may access the system 24 hours per day. There are no time limits and no fees.

Graduates: In 1994–95, 893 bachelor's degrees were awarded. The most popular majors among graduates were nursing (12%), business administration (10%), and English (6%). 50 companies recruited on campus in 1994–95.

Admissions Contact: Susan Campbell, Director of Admissions. E-mail: usmadm@maine.maine.edu.

WESTBROOK COLLEGE
B-6

Portland, ME 04103　　　　　(207) 797-7261; FAX: (207) 797-7318

Full-time: 37 men, 192 women	**Faculty:** 38; IIB, --$
Part-time: 3 men, 36 women	**Ph.D.s:** 39%
Graduate: none	**Student/Faculty:** 6 to 1
Year: semesters	**Tuition:** $11,650
Application Deadline: open	**Room & Board:** $4900
Freshman Class: 269 applied, 235 accepted, 80 enrolled	
SAT I Verbal/Math: 400/440	**ACT:** 18　　**COMPETITIVE**

Westbrook College, founded in 1831, is a private, coeducational, undergraduate institution offering degree programs in health sciences, business, education, and the arts and sciences. In addition to regional accreditation, Westbrook has baccalaureate program accreditation with ADA and NLN. The library contains 50,000 volumes, 1600 microform items, and 1650 audiovisual forms, and subscribes to 500 periodicals. Computerized library sources and services include interlibrary loans and database searching. Special learning facilities include a learning resource center, art gallery, a laboratory school, a dental hygiene clinic, and the Maine Women Writers Collection. The 50-acre campus is in a suburban area 100 miles north of Boston. Including residence halls, there are 20 buildings on campus.

Student Life: 68% of undergraduates are from Maine. Students come from 15 states, 6 foreign countries, and Canada. 90% are from public schools; 10% from private. 99% are white. 57% are Catholic; 42% Protestant. The average age of freshmen is 18; all undergraduates, 21.

Housing: 450 students can be accommodated in college housing. College-sponsored living facilities include dormitories. On-campus housing is guaranteed for all 4 years. 60% of students live on campus. All students may keep cars on campus.

Activities: There are no fraternities or sororities. There are 15 groups on campus, including art, cheerleading, computers, drama, international, musical theater, newspaper, professional, social, social service, student government, and yearbook.

Sports: Athletic and recreation facilities include an athletic center and soccer and softball fields.

Disabled Students: The following facilities are available: wheelchair ramps, special parking, specially equipped rest rooms, special class scheduling, lowered drinking fountains, and lowered telephones.

Services: In addition to many counseling and information services, tutoring is available in most subjects. There is remedial math, reading, and writing.

Campus Safety and Security: Campus safety and security measures include 24-hour foot and vehicle patrol, escort service, informal discussions, and lighted pathways/sidewalks.

Programs of Study: Westbrook confers B.A. and B.S. degrees. Associate degrees are also awarded. Bachelor's degrees are awarded in BUSINESS (accounting, business administration and management, and marketing/retailing/merchandising), COMMUNICATIONS AND THE ARTS (English), EDUCATION (early childhood and elementary), HEALTH PROFESSIONS (dental hygiene, medical laboratory technology, and nursing). Dental hygiene, business, and nursing are the strongest academically and have the largest enrollments.

Required: To graduate, students must complete 120 to 123 credit hours with a GPA of 2.0. A total of 60 to 62 credit hours must be taken in the common core arts and sciences distribution, along with a course in computer science.

Special: A co-op program is offered in nursing, and internships are available in every major. There is 1 national honor society on campus.

Faculty/Classroom: 70% of faculty are male; 30%, female. All teach undergraduates. The average class size in an introductory lecture is 25; in a laboratory, 20; and in a regular course offering, 18.

Admissions: 87% of the 1995–96 applicants were accepted. The SAT I scores for the 1995–96 freshman class were as follows: Verbal—92% below 500, 6% between 500 and 599, and 1% between 600 and 700; Math—74% below 500, 23% between 500 and 599, and 3% between 600 and 700. 27% of the current freshmen were in the top fifth of their class; 77% were in the top two fifths. 2 freshmen graduated first in their class in a recent year.

Requirements: The SAT I or ACT is required. A minimum GPA of 2.0 is required. In addition, applicants should be graduates of an accredited secondary school. The GED is accepted. 16 academic credits are required, including 4 years of English, 3 of mathematics, 2 each of science, social studies, foreign language, and academic electives, and 1 of history. All candidates must submit an essay and recommendations. An interview is encouraged. AP and CLEP credits are accepted. Important factors in the admissions decision are advanced placement or honor courses, recommendations by school officials, and evidence of special talent.

Procedure: Freshmen are admitted in the fall and spring. Entrance exams should be taken by December of the senior year. There is a deferred admissions plan. Application deadlines are open. Application fee is $25. Notification is sent on a rolling basis.

Transfer: Transfer students should have a minimum college GPA of 2.5. The SAT I, with a minimum composite score of 800, is recommended. 60 credits of 120 to 123 must be completed at Westbrook.

Visiting: There are regularly scheduled orientations for prospective students. There are guides for informal visits and visitors may sit in on classes and stay overnight at the school. To schedule a visit, contact the Admissions Office at (207) 797-7261.

Financial Aid: 95% of undergraduate students work part-time. Westbrook is a member of CSS. The FAF and the college's own financial statement are required. The application deadline for fall entry is May 1.

International Students: There were 15 international students enrolled in a recent year. The school actively recruits these students. They must score 450 on the TOEFL and also take SAT I or the ACT.

Computers: The college provides computer facilities for student use. The mainframe is a Data MV 600. Students have access to 3 computer laboratories, each equipped with IBM-compatible microcomputers, printers, and other peripherals. Westbrook also has an extensive library of business and scientific software applications. All students may access the system 24 hours a day in the library study room; from 9 A.M. to 10 P.M. daily in other facilities. There are no time limits. The fees are $25 per semester.

Admissions Contact: David Anthony, Director of Admissions.

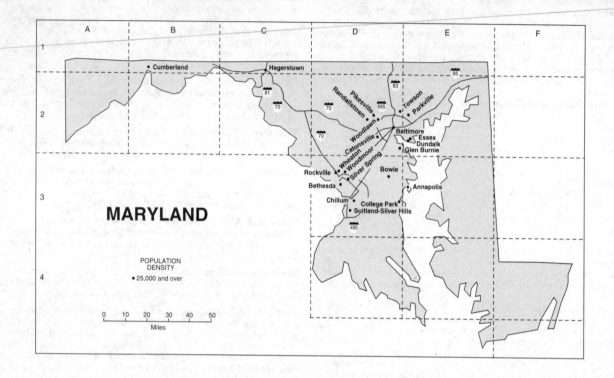

MARYLAND

POPULATION
DENSITY

• 25,000 and over

0 10 20 30 40 50
Miles

BALTIMORE HEBREW UNIVERSITY

D-2

Baltimore, MD 21215–3996

(410) 578-6917
FAX: (410) 578-6940

Full-time: 11 men, 20 women	Faculty: 11
Part-time: 54 men, 127 women	Ph.D.s: 82%
Graduate: 29 men, 68 women	Student/Faculty: 3 to 1
Year: semesters, summer session	Tuition: $12,320
Application Deadline: open	Room & Board: n/app
Freshman Class: n/av	
SAT I or ACT: not required	SPECIAL

Baltimore Hebrew University, founded in 1919, is a private, coeducational, nonsectarian institution of Jewish higher education and a major center of advanced Jewish study in the United States. The library contains 70,000 volumes, 7500 microform items, and 1100 audiovisual forms, and subscribes to 225 periodicals. Computerized library sources and services include database searching. Special learning facilities include a language laboratory. The 2-acre campus is in an urban area in residential northwest Baltimore. There is 1 building on campus.

Student Life: 98% of undergraduates are from Maryland. Students come from 1 state and 4 foreign countries. 99% are white. Most are Jewish. The average age of freshmen is 30; all undergraduates, 45.

Housing: There are no residence halls. All students commute. Alcohol is not permitted. All students may keep cars on campus.

Activities: There are no fraternities or sororities. There are some groups and organizations on campus, including dance. Popular campus events include singles brunches, and concerts.

Sports: There is no sports program at the university.

Disabled Students: 50% of the campus is accessible to disabled students. The following facilities are available: special parking and special class scheduling.

Services: In addition to many counseling and information services, tutoring is available in some subjects, including Hebrew.

Campus Safety and Security: Campus safety and security measures include escort service, pamphlets/posters/films, lighted pathways/sidewalks, a lighted parking lot, and guards during hours of operation.

Programs of Study: The university confers the B.A. degree. Associate, master's, and doctoral degrees are also awarded. Bachelor's degrees are awarded in SOCIAL SCIENCE (Judaic studies).

Required: A total 60 credits of Jewish studies plus 60 credits of general studies, with a GPA of 2.0, is required for graduation.

Special: Cooperative programs with the University of Maryland/Baltimore County, cross-registration with Johns Hopkins and Towson State universities, and study in Israel are available.

Faculty/Classroom: No introductory courses are taught by graduate students. The average class size in an introductory lecture and in a regular course offering is 10.

Requirements: A candidate's high school record, previous college record, additional Jewish education, and Jewish communal activity are reviewed by the dean, who also conducts a personal interview. AP and CLEP credits are accepted. Important factors in the admissions decision are recommendations by school officials, personality/intangible qualities, and evidence of special talent.

Procedure: Freshmen are admitted to all sessions. There are early decision and early admissions plans. Application deadlines are open. Application fee is $20. Notification is sent on a rolling basis.

Transfer: 30 credits of 120 must be completed at the university.

Visiting: There are guides for informal visits and visitors may sit in on classes. To schedule a visit, contact Dean Judy Meltzer.

Financial Aid: In 1995–96, all students received some form of financial and need-based aid. The average freshman award was $4515. Of that total, scholarships or need-based grants averaged $1470 ($2940 maximum); and loans averaged $3045 ($5633 maximum). The university is a member of CSS. The FAFSA and the college's own financial statement are required. The application deadline for fall entry is September 5.

International Students: There are currently 4 international students enrolled. Students must score 500 on the TOEFL or take the college's own test.

Computers: The college provides computer facilities for student use. PCs in the computer room, with Hebrew language software, are available for word processing and computer course assignments. All students may access the system. There are no time limits and no fees.

Graduates: In 1994–95, 5 bachelor's degrees were awarded.

Admissions Contact: Judy Meltzer, Dean.

BOWIE STATE UNIVERSITY
D-3

Bowie, MD 20715
(301) 464-6563

Full-time: 938 men, 1441 women	Faculty: 127; IIA, --$
Part-time: 326 men, 718 women	Ph.D.s: 50%
Graduate: 601 men, 1234 women	Student/Faculty: 19 to 1
Year: semesters, summer session	Tuition: $3019 ($6161)
Application Deadline: April 1	Room & Board: $4136
Freshman Class: 2056 applied, 974 accepted, 486 enrolled	
SAT I Verbal/Math: 376/396	**LESS COMPETITIVE**

Bowie State University, founded in 1865, is a publicly funded institution offering undergraduate and graduate degrees in the liberal arts. The school is a part of the University of Maryland System of Higher Education. In addition to regional accreditation, Bowie State has baccalaureate program accreditation with CSWE, NCATE, and NLN. The library contains 255,282 volumes, 598,007 microform items, and 1055 audiovisual forms, and subscribes to 1287 periodicals. Computerized library sources and services include interlibrary loans. Special learning facilities include an art gallery, radio station, TV station, and the Adler-Dreikurs Institute of Human Relations. The 312-acre campus is in a suburban area 18 miles north of Washington, D.C. Including residence halls, there are 20 buildings on campus.

Student Life: 84% of undergraduates are from Maryland. Students come from 25 states. 74% are African American; 20% white. The average age of freshmen is 20; all undergraduates, 22. 33% do not continue beyond their first year; 20% remain to graduate.

Housing: 965 students can be accommodated in college housing. College-sponsored living facilities include single-sex and coed dormitories. In addition there are honors houses. On-campus housing is available on a first-come, first-served basis. Priority is given to out-of-town students. 77% of students commute. Alcohol is not permitted. All students may keep cars on campus.

Activities: 25% of men belong to 15 local and 11 national fraternities; 18% of women belong to 4 national sororities. There are 40 groups on campus, including art, band, cheerleading, choir, chorale, dance, drama, honors, international, jazz band, literary magazine, marching band, newspaper, pep band, political, professional, radio and TV, religious, social, social service, student government, and yearbook. Popular campus events include Black History Month Convocation, Parents/Founders Day, Fine Arts Festival, Honors Convocation, Commencement, and Fall Convocation.

Sports: There are 5 intercollegiate sports for men and 4 for women, and 2 intramural sports for men and 2 for women. Athletic and recreation facilities include a gymnasium, a stadium, an indoor pool, 6 tennis courts, an exercise room, a baseball field, a track, and 4 outdoor basketball courts.

Disabled Students: The following facilities are available: wheelchair ramps, elevators, special parking, specially equipped rest rooms, lowered telephones, and wide doors.

Services: In addition to counseling and information services, there is a reader service for the blind, and remedial math, reading, and writing.

Campus Safety and Security: Campus safety and security measures include 24-hour foot and vehicle patrol, self-defense education, escort service, and shuttle buses. In addition, there are informal discussions, pamphlets/posters/films, emergency telephones, and lighted pathways/sidewalks.

Programs of Study: Bowie State confers B.A., B.S., B.S.E., and B.S.N. degrees. Master's degrees are also awarded. Bachelor's degrees are awarded in BIOLOGICAL SCIENCE (biology/biological science), BUSINESS (business administration and management), COMMUNICATIONS AND THE ARTS (broadcasting, dramatic arts, fine arts, journalism, music, and public relations), COMPUTER AND PHYSICAL SCIENCE (computer science), EDUCATION (art, early childhood, and elementary), ENGINEERING AND ENVIRONMENTAL DESIGN (computer technology), HEALTH PROFESSIONS (nursing), SOCIAL SCIENCE (criminal justice, history, international studies, political science/government, psychology, social work, and sociology). Business administration, computer science, and elementary education have the largest enrollments.

Required: A total of 120 credit hours is required for graduation. The minimum GPA required is 1.7 to 1.9 for the freshman year and 2.0 from the sophomore year on. The number of hours that must be taken in a student's major varies. All students must complete 48 credits in general studies, including 18 credits in social science, 9 each in communication skills, humanities, science, and mathematics, 2 in education, and 1 in freshman orientation.

Special: The school offers cooperative programs, an internship in practice teaching, work-study programs, B.A.-B.S. degree, dual majors, credit for life experience, and a 3–2 engineering degree. Dual-degree programs in engineering and dentistry are available at the University of Maryland. Cross-registration is offered with Coppin State, Morgan State, and Townson State Colleges, and the Universities of Baltimore and Maryland/Baltimore County. There is a fresh-

man honors program on campus, as well as 12 national honor societies.

Faculty/Classroom: 61% of faculty are male; 39%, female. No introductory courses are taught by graduate students.

Admissions: 47% of the 1995–96 applicants were accepted.

Requirements: The SAT I is required, with a minimum composite score of 700 (350 on the verbal and 350 on the mathematics). A minimum GPA of 2.0 is required. Applicants should be graduates of an accredited secondary school. The GED is accepted. 9 academic credits are required. Secondary school courses should include 4 years of English, 3 of mathematics, 2 each of history and social studies, and 1 each of science and a foreign language. AP and CLEP credits are accepted.

Procedure: Freshmen are admitted in the fall and spring. Entrance exams should be taken before the end of January for fall application. There are early decision and early admissions plans. Applications should be filed by April 1 for fall entry and November 1 for spring entry, along with an application fee of $10.

Transfer: 403 transfer students enrolled in a recent year. Applicants must have a minimum GPA of 2.0. The SAT I is required if fewer than 25 credit hours are being transferred. 30 credits of 120 must be completed at Bowie State.

Visiting: There are regularly scheduled orientations for prospective students. There are guides for informal visits. To schedule a visit, contact Hope Y. Savoy at (301) 464-6560.

Financial Aid: In a recent year, 64% of all freshmen and 68% of continuing students received some form of financial aid. Scholarships or need-based grants averaged $200 ($6000 maximum); loans averaged $200 ($4000 maximum); and work contracts averaged $200 ($1000 maximum). 30% of undergraduate students work part-time. Average earnings from campus work for the school year are $1000. The average financial indebtedness of the recent graduate was $5619. Bowie State is a member of CSS. The FAF and the college's own financial statement are required. The application deadline for fall entry is June 1.

International Students: There were 183 international students enrolled in a recent year. They must take the TOEFL and achieve a minimum score of 500. The student must also take the college's own entrance exam.

Computers: The college provides computer facilities for student use. The mainframe is a DEC VAX 6210. Microcomputers are available in the computing center for academic purposes. Students may request accounts on the mainframe in conjunction with course work. The system may be used by any students requiring access to a computer to complete an academic assignment. Students may access the system 24 hours a day. There are no time limits and no fees.

Graduates: In a recent year, 378 bachelor's degrees were awarded. The most popular majors among graduates were business administration (33%), elementary education (9%), and nursing (7%). Within an average freshman class, 14% graduate in 5 years and 6% in 6 years.

Admissions Contact: Dharmi Chaudhari.

CAPITOL COLLEGE
D-3

Laurel, MD 20708
(301) 953-3200
(800) 950–1992; FAX: (301) 953-1442

Full-time: 292 men, 32 women	Faculty: 21; IIB, -$
Part-time: 306 men, 49 women	Ph.D.s: 1%
Graduate: 78 men, 24 women	Student/Faculty: 15 to 1
Year: semesters, summer session	Tuition: $8766
Application Deadline: open	Room & Board: $2812
Freshman Class: 100 applied, 85 accepted, 45 enrolled	
SAT I Verbal/Math: 345/465	**LESS COMPETITIVE**

Capitol College was originally founded in 1927 as the Capitol Radio Engineering Institute, a correspondence school. Today it is a private coeducational college offering undergraduate programs in engineering. There is 1 graduate school. In addition to regional accreditation, the college has baccalaureate program accreditation with ABET. The library contains 10,000 volumes, and subscribes to 100 periodicals. Computerized library sources and services include the card catalog, interlibrary loans, and database searching. Special learning facilities include a learning resource center and state-of-the-art laboratories. The 52-acre campus is in a rural area 19 miles north of Washington, D.C. Including residence halls, there are 9 buildings on campus.

Student Life: 77% of undergraduates are from Maryland. Students come from 12 states and 17 foreign countries. 57% are white; 26% African American. The average age of freshmen is 24; all undergraduates, 29.

Housing: 100 students can be accommodated in college housing. College-sponsored living facilities include coed on-campus apartments. On-campus housing is available on a first-come, first-served basis. Priority is given to out-of-town students. 87% of students commute. All students may keep cars on campus.

Activities: There are no fraternities or sororities. There are 17 groups on campus, including chess, computers, literary magazine, newspaper, and student government. Popular campus events include Octoberfest and Spring Bash.

Sports: Athletic and recreation facilities include an off-campus gymnasium, a basketball court, a student center, and an athletic field.

Disabled Students: All of the campus is accessible to disabled students. The following facilities are available: wheelchair ramps, elevators, special parking, specially equipped rest rooms, and lowered drinking fountains.

Services: In addition to many counseling and information services, tutoring is available in most subjects, including mathematics, electronics, English, and developmental English.

Campus Safety and Security: Campus safety and security measures include lighted pathways/sidewalks.

Programs of Study: The college confers the B.S. degree. Associate and master's degrees are also awarded. Bachelor's degrees are awarded in COMMUNICATIONS AND THE ARTS (telecommunications), COMPUTER AND PHYSICAL SCIENCE (optics), ENGINEERING AND ENVIRONMENTAL DESIGN (computer engineering, electrical/electronics engineering, and engineering technology). Electrical/electronics engineering is the strongest academically and has the largest enrollment.

Required: A minimum GPA of 2.0 and 130 to 137 credit hours are required for graduation. Additional curriculum requirements vary with the major.

Special: Internships and work-study programs are offered through the school's cooperative education program. There are 2 national honor societies on campus.

Faculty/Classroom: 78% of faculty are male; 22%, female. All teach undergraduates. No introductory courses are taught by graduate students. The average class size in an introductory lecture is 22 and in a regular course offering, 22.

Admissions: 85% of the 1995–96 applicants were accepted. 1 freshman graduated first in his/her class.

Requirements: The SAT I is required, with a minimum composite score of 800. A minimum GPA of 2.5 is required. Applicants should be graduates of an accredited secondary school. The GED is accepted. 20 academic credits or 20 Carnegie units are required. Secondary school courses must include 4 units of English, 3 of mathematics, and 2 each of science and social studies. An essay and an interview are recommended. Applications are accepted on-line at http://www.capcol.edu/capcol. AP and CLEP credits are accepted. Important factors in the admissions decision are advanced placement or honor courses, recommendations by school officials, and extracurricular activities record.

Procedure: Freshmen are admitted to all sessions. Entrance exams should be taken by March 1. Application deadlines are open. Application fee is $25. Notification is sent on a rolling basis.

Transfer: 120 transfer students enrolled in 1995–96. Transfer students must have earned 15 college credits and a minimum GPA of 2.0. 40 credits of 130 to 137 must be completed at the college.

Visiting: There are regularly scheduled orientations for prospective students. There are guides for informal visits and visitors may sit in on classes and stay overnight at the school. To schedule a visit, contact the Admissions Office.

Financial Aid: In a recent year, 46% of all freshmen and 28% of continuing students received some form of financial aid. The average freshman award was $8325. Of that total, scholarships or need-based grants averaged $1900 ($2800 maximum); loans averaged $4625 ($7500 maximum); and work contracts averaged $1800 ($2500 maximum). The average financial indebtedness of a recent graduate was $10,000. the college is a member of CSS. The FAF is required. The application deadline for fall entry is March 15.

International Students: There were 28 international students enrolled in a recent year. The school actively recruits these students. They must take the TOEFL and achieve a minimum score of 500.

Computers: The college provides computer facilities for student use. The mainframe is a DEC VAX 11/750. There are also 25 Tandy, IBM PC, and TRS80 microcomputers available in laboratories. All students may access the system. There are no time limits and no fees. It is recommended that students in computer engineering technology have personal computers.

Admissions Contact: Anthony Miller, Director of Admissions. E-mail: admissions@capcol.edu.

COLLEGE OF NOTRE DAME OF MARYLAND D-2
Baltimore, MD 21210 (410) 532-5330
(800) 435-0200; FAX: (410) 532-6287

Full-time: 1 man, 730 women	**Faculty:** 74; IIB, -$
Part-time: 212 men, 1723 women	**Ph.D.s:** 65%
Graduate: 74 men, 474 women	**Student/Faculty:** 10 to 1
Year: 4–1–4, summer session	**Tuition:** $11,840
Application Deadline: February 15	**Room & Board:** $5845
Freshman Class: 484 applied, 373 accepted, 183 enrolled	
SAT I: required	**COMPETITIVE**

The College of Notre Dame of Maryland, founded in 1873, is a private, liberal arts institution primarily for women and affiliated with the Catholic Church. There is 1 graduate school. In addition to regional accreditation, Notre Dame has baccalaureate program accreditation with NLN. The library contains 290,000 volumes, 378,138 microform items, and 24,000 audiovisual forms, and subscribes to 2000 periodicals. Computerized library sources and services include the card catalog and database searching. Special learning facilities include a learning resource center, art gallery, planetarium, radio station, TV station, graphic arts studio, roof-top greenhouse, and cultural center. The 58-acre campus is in a suburban area 10 miles north of Baltimore. Including residence halls, there are 11 buildings.

Student Life: 70% of undergraduates are from Maryland. Students come from 21 states. 72% are from public schools; 28% from private.

Housing: 450 students can be accommodated in college housing. College-sponsored living facilities include single-sex dormitories. On-campus housing is guaranteed for all 4 years. 65% of students live on campus; of those, 60% remain on campus on weekends. Alcohol is not permitted. All students may keep cars on campus.

Activities: There are no fraternities or sororities. There are 24 groups on campus, including art, choir, dance, drama, ethnic, honors, international, literary magazine, newspaper, political, professional, radio and TV, religious, social, social service, student government, and yearbook. Popular campus events include honors convocation, Notre Dame Day, Tree Trim, and Family Weekend.

Sports: Athletic and recreation facilities include a sports/activities complex that houses racquetball courts, a dance studio, a fitness center, an indoor walking track, a game room, an activities resource center, and a basketball court.

Disabled Students: 98% of the campus is accessible to disabled students. The following facilities are available: wheelchair ramps, elevators, special parking, specially equipped rest rooms, and lowered drinking fountains.

Services: In addition to many counseling and information services, tutoring is available in most subjects.

Campus Safety and Security: Campus safety and security measures include 24-hour foot and vehicle patrol, self-defense education, escort service, and informal discussions. There are pamphlets/posters/films and lighted pathways/sidewalks.

Programs of Study: Notre Dame confers B.A. and B.S. degrees. Master's degrees are also awarded. Bachelor's degrees are awarded in BIOLOGICAL SCIENCE (biology/biological science), BUSINESS (accounting, banking and finance, business administration and management, international business management, and marketing/retailing/merchandising), COMMUNICATIONS AND THE ARTS (art history and appreciation, classics, communications, English, graphic design, modern language, music, photography, and studio art), COMPUTER AND PHYSICAL SCIENCE (chemistry, computer science, information sciences and systems, mathematics, and physics), EDUCATION (art, early childhood, elementary, foreign languages, music, science, secondary, and special), ENGINEERING AND ENVIRONMENTAL DESIGN (preengineering), HEALTH PROFESSIONS (nursing, predentistry, premedicine, and prepharmacy), SOCIAL SCIENCE (economics, history, interdisciplinary studies, international relations, liberal arts/general studies, political science/government, prelaw, psychology, and religion). Business, education, and communication arts are the strongest academically and have the largest enrollments.

Required: To graduate, students must complete a total of 128 credit hours with a GPA of 2.0 (2.5 in many majors). All students must fulfill the distribution requirements in the general education core, the major, and electives, and must demonstrate proficiency in writing, public speaking, computer literacy, and library research. In most majors, a minimum of 42 hours is required. All students must take a speech course and 2 courses in physical education; some majors require senior practicums.

Special: The college offers cross-registration with Johns Hopkins, Towson State, and Morgan State universities; Coppin State, Goucher, and Loyola colleges; and the Maryland Institute College of Art. Study abroad, internships, dual bachelor's degrees in nursing and engineering, 3–2 engineering degrees with Johns Hopkins University and the University of Maryland, and pass/fail opitons are available. Notre Dame's Weekend College offers bachelor's degree programs for employed adults. There is a freshman honors program on campus, as well as 8 national honor societies. 4 departments have honors programs.

Faculty/Classroom: 30% of faculty are male; 70%, female. All teach undergraduates. The average class size in an introductory lecture is 30; in a laboratory, 20; and in a regular course offering, 20.

Admissions: 77% of the 1995–96 applicants were accepted. The SAT I scores for the 1995–96 freshman class were as follows: Verbal—65% below 500, 25% between 500 and 599, 8% between 600 and 700, and 2% above 700; Math—59% below 500, 25% between 500 and 599, 14% between 600 and 700, and 2% above 700. 49% of the current freshmen were in the top fifth of their class; 83% were in the top half. In a recent year, there was 1 National Merit finalist.

Requirements: The SAT I is required. In addition, applicants should be graduates of an accredited secondary school with a 2.5 GPA. 18 academic credits are required, including 4 units of English, 3 each of mathematics and a foreign language, and 2 each of history and science, plus 4 electives. An essay is required and an interview is recommended. AP credits are accepted. Notre Dame offers its viewbook and application on disk; recommendations and essay can also be submitted through this option. Important factors in the admissions decision are recommendations by school officials, advanced placement or honor courses, and leadership record.

Procedure: Freshmen are admitted fall and spring. Entrance exams should be taken no later than January of the senior year. There are early decision, early admissions, and deferred admissions plans. 52 early decision candidates were accepted for the 1995–96 freshman class. Early decision applications should be filed by November 15; regular applications, by February 15 for fall entry and December 15 for spring entry, along with an application fee of $25. Notification of early decision is sent December 1; regular decision, within 2 4o 4 weeks of receipt of the completed application.

Transfer: 35 transfer students enrolled in a recent year. Notre Dame requires a minimum GPA of 2.5 for transfer students but recommends a GPA of 3.0. A combined score of 800 is required for the SAT I and 18 for the ACT. Students must also submit a letter of recommendation and an essay. 60 credits of 128 must be completed at Notre Dame.

Visiting: There are regularly scheduled orientations for prospective students, consisting of programs in June and January, each of which includes a stay in the dormitory, registration, and advisement. There are guides for informal visits and visitors may sit in on classes. To schedule a visit, contact the Office of Admissions.

Financial Aid: In 1995–96, 94% of all freshmen and 86% of continuing students received some form of financial aid. 72% of freshmen and 68% of continuing students received need-based aid. The average freshman award was $12,763. Of that total, scholarships or need-based grants averaged $8500 ($9235 maximum); loans averaged $2625 (maximum); and work contracts averaged $700 (maximum). Average earnings from campus work for the school year are $700. The average financial indebtedness of the recent graduate was $10,000. Notre Dame is a member of CSS. The FAF or FAFSA and the Profile are required. The application deadline for fall entry is February 15.

International Students: There are currently 41 international students enrolled. The school actively recruits these students. They must take the TOEFL and the college's own entrance exam for placement purposes.

Computers: The college provides computer facilities for student use. The mainframe is a DEC MicroVAX II. There are 80 IBM, IBM-compatible, and Apple Macintosh microcomputer workstations located in academic and administrative buildings. Access to the Internet is possible. All students may access the system 7 days a week. There are no time limits and no fees.

Graduates: In 1995–96, 306 bachelor's degrees were awarded. The most popular majors among graduates were business (33%), education (8%), and liberal arts (8%).

Admissions Contact: Terry Boer, Director of Admissions and Enrollment Management.

COLUMBIA UNION COLLEGE   D-3

Takoma Park, MD 20912

Full-time: 225 men, 342 women	(301) 891–4230; (800) 835–4212
Part-time: 191 men, 367 women	Faculty: 39; IIB, --$
Graduate: none	Ph.D.s: 54%
Year: semesters, summer session	Student/Faculty: 15 to 1
Application Deadline: August 1	Tuition: $10,775
Freshman Class: 528 applied, 420 accepted, 166 enrolled	Room & Board: $3850
SAT I Verbal/Math: 420/440	ACT: 22 COMPETITIVE

Columbia Union College, founded in 1904, is a private liberal arts institution affiliated with the Seventh-day Adventist Church. In addition to regional accreditation, CUC has baccalaureate program accreditation with CAHEA and NLN. The library contains 125,000 volumes, 653 microform items, and 1965 audiovisual forms, and subscribes to 437 periodicals. Computerized library sources and services include

the card catalog, interlibrary loans, and database searching. Special learning facilities include a radio station. The 19-acre campus is in a suburban area 7 miles north of Washington, D.C. Including residence halls, there are 10 buildings on campus.

Student Life: 58% of undergraduates are from out-of-state, mostly the Middle Atlantic. Students come from 36 states, 53 foreign countries, and Canada. 31% are from public schools; 69% from private. 40% are white; 37% African American. The average age of freshmen is 18; all undergraduates, 28. 32% do not continue beyond their first year; 36% remain to graduate.

Housing: 440 students can be accommodated in college housing. College-sponsored living facilities include single-sex dormitories. On-campus housing is guaranteed for all 4 years. 73% of students commute. Alcohol is not permitted. All students may keep cars on campus.

Activities: There are no fraternities or sororities. There are 9 groups on campus, including band, choir, honors, newspaper, orchestra, radio and TV, religious, student government, and yearbook.

Sports: There are 6 intercollegiate sports for men and 5 for women, and 5 intramural sports for men and 4 for women. Athletic and recreation facilities include a swimming pool, a gymnasium, racquetball and tennis courts, a sports field, a student lounge, and a weight room.

Disabled Students: 1% of the campus is accessible to disabled students. The following facilities are available: elevators and specially equipped rest rooms.

Services: In addition to many counseling and information services, tutoring is available in some subjects, including all English, mathematics, and accounting courses. There is remedial math and writing.

Campus Safety and Security: Campus safety and security measures include 24-hour foot and vehicle patrol, escort service, informal discussions, and pamphlets/posters/films. In addition, there are lighted pathways/sidewalks.

Programs of Study: CUC confers B.A. and B.S. degrees. Associate degrees are also awarded. Bachelor's degrees are awarded in BIOLOGICAL SCIENCE (biochemistry), BUSINESS (accounting, business administration and management, management science, and personnel management), COMMUNICATIONS AND THE ARTS (communications, English, journalism, and music), COMPUTER AND PHYSICAL SCIENCE (chemistry, computer science, information sciences and systems, and mathematics), EDUCATION (early childhood, elementary, English, and mathematics), HEALTH PROFESSIONS (health care administration, medical laboratory technology, nursing, predentistry, and premedicine), SOCIAL SCIENCE (history, prelaw, psychology, and religion). Nursing and clinical laboratory science are the strongest academically. Business and nursing have the largest enrollments.

Required: To graduate, students must earn 120 to 128 credit hours, including 36 upper division, with a minimum GPA of 2.0, major GPA of 2.5. Students must take 12 hours of religion, 9 of social sciences, 8 of physical sciences, natural sciences, and mathematics, 7 of humanities, 3 of physical education and health, and 6 of practical and applied arts. Courses in English, communication, and computer science are also required.

Special: CUC offers co-op programs in business communication, computer science, English, mathematics, and nursing, internships in counseling psychology, work-study programs, a general studies degree, credit for life experience, nondegree study, and pass/fail options. Dual majors are available in engineering/chemistry, and mathematics with the University of Maryland. Students may study abroad in France, Spain, and Austria. There is an adult evening program for degree completion as well as an external (correspondence) degree. There is a freshman honors program on campus, as well as 6 national honor societies. 1 department has an honors program.

Faculty/Classroom: 65% of faculty are male; 35%, female. All teach undergraduates.

Admissions: 80% of the 1995–96 applicants were accepted. The SAT I scores for the 1995–96 freshman class were as follows: Verbal—76% below 500, 17% between 500 and 599, and 7% between 600 and 700; Math—63% below 500, 23% between 500 and 599, 12% between 600 and 700, and 2% above 700. The ACT scores were 35% below 21, 30% between 21 and 23, 18% between 24 and 26, 5% between 27 and 28, and 11% above 28. 1 freshman graduated first in the class.

Requirements: The SAT I or ACT is recommended, with a minimum composite score of 800, or at least 400 in each section, on the SAT I or 18 on the ACT. CUC requires applicants to be in the upper 50% of their class. A minimum GPA of 2.5 is required. Applicants must be graduates of an accredited secondary school. The GED is accepted. 21 Carnegie units are required, including 4 years of high school English and 2 years each of history, mathematics, and science. An essay is recommended and an interview is required. AP and CLEP credits are accepted. Important factors in the admissions decision are advanced placement or honor courses, leadership record, and recommendations by school officials.

Procedure: Freshmen are admitted to all sessions. Entrance exams should be taken in the fall semester of the senior year. There are early decision, early admissions, and deferred admissions plans. Applications should be filed by August 1 for fall entry, December 1 for spring entry, and May 1 for summer entry, along with an application fee of $15. Notification is sent on a rolling basis. 247 early decision candidates were accepted for the 1995–96 class.

Transfer: 107 transfer students enrolled in 1995–96. Students must have at least 12 hours of college credit and a minimum GPA of 2.0. 30 credits of 120 to 128 must be completed at CUC.

Visiting: There are regularly scheduled orientations for prospective students. There are guides for informal visits and visitors may sit in on classes and stay overnight at the school. To schedule a visit, contact the Office of College Advancement at (800) 492–1715 (in-state) or (800) 835–4212 (out-of-state).

Financial Aid: In 1995–96, 83% of all freshmen and 91% of continuing students received some form of financial aid. 55% of freshmen and 63% of continuing students received need-based aid. The average freshman award was $4975. Of that total, scholarships or need-based grants averaged $2200 ($10,500 maximum); loans averaged $2625 ($6625 maximum); and work contracts averaged $2000 (maximum). 96% of undergraduate students work part-time. The average financial indebtedness of the 1994–95 graduate was $19,230. CUC is a member of CSS. The FAFSA and the college's own financial statement are required. The application deadline for fall entry is March 31.

International Students: There are currently 36 international students enrolled. They must take the TOEFL, the MELAB, or the college's own test.

Computers: The college provides computer facilities for student use. The mainframes are an AT&T 3B2/400 and an HP 932. There are also 20 IBM and AT&T microcomputers available in the computer laboratory and in academic departments. Students in computer classes may access the system 8 A.M. to midnight. There are no time limits and no fees.

Graduates: In 1994–95, 271 bachelor's degrees were awarded. The most popular majors among graduates were business (30%), health care administration (15%), and nursing (11%). Within an average freshman class, 21% graduate in 4 years.

Admissions Contact: Sheila Burnette, Director of Admissions. A campus video is available.

COPPIN STATE COLLEGE
Baltimore, MD 21216

D-2

(410) 383-5990
(800) 635-3674; FAX: (410) 333-7094

Full-time: 581 men, 1482 women	Faculty: 66
Part-time: 252 men, 692 women	Ph.D.s: 64%
Graduate: 140 men, 393 women	Student/Faculty: 31 to 1
Year: semesters, summer session	Tuition: $2749 ($5963)
Application Deadline: July 15	Room & Board: $4640
Freshman Class: 2199 applied, 1039 accepted, 446 enrolled	
SAT I Verbal/Math: 392/405	COMPETITIVE

Coppin State College, founded in 1900, offers undergraduate programs in liberal arts, teacher education, and nursing. There are 3 undergraduate schools and 1 graduate school. In addition to regional accreditation, Coppin has baccalaureate program accreditation with NCATE and NLN. The library contains 200,000 volumes and 233,000 microform items, and subscribes to 715 periodicals. Computerized library sources and services include the card catalog and interlibrary loans. Special learning facilities include a learning resource center, TV station, and an on-campus video production company. The 38-acre campus is in an urban area in Baltimore. Including residence halls, there are 9 buildings on campus.

Student Life: 90% of undergraduates are from Maryland. Students come from 10 states and 5 foreign countries. 90% are from public schools; 10% from private. 80% are African American; 10% white. The average age of freshmen is 19; all undergraduates, 23.

Housing: 300 students can be accommodated in college housing. College-sponsored living facilities include coed dormitories. The housing office maintains lists of community housing available. On-campus housing is guaranteed for all 4 years. 93% of students commute. Alcohol is not permitted. All students may keep cars on campus.

Activities: 45% of men belong to 10 national fraternities; 27% of women belong to 10 national sororities. There are 40 groups on campus, including cheerleading, choir, chorus, computers, dance, drama, ethnic, film, honors, international, newspaper, political, professional, radio and TV, religious, social, social service, student government, and yearbook. Popular campus events include the Lyceum Series.

Sports: There are 7 intercollegiate sports each for men and women, and 5 intramural sports each for men and women. Athletic and recreation facilities include a 2500-seat gymnasium, an indoor swimming pool, handball and racquetball courts, a soccer field, dance studio, weight room, a track, and a baseball field.

Disabled Students: 90% of the campus is accessible to disabled students. The following facilities are available: wheelchair ramps, elevators, special parking, specially equipped rest rooms, lowered drinking fountains, lowered telephones, and individual attention for students requiring specialized materials, equipment, or instructional style accommodation.

Services: There is remedial math, reading, and writing.

Campus Safety and Security: Campus safety and security measures include 24-hour foot and vehicle patrol, escort service, pamphlets/posters/films, and emergency telephones. There are lighted pathways/sidewalks.

Programs of Study: Coppin confers B.A., B.S., and B.S.N. degrees. Master's degrees are also awarded. Bachelor's degrees are awarded in BIOLOGICAL SCIENCE (biology/biological science), BUSINESS (business administration and management and marketing management), COMMUNICATIONS AND THE ARTS (English), COMPUTER AND PHYSICAL SCIENCE (chemistry, computer science, and mathematics), EDUCATION (elementary and special), ENGINEERING AND ENVIRONMENTAL DESIGN (preengineering), HEALTH PROFESSIONS (nursing, predentistry, and prepharmacy), SOCIAL SCIENCE (criminal justice, history, psychology, social science, and social work). Management science and education are the strongest academically and have the largest enrollments.

Required: To graduate, all students must have a 2.0 GPA and a minimum of 120 credit hours, with 36 to 40 hours in the major. Students must complete about 50 hours of liberal arts courses in English, mathematics, speech, history, health, physical education, natural and social sciences, and philosophy. All seniors must take a standardized exit examination relevant to their major.

Special: The college offers co-op programs with Dundalk Community College and Morgan University, internships in criminal justice and sociology, and dual majors in engineering, pharmacy, physical therapy, and dentistry. Internships and work study are also available. There is a freshman honors program on campus, as well as 1 national honor society.

Faculty/Classroom: The average class size in a regular course offering is 25.

Admissions: 47% of the 1995–96 applicants were accepted.

Requirements: The SAT I or ACT is required. Applicants must be graduates of an accredited secondary school with a 2.0 GPA, or have a GED certificate. Students must have completed 4 courses in English, 2 courses each in history, mathematics, science, and social studies, and 1 course in foreign language. Up to 15% of a freshman class may be admitted conditionally without these requirements, and those students who graduated high school more than 5 years ago will be reviewed individually. CLEP credit is accepted. Important factors in the admissions decision are advanced placement or honor courses, extracurricular activities record, and evidence of special talent.

Procedure: Freshmen are admitted to all sessions. There are early decision and early admissions plans. Applications should be filed by July 15 for fall entry and December 15 for spring entry, along with an application fee of $20. Notification is sent on a rolling basis.

Transfer: 76 transfer students enrolled in a recent year. Applicants must have a minimum 2.0 GPA and be in good academic standing at the former institution. Applicants with fewer than 25 credits must meet freshman requirements. 30 credits of 120 must be completed at Coppin.

Visiting: There are regularly scheduled orientations for prospective students. There are guides for informal visits and visitors may sit in on classes. To schedule a visit, contact Admissions.

Financial Aid: In a recent year, 80% of all freshmen and 85% of continuing students received some form of financial aid. 70% of freshmen and 80% of continuing students received need-based aid. The average freshman award was $4500. Of that total, scholarships or need-based grants averaged $3300; and loans averaged $1200. Coppin is a member of CSS. The FAFSA and the college's own financial statement are required. The application deadline for fall entry is May 1.

International Students: They must score 500 on the TOEFL.

Computers: The college provides computer facilities for student use. The mainframe is a DEC VAX 11/780. There are more than 200 personal computers available for students. All students may access the system. There are no time limits and no fees.

Graduates: In a recent year, 258 bachelor's degrees were awarded.

Admissions Contact: Admissions Counselors.

FROSTBURG STATE UNIVERSITY
B-1

Frostburg, MD 21532 (301) 689-4201

Full-time: 4070 men and women	Faculty: 244; IIA, --$
Part-time: 489 men and women	Ph.D.s: 72%
Graduate: 868 men and women	Student/Faculty: 17 to 1
Year: semesters, summer session	Tuition: $3072 ($6548)
Application Deadline: open	Room & Board: $4274
Freshman Class: 2907 applied, 2305 accepted, 915 enrolled	
SAT I: required	**COMPETITIVE**

Frostburg State University, founded in 1898, is a part of the University of Maryland system. The university offers programs through the schools of arts and humanities, business, natural and social science, and education. There are 4 undergraduate and 7 graduate schools. The library contains 245,000 volumes and 31,448 audiovisual forms, and subscribes to 1281 periodicals. Computerized library sources and services include the card catalog, interlibrary loans, and database searching. Special learning facilities include a learning resource center, art gallery, natural history museum, planetarium, and radio station. The 260-acre campus is in a small town about 150 miles west of Baltimore and northwest of Washington D.C. Including residence halls, there are 41 buildings on campus.

Student Life: 85% of undergraduates are from Maryland. Students come from 30 states. 90% are white. The average age of freshmen is 18; all undergraduates, 22. 22% do not continue beyond their first year.

Housing: 1900 students can be accommodated in college housing. College-sponsored living facilities include single-sex and coed dormitories. In addition there are honors houses, special interest houses, and international houses. On-campus housing is guaranteed for all 4 years. All students may keep cars on campus.

Activities: 15% of men belong to 9 national fraternities; 15% of women belong to 6 national sororities. There are 150 groups on campus, including art, band, cheerleading, choir, chorale, chorus, computers, dance, drama, drill team, ethnic, gay, honors, international, jazz band, literary magazine, marching band, musical theater, newspaper, orchestra, pep band, photography, political, professional, radio and TV, religious, social, social service, student government, symphony, and yearbook. Popular campus events include Homecoming, Parents Weekend, Siblings Weekend, and Festival of Africa.

Sports: There are 9 intercollegiate sports for men and 11 for women, and 5 intramural sports for men and 4 for women. Athletic and recreation facilities include a game room, a 3600-seat arena, a practice gymnasium, 5 athletic fields, 2 intramural fields, a swimming pool, a baseball, golf, and archery room, a dance studio, a wellness room, and 6 lighted tennis courts.

Disabled Students: All of the campus is accessible to disabled students. The following facilities are available: wheelchair ramps, elevators, special parking, specially equipped rest rooms, special class scheduling, lowered drinking fountains, and lowered telephones.

Services: In addition to many counseling and information services, tutoring is available in every subject. There is a reader service for the blind, and remedial math, reading, and writing.

Campus Safety and Security: Campus safety and security measures include 24-hour foot and vehicle patrol, escort service, informal discussions, and pamphlets/posters/films. In addition, there are emergency telephones and lighted pathways/sidewalks.

Programs of Study: FSU confers B.A., B.S., and B.F.A. degrees. Master's degrees are also awarded. Bachelor's degrees are awarded in AGRICULTURE (wildlife management), BIOLOGICAL SCIENCE (biology/biological science), BUSINESS (accounting, business administration and management, and recreation and leisure services), COMMUNICATIONS AND THE ARTS (communications, dramatic arts, English, fine arts, graphic design, languages, music, and speech/debate/rhetoric), COMPUTER AND PHYSICAL SCIENCE (chemistry, computer science, mathematics, and physics), EDUCATION (art, business, early childhood, music, and physical), ENGINEERING AND ENVIRONMENTAL DESIGN (environmental science), SOCIAL SCIENCE (economics, geography, history, international studies, philosophy, political science/government, psychology, social science, social work, and sociology). Business, education, and the natural sciences are the strongest academically. Business and education have the largest enrollments.

Required: A minimum GPA of 2.0 and 120 credit hours are required to graduate. All students must complete 6 to 9 credits in humanities and social sciences, 7 to 14 credits in natural science, and 3 to 6 credits in creative and performing arts. Courses in computer science, speech and composition, personalized health fitness, and mathematics are also required.

Special: FSU offers co-op programs with the University of Maryland, internships through individual departments, study abroad through the International Student Exchange Program, work-study and accelerated degree programs, B.A.-B.S. degrees in all majors, and dual majors in engineering. The 3–2 engineering degree is coordinated with the University of Maryland at College Park. Credit for experience, nondegree study, and pass/fail options are also available. There is a freshman honors program on campus, as well as 19 national honor societies. 16 departments have honors programs.

Faculty/Classroom: 65% of faculty are male; 35%, female. No introductory courses are taught by graduate students. The average class size in an introductory lecture is 30; in a laboratory, 15; and in a regular course offering, 25.

Admissions: 79% of the 1995–96 applicants were accepted. The SAT I scores for the 1995–96 freshman class were as follows: Verbal—78% below 500, 18% between 500 and 599, and 3% between 600 and 700; Math—60% below 500, 29% between 500 and 599, 10% between 600 and 700, and 1% above 700.

Requirements: The SAT I is required. A minimum GPA of 2.0 is required. In addition, applicants must be graduates of an accredited secondary school or have the GED. Secondary preparation should include 4 units of English, 3 each of mathematics and social studies, and 2 of science. An interview is recommended. AP and CLEP credits are accepted. Important factors in the admissions decision are recommendations by school officials, extracurricular activities record, and advanced placement or honor courses.

Procedure: Freshmen are admitted to all sessions. Entrance exams should be taken in the junior year. There is an early admissions plan. Application deadlines are open. Application fee is $30. Notification is sent on a rolling basis.

Transfer: 450 transfer students enrolled in 1995–96. Transfer students with 12 to 29 credits must have a minimum GPA of 2.5 and provide an official high school transcript and SAT I scores. Students with 30 or more credits must have a minimum GPA of 2.0. 30 credits of 120 must be completed at FSU.

Visiting: There are regularly scheduled orientations for prospective students, including tours Monday through Friday at 11 A.M. and 1 P.M. There are guides for informal visits and visitors may sit in on classes. To schedule a visit, contact the Office of Admissions.

Financial Aid: In 1995–96, 65% of all freshmen received some form of financial aid. 65% of freshmen and 53% of continuing students received need-based aid. The average freshman award was $3000. Of that total, scholarships or need-based grants averaged $2500 ($5500 maximum); loans averaged $3000 ($4600 maximum); and work contracts averaged $700 ($1000 maximum). 40% of undergraduate students work part-time. Average earnings from campus work for the school year are $700. The average financial indebtedness of the 1994–95 graduate was $5000. The FAFSA and the college's own financial statement are required. The application deadline for fall entry is April 1.

International Students: There are currently 16 international students enrolled. The school actively recruits these students. They must take the TOEFL and achieve a minimum score of 560. The student must also take the SAT I.

Computers: The college provides computer facilities for student use. The mainframe is a VAX/VMS 4300. There are 6 laboratories with microcomputers and word processing equipment in the computer center. All students may access the system by appointment. There are no time limits and no fees.

Graduates: In a recent year, 601 bachelor's degrees were awarded. 61 companies recruited on campus in a recent year.

Admissions Contact: M Edgerton Devel, Dean of Admissions.

GOUCHER COLLEGE
D-2

Baltimore, MD 21204 (410) 337-6100; (800) 638-4278

Full-time: 288 men, 691 women	Faculty: 84; IIB, av$
Part-time: 16 men, 70 women	Ph.D.s: 85%
Graduate: none	Student/Faculty: 12 to 1
Year: semesters	Tuition: $16,655
Application Deadline: February 1	Room & Board: $6260
Freshman Class: 1209 applied, 1030 accepted, 284 enrolled	
SAT I or ACT: required	**COMPETITIVE**

Goucher College, founded in 1885, is a private, coeducational liberal arts college. There are 2 graduate schools. The library contains 269,262 volumes, 58,419 microform items, and 7439 audiovisual forms, and subscribes to 1114 periodicals. Computerized library sources and services include the card catalog, interlibrary loans, and database searching. Special learning facilities include a learning resource center, art gallery, research centers in politics, information technology, and media, and the Public Leadership Institute for Women. The 287-acre campus is in a suburban area 8 miles north of Baltimore. Including residence halls, there are 18 buildings on campus.

Student Life: 57% of undergraduates are from out-of-state, mostly the Middle Atlantic. Students come from 41 states and 14 foreign countries. 71% are from public schools; 29% from private. 78% are white. 41% are Protestant; 40% Catholic; 17% Jewish. The average age of freshmen is 19; all undergraduates, 21. 15% do not continue beyond their first year; 85% remain to graduate.

Housing: 726 students can be accommodated in college housing. College-sponsored living facilities include single-sex and coed dormitories and on-campus apartments. In addition there are language houses and special interest houses. On-campus housing is guaranteed for all 4 years. 75% of students live on campus. Upperclassmen may keep cars on campus.

Activities: There are no fraternities or sororities. There are 43 groups on campus, including art, chorale, chorus, dance, drama, ethnic, film, gay, honors, international, literary magazine, musical theater, newspaper, orchestra, professional, religious, social, social service, student government, symphony, and yearbook. Popular campus events include Get into Goucher Day, Roctober Fest, Spring Fling, and Hot Steel Night.

Sports: There are 7 intercollegiate sports for men and 9 for women, and 12 intramural sports for men and 12 for women.

Disabled Students: 75% of the campus is accessible to disabled students. The following facilities are available: wheelchair ramps, special parking, specially equipped rest rooms, and special class scheduling.

Services: In addition to many counseling and information services, tutoring is available in most subjects. There is a reader service for the blind.

Campus Safety and Security: Campus safety and security measures include 24-hour foot and vehicle patrol, escort service, shuttle buses, and pamphlets/posters/films. In addition, there are emergency telephones, lighted pathways/sidewalks, a whistle-alert program, and a student safety and security committee.

Programs of Study: Goucher confers the B.A. degree. Master's degrees are also awarded. Bachelor's degrees are awarded in BIOLOGICAL SCIENCE (biology/biological science), COMMUNICATIONS AND THE ARTS (communications, dance, English, French, historic preservation, music, Russian, and Spanish), COMPUTER AND PHYSICAL SCIENCE (chemistry and mathematics), EDUCATION (elementary, secondary, and special), SOCIAL SCIENCE (American studies, economics, European studies, history, international relations, philosophy, political science/government, prelaw, psychology, religion, sociology, and women's studies). Science, political science, and English are the strongest academically. English, psychology, and education have the largest enrollments.

Required: To graduate, all students must complete 120 hours, with a minimum GPA of 2.0. Requirements include 2 courses each in the arts and natural sciences, including at least 1 laboratory course, 1 course each in the humanities, social sciences, and mathematics, and the year-long common intellectual experience course for freshmen. Students are also required to demonstrate proficiency in computers, writing, and a foreign language. Other requirements include a 4-class distribution requirement in physical education and at least 3 semester hours of an off-campus experience.

Special: Students may cross-register at Johns Hopkins University, Towson State College, Loyola College, Morgan State University, the College of Notre Dame, and Baltimore Hebrew University. A wide variety of internships are available in such fields as environmental management, scientific research, legislative assistance, and counseling. Study abroad is available in England, Russia, Germany, France, and Spain. A number of field experiences and internships are offered in Washington, D.C. through the Hughes Politics Center. Dual majors are encouraged, and student-designed majors and pass/fail options are also available. There is a freshman honors program on campus, as well as 1 national honor society, Phi Beta Kappa. 18 departments have honors programs.

Faculty/Classroom: 42% of faculty are male; 48%, female. All teach undergraduates, 90% do research, and 90% do both. The average class size in an introductory lecture is 25; in a laboratory, 15; and in a regular course offering, 12.

Admissions: 85% of the 1995–96 applicants were accepted. The SAT I scores for the 1995–96 freshman class were as follows: Verbal—40% below 500, 34% between 500 and 599, 18% between 600 and 700, and 8% above 700; Math—27% below 500, 34% between 500 and 599, 27% between 600 and 700, and 12% above 700. 50% of the current freshmen were in the top fifth of their class; 77% were in the top two fifths. 3 freshmen graduated first in their class.

Requirements: The SAT I or ACT is required. The SAT II: Subject test in writing is required of students taking the SAT I; 2 additional SAT II: Subject tests are encouraged but not required. Applicants should be graduates of an accredited high school or have earned the GED. Secondary preparation should include at least 14 academic units, preferably 4 in English, 3 in mathematics (algebra I and II and geometry), 2 each in the same foreign language and in laboratory science, and 2 or 3 in social studies. A personal essay is required and an interview is recommended. Prospective arts majors are urged to seek an audition or submit a portfolio. AP credits are accepted. Important factors in the admissions decision are extracurricular activities record, recommendations by school officials, and advanced placement or honor courses.

Procedure: Freshmen are admitted fall and spring. Entrance exams should be taken in spring of the junior year or fall of the senior year. There are early admissions and deferred admissions plans. Applications should be filed by February 1 for fall entry and December 1 for spring entry, along with an application fee of $40. Notification is sent April 1.

Transfer: 31 transfer students enrolled in 1995–96. Applicants must present a GPA of at least 2.5 in 30 hours of college work. An interview, a personal essay, and recommendations from college teachers or counselors are also required, as is a graded paper. 60 credits of 120 must be completed at Goucher.

Visiting: There are regularly scheduled orientations for prospective students, including an academic presentation, student panel, discussions, a campus tour, an interview, and an opportunity to sit in on classes and to meet with faculty, coaches, and other staff. There are guides for informal visits and visitors may sit in on classes and stay overnight at the school. To schedule a visit, contact the Office of Admissions.

Financial Aid: In a recent year, 70% of all freshmen and 71% of continuing students received some form of financial aid. 67% of freshmen and 52% of continuing students received need-based aid. The average freshman award was $13,000. Of that total, scholarships or need-based grants averaged $8300 ($13,000 maximum); loans averaged $2700 ($4000 maximum); and work contracts averaged $1010 ($1500 maximum). 46% of undergraduate students work part-time. Average earnings from campus work for the school year are $1200. The average financial indebtedness of a recent graduate was $9000. Goucher is a member of CSS. The FAF or FAFSA and the college's own financial statement are required. The application deadline for fall entry is February 15.

International Students: There were 16 international students enrolled in a recent year. The school actively recruits these students. They must take the TOEFL and achieve a minimum score of 550. The student must also take the SAT I.

Computers: The college provides computer facilities for student use. The mainframe is a Prime 4050. There is an Apple Macintosh computer laboratory as well as 150 PCs available in academic laboratories, dormitories, and the library. Some are available round the clock. There are no time limits and no fees.

Graduates: In a recent year, 216 bachelor's degrees were awarded. The most popular majors among graduates were English (12%), education (10%), and psychology (8%). Within an average freshman class, 75% graduate in 4 years and 85% in 5 years. 18 companies recruited on campus in a recent year.

Admissions Contact: Mr. Carlton E. Surbeck III, Director of Admissions.

HOOD COLLEGE
Frederick, MD 21701-8575
C-2
(301) 696-3400
(800) 922-1599; FAX: (301) 696-3819

Full-time: 48 men, 705 women	Faculty: 77; IIA, --$
Part-time: 97 men, 249 women	Ph.D.s: 89%
Graduate: 308 men, 660 women	Student/Faculty: 10 to 1
Year: semesters, summer session	Tuition: $14,930
Application Deadline: March 15	Room & Board: $6400
Freshman Class: 679 applied, 585 accepted, 177 enrolled	
SAT I Verbal/Math: 484/502	ACT: 22 COMPETITIVE

Hood College, founded in 1893, is an independent, comprehensive college primarily for women. Distinctive for its integration of the liberal arts and professional preparation, Hood offers 33 undergraduate majors. Hood has an especially strong reputation in the natural sciences, and is noted for its application of computing technology to its library, an expanded career center, and throughout the campus. There is 1 undergraduate school. In addition to regional accreditation, Hood has baccalaureate program accreditation with ADA and CAHEA. The library contains 175,000 volumes, 450,000 microform items, and 35,000 audiovisual forms, and subscribes to 920 periodicals. Computerized library sources and services include the card catalog, interlibrary loans, and database searching. Special learning facilities include a learning resource center, art gallery, aquatic center, child development laboratory, observatory, and energy management demonstration facility. The newest facilities include a library and information technology center, the hub of a campuswide computing network. The 50-acre campus is in an urban area 45 miles northwest of Washington, D.C. Including residence halls, there are 31 buildings on campus.

Student Life: 59% of undergraduates are from Maryland. Students come from 29 states and 20 foreign countries. 86% are from public schools; 14% from private. 70% are white; 17% African American. 60% claim no religious affiliation; 20% Protestant; 14% Catholic. The average age of freshmen is 18; all undergraduates, 20. 20% do not continue beyond their first year; 65% remain to graduate.

Housing: 600 students can be accommodated in college housing. College-sponsored living facilities include single-sex dormitories. In addition, there are language houses. Special interest floors in the residence halls may change each year; some have included a wellness floor, current issues floor, athletic floor, and non-smoking floors in each of the 5 large residence halls. On-campus housing is guaranteed for all 4 years. 70% of students live on campus; of those, 75% remain on campus on weekends. All students may keep cars on campus.

Activities: There are no fraternities or sororities. There are 49 groups on campus, including art, choir, chorale, chorus, computers, dance, drama, environmental, ethnic, gay, honors, international, literary magazine, musical theater, newspaper, opera, political, professional, radio and TV, religious, social, social service, student government, and yearbook. Popular campus events include Homecoming Weekend, Ring Formal, Mother-Daughter and Dad-Daughter weekends, performance of 'The Messiah' with the U.S. Naval Academy, Soph Revue, Black History Month, and Liberation of the Black Mind Weekend.

Sports: Athletic and recreation facilities include a weight training room, an aerobics room, indoor and outdoor swimming pools, a dance studio, a mile-long par course, an archery range, a softball diamond, tennis and volleyball courts, and field hockey and soccer fields.

Disabled Students: 35% of the campus is accessible to disabled students. The following facilities are available: wheelchair ramps, elevators, special parking, specially equipped rest rooms, and special class scheduling.

Services: In addition to many counseling and information services, tutoring is available in some subjects. Such services as reader service for the blind and interpreters for the hearing impaired are arranged for individual students. There is remedial math, reading, and writing. There are also services for students with learning disabilities.

Campus Safety and Security: Campus safety and security measures include 24-hour foot and vehicle patrol, escort service, informal discussions, and pamphlets/posters/films. In addition, there are emergency telephones, lighted pathways/sidewalks, and an electronic access control system with 24-hour monitoring in all residence halls.

Programs of Study: Hood confers B.A., B.S., and B.B.A. degrees. Master's degrees are also awarded. Bachelor's degrees are awarded in BIOLOGICAL SCIENCE (biochemistry, biology/biological science, and nutrition), BUSINESS (business administration and management, management science, and retailing), COMMUNICATIONS AND THE ARTS (art history and appreciation, communications, English, French, German, Spanish, and studio art), COMPUTER AND PHYSICAL SCIENCE (chemistry, computer science, information sciences and systems, and mathematics), EDUCATION (art, early childhood, English, foreign languages, home economics, mathematics, science, secondary, and special), ENGINEERING AND ENVIRONMENTAL DESIGN (environmental science), HEALTH PROFESSIONS (medical laboratory technology), SOCIAL SCIENCE (economics, history, Latin American studies, philosophy, political science/government, psychobiology, psychology, religion, social work, and sociology). Biology, chemistry, and mathematics are the strongest academically. Management, biology, and education have the largest enrollments.

Required: To graduate, students must complete a total of 124 credit hours, with a minimum GPA of 2.0. A minimum of 24 hours is required in a student's major, depending on the degree being sought. All students must complete 38 to 40 credits in the core curriculum, which includes basic skills courses, courses in methods in inquiry, and interdisciplinary courses in Western civilization, non-Western civilization and society, science, and technology.

Special: The college offers a Washington semester with American University, dual majors, student-designed majors, credit for life experience, nondegree study, pass/fail options, and cross-registration with area colleges and the Duke University Marine Sciences Education Consortium. Internships of up to 15 credits are available in all majors at more than 1000 sites throughout the United States and abroad. Students may study abroad in the Dominican Republic, Japan, Spain, France, and other countries. A 3–2 engineering degree is offered with George Washington University. Home economics students live in the Marx Resource Management Center for 6 weeks to gain practical experience in energy and water conservation. There is a freshman honors program on campus, as well as 11 national honor societies. All departments have honors programs.

Faculty/Classroom: 45% of faculty are male; 55%, female. All teach undergraduates. The average class size in an introductory lecture is 25; in a laboratory, 12; and in a regular course offering, 15.

Admissions: 86% of the 1995–96 applicants were accepted. The SAT I scores for the 1995–96 freshman class were as follows: Verbal—55% below 500, 31% between 500 and 599, 12% between 600 and 700, and 2% above 700; Math—49% below 500, 30% between 500 and 599, 19% between 600 and 700, and 2% above 700. The ACT scores were 38% below 21, 25% between 21 and 23, 25% between 24 and 26, 8% between 27 and 28, and 5% above 28. 48%

of the current freshmen were in the top fifth of their class; 78% were in the top two fifths. There was 1 National Merit finalist. 3 freshmen graduated first in their class.

Requirements: The SAT I or ACT is required. Hood requires applicants to be in the upper 40% of their class. A minimum GPA of 2.5 is required. In addition, applicants should be graduates of an accredited secondary school. The GED is accepted. Hood recommends the completion of at least 16 academic credits in high school, including courses in English, social sciences, natural sciences, foreign languages, and mathematics. An essay is required and an interview is recommended. Hood accepts applications via CollegeLink and any other IBM-compatible disk. AP and CLEP credits are accepted. Important factors in the admissions decision are advanced placement or honor courses, leadership record, and personality/intangible qualities.

Procedure: Freshmen are admitted in the fall and spring. Entrance exams should be taken in spring of the junior year or fall of the senior year. There are early decision, early admissions, and deferred admissions plans. Early decision applications should be filed by November 15; regular applications, by March 15 for fall entry and December 31 for spring entry, along with an application fee of $30. Notification of early decision is sent December 15; regular decision, April 15. 152 early decision candidates were accepted for the 1995–96 class.

Transfer: 49 transfer students enrolled in 1995–96. Applicants must have at least 12 college credits and a minimum GPA of 2.5. A total of 70 credits may be transferred. 30 credits of 124 must be completed at Hood.

Visiting: There are regularly scheduled orientations for prospective students, including tours and meetings with faculty, students, and administrators. One-day admission seminars offer the opportunity to participate in a faculty-taught seminar and an admissions interview, after which students receive an indication of their admission decision. There are guides for informal visits and visitors may sit in on classes and stay overnight at the school. To schedule a visit, contact the Office of Admissions.

Financial Aid: In 1995–96, 98% of all freshmen and 88% of continuing students received some form of financial aid. 77% of freshmen and 71% of continuing students received need-based aid. The average freshman award was $12,000. Of that total, scholarships or need-based grants averaged $7500 ($14,000 maximum); loans averaged $3000 ($5265 maximum); and work contracts averaged $1500. 35% of undergraduate students work part-time. Average earnings from campus work for the school year are $1500. The average financial indebtedness of the 1994–95 graduate was $12,000. Hood is a member of CSS. The FAFSA and CSS Profile Application are required. The application deadline for fall entry is March 31.

International Students: There are currently 31 international students enrolled. The school actively recruits these students. They must take the TOEFL and achieve a minimum score of 530. SAT I scores may be substituted for the TOEFL.

Computers: The college provides computer facilities for student use. The mainframe is a DEC VAX 4300. Students may use the 12 PCs in a 24-hour computing laboratory or the 16 terminals in the VAX laboratory to access the mainframe or dial in from off campus. There are 67 IBM-compatible microcomputers available in 6 student laboratories and 28 Apple and Macintosh microcomputers available in other laboratories. All students may access the system 24 hours per day from a PC in the 24-hour computing laboratory, from a student's PC in a residence hall, or from the student's home if there is a modem. Otherwise, the system may be accessed weekdays 8:30 A.M. to 12 midnight in the terminal laboratory. Student use is limited to 2 hours in a 24-hour period. There are no time limits for course-related work. There are no fees.

Graduates: In 1994–95, 229 bachelor's degrees were awarded. The most popular majors among graduates were management (20%), education (10%), and biology (9%). Within an average freshman class, 2% graduate in 3 years, 63% in 4 years, 65% in 5 years, and 68% in 6 years. 282 companies recruited on campus in 1994–95. Of the 1994 graduating class, 30% were enrolled in graduate school within 6 months of graduation and 80% had found employment.

Admissions Contact: Nancy Gillece, Director of Admissions. E-mail: admissions@nimue.hood.edu.

JOHNS HOPKINS UNIVERSITY D-2
Baltimore, MD 21218 (410) 516-8171

Full-time: 2126 men, 1301 women	Faculty: 356; I, av$
Part-time: 13 men, 4 women	Ph.D.s: 99%
Graduate: 1226 men, 935 women	Student/Faculty: 10 to 1
Year: 4–1–4, summer session	Tuition: $19,750
Application Deadline: January 1	Room & Board: $6955
Freshman Class: 7877 applied, 3313 accepted, 876 enrolled	
SAT I Verbal/Math: 610/700	ACT: 30 MOST COMPETITIVE

The Johns Hopkins University, founded in 1876, is a private, coeducational, multicampus institution offering undergraduate degrees through the schools of arts and sciences and engineering, and graduate degrees through those and the schools of international studies, nursing, medicine, hygiene and public health, and the Peabody Institute (music). There are 4 undergraduate and 8 graduate schools. In addition to regional accreditation, Johns Hopkins has baccalaureate program accreditation with ABET. The 2 libraries contain 2.3 million volumes and 28,587 audiovisual forms, and subscribe to 20,677 periodicals. Computerized library sources and services include the card catalog, interlibrary loans, and database searching. Special learning facilities include an art gallery, radio station, and TV station. The 140-acre campus is in an urban area 3 miles north of downtown Baltimore. Including residence halls, there are 33 buildings on campus.

Student Life: 85% of undergraduates are from out-of-state, mostly the Middle Atlantic. Students come from 50 states, 32 foreign countries, and Canada. 56% are from public schools; 44% from private. 65% are white; 22% Asian American. 30% are Protestant; 25% claim no religious affiliation; 25% Catholic; 15% Jewish. The average age of freshmen is 18; all undergraduates, 20. 5% do not continue beyond their first year; 88% remain to graduate.

Housing: 2200 students can be accommodated in college housing. College-sponsored living facilities include single-sex and coed dormitories, off-campus apartments, and married-student housing. In addition there are special interest houses. On-campus housing is guaranteed for freshman and sophomore years only. It is available on a lottery system for upperclassmen. 65% of students live on campus. Alcohol is not permitted. Upperclassmen may keep cars on campus.

Activities: 30% of men belong to 13 national fraternities; 25% of women belong to 3 national sororities. There are 150 groups on campus, including art, band, cheerleading, chess, choir, chorale, chorus, computers, dance, drama, ethnic, film, gay, honors, international, jazz band, literary magazine, marching band, musical theater, newspaper, opera, orchestra, pep band, photography, political, professional, radio and TV, religious, social, social service, student government, symphony, and yearbook. Popular campus events include Spring Fair, Fiji Islander, MSE Symposium, Cultural Awareness Week, and Relaxation Week.

Sports: There are 13 intercollegiate sports for men and 13 for women, and 18 intramural sports for men and 16 for women. Athletic and recreation facilities include a 4000-seat stadium, outdoor playing fields, a swimming pool and diving board, wrestling and fencing rooms, a weight room, saunas, and courts for basketball, volleyball, badminton, squash, and handball.

Disabled Students: 80% of the campus is accessible to disabled students. The following facilities are available: wheelchair ramps, elevators, special parking, specially equipped rest rooms, special class scheduling, lowered drinking fountains, and lowered telephones.

Services: In addition to many counseling and information services, tutoring is available in most subjects. There is a reader service for the blind.

Campus Safety and Security: Campus safety and security measures include 24-hour foot and vehicle patrol, self-defense education, escort service, and shuttle buses. In addition, there are informal discussions, pamphlets/posters/films, emergency telephones, and lighted pathways/sidewalks.

Programs of Study: Johns Hopkins confers B.A. and B.S. degrees. Master's and doctoral degrees are also awarded. Bachelor's degrees are awarded in BIOLOGICAL SCIENCE (biology/biological science, biophysics, and neurosciences), COMMUNICATIONS AND THE ARTS (art history and appreciation, classics, English, French, German, and music), COMPUTER AND PHYSICAL SCIENCE (chemistry, computer science, earth science, mathematics, and physics), ENGINEERING AND ENVIRONMENTAL DESIGN (biomedical engineering, chemical engineering, civil engineering, electrical/electronics engineering, engineering, engineering mechanics, environmental engineering, environmental science, materials engineering, and mechanical engineering), HEALTH PROFESSIONS (premedicine and public health), SOCIAL SCIENCE (anthropology, cognitive science, crosscultural studies, East Asian studies, economics, history, history of science, humanities, international studies, Latin American studies, Near Eastern studies, philosophy, political science/government, prelaw, psychology, sociology, and urban studies). The sciences, English, and engineering are the strongest academically. Biology, international studies, and biomedical engineering have the largest enrollments.

Required: Although there is no required core curriculum, all students must take 30 hours outside their major field. The B.A. requires a total of 120 hours; the B.S. in engineering requires 120 to 128 hours, depending on the major. A GPA of least 2.0 is required for graduation. All students must take at least 4 courses (2 for engineers) with a writing-intensive component in order to graduate.

Special: Johns Hopkins offers an extensive array of special programs, including internships, dual majors in music and arts and sciences or engineering, cross-registration with all Baltimore-area colleges and all Johns Hopkins divisions, a cooperative 5-year civil engineering program, a student-designed semester in Washington, D.C., and

various multidisciplinary programs. Students may enroll at Johns Hopkins in Bologna, Italy, or Nanjing, China, or arrange programs in Europe, South America, the Far East, or Australia. Accelerated degrees are available in 21 fields. Students may earn combined B.A.-B.S. degrees in biomedical, computer, or mathematical engineering or a combined B.A.-B.M. through the Peabody Institute. Pass/fail options are available in nonmajor courses. There are 7 national honor societies on campus, including Phi Beta Kappa. 25 departments have honors programs.

Faculty/Classroom: 94% of faculty are male; 6%, female. 99% teach undergraduates, 100% do research, and 99% do both. Graduate students teach 15% of introductory courses. The average class size in an introductory lecture is 300; in a laboratory, 50; and in a regular course offering, 30.

Admissions: 42% of the 1995–96 applicants were accepted. The SAT I scores for the 1995–96 freshman class were as follows: Verbal—5% below 500, 33% between 500 and 599, 51% between 600 and 700, and 11% above 700; Math—1% below 500, 8% between 500 and 599, 45% between 600 and 700, and 46% above 700. The ACT scores were 1% below 21, 3% between 21 and 23, 8% between 24 and 26, 29% between 27 and 28, and 59% above 28. 93% of the current freshmen were in the top fifth of their class; 99% were in the top two fifths. There were 87 National Merit finalists and 11 semifinalists. 91 freshmen graduated first in their class.

Requirements: The SAT I or ACT is required. Applicants should be graduates of an accredited secondary school or have the GED. The university recommends that secondary preparation include 4 years each of English and mathematics, 2 or 3 of social science or history, at least 2, preferably 3, of laboratory science, and 2 of a foreign language. Applicants must submit SAT II: Subject tests in writing and literature and 2 others of their choice. 2 personal essays are required, and an interview is recommended. Common App, CollegeLink, and MacApply computer disk applications are accepted. AP credits are accepted. Important factors in the admissions decision are advanced placement or honor courses, leadership record, and evidence of special talent.

Procedure: Freshmen are admitted in the fall. Entrance exams should be taken by January for regular decision, or November for early decision. There are early decision, early admissions, and deferred admissions plans. Early decision applications should be filed by November 15; regular applications, by January 1 for fall entry, along with an application fee of $50. Notification of early decision is sent December 15; regular decision, by April 15. 196 early decision candidates were accepted for the 1995–96 class. A waiting list is an active part of the admissions procedure, with about 6% of all applicants on the list.

Transfer: 35 transfer students enrolled in 1995–96. Applicants should have sophomore or junior standing and at least a B average in previous college work. Applications must include a written essay and at least 1 letter of recommendation. High school records and standardized test scores will also be considered. 60 credits of 120 to 128 must be completed at Johns Hopkins.

Visiting: There are regularly scheduled orientations for prospective students, including campus tours, group information sessions, and panel discussions with students and faculty. There are guides for informal visits and visitors may sit in on classes and stay overnight at the school. To schedule a visit, contact the Office of Undergraduate Admissions.

Financial Aid: In 1995–96, 55% of all students received some form of financial aid. 42% of all students received need-based aid. The average freshman award was $17,600. Of that total, scholarships or need-based grants averaged $12,200 ($21,000 maximum); loans averaged $3500 ($4600 maximum); and work contracts averaged $1800 ($1900 maximum). 50% of undergraduate students work part-time. Average earnings from campus work for the school year are $1500. The average financial indebtedness of the 1994–95 graduate was $13,000. Johns Hopkins is a member of CSS. The FAFSA and college's own financial statement are required. The application deadline for fall entry is February 1.

International Students: There are currently 155 international students enrolled. They must take the TOEFL and achieve a minimum score of 560. The student must also take the SAT I. Students must take SAT II: Subject Tests in writing and literature.

Computers: The college provides computer facilities for student use. The mainframes are an AT&T 3B4000, a DEC VAX 6410, an IBM 3081, and a UNIX O/S. Microcomputer laboratories are available for student use in academic buildings and in some residence halls. The laboratory in Krieger Hall is open 24 hours a day. All students may access the system 24 hours a day, 7 days a week. There are no time limits and no fees.

Graduates: In 1994–95, 788 bachelor's degrees were awarded. The most popular majors among graduates were biology (18%), biomedical engineering (10%), and international studies (8%). Within an average freshman class, 5% graduate in 3 years, 82% in 4 years, 88% in 5 years, and 88% in 6 years. 110 companies recruited on campus in 1994–95. Of the 1994 graduating class, 65% were enrolled in graduate school within 6 months of graduation and 32% had found employment.

Admissions Contact: Paul T. White, Director of Undergraduate Admissions. A campus video is available.

LOYOLA COLLEGE
D-2

Baltimore, MD 21210   (410) 532–5012; (800) 221–9107
Full-time: 1382 men, 1693 women   Faculty: 221; IIA, av$
Part-time: 77 men, 84 women   Ph.Ds: 89%
Graduate: 1304 men, 1824 women   Student/Faculty: 14 to 1
Year: semesters, summer session   Tuition: $14,260
Application Deadline: January 15   Room & Board: $5230
Freshman Class: 5536 applied, 3461 accepted, 801 enrolled
SAT I Verbal/Math: 523/581   **VERY COMPETITIVE**

Loyola College, founded in 1852, is a private, coeducational, liberal arts college affiliated with the Roman Catholic Church and the Jesuit tradition. It offers degree programs in arts and sciences, and business and management. There are 2 undergraduate schools. In addition to regional accreditation, Loyola has baccalaureate program accreditation with AACSB, ABET, CSAB, and NASDTEC. The library contains 307,276 volumes, 397,871 microform items, and 24,787 audiovisual forms, and subscribes to 2057 periodicals. Computerized library sources and services include interlibrary loans and database searching. Special learning facilities include an art gallery and radio station. The 63-acre campus is in a suburban area 3 miles from downtown Baltimore. Including residence halls, there are 22 buildings on campus.

Student Life: 66% of undergraduates are from out-of-state, mostly the Middle Atlantic. Students come from 36 states. 54% are from public schools; 46% from private. 88% are white. 78% are Catholic; 10% Protestant. The average age of freshmen is 18; all undergraduates, 20. 10% do not continue beyond their first year; 77% remain to graduate.

Housing: 2200 students can be accommodated in college housing. College-sponsored living facilities include single-sex and coed dormitories and on-campus apartments. In addition, there are honors houses and special interest houses. On-campus housing is available on a first-come, first-served basis. 74% of students live on campus. Alcohol is not permitted. Upperclassmen may keep cars on campus.

Activities: There are no fraternities or sororities. There are 80 groups on campus, including art, band, cheerleading, chess, choir, chorale, chorus, computers, dance, drama, ethnic, film, honors, international, jazz band, literary magazine, musical theater, newspaper, orchestra, pep band, photography, political, professional, radio and TV, religious, social, social service, student government, symphony, and yearbook. Popular campus events include Parents Weekend, International Festival, Senior 100 concerts, and SYR Dance.

Sports: There are 7 intercollegiate sports for men and 7 for women, and 11 intramural sports for men and 11 for women. Athletic and recreation facilities include a pool, a sauna, a weight room, racquetball, tennis, and squash courts, a 3000-seat arena, a 2000-seat multipurpose outdoor facility, and a fitness center.

Disabled Students: 95% of the campus is accessible to disabled students. The following facilities are available: wheelchair ramps, elevators, special parking, specially equipped rest rooms, special class scheduling, lowered drinking fountains, and lowered telephones.

Services: In addition to many counseling and information services, tutoring is available in most subjects. There is remedial math.

Campus Safety and Security: Campus safety and security measures include 24-hour foot and vehicle patrol, escort service, shuttle buses, and informal discussions. In addition, there are pamphlets/posters/films, emergency telephones, and lighted pathways/sidewalks.

Programs of Study: Loyola confers B.A., B.S., B.B.A., B.S.E.E., and B.S.E.S. degrees. Master's and doctoral degrees are also awarded. Bachelor's degrees are awarded in BIOLOGICAL SCIENCE (biology/biological science), BUSINESS (accounting and business administration and management), COMMUNICATIONS AND THE ARTS (communications, creative writing, English, fine arts, French, German, Latin, and Spanish), COMPUTER AND PHYSICAL SCIENCE (chemistry, computer science, mathematics, and physics), EDUCATION (elementary and secondary), ENGINEERING AND ENVIRONMENTAL DESIGN (electrical/electronics engineering and engineering), HEALTH PROFESSIONS (speech pathology/audiology), SOCIAL SCIENCE (economics, history, philosophy, political science/government, psychology, sociology, and theological studies). General business, communications, and accounting have the largest enrollments.

Required: All students must complete 120 hours, including 36 in the major, with at least a 2.0 GPA. The required core curriculum includes 3 courses in mathematics, computer science or natural science, 2 courses each in history, literature, philosophy, theology, and social science, 2 to 4 courses in a foreign language, and 1 course each in writing, ethics, and fine arts.

Special: Loyola offers cooperative programs with Johns Hopkins and Towson State Universities, Goucher College, and the College of Notre Dame of Maryland. Credit-bearing internships are available in most majors, and there are study-abroad programs in Thailand and Belgium. Work-study programs and dual majors are also offered. There is a freshman honors program on campus, as well as 18 national honor societies, including Phi Beta Kappa. 1 department has an honors program.

Faculty/Classroom: 61% of faculty are male; 39%, female. 90% teach undergraduates, 94% both teach and do research. No introductory courses are taught by graduate students. The average class size in an introductory lecture is 26; in a laboratory, 24; and in a regular course offering, 23.

Admissions: 63% of the 1995–96 applicants were accepted. The SAT I scores for the 1995–96 freshman class were as follows: Verbal—38% below 500, 43% between 500 and 599, 17% between 600 and 700, and 2% above 700; Math—14% below 500, 42% between 500 and 599, 35% between 600 and 700, and 9% above 700. 58% of the current freshmen were in the top fifth of their class; 87% were in the top two fifths. 13 freshmen graduated first in their class.

Requirements: The SAT I is required. Loyola requires applicants to be in the upper 30% of their class. A minimum GPA of 3.0 is required. Applicants should have graduated from an accredited secondary school or have earned the GED. Secondary preparation should include 4 years of English, 2 to 3 each of mathematics and foreign language, 1 to 2 of natural science, and 1 of history. A personal essay is required; an interview is recommended. AP and CLEP credits are accepted. Important factors in the admissions decision are advanced placement or honor courses, recommendations by school officials, and evidence of special talent.

Procedure: Freshmen are admitted to all sessions. Entrance exams should be taken by December of the senior year. There are early admissions and deferred admissions plans. Applications should be filed by January 15 for fall entry, December 15 for spring entry, and May 1 for summer entry, along with an application fee of $30. Notification is sent April 15. A waiting list is an active part of the admissions procedure, with about 1% of all applicants on the list.

Transfer: 109 transfer students enrolled in 1995–96. Transfer applicants should have at least a 2.5 GPA and should submit SAT I scores. 60 credits of 120 must be completed at Loyola.

Visiting: There are regularly scheduled orientations for prospective students, including a general information session, an interview, and a campus tour. There are guides for informal visits and visitors may sit in on classes. To schedule a visit, contact the Admissions Office at (410) 617–5012 or (800) 221–9107, ext. 5012.

Financial Aid: In 1995–96, 65% of all freshmen and 62% of continuing students received some form of financial aid. 49% of freshmen and 42% of continuing students received need-based aid. Scholarships or need-based grants averaged $5630 ($14,000 maximum); loans averaged $3050 ($3625 maximum); and work contracts averaged $1400 (maximum). 10% of undergraduate students work part-time. Average earnings from campus work for the school year are $1250. Loyola is a member of CSS. The FAF and the college's own financial statement are required. The application deadline for fall entry is March 1.

International Students: There are currently 68 international students enrolled. The school actively recruits these students. They must take the TOEFL and achieve a minimum score of 550. The student must also take the SAT I.

Computers: The college provides computer facilities for student use. There are 2 DEC VAX 11/785 mainframe computers. There are also more than 100 IBM PC, Apple IIe, and Macintosh personal computers available in the science center, library, and dormitories. All students may access the system. There are no time limits and no fees.

Graduates: In 1994–95, 662 bachelor's degrees were awarded. The most popular majors among graduates were business (23%), psychology (11%), and communications (9%). Within an average freshman class, 69% graduate in 4 years, 76% in 5 years, and 77% in 6 years. 214 companies recruited on campus in 1994–95. Of the 1994 graduating class, 25% were enrolled in graduate school within 6 months of graduation and 67% had found employment.

Admissions Contact: William Bossemeyer, Director of Admissions. A campus video is available.

MARYLAND INSTITUTE, COLLEGE OF ART   D-2
Baltimore, MD 21217   (410) 225-2222; FAX: (410) 225-2337

Full-time: 378 men, 416 women	Faculty: 60; IIB, +$
Part-time: 5 men, 18 women	Ph.D.s: 87%
Graduate: 45 men, 62 women	Student/Faculty: 13 to 1
Year: semesters, summer session	Tuition: $15,100
Application Deadline: March 1	Room & Board: $5390
Freshman Class: 811 applied, 538 accepted, 204 enrolled	
SAT I or ACT: see profile	SPECIAL

Maryland Institute, College of Art, founded in 1826, is a private, co-educational institution offering undergraduate and graduate degrees in the fine arts. There are 5 graduate schools. In addition to regional accreditation, Maryland Institute has baccalaureate program accreditation with NASAD. The library contains 51,000 volumes and 400 audiovisual forms, and subscribes to 200 periodicals. Special learning facilities include a learning resource center and 6 large art galleries, open to the public year-round, as well as a number of smaller, student-run galleries. The 12-acre campus is in an urban area in the Mount Royal cultural center of Baltimore. Including residence halls, there are 19 buildings on campus.

Student Life: 71% of undergraduates are from out of state, mostly the Northeast. Students come from 41 states, 44 foreign countries, and Canada. 80% are from public schools; 20% from private. 76% are white. The average age of freshmen is 19; all undergraduates, 21. 23% do not continue beyond their first year; 60% remain to graduate.

Housing: 350 students can be accommodated in college housing. College-sponsored living facilities include coed dormitories and on-campus apartments. All housing includes project rooms where students can do artwork 24 hours a day. On-campus housing is guaranteed for the freshman year only, is available on a first-come, first-served basis, and is available on a lottery system for upperclassmen. 85% of students live on campus; of those, 95% remain on campus on weekends. Alcohol is not permitted. All students may keep cars on campus.

Activities: There are no fraternities or sororities. There are 16 groups on campus, including art, dance, drama, ethnic, film, gay, international, literary magazine, newspaper, photography, political, professional, religious, social, and student government. Popular campus events include dances, exhibition openings, film festivals, and an annual Halloween costume party.

Sports: There is no sports program at Maryland Institute. Athletic and recreation facilities include classes in aerobics, dance, t'ai chi, and yoga, and a nearby recreation center with volleyball, basketball, and weight-training facilities.

Disabled Students: 75% of the campus is accessible to disabled students. The following facilities are available: wheelchair ramps, elevators, special parking, specially equipped rest rooms, and special class scheduling.

Services: In addition to many counseling and information services, tutoring is available in some subjects, including reading and writing.

Campus Safety and Security: Campus safety and security measures include 24-hour foot and vehicle patrol, self-defense education, escort service, and shuttle buses. There are informal discussions, lighted pathways/sidewalks, security guards in every building, and periodic discussions and seminars on safety.

Programs of Study: Maryland Institute confers the B.F.A. degree. Master's degrees are also awarded. Bachelor's degrees are awarded in COMMUNICATIONS AND THE ARTS (ceramic art and design, drawing, fiber/textiles/weaving, fine arts, graphic design, illustration, painting, photography, printmaking, and sculpture), ENGINEERING AND ENVIRONMENTAL DESIGN (interior design). Fine arts, graphic design, and illustration are the strongest academically and have the largest enrollments.

Required: All students must complete a foundation program in their first year, including courses in painting, drawing, 2- and 3-dimensional design, and liberal arts. Of a total 126 to 132 credits, students must take one third of the courses in liberal arts and two thirds in studio arts, with 63 to 69 credits in the major and a minimum 2.0 GPA. Seniors must undertake independent studio and study, a requirement sometimes met by job internships.

Special: Exchange programs are offered with Goucher College, Johns Hopkins University, Peabody Conservatory, Loyola College, and the University of Baltimore. Cross-registration is possible with any member schools in the Alliance of Independent Colleges of Art and the East Coast Art Schools Consortium. A New York studio semester is available. Study abroad in the junior year in any of 7 countries, student-designed majors, and nondegree study in liberal arts are possible. There are work-study programs, and juniors and seniors who meet prerequisites are eligible for credit-earning internships locally and nationally.

Faculty/Classroom: 54% of faculty are male; 46%, female. 95% teach undergraduates. No introductory courses are taught by graduate students. The average class size in an introductory lecture is 20 and in a regular course offering, 20.

Admissions: 66% of the 1995-96 applicants were accepted. The SAT I scores for the 1995-96 freshman class were as follows: Verbal—50% below 500, 36% between 500 and 599, 13% between 600 and 700, and 1% above 700.

Requirements: SAT I or ACT scores are strongly recommended for course placement purposes only; they are not considered in the admissions decision. Applicants should have graduated from accredited secondary schools or earned the GED, but no particular secondary preparation is required or recommended. Emphasis is primarily on the applicant's portfolio, which is reviewed as part of the admissions process. Applicants submit 12 to 20 pieces of their best current work in and out of school, including samples of drawing from observation. AP credits are accepted. Important factors in the admissions decision are evidence of special talent, advanced placement or honor courses, and personality/intangible qualities.

Procedure: Freshmen are admitted fall and spring. There are early decision, early admissions, and deferred admissions plans. Early decision applications should be filed by November 15; regular applications, by March 1 for fall entry and December 15 for spring entry, along with an application fee of $40. Notification of early decision is sent December 1; regular decision, on a rolling basis. 22 early decision candidates were accepted for the 1995-96 class.

Transfer: 67 transfer students enrolled in 1995-96. Transfer applicants must submit high school and college transcripts, a personal essay, and a portfolio. 62 credits of 126 must be completed at Maryland Institute.

Visiting: There are regularly scheduled orientations for prospective students, including a tour of campus facilities, a meeting with an admissions counselor for portfolio review, and an interview. There are guides for informal visits and visitors may sit in on classes. To schedule a visit, contact the Admissions Office at (410) 225-2294.

Financial Aid: In 1995-96, 72% of all freshmen and 70% of continuing students received some form of financial aid. 65% of freshmen and 68% of continuing students received need-based aid. The average freshman award was $11,164. Of that total, scholarships or need-based grants averaged $6073 ($12,000 maximum); loans averaged $2625 ($3625 maximum); and work contracts averaged $1100 ($1650 maximum). 30% of undergraduate students work part-time. Average earnings from campus work for the school year are $1100. The average financial indebtedness of the 1994-95 graduate was $10,500. The FAF and the college's own financial statement are required. The application deadline for fall entry is March 15.

International Students: There are currently 58 international students enrolled. The school actively recruits these students. They must score 500 on the TOEFL.

Computers: The college provides computer facilities for student use. The mainframe is an IBM AS/400. There are 121 IBM PC and Macintosh microcomputers available for student use. Every student has an E-mail address. There are no time limits and no fees. It is recommended that students in visual communication: graphic design/interior architecture and design have personal computers. Macintosh, except for interior design, is recommended.

Graduates: In 1994-95, 186 bachelor's degrees were awarded. The most popular majors among graduates were general fine arts (34%), visual communication (24%), and painting (18%). Within an average freshman class, 41% graduate in 4 years, 48% in 5 years, and 51% in 6 years. Of the 1994 graduating class, 22% were enrolled in graduate school within 6 months of graduation.

Admissions Contact: Theresa Lynch Bedoya, Dean of Admissions.

MORGAN STATE UNIVERSITY   D-2
Baltimore, MD 21239   (410) 319-3000
(800) 332-6674; FAX: (410) 319-3684

Full-time: 1995 men, 2850 women	Faculty: 243; IIA, av$
Part-time: 332 men, 424 women	Ph.D.s: 80%
Graduate: 182 men, 233 women	Student/Faculty: 20 to 1
Year: semesters, summer session	Tuition: $2832 ($6462)
Application Deadline: April 15	Room & Board: $4840
Freshman Class: n/av	
SAT I Verbal/Math: 414/447	LESS COMPETITIVE

Morgan State University, founded in 1867, is a coeducational, comprehensive public institution offering undergraduate and graduate programs leading to liberal arts, preprofessional, and professional degrees. There are 4 undergraduate schools and 1 graduate school. In addition to regional accreditation, Morgan State has baccalaureate program accreditation with ABET, ADA, ASLA, CSWE, NAAB, NASAD, NASM, and NCATE. The library contains 333,101 volumes, 141,733 microform items, and 37,422 audiovisual forms, and subscribes to 2526 periodicals. Computerized library sources and services include the card catalog, interlibrary loans, and database searching. Special learning facilities include a learning resource center, art gallery, radio station, and TV station. The 122-acre campus is in a suburban area in the northeast corner of Baltimore. Including residence halls, there are 30 buildings on campus.

Student Life: 58% of undergraduates are from Maryland. Students come from more than 40 states, more than 20 foreign countries, and Canada. 91% are from public schools; 9% from private. 93% are African American. The average age of freshmen is 19; all undergraduates, 25. 25% do not continue beyond their first year; 35% remain to graduate.

Housing: 1800 students can be accommodated in college housing. College-sponsored living facilities include single-sex and coed dormitories. In addition, there are honors houses. On-campus housing is available on a first-come, first-served basis. 70% of students commute. Alcohol is not permitted. All students may keep cars on campus.

Activities: 4% of men belong to 4 national fraternities; 3% of women belong to 4 national sororities. There are more than 30 groups on campus, including art, band, cheerleading, chess, choir, chorale, chorus, computers, dance, drama, drill team, ethnic, honors, international, jazz band, marching band, musical theater, newspaper, pep band, photography, political, professional, radio and TV, religious, social, social service, student government, and yearbook. Popular campus events include Kwanzaa.

Sports: There are 6 intercollegiate sports for men and 6 for women, and 17 intramural sports for men and 16 for women. Athletic and recreation facilities include a field house, a gymnasium, a weight room, a swimming pool, tennis and racquetball courts, and various playing fields.

Disabled Students: 90% of the campus is accessible to disabled students. The following facilities are available: wheelchair ramps, elevators, special parking, specially equipped rest rooms, special class scheduling, and lowered drinking fountains.

Services: In addition to many counseling and information services, tutoring is available in every subject. There is a reader service for the blind, and remedial math, reading, and writing. There are also note takers and sign language interpreters for disabled students.

Campus Safety and Security: Campus safety and security measures include 24-hour foot and vehicle patrol, self-defense education, escort service, and shuttle buses. In addition, there are informal discussions, pamphlets/posters/films, emergency telephones, and lighted pathways/sidewalks.

Programs of Study: Morgan State confers A.B., B.S., and B.S.Ed. degrees. Master's and doctoral degrees are also awarded. Bachelor's degrees are awarded in BIOLOGICAL SCIENCE (biology/ biological science), BUSINESS (accounting, business administration and management, hospitality management services, and marketing/ retailing/merchandising), COMMUNICATIONS AND THE ARTS (dramatic arts, English, fine arts, music, speech/debate/rhetoric, and telecommunications), COMPUTER AND PHYSICAL SCIENCE (chemistry, computer science, information sciences and systems, mathematics, and physics), EDUCATION (elementary, health, and physical), ENGINEERING AND ENVIRONMENTAL DESIGN (civil engineering, electrical/electronics engineering, engineering physics, and industrial engineering technology), HEALTH PROFESSIONS (medical laboratory technology and mental health/human services), SOCIAL SCIENCE (African American studies, economics, history, home economics, philosophy, political science/government, psychology, religion, social work, and sociology). Engineering, chemistry, and physics are the strongest academically. Business administration, accounting, and electrical engineering have the largest enrollments.

Required: In order to graduate, students must complete 120 credit hours, including 74 in the major, with a 2.0 GPA. All students must pass speech and writing proficiency examinations prior to their senior year. The 46-credit general education requirement includes courses in English, humanities, logic, history, behavioral science, science, mathematics, African American history, and health and physical education. Seniors must pass a proficiency examination in their major.

Special: Co-op programs in public and private institutions may be arranged for pharmacy honors, predentistry, premedicine, and special education students. The university also offers internships for juniors and seniors, work-study programs, preprofessional physical therapy, and prelaw programs. Dual majors may be pursued but do not lead to a dual degree. There is a freshman honors program on campus, as well as 28 national honor societies. 1 department has an honors program.

Faculty/Classroom: 67% of faculty are male; 33%, female. All teach undergraduates; 76% both teach and do research. No introductory courses are taught by graduate students. The average class size in an introductory lecture is 31; in a laboratory, 26; and in a regular course offering, 21.

Admissions: The SAT I scores for a recent freshman class were as follows: Verbal—93% below 500, 7% between 500 and 599, and 1% between 600 and 700; Math—83% below 500, 15% between 500 and 599, and 2% between 600 and 700.

Requirements: The SAT I or ACT is required, with a minimum composite (recentered) score of 870 on the SAT I. A minimum GPA of 2.0 is required. In addition, applicants should be high school graduates, or have earned the GED, and are encouraged to have 4 years of English, 3 of mathematics, 2 each of science, social studies, and history, and 1 of a foreign language. A personal essay is recommended and, when appropriate, an audition. AP and CLEP credits are accepted. Important factors in the admissions decision are recommendations by school officials, evidence of special talent, and parents or siblings attending the school.

Procedure: Freshmen are admitted in the fall and spring. Entrance exams should be taken during the junior or senior year. There is an early admissions plan. Applications should be filed by April 15 for fall entry and December 1 for spring entry, along with an application fee of $25. Notification is sent on a rolling basis.

Transfer: 300 transfer students enrolled in a recent year. Applicants with fewer than 12 credits must submit SAT I scores; those with fewer than 24 credits must also submit high school transcripts. Applicants are expected to have at least a 2.0 GPA in all college work attempted and be in good standing at the last institution attended. 30 credits of 120 must be completed at Morgan State.

Visiting: There are regularly scheduled orientations for prospective students, including placement testing and academic advising. There are guides for informal visits and visitors may sit in on classes and stay overnight at the school. To schedule a visit, contact Delores Moffatt.

Financial Aid: In 1995–96, 80% of all freshmen and 63% of continuing students received some form of financial aid. Morgan State is a member of CSS. FAFSA and the college's own financial statement are required. The application deadline for fall entry is April 1.

International Students: There are currently 158 international students enrolled. They must take the TOEFL and achieve a minimum score of 550. The student must also take the SAT I or ACT and achieve a minimum score of 750 on the SAT I. Students who have not attended any school during the preceding 3 years are not required to submit standardized test scores.

Computers: The college provides computer facilities for student use. The mainframes are a DEC VAX 11/780 and an 8300. There are also IBM and Apple Macintosh microcomputers available. All students may access the system. There are no time limits.

Graduates: Within an average freshman class, 12% graduate in 4 years and 12% in 5 years. More than 200 companies recruited on campus in 1994–95.

Admissions Contact: Chelseia Harold-Miller, Director of Admission and recruitment.

MOUNT SAINT MARY'S COLLEGE D-1
Emmitsburg, MD 21727
(301) 447-5214
(800) 448-4347; FAX: (301) 447-5755

Full-time: 607 men, 697 women	**Faculty:** 95; IIB, -$
Part-time: 65 men, 48 women	**Ph.D.s:** 82%
Graduate: 337 men, 146 women	**Student/Faculty:** 14 to 1
Year: semesters, summer session	**Tuition:** $14,120
Application Deadline: March 1	**Room & Board:** $6250
Freshman Class: 1315 applied, 1130 accepted, 319 enrolled	
SAT I Verbal/Math: 470/510	**COMPETITIVE**

Mount Saint Mary's College, founded in 1808, is a private, coeducational liberal arts institution affiliated with the Roman Catholic Church. There are 3 graduate schools. In addition to regional accreditation, the Mount has baccalaureate program accreditation with NASDTEC. The library contains 193,275 volumes, 19,112 microform items, and 4250 audiovisual forms, and subscribes to 928 periodicals. Computerized library sources and services include the card catalog, interlibrary loans, and database searching. Special learning facilities include a learning resource center, radio station, TV station, and archives. The 1400-acre campus is in a rural area 60 miles northwest of Washington, D.C., and 50 miles west of Baltimore. Including residence halls, there are 25 buildings on campus.

Student Life: 51% of undergraduates are from out-of-state, mostly the Middle Atlantic. Students come from 32 states and 11 foreign countries. 51% are from public schools; 49% from private. 90% are white. Most are Catholic. The average age of freshmen is 18; all undergraduates, 20. 18% do not continue beyond their first year; 72% remain to graduate.

Housing: 1126 students can be accommodated in college housing. College-sponsored living facilities include coed dormitories, on-campus apartments, and married-student housing. In addition there are honors houses, special interest houses, wellness floors, and quiet floors. On-campus housing is guaranteed for all 4 years. 85% of students live on campus; of those, 85% remain on campus on weekends. All students may keep cars on campus.

Activities: There are no fraternities or sororities. There are 53 groups on campus, including art, cheerleading, chess, choir, chorale, chorus, computers, dance, drama, ethnic, honors, international, literary magazine, musical theater, newspaper, pep band, photography, political, professional, radio and TV, religious, social, social service, student government, and yearbook. Popular campus events include Spring Fling, Special Olympics, Founders Day, Open Picnic, Du Bois Lecture, Crab Fest, Mountapalooza, Christmas Dance, and Fall Bonfire.

Sports: There are 9 intercollegiate sports for men and 8 for women, and 31 intramural sports for men and 31 for women. Athletic and recreation facilities include multipurpose indoor courts, a track, a pool, aerobic facilities, a sauna, a weight room, a basketball arena, lighted tennis courts, and playing fields.

Disabled Students: 60% of the campus is accessible to disabled students. The following facilities are available: wheelchair ramps, elevators, special parking, specially equipped rest rooms, lowered drinking fountains, and lowered telephones.

Services: In addition to many counseling and information services, tutoring is available in every subject. In addition, there is a reader service for the blind, remedial math, reading, and writing, study skills and language laboratories, and a writing center. Hearing assistance systems, closed-caption TV, and sight-impaired computer system software are also available.

Campus Safety and Security: Campus safety and security measures include 24-hour foot and vehicle patrol, self-defense education, escort service, and informal discussions. In addition, there are pamphlets/posters/films, emergency telephones, lighted pathways/sidewalks, and access control.

Programs of Study: The Mount confers B.A. and B.S. degrees. Master's degrees are also awarded. Bachelor's degrees are awarded in BIOLOGICAL SCIENCE (biochemistry and biology/biological science), BUSINESS (accounting and business administration and management), COMMUNICATIONS AND THE ARTS (communications, English, fine arts, French, German, and Spanish), COMPUTER AND PHYSICAL SCIENCE (chemistry and mathematics), EDUCATION (elementary), SOCIAL SCIENCE (economics, history, international studies, philosophy, political science/government, psychology, sociology, and theological studies). Government and international studies, education, and science are the strongest academically. Business, biology, and elementary education have the largest enrollments.

Required: Students are required to take a 4-year, 61-credit core curriculum in liberal arts, which includes a freshman seminar, a Western civilization sequence including art and literature, and courses in humanities, science, mathematics, American culture, philosophy, theology, non-Western culture, foreign language, and ethics. Graduation requirements include 120 credits, with 30 to 36 in the major, and a minimum GPA of 2.0.

Special: Mount Saint Mary's College offers co-op programs, cross-registration with area community colleges, study abroad, a Washington semester, and secondary teacher certification in biology, business education, English, foreign languages, mathematics, and social science. Dual and student-designed majors, interdisciplinary majors in biopsychology, American culture, and classical studies, a general studies degree, 3-2 engineering and nursing degrees, and nondegree and accelerated study are possible. A number of independently designed internships and work-study programs and pass/fail options are available. There also is an integrated freshman year program. There is a freshman honors program on campus, as well as 16 national honor societies. 14 departments have honors programs.

Faculty/Classroom: 67% of faculty are male; 33%, female. 96% teach undergraduates and 80% do research. The average class size in an introductory lecture is 22; in a laboratory, 15; and in a regular course offering, 17.

Admissions: 86% of the 1995-96 applicants were accepted. The SAT I scores for the 1995-96 freshman class were as follows: Verbal—64% below 500, 27% between 500 and 599, 8% between 600 and 700, and 1% above 700; Math—43% below 500, 35% between 500 and 599, 19% between 600 and 700, and 3% above 700. 34% of the current freshmen were in the top fifth of their class; 65% were in the top two fifths. There were 3 National Merit semifinalists. 3 freshmen graduated first in their class.

Requirements: The SAT I or ACT is required. The Mount requires applicants to be in the upper 50% of their class. A minimum GPA of 3.0 is required. Applicants should have graduated from an accredited secondary school or earned the GED. Secondary preparation should include 4 years of English, 3 each of mathematics, history, natural science, and social sciences, and 2 of a foreign language. An interview is recommended. AP and CLEP credits are accepted. Important factors in the admissions decision are recommendations by school officials, extracurricular activities record, and leadership record.

Procedure: Freshmen are admitted fall and spring. Entrance exams should be taken by January of the senior year. There are early decision, early admissions, and deferred admissions plans. Early decision applications should be filed by December 1; regular applications, by March 1 for fall entry and December 1 for spring entry, along with an application fee of $25. Notification of early decision is sent December 15; regular decision, on a rolling basis. 142 early decision candidates were accepted for the 1995-96 class. A waiting list is an active part

of the admissions procedure, with about 5% of all applicants on the list.

Transfer: 52 transfer students enrolled in 1995-96. Transfer applicants should have at least a 2.5 GPA in previous college work, be in good academic and disciplinary standing, and account for all time elapsed since graduation from high school. 30 credits of 120 must be completed at the Mount.

Visiting: There are regularly scheduled orientations for prospective students, including campus tours and information sessions on academic programs, community life, admissions, and financial aid. There are guides for informal visits and visitors may sit in on classes and stay overnight at the school. To schedule a visit, contact the Admissions Office.

Financial Aid: In 1995-96, 86% of all freshmen and 78% of continuing students received some form of financial aid. 66% of freshmen and 40% of continuing students received need-based aid. The average freshman award was $12,027. Of that total, scholarships or need-based grants averaged $8355 ($20,370 maximum); loans averaged $2512 ($4125 maximum); and work contracts averaged $1160 ($1500 maximum). 25% of undergraduate students work part-time. Average earnings from campus work for the school year are $1200. The average financial indebtedness of the 1994-95 graduate was $6343. The Mount is a member of CSS. The FAFSA is required. The application deadline for fall entry is March 15.

International Students: There are currently 13 international students enrolled. They must take the TOEFL and achieve a minimum score of 550.

Computers: The college provides computer facilities for student use. The mainframes are comprised of an IBM AS/400 and a Sun SPARC Server 20 SPARC Station IPX. There are 52 microcomputers located in 3 laboratories throughout campus; students have access to the SPARC Server via Telnet. All students may access the system 24 hours per day. There are no time limits and no fees.

Graduates: In 1994-95, 262 bachelor's degrees were awarded. The most popular majors among graduates were business and finance (17%), sociology (15%), and English (9%). Within an average freshman class, 1% graduate in 3 years, 67% in 4 years, 71% in 5 years, and 72% in 6 years. 36 companies recruited on campus in 1994-95. Of the 1994 graduating class, 17% were enrolled in graduate school within 6 months of graduation and 90% had found employment.

Admissions Contact: John Gill, Admissions Director. E-mail: admissions@msmary.edu. A campus video is available.

SAINT JOHN'S COLLEGE E-3
Annapolis, MD 21404 (410) 263-2371, ext. 222; (800) 727-9238

Full-time: 218 men, 200 women	Faculty: 57; IIB, +$
Part-time: 1 man	Ph.D.s: 67%
Graduate: 58 men, 42 women	Student/Faculty: 8 to 1
Year: semesters, summer session	Tuition: $18,830
Application Deadline: see profile	Room & Board: $5890
Freshman Class: 338 applied, 292 accepted, 111 enrolled	
SAT I Verbal/Math: 620/590	VERY COMPETITIVE +

St. John's College, founded as King William's School in 1696 and chartered as St. John's in 1784, is a private, coeducational institution that offers a single all-required curriculum sometimes called the Great Books Program. Students and faculty work together in small discussion classes without lecture courses, written finals, or emphasis on grades. The program is a rigorous interdisciplinary curriculum based on the great works of literature, mathematics, philosophy, theology, sciences, political theory, music, history, and economics. There is also a campus in Santa Fe, New Mexico. The 2 libraries contain 97,266 volumes, 961 microform items, and 9603 audiovisual forms, and subscribe to 125 periodicals. Computerized library sources and services include the card catalog, interlibrary loans, and database searching. Special learning facilities include an art gallery and planetarium. The 36-acre campus is in a small town 35 miles east of Washington, D.C. and 32 miles south of Baltimore. Including residence halls, there are 16 buildings on campus.

Student Life: 86% of undergraduates are from out-of-state, mostly the Middle Atlantic. Students come from 45 states, 20 foreign countries, and Canada. 65% are from public schools; 35% from private. 83% are white. The average age of freshmen is 18; all undergraduates, 21. 19% do not continue beyond their first year; 65% remain to graduate.

Housing: 291 students can be accommodated in college housing. College-sponsored living facilities include coed dormitories. On-campus housing is guaranteed for the freshman year only and is available on a lottery system for upperclassmen. 75% of students live on campus; of those, 90% remain on campus on weekends. Upperclassmen may keep cars on campus.

Activities: There are no fraternities or sororities. There are 32 groups on campus, including art, chorus, computers, dance, drama, film, gay, literary magazine, newspaper, photography, political, religious, social service, student government, and yearbook. Popular campus events include Reality Weekend, Senior Prank, College Navy Croquet Match, concerts, and Friday night lectures.

Sports: There are 2 intercollegiate sports for men and 2 for women, and 19 intramural sports for men and 19 for women. Athletic and recreation facilities include a gymnasium with a weight room, tennis courts, a boathouse, and playing fields.

Disabled Students: 70% of the campus is accessible to disabled students. The following facilities are available: wheelchair ramps, elevators, special parking, specially equipped rest rooms, special class scheduling, lowered drinking fountains, lowered telephones, and ground floor dormitory rooms.

Services: In addition to many counseling and information services, tutoring is available in every subject. There is a reader service for the blind and remedial math and writing.

Campus Safety and Security: Campus safety and security measures include 24-hour foot and vehicle patrol, escort service, informal discussions, and pamphlets/posters/films. In addition, there are emergency telephones and lighted pathways/sidewalks. Adult members of the community living on campus and designated students take responsiblity on freshman floors in dormitories and at student parties and other activities.

Programs of Study: St. John's confers the B.A. degree. Master's degrees are also awarded. Bachelor's degrees are awarded in SOCIAL SCIENCE (liberal arts/general studies, Western civilization/culture, and Western European studies).

Required: The common curriculum, equivalent to 132 credits, covers a range of classic to modern works. Students attend small seminars; 9-week preceptorials on specific works or topics; language, music, and mathematics tutorials; and a 3-year natural sciences laboratory. Active learning occurs through discussion, translations, writing, experiment, mathematical demonstration, and musical analysis. Students take oral examinations each semester and submit annual essays. Sophomores also take a mathematics examination and seniors an oral examination that admits them to degree candidacy. Seniors also present a final essay to the faculty and take a 1-hour public oral examination.

Faculty/Classroom: 73% of faculty are male; 27%, female. All teach undergraduates. No introductory courses are taught by graduate students. The average class size in a laboratory is 15 and in a regular course offering, 15.

Admissions: 86% of the 1995–96 applicants were accepted. The SAT I scores for the 1995–96 freshman class were as follows: Verbal—9% below 500, 27% between 500 and 599, 51% between 600 and 700, and 13% above 700; Math—18% below 500, 35% between 500 and 599, 31% between 600 and 700, and 16% above 700. 54% of the current freshmen were in the top fifth of their class; 74% were in the top two fifths. There were 5 National Merit finalists and 9 semifinalists.

Requirements: Applicants need not be high school graduates; some students are admitted before they complete high school. Test scores may be submitted, but are not required. Secondary preparation should include 4 years of English, 3 years of mathematics, and 2 years each of foreign language, science, and history. Applicants must submit written essays, which are critical to the admissions decision, and are strongly urged to schedule an interview. Important factors in the admissions decision are recommendations by school officials, advanced placement or honor courses, and personality/intangible qualities.

Procedure: Freshmen are admitted in the fall and spring. There are early admissions and deferred admissions plans. Application deadlines are open, but it is recommended that applications be filed by March 1 for fall entry and December 15 for spring entry. Notification is sent on a rolling basis.

Transfer: 21 transfer students enrolled in 1995–96. Transfer students may enter only as freshmen and must complete the entire program at St. John's. The admissions criteria are the same as for regular students. 132 credits of 132 must be completed at St. John's.

Visiting: There are regularly scheduled orientations for prospective students, consisting of an overnight stay on campus, class visits, and a tour. There are guides for informal visits and visitors may sit in on classes and stay overnight at the school. To schedule a visit, contact the Admission Office.

Financial Aid: In 1995–96, 70% of all freshmen and 69% of continuing students received some form of financial aid. 55% of freshmen and 52% of continuing students received need-based aid. The average freshman award was $17,934. Of that total, scholarships or need-based grants averaged $13,609 ($18,000 maximum); loans averaged $2625 ($5625 maximum); and work contracts averaged $1700 (maximum). 75% of undergraduate students work part-time. Average earnings from campus work for the school year are $1800. The average financial indebtedness of the 1994–95 graduate was $15,125. St. John's is a member of CSS. FAFSA, the college's own financial statement, and the CSS Profile Application are required. The application deadline for fall entry is February 15.

International Students: There were 19 international students enrolled in a recent year. The school actively recruits these students. They must take the TOEFL. The student must also take the SAT I.

Computers: The college provides computer facilities for student use. The mainframe is an IBM AS/400. There is a network of 8 Apple Macintosh computers available for student use in a computer room and in the library. They are equipped with word processing programs and a variety of other software. All students may access the system 24 hours a day. There are no time limits and no fees.

Graduates: In 1994–95, 84 bachelor's degrees were awarded. The most popular major among graduates was liberal arts (100%). Within an average freshman class, 60% graduate in 5 years and 65% in 6 years. 6 companies recruited on campus in 1994–95. Of the 1994 graduating class, 18% were enrolled in graduate school within 6 months of graduation and 20% had found employment.

Admissions Contact: John Christensen, Director of Admissions.

SAINT MARY'S COLLEGE OF MARYLAND   E-4

St. Mary's City, MD 20686   (301) 862-0292
(800) 492–7181; FAX: (301) 862-0906

Full-time: 612 men, 789 women	**Faculty:** 105; IIB, +$
Part-time: 88 men, 147 women	**Ph.D.s:** 97%
Graduate: none	**Student/Faculty:** 13 to 1
Year: semesters, summer session	**Tuition:** $5435 ($8735)
Application Deadline: January 15	**Room & Board:** $4970
Freshman Class: 1588 applied, 855 accepted, 352 enrolled	
SAT I Verbal/Math: 580/640	**HIGHLY COMPETITIVE**

St. Mary's College of Maryland, founded in 1840, is a small public liberal arts college in the Maryland State College and University System. In addition to regional accreditation, St. Mary's has baccalaureate program accreditation with NASM. The library contains 152,392 volumes, 32,841 microform items, and 7739 audiovisual forms, and subscribes to 1601 periodicals. Computerized library sources and services include the card catalog, interlibrary loans, and database searching. Special learning facilities include a learning resource center, art gallery, radio station, TV station, historic archaeological site, and estuarine research facilities. The 275-acre campus is in a rural area 70 miles south of Washington, D.C. Including residence halls, there are 34 buildings on campus.

Student Life: 86% of undergraduates are from Maryland. Students come from 38 states, 27 foreign countries, and Canada. 82% are from public schools; 17% from private. 84% are white; 10% African American. 39% are Protestant; 29% Catholic; 23% claim no religious affiliation. The average age of freshmen is 18.5; all undergraduates, 22. 16% do not continue beyond their first year; 74% remain to graduate.

Housing: 1030 students can be accommodated in college housing. College-sponsored living facilities include single-sex and coed dormitories and on-campus apartments. In addition, there are honors houses, language houses, and special interest houses. On-campus housing is guaranteed for all 4 years. 73% of students live on campus; of those, 60% remain on campus on weekends. All students may keep cars on campus.

Activities: There are no fraternities or sororities. There are 45 groups on campus, including art, athletic clubs, band, cheerleading, chess, choir, chorale, chorus, dance, drama, ethnic, film, gay, honors, international, jazz band, literary magazine, musical theater, newspaper, orchestra, philosophy, photography, political, professional, radio and TV, religious, social, social service, student government, symphony, and yearbook. Popular campus events include World Carnival, concerts, and dances.

Sports: There are 7 intercollegiate sports for men and 8 for women, and 9 intramural sports for men and 8 for women. Athletic and recreation facilities include an athletic track, a pool, basketball, volleyball, and tennis courts, training, weight, and exercise rooms, a boat house, pier, and sailing fleet, and baseball, soccer, and lacrosse fields.

Disabled Students: 86% of the campus is accessible to disabled students. The following facilities are available: wheelchair ramps, elevators, special parking, specially equipped rest rooms, lowered drinking fountains, and lowered telephones.

Services: In addition to many counseling and information services, tutoring is available in some subjects, including mathematics, writing, physics, foreign languages, biology, chemistry, and economics. There is a reader service for the blind.

Campus Safety and Security: Campus safety and security measures include 24-hour foot and vehicle patrol, self-defense education, escort service, and informal discussions. In addition, there are pamphlets/posters/films, emergency telephones, lighted pathways/sidewalks, and student security assistant foot patrols.

Programs of Study: St. Mary's confers the B.A. degree. Bachelor's degrees are awarded in BIOLOGICAL SCIENCE (biology/biological science), COMMUNICATIONS AND THE ARTS (dramatic arts, English, fine arts, languages, and music), COMPUTER AND PHYSICAL SCIENCE (chemistry, mathematics, natural sciences, and physics), SOCIAL SCIENCE (anthropology, economics, history, human development, philosophy, political science/government, psychology, and public affairs). Biology is the strongest academically. Economics, psychology, and biology have the largest enrollments.

Required: Students must complete general education requirements in writing, mathematics, foreign language, history, the arts, literature, physical, biological, behavioral, and policy sciences, philosophy, and an interdisciplinary seminar. Students must meet additional requirements in their majors and complete 128 semester hours with at least a 2.0 GPA.

Special: St. Mary's offers an exchange program with Johns Hopkins University, study abroad in 5 countries, dual and student-designed majors, and nondegree study. There are pass/fail options for some courses. Unpaid internships for credit, with placement worldwide, are also permitted. There is a freshman honors program on campus, as well as 4 national honor societies. There is a campuswide honors program.

Faculty/Classroom: 61% of faculty are male; 39%, female. All both teach and do research. The average class size in an introductory lecture is 24; in a laboratory, 17; and in a regular course offering, 14.

Admissions: 54% of the 1995–96 applicants were accepted. The SAT I scores for the 1995–96 freshman class were as follows: Verbal—12% below 500, 41% between 500 and 599, 42% between 600 and 700, and 5% above 700; Math—6% below 500, 21% between 500 and 599, 59% between 600 and 700, and 14% above 700. 68% of the current freshmen were in the top fifth of their class; 89% were in the top two fifths. There were 10 National Merit finalists and 19 semifinalists.

Requirements: The SAT I or ACT is required, with an SAT I score of 1000. Applicants should have graduated from an accredited secondary school with a 2.0 GPA or have earned the GED. Minimum high school preparation should include 4 units of English, 3 each of mathematics, social studies, and science, and 7 electives. An essay and 3 letters of recommendation are required. AP and CLEP credits are accepted. Important factors in the admissions decision are advanced placement or honor courses, recommendations by school officials, and evidence of special talent.

Procedure: Freshmen are admitted fall and spring. Entrance exams should be taken in May of the junior year or November of the senior year. There are early decision and early admissions plans. Early decision applications should be filed by December 1; regular applications, by January 15 for fall entry and October 15 for spring entry, along with an application fee of $25. Notification of early decision is sent February 1; regular decision, April 1. 155 early decision candidates were accepted for the 1995–96 class. A waiting list is an active part of the admissions procedure, with about 5% of all applicants on the list.

Transfer: 70 transfer students enrolled in 1995–96. Applicants with a minimum of 24 credits should have at least a 2.0 GPA; those with fewer credits should have 2.5. 38 credits of 128 must be completed at St. Mary's.

Visiting: There are regularly scheduled orientations for prospective students, including group presentations, interaction with faculty and students, and campus tours. There are guides for informal visits and visitors may sit in on classes and stay overnight at the school. To schedule a visit, contact the Admissions Office.

Financial Aid: In 1995–96, 75% of all freshmen and 59% of continuing students received some form of financial aid. 41% of freshmen and 34% of continuing students received need-based aid. The average freshman award was $4900. Of that total, scholarships or need-based grants averaged $3200 ($4100 maximum); other grants averaged $4300 ($5000 maximum); loans averaged $2298 ($2625 maximum); and work contracts averaged $508 ($1300 maximum). 26% of undergraduate students work part-time. Average earnings from campus work for the school year are $508. The average financial indebtedness of the 1994–95 graduate was $5900. St. Mary's is a member of CSS. The FAF or FAFSA is required. The application deadline for fall entry is March 1.

International Students: There are currently 36 international students enrolled. They must take the TOEFL and achieve a minimum score of 550. The student must also take the SAT I or the ACT.

Computers: The college provides computer facilities for student use. The mainframes are a DEC MicroVAX 3100 and a DEC 6520. Students can access the MicroVAX or use any of the 70 DOS-based systems, 6 NEXTSTEP workstations, or multimedia stand-alone workstations. Access to the Internet, World Wide Web, and E-mail is available. There are several computer laboratories on campus. All students may access the system during all laboratory hours. There are no time limits and no fees.

Graduates: In 1994–95, 318 bachelor's degrees were awarded. The most popular majors among graduates were psychology (16%), biology (13%), and economics (11%). Within an average freshman class, 1% graduate in 3 years, 64% in 4 years, 73% in 5 years, and 74% in 6 years. 8 companies recruited on campus in 1994–95.

Admissions Contact: Richard Edgar, Director of Admissions. E-mail: admissions@honors.smcm.edu. A campus video is available.

SALISBURY STATE UNIVERSITY   F-4

Salisbury, MD 21801	(410) 543-6161; FAX: (410) 543-6138
Full-time: 1842 men, 2414 women	Faculty: 244; IIA, --$
Part-time: 451 men, 629 women	Ph.D.s: 74%
Graduate: 193 men, 481 women	Student/Faculty: 17 to 1
Year: 4-1-4, summer session	Tuition: $3440 ($6554)
Application Deadline: January 15	Room & Board: $4790
Freshman Class: 3840 applied, 1863 accepted, 650 enrolled	
SAT I Verbal/Math: 500/570	ACT: 23 VERY COMPETITIVE

Salisbury State University, founded in 1925, is a public, coeducational institution within the University of Maryland system. SSU offers undergraduate programs in the arts and sciences, business, education, health science, nursing, technology, and professional training. There are 4 undergraduate schools and 1 graduate school. In addition to regional accreditation, SSU has baccalaureate program accreditation with AACSB, CAHEA, CSWE, and NLN. The library contains 254,000 volumes, 600,000 microform items, and 10,569 audiovisual forms, and subscribes to 1800 periodicals. Computerized library sources and services include the card catalog, interlibrary loans, and database searching. Special learning facilities include a learning resource center, art gallery, radio station, the Research Center for Delmarva History and Culture, and the Small Business Development Center Network. The 140-acre campus is in a small town 110 miles southeast of Baltimore and 100 miles east of Washington, D.C. Including residence halls, there are 35 buildings on campus.

Student Life: 75% of undergraduates are from Maryland. Students come from 39 states, 21 foreign countries, and Canada. 75% are from public schools; 25% from private. 90% are white. The average age of freshmen is 18; all undergraduates, 23. 20% do not continue beyond their first year; 56% remain to graduate.

Housing: 1900 students can be accommodated in college housing. College-sponsored living facilities include single-sex and coed dormitories and on-campus apartments. In addition there are honors houses, special-interest houses, and 2 international houses. On-campus housing is guaranteed for all 4 years. 59% of students commute. Upperclassmen may keep cars on campus.

Activities: 7% of men belong to 7 national fraternities; 8% of women belong to 5 national sororities. There are 87 groups on campus, including art, band, cheerleading, choir, chorale, chorus, computers, dance, drama, ethnic, film, gay, honors, international, jazz band, literary magazine, musical theater, newspaper, orchestra, political, professional, radio and TV, religious, social, social service, student government, symphony, and yearbook. Popular campus events include Family Weekend, October Fest, and Spring Fling.

Sports: There are 9 intercollegiate sports for men and 10 for women, and 40 intramural sports for men and 40 for women. Athletic and recreation facilities include a 3000-seat stadium, a 3000-seat gymnasium, a 1000-seat arena, a swimming pool, a wrestling room, a dance studio, racquetball and indoor and outdoor tennis courts, a baseball diamond, varsity and practice fields, an all-weather track, and a Nautilus center.

Disabled Students: 90% of the campus is accessible to disabled students. The following facilities are available: wheelchair ramps, elevators, special parking, specially equipped rest rooms, special class scheduling, lowered drinking fountains, lowered telephones, and special equipment for vision- or hearing-impaired students.

Services: In addition to many counseling and information services, tutoring is available in most subjects. There is a reader service for the blind, and remedial math, reading, and writing.

Campus Safety and Security: Campus safety and security measures include 24-hour foot and vehicle patrol, self-defense education, escort service, and shuttle buses. There are informal discussions, pamphlets/posters/films, emergency telephones, and lighted pathways/sidewalks.

Programs of Study: SSU confers B.A., B.S., B.F.A., B.S.N., and B.S.W. degrees. Master's degrees are also awarded. Bachelor's degrees are awarded in BIOLOGICAL SCIENCE (biology/biological science), BUSINESS (accounting and business administration and management), COMMUNICATIONS AND THE ARTS (art, communications, English, fine arts, French, music, and Spanish), COMPUTER AND PHYSICAL SCIENCE (chemistry, information sciences and systems, mathematics, and physics), EDUCATION (elementary and physical), HEALTH PROFESSIONS (environmental health science, medical laboratory technology, nursing, and respiratory therapy), SOCIAL SCIENCE (economics, geography, history, philosophy, political science/government, psychology, social work, and sociology). The sciences and business are the strongest academically. Biology and elementary education have the largest enrollments.

Required: Students must complete 47 semester hours of general education requirements, including specific courses in English composition and literature, world civilization, and physical education. The bachelor's degree requires completion of at least 120 semester hours, including 30 or more in the major field, with a minimum GPA of 2.0.

Special: Co-operative programs in business and mathematics, cross-registration with schools in the University of Maryland System, and study abroad in numerous countries are offered. SSU also offers an Annapolis semester, a Washington semester, internships, work-study programs, accelerated degree programs, a general studies degree, dual, interdisciplinary, and student-designed majors including physics/microelectronics, a 3–2 engineering degree with the University of Maryland at College Park, Old Dominion University, and Widener University, and pass/fail options. There is a freshman honors program on campus, as well as 16 national honor societies. 11 departments have honors programs.

Faculty/Classroom: 56% of faculty are male; 44%, female. All teach undergraduates and 47% also do research. Graduate students teach 1% of introductory courses. The average class size in an introductory lecture is 29 and in a laboratory, 18.

Admissions: 49% of the 1995–96 applicants were accepted. The SAT I scores for the 1995–96 freshman class were as follows: Verbal—43% below 500, 47% between 500 and 599, and 10% between 600 and 700; Math—11% below 500, 49% between 500 and 599, 36% between 600 and 700, and 4% above 700. The ACT scores were 16% below 21, 49% between 21 and 23, 26% between 24 and 26, 6% between 27 and 28, and 3% above 28. 53% of the current freshmen were in the top fifth of their class; 85% were in the top two fifths. 9 freshmen graduated first in their class.

Requirements: The SAT I or ACT is required, with a recommended score of 1000 on SAT I. Applicants must be graduates of accredited secondary schools with a 2.0 GPA or have earned a GED. The university requires 14 academic credits or 20 Carnegie units, including 4 in English, 3 each in mathematics and social studies, of which U.S. history must be a component, and 2 each in foreign language and science. A portfolio or audition is required for some majors. A campus visit is recommended for all students. AP and CLEP credits are accepted. Important factors in the admissions decision are advanced placement or honor courses, leadership record, and extracurricular activities record.

Procedure: Freshmen are admitted fall and spring. Entrance exams should be taken by November of the senior year. There are early decision and early admissions plans. Early decision applications should be filed by December 15; regular applications, by January 15 for fall entry and January 1 for spring entry, along with an application fee of $30. Notification of early decision is sent January 15; regular decision, March 15. 180 early decision candidates were accepted for the 1995–96 class. A waiting list is an active part of the admissions procedure, with about 8% of all applicants on the list.

Transfer: 520 transfer students enrolled in 1995–96. Applicants must present a minimum GPA of 2.0 in at least 25 transferable credit hours earned. Students with fewer than 25 credit hours must be eligible for freshman admission in addition to maintaining at least a 2.0 GPA in college courses. 30 credits of 120 must be completed at SSU.

Visiting: There are regularly scheduled orientations for prospective students, including presentations, tours, meetings with faculty and staff, and Saturday open house programs. There are guides for informal visits and visitors may sit in on classes and stay overnight at the school. To schedule a visit, contact the Admissions Office.

Financial Aid: In 1995–96, 40% of all students received some form of financial aid. 40% of freshmen and 60% of continuing students received need-based aid. The average freshman award was $2700. Of that total, scholarships or need-based grants averaged $1500 ($9000 maximum); loans averaged $2500 ($4625 maximum); and work contracts averaged $1500 ($2000 maximum). 30% of undergraduate students work part-time. Average earnings from campus work for the school year are $1800. The average financial indebtedness of the 1994–95 graduate was $6000. SSU is a member of CSS. The FAFSA is required. The application deadline for fall entry is March 1.

International Students: There are currently 33 international students enrolled. The school actively recruits these students. They must score 550 on the TOEFL.

Computers: The college provides computer facilities for student use. The mainframes are a DEC VAX 4000–705A, a DEC ALPHA 2100–4/275, a cluster DEC VAX 8350, and a DEC VAX 6310. There are 24 VAX graphics-capable terminals connected to the mainframe that are available for student use. The library has 30 IBM-compatible microcomputers networked to a server. In addition, there are 3 computer laboratories, each containing 30 microcomputers using the Pathworks network with a MicroVAX as a server; a 19-station, networked Macintosh laboratory; and a graphics laboratory with 5 DEC workstations and an academic help room. All students may access the system 24 hours daily via modem. There are no time limits and no fees.

Graduates: In 1994–95, 1091 bachelor's degrees were awarded. The most popular majors among graduates were elementary education (15%), business (11%), and biology (7%). Within an average freshman class, 40% graduate in 4 years, 54% in 5 years, and 56% in 6 years. 100 companies recruited on campus in 1994–95.

Admissions Contact: Jane H. Dane, Dean of Admissions and Financial Aid. E-mail: d3adadm@saa.ssu.umd.edu.

SOJOURNER-DOUGLASS COLLEGE
D-2
Baltimore, MD 21201   (410) 276-0306

Full-time: 30 men, 140 women	**Faculty:** 14
Part-time: 10 men, 30 women	**Ph.D.s:** 18%
Graduate: none	**Student/Faculty:** 13 to 1
Year: trimesters	**Tuition:** $5300
Application Deadline: open	**Room & Board:** n/app
Freshman Class: n/av	
SAT I or ACT: not required	**LESS COMPETITIVE**

Sojourner-Douglas College, established in 1980, is a private institution offering undergraduate programs in administration, human and social resources, and human growth and development to a predominantly black student body. Figures given in the above capsule are approximate. The library contains 20,000 volumes. Special learning facilities include a learning resource center. The campus is in an urban area in Baltimore.

Student Life: All undergraduates are from Maryland.

Housing: There are no residence halls. All students commute.

Activities: There are no fraternities or sororities. There are 5 groups on campus, including newspaper and student government.

Sports: There is no sports program at Sojourner-Douglass.

Disabled Students: Wheelchair ramps, elevators and special parking are available.

Services: In addition to many counseling and information services, tutoring is available in some subjects, including reading, writing, mathematics, and study skills.

Programs of Study: Sojourner-Douglass confers the B.A. degree. Bachelor's degrees are awarded in BUSINESS (business administration and management and tourism), COMMUNICATIONS AND THE ARTS (broadcasting), EDUCATION (early childhood), HEALTH PROFESSIONS (health care administration), SOCIAL SCIENCE (criminal justice, gerontology, psychology, public administration, and social work).

Required: To graduate, students must earn 63 to 66 general education credits, with 15 credits in English literature and composition; 15 in political science, history, economics, sociology, geography, psychology, and anthropology; 12 in the humanities; 9 in natural science and mathematics; and 3 each in career planning and personal development, psychology of the black family in America, and psychology of racism. 12 credits must be earned in a project that demonstrates competence in the major. 6 credits must be earned in the sociology of work. There is also a 3-credit education seminar requirement. A total of 132 credits is needed to graduate, with 54 to 69 in the major.

Special: Credit may be granted for life, military, and work experience. Faculty-supervised independent study is possible for adult students.

Requirements: The SAT I or ACT is not required. Applicants must be graduates of an accredited secondary school or have a GED certificate. They must have completed 4 years of English and 2 years each of mathematics, history, and social studies. Autobiographical essays, resumes, and interviews are required.

Procedure: Freshmen are admitted to all sessions. Application deadlines are open. Check with the school for current fee. Notification is sent on a rolling basis.

Transfer: Transfer criteria are the same as for entering freshmen; however, transfers are not accepted to all classes.

Visiting: There are regularly scheduled orientations for prospective students. To schedule a visit, contact the Office of Admissions.

Financial Aid: The FAF, FAFSA, FFS, or SFS and federal income tax forms are required. Check with the school for current deadlines.

Computers: The college provides computer facilities for student use.

Admissions Contact: LaVerne B. Cawthorne, Coordinator of Admissions.

TOWSON STATE UNIVERSITY
D-2
Towson, MD 21204-7097   (410) 830-2113
(800) CALL-TSU; FAX: (410) 830-3030

Full-time: 3863 men, 5627 women	**Faculty:** 457; IIA, av$
Part-time: 1386 men, 1894 women	**Ph.D.s:** 82%
Graduate: 442 men, 1431 women	**Student/Faculty:** 21 to 1
Year: 4-1-4, summer session	**Tuition:** $3580 ($6982)
Application Deadline: May 1	**Room & Board:** $4510
Freshman Class: 6365 applied, 3555 accepted, 1500 enrolled	
SAT I Verbal/Math: 471/527	**COMPETITIVE**

Towson State University, founded in 1866, is part of the University of Maryland system, offering undergraduate and graduate programs in liberal arts and sciences, allied health sciences, education, fine arts, communication, and business and economics. There are 7 undergraduate schools and 1 graduate school. In addition to regional accreditation, Towson State has baccalaureate program accreditation with AACSB, ASLA, NASAD, NASM, NCATE, and NLN. The library contains 563,751 volumes, 730,925 microform items, and 14,643 audiovisual forms, and subscribes to 2107 periodicals. Computerized library sources and services include the card catalog, interlibrary loans, and database searching. Special learning facilities include a learning resource center, art gallery, planetarium, radio station, TV station, curriculum center, herbarium, animal museum, observatory, and greenhouse. The 321-acre campus is in a suburban area 2 miles north of Baltimore. Including residence halls, there are 40 buildings on campus.

Student Life: 83% of undergraduates are from Maryland. Students come from 48 states, 66 foreign countries, and Canada. 65% are from public schools; 35% from private. 83% are white. The average age of freshmen is 20; all undergraduates, 24. 18% do not continue beyond their first year; 58% remain to graduate.

Housing: 3112 students can be accommodated in college housing. College-sponsored living facilities include coed dormitories, on-campus apartments, and married-student housing. In addition, there are alcohol-free floors and international floors. On-campus housing is available on a first-come, first-served basis and is available on a lottery system for upperclassmen. 78% of students commute. Upperclassmen may keep cars on campus.

Activities: 8% of men belong to 18 national fraternities; 7% of women belong to 13 national sororities. There are 105 groups on campus, including art, band, cheerleading, chess, choir, chorale, chorus, computers, dance, drama, drill team, ethnic, film, gay, honors, international, jazz band, literary magazine, marching band, musical theater, newspaper, orchestra, pep band, photography, political, professional, radio and TV, religious, social, social service, student government, symphony, and yearbook. Popular campus events include Ethics Forum, Tiger Fest, Expo, and Parents Weekend.

Sports: There are 10 intercollegiate sports for men and 11 for women, and 14 intramural sports for men and 14 for women. Athletic and recreation facilities include a gymnasium with basketball and racquetball courts and a dance studio, a fitness center, a pool, a recreation center with a bowling alley and other games, playing fields, a weight room, and indoor and outdoor tracks.

Disabled Students: 95% of the campus is accessible to disabled students. The following facilities are available: wheelchair ramps, elevators, special parking, specially equipped rest rooms, special class scheduling, lowered drinking fountains, lowered telephones, and specially equipped apartments and dormitory rooms.

Services: In addition to many counseling and information services, tutoring is available in most subjects. There is a reader service for the blind, and remedial math, reading, and writing. There are also note takers, English language and tutorial services centers, a writing laboratory, and signers for the hearing impaired.

Campus Safety and Security: Campus safety and security measures include 24-hour foot and vehicle patrol, self-defense education, escort service, and shuttle buses. In addition, there are informal discussions, pamphlets/posters/films, emergency telephones, lighted pathways/sidewalks, and a police dog on campus.

Programs of Study: Towson State confers B.A., B.S., and B.F.A. degrees. Master's degrees are also awarded. Bachelor's degrees are awarded in BIOLOGICAL SCIENCE (biology/biological science), BUSINESS (accounting and business administration and management), COMMUNICATIONS AND THE ARTS (communications, dance, dramatic arts, English, fine arts, French, German, music, Spanish, and speech/debate/rhetoric), COMPUTER AND PHYSICAL SCIENCE (chemistry, computer science, mathematics, natural sciences, and physics), EDUCATION (art, dance, early childhood, education, elementary, music, physical, and secondary), HEALTH PROFESSIONS (health, medical laboratory technology, nursing, occupational therapy, and speech pathology/audiology), SOCIAL SCIENCE (anthropology, economics, geography, history, interdisciplinary studies, international studies, philosophy, political science/government, psychology, social science, sociology, and women's studies). Fine arts, business, and education are the strongest academically. Business disciplines, mass communications, and psychology have the largest enrollments.

Required: A total of 120 credits is required for most majors, including 18 core courses in the disciplines of physical education and writing, fine and performing arts, humanities, natural and mathematical sciences, and social and behavioral sciences/personal development. Students must earn a C or better in basic and advanced writing courses and at least a 2.0 GPA overall.

Special: Towson State offers a cooperative program with other institutions in the University of Maryland system, or at Loyola College, the College of Notre Dame, or Johns Hopkins University, cross-registration at more than 80 colleges through the National Student Exchange, and study abroad in 37 countries. Students may pursue a dual major in physics and engineering, an interdisciplinary studies degree, which allows them to design their own majors, a 3–2 engineering program with the University of Maryland at College Park, or nondegree study. There are pass/fail options, extensive evening offerings, and opportunities to earn credits between semesters. Internships are available in most majors, and work-study programs are offered both on and off campus. There is a freshman honors program on campus, as well as 20 national honor societies, including Phi Beta Kappa. 12 departments have honors programs.

Faculty/Classroom: 66% of faculty are male; 34%, female. 98% teach undergraduates and 2% both teach and do research. No introductory courses are taught by graduate students. The average class size in an introductory lecture is 30; in a laboratory, 24; and in a regular course offering, 25.

Admissions: 56% of the 1995–96 applicants were accepted. The SAT I scores for the 1995–96 freshman class were as follows: Verbal—70% below 500, 25% between 500 and 599, and 5% between 600 and 700; Math—44% below 500, 37% between 500 and 599, 18% between 600 and 700, and 1% above 700. 37% of the current freshmen were in the top fifth of their class; 75% were in the top two fifths. 1 freshman graduated first in the class.

Requirements: The SAT I is required, generally with scores of 500 verbal and 500 math. Towson State requires applicants to be in the upper 50% of their class, with a 2.5 GPA. The ACT will be accepted in lieu of SAT I. Applicants should have graduated from an accredited secondary school or earned the GED. Secondary preparation should include 4 years of English, 3 each of mathematics and social studies, and 2 each of science and foreign language. Prospective music and dance majors must audition. AP and CLEP credits are accepted. Important factors in the admissions decision are advanced placement or honor courses, recommendations by school officials, and ability to finance college education.

Procedure: Freshmen are admitted fall and spring. Entrance exams should be taken in the junior or senior year. There are early admissions and deferred admissions plans. Applications should be filed by May 1 for fall entry and December 1 for spring entry, along with an application fee of $25. Notification is sent on a rolling basis. A waiting list is an active part of the admissions procedure, with about 5% of all applicants on the list.

Transfer: 1718 transfer students enrolled in 1995–96. Applicants should have earned at least 30 academic credits. For those with less than 30 attempted, freshman requirements must be met. Minimum GPA requirements range from 2.0 to 2.5, depending on the number of credits completed. 30 credits of 120 must be completed at Towson State.

Visiting: There are regularly scheduled orientations for prospective students, including campus tours, a session for parents, classroom visitation, a session on the admissions process for transfers and freshmen, and a roundtable discussion. There are guides for informal visits and visitors may sit in on classes. To schedule a visit, contact the Admissions Office at (410) 830–3333 or (800) 225–5878.

Financial Aid: In 1995–96, 41% of all freshmen received some form of financial aid. 31% of freshmen received need-based aid. The average freshman award was $3143. Of that total, scholarships or need-based grants averaged $1752 ($7200 maximum); loans averaged $4035 ($13,500 maximum); and work contracts averaged $1036 ($2500 maximum). 16% of undergraduate students work part-time. Average earnings from campus work for the school year are $1214. The average financial indebtedness of the 1994–95 graduate was $12,000. Towson State is a member of CSS. The FAFSA and the college's own financial statement are required. The application deadline for fall entry is March 15.

International Students: There are currently 235 international students enrolled. The school actively recruits these students. They must take the TOEFL and achieve a minimum score of 500. The student must also take the SAT I or ACT. The school accepts the TOEFL as a substitute for the verbal SAT I. Graduates of the campus English language center are not required to take the TOEFL.

Computers: The college provides computer facilities for student use. The mainframes are 3 SGI Challenge/IRIX systems, 2 DEC VAX/VMS systems, and 2 DEC system 5200/Ultrix systems. About 400 microcomputers are available, 300 of which are networked. Software packages and computer languages include BASIC, Pascal, Lotus 1-2-3, WordPerfect, COBOL, Pagemaker, SAS, and SPSS. Also available are C++ Internet access services, Netscape, Pine, Tin, SGI, and a DEC workstation laboratory. All students may access the system 24 hours daily except 5 P.M. to 9 P.M. Fridays. There are no time limits and no fees.

Graduates: In a recent year, 2744 bachelor's degrees were awarded. The most popular majors among graduates were business administration (17%), mass communications (12%), and elementary education (9%). Within an average freshman class, 24% graduate in 4 years and 54% in 5 years. 112 companies recently recruited on campus.

Admissions Contact: Angel Jackson, Director of Admissions. E-mail: jacque.m@toa.towson.edu. A campus video is available.

UNITED STATES NAVAL ACADEMY E-3

Annapolis, MD 21402-5018 (410) 293-4361

(800) 638-9156; FAX: (410) 293-4348

Full-time: 3400 men, 600 women	Faculty: 600
Part-time: none	Ph.D.s: 90%
Graduate: none	Student/Faculty: 7 to 1
Year: semesters, summer session	Tuition: see profile
Application Deadline: March 1	Room & Board: see profile
Freshman Class: 10,422 applied, 1474 accepted, 1165 enrolled	
SAT I or ACT: required	**MOST COMPETITIVE**

The United States Naval Academy, founded in 1845, is a national military service college offering men and women undergraduate degree programs and professional training in aviation, surface ships, submarines, and various military, maritime, and technical fields. The U.S. Navy pays tuition, room and board, medical and dental care, and a monthly stipend to all Naval Academy students. In addition to regional accreditation, the academy has baccalaureate program accreditation with ABET and CSAB. The library contains 530,000 volumes and subscribes to 2000 periodicals. Computerized library sources and services include the card catalog, interlibrary loans, and database searching. Special learning facilities include a learning resource center, art gallery, planetarium, radio station, TV station, propulsion laboratory, nuclear reactor, oceanographic research vessel, towing tanks, flight simulator, and naval history museum. The 329-acre campus is in a small town 30 miles southeast of Baltimore and 35 miles east of Washington, D.C. Including residence halls, there are 25 buildings on campus.

Student Life: 97% of undergraduates are from out-of-state, mostly the Northeast. Students come from 50 states and 21 foreign countries. 80% are white. 50% are Protestant; 49% Catholic. The average age of freshmen is 18.5; all undergraduates, 20. 11% do not continue beyond their first year; 77% remain to graduate.

Housing: 4100 students can be accommodated in college housing. College-sponsored living facilities include coed dormitories. On-campus housing is guaranteed for all 4 years. All students live on campus; of those, 75% remain on campus on weekends. Alcohol is not permitted. Upperclassmen may keep cars on campus.

Activities: There are no fraternities or sororities. There are 75 groups on campus, including bagpipe band, cheerleading, chess, choir, chorus, computers, drama, drill team, drum and bugle corps, ethnic, honors, international, jazz band, literary magazine, musical theater, pep band, photography, professional, radio and TV, religious, social, social service, student government, and yearbook. Popular campus events include Commissioning Week, which includes the Plebe Recognition Ceremony, Ring Dance, and graduation.

Sports: There are 20 intercollegiate sports for men and 9 for women, and 23 intramural sports for men and 10 for women. Athletic and recreation facilities include a 30,000-seat stadium, a 5000-seat basketball arena, an Olympic pool with a diving well for 10-meter diving boards, a wrestling arena, a 200-meter indoor track, a 400-meter outdoor track, an indoor ice rink, 6 Nautilus and weight rooms, and facilities for gymnastics, boxing, fencing, and other sports.

Disabled Students: The entire campus is accessible to disabled students. The following facilities are available: wheelchair ramps, elevators, special parking, and specially equipped rest rooms.

Services: In addition to many counseling and information services, tutoring is available in most subjects. There is remedial math, reading, and writing.

Campus Safety and Security: Campus safety and security measures include 24-hour foot and vehicle patrol, self-defense education, shuttle buses, and emergency telephones. In addition, there are lighted pathways/sidewalks and gate guards.

Programs of Study: The academy confers the B.S. degree. Bachelor's degrees are awarded in COMMUNICATIONS AND THE ARTS (English), COMPUTER AND PHYSICAL SCIENCE (chemistry, computer science, mathematics, oceanography, physics, and science), ENGINEERING AND ENVIRONMENTAL DESIGN (aeronautical engineering, electrical/electronics engineering, engineering, marine engineering, mechanical engineering, naval architecture and marine engineering, ocean engineering, and systems engineering), SOCIAL SCIENCE (economics, history, and political science/government). Chemistry, aeronautical engineering, and systems engineering are the strongest academically. Mechanical engineering, mathematics, oceanography, and political science have the largest enrollments.

Required: Students must complete 140 semester hours, including core requirements in engineering, natural sciences, humanities, and social sciences. Physical education is required during all 4 years. Physical readiness testing must be passed. During required summer training sessions, students train aboard U.S. ships, submarines, and aircraft. Graduates serve at least 6 years on active duty as commissioned officers of the Navy or Marine Corps.

Special: Study in Washington, D.C., is available during 1 semester of the senior year. A voluntary graduate program is available for those who complete requirements early and wish to begin master's work at nearby institutions, such as Georgetown or Johns Hopkins universities. Trident Scholars may spend their senior year in independent research. There are 10 national honor societies on campus. 5 departments have honors programs.

Faculty/Classroom: 80% of faculty are male; 20%, female. All teach undergraduates. The average class size in an introductory lecture is 23; in a laboratory, 10; and in a regular course offering, 15.

Admissions: 14% of the 1995–96 applicants were accepted. The SAT I scores for the 1995–96 freshman class were as follows: Verbal—15% below 500, 47% between 500 and 599, 34% between 600 and 700, and 4% above 700; Math—1% below 500, 15% between 500 and 599, 53% between 600 and 700, and 31% above 700. 78% of the current freshmen were in the top fifth of their class; 95% were in the top two fifths.

Requirements: The SAT I or ACT is required. Candidates must be unmarried with no dependents, U.S. citizens of good moral character, and between 17 and 21 years of age. Candidates should have a sound secondary school background, including 4 years each of English and mathematics, 2 of a foreign language, and 1 each of U.S. history, world or European history, chemistry, physics, and computer literacy. Candidates must obtain an official nomination from congressional or military sources. An interview is conducted, and medical and physical examinations must be passed to qualify for admission. AP credits are accepted. Important factors in the admissions decision are advanced placement or honor courses, recommendations by school officials, and leadership record.

Procedure: Freshmen are admitted in the summer. Entrance exams should be taken after December of the junior year. Applications should be filed by March 1 for fall entry. Notification is sent on a rolling basis.

Transfer: All students enter as freshmen. 140 credits of 140 must be completed at the academy.

Visiting: There are regularly scheduled orientations for prospective students, including visitation weekends for candidates likely to be accepted, summer seminars, and Admissions Day. Visitors may sit in on classes.

International Students: There are currently 40 international students enrolled. They must take the TOEFL. The student must also take the SAT I or the ACT.

Computers: The college provides computer facilities for student use. The mainframe is a Honeywell DPS8. There are also 1500 microcomputers available in the dormitory, library, computer center, and computer laboratory. All students may access the system. There are no time limits and no fees. In addition, each student is issued a personal computer.

Graduates: Of the 1994 graduating class, 4% were enrolled in graduate school within 6 months of graduation and all had found employment.

Admissions Contact: Candidate Guidance Office. A campus video is available.

UNIVERSITY OF MARYLAND SYSTEM

The University of Maryland System, established in 1807, is a public system in Maryland. It is governed by a board of regents, whose chief administrator is chancellor. The primary goal of the system is research, teaching, and public service, while each campus serves a special mission. The flagship institution of the system is the University of Maryland at College Park, which holds the distinctive mission of enrolling the most academically talented students from the state and across the nation. The combined enrollment of all campuses in the UM system is 127,692; the total of faculty for all campuses is 9,361. Altogether UM system instutions offer more than 600 academic programs leading to 31 undergraduate, master's, doctoral, and pre-professional degrees. More specific profiles for each campus are included in this chapter in alphabetical order with other Maryland schools.

UNIVERSITY OF MARYLAND/BALTIMORE COUNTY D-2

Baltimore, MD 21228 (410) 455-2291

(800) UMBC-4U2; FAX: (410) 455-1094

Full-time: 3135 men, 3176 women	Faculty: 424; I, --$
Part-time: 1188 men, 1400 women	Ph.D.s: 88%
Graduate: 762 men, 796 women	Student/Faculty: 15 to 1
Year: 4-1-4, summer session	Tuition: $3852 ($8680)
Application Deadline: March 15	Room & Board: $4474
Freshman Class: 4131 applied, 2615 accepted, 999 enrolled	
SAT I Verbal/Math: 510/600	ACT: 22 **VERY COMPETITIVE**

University of Maryland/Baltimore County, founded in 1963 as a member of the state university system, offers a wide variety of degree programs. There are 2 undergraduate schools and 1 graduate school. In addition to regional accreditation, UMBC has baccalaureate program accreditation with ABET, CSWE, and NLN. The library contains 610,637 volumes, 854,735 microform items, and 28,694 audiovisual forms, and subscribes to 4067 periodicals. Computerized library sources and services include the card catalog, interlibrary loans, and database searching. Special learning facilities include a learning resource center, art gallery, radio station, TV studio, imaging research center, and the National Center for Structural Biochemistry. The 485-acre campus is in a suburban area 5 miles southwest of Baltimore. Including residence halls, there are 47 buildings on campus.

Student Life: 93% of undergraduates are from Maryland. Students come from 32 states, 62 foreign countries, and Canada. 84% are from public schools; 16% from private. 68% are white; 15% African American; 12% Asian American. The average age of freshmen is 19; all undergraduates, 25. 14% do not continue beyond their first year; 56% remain to graduate.

Housing: 2278 students can be accommodated in college housing. College-sponsored living facilities include single-sex and coed dormitories and on-campus apartments. In addition, there are honors houses and wellness and quiet-study floors. On-campus housing is available on a first-come, first-served basis. Priority is given to out-of-town students. 76% of students commute. Alcohol is not permitted. All students may keep cars on campus.

Activities: 8% of men belong to 12 national fraternities; 7% of women belong to 8 national sororities. There are 180 groups on campus, including band, cheerleading, chess, choir, chorus, computers, dance, drama, ethnic, film, gay, honors, international, jazz band, literary magazine, musical theater, newspaper, opera, orchestra, pep band, political, professional, radio and TV, religious, social, social service, student government, and symphony. Popular campus events include Quadmania, Gospel Extravaganza, Shakespeare-on-Wheels, Jazz Fest, and Fall Frenzy.

Sports: There are 11 intercollegiate sports for men and 11 for women, and 13 intramural sports for men and 12 for women. Athletic and recreation facilities include a multipurpose field house, an aquatic center, a fitness center, tennis courts, a 4500-seat stadium, playing and practice fields, an indoor track, an outdoor cross-country course, and a golf driving range.

Disabled Students: 95% of the campus is accessible to disabled students. The following facilities are available: wheelchair ramps, elevators, special parking, specially equipped rest rooms, special class scheduling, lowered drinking fountains, and lowered telephones.

Services: In addition to many counseling and information services, tutoring is available in most subjects. There is a reader service for the blind, and remedial math, reading, and writing.

Campus Safety and Security: Campus safety and security measures include self-defense education, escort service, shuttle buses, and pamphlets/posters/films. In addition, there are emergency telephones, lighted pathways/sidewalks, a 24-hour police department, and a campus risk management department.

Programs of Study: UMBC confers B.A., B.S., B.S.E., and B.S.N. degrees. Master's and doctoral degrees are also awarded. Bachelor's degrees are awarded in BIOLOGICAL SCIENCE (biochemistry and biology/biological science), BUSINESS (management information systems), COMMUNICATIONS AND THE ARTS (dramatic arts, English, fine arts, French, German, languages, music, Russian, Spanish, and visual and performing arts), COMPUTER AND PHYSICAL SCIENCE (chemistry, computer science, mathematics, and physics), EDUCATION (early childhood, elementary, and secondary), ENGINEERING AND ENVIRONMENTAL DESIGN (chemical engineering, emergency/disaster science, engineering, and mechanical engineering), HEALTH PROFESSIONS (health science and nursing), SOCIAL SCIENCE (African American studies, American studies, classical/ancient civilization, economics, geography, history, interdisciplinary studies, philosophy, political science/government, psychology, social work, and sociology). Chemistry, biology, and engineering are the strongest academically. Information systems management, psychology, and computer science have the largest enrollments.

Required: To graduate, students are required to complete at least 120 credits, including 45 at the upper-division level, with a minimum GPA of 2.0. The core curriculum includes courses in arts and humanities, social sciences, mathematics and natural sciences, physical education, and modern or classical language and culture. Students must pass an English composition course with a C or better.

Special: Dual and student-designed majors, cooperative education programs in all majors, cross-registration with several state schools, internships, study abroad, work-study programs, B.A.-B.S. degrees, pass/fail options, and nondegree study are available. UMBC also offers various opportunities in interdisciplinary studies and in such fields as artificial intelligence and optical communications. There is a freshman honors program on campus, as well as 15 national honor societies. 14 departments have honors programs.

Faculty/Classroom: 65% of faculty are male; 35%, female. All both teach and do research. Graduate students teach 4% of introductory courses. The average class size in an introductory lecture is 200; in a laboratory, 20; and in a regular course offering, 40.

Admissions: 63% of the 1995–96 applicants were accepted. The SAT I scores for the 1995–96 freshman class were as follows: Verbal—41% below 500, 38% between 500 and 599, 20% between 600 and 700, and 1% above 700; Math—11% below 500, 36% between 500 and 599, 43% between 600 and 700, and 10% above 700. The ACT scores were 24% below 21, 50% between 21 and 23, 21% between 24 and 26, 4% between 27 and 28, and 1% above 28. 50% of the current freshmen were in the top fifth of their class; 78% were in the top two fifths. There were 3 National Merit finalists and 11 semifinalists. 11 freshmen graduated first in their class.

Requirements: The SAT I or ACT is required. UMBC recommends that applicants be in the upper 30% of their class with a 2.5 GPA. Minimum high school preparation should include 4 years of English, 3 years each of social science/history and mathematics, including algebra I and II and geometry, and 2 years each of laboratory sciences and a foreign language. An essay is required of all freshman applicants. AP and CLEP credits are accepted. Important factors in the admissions decision are advanced placement or honor courses, evidence of special talent, and recommendations by school officials.

Procedure: Freshmen are admitted to all sessions. Entrance exams should be taken by the fall of the senior year. There is an early admissions plan. Applications should be filed by March 15 for fall entry, December 1 for winter entry, February 1 for spring entry, and May 15 for summer entry, along with an application fee of $25. A waiting list is an active part of the admissions procedure, with about 5% of all applicants on the list.

Transfer: 1279 transfer students enrolled in 1995–96. A 2.5 cumulative GPA for all previous college work is recommended. Applicants with fewer than 28 semester hours should submit SAT I scores and the high school transcript; they must also meet freshman admission requirements. 30 credits of 120 must be completed at UMBC.

Visiting: There are regularly scheduled orientations for prospective students, including a group information session with an admissions counselor followed by a student-guided walking tour of campus. Saturday information sessions and 3 campus open houses are also scheduled each fall. There are guides for informal visits and visitors may sit in on classes and stay overnight at the school. To schedule a visit, contact the Admissions Office.

Financial Aid: In 1995–96, 60% of all freshmen and 45% of continuing students received some form of financial aid. 40% of freshmen and 30% of continuing students received need-based aid. The average freshman award was $3295. Of that total, scholarships or need-based grants averaged $1300 ($4000 maximum); loans averaged $1395 ($3625 maximum); and work contracts averaged $600 ($1200 maximum). 21% of undergraduate students work part-time. Average earnings from campus work for the school year are $1200. UMBC is a member of CSS. The FAFSA is required. The application deadline for fall entry is March 1.

International Students: There are currently 161 international students enrolled. The school actively recruits these students. They must take the TOEFL and achieve a minimum score of 550.

Computers: The college provides computer facilities for student use. The mainframes are a DEC VAX 4000 Model 500 and an SGI CRIMSON. 250 Macintosh and MS-DOS systems microcomputers and 70 SGI graphics workstations are located in student laboratories, with some computer facilities in dormitories and various academic buildings. All are networked to the mainframes, with connectivity to Internet, Bitnet, and Gopher services. All students may access the system. There are no time limits and no fees.

Graduates: In 1994–95, 1553 bachelor's degrees were awarded. The most popular majors among graduates were psychology (12%), information systems (11%), and computer science (7%). Within an average freshman class, 18% graduate in 4 years, 46% in 5 years, and 56% in 6 years. 747 companies recruited on campus in 1994–95.

Admissions Contact: Thomas Taylor, Director of Admissions. E-mail: admissions@umbc.edu.

UNIVERSITY OF MARYLAND/COLLEGE PARK D-3
College Park, MD 20742   (301) 314-8385
(800) 422-5867; FAX: (301) 314-9693

Full-time: 10,635 men, 9709 women	Faculty: 1265; I, -$
Part-time: 1461 men, 1117 women	Ph.D.s: 91%
Graduate: 3985 men, 3739 women	Student/Faculty: 16 to 1
Year: semesters, summer session	Tuition: $3794 ($9738)
Application Deadline: December 1	Room & Board: $5311
Freshman Class: 14,956 applied, 10,143 accepted, 3632 enrolled	
SAT I Verbal/Math: 510/600	VERY COMPETITIVE

University of Maryland/College Park, founded in 1856, is a coeducational, land-grant institution, the flagship campus of the state's university system, offering undergraduate and graduate degrees through

13 undergraduate and 14 graduate schools. There are 13 undergraduate and 14 graduate schools. In addition to regional accreditation, Maryland has baccalaureate program accreditation with AACSB, ABET, ACEJMC, ACPE, ADA, ASLA, CSWE, NAAB, NASM, NCATE, and NLN. The 7 libraries contain 2,464,623 volumes, 5,230,525 microform items, and 155,703 audiovisual forms, and subscribe to 25,974 periodicals. Computerized library sources and services include the card catalog, interlibrary loans, and database searching. Special learning facilities include a learning resource center, art gallery, radio station, and TV station. The 1281-acre campus is in a suburban area 9 miles northeast of Washington, D.C. Including residence halls, there are 350 buildings on campus.

Student Life: 73% of undergraduates are from Maryland. Students come from 50 states, 113 foreign countries, and Canada. 80% are from public schools; 20% from private. 63% are white; 14% Asian American; 13% African American. 32% are Catholic, 19% Jewish, and 17% claim no religious affiliation. The average age of freshmen is 19; all undergraduates, 22.5. 15% do not continue beyond their first year; 66% remain to graduate.

Housing: 7470 students can be accommodated in college housing. College-sponsored living facilities include single-sex and coed dormitories, on-campus apartments, fraternity houses, and sorority houses. In addition there are honors houses, language houses, special interest houses, and an international house. On-campus housing is guaranteed for the freshman year only, is available on a first-come, first-served basis, and is available on a lottery system for upperclassmen. 70% of students commute. Alcohol is not permitted. Upperclassmen may keep cars on campus.

Activities: 13% of men belong to 26 national fraternities; 14% of women belong to 20 national sororities. There are 274 groups on campus, including art, band, cheerleading, chess, choir, chorale, chorus, computers, dance, drama, drill team, ethnic, film, gay, honors, international, jazz band, literary magazine, marching band, musical theater, newspaper, opera, orchestra, pep band, photography, political, professional, radio and TV, religious, social, social service, student government, symphony, and yearbook. Popular campus events include University Talent Show, Panhellenic Council Show, Handel Festival, and Art Attack.

Sports: There are 12 intercollegiate sports for men and 12 for women, and 28 intramural sports for men and 28 for women. Athletic and recreation facilities include swimming pools, intramural fields, tennis, squash, racquetball, and basketball courts, a weight room, a track, a bowling alley, a 50000-seat stadium, a 14500-seat gymnasium, and a golf course.

Disabled Students: 85% of the campus is accessible to disabled students. The following facilities are available: wheelchair ramps, elevators, special parking, specially equipped rest rooms, special class scheduling, lowered drinking fountains, lowered telephones, and a special shuttle service.

Services: In addition to many counseling and information services, tutoring is available in most subjects, including all 100- and 200-level courses. There is a reader service for the blind.

Campus Safety and Security: Campus safety and security measures include 24-hour foot and vehicle patrol, escort service, shuttle buses, and informal discussions. In addition, there are pamphlets/posters/films, emergency telephones, and lighted pathways/sidewalks.

Programs of Study: Maryland confers B.A., B.S., B.L.A., and B.M. degrees. Master's and doctoral degrees are also awarded. Bachelor's degrees are awarded in AGRICULTURE (agricultural economics, agriculture, agronomy, animal science, horticulture, and natural resource management), BIOLOGICAL SCIENCE (biochemistry, biology/biological science, botany, entomology, microbiology, and zoology), BUSINESS (accounting, banking and finance, business administration and management, business economics, management science, marketing/retailing/merchandising, personnel management, recreation and leisure services, and transportation management), COMMUNICATIONS AND THE ARTS (advertising, art history and appreciation, broadcasting, Chinese, classics, dance, design, dramatic arts, English, film arts, fine arts, French, German, Italian, Japanese, journalism, linguistics, music, romance languages, Russian, Spanish, speech/debate/rhetoric, and studio art), COMPUTER AND PHYSICAL SCIENCE (astronomy, chemistry, computer programming, computer science, geology, mathematics, physical sciences, physics, and statistics), EDUCATION (art, business, early childhood, elementary, foreign languages, health, home economics, industrial arts, music, physical, science, secondary, and special), ENGINEERING AND ENVIRONMENTAL DESIGN (aeronautical engineering, agricultural engineering, architecture, chemical engineering, civil engineering, electrical/electronics engineering, engineering, fire protection engineering, interior design, landscape architecture/design, and mechanical engineering), HEALTH PROFESSIONS (predentistry, prepharmacy, and speech pathology/audiology), SOCIAL SCIENCE (African American studies, American studies, anthropology, criminal justice, dietetics, economics, family/consumer studies, food science, geogra-

phy, history, Judaic studies, philosophy, physical fitness/movement, political science/government, psychology, social science, sociology, and women's studies). Engineering, computer science, and physics are the strongest academically. Psychology, English, and accounting have the largest enrollments.

Required: Most programs require a minimum of 120 credits for graduation; the number of hours required in the major varies. All students must take 29 credits in a multidisciplinary core curriculum, including 10 in mathematics and science, 9 each in social science and advanced studies, and 1 diversity course. Freshman and junior composition are also required, and students must maintain a 2.0 GPA.

Special: Each of the 13 undergraduate schools offers special programs, and there is a campuswide cooperative education program. In addition, the university offers cross-registration with other colleges in the Consortium of Universities of the Washington Metropolitan Area, the B.A.-B.S. degree, dual and student-designed majors, nondegree study, an accelerated veterinary medicine program, study abroad, work-study programs with nonprofit organizations, and various internship opportunities with members of Congress and the Maryland State House, with local media, and with various federal agencies. There is a freshman honors program on campus, as well as 46 national honor societies, including Phi Beta Kappa. 30 departments have honors programs.

Faculty/Classroom: In a recent year, 72% of faculty were male; 28%, female. 62% taught undergraduates. Graduate students teach about 40% of introductory courses. The average class size in an introductory lecture is 42; in a laboratory, 18; and in a regular course offering, 30.

Admissions: 68% of the 1995–96 applicants were accepted. The SAT I scores for the 1995–96 freshman class were as follows: Verbal—43% below 500, 40% between 500 and 599, 15% between 600 and 700, and 2% above 700; Math—13% below 500, 33% between 500 and 599, 43% between 600 and 700, and 11% above 700. 53% of the current freshmen were in the top fifth of their class; 83% were in the top two fifths. There were 18 National Merit finalists and 110 semifinalists.

Requirements: The SAT I or ACT is required. The university evaluates examination scores along with other admissions criteria. Applicants should be graduates of accredited secondary schools or have the GED. Secondary preparation should include 4 years of English, 2 of algebra and 1 of plane geometry, 2 of laboratory sciences, and 3 of history or social sciences. Music majors are required to audition. AP and CLEP credits are accepted. Important factors in the admissions decision are advanced placement or honor courses, recommendations by school officials, and evidence of special talent.

Procedure: Freshmen are admitted fall, spring, and summer. Entrance exams should be taken at the end of the junior year or beginning of the senior year. There is an early admissions plan. Applications should be filed by December 1 for fall entry and February 15 for spring entry, along with an application fee of $30. Notification is sent by March 15. A waiting list is an active part of the admissions procedure.

Transfer: 2300 transfer students enrolled in 1995–96. Applicants from regionally accredited institutions should have attempted at least 9 credits and have earned at least a 3.0 GPA, although this requirement varies depending on space available. Applicants from Maryland community colleges may be given special consideration and admitted with lower GPAs. 30 credits of 120 must be completed at Maryland.

Visiting: There are regularly scheduled orientations for prospective students, consisting of an information session followed by a tour. There are guides for informal visits and visitors may sit in on classes and stay overnight at the school. To schedule a visit, contact the Undergraduate Admissions Office.

Financial Aid: In 1995–96, 62% of all freshmen and 55% of continuing students received some form of financial aid. 51% of freshmen and 44% of continuing students received need-based aid. The average freshman award was $5041. Of that total, scholarships or need-based grants averaged $1912 ($17,945 maximum); loans averaged $3128 ($17,945 maximum); and work contracts averaged $822 ($1200 maximum). 23% of undergraduate students work part-time. Average earnings from campus work for the school year are $1249. The average financial indebtedness of the 1994–95 graduate was $15,448. Maryland is a member of CSS. The FAFSA is required. The application deadline for fall entry is February 15.

International Students: There are currently 694 international students enrolled. They must take the TOEFL and achieve a minimum score of 550. The student must also take the SAT I or the ACT.

Computers: The college provides computer facilities for student use. The mainframe is an IBM ES9000. There are also 1700 microcomputers available for student use in academic buildings, computer centers, libraries, and residence halls. IBM and Apple word-processing programs are available to all registered students. The Computer Science Center supports advanced workstation and microcomputer laboratories across campus for day and evening self-study and class projects. Those students with account numbers may access the system at any time. There are no time limits and no fees.

Graduates: In 1994–95, 4537 bachelor's degrees were awarded. The most popular majors among graduates were accounting (6%), English language and literature (5%), and criminology and criminal justice (5%). Within an average freshman class, 1% graduate in 3 years, 30% in 4 years, 54% in 5 years, and 66% in 6 years. 448 companies recruited on campus in 1994–95. Of the 1994 graduating class, 14% were enrolled in graduate school within 6 months of graduation and 36% had found employment.

Admissions Contact: Dr. Linda Clement, Director of Undergraduate Admissions. E-mail: um-admit@uga.umd.edu.

UNIVERSITY OF MARYLAND/EASTERN SHORE
F-4

Princess Anne, MD 21853   (410) 651-6410

(800) 232-UMES; FAX: (410) 651-7922

Full-time: 1000 men, 1310 women	**Faculty:** 88; IIA, --$
Part-time: 47 men, 183 women	**Ph.D.s:** 80%
Graduate: 121 men, 147 women	**Student/Faculty:** 26 to 1
Year: semesters, summer session	**Tuition:** $2855 ($7536)
Application Deadline: May 6	**Room & Board:** $4030
Freshman Class: 2480 applied, 1882 accepted, 830 enrolled	
SAT I Verbal/Math: 387/361	**LESS COMPETITIVE**

University of Maryland/Eastern Shore, founded in 1886, is a public university, part of the University of Maryland System, offering undergraduate and graduate programs in the arts and sciences, professional studies, and agricultural sciences. There are 3 undergraduate schools and one graduate school. The library contains 150,000 volumes. Computerized library sources and services include the card catalog, interlibrary loans, and database searching. Special learning facilities include a learning resource center, art gallery, and radio station. The 600-acre campus is in a rural area 15 miles south of Salisbury. Including residence halls, there are 40 buildings on campus.

Student Life: 71% of undergraduates are from Maryland. Students come from 32 states, 48 foreign countries, and Canada. 85% are from public schools; 15% from private. 76% are African American; 18% white. 90% are Protestant; 10% claim no religious affiliation. The average age of freshmen is 18; all undergraduates, 24. 25% do not continue beyond their first year; 36% remain to graduate.

Housing: 1530 students can be accommodated in college housing. College-sponsored living facilities include single-sex dormitories, on-campus apartments, and off-campus apartments. In addition there are honors houses and a residential complex. On-campus housing is available on a first-come, first-served basis and is available on a lottery system for upperclassmen. 50% of students live on campus; of those, 30% remain on campus on weekends. All students may keep cars on campus.

Activities: 20% of men belong to 4 national fraternities; 20% of women belong to 4 national sororities. There are 25 groups on campus, including art, band, cheerleading, choir, chorale, chorus, computers, dance, drama, drill team, ethnic, honors, international, jazz band, literary magazine, musical theater, newspaper, pep band, photography, political, professional, radio and TV, religious, social, social service, student government, and yearbook. Popular campus events include Parents Day, Spring Festival, Ethnic Festival, and Founder's Day.

Sports: There are 5 intercollegiate sports for men and 5 for women, and 4 intramural sports for men and 4 for women. Athletic and recreation facilities include an indoor swimming pool and a 3000-seat stadium.

Disabled Students: 20% of the campus is accessible to disabled students. The following facilities are available: wheelchair ramps, elevators, special parking, specially equipped rest rooms, special class scheduling, lowered drinking fountains, and lowered telephones.

Services: In addition to many counseling and information services, tutoring is available in every subject. There is remedial math, reading, and writing.

Campus Safety and Security: Campus safety and security measures include 24-hour foot and vehicle patrol, escort service, shuttle buses, and informal discussions. In addition, there are pamphlets/posters/films, emergency telephones, lighted pathways/sidewalks, and a student security team.

Programs of Study: UMES confers B.A., B.S., B.G.S., and B.M. degrees. Master's and doctoral degrees are also awarded. Bachelor's degrees are awarded in AGRICULTURE (agriculture and poultry science), BIOLOGICAL SCIENCE (biology/biological science), BUSINESS (accounting, business administration and management, and hotel/motel and restaurant management), COMMUNICATIONS AND THE ARTS (English), COMPUTER AND PHYSICAL SCIENCE (chemistry, computer science, and mathematics), EDUCATION (agricultural, art, business, elementary, health, home economics, industrial arts, mathematics, music, physical, science, secondary, and social science), ENGINEERING AND ENVIRONMENTAL DESIGN (aeronauti-

cal science, construction technology, engineering technology, and environmental science), HEALTH PROFESSIONS (physical therapy and rehabilitation therapy), SOCIAL SCIENCE (criminal justice, history, home economics, liberal arts/general studies, and sociology). Physical therapy, engineering, and environmental science are the strongest academically. Business, hotel restaurant management, and biology have the largest enrollments.

Required: Students must complete 122 hours, including 36 hours in the major, 15 in communicative and quantitative skills, 9 in humanities, 7 in natural sciences, 6 in social sciences, and 4 in health and physical education. A minimum 2.0 overall GPA is required.

Special: Students may cross-register at Salisbury State University. A cooperative education program, internships, a winter term, work-study programs, a general studies degree, and dual and student-designed majors are offered. Also available are an accelerated degree program and a 3–2 engineering degree with the University of Maryland/College Park. There are pass/fail options. There is a freshman honors program on campus, as well as 1 national honor society. 10 departments have honors programs.

Faculty/Classroom: 45% of faculty are male; 55%, female. 85% teach undergraduates and 15% do research. Graduate students teach 1% of introductory courses. The average class size in an introductory lecture is 75; in a laboratory, 18; and in a regular course offering, 30.

Admissions: 76% of the 1995–96 applicants were accepted. 15% of the current freshmen were in the top fifth of their class; 45% were in the top two fifths.

Requirements: The SAT I is required. UMES requires applicants to be in the upper 40% of their class. A minimum GPA of 2.5 is required. Applicants should be graduates of accredited secondary schools or have the GED. High school preparation should include 4 years of English, 3 each of social science or history and mathematics, including 2 of algebra and 1 of geometry, and 2 of laboratory science. An essay and interview are recommended. UMES recommends that prospective art education majors submit a portfolio. Students may earn credit by examination. AP and CLEP credits are accepted. Important factors in the admissions decision are advanced placement or honor courses, leadership record, and recommendations by school officials.

Procedure: Freshmen are admitted to all sessions. Entrance exams should be taken in April. There are early decision, early admissions, and deferred admissions plans. Applications should be filed by May 6 for fall entry, December for spring entry, and May for summer entry, along with an application fee of $25. Notification is sent on a rolling basis. 6 early decision candidates were accepted for the 1995–96 class.

Transfer: 129 transfer students enrolled in 1995–96. Transfer applicants must have attempted at least 9 credits at another institution and have at least a cumulative GPA of 2.0, or have earned an associate degree or completed 56 hours of community college work. 75 credits of 122 must be completed at UMES.

Visiting: There are regularly scheduled orientations for prospective students, including 2 formal orientation sessions and 9 visitation/open house days. There are guides for informal visits and visitors may sit in on classes and stay overnight at the school. To schedule a visit, contact the Office of Recruitment at (410) 651-6178 or (800) 232-UMES.

Financial Aid: In 1995–96, 80% of all freshmen and 85% of continuing students received some form of financial aid. 75% of freshmen and 80% of continuing students received need-based aid. The average freshman award was $3100. 30% of undergraduate students work part-time. Average earnings from campus work for the school year are $700. UMES is a member of CSS. The college's own financial statement is required. The application deadline for fall entry is April 1.

International Students: There are currently 122 international students enrolled. They must take the TOEFL and achieve a minimum score of 500. The student must also take the SAT I.

Computers: The college provides computer facilities for student use. The mainframe is an IBM 4341. About 80 microcomputers, including IBM PS/2 Models 30, 50, and 502, and AT&T 6300, are available in the library and various departments. A limited number may access the system. There are no fees.

Graduates: In 1994–95, 347 bachelor's degrees were awarded. The most popular majors among graduates were business administration (16%), physical therapy (10%), and hotel and restaurant management (10%). Within an average freshman class, 25% graduate in 6 years. 120 companies recruited on campus in 1994–95.

Admissions Contact: Dr. Rochell Peoples, Assistant Vice President, Student Affairs/Enrollment Management. E-mail: rpeoples@umes3.umd.edu.

UNIVERSITY OF MARYLAND/UNIVERSITY COLLEGE

College Park, MD 20742-1609

D-3

(301) 985-7930
FAX: (301) 985-7364

Full-time: 497 men, 595 women
Part-time: 4183 men, 5076 women
Graduate: 2040 men, 1813 women
Year: semesters, summer session
Application Deadline: open
Freshman Class: n/av
SAT I or ACT: not required

Faculty: 10
Ph.D.s: n/av
Student/Faculty: 16 to 1
Tuition: $5220 ($5850)
Room & Board: n/app

NONCOMPETITIVE

University of Maryland/University College was founded in 1947 to serve the needs of the adult continuing education student. It offers evening and weekend courses in the liberal arts and sciences and in business at more than 30 locations throughout the Washington, D.C.-Baltimore area and the state of Maryland. There is 1 graduate school. Computerized library sources and services include the card catalog and database searching. Special learning facilities include a learning resource center and art gallery. The campus is in an urban area.

Student Life: 78% of undergraduates are from Maryland. Students come from 47 states and Canada. 69% are white; 20% African American. The average age of all undergraduates is 32.

Housing: There are no residence halls. All students commute. Alcohol is not permitted. All students may keep cars on campus.

Activities: There are no fraternities or sororities.

Sports: There is no sports program at UMUC.

Services: In addition to many counseling and information services, tutoring is available in some subjects, including mathematics, writing, and accounting. There is a reader service for the blind. Referrals are available for tutoring in other subjects. There are fees for tutoring.

Programs of Study: UMUC confers B.A. and B.S. degrees. Associate and master's degrees are also awarded. Bachelor's degrees are awarded in BIOLOGICAL SCIENCE (microbiology), BUSINESS (accounting, banking and finance, business administration and management, business law, management science, marketing/retailing/merchandising, and personnel management), COMMUNICATIONS AND THE ARTS (art history and appreciation, broadcasting, communications, English, fine arts, journalism, languages, and speech/debate/rhetoric), COMPUTER AND PHYSICAL SCIENCE (computer science and geology), HEALTH PROFESSIONS (health care administration), SOCIAL SCIENCE (anthropology, behavioral science, criminal justice, economics, geography, history, humanities, interdisciplinary studies, paralegal studies, philosophy, political science/government, psychology, and sociology). Business has the largest enrollment.

Required: A general education requirement of 30 semester hours includes courses in communications, humanities, social sciences, and mathematics/science. The B.A. degree requires 12 semester hours of a foreign language. A minimum 2.0 GPA and 120 credit hours are required to graduate.

Special: There are a number of work-study programs with local employers. Credit by examination, credit for life/work experience, non-degree study, and pass/fail options are available. Through UMUC's open learning program, a number of independent learning courses, including telecourses, are available. There are 4 national honor societies on campus.

Faculty/Classroom: 77% of faculty are male; 23%, female. All teach undergraduates.

Requirements: Students should be graduates of an accredited secondary school or have a GED equivalent. AP and CLEP credits are accepted.

Procedure: Freshmen are admitted to all sessions. Application deadlines are open. Application fee is $25. The college accepts all applicants. Notification is sent on a rolling basis.

Transfer: 30 credits of 120 must be completed at UMUC.

Financial Aid: UMUC is a member of CSS. The FAFSA and SAR (for Pell) are required. Check with the school for current deadlines.

International Students: In a recent year, 17 international students were enrolled. They must take the TOEFL or the college's own test and achieve a minimum score on the TOEFL of 550.

Computers: The college provides computer facilities for student use. The mainframes are 4341 Model N12, a DEC VAX 11/780, a CDC CYBER 180, and an HP 8255. There are also 153 IBM, Zenith, and AT&T microcomputers available at various locations. All students may access the system. There are no time limits and no fees.

Admissions Contact: Anne Rahill, Admissions Office.

VILLA JULIE COLLEGE

Stevenson, MD 21153

D-2

(410) 486-7001

Full-time: 190 men, 870 women
Part-time: 120 men, 680 women
Graduate: none
Year: semesters, summer session
Application Deadline: open
Freshman Class: n/av
SAT I or ACT: required

Faculty: 51; III
Ph.D.s: 36%
Student/Faculty: 21 to 1
Tuition: $6900
Room & Board: $3000

LESS COMPETITIVE

Villa Julie College, founded in 1947, is an independent, comprehensive college offering career preparation with a liberal arts foundation. Figures given in the above capsule are approximate. The library contains 78,534 volumes, 15,450 microform items, and 1350 audiovisual forms, and subscribes to 510 periodicals. Computerized library sources and services include the card catalog and database searching. Special learning facilities include a learning resource center, art gallery, theater, and video studio. The 60-acre campus is in a suburban area 10 miles northwest of Baltimore. There are 6 buildings on campus.

Student Life: 98% of undergraduates are from Maryland. Students come from 5 states and 5 foreign countries. 70% are from public schools; 30% from private. 80% are white; 12% African American. 39% are Catholic; 29% Protestant. The average age of freshmen is 18.1; all undergraduates, 26.7.

Housing: College-sponsored living facilities include coed off-campus apartments, available on a lottery system for upperclassmen. All students commute. Alcohol is not permitted. All students may keep cars on campus.

Activities: 5% of women belong to 1 national sorority. There are no fraternities. There are 20 groups on campus, including art, cheerleading, computers, drama, ethnic, honors, jazz band, literary magazine, newspaper, political, professional, religious, social, social service, and student government. Popular campus events include Welcome Picnic, Naval Academy Mixer, Christmas Party, art receptions, Autumn Bonfire, and All-College Meetings.

Sports: There are 6 intercollegiate sports for men and 7 for women, and 5 intramural sports for men and 5 for women. Athletic and recreation facilities include tennis courts and an athletic field.

Disabled Students: All of the campus is accessible to disabled students. The following facilities are available: wheelchair ramps, elevators, special parking, specially equipped rest rooms, special class scheduling, and lowered drinking fountains.

Services: In addition to many counseling and information services, tutoring is available in every subject. There is remedial math, reading, and writing.

Campus Safety and Security: Campus safety and security measures include self-defense education, escort service, shuttle buses, and pamphlets/posters/films. In addition, there are emergency telephones, lighted pathways/sidewalks. There are also 15-hour foot and vehicle parols during VJC's operating hours.

Programs of Study: VJC confers the B.S. degree. Associate degrees are also awarded. Bachelor's degrees are awarded in BUSINESS (business administration and management), COMPUTER AND PHYSICAL SCIENCE (information sciences and systems), HEALTH PROFESSIONS (nursing), SOCIAL SCIENCE (paralegal studies). Liberal arts and technology, computer information systems, and business information systems are the strongest academically. Paralegal, computer accounting, and computer information systems have the largest enrollments.

Required: General college requirements include courses in writing and literature, communication and fine arts, philosophy and religion, social sciences, mathematics, natural science, computer information systems, physical education, and patterns of thought. A capstone course and an internship are also required. Students must complete 120 hours, including 45 to 50 hours in the major, with at least a 2.0 overall GPA.

Special: A general studies program is offered. There are cooperative education programs in several majors as well as internships and independent study opportunities. Students may earn credit by examination. Study abroad in 4 countries, a work-study program, student-designed majors, interdisciplinary majors, including liberal arts and technology, computer accounting, and business information systems, and education courses for state certification are available. Pass/fail options are also possible. There is a freshman honors program on campus, as well as 3 national honor societies.

Faculty/Classroom: 47% of faculty are male; 53%, female. All teach undergraduates. The average class size in an introductory lecture is 20; in a laboratory, 20; and in a regular course offering, 20.

Requirements: The SAT I or ACT is required. Applicants must be graduates of an accredited secondary school. Although a secondary transcript is required, particular secondary preparation is not stipulated for all programs. Some degree programs do require specific high school courses, however. An essay and an interview are required. AP and CLEP credits are accepted. Important factors in the admissions decision are advanced placement or honor courses, recommendations by school officials, and evidence of special talent.

Procedure: Freshmen are admitted fall and spring. Entrance exams should be taken between September and November of the senior year. There are early admissions and deferred admissions plans. Application deadlines are open. Check with the school for current fee. Notification is sent on a rolling basis. A waiting list is an active part of the admissions procedure, with about 15% of all applicants on the list.

Transfer: 129 transfer students enrolled in a recent year. Transfer applicants must follow freshman application procedures, provide both college and secondary school transcripts, and have a minimum 2.5 GPA. Grades earned at other institutions are not included in calculating the GPA required for graduation. 30 credits of 120 must be completed at VJC.

Visiting: There are regularly scheduled orientations for prospective students, including a general overview, information on how to apply and how to finance a college education, special academic presentations, tours, meetings with faculty and students, and lunch. There are guides for informal visits and visitors may sit in on classes. To schedule a visit, contact the Admissions Office.

Financial Aid: In a recent year, 76% of all freshmen and 80% of continuing students received some form of financial aid. 61% of freshmen and 82% of continuing students received need-based aid. The average freshman award was $4388. Of that total, scholarships or need-based grants averaged $3804 ($6440 maximum); loans averaged $2147 ($2625 maximum); and work contracts averaged $1000 ($1500 maximum). 4% of undergraduate students work part-time. Average earnings from campus work for the school year are $1400. The average financial indebtedness of a recent graduate was $8411. VJC is a member of CSS. The college's own financial statement and the FAFSA are required. Check with the school for current deadlines.

International Students: In a recent year, there were 3 international students enrolled. They must take the TOEFL and achieve a minimum score of 500.

Computers: The college provides computer facilities for student use. The mainframe is an IBM. More than 150 networked microcomputers are available for student use in classrooms and laboratories. The campuswide fiber-optic backbone provides an SNA gateway to the IBM mainframe, library card catalog access via a CD-ROM server, student dial-in from home, Macintosh connectivity, E-mail, and hundreds of software applications in all disciplines. All students may access the system at all times. There are no time limits and no fees.

Graduates: In a recent year, 114 bachelor's degrees were awarded. The most popular majors among graduates were business/accounting (45%), computer information systems (27%), and paralegal (26%). 50 companies recruited on campus in a recent year.

Admissions Contact: Orsia F. Young, Director of Admissions and Financial Aid.

WASHINGTON COLLEGE
Chestertown, MD 21620–1197

E-2

(410) 778-7700
(800) 422-1782; FAX: (410) 778-7287

Full-time: 397 men, 486 women	Faculty: 63; IIB, av$
Part-time: 15 men, 30 women	Ph.D.s: 93%
Graduate: 25 men, 39 women	Student/Faculty: 14 to 1
Year: semesters	Tuition: $16,440
Application Deadline: February 15	Room & Board: $5888
Freshman Class: 1037 applied, 926 accepted, 242 enrolled	
SAT I Verbal/Math: 517/541	ACT: 24	COMPETITIVE +

Washington College, founded in 1782, is an independent college offering programs in the liberal arts and sciences, business management, and teacher preparation. The library contains 201,576 volumes, 159,270 microform items, and 4158 audiovisual forms, and subscribes to 801 periodicals. Computerized library sources and services include the card catalog, interlibrary loans, and database searching. Special learning facilities include a learning resource center. The 112-acre campus is in a small town 75 miles from Baltimore, Philadelphia, and Washington, D.C. Including residence halls, there are 37 buildings on campus.

Student Life: 53% of undergraduates are from out-of-state, mostly the Middle Atlantic. Students come from 30 states and 31 foreign countries. 60% are from public schools; 40% from private. 90% are white. 41% are Protestant; 35% Catholic; 17% claim no religious affiliation. The average age of freshmen is 18; all undergraduates, 22. 11% do not continue beyond their first year; 66% remain to graduate.

Housing: 700 students can be accommodated in college housing. College-sponsored living facilities include single-sex and coed dormitories and on-campus apartments. In addition, there are special interest houses, an international house, and a science house. On-campus housing is guaranteed for the freshman year only and is available on a lottery system for upperclassmen. 80% of students live on campus; of those, 70% remain on campus on weekends. All students may keep cars on campus.

Activities: 20% of men belong to 3 national fraternities; 20% of women belong to 3 national sororities. There are 50 groups on campus, including Amnesty International Studies, cheerleading, chorus, community service, dance, drama, ethnic, gay, honors, international, jazz band, literary magazine, newspaper, opera, political, professional, religious, social, social service, student government, writers' union, and yearbook. Popular campus events include fall and spring convocations, George Washington Birthday Ball, and May Day.

Sports: There are 7 intercollegiate sports for men and 8 for women, and 7 intramural sports for men and 5 for women. Athletic and recreation facilities include a swim center, a gymnasium, a field house, squash and racquetball courts, a fitness center, playing and practice fields, and a boathouse. There are riding facilities nearby.

Disabled Students: 80% of the campus is accessible to disabled students. The following facilities are available: wheelchair ramps, elevators, special parking, specially equipped rest rooms, special class scheduling, lowered drinking fountains, and lowered telephones.

Services: In addition to many counseling and information services, tutoring is available in every subject. There is remedial math and writing, a writing center, a mathematics laboratory, a study skills tutor, and peer tutors.

Campus Safety and Security: Campus safety and security measures include 24-hour foot and vehicle patrol, self-defense education, escort service, and informal discussions. In addition, there are pamphlets/posters/films, emergency telephones, and lighted pathways/sidewalks.

Programs of Study: WC confers B.A. and B.S. degrees. Master's degrees are also awarded. Bachelor's degrees are awarded in BIOLOGICAL SCIENCE (biology/biological science), BUSINESS (business administration and management), COMMUNICATIONS AND THE ARTS (dramatic arts, English, fine arts, French, German, music, and Spanish), COMPUTER AND PHYSICAL SCIENCE (chemistry, mathematics, and physics), SOCIAL SCIENCE (American studies, economics, history, humanities, international studies, philosophy, political science/government, psychology, and sociology). Psychology, English, and chemistry are the strongest academically. Business management, English, and psychology have the largest enrollments.

Required: All students are required to take 2 freshman seminars, 2 sophomore seminars, and 8 courses distributed among the social sciences, natural sciences, and humanities. The senior obligation consists of a comprehensive examination, thesis, or independent project. Students must complete 128 credit hours, including at least 32 in the major in order to graduate. A minimum GPA of 2.0 is required.

Special: Internships are available in all majors. There is study abroad in 6 countries, and a Washington semester at American University. The college offers a 3–2 engineering degree with the University of Maryland at College Park, as well as a 3–2 nursing program with John Hopkins University, credit by exam, and pass/fail options. There are 6 national honor societies on campus.

Faculty/Classroom: 70% of faculty are male; 30%, female. 93% teach undergraduates. No introductory courses are taught by graduate students. The average class size in an introductory lecture is 26; in a laboratory, 16; and in a regular course offering, 17.

Admissions: 89% of the 1995–96 applicants were accepted. The SAT I scores for the 1995–96 freshman class were as follows: Verbal—45% below 500, 35% between 500 and 599, 18% between 600 and 700, and 2% above 700; Math—36% below 500, 34% between 500 and 599, 24% between 600 and 700, and 6% above 700. 55% of the current freshmen were in the top fifth of their class; 75% were in the top two fifths. 5 freshmen graduated first in their class.

Requirements: The SAT I or ACT is required. WC requires applicants to be in the upper 80% of their class. A minimum GPA of 2.3 is required. Applicants must be graduates of an accredited secondary school or have a GED. 16 Carnegie units are required. Applicants should take high school courses in English, foreign language, history, mathematics, science, and social studies. An essay is required, and an interview is recommended. AP and CLEP credits are accepted. Important factors in the admissions decision are advanced placement or honor courses, recommendations by school officials, and leadership record.

Procedure: Freshmen are admitted in the fall and spring. Entrance exams should be taken in the spring of the junior year or fall of the senior year. There are early decision and early admissions plans. Early decision applications should be filed by December 1; regular applications, by February 15 for fall entry and December 1 for spring entry, along with an application fee of $35. Notification of early decision is sent December 15; regular decision, March 1. 50 early decision candidates were accepted for the 1995–96 class. A waiting list is an active part of the admissions procedure, with about 10% of all applicants on the list.

Transfer: 30 transfer students enrolled in a recent year. A minimum GPA of 2.5 is required. An associate degree and interview are recommended. 32 credits of 128 must be completed at WC.

Visiting: There are guides for informal visits and visitors may sit in on classes and stay overnight at the school. To schedule a visit, contact the Admissions Office.

Financial Aid: In 1995–96, 85% of all freshmen and 83% of continuing students received some form of financial aid. 60% of freshmen and 70% of continuing students received need-based aid. The average freshman award was $12,222. Of that total, scholarships or need-based grants averaged $8100 ($14,000 maximum); loans averaged $2625 ($3825 maximum); and work contracts averaged $1145 ($1200 maximum). 65% of undergraduate students work part-time. Average earnings from campus work for the school year are $900. The average financial indebtedness of the 1994–95 graduate was $12,000. WC is a member of CSS. FAFSA, the parents'/students' federal income tax returns, and the CSS Profile Application are required. The application deadline for fall entry is February 15.

International Students: There are currently 73 international students enrolled. The school actively recruits these students. They must take the TOEFL and achieve a minimum score of 500.

Computers: The college provides computer facilities for student use. The mainframe is a Data General Aviion 5500. Students may access the mainframe, the library collection, and the Internet via a campus network of more than 100 Apple Macintosh microcomputers in the library, academic buildings, and dormitories. All students may access the system. There are no time limits and no fees.

Graduates: In 1994–95, 166 bachelor's degrees were awarded. The most popular majors among graduates were business (16%), psychology (16%), and political science (11%). Within an average freshman class, 60% graduate in 4 years and 65% in 5 years. 30 companies recruited on campus in 1994–95.

Admissions Contact: Kevin Coveney, Vice President for Admissions. E-mail: adm-off@washcoll.edu.

WESTERN MARYLAND COLLEGE
D-1
Westminster, MD 21157-4390

(301) 848-7000 ext. 230
(800) 638-5005; FAX: (410) 857-2757

Full-time: 545 men, 643 women	Faculty: 77; IIB, av$
Part-time: 31 men, 56 women	Ph.D.s: 95%
Graduate: 202 men, 893 women	Student/Faculty: 15 to 1
Year: 4-1-4	Tuition: $15,300
Application Deadline: March 15	Room & Board: $5365
Freshman Class: 1565 applied, 1178 accepted, 323 enrolled	
SAT I Verbal/Math: 480/550	**VERY COMPETITIVE**

Western Maryland College, founded in 1867, is a private college offering programs in the liberal arts. In addition to regional accreditation, Western Maryland has baccalaureate program accreditation with CSWE and NASM. The library contains 187,000 volumes, 425,000 microform items, and 2300 audiovisual forms, and subscribes to 823 periodicals. Computerized library sources and services include the card catalog, interlibrary loans, and database searching. Special learning facilities include an art gallery, radio station, and TV station. The 160-acre campus is in a small town 30 miles northwest of Baltimore. Including residence halls, there are 35 buildings on campus.

Student Life: 65% of undergraduates are from Maryland. Students come from 23 states and 19 foreign countries. 89% are white. 37% are Protestant; 27% Catholic; 17% claim no religious affiliation. The average age of freshmen is 18; all undergraduates, 20. 22% do not continue beyond their first year; 60% remain to graduate.

Housing: 1118 students can be accommodated in college housing. College-sponsored living facilities include single-sex and coed dormitories, on-campus apartments, and married-student housing. In addition, there are honors houses, language houses, special interest houses, and fraternity and sorority floors. On-campus housing is guaranteed for all 4 years. 82% of students live on campus; of those, 85% remain on campus on weekends. Upperclassmen may keep cars on campus.

Activities: 17% of men belong to 2 local and 2 national fraternities; 21% of women belong to 2 local and 2 national sororities. There are 70 groups on campus, including art, band, cheerleading, choir, chorale, chorus, computers, drama, ethnic, film, gay, honors, international, jazz band, literary magazine, musical theater, newspaper, orchestra, pep band, photography, political, professional, radio and TV, religious, social, social service, student government, and yearbook. Popular campus events include Homecoming, May Day, and Senior Week.

Sports: There are 10 intercollegiate sports for men and 11 for women, and 9 intramural sports for men and 9 for women. Athletic and recreation facilities include a 9-hole golf course, tennis courts, swimming pool, football stadium with track, squash/racquetball court, weight training center, basketball and volleyball courts, and soccer, softball, and lacrosse fields.

Disabled Students: 60% of the campus is accessible to disabled students. The following facilities are available: wheelchair ramps, elevators, special parking, specially equipped rest rooms, special class scheduling, lowered drinking fountains, and lowered telephones.

Services: In addition to many counseling and information services, tutoring is available in every subject. There is a reader service for the blind, and remedial math, reading, and writing.

Campus Safety and Security: Campus safety and security measures include 24-hour foot and vehicle patrol, escort service, informal discussions, and pamphlets/posters/films. In addition, there are emergency telephones and lighted pathways/sidewalks.

Programs of Study: Western Maryland confers the B.A. degree. Master's degrees are also awarded. Bachelor's degrees are awarded in BIOLOGICAL SCIENCE (biology/biological science), BUSINESS (business administration and management), COMMUNICATIONS AND THE ARTS (communications, English, fine arts, French, German, music, Spanish, and theater design), COMPUTER AND PHYSICAL SCIENCE (chemistry, mathematics, and physics), EDUCATION (physical), SOCIAL SCIENCE (economics, history, philosophy, political science/government, psychology, religion, social work, and sociology). Biology, chemistry, and English are the strongest academically. Biology, psychology, and physical education have the largest enrollments.

Required: Distribution requirements for all students include cross-cultural studies, literature and fine arts, humanities, natural sciences, quantitative analysis, and social sciences. All students must take English composition, foreign language, and physical education (4 courses), and pass a mathematics proficiency examination. A total of 128 credit hours is required for graduation, including 38 to 50 in the major. The college now uses a 4-course system, with most courses earning 4 credits. The minimum GPA for graduation is 2.0.

Special: Internships are available in all majors. Study abroad is available around the world. There is a Washington semester in conjunction with American University, and 3–2 engineering programs with Washington University and the University of Maryland. The college offers work-study programs, dual and student-designed majors, credit by examination (in foreign languages), and pass/fail options. Western Maryland has a 5-year deaf education program and offers certification in elementary and secondary elementary education. The college also offers advanced standing for international baccalaureate recipients. There is a freshman honors program on campus, as well as 12 national honor societies, including Phi Beta Kappa. 22 departments have honors programs.

Faculty/Classroom: 65% of faculty are male; 35%, female. All both teach undergraduates and do research. No introductory courses are taught by graduate students. The average class size in an introductory lecture is 30; in a laboratory, 15; and in a regular course offering, 19.

Admissions: 75% of the 1995–96 applicants were accepted. The SAT I scores for the 1995–96 freshman class were as follows: Verbal—29% below 500, 42% between 500 and 599, 24% between 600 and 700, and 5% above 700; Math—31% below 500, 39% between 500 and 599, 26% between 600 and 700, and 4% above 700. 47% of the current freshmen were in the top fifth of their class; 74% were in the top two fifths. There were 3 National Merit finalists. 33 freshmen graduated first in their class.

Requirements: The SAT I is required, with a minimum composite score of 900. Western Maryland requires applicants to be in the upper 50% of their class. A minimum GPA of 2.5 is required. Applicants must be graduates of an accredited secondary school or have a GED. 16 academic credits are required, including 4 years of English, 3 years each of foreign language, mathematics, and social studies, and 2 years of a laboratory science. SAT II: Subject tests and an interview are recommended. An essay is required. Applications are accepted on computer disk and on-line via CollegeLink and Common App. AP and CLEP credits are accepted. Important factors in the admissions decision are advanced placement or honor courses, leadership record, and evidence of special talent.

Procedure: Freshmen are admitted in the fall and spring. Entrance exams should be taken at the end of the junior year. There are early decision, early admissions, and deferred admissions plans. Early decision applications should be filed by December 15; regular applications, by March 15 for fall entry and January 15 for spring entry, along with an application fee of $30. Notification of early decision is sent December 20; regular decision, February 1. 33 early decision candidates were accepted for the 1995–96 class.

Transfer: 61 transfer students enrolled in 1995–96. A minimum college GPA of 2.0 is required. If fewer than 30 credits transfer, a minimum SAT I score of 900 (composite) is required to transfer. An interview is recommended. 30 credits of 128 must be completed at Western Maryland.

Visiting: There are regularly scheduled orientations for prospective students, including meeting the president, a panel of faculty, and a panel of students. Tours of the campus for parents are conducted by faculty members; students tour with current students. There are guides for informal visits and visitors may sit in on classes and stay overnight at the school. To schedule a visit, contact the Admissions Office at (410) 857–2230 or (800) 638–5005 (out of state).

Financial Aid: In 1995–96, 85% of all freshmen and 78% of continuing students received some form of financial aid. 60% of freshmen and 56% of continuing students received need-based aid. The average freshman award was $13,649. Of that total, scholarships or need-based grants averaged $9338 ($15,300 maximum); loans averaged $3139 ($4625 maximum); and work contracts averaged $1172 ($1600 maximum). 36% of undergraduate students work part-time. Average earnings from campus work for the school year are $615. The average financial indebtedness of the 1994–95 graduate was $9616. Western Maryland is a member of CSS. The FAF, FAFSA, FFS, or SFS and the college's own financial statement are required. The application deadline for fall entry is March 1.

International Students: There were 25 international students enrolled in a recent year. The school actively recruits these students. They must take the TOEFL and achieve a minimum score of 550.

Computers: The college provides computer facilities for student use. The mainframe is a Prime 6650. 4 public-access microcomputer laboratories are available. All students may access the system. Laboratories are open 8:30 A.M. to 11 P.M. daily. Network is available 24 hours per day. There are no time limits and no fees. It is recommended that students have Apple Macintosh, IBM, or IBM-clone personal computers.

Graduates: In 1994–95, 240 bachelor's degrees were awarded. The most popular majors among graduates were sociology (13%), English (10%), and biology (8%). Within an average freshman class, 2% graduate in 3 years, 55% in 4 years, 62% in 5 years, and 60% in 6 years. 49 companies recruited on campus in 1994–95.

Admissions Contact: Martha O'Connell, Director of Admissions. E-mail: admissio@ns1.wmc.car.md.us.

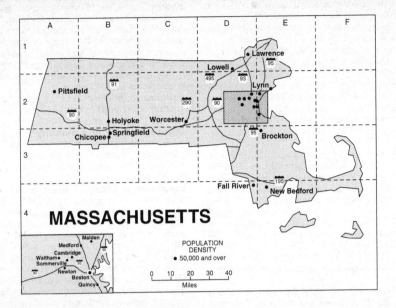

AMERICAN INTERNATIONAL COLLEGE   B-3

Springfield, MA 01109   (413) 747–6201

Full-time: 556 men, 626 women | Faculty: 74
Part-time: 82 men, 162 women | Ph.D.s: 52%
Graduate: 150 men, 337 women | Student/Faculty: 16 to 1
Year: semesters, summer session | Tuition: $9825
Application Deadline: open | Room & Board: $5062
Freshman Class: 1281 applied, 1024 accepted, 315 enrolled
SAT I Verbal/Math: 422/469 | **COMPETITIVE**

American International College, founded in 1885, is an independent, coeducational institution offering programs in liberal arts, business, health science, and teacher preparation. In addition to regional accreditation, AIC has baccalaureate program accreditation with NASDTEC and NLN. The library contains 118,000 volumes, 83,700 microform items, and 1140 audiovisual forms, and subscribes to 390 periodicals. Computerized library sources and services include the card catalog and database searching. Special learning facilities include a learning resource center, art gallery, and radio station. The 58-acre campus is in an urban area 75 miles west of Boston. Including residence halls, there are 22 buildings on campus.

Student Life: 59% of undergraduates are from Massachusetts. Students come from 30 states, 15 foreign countries, and Canada. 83% are from public schools; 17% from private. 75% are white; 13% African American. 54% are Catholic; 32% Protestant; 12% Jewish. The average age of freshmen is 18; all undergraduates, 22. 18% do not continue beyond their first year; 59% remain to graduate.

Housing: 780 students can be accommodated in college housing. College-sponsored living facilities include single-sex and coed dormitories. On-campus housing is guaranteed for all 4 years. 59% of students live on campus; of those, 65% remain on campus on weekends. Alcohol is not permitted. All students may keep cars on campus.

Activities: 10% of women belong to 4 local sororities. There are 40 groups on campus, including cheerleading, choir, chorale, computers, drama, ethnic, honors, international, literary magazine, musical theater, newspaper, political, professional, radio and TV, religious, social, social service, student government, women's, and yearbook. Popular campus events include fall, winter, and spring weekends.

Sports: There are 9 intercollegiate sports for men and 5 for women, and 9 intramural sports for men and 8 for women. Athletic and recreation facilities include a gymnasium, a football stadium, tennis courts, playing fields, and a health and fitness center.

Disabled Students: 70% of the campus is accessible to disabled students. The following facilities are available: wheelchair ramps, elevators, special parking, specially equipped rest rooms, and special class scheduling.

Services: In addition to many counseling and information services, tutoring is available in every subject. There is remedial math and writing.

Campus Safety and Security: Campus safety and security measures include 24-hour foot and vehicle patrol, escort service, shuttle buses, and informal discussions. In addition, there are pamphlets/posters/films and lighted pathways/sidewalks.

Programs of Study: AIC confers B.A., B.S., B.B.A., and B.S.N. degrees. Associate, master's, and doctoral degrees are also awarded. Bachelor's degrees are awarded in BIOLOGICAL SCIENCE (biochemistry and biology/biological science), BUSINESS (accounting, business administration and management, business economics, international business management, marketing/retailing/merchandising, and personnel management), COMMUNICATIONS AND THE ARTS (communications, English, and Spanish), COMPUTER AND PHYSICAL SCIENCE (chemistry, mathematics, and science), EDUCATION (business, early childhood, elementary, foreign languages, middle school, science, secondary, and special), HEALTH PROFESSIONS (medical laboratory technology, nursing, occupational therapy, physical therapy, predentistry, and premedicine), SOCIAL SCIENCE (criminal justice, economics, history, international relations, liberal arts/general studies, philosophy, political science/government, prelaw, psychology, public administration, and sociology). Psychology, preprofessional, accounting, and education are the strongest academically. Criminal justice, prephysical therapy, and nursing have the largest enrollments.

Required: Distribution requirements include 12 credits of social sciences, 9 of English, 8 of laboratory science, and 6 of humanities. A total of 120 credit hours is required for graduation, with 30 to 36 in the major. A minimum 2.0 GPA is required for graduation. Students must take 4 credits of physical education.

Special: Cross-registration with other colleges in the area is permitted. Internships are available in all programs, and study abroad is offered, as is a Washington semester. AIC also offers dual majors, credit by examination, credit for life/military/work experience, nondegree study, and for lower-division students, pass/fail options. There is a freshman honors program on campus, as well as 2 national honor societies.

Faculty/Classroom: 41% of faculty are male; 59%, female. All teach undergraduates; 15% also do research. No introductory courses are taught by graduate students. The average class size in an introductory lecture is 26; in a laboratory, 16; and in a regular course offering, 19.

Admissions: 80% of the 1995–96 applicants were accepted. The SAT I scores for the 1995–96 freshman class were as follows: Verbal—73% below 500, 25% between 500 and 599, and 2% between 600 and 700; Math—69% below 500, 29% between 500 and 599, 1% between 600 and 700, and 1% above 700. 13% of the current freshmen were in the top fifth of their class; 61% were in the top two fifths. 3 freshmen graduated first in their class.

Requirements: The SAT I is required. A minimum GPA of 2.0 is required. In addition, students must be graduates of an accredited secondary school or have a GED. They must have completed 16 academic credits of secondary school work with a minimum of 4 years of English, 2 each of history, mathematics, and science, and 1 of social studies. An interview is recommended. AP and CLEP credits are accepted. Important factors in the admissions decision are recommendations by school officials, advanced placement or honor courses, and personality/intangible qualities.

Procedure: Freshmen are admitted to all sessions. Entrance exams should be taken by March of the senior year. There are early decision, early admissions, and deferred admissions plans. Application deadlines are open. Application fee is $20. Notification of early decision is sent December 15; regular decision, on a rolling basis. 15 early decision candidates were accepted for the 1995–96 class.

Transfer: 170 transfer students enrolled in 1995–96. Transfer applicants must have at least a 2.0 GPA. 45 credits of 120 must be completed at AIC.

Visiting: There are regularly scheduled orientations for prospective students, including open houses with faculty, a student life panel, departmental faculty presentations, a finacial aid presentation, a tour, and brunch. There are guides for informal visits and visitors may sit in on classes and stay overnight at the school. To schedule a visit, contact the Admissions Office.

Financial Aid: In 1995–96, 69% of all freshmen and 71% of continuing students received some form of financial aid. 60% of freshmen and 64% of continuing students received need-based aid. The average freshman award was $6950. Of that total, scholarships or need-based grants averaged $3320 ($9200 maximum); loans averaged $2700 ($5500 maximum); and work contracts averaged $1200 ($1600 maximum). 88% of undergraduate students work part-time. Average earnings from campus work for the school year are $1150. The average financial indebtedness of the 1994–95 graduate was $6400. AIC is a member of CSS. FAFSA and the college's own financial statement are required. The application deadline for fall entry is April 15.

International Students: There are currently 88 international students enrolled. The school actively recruits these students. They must take the TOEFL and achieve a minimum score of 500.

Computers: The college provides computer facilities for student use. The mainframe is a DEC VAX 3100. Students may access the mainframe from the school's computer laboratories or from home via a modem. There is a cluster of DEC VAX station 3100s, DEC VT 320 terminals, and at-class microcomputers, all on an Ethernet network. All students may access the system 7 days per week for a total of 80 hours. There are no time limits. The fees are $25 per semester.

Graduates: In 1994–95, 270 bachelor's degrees were awarded. The most popular majors among graduates were criminal justice (17%), accounting (11%), and nursing (10%). Within an average freshman class, 50% graduate in 4 years, 8% in 5 years, and 1% in 6 years. 42 companies recruited on campus in 1994–95. Of the 1994 graduating class, 25% were enrolled in graduate school within 6 months of graduation and 78% had found employment.

Admissions Contact: Admissions Officer.

AMHERST COLLEGE   B-2
Amherst, MA 01002-5000   (413) 542-2328; FAX: (413) 542-2040
Full-time: 891 men, 709 women   **Faculty:** 173; IIB, ++$
Part-time: none   **Ph.D.s:** 91%
Graduate: none   **Student/Faculty:** 9 to 1
Year: semesters   **Tuition:** $21,065
Application Deadline: December 31   **Room & Board:** $5560
Freshman Class: 4836 applied, 943 accepted, 422 enrolled
SAT I Verbal/Math: 640/690   **MOST COMPETITIVE**

Amherst College, founded in 1821, is a private liberal arts college for undergraduate men and women. The 6 libraries contain 807,106 volumes, 434,437 microform items, and 28,804 audiovisual forms, and subscribe to 4731 periodicals. Computerized library sources and services include the card catalog, interlibrary loans, and database searching. Special learning facilities include an art gallery, natural history museum, planetarium, and radio station. The 1000-acre campus is in a small town 90 miles west of Boston and 165 miles north of New York City. Including residence halls, there are 67 buildings on campus.

Student Life: 82% of undergraduates are from out-of-state, mostly the Middle Atlantic. Students come from 50 states, 25 foreign countries, and Canada. 65% are from public schools; 35% from private. 65% are white; 11% Asian American. The average age of freshmen is 18; all undergraduates, 19. 2% do not continue beyond their first year; 98% remain to graduate.

Housing: 1600 students can be accommodated in college housing. College-sponsored living facilities include single-sex and coed dormitories. In addition there are language houses, special interest houses, and 1 cooperative house. On-campus housing is guaranteed for all 4 years. 98% of students live on campus; of those, 95% remain on campus on weekends. All students may keep cars on campus.

Activities: There are no fraternities or sororities. There are 100 groups on campus, including choir, chorale, chorus, dance, drama, ethnic, film, gay, international, jazz band, literary magazine, musical theater, newspaper, orchestra, pep band, photography, political, professional, radio and TV, religious, social, social service, student government, symphony, and yearbook. Popular campus events include

Homecoming, Triathlon, Parents Weekend, Casino, and various cultural awareness events.

Sports: There are 13 intercollegiate sports for men and 13 for women, and 14 intramural sports for men, 14 for women, and 14 coed. Athletic and recreation facilities include 2 gymnasiums, a pool, a field house, a hockey rink, a track, a Nautilus room, squash and tennis courts, a golf course, and playing fields.

Disabled Students: The following facilities are available: wheelchair ramps, elevators, special parking, specially equipped rest rooms, and special class scheduling.

Services: In addition to many counseling and information services, tutoring is available in every subject. In addition, there is a reader service for the blind and a full-time writing counselor on staff.

Campus Safety and Security: Campus safety and security measures include 24-hour foot and vehicle patrol, escort service, shuttle buses, and informal discussions. In addition, there are pamphlets/posters/films, emergency telephones, and lighted pathways/sidewalks.

Programs of Study: Amherst confers the A.B. degree. Bachelor's degrees are awarded in BIOLOGICAL SCIENCE (biology/biological science and neurosciences), COMMUNICATIONS AND THE ARTS (classics, dance, English, fine arts, French, German, Latin, music, Russian, and Spanish), COMPUTER AND PHYSICAL SCIENCE (astronomy, chemistry, computer science, geology, and physics), SOCIAL SCIENCE (African American studies, American studies, anthropology, Asian/Oriental studies, economics, European studies, history, philosophy, political science/government, psychology, religion, sociology, and women's studies). English, political science, and economics have the largest enrollments.

Required: To earn the B.A., all students must complete 32 courses, equivalent to 128 credits, 8 to 14 of which are in the major, with at least a C average. Other than a 1-semester course in liberal studies, there are no specific course requirements.

Special: Students may cross-register through the Five College Consortium, the other members of which are all within 10 miles of Amherst, or through the Twelve College Exchange Program. A number of interterm and summer internships are available. Many programs are offered abroad. Dual majors, student-designed interdisciplinary majors, and work-study are possible. There are limited pass/fail options. There are 2 national honor societies on campus, including Phi Beta Kappa.

Faculty/Classroom: 68% of faculty are male; 32%, female. All teach undergraduates and also do research. The average class size in a regular course offering is 25.

Admissions: 19% of the 1995–96 applicants were accepted. The SAT I scores for the 1995–96 freshman class were as follows: Verbal—9% below 500, 23% between 500 and 599, 50% between 600 and 700, and 18% above 700; Math—2% below 500, 11% between 500 and 599, 44% between 600 and 700, and 42% above 700. 90% of the current freshmen were in the top fifth of their class; all were in the top two fifths.

Requirements: The SAT I or ACT is required, as well as 3 SAT II: Subject tests, preferably including the writing test. Applicants should be high school graduates or have earned the GED. No specific secondary preparation is required, but Amherst strongly recommends that applicants take 4 years of English, mathematics through precalculus, 3 or 4 years of a foreign language, 2 years of history and social science, and at least 2 years of natural science, including a laboratory science. 2 essays are required. Important factors in the admissions decision are advanced placement or honor courses, recommendations by school officials, and evidence of special talent.

Procedure: Freshmen are admitted in the fall. Entrance exams should be taken no later than December of the senior year. There are early decision and deferred admissions plans. Early decision I applications should be filed by November 15; early decision II applicants, by February 1; regular applications, by December 31 for fall entry, along with an application fee of $50. Notification of early decision I is sent December 15; early decision II, March 1; regular decision, April 1. 147 early decision candidates were accepted for the 1995–96 class. A waiting list is an active part of the admissions procedure.

Transfer: 15 transfer students enrolled in 1995–96. Transfer applicants must have full sophomore standing and a minimum 3.0 GPA in previous college work. Transfers are accepted for the sophomore and junior classes only, and Amherst recommends that they submit SAT I or ACT scores, plus high school and college transcripts, and seek a personal interview. 64 credits of 128 must be completed at Amherst.

Visiting: There are guides for informal visits and visitors may sit in on classes and stay overnight at the school. To schedule a visit, contact the Admission Office.

Financial Aid: In 1995–96, 60% of all freshmen and 55% of continuing students received some form of financial aid. 44% of freshmen and 43% of continuing students received need-based aid. The average freshman award was $20,789. Of that total, scholarships or need-based grants averaged $16,606 ($25,240 maximum); loans averaged $2681 ($4200 maximum); and work contracts averaged $1502 ($2161 maximum). 66% of undergraduate students work part-time. Average earnings from campus work for the school year are $766. The average financial indebtedness of the 1994–95 graduate was $8977. Amherst is a member of CSS. The FAFSA, the college's own financial statement, and the CSS Profile Application are required. The application deadline for fall entry is February 15.

International Students: There are currently 46 international students enrolled. They must take the TOEFL and achieve a minimum score of 600.

Computers: The college provides computer facilities for student use. The mainframes are a DEC VMS and a DEC UNIX. There are 12 IBM and 60 Apple Macintosh microcomputers available in the computer center, and every student has an E-mail account. All students may access the system 24 hours a day. There are no time limits and no fees.

Graduates: In 1994–95, 410 bachelor's degrees were awarded. Within an average freshman class, 97% graduate in 5 years. 112 companies recruited on campus in 1994–95. Of the 1994 graduating class, 34% were enrolled in graduate school within 6 months of graduation and 50% had found employment.

Admissions Contact: Jane Reynolds, Dean of Admission. E-mail: admissions@amherst.edu.

ANNA MARIA COLLEGE
C-2
Paxton, MA 01612-1198   (508) 849-3360
(800) 344-4586, ext. 360; FAX: (508) 849-3362

Full-time: 137 men, 217 women	Faculty: 33; IIB, --$
Part-time: 149 men, 228 women	Ph.D.s: 33%
Graduate: 492 men, 388 women	Student/Faculty: 11 to 1
Year: semesters, summer session	Tuition: $11,875
Application Deadline: March 1	Room & Board: $5200
Freshman Class: 415 applied, 341 accepted, 106 enrolled	
SAT I Verbal/Math: 402/451	**LESS COMPETITIVE**

AMC, founded in 1946, is a small, comprehensive Catholic, coeducational college located 8 miles northwest of Worcester. It offers career-oriented programs in liberal and fine arts, business, and teacher preparation. In addition to regional accreditation, AMC has baccalaureate program accreditation with CSWE and NLN. The library contains 75,000 volumes, and subscribes to 1000 periodicals. Computerized library sources and services include the card catalog, interlibrary loans, and database searching. Special learning facilities include a learning resource center, art gallery, and an audiovisual center. The 180-acre campus is in a rural area 8 miles northwest of Worcester. Including residence halls, there are 11 buildings on campus.

Student Life: 91% of undergraduates are from Massachusetts. Students come from 12 states and 5 foreign countries. 75% are from public schools; 25% from private. 95% are white. The average age of freshmen is 18; all undergraduates, 24. 10% do not continue beyond their first year; 80% remain to graduate.

Housing: 400 students can be accommodated in college housing. College-sponsored living facilities include coed dormitories. On-campus housing is guaranteed for all 4 years. 60% of students live on campus; of those, 50% remain on campus on weekends. All students may keep cars on campus.

Activities: There are no fraternities or sororities. There are 23 groups on campus, including art, cheerleading, choir, chorus, computers, drama, ethnic, honors, international, musical theater, political, professional, religious, social, social service, student government, and yearbook. Popular campus events include Harvest Weekend, Winter Semiformal, and Spring Variety Show.

Sports: There are 4 intercollegiate sports for men and 4 for women, and 5 intramural sports for men and 5 for women. Athletic and recreation facilities include an activities center with a basketball court, locker rooms, and weight and fitness equipment; soccer, baseball, and softball fields, a sand volleyball court, an outdoor basketball court, and a fitness trail.

Disabled Students: 93% of the campus is accessible to disabled students. The following facilities are available: wheelchair ramps, elevators, special parking, specially equipped rest rooms, and special class scheduling.

Services: In addition to many counseling and information services, tutoring is available in every subject, including through a tutoring laboratory. In addition, there is a reader service for the blind, and remedial math, reading, and writing.

Campus Safety and Security: Campus safety and security measures include 24-hour foot and vehicle patrol, escort service, informal discussions, and pamphlets/posters/films. In addition, there are emergency telephones and lighted pathways/sidewalks.

Programs of Study: AMC confers B.A., B.S., B.B.A., B.F.A., B.M., and B.S.N. degrees. Associate and master's degrees are also awarded. Bachelor's degrees are awarded in BIOLOGICAL SCIENCE (biology/biological science), BUSINESS (business administration and management), COMMUNICATIONS AND THE ARTS (art, English, music, music performance, and studio art), EDUCATION (art, early

childhood, elementary, and music), HEALTH PROFESSIONS (art therapy, medical laboratory technology, medical technology, and music therapy), SOCIAL SCIENCE (criminal justice, human development, liberal arts/general studies, paralegal studies, political science/government, psychology, social science, and social work). Criminal justice, education, and business have the largest enrollments.

Required: The 60-credit core curriculum consists of classes in English, literature, mathematics, computers, natural science, foreign language, fine arts, history, philosophy, social/behavioral sciences, and religious studies. A total of 120 credits is required for graduation, with a minimum of 30 in the major, and a 2.0 GPA.

Special: Cross-registration with the Colleges of the Worcester Consortium, internships in all majors, and a 3–2 engineering degree in conjunction with the Worcester Polytechnic Institute are available. The art and business major results in a B.F.A. degree. There are pre-professional concentrations in prelaw, predentistry, premedicine, and preveterinary science. The college offers study abroad, a Washington semester, accelerated degree programs, a general studies degree, credit by exam, work-study programs and 5-year BBA/MBA, BA/MA, and BA/MS programs.

Faculty/Classroom: 50% of faculty are male; 50%, female. All teach undergraduates. 10% both teach and do research. No introductory courses are taught by graduate students. The average class size in an introductory lecture is 20; in a laboratory, 15; and in a regular course offering, 13.

Admissions: 82% of the 1995–96 applicants were accepted. The SAT I scores for the 1995–96 freshman class were as follows: Verbal—71% below 500, 21% between 500 and 599, and 8% between 600 and 700; Math—70% below 500, 20% between 500 and 599, and 10% between 600 and 700. 25% of the current freshmen were in the top fifth of their class; 46% were in the top two fifths. One freshman graduated first in their class.

Requirements: The SAT I or ACT is required. A GED is accepted. 16 academic units are recommended, including 4 years of English, 2 years each of foreign language, history, mathematics, and sciences, and 1 year of social studies. An interview is recommended. When applicable, an audition and portfolio are required. Students who have been out of high school for 3 or more years, or transfer students with 10 or more college level courses, do not need to submit standardized test scores. Applications are accepted on computer disk. AP and CLEP credits are accepted. Important factors in the admissions decision are advanced placement or honor courses, evidence of special talent, and leadership record.

Procedure: Freshmen are admitted fall and spring. Entrance exams should be taken in the spring of the junior year and in the fall of the senior year. There are early admissions and deferred admissions plans. The priority application deadline is March 1. Application fee is $30. Notification is sent on a rolling basis.

Transfer: 29 transfer students enrolled in 1995–96. Transfers with a minimum GPA of 2.0 are accepted for upper-division work. 45 credits of 120 must be completed at AMC.

Visiting: There are regularly scheduled orientations for prospective students, including on-campus interviews, campus tours, and day visitation program by appointment, and a fall open house. There are guides for informal visits and visitors may sit in on classes. To schedule a visit, contact the Undergraduate Admission Office.

Financial Aid: In 1995–96, 95% of all students received some form of financial aid; 90% received need-based aid. The average freshman award was $11,853. Of that total, scholarships or need-based grants averaged $5913 ($6800 maximum); loans averaged $5040; and work contracts averaged $900 (maximum). 43% of undergraduate students work part-time. Average earnings from campus work for the school year are $673. The average financial indebtedness of the 1994–95 graduate was $17,336. AMC is a member of CSS. The FAF, the college's own financial statement, and the income tax form 1040 and accompanying schedules are required. The application deadline for fall entry is March 1.

International Students: There are currently 20 international students enrolled. The school actively recruits these students. They must score 500 on the TOEFL; students scoring lower than 500 may be admitted to the college's ESL program.

Computers: The college provides computer facilities for student use. The mainframe is a Novell 3.12 Network. There is a main computer laboratory in the library with more than 21 computers, a mini laboratory in the learning center, and access to the network in every dorm room along with a mini laboratory in the dorm. Available programs include E-mail, Internet, Lotus Suite, CD-ROMS, accounting software, and an on-line legal database. All students may access the system. There are no time limits and no fees.

Graduates: In 1994–95, 170 bachelor's degrees were awarded. The most popular majors among graduates were criminal justice (48%), business (11%), and education (7%). Within an average freshman class, 1% graduate in 3 years, 93% in 4 years, and 6% in 5 years. Of the 1994 graduating class, 10% were enrolled in graduate school

within 6 months of graduation and 70% had found employment.
Admissions Contact: David M. Pirani, Director of Admission.

ASSUMPTION COLLEGE
C-2

Worcester, MA 01615   (508) 767-7285; FAX: (508) 799-4412

Full-time: 673 men, 980 women	Faculty: 108; IIB, av$
Part-time: 154 men, 450 women	Ph.D.s: 96%
Graduate: 121 men, 228 women	Student/Faculty: 15 to 1
Year: semesters, summer session	Tuition: $12,825
Application Deadline: March 1	Room & Board: $5780
Freshman Class: 2200 applied, 1600 accepted, 453 enrolled	
SAT I Verbal/Math: 460/470	COMPETITIVE

Assumption College, founded in 1904, is a private coeducational institution affiliated with the Roman Catholic Church offering undergraduate and graduate programs in the liberal arts, rehabilitation, and business. There are 4 graduate schools. In addition to regional accreditation, Assumption has baccalaureate program accreditation with NLN. The library contains 198,000 volumes, 9000 microform items, and more than 1000 audiovisual forms, and subscribes to 1200 periodicals. Computerized library sources and services include the card catalog, interlibrary loans, and database searching. Special learning facilities include a learning resource center. The 150-acre campus is in a suburban area 45 miles west of Boston. Including residence halls, there are 37 buildings on campus.

Student Life: 60% of undergraduates are from Massachusetts. Students come from 15 states, 14 foreign countries, and Canada. 60% are from public schools; 40% from private. 93% are white. 80% are Catholic; 18% Protestant. The average age of freshmen is 19; all undergraduates, 20. 14% do not continue beyond their first year; 78% remain to graduate.

Housing: 1450 students can be accommodated in college housing. College-sponsored living facilities include single-sex dormitories, dormitories with coed floors, and on-campus apartments. In addition there are special interest houses and substance-free housing. On-campus housing is guaranteed for all 4 years. 90% of students live on campus; of those, 75% remain on campus on weekends. All students may keep cars on campus.

Activities: There are no fraternities or sororities. There are 40 groups on campus, including art, band, cheerleading, choir, chorale, chorus, computers, dance, drama, ethnic, honors, international, literary magazine, newspaper, pep band, political, professional, religious, social, social service, student government, and yearbook. Popular campus events include Pup Cup Weekend, Christmas Ball, Spring Semiformal, and Sibling Weekend.

Sports: There are 10 intercollegiate sports for men and 8 for women, and 12 intramural sports for men and 12 for women. Athletic and recreation facilities include a 3000-seat gymnasium, baseball and softball diamonds, a field hockey area, a soccer field, and tennis courts. A new recreation center houses a 6-lane swimming pool, a jogging/walking track, 4 racquetball courts, an aerobics/dance studio, fully-equipped Bodymaster and free-weight rooms, a fitness center, and a field house with 3 multipurpose courts for basketball, volleyball, and floor hockey.

Disabled Students: 90% of the campus is accessible to disabled students. The following facilities are available: wheelchair ramps, elevators, special parking, specially equipped rest rooms, special class scheduling, lowered drinking fountains, and lowered telephones.

Services: In addition to many counseling and information services, tutoring is available in every subject. There is a reader service for the blind, and remedial math, reading, and writing.

Campus Safety and Security: Campus safety and security measures include 24-hour foot and vehicle patrol, escort service, shuttle buses, and informal discussions. In addition, there are pamphlets/posters/films and lighted pathways/sidewalks.

Programs of Study: Assumption confers the B.A. degree. Associate and master's degrees are also awarded. Bachelor's degrees are awarded in BIOLOGICAL SCIENCE (biology/biological science), BUSINESS (accounting, business administration and management, international business management, and marketing management), COMMUNICATIONS AND THE ARTS (classics, communications, English, French, languages, and Spanish), COMPUTER AND PHYSICAL SCIENCE (chemistry, computer science, and mathematics), HEALTH PROFESSIONS (rehabilitation therapy), SOCIAL SCIENCE (economics, history, international studies, philosophy, political science/government, psychology, religion, and sociology). Business, English, and political science are the strongest programs academically and have the largest enrollments.

Required: Students must complete a core curriculum of 2 courses each of English composition, philosophy, and religious studies; 2 of the following 3: mathematics, a laboratory science, and a third year of a foreign language; and 1 each of literature, history, social science, and either art, music, or theater. A total of 120 semester credit hours must be completed, with 9 to 12 in the upper division of the major. A minimum 2.0 GPA is required.

Special: There are co-op programs in optometry and marine studies. Cross-registration with the Worcester Consortium and a 3-2 engineering program with Worcester Polytechnic Institute are permitted. The college offers internships, study abroad, a Washington semester, work-study, a general studies degree, student-designed and dual majors, credit by examination, and credit for life, military, and work experience. There are 5 national honor societies on campus.

Faculty/Classroom: 64% of faculty are male; 36%, female. All teach undergraduates. No introductory courses are taught by graduate students. The average class size in an introductory lecture is 40; in a laboratory, 15; and in a regular course offering, 23.

Admissions: 73% of the 1995-96 applicants were accepted. The SAT I scores for the 1995-96 freshman class were as follows: Verbal—70% below 500, 28% between 500 and 599, and 2% between 600 and 700; Math—45% below 500, 39% between 500 and 599, and 16% between 600 and 700. 25% of the current freshmen were in the top fifth of their class; 50% were in the top two fifths. There was 1 National Merit finalist and 10 semifinalists. 7 freshmen graduated first in their class.

Requirements: The SAT I is required. In addition, all applicants must graduate from an accredited secondary school or have a GED. 16 academic units are required, including 4 years of English, 3 each of mathematics and foreign language, and 1 each of history and science. An essay and an interview are recommended. AP and CLEP credits are accepted. Important factors in the admissions decision are advanced placement or honor courses, parents or siblings attending the school, and evidence of special talent.

Procedure: Freshmen are admitted fall and spring. Entrance exams should be taken in May of the junior year or November of the senior year. There are early decision, early admissions, and deferred admissions plans. Early decision applications should be filed by November 1; regular applications, by March 1 for fall entry and December 1 for spring entry, along with an application fee of $30. Notification of early decision is sent December 15; regular decision, on a rolling basis. 30 early decision candidates were accepted for the 1995-96 class.

Transfer: 70 transfer students enrolled in 1995-96. Transfer students must have maintained a minimum 2.5 GPA at their previous college. SAT I scores and high school and college transcripts are required. 60 credits of 120 must be completed at Assumption.

Visiting: There are regularly scheduled orientations for prospective students, consisting of new student orientation, a program that includes meetings with future classmates, choosing roommates, registration, testing, conferences with academic advisers, and discussions of aspects of college life. There are guides for informal visits and visitors may sit in on classes. To schedule a visit, contact the Admissions Office.

Financial Aid: In 1995-96, 69% of all freshmen and 65% of continuing students received some form of financial aid including need-based aid. The average freshman award was $8400. Of that total, scholarships or need-based grants averaged $5300; loans averaged $2625; and work contracts averaged $1000. 45% of undergraduate students work part-time. Average earnings from campus work for the school year are $1000. The average financial indebtedness of the 1994-95 graduate was $12,000. Assumption is a member of CSS. The CSS Profile Application financial statement is required. The application deadline for fall entry is February 1.

International Students: There were 20 international students enrolled in a recent year. The school actively recruits these students. They must take the TOEFL and achieve a minimum score of 550. Students may be requested to submit SAT I scores as well.

Computers: The college provides computer facilities for student use. The mainframes are a DEC VAX 3900 and 4000/100. Students may use the Apple Macintosh and IBM microcomputers, located in microcomputer laboratory areas throughout the campus, as well as a student-dedicated mainframe. All students may access the system. There are no time limits and no fees.

Graduates: In 1994-95, 454 bachelor's degrees were awarded. The most popular majors among graduates were social and rehabilitation services (18%), business management (16%), and English (13%). Within an average freshman class, 72% graduate in 4 years, 76% in 5 years, and 78% in 6 years. 400 companies recruited on campus in 1994-95. Of the 1994 graduating class, 20% were enrolled in graduate school within 6 months of graduation and 75% had found employment.

Admissions Contact: Dean of Admissions. A campus video is available.

ATLANTIC UNION COLLEGE
South Lancaster, MA 01561

C-2

(508) 368-2258
(800) 282-2030; FAX: (508) 368-2015

Full-time, part-time: 461 men and women	**Faculty:** 49
	Ph.D.s: 51%
Graduate: none	**Student/Faculty:** 8 to 1
Year: semesters, summer session	**Tuition:** $11,150
Application Deadline: August 1	**Room & Board:** $3600
Freshman Class: n/av	
SAT I or ACT: required	**LESS COMPETITIVE**

Atlantic Union College, founded in 1882, is a private coeducational institution affiliated with the Seventh-Day Adventist Church, offering undergraduate programs in the arts and sciences, business, education, health science, nursing, and religious studies. In addition to regional accreditation, AUC has baccalaureate program accreditation with CSWE, NASM, and NLN. The library contains 121,338 volumes, 9504 microform items, and 3372 audiovisual forms, and subscribes to 840 periodicals. Computerized library sources and services include interlibrary loans and database searching. Special learning facilities include a learning resource center, art gallery, model elementary and secondary schools, and a music conservatory. The 314-acre campus is in a small town 50 miles west of Boston. Including residence halls, there are 35 buildings on campus.

Housing: College-sponsored living facilities include single-sex dormitories, on-campus apartments, off-campus apartments, and married-student housing. On-campus housing is guaranteed for all 4 years. Alcohol is not permitted. All students may keep cars on campus.

Activities: There are no fraternities or sororities. There are 20 groups on campus, including art, band, choir, chorale, drama, ethnic, honors, literary magazine, newspaper, orchestra, religious, student government, and yearbook. Popular campus events include Fall Picnic, Cultural Heritage Weeks, Fine Arts Week, and Interschool Ethics Weekend.

Sports: There are 3 intercollegiate sports for men and 2 for women, and 5 intramural sports for men and 5 for women. Athletic and recreation facilities include a gymnasium, a field house, a swimming pool, tennis courts, a racquetball court, and softball and soccer fields.

Disabled Students: The following facilities are available: wheelchair ramps, elevators, special parking, and specially equipped rest rooms.

Services: In addition to many counseling and information services, tutoring is available in most subjects. There is remedial math, reading, and writing.

Campus Safety and Security: Campus safety and security measures include self-defense education, informal discussions, and lighted pathways/sidewalks.

Programs of Study: AUC confers B.A., B.S., and B.M. degrees. Associate and master's degrees are also awarded. Bachelor's degrees are awarded in BIOLOGICAL SCIENCE (biochemistry and biology/biological science), BUSINESS (accounting, business administration and management, and office supervision and management), COMMUNICATIONS AND THE ARTS (art, English, French, music, and Spanish), COMPUTER AND PHYSICAL SCIENCE (chemistry, computer science, and mathematics), EDUCATION (art, business, early childhood, elementary, music, physical, and secondary), ENGINEERING AND ENVIRONMENTAL DESIGN (interior design), HEALTH PROFESSIONS (medical laboratory technology and nursing), SOCIAL SCIENCE (history, psychology, religion, and social work). Nursing, English, and business are the strongest academically. Business, psychology, and education have the largest enrollments.

Required: Students must complete 12 hours each in humanities, religion/ethics, science, and social science. Foreign language proficiency, a physical education requirement, and a course in freshman rhetoric must also be fulfilled. AUC requires 128 credit hours for the bachelor's degree, with 30 to 50 in the major, and a 2.0 GPA.

Special: There is cross-registration with Mount Wachusett Community College. Students may study abroad in 4 countries. AUC also offers newspaper and biology research internships, cooperative programs in several majors, pass/fail options and nondegree study. The Summer Advantage in New England program offers precollege credit to high school honor students. There is also an adult degree program, in which most study is done at home, and in which student-designed majors are permitted. Dual majors, an accelerated degree in management and professional studies, a 1-3 engineering degree with Walla Walla College, and preprofessional curricula in dentistry, dental hygiene, medicine, respiratory therapy, radiologic technology, and veterinary medicine in conjunction with Loma Linda University are offered. There is a freshman honors program on campus, as well as 2 national honor societies. 2 departments have honors programs.

Faculty/Classroom: 54% of faculty are male; 46%, female. All teach undergraduates and 2% do research. The average class size in an introductory lecture is 20 and in a laboratory, 10.

Requirements: The SAT I or ACT is required. Applicants should be graduates of an accredited secondary school with a 2.0 GPA or hold a GED. Required academic credits include 4 years of high school English and 2 years each of a foreign language, mathematics, history, and science. AP and CLEP credits are accepted. Important factors in the admissions decision are recommendations by school officials, recommendations by alumni, and personality/intangible qualities.

Procedure: Freshmen are admitted fall and spring. Entrance exams should be taken during the senior year of high school. Applications should be filed by August 1 for fall entry and January 1 for spring entry, along with an application fee of $25. Notification is sent on a rolling basis.

Transfer: Applicants who have completed at least 24 semester hours are not required to submit SAT I or ACT scores. Applicants from junior colleges may receive credit for up to 72 semester hours. Only a grade of C or better transfers for credit. 30 credits of 128 must be completed at AUC.

Visiting: There are regularly scheduled orientations for prospective students, including campus tours, class visits, and financial aid information sessions. There are guides for informal visits and visitors may sit in on classes and stay overnight at the school. To schedule a visit, contact Julie Lee.

Financial Aid: In 1995-96, 85% of all freshmen and 80% of continuing students received some form of financial aid. 70% of freshmen and 70% of continuing students received need-based aid. The average freshman award was $7000. Of that total, scholarships or need-based grants averaged $1200 ($3000 maximum); and loans averaged $2500 ($2625 maximum). 80% of undergraduate students work part-time. Average earnings from campus work for the school year are $1500. The average financial indebtedness of the 1994-95 graduate was $15,000. The FAFSA and the college's own financial statement are required. The application deadline for fall entry is April 15.

International Students: The school actively recruits these students. They must take the TOEFL and achieve a minimum score of 525 or 550 for nursing students. The student must also take the SAT I or the ACT and achieve a minimum score of 17 on the ACT.

Computers: The college provides computer facilities for student use. The mainframes are a DEC MicroVAX II and a Novell Network. Some 40 computers and terminals are available for student use in the computer laboratory. All students may access the system. There are no time limits and no fees.

Graduates: In 1994-95, 128 bachelor's degrees were awarded.

Admissions Contact: Julie Lee, Associate Director of Enrollment Management. E-mail: enroll@atlanticuc.edu.

BABSON COLLEGE
Babson Park, MA 02157

D-2

(617) 239-5522
(800) 488-3696; (617) 239-4006

Full-time: 1093 men, 632 women	**Faculty:** 114; IIB, + +$
Part-time: none	**Ph.D.s:** 89%
Graduate: 1653 men and women	**Student/Faculty:** 15 to 1
Year: semesters, summer session	**Tuition:** $18,115
Application Deadline: February 1	**Room & Board:** $7275
Freshman Class: 2242 applied, 1066 accepted, 399 enrolled	
SAT I or ACT: required	**VERY COMPETITIVE**

Babson College, founded in 1919, is a private, coeducational institution offering programs in business. There is 1 graduate school. In addition to regional accreditation, Babson has baccalaureate program accreditation with AACSB. The library contains 124,125 volumes, 346,089 microform items, and 2456 audiovisual forms, and subscribes to 1482 periodicals. Computerized library sources and services include the card catalog, interlibrary loans, and database searching. Special learning facilities include a learning resource center, art gallery, TV station, and a cable channel. The 450-acre campus is in a suburban area 14 miles west of Boston. Including residence halls, there are 52 buildings on campus.

Student Life: 63% of undergraduates are from out-of-state, mostly the Northeast. Students come from 43 states, 70 foreign countries, and Canada. 58% are from public schools; 42% from private. 61% are white; 18% foreign nationals. The average age of freshmen is 18; all undergraduates, 20. 9% do not continue beyond their first year; 83% remain to graduate.

Housing: 1230 students can be accommodated in college housing. College-sponsored living facilities include single-sex and coed dormitories, on-campus apartments, and married-student housing. In addition, there are special interest houses and substance-free living, fraternity and sorority towers, and a cultural house. On-campus housing is guaranteed for all 4 years. 85% of students live on campus; of those, 75% remain on campus on weekends. All students may keep cars on campus.

Activities: 11% of men and about 1% of women belong to 5 national fraternities; 8% of women belong to 2 national sororities. There are 57 groups on campus, including art, billiards, chess, computers, dance, debate, drama, emergency services, environmental, ethnic, film, gay, health, honors, international, jazz band, literary magazine, musical theater, newspaper, political, professional, radio and TV, religious, social, social service, student government, and yearbook. Popular campus events include Multicultural Week, Winter Weekend, Spring Weekend, and Octoberfest Weekend.

Sports: There are 10 intercollegiate sports for men and 10 for women, and 12 intramural sports for men and 6 for women. Athletic and recreation facilities include a sports complex with an indoor pool, a 200-meter, 6-lane indoor track, a 1500-seat field house, a 600-seat gymnasium with 3 basketball courts, 5 squash and 2 racquetball courts, a fitness center, a dance aerobics studio, locker rooms with saunas, and a sports medicine facility.

Disabled Students: 98% of the campus is accessible to disabled students. The following facilities are available: wheelchair ramps, elevators, special parking, specially equipped rest rooms, special class scheduling, lowered drinking fountains, and lowered telephones.

Services: In addition to many counseling and information services, tutoring is available in most subjects. There are writing/speech skills and mathematics/science skills centers.

Campus Safety and Security: Campus safety and security measures include 24-hour foot and vehicle patrol, escort service, shuttle buses, and informal discussions. There are pamphlets/posters/films, emergency telephones, lighted pathways/sidewalks, and a motorist assist program.

Programs of Study: Babson confers the B.S.M. degree. Master's degrees are also awarded. Bachelor's degrees are awarded in BUSINESS (accounting, banking and finance, business administration and management, international business management, investments and securities, management information systems, management science, and marketing/retailing/merchandising), COMMUNICATIONS AND THE ARTS (communications), COMPUTER AND PHYSICAL SCIENCE (quantitative methods), SOCIAL SCIENCE (American studies and economics). Management is the strongest academically and has the largest enrollment.

Required: Students must complete a curriculum of general management and liberal arts, with 40% in management, 40% in liberal arts, and 20% in course work in either area. A total of 128 semester hours is required for graduation. A minimum GPA of 2.0 is required. Students must take 2 semesters of physical education, a course on introduction to information processing, and a fundamental science course. Students must also fulfill a liberal arts concentration in 1 of 16 different areas.

Special: There is cross-registration with Brandeis University and Pine Manor, Wellesley, and Regis colleges. Internships in management, study abroad in 11 countries, dual and student-designed majors, credit by exam, and up to 8 semester hours of credit for significant work/life experience are possible. There is a freshman honors program on campus, as well as 7 national honor societies. There is 1 general an honors program.

Faculty/Classroom: 75% of faculty are male; 25%, female. No introductory courses are taught by graduate students.

Admissions: 48% of the 1995–96 applicants were accepted. The SAT I scores for the 1995–96 freshman class were as follows: Verbal—51% below 500, 38% between 500 and 599, 9% between 600 and 700, and 2% above 700; Math—12% below 500, 36% between 500 and 599, 37% between 600 and 700, and 15% above 700.

Requirements: The SAT I or ACT is required along with SAT II: Subject tests in writing and mathematics. Applicants must be graduates of an accredited secondary school or have a GED. 16 academic courses are required, including 4 credits of English, 3 of mathematics, 2 of social studies, and 1 of science. A fourth year of mathematics is strongly recommended. An essay and a graded paper are required. An interview is recommended. Applications are accepted on computer disk via CollegeLink, ExPAN, CollegeView, and Apply. AP and CLEP credits are accepted. Important factors in the admissions decision are academic performance, advanced placement or honor courses, and leadership record.

Procedure: Freshmen are admitted fall and spring. Entrance exams should be taken prior to application (SAT I or ACT). SAT II: Subject tests should be taken by June of the senior year. There are early decision and deferred admissions plans. Early decision applications should be filed by November 15; regular applications, by February 1 for fall entry and November 1 for spring entry, along with an application fee of $50. Notification of early decision is sent January 1; regular decision, April 1. 49 early decision candidates were accepted for the 1995–96 class. A waiting list is an active part of the admissions procedure.

Transfer: 89 transfer students enrolled in 1995–96. Applicants are expected to demonstrate solid academic performance at their prior institution and must submit an essay. 64 credits of 128 must be completed at Babson.

Visiting: There are regularly scheduled orientations for prospective students, usually consisting of personal interviews and campus tours. Group information sessions may also be available. There are guides for informal visits and visitors may sit in on classes and stay overnight at the school. To schedule a visit, contact the Admission Office at least 2 weeks beforehand.

Financial Aid: In 1995–96, 52% of all freshmen and 48% of continuing students received some form of financial aid. 50% of freshmen and 46% of continuing students received need-based aid. The average freshman award was $14,600. Of that total, scholarships or need-based grants averaged $9800 ($22,430 maximum); loans averaged $3000 ($3625 maximum); and work contracts averaged $1800 (maximum). 35% of undergraduate students work part-time. Average earnings from campus work for the school year are $1200. The average financial indebtedness of the 1994–95 graduate was $16,125. Babson is a member of CSS. The FAFSA and CSS Profile Application are required. The application deadline for fall entry is February 15.

International Students: There are currently 362 international students enrolled. The school actively recruits these students. They must score 550 on the TOEFL and take SAT I or the ACT and SAT II: Subject tests in mathematics and English composition.

Computers: The college provides computer facilities for student use. The mainframe is a MicroVAX 4000–600A. Residence hall rooms have access to GlobeNet through a 10-Base-T Ethernet connection. Access to the Internet, including NetScape for browsing the World Wide Web, and E-mail are also provided. All students may access the system. There are no time limits and no fees.

Graduates: In 1994–95, 399 bachelor's degrees were awarded. Within an average freshman class, 83% graduate in 5 years and 85% in 6 years. More than 300 companies recruited on campus in 1994–95. Of the 1994 graduating class, 4% were enrolled in graduate school within 6 months of graduation and 79% had found employment.

Admissions Contact: Charles S. Nolan, Dean of Admissions. A campus video is available.

BENTLEY COLLEGE
D-2

Waltham, MA 02154–4705   (617) 891–2244; (800) 523–2354

Full-time: 1789 men, 1287 women	Faculty: 191; IIA, + +$
Part-time: 643 men, 754 women	Ph.D.s: 87%
Graduate: 1200 men, 926 women	Student/Faculty: 16 to 1
Year: semesters, summer session	Tuition: $14,835
Application Deadline: February 15	Room & Board: $6340
Freshman Class: 3631 applied, 2410 accepted, 720 enrolled	
SAT I or ACT: required	**VERY COMPETITIVE**

Bentley College, founded in 1917, is a private coeducational institution offering instruction in business and the liberal arts. There is 1 graduate school. In addition to regional accreditation, Bentley has baccalaureate program accreditation with AACSB. The library contains 192,566 volumes, 217,778 microform items, and 4400 audiovisual forms, and subscribes to 2606 periodicals. Computerized library sources and services include interlibrary loans and database searching. Special learning facilities include a learning resource center, art gallery, planetarium, radio station, and 6 academic learning centers. The 110-acre campus is in a suburban area 9 miles west of Boston. Including residence halls, there are 43 buildings on campus.

Student Life: 58% of undergraduates are from Massachusetts. Students come from 42 states, 75 foreign countries, and Canada. 70% are from public schools; 30% from private. 78% are white; 12% foreign nationals. 56% are Catholic; 16% Protestant; 14% claim no religious affiliation. The average age of freshmen is 18; all undergraduates, 20. 12% do not continue beyond their first year; 76% remain to graduate.

Housing: 2829 students can be accommodated in college housing. College-sponsored living facilities include single-sex and coed dormitories, on-campus apartments, off-campus apartments, and married-student housing. In addition there are special interest houses and substance-free housing. On-campus housing is available on a first-come, first-served basis and is available on a lottery system for upperclassmen. Priority is given to out-of-town students. 84% of students live on campus; of those, 60% remain on campus on weekends. Upperclassmen may keep cars on campus.

Activities: 15% of men belong to 3 local and 4 national fraternities; 13% of women belong to 2 local and 4 national sororities. There are 74 groups on campus, including art, band, cheerleading, chorus, computers, dance, drama, ethnic, gay, honors, international, jazz band, literary magazine, musical theater, newspaper, photography, political, professional, radio and TV, religious, social, social service, student government, and yearbook. Popular campus events include Monte Carlo Night, Spring Weekend, and Spring Concert.

Sports: There are 10 intercollegiate sports for men and 9 for women, and 10 intramural sports for men and 9 for women. Athletic and recreation facilities include an 86,000-square-foot multipurpose facility with 8 basketball hoops and 3 full-size basketball courts, 3 volleyball courts, a batting cage, 2 golf cages, 2 racquetball/handball courts, a therapy room, saunas, a steam bath, a dance studio; a natatorium with a competition-size swimming pool and a separate diving tank; a fitness center with state-of-the-art fitness equipment; and 2 lighted playing fields, a softball field, and 6 lighted tennis courts.

Disabled Students: 95% of the campus is accessible to disabled students. The following facilities are available: wheelchair ramps, elevators, special parking, specially equipped rest rooms, and special class scheduling.

Services: In addition to many counseling and information services, tutoring is available in most subjects. There is remedial math, reading, and writing.

Campus Safety and Security: Campus safety and security measures include 24-hour foot and vehicle patrol, self-defense education, escort service, and shuttle buses. In addition, there are informal discussions, pamphlets/posters/films, emergency telephones, and lighted pathways/sidewalks.

Programs of Study: Bentley confers B.A. and B.S. degrees. Associate and master's degrees are also awarded. Bachelor's degrees are awarded in BUSINESS (accounting, banking and finance, business economics, international economics, management science, and marketing management), COMMUNICATIONS AND THE ARTS (communications and English), COMPUTER AND PHYSICAL SCIENCE (information sciences and systems and mathematics), SOCIAL SCIENCE (economics, history, liberal arts/general studies, and philosophy). Accountancy, marketing, and management have the largest enrollments.

Required: Students majoring in the B.S. degree programs take a common business core of 10 courses covering major business areas such as accounting, business law, and marketing. Students working toward the B.A. must take English composition, literature, philosophy, history, government, economics, behavioral science, mathematical science, natural science, and computer information systems. A total of 120 credit hours is required for graduation, with a minimum GPA of 2.0. Freshmen must take physical education.

Special: There is cross-registration with Regis College and Brandeis University, and internships are available in all departments. The college offers study abroad in 7 countries, student-designed majors, credit by exam, and nondegree study. There is also a minor concentration program through which business majors can broaden their exposure to the arts and sciences, and arts and science majors can minor in business or interdisciplinary topics. There is a freshman honors program on campus, as well as 2 national honor societies. 3 departments have honors programs.

Faculty/Classroom: 67% of faculty are male; 33%, female. The average class size in a regular course offering is 30.

Admissions: 66% of the 1995–96 applicants were accepted. The SAT I scores for the 1995–96 freshman class were as follows: Verbal—31% below 500, 48% between 500 and 599, 19% between 600 and 700, and 2% above 700; Math—17% below 500, 48% between 500 and 599, 32% between 600 and 700, and 3% above 700. 45% of the current freshmen were in the top fifth of their class; 76% were in the top two fifths.

Requirements: The SAT I or ACT is required. Applicants must be graduates of an accredited high school or have a GED. The SAT II: Subject tests in writing, mathematics I or II, and a third subject of the student's chioce may be substituted for the SAT I or ACT. The recommended high school preparation is 4 units each in English and mathematics, including algebra I and II and geometry; 3 units in laboratory science; 2 to 3 units in a foreign langauage; 2 units in social science; and 2 additional units in English, mahtematics, social science or laboratory science, foreign langauage, speech, or advanced accounting. AP and CLEP credits are accepted. Important factors in the admissions decision are recommendations by alumni, recommendations by school officials, and advanced placement or honor courses.

Procedure: Freshmen are admitted fall and spring. Entrance exams should be taken no later than the January test date. There are early decision, early admissions, and deferred admissions plans. Early decision applications should be filed by December 1; regular applications, by February 15 for fall entry and December 1 for spring entry, along with an application fee of $35. Notification of early decision is sent December 20; regular decision, April 1. 35 early decision candidates were accepted for the 1995–96 class. A waiting list is an active part of the admissions procedure.

Transfer: 190 transfer students enrolled in 1995–96. The SAT I, ACT, or SAT II: Subject tests is required of all applicants who have completed fewer than 10 college courses. To be considered, students must have a minimum GPA of 2.5. All official college transcripts must be submitted. 45 credits of 120 must be completed at Bentley.

Visiting: There are regularly scheduled orientations for prospective students, including fall, spring, and summer open house programs. Interviews are arranged by appointment; campus tours take place at regularly scheduled times each weekday. There are guides for informal visits and visitors may sit in on classes. To schedule a visit, contact the Office of Undergraduate Admissions.

Financial Aid: In 1995–96, 71% of all freshmen and 63% of continuing students received some form of financial aid. 88% of freshmen and 98% of continuing students received need-based aid. The average freshman award was $12,600. Of that total, scholarships or need-based grants averaged $8800; loans averaged $4600; and work contracts averaged $1500. 96% of undergraduate students work part-time. Average earnings from campus work for the school year are $700. Bentley is a member of CSS. The FAF is required. The application deadline for fall entry is February 1.

International Students: There are currently 363 international students enrolled. The school actively recruits these students. They must take the TOEFL and achieve a minimum score of 550. The student must also take the SAT I or the ACT.

Computers: The college provides computer facilities for student use. The mainframes are a DEC VAX 6620 and a DEC VAX 6510. The mainframes are linked to more than 3,000 microcomputers and terminals across the campus. The network also provides worldwide access to databases and other services via the Internet and dial-out modems. All students must have personal computers, and 5 student computer laboratories contain 130 IBM-compatible and 50 Apple Macintosh microcomputers, all with network access. All students may access the system during laboratory hours, 7 days a week. There are no time limits and no fees.

Graduates: In 1994–95, 827 bachelor's degrees were awarded. The most popular majors among graduates were accountancy (28%), marketing (19%), and finance (17%). Within an average freshman class, 61% graduate in 4 years, 70% in 5 years, and 72% in 6 years. Of the 1994 graduating class, 4% were enrolled in graduate school within 6 months of graduation and 88% had found employment.

Admissions Contact: Joann McKenna, Director of Admissions. A campus video is available.

BERKLEE COLLEGE OF MUSIC E-2

Boston, MA 02215-3693

(617) 266-1400
(800) 421-0084; FAX: (617) 536-2632

Full-time: 1923 men, 409 women	**Faculty:** 146; IIB, av$
Part-time: 257 men, 78 women	**Ph.D.s:** 5%
Graduate: 12 men and women	**Student/Faculty:** 16 to 1
Year: semesters, summer session	**Tuition:** $12,400
Application Deadline: open	**Room & Board:** $7190
Freshman Class: 2150 applied, 1681 accepted, 737 enrolled	
SAT I or ACT: required	**SPECIAL**

Berklee College of Music, founded in 1945, is a private coeducational institution offering programs in all areas of contemporary music, primarily American jazz, pop, Latin, fusion, rhythm and blues, and reggae. There is one graduate school. The library contains 34,982 volumes, 3303 microform items, and 8188 audiovisual forms. Special learning facilities include a learning resource center and 9 recording studios, 5 performance venues, and film editing, music synthesis, and home recording laboratories. The campus is in an urban area in the Back Bay section of Boston. Including residence halls, there are 9 buildings on campus.

Student Life: 76% of undergraduates are from out-of-state, mostly the Northeast. Students come from 46 states, 75 foreign countries, and Canada. 85% are white; 34% foreign nationals. The average age of freshmen is 21; all undergraduates, 23. 40% do not continue beyond their first year; 60% remain to graduate.

Housing: 800 students can be accommodated in college housing. College-sponsored living facilities include coed dormitories. On-campus housing is available on a first-come, first-served basis and is available on a lottery system for upperclassmen. 70% of students commute. Alcohol is not permitted. All students may keep cars on campus.

Activities: There are no fraternities or sororities. There are 45 groups on campus, including art, band, choir, chorale, chorus, computers, drama, ethnic, gay, international, jazz band, orchestra, professional, religious, and social. Popular campus events include International Students Fair and Concert, film festivals, and Singer Showcase.

Sports: There are 5 intramural sports for men and women. Discount memberships at the YMCA and a student rate at the Massachusetts College of Art fitness room are available.

Disabled Students: The following facilities are available: wheelchair ramps, elevators, specially equipped rest rooms, and special class scheduling.

Services: In addition to many counseling and information services, tutoring is available in every subject. There is a reader service for the blind, tape recorders, untimed testing, and learning center resources.

Campus Safety and Security: Campus safety and security measures include 24-hour foot and vehicle patrol, informal discussions, pamphlets/posters/films, and lighted pathways/sidewalks.

Programs of Study: Berklee confers the B.M. degree. Master's degrees are also awarded. Bachelor's degrees are awarded in COMMUNICATIONS AND THE ARTS (audio technology, film arts, jazz, music, music business management, music performance, and music theory and composition), EDUCATION (music) and HEALTH PROFESSIONS (music therapy). Performance, professional music, and music production and engineering have the largest enrollments.

Required: Students working toward a degree must take general education courses in English composition/literature, history, physical science, and social sciences. Music course programs vary by specialization. A total of 120 credits must be completed with a minimum GPA of 2.0.

Special: Berklee offers cross-registration with the Pro-Arts Consortium, study abroad in the Netherlands, and internships in music education and music production' and engineering, 5-year dual majors, and a 4-year professional (nondegree) diploma program. Work-study programs, an accelerated-degree program, student-designed majors, and credit by examination are available.

Faculty/Classroom: 86% of faculty are male; 14%, female. All teach undergraduates. The average class size in an introductory lecture is 14; in a laboratory, 8; and in a regular course offering, 15.

Admissions: 78% of the 1995–96 applicants were accepted. The SAT I scores for a recent freshman class were as follows: Verbal—34% below 500, 60% between 500 and 599, 5% between 600 and 700, and 1% above 700; Math—22% below 500, 54% between 500 and 599, 20% between 600 and 700, and 4% above 700.

Requirements: The SAT I or ACT is required. Applicants must be graduates of an accredited secondary school or have their GED. An audition and interview are recommended. Applicants must also submit a detailed reference letter regarding their training and experience in music, a letter from a private instructor, school music director, or professional musician. A letter of character reference is also required. AP credits are accepted. Important factors in the admissions decision are evidence of special talent, extracurricular activities record, and recommendations by alumni.

Procedure: Freshmen are admitted to all sessions. Entrance exams should be taken in the fall of the senior year. There are early decision and deferred admissions plans. Application deadlines are open. Application fee is $50. Notification is sent on a rolling basis.

Transfer: 287 transfer students enrolled in a recent year. Applicants must go through the same application procedures as entering freshmen, as well as submit all previous college records. 60 credits of 120 must be completed at Berklee.

Visiting: There are regularly scheduled orientations for prospective students, consisting of 2 tours scheduled daily during semesters, with the morning tour followed by an information session given by an admissions counselor. There are guides for informal visits. To schedule a visit, contact the Admissions Office.

Financial Aid: In a recent year, 72% of all students received some form of financial aid. The average freshman award was $9183. 13% of undergraduate students work part-time. The FAF or FFS and the college's own financial statement are required. The application deadline for fall entry is March 31.

International Students: There are currently 911 international students enrolled. The school actively recruits these students.

Computers: The college provides computer facilities for student use. The mainframe is an IBM/AS400. There are more than 40 networked Apple Macintosh computers in the learning center. There are no time limits and no fees.

Graduates: In a recent class, 385 bachelor's degrees were awarded.

Admissions Contact: Director of Admissions. A campus video is available.

BOSTON ARCHITECTURAL CENTER

E-2

Boston, MA 02115   (617) 536–3170; FAX: (617) 536–5829

Full-time: 459 men and women	Faculty: 275
Part-time: 121 men and women	Ph.D.s: 80%
Graduate: none	Student/Faculty: 2 to 1
Year: semesters, summer session	Tuition: $4620
Application Deadline: open	Room & Board: n/app
Freshman Class: 322 applied, 302 accepted, 137 enrolled	
SAT I or ACT: not required	SPECIAL

Boston Architectural Center, founded in 1889 as the Boston Architectural Club, is an independent, coeducational, commuter institution offering 6-year programs in architecture and interior design. Students work in professional offices during the day and attend classes at night. In addition to regional accreditation, BAC has baccalaureate program accreditation with NAAB. The library contains 23,000 volumes and subscribes to 140 periodicals. The campus is in an urban area in Boston. There is one building on campus.

Student Life: 60% of undergraduates are from Massachusetts. Students come from 35 states, 4 foreign countries, and Canada. 93% are white. The average age of freshmen is 25; all undergraduates, 27. 30% do not continue beyond their first year; 25% remain to graduate.

Housing: There are no residence halls. Arrangements for housing may be made through consortium schools on a space-available basis. All of students commute. Alcohol is not permitted.

Activities: There are no fraternities or sororities. There are several groups and organizations on campus, including newspaper, professional, and student government.

Sports: There is no sports program at BAC.

Disabled Students: All of the campus is accessible to disabled students. The following facilities are available: wheelchair ramps, elevators, special parking, and specially equipped rest rooms.

Programs of Study: BAC confers B.Arch. and B.Int.Design. degrees. Bachelor's degrees are awarded in ENGINEERING AND ENVIRONMENTAL DESIGN (architecture and interior design).

Required: In order to graduate, all students must complete 177 credits. Academic credits must total 123, 93 of which must be in professional subjects and 30 in general education courses. 21 credits must be earned in outside liberal arts courses, which may be taken by special arrangement at Metropolitan College of Boston University and Harvard University Extension. Students must earn 54 credits by working in architectural or interior-design offices or in related fields. Academic study is divided into 3 segments, the final segment being the thesis year, which consists of 2 semesters of student-designed study under the guidance of a faculty adviser. A minimum 2.5 GPA is required.

Special: The center offers cross-registration with schools in the Professional Arts Consortium in Boston and with the Art Institute of Boston for studio and professional courses.

Faculty/Classroom: 86% of faculty are male; 14%, female. All teach undergraduates. The average class size in an introductory lecture is 33 and in a laboratory, 8.

Admissions: 94% of the 1995–96 applicants were accepted.

Requirements: All applicants who have graduated from high school or have a college degree are admitted on a first-come, first-served basis. Official transcripts from previously attended secondary schools and colleges must be submitted to determine qualification for admission and advanced placement. AP and CLEP credits are accepted.

Procedure: Freshmen are admitted fall and spring. Application deadlines are open. Application fee is $50. The college accepts all applicants. Notification is sent on a rolling basis. A waiting list is an active part of the admissions procedure, with about 5% of all applicants on the list.

Transfer: 69 transfer students enrolled in a recent year. Applicants for transfer must have a 2.0 GPA to receive transfer credit. 47 credits of 123 must be completed at BAC.

Visiting: There are regularly scheduled orientations for prospective students, consisting of monthly presentations. There are guides for informal visits and visitors may sit in on classes. To schedule a visit, contact the Admissions Office.

Financial Aid: In a recent year, 45% of all freshmen and 40% of continuing students received some form of financial aid. 45% of freshmen and 37% of continuing students received need-based aid. The average freshman award was $4234. Of that total, scholarships or need-based grants averaged $1265 ($2300 maximum); and loans averaged $3928 ($5500 maximum). BAC is a member of CSS. The FAFSA and the college's own financial statement are required.

International Students: In a recent year, 7 international students were enrolled.

Computers: The college provides Macintosh and IBM microcomputers for student use. All students may access the system. There are no time limits. The fee is $44 per semester.

Graduates: In 1994–95, 42 bachelor's degrees were awarded.

Admissions Contact: Kristen Keefe, Admissions Coordinator.

BOSTON COLLEGE

E-2

Chestnut Hill, MA 02167   (617) 552–3100

(800) 360–2522; FAX: (617) 552–0798

Full-time: 4220 men, 4676 women	Faculty: 591; I, +$
Part-time: none	Ph.D.s: 95%
Graduate: 1928 men, 2631 women	Student/Faculty: 15 to 1
Year: semesters, summer session	Tuition: $18,356
Application Deadline: January 1	Room & Board: $7270
Freshman Class: 16,680 applied, 6399 accepted, 2140 enrolled	
SAT I or ACT: required	MOST COMPETITIVE

Boston College, founded in 1863, is an independent institution affiliated with the Roman Catholic Church and the Jesuit Order. It offers undergraduate programs in the arts and sciences, business, nursing, and education. There are 4 undergraduate and 6 graduate schools. In addition to regional accreditation, BC has baccalaureate program accreditation with AACSB, CSWE, NCATE, and NLN. The 6 libraries contain 1,591,801 volumes, 2,540,309 microform items, and 83,791 audiovisual forms, and subscribe to 17,489 periodicals. Computerized library sources and services include the card catalog, interlibrary loans, and database searching. Special learning facilities include a learning resource center, art gallery, radio station, and TV station. The 240-acre campus is in a suburban area 6 miles west of Boston. Including residence halls, there are 88 buildings on campus.

Student Life: 71% of undergraduates are from out-of-state, mostly the Northeast. Students come from 50 states, 68 foreign countries, and Canada. 60% are from public schools; 40% from private. 78% are white. 80% are Catholic; 10% claim no religious affiliation. The average age of freshmen is 19; all undergraduates, 20. 7% do not continue beyond their first year; 91% remain to graduate.

Housing: 6482 students can be accommodated in college housing. College-sponsored living facilities include single-sex and coed dormitories and on-campus apartments. In addition, there are honors houses, language houses, special interest houses, and community and multicultural housing, quiet residences, single-sex freshman halls, perspectives academic program housing, and a substance-free floor. On-campus housing is guaranteed for all 4 years. 73% of students live on campus; of those, 75% remain on campus on weekends. Upperclassmen may keep cars on campus.

Activities: There are no fraternities or sororities. There are 120 groups on campus, including art, band, cheerleading, chess, choir, chorale, chorus, computers, dance, drama, ethnic, film, honors, international, jazz band, literary magazine, marching band, musical theater, newspaper, orchestra, pep band, photography, political, professional, radio and TV, religious, social, social service, student government, symphony, and yearbook. Popular campus events include Middlemarch Ball, Christmas Chorale, and Senior Week.

Sports: There are 17 intercollegiate sports for men and 16 for women, and 16 intramural sports for men and 14 for women. Athletic and recreation facilities include a 32,000-seat stadium, a forum that seats 8604 for basketball and 7800 for ice hockey, a field, a track, and a student recreation complex.

Disabled Students: All of the campus is accessible to disabled students. The following facilities are available: wheelchair ramps, elevators, special parking, specially equipped rest rooms, special class scheduling, lowered drinking fountains, and lowered telephones.

Services: In addition to many counseling and information services, tutoring is available in most subjects. There is a reader service for the blind and an academic development center.

Campus Safety and Security: Campus safety and security measures include 24-hour foot and vehicle patrol, self-defense education, escort service, and shuttle buses. There are informal discussions, pamphlets/posters/films, emergency telephones, lighted pathways/sidewalks, safety seminars, safety walking tours, and whistles distributed to incoming students.

Programs of Study: BC confers B.A. and B.S. degrees. Master's and doctoral degrees are also awarded. Bachelor's degrees are awarded in BIOLOGICAL SCIENCE (biochemistry and biology/biological science), BUSINESS (accounting, banking and finance, business administration and management, business economics, human resources, management science, marketing/retailing/merchandising, and operations research), COMMUNICATIONS AND THE ARTS (art history and appreciation, classics, communications, dramatic arts, English, French, German, Greek, Italian, Latin, linguistics, music, romance languages, Spanish, and studio art), COMPUTER AND PHYSICAL SCIENCE (chemistry, computer science, geology, geophysics and seismology, information sciences and systems, mathematics, and physics), EDUCATION (early childhood, elementary, secondary, and special), ENGINEERING AND ENVIRONMENTAL DESIGN (environmental science), HEALTH PROFESSIONS (nursing), SOCIAL SCIENCE (classical/ancient civilization, economics, history, human development, philosophy, political science/government, psychology, Russian and Slavic studies, sociology, and theological studies). Humanities and social sciences are the strongest academically. English, biology, political science, and psychology have the largest enrollments.

Required: Core requirements include 2 courses each in natural science, social science, history, philosophy, and theology, and 1 course each in literature, writing, mathematics, cultural diversity, and the arts. To graduate, students must complete 114 credits (121 in nursing), including at least 30 in the major, with a minimum 1.667 GPA (1.5 in management). Computer science is required for management majors, intermediate-level foreign language proficiency for arts and sciences and management students, and a freshman writing seminar for all students except Honors and AP students.

Special: There are internship programs in communications and political science. Students may cross-register with Boston University, Brandeis University, Hebrew College, Pine Manor College, Regis College, and Tufts University. BC also offers a Washington semester with American University, work-study programs with nonprofit agencies, study abroad, dual and student-designed majors, credit by exam, and pass/fail options. Students may pursue a 3–2 engineering program with Boston University and accelerated programs in business, social work, and education. There are also special programs in social work and philosophy/theology, in language immersion, capstone courses, and in exploring fundamental questions of faith, peace, and justice. There is a freshman honors program on campus, as well as 12 national honor societies, including Phi Beta Kappa. 8 departments have honors programs.

Faculty/Classroom: 68% of faculty are male; 32%, female. All both teach and do research. Graduate students teach 15% of introductory courses. The average class size in an introductory lecture is 100; in a laboratory, 15; and in a regular course offering, 30.

Admissions: 38% of the 1995–96 applicants were accepted. The SAT I scores for the 1995–96 freshman class were as follows: Verbal—18% below 500, 46% between 500 and 599, 33% between 600 and 700, and 4% above 700; Math—2% below 500, 18% between 500 and 599, 56% between 600 and 700, and 25% above 700. There were 7 National Merit finalists.

Requirements: The SAT I or ACT is required. Students must also take SAT II: Subject tests in writing, mathematics level I or II, and any third test. Applicants must be graduates of an accredited high school, completing 4 units each of English, foreign language, and mathematics, and 3 units of science. Those students applying to the School of Nursing must complete at least 2 years of a laboratory science, including 1 year of chemistry. Applicants to the School of Management are strongly encouraged to take 4 years of mathematics. An essay is required and an interview is recommended. Applications are accepted on diskette or on-line via Apply, CollegeLink, and ExPAN. Important factors in the admissions decision are advanced placement or honor courses, evidence of special talent, and leadership record.

Procedure: Freshmen are admitted fall and spring. Entrance exams should be taken no later than January of the senior year. There are early action, early admissions, and deferred admissions plans. Early action applications should be filed by October 15; regular applications, by January 1 for fall entry and November 1 for spring entry, along with an application fee of $50. Notification of early action is sent December 15; regular decision, April 15. 137 early decision candidates were accepted for the 1995–96 class. A waiting list is an active part of the admissions procedure, with about 10% of all applicants on the list.

Transfer: 216 transfer students enrolled in 1995–96. Applicants must have a current GPA of at least 2.5 and must have earned a minimum of 9 semester hours. High school transcripts, letters of recommendation, and SAT I or ACT scores are required. 54 credits of 114 to 121 must be completed at BC.

Visiting: There are regularly scheduled orientations for prospective students, consisting of group information sessions and campus tours Monday through Friday. Interviews should be scheduled 10 to 12 weeks in advance. There are guides for informal visits and visitors may sit in on classes. To schedule a visit, contact the Office of Undergraduate Admission.

Financial Aid: In 1995–96, 68% of all freshmen and 62% of continuing students received some form of financial aid. 65% of freshmen and 51% of continuing students received need-based aid. The average freshman award was $18,266. Of that total, scholarships or need-based grants averaged $11,110 ($17,890 maximum); loans averaged $3099 ($4625 maximum); and work contracts averaged $1048. 19% of undergraduate students work part-time. Average earnings from campus work for the school year are $1200. The average financial indebtedness of the 1994–95 graduate was $5434. BC is a member of CSS. The FAF or FAFSA, the college's own financial statement and the federal IRS income tax form, W-2s, and Divorced/Separated Statement (when applicable) are required. The application deadline for fall entry is February 1.

International Students: There are currently 314 international students enrolled. They must score 550 on the TOEFL and also take the SAT I or the ACT, and SAT II: Subject tests in writing, mathematics level I or II, and any third test.

Computers: The college provides computer facilities for student use. The mainframes are an IBM 3090 and DEC VAX 11/785 and 8700 units. More than 200 microcomputers are available, providing database searches, optical disk references, and on-line access to catalog services. Project AGORA brings voice, data, and video to every student through a campus computing center that manages the phone system and includes cable access, satellite and video conferencing, cable casting of university events, and video program production and training. All students may access the system at all times. There are no time limits and no fees.

Graduates: In 1994–95, 2276 bachelor's degrees were awarded. The most popular majors among graduates were English (11%), finance (10%), and political science and psychology (8%). Within an average freshman class, 91% graduate in 6 years. 250 to 300 companies recruited on campus in 1994–95. Of the 1994 graduating class, 26% were enrolled in graduate school within 6 months of graduation.

Admissions Contact: John L. Mahoney, Jr., Director of Undergraduate Admission. E-mail: admissions@bc.edu. A campus video is available.

BOSTON CONSERVATORY

E-2

Boston, MA 02215   (617) 536-6340; FAX: (617) 536-3176

Full-time: 300 men and women	Faculty: 17
Part-time: 32 men and women	Ph.D.s: 1%
Graduate: 125 men and women	Student/Faculty: 15 to 1
Year: semesters, summer session	Tuition: $13,975
Application Deadline: see profile	Room & Board: $6280
Freshman Class: 336 applied, 167 accepted, 99 enrolled	
SAT I or ACT: recommended	SPECIAL

The Boston Conservatory, founded in 1867, is a private, coeducational college providing degree programs in music, musical theater, and dance. There are 3 graduate schools. In addition to regional accreditation, the conservatory has baccalaureate program accreditation with NASM. The library contains 40,000 volumes and subscribes to 120 periodicals. Computerized library sources and services include interlibrary loans and database searching. The campus is in an urban area in Boston's Back Bay. Including residence halls, there are 7 buildings on campus.

Student Life: 20% of undergraduates are from Massachusetts. Students come from 36 states, 29 foreign countries, and Canada. 90% are white. The average age of freshmen is 18. 23% do not continue beyond their first year; 44% remain to graduate.

Housing: 164 students can be accommodated in college housing. College-sponsored living facilities include single-sex and coed dormitories. In addition, there are special interest and international houses. On-campus housing is guaranteed for all 4 years. 67% of students commute. Alcohol is not permitted. All students may keep cars on campus.

Activities: There are 1 national fraternity and 2 national sororities. There are 19 groups on campus, including band, choir, chorale, chorus, dance, drama, ethnic, gay, international, musical theater, newspaper, opera, orchestra, political, professional, religious, social service, student government, and yearbook. Popular campus events include Parents Weekend.

Sports: There is no sports program at the conservatory.

Disabled Students: 20% of the campus is accessible to disabled students. Elevators are available for these students.

Services: In addition to many counseling and information services, tutoring is available in every subject for a fee.

Campus Safety and Security: Campus safety and security measures include 24-hour foot and vehicle patrol, self-defense education, and informal discussions.

Programs of Study: The conservatory confers B.F.A. and B.Mus. degrees. Bachelor's degrees are awarded in COMMUNICATIONS AND THE ARTS (dance, guitar, music, music performance, music theory and composition, musical theater, opera, and piano/organ), EDUCATION (music). Music has the largest enrollment.

Required: All students must successfully complete the curriculum with no more than 12 credit hours of D-grade work. In addition, music performance majors must present recitals, music education majors must present a recital from memory, and composition majors must pass an examination on their primary instrument, present a portfolio of original composition, and perform a recital.

Special: There are 3 national honor societies on campus. 1 department has an honors program.

Faculty/Classroom: All teach undergraduates. No introductory courses are taught by graduate students. The average class size in an introductory lecture is 15; in a laboratory, 5; and in a regular course offering, 15.

Admissions: 50% of the 1995–96 applicants were accepted. The SAT I scores for a recent freshman class were as follows: Verbal—95% below 500 and 5% between 500 and 599; Math—98% below 500 and 2% between 500 and 599.

Requirements: The SAT I or ACT is recommended, and scores are reviewed. An audition is required. An academic high school diploma with a 2.0 GPA or GED also is required. AP and CLEP credits are accepted. Important factors in the admissions decision are evidence of special talent, extracurricular activities record, and personality/intangible qualities.

Procedure: Freshmen are admitted in the fall. Entrance exams should be taken as early as possible. There is a deferred admissions plan. Application deadlines are February 15 (priority) and April 1 for fall entry and September 1 for winter entry. The application fee is $60. Notification is sent on a rolling basis.

Transfer: A successful audition and a 2.0 GPA are required. Transfer credits are determined by examination or review by the division head and the dean. The high school transcript is required if fewer than 30 college credits have been earned.

Visiting: Visitors may sit in on classes. To schedule a visit, contact the Admissions Office.

Financial Aid: The conservatory is a member of CSS. The FAF and the college's own financial statement are required. The application deadline for fall entry is March 1.

International Students: There were 101 international students enrolled in a recent year. The school actively recruits these students. They must take the TOEFL, with a recommended minimum score of 530, the MELAB, or the college's own test. The student must also take the SAT I and achieve a minimum composite score of 950. An audition also is required.

Computers: The college provides computer facilities for student use. Apple Macintosh microcomputers are available to all students when the library is open.

Admissions Contact: Richard S. Wallace, Director of Enrollment Management.

BOSTON UNIVERSITY

E-2

Boston, MA 02215   (617) 353-2300

Full-time: 6456 men, 8142 women	Faculty: 1099
Part-time: 243 men, 256 women	Ph.D.s: 81%
Graduate: 5020 men, 5512 women	Student/Faculty: 13 to 1
Year: semesters, summer session	Tuition: $19,700
Application Deadline: January 15	Room & Board: $7100
Freshman Class: 25,617 applied, 14,929 accepted, 4348 enrolled	
SAT I Verbal/Math: 550/610	ACT: 27 HIGHLY COMPETITIVE

Boston University, founded in 1839, is a private, coeducational institution offering undergraduate and graduate programs in basic studies, liberal arts, communication, hotel and food administration, allied health education management, and fine arts. There are 10 undergraduate and 15 graduate schools. In addition to regional accreditation, BU has baccalaureate program accreditation with AACSB, ABET, NASM, and NCATE. The 23 libraries contain 2 million volumes, 3.4 million microform items, 65,870 audiovisual forms, over 350 CD-ROMs, and subscribe to 28,858 periodicals. Computerized library sources and services include the card catalog, interlibrary loans, and database searching. Special learning facilities include a learning resource center, art gallery, planetarium, radio station, TV station, astronomy observatory, 20th century archives, a theater and theater company in residence, a scientific computing and visualization laboratory, the Geddes language laboratory, a speech, language, and hearing clinic, a hotel/food administration culinary center, a performance center, and a multimedia center. The 123-acre campus is in an urban area on the Charles River in Boston's Back Bay. Including residence halls, there are 319 buildings on campus.

Student Life: 73% of undergraduates are from out-of-state, mostly the Middle Atlantic. Students come from 50 states, 133 foreign countries, and Canada. 70% are from public schools; 30% from private. 67% are white; 13% Asian American; 11% foreign nationals. 39% are Catholic; 21% Protestant; 15% Jewish; and 15% claim no religious affiliation. The average age of freshmen is 18.8; all undergraduates, 20.7. 16% do not continue beyond their first year; 71% remain to graduate.

Housing: 9023 students can be accommodated in college housing. College-sponsored living facilities include single-sex and coed dormitories, on-campus apartments, off-campus apartments, and married-student housing. In addition, there are honors houses, language houses, special interest houses, and international floors and houses. On-campus housing is guaranteed for all 4 years. 60% of students live on campus; of those, 80% remain on campus on weekends. All students may keep cars on campus.

Activities: 6% of men belong to 6 national fraternities; 8% of women belong to 9 national sororities. There are 325 groups on campus, including art, band, cheerleading, chess, choir, chorale, chorus, computers, dance, drama, ethnic, film, honors, international, jazz band, literary magazine, marching band, musical theater, newspaper, opera, orchestra, pep band, photography, political, professional, radio and TV, religious, social, social service, student government, symphony, and yearbook. Popular campus events include World Fair, Head of the Charles River Regatta, and the Boston Marathon.

Sports: There are 12 intercollegiate sports for men and 12 for women, and 10 intramural sports for men and 10 for women. Athletic and recreation facilities include 2 gymnasiums, an ice-skating rink, saunas, a pool, a dance studio, a crew tank, a weight room, indoor and outdoor tracks, tennis and volleyball courts, and multipurpose playing fields.

Disabled Students: 87% of the campus is accessible to disabled students. The following facilities are available: wheelchair ramps, elevators, special parking, specially equipped rest rooms, special class scheduling, lowered drinking fountains, lowered telephones, tactile and access maps, visual fire alarms, adaptive computers, and ASL interpreters.

Services: In addition to many counseling and information services, tutoring is available in most subjects, including liberal arts, science, engineering, and management. There is a reader service for the blind. Interpreters are available for the hearing impaired.

Campus Safety and Security: Campus safety and security measures include 24-hour foot and vehicle patrol, self-defense education, escort service, and shuttle buses. In addition, there are informal discussions, pamphlets/posters/films, emergency telephones, lighted pathways/sidewalks, and a mountain bicycle patrol system. There is a uniformed safety/security assistant on duty 24 hours a day in large residence halls and there are 48 academy-trained officers in the university police department.

Programs of Study: BU confers B.A., B.S., B.F.A., B.L.S., B.Mus., and B.S.B.A. degrees. Master's and doctoral degrees are also awarded. Bachelor's degrees are awarded in BIOLOGICAL SCIENCE (biochemistry, biology/biological science, biophysics, marine biology, molecular biology, and physiology), BUSINESS (accounting, banking and finance, business administration and management, business economics, hotel/motel and restaurant management, international business management, management information systems, marketing/retailing/merchandising, operations research, and recreation and leisure services), COMMUNICATIONS AND THE ARTS (advertising, art history and appreciation, broadcasting, classics, communications, dramatic arts, film arts, fine arts, French, German, graphic design, Greek (classical), Greek (modern), Italian, journalism, Latin, linguistics, music history and appreciation, music performance, music theory and composition, painting, Portuguese, public relations, Russian, sculpture, Spanish, and theater design), COMPUTER AND PHYSICAL SCIENCE (astronomy, astrophysics, chemistry, computer science, geology, information sciences and systems, mathematics, physics, planetary and space science, and statistics), EDUCATION (art, athletic training, bilingual/bicultural, business, drama, early childhood, education of the deaf and hearing impaired, elementary, English, foreign languages, mathematics, music, physical, school psychology, science, secondary, social foundations, social studies, special, speech correction, and teaching English as a second/foreign language (TESOL/TEFOL)), ENGINEERING AND ENVIRONMENTAL DESIGN (aeronautical engineering, biomedical engineering, computer engineering, electrical/electronics engineering, engineering, engineering management, environmental science, industrial engineering, manufacturing engineering, mechanical engineering, and systems engineering), HEALTH PROFESSIONS (dental laboratory technology, health, health science, medical laboratory technology, occupational therapy, physical therapy, predentistry, premedicine, rehabilitation therapy, speech pathology/audiology, and sports medicine), SOCIAL SCIENCE (American studies, anthropology, archeology, East Asian studies, Eastern European studies, economics, European studies, geography, history, human services, interdisciplinary studies, international relations, Latin American studies, Luso-Brazilian studies, paralegal studies, philosophy, physical fitness/movement, political science/government, prelaw, psychology, religion, Russian and Slavic studies, social science, social work, sociology, urban studies, and Western European studies). The University Professors Program and accelerated medical program are the strongest academically. Business administration and management and biology have the largest enrollments.

Required: Most students are required to complete 128 credit hours to qualify for graduation. Hours in the major, specific disciplines, curricula, distribution requirements, and minimum GPA vary, depending on the school or college of BU attended. All freshmen students must take an English composition course unless exempted by their SAT I verbal or AP scores.

Special: Cross-registration is permitted with Brandeis University, Tufts University, Boston College, and Hebrew College in Massachusetts. Opportunities are provided for internships, co-op programs in engineering, a Washington semester, on- and off-campus work-study, accelerated degrees in medicine and dentistry, B.A.-B.S. degrees, dual majors, student-designed majors, credit by exam, nondegree studies, pass/fail options, and study abroad in more than 10 countries. A 3–2 engineering degree is offered with 18 schools and 2–2 engineering agreements with 15, plus 10 other 2–2 agreements. The University Professors Program offers a creative cross-disciplinary approach, and the College of Basic Studies offers team teaching. There is a freshman honors program on campus, as well as 12 national honor societies, including Phi Beta Kappa. All departments have honors programs.

Faculty/Classroom: 72% of faculty are male; 28%, female. 73% teach undergraduates. Graduate students teach 13% of introductory courses. The average class size in an introductory lecture is 41; in a laboratory, 25; and in a regular course offering, 25.

Admissions: 58% of the 1995–96 applicants were accepted. The SAT I scores for the 1995–96 freshman class were as follows: Verbal—26% below 500, 47% between 500 and 599, 25% between 600 and 700, and 2% above 700; Math—7% below 500, 33% between 500 and 599, 44% between 600 and 700, and 16% above 700. The ACT scores were 4% below 21, 14% between 21 and 23, 35% between 24 and 26, 19% between 27 and 28, and 28% above 28. 71% of the current freshmen were in the top fifth of their class; 94% were in the top two fifths. There were 32 National Merit finalists. 77 freshmen graduated first in their class.

Requirements: The SAT I or ACT is required. SAT II: Subject tests are required for some programs and majors. Graduation from an accredited secondary school is required; a GED will be accepted. It is recommended that applicants have successfully completed 4 years each of English, mathematics, science, and social studies, and at least 3 of a foreign language. Medical, dental, management, and engineering programs require additional preparatory courses in high school. Applicants are evaluated on an individual basis. Emphasis is placed on strong academic performance in a solid college preparatory curriculum. An essay is required along with, for some programs, an interview, portfolio, or audition. AP and CLEP credits are accepted. Important factors in the admissions decision are parents or siblings attending the school, advanced placement or honor courses, and personality/intangible qualities.

Procedure: Freshmen are admitted fall and spring. Entrance exams should be taken in the junior year or early in the senior year. There are early decision, early admissions, and deferred admissions plans. Early decision applications should be filed by November 15; regular applications, by January 15 (priority) for fall entry and November 15 for spring entry, along with an application fee of $50. Notification of early decision is sent December 31; regular decision by March 15. 256 early decision candidates were accepted for the 1995–96 class. A waiting list is an active part of the admissions procedure.

Transfer: 445 transfer students enrolled in 1995–96. SAT I or ACT scores and a complete high school transcript (or GED) should be submitted. Recommendations and an essay are also recommended.

Visiting: There are regularly scheduled orientations for prospective students, consisting of personal interviews, class visits, lunch with current students, campus tours, and information sessions. Appointments must be made in advance. There are guides for informal visits and visitors may sit in on classes and stay overnight at the school. To schedule a visit, contact the Admissions Reception Center at (617) 353–2318.

Financial Aid: In 1995–96, 71% of all freshmen received some form of financial aid. 61% of freshmen received need-based aid. The average freshman award was $19,908. Of that total, scholarships or need-based grants averaged $12,203 ($27,000 maximum); loans averaged $3754 ($5625 maximum); and work contracts averaged $1971 ($2000 maximum). 60% of undergraduate students work part-time. Average earnings from campus work for the school year are $1720. The average student loan indebtedness of the 1994–95 graduate was $14,463. BU is a member of CSS. The FAF or FAFSA is required. The application deadline for fall entry is February 1.

International Students: There are currently 1619 international students enrolled. The school actively recruits these students. They must take the TOEFL and achieve a minimum score of 550. The student must also take the SAT I or the ACT; there are no minimum scores except for select programs.

Computers: The college provides computer facilities for student use. The mainframe is an IBM RS/6000 cluster. A 2800-port high-speed campus network with more than 800 public acccess terminals provides access to the mainframe, to the Internet, and to a Connection CM 5 via terminal and workstation clusters situated throughout the campus, and via dial-up facilities. A state-of-the-art computer graphics laboratory and a personal computing support center are also available to students. All students may access the system 24 hours a day. There are no time limits and no fees.

Graduates: In 1994–95, 3249 bachelor's degrees were awarded. The most popular majors among graduates were business and management (18%), social sciences (17%), and communications (16%). Within an average freshman class, 71% graduate in 6 years. More than 300 companies recruited on campus in 1994–95.

Admissions Contact: Thomas Rajala, Director, Office of Undergraduate Admissions. A campus video is available.

BRADFORD COLLEGE   **D-1**
Bradford, MA 01830   (508) 372-7161
                              (800) 336-6448; FAX: (508) 372-5240

Full-time: 220 men, 343 women	**Faculty:** 35; IIB, --$
Part-time: none	**Ph.D.s:** 80%
Graduate: none	**Student/Faculty:** 16 to 1
Year: semesters, summer session	**Tuition:** $15,455
Application Deadline: open	**Room & Board:** $6490
Freshman Class: 1029 applied, 803 accepted, 223 enrolled	
SAT I or ACT: not required	**COMPETITIVE**

Bradford College, founded in 1803, is a private coeducational institution offering programs in liberal arts and teacher preparation. In addition to regional accreditation, Bradford has baccalaureate program accreditation with NASDTEC. The library contains 58,000 volumes and 86 microform items, and subscribes to 236 periodicals. Computerized library sources and services include the card catalog and interlibrary loans. Special learning facilities include a learning resource center, art gallery, and radio station. The 70-acre campus is in a suburban area 35 miles north of Boston. Including residence halls, there are 14 buildings on campus.

Student Life: 60% of undergraduates are from out-of-state, mostly the Northeast. Students come from 30 states and 35 foreign countries. 80% are from public schools; 20% from private. 76% are white; 15% foreign nationals. The average age of freshmen is 18; all undergraduates, 21. 20% do not continue beyond their first year; 50% remain to graduate.

Housing: 442 students can be accommodated in college housing. College-sponsored living facilities include single-sex and coed dormitories and on-campus apartments. In addition there are special interest houses. On-campus housing is guaranteed for all 4 years. 75% of students live on campus; of those, 75% remain on campus on weekends. Alcohol is not permitted. All students may keep cars on campus.

Activities: There are no fraternities or sororities. There are 23 groups on campus, including chorale, dance, drama, ethnic, film, gay, honors, international, literary magazine, musical theater, newspaper, photography, political, radio and TV, social, social service, student government, and yearbook. Popular campus events include Spring Ball, Christmas Step Singing, Faculty/Staff Variety Show, and Student Talent Show.

Sports: There are 3 intercollegiate sports for men and 3 for women, and 8 intramural sports for men and 8 for women. Each student has a membership in the multipurpose athletic club located one mile from the campus. Its facilities include an exercise room, a swimming pool, and squash, tennis, and basketball courts.

Disabled Students: The following facilities are available: wheelchair ramps, elevators, and special class scheduling.

Services: In addition to many counseling and information services, tutoring is available in most subjects. There is remedial writing.

Campus Safety and Security: Campus safety and security measures include 24-hour foot and vehicle patrol, self-defense education, escort service, and emergency telephones. In addition, there are lighted pathways/sidewalks.

Programs of Study: Bradford confers the B.A. degree. Bachelor's degrees are awarded in BUSINESS (management science), COMMUNICATIONS AND THE ARTS (fine arts), COMPUTER AND PHYSICAL SCIENCE (mathematics and natural sciences), SOCIAL SCIENCE (human development and humanities).

Required: Students must complete courses in critical inquiry, human heritage, the individual and the community, perspective on the arts, language of numbers, global perspective, nature of work, individual science and the environment, personal health and fitness, and a senior seminar in ethics and values. A total of 121 credit hours and a minimum GPA of 2.0 are required for graduation.

Special: Bradford offers cross-registration with 10 area colleges, 9 internships, study abroad in 100 countries, a Washington semester, and work-study programs. Student-designed majors, credit by exam, nondegree study, and pass/fail options are also available. There is a freshman honors program on campus

Faculty/Classroom: 65% of faculty are male; 35%, female. All teach undergraduates. The average class size in an introductory lecture is 20; in a laboratory, 10; and in a regular course offering, 15.

Admissions: 78% of the 1995–96 applicants were accepted. 25% of the current freshmen were in the top fifth of their class; 60% were in the top two fifths.

Requirements: Bradford requires applicants to be in the upper 70% of their class. A minimum GPA of 2.0 is required. Applicants must be graduates of an accredited secondary school or have a GED. 16 academic credits are required, including 4 in English, 3 in mathematics, 2 in foreign language, and 1 each in science, social studies, and history. An essay is required and an interview is recommended. A portfolio is required of art and creative writing applicants. Applications are accepted on computer disk and on-line. AP and CLEP credits are accepted. Important factors in the admissions decision are advanced placement or honor courses, evidence of special talent, and recommendations by school officials.

Procedure: Freshmen are admitted fall and spring. Entrance exams should be taken by November of the senior year. There are early admissions and deferred admissions plans. Application deadlines are open. Notification is sent on a rolling basis.

Transfer: 45 transfer students enrolled in 1995–96. The high school transcript, official transcripts of all previous college work, and a recommendation from a faculty adviser, instructor, or dean must be submitted. Students must provide a catalog from each institution from which they wish to transfer credit. Bradford will accept a maximum of 72 credit hours from 2-year institutions for courses graded C and above. All transfer students will be expected to meet the requirements of the Bradford plan. A minimum GPA of 2.0 is required. 46 credits of 121 must be completed at Bradford.

Visiting: There are regularly scheduled orientations for prospective students, including an orientation program in June and also at the beginning of the fall term. There are guides for informal visits and visi-

tors may sit in on classes and stay overnight at the school. To schedule a visit, contact the Admissions Office.

Financial Aid: In 1995–96, 75% of all freshmen and 70% of continuing students received some form of financial aid. 75% of freshmen and 65% of continuing students received need-based aid. The average freshman award was $15,000. 70% of undergraduate students work part-time. Average earnings from campus work for the school year are $1000. The average financial indebtedness of the 1994–95 graduate was $13,250. Bradford is a member of CSS. The FAFSA and CSS Profile Application financial statement are required. The application deadline for fall entry is February 15.

International Students: There are currently 110 international students enrolled. The school actively recruits these students. They must take the TOEFL and achieve a minimum score of 500.

Computers: The college provides computer facilities for student use. The mainframe is a DEC VAX. IBM and Epson microcomputers are available in the library, in 1 dormitory, and in a dedicated computer laboratory. There are no time limits and no fees.

Graduates: In 1994–95, 90 bachelor's degrees were awarded. Within an average freshman class, 50% graduate in 5 years. 25 companies recruited on campus in 1994–95.

Admissions Contact: William Dunfey, Dean of Admission. E-mail: bradcoll@aol.com.

BRANDEIS UNIVERSITY D-2

Waltham, MA 02254–9110	(617) 736–3500; (800) 622–0622
Full-time: 1330 men, 1599 women	Faculty: 361; I, –$
Part-time: 69 men and women	Ph.D.s: 95%
Graduate: 1194 men and women	Student/Faculty: 8 to 1
Year: semesters, summer session	Tuition: $20,934
Application Deadline: February 1	Room & Board: $6950
Freshman Class: 4539 applied, 2998 accepted, 876 enrolled	
SAT I or ACT: required	**VERY COMPETITIVE**

Brandeis University, founded in 1948, is a private, coeducational liberal arts institution. There are 4 undergraduate and 2 graduate schools. The 3 libraries contain 981,911 volumes, 834,668 microform items, and 23,166 audiovisual forms, and subscribe to 7064 periodicals. Computerized library sources and services include the card catalog, interlibrary loans, and database searching. Special learning facilities include a learning resource center, a radio station, a TV station, an astronomical observatory, a cultural center, a treasure hall, an art museum, and an audiovisual center. The 235-acre campus is in a suburban area 10 miles west of Boston. Including residence halls, there are 98 buildings on campus.

Student Life: 25% of undergraduates are from Massachusetts. Students come from 50 states and 55 foreign countries. 75% are from public schools. 80% are white. The average age of freshmen is 18.1; all undergraduates, 20.6. 13% do not continue beyond their first year.

Housing: 2600 students can be accommodated in college housing. College-sponsored living facilities include coed dormitories, on-campus apartments, off-campus apartments, and married-student housing. In addition, there are special interest houses. On-campus housing is guaranteed for the freshman and sophmore years only, is available on a first-come, first-served basis, and is available on a lottery system for upperclassmen. 90% of students live on campus. All students may keep cars on campus.

Activities: There are no fraternities or sororities. There are 150 groups on campus, including art, cheerleading, chess, choir, chorale, chorus, computers, dance, drama, ethnic, film, gay, honors, international, jazz band, literary magazine, musical theater, newspaper, orchestra, pep band, photography, political, professional, radio and TV, religious, social, social service, student government, symphony, and yearbook. Popular campus events include Octoberfest, Tropics Night, Divali, and Chinese New Year.

Sports: There are 11 intercollegiate sports for men and 11 for women, and 10 intramural sports for men and 9 for women. Athletic and recreation facilities include a 6000-seat field house, a basketball arena, an indoor swimming pool, 3 indoor tennis courts, 10 squash and racquetball courts, an indoor track, several multipurpose rooms for fencing, aerobics, dance, and wrestling, sauna and steam rooms, Nautilus and free weight rooms, soccer and practice fields, baseball and softball diamonds, a cross-country and fitness trail, and 10 outdoor tennis courts.

Disabled Students: 65% of the campus is accessible to disabled students. The following facilities are available: wheelchair ramps, elevators, special parking, specially equipped rest rooms, special class scheduling, lowered drinking fountains, and lowered telephones.

Services: In addition to many counseling and information services, tutoring is available in most subjects. There is a reader service for the blind, and remedial math, reading, and writing.

Campus Safety and Security: Campus safety and security measures include 24-hour foot and vehicle patrol, self-defense education, escort service, and shuttle buses. In addition, there are informal discussions, pamphlets/posters/films, emergency telephones, lighted pathways/sidewalks, and a 25-member campus police force.

Programs of Study: Brandeis confers the B.A. degree. Master's and doctoral degrees are also awarded. Bachelor's degrees are awarded in BIOLOGICAL SCIENCE (biochemistry, biology/biological science, and neurosciences), COMMUNICATIONS AND THE ARTS (American literature, classics, comparative literature, dramatic arts, English, English literature, fine arts, French, German, linguistics, music, Russian, and Spanish), COMPUTER AND PHYSICAL SCIENCE (chemistry, computer science, mathematics, physics, and science), SOCIAL SCIENCE (African American studies, African studies, American studies, anthropology, economics, European studies, history, history of philosophy, Judaic studies, Latin American studies, Near Eastern studies, philosophy, political science/government, psychology, and sociology). Sciences, economics, and psychology are the strongest academically. Economics, politics, and English have the largest enrollments.

Required: For the bachelor's degree, all students must complete 3 interrelated semester courses from an approved cluster, including selections from at least 2 different schools of the university. They must also complete 1 course from the University Seminar in Humanistic Inquiries and 1 in non-Western or cross-cultural studies, as well as a 1-semester course in each of the university's schools of creative arts, humanities, science, and social science. Writing, quantitative reasoning, and foreign language requirements also must be met. A total of 32 semester courses must be completed to graduate.

Special: Students may pursue interdepartmental programs in 10 different fields. Students may cross-register with Boston College, Boston University, Tufts University, and Wellesley College. Study abroad is possible in 39 countries. Internships are available in virtually every field, and a work-study program is also provided. Dual and student-designed majors can be arranged. The university also offers credit by examination, nondegree study, and pass/fail options. In the Mount Sinai Humanities and Medicine Program, students are accepted to the Mount Sinai School of Medicine for entry after freshman year and successful completion of a Brandeis degree. There is a chapter of Phi Beta Kappa on campus.

Faculty/Classroom: 68% of faculty are male; 32%, female. All both teach and do research. Graduate students teach 10% of introductory courses. The average class size in an introductory lecture is 30; in a laboratory, 20; and in a regular course offering, 15.

Admissions: 66% of the 1995–96 applicants were accepted. 78% of the current freshmen were in the top fifth of their class; 98% were in the top half.

Requirements: The SAT I or ACT is required. Students submitting the SAT I score must also take 3 SAT II: Subject tests, including writing. Applicants should prepare with 4 years of high school English, 3 each of foreign language and mathematics, and at least 1 each of science and social studies. An essay is required, and an interview is recommended. Brandeis accepts applications on-line and on computer disk via Common Application, CollegeLink, and Apply. AP credits are accepted. Important factors in the admissions decision are advanced placement or honor courses, leadership record, and evidence of special talent.

Procedure: Freshmen are admitted fall and spring. Entrance exams should be taken by the fall of the senior year. There are early decision, early admissions, and deferred admissions plans. Early decision applications should be filed by January 1; regular applications, by February 1 for fall entry and December 1 for spring entry, along with an application fee of $50. Notification is sent April 15. 127 early decision candidates were accepted for the 1995–96 class. A waiting list is an active part of the admissions procedure.

Transfer: 39 transfer students enrolled in 1995–96. Major consideration is given to the quality of college-level work completed, the secondary school record, testing, professors' and deans' evaluations, and the impression made by the candidate. Because there is a 2-year residence requirement, students should apply before entering their junior year. 16 semester courses of 32 must be completed at Brandeis.

Visiting: There are regularly scheduled orientations for prospective students. There are year-round student-led campus tours, and in the summer there are information sessions given by the admissions staff. There are guides for informal visits and visitors may sit in on classes and stay overnight at the school. To schedule a visit, contact the Office of Admissions.

Financial Aid: In 1995–96, 59% of all students received some form of financial and need-based aid. The average freshman award was $18,566. 45% of undergraduate students work part-time. Average earnings from campus work for the school year are $1385. Brandeis is a member of CSS. The FAF or FAFSA, the college's own financial statement, and copies of student and parent income tax returns are required. The application deadline for fall entry is February 15.

International Students: There are currently 165 international students enrolled. The school actively recruits these students. They must take the TOEFL and achieve a minimum score of 600. The student must also take the SAT I.

Computers: The college provides computer facilities for student use. The mainframe is a DEC VAX cluster for undergraduate network services. There are 3 clusters located throughout the campus containing more than 100 Macintosh and IBM-compatible computers and printers for both. All Macintoshes and some IBM-compatibles are connected to the campus network via an Ethernet Gateway, giving students access to Student Network Services accounts. Access to the mainframe is also available from students' rooms. All students may access the system. Students may access the system 3 hours when other students are waiting. There are no fees.

Graduates: In a recent year, 704 bachelor's degrees were awarded. The most popular majors among graduates were politics (13%), psychology (13%), and English (11%). Within an average freshman class, 2% graduate in 3 years, 73% in 4 years, and 81% in 5 years. 40 companies recruited on campus in a recent year.

Admissions Contact: David L. Gould, Dean of Admissions. E-mail: admitme@brandeis.edu.

BRIDGEWATER STATE COLLEGE E-3

Bridgewater, MA 02325   (508) 697–1237; FAX: (508) 697–1746

Full-time: 2289 men, 3072 women	**Faculty:** 258; IIA, av$
Part-time: 656 men, 1023 women	**Ph.D.s:** 75%
Graduate: 347 men, 1006 women	**Student/Faculty:** 21 to 1
Year: semesters, summer session	**Tuition:** $3462 ($7596)
Application Deadline: March 1	**Room & Board:** $4221

Freshman Class: 4938 applied, 3461 accepted, 1115 enrolled
SAT I Verbal/Math: 430/460   **COMPETITIVE**

Bridgewater State College, founded in 1840, is a state-supported college offering undergraduate and graduate programs in liberal arts, education, business, aviation science, and preprofessional studies. There are 2 undergraduate schools and 1 graduate school. In addition to regional accreditation, The college has baccalaureate program accreditation with CSWE and NCATE. The library contains 337,723 volumes, 611,518 microform items, and 23,094 audiovisual forms, and subscribes to 1380 periodicals. Computerized library sources and services include the card catalog, interlibrary loans, and database searching. Special learning facilities include a learning resource center, art gallery, radio station, TV station, an astronomical observatory, a human performance laboratory and flight simulators, electronic classrooms, a teleconferencing facility with a satellite dish, a children's developmental clinic, and an outdoor classroom. The 220-acre campus is in a small town 28 miles south of Boston. Including residence halls, there are 29 buildings on campus.

Student Life: 97% of undergraduates are from Massachusetts. Students come from 22 states, 21 foreign countries, and Canada. 86% are from public schools; 14% from private. 87% are white. 63% are Catholic; 18% Protestant; 12% claim no religious affiliation. The average age of freshmen is 19; all undergraduates, 24. 30% do not continue beyond their first year; 49% remain to graduate.

Housing: 1900 students can be accommodated in college housing. College-sponsored living facilities include single-sex and coed dormitories and on-campus apartments. On-campus housing is guaranteed for all 4 years. 66% of students commute. All students may keep cars on campus.

Activities: 9% of men and about 2% of women belong to 2 local and 5 national fraternities; 4% of women belong to 3 national sororities. There are more than 100 groups and organizations on campus, including band, cheerleading, choir, chorale, computers, dance, drama, ethnic, gay, honors, international, jazz band, literary magazine, newspaper, pep band, photography, political, professional, radio and TV, religious, social, social service, student government, and yearbook. Popular campus events include Convocation, Multiculture Day, and the Christmas and spring balls.

Sports: There are 9 intercollegiate sports for men and 11 for women, and 11 intramural sports for men and 9 for women. Athletic and recreation facilities include 2 gymnasiums, an Olympic-size swimming pool, tennis courts, a football stadium, a 9-lane track, soccer, lacrosse, and field hockey fields, and a new baseball and softball complex.

Disabled Students: 90% of the campus is accessible to disabled students. The following facilities are available: wheelchair ramps, elevators, special parking, specially equipped rest rooms, special class scheduling, lowered drinking fountains, lowered telephones, handicapped van service, and college-operated transit system.

Services: In addition to many counseling and information services, tutoring is available in most subjects. There is a reader service for the blind, and remedial math, reading, and writing, taped texts, classroom interpreters, scribes/note takers, testing accommodations, and a speech/hearing/language center.

Campus Safety and Security: Campus safety and security measures include 24-hour foot and vehicle patrol, self-defense education, escort service, and shuttle buses. In addition, there are informal discussions, pamphlets/posters/films, emergency telephones, lighted pathways/sidewalks, and a college-operated transit system that runs from 7 A.M. to 12 midnight, Monday through Friday, and a safety-escort van that runs from 6 P.M. to 3 A.M.

Programs of Study: The college confers B.A., B.S., and B.S.Ed. degrees. Master's degrees are also awarded. Bachelor's degrees are awarded in BIOLOGICAL SCIENCE (biochemistry and biology/biological science), BUSINESS (accounting, banking and finance, management science, marketing/retailing/merchandising, and transportation management), COMMUNICATIONS AND THE ARTS (communications, crafts, English, fine arts, French, and Spanish), COMPUTER AND PHYSICAL SCIENCE (chemistry, computer science, earth science, geology, information sciences and systems, mathematics, and physics), EDUCATION (art, early childhood, elementary, foreign languages, health, middle school, physical, recreation, science, and secondary), ENGINEERING AND ENVIRONMENTAL DESIGN (aviation administration/management, energy management technology, and graphic arts technology), HEALTH PROFESSIONS (speech pathology/audiology), SOCIAL SCIENCE (anthropology, archeology, criminology, crosscultural studies, geography, history, industrial and organizational psychology, international relations, paralegal studies, philosophy, physical fitness/movement, political science/government, psychology, social work, and sociology). Management science, aviation science, and education are the strongest academically. Management science, psychology, and education have the largest enrollments.

Required: Students are required to complete a minimum of 120 semester hours, with 30 to 39 of these hours in the major and 49 to 55 hours in general education courses. Students must maintain a minimum GPA of 2.0 and must complete an introduction to information resources course.

Special: Opportunities are provided for cross-registration programs with other schools, internships in most majors, dual majors in any subject, student-designed majors, core requirement credit for military service and work experience, nondegree study, and study abroad in China, England, Canada and West Germany, as well as with other countries with a consortium agreement. A Washington semester offers possible internship experience with the political sciences. There is a freshman honors program on campus, as well as 5 national honor societies. 14 departments have honors programs.

Faculty/Classroom: 61% of faculty are male; 39%, female. All both teach and do research. No introductory courses are taught by graduate students. The average class size in an introductory lecture is 40; in a laboratory, 21; and in a regular course offering, 35.

Admissions: 70% of the 1995–96 applicants were accepted. The SAT I scores for the 1995–96 freshman class were as follows: Verbal—82% below 500, 17% between 500 and 599, and 2% between 600 and 700; Math—64% below 500, 28% between 500 and 599, and 8% between 600 and 700. 15% of the current freshmen were in the top fifth of their class; 46% were in the top two fifths. There were 18 National Merit semifinalists. One freshman graduated first in their class.

Requirements: The SAT I or ACT is required. Graduation from an accredited secondary school is required; a GED will be accepted. Applicants must have successfully completed 16 Carnegie units, including 4 years of English, 3 of mathematics, 2 each of a foreign language, history, and science, and 3 in other college preparatory electives. An essay is recommended. Applications are accepted on-line via College Link and ExPAN. AP and CLEP credits are accepted. Important factors in the admissions decision are advanced placement or honor courses, recommendations by school officials, and leadership record.

Procedure: Freshmen are admitted fall and spring. Entrance exams should be taken no later than January. There are early decision, early admissions, and deferred admissions plans. Early decision applications should be filed by November 15; regular applications, by March 1 for fall entry and December 1 for spring entry, along with an application fee of $10. Notification of early decision is sent December 15; regular decision, on a rolling basis. 73 early decision candidates were accepted for the 1995–96 class. A waiting list is an active part of the admissions procedure, with about 2% of all applicants on the list.

Transfer: 1080 transfer students enrolled in 1995–96. Transfer students must have maintained a minimum GPA of 2.0 at the previous college, although this alone does not guarantee admission. Priority is given to community college graduates. 30 credits of 120 must be completed at the college.

Visiting: There are regularly scheduled orientations for prospective students, Tours are available Monday through Friday at 11 A.M. and 3 P.M., and information sessions are scheduled on Fridays at 10 A.M. when college is in session. Visitations are available on a limited basis Saturdays during the fall. Campus tours are available year round.

There are guides for informal visits and visitors may sit in on classes. To schedule a visit, contact the Office of Admissions at (508) 697–1237.

Financial Aid: In 1995–96, 76% of all freshmen and 78% of continuing students received some form of financial aid. 63% of freshmen and 65% of continuing students received need-based aid. The average freshman award was $3901. Of that total, scholarships or need-based grants averaged $500 ($1400 maximum); loans averaged $1000 ($2625 maximum); and work contracts averaged $1200 ($1800 maximum). 18% of undergraduate students work part-time. Average earnings from campus work for the school year are $1083. The average financial indebtedness of the 1994–95 graduate was $4800. The college is a member of CSS. The FAF, the college's own financial statement, and the parents' tax returns are required. The application deadline for fall entry is March 1.

International Students: There are currently 80 international students enrolled. They must take the TOEFL and achieve a minimum score of 500.

Computers: The college provides computer facilities for student use. The mainframes are a DEC VAX 8530 and 4000/500, a DEC Microvax II, a DEC Station 5000–240, a CDC Cyber 180/310, and a Wang V565. There are 400 terminals and PCs available in various laboratories and residence halls, and modem access is possible from the students' homes or offices. All students may access the system 90 hours a week in the laboratories and 7 days a week, 24 hours a day by dial-up. There are no time limits and no fees.

Graduates: In 1994–95, 1149 bachelor's degrees were awarded. The most popular majors among graduates were management science (23%), physical education (11%), and psychology (11%). Within an average freshman class, 30% graduate in 4 years, 50% in 5 years, and 51% in 6 years. 40 companies recruited on campus in 1994–95.

Admissions Contact: James F. Plotner, Jr., Dean of Admissions. E-mail: jplotner@bridgew.edu.

CLARK UNIVERSITY
C-2
Worcester, MA 01610–1477   (508) 793–7431
(800) 462–5275; FAX: (508) 793–8821

Full-time: 766 men, 1084 women	Faculty: 170; IIA, +$
Part-time: 24 men, 10 women	Ph.D.s: 99%
Graduate: 355 men, 384 women	Student/Faculty: 11 to 1
Year: semesters, summer session	Tuition: $19,140
Application Deadline: February 15	Room & Board: $4250
Freshman Class: 2439 applied, 2001 accepted, 517 enrolled	
SAT I Verbal/Math: 510/560	VERY COMPETITIVE

Clark University, founded in 1887, is an independent liberal arts and research institution. There are 3 graduate schools. In addition to regional accreditation, Clark has baccalaureate program accreditation with AACSB. The 4 libraries contain 535,000 volumes, 60,000 microform items, and 1000 audiovisual forms, and subscribe to 1900 periodicals. Computerized library sources and services include the card catalog, interlibrary loans, and database searching. Special learning facilities include a learning resource center, art gallery, and center for music with 2 studios for electronic music, 2 theaters, magnetic resonance imaging facility, and arboretum. The 50-acre campus is in an urban area 40 miles west of Boston. Including residence halls, there are 56 buildings on campus.

Student Life: 63% of undergraduates are from out-of-state, mostly the Northeast. Students come from 38 states, 70 foreign countries, and Canada. 75% are from public schools; 25% from private. 63% are white; 15% foreign nationals. 27% claim no religious affiliation; 25% Catholic; 18% Jewish; 16% Protestant. The average age of freshmen is 18.4; all undergraduates, 20.2. 16% do not continue beyond their first year; 76% remain to graduate.

Housing: 1400 students can be accommodated in college housing. College-sponsored living facilities include single-sex and coed dormitories and on-campus apartments. In addition there are language houses, special interest houses, and nonsmoking, quiet, substance awareness, global environment, and year-round houses. On-campus housing is guaranteed for all 4 years (unless demand exceeds capacity). 70% of students live on campus. All students may keep cars on campus.

Activities: There are no fraternities or sororities. There are 80 groups on campus, including chess, choir, chorale, chorus, computers, dance, departmental, debate, drama, ethnic, film, gay, honors, international, jazz band, literary magazine, musical theater, newspaper, photography, political, professional, radio and TV, religious, social, social service, student government, and yearbook. Popular campus events include Fall Fest, Martin Luther King Commemoration, Academic Spree Day, and Clark University United Nations.

Sports: There are 8 intercollegiate sports for men and 9 for women, and 15 intramural sports for men and 15 for women. Athletic and recreation facilities include an athletic center, with a 2000-seat gymnasium, a pool, a fitness center, tennis courts, outdoor fields, baseball and softball diamonds, and a boat house.

Disabled Students: 75% of the campus is accessible to disabled students. The following facilities are available: wheelchair ramps, elevators, special parking, specially equipped rest rooms, special class scheduling, lowered drinking fountains, lowered telephones, and specially equipped residence rooms.

Services: In addition to many counseling and information services, tutoring is available in some subjects, including computer science, mathematics, biology, chemistry, economics, and psychology. There is remedial math and writing. For learning-disabled students, the university provides early orientation, alternative test-taking accommodations, individual sessions with a learning specialist, compensatory skill training in written expression, mathematics application, and learning strategies.

Campus Safety and Security: Campus safety and security measures include 24-hour foot and vehicle patrol, self-defense education, escort service, and shuttle buses. In addition, there are informal discussions, pamphlets/posters/films, emergency telephones, and lighted pathways/sidewalks.

Programs of Study: Clark confers the B.A. degree. Master's and doctoral degrees are also awarded. Bachelor's degrees are awarded in BIOLOGICAL SCIENCE (biochemistry and biology/biological science), BUSINESS (business administration and management), COMMUNICATIONS AND THE ARTS (art history and appreciation, comparative literature, dramatic arts, English, film arts, fine arts, French, German, languages, music, romance languages, Spanish, studio art, and visual and performing arts), COMPUTER AND PHYSICAL SCIENCE (chemistry, computer science, mathematics, and physics), ENGINEERING AND ENVIRONMENTAL DESIGN (environmental science), HEALTH PROFESSIONS (predentistry and premedicine) and SOCIAL SCIENCE (classical/ancient civilization, economics, geography, history, human ecology, international relations, philosophy, political science/government, prelaw, psychology, and sociology). Psychology, geography, and environmental studies are the strongest academically. Psychology and government, and international relations have the largest enrollments.

Required: Each student is required to complete 2 critical thinking courses in 2 categories of verbal expression and formal analysis, and 6 perspectives courses, representing the categories of aesthetics, comparative, historical, language and culture, science, and values. A student must receive passing grades in a minimum of 32 full courses, with a C- or better in at least 24 of these courses, and maintain a minimum 2.0 GPA to graduate.

Special: For-credit internships are available in all disciplines with private corporations and small businesses, medical centers, and government agencies. There is cross-registration with members of the Worcester Consortium, including Holy Cross and Worcester Polytechnic Institute. Clark also offers study abroad in 12 countries, a Washington semester with American University, work-study programs, dual and student-designed majors, pass/no record options, and a 3-2 engineering degree with Columbia University, Washington University, and Worcester Polytechnic Institute. A gerontology certificate is offered with the Worcester Consortium for Higher Education. Integrated undergraduate/graduate programs are available in environmental science and policy, international development and social change, management, biology, chemistry, communications, education, health administration, history, and physics. High-achieving, 4-year degree students at Clark are eligible for a tuition-free fifth year, to combine an undergraduate major with a master's degree in 10 possible areas. There are 7 national honor societies on campus, including Phi Beta Kappa. Almost all departments have honors programs.

Faculty/Classroom: 70% of faculty are male; 30%, female. 95% both teach and do research. Graduate students teach 1% of introductory courses. The average class size in an introductory lecture is 23; in a laboratory, 10; and in a regular course offering, 20.

Admissions: 82% of the 1995–96 applicants were accepted. 52% of the current freshmen were in the top fifth of their class; 84% were in the top two fifths. 20 freshmen graduated first in their class.

Requirements: The SAT I or ACT is required. The SAT II: Writing test is also required. Applicants must graduate from an accredited secondary school or have a GED. 16 Carnegie units are required, including 4 years of English, 3 each of mathematics and science, and 2 each of foreign language, history, and social studies. An interview is recommended. AP credits are accepted. Important factors in the admissions decision are advanced placement or honor courses, recommendations by alumni, and recommendations by school officials.

Procedure: Freshmen are admitted fall and spring. Entrance exams should be taken by November of the senior year. There are early decision, early admissions, and deferred admissions plans. Early decision applications should be filed by either December 1 or January 1; regular applications, by February 15 for fall entry and November 15 for spring entry, along with an application fee of $40. Notification of early decision is sent either January 15 or February 1; regular decision, April 1. 47 early decision candidates were accepted for the 1995–96 class. A waiting list is an active part of the admissions procedure, with about 1% of all applicants on the list.

Transfer: 78 transfer students enrolled in 1995–96. Transfers should have a minimum GPA of about 2.8. A full semester of college course work is recommended. 16 courses of 32 must be completed at Clark.

Visiting: There are regularly scheduled orientations for prospective students. Students can make advance arrangements for visits, tours, and overnight stays; they can also talk with coaches and professors. There are guides for informal visits and visitors may sit in on classes. To schedule a visit, contact the Admissions Office.

Financial Aid: In 1995–96, 67% of all freshmen and 71% of continuing students received some form of financial aid. 63% of freshmen and 57% of continuing students received need-based aid. The average freshman award was $15,600. Of that total, scholarships or need-based grants averaged $10,595 ($21,050 maximum); loans averaged $2976 ($4825 maximum); and work contracts averaged $1249 ($1300 maximum). 47% of undergraduate students work part-time. Average earnings from campus work for the school year were $1100. The average financial indebtedness of the 1994–95 graduate was $17,100. Clark is a member of CSS. The FAFSA or CSS Profile Application financial statement is required. The application deadline for fall entry is February 15.

International Students: There are currently 536 international students enrolled. The school actively recruits these students. They must take the TOEFL and achieve a minimum score of 550.

Computers: The college provides computer facilities for student use. The mainframes are a cluster including the DEC VAX 8530, 6420, and 6410, the VAX Station 3100/76, and the DEC ALPHA Systems 3000/400, 2000/233, and 4000/710. There are networked departmental systems in various buildings throughout campus and DOS-compatible and Macintosh microcomputers in 2 public computer laboratories, with campuswide connections to the Internet and Bitnet. All students may access the system 7 days per week during scheduled hours. There are no time limits and no fees.

Graduates: In 1994–95, 444 bachelor's degrees were awarded. The most popular majors among graduates were psychology (20%), business management (10%), and government and international relations (10%). Within an average freshman class, 1% graduate in 3 years, 68% in 4 years, 73% in 5 years, and 76% in 6 years. 80 companies recruited on campus in 1994–95.

Admissions Contact: Harold M. Wingood, Dean of Admissions. E-mail: admissions@vax.clarku.edu. A campus video is available.

COLLEGE OF OUR LADY OF THE ELMS   B-3
Chicopee, MA 01013
(413) 592-3189
(800) 255-ELMS; FAX: (413) 594-2781

Full-time: 10 men, 604 women	Faculty: 57; IIB, --$
Part-time: 41 men, 448 women	Ph.D.s: 73%
Graduate: 10 men, 144 women	Student/Faculty: 11 to 1
Year: semesters	Tuition: $12,470
Application Deadline: open	Room & Board: $5000
Freshman Class: 285 applied, 238 accepted, 133 enrolled	
SAT I Verbal/Math: 440/440	COMPETITIVE

Elms College, founded in 1928, is a Catholic women's college offering undergraduate degrees in liberal arts and sciences, nursing, and social work, and graduate degrees in education and theology. In addition to regional accreditation, Elms College has baccalaureate program accreditation with CSWE and NLN. The library contains 98,700 volumes and 77,784 microform items, and subscribes to 730 periodicals. Computerized library sources and services include the card catalog, interlibrary loans, and database searching. Special learning facilities include a learning resource center, art gallery, and rare book collection. The 65-acre campus is in a suburban area 2 miles north of Springfield. Including residence halls, there are 11 buildings on campus.

Student Life: 91% of undergraduates are from Massachusetts. Students come from 9 states and 7 foreign countries. 60% are from public schools; 40% from private. 85% are white. 70% are Catholic; 13% Protestant. The average age of freshmen is 18; all undergraduates, 24. 15% do not continue beyond their first year; 85% remain to graduate.

Housing: 315 students can be accommodated in college housing. College-sponsored living facilities include dormitories. On-campus housing is guaranteed for all 4 years. 58% of students commute. All students may keep cars on campus.

Activities: There are no sororities. There are 41 groups on campus, including art, choir, chorale, chorus, computers, dance, drama, ethnic, honors, international, musical theater, newspaper, photography, professional, religious, social, social service, student government, and yearbook. Popular campus events include Soph Show, Cap and Gown Ring Ceremony, Spring Week, Winter Fest, Family Weekend, Christmas Vespers, lecture series, and Elms Night.

Sports: Athletic and recreation facilities include a new athletic facility that includes an aerobic and weight training area, 6-lane, 25-meter pool, multipurpose gymnasium with a suspended indoor track, health science laboratory, locker rooms, and showers.

Disabled Students: 40% of the campus is accessible to disabled students. The following facilities are available: wheelchair ramps, elevators, special parking, specially equipped rest rooms, special class scheduling, lowered drinking fountains, lowered telephones, and automated doors.

Services: In addition to many counseling and information services, tutoring is available in every subject. There is a reader service for the blind, and remedial math, reading, and writing, an academic advising center and resource center, a counseling service office, wellness services, a campus ministry office, and resident advisers.

Campus Safety and Security: Campus safety and security measures include 24-hour foot and vehicle patrol, self-defense education, escort service, and informal discussions. In addition, there are pamphlets/posters/films, emergency telephones, and lighted pathways/sidewalks. A safety and security manual is published each year, and there is a safety and security committee of administrators, students, faculty, and staff.

Programs of Study: Elms College confers B.A., B.S., B.S.N., and B.S.W. degrees. Associate and master's degrees are also awarded. Bachelor's degrees are awarded in BIOLOGICAL SCIENCE (biology/biological science), BUSINESS (accounting, international business management, and marketing/retailing/merchandising), COMMUNICATIONS AND THE ARTS (arts administration/management, English, fine arts, French, and Spanish), COMPUTER AND PHYSICAL SCIENCE (chemistry, computer science, and mathematics), EDUCATION (art, bilingual/bicultural, early childhood, elementary, foreign languages, middle school, science, secondary, special, and teaching English as a second/foreign language (TESOL/TEFOL)), ENGINEERING AND ENVIRONMENTAL DESIGN (commercial art), HEALTH PROFESSIONS (art therapy, health science, medical laboratory technology, nursing, predentistry, premedicine, and speech pathology/audiology), SOCIAL SCIENCE (American studies, international studies, paralegal studies, prelaw, psychology, religion, social work, and sociology). Nursing, education, and biology are the strongest academically. Education, business, and nursing have the largest enrollments.

Required: All students must complete 120 hours with a 2.0 GPA. 30 hours are required in courses in rhetoric, computer science, history, religion, physical education, philosophy, sociology, fine arts, humanities, language, mathematics, and senior seminar.

Special: Students may cross-register at any of the Cooperating Colleges of Greater Springfield or the Consortium of Sisters of St. Joseph Schools, or study abroad in Ireland, France, and Spain. Internships are available with local hospitals, businesses, and schools. Student-designed interdepartmental majors, accelerated degree programs, work-study, dual majors, nondegree study, and pass/fail options are offered. There are 5 national honor societies on campus, including Phi Beta Kappa.

Faculty/Classroom: 28% of faculty are male; 72%, female. All teach undergraduates and 89% also do research. No introductory courses are taught by graduate students. The average class size in an introductory lecture is 16; in a laboratory, 11; and in a regular course offering, 12.

Admissions: 84% of the 1995–96 applicants were accepted. The SAT I scores for the 1995–96 freshman class were as follows: Verbal—80% below 500, 16% between 500 and 599, and 4% between 600 and 700; Math—77% below 500, 18% between 500 and 599, 5% between 600 and 700, and 1% above 700. 50% of the current freshmen were in the top fifth of their class; 50% were in the top two fifths. There were 2 National Merit semifinalists. 3 freshmen graduated first in their class.

Requirements: The SAT I or ACT is required. Elms College requires applicants to be in the upper 50% of their class. A minimum GPA of 2.0 is required. The college prefers SAT I composite scores of at least 900. Applicants should be graduates of accredited high schools or have earned the GED. Secondary preparation should include 4 units of English, 3 each of mathematics and science, and 2 each of foreign language, history, and social studies. The college recommends that potential art majors submit a portfolio. A personal essay is required; an interview is recommended. Elms College accepts applications on computer disk and on-line via CollegeLink. AP and CLEP credits are accepted. Important factors in the admissions decision are advanced placement or honor courses, recommendations by school officials, and extracurricular activities record.

Procedure: Freshmen are admitted fall and spring. Entrance exams should be taken by no later than November of the senior year. There are early admissions and deferred admissions plans. Application deadlines are open. Application fee is $30. Notification is sent on a rolling basis.

Transfer: 87 transfer students enrolled in 1995–96. Transfer applicants must have a minimum 2.0 GPA. 45 credits of 120 must be completed at Elms College.

Visiting: There are regularly scheduled orientations for prospective students, including inteviews and tours. The college also offers an overnight program, an open house, and Applicant Day. There are guides for informal visits and visitors may sit in on classes and stay overnight at the school. To schedule a visit, contact the Admissions Office.

Financial Aid: In 1995–96, 87% of all freshmen and 88% of continuing students received some form of financial aid. 80% of all students received need-based aid. The average freshman award was $9000. Of that total, scholarships or need-based grants averaged $4000 ($7000 maximum); loans averaged $3500 ($5025 maximum); and work contracts averaged $1000 ($2000 maximum). 30% of undergraduate students work part-time. Average earnings from campus work for the school year are $1200. The average financial indebtedness of the 1994–95 graduate was $18,250. Elms College is a member of CSS. The FAF and the college's own financial statement are required. The application deadline for fall entry is February 15.

International Students: There are currently 22 international students enrolled. The school actively recruits these students. They must take the TOEFL, and achieve a minimum score of 500, or the SAT I.

Computers: The college provides computer facilities for student use. The mainframe is a DEC VAX VT440. There are 4 computer laboratories for student use: 1 in the library, 2 in the main building, and 1 in a residence hall. All students may access the system Monday through Friday, 8 A.M. to 10 P.M.; Saturday and Sunday, 12 noon to 9 P.M. There are no time limits and no fees.

Graduates: In a recent year, 198 bachelor's degrees were awarded. The most popular majors among graduates were nursing (25%), education (17%), and paralegal/business (10%). Within an average freshman class, 1% graduate in 3 years, 76% in 4 years, 77% in 5 years, and 77% in 6 years. 20 companies recruited on campus in 1994–95.

Admissions Contact: Betty Broughan, SSJ, Dean of Admissions and Financial Aid. E-mail: broughanb@elms.edu.

COLLEGE OF THE HOLY CROSS
Worcester, MA 01610

C-2

(508) 793-2443
(800) 442-2421; FAX: (508) 793-3888

Full-time: 1274 men, 1464 women	**Faculty:** 212; IIB, +$
Part-time: none	**Ph.D:** 94%
Graduate: none	**Student/Faculty:** 13 to 1
Year: semesters	**Tuition:** $19,265
Application Deadline: February 1	**Room & Board:** $6500
Freshman Class: 3536 applied, 1774 accepted, 712 enrolled	
SAT I Verbal/Math: 560/620	**HIGHLY COMPETITIVE**

College of the Holy Cross, founded in 1843, is a private college affiliated with the Roman Catholic Church and the Jesuit order offering programs in the liberal arts. The 3 libraries contain 512,000 volumes, 22,000 microform items, and 19,500 audiovisual forms, and subscribe to 2057 periodicals. Computerized library sources and services include the card catalog, interlibrary loans, and database searching. Special learning facilities include an art gallery, radio station, greenhouses, facilities for aquatic research, and a multimedia resource center. The 174-acre campus is in a suburban area 45 miles west of Boston. Including residence halls, there are 27 buildings on campus.

Student Life: 60% of undergraduates are from out-of-state, mostly the Northeast. Students come from 46 states, 20 foreign countries, and Canada. 50% are from public schools; 50% from private. 91% are white. Most are Catholic. The average age of freshmen is 18; all undergraduates, 20. 6% do not continue beyond their first year; 87% remain to graduate.

Housing: 2092 students can be accommodated in college housing. College-sponsored living facilities include coed dormitories and off-campus apartments. In addition there are special interest houses, a Fit-for-Life program housing, and First-Year program housing. On-campus housing is guaranteed for all 4 years. 85% of students live on campus; of those, 95% remain on campus on weekends. Upperclassmen may keep cars on campus.

Activities: There are no fraternities or sororities. There are 79 groups on campus, including art, band, cheerleading, chess, choir, chorale, chorus, computers, dance, drama, drill team, ethnic, film, gay, honors, international, jazz band, literary magazine, marching band, musical theater, newspaper, opera, orchestra, pep band, photography, political, professional, radio and TV, religious, social, social service, student government, and yearbook. Popular campus events include Spring Weekend, and Easy Street Night.

Sports: There are 15 intercollegiate sports for men and 15 for women, and 6 intramural sports for men and 4 for women. Athletic and recreation facilities include an omniturf playing field, baseball and football fields, an indoor and outdoor running track, tennis, squash, and racquetball courts, a swimming pool, an ice rink, indoor crew tanks, a basketball arena, and weight and exercise rooms.

Disabled Students: 74% of the campus is accessible to disabled students. The following facilities are available: wheelchair ramps, elevators, special parking, specially equipped rest rooms, special class scheduling, lowered drinking fountains, and lowered telephones.

Services: In addition to many counseling and information services, tutoring is available in every subject. Mathematics and writing workshops and language laboratories are available.

Campus Safety and Security: Campus safety and security measures include 24-hour foot and vehicle patrol, self-defense education, escort service, and shuttle buses. In addition, there are informal discussions, pamphlets/posters/films, emergency telephones, and lighted pathways/sidewalks.

Programs of Study: Holy Cross confers the A.B. degree. Bachelor's degrees are awarded in BIOLOGICAL SCIENCE (biology/biological science), COMMUNICATIONS AND THE ARTS (classics, dramatic arts, English, fine arts, French, German, Greek, Latin, music, Russian, and Spanish), COMPUTER AND PHYSICAL SCIENCE (chemistry, mathematics, and physics), SOCIAL SCIENCE (economics, European studies, history, philosophy, political science/government, psychology, religion, and sociology). English, economics, and political science have the largest enrollments.

Required: Distribution requirements include social science, natural and mathematical science, cross-cultural studies, religious and philosophical studies, historical studies and the arts, and literature. In addition, students must demonstrate competence in a classical or modern language. A total of 128 credit hours is required for graduation, with 10 to 14 in the major. The minimum GPA for graduation is 2.0.

Special: Local internships are available in health and education, law and business, journalism, social service, state and local government, scientific research, and cultural affairs. Student-designed majors, a Washington semester, and study abroad are possible. There is a 3–2 engineering program with Columbia University, Dartmouth College, and Washington University (St. Louis), and premedicine and predentistry programs are available. Students may cross-register with other universities in the Worcester Consortium for Higher Education. Non-degree study is possible. There are 11 national honor societies on campus, including Phi Beta Kappa. 3 departments have honors programs.

Faculty/Classroom: 67% of faculty are male; 33%, female. All both teach and do research. The average class size in an introductory lecture is 27; in a laboratory, 20; and in a regular course offering, 30.

Admissions: 50% of the 1995–96 applicants were accepted. The SAT I scores for the 1995–96 freshman class were as follows: Verbal—17% below 500, 51% between 500 and 599, 29% between 600 and 700, and 3% above 700; Math—5% below 500, 32% between 500 and 599, 51% between 600 and 700, and 12% above 700. 84% of the current freshmen were in the top fifth of their class; 98% were in the top two fifths. There were 6 National Merit finalists and 10 semifinalists. 15 freshmen graduated first in their class.

Requirements: The SAT I or ACT is required. Applicants should be graduates of an accredited secondary school, or a GED is accepted. Applicants are recommended to prepare with courses in English, foreign language, history, mathematics, and science. An essay and the SAT II: Subject tests in writing and in 2 other areas are required. An interview is recommended. AP credits are accepted. Important factors in the admissions decision are advanced placement or honor courses, extracurricular activities record, and recommendations by school officials.

Procedure: Freshmen are admitted in the fall. Entrance exams should be taken by January of the senior year. There are early decision, early admissions, and deferred admissions plans. Early decision applications should be filed by January 15; regular applications, by February 1 for fall entry, along with an application fee of $50. Notification of early decision is sent December 15; regular decision, April 1. 176 early decision candidates were accepted for the 1995–96 class. A waiting list is an active part of the admissions procedure, with about 9% of all applicants on the list.

Transfer: 10 transfer students enrolled in 1995–96. Transfer students must have a minimum GPA of 3.2. The SAT I is required, as are transcripts and 2 teacher recommendations. Personal interviews are highly recommended. 64 credits of 128 must be completed at Holy Cross.

Visiting: There are regularly scheduled orientations for prospective students, including fall open houses in October and November consisting of informational panels on academics, admissions, financial aid, and student life, as well as tours of the facilities. There are guides for informal visits and visitors may sit in on classes and stay overnight at the school. To schedule a visit, contact the Admissions Office.

Financial Aid: In 1995–96, 58% of all freshmen and 63% of continuing students received some form of financial aid. 58% of freshmen and 53% of continuing students received need-based aid. The average freshman award was $14,070. Of that total, scholarships or need-based grants averaged $10,681 ($17,200 maximum); loans averaged $3255 ($4025 maximum); outside sources averaged $2688; and work contracts averaged $1391 ($1500 maximum). 48% of undergraduate students work part-time. Average earnings from campus work for the school year are $1200. The average financial indebtedness of the 1994–95 graduate was $12,634. Holy Cross is a member of CSS. The CSS Profile Application financial statement is required. The application deadline for fall entry is February 1.

International Students: There are currently 16 international students enrolled. The school actively recruits these students. They must take the TOEFL and achieve a minimum score of 550. The student must also take the SAT I or the ACT. Students must take SAT II: Subject tests in writing and 2 others of the student's choice.

Computers: The college provides computer facilities for student use. The mainframe is a DEC ALPHA 3100. There are 4 public laboratories on campus housing 100 Intel microcomputers, 12 Macintoshes, 15 ALPHA terminals. Every residence hall has access to the college computer network. All students may access the system 24 hours per day. There are no time limits and no fees.

Graduates: In 1994–95, 648 bachelor's degrees were awarded. The most popular majors among graduates were English (18%), economics (14%), and history (11%). Within an average freshman class, 87% graduate in 4 years and 1% in 5 years. 57 companies recruited on campus in 1994–95.

Admissions Contact: Admissions Office. E-mail: admissions@holycross.edu Web: www.holycross.edu. A campus video is available.

CURRY COLLEGE
E-2

Milton, MA 02186–9984   (617) 333–2210; (800) 669–0686

Full-time: 525 men, 545 women	Faculty: 68
Part-time: 279 men, 418 women	Ph.D.s: 67%
Graduate: 7 men, 37 women	Student/Faculty: 16 to 1
Year: semesters, summer session	Tuition: $14,735
Application Deadline: April 1	Room & Board: $5900
Freshman Class: 1202 applied, 972 accepted, 313 enrolled	
SAT I Verbal/Math: 420/420	COMPETITIVE

Curry College, founded in 1879, is a private, coeducational liberal arts institution. There is one graduate school. In addition to regional accreditation, Curry has baccalaureate program accreditation with NLN. The library contains 110,000 volumes and 10,000 microform items, and subscribes to 650 periodicals. Computerized library sources and services include the card catalog, interlibrary loans, and database searching. Special learning facilities include a learning resource center and radio station. The 120-acre campus is in a suburban area 7 miles southwest of Boston. Including residence halls, there are 40 buildings on campus.

Student Life: 63% of undergraduates are from Massachusetts. Students come from 26 states, 34 foreign countries, and Canada. 70% are from public schools; 30% from private. 75% are white. The average age of freshmen is 18; all undergraduates, 20. 30% do not continue beyond their first year; 51% remain to graduate.

Housing: 662 students can be accommodated in college housing. College-sponsored living facilities include coed dormitories. On-campus housing is guaranteed for all 4 years. 67% of students live on campus; of those, 80% remain on campus on weekends. All students may keep cars on campus.

Activities: There are no fraternities or sororities. There are 21 groups on campus, including cheerleading, chorale, dance, drama, ethnic, film, honors, international, jazz band, literary magazine, musical theater, newspaper, photography, political, professional, radio and TV, religious, social, social service, student government, and yearbook. Popular campus events include formal dances, Career Day, and Spring Fling.

Sports: There are 7 intercollegiate sports for men and 4 for women, and 5 intramural sports for men and 5 for women. Athletic and recreation facilities include a 500-seat gymnasium, a dance studio, 13 outdoor tennis courts, an outdoor pool, 5 athletic fields, a 1000-seat stadium, a 500-seat auditorium, and a 5000-meter cross-country trail.

Disabled Students: The following facilities are available: wheelchair ramps, elevators, special parking, specially equipped rest rooms, and special class scheduling.

Services: In addition to many counseling and information services, tutoring is available in most subjects. LD tutoring and the Program for Advancement of Learning are also available. In addition, there is a reader service for the blind, and remedial math, reading, and writing. General development courses in writing, reading, and mathematics are designed to develop the student's basic skills.

Campus Safety and Security: Campus safety and security measures include 24-hour foot and vehicle patrol, escort service, shuttle buses, and informal discussions. In addition, there are pamphlets/posters/films, emergency telephones, and lighted pathways/sidewalks. A campus safety office offers security services.

Programs of Study: Curry confers B.A. and B.S.N. degrees. Master's degrees are also awarded. Bachelor's degrees are awarded in BIOLOGICAL SCIENCE (biology/biological science), BUSINESS (business administration and management), COMMUNICATIONS AND THE ARTS (communications, English, and visual and performing arts), COMPUTER AND PHYSICAL SCIENCE (chemistry and physics), EDUCATION (elementary), ENGINEERING AND ENVIRONMENTAL DESIGN (environmental science), HEALTH PROFESSIONS (nursing), SOCIAL SCIENCE (criminal justice, history, philosophy, psychology, and sociology). Nursing is the strongest academically. Business and communications have the largest enrollments.

Required: Successful completion of the liberal arts core curriculum and a total of 120 semester hours (121 for nurses), with at least 30 in the major, and a minimum 2.0 GPA, are required for graduation.

Special: Curry offers internships in all majors, an accelerated degree with approval of the dean, study abroad, work-study programs, dual and student-designed majors, credit by exam and for life, work, and military experience, nondegree study, and pass/fail options. There are 2 national honor societies on campus.

Faculty/Classroom: 44% of faculty are male; 56%, female. All teach undergraduates. No introductory courses are taught by graduate students. The average class size in an introductory lecture is 30; in a laboratory, 16; and in a regular course offering, 21.

Admissions: 81% of the 1995–96 applicants were accepted. 10% of the current freshmen were in the top fifth of their class; 14% were in the top two fifths.

Requirements: The SAT I is required, with average scores of 400 verbal and 400 mathematics. A minimum GPA of 2.0 is required. Applicants must be graduates of an accredited secondary school or have a GED. Sixteen credits and Carnegie units are required, including 4 years of English, 2 each of foreign language, history, science, and social studies, and 3 of mathematics. An essay is required, and an interview recommended. A portfolio, where appropriate, is also advised. Applications are accepted on computer disk. AP and CLEP credits are accepted. Important factors in the admissions decision are recommendations by school officials, extracurricular activities record, and evidence of special talent.

Procedure: Freshmen are admitted fall and spring. Entrance exams should be taken in the junior year or in November of the senior year. There are early decision, early admissions, and deferred admissions plans. Early decision applications should be filed by December 1; regular applications, by April 1 for fall entry and December 1 for spring entry, along with an application fee of $40. Notification of early decision is sent December 15; regular decision, on a rolling basis beginning January 15. 10 early decision candidates were accepted for the 1995–96 class.

Transfer: 99 transfer students enrolled in 1995–96. Transfer applicants must be in good academic standing at their previous college, with a minimum GPA of 2.0. An interview is recommended. 30 credits of 120 must be completed at Curry.

Visiting: There are regularly scheduled orientations for prospective students, consisting of interviews with an admissions counselor and tours with a student. There are guides for informal visits and visitors may sit in on classes and stay overnight at the school. To schedule a visit, contact the Admissions Office.

Financial Aid: In 1995–96, 49% of all freshmen and 50% of continuing students received some form of financial aid. The average freshman award was $8825. Of that total, scholarships or need-based grants averaged $5000 ($10,000 maximum); and work contracts averaged $1200. 10% of undergraduate students work part-time. Average earnings from campus work for the school year are $1500. The average financial indebtedness of the 1994–95 graduate was $12,000. Curry is a member of CSS. The FAF and the college's own financial statement are required. The application deadline for fall entry is March 15.

International Students: There are currently 36 international students enrolled. The school actively recruits these students. They must take the TOEFL and achieve a minimum score of 500. The student must also take the SAT I or the ACT.

Computers: The college provides computer facilities for student use. The mainframe is a DEC PDP 11/86. There are also 70 Macintosh Plus, SE, IIe, and IICX PCs in 2 library laboratories and in the learning center laboratory. Four laser printers are available. All students have access to the Internet from residence hall rooms. All students may access the system. There are no time limits and no fees.

Admissions Contact: Janet Cromie Kelly, Dean of Admissions and Financial Aid.

EASTERN NAZARENE COLLEGE   E-2

Quincy, MA 02170   (617) 745-3711
(800) 883-6288; (617) 745-3410

Full-time: 1104 men and women	Faculty: 51
Part-time: 32 men and women	Ph.D.s: 57%
Graduate: 124 men and women	Student/Faculty: 22 to 1
Year: 4–1–4, summer session	Tuition: $10,160
Application Deadline: open	Room & Board: $3600
Freshman Class: 702 applied, 535 accepted, 210 enrolled	
SAT I Verbal/Math: 500/500	COMPETITIVE

Eastern Nazarene College, founded in 1918, is a private, coeducational college affiliated with the Church of the Nazarene. It offers a program in the liberal arts. There is 1 graduate school. In addition to regional accreditation, ENC has baccalaureate program accreditation with CSWE. The library contains 115,000 volumes and subscribes to 600 periodicals. Computerized library sources and services include interlibrary loans and database searching. Special learning facilities include a learning resource center and radio station. The 15-acre campus is in a suburban area 6 miles south of Boston. Including residence halls, there are 16 buildings on campus.

Student Life: 55% of undergraduates are from out-of-state, mostly the Northeast. Students come from 27 states, 24 foreign countries, and Canada. 88% are white. Most are Protestant. The average age of freshmen is 18; all undergraduates, 20. 25% do not continue beyond their first year; 60% remain to graduate.

Housing: 638 students can be accommodated in college housing. College-sponsored living facilities include single-sex dormitories and married-student housing. On-campus housing is guaranteed for all 4 years. 75% of students live on campus; of those, 75% remain on campus on weekends. Alcohol is not permitted. All students may keep cars on campus.

Activities: There are no fraternities or sororities. There are 34 groups on campus, including band, cheerleading, choir, chorale, chorus, drama, jazz band, literary magazine, musical theater, newspaper, pep band, photography, professional, radio and TV, religious, social service, student government, and yearbook. Popular campus events include Freshmen Breakout, All-School Outing, and Junior/Senior Banquet.

Sports: There are 5 intercollegiate sports for men and 5 for women, and 4 intramural sports for men and 5 for women. Athletic and recreation facilities include a physical education center equipped with a basketball area, batting cage, and playing courts.

Disabled Students: 65% of the campus is accessible to disabled students. The following facilities are available: wheelchair ramps, elevators, special parking, and specially equipped rest rooms.

Services: In addition to many counseling and information services, tutoring is available in most subjects. There is remedial math, reading, and writing.

Campus Safety and Security: Campus safety and security measures include 24-hour foot and vehicle patrol, self-defense education, escort service, and informal discussions. There are pamphlets/posters/films, emergency telephones, and lighted pathways/sidewalks.

Programs of Study: ENC confers B.A. and B.S. degrees. Associate and master's degrees are also awarded. Bachelor's degrees are awarded in BIOLOGICAL SCIENCE (biology/biological science and marine biology), BUSINESS (accounting and business administration and management), COMMUNICATIONS AND THE ARTS (advertising, broadcasting, communications, dramatic arts, English, French, journalism, literature, music, music performance, Spanish, and speech/debate/rhetoric), COMPUTER AND PHYSICAL SCIENCE (chemistry, computer science, mathematics, physics, and science), EDUCATION (athletic training, education, elementary, music, science, and social science), ENGINEERING AND ENVIRONMENTAL DESIGN (computer engineering, engineering physics, and environmental science), HEALTH PROFESSIONS (sports medicine), SOCIAL SCIENCE (child psychology/development, Christian studies, clinical psychology, history, ministries, physical fitness/movement, psychology, religion, religious music, social studies, social work, and sociology). Chemistry, physics, and history are the strongest academically. Education, business, and psychology have the largest enrollments.

Required: All students must complete the core curriculum of writing and rhetoric, biblical history, social science, science or mathematics, symbolic systems and intercultural awareness, philosophy and religion, and physical education. A total of 130 credits is required for the B.A. or B.S., with 32 to 40 in the major. Minimum GPA for graduation is 2.0.

Special: Internships are available in the metropolitan Boston area. Study abroad in Costa Rica, a Washington semester, a 3–2 engineering degree with Boston University, and a cooperative program with the Massachusetts College of Pharmacy are offered. Work-study programs, dual majors, credit for life/military/work experience, and pass/fail options are available. An off-campus degree-completion program for adults in business administration is offered. There is 1 national honor society on campus.

Faculty/Classroom: 72% of faculty are male; 28%, female. 83% teach undergraduates. No introductory courses are taught by graduate students. The average class size in an introductory lecture is 75; in a laboratory, 20; and in a regular course offering, 22.

Admissions: 76% of the 1995–96 applicants were accepted. The SAT I scores for the 1995–96 freshman class were as follows: Verbal—46% below 500, 31% between 500 and 599, 19% between 600 and 700, and 4% above 700; Math—49% below 500, 30% between 500 and 599, 16% between 600 and 700, and 5% above 700. 21% of the current freshmen were in the top fifth of their class; 41% were in the top two fifths.

Requirements: The ACT is recommended. Applicants must be graduates of an accredited secondary school or have a GED. They must have a minimum of 16 academic credits including 4 of English, 2 to 4 each of mathematics and foreign language, 1 to 4 of science, and 1 to 2 each of history and social studies. Music students must audition. An essay and interview are recommended. AP and CLEP credits are accepted. Important factors in the admissions decision are advanced placement or honor courses, recommendations by school officials, and leadership record.

Procedure: Freshmen are admitted to all sessions. Entrance exams should be taken in the spring of the junior year. There is a deferred admissions plan. Application deadlines are open. Application fee is $20. Notification is sent on a rolling basis.

Transfer: 32 transfer students enrolled in a recent year. A minimum 2.0 GPA is required. An interview is recommended, as is submission of a composite SAT score of at least 800. 60 credits of 130 must be completed at ENC.

Visiting: There are regularly scheduled orientations for prospective students. There are guides for informal visits and visitors may sit in on classes and stay overnight at the school. To schedule a visit, contact the Office of Admissions at (617) 773–2373 or (800) 883–6288.

Financial Aid: Average earnings from campus work for the school year are $2000. ENC is a member of CSS. The FAFSA and the college's own financial statement are required. Check with the school for current application deadlines.

International Students: In a recent year, 45 international students were enrolled. They must score 500 on the TOEFL.

Computers: The college provides computer facilities for student use. The mainframes are a DEC VAX 11/750 and a Plexus P/60. There are more than 30 microcomputers available for student use in the library. Access to the mainframe computers is gained by assigned password, and terminals are plentiful. All students may access the system. There are no time limits. The fee is $5.

Graduates: In a recent year, 129 bachelor's degrees were awarded. The most popular majors among graduates were education (18%), business administration (16%), and psychology (9%). Within an average freshman class, 44% graduate in 4 years and 51% in 5 years.

Admissions Contact: Bill Nichols, Executive Director of Enrollment Management.

EMERSON COLLEGE
E-2

Boston, MA 02116	(617) 824–8600; FAX: (617) 824–8609
Full-time: 999 men, 1276 women	Faculty: 84; IIA, +$
Part-time: 55 men, 80 women	Ph.D.s: 73%
Graduate: 255 men, 633 women	Student/Faculty: 27 to 1
Year: semesters, summer session	Tuition: $16,346
Application Deadline: February 1	Room & Board: $7850
Freshman Class: 2149 applied, 1493 accepted, 529 enrolled	
SAT I Verbal/Math: 530/520	ACT: 24 **VERY COMPETITIVE**

Emerson College, founded in 1880, is a private, independent, coeducational college devoted to the study of communications and performing arts. There are 5 graduate schools. The library contains 175,012 volumes, 11,994 microform items, and 7300 audiovisual forms, and subscribes to 1102 periodicals. Computerized library sources and services include the card catalog, interlibrary loans, and database searching. Special learning facilities include a learning resource center, 2 radio stations, TV station, film production facilities, computerized newsroom, speech-language-hearing clinic and proscenium stage theater. The campus is in Boston's Beacon Hill neighborhood. Including residence halls, there are 18 buildings on campus.

Student Life: 60% of undergraduates are from out-of-state, mostly the Northeast. Students come from 50 states, 70 foreign countries, and Canada. 79% are white; 12% foreign nationals. The average age of freshmen is 18; all undergraduates, 20. 20% do not continue beyond their first year; 68% remain to graduate.

Housing: 1160 students can be accommodated in college housing. College-sponsored living facilities include coed dormitories. In addition, there are honors and special interest floors. On-campus housing is guaranteed for the freshman year only, is available on a first-come,

first-served basis, and is available on a lottery system for upperclassmen. 51% of students live on campus; of those, 75% remain on campus on weekends.

Activities: 8% of men belong to 4 local and 2 national fraternities; 5% of women belong to 3 local and 2 national sororities. There are 48 groups on campus, including dance, drama, ethnic, film, gay, honors, international, literary magazine, musical theater, newspaper, photography, political, professional, radio and TV, religious, social, social service, student government, and yearbook. Popular campus events include Black History Month, Spring Musical, International Student Thanksgiving and Family Weekend.

Sports: There are 5 intercollegiate sports for men and 6 for women, and 3 intramural sports for men and 2 for women. Athletic and recreation facilities include a fitness center and a gymnasium.

Disabled Students: 50% of the campus is accessible to disabled students. The following facilities are available: elevators, specially equipped rest rooms, special class scheduling, and residence halls accommodation.

Services: In addition to many counseling and information services, tutoring is available in most subjects. There is remedial math, reading, and writing.

Campus Safety and Security: Campus safety and security measures include 24-hour foot and vehicle patrol, self-defense education, escort service, and shuttle buses. In addition, there are informal discussions, pamphlets/posters/films, emergency telephones, and lighted pathways/sidewalks.

Programs of Study: Emerson confers B.A., B.S., B.F.A., B.L.I., B.M., and B.S.Sp. degrees. Master's and doctoral degrees are also awarded. Bachelor's degrees are awarded in COMMUNICATIONS AND THE ARTS (advertising, broadcasting, communications, creative writing, dramatic arts, film arts, journalism, public relations, publishing, and speech/debate/rhetoric), HEALTH PROFESSIONS (speech pathology/audiology), SOCIAL SCIENCE (prelaw). Creative writing, communication disorders, and mass communication are the strongest academically. Mass communication, film, and advertising have the largest enrollments.

Required: All students must complete 128 credit hours, with 40 to 64 in the major, with a minimum GPA of 2.0. The required general education curriculum consists of 12 credits in communications and 40 in liberal arts, for a total of 52 credits. A course in voice and articulation is required.

Special: Student-designed, interdisciplinary, and dual majors are available. Cross-registration is offered with the Berklee College of Music, Boston Conservatory, Massachusetts College of Art, Museum of Fine Arts School, and other Boston area schools. Many internships are possible in Boston and in Los Angeles. Emerson has nondegree study and pass/fail options, as well as study abroad in the Netherlands. There is a freshman honors program on campus, as well as 3 national honor societies.

Faculty/Classroom: 66% of faculty are male; 34%, female. 89% teach undergraduates. Graduate students teach 11% of introductory courses. The average class size in an introductory lecture is 50; in a laboratory, 15; and in a regular course offering, 20.

Admissions: 69% of the 1995–96 applicants were accepted. The SAT I scores for the 1995–96 freshman class were as follows: Verbal—36% below 500, 43% between 500 and 599, 19% between 600 and 700, and 2% above 700; Math—37% below 500, 40% between 500 and 599, 20% between 600 and 700, and 3% above 700. The ACT scores were 17% below 21, 30% between 21 and 23, 23% between 24 and 26, 24% between 27 and 28, and 6% above 28. 41% of the current freshmen were in the top fifth of their class; 78% were in the top two fifths. 5 freshmen graduated first in their class.

Requirements: The SAT I or ACT is required. In addition, candidates must be graduates of an accredited secondary school or hold a GED certificate. They must have completed 16 Carnegie units, including 4 in English and 2 each in science, social studies, and mathematics. An essay is required. Auditions and interviews are recommended. Applications are accepted on computer disk. AP and CLEP credits are accepted. Important factors in the admissions decision are advanced placement or honor courses, evidence of special talent, and recommendations by school officials.

Procedure: Freshmen are admitted fall and spring. Entrance exams should be taken before January of the senior year. There are early action, early admissions, and deferred admissions plans. Early action applications should be filed by November 15; regular applications, by February 1 for fall entry and November 15 for spring entry, along with an application fee of $45. Notification of early action is sent December 15; regular decision, the end of March. A waiting list is an active part of the admissions procedure, with about 8% of all applicants on the list.

Transfer: 238 transfer students enrolled in 1995–96. The SAT I or ACT is required for some classes and recommended for others. Applicants must have a minimum 2.5 GPA and 2 letters of reference. 32 credits of 128 must be completed at Emerson.

Visiting: There are regularly scheduled orientations for prospective students, including a video, a bus/walking tour of the campus, and an information session with admissions representative and a currently enrolled student. There are guides for informal visits. Visitors may sit in on classes and admitted students may stay overnight at the school. To schedule a visit, contact the Admission Office.

Financial Aid: In 1995–96, 77% of all freshmen and 73% of continuing students received some form of financial aid. 73% of freshmen and 77% of continuing students received need-based aid. The average freshman award was $13,290. Of that total, scholarships or need-based grants averaged $8973 ($16,500 maximum); loans averaged $3002 ($4125 maximum); and work contracts averaged $1300 ($1700 maximum). 55% of undergraduate students work part-time. Average earnings from campus work for the school year are $1400. The average financial indebtedness of the 1994–95 graduate was $17,125. Emerson is a member of CSS. The FAFSA, the college's own financial statement, and the CSS Profile are required. The application deadline for fall entry is March 1.

International Students: There are currently 393 international students enrolled. The school actively recruits these students. They must take the TOEFL and achieve a minimum score of 550.

Computers: The college provides computer facilities for student use. The mainframe is a Digital VAX 4500. Many microcomputers are available in the academic computing center and new media center. All campus buildings, including residence halls, are networked and have direct access to the college server. All students may access the system 24 hours a day. There are no time limits and no fees.

Graduates: In 1994–95, 521 bachelor's degrees were awarded. The most popular majors among graduates were mass communication (53%), communication studies (19%), and performing arts (15%). Within an average freshman class, 1% graduate in 3 years, 60% in 4 years, 64% in 5 years, and 68% in 6 years. Of the 1994 graduating class, 72% had found employment within 6 months of graduation.

Admissions Contact: Gerald Doyle, Director of Admission. E-mail: admission@emerson.edu. A campus video is available.

EMMANUEL COLLEGE
E-2
Boston, MA 02115   (617) 735-9715; FAX: (617) 735-9801

Full-time: 7 men, 495 women	Faculty: 51; IIB, av$
Part-time: 141 men, 622 women	Ph.D.s: 70%
Graduate: 26 men, 118 women	Student/Faculty: 10 to 1
Year: semesters, 2 summer sessions	Tuition: $13,450
Application Deadline: open	Room & Board: $6275
Freshman Class: 271 applied, 236 accepted, 113 enrolled	
SAT I Verbal/Math: 400/420	ACT: 19 LESS COMPETITIVE

Emmanuel College, founded in 1919, is a primarily women's liberal arts college affiliated with the Roman Catholic Church. It offers programs in the fine arts, liberal arts, health sciences, engineering, business, and teacher's preparation. There are 6 graduate schools. In addition to regional accreditation, the college has baccalaureate program accreditation with NLN. The library contains 98,385 volumes, 12 microform items, and 1653 audiovisual forms, and subscribes to 825 periodicals. Computerized library sources and services include interlibrary loans and database searching. Special learning facilities include a learning resource center and art gallery. The 16-acre campus is in an urban area. Including residence halls, there are 8 buildings on campus.

Student Life: 91% of undergraduates are from Massachusetts. Students come from 18 states, 55 foreign countries, and Canada. 72% are from public schools; 28% from private. 75% are white. 55% claim no religious affiliation; 34% Catholic. The average age of freshmen is 18; all undergraduates, 21. 23% do not continue beyond their first year; 56% remain to graduate.

Housing: 855 students can be accommodated in college housing. College-sponsored living facilities include single-sex dormitories. In addition, there are special interest houses. On-campus housing is guaranteed for all 4 years. 70% of students live on campus; of those, 40% remain on campus on weekends. Alcohol is not permitted. Upperclassmen may keep cars on campus.

Activities: There are no fraternities or sororities. There are 20 groups on campus, including art, chorus, dance, drama, ethnic, honors, international, literary magazine, political, professional, religious, social, social service, student government, and yearbook. Popular campus events include Fall Carnival, Commencement Ball, and Spring Clambake.

Sports: There are 4 intercollegiate sports for women and 4 intramural sports for women. Athletic and recreation facilities include a 500-seat gymnasium, a training room/locker room, a fitness center, and a 500-seat auditorium. Students have access to a swimming pool and aerobic facilities.

Disabled Students: 75% of the campus is accessible to disabled students. The following facilities are available: wheelchair ramps, elevators, special parking, specially equipped rest rooms, special class scheduling, and lowered telephones.

Services: In addition to many counseling and information services, tutoring is available in every subject. There is also remedial math, reading, and writing.

Campus Safety and Security: Campus safety and security measures include 24-hour foot and vehicle patrol, self-defense education, escort service, and shuttle buses. In addition, there are informal discussions, pamphlets/posters/films, emergency telephones, and lighted pathways/sidewalks.

Programs of Study: The college confers B.A., B.S., and B.F.A. degrees. Associate and master's degrees are also awarded. Bachelor's degrees are awarded in BIOLOGICAL SCIENCE (biochemistry and biology/biological science), BUSINESS (accounting and business administration and management), COMMUNICATIONS AND THE ARTS (art history and appreciation, communications, English, fine arts, French, languages, Spanish, and studio art), COMPUTER AND PHYSICAL SCIENCE (chemistry, mathematics, and physics), EDUCATION (art, elementary, music, and secondary), ENGINEERING AND ENVIRONMENTAL DESIGN (preengineering), HEALTH PROFESSIONS (art therapy, health care administration, medical laboratory technology, nursing, predentistry, premedicine, and preveterinary science), SOCIAL SCIENCE (economics, political science/government, prelaw, psychology, and sociology). Education, sciences, and liberal arts are the strongest academically. Education and liberal arts have the largest enrollments.

Required: Students must complete a broad range of distribution requirements including fine arts, mathematics, writing, humanities, foreign language, philosophy, science, social science, and religious studies. A total of 128 credit hours is required, with 10 to 21 courses in the major and a minimum GPA of 2.0 for graduation.

Special: There is cross-registration with Northeastern University, Simmons College, Wentworth Institute, and Andover-Newton Theological School. The college offers internships, study abroad, a Washington semester, work-study programs, an accelerated degree program in business administration, dual and student-designed majors, a general studies degree, a 3–2 engineering degree, and pass/fail options. The adult learner degree program offers learning opportunities at off-campus sites for men and women age 23 and older. There are 4 national honor societies on campus. 5 departments have honors programs.

Faculty/Classroom: 38% of faculty are male; 62%, female. All both teach and do research. The average class size in an introductory lecture is 22; in a laboratory, 15; and in a regular course offering, 18.

Admissions: 87% of the 1995–96 applicants were accepted. The SAT I scores for the 1995–96 freshman class were as follows: Verbal—59% below 500, 23% between 500 and 599, 15% between 600 and 700, and 3% above 700; Math—49% below 500, 34% between 500 and 599, 14% between 600 and 700, and 3% above 700. The ACT scores were 58% below 21, 14% between 21 and 23, 14% between 24 and 26, and 14% above 28. 20% of the current freshmen were in the top fifth of their class; 37% were in the top two fifths.

Requirements: The SAT I or ACT is required. Applicants must be graduates of an accredited secondary school with a 2.3 GPA or have a GED. 16 academic credits are required, including 4 years of English, 3 each of foreign language and mathematics, and 2 each of laboratory science and social studies. An essay and an interview are required. AP and CLEP credits are accepted. Important factors in the admissions decision are advanced placement or honor courses, recommendations by school officials, and leadership record.

Procedure: Freshmen are admitted fall and spring. Entrance exams should be taken by November of the senior year. There are early decision, early admissions, and deferred admissions plans. Early decision applications should be filed by November 1. Regular application filing is open for fall entry. The application fee is $40. Notification of early decision is sent December 1; regular decision, on a rolling basis.

Transfer: 30 transfer students enrolled in a recent year. Students must submit essays, college and high school transcripts, and 2 letters of recommendation. They must be financially and academically eligible to return to previously attended institution. 72 credits of 128 must be completed at the college.

Visiting: There are regularly scheduled orientations for prospective students. There are guides for informal visits and visitors may sit in on classes and stay overnight at the school. To schedule a visit, contact the Admissions Office.

Financial Aid: In a recent year, 81% of all freshmen and 73% of continuing students received some form of financial aid. 77% of freshmen and 72% of continuing students received need-based aid. The average freshman award was $10,900. Of that total, scholarships or need-based grants averaged $6669 ($16,498 maximum); loans averaged $2900 ($4625 maximum); and work contracts averaged $1400. 32% of undergraduate students work part-time. Average earnings from campus work for the school year are $1223. The average financial indebtedness of the recent graduate was $6700. The college is a member of CSS. The FAF or FAFSA and parents' and student's income tax forms are required. The application deadline for fall entry is March 1.

International Students: In a recent year, 69 international students were enrolled. The school actively recruits these students. They must score 500 on the TOEFL or take ELS level 109 or others. The student must also take SAT I or the ACT.

Computers: The college provides computer facilities for student use. The mainframe is a Prime 4050. IBM microcomputers are available in the computer and academic resource centers. A campuswide network permits access to the Internet and other services from the library, dormitory rooms, and other locations. All students may access the system. There are no time limits and no fees.

Graduates: In a recent year, 193 bachelor's degrees were awarded. The most popular majors among graduates were interdepartmental (14%), education (14%), and psychology (11%). Within an average freshman class, 76% graduate in 4 years, 87% in 5 years, and 92% in 6 years.

Admissions Contact: Mary Ellen Ackerson, Director of Admissions. E-mail: enroll@emmanuel.edu.

ENDICOTT COLLEGE   E-2
Beverly, MA 01915

(508) 921-1000
(800) 325-1114; FAX: (508) 927-0084

Full-time: 800 men and women	Faculty: 42; III, --$
Part-time: 300 men and women	Ph.Ds: 28%
Graduate: none	Student/Faculty: 19 to 1
Year: 4-1-4, summer session	Tuition: $12,220
Application Deadline: open	Room & Board: $6400
Freshman Class: 1378 applied, 1117 accepted, 406 enrolled	
SAT I or ACT: recommended	**COMPETITIVE**

Endicott College, founded in 1939, is a private coeducational institution offering programs in the arts, business, fine arts, and nursing. There is 1 graduate school. In addition to regional accreditation, Endicott College has baccalaureate program accreditation with FIDER. The library contains 45,000 volumes, 4 microform items, and 1922 audiovisual forms, and subscribes to 950 periodicals. Computerized library sources and services include the card catalog, interlibrary loans, and database searching. Special learning facilities include a learning resource center, art gallery, radio station, and TV station. The 150-acre campus is in a suburban area 20 miles north of Boston. Including residence halls, there are 31 buildings on campus.

Student Life: 55% of undergraduates are from Massachusetts. Students come from 25 states and 43 foreign countries. 88% are white. 16% do not continue beyond their first year; 78% remain to graduate.

Housing: 650 students can be accommodated in college housing. College-sponsored living facilities include single-sex and coed dormitories and on-campus apartments. On-campus housing is guaranteed for all 4 years and is available on a lottery system for upperclassmen. 80% of students live on campus; of those, 70% remain on campus on weekends. All students may keep cars on campus.

Activities: There are no fraternities or sororities. There are 35 groups on campus, including choir, chorale, chorus, drama, international, literary magazine, newspaper, photography, radio and TV, student government, and yearbook.

Sports: There are 5 intercollegiate sports for men and 8 for women, and 3 intramural sports for men and 3 for women. Athletic and recreation facilities include a 500-seat gymnasium with a basketball court, weight room, and aerobics room. Outdoor facilities include field hockey, softball, baseball, lacrosse, soccer fields, and 6 tennis courts.

Disabled Students: The following facilities are available: wheelchair ramps, elevators, special parking, specially equipped rest rooms, special class scheduling, and lowered drinking fountains.

Services: In addition to many counseling and information services, tutoring is available in every subject. There is a reader service for the blind, and remedial math, reading, and writing.

Campus Safety and Security: Campus safety and security measures include 24-hour foot and vehicle patrol, self-defense education, escort service, and shuttle buses. In addition, there are informal discussions, pamphlets/posters/films, emergency telephones, and lighted pathways/sidewalks.

Programs of Study: Endicott College confers B.A., B.F.A., and B.S.N. degrees. Associate and master's degrees are also awarded. Bachelor's degrees are awarded in BUSINESS (business administration and management, entrepreneurial studies, fashion merchandising, hotel/motel and restaurant management, retailing, and sports management), COMMUNICATIONS AND THE ARTS (advertising, communications, fine arts, and graphic design), EDUCATION (athletic training, elementary, and physical), ENGINEERING AND ENVIRONMENTAL DESIGN (interior design), HEALTH PROFESSIONS (nursing), SOCIAL SCIENCE (criminal justice, liberal arts/general studies, and psychology).

Required: To graduate, students must complete 126 credit hours with a minimum GPA of 1.8. Core requirements include 8 credits in science and 6 each in English, mathematics, social science, and humanities.

Special: Cross registration is available with NECCUM and internships are offered in every major. Students may study abroad in 3 countries. There is a freshman honors program on campus, as well as 2 national honor societies, including Phi Beta Kappa. 1 department has an honors program.

Faculty/Classroom: All teach undergraduates. The average class size in an introductory lecture is 22.

Admissions: 81% of the 1995–96 applicants were accepted. 12% of the current freshmen were in the top fifth of their class; 65% were in the top two fifths.

Requirements: The SAT I or ACT is recommended. AP and CLEP credits are accepted.

Procedure: Freshmen are admitted fall and spring. There are early admissions and deferred admissions plans. Application deadlines are open. Application fee is $25. Notification is sent on a rolling basis.

Visiting: There are regularly scheduled orientations for prospective students, including testing, preregistration, and an introduction to general student life. There are guides for informal visits and visitors may sit in on classes and stay overnight at the school. To schedule a visit, contact the Admission Office.

Financial Aid: In 1995–96, 86% of all freshmen received some form of financial aid. 80% of freshmen received need-based aid. 42% of undergraduate students work part-time. Average earnings from campus work for the school year are $800. Endicott College is a member of CSS. The FAFSA, the college's own financial statement, and the CSS Profile Application are required. The preferred application deadline for fall entry is March 15.

International Students: There are currently 86 international students enrolled. The school actively recruits these students. They must take the TOEFL and achieve a minimum score of 475.

Computers: The college provides computer facilities for student use. There are 5 academic computer laboratories that house IBM, Macintosh, and IBM-compatible computers. Students have access to the Internet and E-mail. All students may access the system Monday to Thursday, 9 A.M. to 11 P.M.; Friday, 9 A.M. to 5 P.M.; Saturday, 11 A.M. to 5 P.M., and Sunday, 11 A.M. to 11 P.M. There are no fees. It is recommended that all students have personal computers.

Graduates: In 1994–95, 52 bachelor's degrees were awarded. Within an average freshman class, 78% graduate in 4 years. 50 companies recruited on campus in 1994–95.

Admissions Contact: Thomas J. Redman, Vice President of Admission. A campus video is available.

FITCHBURG STATE COLLEGE   C-2
Fitchburg, MA 01420-2697

(508) 665-3144

Full-time: 1100 men, 1650 women	Faculty: 211; IIA, -$
Part-time: 600 men, 900 women	Ph.Ds: 68%
Graduate: 825 men, 1625 women	Student/Faculty: 13 to 1
Year: semesters, summer session	Tuition: $3316 ($7450)
Application Deadline: March 1	Room & Board: $4060
Freshman Class: 2655 applied, 2064 accepted, 606 enrolled	
SAT I Verbal/Math: 420/450	**LESS COMPETITIVE**

Fitchburg State College, founded in 1894, is a coeducational institution in the state system, offering programs in liberal arts, business, health sciences, and education. In addition to regional accreditation, Fitchburg has baccalaureate program accreditation with NASDTEC, NCATE, and NLN. The library contains 194,375 volumes, 409,069 microform items, and 3317 audiovisual forms, and subscribes to 1822 periodicals. Computerized library sources and services include the card catalog, interlibrary loans, and database searching. Special learning facilities include a learning resource center, art gallery, radio station, campus school, graphics center, and TV studio. The 45-acre campus is in a small town 45 miles west of Boston. Including residence halls, there are 33 buildings on campus.

Student Life: 96% of undergraduates are from Massachusetts. Students come from 16 states and 19 foreign countries. 80% are from public schools; 20% from private. 92% are white. The average age of freshmen is 19; all undergraduates, 20. 32% do not continue beyond their first year; 54% remain to graduate.

Housing: 1467 students can be accommodated in college housing. College-sponsored living facilities include single-sex and coed dormitories and on-campus apartments. On-campus housing is guaranteed for all 4 years. 55% of students commute. All students may keep cars on campus.

Activities: 10% of men belong to 5 local and 2 national fraternities; 15% of women belong to 3 local and 2 national sororities. There are 70 groups on campus, including art, band, cheerleading, chorus, computers, dance, drama, ethnic, film, gay, honors, international, jazz band, literary magazine, newspaper, photography, political, professional, radio and TV, religious, social, social service, student government, and yearbook. Popular campus events include the visiting lecture Series.

Sports: There are 8 intercollegiate sports for men and 8 for women, and 5 intramural sports for men and 5 for women. Athletic and recreation facilities include a 500-seat gymnasium, a track, volleyball, basketball, and tennis courts, a weight room, intramural fields, and the student union.

Disabled Students: 80% of the campus is accessible to disabled students. The following facilities are available: wheelchair ramps, elevators, special parking, specially equipped rest rooms, special class scheduling, lowered drinking fountains, lowered telephones, and an adaptive computer laboratory.

Services: In addition to many counseling and information services, tutoring is available in most subjects. There is a reader service for the blind, and remedial math, reading, and writing.

Campus Safety and Security: Campus safety and security measures include 24-hour foot and vehicle patrol, self-defense education, escort service, and informal discussions. In addition, there are pamphlets/posters/films, emergency telephones, and lighted pathways/sidewalks.

Programs of Study: Fitchburg confers B.A., B.S., and B.S.Ed. degrees. Master's degrees are also awarded. Bachelor's degrees are awarded in BIOLOGICAL SCIENCE (biology/biological science), BUSINESS (accounting, business administration and management, and marketing/retailing/merchandising), COMMUNICATIONS AND THE ARTS (communications, English, photography, and telecommunications), COMPUTER AND PHYSICAL SCIENCE (chemistry, computer science, earth science, and mathematics), EDUCATION (early childhood, elementary, industrial arts, middle school, secondary, and special), ENGINEERING AND ENVIRONMENTAL DESIGN (industrial engineering technology), HEALTH PROFESSIONS (medical laboratory technology and nursing), SOCIAL SCIENCE (economics, geography, history, human services, psychology, and sociology). Computer science, clinical laboratory sciences, and nursing are the strongest academically. Business administration, communications, and nursing have the largest enrollments.

Required: All students must complete a minimum of 120 credit hours with a GPA of at least 2.0 overall and in the major. Distribution requirements include courses from the categories of ideas and events, human behavior, literature/language arts, and the quantitative/scientific area. 2 introductory semesters of writing, plus junior/senior Writing in the Major, 1 semester of health and fitness, and a computer literacy course are also required.

Special: Students may cross-register at any other Massachusetts state college. Internships in a variety of fields, study abroad, B.A.-B.S. degrees, dual majors, and a student-designed general studies major are offered. There is a freshman honors program on campus, as well as 3 national honor societies.

Faculty/Classroom: 58% of faculty are male; 42%, female. All teach undergraduates; 20% also do research. No introductory courses are taught by graduate students. The average class size in an introductory lecture is 30; in a laboratory, 20; and in a regular course offering, 25.

Admissions: 78% of the 1995–96 applicants were accepted. The SAT I scores for the 1995–96 freshman class were as follows: Verbal—81% below 500, 16% between 500 and 599, and 3% between 600 and 700; Math—68% below 500, 23% between 500 and 599, 7% between 600 and 700, and 2% above 700. 16% of the current freshmen were in the top fifth of their class; 46% were in the top two fifths. There was 1 National Merit finalist and 5 semifinalists.

Requirements: The SAT I or ACT is required. Applicants should be graduates of accredited high schools or have the GED. Secondary preparation should include 4 years of English, 3 each of mathematics and liberal arts or physical education, and 2 each of a foreign language, social studies including U.S. history, and science. A personal interview is recommended. AP and CLEP credits are accepted. Important factors in the admissions decision are evidence of special talent, leadership record, and parents or siblings attending the school.

Procedure: Freshmen are admitted in the fall and spring. Entrance exams should be taken in the junior or senior year. There are early admissions and deferred admissions plans. Applications should be filed by March 1 for fall entry and December 1 for spring entry, along with an application fee of $10. Notification is sent on a rolling basis. A waiting list is an active part of the admissions procedure.

Transfer: 286 transfer students enrolled in 1995–96. Applicants should present a minimum GPA of 2.0 in at least 12 credits of transferable college work. An associate degree and personal interview are recommended. 45 credits of 120 must be completed at Fitchburg.

Visiting: There are regularly scheduled orientations for prospective students, including tours of the campus and residence halls, admissions/financial aid information, and academic major discussions. There are guides for informal visits and visitors may sit in on classes. To schedule a visit, contact the Admissions Office.

Financial Aid: Fitchburg is a member of CSS. FAFSA and the college's own financial statement are required. The application deadline for fall entry is March 30.

International Students: There are currently 64 international students enrolled. They must score 500 on the TOEFL and take SAT I, and the Listening and Structure sections of the CELT.

Computers: The college provides computer facilities for student use. The mainframes are a DEC Alpha 4/275, CDC CYBER 932/32, and Tricord ES8000. Some 225 microcomputers are available for student use in the residence halls and in various laboratories throughout the campus. All students may access the system 24 hours per day. There are no time limits and no fees.

Graduates: In 1994–95, 638 bachelor's degrees were awarded. The most popular majors among graduates were nursing (12%), communications (11%), and education (11%). Within an average freshman class, 32% graduate in 4 years, 53% in 5 years, and 54% in 6 years. 30 companies recruited on campus in 1994–95. Of the 1994 graduating class, 12% were enrolled in graduate school within 6 months of graduation and 92% had found employment.

Admissions Contact: Marke Miller Vickers, Director of Admissions. A campus video is available.

FRAMINGHAM STATE COLLEGE D-2

Framingham, MA 01701	(508) 626-4500; FAX: (508) 626-4592
Full-time: 1058 men, 1973 women	Faculty: 159
Part-time: 628 men, 951 women	Ph.D.s: 66%
Graduate: 134 men, 391 women	Student/Faculty: 19 to 1
Year: semesters, summer session	Tuition: $3394 ($7528)
Application Deadline: March 1	Room & Board: $3719
Freshman Class: 2730 applied, 1947 accepted, 625 enrolled	
SAT I: required	COMPETITIVE

Framingham State College, founded in 1839, is a comprehensive, coeducational public college offering 28 undergraduate majors and 14 graduate programs based on a liberal arts foundation that includes career and professional programs. There is 1 graduate school. In addition to regional accreditation, the college has baccalaureate program accreditation with ADA, AHEA, and NLN. The library contains 171,000 volumes, 454,000 microform items, and 5364 audiovisual forms, and subscribes to 1205 periodicals. Computerized library sources and services include the card catalog, interlibrary loans, and database searching. Special learning facilities include a learning resource center, art gallery, planetarium, radio station, greenhouse, TV studio, and early childhood demonstration laboratory. The 73-acre campus is in a suburban area 20 miles west of Boston. Including residence halls, there are 19 buildings on campus.

Student Life: 92% of undergraduates are from Massachusetts. Students come from 19 states, 15 foreign countries, and Canada. 80% are from public schools; 20% from private. 90% are white. The average age of freshmen is 19; all undergraduates, 21. 28% do not continue beyond their first year; 55% remain to graduate.

Housing: 1450 students can be accommodated in college housing. College-sponsored living facilities include single-sex and coed dormitories. On-campus housing is guaranteed for all 4 years. 60% of students commute. Alcohol is not permitted. Upperclassmen may keep cars on campus.

Activities: There are no fraternities or sororities. There are 40 groups on campus, including art, cheerleading, chorale, chorus, computers, drama, ethnic, gay, honors, international, literary magazine, newspaper, professional, radio and TV, religious, social, social service, student government, and yearbook. Popular campus events include Homecoming, Arts and Humanities Program, and New England Philharmonic Concerts (orchestra in residence).

Sports: There are 6 intercollegiate sports for men and 6 for women, and 6 intramural sports for men and 6 for women. Athletic and recreation facilities include a gymnasium, a football field, soccer field, tennis courts, and basketball courts.

Disabled Students: 80% of the campus is accessible to disabled students. The following facilities are available: wheelchair ramps, elevators, special parking, specially equipped rest rooms, special class scheduling, lowered drinking fountains, and lowered telephones.

Services: In addition to many counseling and information services, there is a reader service for the blind, and free remedial math, reading, and writing. Subject tutoring may be arranged for an hourly fee.

Campus Safety and Security: Campus safety and security measures include 24-hour foot and vehicle patrol, self-defense education, escort service, and shuttle buses. In addition, there are informal discussions, pamphlets/posters/films, emergency telephones, and lighted pathways/sidewalks.

Programs of Study: The college confers B.A. and B.S. degrees. Master's degrees are also awarded. Bachelor's degrees are awarded in BIOLOGICAL SCIENCE (biology/biological science), BUSINESS (business administration and management), COMMUNICATIONS AND THE ARTS (art history and appreciation, communications, English, fine arts, French, and Spanish), COMPUTER AND PHYSICAL

SCIENCE (chemistry, computer science, earth science, and mathematics), EDUCATION (early childhood and elementary), ENGINEERING AND ENVIRONMENTAL DESIGN (preengineering), HEALTH PROFESSIONS (medical laboratory technology and nursing), SOCIAL SCIENCE (clothing and textiles management/production/services, dietetics, economics, family/consumer studies, food science, geography, history, philosophy, political science/government, psychology, sociology, and textiles and clothing). Business administration, elementary/early childhood education, and food and nutrition have the largest enrollments.

Required: Students must complete 32 courses, 20 of which must be in the major and related electives, for a total of 128 credits. General education courses include writing, mathematics, study of federal and state constitutions, 3 humanities courses, 3 social science courses, and 2 science/mathematics courses. A 2.0 GPA is required for graduation.

Special: The college offers a 2–3 preengineering program in cooperation with the universities of Massachusetts at Amherst, Lowell, and Dartmouth. Cross-registration is possible at any of the state colleges. Study abroad in 5 countries, a Washington semester, and various internships are available. Pass/fail options are limited to 2 courses. A liberal studies program may be designed by the student. There is a freshman honors program on campus, as well as 6 national honor societies. 6 departments have honors programs.

Faculty/Classroom: 55% of faculty are male; 45%, female. All teach undergraduates. No introductory courses are taught by graduate students. The average class size in an introductory lecture is 25 and in a laboratory, 25.

Admissions: 71% of the 1995–96 applicants were accepted. SAT I scores for the 1995–96 freshman class were as follows: Verbal—83% below 500, 14% between 500 and 599, and 3% between 600 and 700; Math—66% below 500, 28% between 500 and 599, and 6% between 600 and 700. 17% of the current freshmen were in the top fifth of their class; 55% were in the top two fifths. 2 freshmen graduated first in their class.

Requirements: The SAT I is required. A minimum GPA of 2.0 is required. In addition, applicants must have a high school diploma or the GED. Secondary preparation must total 16 college preparatory credits, including 4 years of English, 3 of mathematics, 2 each of a foreign language and science, and 1 each of history and social science. The recommended 3 years of electives may include additional academic subjects or art, music, or computer courses. Prospective art majors must submit a portfolio. FSU accepts applications on-line and on computer disk via ExPAN and CollegeLink. AP and CLEP credits are accepted. Important factors in the admissions decision are advanced placement or honor courses, leadership record, and recommendations by school officials.

Procedure: Freshmen are admitted fall and spring. Entrance exams should be taken in spring of the junior year or fall of the senior year. There are early admissions and deferred admissions plans. Applications should be filed by March 1 for fall entry and December 1 for spring entry, along with an application fee of $10 (in-state) or $20 (out-of-state). Notification is sent on a rolling basis.

Transfer: 454 transfer students enrolled in 1995–96. Applicants with more than 30 college credits must present a college GPA of at least 2.5. Those with fewer than 30 credits must meet freshman admission requirements. 32 credits of 128 must be completed at the college.

Visiting: There are regularly scheduled orientations for prospective students, including campus tours and information sessions. There are guides for informal visits, and visitors may sit in on classes and stay overnight at the school. To schedule a visit, contact the Admissions Office.

Financial Aid: In 1995–96, 72% of all freshmen and 55% of continuing students received some form of financial aid. 52% of freshmen and 42% of continuing students received need-based aid. The average freshman award was $4208. Of that total, scholarships or need-based grants averaged $1369 ($4600 maximum); loans averaged $2612 ($3625 maximum); and work contracts averaged $226 ($1000 maximum). 50% of undergraduate students work part-time. Average earnings from campus work for the school year are $1000. The average financial indebtedness of the 1994–95 graduate was $7869. The college is a member of CSS. The college's own financial statement and the FAFSA are required. The application deadline for fall entry is April 1.

International Students: There are currently 65 international students enrolled. They must score 550 on the TOEFL, and also take the SAT I.

Computers: The college provides computer facilities for student use. The mainframe is an NEC ExpressII/466ST server running Novell 3.11. There are 100 connections to the server spread between 2 computer classrooms and 2 general laboratories and faculty offices. There are also 9 departmental LANs with 64 MACs and PCs. The student residence halls also have small LANs, not connected to the main network, with approximately 34 PCs. All students may access the system at any time. There are no time limits and no fees.

Graduates: In 1994–95, 669 bachelor's degrees were awarded. The most popular majors among graduates were business and management (14%), psychology (13%), and English (11%). Within an average freshman class, 45% graduate in 4 years, 50% in 5 years, and 55% in 6 years. 30 companies recruited on campus in 1994–95. Of the 1994 graduating class, 12% were enrolled in graduate school within 6 months of graduation and 95% had found employment.

Admissions Contact: Dr. Philip M. Dooher, Dean of Admissions. A campus video is available.

GORDON COLLEGE
E-2

Wenham, MA 01984

Full-time: 421 men, 755 women	Faculty: 73; IIB, av$
Part-time: 16 men, 37 women	Ph.D.s: 85%
Graduate: none	Student/Faculty: 16 to 1
Year: semesters	Tuition: $13,950
Application Deadline: April 15	Room & Board: $4440
Freshman Class: 694 applied, 571 accepted, 333 enrolled	
SAT I Verbal/Math: 500/520	COMPETITIVE

Phone: (508) 927-2300; (800) 343-1379

Gordon College, founded in 1889, is an independent Christian college emphasizing a Christian approach to the liberal arts and sciences. In addition to regional accreditation, Gordon has baccalaureate program accreditation with CSWE and NASM. The library contains 238,459 volumes, 29,522 microform items, and 9234 audiovisual forms, and subscribes to 593 periodicals. Computerized library sources and services include the card catalog, interlibrary loans, and database searching. Special learning facilities include a learning resource center and art gallery. The 730-acre campus is in a small town 25 miles north of Boston. Including residence halls, there are 26 buildings on campus.

Student Life: 69% of undergraduates are from out-of-state, mostly the Northeast. Students come from 38 states, 28 foreign countries, and Canada. 90% are white. Most are Protestant. The average age of freshmen is 18.2; all undergraduates, 20.3. 16% do not continue beyond their first year; 66% remain to graduate.

Housing: 1039 students can be accommodated in college housing. College-sponsored living facilities include single-sex dormitories and on-campus apartments. In addition, there are special interest houses. On-campus housing is guaranteed for all 4 years. 87% of students live on campus; of those, 80% remain on campus on weekends. Alcohol is not permitted. All students may keep cars on campus.

Activities: There are no fraternities or sororities. There are 35 groups on campus, including art, band, cheerleading, chess, choir, chorus, computers, drama, ethnic, honors, international, jazz band, literary magazine, musical theater, newspaper, orchestra, photography, political, professional, religious, social, social service, student government, student outreach, symphony, and yearbook. Popular campus events include Genesis Week, International Week, dances, and concerts.

Sports: There are 5 intercollegiate sports for men and 7 for women, and 19 intramural sports for men and 14 for women. Athletic and recreation facilities include a gymnasium, weight room, tennis courts, athletic fields, and a training room.

Disabled Students: 85% of the campus is accessible to disabled students. The following facilities are available: wheelchair ramps, elevators, special parking, specially equipped rest rooms, special class scheduling, lowered drinking fountains, and electric doors.

Services: In addition to many counseling and information services, tutoring is available in some subjects, including mathematics, writing, and core science. There is remedial math, reading, and writing, as well as writing and academic support centers. Gordon also provides special advising, study skills help, support groups for some liberal arts core courses, walk-in help, and assistance finding volunteer note takers.

Campus Safety and Security: Campus safety and security measures include 24-hour foot and vehicle patrol, escort service, informal discussions, and pamphlets/posters/films. In addition, there are emergency telephones and lighted pathways/sidewalks.

Programs of Study: Gordon confers A.B., B.S., and B.Mu. degrees. Bachelor's degrees are awarded in BIOLOGICAL SCIENCE (biology/biological science), BUSINESS (accounting, business administration and management, and recreation and leisure services), COMMUNICATIONS AND THE ARTS (art, English, French, music, and Spanish), COMPUTER AND PHYSICAL SCIENCE (chemistry, computer science, mathematics, and physics), EDUCATION (early childhood, elementary, middle school, and special), SOCIAL SCIENCE (biblical studies, economics, history, international studies, philosophy, physical fitness/movement, political science/government, psychology, social work, sociology, and youth ministry). English, biology, and psychology are the strongest academically. Biblical studies, English, and psychology have the largest enrollments.

Required: All students must demonstrate competency in writing, speech, and foreign language. The core curriculum consists of 8 credits in biblical studies, 8 in social and behavioral sciences, 8 in natural sciences, mathematics, and computer science, 6 in humanities, and 4 each in fine arts and freshman seminar. A total of 128 credits is required for graduation, with 18 or more in the major and a minimum GPA of 2.0.

Special: Gordon offers cooperative education, internships, and cross-registration with other institutions in the Northeast Consortium of Colleges and Universities in Massachusetts. There is a 3-2 engineering program with the University of Massachusetts at Lowell and a 2-2 program in allied health with the Thomas Jefferson College of Allied Health Science in Philadelphia. B.A.-B.S. degrees, dual majors, student-designed majors, nondegree study, and pass/fail options are all available. Off-campus study opportunities include a Washington semester, the Christian College Consortium Visitor Program, The British Education Semester, the LaVida Wilderness Expedition, the Nova Scotia Student Exchange Program, the Tropical Coastal Waters Program, and study abroad in Europe, the Middle East, and Latin America. There are 2 national honor societies on campus.

Faculty/Classroom: 71% of faculty are male; 29%, female. All teach undergraduates. The average class size in an introductory lecture is 35; in a laboratory, 18; and in a regular course offering, 21.

Admissions: 82% of the 1995-96 applicants were accepted. The SAT I scores for the 1995-96 freshman class were as follows: Verbal—39% below 500, 37% between 500 and 599, 19% between 600 and 700, and 5% above 700; Math—49% below 500, 33% between 500 and 599, 16% between 600 and 700, and 2% above 700. 46% of the current freshmen were in the top fifth of their class; 80% were in the top two fifths. There were 3 National Merit finalists and 1 semifinalist.

Requirements: The SAT I or ACT is required; the SAT I is preferred. In addition, applicants must graduate from an accredited secondary school or have a GED. 17 Carnegie units are required, including 4 English courses and 2 courses each in mathematics, science, and social studies. Foreign language is a preferred elective. An essay, a personal reference, and an interview are required. Music majors must audition. Applications are accepted on-line through CollegeLink. AP and CLEP credits are accepted. Important factors in the admissions decision are personality/intangible qualities, leadership record, and evidence of special talent.

Procedure: Freshmen are admitted to all sessions. Entrance exams should be taken in the spring of the junior year or the fall of the senior year. There are early decision, early admissions, and deferred admissions plans. Early decision applications should be filed by December 1; regular applications, by April 15 for fall entry and November 1 for spring entry, along with an application fee of $40. Notification of early decision is sent January 15; regular decision, on a rolling basis.

Transfer: 62 transfer students enrolled in 1995-96. Applicatns must have a minimum GPA of 2.5. College transcripts, and high school transcripts if the applicant has completed less than 1 year of full-time study, SAT I or ACT scores, an essay, and an interview are required. 32 credits of 128 must be completed at Gordon.

Visiting: There are regularly scheduled orientations for prospective students, consisting of 5 open house programs throughout the fall, winter, and spring. There are guides for informal visits and visitors may sit in on classes and stay overnight at the school. To schedule a visit, contact Kristen Hopkins, Visitation Coordinator.

Financial Aid: In 1995-96, 70% of all freshmen and 89% of continuing students received some form of financial aid. 73% of freshmen and 70% of continuing students received need-based aid. The average freshman award was $11,000. Of that total, scholarships or need-based grants averaged $6800 ($10,000 maximum); loans averaged $2500 ($4000 maximum); and work contracts averaged $1500 ($1700 maximum). 90% of undergraduate students work part-time. Average earnings from campus work for the school year are $1200. Gordon is a member of CSS. The FAFSA and CSS Profile Application are required. The application deadline for fall entry is March 15.

International Students: There are currently 51 international students enrolled. They must take the TOEFL or SAT I or the ACT.

Computers: The college provides computer facilities for student use. The mainframes are a DEC VAX 4000 and a DEC VAX 6420. There are also a number of Apple Macintosh and IBM microcomputers available in student laboratories and the computer center. The campus network may be accessed from residence halls, and there is access to the Internet and the World Wide Web. All students may access the system 24 hours a day, 7 days a week. There are no time limits and no fees.

Graduates: In 1994-95, 276 bachelor's degrees were awarded. The most popular majors among graduates were psychology (12%), business administration (9%), and history (8%). Within an average freshman class, 52% graduate in 4 years.

Admissions Contact: Pamela B. Lazarakis, Dean of Admissions. A campus video is available.

HAMPSHIRE COLLEGE B-2

Amherst, MA 01002 (413) 582-5471; FAX: (413) 582-5631

Full-time: 462 men, 636 women	Faculty: 87; IIB, +$
Part-time: none	Ph.D.s: 82%
Graduate: none	Student/Faculty: 13 to 1
Year: 4-1-4	Tuition: $22,535
Application Deadline: February 1	Room & Board: $5740
Freshman Class: 1635 applied, 1110 accepted, 309 enrolled	
SAT I or ACT: not required	**VERY COMPETITIVE +**

Hampshire College, founded in 1965, is a private coeducational institution offering a liberal arts education with an emphasis on independent research, creative work, and multidisciplinary study. The library contains 111,000 volumes, 400 microform items, and 29,000 audiovisual forms, and subscribes to 800 periodicals. Computerized library sources and services include the card catalog and interlibrary loans. Special learning facilities include an art gallery, TV station, multimedia center, farm center, music and dance studios, optics laboratory, electronics shop, integrated greenhouse and aquaculture facility, fabrication shop, and performing arts center. The 800-acre campus is in a rural area 20 miles north of Springfield. Including residence halls, there are 28 buildings on campus.

Student Life: 81% of undergraduates are from out-of-state, mostly the Northeast. Students come from 47 states, 24 foreign countries, and Canada. 73% are from public schools; 27% from private. 80% are white. The average age of freshmen is 18; all undergraduates, 20. 16% do not continue beyond their first year; 63% remain to graduate.

Housing: 1100 students can be accommodated in college housing. College-sponsored living facilities include single-sex and coed dormitories and on-campus apartments. In addition, there are special interest halls and special interest on-campus apartments. On-campus housing is guaranteed for all 4 years. 95% of students live on campus. All students may keep cars on campus.

Activities: There are no fraternities or sororities. There are about 100 groups on campus, including art, chess, chorus, computers, dance, drama, ethnic, film, gay, international, literary magazine, musical theater, newspaper, orchestra, photography, political, radio and TV, religious, social, social service, and student government. Popular campus events include Southern Exposure, Spring Jam, Casino Night, and Family and Friends Weekend.

Sports: There are coed intercollegiate sports and 11 intramural sports for men and 11 for women. Athletic and recreation facilities include 2 multipurpose sports centers housing a glass-enclosed swimming pool, a 12,000-square-foot playing floor, a 30-foot climbing wall, a weight lifting area, 4 indoor tennis courts, and a jogging track. Other facilities include soccer fields, 10 outdoor tennis courts, 2 softball diamonds, and a 2-mile nature trail.

Disabled Students: 90% of the campus is accessible to disabled students. The following facilities are available: wheelchair ramps, elevators, special parking, specially equipped rest rooms, special class scheduling, lowered drinking fountains, and lowered telephones. The college provides a variety of support services to meet individual special needs.

Services: In addition to many counseling and information services, tutoring is available in most subjects. There is a reader service for the blind, an advising center, a writing and reading program, and a laboratory quantitative skills program.

Campus Safety and Security: Campus safety and security measures include 24-hour foot and vehicle patrol, escort service, informal discussions, and pamphlets/posters/films. In addition, there are lighted pathways/sidewalks, an EMT on-call program, and dormitory doors accessible by students only.

Programs of Study: Hampshire confers the B.A. degree. Bachelor's degrees are awarded in AGRICULTURE (agriculture and animal science), BIOLOGICAL SCIENCE (biology/biological science, botany, ecology, marine biology, nutrition, and physiology), COMMUNICATIONS AND THE ARTS (art history and appreciation, communications, comparative literature, creative writing, dance, dramatic arts, film arts, fine arts, journalism, linguistics, literature, music, performing arts, photography, and video), COMPUTER AND PHYSICAL SCIENCE (chemistry, computer science, geology, mathematics, physics, and science), EDUCATION (education), ENGINEERING AND ENVIRONMENTAL DESIGN (architecture, environmental design, and environmental science), HEALTH PROFESSIONS (health science and premedicine), SOCIAL SCIENCE (African American studies, African studies, American studies, anthropology, Asian/Oriental studies, cognitive science, crosscultural studies, economics, family/consumer studies, geography, history, humanities, international relations, international studies, Judaic studies, Latin American studies, law, Middle Eastern studies, peace studies, philosophy, political science/government, psychology, religion, sociology, urban studies, and women's studies). Film/photography/video is the strongest academically. Social sciences has the largest enrollment.

Required: All students must complete 3 divisions of study. In Division I, Basic Studies, students work in each of Hampshire's 4 schools: Cognitive Science and Cultural Studies, Humanities and the Arts, Natural Science, and Social Science. In Division II, the Concentration, students explore their field or fields of emphasis through individually designed internships or field studies. In Division III, Advanced Studies, students complete a major independent study project centered on a specific topic, question, or idea. Students must also include service to the college or the surrounding community and consider some aspect of their work from a non-Western perspective.

Special: Cross-registration is possible with other members of the Five-College Consortium (Amherst College, the University of Massachusetts, Smith College, and Mount Holyoke). Internships, multidisciplinary dual majors, and study abroad are offered. All majors are student-designed. Students may complete their programs in fewer than 4 years.

Faculty/Classroom: 53% of faculty are male; 47%, female. All both teach and do research. The average class size in a regular course offering is 17.

Admissions: 68% of the 1995–96 applicants were accepted. 46% of the current freshmen were in the top fifth of their class; 80% were in the top two fifths. There were 5 National Merit semifinalists. 2 freshmen graduated first in their class.

Requirements: Applicants must submit all transcripts from 9th grade on or GED/state equivalency examination results. Students are required to submit a personal statement and an analytic essay or academic paper. An interview is recommended. Samples of creative work in a single medium are accepted. AP credits are accepted. Important factors in the admissions decision are personality/intangible qualities, evidence of special talent, and extracurricular activities record.

Procedure: Freshmen are admitted in the fall and spring. There are early decision, early admissions, and deferred admissions plans. Early decision applications should be filed by November 15; regular applications, by February 1 for fall entry and November 15 for spring entry, along with an application fee of $45. Notification of early decision is sent December 15; regular decision, April 1. 41 early decision candidates were accepted for the 1995–96 class. A waiting list is an active part of the admissions procedure, with about 13% of all applicants on the list.

Transfer: 40 transfer students enrolled in 1995–96. A proposed program of study, high school and college transcripts, and 1 recommendation must be submitted.

Visiting: There are regularly scheduled orientations for prospective students, including interviews, information sessions, campus tours, open houses, and an overnight program. There are guides for informal visits and visitors may sit in on classes and stay overnight at the school. To schedule a visit, contact the Admissions Office.

Financial Aid: In 1995–96, 55% of all freshmen and 63% of continuing students received some form of financial aid, including need-based aid. The average freshman award was $17,125. Of that total, scholarships or need-based grants averaged $13,000 ($21,900 maximum); loans averaged $2625; and work contracts averaged $1500. 66% of undergraduate students work part-time. Average earnings from campus work for the school year are $1600. The average financial indebtedness of the 1994–95 graduate was $15,000. Hampshire is a member of CSS. FAFSA, the college's own financial statement, and the CSS Profile Application are required. The application deadline for fall entry is February 15.

International Students: There are currently 41 international students enrolled. The school actively recruits these students. They must take the TOEFL and achieve a minimum score of 577.

Computers: The college provides computer facilities for student use. Hampshire uses a variety of computers as file servers. Several computing laboratories on campus allow students access to microcomputers and networked systems. In addition, all student rooms are networked and many students own personal computers. All students may access the system 24 hours per day via their own personal computers or at designated hours in the laboratories, generally 8 A.M. to midnight but up to 24 hours daily at the end of each semester. There are no time limits and no fees.

Graduates: In 1994–95, 222 bachelor's degrees were awarded. The most popular majors among graduates were creative writing (9%), film/photo (7%), education (5%), and art (5%). Within an average freshman class, 11% graduate in 3 years, 86% in 4 years, 99% in 5 years, and 1% in 6 years. 5 companies recruited on campus in 1994–95.

Admissions Contact: Audrey Y. Smith, Director of Admissions. E-mail: admissions@hamp.hampshire.edu.

HARVARD UNIVERSITY/HARVARD AND RADCLIFFE COLLEGES

D-2

Cambridge, MA 02138 (617) 495-1551

Full-time, part-time: 3739 men, 2904 women	Faculty: I, ++$
	Ph.D.s: 96%
Graduate: 6268 men, 4854 women	Student/Faculty: n/av
Year: semesters, summer session	Tuition: $20,865
Application Deadline: see profile	Room & Board: $6710
Freshman Class: 17,852 applied, 2150 accepted, 1618 enrolled	
SAT I or ACT: required	MOST COMPETITIVE

Harvard and Radcliffe Colleges are the undergraduate colleges of Harvard University. Harvard College was founded in 1636. There are 10 graduate schools. In addition to regional accreditation, Harvard/Radcliffe has baccalaureate program accreditation with ABET. The 97 libraries contain 13 million volumes, and subscribe to 100,000 periodicals. Computerized library sources and services include the card catalog, interlibrary loans, and database searching. Special learning facilities include a learning resource center, art gallery, natural history museum, planetarium, and radio station. The 380-acre campus is in an urban area across the Charles River from Boston. Including residence halls, there are 400 buildings on campus.

Student Life: 81% of undergraduates are from out-of-state, mostly the Middle Atlantic. Students come from 50 states, 118 foreign countries, and Canada. 67% are from public schools; 33% from private. 45% are white; 19% Asian American. The average age of freshmen is 18; all undergraduates, 20. 96% of freshmen remain to graduate.

Housing: 6325 students can be accommodated in college housing. College-sponsored living facilities include coed dormitories and on-campus apartments. On-campus housing is guaranteed for all 4 years. 97% of students live on campus. All students may keep cars on campus.

Activities: There are no fraternities or sororities. There are more than 250 groups on campus, including art, band, cheerleading, chess, choir, chorale, chorus, computers, dance, drama, ethnic, film, gay, honors, international, jazz band, literary magazine, marching band, musical theater, newspaper, opera, orchestra, pep band, photography, political, professional, radio and TV, religious, social, social service, student government, symphony, and yearbook. Popular campus events include Harvard/Yale football, Head-of-the-Charles crew regatta, and Cultural Rhythms Festival.

Sports: There are 21 intercollegiate sports for men and 20 for women, and 16 intramural sports for men and 16 for women. Athletic and recreation facilities include several gymnasiums and athletic centers, pools, a track, boat houses, a sailing center, a hockey rink, and various courts and playing fields.

Disabled Students: The following facilities are available: wheelchair ramps, elevators, special parking, specially equipped rest rooms, special class scheduling, lowered drinking fountains, and lowered telephones. There are also tutors, adaptive equipment in the field of information technology, TDD/TTY, shuttle van service, a student support organization called ABLE, and an adaptive technology laboratory.

Services: In addition to many counseling and information services, tutoring is available in every subject. There is a reader service for the blind.

Campus Safety and Security: Campus safety and security measures include 24-hour foot and vehicle patrol, self-defense education, escort service, and shuttle buses. In addition, there are informal discussions, pamphlets/posters/films, emergency telephones, and lighted pathways/sidewalks.

Programs of Study: Harvard/Radcliffe confers A.B. and S.B. degrees. Master's and doctoral degrees are also awarded. Bachelor's degrees are awarded in BIOLOGICAL SCIENCE (biochemistry, biology/biological science, and biophysics), COMMUNICATIONS AND THE ARTS (art history and appreciation, Chinese, classics, creative writing, English, fine arts, folklore and mythology, French, German, Greek, Hebrew, Italian, Japanese, Latin, linguistics, literature, music, Portuguese, Russian, and Spanish), COMPUTER AND PHYSICAL SCIENCE (applied mathematics, astronomy, chemistry, computer science, geology, geophysics and seismology, mathematics, physical sciences, physics, and statistics), ENGINEERING AND ENVIRONMENTAL DESIGN (engineering, environmental design, environmental science, and preengineering), SOCIAL SCIENCE (African American studies, American studies, anthropology, Asian/Oriental studies, economics, European studies, history, humanities, Middle Eastern studies, philosophy, political science/government, psychology, religion, Russian and Slavic studies, Sanskrit and Indian studies, social science, social studies, sociology, and women's studies). Economics, government, and biology have the largest enrollments.

Required: In 8 semesters, students must pass a minimum of 32 1-semester courses. The average course load is 4 courses per semester, but the course rate may be varied for special reasons. A typical balanced program devotes about one fourth of its courses to core curriculum requirements, one half to the concentration (or major field), and the remaining one fourth to electives.

Special: Undergraduates may cross-register at MIT and for certain courses in other schools of the university. Students may design their own concentrations or enroll for nondegree study. Study abroad may be arranged. A combined A.B.-S.B. in engineering is offered. There are pass/fail options. There is a chapter of Phi Beta Kappa on campus. All departments have honors programs.

Faculty/Classroom: 76% of faculty are male; 24%, female. 98% teach undergraduates, 97% do research, and 95% do both. No introductory courses are taught by graduate students. The average class size in a regular course offering is 25.

Admissions: 12% of the 1995–96 applicants were accepted. 98% of the current freshmen were in the top fifth of their class; 100% were in the top two fifths. There were 393 National Merit finalists. 474 freshmen graduated first in their class.

Requirements: The SAT I or ACT is required, as well as 3 SAT II: Subject tests. Applicants need not be high school graduates but are expected to be well prepared academically. An essay and an interview are required, in addition to a transcript, counselor report, and 2 teacher recommendations from academic disciplines. AP credits are accepted. Important factors in the admissions decision are evidence of special talent, personality/intangible qualities, and recommendations by school officials.

Procedure: Freshmen are admitted in the fall. Entrance exams should be taken by January of the senior year. There are early decision and deferred admissions plans. Early decision applications should be filed by November 1; regular decision, December 15 (preferred) and January 1 (final), along with an application fee of $60. Notification of early decision is sent in early December; regular decision, April 3. A waiting list is an active part of the admissions procedure.

Transfer: 101 transfer students enrolled in 1995–96. Transfer applicants must have completed at least 1 full year of daytime study in a degree-granting program at 1 institution. Students are required to submit the SAT I or ACT, 2 letters of recommendation, high school and college transcripts with a dean's report, and several essays. 16 semester courses of 32 must be completed at Harvard/Radcliffe.

Visiting: There are regularly scheduled orientations for prospective students, consisting of group information sessions and tours. There are guides for informal visits and visitors may sit in on classes and stay overnight at the school. To schedule a visit, contact the Undergraduate Admissions Office.

Financial Aid: In 1995–96, 79% of all freshmen and 65% of continuing students received some form of financial aid. 61% of freshmen and 52% of continuing students received need-based aid. The average freshman award was $19,705. Of that total, scholarships or need-based grants averaged $14,174 ($13,699 maximum); loans averaged $3761 ($4184 maximum); and work contracts averaged $1770 ($1844 maximum). 64% of undergraduate students work part-time. Average earnings from campus work for the school year are $1450. The average financial indebtedness of the 1994–95 graduate was $11,641. Harvard/Radcliffe is a member of CSS. FAFSA, the college's own financial statement, federal tax forms, and CSS Profile Application are required. The application deadline for fall entry is February 15.

International Students: There are currently 446 international students enrolled. The school actively recruits these students. They must take the TOEFL and achieve a minimum score of 600. The student must also take the SAT I or the ACT. Students must take any 3 SAT II: Subject Tests.

Computers: The college provides computer facilities for student use. All residences have Internet network access. There are also microcomputers available for use in the science center and all residence halls. All students may access the system 24 hours per day. There are no time limits and no fees.

Graduates: In 1994–95, 1740 bachelor's degrees were awarded. The most popular majors among graduates were economics (11%), government (11%), and biology (10%). Within an average freshman class, 97% graduate in 5 years and 7% in 6 years. 313 companies recruited on campus in 1994–95.

Admissions Contact: Dr. Marlyn McGrath Lewis, Director of Admissions. A campus video is available.

HEBREW COLLEGE

D-2

Brookline, MA 02146   (617) 278-4944
(800) 866-4814; FAX: (617) 264-9264

Full-time: 8 men and women	Faculty: 4
Part-time: 16 men and women	Ph.D.s: 100%
Graduate: 85 men and women	Student/Faculty: 2 to 1
Year: semesters, summer session	Tuition: $6690
Application Deadline: open	Room & Board: n/app
Freshman Class: n/av	
SAT I: required	**LESS COMPETITIVE**

Hebrew College, founded in 1921, is a private, coeducational institution of Hebrew and Jewish studies providing undergraduate and graduate degrees in Judaic disciplines with an external liberal arts foundation. There are 2 graduate schools. The school is in the process of restructuring and enlarging its undergraduate program. The library contains 100,000 volumes, 2200 microform items, and 1000 audiovisual forms, and subscribes to 255 periodicals. Computerized library sources and services include database searching. Special learning facilities include an art gallery. The 4-acre campus is in a suburban area 2 miles west of Boston. There is 1 building on campus.
Student Life: 99% of undergraduates are from Massachusetts. Students come from 6 states, 3 foreign countries, and Canada.
Housing: There are no residence halls. The college assists in finding nearby housing. Undergraduates may live in dormitories on an adjacent campus. All students commute. Alcohol is not permitted.
Sports: There is no sports program at the college.
Disabled Students: 75% of the campus is accessible to disabled students.
Programs of Study: The college confers B.A. and B.J.Ed. degrees. Master's degrees are also awarded. Bachelor's degrees are awarded in SOCIAL SCIENCE (Judaic studies and religious education).
Required: All students must complete a total of 120 credit hours, including 78 in Hebrew/Jewish studies, 12 electives, and 30 in liberal arts and sciences outside the college through cross-registration agreements, and maintain a minimum 2.0 GPA.
Special: To fulfill the liberal arts requirements, students have the opportunity to cross-register through Hebrew College at Boston College, Boston University, Northeastern University, University of Massachusetts, Simmons College, and Brandeis University. At several of these schools, cross-registered students may also participate in campus activities.
Faculty/Classroom: No introductory courses are taught by graduate students.
Requirements: The SAT I is required. Admission criteria include the secondary school record and recommendations. Applicants must have a high school diploma or equivalent. A personal statement is required and an interview is encouraged. Important factors in the admissions decision are personality/intangible qualities, extracurricular activities record, and leadership record.
Procedure: Freshmen are admitted fall, spring, and summer. Application deadlines are open. Application fee is $25. Notification is sent on a rolling basis.
Transfer: Courses in Hebrew and Jewish studies applicable to the college's curriculum are accepted for transfer credit. 54 credits of 120 must be completed at the college.
Visiting: There are guides for informal visits and visitors may sit in on classes. To schedule a visit, contact Norma Frankel at (617) 278-4944.
Financial Aid: The college is a member of CSS. The college's own financial statement is required.
International Students: The school actively recruits these students. Students must score 550 on the TOEFL.
Admissions Contact: Norma Frankel, Registrar.

HELLENIC COLLEGE/HOLY CROSS GREEK ORTHODOX SCHOOL OF THEOLOGY

D-2

Brookline, MA 02146   (617) 731-3500, ext. 260
FAX: (617) 232-7819

Full-time: 48 men, 29 women	Faculty: 9
Part-time: 2 men, 1 women	Ph.D.s: 100%
Graduate: 80 men, 9 women	Student/Faculty: 9 to 1
Year: semesters	Tuition: $7680
Application Deadline: open	Room & Board: $5360
Freshman Class: n/av	
SAT I Verbal/Math: 450/500	**COMPETITIVE**

Hellenic College, founded in 1937, is a private coeducational college affiliated with the Greek Orthodox Church. It offers programs in the classics, elementary education, religious studies, and human development. There is 1 undergraduate school. The library contains 102,100 volumes, 85 microform items, and 125 audiovisual forms, and subscribes to 684 periodicals. Computerized library sources and services include the card catalog and database searching. Special learning facilities include a Greek cultural center and a language laboratory. The 52-acre campus is in an urban area 4 miles southwest of Boston. Including residence halls, there are 7 buildings on campus.

Student Life: 54% of undergraduates are from out-of-state, mostly the Midwest. Students come from 15 states, 4 foreign countries, and Canada. 97% are white. Most are Greek or Eastern Orthodox. The average age of freshmen is 22. 3% do not continue beyond their first year; 93% remain to graduate.

Housing: 220 students can be accommodated in college housing. College-sponsored living facilities include single-sex dormitories, on-campus apartments, and married-student housing. On-campus housing is guaranteed for all 4 years. 79% of students live on campus. All students may keep cars on campus.

Activities: There are no fraternities or sororities. There are 9 groups on campus, including choir, ethnic, photography, religious, social, social service, student government, and yearbook. Popular campus events include Feast of the Holy Cross, Campus Christmas Party, and Easter dinner.

Sports: There are 4 intramural sports for men and 3 for women. Athletic and recreation facilities include a gymnasium, tennis courts, racquetball courts, and a football field.

Disabled Students: 10% of the campus is accessible to disabled students. The following facilities are available: wheelchair ramps and special parking.

Services: In addition to many counseling and information services, tutoring is available in some subjects, including Greek and music writing and composition. There is remedial math, reading, and writing.

Campus Safety and Security: Campus safety and security measures include informal discussions, pamphlets/posters/films, lighted pathways/sidewalks, and a 16-hour security patrol.

Programs of Study: The school confers the B.A. degree. Master's degrees are also awarded. Bachelor's degrees are awarded in COMMUNICATIONS AND THE ARTS (classics), EDUCATION (elementary), SOCIAL SCIENCE (human development and religion). Religious studies is the strongest academically.

Required: To graduate, students must complete 129 credits, with 39 in the major, and maintain a minimum overall GPA of 2.0. General education requirements include 72 credits, with courses in English language and literature, music, history, science, philosophy, and social science.

Special: The college offers cross-registration with Boston Theological Institute and credit by examination.

Faculty/Classroom: 76% of faculty are male; 24%, female. No introductory courses are taught by graduate students. The average class size in an introductory lecture is 75; in a laboratory, 20; and in a regular course offering, 22.

Requirements: The SAT I is required. Applicants should graduate from an accredited secondary school with a 2.5 GPA or have a GED. 15 academic credits are required, including 4 units of English, 2 each of mathematics, foreign language, and social studies, and 1 of science. An essay is required. AP and CLEP credits are accepted. Important factors in the admissions decision are recommendations by school officials, recommendations by alumni, and advanced placement or honor courses.

Procedure: Freshmen are admitted to all sessions. There is a deferred admissions plan. Application deadlines are open. Application fee is $35. Notification is sent on a rolling basis.

Transfer: 6 transfer students enrolled in 1995–96. The SAT I, an autobiographical statement, recommendation letters, high school transcripts, and a health certificate are required. 60 credits of 129 must be completed at the school.

Visiting: There are regularly scheduled orientations for prospective students, including observation of classroom and student life. There are guides for informal visits and visitors may sit in on classes and stay overnight at the school. To schedule a visit, contact Agnes Desses, Office of Admissions.

Financial Aid: In 1995–96, 72% of all freshmen and 75% of continuing students received some form of financial aid. 33% of freshmen and 40% of continuing students received need-based aid. The average freshman award was $5000. Of that total, scholarships or need-based grants averaged $1500 ($2500 maximum); loans averaged $3500 ($5500 maximum); and work contracts averaged $1500 ($2000 maximum). 15% of undergraduate students work part-time. Average earnings from campus work for the school year are $1500. The average financial indebtedness of the 1994–95 graduate was $15,000. The school is a member of CSS. The FAF, FAFSA, and the college's own financial statement are required. The application deadline for fall entry is May 1.

International Students: There are currently 32 international students enrolled. They must take the TOEFL and achieve a minimum score of 500.

Computers: The mainframe is a 9404 AS/400 IBM Model C20.

Graduates: In 1994–95, 16 bachelor's degrees were awarded.
Admissions Contact: Agnes Desses, Assistant Director of Admissions.

HOLY CROSS
(See College of the Holy Cross)

LESLEY COLLEGE   D-2
Cambridge, MA 02138–2790   (617) 349-8800
                                  (800) 541-8486; FAX: (617) 349-8150

Full-time: 466 women	Faculty: 30; IIA, --$
Part-time: 28 women	Ph.D.s: 59%
Graduate: 1083 men, 4929 women	Student/Faculty: 16 to 1
Year: semesters, summer session	Tuition: $13,050
Application Deadline: March 15	Room & Board: $6075
Freshman Class: 326 applied, 252 accepted, 98 enrolled	
SAT I Verbal/Math: 420/460	**LESS COMPETITIVE**

Lesley College, founded in 1909, is a private, primarily women's institution. Within Lesley's School of Undergraduate Studies, the Women's college offers degree programs in education, human services, management, liberal arts, and interdisciplinary studies. Bachelor's programs in alternative formats are offered to returning students through the coeducational Baccalaureate College and the School of Management. There are 3 graduate schools. The library contains 89,749 volumes, 700,000 microform items, and 855 audiovisual forms, and subscribes to 740 periodicals. Computerized library sources and services include the card catalog, interlibrary loans, and database searching. Special learning facilities include a center for teaching resources. The 5-acre campus is in an urban area 3 miles northwest of Boston. Including residence halls, there are 45 buildings on campus.

Student Life: 60% of undergraduates are from Massachusetts. Students come from 31 states, 5 foreign countries, and Canada. 70% are from public schools; 30% from private. 81% are white. The average age of freshmen is 18. 20% do not continue beyond their first year; 60% remain to graduate.

Housing: 432 students can be accommodated in college housing. College-sponsored living facilities include dormitories. In addition, there are special interest houses, an England exchange program house, a community service floor, and a wellness floor. On-campus housing is guaranteed for all 4 years. 67% of students live on campus.

Activities: There are no fraternities or sororities. There are 20 groups on campus, including choir, chorus, commuter, disabilities awareness, drama, environmental, ethnic, feminist, gay, international, literary magazine, professional, religious, social, social service, student government, and yearbook. Popular campus events include Family and Friends Weekend, School Spirit Days, and Honors Assembly.

Sports: Athletic and recreation facilities include a gymnasium, outdoor tennis courts, a fitness center with Nautilus circuit, free weights, and cardiovascular equipment. Students may also use an Olympic-size swimming pool at a nearby school and local playing field facilities.

Disabled Students: 80% of the campus is accessible to disabled students. The following facilities are available: wheelchair ramps, elevators, special parking, specially equipped rest rooms, special class scheduling, and lowered drinking fountains.

Services: In addition to many counseling and information services, tutoring is available in most subjects. There is remedial math, reading, and writing. study skills.

Campus Safety and Security: Campus safety and security measures include 24-hour foot and vehicle patrol, self-defense education, escort service, and informal discussions. In addition, there are pamphlets/posters/films, emergency telephones, and lighted pathways/sidewalks.

Programs of Study: Lesley's Women's College confers the B.S. degree. Associate, master's, and doctoral degrees are also awarded. Bachelor's degrees are awarded in BUSINESS (management science), COMPUTER AND PHYSICAL SCIENCE (natural sciences), EDUCATION (early childhood, elementary, middle school, and special), SOCIAL SCIENCE (human services, humanities, and social science). Education has the largest enrollment.

Required: Students must complete 45 hours of general education requirements, including 15 of humanities, 12 of natural science, 9 of social science, 6 of multicultural perspectives, and 3 of freshman seminar; emphasis is given to cross-cultural components in writing, critical and quantitative reasoning, global perspectives, and leadership and ethics. To graduate, students need 128 total credit hours, including 30 in the liberal arts majors or 34 to 49 in preprofessional majors, with a minimum 2.0 GPA.

Special: Cross-registration with Harvard University Extension, study abroad in England, a Washington Justice semester, and on-campus work-study programs are offered. All students participate in at least 3 field placement experiences. There are joint bachelor's/master's degree programs in clinical mental health counseling, counseling psychology, early childhood education, and special education. Accelerated and weekend course programs are offered for Adult Baccalaureate College and School of Management degree programs.

Faculty/Classroom: 26% of faculty are male; 74%, female. All both teach and do research. No introductory courses are taught by graduate students. The average class size in an introductory lecture is 15 and in a regular course offering, 16.

Admissions: 77% of the 1995–96 applicants were accepted. The SAT I scores for the 1995–96 freshman class were as follows: Verbal—82% below 500, 15% between 500 and 599, 2% between 600 and 700, and 1% above 700. 18% of the current freshmen were in the top fifth of their class; 54% were in the top two fifths. 1 freshman graduated first in her class.

Requirements: The SAT I or ACT is required. Applicants must be graduates of an accredited secondary school or have a GED. Students must have completed 15 academic units, including 4 in English, 2 to 3 in science with a laboratory course, 2 in mathematics, and 1 in U.S. history. A writing sample and 3 recommendations are required; an interview is recommended. AP and CLEP credits are accepted. Important factors in the admissions decision are extracurricular activities record, recommendations by school officials, and advanced placement or honor courses.

Procedure: Freshmen are admitted in the fall and spring. Entrance exams should be taken by November of the senior year. There are early decision and deferred admissions plans. Early decision applications should be filed by December 1; regular applications, by March 15 for fall entry and December 15 for spring entry, along with an application fee of $35. Notification of early decision is sent December 15; regular decision, within 3 weeks of completed application after January 15. 25 early decision candidates were accepted for the 1995–96 class.

Transfer: 61 transfer students enrolled in 1995–96. Applicants must have at least 12 credit hours earned and a minimum 2.0 GPA. Recommendations are required and an interview is recommended. 63 credits of 128 must be completed at Lesley.

Visiting: There are regularly scheduled orientations for prospective students, including personal interviews with professional staff and student campus tours. There are guides for informal visits and visitors may sit in on classes and stay overnight at the school. To schedule a visit, contact Valerie Brown at (617) 349–8800.

Financial Aid: In 1995–96, 73% of all freshmen and 74% of continuing students received some form of financial aid. 67% of freshmen and 69% of continuing students received need-based aid. The average freshman award was $12,766. Of that total, scholarships or need-based grants averaged $7542 ($13,730 maximum); loans averaged $4009 ($5500 maximum); and work contracts averaged $1215 ($1800 maximum). 45% of undergraduate students work part-time. Average earnings from campus work for the school year are $1700. The average financial indebtedness of the 1994–95 graduate was $17,125. Lesley is a member of CSS. FAFSA, the college's own financial statement, the state scholarship/grant form, and parent and student federal tax returns are required. The application deadline for fall entry is February 15 for first-year students and May 1 for returning students.

International Students: There are currently 20 international students enrolled. The school actively recruits these students. They must take the TOEFL and achieve a minimum score of 500. The student must also take the SAT I or the ACT.

Computers: The college provides computer facilities for student use. The mainframe is an IBM. More than 120 Apple II, Apple Macintosh, and IBM microcomputers are available in the microcomputer center, computer laboratories, the learning center, the library, classrooms, and some dormitories. There is also a word processing center. The library is part of an on-line Internet network and OCLC. All students may access the system during library hours primarily; the word processing center is available 24 hours a day. There are no time limits and no fees.

Graduates: In 1994–95, 118 bachelor's degrees were awarded. The most popular majors among graduates were education (60%), human services (30%), and management (10%). Within an average freshman class, 60% graduate in 5 years. 63 companies recruited on campus in a recent year. Of the 1994 graduating class, 13% were enrolled in graduate school within 6 months of graduation and 79% had found employment.

Admissions Contact: Jane A. Raley, Director of Women's College Admissions.

MASSACHUSETTS BOARD OF REGENTS OF HIGHER EDUCATION

The Massachusetts Board of Regents of Higher Education was established in 1980. It is governed by a 16-member board of regents appointed by the governor, whose chief administrator is the chancellor.

The system is the central governing authority for the state's public higher education system. The total enrollment of all 29 campuses is approximately 170,000. Profiles of the 4-year campuses, located in Amherst, Buzzard's Bay, Bridgewater, Fitchburg, Farmingham, North Salem, North Dartmouth, Westfield, and Worcester, are included in this chapter.

MASSACHUSETTS COLLEGE OF ART

E-2

Boston, MA 02115 (617) 232–1555, ext. 236; FAX: (617) 739–9744

Full-time: 471 men, 685 women	Faculty: 63; IIB, +$
Part-time: 52 men, 75 women	Ph.Ds: 75%
Graduate: 32 men, 80 women	Student/Faculty: 18 to 1
Year: semesters, summer session	Tuition: $4774 ($9733)
Application Deadline: March 1	Room & Board: $5652
Freshman Class: 1083 applied, 542 accepted, 327 enrolled	
SAT I Verbal/Math: 481/488	SPECIAL

Massachusetts College of Art, founded in 1873, is a public coeducational institution offering undergraduate and graduate programs in art, design, and education. In addition to regional accreditation, MassArt has baccalaureate program accreditation with NASAD. The library contains 95,000 volumes, 65,000 microform items, and 1165 audiovisual forms, and subscribes to 400 periodicals. Computerized library sources and services include the card catalog and interlibrary loans. Special learning facilities include an art gallery, a computer arts center, performance spaces, and film viewing rooms. The 5-acre campus is in an urban area in Boston. Including residence halls, there are 7 buildings on campus.

Student Life: 74% of undergraduates are from Massachusetts. Students come from 21 states, 30 foreign countries, and Canada. 85% are from public schools; 15% from private. 81% are white. The average age of freshmen is 21; all undergraduates, 24. 15% do not continue beyond their first year; 50% remain to graduate.

Housing: 300 students can be accommodated in college housing. College-sponsored living facilities include coed dormitories. In addition, there is a visual art college residence hall with ventilated workrooms, a visiting artist suite, and gallery space. On-campus housing is available on a first-come, first-served basis and is available on a lottery system for upperclassmen. 74% of students commute. All students may keep cars on campus.

Activities: There are no fraternities or sororities. There are 30 groups on campus, including art, computers, ethnic, film, gay, international, literary magazine, newspaper, photography, political, professional, radio and TV, social, social service, student government, and yearbook. Popular campus events include Eventworks, First Night Ice Sculpture, and gallery exhibitions and openings.

Sports: There are 7 intercollegiate sports for men and 6 for women, and 8 intramural sports for men and 6 for women. Athletic and recreation facilities include a gymnasium, a fitness center, and courts for squash, volleyball, and basketball.

Disabled Students: 95% of the campus is accessible to disabled students. The following facilities are available: wheelchair ramps, elevators, special parking, specially equipped rest rooms, special class scheduling, lowered drinking fountains, and lowered telephones.

Services: There is remedial reading and writing.

Campus Safety and Security: Campus safety and security measures include 24-hour foot and vehicle patrol, self-defense education, escort service, and shuttle buses. In addition, there are informal discussions, pamphlets/posters/films, emergency telephones, and lighted pathways/sidewalks.

Programs of Study: MassArt confers the B.F.A. degree. Master's degrees are also awarded. Bachelor's degrees are awarded in COMMUNICATIONS AND THE ARTS (art history and appreciation, design, film arts, fine arts, industrial design, photography, and studio art), EDUCATION (art), ENGINEERING AND ENVIRONMENTAL DESIGN (architecture), SOCIAL SCIENCE (fashion design and technology). Painting, illustration, and graphic design have the largest enrollments.

Required: A total of 132 semester credits is required for graduation; the minimum GPA varies by major. Typically, students take 45 credits in liberal arts, 39 in the major, 18 in studio foundations, and 30 in electives. Beginning in the sophomore year, the student's work is reviewed by panels of faculty and visiting artists.

Special: MassArt offers cross-registration with several consortiums, internships for advanced students, on- and off-campus work-study programs, study-abroad and foreign-exchange programs, an open major for exceptional students, and dual majors in any combination of concentrations.

Faculty/Classroom: 51% of faculty are male; 49%, female. All teach undergraduates. No introductory courses are taught by graduate students. The average class size in an introductory lecture is 23; in a laboratory, 12; and in a regular course offering, 14.

Admissions: 50% of the 1995–96 applicants were accepted. 31% of the current freshmen were in the top fifth of their class; 58% were in the top two fifths. There were 2 National Merit finalists and 7 semifinalists. 2 freshmen graduated first in their class.

Requirements: The SAT I is required. In addition, applicants should be graduates of an accredited secondary school or have earned the GED. College-preparatory studies should include as a minimum 4 years of English, 3 each of mathematics and science, 2 each of social studies and a foreign language, plus 2 academic electives. A personal essay and portfolio are required, and an interview and letters of reference are recommended. AP and CLEP credits are accepted. Important factors in the admissions decision are evidence of special talent, recommendations by school officials, and personality/intangible qualities.

Procedure: Freshmen are admitted in the fall and spring. Entrance exams should be taken in the early fall of the senior year. There are early decision, early admissions, and deferred admissions plans. Early decision applications should be filed by December 1; regular applications, by March 1 for fall entry and November 1 for spring entry, along with an application fee of $10 in-state, $40 out-of-state. Notification of early decision is sent December 20; regular decision, on a rolling basis. 4 early decision candidates were accepted for the 1995–96 class. A waiting list is an active part of the admissions procedure, with about 10% of all applicants on the list.

Transfer: 163 transfer students enrolled in 1995–96. Applicants must submit secondary school and postsecondary school transcripts, a statement of purpose, and a portfolio of at least 15 pieces, preferably in slides. An interview is recommended. 66 credits of 132 must be completed at MassArt.

Visiting: There are regularly scheduled orientations for prospective students, including an information session and a campus tour. There are guides for informal visits and visitors may sit in on classes. To schedule a visit, contact the Admissions Office at (617) 232-1555, ext. 236 or 238.

Financial Aid: In a recent year, 38% of all freshmen and 55% of continuing students received some form of financial aid. 37% of freshmen and 52% of continuing students received need-based aid. The average freshman award was $3603. Of that total, scholarships or need-based grants averaged $1683 ($2700 maximum); and loans averaged $1916 ($2400 maximum). 84% of undergraduate students work part-time. Average earnings from campus work for the school year are $800. The average financial indebtedness of a recent graduate was $14,000. MassArt is a member of CSS. The FAF, FAFSA, FFS, or SFS is required. The application deadline for fall entry is May 1.

International Students: There are currently 87 international students enrolled. They must take the TOEFL and achieve a minimum score of 550.

Computers: The college provides computer facilities for student use. MassArt provides Amiga, Apple, Apple Macintosh, IBM, and NEC microcomputers for academic use. They are located in the computer center. All students may access the system. There are no time limits. The fees are $100 per semester for students not enrolled in computer courses.

Graduates: In 1994–95, 163 bachelor's degrees were awarded. The most popular majors among graduates were design (28%), painting (22%), and photography (7%). Within an average freshman class, 6% graduate in 3 years, 22% in 4 years, 15% in 5 years, and 7% in 6 years. 35 companies recruited on campus in 1994–95.

Admissions Contact: Kay Ransdell, Associate Dean for Admissions and Retention. A campus video is available.

dio station. The 2-acre campus is in an urban area 1 mile from Boston's center. There are 2 buildings on campus.

Student Life: 60% of undergraduates are from Massachusetts. The average age of freshmen is 18; all undergraduates, 21. 21% do not continue beyond their first year; 75% remain to graduate.

Housing: There are no residence halls.

Activities: There are 9 groups on campus, including drama, ethnic, international, newspaper, professional, student government, and yearbook.

Sports: There are 4 intercollegiate sports for men and 4 for women, and 2 intramural sports for men and 2 for women.

Disabled Students: 90% of the campus is accessible to disabled students. The following facilities are available: wheelchair ramps, elevators, special parking, specially equipped rest rooms, and lowered drinking fountains.

Services: In addition to some personal counseling services, tutoring is provided free of charge.

Programs of Study: The college confers B.S., B.S.Ch., B.S.H., B.S.N., B.S.Nuc.T., B.S.P., and B.S.Rad.Tech. degrees. Associate, master's, and doctoral degrees are also awarded. Bachelor's degrees are awarded in COMPUTER AND PHYSICAL SCIENCE (chemistry and radiological technology), HEALTH PROFESSIONS (allied health, nuclear medical technology, nursing, pharmacy, and premedicine), SOCIAL SCIENCE (psychology).

Required: Graduation requirements vary by program. Students must complete course work in expository writing, history and politics, psychology, sociology, interpersonal communications in the health professions, evolution of the health professions, biomedical ethics, and humanities. Quarter hours required for graduation range from 190 to 274, depending on the degree. Students must maintain a minimum quality point average of 2.0.

Special: Cooperative programs are available with Simmons College and Western New England College. The college offers an externship program in radiopharmacy in conjunction with Massachusetts General Hospital. Internships and work-study are possible. There are 2 national honor societies on campus.

Admissions: 66% of the 1995–96 applicants were accepted.

Requirements: The SAT I is required. Applicants must have been in the upper 30% of their class with a 3.0 GPA, and must have graduated from an accredited secondary school with 16 units, including 4 of English, 3 of math, and 2 of laboratory science. The college additionally advises advanced chemistry or physics with laboratory and an extra unit of mathematics. Interviews are recommended. AP and CLEP credits are accepted.

Procedure: There are early decision, early admissions, and deferred admissions plans. Early decision applications should be filed by November 1; regular applications, by March 1 for fall entry, along with an application fee of $25. Notification is sent on a rolling basis.

Transfer: Transfer applicants must have a GPA of 2.5. Those with 1 year or less of college must submit secondary school transcripts. 135 quarter hours of 190 to 274 must be completed at the college.

Visiting: There are regularly scheduled orientations for prospective students. To schedule a visit, contact the Admissions Office.

Financial Aid: The FAFSA, the college's own financial statement and the parents' and students' most recent federal tax form are required. Check with the school for current application deadlines.

International Students: They must take the TOEFL or the college's own test.

Computers: The college provides IBM and Leading Edge PCs for academic use by all students. They are available in the library and the laboratory and research facility.

Admissions Contact: Admissions representative.

MASSACHUSETTS COLLEGE OF PHARMACY AND ALLIED HEALTH SCIENCES   E-2

Boston, MA 02115   (617) 732-2850
(800) 225-5506; FAX: (617) 732-2801

Full-time: 468 men, 767 women	Faculty: 67; IIB, av$
Part-time: 43 men, 108 women	Ph.D.s: 38%
Graduate: 30 men, 35 women	Student/Faculty: 18 to 1
Year: quarters, summer session	Tuition: $12,676
Application Deadline: March 1	Room & Board: $6900
Freshman Class: 567 applied, 372 accepted, 131 enrolled	
SAT I: required	VERY COMPETITIVE

The Massachusetts College of Pharmacy and Allied Health Sciences, established in 1823, is a private, independent institution offering undergraduate and graduate programs in chemistry, pharmacy, nursing, and allied health sciences. In addition to regional accreditation, the college has baccalaureate program accreditation with ACPE, CAHEA, and NLN. The library contains 70,000 volumes and subscribes to 800 periodicals. Computerized library sources and services include the card catalog, interlibrary loans, and database searching. Special learning facilities include a learning resource center and ra-

MASSACHUSETTS INSTITUTE OF TECHNOLOGY   D-2

Cambridge, MA 02139   (617) 253-4791

Full-time: 2753 men, 1690 women	Faculty: 938; I, + +$
Part-time: 37 men, 15 women	Ph.D.s: 99%
Graduate: 4157 men, 1308 women	Student/Faculty: 5 to 1
Year: 4-1-4	Tuition: $21,612
Application Deadline: January 1	Room & Board: $6150
Freshman Class: 7958 applied, 2113 accepted, 1116 enrolled	
SAT I or ACT: required	MOST COMPETITIVE

Massachusetts Institute of Technology, founded in 1861, is a coeducational land-grant institution offering programs in architecture and planning, engineering, humanities and social science, science, health sciences, technology, and management. There are 6 undergraduate and 6 graduate schools. In addition to regional accreditation, MIT has baccalaureate program accreditation with AACSB, ABET, and NAAB. The 22 libraries contain 2,409,136 volumes, 2,105,096 microform items, and 545,957 audiovisual forms, and subscribe to 21,453 periodicals. Computerized library sources and services include the card catalog, interlibrary loans, and database searching.

Special learning facilities include an art gallery, radio station, and TV station. The 154-acre campus is in an urban area 1 mile north of Boston. Including residence halls, there are 148 buildings on campus.

Student Life: 92% of undergraduates are from out-of-state, mostly the Northeast. Students come from 50 states, 100 foreign countries, and Canada. 79% are from public schools; 13% from private. 48% are white; 29% Asian American. The average age of freshmen is 18; all undergraduates, 19.5. 4% do not continue beyond their first year; 91% remain to graduate.

Housing: 4238 students can be accommodated in college housing. College-sponsored living facilities include single-sex and coed dormitories, on-campus apartments, married-student housing, fraternity houses, and sorority houses. In addition, there are language houses, special interest houses, coed fraternity houses, a cooperative house, and off-campus independent living groups, including 2 for women. On-campus housing is guaranteed for all 4 years. 94% of students live on campus. Upperclassmen may keep cars on campus.

Activities: 50% of men and 2% of women belong to 2 local and 28 national fraternities; 26% of women belong to 1 local and 4 national sororities. There are 210 groups on campus, including art, band, cheerleading, chess, choir, chorale, chorus, computers, dance, drama, ethnic, film, gay, honors, international, jazz band, literary magazine, marching band, musical theater, newspaper, orchestra, photography, political, professional, radio and TV, religious, social, social service, student government, symphony, and yearbook. Popular campus events include Campus Preview Weekend, Spring Weekend, and 2.70 Contest.

Sports: There are 24 intercollegiate sports for men and 15 for women, and 18 coed intramural sports for men and women. Athletic and recreation facilities include an athletic center with an indoor track, an ice rink, and an indoor swimming pool, a sailing pavilion and boat house, indoor and outdoor tennis courts, and softball diamonds.

Disabled Students: The following facilities are available: wheelchair ramps, elevators, special parking, specially equipped rest rooms, special class scheduling, lowered drinking fountains, lowered telephones, wheelchair lifts, and automatic doors.

Services: In addition to many counseling and information services, tutoring is available in every subject. There is also a reader service for the blind.

Campus Safety and Security: Campus safety and security measures include 24-hour foot and vehicle patrol, self-defense education, escort service, and shuttle buses. There are informal discussions, pamphlets/posters/films, emergency telephones, and lighted pathways/sidewalks.

Programs of Study: MIT confers the S.B. degree. Master's and doctoral degrees are also awarded. Bachelor's degrees are awarded in BIOLOGICAL SCIENCE (biology/biological science), BUSINESS (business administration and management), COMMUNICATIONS AND THE ARTS (literature, modern language, music, and technical and business writing), COMPUTER AND PHYSICAL SCIENCE (atmospheric sciences and meteorology, chemistry, computer science, earth science, mathematics, physics, planetary and space science, and science technology), ENGINEERING AND ENVIRONMENTAL DESIGN (aeronautical engineering, architecture, chemical engineering, civil engineering, electrical/electronics engineering, environmental engineering, materials engineering, mechanical engineering, nuclear engineering, and ocean engineering), SOCIAL SCIENCE (anthropology, cognitive science, economics, history, humanities, philosophy, political science/government, and urban studies). Architecture, management, and science are the strongest academically. Engineering has the largest enrollment.

Required: To graduate, students must fulfill General Institute Requirements, as well as writing and physical education requirements, and earn an additional 180 to 198 credit units, while fulfilling departmental program requirements. A 3.0 GPA on a scale of 5.0 should be maintained. The General Institute Requirements consist of 8 courses in humanities, arts, and social sciences, 6 in science, including chemistry, physics, calculus, and biology, science and technology electives, and 1 laboratory, for a total of 17 courses.

Special: MIT offers cross-registration with Wellesley and Harvard, cooperative programs, engineering internships, junior year abroad, work-study in on- and some off-campus research laboratories, accelerated degree programs and dual majors in all fields, and student-designed majors. A general studies degree, credit by examination, and pass/fail options are possible. Alternative programs are available to a limited number of freshmen, providing for smaller academic communities within MIT. There are 7 national honor societies on campus, including Phi Beta Kappa. 5 departments have honors programs.

Faculty/Classroom: 87% of faculty are male; 13%, female. All both teach and do research. No introductory courses are taught by graduate students.

Admissions: 27% of the 1995–96 applicants were accepted. The ACT scores for the 1995–96 freshman class were as follows: 8% between 24 and 26, 19% between 27 and 28, and 73% above 28. All of the current freshmen were in the top fifth of their class. 264 fresh-

men graduated first in their class. There were 129 National Merit Scholars.

Requirements: The SAT I or ACT is required, along with 3 SAT II: Subject tests, including mathematics, science, and writing/literature or history. 14 academic units are recommended, including 4 of English and mathematics, 3 of laboratory science, 2 of social studies, and 1 of foreign language. The GED is accepted. An essay, 2 teacher evaluations, and an interview are required. AP credits are accepted. Important factors in the admissions decision are extracurricular activities record, personality/intangible qualities, and parents or siblings attending the school.

Procedure: Freshmen are admitted in the fall. Entrance exams should be taken by January of the senior year. There are early action, early admissions, and deferred admissions plans. Early action applications should be filed by November 1; regular applications, by January 1 for fall entry, along with an application fee of $50. Notification of early decision is sent in late December; regular decision, April 1. 513 early action candidates were accepted for the 1995–96 class. A waiting list is an active part of the admissions procedure, with about 6% of all applicants on the list.

Transfer: 12 transfer students enrolled in 1995–96. Transfer applicants must have completed at least 2 terms of an accredited college, university, engineering school, or community college and be in good standing at the previously attended institution. They must have taken a year of college-level calculus and calculus-based physics and 1 semester each of biology and chemistry. They must also take or have taken 3 SAT II: Subject tests in mathematics, sciences, and writing, literature, or history. 3 terms must be completed at MIT.

Visiting: There are regularly scheduled orientations for prospective students, including daily tours followed by an information session with an admissions officer. Visitors may sit in on classes and stay overnight at the school. To schedule a visit, contact Robin Dey at (617) 258-5515.

Financial Aid: 61% of freshmen and 58% of continuing students received need-based aid in 1995–96. The average freshman award was $19,380. Of that total, scholarships or need-based grants averaged $11,230 ($29,600 maximum); loans averaged $6120 ($29,600 maximum); and work contracts averaged $2030. 60% of undergraduate students work part-time. Average earnings from campus work for the school year are $2100. The average financial indebtedness of the 1994–95 graduate was $18,714. MIT is a member of CSS. The FAF, FAFSA, the college's own financial statement, and tax returns are required. The application deadline for fall entry is January 19.

International Students: There are currently 340 international students enrolled. Students whose native language is not English may take the TOEFL in place of SAT I or the ACT and the SAT II: Subject test in writing, literature, or history. A 577 score is required on the TOEFL. Students must also take SAT II: Subject tests in mathematics and chemistry, physics, or biology.

Computers: The college provides computer facilities for student use. The mainframe is an IBM ES9000 Model 480. An Athena Computing Environment provides approximately 700 public workstations distributed across campus. Specialized departmental computing facilities are also available. Digital-network connections are provided to dormitory rooms and living groups. All students may access the system at all times. There are no time limits and no fees.

Graduates: In 1994–95, 1104 bachelor's degrees were awarded. The most popular majors among graduates were mechanical engineering (16%), electrical engineering (13%), and computer science (10%). Within an average freshman class, 2% graduate in 3 years, 80% in 4 years, 89% in 5 years, and 91% in 6 years. 440 companies recruited on campus in 1994–95.

Admissions Contact: Admissions Officers. A campus video is available.

MASSACHUSETTS MARITIME ACADEMY   E-4

Buzzards Bay, MA 02532-1803	(508) 830-5000; (800) 544-3411
Full-time: 670 men, 80 women	Faculty: 50; IIB, +$
Part-time: 17 men, 2 women	Ph.D.s: 70%
Graduate: none	Student/Faculty: 15 to 1
Year: semesters (see profile)	Tuition: $4340 ($9299)
Application Deadline: open	Room & Board: $3680
Freshman Class: 500 applied, 374 accepted, 232 enrolled	
SAT I or ACT: required	LESS COMPETITIVE

The Massachusetts Maritime Academy, founded in 1891, is a public, coeducational institution that prepares graduates for qualification as officers in the U.S. Merchant Marine, U.S. Coast Guard, or U.S. Naval Reserve. A 6- to 8-week winter sea term involves the majority of students in a professional setting with travel to foreign countries included. The library contains 40,171 volumes, 11,674 microform items, and 1113 audiovisual forms, and subscribes to 505 periodicals. Computerized library sources and services include interlibrary loans and database searching. Special learning facilities include a planetarium, a full bridge-training simulator, an oil-spill management simulator, and a liquid cargo-handling simulator. The 55-acre campus is in a small town 60 miles south of Boston. Including residence halls, there are 9 buildings on campus.

Student Life: 72% of undergraduates are from Massachusetts. Students come from 26 states and 11 foreign countries. 73% are from public schools; 27% from private. 90% are white. The average age of freshmen is 18; all undergraduates, 21. 15% do not continue beyond their first year; 70% remain to graduate.

Housing: 800 students can be accommodated in college housing. College-sponsored living facilities include coed dormitories. On-campus housing is guaranteed for all 4 years. 97% of students live on campus; of those, 25% remain on campus on weekends. Alcohol is not permitted. All students may keep cars on campus.

Activities: There are no fraternities or sororities. There are 15 groups on campus, including band, choir, computers, drill team, jazz band, marching band, newspaper, photography, professional, religious, social service, student government, and yearbook. Popular campus events include Homecoming and Ring Dance.

Sports: There are 7 intercollegiate sports for men and 3 for women, and 13 intramural sports for men and 2 for women. Athletic and recreation facilities include football and baseball fields, a pistol range, outdoor tennis and basketball courts, a sailing center, an Olympic-size swimming pool, 2 weight rooms, 3 multipurpose handball courts, and wrestling courts and fitness rooms. An indoor gymnasium/auditorium seats 2500.

Disabled Students: 75% of the campus is accessible to disabled students. The following facilities are available: wheelchair ramps, elevators, special parking, and specially equipped rest rooms.

Services: In addition to many counseling and information services, tutoring is available in most subjects.

Campus Safety and Security: Campus safety and security measures include 24-hour foot and vehicle patrol and lighted pathways/sidewalks.

Programs of Study: MMA confers the B.S. degree. Bachelor's degrees are awarded in BUSINESS (transportation management) and ENGINEERING AND ENVIRONMENTAL DESIGN (environmental engineering, industrial engineering, and marine engineering). Marine engineering is the strongest academically and has the largest enrollment.

Required: All students must complete 164 credit hours with a minimum of 60 hours in the major and a minimum GPA of 2.0. Requirements include 4 courses in physical education, 2 each in chemistry and naval science, and 1 each in algebra/trigonometry, introduction to computers, English composition, American literature, Western civilization, economics, analysis, American government, first aid, admiralty law, introduction to marine transportation, introduction to marine engineering, sea term/deck, sea term/engine, and calculus.

Special: MMA offers a junior-year internship in a commercial shipping program. Educational experience includes a minimum of 120 days aboard a training ship, with visits to foreign ports. There are cooperative programs in facilities and plant engineering and in marine safety and environmental protection. A dual major is available in marine engineering and marine transportation.

Faculty/Classroom: 96% of faculty are male; 4%, female. 98% teach undergraduates and 3% do research. The average class size in an introductory lecture is 25; in a laboratory, 12; and in a regular course offering, 22.

Admissions: 75% of the 1995–96 applicants were accepted.

Requirements: The SAT I or ACT is required. Applicants must have graduated from an accredited secondary school or hold a GED certificate. They should have completed 16 Carnegie units, including 4 in English, 3 in mathematics, and 2 each in a foreign language, science, and social science. An essay is required, and an interview is strongly recommended. AP and CLEP credits are accepted. Important factors in the admissions decision are advanced placement or honor courses, recommendations by school officials, and extracurricular activities record.

Procedure: Freshmen are admitted in the fall. There are early decision and deferred admissions plans. Early decision applications should be filed by November 1; regular application deadlines are open. Notification is sent on a rolling basis.

Transfer: 65 transfer students enrolled in 1995–96. Students must have a minimum GPA of 2.0. 30 credits of 164 must be completed at MMA.

Visiting: There are regularly scheduled orientations for prospective students, including a campus tour and an admissions interview. There are guides for informal visits and visitors may sit in on classes and stay overnight at the school. To schedule a visit, contact Lieutenant Commander Fulgueras.

Financial Aid: In a recent year, 80% of all freshmen and 60% of continuing students received some form of financial aid. Loans averaged $200 ($2625 maximum) and work contracts averaged $500 ($1000 maximum). MMA is a member of CSS. The FAF, FAFSA, and the academy's own financial statement are required. The application deadline for fall entry is May 1.

International Students: There are currently 20 international students enrolled. They must take the TOEFL and achieve a minimum score of 500. The student must also take the SAT I or the ACT.

Computers: The academy provides computer facilities for student use. The mainframe is a CDC Cyber 172. Microcomputers are provided for student use in the computer laboratory and dormitory. All students may access the system from 8 A.M. to 11 P.M. There are no time limits and no fees.

Graduates: In a recent year, 130 bachelor's degrees were awarded. Within an average freshman class, 70% graduate in 4 years. 60 companies recruited on campus.

Admissions Contact: Keith D. Rabine, Dean of Enrollment Services. A campus video is available.

MERRIMACK COLLEGE   E-2

North Andover, MA 01845   (508) 837–5100; FAX: (508) 837–5222

Full-time: 911 men, 942 women	**Faculty:** 126; IIB, av$
Part-time: 411 men, 450 women	**Ph.D.s:** 67%
Graduate: none	**Student/Faculty:** 15 to 1
Year: semesters, summer session	**Tuition:** $13,350
Application Deadline: March 1	**Room & Board:** $6600
Freshman Class: 2100 applied, 1600 accepted, 500 enrolled	
SAT I Verbal/Math: 440/450	**ACT:** 23 **COMPETITIVE**

Merrimack College, founded in 1947 by the Augustinian clergy of the Roman Catholic Church, offers undergraduate programs in science, engineering, business administration, and liberal arts. In addition to regional accreditation, Merrimack has baccalaureate program accreditation with ABET. The library contains 150,000 volumes, 7200 microform items, and 1000 audiovisual forms, and subscribes to 900 periodicals. Computerized library sources and services include the card catalog, interlibrary loans, and database searching. Special learning facilities include a learning resource center, art gallery, planetarium, TV station, the National Microscale Chemistry Center, and the Urban Institute. The 220-acre campus is in a suburban area 25 miles north of Boston. Including residence halls, there are 32 buildings on campus.

Student Life: 70% of undergraduates are from Massachusetts. Students come from 23 states, 18 foreign countries, and Canada. 60% are from public schools; 40% from private. 95% are white. 75% are Catholic; 15% Protestant. The average age of freshmen is 18; all undergraduates, 20. 10% do not continue beyond their first year; 70% remain to graduate.

Housing: 1171 students can be accommodated in college housing. College-sponsored living facilities include single-sex and coed dormitories and on-campus apartments. In addition there are special interest houses and international, wellness, and engineering houses. On-campus housing is guaranteed for all 4 years. 53% of students live on campus; of those, 75% remain on campus on weekends. Alcohol is not permitted. All students may keep cars on campus.

Activities: 10% of men belong to 5 local fraternities; 5% of women belong to 3 local sororities. There are 43 groups on campus, including art, cheerleading, chess, chorale, chorus, computers, dance, drama, ethnic, international, literary magazine, musical theater, newspaper, photography, political, radio and TV, religious, social, social service, student government, and yearbook. Popular campus events include Autumn Interlude, Springfest, Greek Week, and Family Weekend.

Sports: There are 8 intercollegiate sports for men and 8 for women, and 13 intramural sports for men and 13 for women. Athletic and recreation facilities include an athletic complex with a wide variety of facilities including an ice rink, basketball and racquetball courts, an aerobics studio, and a well-equipped exercise room. The outdoor facilities include 2 sets of tennis courts and baseball, softball, soccer, lacrosse, and field hockey fields.

Disabled Students: All of the campus is accessible to disabled students. The following facilities are available: wheelchair ramps, elevators, special parking, specially equipped rest rooms, special class scheduling, lowered drinking fountains, and lowered telephones.

Services: In addition to many counseling and information services, tutoring is available in every subject. There are mathematics, science, and writing resource centers available to all students.

Campus Safety and Security: Campus safety and security measures include 24-hour foot and vehicle patrol, escort service, informal discussions, and pamphlets/posters/films. In addition, there are emergency telephones and lighted pathways/sidewalks.

Programs of Study: Merrimack confers B.A. and B.S. degrees. Bachelor's degrees are awarded in BIOLOGICAL SCIENCE (biochemistry and biology/biological science), BUSINESS (accounting, business administration and management, business economics, international business management, and marketing/retailing/merchandising), COMMUNICATIONS AND THE ARTS (English and modern language), COMPUTER AND PHYSICAL SCIENCE (chemistry, computer science, mathematics, and physics), EDUCATION (elementary, science, and secondary), ENGINEERING AND ENVIRON-

MENTAL DESIGN (civil engineering, computer engineering, electrical/electronics engineering, engineering, and environmental science), HEALTH PROFESSIONS (allied health, predentistry, and premedicine), SOCIAL SCIENCE (economics, history, philosophy, political science/government, prelaw, psychology, religion, and sociology). Science, engineering, and business are the strongest academically. Business, psychology, and liberal arts have the largest enrollments.

Required: All students are required to emphasize liberal arts with a variety of courses that must include 3 each in humanities, social science, and mathematics and science, 2 each in theology and philosophy, and 1 each in English composition and freshman seminar. Students also must maintain a minimum GPA of 2.0 while taking a total of 120 credit hours.

Special: Merrimack offers cooperative programs in business, engineering, and computer science, cross-registration through the Northeast consortium, internships in all arts and science programs, study abroad in numerous countries, and a Washington semester at American University. Work-study programs, a 5-year combined B.A.-B.S. degree in many major fields, and dual and self-designed majors are available. General studies, nondegree study, and pass/fail options are possible.

Faculty/Classroom: 72% of faculty are male; 28%, female. All teach undergraduates. The average class size in an introductory lecture is 25; in a laboratory, 20; and in a regular course offering, 15.

Admissions: 76% of the 1995–96 applicants were accepted. The SAT I scores for the 1995–96 freshman class were as follows: Verbal—75% below 500, 20% between 500 and 599, and 5% between 600 and 700; Math—72% below 500, 25% between 500 and 599, and 2% between 600 and 700. The ACT scores were 70% below 21, 25% between 21 and 23, and 5% between 24 and 26. 40% of the current freshmen were in the top fifth of their class; 75% were in the top two fifths. 7 freshmen graduated first in their class.

Requirements: The SAT I or ACT is required. Merrimack requires applicants to be in the upper 50% of their class. A minimum GPA of 2.5 is required. For business administration, humanities, and social science majors, Merrimack recommends that applicants complete 4 units of English, 3 of mathematics, 2 of social studies, and 1 of science. For other majors, an additional mathematics course and 2 additional courses in science are needed. An essay is required and an interview is recommended. Applicants should have completed 16 Carnegie units. Applications are accepted on computer disk and online via ExPAN, Mac Apply, and CollegeLink. AP and CLEP credits are accepted. Important factors in the admissions decision are advanced placement or honor courses, recommendations by school officials, and leadership record.

Procedure: Freshmen are admitted fall and spring. Entrance exams should be taken during the spring of the junior year and the fall of the senior year. There are early decision, early admissions, and deferred admissions plans. Early decision applications should be filed by November 30; regular applications, by March 1 for fall entry and December 1 for spring entry, along with an application fee of $40. Notification of early decision is sent by December 15; regular decision, from January 15 to April 15. 27 early decision candidates were accepted for a recent class.

Transfer: 120 transfer students enrolled in a recent year. Transfer applicants must have maintained a minimum 2.0 GPA while accumulating 30 credits. The SAT I, an interview, and a letter of recommendation are recommended. 60 credits of 120 must be completed at Merrimack.

Visiting: There are regularly scheduled orientations for prospective students, including 10 information sessions on Saturdays in the fall and 4 financial aid information sessions throughout the year. There are guides for informal visits and visitors may sit in on classes and stay overnight at the school. To schedule a visit, contact the Office of Admissions.

Financial Aid: In a recent year, 82% of all freshmen and 65% of continuing students received some form of financial aid. 63% of freshmen and 52% of continuing students received need-based aid. The average freshman award was $10,107. Of that total, scholarships or need-based grants averaged $7300 ($17,800 maximum); loans averaged $1500 ($4125 maximum); and work contracts averaged $1000 ($2000 maximum). 68% of undergraduate students work part-time. Average earnings from campus work for the school year are $1300. The average financial indebtedness of a recent graduate was $15,715. Merrimack is a member of CSS. The FAFSA and CSS Profile Application are required. The application deadline for fall entry is March 1.

International Students: There were 35 international students enrolled in a recent year. The school actively recruits these students. They must take the TOEFL and achieve a minimum score of 550.

Computers: The college provides computer facilities for student use. The mainframe is a DEC VAX 11/785. Microcomputers for academic use are available in the library, classrooms, and dormitories. All students may access the system. There are no time limits and no fees.

Merrimack recommends students have Macintosh or IBM-compatible PCs.

Graduates: In a recent year, 571 bachelor's degrees were awarded. The most popular majors among graduates were marketing (14%), psychology (9%), and English (7%). Within an average freshman class, 70% graduate in 4 years, 75% in 5 years, and 80% in 6 years. 265 companies recruited on campus in a recent year.

Admissions Contact: Mary Lou Retelle, Dean of Admission and Financial Aid.

MONTSERRAT COLLEGE OF ART   E-2
Beverly, MA 01915   (508) 921-2350
          (800) 836-0487; FAX: (508) 922-4268

Full-time: 149 men, 123 women	Faculty: 13
Part-time: 14 men, 26 women	Ph.Ds: 54%
Graduate: none	Student/Faculty: 21 to 1
Year: terms	Tuition: $9730
Application Deadline: open	Room & Board: $4500
Freshman Class: 281 applied, 256 accepted, 101 enrolled	
SAT I: required	ACT: recommended SPECIAL

Montserrat College of Art, founded in 1970, is an independent, private professional college of art and design offering bachelor's degrees in painting and drawing, printmaking, graphic design, illustration, photography, sculpture, and certification in art education. In addition to regional accreditation, Montserrat has baccalaureate program accreditation with NASAD. The library contains 12,000 volumes and 100 audiovisual forms, and subscribes to 55 periodicals. Computerized library sources and services include the card catalog, interlibrary loans, and database searching. Special learning facilities include a learning resource center and art gallery. The 10-acre campus is in a suburban area 26 miles north of Boston. Including residence halls, there are 9 buildings on campus.

Student Life: 56% of undergraduates are from Massachusetts. Students come from 17 states, 8 foreign countries, and Canada. 93% are white. The average age of freshmen is 19; all undergraduates, 23. 10% do not continue beyond their first year; 46% remain to graduate.

Housing: 150 students can be accommodated in college housing. College-sponsored living facilities include single-sex and coed off-campus apartments. In addition there are special interest houses and and smoke-free buildings. On-campus housing is guaranteed for the freshman year only, is available on a first-come, first-served basis, and is available on a lottery system for upperclassmen. Priority is given to out-of-town students. 50% of students live on campus; of those, 30% remain on campus on weekends. Alcohol is not permitted. All students may keep cars on campus.

Activities: There are no fraternities or sororities. There are some groups and organizations on campus, including art, literary magazine, newspaper, social, and student government. Popular campus events include Forum Days, year-end picnic, and gallery openings.

Sports: There is no sports program at Montserrat.

Disabled Students: 50% of the campus is accessible to disabled students. The following facilities are available: elevators, special parking, and specially equipped rest rooms. All rooms are accessible to persons in wheelchairs.

Services: In addition to many counseling and information services, tutoring is available in every subject.

Campus Safety and Security: Campus safety and security measures include self-defense education, informal discussions, pamphlets/posters/films, and emergency telephones.

Programs of Study: Montserrat confers the B.F.A. degree. Bachelor's degrees are awarded in COMMUNICATIONS AND THE ARTS (fine arts, graphic design, illustration, painting, photography, printmaking, and sculpture).

Required: All students are required to take at least 78 credits in studio courses, and the freshman program or equivalent, which includes 42 liberal arts credits for a total of 120 credits. To enter the senior program, Montserrat students must have a portfolio. During semester-end evaluations, each student displays work from all courses and is evaluated by a faculty panel.

Special: Montserrat is a member of the Northeast Consortium of Colleges and Universities in Massachusetts, which allows students to take classes at any member college for the same cost. Credit study is available through the continuing education department. In addition, internships, study abroad in Italy, and dual majors are available. Students can also participate in a mobility program through the Association of Independent Colleges of Art and Design.

Faculty/Classroom: 52% of faculty are male; 48%, female. The average class size in an introductory lecture is 20 and in a regular course offering, 18.

Admissions: 91% of the 1995–96 applicants were accepted. 3 freshmen graduated first in their class.

Requirements: The SAT I is required and the ACT is recommended. A minimum GPA of 2.0 is required. Applicants must submit a statement of purpose, a portfolio, and a high school degree, although no specific program is required. A portfolio interview is generally required. AP credits are accepted. Important factors in the admissions decision are evidence of special talent and advanced placement or honor courses.

Procedure: Freshmen are admitted in the fall and winter. There is a deferred admissions plan. Application deadlines are open. Application fee is $30. Notification is sent on a rolling basis.

Transfer: 30 transfer students enrolled in 1995–96. Applicants are required to submit a portfolio, transcripts from a previous college, and a statement of purpose. They also must be interviewed. 60 credits of 120 must be completed at Montserrat.

Visiting: There are regularly scheduled orientations for prospective students, including tours of college studios, observation of classes, and portfolio consultations. There are guides for informal visits and visitors may sit in on classes. To schedule a visit, contact Lena Hill, Admissions Secretary.

Financial Aid: In 1995–96, 60% of all freshmen and 80% of continuing students received some form of financial aid. 55% of freshmen and 75% of continuing students received need-based aid. The average freshman award was $4825. Of that total, scholarships or need-based grants averaged $1400 ($3000 maximum); loans averaged $2625 (maximum); and work contracts averaged $800 ($1000 maximum). 10% of undergraduate students work part-time. Average earnings from campus work for the school year are $800. The average financial indebtedness of the 1994–95 graduate was $10,300. Montserrat is a member of CSS. The FAFSA and FAF are required. The application deadline for fall entry is April 15.

International Students: There are currently 12 international students enrolled. The school actively recruits these students. They must take the TOEFL and achieve a minimum score of 500. The applicant must also take the SAT I or the ACT, with a score of 480 on SAT I verbal.

Computers: The college provides computer facilities for student use. The graphic design department provides 27 Apple Macintosh computers, digital photography capabilities, and CD-ROM. Students enrolled in graphic design or photography courses may access the system 8 A.M. to 11 P.M. daily. There are no time limits and no fees.

Graduates: In 1994–95, 40 bachelor's degrees were awarded. The most popular majors among graduates were fine arts (52%), graphic design (25%), and illustration (23%). Of the 1994 graduating class, 1% were enrolled in graduate school within 6 months of graduation and 31% had found employment.

Admissions Contact: Carol Lee Conchar, Director of Admissions.

MOUNT HOLYOKE COLLEGE
B-3
South Hadley, MA 01075 (413) 538-2023; FAX: (413) 538-2409

Full-time: 1848 women	Faculty: 181; IIB, + +$
Part-time: 36 women	Ph.D.s: 96%
Graduate: 11 women	Student/Faculty: 10 to 1
Year: 4-1-4	Tuition: $20,290
Application Deadline: January 15	Room & Board: $5950
Freshman Class: 2033 applied, 1328 accepted, 500 enrolled	
SAT I Verbal/Math: 553/588	ACT: 26　HIGHLY COMPETITIVE

Mount Holyoke, founded in 1837, is one of the oldest institutions of higher learning for women in the United States. An independent, liberal arts college, it affords students great freedom in selecting course studies. The library contains 623,336 volumes, 15,120 microform items, and 4411 audiovisual forms, and subscribes to 1800 periodicals. Special learning facilities include a learning resource center, art gallery, radio station, observatory, child study and language centers, and arboretum. The 800-acre campus is in a small town 90 miles west of Boston and 160 miles north of New York City. Including residence halls, there are 40 buildings on campus.

Student Life: 78% of undergraduates are from out-of-state, mostly the Northeast. Students come from 49 states, 55 foreign countries, and Canada. 68% are from public schools; 24% from private. 71% are white; 13% foreign nationals. The average age of freshmen is 18; all undergraduates, 20. 5% do not continue beyond their first year; 85% remain to graduate.

Housing: 1871 students can be accommodated in college housing. College-sponsored living facilities include dormitories. In addition, there is a language house. On-campus housing is guaranteed for all 4 years. 99% of students live on campus. All students may keep cars on campus.

Activities: There are no sororities. There are 70 groups on campus, including art, band, choir, chorale, chorus, computers, dance, drama, ethnic, film, gay, honors, international, literary magazine, musical theater, newspaper, orchestra, photography, political, radio and TV, religious, social, social service, student government, symphony, and yearbook. Popular campus events include Festival of Diversity, Glascock Intercollegiate Poetry Contest, Las Vegas Night, and the Junior Show.

Sports: There are 15 intercollegiate and 7 intramural sports. Athletic and recreation facilities include a sports complex area with indoor and outdoor tracks, playing fields, basketball, racquetball, squash, and volleyball courts, a dance studio, weight training rooms, a 25-meter, 8-lane swimming pool, a diving pool, a hydra-gymnasium, an equestrian center, an 18-hole golf course, field and canoe houses, a 2500-seat amphitheater, and 6 indoor tennis courts.

Disabled Students: The following facilities are available: wheelchair ramps, elevators, special parking, specially equipped rest rooms, and special class scheduling.

Services: In addition to many counseling and information services, tutoring is available in every subject. There is a reader service for the blind. The Writing Center helps students at all levels.

Campus Safety and Security: Campus safety and security measures include 24-hour foot and vehicle patrol, self-defense education, escort service, and shuttle buses. In addition, there are pamphlets/posters/films, emergency telephones, and lighted pathways/sidewalks.

Programs of Study: Mount Holyoke confers the B.A. degree. Master's and doctoral degrees are also awarded. Bachelor's degrees are awarded in BIOLOGICAL SCIENCE (biochemistry and biology/biological science), COMMUNICATIONS AND THE ARTS (art history and appreciation, classical languages, dance, dramatic arts, English, French, German, Greek, Italian, Latin, music, romance languages, Russian, Spanish, and studio art), COMPUTER AND PHYSICAL SCIENCE (astronomy, chemistry, computer science, geology, mathematics, physics, and statistics), EDUCATION (bilingual/bicultural, early childhood, elementary, mathematics, science, and social science), SOCIAL SCIENCE (African American studies, American studies, anthropology, Asian/Oriental studies, economics, European studies, geography, history, international relations, Judaic studies, Latin American studies, medieval studies, philosophy, political science/government, psychobiology, psychology, religion, sociology, and women's studies). Sciences and mathematics are the strongest academically. English, politics, and biology have the largest enrollments.

Required: Students must maintain a minimum GPA of 2.0 while taking 128 total credits, with 32 to 46 in the major. Students must complete 2 courses each in the humanities, science/mathematics, and social studies, course work in a foreign language, a course with multicultural perspective, and 6 credits in physical education. A minor field of study is necessary for those not pursuing a double major.

Special: Mount Holyoke offers students cross-registration through a 12- and 5-college exchange plan. Internships, including those in science and international studies, study abroad in 16 countries, a Washington semester, work-study, student-designed majors, dual majors, a January program, B.A-B.S and accelerated degrees, nondegree study, and pass/fail options also are offered. The school, in addition, emphasizes humanities and mathematics. There is a 3–2 engineering degree available with Dartmouth College. There is a freshman honors program on campus, as well as 2 national honor societies, including Phi Beta Kappa.

Faculty/Classroom: 50% of faculty are male; 50%, female. All teach undergraduates. No introductory courses are taught by graduate students. The average class size in a laboratory is 12 and in a regular course offering, 15.

Admissions: 65% of the 1995–96 applicants were accepted. The SAT I scores for the 1995–96 freshman class were as follows: Verbal—27% below 500, 42% between 500 and 599, 26% between 600 and 700, and 5% above 700; Math—16% below 500, 36% between 500 and 599, 37% between 600 and 700, and 11% above 700. 83% of the current freshmen were in the top fifth of their class; 98% were in the top two fifths. There were 5 National Merit finalists. 19 freshmen graduated first in their class.

Requirements: The SAT I or ACT is required. Three SAT II: Subject tests, with 1 in writing, are required. The school recommends that applicants have 4 years each of English and foreign language, 3 each of mathematics and science, and 2 of social studies. An essay is required and an interview is strongly recommended. AP credits are accepted.

Procedure: Freshmen are admitted in the fall. Entrance exams should be taken before the application deadline. There are early decision, early admissions, and deferred admissions plans. Early decision applications should be filed by December 1 or January 1; regular applications, by January 15 for fall entry, along with an application fee of $50. Notification of early decision is sent January 1 or February 1; regular decision, April 1. 97 early decision candidates were accepted for the 1995–96 class. A waiting list is an active part of the admissions procedure, with about 8% of all applicants on the list.

Transfer: 45 transfer students enrolled in 1995–96. A minimum GPA of 3.0, SAT I scores, transcripts of secondary school or college-level work, an interview, and an essay are required of applicants. 64 credits of 128 must be completed at Mount Holyoke.

Visiting: There are regularly scheduled orientations for prospective students. There are guides for informal visits and visitors may sit in on classes and stay overnight at the school. To schedule a visit, contact the Admissions Office.

Financial Aid: In a recent year, 69% of all freshmen and 71% of continuing students received some form of financial aid, including need-based aid. The average freshman award was $18,100. Of that total, scholarships or need-based grants averaged $9000 ($14,200 maximum); loans averaged $2400 ($2500 maximum); and work contracts averaged $1300 ($1400 maximum). 60% of undergraduate students work part-time. Average earnings from campus work for the school year are $925. The average financial indebtedness of a recent graduate was $9400. Mount Holyoke is a member of CSS. The FAF, FAFSA, college's own financial statement, and parent and student tax returns are required. The application deadline for fall entry is February 1.

International Students: There are currently 243 international students enrolled. The school actively recruits these students. They must take the TOEFL if English is not their first language and achieve a minimum score of 600. The student must also take the SAT I and 3 SAT II: Subject tests, with 1 in writing, or the ACT alone.

Computers: The college provides computer facilities for student use. The mainframes are a DEC MicroVAX and a Sun system. A computer center houses several laboratories containing various PCs and workstations. There are 4 other laboratories distributed elsewhere. Most residence halls contain word-processing facilities with 3 to 6 computers. The mainframes may be accessed via PCs connected to Ethernet or by modem. Network connections beyond the campus are through a DECnet to neighbor schools and through Bitnet and Internet to the world. All students may access the system. There are no time limits and no fees.

Graduates: In 1994–95, 501 bachelor's degrees were awarded. The most popular majors among graduates were English (14%), biological science (12%), and psychology (7%). 100 companies recruited on campus in 1994–95.

Admissions Contact: Anita Smith, Director of Admissions. A campus video is available.

MOUNT IDA COLLEGE

Newton Center, MA 02159 (617) 928-4506; FAX: (617) 928-4760

D-2

Full-time: 644 men, 945 women	Faculty: 66
Part-time: 131 men, 297 women	Ph.Ds: 25%
Graduate: none	Student/Faculty: 24 to 1
Year: semesters, summer session	Tuition: $10,888
Application Deadline: open	Room & Board: $7718
Freshman Class: 4800 applied, 4000 accepted, 830 enrolled	
SAT I: recommended	LESS COMPETITIVE

Mount Ida College, founded in 1899, is a private, liberal arts institution offering associate degrees in more than 40 programs that transfer to the school's senior college division's 4-year program. In addition to regional accreditation, Mount Ida has baccalaureate program accreditation with ABFSE, ADA, and FIDER. The 2 libraries contain 62,500 volumes, 68 microform items, and 2000 audiovisual forms, and subscribe to 530 periodicals. Computerized library sources and services include the card catalog, interlibrary loans, and database searching. Special learning facilities include a learning resource center, radio station, TV station, a communication laboratory, dark room, sewing rooms, a blueprint-making facility, and optical and dental laboratories. The 85-acre campus is in a suburban area 8 miles west of Boston. Including residence halls, there are 18 buildings on campus.

Student Life: 50% of undergraduates are from out-of-state, mostly the Northeast. Students come from 27 states, 41 foreign countries, and Canada. 80% are from public schools. 74% are white; 10% African American. The average age of freshmen is 18; all undergraduates, 19. 20% do not continue beyond their first year; 60% remain to graduate.

Housing: 850 students can be accommodated in college housing. College-sponsored living facilities include single-sex and coed dormitories. In addition, there are honors houses. On-campus housing is guaranteed for all 4 years. 50% of students live on campus; of those, 60% remain on campus on weekends. All students may keep cars on campus.

Activities: 3% of men belong to 1 national fraternity; 3% of women belong to 1 national sorority. There are 25 groups on campus, including cheerleading, chess, choir, drama, commuter council, dental, equestrian, ethnic, fashion, honors, international, literary magazine, newspaper, professional, radio and TV, residence hall council, social, student government, travel, veterinary technician, and yearbook. Popular campus events include a fashion show, formal dances, senior week, and Spring Fling.

Sports: There are 4 intercollegiate sports for men and 4 for women, and 10 intramural sports for men and 10 for women. Athletic and recreation facilities include a gymnasium, playing fields, and a new fitness center.

Disabled Students: 75% of the campus is accessible to disabled students. The following facilities are available: wheelchair ramps, elevators, special parking, specially equipped rest rooms, and special class scheduling.

Services: In addition to many counseling and information services, tutoring is available in most subjects. There is also a program for learning disabled students, for which a fee is charged. Studies skills courses are also available.

Campus Safety and Security: Campus safety and security measures include 24-hour foot and vehicle patrol, self-defense education, escort service, and shuttle buses. In addition, there are informal discussions, pamphlets/posters/films, and lighted pathways/sidewalks.

Programs of Study: Mount Ida confers B.A., B.S., and B.L.S. degrees. Associate degrees are also awarded. Bachelor's degrees are awarded in AGRICULTURE (equine science), BUSINESS (business administration and management, fashion merchandising, funeral home services, hospitality management services, retailing, and small business management), COMMUNICATIONS AND THE ARTS (graphic design, journalism, and media arts), EDUCATION (early childhood), ENGINEERING AND ENVIRONMENTAL DESIGN (interior design), HEALTH PROFESSIONS (veterinary science), SOCIAL SCIENCE (counseling psychology, criminal justice, fashion design and technology, liberal arts/general studies, and public administration). Veterinary technology is the strongest academically. Liberal arts studies and occupational therapy assistant have the largest enrollments.

Required: Candidates for a bachelor's degree require 128 credits with a 2.0 GPA. All students in the junior college must complete a freshman core and physical education requirement.

Special: Internships in the form of work experience are available in each department. Work-study provided by the college, student-designed majors, study abroad in England and France, a general studies degree, an interdisciplinary major in legal studies, nondegree study, and a combined B.A.-B.S. degree also are available. There is a freshman honors program on campus, as well as 2 national honor societies, including Phi Beta Kappa. 5 departments have honors programs.

Faculty/Classroom: 41% of faculty are male; 59%, female. The average class size in an introductory lecture is 25; in a laboratory, 16; and in a regular course offering, 20.

Admissions: 83% of the 1995–96 applicants were accepted.

Requirements: The SAT I is recommended. Applicants are required to have 4 units of English, 3 of social studies, and 2 each of mathematics and science. A portfolio is recommended for certain programs, an interview for all applicants. The GED is accepted. CLEP credit is accepted. Important factors in the admissions decision are recommendations by school officials, evidence of special talent, and extracurricular activities record.

Procedure: Freshmen are admitted in the fall and spring. Entrance exams should be taken as early as possible. There are early admissions and deferred admissions plans. Application deadlines are open. Application fee is $25. Notification is sent on a rolling basis.

Transfer: 193 transfer students enrolled in 1995–96. Transfer students need a minimum GPA of C, and must submit college and high school transcripts. 32 credits of 128 must be completed at Mount Ida.

Visiting: There are regularly scheduled orientations for prospective students, consisting of fall and spring open houses. There are guides for informal visits and visitors may sit in on classes. To schedule a visit, contact the Admissions Office at (617) 928-4506.

Financial Aid: In 1995–96, 70% of all freshmen and 60% of continuing students received some form of financial aid. 70% of freshmen and 60% of continuing students received need-based aid. The average freshman award was $7000. Of that total, scholarships or need-based grants averaged $3000 ($7000 maximum); state scholarships averaged $1000 ($2300 maximum); loans averaged $3500 ($5500 maximum); and work contracts averaged $1500. 65% of undergraduate students work part-time. Average earnings from campus work for the school year are $1500. The average financial indebtedness of the 1994–95 graduate was $6000. The FAF, the college's own financial statement, and tax returns are required. The application deadline for fall entry is September 13.

International Students: There are currently 220 international students enrolled. The school actively recruits these students. They must take the TOEFL.

Computers: The college provides computer facilities for student use. The mainframe is an IBM AS 400. There are 80 microcomputers for student use, including IBM and Apple Macintosh. World Wide Web terminals are also available. All students may access the system. There are no time limits and no fees.

Graduates: In 1994–95, 90 bachelor's degrees were awarded. The most popular majors among graduates were occupational therapy assistant (12%), liberal studies (10%), and veterinary technology (8%). 40 companies recruited on campus in 1994–95.

Admissions Contact: Harold Duvall or Judy Kaufmann, Co-Directors of Admissions.

NEW ENGLAND CONSERVATORY OF MUSIC   E-2
Boston, MA 02115   (617) 262-1120, ext. 431

Full-time: 150 men, 170 women	Faculty: 54
Part-time: 20 men, 40 women	Ph.D.s: 22%
Graduate: 150 men, 220 women	Student/Faculty: 6 to 1
Year: semesters	Tuition: $15,000
Application Deadline: see profile	Room & Board: $7000
Freshman Class: n/av	
SAT I or ACT: required	SPECIAL

The New England Conservatory of Music, founded in 1867, is the oldest private school of its kind in the United States. It combines classroom study of music with an emphasis on performance for talented young musicians. There is 1 graduate school. Figures given in the above capsule are approximate. In addition to regional accreditation, NEC has baccalaureate program accreditation with NASM. The 3 libraries contain 70,000 volumes, 500 microform items, and 20,000 audiovisual forms, and subscribe to 250 periodicals. Computerized library sources and services include interlibrary loans. Special learning facilities include an electronic music studio. The 8-acre campus is in an urban area 2 miles south of downtown Boston. Including residence halls, there are 4 buildings on campus.

Student Life: 71% of undergraduates are from out-of-state, mostly the Northeast. Students come from 42 states, 32 foreign countries, and Canada. 75% are from public schools. 50% are white; 10% foreign nationals. The average age of freshmen is 18; all undergraduates, 21.

Housing: 168 students can be accommodated in college housing. College-sponsored living facilities include coed dormitories. On-campus housing is guaranteed for the freshman year only. Alcohol is not permitted. All students may keep cars on campus.

Activities: 3% of men belong to fraternities; 2% of women belong to 1 national sorority. There are 12 groups on campus, including band, choir, chorale, chorus, computers, jazz band, opera, orchestra, political, religious, student government, and symphony. Popular campus events include the NEC/Juilliard Hockey Match, NEC concerts, the Halloween Dance, and GradFest.

Disabled Students: The following facilities are available: elevators, special parking, specially equipped rest rooms, and lowered drinking fountains.

Services: In addition to many counseling and information services, tutoring is available in most subjects.

Campus Safety and Security: Campus safety and security measures include escort service and 24-hour security at the residence hall.

Programs of Study: NEC confers the B.Mus. degree. Master's and doctoral degrees are also awarded. Bachelor's degrees are awarded in COMMUNICATIONS AND THE ARTS (applied music, jazz, music, music history and appreciation, music performance, music theory and composition, and visual and performing arts), EDUCATION (music).

Required: Requirements for graduation include a minimum 2.0 GPA and an average of 120 total credits, including at least 14 in music education.

Special: NEC offers cross-registration with Northeastern and Tufts universities and Simmons College, a 5-year, double-degree program with Tufts, a double major combining a performance major with a nonperformance area, and a diploma program in which students can focus on studio instruction in instruments or voice. Work-study also is possible, along with pass/fail options in ensemble work or recitals.

Faculty/Classroom: 72% of faculty are male; 28%, female. The average class size in an introductory lecture is 30 and in a regular course offering, 15.

Requirements: The SAT I or ACT is required. In addition, applicants must be graduates of an accredited secondary school or have a GED. An essay is required, as is an audition after submitting the formal application. In some cases, taped auditions are accepted; these must be submitted with the admissions application. Applicants are expected to have reached an advanced level of performance accomplishment. AP and CLEP credits are accepted. Evidence of special talent is an important factor in the admissions decision.

Procedure: Freshmen are admitted to all sessions. There is a deferred admissions plan. Check with the school for current application deadlines and fee. A waiting list is an active part of the admissions procedure.

Transfer: 24 transfer students enrolled in a recent year. Students must audition and submit all college-level transcripts and a transfer statement. 60 credits of 120 must be completed at NEC.

Visiting: There are regularly scheduled orientations for prospective students, consisting of a full range of scheduled events on audition days. Visitors may sit in on classes. To schedule a visit, contact the Admissions Office.

Financial Aid: In a recent year, 56% of all freshmen and 80% of continuing students received some form of financial aid. Scholarships or need-based grants averaged $6850; loans averaged $2500

($4000 maximum); and work contracts averaged $1500. 80% of undergraduate students work part-time. The average financial indebtedness of a recent graduate was $17,000. NEC is a member of CSS. The FAFSA and the college's own financial statement are required. Check with the school for current deadlines.

International Students: In a recent year, there were 150 international students enrolled. The school actively recruits these students. They must take the TOEFL and SAT I or the ACT.

Computers: The college provides computer facilities for student use. Macintosh PCs, a library of music software, and synthesizers are available in the computer studio. All students may access the system. There are no time limits and no fees.

Admissions Contact: Rachael Noyes, Assistant to Dean of Enrollment Services.

NICHOLS COLLEGE   C-3
Dudley, MA 01571   (508) 943-2055
                            (800) 470-3379; FAX: (508) 943-9885

Full-time: 485 men, 264 women	Faculty: 36
Part-time: 385 men, 217 women	Ph.D.s: 67%
Graduate: 197 men, 140 women	Student/Faculty: 21 to 1
Year: semesters, summer session	Tuition: $10,332
Application Deadline: open	Room & Board: $5904
Freshman Class: 960 applied, 825 accepted, 288 enrolled	
SAT I Verbal/Math: 404/447	LESS COMPETITIVE

Nichols College, founded in 1930 as a private institution for men, became coeducational in 1971. It emphasizes business and liberal arts. There are campuses in Dudley, Southboro, Auburn, and Leominster. There is 1 undergraduate school. The library contains 60,000 volumes, 8000 microform items, and 544 audiovisual forms, and subscribes to 450 periodicals. Computerized library sources and services include the card catalog, interlibrary loans, and database searching. Special learning facilities include a learning resource center, art gallery, and radio station. The 210-acre campus is in a rural area 20 miles south of Worcester. Including residence halls, there are 44 buildings on campus.

Student Life: 59% of undergraduates are from Massachusetts. Students come from 22 states, 8 foreign countries, and Canada. 79% are from public schools; 21% from private. 97% are white. Most are Catholic. The average age of freshmen is 18; all undergraduates, 20. 20% do not continue beyond their first year; 43% remain to graduate.

Housing: 602 students can be accommodated in college housing. College-sponsored living facilities include single-sex dormitories. On-campus housing is guaranteed for all 4 years. 80% of students live on campus; of those, 50% remain on campus on weekends. Alcohol is not permitted. All students may keep cars on campus.

Activities: There are no fraternities or sororities. There are 28 groups on campus, including cheerleading, computers, drama, ecumenical, honors, international, literary magazine, newspaper, professional, radio and TV, student government, and yearbook. Popular campus events include Parents Weekend, Spring Weekend, and 100-Days Social.

Sports: There are 9 intercollegiate sports for men and 6 for women, and 7 intramural sports for men and 3 for women. Athletic and recreation facilities include a field house with basketball courts, swimming pool, sauna, and weight-training room as well as athletic training facilities. There is also a 9-hole golf course, 6 outdoor tennis courts, a volleyball court, and an outdoor basketball court.

Disabled Students: 67% of the campus is accessible to disabled students. The following facilities are available: wheelchair ramps, elevators, special parking, specially equipped rest rooms, special class scheduling, and lowered drinking fountains. The college makes every effort to accommodate students with special needs.

Services: In addition to many counseling and information services, tutoring is available in most subjects.

Campus Safety and Security: Campus safety and security measures include 24-hour foot and vehicle patrol, self-defense education, escort service, and informal discussions. There are also pamphlets/posters/films and lighted pathways/sidewalks.

Programs of Study: Nichols confers B.A., B.S., and B.S. in Public Administration degrees. Associate and master's degrees are also awarded. Bachelor's degrees are awarded in BUSINESS (accounting, banking and finance, business administration and management, business economics, management information systems, and marketing/retailing/merchandising), SOCIAL SCIENCE (American studies, history, industrial and organizational psychology, psychology, public administration, and social science). Accounting, finance, and management are the strongest academically and have the largest enrollments.

Required: All students must complete a program of study within 10 semesters and maintain a GPA of 2.0 overall and in their major. Students also must complete The Cultural Experience: The Arts, Sciences, and Public Policy Program, which provides cultural events each year. Business students need 33 hours of business core classes out of the total 122 hours required of all students.

Special: Internships designed with the approval of the department, study abroad at Regents College in London, a Washington semester, and a general business degree are available. Nondegree study also is offered. There are 2 national honor societies on campus. 8 departments have honors programs.

Faculty/Classroom: 77% of faculty are male; 23%, female. All teach undergraduates. No introductory courses are taught by graduate students. The average class size in a laboratory is 18 and in a regular course offering, 26.

Admissions: 86% of the 1995–96 applicants were accepted. The SAT I scores for the 1995–96 freshman class were as follows: Verbal—88% below 500, 11% between 500 and 599, and 1% between 600 and 700; Math—73% below 500, 21% between 500 and 599, and 6% between 600 and 700. 8% of the current freshmen were in the top fifth of their class; 32% were in the top two fifths.

Requirements: The SAT I is required. A minimum GPA of 2.0 is required. Four years of high school English, 3 years of mathematics, and 2 years each in science and social studies are recommended. AP and CLEP credits are accepted. Important factors in the admissions decision are advanced placement or honor courses, recommendations by school officials, and personality/intangible qualities.

Procedure: Freshmen are admitted in the fall and spring. Entrance exams should be taken by November of the senior year. There are early decision, early admissions, and deferred admissions plans. Application deadlines are open. Application fee is $25. Notification is sent on a rolling basis.

Transfer: 57 transfer students enrolled in 1995–96. Applicants need a minimum GPA of 2.0 in courses to be transferred. 30 credits of 122 must be completed at Nichols.

Visiting: There are regularly scheduled orientations for prospective students. There are guides for informal visits and visitors may sit in on classes and stay overnight at the school. To schedule a visit, contact the Admissions Office.

Financial Aid: In 1995–96, 90% of all freshmen and 85% of continuing students received some form of financial aid. 67% of freshmen and 40% of continuing students received need-based aid. The average freshman award was $12,668. Nichols is a member of CSS. The FAFSA is required.

International Students: There were 9 international students enrolled in a recent year. The school actively recruits these students. They must take the TOEFL and achieve a minimum score of 500.

Computers: The college provides computer facilities for student use. The mainframe is a DEC VAX 3800. A Novelle Token Ring Network supplies programs to all students via modem. There are 246 connections in the academic center and 2 connections in every dorm room in Shamie Hall. All students may access the system 24 hours a day. There are no time limits and no fees. It is recommended that students in all programs have personal computers. NEC 186F Ultralite Notebook, Panasonic CF-1000 Notebook, or compatible computer is recommended.

Graduates: Of the 1994 graduating class, 68% had found employment within 6 months of graduation.

Admissions Contact: Tracey Dysart, Director of Admissions and Financial Aid. A campus video is available.

NORTH ADAMS STATE COLLEGE
A-1
North Adams, MA 01247
(413) 662-5410
(800) 292-6632, ext. 5410; FAX: (413) 662-5179

Full-time: 683 men, 697 women	Faculty: 98; IIB, av$
Part-time: 53 men, 83 women	Ph.D.s: 70%
Graduate: none	Student/Faculty: 14 to 1
Year: semesters	Tuition: $3817 ($7734)
Application Deadline: June 1	Room & Board: $4340 ($4602)
Freshman Class: 1554 applied, 977 accepted, 313 enrolled	
SAT I Verbal/Math: 446/470	COMPETITIVE

North Adams State College, founded in 1894, is a coeducational liberal arts college emphasizing business and education courses. In addition to regional accreditation, NASC has baccalaureate program accreditation with NCATE. The library contains 175,000 volumes, more than 200,000 microform items, and 4825 audiovisual forms, and subscribes to 510 periodicals. Computerized library sources and services include the card catalog, interlibrary loans, and database searching. Special learning facilities include a learning resource center, art gallery, radio station, and TV station. The 80-acre campus is in a rural area 45 miles east of Albany, New York, and 130 miles west of Boston. Including residence halls, there are 15 buildings on campus.

Student Life: 82% of undergraduates are from Massachusetts. Students come from 16 states and Canada. 80% are from public schools; 20% from private. 94% are white. Most are Catholic. The average age of freshmen is 18; all undergraduates, 23. 18% do not continue beyond their first year; 58% remain to graduate.

Housing: 1100 students can be accommodated in college housing. College-sponsored living facilities include single-sex and coed dormitories and on-campus apartments. In addition, there are honors houses. On-campus housing is guaranteed for all 4 years. 60% of students live on campus; of those, 80% remain on campus on weekends. Upperclassmen may keep cars on campus.

Activities: 5% of men belong to 4 local and 2 national fraternities; 10% of women belong to 4 local and 3 national sororities. There are 48 groups on campus, including chorale, chorus, computers, dance, drama, ethnic, gay, honors, jazz band, literary magazine, musical theater, newspaper, photography, political, professional, radio and TV, religious, social, social service, student government, and yearbook. Popular campus events include Homecoming, Parents Weekend, and Winter Carnival.

Sports: There are 5 intercollegiate sports for men and 5 for women, and 10 intramural sports for men and 10 for women. Athletic and recreation facilities include a campus center, with a swimming pool, weight rooms, and handball, squash, and racquetball courts, an outdoor complex, with tennis courts and soccer, baseball, and softball fields, a 450-seat gymnasium, and a 5-mile cross-country running trail.

Disabled Students: 80% of the campus is accessible to disabled students. The following facilities are available: wheelchair ramps, elevators, special parking, specially equipped rest rooms, and special class scheduling.

Services: In addition to many counseling and information services, tutoring is available in some subjects. There is remedial math, reading, and writing, and the Tutoring Exchange Network has qualified peers tutoring small groups.

Campus Safety and Security: Campus safety and security measures include 24-hour foot and vehicle patrol, escort service, informal discussions, and pamphlets/posters/films. In addition, there are lighted pathways/sidewalks.

Programs of Study: NASC confers B.A. and B.S. degrees. Master's degrees are also awarded. Bachelor's degrees are awarded in BIOLOGICAL SCIENCE (biology/biological science), BUSINESS (business administration and management), COMMUNICATIONS AND THE ARTS (English and fine arts), COMPUTER AND PHYSICAL SCIENCE (chemistry, computer science, mathematics, and physics), EDUCATION (education), HEALTH PROFESSIONS (health science), SOCIAL SCIENCE (history, philosophy, psychology, and sociology). Business, English, and education are the strongest academically. Business and education have the largest enrollments.

Required: All students must complete at least 120 credits, including 50 in a core curriculum, and maintain a GPA of at least 2.0. Physical education and computer science courses are required.

Special: The college offers cross-registration with Williams College and Berkshire Community College, dual majors, internships, and study abroad in many countries within the International College Program. Student-designed majors, pass/fail options, nondegree study, and independent study also are available. There is a freshman honors program on campus, as well as 2 national honor societies. 1 department has an honors program.

Faculty/Classroom: 69% of faculty are male; 31%, female. All teach undergraduates. The average class size in an introductory lecture is 75; in a laboratory, 15; and in a regular course offering, 25.

Admissions: 63% of the 1995–96 applicants were accepted. 12% of the current freshmen were in the top fifth of their class; 50% were in the top two fifths.

Requirements: The SAT I is required, with an SAT eligibility index used to determine a minimum score. NASC requires applicants to be in the upper 40% of their class, with a 2.0 GPA. Applicants should have completed 16 Carnegie units, including 4 courses in English, 3 each in electives and mathematics, and 2 each in foreign language, science, and history/social science. The GED is accepted. AP and CLEP credits are accepted. Important factors in the admissions decision are advanced placement or honor courses, evidence of special talent, and parents or siblings attending the school.

Procedure: Freshmen are admitted in the fall and spring. Entrance exams should be taken by January of the senior year. There are early admissions and deferred admissions plans. Applications should be filed by June 1 for fall entry and January 1 for spring entry, along with an application fee of $10. Notification is sent on a rolling basis. A waiting list is an active part of the admissions procedure, with about 5% of all applicants on the list.

Transfer: 175 transfer students enrolled in 1995–96. Applicants who have a minimum of 12 semester hours from an accredited college are eligible. Students are evaluated on the basis of past college records, which must include a GPA of at least 2.0. 30 credits of 120 must be completed at NASC.

Visiting: There are regularly scheduled orientations for prospective students, including a 2-day, overnight program for students who have been accepted. There are guides for informal visits and visitors may sit in on classes. To schedule a visit, contact the Admissions Office.

Financial Aid: In 1995–96, 60% of all students received some form of financial aid. 50% of all students received need-based aid. Average earnings from campus work for the school year are $1300. NASC is a member of CSS. The FAFSA and the college's own financial statement are required. The application deadline for fall entry is April 1.

International Students: There are currently 2 international students enrolled. They must take the TOEFL and achieve a minimum score of 550. The student must also take the SAT I.

Computers: The college provides computer facilities for student use. The mainframes are a CDC Cyber 815 and a DEC VAX 1850. There are also AT&T, Zenith, IBM, and Apple microcomputers available in the computer services facility. All students may access the system. Limits on student access to the system vary with the time of year. The fees are $25 per year.

Graduates: In 1994–95, 429 bachelor's degrees were awarded. The most popular majors among graduates were business (31%), psychology (21%), and English communications (14%). Within an average freshman class, 1% graduate in 3 years, 45% in 4 years, 48% in 5 years, and 50% in 6 years.

Admissions Contact: Denise C. Richardello, Director of Admissions. A campus video is available.

NORTHEASTERN UNIVERSITY

E-2

Boston, MA 02115 — (617) 373-2200

Full-time: 6123 men, 4899 women	Faculty: 754; I, -$
Part-time: 4057 men, 4658 women	Ph.D.s: 84%
Graduate: 2459 men, 2409 women	Student/Faculty: 15 to 1
Year: quarters, summer session	Tuition: $14,241
Application Deadline: open	Room & Board: $7710
Freshman Class: 13,609 applied, 9960 accepted, 2783 enrolled	
SAT I Verbal/Math: 470/530	ACT: 23 **COMPETITIVE**

Northeastern University, founded in 1898, is a private, nonsectarian institution offering programs that include an experiential learning component and that integrate professional work experience with classroom study. The academic program requires 5 years to complete. There are 7 undergraduate and 9 graduate schools. In addition to regional accreditation, Northeastern has baccalaureate program accreditation with AACSB, ABET, ACPE, APTA, CAHEA, CSAB, and NLN. The 6 libraries contain 808,509 volumes, 1,879,678 microform items, and 16,301 audiovisual forms, and subscribe to 8963 periodicals. Computerized library sources and services include the card catalog, interlibrary loans, and database searching. Special learning facilities include a learning resource center, art gallery, and radio station. The 55-acre campus is in an urban area in Boston. Including residence halls, there are 54 buildings on campus.

Student Life: 65% of undergraduates are from Massachusetts. Students come from 50 states, 127 foreign countries, and Canada. 81% are white. The average age of freshmen is 18; all undergraduates, 22. 27% do not continue beyond their first year; 43% remain to graduate.

Housing: 3204 students can be accommodated in college housing. College-sponsored living facilities include single-sex and coed dormitories, on-campus apartments, and fraternity houses. In addition, there are honors houses, special interest houses, and quiet, engineering, living and learning, international, and wellness halls. On-campus housing is guaranteed for the freshman year only and is available on a first-come, first-served basis. 65% of students live on campus. All students may keep cars on campus.

Activities: 9% of men belong to 5 local and 13 national fraternities; 5% of women belong to 8 national sororities. There are 187 groups on campus, including art, band, cheerleading, chess, chorale, chorus, computers, dance, drama, ethnic, gay, honors, international, jazz band, literary magazine, marching band, newspaper, orchestra, pep band, photography, political, professional, radio and TV, religious, social, social service, student government, and yearbook. Popular campus events include NUAlive!, and International, Greek, and Unity weeks.

Sports: There are 12 intercollegiate sports for men and 10 for women, and 10 intramural sports for men and 10 for women. Athletic and recreation facilities include outdoor and indoor tracks, a football stadium, an indoor hockey arena, a swimming pool, indoor and outdoor tennis courts, and racquetball, volleyball, and basketball courts.

Disabled Students: 95% of the campus is accessible to disabled students. The following facilities are available: wheelchair ramps, elevators, special parking, specially equipped rest rooms, special class scheduling, lowered drinking fountains, and lowered telephones.

Services: In addition to many counseling and information services, tutoring is available in most subjects. The Academic Assistance Center offers assistance in reading, language problems, vocabulary, note taking, test preparation, and related study skills. There is also a reader service for the blind, and remedial math, reading, and writing.

Campus Safety and Security: Campus safety and security measures include 24-hour foot and vehicle patrol, escort service, pamphlets/posters/films, and emergency telephones. In addition,

there are lighted pathways/sidewalks and awareness programs on rape prevention, alcohol abuse, personal safety, and crime prevention. A state-of-the-art fire and security alarm center monitors residence halls, academic buildings, and athletic facilities.

Programs of Study: Northeastern confers B.A., B.S., and B.Ed. degrees. Associate, master's, and doctoral degrees are also awarded. Bachelor's degrees are awarded in BIOLOGICAL SCIENCE (biology/biological science, neurosciences, and toxicology), BUSINESS (accounting, business administration and management, human resources, insurance, international business management, management information systems, marketing/retailing/merchandising, small business management, and transportation management), COMMUNICATIONS AND THE ARTS (art, communications, dramatic arts, English, French, journalism, linguistics, music, and Spanish), COMPUTER AND PHYSICAL SCIENCE (chemistry, computer programming, geology, information sciences and systems, mathematics, and physics), EDUCATION (athletic training, early childhood, and elementary), ENGINEERING AND ENVIRONMENTAL DESIGN (chemical engineering, civil engineering, computer engineering, electrical/electronics engineering, electrical/electronics engineering technology, engineering, engineering technology, industrial engineering, mechanical engineering, and mechanical engineering technology), HEALTH PROFESSIONS (medical laboratory science, medical laboratory technology, nursing, pharmacy, physical therapy, and respiratory therapy), SOCIAL SCIENCE (African American studies, anthropology, criminal justice, economics, history, human services, interpreter for the deaf, philosophy, physical fitness/movement, political science/government, psychology, and sociology). Engineering, computer science, and business administration are the strongest academically. Arts and sciences, business administration, and engineering have the largest enrollments.

Required: Although each college has its own requirements, students must generally complete an upper-division writing proficiency requirement in addition to at least 176 quarter hours with a minimum GPA of 2.0.

Special: Northeastern offers many paid professional internships with area companies to integrate classroom instruction with professional experience. Cross-registration with the New England Conservatory of Music and Hebrew College, study abroad in numerous countries, a Washington semester, work-study through the university and public or private agencies, and student-designed majors in arts and sciences are offered. Nondegree adult and continuing education, and limited pass/fail options are possible. Also available are the Alternative Freshman Year Program and Project Ujima, an academic support program designed to assist minority students. The Women in Engineering Program Office maintains a database for academic support and networking. Accelerated degrees in engineering, nursing, and business are available. There is a freshman honors program on campus, as well as 26 national honor societies. All departments have honors programs.

Faculty/Classroom: 67% of faculty are male; 33%, female. The average class size in a regular course offering is 26.

Admissions: 73% of the 1995–96 applicants were accepted. The SAT I scores for the 1995–96 freshman class were as follows: Verbal—65% below 500, 28% between 500 and 599, 7% between 600 and 700, and 1% above 700; Math—34% below 500, 39% between 500 and 599, 23% between 600 and 700, and 4% above 700. The ACT scores were 22% below 21, 37% between 21 and 23, 23% between 24 and 26, 12% between 27 and 28, and 6% above 28. 37% of the current freshmen were in the top fifth of their class; 70% were in the top two fifths.

Requirements: The SAT I or ACT is required. Northeastern recommends that applicants have 17 academic units, including 4 each in English and mathematics, and 2 each in foreign language, science, and social studies. An essay is required and an interview is recommended. Applications are accepted on-line. AP and CLEP credits are accepted. Important factors in the admissions decision are recommendations by school officials, advanced placement or honor courses, and leadership record.

Procedure: Freshmen are admitted fall and winter. Entrance exams should be taken between October of the junior year and December of the senior year. There are early admissions and deferred admissions plans. Application deadlines are open. Application fee is $40. Notification is sent on a rolling basis.

Transfer: 519 transfer students enrolled in 1995–96. Candidates applying for transfer must have a satisfactory college record. Credit is generally granted for a grade of C or better in any reasonably equivalent course. Candidates must be in good standing and must be eligible to continue in the institution they are currently attending. Emphasis is placed on the college record, but the high school record will be considered. SAT I or ACT scores are required of transfer applicants with fewer than 2 years of college. 48 quarter units of 176 must be completed at Northeastern.

Visiting: There are regularly scheduled orientations for prospective students. There are guides for informal visits and visitors may sit in on classes. To schedule a visit, contact the Department of Undergraduate Admissions at (617) 373-2211.

Financial Aid: In 1995–96, 76% of all freshmen and 68% of continuing students received some form of financial aid. 72% of freshmen and 64% of continuing students received need-based aid. The average freshman award was $10,199. Of that total, scholarships or need-based grants averaged $7678 ($21,834 maximum); loans averaged $2815 ($5625 maximum); and work contracts averaged $1806 ($2100 maximum). Average earnings from campus work for the school year are $1886. The average financial indebtedness of the 1994–95 graduate was $20,543. Northeastern is a member of CSS. The FAFSA and the CSS Profile Application are required; upperclassmen must submit the university's own financial statement as well. The application deadline for all sessions is March 1.

International Students: There are currently 1005 international students enrolled. The school actively recruits these students. They must take the TOEFL and achieve a minimum score of 550. The student must also take the SAT I or the ACT; minimum scores vary by or within program.

Computers: The college provides computer facilities for student use. The mainframe is a super-miniVAXcluster consisting of 2 DEC VAX 6000–440 computers. Students may gain access to the mainframe systems from on-campus computer laboratories or off-campus dial-in modems. The computers accessed are utilized for various computer courses, E-mail, computer conferencing, and bulletin board purposes. All students may access the system 24 hours daily. There are no time limits and no fees.

Graduates: In 1994–95, 2370 bachelor's degrees were awarded. The most popular majors among graduates were criminal justice (11%), physical therapy (6%), and finance and insurance (5%). Northeastern is a 5-year cooperative education school. Within an average freshman class, 38% graduate in 5 years and 43% in 6 years. 200 companies recruited on campus in 1994–95. Of the 1994 graduating class, 10% were enrolled in graduate school within 6 months of graduation and 77% had found employment.

Admissions Contact: Gary Bracken, Interim Dean and Director of Admissions. E-mail: http://www.neu.edu.

PINE MANOR COLLEGE

Chestnut Hill, MA 02167
E-2
(617) 731-7104
(800) PMC-1357; FAX: (617) 731-7199

Full-time: 290 women	Faculty: 27
Part-time: 43 women	Ph.D.s: 56%
Graduate: 10 women	Student/Faculty: 11 to 1
Year: semesters, summer session	Tuition: $16,355
Application Deadline: open	Room & Board: $6660
Freshman Class: 237 applied, 189 accepted, 96 enrolled	
SAT I Verbal/Math: 377/393	LESS COMPETITIVE

Pine Manor College, established in 1911, is a private liberal arts college for women. The library contains 83,400 volumes and 8000 microform items, and subscribes to 468 periodicals. Computerized library sources and services include the card catalog, interlibrary loans, and database searching. Special learning facilities include a learning resource center, radio station, TV station, and language laboratory. The 79-acre campus is in a suburban area 5 miles west of Boston. Including residence halls, there are 28 buildings on campus.

Student Life: 79% of undergraduates are from out-of-state, mostly the Northeast. Students come from 31 states, 15 foreign countries, and Canada. 51% are from public schools; 49% from private. 67% are white; 22% foreign nationals. 22% do not continue beyond their first year.

Housing: 510 students can be accommodated in college housing. College-sponsored living facilities include dormitories and on-campus apartments. In addition, there are language houses, special interest houses, nonsmoking dormitories, and a quiet dormitory. On-campus housing is guaranteed for all 4 years. 85% of students live on campus; of those, 80% remain on campus on weekends. All students may keep cars on campus.

Activities: There are no sororities. There are 15 groups on campus, including chorus, dance, drama, ethnic, honors, international, literary magazine, musical theater, newspaper, political, professional, radio and TV, social service, student government, and yearbook. Popular campus events include Holiday Formal, Spring Formal, and First and Last Hurrahs.

Sports: Athletic and recreation facilities include a modern gym, outdoor fields, a cross-country track, tennis courts, dance studios, and a weight room.

Disabled Students: 40% of the campus is accessible to disabled students. The following facilities are available: wheelchair ramps, elevators, and specially equipped rest rooms.

Services: In addition to many counseling and information services, tutoring is available in every subject. There is also remedial math, reading, and writing. The learning resource center has professional and peer tutoring and workshops.

Campus Safety and Security: Campus safety and security measures include escort service and shuttle buses.

Programs of Study: Pine Manor confers the B.A. degree. Associate and master's degrees are also awarded. Bachelor's degrees are awarded in BIOLOGICAL SCIENCE (biology/biological science), BUSINESS (management science), COMMUNICATIONS AND THE ARTS (art history and appreciation, communications, English, fine arts, and visual and performing arts), EDUCATION (early childhood and elementary), SOCIAL SCIENCE (American studies, psychobiology, and psychology). Management, English, and psychology are the strongest academically. Management, communications, and psychology have the largest enrollments.

Required: All students must take 2 courses each in humanities, fine and performing arts, social sciences, and natural and behavioral science, plus a mathematics competency course and 2 semesters of freshman composition. In addition, students must maintain a minimum GPA of 2.0 and take a total of 128 semester hours.

Special: Pine Manor offers cross-registration with Boston and Babson colleges, internships at more than 600 sites, and study abroad in France, England, Italy, Spain, and at sea. A Washington semester, work-study programs, dual majors, student-designed majors, nondegree study within continuing education, and pass/fail options for 2 courses each semester (except the first freshman semester) also are available. There is 1 national honor society on campus.

Faculty/Classroom: 40% of faculty are male; 60%, female. 95% teach undergraduates. The average class size in an introductory lecture is 30; in a laboratory, 20; and in a regular course offering, 20.

Admissions: 80% of the 1995–96 applicants were accepted. The SAT I scores for the 1995–96 freshman class were as follows: Verbal—86% below 500, 11% between 500 and 599, and 1% between 600 and 700; Math—84% below 500 and 15% between 500 and 599. 35% of the current freshmen were in the top half of their class.

Requirements: The SAT I or ACT is required. Applicants are required to have taken 4 courses in English and 2 in mathematics. Additional courses in foreign language, social science, natural science, and elective areas are recommended. An essay is also required. An interview is recommended. The GED is accepted, and the number of Carnegie units required is 16. AP and CLEP credits are accepted. Important factors in the admissions decision are recommendations by school officials, leadership record, and advanced placement or honor courses.

Procedure: Freshmen are admitted fall and spring. There are early decision and deferred admissions plans. Early decision applications should be filed by November 15. Regular application dates are open for fall entry. The application fee is $40. Notification is sent on a rolling basis.

Transfer: 26 transfer students enrolled in a recent year. Pine Manor requires transfer students to submit 2 letters of recommendation (1 from a professor) and college and high school transcripts. The SAT I or ACT also is necessary. 32 credits of 128 must be completed at Pine Manor.

Visiting: There are regularly scheduled orientations for prospective students, including a campus tour. There are guides for informal visits and visitors may sit in on classes and stay overnight at the school. To schedule a visit, contact the Admissions Office.

Financial Aid: 15% of undergraduate students work part-time. Average earnings from campus work for the school year are $1100. Pine Manor is a member of CSS. The FAF and the college's own financial statement are required. The application deadline for fall entry is March 1.

International Students: In a recent year, 105 international students were enrolled. The school actively recruits these students. They must take the TOEFL.

Computers: The college provides computer facilities for student use. IBM, IBM-compatible, and Apple microcomputers are available for student use in computer centers in the library and in the science, management, and art buildings. The communications center houses a computerized print media room. All students may access the system. There are no time limits. The fee is $35.

Graduates: In a recent year, 107 bachelor's degrees were awarded. The most popular majors among graduates were management (21%), communication (20%), and psychology (16%). Within an average freshman class, 55% graduate in 4 years and 60% in 5 years.

Admissions Contact: Leslie Miles, Dean of Admissions.

REGIS COLLEGE
Weston, MA 02193–1571

D-2

(617) 768–7065
(800) 456–1820; FAX: (617) 768–7071

Full-time: 706 women	Faculty: 57; IIB, av$
Part-time: 496 women	Ph.D.s: 85%
Graduate: 134 women	Student/Faculty: 12 to 1
Year: semesters, summer session	Tuition: $13,700
Application Deadline: May 1	Room & Board: $6250
Freshman Class: 601 applied, 542 accepted, 228 enrolled	
SAT I Verbal/Math: 450/460	**COMPETITIVE**

Regis College, founded in 1927, is a private liberal arts institution for women, affiliated with the Roman Catholic Church. There is 1 undergraduate school. In addition to regional accreditation, Regis has baccalaureate program accreditation with CSWE and NLN. The library contains 147,577 volumes, 35,721 microform items, and 3628 audiovisual forms, and subscribes to 842 periodicals. Computerized library sources and services include the card catalog, interlibrary loans, and database searching. Special learning facilities include a learning resource center, art gallery, radio station, philatelic museum, and fine arts center. The 168-acre campus is in a suburban area 12 miles west of Boston. Including residence halls, there are 15 buildings on campus.

Student Life: 84% of undergraduates are from Massachusetts. Students come from 21 states and 9 foreign countries. 67% are from public schools; 33% from private. 87% are white. 72% are Catholic; 11% Protestant. The average age of freshmen is 18; all undergraduates, 24. 19% do not continue beyond their first year; 69% remain to graduate.

Housing: 650 students can be accommodated in college housing. College-sponsored living facilities include dormitories. On-campus housing is guaranteed for all 4 years. 72% of students live on campus; of those, 50% remain on campus on weekends. All students may keep cars on campus.

Activities: There are 39 groups on campus, including art, choir, chorale, chorus, computers, dance, drama, ethnic, film, honors, international, jazz band, literary magazine, musical theater, photography, political, professional, radio and TV, religious, social, social service, student government, and yearbook. Popular campus events include orientation, Father/Daughter Dance, Comedy Night, Oktoberfest, and Family Weekend.

Sports: There are 11 intercollegiate sports and 6 to 8 intramural sports. Athletic and recreation facilities include a softball diamond, a soccer field, 4 tennis courts, an athletic facility with a gymnasium, an aerobics and dance studio, a Nautilus weight room, racquetball and squash courts, a pool, a sauna, and a Jacuzzi.

Disabled Students: The following facilities are available: wheelchair ramps, elevators, special parking, specially equipped rest rooms, special class scheduling, lowered drinking fountains, and lowered telephones.

Services: In addition to many counseling and information services, tutoring is available in every subject. There is a reader service for the blind, remedial math and writing, and academic support services for learning-disabled students.

Campus Safety and Security: Campus safety and security measures include 24-hour foot and vehicle patrol, self-defense education, escort service, and shuttle buses. In addition, there are informal discussions, pamphlets/posters/films, emergency telephones, and lighted pathways/sidewalks.

Programs of Study: Regis confers B.A. and B.S.N. degrees. Master's degrees are also awarded. Bachelor's degrees are awarded in BIOLOGICAL SCIENCE (biochemistry and biology/biological science), BUSINESS (management science), COMMUNICATIONS AND THE ARTS (art, classics, communications, English, French, German, and Spanish), COMPUTER AND PHYSICAL SCIENCE (chemistry and mathematics), HEALTH PROFESSIONS (nursing), SOCIAL SCIENCE (economics, history, political science/government, psychology, social work, and sociology). Communication, English, and political science have the largest enrollments.

Required: General education requirements include course work in mathematics, global economy, writing, sacred tradition, natural sciences, ethical approaches, literature, second language, fitness and health, fine arts, individuals in social context, and individuals in historical and political context. To graduate, students must complete a total of 38 credit courses, including 8 to 12 in the major, with a minimum GPA of 2.0.

Special: Cross-registration with Boston, Babson, and Bentley colleges and through the Sisters of St. Joseph Consortium is offered. Students may study abroad at Regis afflates in London and in Kyoto, Japan, or through programs of other American colleges. Regis also offers internships, study abroad, a Washington semester at American University, dual and self-designed majors, work-study, nondegree study, and pass/fail options. There are special programs in American studies; communication; computer science; graphics; Greek, interna-

tional, legal, and women's studies; and teacher-training programs. A 3–2 engineering degree is available with Worcester Polytechnic Institute. There is a freshman honors program on campus, as well as 6 national honor societies. 18 departments have honors programs.

Faculty/Classroom: 18% of faculty are male; 82%, female. All teach undergraduates. No introductory courses are taught by graduate students. The average class size in an introductory lecture is 21; in a laboratory, 17; and in a regular course offering, 15.

Admissions: 90% of the 1995–96 applicants were accepted. The SAT I scores for the 1995–96 freshman class were as follows: Verbal—66% below 500, 26% between 500 and 599, 7% between 600 and 700, and 1% above 700; Math—66% below 500, 22% between 500 and 599, 11% between 600 and 700, and 1% above 700. 40% of the current freshmen were in the top fifth of their class; 75% were in the top two fifths. 3 freshmen graduated first in their class.

Requirements: The SAT I is required. The minimum score needed is 400 each on verbal and mathematics. Regis requires applicants to be in the upper 50% of their class with a 2.5 GPA. Applicants should have 4 years of English, 3 or 4 electives, 3 of mathematics, and 2 each of foreign language, social studies, and natural science, including a laboratory science. An essay and 2 letters of recommendation are required. An interview is strongly encouraged. The GED is accepted. Application may be made via Macintosh disk, which must be accompanied by the transcript, letters of recommendation, and signed copy of the college's paper application. AP and CLEP credits are accepted. Important factors in the admissions decision are recommendations by school officials, ability to finance college education, and extracurricular activities record.

Procedure: Freshmen are admitted in the fall and spring. Entrance exams should be taken during the fall before enrollment. There are early admissions and deferred admissions plans. Applications for priority consideration should be filed by May 1 for fall entry and December 1 for spring entry, along with an application fee of $30. Notification is sent within 1 month of receipt of the completed application. A waiting list is an active part of the admissions procedure, with about 8% of all applicants on the list.

Transfer: 42 transfer students enrolled in 1995–96. Applicants need an admission application and fee; an official high school transcript if fewer than 9 college courses have been completed; an official college transcript; 1 letter of recommendation from a professor at the previous college attended; the academic catalog of the previous college; an essay; SAT I scores if fewer than 16 courses have been completed; and health records. 18 courses of 38 must be completed at Regis.

Visiting: There are regularly scheduled orientations for prospective students, consisting of programs hosted 3 times during the summer prior to fall enrollment and once during January before second semester enrollment. There are guides for informal visits and visitors may sit in on classes and stay overnight at the school. To schedule a visit, contact the Admissions Office at (800) 456–1820.

Financial Aid: In 1995–96, 90% of all freshmen and 40% of continuing students received some form of financial aid. 81% of freshmen and 30% of continuing students received need-based aid. The average freshman award was $13,000. Of that total, scholarships or need-based grants averaged $8000 ($16,500 maximum); loans averaged $4205 ($5625 maximum); and work contracts averaged $800 ($1500 maximum). 56% of undergraduate students work part-time. Average earnings from campus work for the school year are $840. The average financial indebtedness of the 1994–95 graduate was $14,304. Regis is a member of CSS. The FAFSA and the CSS Profile Application are required. The application deadline for fall entry is February 15.

International Students: There are currently 40 international students enrolled. The school actively recruits these students. They must take the TOEFL and achieve a minimum score of 500. The student must also take the SAT I.

Computers: The college provides computer facilities for student use. The mainframes are a Prime 9955 Model 2 and an HP 9000/G50. There are also 86 IBM and Apple Macintosh microcomputers available in the academic computer center and in various departments. All students may access the system daily at posted hours in the academic computing center or by permission in the individual departments. There are no time limits and no fees.

Graduates: In 1994–95, 146 bachelor's degrees were awarded. The most popular majors among graduates were nursing (21%), communication (12%), and psychology (10%). Within an average freshman class, 60% graduate in 4 years, 66% in 5 years, and 68% in 6 years. 21 companies recruited on campus in 1994–95. Of the 1994 graduating class, 11% were enrolled in graduate school within 6 months of graduation and 36% had found employment.

Admissions Contact: Valerie L. Brown, Director of Admissions. A campus video is available.

SALEM STATE COLLEGE
E-2
Salem, MA 01970 (508) 740-7068

Full-time: 2400 men, 3230 women	Faculty: 292; IIA, -$
Part-time: 3400 men, 6200 women	Ph.D.s: 65%
Graduate: 140 men, 400 women	Student/Faculty: 19 to 1
Year: semesters, summer session	Tuition: $3198 ($7332)
Application Deadline: March 1	Room & Board: $3514
Freshman Class: n/av	
SAT I or ACT: required	LESS COMPETITIVE

Salem State College, founded in 1854, is a public coeducational institution offering programs in liberal arts, business, education, and nursing. There are 5 undergraduate schools and 1 graduate school. In addition to regional accreditation, Salem State has baccalaureate program accreditation with CSWE, NASAD, NCATE, and NLN. The library contains 225,000 volumes and 300,000 microform items, and subscribes to 1340 periodicals. Special learning facilities include a learning resource center, art gallery, radio station, and TV station. The 62-acre campus is in an urban area 18 miles northeast of Boston. Including residence halls, there are 19 buildings on campus.

Student Life: 98% of undergraduates are from Massachusetts. Students come from 20 states, 15 foreign countries, and Canada. 98% are from public schools; 2% from private. 90% are white.

Housing: 950 students can be accommodated in college housing. College-sponsored living facilities include coed dormitories and on-campus apartments. On-campus housing is guaranteed for all 4 years. Priority is given to out-of-town students. 60% of students commute. All students may keep cars on campus.

Activities: There are no fraternities or sororities. There are 44 groups on campus, including band, cheerleading, choir, chorale, chorus, computers, dance, drama, ethnic, gay, honors, jazz band, musical theater, newspaper, photography, political, radio and TV, religious, social, social service, student government, and yearbook. Popular campus events include Homecoming, Welcome Week, Halloween, Arts Festival, and Senior Week.

Sports: There are 8 intercollegiate sports for men and 8 for women, and 15 intramural sports for men and 15 for women. Athletic and recreation facilities include an athletic center with 27 facilities, including a 2200-seat gymnasium, a 2800-seat auditorium, an 8-lane swimming pool, 4 tennis courts, a weight room, and a dance studio.

Disabled Students: 90% of the campus is accessible to disabled students. The following facilities are available: wheelchair ramps, elevators, special parking, specially equipped rest rooms, lowered drinking fountains, and lowered telephones.

Services: In addition to many counseling and information services, tutoring is available in every subject. There is a reader service for the blind, and remedial math, reading, and writing.

Campus Safety and Security: Campus safety and security measures include shuttle buses, pamphlets/posters/films, emergency telephones, and lighted pathways/sidewalks.

Programs of Study: Salem State confers B.A., B.S., B.S.B.A., B.F.A., B.G.S., B.S.Ed., B.S.N., B.S.O.A., and B.S.W. degrees. Master's degrees are also awarded. Bachelor's degrees are awarded in BIOLOGICAL SCIENCE (biology/biological science), BUSINESS (accounting, banking and finance, business administration and management, and marketing/retailing/merchandising), COMMUNICATIONS AND THE ARTS (advertising, communications, design, dramatic arts, English, fine arts, and photography), COMPUTER AND PHYSICAL SCIENCE (chemistry, computer programming, earth science, geology, and mathematics), EDUCATION (art, business, education, science, and secondary), ENGINEERING AND ENVIRONMENTAL DESIGN (cartography), HEALTH PROFESSIONS (medical laboratory technology and nursing), SOCIAL SCIENCE (criminal justice, economics, geography, history, psychology, social work, and sociology). Sciences are the strongest academically. Business administration has the largest enrollment.

Required: All students must demonstrate basic competence in reading, mathematics, and computer literacy, and are required to take a distribution of classes that includes 36 to 38 credits in humanities, sciences, and social sciences. Specific courses required are English composition, speech, physical education, and the first year seminar. All core and distribution requirements may be waived if the student passes a departmentally prescribed exemption examination. A minimum GPA of 2.0 and a total of 127 credits, with 36 in the major, are needed to graduate.

Special: Study abroad is available in 3 countries. Cross-registration through a consortium, internships, work-study programs, student-designed and dual majors, B.A.-B.S. degrees, and a general studies degree are offered. Life experience credit, nondegree study, and pass/fail options also are possible. There is a freshman honors program on campus, as well as 11 national honor societies. 9 departments have honors programs.

Faculty/Classroom: 64% of faculty are male; 36%, female. The average class size in an introductory lecture is 35; in a laboratory, 20; and in a regular course offering, 30.

Admissions: In a recent year, 20% of the freshmen were in the top fifth of their class; 60% were in the top two fifths.

Requirements: The SAT I or ACT is required. Salem State requires applicants to be in the upper 50% of their class. A minimum GPA of 2.0 is required. Salem State recommends that applicants have earned 16 credits, including 4 years of English, 3 of mathematics, and 2 each of foreign language, history, and laboratory science. Courses in music, art, drama, computer science, and psychology are suggested. Art majors must provide a portfolio. A GED is acceptable. Students with a GED, those out of school more than 3 years, and the learning disabled do not need the SAT I. AP and CLEP credits are accepted. Important factors in the admissions decision are advanced placement or honor courses, evidence of special talent, and leadership record.

Procedure: Freshmen are admitted in the fall. Entrance exams should be taken by December of the senior year. There is a deferred admissions plan. Applications should be filed by March 1 for fall entry and December 1 for winter entry, along with an application fee of $10. Notification is sent on a rolling basis.

Transfer: Transfer students are required to have a minimum GPA of 2.0. 30 credits of 127 must be completed at Salem State.

Visiting: There are regularly scheduled orientations for prospective students. To schedule a visit, contact the Admissions Office at (508) 741-6200.

Financial Aid: Salem State is a member of CSS. The FAF is required. The application deadline for fall entry is April 15.

International Students: In a recent year, there were 65 international students enrolled. Students must take the TOEFL.

Computers: The college provides computer facilities for student use. The mainframe is a CDC CYBER 170. Numerous microcomputers are available throughout the campus. Students enrolled in computer courses may access the system. There are no time limits and no fees.

Admissions Contact: Nate Bryant, Acting Director of Admissions.

SIMMONS COLLEGE
E-2
Boston, MA 02115 (617) 521-2051; (800) 345-8468

Full-time: 1106 women	Faculty: 111; IIA, av$
Part-time: 246 women	Ph.D.s: 78%
Graduate: 273 men, 1989 women	Student/Faculty: 10 to 1
Year: semesters, summer session	Tuition: $17,496
Application Deadline: February 1	Room & Board: $7228
Freshman Class: 1144 applied, 770 accepted, 240 enrolled	
SAT I Verbal/Math: 470/500	ACT: 23 COMPETITIVE

Simmons College, founded in 1899, is a private institution primarily for women that offers a comprehensive education combining the arts, sciences, and humanities with preprofessional training. There are 5 graduate schools. In addition to regional accreditation, Simmons has baccalaureate program accreditation with ADA, APTA, CSWE, and NLN. The 5 libraries contain 271,990 volumes, 1393 microform items, and 2106 audiovisual forms, and subscribe to 2040 periodicals. Computerized library sources and services include the card catalog, interlibrary loans, and database searching. Special learning facilities include an art gallery and TV studio, microcomputer laboratory, foreign language laboratory, physical therapy sports laboratory, nursing laboratory, and library science technology center. The 12-acre campus is in an urban area of Boston. Including residence halls, there are 26 buildings on campus.

Student Life: 65% of undergraduates are from Massachusetts. Students come from 39 states, 40 foreign countries, and Canada. 78% are from public schools; 22% from private. 76% are white. 38% claim no religious affiliation; 30% Catholic; 16% Protestant; 16% Jewish. The average age of freshmen is 18; all undergraduates, 20. 17% do not continue beyond their first year; 70% remain to graduate.

Housing: 1031 students can be accommodated in college housing. College-sponsored living facilities include dormitories and off-campus apartments. In addition, there are special interest houses. On-campus housing is guaranteed for all 4 years. 87% of students live on campus; of those, 75% remain on campus on weekends.

Activities: There are no fraternities or sororities. There are 70 groups on campus, including chorale, dance, drama, ethnic, film, gay, honors, international, literary magazine, newspaper, political, professional, religious, social, social service, student government, and yearbook. Popular campus events include Friday Teas, Family Weekend, Spring Spree, May Breakfast, and Head of the Charles.

Sports: There are 10 intercollegiate sports and 2 intramural sports. Athletic and recreation facilities include an 8-lane pool, a spa and sauna, 2 racquetball and 2 squash courts, 2 rowing tanks, 3 fitness rooms, a dance studio, an indoor track, and a gymnasium with 3 badminton courts, 2 volleyball courts, and a basketball court.

Disabled Students: The entire campus is accessible to disabled students. The following facilities are available: wheelchair ramps, elevators, special parking, specially equipped rest rooms, special class scheduling, lowered drinking fountains, and lowered telephones.

Services: In addition to many counseling and information services, tutoring is available in some subjects, including basic freshman courses, languages, biology, chemistry, and psychology. There is remedial math and writing. The school also provides study groups, individual tutoring, help with study skills and time management, and assistance for learning-disabled and special-needs students.

Campus Safety and Security: Campus safety and security measures include 24-hour foot and vehicle patrol, self-defense education, escort service, and shuttle buses. In addition, there are informal discussions, pamphlets/posters/films, emergency telephones, lighted pathways/sidewalks, closed-circuit TV, ID card access, and security training in first response and crisis intervention.

Programs of Study: Simmons confers B.A. and B.S. degrees. Master's and doctoral degrees are also awarded. Bachelor's degrees are awarded in BIOLOGICAL SCIENCE (biochemistry, biology/biological science, and nutrition), BUSINESS (accounting, banking and finance, international business management, management information systems, marketing management, and retailing), COMMUNICATIONS AND THE ARTS (advertising, art, arts administration/management, communications, English, French, graphic design, music, public relations, and Spanish), COMPUTER AND PHYSICAL SCIENCE (chemistry, computer science, and mathematics), EDUCATION (education, secondary, and special), ENGINEERING AND ENVIRONMENTAL DESIGN (environmental science), HEALTH PROFESSIONS (nursing and premedicine), SOCIAL SCIENCE (American studies, economics, history, human services, international relations, philosophy, political science/government, prelaw, psychobiology, psychology, sociology, and women's studies). International relations is the strongest academically. Nursing, biology, and psychology have the largest enrollments.

Required: To graduate, students must complete 128 semester hours, including 20 to 40 in the major, and maintain a minimum GPA of 1.7. They must complete a total of 40 hours in the humanities, social sciences, and sciences, including 1 course each in internationalization and diversity, as well as Writing and Thinking 101 and 102 or the equivalent, another designated writing course, 1 year of physical education, and 8 semester hours in a supervised independent learning experience or an internship. They must also show proficiency in a foreign language and in mathematics.

Special: Cross-registration is available with the New England Conservatory of Music, and Hebrew, Emmanuel, and Wheelock colleges. Simmons also offers study abroad in Europe, a 6-year B.S.-M.S. program in physical therapy, a Washington semester at American University, internship programs, a B.A.-B.S. degree, dual majors, interdisciplinary majors such as chemistry management, student-designed majors, work-study programs, and pass/fail options. A dual-degree program in chemistry and pharmacy with Massachusetts College of Pharmacy and Allied Health Sciences is also possible. There is a freshman honors program on campus. Most departments have honors programs.

Faculty/Classroom: 36% of faculty are male; 64%, female. All both teach and do research. No introductory courses are taught by graduate students. The average class size in an introductory lecture is 50; in a laboratory, 12; and in a regular course offering, 16.

Admissions: 67% of the 1995–96 applicants were accepted. The SAT I scores for the 1995–96 freshman class were as follows: Verbal—61% below 500, 31% between 500 and 599, 7% between 600 and 700, and 1% above 700; Math—49% below 500, 35% between 500 and 599, 14% between 600 and 700, and 2% above 700. The ACT scores were 18% below 21, 55% between 21 and 23, and 27% between 24 and 26. 47% of the current freshmen were in the top fifth of their class; 86% were in the top two fifths. 2 freshmen graduated first in their class.

Requirements: The SAT I or ACT is required. Simmons recommends that applicants have a 3.0 GPA and 4 years of English, 3 each of mathematics, science, and social studies, and 2 of foreign language. An essay is required, and an interview is strongly recommended. AP and CLEP credits are accepted. Important factors in the admissions decision are advanced placement or honor courses, recommendations by school officials, and extracurricular activities record.

Procedure: Freshmen are admitted in the fall and spring. Entrance exams should be taken by February 1 of senior year. There are early decision, early admissions, and deferred admissions plans. Early decision applications should be filed by November 15 or January 1; regular applications, by February 1 for fall entry and December 1 for spring entry, along with an application fee of $35. Notification of early decision is sent December 15 or February 1; regular decision, April 15. 54 early decision candidates were accepted for the 1995–96 class. A waiting list is an active part of the admissions procedure.

Transfer: 35 transfer students enrolled in 1995–96. Applicants need a minimum GPA of 2.7, either the SAT I or ACT, at least 9 college-level credit hours, and a faculty recommendation and dean's report from the previous college attended. 48 credits of 128 must be completed at Simmons.

Visiting: There are regularly scheduled orientations for prospective students, including a campus tour, an interview, and meetings with faculty and students. There are guides for informal visits and visitors may sit in on classes and stay overnight at the school. To schedule a visit, contact the Admissions Office.

Financial Aid: In 1995–96, 95% of all freshmen and 74% of continuing students received some form of financial aid. 76% of freshmen and 72% of continuing students received need-based aid. The average freshman award was $15,265. Of that total, scholarships or need-based grants averaged $11,476 ($18,500 maximum); loans averaged $3825 (maximum); and work contracts averaged $1500 (maximum). 60% of undergraduate students work part-time. Average earnings from campus work for the school year are $1080. The average financial indebtedness of the 1994–95 graduate was $14,047. Simmons is a member of CSS. The college's own financial statement and federal tax returns are required. The application deadline for fall entry is February 1.

International Students: There are currently 55 international students enrolled. The school actively recruits these students. They must take the TOEFL and achieve a minimum score of 550. The student must also take the SAT I.

Computers: The college provides computer facilities for student use. The mainframes are a DEC VAX and RISC network. There are 40 terminals on the academic network, including 8 in the residence halls. In addition, there are 29 microcomputers in the library. Students use the mainframe for programming, statistics, and other computations. Microcomputers are used for personal information management, including word processing, graphics, and Internet access. All students may access the system. There are no time limits and no fees.

Graduates: In 1994–95, 243 bachelor's degrees were awarded. The most popular majors among graduates were nursing (16%), psychology (9%), and communication (7%). Within an average freshman class, 59% graduate in 4 years, 60% to 66% in 6 years. 37 companies recruited on campus in 1994–95.

Admissions Contact: Deborah Wright, Dean of Admission.

SIMON'S ROCK COLLEGE OF BARD
A-2
Great Barrington, MA 01230–9702
(413) 528-7313
(800) 235-7186

Full-time: 114 men, 185 women	**Faculty:** 36
Part-time: 6 men, 12 women	**Ph.D.s:** 94%
Graduate: none	**Student/Faculty:** 8 to 1
Year: 4–1–4	**Tuition:** $20,270
Application Deadline: June 1	**Room & Board:** $5860
Freshman Class: 382 applied, 229 accepted, 124 enrolled	
SAT I Verbal/Math: 600/600	**VERY COMPETITIVE +**

Simon's Rock College of Bard, founded in 1964, is a private, coeducational liberal arts school especially designed to permit students who have completed the 10th or 11th grades to enroll for collegiate studies. The library contains 60,000 volumes, 7000 microform items, and 3000 audiovisual forms, and subscribes to 325 periodicals. Computerized library sources and services include the card catalog, interlibrary loans, and database searching. Special learning facilities include an art gallery, radio station, and language laboratory. The 275-acre campus is in a small town 50 miles west of Springfield. Including residence halls, there are 10 buildings on campus.

Student Life: 87% of undergraduates are from out-of-state, mostly the Northeast and Middle Atlantic. Students come from 41 states, 5 foreign countries, and Canada. 82% are from public schools; 18% from private. 65% are white. The average age of freshmen is 16.5; all undergraduates, 18. 15% do not continue beyond their first year; 85% remain to graduate.

Housing: 300 students can be accommodated in college housing. College-sponsored living facilities include single-sex and coed dormitories and on-campus apartments. In addition, there are special interest houses. On-campus housing is guaranteed for all 4 years. 90% of students live on campus; of those, 95% remain on campus on weekends. Alcohol is not permitted. Upperclassmen may keep cars on campus.

Activities: There are no fraternities or sororities. There are 21 groups on campus, including chorale, chorus, computers, dance, drama, ethnic, film, gay, honors, international, jazz band, literary magazine, newspaper, political, radio and TV, religious, social, social service, student government, women's, and yearbook. Popular campus events include Founders Day, May Fest, and the Winter Dance Festival.

Sports: There are 5 intercollegiate sports for men and 3 for women, and 10 intramural sports for men and 10 for women. Athletic and recreation facilities include a gymnasium, tennis courts, athletic fields, skating ponds, and hiking trails.

Disabled Students: 80% of the campus is accessible to disabled students. The following facilities are available: wheelchair ramps, special parking, specially equipped rest rooms, special class scheduling, and lowered telephones.

Services: In addition to many counseling and information services, tutoring is available in most subjects. Study skills instruction is available upon request.

Campus Safety and Security: Campus safety and security measures include informal discussions, pamphlets/posters/films, emergency telephones, and lighted pathways/sidewalks.

Programs of Study: Simon's Rock confers the B.A. degree. Associate degrees are also awarded. Bachelor's degrees are awarded in COMPUTER AND PHYSICAL SCIENCE (natural sciences and quantitative methods), ENGINEERING AND ENVIRONMENTAL DESIGN (environmental science), SOCIAL SCIENCE (interdisciplinary studies, social science, and women's studies).

Required: Students must complete a writing and thinking workshop, a freshman composition course and seminar, and a cultural perspectives seminar. The core curriculum, which includes distribution requirements in the arts, mathematics, natural sciences, and foreign language courses, is completed in the first 2 years. A total of 120 credits, including an 8-credit senior thesis, and a minimum 2.0 GPA are needed to graduate.

Special: All majors are interdisciplinary: arts and aesthetics, environmental studies, intercultural studies, literary studies, natural science, quantitative studies, and social science. Independent study, internships in many fields, study abroad, a cooperative program with Bard College, and pass/fail options are offered.

Faculty/Classroom: 63% of faculty are male; 37%, female. All teach undergraduates. The average class size in a regular course offering is 11.

Admissions: 60% of the 1995–96 applicants were accepted.

Requirements: The SAT I is required. The admissions committee looks more toward the required interview, essay, recommendations, and special talent. The school recommends that prospective students finish 2 years each of English, foreign languages, history, mathematics, science, and social studies. Important factors in the admissions decision are advanced placement or honor courses, recommendations by school officials, and personality/intangible qualities.

Procedure: Freshmen are admitted in the fall and spring. Entrance exams should be taken prior to March 30. There are early admissions and deferred admissions plans. Applications should be filed by June 1 for fall entry and December 15 for spring entry, along with an application fee of $25. Notification is sent on a rolling basis.

Transfer: Transfer students must be evaluated by the dean and registrar. 72 credits of 120 must be completed at Simon's Rock.

Visiting: There are regularly scheduled orientations for prospective students, including class visits, a campus tour, and an interview. There are guides for informal visits and visitors may sit in on classes. To schedule a visit, contact Brian R. Hopewell, Director of Admissions.

Financial Aid: In 1995–96, 90% of all freshmen and 81% of continuing students received some form of financial aid. 60% of all students received need-based aid. The average freshman award was $12,081. 50% of undergraduate students work part-time. Average earnings from campus work for the school year are $1000. The average financial indebtedness of the 1994–95 graduate was $17,000. Simon's Rock is a member of CSS. The FAFSA and FAF are required. The application deadline for fall entry is June 15.

International Students: There were 4 international students enrolled in a recent year. The school actively recruits these students. They must take the TOEFL and achieve a minimum score of 500.

Computers: The college provides computer facilities for student use. The mainframe is a UNIX. Students may access the mainframe from PCs in their dorm or from 2 computer laboratories. All students should, if possible, have their own PCs with modems. All students may access the system. There are no time limits and no fees.

Admissions Contact: Brian R. Hopewell, Director of Admissions.

SMITH COLLEGE

		B-2
Northampton, MA 01063	(413) 585-2500; FAX: (413) 585-2527	
Full-time: 2592 women	Faculty: 254; IIA, + +$	
Part-time: 76 women	Ph.D.s: 97%	
Graduate: 82 men, 422 women	Student/Faculty: 10 to 1	
Year: semesters	Tuition: $19,814	
Application Deadline: January 15	Room & Board: $6670	
Freshman Class: 3334 applied, 1635 accepted, 631 enrolled		
SAT I or ACT: required		MOST COMPETITIVE

Smith College, founded in 1871, is the largest independent women's college in the United States, and offers a liberal arts education. There are 2 graduate schools. The 4 libraries contain 1,128,550 volumes, 88,364 microform items, and 54,245 audiovisual forms, and subscribe to 3050 periodicals. Computerized library sources and services include the card catalog, interlibrary loans, and database

searching. Special learning facilities include a learning resource center, art gallery, radio station, TV studio, astronomy observatories, center for foreign languages and culture, digital design studio, plant and horticultural laboratories, art studios with casting, printmaking, and darkroom facilities, and specialized libraries for science, music, and art. The 125-acre campus is in a small town 90 miles west of Boston. Including residence halls, there are 105 buildings on campus.

Student Life: 82% of undergraduates are from out-of-state, mostly the Middle Atlantic. Students come from 50 states, 68 foreign countries, and Canada. 73% are white; 11% Asian American. 32% are Protestant; 31% claim no religious affiliation; 23% Catholic. The average age of freshmen is 18; all undergraduates, 20. 13% do not continue beyond their first year; 85% remain to graduate.

Housing: 2348 students can be accommodated in college housing. College-sponsored living facilities include dormitories and on-campus apartments. In addition there are language houses, nonsmoking wings, a cooperative house, and housing for nontraditional-age students. On-campus housing is guaranteed for all 4 years. 90% of students live on campus; of those, 80% remain on campus on weekends. Upperclassmen may keep cars on campus.

Activities: There are no sororities. There are 93 groups on campus, including art, choir, chorale, chorus, computers, dance, drama, ethnic, film, gay, international, literary magazine, newspaper, orchestra, photography, political, professional, radio and TV, religious, social, social service, student government, symphony, and yearbook. Popular campus events include Mountain Day, International Student Day, Spring and Winter Weekends, Rally Day, Otelia Cromwell Day, and Rhythm Nations.

Sports: There are 14 intercollegiate sports for women and 13 intramural sports for women. Athletic and recreation facilities include indoor and outdoor tracks and tennis courts, riding rings, 2 gymnasiums, an indoor swimming pool with 1- and 3-meter diving boards, 2 weight-training rooms, a dance studio, an athletic training room, a human performance laboratory, squash courts, and field hockey, soccer, lacrosse, and softball fields. There is a performing arts center and a concert hall.

Disabled Students: 50% of the campus is accessible to disabled students. The following facilities are available: wheelchair ramps, elevators, special parking, specially equipped rest rooms, special class scheduling, lowered drinking fountains, and lowered telephones.

Services: In addition to many counseling and information services, tutoring is available in every subject. There is a reader service for the blind. Numerous services are provided for learning-disabled students, including note taking, oral tests, readers, tutors, talking books, reading machines, tape recorders, untimed tests, and writing counselors.

Campus Safety and Security: Campus safety and security measures include 24-hour foot and vehicle patrol, self-defense education, escort service, and shuttle buses. In addition, there are informal discussions, pamphlets/posters/films, emergency telephones, and lighted pathways/sidewalks. First-year students are required to attend panel discussions on campus safety. Specialized personal safety presentations are provided to various houses and organizations.

Programs of Study: Smith confers the A.B. degree. Master's and doctoral degrees are also awarded. Bachelor's degrees are awarded in BIOLOGICAL SCIENCE (biochemistry and biology/biological science), COMMUNICATIONS AND THE ARTS (art history and appreciation, classics, comparative literature, dance, dramatic arts, English, French, Germanic languages and literature, Greek, Italian, Latin, music, Russian, Spanish, and studio art), COMPUTER AND PHYSICAL SCIENCE (astronomy, chemistry, computer science, geology, mathematics, and physics), EDUCATION (early childhood and elementary), ENGINEERING AND ENVIRONMENTAL DESIGN (architecture), SOCIAL SCIENCE (African American studies, American studies, anthropology, classical/ancient civilization, economics, French studies, history, Latin American studies, Luso-Brazilian studies, medieval studies, philosophy, political science/government, psychology, religion, Russian and Slavic studies, sociology, and women's studies). Biological sciences, psychology, and economics are the strongest academically. Government, psychology, and art have the largest enrollments.

Required: All students planning individual programs in consultation with faculty advisers take 64 credits outside their major and 36 to 48 credits in the major. Students must maintain a minimum 2.0 GPA in all academic work and during the senior year. A total of 128 credits is needed to graduate.

Special: Smith offers a junior year co-op program called the Twelve College Exchange, and cross-registration with 5 area colleges and universities. Internships, including one at the Smithsonian Institution, study abroad in Rome, Geneva, Hamburg, and Paris, consortial programs in Spain, China, Russia, Italy, Japan, and South India, and a Washington semester are available. An accelerated degree program, student-designed majors, nondegree study, and satisfactory/unsatisfactory options are possible. There are 3 national honor societies on campus, including Phi Beta Kappa.

Faculty/Classroom: 54% of faculty are male; 46%, female. All teach undergraduates and do research. No introductory courses are taught by graduate students. The average class size in an introductory lecture is 25; in a laboratory, 10; and in a regular course offering, 15.

Admissions: 49% of the 1995–96 applicants were accepted. The SAT I scores for the 1995–96 freshman class were as follows: Verbal—9% below 500, 38% between 500 and 599, 46% between 600 and 700, and 8% above 700; Math—6% below 500, 28% between 500 and 599, 53% between 600 and 700, and 13% above 700. 84% of the current freshmen were in the top fifth of their class; 97% were in the top two fifths. 25 freshmen graduated first in their class.

Requirements: The SAT I or ACT is required. Smith highly recommends that applicants have 4 years of English, 3 years each of mathematics and a foreign language, and 2 years each of science and history. SAT II: Subject tests, especially in writing, are strongly recommended, as are personal interviews. The GED is accepted. AP credits are accepted. Important factors in the admissions decision are advanced placement or honor courses, leadership record, and recommendations by school officials.

Procedure: Freshmen are admitted in the fall. Entrance exams should be taken before January of the senior year. There are early decision, early admissions, and deferred admissions plans. Early decision applications should be filed by November 15; regular applications, by January 15 for fall entry, along with an application fee of $45. Notification of early decision is sent December 15; regular decision, March 30. 142 early decision candidates were accepted for the 1995–96 class. A waiting list is an active part of the admissions procedure.

Transfer: 102 transfer students enrolled in 1995–96. Criteria for transfer students are similar to those for entering freshmen, with more emphasis on the college record. 64 credits of 128 must be completed at Smith.

Visiting: There are regularly scheduled orientations for prospective students. Student-guided tours are available 6 times a day, Monday through Friday, when school is in full session and on Saturday mornings from September to January. Interviews may also be scheduled during these times. There are guides for informal visits and visitors may sit in on classes and stay overnight at the school. To schedule a visit, contact Michelle LaPlante, Receptionist.

Financial Aid: In 1995–96, 60% of all freshmen and 56% of continuing students received some form of financial aid. 60% of freshmen and 56% of continuing students received need-based aid. The average freshman award was $17,837. Of that total, scholarships or need-based grants averaged $14,018 ($25,050 maximum); loans averaged $2657 ($3625 maximum); and work contracts averaged $1162 ($1475 maximum). 45% of undergraduate students work part-time. Average earnings from campus work for the school year are $966. The average financial indebtedness of the 1994–95 graduate was $11,653. Smith is a member of CSS. The college's own financial statement and the CSS Profile Application are required. The application deadline for fall entry is February 1.

International Students: There are currently 203 international students enrolled. The school actively recruits these students. They must take the TOEFL. The student must also take the SAT I if the language of instruction in school is English.

Computers: The college provides computer facilities for student use. The mainframe is comprised of 4 DEC MicroVAX 3100s. Computing facilities span the campus with public computing laboratories in several buildings joined by a campuswide local area network (LAN). Resources include more than 230 IBM and Macintosh personal computers. Internet access is available. All students may access the system. There are no time limits and no fees.

Graduates: In 1994–95, 672 bachelor's degrees were awarded. The most popular majors among graduates were government (13%), psychology (10%), and art (8%). Within an average freshman class, 2% graduate in 3 years, 80% in 4 years, 85% in 5 years, and 86% in 6 years. 58 companies recruited on campus in 1994–95. Of the 1994 graduating class, 20% were enrolled in graduate school within 6 months of graduation.

Admissions Contact: Nanci Tessier, Director of Admissions. E-mail: admission@smith.edu. A campus video is available.

SPRINGFIELD COLLEGE
Springfield, MA 01109

B-3

(413) 748-3136
(800) 343-1257; FAX: (413) 748-3694

Full-time: 991 men, 1033 women	**Faculty:** IIA, --$
Part-time: none	**Ph.D.s:** n/av
Graduate: 157 men, 367 women	**Student/Faculty:** n/av
Year: semesters, summer session	**Tuition:** $11,900
Application Deadline: April 1	**Room & Board:** $5400
Freshman Class: 2150 applied, 1327 accepted, 503 enrolled	
SAT I: required	**LESS COMPETITIVE**

Springfield College, established in 1885, is a private liberal arts institution. There is 1 graduate school. In addition to regional accreditation, the college has baccalaureate program accreditation with APTA, CAHEA, and NRPA. The library contains 145,000 volumes, 500,000 microform items, and 3200 audiovisual forms, and subscribes to 925 periodicals. Special learning facilities include a radio station. The 160-acre campus is in a suburban area 26 miles north of Hartford, Connecticut. Including residence halls, there are 38 buildings on campus.

Student Life: 70% of undergraduates are from out-of-state, mostly the Northeast. Students come from 30 states and 12 foreign countries. 83% are from public schools; 17% from private. 93% are white. The average age of freshmen is 18; all undergraduates, 21. 12% do not continue beyond their first year; 83% remain to graduate.

Housing: 1967 students can be accommodated in college housing. College-sponsored living facilities include dormitories and off-campus apartments. In addition there is a wellness dormitory. On-campus housing is guaranteed for all 4 years. 85% of students live on campus; of those, 75% remain on campus on weekends. Alcohol is not permitted. Upperclassmen may keep cars on campus.

Activities: There are no fraternities or sororities. There are 45 groups on campus, including band, cheerleading, choir, chorus, computers, dance, drama, jazz band, musical theater, newspaper, pep band, religious, social service, student government, and yearbook. Popular campus events include Parents Weekend, Homecoming, and Stepping Up Day.

Sports: There are 14 intercollegiate sports for men and 13 for women, and 10 intramural sports for men and 10 for women. Athletic and recreation facilities include a 2000-seat stadium, a 2000-seat gymnasium, a superturf football/soccer/lacrosse/field hockey field, 8 tennis courts, baseball and softball fields, and free weight and Nautilus rooms.

Disabled Students: 75% of the campus is accessible to disabled students. The following facilities are available: wheelchair ramps, elevators, special parking, specially equipped rest rooms, and lowered drinking fountains.

Services: In addition to many counseling and information services, tutoring is available in most subjects. There is remedial writing.

Campus Safety and Security: Campus safety and security measures include 24-hour foot and vehicle patrol, self-defense education, escort service, and informal discussions. In addition, there are pamphlets/posters/films, emergency telephones, and lighted pathways/sidewalks.

Programs of Study: The college confers B.A. and B.S. degrees. Master's and doctoral degrees are also awarded. Bachelor's degrees are awarded in BIOLOGICAL SCIENCE (biochemistry and biology/biological science), BUSINESS (business administration and management and sports management), COMMUNICATIONS AND THE ARTS (English and fine arts), COMPUTER AND PHYSICAL SCIENCE (chemistry, information sciences and systems, and mathematics), EDUCATION (early childhood, elementary, health, middle school, physical, science, and secondary), HEALTH PROFESSIONS (art therapy, emergency medical technologies, environmental health science, health care administration, medical laboratory technology, physical therapy, physician's assistant, predentistry, premedicine, recreation therapy, and rehabilitation therapy), SOCIAL SCIENCE (gerontology, history, human services, parks and recreation management, physical fitness/movement, political science/government, prelaw, psychology, and sociology). Physical therapy and athletic training are the strongest academically. Physical education, business, and health/fitness have the largest enrollments.

Required: To graduate, students must complete a total of 130 credits with a 2.0 GPA. Core requirements include 30 semester hours in English, social and natural sciences, health, religion, philosophy, and art, and 4 credits in physical education.

Special: Cross-registration may be arranged with cooperating colleges in the greater Springfield area. There is 1 national honor society on campus.

Faculty/Classroom: 54% of faculty are male; 46%, female. The average class size in an introductory lecture is 250; in a laboratory, 35; and in a regular course offering, 30.

Admissions: 62% of the 1995–96 applicants were accepted. 26% of the current freshmen were in the top fifth of their class.

Requirements: The SAT I is required. Applicants must be graduates of an accredited secondary school and have completed 4 years of English, 2 years each of history, mathematics, and science, and 6 electives. The school accepts the GED. An essay and an interview are required. AP credits are accepted. Important factors in the admissions decision are advanced placement or honor courses, leadership record, and extracurricular activities record.

Procedure: Freshmen are admitted fall and spring. Entrance exams should be taken in November of the senior year. There are early decision, early admissions, and deferred admissions plans. Early decision applications should be filed by December 1; regular applications, by April 1 for fall entry and December 1 for spring entry, along with an application fee of $35. Notification is sent on a rolling basis. A waiting list is an active part of the admissions procedure.

Transfer: Grades of 2.0 transfer for credit. Applicants are admitted in the fall and spring.

Visiting: There are guides for informal visits and visitors may sit in on classes and stay overnight at the school. To schedule a visit, contact the Admissions Office.

Financial Aid: The FAF, the college's own financial statement, and tax returns for parents and the student are required. The application deadline for fall entry is April 1.

International Students: There were 57 international students enrolled in a recent year. They must take the TOEFL and achieve a minimum score of 500. The student must also take the SAT I.

Computers: The college provides computer facilities for student use. The mainframe is an IBM AS/400. There are also 30 Apple IIe, IBM PS/2 Model 30, and IBM PS/2 Model 25 microcomputers available for academic use. All students may access the system. There are no time limits and no fees.

Graduates: Within an average freshman class, 1% graduate in 3 years.

Admissions Contact: Fred Bartlett, Director of Admissions. E-mail: admissions@spfldcol.edu.

STONEHILL COLLEGE   E-3

North Easton, MA 02357   (508) 230-1373; FAX: (508) 230-3732

Full-time: 836 men, 1146 women	Faculty: 118; IIB, av$
Part-time: 11 men, 12 women	Ph.D.s: 81%
Graduate: none	Student/Faculty: 17 to 1
Year: semesters, summer session	Tuition: $13,284
Application Deadline: February 1	Room & Board: $6350
Freshman Class: 3796 applied, 2292 accepted, 547 enrolled	
SAT I Verbal/Math: 480/540	ACT: 23 **VERY COMPETITIVE**

Stonehill College, founded in 1948 by the Holy Cross Fathers, is a private Roman Catholic college offering undergraduate degrees in business administration, liberal arts, and the sciences. In addition to regional accreditation, Stonehill has baccalaureate program accreditation with NCATE. The 2 libraries contain 154,898 volumes, 53,576 microform items, and 2785 audiovisual forms, and subscribe to 1145 periodicals. Computerized library sources and services include the card catalog, interlibrary loans, and database searching. Special learning facilities include a learning resource center, radio station, an observatory, and an institute for the study of law and society. The 375-acre campus is in a suburban area 20 miles south of Boston. Including residence halls, there are 58 buildings on campus.

Student Life: 63% of undergraduates are from Massachusetts. Students come from 25 states, 17 foreign countries, and Canada. 76% are from public schools; 24% from private. 93% are white. 79% are Catholic; 10% Protestant. The average age of freshmen is 18; all undergraduates, 19.5. 15% do not continue beyond their first year; 79% remain to graduate.

Housing: 1500 students can be accommodated in college housing. College-sponsored living facilities include single-sex and coed dormitories. In addition, there are special interest houses, international experience housing, and substance free/wellness housing. On-campus housing is guaranteed for all 4 years. 79% of students live on campus; of those, 70% remain on campus on weekends. All students may keep cars on campus.

Activities: There are no fraternities or sororities. There are 56 groups on campus, including academic, cheerleading, choir, computers, dance, drama, environmental, ethnic, film, honors, international, literary magazine, newspaper, political, radio and TV, religious, social, social service, student government, and yearbook. Popular campus events include Fall Concert, Spring Weekend, Octoberfest, and Spring Semiformals.

Sports: There are 10 intercollegiate sports for men and 9 for women, and 15 intramural sports for men and 15 for women. Athletic and recreation facilities include a 55,000-square-foot complex that houses a fitness center, a jogging track, courts for basketball, volleyball, tennis, racquetball, and squash, and an instructional program area. There are outdoor practice and playing fields, and a 2,000-seat stadium.

Disabled Students: 85% of the campus is accessible to disabled students. The following facilities are available: wheelchair ramps, elevators, special parking, specially equipped rest rooms, special class scheduling, lowered drinking fountains, lowered telephones, telecommunication devices for the deaf, and 8 dormitory rooms designed specifically for disabled students.

Services: In addition to many counseling and information services, tutoring is available in most subjects. There is a reader service for the blind and remedial writing.

Campus Safety and Security: Campus safety and security measures include 24-hour foot and vehicle patrol, self-defense education, escort service, and informal discussions. In addition, there are pamphlets/posters/films, emergency telephones, lighted pathways/sidewalks, bicycle patrols, and a weekend guest sign-in policy.

Programs of Study: Stonehill confers B.A., B.S., and B.S.B.A. degrees. Master's degrees are also awarded. Bachelor's degrees are awarded in BIOLOGICAL SCIENCE (biology/biological science), BUSINESS (accounting, banking and finance, business economics, management science, and marketing/retailing/merchandising), COMMUNICATIONS AND THE ARTS (communications, English, and languages), COMPUTER AND PHYSICAL SCIENCE (chemistry, computer science, and mathematics), EDUCATION (education), HEALTH PROFESSIONS (health care administration and medical technology), SOCIAL SCIENCE (American studies, criminal justice, economics, history, interdisciplinary studies, international studies, philosophy, political science/government, psychology, public administration, religion, and sociology). Biology, chemistry, and accounting are the strongest academically. Psychology, biology, and education studies have the largest enrollments.

Required: All students must complete a Western heritage core, which consists of 2 semesters each in the following 5 areas: religious studies, philosophy, social institutions, literature and fine arts, and scientific inquiry. They must also take 1 semester each of writing and quantitative techniques, and 1 year of foreign language. Students must complete 40 3- or 4- credit courses, while maintaining a minimum GPA of 2.0.

Special: On-campus work-study, international and domestic internships, and a Washington semester through the Washington Center and the Washington Internship Program are available. Cross-registration with 8 other Massachusetts schools in the SACHEM consortium is also available. Opportunities for study abroad include an exchange program with Yaroslavl State University in the Russian Federation, Stonehill-Quebec Exchange, a semester in Irish studies at University College Dublin, and a worldwide Foreign Studies Program. Non-degree, directed, and field study are available as well as a pass/fail option for upperclassmen. Programs in early childhood, elementary, and secondary education lead to the state's provisional teacher certification. Stonehill is also a member of the Massachusetts Bay Marine Studies Consortium. There is a freshman honors program on campus, as well as 9 national honor societies. 5 departments have honors programs.

Faculty/Classroom: 69% of faculty are male; 31%, female. All teach undergraduates. The average class size in an introductory lecture is 25; in a laboratory, 19; and in a regular course offering, 22.

Admissions: 60% of the 1995–96 applicants were accepted. The SAT I scores for the 1995–96 freshman class were as follows: Verbal—57% below 500, 36% between 500 and 599, and 7% between 600 and 700; Math—32% below 500, 45% between 500 and 599, 21% between 600 and 700, and 2% above 700. 58% of the current freshmen were in the top fifth of their class; 89% were in the top two fifths. 5 freshmen graduated first in their class.

Requirements: The SAT I or ACT is required. Applicants should be graduates of an accredited high school or have earned the GED. Secondary preparation should include 4 units of English, at least 2 units of the same foreign language, 1 each in algebra, geometry, science, and history, as well as 6 electives with no more than 3 in business subjects. An essay and guidance counselor recommendation are also required. AP and CLEP credits are accepted. Important factors in the admissions decision are advanced placement or honor courses, evidence of special talent, and leadership record.

Procedure: Freshmen are admitted in the fall and spring. Entrance exams should be taken in October. There are early admissions and deferred admissions plans. Applications should be filed by February 1 for fall entry and November 1 for spring entry, along with an application fee of $40. Notification is sent by April 1. A waiting list is an active part of the admissions procedure, with about 9% of all applicants on the list.

Transfer: 52 transfer students enrolled in 1995–96. Applicants must have a minimum GPA of 2.0. Official high school transcripts and college transcripts, along with catalogs with course descriptions from all colleges attended, are required. SAT I or ACT scores are required and an interview is recommended. 60 credits of 120 must be completed at Stonehill.

Visiting: There are regularly scheduled orientations for prospective students, consisting of group information sessions and guided campus tours available by appointment throughout the year. Visitors may sit in on classes. To schedule a visit, contact the Admissions Office.

Financial Aid: In 1995–96, 81% of all freshmen and 82% of continuing students received some form of financial aid. 62% of freshmen and 55% of continuing students received need-based aid. The average freshman award was $9055. Of that total, scholarships or need-based grants averaged $6315 ($19,882 maximum); loans averaged $3081 ($5625 maximum); and work contracts averaged $1110 ($1200 maximum). 29% of undergraduate students work part-time. Average earnings from campus work for the school year are $830. The average financial indebtedness of the 1994–95 graduate was $13,996. Stonehill is a member of CSS. FAFSA and the CSS Profile Application are required. The application deadline for fall entry is February 1.

International Students: There are currently 46 international students enrolled. The school actively recruits these students. They must take the TOEFL and achieve a minimum score of 550. The student must also take the SAT I or the ACT.

Computers: The college provides computer facilities for student use. The mainframe is a DEC VAX 4000–300. Some 36 terminals, 60 microcomputers, and 12 printers are accessible to students. A variety of software, word processors, statistics, spreadsheets, and databases are available for student use. All students may access the system from 8 A.M. to 11:30 P.M. weekdays, from 8 A.M. to 4 P.M on Saturday, and from 1 P.M. to midnight on Sunday. There are no time limits. The fees are $100 per computer laboratory course per semester, not to exceed $200 per semester, or $50 per semester for word processing.

Graduates: In 1994–95, 504 bachelor's degrees were awarded. The most popular majors among graduates were psychology (12%), criminal justice (11%), and accounting (10%). Within an average freshman class, 75% graduate in 4 years, 79% in 5 years, and 79% in 6 years. 57 companies recruited on campus in 1994–95. Of the 1994 graduating class, 16% were enrolled in graduate school within 6 months of graduation and 89% had found employment.

Admissions Contact: Brian P. Murphy, Dean of Admissions and Enrollment.

SUFFOLK UNIVERSITY

E-2

Boston, MA 02108-2770

(617) 573-8460

(800) 6 SUFFOLK; FAX: (617) 742-4291

Full-time: 1021 men, 1143 women	**Faculty:** 169; IIA, av$
Part-time: 243 men, 354 women	**Ph.D.s:** 91%
Graduate: 781 men, 684 women	**Student/Faculty:** 13 to 1
Year: semesters, summer session	**Tuition:** $11,360
Application Deadline: open	**Room & Board:** $6000
Freshman Class: 1526 applied, 1114 accepted, 402 enrolled	
SAT I Verbal/Math: 410/430	**COMPETITIVE**

Suffolk University, founded in 1906, is a private coeducational institution offering undergraduate and graduate degrees in the arts and sciences, business, and law. There are 2 undergraduate and 3 graduate schools. In addition to regional accreditation, Suffolk has baccalaureate program accreditation with AACSB. The 2 libraries contain 283,620 volumes, 221,923 microform items, and 213 audiovisual forms, and subscribe to 1370 periodicals. Computerized library sources and services include the card catalog, interlibrary loans, and database searching. Special learning facilities include a learning resource center, radio station, TV station, and satellite hookups. The 2-acre campus is in an urban area in the Beacon Hill area of downtown Boston. Including residence halls, there are 9 buildings on campus.

Student Life: 84% of undergraduates are from Massachusetts. Students come from 22 states, 81 foreign countries, and Canada. 70% are from public schools; 30% from private. 63% are white; 11% foreign nationals. The average age of freshmen is 20; all undergraduates, 23. 24% do not continue beyond their first year; 54% remain to graduate.

Housing: 400 students can be accommodated in college housing. College-sponsored living facilities include coed dormitories and off-campus apartments. On-campus housing is guaranteed for the freshman year only and is available on a first-come, first-served basis. 95% of students commute. Alcohol is not permitted.

Activities: 2% of men and about 2% of women belong to 1 local and 2 national fraternities; 2% of women belong to 1 national sorority. There are 40 groups on campus, including art, cheerleading, computers, drama, ethnic, film, gay, honors, international, literary magazine, literary society, musical theater, newspaper, photography, political, professional, radio and TV, religious, social, social service, student government, women's center, and yearbook. Popular campus events include Hispanic Fiesta, Springfest Talent Show, Holiday Party, and Commencement Ball.

Sports: There are 6 intercollegiate sports for men and 5 for women, and 2 intramural sports for men and 2 for women. Athletic and recreation facilities include a gymnasium for basketball, volleyball, aerobics, intramurals, and indoor baseball/softball practice as well as a fully equipped fitness center.

Disabled Students: 90% of the campus is accessible to disabled students. The following facilities are available: wheelchair ramps, elevators, specially equipped rest rooms, special class scheduling, lowered drinking fountains, and lowered telephones.

Services: In addition to many counseling and information services, tutoring is available in most subjects. There is a reader service for the blind, and remedial math, reading, and writing.

Campus Safety and Security: Campus safety and security measures include 24-hour foot and vehicle patrol, escort service, informal discussions, and pamphlets/posters/films. In addition, there are emergency telephones and lighted pathways/sidewalks.

Programs of Study: Suffolk confers B.A., B.S., B.F.A., B.S.B.A., B.S.G.S., and B.S.J. degrees. Associate, master's, and doctoral degrees are also awarded. Bachelor's degrees are awarded in BIO-

LOGICAL SCIENCE (biochemistry, biology/biological science, and marine science), BUSINESS (accounting, banking and finance, international economics, management science, and marketing/retailing/merchandising), COMMUNICATIONS AND THE ARTS (broadcasting, communications, dramatic arts, English, French, journalism, public relations, Spanish, and speech/debate/rhetoric), COMPUTER AND PHYSICAL SCIENCE (chemistry, computer programming, computer science, mathematics, and physics), EDUCATION (business and elementary), ENGINEERING AND ENVIRONMENTAL DESIGN (computer engineering and electrical/electronics engineering), HEALTH PROFESSIONS (cytotechnology and medical laboratory technology), SOCIAL SCIENCE (criminal justice, economics, history, human development, humanities, industrial and organizational psychology, paralegal studies, philosophy, political science/government, public administration, social science, and sociology). Medical biophysics and radiation biology are the strongest academically. Business subjects, sociology, and communications and speech have the largest enrollments.

Required: All students must complete 122 semester hours with at least a 2.0 GPA. Distribution requirements vary by degree program.

Special: Numerous cooperative education and work-study programs are available in the Boston area. Cross-registration is offered with New England School of Art and Design (B.F.A.), Suffolk University, Madrid campus, Northeast Broadcasting School, International University in Moscow, and Stilwell School for International Studies in Chongoing, China. Study abroad in 25 countries and a semester internship in Washington, D.C., as well as local and international internships, are possible. A combined 3–2 engineering degree with Boston University and Case Western Reserve University, majors in medical biophysics and radiation biology taught in collaboration with Massachusetts General Hospital, dual and student-designed majors, and a lawyer's assistant certificate program are also available. There is a freshman honors program on campus, as well as 19 national honor societies. 8 departments have honors programs.

Faculty/Classroom: 66% of faculty are male; 34%, female. 92% teach undergraduates, 86% both teach and do research. No introductory courses are taught by graduate students. The average class size in an introductory lecture is 24; in a laboratory, 14; and in a regular course offering, 21.

Admissions: 73% of the 1995–96 applicants were accepted. The SAT I scores for the 1995–96 freshman class were as follows: Verbal—81% below 500, 13% between 500 and 599, and 6% between 600 and 700; Math—71% below 500, 23% between 500 and 599, 5% between 600 and 700, and 1% above 700. 24% of the current freshmen were in the top fifth of their class; 53% were in the top two fifths. There was 1 National Merit finalist and 8 semifinalists. 6 freshmen graduated first in their class.

Requirements: The SAT I is required. Suffolk requires applicants to be in the upper 60% of their class. Applicants should have a high school diploma with a 2.0 GPA or the GED. Recommended secondary preparation includes 4 years of English, 3 of mathematics, 2 each of a foreign language, history, and social studies, and 1 of science. Exact requirements differ by degree program. A personal essay is required, and an interview is recommended. AP and CLEP credits are accepted. Important factors in the admissions decision are recommendations by school officials, advanced placement or honor courses, and leadership record.

Procedure: Freshmen are admitted to all sessions. Entrance exams should be taken by December of the senior year. There are early admissions and deferred admissions plans. Application deadlines are open. Application fee is $40. Notification is sent on a rolling basis.

Transfer: 389 transfer students enrolled in 1995–96. Applicants should have a minimum 2.2 GPA from an accredited college. Those with fewer than 15 college credits must submit a high school transcript. 30 credits of 122 must be completed at Suffolk.

Visiting: There are regularly scheduled orientations for prospective students, including a general presentation and overview, panel presentation of student life, career and co-op, learning center services, athletics, academic department meetings, and campus tours. There are guides for informal visits and visitors may sit in on classes. To schedule a visit, contact the Admissions Office.

Financial Aid: In 1995–96, 68% of all freshmen and 43% of continuing students received some form of financial aid. 61% of freshmen and 44% of continuing students received need-based aid. The average freshman award was $9315. Of that total, scholarships or need-based grants averaged $4937 ($9200 maximum); loans averaged $4825 ($6625 maximum); and work contracts averaged $1181 ($1500 maximum). Most undergraduates work part time. Average earnings from campus work for the school year are $1200. The average financial indebtedness of the 1994–95 graduate was $13,560. Suffolk is a member of CSS. FAFSA, the college's own financial statement, and verification of income are required. The application deadline for fall entry is March 1.

International Students: There are currently 392 international students enrolled. The school actively recruits these students. They must take the TOEFL or the college's own test and achieve a minimum score on the TOEFL of 525.

Computers: The college provides computer facilities for student use. The mainframe is an IBM RS/6000. Various computer laboratories on campus house more than 200 microcomputers with access to the mainframe. Students have access to the Internet, LEXIS/NEXIS database, the Suffolk on-line library system, CD-ROM library and information systems, as well as Sun and DEC UNIX workstations. All students may access the system. There are no time limits and no fees.

Graduates: In 1994–95, 607 bachelor's degrees were awarded. The most popular majors among graduates were sociology (17%), management (15%), and accounting (9%). Within an average freshman class, 1% graduate in 3 years, 40% in 4 years, 50% in 5 years, and 55% in 6 years. 73 companies recruited on campus in 1994–95. Of the 1994 graduating class, 12% were enrolled in graduate school within 6 months of graduation and 85% had found employment.

Admissions Contact: Katherine Teehan, Director of Admissions. E-mail: admission@admin.suffolk.edu. A campus video is available.

TUFTS UNIVERSITY   D-2

Medford, MA 02155   (617) 627-3170; FAX: (617) 627-3860

Full-time: 2169 men, 2362 women	Faculty: 341; I, av$
Part-time: 16 men, 11 women	Ph.D.s: 99%
Graduate: 1637 men, 1902 women	Student/Faculty: 13 to 1
Year: semesters, summer session	Tuition: $21,086
Application Deadline: January 1	Room & Board: $6250
Freshman Class: 8510 applied, 3649 accepted, 1158 enrolled	
SAT I Verbal/Math: 580/660	ACT: 28 MOST COMPETITIVE

Tufts University, founded in 1852, is a private coeducational institution offering undergraduate programs in liberal arts and sciences and engineering. There are 2 undergraduate and 9 graduate schools. In addition to regional accreditation, Tufts has baccalaureate program accreditation with ABET, ADA, and CAHEA. The 2 libraries contain 864,000 volumes, 1,066,000 microform items, and 24,000 audiovisual forms, and subscribe to 5030 periodicals. Computerized library sources and services include the card catalog, interlibrary loans, and database searching. Special learning facilities include a learning resource center, art gallery, radio station, TV station, and theater. The 140-acre campus is in a suburban area 5 miles northwest of Boston. Including residence halls, there are 167 buildings on campus.

Student Life: 73% of undergraduates are from out-of-state, mostly the Middle Atlantic. Students come from 50 states, 64 foreign countries, and Canada. 65% are from public schools; 35% from private. 69% are white; 14% Asian American. The average age of freshmen is 18; all undergraduates, 20. 2% do not continue beyond their first year; 89% remain to graduate.

Housing: 3550 students can be accommodated in college housing. College-sponsored living facilities include single-sex and coed dormitories, on-campus apartments, fraternity houses, and sorority houses. In addition, there are language houses, special interest houses, and cooperative houses. On-campus housing is guaranteed for the freshman and sophomore years only and is available on a lottery system for upperclassmen. 80% of students live on campus. Upperclassmen may keep cars on campus.

Activities: 15% of men belong to 9 national fraternities; 4% of women belong to 4 national sororities. There are 130 groups on campus, including art, band, cheerleading, chess, choir, chorale, chorus, computers, dance, drama, ethnic, gay, honors, international, jazz band, literary magazine, marching band, musical theater, newspaper, orchestra, outdoor, pep band, photography, political, professional, radio and TV, religious, social, social service, student government, symphony, and yearbook. Popular campus events include a dramatic arts series and national and international forums.

Sports: There are 17 intercollegiate sports for men and 16 for women, and 11 intramural sports for men, 9 for women, and 4 for both men and women. Athletic and recreation facilities include a football stadium, 2 gymnasiums, an 8-lane all-weather track, baseball, softball, and playing fields, 9 tennis courts, a field house, an indoor cage, an indoor track, 7 squash courts, a swimming pool, a dance room, a weight room, a sauna, a sailing center, and an exercise center.

Disabled Students: 90% of the campus is accessible to disabled students. The following facilities are available: wheelchair ramps, elevators, special parking, specially equipped rest rooms, special class scheduling, lowered drinking fountains, lowered telephones, and other special services as needed.

Services: In addition to many counseling and information services, tutoring is available in some subjects as needed through the Academic Resources Center. There is a reader service for the blind. There are women's, African American, Hispanic American, Asian American, international, and lesbian-gay-bisexual centers.

Campus Safety and Security: Campus safety and security measures include 24-hour foot and vehicle patrol, escort service, shuttle buses, and informal discussions. In addition, there are pamphlets/posters/films, emergency telephones, and lighted pathways/sidewalks.

Programs of Study: Tufts confers B.A., B.S., B.S.C.E., B.S.ChE., B.S.E., B.S.E.E., B.S.E.S., and B.S.M.E. degrees. Master's and doctoral degrees are also awarded. Bachelor's degrees are awarded in BIOLOGICAL SCIENCE (biology/biological science), COMMUNICATIONS AND THE ARTS (art history and appreciation, classics, dramatic arts, English, French, German, Greek, Latin, music, Russian, and Spanish), COMPUTER AND PHYSICAL SCIENCE (chemistry, computer science, geology, mathematics, and physics), EDUCATION (early childhood), ENGINEERING AND ENVIRONMENTAL DESIGN (chemical engineering, civil engineering, computer engineering, electrical/electronics engineering, engineering, engineering and applied science, engineering physics, environmental science, and mechanical engineering), SOCIAL SCIENCE (American studies, anthropology, archeology, Asian/Oriental studies, clinical psychology, economics, experimental psychology, history, international relations, philosophy, political science/government, psychobiology, psychology, religion, Russian and Slavic studies, social psychology, and sociology). English, international relations, and biology have the largest enrollments.

Required: Liberal arts students must complete 34 courses, 10 of which are in the area of concentration. Requirements include foundation courses in writing and foreign language or culture and courses in humanities, arts, social sciences, mathematics, and natural sciences. Requirements for engineering students include a total of 38 courses, 12 of which are in the area of concentration, and distribution requirements in English, mathematics and science, humanities, and social sciences.

Special: The university offers cross-registration at Swarthmore College, Boston University, Boston College, and Brandeis University, a Washington semester, and study abroad in England, Spain, France, Moscow, Ghana, and Germany. Many internships are available. Double majors in the liberal arts are common; student-designed majors are possible. There is a 5-year B.A.-B.S. program in engineering and liberal arts, a B.A.-B.F.A. program with the Museum School of Fine Arts, and a B.A.-B.M. program with the New England Conservatory of Music. Pass/fail options are offered. There are 4 national honor societies on campus, including Phi Beta Kappa.

Faculty/Classroom: 60% of faculty are male; 40%, female. All both teach and do research. No introductory courses are taught by graduate students. The average class size in a regular course offering is 25.

Admissions: 43% of the 1995–96 applicants were accepted. The SAT I scores for the 1995–96 freshman class were Verbal—17% below 500, 40% between 500 and 599, 37% between 600 and 700, and 6% above 700; Math—1% below 500, 16% between 500 and 599, 51% between 600 and 700, and 32% above 700. The ACT scores were 2% below 21, 8% between 21 and 23, 22% between 24 and 26, 27% between 27 and 28, and 41% above 28. 86% of the current freshmen were in the top fifth of their class; 98% were in the top two fifths.

Requirements: The university accepts either the SAT I and the results of 3 SAT II: Subject tests, or the ACT. Liberal arts applicants should take the SAT II: Subject test in writing and 2 others; engineering applicants should take writing, mathematics level I or II, and either physics or chemistry. In addition, all applicants should be high school graduates or hold the GED. Academic preparation is expected to include 4 years of English, 3 years each of humanities and a foreign language, 2 years each of social and natural sciences, and 1 year of history. A personal essay is required. Tufts provides its own on-disk application, which can be downloaded from its World Wide Web site, http://www.tufts.edu. AP credits are accepted. Important factors in the admissions decision are advanced placement or honor courses, recommendations by school officials, and extracurricular activities record.

Procedure: Freshmen are admitted in the fall. Entrance exams should be taken by January of the senior year. There are early decision, early admissions, and deferred admissions plans. Early decision applications should be filed by November 15 and January 1; regular applications, by January 1 for fall entry, along with an application fee of $50. Notification of early decision is sent December 15 and February 1; regular decision, April 1. 300 early decision candidates were accepted for the 1995–96 class. A waiting list is an active part of the admissions procedure.

Transfer: 65 transfer students enrolled in 1995–96. Admission is competitive. Primary consideration is given to college and secondary school achievement and record of personal involvement. 17 courses of 34 must be completed at Tufts.

Visiting: There are regularly scheduled orientations for prospective students, including orientation sessions twice a day, Monday through Friday, April 1 to December 10, followed by campus tours. There are additional orientation sessions and tours on selected Saturday mornings during the fall. There are guides for informal visits and visitors may sit in on classes and stay overnight at the school. To schedule a visit, contact the Admissions Office.

Financial Aid: In 1995–96, 48% of all freshmen and 41% of continuing students received some form of financial aid. 44% of freshmen and 37% of continuing students received need-based aid. The average freshman award was $17,400. Of that total, scholarships or need-based grants averaged $15,000 ($25,500 maximum); loans averaged $3200 ($3625 maximum); and work contracts averaged $1560 ($1800 maximum). 42% of undergraduate students work part-time. Average earnings from campus work for the school year are $1350. The average financial indebtedness of the 1994–95 graduate was $12,227. Tufts is a member of CSS. The FAFSA and CSS Profile Application are required. The application deadline for fall entry is February 1.

International Students: There are currently 336 international students enrolled. The school actively recruits these students. They must take the TOEFL if English is not their first language, and must also take the ACT, or SAT I and 3 SAT II: Subject tests, including writing.

Computers: The college provides computer facilities for student use. The mainframes are a DEC VAX 4300 and a DEC MicroVAX 3600 running VMS, and a Convex 3220 minisupercomputer running UNIX. Mainframes and PC laboratories are networked on a university-wide computer network called Jumbonet. There are 254 terminals and microcomputers in 5 locations across campus, supported by 45 printers in various locations. A special computer-aided design (CAD) laboratory is available to undergraduates. All campus residence rooms are hard-wired for access to the university computer facilities and the Internet. All students may access the system 24 hours a day. There are no time limits and no fees.

Graduates: In 1994–95, 1118 bachelor's degrees were awarded. The most popular majors among graduates were international relations (10%), English (10%), and biology (8%). Within an average freshman class, 89% graduate in 4 years. 153 companies recruited on campus in 1994–95.

Admissions Contact: David Cuttino, Dean of Admissions. E-mail: uadmiss_inquiry@infonet.tufts.edu.

UNIVERSITY OF LOWELL
(See University of Massachusetts Lowell)

UNIVERSITY OF MASSACHUSETTS SYSTEM

The University of Massachusetts, established in 1863, is the public university system in Massachusetts. It is governed by a board of trustees and its CEO is the president. The primary goal of the university system is the coordination of campus teaching, research, and service. The main priorities are fiscal management, legal counsel, and academic and student affairs coordination and collaberation. The total enrollment for fall 1994 of all 5 campuses was 58,271; there were 3,378 faculty members. Altogether there are 245 baccalaureate, 147 master's, and 76 doctoral programs offered in the University of Massachusetts System. Profiles of the 4-year campuses are included in this chapter.

UNIVERSITY OF MASSACHUSETTS AMHERST   B-2
Amherst, MA 01003   (413) 545-0222; FAX: (413) 545-4312

Full-time: 8599 men, 8147 women	Faculty: 1146; I, av$
Part-time: 496 men, 488 women	Ph.D.s: 96%
Graduate: 3003 men, 3101 women	Student/Faculty: 15 to 1
Year: semesters, summer session	Tuition: $5514 ($11,860)
Application Deadline: February 15	Room & Board: $4188
Freshman Class: 17,562 applied, 13,780 accepted, 3861 enrolled	
SAT I or ACT: required	COMPETITIVE

University of Massachusetts Amherst, established in 1863, is a public, land-grant, coeducational institution offering undergraduate and graduate degrees in its 9 schools and colleges. In addition to regional accreditation, the university has baccalaureate program accreditation with AACSB, ABET, ADA, ASLA, FIDER, NASM, NCATE, NLN, NRPA, and SAF. The 4 libraries contain 2,710,040 volumes, 2,131,229 microform items, and 13,348 audiovisual forms, and subscribe to 15,641 periodicals. Computerized library sources and services include the card catalog, interlibrary loans, and database searching. Special learning facilities include a learning resource center, art gallery, radio station, and TV station. The 1405-acre campus is in a small town 90 miles west of Boston and 60 miles north of Hartford, Connecticut. Including residence halls, there are 349 buildings on campus.

Student Life: 75% of undergraduates are from Massachusetts. Students come from 48 states, 72 foreign countries, and Canada. 84% are from public schools; 16% from private. 80% are white. 24% are Catholic. The average age of freshmen is 18; all undergraduates, 21. 24% do not continue beyond their first year; 67% remain to graduate.

Housing: 10,557 students can be accommodated in college housing. College-sponsored living facilities include single-sex and coed dormitories, on-campus apartments, married-student housing, fraternity houses, and sorority houses. In addition there are honors houses, special-interest houses, language corridors, a social awareness corridor, and family housing. On-campus housing is guaranteed for the freshman and sophomore years only and is available on a lottery system for upperclassmen. 58% of students live on campus; of those, 80% remain on campus on weekends. All students may keep cars on campus.

Activities: 8% of men belong to 1 local and 21 national fraternities; 6% of women belong to 1 local and 12 national sororities. There are 190 groups on campus, including art, band, cheerleading, chess, choir, chorale, chorus, computers, dance, drama, ethnic, film, gay, honors, international, jazz band, literary magazine, marching band, musical theater, newspaper, opera, orchestra, pep band, photography, political, professional, radio and TV, religious, social, social service, student government, symphony, and yearbook. Popular campus events include basketball games, Spring Pond Concert, Asian Night, and International Fair.

Sports: There are 14 intercollegiate sports for men and 14 for women, and 20 intramural sports for men and 20 for women. Athletic and recreation facilities include 120 acres of playing fields, a 20000-seat outdoor stadium, and lighted tennis courts. Indoor facilities include 3 pools, handball/squash/racquetball courts, 2 gymnastics centers, a wrestling room, a physiotherapy laboratory with steam bath and whirlpool for visiting athletes, 2 dance studios, fencing facilities, an indoor track, universals, crew tanks, weight-training rooms, and a 10500-seat indoor sports arena that houses 2 Olympic-size ice sheets, 7 racquetball courts, and additional athletic training facilities.

Disabled Students: The following facilities are available: wheelchair ramps, elevators, special parking, specially equipped rest rooms, special class scheduling, lowered drinking fountains, and lowered telephones. All programs are made accessible through accommodations.

Services: In addition to many counseling and information services, tutoring is available in most subjects. There is a reader service for the blind and remedial math and reading.

Campus Safety and Security: Campus safety and security measures include 24-hour foot and vehicle patrol, self-defense education, escort service, and shuttle buses. There are informal discussions, pamphlets/posters/films, emergency telephones, lighted pathways/sidewalks, and strictly enforced restrictions on residence hall access.

Programs of Study: The university confers B.A., B.S., B.B.A., B.F.A., B.G.S., B.Mus., B.S.C.E., B.S.C.H.E., B.S.C.S.E., B.S.E.E., B.S.I.E.O.R., and B.S.M.E. degrees. Associate, master's, and doctoral degrees are also awarded. Bachelor's degrees are awarded in AGRICULTURE (animal science, conservation and regulation, forestry and related sciences, natural resource management, plant science, soil science, wildlife management, and wood science), BIOLOGICAL SCIENCE (biochemistry, biology/biological science, entomology, microbiology, nutrition, and plant pathology), BUSINESS (accounting, apparel and accessories marketing, business administration and management, hotel/motel and restaurant management, management science, and sports management), COMMUNICATIONS AND THE ARTS (art history and appreciation, Chinese, classics, communications, comparative literature, dance, design, dramatic arts, English, French, German, Italian, Japanese, journalism, linguistics, music, Portuguese, Russian, Spanish, and studio art), COMPUTER AND PHYSICAL SCIENCE (astronomy, chemistry, computer science, geology, mathematics, and physics), EDUCATION (art, athletic training, early childhood, elementary, middle school, and secondary), ENGINEERING AND ENVIRONMENTAL DESIGN (chemical engineering, civil engineering, computer engineering, electrical/electronics engineering, environmental design, environmental science, industrial engineering, landscape architecture/design, and mechanical engineering), HEALTH PROFESSIONS (medical laboratory technology, nursing, predentistry, premedicine, and speech pathology/audiology), SOCIAL SCIENCE (African American studies, anthropology, economics, ethics, politics, and social policy, European studies, family/consumer studies, food science, geography, history, Judaic studies, law, liberal arts/general studies, Middle Eastern studies, philosophy, political science/government, psychology, Russian and Slavic studies, sociology, and women's studies). Psychology, chemical engineering, and computer science are the strongest academically. Psychology, communication, and hotel, restaurant, and travel administration have the largest enrollments.

Required: To graduate, students must complete 120 credit hours and maintain a minimum GPA of 2.0 with at least 2 courses fulfilling a diversity requirement. The general education requirements for all students include courses in writing, the social world, the biological and physical world, mathematics, and analytic reasoning.

Special: Cross-registration is possible with other University of Massachusetts campuses and with the other schools of the Five-College Consortium (Smith, Mount Holyoke, Hampshire, and Amherst). Students may participate in co-op programs, internships in every major, study abroad in 31 countries, a Washington semester, work-study programs in various university departments, dual majors in most subjects, and student-designed majors. The University Without Walls program gives credit for life, military, and work experience. Other special programs include the National and International Exchange Programs, Learning Resources Center, Honors Program, Minority and Women Engineering Programs, Bilingual Collegiate Program, Committee for the College Education of Black and Other Minority Students, the United Asian Learning Resource Center, and Talent Advancement Programs. There is a freshman honors program on campus, as well as 15 national honor societies, including Phi Beta Kappa. 76 departments have honors programs.

Faculty/Classroom: 73% of faculty are male; 27%, female. All do research. The average class size in an introductory lecture is 46; in a laboratory, 23; and in a regular course offering, 41.

Admissions: 78% of the 1995–96 applicants were accepted. The SAT I scores for the 1995–96 freshman class were as follows: Verbal—63% below 500, 28% between 500 and 599, 8% between 600 and 700, and 1% above 700; Math—32% below 500, 40% between 500 and 599, 23% between 600 and 700, and 5% above 700. 28% of the current freshmen were in the top fifth of their class; 63% were in the top two fifths. 20 freshmen graduated first in their class.

Requirements: The SAT I or ACT is required. In addition, applicants must be graduates of an accredited secondary school, or have the GED. The university recommends that students complete 16 Carnegie units, including 4 years of English, 3 of mathematics, and 2 of foreign language and laboratory science, plus 3 of electives. Students must present a portfolio for admission to the art program and must audition for admission to music and dance. AP and CLEP credits are accepted. Important factors in the admissions decision are advanced placement or honor courses, evidence of special talent, and recommendations by school officials.

Procedure: Freshmen are admitted fall and spring. Entrance exams should be taken before February 15. There are early admissions and deferred admissions plans. Applications should be filed by February 15 for fall entry and October 15 for spring entry, along with an application fee of $25 ($40 for out-of-state applicants). Notification is sent on a rolling basis.

Transfer: 1312 transfer students enrolled in 1995–96. Transfer applicants with fewer than 30 credits must take the SAT I and submit an essay. Priority is given to students with an associate degree. Grades of C or better transfer for credit. 45 credits of 120 must be completed at the university.

Visiting: There are regularly scheduled orientations for prospective students, during which accepted freshmen and transfers may make residence hall choices, take placement exams, register for classes, meet their advisers, live in dormitories with current students, and enjoy a number of social activities. There are guides for informal visits and visitors may sit in on classes and stay overnight at the school. To schedule a visit, call the New Students Program at (413) 545–2621.

Financial Aid: In 1995–96, 60% of all students received some form of financial aid. 55% of all students received need-based aid. The average undergraduate award was $8100. Of that total, scholarships or need-based grants averaged $3100 ($6200 maximum); loans averaged $3100 ($7000 maximum); and work contracts averaged $1500 ($1800 maximum). 80% of undergraduate students work part-time. Average earnings from campus work for the school year are $2500. The average financial indebtedness of the 1994–95 graduate was $9184. The university is a member of CSS. The FAFSA is required. The application deadline for fall entry is March 1.

International Students: There are currently 462 international students enrolled. They must score 550 on the TOEFL and also take SAT I or the ACT.

Computers: The college provides computer facilities for student use. The mainframes are a VAX cluster (2 VAX 6420s) running VMS, 2 DEC/system 5500s running ULTRIX, a CDC 840 running NOS/VE, and a CDC 830 providing access to the CYBIS computer-aided instruction system. There are 70 IBM-compatible and 65 Macintosh computers available in 4 computer classrooms that are open most of the day for walk-in use. There are also 70 terminals accessing the mainframe. Computers are also available through numerous academic departments, and the mainframe is accessible in residence halls to students who own computers. All students may access the system. There are no time limits. The fees are $20 per semester.

Graduates: In 1994–95, 3311 bachelor's degrees were awarded. The most popular majors among graduates were psychology (7%), hotel, restaurant, and travel administration (5%), and communication (5%). Within an average freshman class, 47% graduate in 4 years, 64% in 5 years, and 67% in 6 years. 270 companies recruited on campus in 1994–95. Of the 1994 graduating class, 26% were enrolled in graduate school within 6 months of graduation and 70% had found employment.

Admissions Contact: Arlene Cash, Director of University Admissions. E-mail: amh.admis@dpc.umassp.edu. A campus video is available.

UNIVERSITY OF MASSACHUSETTS BOSTON   E-2

Boston, MA 02125–3393   (617) 287–6000; FAX: (617) 287–6242

Full-time: 2536 men, 2817 women	Faculty: 470; IIA, +$
Part-time: 1631 men, 2013 women	Ph.D.s: 89%
Graduate: 982 men, 1623 women	Student/Faculty: 11 to 1
Year: semesters, summer session	Tuition: $4405 ($10,753)
Application Deadline: March 1	Room & Board: n/app
Freshman Class: 2110 applied, 1363 accepted, 691 enrolled	
SAT I Verbal/Math: 430/470	COMPETITIVE

The University of Massachusetts Boston, established in 1964, is a public, coeducational commuter institution offering undergraduate studies in arts and sciences and in preprofessional training. There are 4 undergraduate schools. In addition to regional accreditation, UMass Boston has baccalaureate program accreditation with NLN. The library contains 559,885 volumes, 727,750 microform items, and 1939 audiovisual forms, and subscribes to 3120 periodicals. Computerized library sources and services include the card catalog, interlibrary loans, and database searching. Special learning facilities include a learning resource center, art gallery, radio station, tropical greenhouse, observatory, adaptive computer laboratory, languages laboratory, and applied language and mathematics center. The 177-acre campus is in an urban area 5 miles south of downtown Boston. There are 10 buildings on campus.

Student Life: 96% of undergraduates are from Massachusetts. Students come from 22 states, 51 foreign countries, and Canada. 66% are white; 15% African American; 10% Asian American. The average age of freshmen is 23; all undergraduates, 29. 29% do not continue beyond their first year; 45% remain to graduate.

Housing: There are no residence halls. All students commute. Alcohol is not permitted. All students may keep cars on campus.

Activities: There are no fraternities or sororities. There are about 70 groups on campus, including art, band, cheerleading, chess, chorale, chorus, computers, dance, drama, ethnic, film, gay, honors, international, jazz band, literary magazine, musical theater, newspaper, photography, political, professional, radio and TV, religious, social, social service, student government, and yearbook. Popular campus events include Convocation Day, seasonal festivals, and senior events.

Sports: There are 9 intercollegiate sports for men and 7 for women, and 15 intramural sports for men and 13 for women. Athletic and recreation facilities include an athletic center with a 3500-seat gymnasium with 4 basketball courts and 2 volleyball courts, an ice rink which seats 1000, an Olympic-size swimming pool with high dive area, a multipurpose weight room, and a sports medicine area; an 8-lane 400-meter track; 8 tennis courts; a softball diamond, 3 multipurpose fields primarily used for football, soccer and lacrosse, and several other recreational fields; a boat house, dock, and fleet of sailboats and rowing dories; and a newly constructed fitness center with strength training equipment, cardiovascular machines, and racquetball and squash courts.

Disabled Students: The entire campus is accessible to disabled students. The following facilities are available: wheelchair ramps, elevators, special parking, specially equipped rest rooms, special class scheduling, lowered drinking fountains, lowered telephones, amplified phones, powered doors, indoor-connected building access, accessible shuttle bus, adaptive computer laboratory, and center for students with disabilities.

Services: In addition to many counseling and information services, tutoring is available in every subject. There is a reader service for the blind, and remedial math, reading, and writing. There are also reading study skills workshops and a mathematics resource center available.

Campus Safety and Security: Campus safety and security measures include 24-hour foot and vehicle patrol, self-defense education, escort service, and shuttle buses. In addition, there are pamphlets/posters/films, emergency telephones, lighted pathways/sidewalks, Operation ID, motorist assistance, and crime prevention programs.

Programs of Study: UMass Boston confers B.A. and B.S. degrees. Master's and doctoral degrees are also awarded. Bachelor's degrees are awarded in BIOLOGICAL SCIENCE (biochemistry and biology/biological science), BUSINESS (management science), COMMUNICATIONS AND THE ARTS (classics, dramatic arts, English, fine arts, French, German, Greek (classical), Italian, Latin, music, Russian, and Spanish), COMPUTER AND PHYSICAL SCIENCE (applied mathematics, chemistry, computer science, mathematics, and physics), EDUCATION (physical), ENGINEERING AND ENVIRONMENTAL DESIGN (engineering physics), HEALTH PROFESSIONS (medical laboratory technology and nursing), SOCIAL SCIENCE (African American studies, anthropology, community services, criminal justice, economics, geography, gerontology, history, human services, philosophy, political science/government, psychology, sociology, and women's studies). Management, nursing, and psychology have the largest enrollments.

Required: For graduation, students must complete 120 credit hours (123 hours in the College of Nursing) and maintain a minimum GPA of 2.0. Distribution requirements vary by college. All students must demonstrate writing proficiency.

Special: Students may cross-register with Massachusetts College of Art, Bunker Hill Community College, Roxbury Community College, and Hebrew College. UMass Boston also offers cooperative programs, internships, study abroad, work-study programs, student-designed majors, B.A.-B.S. degrees, nondegree study, pass/fail options, and dual and interdisciplinary majors, including anthropology/history, biology/medical technology, philosophy/public policy, and psychology/sociology. A 2-2 engineering program is possible with various area institutions, and the College of Public and Community Service provides social-oriented education, generally to older students. There is a freshman honors program on campus, as well as 3 national honor societies. Most departments have honors programs.

Faculty/Classroom: 65% of faculty are male; 35%, female. All both teach and do research. Graduate students teach 4% of introductory courses. The average class size in an introductory lecture is 31 and in a laboratory, 27.

Admissions: 65% of the 1995-96 applicants were accepted. The SAT I scores for the 1995-96 freshman class were as follows: Verbal—80% below 500, 15% between 500 and 599, and 5% between 600 and 700; Math—60% below 500, 28% between 500 and 599, 11% between 600 and 700, and 1% above 700. 23% of the current freshmen were in the top fifth of their class; 53% were in the top two fifths.

Requirements: The SAT I is required, with a minimum composite score of 800. The ACT may be substituted for the SAT I, and SAT I scores are not required of students who have been out of high school for 3 or more years. UMass Boston requires applicants to be in the upper 50% of their class. Applicants should be graduates of an accredited secondary school with a 2.0 GPA. The GED is accepted. The university requires the completion of 16 Carnegie units, including 4 years of English, 3 of college preparatory mathematics, 2 each of foreign language, science, and social studies, and 3 electives in the above academic areas or in humanities, arts, or computer science. An essay is recommended. AP and CLEP credits are accepted. Important factors in the admissions decision are advanced placement or honor courses, recommendations by school officials, and personality/intangible qualities.

Procedure: Freshmen are admitted in the fall and spring. Entrance exams should be taken no later than fall of the senior year in high school. There is a deferred admissions plan. Applications should be filed by March 1 for priority consideration for fall entry and November 1 for spring entry, along with an application fee of $20 ($35 for nonresidents). Notification is sent on a rolling basis.

Transfer: 1225 transfer students enrolled in 1995-96. Applicants with fewer than 30 credits must meet freshman requirements. To transfer, students must have a minimum GPA of 2.25 (2.75 for management, nursing, and engineering). Grades of C or better transfer for credit. 30 credits of 120 must be completed at UMass Boston.

Visiting: There are regularly scheduled orientations for prospective students, include general information about the university and the admissions process and a tour of the campus. There are guides for informal visits and visitors may sit in on classes. To schedule a visit, contact the Admissions Information Service.

Financial Aid: In 1995-96, 92% of all freshmen and 72% of continuing students received some form of financial aid. 83% of freshmen and 64% of continuing students received need-based aid. The average freshman award was $7334. Of that total, scholarships or need-based grants averaged $2507 ($4405 maximum); loans averaged $3320 ($5500 maximum); and work contracts averaged $1507 ($2500 maximum). 19% of undergraduate students work part-time. Average earnings from campus work for the school year was $1507. The average financial indebtedness of the 1994-95 graduate was $7983. FAFSA, the college's own financial statement, and SAFA are required. The application deadline for fall entry is March 1.

International Students: There are currently 187 international students enrolled. They must take the TOEFL and achieve a minimum score of 500.

Computers: The college provides computer facilities for student use. The mainframes are DEC VAX models 8800, 6000-410, and 6000-510. Students may access the mainframe through terminals located in the terminal room. There are also a number of microcomputer laboratories containing Apple Macintosh, IBM, and/or IBM-compatible microcomputers. Most of the 390 terminals and microcomputers are located in the library, with the remainder in classroom buildings. All students may access the system 24 hours a day. There are no time limits and no fees.

Graduates: In 1994-95, 1468 bachelor's degrees were awarded. The most popular majors among graduates were management (16%), psychology (12%), and nursing (11%). Within an average freshman class, 1% graduate in 3 years, 13% in 4 years, 17% in 5 years, and 7% in 6 years. 42 companies recruited on campus in 1994-95.

Admissions Contact: Office of Admissions Information Service.

UNIVERSITY OF MASSACHUSETTS DARTMOUTH   E-4
North Dartmouth, MA 02747-2300

(508) 999-8605
FAX: (508) 999-8755

Full-time: 2185 men, 2186 women	**Faculty:** 319; IIA, +$
Part-time: 201 men, 304 women	**Ph.D.s:** 90%
Graduate: 249 men, 318 women	**Student/Faculty:** 14 to 1
Year: 4-1-4, summer session	**Tuition:** $4122 ($10,219)
Application Deadline: open	**Room & Board:** $4855
Freshman Class: 3838 applied, 2703 accepted, 1009 enrolled	
SAT I Verbal/Math: 430/482	**COMPETITIVE**

University of Massachusetts Dartmouth is a public coeducational institution that was founded in 1895 to meet the needs of the area's textile industry. Undergraduate programs now emphasize a comprehensive college curriculum. There are 5 undergraduate schools. In addition to regional accreditation, UMass Dartmouth has baccalaureate program accreditation with ABET, CSAB, NASAD, and NLN. The library contains 341,165 volumes, 43,505 microform items, and 107,659 audiovisual forms, and subscribes to 2083 periodicals. Computerized library sources and services include the card catalog, interlibrary loans, and database searching. Special learning facilities include a learning resource center, art gallery, radio station, an observatory, marine research vessels, and a number of cultural and research centers. The 710-acre campus is in a suburban area 60 miles south of Boston. Including residence halls, there are 20 buildings on campus.

Student Life: 95% of undergraduates are from Massachusetts. Students come from 29 states, 37 foreign countries, and Canada. 85% are from public schools; 15% from private. 82% are white. The average age of freshmen is 18; all undergraduates, 20. 29% do not continue beyond their first year; 50% remain to graduate.

Housing: 2100 students can be accommodated in college housing. College-sponsored living facilities include coed dormitories and on-campus apartments. In addition there are honors houses, a quiet house, and substance-free apartments. On-campus housing is guaranteed for all 4 years. 58% of students commute. All students may keep cars on campus.

Activities: There are no fraternities or sororities. There are 100 groups on campus, including art, band, cheerleading, choir, chorale, chorus, computers, drama, ethnic, gay, honors, international, jazz band, literary magazine, musical theater, newspaper, orchestra, pep band, photography, political, professional, radio and TV, religious, social, social service, student government, symphony, and yearbook. Popular campus events include Winterfest, Spring Fling Week, Cultural Awareness Week, and Eisteddfod Traditional Arts Festival.

Sports: There are 10 intercollegiate sports for men and 10 for women, and 7 intramural sports for men and 7 for women. Athletic and recreation facilities include a 3000-seat gymnasium, an 1850-seat football stadium, an aquatic sports center, and 13 tennis courts.

Disabled Students: 90% of the campus is accessible to disabled students. The following facilities are available: wheelchair ramps, elevators, special parking, specially equipped rest rooms, special class scheduling, lowered drinking fountains, lowered telephones, mobility assistance, note-takers/readers, alternative testing, and an office of disabled student services.

Services: In addition to many counseling and information services, tutoring is available in most subjects through the writing/reading, science/engineering, and mathematics/business centers. There is a reader service for the blind, and remedial math, reading, and writing.

Campus Safety and Security: Campus safety and security measures include 24-hour foot and vehicle patrol, self-defense education, escort service, and shuttle buses. In addition, there are pamphlets/posters/films, emergency telephones, lighted pathways/sidewalks, and bicycle patrol.

Programs of Study: UMass Dartmouth confers B.A., B.S., B.F.A., and B.Mus. degrees. Master's and doctoral degrees are also awarded. Bachelor's degrees are awarded in BIOLOGICAL SCIENCE (biology/biological science and marine biology), BUSINESS (accounting, banking and finance, business administration and management, and marketing/retailing/merchandising), COMMUNICATIONS AND THE ARTS (art history and appreciation, ceramic art and design, design, English, fiber/textiles/weaving, fine arts, French, graphic design, illustration, music, painting, photography, Portuguese, printmaking, sculpture, and Spanish), COMPUTER AND PHYSICAL SCIENCE (chemistry, computer science, information sciences and systems, mathematics, and physics), EDUCATION (art and foreign languages), ENGINEERING AND ENVIRONMENTAL DESIGN (civil engineering, computer engineering, electrical/electronics engineering, electrical/electronics engineering technology, engineering, mechanical engineering, mechanical engineering technology, and textile technology), HEALTH PROFESSIONS (medical laboratory science, nursing, and premedicine), SOCIAL SCI-

ENCE (criminal justice, economics, history, humanities, interdisciplinary studies, philosophy, political science/government, psychology, and sociology). Engineering, biology, and English are the strongest academically. Psychology, sociology, and English have the largest enrollments.

Required: Distribution requirements vary within the individual colleges, but all students must maintain a minimum 2.0 GPA and complete 120 to 132 credit hours. Freshman English and writing and electives in the humanities, social sciences, and physical sciences are required.

Special: The school permits cross-registration through the SACHEM Consortium of 9 schools in Massachusetts. Study abroad in 9 countries, an engineering co-op program, a Washington semester, internships, numerous work-study programs, dual majors, a B.A.-B.S. degree program in chemistry, and student-designed majors are available. Teacher certification in elementary and secondary education is available. Nondegree study and pass/fail options are possible. Students also may receive credit for life experiences. There is a freshman honors program on campus, as well as 1 national honor society. All departments have honors programs.

Faculty/Classroom: 69% of faculty are male; 31%, female. All teach undergraduates and 50% do research. Graduate students teach 3% of introductory courses. The average class size in an introductory lecture is 45; in a laboratory, 20; and in a regular course offering, 23.

Admissions: 70% of the 1995–96 applicants were accepted. The SAT I scores for the 1995–96 freshman class were as follows: Math—56% below 500, 28% between 500 and 599, 13% between 600 and 700, and 1% above 700. 28% of the current freshmen were in the top fifth of their class; 70% were in the top two fifths.

Requirements: The SAT I is required. UMass Dartmouth requires applicants to be in the upper 50% of their class. A minimum GPA of 2.5 is required. Applicants should have 4 years of English, 3 each of mathematics and electives, 2 each of science and foreign language, and 1 each of social studies and U.S. history. The GED is accepted. An audition is necessary for music majors, and a portfolio is recommended for studio arts and design applicants. All applicants must submit an essay. AP and CLEP credits are accepted. Important factors in the admissions decision are recommendations by school officials, advanced placement or honor courses, and evidence of special talent.

Procedure: Freshmen are admitted fall and spring. Entrance exams should be taken during the spring of the junior year or early fall of the senior year. There are early decision, early admissions, and deferred admissions plans. Early decision applications should be filed by November 15. The application fee is $20 in-state, $40 out-of-state. Notification of early decision is sent December 15; regular decision, on a rolling basis. 28 early decision candidates were accepted for the 1995–96 class.

Transfer: 415 transfer students enrolled in 1995–96. Transfer applicants must take the SAT I unless they graduated from high school more than 3 years prior to applying or have 30 transferable credits. They must also submit previous course descriptions. 60 credits of 120 to 132 must be completed at UMass Dartmouth.

Visiting: There are regularly scheduled orientations for prospective students, including scheduled campus tours Monday through Friday and most Saturdays. There are guides for informal visits and visitors may sit in on classes. To schedule a visit, contact the Admissions Office.

Financial Aid: In 1995–96, 60% of all freshmen and 52% of continuing students received some form of financial aid. 55% of freshmen and 50% of continuing students received need-based aid. The average freshman award was $5552. Of that total, scholarships or need-based grants averaged $2165; loans averaged $3109; and work contracts averaged $278. 30% of undergraduate students work part-time. The average financial indebtedness of the 1994–95 graduate was $8301. UMass Dartmouth is a member of CSS. The FAFSA is required. The priority application deadline for fall entry is March 1.

International Students: There are currently 188 international students enrolled. They must take the TOEFL and achieve a minimum score of 500. The student must also take the SAT I.

Computers: The college provides computer facilities for student use. The mainframes are a DEC VAX 8650 and a DEC VAX 11/785. There are several computer laboratories on campus that have more than 200 microcomputers available, and computer ports are in every dormitory room for students with their own terminal to hook into the university mainframe. All students may access the system during the day and evening as well as on weekends. There are no time limits and no fees.

Graduates: In 1994–95, 976 bachelor's degrees were awarded. The most popular majors among graduates were accounting (10%), management (8%), and humanities/social studies (8%). Within an average freshman class, 34% graduate in 4 years and 49% in 5 years. 400 companies recruited on campus in 1994–95.

Admissions Contact: Raymond M. Barrows, Admissions Director. E-mail: athompson@umassd.edu. A campus video is available.

UNIVERSITY OF MASSACHUSETTS LOWELL   D-1
(Formerly University of Lowell)
Lowell, MA 01854

(508) 934–3930
(800) 410–4607; FAX: (508) 934–3086

Full-time: 3866 men, 2469 women	Faculty: 445; I, av$
Part-time: n/av	Ph.D.s: 79%
Graduate: n/av	Student/Faculty: 14 to 1
Year: semesters, summer session	Tuition: $4735 ($9879)
Application Deadline: open	Room & Board: $4254
Freshman Class: 3578 applied, 2848 accepted, 1144 enrolled	
SAT I Verbal/Math: 450/500	COMPETITIVE

The University of Massachussets Lowell, founded in 1895, is a public institution offering undergraduate programs through the schools of arts and sciences, engineering, health professions, management science, and music, and graduate programs in education. There are 5 undergraduate schools and one graduate school. In addition to regional accreditation, UMass Lowell has baccalaureate program accreditation with AACSB, ABET, APTA, CAHEA, NASAD, NASM, NCATE, and NLN. The 3 libraries contain 400,000 volumes, 625,000 microform items, and 17,100 audiovisual forms, and subscribe to 3400 periodicals. Computerized library sources and services include the card catalog, interlibrary loans, and database searching. Special learning facilities include a radio station and many experimental and investigative laboratories, and the Research Foundation, which includes a materials testing division and centers for atmospheric research and tropical disease. The 100-acre campus is in an urban area 30 miles northwest of Boston. Including residence halls, there are 37 buildings on campus.

Student Life: 90% of undergraduates are from Massachusetts. Students come from 20 states and 48 foreign countries. 79% are white. The average age of freshmen is 18.

Housing: 2536 students can be accommodated in college housing. College-sponsored living facilities include dormitories, off-campus apartments, and married-student housing. In addition there are special interest houses. On-campus housing is available on a first-come, first-served basis. All students may keep cars on campus.

Activities: There are no fraternities or sororities. There are 85 groups on campus, including art, cheerleading, computers, drama, ethnic, international, marching band, newspaper, photography, political, professional, radio and TV, religious, social, social service, student government, and yearbook.

Sports: There are 15 intercollegiate sports for men and 10 for women, and 34 intramural sports for men and 34 for women. Athletic and recreation facilities include a gymnasium seating 2000, a pool, weight-training facilities, and areas for gymnastics, wrestling, and judo. There are also courts for handball, squash, and tennis, and various playing fields.

Disabled Students: The following facilities are available: wheelchair ramps, elevators, special parking, specially equipped rest rooms, special class scheduling, lowered drinking fountains, and lowered telephones.

Services: In addition to many counseling and information services, tutoring is available in most subjects. There is a reader service for the blind, and remedial math, reading, and writing.

Programs of Study: UMass Lowell confers B.A., B.S., B.F.A., B.L.A., B.M., B.S.B.A., B.S.E., B.S.E.T., B.S.I.M., and B.S.I.T. degrees. Associate, master's, and doctoral degrees are also awarded. Bachelor's degrees are awarded in BIOLOGICAL SCIENCE (biology/biological science and biotechnology), BUSINESS (accounting, banking and finance, business administration and management, business economics, marketing/retailing/merchandising, and personnel management), COMMUNICATIONS AND THE ARTS (English, fine arts, French, modern language, music, and Spanish), COMPUTER AND PHYSICAL SCIENCE (atmospheric sciences and meteorology, chemistry, computer science, geology, mathematics, physics, and statistics), EDUCATION (health and music), ENGINEERING AND ENVIRONMENTAL DESIGN (chemical engineering, civil engineering, electrical/electronics engineering, engineering technology, environmental science, industrial engineering technology, mechanical engineering, nuclear engineering, and plastics engineering), HEALTH PROFESSIONS (clinical science, medical laboratory technology, nursing, radiograph medical technology, and sports medicine), SOCIAL SCIENCE (American studies, criminal justice, economics, history, philosophy, political science/government, psychology, and sociology). Engineering and management have the largest enrollments.

Required: All students must complete a minimum of 120 credits with a 2.0 GPA. Core requirements include 6 credits of English composition, 3 credits of human values, and an area distribution requirement of 27 to 29 credits outside the major in behavioral and social science, fine arts and the humanities, and mathematics and the sciences.

Special: Cross-registration and cooperative and work-study programs are available, as are opportunities for study abroad. The university offers a combined B.A.-B.S. degree in engineering, and dual majors and nondegree study, as well as pass/fail options. There is a freshman honors program on campus, as well as 2 national honor societies.

Faculty/Classroom: 78% of faculty are male; 22%, female. All teach undergraduates.

Admissions: 80% of the 1995-96 applicants were accepted. The SAT I scores for the 1995-96 freshman class were as follows: Verbal—50% below 500, 30% between 500 and 599, 18% between 600 and 700, and 2% above 700; Math—30% below 500, 41% between 500 and 599, 24% between 600 and 700, and 5% above 700. 30% of the current freshmen were in the top fifth of their class; 64% were in the top two fifths.

Requirements: The SAT I or ACT is required. The SAT I is preferred. In addition, applicants should have a high school diploma or the GED. The university recommends that secondary preparation include 4 courses in English, 3 each in social science/history and mathematics, 2 each in science and a foreign language, and 2 academic electives. Prospective music majors must audition, and an interview is recommended for all students. AP and CLEP credits are accepted.

Procedure: Freshmen are admitted fall and spring. Entrance exams should be taken by January of the senior year. There is a deferred admissions plan. Application deadlines are open. Application fee is $20. Notification is sent on a rolling basis.

Transfer: Transfer applicants must present at least a 2.0 GPA in previous college work, and must complete at least 30 credits in residence for a bachelor's degree. Those with fewer than 30 credits must meet freshman admission requirements. 30 credits of 120 must be completed at UMass Lowell.

Financial Aid: UMass Lowell is a member of CSS. The FAF is required. The application deadline for fall entry is May 1.

International Students: Students must take the TOEFL as well as the SAT I or the ACT.

Computers: The college provides computer facilities for student use. The mainframes are a comprised of a cluster of DEC VAX 6420s, 8700s, and 8800s. 2500 terminals, microcomputers, and workstations are linked to more than 150 multiuser systems in a campuswide communications network. All students may access the system. There are no time limits and no fees.

Admissions Contact: Lawrence R. Martin, Director. E-mail: admissions@woods.uml.edu.

WELLESLEY COLLEGE
Wellesley, MA 02181

D-2
(617) 283-2270

Full-time: 2217 women	Faculty: 241; IIB, ++$
Part-time: 82 women	Ph.D.s: 97%
Graduate: none	Student/Faculty: 9 to 1
Year: semesters	Tuition: $19,610
Application Deadline: January 15	Room & Board: $6200
Freshman Class: 3411 applied, 1370 accepted, 587 enrolled	
SAT I Verbal/Math: 630/670	MOST COMPETITIVE

Wellesley College, established in 1870, is an independent liberal arts college for women. The 5 libraries contain more than 1 million volumes, 60,898 microform items, and 15,092 audiovisual forms, and subscribe to 4000 periodicals. Computerized library sources and services include the card catalog, interlibrary loans, and database searching. Special learning facilities include a learning resource center, art gallery, radio station, science center, greenhouse, observatory, center for developmental studies and services, and centers for research on women and children. The 500-acre campus is in a suburban area 12 miles west of Boston. Including residence halls, there are 64 buildings on campus.

Student Life: 79% of students are from out of state, mostly the Middle Atlantic. Students come from 50 states, 69 foreign countries, and Canada. 68% are from public schools; 31% from private. 48% are white; 25% Asian American. The average age of freshmen is 18; all undergraduates, 20. 3% do not continue beyond their first year; 87% remain to graduate.

Housing: 2120 students can be accommodated in college housing. College-sponsored living facilities include dormitories. In addition there are special-interest houses and language corridors and co-ops. On-campus housing is guaranteed for all 4 years. 98% of students live on campus. Upperclassmen may keep cars on campus.

Activities: There are no sororities. There are 139 groups on campus, including art, choir, chorus, computers, dance, drama, ethnic, film, gay, honors, international, jazz band, literary magazine, musical theater, newspaper, orchestra, photography, political, professional, radio and TV, religious, social, social service, student government, symphony, and yearbook. Popular campus events include Step-Singing, Spring Weekend, and Christmas Vespers.

Sports: Athletic and recreation facilities include an indoor pool, dance studios, a weight room, an indoor track, and courts for racquetball, squash, tennis, and volleyball.

Disabled Students: All of the campus is accessible to disabled students. The following facilities are available: wheelchair ramps, elevators, special parking, specially equipped rest rooms, special class scheduling, lowered drinking fountains, lowered telephones, specially equipped dormitories, and signage in Braille.

Services: In addition to many counseling and information services, tutoring is available in every subject. There is a reader service for the blind.

Campus Safety and Security: Campus safety and security measures include 24-hour foot and vehicle patrol, self-defense education, escort service, and shuttle buses. There are informal discussions, pamphlets/posters/films, emergency telephones, and lighted pathways/sidewalks.

Programs of Study: Wellesley confers the B.A. degree. Bachelor's degrees are awarded in BIOLOGICAL SCIENCE (biochemistry, biology/biological science, and biophysics), COMMUNICATIONS AND THE ARTS (art history and appreciation, Chinese, dramatic arts, English, fine arts, French, German, Greek, Italian, Japanese, languages, Latin, music, Russian, Spanish, and studio art), COMPUTER AND PHYSICAL SCIENCE (astronomy, chemistry, computer science, geology, mathematics, and physics), EDUCATION (secondary), ENGINEERING AND ENVIRONMENTAL DESIGN (architectural engineering), SOCIAL SCIENCE (African American studies, American studies, anthropology, Asian/Oriental studies, classical/ancient civilization, cognitive science, economics, European studies, history, international relations, Judaic studies, Latin American studies, medieval studies, peace studies, philosophy, political science/government, psychobiology, psychology, religion, sociology, and women's studies). Psychology, English, and art history have the largest enrollments.

Required: All students must complete 32 units, at least 8 of which are in the major field, with a minimum 2.0 GPA. Requirements include 3 courses each in humanities, social science, and natural science and mathematics; 1 multicultural course; 1 semester of expository writing in any department; and 8 credits in physical education. Students must also demonstrate proficiency in a modern or ancient foreign language. A thesis is required for departmental honors.

Special: Students may cross-register at MIT, Brandeis University, or Babson College. Exchange programs are available with Spelman College in Georgia and Mills College in California, with members of the 12-College Exchange, with Williams College in maritime studies, and with the National Theatre Institute. Study abroad is possible in Wellesley-administered programs in various countries, in exchange programs in Russia and Japan, and at Cambridge and Oxford in England. There are summer internship programs in Boston and Washington, D.C. Dual majors, student-designed majors, nondegree study, and pass/fail options are possible. A 3-2 program with MIT awards a B.A.-B.S. degree. There are 2 national honor societies on campus, including Phi Beta Kappa. 10 departments have honors programs.

Faculty/Classroom: 48% of faculty are male; 52%, female. All teach and do research. The average class size in an introductory lecture is 25; in a laboratory, 15; and in a regular course offering, 21.

Admissions: 40% of the 1995-96 applicants were accepted. The SAT I scores for the 1995-96 freshman class were as follows: Verbal—8% below 500, 28% between 500 and 599, 50% between 600 and 700, and 14% above 700; Math—4% below 500, 15% between 500 and 599, 49% between 600 and 700, and 32% above 700. 96% of the current freshmen were in the top fifth of their class; all were in the top two fifths.

Requirements: The SAT I is required, as are 3 SAT II: Subject tests, including writing and any 2 others. Most successful applicants are high school graduates or those who have earned the GED and taken college preparatory courses. The college expects training in writing and interpretation of literature, at least 4 years each of mathematics and a modern or ancient language, 2 of natural science, and 1 of a social science. A personal essay is required and an interview is recommended. Disk applications are accepted through CollegeLink and Mac Apply. AP credits are accepted.

Procedure: Freshmen are admitted in the fall. Entrance exams should be taken during the spring of the junior year or fall of the senior year. There are early decision, early admissions, and deferred admissions plans. Early decision applications should be filed by November 1; regular applications, by January 15 for fall entry, along with an application fee of $50. Notification of early decision is sent December 15; regular decision, April 1. 90 early decision candidates were accepted for the 1995-96 class. A waiting list is an active part of the admissions procedure.

Transfer: 26 transfer students enrolled in a recent year. Applicants must provide high school and college transcripts and SAT I scores. An interview is required. 16 units of 32 must be completed at Wellesley.

Visiting: There are guides for informal visits and visitors may sit in on classes and stay overnight at the school. To schedule a visit, contact the Admissions Office.

Financial Aid: In 1995–96, over 50% of all students received some form of financial aid. 53% of freshmen and 55% of continuing students received need-based aid. The average freshman award was $15,959. Of that total, scholarships or need-based grants averaged $13,660 ($23,506 maximum); loans averaged $2870 ($5295 maximum); and work contracts averaged $1800 ($2000 maximum). 38% of undergraduate students work part-time. Estimated average earnings from campus work for the school year are $1250. The average financial indebtedness of the 1994–95 graduate was $15,817. Wellesley is a member of CSS. The FAFSA, the college's own financial statement, and the most recent income tax returns of parents and student are required. The application deadline for fall entry is February 1.

International Students: There were 194 international students enrolled in a recent year. The school actively recruits these students. They must score 600 on the TOEFL and also take SAT I and SAT II: Subject tests in writing and 2 others.

Computers: The college provides computer facilities for student use. The mainframes are a DEC VAX 8550 and a Digital AXP. Students may access the mainframe through more than 200 microcomputers located in the science center, library, and dormitories. All students may access the system. There are no time limits and no fees.

Graduates: In 1994–95, 610 bachelor's degrees were awarded. The most popular majors among graduates were political science (11%), psychology (10%), and English (10%). Within an average freshman class, 82% graduate in 4 years, 86% in 5 years, and 87% in 6 years. 124 companies recruited on campus in 1994–95.

Admissions Contact: Janet A. Lavin, Director of Admissions. A campus video is available.

WENTWORTH INSTITUTE OF TECHNOLOGY   E-2
Boston, MA 02115

(617) 442–9010, ext. 219
(800) 556–0610; FAX: (617) 427–0276

Full-time: 1786 men, 315 women	Faculty: 116
Part-time: 12 men, 3 women	Ph.Ds: 90%
Graduate: none	Student/Faculty: 18 to 1
Year: semesters, summer session	Tuition: $10,500
Application Deadline: June 1	Room & Board: $6050
Freshman Class: 1808 applied, 1506 accepted, 643 enrolled	

LESS COMPETITIVE

Wentworth Institute of Technology, founded in 1904, is a private co-educational college specializing in architecture, design, engineering, technology, and management. In addition to regional accreditation, WIT has baccalaureate program accreditation with ABET, FIDER, and NAAB. The library contains 77,000 volumes, 90 microform items, and 750 audiovisual forms, and subscribes to 500 periodicals. Computerized library sources and services include the card catalog, interlibrary loans, and database searching. Special learning facilities include a learning resource center, a welding shop, a printed-circuit laboratory, CAD/CAM/CAE laboratories, design studios, and numerically controlled manufacturing systems. The 30-acre campus is in an urban area in Boston. Including residence halls, there are 21 buildings on campus.

Student Life: 71% of undergraduates are from Massachusetts. Students come from 22 states, 68 foreign countries, and Canada. 72% are white. The average age of freshmen is 20; all undergraduates, 22. 33% do not continue beyond their first year; 50% remain to graduate.

Housing: 613 students can be accommodated in college housing. College-sponsored living facilities include coed dormitories and on-campus apartments. On-campus housing is available on a first-come, first-served basis. Priority is given to out-of-town students. 70% of students commute. Alcohol is not permitted. All students may keep cars on campus.

Activities: There are no fraternities or sororities. There are 35 groups on campus, including cheerleading, computers, ethnic, honors, international, literary magazine, newspaper, professional, religious, social, student government, and yearbook. Popular campus events include Design Lecture Series, Beaux Arts Ball, and Campus Carnival.

Sports: There are 9 intercollegiate sports for men and 5 for women, and 9 intramural sports for men and 9 for women. Athletic and recreation facilities include gymnasiums, tennis courts, a riflery range, a weight-lifting room, and an outdoor basketball court.

Disabled Students: 30% of the campus is accessible to disabled students. The following facilities are available: wheelchair ramps, elevators, special parking, specially equipped rest rooms, special class scheduling, lowered drinking fountains, and lowered telephones.

Services: In addition to many counseling and information services, free tutoring is available to all students through the learning center. A 1-year preparatory curriculum is available for students who need additional preparation before starting college.

Campus Safety and Security: Campus safety and security measures include 24-hour foot and vehicle patrol, escort service, informal discussions, and pamphlets/posters/films. There are emergency telephones and lighted pathways/sidewalks. All campus police officers have emergency medical training.

Programs of Study: WIT confers B.S. and B.Arch. degrees. Associate degrees are also awarded. Bachelor's degrees are awarded in COMMUNICATIONS AND THE ARTS (industrial design and technical and business writing), COMPUTER AND PHYSICAL SCIENCE (computer science), ENGINEERING AND ENVIRONMENTAL DESIGN (architectural engineering, architecture, civil engineering technology, computer engineering, construction management, construction technology, electrical/electronics engineering technology, electromechanical technology, environmental engineering, interior design, manufacturing engineering, mechanical engineering technology, and technological management). Architectural engineering technology, electronics engineering technology, and building construction technology have the largest enrollments.

Required: For a bachelor's degree, students must complete a total of 148 hours in most majors, with a minimum GPA of 2.5 in the major and 2.0 overall. An introductory computer course is required of all students.

Special: Cooperative programs, study abroad, student-designed majors, interdisciplinary majors, including engineering technology and facilities planning and management, and nondegree study are possible. Most students at the bachelor's level attend school in the summer, as most cooperative work occurs during the academic year. There is 1 national honor society on campus.

Faculty/Classroom: All faculty teach undergraduates. The average class size in an introductory lecture is 28; in a laboratory, 28; and in a regular course offering, 25.

Admissions: 83% of the 1995–96 applicants were accepted. The SAT I scores for a recent freshman class were as follows: Verbal—92% below 500, 7% between 500 and 599, and 1% between 600 and 700; Math—62% below 500, 28% between 500 and 599, and 10% between 600 and 700. 17% of the current freshmen were in the top fifth of their class; 42% were in the top two fifths.

Requirements: SAT I or ACT scores are required of freshmen for all programs except Tech One, the 1-year preparatory curriculum. Applicants must be graduates of an accredited secondary school or have the GED. High school course requirements vary by major. AP and CLEP credits are accepted.

Procedure: Freshmen are admitted fall and winter. Entrance exams should be taken in the spring of the junior year and/or fall of the senior year. There is a deferred admissions plan. Applications should be filed by June 1 for fall entry and December 1 for winter entry, along with an application fee of $30. Notification is sent on a rolling basis.

Transfer: 203 transfer students enrolled in a recent year. Requirements vary by program. Grades of C or better transfer for credit. Transfer students are admitted for fall or winter semesters. Transfer students must take 50% of the course work in their degree program at Wentworth to graduate. Portfolios and faculty reviews are required of applicants to industrial design, interior design, and architecture programs.

Visiting: There are regularly scheduled orientations for prospective students, including a 2-day orientation with optional overnight stay. There are guides for informal visits and visitors may sit in on classes and stay overnight at the school. To schedule a visit, contact Beth Canter at the Admissions Office.

Financial Aid: In a recent year, 52% of all freshmen and 26% of continuing students received some form of financial aid. 51% of freshmen and 26% of continuing students received need-based aid. The average freshman award was $5527. Of that total, scholarships or need-based grants averaged $2246 ($9250 maximum); loans averaged $2539 ($4825 maximum); and work contracts averaged $1360 ($1600 maximum). 17% of undergraduate students work part-time. Average earnings from campus work for the school year are $960. The average financial indebtedness of the 1994–95 graduate was $6206. WIT is a member of CSS. The FAFSA is required. The application deadline for fall entry is March 1.

International Students: There were 211 international students enrolled in a recent year. The school actively recruits these students. They must score 525 on the TOEFL or take the MELAB as well as SAT I or the ACT.

Computers: The college provides computer facilities for student use. The mainframe is a DEC VAX 400/300. The academic VAX may be accessed via 30 terminals and several modems, as well as from 115 networked microcomputers in various student laboratories. In addition, 122 Pentium systems and 47 Macintosh and Power Macintosh systems, all networked, are available in student laboratories throughout the institute. All students may access the system. There are no time limits.

Graduates: In a recent year, 542 bachelor's degrees were awarded. The most popular majors among graduates were electronic engineering technology (19%), architectural engineering technology (11%), and mechanical engineering technology (10%). 20 companies recruited on campus in a recent year.

Admissions Contact: Patrick Deskin, Assistant Director of Admissions. E-mail: admissions@wit.edu.

WESTERN NEW ENGLAND COLLEGE B-3
Springfield, MA 01119 (413) 782-1321
(800) 325-1122; FAX: (413) 782-1777

Full-time: 1031 men, 707 women	Faculty: 105; IIA, +$
Part-time: 647 men, 384 women	Ph.D.s: 69%
Graduate: 971 men, 745 women	Student/Faculty: 17 to 1
Year: semesters, summer session	Tuition: $10,310
Application Deadline: open	Room & Board: $5740
Freshman Class: 2489 applied, 1934 accepted, 588 enrolled	
SAT I Verbal/Math: 410/450	LESS COMPETITIVE

Western New England College, founded in 1919, is a private, coeducational institution offering programs in business, engineering, liberal arts, teacher preparation, and pharmacy. There are 3 undergraduate and 2 graduate schools. In addition to regional accreditation, WNEC has baccalaureate program accreditation with ABET and CSWE. The 2 libraries contain 277,407 volumes, 2128 microform items, and 1832 audiovisual forms, and subscribe to 4602 periodicals. Computerized library sources and services include the card catalog, interlibrary loans, and database searching. Special learning facilities include an art gallery and radio station. The 131-acre campus is in a suburban area 90 miles west of Boston. Including residence halls, there are 29 buildings on campus.

Student Life: 50% of undergraduates are from out-of-state, mostly the Northeast. Students come from 26 states, 18 foreign countries, and Canada. 92% are white. 13% are Catholic. The average age of freshmen is 18; all undergraduates, 21.7. 24% do not continue beyond their first year; 55% remain to graduate.

Housing: 1254 students can be accommodated in college housing. College-sponsored living facilities include single-sex and coed dormitories and on-campus apartments. In addition, there are special interest houses and healthful living and community service floors. On-campus housing is guaranteed for all 4 years. 72% of students live on campus; of those, 78% remain on campus on weekends. All students may keep cars on campus.

Activities: 1% of men and about 1% of women belong to 1 local fraternity; 1% of women belong to 1 local sorority. There are 44 groups on campus, including art, cheerleading, computers, drama, ethnic, film, honors, international, literary magazine, musical theater, newspaper, pep band, photography, political, professional, radio and TV, religious, social, social service, student government, and yearbook. Popular campus events include Parents Weekend, Community Festival, Sibling Weekend, and Spring Week.

Sports: There are 12 intercollegiate sports for men and 7 for women, and 6 intramural sports for men and 4 for women. Athletic and recreation facilities include a healthful living center with facilities for basketball (2000 seats), wrestling, racquetball, squash, aerobics, fitness and volleyball, as well as a weight room, an 8-lane pool, and a track. There is also a 1200-seat football stadium.

Disabled Students: 90% of the campus is accessible to disabled students. The following facilities are available: wheelchair ramps, elevators, special parking, specially equipped rest rooms, special class scheduling, lowered drinking fountains, and lowered telephones.

Services: In addition to many counseling and information services, tutoring is available in most subjects.

Campus Safety and Security: Campus safety and security measures include 24-hour foot and vehicle patrol, self-defense education, escort service, and informal discussions. In addition, there are pamphlets/posters/films, emergency telephones, lighted pathways/sidewalks, security cameras, medical response, fire response, and a comprehensive public safety awareness program.

Programs of Study: WNEC confers B.A., B.S., B.S.B.A., B.S.E., B.S.E.E., B.S.I.E., B.S.M.E., and B.S.W. degrees. Associate, master's, and doctoral degrees are also awarded. Bachelor's degrees are awarded in BIOLOGICAL SCIENCE (biology/biological science), BUSINESS (accounting, banking and finance, business administration and management, management science, marketing/retailing/merchandising, personnel management, and sports management), COMMUNICATIONS AND THE ARTS (advertising, communications, and English), COMPUTER AND PHYSICAL SCIENCE (chemistry, computer science, information sciences and systems, and mathematics), ENGINEERING AND ENVIRONMENTAL DESIGN (bioengineering, computer engineering, electrical/electronics engineering, environmental science, industrial administration/management, industrial engineering, and mechanical engineering), HEALTH PROFESSIONS (prepharmacy), SOCIAL SCIENCE (criminal justice, economics, history, law enforcement and corrections, political science/government,

psychology, social work, and sociology). Engineering, prepharmacy, and sciences are the strongest academically. Criminal justice, marketing, and accounting have the largest enrollments.

Required: To graduate, students must complete 120 credit hours with a minimum GPA of 2.0. Required courses include 2 courses each in English, mathematics, laboratory science, and physical education, 1 each in history and culture, and computer and college success skills courses. Other requirements vary according to the major.

Special: Students may cross-register with the cooperating colleges of Greater Springfield. The college offers a 5-year prepharmacy program with Massachusetts College of Pharmacy and Allied Health Sciences, internships, study abroad, a Washington semester, work-study programs, B.A.-B.S. degrees, an accelerated degree program, dual majors, student-designed majors, credit for life, military, work experience, and nondegree study. Engineering students must complete a senior project. There are 6 national honor societies on campus.

Faculty/Classroom: 70% of faculty are male; 30%, female. All teach undergraduates. No introductory courses are taught by graduate students. The average class size in an introductory lecture is 24 and in a regular course offering, 24.

Admissions: 78% of the 1995–96 applicants were accepted. The SAT I scores for the 1995–96 freshman class were as follows: Verbal—88% below 500, 11% between 500 and 599, and 1% between 600 and 700; Math—62% below 500, 27% between 500 and 599, 10% between 600 and 700, and 1% above 700. 15% of the current freshmen were in the top fifth of their class; 40% were in the top two fifths.

Requirements: The SAT I or ACT is required. Applicants must be graduates of an accredited secondary school with a 2.0 GPA and have completed 4 years of high school English, 2 or more years of mathematics, 1 or more of science, and 1 of history. An interview is recommended. AP and CLEP credits are accepted. Important factors in the admissions decision are advanced placement or honor courses, extracurricular activities record, and recommendations by school officials.

Procedure: Freshmen are admitted fall and spring. Entrance exams should be taken in the senior year. There is a deferred admissions plan. Application deadlines are open. Application fee is $30. Notification is sent on a rolling basis.

Transfer: 91 transfer students enrolled in 1995–96. Applicants must have a minimum GPA of 2.0. Grades of C or better transfer for credit. The college admits transfer students in the fall and spring. 30 credits of 120 must be completed at WNEC.

Visiting: There are regularly scheduled orientations for prospective students, including 7 open houses. There are guides for informal visits and visitors may sit in on classes and stay overnight at the school. To schedule a visit, contact the Undergraduate Admissions Office.

Financial Aid: In 1995–96, 77% of all freshmen and 74% of continuing students received need-based aid. The average freshman award was $9854. Of that total, scholarships or need-based grants averaged $3079 ($5500 maximum); loans averaged $3364 ($5625 maximum); and work contracts averaged $1729 ($2000 maximum). 30% of undergraduate students work part-time. Average earnings from campus work for the school year are $720. The average financial indebtedness of the 1994–95 graduate was $16,000. WNEC is a member of CSS. The FAFSA, the college's own financial statement, and federal tax returns are required. The application deadline for fall entry is April 1.

International Students: There are currently 30 international students enrolled. They must score 500 on the TOEFL.

Computers: The college provides computer facilities for student use. The mainframe is a Data General MV/40,000 HAII. There are 275 microcomputers/terminals available in 6 laboratories in various locations on campus. Access to the Internet is possible. All students may access the system 8 A.M. to 11 P.M. Monday through Thursday, 8 A.M. to 5 P.M. on Friday, noon to 5 P.M. on Saturday, and noon to 11 P.M. on Sunday. There are no time limits and no fees.

Graduates: In 1994–95, 548 bachelor's degrees were awarded. 32 companies recruited on campus in 1994–95. Of the 1994 graduating class, 11% were enrolled in graduate school within 6 months of graduation and 80% had found employment.

Admissions Contact: Dr. Charles R. Pollock, Dean of Enrollment Management. A campus video is available.

WESTFIELD STATE COLLEGE
B-3

Westfield, MA 01086   (413) 572-5218; (800) 322-8401

Full-time: 1553 men, 1614 women	Faculty: 168; IIA, -$
Part-time: 479 men, 406 women	Ph.D.s: 75%
Graduate: 225 men, 494 women	Student/Faculty: 19 to 1
Year: semesters, summer session	Tuition: $3193 ($7327)
Application Deadline: March 1	Room & Board: $4115
Freshman Class: 2972 applied, 1855 accepted, 745 enrolled	
SAT I Verbal/Math: 420/450	COMPETITIVE

Westfield State College, founded in 1838, is a public coeducational college with liberal arts and teacher preparation programs and professional training. There is 1 undergraduate school. In addition to regional accreditation, Westfield State has baccalaureate program accreditation with NCATE. The library contains 163,500 volumes and 455,000 microform items, and subscribes to 1519 periodicals. Special learning facilities include an art gallery, radio station, and TV station. The 227-acre campus is in a rural area 15 miles west of Springfield. Including residence halls, there are 13 buildings on campus.

Student Life: 94% of undergraduates are from Massachusetts. Students come from 15 states and 1 foreign country. 83% are white. The average age of freshmen is 18; all undergraduates, 20. 27% do not continue beyond their first year; 60% remain to graduate.

Housing: 1900 students can be accommodated in college housing. College-sponsored living facilities include single-sex and coed dormitories and on-campus apartments. On-campus housing is guaranteed for all 4 years. 65% of students live on campus; of those, 70% remain on campus on weekends. Upperclassmen may keep cars on campus.

Activities: There are no fraternities or sororities. There are 50 groups on campus, including art, band, cheerleading, choir, chorale, chorus, drama, ethnic, honors, jazz band, literary magazine, musical theater, newspaper, orchestra, pep band, photography, political, professional, radio and TV, religious, social service, student government, and yearbook. Popular campus events include Halloween Dance, Spring Weekend, Comedy Night, and Student Senate Banquet.

Sports: There are 7 intercollegiate sports for men and 7 for women, and 24 intramural sports for men and 24 for women. Athletic and recreation facilities include a track, baseball and softball fields, tennis courts, a 400-seat gymnasium, and a 5000-seat stadium.

Disabled Students: The following facilities are available: wheelchair ramps, elevators, special parking, specially equipped rest rooms, special class scheduling, and lowered telephones.

Services: In addition to many counseling and information services, tutoring is available in every subject. There is a reader service for the blind, and remedial math, reading, and writing.

Campus Safety and Security: Campus safety and security measures include 24-hour foot and vehicle patrol, escort service, shuttle buses, and emergency telephones. In addition, there are lighted pathways/sidewalks.

Programs of Study: Westfield State confers B.A., B.S., and B.S.E degrees. Master's degrees are also awarded. Bachelor's degrees are awarded in BIOLOGICAL SCIENCE (biology/biological science), BUSINESS (business administration and management), COMMUNICATIONS AND THE ARTS (communications, English, fine arts, French, music, and Spanish), COMPUTER AND PHYSICAL SCIENCE (chemistry, computer science, information sciences and systems, and mathematics), EDUCATION (art, business, early childhood, elementary, foreign languages, middle school, music, science, secondary, and special), SOCIAL SCIENCE (criminal justice, economics, geography, history, political science/government, psychology, social science, and urban studies). Computer science, English, and psychology are the strongest academically. Criminal justice, education, and business have the largest enrollments.

Required: Students must complete a total of 120 credit hours, with 40 credits in 7 specified areas and 30 to 40 hours in the major. The college requires a 2.0 GPA overall and 2.0 in major courses. U.S. history is a required course.

Special: Students may cross-register with Cooperating Colleges of Greater Springfield. Internships are for credit only in conjunction with all major programs. The college offers study abroad in 3 countries, a Washington semester for political science majors, dual majors, and some credit for military experience.

Faculty/Classroom: 68% of faculty are male; 32%, female. All teach undergraduates. No introductory courses are taught by graduate students. The average class size in an introductory lecture is 30; in a laboratory, 12; and in a regular course offering, 25.

Admissions: 62% of the 1995-96 applicants were accepted. The SAT I scores for the 1995-96 freshman class were as follows: Verbal—87% below 500, 12% between 500 and 599, and 1% between 600 and 700; Math—70% below 500, 25% between 500 and 599, 5% between 600 and 700, and 1% above 700. 14% of the current freshmen were in the top fifth of their class; 46% were in the top two fifths.

Requirements: The SAT I is required, with a recommended combined score of 880, 480 verbal and 400 mathematics (recentered). Westfield State requires applicants to be in the upper 60% of their class. Applicants must be graduates of an accredited secondary school with a 2.0 GPA and must have completed 4 years of college preparatory level English, 3 of mathematics (algebra I and II and geometry), 2 each of social sciences (including 1 year of U.S. history), laboratory sciences, and foreign language, and 3 of electives. The GED is accepted. A portfolio is required for admission to the art program, and an audition is necessary for admission to the music program. AP and CLEP credits are accepted. Important factors in the admissions decision are advanced placement or honor courses, leadership record, and extracurricular activities record.

Procedure: Freshmen are admitted in the fall and spring. Entrance exams should be taken in spring of the junior year and fall of the senior year. Applications should be filed by March 1 for fall entry and November 15 for spring entry, along with an application fee of $10. Notification is sent on a rolling basis.

Transfer: 280 transfer students enrolled in 1995-96. Applicants must have more than 24 transferable credits with a minimum GPA of 2.0 (higher for some majors). A grade of D or better with a 2.0 GPA will transfer for credit. Of the 120 credits required for a bachelor's degree, a minimum of 30 credits must be completed at the college. Transfer students are admitted in the fall and spring. 30 credits of 120 must be completed at Westfield State.

Visiting: There are regularly scheduled orientations for prospective students, including a campus tour, classroom observation, academic department presentations, lunch with faculty, staff, and students, and a question-and-answer session moderated by a panel of administrators. There are guides for informal visits. To schedule a visit, contact the Admission Office.

Financial Aid: In a recent year, 71% of all freshmen and 69% of continuing students received some form of financial aid. 70% of all students received need-based aid. The average freshman award was $4686. Of that total, scholarships or need-based grants averaged $1150 ($4400 maximum); loans averaged $2435 ($3625 maximum); supplemented loans averaged $800 ($6384 maximum); and work contracts averaged $300 ($1000 maximum). 21% of undergraduate students work part-time. The average financial indebtedness of a recent graduate was $3200. Westfield State is a member of CSS. FAFSA and the college's own financial statement are required. The application deadline for fall entry is April 1.

International Students: There are currently 2 international students enrolled. They must take the TOEFL and achieve a minimum score of 550. The student must also take the SAT I.

Computers: The college provides computer facilities for student use. The mainframes are a CDC Cyber 172 and 2 DEC MicroVAX IIs. There are also a number of microcomputers available for student use in laboratories. All students may access the system. There are no time limits and no fees.

Graduates: In 1994-95, 752 bachelor's degrees were awarded. The most popular majors among graduates were criminal justice (23%), business management (14%), and elementary education (10%). Within an average freshman class, 50% graduate in 4 years, 58% in 5 years, and 60% in 6 years. 28 companies recruited on campus in 1994-95.

Admissions Contact: Director of Admission.

WHEATON COLLEGE
D-3

Norton, MA 02766   (508) 285-8251

(800) 394-6003; FAX: (508) 285-8271

Full-time: 417 men, 883 women	Faculty: 88; IIB, +$
Part-time: 2 men, 17 women	Ph.D.s: 96%
Graduate: none	Student/Faculty: 15 to 1
Year: semesters	Tuition: $19,140
Application Deadline: February 1	Room & Board: $6050
Freshman Class: 1830 applied, 1330 accepted, 372 enrolled	
SAT I Verbal/Math: 560/580	VERY COMPETITIVE +

Wheaton College, established in 1834, is an independent, coeducational, liberal arts institution. The library contains 327,213 volumes, 61,392 microform items, and 9659 audiovisual forms, and subscribes to 1373 periodicals. Computerized library sources and services include the card catalog, interlibrary loans, and database searching. Special learning facilities include an art gallery, planetarium, radio station, and TV station. The 140-acre campus is in a rural area 35 miles south of Boston and 15 miles north of Providence, Rhode Island. Including residence halls, there are 84 buildings on campus.

Student Life: 60% of undergraduates are from out-of-state, mostly the Northeast. Students come from 44 states, 30 foreign countries, and Canada. 60% are from public schools; 27% from private. 83% are white. The average age of freshmen is 18; all undergraduates, 20. 15% do not continue beyond their first year; 85% remain to graduate.

Housing: 1300 students can be accommodated in college housing. College-sponsored living facilities include single-sex and coed dormitories. In addition, there are special interest houses and substance-awareness, multicultural-awareness, and international-understanding houses. On-campus housing is guaranteed for all 4 years. 98% of students live on campus; of those, 75% remain on campus on weekends. All students may keep cars on campus.

Activities: There are no fraternities or sororities. There are 50 groups on campus, including art, choir, chorale, chorus, dance, drama, ethnic, film, gay, honors, international, literary magazine, musical theater, newspaper, photography, political, radio and TV, religious, social, social service, student government, and yearbook. Popular campus events include Academic Festival, AutumnFest, Parents Weekend, and Spring Weekend.

Sports: There are 9 intercollegiate sports for men and 13 for women, and 16 intramural sports for men and 16 for women. Athletic and recreation facilities include an 8-lane stretch pool; a field house with 5 tennis courts; 3 indoor basketball courts; 1 outdoor basketball court; 200 meter track; a golf/archery range and batting cage; an 850-seat gymnasium; 7 outdoor tennis courts; a running course; a baseball stadium; 2 athletic fields; an aerobics/dance studio; and a fitness center.

Disabled Students: 50% of the campus is accessible to disabled students. The following facilities are available: wheelchair ramps, elevators, special parking, specially equipped rest rooms, special class scheduling, and lowered telephones.

Services: In addition to many counseling and information services, tutoring is available in most subjects, including peer tutoring. There is also a reader service for the blind and remedial writing. Note takers for hearing-impaired students are available.

Campus Safety and Security: Campus safety and security measures include 24-hour foot and vehicle patrol, self-defense education, escort service, and informal discussions. In addition, there are pamphlets/posters/films, emergency telephones, and lighted pathways/sidewalks.

Programs of Study: Wheaton confers the A.B. degree. Bachelor's degrees are awarded in BIOLOGICAL SCIENCE (biochemistry and biology/biological science), COMMUNICATIONS AND THE ARTS (art history and appreciation, classics, creative writing, English, fine arts, French, German, Italian, literature, music, Russian, and Spanish), COMPUTER AND PHYSICAL SCIENCE (chemistry, computer mathematics, mathematics, and physics), ENGINEERING AND ENVIRONMENTAL DESIGN (environmental science), SOCIAL SCIENCE (American studies, anthropology, Asian/Oriental studies, classical/ancient civilization, economics, Hispanic American studies, history, international relations, philosophy, political science/government, psychobiology, psychology, religion, Russian and Slavic studies, social psychology, and sociology). Arts and sciences are the strongest academically. Psychology has the largest enrollment.

Required: Among the requirements for graduation are 32 credits (4 semester hours equals a course credit), with a minimum of 10 credits in the major, at least 3 of which are at the 300 level or above. Students must also fulfill general education requirements and complete 2 physical education courses. The college requires a minimum GPA of 2.0 (C-) in all courses taken to remain in academic good standing.

Special: Students may cross-register at Brown University, the Southeastern Association for Cooperation in Higher Education in Massachusetts, and several other schools. The school offers study abroad in 25 countries, internship programs, nondegree study, dual majors, student-designed majors, interdisciplinary majors, including mathematics and economics, mathematics and computer science, and theater and English dramatic literature, and a Washington semester at American University. 3–2 engineering degrees are offered with George Washington University, Dartmouth College, and Worcester Polytechnic Institute. Pass/fail options are possible. There is a freshman honors program on campus, as well as 8 national honor societies, including Phi Beta Kappa. All departments have honors programs.

Faculty/Classroom: 50% of faculty are male; 50%, female. All both teach and do research. The average class size in an introductory lecture is 40; in a laboratory, 20; and in a regular course offering, 19.

Admissions: 73% of the 1995–96 applicants were accepted. The SAT I scores for the 1995–96 freshman class were as follows: Verbal—25% below 500, 55% between 500 and 599, and 20% between 600 and 700; Math—26% below 500, 48% between 500 and 599, 25% between 600 and 700, and 1% above 700. 42% of the current freshmen were in the top fifth of their class; 78% were in the top two fifths. 5 freshmen graduated first in their class.

Requirements: Submission of SAT I or ACT scores is optional. Upon enrollment, all students are required to submit results of the SAT II: Subject tests in writing or the ACT for placement purposes. Applicants must be graduates of an accredited secondary school. Recommended courses include English with emphasis on composition skills, 4 years; foreign language and mathematics, 3 to 4 years each; social studies, 3 years; and laboratory science, 2 to 3 years. The GED is accepted. The college requires an essay and strongly recom-

mends an interview. Applications can be submitted on computer disk via Apply or CollegeLink. AP credits are accepted. Important factors in the admissions decision are advanced placement or honor courses, extracurricular activities record, and leadership record.

Procedure: Freshmen are admitted to all sessions. Entrance exams should be taken in October and/or November. There are early decision, early admissions, and deferred admissions plans. Early decision applications should be filed by November 15; regular applications, by February 1 for fall entry and November 15 for spring entry, along with an application fee of $50. Notification of early decision is sent late December; early action, February 1; regular decision, April 1. 31 early decision candidates were accepted for the 1995–96 class. A waiting list is an active part of the admissions procedure, with about 6% of all applicants on the list.

Transfer: 21 transfer students enrolled in 1995–96. Transfer students are encouraged to present a strong B average in their college work to date. Preference will be given to college over high school work. The college transcript is evaluated individually for transfer of credit. 16 course credits of 32 must be completed at Wheaton.

Visiting: There are regularly scheduled orientations for prospective students, including class visits; tours; panels on financial aid, student life, and athletics; lunch with faculty; and department open houses. There are guides for informal visits and visitors may sit in on classes and stay overnight at the school. To schedule a visit, contact the Admission Office.

Financial Aid: In 1995–96, 60% of all freshmen and 67% of continuing students received some form of financial aid. 60% of freshmen and 67% of continuing students received need-based aid. The average freshman award was $16,834. Of that total, scholarships or need-based grants averaged $12,190 ($20,650 maximum); loans averaged $3120 ($5125 maximum); and work contracts averaged $1260 ($1300 maximum). 85% of undergraduate students work part-time. Average earnings from campus work for the school year were $850. The average financial indebtedness of the 1994–95 graduate was $13,250. Wheaton is a member of CSS. The FAFSA and the college's own financial statement are required. The application deadline for fall entry is February 15 (early decision, November 15; early action, February 1).

International Students: There are currently 56 international students enrolled. The school actively recruits these students. They must take the TOEFL and achieve a minimum score of 550.

Computers: The college provides computer facilities for student use. The mainframe is a DEC Server 5000, Model 240. There are 40 Internet connected computers in the academic computer center available for student use. E-mail is also available through 20 public access terminals and by dial-in. All students may access the system Monday through Thursday, 8:30 A.M. to 2 A.M.; Friday, 8:30 A.M. to 10 P.M.; Saturday, 10 A.M. to 10 P.M.; Sunday, 10 A.M. to 2 A.M. There are no time limits and no fees.

Graduates: In 1994–95, 258 bachelor's degrees were awarded. The most popular majors among graduates were English literature (14%), psychology (14%), and political science (7%). Within an average freshman class, 70% graduate in 4 years, 71% in 5 years, and 72% in 6 years. 22 companies recruited on campus in 1994–95. Of the 1994 graduating class, 20% were enrolled in graduate school within 6 months of graduation and 40% had found employment.

Admissions Contact: Gail Berson, Dean of Admission and Student Aid. E-mail: admission@wheatonma.edu. A campus video is available.

WHEELOCK COLLEGE
E-2
Boston, MA 02215-4176

(617) 734-5200, ext. 206
FAX: (617) 566-4453

Full-time: 26 men, 669 women	Faculty: 47; IIA, --$
Part-time: 2 men, 42 women	Ph.D.s: 73%
Graduate: 20 men, 525 women	Student/Faculty: 15 to 1
Year: semesters	Tuition: $14,368
Application Deadline: February 15	Room & Board: $5772
Freshman Class: 442 applied, 356 accepted, 151 enrolled	
SAT I Verbal/Math: 400/420	LESS COMPETITIVE

Wheelock College, established in 1888, is a private institution with programs in education and human services. There is one graduate school. In addition to regional accreditation, Wheelock College has baccalaureate program accreditation with CSWE and NCATE. The library contains 90,394 volumes, 346,411 microform items, and 4789 audiovisual forms, and subscribes to 557 periodicals. Computerized library sources and services include the card catalog, interlibrary loans, and database searching. Special learning facilities include an art gallery and the Wheelock Family Theater. The 9-acre campus is in an urban area in Boston. Including residence halls, there are 10 buildings on campus.

Student Life: 54% of undergraduates are from Massachusetts. Students come from 17 states and 6 foreign countries. 77% are from public schools; 23% from private. 88% are white. The average age of freshmen is 18; all undergraduates, 19.5. 15% do not continue beyond their first year; 60% remain to graduate.

Housing: 508 students can be accommodated in college housing. College-sponsored living facilities include single-sex and coed dormitories. In addition there is a cooperative living house. On-campus housing is guaranteed for all 4 years. 71% of students live on campus. Upperclassmen may keep cars on campus.

Activities: There are no fraternities or sororities. There are 37 groups on campus, including choir, chorale, drama, ethnic, honors, international, literary magazine, musical theater, newspaper, professional, religious, social, social service, student government, and yearbook. Popular campus events include Senior/Sophomore Banquet, Kids Day, Winter Weekend, and Freshman Dinner.

Sports: There are 4 intercollegiate sports for women, and 4 intramural sports for men and 4 for women. Athletic and recreation facilities include a sports complex at a neighboring college with a pool and diving board, racquetball courts, a weight room, an indoor track, a basketball court, crew tanks, and cardiovascular equipment.

Disabled Students: The following facilities are available: wheelchair ramps, elevators, special parking, specially equipped rest rooms, special class scheduling, and lowered drinking fountains.

Services: In addition to many counseling and information services, tutoring is available in every subject. There is a reader service for the blind and remedial math and writing. Academic support services provide individualized programs upon request.

Campus Safety and Security: Campus safety and security measures include escort service, informal discussions, lighted pathways/sidewalks, and 24-hour foot patrol.

Programs of Study: Wheelock College confers B.A., B.S., and B.S.W. degrees. Master's degrees are also awarded. Bachelor's degrees are awarded in EDUCATION (early childhood, elementary, and special), SOCIAL SCIENCE (child care/child and family studies, human development, and social work). Teaching, social work, and child life are the strongest academically and have the largest enrollments.

Required: To graduate, students must complete between 132 and 140 credit hours, with a minimum GPA of 2.0. Wheelock requires at least a 32-credit major combined with a 36-credit professional studies program. Students must earn 24 credits in English composition, mathematics, human growth and development, children and their environments, first-year seminar, visual and performing arts, and 1 course in first aid. Some majors require a thesis.

Special: Wheelock offers cross-registration with Simmons College and internships that include student teaching and social work practice. Dual majors, study-abroad programs, and pass/fail options are available. Students may receive credit for life and work experience. Students begin practical field work their freshman year and continue for all 4 years. There is a freshman honors program on campus, as well as 1 national honor society.

Faculty/Classroom: 23% of faculty are male; 77%, female. 75% teach undergraduates. No introductory courses are taught by graduate students. The average class size in an introductory lecture is 22; in a laboratory, 16; and in a regular course offering, 16.

Admissions: 81% of the 1995–96 applicants were accepted. The SAT I scores for the 1995–96 freshman class were as follows: Verbal—89% below 500, 8% between 500 and 599, and 3% between 600 and 700; Math—82% below 500, 15% between 500 and 599, and 3% between 600 and 700. 21% of the current freshmen were in the top fifth of their class; 46% were in the top two fifths.

Requirements: The SAT I or ACT is required. In addition, applicants must be graduates of an accredited secondary school and must have completed 4 years of English, 3 of mathematics, and 2 each of science and history. The GED is accepted. The college requires an essay and an interview. AP and CLEP credits are accepted. Important factors in the admissions decision are advanced placement or honor courses, evidence of special talent, and personality/intangible qualities.

Procedure: Freshmen are admitted fall and spring. Entrance exams should be taken in the spring of the junior year and/or fall of the senior year. There are early decision and deferred admissions plans. Early decision applications should be filed by December 1; regular applications, by February 15 for fall entry and December 1 for spring entry, along with an application fee of $30. Notification of early decision is sent January 1; regular decision, on a rolling basis. 37 early decision candidates were accepted for the 1995–96 class.

Transfer: 87 transfer students enrolled in 1995–96. Transfer students must have a minimum GPA of 2.0 and must present 2 letters of recommendation. Grades of C- or better transfer for credit. 66 credits of 132 to 140 must be completed at Wheelock College.

Visiting: There are guides for informal visits and visitors may sit in on classes and stay overnight at the school. To schedule a visit, contact the Undergraduate Admissions Office.

Financial Aid: In 1995–96, 88% of all freshmen and 80% of continuing students received some form of financial aid, including need-based aid. The average freshman award was $12,170. Of that total,

scholarships or need-based grants averaged $7950 ($12,700 maximum); loans averaged $3736 ($3825 maximum); and work contracts averaged $890 ($1200 maximum). 33% of undergraduate students work part-time. Average earnings from campus work for the school year are $890. The average financial indebtedness of the 1994–95 graduate was $16,000. Wheelock College is a member of CSS. The FAFSA, the college's own financial statement, and the CSS Profile Application are required. The application deadline for fall entry is March 1.

International Students: They must take the TOEFL and achieve a minimum score of 500.

Computers: The college provides computer facilities for student use. The college's 56 microcomputers are located in the computer center and in the residence halls. All students may access the system 24 hours a day any time school is in session. There are no time limits and no fees.

Graduates: The most popular majors among graduates were teacher education (65%), child life (19%), and social work (15%). Within an average freshman class, 60% graduate in 4 years, 62% in 5 years, and 65% in 6 years. 29 companies recruited on campus in 1994–95. Of the 1994 graduating class, 9% were enrolled in graduate school within 6 months of graduation and 98% had found employment.

Admissions Contact: Lynne E. Dailey, Dean of Admissions. A campus video is available.

WILLIAMS COLLEGE
A-1
Williamstown, MA 01267
(413) 597-2211

Full-time: 998 men, 962 women	Faculty: 226; IIB, + +$
Part-time: 10 men, 12 women	Ph.D.s: 95%
Graduate: 14 men, 27 women	Student/Faculty: 9 to 1
Year: 4–1–4	Tuition: $20,790
Application Deadline: January 1	Room & Board: $5990
Freshman Class: 4996 applied, 1300 accepted, 525 enrolled	
SAT I or ACT: required	MOST COMPETITIVE

Williams College, founded in 1793, is a private coeducational institution offering undergraduate degrees in liberal arts and graduate degrees in art history and development economics. There are 2 graduate schools. The 9 libraries contain 748,711 volumes, 448,711 microform items, and 27,464 audiovisual forms, and subscribe to 2678 periodicals. Computerized library sources and services include the card catalog, interlibrary loans, and database searching. Special learning facilities include a learning resource center, art gallery, planetarium, radio station, a 2500-acre experimental forest, an environmental studies center, a center for foreign languages, literatures, and cultures, a rare book library, and a studio art center. The 450-acre campus is in a small town 150 miles north of New York City and west of Boston. Including residence halls, there are 97 buildings on campus.

Student Life: 89% of undergraduates are from out-of-state, mostly the Middle Atlantic. Students come from 50 states, 40 foreign countries, and Canada. 55% are from public schools; 45% from private. 73% are white; 11% Asian American. The average age of freshmen is 18; all undergraduates, 20. 4% do not continue beyond their first year; 94% remain to graduate.

Housing: 1908 students can be accommodated in college housing. College-sponsored living facilities include single-sex and coed dormitories and on-campus apartments. In addition, there is cooperative housing, in which students prepare their own meals. On-campus housing is guaranteed for all 4 years. 96% of students live on campus; of those, 90% remain on campus on weekends. Upperclassmen may keep cars on campus.

Activities: There are no fraternities or sororities. There are 115 groups on campus, including a capella singing, art, band, chess, choir, chorale, chorus, comedy, computers, dance, drama, ethnic, film, gay, hand bell choir, honors, international, jazz band, literary magazine, marching band, musical theater, newspaper, orchestra, pep band, photography, political, radio and TV, religious, social service, student government, symphony, and yearbook. Popular campus events include Winter Carnival, Mountain Day, and Multicultural Center-sponsored activities.

Sports: There are 16 intercollegiate sports for men and 15 for women, and 17 intramural sports for men and 17 for women. Athletic and recreation facilities include 2 gymnasiums, a 50-meter pool, a dance studio, a weight room, rowing tanks, a boathouse, a golf course, playing fields, and courts for tennis, squash, and paddle tennis. The campus stadium seats 6795.

Disabled Students: 45% of the campus is accessible to disabled students. The following facilities are available: wheelchair ramps, elevators, special parking, specially equipped rest rooms, special class scheduling, lowered drinking fountains, lowered telephones, wheelchair lifts, and special laundry and kitchen facilities.

Services: In addition to many counseling and information services, tutoring is available in every subject. There is a reader service for the blind, and remedial math, reading, and writing. Other services include a peer health program, rape and sexual assault hotline, and 10–1 counseling service.

Campus Safety and Security: Campus safety and security measures include 24-hour foot and vehicle patrol, self-defense education, escort service, and informal discussions. In addition, there are pamphlets/posters/films, emergency telephones, and lighted pathways/sidewalks.

Programs of Study: Williams confers the B.A. degree. Master's degrees are also awarded. Bachelor's degrees are awarded in BIOLOGICAL SCIENCE (biology/biological science), COMMUNICATIONS AND THE ARTS (art, art history and appreciation, classics, dramatic arts, English, fine arts, French, German, literature, music, Russian, and Spanish), COMPUTER AND PHYSICAL SCIENCE (astronomy, astrophysics, chemistry, computer science, geology, mathematics, and physics), SOCIAL SCIENCE (American studies, anthropology, Asian/Oriental studies, economics, history, philosophy, political science/government, psychology, religion, and sociology). English, history, and economics have the largest enrollments.

Required: All students must complete 4 winter studies and 32 courses, 9 of which are in the major field, with a C- or higher. Requirements include 3 semester-long courses in each of 3 academic divisions: languages and arts, social sciences, and science and mathematics. Also required are 1 course in cultural pluralism and 4 semesters of physical education.

Special: Students may cross-register at Bennington or North Adams State and study abroad in Madrid, Oxford, Cairo, Beijing, and Kyoto, or any approved program with another college or university. Teaching and medical field experiences, dual and student-designed majors, internships, and a 3–2 engineering program with Columbia University, Rensselaer Polytechnic Institute, Massachusetts Institute of Technology, and Washington University are offered. There are pass/fail options during the Winter Term. Each department offers at least one Oxford-model tutorial every year. There are 2 national honor societies on campus, including Phi Beta Kappa.

Faculty/Classroom: 65% of faculty are male; 35%, female. All both teach and do research. No introductory courses are taught by graduate students. The average class size in an introductory lecture is 20; in a laboratory, 17; and in a regular course offering, 18.

Admissions: 26% of the 1995–96 applicants were accepted. The SAT I scores for the 1995–96 freshman class were as follows: Verbal—6% below 500, 21% between 500 and 599, 44% between 600 and 700, and 29% above 700; Math—1% below 500, 10% between 500 and 599, 30% between 600 and 700, and 59% above 700. The ACT scores were 4% between 21 and 23, 12% between 24 and 26, 17% between 27 and 28, and 67% above 28. 95% of the current freshmen were in the top fifth of their class; 99% were in the top two fifths. There were 59 National Merit finalists.

Requirements: The SAT I or ACT is required, as well as SAT II: Subject tests in 3 subjects. Applicants should be graduates of an accredited high school or have earned the GED. Secondary preparation should include 4 years each of English and mathematics, 3 to 4 years of foreign language, and at least 2 years each of science and social studies. A personal essay must be submitted. Williams accepts applications via ExPAN, Apply, and CollegeLink. AP credits are accepted. Important factors in the admissions decision are advanced placement or honor courses, recommendations by school officials, and evidence of special talent.

Procedure: Freshmen are admitted in the fall. There are early decision and deferred admissions plans. Early decision applications should be filed by November 15; regular applications, by January 1 for fall entry, along with an application fee of $50. Notification of early decision is sent December 15; regular decision, April 10. 171 early decision candidates were accepted for the 1995–96 class. A waiting list is an active part of the admissions procedure, with about 18% of all applicants on the list.

Transfer: 23 transfer students enrolled in a recent year. Transfer applicants should present a 3.5 GPA in previous college work and must submit either SAT I or ACT scores. 4 semesters must be completed at Williams.

Visiting: There are regularly scheduled orientations for prospective students, consisting of panels, forums, class visits, and campus tours. There are guides for informal visits and visitors may sit in on classes and stay overnight at the school. To schedule a visit, contact the Purple Key Society office at (413) 597-3148.

Financial Aid: In 1995–96, 47% of all freshmen and 38% of continuing students received some form of financial aid. 40% of freshmen and 34% of continuing students received need-based aid. The average freshman award was $18,430. Of that total, scholarships or need-based grants averaged $15,560 ($29,100 maximum); loans averaged $2110 ($2625 maximum); and work contracts averaged $1450 ($1550 maximum). Summer work averaged $1200 (maximum). 46% of undergraduate students work part-time. Average earnings from campus work for the school year are $850. The average financial indebtedness of the 1994–95 graduate was $12,000. Williams is a member of CSS. FAFSA, the college's own financial statement, and CSS Profile Application are required. The application deadline for fall entry is February 1.

International Students: There were 56 international students enrolled in a recent year. The school actively recruits these students. They must take the TOEFL and achieve a minimum score of 600. The applicant must also take SAT I or the ACT and SAT II: Subject tests in writing and 2 other subjects.

Computers: The college provides computer facilities for student use. The mainframe is a DEC VAX 11/785. The Computer Center houses the mainframe, which has 40 ports, as well as 7 Sun Microsystems workstations and 100 assorted IBM PCs, Apple Macintoshes, and graphics terminals. Additional PCs are located in the library and other academic buildings. All public-access DEC terminals and PCs are networked. All students may access the system. There are no time limits and no fees.

Graduates: In 1994–95, 518 bachelor's degrees were awarded. The most popular majors among graduates were history (15%), English (15%), and political science (14%). Within an average freshman class, 93% graduate in 4 years, 96% in 5 years, and 96% in 6 years. 100 companies recruited on campus in 1994–95. Of the 1994 graduating class, 18% were enrolled in graduate school within 6 months of graduation and 63% had found employment.

Admissions Contact: Director of Admissions. E-mail: admission@williams.edu. A campus video is available.

WORCESTER POLYTECHNIC INSTITUTE   C-2
Worcester, MA 01609–2280
(508) 831-5286
FAX: (508) 831-5875

Full-time: 2005 men, 524 women	**Faculty:** 205; IIA, +$
Part-time: 44 men and women	**Ph.D:s:** 95%
Graduate: 846 men, 208 women	**Student/Faculty:** 12 to 1
Year: quarters, summer session	**Tuition:** $17,160
Application Deadline: February 15	**Room & Board:** $5640
Freshman Class: 2481 applied, 2112 accepted, 593 enrolled	
SAT I Verbal/Math: 590/700	**ACT:** 28 **HIGHLY COMPETITIVE**

Worcester Polytechnic Institute, founded in 1865, is a private, coeducational institution with a unique, project-oriented program of study in engineering and other technical fields. There is 1 undergraduate school. In addition to regional accreditation, WPI has baccalaureate program accreditation with ABET. The library contains 330,000 volumes, 785,000 microform items, and 3342 audiovisual forms, and subscribes to 1300 periodicals. Computerized library sources and services include the card catalog, interlibrary loans, and database searching. Special learning facilities include a radio station, TV station, a nuclear reactor, and a robotics laboratory. The 80-acre campus is in a suburban area 40 miles west of Boston. Including residence halls, there are 30 buildings on campus.

Student Life: 53% of undergraduates are from Massachusetts. Students come from 47 states, 57 foreign countries, and Canada. 77% are from public schools; 23% from private. 84% are white. The average age of freshmen is 18; all undergraduates, 20. 6% do not continue beyond their first year; 80% remain to graduate.

Housing: 1247 students can be accommodated in college housing. College-sponsored living facilities include single-sex and coed dormitories, on-campus apartments, and fraternity houses. In addition, there are special interest houses. On-campus housing is guaranteed for the freshman year only and is available on a lottery system for upperclassmen. 50% of students live on campus; of those, 75% remain on campus on weekends. Upperclassmen may keep cars on campus.

Activities: 39% of men belong to 12 national fraternities; 31% of women belong to 2 national sororities. There are more than 100 groups on campus, including art, band, cheerleading, chess, choir, chorale, chorus, computers, dance, drama, ethnic, gay, international, jazz band, literary magazine, musical theater, newspaper, orchestra, pep band, photography, political, professional, radio and TV, religious, social, social service, student government, symphony, and yearbook. Popular campus events include Traditions Day and New Voices Festival.

Sports: There are 11 intercollegiate sports for men and 10 for women, and 15 intramural sports for men and 9 for women. Athletic and recreation facilities include an aerobics area, softball and baseball fields, bowling alleys, 8-lane synthetic surface track, a fitness center, a crew center, a playing field with artificial turf, a pool, basketball, racquetball, tennis, and squash courts, and a 2800-seat gymnasium.

Disabled Students: 90% of the campus is accessible to disabled students. The following facilities are available: wheelchair ramps, elevators, special parking, specially equipped rest rooms, special class scheduling, and lowered drinking fountains.

Services: In addition to many counseling and information services, tutoring is available in every subject.

Campus Safety and Security: Campus safety and security measures include 24-hour foot and vehicle patrol, self-defense education, escort service, and shuttle buses. In addition, there are informal discussions, pamphlets/posters/films, emergency telephones, lighted pathways/sidewalks, and a student-run emergency medical service supervised by the campus police department.

Programs of Study: WPI confers the B.S. degree. Master's and doctoral degrees are also awarded. Bachelor's degrees are awarded in BIOLOGICAL SCIENCE (biochemistry, biology/biological science, and biotechnology), BUSINESS (management engineering, management information systems, management science, and operations research), COMMUNICATIONS AND THE ARTS (English), COMPUTER AND PHYSICAL SCIENCE (actuarial science, chemistry, computer science, mathematics, physics, and statistics), ENGINEERING AND ENVIRONMENTAL DESIGN (aeronautical engineering, biomedical engineering, chemical engineering, civil engineering, computer engineering, construction management, electrical/electronics engineering, engineering, engineering physics, environmental science, fire protection engineering, industrial engineering, manufacturing engineering, materials engineering, mechanical engineering, and nuclear engineering), HEALTH PROFESSIONS (biomedical science, predentistry, premedicine, and preveterinary science), SOCIAL SCIENCE (economics, history, humanities, interdisciplinary studies, philosophy, and social science). Engineering has the largest enrollment.

Required: For a B.S. degree, WPI requires that students in science and engineering complete a minor in the humanities. Students must also complete 2 major individual projects. Distribution requirements vary according to the major, and all students must take courses in social sciences and physical education.

Special: WPI offers study abroad in 8 countries. Students may cross-register with 9 colleges in the Worcester Area College Consortium. Co-op programs in all majors, internships, work-study programs, dual majors in every subject, student-designed majors, 3–2 engineering degrees, nondegree study, and pass/fail options are all available. There is a 7-year veterinary medicine program with Tufts Medical School and an accelerated degree program in fire protection engineering. There are special project centers in Europe and Latin America, as well as a Washington semester. There are 10 national honor societies on campus.

Faculty/Classroom: 90% of faculty are male; 10%, female. 96% teach undergraduates and 50% do research. No introductory courses are taught by graduate students. The average class size in an introductory lecture is 35; in a laboratory, 20; and in a regular course offering, 25.

Admissions: 85% of the 1995–96 applicants were accepted. 79% of the current freshmen were in the top fifth of their class; 98% were in the top two fifths. There were 13 National Merit finalists and 13 semifinalists. 19 freshmen graduated first in their class.

Requirements: The SAT I or ACT is required. SAT II: Subject tests in writing, mathematics I or II, and a science are also required. Applicants must have completed 4 years of English, precalculus, chemistry, and physics. The GED is accepted if the applicant has taken precalculus, chemistry, and physics. Students should submit an essay, and an interview is recommended. Students may apply by disk, modem, Internet, World Wide Web, ExPAN, CollegeLink, and CollegeView. AP credits are accepted. Important factors in the admissions decision are advanced placement or honor courses, recommendations by school officials, and extracurricular activities record.

Procedure: Freshmen are admitted in the fall and spring. Entrance exams should be taken between April and December. There are early decision, early admissions, and deferred admissions plans. Early decision applications should be filed by December 1; regular applications, by February 15 for fall entry and November 15 for spring entry, along with an application fee of $40. Notification is sent April 1. 151 early decision candidates were accepted for the 1995–96 class. A waiting list is an active part of the admissions procedure.

Transfer: 100 transfer students enrolled in a recent year. Grades of C or better transfer for credit. 8 units of 45 must be completed at WPI.

Visiting: There are regularly scheduled orientations for prospective students, consisting of meetings and presentations from various academic and extracurricular groups. There are guides for informal visits and visitors may sit in on classes and stay overnight at the school. To schedule a visit, contact the Admissions Office.

Financial Aid: In 1995–96, 85% of all freshmen and 78% of continuing students received some form of financial aid. 76% of all students received need-based aid. The average freshman award was $14,200. Of that total, scholarships or need-based grants averaged $9500 ($16,500 maximum); outside scholarships averaged $1,800 ($18,000 maximum); loans averaged $4680 ($5375 maximum); and work contracts averaged $1050 ($1200 maximum). 55% of undergraduate students work part-time. Average earnings from campus work for the school year are $850. The average financial indebtedness of the 1994–95 graduate was $16,000. WPI is a member of CSS. FAFSA and the College Scholarship Service Profile are required. The application deadline for fall entry is March 1.

International Students: There are currently 152 international students enrolled. The school actively recruits these students. They must take the TOEFL and achieve a minimum score of 550. The student must also take SAT I or the ACT and SAT II: Subject tests in writing, mathematics, and science.

Computers: The college provides computer facilities for student use. The UNIX-based mainframe is accessible via 8 parallel processors and a campuswide data network available in many locations, including the College Computer Center. The center also features 56 X terminals. More than 1,000 IBM-compatible PC-6300 computers are available throughout the campus in general-access and specialized laboratories and computer classrooms. There is also a 32-PC documentation preparation laboratory for typesetting and desktop publishing applications. All residence halls provide access to campus network for students bringing a computer. All students may access the system 24 hours daily. There are no time limits and no fees.

Graduates: In 1994–95, 628 bachelor's degrees were awarded. The most popular majors among graduates were mechanical engineering (33%), electrical engineering (18%), and civil engineering (14%). Within an average freshman class, 1% graduate in 3 years, 71% in 4 years, 8% in 5 years, and 2% in 6 years. 200 companies recruited on campus in 1994–95. Of the 1994 graduating class, 15% were enrolled in graduate school within 6 months of graduation and 75% had found employment.

Admissions Contact: Kay Dietrich, Director of Admissions. A campus video is available.

WORCESTER STATE COLLEGE · C-2

Worcester, MA 01605 · (508) 793–8040; FAX: (508) 793–8191

Full-time: 1190 men, 1661 women	Faculty: 164
Part-time: 11 men, 37 women	Ph.D.s: 62%
Graduate: 821 men, 1785 women	Student/Faculty: 17 to 1
Year: semesters, summer session	Tuition: $2753 ($6887)
Application Deadline: open	Room & Board: $4000
Freshman Class: 2283 applied, 1406 accepted, 485 enrolled	
SAT I or ACT: not required	COMPETITIVE

Worcester State College, established in 1874, is a public, primarily commuter institution offering undergraduate degrees in education and liberal arts and sciences. In addition to regional accreditation, the college has baccalaureate program accreditation with CAHEA and NLN. The library contains 160,000 volumes, and subscribes to 1000 periodicals. Special learning facilities include a learning resource center, radio station, TV station, photographic laboratories, and audiovisual center. The 58-acre campus is in a suburban area 40 miles west of Boston. Including residence halls, there are 6 buildings on campus.

Student Life: 98% of undergraduates are from Massachusetts. 86% are from public schools. The average age of freshmen is 19; all undergraduates, 24. 15% do not continue beyond their first year; 40% remain to graduate.

Housing: 700 students can be accommodated in college housing. College-sponsored living facilities include dormitories and on-campus apartments. 85% of students commute. All students may keep cars on campus.

Activities: There are no fraternities or sororities. There are 20 groups on campus, including drama, newspaper, radio and TV, religious, social, social service, student government, and yearbook. Popular campus events include Homecoming, Winter Carnival, Senior Week, lecture series, and Academic Honors Convocation.

Sports: Athletic and recreation facilities include an auditorium, a gymnasium, a fitness center, tennis courts, a track, baseball and softball diamonds, and football, field hockey, and all-purpose fields.

Disabled Students: 75% of the campus is accessible to disabled students. The following facilities are available: wheelchair ramps, elevators, special parking, and specially equipped rest rooms.

Services: There is remedial math, reading, and writing.

Campus Safety and Security: Security is provided 24 hours a day throughout the calendar year by full-time officers. The dormitory is protected by a state-of-the-art security system.

Programs of Study: The college confers B.A., B.S., and B.S.Ed. degrees. Master's degrees are also awarded. Bachelor's degrees are awarded in BIOLOGICAL SCIENCE (biology/biological science), BUSINESS (business administration and management), COMMUNICATIONS AND THE ARTS (English, French, media arts, and Spanish), COMPUTER AND PHYSICAL SCIENCE (chemistry, computer science, mathematics, natural sciences, and physics), EDUCATION (early childhood and elementary), HEALTH PROFESSIONS (nursing, occupational therapy, and speech pathology/audiology), SOCIAL SCIENCE (economics, geography, history, psychology, sociology, and urban studies).

Required: To graduate, students must complete a foundation requirement, including English composition, the study of the U.S. and Massachusetts constitutions, physical education, and, if necessary, developmental reading, English, and mathematics. Distribution requirements include 12 credits each in humanities, social sciences, and natural sciences and mathematics, and 9 in fine arts. Students must complete 128 credits, 30 to 48 in the major, with a minimum 2.0 GPA overall and in the major.

Special: There is cross-registration with the Worcester Consortium for Higher Education, internships, work-study, B.A.-B.S. degrees, dual majors, a 3–2 engineering degree with Worcester Polytechnic Institute, nondegree study, and a pass/fail option. There is 1 national honor society on campus.

Faculty/Classroom: 97% teach undergraduates.

Admissions: 62% of the 1995–96 applicants were accepted. The SAT I scores for the 1995–96 freshman class were as follows: Verbal—86% below 500, 11% between 500 and 599, and 3% between 600 and 700; Math—69% below 500, 24% between 500 and 599, 6% between 600 and 700, and 1% above 700. 21% of the current freshmen were in the top fifth of their class; 60% were in the top two fifths.

Requirements: The college requires applicants to be in the upper 90% of their class. Applicants must graduate from an accredited secondary school or have a GED. They should have completed 4 years of English, 3 of mathematics, 2 each of a foreign language, a laboratory science, and social studies, including 1 year of U.S. history and government, and 3 electives. The College Board Student Descriptive questionnaire must be submitted. AP and CLEP credits are accepted.

Procedure: Entrance exams should be taken in May of the junior year or December of the senior year. Application deadlines are open. Application fee is $10 (in-state); $40 (out-of-state). Notification is sent on a rolling basis.

Transfer: Transfer applicants must have earned a minimum of 12 college credits. 30 credits of 128 must be completed at the college.

Visiting: There are regularly scheduled orientations for prospective students. To schedule a visit, contact the Director of Admissions.

Financial Aid: In a recent year, scholarships or need-based grants averaged $400; loans averaged $600; and work contracts averaged $500. The college is a member of CSS. The FAF is required. The application deadline for fall entry is March 1.

International Students: There were 70 international students enrolled in a recent year.

Computers: The college provides computer facilities for student use. The mainframes are comprised of a CYBER CDC, Control Data, and a DEC MicroVAX 3900. There are also PC laboratories available.

Admissions Contact: E. Jay Tierney, Director of Admissions.

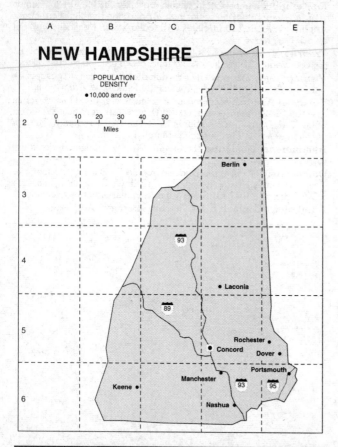

NEW HAMPSHIRE

POPULATION
DENSITY
● 10,000 and over

0 10 20 30 40 50
Miles

Berlin

93

Laconia

89

Rochester
Concord
Dover

Keene   Manchester   Portsmouth
93   95

Nashua

COLBY-SAWYER COLLEGE
New London, NH 03257

C-5

(603) 526-3700
(800) 272-1015; FAX: (603) 526-3452

Full-time: 262 men, 423 women	Faculty: 40; IIB, -$
Part-time: 5 men, 22 women	Ph.D.s: 70%
Graduate: none	Student/Faculty: 17 to 1
Year: semesters	Tuition: $14,720
Application Deadline: May 1	Room & Board: $5640
Freshman Class: 1040 applied, 840 accepted, 276 enrolled	
SAT I Verbal/Math: 410/450	**COMPETITIVE**

Colby-Sawyer College, established in 1837, is an independent coeducational college offering a variety of undergraduate majors, including fine arts, nursing, business, and communications, as well as education certification. In addition to regional accreditation, Colby-Sawyer has baccalaureate program accreditation with NLN. The library contains 72,230 volumes, 155,700 microform items, and 1120 audiovisual forms, and subscribes to 580 periodicals. Computerized library sources and services include the card catalog, interlibrary loans, and database searching. Special learning facilities include a learning resource center, art gallery, radio station, academic development center, and laboratory school (K-3). The 80-acre campus is in a small town 100 miles northwest of Boston. Including residence halls, there are 23 buildings on campus.

Student Life: 66% of undergraduates are from out of state, mostly the Northeast. Students come from 22 states, 9 foreign countries, and Canada. 75% are from public schools; 25% from private. 95% are white. The average age of freshmen is 18; all undergraduates, 20. 20% do not continue beyond their first year; 61% remain to graduate.

Housing: 600 students can be accommodated in college housing. College-sponsored living facilities include single-sex and coed dormitories and on-campus apartments. In addition there is a substance-free residence hall. On-campus housing is guaranteed for all 4 years. 82% of students live on campus; of those, 70% remain on campus on weekends. All students may keep cars on campus.

Activities: There are no fraternities or sororities. There are 22 groups on campus, including art, dance, drama, film, honors, jazz band, literary magazine, musical theater, newspaper, photography, radio and TV, social, social service, student government, and yearbook. Popular campus events include Fall and Spring Weekends and Mountain Day.

Sports: There are 7 intercollegiate sports for men and 8 for women, and 8 intramural sports for men and 8 for women. Athletic and recreation facilities include 6 outdoor and 3 indoor tennis courts, a fitness center, an NCAA-approved swimming pool, a suspended track, squash and racquetball courts, and 3 outdoor competitive fields.

Disabled Students: 20% of the campus is accessible to disabled students. Special parking and special class scheduling are available.

Services: In addition to many counseling and information services, tutoring is available in every subject. There is a reader service for the blind, and remedial math, reading, and writing.

Campus Safety and Security: Campus safety and security measures include 24-hour foot and vehicle patrol, self-defense education, escort service, and shuttle buses. In addition, there are informal discussions, pamphlets/posters/films, emergency telephones, lighted pathways/sidewalks, and monthly meetings of students with campus safety personnel.

Programs of Study: Colby-Sawyer confers B.A., B.S., and B.F.A. degrees. Associate degrees are also awarded. Bachelor's degrees are awarded in BIOLOGICAL SCIENCE (biology/biological science), BUSINESS (business administration and management and sports management), COMMUNICATIONS AND THE ARTS (art, communications, design, English, and fine arts), EDUCATION (athletic training), HEALTH PROFESSIONS (nursing), SOCIAL SCIENCE (child psychology/development and psychology). Biology and nursing are the strongest academically. Sports science, nursing, and child development have the largest enrollments.

Required: Required courses include first-year colloquium, writing, mathematics, and computer literacy. Required interdisciplinary core courses include Creative Expression, Process of Discovery, Social Analysis, and Judgment and Belief. Required electives include 1 each in fine and performing arts and natural sciences, and 2 each in social sciences and humanities. A total of 120 credit hours with a minimum GPA of 2.0 is needed for graduation.

Special: There is cross-registration through the New Hampshire College and University Council. Students may choose internships (required in some majors) and study abroad in Greece, England, and various other countries. A Washington semester with American University is available. Other options include student-designed majors, education certification, credit by examination, and a general studies degree. There is a freshman honors program on campus, as well as 1 national honor society.

Faculty/Classroom: 52% of faculty are male; 48%, female. All teach undergraduates, and 4% both teach and do research. The average class size in a regular course offering is 17.

Admissions: 81% of the 1995–96 applicants were accepted.

Requirements: The SAT I or ACT is required. Applicants need a 2.0 GPA. The GED is accepted. A total of 15 college preparatory credits is recommended for admission, including 4 years of English, 3 of mathematics, and 2 each of history, a foreign language, and a science. An essay is required, as are 2 letters of recommendation. Interviews are strongly recommended. AP and CLEP credits are accepted. Important factors in the admissions decision are advanced placement or honor courses, recommendations by school officials, and evidence of special talent.

Procedure: Freshmen are admitted fall and spring. Entrance exams should be taken in the fall of the senior year. There is a deferred admissions plan. Applications should be filed by May 1 for fall entry and November 1 for spring entry, along with an application fee of $40. Notification is sent on a rolling basis.

Transfer: 31 transfer students enrolled in 1995–96. College-level work will be emphasized. College transcripts, course descriptions, and a dean's form are required in addition to the standard requirements. 30 credits of 120 must be completed at Colby-Sawyer.

Visiting: There are regularly scheduled orientations for prospective students, including tours and interviews. 2 open house programs offer tours as well as academic, athletic, campus life, career development, and academic development presentations. 4 1-day visit day programs offer tours, interviews, and class visits. There are guides for informal visits, and visitors may sit in on classes. To schedule a visit, contact the Admissions Office.

Financial Aid: In 1995–96, 66% of all freshmen and 69% of continuing students received some form of financial aid. 54% of freshmen and 61% of continuing students received need-based aid. The average freshman award was $12,297. Of that total, scholarships or need-based grants averaged $9223 ($16,340 maximum); and loans averaged $2603 ($4125 maximum). 43% of undergraduate students work part-time. Average earnings from campus work for the school year are $1100. The average financial indebtedness of the 1994–95 graduate was $9850. Colby-Sawyer is a member of CSS. The college's own financial statement and the FAFSA are required. The application deadline for fall entry is March 1.

International Students: There are currently 25 international students enrolled. The school actively recruits these students. They must score 500 on the TOEFL.

Computers: The college provides computer facilities for student use. The mainframe is a DEC ALPHA 2100. Three student computer laboratories, housing 45 IBM-compatible and 15 Apple Macintosh microcomputers, are available on campus. All students may access the system. There are no time limits and no fees.

Graduates: In 1994–95, 151 bachelor's degrees were awarded. The most popular majors among graduates were sports science (19%), business administration (15%), and child development (15%). Within an average freshman class, 53% graduate in 4 years and 61% in 5 years. 2 companies recruited on campus in 1994–95. Of the 1994 graduating class, 9% were enrolled in graduate school within 6 months of graduation and 89% had found employment.

Admissions Contact: Office of Admissions and Financial Aid. A video of the campus is available.

COLLEGE FOR LIFELONG LEARNING   E-5

Concord, NH 03301-6430	(603) 228-3000, ext. 308
	(800) 582-7248; FAX: (603) 229-0964
Full-time: 179 men, 409 women	Faculty: 365
Part-time: 269 men, 901 women	Ph.D.s: n/av
Graduate: none	Student/Faculty: 5 to 1
Year: trimesters, summer session	Tuition: $3204 ($3540)
Application Deadline: open	Room & Board: n/app
Freshman Class: n/av	
SAT I or ACT: not required	SPECIAL

The College for Lifelong Learning, established as part of the University System of New Hampshire in 1972, is a state-supported, commuter institution offering undergraduate programs in general and professional studies for adults. Computerized library sources and services include the card catalog, interlibrary loans, and database searching. The campus is in a small town.

Student Life: 92% of undergraduates are from New Hampshire. Students come from 4 states and 1 foreign country. 91% are white.

Housing: There are no residence halls. All students commute. Alcohol is not permitted. All students may keep cars on campus.

Activities: There are no fraternities or sororities.

Sports: There is no sports program at CLL.

Disabled Students: 80% of the campus is accessible to disabled students. The following facilities are available: wheelchair ramps, special parking, and specially equipped rest rooms.

Services: In addition to many counseling and information services, tutoring is available in every subject. There is a reader service for the blind, and remedial math, reading, and writing.

Campus Safety and Security: Campus safety and security measures include self-defense education, informal discussions, and pamphlets/posters/films.

Programs of Study: CLL confers B.G.S. and B.P.S. degrees. Associate degrees are also awarded. Bachelor's degrees are awarded in BUSINESS (management science), SOCIAL SCIENCE (behavioral science). Behavioral science has the largest enrollment.

Required: Students must complete 124 credits, 30 to 36 in the major, and must maintain a minimum GPA of 2.0. All students are required to complete courses in functional understanding, computer literacy, critical thinking, writing, mathematics, and communications.

Special: Opportunities are provided for internships through the Washington Center, cross-registration with all USNH schools, student-designed and dual majors, credit by examination, nondegree study, and pass/fail options. CLL offers programs throughout the state, in 4 regions and 12 local sites. There is 1 national honor society on campus.

Faculty/Classroom: 40% of faculty are male. All teach undergraduates. The average class size in a regular course offering is 11.

Requirements: A GED will be considered if submitted for admission evaluation. An interview is recommended. AP and CLEP credits are accepted.

Procedure: Freshmen are admitted to all sessions. Application deadlines are open. Application fee is $35. The college accepts all applicants. Notification is sent on a rolling basis.

Transfer: An interview is recommended. 30 credits of 124 must be completed at CLL.

Visiting: Visitors may sit in on classes.

Financial Aid: The average freshman award for 1995–96 was $3615. 1% of undergraduate students work part-time. Average earnings from campus work for the school year are $4000. The FAFSA is required. The application deadline for fall entry is August 27.

International Students: There are currently 3 international students enrolled. They must take the TOEFL and achieve a minimum score of 500.

Computers: The college provides computer facilities for student use. The mainframe is a DEC VAX. Students have no mainframe access, but may use microcomputers in 5 laboratories. There are no time limits and no fees.

Graduates: In 1994–95, 138 bachelor's degrees were awarded. The most popular majors among graduates were management (38%), behavioral science (35%), and self-designed studies (27%).

Admissions Contact: Tessa McDonnell, Admissions Office. E-mail: t_mcdonnell@unhf.unh.edu.

DANIEL WEBSTER COLLEGE   D-6

Nashua, NH 03063-1300	(603) 577-6602
	(800) 325-6876; FAX: (603) 577-6001
Full-time: 346 men, 95 women	Faculty: 23; IIB, -$
Part-time: 29 men, 6 women	Ph.D.s: 44%
Graduate: none	Student/Faculty: 19 to 1
Year: semesters	Tuition: $13,197
Application Deadline: open	Room & Board: $5262
Freshman Class: 653 applied, 563 accepted, 178 enrolled	
SAT I Verbal/Math: 434/505	COMPETITIVE

Daniel Webster College, founded in 1965, is a private coeducational college offering study in the fields of aviation, business, computer sciences, engineering, and sports management. The library contains 35,000 volumes, 410 microform items, and 432 audiovisual forms, and subscribes to 250 periodicals. Computerized library sources and services include the card catalog, interlibrary loans, and database searching. Special learning facilities include a learning resource center and a flight center, a flight tower, air traffic control laboratories, flight simulators, a hangar, and 26 airplanes. The 50-acre campus is in a suburban area 45 miles northwest of Boston, Massachusetts. Including residence halls, there are 12 buildings on campus.

Student Life: 74% of undergraduates are from out-of-state, mostly the Northeast. Students come from 25 states, 7 foreign countries, and Canada. 80% are from public schools; 20% from private. 87% are white. The average age of freshmen is 18; all undergraduates, 21. 25% do not continue beyond their first year; 49% remain to graduate.

Housing: 380 students can be accommodated in college housing. College-sponsored living facilities include single-sex dormitories and on-campus apartments. In addition, there are quiet floors in residence halls, smoke-free areas, and a substance-free, 10-month housing option. On-campus housing is guaranteed for all 4 years. 70% of students live on campus; of those, 80% remain on campus on weekends. All students may keep cars on campus.

Activities: There are no fraternities or sororities. There are 16 groups on campus, including computers, honors, jazz band, literary magazine, newspaper, professional, religious, social, social service, student government, and yearbook. Popular campus events include Spring Weekend and Ski Day.

Sports: There are 6 intercollegiate sports for men and 5 for women, and 15 intramural sports for men and 10 for women. Athletic and recreation facilities include an indoor basketball/volleyball court, a weight room, tennis courts, soccer and softball fields, and cross-country trails.

Disabled Students: 60% of the campus is accessible to disabled students. The following facilities are available: wheelchair ramps, elevators, special parking, specially equipped rest rooms, and lowered drinking fountains.

Services: In addition to many counseling and information services, tutoring is available in every subject. There is remedial math and writing, study skills and test skills workshops, and study groups. Facilities include a mathematics center and a writing center.

Campus Safety and Security: Campus safety and security measures include 24-hour foot and vehicle patrol, informal discussions, pamphlets/posters/films, and lighted pathways/sidewalks.

Programs of Study: DWC confers the B.S. degree. Associate degrees are also awarded. Bachelor's degrees are awarded in BUSINESS (accounting, business administration and management, and sports management), COMPUTER AND PHYSICAL SCIENCE (computer science), ENGINEERING AND ENVIRONMENTAL DESIGN (aviation administration/management and computer technology). Aviation, computer science, and computer systems are the strongest academically. Aviation has the largest enrollment.

Required: Students must complete general education courses in communication, computer science, mathematics, natural science, the humanities, and the social sciences. At least 120 credits, with a minimum of 30 in the major, are required for graduation. Students must maintain a minimum GPA of 2.0.

Special: There is cross-registration with the New Hampshire College and University Council. All programs offer credit by examination. Interdisciplinary majors, including aviation management/flight operations and aviation management/air traffic control are available. There are internships in aviation, business, computer sciences, and sports management. Study abroad, a general studies degree, and a 2–2 engineering program with the universities of New Hampshire and Massachusetts at Lowell and Clarkson University are additional options. There is 1 national honor society on campus, Phi Beta Kappa.

Faculty/Classroom: 82% of faculty are male; 18%, female. All teach undergraduates. The average class size in an introductory lecture is 25; in a laboratory, 12; and in a regular course offering, 20.

Admissions: 86% of the 1995–96 applicants were accepted. 23% of the current freshmen were in the top fifth of their class; 52% were in the top two fifths. 4 freshmen graduated first in their class.

Requirements: The SAT I or ACT is required. DWC requires applicants to be in the upper 60% of their class. A minimum GPA of 2.0 is required. Applicants must be graduates of an accredited secondary school or submit the GED. Students should have taken 4 years of English, 3 of mathematics, 2 each of social studies and science, and 1 of history. An essay and an interview are recommended. AP and CLEP credits are accepted. Important factors in the admissions decision are advanced placement or honor courses, recommendations by school officials, and leadership record.

Procedure: Freshmen are admitted to all sessions. Entrance exams should be taken in early fall. There are early admissions and deferred admissions plans. Application deadlines are open. Application fee is $35. Notification is sent on a rolling basis.

Transfer: 27 transfer students enrolled in 1995–96. Students must have a minimum college GPA of 2.0. The SAT I is required. Grades of C or better transfer for credit. 30 credits of 120 must be completed at DWC.

Visiting: There are regularly scheduled orientations for prospective students, including a tour and an admissions interview; also available are meetings with faculty and meals. There are guides for informal visits and visitors may sit in on classes and stay overnight at the school. To schedule a visit, contact Kent Ericson, Dean of Enrollment Management.

Financial Aid: In 1995–96, 93% of all freshmen and 84% of continuing students received some form of financial aid. 84% of freshmen and 75% of continuing students received need-based aid. The average freshman award was $13,218. Of that total, scholarships or need-based grants averaged $8665 ($14,240 maximum); loans averaged $3680 ($4625 maximum); and work contracts averaged $1560 ($2000 maximum). 33% of undergraduate students work part-time. Average earnings from campus work for the school year are $980. The average financial indebtedness of the 1994–95 graduate was $15,324. DWC is a member of CSS. The FAFSA is required.

International Students: There are currently 8 international students enrolled. They must take the TOEFL and achieve a minimum score of 500.

Computers: The college provides computer facilities for student use. The mainframes are a DEC MicroVAX 3800, a DEC System 5400, and an IBM RS/6000. The 3 mainframes and more than 40 PCs, 25 of which are part of a Novell Ethernet local area network, are available to all students when the computer center is open. There are no time limits and no fees.

Graduates: In 1994–95, 96 bachelor's degrees were awarded. The most popular majors among graduates were aviation management/flight operations (37%), aviation management (26%), and business management (20%). Within an average freshman class, 5% graduate in 3 years, 29% in 4 years, 13% in 5 years, and 2% in 6 years. Of the 1994 graduating class, 10% were enrolled in graduate school within 6 months of graduation and 81% had found employment.

Admissions Contact: Kent Ericson, Dean of Enrollment Management. E-mail: postmasteradmissions.disney.dwc.edu.

DARTMOUTH COLLEGE
Hanover, NH 03755

B-4
(603) 646-2875

Full-time: 2300 men, 1970 women	Faculty: 344; I, +$
Part-time: none	Ph.Ds: 98%
Graduate: 930 men and women	Student/Faculty: 12 to 1
Year: see profile, summer session	Tuition: $19,650
Application Deadline: January 1	Room & Board: $5865
Freshman Class: 10,006 applied, 2281 accepted, 1048 enrolled	
SAT I or ACT: required	**MOST COMPETITIVE**

Dartmouth College, chartered in 1769, is a private liberal arts institution offering a wide range of graduate and undergraduate programs. There is a year-round academic calendar of 4 10-week terms. There are 4 graduate schools. The 9 libraries contain 2 million volumes and 2.3 million microform items, and subscribe to 21,000 periodicals. Computerized library sources and services include the card catalog, interlibrary loans, and database searching. Special learning facilities include a learning resource center, an art gallery, a radio station, a TV station, a center for performing arts, a life sciences laboratory, a physical sciences center, and an observatory. The 265-acre campus is in a rural area 140 miles northwest of Boston. Including residence halls, there are 100 buildings on campus.

Student Life: 97% of undergraduates are from out-of-state, mostly the Middle Atlantic. Students come from 50 states, 54 foreign countries, and Canada. 65% are from public schools; 35% from private. 57% are white. The average age of freshmen is 18; all undergraduates, 21. 1% do not continue beyond their first year; 97% remain to graduate.

Housing: 3500 students can be accommodated in college housing. College-sponsored living facilities include coed dormitories, on-campus apartments, married-student housing, fraternity houses, and sorority houses. In addition there are language houses and special interest houses. On-campus housing is guaranteed for the freshman year only, is available on a first-come, first-served basis, and is available on a lottery system for upperclassmen. 95% of students live on campus; of those, 90% remain on campus on weekends. Upperclassmen may keep cars on campus.

Activities: 41% of men belong to 7 local and 10 national fraternities; 28% of women belong to 3 local and 4 national sororities. There are 290 groups on campus, including art, band, cheerleading, chess, choir, chorale, chorus, computers, dance, drama, ethnic, film, gay, honors, international, jazz band, literary magazine, marching band, musical theater, newspaper, opera, orchestra, pep band, photography, political, radio and TV, religious, social, social service, student government, symphony, and yearbook. Popular campus events include Dartmouth Night/Homecoming, Winter and Summer Carnivals, and Green Key Service Weekend.

Sports: There are 16 intercollegiate sports for men and 16 for women, and 25 intramural sports for men and 25 for women. Athletic and recreation facilities include a 2100-seat stadium, a fitness center, squash and racquetball courts, a dance studio, a 5000-seat arena, a gymnasium, a 21,000-seat football stadium, a boathouse, indoor and outdoor tennis courts, a golf course, a ski slope with 3 chairlifts, and a riding farm.

Disabled Students: The following facilities are available: wheelchair ramps, elevators, special parking, specially equipped rest rooms, special class scheduling, lowered drinking fountains, lowered telephones, and accessible residence halls.

Services: In addition to many counseling and information services, tutoring is available in every subject. There is a reader service for the blind. There is an academic skills center for all students, and readers, note takers, and tape recorders are available.

Campus Safety and Security: Campus safety and security measures include 24-hour foot and vehicle patrol, self-defense education, escort service, and shuttle buses. There are informal discussions, pamphlets/posters/films, emergency telephones, and lighted pathways/sidewalks.

Programs of Study: Dartmouth confers B.A. and B.Eng. degrees. Master's and doctoral degrees are also awarded. Bachelor's degrees are awarded in BIOLOGICAL SCIENCE (biochemistry, biology/biological science, evolutionary biology, and genetics), COMMUNICATIONS AND THE ARTS (art history and appreciation, Chinese, classics, comparative literature, creative writing, dramatic arts, English, film arts, fine arts, French, German, Greek, Italian, languages, Latin, linguistics, literature, music, romance languages, Russian, Spanish, studio art, and visual and performing arts), COMPUTER AND PHYSICAL SCIENCE (chemistry, computer science, earth science, geology, mathematics, and physics), EDUCATION (education), ENGINEERING AND ENVIRONMENTAL DESIGN (engineering and environmental science), SOCIAL SCIENCE (African American studies, African studies, anthropology, archeology, Asian/Oriental studies, Caribbean studies, cognitive science, economics, geography, history, Latin American studies, Native American studies, philosophy, political science/government, psychology, religion, Russian and Slavic studies, social science, sociology, and women's studies). History, government, and engineering have the largest enrollments.

Required: All students must take 35 courses, 10 of which must be distributed in the following fields: arts; social analysis; literature; quantitative or deductive science; philosophical, religious, or historical analysis; natural science; technology or applied science; and international or comparative study. 3 world culture courses are required from the U.S., Europe, and at least 1 non-Western society. A multidisciplinary or interdisciplinary course is also required.

Special: Students may design programs using the college's unique Dartmouth Plan, which divides the academic calendar into 4 10-week terms, based on the seasons. The plan permits greater flexibility for vacations and for the 45 study abroad programs in 18 countries, including Italy, France, Scotland, the former U.S.S.R., and Brazil. Cross-registration is offered through the Twelve College Exchange Network, which includes Amherst and Mt. Holyoke. Exchange programs also exist with the University of California at San Diego, McGill University in Montreal, selected German universities, Keio University in Tokyo, and Beijing Normal University in China. There are special academic programs in Washington, D.C., and Tucson, Arizona. Students may design their own interdisciplinary majors, involving multiple departments if desired, take dual majors in all fields, or satisfy a modified major involving 2 departments, with emphasis in one. Hands-on computer science education, internships, combined B.A.-B.S. degrees, and work-study programs also are available. A 3–2 engineering degree is offered with Dartmouth's Thayer School of Engineering. There are 2 national honor societies on campus, including Phi Beta Kappa. All departments have honors programs.

Faculty/Classroom: 65% of faculty are male; 35%, female. All both teach and do research. No introductory courses are taught by graduate students. The average class size in a regular course offering is 23.

Admissions: 23% of the 1995–96 applicants were accepted. The SAT I scores for a recent freshman class were as follows: Verbal—4% below 500, 24% between 500 and 599, 55% between 600 and 700, and 17% above 700; Math—1% below 500, 9% between 500 and 599, 34% between 600 and 700, and 56% above 700. 95% of recent freshmen were in the top fifth of their class; 99% were in the top two fifths. 179 freshmen graduated first in their class.

Requirements: The SAT I or ACT is required, as are 3 SAT II: Subject tests. Evidence of intellectual capacity, motivation, and personal integrity are prime considerations in the highly competitive admissions process, which also considers talent, accomplishment, and involvement in nonacademic areas. Course requirements are flexible, but students are urged to take English, foreign language, mathematics, laboratory science, and history. The GED is accepted. AP credits are accepted.

Procedure: Freshmen are admitted in the fall. Entrance exams should be taken no later than January of the senior year. There are early decision and deferred admissions plans. Early decision applications should be filed by November 1; regular applications, by January 1 for fall entry, along with an application fee of $60. Notification of early decision is sent December 15; regular decision, April 15. 334 early decision candidates were accepted for the 1995–96 class. A waiting list is an active part of the admissions procedure.

Transfer: Transfers must demonstrate high achievement and intellectual motivation through college transcripts as well as standardized test scores and high school transcripts.

Visiting: There are regularly scheduled orientations for prospective students, including tours, group information sessions, and interviews. There are guides for informal visits and visitors may sit in on classes and stay overnight at the school. To schedule a visit, contact the Office of Admissions.

Financial Aid: In a recent year, 47% of all freshmen and 44% of continuing students received some form of financial aid. 47% of freshmen and 44% of continuing students received need-based aid. The average freshman award was $17,369. Of that total, scholarships or need-based grants averaged $12,614 ($24,000 maximum); loans averaged $2300; and work contracts averaged $2300. Dartmouth is a member of CSS. The FAF or FAFSA and the college's own financial statement are required. The application deadline for fall entry is February 1.

International Students: In a recent year there were 234 international students enrolled. The school actively recruits these students. They must take the TOEFL, SAT I or the ACT, and SAT II: Subject tests in any 3 subjects.

Computers: The college provides computer facilities for student use. The mainframes are an IBM, a DEC, and a Honeywell. More than 7000 PCs are available for student use. The computer network links dormitory rooms, administrative and academic buildings, and mainframe computers on and off campus. Students can access scholarly databases, a collegewide E-mail system, and the Internet. All students may access the system 24 hours daily. There are no time limits and no fees. All students are required to have personal computers. Apple Macintoshes are offered at a substantial discount.

Graduates: In a recent year, 994 bachelor's degrees were awarded. The most popular majors among graduates were government (17%), history (12%), and English (8%). Within an average freshman class, 97% graduate in 4 years. 219 companies recruited on campus in 1994–95.

Admissions Contact: Karl Furstenberg, Dean of Admissions. A campus video is available.

FRANKLIN PIERCE COLLEGE

C-6

Rindge, NH 03461-0060   (603) 899-4050

(800) 437-0048; FAX: (603) 899-4372

Full-time: 654 men, 584 women	Faculty: 61; IIB, -$
Part-time: 24 men, 14 women	Ph.Ds: 72%
Graduate: none	Student/Faculty: 20 to 1
Year: semesters, summer session	Tuition: $14,095
Application Deadline: open	Room & Board: $4900
Freshman Class: 5011 applied, 4188 accepted, 493 enrolled	
SAT I Verbal/Math: 403/418	**LESS COMPETITIVE**

Franklin Pierce College, founded in 1962, is a private, coeducational liberal arts institution that also has an extensive continuing education program, which offers bachelor's degrees from locations in Concord, Keene, Salem, Nashua, and Portsmouth in New Hampshire. The library contains 78,764 volumes, 25,600 microform items, and 1394 audiovisual forms, and subscribes to 650 periodicals. Computerized library sources and services include the card catalog, interlibrary loans, and database searching. Special learning facilities include a learning resource center, art gallery, radio station, and TV station. The 1000-acre campus is in a rural area 65 miles northwest of Boston, Massachusetts. Including residence halls, there are 30 buildings on campus.

Student Life: 87% of undergraduates are from out-of-state, mostly the Northeast. Students come from 26 states, 22 foreign countries, and Canada. 85% are from public schools; 15% from private. 90% are white. 38% are Catholic; 36% Protestant; 22% Jewish. The average age of freshmen is 18; all undergraduates, 20. 34% do not continue beyond their first year; 42% remain to graduate.

Housing: 1075 students can be accommodated in college housing. College-sponsored living facilities include single-sex and coed dormitories, on-campus apartments, and off-campus apartments. On-campus housing is guaranteed for all 4 years. 86% of students live on campus; of those, 70% remain on campus on weekends. All students may keep cars on campus.

Activities: There are no fraternities or sororities. There are 34 groups on campus, including art, cheerleading, chess, choir, chorale, computers, dance, drama, ethnic, gay, honors, international, jazz band, literary magazine, musical theater, newspaper, photography, political,

professional, radio and TV, religious, social, social service, student government, and yearbook. Popular campus events include Winter Carnival, Spring and Fall Weekends, the performance of the Messiah, and cultural and lecture series.

Sports: There are 6 intercollegiate sports for men and 6 for women, and 6 intramural sports for men and 3 for women. Athletic and recreation facilities include a field house, a fitness center, an 800-seat gymnasium, playing fields, a lake with a beach, a fleet of sailboats, cross-country trails, and courts for tennis, basketball, and volleyball.

Disabled Students: 90% of the campus is accessible to disabled students. The following facilities are available: wheelchair ramps, elevators, special parking, specially equipped rest rooms, special class scheduling, lowered drinking fountains, and lowered telephones.

Services: In addition to many counseling and information services, tutoring is available in every subject. There is a reader service for the blind, and remedial math, reading, and writing. Note takers, a professional reading specialist, alternative testing, reduced course loads, study skills workshops, and content-area study skills courses are also available.

Campus Safety and Security: Campus safety and security measures include 24-hour foot and vehicle patrol, escort service, shuttle buses, and informal discussions. In addition, there are pamphlets/posters/films, emergency telephones, and lighted pathways/sidewalks.

Programs of Study: FPC confers B.A. and B.S. degrees. Bachelor's degrees are awarded in BIOLOGICAL SCIENCE (biology/biological science), BUSINESS (accounting, banking and finance, business administration and management, international business management, management science, marketing/retailing/merchandising, and recreational facilities management), COMMUNICATIONS AND THE ARTS (advertising, broadcasting, communications, dramatic arts, English, fine arts, graphic design, music, and theater design), COMPUTER AND PHYSICAL SCIENCE (computer science and mathematics), EDUCATION (art, elementary, foreign languages, science, secondary, and social science), ENGINEERING AND ENVIRONMENTAL DESIGN (environmental science), HEALTH PROFESSIONS (predentistry, premedicine, and preveterinary science), SOCIAL SCIENCE (anthropology, archeology, criminal justice, economics, history, prelaw, psychology, social work, and sociology). Anthropology, biology, and English are the strongest academically. Communications, graphics, and business have the largest enrollments.

Required: To graduate, students must complete 120 semester hours with a cumulative GPA of at least 2.0 and pass examinations for writing and mathematics competency. Individual and Community core requirements total 11 courses, including Individual and Community, College Writing, Integrated Science, American Experience, Twentieth Century, Foundations of Mathematics, Experiencing the Arts, Ancient and Medieval Worlds, Reason and Romanticism, Science of Society, and a senior liberal arts seminar.

Special: Cross-registration is offered in nearly every subject through the New Hampshire College and University Council, a 13-member consortium of area institutions. Study at Richmond College in London, on- and off-campus internships in most majors, and work-study through the college are possible. In addition, accelerated degree programs in all majors, dual majors in most fields, student-designed majors, credit for life experience, and nondegree study are available. There is a freshman honors program on campus, as well as 5 national honor societies.

Faculty/Classroom: 70% of faculty are male; 30%, female. All teach undergraduates. The average class size in an introductory lecture is 25; in a laboratory, 20; and in a regular course offering, 18.

Admissions: 84% of the 1995–96 applicants were accepted. The SAT I scores for the 1995–96 freshman class were as follows: Verbal—86% below 500, 12% between 500 and 599, and 2% between 600 and 700; Math—80% below 500, 16% between 500 and 599, 3% between 600 and 700, and 1% above 700. 12% of the current freshmen were in the top fifth of their class; 31% were in the top two fifths.

Requirements: The SAT I or ACT is required, but with no minimum score. A minimum GPA of 1.5 is required. Applicants must have earned 10 academic units or 16 Carnegie units in high school, including 4 years of English, 2 each of mathematics and science, and 1 each of history and social studies. An interview is recommended. The GED is accepted. AP and CLEP credits are accepted. Important factors in the admissions decision are recommendations by school officials, advanced placement or honor courses, and leadership record.

Procedure: Freshmen are admitted to all sessions. Entrance exams should be taken in the fall of the senior year. There are early admissions and deferred admissions plans. Application deadlines are open. Notification is sent on a rolling basis.

Transfer: 36 transfer students enrolled in a recent year. A minimum 2.0 GPA in college work is required. Students with fewer than 30 credits must submit SAT I results (no minimum score) and official high school transcripts. A personal recommendation is necessary and an interview recommended. 30 credits of 120 must be completed at FPC.

Visiting: There are regularly scheduled orientations for prospective students, including open houses held each spring and fall, and interviews and tours available weekdays and most Saturdays. There are guides for informal visits and visitors may sit in on classes. To schedule a visit, contact Admissions.

Financial Aid: In 1995–96, 93% of all freshmen and 81% of continuing students received some form of financial aid. 90% of freshmen and 80% of continuing students received need-based aid. The average freshman award was $11,800. Of that total, scholarships or need-based grants averaged $7100 ($9940 maximum); private scholarships averaged $277 ($7975 maximum); loans averaged $3438 ($5025 maximum); and work contracts averaged $984 ($2100 maximum). 46% of undergraduate students work part-time. Average earnings from campus work for the school year are $760. The average financial indebtedness of the 1994–95 graduate was $18,000. FPC is a member of CSS. The FAFSA is required.

International Students: In a recent year, there were 43 international students enrolled. The school actively recruits these students. They must take the TOEFL, achieving a minimum score of 500, and ELS Level 109. The SAT I or ACT may be substituted for the TOEFL.

Computers: The college provides computer facilities for student use. There are 2 DOS laboratories and 1 Apple Macintosh laboratory, both enhanced with a Novell network, forming a campuswide academic network, with 96 computers available to students. Internet access, campuswide E-mail, word processing, spreadsheets, database management, and statistics are available. All students may access the system 16 hours daily. There are no time limits and no fees. It is recommended that all students have personal computers.

Graduates: In 1994–95, 217 bachelor's degrees were awarded. The most popular majors among graduates were history (10%), education (10%), and mass communication (8%). Within an average freshman class, 4% graduate in 3 years, 37% in 4 years, and 42% in 5 years. 47 companies recruited on campus in 1994–95.

Admissions Contact: Thomas E. Desrosiers, Director of Admissions. A campus video is available.

KEENE STATE COLLEGE

Keene, NH 03435   (603) 358–2276; (800) 833–4800 (tri-state area)

B-6

Full-time: 1516 men, 2043 women	Faculty: 181; IIB, +$
Part-time: 156 men, 244 women	Ph.Ds: 73%
Graduate: 24 men, 59 women	Student/Faculty: 20 to 1
Year: semesters, summer session	Tuition: $3604 ($9094)
Application Deadline: March 1	Room & Board: $4350 ($4350)
Freshman Class: 3541 applied, 2847 accepted, 995 enrolled	
SAT I Verbal/Math: 418/452	ACT: 19 COMPETITIVE

Keene State College, founded in 1909, is part of the public University System of New Hampshire and offers a liberal arts program that includes teacher preparation, art, and business emphases. There is 1 graduate school. In addition to regional accreditation, KSC has baccalaureate program accreditation with NASM and NCATE. The library contains 272,523 volumes, 567,530 microform items, and 2 audiovisual forms, and subscribes to 1008 periodicals. Computerized library sources and services include the card catalog, interlibrary loans, and database searching. Special learning facilities include a learning resource center, art gallery, planetarium, radio station, TV station, and the Holocaust Resource Center. The 150-acre campus is in a suburban area 90 miles northwest of Boston, Massachusetts. Including residence halls, there are 36 buildings on campus.

Student Life: 57% of undergraduates are from New Hampshire. Students come from 32 states, 33 foreign countries, and Canada. 80% are from public schools; 20% from private. 93% are white. 48% are Catholic; 21% claim no religious affiliation; 20% are Protestant. The average age of freshmen is 18; all undergraduates, 22. 28% do not continue beyond their first year; 58% remain to graduate.

Housing: 2007 students can be accommodated in college housing. College-sponsored living facilities include single-sex and coed dormitories, on-campus apartments, married-student housing, fraternity houses, and sorority houses. In addition, there are honors houses, language houses, special interest houses, wellness areas, and drug-free areas. On-campus housing is guaranteed for the freshman year only and is available on a lottery system for upperclassmen. 56% of students live on campus. Upperclassmen may keep cars on campus.

Activities: 20% of men belong to 3 local and 3 national fraternities; 20% of women belong to 2 local and 4 national sororities. There are 60 groups on campus, including art, band, cheerleading, choir, chorale, chorus, computers, dance, drama, ethnic, film, gay, honors, jazz band, musical theater, newspaper, orchestra, pep band, photography, political, professional, radio and TV, religious, social, student government, and yearbook. Popular campus events include Homecoming, Winter Carnival, Spring Weekend, and Diversity Day.

Sports: There are 7 intercollegiate sports for men and 8 for women, and 10 intramural sports for men and 7 for women. Athletic and recreation facilities include a 1500-seat gymnasium, a 1000-seat stadium for soccer and field hockey, an indoor pool, a fitness center, racquetball, tennis, and squash courts, and a training room.

Disabled Students: 90% of the campus is accessible to disabled students. The following facilities are available: wheelchair ramps, elevators, special parking, specially equipped rest rooms, lowered drinking fountains, and lowered telephones.

Services: In addition to many counseling and information services, tutoring is available in most subjects. There are also writing process, reading, and math centers, a reader service for the blind, and remedial math and reading.

Campus Safety and Security: Campus safety and security measures include 24-hour foot and vehicle patrol, escort service, shuttle buses, and informal discussions. In addition, there are pamphlets/posters/films, emergency telephones, and lighted pathways/sidewalks.

Programs of Study: KSC confers B.A., B.S., and B.M. degrees. Associate and master's degrees are also awarded. Bachelor's degrees are awarded in BIOLOGICAL SCIENCE (biology/biological science), BUSINESS (sports management), COMMUNICATIONS AND THE ARTS (dramatic arts, English, fine arts, French, journalism, music, music performance, and Spanish), COMPUTER AND PHYSICAL SCIENCE (chemistry, computer mathematics, computer science, geology, and mathematics), EDUCATION (early childhood, elementary, foreign languages, home economics, industrial arts, mathematics, music, physical, science, secondary, special, and vocational), ENGINEERING AND ENVIRONMENTAL DESIGN (environmental science, industrial engineering technology, and occupational safety and health), HEALTH PROFESSIONS (sports medicine), SOCIAL SCIENCE (American studies, dietetics, geography, history, political science/government, psychology, safety management, and sociology). Education, safety studies, and sports medicine are the strongest academically. Education, management, and psychology have the largest enrollments.

Required: All students must take 120 to 142 credits, with at least 30 hours in their major, while maintaining a 2.0 GPA. Distribution requirements include 5 courses in the arts and humanities, 4 each in the social sciences, mathematics, and sciences, and 1 in English composition. Students also must demonstrate competence in mathematics.

Special: Cross-registration through New Hampshire College and University Council, internships and co-op programs in all areas of study, study abroad anywhere in the world, and work-study at the college are available. Students also may pursue dual majors, a general studies degree, individualized majors, accelerated degrees in the honors program, and a 3–2 engineering degree in an agreement with Clarkson University or the University of New Hampshire. In addition, there are pass/fail options and credit for life experience. There is a freshman honors program on campus, as well as 12 national honor societies. 1 department has an honors program.

Faculty/Classroom: 54% of faculty are male; 46%, female. All teach undergraduates. No introductory courses are taught by graduate students. The average class size in an introductory lecture is 28; in a laboratory, 12; and in a regular course offering, 20.

Admissions: 80% of the 1995–96 applicants were accepted. The SAT I scores for the 1995–96 freshman class were as follows: Verbal—83% below 500, 13% between 500 and 599, 2% between 600 and 700, and 2% above 700; Math—70% below 500, 23% between 500 and 599, 6% between 600 and 700, and 1% above 700. The ACT scores were 72% below 21, 17% between 21 and 23, and 10% between 24 and 26. 10% of the current freshmen were in the top fifth of their class; 32% were in the top two fifths. 1 freshman graduated first in the class.

Requirements: The SAT I is recommended, with scores of 450 verbal and 450 mathematics. KSC requires applicants to be in the upper 50% of their class. A minimum GPA of 2.3 is required. Applicants need at least 11 academic credits, including 4 years of English, 3 each of mathematics, science, and social studies, and 1 of history. An essay, portfolio, and audition are required for certain programs, and an interview is recommended. AP and CLEP credits are accepted. Important factors in the admissions decision are advanced placement or honor courses, recommendations by school officials, and evidence of special talent.

Procedure: Freshmen are admitted in the fall and spring. Entrance exams should be taken during the spring of the junior year or fall of the senior year. There is a deferred admissions plan. Applications should be filed by March 1 for fall entry and December 1 for spring entry, along with an application fee of $25 (in-state), $35 (out-of-state). Notification is sent on a rolling basis.

Transfer: 253 transfer students enrolled in 1995–96. Applicants must have a 2.0 cumulative GPA and at least 12 college credits. An interview is recommended. 24 credits of 120 to 142 must be completed at KSC.

Visiting: There are regularly scheduled orientations for prospective students, consisting of a personal interview with the professional staff and a tour. There are guides for informal visits and visitors may sit in on classes. To schedule a visit, contact the Admissions Office at (603) 358–2276 or (800) 833–4800.

Financial Aid: In 1995–96, 58% of all freshmen and 66% of continuing students received some form of financial aid. 75% of freshmen and 78% of continuing students received need-based aid. The average freshman award was $6874. Of that total, scholarships or need-based grants averaged $3116 ($13,926 maximum); loans averaged $3829 ($15,420 maximum); and work contracts averaged $1284 ($2500 maximum). 22% of undergraduate students work part-time. Average earnings from campus work for the school year are $443. The average financial indebtedness of the 1994–95 graduate was

$9119. KSC is a member of CSS. The FAFSA and IRS tax returns are required. The application deadline for fall entry is March 1.

International Students: There are currently 83 international students enrolled. They must score 500 on the TOEFL.

Computers: The college provides computer facilities for student use. The mainframe is a DEC VAX. 145 microcomputers are available in special interest and general purpose laboratories. All students may access the system 24 hours per day. There are no time limits and no fees.

Graduates: In 1994–95, 905 bachelor's degrees were awarded. The most popular majors among graduates were business management (9%), elementary education (8%), and psychology (7%). Within an average freshman class, 41% graduate in 4 years, 55% in 5 years, and 54% in 6 years. 6 companies recruited on campus in 1994–95. Of the 1994 graduating class, 10% were enrolled in graduate school within 6 months of graduation and 49% had found employment.

Admissions Contact: Kathryn Dodge, Director of Admissions. A campus video is available.

NEW ENGLAND COLLEGE C-5

Henniker, NH 03242	(603) 428–2223; (800) 521–7642
Full-time: 375 men, 325 women	**Faculty:** 47
Part-time: 12 men, 38 women	**Ph.D.s:** 53%
Graduate: 64 men, 136 women	**Student/Faculty:** 15 to 1
Year: semesters, summer session	**Tuition:** $14,226
Application Deadline: open	**Room & Board:** $5620
Freshman Class: 943 applied, 725 accepted, 210 enrolled	
SAT I or ACT: not required	**COMPETITIVE**

New England College, founded in 1946, is an independent, coeducational liberal arts institution with campuses in New Hampshire and Britain. Students may pursue numerous majors while studying at either campus. In addition to regional accreditation, NEC has baccalaureate program accreditation with ABET. The library contains 100,000 volumes, 34,000 microform items, and 2000 audiovisual forms, and subscribes to 650 periodicals. Computerized library sources and services include the card catalog, interlibrary loans, and database searching. Special learning facilities include a learning resource center, art gallery, radio station, and an island off the Maine coast for environmental research. The 212-acre campus is in a rural area 17 miles west of Concord and 80 miles north of Boston, Massachusetts. Including residence halls, there are 30 buildings on campus.

Student Life: 85% of undergraduates are from out-of-state, mostly the Northeast. Students come from 35 states, 25 foreign countries, and Canada. 70% are from public schools; 30% from private. 92% are white. 40% are Protestant; 30% Jewish; 25% Catholic. The average age of freshmen is 18; all undergraduates, 20. 24% do not continue beyond their first year; 55% remain to graduate.

Housing: College-sponsored living facilities include coed dormitories, on-campus apartments, fraternity houses, and sorority houses. In addition, there are special interest houses. Students may choose to live in cooperative substance-free housing or international housing. On-campus housing is guaranteed for all 4 years. 60% of students live on campus; of those, 80% remain on campus on weekends. All students may keep cars on campus.

Activities: 12% of men and about 3% of women belong to 3 local fraternities; 8% of women belong to 2 local and 1 national sororities. There are 35 groups on campus, including chorus, dance, drama, ethnic, film, honors, international, literary magazine, newspaper, photography, political, professional, radio and TV, social, social service, student government, and yearbook. Popular campus events include Homecoming, International Week, and Spring Weekend.

Sports: There are 6 intercollegiate sports for men and 6 for women, and 15 intramural sports for men and 15 for women. Athletic and recreation facilities include a gymnasium, a field house, a weight room, 26 acres of playing fields, indoor and outdoor basketball and tennis courts, cross-country ski trails, and a local ski area for Alpine skiing.

Disabled Students: 70% of the campus is accessible to disabled students. The following facilities are available: wheelchair ramps, elevators, special parking, specially equipped rest rooms, and special class scheduling.

Services: In addition to many counseling and information services, tutoring is available in every subject.

Campus Safety and Security: Campus safety and security measures include 24-hour foot and vehicle patrol, escort service, shuttle buses, and informal discussions. In addition, there are pamphlets/posters/films and lighted pathways/sidewalks.

Programs of Study: NEC confers the B.A. degree. Master's degrees are also awarded. Bachelor's degrees are awarded in BIOLOGICAL SCIENCE (biology/biological science), BUSINESS (business administration and management), COMMUNICATIONS AND THE ARTS (communications, dramatic arts, English, and fine arts), EDUCATION (elementary, physical, and secondary), ENGINEERING AND ENVIRONMENTAL DESIGN (environmental science), SOCIAL SCIENCE (philosophy, political science/government, and psychology). Art, theater, and environmental science are the strongest academically. Business, communications, and psychology have the largest enrollments.

Required: To graduate, all students must earn a minimum GPA of 2.0 and take 120 credit hours, including an average of 30 in their major. Distribution requirements cover 9 general education areas, including English, humanities, mathematics, and world culture and awareness. Specific requirements include a senior project, College Writing I and II, communications skills, and a mathematics course (or passing grade on a placement test).

Special: Cross-registration is available with the New Hampshire Consortium of Universities and Colleges. Also available are internships for juniors and seniors with a GPA of 2.5, study abroad in 4 countries, work-study programs, dual majors, student-designed majors, interdisciplinary majors, nondegree study, and pass/fail options. There is a freshman honors program on campus.

Faculty/Classroom: 51% of faculty are male; 49%, female. All teach undergraduates. The average class size in an introductory lecture is 22; in a laboratory, 15; and in a regular course offering, 16.

Admissions: 77% of the 1995–96 applicants were accepted. 18% of the current freshmen were in the top fifth of their class; 36% were in the top two fifths.

Requirements: A minimum GPA of 2.0 is required. 4 years of English, 3 each of mathematics and social studies, and 2 each of science and electives are recommended. An essay is required and an interview is recommended. AP and CLEP credits are accepted. Important factors in the admissions decision are academic record, recommendations by school officials, and extracurricular activities record.

Procedure: Freshmen are admitted fall and spring. There is a deferred admissions plan. Application deadlines are open. Application fee is $30. Notification is sent on a rolling basis.

Transfer: 45 transfer students enrolled in 1995–96. Students should have a 2.0 minimum GPA from the previous college. Academic recommendations are required from a professor, and from the academic adviser. An interview is recommended. 60 credits of 120 must be completed at NEC.

Visiting: There are regularly scheduled orientations for prospective students, including class registration and meeting faculty and other students. There are guides for informal visits and visitors may sit in on classes and stay overnight at the school. To schedule a visit, contact Lois Richards at the Admissions Office.

Financial Aid: In 1995–96, 64% of all students received some form of financial aid. 63% of all students received need-based aid. The average freshman award was $11,000. Of that total, scholarships or need-based grants averaged $5835; loans averaged $4030; and work contracts averaged $1135. 35% of undergraduate students work part-time. Average earnings from campus work for the school year are $1200. NEC is a member of CSS. The FAFSA and the college's own financial statement are required. The application deadline for fall entry is March 1.

International Students: In a recent year, there were 85 international students enrolled. The school actively recruits these students. They must take the TOEFL and achieve a minimum score of 450.

Computers: The college provides computer facilities for student use. The mainframes are 2 DEC 5000s. 24 IBM 486 PCs are available in the computer laboratory. More than 40 Apple II microcomputers are available in the skills center and writing laboratory. All students may access the system. There are no time limits and no fees.

Admissions Contact: Office of Admissions.

NEW HAMPSHIRE COLLEGE D-6

Manchester, NH 03106-1045	(603) 645–9611; (800) 642–4968
Full-time: 733 men, 494 women	**Faculty:** 70; IIA, av$
Part-time: 1209 men, 1615 women	**Ph.D.s:** 65%
Graduate: 999 men, 794 women	**Student/Faculty:** 18 to 1
Year: semesters, summer session	**Tuition:** $11,622
Application Deadline: March 15	**Room & Board:** $4824
Freshman Class: 1457 applied, 1212 accepted, 314 enrolled	
SAT I Verbal/Math: 386/431	**LESS COMPETITIVE**

New Hampshire College, founded in 1932, is a private coeducational institution offering business, liberal arts, hospitality, and teacher education disciplines. There is one graduate school. In addition to regional accreditation, NHC has baccalaureate program accreditation with ACBSP. The library contains 76,269 volumes, 238,730 microform items, and 1710 audiovisual forms, and subscribes to 863 periodicals. Computerized library sources and services include the card catalog, interlibrary loans, and database searching. Special learning facilities include a learning resource center, art gallery, TV station, and an audiovisual studio. The 200-acre campus is in a suburban area 55 miles north of Boston, Massachusetts. Including residence halls, there are 22 buildings on campus.

Student Life: 80% of undergraduates are from out-of-state, mostly the Northeast. Students come from 23 states, 67 foreign countries, and Canada. 80% are from public schools; 20% from private. 60% are white. 50% are Catholic; 35% Protestant; 10% Jewish. The average age of freshmen is 19; all undergraduates, 21. 25% do not continue beyond their first year; 55% remain to graduate.

Housing: 811 students can be accommodated in college housing. College-sponsored living facilities include single-sex and coed dormitories, on-campus apartments, fraternity houses, and sorority houses.

In addition, there are special interest houses and and a wellness housing area. On-campus housing is guaranteed for all 4 years. 80% of students live on campus; of those, 65% remain on campus on weekends. All students may keep cars on campus.

Activities: 15% of men belong to 4 national fraternities; 15% of women belong to 1 national and 3 local sororities. There are 40 groups on campus, including cheerleading, dance, drama, ethnic, honors, international, musical theater, newspaper, professional, radio and TV, religious, social, social service, student government, and yearbook. Popular campus events include Fall and Spring weekends, Alumni Weekend, and International Bazaar.

Sports: There are 5 intercollegiate sports for men and 5 for women, and 8 intramural sports for men and 8 for women. Athletic and recreation facilities include an Olympic-sized swimming pool, racquetball and tennis courts, a weight room, a hockey rink, 2 gymnasiums, several baseball fields, and soccer and softball fields.

Disabled Students: 70% of the campus is accessible to disabled students. The following facilities are available: wheelchair ramps, special parking, specially equipped rest rooms, special class scheduling, lowered drinking fountains, lowered telephones, and automatic door openers.

Services: In addition to many counseling and information services, tutoring is available in every subject.

Campus Safety and Security: Campus safety and security measures include 24-hour foot and vehicle patrol, self-defense education, escort service, and shuttle buses. In addition, there are informal discussions, pamphlets/posters/films, emergency telephones, lighted pathways/sidewalks, and winter driving seminars for international students.

Programs of Study: NHC confers B.A. and B.S. degrees. Associate and master's degrees are also awarded. Bachelor's degrees are awarded in BUSINESS (accounting, business administration and management, hospitality management services, hotel/motel and restaurant management, international business management, management science, marketing/retailing/merchandising, retailing, and sports management), COMMUNICATIONS AND THE ARTS (communications and English), COMPUTER AND PHYSICAL SCIENCE (computer programming), EDUCATION (business, English, marketing and distribution, and mathematics), ENGINEERING AND ENVIRONMENTAL DESIGN (technological management), SOCIAL SCIENCE (economics, humanities, and social science). Accounting, hotel management, and computer information systems are the strongest academically. Business administration, accounting, and sport management have the largest enrollments.

Required: Students must take 120 credit hours, including a maximum of 36 in their major, while maintaining a GPA of 2.0. Distribution requirements total 69 credits from the college core, including 3 courses in writing, 2 courses each in mathematics, accounting, economics, and computer science, and other courses in communications, public speaking, statistics, and marketing.

Special: Co-op programs with the area business community are strongly promoted, as is cross-registration through the New Hampshire College and University Council. Study abroad in London, a general business studies degree with 10 different concentrations, work-study programs, dual majors, accelerated degree programs in all majors, combined B.A.-B.S. degrees, credit for life experience, and nondegree study are available. There is a freshman honors program on campus, as well as 4 national honor societies.

Faculty/Classroom: 64% of faculty are male; 36%, female. All teach undergraduates. No introductory courses are taught by graduate students. The average class size in an introductory lecture is 20 and in a regular course offering, 22.

Admissions: 83% of the 1995–96 applicants were accepted. The SAT I scores for the 1995–96 freshman class were as follows: Verbal—90% below 500, 7% between 500 and 599, and 1% between 600 and 700; Math—76% below 500, 17% between 500 and 599, 4% between 600 and 700, and 1% above 700. 9% of the current freshmen were in the top fifth of their class; 25% were in the top two fifths.

Requirements: The SAT I is required. NHC requires applicants to be in the upper 50% of their class. A minimum GPA of 2.0 is required. Students must have completed 4 years of English and 3 of mathematics. An essay is required and an interview is strongly recommended. The GED is accepted. Applications are accepted on computer disk. AP and CLEP credits are accepted. Important factors in the admissions decision are advanced placement or honor courses, recommendations by school officials, and parents or siblings attending the school.

Procedure: Freshmen are admitted fall and spring. There are early admissions and deferred admissions plans. Early action applications should be filed by November 15; regular applications are open, but it is recommended that students apply by March 15 for fall entry and December 1 for spring entry. Notification is sent on a rolling basis.

Transfer: 103 transfer students enrolled in 1995–96. Transfer applicants must have a minimum GPA of 2.0. An interview is recommended. 30 credits of 120 must be completed at NHC.

Visiting: There are regularly scheduled orientations for prospective students, including a greeting from college administrators, campus tours with students, and informal discussions with faculty. There are

guides for informal visits and visitors may sit in on classes. To schedule a visit, contact the Admission Office.

Financial Aid: In 1995–96, 73% of all freshmen and 72% of continuing students received some form of financial aid. 70% of all students received need-based aid. The average freshman award was $9000. Of that total, scholarships or need-based grants averaged $2800 ($6300 maximum); loans averaged $3200 ($5500 maximum); and work contracts averaged $1500 ($2000 maximum). 65% of undergraduate students work part-time. Average earnings from campus work for the school year are $1780. The average financial indebtedness of the 1994–95 graduate was $13,000. NHC is a member of CSS. The FAFSA and Profile are required. The application deadline for fall entry is March 15.

International Students: In a recent year, 173 international students were enrolled. The school actively recruits these students. They must take the TOEFL and achieve a minimum score of 500.

Computers: The mainframe is an IBM 4381 and there are also 71 IBM compatibles and 4 Macintoshes in 2 laboratories on campus. All students may access the system 16 hours daily. Students are also required to have their own IBM-compatible PC. There are no time limits and no fees.

Graduates: In 1994–95, 704 bachelor's degrees were awarded. The most popular majors among graduates were business administration (56%), accounting (10%), and hotel and restaurant management (9%). 160 companies recruited on campus in 1994–95.

Admissions Contact: Brad Poznanski, Director of Admission and Financial Aid. A campus video is available.

NOTRE DAME COLLEGE
D-6
Manchester, NH 03104

(603) 669–4298, ext. 163
FAX: (603) 644–8316

Full-time: 146 men, 382 women	**Faculty:** 42; IIB, --$
Part-time: 66 men, 233 women	**Ph.D.s:** 40%
Graduate: 92 men, 405 women	**Student/Faculty:** 13 to 1
Year: semesters, summer session	**Tuition:** $10,927
Application Deadline: open	**Room & Board:** $5050
Freshman Class: 472 applied, 421 accepted, 148 enrolled	
SAT I Verbal/Math: 432/448	**LESS COMPETITIVE**

Notre Dame College, founded in 1950, is a private, Catholic institution providing a liberal arts education. There is 1 graduate school. The library contains 52,000 volumes, 3200 microform items, and 24,000 audiovisual forms, and subscribes to 270 periodicals. Computerized library sources and services include interlibrary loans. Special learning facilities include a learning resource center and radio station. The 7-acre campus is in a suburban area 2 miles north of Manchester. Including residence halls, there are 17 buildings.

Student Life: 50% of undergraduates are from out-of-state, mostly the Northeast. Students come from 12 states and 3 foreign countries. 65% are from public schools; 35% from private. 90% are white. 80% are Catholic; 16% Protestant. The average age of freshmen is 19; all undergraduates, 24. 20% do not continue beyond their first year; 65% remain to graduate.

Housing: 210 students can be accommodated in college housing. College-sponsored living facilities include single-sex dormitories. In addition, there are substance-free facilities. On-campus housing is guaranteed for all 4 years. 60% of students commute. Upperclassmen may keep cars on campus.

Activities: There are no fraternities or sororities. There are 34 groups on campus, including art, choir, chorale, drama, honors, literary magazine, musical theater, newspaper, photography, political, professional, radio and TV, religious, social, social service, student government, and yearbook. Popular campus events include Family Weekend, Octoberfest, and Winter Weekend.

Sports: There are 3 intercollegiate sports each for men and women, and 3 intramural sports each for men and women. Athletic and recreation facilities include a gymnasium, tennis courts, and a weight room.

Disabled Students: 90% of the campus is accessible to disabled students. The following facilities are available: wheelchair ramps, elevators, special parking, specially equipped rest rooms, special class scheduling, and lowered telephones.

Services: In addition to many counseling and information services, tutoring is available in most subjects. There is remedial math, reading, and writing.

Campus Safety and Security: Campus safety and security measures include 24-hour foot and vehicle patrol, escort service, shuttle buses, and informal discussions. There are pamphlets/posters/films and lighted pathways/sidewalks.

Programs of Study: NDC confers B.A., B.S., and B.S.Ed. degrees. Associate and master's degrees are also awarded. Bachelor's degrees are awarded in BIOLOGICAL SCIENCE (biology/biological science and microbiology), BUSINESS (business administration and management), COMMUNICATIONS AND THE ARTS (communications, English, and fine arts), COMPUTER AND PHYSICAL SCIENCE (science), EDUCATION (art, early childhood, elementary, middle school, science, secondary, special, and teaching English as a second/foreign language (TESOL/TEFOL)), ENGINEERING AND ENVIRONMENTAL DESIGN (commercial art), HEALTH PROFES-

SIONS (prepharmacy), SOCIAL SCIENCE (child psychology/ development, history, paralegal studies, prelaw, psychology, and religion). Paralegal, prepharmacy, and education are the strongest academically. Education, commercial art, and communications have the largest enrollments.

Required: All students must maintain a GPA of at least 2.0 and complete 124 credit hours, with 30 in the major. Distribution requirements include 3 courses in English, 2 each in Western civilization, religious studies, natural science, foreign language, and electives, and 1 each in art, music, philosophy, mathematics logic or computer science, and social science.

Special: Cross-registration is available with the New Hampshire College and University Council. Internships in commercial art, communications, and management, and study abroad in England and France are also available. In addition, work-study, dual majors, a general studies degree, credit for life and work experience, and nondegree study are possible. There are 2 national honor societies on campus, including Phi Beta Kappa.

Faculty/Classroom: 30% of faculty are male; 70%, female. All teach undergraduates. No introductory courses are taught by graduate students. The average class size in an introductory lecture is 25; in a laboratory, 20; and in a regular course offering, 20.

Admissions: 89% of the 1995–96 applicants were accepted. The SAT I scores for the 1995–96 freshman class were as follows: Verbal—82% below 500, 14% between 500 and 599, 3% between 600 and 700, and 1% above 700; Math—76% below 500, 17% between 500 and 599, 6% between 600 and 700, and 1% above 700. 13% of the current freshmen were in the top fifth of their class; 42% were in the top two fifths. 2 freshmen graduated first in their class.

Requirements: The SAT I is required and the ACT is recommended. A 2.0 GPA is required. In addition, applicants are expected to have completed 16 academic units in high school, including 4 years of English and 2 each of foreign language, history, mathematics, science, and social studies. An essay and a portfolio are required, and an interview is recommended. The GED is accepted. AP and CLEP credits are accepted. Important factors in the admissions decision are recommendations by school officials, advanced placement or honor courses, and personality/intangible qualities.

Procedure: Freshmen are admitted fall and spring. Entrance exams should be taken by December of the senior year. There is a deferred admissions plan. Application deadlines are open. The application fee is $25. Notification is sent on a rolling basis.

Transfer: 53 transfer students enrolled in a recent year. Transfer applicants must have earned a cumulative GPA of 2.0 for 30 credit hours, or take SAT I. An interview and a recommendation from an official from the previous school are required, and an associate degree is recommended. 30 credits of 124 must be completed at NDC.

Visiting: There are regularly scheduled orientations for prospective students. There are guides for informal visits and visitors may sit in on classes and stay overnight at the school. To schedule a visit, contact Jane Murray.

Financial Aid: 90% of undergraduate students work part-time. Average earnings from campus work for the school year are $1000. NDC is a member of CSS. The FAF and the college's own financial statement are required. The application deadline for fall entry is March 15.

International Students: In a recent year, 11 international students were enrolled. They must score 500 on the TOEFL and also take SAT I or the ACT.

Computers: The college provides computer facilities for student use. Microcomputers are available for student use in the computer room. All students may access the system whenever the computer room is open, usually at least 14 hours per day. There are no time limits and no fees.

Graduates: In a recent year, 112 bachelor's degrees were awarded. The most popular majors among graduates were education (45%), commercial art (15%), and paralegal (10%). Within an average freshman class, 60% graduate in 4 years and 15% in 5 years.

Admissions Contact: Joseph P. Wagner, Dean of Admissions.

PLYMOUTH STATE COLLEGE
Plymouth, NH 03264

D-4
(603) 535-2237
(800) 842-6900; FAX: (603) 535-2714

Full-time: 1750 men, 1750 women	Faculty: 200; IIB, +$
Part-time: 250 men, 250 women	Ph.D.s: 80%
Graduate: 150 men, 50 women	Student/Faculty: 18 to 1
Year: semesters, summer session	Tuition: $3754 ($9244)
Application Deadline: April 1	Room & Board: $4192
Freshman Class: 3202 applied, 2598 accepted, 879 enrolled	
SAT I: required	COMPETITIVE

Plymouth State College, founded in 1871, is a public coeducational institution and part of the university system of New Hampshire. Although historically a teacher preparation institution, it now emphasizes a liberal arts education. There are 2 graduate schools. In addition to regional accreditation, PSC has baccalaureate program accreditation with NCATE and NLN. The library contains 750,000 volumes and 500,000 microform items, and subscribes to 1200 peri-

odicals. Computerized library sources and services include the card catalog, interlibrary loans, and database searching. Special learning facilities include a learning resource center, art gallery, planetarium, and radio station. The 150-acre campus is in a small town 40 miles north of Concord. Including residence halls, there are 42 buildings.

Student Life: 60% of undergraduates are from New Hampshire. Students come from 30 states and 10 foreign countries. 95% are from public schools. 99% are white. The average age of freshmen is 18; all undergraduates, 20. 15% do not continue beyond their first year; 70% remain to graduate.

Housing: 2200 students can be accommodated in college housing. College-sponsored living facilities include single-sex and coed dormitories, on-campus apartments, married-student housing, fraternity houses, and sorority houses. In addition, there are honor houses, language houses, and special interest houses. On-campus housing is guaranteed for all 4 years. 70% of students live on campus; of those, 70% remain on campus on weekends. All students may keep cars on campus.

Activities: 10% of men belong to 5 local and 2 national fraternities; 10% of women belong to 7 local and 2 national sororities. There are 50 groups on campus, including art, band, cheerleading, choir, chorale, chorus, computers, dance, drama, gay, honors, international, jazz band, literary magazine, musical theater, newspaper, pep band, political, professional, radio and TV, religious, social, social service, student government, and yearbook. Popular campus events include Homecoming, Winter Carnival, and Medieval Forum.

Sports: There are 9 intercollegiate sports for men and 8 for women, and 17 intramural sports each for men and women. Athletic and recreation facilities include a 5000-seat stadium, a 2000-seat gymnasium, playing fields, and facilities for basketball, handball, racquetball, indoor soccer, swimming, tennis, volleyball, and softball.

Disabled Students: 75% of the campus is accessible to disabled students. The following facilities are available: wheelchair ramps, elevators, special parking, specially equipped rest rooms, lowered drinking fountains, and lowered telephones.

Services: In addition to many counseling and information services, tutoring is available in most subjects. There is a reader service for the blind, and remedial math, reading, and writing.

Campus Safety and Security: Campus safety and security measures include 24-hour foot and vehicle patrol, self-defense education, escort service, and shuttle buses. There are informal discussions, pamphlets/posters/films, emergency telephones, and lighted pathways/sidewalks.

Programs of Study: PSC confers B.A., B.S., B.F.A., B.H.E., and B.S.Ed. degrees. Associate and master's degrees are also awarded. Bachelor's degrees are awarded in BIOLOGICAL SCIENCE (biology/biological science and environmental biology), BUSINESS (accounting, business administration and management, business economics, management science, and marketing/retailing/ merchandising), COMMUNICATIONS AND THE ARTS (art history and appreciation, dramatic arts, drawing, English, fine arts, French, graphic design, literature, music, painting, printmaking, sculpture, Spanish, and studio art), COMPUTER AND PHYSICAL SCIENCE (actuarial science, atmospheric sciences and meteorology, chemistry, computer programming, computer science, and mathematics), EDUCATION (art, early childhood, elementary, English, foreign languages, guidance, health, mathematics, middle school, music, physical, recreation, science, secondary, social science, and special), ENGINEERING AND ENVIRONMENTAL DESIGN (city/community/ regional planning), SOCIAL SCIENCE (anthropology, geography, history, humanities, interdisciplinary studies, medieval studies, philosophy, political science/government, psychology, public administration, social science, social work, and sociology). Business, education, and health and physical education have the largest enrollments.

Required: All students must maintain a 2.0 GPA while taking 122 semester hours, including 1 hour of introduction to the academic community, 2 in physical education, and 1 each in composition and mathematics proficiency. Distribution requirements stem from the general education program requiring 3 credits each in the perspectives of the fine and performing arts, global history, literacy, philosophy, quantitative reasoning, science, sociology, psychology, and technology.

Special: Co-op programs with the university system of New Hampshire and cross-registration with the New Hampshire College and University Council are provided. Internships both on and off campus, study abroad in 5 countries, and college work-study programs are available. Dual majors, a general studies degree, and student-designed majors are possible. There also is credit for life experience, nondegree study, and pass/fail options. There are 3 national honor societies on campus.

Faculty/Classroom: 69% of faculty are male; 31%, female. No introductory courses are taught by graduate students.

Admissions: 81% of the 1995–96 applicants were accepted. 20% of the current freshmen were in the top fifth of their class.

Requirements: The SAT I is required. PSC recommends that applicants be in the upper 50% of their class. A 2.4 GPA is recommended. PSC also recommends that applicants have completed 4 units of English, 3 of mathematics, 2 each in foreign language, science, social studies, and history, and 1 in art. An audition for certain programs is required, and an essay is recommended. The GED is accepted. AP and CLEP credits are accepted. Important factors in the admissions decision are advanced placement or honor courses, leadership record, and recommendations by school officials.

Procedure: Freshmen are admitted fall and spring. Entrance exams should be taken in November. Applications should be filed by April 1 for fall entry and January 1 for spring entry, along with an application fee of $25 for in-state students, or $30 for out-of-state students. Notification is sent on a rolling basis.

Transfer: Transfer students must have a 2.0 GPA on prior work. The SAT I is required. 30 credits of 122 must be completed at PSC.

Visiting: There are regularly scheduled orientations for prospective students. There are guides for informal visits and visitors may sit in on classes. To schedule a visit, contact the Admissions Office.

Financial Aid: In a recent year, 73% of all freshmen and 49% of continuing students received some form of financial aid. 64% of freshmen and 43% of continuing students received need-based aid. The average freshman award was $5400. Of that total, scholarships or need-based grants averaged $2000 ($2800 maximum); loans averaged $2100 ($2750 maximum); and work contracts averaged $500 ($1300 maximum). 31% of undergraduate students work part-time. Average earnings from campus work for the school year are $820. PSC is a member of CSS. The FAF and parent and student tax returns are required. The application deadline for fall entry is March 1.

International Students: In an earlier year, 75 international students were enrolled. They must score 520 on the TOEFL.

Computers: The college provides computer facilities for student use. The mainframe is a DEC VAX. There are also 125 IBM, Apple IIe, Macintosh, Zenith 150, and other microcomputers available. All students may access the system. There are no time limits and no fees.

Graduates: In a recent year, 732 bachelor's degrees were awarded. The most popular majors among graduates were management (15%), elementary education (15%), and marketing (10%).

Admissions Contact: Eugene D. Fahey, Director of Admissions. E-mail: pscadmit@psc.plymouth.edu.

RIVIER COLLEGE

Nashua, NH 03060-5086   **D-6**

                  (603) 888–1311, ext. 8507
      (800) 44-RIVIER; FAX: (603) 891-1799

Full-time: 108 men, 545 women	Faculty: 66; IIA, --$
Part-time: 158 men, 915 women	Ph.D.s: 60%
Graduate: 321 men, 751 women	Student/Faculty: 10 to 1
Year: semesters, summer session	Tuition: $11,210
Application Deadline: open	Room & Board: $5250
Freshman Class: n/av	
SAT I Verbal/Math: 410/440	**LESS COMPETITIVE**

Rivier College, founded in 1933, is a coeducational, liberal arts college affiliated with the Roman Catholic Church. There are 3 undergraduate schools and 1 graduate school. In addition to regional accreditation, Rivier has baccalaureate program accreditation with NLN. The library contains 130,000 volumes, 26,350 microform items, and 17,465 audiovisual forms, and subscribes to 750 periodicals. Computerized library sources and services include the card catalog and interlibrary loans. Special learning facilities include a learning resource center and art gallery. The 60-acre campus is in a suburban area 40 miles north of Boston, Massachusetts. Including residence halls, there are 37 buildings on campus.

Student Life: 78% of undergraduates are from New Hampshire. Students come from 10 states and 12 foreign countries. 80% are from public schools; 20% from private. 78% are white. The average age of freshmen is 18; all undergraduates, 30. 9% do not continue beyond their first year.

Housing: 250 students can be accommodated in college housing. College-sponsored living facilities include coed dormitories. On-campus housing is guaranteed for all 4 years. 60% of students commute. All students may keep cars on campus.

Activities: There are no fraternities or sororities. There are 25 groups on campus, including art, chorus, drama, honors, international, literary magazine, newspaper, political, professional, religious, social, social service, student government, and yearbook. Popular campus events include Global Awareness Week, Spirit Week, and Parents and Homecoming weekends.

Sports: There are 5 intercollegiate sports for men and 5 for women, and 7 intramural sports for men and 7 for women. Athletic and recreation facilities include a 300-seat gymnasium, a weight room, tennis courts, and soccer and softball fields.

Disabled Students: 75% of the campus is accessible to disabled students. The following facilities are available: wheelchair ramps, elevators, special parking, specially equipped rest rooms, and lowered drinking fountains.

Services: In addition to many counseling and information services, tutoring is available in some subjects, including mathematics, English, business, and languages. There is remedial math and writing.

Campus Safety and Security: Campus safety and security measures include 24-hour foot and vehicle patrol, escort service, informal discussions, and pamphlets/posters/films. There are lighted pathways/sidewalks, 24-hour access by beeper or walkie-talkie, and electronically operated dorm entrances using security cards.

Programs of Study: Rivier confers B.A., B.S., and B.F.A. degrees. Associate and master's degrees are also awarded. Bachelor's degrees are awarded in BIOLOGICAL SCIENCE (biology/biological science), BUSINESS (accounting, business administration and management, management science, and marketing/retailing/merchandising), COMMUNICATIONS AND THE ARTS (communications, design, English, French, Spanish, and studio art), COMPUTER AND PHYSICAL SCIENCE (chemistry, computer science, and mathematics), EDUCATION (art, business, early childhood, elementary, English, foreign languages, mathematics, science, secondary, social studies, and special), HEALTH PROFESSIONS (nursing, predentistry, premedicine, and preveterinary science), SOCIAL SCIENCE (human development, liberal arts/general studies, paralegal studies, political science/government, prelaw, psychology, and sociology). Education, business, and paralegal studies have the largest enrollments.

Required: A writing sample is required at entry, and a demonstration of writing proficiency must be shown prior to graduation. Students must complete at least 120 credit hours to graduate, ordinarily consisting of 40 3-credit courses with 35 to 60 credits in the student's major, and must maintain a minimum GPA of 2.0. Distribution requirements include 19 core courses in basic skills of writing and reasoning, the humanities, and the sciences. These courses include religious studies, philosophy, physical and life sciences, fine arts, modern languages, literature, behavioral and social sciences, and Western civilization.

Special: Rivier offers cross-registration through the New Hampshire College and University Council, internships in most majors, a B.A.-B.S. degree in chemistry, dual majors, a liberal studies degree, credit by challenge examination, nondegree study, and pass/fail options. There is a freshman honors program on campus, as well as 1 national honor society.

Faculty/Classroom: 38% of faculty are male; 62%, female. All teach undergraduates. No introductory courses are taught by graduate students. The average class size in an introductory lecture, in a laboratory, and in a regular course offering is 15.

Admissions: The SAT I scores for the 1995–96 freshman class were as follows: Verbal—81% below 500, 15% between 500 and 599, 3% between 600 and 700, and 1% above 700; Math—73% below 500, 19% between 500 and 599, and 8% between 600 and 700. 16% of the freshmen in a recent class were in the top fifth of their class; 30% were in the top two fifths.

Requirements: The SAT I is required. In addition, it is recommended that students rank in the top third to top half of their class, depending on its size, and that they maintain a strong college preparatory curriculum. Applicants must have earned 16 academic credits, including 4 units of English, 2 each of social sciences, foreign language, and mathematics, 1 of science with a laboratory course, and 5 of electives. An essay and a portfolio (for art majors) also are required, and an interview is recommended. Students should consult the Office of Admissions about whether the GED is accepted. AP and CLEP credits are accepted. Important factors in the admissions decision are advanced placement or honor courses, leadership record, and extracurricular activities record.

Procedure: Freshmen are admitted fall and spring. Entrance exams should be taken in the junior or senior year. There are early admissions and deferred admissions plans. Application deadlines are open. Application fee is $25. Notification is sent on a rolling basis. A waiting list is an active part of the admissions procedure, with about 10% of all applicants on the list.

Transfer: 92 transfer students enrolled in a recent year. Transfer students must have a minimum GPA of 2.0 and submit an official high school transcript and the SAT I if they have earned fewer than 60 credits at the previous institution. A college transcript is required and an interview is recommended. 30 credits of 120 must be completed at Rivier.

Visiting: There are regularly scheduled orientations for prospective students, including a tour, class visits, and an interview with department chairs. There are guides for informal visits and visitors may sit in on classes and stay overnight at the school. To schedule a visit, contact the Office of Admissions.

Financial Aid: 35% of undergraduate students work part-time. Average earnings from campus work for the school year are $1000. Rivier is a member of CSS. The FAFSA is required. The application deadline for fall entry is March 16.

International Students: There were 38 international students enrolled in a recent year. The school actively recruits these students. They must score 500 on the TOEFL.

Computers: The college provides computer facilities for student use. The mainframes are a DEC VAX 8550, a DEC MicroVAX II, and a DEC VAX Server 3100. There are 30 terminals and 14 Apple Macintosh, 19 Apple IIgs, and 30 DOS-based microcomputers available for student use in programming, word processing, accessing the Ethernet/DECNET Network, and other applications. All students may access the system Monday through Saturday and on Sundays via modem. There are no time limits and no fees.

Graduates: In a recent year, 157 bachelor's degrees were awarded. The most popular majors among graduates were accounting (30%), education (24%), and paralegal studies (24%).

Admissions Contact: Office of Admissions. E-mail: rivadmit@mighty.riv.edu.

SAINT ANSELM COLLEGE D-6

Manchester, NH 03102	(603) 641-7500; FAX: (603) 641-7550
Full-time: 817 men, 1093 women	**Faculty:** 111; IIB, av$
Part-time: 38 men, 53 women	**Ph.D.s:** 87%
Graduate: none	**Student/Faculty:** 17 to 1
Year: semesters, summer session	**Tuition:** $14,020
Application Deadline: March 15	**Room & Board:** $5550
Freshman Class: 2079 applied, 1729 accepted, 630 enrolled	
SAT I Verbal/Math: 480/519	**COMPETITIVE**

Saint Anselm College, founded in 1889, is a private, coeducational Roman Catholic institution offering a liberal arts education. In addition to regional accreditation, Saint Anselm has baccalaureate program accreditation with NLN. The library contains 192,000 volumes, 16,000 microform items, and 7100 audiovisual forms, and subscribes to 1350 periodicals. Computerized library sources and services include interlibrary loans and database searching. Special learning facilities include a learning resource center, art gallery, and planetarium. The 450-acre campus is in a suburban area 50 miles north of Boston, Massachusetts. Including residence halls, there are 38 buildings on campus.

Student Life: 80% of undergraduates are from out-of-state, mostly the Northeast. Students come from 24 states, 15 foreign countries, and Canada. 65% are from public schools; 35% from private. 97% are white. Most are Catholic. The average age of freshmen is 18; all undergraduates, 20. 12% do not continue beyond their first year; 75% remain to graduate.

Housing: 1300 students can be accommodated in college housing. College-sponsored living facilities include single-sex dormitories and on-campus apartments. On-campus housing is guaranteed for all 4 years. 68% of students live on campus; of those, 75% remain on campus on weekends. All students may keep cars on campus.

Activities: 3% of men belong to 1 local and 1 national fraternities; 3% of women belong to 1 local sorority. There are 51 groups on campus, including art, cheerleading, chess, choir, chorale, computers, drama, jazz band, literary magazine, newspaper, photography, political, professional, religious, social, social service, student government, and yearbook. Popular campus events include Fall Fest, Spring Olympics, New Hampshire Philharmonic Orchestra performances, Family Weekend, Jazz Festival, presidential debates sponsored by the League of Women Voters, and Bean Lecture Series.

Sports: There are 9 intercollegiate sports for men and 7 for women, and 14 intramural sports for men and 14 for women. Athletic and recreation facilities include a 1500-seat gymnasium; a multipurpose complex providing basketball, volleyball, tennis, and racquetball courts; a swimming pool; athletic fields; and weight and training rooms.

Disabled Students: 85% of the campus is accessible to disabled students. The following facilities are available: wheelchair ramps, elevators, special parking, specially equipped rest rooms, special class scheduling, and lowered drinking fountains.

Services: In addition to many counseling and information services, tutoring is available in every subject. There is a reader service for the blind.

Campus Safety and Security: Campus safety and security measures include 24-hour foot and vehicle patrol and lighted pathways/sidewalks.

Programs of Study: Saint Anselm confers B.A. and B.S.N. degrees. Associate degrees are also awarded. Bachelor's degrees are awarded in BIOLOGICAL SCIENCE (biochemistry and biology/biological science), BUSINESS (accounting, banking and finance, and business economics), COMMUNICATIONS AND THE ARTS (classics, English, fine arts, French, languages, and Spanish), COMPUTER AND PHYSICAL SCIENCE (chemistry, computer science, mathematics, and natural sciences), EDUCATION (secondary), ENGINEERING AND ENVIRONMENTAL DESIGN (environmental science), HEALTH PROFESSIONS (nursing, predentistry, and premedicine), SOCIAL SCIENCE (criminal justice, economics, history, liberal arts/general studies, philosophy, political science/government, prelaw, psychology, social work, sociology, and theological studies). Business economics, biology, and nursing have the largest enrollments.

Required: To graduate, students must maintain a GPA of 2.0 while completing at least 40 semester courses, including 10 to 13 in the major. Core requirements include 4 semesters in the humanities, 3 each in philosophy and theology, 2 to 4 in foreign language, and 2 each in English and laboratory science.

Special: Saint Anselm offers a 5-year liberal arts and a 3–2 engineering program in cooperation with Manhattan College, Notre Dame University, University of Massachusetts at Lowell, and Catholic University of America. Cross-registration is possible through the New Hampshire College and University Council. In addition, Saint Anselm offers internships in most departments, a Washington semester to qualified students, study abroad in Europe, nondegree study, and dual majors in computer science/business, computer science/mathematics, and mathematics/economics. There is a freshman honors program on campus, as well as 8 national honor societies.

Faculty/Classroom: 63% of faculty are male; 37%, female. All teach undergraduates. The average class size in an introductory lecture is 22; in a laboratory, 20; and in a regular course offering, 24.

Admissions: 83% of the 1995–96 applicants were accepted. The SAT I scores for the 1995–96 freshman class were as follows: Verbal—61% below 500, 32% between 500 and 599, and 6% between 600 and 700; Math—42% below 500, 44% between 500 and 599, 12% between 600 and 700, and 3% above 700. 34% of the current freshmen were in the top fifth of their class; 67% were in the top two fifths. There were 13 National Merit semifinalists. 4 freshmen graduated first in their class.

Requirements: The SAT I is required. A minimum GPA of 2.0 is required. Applicants must have 16 academic credits and 16 Carnegie units, including 4 years of English, 3 each of mathematics and science, 2 of history and social studies, 2 of foreign language, and 1 each of history and social studies. An essay is required and an interview is recommended. The GED is accepted. AP and CLEP credits are accepted. Important factors in the admissions decision are advanced placement or honor courses, leadership record, and recommendations by school officials.

Procedure: Freshmen are admitted fall and spring. Entrance exams should be taken during the spring of the junior year or the fall of the senior year. There are early decision and deferred admissions plans. Early decision applications should be filed by December 1; regular applications, by March 15 for fall entry and December 1 for spring entry, along with an application fee of $25. Notification of early decision is sent December 15; regular decision, on a rolling basis beginning mid- to late January. 67 early decision candidates were accepted for the 1995–96 class. A waiting list is an active part of the admissions procedure, with about 3% of all applicants on the list.

Transfer: 36 transfer students enrolled in 1995–96. Students must have a minimum GPA of 2.5 after earning at least 30 college credit hours. The SAT I is required and an interview is recommended. In addition, 2 letters of recommendation are necessary. 20 semester courses of 40 must be completed at Saint Anselm.

Visiting: There are regularly scheduled orientations for prospective students, consisting of daily individual interviews followed by a campus tour. There are guides for informal visits and visitors may sit in on classes and stay overnight at the school. To schedule a visit, contact the Admissions Office.

Financial Aid: In 1995–96, 82% of all freshmen and 78% of continuing students received some form of financial aid. 59% of freshmen and 63% of continuing students received need-based aid. The average freshman award was $13,140. Of that total, scholarships or need-based grants averaged $8640 ($13,750 maximum); loans averaged $2400 ($5125 maximum); and work contracts averaged $800 (maximum). 55% of undergraduate students work part-time. Average earnings from campus work for the school year are $682. The average financial indebtedness of the 1994–95 graduate was $8115. Saint Anselm is a member of CSS. The FAFSA and the CSS Profile Application are required. The application deadline for fall entry is March 15.

International Students: There are currently 16 international students enrolled. They must take the TOEFL and achieve a minimum score of 600. The student must also take the SAT I or the ACT.

Computers: The college provides computer facilities for student use. The mainframes are 2 DEC ALPHA systems. 2 main computer centers on campus contain 55 Apple Macintosh, 50 MS-DOS, and 11 dumb terminals. All have access to the mainframe; some are connected to the Novell Network. There are additional small centers located in the departments of psychology, biology, physics, and nursing. All students may access the system weekdays from 8:30 A.M. and weekends from 10 A.M. Those students with dorm connections to the system have 24-hour access. There are no time limits. The fees are $25.

Graduates: In 1994–95, 424 bachelor's degrees were awarded. The most popular majors among graduates were nursing (14%), business (10%), and history (9%). Within an average freshman class, 75% graduate in 4 years and 78% in 5 years. 94 companies recruited on campus in 1994–95. Of the 1994 graduating class, 22% were enrolled in graduate school within 6 months of graduation.

Admissions Contact: Donald Healy, Director of Admissions. E-mail: admissions@anselm.edu.

THOMAS MORE COLLEGE OF LIBERAL ARTS D-6

Merrimack, NH 03054	(603) 880-8308; FAX: (603) 880-9280
Recognized candidate for accreditation	
Full-time: 30 men, 30 women	**Faculty:** 5
Part-time: none	**Ph.D.s:** 80%
Graduate: none	**Student/Faculty:** 12 to 1
Year: semesters	**Tuition:** $7400
Application Deadline: open	**Room & Board:** $5600
Freshman Class: n/av	
SAT I or ACT: required	**LESS COMPETITIVE**

Thomas More College of Liberal Arts, founded in 1978 by Roman Catholic educators, is a coeducational, undergraduate institution. Current faculty and enrollment figures are approximate. The 11-acre campus is in a rural area between Nashua and Manchester, 40 miles north of Boston. Including residence halls, there are 5 buildings on campus.

Student Life: 79% of undergraduates are from out-of-state, mostly the Northeast. Students come from 17 states, 3 foreign countries, and Canada. The average age of freshmen is 18; all undergraduates, 20.

Housing: 60 students can be accommodated in college housing. College-sponsored living facilities include single-sex dormitories. On-campus housing is guaranteed for all 4 years. All students live on campus and all remain on campus on weekends. Alcohol is not permitted. All students may keep cars on campus.

Activities: There are no fraternities or sororities. Popular campus events include Mardi Gras, Halloween and a film series.

Sports: Athletic and recreation facilities include a pool, a weight room, a jogging track, and tennis, basketball, volleyball, and racquetball courts.

Disabled Students: Wheelchair ramps are available.

Programs of Study: Thomas More College of Liberal Arts confers the B.A. degree. Bachelor's degrees are awarded in COMMUNICATIONS AND THE ARTS (literature), SOCIAL SCIENCE (philosophy and political science/government).

Required: To graduate, students must complete 120 credit hours, including 48 in humanities, 12 in writing workshop, 12 in classical languages, 12 in mathematics and science, 6 in theology, and 3 in fine arts. At least 24 hours in the major are required. In addition, students must complete the junior project, a senior thesis, and the modern language examination.

Special: A semester in Rome for sophomores is possible.

Faculty/Classroom: 80% of faculty are male; 20%, female. All teach undergraduates.

Admissions: The SAT I scores for a recent freshman class were as follows: Verbal—35% below 500, 35% between 500 and 599, 24% between 600 and 700, and 6% above 700; Math—53% below 500, 18% between 500 and 599, 18% between 600 and 700, and 11% above 700.

Requirements: The SAT I or ACT is required. Applicants should be high school graduates with a 2.0 GPA and with 4 college preparatory units of English, 3 of mathematics, and 2 each of foreign language, social science, and laboratory science. The GED is accepted. An essay and 2 letters of recommendation are required. An interview is strongly recommended. Important factors in the admissions decision are personality/intangible qualities, evidence of special talent, and leadership record.

Procedure: Freshmen are admitted to all sessions. Application deadlines are open. Application fee is $15. Notification is sent on a rolling basis.

Transfer: 2 transfer students enrolled in a recent year. Transfer applicants must submit a transcript from all higher institutions attended.

Visiting: There are guides for informal visits and visitors may sit in on classes and stay overnight at the school. To schedule a visit, contact Peter O'Connor, Director of Admissions.

Financial Aid: In a recent year, 83% of all freshmen and 91% of continuing students received some form of financial aid, including need-based aid. 66% of undergraduate students work part-time. Average earnings from campus work for the school year are $2400. Thomas More College of Liberal Arts is a member of CSS. The FAFSA is required.

International Students: In a recent year, 6 international students were enrolled. The school actively recruits these students, who must take the SAT I or the ACT.

Computers: The college provides computer facilities for student use.

Graduates: In a recent year, 15 bachelor's degrees were awarded. The most popular majors among graduates were literature (60%), philosophy (27%), and political science (13%). Within an average freshman class, 33% graduate in 3 years and 67% in 4 years.

Admissions Contact: Peter I. O'Connor, Director of Admissions.

UNIVERSITY OF NEW HAMPSHIRE
Durham, NH 03824 E-5
(603) 862-1360; FAX: (603) 862-0077

Full-time: 4369 men, 5632 women	Faculty: 629; I, -$
Part-time: 217 men, 402 women	Ph.D.s: 85%
Graduate: 773 men, 1021 women	Student/Faculty: 16 to 1
Year: semesters, summer session	Tuition: $5054 ($13,724)
Application Deadline: February 1	Room & Board: $4150
Freshman Class: 10,026 applied, 2440 enrolled	
SAT I Verbal/Math: 477/536	COMPETITIVE

The University of New Hampshire, founded in 1866, is part of the public university system of New Hampshire and offers a wide range of undergraduate and graduate programs, including liberal arts, engineering, physical sciences, business, economics, life sciences, agriculture, and health and human services. There are 7 undergraduate schools and 1 graduate school. In addition to regional accreditation, UNH has baccalaureate program accreditation with AACSB, ABET, ADA, AHEA, CAHEA, NCATE, NLN, and SAF. The 5 libraries contain more than 1 million volumes, 615,000 microform items, and 10,000 audiovisual forms, and subscribe to 6500 periodicals. Computerized library sources and services include the card catalog, interlibrary loans, and database searching. Special learning facilities include a learning resource center, art gallery, radio station, TV station, and observatory. The 188-acre campus is in a rural area 60 miles north of Boston, Massachusetts. Including residence halls, there are about 100 buildings on campus.

Student Life: 60% of undergraduates are from New Hampshire. Students come from 44 states, 30 foreign countries, and Canada. 91% are white. The average age of freshmen is 19; all undergraduates, 21. 15% do not continue beyond their first year; 85% remain to graduate.

Housing: 5297 students can be accommodated in college housing. College-sponsored living facilities include single-sex and coed dormitories, on-campus apartments, and married-student housing. In addition, there are honors houses, special interest houses, and an international dormitory. On-campus housing is guaranteed for the freshman year only, is available on a first-come, first-served basis, and is available on a lottery system for upperclassmen. 50% of students live on campus. Upperclassmen may keep cars on campus.

Activities: 10% of men belong to 2 local and 8 national fraternities; 10% of women belong to 6 national sororities. There are 100 groups on campus, including art, band, cheerleading, chess, choir, chorale, chorus, computers, dance, drama, drill team, ethnic, film, gay, honors, international, jazz band, literary magazine, marching band, musical theater, newspaper, opera, orchestra, pep band, photography, political, professional, radio and TV, religious, social, social service, student government, symphony, and yearbook. Popular campus events include International Day, concert series, Homecoming, and Winter Carnival.

Sports: There are 13 intercollegiate sports for men and 15 for women, and 16 intramural sports for men and 14 for women. Athletic and recreation facilities include indoor and outdoor swimming pools, tracks, tennis courts, gymnasiums, weight training, wrestling, and gymnastics rooms, a dance studio, playing fields, an indoor ice rink, and cross-country ski trails. A new 3-story recreation and sports complex seats 6000 at hockey and basketball games and special events. It also includes a fitness center, jogging track, weight room, racquetball courts, an international squash court, aerobics and martial arts studios, multipurpose courts, and basketball courts.

Disabled Students: 75% of the campus is accessible to disabled students. The following facilities are available: wheelchair ramps, elevators, special parking, specially equipped rest rooms, special class scheduling, lowered drinking fountains, and lowered telephones. Accommodations made on a case-by-case basis include reduced course loads, extended examination time, academic modifications, and accessible transportation.

Services: In addition to many counseling and information services, tutoring is available in most subjects, along with learning skills training. There is a reader service for the blind, and remedial math, reading, and writing. Sign language interpreters and note takers can be provided.

Campus Safety and Security: Campus safety and security measures include 24-hour foot and vehicle patrol, self-defense education, escort service, and shuttle buses. In addition, there are informal discussions, pamphlets/posters/films, emergency telephones, and lighted pathways/sidewalks.

Programs of Study: UNH confers B.A., B.S., B.F.A., B.M., and B.S.F. degrees. Associate, master's, and doctoral degrees are also awarded. Bachelor's degrees are awarded in AGRICULTURE (animal science, dairy science, equine science, forestry and related sciences, horticulture, natural resource management, plant science, soil science, and wildlife management), BIOLOGICAL SCIENCE (biochemistry, biology/biological science, biotechnology, ecology, marine biology, microbiology, molecular biology, nutrition, and zoology), BUSINESS (business administration and management, hotel/motel and restaurant management, recreation and leisure services, and tourism), COMMUNICATIONS AND THE ARTS (art history and appreciation, classics, communications, dramatic arts, English, fine arts, French, German, Greek, journalism, Latin, linguistics, music, music history and appreciation, music performance, music theory and composition, performing arts, Russian, Spanish, studio art, and voice), COMPUTER AND PHYSICAL SCIENCE (chemistry, computer science, earth science, geology, hydrology, mathematics, and physics), EDUCATION (English, industrial arts, mathematics, music, physical, science, and vocational), ENGINEERING AND ENVIRONMENTAL DESIGN (chemical engineering, city/community/regional planning, civil engineering, computer engineering, electrical/electronics engineering, energy management technology, engineering technology, environmental engineering, environmental science, mechanical engineering, and mechanical engineering technology), HEALTH PROFESSIONS (health care administration, medical laboratory technology, nursing, occupational therapy, preveterinary science, and speech pathology/audiology), SOCIAL SCIENCE (anthropology, economics, family/consumer studies, geography, history, humanities, international studies, liberal arts/general studies, philosophy, political science/government, psychology, social work, sociology, water resources, and women's studies). English and business administration have the largest enrollments.

Required: All students must maintain a GPA of 2.0 and complete at least 128 credits, with a minimum of 36 credits and 10 classes in the major. Students must also complete general education requirements and, in the freshman year, an introductory prose writing course. Honors students and most seniors write a thesis or complete a project.

Special: Co-op programs with Cornell University in marine science are available. Extensive cross-registration is possible through the New Hampshire College and University Council, the University of New Hampshire at Manchester, and the University of California, Santa Cruz. There also is nationwide study through the National Student Exchange. Internships, study abroad throughout the world, a Washington semester, and work-study are possible. Also available are B.A.-B.S. degrees, dual majors, a general studies degree, student-designed majors, extensive 3-2 B.S./M.B.A. programs and other bachelor's/graduate degree plans, nondegree study, and pass/fail options. A 3-2 engineering degree is offered with the New Hampshire Technical Institute, Vermont Technical College, Keene State College, and other institutions. There is a freshman honors program on campus, as well as 21 national honor societies, including Phi Beta Kappa. 49 departments have honors programs.

Faculty/Classroom: 71% of faculty are male; 29%, female. All both teach and do research. Graduate students teach 6% of introductory courses. The average class size in an introductory lecture is 34; in a laboratory, 17; and in a regular course offering, 22.

Admissions: The SAT I scores for the 1995-96 freshman class were as follows: Verbal—62% below 500, 29% between 500 and 599, and 8% between 600 and 700; Math—33% below 500, 39% between 500 and 599, 24% between 600 and 700, and 4% above 700. 49% of the current freshmen were in the top fifth of their class; 86% were in the top two fifths.

Requirements: The SAT I or ACT is required, with a composite SAT I score of 1080 recommended. A grade average of B is recommended. Applicants should have 17 academic credits, including 4 years each of English and mathematics, 3 each of science and foreign language, and 2 of social studies. Students with a specific major in mind are encouraged to take SAT II: Subject tests relating to that major. An essay is required for all students and an informational interview recommended. For art students, a portfolio is required, as is an audition for music students. The GED is accepted. AP and CLEP credits are accepted. Important factors in the admissions decision are advanced placement or honor courses, recommendations by school officials, and personality/intangible qualities.

Procedure: Freshmen are admitted fall and spring. Entrance exams should be taken before February 1 of the senior year. There are early decision and deferred admissions plans. Early decision applications should be filed by December 1; regular applications, by February 1 for fall entry and November 1 for spring entry, along with an application fee of $25 ($45 for nonresidents). Notification of early decision is sent January 15; regular decision, April 15. 925 early decision candidates were accepted for the 1995-96 class.

Transfer: 499 transfer students enrolled in 1995-96. Students must submit a GPA of 3.0 in a general education curriculum and an overall minimum GPA of 2.8. The SAT I or ACT is required. 32 credits of 128 must be completed at UNH.

Visiting: There are regularly scheduled orientations for prospective students, including campus tours, a student panel, and general information sessions. There are guides for informal visits and visitors may sit in on classes. To schedule a visit, contact the Admissions Office.

Financial Aid: In 1995-96, 74% of all freshmen and 69% of continuing students received some form of financial aid. 71% of freshmen and 63% of continuing students received need-based aid. The average freshman award was $8047. Of that total, scholarships or need-based grants averaged $4677 ($12,840 maximum); loans averaged $3474 ($4000 maximum); and work contracts averaged $1877 ($2500 maximum). 80% of undergraduate students work part-time. Average earnings from campus work for the school year are $1209. The average financial indebtedness of the 1994-95 graduate was $14,406. UNH is a member of CSS. The FAFSA is required. The application deadline for fall entry is March 1.

International Students: There are currently 70 international students enrolled. The school actively recruits these students. They must take the TOEFL and achieve a minimum score of 550. The student must also take the SAT I or the ACT.

Computers: The college provides computer facilities for student use. The mainframes are a DEC 5500, 8820, and 4000. Each dormitory is fitted with telephone lines to enable students to access the university's mainframe. In addition, there are nearly 200 computers located in 5 clusters on the campus and open to all UNH students. There are no time limits and no fees.

Graduates: In 1994-95, 2322 bachelor's degrees were awarded. The most popular majors among graduates were English (9%), business administration (9%), and political science (7%). Within an average freshman class, 55% graduate in 4 years, 70% in 5 years, and 73% in 6 years. 200 companies recruited on campus in 1994-95.

Admissions Contact: Davod Kraus, Director of Admissions.

UNIVERSITY SYSTEM OF NEW HAMPSHIRE

The University System of New Hampshire, established in 1963, is the public university system in New Hampshire. It is governed by a board of trustees, whose chief administrator is the chancellor. The primary goal of the system is to serve the higher educational needs of the people of New Hampshire. The main priorities are to provide a well-coordinated system of higher education, student access and diversity, and quality programs through a commitment to excellence. In addition, the University System of New Hampshire institutions carry on research, which contributes to the welfare of humanity, to the development of faculty, and to the educational experiences of students. The total enrollment in fall 1994 of all campuses was 29,533. There were 1,101 faculty members. Altogether there are 174 baccalaureate, 69 master's and 21 doctoral programs offered in the University System of New Hampshire. Four-year campuses in the University System of New Hampshire are located in Durham, Keene and Plymouth. Profiles of these campuses are included in this chapter.

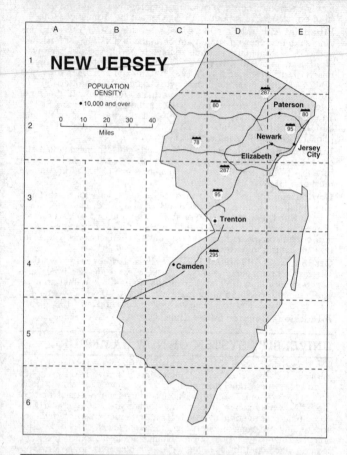

NEW JERSEY

POPULATION DENSITY
• 10,000 and over

0 10 20 30 40
Miles

BLOOMFIELD COLLEGE
E-2

Bloomfield, NJ 07003   (201) 748-9000, ext. 230; (800) 216-1212

Full-time: 393 men, 982 women	**Faculty:** 56; IIB, av$
Part-time: 288 men, 510 women	**Ph.Ds:** 61%
Graduate: none	**Student/Faculty:** 25 to 1
Year: semesters, summer session	**Tuition:** $8450
Application Deadline: open	**Room & Board:** $4325
Freshman Class: n/av	
SAT I or ACT: required	**LESS COMPETITIVE**

Bloomfield College, founded in 1868 and affiliated with the Presbyterian Church, USA, is an independent coeducational institution offering programs in liberal arts and sciences, creative arts and technology, professional studies, and the clinical and health sciences. In addition to regional accreditation, Bloomfield has baccalaureate program accreditation with NLN. The library contains 64,000 volumes, 546 microform items, and 3000 audiovisual forms, and subscribes to 385 periodicals. Computerized library sources and services include interlibrary loans and database searching. Special learning facilities include a learning resource center and art gallery. The 11-acre campus is in a suburban area 15 miles from New York City. Including residence halls, there are 28 buildings on campus.

Student Life: 95% of undergraduates are from New Jersey. Students come from 11 states and 6 foreign countries. 46% are African American; 33% white; 13% Hispanic. The average age of freshmen is 19; all undergraduates, 25. 66% do not continue beyond their first year; 29% remain to graduate.

Housing: 250 students can be accommodated in college housing. College-sponsored living facilities include single-sex and coed dormitories, fraternity houses, and sorority houses. In addition, there are honors houses and special interest houses. On-campus housing is available on a first-come, first-served basis. Priority is given to out-of-town students. 75% of students commute. All students may keep cars on campus.

Activities: 25% of men and about 38% of women belong to 5 local and 6 national fraternities; 20% of women belong to 2 local and 3 national sororities. There are 36 groups on campus, including cheerleading, choir, chorale, chorus, drama, ethnic, honors, international, literary magazine, newspaper, professional, religious, social service, student government, and yearbook. Popular campus events include Spring Festival and Broadway theater trips.

Sports: There are 6 intercollegiate sports for men and 6 for women, and 5 intramural sports for men and 5 for women. Athletic and recreation facilities include a 750-seat gymnasium.

Disabled Students: The following facilities are available: wheelchair ramps, elevators, special parking, specially equipped rest rooms, and lowered telephones.

Services: In addition to many counseling and information services, tutoring is available in some subjects, including English, accounting, mathematics, biology, and chemistry. There is remedial math, reading, and writing.

Campus Safety and Security: Campus safety and security measures include 24-hour foot and vehicle patrol, informal discussions, and pamphlets/posters/films.

Programs of Study: Bloomfield confers B.A. and B.S. degrees. Bachelor's degrees are awarded in BIOLOGICAL SCIENCE (biology/biological science), BUSINESS (accounting and business administration and management), COMMUNICATIONS AND THE ARTS (English, fine arts, French, and Spanish), COMPUTER AND PHYSICAL SCIENCE (chemistry), HEALTH PROFESSIONS (nursing), SOCIAL SCIENCE (economics, history, interdisciplinary studies, philosophy, political science/government, psychology, religion, and sociology). Nursing, prechiropractic, and business are the strongest academically and have the largest enrollments.

Required: To graduate, all students must maintain a minimum GPA of 2.0 while taking 132 credits. Distribution requirements include 16 courses from a general education group, 8 courses from culture and the arts, humanistic studies, social and behavioral science, and natural science, and 4 courses from English/humanities and mathematics areas.

Special: Student-designed majors through independent study programs and a contract program, study abroad in 6 countries, including England and Puerto Rico, combined B.A.-B.S. degrees, internships, pass/fail options, dual majors, nondegree study, and work-study programs are available. Cross-registration with the University of Medicine and Dentistry of New Jersey is permitted. There are 3 national honor societies on campus. One department has an honors program.

Faculty/Classroom: 54% of faculty are male; 46%, female. All teach undergraduates and 21% also do research. The average class size in an introductory lecture is 25; in a laboratory, 18; and in a regular course offering, 25.

Requirements: The SAT I or ACT is required. In addition, the college requires at least 14 academic units, which should include English, mathematics, history, foreign language, and laboratory science. Candidates for the nursing major also should have a biology and a chemistry course. A personal recommendation is required. AP and CLEP credits are accepted. Important factors in the admissions decision are leadership record, recommendations by school officials, and advanced placement or honor courses.

Procedure: Freshmen are admitted to all sessions. Entrance exams should be taken by December of the senior year. There are early decision, early admissions, and deferred admissions plans. Application deadlines are open. Application fee is $25. Notification is sent on a rolling basis.

Transfer: 291 transfer students enrolled in 1995–96. Applicants must present a minimum GPA of 2.0 from an accredited institution and submit official transcripts from all previously attended colleges. 32 credits of 132 must be completed at Bloomfield.

Visiting: There are regularly scheduled orientations for prospective students, consisting of a campus tour, an admissions interview, and other activities by request. There are guides for informal visits and visitors may sit in on classes and stay overnight at the school. To schedule a visit, contact the Office of Admission.

Financial Aid: In 1995–96, 90% of all students received some form of financial aid. 89% of all students received need-based aid. The average freshman award was $7404. Of that total, scholarships or need-based grants averaged $5836 ($13,350 maximum); loans averaged $2100 ($2625 maximum); and work contracts averaged $1200 ($1500 maximum). 5% of undergraduate students work part-time. Average earnings from campus work for the school year are $1525. The average financial indebtedness of the 1994–95 graduate was $12,000. Bloomfield is a member of CSS. The FAF, FAFSA, and the college's own financial statement are required. The application deadline for fall entry is June 1.

International Students: They must take the TOEFL, the Comprehensive English Language Test, or the college's own test and achieve a minimum score on the TOEFL of 500.

Computers: The college provides computer facilities for student use. The mainframe is a DEC VAX 5400. Students have access to an 18-station networked laboratory, as well as 54 computers in 2 public-access facilities. All students may access the system 70 hours a week. There are no time limits. The fees are $50.

Graduates: The most popular majors among graduates were business administration (29%), sociology (15%), and psychology (14%). 45 companies recruited on campus in 1994–95.

Admissions Contact: George P. Lynes, II, Dean of Admission.

CALDWELL COLLEGE
E-2

Caldwell, NJ 07006   (201) 228-4424, ext. 220; (800) 831-9178

Full-time: 280 men, 453 women	**Faculty:** 56; IIB, -$
Part-time: 216 men, 663 women	**Ph.D:** 65%
Graduate: 19 men, 74 women	**Student/Faculty:** 13 to 1
Year: semesters, summer session	**Tuition:** $9560
Application Deadline: open	**Room & Board:** $4900
Freshman Class: 958 applied, 682 accepted, 185 enrolled	
SAT I Verbal/Math: 433/465	**COMPETITIVE**

Caldwell College, founded in 1939, is a private coeducational school offering programs in liberal arts, science, business, fine arts, and education. It is affiliated with the Roman Catholic Church. The library contains 109,809 volumes, 2909 microform items, and 6959 audiovisual forms, and subscribes to 390 periodicals. Computerized library sources and services include the card catalog, interlibrary loans, and database searching. Special learning facilities include a learning resource center, art gallery, and TV station. The 100-acre campus is in a suburban area 20 miles west of New York City. Including residence halls, there are 6 buildings on campus.

Student Life: 87% of undergraduates are from New Jersey. Students come from 10 states, 14 foreign countries, and Canada. 70% are from public schools; 30% from private. 68% are white; 11% foreign nationals; 11% African American. 66% are Catholic; 20% Protestant. The average age of freshmen is 18; all undergraduates, 20. 28% do not continue beyond their first year; 46% remain to graduate.

Housing: 264 students can be accommodated in college housing. College-sponsored living facilities include coed dormitories. On-campus housing is guaranteed for all 4 years. 66% of students commute. Alcohol is not permitted. All students may keep cars on campus.

Activities: There are no fraternities or sororities. There are 28 groups on campus, including art, cheerleading, choir, drama, ethnic, honors, international, literary magazine, professional, radio and TV, religious, social, social service, student government, and yearbook. Popular campus events include Founders Day, Christmas Banquet, Junior Ring Ceremony, and Freshman Investiture.

Sports: There are 5 intercollegiate sports for men and 5 for women, and 8 intramural sports for men and 8 for women. Athletic and recreation facilities include a multipurpose gymnasium, a training room, tennis courts, weight rooms, playing fields, and a pool.

Disabled Students: 80% of the campus is accessible to disabled students. The following facilities are available: wheelchair ramps, elevators, special parking, specially equipped rest rooms, special class scheduling, and lowered drinking fountains.

Services: In addition to many counseling and information services, tutoring is available in most subjects. There is a reader service for the blind, and remedial math, reading, and writing.

Campus Safety and Security: Campus safety and security measures include 24-hour foot and vehicle patrol, informal discussions, pamphlets/posters/films, and emergency telephones. In addition, there are lighted pathways/sidewalks.

Programs of Study: Caldwell confers B.A., B.S., and B.F.A. degrees. Master's degrees are also awarded. Bachelor's degrees are awarded in BIOLOGICAL SCIENCE (biology/biological science), BUSINESS (business administration and management and international business management), COMMUNICATIONS AND THE ARTS (art, communications, English, fine arts, French, music, and Spanish), COMPUTER AND PHYSICAL SCIENCE (chemistry, computer management, computer science, and mathematics), EDUCATION (elementary), HEALTH PROFESSIONS (medical laboratory technology), SOCIAL SCIENCE (criminal justice, history, psychology, religion, social studies, and sociology). Biological science and liberal arts are the strongest academically. Business and education have the largest enrollments.

Required: To graduate, students must maintain a minimum GPA of 2.0 while taking 122 credit hours, including 30 in the major. The 55-credit core includes 15 credits in religion/philosophy, 6 each in history, English, language, social science, and mathematics, 4 in fine arts, 3 in science, 2 in communication arts, and 1 in physical education. A 3-credit course in computer science is also required. A comprehensive examination is required in the senior year.

Special: Caldwell offers co-op programs in all majors except education and medical technology, study abroad in 3 countries, a Washington semester, 1-semester internships, and work-study with Mt. St. Dominic, Hill Top Day Care, and Family and Child Services of North Essex. B.A.-B.S. degrees in 22 fields, dual majors in all majors, credit for life experience in adult education, nondegree study, and pass/fail

options are possible. The Continuing Education Program offers adults (23 years or older) a chance to complete degree requirements in the evening and Saturdays, and the External Degree Program gives adults an opportunity to earn a degree off campus. There is a freshman honors program on campus, as well as 10 national honor societies. All departments have honors programs.

Faculty/Classroom: 44% of faculty are male; 56%, female. All teach undergraduates. No introductory courses are taught by graduate students. The average class size in an introductory lecture is 23; in a laboratory, 13; and in a regular course offering, 16.

Admissions: 71% of the 1995–96 applicants were accepted. The SAT I scores for the 1995–96 freshman class were as follows: Verbal—80% below 500, 14% between 500 and 599, and 6% between 600 and 700; Math—72% below 500, 17% between 500 and 599, 8% between 600 and 700, and 3% above 700. 13% of the current freshmen were in the top fifth of their class; 40% were in the top two fifths. One freshman graduated first in the class.

Requirements: The SAT I is required; a composite score of 900 is recommended. Caldwell requires applicants to be in the upper 50% of their class. A minimum GPA of 2.0 is required. Applicants need 16 academic credits or 16 Carnegie units, including 4 years in English, 2 each in foreign language, mathematics, and science, and 1 in history. A written recommendation from a high school counselor is required. A portfolio, audition, and interview are recommended, depending on the field of study. The GED is accepted. AP and CLEP credits are accepted. Important factors in the admissions decision are academic record, standardized test scores, and recommendations by school officials.

Procedure: Freshmen are admitted to all sessions. Entrance exams should be taken in the fall of the senior year. Application deadlines are open. Application fee is $25. Notification is sent on a rolling basis.

Transfer: 64 transfer students enrolled in 1995–96. Students must have a minimum GPA of 2.0 (2.5 in teacher education). 45 credits of 122 must be completed at Caldwell.

Visiting: There are regularly scheduled orientations for prospective students, including a brief presentation by faculty and students, followed by a tour. There are guides for informal visits and visitors may sit in on classes and stay overnight at the school. To schedule a visit, contact Admissions.

Financial Aid: In 1995–96, 84% of all freshmen and 76% of continuing students received some form of financial aid. 65% of freshmen and 60% of continuing students received need-based aid. The average freshman award was $8461. Of that total, scholarships or need-based grants averaged $6331 ($8400 maximum); loans averaged $2424 ($2625 maximum); and work contracts averaged $815 ($1000 maximum). 35% of undergraduate students work part-time. Average earnings from campus work for the school year are $600. The average financial indebtedness of the 1994–95 graduate was $9000. The FAFSA and the college's own financial statement are required. The application deadline for fall entry is May 1.

International Students: There are currently 83 international students enrolled. The school actively recruits these students. They must take the TOEFL and achieve a minimum score of 500.

Computers: The college provides computer facilities for student use. The mainframe is an IBM AS/400. There are 110 IBM PC, Tandy 1000 SX, DTK, and Apple IIe and IIgs microcomputers available in the academic computing center. All students may access the system Monday to Thursday 9 A.M. to 9:30 P.M., Friday 10:30 A.M. to 4 P.M., and weekends 1 to 5 P.M. There are no time limits and no fees.

Graduates: In 1994–95, 214 bachelor's degrees were awarded. The most popular majors among graduates were business administration (39%), psychology (14%), and education (12%). Within an average freshman class, 31% graduate in 4 years, 43% in 5 years, and 46% in 6 years. 10 companies recruited on campus in 1994–95.

Admissions Contact: J. Raymond Sheenan, Director of Admissions. A campus video is available.

CENTENARY COLLEGE
C-2

Hackettstown, NJ 07840   (908) 852-4696
(800) 236-8679; FAX: (908) 852-3454

Full-time: 128 men, 357 women	**Faculty:** 36; IIB, --$
Part-time: 93 men, 374 women	**Ph.D:** 75%
Graduate: 16 women	**Student/Faculty:** 13 to 1
Year: semesters, summer session	**Tuition:** $12,119
Application Deadline: open	**Room & Board:** $5500
Freshman Class: 245 applied, 214 accepted, 77 enrolled	
SAT I Verbal/Math: 420/460 **ACT:** 18	**LESS COMPETITIVE**

Centenary College, founded in 1867, is a private coeducational institution affiliated with the United Methodist Church. The college offers undergraduate programs in liberal arts, business, international studies, education, equine studies, fashion, and fine arts. In addition to regional accreditation, Centenary has baccalaureate program accreditation with NASDTEC. The library contains 65,000 volumes, 12,400 microform items, and 2600 audiovisual forms, and subscribes to 375 periodicals. Computerized library sources and services include interlibrary loans and database searching. Special learning facilities include a learning resource center, art gallery, radio station, children's center, an equestrian center, and language laboratory. The 42-acre campus is in a suburban area 55 miles west of New York City. Including residence halls, there are 14 buildings on campus.

Student Life: 88% of undergraduates are from New Jersey. Students come from 12 states and 10 foreign countries. 76% are from public schools; 24% from private. 67% are white; 12% African American; 11% Hispanic. The average age of freshmen is 18; all undergraduates, 36. 40% do not continue beyond their first year; 60% remain to graduate.

Housing: 460 students can be accommodated in college housing. College-sponsored living facilities include single-sex and coed dormitories. In addition, there are wellness wings. On-campus housing is guaranteed for all 4 years. 51% of students commute. All students may keep cars on campus.

Activities: 20% of men belong to 1 local fraternity; 60% of women belong to 3 local sororities. There are 27 groups on campus, including art, cheerleading, chorus, dance, drama, ethnic, honors, international, literary magazine, newspaper, photography, professional, radio and TV, religious, social, social service, student government, and yearbook. Popular campus events include Presidents Ball, Centenary Weekend, and Spring Fling Weekend.

Sports: There are 4 intercollegiate sports for men and 5 for women, and 3 intramural sports for men and 4 for women. Athletic and recreation facilities include a gymnasium, a fitness center and indoor pool, tennis courts, playing fields, and an equine center and stables.

Disabled Students: 20% of the campus is accessible to disabled students. The following facilities are available: wheelchair ramps, special parking, specially equipped rest rooms, special class scheduling, and lowered telephones.

Services: In addition to many counseling and information services, tutoring is available in every subject. There is remedial math, reading, and writing.

Campus Safety and Security: Campus safety and security measures include self-defense education, escort service, informal discussions, and pamphlets/posters/films. In addition, there are lighted pathways/sidewalks.

Programs of Study: Centenary confers B.A., B.S., and B.F.A. degrees. Associate and master's degrees are also awarded. Bachelor's degrees are awarded in AGRICULTURE (equine science), BUSINESS (accounting and business administration and management), COMMUNICATIONS AND THE ARTS (communications, design, and English), COMPUTER AND PHYSICAL SCIENCE (mathematics), EDUCATION (elementary and secondary), ENGINEERING AND ENVIRONMENTAL DESIGN (interior design), SOCIAL SCIENCE (American studies, fashion design and technology, history, interdisciplinary studies, international studies, political science/government, and psychology). Equine studies, business, and education certification are the strongest academically and have the largest enrollments.

Required: Students must complete a distribution of 52 semester hours in core courses, including college seminars, as well as the required number of credits, usually 48, for their major. At least 128 semester hours and a minimum GPA of 2.0 are needed to earn the bachelor's degree.

Special: Centenary requires internships in some majors. The college offers study abroad in England and other countries, student-designed majors, work-study, and a pass/fail option. Students aged 25 or older may earn life experience credits. There is a freshman honors program on campus, as well as 1 national honor society. 10 departments have honors programs.

Faculty/Classroom: 48% of faculty are male; 52%, female. All both teach and do research. No introductory courses are taught by graduate students. The average class size in an introductory lecture is 25; in a laboratory, 20; and in a regular course offering, 15.

Admissions: 87% of the 1995–96 applicants were accepted. The SAT I scores for the 1995–96 freshman class were as follows: Verbal—77% below 500, 19% between 500 and 599, and 4% between 600 and 700; Math—66% below 500, 30% between 500 and 599, and 4% between 600 and 700. The ACT scores were 50% below 21 and 50% between 21 and 23. 27% of the current freshmen were in the top fifth of their class; 58% were in the top two fifths.

Requirements: The SAT I or ACT is required. Minimum scores include an SAT I composite of 810, 410 verbal and 400 mathematics, and an ACT composite of 19. Centenary requires applicants to be in the upper 50% of their class. A minimum GPA of 2.0 is required. Applicants must be graduates of accredited secondary schools or have earned a GED. Secondary preparation requires 16 academic credits or Carnegie units, based on 4 years of English, mathematics, and science, and 2 each of foreign language and history. An essay is required, and an interview is recommended. Applicants to specific fine arts programs must also submit a portfolio. AP and CLEP credits are accepted. Important factors in the admissions decision are advanced placement or

honor courses, leadership record, and ability to finance college education.

Procedure: Freshmen are admitted fall and spring. Entrance exams should be taken as early as possible in the senior year. There is a deferred admissions plan. Application deadlines are open. Application fee is $25 ($50 for international students). Notification is sent on a rolling basis.

Transfer: 120 transfer students enrolled in 1995–96. Applicants must have a minimum college GPA of 2.0 and submit proof of high school graduation or the equivalent. 32 credits of 128 must be completed at Centenary.

Visiting: There are regularly scheduled orientations for prospective students, including basic skills testing, advising, registration, and social events. Visitors may sit in on classes and stay overnight at the school. To schedule a visit, contact the Admissions Office.

Financial Aid: In 1995–96, 86% of all freshmen and 94% of continuing students received some form of financial aid. 69% of freshmen and 72% of continuing students received need-based aid. The average freshman award was $12,597. Of that total, scholarships or need-based grants averaged $7113 ($19,394 maximum); loans averaged $3132 ($6625 maximum); grants for institutional service/community project averaged $1164 ($19,394 maximum); and work contracts averaged $561 ($1000 maximum). 75% of undergraduate students work part-time. Average earnings from campus work for the school year are $800. The average financial indebtedness of the 1994–95 graduate was $7000. Centenary is a member of CSS. The FAFSA and the college's own financial statement are required. The application deadline for fall entry is May 1.

International Students: There are currently 41 international students enrolled. The school actively recruits these students. They must take the TOEFL and achieve a minimum score of 500. The student must take the SAT I or ACT if the TOEFL is not taken.

Computers: The college provides computer facilities for student use. The mainframe is an IBM/36. Microcomputer and CAD laboratories are available. Those students enrolled in computer courses may access the mainframe during the laboratory hours specified by their course. All students have access to the microcomputer laboratory. There are no fees.

Graduates: In 1994–95, 134 bachelor's degrees were awarded. Within an average freshman class, 50% graduate in 4 years and 10% in 5 years.

Admissions Contact: Dennis M. Kelly, Dean of Admissions. A campus video is available.

COLLEGE OF SAINT ELIZABETH
E-2
Morristown, NJ 07960–6989

(201) 605-7700
(800) 210-7900; FAX: (201) 605-7070

Full-time: 1 man, 532 women	Faculty: 48; IIB, av$
Part-time: 159 men, 812 women	Ph.D.s: 73%
Graduate: 14 men, 245 women	Student/Faculty: 11 to 1
Year: semesters, summer session	Tuition: $11,950
Application Deadline: August 15	Room & Board: $5400
Freshman Class: 389 applied, 311 accepted, 130 enrolled	
SAT I Verbal/Math: 460/490	COMPETITIVE

The College of St. Elizabeth, founded in 1899, is a private Roman Catholic college primarily for women. Undergraduate programs are offered in the arts and sciences, business administration, education, home economics, and upper-level nursing. There are graduate programs in education, nutrition, psychology, and theology. In addition to regional accreditation, CSE has baccalaureate program accreditation with NLN. The library contains 187,931 volumes, 37,195 microform items, and 5618 audiovisual forms, and subscribes to 769 periodicals. Computerized library sources and services include interlibrary loans and database searching. Special learning facilities include a learning resource center and a television studio. The 188-acre campus is in a suburban area 40 miles west of New York City. Including residence halls, there are 12 buildings on campus.

Student Life: 94% of undergraduates are from New Jersey. Students come from 7 states and 16 foreign countries. 66% are from public schools; 34% from private. 73% are white; 10% Hispanic. 70% are Catholic; 21% claim no religious affiliation. The average age of freshmen is 18; all undergraduates, 29. 23% do not continue beyond their first year; 60% remain to graduate.

Housing: 346 students can be accommodated in college housing. College-sponsored living facilities include single-sex dormitories. On-campus housing is guaranteed for all 4 years. 63% of students live on campus; of those, 35% remain on campus on weekends. All students may keep cars on campus.

Activities: There are no fraternities or sororities. There are 24 groups on campus, including chorale, drama, ethnic, film, honors, international, literary magazine, newspaper, professional, religious, social, student government, and yearbook. Popular campus events include Oktoberfest, International Night, and Junior Class Ring Ceremony.

Sports: There are 7 intercollegiate and 7 intramural sports for women. Athletic and recreation facilities include a student center that houses a swimming pool, a sauna, a weight room, an archery range, and a gymnasium. Tennis courts are also available, as is a bike or hiking trail.

Disabled Students: 75% of the campus is accessible to disabled students. The following facilities are available: wheelchair ramps, elevators, special parking, specially equipped rest rooms, and special class scheduling.

Services: In addition to many counseling and information services, tutoring is available in most subjects. There is remedial math, reading, and writing.

Campus Safety and Security: Campus safety and security measures include 24-hour foot and vehicle patrol, escort service, and lighted pathways/sidewalks.

Programs of Study: CSE confers B.A., B.S., and B.S.N. degrees. Master's degrees are also awarded. Bachelor's degrees are awarded in BIOLOGICAL SCIENCE (biology/biological science and nutrition), BUSINESS (accounting and business administration and management), COMMUNICATIONS AND THE ARTS (art, communications, English, fine arts, French, music, and Spanish), COMPUTER AND PHYSICAL SCIENCE (chemistry, computer science, and mathematics), EDUCATION (early childhood, elementary, home economics, and special), HEALTH PROFESSIONS (nursing, predentistry, and premedicine), SOCIAL SCIENCE (American studies, economics, history, liberal arts/general studies, philosophy, prelaw, psychology, religion, and sociology). Mathematics, chemistry, and education are the strongest academically. Business administration, nursing, and education have the largest enrollments.

Required: To graduate, students must complete 128 semester hours, with a minimum of 32 in the major, while maintaining a GPA of 2.0, or 2.5 for education majors. Core requirements include 27 credits in specific humanities courses focusing on religion, philosophy, literature, history, foreign language, and fine arts, 6 to 8 in mathematics and science, and 6 in social science. In addition, 2 credits in fitness/wellness and an interdisciplinary course are required. Students must also demonstrate proficiency in writing.

Special: There is cross-registration with Drew and Fairleigh Dickinson universities. CSE also offers internships in business, health, government, sports, and television, study abroad, and a Washington semester, including internships and seminars through the American University Justice Semester program. On-campus work-study, accelerated degree programs, dual majors, student-designed majors, credit for life experience, pass/fail options, and nondegree study are also available. Weekend College is a program geared to the working student. There is a freshman honors program on campus, as well as 5 national honor societies.

Faculty/Classroom: 27% of faculty are male; 73%, female. 94% teach undergraduates. No introductory courses are taught by graduate students. The average class size in an introductory lecture is 25; in a laboratory, 16; and in a regular course offering, 16.

Admissions: 80% of the 1995–96 applicants were accepted. The SAT I scores for the 1995–96 freshman class were as follows: Verbal—62% below 500, 30% between 500 and 599, 7% between 600 and 700, and 1% above 700; Math—52% below 500, 36% between 500 and 599, and 12% between 600 and 700. 28% of the current freshmen were in the top fifth of their class; 52% were in the top two fifths. 3 freshmen graduated first in their class.

Requirements: The SAT I or ACT is required, with a minimum composite SAT I score of 800, 400 on each part recommended. CSE requires applicants to be in the upper 80% of their class with a 2.0 GPA. Applicants must be graduates of accredited secondary schools or have earned a GED. The college requires 16 academic units, including 3 each in English, mathematics, and science and 2 each in foreign language and history. An essay is required and an interview is recommended. AP and CLEP credits are accepted. Important factors in the admissions decision are leadership record, recommendations by school officials, and advanced placement or honor courses.

Procedure: Freshmen are admitted fall and spring. Entrance exams should be taken early in the senior year. There are early decision, early admissions, and deferred admissions plans. Early decision applications should be filed by November 15; regular applications, by August 15 for fall entry and December 15 for spring entry, along with an application fee of $35. Notification of early decision is sent December 1; regular decision, on a rolling basis. 5 early decision candidates were accepted for the 1995–96 class.

Transfer: 32 transfer students enrolled in 1995–96. Applicants must present a minimum GPA of 2.0 in course work from an accredited college. SAT I or ACT scores, an associate degree, and an interview are also recommended. 64 credits of 128 must be completed at CSE.

Visiting: There are regularly scheduled orientations for prospective students, including interviews, tours, and class visitation. There are guides for informal visits and visitors may sit in on classes and stay overnight at the school. To schedule a visit, contact Donna Yamanis, Dean of Admission and Financial Aid.

Financial Aid: In 1995–96, 94% of all freshmen and 90% of continuing students received some form of financial aid. 46% of freshmen and 75% of continuing students received need-based aid. The average freshman award was $7908. Of that total, scholarships or need-based grants averaged $5000 ($11,400 maximum); loans averaged $3100 ($7500 maximum); and work contracts averaged $1000 ($1330 maximum). 95% of undergraduate students work part-time. Average earnings from campus work for the school year are $1000. The average financial indebtedness of the 1994–95 graduate was $14,000. CSE is a member of CSS. The FAFSA is required. The application deadline for fall entry is April 15.

International Students: There are currently 61 international students enrolled. The school actively recruits these students. They must score 500 on the TOEFL. Applicants from English-speaking countries may submit scores from either the TOEFL or SAT I.

Computers: The college provides computer facilities for student use. The mainframe is an AT&T 3B2 1000 Model 60 minicomputer. There are also 142 IBM, Apple IIC, and Apple Macintosh microcomputers in various laboratories throughout the campus. Science departments have computers interfacing with equipment, and the foods and nutrition department has computers for nutrition analysis. Those students enrolled in computer courses may access the minicomputer 72 hours per week, when the main laboratory is open. There are no time limits and no fees.

Graduates: In 1994–95, 185 bachelor's degrees were awarded. The most popular majors among graduates were business (41%), psychology (11%), and education (11%). Within an average freshman class, 1% graduate in 3 years, 49% in 4 years, 57% in 5 years, and 61% in 6 years. 23 companies recruited on campus in 1994–95.

Admissions Contact: Donna Yamanis, Dean of Admission and Financial Aid. E-mail: apply@liza.st-elizabeth.edu.

DREW UNIVERSITY/COLLEGE OF LIBERAL ARTS   D-2

Madison, NJ 07940   (201) 408-DREW

Full-time: 544 men, 804 women	**Faculty:** 106; IIA, +$
Part-time: 29 men, 44 women	**Ph.D.s:** 95%
Graduate: 372 men, 318 women	**Student/Faculty:** 13 to 1
Year: semesters, summer session	**Tuition:** $19,638
Application Deadline: February 15	**Room & Board:** $5834
Freshman Class: 2523 applied, 2032 accepted, 433 enrolled	
SAT I Verbal/Math: 560/620	**VERY COMPETITIVE +**

The College of Liberal Arts was added to Drew University in 1928 and is part of an educational complex that includes a theological school and a graduate school. Drew is a private, independent, coeducational university affiliated with the United Methodist Church. The library contains 429,636 volumes, 296,414 microform items, and 3320 audiovisual forms, and subscribes to 2049 periodicals. Computerized library sources and services include the card catalog, interlibrary loans, and database searching. Special learning facilities include an art gallery, a radio station, an observatory, a photography gallery, and a TV satellite dish. The 186-acre campus is in a small town 30 miles west of New York City. Including residence halls, there are 57 buildings on campus.

Student Life: 57% of undergraduates are from New Jersey. Students come from 37 states and 15 foreign countries. 66% are from public schools; 34% from private. 64% are white. The average age of freshmen is 18; all undergraduates, 20. 10% do not continue beyond their first year.

Housing: 1245 students can be accommodated in college housing. College-sponsored living facilities include single-sex and coed dormitories, on-campus apartments, and married-student housing. In addition, there are language houses and special interest houses. On-campus housing is guaranteed for all 4 years. 87% of students live on campus; of those, 70% remain on campus on weekends. Upperclassmen may keep cars on campus.

Activities: There are no fraternities or sororities. There are 64 groups on campus, including art, cheerleading, choir, chorale, computers, dance, drama, ethnic, gay, honors, international, literary magazine, newspaper, orchestra, photography, political, professional, radio and TV, religious, social, social service, student government, and yearbook. Popular campus events include Holiday Semiformal, Annual Picnic, and the New Jersey Shakespeare Festival.

Sports: There are 9 intercollegiate sports for men and 10 for women, and 16 intramural sports for men and 16 for women. Athletic and recreation facilities include an artificial turf athletic field with a 1000-seat gymnasium, a 1000-seat auditorium, swimming pool, lighted tennis complex, weight training room, forest preserve, arboretum, game room, and indoor track.

Disabled Students: The following facilities are available: wheelchair ramps, elevators, special parking, specially equipped rest rooms, and special class scheduling. The main dining facility, the student center and commons, and the ground floor of every dormitory and class-room building are accessible to physically disabled students.

Services: In addition to many counseling and information services, tutoring is available in every subject.

Campus Safety and Security: Campus safety and security measures include 24-hour foot and vehicle patrol, escort service, informal discussions, and emergency telephones. In addition, there are lighted pathways/sidewalks.

Programs of Study: Drew confers the B.A. degree. Master's and doctoral degrees are also awarded. Bachelor's degrees are awarded in BIOLOGICAL SCIENCE (biology/biological science), COMMUNICATIONS AND THE ARTS (classics, dramatic arts, English, fine arts, French, German, music, Russian, and Spanish), COMPUTER AND PHYSICAL SCIENCE (chemistry, computer science, mathematics, and physics), SOCIAL SCIENCE (American studies, anthropology, behavioral science, economics, history, philosophy, political science/government, psychobiology, psychology, religion, Russian and Slavic studies, and sociology). Biological and other physical sciences are the strongest academically. Social sciences have the largest enrollments.

Required: General education requirements include a freshman seminar, 6 credits in foreign language, 6 in natural science/mathematics distribution, 4 in performing or fine arts, and 3 each in history, religion/philosophy, economics and political systems, behavioral science, and non-Western/Third World perspectives. Students must also demonstrate computer literacy and writing proficiency. To graduate, students must complete at least 120 semester hours, including the required number in their particular major, with a GPA of 2.0.

Special: Drew offers co-op programs with the University of Miami, the University of Hawaii, and Duke University, as well as cross-registration with the College of Saint Elizabeth and Fairleigh Dickinson University. There are also dual majors, study abroad, a Washington semester, student-designed majors, internships, field work, and 3-2 engineering programs with Washington University in St. Louis and the Stevens Institute of Technology. There are 11 national honor societies on campus, including Phi Beta Kappa. 12 departments have honors programs.

Faculty/Classroom: 60% of faculty are male; 40%, female. All both teach and do research. No introductory courses are taught by graduate students. The average class size in an introductory lecture is 25; in a laboratory, 20; and in a regular course offering, 18.

Admissions: 81% of the 1995–96 applicants were accepted. The SAT I scores for the 1995–96 freshman class were Verbal—26% below 500, 37% between 500 and 599, 29% between 600 and 700, and 8% above 700; Math—10% below 500, 29% between 500 and 599, 42% between 600 and 700, and 19% above 700. 69% of the current freshmen were in the top fifth of their class; 89% were in the top two fifths. There were 9 National Merit finalists. 17 freshmen graduated first in their class.

Requirements: The SAT I is required. Applicants must be graduates of accredited secondary schools or have earned a GED. The university strongly recommends 16 academic credits or Carnegie units, including 4 in English, 2 in mathematics, and 2 each in foreign language, science, and history, with the remaining 3 in additional academic courses. 3 SAT II: Subject tests are recommended, including writing. An essay is also required, and an interview is recommended. AP and CLEP credits are accepted. Important factors in the admissions decision are advanced placement or honor courses, evidence of special talent, and leadership record.

Procedure: Freshmen are admitted fall and spring. Entrance exams should be taken by January of the senior year. There are early decision, early admissions, and deferred admissions plans. Early decision applications should be filed by January 15; regular applications, by February 15 for fall entry and December 1 for spring entry, along with an application fee of $30. Notification is sent March 15. 58 early decision candidates were accepted for the 1995–96 class. A waiting list is an active part of the admissions procedure, with about 2% of all applicants on the list.

Transfer: 50 transfer students enrolled in 1995–96. Applicants must submit satisfactory high school and college academic records and either SAT I or ACT scores. An interview is also required. 60 credits of 120 must be completed at Drew.

Visiting: There are regularly scheduled orientations for prospective students. There are guides for informal visits and visitors may sit in on classes and stay overnight at the school. To schedule a visit, contact the Admissions Office.

Financial Aid: In 1995–96, 89% of all freshmen and 80% of continuing students received some form of financial aid. 59% of freshmen and 55% of continuing students received need-based aid. The average freshman award was $14,400. Of that total, scholarships or need-based grants averaged $11,190 ($19,130 maximum); loans averaged $3080 ($4000 maximum); and work contracts averaged $1180 ($1300 maximum). 80% of undergraduate students work part-time. Average earnings from campus work for the school year are $1300. The average financial indebtedness of the 1994–95 graduate was

$9200. The FAF or FFS and the college's own financial statement are required. The application deadline for fall entry is March 1.

International Students: There are currently 23 international students enrolled. They must take the TOEFL and achieve a minimum score of 550.

Computers: The college provides computer facilities for student use. The mainframes are 2 DEC VAX 11/750s and a 6330. All full-time students are provided with a laptop PC, a dot-matrix printer, and accompanying software, including DOS 6.0 and WordPerfect 5.1. An extensive software library and additional computers are located on campus. Students also have access to the Internet. All students may access the system. There are no time limits and no fees.

Graduates: In 1994–95, 268 bachelor's degrees were awarded. The most popular majors among graduates were political science (19%), English (12%), and psychology (11%). Within an average freshman class, 1% graduate in 3 years, 71% in 4 years, and 76% in 5 years. 22 companies recruited on campus in 1994–95. Of the 1994 graduating class, 25% were enrolled in graduate school within 6 months of graduation and 64% had found employment.

Admissions Contact: Roberto Noya, Dean of Admissions.

FAIRLEIGH DICKINSON UNIVERSITY SYSTEM

Established in 1942, Fairleigh Dickinson University is an independent, nonsectarian institution of higher education offering career-oriented undergraduate and graduate programs. It is governed by a Board of Trustees, whose chief administrator is the president. The two northern New Jersey campuses are in Florham-Madison and Teaneck-Hackensack; the Wroxton College campus is in Oxfordshire, England. Teaching and research are the primary goals of the institution, with a student-faculty ratio of 15:1. All courses are taught by full- or part-time faculty. The university seeks to provide an academically challenging learning experience to prepare students for employment or enrollment in graduate or professional schools. The university offers 52 undergraduate programs and 53 graduate programs including the Ph.D. in clinical psychology.

FAIRLEIGH DICKINSON UNIVERSITY (TEANECK/HACKENSACK AND FLORHAM/MADISON CAMPUSES)   E-2

Teaneck, NJ 07666   (800) 338–8803; **FAX:** (201) 692–7319

Full-time: 1221 men, 1327 women	**Faculty:** 256; IIA, av$
Part-time: 775 men, 1008 women	**Ph.D.s:** 79%
Graduate: 1567 men, 1916 women	**Student/Faculty:** 10 to 1
Year: semesters, summer session	**Tuition:** $12,370
Application Deadline: June 1	**Room & Board:** $5550
Freshman Class: 3172 applied, 1814 accepted, 504 enrolled	
SAT I Verbal/Math: 460/530	**COMPETITIVE**

Fairleigh Dickinson University, founded in 1942, is an independent coeducational institution comprised of 2 campuses, Teaneck/Hackensack and Florham/Madison, offering undergraduate and graduate degrees in business, arts and sciences, professional studies, public administration, and hotel, restaurant, and tourism management. There are 6 undergraduate and 6 graduate schools. In addition to regional accreditation, FDU has baccalaureate program accreditation with ABET, APTA, and NLN. The 3 libraries contain 457,188 volumes, 258,681 microform items, and 4868 audiovisual forms, and subscribe to 2510 periodicals. Computerized library sources and services include the card catalog, interlibrary loans, and database searching. Special learning facilities include a learning resource center, art gallery, radio station, TV station, ITV multimedia classrooms, photonics laboratory, and regional center for learning disabilities. The 125-acre Teaneck/Hackensack campus is located in a suburban area 5 miles from New York City; the 177-acre Florham/Madison campus is located 33 miles from New York City. Including residence halls, there are 82 buildings on the combined campuses.

Student Life: 83% of undergraduates are from New Jersey. Students come from 26 states, 42 foreign countries, and Canada. 73% are white. 49% are Catholic; 27% Protestant; 12% claim no religious affiliation. The average age of freshmen is 19; all undergraduates, 27. 24% do not continue beyond their first year; 37% remain to graduate.

Housing: 1790 students can be accommodated in college housing. College-sponsored living facilities include single-sex and coed dormitories. In addition, there are special interest houses and sports, sorority and fraternity communal living, Greek life, and major houses. On-campus housing is guaranteed for all 4 years. 74% of students commute. All students may keep cars on campus.

Activities: 20% of men belong to 12 national fraternities; 20% of women belong to 12 national sororities. There are 65 groups on campus, including art, cheerleading, choir, drama, drill team, ethnic, film, gay, honors, international, jazz band, literary magazine, newspaper, photography, political, professional, radio and TV, religious, social, social service, student government, and yearbook. Popular campus events include Welcome Back Week, Home-Coming, Greek Week,

Spring Fling, Senior Week, Spring Jam, MultiCultural Week, SGA Awards Dinner, Senior Dinner Dance, and University Day.

Sports: At the Teaneck campus, there are 8 intercollegiate sports for men and 7 for women, and 14 intramural sports for men and 4 for women. The Madison campus has 7 intercollegiate sports for men and 7 for women, and 12 intramural sports for men and 12 for women. Athletic and recreation facilities at Teaneck include a 5000-seat facility with a 6-lane, 200-meter track, 4 full basketball courts, and 2 volleyball courts; a soccer field; a fully equipped weight room; 6 tennis courts; a baseball field; outdoor basketball courts; and a billiards area. Madison facilities include football, baseball, men's and women's soccer, softball, lacrosse, and field hockey fields, 5 tennis courts, and 2 full outdoor basketball courts. There is an 82,000-square-foot recreation center, a 6000-square-foot fitness center, 2 racquetball courts, basketball seating for 2500, an 8-lane competition pool, an aerobics room, and a training room.

Disabled Students: 27% of the campus is accessible to disabled students. The following facilities are available: wheelchair ramps, elevators, special parking, specially equipped rest rooms, special class scheduling, lowered drinking fountains, and lowered telephones.

Services: In addition to many counseling and information services, tutoring is available in every subject. There is a reader service for the blind, and remedial math, reading, and writing. Interpretation assistance is available for hearing-impaired students. Workshops also offer assistance with study skills and time management, and support services for basic-skills students and freshmen are available. There is also a regional center for learning-disabled students.

Campus Safety and Security: Campus safety and security measures include 24-hour foot and vehicle patrol, self-defense education, escort service, and informal discussions. In addition, there are pamphlets/posters/films, emergency telephones, lighted pathways/sidewalks, an active crime prevention program, and bike patrol.

Programs of Study: FDU confers B.A., B.S., B.S.C.L.S., B.S.Civ.E.T., B.S.Con.E.T., B.S.E.E., B.S.E.E.T., B.S.M.E.T., and B.S.N. degrees. Associate, master's, and doctoral degrees are also awarded. Bachelor's degrees are awarded in BIOLOGICAL SCIENCE (biochemistry, biology/biological science, and marine biology), BUSINESS (accounting, business administration and management, hotel/motel and restaurant management, management science, and marketing/retailing/merchandising), COMMUNICATIONS AND THE ARTS (English and fine arts), COMPUTER AND PHYSICAL SCIENCE (chemistry, computer science, mathematics, and science), ENGINEERING AND ENVIRONMENTAL DESIGN (civil engineering technology, construction technology, electrical/electronics engineering, electrical/electronics engineering technology, environmental science, and mechanical engineering technology), HEALTH PROFESSIONS (clinical science, medical laboratory technology, nursing, predentistry, premedicine, and preveterinary science), SOCIAL SCIENCE (economics, French studies, history, humanities, international studies, liberal arts/general studies, philosophy, political science/government, prelaw, psychology, sociology, and Spanish studies). Business management, administrative services, and psychology have the largest enrollments.

Required: To graduate, students must complete a minimum of 128 credits, including 30 to 44 in the major, with an overall minimum 2.0 GPA. Distribution requirements include courses in English, communications, mathematics, physical education, foreign language, humanities, social and behavioral sciences, laboratory and computer science, and an integrated, interdisciplinary university core sequence.

Special: FDU offers co-op programs in all majors, cross-registration, internships, study abroad, a Washington semester, work-study, accelerated degrees, and student-designed majors in the humanities and general studies. A prepharmacy program as well as joint baccalaureate/dental programs are available. There is a freshman honors program on campus, as well as 14 national honor societies. 19 departments have honors programs.

Faculty/Classroom: 68% of faculty are male; 32%, female. All teach undergraduates and 60% also do research. No introductory courses are taught by graduate students. The average class size in an introductory lecture is 24; in a laboratory, 16; and in a regular course offering, 22.

Admissions: 57% of the 1995–96 applicants were accepted. The SAT I scores for the 1995–96 freshman class were as follows: Verbal—69% below 500, 24% between 500 and 599, and 7% between 600 and 700; Math—36% below 500, 37% between 500 and 599, 21% between 600 and 700, and 6% above 700. 37% of the current freshmen were in the top fifth of their class; 66% were in the top two fifths. 13 freshmen graduated first in their class.

Requirements: The SAT I or ACT is required. FDU requires applicants to be in the upper 50% of their class. A minimum GPA of 2.0 is required. Applicants should be graduates of an accredited high school or have a GED certificate. They should have completed a minimum of 16 academic units, including 4 in English, 3 in mathematics, 2 each in history, foreign language, and laboratory science (3 are recommended), and 3 in electives. Those students applying to science,

engineering, and health sciences programs must meet additional requirements. An interview may be requested by the university. AP and CLEP credits are accepted. Important factors in the admissions decision are advanced placement or honor courses, recommendations by school officials, and leadership record.

Procedure: Freshmen are admitted to all sessions. There are early decision, early admissions, and deferred admissions plans. Early decision applications should be filed by December 1; regular applications, by June 1 for fall entry and October 15 for spring entry, along with an application fee of $35. Notification of early decision is sent December 15; regular decision, on a rolling basis. 25 early decision candidates were accepted for the 1995–96 class.

Transfer: 406 transfer students enrolled in 1995–96. All applicants must submit official transcripts for all college work taken. Those students with fewer than 24 credits must also submit a high school transcript or a copy of their state department of education's equivalency score. 32 credits of 128, including 50% of the major, must be completed at FDU.

Visiting: There are regularly scheduled orientations for prospective students, including an overnight stay during the summer, standardized placement testing, faculty advisement, class registration, and educational and social activities to prepare students for entrance in the fall. There are guides for informal visits and visitors may sit in on classes and stay overnight at the school. To schedule a visit, contact the Admissions Office.

Financial Aid: In 1995–96, 87% of all freshmen and 62% of continuing students received some form of financial aid. 46% of freshmen received need-based aid. The average freshman award was $12,264. Of that total, scholarships or need-based grants averaged $4656 ($11,610 maximum); loans averaged $2741 ($4625 maximum); and work contracts averaged $1119 ($1600 maximum). 18% of undergraduate students work part-time. Average earnings from campus work for the school year are $639. FDU is a member of CSS. The FAF and FAFSA are required. The application deadline for fall entry is March 15.

International Students: In a recent year, there were 602 international students enrolled. The school actively recruits these students. They must take the TOEFL and achieve a minimum score of 500.

Computers: The college provides computer facilities for student use. The mainframes are a DEC ALPHA 2100, a DEC VAX 4000/500, a Sun 4/490, an IBM 4381, and an HP 9000/G70. There are 10 PC laboratories at Teaneck and 6 at Madison. Each laboratory consists of 20 or more NEC 486 or Pentium PCs connected to a central Novell file server and to the universitywide network, which is connected to the Internet. All students may access the system. There are no time limits and no fees.

Graduates: In 1994–95, 717 bachelor's degrees were awarded. The most popular majors among graduates were business management (16%), psychology (10%), and nursing (9%). Within an average freshman class, 1% graduate in 3 years, 27% in 4 years, 64% in 5 years, and 7% in 6 years. 56 companies recruited on campus in 1994–95.

Admissions Contact: Dale Herold, Dean of Enrollment Management.

FELICIAN COLLEGE	**E-2**
Lodi, NJ 07644	**(201) 778-1029**
Full-time: 56 men, 387 women	**Faculty:** 45; IIB, --$
Part-time: 73 men, 505 women	**Ph.D.s:** 75%
Graduate: 15 men, 100 women	**Student/Faculty:** 10 to 1
Year: semesters, summer session	**Tuition:** $7900
Application Deadline: open	**Room & Board:** n/app
Freshman Class: 774 applied, 473 accepted, 312 enrolled	
SAT I: required	**COMPETITIVE**

Felician College, founded in 1942, is a private, Roman Catholic, liberal arts school with concentrations in health science, teacher education, and arts and sciences. In addition to regional accreditation, Felician has baccalaureate program accreditation with CAHEA and NLN. The library contains 110,000 volumes, 10,860 microform items, and 4870 audiovisual forms, and subscribes to 553 periodicals. Computerized library sources and services include interlibrary loans and database searching. Special learning facilities include a learning resource center and a nursing clinical laboratory. The 32-acre campus is in a suburban area 10 miles east of New York City. There are 6 buildings on campus.

Student Life: 99% of undergraduates are from New Jersey. Students come from 2 states, 6 foreign countries, and Canada. 65% are from public schools; 35% from private. 74% are white; 11% Hispanic. The average age of freshmen is 19; all undergraduates, 24. 9% do not continue beyond their first year.

Housing: There are no residence halls. All students commute. Alcohol is not permitted. All students may keep cars on campus.

Activities: 25% of men belong to 1 local fraternity; 10% of women belong to 2 local sororities. There are 17 groups on campus, including art, choir, drama, honors, literary magazine, political, professional, religious, social, social service, and student government. Popular campus events include holiday dances, a variety show, and commencement week activities.

Sports: Athletic and recreation facilities include a fitness center and a gymnasium.

Disabled Students: 90% of the campus is accessible to disabled students. The following facilities are available: wheelchair ramps, elevators, special parking, specially equipped rest rooms, lowered drinking fountains, lowered telephones, and wheelchair lifts.

Services: In addition to many counseling and information services, tutoring is available in every subject. There is remedial math, reading, and writing.

Campus Safety and Security: Campus safety and security measures include 24-hour foot and vehicle patrol, lighted pathways/sidewalks, and guards on duty when school is open.

Programs of Study: Felician confers B.A., B.S., and B.S.N. degrees. Associate and master's degrees are also awarded. Bachelor's degrees are awarded in BIOLOGICAL SCIENCE (biochemistry and biology/biological science), BUSINESS (business administration and management), COMMUNICATIONS AND THE ARTS (English and fine arts), COMPUTER AND PHYSICAL SCIENCE (computer programming and mathematics), EDUCATION (elementary and special), ENGINEERING AND ENVIRONMENTAL DESIGN (environmental science), HEALTH PROFESSIONS (clinical science, medical laboratory technology, and nursing), SOCIAL SCIENCE (history, humanities, psychology, and religion). Education and nursing are the strongest academically and have the largest enrollments.

Required: All students must earn a minimum GPA of 2.0 (2.5 in medical laboratory technology, nursing, and education), while taking 120 credit hours (128 to 130 in education), with 39 to 57 hours in their majors. Distribution requirements include 42 hours from a core curriculum, including courses in English, philosophy, religious studies, humanities, historical tradition, science, and social-cultural studies.

Special: Co-op programs are available in clinical laboratory sciences with the University of Medicine and Dentistry of New Jersey. In addition, internships for credit, work-study at the college, dual majors in education, an interdisciplinary studies degree, student-designed majors within humanities and social and behavioral sciences, weekend college, and pass/fail options are possible. There is a freshman honors program on campus.

Faculty/Classroom: 30% of faculty are male; 70% female. 90% teach undergraduates. The average class size in an introductory lecture is 18; in a laboratory, 20; and in a regular course offering, 11.

Admissions: 61% of the 1995–96 applicants were accepted. In a recent year, 11% of freshmen were in the top fifth of their class; 31% were in the top two fifths.

Requirements: The SAT I is required, with a recommended composite score of 850. A 2.0 GPA is required. The college recommends that applicants have 16 academic credits, including 4 in English, 3 each in mathematics and science, 2 each in foreign language and history, and 1 in social studies. An interview is required. The GED is accepted. AP and CLEP credits are accepted. Important factors in the admissions decision are personality/intangible qualities, advanced placement or honor courses, and extracurricular activities record.

Procedure: Freshmen are admitted fall and spring. Application deadlines are open. Application fee is $25. Notification is sent on a rolling basis.

Transfer: 194 transfer students enrolled in 1995–96. Transfer students must have maintained a minimum GPA of 2.0 (2.5 in medical laboratory technology, nursing, and education). An interview is recommended. Nursing majors require previous college-level laboratory science. 30 credits of 120 must be completed at Felician.

Visiting: There are guides for informal visits and visitors may sit in on classes. To schedule a visit, contact the Admissions Office.

Financial Aid: In a recent year, 38% of all freshmen and 26% of continuing students received some form of financial and need-based aid. Scholarships or need-based grants averaged $1000; and work contracts averaged $500. 90% of undergraduate students work part-time. Felician is a member of CSS. The FAF and the college's own financial statement are required. The application deadline for fall entry is June 1.

International Students: There were 23 international students enrolled in a recent year. They must take the TOEFL and achieve a minimum score of 500.

Computers: The college provides computer facilities for student use. There are 50 IBM and Apple microcomputers available for academic use. All students may access the system. There are no time limits and no fees.

Graduates: In a recent year, 106 bachelor's degrees were awarded. The most popular majors among graduates were nursing (43%), arts and sciences (30%), and education (12%).

Admissions Contact: Susan M. Chalfin, M.S.Ed., Director of Admissions.

GEORGIAN COURT COLLEGE   E-4

Lakewood, NJ 08701–2697   (908) 364–2200, ext. 760
(800) 458–8422; FAX: (908) 364–4442

Full-time: 57 men, 1057 women	Faculty: 82; IIB, av$
Part-time: 117 men, 566 women	Ph.D.s: 63%
Graduate: 91 men, 621 women	Student/Faculty: 14 to 1
Year: semesters, summer session	Tuition: $10,075
Application Deadline: August 1	Room & Board: $4150
Freshman Class: 387 applied, 331 accepted, 143 enrolled	
SAT I Verbal/Math: 430/460	COMPETITIVE

Georgian Court College, founded in 1908, is an independent Roman Catholic college. The day division matriculates only women; the evening and graduate divisions are coeducational. Undergraduate programs are offered in the arts and sciences, business administration, religion, social work, and teacher preparation. In addition to regional accreditation, Georgian Court has baccalaureate program accreditation with ACBSP and NASDTEC. The library contains 153,637 volumes, 509,717 microform items, and 3574 audiovisual forms, and subscribes to 1030 periodicals. Computerized library sources and services include the card catalog, interlibrary loans, and database searching. Special learning facilities include a learning resource center, an art gallery, and an arboretum. The 150-acre campus is in a suburban area 60 miles south of New York City and 60 miles east of Philadelphia. Including residence halls, there are 17 buildings on campus.

Student Life: 98% of undergraduates are from New Jersey. Students come from 8 states and 1 foreign country. 77% are from public schools; 23% from private. 84% are white. The average age of freshmen is 21; all undergraduates, 29. 23% do not continue beyond their first year; 57% remain to graduate.

Housing: 308 students can be accommodated in college housing. College-sponsored living facilities include single-sex dormitories. On-campus housing is guaranteed for all 4 years. 75% of students commute. All students may keep cars on campus.

Activities: There are no fraternities or sororities. There are 31 groups on campus, including art, band, chorale, chorus, computers, ethnic, honors, international, literary magazine, newspaper, professional, religious, social, social service, student government, and yearbook. Popular campus events include Irish Afternoon, Court Singers Concerts, Christmas Reception, and SGA Bonfire.

Sports: There are 4 intercollegiate sports and 4 intramural sports for women. Athletic and recreation facilities include a porcelain-faced swimming pool, basketball, squash, badminton, and volleyball courts, a bowling alley, a 300-seat gymnasium, a fitness center, athletic fields, and a Royal Court tennis court.

Disabled Students: 90% of the campus is accessible to disabled students. The following facilities are available: wheelchair ramps, elevators, special parking, specially equipped rest rooms, special class scheduling, lowered drinking fountains, lowered telephones, and special equipment for the visually and hearing impaired.

Services: In addition to many counseling and information services, tutoring is available in most subjects. There is remedial math, reading, and writing.

Campus Safety and Security: Campus safety and security measures include 24-hour foot and vehicle patrol, escort service, informal discussions, and pamphlets/posters/films. There are emergency telephones and lighted pathways/sidewalks.

Programs of Study: The Court confers B.A., B.S., B.F.A., and B.S.W. degrees. Master's degrees are also awarded. Bachelor's degrees are awarded in BIOLOGICAL SCIENCE (biochemistry and biology/biological science), BUSINESS (accounting and business administration and management), COMMUNICATIONS AND THE ARTS (applied music, art, art history and appreciation, English, French, and Spanish), COMPUTER AND PHYSICAL SCIENCE (chemistry, mathematics, and physics), EDUCATION (special), SOCIAL SCIENCE (history, humanities, psychology, religion, social work, and sociology). Accounting, business administration, and psychology have the largest enrollments.

Required: General education requirements include 9 semester courses in humanities, 5 in social science, and 3 in natural science/mathematics. Students under 25 also must complete a semester course in physical education. The bachelor's degree requires completion of at least 132 credit hours, including a minimum of 30 in a major field. Students must maintain a GPA of at least 2.0 overall and 2.5 in all majors but social work, which requires a 3.0.

Special: Business administration majors may participate in cooperative programs and work-study programs with various employers. A 3–2 degree program in engineering is offered in conjunction with George Washington University. Georgian Court also offers study abroad through the College Consortium for International Studies, internships in history, social work, and political science, dual majors in education, a general studies degree in humanities, field experience externships in art, psychology, education, and social work, credit for life experience, and pass/fail options. Nondegree study is possible. There are 12 national honor societies on campus.

Faculty/Classroom: 33% of faculty are male; 67%, female. 83% teach undergraduates. No introductory courses are taught by graduate students. The average class size in an introductory lecture is 16 and in a regular course offering, 16.

Admissions: 86% of the 1995–96 applicants were accepted. The SAT I scores for the 1995–96 freshman class were as follows: Verbal—85% below 500, 13% between 500 and 599, and 2% between 600 and 700; Math—66% below 500, 27% between 500 and 599, and 7% between 600 and 700. 38% of the current freshmen were in the top fifth of their class; 80% were in the top two fifths.

Requirements: The SAT I or ACT is required, with a composite score of 860 (recentered) on the SAT I or 18 on the ACT. The Court requires applicants to be in the upper 50% of their class and have a 2.7 GPA. Applicants must be graduates of accredited secondary schools or have earned a GED. The college requires 16 academic credits or Carnegie units, based on 4 years of English, 2 each of foreign language and mathematics, 1 each of history and a laboratory science, and 6 of academic electives. An interview is recommended for all students, and an audition is required for applied music majors. AP and CLEP credits are accepted. Important factors in the admissions decision are advanced placement or honor courses, leadership record, and extracurricular activities record.

Procedure: Freshmen are admitted fall and spring. Entrance exams should be taken by January of the senior year. There are early decision and early admissions plans. Early decision applications should be filed by November 15; regular applications, by August 1 for fall entry and January 1 for spring entry, along with an application fee of $30. Notification of early decision is sent December 1; regular decision, on a rolling basis. 20 early decision candidates were accepted for the 1995–96 class.

Transfer: 291 transfer students enrolled in 1995–96. Applicants with fewer than 24 credits must fulfill all requirements for admission to the freshman class. 50 credits of 132 must be completed at Georgian Court.

Visiting: There are regularly scheduled orientations for prospective students, including visits with faculty and students and a tour of facilities. There are guides for informal visits and visitors may sit in on classes and stay overnight at the school. To schedule a visit, contact Nancy G. Hazelgrove, Director of Admissions.

Financial Aid: In 1995–96, 97% of freshmen and 90% of continuing students received need-based aid. The average freshman award was $6252. Of that total, scholarships or need-based grants averaged $3000 ($9750 maximum); loans averaged $2300 ($3625 maximum); and work contracts averaged $1000 ($1200 maximum). Average earnings from campus work for the school year are $1000. The average financial indebtedness of the 1994–95 graduate was $10,000. The Court is a member of CSS. The FAFSA, parent and student 1040 tax forms, and the CSS Profile Application for full-time students are required. The application deadline for fall entry is October 1.

International Students: There was 1 international student enrolled in a recent year. The school actively recruits these students. They must take the TOEFL and achieve a minimum score of 550.

Computers: The college provides computer facilities for student use. 6 modern computer laboratories with 124 networked computers are available to all students. In addition, student rooms in residence halls all have network connectivity. Commuter students also have dial-in access to the campus network. All students may access the system from 8 A.M. to 10 P.M. daily. There are no time limits and no fees.

Graduates: In 1994–95, 348 bachelor's degrees were awarded. The most popular majors among graduates were psychology (16%), business (16%), and special education (12%). Within an average freshman class, 57% graduate in 4 years, 61% in 5 years, and 62% in 6 years. 63 companies recruited on campus in 1994–95. Of the 1994 graduating class, 15% were enrolled in graduate school within 6 months of graduation and 83% had found employment.

Admissions Contact: Nancy G. Hazelgrove, Director of Admissions. A campus video is available.

JERSEY CITY STATE COLLEGE
E-2
Jersey City, NJ 07305

(201) 200-3234
(800) 441-JCSC; FAX: (201) 200-2044

Full-time: 1783 men, 2272 women	Faculty: 243; IIB, + +$
Part-time: 724 men, 1256 women	Ph.D.s: 72%
Graduate: 351 men, 970 women	Student/Faculty: 17 to 1
Year: semesters, summer session	Tuition: $3158 ($4448)
Application Deadline: April 1	Room & Board: $4800
Freshman Class: 3166 applied, 1419 accepted, 668 enrolled	
SAT I Verbal/Math: 414/440	COMPETITIVE +

Jersey City State College, founded in 1927, is a public coeducational institution offering undergraduate programs in the arts and sciences, business administration, education, health science, upper-level nursing, and preprofessional fields. There are 2 undergraduate schools and 1 graduate school. In addition to regional accreditation, JCSC has baccalaureate program accreditation with NASAD, NASM, NCATE, and NLN. The library contains more than 250,000 volumes, 597,191 microform items, and 850 audiovisual forms, and subscribes to 1445 periodicals. Computerized library sources and services include the card catalog, interlibrary loans, and database searching. Special learning facilities include a learning resource center, art gallery, radio station, TV station, media arts center, and laboratory school for special-education instruction. The 17-acre campus is in an urban area 10 miles west of New York City. Including residence halls, there are 14 buildings on campus.

Student Life: 96% of undergraduates are from New Jersey. Students come from 14 states, 50 foreign countries, and Canada. 60% are from public schools; 40% from private. 44% are white; 24% Hispanic; 20% African American. The average age of freshmen is 23; all undergraduates, 25. 25% do not continue beyond their first year; 75% remain to graduate.

Housing: 267 students can be accommodated in college housing. College-sponsored living facilities include coed dormitories. On-campus housing is guaranteed for all 4 years. 95% of students commute. Alcohol is not permitted. All students may keep cars on campus.

Activities: 4% of men belong to 4 local and 4 national fraternities; 3% of women belong to 7 local and 1 national sororities. There are 42 groups on campus, including art, band, cheerleading, choir, chorale, chorus, computers, dance, drama, ethnic, film, honors, international, jazz band, literary magazine, musical theater, newspaper, orchestra, photography, political, professional, radio and TV, religious, social, social service, student government, symphony, and yearbook. Popular campus events include Dean's Picnic, summer concert series, lecture series, films, coffee house entertainment, day trips to New York City for Broadway shows, winter and spring semiformals, and Club Fair.

Sports: There are 6 intercollegiate sports for men and 5 for women, and 14 intramural sports for men and 14 for women. Athletic and recreation facilities include a new athletic and fitness center with a 2000-seat arena, jogging track, fitness facilities, 6-lane pool, and racquetball courts.

Disabled Students: All of the campus is accessible to disabled students. The following facilities are available: wheelchair ramps, elevators, special parking, specially equipped rest rooms, special class scheduling, lowered drinking fountains, and lowered telephones.

Services: In addition to many counseling and information services, tutoring is available in most subjects. There is remedial math, reading, and writing.

Campus Safety and Security: Campus safety and security measures include 24-hour foot and vehicle patrol, escort service, shuttle buses, and informal discussions. In addition, there are pamphlets/posters/films, emergency telephones, and lighted pathways/sidewalks.

Programs of Study: JCSC confers B.A., B.S., B.F.A., and B.S.N. degrees. Master's degrees are also awarded. Bachelor's degrees are awarded in BIOLOGICAL SCIENCE (biology/biological science), BUSINESS (accounting, banking and finance, business administration and management, marketing/retailing/merchandising, and retailing), COMMUNICATIONS AND THE ARTS (design, English, fine arts, media arts, music, photography, and Spanish), COMPUTER AND PHYSICAL SCIENCE (chemistry, computer science, earth science, geology, mathematics, and physics), EDUCATION (art, early childhood, elementary, health, music, secondary, and special), HEALTH PROFESSIONS (medical laboratory technology, nuclear medical technology, nursing, predentistry, premedicine, and public health), SOCIAL SCIENCE (criminal justice, economics, geography, history, philosophy, political science/government, prelaw, psychology, and sociology). Music, criminal justice, and business are the strongest academically. Art, music, and media arts have the largest enrollments.

Required: Students must complete 66 semester hours in general education courses, satisfy college requirements in English, communication, and mathematics, and complete the introductory career exploration and computer usage courses. The bachelor's degree requires completion of at least 128 semester hours, including 36 to 54 in a major, with a minimum GPA of 2.0. Distribution requirements include 9 credits each in natural science, social science, humanities, and fine and performing arts, and 6 credits in communications and contemporary world.

Special: Co-op programs and internships in all majors are available. JCSC also offers study abroad in Europe, Africa, and South America, a Washington semester, work-study programs, numerous health science programs affiliated with New Jersey College of Medicine and Dentistry in Newark, a B.A.-B.S. degree program in biology, chemistry, or geoscience, and pass/fail options. Nondegree study is possible. There is a freshman honors program on campus, as well as 4 national honor societies. One department has an honors program.

Faculty/Classroom: 57% of faculty are male; 43%, female. All teach undergraduates. No introductory courses are taught by graduate students. The average class size in an introductory lecture is 25; in a laboratory, 15; and in a regular course offering, 16.

Admissions: 45% of the 1995–96 applicants were accepted. The SAT I scores for the 1995–96 freshman class were as follows: Verbal—88% below 500 and 11% between 500 and 599; Math—80% below 500, 17% between 500 and 599, and 3% between 600 and 700. 22% of the current freshmen were in the top fifth of their class; 53% were in the top two fifths. 2 freshmen graduated first in their class.

Requirements: The SAT I is required, with a recommended minimum score of 400 on each section. JCSC requires applicants to be in the upper 50% of their class. A minimum GPA of 2.5 is required. Applicants must be graduates of accredited secondary schools or have earned a GED. The college requires 16 Carnegie units, including 4 in English, 3 in mathematics, and 2 each in social studies and a laboratory science, with the remaining 5 units in a foreign language and additional academic courses. An essay is also required and an interview is recommended. AP and CLEP credits are accepted. Important factors in the admissions decision are advanced placement or honor courses, evidence of special talent, and extracurricular activities record.

Procedure: Freshmen are admitted fall and spring. Entrance exams should be taken in the spring of the junior year or the fall of the senior year. There are early admissions and deferred admissions plans. Applications should be filed by April 1 for fall entry and November 1 for spring entry, along with an application fee of $35. Notification is sent on a rolling basis.

Transfer: 728 transfer students enrolled in 1995–96. Applicants must present a minimum GPA of 2.5 in at least 12 credit hours completed at the college level. Students transferring fewer than 12 credits must also submit SAT I scores of at least 400 on each part. An interview is recommended for all transfers. A basic skills test is required for transfers with fewer than 30 credits or who have not taken English or mathematics at their previous school. 36 credits of 128 must be completed at JCSC.

Visiting: There are regularly scheduled orientations for prospective students, including a financial aid workshop, guided tours, and open house. There is a summer orientation. There are guides for informal visits and visitors may sit in on classes. To schedule a visit, contact the Admissions Office.

Financial Aid: In 1995–96, 57% of all freshmen and 44% of continuing students received some form of financial aid, including need-based aid. The average freshman award was $4008. Of that total, scholarships or need-based grants averaged $3195 ($5242 maximum); loans averaged $2580 ($6625 maximum); and work contracts averaged $1606 ($2000 maximum). 12% of undergraduate students work part-time. Average earnings from campus work for the school year are $1250. The average financial indebtedness of the 1994–95 graduate was $6836. JCSC is a member of CSS. The FAFSA is required. The application deadline for fall entry is April 15.

International Students: There are currently 326 international students enrolled. They must take the TOEFL and achieve a minimum score of 400. The student must also take the SAT I, scoring a minimum composite of 800, or the ACT.

Computers: The college provides computer facilities for student use. The mainframes are a DEC VAX 6510, a DEC VAX 8530, 3 DEC MicroVax 3100s, and a DEC MicroVax 3800. Students are able to use the BITNET and Internet systems as well as other network systems, and a toll-free dial-up system whereby they may use home computers and the mainframe. There are 3 computer laboratories with 75 terminals. Those students enrolled in computer science classes may access the system 24 hours a day. There are no time limits and no fees.

Graduates: In 1994–95, 765 bachelor's degrees were awarded. The most popular majors among graduates were business administration (29%), criminal justice (13%), and psychology/sociology (6%). 350 companies recruited on campus in 1994–95.

Admissions Contact: Samuel T. McGhee, Director of Admissions. A campus video is available.

KEAN COLLEGE OF NEW JERSEY   E-2

Union, NJ 07083–0411   (908) 527–2195; FAX: (908) 351–5187

Full-time: 2718 men, 3855 women	Faculty: 341
Part-time: 1116 men, 2377 women	Ph.Ds: 85%
Graduate: 345 men, 1323 women	Student/Faculty: 19 to 1
Year: semesters, summer session	Tuition: $3089 ($4288)
Application Deadline: June 15	Room & Board: $4820
Freshman Class: 4167 applied, 2814 accepted, 1243 enrolled	
SAT I Verbal/Math: 405/453	COMPETITIVE

Kean College of New Jersey, founded in 1855, is a public, coeducational institution offering undergraduate programs in the arts and sciences, business, education, government, nursing, and technology. Kean is primarily a commuter college. There are 4 undergraduate and 4 graduate schools. The library contains 265,000 volumes, 792,000 microform items, and 6000 audiovisual forms, and subscribes to 1200 periodicals. Special learning facilities include a learning resource center, art gallery, planetarium, radio station, and TV station. The 151-acre campus is in a suburban area 20 miles west of New York City. Including residence halls, there are 23 buildings on campus.

Student Life: 97% of undergraduates are from New Jersey. 68% are white; 13% African American; 12% Hispanic. The average age of freshmen is 18; all undergraduates, 24. 23% do not continue beyond their first year; 77% remain to graduate.

Housing: 1400 students can be accommodated in college housing. College-sponsored living facilities include coed dormitories and on-campus apartments. On-campus housing is guaranteed for all 4 years. 88% of students commute. All students may keep cars on campus.

Activities: 9 local and 4 national fraternities and 13 local and 5 national sororities are available. There are 80 groups on campus, including cheerleading, chorus, computers, dance, drama, ethnic, gay, honors, international, jazz band, literary magazine, musical theater, newspaper, pep band, political, professional, radio and TV, religious, social, social service, student government, and yearbook. Popular campus events include Campus Awareness Festival and Homecoming.

Sports: There are 8 intercollegiate sports for men and 7 for women, and 8 intramural sports for men and 8 for women. Athletic and recreation facilities include a 2000-seat stadium, 7 playing fields, 4 gymnasiums, basketball courts, 22 tennis courts, swimming pools, a track, a weight-training room, pool tables, and pinball and video machines.

Disabled Students: All of the campus is accessible to disabled students. The following facilities are available: wheelchair ramps, elevators, special parking, and specially equipped rest rooms.

Services: In addition to many counseling and information services, tutoring is available in most subjects. There is remedial math, reading, and writing.

Campus Safety and Security: Campus safety and security measures include 24-hour foot and vehicle patrol, escort service, shuttle buses, and informal discussions. There are pamphlets/posters/films, emergency telephones, and lighted pathways/sidewalks.

Programs of Study: Kean confers B.A., B.S., and B.F.A. degrees. Master's degrees are also awarded. Bachelor's degrees are awarded in BIOLOGICAL SCIENCE (biology/biological science), BUSINESS (accounting, banking and finance, business administration and management, business economics, international business management, and marketing/retailing/merchandising), COMMUNICATIONS AND THE ARTS (communications, design, dramatic arts, English, fine arts, French, music, Spanish, and studio art), COMPUTER AND PHYSICAL SCIENCE (chemistry, computer science, earth science, geology, information sciences and systems, and mathematics), EDUCATION (art, bilingual/bicultural, early childhood, elementary, foreign languages, health, industrial arts, music, science, secondary, special, and technical), ENGINEERING AND ENVIRONMENTAL DESIGN (electrical/electronics engineering and engineering management), HEALTH PROFESSIONS (medical laboratory technology, medical records administration/services, nursing, occupational therapy, and physical therapy), SOCIAL SCIENCE (criminal justice, economics, history, philosophy, political science/government, psychology, public administration, social work, and sociology). Allied health and technology are the strongest academically. Business has the largest enrollment.

Required: Students must complete a freshman seminar, 18 credits of core requirements, 2 upper-level writing courses, and at least 30 credits in a major field. The bachelor's degree requires completion of 124 to 129 semester hours with a minimum GPA of 2.0.

Special: Students may study abroad in 7 countries, and Kean offers cooperative programs and cross-registration with other members of the Consortium of East New Jersey. There are also dual majors in elementary education, internships in selected majors, credit for life experience, and pass/fail options. There is a freshman honors program on campus, as well as 3 national honor societies. 15 departments have honors programs.

Faculty/Classroom: 59% of faculty are male; 41%, female. The average class size in an introductory lecture is 25; in a laboratory, 15; and in a regular course offering, 17.

Admissions: 68% of the 1995–96 applicants were accepted. The SAT I scores for the 1995–96 freshman class were as follows: Verbal—92% below 500, 7% between 500 and 599, and 1% between 600 and 700; Math—74% below 500, 22% between 500 and 599, and 5% between 600 and 700. 19% of the current freshmen were in the top fifth of their class; 52% were in the top two fifths.

Requirements: The SAT I is required, with a minimum composite score of 900. Applicants must be graduates of accredited secondary schools in the top 50% of their class or have earned a GED. College preparatory study includes 4 courses in English, 3 in mathematics, 2 each in science and social studies, and 5 in academic electives. An essay is required and an interview is recommended. AP and CLEP credits are accepted. Important factors in the admissions decision are leadership record, advanced placement or honor courses, and recommendations by school officials.

Procedure: Freshmen are admitted fall and spring. Applications should be filed by June 15 for fall entry and November 1 for spring entry, along with an application fee of $35. Notification is sent on a rolling basis.

Transfer: 1269 transfer students enrolled in a recent year. Applicants must present a minimum GPA of 2.0. Those students tranferring fewer than 15 credits must also submit SAT I scores. 32 credits of 124 to 129 must be completed at Kean.

Visiting: There are regularly scheduled orientations for prospective students. To schedule a visit, contact the Admissions Office.

Financial Aid: Kean is a member of CSS. The FAF, the college's own financial statement, and a tax return are required. Check with the school for the deadlines.

International Students: There were 224 international students enrolled in a recent year. They must take the TOEFL.

Computers: The college provides computer facilities for student use. The mainframe is a Prime 6350. The Computer Services Department operates a Prime 6550 for academic use and a Prime 5340 for CAD/CAM use by the Technology Department. Major buildings are connected by a campuswide fiber-optic backbone. This network allows access to the college's Prime super minicomputers and Novell Netware file servers. More than 30 discipline-based microcomputer labs with software packages are located throughout the campus. All students may access the system. There are no time limits and no fees.

Graduates: In a recent year, 1682 bachelor's degrees were awarded. The most popular majors among graduates were management science (26%), accounting (8%), and elementary education (7%). Within an average freshman class, 15% graduate in 4 years, 35% in 5 years, and 43% in 6 years.

Admissions Contact: Audley Bridges, Director of Admissions. E-mail: admitme@turbo.kean.edu.

MONMOUTH COLLEGE
(See Monmouth University)

MONMOUTH UNIVERSITY   E-3
(Formerly Monmouth College)
West Long Branch, NJ 07764–1898   **(908) 571-3456**
                                 (800) 543-9671; FAX: (908) 571-7589

Full-time: 1291 men, 1566 women	Faculty: 162; IIA, av$
Part-time: 233 men, 500 women	Ph.D.s: 70%
Graduate: 497 men, 638 women	Student/Faculty: 18 to 1
Year: semesters, summer session	Tuition: $13,140
Application Deadline: March 1	Room & Board: $4710
Freshman Class: 4595 applied, 3758 accepted, 764 enrolled	
SAT I Verbal/Math: 440/500	COMPETITIVE

Monmouth University, founded in 1933, is a private, comprehensive, coeducational institution offering both undergraduate and graduate programs in the arts and sciences, business, education, upper-level nursing, technology, and professional training. There are 4 undergraduate schools and 1 graduate school. In addition to regional accreditation, Monmouth has baccalaureate program accreditation with ABET, CSWE, and NLN. The library contains 246,046 volumes and 306,861 microform items, and subscribes to 1295 periodicals. Computerized library sources and services include the card catalog, interlibrary loans, and database searching. Special learning facilities include a learning resource center, art gallery, radio station, and TV station. The 138-acre campus is in a suburban area 60 miles south of New York City. Including residence halls, there are 39 buildings on campus.

Student Life: 92% of undergraduates are from New Jersey. Students come from 18 states, 29 foreign countries, and Canada. 78% are white. The average age of freshmen is 18.3; all undergraduates, 23.9. 27% do not continue beyond their first year; 50% remain to graduate.

Housing: 1200 students can be accommodated in college housing. College-sponsored living facilities include single-sex and coed dormitories and on-campus apartments. On-campus housing is available on a first-come, first-served basis. Priority is given to out-of-town students. 65% of students commute. Alcohol is not permitted. All students may keep cars on campus.

Activities: There are 7 national fraternities and 5 national sororities. There are 72 groups on campus, including art, band, cheerleading, choir, computers, dance, drama, ethnic, film, gay, honors, international, jazz band, literary magazine, musical theater, newspaper, pep band, photography, political, professional, radio and TV, religious, social, social service, student government, symphony, and yearbook. Popular campus events include Springfest, Ebony Night, Homecoming, and Winter Ball.

Sports: There are 8 intercollegiate sports for men and 7 for women, and 7 intramural sports for men and 7 for women. Athletic and recreation facilities include a 2800-seat gymnasium, outdoor tennis courts, 3 basketball courts, an 8-lane all-weather track, an indoor Olympic-size pool, exercise, wrestling, and weight rooms, and baseball, softball, and soccer fields.

Disabled Students: 90% of the campus is accessible to disabled students. The following facilities are available: wheelchair ramps, elevators, special parking, specially equipped rest rooms, special class scheduling, and lowered drinking fountains.

Services: In addition to many counseling and information services, tutoring is offered in every subject for learning-disabled and physically challenged students. It is available upon request for others. There is a reader service for the blind, and remedial math, reading, and writing.

Campus Safety and Security: Campus safety and security measures include 24-hour foot and vehicle patrol, self-defense education, escort service, and informal discussions. In addition, there are pamphlets/posters/films, emergency telephones, lighted pathways/sidewalks, an official Monmouth University police force, and a student watch organization.

Programs of Study: Monmouth confers B.A., B.S., B.S.N., and B.S.W. degrees. Master's degrees are also awarded. Bachelor's degrees are awarded in BIOLOGICAL SCIENCE (biology/biological science), BUSINESS (accounting, banking and finance, business administration and management, business economics, and marketing/retailing/merchandising), COMMUNICATIONS AND THE ARTS (communications, English, fine arts, French, music, and Spanish), COMPUTER AND PHYSICAL SCIENCE (chemistry, computer science, and mathematics), EDUCATION (art, early childhood, elementary, foreign languages, middle school, music, science, and secondary), HEALTH PROFESSIONS (medical laboratory technology, nursing, and premedicine), SOCIAL SCIENCE (anthropology, criminal justice, history, political science/government, prelaw, psychology, and social work). Business, education, and communication have the largest enrollments.

Required: General education requirements include 6 credits each of English composition, literature, history, science/mathematics, social science, and global studies; 3 each of computer science, critical discourse, and perspectives; and 2 of physical education. Students must also pass a writing proficiency examination. To graduate, students must earn at least 128 credits, including 30 or more in a major, with a minimum GPA of 2.0 overall and 2.1 in the major.

Special: Students may study abroad. There are cooperative and internship programs and a Washington semester. Qualified students may pursue a 5-year B.S.-M.B.A. degree program. Monmouth also offers work-study programs, dual majors, flexible studies programs, credit for life experience, and nondegree study. There is a freshman honors program on campus, as well as 7 national honor societies.

Faculty/Classroom: 67% of faculty are male; 33%, female. All teach undergraduates. No introductory courses are taught by graduate students. The average class size in a regular course offering is 23.

Admissions: 82% of the 1995–96 applicants were accepted. The SAT I scores for the 1995–96 freshman class were as follows: Verbal—80% below 500, 17% between 500 and 599, 3% between 600 and 700; and fewer than 1% above 700; Math—47% below 500, 40% between 500 and 599, 11% between 600 and 700, and 2% above 700.

Requirements: The SAT I or ACT is required. For the SAT I, the required minimum verbal score is 450; the recommended minimum mathematics score is 450 and the composite, 900. A minimum GPA of 2.25 is required. Applicants must be graduates of accredited secondary schools or have earned a GED. Monmouth requires 16 Carnegie units, based on 4 years of English, 3 of mathematics, and 2 each of social studies and science, with the remaining units in any additional combination of the above. An essay and an interview are also recommended. AP and CLEP credits are accepted. Important factors in the admissions decision are advanced placement or honor courses, recommendations by school officials, and personality/intangible qualities.

Procedure: Freshmen are admitted to all sessions. Entrance exams should be taken by December of the senior year. There is a deferred admissions plan. Applications should be filed by March 1 for fall entry and January 1 for spring entry, along with an application fee of $30. Notification is sent January 19.

Transfer: 334 transfer students enrolled in 1995–96. Applicants with fewer than 24 transferable college credits must provide a high school transcript and SAT I scores. 32 credits of 128 must be completed at Monmouth.

Visiting: There are regularly scheduled orientations for prospective students, including campus tours and interviews. There are guides for informal visits and visitors may sit in on classes. To schedule a visit, contact the Admissions Office.

Financial Aid: In 1995–96, 91% of all freshmen and 88% of continuing students received some form of financial aid. 70% of freshmen and 55% of continuing students received need-based aid. The average freshman award was $10,621. Of that total, scholarships or need-based grants averaged $6500; loans averaged $2600; and work contracts averaged $1800. 17% of undergraduate students work part-time. The average financial indebtedness of the 1994–95 graduate was $14,800. Monmouth is a member of CSS. The FAFSA, college's own financial statement, and parent and student 1040 federal tax forms are required. The application deadline for fall entry is May 1.

International Students: There are currently 78 international students enrolled. The school actively recruits these students. They must take the TOEFL and achieve a minimum score of 500.

Computers: The college provides computer facilities for student use. Microcomputers are available in the computer center and the college center. Residence halls are wired for computer network access. All students may access the system. There are no time limits and no fees.

Graduates: In 1994–95, 426 bachelor's degrees were awarded. The most popular majors among graduates were business (28%), communication (13%), and education (11%). Within an average freshman class, 31% graduate in 4 years, 15% in 5 years, and 4% in 6 years.

Admissions Contact: Christine L. Barsony, Associate Director of Admissions. E-mail: barson@mondec.monmouth.edu or http://www.monmouth.edu/.

MONTCLAIR STATE COLLEGE
(See Montclair State University)

MONTCLAIR STATE UNIVERSITY
(Formerly Montclair State College)
Upper Montclair, NJ 07043-1624

E-2

(201) 655-4444
(800) 331-9205

Full-time: 2505 men, 3807 women	Faculty: 418; IIA, + +$
Part-time: 1024 men, 2027 women	Ph.D.s: 84%
Graduate: 1064 men, 2403 women	Student/Faculty: 15 to 1
Year: semesters, summer session	Tuition: $3162 ($4474)
Application Deadline: March 1	Room & Board: $5060
Freshman Class: 5798 applied, 1511 accepted, 1070 enrolled	
SAT I Verbal/Math: 460/520	COMPETITIVE +

Montclair State University, established in 1908, is a public coeducational institution offering programs in liberal arts and sciences, business administration, fine and performing arts, and professional studies. There are 5 undergraduate schools and 1 graduate school. In addition to regional accreditation, Montclair has baccalaureate program accreditation with ADA, AHEA, CSAB, NASAD, NASM, NCATE, and NRPA. The library contains 409,967 volumes, 1,040,442 microform items, and 13,050 audiovisual forms, and subscribes to 2663 periodicals. Computerized library sources and services include the card catalog, interlibrary loans, and database searching. Special learning facilities include a learning resource center, art gallery, radio station, and psychoeducational center. The 200-acre campus is in a suburban area 15 miles west of New York City. Including residence halls, there are 35 buildings on campus.

Student Life: 97% of undergraduates are from New Jersey. Students come from 15 states, 76 foreign countries, and Canada. 80% are from public schools; 20% from private. 74% are white; 12% Hispanic. The average age of freshmen is 18; all undergraduates, 20. 20% do not continue beyond their first year; 58% remain to graduate.

Housing: 1985 students can be accommodated in college housing. College-sponsored living facilities include single-sex and coed dormitories and on-campus apartments. On-campus housing is guaranteed for the freshman year only and is available on a lottery system for upperclassmen. Priority is given to out-of-town students. 79% of students commute. Alcohol is not permitted. All students may keep cars on campus.

Activities: There are 5 local and 16 national fraternities, and 8 local and 11 national sororities. There are 113 groups on campus, including band, cheerleading, choir, chorus, drama, ethnic, gay, honors, international, jazz band, literary magazine, marching band, newspaper, orchestra, professional, radio and TV, religious, social, social service, student government, and yearbook. Popular campus events include Carnival, Homecoming, Spring Week, and Greek Week.

Sports: There are 11 intercollegiate sports for men and 9 for women, and 10 intramural sports for men and 9 for women. Athletic and recreation facilities include a gymnasium complex with a pool, wrestling and weight rooms, a basketball court, and an auxiliary gymnasium, a 6000-seat field, a baseball diamond, tennis and platform tennis courts, 2 softball fields, a multipurpose field, an all-weather track, a field house, and a fitness center.

Disabled Students: 85% of the campus is accessible to disabled students. The following facilities are available: wheelchair ramps, elevators, special parking, specially equipped rest rooms, lowered drinking fountains, lowered telephones, curb cuts, speaker phones, and special building signs.

Services: In addition to many counseling and information services, tutoring is available in most subjects. There is remedial math, reading, and writing.

Campus Safety and Security: Campus safety and security measures include 24-hour foot and vehicle patrol, self-defense education, escort service, and shuttle buses. In addition, there are informal discussions, pamphlets/posters/films, emergency telephones, lighted pathways/sidewalks, a full-time campus police force, a crime prevention officer, and crime prevention programs.

Programs of Study: Montclair confers B.A., B.S., B.F.A., and B.Mus. degrees. Master's degrees are also awarded. Bachelor's degrees are awarded in BIOLOGICAL SCIENCE (biochemistry, biology/biological science, and molecular biology), BUSINESS (business administration and management), COMMUNICATIONS AND THE ARTS (classics, dance, dramatic arts, English, fine arts, French, German, Italian, Latin, linguistics, music, and Spanish), COMPUTER AND PHYSICAL SCIENCE (chemistry, computer science, geoscience, mathematics, and physics), EDUCATION (business, health, physical, and technical), HEALTH PROFESSIONS (allied health and music therapy), SOCIAL SCIENCE (anthropology, economics, geography, history, home economics, humanities, parks and recreation management, philosophy, political science/government, psychology, and sociology). Business administration, psychology, and home economics have the largest enrollments.

Required: To graduate, students must successfully complete a minimum of 128 semester hours, with 33 to 82 in the major, while maintaining a minimum GPA of 2.0. General education requirements include courses in communications, contemporary issues, art appreciation, a foreign language, humanities, mathematics, natural/physical science, social sciences, and multicultural awareness, as well as 1 semester hour in physical education and 2 semester hours in computer science.

Special: Internships, co-op programs in all majors, credit by examination, pass/fail options, work-study, credit for life experience, independent study, weekend study, and study abroad in 33 countries are offered. A 5-year joint-degree program in practical anthropology is possible, and a 5-year B.A.-B.Mus. program in music is available. There is a freshman honors program on campus, as well as 2 national honor societies. 5 departments have honors programs.

Faculty/Classroom: 63% of faculty are male; 37%, female.

Admissions: 26% of the 1995–96 applicants were accepted. The SAT I scores for the 1995–96 freshman class were as follows: Verbal—72% below 500, 22% between 500 and 599, and 6% between 600 and 700; Math—44% below 500, 39% between 500 and 599, 16% between 600 and 700, and 2% above 700. 46% of the current freshmen were in the top fifth of their class; 90% were in the top two fifths.

Requirements: The SAT I or ACT is required. Applicants must submit 16 Carnegie units, including 4 in English, 3 to 4 in mathematics, 2 each in science, social studies, and a foreign language, and the remainder in additional courses in these fields. The GED is accepted. A portfolio, audition, or interview are required for students planning to major in fine arts, music, speech, or theater. AP and CLEP credits are accepted. Important factors in the admissions decision are recommendations by school officials, extracurricular activities record, and ability to finance college education.

Procedure: Freshmen are admitted fall and spring. Entrance exams should be taken in November or December of the senior year. Applications should be filed by March 1 for fall entry and October 15 for spring entry, along with an application fee of $40. Notification is sent on a rolling basis. A waiting list is an active part of the admissions procedure, with about 5% of all applicants on the list.

Transfer: 718 transfer students enrolled in 1995–96. Applicants must have completed a minimum of 15 credits from an accredited college. A cumulative GPA of 2.5 is required; a GPA of 3.0 is required for business and computer science majors. 32 credits of 128 must be completed at Montclair.

Visiting: There are regularly scheduled orientations for prospective students. There are guides for informal visits. To schedule a visit, contact the Admissions Office.

Financial Aid: In 1995–96, 75% of all students received some form of financial aid. 38% of all students received need-based aid. The average freshman award was $3500. Of that total, scholarships or need-based grants averaged $1000 ($2000 maximum); loans averaged $1250 ($2500 maximum); and work contracts averaged $500 ($1000 maximum). 10% of undergraduate students work part-time. Average earnings from campus work for the school year are $800. The average financial indebtedness of the 1994–95 graduate was $5000. Montclair is a member of CSS. The FAFSA is required. The application deadline for fall entry is February 15.

International Students: There are currently 208 international students enrolled. They must take the TOEFL and achieve a minimum score of 500.

Computers: The college provides computer facilities for student use. The mainframes are a DEC VAX cluster and a DEC ALPHA cluster. PC and Apple Macintosh laboratories are located throughout the campus, with about 400 computers and PC printers. A network of Sun workstations is also available. A wide variety of general and discipline-specific software is offered. All students may ccess the system. There are no time limits and no fees.

Graduates: In 1994–95, 1588 bachelor's degrees were awarded. The most popular majors among graduates were business administration (22%), psychology (11%), and home economics (10%). Within an average freshman class, 1% graduate in 3 years, 19% in 4 years, 44% in 5 years, and 53% in 6 years.

Admissions Contact: Dr. Alan L. Buechler, Director of Admissions.

NEW JERSEY INSTITUTE OF TECHNOLOGY   E-2

Newark, NJ 07102–1982	(201) 596-3300; (800) 222-NJIT
Full-time: 2741 men, 613 women	Faculty: 243; I, +$
Part-time: 1414 men, 274 women	Ph.D.s: 98%
Graduate: 2111 men, 732 women	Student/Faculty: 14 to 1
Year: semesters, summer session	Tuition: $5220 ($9564)
Application Deadline: April 1	Room & Board: $5500
Freshman Class: 1916 applied, 1277 accepted, 564 enrolled	
SAT I Verbal/Math: 480/610	VERY COMPETITIVE

New Jersey Institute of Technology is a coeducational, public research university providing instruction, research, and public service in engineering, computer science, management, architecture, engineering technology, applied sciences, and related fields. There are 5 undergraduate schools and 1 graduate school. In addition to regional accreditation, NJIT has baccalaureate program accreditation with ABET, CSAB, and NAAB. The 2 libraries contain 157,000 volumes, 3730 microform items, and 700 audiovisual forms, and subscribe to 1129 periodicals. Computerized library sources and services include the card catalog, interlibrary loans, and database searching. Special learning facilities include a learning resource center, art gallery, radio station, and 3 TV studios. NJIT is home to many government- and industry-sponsored laboratories and research centers, including the EPA Northeast Hazardous Substance Research Center, the National Center for Transportation and Industrial Productivity, the Center for Manufacturing Systems, the Emission Reduction Research Center, the Microelectronics Research Center, the Center for Microwave and Lightwave Engineering, and the Multi-Lifecycle Engineering Center. The 45-acre campus is in an urban area 10 miles west of New York City. Including residence halls, there are 24 buildings on campus.

Student Life: 90% of undergraduates are from New Jersey. Students come from 19 states, 66 foreign countries, and Canada. 80% are from public schools; 20% from private. 53% are white; 15% Asian American; 11% foreign nationals; 11% Hispanic; 10% African American. 38% are Catholic; 36% Islamic, Buddhist, Eastern Orthodox, or other; 25% are Protestant. The average age of freshmen is 18; all undergraduates, 24. 15% do not continue beyond their first year; 80% remain to graduate.

Housing: 870 students can be accommodated in college housing. College-sponsored living facilities include coed dormitories. On-campus housing is available on a first-come, first-served basis and is available on a lottery system for upperclassmen. Priority is given to out-of-town students. 75% of students commute. All students may keep cars on campus.

Activities: 15% of men belong to 4 local and 10 national fraternities; 8% of women belong to 4 local and 5 national sororities. There are 50 groups on campus, including art, chess, computers, drama, drum and bugle corps, ethnic, gay, honors, international, musical theater, newspaper, photography, professional, radio and TV, religious, social, social service, student government, and yearbook. Popular campus events include Alcohol Awareness Week, Fall Holiday Celebration, Miniversity, International Students Food Festival, World Week, Leadership Training Weekend, Black History Month, Women's History Month, Hispanic Heritage Month, Winter Holiday Celebration, Spring Week, off-campus trips on weekends and breaks, Greek Week, Senior Semiformal, Gay/Lesbian Bisexual Awareness Day, Asian American Heritage Month, Indian Dewali, Caribbean Nite, Chinese New Year, regularly scheduled movies, and other ongoing cultural events.

Sports: There are 9 intercollegiate sports for men and 6 for women, and 13 intramural sports for men and 7 for women. Athletic and recreation facilities include a 1000-seat stadium, a fitness center with an indoor track, a 6-lane swimming pool, 4 tennis courts, 4 racquet-sport courts, playing fields, bowling lanes, a table tennis and billiards area, and 3 gymnasiums, the largest of which seats 1200.

Disabled Students: 95% of the campus is accessible to disabled students. The following facilities are available: wheelchair ramps, elevators, special parking, specially equipped rest rooms, special class scheduling, lowered drinking fountains, and lowered telephones.

Services: In addition to many counseling and information services, tutoring is available in most subjects. There is a reader service for the blind, and remedial math, reading, and writing.

Campus Safety and Security: Campus safety and security measures include 24-hour foot and vehicle patrol, self-defense education, escort service, and shuttle buses. In addition, there are informal discussions, pamphlets/posters/films, emergency telephones, and lighted pathways/sidewalks.

Programs of Study: NJIT confers B.A., B.S., and B.Arch. degrees. Master's and doctoral degrees are also awarded. Bachelor's degrees are awarded in BUSINESS (management science), COMPUTER AND PHYSICAL SCIENCE (actuarial science, applied mathematics, applied physics, chemical technology, computer science, information sciences and systems, science technology, and statistics), ENGINEERING AND ENVIRONMENTAL DESIGN (architecture, chemical engineering, civil engineering, computer engineering, electrical/electronics engineering, engineering and applied science, engineering technology, industrial engineering, manufacturing engineering, and mechanical engineering). Engineering, computer science, and architecture are the strongest academically. Engineering has the largest enrollment.

Required: General university requirements include 9 credits of humanities and social science electives, 7 of natural sciences, 6 each of mathematics, cultural history, basic social sciences, and engineering technology, 3 each of English and management, and 2 of computer science. Students must also complete 2 courses in physical education. To graduate, students must earn between 124 and 164 credits, depending on the program, including 50 in the major, with a minimum GPA of 2.0 in upper-level major courses.

Special: Cross-registration is offered in conjunction with Essex County College, Rutgers University's Newark campus, and the University of Medicine and Dentistry of New Jersey. Cooperative programs, available in all majors, include two 6-month internships. There are 3–2 engineering degree programs with Stockton State College and Lincoln and Seton Hall universities. NJIT also offers work-study programs, study abroad in 5 countries, dual and interdisciplinary majors, accelerated degree programs, distance learning, and nondegree study. There is a freshman honors program on campus, as well as 1 national honor society. All departments have honors programs.

Faculty/Classroom: 83% of faculty are male; 17%, female. 74% teach undergraduates, 64% do research, and 38% do both. Graduate students teach 8% of introductory courses. The average class size in an introductory lecture is 30; in a laboratory, 27; and in a regular course offering, 25.

Admissions: 67% of the 1995–96 applicants were accepted. The SAT I scores for the 1995–96 freshman class were as follows: Verbal—57% below 500, 31% between 500 and 599, 11% between 600 and 700, and 1% above 700; Math—7% below 500, 38% between 500 and 599, 42% between 600 and 700, and 13% above 700. 45% of the current freshmen were in the top fifth of their class; 75% were in the top two fifths. There was 1 National Merit finalist and 4 semifinalists. 3 freshmen graduated first in their class.

Requirements: The SAT I or ACT is required; the SAT I is preferred. The SAT II: Subject test in mathematics I or II is also required. Applicants should have completed 16 secondary school units, including 4 each in English and mathematics, 2 in a laboratory science, and 6 in a distribution of social studies, foreign language, mathematics, and science courses. Applications are accepted on-line via the World Wide Web: http://www.njit.edu. AP and CLEP credits are accepted. Important factors in the admissions decision are advanced placement or honor courses, extracurricular activities record, and leadership record.

Procedure: Freshmen are admitted to all sessions. Entrance exams should be taken in May of the junior year or November of the senior year. There are early decision and early admissions plans. Early decision applications should be filed by December 1; regular applications, by April 1 for fall entry and December 1 for spring entry, along with an application fee of $35. Notification of early decision is sent December 31; regular decision, on a rolling basis. 30 early decision candidates were accepted for the 1995–96 class. A waiting list is an active part of the admissions procedure, with about 2% of all applicants on the list.

Transfer: 462 transfer students enrolled in 1995–96. A minimum college GPA of 2.0 is required, but 2.5 or higher is recommended. Students must submit transcripts of all attempted postsecondary academic work. Applicants with fewer than 30 credits may be asked to provide SAT I scores, SAT II: Subject test in mathematics scores, and a high school transcript. Engineering technology students must present an associate degree. Admission to the School of Architecture is very competitive for transfer students. 33 credits of 124 to 164 must be completed at NJIT.

Visiting: There are regularly scheduled orientations for prospective students, including tours and meetings with admissions personnel, students, and faculty. There are guides for informal visits and visitors may sit in on classes and stay overnight at the school. To schedule a visit, contact Kathy Kelly, Director of Admissions.

Financial Aid: In 1995–96, 79% of all freshmen and 61% of continuing students received some form of financial aid. 58% of freshmen and 54% of continuing students received need-based aid. The average freshman award was $8246. Of that total, scholarships or need-based grants averaged $6100; loans averaged $1494; and work contracts averaged $652. 70% of undergraduate students work part-time. Average earnings from campus work for the school year are $2150. The average financial indebtedness of the 1994–95 graduate was $10,000. NJIT is a member of CSS. The FAF and the college's own financial statement are required. The application deadline for fall entry is March 15.

International Students: There are currently 173 international students enrolled. The school actively recruits these students. They must take the TOEFL and achieve a minimum score of 520. The student must also take the SAT I or the ACT. Students must take SAT II: Subject tests in mathematics I or II.

Computers: The college provides computer facilities for student use. The mainframes are comprised of a DEC VAX 6430, which serves as the main VMS computer, and a DEC 5900, which serves as the UNIX engine for academic work. All computing facilities are connected to a campuswide network, which has a fiber-optic spine between buildings, including all dormitory rooms; 150 computer nodes can be accessed from 2500 on-campus locations. All students may access the system. There are no time limits and no fees. All full-time freshmen are given a 486 computer and a variety of software packages to use while at NJIT. The computer and software may be purchased for a nominal fee upon graduation.

Graduates: In 1994–95, 671 bachelor's degrees were awarded. The most popular majors among graduates were engineering technology (18%), electrical engineering (15%), and mechanical engineering (11%). Within an average freshman class, 35% graduate in 4 years, 60% in 5 years, and 70% in 6 years. 100 companies recruited on campus in 1994–95. Of the 1994 graduating class, 20% were enrolled in graduate school within 6 months of graduation and 70% had found employment.

Admissions Contact: Kathy Kelly, Director of Admissions. E-mail: kelly@admin.njit.edu.

PRINCETON UNIVERSITY   D-3

Princeton, NJ 08544-0430	(609) 258-3060; FAX: (609) 258-6743
Full-time: 2486 men, 2123 women	Faculty: 728; I, ++$
Part-time: none	Ph.D.s: 99%
Graduate: 1150 men, 660 women	Student/Faculty: 6 to 1
Year: semesters	Tuition: $22,000
Application Deadline: January 2	Room & Board: $6325
Freshman Class: 14,311 applied, 2013 accepted, 1209 enrolled	
SAT I: required	MOST COMPETITIVE

Princeton University, established in 1746, is a private institution offering degrees in the liberal arts and sciences, engineering, applied science, architecture, public and international affairs, interdisciplinary and regional studies, and the creative arts. There are 4 graduate schools. In addition to regional accreditation, Princeton has baccalaureate program accreditation with ABET and NAAB. The 20 libraries contain 5,000,000 volumes, 3,000,000 microform items, and 52,000 audiovisual forms, and subscribe to 30,000 periodicals. Computerized library sources and services include the card catalog. Special learning facilities include an art gallery, natural history museum, radio station, a music center, a visual and performing arts center, several theaters, an observatory, a plasma physics laboratory, and a center for environmental and energy studies. The 600-acre campus is in a small town 50 miles south of New York City. Including residence halls, there are 140 buildings on campus.

Student Life: 86% of undergraduates are from out-of-state, mostly the Middle Atlantic. Students come from 50 states, 70 foreign countries, and Canada. 71% are white; 10% Asian American. The average age of freshmen is 18; all undergraduates, 20. 2% do not continue beyond their first year; 96% remain to graduate.

Housing: 4400 students can be accommodated in college housing. College-sponsored living facilities include coed dormitories, on-campus apartments, and married-student housing. In addition, freshmen and sophomores are assigned to 1 of 5 residential colleges; most juniors and seniors live in upperclass dormitories and select from among such dining options as co-ops and private clubs. On-campus housing is guaranteed for all 4 years. 98% of students live on campus. Alcohol is not permitted. All students may keep cars on campus.

Activities: There are no fraternities or sororities. There are 200 groups on campus, including art, band, cheerleading, chess, choir, chorale, chorus, dance, drama, ethnic, film, gay, international, jazz band, literary magazine, musical theater, newspaper, opera, orchestra, pep band, photography, political, professional, radio and TV, religious, social, social service, student government, symphony, and

yearbook. Popular campus events include recitals and theater productions.

Sports: There are 17 intercollegiate sports for men and 16 for women, and 53 intramural sports each for men and women. Athletic and recreation facilities include a 45,000-seat football and track stadium, an 18-hole golf course, 2 gymnasiums, an Olympic swimming and diving complex, playing fields, a boathouse and Olympic-level racing course for crew and sailing, a health fitness center, an ice rink, dance studios, and tennis, squash, and volleyball courts.

Disabled Students: The following facilities are available: wheelchair ramps, elevators, special parking, specially equipped rest rooms, special class scheduling, and lowered telephones.

Services: In addition to many counseling and information services, tutoring is available in every subject. There is a reader service for the blind.

Campus Safety and Security: Campus safety and security measures include 24-hour foot and vehicle patrol, self-defense education, escort service, and shuttle buses. There are informal discussions, pamphlets/posters/films, emergency telephones, and lighted pathways/sidewalks.

Programs of Study: Princeton confers A.B. and B.S.E. degrees. Master's and doctoral degrees are also awarded. Bachelor's degrees are awarded in BIOLOGICAL SCIENCE (biology/biological science), COMMUNICATIONS AND THE ARTS (classics, comparative literature, English, Germanic languages and literature, music, romance languages, and Slavic languages), COMPUTER AND PHYSICAL SCIENCE (astrophysics, chemistry, computer science, geology, mathematics, and physics), ENGINEERING AND ENVIRONMENTAL DESIGN (aeronautical engineering, architectural engineering, architecture, chemical engineering, civil engineering, electrical/electronics engineering, and mechanical engineering), SOCIAL SCIENCE (anthropology, archeology, East Asian studies, economics, history, international relations, Near Eastern studies, philosophy, political science/government, psychology, religion, and sociology). History, political science, and English have the largest enrollments.

Required: To graduate, students must complete 8 semesters, or academic units. Candidates for the A.B. degree must demonstrate proficiency in English composition and a foreign language and complete distribution requirements in the areas of arts and letters, natural science, social science, and history, philosophy, and religion. Candidates for the B.S.E. must satisfy the English composition requirement and, by the end of the sophomore year, complete 4 terms of mathematics, 2 of physics, and 1 each of chemistry and computer programming. A junior project and senior thesis are required of virtually all students.

Special: Princeton offers independent study, preceptorials, accelerated degree programs, a program in teacher preparation, student-proposed courses and majors, field study, study abroad, seminars, and internships in public affairs. The university operates on an honor code whereby examinations are not proctored by faculty members. There are 2 national honor societies on campus, including Phi Beta Kappa.

Faculty/Classroom: 76% of faculty are male; 24%, female. All teach undergraduates and 90% do research. Graduate students teach 1% of introductory courses.

Admissions: 14% of the applicants in a recent freshman class were accepted. The SAT I scores for a recent freshman class were as follows: Verbal—2% below 500, 19% between 500 and 599, 52% between 600 and 700, and 27% above 700; Math—6% between 500 and 599, 31% between 600 and 700, and 63% above 700. All of a recent freshmen class were in the top fifth of their class.

Requirements: The SAT I is required but the ACT is accepted. SAT II: Subject tests are also required. Applicants must be graduates of an accredited secondary school. Recommended college preparatory courses include 4 years each of English, mathematics, and a foreign language; 2 each of laboratory science and history; and some study of art, music, and, if possible, a second foreign language. An essay is required and an interview is recommended. Fine arts majors should submit an audition tape or portfolio. AP credits are accepted.

Procedure: Freshmen are admitted in the fall. Entrance exams should be taken by January of the senior year. There are early decision, early admissions, and deferred admissions plans. Early decision applications should be filed by November 1; regular applications, by January 2 for fall entry, along with an application fee of $55. Notification of early decision is sent in December; regular decision, early April. A waiting list is an active part of the admissions procedure, with about 3% of all applicants on the list.

Transfer: Since space is limited, only those students with excellent academic records and compelling academic reasons for transferring should apply.

Visiting: There are regularly scheduled orientations for prospective students. There are guides for informal visits and visitors may sit in on classes and stay overnight at the school. To schedule a visit, contact Orange Key Guide Service at (609) 258-3603.

Financial Aid: In a recent year, 43% of all freshmen and 42% of continuing students received some form of financial aid, including need-based aid. The average freshman award was $15,870. Of that total, scholarships or need-based grants averaged $11,830 ($20,000 maximum); loans averaged $2660 ($3500 maximum); and work contracts averaged $1380 ($1750 maximum). 67% of undergraduate students work part-time. Average earnings from campus work for the school year are $1200. The average financial indebtedness of a recent year's graduate was $13,000. Princeton is a member of CSS. The FAF and the college's own financial statement are required. The application deadline for fall entry is February 1.

International Students: In a recent year, 273 international students were enrolled. The school actively recruits these students. They must take the TOEFL and also take the SAT I.

Computers: The college provides computer facilities for student use. The mainframes are an IBM 3081 and a DEC VAX 8700. There are also 450 microcomputers, including Apple Macintoshes and IBM PCs, connected to a central TigerNet system. NeXT, Silicon Graphics, Bitnet, and Internet are available through SUN workstations. All students may access the system and receive a $500 account.

Graduates: In a recent year, 1097 bachelor's degrees were awarded.

Admissions Contact: Fred A. Hargadon, Dean of Admissions.

RAMAPO COLLEGE OF NEW JERSEY   D-2

Mahwah, NJ 07430   **(201) 529-7600**

Full-time: 1254 men, 1354 women	Faculty: 141; IIB, + +$
Part-time: 847 men, 1088 women	Ph.D.s: 97%
Graduate: 13 men, 37 women	Student/Faculty: 18 to 1
Year: semesters, summer session	Tuition: $3521 ($4878)
Application Deadline: March 15	Room & Board: $5186
Freshman Class: 1711 applied, 750 accepted, 340 enrolled	
SAT I Verbal/Math: 475/520	**COMPETITIVE +**

Ramapo College founded in 1971, is a public, coeducational institution offering undergraduate programs in the arts and sciences, American and international studies, business administration, and human services. Incorporated throughout the curriculum is an international, multicultural component including telecommunications and computer technology. There are 5 undergraduate schools and 1 graduate school. In addition to regional accreditation, Ramapo has baccalaureate program accreditation with CSWE. The library contains 145,614 volumes, 21,948 microform items, and 19,057 audiovisual forms, and subscribes to 1283 periodicals. Computerized library sources and services include the card catalog, interlibrary loans, and database searching. Special learning facilities include an art gallery, radio station, and international telecommunications satellite center. The 314-acre campus is in a suburban area 25 miles northwest of New York City. Including residence halls, there are 20 buildings on campus.

Student Life: 82% of undergraduates are from New Jersey. Students come from 15 states and 42 foreign countries. 94% are from public schools; 6% from private. 81% are white. The average age of freshmen is 18; all undergraduates, 20. 24% do not continue beyond their first year.

Housing: 1100 students can be accommodated in college housing. College-sponsored living facilities include coed dormitories and on-campus apartments. In addition, there are honors houses, special interest houses, and an international house. On-campus housing is guaranteed for all 4 years. 62% of students commute. All students may keep cars on campus.

Activities: 11% of men belong to 7 national fraternities; 8% of women belong to 8 national sororities. There are 77 groups on campus, including art, cheerleading, choir, chorus, computers, drama, ethnic, gay, honors, international, jazz band, literary magazine, newspaper, political, professional, radio and TV, religious, social, social service, student government, and yearbook. Popular campus events include Welcome Week, Homecoming, African Ancestry Month, Springfest, Spring Semiformal, Earth Days, Hispanic Latino Heritage Month, International Celebration, Senior Gala, and Summer Block Party.

Sports: There are 8 intercollegiate sports for men and 7 for women, and 13 intramural sports for men and 12 for women. Athletic and recreation facilities include a 1000-seat stadium, 12 lighted tennis courts, playing fields, a 300-seat arena, a track, a 1000-seat gymnasium with a basketball court, an Olympic-size pool, and fitness and weight training rooms.

Disabled Students: The entire campus is accessible to disabled students. The following facilities are available: wheelchair ramps, elevators, special parking, specially equipped rest rooms, special class scheduling, lowered drinking fountains, lowered telephones, and specially equipped residence hall units.

Services: In addition to many counseling and information services, tutoring is available in every subject. There is a reader service for the blind, and remedial math, reading, and writing.

Campus Safety and Security: Campus safety and security measures include 24-hour foot and vehicle patrol, shuttle buses, informal discussions, and pamphlets/posters/films. In addition, there are emergency telephones and lighted pathways/sidewalks.

Programs of Study: Ramapo confers B.A., B.S., B.S.N., and B.S.W. degrees. Master's degrees are also awarded. Bachelor's degrees are awarded in BIOLOGICAL SCIENCE (biology/biological science), BUSINESS (accounting, business administration and management, international business management, and management information systems), COMMUNICATIONS AND THE ARTS (communications, literature, music, and visual and performing arts), COMPUTER AND PHYSICAL SCIENCE (chemistry, computer science, mathematics, and physics), ENGINEERING AND ENVIRONMENTAL DESIGN (environmental science), HEALTH PROFESSIONS (nursing), SOCIAL SCIENCE (American studies, economics, history, human ecology, international studies, law, political science/government, psychology, social work, sociology, and urban studies). Business, liberal arts, and social sciences are the strongest academically. Communications and business administration have the largest enrollments.

Required: Students must complete general education requirements of approximately 50 credits in science, social science, humanities, and English composition, as well as core requirements in their school of study and their particular major. A senior seminar is also required. To graduate, students must earn at least 128 credits with a minimum GPA of 2.0.

Special: Ramapo's curriculum emphasizes the interdependence of global society and includes an international dimension in all academic programs. Students may study abroad in 10 countries. Cooperative programs are available with various corporations and in 12 foreign countries. Cross-registration is possible with local state colleges. Ramapo also offers a winter session, accelerated degree programs, credit for life experience, pass/fail options, nondegree study, and dual, student-designed, and interdisciplinary majors, including law and society. There is a freshman honors program on campus, as well as 5 national honor societies. 10 departments have honors programs.

Faculty/Classroom: 65% of faculty are male; 35%, female. All teach undergraduates. The average class size in an introductory lecture is 28; in a laboratory, 18; and in a regular course offering, 22.

Admissions: 44% of the 1995–96 applicants were accepted. The SAT I scores for the 1995–96 freshman class were as follows: Verbal—64% below 500, 29% between 500 and 599, 6% between 600 and 700, and 1% above 700; Math—41% below 500, 37% between 500 and 599, 19% between 600 and 700, and 3% above 700. 22% of the current freshmen were in the top fifth of their class; 61% were in the top two fifths. 2 freshmen graduated first in their class.

Requirements: The SAT I or ACT is required. Ramapo requires applicants to be in the upper 50% of their class. A minimum GPA of 3.0 is required. Applicants must be graduates of accredited secondary schools or have earned a GED. The college requires 16 academic credits, including 4 in English, 3 in mathematics, 2 each in science and social studies, and the remaining 5 in academic electives. Students are encouraged to take 2 years of a foreign language. An essay is required, and an interview is recommended. AP and CLEP credits are accepted. Important factors in the admissions decision are advanced placement or honor courses, recommendations by school officials, and extracurricular activities record.

Procedure: Freshmen are admitted fall and spring. Entrance exams should be taken by January of the senior year. Applications should be filed by March 15 for fall entry and December 1 for spring entry, along with an application fee of $35. Notification is sent on a rolling basis. A waiting list is an active part of the admissions procedure, with about 4% of all applicants on the list.

Transfer: 426 transfer students enrolled in 1995–96. Applicants must present a minimum GPA of 2.0; however, students applying to the School of Business with at least 45 credits must submit a GPA of 2.5. There are special requirements for social work, nursing, and communications majors. Any applicant transferring fewer than 30 credits must provide a high school transcript. SAT I scores are recommended. Associate degree recipients are encouraged to apply. 45 credits of 128 must be completed at Ramapo.

Visiting: There are regularly scheduled orientations for prospective students, including orientation, advisement, and registration. There are guides for informal visits and visitors may sit in on classes. To schedule a visit, contact the Admissions Office.

Financial Aid: In 1995–96, 45% of all students received some form of financial aid. 59% of freshmen and 37% of continuing students received need-based aid. The average freshman award was $6845. Of that total, scholarships or need-based grants averaged $5876 ($9498 maximum); loans averaged $2809 ($9625 maximum); and work contracts averaged $1243 ($1400 maximum). 93% of undergraduate students work part-time. Average earnings from campus work for the school year are $1104. The average financial indebtedness of the 1994–95 graduate was $9981. Ramapo is a member of CSS. The FAFSA is required. The application deadline for fall entry is March 15.

International Students: There are currently 132 international students enrolled. They must take the TOEFL and achieve a minimum score of 500.

Computers: The college provides computer facilities for student use. The mainframe is a DEC 5500 running UNIX. In addition, 250 microcomputers are located in the residence halls and the computing laboratory. All students may access the system according to a posted schedule. There are no time limits and no fees.

Graduates: In 1994–95, 739 bachelor's degrees were awarded. The most popular majors among graduates were business administration (27%), communications (13%), and psychology (10%). Within an average freshman class, 20% graduate in 4 years, 36% in 5 years, and 40% in 6 years. 110 companies recruited on campus in 1994–95.

Admissions Contact: Nancy E. Jaeger, Director of Admissions. A campus is available.

RICHARD STOCKTON COLLEGE OF NEW JERSEY

Pomona, NJ 08240–9988

(609) 652-4261

Full-time: 2089 men, 2495 women	Faculty: 178; IIB, + +$
Part-time: 568 men, 720 women	Ph.D.s: 94%
Graduate: none	Student/Faculty: 26 to 1
Year: semesters, summer session	Tuition: $3152 ($3968)
Application Deadline: May 1	Room & Board: $4456
Freshman Class: 3592 applied, 1595 accepted, 763 enrolled	
SAT I Verbal/Math: 500/560	**VERY COMPETITIVE**

Richard Stockton College of New Jersey, founded in 1969, is a public, coeducational liberal arts, preprofessional, business, and teachers' college. In addition to regional accreditation, Stockton has baccalaureate program accreditation with APTA, CSWE, NASDTEC, NCATE, and NLN. The library contains 236,945 volumes, 316,563 microform items, and 9587 audiovisual forms, and subscribes to 1881 periodicals. Computerized library sources and services include the card catalog, interlibrary loans, and database searching. Special learning facilities include a learning resource center, art gallery, radio station, TV station, astronomical observatory, marine science field laboratory, and a marina with a fleet of small boats. The 1600-acre campus is in a suburban area 12 miles northwest of Atlantic City. Including residence halls, there are 51 buildings on campus.

Student Life: 97% of undergraduates are from New Jersey. Students come from 22 states, 29 foreign countries, and Canada. 70% are from public schools; 30% from private. 85% are white. The average age of freshmen is 18; all undergraduates, 22. 15% do not continue beyond their first year; 57% remain to graduate.

Housing: 1862 students can be accommodated in college housing. College-sponsored living facilities include single-sex and coed dormitories and on-campus apartments. In addition, there are honors houses and special interest houses. On-campus housing is guaranteed for the freshman year only and is available on a first-come, first-served basis. Priority is given to out-of-town students. 68% of students commute. All students may keep cars on campus.

Activities: 19% of men belong to 12 national fraternities; 5% of women belong to 9 national sororities. There are 82 groups on campus, including art, band, cheerleading, chess, choir, chorale, chorus, computers, dance, drama, ethnic, honors, international, jazz band, literary magazine, newspaper, orchestra, photography, political, professional, radio and TV, religious, social, social service, and student government. Popular campus events include Comedy Club, Kwanzaa, Spring Challenge, Alumni Picnic, and Family Day.

Sports: There are 7 intercollegiate sports for men and 7 for women, and 6 intramural sports for men and 6 for women. Athletic and recreation facilities include an indoor 6-lane swimming pool, a weightlifting gymnasium, a multipurpose gymnasium, a sauna, steam baths, and dance studios, as well as playing fields, a 60-acre lake for fishing and canoeing, cross-country courses, bike trails, an all-weather track, and tennis, racquetball, and basketball courts. There are 9 club sports in addition to intramurals.

Disabled Students: The entire campus is accessible to persons with physical disabilities. The following facilities are available: wheelchair ramps, elevators, special parking, specially equipped rest rooms, special class scheduling, lowered drinking fountains, and lowered telephones.

Services: In addition to many counseling and information services, tutoring is available in most subjects. There is also a reader service for the blind, remedial math, reading, and writing, a skills center, and a learning access program for learning disabled students.

Campus Safety and Security: Campus safety and security measures include 24-hour foot and vehicle patrol, self-defense education, escort service, and shuttle buses. In addition, there are informal discussions, pamphlets/posters/films, emergency telephones, and lighted pathways/sidewalks.

Programs of Study: Stockton confers B.A., B.S., and B.S.N. degrees. Master's degrees are also awarded. Bachelor's degrees are awarded in BIOLOGICAL SCIENCE (biology/biological science and marine science), BUSINESS (accounting, banking and finance, management science, and marketing/retailing/merchandising), COMMUNICATIONS AND THE ARTS (dance, design, dramatic arts, fine arts, and music), COMPUTER AND PHYSICAL SCIENCE (chemistry, computer programming, computer science, information sciences and systems, mathematics, and physics), ENGINEERING AND ENVIRONMENTAL DESIGN (environmental science and preengineering), HEALTH PROFESSIONS (nursing, physical therapy, public health, and speech pathology/audiology), SOCIAL SCIENCE (anthropology, criminal justice, economics, history, liberal arts/general studies, philosophy, political science/government, psychology, and social work). The sciences are the strongest academically. Business has the largest enrollment.

Required: To graduate, students must earn 128 credit hours, 32 in the general studies curriculum and at least 40 in the major, with a minumum GPA of 2.0. General studies includes 1 quantitative and 3 writing courses as well as freshman and senior seminars. Graduates must also satisfy writing and basic skills requirements.

Special: Stockton offers co-op programs in business, computers, and computer science, internships in all fields with a wide variety of companies, work-study with various government agencies and corporations, a Washington semester, independent study, and study abroad in 10 countries. Dual majors in all programs, student-designed majors, an accelerated degree in medicine, 3–2 engineering degrees with the New Jersey Institute of Technology and Rutgers University, and general studies degrees are offered. Nondegree study, pass/fail options, and credit for life, military, and work experience are possible. There is a freshman honors program on campus, as well as 5 national honor societies. One department has an honors program.

Faculty/Classroom: 65% of faculty are male; 35%, female. All teach undergraduates; 70% both teach and do research. The average class size in an introductory lecture is 35; in a laboratory, 12; and in a regular course offering, 26.

Admissions: 44% of the 1995–96 applicants were accepted. The SAT I scores for the 1995–96 freshman class were as follows: Verbal—55% below 500, 35% between 500 and 599, 9% between 600 and 700, and 1% above 700; Math—16% below 500, 51% between 500 and 599, 30% between 600 and 700, and 3% above 700. 55% of the current freshmen were in the top fifth of their class; 91% were in the top two fifths.

Requirements: The SAT I or ACT is required. Stockton requires applicants to be in the upper 50% of their class with a 2.5 GPA. Applicants must be high school graduates; the GED is accepted. Sixteen academic credits are required, including 4 years in English, 3 each in mathematics and social studies, 2 in science, and 4 additional years of any of the above or a foreign language, or both. An essay and an interview are recommended and a portfolio or audition is necessary where appropriate. AP and CLEP credits are accepted. Important factors in the admissions decision are advanced placement or honor courses, leadership record, and evidence of special talent.

Procedure: Freshmen are admitted fall and spring. Entrance exams should be taken once in the junior year, and again before January in the senior year. There is an early admissions plan. Early decision applications should be filed by January 15; regular applications, by May 1 for fall entry and December 1 for spring entry, along with an application fee of $25. Notification of early decision is sent January 31; regular decision, May 15. A waiting list is an active part of the admissions procedure, with about 15% of all applicants on the list.

Transfer: 658 transfer students enrolled in 1995–96. Transfer students must have earned at least 16 credits at other colleges and must submit college and high school transcripts as well as SAT I scores. 32 credits of 128 must be completed at Stockton.

Visiting: There are regularly scheduled orientations for prospective students. There are guides for informal visits and visitors may sit in on classes. To schedule a visit, contact Enrollment Management.

Financial Aid: In a recent year, 64% of all freshmen and 39% of continuing students received some form of financial aid. 42% of freshmen and 35% of continuing students received need-based aid. The average freshman award was $4658. Of that total, scholarships or need-based grants averaged $1159 ($5700 maximum); loans averaged $2455 ($3000 maximum); and work contracts averaged $1044 ($2400 maximum). 46% of undergraduate students work part-time. Average earnings from campus work for the school year are $985. The FAFSA is required. The application deadline for fall entry is March 1.

International Students: In a recent year, 123 international students were enrolled. The school actively recruits these students. They must take the TOEFL and achieve a minimum score of 525.

Computers: The college provides computer facilities for student use. The mainframes are a DEC VAX 8600 and 6300, and an IBM 3090. There are also 2 Alpha 2104/275 servers, 1 Alpha 2000/233 server, a DEC 5500 processor, and 26 UNIX workstations. Students may access a network called Co Sy for conferencing and linkage to the mainframe and Internet. There are also more than 560 microcomputers dispersed in 20 computer laboratories, 15 electronic classrooms, the library, faculty offices, and academic support facilities. All students may access the system between 8 A.M. and midnight. There are no time limits and no fees.

Graduates: In a recent year, 1089 bachelor's degrees were awarded. The most popular majors among graduates were business and management (35%), social sciences (26%), and health professions (8%). Within an average freshman class, 49% graduate in 4 years, 52% in 5 years, and 56% in 6 years. 156 companies recruited on campus.

Admissions Contact: Sal Catalfamo, Dean of Enrollment Management.

RIDER COLLEGE
(See Rider University)

RIDER UNIVERSITY
D-3

(Formerly Rider College)
Lawrenceville, NJ 08648-3099
(609) 896-5042
(800) 257-9026; FAX: (609) 895-6645

Full-time: 1090 men, 1441 women	Faculty: 174; IIA, +$
Part-time: 428 men, 711 women	Ph.D.s: 92%
Graduate: 460 men, 811 women	Student/Faculty: 15 to 1
Year: semesters, summer session	Tuition: $14,065
Application Deadline: open	Room & Board: $5630
Freshman Class: 3011 applied, 2594 accepted, 552 enrolled	
SAT I Verbal/Math: 435/499	COMPETITIVE

Rider University, founded in 1865, is a private coeducational institution offering undergraduate programs through its colleges of business, education and human services, liberal arts and science, and continuing studies. Westminster Choir College, located in nearby Princeton, is Rider's fifth college. There are 5 undergraduate and 2 graduate schools. In addition to regional accreditation, Rider has baccalaureate program accreditation with AACSB and NCATE. The library contains 350,000 volumes and 450,000 microform items, and subscribes to 2000 periodicals. Computerized library sources and services include the card catalog, interlibrary loans, and database searching. Special learning facilities include a learning resource center, art gallery, radio station, TV station, journalism and sociology laboratories, and holocaust/genocide center. The 340-acre campus is in a suburban area 3 miles north of Trenton. Including residence halls, there are 37 buildings on campus.

Student Life: 77% of undergraduates are from New Jersey. Students come from 23 states, 19 foreign countries, and Canada. 75% are white. 42% are Catholic; 16% Protestant. The average age of freshmen is 18; all undergraduates, 21. 18% do not continue beyond their first year; 60% remain to graduate.

Housing: 2264 students can be accommodated in college housing. College-sponsored living facilities include single-sex and coed dormitories, on-campus apartments, fraternity houses, and sorority houses. In addition, there are special interest houses. On-campus housing is guaranteed for all 4 years and is available on a lottery system for upperclassmen. 70% of students live on campus; of those, 65% remain on campus on weekends. All students may keep cars on campus.

Activities: 16% of men belong to 4 national fraternities; 12% of women belong to 1 local and 6 national sororities. There are 80 groups on campus, including art, band, cheerleading, choir, chorus, computers, drama, ethnic, film, gay, honors, international, jazz band, literary magazine, musical theater, newspaper, orchestra, pep band, photography, political, professional, radio and TV, religious, social, social service, student government, and yearbook. Popular campus events include Cranberry Day, Cranberry and White Night, movie nights, Homecoming, Spring Fling, and Parents Day.

Sports: There are 9 intercollegiate sports for men and 9 for women, and 12 intramural sports for men and 12 for women. Athletic and recreation facilities include a gymnasium, a swimming pool, a fitness center and spa, lighted outdoor multipurpose courts, outdoor varsity and intramural fields, and an outdoor track.

Disabled Students: 30% of the campus is accessible to disabled students. The following facilities are available: wheelchair ramps, elevators, special parking, specially equipped rest rooms, special class scheduling, lowered drinking fountains, and lowered telephones.

Services: In addition to many counseling and information services, tutoring is available in most subjects. There is remedial math, reading, and writing.

Campus Safety and Security: Campus safety and security measures include 24-hour foot and vehicle patrol, self-defense education, escort service, and informal discussions. In addition, there are pamphlets/posters/films, emergency telephones, lighted pathways/sidewalks, shuttle car, staffed kiosk at entrance, and security system in residence halls.

Programs of Study: Rider confers B.A., B.S., and B.S.B.A. degrees. Associate and master's degrees are also awarded. Bachelor's degrees are awarded in BIOLOGICAL SCIENCE (biochemistry, biology/biological science, and marine science), BUSINESS (accounting, banking and finance, business administration and management, business economics, marketing/retailing/merchandising, organizational behavior, and personnel management), COMMUNICATIONS AND THE ARTS (advertising, communications, English, fine arts, French, German, journalism, Russian, Spanish, and speech/debate/rhetoric), COMPUTER AND PHYSICAL SCIENCE (actuarial science, chemistry, computer management, geology, mathematics, and physics), EDUCATION (business, early childhood, elementary, foreign languages, marketing and distribution, science, secondary, social studies, and teaching English as a second/foreign language, HEALTH PROFESSIONS (predentistry and premedicine), SOCIAL SCIENCE (American studies, economics, history, philosophy, political science/government, prelaw, psychology, and sociology). Business, actuarial science, and education are the strongest academically. Accounting, finance, and elementary education have the largest enrollments.

Required: To graduate, all students must maintain a minimum GPA of 2.0 while taking 120 semester hours. Students also must fulfill core curriculum requirements, including 9 hours in humanities, 7 to 8 in science, 6 each in English writing and foreign language (may be waived if proficiency is demonstrated), social sciences/communications, and history, and 3 in mathematics.

Special: Internships in many programs, a co-op program in marketing, work-study, study abroad in 6 countries, a B.A.-B.S. degree in all liberal arts and sciences, dual majors in education, liberal studies degree, and nondegree study are possible. There is a freshman honors program on campus, as well as 28 national honor societies. 19 departments have honors programs.

Faculty/Classroom: 51% of faculty are male; 49%, female. All teach undergraduates. No introductory courses are taught by graduate students. The average class size in an introductory lecture is 35; in a laboratory, 20; and in a regular course offering, 25.

Admissions: 86% of the 1995-96 applicants were accepted. The SAT I scores for the 1995-96 freshman class were as follows: Verbal—86% below 500, 11% between 500 and 599, 2% between 600 and 700, and 1% above 700; Math—54% below 500, 31% between 500 and 599, 12% between 600 and 700, and 3% above 700. 20% of the current freshmen were in the top fifth of their class; 40% were in the top two fifths. 2 freshmen graduated first in their class.

Requirements: The SAT I or ACT is required. Rider requires applicants to be in the upper 50% of their class. A minimum GPA of 2.5 is required. Applicants need 16 Carnegie units, including 4 years of English. 3 units of mathematics are required for prospective mathematics, science, and business majors. An essay and interview are recommended. An audition is required for theater scholarships. The GED is accepted. AP and CLEP credits are accepted. Important factors in the admissions decision are advanced placement or honor courses, extracurricular activities record, and leadership record.

Procedure: Freshmen are admitted fall and spring. Entrance exams should be taken by January of the senior year. There is a deferred admissions plan. Application deadlines are open. Application fee is $35. Notification is sent on a rolling basis.

Transfer: 199 transfer students enrolled in 1995-96. A minimum GPA of 2.5 or better is required for applicants. If students have fewer than 30 credits, they also must submit high school transcripts and SAT I scores. An interview is recommended. 30 credits of 120 must be completed at Rider.

Visiting: There are regularly scheduled orientations for prospective students, including 3 fall open houses with programs that consist of a welcome, a campus tour, and a variety of formal and informal activities to meet faculty, staff, current students, and alumni. There are guides for informal visits and visitors may sit in on classes. To schedule a visit, contact the Admissions Office.

Financial Aid: In 1995-96, 83% of all freshmen and 63% of continuing students received some form of financial aid. 77% of freshmen and 69% of continuing students received need-based aid. The average freshman award was $12,673. Of that total, scholarships or need-based grants averaged $7148 ($13,800 maximum); loans averaged $2432 ($2625 maximum); and work contracts averaged $997 ($1500 maximum). 35% of undergraduate students work part-time. Average earnings from campus work for the school year are $1000. Rider is a member of CSS. The FAFSA is required. The application deadline for fall entry is March 1.

International Students: There are currently 53 international students enrolled. The school actively recruits these students. They must take the TOEFL and achieve a minimum score of 550. The student must also take the SAT I or the ACT.

Computers: The college provides computer facilities for student use. The mainframes are 2 DEC VAX 4000s and a MicroVAX 3400. The microcomputer laboratories have 62 IBM PCs available for general use and more than 200 microcomputers in departmental laboratories, many of which are networked. Workstations are available in each laboratory. In addition, students have assigned voice mail and E-mail accounts. The campus has a comprehensive light guide voice, data, and video network linking residence halls, classrooms, and faculty/administrative offices. All students may access the system during regular laboratory hours and at any time in residence halls. There are no time limits.

Graduates: In 1994–95, 678 bachelor's degrees were awarded. The most popular majors among graduates were accounting (15%), elementary education (10%), and marketing (9%). Within an average freshman class, 48% graduate in 4 years, 13% in 5 years, and 2% in 6 years. 128 companies recruited on campus in 1994–95. Of the 1994 graduating class, 13% were enrolled in graduate school within 6 months of graduation.

Admissions Contact: Susan C. Christian, Director of Admissions. E-mail: admissions@rider.edu. A campus video is available.

ROWAN COLLEGE OF NEW JERSEY
Glassboro, NJ 08028

C-4

(609) 256-4200
(800) 447-1165; FAX: (609) 256-4430

Full-time: 2329 men, 2933 women	**Faculty:** 323
Part-time: 864 men, 1416 women	**Ph.D.s:** 80%
Graduate: 404 men, 1084 women	**Student/Faculty:** 16 to 1
Year: semesters, summer session	**Tuition:** $3393 ($5883)
Application Deadline: March 15	**Room & Board:** $4735
Freshman Class: 4785 applied, 2106 accepted, 931 enrolled	
SAT I Verbal/Math: 491/545	**COMPETITIVE +**

Rowan College, founded in 1923, is a public coeducational institution offering undergraduate programs in the arts and sciences, business administration, education, fine and performing arts, and engineering. There are 4 undergraduate schools and 1 graduate school. In addition to regional accreditation, the college has baccalaureate program accreditation with NASM and NCATE. The library contains 350,800 volumes, 77,000 microform items, and 43,500 audiovisual forms, and subscribes to 1725 periodicals. Computerized library sources and services include database searching. Special learning facilities include an art gallery, planetarium, and radio station. The 200-acre campus is in a small town 20 miles southeast of Philadelphia. Including residence halls, there are 40 buildings on campus.

Student Life: 98% of undergraduates are from New Jersey. Students come from 11 states, 13 foreign countries, and Canada. 65% are from public schools; 35% from private. 82% are white; 10% African American. The average age of freshmen is 19.6; all undergraduates, 24.8. 11% do not continue beyond their first year; 55% remain to graduate.

Housing: 2224 students can be accommodated in college housing. College-sponsored living facilities include single-sex and coed dormitories, on-campus apartments, off-campus apartments, and married-student housing. In addition, there are honors houses. On-campus housing is available on a lottery system for upperclassmen. Priority is given to out-of-town students. Alcohol is not permitted. Upperclassmen may keep cars on campus.

Activities: 9% of men belong to 1 local and 11 national fraternities; 9% of women belong to 5 local and 8 national sororities. There are 150 groups on campus, including art, band, cheerleading, chess, choir, chorale, chorus, computers, dance, drama, ethnic, film, honors, international, jazz band, literary magazine, marching band, musical theater, newspaper, opera, orchestra, political, professional, radio and TV, religious, social, social service, student government, symphony, and yearbook.

Sports: There are 7 intercollegiate sports for men and 9 for women, and 7 intramural sports for men and 6 for women. Athletic and recreation facilities include a 3000-seat stadium, an 1800-seat gymnasium, a 1000-seat auditorium, a swimming pool, tennis courts, and playing fields.

Disabled Students: 95% of the campus is accessible to disabled students. The following facilities are available: wheelchair ramps, elevators, special parking, specially equipped rest rooms, special class scheduling, lowered drinking fountains, and lowered telephones.

Services: In addition to many counseling and information services, tutoring is available in some subjects. There is remedial math, reading, and writing.

Campus Safety and Security: Campus safety and security measures include 24-hour foot and vehicle patrol, escort service, informal discussions, and pamphlets/posters/films. In addition, there are emergency telephones and lighted pathways/sidewalks.

Programs of Study: Rowan College of New Jersey confers B.A., B.S., B.F.A., B.M. degrees. Master's degrees are also awarded. Bachelor's degrees are awarded in BIOLOGICAL SCIENCE (biology/biological science), BUSINESS (accounting, business administration and management, marketing/retailing/merchandising, personnel management, and small business management), COMMUNICATIONS AND THE ARTS (broadcasting, communications, dramatic arts, English, fine arts, journalism, music, Spanish, and speech/debate/rhetoric), COMPUTER AND PHYSICAL SCIENCE (chemistry

and physics), EDUCATION (early childhood, elementary, foreign languages, music, and science), ENGINEERING AND ENVIRONMENTAL DESIGN (engineering), SOCIAL SCIENCE (criminal justice, economics, history, liberal arts/general studies, political science/government, psychology, and sociology). Communications, business administration, and elementary education are the strongest academically and have the largest enrollments.

Required: General education requirements include 12 to 18 semester hours of social and behavioral sciences, 12 to 16 of science and mathematics, 6 to 9 of communications, 6 of fine and performing arts, and 3 to 6 of history/humanities/language/arts. Students must also complete 6 semester hours of writing and 3 of physical education. The bachelor's degree requires completion of at least 120 semester hours, including 30 to 39 in a major, with a minimum GPA of 2.0.

Special: Students may study abroad in 8 countries. Internships are available both with and without pay. The college also offers accelerated degree programs and 3–2 degrees in engineering, optometry, podiatry, and pharmacy. There are also dual majors, pass/fail options and credit for military experience. There is a freshman honors program on campus, as well as a chapter of Phi Beta Kappa.

Faculty/Classroom: 71% of faculty are male; 29%, female. All teach undergraduates. No introductory courses are taught by graduate students. The average class size in an introductory lecture is 25; in a laboratory, 20; and in a regular course offering, 25.

Admissions: 44% of the 1995–96 applicants were accepted. The SAT I scores for the 1995–96 freshman class were as follows: Verbal—68% below 500, 26% between 500 and 599, 5% between 600 and 700, and 1% above 700; Math—43% below 500, 39% between 500 and 599, 17% between 600 and 700, and 1% above 700. 30% of the current freshmen were in the top fifth of their class; 66% were in the top two fifths. There was 1 National Merit finalist and 27 semifinalists. 29 freshmen graduated first in their class.

Requirements: The SAT I is required, with a recommended minimum composite score of 950, or no less than 450 on either part. Students submitting ACT scores should have a minimum composite score of 19. A minimum GPA of 3.0 is required. Applicants must be graduates of accredited secondary schools or have earned a GED. The college requires 16 academic credits or Carnegie units, including 4 in English, 3 in mathematics, 2 in foreign language, history, and a laboratory science, and 3 in college preparatory electives. An essay is required of all students, and a portfolio or audition is required for specific majors. AP and CLEP credits are accepted. Important factors in the admissions decision are advanced placement or honor courses, evidence of special talent, and leadership record.

Procedure: Freshmen are admitted fall and spring. Entrance exams should be taken in November or December of the senior year. There is a deferred admissions plan. Applications should be filed by March 15 for fall entry and November 15 for spring entry, along with an application fee of $30. Notification is sent on a rolling basis. A waiting list is an active part of the admissions procedure, with about 5% of all applicants on the list.

Transfer: 1267 transfer students enrolled in 1995–96. Applicants must present a minimum GPA of 2.0, but should present a GPA of 2.5 to be competitive. An associate degree is recommended. Students who have earned less than 24 semester hours must also submit a high school transcript and SAT I results. 30 credits of 120 must be completed at Rowan College of New Jersey.

Visiting: There are regularly scheduled orientations for prospective students, consisting of a 2-day summer program providing schedule confirmation/adjustment, student activities updates, and workshops for students and parents. There are guides for informal visits and visitors may sit in on classes. To schedule a visit, contact the Admissions Office.

Financial Aid: In 1995–96, 55% of all freshmen and 50% of continuing students received some form of financial aid, including need-based aid. The average freshman award was $4600. Of that total, scholarships or need-based grants averaged $3190 ($2000 maximum); loans averaged $2185 ($2500 maximum); other grants averaged $900 ($1900 maximum); and work contracts averaged $900 ($1500 maximum). 10% of undergraduate students work part-time. Average earnings from campus work for the school year are $1200. The average financial indebtedness of the 1994–95 graduate was $6000. The college is a member of CSS. The FAF, the college's own financial statement, and financial aid transcripts are required. The application deadline for fall entry is April 1.

International Students: There are currently 69 international students enrolled. They must take the TOEFL or the MELAB and achieve a minimum score on the TOEFL of 550. Applicants from English-speaking countries must also submit an SAT I score.

Computers: The college provides computer facilities for student use. The mainframes are 2 DEC VAX 8650, series 6000–410 models. Microcomputers are available in academic laboratories. Students enrolled in computer science courses and seniors working on research projects may access the mainframe from 8:30 A.M. to 4:30 P.M. There are no fees.

Graduates: In 1994–95, 1639 bachelor's degrees were awarded. The most popular majors among graduates were business administration (17%), communications (14%), and elementary education (10%). Within an average freshman class, 20% graduate in 4 years, 46% in 5 years, and 55% in 6 years. 110 companies recruited on campus in 1994–95.

Admissions Contact: Marvin G. Sills, Director of Admissions. E-mail: admissions@rowan.edu.

RUTGERS, THE STATE UNIVERSITY OF NEW JERSEY

Rutgers, the State University of New Jersey, established in 1766, is a public system governed by a board of governors. Its chief administrator is the president. The primary goal of the system is instruction, research, and service. The main priorities are to continue development as a distinguished comprehensive public university, to enhance undergraduate education, to strengthen graduate educaction and research, and to develop and improve programs to better serve New Jersey's and society's needs. Four-year campuses are located in New Brunswick, Newark, and Camden. There are more than 100 baccalaureate, 100 master's, and 80 doctoral programs offered through the Rutgers system.

RUTGERS, THE STATE UNIVERSITY OF NEW JERSEY/CAMDEN COLLEGE OF ARTS AND SCIENCES   C-4

Camden, NJ 08102	(609) 225-6104
Full-time: 798 men, 1128 women	Faculty: 133; IIA, ++$
Part-time: 182 men, 253 women	Ph.D.s: 98%
Graduate: none	Student/Faculty: 14 to 1
Year: semesters, summer session	Tuition: $4681 ($8602)
Application Deadline: May 1	Room & Board: $4936
Freshman Class: 3053 applied, 1798 accepted, 250 enrolled	
SAT I Verbal/Math: 483/547	VERY COMPETITIVE

Rutgers University, The State University of New Jersey/Camden College of Arts and Sciences, established in 1927, is a coeducational liberal arts institution. In addition to regional accreditation, Camden College of Arts and Sciences has baccalaureate program accreditation with CSWE, NASDTEC, and NLN. The 2 libraries contain 377,416 volumes, 227,463 microform items, and 190 audiovisual forms, and subscribe to 2039 periodicals. Computerized library sources and services include the card catalog, interlibrary loans, and database searching. Special learning facilities include a learning resource center, art gallery, and radio station. The 25-acre campus is in an urban area 1 mile from Philadelphia, Pennsylvania. Including residence halls, there are 22 buildings on campus.

Student Life: 97% of undergraduates are from New Jersey. Students come from 14 states and 4 foreign countries. 67% are white; 14% African American. The average age of freshmen is 18.5; all undergraduates, 24. 23% do not continue beyond their first year; 53% remain to graduate.

Housing: College-sponsored living facilities include coed dormitories and on-campus apartments. In addition there are special interest houses and substance-free housing. On-campus housing is available on a first-come, first-served basis and is available on a lottery system for upperclassmen. Alcohol is not permitted. All students may keep cars on campus.

Activities: 3% of men belong to 1 local and 5 national fraternities; 3% of women belong to 4 local and 5 national sororities. There are 70 groups on campus, including cheerleading, choir, computers, drama, ethnic, gay, honors, international, literary magazine, newspaper, orchestra, political, professional, radio and TV, religious, social, social service, student government, theater, and yearbook. Popular campus events include Pioneer Pride Night, Springfest, Fallfest, and Diversity Week.

Sports: There are 9 intercollegiate sports for men and 5 for women, and 8 intramural sports for men and 6 for women. Athletic and recreation facilities include a 2000-seat gymnasium; a swimming pool; soccer, baseball, and softball fields; basketball, handball, racquetball, and squash courts; a weight room; and tennis courts.

Disabled Students: 95% of the campus is accessible to disabled students. The following facilities are available: wheelchair ramps, elevators, special parking, specially equipped rest rooms, special class scheduling, lowered drinking fountains, and lowered telephones. Facilities vary from building to building. However, all classes are scheduled in accessible locations for disabled students, and adaptations are made to individual needs in dormitory rooms.

Services: In addition to many counseling and information services, tutoring is available in some subjects, including introductory-level courses. There is a reader service for the blind, and remedial math, reading, and writing.

Campus Safety and Security: Campus safety and security measures include 24-hour foot and vehicle patrol, self-defense education, escort service, and shuttle buses. In addition, there are informal discussions, pamphlets/posters/films, emergency telephones, and lighted pathways/sidewalks. The police department and security guards offer additional security.

Programs of Study: Camden College of Arts and Sciences confers B.A. and B.S. degrees. Bachelor's degrees are awarded in BIOLOGICAL SCIENCE (biochemistry and biology/biological science), BUSINESS (accounting, banking and finance, management science, and marketing/retailing/merchandising), COMMUNICATIONS AND THE ARTS (art, art history and appreciation, dramatic arts, English, fine arts, French, German, music, and Spanish), COMPUTER AND PHYSICAL SCIENCE (chemistry, computer science, mathematics, physics, and science), EDUCATION (elementary and secondary), ENGINEERING AND ENVIRONMENTAL DESIGN (ceramic engineering, chemical engineering, civil engineering, electrical/electronics engineering, engineering and applied science, environmental engineering, industrial engineering, and mechanical engineering), HEALTH PROFESSIONS (medical laboratory technology, nursing, predentistry, and premedicine), SOCIAL SCIENCE (African American studies, economics, history, philosophy, political science/government, prelaw, psychology, social work, sociology, and urban studies). Psychology, business, and English have the largest enrollments.

Required: For graduation, students must complete a total of 120 credits, with 30 to 48 credits in the major and a minimum GPA of 2.0. General curriculum requirements include 9 credits in social science, 6 credits each in English composition and history, philosophy, or religion; 6 credits in the natural science disciplines; 3 credits in mathematics and 3 additional credits in mathematics, computer science, or statistics; 3 credits in one interdisciplinary course; 9 additional credits in courses offered outside the major department; 3 credits each in literary masterpieces and a foreign language, and an additional 3 credits in English or a foreign language; and 3 credits in art, music, or theater arts.

Special: The college offers study abroad in 8 countries, some B.A.-B.S. degrees, and student-designed majors. Pass/fail options are available for two courses during matriculation. Students may take 2–2 and 2–3 (dual majors) programs with the College of Engineering, a 1–3 program with Cook College (agriculture), and a 2–3 program with the College of Pharmacy. There is a freshman honors program on campus, as well as 11 national honor societies. Almost all departments have honors programs.

Faculty/Classroom: 65% of faculty are male; 35%, female. All both teach and do research. The average class size in an introductory lecture is 37; in a laboratory, 24; and in a regular course offering, 31.

Admissions: 59% of the 1995–96 applicants were accepted. The SAT I scores for the 1995–96 freshman class were as follows: Verbal—58% below 500, 29% between 500 and 599, 11% between 600 and 700, and 2% above 700; Math—29% below 500, 42% between 500 and 599, 23% between 600 and 700, and 6% above 700. 51% of the current freshmen were in the top fifth of their class; 88% were in the top two fifths. 3 freshmen graduated first in their class.

Requirements: The SAT I or ACT is required. Applicants must be graduates of an accredited secondary school. The GED is also accepted. Students must have completed 16 academic credits or Carnegie units, including 4 years of English, 3 years of mathematics (algebra I and II and geometry), 2 years each of a foreign language and science, and 5 other approved academic subjects. AP and CLEP credits are accepted. Important factors in the admissions decision are advanced placement or honor courses, evidence of special talent, and leadership record.

Procedure: Freshmen are admitted fall and spring. Entrance exams should be taken early in the junior year. There are early admissions and deferred admissions plans. Applications should be filed by May 1 for fall entry and November 15 for spring entry, along with an application fee of $50. Notification is sent on a rolling basis.

Transfer: 387 transfer students enrolled in 1995–96. Applicants must have completed a minimum of 12 college credits with a GPA of 2.5 or better. Grades of C or better in courses that correspond in content and credit to those offered by the college transfer for credit. 30 credits of 120 must be completed at Camden College of Arts and Sciences.

Visiting: There are regularly scheduled orientations for prospective students, including an information session with an admissions officer and a tour of the campus. Visitors may sit in on classes. To schedule a visit, contact the Office of University Undergraduate Admissions (Camden).

Financial Aid: In 1995–96, 77% of all freshmen and 59% of continuing students received some form of financial aid. 66% of freshmen and 52% of continuing students received need-based aid. The average freshman award was $5398. Of that total, scholarships or need-based grants averaged $4495 ($9502 maximum); loans averaged $2364 ($3000 maximum); outside scholarships averaged $1109

($2600 maximum); and work contracts averaged $1231 ($1500 maximum). 6% of undergraduate students work part-time. Average earnings from campus work for the school year are $809. The average financial indebtedness of the 1994–95 graduate was $6646. The FAFSA is required. The application deadline for fall entry is March 1.

International Students: There were 26 international students enrolled in a recent year. They must take the TOEFL and achieve a minimum score of 550. The student must also take the SAT I or the ACT.

Computers: The college provides computer facilities for student use. The mainframes are a Sun SPARC Server 10/41 and a 10/51 MP. Terminals or networked microcomputers are located in two major academic buildings, the library, the Campus Center, and dorms, and provide access to the central systems as well as to the local Camden campus computers. The on-campus computer network services include on-line registration, E-mail, and access to the Internet and Bitnet. All students may access the system Monday through Thursday, 8:30 A.M. to 11 P.M.; Friday and Saturday, 9 A.M. to 5 P.M.; Sunday 2 P.M. to 10 P.M. (24 hours/day 7 days/week through modem access). There are no time limits. The fees are $100 per year.

Graduates: In 1994–95, 504 bachelor's degrees were awarded. The most popular majors among graduates were psychology (16%), English (12%), and sociology (9%). Within an average freshman class, 21% graduate in 4 years, 47% in 5 years, and 53% in 6 years. 90 companies recruited on campus in 1994–95. Of the 1994 graduating class, 18% were enrolled in graduate school within 6 months of graduation and 71% had found employment.

Admissions Contact: Dr. Deborah Bowles, Director of Admissions-Camden.

RUTGERS, THE STATE UNIVERSITY OF NEW JERSEY/COLLEGE OF ENGINEERING   D-3

New Brunswick, NJ 08903   (908) 445-3770

Full-time: 1807 men, 395 women	Faculty: 127; I, + +$
Part-time: 62 men, 14 women	Ph.D.s: 98%
Graduate: none	Student/Faculty: 17 to 1
Year: semesters, summer session	Tuition: $5244 ($9592)
Application Deadline: January 15	Room & Board: $4936
Freshman Class: 3005 applied, 2281 accepted, 542 enrolled	
SAT I Verbal/Math: 508/657	**HIGHLY COMPETITIVE**

Rutgers, The State University of New Jersey/College of Engineering, founded in 1864, offers bachelor of science programs in engineering. In addition to regional accreditation, College of Engineering has baccalaureate program accreditation with ABET. The 14 libraries contain 4,480,097 volumes, 2,839,735 microform items, and 76,968 audiovisual forms, and subscribe to 18,274 periodicals. Computerized library sources and services include the card catalog, interlibrary loans, and database searching. Special learning facilities include a learning resource center, art gallery, radio station, TV station, and fiber optics drawing towers, a center for ceramics research that has ongoing projects for the Space Shuttle, research laboratories for artificial intelligence and virtual reality, the Nabisco Center for Advanced Food Technology for chemical and mechanical engineering research, and automated manufacturing laboratories for robotics. The 2694-acre campus is in a suburban area 33 miles south of New York City. Including residence halls, there are 7 buildings on campus.

Student Life: 86% of undergraduates are from New Jersey. Students come from 22 states, 37 foreign countries, and Canada. 55% are white; 23% Asian American. The average age of freshmen is 18.2; all undergraduates, 21. 13% do not continue beyond their first year; 70% remain to graduate.

Housing: College-sponsored living facilities include single-sex and coed dormitories and on-campus apartments. In addition there are language houses, special interest houses, a special dorm for women interested in math and sciences, and substance-free housing. Housing is guaranteed for the first 2 years. On-campus housing is available on a lottery system for upperclassmen. 64% of students live on campus. Alcohol is not permitted.

Activities: 11% of men belong to 31 national fraternities; 7% of women belong to 4 local and 11 national sororities. There are 400 groups on campus, including art, band, cheerleading, chess, choir, chorale, chorus, computers, dance, drama, drill team, ethnic, film, gay, honors, international, jazz band, literary magazine, marching band, musical theater, newspaper, orchestra, pep band, photography, political, professional, radio and TV, religious, social, social service, student government, symphony, and yearbook. Popular campus events include Open House, Springfest, Semi-Formal, Freshman Picnic, and Career Fair.

Sports: There are 15 intercollegiate sports for men and 15 for women, and 28 intramural sports for men and 28 for women. Athletic and recreation facilities include a 41000-seat stadium, an athletic center, a gymnasium, a swimming pool, tennis courts, beach volleyball courts, and a recreation center.

Disabled Students: 51% of the campus is accessible to disabled students. The following facilities are available: wheelchair ramps, elevators, special parking, specially equipped rest rooms, special class scheduling, lowered drinking fountains, and lowered telephones. Facilities available vary widely from building to building. However, all classes are scheduled in accessible locations for students with disabilities.

Services: In addition to many counseling and information services, tutoring is available in most subjects. The academic tutoring service provides specific course assistance in first- and second-level difficult courses. There is a reader service for the blind, and remedial math, reading, and writing.

Campus Safety and Security: Campus safety and security measures include 24-hour foot and vehicle patrol, self-defense education, escort service, and shuttle buses. In addition, there are informal discussions, pamphlets/posters/films, emergency telephones, and lighted pathways/sidewalks. The police department is supplemented by security guards and student safety offices.

Programs of Study: College of Engineering confers the B.S. degree. Bachelor's degrees are awarded in ENGINEERING AND ENVIRONMENTAL DESIGN (bioengineering, ceramic engineering, chemical engineering, civil engineering, electrical/electronics engineering, engineering and applied science, industrial engineering, and mechanical engineering). Electrical engineering, mechanical engineering, and chemical engineering have the largest enrollments.

Required: In order to graduate, 131 credits are required with a minimum GPA of 2.0. The core curriculum includes 12 credits of calculus for engineering; 12 credits each of analytical physics and humanities/social sciences; 6 credits of general chemistry for engineers; 3 credits each of expository writing, introduction to computers for engineers, engineering mechanics/statics, and 1 credit each of introduction to experimentation and engineering orientation lectures.

Special: The college offers study abroad in England, 2–3 dual degree programs in conjunction with other undergraduate colleges of Rutgers, and B.A.-B.S. degrees in all engineering majors and all B.A. majors offered on the New Brunswick campus. Pass/fail options are limited to 2 elective courses. Internships are offered through the engineering departments and Career Services. An extended business degree is offered wih the Graduate School of Management, and an 8-year medical degree is available with the University of Medicine and Dentistry of New Jersey. There is a freshman honors program on campus, as well as 7 national honor societies. 7 departments have honors programs.

Faculty/Classroom: 94% of faculty are male; 6%, female. All both teach and do research. The average class size in an introductory lecture is 81; in a laboratory, 24; and in a regular course offering, 67.

Admissions: 76% of the 1995–96 applicants were accepted. The SAT I scores for the 1995–96 freshman class were as follows: Verbal—46% below 500, 41% between 500 and 599, and 13% between 600 and 700; Math—16% between 500 and 599, 57% between 600 and 700, and 27% above 700. 63% of the current freshmen were in the top fifth of their class; 95% were in the top two fifths. There were 3 National Merit finalists. 14 freshmen graduated first in their class.

Requirements: The SAT I or ACT is required. Applicants usually must be graduates of an accredited secondary school, but the GED is accepted. Students must have completed 16 academic credits or Carnegie units, including 4 years each of English and mathematics (through precalculus), 1 year each of chemistry and physics, plus 6 other approved academic subjects. Computer programming is recommended. Students without a high school diploma, those from nonaccredited high schools, and those with academic unit entrance deficiencies must take SAT II: Subject tests in writing, mathematics, and a science. AP credits are accepted. Important factors in the admissions decision are advanced placement or honor courses, evidence of special talent, and leadership record.

Procedure: Freshmen are admitted in the fall. Entrance exams should be taken by December of the senior year. There are early admissions and deferred admissions plans. Applications should be filed by January 15 for fall entry, along with an application fee of $50. Notification is sent by April 15. A waiting list is an active part of the admissions procedure, with about 5% of all applicants on the list.

Transfer: 106 transfer students enrolled in 1995–96. Students with a minimum of 12 college credits are considered for transfer. Grades of C or better in courses that correspond in content and credit to ones offered at the college transfer for credit. Transfer students are admitted in both the fall and spring semesters. 30 credits of 131 must be completed at College of Engineering.

Visiting: There are regularly scheduled orientations for prospective students, including an information session with an admissions officer followed by a bus tour with a student guide. Student-guided walking tours are also available, which include a meeting with the dean. Visitors may sit in on classes with prior arrangement. To schedule a visit, contact the Office of University Undergraduate Admissions.

Financial Aid: In 1995–96, 73% of all freshmen and 68% of continuing students received some form of financial aid. 53% of freshmen and 45% of continuing students received need-based aid. The average freshman award was $6506. Of that total, scholarships or need-based grants averaged $4061 ($9000 maximum); loans averaged $2334 ($6000 maximum); outside scholarships averaged $1573 ($6300 maximum); and work contracts averaged $1211 ($1500 maximum). 6% of undergraduate students work part-time. Average earnings from campus work for the school year are $818. The average financial indebtedness of the 1994–95 graduate was $7691. The FAFSA is required. The application deadline for fall entry is March 1.

International Students: There are currently 124 international students enrolled. They must take the TOEFL and achieve a minimum score of 550. The student must also take the SAT I or the ACT.

Computers: The college provides computer facilities for student use. Central computer systems include a cluster of 2 DEC VAX 8650 systems, 3 Sun SPARC Server 1000s, and 1 Sun SPARC 2000 UNIX system. Individual departments have a variety of minicomputers. The central systems may be accessed from Windows/DOS and Apple Macintosh personal computers, and X-terminals located in several large public laboratories. Services available include E-mail, newsgroups, software applications, a campuswide information system, and access to the Internet. All students may access the system 24 hours a day. There are no time limits. The fees are $100 per year.

Graduates: In 1994–95, 408 bachelor's degrees were awarded. The most popular majors among graduates were mechanical engineering (27%), electrical engineering (24%), and civil and environmental engineering (13%). Within an average freshman class, 35% graduate in 4 years, 65% in 5 years, and 70% in 6 years. 500 companies recruited on campus in 1994–95.

Admissions Contact: Dr. Elizabeth Mitchell, Assistant Vice President for University Undergraduate Admissions.

RUTGERS, THE STATE UNIVERSITY OF NEW JERSEY/COLLEGE OF NURSING E-2

Newark, NJ 07102 (201) 648-5205

Full-time: 33 men, 306 women	Faculty: 38; IIA, + +$
Part-time: 7 men, 25 women	Ph.Ds: 95%
Graduate: none	Student/Faculty: 9 to 1
Year: semesters, summer session	Tuition: $4627 ($8548)
Application Deadline: January 15	Room & Board: $4936
Freshman Class: 631 applied, 177 accepted, 48 enrolled	
SAT I Verbal/Math: 490/540	SPECIAL

Rutgers, The State University of New Jersey/College of Nursing, founded in 1952, is a four-year coeducational institution. In addition to regional accreditation, the College of Nursing has baccalaureate program accreditation with NLN. The 4 libraries contain 624,875 volumes, 733,742 microform items, and 27,123 audiovisual forms, and subscribe to 3680 periodicals. Computerized library sources and services include the card catalog, interlibrary loans, and database searching. Special learning facilities include a learning resource center, art gallery, radio station, and center for molecular and behavioral neuroscience. The 34-acre campus is in an urban area 7 miles west of New York City, in downtown Newark. Including residence halls, there are 18 buildings on campus.

Student Life: 97% of undergraduates are from New Jersey. Students come from 5 states and 4 foreign countries. 45% are white; 21% Asian American; 17% African American; 12% Hispanic. The average age of freshmen is 18.2; all undergraduates, 23.8. 14% do not continue beyond their first year; 66% remain to graduate.

Housing: College-sponsored living facilities include coed dormitories, on-campus apartments, and married-student housing. On-campus housing is available on a first-come, first-served basis. Alcohol is not permitted. All students may keep cars on campus.

Activities: There are 2 local and 5 national fraternities and 4 local and 3 national sororities. There are 85 groups on campus, including art, band, cheerleading, chess, choir, chorale, chorus, computers, drama, ethnic, gay, honors, international, jazz band, literary magazine, musical theater, newspaper, orchestra, photography, political, professional, radio and TV, religious, social, social service, student government, and yearbook. Popular campus events include holiday party, Research and Career Day, and end-of-the-year picnic in May.

Sports: There are 5 intercollegiate sports for men and 4 for women, and 5 intramural sports for men and 4 for women. Athletic and recreation facilities include a 1300-seat athletic center, tennis complex, swimming pool, soccer, softball, and baseball fields, racquetball courts, and dance room.

Disabled Students: 80% of the campus is accessible to disabled students. The following facilities are available: wheelchair ramps, elevators, special parking, specially equipped rest rooms, special class scheduling, lowered drinking fountains, and lowered telephones. Facilities vary widely from building to building. However, all classes will

be scheduled in accessible locations for disabled students, and adaptations will be made to individual needs in dormitory rooms.

Services: In addition to many counseling and information services, tutoring is available in most subjects. There is a reader service for the blind, and remedial math, reading, and writing.

Campus Safety and Security: Campus safety and security measures include 24-hour foot and vehicle patrol, self-defense education, escort service, and shuttle buses. In addition, there are informal discussions, pamphlets/posters/films, emergency telephones, and lighted pathways/sidewalks. Security guards assist Rutgers police in providing public safety services. There is also a student marshal program.

Programs of Study: The College of Nursing confers the B.S degree. Bachelor's degrees are awarded in HEALTH PROFESSIONS (nursing).

Required: To graduate, students must complete 125 credits, including 70 credits in nursing, and maintain a minimum GPA of 2.0. The college also requires 27 liberal arts credits and 19 science credits.

Special: There is a freshman honors program on campus

Faculty/Classroom: The faculty is entirely female. The average class size in an introductory lecture is 36; in a laboratory, 24; and in a regular course offering, 13.

Admissions: 28% of the 1995–96 applicants were accepted. The SAT I scores for the 1995–96 freshman class were as follows: Verbal—58% below 500, 38% between 500 and 599, and 4% between 600 and 700; Math—16% below 500, 63% between 500 and 599, and 21% between 600 and 700. 88% of the current freshmen were in the top fifth of their class; all were in the top two fifths.

Requirements: The SAT I or ACT is required. Applicants must be graduates of an accredited secondary school; the GED is accepted. Secondary school courses must include 4 years of English, 3 years of mathematics (algebra I and II and plane geometry), 1 year each of biology and chemistry, and 7 other approved academic subjects. AP and CLEP credits are accepted. Important factors in the admissions decision are advanced placement or honor courses, evidence of special talent, and leadership record.

Procedure: Freshmen are admitted in the fall. Entrance exams should be taken by December of the senior year. There are early admissions and deferred admissions plans. Applications should be filed by January 15 for fall entry, along with an application fee of $50. Notification is sent on a rolling basis. A waiting list is an active part of the admissions procedure, with about 6% of all applicants on the list.

Transfer: 46 transfer students enrolled in 1995–96. Applicants must have earned a minimum of 12 credits. Transfer students are admitted in the fall. Grades of C or better in courses that correspond in content and credit to those offered by the college transfer for credit. 30 credits of 125 must be completed at the College of Nursing.

Visiting: There are regularly scheduled orientations for prospective students, including an information session with admissions representatives and a tour of the campus. There are guides for informal visits and visitors may sit in on classes. To schedule a visit, contact the Office of University Undergraduate Admissions.

Financial Aid: In 1995–96, 82% of all freshmen and 68% of continuing students received some form of financial aid. 71% of freshmen and 56% of continuing students received need-based aid. The average freshman award was $8079. Of that total, scholarships or need-based grants averaged $4920 ($8000 maximum); loans averaged $2246 ($2625 maximum); outside scholarships averaged $900 ($1800 maximum); and work contracts averaged $1200 (maximum). 1% of undergraduate students work part-time. Average earnings from campus work for the school year are $885. The average financial indebtedness of the 1994–95 graduate was $7708. The FAFSA is required. The application deadline for fall entry is March 1.

International Students: There are currently 6 international students enrolled. They must take the TOEFL or the college's own test and achieve a minimum score on the TOEFL of 600. The student must also take the SAT I or the ACT.

Computers: The college provides computer facilities for student use. The mainframes are a DEC VAX 8550 and a Sun SPARC 1000; individual departments also have a variety of minicomputers. All students on the Newark campus can generate their own accounts on this system. Access to the local systems, as well as to the New Brunswick central systems, is provided through networked micro laboratories in major buildings on campus. All students may access the system. There are no time limits. The fees are $100 per year.

Graduates: In 1994–95, 87 bachelor's degrees were awarded. Within an average freshman class, 44% graduate in 4 years, 57% in 5 years, and 66% in 6 years. 60 companies recruited on campus in 1994–95. Of the 1994 graduating class, 5% were enrolled in graduate school within 6 months of graduation and 85% had found employment.

Admissions Contact: John Scott, Director of Admissions—Newark.

RUTGERS, THE STATE UNIVERSITY OF NEW JERSEY/COLLEGE OF PHARMACY   D-3

New Brunswick, NJ 08903   (908) 445-3770

Full-time: 340 men, 561 women	Faculty: 54; I, + +$
Part-time: 3 men, 10 women	Ph.D.s: 98%
Graduate: 16 men, 53 women	Student/Faculty: 17 to 1
Year: semesters, summer session	Tuition: $5244 ($9592)
Application Deadline: January 15	Room & Board: $4936
Freshman Class: 1567 applied, 583 accepted, 198 enrolled	
SAT I Verbal/Math: 543/676	**HIGHLY COMPETITIVE**

Rutgers, The State University of New Jersey/College of Pharmacy, founded in 1892, provides undergraduates with a 5-year pharmacy program. In addition to regional accreditation, the College of Pharmacy has baccalaureate program accreditation with ACPE. The 14 libraries contain 4,480,097 volumes, 2,839,739 microform items, and 76,968 audiovisual forms, and subscribe to 18,274 periodicals. Computerized library sources and services include the card catalog, interlibrary loans, and database searching. Special learning facilities include a learning resource center, art gallery, radio station, TV station, a geology museum, a controlled drug delivery research center, and a pharmaceutical manufacturing laboratory. The 2694-acre campus is in a suburban area 33 miles south of New York City. Including residence halls, there is 1 building on campus.

Student Life: 86% of undergraduates are from New Jersey. Students come from 19 states, 11 foreign countries, and Canada. 41% are white; 40% Asian American. The average age of freshmen is 18; all undergraduates, 21. 8% do not continue beyond their first year; 77% remain to graduate.

Housing: College-sponsored living facilities include single-sex and coed dormitories, on-campus apartments, and off-campus apartments. In addition there are language houses, special interest houses, a special math/science house for women, and substance-free housing. Housing is guaranteed for the first 2 years. On-campus housing is available on a lottery system for upperclassmen. 65% of students live on campus. Alcohol is not permitted.

Activities: 11% of men belong to 31 national fraternities; 7% of women belong to 4 local and 11 national sororities. There are 400 groups on campus, including art, band, cheerleading, chess, choir, chorale, chorus, computers, dance, drama, drill team, ethnic, film, gay, honors, international, jazz band, literary magazine, marching band, musical theater, newspaper, orchestra, pep band, photography, political, professional, radio and TV, religious, social, social service, student government, symphony, and yearbook. Popular campus events include 2 career fairs in the fall and an open house in the spring.

Sports: There are 15 intercollegiate sports for men and 15 for women, and 28 intramural sports for men and 28 for women. Athletic and recreation facilities include a 41000-seat stadium, an athletic center, a gymnasium, a swimming pool, tennis courts, and a recreation center.

Disabled Students: 55% of the campus is accessible to disabled students. The following facilities are available: wheelchair ramps, elevators, special parking, specially equipped rest rooms, special class scheduling, lowered drinking fountains, and lowered telephones. Facilities vary widely from building to building. However, all classes will be scheduled in accessible locations for disabled students, and adaptations will be made to individual needs in dormitory rooms.

Services: In addition to many counseling and information services, tutoring is available in most subjects. The academic tutoring service provides specific assistance in first- and second- level difficult courses. There is remedial math, reading, and writing.

Campus Safety and Security: Campus safety and security measures include 24-hour foot and vehicle patrol, self-defense education, escort service, and shuttle buses. In addition, there are informal discussions, pamphlets/posters/films, emergency telephones, and lighted pathways/sidewalks. The police department is supplemented by security guards and student safety officers.

Programs of Study: College of Pharmacy confers the B.S. degree. Doctoral degrees are also awarded. Bachelor's degrees are awarded in HEALTH PROFESSIONS (pharmacy).

Required: To graduate, students must complete 172 credit hours with a 2.0 GPA and a professional course average. Students must complete 21 credits in humanities and social sciences. Required courses include microeconomics, physiology, biochemistry, general chemistry and biology, calculus, statistics, organic chemistry, physics, English composition, and professional pharmaceutical sciences. All students must complete an externship in pharmacy practice, in industry, community, and hospitals.

Special: Internships include 4- or 8-week rotations in community and hospital pharmacies and in industrial research laboratories. This is the only college of pharmacy to provide industrial experience for all students. A 6-year advanced pharmacy program is also available. There

is a freshman honors program on campus, as well as 3 national honor societies. One department has an honors program.

Faculty/Classroom: 61% of faculty are male; 39%, female. All both teach and do research. The average class size in an introductory lecture is 72; in a laboratory, 24; and in a regular course offering, 113.

Admissions: 37% of the 1995–96 applicants were accepted. The SAT I scores for the 1995–96 freshman class were as follows: Verbal—29% below 500, 46% between 500 and 599, and 25% between 600 and 700; Math—1% below 500, 13% between 500 and 599, 50% between 600 and 700, and 36% above 700. 97% of the current freshmen were in the top fifth of their class; all were in the top two fifths. There were 2 National Merit finalists. 9 freshmen graduated first in their class.

Requirements: The SAT I or ACT is required. Applicants must have completed 16 high school academic credits or Carnegie units, including 4 years of English, 3 years of mathematics (algebra I and II and plane geometry), 2 years of a foreign language, 1 year each of biology and chemistry, and 5 other academic subjects. Physics is recommended. The GED is accepted. Students without a high school diploma, those from nonaccredited high schools, or those with academic unit entrance deficiencies must take SAT II: Subject tests, in writing, mathematics, and 1 science. AP and CLEP credits are accepted. Important factors in the admissions decision are advanced placement or honor courses, evidence of special talent, and leadership record.

Procedure: Freshmen are admitted in the fall. Entrance exams should be taken by December of the senior year. There are early admissions and deferred admissions plans. Applications should be filed by January 15 for fall entry, along with an application fee of $50. Notification is sent by April 15. A waiting list is an active part of the admissions procedure, with about 15% of all applicants on the list.

Transfer: 32 transfer students enrolled in 1995–96. Applicants must have completed a minimum of 12 college credits. Grades of C or better in courses that correspond in content and credit to those offered by the college transfer for credit. Transfer students are admitted only in the fall.

Visiting: There are regularly scheduled orientations for prospective students, including an information session with an admissions officer followed by a bus tour with a student guide. Student-guided walking tours are also available. Visitors may sit in on classes with prior approval. To schedule a visit, contact the Undergraduate Admissions Office.

Financial Aid: In 1995–96, 96% of all freshmen and 81% of continuing students received some form of financial aid. 63% of freshmen and 51% of continuing students received need-based aid. The average freshman award was $6600. Of that total, scholarships or need-based grants averaged $3644 ($8550 maximum); loans averaged $2119 ($3000 maximum); outside scholarships averaged $1952 ($8000 maximum); and work contracts averaged $1301 ($1500 maximum). 2% of undergraduate students work part-time. Average earnings from campus work for the school year are $706. The average financial indebtedness of the 1994–95 graduate was $7708. The FAFSA is required. The application deadline for fall entry is March 1.

International Students: There are currently 17 international students enrolled. They must take the TOEFL and achieve a minimum score of 550. The student must also take the SAT I or the ACT.

Computers: The college provides computer facilities for student use. Central computer systems include a cluster of 2 DEC VAX 8650 systems, 3 Sun SPARC 1000s, and 1 Sun SPARC 2000 UNIX system. Individual departments have a variety of minicomputers. The central systems may be accessed from Windows/DOS, Apple Macintosh personal computers, and X-terminals located in several large public laboratories. Services available include E-mail, newsgroups, software applications, a campuswide information system, and access to the Internet. All students may access the system 24 hours a day. There are no time limits. The fees are $100 per year.

Graduates: In 1994–95, 143 bachelor's degrees were awarded. Within an average freshman class, 62% graduate in 5 years and 77% in 6 years. 500 companies recruited on campus in 1994–95.

Admissions Contact: Dr. Elizabeth Mitchell, Assistant Vice President for University Undergraduate Admissions.

RUTGERS, THE STATE UNIVERSITY OF NEW JERSEY/COOK COLLEGE   D-3

New Brunswick, NJ 08903   (908) 445-3770

Full-time: 1432 men, 1382 women	Faculty: 95; I, + +$
Part-time: 143 men, 190 women	Ph.D.s: 98%
Graduate: none	Student/Faculty: 30 to 1
Year: semesters, summer session	Tuition: $5231 ($9579)
Application Deadline: January 15	Room & Board: $4936
Freshman Class: 6919 applied, 4428 accepted, 629 enrolled	
SAT I Verbal/Math: 498/590	**VERY COMPETITIVE**

Rutgers, The State University of New Jersey/Cook College, founded in 1864, is a coeducational residential college offering a program that emphasizes life, environmental, marine and coastal, and agricultural sciences. In addition to regional accreditation, Cook College has baccalaureate program accreditation with ASLA and NASDTEC. The 14 libraries contain 4,480,097 volumes, 2,839,739 microform items, and 76,968 audiovisual forms, and subscribe to 18,274 periodicals. Computerized library sources and services include the card catalog, interlibrary loans, and database searching. Special learning facilities include a learning resource center, art gallery, radio station, TV station, a geology museum, and various research centers and institutes. The 2694-acre campus is in a small town 33 miles south of New York City. Including residence halls, there are 100 buildings on campus.

Student Life: 91% of undergraduates are from New Jersey. Students come from 25 states, 19 foreign countries, and Canada. 73% are white; 11% Asian American. The average age of freshmen is 18; all undergraduates, 22. 8% do not continue beyond their first year; 75% remain to graduate.

Housing: College-sponsored living facilities include single-sex and coed dormitories and on-campus apartments. In addition there are special interest houses and a substance-free house. In addition, there is a small modern residence hall where male students can reduce college expenses by helping with maintenance, ordering supplies, and preparing meals; residents are selected on the basis of financial need. Housing is guaranteed for the first 2 years. On-campus housing is available on a lottery system for upperclassmen. 56% of students live on campus. Upperclassmen may keep cars on campus.

Activities: 11% of men belong to 31 national fraternities; 7% of women belong to 4 local and 11 national sororities. There are 400 groups on campus, including art, band, cheerleading, chess, choir, chorale, chorus, computers, dance, drama, drill team, ethnic, film, gay, honors, international, jazz band, literary magazine, marching band, musical theater, newspaper, orchestra, pep band, photography, political, professional, radio and TV, religious, social, social service, student government, symphony, and yearbook. Popular campus events include Agricultural Field Day, Intramural/Recreation Sports, and Parents Day.

Sports: There are 15 intercollegiate sports for men and 15 for women, and 28 intramural sports for men and 25 for women. Athletic and recreation facilities include a 41000-seat stadium, an athletic center, a gymnasium, a swimming pool, a recreation center, a weight room, and tennis and racquetball courts.

Disabled Students: 55% of the campus is accessible to disabled students. The following facilities are available: wheelchair ramps, elevators, special parking, specially equipped rest rooms, special class scheduling, lowered drinking fountains, and lowered telephones. Facilities available vary widely from building to building. However, all classes will be scheduled in accessible locations for disabled students, and adaptations will be made to individual needs in dormitory rooms.

Services: In addition to many counseling and information services, tutoring is available in most subjects. The academic tutoring provides specific course assistance in first- and second- level difficult courses. There is a reader service for the blind, and remedial math, reading, and writing.

Campus Safety and Security: Campus safety and security measures include 24-hour foot and vehicle patrol, self-defense education, escort service, and shuttle buses. In addition, there are informal discussions, pamphlets/posters/films, emergency telephones, and lighted pathways/sidewalks. The police department is supplemented by security guards and student safety officers.

Programs of Study: Cook College confers B.A. and B.S. degrees. Bachelor's degrees are awarded in AGRICULTURE (agriculture, animal science, fishing and fisheries, horticulture, natural resource management, plant science, and wildlife management), BIOLOGICAL SCIENCE (biochemistry, biology/biological science, biotechnology, botany, cell biology, ecology, evolutionary biology, genetics, microbiology, molecular biology, nutrition, and physiology), BUSINESS (business economics), COMMUNICATIONS AND THE ARTS (communications and journalism), COMPUTER AND PHYSICAL SCIENCE (atmospheric sciences and meteorology, chemistry, computer science, earth science, and geology), EDUCATION (health, physical, and vocational), ENGINEERING AND ENVIRONMENTAL DESIGN (environmental design, environmental science, and landscape architecture/design), HEALTH PROFESSIONS (biomedical science, predentistry, premedicine, preveterinary science, and public health), SOCIAL SCIENCE (food science, geography, human ecology, international studies, and physical fitness/movement). Nutritional sciences, environmental science, and human ecology have the largest enrollments.

Required: To graduate, students must complete 128 credit hours (163 credits for the 5-year bioresource engineering program), with a minimum GPA of 2.0. In addition to achieving competency in one of the programs of study offered at Cook College, all students are required to complete course work in introductory life and physical sciences, interdisciplinary/ethical analysis, the arts, human diversity, economic and political systems, oral and written communication, and experience-based education. Competence in a field includes course work in quantitative skills, computer use, and professional ethics.

Special: Cook College offers an extensive cooperative education program, independent study programs, B.A.-B.S. degrees, a 2–3 engineering degree, and an 8-year medical degree with the University of Medicine and Dentistry of New Jersey. Seniors may elect to take 1 course each semester on a pass/fail basis. Study abroad is offered in 8 countries. A wide variety of professionally oriented majors in the life, environmental, marine, and coastal, and agricultural sciences is offered. There is a freshman honors program on campus, as well as 8 national honor societies. 5 departments have honors programs.

Faculty/Classroom: 80% of faculty are male; 20%, female. All both teach and do research. Graduate students teach 10% of introductory courses. The average class size in an introductory lecture is 57; in a laboratory, 24; and in a regular course offering, 39.

Admissions: 64% of the 1995–96 applicants were accepted. The SAT I scores for the 1995–96 freshman class were as follows: Verbal—51% below 500, 37% between 500 and 599, 11% between 600 and 700, and 1% above 700; Math—11% below 500, 44% between 500 and 599, 36% between 600 and 700, and 9% above 700. 60% of the current freshmen were in the top fifth of their class; 98% were in the top two fifths. 7 freshmen graduated first in their class.

Requirements: The SAT I or ACT is required. Applicants must have completed 16 high school academic credits or Carnegie units, including 4 years of English, 3 years of mathematics (algebra I and II and geometry), and 9 other approved academic subjects. The GED is accepted. Students without a high school diploma, those from a nonaccredited high school, or those with academic unit entrance deficiences must take SAT II: Subject tests in writing, mathematics, and 1 other subject. AP and CLEP credits are accepted. Important factors in the admissions decision are advanced placement or honor courses, evidence of special talent, and leadership record.

Procedure: Freshmen are admitted in the fall. Entrance exams should be taken by December of the senior year. There are early admissions and deferred admissions plans. Applications should be filed by January 15 for fall entry, along with an application fee of $50. Notification is sent by April 15. A waiting list is an active part of the admissions procedure, with about 8% of all applicants on the list.

Transfer: 192 transfer students enrolled in 1995–96. Applicants must have completed a minimum of 12 college credits. Grades of C or better in courses that correspond in content and credit to those offered by the college transfer for credit. Transfer students are admitted in both the fall and spring semesters. 40 credits of 128 must be completed at Cook College.

Visiting: There are regularly scheduled orientations for prospective students, including an information session with an admissions officer and a bus tour with a student guide. Walking tours are also available. Visitors may sit in on classes with prior arrangement. To schedule a visit, contact the Office of University Undergraduate Admissions.

Financial Aid: In 1995–96, 75% of all freshmen and 64% of continuing students received some form of financial aid. 54% of freshmen and 47% of continuing students received need-based aid. The average freshman award was $5914. Of that total, scholarships or need-based grants averaged $4038 ($14,796 maximum); loans averaged $2388 ($7500 maximum); outside scholarships averaged $1100 ($5932 maximum); and work contracts averaged $1222 ($1500 maximum). 8% of undergraduate students work part-time. Average earnings from campus work for the school year are $846. The average financial indebtedness of the 1994–95 graduate was $7209. The FAFSA is required. The application deadline for fall entry is March 1.

International Students: There are currently 29 international students enrolled. They must take the TOEFL and achieve a minimum score of 550. The student must also take the SAT I or the ACT.

Computers: The college provides computer facilities for student use. Central computer systems include a cluster of 2 DEC VAX 8650 systems, 3 Sun SPARC Server 1000s, and 1 Sun SPARC Server 2000 UNIX system. Individual departments have a variety of minicomputers. The central systems may be accessed from Windows/DOS and Apple Macintosh personal computers, and X-terminals located in several large laboratories. Services available includ E-mail, newsgroups, software applications, a campuswide information system, and access to the Internet. All students may access the system 24 hours a day. There are no time limits. The fees are $100 per year.

Graduates: In 1994–95, 609 bachelor's degrees were awarded. The most popular majors among graduates were environmental science (19%), biological sciences (13%), and environmental and business economics (9%). Within an average freshman class, 36% graduate in 4 years, 62% in 5 years, and 72% in 6 years. 500 companies recruited on campus in 1994–95. Of the 1994 graduating class, 15% were enrolled in graduate school within 6 months of graduation and 66% had found employment.

Admissions Contact: Dr. Elizabeth Mitchell, Assistant Vice President for University Undergraduate Admissions.

RUTGERS, THE STATE UNIVERSITY OF NEW JERSEY/DOUGLASS COLLEGE
D-3

New Brunswick, NJ 08903 (908) 445-3770; FAX: (908) 445-0237

Full-time: 2783 women	Faculty: 763; I, ++$
Part-time: 190 women	Ph.D.s: 98%
Graduate: none	Student/Faculty: 4 to 1
Year: semesters, summer session	Tuition: $4798 ($8719)
Application Deadline: January 15	Room & Board: $4936
Freshman Class: 5319 applied, 3861 accepted, 603 enrolled	
SAT I Verbal/Math: 494/551	VERY COMPETITIVE

Rutgers, The State University of New Jersey/Douglass College, founded in 1918, is a women's liberal arts institution. In addition to regional accreditation, Douglass College has baccalaureate program accreditation with AACSB, NASDTEC, and NASM. The 14 libraries contain 4,480,097 volumes, 2,839,739 microform items, and 76,968 audiovisual forms, and subscribe to 18,274 periodicals. Computerized library sources and services include the card catalog, interlibrary loans, and database searching. Special learning facilities include a learning resource center, art gallery, radio station, TV station, a geology museum, and various research institutes and centers including the Center for Women and Work, the Eagleton Institute of Politics, and the Institute for Research on Women. The 2694-acre campus is in a suburban area 33 miles south of New York City. Including residence halls, there are 96 buildings on campus.

Student Life: 94% of undergraduates are from New Jersey. Students come from 25 states, 21 foreign countries, and Canada. 62% are white; 14% Asian American; 11% African American. The average age of freshmen is 18; all undergraduates, 21. 11% do not continue beyond their first year; 83% remain to graduate.

Housing: College-sponsored living facilities include dormitories and on-campus apartments. In addition there are language houses, special interest houses, a substance-free house, 7 cultural houses, and a math-science house. Housing is guaranteed for the first 2 years. 56% of students live on campus. Alcohol is not permitted. Upperclassmen may keep cars on campus.

Activities: 7% of women belong to 4 local and 11 national sororities. There are no fraternities. There are 400 groups on campus, including art, band, cheerleading, chess, choir, chorale, chorus, computers, dance, drama, drill team, ethnic, film, gay, honors, international, jazz band, literary magazine, marching band, musical theater, newspaper, orchestra, pep band, photography, political, professional, radio and TV, religious, social, social service, student government, symphony, and yearbook. Popular campus events include Spring Spectacolor, Sacred Path, Campus Night, and Commencement.

Sports: There are 15 intercollegiate sports and 28 intramural sports. Athletic and recreation facilities include a 41000-seat stadium, an athletic center, a gymnasium, a swimming pool, tennis courts, and a recreation center.

Disabled Students: 55% of the campus is accessible to disabled students. The following facilities are available: wheelchair ramps, elevators, special parking, specially equipped rest rooms, special class scheduling, lowered drinking fountains, and lowered telephones. Facilities vary widely from building to building. However, all classes will be scheduled in accessible locations for disabled students, and adaptations will be made to individual needs in dormitory rooms.

Services: In addition to many counseling and information services, tutoring is available in most subjects. The academic tutoring service provides specific course assistance in first and second-level difficult courses. In addition, there is remedial math, reading, and writing.

Campus Safety and Security: Campus safety and security measures include 24-hour foot and vehicle patrol, self-defense education, escort service, and shuttle buses. In addition, there are informal discussions, pamphlets/posters/films, emergency telephones, and lighted pathways/sidewalks. The police department is supplemented by security guards and student safety officers.

Programs of Study: Douglass College confers B.A. and B.S. degrees. Bachelor's degrees are awarded in BIOLOGICAL SCIENCE (biochemistry, biology/biological science, biometrics and biostatistics, biotechnology, botany, cell biology, ecology, evolutionary biology, genetics, microbiology, neurosciences, nutrition, and physiology), BUSINESS (accounting, banking and finance, business administration and management, labor studies, management information systems, and marketing/retailing/merchandising), COMMUNICATIONS AND THE ARTS (art history and appreciation, Chinese, classical languages, classics, communications, comparative literature, dance, dramatic arts, English, fine arts, French, German, Greek, Italian, journalism, Latin, linguistics, music, Portuguese, Russian, Spanish, and visual and performing arts), COMPUTER AND PHYSICAL SCIENCE (atmospheric sciences and meteorology, chemistry, computer science, geology, mathematics, physics, and statistics), EDUCATION (physical), HEALTH PROFESSIONS (biomedical science, medical laboratory technology, predentistry, premedicine, and public health), SOCIAL SCIENCE (African American studies, American studies, anthropolo-

gy, East Asian studies, Eastern European studies, economics, food science, geography, Hispanic American studies, history, Judaic studies, Latin American studies, medieval studies, Middle Eastern studies, philosophy, physical fitness/movement, political science/government, prelaw, psychology, religion, sociology, urban studies, and women's studies). Biological sciences, psychology, and English have the largest enrollments.

Required: To graduate, students must complete 120 credits, with a minimum GPA of 1.95. Nine credits are required in each of 3 areas: mathematics and science, history and social science, and humanities. In addition, students must take 3 credits each in women's experience, cross-cultural perspectives, and English composition. Demonstrated proficiency must be achieved in a foreign language on the intermediate level, and in elementary algebra.

Special: Douglass offers an alumnae-sponsored externship program, a Washington semester, B.A.-B.S. degrees in liberal arts and engineering, dual majors, student-designed majors, an environmental policy major through Cook College, 2–3 degrees with the College of Engineering, and pass/fail options. Students may study abroad in 8 countries. The following are also available: an 8-year medical degree with the University of Medicine and Dentistry of New Jersey, a 5-year advanced business degree with the Graduate School of Management, and a 5-year advanced education degree with the Graduate School of Education. There is also a certificate program in international studies. There is a freshman honors program on campus, as well as 1 national honor society, Phi Beta Kappa. Almost all departments have honors programs.

Faculty/Classroom: 73% of faculty are male; 27%, female. All both teach and do research. Graduate students teach 32% of introductory courses. The average class size in an introductory lecture is 60; in a laboratory, 24; and in a regular course offering, 46.

Admissions: 73% of the 1995–96 applicants were accepted. The SAT I scores for the 1995–96 freshman class were as follows: Verbal—53% below 500, 35% between 500 and 599, 10% between 600 and 700, and 2% above 700; Math—24% below 500, 46% between 500 and 599, 27% between 600 and 700, and 3% above 700. 48% of the current freshmen were in the top fifth of their class; 94% were in the top two fifths. There were 4 National Merit finalists. 6 freshmen graduated first in their class.

Requirements: The SAT I or ACT is required. Applicants must have completed 16 high school academic credits or Carnegie units, including 4 years of English, 3 years of mathematics (algebra I and II and geometry), 2 years each of science and foreign language, and 5 other academic subjects. Students without a high school diploma, those from a nonaccredited high school, or those with academic deficiencies must take SAT II: Subject tests in writing, mathematics, and 1 other subject. AP credits are accepted. Important factors in the admissions decision are advanced placement or honor courses, evidence of special talent, and leadership record.

Procedure: Freshmen are admitted in the fall. Entrance exams should be taken by December of the senior year. There are early admissions and deferred admissions plans. Applications should be filed by January 15 for fall entry, along with an application fee of $50. Notification is sent on a rolling basis. A waiting list is an active part of the admissions procedure, with about 7% of all applicants on the list.

Transfer: 203 transfer students enrolled in 1995–96. Applicants must have a minimum of 12 college credits. Grades of C or better in courses that correspond in content and credit to those offered at the college transfer for credit. Transfer students are admitted in both the fall and spring semesters. 30 credits of 120 must be completed at Douglass College.

Visiting: There are regularly scheduled orientations for prospective students, including an information session with an admissions officer followed by a bus tour with a student guide. Student-guided walking tours are also available and include a meeting with the dean prior to the tour. Visitors may sit in on classes with prior arrangement. To schedule a visit, contact the Office of University Undergraduate Admissions.

Financial Aid: In 1995–96, 77% of all freshmen and 66% of continuing students received some form of financial aid. 58% of freshmen and 50% of continuing students received need-based aid. The average freshman award was $6102. Of that total, scholarships or need-based grants averaged $4231 ($14,633 maximum); loans averaged $2534 ($6625 maximum); outside scholarships averaged $1582 ($14,633 maximum); and work contracts averaged $1236 ($1500 maximum). 13% of undergraduate students work part-time. Average earnings from campus work for the school year are $902. The average financial indebtedness of the 1994–95 graduate was $6916. Douglass College is a member of CSS. The FAFSA is required. The application deadline for fall entry is March 1.

International Students: There are currently 35 international students enrolled. They must take the TOEFL and achieve a minimum score of 550. The student must also take the SAT I or the ACT.

Computers: The college provides computer facilities for student use. Central computer systems include a cluster of 2 DEC VAX 8650 systems, 3 Sun SPARC Server 1000s, and 1 Sun SPARC Server 2000 UNIX system. Individual departments have a variety of minicomputers. The central systems may be accessed from Windows/DOS and Apple Macintosh personal computers, and X-terminals located in several large public laboratories. Services available include E-mail, newsgroups, software applications, a campuswide information system, and access to the Internet. All students may access the system 24 hours a day. There are no time limits. The fees are $100 per year.

Graduates: In 1994–95, 778 bachelor's degrees were awarded. The most popular majors among graduates were psychology (17%), English (11%), and political science (7%). Within an average freshman class, 53% graduate in 4 years, 72% in 5 years, and 83% in 6 years. 500 companies recruited on campus in 1994–95. Of the 1994 graduating class, 15% were enrolled in graduate school within 6 months of graduation and 66% had found employment.

Admissions Contact: Dr. Elizabeth Mitchell, Assistant Vice President for University Undergraduate Admissions.

RUTGERS, THE STATE UNIVERSITY OF NEW JERSEY/LIVINGSTON COLLEGE

D-3

New Brunswick, NJ 08903	(908) 445-3770; FAX: (908) 445-0237
Full-time: 1765 men, 1184 women	Faculty: 763; I, + +$
Part-time: 116 men, 84 women	Ph.D.s: 98%
Graduate: none	Student/Faculty: 4 to 1
Year: semesters, summer session	Tuition: $4862 ($8783)
Application Deadline: January 15	Room & Board: $4936
Freshman Class: 11,208 applied, 7060 accepted, 561 enrolled	
SAT I Verbal/Math: 473/557	COMPETITIVE +

Rutgers, The State University of New Jersey/Livingston College, founded in 1969, is a coeducational, liberal arts, residential college. In addition to regional accreditation, Livingston College has baccalaureate program accreditation with AACSB, CAHEA, CSWE, NASDTEC, and NASM. The 14 libraries contain 4,480,097 volumes, 2,839,739 microform items, and 76,968 audiovisual forms, and subscribe to 18,274 periodicals. Computerized library sources and services include the card catalog, interlibrary loans, and database searching. Special learning facilities include a learning resource center, art gallery, radio station, TV station, a geology museum, and various research institutes and centers. The 2694-acre campus is in a suburban area 33 miles south of New York City. Including residence halls, there are 41 buildings on campus.

Student Life: 89% of undergraduates are from New Jersey. Students come from 30 states, 26 foreign countries, and Canada. 59% are white; 15% Asian American; 12% African American. The average age of freshmen is 18; all undergraduates, 21. 13% do not continue beyond their first year; 66% remain to graduate.

Housing: College-sponsored living facilities include coed dormitories and on-campus apartments. In addition there are special interest houses and substance-free housing. Housing is guaranteed for the first 2 years. On-campus housing is available on a lottery system for upperclassmen. All students may keep cars on campus.

Activities: 11% of men belong to 31 national fraternities; 7% of women belong to 4 local and 11 national sororities. There are 400 groups on campus, including art, band, cheerleading, chess, choir, chorale, chorus, computers, dance, drama, drill team, ethnic, film, gay, honors, international, jazz band, literary magazine, marching band, musical theater, newspaper, orchestra, pep band, photography, political, professional, radio and TV, religious, social, social service, student government, symphony, and yearbook. Popular campus events include Boardwalk Beach Party, Helmet Concert, Rock'n Roll Bowl, and Springfest.

Sports: There are 15 intercollegiate sports for men and 15 for women, and 28 intramural sports for men and 28 for women. Athletic and recreation facilities include a 41000-seat stadium, an athletic center, a gymnasium, a swimming pool, tennis courts, and a recreation center.

Disabled Students: 55% of the campus is accessible to disabled students. The following facilities are available: wheelchair ramps, elevators, special parking, specially equipped rest rooms, special class scheduling, lowered drinking fountains, and lowered telephones. Facilities vary widely from building to building. However, all classes will be scheduled in accessible locations for disabled students, and adaptations will be made to individual needs in dormitory rooms.

Services: In addition to many counseling and information services, tutoring is available in most subjects. The academic tutoring service provides specific course assistance in first- and second-level difficult courses. There is a reader service for the blind, and remedial math, reading, and writing.

Campus Safety and Security: Campus safety and security measures include 24-hour foot and vehicle patrol, self-defense education, escort service, and shuttle buses. In addition, there are informal discussions, pamphlets/posters/films, emergency telephones, and lighted pathways/sidewalks. The police department is supplemented by security guards and student safety officers.

Programs of Study: Livingston College confers B.A. and B.S. degrees. Bachelor's degrees are awarded in BIOLOGICAL SCIENCE (biochemistry, biology/biological science, biometrics and biostatistics, botany, cell biology, ecology, genetics, microbiology, and physiology), BUSINESS (accounting, banking and finance, business administration and management, labor studies, management information systems, management science, and marketing/retailing/merchandising), COMMUNICATIONS AND THE ARTS (art history and appreciation, Chinese, classical languages, classics, communications, comparative literature, dance, dramatic arts, English, French, German, Greek, Italian, journalism, Latin, linguistics, music, Portuguese, Russian, Spanish, and visual and performing arts), COMPUTER AND PHYSICAL SCIENCE (chemistry, computer science, geology, mathematics, physics, and statistics), HEALTH PROFESSIONS (biomedical science, medical laboratory technology, predentistry, premedicine, and public health), SOCIAL SCIENCE (African American studies, American studies, anthropology, Asian/Oriental studies, criminal justice, East Asian studies, Eastern European studies, economics, geography, Hispanic American studies, history, humanities, Judaic studies, Latin American studies, medieval studies, Middle Eastern studies, philosophy, physical fitness/movement, political science/government, prelaw, psychology, religion, social work, sociology, urban studies, and women's studies). Biological sciences, psychology, and English have the largest enrollments.

Required: To graduate, students must complete 120 credit hours, with a minimum GPA of 1.93. Distribution requirements include 2 courses each in cultural perspectives, contemporary issues, and arts and humanities, and 1 course each in social science, natural sciences, and analytical/quantitative skills. All students must take at least 2 semesters of English composition, and must show proficiency through intermediate algebra. All students must accumulate at least 30 credits at the 300/400 level.

Special: Internships, a Washington semester, accelerated degree programs, B.A.-B.S. degrees, student-designed majors, a 2–3 engineering degree, and nondegree study are available. Credit for life, military, and work experience (including summer work) is available. There are pass/fail options under certain circumstances. Students may study abroad in 8 countries. Dual degrees are offered in statistics/mathematics and history/political science. A 3–3 physician's assistant program is offered jointly with the University of Medicine and Dentistry of New Jersey. There is a freshman honors program on campus, as well as 1 national honor society, Phi Beta Kappa. All departments have honors programs.

Faculty/Classroom: 73% of faculty are male; 27%, female. All both teach and do research. Graduate students teach 32% of introductory courses. The average class size in an introductory lecture is 60; in a laboratory, 24; and in a regular course offering, 46.

Admissions: 63% of the 1995–96 applicants were accepted. The SAT I scores for the 1995–96 freshman class were as follows: Verbal—67% below 500, 27% between 500 and 599, and 6% between 600 and 700; Math—24% below 500, 45% between 500 and 599, 29% between 600 and 700, and 2% above 700. 32% of the current freshmen were in the top fifth of their class; 93% were in the top two fifths.

Requirements: The SAT I or ACT is required. Students should have completed 16 high school academic credits or Carnegie units including 4 years of English, 3 years of mathematics (algebra I and II and geometry), 2 years each of 1 foreign language and science, and 5 other approved academic subjects. The GED is accepted. Students without a high school diploma, those from a nonaccredited high school, or those with academic unit deficiencies must take SAT II: Subject tests in writing, mathematics, and 1 other subject. AP and CLEP credits are accepted. Important factors in the admissions decision are advanced placement or honor courses, evidence of special talent, and leadership record.

Procedure: Freshmen are admitted in the fall. Entrance exams should be taken by December of the senior year. There are early admissions and deferred admissions plans. Applications should be filed by January 15 for fall entry, along with an application fee of $50. Notification is sent by April 15. A waiting list is an active part of the admissions procedure, with about 8% of all applicants on the list.

Transfer: 291 transfer students enrolled in 1995–96. Students with a minimum of 12 credit hours at another institution are considered for transfer. Grades of C or better in courses that correspond in content and credit to those offered by the college transfer for credit. Transfer students are usually admitted in both the fall and spring semesters. 30 credits of the last 42 must be completed at Livingston College.

Visiting: There are regularly scheduled orientations for prospective students, including an information session with an admissions officer followed by a bus tour with a student guide. Student-guided walking tours are also available. Visitors may sit in on classes with prior arrangement. To schedule a visit, contact the Office of University Undergraduate Admissions.

Financial Aid: In 1995–96, 69% of all freshmen and 59% of continuing students received some form of financial aid. 58% of freshmen and 50% of continuing students received need-based aid. The average freshman award was $7457. Of that total, scholarships or need-based grants averaged $4512 ($14,284 maximum); loans averaged $2244 ($3542 maximum); outside scholarships averaged $1433 ($6810 maximum); and work contracts averaged $1249 ($1500 maximum). 14% of undergraduate students work part-time. Average earnings from campus work for the school year are $893. The average financial indebtedness of the 1994–95 graduate was $7681. The FAFSA is required. The application deadline for fall entry is March 1.

International Students: There are currently 64 international students enrolled. They must take the TOEFL and achieve a minimum score of 550. The student must also take the SAT I or the ACT.

Computers: The college provides computer facilities for student use. Central computer systems include a cluster of 2 DEC VAX 8650 systems, 3 Sun SPARC Server 1000s, and 1 Sun SPARC Server 2000 UNIX systems. Individual departments have a variety of minicomputers. The central systems may be accessed from Windows/DOS, and Apple Macintosh personal computers, and X-terminals located in several large public laboratories. Services available include E-mail, newsgroups, software applications, a campuswide information system, and access to the Internet. All students may access the system 24 hours a day. There are no time limits. The fees are $100 per year.

Graduates: In 1994–95, 842 bachelor's degrees were awarded. The most popular majors among graduates were psychology (13%), economics (10%), and administration of justice (8%). Within an average freshman class, 39% graduate in 4 years, 60% in 5 years, and 66% in 6 years. 500 companies recruited on campus in 1994–95. Of the 1994 graduating class, 15% were enrolled in graduate school within 6 months of graduation and 66% had found employment.

Admissions Contact: Dr. Elizabeth Mitchell, Assistant Vice President for University Undergraduate Admissions.

RUTGERS, THE STATE UNIVERSITY OF NEW JERSEY/MASON GROSS SCHOOL OF THE ARTS

D-3

New Brunswick, NJ 08903

(908) 445-3770

Full-time: 190 men, 244 women	Faculty: 79; I, ++$
Part-time: 6 men, 12 women	Ph.D.s: 98%
Graduate: 114 men, 116 women	Student/Faculty: 5 to 1
Year: semesters, summer session	Tuition: $4828 ($8749)
Application Deadline: see profile	Room & Board: $4936
Freshman Class: 902 applied, 248 accepted, 106 enrolled	
SAT I Verbal/Math: 497/535	SPECIAL

Rutgers, The State University of New Jersey/Mason Gross School of the Arts, founded in 1976, offers programs to students of special talent and ability who wish to pursue careers in theater arts, visual arts, dance, and music. In addition to regional accreditation, Mason Gross School of the Arts has baccalaureate program accreditation with NASAD, NASDTEC, and NASM. The 14 libraries contain 4,480,097 volumes, 2,839,739 microform items, and 76,968 audiovisual forms, and subscribe to 18,274 periodicals. Computerized library sources and services include the card catalog, interlibrary loans, and database searching. Special learning facilities include a learning resource center, art gallery, radio station, TV station, a geology museum; dance, music, and art studios; concert and recital halls; and black-box and proscenium theaters. The 2694-acre campus is in a small town 33 miles south of New York City.

Student Life: 86% of undergraduates are from New Jersey. Students come from 19 states and 4 foreign countries. 74% are white. The average age of freshmen is 18; all undergraduates, 21. 18% do not continue beyond their first year; 64% remain to graduate.

Housing: College-sponsored living facilities include single-sex and coed dormitories and on-campus apartments. In addition there are language houses, special interest houses, and substance-free housing. Housing is guaranteed for the first 2 years. On-campus housing is available on a lottery system for upperclassmen.

Activities: 11% of men belong to 31 national fraternities; 7% of women belong to 4 local and 11 national sororities. There are 400 groups on campus, including art, band, cheerleading, chess, choir, chorale, chorus, computers, dance, drama, drill team, ethnic, film, gay, honors, international, jazz band, literary magazine, marching band, musical theater, newspaper, orchestra, pep band, photography, political, professional, radio and TV, religious, social, social service, student government, symphony, and yearbook. Popular campus events include concerts, opera, and dance faculty performances.

Sports: There are 15 intercollegiate sports for men and 15 for women, and 28 intramural sports for men and 28 for women. Athletic and recreation facilities include a 41000-seat stadium, an athletic center, a gymnasium, a swimming pool, tennis courts, and a recreation center.

Disabled Students: 55% of the campus is accessible to disabled students. The following facilities are available: wheelchair ramps, elevators, special parking, specially equipped rest rooms, special class scheduling, lowered drinking fountains, and lowered telephones. Facilities vary widely from building to building. However, all classes will be scheduled in accessible locations for students with disabilities, and adaptations will be made to individual needs in dormitory rooms.

Services: In addition to many counseling and information services, tutoring is available in most subjects. The academic tutoring service provides specific course assistance in first and second-level difficult courses. There is a reader service for the blind, and remedial math, reading, and writing.

Campus Safety and Security: Campus safety and security measures include 24-hour foot and vehicle patrol, self-defense education, escort service, and shuttle buses. In addition, there are informal discussions, pamphlets/posters/films, emergency telephones, and lighted pathways/sidewalks. The police department is supplemented by security guards and student safety officers.

Programs of Study: Mason Gross School of the Arts confers B.F.A and B.Mus. degrees. Master's and doctoral degrees are also awarded. Bachelor's degrees are awarded in COMMUNICATIONS AND THE ARTS (dance, dramatic arts, music, and visual and performing arts), EDUCATION (music). Visual arts, theater arts, and music have the largest enrollments.

Required: To graduate, students must complete 120 to 129 credits with a cumulative GPA of 2.0. The college requires 36 credits of liberal arts courses, in addition to the requirements of the major. All students must take expository writing.

Special: Mason Gross is a creative and performing arts school. Three-fourths of the courses are performance, studio, or critical studies classes within the chosen discipline. The college offers study abroad in 8 countries.

Faculty/Classroom: 63% of faculty are male; 37%, female. All both teach and do research. Graduate students teach 34% of introductory courses. The average class size in an introductory lecture is 63; in a laboratory, 24; and in a regular course offering, 11.

Admissions: 27% of the 1995–96 applicants were accepted. The SAT I scores for the 1995–96 freshman class were as follows: Verbal—51% below 500, 32% between 500 and 599, 16% between 600 and 700, and 1% above 700; Math—41% below 500, 32% between 500 and 599, 18% between 600 and 700, and 9% above 700. 27% of the current freshmen were in the top fifth of their class; 60% were in the top two fifths.

Requirements: The SAT I or ACT is required. Applicants should have completed 16 high school academic credits or Carnegie units, including 4 years of English, 3 years of mathematics (algebra I and II and geometry), and 9 other approved academic subjects. The GED is accepted. Students without a high school diploma, those from non-accredited high schools, or those with academic unit entrance deficiencies must take SAT II: Subject tests in writing, mathematics, and 1 other subject. Two years of a foreign language are recommended. All students must audition or present a portfolio for admission. AP credits are accepted. Important factors in the admissions decision are evidence of special talent, advanced placement or honor courses, and extracurricular activities record.

Procedure: Freshmen are admitted in the fall. Entrance exams should be taken by December of the senior year. There are early admissions and deferred admissions plans. Applications should be filed by January 15 for visual arts; February 15 for music, dance, and theater. Application fee is $50. Notification is sent by April 15. A waiting list is an active part of the admissions procedure, with about 13% of all applicants on the list.

Transfer: 38 transfer students enrolled in 1995–96. Applicants should have earned a minimum of 12 credit hours at another college. A portfolio and/or audition is required for admission. Grades of C or better in courses that correspond in content and credit to those offered by the college transfer for credit. Transfer students are usually admitted in the fall, but applicants may contact the Admissions Office in early October to see if spring admission is available. 30 credits of 120 must be completed at Mason Gross School of the Arts.

Visiting: There are regularly scheduled orientations for prospective students, including an information session with an admissions officer followed by a bus tour with a student guide. Walking tours are also available. Visitors may sit in on classes with prior arrangement. To schedule a visit, contact the Office of University Undergraduate Admissions.

Financial Aid: In 1995–96, 77% of all freshmen and 65% of continuing students received some form of financial aid. 62% of freshmen and 50% of continuing students received need-based aid. The average freshman award was $5808. Of that total, scholarships or need-based grants averaged $3635 ($5000 maximum); loans averaged $2315 ($3000 maximum); outside scholarships averaged $1129 ($2418 maximum); and work contracts averaged $1303 ($1500 maximum). 1% of undergraduate students work part-time. Average earnings from campus work for the school year are $883. The average financial indebtedness of the 1994–95 graduate was $7361. The FAFSA is required. The application deadline for fall entry is March 1.

International Students: There are currently 5 international students enrolled. They must take the TOEFL and achieve a minimum score of 550.

Computers: The college provides computer facilities for student use. Central Computer systems include a cluster of 2 DEC VAX 8650 systems, 3 Sun SPARC Server 1000s, and 1 Sun SPARC Server 2000 UNIX system. Individual departments have a variety of minicompuers. The central systems may be accessed from Windows/DOS and Apple Macintosh personal computers, and X-terminals located in several large public laboratories. Services available include E-mail, newsgroups, software applications, a campuswide information system, and access to the Internet. All students may access the system 24 hours a day. There are no time limits. The fees are $100 per year.

Graduates: In 1994–95, 64 bachelor's degrees were awarded. The most popular majors among graduates were visual arts (63%), music (27%), and theater arts (6%). Within an average freshman class, 33% graduate in 4 years, 49% in 5 years, and 64% in 6 years. 500 companies recruited on campus in 1994–95.

Admissions Contact: Dr. Elizabeth Mitchell, Assistant Vice President for University Undergraduate Admissions.

RUTGERS, THE STATE UNIVERSITY OF NEW JERSEY/NEWARK COLLEGE OF ARTS AND SCIENCES
E-2

Newark, NJ 07102   (201) 648-5205

Full-time: 1498 men, 1584 women	Faculty: 189; IIA, + +$
Part-time: 326 men, 318 women	Ph.D.s: 98%
Graduate: none	Student/Faculty: 16 to 1
Year: semesters, summer session	Tuition: $4644 ($8565)
Application Deadline: May 1	Room & Board: $4936
Freshman Class: 4538 applied, 2453 accepted, 454 enrolled	
SAT I Verbal/Math: 437/520	COMPETITIVE

Rutgers, The State University of New Jersey/Newark College of Arts and Science, a coeducational liberal arts institution, became part of Rutgers in 1946. In addition to regional accreditation, Newark College of Arts and Sciences has baccalaureate program accreditation with AACSB, CSWE, NASDTEC, and NASM. The 4 libraries contain 624,875 volumes, 733,742 microform items, and 27,123 audiovisual forms, and subscribe to 3680 periodicals. Computerized library sources and services include the card catalog, interlibrary loans, and database searching. Special learning facilities include a learning resource center, art gallery, and a TV and radio media center, a molecular and behavioral neuroscience center, and institutes of jazz studies and animal behavior. The 34-acre campus is in an urban area 7 miles west of New York City, in downtown Newark. Including residence halls, there are 18 buildings on campus.

Student Life: 94% of undergraduates are from New Jersey. Students come from 13 states, 46 foreign countries, and Canada. 34% are white; 19% Hispanic; 18% African American; 16% Asian American. The average age of freshmen is 19; all undergraduates, 23. 19% do not continue beyond their first year; 57% remain to graduate.

Housing: College-sponsored living facilities include coed dormitories and on-campus apartments. On-campus housing is available on a first-come, first-served basis. All students may keep cars on campus.

Activities: There are 2 local and 5 national fraternities and 4 local and 3 national sororities. There are 85 groups on campus, including art, band, cheerleading, chess, choir, chorale, chorus, computers, drama, ethnic, gay, honors, international, jazz band, literary magazine, musical theater, newspaper, orchestra, photography, political, professional, radio and TV, religious, social, social service, student government, and yearbook. Popular campus events include Latin Night Bash, Puerto Rican Quatro Festival, and gallery exhibitions.

Sports: There are 5 intercollegiate sports for men and 4 for women, and 5 intramural sports for men and 4 for women. Athletic and recreation facilities include an athletic center, a tennis complex, a swimming pool, soccer, softball, and baseball fields, racquetball courts, and a dance room.

Disabled Students: 80% of the campus is accessible to disabled students. The following facilities are available: wheelchair ramps, elevators, special parking, specially equipped rest rooms, special class scheduling, lowered drinking fountains, and lowered telephones. Facilities vary from building to building. However, all classes are scheduled in accessible locations for disabled students, and adaptations are made to individual needs in dormitory rooms.

Services: In addition to many counseling and information services, tutoring is available in most subjects. There is a reader service for the blind, and remedial math, reading, and writing.

Campus Safety and Security: Campus safety and security measures include 24-hour foot and vehicle patrol, self-defense education, escort service, and shuttle buses. In addition, there are informal discussions, pamphlets/posters/films, emergency telephones, and lighted pathways/sidewalks. Security guards assist Rutgers police in providing public safety services. There is also a student marshal program.

Programs of Study: Newark College of Arts and Sciences confers B.A. and B.S. degrees. Bachelor's degrees are awarded in BIOLOGICAL SCIENCE (biology/biological science, botany, and zoology), BUSINESS (accounting, banking and finance, business administration and management, management science, and marketing/retailing/merchandising), COMMUNICATIONS AND THE ARTS (art, art history and appreciation, dramatic arts, English, fine arts, French, German, Italian, journalism, music, Russian, and Spanish), COMPUTER AND PHYSICAL SCIENCE (applied mathematics, applied physics, chemistry, computer science, geology, information sciences and systems, mathematics, physics, and science), ENGINEERING AND ENVIRONMENTAL DESIGN (ceramic engineering, chemical engineering, civil engineering, electrical/electronics engineering, industrial engineering, and mechanical engineering), HEALTH PROFESSIONS (clinical science, medical laboratory technology, predentistry, and premedicine), SOCIAL SCIENCE (African American studies, American studies, anthropology, classical/ancient civilization, criminal justice, economics, Hispanic American studies, history, philosophy, political science/government, prelaw, psychology, Russian and Slavic studies, social work, sociology, and women's studies). Business, biology, and psychology have the largest enrollments.

Required: To graduate, students must complete 124 credit hours, including 30 or more in the major, and have a minimum GPA of 2.0. Distribution requirements include 8 credits of natural sciences, 6 credits each of history, literature, and social science; 3 additional credits in mathematics or natural science, and 3 credits each in fine arts and interdisciplinary study. English composition is also required.

Special: Students may cross-register at the New Jersey Institute of Technology and the University of Medicine and Dentistry of New Jersey. Study abroad is offered in 8 countries. Internships, dual majors, student-designed majors, pass-fail options, and nondegree study are available. The college offers accelerated degree programs in business administration and criminal justice and 2–2 and 2–3 engineering degrees with the College of Engineering in New Brunswick. There is a freshman honors program on campus, as well as 12 national honor societies, including Phi Beta Kappa. Almost all departments have honors programs.

Faculty/Classroom: 68% of faculty are male; 32%, female. All both teach and do research. Graduate students teach 10% of introductory courses. The average class size in an introductory lecture is 37; in a laboratory, 24; and in a regular course offering, 30.

Admissions: 54% of the 1995–96 applicants were accepted. The SAT I scores for the 1995–96 freshman class were as follows: Verbal—81% below 500, 18% between 500 and 599, and 1% between 600 and 700; Math—38% below 500, 43% between 500 and 599, 16% between 600 and 700, and 3% above 700. 47% of the current freshmen were in the top fifth of their class; 88% were in the top two fifths.

Requirements: The SAT I or ACT is required. Applicants must be graduates of an accredited secondary school. The GED is accepted. 16 academic credits or Carnegie units are required, including 4 years of English, 3 of mathematics (alegbra I and II and geometry), 2 each of a foreign language and science, plus 5 other approved academic subjects. AP and CLEP credits are accepted. Important factors in the admissions decision are advanced placement or honor courses, evidence of special talent, and leadership record.

Procedure: Freshmen are admitted fall and spring. Entrance exams should be taken by February of the senior year. There are early admissions and deferred admissions plans. Applications should be filed by May 1 for fall entry and November 15 for spring entry, along with an application fee of $50. Notification is sent on a rolling basis. A waiting list is an active part of the admissions procedure, with about 3% of all applicants on the list.

Transfer: 473 transfer students enrolled in 1995–96. Applicants must have a minimum GPA of 2.5 with a minimum of 12 credit hours earned. Grades of C or better in courses that correspond in content and credit to those offered by the college transfer for credit. Transfer students are admitted in the fall and spring semesters. 30 credits of 124 must be completed at Newark College of Arts and Sciences.

Visiting: There are regularly scheduled orientations for prospective students, including an information session with an admissions officer and a tour of the campus. There are guides for informal visits and visitors may sit in on classes. To schedule a visit, contact the Office of University Undergraduate Admissions.

Financial Aid: In 1995–96, 71% of all freshmen and 56% of continuing students received some form of financial aid. 64% of freshmen and 52% of continuing students received need-based aid. The average freshman award was $6799. Of that total, scholarships or need-based grants averaged $4510 ($8000 maximum); loans averaged $2356 ($6625 maximum); outside scholarships averaged $1350 ($4500 maximum); and work contracts averaged $1259 ($3700 maximum). 9% of undergraduate students work part-time. Average earnings from campus work for the school year are $981. The average financial indebtedness of the 1994-95 graduate was $6360. The FAFSA is required. The application deadline for fall entry is March 1.

International Students: There are currently 152 international students enrolled. They must take the TOEFL or the college's own test and achieve a minimum score on the TOEFL of 550. The student must also take the SAT I or the ACT.

Computers: The college provides computer facilities for student use. The mainframes are a Sun SPARC 1000 and a DEC VAX 8550. Individual departments also have a variety of minicomputers. All students on the Newark campus can generate their own accounts on this system. Access to the local systems, as well as to the New Brunswick central system, is provided through networked micro laboratories in major buildings on the campus. Stand-alone microcomputers are also available in one of the dorms. All students may access the system. There are no time limits. The fees are $100 per year.

Graduates: In 1994-95, 794 bachelor's degrees were awarded. The most popular majors among graduates were accounting (20%), management (9%), and psychology (9%). Within an average freshman class, 33% graduate in 4 years, 49% in 5 years, and 64% in 6 years. 194 companies recruited on campus in 1994-95.

Admissions Contact: John Scott, Director of Admissions.

RUTGERS, THE STATE UNIVERSITY OF NEW JERSEY/RUTGERS COLLEGE　　D-3

New Brunswick, NJ 08903　　(908) 445-3770; FAX: (908) 445-0237

Full-time: 4562 men, 4659 women	Faculty: 763; I, ++$
Part-time: 213 men, 139 women	Ph.D.s: 98%
Graduate: none	Student/Faculty: 12 to 1
Year: semesters, summer session	Tuition: $4836 ($8757)
Application Deadline: January 15	Room & Board: $4936
Freshman Class: 15,978 applied, 8510 accepted, 2056 enrolled	
SAT I Verbal/Math: 541/629	HIGHLY COMPETITIVE

Rutgers, The State University of New Jersey/Rutgers College, founded in 1766, is a coeducational liberal arts institution and the largest residential college in the Rutgers system. In addition to regional accreditation, Rutgers College has baccalaureate program accreditation with AACSB, NASDTEC, and NASM. The 14 libraries contain 4,480,097 volumes, 2,839,739 microform items, and 76,968 audiovisual forms, and subscribe to 18,274 periodicals. Computerized library sources and services include the card catalog, interlibrary loans, and database searching. Special learning facilities include a learning resource center, art gallery, radio station, TV station, a geology museum, and various research institutes and centers. The 2694-acre campus is in a suburban area 33 miles south of New York City. Including residence halls, there are 90 buildings on campus.

Student Life: 88% of undergraduates are from New Jersey. Students come from 41 states, 51 foreign countries, and Canada. 58% are white; 18% Asian American; 11% Hispanic. The average age of freshmen is 18.2; all undergraduates, 20.3. 9% do not continue beyond their first year; 81% remain to graduate.

Housing: College-sponsored living facilities include coed dormitories and on-campus apartments. Special living facilities include honors houses and special interest houses that have Latin Image (Hispanic) Paul Robeson (black experience), and language sections. Substance-free housing is also available. On-campus housing is available on a lottery system for upperclassmen. 54% of students live on campus. Alcohol is not permitted. Upperclassmen may keep cars on campus.

Activities: 11% of men belong to 31 national fraternities; 7% of women belong to 4 local and 11 national sororities. There are 400 groups on campus, including art, band, cheerleading, chess, choir, chorale, chorus, computers, dance, drama, drill team, ethnic, film, gay, honors, international, jazz band, literary magazine, marching band, musical theater, newspaper, orchestra, pep band, photography, political, professional, radio and TV, religious, social, social service, student government, symphony, and yearbook. Popular campus events include Rutgers Fest, International Festival, Unity Day Picnic, and Student Activities Fair.

Sports: There are 15 intercollegiate sports for men and 15 for women, and 28 intramural sports for men and 28 for women. Athletic and recreation facilities include a 41000-seat stadium, an athletic center, a gymnasium, a swimming pool, tennis courts, and a recreation center.

Disabled Students: 55% of the campus is accessible to disabled students. The following facilities are available: wheelchair ramps, elevators, special parking, specially equipped rest rooms, special class scheduling, lowered drinking fountains, and lowered telephones. Facilities available vary widely from building to building. However,

classes will be scheduled in accessible locations for disabled students, and adaptations will be made to individual needs in dormitories.

Services: In addition to many counseling and information services, tutoring is available in most subjects. The academic tutoring service provides specific course assistance in first- and second-level difficult courses. There is a reader service for the blind, and remedial math, reading, and writing.

Campus Safety and Security: Campus safety and security measures include 24-hour foot and vehicle patrol, self-defense education, escort service, and shuttle buses. In addition, there are informal discussions, pamphlets/posters/films, emergency telephones, and lighted pathways/sidewalks. The police department is supplemented by security guards and student safety officers.

Programs of Study: Rutgers College confers B.A. and B.S. degrees. Bachelor's degrees are awarded in BIOLOGICAL SCIENCE (biochemistry, biology/biological science, biometrics and biostatistics, botany, cell biology, ecology, evolutionary biology, genetics, microbiology, molecular biology, and physiology), BUSINESS (accounting, banking and finance, labor studies, management information systems, management science, and marketing/retailing/merchandising), COMMUNICATIONS AND THE ARTS (art history and appreciation, Chinese, classical languages, classics, communications, comparative literature, dance, dramatic arts, English, fine arts, French, German, Greek (classical), Italian, journalism, Latin, linguistics, music, Portuguese, Russian, Spanish, and visual and performing arts), COMPUTER AND PHYSICAL SCIENCE (chemistry, computer science, geology, mathematics, physics, and statistics), HEALTH PROFESSIONS (biomedical science, predentistry, premedicine, and public health), SOCIAL SCIENCE (African studies, American studies, anthropology, criminal justice, East Asian studies, economics, geography, Hispanic American studies, history, humanities, Judaic studies, Latin American studies, medieval studies, Middle Eastern studies, philosophy, physical fitness/movement, political science/government, prelaw, psychology, religion, Russian and Slavic studies, sociology, urban studies, and women's studies). Biological sciences, psychology, and English have the largest enrollments.

Required: To graduate, students must complete a total of 120 credit hours, including 30 hours in the major, with a minimum GPA of 2.0. The general education requirements include 2 courses each in writing skills, quantitative skills, natural science, social science, and humanities, and 1 each in non-Western world statistics. A major and a minor are required.

Special: Rutgers College offers internships, a Washington semester, study abroad in 8 countries, student-designed majors, accelerated degree programs in business and engineering, and dual majors in statistics and mathematics, and history and political science. A 2-3 degree with the College of Engineering is available, as are a 5-year business degree with the Graduate School of Management, a 5-year education degree with the Graduate School of Education, and an 8-year medical degree with the University of Medicine and Dentistry of New Jersey. There is a freshman honors program on campus, as well as 1 national honor society, Phi Beta Kappa. Almost all departments have honors programs.

Faculty/Classroom: 73% of faculty are male; 27%, female. All both teach and do research. Graduate students teach 32% of introductory courses. The average class size in an introductory lecture is 60; in a laboratory, 24; and in a regular course offering, 46.

Admissions: 53% of the 1995-96 applicants were accepted. The SAT I scores for the 1995-96 freshman class were as follows: Verbal—32% below 500, 44% between 500 and 599, 22% between 600 and 700, and 2% above 700; Math—8% below 500, 28% between 500 and 599, 47% between 600 and 700, and 17% above 700. 76% of the current freshmen were in the top fifth of their class; 98% were in the top two fifths. There were 14 National Merit finalists. 22 freshmen graduated first in their class.

Requirements: The SAT I or ACT is required. Applicants must have completed 16 high school credits or Carnegie units, including 4 years of English, 3 years of mathematics (algebra I and II and plane geometry), 2 years each of a foreign language and science, and 5 other academic subjects. Students without a high school diploma, those from a nonaccredited high school, or those with academic unit deficiencies, must take SAT II: Subject tests in writing, mathematics, and 1 other subject. AP credits are accepted. Important factors in the admissions decision are advanced placement or honor courses, evidence of special talent, and leadership record.

Procedure: Freshmen are admitted in the fall. Entrance exams should be taken by December of the senior year. There are early admissions and deferred admissions plans. Applications should be filed by January 15 for fall entry, along with an application fee of $50. Notification is sent by April 15. A waiting list is an active part of the admissions procedure, with about 6% of all applicants on the list.

Transfer: 634 transfer students enrolled in 1995-96. Students who have completed a minimum of 12 college credits are considered for transfer. Grades of C or better in courses that correspond in content and credit to those offered by the college transfer for credit. Transfer students are admitted in both the fall and spring semesters. 30 credits of 120 must be completed at Rutgers College.

Visiting: There are regularly scheduled orientations for prospective students, including an information session with an admissions officer followed by a bus tour with a student guide. Students-guided walking tours are also available, which include a meeting with a dean prior to the tour. Visitors may sit in on classes with prior arrangement. To schedule a visit, contact the Office of University Undergraduate Admissions.

Financial Aid: In 1995–96, 78% of all freshmen and 69% of continuing students received some form of financial aid. 50% of freshmen and 46% of continuing students received need-based aid. The average freshman award was $6157. Of that total, scholarships or need-based grants averaged $3894 ($14,050 maximum); loans averaged $2379 ($10,000 maximum); outside scholarships averaged $1283 ($9000 maximum); and work contracts averaged $1253 ($1500 maximum). 9% of undergraduate students work part-time. Average earnings from campus work for the school year are $825. The average financial indebtedness of the 1994–95 graduate was $7059. The FAFSA is required. The application deadline for fall entry is March 1.

International Students: There are currently 212 international students enrolled. They must take the TOEFL and achieve a minimum score of 550. The student must also take the SAT I or the ACT.

Computers: The college provides computer facilities for student use. Central computer systems include a cluster of 2 DEC VAX 8650 systems, 3 Sun SPARC Server 1000s, and 1 Sun SPARC Server 2000 UNIX system. Individual departments have a variety of minicomputers. The central systems may be accessed from Windows/DOS and Apple Macintosh personal computers, and X-terminals located in several large public laboratories. Services include E-mail, newsgroups, software applications, a campuswide information system, and access to the Internet. All students may access the system 24 hours a day. There are no time limits. The fees are $100 per year.

Graduates: In 1994–95, 2348 bachelor's degrees were awarded. The most popular majors among graduates were psychology (13%), English (9%), and political science (8%). Within an average freshman class, 57% graduate in 4 years, 76% in 5 years, and 81% in 6 years. 500 companies recruited on campus in 1994–95. Of the 1994 graduating class, 15% were enrolled in graduate school within 6 months of graduation and 66% had found employment.

Admissions Contact: Dr. Elizabeth Mitchell, Assistant Vice President for University Undergraduate Admissions.

RUTGERS, THE STATE UNIVERSITY OF NEW JERSEY/UNIVERSITY COLLEGE—CAMDEN

C-4

Camden, NJ 08102   (609) 225-6104

Full-time: 156 men, 142 women	Faculty: 133; IIA, + +$
Part-time: 193 men, 238 women	Ph.D.s: 98%
Graduate: none	Student/Faculty: 5 to 1
Year: semesters	Tuition: see profile
Application Deadline: May 1	Room & Board: n/app
Freshman Class: n/av	
SAT I or ACT: required	**SPECIAL**

Rutgers, The State University of New Jersey/University College-Camden, established in 1934, is a coeducational, liberal arts college serving part-time and evening adult students. Tuition is $122 per credit plus a $131 fee per semester for New Jersey residents; $250 per credit, plus a $131 fee per semester for out-of-state residents. In addition to regional accreditation, University College—Camden has baccalaureate program accreditation with CSWE and NASDTEC. The 2 libraries contain 377,416 volumes, 227,463 microform items, and 190 audiovisual forms, and subscribe to 2039 periodicals. Computerized library sources and services include the card catalog, interlibrary loans, and database searching. Special learning facilities include a learning resource center and art gallery. The 25-acre campus is in an urban area 1 mile east of Philadelphia, Pennsylvania. There are 22 buildings on campus.

Student Life: 98% of undergraduates are from New Jersey. Students come from 2 states. 67% are white; 16% African American. The average age of all undergraduates is 30.

Housing: There are no residence halls. Alcohol is not permitted.

Activities: There are no fraternities or sororities. There are 70 groups on campus, including choir, computers, drama, ethnic, gay, honors, international, literary magazine, newspaper, orchestra, political, professional, radio and TV, religious, social, social service, student government, theater, and yearbook. Popular campus events include Pioneer Pride Night, Springfest, Fallfest, and Diversity Week.

Sports: There is no sports program at University College—Camden.

Disabled Students: 95% of the campus is accessible to disabled students. The following facilities are available: wheelchair ramps, elevators, special parking, specially equipped rest rooms, special class scheduling, lowered drinking fountains, and lowered telephones. Facilities vary from building to building. However, all classes are scheduled in accessible locations for disabled students.

Services: In addition to many counseling and information services, tutoring is available in some subjects, including introductory classes. There is a reader service for the blind, and remedial math, reading, and writing.

Campus Safety and Security: Campus safety and security measures include 24-hour foot and vehicle patrol, self-defense education, escort service, and shuttle buses. In addition, there are informal discussions, pamphlets/posters/films, emergency telephones, and lighted pathways/sidewalks. The police department is supplemented by security guards.

Programs of Study: University College—Camden confers B.A. and B.S. degrees. Bachelor's degrees are awarded in BIOLOGICAL SCIENCE (biochemistry and biology/biological science), BUSINESS (accounting, banking and finance, management science, and marketing/retailing/merchandising), COMMUNICATIONS AND THE ARTS (art history and appreciation, dramatic arts, English, French, German, music, Spanish, and visual and performing arts), COMPUTER AND PHYSICAL SCIENCE (chemistry, computer science, mathematics, physics, and science), EDUCATION (elementary and secondary), HEALTH PROFESSIONS (medical laboratory technology, nursing, predentistry, and premedicine), SOCIAL SCIENCE (African American studies, American studies, economics, history, philosophy, political science/government, prelaw, psychology, social work, sociology, and urban studies). Psychology, business, and English have the largest enrollments.

Required: To graduate, students must complete 120 credits, with 30 to 48 in the major, and maintain a minimum GPA of 2.0. A core curriculum of 60 credits is required, including 3 credits each in literary masterpieces, art, music or theater arts, and a foreign language, with an additional 3 credits in English or a foreign language; and mathematics, with an additional 3 credits in mathematics, computer science or statistics. One interdisciplinary course is required, as are 9 credits from social science disciplines, 6 credits in English composition, 6 credits in history, 6 credits in the natural science disciplines, and an additional 9 credits in courses offered by a department(s) other than the major department.

Special: The college offers student-designed majors, dual majors, nondegree study, and pass/fail options. Students may study abroad in 8 countries. There is a freshman honors program on campus, as well as 1 national honor society. Almost all departments have honors programs.

Faculty/Classroom: 65% of faculty are male; 35%, female. All both teach and do research. The average class size in an introductory lecture is 37; in a laboratory, 24; and in a regular course offering, 31.

Requirements: The SAT I or ACT is required, but not for students who have been out of high school for two years or more. Applicants for admission must be graduates of an accredited secondary school. The GED is accepted. Students must have completed 16 academic credits or Carnegie units, including 4 years of English, 3 years of mathematics (algebra I and II and geometry), and 2 years of a foreign language, plus 7 additional academic units. AP and CLEP credits are accepted. Important factors in the admissions decision are advanced placement or honor courses, evidence of special talent, and leadership record.

Procedure: Freshmen are admitted fall and spring. There is a deferred admissions plan. Applications should be filed by May 1 for fall entry and November 15 for spring entry, along with an application fee of $40. Notification is sent on a rolling basis.

Transfer: 194 transfer students enrolled in 1995–96. Applicants must have a minimum GPA of 2.5 and a minimum of 12 credit hours. Grades of C or better in courses that correspond in content and credit to those offered by the college transfer for credit. Transfer students are admitted in the fall and spring semesters. 30 credits of 120 must be completed at University College—Camden.

Visiting: There are regularly scheduled orientations for prospective students, including an information session with an admissions officer and a campus tour. Visitors may sit in on classes. To schedule a visit, contact the Office of University Undergraduate Admission.

Financial Aid: In 1995–96, 53% of all freshmen and 34% of continuing students received some form of financial aid. 45% of freshmen and 29% of continuing students received need-based aid. The average freshman award was $5444. Of that total, scholarships or need-based grants averaged $3832 ($5700 maximum); loans averaged $2127 ($2625 maximum); work contracts averaged $1200 (maximum); and $750 (maximum) in other aid. Average earnings from campus work for the school year are $671. The average financial indebtedness of the 1994–95 graduate was $6943. The FAFSA is required. The application deadline for fall entry is March 1.

International Students: They must take the TOEFL and achieve a minimum score of 550. The student must also take the SAT I or the ACT.

Computers: The college provides computer facilities for student use. The mainframes are a Sun SPARC Server 10/41 and a 10/51 MP. Terminals or networked microcomputers are located in two major academic buildings, the library, the Campus Center, and dorms, and provide access to the central system, as well as to the Camden campus computers. The on-campus computer network includes on-line registration, E-mail, and access to the Internet and Bitnet. All students may access the system Monday through Thursday, 8:30 A.M. to 11 P.M.; Friday and Saturday, 9 A.M. to 5 P.M.; Sunday 2 P.M. to 10 P.M. (24 hours a day, 7 days a week through modem access.). There are no time limits. The fees are $10 per semester.

Graduates: In 1994–95, 59 bachelor's degrees were awarded. The most popular majors among graduates were psychology (24%), computer science (22%), and history (17%). 90 companies recruited on campus in 1994–95.

Admissions Contact: Dr. Deborah Bowles, Director of Admissions-Camden.

RUTGERS, THE STATE UNIVERSITY OF NEW JERSEY/UNIVERSITY COLLEGE—NEW BRUNSWICK

D-3

New Brunswick, NJ 08903

(908) 932-8093

Full-time: 361 men, 331 women	Faculty: 763; I, + +$
Part-time: 1036 men, 1251 women	Ph.D.s: 98%
Graduate: none	Student/Faculty: 4 to 1
Year: semesters, summer session	Tuition: see profile
Application Deadline: July 15	Room & Board: n/app
Freshman Class: n/av	
SAT I or ACT: not required	SPECIAL

Rutgers, The State University of New Jersey/University College—New Brunswick, founded in 1934, is a coeducational, liberal arts school for adult part-time students. Tuition is $122 per credit, plus a $102 fee per semester for New Jersey residents; $250 per credit, plus a $102 fee per semester for out-of-state residents. In addition to regional accreditation, University College—New Brunswick has baccalaureate program accreditation with AACSB, NASDTEC, and NASM. The 14 libraries contain 4,480,097 volumes, 2,839,739 microform items, and 76,968 audiovisual forms, and subscribe to 18,274 periodicals. Computerized library sources and services include the card catalog, interlibrary loans, and database searching. Special learning facilities include a learning resource center, art gallery, radio station, TV station, a geology museum, and various research centers. The 2694-acre campus is in a small town 33 miles south of New York City. There are 100 buildings on campus.

Student Life: 98% of undergraduates are from New Jersey. Students come from 8 states. 73% are white. The average age of all undergraduates is 31.

Housing: There are no residence halls.

Activities: There are no fraternities or sororities. There are 400 groups on campus, including art, band, cheerleading, chess, choir, chorale, chorus, computers, dance, drama, drill team, ethnic, film, gay, honors, international, jazz band, literary magazine, marching band, musical theater, newspaper, orchestra, pep band, photography, political, professional, radio and TV, religious, social, social service, student government, symphony, and yearbook. Popular campus events include Homecoming, theater trips, and a picnic.

Sports: There is no sports program at University College—New Brunswick.

Disabled Students: 55% of the campus is accessible to disabled students. The following facilities are available: wheelchair ramps, elevators, special parking, specially equipped rest rooms, special class scheduling, lowered drinking fountains, and lowered telephones. Facilities vary from building to building. However, all classes will be scheduled in accessible locations for disabled students.

Services: In addition to many counseling and information services, tutoring is available in most subjects. The academic tutoring service provides specific course assistance in first- and second-level difficult courses. There is remedial math, reading, and writing.

Campus Safety and Security: Campus safety and security measures include 24-hour foot and vehicle patrol, self-defense education, escort service, and shuttle buses. In addition, there are informal discussions, pamphlets/posters/films, emergency telephones, and lighted pathways/sidewalks. The police department is supplemented by security guards and student safety officers.

Programs of Study: University College—New Brunswick confers B.A. and B.S. degrees. Bachelor's degrees are awarded in BIOLOGICAL SCIENCE (biochemistry, biology/biological science, botany, cell biology, ecology, evolutionary biology, genetics, microbiology, molecular biology, nutrition, and physiology), BUSINESS (accounting, banking and finance, business administration and management, labor studies, management science, and marketing/retailing/merchandising), COMMUNICATIONS AND THE ARTS (art, art history and appreciation, Chinese, classics, communications, comparative literature, dance, dramatic arts, English, fine arts, French, German, Greek, Italian, journalism, Latin, linguistics, music, Portuguese, Russian, Spanish, and visual and performing arts), COMPUTER AND PHYSICAL SCIENCE (chemistry, computer science, geology, mathematics, physics, and statistics), EDUCATION (vocational), HEALTH PROFESSIONS (biomedical science, predentistry, premedicine, and public health), SOCIAL SCIENCE (African American studies, American studies, anthropology, Asian/Oriental studies, criminal justice, economics, food science, geography, Hispanic American studies, history, humanities, Judaic studies, Latin American studies, Middle Eastern studies, philosophy, physical fitness/movement, political science/government, prelaw, psychology, religion, Russian and Slavic studies, sociology, urban studies, and women's studies). Biological sciences, psychology, and English have the largest enrollments.

Required: To graduate, students must complete 120 credits, with a minimum GPA of 2.0. A liberal arts core requirement includes 6 credits of English composition and 12 credits each of humanities, social sciences, mathematics, and science.

Special: Internships are available. The college offers study abroad in 8 countries. A Washington semester, B.A.-B.S. degrees, student-designed majors, nondegree study, and pass/fail options are available. There is a freshman honors program on campus, as well as 2 national honor societies, including Phi Beta Kappa. Almost all departments have honors programs.

Faculty/Classroom: 73% of faculty are male; 27%, female. All both teach and do research. The average class size in an introductory lecture is 60; in a laboratory, 24; and in a regular course offering, 46.

Requirements: Applicants must be graduates of an accredited secondary school. The GED is accepted. Students must have completed 16 academic credits or Carnegie units, including 4 years of English, 3 years of mathematics (algebra I and II and geometry), 2 years of a foreign language, and 7 additional academic units. Ordinarily, University College-New Brunswick does not admit applicants who apply within 2 years of high school graduation unless they have completed 24 transferable credits with a 2.5 GPA at another college. AP and CLEP credits are accepted. Important factors in the admissions decision are evidence of special talent, extracurricular activities record, and ability to finance college education.

Procedure: Applications should be filed by July 15 for fall entry and December 1 for spring entry, along with an application fee of $50. Notification is sent on a rolling basis.

Transfer: 809 transfer students enrolled in 1995–96. Applicant must have a 2.5 GPA with a minimum of 24 credit hours earned. Grades of C or better transfer for credit. Transfers are admitted in the fall or spring. 30 credits of 120 must be completed at University College—New Brunswick.

Visiting: There are regularly scheduled orientations for prospective students, including a preadmission orientation for prospective students. To schedule a visit, contact University College Admissions.

Financial Aid: In 1995–96, 14% of all freshmen and 23% of continuing students received some form of financial aid. 12% of freshmen and 20% of continuing students received need-based aid. The average freshman award was $6717. Of that total, scholarships or need-based grants averaged $3397 ($8605 maximum); and loans averaged $2625 (maximum). Average earnings from campus work for the school year are $752. The average financial indebtedness of the 1994–95 graduate was $6348. The FAFSA is required. The application deadline for fall entry is March 1.

International Students: There are currently 4 international students enrolled. They must take the TOEFL or the college's own test and achieve a minimum score on the TOEFL of 550.

Computers: The college provides computer facilities for student use. Central systems include a cluster of 2 DEC VAX 8650 systems, 3 Sun SPARC Server 1000s, and a Sun SPARC Server 2000 UNIX system. Individual departments have a variety of minicomputers. The central systems may be accessed from Windows/DOS and Apple Macintosh personal computers, and X-terminals located in several large public laboratories. Services include E-mail, newsgroups, software applications, a campuswide information system, and access to the Internet. All students may access the system 24 hours per day. There are no time limits. The fees are $10 per semester.

Graduates: In 1994–95, 441 bachelor's degrees were awarded. The most popular majors among graduates were psychology (11%), economics (8%), and English (8%). 500 companies recruited on campus in 1994–95.

Admissions Contact: Loretta Daniel, Director of Admissions.

RUTGERS, THE STATE UNIVERSITY OF NEW JERSEY/UNIVERSITY COLLEGE—NEWARK

E-2

Newark, NJ 07102
(201) 648-5205

Full-time: 303 men, 340 women	Faculty: 189; IIA, + +$
Part-time: 660 men, 612 women	Ph.D.s: 98%
Graduate: none	Student/Faculty: 10 to 1
Year: semesters, summer session	Tuition: see profile
Application Deadline: August 1	Room & Board: n/app
Freshman Class: n/av	
SAT I or ACT: required	**LESS COMPETITIVE**

Rutgers, The State University of New Jersey/University College—Newark, founded in 1934, is a liberal arts evening school designed for part-time adult students. Tuition is $122 per credit, plus a $108 fee per semester for New Jersey residents; $250 per credit, plus a $108 fee per semester for out-of-state residents. In addition to regional accreditation, University College—Newark has baccalaureate program accreditation with AACSB, CSWE, and NASDTEC. The 4 libraries contain 624,875 volumes, 733,742 microform items, and 27,123 audiovisual forms, and subscribe to 3680 periodicals. Computerized library sources and services include the card catalog, interlibrary loans, and database searching. Special learning facilities include a learning resource center, art gallery, a molecular and behavioral neuroscience center, and institutes of jazz and animal behavior. The 34-acre campus is in an urban area 7 miles west of New York City, in downtown Newark. There are 18 buildings on campus.

Student Life: 93% of undergraduates are from New Jersey. Students come from 5 states and 5 foreign countries. 33% are African American; 32% white; 14% Hispanic; 11% Asian American. The average age of freshmen is 23.2; all undergraduates, 28.6.

Housing: There are no residence halls. Alcohol is not permitted.

Activities: There are no fraternities or sororities. There are 85 groups on campus, including art, band, chess, choir, chorale, chorus, computers, drama, ethnic, gay, honors, international, jazz band, literary magazine, musical theater, newspaper, orchestra, political, professional, radio and TV, religious, social, social service, student government, and yearbook. Popular campus events include Latin Night Bash, Puerto Rican Quatro Festival, and gallery exhibitions.

Sports: There is no sports program at University College—Newark.

Disabled Students: 80% of the campus is accessible to disabled students. The following facilities are available: wheelchair ramps, elevators, special parking, specially equipped rest rooms, special class scheduling, lowered drinking fountains, and lowered telephones. Facilities vary from building to building. However, all classes will be scheduled in accessible locations for disabled students.

Services: In addition to many counseling and information services, tutoring is available in most subjects. There is a reader service for the blind, and remedial math, reading, and writing.

Campus Safety and Security: Campus safety and security measures include 24-hour foot and vehicle patrol, self-defense education, escort service, and shuttle buses. In addition, there are informal discussions, pamphlets/posters/films, emergency telephones, and lighted pathways/sidewalks. Security guards assist Rutgers police in providing public safety services. There is also a student marshal program.

Programs of Study: University College—Newark confers B.A. and B.S. degrees. Bachelor's degrees are awarded in BUSINESS (accounting, banking and finance, business administration and management, management science, and marketing/retailing/merchandising), COMMUNICATIONS AND THE ARTS (English), COMPUTER AND PHYSICAL SCIENCE (computer science and information sciences and systems), HEALTH PROFESSIONS (predentistry and premedicine), SOCIAL SCIENCE (criminal justice, economics, history, philosophy, political science/government, prelaw, psychology, social work, and sociology). Business, English, and psychology have the largest enrollments.

Required: To graduate, students must complete 124 credits with a minimum GPA of 2.0. Distribution requirements include 8 credits in natural science/mathematics or 3 courses in nonlaboratory science, mathematics, or computer science; 6 credits each in history, literature, social sciences, humanities, and fine arts; 1 course in critical thinking; and 15 credits of electives. All students must take English composition and demonstrate mathematics proficiency either by examination, by successfully completing a college algebra course or any other advanced course in mathematics, or by successfully completing (with a grade of C or better) a college-level calculus course, or (with a grade of B or better) a precalculus course.

Special: Students may cross-register with the New Jersey Institute of Technology and the University of Medicine and Dentistry of New Jersey. Internships are available. The school offers study abroad, accelerated degree programs in business administration and criminal justice, dual majors, student-designed majors, nondegree study, and pass/fail options. There is a freshman honors program on campus, as well as 12 national honor societies, including Phi Beta Kappa. Almost all departments have honors programs.

Faculty/Classroom: 68% of faculty are male; 32%, female. All both teach and do research. The average class size in an introductory lecture is 26; in a laboratory, 24; and in a regular course offering, 28.

Requirements: The SAT I or ACT is required. Students must be graduates of an accredited high school. The GED is accepted. Students should have completed 16 high school academic credits or Carnegie units, including 4 years of English, 3 years of mathematics, 2 years of a foreign language, and 7 other academic units. AP and CLEP credits are accepted. Important factors in the admissions decision are advanced placement or honor courses, evidence of special talent, and leadership record.

Procedure: Freshmen are admitted fall and spring. There is a deferred admissions plan. Applications should be filed by August 1 for fall entry and December 1 for spring entry, along with an application fee of $50. Notification is sent on a rolling basis.

Transfer: 345 transfer students enrolled in 1995–96. Students who have completed at least 12 credit hours at another college with a cumulative GPA of 2.0 are considered for admission as transfer students. Transfers are admitted in the fall and spring. 30 credits of 124 must be completed at University College—Newark.

Visiting: There are regularly scheduled orientations for prospective students, including an information session with an admissions counselor and a tour of the campus. There are guides for informal visits and visitors may sit in on classes. To schedule a visit, contact the Office of University Undergraduate Admissions-Newark.

Financial Aid: In 1995–96, 58% of all freshmen and 39% of continuing students received some form of financial aid. 52% of freshmen and 35% of continuing students received need-based aid. The average freshman award was $5729. Of that total, scholarships or need-based grants averaged $3991 ($8999 maximum); loans averaged $2328 ($2625 maximum); and work contracts averaged $1306 ($1500 maximum). 1% of undergraduate students work part-time. Average earnings from campus work for the school year are $821. The average financial indebtedness of the 1994–95 graduate was $7501. The FAFSA is required. The application deadline for fall entry is March 1.

International Students: There are currently 19 international students enrolled. They must take the TOEFL or the college's own test and achieve a minimum score on the TOEFL of 550.

Computers: The college provides computer facilities for student use. The mainframes are a Sun SPARC 1000 and a DEC VAX 8550. Individual departments also have a variety of minicomputers. All students on the Newark campus can generate their own accounts on this system. Access to the local systems, as well as to the New Brunswick central system, is provided through networked micro laboratories in major buildings on the campus. All students may access the system. There are no time limits. The fees are $10 per semester.

Graduates: In 1994–95, 221 bachelor's degrees were awarded. The most popular majors among graduates were accounting (32%), management (13%), and criminal justice (9%). 194 companies recruited on campus in 1994–95.

Admissions Contact: John Scott, Director of Admissions-Newark.

SAINT PETER'S COLLEGE

E-2

Jersey City, NJ 07306
(201) 915-9213; FAX: (201) 432-5860

Full-time: 1033 men, 1166 women	Faculty: 111; IIB, av$
Part-time: 275 men, 743 women	Ph.D.s: 81%
Graduate: 220 men, 217 women	Student/Faculty: 20 to 1
Year: semesters, summer session	Tuition: $10,965
Application Deadline: open	Room & Board: $5440
Freshman Class: 1891 applied, 1576 accepted, 602 enrolled	
SAT I Verbal/Math: 430/470	**COMPETITIVE**

Saint Peter's College, founded in 1872, is a coeducational liberal arts and business college affiliated with the Roman Catholic Church and known as New Jersey's Jesuit College. There are 2 undergraduate and 2 graduate schools. In addition to regional accreditation, SPC has baccalaureate program accreditation with NLN. The 2 libraries contain 320,958 volumes, 636 microform items, and 5169 audiovisual forms, and subscribe to 1455 periodicals. Computerized library sources and services include the card catalog, interlibrary loans, and database searching. Special learning facilities include a learning resource center, art gallery, radio station, and TV station. The 10-acre campus is in an urban area 2 miles west of New York City. Including residence halls, there are 24 buildings on campus.

Student Life: 84% of undergraduates are from New Jersey. Students come from 10 states, 15 foreign countries, and Canada. 50% are from public schools; 50% from private. 57% are white; 21% Hispanic; 12% African American. Most are Catholic. 27% do not continue beyond their first year; 53% remain to graduate.

Housing: 485 students can be accommodated in college housing. College-sponsored living facilities include single-sex and coed dormitories and on-campus apartments. On-campus housing is guaranteed for all 4 years. 78% of students commute. Upperclassmen may keep cars on campus.

Activities: There are no fraternities or sororities. There are 50 groups on campus, including cheerleading, chess, chorus, computers, drama, ethnic, honors, international, literary magazine, newspaper, pep band, political, professional, radio and TV, religious, social, social service, student government, and yearbook. Popular campus events include International Day, career fairs, and SpringFest.

Sports: There are 11 intercollegiate sports for men and 9 for women, and 19 intramural sports for men and 19 for women. Athletic and recreation facilities include a recreational center, a 2000-seat gymnasium, and an athletic field.

Disabled Students: 80% of the campus is accessible to disabled students. The following facilities are available: wheelchair ramps, elevators, special parking, specially equipped rest rooms, lowered drinking fountains, lowered telephones, and specially equipped rooms in residence halls.

Services: In addition to many counseling and information services, tutoring is available in every subject. There is a reader service for the blind, and remedial math, reading, and writing.

Campus Safety and Security: Campus safety and security measures include 24-hour foot and vehicle patrol, self-defense education, escort service, and shuttle buses. There are informal discussions, pamphlets/posters/films, and emergency telephones.

Programs of Study: SPC confers B.A., B.S., and B.S.N. degrees. Associate and master's degrees are also awarded. Bachelor's degrees are awarded in BIOLOGICAL SCIENCE (biochemistry and biology/biological science), BUSINESS (accounting, business administration and management, international business management, and marketing/retailing/merchandising), COMMUNICATIONS AND THE ARTS (classical languages, classics, English, fine arts, and Spanish), COMPUTER AND PHYSICAL SCIENCE (chemistry, computer science, mathematics, natural sciences, and physics), EDUCATION (elementary and secondary), HEALTH PROFESSIONS (health care administration, medical laboratory technology, nursing, predentistry, and premedicine), SOCIAL SCIENCE (American studies, economics, history, humanities, philosophy, political science/government, prelaw, psychology, social science, sociology, theological studies, and urban studies). Natural sciences and accounting are the strongest academically. Business administration, accounting, computer sciences, and education have the largest enrollments.

Required: To graduate, students must complete 129 credit hours, including 57 in the core curriculum, 12 in core electives, between 30 and 45 in the major, and the rest in subjects related to the major. The core curriculum consists of courses in communications, literature, mathematics, natural sciences, social science, philosophy, history, theology, fine arts, and a modern language. Students must earn a GPA of 2.0.

Special: There are co-op programs with local companies, as well as departmental programs. A Washington semester and study abroad in any of 60 countries are offered. The college also offers dual majors and student-designed majors, credit for life, military, and work experience, nondegree study, and pass/fail options. There is a freshman honors program on campus, as well as 9 national honor societies. One department has an honors program.

Faculty/Classroom: 74% of faculty are male; 26%, female. All teach undergraduates. No introductory courses are taught by graduate students. The average class size in an introductory lecture is 21 and in a regular course offering, 19.

Admissions: 83% of the 1995–96 applicants were accepted. The SAT I scores for the 1995–96 freshman class were as follows: Verbal—83% below 500, 14% between 500 and 599, and 3% between 600 and 700; Math—61% below 500, 25% between 500 and 599, 12% between 600 and 700, and 1% above 700. 43% of the current freshmen were in the top fifth of their class; 67% were in the top two fifths. 6 freshmen graduated first in their class.

Requirements: The SAT I is required. Applicants must be high school graduates or submit the GED certificate. Students should have completed 16 Carnegie units of high school study, including 4 years of English, 3 of mathematics, 2 each of science, history, and a foreign language, and another 3 of additional work in any of these subjects. They must be in the top 50% of their high school class, and present an essay and letters of recommendation. The school recommends an interview. AP and CLEP credits are accepted. Important factors in the admissions decision are advanced placement or honor courses, extracurricular activities record, and recommendations by school officials.

Procedure: Freshmen are admitted fall and spring. Entrance exams should be taken by the fall of the senior year. There are early admissions and deferred admissions plans. Application deadlines are open. The fee is $30. Notification is sent on a rolling basis.

Transfer: The school requires a 2.0 college GPA of transfer students, as well as a high school transcript and an 800 composite SAT I score for students less than 2 years out of high school. An interview is recommended. 30 credits of 129 must be completed at SPC.

Visiting: There are regularly scheduled orientations for prospective students, including open houses, weekend and weekday visit days with a tour and class and information sessions, as well as tours and interviews by appointment. There are guides for informal visits and visitors may sit in on classes. To schedule a visit, contact the Admissions Office.

Financial Aid: In 1995–96, 85% of all freshmen and 80% of continuing students received some form of financial aid. 80% of freshmen and 75% of continuing students received need-based aid. The average freshman award was $8700. Of that total, scholarships or need-based grants averaged $4000 ($14,500 maximum); loans averaged $2000 ($2625 maximum); and work contracts averaged $1000 ($2000 maximum). 18% of undergraduate students work part-time. Average earnings from campus work for the school year are $1500. The average financial indebtedness of the 1994–95 graduate was $4812. SPC is a member of CSS. The FAFSA is required.

International Students: There were 46 international students enrolled in a recent year. The school actively recruits these students. They must score 500 on the TOEFL.

Computers: The college provides computer facilities for student use. The mainframes are an IBM 9370, a DEC VAX 780, 2 DEC PDP-11/44, and a DEC PDP-11/24. There are also a number of microcomputers available in computer laboratories, and the VAX can be accessed from outside computers by modem. All students may access the system. It may be used for remote access 24 hours a day; for local access, about 70 hours a week. There are no time limits and no fees.

Graduates: In 1994–95, 421 bachelor's degrees were awarded. The most popular majors among graduates were business management (22%), accountancy (18%), and elementary education (10%). Within an average freshman class, 30% graduate in 4 years, 46% in 5 years, and 48% in 6 years. 75 companies recruited on campus in 1994–95.

Admissions Contact: Jay Leiendecker, Associate Vice President for Enrollment.

SETON HALL UNIVERSITY
E-2
South Orange, NJ 07079–2691
(201) 761–9332
(800) THE-HALL; FAX: (201) 761–9452

Full-time: 1906 men, 2266 women	Faculty: 299; IIA, +$
Part-time: 401 men, 514 women	Ph.D.s: 87%
Graduate: 2044 men, 2486 women	Student/Faculty: 14 to 1
Year: semesters, summer session	Tuition: $12,250
Application Deadline: March 1	Room & Board: $6710
Freshman Class: 4941 applied, 3667 accepted, 966 enrolled	
SAT I or ACT: required	COMPETITIVE

Seton Hall University, founded in 1856 by the first bishop of Newark and affiliated with the Roman Catholic Church, has undergraduate programs in the colleges of arts and sciences, business, education and human services, and nursing. There are 4 undergraduate and 7 graduate schools. In addition to regional accreditation, Seton Hall has baccalaureate program accreditation with AACSB, CSWE, and NLN. The 2 libraries contain 501,153 volumes, 369,722 microform items, and 16,035 audiovisual forms, and subscribe to 3047 periodicals. Computerized library sources and services include the card catalog, interlibrary loans, and database searching. Special learning facilities include a learning resource center, art gallery, natural history museum, radio station, and TV station. The 58-acre campus is in a suburban area 14 miles west of New York City. Including residence halls, there are 34 buildings on campus.

Student Life: 84% of undergraduates are from New Jersey. Students come from 36 states, 43 foreign countries, and Canada. 60% are from public schools; 40% from private. 58% are white; 12% African American. The average age of freshmen is 18; all undergraduates, 20. 15% do not continue beyond their first year; 64% remain to graduate.

Housing: 2000 students can be accommodated in college housing. College-sponsored living facilities include single-sex and coed dormitories and off-campus apartments. In addition, there are special interest houses and an all-quiet residence hall, an all-female residence hall, and modern language and transfers floors. On-campus housing is guaranteed for the freshman year only, is available on a first-come, first-served basis, and is available on a lottery system for upperclassmen. Priority is given to out-of-town students. 50% of students live on campus; of those, 70% remain on campus on weekends. Upperclassmen may keep cars on campus.

Activities: 25% of men belong to 12 national fraternities; 25% of women belong to 10 national sororities. There are 100 groups on campus, including art, cheerleading, choir, chorus, computers, drama, drill team, ethnic, honors, international, literary magazine, musical theater, newspaper, pep band, photography, political, professional, radio and TV, religious, social, social service, student government, and yearbook. Popular campus events include Theatre-in-the-Round, lawn parties, International Students Day, and Welcome Weekend.

Sports: There are 10 intercollegiate sports for men and 9 for women, and 25 intramural sports for men and 25 for women. Athletic and recreation facilities include a 3400-seat gymnasium, an indoor track, an indoor pool, a dance studio, a weight room, a soccer and baseball field, a softball field, and tennis and racquetball courts. School teams also use the Meadowlands Arena, which seats 19,759.

Disabled Students: The entire campus is accessible to persons with physical disabilities. The following facilities are available: wheelchair ramps, elevators, special parking, specially equipped rest rooms, special class scheduling, lowered drinking fountains, and lowered telephones.

Services: In addition to many counseling and information services, tutoring is available in most subjects. There is also a reader service for the blind, remedial math, reading, and writing, and tutorial assistance for disabled students.

Campus Safety and Security: Campus safety and security measures include 24-hour foot and vehicle patrol, informal discussions, pamphlets/posters/films, and emergency telephones. In addition, there are lighted pathways/sidewalks. Paid student security attendants are posted at residence hall entrances.

Programs of Study: Seton Hall confers B.A., B.S., B.S.Ed., and B.S.N. degrees. Master's and doctoral degrees are also awarded. Bachelor's degrees are awarded in BIOLOGICAL SCIENCE (biology/biological science), BUSINESS (accounting, banking and finance, business administration and management, business economics, marketing/retailing/merchandising, and sports management), COMMUNICATIONS AND THE ARTS (art, communications, English, French, Italian, modern language, music, and Spanish), COMPUTER AND PHYSICAL SCIENCE (chemistry, computer science, information sciences and systems, mathematics, and physics), EDUCATION (elementary, physical, and secondary), HEALTH PROFESSIONS (nursing, predentistry, and premedicine), SOCIAL SCIENCE (African American studies, anthropology, Asian/Oriental studies, classical/ancient civilization, criminal justice, economics, history, liberal arts/general studies, philosophy, political science/government, prelaw, psychology, religion, social science, social work, and sociology). Business (accounting, finance), premedical, and predental are the strongest academically. Communications, accounting, and political science have the largest enrollments.

Required: To graduate, students must complete at least 128 hours, including a minimum of 36 hours in the major, both varying by major. Students must take freshman composition as well as courses in English, mathematics, social science, natural sciences, religious studies, and philosophy, earning a minimum GPA of 2.0 (2.5 in the College of Education and Human Services).

Special: Co-op and work-study are possible through the College of Arts and Sciences and the School of Business, and internships are available in many arts and sciences majors. Education majors go into the field during their sophomore year. There is a 3-week optional winter session. Cross-registration in engineering and 3–2 engineering degrees are offered with the New Jersey Institute of Technology and Stevens Institute of Technology. Students may take a Washington semester or study abroad in more than 100 countries. An accelerated B.S.N. degree, a 5-year B.A.-M.B.A., and a 5-year B.A.-B.S. degree in engineering are offered. Nondegree study is permitted, as are pass/fail options in electives. There is a freshman honors program on campus, as well as 20 national honor societies. 10 departments have honors programs.

Faculty/Classroom: 67% of faculty are male; 33%, female. No introductory courses are taught by graduate students. The average class size in an introductory lecture is 50; in a laboratory, 20; and in a regular course offering, 25.

Admissions: 74% of the 1995–96 applicants were accepted. The SAT I scores for the 1995–96 freshman class were as follows: Verbal—71% below 500, 23% between 500 and 599, 5% between 600 and 700, and 1% above 700; Math—47% below 500, 38% between 500 and 599, 13% between 600 and 700, and 2% above 700. 28% of the current freshmen were in the top fifth of their class; 51% were in the top two fifths.

Requirements: The SAT I or ACT is required. Seton Hall recommends a composite score higher than 1050 on SAT I, with at least 500 on each part, or a composite score of 24 on the ACT. Applicants must supply high school transcripts or a GED certificate. Students should have completed 16 Carnegie units of high school study, including 4 years of English, 3 of mathematics, 2 each of a foreign language and either history or social studies, and 1 of science. An essay is optional, and an interview is recommended. AP and CLEP credits are accepted. Important factors in the admissions decision are advanced placement or honor courses, leadership record, and parents or siblings attending the school.

Procedure: Freshmen are admitted fall and spring. Entrance exams should be taken by January of the senior year. There is a deferred admissions plan. Applications should be filed by March 1 for fall entry and December 1 for spring entry, along with an application fee of $25. Notification is sent on a rolling basis. A waiting list is an active part of the admissions procedure, with about 7% of all applicants on the list.

Transfer: 365 transfer students enrolled in 1995–96. Transfer students should have earned 30 hours of college credit, with a minimum GPA of 2.5, or 2.8 for the business and science schools. The SAT I is required for students with fewer than 30 credits of college-level work at the time of application, and an interview is recommended. 30 credits of 128 must be completed at Seton Hall.

Visiting: There are regularly scheduled orientations for prospective students, including Freshmen Preview (accepted students only), tours, meetings with departments, student talk, Freshman Studies talk, and financial aid and housing information. Visitors may sit in on classes. To schedule a visit, contact the Office of Admissions.

Financial Aid: In 1995–96, 93% of all freshmen and 83% of continuing students received some form of financial aid. 74% of freshmen and 63% of continuing students received need-based aid. The average freshman award was $13,500. Of that total, scholarships or need-based grants averaged $7500 ($15,200 maximum); loans averaged $4000 ($4400 maximum); and work contracts averaged $2000 ($3000 maximum). 20% of undergraduate students work part-time. Average earnings from campus work for the school year are $1200. The average financial indebtedness of the 1994–95 graduate was $20,000. Seton Hall is a member of CSS. The FAFSA is required. The application deadline for fall entry is April 15.

International Students: There are currently 72 international students enrolled. The school actively recruits these students. They must take the TOEFL and achieve a minimum score of 550. The student must also take the SAT I or the ACT.

Computers: The college provides computer facilities for student use. The mainframe is an IBM 4381. Approximately 300 microcomputers in public laboratories may be used to access the mainframe, networked file servers, the campuswide information system, the library catalog, and the Internet. All students may access the system. Public laboratories are available until 11 P.M.; there is 24-hour remote connection availability. There are no time limits and no fees.

Graduates: In 1994–95, 1030 bachelor's degrees were awarded. The most popular majors among graduates were communications (11%), accounting (9%), and finance (7%). Within an average freshman class, 1% graduate in 3 years, 45% in 4 years, 61% in 5 years, and 64% in 6 years. 1000 companies recruited on campus in 1994–95. Of the 1994 graduating class, 20% were enrolled in graduate school within 6 months of graduation and 50% had found employment.

Admissions Contact: Edward A. Blankmeyer, Director of Admissions. A campus video is available.

STEVENS INSTITUTE OF TECHNOLOGY E-2
Hoboken, NJ 07030 (201) 216-5194
(800) 247-7722; FAX: (201) 216-8348

Full-time: 1035 men, 278 women	Faculty: 90
Part-time: 9 men, 2 women	Ph.D.s: 90%
Graduate: 1326 men and women	Student/Faculty: 15 to 1
Year: semesters, summer session	Tuition: $17,980
Application Deadline: March 1	Room & Board: $5290
Freshman Class: 1935 applied, 1345 accepted, 405 enrolled	
SAT I Verbal/Math: 530/670	VERY COMPETITIVE +

Stevens Institute of Technology, founded in 1870, is a private coeducational institution offering programs of study in science, computer science, engineering, and humanities. There is one graduate school. In addition to regional accreditation, Stevens has baccalaureate program accreditation with ABET. The library contains 106,288 volumes, 850 microform items, and 1450 audiovisual forms, and subscribes to 2640 periodicals. Computerized library sources and services include the card catalog, interlibrary loans, and database searching. Special learning facilities include an art gallery, radio station, TV station, laboratory for ocean and coastal engineering, environmental laboratory, design and manufacturing institute, and telecommunications institute. The 55-acre campus is in an urban area 1 mile west of New York City. Including residence halls, there are 30 buildings on campus.

Student Life: 63% of undergraduates are from New Jersey. Students come from 33 states and 40 foreign countries. 73% are from public schools; 26% from private. 57% are white; 25% Asian American; 11% Hispanic. The average age of freshmen is 18; all undergraduates, 20. 17% do not continue beyond their first year; 70% remain to graduate.

Housing: 1015 students can be accommodated in college housing. College-sponsored living facilities include single-sex and coed dormitories, off-campus apartments, married-student housing, fraternity houses, and sorority houses. On-campus housing is guaranteed for all 4 years. 80% of students live on campus; of those, 80% remain on campus on weekends. Upperclassmen may keep cars on campus.

Activities: 40% of men and about 30% of women belong to 10 national fraternities; 40% of women belong to 3 national sororities. There are 50 groups on campus, including art, band, cheerleading, chess, chorus, computers, drama, ethnic, international, jazz band, literary magazine, musical theater, newspaper, pep band, photography, political, professional, radio and TV, religious, social, social service, student government, and yearbook. Popular campus events include Fall Tech Fest and Spring Boken Festival.

Sports: There are 10 intercollegiate sports for men and 4 for women, and 18 intramural sports for men and 18 for women. Athletic and recreation facilities include a 60,000-square-foot complex with an NCAA regulation swimming pool convertible to international size, squash courts, a 1000-seat basketball arena, fitness rooms, racquetball courts, a playing field, a student union, and several outdoor courts.

Disabled Students: 25% of the campus is accessible to disabled students. The following facilities are available: wheelchair ramps, elevators, special parking, specially equipped rest rooms, and lowered drinking fountains.

Services: In addition to many counseling and information services, tutoring is available in every subject.

Campus Safety and Security: Campus safety and security measures include 24-hour foot and vehicle patrol, self-defense education, escort service, and informal discussions. In addition, there are pamphlets/posters/films, emergency telephones, and lighted pathways/sidewalks.

Programs of Study: Stevens confers B.A., B.S., and B.E. degrees. Master's and doctoral degrees are also awarded. Bachelor's degrees are awarded in BIOLOGICAL SCIENCE (biochemistry), BUSINESS (management science), COMMUNICATIONS AND THE ARTS (literature), COMPUTER AND PHYSICAL SCIENCE (chemistry, computer science, mathematics, physics, polymer science, science, and statistics), ENGINEERING AND ENVIRONMENTAL DESIGN (chemical engineering, civil engineering, computer engineering, electrical/electronics engineering, engineering management, engineering physics, environmental engineering, materials engineering, and mechanical engineering), SOCIAL SCIENCE (history and philosophy). Engineering is the strongest academically and has the largest enrollment.

Required: To graduate, the student must have earned at least 145 credit hours with a minimum 2.0 GPA; the total hours in the major varies by program. The core curriculum includes courses in engineering, science, computer science, mathematics, liberal arts, and physical education.

Special: Stevens offers a 3–2 engineering degree with New York University, a work-study program within the school, co-op programs, corporate and research internships through the Undergraduate Projects in Technology and Medicine, study abroad in Scotland or Germany, and pass/fail options for extra courses. Students may undertake dual majors as well as accelerated degree programs in medicine, dentistry, and law, and can receive a B.A.-B.E. degree or a B.A.-B.S. degree in all majors. Undergraduates may take graduate courses. There is a freshman honors program on campus, as well as 3 national honor societies. All departments have honors programs.

Faculty/Classroom: 95% of faculty are male; 5%, female. 90% teach undergraduates, 80% do research, and 80% do both. No introductory courses are taught by graduate students. The average class size in an introductory lecture is 100; in a laboratory, 50; and in a regular course offering, 20.

Admissions: 70% of the 1995–96 applicants were accepted. There were 3 National Merit finalists and 15 semifinalists. 30 freshmen graduated first in their class.

Requirements: The SAT I is required. A minimum GPA of 3.0 is required. Stevens recommends either 2 or 3 SAT II: Subject tests, depending on the intended major. In addition, applicants must provide high school transcripts. Students should have taken 4 years of both English and mathematics, or 3 of mathematics for the management or liberal arts major. An interview is required. Stevens's application and catalog are on diskette, and students may apply on-line via ExPAN. AP credits are accepted. Important factors in the admissions decision are advanced placement or honor courses, recommendations by school officials, and extracurricular activities record.

Procedure: Freshmen are admitted in the fall. Entrance exams should be taken by March of the senior year. There are early decision, early admissions, and deferred admissions plans. Early decision applications should be filed by December 1; regular applications, by March 1 for fall entry, November 1 for spring entry, and March 1 for summer entry, along with an application fee of $45. Notification of early decision is sent December 15; regular decision, on a rolling basis. 23 early decision candidates were accepted for the 1995–96 class. A waiting list is an active part of the admissions procedure.

Transfer: 60 transfer students enrolled in 1995–96. Applicants should have a minimum GPA of 3.0. They must submit all college transcripts, including course descriptions; SAT I or ACT scores are required of those students with fewer than 30 hours of college credit.

Visiting: There are regularly scheduled orientations for prospective students, including interviews and campus tours. There are guides for informal visits and visitors may sit in on classes and stay overnight at the school. To schedule a visit, contact the Admissions Office.

Financial Aid: In 1995–96, 85% of all freshmen and 82% of continuing students received some form of financial aid. 70% of all students received need-based aid. The average freshman award was $17,850. Of that total, scholarships or need-based grants averaged $12,150 ($26,500 maximum); loans averaged $4000 ($8100 maximum); and work contracts averaged $1700 (maximum). 95% of undergraduate students work part-time. Average earnings from campus work for the school year are $1500. The average financial indebtedness of the 1994–95 graduate was $16,000. Stevens is a member of CSS. The FAFSA and the college's own financial statement are required. The application deadline for priority consideration is May 1.

International Students: In a recent year, 142 international students were enrolled. The school actively recruits these students. They must take the TOEFL and achieve a minimum score of 550. The student must also take the SAT I.

Computers: The college provides computer facilities for student use. The mainframes are a DEC VAX 6320, an 11/785, an 8700, and an 11/780, a MicroVAX II, and several VAX 3600s. All students may access the mainframe anytime using their own computers connected to a campuswide network. There are no time limits and no fees. It is recommended that students in all programs have personal computers. An IBM-compatible 486 DX, 33 MHz or 66 MHz is recommended.

Graduates: In 1994–95, 206 bachelor's degrees were awarded. The most popular majors among graduates were electrical engineering (23%), mechanical engineering (21%), and computer engineering (9%). Within an average freshman class, 73% graduate in 4 years and 78% in 5 years. 300 companies recruited on campus in 1994–95.

Admissions Contact: Maureen Weatherall, Dean of Admissions and Financial Aid. E-mail: admissions@stevens-tech.edu.

THOMAS A. EDISON STATE COLLEGE D-3
Trenton, NJ 08608–1176   (609) 633–6472; FAX: (609) 984-8447

Full-time: none	Faculty: n/app
Part-time: 5076 men, 3473 women	Ph.D.s: n/app
Graduate: none	Student/Faculty: n/app
Year: see profile	Tuition: $490 ($843)
Application Deadline: open	Room & Board: n/app
Freshman Class: 4899 applied, 4899 accepted, 2822 enrolled	
SAT I or ACT: not required	SPECIAL

Thomas A. Edison State College, founded in 1972, is a public learner-centered institution serving the educational needs of adults in a rigorous academic program without interrupting their professional or personal lives. Students have numerous degree-completion options, including transfer of credit from other colleges, credit by examination, assessment of experiential learning, guided independent study, and credit from approved licenses, certificates, and training programs. The college has no classrooms or regular semesters; attendance is not required in the traditional college way. In addition to regional accreditation, Thomas Edison has baccalaureate program accreditation with NLN. The 2-acre campus is in an urban area 40 miles north of Philadelphia. There are 3 buildings on campus.

Student Life: 70% of undergraduates are from New Jersey. Students come from 50 states, 74 foreign countries, and Canada. 84% are white. The average age of all undergraduates is 39.

Housing: There are no residence halls.

Sports: There is no sports program at Thomas Edison.

Disabled Students: All of the campus is accessible to disabled students. The following facilities are available: wheelchair ramps, elevators, special parking, specially equipped rest rooms, and lowered drinking fountains.

Services: Alumni peer counseling and study groups for the nursing degree are among the counseling and tutorial services available.

Campus Safety and Security: Campus safety and security measures include lighted pathways/sidewalks. There is a guard on the premises 7 A.M. to 11 P.M.; the outside is patrolled by Trenton police.

Programs of Study: Thomas Edison confers B.A., B.S., B.S.B.A., and B.S.N. degrees. Associate degrees are also awarded. Bachelor's degrees are awarded in BIOLOGICAL SCIENCE (biology/biological science), BUSINESS (business administration and management and labor studies), COMMUNICATIONS AND THE ARTS (communications, dance, dramatic arts, fine arts, journalism, languages, literature, music, and photography), COMPUTER AND PHYSICAL SCIENCE (chemistry, computer science, geology, mathematics, natural sciences, physics, and science technology), ENGINEERING AND ENVIRONMENTAL DESIGN (environmental science), HEALTH PROFESSIONS (nursing), SOCIAL SCIENCE (anthropology, archeology, economics, geography, history, human services, humanities, philosophy, political science/government, psychology, religion, social science, and sociology). Applied science and technology has the largest enrollment.

Required: The baccalaureate student must complete at least 9 semester hours in each of 3 liberal arts areas (humanities, social sciences, and natural science/mathematics), including 1 year of English composition, and a mathematics or computer science course; 120 semester hours, 33 in the major, are required, with a minimum GPA of 2.0.

Special: Students may design their own majors and take dual majors in all degree programs except nursing. Credit for college-level knowledge gained through life, military, and work experience is readily granted. Students may receive pass/fail grades. The college will develop new programs of study when requested by students, if they fit into the school's aims and requirements. Students work on their own, proceeding at their own pace, depending on the option selected for earning credit. Thomas Edison has no semesters, though the Guided Study program is on a traditional semester calendar; the school holds 6 graduations a year.

Admissions: All of the 1995–96 applicants were accepted.

Requirements: Applicants must have a high school diploma or the equivalent and be at least 21 years old. AP and CLEP credits are accepted.

Procedure: Application deadlines are open. The application fee is $75. The college accepts all applicants. Notification is sent on a rolling basis.

Transfer: 2840 transfer students enrolled in a recent year. Applicants must be at least 21 and be high school graduates or the equivalent. The granting of credit for coursework successfully completed elsewhere is an intrinsic part of the school's system. Transfer credits are awarded with the grades earned.

Visiting: There are regularly scheduled orientations for prospective students, including group information sessions and seminars. To schedule a visit, contact Janice Toliver, Director of Admissions.

Financial Aid: In 1995–96, 1% of continuing students received some form of financial aid or need-based aid. The average freshman award was $1000. Of that total, scholarships or need-based grants averaged $1000 ($2340 maximum); and loans averaged $1000 ($2625 maximum). All undergraduate students work part-time. Thomas Edison is a member of CSS. The FAF is required. The application deadline for fall entry is September 1.

International Students: There are currently 37 international students enrolled. They must score 500 on the TOEFL.

Computers: The college provides computer facilities for student use. The mainframes are a Wang VS 300 and a DEC VAX 4000. The Computer Assisted Lifelong Learning (CALL) network allows students to access the college via the WWW. Students may use electronic mail to communicate with the college, interactively register and pay fees, view copies of their records, and access informational software. Nonstudents may access information via the public bulletin board of the CALL network. All students may access the system at the student's convenience. There are no time limits and no fees.

Graduates: In 1994–95, 747 bachelor's degrees were awarded. The most popular majors among graduates were general management (7%), social sciences (7%), and aviation (6%).

Admissions Contact: Janice Toliver, Director of Admissions. E-mail: info@call.tesc.edu.

TRENTON STATE COLLEGE
D-3

Trenton, NJ 08650–4700   (609) 771–2131; (800) 345–7354

Full-time: 2124 men, 3174 women	Faculty: 306; IIB, + +$
Part-time: 233 men, 434 women	Ph.D.s: 84%
Graduate: 189 men, 830 women	Student/Faculty: 17 to 1
Year: semesters, summer session	Tuition: $4168 ($6585)
Application Deadline: March 1	Room & Board: $5600
Freshman Class: 5946 applied, 2683 accepted, 1088 enrolled	
SAT I Verbal/Math: 610/620	HIGHLY COMPETITIVE +

Trenton State College, founded in 1855, is a public coeducational institution offering programs in the liberal arts, sciences, business, engineering, nursing, and education. There are 5 undergraduate schools and 1 graduate school. In addition to regional accreditation, TSC has baccalaureate program accreditation with ABET, FIDER, NASDTEC, NASM, NCATE, and NLN. The library contains 484,000 volumes, 558,000 microform items, and 10,344 audiovisual forms, and subscribes to 1428 periodicals. Computerized library sources and services include the card catalog, interlibrary loans, and database searching. Special learning facilities include a learning resource center, art gallery, planetarium, radio station, TV station, and microscopy lab. The 250-acre campus is in a suburban area 6 miles northwest of Trenton in central New Jersey; it is 60 miles from New York City and 30 miles from Philadelphia, Pennsylvania. Including residence halls, there are 36 buildings on campus.

Student Life: 92% of undergraduates are from New Jersey. Students come from 23 states and 19 foreign countries. 65% are from public schools; 35% from private. 82% are white. 51% are Catholic; 26% Protestant; 12% claim no religious affiliation. The average age of freshmen is 18; all undergraduates, 21.5. 9% do not continue beyond their first year; 68% remain to graduate.

Housing: 3133 students can be accommodated in college housing. College-sponsored living facilities include single-sex and coed dormitories. In addition, there are honors houses, special interest houses, a music house, study floors with extended quiet hours, and a living-learning center for the First-Year Experience taken by all entering stu-

dents. On-campus housing is guaranteed for the freshman and sophomore years and is available on a lottery system for upperclassmen. 59% of students live on campus; of those, 40% remain on campus on weekends. Upperclassmen may keep cars on campus.

Activities: 18% of men belong to 3 local and 12 national fraternities; 18% of women belong to 4 local and 13 national sororities. There are 140 groups on campus, including art, band, cheerleading, choir, chorale, chorus, computers, dance, drama, ethnic, film, foreign language, gay, honors, international, jazz band, literary magazine, musical theater, newspaper, opera, orchestra, photography, political, professional, radio and TV, recreational, religious, social, social service, student government, symphony, and yearbook. Popular campus events include Family Fest (Parents Day), Convocation, Homecoming, Welcome Week, Handicapable Awareness Week, Holiday Marketplace, Government Jam, TSC Holidays-Share the Spirit, Feast of the Golden Lion (honoring student leaders), Women's History Month, and cultural awareness events.

Sports: There are 11 intercollegiate sports for men and 16 for women, and 10 intramural sports for men and 13 for women. Athletic and recreation facilities include a 5000-seat stadium with an astroturf field, an aquatic center, baseball and softball diamonds, an NCAA-approved all-weather track, lighted tennis courts, a sand volleyball court, a 1200-seat gymnasium, and a student recreation center with tennis and racquetball courts and a weight room.

Disabled Students: 90% of the campus is accessible to disabled students. The following facilities are available: wheelchair ramps, elevators, special parking, specially equipped rest rooms, special class scheduling, lowered drinking fountains, lowered telephones, TDD machines for the deaf, and a library room equipped for the hearing-impaired, visually impaired, and motor-impaired.

Services: In addition to many counseling and information services, tutoring is available in most subjects. There is a reader service for the blind, and remedial math, reading, and writing. The school also offers science laboratory tutoring and evaluative testing services.

Campus Safety and Security: Campus safety and security measures include 24-hour foot and vehicle patrol, escort service, informal discussions, and pamphlets/posters/films. In addition, there are emergency telephones and lighted pathways/sidewalks.

Programs of Study: TSC confers B.A., B.S., B.F.A., B.M., and B.S.N. degrees. Master's degrees are also awarded. Bachelor's degrees are awarded in BIOLOGICAL SCIENCE (biology/biological science), BUSINESS (accounting, banking and finance, business administration and management, business economics, management science, and marketing/retailing/merchandising), COMMUNICATIONS AND THE ARTS (communications, dramatic arts, English, fine arts, music, and Spanish), COMPUTER AND PHYSICAL SCIENCE (chemistry, computer science, mathematics, physics, and statistics), EDUCATION (art, early childhood, education of the deaf and hearing impaired, elementary, music, physical, and special), ENGINEERING AND ENVIRONMENTAL DESIGN (engineering and applied science), HEALTH PROFESSIONS (nursing), SOCIAL SCIENCE (criminal justice, economics, history, philosophy, political science/government, psychology, and sociology). History, biology, and English are the strongest academically. Art, biology, and business administration have the largest enrollments.

Required: To graduate, the student must earn 128 semester hours, with a minimum GPA of 2.0. The general education curriculum includes 26 hours in perspectives on the world, 3 to 21 hours in intellectual skills, and 6 hours in an interdisciplinary core. A college seminar is required of first-time freshmen. The credits required in the major varies by program.

Special: TSC offers cross-registration with the New Jersey Marine Science Consortium, numerous internships in the public and private sectors, and study abroad through the International Student Exchange Program (ISEP). Pass/fail options are possible. The Oxford tutorial is offered in the history department. Combined advanced-degree professional programs are offered in law and justice, medicine, and optometry with other area schools. There is a freshman honors program on campus, as well as 9 national honor societies. 17 departments have honors programs.

Faculty/Classroom: 63% of faculty are male; 37%, female. 98% teach undergraduates and 25% both teach and do research. No introductory courses are taught by graduate students. The average class size in an introductory lecture is 25; in a laboratory, 24; and in a regular course offering, 19.

Admissions: 45% of the 1995–96 applicants were accepted. The SAT I scores for the 1995–96 freshman class were as follows: Verbal—3% below 500, 33% between 500 and 599, 53% between 600 and 700, and 11% above 700; Math—1% below 500, 31% between 500 and 599, 58% between 600 and 700, and 10% above 700. 60% of the current freshmen were in the top fifth of their class; 85% were in the top two fifths. There was 1 National Merit finalist and 2 semifinalists. 19 freshmen graduated first in their class.

Requirements: The SAT I is required. Applicants must have earned 16 academic credits in high school, consisting of 4 in English, 2 each in mathematics, science, and social studies, and 6 others distributed among mathematics, science, social studies, and a foreign language. An essay is required. Art majors must submit a portfolio, and music majors must audition. The GED is accepted. The SAT II: Writing test is required for placement purposes. AP and CLEP credits are accepted. Important factors in the admissions decision are advanced placement or honor courses, leadership record, and evidence of special talent.

Procedure: Freshmen are admitted fall and spring. Entrance exams should be taken by the end of the junior year or early in the senior year. There are early decision and early admissions plans. Early decision applications should be filed by November 15; regular applications, by March 1 for fall entry, November 1 for spring entry, and May 1 for summer entry, along with an application fee of $50. Notification of early decision is sent December 15; regular decision, April 1. 163 early decision candidates were accepted for the 1995–96 class. A waiting list is an active part of the admissions procedure, with about 8% of all applicants on the list.

Transfer: 493 transfer students enrolled in 1995–96. Students must have a minimum GPA of 3.0 and submit high school transcripts; those applicatns with fewer than 33 credits must also submit SAT I scores. An associate's degree is recommended. 45 credits of 128 must be completed at TSC.

Visiting: There are regularly scheduled orientations for prospective students, consisting of campus tours. There are guides for informal visits and visitors may sit in on classes and stay overnight at the school. To schedule a visit, contact the Admissions Office.

Financial Aid: In 1995–96, 57% of all freshmen and 52% of continuing students received some form of financial aid. 44% of freshmen and 42% of continuing students received need-based aid. The average freshman award was $4600. Of that total, scholarships or need-based grants averaged $2600 ($9500 maximum); loans averaged $3200 ($9500 maximum); and work contracts averaged $1000 ($2000 maximum). 25% of undergraduate students work part-time. Average earnings from campus work for the school year are $850. The average financial indebtedness of the 1994–95 graduate was $4850. TSC is a member of CSS. The FAF, the college's own financial statement, and copies of student and parent tax returns are required. The application deadline for fall entry is May 1.

International Students: There are currently 29 international students enrolled. They must take the TOEFL and achieve a minimum score of 550. The student must also take the SAT I. Students must take the SAT II: Writing test. Engineering technology students must pass a mathematics aptitude test.

Computers: The college provides computer facilities for student use. The mainframe is an IBM ES9000–210. There are 600 networked microcomputers and workstations available in 18 academic computing laboratories throughout the campus, including 3 in residence halls. Students have access to the campuswide network from their residence hall rooms. All students may access the system. There are no time limits and no fees. It is recommended that all students have personal computers.

Graduates: In 1994–95, 1235 bachelor's degrees were awarded. The most popular majors among graduates were elementary/early childhood education (12%), art (7%), and English (7%). Within an average freshman class, 42% graduate in 4 years, 67% in 5 years, and 72% in 6 years. 200 companies recruited on campus in 1994–95.

Admissions Contact: Frank Cooper, Acting Director of Admissions.

WESTMINSTER CHOIR COLLEGE
(See Westminster Choir College of Rider University)

WESTMINSTER CHOIR COLLEGE OF RIDER UNIVERSITY   D-3
(Formerly Westminster Choir College)

Princeton, NJ 08540

	(609) 921-7144; (800) 96-CHOIR
Full-time: 117 men, 155 women	Faculty: 37
Part-time: 15 men, 23 women	Ph.D.s: 80%
Graduate: 87 men and women	Student/Faculty: 7 to 1
Year: semesters, summer session	Tuition: $14,186
Application Deadline: open	Room & Board: $6100
Freshman Class: 91 enrolled	
SAT I Verbal/Math: 458/479	ACT: 24 SPECIAL

Westminster Choir College, founded in 1926, is a private, coeducational school of music within Rider University, that focuses on undergraduate and graduate students seeking positions of music leadership in churches, schools, and communities. There is one graduate school. In addition to regional accreditation, Westminster Choir College has baccalaureate program accreditation with NASM. The library contains 56,260 volumes, 414 microform items, and 9000 audiovisual forms, and subscribes to 160 periodicals. Computerized

library sources and services include the card catalog, interlibrary loans, and database searching. Special learning facilities include a learning resource center, a music computer laboratory, and a vocal laboratory. The 23-acre campus is in a suburban area 50 miles south of New York City. Including residence halls, there are 12 buildings on campus.

Student Life: 63% of undergraduates are from out-of-state, mostly the Middle Atlantic. Students come from 38 states, 11 foreign countries, and Canada. 77% are white; 13% foreign nationals. The average age of freshmen is 18; all undergraduates, 20.6. 18% do not continue beyond their first year; 50% remain to graduate.

Housing: 206 students can be accommodated in college housing. College-sponsored living facilities include single-sex and coed dormitories. In addition there are language houses. On-campus housing is guaranteed for all 4 years. 70% of students live on campus; of those, 85% remain on campus on weekends. All students may keep cars on campus.

Activities: There are no fraternities or sororities. There are 12 groups on campus, including choir, chorus, drama, ethnic, gay, honors, musical theater, newspaper, opera, orchestra, professional, radio and TV, religious, social, student government, and yearbook. Popular campus events include Spring Fling, Christmas at Westminster, Homecoming Dance, and concerts.

Sports: There are 2 intramural sports for men and 2 for women.

Disabled Students: 42% of the campus is accessible to disabled students. The following facilities are available: wheelchair ramps, elevators, special parking, specially equipped rest rooms, and lowered telephones.

Services: In addition to many counseling and information services, tutoring is available in every subject. There is remedial math, reading, and writing.

Campus Safety and Security: Campus safety and security measures include escort service, shuttle buses, pamphlets/posters/films, and emergency telephones. In addition, there are lighted pathways/sidewalks and increased campus security from 6 P.M. to 6 A.M.

Programs of Study: Westminster Choir College confers B.A. and B.M. degrees. Master's degrees are also awarded. Bachelor's degrees are awarded in COMMUNICATIONS AND THE ARTS (music, music performance, music theory and composition, piano/organ, and voice), EDUCATION (music), SOCIAL SCIENCE (religious music). Music education has the largest enrollment.

Required: All students must maintain a minimum GPA of 2.0 (2.5 for music education majors) while completing 124 semester hours, including 92 to 100 in their majors. All students also must meet English reading and writing proficiency requirements. Distribution requirements include 33 semester hours in arts and sciences with at least 1 course from each of the divisions of the department. Satisfactory performance in recital also is needed.

Special: Cross-registration with Princeton University, Rider University, and Princeton Theological Seminary, internships in the arts, church, box office management, and arts administration, work-study programs, dual majors in any combination of 7 majors in music, and pass/fail options are all available. In addition, individualized programs of study in Europe may be pursued. There is 1 national honor society on campus.

Faculty/Classroom: All teach undergraduates. No introductory courses are taught by graduate students. The average class size in an introductory lecture is 18; in a laboratory, 8; and in a regular course offering, 12.

Admissions: The SAT I scores for the 1995–96 freshman class were as follows: Verbal—64% below 500, 21% between 500 and 599, and 15% between 600 and 700; Math—57% below 500, 25% between 500 and 599, 15% between 600 and 700, and 4% above 700. 34% of a recent freshmen class were in the top fifth of their class; 64% were in the top two fifths.

Requirements: The SAT I or ACT is required. Westminster Choir College requires applicants to be in the upper 50% of their class. A minimum GPA of 2.0 is required. SAT I minimum scores should be 700 (recentered) composite, 300 verbal and 350 mathematics. Applicants must present 4 years each of credits in English and history, 2 in mathematics, and 1 in science. An essay and music audition are required, while an interview is recommended. The GED is accepted. AP credits are accepted. Important factors in the admissions decision are evidence of special talent, recommendations by alumni, and recommendations by school officials.

Procedure: Freshmen are admitted fall and spring. Entrance exams should be taken at the time of the audition. There are early decision, early admissions, and deferred admissions plans. Application deadlines are open. Application fee is $35. Notification is sent on a rolling basis.

Transfer: Transfer applicants must submit high school and college transcripts and 3 letters of recommendation. An audition is required. 65 credits of 124 must be completed at Westminster Choir College.

Visiting: There are regularly scheduled orientations for prospective students. There are guides for informal visits and visitors may sit in on classes. To schedule a visit, contact the Admissions Office.

Financial Aid: In a recent year, more than 80% of all students received some form of financial aid. Westminster Choir College is a member of CSS. The FAFSA is required. The application deadline for fall entry is March 15.

International Students: There were 46 international students enrolled in a recent year. They must take the TOEFL and achieve a minimum score of 550.

Computers: The college provides computer facilities for student use. Microcomputers are available for academic use in the Music, Arts and Sciences, and Learning Center computer laboratories. All students may access the system. There are no time limits and no fees.

Graduates: In a recent year, 38 bachelor's degrees were awarded. The most popular majors among graduates were music education (47%), voice performance (18%), and church music (18%). Within an average freshman class, 36% graduate in 4 years, 47% in 5 years, and 50% in 6 years.

Admissions Contact: Anne Meservey, Director of Admissions.

WILLIAM PATERSON COLLEGE E-2

Wayne, NJ 07470	(201) 595-2126; FAX: (201) 595-2910
Full-time: 2484 men, 3333 women	**Faculty:** 309; IIB, + +$
Part-time: 754 men, 1323 women	**Ph.D.s:** 79%
Graduate: 289 men, 907 women	**Student/Faculty:** 19 to 1
Year: semesters, summer session	**Tuition:** $3120 ($5000)
Application Deadline: May 1	**Room & Board:** $4830
Freshman Class: 5460 applied, 2388 accepted, 855 enrolled	
SAT I Verbal/Math: 450/453	**ACT:** 21 **COMPETITIVE +**

William Paterson College, founded in 1855, is a public coeducational institution offering degree programs in the arts and sciences, communication, education, management, and health fields. There are 4 undergraduate and 4 graduate schools. In addition to regional accreditation, WPC has baccalaureate program accreditation with ASLA, NASM, NCATE, and NLN. The library contains 307,000 volumes, 102,000 microform items, and 5300 audiovisual forms, and subscribes to 1400 periodicals. Computerized library sources and services include the card catalog, interlibrary loans, and database searching. Special learning facilities include a learning resource center, art gallery, radio station, TV station, speech and hearing clinic, and teleconference center. The 250-acre campus is in a suburban area 25 miles west of New York City. Including residence halls, there are 35 buildings on campus.

Student Life: 98% of undergraduates are from New Jersey. Students come from 22 states, 58 foreign countries, and Canada. 75% are from public schools; 25% from private. 77% are white. The average age of freshmen is 18; all undergraduates, 24. 23% do not continue beyond their first year.

Housing: 1800 students can be accommodated in college housing. College-sponsored living facilities include coed dormitories and on-campus apartments. On-campus housing is guaranteed for all 4 years. 81% of students commute. All students may keep cars on campus.

Activities: 10% of men belong to 3 local and 8 national fraternities; 12% of women belong to 3 local and 11 national sororities. There are 50 groups on campus, including art, cheerleading, chorus, computers, dance, drama, ethnic, film, gay, honors, international, jazz band, literary magazine, musical theater, newspaper, opera, orchestra, photography, political, professional, radio and TV, religious, student government, and yearbook. Popular campus events include distinguished lecturer series, Wayne Chamber Orchestra, Midday Artist Series, Kwanzaa, Freshman Convocation, Homecoming, African Heritage Month, Puerto Rican Heritage Month, Latin American Week, and Springfest.

Sports: There are 7 intercollegiate sports for men and 7 for women, and 24 intramural sports for men and 24 for women. Athletic and recreation facilities include a recreation center with courts for basketball, tennis, racquetball, volleyball, and badminton, weight and exercise rooms, saunas and whirlpools, and a 4000-seat auditorium. The college also offers an Olympic-size pool, 8 additional tennis courts, and an athletic complex with fields for baseball, field hockey, football, soccer, softball, and track.

Disabled Students: The following facilities are available: wheelchair ramps, elevators, special parking, specially equipped rest rooms, special class scheduling, and lowered drinking fountains.

Services: In addition to many counseling and information services, tutoring is available in most subjects. There is a reader service for the blind, and remedial math, reading, and writing. Facilities include an academic support center, a science enrichment center, and a computerized writing center.

Campus Safety and Security: Campus safety and security measures include 24-hour foot and vehicle patrol, shuttle buses, informal discussions, and pamphlets/posters/films. In addition, there are emergency telephones and lighted pathways/sidewalks.

Programs of Study: WPC confers B.A., B.S., B.F.A., and B.M. degrees. Master's degrees are also awarded. Bachelor's degrees are awarded in BIOLOGICAL SCIENCE (biology/biological science and biotechnology), BUSINESS (accounting, banking and finance, and business administration and management), COMMUNICATIONS AND THE ARTS (art history and appreciation, communications, dramatic arts, English, fine arts, music, Spanish, and studio art), COMPUTER AND PHYSICAL SCIENCE (chemistry, computer science, and mathematics), EDUCATION (health, music, physical, and special), ENGINEERING AND ENVIRONMENTAL DESIGN (environmental science), HEALTH PROFESSIONS (community health work, health science, and nursing), SOCIAL SCIENCE (African American studies, anthropology, economics, geography, history, philosophy, political science/government, psychology, and sociology). Biology/biotechnology, management, and English are the strongest academically. Management, communications, and education have the largest enrollments.

Required: To graduate, all students must maintain a cumulative GPA of at least 2.0 and take 128 credit hours, typically including 30 to 40 in their major. General education requirements include 21 credits in the humanities, 11 to 12 in science, 9 in the social sciences, 6 in art and communication, and 6 in electives. Also required are 1 course in health or movement science, 1 course dealing with racism or sexism, 1 course in non-Western culture, and a minimum of 9 credits of upper-level elective courses.

Special: Study abroad in 33 countries, cross-registration, internships, work-study programs on campus, accelerated degree programs, dual majors, individual curriculum design, and credit for military experience are available. Nondegree study and some pass/fail options are also possible. In the Learning Clusters Project, students experience how 3 general education courses, taken together, reinforce and better integrate each other. There is a professional program in teacher education leading to certification in early childhood, elementary, middle, and secondary education. There are 6 national honor societies on campus. 4 departments have honors programs.

Faculty/Classroom: 62% of faculty are male; 38%, female. All teach undergraduates and 40% also do research. No introductory courses are taught by graduate students. The average class size in an introductory lecture is 32; in a laboratory, 24; and in a regular course offering, 19.

Admissions: 44% of the 1995–96 applicants were accepted. The SAT I scores for the 1995–96 freshman class were as follows: Verbal—53% below 500, 38% between 500 and 599, and 9% between 600 and 700; Math—53% below 500, 37% between 500 and 599, and 10% between 600 and 700. 25% of the current freshmen were in the top fifth of their class; 67% were in the top two fifths.

Requirements: The SAT I or ACT is required. WPC requires applicants to be in the upper 50% of their class. A minimum GPA of 2.5 is required. Applicants must have 16 academic credits or Carnegie units, including 4 in English, 3 in mathematics, 2 each in science laboratory and social studies, and 5 electives such as foreign language and history. An essay and interview are recommended for some applicants, as are a portfolio and audition. The GED is accepted. AP and CLEP credits are accepted. Important factors in the admissions decision are advanced placement or honor courses, recommendations by school officials, and evidence of special talent.

Procedure: Freshmen are admitted fall and spring. Entrance exams should be taken by January 31 of the senior year. There are early decision, early admissions, and deferred admissions plans. Early decision applications should be filed by April 1; regular applications, by May 1 for fall entry and November 1 for spring entry, along with an application fee of $35. Notification of early decision is sent January 15; regular decision, on a rolling basis. 84 early decision candidates were accepted for the 1995–96 class. A waiting list is an active part of the admissions procedure, with about 5% of all applicants on the list.

Transfer: 822 transfer students enrolled in 1995–96. Students need a minimum 2.0 GPA (business, nursing, computer science, and education students need a 2.5 GPA) and at least 12 credit hours earned. At least 38 credits of 128 must be completed at WPC.

Visiting: There are regularly scheduled orientations for prospective students, including a campus tour, guest speakers, and dissemination of printed information. There are guides for informal visits and visitors may sit in on classes. To schedule a visit, contact the Admissions Office at (201) 595-2125.

Financial Aid: WPC is a member of CSS. The FAFSA and parent and student federal income tax forms are required. The application deadline for fall entry is open.

International Students: In a recent year, there were 50 international students enrolled. They must take the TOEFL and achieve a minimum score of 550.

Computers: The college provides computer facilities for student use. The mainframe is an IBM 3099. There are also Zenith, Apple II, and AST Bravo/286 microcomputers available. All students may access the system at all times. There are no time limits. The fees are $30.

Graduates: In 1994–95, 1250 bachelor's degrees were awarded. The most popular majors among graduates were education (15%), communication (14%), and business administration (8%). Within an average freshman class, 14% graduate in 4 years, 39% in 5 years, and 48% in 6 years. 46 companies recruited on campus in 1994–95. Of the 1994 graduating class, 18% were enrolled in graduate school within 1 year of graduation and 88% had found employment.

Admissions Contact: Director of Admissions. A campus video is available.

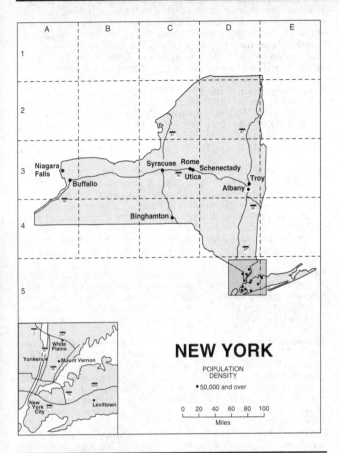

NEW YORK

POPULATION DENSITY

● 50,000 and over

0 20 40 60 80 100

Miles

ADELPHI UNIVERSITY
Garden City, NY 11530

D-5

(516) 663-1100
(800) ADELPHI (in-state)

Full-time: 950 men, 1750 women	Faculty: 264
Part-time: 340 men, 890 women	Ph.D.s: 75%
Graduate: 1065 men, 3200 women	Student/Faculty: 10 to 1
Year: semesters, summer session	Tuition: $13,000
Application Deadline: March 1	Room & Board: $6500
Freshman Class: n/av	
SAT I or ACT: required	**LESS COMPETITIVE**

Adelphi University, founded in 1896, is a private, coeducational liberal arts institution. There are 6 undergraduate and 6 graduate schools. Figures given in the above capsule are approximate. In addition to regional accreditation, Adelphi has baccalaureate program accreditation with CSWE and NLN. The 2 libraries contain 624,000 volumes, 700,000 microform items, and 40,000 audiovisual forms, and subscribe to 1600 periodicals. Computerized library sources and services include the card catalog, interlibrary loans, and database searching. Special learning facilities include a learning resource center, art gallery, radio station, and observatory. The 75-acre campus is in a suburban area 20 miles east of New York City. Including residence halls, there are 22 buildings on campus.

Student Life: 87% of undergraduates are from New York. Students come from 34 states, 40 foreign countries, and Canada. 75% are from public schools; 9% from private. 80% are white; 11% African American. 63% are Catholic; 13% Jewish; 10% Protestant. The average age of freshmen is 21; all undergraduates, 27. 12% do not continue beyond their first year; 56% remain to graduate.

Housing: 1112 students can be accommodated in college housing. College-sponsored living facilities include single-sex and coed dormitories and off-campus apartments. On-campus housing is guaranteed for all 4 years. 78% of students commute. Alcohol is not permitted. All students may keep cars on campus.

Activities: 10% of men belong to 8 national fraternities; 8% of women belong to 1 local and 6 national sororities. There are 77 groups on campus, including cheerleading, chorale, computers, dance, drama, ethnic, film, honors, international, literary magazine, musical theater, newspaper, opera, orchestra, pep band, political, professional, radio and TV, religious, social, social service, student government, symphony, and yearbook. Popular campus events include Halloween Party, Spring Fest, and Kwanzaa.

Sports: There are 7 intercollegiate sports for men and 7 for women, and 25 intramural sports for men and 25 for women. Athletic and recreation facilities include a 3000-seat stadium, a 600-seat gymnasium, a swimming pool, racquetball, squash, tennis, and handball courts, exercise rooms, a dance studio, a track, and playing fields for baseball, softball, and soccer.

Disabled Students: 80% of the campus is accessible to disabled students. The following facilities are available: wheelchair ramps, elevators, special parking, specially equipped rest rooms, special class scheduling, lowered drinking fountains, and lowered telephones.

Services: In addition to many counseling and information services, tutoring is available in most subjects. There is a reader service for the blind, and remedial math, reading, and writing.

Campus Safety and Security: Campus safety and security measures include 24-hour foot and vehicle patrol, self-defense education, escort service, and shuttle buses. There are informal discussions, pamphlets/posters/films, emergency telephones, and lighted pathways/sidewalks. All dormitory main entrances are videotaped and all dormitory doors locked 24 hours a day.

Programs of Study: Adelphi confers B.A., B.S., B.B.A., B.F.A., B.S.Ed., and B.S.S.W. degrees. Associate, master's, and doctoral degrees are also awarded. Bachelor's degrees are awarded in BIOLOGICAL SCIENCE (biochemistry and biology/biological science), BUSINESS (accounting, banking and finance, business administration and management, and management information systems), COMMUNICATIONS AND THE ARTS (art history and appreciation, communications, dance, design, dramatic arts, English, fine arts, French, languages, music, performing arts, and Spanish), COMPUTER AND PHYSICAL SCIENCE (chemistry, computer science, earth science, mathematics, natural sciences, and physics), EDUCATION (art, education of the deaf and hearing impaired, elementary, English, foreign languages, mathematics, music, physical, science, secondary, and social studies), HEALTH PROFESSIONS (nursing and speech pathology/audiology), SOCIAL SCIENCE (anthropology, economics, history, Latin American studies, liberal arts/general studies, philosophy, physical fitness/movement, political science/government, psychology, social science, social work, and sociology). Business management, nursing, and psychology have the largest enrollments.

Required: To graduate, students need at least a 2.0 cumulative GPA (higher in some programs) and 120 credit hours. Adelphi's core curriculum requires 8 credits in Modern Condition, 3 each in composition and senior seminar, and 2 in Origin of the Modern Condition, as well as 7 courses pertaining to nature, society and culture, and art and expression.

Special: Internships are available in accounting, banking and money management, and communications, among others. Study abroad is available in more than 30 countries, including Spain, France, Denmark, and England. A 5-year bachelor's/master's degree in a number of fields, including business, nursing, physics, social work, and applied psychology, is offered. In addition, work-study programs, double majors, the B.A.-B.S. degree, a general studies degree, a 3–2 engineering degree, credit for life experience for adult students, nondegree study in special cases, and pass/fail options are possible. There is a freshman honors program on campus, as well as 15 national honor societies. 3 departments have honors programs.

Faculty/Classroom: 63% of faculty are male; 37%, female. The average class size in a regular course offering is 22.

Admissions: The SAT I scores for a recent freshman class were as follows: Verbal—74% below 500, 25% between 500 and 599, and 1% between 600 and 700; Math—75% below 500, 23% between 500 and 599, and 2% between 600 and 700.

Requirements: The SAT I or ACT is required. Scores should be 950 on SAT I or 24 on the ACT. Applicants should have 16 academic credits, including a recommended 4 units of English, 3 each of mathematics and science, 2 or 3 of foreign language, and 4 each from history, social studies, and the fields named above. An essay is required and an interview recommended for all applicants. A portfolio for art and technical theater candidates, an audition for music, dance, and theater candidates, or an interview for nursing candidates is required. AP and CLEP credits are accepted. Important factors in the admissions decision are advanced placement or honor courses, leadership record, and personality/intangible qualities.

Procedure: Freshmen are admitted fall and spring. Entrance exams should be taken in December of the senior year. There are early admissions and deferred admissions plans. Applications should be filed by March 1 for fall entry and November 30 for spring entry, along with an application fee of $35. Notification is sent on a rolling basis.

Transfer: 600 transfer students enrolled in a recent year. A GPA of 2.5 is preferred in addition to an essay, an official high school transcript, and official records of all work completed or in progress from all previous colleges and universities. An interview is recommended for students in social work and nursing, while an audition is needed for music, dance, and theater students, and a portfolio for art and technical theater students. 30 credits of 120 must be completed at Adelphi.

Visiting: There are guides for informal visits and visitors may sit in on classes and stay overnight at the school. To schedule a visit, contact Undergraduate Admissions at (516) 877–3050.

Financial Aid: In a recent year, 75% of all freshmen and 60% of continuing students received some form of financial aid. 86% of freshmen and 50% of continuing students received need-based aid. The average freshman award was $10,110. Of that total, scholarships or need-based grants averaged $4991 ($17,000 maximum); loans averaged $2525 ($2625 maximum); and work contracts averaged $1662 ($2500 maximum). 26% of undergraduate students work part-time. Average earnings from campus work for the school year are $1000. The FAFSA and the college's own financial statement are required. The application deadline for fall entry is February 15.

International Students: In a recent year, there were 180 international students enrolled. The school actively recruits these students. They must score 500 on the TOEFL.

Computers: The college provides computer facilities for student use. The mainframes are a DEC VAX 6420 and DEC System 5500. Students use the mainframe for course work and research. Approximately 125 terminals and microcomputers are available in various public, private, and departmental laboratories, all with access to the mainframes and PC service networks. All students may access the system. There are no time limits and no fees.

Graduates: In a recent class, 1026 bachelor's degrees were awarded. The most popular majors among graduates were management (15%), management/communications (12%), and elementary education (8%). Within an average freshman class, 1% graduate in 3 years, 44% in 4 years, 9% in 5 years, and 2% in 6 years. 74 companies recruited on campus in a recent year.

Admissions Contact: Office of University Admissions.

ALBANY COLLEGE OF PHARMACY D-3

Albany, NY 12208   (518) 445–7221; FAX: (518) 445–7202

Full-time: 272 men, 384 women	Faculty: 40
Part-time: 11 men, 15 women	Ph.D.s: 75%
Graduate: 9 men, 18 women	Student/Faculty: 16 to 1
Year: semesters	Tuition: $9765
Application Deadline: rolling	Room & Board: $4600
Freshman Class: 448 applied, 287 accepted, 133 enrolled	
SAT I Verbal/Math: 484/588	SPECIAL

Albany College of Pharmacy, founded in 1881, is a private, coeducational, 5-year institution, a division of Union University. In addition to regional accreditation, ACP has baccalaureate program accreditation with ACPE. The library contains 8000 volumes and subscribes to 155 periodicals. Computerized library sources and services include interlibrary loans and database searching. Special learning facilities include a learning resource center. The 1-acre campus is in an urban area in downtown Albany. Including residence halls, there are 3 buildings on campus.

Student Life: 87% of undergraduates are from New York. Students come from 9 states, 9 foreign countries, and Canada. About 75% are from public schools; 25% from private. 86% are white; 10% Asian American. The average age of freshmen is 18; all undergraduates, 21. 15% do not continue beyond their first year; 81% remain to graduate.

Housing: 110 students can be accommodated in college housing. College-sponsored living facilities include coed off-campus apartments. On-campus housing is guaranteed for the freshman year only. Priority is given to out-of-town students. Alcohol is not permitted. Upperclassmen may keep cars on campus.

Activities: 45% of men and about 43% of women belong to 3 national fraternities; 30% of women belong to 1 national sorority. There are 10 groups on campus, including cheerleading, ethnic, honors, international, newspaper, photography, professional, social service, student government, and yearbook. Popular campus events include Parents Weekend, Open House, and Interview Day.

Sports: There are 5 intercollegiate sports for men and 5 for women, and 3 intramural sports for men and 3 for women. Athletic and recreation facilities include a small gymnasium on campus.

Disabled Students: The entire campus is accessible to disabled students. The following facilities are available: wheelchair ramps, elevators, special parking, and specially equipped rest rooms.

Services: In addition to many counseling and information services, tutoring is available in most subjects.

Campus Safety and Security: Campus safety and security measures include informal discussions, pamphlets/posters/films, and lighted pathways/sidewalks.

Programs of Study: ACP confers the B.S.Pharm. degree. Master's and doctoral degrees are also awarded. Bachelor's degrees are awarded in HEALTH PROFESSIONS (pharmacy).

Required: To graduate, students must complete 162 credits, including core curriculum courses, with a minimum GPA of 2.0.

Special: The college offers cross-registration with other area colleges, dual majors leading to master's and doctoral degrees, and work-study programs. There is 1 national honor society on campus.

Faculty/Classroom: 75% of faculty are male; 25%, female. All teach undergraduates. No introductory courses are taught by graduate students. The average class size in an introductory lecture is 120; in a laboratory, 30; and in a regular course offering, 125.

Admissions: 64% of the 1995–96 applicants were accepted. The SAT I scores for the 1995–96 freshman class were as follows: Verbal—57% below 500, 40% between 500 and 599, and 3% between 600 and 700; Math—10% below 500, 45% between 500 and 599, 41% between 600 and 700, and 4% above 700. 74% of the current freshmen were in the top fifth of their class; 92% were in the top two fifths.

Requirements: The SAT I is required. ACP requires applicants to be in the upper 50% of their class. A minimum GPA of 3.0 is required. Applicants must be graduates of an accredited high school, with at least 17 credits consisting of 4 each of English and mathematics, including precalculus, and 3 of science, including chemistry. The GED is accepted. AP and CLEP credits are accepted. Important factors in the admissions decision are advanced placement or honor courses, extracurricular activities record, and recommendations by alumni.

Procedure: Freshmen are admitted in the fall. Entrance exams should be taken in the junior year. There are early decision and early admissions plans. Early decision applications should be filed by December 1, along with an application fee of $50. Notification is sent on a rolling basis. 52 early decision candidates were accepted for the 1995–96 class.

Transfer: 55 transfer students enrolled in 1995–96. Applicants must have a GPA of 3.2, 83 credits of 162 must be completed at ACP.

Visiting: There are regularly scheduled orientations for prospective students, including a tour of the school and residence halls and a discussion of admissions requirements, financial aid, and student activities. There are guides for informal visits and visitors may sit in on classes and stay overnight at the school. To schedule a visit, contact the Admissions Office.

Financial Aid: In 1995–96, 82% of all freshmen and 83% of continuing students received some form of financial aid. 78% of freshmen and 74% of continuing students received need-based aid. The average freshman award was $6300. Of that total, scholarships or need-based grants averaged $1000 ($2500 maximum); loans averaged $2900 ($4400 maximum); work contracts averaged $800 ($1500 maximum); and state grants averaged $1900 ($3900 maximum). 95% of undergraduate students work part-time. Average earnings from campus work for the school year are $800. The average financial indebtedness of the 1994–95 graduate was $14,000. ACP is a member of CSS. The FAFSA is required. The application deadline for fall entry is March 1.

International Students: There are currently 14 international students enrolled. They must take the TOEFL and achieve a minimum score of 550. The student must also take the SAT I or the ACT.

Computers: The college provides computer facilities for student use. The mainframe is a DEC VAX 11/750. A number of microcomputers are also available. All students may access the system 24 hours a day. There are no time limits and no fees.

Graduates: In 1994–95, 119 bachelor's degrees were awarded. Within an average freshman class, 86% graduate in 5 years and 1% in 6 years. 50 companies recruited on campus in 1994–95. Of the 1994 graduating class, 12% were enrolled in graduate school within 6 months of graduation and all had found employment.

Admissions Contact: Janis L. Fisher, Director of Admissions. A campus video is available.

ALFRED UNIVERSITY B-4

Alfred, NY 14802–1205   (607) 871–2115

(800) 541–9229; FAX: (607) 871–2198

Full-time: 1013 men, 898 women	Faculty: 168; IIA, -$
Part-time: 33 men, 50 women	Ph.D.s: 90%
Graduate: 197 men, 214 women	Student/Faculty: 11 to 1
Year: semesters, summer session	Tuition: $7652–17,948 ($10,624–$17,948)
Application Deadline: February 15	Room & Board: $5716
Freshman Class: 1648 applied, 1408 accepted, 495 enrolled	
SAT I Verbal/Math: 485/555 (mean)	ACT: 24 (mean) COMPETITIVE +

Alfred University, founded in 1836, is a private, coeducational institution offering programs in business administration, liberal arts and sciences, engineering, and professional studies, and in art and design and ceramic engineering through the New York State College of Ceramics. Tuition is lower in the public division. There are 5 undergraduate and 6 graduate schools. In addition to regional accreditation, Alfred has baccalaureate program accreditation with AACSB, ABET, and NASAD. The 2 libraries contain 323,234 volumes, 92,693 microform items, and 5149 audiovisual forms, and subscribe to 2527 periodicals. Computerized library sources and services include the card catalog, interlibrary loans, and database searching. Special learning facilities include a learning resource center, art gallery, radio station, TV station, and observatory. The 232-acre campus is in a rural area 70 miles south of Rochester. Including residence halls, there are 54 buildings on campus.

Student Life: 69% of undergraduates are from New York. Students come from 43 states, 31 foreign countries, and Canada. 84% are from public schools; 16% from private. 89% are white. The average age of freshmen is 18; all undergraduates, 20.5. 15% do not continue beyond their first year; 65% remain to graduate.

Housing: 1330 students can be accommodated in college housing. College-sponsored living facilities include coed dormitories, on-campus apartments, fraternity houses, and sorority houses. In addition, there are honors houses, language houses, and special interest houses. On-campus housing is available on a first-come, first-served basis and is available on a lottery system for upperclassmen. 65% of students live on campus; of those, 90% remain on campus on weekends. All students may keep cars on campus.

Activities: 30% of men belong to 2 local and 5 national fraternities; 17% of women belong to 1 national and 4 local sororities. There are 72 groups on campus, including art, band, cheerleading, chess, chorale, chorus, dance, drama, ethnic, film, gay, honors, international, jazz band, literary magazine, newspaper, orchestra, pep band, photography, political, professional, radio and TV, religious, social, social service, student government, and yearbook. Popular campus events include Alumni Weekend, Hot Dog Day, and Family Weekend.

Sports: There are 9 intercollegiate sports for men and 9 for women, and 17 intramural sports for men and 17 for women. Athletic and recreation facilities include an omniturf football surface, a soccer and lacrosse field, an Olympic-size pool, a weight room, a dance and exercise studio, and tennis courts, racquetball and squash courts. The campus stadium seats 4200, the indoor gymnasium, 3000. There is also a fitness center and facilities for horseback riding nearby.

Disabled Students: 50% of the campus is accessible to disabled students. The following facilities are available: wheelchair ramps, elevators, special parking, specially equipped rest rooms, and special class scheduling.

Services: In addition to many counseling and information services, tutoring is available in most subjects. There is a reader service for the blind, and remedial math, reading, and writing. Time management and study skills workshops and advocacy and support for students with learning and physical disabilities are available.

Campus Safety and Security: Campus safety and security measures include escort service, informal discussions, pamphlets/posters/films, and emergency telephones. In addition, there are lighted pathways/sidewalks.

Programs of Study: Alfred confers B.A., B.S., and B.F.A. degrees. Master's and doctoral degrees are also awarded. Bachelor's degrees are awarded in BIOLOGICAL SCIENCE (biology/biological science), BUSINESS (accounting, banking and finance, business administration and management, business economics, international business management, and marketing/retailing/merchandising), COMMUNICATIONS AND THE ARTS (broadcasting, communications, design, dramatic arts, English, fine arts, French, photography, and Spanish), COMPUTER AND PHYSICAL SCIENCE (chemistry, computer science, geology, mathematics, physics, and science), EDUCATION (art, elementary, secondary, and special), ENGINEERING AND ENVIRONMENTAL DESIGN (ceramic engineering, electrical/electronics engineering, engineering, environmental science, and mechanical engineering), HEALTH PROFESSIONS (health care administration, medical laboratory technology, predentistry, premedicine, and preveterinary science), SOCIAL SCIENCE (criminal justice, economics, gerontology, history, international studies, philosophy, political science/government, prelaw, psychology, public administration, and sociology). Ceramic engineering, electrical engineering, and business are the strongest academically. Ceramic engineering, accounting, and psychology have the largest enrollments.

Required: To graduate, students must complete 120 to 137 credits, depending on the major, with 36 to 48 credits in the major. Students must demonstrate basic competencies in writing, oral communication, mathematics, and computers. Freshmen must attend 10 freshman forums. Distribution requirements include 8 credits each of social studies and natural science, and 4 credits each of philosophy or religion, literature, art, and history. A minimum GPA of 2.0 is required.

Special: There are cooperative programs in engineering and business with Duke, Clarkson, and Columbia universities and SUNY/Brockport. There is cross-registration with the SUNY College of Technology and a 5-year program in environmental management/forestry with Duke. Alfred offers internships in all programs, extensive study abroad, Washington and Albany semesters, work-study, accelerated degree programs, a general studies degree, student-designed majors, dual majors, credit by examination, and pass/fail options. A special feature is the New York State College of Ceramics, which offers programs and facilities in ceramic engineering and science as well as art and design. There is a freshman honors program on campus, as well as 14 national honor societies.

Faculty/Classroom: 70% of faculty are male; 30%, female. All teach undergraduates and 90% also do research. The average class size in an introductory lecture is 18; in a laboratory, 18; and in a regular course offering, 18.

Admissions: 85% of the 1995–96 applicants were accepted. The SAT I recentered scores for the 1995–96 freshman class were as follows: Verbal—20% below 500, 43% between 500 and 599, 31% between 600 and 700, and 6% above 700; Math—20% below 500, 44% between 500 and 599, 32% between 600 and 700, and 4% above 700. The ACT scores were 26% below 22, 32% between 22 and 24, 25% between 25 and 27, and 17% above 27. 40% of the current freshmen were in the top fifth of their class; 70% were in the top two fifths. There were 10 National Merit finalists.

Requirements: The SAT I or ACT is required. A GED is accepted. A minimum of 16 Carnegie units is required, including 4 years of English and 2 to 3 years each of mathematics, history/social studies, and science. The remaining units may be either in a foreign language or any of the previously mentioned fields. An essay is required, and applicants to B.F.A. programs must submit a portfolio. Interviews are encouraged. AP and CLEP credits are accepted. Important factors in the admissions decision are advanced placement or honor courses, personality/intangible qualities, and extracurricular activities record.

Procedure: Freshmen are admitted fall and spring. Entrance exams should be taken in the junior year. There are early decision, early admissions, and deferred admissions plans. Early decision applications should be filed by December 1; regular applications, by February 15 for fall entry and December 1 for spring entry, along with an application fee of $40. Notification of early decision is sent December 15; regular decision, March 15. A waiting list is an active part of the admissions procedure, with about 5% of all applicants on the list.

Transfer: 96 transfer students enrolled in 1995–96. Transfer applicants must have a GPA of at least 2.5. They must submit at least 1 letter of recommendation and official high school and college transcripts. Art students must submit a portfolio. 30 credits of 120 to 137 must be completed at Alfred.

Visiting: There are regularly scheduled orientations for prospective students, including a campus tour, social activities panel, financial aid presentation, faculty discussions, and on-campus interviews. There are guides for informal visits and visitors may sit in on classes and stay overnight at the school. To schedule a visit, contact Laurie A. Richer, Director of Admissions.

Financial Aid: 50% of undergraduate students work part-time. Average earnings from campus work for the school year are $500. Alfred is a member of CSS. The FAF and the college's own financial statement are required. The application deadline for fall entry is May 1.

International Students: There were 90 international students enrolled in a recent year. The school actively recruits these students. They must take the TOEFL and achieve a minimum score of 550.

Computers: The college provides computer facilities for student use. The mainframes are 2 DEC VAX 11/785s, a VAX 8530, and 2 VAX 3100 systems. All academic and administration buildings are connected to the VAX network. There are numerous high-speed and laser printers, 4 tape drives, and multicolor pen plotters. More than 300 terminals are located across campus for student use. All students may access the system 24 hours a day, 7 days a week. There are no time limits and no fees.

Graduates: In 1994–95, 239 bachelor's degrees were awarded. The most popular majors among graduates were business administration (19%), psychology (14%), and criminal justice studies (6%). Within an average freshman class, 1% graduate in 3 years, 50% in 4 years, and 15% in 5 years. 56 companies recruited on campus in 1994–95. Of the 1994 graduating class, 82% had found employment within 1 year of graduation.

Admissions Contact: Laurie A. Richer, Director of Admissions.

AUDREY COHEN COLLEGE

	D-5
New York, NY 10013	(212) 343-1234, ext. 5001
	(800) 33-THINK (in-state); FAX: (212) 343-8470

Full-time: 297 men, 720 women	Faculty: 15
Part-time: 12 men, 42 women	Ph.Ds: 90%
Graduate: 30 men, 49 women	Student/Faculty: 68 to 1
Year: trimesters, summer session	Tuition: $12,360
Application Deadline: August 1	Room & Board: n/app
Freshman Class: 436 applied, 348 accepted, 179 enrolled	
SAT I or ACT: not required	**LESS COMPETITIVE**

Audrey Cohen College, founded in 1964, is a private, coeducational institution offering programs in human services and business management. All bachelor degree programs involve a combination of class work and field work and may be completed in two years and eight months. There are 2 undergraduate schools and one graduate school. The library contains 22,200 volumes and 310 microform items, and subscribes to 1000 periodicals. Computerized library sources and services include the card catalog and database searching. Special learning facilities include a learning resource center. The campus is in an urban area in New York City. There is one building on campus.

Student Life: 95% of undergraduates are from New York. Students come from 4 states and 3 foreign countries. 68% are from public schools; 32% from private. 60% are African American; 21% Hispanic; 12% white. The average age of freshmen is 29; all undergraduates, 32. 28% do not continue beyond their first year; 59% remain to graduate.

Housing: There are no residence halls. All students commute. Alcohol is not permitted.

Activities: There are no fraternities or sororities. There are 6 groups on campus, including computers, gay, professional, social, social service, student government, and yearbook. Popular campus events include career fairs, admissions open house, and dean's ceremonies.

Sports: There is no sports program at the college.

Disabled Students: All of the campus is accessible to disabled students. The following facilities are available: wheelchair ramps, elevators, specially equipped rest rooms, special class scheduling, lowered drinking fountains, and lowered telephones.

Services: In addition to many counseling and information services, tutoring is available in every subject. There is remedial math, reading, and writing.

Campus Safety and Security: Campus safety and security measures include 24-hour foot and vehicle patrol and lighted pathways/sidewalks.

Programs of Study: The college confers the B.P.S. degree. Master's degrees are also awarded. Bachelor's degrees are awarded in BUSINESS (business administration and management), EDUCATION (early childhood), HEALTH PROFESSIONS (mental health/human services), SOCIAL SCIENCE (child care/child and family studies, community services, gerontology, human services, prelaw, psychology, and social work). Human services has the largest enrollment.

Required: To graduate, students must complete 128 credit hours with a minimum GPA of 2.0. The curriculum is prescribed and no electives are featured. A constructive action document based on performance in the field and mastery of course work is required each semester.

Special: Internships, work-study programs, an accelerated degree program, credit by examination, and credit for life experience are offered.

Faculty/Classroom: 40% of faculty are male; 60%, female. All teach undergraduates. The average class size in an introductory lecture is 25; in a laboratory, 18; and in a regular course offering, 20.

Admissions: 80% of the 1995–96 applicants were accepted. 15% of the current freshmen were in the top fifth of their class; 50% were in the top two fifths.

Requirements: Students must take the Test of Adult Basic Education (TABE) in English, reading, and mathematics; recent high school graduates who have a minimum composite SAT I score of 1000 (recentered) may present the SAT I instead. Applicants must have graduated from an accredited secondary school. The GED is accepted. An essay and an interview are required. Important factors in the admissions decision are evidence of special talent, leadership record, and personality/intangible qualities.

Procedure: Freshmen are admitted to all sessions. Entrance exams should be taken in the senior year. Applications should be filed by August 1 for fall entry, December 1 for spring entry, and April 1 for summer entry, along with an application fee of $20. Notification is sent on a rolling basis.

Transfer: 115 transfer students enrolled in a recent year. Admission is based on current skills and abilities as measured on the entrance examination and essay. 64 credits of 128 must be completed at the college.

Visiting: There are regularly scheduled orientations for prospective students. There are guides for informal visits and visitors may sit in on classes. To schedule a visit, contact the Admissions Office.

Financial Aid: In a recent year, 80% of all students received some form of financial aid. Scholarships or need-based grants averaged $900 ($1000 maximum); loans averaged $1500 ($6625 maximum); and work contracts averaged $1500 ($3000 maximum). 8% of undergraduate students work part-time. The FAF and the New York State Higher Education Financial statement are required. The application deadline for fall entry is August 15.

International Students: They must take the TOEFL and achieve a minimum score of 550. The student must also take TABE.

Computers: The college provides computer facilities for student use. The mainframe is a Sun 3/260. There are also 32 Unisys PW300 microcomputers available in the computer laboratory. All students may access the system whenever the college is open. There are no time limits and no fees.

Graduates: In 1994–95, 159 bachelor's degrees were awarded. Within an average freshman class, 40% graduate in 4 years. 35 companies recruited on campus in 1994–95. Of the 1994 graduating class, 50% were enrolled in graduate school within 6 months of graduation and 90% had found employment.

Admissions Contact: Steven Lenhart, Admissions Office. A campus video is available.

BARD COLLEGE
D-4

Annandale-on-Hudson, NY 12504   (914) 758-7472

Full-time: 496 men, 536 women	Faculty: 96; IIB, +$
Part-time: 20 men, 20 women	Ph.D.s: 95%
Graduate: 94 men, 83 women	Student/Faculty: 11 to 1
Year: 4–1–4	Tuition: $20,552
Application Deadline: January 31	Room & Board: $6382
Freshman Class: 1903 applied, 1014 accepted, 296 enrolled	
SAT I or ACT: not required	VERY COMPETITIVE

Bard College, founded in 1860, is an independent, coeducational liberal arts and sciences institution, affiliated historically with the Association of Episcopal Colleges. Discussion-oriented seminars and independent study are encouraged, tutorials are on a one-to-one basis, and most classes are kept small, with fewer than 20 students. There is 1 undergraduate and 4 graduate schools. The library contains 260,000 volumes, 5670 microform items, and 5600 audiovisual forms, and subscribes to 850 periodicals. Computerized library services and services include the card catalog, interlibrary loans, and database searching. Special learning facilities include an art gallery, a radio station, an ecology field station, the Jerome Levy International Economics Institute, the Institute for Writing and Thinking, the International Academy for Scholarship and the Arts, the Center for Curatorial Studies and Art in Contemporary Culture, and an archaeological field school. The 600-acre campus is in a rural area 100 miles north of New York City. Including residence halls, there are 70 buildings on campus.

Student Life: 74% of undergraduates are from out-of-state, mostly the Northeast. Students come from 50 states, 45 foreign countries, and Canada. 70% are from public schools; 30% from private. 74% are white; 10% foreign nationals. The average age of freshmen is 18; all undergraduates, 20. 10% do not continue beyond their first year; 77% remain to graduate.

Housing: 820 students can be accommodated in college housing. College-sponsored living facilities include single-sex and coed dormitories. In addition, there are special interest houses. On-campus housing is guaranteed for all 4 years. 85% of students live on campus; of those, 75% remain on campus on weekends. All students may keep cars on campus.

Activities: There are no fraternities or sororities. There are 60 groups on campus, including art, band, chamber groups, chess, choir, chorus, computers, dance, drama, ethnic, film, gay, international, jazz band, literary magazine, newspaper, opera, orchestra, photography, political, radio and TV, religious, social, social service, student government, and yearbook. Popular campus events include Winter Carnival, Spring Festival, musical events, and senior project shows.

Sports: There are 7 intercollegiate sports for men and 6 for women, and 13 intramural sports for men and 13 for women. Athletic and recreation facilities include a gymnasium and pool, a student center, soccer and softball fields, squash and tennis courts, cross-country trails, bike paths, a 300-seat auditorium, and a film center.

Disabled Students: 70% of the campus is accessible to disabled students. The following facilities are available: wheelchair ramps, elevators, special parking, specially equipped rest rooms, lowered drinking fountains, and lowered telephones.

Services: In addition to many counseling and information services, tutoring is available in most subjects. There is a reader service for the blind.

Campus Safety and Security: Campus safety and security measures include 24-hour foot and vehicle patrol, self-defense education, escort service, and shuttle buses. In addition, there are informal discussions, pamphlets/posters/films, emergency telephones, lighted pathways/sidewalks, volunteer emergency medical technicians on call 24 hours a day, and Bard Response to Rape and Associated Violence Education (BRAVE) volunteers.

Programs of Study: Bard confers the B.A. degree. Master's degrees are also awarded. Bachelor's degrees are awarded in BIOLOGICAL SCIENCE (biology/biological science), COMMUNICATIONS AND THE ARTS (art history and appreciation, dance, dramatic arts, English, film arts, fine arts, languages, music, and photography), COMPUTER AND PHYSICAL SCIENCE (chemistry, mathematics, and physics), ENGINEERING AND ENVIRONMENTAL DESIGN (environmental science), HEALTH PROFESSIONS (predentistry and premedicine), SOCIAL SCIENCE (American studies, anthropology, Asian/Oriental studies, economics, history, history of science, philosophy, political science/government, prelaw, psychology, religion, social science, and sociology). Language and literature, the arts, and social studies have the largest enrollments.

Required: All students must complete a year-long freshman seminar, a 3-week workshop in language and thinking, and a senior project. A conference in the junior year is required, and through a moderation process in the sophomore year, the student chooses a concentration in an academic department. A distribution of at least 1 course in each of the 7 academic areas, including a quantitative analysis course, is required, with a maximum of 84 hours in the student's major and a total of 124 credit hours needed to graduate.

Special: Bard offers opportunities for study abroad, internships (no academic credit), a Washington semester, dual majors, student-designed majors, and pass/fail options. Cross-registration is available with Vassar College and SUNY/New Paltz. A 3–2 engineering degree is available with the Columbia University School of Engineering. Other 3–2 degrees are available in forestry and environmental studies, social work, architecture, city and regional planning, public health, and business administration. There are also opportunities for independent study; multicultural and ethnic studies; community, regional, and environmental studies; area studies; and the International Honors Program.

Faculty/Classroom: 60% of faculty are male; 40%, female. All both teach and do research. No introductory courses are taught by graduate students. The average class size in an introductory lecture is 20; in a laboratory, 15; and in a regular course offering, 15.

Admissions: 53% of the 1995–96 applicants were accepted. The SAT I scores for a recent freshman class were as follows: Verbal—1% below 500, 43% between 500 and 599, 46% between 600 and 700, and 10% above 700; Math—1% below 500, 40% between 500 and 599, 51% between 600 and 700, and 8% above 700. 70% of the current freshmen were in the top fifth of their class; 90% were in the top two fifths.

Requirements: Bard requires applicants to be in the upper 50% of their class. A minimum GPA of 2.5 is required. Bard places strong emphasis on the academic background and intellectual curiosity of applicants, as well as indications of the student's commitment to social and environmental concerns, independent research, volunteer work, and other important extracurricular activities. Students applying for admission are expected to have graduated from an accredited secondary school (the GED is accepted) and must submit written essays with the application. The high school record should include a full complement of college-preparatory courses. An interview is recommended. AP credits are accepted. Important factors in the admissions decision are advanced placement or honor courses, evidence of special talent, and leadership record.

Procedure: Freshmen are admitted fall and spring. There are early decision, early admissions, and deferred admissions plans. Early decision applications should be filed by December 1; regular applications, by January 31 for fall entry and December 1 for spring entry, along with an application fee of $40. Notification of early decision is sent January 1; regular decision, April 1. 169 early decision candidates were accepted for the 1995–96 class. A waiting list is an active part of the admissions procedure, with about 10% of all applicants on the list.

Transfer: Admission requirements are the same as for regular applicants. A minimum GPA of 3.0 and an interview are recommended. 60 credits of 124 must be completed at Bard.

Visiting: There are regularly scheduled orientations for prospective students, consisting of regularly scheduled, daily tours and interviews (each 1 hour), which are strongly recommended. There are guides for informal visits and visitors may sit in on classes. To schedule a visit, contact the Admissions Office.

Financial Aid: In 1995–96, 72% of all freshmen and 70% of continuing students received some form of financial aid. 70% of freshmen and 68% of continuing students received need-based aid. The average freshman award was $17,604. Of that total, scholarships or need-based grants averaged $12,950 ($20,614 maximum); loans averaged $3154 ($4125 maximum); and work contracts averaged $1500 (maximum). 60% of undergraduate students work part-time. Average earnings from campus work for the school year are $1200. The average financial indebtedness of the 1994–95 graduate was $14,700. Bard is a member of CSS. The CSS Profile Application is required. The application deadline for fall entry is February 15.

International Students: There are currently 124 international students enrolled. The school actively recruits these students. They must take the TOEFL and achieve a minimum score of 550.

Computers: The college provides computer facilities for student use. The computer center houses more than 65 networked IBM and Apple microcomputers as well as some 50 additional terminals and PCs. Others are located in the library and academic departments. All students may access the system. There are no time limits and no fees.

Graduates: In 1994–95, 190 bachelor's degrees were awarded. The most popular majors among graduates were social studies (33%), arts (32%), and language and literature (23%). Within an average freshman class, 77% graduate in 5 years. 100 companies recruited on campus in 1994–95.

Admissions Contact: Mary Backlund, Director of Admissions.

BORICUA COLLEGE   D-5

New York, NY 10032	(212) 694–1000; FAX: (212) 694–1015
Full-time: 350 men, 860 women	Faculty: 50
Part-time: none	Ph.D.s: n/av
Graduate: none	Student/Faculty: 24 to 1
Year: trimesters, summer session	Tuition: $6125
Application Deadline: open	Room & Board: n/app
Freshman Class: 457 applied, 438 accepted, 344 enrolled	
SAT I or ACT: accepted	LESS COMPETITIVE

Boricua College, founded in 1974, is a private college for bilingual students, designed to meet the needs of a Spanish-speaking population. Special learning facilities include a learning resource center and art gallery. The campus is in an urban area in Manhattan. There are 4 buildings on campus.

Student Life: All undergraduates are from New York.

Housing: There are no residence halls.

Activities: There are 5 groups on campus, including chorus, drama, newspaper, and student government. Popular campus events include cultural programs.

Sports: There is no sports program at Boricua.

Services: In addition to many counseling and information services, tutoring is available in most subjects.

Campus Safety and Security: Campus safety and security measures include informal discussions, pamphlets/posters/films, emergency telephones, and lighted pathways/sidewalks.

Programs of Study: Boricua confers B.A. and B.S. degrees. Associate degrees are also awarded. Bachelor's degrees are awarded in BUSINESS (business administration and management), EDUCATION (elementary), SOCIAL SCIENCE (human services and liberal arts/general studies).

Required: To graduate, students must complete 124 credits, including a computer course.

Special: Nontraditional methods of teaching include individualized instruction, small learning groups, and independent study. Students take part in directed internships throughout their 4 years; the internships are related to human services, business administration, and elementary education. Study abroad in Mexico is permitted.

Faculty/Classroom: 51% of faculty are male; 49%, female.

Admissions: 96% of the 1995–96 applicants were accepted.

Requirements: Boricua administers its own tests to prospective students, although the SAT I or ACT is accepted. Applicants must be graduates of an accredited secondary school. Two letters of recommendation are required. Applicants must demonstrate a working knowledge of English and Spanish to a faculty panel. Important factors in the admissions decision are leadership record, personality/intangible qualities, and recommendations by school officials.

Procedure: Freshmen are admitted fall, spring, and summer. There is an early decision plan. Application deadlines are open. The application fee is $25. Notification is sent on a rolling basis.

Transfer: Applicants with associate degrees may transfer up to 60 credits, others up to 30 credits. 64 credits of 124 must be completed at Boricua.

Visiting: There are regularly scheduled orientations for prospective students. Letters are sent to prospective students advising them of scheduled orientations. To schedule a visit, contact the Admissions Department.

Financial Aid: Boricua is a member of CSS. The FAFSA is required. The application deadline for fall entry is March 31.

International Students: The student must take the college's own entrance exam.

Computers: The college provides computer facilities for student use. The mainframe is an IBM. There are computers available for student use in the computer laboratory. Those students registered in computer courses may access the system. There are no fees.

Admissions Contact: Abraham Cruz, Director of Student Services.

BROOKLYN CAMPUS OF LONG ISLAND   D-5
UNIVERSITY

Brooklyn, NY 11201	(718) 488–1292; FAX: (718) 797–2399
Full-time: 1715 men, 3619 women	Faculty: 211; IIA, +$
Part-time: 298 men, 672 women	Ph.D.s: 76%
Graduate: 632 men, 1145 women	Student/Faculty: 25 to 1
Year: semesters, summer session	Tuition: $11,810
Application Deadline: open	Room & Board: $6800
Freshman Class: 2775 applied, 2290 accepted, 1106 enrolled	
SAT I: recommended	COMPETITIVE

Long Island University/Brooklyn Campus, founded in 1926, is part of the Long Island University system. It is a private, coeducational institution offering programs in liberal arts and sciences, pharmacy, health professions, education, business, nursing, and special programs. It is largely a commuter school. There are 6 undergraduate and 5 graduate schools. In addition to regional accreditation, LIU has baccalaureate program accreditation with ACPE and NLN. The library contains 2,100,000 volumes, 813,544 microform items, and 7902 audiovisual forms, and subscribes to 8042 periodicals. Computerized library sources and services include the card catalog and interlibrary loans. Special learning facilities include a learning resource center, art gallery, radio station, and TV station. The 10-acre campus is in an urban area. Including residence halls, there are 8 buildings on campus.

Student Life: 91% of undergraduates are from New York. Students come from 35 states, 21 foreign countries, and Canada. 75% are from public schools; 25% from private. 43% are African American; 29% white; 17% Hispanic; 11% Asian American. The average age of freshmen is 21; all undergraduates, 25. 36% do not continue beyond their first year; 61% remain to graduate.

Housing: 525 students can be accommodated in college housing. College-sponsored living facilities include single-sex and coed dormitories and married-student housing. On-campus housing is available on a first-come, first-served basis. 89% of students commute. Alcohol is not permitted.

Activities: There are 75 groups on campus, including band, cheerleading, chess, chorale, computers, dance, ethnic, honors, international, literary magazine, newspaper, photography, political, radio and TV, religious, student government, and yearbook.

Sports: There are 7 intercollegiate sports for men and 6 for women. Athletic and recreation facilities include a baseball/soccer field and a basketball gymnasium.

Disabled Students: All of the campus is accessible to disabled students. The following facilities are available: wheelchair ramps, elevators, specially equipped rest rooms, special class scheduling, lowered drinking fountains, and lowered telephones.

Services: In addition to many counseling and information services, tutoring is available in most subjects. There is remedial math, reading, and writing.

Programs of Study: LIU confers B.A., B.S., and B.F.A. degrees. Associate, master's, and doctoral degrees are also awarded. Bachelor's degrees are awarded in BIOLOGICAL SCIENCE (biology/biological science), BUSINESS (accounting, banking and finance, business administration and management, and marketing/retailing/merchandising), COMMUNICATIONS AND THE ARTS (broadcasting, communications, English, fine arts, journalism, languages, music, and speech/debate/rhetoric), COMPUTER AND PHYSICAL SCIENCE (chemistry, computer science, information sciences and systems, and mathematics), EDUCATION (art, business, early childhood, elementary, music, science, secondary, special, and teaching English as a second/foreign language (TESOL/TEFOL)), HEALTH PROFESSIONS (nursing, pharmacy, physical therapy, predentistry, and premedicine), SOCIAL SCIENCE (anthropology, economics, history, philosophy, political science/government, prelaw, psychology, social science, and sociology). Health professions, pharmacy, and liberal arts are the strongest academically. Health professions, liberal arts, and business have the largest enrollments.

Required: Proficiency courses include basic English and mathematics, English composition, and speech. Distribution requirements are 6 credits each in foreign language, mathematics, and science. Students must complete a core curriculum of 18 credits in the humanities, 12 in social sciences, 8 in natural sciences, and 6 in mathematics. A total of 128 credits is required for graduation, with 40 to 50 credits in the major, and a GPA of 2.0.

Special: Accelerated degree programs are available in all majors. Students may cross-register with other LIU campuses. Internships in career-related jobs provide cooperative education credits. Study abroad, dual-majors, credit for life, military, and work experience, and pass/fail options are also offered. There is a freshman honors program on campus.

Faculty/Classroom: All teach undergraduates. The average class size in a regular course offering is 22.

Admissions: 83% of the 1995–96 applicants were accepted. 18% of the current freshmen were in the top fifth of their class; 36% were in the top two fifths.

Requirements: The SAT I is recommended. A minimum GPA of 2.0 is required. AP and CLEP credits are accepted. Important factors in the admissions decision are recommendations by school officials, advanced placement or honor courses, and evidence of special talent.

Procedure: Freshmen are admitted to all sessions. Entrance exams should be taken by January of the senior year. There is a deferred admissions plan. Application deadlines are open. Application fee is $30. Notification is sent on a rolling basis.

Transfer: A GPA of 2.5 and 64 earned credit hours are required to transfer. The SAT I, an associate degree, and an interview are recommended. 32 credits of 128 must be completed at LIU.

Visiting: There are regularly scheduled orientations for prospective students. Visitors may sit in on classes. To schedule a visit, contact the Admissions Office at (718) 488-1292.

Financial Aid: Average earnings from campus work for the school year are $750. LIU is a member of CSS. The FAF and the college's own financial statement are required. The application deadline for fall entry is November 15.

International Students: There were 175 international students enrolled in a recent year. The school actively recruits these students. They must score 500 on the TOEFL and also take SAT I or the ACT.

Computers: The college provides computer facilities for student use. The mainframe is a DEC VAX 8600. Microcomputers are available in the library for academic use. All students may access the system during library hours. There are no time limits and no fees.

Admissions Contact: Alan B. Chaves, Dean of Admissions.

CANISIUS COLLEGE
Buffalo, NY 14208   A-3

(716) 888-2200
(800) 843-1517; FAX: (716) 888-2377

Full-time: 1578 men, 1333 women	**Faculty:** 190; IIA, av$
Part-time: 254 men, 244 women	**Ph.D.s:** 92%
Graduate: 583 men, 844 women	**Student/Faculty:** 15 to 1
Year: semesters, summer session	**Tuition:** $11,976
Application Deadline: open	**Room & Board:** $5500
Freshman Class: 2515 applied, 2128 accepted, 719 enrolled	
SAT I Verbal/Math: 450/510	**ACT:** 24 COMPETITIVE

Canisius College, founded in 1870, is a private, coeducational Roman Catholic college in the Jesuit tradition. It offers undergraduate programs in the liberal arts and sciences, business, education, and human services. There are 3 undergraduate and 2 graduate schools. In addition to regional accreditation, Canisius has baccalaureate program accreditation with AACSB and NCATE. The library contains 295,843 volumes, 527,366 microform items, and 4530 audiovisual forms, and subscribes to 1885 periodicals. Computerized library sources and services include the card catalog, interlibrary loans, and database searching. Special learning facilities include a learning resource center, planetarium, radio station, television studio, foreign language laboratory, and 6 media-assisted classrooms. The 25-acre campus is in an urban area. Including residence halls, there are 39 buildings on campus.

Student Life: 93% of undergraduates are from New York. Students come from 27 states, 21 foreign countries, and Canada. 72% are from public schools; 28% from private. 84% are white. 53% are Catholic; 27% claim no religious affiliation. The average age of freshmen is 19; all undergraduates, 22. 18% do not continue beyond their first year; 55% remain to graduate.

Housing: 928 students can be accommodated in college housing. College-sponsored living facilities include single-sex and coed dormitories and off-campus apartments. In addition, there are special interest houses and an international students house. On-campus housing is guaranteed for all 4 years. 70% of students commute. All students may keep cars on campus.

Activities: 4% of men belong to 2 national fraternities; 4% of women belong to 2 national sororities. There are 90 groups on campus, including art, cheerleading, chess, chorale, computers, dance, drama, drill team, ethnic, honors, international, jazz band, literary magazine, newspaper, pep band, political, professional, radio and TV, religious, social, social service, student government, and yearbook. Popular campus events include Quad Parties, Buffalo Philharmonic on Campus, Carnivale, International Fest, and Multicultural Week.

Sports: There are 16 intercollegiate sports for men and 12 for women, and 17 intramural sports for men and 17 for women. Athletic and recreation facilities include an 1800-seat athletic center with a 24-yard pool, racquetball courts, and training rooms, a 1000-seat sports complex with Astroturf playing fields and perimeter track, a rifle range, a mirrored dance studio, and outdoor tennis courts.

Disabled Students: 95% of the campus is accessible to disabled students. The following facilities are available: wheelchair ramps, elevators, special parking, specially equipped rest rooms, special class scheduling, lowered drinking fountains, lowered telephones, automatic doors, and TDD.

Services: In addition to many counseling and information services, tutoring is available in some subjects, including in most introductory courses. There is a reader service for the blind and remedial math and writing.

Campus Safety and Security: Campus safety and security measures include 24-hour foot and vehicle patrol, escort service, shuttle buses, and informal discussions. In addition, there are pamphlets/posters/films, emergency telephones, lighted pathways/sidewalks, a crime prevention officer, and crime prevention programs.

Programs of Study: Canisius confers B.A. and B.S. degrees. Associate and master's degrees are also awarded. Bachelor's degrees are awarded in BIOLOGICAL SCIENCE (biochemistry and biology/biological science), BUSINESS (accounting, banking and finance, business administration and management, hotel/motel and restaurant management, management information systems, and marketing/retailing/merchandising), COMMUNICATIONS AND THE ARTS (art history and appreciation, communications, English, French, German, languages, and Spanish), COMPUTER AND PHYSICAL SCIENCE (chemistry, computer science, mathematics, and physics), EDUCATION (athletic training, business, elementary, English, foreign languages, mathematics, physical, science, secondary, and social studies), HEALTH PROFESSIONS (medical laboratory technology), SOCIAL SCIENCE (anthropology, economics, history, international relations, philosophy, political science/government, psychology, religion, sociology, and urban studies). Accounting, chemistry, and computer science are the strongest academically. Accounting, psychology, and management have the largest enrollments.

Required: All students must complete a core curriculum consisting of 4 courses in general studies (literature, philosophy, and religion) and 14 courses in area studies (natural sciences, social studies, art and literature, history, philosophy, religious studies, mathematics, and languages). In addition, students must take 10 courses in the major. A minimum of 120 credit hours and a minimum GPA of 2.0 are required for graduation.

Special: Canisius offers internships, credit by examination, pass/fail options, nondegree studies, dual majors, including anthropology/sociology, a Washington semester, work-study programs, and study abroad in 6 countries. Cooperative programs are available with the Fashion Institute of Technology in New York City and the SUNY College of Environmental Science and Forestry in Syracuse. Cross-registration is permitted with 14 schools in the Western New York Consortium of Higher Education. Canisius also offers early assurance programs with SUNY health professions schools in Buffalo and Syracuse. There is a freshman honors program on campus, as well as 8 national honor societies. 3 departments have honors programs.

Faculty/Classroom: 72% of faculty are male; 28%, female. 99% teach undergraduates, 75% do research, and 65% do both. The average class size in an introductory lecture is 26; in a laboratory, 20; and in a regular course offering, 28.

Admissions: 85% of the 1995–96 applicants were accepted. The SAT I scores for the 1995–96 freshman class were as follows: Verbal—68% below 500, 24% between 500 and 599, 7% between 600 and 700, and 1% above 700; Math—42% below 500, 32% between 500 and 599, 21% between 600 and 700, and 5% above 700. The ACT scores were 33% below 21, 28% between 21 and 23, 19% between 24 and 26, 11% between 27 and 28, and 9% above 28. 38% of the current freshmen were in the top fifth of their class; 66% were in the top two fifths. 14 freshmen graduated first in their class.

Requirements: The SAT I or ACT is required; minimum scores recommended are SAT I composite 800 and 21 ACT. A minimum GPA of 2.0 is required. Applicants must have graduated from an accredited secondary school (a GED will be accepted) and have acquired 4 credits in English, 2 in a foreign language, 3 to 3 1/2 in mathematics, 1 to 2 in science, 2 in social studies, and 2 1/2 to 4 in other electives. An essay and an interview are recommended. Applications are accepted on-line via ExPAN. AP and CLEP credits are accepted. Important factors in the admissions decision are advanced placement or honor courses, recommendations by school officials, and evidence of special talent.

Procedure: Freshmen are admitted fall and spring. Entrance exams should be taken during the student's junior or senior year. There are early admissions and deferred admissions plans. Application deadlines are open. The fee is $25. Notification is sent on a rolling basis.

Transfer: 184 transfer students enrolled in 1995–96. Transfer students must present a minimum GPA of 2.0. 30 credits of 120 must be completed at Canisius.

Visiting: There are regularly scheduled orientations for prospective students, including campus weekends, single-day visits, and overnights. Also available are summer visitations for families and an open house in the fall. There are guides for informal visits and visitors may sit in on classes and stay overnight at the school. To schedule a visit, contact the Admissions Office.

Financial Aid: In 1995–96, 90% of all freshmen and 80% of continuing students received some form of financial aid. 88% of freshmen and 77% of continuing students received need-based aid. The average freshman award was $10,445. Of that total, scholarships or need-based grants averaged $7918 ($11,650 maximum); loans averaged $2805; and work contracts averaged $721 ($1600 maximum). 22% of undergraduate students work part-time. Average earnings from campus work for the school year are $1050. The average financial indebtedness of the 1994–95 graduate was $14,824. Canisius is a member of CSS. The FAFSA and the college's own financial statement are required. The application deadline for fall entry is February 1.

International Students: There are currently 80 international students enrolled. The school actively recruits these students. They must take the TOEFL and achieve a minimum score of 500.

Computers: The college provides computer facilities for student use. The mainframes are a DEC VAX 4000 and a Sun SPARC 10. 5 computer laboratories contain 84 networked Macintoshes, 61 networked IBM-compatibles, and 9 VAX terminals. The laboratories are open to all registered students. Personal network accounts with E-mail are available to all students. All students may access the system 24 hours a day, 7 days a week. Students may access the system for 1 hour if others are waiting. There are no fees.

Graduates: In 1994–95, 638 bachelor's degrees were awarded. The most popular majors among graduates were psychology (11%), management (9%), and English (8%). Within an average freshman class, 45% graduate in 4 years and 55% in 5 years. 35 companies recruited on campus in 1994–95.

Admissions Contact: Penelope H. Lips, Director of Admissions. E-mail: lips@canisius.edu. A campus video is available.

CAZENOVIA COLLEGE   C-3

Cazenovia, NY 13035	(315) 655–8005; (800) 654-3210
Full-time: 306 men, 519 women	Faculty: 46; IIB, --$
Part-time: 6 men, 23 women	Ph.D.s: 40%
Graduate: none	Student/Faculty: 18 to 1
Year: 12–12–6	Tuition: $10,200
Application Deadline: open	Room & Board: $5100
Freshman Class: 3076 applied, 2764 accepted, 299 enrolled	
SAT I Verbal/Math: 398/468	ACT: 18 LESS COMPETITIVE

Cazenovia College, founded in 1824, is a private coeducational institution offering undergraduate programs in applied arts and sciences and professional studies. The library contains 52,095 volumes, 210 microform items, and 2704 audiovisual forms, and subscribes to 456 periodicals. Computerized library sources and services include interlibrary loans and database searching. Special learning facilities include a learning resource center, art gallery, and radio station. The 40-acre campus is in a small town 18 miles southeast of Syracuse. Including residence halls, there are 19 buildings on campus.

Student Life: 91% of undergraduates are from New York. Students come from 15 states and 1 foreign country. 91% are from public schools; 9% from private. 76% are white; 15% African American. The average age of freshmen is 18. 47% do not continue beyond their first year; 32% remain to graduate.

Housing: 600 students can be accommodated in college housing. College-sponsored living facilities include single-sex and coed dormitories and on-campus apartments. On-campus housing is guaranteed for all 4 years. 86% of students live on campus; of those, 60% remain on campus on weekends. Alcohol is not permitted. All students may keep cars on campus.

Activities: There are no fraternities or sororities. There are many groups and organizations on campus, including cheerleading, computers, drama, ethnic, gay, honors, musical theater, newspaper, political, social service, student government, and yearbook. Popular campus events include Spring Day, Parents Weekend, and athletic events.

Sports: There are 6 intercollegiate sports for men and 6 for women, and 8 intramural sports for men and 9 for women. Athletic and recreation facilities include an athletic center that houses an Olympic-size pool, a weight room, racquetball courts, tennis courts, and a main gymnasium.

Disabled Students: 86% of the campus is accessible to disabled students. The following facilities are available: wheelchair ramps, elevators, special parking, specially equipped rest rooms, special class scheduling, lowered telephones, and special dormitory facilities.

Services: In addition to many counseling and information services, tutoring is available in every subject. There is a reader service for the blind, and remedial math, reading, and writing.

Campus Safety and Security: Campus safety and security measures include escort service, informal discussions, pamphlets/posters/films, and emergency telephones. In addition, there are lighted pathways/sidewalks and night foot patrol.

Programs of Study: Cazenovia confers B.A., B.S., B.F.A., and B.P.S. degrees. Associate degrees are also awarded. Bachelor's degrees are awarded in BUSINESS (management science and retailing), COMMUNICATIONS AND THE ARTS (fine arts and graphic design), COMPUTER AND PHYSICAL SCIENCE (science technology), ENGINEERING AND ENVIRONMENTAL DESIGN (interior design), SOCIAL SCIENCE (humanities and social science). Interior design, liberal arts, and human services are the strongest academically. Art and design have the largest enrollments.

Required: A total of 126 semester credits and a GPA of 2.0 are required for the bachelor's degree. All students must take courses in speech, English composition, and physical education.

Special: Cazenovia offers internships in human services and child studies, student-designed majors, work-study, B.A.-B.S. degrees in liberal studies and liberal and professional studies, and study abroad. There is a freshman honors program on campus, as well as 1 national honor society. 2 departments have honors programs.

Faculty/Classroom: 39% of faculty are male; 61%, female. All teach undergraduates and 1% also do research. The average class size in an introductory lecture is 45; in a laboratory, 20; and in a regular course offering, 35.

Admissions: 90% of the 1995–96 applicants were accepted. The SAT I scores for the 1995–96 freshman class were as follows: Math—84% below 500, 13% between 500 and 599, 2% between 600 and 700, and 1% above 700. The ACT scores were 78% below 21, 9% between 21 and 23, 11% between 24 and 26, 1% between 27 and 28, and 1% above 28. 6% of the current freshmen were in the top fifth of their class; 22% were in the top two fifths. 1 freshman graduated first in the class.

Requirements: The SAT I or ACT is required. Applicants should be graduates of an accredited secondary school with a 2.0 GPA or the equivalent. AP and CLEP credits are accepted. Important factors in the admissions decision are evidence of special talent, personality/intangible qualities, and recommendations by school officials.

Procedure: Freshmen are admitted fall and winter. Entrance exams should be taken by the fall of the senior year. There is a deferred admissions plan. Application deadlines are open. Application fee is $25. Notification is sent on a rolling basis. A waiting list is an active part of the admissions procedure, with about 5% of all applicants on the list.

Transfer: Applicants must present at least 12 college credits and a minimum GPA of 2.0. 30 credits of 126 must be completed at Cazenovia.

Visiting: There are regularly scheduled orientations for prospective students, through an information mall on campus. There are guides for informal visits and visitors may sit in on classes and stay overnight at the school. To schedule a visit, contact the Director of Admissions.

Financial Aid: 28% of undergraduate students work part-time. Average earnings from campus work for the school year are $800. Cazenovia is a member of CSS. The FAF is required. The application deadline for fall entry is September 15.

International Students: There were 5 international students enrolled in a recent year. They must take the TOEFL and achieve a minimum score of 500. The student must also take the SAT I or the ACT.

Computers: The college provides computer facilities for student use. The mainframe is a networked IBM-type LAN. Students access a network designed for the computer laboratory, which houses approximately 70 microcomputers. All students may access the system daily from 8 A.M. to midnight. There are no time limits. The fees are $100.

Graduates: In 1994–95, 51 bachelor's degrees were awarded. The most popular majors among graduates were professional studies (82%) and applied arts and sciences (18%). 23 companies recruited on campus in 1994–95. Of the 1994 graduating class, 68% were enrolled in continuing education within 6 months of graduation and 30% had found employment.

Admissions Contact: Director of Admissions.

CITY UNIVERSITY OF NEW YORK

The City University of New York (CUNY), established in 1847, is a public system in New York City. It is governed by a Board of Trustees, whose chief administrator is the chancellor. The primary goal of the system is to maintain and expand its commitment to academic excellence and to the provision of equal access and opportunity. The main priorities are providing access for all students who seek to enroll, ensuring student success, and enhancing instructional and research excellence. The total enrollment of all 21 campuses is about 208,000, with some 5691 faculty members. Altogether, there are 598 baccalaureate, 343 master's, and 46 doctoral programs offered within the City University of New York. Profiles of the 4-year campuses, located in New York's 5 boroughs of Manhattan, Brooklyn, Queens, Staten Island, and the Bronx, are included in this chapter.

CITY UNIVERSITY OF NEW YORK/BARUCH COLLEGE

D-5

New York, NY 10010-5585 (212) 802-2300

Full-time: 3652 men, 4849 women	Faculty: 455
Part-time: 1675 men, 2517 women	Ph.D.s: 87%
Graduate: 1230 men, 1105 women	Student/Faculty: 19 to 1
Year: semesters, summer session	Tuition: $3312 ($6912)
Application Deadline: January 16	Room & Board: n/app
Freshman Class: 5377 applied, 3059 accepted, 1480 enrolled	
SAT I: recommended	VERY COMPETITIVE

Baruch College was founded in 1919 and became a separate unit of the City University of New York in 1968. It offers undergraduate programs in business and public administration, liberal arts and sciences, and education. There are 2 undergraduate and 3 graduate schools. In addition to regional accreditation, Baruch has baccalaureate program accreditation with AACSB. The library contains 270,000 volumes, 1.6 million microform items, and 500 audiovisual forms, and subscribes to 2100 periodicals. Computerized library sources and services include the card catalog, interlibrary loans, and database searching. Special learning facilities include a learning resource center, art gallery, and radio station. The campus is in an urban area. There are 6 buildings on campus.

Student Life: 90% of undergraduates are from New York. Students come from 93 foreign countries and Canada. 25% are Asian American; 24% African American; 23% white; 20% Hispanic. 16% do not continue beyond their first year.

Housing: There are no residence halls. All students commute. Alcohol is not permitted.

Activities: There are no fraternities or sororities. There are 97 groups on campus, including cheerleading, chess, chorus, computers, drama, ethnic, film, gay, honors, international, jazz band, literary magazine, musical theater, newspaper, photography, political, professional, radio and TV, religious, social, social service, student government, and yearbook. Popular campus events include club fairs and street fairs.

Sports: There are 5 intercollegiate sports each for men and women, and 6 intramural sports for men and 5 for women. Athletic and recreation facilities include a gymnasium, a swimming pool, a weight room, and an exercise room.

Disabled Students: All of the campus is accessible to disabled students. The following facilities are available: wheelchair ramps, elevators, specially equipped rest rooms, and special class scheduling.

Services: In addition to many counseling and information services, tutoring is available in most subjects. There is a reader service for the blind, and remedial math, reading, and writing. Note takers and large-print computer screens are available.

Campus Safety and Security: Campus safety and security measures include pamphlets/posters/films, emergency telephones, and lighted pathways/sidewalks.

Programs of Study: Baruch confers B.A. and B.B.A. degrees. Master's and doctoral degrees are also awarded. Bachelor's degrees are awarded in BUSINESS (accounting, investments and securities, management science, marketing management, marketing/retailing/merchandising, operations research, and personnel management), COMMUNICATIONS AND THE ARTS (advertising, communications, English, journalism, music, and Spanish), COMPUTER AND PHYSICAL SCIENCE (actuarial science, computer management, mathematics, and statistics), EDUCATION (early childhood and elementary), SOCIAL SCIENCE (economics, history, industrial and organizational psychology, philosophy, political science/government, psychology, public administration, and sociology). Economics, English, and mathematics are the strongest academically. Accounting has the largest enrollment.

Required: Students must complete a minimum of 128 credit hours, with at least 24 hours in the major, and maintain a GPA of 2.0.

Special: The college offers internships and study abroad in Great Britain, France, Germany, Mexico, and Israel. Students may design their own liberal arts major. A federal work-study program is available, and pass/fail options are permitted for liberal arts majors. There is 1 national honor society on campus.

Faculty/Classroom: 67% of faculty are male; 33%, female.

Admissions: 57% of the 1995–96 applicants were accepted.

Requirements: The SAT I is recommended, with a minimum composite score of 1020 (recentered). Baruch requires applicants to be in the upper 33% of their class. Applicants must present an official high school transcript (a GED will be accepted) indicating a minimum high school average grade of 80% in academic subjects. AP and CLEP credits are accepted.

Procedure: Freshmen are admitted fall and spring. There is an early admissions plan. Applications should be filed by January 16 for fall entry and October 15 for spring entry, along with an application fee of $40. Notification is sent in March and November.

Transfer: 1465 transfer students enrolled in 1995–96. Transfer students must have a minimum GPA of 2.5 for 12 to 34.9 credits submitted, a minimum GPA of 2.25 for 35 to 59.9 credits, and a minimum GPA of 2.0 for 60 or more credits. Students applying for transfer with fewer than 12 credits earned must have a minimum GPA of 2.5 and a minimum high school average of 80%. 32 credits of 128 must be completed at Baruch.

Visiting: There are regularly scheduled orientations for prospective students, including a meeting with an admissions counselor. There are guides for informal visits. To schedule a visit, contact the Admissions Office.

Financial Aid: In 1995–96, 63% of all freshmen and 61% of continuing students received some form of financial aid. The average freshman award was $6900. Of that total, scholarships or need-based grants averaged $5400; loans averaged $1500; and work contracts averaged $900. 5% of undergraduate students work part-time. Average earnings from campus work for the school year are $2500. The FAFSA is required. The application deadline for fall entry is May 1.

International Students: There are currently 1035 international students enrolled. They must take the TOEFL and achieve a minimum score of 500.

Computers: The college provides computer facilities for student use. There are 469 microcomputers available in the computer center, media center, resource center, library, computer laboratories, and classrooms. All students may access the system. There are no fees.

Graduates: In 1994–95, 1918 bachelor's degrees were awarded. The most popular majors among graduates were accounting (29%), finance and investments (15%), and human resource management (9%). Within an average freshman class, 5% graduate in 4 years, 23% in 5 years, and 35% in 6 years. 350 companies recruited on campus in 1994–95.

Admissions Contact: Undergraduate Admissions Office.

CITY UNIVERSITY OF NEW YORK/BROOKLYN COLLEGE   D-5

Brooklyn, NY 11210–2889   (718) 951-5001

Full-time: 8450 men and women	**Faculty:** 716
Part-time: 3820 men and women	**Ph.D.s:** 79%
Graduate: 3880 men and women	**Student/Faculty:** 12 to 1
Year: semesters, summer session	**Tuition:** $3200 ($6500)
Application Deadline: June 1	**Room & Board:** n/app
Freshman Class: n/av	
SAT I: recommended	**VERY COMPETITIVE**

Brooklyn College, established in 1930, is a publicly supported college of liberal arts, sciences, preprofessional, and professional studies. It is part of the City University of New York and serves the commuter student. There are 2 undergraduate schools and 1 graduate school. The library contains 1 million volumes, 439 microform items, and 18,000 audiovisual forms, and subscribes to 4900 periodicals. Computerized library sources and services include the card catalog, interlibrary loans, and database searching. Special learning facilities include a learning resource center, art gallery, radio station, TV station, 3 color studios, and a speech and hearing clinic. The 26-acre campus is in an urban area. There are 8 buildings on campus.

Student Life: 92% of undergraduates are from New York. Students come from 15 states, 22 foreign countries, and Canada. 60% are from public schools; 40% from private. 54% are white; 23% African American; 10% Hispanic. The average age of freshmen is 19; all undergraduates, 21.

Housing: There are no residence halls. All students commute. Alcohol is not permitted.

Activities: 2% of men belong to 7 national fraternities; 2% of women belong to 2 national sororities. There are 150 groups on campus, including art, choir, chorus, computers, dance, drama, ethnic, film, gay, honors, literary magazine, musical theater, newspaper, orchestra, photography, political, professional, radio and TV, religious, social, social service, student government, symphony, and yearbook. Popular campus events include Country Fair, Fall Festival, and Black Solidarity Day.

Sports: Athletic and recreation facilities include swimming pools, a soccer field, volleyball, racquetball, squash, tennis, and basketball courts, a weight-training room, and a jogging track.

Disabled Students: The entire campus is accessible to disabled students. The following facilities are available: wheelchair ramps, elevators, special parking, specially equipped rest rooms, special class scheduling, and lowered drinking fountains.

Services: In addition to many counseling and information services, tutoring is available in every subject. There is a reader service for the blind, and remedial math, reading, and writing.

Campus Safety and Security: Campus safety and security measures include 24-hour foot and vehicle patrol, informal discussions, pamphlets/posters/films, and emergency telephones. In addition, there are lighted pathways/sidewalks.

Programs of Study: Brooklyn College confers B.A., B.S., B.F.A., and B.M. degrees. Master's degrees are also awarded. Bachelor's degrees are awarded in BIOLOGICAL SCIENCE (biology/biological science), BUSINESS (accounting, banking and finance, and business administration and management), COMMUNICATIONS AND THE ARTS (art, art history and appreciation, broadcasting, classics, comparative literature, creative writing, dance, dramatic arts, English, film arts, French, German, Greek, Hebrew, Italian, journalism, languages, Latin, linguistics, music, Russian, Spanish, and speech/debate/rhetoric), COMPUTER AND PHYSICAL SCIENCE (chemistry, computer science, geology, information sciences and systems, mathematics, and physics), EDUCATION (art, bilingual/bicultural, early childhood, education of the deaf and hearing impaired, elementary, mathematics, music, physical, secondary, and special), HEALTH PROFESSIONS (health science, predentistry, premedicine, and speech pathology/audiology), SOCIAL SCIENCE (African studies, American studies, anthropology, archeology, Caribbean studies, economics, Hispanic American studies, history, Judaic studies, philosophy, political science/government, prelaw, psychology, religion, sociology, urban studies, and women's studies). Education, TV/radio, and premedicine are the strongest academically. Education, business, and computer science have the largest enrollments.

Required: 10 required, interrelated courses cover the following core curriculum areas: classics, art, music, political science, sociology, history, literature, mathematics, computer science, chemistry, physics, biology, geology, philosophy, and comparative cultures. There are ba-

sic skills requirements in reading, composition, speech, and mathematics, as well as a foreign language requirement. A 2.0 GPA and a minimum of 128 credit hours, with 31 to 36 in the major, are required to graduate.

Special: There are numerous cooperative and cross-registration programs with colleges and universities in the area. Many internships and work-study programs are available. Study abroad is possible in Israel, Paris, Puerto Rico, and Africa. Summer programs are available in London, Florence, Madrid, Tokyo, and Ireland. A B.A.-M.D. and accelerated B.A.-M.A. programs are available. A number of B.A.-B.S. degrees, dual majors, and student-designed majors are possible. Credit by examination, credit for life experience, nondegree study, and pass/fail options are offered. There is a freshman honors program on campus, as well as 11 national honor societies, including Phi Beta Kappa.

Faculty/Classroom: 70% of faculty are male; 30% female. All teach undergraduates and 80% do research. The average class size in a laboratory is 15 and in a regular course offering, 35.

Requirements: The SAT I is recommended, with a composite score of 1020. Brooklyn College requires applicants to be in the upper 67% of their class. A minimum grade average of 80 is required. The GED, with a score of 300 or higher, is accepted. Requirements are higher for B.A.-M.D. entrants and for the scholars program. Applicants not meeting the standard requirements are eligible for admission to the City University's community colleges. AP and CLEP credits are accepted.

Procedure: Freshmen are admitted fall and spring. There are early admissions and deferred admissions plans. Applications should be filed by June 1 for fall entry and November 15 for spring entry, along with an application fee of $35. Notification is sent on a rolling basis.

Transfer: 1150 transfer students enrolled in 1995–96. Transfer students must have a minimum 2.0 GPA with 24 or more credits; 2.25 with 15 to 23 credits; and 2.5 with 7 to 14 credits. 48 credits of 128 must be completed at Brooklyn College.

Visiting: There are regularly scheduled orientations for prospective students. There are guides for informal visits and visitors may sit in on classes. To schedule a visit, contact the Office of Admissions.

Financial Aid: In a recent year, 35% of all students received some form of financial aid. 33% of freshmen and 37% of continuing students received need-based aid. The average freshman award was $4674. The average financial indebtedness of a recent graduate was $7000. Brooklyn College is a member of CSS. The college's own financial statement is required. The application deadline for fall entry is March 31.

International Students: There were 572 international students enrolled in a recent year. They must take the TOEFL and achieve a minimum score of 500.

Computers: The college provides computer facilities for student use. The mainframe is an IBM 4381. A 150-workstation microcomputer facility includes 36 Apple Macintosh IIci computers, 82 IBM PS2/55sx computers, and 36 Sun workstations networked across 5 file servers and 3 mainframe gateways. Computer science students may access the mainframe at any time. Students may access the system with a 1-hour limit. There are no fees.

Admissions Contact: John Fraire, Director of Admissions.

CITY UNIVERSITY OF NEW YORK/CITY COLLEGE   D-5

New York, NY 10031   (212) 650-6977; FAX: (212) 650-6417

Full-time: 3683 men, 3518 women	**Faculty:** 554
Part-time: 1707 men, 1778 women	**Ph.D.s:** 85%
Graduate: 1451 men, 2020 women	**Student/Faculty:** 13 to 1
Year: semesters, summer session	**Tuition:** $3295 ($6895)
Application Deadline: January 15	**Room & Board:** n/app
Freshman Class: 3499 applied, 1989 accepted, 939 enrolled	
SAT I or ACT: recommended	**VERY COMPETITIVE**

City College, founded in 1847, is a public, coeducational liberal arts institution that is part of the City University of New York. The college offers programs through 5 undergraduate and 4 graduate schools and 2 professional centers. In addition to regional accreditation, CCNY has baccalaureate program accreditation with ABFSE, NAAB, NCATE, and NLN. The 4 libraries contain 1,199,342 volumes, 644 microform items, and 15,270 audiovisual forms, and subscribe to 3401 periodicals. Computerized library sources and services include the card catalog, interlibrary loans, and database searching. Special learning facilities include an art gallery, planetarium, radio station, TV station, weather station, laser laboratories, and microwave laboratories. The 34-acre campus is in an urban area in New York City. There are 14 buildings on campus.

Student Life: 85% of undergraduates are from New York. Students come from 52 states, 60 foreign countries, and Canada. 90% are from public schools; 10% from private. 38% are African American; 27% Hispanic; 16% Asian American; 11% white; 10% foreign nationals.

The average age of freshmen is 18; all undergraduates, 26. 20% do not continue beyond their first year.

Housing: There are no residence halls; all students commute. Alcohol is not permitted.

Activities: There are 4 local fraternities. There are no sororities. There are 100 groups on campus, including art, band, cheerleading, chess, chorus, computers, drama, ethnic, gay, honors, international, jazz band, literary magazine, newspaper, orchestra, political, professional, radio and TV, religious, social, social service, student government, and yearbook. Popular campus events include Langston Hughes Poetry Contest and Dance Theater of Harlem performances at Davis Center.

Sports: There are 11 intercollegiate sports for men and 8 for women, as well as intramural sports. Athletic and recreation facilities include swimming pools, 3 gymnasiums, and a weight room.

Disabled Students: 90% of the campus is accessible to disabled students. The following facilities are available: wheelchair ramps, elevators, special parking, specially equipped rest rooms, special class scheduling, lowered drinking fountains, and lowered telephones.

Services: In addition to many counseling and information services, tutoring is available in most subjects, including science, economics, and engineering. There is a reader service for the blind, and remedial math, reading, and writing.

Campus Safety and Security: Campus safety and security measures include shuttle buses, informal discussions, pamphlets/posters/films, and emergency telephones.

Programs of Study: CCNY confers B.A., B.S., B.Arch., B.E., B.F.A., B.S.Ed., and B.S.N. degrees. Master's degrees are also awarded. Bachelor's degrees are awarded in BIOLOGICAL SCIENCE (biochemistry, biology/biological science, and marine science), BUSINESS (business administration and management), COMMUNICATIONS AND THE ARTS (communications, comparative literature, creative writing, dramatic arts, English, film arts, fine arts, French, languages, music, photography, and Spanish), COMPUTER AND PHYSICAL SCIENCE (chemistry, computer science, earth science, geology, mathematics, and physics), EDUCATION (art, early childhood, elementary, foreign languages, music, physical, science, secondary, and special), ENGINEERING AND ENVIRONMENTAL DESIGN (chemical engineering, civil engineering, electrical/electronics engineering, and mechanical engineering), HEALTH PROFESSIONS (predentistry and premedicine), SOCIAL SCIENCE (African American studies, anthropology, Asian/Oriental studies, economics, geography, Hispanic American studies, history, international studies, Judaic studies, Latin American studies, philosophy, political science/government, prelaw, psychology, and sociology). Engineering, architecture, and sciences are the strongest academically. Engineering, architecture, and psychology have the largest enrollments.

Required: To graduate, students must successfully complete 128 credits, with 32 to 48 in the major, and must maintain a minimum GPA of 2.0. A core curriculum must be met, and students must complete courses in basic writing, world humanities, world civilizations, computer literacy, world arts, and United States society.

Special: Cross-registration is permitted with other City University colleges. A 6-year urban legal studies degree and a 7-year biomedical education degree are available. Opportunities are provided for internships, a Washington semester, work-study programs, a wide variety of accelerated degree programs, credit by examination, credit for life experience, and study abroad in Europe, China, Africa, the Dominican Republic, and Japan. There is a freshman honors program on campus, as well as a chapter of Phi Beta Kappa.

Faculty/Classroom: The average class size in an introductory lecture is 135 and in a regular course offering, 25.

Admissions: 57% of the 1995–96 applicants were accepted.

Requirements: The SAT I or ACT is recommended, with a minimum composite SAT I score of 1020 or an ACT score of 22 recommended. Graduation from an accredited secondary school is generally required, but a GED will be accepted. 12 academic credits should be presented, with a minimum grade average of 80 or graduation in the top third of the current senior class. AP credits are accepted.

Procedure: Freshmen are admitted fall and spring. Entrance exams should be taken prior to registration. There is an early admissions plan. Applications should be filed by January 15 for fall entry and October 15 for spring entry, along with an application fee of $40. Notification is sent on a rolling basis.

Transfer: 866 transfer students enrolled in 1995–96. Applicants must have earned at least 24 credit hours and maintained a GPA of 2.0. Selected programs have more competitive requirements. 32 credits of 128 must be completed at CCNY.

Visiting: There are regularly scheduled orientations for prospective students. There are guides for informal visits and visitors may sit in on classes. To schedule a visit, contact the Admissions Office.

Financial Aid: The college's own financial statement is required.

International Students: There are currently 1481 international students enrolled. They must take the TOEFL and achieve a minimum score of 500.

Computers: The college provides computer facilities for student use. The mainframes are an IBM 4381, a DEC VAX, and a Sun. A campus-wide fiber-optics network is the backbone of the network; more than 1000 microcomputers are networked throughout campus, along with 500 dumb workstations; 50 computer languages are available. All students may access the system. There are no time limits. It is recommended that all students have personal computers.

Graduates: 100 companies recruited on campus in 1994–95.

Admissions Contact: Laurie Austin, Director of Admissions. E-mail: adocc@cunyvm.cuny.edu.

CITY UNIVERSITY OF NEW YORK/COLLEGE OF STATEN ISLAND D-5

Staten Island, NY 10314   (718) 982-2010

Full-time: 3004 men, 3460 women	Faculty: 269
Part-time: 1525 men, 2685 women	Ph.D.s: 78%
Graduate: 319 men, 1203 women	Student/Faculty: 24 to 1
Year: semesters, summer session	Tuition: $3316 ($6916)
Application Deadline: September 1	Room & Board: n/app
Freshman Class: 3528 applied, 3528 accepted, 1708 enrolled	
SAT I or ACT: not required	NONCOMPETITIVE

The College of Staten Island, founded in 1955, is a public coeducational institution offering programs in liberal arts and sciences, professional studies, health sciences, and the technologies. In addition to regional accreditation, CSI has baccalaureate program accreditation with ABET, CAHEA, and NLN. The library contains 190,764 volumes, 469,597 microform items, and 7942 audiovisual forms, and subscribes to 1374 periodicals. Computerized library sources and services include the card catalog, interlibrary loans, and database searching. Special learning facilities include an art gallery, planetarium, and radio station. The 204-acre campus is in an urban area in New York City's borough of Staten Island. There are 19 buildings on campus.

Student Life: 95% of undergraduates are from New York. Students come from 4 states, 75 foreign countries, and Canada. 73% are white. The average age of freshmen is 20; all undergraduates, 27.1. 21% do not continue beyond their first year; 40% remain to graduate.

Housing: There are no residence halls; all students commute. Alcohol is not permitted. All students may keep cars on campus.

Activities: There are no fraternities or sororities. There are 56 groups on campus, including art, cheerleading, chorus, drama, ethnic, film, gay, honors, international, jazz band, literary magazine, newspaper, photography, professional, radio and TV, religious, social, student government, and yearbook. Popular campus events include International Festival, Holiday Hip-Hop Party, Kwanzaa, and World Beat Festival.

Sports: There are 4 intercollegiate sports for men and 4 for women, and 13 intramural sports for men and 13 for women. Athletic and recreation facilities include a 1200-seat gymnasium, an indoor pool, outdoor baseball, soccer, and football fields, tennis courts, outdoor recreational basketball courts, shuffleboard and bocce courts, outdoor track and field facilities, and 4 volleyball fields.

Disabled Students: 90% of the campus is accessible to disabled students. The following facilities are available: wheelchair ramps, elevators, special parking, specially equipped rest rooms, special class scheduling, lowered drinking fountains, and lowered telephones.

Services: In addition to many counseling and information services, tutoring is available in most subjects. There is a reader service for the blind, and remedial math, reading, and writing.

Campus Safety and Security: Campus safety and security measures include 24-hour foot and vehicle patrol, escort service, shuttle buses, and informal discussions. In addition, there are pamphlets/posters/films, emergency telephones, lighted pathways/sidewalks, and formal talks by the security director.

Programs of Study: CSI confers B.A. and B.S. degrees. Associate, master's, and doctoral degrees are also awarded. Bachelor's degrees are awarded in BIOLOGICAL SCIENCE (biochemistry and biology/biological science), BUSINESS (accounting and business administration and management), COMMUNICATIONS AND THE ARTS (communications, dramatic arts, English, film arts, fine arts, languages, music, and Spanish), COMPUTER AND PHYSICAL SCIENCE (chemistry, computer science, mathematics, and physics), EDUCATION (education), ENGINEERING AND ENVIRONMENTAL DESIGN (engineering), HEALTH PROFESSIONS (medical laboratory technology, medical technology, nursing, physical therapy, and physician's assistant), SOCIAL SCIENCE (African American studies, American studies, economics, history, international studies, liberal arts/general studies, philosophy, political science/government, psychology, and women's studies). Business, education, and psychology have the largest enrollments.

Required: The curriculum varies for each degree, but physical education and English are required for all, as are courses from each of three areas: science/technology/mathematics; social sciences/

history/philosophy; and humanities. A minimum 2.0 GPA and 128 to 136 credit hours are required to graduate.

Special: Internships are available in most fields. Study abroad is possible in Italy, Israel, France, Spain, Ecuador, Denmark, England, and Greece. There are student-designed majors and interdisciplinary majors, including computer science-mathematics, sociology-anthropology, and science, letters, and society. Credit by examination, credit for life experience, and nondegree study are available. There are 4 national honor societies on campus. 18 departments have honors programs.

Faculty/Classroom: 64% of faculty are male; 36%, female. All teach undergraduates and 80% also do research. No introductory courses are taught by graduate students. The average class size in an introductory lecture is 40; in a laboratory, 24; and in a regular course offering, 28.

Admissions: All of the 1995–96 applicants were accepted.

Requirements: CSI requires applicants to be in the upper 67% of their class. All graduates of an accredited secondary school or GED equivalent are accepted for admission. Applicants must have a minimum grade average of 80 or graduate in the upper two thirds of their class to be eligible for admission to the 4-year programs. AP and CLEP credits are accepted.

Procedure: Freshmen are admitted to all sessions. Applications should be filed by September 1 for fall entry and February 1 for spring entry, along with an application fee of $40. The college accepts all applicants. Notification is sent on a rolling basis.

Transfer: 644 transfer students enrolled in 1995–96. Applicants must have a minimum 2.0 GPA. 30 credits of 128 to 136 must be completed at CSI.

Visiting: There are regularly scheduled orientations for prospective students, including campus tours, presentations, and lunch. There are guides for informal visits and visitors may sit in on classes. To schedule a visit, contact the Office of Student Recruitment at (718) 982–2259.

Financial Aid: Average earnings from campus work for the school year are $1300. CSI is a member of CSS. The college's own financial statement is required. The application deadline for fall entry is May 31.

International Students: There are currently 496 international students enrolled. They must take the TOEFL and achieve a minimum score of 450.

Computers: The college provides computer facilities for student use. The mainframes are an IBM 3090/200, an IBM 3081KX, and an IBM 4341. Approximately 300 microcomputers and 25 terminals are located in 14 laboratories, which vary in size from 7 workstations to 36 units. Students receive computer accounts to use the mainframe computers. All students may access the system 24 hours a day, up to a total time limit valued at $5000 per semester. The fees are $25.

Graduates: In 1994–95, 869 bachelor's degrees were awarded. The most popular majors among graduates were business (32%), psychology (17%), and education (10%). Within an average freshman class, 8% graduate in 3 years, 23% in 4 years, 35% in 5 years, and 40% in 6 years. 70 companies recruited on campus in 1994–95. Of the 1994 graduating class, 39% were enrolled in graduate school within 6 months of graduation and 75% had found employment.

Admissions Contact: Raymon Hulsey, Director of Admissions.

CITY UNIVERSITY OF NEW YORK/HERBERT H. LEHMAN COLLEGE
D-5

Bronx, NY 10468

Full-time: 1540 men, 3350 women	(718) 960–8131; FAX: (718) 960–8712
Part-time: 1140 men, 2640 women	Faculty: n/av
Graduate: 470 men, 1220 women	Ph.D.s: 83%
Year: semesters, summer session	Student/Faculty: 13 to 1
Application Deadline: see profile	Tuition: $3000 ($5500)
Freshman Class: n/av	Room & Board: n/app
SAT I or ACT: recommended	**LESS COMPETITIVE**

Lehman College, established in 1968 as an independent unit of the City University of New York, is a coeducational commuter institution offering programs in the arts and humanities, natural and social sciences, nursing, and preprofessional studies. There are 5 undergraduate and 4 graduate schools. Figures given in the above capsule are approximate. In addition to regional accreditation, Lehman has baccalaureate program accreditation with ADA, CSWE, NCATE, and NLN. The library contains 500,000 volumes and 450,000 microform items, and subscribes to 2000 periodicals. Computerized library sources and services include the card catalog. Special learning facilities include a learning resource center, art gallery, radio station, and center for performing arts. The 37-acre campus is in an urban area 8 miles north of midtown Manhattan. There are 15 buildings on campus.

Student Life: 95% of undergraduates are from New York. Students come from 4 states and 70 foreign countries. 74% are from public schools; 26% from private. 38% are Hispanic; 30% white; 30% Afri-

can American. 54% are Catholic; 14% claim no religious affiliation. The average age of freshmen is 18; all undergraduates, 25.

Housing: There are no residence halls. All students commute.

Activities: There is 1 national sorority. There are no fraternities. There are 54 groups on campus, including art, band, chess, choir, chorus, computers, dance, drama, ethnic, film, honors, international, literary magazine, musical theater, newspaper, professional, radio and TV, religious, social, social service, student government, and yearbook.

Sports: There are 7 intercollegiate sports for men and 6 for women, and 4 intramural sports for men and 4 for women. Athletic and recreation facilities include 3 gymnasiums, an exercise room, a swimming pool, outdoor tennis courts, soccer and baseball fields, and a dance studio.

Disabled Students: All of the campus is accessible to disabled students. The following facilities are available: wheelchair ramps, elevators, special parking, specially equipped rest rooms, and special class scheduling.

Services: In addition to many counseling and information services, tutoring is available in every subject. There is a reader service for the blind, and remedial math, reading, and writing. A writing center offers individual and small group tutorials and workshops.

Programs of Study: Lehman confers B.A., B.S., and B.F.A. degrees. Master's degrees are also awarded. Bachelor's degrees are awarded in BIOLOGICAL SCIENCE (biology/biological science), BUSINESS (accounting, business administration and management, and management science), COMMUNICATIONS AND THE ARTS (communications, comparative literature, dance, English, fine arts, French, German, Greek, Hebrew, Italian, languages, Latin, linguistics, music, Russian, Spanish, and speech/debate/rhetoric), COMPUTER AND PHYSICAL SCIENCE (chemistry, computer science, geology, mathematics, and physics), EDUCATION (art, business, early childhood, elementary, foreign languages, health, home economics, music, science, and secondary), HEALTH PROFESSIONS (health care administration, nursing, predentistry, premedicine, public health, and speech pathology/audiology), SOCIAL SCIENCE (African American studies, American studies, anthropology, classical/ancient civilization, criminal justice, crosscultural studies, dietetics, economics, family/consumer studies, geography, Hispanic American studies, history, international relations, Latin American studies, philosophy, political science/government, prelaw, psychology, social work, and sociology). Economics and accounting have the largest enrollments.

Required: To graduate, students must successfully complete 128 credits, including 64 in the major, with a minimum GPA of 2.0. Requirements include 17 credits of core courses, 8 of English composition, 3 to 10 of a foreign language, 3 of oral communication, and 2 of physical fitness, as well as 22 credits distributed among courses in comparative culture, historical studies, social science, natural science, literature, art, and knowledge, self, and values. Students must demonstrate proficiency in basic reading, writing, and mathematics skills before entering the upper division.

Special: Lehman offers internships, study abroad, work-study programs, dual and student-designed majors, nondegree study, pass/fail options, and credit for life experience. A 3–2 social work degree is offered in conjunction with the senior college of CUNY, Bard, and Sarah Lawrence. Transfer programs in preengineering, prepharmacy, and preenvironmental science and forestry allow students to complete their degrees at specialized colleges of other New York universities. There is a freshman honors program on campus, as well as 21 national honor societies, including Phi Beta Kappa.

Faculty/Classroom: 58% of faculty are male; 42%, female. No introductory courses are taught by graduate students. The average class size in an introductory lecture is 25; in a laboratory, 12; and in a regular course offering, 18.

Admissions: 54% of the applicants in a recent year were accepted.

Requirements: A minimum grade average of 80 is required. This requirement may also be satisfied by an SAT I composite score of 900. The SAT I or ACT is recommended; the SAT I is preferred. Graduation from an accredited secondary school is required; a GED will be accepted. AP and CLEP credits are accepted.

Procedure: Freshmen are admitted to all sessions. There are early admissions and deferred admissions plans. Check with the school for current application deadlines and fee. Notification is sent on a rolling basis.

Transfer: Transfer students must submit all educational records and show a minimum GPA of 2.0 in previous college work. Applicants with fewer than 12 college credits must also have a high school average of 80 in academic subjects. 38 credits of 128 must be completed at Lehman.

Visiting: There are regularly scheduled orientations for prospective students. There are guides for informal visits and visitors may sit in on classes. To schedule a visit, contact the Office of Enrollment Management at (718) 960–8713.

Financial Aid: The college's own financial statement is required. Check with the school for current deadlines.

International Students: In a recent year, there were 72 international students enrolled. They must score 500 on the TOEFL or take the college's own test.

Computers: The college provides computer facilities for student use. The mainframe is a DEC VAX 11/750. There are also Apple Macintosh and IBM microcomputers located in the Academic Computer Center and specific classrooms. A UNIX-based network includes an IBM PC/RT file server and 8 IBM 6152 RISC workstations. All students may access the system. There are no time limits and no fees.

Admissions Contact: Alberto G. Forbes, Director of Admission.

CITY UNIVERSITY OF NEW YORK/HUNTER COLLEGE
D-5

New York, NY 10021	(212) 772-4490; (800) 772-4000
Full-time: 2154 men, 5962 women	**Faculty:** 674
Part-time: 1697 men, 4168 women	**Ph.D.s:** 85%
Graduate: 972 men, 3298 women	**Student/Faculty:** 18 to 1
Year: semesters, summer session	**Tuition:** $3313 ($6913)
Application Deadline: January 15	**Room & Board:** $1800
Freshman Class: 2816 accepted, 1186 enrolled	
SAT I: recommended	**VERY COMPETITIVE**

Hunter College, a comprehensive, nonprofit, coeducational institution established in 1870, is part of the City University of New York, and is both city- and state-supported. Primarily a commuter college, it emphasizes liberal arts in its undergraduate and graduate programs. There are 6 undergraduate and 7 graduate schools. In addition to regional accreditation, Hunter has baccalaureate program accreditation with ADA, APTA, CSWE, NCATE, and NLN. The library contains 725,000 volumes and 1,023,500 microform items, and subscribes to 2160 periodicals. Computerized library sources and services include the card catalog and database searching. Special learning facilities include a learning resource center, art gallery, radio station, geography/geology laboratory, on-campus elementary and secondary schools, and theater. The 3-acre campus is in an urban area in New York City. Including the residence hall, there are 6 buildings on campus.

Student Life: 93% of undergraduates are from New York. Students come from 9 foreign countries and Canada. 41% are white; 23% Hispanic; 21% African American; 15% Asian American. The average age of freshmen is 19; all undergraduates, 28. 23% do not continue beyond their first year; 34% remain to graduate.

Housing: 500 students can be accommodated in college housing. College-sponsored living facilities include a coed dormitory. On-campus housing is available on a first-come, first-served basis and is available on a lottery system for upperclassmen. 99% of students commute.

Activities: 2% of men belong to 1 local and 1 national fraternities; 1% of women belong to 2 sororities. There are 130 groups on campus, including art, band, cheerleading, choir, chorale, chorus, drama, ethnic, film, gay, honors, international, jazz band, literary magazine, musical theater, newspaper, orchestra, political, professional, radio and TV, religious, social, social service, student government, symphony, and yearbook. Popular campus events include Major Day Fair.

Sports: Athletic and recreation facilities include fencing, dance, and weight rooms, racquetball courts, a pool, outdoor tennis courts, and a gymnasium.

Disabled Students: All of the campus is accessible to disabled students. The following facilities are available: wheelchair ramps, elevators, special parking, specially equipped rest rooms, special class scheduling, lowered drinking fountains, and lowered telephones. A special advisement office and a student organization are also available.

Services: In addition to many counseling and information services, tutoring is available in every subject. There is a reader service for the blind, and remedial math, reading, and writing. Review of graduate-level papers through the writing center and advanced tutoring in the mathematics center are available.

Campus Safety and Security: Campus safety and security measures include self-defense education, shuttle buses, pamphlets/posters/films, and emergency telephones. In addition, there is 24-hour foot patrol.

Programs of Study: Hunter confers B.A., B.S., B.F.A., B.Mus., and B.S.Ed. degrees. Master's degrees are also awarded. Bachelor's degrees are awarded in BIOLOGICAL SCIENCE (biology/biological science and nutrition), BUSINESS (accounting), COMMUNICATIONS AND THE ARTS (Chinese, classics, communications, comparative literature, creative writing, dance, dramatic arts, English, English literature, film arts, fine arts, French, German, Greek, Hebrew, Italian, languages, Latin, media arts, music, Russian, and Spanish), COMPUTER AND PHYSICAL SCIENCE (chemistry, computer science, mathematics, physics, and statistics), EDUCATION (art, early childhood, elementary, foreign languages, health, middle school, music, science, and secondary), ENGINEERING AND ENVIRONMENTAL

DESIGN (energy management technology, environmental science, and preengineering), HEALTH PROFESSIONS (medical laboratory technology, nursing, physical therapy, predentistry, premedicine, and public health), SOCIAL SCIENCE (African American studies, anthropology, archeology, economics, geography, Hispanic American studies, history, international relations, Judaic studies, Latin American studies, philosophy, political science/government, prelaw, psychology, religion, social science, sociology, urban studies, and women's studies). Physical therapy is the strongest academically. Psychology has the largest enrollment.

Required: To graduate, students must complete 125 (up to 131 for the B.S. degree). The total number of hours in a major varies from 24 credits for a liberal arts major to 63 credits for a professional concentration; a minimum GPA of 2.0 is needed overall and in the major. Distribution requirements include 12 credits of social sciences, up to 12 of a foreign language, 10 or more of mathematics and science, 9 of humanities and the arts, 6 of literature, and 3 of English composition.

Special: Special academic programs include internships, student-designed majors, work-study, study abroad, and dual majors. There is cross-registration with the Brooklyn School of Law, the Mannes College of Music, Marymount Manhattan College, and the YIVO Institute. Accelerated degree programs are offered in anthropology, biopharmacology, economics, English, history, mathematics, physics, sociology, and social research. A 2–3 engineering degree with City College is also offered. Exchange programs in Paris or Puerto Rico are possible. There is a freshman honors program on campus, as well as 2 national honor societies, including Phi Beta Kappa. 19 departments have honors programs.

Requirements: The SAT I is recommended. Although the City University of New York accepts all New York State residents having a high school diploma from an accredited secondary school and meeting the university's health standards, applicants must have completed 15 academic credits in that secondary school, as well as have a minimum grade average of 80, be in the top third of their class, or score a minimum composite of 1020 on the recentered SAT I to be eligible for admission to the senior colleges. Those with lower averages or class ranks are eligible for admission to the university's community colleges and technical college. The GED is also accepted. AP and CLEP credits are accepted.

Procedure: Freshmen are admitted fall and spring. There are early admissions and deferred admissions plans. Applications should be filed by January 15 for fall entry and October 15 for spring entry, along with an application fee of $40.

Transfer: 1346 transfer students enrolled in 1995–96. Students must have at least a 2.0 GPA. All students must complete 30 of the 125 to 131 credits required for a bachelor's degree at the college, including half of those needed for both the major and the minor.

Visiting: Visitors may sit in on classes. To schedule a visit, contact the Office of Admissions.

Financial Aid: 25% of undergraduate students work part-time. The college's own financial statement is required. The application deadline for fall entry is May 1.

International Students: There are currently 769 international students enrolled. They must take the TOEFL or the college's own test and achieve a minimum score on the TOEFL of 500.

Computers: The college provides computer facilities for student use. The mainframes are an IBM 3090 and a Sun. There are 400 microcomputers networked in 10 computer laboratories. All students may access the system 24 hours a day, with a time limit of 1 hour when students are waiting. The fees are $25.

Graduates: In 1994–95, 1613 bachelor's degrees were awarded. The most popular majors among graduates were psychology (18%), sociology (10%), and English (9%).

Admissions Contact: Office of Admissions.

CITY UNIVERSITY OF NEW YORK/JOHN JAY COLLEGE OF CRIMINAL JUSTICE
D-5

New York, NY 10019	(212) 237-8873; FAX: (212) 237-8777
Full-time: 3044 men, 3819 women	**Faculty:** 238
Part-time: 1316 men, 1090 women	**Ph.D.s:** 85%
Graduate: 368 men, 393 women	**Student/Faculty:** 29 to 1
Year: semesters, summer session	**Tuition:** $3251 ($6851)
	Room & Board: n/app
Freshman Class: 3108 accepted, 1624 enrolled	
SAT I: recommended	**LESS COMPETITIVE**

John Jay College of Criminal Justice, established in 1964, is a liberal arts college and part of the City University of New York, with special emphasis in the fields of criminology, forensic science, correction administration, and other areas of the criminal justice system. There are 5 graduate schools. The library contains 200,000 volumes, 30,000 microform items, and 3000 audiovisual forms, and subscribes to 1300 periodicals. Computerized library sources and services include the card catalog, interlibrary loans, and database searching. Special learning facilities include an art gallery, radio station, TV station, fire science laboratory, security technology laboratory, and explosion-proof forensic science/toxicology laboratory. The 1-acre campus is in an urban area in midtown Manhattan. There are 2 buildings on campus.

Student Life: 97% of undergraduates are from New York. 80% are from public schools; 20% from private. 35% are white; 32% Hispanic; 29% African American. The average age of freshmen is 17; all undergraduates, 27. 20% do not continue beyond their first year; 40% remain to graduate.

Housing: There are no residence halls. 100% of students commute. All students may keep cars on campus.

Activities: There are no fraternities or sororities. There are many groups and organizations on campus, including art, cheerleading, chess, choir, chorale, chorus, computers, dance, drama, ethnic, film, gay, honors, international, literary magazine, musical theater, newspaper, photography, political, professional, radio and TV, religious, social, social service, student government, and yearbook.

Sports: There are 5 intercollegiate sports for men and 5 for women, and 15 intramural sports for men and 15 for women. Athletic and recreation facilities include 2 gymnasiums, 2 racquetball courts, a fitness center, a swimming pool, a strength training center, and a rooftop outdoor tennis court and jogging track.

Disabled Students: 99% of the campus is accessible to disabled students. The following facilities are available: wheelchair ramps, elevators, special parking, specially equipped rest rooms, special class scheduling, lowered drinking fountains, and lowered telephones.

Services: In addition to many counseling and information services, tutoring is available in most subjects, including English, mathematics and reading. There is also a reader service for the blind, and remedial math, reading, and writing.

Campus Safety and Security: Campus safety and security measures include 24-hour foot and vehicle patrol, self-defense education, informal discussions, and pamphlets/posters/films. In addition, there are emergency telephones and lighted pathways/sidewalks.

Programs of Study: John Jay confers B.A. and B.S. degrees. Associate, master's, and doctoral degrees are also awarded. Bachelor's degrees are awarded in BIOLOGICAL SCIENCE (toxicology), COMPUTER AND PHYSICAL SCIENCE (information sciences and systems), SOCIAL SCIENCE (corrections, criminal justice, criminology, fire science, forensic studies, law enforcement and corrections, political science/government, public administration, and safety management). Forensic science is the strongest academically. Criminal justice, police science, and legal studies have the largest enrollments.

Required: Students are required to complete 128 credit hours, with 36 to 42 of these hours in the student's major, and must maintain a minimum GPA of 2.0. One credit in physical education is required of all students.

Special: The school offers cross-registration with other schools in the City University of New York. Internships are available with the Manhattan District Attorney, the Queens Supreme Court, the New York City Police Department, the United States Marshal's Service, and the New York City Corrections Department. Opportunities are provided for work-study programs, interdisciplinary majors, including forensic psychology, pass/fail options, nondegree study, credit for life experience, and study abroad in England, Barbados, and Israel. There is a freshman honors program on campus, as well as 1 national honor society.

Faculty/Classroom: 65% of faculty are male; 35%, female. All teach undergraduates; 80% also do research. Graduate students teach 5% of introductory courses. The average class size in an introductory lecture is 25; in a laboratory, 15; and in a regular course offering, 20.

Requirements: The SAT I is recommended. John Jay requires applicants to be in the upper 50% of their class. A minimum grade average of 75% is required. Applicants must have graduated from an accredited secondary school or hold a GED certificate. AP and CLEP credits are accepted.

Procedure: Freshmen are admitted fall and spring. There is an early admissions plan. Application fee is $40 for freshmen, $50 for transfers. Notification is sent on a rolling basis.

Transfer: Transfer applicants must have completed 24 credits with a cumulative GPA of 2.0. If fewer than 24 credits are presented, a high school transcript should be presented. Half of the credits required for the major must be completed at John Jay. 32 credits of 128 must be completed at John Jay.

Visiting: There are regularly scheduled orientations for prospective students, consisting of a freshman/transfer workshop. There are guides for informal visits and visitors may sit in on classes. To schedule a visit, contact Christopher Williams at (212) 237-8868.

Financial Aid: The average freshman award was $1500. 5% of undergraduate students work part-time. Average earnings from campus work for the school year are $1000. The college's own financial statement is required.

International Students: There are currently 90 international students enrolled. They must take the TOEFL and achieve a minimum score of 500.

Computers: The college provides computer facilities for student use. The mainframe is an IBM 3090/400. All students may access the system. There are no time limits. The fee is $25 per year.

Graduates: In 1994–95, 693 bachelor's degrees were awarded. The most popular majors among graduates were criminal justice (39%), legal studies (14%), and forensic psychology (12%). 75 companies recruited on campus in 1994–95.

Admissions Contact: Dean Frank W. Marousek.

CITY UNIVERSITY OF NEW YORK/MEDGAR EVERS COLLEGE D-5

Brooklyn, NY 11225–2201   (718) 270-6076, ext. 3022

Full-time: 660 men, 2399 women	Faculty: 113
Part-time: 454 men, 1905 women	Ph.D.s: 72%
Graduate: none	Student/Faculty: 49 to 1
Year: semesters, summer session	Tuition: $1636 ($3436)
Application Deadline: open	Room & Board: n/app
Freshman Class: n/av	
SAT I or ACT: not required	NONCOMPETITIVE

Medgar Evers College, established in 1969 as part of the City University of New York, is an undergraduate commuter institution offering programs in business, education, environmental science, biology, mathematics, nursing, and social sciences. There are 6 undergraduate schools. The library contains 74,000 volumes, 40,000 microform items, and 13,000 audiovisual forms, and subscribes to 700 periodicals. Computerized library sources and services include the card catalog and interlibrary loans. Special learning facilities include a learning resource center and radio station. The campus is in an urban area in the Crown Heights section of Brooklyn.

Student Life: 98% of undergraduates are from New York. The average age of freshmen is 22; all undergraduates, 27. 25% do not continue beyond their first year.

Housing: There are no residence halls.

Activities: There are no fraternities or sororities. There are 5 groups on campus, including dance, ethnic, political, religious, and student government. Popular campus events include Kwaanza and Black Solidarity Day.

Sports: There are 4 intercollegiate sports for men and 3 for women, and 5 intramural sports for men and 3 for women. Athletic and recreation facilities include a swimming pool, a gymnasium, and an exercise room.

Disabled Students: Wheelchair ramps and elevators are available.

Services: There is remedial math, reading, and writing.

Programs of Study: MEC confers the B.A. and B.S. degrees. Associate degrees are also awarded. Bachelor's degrees are awarded in BIOLOGICAL SCIENCE (biology/biological science), BUSINESS (accounting and business administration and management), EDUCATION (elementary and special), ENGINEERING AND ENVIRONMENTAL DESIGN (environmental science), HEALTH PROFESSIONS (nursing), SOCIAL SCIENCE (liberal arts/general studies, psychology, and public administration).

Required: To graduate, students must complete 128 credits with a minimum GPA of 2.0. The core curriculum requires a total of 42 credits in English, philosophy, speech, mathematics, liberal arts, career planning, and physical education. Students must demonstrate proficiency in basic reading, writing, and mathematics skills prior to entering their junior year.

Special: MEC offers exchange programs with other CUNY institutions, evening and weekend classes, credit for military and prior learning experience, pass/fail options, and nondegree study.

Requirements: MEC accepts all applicants who either are graduates of an accredited secondary school or have earned a GED with a score of 225 or higher. Students must meet the university's health standards. CLEP credit is accepted.

Procedure: Application deadlines are open. Application fee is $40.

Transfer: Applicants must have a 2.0 GPA. Those students with fewer than 24 college credits must also submit a high school transcript. 32 credits of 128 must be completed at MEC.

Financial Aid: The CUNY Student Aid Form (CSAF) financial statement is required. The application deadline for fall entry is August 15.

International Students: Students must score 475 on the TOEFL.

Computers: The college provides computer facilities for student use. The mainframe is an IBM 3033. There are also IBM PCs and Apple microcomputers available in the data processing center. All students may access the system.

Admissions Contact: Edward Collier, Admissions Counselor.

CITY UNIVERSITY OF NEW YORK/NEW YORK D-5
CITY TECHNICAL COLLEGE
Brooklyn, NY 11201-2983

	(718) 260-5500
	FAX: (718) 260-5504/5198
Full-time: 3429 men, 3376 women	Faculty: 281
Part-time: 1819 men, 1532 women	Ph.D.s: n/av
Graduate: none	Student/Faculty: 24 to 1
Year: semesters, summer session	Tuition: $3260 ($6860)
Application Deadline: open	Room & Board: n/app
Freshman Class: n/av	
SAT I or ACT: recommended	**NONCOMPETITIVE**

New York City Technical College, founded in 1946 and made part of the City University of New York system in 1964, is a commuter college offering day and evening programs in technology. The library contains 150,000 volumes and subscribes to 700 periodicals. Special learning facilities include a learning resource center and art gallery. The campus is in an urban area. There are 9 buildings on campus.

Housing: There are no residence halls. Alcohol is not permitted on campus.

Activities: There are no fraternities or sororities. There are 70 groups on campus, including drama, ethnic, newspaper, and professional. Popular campus events include concerts, film series, and the Presidential Lecture series.

Sports: There is no sports program at City Tech.

Services: In addition to career and personal counseling, tutoring is available in basic skills and study skills.

Programs of Study: City Tech confers the B.T. degree. Associate degrees are also awarded. Bachelor's degrees are awarded in BUSINESS (hotel/motel and restaurant management), ENGINEERING AND ENVIRONMENTAL DESIGN (graphic and printing production).

Required: Students must receive CUNY certification in reading, writing, and mathematics and complete associate degree requirements. General education requirements include selections from African-American, Puerto Rican, and Latin American studies, sciences, humanities, social sciences, and education. A total of 128 credits is required for the B.T. degree.

Special: B.A. and B.S. degrees are offered through CUNY's universitywide bachelor's exchange credits program. An alternative format program for adults offers credit for life/work experience. Nondegree study and work-study are possible.

Requirements: The SAT I or ACT is recommended. Applicants should be graduates of an accredited secondary school or have the GED equivalent and meet the university's health standards. Students must first apply to the associate degree program and later to the specific bachelor degree program. AP and CLEP credits are accepted.

Procedure: Application deadlines are open. Application fee is $40 ($50 for transfer applicants). The college accepts all applicants. Notification is sent on a rolling basis.

Transfer: Candidates must have an associate degree in hotel and restaurant management or graphic arts, lithographic offset technology, or the equivalent. They must meet CUNY requirements in reading, writing, and mathematics. 34 credits of 128 must be completed at City Tech.

Financial Aid: The CUNY Students Aid Form (CSAF) is required.

Admissions Contact: Arlene Matsumoto Floyd, Director of Admissions.

CITY UNIVERSITY OF NEW YORK/QUEENS D-5
COLLEGE
Flushing, NY 11367-1597

	(718) 997-5600
Full-time: 14,100 men and women	Faculty: 665
Part-time: none	Ph.D.s: 87%
Graduate: 3300 men and women	Student/Faculty: n/av
Year: semesters, summer session	Tuition: $2700 ($5300)
Application Deadline: see profile	Room & Board: n/app
Freshman Class: n/av	
SAT I or ACT: see profile	**COMPETITIVE**

Queens College, founded in 1937, is a public, coeducational, commuter institution within the City University of New York system. Figures given in the above capsule are approximate. The 2 libraries contain 630,000 volumes, 631,000 microform items, and 25,000 audiovisual forms, and subscribe to 4100 periodicals. Computerized library sources and services include the card catalog, interlibrary loans, and database searching. Special learning facilities include a learning resource center, art gallery, center for the performing arts, and center for environmental teaching and research located on Long Island. The 76-acre campus is in an urban area 10 miles from Manhattan. There are 20 buildings on campus.

Student Life: 90% of undergraduates are from New York. Students come from Canada. 65% are from public schools; 35% from private. 60% are white; 14% Asian American; 10% Hispanic. 44% are Catholic; 23% Jewish; 11% claim no religious affiliation; 11% Protestant. The average age of freshmen is 18; all undergraduates, 22. 30% do not continue beyond their first year; 40% remain to graduate.

Housing: There are no residence halls. All students commute. All students may keep cars on campus.

Activities: 1% of men belong to 1 national fraternity. There are 20 groups on campus, including band, choir, chorus, ethnic, honors, jazz band, literary magazine, musical theater, newspaper, orchestra, radio and TV, religious, social service, student government, and yearbook.

Sports: There are 10 intercollegiate sports for men and 7 for women, and 7 intramural sports for men and 4 for women. Athletic and recreation facilities include a gymnasium complex, a swimming pool, dance studios, weight rooms, outdoor quarter-mile track, soccer, lacrosse and baseball fields, and 18 tennis courts.

Disabled Students: 80% of the campus is accessible to disabled students. The following facilities are available: wheelchair ramps, elevators, special parking, specially equipped rest rooms, and special class scheduling.

Services: In addition to many counseling and information services, tutoring is available in most subjects. There is a reader service for the blind, and remedial math, reading, and writing.

Campus Safety and Security: Campus safety and security measures include pamphlets/posters/films, emergency telephones, and lighted pathways/sidewalks.

Programs of Study: Queens confers B.A., B.S., B.F.A., and B.Mus. degrees. Master's degrees are also awarded. Bachelor's degrees are awarded in BIOLOGICAL SCIENCE (biochemistry and biology/biological science), BUSINESS (accounting and labor studies), COMMUNICATIONS AND THE ARTS (communications, dance, dramatic arts, English, English as a second/foreign language, film arts, fine arts, French, German, Greek, Hebrew, Italian, Latin, music, Portuguese, Russian, Spanish, and Yiddish), COMPUTER AND PHYSICAL SCIENCE (chemistry, computer science, geology, mathematics, and physics), EDUCATION (art, early childhood, elementary, foreign languages, health, home economics, mathematics, music, physical, science, secondary, and social studies), HEALTH PROFESSIONS (predentistry, premedicine, and speech pathology/audiology), SOCIAL SCIENCE (anthropology, dietetics, economics, history, philosophy, political science/government, prelaw, psychology, sociology, and urban studies). Anthropology, biology, and chemistry are the strongest academically. Accounting, elementary education, and computer science have the largest enrollments.

Required: To graduate, students must complete 128 credits with a minimum GPA of 2.0. They must fulfill requirements in the major and 35 to 40 credits of a liberal arts core curriculum.

Special: Queens offers cooperative programs in all majors, study abroad, independent study, interdisciplinary and dual majors, internships in business and liberal arts fields, a 3-2 engineering degree with Columbia University or CCNY/CUNY, pass/fail options, work-study, and nondegree study. The SEEK program provides financial and educational resources for underprepared freshmen. There is a freshman honors program on campus.

Faculty/Classroom: 61% of faculty are male; 39%, female. The average class size in an introductory lecture is 100 and in a regular course offering, 27.

Requirements: A minimum high school average of 80 is required. If the high school average is less than 80, the SAT I or ACT is required, with a composite score of 900 or 20 respectively. Either of the tests and an interview are required for scholarship and honors program candidates. Music students must audition. AP and CLEP credits are accepted.

Procedure: Freshmen are admitted fall and spring. Entrance exams should be taken in the spring of the junior year or the fall of the senior year. There is an early admissions plan. Check with the school for current application deadlines and fee.

Transfer: Applicants should have a minimum GPA of 2.5. 45 credits of 128 must be completed at Queens.

Visiting: There are regularly scheduled orientations for prospective students, including information sessions and a campus tour. To schedule a visit, contact the Admissions Office.

Financial Aid: 35% of undergraduate students work part-time. The FAFSA is required. The application deadline for fall entry is May 1.

International Students: They must take the TOEFL or the college's own test and achieve a minimum score on the TOEFL of 500.

Computers: The college provides computer facilities for student use. The mainframe is a Hitachi Data Systems Model 8023. A computer center has DEC VAX and IBM systems. Extensive microcomputer facilities are also provided throughout the campus, and there are a variety of support services for PC users. Those students enrolled in computer science courses may access the system during day and evening hours. There are no fees.

Admissions Contact: Diane Warmsley, Admissions Office.

CITY UNIVERSITY OF NEW YORK/YORK COLLEGE   D-5

Jamaica, NY 11451	(718) 262-2165; FAX: (718) 262-2601
Full-time: 1367 men, 2310 women	Faculty: 138
Part-time: 928 men, 1885 women	Ph.D.s: 67%
Graduate: none	Student/Faculty: 27 to 1
Year: semesters, summer session	Tuition: $3282 ($6882)
Application Deadline: March 1	Room & Board: n/app
Freshman Class: 1200 accepted, 542 enrolled	
SAT I or ACT: recommended	NONCOMPETITIVE

York College, established in 1966, is a public liberal arts commuter college and part of the City University of New York. In addition to regional accreditation, York has baccalaureate program accreditation with CAHEA, CSWE, and NLN. The library contains 180,000 volumes, 135,600 microform items, and 4613 audiovisual forms, and subscribes to 1425 periodicals. Computerized library sources and services include the card catalog, interlibrary loans, and database searching. Special learning facilities include a learning resource center and art gallery. The 50-acre campus is in an urban area in New York City. There are 5 buildings on campus.

Student Life: 89% of undergraduates are from New York. Students come from 20 foreign countries and Canada. 75% are from public schools; 25% from private. 42% are African American; 20% Hispanic; 15% Asian American. The average age of freshmen is 19; all undergraduates, 32.

Housing: There are no residence halls. All students commute. Alcohol is not permitted. All students may keep cars on campus.

Activities: There are 64 groups on campus, including art, band, cheerleading, choir, chorus, computers, dance, drama, ethnic, honors, international, jazz band, literary magazine, musical theater, newspaper, political, professional, radio and TV, religious, social, social service, student government, and yearbook.

Sports: There are 6 intercollegiate sports for men and 5 for women, and 5 intramural sports each for men and women. Athletic and recreation facilities include a 1200-seat gymnasium, a 25-meter, 6-lane swimming pool with diving boards, a fitness center, a health risk appraisal center, and an exercise therapy room.

Disabled Students: All of the campus is accessible to disabled students. The following facilities are available: wheelchair ramps, elevators, special parking, specially equipped rest rooms, special class scheduling, lowered drinking fountains, and lowered telephones.

Services: In addition to many counseling and information services, tutoring is available in every subject. There is a reader service for the blind, and remedial math, reading, and writing.

Campus Safety and Security: Campus safety and security measures include escort service, informal discussions, pamphlets/posters/films, and lighted pathways/sidewalks.

Programs of Study: York confers B.A. and B.S. degrees. Bachelor's degrees are awarded in BIOLOGICAL SCIENCE (biology/biological science), BUSINESS (accounting, business administration and management, and marketing/retailing/merchandising), COMMUNICATIONS AND THE ARTS (English, French, Italian, music, Spanish, and speech/debate/rhetoric), COMPUTER AND PHYSICAL SCIENCE (chemistry, computer science, earth science, geology, information sciences and systems, mathematics, and physics), EDUCATION (art, business, early childhood, elementary, foreign languages, middle school, and secondary), HEALTH PROFESSIONS (medical laboratory technology, nursing, occupational therapy, predentistry, and premedicine), SOCIAL SCIENCE (anthropology, economics, geography, history, philosophy, political science/government, prelaw, psychology, social work, and sociology). Business, accounting, and information systems management have the largest enrollments.

Required: All students are required to complete 128 credits and maintain a minimum GPA of 2.0. The core curriculum of 61 credits includes courses in humanities, behavioral science, cultural diversity, mathematics, and natural science. Students must also take a 2-credit physical education course and complete 2 semesters of English.

Special: Cross-registration with all schools in the City University of New York is permitted. Also provided are work-study programs, credit by examination, nondegree study, pass/fail options, credit for life experience, internships, cooperative programs with other schools, and study abroad in Paris.

Faculty/Classroom: 60% of faculty are male; 40%, female. The average class size in an introductory lecture is 35; in a laboratory, 20; and in a regular course offering, 35.

Requirements: The SAT I or ACT is recommended. York requires applicants to be in the upper 66% of their class. A minimum high school average of 75% is required. Applicants must have graduated from an accredited secondary school or present a GED certificate. Students should achieve a minimum composite score of 1050 on the SAT I. An audition is recommended for music majors. AP and CLEP credits are accepted.

Procedure: Freshmen are admitted fall and spring. There are early decision, early admissions, and deferred admissions plans. Applications should be filed by March 1 for fall entry and November 1 for spring entry, along with an application fee of $40. The college accepts all applicants. Notification is sent on a rolling basis.

Transfer: 593 transfer students enrolled in 1995-96. Transfer students must present a minimum GPA of 2.0. 30 credits of 128 must be completed at York.

Visiting: There are regularly scheduled orientations for prospective students. To schedule a visit, contact Sally Nelson, Director of Admissions.

Financial Aid: The FAFSA and the college's own financial statement are required. The application deadline for fall entry is March 15.

International Students: There are currently 306 international students enrolled. They must take the TOEFL or the college's own test and achieve a minimum score on the TOEFL of 400.

Computers: The college provides computer facilities for student use. The mainframes are an IBM 3090, 3081KX, and 4361-5. There are also 353 IBM, Apple, and Apple Macintosh microcomputers available throughout the school. Information systems management majors only may access the system. There are no time limits and no fees.

Graduates: In a recent year, 564 bachelor's degrees were awarded.

Admissions Contact: Sally Nelson, Director of Admissions.

CLARKSON UNIVERSITY   D-2

Potsdam, NY 13699	(315) 268-6479
	(800) 527-6577; FAX: (315) 268-7647
Full-time: 1679 men, 533 women	Faculty: 147; I, -$
Part-time: 20 men, 17 women	Ph.D.s: 94%
Graduate: 247 men, 87 women	Student/Faculty: 15 to 1
Year: semesters, summer session	Tuition: $17,113
Application Deadline: February 1	Room & Board: $5830
Freshman Class: 2334 applied, 2068 accepted, 645 enrolled	
SAT I Verbal/Math: 535/619	VERY COMPETITIVE +

Clarkson University, founded in 1896, is a private, coeducational institution offering undergraduate programs in engineering, business, science, and the liberal arts. There are 4 undergraduate and 4 graduate schools. In addition to regional accreditation, Clarkson has baccalaureate program accreditation with AACSB and ABET. The library contains 224,306 volumes, 269,289 microform items, and 676 audiovisual forms, and subscribes to 2716 periodicals. Computerized library sources and services include the card catalog, interlibrary loans, and database searching. Special learning facilities include a learning resource center, natural history museum, radio station, and TV station. The 640-acre campus is in a rural area 70 miles north of Watertown and 75 miles south of Ottawa, Canada. Including residence halls, there are 39 buildings on campus.

Student Life: 69% of undergraduates are from New York. Students come from 38 states, 25 foreign countries, and Canada. 88% are from public schools; 8% from private. 91% are white. 33% claim no religious affiliation; 33% Catholic; 22% Protestant; 10% Buddhist, Hindu, Muslim, Mormon, or Orthodox. The average age of freshmen is 18; all undergraduates, 20. 17% do not continue beyond their first year; 71% remain to graduate.

Housing: 1993 students can be accommodated in college housing. College-sponsored living facilities include single-sex and coed dormitories, on-campus apartments, married-student housing, fraternity houses, and sorority houses. In addition there are special interest houses. On-campus housing is guaranteed for all 4 years. 78% of students live on campus; of those, 90% remain on campus on weekends. Alcohol is not permitted. All students may keep cars on campus.

Activities: 25% of men belong to 5 local and 11 national fraternities; 30% of women belong to 3 national sororities. There are 36 groups on campus, including cheerleading, chess, chorus, computers, drama, ethnic, honors, international, jazz band, literary magazine, musical theater, newspaper, orchestra, pep band, photography, professional, radio and TV, religious, social, social service, student government, and yearbook. Popular campus events include Ice Carnival.

Sports: There are 9 intercollegiate sports for men and 6 for women, and 11 intramural sports for men and 9 for women. Athletic and recreation facilities include a 3000-seat multipurpose ice arena, a gymnasium, a swimming pool, a weight room, a field house, and racquetball, paddleball, and tennis courts.

Disabled Students: 85% of the campus is accessible to disabled students. The following facilities are available: wheelchair ramps, elevators, special parking, specially equipped rest rooms, special class scheduling, lowered drinking fountains, lowered telephones, and special residence hall rooms.

Services: In addition to many counseling and information services, tutoring is available in most subjects, including all freshman- and sophomore-level courses and some junior-level courses.

Campus Safety and Security: Campus safety and security measures include 24-hour foot and vehicle patrol, escort service, shuttle buses, and informal discussions. In addition, there are pamphlets/posters/films, emergency telephones, and lighted pathways/sidewalks.

Programs of Study: Clarkson confers B.S. and B.P.S. degrees. Master's and doctoral degrees are also awarded. Bachelor's degrees are awarded in BIOLOGICAL SCIENCE (biology/biological science), BUSINESS (accounting, banking and finance, management information systems, management science, and marketing/retailing/merchandising), COMMUNICATIONS AND THE ARTS (technical and business writing), COMPUTER AND PHYSICAL SCIENCE (chemistry, computer science, mathematics, and physics), ENGINEERING AND ENVIRONMENTAL DESIGN (aeronautical engineering, chemical engineering, civil engineering, computer engineering, electrical/electronics engineering, engineering management, industrial administration/management, and mechanical engineering), HEALTH PROFESSIONS (industrial hygiene), SOCIAL SCIENCE (economics, history, humanities, political science/government, psychology, social science, and sociology). Engineering, business, and sciences are the strongest academically. Engineering has the largest enrollment.

Required: Students must complete at least 120 credit hours, with a minimum GPA of 2.0, to graduate. Students must meet a foundation curriculum requirement, take the Personal Wellness unit, and meet the requirement for courses in physical education, military science, or aerospace studies.

Special: Clarkson offers cross-registration with the Associate Colleges of the St. Lawrence Valley: St. Lawrence University and Potsdam and Canton colleges. Co-op programs with industry, work-study programs, dual majors in business and liberal arts, interdisciplinary majors in engineering and management and professional studies, internships for premedical students at local hospitals, and study abroad in England, Sweden, Scotland, Germany, Australia, China, and Canada are possible. There are 3–2 engineering programs with many institutions in the Northeast; students who participate take the first 3 years of the prescribed program at a 4-year liberal arts institution and then transfer with junior standing into one of Clarkson's 4-year engineering curricula. There are 15 national honor societies on campus, including Phi Beta Kappa. 1 department has an honors program.

Faculty/Classroom: 86% of faculty are male; 14%, female. 94% teach undergraduates and 51% do research. The average class size in an introductory lecture is 85; in a laboratory, 26; and in a regular course offering, 35.

Admissions: 89% of the 1995–96 applicants were accepted. The SAT I scores for the 1995–96 freshman class were as follows: Verbal—36% below 500, 35% between 500 and 599, 23% between 600 and 700, and 7% above 700; Math—4% below 500, 29% between 500 and 599, 53% between 600 and 700, and 15% above 700. 61% of the current freshmen were in the top fifth of their class; 85% were in the top two fifths. There were 3 National Merit finalists. 11 freshmen graduated first in their class.

Requirements: The SAT I is required and the ACT is recommended. A minimum GPA of 3.0 is required. SAT II: Subject tests are also recommended. Applicants must have graduated from an accredited secondary school or have the GED. An essay and interview are also recommended. AP and CLEP credits are accepted. Important factors in the admissions decision are advanced placement or honor courses, recommendations by school officials, and extracurricular activities record.

Procedure: Freshmen are admitted fall and spring. There are early decision, early admissions, and deferred admissions plans. Early decision applications should be filed by December 1; regular applications, by February 1 for fall entry and December 1 for spring entry, along with an application fee of $25. Notification is sent in February. 124 early decision candidates were accepted for the 1995–96 class.

Transfer: 142 transfer students enrolled in 1995–96. Transfer students should submit transcripts from all colleges attended and must present a minimum GPA of 2.8. An associate degree will be considered, and an interview is recommended. 30 credits of 120 must be completed at Clarkson.

Visiting: There are regularly scheduled orientations for prospective students, including meetings with administration and faculty. There are guides for informal visits and visitors may sit in on classes and stay overnight at the school. To schedule a visit, contact the Admissions Office.

Financial Aid: In 1995–96, 95% of all freshmen and 90% of continuing students received some form of financial aid. 78% of freshmen and 75% of continuing students received need-based aid. The average freshman award was $14,048. Of that total, scholarships or need-based grants averaged $7400 ($25,000 maximum); loans averaged $3848 ($5125 maximum); federal and state awards averaged $2000; and work contracts averaged $800 ($1000 maximum). 45% of undergraduate students work part-time. Average earnings from campus work for the school year are $900. The average financial indebtedness of the 1994–95 graduate was $20,000. Clarkson is a member of CSS. The FAFSA is required. The application deadline for fall entry is February 15.

International Students: There are currently 70 international students enrolled. The school actively recruits these students. They must take the TOEFL and achieve a minimum score of 500. Students for whom English is a second language must take a placement examination.

Computers: The college provides computer facilities for student use. The mainframes are an IBM 4381 and an RS 6000. About 100 terminals are available in clusters throughout the campus. All students may access the system. There are no time limits and no fees.

Graduates: In 1994–95, 593 bachelor's degrees were awarded. The most popular majors among graduates were civil engineering (21%), mechanical engineering (20%), and engineering and management (11%). Within an average freshman class, 62% graduate in 4 years and 73% in 5 years. 122 companies recruited on campus in 1994–95. Of the 1994 graduating class, 19% were enrolled in graduate school within 6 months of graduation and 75% had found employment.

Admissions Contact: Robert A. Croot, Executive Director of Freshman Admissions. E-mail: crootra@agent.clarkson.educ.

COLGATE UNIVERSITY
C-3

Hamilton, NY 13346   (315) 824-7401; FAX: (315) 824-7544

Full-time: 1394 men, 1481 women	Faculty: 198; IIB, + +$
Part-time: 14 men, 36 women	Ph.D.s: 99%
Graduate: 8 men, 6 women	Student/Faculty: 15 to 1
Year: semesters	Tuition: $20,650
Application Deadline: January 16	Room & Board: $5765
Freshman Class: 6037 applied, 2465 accepted	
SAT I Verbal/Math: 583/645 (mean)	ACT: 28 MOST COMPETITIVE

Colgate University, founded in 1819, is a private, coeducational, liberal arts institution. There is 1 graduate school. The 2 libraries contain 550,000 volumes, 67,200 microform items, and 6900 audiovisual forms, and subscribe to 2200 periodicals. Computerized library sources and services include the card catalog, interlibrary loans, and database searching. Special learning facilities include an art gallery, radio station, TV station, anthropology museum, and observatory. The 550-acre campus is in a small town 45 miles southeast of Syracuse. Including residence halls, there are 70 buildings on campus.

Student Life: 66% of undergraduates are from out of state, mostly the Northeast. Students come from 48 states, 44 foreign countries, and Canada. 61% are from public schools; 27% from private. 88% are white. 84% claim no religious affiliation; 10% Catholic. The average age of freshmen is 18; all undergraduates, 20. 4% do not continue beyond their first year; 89% remain to graduate.

Housing: 1971 students can be accommodated in college housing. College-sponsored living facilities include coed dormitories, on-campus apartments, fraternity houses, and sorority houses. In addition there are language houses and special interest houses. On-campus housing is guaranteed for the freshman and sophomore years only and is available on a lottery system for upperclassmen. 74% of students live on campus; of those, 90% remain on campus on weekends. All students may keep cars on campus.

Activities: 39% of men belong to 2 local and 8 national fraternities; 30% of women belong to 4 national sororities. There are 90 groups on campus, including art, band, cheerleading, chess, choir, chorale, chorus, computers, dance, drama, ethnic, film, gay, honors, international, jazz band, literary magazine, marching band, musical theater, newspaper, orchestra, pep band, photography, political, professional, radio and TV, religious, social, social service, student government, symphony, and yearbook. Popular campus events include Peace Jam, Winter Carnival, and Spring Party Weekend.

Sports: There are 12 intercollegiate sports for men and 11 for women, and 26 intramural sports for men and 26 for women. Athletic and recreation facilities include numerous athletic fields, an athletic center, a 3000-seat gymnasium, tennis courts and a golf course, a field house, a ski center, and a 50-meter pool. Recreational facilities include a woodworking shop, a 9000-square-foot fitness center, running trails, and a trap range.

Disabled Students: 20% of the campus is accessible to disabled students. The following facilities are available: wheelchair ramps, elevators, special parking, specially equipped rest rooms, special class scheduling, and lowered drinking fountains.

Services: In addition to many counseling and information services, tutoring is available in most subjects. There is a reader service for the blind, remedial writing, and a note taker service for students with learning and sensory disabilities.

Campus Safety and Security: Campus safety and security measures include 24-hour foot and vehicle patrol, self-defense education, escort service, and shuttle buses. There are informal discussions, pamphlets/posters/films, emergency telephones, and lighted pathways/sidewalks.

Programs of Study: Colgate confers the B.A. degree. Master's degrees are also awarded. Bachelor's degrees are awarded in BIOLOGICAL SCIENCE (biochemistry, biology/biological science, molecular biology, and neurosciences), COMMUNICATIONS AND THE ARTS (dramatic arts, English, fine arts, French, German, Greek, Latin, music, Russian, and Spanish), COMPUTER AND PHYSICAL SCIENCE (astronomy, chemistry, computer science, geology, geophysics and seismology, mathematics, and physics), EDUCATION (education), SOCIAL SCIENCE (anthropology, Asian/Oriental studies, economics, geography, history, international relations, Native American studies, peace studies, philosophy, political science/government, psychology, religion, Russian and Slavic studies, social science, sociology, and women's studies). Geology, psychology, and chemistry are the strongest academically. English, economics, and political science have the largest enrollments.

Required: To graduate, students must complete courses in a core curriculum, including 4 general education courses and 2 courses each in the natural sciences, social sciences, and humanities. A total of 32 courses is required, with 8 courses in the major. Study in a foreign language, physical education, and a swimming test are also required. Students need a 1.8 GPA overall for graduation, with a 2.0 GPA in the major.

Special: Various internships, work-study, and study abroad in 15 countries are available. Students may choose accelerated degree programs, dual majors, and student-designed majors. Cross-registration is possible with Hamilton College. A 3-2 engineering degree with Columbia and Washington universities and Rensselaer Polytechnic Institute, a 3-4 architecture degree with Washington University, credit by exam, pass/fail options, co-op programs in preengineering and prearchitecture, and a Washington semester are offered. There is a freshman honors program on campus, as well as 8 national honor societies, including Phi Beta Kappa. All departments have honors programs.

Faculty/Classroom: 63% of faculty are male; 37%, female. All teach and do research. No introductory courses are taught by graduate students. The average class size in an introductory lecture is 30; in a laboratory, 15; and in a regular course offering, 21.

Admissions: 41% of the 1995–96 applicants were accepted. The mean SAT I scores for the 1995–96 freshman class were as follows: Verbal—9% below 500, 45% between 500 and 599, 41% between 600 and 700, and 4% above 700; Math—2% below 500, 18% between 500 and 599, 57% between 600 and 700, and 23% above 700. 89% of the current freshmen were in the top fifth of their class; 100% were in the top two fifths. 24 freshmen graduated first in their class.

Requirements: The SAT I or ACT is required. Students may submit SAT I and SAT II: Subject tests in writing and 2 subject tests; SAT II: Subject tests in writing and 4 subject tests (one of which must be mathematics); or the ACT. 2 teacher recommendations and a counselor's report are required. An interview, though not evaluated, is recommended, and 16 or more Carnegie credits, including humanities, social science, mathematics, physical science, and biology, are also recommended. Colgate accepts applications via MacApply and College Link. AP and CLEP credits are accepted. Important factors in the admissions decision are advanced placement or honor courses, recommendations by school officials, and evidence of special talent.

Procedure: Freshmen are admitted fall and spring. Entrance exams should be taken in time for score reports to reach the university by January 16. There are early decision, early admissions, and deferred admissions plans. Early decision applications should be filed by March 1; regular applications, by January 16 for fall entry, along with an application fee of $50. Notification is sent for early decision 3 to 4 weeks after receipt; for regular decision, April 1. 200 early decision candidates were accepted for the 1995–96 class. A waiting list is an active part of the admissions procedure, with about 16% of all applicants on the list.

Transfer: 19 transfer students enrolled in 1995–96. Either the SAT I or the ACT is required, as well as high school transcripts, a dean's report, faculty recommendations and college transcripts. 16 courses of 32 must be completed at Colgate.

Visiting: There are regularly scheduled orientations for prospective students, including interviews and group sessions and tours available throughout the year, except during final examinations and holiday recesses. There are guides for informal visits, and visitors may sit in on classes and stay overnight at the school. To schedule a visit, contact the Office of Admissions.

Financial Aid: In 1995–96, 50% of all freshmen and 62% of continuing students received some form of financial aid. 46% of freshmen and 44% of continuing students received need-based aid. The average freshman award was $15,160. Of that total, scholarships or need-based grants averaged $12,440 ($26,500 maximum); loans averaged $1850 ($2625 maximum); and work contracts averaged $870 ($1300 maximum). 55% of undergraduate students work part-time. Average earnings from campus work for the school year are $1100. The average financial indebtedness of the 1994–95 graduate was

$8918. Colgate is a member of CSS. The college's own financial statement, the FAFSA, and CSS Profile Application are required. The application deadline for fall entry is February 1.

International Students: There are currently 67 international students enrolled. The school actively recruits these students. They must score 600 on the TOEFL and also take SAT I or the ACT.

Computers: The college provides computer facilities for student use. The mainframe is a DEC VAX 11/780. There are 250 terminals on campus offering a wide variety of applications software. In addition, all residence halls are wired for networked computers. All students may access the system. There are no time limits and no fees.

Graduates: In 1994–95, 617 bachelor's degrees were awarded. The most popular majors among graduates were English (12%), economics (9%), and history (8%). Within an average freshman class, 81% graduate in 4 years, 5% in 5 years, and 2% in 6 years. 82 companies recruited on campus in 1994–95. Of the 1994 graduating class, 29% were enrolled in graduate school within 6 months of graduation and 70% had found employment.

Admissions Contact: Mary F. Hill, Dean of Admission. E-mail: admission@center.colgate.edu or http://www.colgate.edu.

COLLEGE OF AERONAUTICS
Flushing, NY 11371

(718) 429-6600
(800) 776-2376; FAX: (718) 429-0256

Full-time: 850 men, 85 women	Faculty: 57; III, av$
Part-time: 80 men, 15 women	Ph.Ds: 15%
Graduate: none	Student/Faculty: 16 to 1
Year: semesters, summer session	Tuition: $7650
Application Deadline: open	Room & Board: n/app
Freshman Class: 400 applied, 375 accepted, 250 enrolled	
SAT I: recommended	**NONCOMPETITIVE**

The College of Aeronautics, founded in 1932, is a private, coeducational aviation school offering undergraduate degrees in aeronautical engineering technology. In addition to regional accreditation, COA has baccalaureate program accreditation with ABET. The library contains 60,000 volumes and 10,000 microform items. Computerized library sources and services include the card catalog and database searching. Special learning facilities include a learning resource center. The 6-acre campus is in an urban area at LaGuardia Airport, 4 miles east of Manhattan. There are 2 buildings on campus.

Student Life: 95% of undergraduates are from New York. Students come from 9 states, 19 foreign countries, and Canada. 96% are from public schools; 4% from private. 40% are white; 25% Hispanic; 25% African American. The average age of freshmen is 21.5; all undergraduates, 23. 27% do not continue beyond their first year; 59% remain to graduate.

Housing: There are no residence halls. College-sponsored living facilities include off-campus apartments. On-campus housing is available on a first-come, first-served basis. Priority is given to out-of-town students. 98% of students commute. Alcohol is not permitted. All students may keep cars on campus.

Activities: There are no fraternities or sororities. There are some groups and organizations on campus, including newspaper, student government, and yearbook. Popular campus events include Open House and Dance Party.

Sports: There are 3 intramural sports for men and 3 for women. Athletic and recreation facilities include nearby areas for softball, flag football, and bowling.

Disabled Students: 95% of the campus is accessible to disabled students. The following facilities are available: wheelchair ramps, elevators, special parking, specially equipped rest rooms, special class scheduling, lowered drinking fountains, and lowered telephones.

Services: In addition to many counseling and information services, tutoring is available in most subjects. There is remedial math, reading, and writing.

Campus Safety and Security: Campus safety and security measures include 24-hour foot and vehicle patrol, informal discussions, and pamphlets/posters/films.

Programs of Study: COA confers the B.Tech. degree. Associate degrees are also awarded. Bachelor's degrees are awarded in ENGINEERING AND ENVIRONMENTAL DESIGN (aeronautical technology). Maintenance technology is the strongest academically and has the largest enrollment.

Required: All students must satisfy English, mathematics, and science requirements and fulfill appropriate licensing requirements while maintaining a GPA of at least 2.0. Students with advanced credit must complete 30 credits in residency. A total of 134 credits is required to graduate.

Faculty/Classroom: 90% of faculty are male; 10%, female. All teach undergraduates. The average class size in an introductory lecture is 25; in a laboratory, 20; and in a regular course offering, 20.

Admissions: 94% of the 1995–96 applicants were accepted. The SAT I scores for a recent freshman class were as follows: Verbal—60% below 500, 30% between 500 and 599, and 8% between

600 and 700; Math—70% below 500, 23% between 500 and 599, and 5% between 600 and 700. 18% of the current freshmen were in the top fifth of their class; 45% were in the top two fifths. 2 freshmen graduated first in their class.

Requirements: The SAT I is recommended, with scores of 400 verbal and 400 mathematics. Applicants are required to have 2 years each of English and science and 3 of mathematics. An interview is also recommended. AP credits are accepted. Important factors in the admissions decision are evidence of special talent, advanced placement or honor courses, and personality/intangible qualities.

Procedure: Freshmen are admitted to all sessions. There are early decision and early admissions plans. Application deadlines are open. Application fee is $25. The college accepts all applicants. Notification is sent on a rolling basis. 60 early decision candidates were accepted for the 1995–96 class.

Transfer: 45 transfer students enrolled in 1995–96. A minimum 2.0 GPA is required. 30 credits of 134 must be completed at COA.

Visiting: There are regularly scheduled orientations for prospective students, scheduled prior to registration, which include a tour and academic advisement. There are guides for informal visits and visitors may sit in on classes. To schedule a visit, contact the Admissions Office.

Financial Aid: 85% of undergraduate students work part-time. Average earnings from campus work for the school year are $1500. The FAF and the college's own financial statement are required. The application deadline for fall entry is April 15.

International Students: In a recent year, 50 international students enrolled. The school actively recruits these students. They must take the TOEFL and achieve a minimum score of 500, and have an English Proficiency Certificate.

Computers: The college provides computer facilities for student use. The mainframe is an IBM networked for both PC and Macintosh use. All students may access the system. There are no time limits and no fees.

Graduates: The most popular majors among graduates were aeronautical technology-maintenance (90%) and aeronautical technology-manufacturing (10%). Within an average freshman class, 30% graduate in 3 years, 30% in 4 years, 20% in 5 years, and 20% in 6 years. 25 companies recruited on campus in 1994–95.

Admissions Contact: Donald J. Whitman, Direct of Admissions.

COLLEGE OF INSURANCE D-5
New York, NY 10007 (212) 815-9232
(800) 356-5146; FAX: (212) 964-3381

Full-time: 59 men, 38 women	Faculty: 22
Part-time: 211 men, 303 women	Ph.D.s: 25%
Graduate: 104 men, 61 women	Student/Faculty: 4 to 1
Year: semesters, summer session	Tuition: $12,260
Application Deadline: May 1	Room & Board: $8200
Freshman Class: 180 applied, 98 accepted, 70 enrolled	
SAT I or ACT: required	**VERY COMPETITIVE**

The College of Insurance, founded in 1962, is a private college established and supported by insurance and financial service organizations. There is 1 graduate school. The library contains 96,506 volumes, 3894 microform items, and 43 audiovisual forms, and subscribes to 381 periodicals. Computerized library sources and services include database searching. Special learning facilities include a learning resource center. The campus is in an urban area in Manhattan. Including residence halls, there is 1 building on campus.

Student Life: Students come from 15 foreign countries and Canada. 59% are white; 13% African American; 10% foreign nationals; 10% Hispanic. The average age of freshmen is 18; all undergraduates, 21.

Housing: 120 students can be accommodated in college housing. College-sponsored living facilities include coed dormitories. On-campus housing is available on a first-come, first-served basis. 60% of students live on campus; of those, 50% remain on campus on weekends. Alcohol is not permitted.

Activities: There are no sororities. There are 15 groups on campus, including band, chess, drama, international, newspaper, photography, professional, student government, and yearbook. Popular campus events include the Kick-Off Dance, Halloween Celebration, Senior Week, and a ski trip.

Sports: There is 1 intercollegiate sport for men and 1 for women, and 2 intramural sports for men and 2 for women. Athletic and recreation facilities include a weight and exercise room and a game room.

Disabled Students: All of the campus is accessible to disabled students. The following facilities are available: elevators, specially equipped rest rooms, and lowered drinking fountains.

Services: In addition to many counseling and information services, tutoring is available in most subjects. All tutoring is provided by professors or fellow students via a Tutorial Network Program.

Campus Safety and Security: Campus safety and security measures include 24-hour foot and vehicle patrol, emergency telephones, and lighted pathways/sidewalks.

Programs of Study: TCI confers B.S. and B.B.A. degrees. Associate and master's degrees are also awarded. Bachelor's degrees are awarded in BUSINESS (business administration and management and insurance), COMPUTER AND PHYSICAL SCIENCE (actuarial science).

Required: Students must successfully complete a total of 126 credits and maintain a minimum GPA of 2.3. A liberal arts requirement must be met, as well as a business core, which includes accounting, finance, information systems, insurance, law, management, and marketing.

Special: Many students take part in a cooperative education program that allows them to work alternate semesters of full-time study and full-time work in various business companies. B.A.-B.S. degrees in insurance, finance, business, and actuarial science are available. With advance permission, students may cross-register at other accredited 4-year colleges.

Admissions: 54% of the 1995–96 applicants were accepted. The SAT I scores for the 1995–96 freshman class were as follows: Verbal—43% below 500 and 57% between 500 and 599; Math—11% below 500, 23% between 500 and 599, 33% between 600 and 700, and 33% above 700. 60% of the current freshmen were in the top fifth of their class.

Requirements: The SAT I or ACT is required, with SAT I scores of 900 to 1200 (450 to 600 in each section). Alternatively, a score of 25 on the ACT is recommended. In addition, applicants must have graduated in the upper 50% from an accredited secondary school or have the GED. Applicants must have completed 19 academic units, including 4 years of English and at least 3 of college-preparatory mathematics. An essay and interview are also recommended. AP credits are accepted. Important factors in the admissions decision are advanced placement or honor courses, leadership record, and extracurricular activities record.

Procedure: Freshmen are admitted to all sessions. There are early decision and deferred admissions plans. Early decision applications should be filed by December 1; regular applications, by May 1 for fall entry, October 15 for spring entry, and February 15 for summer entry, along with an application fee of $30. Notification of early decision is sent December 15; regular decision, on a rolling basis.

Transfer: 21 transfer students enrolled in 1995–96. Transfer applicants must submit a high school transcript with a GPA of 3.0, combined SAT I scores of 900 to 1200, and a college transcript with a GPA of 2.5. 57 credits of 126 must be completed at TCI.

Visiting: There are regularly scheduled orientations for prospective students, consisting of an interview, a tour of the school, and a chance to sit in on a class. There are guides for informal visits and visitors may sit in on classes and stay overnight at the school. To schedule a visit, contact Theresa Marro, Director of Admissions.

Financial Aid: In 1995–96, 78% of all freshmen and 73% of continuing students received some form of financial aid. 86% of freshmen and 70% of continuing students received need-based aid. The average freshman award was $18,328. Of that total, scholarships or need-based grants averaged $15,482 ($23,116 maximum); loans averaged $1134 ($2625 maximum); and work contracts averaged $1712 ($1900 maximum). Average earnings from campus work for the school year are $2176. The average financial indebtedness of the 1994–95 graduate was $5559. The FAFSA is required, and full-time undergraduate applicants who are in-state residents must also submit the NYS TAP. The application deadline for fall entry is July 5.

International Students: There are currently 50 international students enrolled. They must score 550 on the TOEFL and must also take SAT I or the ACT.

Computers: The college provides computer facilities for student use. The mainframe is a Prime. A microcomputer laboratory is available 24 hours a day. All students may access the system. There are no time limits and no fees.

Graduates: In 1994–95, 31 bachelor's degrees were awarded.

Admissions Contact: Theresa Marro, Director of Admissions.

COLLEGE OF MOUNT SAINT VINCENT D-5
Riverdale, NY 10471 (718) 405-3267
(800) 665-CMSV; FAX: (718) 549-7945

Full-time: 178 men, 662 women	Faculty: 70; IIB, -$
Part-time: 47 men, 398 women	Ph.D.s: 68%
Graduate: 14 men, 155 women	Student/Faculty: 12 to 1
Year: semesters, summer session	Tuition: $12,440
Application Deadline: February 1	Room & Board: $5944
Freshman Class: 920 applied, 669 accepted, 218 enrolled	
SAT I Verbal/Math: 437/461	ACT: 21	**COMPETITIVE**

The College of Mount Saint Vincent, founded as an academy in 1847 and chartered as a college in 1911, is a private, coeducational liberal arts institution in the Catholic tradition. There are 2 graduate schools. In addition to regional accreditation, CMSV has baccalaureate program accreditation with ACBSP and NLN. The library contains 151,308 volumes, 5717 microform items, and 5421 audiovisual forms, and subscribes to 618 periodicals. Computerized library sources and services include the card catalog, interlibrary loans, and database searching. Special learning facilities include a learning resource center, radio station, and TV station. The 70-acre campus is in a suburban area 11 miles north of midtown Manhattan. Including residence halls, there are 11 buildings on campus.

Student Life: 93% of undergraduates are from New York. Students come from 10 states and 10 foreign countries. 39% are from public schools; 61% from private. 55% are white; 17% Hispanic; 12% African American; 10% Asian American. Most are Catholic. The average age of freshmen is 18; all undergraduates, 20. 15% do not continue beyond their first year; 67% remain to graduate.

Housing: 556 students can be accommodated in college housing. College-sponsored living facilities include single-sex and coed dormitories. On-campus housing is guaranteed for all 4 years. 55% of students live on campus; of those, 75% remain on campus on weekends. Upperclassmen may keep cars on campus.

Activities: There are no fraternities or sororities. There are 30 groups on campus, including art, cheerleading, choir, chorus, computers, dance, drama, ethnic, film, honors, international, literary magazine, newspaper, photography, professional, radio and TV, religious, social, social service, student government, and yearbook. Popular campus events include Annual Block Party, Battle of the Dorms, International Festival, Bachelor Auction, Spring Week, Senior Week, Talent Night, Ring Night, Family Day, and Siblings Weekend.

Sports: There are 5 intercollegiate sports for men and 7 for women, and 6 intramural sports for men and 6 for women. Athletic and recreation facilities include a gymnasium, a swimming pool, a weight room, a dance studio, a recreation room, a new fitness center with aerobic and nautilus facilities, and basketball, squash, and tennis courts.

Disabled Students: The following facilities are available: wheelchair ramps, elevators, special parking, specially equipped rest rooms, lowered drinking fountains, and lowered telephones.

Services: In addition to many counseling and information services, tutoring is available in most subjects, including computer science, mathematics, chemistry, biology, languages, psychology, sociology, writing, and economics. There is a reader service for the blind, and remedial math, reading, and writing.

Campus Safety and Security: Campus safety and security measures include 24-hour foot and vehicle patrol, escort service, shuttle buses, and informal discussions. In addition, there are pamphlets/posters/films, emergency telephones, lighted pathways/sidewalks, and a college committee on safety and security on campus.

Programs of Study: CMSV confers B.A. and B.S. degrees. Associate and master's degrees are also awarded. Bachelor's degrees are awarded in BIOLOGICAL SCIENCE (biochemistry and biology/biological science), BUSINESS (business administration and management), COMMUNICATIONS AND THE ARTS (communications, English, French, modern language, and Spanish), COMPUTER AND PHYSICAL SCIENCE (chemistry, computer science, and mathematics), EDUCATION (health and special), HEALTH PROFESSIONS (allied health and nursing), SOCIAL SCIENCE (economics, history, liberal arts/general studies, psychology, and sociology). Nursing, biology, and communications are the strongest academically. Nursing, communications, and business have the largest enrollments.

Required: All students must complete a 56-credit core curriculum with courses in humanities, social sciences, mathematics and computers, and natural sciences. A total of 120 credits for a B.A. or 126 credits for a B.S., with a minimum of 30 credits in the major, and a minimum GPA of 2.0, are required.

Special: Cross-registration with Manhattan College offers cooperative B.A. programs in international studies, philosophy, physical education, physics, religious studies, and urban affairs. Internships, work-study, study abroad in 6 countries, a 3–2 engineering degree with Manhattan College, dual majors and student-designed majors in liberal arts are available. B.A.-B.S. degrees in computer science, health education, mathematics, and psychology, and teacher certification programs in elementary, middle school, and secondary education, are possible. There is a freshman honors program on campus, as well as 15 national honor societies. 5 departments have honors programs.

Faculty/Classroom: 49% of faculty are male; 51%, female. 99% teach undergraduates. No introductory courses are taught by graduate students. The average class size in an introductory lecture is 25; in a laboratory, 15; and in a regular course offering, 18.

Admissions: 73% of the 1995–96 applicants were accepted. The SAT I scores for the 1995–96 freshman class were as follows: Verbal—80% below 500, 18% between 500 and 599, and 2% between 600 and 700; Math—71% below 500, 24% between 500 and 599, 5% between 600 and 700, and 1% above 700. The ACT scores were 28% below 21, 43% between 21 and 23, and 29% between 24 and 26. 34% of the current freshmen were in the top fifth of their class; 64% were in the top two fifths. 4 freshmen graduated first in their class.

Requirements: The SAT I or ACT is required. CMSV requires applicants to be in the upper 50% of their class. A minimum GPA of 2.5 is required. Applicants should have completed 4 high school academic units of English, 3 of science, 2 of mathematics, foreign language, and social sciences, as well as electives. An essay is required, and an interview is recommended. One letter of recommendation is required, while additional letters are encouraged. AP and CLEP credits are accepted. Important factors in the admissions decision are advanced placement or honor courses, recommendations by school officials, and leadership record.

Procedure: Freshmen are admitted fall and spring. Entrance exams should be taken during the junior year and/or fall of senior year. There are early decision and early admissions plans. Early decision applications should be filed by November 15; regular applications, by February 1 for fall entry, along with an application fee of $25. Notification of early decision is sent December 15; regular decision, on a rolling basis. 5 early decision candidates were accepted for the 1995–96 class.

Transfer: 158 transfer students enrolled in a recent year. Transfer applicants should have a minimum GPA of 2.0. Those majoring in nursing, the sciences, mathematics or computer science need at least a 2.5 GPA. An interview is recommended. 45 to 51 credits of 120 to 126 must be completed at CMSV.

Visiting: There are regularly scheduled orientations for prospective students. Upon request students can have an interview with an admissions counselor, sit in on classes, and tour the campus. All students are invited to an open house. Accepted students can have a one-on-one with a student on campus, staying overnight at the college. There are guides for informal visits and visitors may sit in on classes and stay overnight at the school. To schedule a visit, contact the Admissions Office.

Financial Aid: In 1995–96, 88% of all freshmen and 75% of continuing students received some form of financial aid. 80% of freshmen and 75% of continuing students received need-based aid. The average freshman award was $7086. Of that total, scholarships or need-based grants averaged $4000 ($18,774 maximum); loans averaged $2625 ($6625 maximum); and work contracts averaged $700 ($1000 maximum). 70% of undergraduate students work part-time. Average earnings from campus work for the school year are $800. The average financial indebtedness of the 1994–95 graduate was $9000. CMSV is a member of CSS. The FAFSA, the college's own financial statement, and TAP application for New York state residents are required. The application deadline for fall entry is March 15.

International Students: There are currently 24 international students enrolled. The school actively recruits these students. They must take the TOEFL and achieve a minimum score of approximately 550. The student must also take the SAT I, ACT, or TOEFL.

Computers: The college provides computer facilities for student use. The mainframe is a DEC VAX 11/780 in conjunction with Manhattan College. Two terminals are connected to Manhattan College's DEC VAX system via modem. Students whose course work requires mainframe use may access the system 9:30 A.M. to 10 P.M. Monday through Thursday and 9:30 A.M. to 4 P.M. Friday and Saturday. There are no time limits and no fees.

Graduates: In 1994–95, 175 bachelor's degrees were awarded. The most popular majors among graduates were nursing (31%), business (12%), and communications (11%). Within an average freshman class, 57% graduate in 4 years, 64% in 5 years, and 68% in 6 years. 10 companies recruited on campus in 1994–95. Of the 1994 graduating class, 30% were enrolled in graduate school within 6 months of graduation and 72% had found employment.

Admissions Contact: Lenore Mott, Dean of Admissions and Financial Aid. A campus video is available.

COLLEGE OF NEW ROCHELLE
New Rochelle, NY 10805

D-5
(914) 654-5452
(800) 933-5923; FAX: (914) 654-5554

Full-time: 12 men, 656 women	Faculty: 50; IIA, -$
Part-time: 16 men, 352 women	Ph.Ds: 70%
Graduate: 201 men, 1374 women	Student/Faculty: 13 to 1
Year: semesters, summer session	Tuition: $12,300
Application Deadline: August 15	Room & Board: $5550
Freshman Class: 661 applied, 396 accepted, 146 enrolled	
SAT I Verbal/Math: 430/420	COMPETITIVE

The College of New Rochelle was founded in 1904 by the Ursuline order as the first Catholic college for women in New York State and is now independent. There are 3 undergraduate schools, and 1 graduate school. The School of Arts and Sciences offers liberal arts baccalaureate education for women only; the School of Nursing is coeducational. The School of New Resources is described on these pages. In addition to regional accreditation, CNR has baccalaureate program accreditation with CSWE and NLN. The library contains 224,000 volumes, 277 microform items, and 5700 audiovisual forms, and subscribes to 1432 periodicals. Computerized library sources and services include the card catalog, interlibrary loans, and database searching. Special learning facilities include a learning resource center, art gallery, and the Learning Center for Nursing. The 20-acre campus is in a suburban area 12 miles north of New York City. Including residence halls, there are 20 buildings on campus.

Student Life: 90% of undergraduates are from New York. Students come from 13 states and 4 foreign countries. 73% are from public schools; 27% from private. 49% are white; 25% African American; 18% Hispanic. 77% are Catholic; 18% Protestant. The average age of freshmen is 18; all undergraduates, 21. 23% do not continue beyond their first year; 55% remain to graduate.

Housing: 550 students can be accommodated in college housing. College-sponsored living facilities include single-sex dormitories. On-campus housing is guaranteed for all 4 years. 55% of students live on campus; of those, 50% remain on campus on weekends.

Activities: There are no fraternities or sororities. There are 20 groups on campus, including art, choir, chorus, drama, ethnic, film, honors, international, literary magazine, musical theater, newspaper, photography, political, professional, radio and TV, religious, social, social service, student government, and yearbook. Popular campus events include Junior Ring Dance, Parents Weekend, Founders Day, World Food Day, Swimphony, and honors convocation.

Sports: Athletic and recreation facilities include a gymnasium, a dance studio, a swimming pool, a tennis court, and a Nautilus room.

Disabled Students: 25% of the campus is accessible to disabled students. The following facilities are available: wheelchair ramps, elevators, special parking, specially equipped rest rooms, and special class scheduling.

Services: In addition to many counseling and information services, tutoring is available in some subjects, including science and languages. There is remedial math, reading, and writing. Individual counseling and educational workshops about self-development and personal concerns are available, as are self-help materials.

Campus Safety and Security: Campus safety and security measures include 24-hour foot and vehicle patrol, self-defense education, escort service, and shuttle buses. In addition, there are informal discussions, pamphlets/posters/films, emergency telephones, lighted pathways/sidewalks, card access into dormitories, and surveillance cameras.

Programs of Study: CNR confers B.A., B.S., B.F.A., and B.S.N. degrees. Master's degrees are also awarded. Bachelor's degrees are awarded in BIOLOGICAL SCIENCE (biology/biological science), BUSINESS (business administration and management), COMMUNICATIONS AND THE ARTS (art history and appreciation, classics, communications, English, fine arts, French, and Spanish), COMPUTER AND PHYSICAL SCIENCE (chemistry, mathematics, and physics), EDUCATION (art, early childhood, elementary, foreign languages, middle school, and secondary), HEALTH PROFESSIONS (art therapy, nursing, predentistry, and premedicine), SOCIAL SCIENCE (economics, history, international studies, philosophy, political science/government, prelaw, psychology, religion, social work, and sociology). Nursing, art, and psychology have the largest enrollments.

Required: Students must complete 120 credit hours, 60 to 90 in liberal arts courses, depending on the major, meet specific course distribution requirements, and maintain a minimum GPA of 2.0 to graduate. 4 physical education courses are also required.

Special: CNR provides cooperative programs in all disciplines, cross-registration with Iona College, work-study programs, dual majors in all majors, interdisciplinary studies, an accelerated degree program in nursing, a Washington semester, internships, study abroad in 9 countries, nondegree study, pass/fail options, student-designed majors, and a general studies degree. There is a freshman honors program on campus, as well as 1 national honor society. All departments have honors programs.

Faculty/Classroom: 34% of faculty are male; 66%, female. All both teach and do research. No introductory courses are taught by graduate students. The average class size in an introductory lecture is 15; in a laboratory, 10; and in a regular course offering, 15.

Admissions: 60% of the 1995–96 applicants were accepted. The SAT I scores for the 1995–96 freshman class were as follows: Verbal—85% below 500, 11% between 500 and 599, 3% between 600 and 700, and 1% above 700; Math—78% below 500, 17% between 500 and 599, and 5% between 600 and 700. 41% of the current freshmen were in the top fifth of their class; 88% were in the top two fifths.

Requirements: The SAT I is required. Graduation from an accredited secondary school is required; the GED is accepted. Applicants must have completed 15 academic credits, with 4 in English, 3 each in mathematics, science, and social studies, and 2 in a foreign language. A portfolio is required for art majors. An essay and an interview are recommended. AP credits are accepted. Important factors in the admissions decision are advanced placement or honor courses, recommendations by school officials, and leadership record.

Procedure: Freshmen are admitted to all sessions. Entrance exams should be taken in the junior year or fall of the senior year. There are early decision, early admissions, and deferred admissions plans. Early decision applications should be filed by November 1; regular applications, by August 15 for fall entry and January 10 for spring entry, along with an application fee of $20. Notification of early decision is sent December 15; regular decision, on a rolling basis.

Transfer: 57 transfer students enrolled in 1995–96. Students must submit a transcript from their previous college showing courses completed and a minimum GPA of 2.0. High school records and SAT I scores are required. An interview is recommended. 30 credits of 120 must be completed at CNR.

Visiting: There are guides for informal visits and visitors may sit in on classes and stay overnight at the school. To schedule a visit, contact the Office of Admissions.

Financial Aid: In 1995–96, 90% of all students received some form of financial aid. 80% of all students received need-based aid. The average freshman award was $12,710. Of that total, scholarships or need-based grants averaged $8166; loans averaged $3625; and work contracts averaged $781. 60% of undergraduate students work part-time. Average earnings from campus work for the school year are $780. The average financial indebtedness of the 1994–95 graduate was $20,000. The FAF, FAFSA, FFS, or SFS, the college's own financial statement, and income documentation are required. The application deadline for fall entry is open.

International Students: There are currently 4 international students enrolled. The school actively recruits these students. They must take the TOEFL and achieve a minimum score of 550. The student must also take the SAT I or ACT; the SAT I is preferred.

Computers: The college provides computer facilities for student use. The mainframe is an IBM PS 80. The computer center contains 69 PCs for student use. All students may access the system from 8:30 A.M. to 11 P.M. daily. Students may access the system 2 hours during peak usage. There are no fees.

Graduates: In 1994–95, 207 bachelor's degrees were awarded. The most popular majors among graduates were nursing (School of Nursing) (100%), psychology (18%), art (17%), and business (14%). Within an average freshman class, 76% graduate in 4 years, 23% in 5 years, and 2% in 6 years. 27 companies recruited on campus in 1994–95. Of the 1994 graduating class, 20% were enrolled in graduate school within 6 months of graduation and 60% had found employment.

Admissions Contact: John Hine, Director of Admission. A campus video is available.

COLLEGE OF NEW ROCHELLE - SCHOOL OF NEW RESOURCES   D-5
New Rochelle, NY 10805

(914) 654–5522
(800) 288–4767; FAX: (914) 654–5664

Full-time: 650 men, 3028 women	Faculty: 18; IIA, -$
Part-time: 83 men, 389 women	Ph.D.s: 16%
Graduate: none	Student/Faculty: 8 to 1
Year: semesters, summer session	Tuition: $4234
Application Deadline: August 15	Room & Board: $5550
Freshman Class: 1700 applied, 1500 accepted, 910 enrolled	SPECIAL

The College of New Rochelle's School of New Resources is a coeducational liberal arts institution serving adult baccalaureate students. The main campus library contains 224,000 volumes, 277 microform items, and 5700 audiovisual forms, and subscribes to 1432 periodicals. Computerized library sources and services include the card catalog, interlibrary loans, and database searching. Special learning facilities on the main campus include a learning resource center, art gallery, and TV station. The main campus is in a suburban area 12 miles north of New York City. 6 additional campuses are located within New York City. Including residence halls, there are 20 buildings on campus.

Student Life: 98% of undergraduates are from New York. Students come from 3 states and 3 foreign countries. 73% are African American; 18% Hispanic. 79% are Catholic; 18% Protestant. The average age of all undergraduates is 33.

Housing: 550 students can be accommodated in college housing. College-sponsored living facilities include single-sex dormitories on the main campus. All students may keep cars on campus.

Activities: There are no fraternities or sororities. There is an organization for student government on campus.

Sports: There is no sports program at SNR.

Disabled Students: Each of the 7 campuses has different facilities.

Services: There is remedial math, reading, and writing. Individual counseling and educational workshops about self-development and personal concerns are available, as are self-help materials.

Campus Safety and Security: Campus safety and security measures include 24-hour foot and vehicle patrol, self-defense education, escort service, and shuttle buses. In addition, there are informal discussions, pamphlets/posters/films, emergency telephones, lighted pathways/sidewalks, card access into dormitories, and surveillance cameras.

Programs of Study: SNR confers the B.A. degree. Bachelor's degrees are awarded in SOCIAL SCIENCE (liberal arts/general studies).

Required: Students must complete 120 credit hours, meet specific course distribution requirements, and maintain a minimum GPA of 2.0 to graduate. Entrance, core, and exit seminars are required, as are degree-planning courses.

Special: There are concentrations available in communications, letters, psychology, and social sciences.

Faculty/Classroom: 47% of faculty are male; 53%, female. All teach undergraduates. The average class size in an introductory lecture is 15; in a laboratory, 10; and in a regular course offering, 15.

Admissions: 88% of the 1995–96 applicants were accepted.

Requirements: Applicants must place in college-level English. AP credits are accepted.

Procedure: Freshmen are admitted to all sessions. Entrance exams should be taken in the junior year or fall of the senior year. Early decision applications should be filed by November 1; regular applications, by August 15 for fall entry and January 10 for spring entry, along with an application fee of $20. Notification of early decision is sent December 15; regular decision, on a rolling basis.

Transfer: 492 transfer students enrolled in 1995–96. Students must submit a transcript from their previous college, showing courses completed and a minimum GPA of 2.0. An interview is required. 30 credits of 120 must be completed at SNR.

Financial Aid: In 1995–96, more than 90% of all students received need-based or other financial aid. Scholarships or need-based grants averaged $6300; loans averaged $2000; work contracts averaged $100; and external aid averaged $200. 5% of undergraduate students work part-time. Average earnings from campus work for the school year are $100. The FAFSA, the college's own financial statement, and income documentation are required. The application deadline for fall entry is open.

International Students: There are currently 3 international students enrolled. They must take the TOEFL.

Computers: The college provides computer facilities for student use. The mainframe is an IBM PS 80. The main campus computer center contains 69 PCs for student use. All students may access the system from 8:30 A.M. to 11 P.M. daily. Students may access the system 2 hours during peak usage. There are no fees.

Graduates: In 1994–95, 588 bachelor's degrees were awarded.

Admissions Contact: Donna Tyler, Assistant Dean.

COLLEGE OF SAINT ROSE

D-5

Albany, NY 12203

(518) 454-5150
(800) 637-8556; FAX: (518) 454-2013

Full-time: 453 men, 1246 women	Faculty: 129; IIA, --$
Part-time: 218 men, 536 women	Ph.D.s: 73%
Graduate: 306 men, 967 women	Student/Faculty: 13 to 1
Year: semesters, summer session	Tuition: $10,730
Application Deadline: open	Room & Board: $5095–5836
Freshman Class: 898 applied, 652 accepted, 259 enrolled	
SAT I Verbal/Math: 480/500	COMPETITIVE

The College of Saint Rose, established in 1920, is an independent liberal arts institution sponsored by the Sisters of St. Joseph of Carondelet. There are 4 undergraduate schools and 1 graduate school. The library contains 170,000 volumes and 100,000 microform items, and subscribes to 1025 periodicals. Computerized library sources and services include interlibrary loans. Special learning facilities include a learning resource center, art gallery, and TV station. The 22-acre campus is in a suburban area in a residential section, 1 1/2 miles from downtown Albany.

Student Life: Students come from 16 states, 30 foreign countries, and Canada. 60% are from public schools. 61% are Catholic; 38% Protestant. The average age of freshmen is 18; all undergraduates, 22. 65% of freshmen remain to graduate.

Housing: 725 students can be accommodated in college housing. College-sponsored living facilities include single-sex and coed dormitories, on-campus apartments, and married-student housing. In addition there are language houses. On-campus housing is available on a first-come, first-served basis and is available on a lottery system for upperclassmen. All students may keep cars on campus.

Activities: There are no fraternities or sororities. There are 34 groups on campus, including art, cheerleading, chorale, computers, drama, ethnic, gay, international, jazz band, literary magazine, newspaper, orchestra, political, professional, religious, social, social service, student government, and yearbook.

Sports: There are 7 intercollegiate sports for men and 8 for women, and 3 intramural sports for men and 3 for women. Athletic and recreation facilities include an activities center, a basketball court, a weight room, and an Olympic-size swimming pool.

Disabled Students: 98% of the campus is accessible to disabled students. The following facilities are available: wheelchair ramps, elevators, special parking, specially equipped rest rooms, lowered drinking fountains, lowered telephones, and automatic-open doors and braille-numbered doors and elevators.

Services: In addition to many counseling and information services, tutoring is available in most subjects, including writing, mathematics, accounting, computer, and others as needed. There is remedial math, reading, and writing. There is also a full-time coordinator of disabled student services.

Campus Safety and Security: Campus safety and security measures include 24-hour foot and vehicle patrol, self-defense education, shuttle buses, and informal discussions. There are pamphlets/posters/films, emergency telephones, lighted pathways/sidewalks, and a student volunteer escort service.

Programs of Study: CSR confers B.A. and B.S. degrees. Master's degrees are also awarded. Bachelor's degrees are awarded in BIOLOGICAL SCIENCE (biology/biological science), BUSINESS (accounting and business administration and management), COMMUNICATIONS AND THE ARTS (English, graphic design, music, public relations, Spanish, and studio art), COMPUTER AND PHYSICAL SCIENCE (chemistry, computer programming, and mathematics), EDUCATION (art, elementary, English, foreign languages, mathematics, music, science, social studies, and special), HEALTH PROFESSIONS (medical laboratory technology and speech pathology/audiology), SOCIAL SCIENCE (American studies, history, interdisciplinary studies, religion, and sociology).

Required: To graduate, students must complete 122 credits with a 2.0 GPA, overall and in the major; these requirements are higher for education majors. Liberal education requirements consist of 6 credits in college writing and speech and 30 credits in the humanities, science and mathematics, social science and business, and the arts. Students must also complete 2 credits in physical education.

Special: CSR offers cross-registration with the Hudson-Mohawk Consortium and the Sisters of Saint Joseph College Consortium, internships, work-study programs, study abroad in China and Italy, dual and student-designed majors, nondegree study, and pass/fail options. There are 3–2 engineering degree programs with Alfred and Clarkson universities and Union College, as well as a 6-year law program with Albany Law School. There are 3 national honor societies on campus.

Admissions: 73% of the 1995–96 applicants were accepted. The SAT I scores for the 1995–96 freshman class were as follows: Verbal—71% below 500, 24% between 500 and 599, and 4% between 600 and 700

Requirements: The SAT I or ACT is required. CSR requires applicants to be in the upper 50% of their class and have graduated from an accredited secondary school or have a GED certificate. They should have completed 16 college preparatory units. All students must submit a letter of recommendation. Art students must submit portfolios, and music students must audition. CLEP credit is accepted.

Procedure: Freshmen are admitted fall and spring. There are early admissions and deferred admissions plans. Application deadlines are open. Application fee is $25. Notification is sent on a rolling basis.

Transfer: 454 transfer students enrolled in a recent year. Applicants must submit official transcripts and catalogs from each college attended, along with a statement of honorable dismissal, a letter of recommendation, and a personal statement of the reasons for seeking transfer. Art majors must submit a portfolio and music majors must audition. 60 credits of 122 must be completed at CSR.

Visiting: There are guides for informal visits and visitors may sit in on classes and stay overnight at the school. To schedule a visit, contact the Admissions Office.

Financial Aid: In a recent year, 90% of all freshmen and 85% of continuing students received some form of financial aid. 85% of all students received need-based aid. The average freshman award was $13,575. Of that total, scholarships or need-based grants averaged $9575 ($12,000 maximum); loans averaged $3250 ($3700 maximum); and work contracts averaged $750 ($1000 maximum). 20% of undergraduate students work part time. The average financial indebtedness of the 1994–95 graduate was $12,000. CSR is a member of CSS. The FAFSA and the college's own financial statement are required. The application deadline for fall entry is February 1.

International Students: There were 69 international students enrolled in a recent year. They must score 500 on the TOEFL.

Computers: The college provides computer facilities for student use. The mainframe is a Sperry 2200/100. There is 24-hour access via modem from home or through 34 PCs located on campus. All students may access the system 24 hours a day Monday through Saturday, and additional hours on Sunday. There are no time limits and no fees.

Admissions Contact: Mary Grondahl, Dean of Admissions and Enrollment Services. E-mail: admit@rosnet.strose.edu.

COLUMBIA UNIVERSITY SYSTEM

Columbia University, established in 1754, is a private system in New York. It is governed by a board of trustees, whose chief administrator is president. The primary goals of the sytem are teaching and research. The main priorities are providing outstanding undergraduate instruction; conducting research to develop new knowledge and methods; and training of professionals in law, business, social work, and medicine. Graduate and professional programs include architecture, fine arts, public health, international affairs, public affairs, dentistry, education, and engineering. The total enrollment of both campuses is about 19,000, with 2100 faculty members. There are approximately 110 baccalaureate, 160 master's, and 80 doctoral programs offered at Columbia University. Profiles of the 4-year campuses are included in this chapter.

COLUMBIA UNIVERSITY/BARNARD COLLEGE D-5
New York, NY 10027-6598

	(212) 854-2014
	FAX: (212) 854-6220
Full-time: 2217 women	Faculty: 181; IIB, +$
Part-time: 59 women	Ph.D.s: 98%
Graduate: none	Student/Faculty: 12 to 1
Year: semesters	Tuition: $19,480
Application Deadline: January 15	Room & Board: $8172
Freshman Class: 2973 applied, 1335 accepted, 531 enrolled	
SAT I Verbal/Math: 600/640	ACT: 28 MOST COMPETITIVE

Barnard College, founded in 1889, is an independent affiliate of Columbia University. It is an undergraduate women's liberal arts college. The library contains 175,019 volumes, 14,607 microform items, and 7300 audiovisual forms, and subscribes to 472 periodicals. Computerized library sources and services include the card catalog, interlibrary loans, and database searching. Special learning facilities include a learning resource center, art gallery, radio station, greenhouse, history of physics laboratory, child development research and study center, dance studio, modern theater, and women's research archives within a women's center. The 4-acre campus occupies 4 city blocks of Manhattan's Upper West Side. Including residence halls, there are 15 buildings on campus.

Student Life: 61% of undergraduates are from out-of-state, mostly the Middle Atlantic. Students come from 48 states, 27 foreign countries, and Canada. 56% are from public schools; 44% from private. 62% are white; 25% Asian American. The average age of freshmen is 18; all undergraduates, 20. 5% do not continue beyond their first year; 87% remain to graduate.

Housing: 1900 students can be accommodated in college housing. College-sponsored living facilities include dormitories, on-campus apartments, and off-campus apartments. In addition there are special interest houses. On-campus housing is guaranteed for all 4 years. 87% of students live on campus; of those, 75% remain on campus on weekends. Alcohol is not permitted. All students may keep cars on campus.

Activities: There are no fraternities. There are 80 groups on campus, including art, band, choir, chorale, chorus, dance, drama, ethnic, film, gay, international, jazz band, literary magazine, marching band, musical theater, newspaper, opera, orchestra, photography, political, professional, radio and TV, religious, social, social service, student government, symphony, and yearbook. Popular campus events include Spring Festival, Winter Festival, Women Poets Series, The Scholar and the Feminist Conference, Celebration of Black Women, Women's History Month, Latina Month, and Founders Day.

Sports: Athletic and recreation facilities include pools, weight rooms, gymnasiums, tennis courts, an indoor track, a boat slip, and a bowling alley.

Disabled Students: The entire campus is accessible to disabled students. The following facilities are available: wheelchair ramps, elevators, specially equipped rest rooms, lowered drinking fountains, and lowered telephones.

Services: In addition to many counseling and information services, tutoring is available in every subject. A writing room is available for students of all levels of writing ability.

Campus Safety and Security: Campus safety and security measures include 24-hour foot and vehicle patrol, escort service, shuttle buses, and informal discussions. In addition, there are pamphlets/posters/films, emergency telephones, lighted pathways/sidewalks, and safety and security education programs.

Programs of Study: Barnard confers the B.A. degree. Bachelor's degrees are awarded in BIOLOGICAL SCIENCE (biochemistry and biology/biological science), COMMUNICATIONS AND THE ARTS (art history and appreciation, classics, comparative literature, dance, dramatic arts, English, French, German, Greek, Italian, Latin, linguistics, music, Russian, and Spanish), COMPUTER AND PHYSICAL SCIENCE (astronomy, chemistry, computer science, mathematics, physics, and statistics), EDUCATION (elementary and secondary), ENGINEERING AND ENVIRONMENTAL DESIGN (architecture and environmental science), SOCIAL SCIENCE (African American studies, American studies, anthropology, biopsychology, classical/ancient civilization, East Asian studies, economics, European studies, history, international studies, medieval studies, Middle Eastern studies, philosophy, political science/government, psychology, religion, sociology, urban studies, and women's studies). English, biology, psychology, art history, and political science are the strongest academically. English, political science, psychology, history, and economics have the largest enrollments.

Required: A total of 120 credits is required, with a minimum GPA of 2.0. All students must take 4 semesters each of a foreign language, humanities, or social sciences outside the major, and geographic and cultural diversity courses that may satisfy the major or other requirements, 2 semesters each of laboratory science and physical education, and 1 semester each in first-year seminar, first-year English, and quantitative reasoning.

Special: Barnard offers cross-registration with Columbia College, more than 1000 internships with New York City firms, and study abroad worldwide. A 3-2 engineering program with the Columbia School of Engineering and double degree programs with the Columbia University School of International and Public Affairs, School of Law, School of Dentistry, the Juilliard School, and the Jewish Theological Seminary are possible. The college offers dual and student-designed majors and multidisciplinary majors, including economic history. There is 1 national honor society on campus, Phi Beta Kappa.

Faculty/Classroom: 40% of faculty are male; 60%, female. All both teach and do research. Graduate students teach 5% of introductory courses. The average class size in an introductory lecture is 30; in a laboratory, 14; and in a regular course offering, 22.

Admissions: 45% of the 1995-96 applicants were accepted. The SAT I scores for the 1995-96 freshman class were as follows: Verbal—7% below 500, 42% between 500 and 599, 46% between 600 and 700, and 5% above 700; Math—2% below 500, 24% between 500 and 599, 60% between 600 and 700, and 14% above 700. The ACT scores were 5% between 21 and 23, 23% between 24 and 26, 35% between 27 and 28, and 36% above 28. 89% of the current freshmen were in the top fifth of their class; 100% were in the top two fifths. There were 2 National Merit finalists and 14 semifinalists.

Requirements: The SAT I or ACT is required. If taking the SAT I, an applicant must also take 3 SAT II: Subject tests, one of which must be in writing or literature. A GED is accepted. Applicants should prepare with 4 years of English, 3 of mathematics, 3 or 4 of a foreign language, 2 of a laboratory science, and 1 of history. An interview is recommended. AP credits are accepted. Important factors in the admissions decision are advanced placement or honor courses, recommendations by school officials, and extracurricular activities record.

Procedure: Freshmen are admitted fall and spring. Entrance exams should be taken by January of the senior year. There are early decision, early admissions, and deferred admissions plans. Early decision applications should be filed by November 15 and January 2; regular applications, by January 15 for fall entry and November 1 for spring entry, along with an application fee of $45. Notification of early decision is sent December 15 and February 2; regular decision, April 1. 89 early decision candidates were accepted for the 1995-96 class. A waiting list is an active part of the admissions procedure, with about 19% of all applicants on the list.

Transfer: 102 transfer students enrolled in 1995-96. Transfer applicants must complete at least one college course with a GPA of 3.0. The SAT I or ACT is required. An interview is recommended. 60 credits of 120 must be completed at Barnard.

Visiting: There are regularly scheduled orientations for prospective students, consisting of open house programs regularly scheduled throughout the fall. There are guides for informal visits and visitors may sit in on classes and stay overnight at the school. To schedule a visit, contact the Office of Admissions at (212) 854-2014 or E-mail: admissions@barnard.columbia.edu.

Financial Aid: In 1995-96, 60% of all students received some form of financial aid. 49% of freshmen and 48% of continuing students received need-based aid. The average freshman award was $20,242. Of that total, scholarships or need-based grants averaged $16,362 ($28,442 maximum); loans averaged $2400 ($2625 maximum); and work contracts averaged $900 ($1600 maximum). 41% of undergraduate students work part-time. The average financial indebtedness of the 1994-95 graduate was $11,000. Barnard is a member of CSS. The FAFSA, the college's own financial statement, the CSS Profile Application, and the parents' and student's federal tax returns and appropriate supplements are required. The application deadline for fall entry is February 1.

International Students: There are currently 75 international students enrolled. The school actively recruits these students. They must take the TOEFL and achieve a minimum score of 600. The student must also take the SAT I or ACT. Applicants who take the SAT I must also take SAT II: Subject tests in writing or literature and 2 others.

Computers: The college provides computer facilities for student use. The mainframe is an IBM RS/6000. All students have access to 3 academic computer laboratories that provide networked access to software, bibliographic searching, and Columbia University mainframe links. Several academic departments maintain computer laboratories for student use. All students may access the system. There are no time limits and no fees.

Graduates: In 1994–95, 528 bachelor's degrees were awarded. The most popular majors among graduates were English (14%), psychology (12%), and political science (11%). Within an average freshman class, 3% graduate in 3 years, 82% in 4 years, 84% in 5 years, and 88% in 6 years. 46 companies recruited on campus in 1994–95. Of the 1994 graduating class, 28% were enrolled in graduate school within 6 months of graduation and 67% had found employment.

Admissions Contact: Doris Davis, Director of Admissions. E-mail: admissions@barnard.columbia.edu.

COLUMBIA UNIVERSITY/COLUMBIA COLLEGE

D-5

New York, NY 10027 (212) 854-2521; FAX: (212) 854-1209

Full-time: 1825 men, 1748 women	Faculty: 571; I, +$
Part-time: none	Ph.D.s: 100%
Graduate: none	Student/Faculty: 6 to 1
Year: semesters, summer session	Tuition: $20,452
Application Deadline: January 1	Room & Board: $6864
Freshman Class: 8714 applied, 2045 accepted, 883 enrolled	
SAT I or ACT: required	MOST COMPETITIVE

Columbia College of Columbia University, founded in 1754, is a private college offering programs in the liberal arts. There are 2 undergraduate schools. The libraries contain 6.6 million volumes and 4.9 million microform items, and subscribe to 66,000 periodicals. Computerized library sources and services include the card catalog and interlibrary loans. Special learning facilities include an art gallery, planetarium, radio station, TV station, geological research center, and the Nevis Laboratory Center for study of high energy particle physics. The 36-acre campus is in an urban area of New York City. Including residence halls, there are 37 buildings on campus.

Student Life: Students come from 49 states, more than 40 foreign countries, and Canada. 56% are from public schools; 44% from private. 64% are white; 22% Asian American. The average age of freshmen is 17; all undergraduates, 19. 4% do not continue beyond their first year; 90% remain to graduate.

Housing: College-sponsored living facilities include coed dormitories, on-campus apartments, fraternity houses, and sorority houses. In addition, there are language houses and special interest houses. On-campus housing is guaranteed for all 4 years. 90% of students live on campus.

Activities: 13% of men belong to 19 national fraternities; 6% of women belong to 5 national sororities. There are 120 groups on campus, including art, band, cheerleading, chess, choir, chorale, chorus, computers, dance, drama, ethnic, film, gay, honors, international, jazz band, literary magazine, marching band, musical theater, newspaper, opera, orchestra, pep band, photography, political, professional, radio and TV, religious, social, social service, student government, symphony, and yearbook. Popular campus events include Columbia Fest, and United Minorities Board Ethnic Festival.

Sports: There are 12 intercollegiate sports for men and 12 for women, and 44 intramural sports for men and 44 for women. Athletic and recreation facilities include a football stadium, indoor and outdoor track and field facilities, a baseball field, a soccer stadium, a recreational gymnasium with a swimming pool, basketball/volleyball courts, aerobic, martial arts, and weight rooms, tennis, squash, handball, and racquetball courts, and a boat house.

Disabled Students: The entire campus is accessible to disabled students. The following facilities are available: wheelchair ramps, elevators, special parking, specially equipped rest rooms, special class scheduling, lowered drinking fountains, lowered telephones, and chair lifts.

Services: In addition to many counseling and information services, tutoring is available in every subject. There is a reader service for the blind.

Campus Safety and Security: Campus safety and security measures include 24-hour foot and vehicle patrol, self-defense education, escort service, and shuttle buses. In addition, there are informal discussions, pamphlets/posters/films, emergency telephones, and lighted pathways/sidewalks.

Programs of Study: Columbia confers the A.B. degree. Bachelor's degrees are awarded in BIOLOGICAL SCIENCE (biochemistry, biology/biological science, biophysics, and neurosciences), COMMUNICATIONS AND THE ARTS (art history and appreciation, classics, comparative literature, dance, dramatic arts, English, film arts, French, German, Germanic languages and literature, Greek, Latin, music, Russian, Spanish, and visual and performing arts), COMPUT-ER AND PHYSICAL SCIENCE (astronomy, astrophysics, chemistry, computer science, earth science, geochemistry, geology, geophysics and seismology, mathematics, physics, and statistics), ENGINEERING AND ENVIRONMENTAL DESIGN (architecture and environmental science), SOCIAL SCIENCE (African American studies, anthropology, archeology, Asian/Oriental studies, classical/ancient civilization, East Asian studies, economics, Hispanic American studies, history, Italian studies, Latin American studies, medieval studies, Middle Eastern studies, philosophy, political science/government, psychology, religion, Russian and Slavic studies, sociology, urban studies, and women's studies). English, political science, and history have the largest enrollments.

Required: All students complete a core curriculum consisting of classes in moral and religious philosophy, history, social science, art, sculpture and architecture, literature, and music of the Western tradition; additionally, 2 courses in non-Western areas are required. Distribution requirements include half a year of writing, 2 years of foreign language (unless competency can be demonstrated), 3 semesters of science, and 1 year of physical education. A total of 124 credit hours is required; usually 42 of these are in the major. The minimum required GPA is 2.0.

Special: There is a co-op program with Oxford and Cambridge universities in England and the Kyoto Center for Japanese Studies in Japan, and cross-registration with the Juilliard School and Barnard College. Combined B.A.-B.S. degrees are offered via 3-2 or 4-1 engineering programs. The college also offers study abroad in France, work-study, dual, student-designed, and interdisciplinary majors, including regional studies and ancient studies, internships, credit by examination, and pass/fail options. There is also a 3-2 program in international affairs with the School of International and Public Affairs, and a joint 5-year program with the School of Arts, both other units of the university. There is a chapter of Phi Beta Kappa on campus.

Faculty/Classroom: 69% of faculty are male; 31%, female. All both teach and do research. The average class size in an introductory lecture is 70; in a laboratory, 15; and in a regular course offering, 25.

Admissions: 23% of the 1995–96 applicants were accepted. 95% of the current freshmen were in the top fifth of their class.

Requirements: The SAT I or ACT is required, and 3 SAT II: Subject tests, 1 of which must be writing, are also required. A GED is accepted. Students should prepare with 4 years of English and 3 years each of foreign language, history, mathematics, and science. An essay is required, and an interview is recommended. 2 academic faculty recommendations and a written evaluation or recommendation from a school official are also required. AP credits are accepted. Important factors in the admissions decision are advanced placement or honor courses, recommendations by school officials, and leadership record.

Procedure: Freshmen are admitted in the fall. Entrance exams should be taken in the summer of the junior year or fall of the senior year. There are early decision, early admissions, and deferred admissions plans. Early decision applications should be filed by November 1; regular applications, by January 1 for fall entry, along with an application fee of $45. Notification of early decision is sent in December; regular decision, April 3. 248 early decision candidates were accepted for the 1995–96 class. A waiting list is an active part of the admissions procedure, with about 4% of all applicants on the list.

Transfer: 85 transfer students enrolled in a recent year. Transfer applicants must have completed 1 full year of college (24 credits) with a GPA of at least 3.0. They must submit high school and college transcripts. 60 credits of 124 must be completed at Columbia.

Visiting: There are regularly scheduled orientations for prospective students, consisting of group information sessions at 11 A.M. and 2 P.M., and student-led tours. There are guides for informal visits and visitors may sit in on classes and stay overnight at the school. To schedule a visit, contact the Admissions Office.

Financial Aid: In 1995–96, 80% of all freshmen received some form of financial aid. 80% of freshmen and more than 50% of continuing students received need-based aid. The average freshman award was $14,338. Columbia is a member of CSS. The FFS, the college's own financial statement, and the business and/or divorced parents statement are required. The application deadline for fall entry is January 30.

International Students: There are currently 103 international students enrolled. The school actively recruits these students. They must take the TOEFL and achieve a minimum score of 600. The student must also take the SAT I or ACT, and 3 SAT II: Subject tests, 1 of them in writing.

Computers: The college provides computer facilities for student use. The mainframes are 3 Sun 4/280s, a DEC VAX 8700, and an IBM 4341. Computer terminals are accessible throughout the campus. All students may access the system, and extra time can be bought.

Graduates: In 1994–95, 852 bachelor's degrees were awarded. Within an average freshman class, 80% graduate in 4 years and 90% in 6 years. 375 companies recruited on campus in a recent year.

Admissions Contact: E-mail: ugrad-admiss@columbia.edu.

COLUMBIA UNIVERSITY/SCHOOL OF ENGINEERING AND APPLIED SCIENCE
D-5

New York, NY 10027   (212) 854-2521; FAX: (212) 854-1209

Full-time: 814 men, 230 women	Faculty: 93
Part-time: none	Ph.D.s: 100%
Graduate: n/av	Student/Faculty: 11 to 1
Year: semesters	Tuition: $20,292
Application Deadline: January 1	Room & Board: $6864
Freshman Class: 1351 applied, 671 accepted, 278 enrolled	
SAT I or ACT: required	**MOST COMPETITIVE**

The School of Engineering and Applied Science of Columbia University offers undergraduate and graduate degree programs in engineering. There are 2 undergraduate and 15 graduate schools. In addition to regional accreditation, Columbia Engineering has baccalaureate program accreditation with ABET. The libraries contain more than 6 million volumes and more than 4 million microform items, and subscribe to more than 59,000 periodicals. Computerized library sources and services include the card catalog, interlibrary loans, and database searching. Special learning facilities include an art gallery, planetarium, radio station, and TV station. The approximately 25-acre campus is in an urban area in New York City.

Student Life: Many undergraduates are from out-of-state, mostly the Northeast. Students come from 40 states, more than 30 foreign countries, and Canada. 66% are from public schools; 34% from private. 49% are Asian American; 38% white. The average age of freshmen is 17.7; all undergraduates, 20.5. 11% do not continue beyond their first year; 84% remain to graduate.

Housing: All students can be accommodated in college housing. College-sponsored living facilities include coed dormitories, on-campus apartments, off-campus apartments, married-student housing, fraternity houses, and sorority houses. In addition, there are language houses and special interest houses. On-campus housing is guaranteed for all 4 years. 97% of students live on campus.

Activities: 18% of men belong to 17 fraternities; 8% of women belong to fraternities and 7 sororities. There are many groups and organizations on campus, including band, cheerleading, chess, choir, chorus, computers, dance, drama, ethnic, film, gay, honors, international, jazz band, literary magazine, marching band, musical theater, newspaper, orchestra, political, professional, radio and TV, religious, social service, student government, and yearbook. Popular campus events include Columbiafest-Spring.

Sports: There are 12 intercollegiate sports for men and 12 for women, and 20 intramural sports for men and 21 for women. Athletic and recreational facilities of Columbia University are available to students.

Disabled Students: 70% of the campus is accessible to disabled students. The following facilities are available: wheelchair ramps, elevators, special parking, and specially equipped rest rooms.

Services: In addition to many counseling and information services, tutoring is available in every subject. There is a reader service for the blind, and remedial math, reading, and writing.

Campus Safety and Security: Campus safety and security measures include 24-hour foot and vehicle patrol, self-defense education, escort service, and shuttle buses. In addition, there are pamphlets/posters/films, emergency telephones, and lighted pathways/sidewalks.

Programs of Study: Columbia Engineering confers the B.S. degree. Master's and doctoral degrees are also awarded. Bachelor's degrees are awarded in BUSINESS (operations research), COMPUTER AND PHYSICAL SCIENCE (applied mathematics, applied physics, and computer science), ENGINEERING AND ENVIRONMENTAL DESIGN (bioengineering, biomedical engineering, chemical engineering, civil engineering, computer engineering, electrical/electronics engineering, engineering management, engineering mechanics, geological engineering, industrial engineering technology, materials science, mechanical engineering, metallurgical engineering, and mining and mineral engineering). Computer science, electrical engineering, and mechanical engineering have the largest enrollments.

Required: All students must complete 128 semester hours, including calculus I to III, ordinary differential equations, 3 credits in computer science, 9 in chemistry, 15 in physics, 2 in physical education, and 28 in humanities. They must take 66 hours in the major and maintain a 2.5 GPA.

Special: Students may study at Columbia College or any of more than 80 other liberal arts colleges throughout the country in a 5-year program leading to the combined B.A.-B.S. degree. There is cross-registration with Barnard College, Teacher's College, and the Juilliard School. The school offers study abroad, internships, work-study, and pass/fail options. There is a chapter of Phi Beta Kappa on campus.

Faculty/Classroom: All faculty both teach and do research.

Admissions: 50% of the 1995–96 applicants were accepted. 91% of the current freshmen were in the top fifth of their class; all were in the top two fifths.

Requirements: The SAT I or ACT is required, as are SAT II: Subject tests in mathematics I or II, chemistry or physics, and writing. Applicants must be graduates of an accredited secondary school with preparation including 4 years of English, 3 or 4 of history or social science, 2 or 3 of a foreign language, 1 each of physics and chemistry, and mathematics courses through calculus. Also required are a written evaluation or recommendation from a school official (college adviser, guidance counselor) and 2 recommendations from teachers of academic classroom subjects (1 of these must be from a teacher of mathematics). An essay is required, and an interview is recommended. Applications on computer disk are accepted. AP credits are accepted. Important factors in the admissions decision are advanced placement or honor courses, evidence of special talent, and extracurricular activities record.

Procedure: Freshmen are admitted in the fall. Entrance exams should be taken in the spring of the junior year and/or fall of the senior year. There are early decision and deferred admissions plans. Early decision applications should be filed by November 1; regular applications, by January 1 for fall entry, along with an application fee of $60. Notification of early decision is sent December 15; regular decision, April 3. 34 early decision candidates were accepted for the 1995–96 class. A waiting list is an active part of the admissions procedure.

Transfer: 14 transfer students enrolled in a recent year. Transfer applicants should have completed 1 year each of calculus, physics, and chemistry with laboratory, in addition to appropriate liberal arts courses. 60 credits of 128 must be completed at Columbia Engineering.

Visiting: There are regularly scheduled orientations for prospective students, consisting of group information sessions and student-led tours. There are guides for informal visits and visitors may sit in on classes and stay overnight at the school. To schedule a visit, contact the Admissions Office.

Financial Aid: In a recent year, 93% of all freshmen and 63% of continuing students received some form of financial aid. The average freshman award was $18,000. Of that total, scholarships or need-based grants averaged $12,000. 49% of undergraduate students work part-time. Average earnings from campus work for the school year are $1600. The average financial indebtedness of a recent year's graduate was $11,000. Columbia Engineering is a member of CSS. The FAFSA and the college's own financial statement are required. The application deadline for fall entry is February 1.

International Students: There are currently 489 international students enrolled. The school actively recruits these students. They must take the TOEFL or the college's own test and achieve a minimum score on the TOEFL of 600. The student must also take the SAT I or the ACT. Students must take SAT II: Subject tests in writing, mathematics I or II, and physics or chemistry.

Computers: The college provides computer facilities for student use. The mainframes are a Prime, 13 DEC VAX 11/750s, 3 AT&T 3B20s, 75 AT&T 3B2 supermicros, an HP 9050, a system of HP 9900s, 2 IRIS computers, and an IBM Interactive Graphics Lab. There are also microcomputers available in laboratories and classrooms. All students may access the system 24 hours a day. There are no time limits. The fees are $34.

Graduates: In 1994–95, 210 bachelor's degrees were awarded. The most popular majors among graduates were electrical engineering (21%), industrial engineering (18%), and mechanical engineering (18%).

Admissions Contact: Admissions Officer, Office of Undergraduate Admissions. E-mail: ugrad-admiss@columbia.edu.

COLUMBIA UNIVERSITY/SCHOOL OF GENERAL STUDIES
D-5

New York, NY 10027   (212) 854-5364; FAX: (212) 854-6316

Full-time and part-time: 950 men and women	Faculty: n/av
	Ph.D.s: n/av
Graduate: none	Student/Faculty: n/av
Year: semesters, summer session	Tuition: $17,384
Application Deadline: July 15	Room & Board: $9000
Freshman Class: 624 applied, 324 accepted, 226 enrolled	
SAT I or ACT: recommended	**VERY COMPETITIVE**

The School of General Studies of Columbia University, founded in 1947, offers liberal arts degree programs and postgraduate studies for adult men and women whose post-high school education has been interrupted or postponed by at least 1 year. The 22 Columbia University libraries contain 6 million volumes and 4 million microform items. Computerized library sources and services include the card catalog, interlibrary loans, and database searching. Special learning facilities include a learning resource center, art gallery, and radio station. The campus is in an urban area in New York City.

Student Life: 65% of students are white; 10% foreign nationals. The average age of all undergraduates is 28.

Housing: College-sponsored living facilities include off-campus apartments, married-student housing, and fraternity houses.

Activities: There are many groups and organizations on campus, including band, choir, drama, film, jazz band, literary magazine, marching band, musical theater, newspaper, orchestra, photography, radio and TV, student government, symphony, and yearbook.

Sports: There is a universitywide sports program.

Disabled Students: The following facilities are available: wheelchair ramps, elevators, specially equipped rest rooms, lowered drinking fountains, and lowered telephones.

Services: In addition to many counseling and information services, tutoring is available in some subjects, including English composition, mathematics, languages, and sciences.

Campus Safety and Security: Campus safety and security measures include 24-hour foot and vehicle patrol, escort service, pamphlets/posters/films, and emergency telephones. In addition, there are lighted pathways/sidewalks.

Programs of Study: General Studies confers B.A. and B.S. degrees. Bachelor's degrees are awarded in BIOLOGICAL SCIENCE (biology/biological science), COMMUNICATIONS AND THE ARTS (art history and appreciation, classics, comparative literature, dance, dramatic arts, East Asian languages and literature, English literature, film arts, French, German, Germanic languages and literature, Greek, Italian, Latin, literature, music, Russian, Slavic languages, Spanish, and visual and performing arts), COMPUTER AND PHYSICAL SCIENCE (applied mathematics, astronomy, chemistry, computer science, geoscience, mathematics, physics, and statistics), ENGINEERING AND ENVIRONMENTAL DESIGN (architecture and environmental science), SOCIAL SCIENCE (African studies, anthropology, economics, Hispanic American studies, history, Middle Eastern studies, philosophy, political science/government, psychology, religion, sociology, urban studies, and women's studies).

Required: All students must complete 124 credit hours, including 56 distribution requirement credits in literature, humanities, foreign language or literature, social science, science, and cultural diversity. Proficiency in English composition and mathematics is required. A GPA of 2.0 is necessary to graduate.

Special: Preprofessional studies in allied health and medical fields and interdisciplinary majors, minors, and concentrations are offered. Internships in New York City, work-study programs on campus, study abroad, a 3–2 engineering degree at Columbia University School of Engineering and Applied Science, B.A.-B.S. degrees, and dual majors are available. There is a chapter of Phi Beta Kappa on campus. Many departments have honors programs.

Admissions: 52% of the 1995–96 applicants were accepted. 70% of the current freshmen were in the top two fifths of their class.

Requirements: The SAT I or ACT is recommended. SAT I, ACT, or Columbia's General Studies Admissions Examination scores should be submitted along with high school and all college transcripts. An autobiographical statement is required. An interview is encouraged. AP credits are accepted. Important factors in the admissions decision are advanced placement or honor courses, personality/intangible qualities, and evidence of special talent.

Procedure: Freshmen are admitted to all sessions. Entrance exams should be taken as early as possible. Applications should be filed by July 15 for fall entry, December 1 for spring entry, and May 1 for summer entry, along with an application fee of $35. Notification is sent on a rolling basis.

Transfer: 188 transfer students enrolled in 1995–96. 60 credits of 124 must be completed at General Studies.

Visiting: There are regularly scheduled orientations for prospective students, consisting of 4 evening open houses each year.

Financial Aid: 25% of freshmen and 30% of continuing students received need-based aid. The average freshman award was $2100. Of that total, scholarships or need-based grants averaged $4000 ($8500 maximum); the maximum for loans is $10,500 to $13,500. The average financial indebtedness of the 1994–95 graduate was $30,000. The FAFSA and the college's own financial statement are required. The application deadline for fall entry is May 30.

International Students: The school actively recruits international students. They must take the college's own test.

Computers: The mainframe is an IBM. All students may access the system. Students may access the system 1 hour.

Graduates: In 1994–95, 215 bachelor's degrees were awarded.

Admissions Contact: Dr. Barbara Tischler, Director of Admissions and Financial Aid. E-mail: blt1@columbia.edu. A campus video is available.

CONCORDIA COLLEGE
D-5

Bronxville, NY 10708 (914) 337-9300
(800) YES-COLLege; FAX: (914) 395-4500

Full-time: 221 men, 275 women	Faculty: 37; IIB, --$
Part-time: 33 men, 91 women	Ph.D.s: 60%
Graduate: none	Student/Faculty: 13 to 1
Year: semesters	Tuition: $10,696
Application Deadline: March 15	Room & Board: $5220
Freshman Class: 273 applied, 210 accepted, 179 enrolled	
SAT I Verbal/Math: 414/437	ACT: 20 LESS COMPETITIVE

Concordia College, founded in 1881, is a private institution affiliated with the Lutheran Church-Missouri Synod and offering undergraduate programs in business, education, music, social work, and professional training in ministry. In addition to regional accreditation, Concordia has baccalaureate program accreditation with CSWE. The library contains 45,000 volumes and 20,000 microform items, and subscribes to 450 periodicals. Computerized library sources and services include the card catalog, interlibrary loans, and database searching. Special learning facilities include a learning resource center and art gallery. The 33-acre campus is in a suburban area 17 miles north of New York City. Including residence halls, there are 21 buildings on campus.

Student Life: 69% of undergraduates are from New York. Students come from 16 states and 38 foreign countries. 65% are white; 17% foreign nationals; 10% African American. 40% are Protestant; 38% Catholic; 18% unknown. The average age of freshmen is 18.5; all undergraduates, 25. 34% do not continue beyond their first year; 44% remain to graduate.

Housing: 350 students can be accommodated in college housing. College-sponsored living facilities include single-sex dormitories. On-campus housing is guaranteed for all 4 years. 65% of students live on campus; of those, 65% remain on campus on weekends. Upperclassmen may keep cars on campus.

Activities: There are no fraternities or sororities. There are 20 groups on campus, including choir, chorus, drama, ethnic, honors, literary magazine, photography, professional, religious, social service, student government, and yearbook. Popular campus events include guest lectures, dances, and dramatic presentations.

Sports: There are 6 intercollegiate sports for men and 6 for women, and 10 intramural sports for men and 10 for women. Athletic and recreation facilities include an athletic center, a field house, indoor and outdoor tennis courts, squash/racquetball courts, a weight room, and 3 athletic fields.

Disabled Students: 50% of the campus is accessible to disabled students. The following facilities are available: wheelchair ramps, special parking, specially equipped rest rooms, lowered telephones, and elevators in the library, student center, and 1 academic building.

Services: In addition to many counseling and information services, tutoring is available in some subjects, including reading, writing, and mathematics.

Campus Safety and Security: Campus safety and security measures include escort service, informal discussions, emergency telephones, and lighted pathways/sidewalks.

Programs of Study: Concordia confers B.A., B.S., and B.M. degrees. Associate degrees are also awarded. Bachelor's degrees are awarded in BIOLOGICAL SCIENCE (biology/biological science), BUSINESS (business administration and management), COMMUNICATIONS AND THE ARTS (applied music, English, and music), COMPUTER AND PHYSICAL SCIENCE (mathematics), EDUCATION (business, early childhood, education, elementary, music, and secondary), ENGINEERING AND ENVIRONMENTAL DESIGN (environmental science), SOCIAL SCIENCE (behavioral science, history, interdisciplinary studies, international studies, Judaic studies, ministries, religious music, and social work). Education, business administration, and social work have the largest enrollments.

Required: To graduate, students must complete 122 semester hours with a minimum GPA of 2.0. General education requirements include 39 semester hours of liberal arts, 12 of integrated studies, and 18 of foundation courses in basic skills and values. Students are required to take 3 credits each of physical education and computers.

Special: A registered professional nurse program is offered in cooperation with Mount Vernon Hospital School of Nursing. Concordia also offers a dual degree program in physical therapy, cross-registration with a consortium of nearby colleges, internships, study abroad in England, an interdisciplinary studies degree, and credit for life experience. Accelerated degree programs are available in business administration and behavioral studies. There is a freshman honors program on campus, as well as 1 national honor society. All departments have honors programs.

Faculty/Classroom: 62% of faculty are male; 38%, female. All teach undergraduates. The average class size in an introductory lecture is 28; in a laboratory, 12; and in a regular course offering, 17.

Admissions: 77% of the 1995–96 applicants were accepted. The SAT I scores for the 1995–96 freshman class were as follows: Verbal—80% below 500, 15% between 500 and 599, and 5% between 600 and 700; Math—70% below 500, 25% between 500 and 599, and 5% between 600 and 700. The ACT scores were 50% below 21, 31% between 21 and 23, 5% between 24 and 26, 5% between 27 and 28, and 9% above 28. 17% of the current freshmen were in the top fifth of their class; 37% were in the top two fifths.

Requirements: The SAT I or ACT is required. Concordia requires applicants to be in the upper 50% of their class. Applicants should be graduates of an accredited secondary school or have a GED certificate. Concordia prefers completion of 16 academic units, including 4 of English, 2 of mathematics, 2 of history or social studies, 2 of science (at least 1 with laboratory), and 2 years of a foreign language. An interview is required, and those students applying to the music program must audition. AP and CLEP credits are accepted. Important factors in the admissions decision are advanced placement or honor courses, personality/intangible qualities, and leadership record.

Procedure: Freshmen are admitted fall and spring. There are early admissions and deferred admissions plans. Applications should be filed by March 15 for fall entry. Notification is sent on a rolling basis within 3 weeks of receipt of the completed application.

Transfer: 40 transfer students enrolled in 1995–96. A 2.5 GPA is recommended. Applicants must submit official transcripts from previous colleges attended. Students must complete the last 30 credits of 122 at Concordia.

Visiting: There are regularly scheduled orientations for prospective students. There are guides for informal visits and visitors may sit in on classes and stay overnight at the school. To schedule a visit, contact the Office of Admission at (914) 337–9300, ext. 2155.

Financial Aid: In 1995–96, 92% of all freshmen and 66% of continuing students received some form of financial aid. 79% of freshmen and 71% of continuing students received need-based aid. The average freshman award was $9278. Of that total, scholarships or need-based grants averaged $6438 ($10,500 maximum); loans averaged $1908 ($2625 maximum); and work contracts averaged $845 ($1800 maximum). 36% of undergraduate students work part-time. Average earnings from campus work for the school year are $1275. The average financial indebtedness of the 1994–95 graduate was $11,655. Concordia is a member of CSS. The application deadline for fall entry is April 1.

International Students: The school actively recruits these students. They must take the TOEFL and achieve a minimum score of 500, or the SAT I.

Computers: The college provides computer facilities for student use. There are 2 computer laboratories available with 33 computers.

Graduates: In 1994–95, 107 bachelor's degrees were awarded. The most popular majors among graduates were business administration (50%), elementary education (16%), and social work (6%). Within an average freshman class, 2% graduate in 3 years, 35% in 4 years, 41% in 5 years, and 45% in 6 years. Of the 1994 graduating class, 20% were enrolled in graduate school within 6 months of graduation and 70% had found employment.

Admissions Contact: Thomas Weede, Dean of Enrollment Management.

COOPER UNION FOR THE ADVANCEMENT OF SCIENCE AND ART
D-5

New York, NY 10003–7183

(212) 353–4120
FAX: (212) 353–4343

Full-time: 563 men, 329 women	Faculty: 56; IIB, + +$
Part-time: 18 men, 14 women	Ph.D.s: n/av
Graduate: 72 men, 8 women	Student/Faculty: 16 to 1
Year: semesters, summer session	Tuition: see profile
Application Deadline: see profile	Room & Board: $5150
Freshman Class: 2244 applied, 281 accepted, 193 enrolled	
SAT I: required	MOST COMPETITIVE

The Cooper Union for the Advancement of Science and Art, founded in 1859, is a privately endowed, coeducational institution. Students who are U.S. residents are admitted under full scholarship, which covers the tuition of $8300. There is an additional fee of $400. Cooper Union offers undergraduate degrees in architecture, art, and engineering and graduate degrees in engineering. There are 3 undergraduate schools and 1 graduate school. In addition to regional accreditation, Cooper Union has baccalaureate program accreditation with ABET, NAAB, and NASAD. The library contains 88,000 volumes and 300 audiovisual forms, and subscribes to 290 periodicals. Computerized library sources and services include the card catalog, interlibrary loans, and database searching. Special learning facilities include a learning resource center and an art gallery. The campus is in an urban area. Including residence halls, there are 5 buildings on campus.

Student Life: 70% of undergraduates are from New York. Students come from 39 states, 12 foreign countries, and Canada. 75% are from public schools; 25% from private. 55% are white; 27% Asian American; 11% Hispanic. The average age of freshmen is 18; all undergraduates, 20. 8% do not continue beyond their first year; 77% remain to graduate.

Housing: 183 students can be accommodated in college housing. College-sponsored living facilities include coed off-campus apartments. On-campus housing is available on a lottery system for upperclassmen. 80% of students commute. All students may keep cars on campus.

Activities: 20% of men belong to 2 national fraternities; 10% of women belong to 1 local sorority. There are 60 groups on campus, including chorale, computers, ethnic, honors, international, literary magazine, newspaper, political, professional, religious, social, social service, student government, and yearbook. Popular campus events include an end-of-the-year student art and architecture exhibit.

Sports: There are 5 intercollegiate sports for men and 2 for women, and 12 intramural sports for men and 12 for women. Athletic and recreation facilities include weight, martial arts, and fencing rooms, a swimming pool, and basketball courts.

Disabled Students: 60% of the campus is accessible to disabled students. The following facilities are available: wheelchair ramps, elevators, and specially equipped rest rooms.

Services: In addition to many counseling and information services, tutoring is available in some subjects, including mathematics, physics, speech, and writing.

Campus Safety and Security: Campus safety and security measures include pamphlets/posters/films, emergency telephones, lighted pathways/sidewalks, and community security and police.

Programs of Study: Cooper Union confers B.S., B.Arch., B.E., and B.F.A. degrees. Master's degrees are also awarded. Bachelor's degrees are awarded in COMMUNICATIONS AND THE ARTS (fine arts and graphic design), ENGINEERING AND ENVIRONMENTAL DESIGN (architecture, chemical engineering, civil engineering, electrical/electronics engineering, engineering, and mechanical engineering). Engineering is the strongest academically and has the largest enrollment.

Required: The 5-year architecture program requires 169 credits for graduation, including 30 in liberal arts and electives. Art students must complete 128 credits, including 38 in liberal arts and electives, with a minimum overall GPA of 2.0 to graduate. A higher GPA is expected in studio work. Engineering students are required to complete a minimum of 135 credits, including a computer literacy course and 24 credits in humanities and social sciences, with a minimum GPA of 2.0.

Special: Cross-registration with the New School for Social Research, internships, study abroad for art students in 8 countries, and some pass/fail options are available. Nondegree study is possible. An accelerated degree in engineering is also available. There are 4 national honor societies on campus. 1 department has an honors program.

Faculty/Classroom: 74% of faculty are male; 26%, female. All both teach and do research. No introductory courses are taught by graduate students. The average class size in an introductory lecture is 28; in a laboratory, 20; and in a regular course offering, 28.

Admissions: 13% of the 1995–96 applicants were accepted.

Requirements: The SAT I is required. Engineering applicants must take SAT II: Subject tests in mathematics I or II and physics or chemistry. Graduation from an approved secondary school is required. Applicants should have completed 16 to 18 high school academic credits, depending on their major. An essay is part of the application process, and art students must submit a portfolio. Art and architecture applicants must complete a project called the hometest. AP credits are accepted. Important factors in the admissions decision are evidence of special talent, advanced placement or honor courses, and leadership record.

Procedure: Freshmen are admitted in the fall. Entrance exams should be taken before February 1. There are early admissions and deferred admissions plans and an early decision plan in art and engineering. Early decision applications for art and engineering should be filed by December 1; regular applications, by January 1 for fall entry for architecture, January 10 for art, and February 1 for engineering. The application fee is $35. Notification of early decision is sent December 20 for engineering and February 1 for art; regular decision, early April. 40 early decision candidates were accepted for the 1995–96 class. A waiting list is an active part of the admissions procedure, with about 2% of all applicants on the list.

Transfer: 27 transfer students enrolled in 1995–96. Art and architecture transfer applicants must present a portfolio and a minimum of 24 credits in studio classes. Engineering transfer applicants must submit a transcript with grades of B or better in at least 24 credits of appropriate courses.

Visiting: There are regularly scheduled orientations for prospective students, consisting of open houses and portfolio review days. To schedule a visit, contact the Office of Admissions and Records.

Financial Aid: In 1995–96, 44% of all freshmen and 36% of continuing students received some form of financial and need-based aid, to help with living expenses and fees. The average freshman award was $3400. Of that total, scholarships or need-based grants averaged $2700 ($3500 maximum); loans averaged $2470 ($2625 maximum); and work contracts averaged $1000 ($2000 maximum). The average financial indebtedness of the 1994–95 graduate was $8184. Cooper Union is a member of CSS. The FAFSA is required. The application deadline for fall entry is May 1.

International Students: There are currently 84 international students enrolled. Those whose first language is not English must take the TOEFL and achieve a minimum score of 550. All freshman applicants must take the SAT I; art or architecture students must also take the hometest. Engineering students must take SAT II: Subject tests in mathematics I or II and physics or chemistry.

Computers: The college provides computer facilities for student use. The mainframe is a DEC VAX 11/780. A centralized computer center, located in the Engineering Building, contains a UNIX-based time-sharing network with Sun SPARC, DEC, and SGI workstations, and more than 45 PCs and 15 Apple Macintosh microcomputers, all available for student use. Students have access to E-mail and the World Wide Web via the Internet. All students may access the system whenever the Engineering Building is open. There are no time limits and no fees.

Graduates: In 1994–95, 202 bachelor's degrees were awarded. The most popular majors among graduates were fine arts (27%), chemical engineering (16%), and architecture (14%). Within an average freshman class, 50% graduate in 4 years, 20% in 5 years, and 4% in 6 years. 35 companies recruited on campus in 1994–95. Of the 1994 graduating class, 29% were enrolled in graduate school within 6 months of graduation and 25% had found employment.

Admissions Contact: Admissions Representative. E-mail: admissions@cooper.edu.

CORNELL UNIVERSITY

C-3

Ithaca, NY 14850

(607) 255-5241

Full-time: 7092 men, 6280 women	Faculty: 1532; I, +$
Part-time: none	Ph.D.s: 95%
Graduate: 3337 men, 2205 women	Student/Faculty: 9 to 1
Year: semesters, summer session	Tuition: $8556 to $20,066
Application Deadline: January 1	Room & Board: $6762
Freshman Class: 20,603 applied, 7050 accepted, 3204 enrolled	
SAT I or ACT: required	**MOST COMPETITIVE**

Cornell University was founded in 1865 as a land-grant institution. Privately supported undergraduate divisions include the College of Architecture, Art, and Planning; the College of Arts and Sciences; the College of Engineering; and the School of Hotel Administration. State-assisted undergraduate divisions include the College of Agriculture and Life Sciences, the College of Human Ecology, and the School of Industrial and Labor Relations. There are 7 undergraduate and 4 graduate schools. In addition to regional accreditation, Cornell has baccalaureate program accreditation with AACSB, ABET, ASLA, CSWE, and FIDER. The 17 libraries contain 5,835,235 volumes, 6,773,020 microform items, and 114,890 audiovisual forms, and subscribe to 61,705 periodicals. Computerized library sources and services include the card catalog, interlibrary loans, and database searching. Special learning facilities include a learning resource center, art gallery, planetarium, radio station, and bird sanctuary, 5 designated national resource centers, and 2 local optical observatories. The 745-acre campus is in a rural area 60 miles south of Syracuse. Including residence halls, there are 457 buildings on campus.

Student Life: 58% of undergraduates are from out-of-state, mostly the Middle Atlantic. Students come from 50 states, 123 foreign countries, and Canada. 67% are white; 17% Asian American. The average age of freshmen is 18; all undergraduates, 20. 5% do not continue beyond their first year; 88% remain to graduate.

Housing: 6620 students can be accommodated in college housing. College-sponsored living facilities include single-sex and coed dormitories, on-campus apartments, married-student housing, fraternity houses, and sorority houses. In addition there are language houses and special interest houses. On-campus housing is guaranteed for the freshman year only and is available on a lottery system for upperclassmen. 58% of students live on campus; of those, 90% remain on campus on weekends. All students may keep cars on campus.

Activities: 32% of men belong to 2 local and 43 national fraternities; 27% of women belong to 19 national sororities. There are 400 groups on campus, including art, band, cheerleading, choir, chorale, chorus, computers, dance, drama, drill team, drum and bugle corps, ethnic, film, gay, honors, international, literary magazine, marching band, musical theater, newspaper, orchestra, pep band, photography, political, professional, radio and TV, religious, social, social service, student government, symphony, and yearbook. Popular campus events include Festival of Black Gospel, Springfest, Third World Festival of the Arts, and College Bowl.

Sports: There are 18 intercollegiate sports for men and 16 for women, and 46 intramural sports for men and 45 for women. Athletic and recreation facilities include indoor and outdoor tracks, a 5000-seat indoor gymnasium, 3 swimming pools, a 25000-seat stadium, 16 intercollegiate fields, a bowling alley, intramural fields, a boat house, and indoor and outdoor tennis courts.

Disabled Students: 85% of the campus is accessible to disabled students. The following facilities are available: wheelchair ramps, elevators, special parking, specially equipped rest rooms, special class scheduling, lowered drinking fountains, lowered telephones, and alternative test arrangements.

Services: In addition to many counseling and information services, tutoring is available in most subjects. There are reader services for the blind, note takers, biology and mathematics student support centers, and writing workshops.

Campus Safety and Security: Campus safety and security measures include 24-hour foot and vehicle patrol, self-defense education, escort service, and shuttle buses. In addition, there are informal discussions, pamphlets/posters/films, emergency telephones, and lighted pathways/sidewalks.

Programs of Study: Cornell confers B.A., B.S., B.Arch., and B.F.A. degrees. Master's and doctoral degrees are also awarded. Bachelor's degrees are awarded in AGRICULTURE (agricultural economics, agriculture, animal science, international agriculture, natural resource management, plant science, and soil science), BIOLOGICAL SCIENCE (biology/biological science, botany, entomology, evolutionary biology, genetics, microbiology, neurosciences, and nutrition), BUSINESS (business administration and management, hotel/motel and restaurant management, labor studies, and operations research), COMMUNICATIONS AND THE ARTS (art history and appreciation, classics, communications, comparative literature, dance, design, dramatic arts, English, fine arts, French, German, Greek, Italian, languages, Latin, linguistics, music, photography, Russian, and Spanish), COMPUTER AND PHYSICAL SCIENCE (astronomy, atmospheric sciences and meteorology, chemistry, computer science, geology, mathematics, physics, and statistics), EDUCATION (agricultural), ENGINEERING AND ENVIRONMENTAL DESIGN (architecture, chemical engineering, city/community/regional planning, civil engineering, electrical/electronics engineering, engineering physics, environmental engineering technology, landscape architecture/design, materials science, and mechanical engineering), SOCIAL SCIENCE (African studies, American studies, anthropology, archeology, Asian/Oriental studies, classical/ancient civilization, economics, family/consumer studies, food production/management/services, food science, German area studies, history, human development, human services, Near Eastern studies, philosophy, political science/government, psychology, public affairs, religion, rural sociology, Russian and Slavic studies, social science, sociology, textiles and clothing, and women's studies). Hotel administration, industrial and labor relations, and biological sciences have the largest enrollments.

Required: Entering freshmen must meet basic swimming and water safety competency requirements. All undergraduates must take 2 semesters each of freshman writing seminar and physical education. Graduation requirements vary by program, including a minimum of 120 credits.

Special: Co-op programs are offered in the College of Engineering and the School of Industrial and Labor Relations. Cross-registration is available with Ithaca College. Public-policy internships are available in Washington, D.C., Albany, and New York City. Cornell also offers study abroad in more than 50 countries, B.A.-B.S. and B.A.-B.F.A. degrees, interdisciplinary/intercollegiate options, student-designed and dual majors, work-study programs, accelerated degree programs, pass/fail options, and limited nondegree study. There are 3 national honor societies on campus, including Phi Beta Kappa.

Faculty/Classroom: 81% of faculty are male; 19%, female. All teach and do research. Graduate students teach 1% of introductory courses. The average class size in an introductory lecture is 82; in a laboratory, 11; and in a regular course offering, 37.

Admissions: 34% of the 1995–96 applicants were accepted. The SAT I scores for the 1995–96 freshman class were as follows: Verbal—11% below 500, 36% between 500 and 599, 44% between 600 and 700, and 9% above 700; Math—2% below 500, 9% between 500 and 599, 37% between 600 and 700, and 52% above 700. 94% of the current freshmen were in the top fifth of their class; 99% were in the top two fifths. There were 60 National Merit finalists. 242 freshmen graduated first in their class.

Requirements: The SAT I or ACT is required. An essay is required as part of the application process. Other requirements vary by division or program, including specific SAT II: Subject tests and selection of courses within the minimum 16 secondary-school academic units needed. An interview and/or portfolio is required for specific majors. Applications are accepted on-line via ExPAN. AP credits are accepted. Important factors in the admissions decision are advanced placement or honor courses, evidence of special talent, and leadership record.

Procedure: Freshmen are admitted fall and spring. Entrance exams should be taken by December of the senior year. There are early decision, early admissions, and deferred admissions plans. Early decision applications should be filed by November 10; regular applications, by January 1 for fall entry and November 10 for spring entry, along with an application fee of $65. Notification of early decision is sent mid-December; regular decision, mid-April. 752 early decision candidates were accepted for the 1995–96 class. A waiting list is an active part of the admissions procedure.

Transfer: 470 transfer students enrolled in 1995–96. All applicants must submit high school and college transcripts, as well as scores from the SAT I or ACT if taken previously. Other admission requirements vary by program, including the number of credits that must be completed at Cornell.

Visiting: There are regularly scheduled orientations for prospective students, including campus tours and information sessions. There are guides for informal visits and visitors may sit in on classes and stay overnight at the school. To schedule a visit, contact the Red Carpet Society at (607) 255-3447.

Financial Aid: In 1995–96, 65% of all students received some form of financial aid and 50% of all students received need-based aid. The average freshman award was $17,400. Of that total, scholarships or need-based grants averaged $11,200 ($28,400 maximum); loans averaged $4900 ($5520 maximum); and work contracts averaged $1300 ($1600 maximum). 60% of undergraduate students work part-time. Average earnings from campus work for the school year are $1215. The average financial indebtedness of the 1994–95 graduate was $12,900. Cornell is a member of CSS. The college's own financial statement and the CSS Profile Application are required. The IRS form is required after enrollment. The application deadline for fall entry is February 15.

International Students: There are currently 2624 international students enrolled. The school actively recruits these students. They must take the TOEFL and achieve a minimum score of 550. The student must also take the SAT I or the ACT. Some divisions require SAT II:Subject tests.

Computers: The college provides computer facilities for student use. The mainframes are 2 IBM 3090/600s. Students have access to 7 campuswide computer centers and more than 20 departmental facilities with more than 700 microcomputers/terminals, as well as networks in the residence halls. All students may access the system. There are no time limits and no fees. It is recommended that students in engineering have personal computers.

Graduates: In 1994–95, 3392 bachelor's degrees were awarded. The most popular majors among graduates were biological sciences (10%), mechanical engineering (5%), and applied economics and business management (4%). Within an average freshman class, 1% graduate in 3 years, 79% in 4 years, 88% in 5 years, and 89% in 6 years. 400 to 500 companies recruited on campus in 1994–95.

Admissions Contact: Nancy Hargrave Meislahn, Director of Admissions. E-mail: admissions@cornell.edu or http://www.cornell.edu/u. A campus video is available.

D'YOUVILLE COLLEGE

Buffalo, NY 14201 A-3

(716) 881-7600
(800) 777-3921; FAX: (716) 881-7790

Full-time: 314 men, 880 women	Faculty: 81; IIB, -$
Part-time: 46 men, 193 women	Ph.D.s: 72%
Graduate: 76 men, 396 women	Student/Faculty: 15 to 1
Year: semesters, summer session	Tuition: $9420
Application Deadline: August	Room & Board: $4470
Freshman Class: 995 applied, 643 accepted, 198 enrolled	
SAT I Verbal/Math: 440/490	ACT: 21 COMPETITIVE

D'Youville College, founded in 1908, is a private, nonsectarian, co-educational liberal arts institution. In addition to regional accreditation, D'Youville has baccalaureate program accreditation with ADA, APTA, CAHEA, CSWE, and NLN. The library contains 114,411 volumes, 138,224 microform items, and 2071 audiovisual forms, and subscribes to 723 periodicals. Computerized library sources and services include the card catalog and database searching. Special learning facilities include a learning resource center. The 7-acre campus is in an urban area 1 mile north of Buffalo. Including residence halls, there are 8 buildings on campus.

Student Life: 74% of undergraduates are from New York. Students come from 17 states, 4 foreign countries, and Canada. 80% are from public schools; 20% from private. 71% are white; 16% foreign nationals. The average age of freshmen is 18. 23% do not continue beyond their first year; 43% remain to graduate.

Housing: 390 students can be accommodated in college housing. College-sponsored living facilities include coed dormitories. In addition there are honors floors. On-campus housing is guaranteed for all 4 years. 85% of students commute. All students may keep cars on campus.

Activities: There are no fraternities or sororities. There are 16 groups on campus, including computers, ethnic, honors, international, literary magazine, newspaper, professional, religious, social, social service, student government, and yearbook. Popular campus events include Moving Up Days, Sibling Weekend, Senior Week, Compete-A-Thon, and Family Weekend.

Sports: There is 1 intercollegiate sport for men and 2 for women, and 11 intramural sports for men and 9 for women. Athletic and recreation facilities include a 125-seat indoor gymnasium, a basketball court, a swimming pool, and a weight training room.

Disabled Students: The entire campus is accessible to disabled students. The following facilities are available: wheelchair ramps, elevators, special parking, specially equipped rest rooms, and lowered telephones.

Services: In addition to many counseling and information services, tutoring is available in some subjects, and is based on tutor accessibility. There is a reader service for the blind, and remedial math, reading, and writing.

Campus Safety and Security: Campus safety and security measures include 24-hour foot and vehicle patrol, self-defense education, escort service, and informal discussions. In addition, there are pamphlets/posters/films, emergency telephones, lighted pathways/sidewalks, a special focus program, a security committee, and a K-9 patrol.

Programs of Study: D'Youville confers B.A., B.S., B.S.N., and B.S.W. degrees. Master's degrees are also awarded. Bachelor's degrees are awarded in BIOLOGICAL SCIENCE (biology/biological science), BUSINESS (accounting, business administration and management, and marketing/retailing/merchandising), COMMUNICATIONS AND THE ARTS (English and literature), EDUCATION (business, education of the visually handicapped, elementary, secondary, and special), HEALTH PROFESSIONS (nursing, occupational therapy, physical therapy, physician's assistant, predentistry, and premedicine), SOCIAL SCIENCE (dietetics, history, liberal arts/general studies, philosophy, prelaw, social work, and sociology). Education and health professions are the strongest academically. Health professions, business, and nursing have the largest enrollments.

Required: All students must complete general program and core curriculum requirements including 5 courses in humanities, 2 each in English and natural sciences, and 1 each in philosophy or religion, history, sociology, psychology, economics or political science, mathematics, and computer science. A minimum of 120 to 129 credit hours, varying by major, with a minimum GPA of 2.0, is required in order to graduate.

Special: D'Youville has cross-registration with member colleges of the Western New York Consortium. Internships, work-study programs, dual majors, and pass/fail options are available. Accelerated 5-year B.S.-M.S. programs in physical therapy, occupational therapy, and dietetics are offered. For freshman with undecided majors, the Career Discovery Program offers special courses, internships, and faculty advisers. There is a freshman honors program on campus, as well as 1 national honor society. 6 departments have honors programs.

Faculty/Classroom: 43% of faculty are male; 56%, female. All teach undergraduates. No introductory courses are taught by graduate students. The average class size in an introductory lecture is 30; in a laboratory, 12; and in a regular course offering, 23.

Admissions: 65% of the 1995–96 applicants were accepted. The SAT I scores for the 1995–96 freshman class were as follows: Verbal—74% below 500, 23% between 500 and 599, and 3% between 600 and 700; Math—50% below 500, 35% between 500 and 599, 14% between 600 and 700, and 1% above 700. The ACT scores were 32% below 21, 35% between 21 and 23, 26% between 24 and 26, and 7% between 27 and 28. 43% of the current freshmen were in the top fifth of their class; 77% were in the top two fifths. There were 3 National Merit semifinalists.

Requirements: The SAT I or ACT is required. D'Youville requires applicants to be in the upper 50% of their class. A minimum GPA of 2.5 is required. Applicants should have completed 16 Carnegie units, including 4 years of high school English, 3 of social studies, and 1 each of mathematics and science; some majors require additional years of mathematics and science. The GED is accepted. An interview is recommended. AP and CLEP credits are accepted. Important factors in the admissions decision are advanced placement or honor courses, evidence of special talent, and leadership record.

Procedure: Freshmen are admitted fall and spring. There is a deferred admissions plan. Application deadlines are August for fall entry and January for spring entry. Application fee is $20. Notification is sent on a rolling basis.

Transfer: 243 transfer students enrolled in a recent year. Transfer applicants need a minimum GPA of 2.0, or 2.5 for some programs. An interview is recommended. There are very limited openings for transfers seeking part-time studies. 30 credits of 120 to 129 must be completed at D'Youville.

Visiting: There are regularly scheduled orientations for prospective students. There are guides for informal visits and visitors may sit in on classes. To schedule a visit, contact the Admissions Office.

Financial Aid: In 1995–96, 93% of all freshmen and 88% of continuing students received some form of financial aid. 85% of freshmen and 80% of continuing students received need-based aid. The average freshman award was $5844. Of that total, scholarships or need-based grants averaged $5000 ($10,000 maximum); loans averaged $3400 ($5125 maximum); and work contracts averaged $800 (maximum). 26% of undergraduate students work part-time. Average earnings from campus work for the school year are $800. The average financial indebtedness of the 1994–95 graduate was $14,000. D'Youville is a member of CSS. The FAFSA and the New York State TAP financial statement are required. The application deadline for fall entry is April 15.

International Students: 323 international students were enrolled in a recent year. The school actively recruits these students. They must take the TOEFL and achieve a minimum score of 500.

Computers: The college provides computer facilities for student use. There are 3 computer laboratories as well as computers located in the residence hall. Apple Macintosh and DOS computers are nonnetworked. All students may access the system. There are no time limits and no fees.

Graduates: In a recent year, 217 bachelor's degrees were awarded. The most popular majors among graduates were nursing (25%), education (16%), and physical therapy (15%). Within an average freshman class, 1% graduate in 3 years, 24% in 4 years, 16% in 5 years, and 2% in 6 years. 92 companies recruited on campus in a recent year. Of a recent year's graduating class, 10% were enrolled in graduate school within 6 months of graduation and 96% had found employment.

Admissions Contact: Ronald H. Dannecker, Director of Admissions and Financial Aid.

DAEMEN COLLEGE
A-3

Amherst, NY 14226

(716) 839–8225; (800) 462–7652

Full-time: 462 men, 858 women	Faculty: 70
Part-time: 119 men, 455 women	Ph.D.s: 81%
Graduate: 13 men, 31 women	Student/Faculty: 19 to 1
Year: semesters, summer session	Tuition: $9720
Application Deadline: see profile	Room & Board: $4900
Freshman Class: n/av	
SAT I or ACT: required	COMPETITIVE

Daemen College, founded in 1947, is a private, coeducational institution offering programs in the liberal and fine arts, business, education, health sciences, and professional training. There is 1 graduate school. In addition to regional accreditation, Daemen has baccalaureate program accreditation with APTA, CAHEA, CSWE, and NLN. The library contains 135,000 volumes, 2000 microform items, and 4500 audiovisual forms, and subscribes to 850 periodicals. Computerized library sources and services include interlibrary loans and database searching. Special learning facilities include a learning resource center and art gallery. The 37-acre campus is in a suburban area 15 miles north of Buffalo. Including residence halls, there are 35 buildings on campus.

Student Life: 89% of undergraduates are from New York. Students come from 17 states, 7 foreign countries, and Canada. 90% are white. The average age of freshmen is 18; all undergraduates, 20.

Housing: 609 students can be accommodated in college housing. College-sponsored living facilities include single-sex dormitories and on-campus apartments. In addition, there is a quiet dormitory. On-campus housing is guaranteed for all 4 years. 60% of students commute. Alcohol is not permitted. All students may keep cars on campus.

Activities: There is 1 local and 1 national fraternity and 4 local sororities. There are 26 groups on campus, including art, cheerleading, computers, drama, ethnic, honors, international, literary magazine, newspaper, political, professional, religious, social, social service, student government, and yearbook.

Sports: There is 1 intercollegiate sport for men and 1 for women, and 4 intramural sports for men and 4 for women. Athletic and recreation facilities include a gymnasium, weight and exercise rooms, and saunas.

Disabled Students: The entire campus is accessible to disabled students. The following facilities are available: wheelchair ramps, elevators, special parking, specially equipped rest rooms, lowered drinking fountains, and lowered telephones.

Services: In addition to many counseling and information services, tutoring is available in every subject. There is remedial math, reading, and writing.

Campus Safety and Security: Campus safety and security measures include 24-hour foot and vehicle patrol, escort service, informal discussions, and pamphlets/posters/films. In addition, there are emergency telephones, lighted pathways/sidewalks, and video monitors.

Programs of Study: Daemen confers B.A., B.S., and B.F.A. degrees. Master's degrees are also awarded. Bachelor's degrees are awarded in BIOLOGICAL SCIENCE (biology/biological science), BUSINESS (accounting, business administration and management, and transportation management), COMMUNICATIONS AND THE ARTS (design, English, fine arts, French, graphic design, languages, and Spanish), COMPUTER AND PHYSICAL SCIENCE (chemistry, mathematics, and natural sciences), EDUCATION (art, business, elementary, English, mathematics, science, secondary, social studies, and special), HEALTH PROFESSIONS (medical laboratory technology, nursing, physical therapy, and physician's assistant), SOCIAL SCIENCE (history, humanities, psychology, religion, and social work). Physical therapy, medical technology, natural science, and physician assistant are the strongest academically. Business, physical therapy, education, and physician assistant have the largest enrollments.

Required: To graduate, students must complete 122 to 144 hours with a minimum GPA of 2.0. The core curriculum includes 6 credit hours each in literature, philosophy/religion, and history/government; 3 each in composition, fine or performing arts, mathematics, science, economics/sociology, psychology, and Liberal Arts Colloquium; and 6 additional hours outside the major for most programs.

Special: Daemen offers cooperative programs in all majors, internships, cross-registration within the Western New York Consortium of Colleges and Universities, work-study programs, and study abroad in Spain, France, Canada, England, Mexico, and Poland. There are 2 national honor societies on campus, including Phi Beta Kappa.

Faculty/Classroom: 56% of faculty are male; 44%, female. No introductory courses are taught by graduate students. The average class size in an introductory lecture is 50; in a laboratory, 16; and in a regular course offering, 23.

Requirements: The SAT I or ACT is required. Applicants must be graduates of an accredited secondary school or have the GED equivalent. Some departments have further admissions requirements, including a portfolio review for art majors, 3-year sequences of mathematics and science for all natural science programs, and 2 essays, 3 letters of recommendation, and a supplemental application for the physician assistant program. AP and CLEP credits are accepted. Important factors in the admissions decision are advanced placement or honor courses, leadership record, and evidence of special talent.

Procedure: Freshmen are admitted to all sessions. Entrance exams should be taken by the summer following the senior year. There are early decision, early admissions, and deferred admissions plans. Early decision applications should be filed by August; applications for the physician assistant or physical therapy programs, by January 15, along with an application fee of $25. Notification of early decision is sent August; regular decision, on a rolling basis. A waiting list is an active part of the admissions procedure.

Transfer: 258 transfer students enrolled in a recent year. Applicants must have a minimum GPA of 2.0 for most programs. 30 credits of 122 to 144 must be completed at Daemen.

Visiting: There are regularly scheduled orientations for prospective students, including a campus tour and interviews. There are guides for informal visits and visitors may sit in on classes and stay overnight at the school. To schedule a visit, contact the Admissions Office.

Financial Aid: In 1995–96, 95% of all students received some form of financial aid. 91% of freshmen and 89% of continuing students received need-based aid. The average freshman award was $8910. Of that total, scholarships or need-based grants averaged $4885 ($9240 maximum); loans averaged $2625 (maximum); and work contracts averaged $1400 (maximum). 25% of undergraduate students work part-time. Average earnings from campus work for the school year are $1400. The FAFSA and the college's own financial statement are required. The application deadline for fall entry is March 15.

International Students: The school actively recruits these students. They must take the TOEFL and achieve a minimum score of 550.

Computers: The college provides computer facilities for student use. About 80 microcomputers are available in the Academic Resources Center and departmental computer laboratories. All students may access the system. There are no time limits and no fees.

Graduates: In 1994–95, 255 bachelor's degrees were awarded. The most popular majors among graduates were physical therapy (36%), nursing (22%), and education (9%). 22 companies recruited on campus in 1994–95.

Admissions Contact: Maria P. Dillard, Director of Enrollment Management. A campus video is available.

DOMINICAN COLLEGE
D-5

Orangeburg, NY 10962

(914) 359-7800, ext. 271
FAX: (914) 359-2313

Full-time: 225 men, 551 women	Faculty: 40; IIB, -$
Part-time: 212 men, 771 women	Ph.D.s: 55%
Graduate: none	Student/Faculty: 19 to 1
Year: semesters, summer session	Tuition: $9230
Application Deadline: open	Room & Board: $5740
Freshman Class: 375 applied, 358 accepted, 104 enrolled	
SAT I Verbal/Math: 400/420	**LESS COMPETITIVE**

Dominican College, founded in 1952, is an independent, coeducational Catholic institution offering undergraduate programs in business, biology, education, liberal arts, nursing, premedicine, occupational therapy, and social sciences. In addition to regional accreditation, Dominican has baccalaureate program accreditation with CSWE and NLN. The library contains 99,735 volumes, 12,750 microform items, and 1032 audiovisual forms, and subscribes to 637 periodicals. Computerized library sources and services include interlibrary loans. Special learning facilities include a learning resource center. The 14-acre campus is in a suburban area 17 miles north of New York City. Including residence halls, there are 7 buildings on campus.

Student Life: 70% of undergraduates are from New York. Students come from 10 states and 5 foreign countries. 70% are from public schools; 30% from private. 79% are white; 11% African American. 80% are Catholic; 10% Jewish; 10% Protestant. The average age of freshmen is 19; all undergraduates, 23. 30% do not continue beyond their first year; 45% remain to graduate.

Housing: 250 students can be accommodated in college housing. College-sponsored living facilities include coed dormitories. On-campus housing is guaranteed for all 4 years. Priority is given to out-of-town students. 92% of students commute. Alcohol is not permitted. All students may keep cars on campus.

Activities: There are no fraternities or sororities. There are 17 groups on campus, including cheerleading, chorus, computers, drama, honors, international, literary magazine, musical theater, newspaper, professional, religious, social service, student government, and yearbook. Popular campus events include Family Day, craft fair, Dominican Cup Tournament (soccer), Springfest, Alumni Day, Founders Day, Nursing Pinning Ceremony, Career Day, Players Production, and Senior Night.

Sports: Athletic and recreation facilities include a baseball field and a basketball court.

Disabled Students: All of the campus is accessible to disabled students. The following facilities are available: wheelchair ramps, special parking, specially equipped rest rooms, lowered drinking fountains, and lowered telephones.

Services: In addition to many counseling and information services, tutoring is available in some subjects, including English and mathematics. There is remedial math, reading, and writing. There is a writing center.

Campus Safety and Security: Campus safety and security measures include shuttle buses, informal discussions, emergency telephones, and lighted pathways/sidewalks. In addition, there are night security guards in dormitories.

Programs of Study: Dominican confers B.A., B.S., B.S.Ed., and B.S.N. degrees. Associate and master's degrees are also awarded. Bachelor's degrees are awarded in BIOLOGICAL SCIENCE (biology/biological science), BUSINESS (accounting, business administration and management, business economics, international business management, and marketing/retailing/merchandising), COMMUNICATIONS AND THE ARTS (English, languages, and Spanish), COMPUTER AND PHYSICAL SCIENCE (actuarial science and mathematics), EDUCATION (elementary, science, secondary, and special), ENGINEERING AND ENVIRONMENTAL DESIGN (preengineering), HEALTH PROFESSIONS (nursing, occupational therapy, and premedicine), SOCIAL SCIENCE (American studies, history, humanities, prelaw, psychology, public administration, social science, and social work). Business and nursing are the strongest academically. Business, nursing, and occupational therapy have the largest enrollments.

Required: Computer courses are required for business majors. In order to graduate, all students must complete 120 semester hours, including a general education curriculum of 36 to 39 credits. Nursing and occupational therapy majors must maintain a minimum GPA of 2.5, while all other majors require at least a 2.0.

Special: Accelerated degree programs are available in business majors, as well as co-op programs in business administration, arts and sciences, nursing, social sciences, education, and social work. Individualized internships in all fields, work-study programs, B.A.-B.S. degrees, dual majors, and a 3-2 engineering degree with Manhattan College are also offered. Dual teacher certification in elementary and special education is available. Credit for life experience is granted

through submission of a portfolio. Weekend College, offered on a trimester basis, is designed to meet the needs of working adults. There is a freshman honors program on campus, as well as 3 national honor societies. 3 departments have honors programs.

Faculty/Classroom: 40% of faculty are male; 60%, female. All teach undergraduates. The average class size in a regular course offering is 16.

Admissions: 95% of the 1995-96 applicants were accepted. The SAT I scores for the 1995-96 freshman class were as follows: Verbal—67% below 500, 30% between 500 and 599, and 2% between 600 and 700. 15% of the current freshmen were in the top fifth of their class; 30% were in the top two fifths. 2 freshmen graduated first in their class.

Requirements: The SAT I or ACT is required. Dominican requires applicants to be in the upper 80% of their class. A minimum grade average of 70% is required. Applicants should be graduates of an accredited secondary school or possess a GED equivalent. An interview and an essay are recommended. AP and CLEP credits are accepted. Important factors in the admissions decision are advanced placement or honor courses, recommendations by school officials, and extracurricular activities record.

Procedure: Freshmen are admitted to all sessions. Entrance exams should be taken by November of the senior year. There are early decision and deferred admissions plans. Application deadlines are open. Application fee is $25. Notification is sent on a rolling basis.

Transfer: Transfer applicants must submit a transcript from their previous school. A minimum GPA of 2.0 is required. An interview should be scheduled. Those applying to the upper-division occupational therapy program should have completed an associate degree. 30 credits of 120 must be completed at Dominican.

Visiting: There are regularly scheduled orientations for prospective students. There are guides for informal visits and visitors may sit in on classes. To schedule a visit, contact Colleen M. O'Connor, Director of Admissions.

Financial Aid: In 1995-96, 88% of all freshmen and 79% of continuing students received some form of financial aid. 76% of freshmen and 68% of continuing students received need-based aid. The average freshman award was $9850. Of that total, scholarships or need-based grants averaged $3500 ($8940 maximum); loans averaged $2365 ($2830 maximum); and work contracts averaged $1000 ($1200 maximum). 36% of undergraduate students work part-time. Average earnings from campus work for the school year are $1350. The average financial indebtedness of the 1994-95 graduate was $13,650. Dominican is a member of CSS. The FAF and the college's own financial statement are required.

International Students: 20 international students were enrolled in a recent year. They must take the TOEFL and achieve a minimum score of 500. The student must also take the SAT I.

Computers: The college provides computer facilities for student use. The mainframe is a DEC MicroVAX 3100-40. There are 4 PC computer laboratories on campus. Two are networked to the mainframe. One laboratory is located in the residence hall. All students may access the system. There are no time limits.

Admissions Contact: Colleen M. O'Connor, Director of Admissions. A campus video is available.

DOWLING COLLEGE
E-5

Oakdale, NY 11769-1999

(516) 244-3030
(800) DOWLING; FAX: (516) 563-3827

Full-time: 379 men, 545 women	Faculty: 106
Part-time: 1129 men, 1589 women	Ph.D.s: 92%
Graduate: 831 men, 1382 women	Student/Faculty: 9 to 1
Year: 4-1-4, summer session	Tuition: $10,860
Application Deadline: open	Room: $3150
Freshman Class: 1296 applied, 1194 accepted, 376 enrolled	
SAT I Verbal/Math: 380/430	ACT: 18 **LESS COMPETITIVE**

Dowling College, founded in 1955, is a small, independent, coeducational institution offering programs in the arts and sciences, aviation and transportation, business, and education. There are 4 undergraduate and 2 graduate schools. The library contains 170,517 volumes, 381,706 microform items, and 108 audiovisual forms, and subscribes to 1242 periodicals. Computerized library sources and services include the card catalog, interlibrary loans, and database searching. Special learning facilities include a learning resource center, art gallery, and radio station. The 156-acre campus is in a suburban area 50 miles east of New York City. Including residence halls, there are 10 buildings on campus.

Student Life: 95% of undergraduates are from New York. Students come from 12 states, 31 foreign countries, and Canada. 89% are from public schools; 11% from private. 91% are white. The average age of freshmen is 20; all undergraduates, 26. 17% do not continue beyond their first year; 39% remain to graduate.

Housing: 438 students can be accommodated in college housing. College-sponsored living facilities include coed on-campus apartments. Priority for on-campus housing is given to out-of-town students. 94% of students commute. Alcohol is not permitted. All students may keep cars on campus.

Activities: There are no fraternities or sororities. There are 28 groups on campus, including chorus, drama, ethnic, honors, international, literary magazine, newspaper, orchestra, professional, radio and TV, religious, student government, and yearbook. Popular campus events include Freshman Mixer, Holiday Party, Senior Picnic, and Spring Cotillion.

Sports: Athletic and recreation facilities include a basketball court, a weight room, tennis courts, and a fitness center.

Disabled Students: 90% of the campus is accessible to disabled students. The following facilities are available: wheelchair ramps, elevators, special parking, specially equipped rest rooms, special class scheduling, lowered drinking fountains, and lowered telephones.

Services: In addition to many counseling and information services, tutoring is available in most subjects. There is remedial math, reading, and writing.

Campus Safety and Security: Campus safety and security measures include 24-hour foot and vehicle patrol, escort service, shuttle buses, and informal discussions. In addition, there are pamphlets/posters/films, emergency telephones, and lighted pathways/sidewalks.

Programs of Study: Dowling confers B.A., B.S., and B.B.A. degrees. Master's degrees are also awarded. Bachelor's degrees are awarded in BIOLOGICAL SCIENCE (biology/biological science and marine biology), BUSINESS (accounting, banking and finance, business administration and management, international business management, marketing/retailing/merchandising, tourism, and transportation management), COMMUNICATIONS AND THE ARTS (English, fine arts, languages, music, romance languages, speech/debate/rhetoric, and visual and performing arts), COMPUTER AND PHYSICAL SCIENCE (applied mathematics, computer programming, computer science, information sciences and systems, mathematics, and natural sciences), EDUCATION (elementary, secondary, and special), ENGINEERING AND ENVIRONMENTAL DESIGN (aeronautical science and aeronautical technology), SOCIAL SCIENCE (anthropology, economics, history, humanities, political science/government, psychology, social science, and sociology). Business, education, and computer sciences have the largest enrollments.

Required: To graduate, students must complete 122 credits with a minimum GPA of 2.0. The required 36-credit general education core includes a senior seminar.

Special: Dowling offers a B.S. in professional and liberal studies, internships, independent study, and nondegree study. There are cooperative programs in several majors, including aeronautics and airway science majors with the FAA. There is a freshman honors program on campus, as well as 10 national honor societies. 3 departments have honors programs.

Faculty/Classroom: 70% of faculty are male; 30%, female. All teach undergraduates. No introductory courses are taught by graduate students. The average class size in an introductory lecture is 20; in a laboratory, 15; and in a regular course offering, 17.

Admissions: 92% of the 1995–96 applicants were accepted. The SAT I scores for the 1995–96 freshman class were as follows: Verbal—90% below 500 and 10% between 500 and 599; Math—74% below 500, 23% between 500 and 599, and 2% between 600 and 700.

Requirements: The SAT I or ACT is required; the SAT I is recommended. Applicants should be graduates of an accredited secondary school and have completed at least 16 Carnegie units, including 4 in English. An interview is strongly recommended. Applicants can apply on-line at http://www.dowling.edu. AP and CLEP credits are accepted. Important factors in the admissions decision are advanced placement or honor courses, evidence of special talent, and recommendations by school officials.

Procedure: Freshmen are admitted to all sessions. Entrance exams should be taken by January of the senior year. There are early admissions and deferred admissions plans. Application deadlines are open. Application fee is $25. Notification is sent on a rolling basis.

Transfer: 518 transfer students enrolled in 1995–96. Applicants must submit official transcripts from all colleges attended. 30 credits of 122 must be completed at Dowling.

Visiting: There are regularly scheduled orientations for prospective students, including a campus tour and meetings with enrollment services members. There are guides for informal visits and visitors may sit in on classes. To schedule a visit, contact the Enrollment Services Office at (516) 244–3030, (516) 369–5464, or (800) DOWLING.

Financial Aid: In 1995–96, 63% of all freshmen and 76% of continuing students received some form of financial aid. 68% of freshmen and 70% of continuing students received need-based aid. The average freshman award was $5093. Of that total, scholarships or need-based grants averaged $1480 ($10,170 maximum); loans averaged $2500 ($6625 maximum); and work contracts averaged $1113 ($3000 maximum). 100% of undergraduate students work part-time. Average earnings from campus work for the school year are $3000. The average financial indebtedness of the 1994–95 graduate was $5875. Dowling is a member of CSS. The FAFSA and the college's own financial statement are required. The application deadline for fall entry is May 1.

International Students: There are currently 79 international students enrolled. The school actively recruits these students. They must take the TOEFL. The student must also take the SAT I or the ACT.

Computers: The college provides computer facilities for student use. The mainframe is an IBM AIX. There are Apple II, Macintosh, and IBM-compatible microcomputers in the academic computing center and library. All students may access the system 7 A.M. to 10:45 P.M., Monday through Thursday and 7 A.M. to 5 P.M., Friday through Sunday. There are no time limits and no fees.

Graduates: In 1994–95, 813 bachelor's degrees were awarded. The most popular majors among graduates were business (33%), liberal arts (28%), and education (12%). Within an average freshman class, 23% graduate in 4 years, 28% in 5 years, and 31% in 6 years. 115 companies recruited on campus in 1994–95.

Admissions Contact: Kate Rowe, Director of Admissions. E-mail: rowek@dowling.edu. A campus video is available.

EASTMAN SCHOOL OF MUSIC

B-3

Rochester, NY 14604   (716) 274–1060

Full-time: 227 men, 266 women	**Faculty:** 89
Part-time: 1 man, 2 women	**Ph.D.s:** 80%
Graduate: 175 men, 170 women	**Student/Faculty:** 6 to 1
Year: semesters	**Tuition:** $17,373
Application Deadline: January 15	**Room & Board:** $6730
Freshman Class: 730 applied, 304 accepted, 142 enrolled	
SAT I or ACT: not required	**SPECIAL**

Eastman School of Music, founded in 1921, is a private, professional, coeducational school of music within the University of Rochester. In addition to regional accreditation, Eastman has baccalaureate program accreditation with NASM. The library contains 500,000 volumes, 3800 microform items, and 60,000 audiovisual forms, and subscribes to 600 periodicals. Computerized library resources and services include the card catalog, interlibrary loans, and database searching. Special learning facilities include a learning resource center, art gallery, recording studios, a music library, a theater, and 3 recital halls. The 3-acre campus is in an urban area in downtown Rochester. Including residence halls, there are 5 buildings on campus.

Student Life: 73% of undergraduates are from out-of-state, mostly the Midwest. Students come from 47 states, 22 foreign countries, and Canada. 90% are from public schools; 10% from private. 70% are white; 15% foreign nationals. The average age of freshmen is 18; all undergraduates, 20. 12% do not continue beyond their first year; 80% remain to graduate.

Housing: 360 students can be accommodated in college housing. College-sponsored living facilities include single-sex and coed dormitories. On-campus housing is guaranteed for all 4 years. 77% of students live on campus. Alcohol is not permitted. All students may keep cars on campus.

Activities: 10% of men and about 6% of women belong to 2 national fraternities; 5% of women belong to 1 national sorority. There are many groups on campus, including band, chorale, chorus, computers, gay, international, jazz band, literary magazine, musical theater, newspaper, opera, orchestra, religious, student government, symphony, and yearbook. Popular campus events include Christmas Sing, Spring Formal, and Halloween party.

Sports: There is no sports program at Eastman. All athletic facilities of the University of Rochester, as well as a nearby YMCA, are available to students.

Disabled Students: The entire campus is accessible to disabled students. The following facilities are available: wheelchair ramps, elevators, special parking, specially equipped rest rooms, lowered drinking fountains, and lowered telephones.

Services: In addition to many counseling and information services, tutoring is available in every subject. There is a reader service for the blind and remedial writing.

Campus Safety and Security: Campus safety and security measures include 24-hour foot and vehicle patrol, self-defense education, escort service, and shuttle buses. In addition, there are informal discussions, pamphlets/posters/films, emergency telephones, and lighted pathways/sidewalks.

Programs of Study: Eastman confers B.M. and B.A. degrees. Master's and doctoral degrees are also awarded. Bachelor's degrees are awarded in COMMUNICATIONS AND THE ARTS (jazz, music, music performance, and music theory and composition) and EDUCATION (music). Performance has the largest enrollment.

Required: All students must complete core requirements in a major instrument or voice, music theory, music history, and Western cultural tradition, as well as English and humanities electives. A total of 122 to 136 credit hours, varying by program, with a minimum GPA of 2.0, is required in order to graduate.

Special: The school and the University of Rochester cooperatively offer the B.A. degree with a music concentration. All the facilities of the university are open to Eastman students. Cross-registration is also available with colleges in the Rochester Consortium. Dual majors are available in composition, music education, theory, performance, and jazz studies.

Faculty/Classroom: 60% of faculty are male; 40%, female. All both teach and do research. Graduate students teach 10% of introductory courses. The average class size in an introductory lecture is 30 and in a regular course offering, 15.

Admissions: 42% of the 1995–96 applicants were accepted.

Requirements: Applicants should be graduates of an accredited secondary school with 16 academic credits, including 4 years of English. The GED is accepted. An audition and an interview are required. Important factors in the admissions decision are evidence of special talent, recommendations by alumni, and personality/ intangible qualities.

Procedure: Freshmen are admitted fall and spring. Applications should be filed by January 15 for fall entry and December 1 for spring entry, along with an application fee of $50. Notification is sent on a rolling basis. A waiting list is an active part of the admissions procedure, with about 4% of all applicants on the list.

Transfer: 23 transfer students enrolled in 1995–96. Transfer requirements include satisfactory academic standing at the previous institution, a GPA of at least 2.0, a successful audition, and an interview.

Visiting: To schedule a visit, contact the Admissions Office.

Financial Aid: In 1995–96, 87% of all freshmen and 85% of continuing students received some form of financial aid. 66% of freshmen and 64% of continuing students received need-based aid. The average freshman award was $11,850. Of that total, scholarships or need-based grants averaged $7475 ($14,000 maximum); loans averaged $2625 ($4000 maximum); external grants and awards averaged $1000 ($6000 maximum); and work contracts averaged $750 ($1500 maximum). 65% of undergraduate students work part-time. Average earnings from campus work for the school year was $800. The average financial indebtedness of the 1994–95 graduate was $10,000. Eastman is a member of CSS. The FAFSA and the college's own financial statement are required. The application deadline for fall entry is February 1.

International Students: There are currently 103 international students enrolled. The school actively recruits these students. They must take the TOEFL or the college's own test and achieve a minimum score on the TOEFL of 500.

Computers: The college provides computer facilities for student use. The mainframes are a DEC VAX 8650, a DEC VAX 750, and an IBM 4381/P2. IBM and Macintosh microcomputer systems are located in residence halls, the library, and the main building. There is also a computer music center with Musical Instrument Digital Interface. All students may access the system 2 hours during peak periods. There are no fees.

Graduates: In 1994–95, 110 bachelor's degrees were awarded. The most popular majors among graduates were performance (81%), music education (12%), and composition (5%). Within an average freshman class, 71% graduate in 4 years and 9% in 5 years. 15 companies recruited on campus in 1994–95.

Admissions Contact: Charles Krusenstjerna, Director of Admissions..

ELMIRA COLLEGE
Elmira, NY 14901

C-4

(607) 735-1724
(800) 935-6472; FAX: (607) 735-1745

Full-time: 409 men, 695 women	Faculty: 66; IIB, -$
Part-time: none	Ph.D.s: 98%
Graduate: none	Student/Faculty: 17 to 1
Year: modified (4–4–1), summer session	Tuition: $16,700
	Room & Board: $5380
Application Deadline: see profile	
Freshman Class: 1394 applied, 1054 accepted, 296 enrolled	
SAT I Verbal/Math: 480/520	ACT: 23	COMPETITIVE

Elmira College, founded in 1855, is a private, coeducational liberal arts institution offering general and preprofessional programs. In addition to regional accreditation, Elmira has baccalaureate program accreditation with NLN. The library contains 377,000 volumes, 770,000 microform items, and 6059 audiovisual forms, and subscribes to 851 periodicals. Computerized library sources and services include the card catalog, interlibrary loans, and database searching. Special learning facilities include a learning resource center, art gallery, radio station, speech and hearing clinic, and Mark Twain's study. The 42-acre campus is in a suburban area 90 miles southwest of Syracuse. Including residence halls, there are 25 buildings on campus.

Student Life: 57% of undergraduates are from New York. Students come from 28 states, 23 foreign countries, and Canada. 65% are from public schools; 35% from private. 84% are white. The average age of freshmen is 18; all undergraduates, 21. 12% do not continue beyond their first year; 65% remain to graduate.

Housing: 1100 students can be accommodated in college housing. College-sponsored living facilities include single-sex and coed dormitories and on-campus apartments. In addition there are honors floors. On-campus housing is guaranteed for all 4 years. 86% of students live on campus; of those, 90% remain on campus on weekends. All students may keep cars on campus.

Activities: There are no fraternities or sororities. There are 55 groups on campus, including art, band, cheerleading, chorale, chorus, dance, drama, film, honors, international, literary magazine, musical theater, newspaper, orchestra, pep band, political, professional, radio, religious, social, social service, student government, and yearbook. Popular campus events include Mountain Day, Holiday Banquet, Holiday Ball, Midnight Breakfast, and Spring Weekend.

Sports: There are 6 intercollegiate sports for men and 6 for women, and 21 intramural sports for men and 21 for women. Athletic and recreation facilities include 2500-seat and 950-seat gymnasiums, indoor tennis facilities, a 3500-seat hockey arena, racquetball courts, a weight room, a dance studio, and a swimming pool.

Disabled Students: 25% of the campus is accessible to disabled students. The following facilities are available: wheelchair ramps, elevators, special parking, specially equipped rest rooms, and special class scheduling.

Services: In addition to many counseling and information services, tutoring is available in most subjects. Tutoring in mathematics and freshman English is available in each freshman dormitory.

Campus Safety and Security: Campus safety and security measures include 24-hour foot and vehicle patrol, escort service, informal discussions, and pamphlets/posters/films. In addition, there are lighted pathways/sidewalks.

Programs of Study: Elmira confers B.A. and B.S. degrees. Bachelor's degrees are awarded in BIOLOGICAL SCIENCE (biochemistry and biology/biological science), BUSINESS (accounting, business administration and management, business economics, international business management, and marketing/retailing/merchandising), COMMUNICATIONS AND THE ARTS (classics, dramatic arts, English literature, fine arts, French, music, and Spanish), COMPUTER AND PHYSICAL SCIENCE (chemistry and mathematics), EDUCATION (art, elementary, foreign languages, science, and secondary), ENGINEERING AND ENVIRONMENTAL DESIGN (environmental science), HEALTH PROFESSIONS (medical laboratory technology, nursing, predentistry, and premedicine), SOCIAL SCIENCE (American studies, anthropology, criminal justice, history, human services, international studies, philosophy, political science/government, prelaw, psychology, and sociology). History, theater, and premedicine are the strongest academically. Psychology, management, and education have the largest enrollments.

Required: All students must complete general degree requirements, including communication skills, writing courses, mathematical competency, and computer literacy; a core curriculum; distribution requirements in culture and civilization, contemporary social institutions, the scientific method, the creative process, and physical education; and a field experience program. A total of 120 credit hours with a minimum GPA of 2.0 overall and in the major is required to graduate.

Special: The required field experience program provides a career-related internship as well as community service. A junior year abroad program, a Washington semester, an accelerated degree program, a general studies degree, student-designed majors, and pass/fail options are available. A 3–2 chemical engineering degree is offered with Clarkson University. B.A.-B.S. degrees are offered in biochemistry, biology, chemistry, economics, education, environmental studies, history, mathematics, political science, and psychology. Elmira is a member of the Spring Term Consortium enabling students to take 6-week courses at participating institutions. There are 7 national honor societies on campus, including Phi Beta Kappa.

Faculty/Classroom: 64% of faculty are male; 36%, female. All both teach and do research. The average class size in an introductory lecture is 35; in a laboratory, 10; and in a regular course offering, 20.

Admissions: 76% of the 1995–96 applicants were accepted. The SAT I scores for the 1995–96 freshman class were as follows: Verbal—62% below 500, 30% between 500 and 599, 7% between 600 and 700, and 1% above 700; Math—38% below 500, 37% between 500 and 599, 22% between 600 and 700, and 3% above 700. The ACT scores were 30% below 21, 22% between 21 and 23, 29% between 24 and 26, 12% between 27 and 28, and 7% above 28. 48% of the current freshmen were in the top fifth of their class; 77% were in the top two fifths. There were 4 National Merit semifinalists. 36 freshmen graduated first in their class.

Requirements: The SAT I or ACT is required. In addition, applicants should have completed 4 years of high school English, 3 of mathematics, and 2 of science, or GED equivalent. An essay is part of the application process. An interview is strongly recommended. AP and CLEP credits are accepted. Important factors in the admissions decision are advanced placement or honor courses, extracurricular activities record, and recommendations by school officials.

Procedure: Freshmen are admitted fall and winter. Entrance exams should be taken by January of the entry year. There are early decision, early admissions, and deferred admissions plans. Early decision applications should be filed by January 15; other application deadlines are open. Application fee is $40. Notification of early decision is sent January 31; regular decision, on a rolling basis. 44 early decision candidates were accepted for the 1995–96 class. A waiting list is an active part of the admissions procedure, with about 11% of all applicants on the list.

Transfer: 74 transfer students enrolled in 1995–96. Applicants should have a minimum GPA of 2.0. An interview is strongly recommended. 30 credits of 120 must be completed at Elmira.

Visiting: There are regularly scheduled orientations for prospective students, consisting of an open house format and overview, a tour, lunch, a student panel, a faculty panel, general admissions and scholarship information, and an optional interview. Individual visits or interviews and tours are available year-round, including Saturday mornings. There are guides for informal visits and visitors may sit in on classes and stay overnight at the school. To schedule a visit, contact the Office of Admissions.

Financial Aid: In 1995–96, 80% of all students received some form of financial aid. 70% of all students received need-based aid. The average freshman award was $14,350. Of that total, scholarships or need-based grants averaged $8450 ($16,300 maximum); loans averaged $3950 ($4125 maximum); federal and state grants averaged $1200 ($6240 maximum); and work contracts averaged $750 ($1500 maximum). 45% of undergraduate students work part-time. Average earnings from campus work for the school year are $900. The average financial indebtedness of the 1994–95 graduate was $13,749. Elmira is a member of CSS. The FAFSA and the CSS Profile Application financial statement are required. The priority date for financial application for fall entry is March 1.

International Students: There are currently 78 international students enrolled. The school actively recruits these students. They must take the TOEFL and achieve a minimum score of 500.

Computers: The college provides computer facilities for student use. The mainframe is a DEC VAX 4000–600 minicomputer. 20 terminals provide access to the mainframe. About 50 microcomputers are also available at various locations on the campus. All students may access the system weekdays 15 hours per day, and weekends 8 to 10 hours per day. There are no time limits and no fees.

Graduates: In 1994–95, 270 bachelor's degrees were awarded. The most popular majors among graduates were psychology (15%), business (14%), and elementary education (13%). Within an average freshman class, 1% graduate in 3 years, 60% in 4 years, 65% in 5 years, and 65% in 6 years. 40 companies recruited on campus in 1994–95. Of the 1994 graduating class, 40% were enrolled in graduate school within 6 months of graduation and 58% had found employment.

Admissions Contact: William S. Neal, Dean of Admissions. A campus video is available.

EUGENE LANG COLLEGE OF THE NEW SCHOOL FOR SOCIAL RESEARCH D-3

New York, NY 10011 (212) 229-5665; **FAX:** (212) 229-5355

Full-time: 95 men, 225 women	Faculty: 15
Part-time: 13 men, 17 women	Ph.D.s: 100%
Graduate: none	Student/Faculty: 21 to 1
Year: semesters	Tuition: $16,119
Application Deadline: February 1	Room & Board: n/app

Freshman Class: 306 applied, 255 accepted, 80 enrolled
SAT I Verbal/Math: 530/520   **COMPETITIVE +**

Eugene Lang College, established in 1978, is the liberal arts undergraduate division of the New School for Social Research. There are 4 undergraduate and 6 graduate schools. The 4 libraries contain 142,000 volumes and 65,000 microform items, and subscribe to 750 periodicals. Computerized library sources and services include the card catalog, interlibrary loans, and database searching. Special learning facilities include a learning resource center, art gallery, and an environmental simulation center for urban planning and research. The 5-acre campus is in an urban area in the heart of Greenwich Village. Including residence halls, there are 14 buildings on campus.

Student Life: 58% of undergraduates are from out-of-state, mostly the Northeast. Students come from 26 states, 12 foreign countries, and Canada. 60% are from public schools; 30% from private. 44%

are white. The average age of freshmen is 19; all undergraduates, 20. 15% do not continue beyond their first year; 85% remain to graduate.

Housing: 500 students can be accommodated in college housing. College-sponsored living facilities include coed dormitories and off-campus apartments. On-campus housing is guaranteed for the freshman year only, is available on a first-come, first-served basis, and is available on a lottery system for upperclassmen. Priority is given to out-of-town students. 50% of students live on campus; of those, 95% remain on campus on weekends. Alcohol is not permitted. All students may keep cars on campus.

Activities: There are no fraternities or sororities. There are 10 groups on campus, including chorus, dance, drama, ethnic, gay, international, jazz band, literary magazine, newspaper, photography, political, social, social service, and student government. Popular campus events include Lang in the City, a cultural program that makes dance, opera, Broadway, theater, and other events available to students for $5 or less.

Sports: The intramural program is offered in conjunction with Cooper Union. A nearby gymnasium is rented or various city parks are used.

Disabled Students: All of the campus is accessible to disabled students. The following facilities are available: elevators, specially equipped rest rooms, and lowered telephones.

Services: In addition to many counseling and information services, tutoring is available in most subjects. There is also a writing center.

Campus Safety and Security: Campus safety and security measures include informal discussions, pamphlets/posters/films, and and 24-hour dormitory security.

Programs of Study: Eugene Lang College confers the B.A. degree. Master's and doctoral degrees are also awarded. Bachelor's degrees are awarded in COMMUNICATIONS AND THE ARTS (creative writing, dramatic arts, and English), EDUCATION (education), SOCIAL SCIENCE (crosscultural studies, economics, history, political science/government, prelaw, psychology, social science, sociology, urban studies, and women's studies). Creative writing, history, urban studies, and education are the strongest academically. Writing and drama have the largest enrollments.

Required: To graduate, students must complete 120 credit hours, with a GPA of 2.0 and a minimum of 36 hours in 1 of 5 areas of concentration: writing, literature, and the arts; urban studies; social and historical inquiry; cultural studies; and mind, nature, and value. Also required are 88 credit hours in Lang College courses and 4 credits of senior work. Required courses include a first-year writing seminar and a freshman workshop program. A senior project must be completed.

Special: Lang College offers a concentration rather than a traditional major; there is no core curriculum and students are instructed in small seminars. Students may cross-register with other New School divisions and with Mannes School of Music, Parsons School of Design, Cooper Union, and Bank Street College. A large variety of internships for credit, study abroad, a B.A./B.F.A. degree with Parsons School of Design, and the Mannes College of Music's Jazz and Contemporary Music Program, student-designed majors, and nondegree study are available.

Faculty/Classroom: 50% of faculty are male; 50%, female. All teach undergraduates. The average class size in a laboratory is 15 and in a regular course offering, 15.

Admissions: 83% of the 1995–96 applicants were accepted. 22% of the current freshmen were in the top fifth of their class; 70% were in the top two fifths.

Requirements: The SAT I or ACT is required, or 4 SAT II: Subject tests may be substituted for either test. Applicants must be enrolled in a strong college preparatory program. The GED is accepted. An essay and an interview are required. Art students must present a portfolio and complete a home exam and jazz students are required to audition. AP credits are accepted. Important factors in the admissions decision are advanced placement or honor courses, personality/intangible qualities, and recommendations by school officials.

Procedure: Freshmen are admitted fall and spring. Entrance exams should be taken in May of the junior year or October of the senior year. There are early decision, early admissions, and deferred admissions plans. Early decision applications should be filed by November 15; regular applications, by February 1 for fall entry and November 15 for spring entry, along with an application fee of $30. Notification of early decision is sent December 15; regular decision, April 1. 15 early decision candidates were accepted for the 1995–96 class. A waiting list is an active part of the admissions procedure.

Transfer: 60 transfer students enrolled in a recent year. Applicants must have a minimum college GPA of 2.5 and must submit their high school transcript, their ACT or SAT I scores (if taken in the last 5 years), and 2 recommendations. An interview is required. Grades of C or better transfer for credit. 60 credits of 120 must be completed at Eugene Lang College.

Visiting: There are regularly scheduled orientations for prospective students, including a campus tour, visits to classes, and panel discussions. There are guides for informal visits and visitors may sit in on classes. To schedule a visit, contact the Admissions Office.

Financial Aid: In 1995–96, 77% of all freshmen and 40% of continuing students received some form of financial aid. 77% of freshmen and 40% of continuing students received need-based aid. The average freshman award was $12,226. Of that total, scholarships or need-based grants averaged $7749; loans averaged $7500; and work contracts averaged $1531. 40% of undergraduate students work part-time. Average earnings from campus work for the school year are $1531. The average financial indebtedness of the 1994–95 graduate was $13,000. The FAFSA, the college's own financial statement, and the CSS Profile Application are required. The application deadline for fall entry is March 1.

International Students: In a recent year, 20 international students were enrolled. The school actively recruits these students. They must take the TOEFL and achieve a minimum score of 600. The student must also take the SAT I or the ACT.

Computers: The college provides computer facilities for student use. The mainframe is a Hewlett Packard. IBM and Apple microcomputers are available for student use in an academic computing center. Students can arrange for access for statistical course work and dissertation research. There are no time limits and no fees.

Admissions Contact: Jennifer Gill Fondiller, Director of Admissions. E-mail: lang@newschool.edu.

FASHION INSTITUTE OF TECHNOLOGY/ STATE UNIVERSITY OF NEW YORK
D-5

New York, NY 10001–5992	(212) 760–7675; (800) Go-To-FIT
Full-time: 974 men, 4271 women	Faculty: 159; III, + +$
Part-time: 1591 men, 5684 women	Ph.D.s: n/av
Graduate: 7 men, 52 women	Student/Faculty: 33 to 1
Year: 4-1-4, summer session	Tuition: $2995 ($6610)
Application Deadline: January 15	Room & Board: $5174
Freshman Class: 5052 applied, 2425 accepted, 1732 enrolled	
SAT I or ACT: not required	**VERY COMPETITIVE**

The Fashion Institute of Technology, founded in 1944 as part of the State University of New York, is an art and design, business, and technology college that prepares students for careers in fashion and related design professions and industries. There is one graduate school. In addition to regional accreditation, FIT has baccalaureate program accreditation with FIDER and NASAD. The library contains 122,780 volumes, 2037 microform items, and 12,040 audiovisual forms, and subscribes to 850 periodicals. Special learning facilities include an art gallery, radio station, a design laboratory, a lighting laboratory, a quick response center, a computer-aided design and communications facility, and the Annette Green Fragrance Foundation Studio Collections of the Museum at F.I.T. The 5-acre campus is in an urban area in Manhattan. Including residence halls, there are 8 buildings on campus.

Student Life: 81% of undergraduates are from New York. Students come from 50 states, 65 foreign countries, and Canada. 75% are from public schools; 25% from private. 48% are white; 24% Asian American; 14% Hispanic; 12% African American. The average age of freshmen is 19; all undergraduates, 20.

Housing: 1200 students can be accommodated in college housing. College-sponsored living facilities include single-sex and coed dormitories and on-campus apartments. On-campus housing is available on a lottery system for upperclassmen. Priority is given to out-of-town students. 88% of students commute. Alcohol is not permitted.

Activities: There are no fraternities or sororities. There are more than 60 groups on campus, including art, cheerleading, chess, dance, drama, ethnic, gay, literary magazine, musical theater, newspaper, photography, political, professional, radio and TV, religious, social, social service, student government, and yearbook. Popular campus events include fashion shows, craft center events, a carnival, and Monday night movies.

Sports: There are 4 intercollegiate sports for men and 4 for women, and 4 intramural sports for men and 4 for women. Athletic and recreation facilities include 2 gymnasiums, a dance studio, and a weight room.

Disabled Students: 95% of the campus is accessible to disabled students. The following facilities are available: wheelchair ramps, elevators, special parking, specially equipped rest rooms, lowered drinking fountains, lowered telephones, and services/facilities for hearing impaired, and library tapes.

Services: In addition to many counseling and information services, tutoring is available in every subject. There is remedial math, reading, and writing. The school has a special program for the learning disabled.

Campus Safety and Security: Campus safety and security measures include 24-hour foot and vehicle patrol, self-defense education, informal discussions, and emergency telephones. There are lighted pathways/sidewalks.

Programs of Study: FIT confers the B.F.A. and B.S. degree. Associate and master's degrees are also awarded. Bachelor's degrees are awarded in BUSINESS (apparel and accessories marketing, business administration and management, fashion merchandising, and marketing/retailing/merchandising), COMMUNICATIONS AND THE ARTS (advertising, communications, design, fiber/textiles/ weaving, fine arts, graphic design, historic preservation, illustration, photography, and toy design), ENGINEERING AND ENVIRONMENTAL DESIGN (interior design, manufacturing technology, and textile technology), SOCIAL SCIENCE (fashion design and technology and textiles and clothing). Advertising and communications, interior design, and advertising design are the strongest academically. Fashion buying and merchandising, and fashion design have the largest enrollments.

Required: To graduate, students must complete the credit and course requirements for their majors with a 2.0 GPA. Students may qualify for a degree in two ways: by earning 60 credits, with half in the major while in residence at the upper-division level; or by earning 30 credits at the upper-division level, in addition to an F.I.T. associate degree. There is a 2-credit physical education requirement.

Special: Internships are offered, and students may study abroad in England, France, Canada, Spain, and Italy. Nondegree study is available. 1 department has an honors program.

Faculty/Classroom: 51% of faculty are male; 49%, female. All teach undergraduates. No introductory courses are taught by graduate students. The average class size in a regular course offering is 25.

Admissions: 48% of the 1995–96 applicants were accepted. 9% of a recent freshmen class were in the top fifth of their class; 70% were in the top two fifths.

Requirements: FIT requires applicants to be in the upper 50% of their class with a 2.5 GPA. Applicants must be high school graduates, or have a GED certificate. An essay and, when appropriate, a portfolio are required. AP and CLEP credits are accepted. Important factors in the admissions decision are evidence of special talent, leadership record, and personality/intangible qualities.

Procedure: Freshmen are admitted fall and spring. There is an early decision plan. Applications should be filed by January 15 for fall entry and October 15 for spring entry, along with an application fee of $20. Notification is sent beginning March 15. A waiting list is an active part of the admissions procedure, with about 5% of all applicants on the list.

Transfer: Applicants must have a GPA of 2.0 and at least 30 college credits. An interview is required for art and design applicants, as well as a portfolio when appropriate.

Visiting: There are regularly scheduled orientations for prospective students, including a presentation and group information session with a counselor. To schedule a visit, contact the Admissions Office.

Financial Aid: In a recent year, 54% of all freshmen and 52% of continuing students received some form of financial aid. 52% of freshmen and 51% of continuing students received need-based aid. The average freshman award was $3904. Of that total, scholarships or need-based grants averaged $3181 ($6400 maximum); loans averaged $2164 ($5125 maximum); and work contracts averaged $1060 ($1400 maximum). 18% of undergraduate students work part-time. Average earnings from campus work for the school year are $1331. The average financial indebtedness of a recent graduate was $2259. FIT is a member of CSS. The FAF is required. The application deadline for fall entry is March 15.

International Students: There were 252 international students enrolled in a recent year. They must score 550 on the TOEFL.

Computers: The college provides computer facilities for student use. The mainframe is a DEC VAX 11/785. There are also 120 Epson, Zenith, ITT, Apple, and IBM PCs available in various academic computer laboratories. Those students enrolled in the computer course may access the system. There are no fees.

Graduates: In a recent year, 640 bachelor's degrees were awarded. 90 companies recruited on campus in 1994–95.

Admissions Contact: James C. Pidgeon, Director of Admissions.

FIVE TOWNS COLLEGE
Dix Hills, NY 11746

E-5

(516) 424-7000, ext. 110
FAX: (516) 424-7006

Full-time: 451 men, 163 women	Faculty: 29
Part-time: 32 men, 12 women	Ph.D.s: 38%
Graduate: none	Student/Faculty: 21 to 1
Year: semesters, summer session	Tuition: $8400
Application Deadline: open	Room & Board: $4800
Freshman Class: 383 applied, 354 accepted, 250 enrolled	
SAT I Verbal/Math: 450/440	SPECIAL

Five Towns College, founded in 1972, is a private coeducational institution offering undergraduate programs in music, business, and liberal arts. The library contains 26,686 volumes, 41 microform items, and 5404 audiovisual forms, and subscribes to 380 periodicals. Computerized library sources and services include interlibrary loans and database searching. Special learning facilities include a learning resource center, 48- and 24-track recording studios, a midi studio, and a video/TV studio. The 34-acre campus is in a suburban area 18 miles east of New York City. There is 1 building on campus.

Student Life: 94% of undergraduates are from New York. Students come from 6 states and 5 foreign countries. 88% are from public schools; 12% from private. 62% are white; 23% African American; 11% Hispanic. The average age of freshmen is 19; all undergraduates, 21. 37% do not continue beyond their first year; 45% remain to graduate.

Housing: 100 students can be accommodated in college housing. College-sponsored living facilities include coed off-campus apartments. On-campus housing is guaranteed for all 4 years. 91% of students commute. Alcohol is not permitted. All students may keep cars on campus.

Activities: There are no fraternities or sororities. There are numerous groups and organizations on campus, including art, band, barbershop, booster, choir, chorale, chorus, concert, dance, drama, gospel, honors, international, jazz band, live audio, musical theater, newspaper, photography, professional, radio and TV, social, student government, and yearbook. Popular campus events include the Cultural Hour, the Annual Picnic, and the Annual Ski Trip.

Sports: Athletic and recreation facilities include a gymnasium with basketball and volleyball courts and an outdoor baseball/football field.

Disabled Students: 20% of the campus is accessible to disabled students. The following facilities are available: wheelchair ramps, special parking, special class scheduling, lowered drinking fountains, and lowered telephones.

Services: In addition to many counseling and information services, tutoring is available in most subjects. There is also remedial math, reading, and writing.

Campus Safety and Security: Campus safety and security measures include 24-hour foot and vehicle patrol, shuttle buses, informal discussions, and pamphlets/posters/films. In addition, there are lighted pathways/sidewalks.

Programs of Study: Five Towns College confers B.Mus. and B.P.S. degrees. Associate degrees are also awarded. Bachelor's degrees are awarded in COMMUNICATIONS AND THE ARTS (audio technology, jazz, music business management, music performance, and music theory and composition), EDUCATION (music). Music education is the strongest academically. Audio recording technology has the largest enrollment.

Required: To graduate, all students must complete 128 credits for a B.Mus. degree or 120 credits for a B.P.S. degree. Students must maintain at least a C average in their major concentration and have a minimum GPA of 2.0 to graduate. Distribution requirements include 45 credits in applied music or business, 33 in liberal arts, 12 in music history, 24 in the concentration, and either 14 or 6 elective credits. The core curriculum consists of English Composition 101 and 102, Speech 101, 3 credits each of either psychology or sociology, and various upper-division liberal arts and social science courses. All music students must pass a jury examination.

Special: Cross-registration is available with schools in the Long Island Regional Advisory Council on Higher Education. Co-op programs in audio recording technology, music business, video arts, and broadcasting, and internships are possible. Work-study programs are offered on campus. Students can have dual majors in music, audio recording technology, business, and music business. There is 1 national honor society on campus.

Faculty/Classroom: 62% of faculty are male; 38%, female. All both teach and do research. The average class size in an introductory lecture is 25; in a laboratory, 15; and in a regular course offering, 25.

Admissions: 92% of the 1995–96 applicants were accepted. The SAT I scores for the 1995–96 freshman class were as follows: Verbal—74% below 500, 21% between 500 and 599, and 5% between 600 and 700; Math—76% below 500, 19% between 500 and 599,

and 5% between 600 and 700. 10% of the current freshmen were in the top fifth of their class; 28% were in the top two fifths.

Requirements: The SAT I is recommended. A minimum GPA of 2.5 is required. A minimum high school average of 75 is required. A GED with a minimum score of 250 is accepted. An interview is required for all students, and music students are required to audition. AP and CLEP credits are accepted. Important factors in the admissions decision are advanced placement or honor courses, evidence of special talent, and personality/intangible qualities.

Procedure: Freshmen are admitted to all sessions. Entrance exams should be taken prior to admission. There are early admissions and deferred admissions plans. Application deadlines are open. Application fee is $25. Notification is sent on a rolling basis. A waiting list is an active part of the admissions procedure, with about 5% of all applicants on the list.

Transfer: 97 transfer students enrolled in 1995–96. Students must be in good academic standing at their former school. 45 credits of 128 must be completed at Five Towns College.

Visiting: There are regularly scheduled orientations for prospective students, including a campus tour, academic counseling, and financial aid counseling. There are guides for informal visits and visitors may sit in on classes. To schedule a visit, contact the Admissions Office.

Financial Aid: In a recent year, 77% of all freshmen and 80% of continuing students received some form of financial aid. 75% of all students received need-based aid. The average freshman award was $4900. Of that total, scholarships or need-based grants averaged $1820 ($6500 maximum); loans averaged $2467 ($2625 maximum); and work contracts averaged $600 ($3000 maximum). 53% of undergraduate students work part-time. Average earnings from campus work for the school year are $1000. The average financial indebtedness of the recent graduate was $4000. The FAFSA and the college's own financial statement are required.

International Students: There are currently 12 international students enrolled. The school actively recruits these students. They must take the TOEFL and achieve a minimum score of 500. The student must also take the college's own entrance exam.

Computers: The college provides computer facilities for student use. The mainframe is an IBM AS/400. There are 25 terminals available in a computer laboratory. All students may access the system during school hours. There are no time limits and no fees.

Graduates: In 1994–95, 29 bachelor's degrees were awarded. The most popular majors among graduates were music education (35%), audio recording (30%), and music performance (23%).

Admissions Contact: Jennifer Roemer, Director of Admissions.

FORDHAM UNIVERSITY SYSTEM

The Fordham University system, established in 1841, is a private system in New York City in the Jesuit tradition. It is governed by a board of trustees, whose chief administrator is the president. The primary goal of the system is to educate talented men and women in the liberal arts and basic sciences. The main priorities are excellence in undergraduate and selected graduate/professional programs, and commitment to teaching, research, and service. The total enrollment of all 3 campuses was about 4600, with more than 500 faculty members. There are 69 baccalaureate, 71 master's, and 25 doctoral programs offered through Fordham University. Profiles of the 4-year campuses are included in this chapter.

FORDHAM UNIVERSITY/COLLEGE AT LINCOLN CENTER
(See Fordham University/Fordham College at Lincoln Center)

FORDHAM UNIVERSITY/COLLEGE OF BUSINESS ADMINISTRATION

D-5

Bronx, NY 10458

(718) 817-4000

Full-time: 1596 men, 1669 women	Faculty: 351; I, av$
Part-time: 221 men, 257 women	Ph.D.s: 97%
Graduate: 603 men, 555 women	Student/Faculty: 9 to 1
Year: semesters, summer session	Tuition: $15,050
Application Deadline: February 1	Room & Board: $7000
Freshman Class: 836 applied, 582 accepted, 206 enrolled	
SAT I Verbal/Math: 511/550	VERY COMPETITIVE

The College of Business Administration, founded in 1926, is a coeducational undergraduate school of business that maintains its independent status within Fordham University, a private institution founded in 1841 in the Jesuit tradition. There are 3 undergraduate and 2 graduate schools. In addition to regional accreditation, CBA has baccalaureate program accreditation with AACSB. The 2 libraries contain 1,592,621 volumes, 1,895,489 microform items, and 409 audiovisual forms, and subscribe to 10,553 periodicals. Computerized library sources and services include the card catalog, interlibrary loans, and database searching. Special learning facilities include a radio station. The 86-acre campus is in an urban area in the Bronx, adjacent to the Bronx Zoo and New York Botanical Garden. Including residence halls, there are 31 buildings on campus.

Student Life: 67% of undergraduates are from New York. Students come from 43 states, 48 foreign countries, and Canada. 36% are from public schools; 64% from private. 71% are white; 15% Hispanic. 85% are Catholic; 14% Protestant. The average age of freshmen is 18; all undergraduates, 20. 7% do not continue beyond their first year; 77% remain to graduate.

Housing: 2508 students can be accommodated in college housing. College-sponsored living facilities include coed dormitories, on-campus apartments, and off-campus apartments. In addition, there is a residential college. On-campus housing is guaranteed for all 4 years. 70% of students live on campus; of those, 90% remain on campus on weekends. Upperclassmen may keep cars on campus.

Activities: There are no fraternities or sororities. There are 130 groups on campus, including art, band, cheerleading, choir, chorus, computers, dance, drama, ethnic, film, honors, international, literary magazine, marching band, musical theater, newspaper, pep band, photography, political, professional, radio and TV, religious, social, social service, student government, and yearbook. Popular campus events include Spring Weekend, Christmas Formal, Spring Semiformal, and Senior Week.

Sports: There are 11 intercollegiate sports for men and 10 for women, and 11 intramural sports for men and 10 for women. Athletic and recreation facilities include a 6000-seat football stadium, an Olympic-size pool with a separate diving area, an indoor track, a 3200-seat gymnasium, and tennis, squash, and racquetball courts.

Disabled Students: 80% of the campus is accessible to disabled students. The following facilities are available: wheelchair ramps, elevators, special parking, specially equipped rest rooms, and lowered drinking fountains.

Services: In addition to many counseling and information services, tutoring is available in most subjects.

Campus Safety and Security: Campus safety and security measures include 24-hour foot and vehicle patrol, escort service, shuttle buses, and informal discussions. In addition, there are pamphlets/posters/films, emergency telephones, and lighted pathways/sidewalks.

Programs of Study: CBA confers B.A. and B.S. degrees. Master's and doctoral degrees are also awarded. Bachelor's degrees are awarded in BUSINESS (accounting, banking and finance, business economics, international business management, management science, and marketing/retailing/merchandising), COMPUTER AND PHYSICAL SCIENCE (information sciences and systems). Accounting, finance, and information systems are the strongest academically and have the largest enrollments.

Required: All students must complete a core curriculum of liberal arts courses at Fordham College on Rose Hill campus. About half the program is in liberal arts; business requirements and concentration with electives constitute the remainder of the 124 credit hours needed to graduate. A minimum GPA of 2.0 is required.

Special: Career-oriented internships are offered by the college during the junior or senior year with New York City companies and institutions. Study abroad, a Washington semester, student-designed majors, and pass/fail options are available. An evening program leading to the undergraduate degree is also offered. There is a freshman honors program on campus, as well as 3 national honor societies, including Phi Beta Kappa.

Faculty/Classroom: All teach undergraduates. The average class size in an introductory lecture is 28 and in a regular course offering, 24.

Admissions: 70% of the 1995–96 applicants were accepted. The SAT I scores for the 1995–96 freshman class were as follows: Verbal—58% below 500, 32% between 500 and 599, 9% between 600 and 700, and 1% above 700; Math—17% below 500, 52% between 500 and 599, 26% between 600 and 700, and 5% above 700. 57% of the current freshmen were in the top fifth of their class; 84% were in the top two fifths.

Requirements: The SAT I or ACT is required. Applicants should be graduates of an accredited secondary school or have the GED equivalent, with 4 years of English and 3 each of mathematics, science, history, social studies, and foreign language. An essay is part of the application process. An interview is recommended. AP and CLEP credits are accepted. Important factors in the admissions decision are advanced placement or honor courses, recommendations by school officials, and extracurricular activities record.

Procedure: Freshmen are admitted fall and spring. Entrance exams should be taken by November of the senior year. There are early decision, early admissions, and deferred admissions plans. Early decision applications should be filed by November 1; regular applications, by February 1 for fall entry and December 1 for spring entry, along with an application fee of $50. Notification of early decision is

sent December 15; regular decision, March 1. 4 early decision candidates were accepted for the 1995–96 class. A waiting list is an active part of the admissions procedure.

Transfer: 38 transfer students enrolled in 1995–96. A minimum 3.0 GPA is recommended. Transfer applicants under age 21 should submit SAT I or ACT scores. An interview is recommended. 64 credits of 124 must be completed at CBA.

Visiting: There are regularly scheduled orientations for prospective students. There are guides for informal visits and visitors may sit in on classes and stay overnight at the school. To schedule a visit, contact Joseph Giglio, Assistant Director of Admissions.

Financial Aid: In a recent year, 90% of all freshmen and 88% of continuing students received some form of financial aid. 90% of freshmen and 83% of continuing students received need-based aid. The average freshman award was $9500. Of that total, scholarships or need-based grants averaged $6600 ($11,000 maximum); loans averaged $700 ($2200 maximum); and work contracts averaged $700 ($1600 maximum). 95% of undergraduate students work part-time. Average earnings from campus work for the school year are $1600. The average financial indebtedness of a recent year's graduate was $8170. CBA is a member of CSS. The FAFSA, the college's own financial statement, and the CSS Profile Application are required. The application deadline for fall entry is February 1.

International Students: The school actively recruits these students. They must take the TOEFL or the college's own test and achieve a minimum score on the TOEFL of 550. The student must also take the SAT I or the ACT.

Computers: The college provides computer facilities for student use. The mainframe is a DEC VAX system. All students may access the system. There are no time limits and no fees.

Graduates: Within an average freshman class, 77% graduate in 4 years, 82% in 5 years, and 87% in 6 years. 500 companies recruited on campus in a recent year.

Admissions Contact: John W. Buckley, Director of Admissions.

FORDHAM UNIVERSITY/FORDHAM COLLEGE

(See Fordham University/Fordham College at Rose Hill)

FORDHAM UNIVERSITY/FORDHAM COLLEGE AT LINCOLN CENTER   D-5

(Formerly Fordham University/College at Lincoln Center)
New York, NY 10023   (718) 817-4000

Full-time: 369 men, 740 women	Faculty: 92; I, av$
Part-time: 271 men, 673 women	Ph.D.s: 95%
Graduate: 2719 men, 4242 women	Student/Faculty: 12 to 1
Year: semesters	Tuition: $12,900
Application Deadline: February 1	Room & Board: $7900
Freshman Class: 1126 applied, 723 accepted, 240 enrolled	
SAT I Verbal/Math: 513/555	VERY COMPETITIVE

Fordham College at Lincoln Center, established in 1968, is a private, coeducational institution within Fordham University's Jesuit tradition, offering liberal arts and preprofessional studies. There is 1 undergraduate and 4 graduate schools. In addition to regional accreditation, Fordham College at Lincoln Center has baccalaureate program accreditation with AACSB. The library contains 1,592,621 volumes, 1,895,489 microform items, and 409 audiovisual forms, and subscribes to 10,553 periodicals. Computerized library sources and services include the card catalog, interlibrary loans, and database searching. Special learning facilities include an art gallery and radio station. The 8-acre campus is in an urban area in New York City. Including residence halls, there are 3 buildings on campus.

Student Life: 67% of undergraduates are from New York. Students come from 43 states, 48 foreign countries, and Canada. 36% are from public schools; 64% from private. 76% are white; 15% Hispanic. 85% are Catholic; 14% Protestant. The average age of freshmen is 18; all undergraduates, 21. 8% do not continue beyond their first year; 77% remain to graduate.

Housing: 850 students can be accommodated in college housing. College-sponsored living facilities include coed on-campus apartments. On-campus housing is guaranteed for all 4 years. 55% of students live on campus; of those, 90% remain on campus on weekends.

Activities: There are no fraternities or sororities. There are 130 groups on campus, including art, band, cheerleading, chorus, computers, drama, ethnic, film, honors, international, literary magazine, marching band, musical theater, newspaper, pep band, photography, political, professional, radio and TV, religious, social, social service, student government, and yearbook. Popular campus events include Homecoming, Spring Weekend, and Senior Week.

Sports: There are 11 intercollegiate sports for men and 10 for women, and 11 intramural sports for men and 10 for women. Athletic and recreation facilities include a 6000-seat football stadium, an

Olympic-sized pool with a separate diving area, an indoor track, a 3200-seat gymnasium, and tennis, squash, and racquetball courts. All facilities are at the Rose Hill (Bronx) campus of the university.

Disabled Students: All of the campus is accessible to disabled students. The following facilities are available: wheelchair ramps, elevators, special parking, specially equipped rest rooms, lowered drinking fountains, and lowered telephones.

Services: In addition to many counseling and information services, tutoring is available in most subjects.

Campus Safety and Security: Campus safety and security measures include 24-hour foot and vehicle patrol, informal discussions, emergency telephones, and lighted pathways/sidewalks.

Programs of Study: Fordham College at Lincoln Center confers B.A. and B.S. degrees. Master's and doctoral degrees are also awarded. Bachelor's degrees are awarded in COMMUNICATIONS AND THE ARTS (art history and appreciation, comparative literature, creative writing, dramatic arts, English, film arts, French, Italian, journalism, modern language, Spanish, and studio art), COMPUTER AND PHYSICAL SCIENCE (computer science, mathematics, and natural sciences), EDUCATION (elementary and secondary), HEALTH PROFESSIONS (predentistry and premedicine), SOCIAL SCIENCE (African American studies, anthropology, economics, Hispanic American studies, history, Middle Eastern studies, philosophy, political science/government, prelaw, psychology, religion, social science, sociology, and urban studies). Philosophy, media studies, social sciences, and English are the strongest academically. Media studies, political science, and philosophy have the largest enrollments.

Required: All students must complete a core curriculum, including English literature and composition, history, philosophy, mathematics, science, theology, and foreign language. A total of 124 credit hours with a minimum GPA of 2.0 is required in order to graduate.

Special: The college offers career-oriented internships during the junior or senior year with New York City companies and institutions. Study abroad, a Washington semester, student-designed majors, and pass/fail options are available. A combined 3–2 engineering program is available with Columbia University and Case Western Reserve University. Other cooperative programs include a 3–2 in nursing with Columbia University and a 3–2 in pharmacy with Long Island University. The Life Experience program provides credit for outside learning. There is a freshman honors program on campus, as well as 2 national honor societies, including Phi Beta Kappa.

Faculty/Classroom: All teach undergraduates. The average class size in an introductory lecture is 28 and in a regular course offering, 24.

Admissions: 64% of the 1995–96 applicants were accepted. The SAT I scores for the 1995–96 freshman class were Verbal—45% below 500, 42% between 500 and 599, 12% between 600 and 700, and 1% above 700; Math—32% below 500, 41% between 500 and 599, 23% between 600 and 700, and 4% above 700. 50% of the current freshmen were in the top fifth of their class; 83% were in the top two fifths.

Requirements: The SAT I or ACT is required. Applicants should be graduates of an accredited high school or have a GED equivalent, with 4 years of English and 3 each of mathematics, science, social studies, history, and foreign language. An essay is part of the application process, and an audition is required for theater majors. An interview is recommended. AP and CLEP credits are accepted. Important factors in the admissions decision are advanced placement or honor courses, recommendations by school officials, and leadership record.

Procedure: Freshmen are admitted in the fall and spring. Entrance exams should be taken by November of the senior year. There are early decision and early admissions plans. Early decision applications should be filed by November 1; regular applications, by February 1 for fall entry and December 1 for spring entry, along with an application fee of $50. Notification of early decision is sent December 15; regular decision, March 1. 8 early decision candidates were accepted for the 1995–96 class. A waiting list is an active part of the admissions procedure.

Transfer: 85 transfer students enrolled in 1995–96. A minimum 3.0 GPA is recommended. Applicants under age 21 should submit SAT I or ACT scores. An interview is recommended. 64 credits of 124 must be completed at Fordham College at Lincoln Center.

Visiting: There are regularly scheduled orientations for prospective students. There are guides for informal visits and visitors may sit in on classes and stay overnight at the school. To schedule a visit, contact Elizabeth Roper, Associate Director of Admissions at (212) 636–6710.

Financial Aid: In a recent year, 90% of all freshmen and 88% of continuing students received some form of financial aid. 90% of freshmen and 83% of continuing students received need-based aid. The recent average freshman award was $9500. Of that total, scholarships or need-based grants averaged $6600 ($11,000 maximum); Pell grants averaged $780 ($2400 maximum); loans averaged $700 ($2200 maximum); and work contracts averaged $700 ($1600 maximum). 95% of undergraduate students work part-time. Average earnings from campus work for the school year are $1600. The average

financial indebtedness of a recent graduate was $8170. Fordham College at Lincoln Center is a member of CSS. The FAF, FAFSA, and the college's own financial statement are required. The application deadline for fall entry is February 1.

International Students: The school actively recruits these students. They must take the TOEFL and achieve a minimum score of 550. The student must also take the SAT I or the ACT.

Computers: The college provides computer facilities for student use. The mainframe is a DEC VAX. All students may access the system. There are no time limits and no fees.

Graduates: Within an average freshman class, 77% graduate in 4 years, 82% in 5 years, and 87% in 6 years. 500 companies recruited on campus in a recent year.

Admissions Contact: John W. Buckley, Director of Admissions.

FORDHAM UNIVERSITY/FORDHAM COLLEGE AT ROSE HILL   D-5
(Formerly Fordham University/Fordham College)

Bronx, NY 10458   (718) 817–4000

Full-time: 1596 men, 1669 women	**Faculty:** 351; I, av$
Part-time: 221 men, 257 women	**Ph.D.s:** 97%
Graduate: 603 men, 555 women	**Student/Faculty:** 9 to 1
Year: semesters, summer session	**Tuition:** $15,050
Application Deadline: February 1	**Room & Board:** $7000
Freshman Class: 2718 applied, 1984 accepted, 652 enrolled	
SAT I Verbal/Math: 520/557	**ACT:** 25 **VERY COMPETITIVE**

Fordham College at Rose Hill, founded in 1841, is a private, independent, coeducational, liberal arts college within Fordham University's Jesuit tradition. There are 3 undergraduate and 2 graduate schools. In addition to regional accreditation, Fordham College at Rose Hill has baccalaureate program accreditation with AACSB. The 2 libraries contain 1,592,621 volumes, 1,895,489 microform items, and 409 audiovisual forms, and subscribe to 10,553 periodicals. Computerized library sources and services include the card catalog, interlibrary loans, and database searching. Special learning facilities include a radio station. The 86-acre campus is in an urban area in the Bronx, adjacent to the Bronx Zoo and New York Botanical Garden. Including residence halls, there are 31 buildings on campus.

Student Life: 67% of undergraduates are from New York. Students come from 43 states, 48 foreign countries, and Canada. 36% are from public schools; 64% from private. 71% are white; 15% Hispanic. 85% are Catholic; 14% Protestant. The average age of freshmen is 18; all undergraduates, 20. 7% do not continue beyond their first year; 77% remain to graduate.

Housing: 2508 students can be accommodated in college housing. College-sponsored living facilities include coed dormitories, on-campus apartments, and off-campus apartments. In addition, there is a residential college. On-campus housing is guaranteed for all 4 years. 70% of students live on campus; of those, 90% remain on campus on weekends. Upperclassmen may keep cars on campus.

Activities: There are no fraternities or sororities. There are 130 groups on campus, including art, band, cheerleading, choir, chorus, computers, dance, drama, ethnic, film, honors, international, literary magazine, marching band, musical theater, newspaper, pep band, photography, political, professional, radio and TV, religious, social, social service, student government, and yearbook. Popular campus events include Spring Weekend, Christmas Formal, and Senior Week.

Sports: There are 11 intercollegiate sports for men and 10 for women, and 11 intramural sports for men and 10 for women. Athletic and recreation facilities include a 6000-seat football stadium, an Olympic-size pool with a separate diving area, an indoor track, a 3200-seat gymnasium, and tennis, squash, and racquetball courts.

Disabled Students: 80% of the campus is accessible to disabled students. The following facilities are available: wheelchair ramps, elevators, special parking, specially equipped rest rooms, and lowered drinking fountains.

Services: In addition to many counseling and information services, tutoring is available in most subjects.

Campus Safety and Security: Campus safety and security measures include 24-hour foot and vehicle patrol, escort service, shuttle buses, and informal discussions. In addition, there are pamphlets/posters/films, emergency telephones, and lighted pathways/sidewalks.

Programs of Study: Fordham College at Rose Hill confers B.A. and B.S. degrees. Master's and doctoral degrees are also awarded. Bachelor's degrees are awarded in BIOLOGICAL SCIENCE (biology/biological science), COMMUNICATIONS AND THE ARTS (art history and appreciation, broadcasting, classical languages, communications, English, film arts, fine arts, French, German, Greek, Italian, journalism, Latin, modern language, music, Russian, and Spanish), COMPUTER AND PHYSICAL SCIENCE (chemistry, computer science, information sciences and systems, mathematics, and physics),

SOCIAL SCIENCE (African American studies, American studies, anthropology, criminal justice, economics, history, medieval studies, Middle Eastern studies, peace studies, philosophy, political science/government, psychology, Russian and Slavic studies, sociology, theological studies, urban studies, and women's studies). Communications, philosophy, history, and political science are the strongest academically. Communications, political science, and economics have the largest enrollments.

Required: All students must complete a core curriculum, including 2 courses each in English, history, philosophy, theology, and language, and 1 each in life science, physical science, composition, and social science. A total of 124 credits with 30 in the major and a 2.0 minimum GPA are required. A thesis is required for the honors program.

Special: Fordham College offers career-oriented internships in communications and other majors during the junior or senior year with New York City companies and institutions. A combined 3-2 engineering program is available with Columbia University and Case Western University. Study abroad, a Washington semester, dual and student-designed majors, and pass/fail options are available. There is a freshman honors program on campus, as well as 6 national honor societies, including Phi Beta Kappa.

Faculty/Classroom: All teach undergraduates. The average class size in an introductory lecture is 28 and in a regular course offering, 24.

Admissions: 73% of the 1995–96 applicants were accepted. The SAT I scores for the 1995–96 freshman class were as follows: Verbal—41% below 500, 42% between 500 and 599, 14% between 600 and 700, and 3% above 700; Math—25% below 500, 40% between 500 and 599, 29% between 600 and 700, and 6% above 700. 51% of the current freshmen were in the top fifth of their class; 79% were in the top two fifths.

Requirements: The SAT I or ACT is required, and applicants should have completed 4 years of high school English and 3 each of mathematics, science, social studies, history, and foreign language. An essay is part of the application process. An interview is recommended. AP and CLEP credits are accepted. Important factors in the admissions decision are advanced placement or honor courses, recommendations by school officials, and parents or siblings attending the school.

Procedure: Freshmen are admitted in the fall and spring. Entrance exams should be taken by November of the senior year. There are early decision, early admissions, and deferred admissions plans. Early decision applications should be filed by November 1; regular applications, by February 1 for fall entry and December 1 for spring entry, along with an application fee of $50. Notification of early decision is sent December 15; regular decision, March 1. 30 early decision candidates were accepted for the 1995–96 class. A waiting list is an active part of the admissions procedure.

Transfer: 96 transfer students enrolled in 1995–96. A 3.0 minimum GPA is recommended. Applicants under age 21 should submit SAT I or ACT scores. An interview is recommended. 64 credits of 124 must be completed at Fordham College at Rose Hill.

Visiting: There are regularly scheduled orientations for prospective students. There are guides for informal visits and visitors may sit in on classes and stay overnight at the school. To schedule a visit, contact Robert Doslerberg, Assistant Director of Admissions.

Financial Aid: In a recent year, 90% of all freshmen and 88% of continuing students received some form of financial aid. 90% of freshmen and 83% of continuing students received need-based aid. The recent average freshman award was $9500. Of that total, scholarships or need-based grants averaged $6600 ($11,000 maximum); Pell grants averaged $780 ($2400 maximum); loans averaged $700 ($2200 maximum); and work contracts averaged $700 ($1600 maximum). 95% of undergraduate students work part-time. Average earnings from campus work for the school year are $1600. The average financial indebtedness of a recent graduate was $8170. Fordham College at Rose Hill is a member of CSS. The FAF, FAFSA, and the college's own financial statement are required. The application deadline for fall entry is February 1.

International Students: The school actively recruits these students. They must score 550 on the TOEFL and also take SAT I or the ACT.

Computers: The college provides computer facilities for student use. The mainframe is a DEC VAX system. All students may access the system. There are no time limits and no fees.

Graduates: The most popular majors among recent graduates were communications (8%), political science (7%), and English (6%). Within an average freshman class, 77% graduate in 4 years, 82% in 5 years, and 87% in 6 years. 500 companies recruited on campus in a recent year.

Admissions Contact: John W. Buckley, Director of Admissions.

FRIENDS WORLD PROGRAM   E-5

Southampton, NY 11968   (516) 287-8465; (800) LIU-PLAN

Full-time: 53 men, 99 women	Faculty: 17
Part-time: 4 men, 4 women	Ph.D.s: 70%
Graduate: none	Student/Faculty: 9 to 1
Year: semesters	Tuition: $12,900
Application Deadline: open	Room & Board: $1000-$3000
Freshman Class: 110 applied, 45 enrolled	
SAT I or ACT: not required	**LESS COMPETITIVE**

Friends World Program, founded in 1965, offers student-designed majors in the liberal arts and is located on the campus of Southampton College. It has campuses in Costa Rica, England, Israel, Kenya, India, China, and Japan, and during the 4-year program, students study at 2 or 3 of them. Much of the learning is through individually designed off-campus field experience and internships in 2 or more cultures. Students attend the Southampton campus only during their first semester. The library contains 1 million volumes, 1000 microform items, and 500 audiovisual forms, and subscribes to 690 periodicals. Computerized library sources and services include the card catalog, interlibrary loans, and database searching. Special learning facilities include a learning resource center, art gallery, radio station, and a marine laboratory. The 110-acre campus is in a rural area 90 miles east of New York City. Including residence halls, there are 33 buildings on campus.

Student Life: 75% of undergraduates are from out-of-state, mostly the Northwest. Students come from 20 states, 10 foreign countries, and Canada. 75% are from public schools; 25% from private. 85% are white; 10% foreign nationals. Most claim no religious affiliation. The average age of freshmen is 19; all undergraduates, 22. 20% do not continue beyond their first year; 60% remain to graduate.

Housing: 700 students can be accommodated in college housing. College-sponsored living facilities include coed dormitories and off-campus apartments. On-campus housing is guaranteed for the freshman year only. Priority is given to out-of-town students. 95% of students live on campus; of those, 80% remain on campus on weekends. All students may keep cars on campus.

Activities: There are no fraternities or sororities. There are 50 groups on campus, including art, drama, environmental, ethnic, honors, international, literary magazine, newspaper, photography, political, radio and TV, religious, social service, student government, and yearbook. Popular campus events include 'Ingatherings'—weekend events where students on field internships return to campus for sharing and community meetings for college governance. There are also multicultural awareness activities.

Sports: There is no sports program at Friends World.

Disabled Students: 15% of the campus is accessible to disabled students. Wheelchair ramps and special parking are available.

Services: In addition to many counseling and information services, tutoring is available in every subject in the study center with trained faculty. There is remedial math, reading, and writing.

Campus Safety and Security: Campus safety and security measures include 24-hour foot and vehicle patrol, self-defense education, informal discussions, and pamphlets/posters/films. In addition, there are emergency telephones and lighted pathways/sidewalks.

Programs of Study: Friends World confers the B.A. in Interdisciplinary Studies degree. Bachelor's degrees are awarded in SOCIAL SCIENCE (interdisciplinary studies).

Required: All students must complete the core curriculum of 1 writing course and the Friends World Education Seminar. Distribution requirements include 12 credits each in area studies, human issues, and languages and writing and 24 credits in liberal arts. Students are required to study 2 cultures other than their own. All students demonstrate learning by keeping journals. Submission of a completed journal is required to advance to the next year of study. A senior thesis is required. There are no grades. A total of 120 credit hours is required, with at least 24 in the major subject area.

Special: There is cross-registration with Long Island University. All students carry out fieldwork and internships and live abroad. The college offers a general studies degree, and students may study a wide range of subjects that include women's studies, anthropology, politics, archaeology, comparative religions, music, education, holistic medicine and healing, alternative agriculture, ecology, the arts, and peace studies. There is a freshman honors program on campus.

Faculty/Classroom: 50% of faculty are male; 50%, female. All teach undergraduates and 60% both teach and do research. The average class size in an introductory lecture is 20 and in a regular course offering, 10.

Admissions: 2 freshmen graduated first in their class.

Requirements: A minimum grade average of 75 is required. The SAT I or ACT is not required for regular admission, but is considered if submitted. The SAT I or ACT is required for Merit Scholarship consideration. The GED is accepted, as is evidence of equivalent life experience. An essay and interview are required. AP and CLEP credits are accepted. Important factors in the admissions decision are personality/intangible qualities, extracurricular activities record, and evidence of special talent.

Procedure: Freshmen are admitted in the fall. There are early admissions and deferred admissions plans. Application deadlines are open. Application fee is $30. Notification is sent on a rolling basis.

Transfer: 25 transfer students enrolled in 1995–96. Transfer applicants must have earned at least 15 academic credits with a GPA of at least 2.0. An interview is required. 60 credits of 120 must be completed at Friends World.

Visiting: There are guides for informal visits and visitors may sit in on classes. To schedule a visit, contact the Admissions Office.

Financial Aid: In 1995–96, 85% of all students received some form of financial aid; 70% of students received need-based aid. The average freshman award was $4000. Of that total, scholarships or need-based grants averaged $1200 ($10,000 maximum); loans averaged $2600 ($4000 maximum); and work contracts averaged $400 ($600 maximum). All undergraduate students work part-time. Average earnings from campus work for the school year are $700. The average financial indebtedness of the 1994–95 graduate was $9000. Friends World is a member of CSS. The FAFSA and the college's own financial statement is required. The application deadline for fall entry is April 1.

International Students: There are currently 15 international students enrolled. They must take the TOEFL and achieve a minimum score of 500. They must take the SAT I or ACT to be considered for Merit Scholarships.

Computers: The college provides computer facilities for student use. The LIU network is a node on the Internet connecting Friends World students to computers worldwide. There are 125 PCs in 6 campus locations, a 12 to 1 student/computer ratio, and computer hook-up in all dormitory rooms. Overseas, students have access to a Friends World administrative computer. All students may access the system 24 hours a day. There are no time limits and no fees. It is recommended that students in foreign centers have personal computers.

Graduates: Within an average freshman class, 70% graduate in 4 years, 20% in 5 years, and 10% in 6 years. Of the 1994 graduating class, 5% were enrolled in graduate school within 6 months of graduation and 70% had found employment.

Admissions Contact: Kristen Kapp, Admissions Counselor.

HAMILTON COLLEGE

C-3

Clinton, NY 13323

(315) 859-4421
(800) 843-2655; FAX: (315) 859-4457

Full-time: 904 men, 742 women	Faculty: 176; IIB, +$
Part-time: 6 men, 18 women	Ph.D.s: 96%
Graduate: none	Student/Faculty: 9 to 1
Year: semesters	Tuition: $20,700
Application Deadline: January 15	Room & Board: $5250
Freshman Class: 3649 applied, 1753 accepted, 472 enrolled	
SAT I Verbal/Math: 536/603	**HIGHLY COMPETITIVE**

Hamilton College, founded in 1793, is a private, nonsectarian, liberal arts school, offering undergraduate programs in the arts and sciences. The 3 libraries contain 484,634 volumes, 368,587 microform items, and 15,505 audiovisual forms, and subscribe to 1870 periodicals. Computerized library sources and services include the card catalog and database searching. Special learning facilities include an art gallery, radio station, and an observatory. The 1200-acre campus is in a rural area 9 miles southwest of Utica. Including residence halls, there are 51 buildings on campus.

Student Life: 53% of undergraduates are from out-of-state, mostly the Northeast. Students come from 43 states, 35 foreign countries, and Canada. 60% are from public schools; 40% from private. 85% are white. 33% are Catholic; 32% Protestant; 20% claim no religious affiliation. The average age of freshmen is 18; all undergraduates, 20. 5% do not continue beyond their first year; 90% remain to graduate.

Housing: 1449 students can be accommodated in college housing. College-sponsored living facilities include coed dormitories, on-campus apartments, fraternity houses, and sorority houses. In addition there are language houses, special interest houses, quiet floors, substance-free areas, and a cooperative. On-campus housing is guaranteed for all 4 years. 99% of students live on campus; of those, 95% remain on campus on weekends. Upperclassmen may keep cars on campus.

Activities: 48% of men belong to 8 national fraternities; 12% of women belong to 1 local and 1 national sorority. There are 60 groups on campus, including art, band, chess, choir, chorale, chorus, computers, dance, drama, ethnic, film, gay, honors, international, jazz band, literary magazine, newspaper, orchestra, photography, political, professional, radio and TV, religious, social, social service, student government, and yearbook. Popular campus events include Class and Charter Day, Winterfest, and Springfest.

Sports: There are 12 intercollegiate sports for men and 11 for women, and 26 intramural sports for men and 29 for women. Athletic and recreation facilities include a gymnasium, a field house, squash and racquetball courts, indoor and outdoor tennis courts, a football stadium, a 9-hole golf course, a swimming pool, indoor and outdoor tracks, numerous grass fields, paddle tennis courts, and an ice rink.

Disabled Students: 30% of the campus is accessible to disabled students. The following facilities are available: wheelchair ramps, elevators, special parking, specially equipped rest rooms, and special class scheduling.

Services: In addition to many counseling and information services, tutoring is available in some subjects through the New York State Higher Education Opportunity Program (HEOP).

Campus Safety and Security: Campus safety and security measures include 24-hour foot and vehicle patrol, escort service, shuttle buses, and emergency telephones. There are lighted pathways/sidewalks.

Programs of Study: Hamilton confers the B.A. degree. Bachelor's degrees are awarded in BIOLOGICAL SCIENCE (biochemistry and biology/biological science), COMMUNICATIONS AND THE ARTS (classics, comparative literature, creative writing, dance, dramatic arts, English, fine arts, French, German, languages, linguistics, music, and Spanish), COMPUTER AND PHYSICAL SCIENCE (chemistry, computer science, geology, mathematics, and physics), SOCIAL SCIENCE (American studies, anthropology, Asian/Oriental studies, classical/ancient civilization, economics, history, international relations, philosophy, political science/government, psychobiology, psychology, public affairs, religion, Russian and Slavic studies, sociology, and women's studies). English, government, and history have the largest enrollments.

Required: Students must successfully complete 128 credits, with 32 to 40 of these in the student's major, and must maintain at least a 72 average in half the courses taken. Students are required to take 2 courses in each academic division, 3 courses designated as writing-intensive, and at least 2 courses covering human diversity and ethical issues, as well as 2 semesters of physical education. A senior project in the student's major is also required.

Special: Cross-registration is permitted with Colgate University, Syracuse University, and Utica College. Opportunities are provided for internships, a cooperative program through the Williams College Mystic Seaport Program in Connecticut, and a Washington semester. Accelerated degree programs, dual majors, 3–2 engineering degrees, nondegree study, pass/fail options, student-designed majors, a program for early assurance of acceptance to medical school, and study abroad in many countries are offered. There are 4 national honor societies on campus, including Phi Beta Kappa.

Faculty/Classroom: 61% of faculty are male; 39% female. All teach undergraduates.

Admissions: 48% of the 1995–96 applicants were accepted. The SAT I scores for the 1995–96 freshman class were as follows: Verbal—28% below 500, 49% between 500 and 599, 18% between 600 and 700, and 3% above 700; Math—6% below 500, 36% between 500 and 599, 47% between 600 and 700, and 9% above 700. 73% of the current freshmen were in the top fifth of their class. 8 freshmen graduated first in their class.

Requirements: The SAT I or ACT is required. Although graduation from an accredited secondary school with a 3.0 GPA or a GED is desirable, and a full complement of college-preparatory courses is recommended, Hamilton will consider all highly recommended candidates who demonstrate an ability and desire to perform at intellectually demanding levels. An essay is required and an interview is recommended. AP credits are accepted. Important factors in the admissions decision are advanced placement or honor courses, recommendations by school officials, and parents or siblings attending the school.

Procedure: Freshmen are admitted in the fall. Entrance exams should be taken prior to February of the senior year. There are early decision, early admissions, and deferred admissions plans. Early decision applications should be filed by November 15; regular applications, by January 15 for fall entry, along with an application fee of $50. Notification of early decision is sent December 15; regular decision, April 15. A waiting list is an active part of the admissions procedure, with about 7% of all applicants on the list.

Transfer: 64 credits of 128 must be completed at Hamilton.

Visiting: There are regularly scheduled orientations for prospective students, consisting of an interview, tour, and class visit. There are guides for informal visits and visitors may sit in on classes and stay overnight at the school. To schedule a visit, contact the Admissions Office.

Financial Aid: In a recent year, 60% of all freshmen and 65% of continuing students received some form of financial aid. 60% of freshmen and 61% of continuing students received need-based aid. The average freshman award was $14,600. Of that total, scholarships or need-based grants averaged $11,200 ($20,800 maximum); loans averaged $2200 ($2500 maximum); and work contracts averaged

$1200 ($1400 maximum). 45% of undergraduate students work part-time. Average earnings from campus work for the school year are $1400. Hamilton is a member of CSS. The FAF, FFS, or FAFSA, and the college's own financial statement are required. The application deadline for fall entry is February 1.

International Students: There were 88 international students enrolled in a recent year. The school actively recruits these students. They must score 580 on the TOEFL and also take SAT I or the ACT.

Computers: The college provides computer facilities for student use. The mainframes are comprised of a DEC 5100, DEC 5000/25, DEC 5500. Hamilton is connected to Internet and there are 100 Apple Macintosh PCs and 50 MS-DOS PCs in public computer laboratories. Students have full access to Internet. All students may access the system more than 100 hours per week. There are no time limits and no fees.

Graduates: In a recent year, 412 bachelor's degrees were awarded. The most popular majors among graduates were history (12%), English (11%), and government (10%). Within an average freshman class, 85% graduate in 4 years, 91% in 5 years, and 91% in 6 years. 50 companies recruited on campus in a recent year.

Admissions Contact: Richard M. Fuller, Dean of Admissions. E-mail: admission@hamilton.edu.

HARTWICK COLLEGE
D-3
Oneonta, NY 13820-4020

(607) 431-4150
(800) 828-2200; FAX: (607) 431-4154

Full-time: 701 men, 762 women	Faculty: 105; IIB, +$
Part-time: 15 men, 44 women	Ph.D.s: 89%
Graduate: none	Student/Faculty: 14 to 1
Year: 4-1-4	Tuition: $19,300
Application Deadline: February 15	Room & Board: $5310
Freshman Class: 2631 applied, 2311 accepted, 451 enrolled	
SAT I Verbal/Math: 470/530	ACT: 24 COMPETITIVE

Hartwick College, founded in 1797, is a private undergraduate liberal arts college. In addition to regional accreditation, Hartwick has baccalaureate program accreditation with NASAD, NASM, and NLN. The library contains 244,266 volumes, 56,402 microform items, and 6123 audiovisual forms, and subscribes to 1041 periodicals. Computerized library sources and services include the card catalog, interlibrary loans, and database searching. Special learning facilities include an art gallery, radio station, TV station, 3 museums, a 914-acre environmental study center, an observatory, and an environmental field station. The 375-acre campus is in a small town 75 miles southwest of Albany. Including residence halls, there are 27 buildings on campus.

Student Life: 56% of undergraduates are from New York. Students come from 36 states, 20 foreign countries, and Canada. 75% are from public schools; 25% from private. 93% are white. 45% are Catholic; 27% Protestant; 14% claim no religious affiliation. The average age of freshmen is 18; all undergraduates, 20. 20% do not continue beyond their first year; 67% remain to graduate.

Housing: 1300 students can be accommodated in college housing. College-sponsored living facilities include single-sex and coed dormitories, on-campus apartments, fraternity houses, and sorority houses. In addition there are special interest houses and substance-free housing. On-campus housing is guaranteed for all 4 years. 74% of students live on campus; of those, 90% remain on campus on weekends. Alcohol is not permitted. All students may keep cars on campus.

Activities: 23% of men belong to 1 local fraternity and 3 national fraternities; 26% of women belong to 3 local sororities and 1 national sorority. There are 64 groups on campus, including art, band, cheerleading, choir, chorale, chorus, computers, dance, drama, ethnic, film, gay, honors, international, jazz band, literary magazine, musical theater, newspaper, orchestra, pep band, photography, political, professional, radio and TV, religious, social, social service, student government, and yearbook. Popular campus events include a concert series, Winter, Spring, and Fall Weekends, the Holiday Ball, Earth Day, and Multicultural Month.

Sports: There are 11 intercollegiate sports for men and 11 for women, and 14 intramural sports for men and 13 for women. Athletic and recreation facilities include 2 gymnasiums, an indoor pool, a dance room, athletic and training facilities, a track, courts for handball, racquetball, squash, and tennis, a Nautilus exercise gym, a fitness center, and a lighted all-weather playing field.

Disabled Students: 50% of the campus is accessible to disabled students. The following facilities are available: wheelchair ramps, elevators, special parking, specially equipped rest rooms, special class scheduling, lowered drinking fountains, and lowered telephones.

Services: In addition to many counseling and information services, tutoring is available in every subject. There is a reader service for the blind, writing and mathematics centers, and an academic support center.

Campus Safety and Security: Campus safety and security measures include 24-hour foot and vehicle patrol, self-defense education, escort service, and shuttle buses. In addition, there are informal discussions, pamphlets/posters/films, emergency telephones, and lighted pathways/sidewalks.

Programs of Study: Hartwick confers B.A. and B.S. degrees. Bachelor's degrees are awarded in BIOLOGICAL SCIENCE (biochemistry and biology/biological science), BUSINESS (accounting and business administration and management), COMMUNICATIONS AND THE ARTS (dramatic arts, English, fine arts, languages, and music), COMPUTER AND PHYSICAL SCIENCE (chemistry, computer science, geology, information sciences and systems, mathematics, and physics), EDUCATION (music), HEALTH PROFESSIONS (medical technology and nursing), SOCIAL SCIENCE (anthropology, economics, history, philosophy, political science/government, psychology, religion, and sociology). Anthropology, art, and biology are the strongest academically. Psychology, English, and language have the largest enrollments.

Required: Students must complete 36 course units with at least a 2.0 GPA. Core requirements are in the study areas of continuity, interdependence, science and technology, critical thinking, effective communication, and electives. Courses are chosen from offerings in humanities, science and mathematics, social and behavioral sciences, foreign language, and physical education. A first-year seminar, and a contemporary issues seminar for juniors and seniors are required. Students are strongly urged to include an off-campus learning experience.

Special: Students may design their own majors and choose independent study. Cross-registration with SUNY College at Oneonta is possible and local internships are available. There is a January thematic term, a Washington semester, and study abroad in 30 countries. Experiential programs include Outward Bound and the National Outdoor Leadership School. All departments offer dual majors. There is a 3-2 engineering program with Clarkson University or Columbia University, a 3-3 program with Albany Law School, and a 4-1 business program with Clarkson University. There is a freshman honors program on campus, as well as 9 national honor societies. 30 departments have honors programs.

Faculty/Classroom: 65% of faculty are male; 35%, female. All teach undergraduates. The average class size in an introductory lecture is 35; in a laboratory, 20; and in a regular course offering, 18.

Admissions: 88% of the 1995-96 applicants were accepted. The SAT I scores for the 1995-96 freshman class were as follows: Verbal—61% below 500, 28% between 500 and 599, 10% between 600 and 700, and 1% above 700; Math—38% below 500, 38% between 500 and 599, 23% between 600 and 700, and 1% above 700. The ACT scores were 21% below 21, 25% between 21 and 23, 30% between 24 and 26, 13% between 27 and 28, and 11% above 28. 45% of the current freshmen were in the top fifth of their class; 69% were in the top two fifths. 12 freshmen graduated first in their class.

Requirements: Reporting of SAT I and ACT scores is optional. The recommended secondary course of study includes 4 years of English and social studies, 3 years of a foreign language, and 3 to 4 years of mathematics and laboratory science. Hartwick strongly recommends that applicants plan a campus visit and interview. Prospective art majors should submit a portfolio, and music majors must audition. Computer disks are offered to all prospective students, providing information about the college as well as an application. Students may also use the CollegeLink application. AP and CLEP credits are accepted. Important factors in the admissions decision are advanced placement or honor courses and recommendations by school officials.

Procedure: Freshmen are admitted to all sessions. Entrance exams should be taken in the spring of the junior year and/or the fall of the senior year. There are early decision, early admissions, and deferred admissions plans. Early decision applications should be filed by December 1 and January 15; regular applications, by February 15 for fall entry, December 1 for winter entry, and January 1 for spring entry, along with an application fee of $35. Notification of early decision is on a rolling basis; regular decision, March 15. 95 early decision candidates were accepted for the 1995-96 class.

Transfer: 33 transfer students enrolled in 1995-96. Transfer applicants should present a minimum GPA of 2.0. 18 course units of 36 must be completed at Hartwick.

Visiting: There are regularly scheduled orientations for prospective students, consisting of an interview and tour, lunch, class visits, and individual meetings with financial aid representatives. There are guides for informal visits and visitors may sit in on classes and stay overnight at the school. To schedule a visit, contact the Admissions Office.

Financial Aid: In 1995-96, 88% of all freshmen and 74% of continuing students received some form of financial aid. 70% of freshmen and 68% of continuing students received need-based aid. The average freshman award was $12,907. Of that total, scholarships or need-based grants averaged $7810 ($18,000 maximum); loans averaged $5850 ($11,700 maximum); and work contracts averaged $1200

($1400 maximum). 66% of undergraduate students work part-time. Average earnings from campus work for the school year are $1400. The average financial indebtedness of the 1994–95 graduate was $13,973. Hartwick is a member of CSS. The FAFSA and the college's own financial statement are required. The application deadline for fall entry is February 15.

International Students: There are currently 60 international students enrolled. The school actively recruits these students. They must take the TOEFL and achieve a minimum score of 500.

Computers: The college provides computer facilities for student use. The mainframes are a DEC VAX 6410, 2 DEC MicroVAX 3100s, and a MicroVAX II. There are 2 laboratories with 26 IBM-compatible 486sx computers with VGA graphics, and some Apple Macintosh microcomputers. Computers are available throughout academic buildings, all connected with a campus local area network. All students may access the system 8 A.M. to 1 A.M. weekdays, noon to 10 P.M. Saturday, noon to 1 A.M. Sunday, as well as 24-hour network connection. There are no time limits and no fees. It is recommended that students in all programs have personal computers. Each first-year student receives a notebook computer with software and printer.

Graduates: In 1994–95, 309 bachelor's degrees were awarded. The most popular majors among graduates were psychology (12%), nursing (10%), and English (10%). Within an average freshman class, 54% graduate in 4 years, 63% in 5 years, and 66% in 6 years. 30 companies recruited on campus in 1994–95. Of the 1994 graduating class, 20% were enrolled in graduate school within 6 months of graduation and 67% had found employment.

Admissions Contact: Gary E. Johnson, Director of Admission.

HOBART AND WILLIAM SMITH COLLEGES C-3
Geneva, NY 14456-3397   (315) 781-3622 (H) or (315) 781-3472 (WS)

(800) 852-2256 (H) or 245-0100 (WS); FAX: (315) 781-3471

Full-time: 866 men, 898 women	Faculty: 128; IIB, +$
Part-time: 2 men, 4 women	Ph.Ds: 97%
Graduate: none	Student/Faculty: 14 to 1
Year: trimesters	Tuition: $20,393
Application Deadline: February 1	Room & Board: $6075
Freshman Class: 2786 applied, 2117 accepted, 475 enrolled	
SAT I Verbal/Math: 505/555	**VERY COMPETITIVE**

Hobart College, a men's college founded in 1822, shares campus, classes, and faculty with William Smith College, a women's college founded in 1908. Together, these coordinate colleges offer degree programs in the liberal arts. There are 2 undergraduate schools. The library contains 318,000 volumes, 66,438 microform items, and 17,000 audiovisual forms, and subscribes to 1872 periodicals. Computerized library sources and services include the card catalog, interlibrary loans, and database searching. Special learning facilities include a learning resource center, art gallery, radio station, 100-acre natural preserve, and 70-foot research vessel. The 170-acre campus is in a small town 50 miles west of Syracuse and 50 miles east of Rochester, on the north shore of Seneca Lake. Including residence halls, there are 75 buildings on campus.

Student Life: 51% of undergraduates are from out-of-state, mostly the Northeast. Students come from 41 states, 19 foreign countries, and Canada. 62% are from public schools; 38% from private. 89% are white. 30% are Protestant; 30% Catholic; 20% claim no religious affiliation; 15% Jewish. The average age of freshmen is 18; all undergraduates, 20. 14% do not continue beyond their first year; 82% remain to graduate.

Housing: 1450 students can be accommodated in college housing. College-sponsored living facilities include single-sex and coed dormitories and fraternity houses. In addition there are honors houses, language houses, special interest houses, and cooperative houses in which students plan and prepare their own meals. On-campus housing is guaranteed for all 4 years. 80% of students live on campus; of those, 93% remain on campus on weekends. All students may keep cars on campus.

Activities: 30% of men belong to 7 national fraternities. There are no sororities. There are 70 groups on campus, including art, choir, chorale, chorus, computers, dance, drama, ethnic, film, gay, honors, international, jazz band, literary magazine, musical theater, newspaper, orchestra, photography, political, professional, radio and TV, religious, social, social service, student government, and yearbook. Popular campus events include Folk Festival, Air Band Contest, Charter Day, Moving-up Day, Winter Carnival, and Celebrate Geneva Day of Service.

Sports: There are 9 intercollegiate sports for men and 8 for women, and 23 intramural sports for men and 23 for women. Athletic and recreation facilities include a sport and recreation center, 2 gymnasiums, numerous athletic fields, a swimming pool, 5 indoor tennis courts, 2 weight rooms, basketball and racquetball courts, and an indoor track.

Disabled Students: The following facilities are available: wheelchair ramps, elevators, special parking, specially equipped rest rooms, special class scheduling, and lowered drinking fountains.

Services: In addition to many counseling and information services, tutoring is available in every subject. In addition, there is a reader service for the blind, and remedial math, reading, and writing. There is a counseling center staffed by 5 therapists/counselors as well as various support groups and educational workshops.

Campus Safety and Security: Campus safety and security measures include 24-hour foot and vehicle patrol, self-defense education, escort service, and shuttle buses. In addition, there are informal discussions, pamphlets/posters/films, emergency telephones, and lighted pathways/sidewalks.

Programs of Study: HWS confers B.A. and B.S. degrees. Bachelor's degrees are awarded in BIOLOGICAL SCIENCE (biology/biological science), COMMUNICATIONS AND THE ARTS (Chinese, classics, dance, English, fine arts, French, German, Japanese, music, Russian, and Spanish), COMPUTER AND PHYSICAL SCIENCE (chemistry, computer science, geoscience, mathematics, and physics), ENGINEERING AND ENVIRONMENTAL DESIGN (architecture and environmental science), SOCIAL SCIENCE (American studies, anthropology, Asian/Oriental studies, economics, history, philosophy, political science/government, psychology, religion, Russian and Slavic studies, sociology, urban studies, and women's studies). Natural sciences, environmental studies, and creative writing are the strongest academically. English, economics, and political science have the largest enrollments.

Required: All first-year students take a seminar; sophomores take at least 1 bidisciplinary course. All students must fulfill distribution requirements consisting of 2 courses each in humanities (1 in fine or applied arts), natural sciences (1 in a laboratory science), and social sciences by the end of the sophomore year. The Third Tier requirement may be satisfied by study abroad, upper-level bidisciplinary work, or substantial independent study of an interdisciplinary nature. A total of 36 courses is required for graduation, including 10 to 12 in the major, with a minimum GPA of 2.0.

Special: In their junior year, all students are encouraged to spend at least 1 term in a study-abroad program, offered in more than 15 countries, or in some other form of off-campus work. Options include a United Nations term, a Washington semester, an urban semester, and prearchitecture semesters in New York, Paris, or Florence. There is cross-registration with the 15 members of the Rochester Area Colleges Consortium. HWS offers dual and student-designed majors, credit for life/military/work experience, nondegree study, and pass/fail options. There are also M.B.A. degrees with Clarkson University, 3–4 architecture degrees with Washington University, and 3–2 engineering degrees with Columbia University, the University of Rochester, Rensselaer Polytechnic Institute, and Dartmouth College. There are 9 national honor societies on campus, including Phi Beta Kappa. All departments have honors programs.

Faculty/Classroom: 57% of faculty are male; 43%, female. All both teach and do research. The average class size in an introductory lecture is 45; in a laboratory, 25; and in a regular course offering, 23.

Admissions: 76% of the 1995–96 applicants were accepted. The SAT I scores for the 1995–96 freshman class were as follows: Verbal—47% below 500, 40% between 500 and 599, 12% between 600 and 700, and 1% above 700; Math—21% below 500, 47% between 500 and 599, 28% between 600 and 700, and 4% above 700. The ACT scores in a recent year were 14% below 21, 33% between 21 and 23, 28% between 24 and 26, 13% between 27 and 28, and 12% above 28. 51% of the current freshmen were in the top fifth of their class; 82% were in the top two fifths. 2 freshmen graduated first in their class.

Requirements: The SAT I or ACT is required. SAT II: Subject tests are not required but may be considered. A GED is accepted. A total of 18 academic credits is required, including 4 years of English, 3 of mathematics, and at least 2 each of laboratory science, foreign language, and history. An essay is required; an interview is recommended. Applications are accepted on computer disk. AP credits are accepted. Important factors in the admissions decision are advanced placement or honor courses, evidence of special talent, and leadership record.

Procedure: Freshmen are admitted in the fall. Entrance exams should be taken in the junior or senior year. There are early decision, early admissions, and deferred admissions plans. Early decision applications should be filed by January 1; regular applications, by February 1 for fall entry, along with an application fee of $45. Notification of early decision is sent February 1; regular decision, April 1. 101 early decision candidates were accepted for the 1995–96 class. A waiting list is an active part of the admissions procedure, with about 10% of all applicants on the list.

Transfer: 35 transfer students enrolled in 1995–96. Applicants must have a 3.0 GPA and have completed 1 year of college study. They are required to take the SAT I or ACT. An interview is recommended. 18 courses of 36 must be completed at HWS.

Visiting: There are regularly scheduled orientations for prospective students. There are guides for informal visits and visitors may sit in on classes and stay overnight at the school. To schedule a visit, contact the Offices of Admissions.

Financial Aid: In 1995–96, 74% of all freshmen and 67% of continuing students received some form of financial aid. 72% of freshmen and 66% of continuing students received need-based aid. The average freshman award was $17,555. Of that total, scholarships or need-based grants averaged $13,290 ($20,000 maximum); loans averaged $2713 ($3000 maximum); and work contracts averaged $1100 ($2800 maximum). 56% of undergraduate students work part-time. Average earnings from campus work for the school year are $765. The average financial indebtedness of the 1994–95 graduate was $11,315. HWS is a member of CSS. The FAFSA and the CSS Profile Application are required. The application deadline for fall entry is February 15.

International Students: There are currently 42 international students enrolled. The school actively recruits these students. They must take the TOEFL and achieve a minimum score of 500. The student must also take the SAT I or the ACT.

Computers: The college provides computer facilities for student use. The mainframes are a DEC ALPHA 2100 and a DEC VAX 6520. There are 122 microcomputers, and 60 terminals directly connected to the mainframe, with 114 microcomputers networked. The 4 microcomputer laboratories provide access to the on-line library catalog system, E-mail, and Internet. All students have E-mail accounts. All students may access the system from 9 A.M. to midnight, 7 days a week. There are no time limits and no fees.

Graduates: In 1994–95, 404 bachelor's degrees were awarded. The most popular majors among graduates were English (21%), individual majors (12%), and history (12%). Within an average freshman class, 78% graduate in 4 years and 80% in 5 years. 224 companies recruited on campus in 1994–95. Of the 1994 graduating class, 25% were enrolled in graduate school within 6 months of graduation.

Admissions Contact: Mara O'Laughlin, Director of Admissions. E-mail: olaughlin@hws.edu. A campus video is available.

HOFSTRA UNIVERSITY
Hempstead, NY 11550　　　　　　　　　　　　　**D-5**

(516) 463-6700
(800) HOFSTRA; FAX: (516) 560-7660

Full-time: 3079 men, 3510 women	Faculty: 348; I, av$
Part-time: 613 men, 644 women	Ph.D.s: 90%
Graduate: 1521 men, 2410 women	Student/Faculty: 19 to 1
Year: semesters, summer session	Tuition: $12,360
Application Deadline: February 15	Room & Board: $6180
Freshman Class: 7610 applied, 6210 accepted, 1516 enrolled	
SAT I Verbal/Math: 460/530	ACT: 23　　COMPETITIVE

Hofstra University, founded in 1935, is an independent university offering programs in liberal arts and sciences, business, communications, and education. There are 5 undergraduate and 5 graduate schools. In addition to regional accreditation, Hofstra has baccalaureate program accreditation with AACSB, ABET, ASLA, and NCATE. The 2 libraries contain 1,422,523 volumes and 4737 audiovisual forms, and subscribe to 7017 periodicals. Computerized library sources and services include the card catalog and database searching. Special learning facilities include a learning resource center, art gallery, radio station, TV station, museum, arboretum, and bird sanctuary. The 238-acre campus is in a suburban area 25 miles east of New York City. Including residence halls, there are 104 buildings on campus.

Student Life: 83% of undergraduates are from New York. Students come from 45 states, 67 foreign countries, and Canada. 70% are from public schools; 30% from private. 80% are white. 51% are Catholic; 15% Jewish; 15% Protestant. The average age of freshmen is 19; all undergraduates, 21. 15% do not continue beyond their first year; 57% remain to graduate.

Housing: 3375 students can be accommodated in college housing. College-sponsored living facilities include single-sex and coed dormitories and off-campus apartments. In addition, there are special interest houses, a living/learning center, an international house, and a freshman center. On-campus housing is available on a first-come, first-served basis (freshmen are given priority) and is available on a lottery system for upperclassmen. 50% of students live on campus; of those, 90% remain on campus on weekends. All students may keep cars on campus.

Activities: 16% of men belong to 6 local and 13 national fraternities; 16% of women belong to 3 local and 10 national sororities. There are 120 groups on campus, including art, band, cheerleading, choir, chorale, chorus, computers, dance, drama, drill team, ethnic, film, gay, honors, international, jazz band, literary magazine, musical theater, newspaper, opera, orchestra, organization of commuter students, pep band, photography, political, professional, radio and TV, religious, resident students association, social, social service, student government, symphony, and yearbook. Popular campus events include Spring Shakespeare Festival, May Dutch Tulip Festival, Italian American Festival, Homecoming, and Parents Weekend.

Sports: There are 9 intercollegiate sports for men and 8 for women, and 7 intramural sports for men and 7 for women. Athletic and recreation facilities include a physical fitness center, a recreation center, playing fields, a 15,000-seat stadium, a gymnasium, an indoor jogging track, and an Olympic-size swimming pool.

Disabled Students: The entire campus is accessible to disabled students. The following facilities are available: wheelchair ramps, elevators, special parking, specially equipped rest rooms, special class scheduling, lowered drinking fountains, lowered telephones, automated door openers, and TTY visual telephones.

Services: In addition to many counseling and information services, tutoring is available in every subject. There is a reader service for the blind, and remedial math, reading, and writing.

Campus Safety and Security: Campus safety and security measures include 24-hour foot and vehicle patrol, self-defense education, escort service, and shuttle buses. In addition, there are informal discussions, pamphlets/posters/films, emergency telephones, lighted pathways/sidewalks, and security cameras in residence halls.

Programs of Study: Hofstra confers B.A., B.S., B.B.A., B.E., B.F.A., and B.S.Ed. degrees. Associate, master's, and doctoral degrees are also awarded. Bachelor's degrees are awarded in AGRICULTURE (natural resource management), BIOLOGICAL SCIENCE (biochemistry and biology/biological science), BUSINESS (accounting, banking and finance, business administration and management, international business management, management information systems, and marketing/retailing/merchandising), COMMUNICATIONS AND THE ARTS (art history and appreciation, broadcasting, classics, communications, dance, dramatic arts, English, film arts, fine arts, journalism, languages, music, and speech/debate/rhetoric), COMPUTER AND PHYSICAL SCIENCE (chemistry, computer programming, computer science, geology, mathematics, natural sciences, and physics), EDUCATION (art, athletic training, bilingual/bicultural, business, early childhood, elementary, foreign languages, music, physical, science, and secondary), ENGINEERING AND ENVIRONMENTAL DESIGN (electrical/electronics engineering, engineering, industrial engineering, and mechanical engineering), HEALTH PROFESSIONS (community health work and speech pathology/audiology), SOCIAL SCIENCE (African studies, American studies, anthropology, Asian/Oriental studies, crosscultural studies, economics, geography, history, humanities, interdisciplinary studies, Judaic studies, liberal arts/general studies, philosophy, physical fitness/movement, political science/government, psychology, social science, and sociology). Engineering, accounting, communications, and drama and dance are the strongest academically. Accounting, communications, and psychology have the largest enrollments.

Required: Students must take 2 semesters of English and pass a writing proficiency test. A minimum of 9 semester hours each is required in humanities, natural sciences/mathematics, and social science. A total of 124 to 135 credit hours is required for graduation, with 30 to 84 in the major and a minimum GPA of 2.0. Foreign language study is required for the B.A. and B.B.A. in international business, and students in New College must submit a thesis.

Special: Internships, a 3–2 engineering program with Columbia University, a Washington semester, study abroad in 7 countries, and dual and student-designed majors are offered. Credit for military and work experience and credit by examination are given. Hofstra offers nondegree study and pass/fail options. There is a freshman honors program on campus, as well as 17 national honor societies, including Phi Beta Kappa.

Faculty/Classroom: 59% of faculty are male; 41%, female. 96% teach undergraduates and 65% both teach and do research. No introductory courses are taught by graduate students. The average class size in a laboratory is 19 and in a regular course offering, 25.

Admissions: 82% of the 1995–96 applicants were accepted. The SAT I scores for the 1995–96 freshman class were as follows: Math—41% below 500, 39% between 500 and 599, 17% between 600 and 700, and 3% above 700. The ACT scores were 28% below 21, 34% between 21 and 23, 26% between 24 and 26, 6% between 27 and 28, and 6% above 28. 50% of the current freshmen were in the top fifth of their class; 84% were in the top two fifths. 40 freshmen graduated first in their class.

Requirements: The SAT I or ACT is required. Applicants should graduate from an accredited secondary school or have a GED. Preparatory work should include 4 years of English, 3 of history and social studies, 2 each of mathematics and foreign language, and 1 of science, plus 4 academic electives. An essay and interview are recommended. AP and CLEP credits are accepted. Important factors in the admissions decision are advanced placement or honor courses, recommendations by school officials, and leadership record.

Procedure: Freshmen are admitted fall and spring. Entrance exams should be taken in the junior or senior year. There are early decision, early admissions, and deferred admissions plans. Early decision applications should be filed by December 1; regular applications, by

February 15 for fall entry and December 15 for spring entry, along with an application fee of $25. Notification of early decision is sent December 30; regular decision, on a rolling basis. 52 early decision candidates were accepted for the 1995–96 class. A waiting list is an active part of the admissions procedure, with about 5% of all applicants on the list.

Transfer: 822 transfer students enrolled in 1995–96. Admission is based primarily on prior college work in appropriate courses within the study area. A maximum of 64 credits from a 2-year school and 94 credits from a 4-year school are accepted. The minimum GPA is 2.5. 30 credits of 124 to 135 must be completed at Hofstra.

Visiting: There are regularly scheduled orientations for prospective students, including an open house, a tour of the campus, and a program in which a prospective student spends the day with a current student in a similar major. There are guides for informal visits and visitors may sit in on classes and stay overnight at the school. To schedule a visit, contact the Ambassador Program at (516) 463-6796.

Financial Aid: In 1995–96, 78% of all freshmen and 72% of continuing students received some form of financial aid. 61% of all students received need-based aid. The average freshman award was $8314. Of that total, scholarships or need-based grants averaged $3825 ($18,846 maximum); loans averaged $2625 ($6625 maximum); and work contracts averaged $1200 ($2500 maximum). 8% of undergraduate students work part-time. Average earnings from campus work for the school year are $1250. The average financial indebtedness of the 1994–95 graduate was $15,700. Hofstra is a member of CSS. The FAFSA is required. The recommended application deadline for fall entry is May 1.

International Students: There are currently 298 international students enrolled. The school actively recruits these students. They must take the TOEFL or the college's own test and achieve a minimum score on the TOEFL of 550. The student must also take the SAT I or the ACT.

Computers: The college provides computer facilities for student use. The mainframes are an IBM 9121, a DEC VAX 8530, and a DEC VAX 6410. These systems provide central computing resources for teaching and research, including E-mail, Bitnet and Internet access via the World Wide Web and gopher, and databases. Systems are accessible from the 300 PCs and terminals in 3 computer laboratories on campus. All students may access the system. There are no time limits and no fees.

Graduates: In 1994–95, 1621 bachelor's degrees were awarded. The most popular majors among graduates were psychology (14%), accounting (12%), and marketing (8%). Within an average freshman class, 57% graduate in 6 years. 158 companies recruited on campus in 1994–95.

Admissions Contact: Mary Beth Carey, Assistant Vice President and Dean of Admissions. E-mail: hofstra@hofstra.edu.

HOUGHTON COLLEGE
B-3

Houghton, NY 14744

(716) 567-9353
(800) 777-2556; FAX: (716) 567-9522

Full-time: 443 men, 789 women	Faculty: 74; IIB, --$
Part-time: 10 men, 29 women	Ph.D.s: 77%
Graduate: none	Student/Faculty: 17 to 1
Year: semesters, summer session	Tuition: $10,910
Application Deadline: August 1	Room & Board: $3720
Freshman Class: 1024 applied, 809 accepted, 294 enrolled	
SAT I Verbal/Math: 519/556	ACT: 26 **VERY COMPETITIVE**

Houghton College, founded in 1883, is a private coeducational college affiliated with the Wesleyan Church. It offers programs in the liberal arts and music. In addition to regional accreditation, Houghton has baccalaureate program accreditation with NASM. The library contains 220,000 volumes and 18,131 microform items, and subscribes to 822 periodicals. Computerized library sources and services include the card catalog, interlibrary loans, and database searching. Special learning facilities include an art gallery, radio station, and an equestrian center. The 1300-acre campus is in a rural area 60 miles southeast of Buffalo. Including residence halls, there are 32 buildings on campus.

Student Life: 61% of undergraduates are from New York. Students come from 40 states, 18 foreign countries, and Canada. 78% are from public schools; 22% from private. 89% are white. Most are Protestant. The average age of freshmen is 18; all undergraduates, 20.6. 11% do not continue beyond their first year; 63% remain to graduate.

Housing: 930 students can be accommodated in college housing. College-sponsored living facilities include single-sex dormitories and on-campus apartments. In addition there are language houses and special interest houses. On-campus housing is guaranteed for the freshman year only and is available on a lottery system for upperclassmen. Priority is given to out-of-town students. 92% of students live on campus; of those, 80% remain on campus on weekends. Alcohol is not permitted. All students may keep cars on campus.

Activities: There are no fraternities or sororities. There are 40 groups on campus, including art, band, cheerleading, choir, chorale, chorus, drama, ethnic, honors, international, jazz band, literary magazine, musical theater, newspaper, opera, orchestra, political, professional, radio and TV, religious, social service, student government, and yearbook. Popular campus events include Christian Life Emphasis Week, Homecoming, Winter Weekend, Senate Spots, and artist series.

Sports: There are 4 intercollegiate sports for men and 7 for women, and 9 intramural sports for men and 8 for women. Athletic and recreation facilities include 3 basketball and 4 racquetball courts, a swimming pool, an indoor track, a downhill ski slope, cross-country ski trails, 8 tennis courts, and an equestrian farm with an indoor riding ring. The gymnasium seats 1800; the largest auditorium/arena, 1300.

Disabled Students: 80% of the campus is accessible to disabled students. The following facilities are available: wheelchair ramps, elevators, special parking, specially equipped rest rooms, special class scheduling, lowered drinking fountains, and lowered telephones.

Services: In addition to many counseling and information services, tutoring is available in some subjects, including mathematics, writing, and history. There is a reader service for the blind, and support for learning disabled students.

Campus Safety and Security: Campus safety and security measures include 24-hour foot and vehicle patrol, escort service, shuttle buses, and informal discussions. In addition, there are pamphlets/posters/films, emergency telephones, and lighted pathways/sidewalks.

Programs of Study: Houghton confers B.A., B.S., and B.M. degrees. Associate degrees are also awarded. Bachelor's degrees are awarded in BIOLOGICAL SCIENCE (biology/biological science), BUSINESS (accounting, business administration and management, and recreation and leisure services), COMMUNICATIONS AND THE ARTS (art, communications, creative writing, English, fine arts, French, music, and Spanish), COMPUTER AND PHYSICAL SCIENCE (chemistry, mathematics, physics, and science), EDUCATION (art, elementary, foreign languages, music, science, and secondary), HEALTH PROFESSIONS (medical laboratory technology, predentistry, and premedicine), SOCIAL SCIENCE (biblical studies, history, humanities, international studies, philosophy, political science/government, prelaw, psychology, religion, social science, and sociology). Biology, chemistry, and religion are the strongest academically. Elementary education, psychology, and business administration have the largest enrollments.

Required: Required courses include 12 hours of language, 10 each of religion, mathematics and science, English and speech, and social science, 3 of fine arts, and 2 of physical education. A total of 125 credits with at least 25 in the major and a minimum GPA of 2.0 are required to graduate.

Special: Students may cross-register with members of the Western New York Consortium. Internships are available in psychology, social work, business, and Christian education. Study abroad in 7 countries, a Washington semester, dual majors, and a 3–2 engineering degree with Clarkson University are offered. Credit for military experience and nondegree study are possible. There are 2 national honor societies on campus.

Faculty/Classroom: 64% of faculty are male; 36%, female. All teach undergraduates and 20% do research. The average class size in an introductory lecture is 45; in a laboratory, 22; and in a regular course offering, 20.

Admissions: 79% of the 1995–96 applicants were accepted. The SAT I scores for the 1995–96 freshman class were as follows: Verbal—42% below 500, 40% between 500 and 599, 16% between 600 and 700, and 2% above 700; Math—26% below 500, 40% between 500 and 599, 30% between 600 and 700, and 4% above 700. The ACT scores were 7% below 21, 25% between 21 and 23, 33% between 24 and 26, 16% between 27 and 28, and 18% above 28. 54% of the current freshmen were in the top fifth of their class; 85% were in the top two fifths. 19 freshmen graduated first in their class.

Requirements: The SAT I or ACT is required. Houghton requires applicants to be in the upper 50% of their class. A minimum GPA of 2.5 is required. A minimum composite score of 800 on the SAT I or 20 on the ACT is recommended. Applicants must graduate from an accredited secondary school or have a GED. A total of 16 academic credits is required, including 4 of English, 3 of social studies, and 2 each of foreign language, mathematics, and science. An essay is required. Music students must audition. An interview is recommended. AP and CLEP credits are accepted. Important factors in the admissions decision are personality/intangible qualities, recommendations by school officials, and advanced placement or honor courses.

Procedure: Freshmen are admitted fall and spring. Entrance exams should be taken in the spring of the junior year or fall of the senior year. There is a deferred admissions plan. Applications should be filed by August 1 for fall entry and December 1 for spring entry, along with an application fee of $25. A waiting list is an active part of the admissions procedure, with about 5% of all applicants on the list.

Transfer: 54 transfer students enrolled in 1995–96. Transfer applicants should have completed at least 12 credit hours of college work with a 2.5 or better GPA. A pastor's recommendation and high school transcripts must be submitted. The SAT I or ACT and an interview are recommended. 30 credits of 125 must be completed at Houghton.

Visiting: There are regularly scheduled orientations for prospective students, including a tour, admissions interview, financial aid session, class visit, and academic program sessions. There are guides for informal visits and visitors may sit in on classes and stay overnight at the school. To schedule a visit, contact Diane Galloway, Campus Visit Coordinator.

Financial Aid: In 1995–96, 94% of all freshmen and 91% of continuing students received some form of financial aid. 83% of freshmen and 82% of continuing students received need-based aid. The average freshman award was $9017. Of that total, scholarships or need-based grants averaged $2446 ($4718 maximum); loans averaged $2421 ($4125 maximum); federal and state grants averaged $3250 ($6875 maximum); and work contracts averaged $900 ($1200 maximum). 55% of undergraduate students work part-time. Average earnings from campus work for the school year are $989. The average financial indebtedness of the 1994–95 graduate was $11,250. Houghton is a member of CSS. The FAF and the college's own financial statement are required. The application deadline for fall entry is March 15.

International Students: 55 international students were enrolled in a recent year. The school actively recruits these students. They must take the TOEFL and achieve a minimum score of 500.

Computers: The college provides computer facilities for student use. The mainframe is a DEC VAX 8200. There are 2 terminal laboratories, 3 microcomputer laboratories, and terminals in each residence hall. All students may access the system 24 hours a day in the residence halls, 15 hours a day in the computer laboratories. There are no time limits. The fees are $30.

Graduates: In 1994–95, 300 bachelor's degrees were awarded. The most popular majors among graduates were elementary education (22%), biology (17%), and psychology (16%). Within an average freshman class, 2% graduate in 3 years, 62% in 4 years, 65% in 5 years, and 66% in 6 years. 15 companies recruited on campus in 1994–95. Of the 1994 graduating class, 33% were enrolled in graduate school within 6 months of graduation and 84% had found employment.

Admissions Contact: Timothy R. Fuller, Vice President for Alumni and Admissions. E-mail: admissions@houghton.edu. A campus video is available.

IONA COLLEGE

D-5

New Rochelle, NY 10801–1890 (914) 633–2503; (800) 231-IONA

Full-time: 1392 men, 1604 women	Faculty: 175
Part-time: 351 men, 733 women	Ph.D.s: 76%
Graduate: 639 men, 869 women	Student/Faculty: 17 to 1
Year: semesters, summer session	Tuition: $11,590
Application Deadline: March 15	Room & Board: $7000
Freshman Class: 2974 applied, 2377 accepted, 593 enrolled	
SAT I Verbal/Math: 402/445	COMPETITIVE

Iona College, founded in 1940, is an independent, largely commuter college offering programs through schools of general studies, arts and science, and business. It has campuses in Rockland County and Manhattan in addition to the main campus in New Rochelle. There are 3 undergraduate and 2 graduate schools. In addition to regional accreditation, Iona has baccalaureate program accreditation with CSWE and NLN. The library contains 309,518 volumes, 90,000 microform items, and 13,399 audiovisual forms, and subscribes to 1260 periodicals. Computerized library sources and services include the card catalog, interlibrary loans, and database searching. Special learning facilities include a learning resource center, radio station, TV station, electron microscope, and a speech and hearing clinic. The 35-acre campus is in a suburban area 20 miles northeast of New York City. Including residence halls, there are 47 buildings on campus.

Student Life: 91% of undergraduates are from New York. Students come from 22 states, 46 foreign countries, and Canada. 32% are from public schools; 68% from private. 70% are white; 16% African American; 10% Hispanic. Most are Catholic. The average age of freshmen is 18; all undergraduates, 20. 21% do not continue beyond their first year; 63% remain to graduate.

Housing: 600 students can be accommodated in college housing. College-sponsored living facilities include single-sex and coed dormitories. On-campus housing is available on a first-come, first-served basis and is available on a lottery system for upperclassmen. Priority is given to out-of-town students. 83% of students commute. Alcohol is not permitted. All students may keep cars on campus.

Activities: 5% of men belong to 8 local and 2 national fraternities; 5% of women belong to 7 local and 2 national sororities. There are 74 groups on campus, including bagpipe band, cheerleading, choir,

chorale, computers, dance, drama, ethnic, honors, international, literary magazine, musical theater, newspaper, pep band, photography, political, professional, radio and TV, religious, social, social service, student government, and yearbook. Popular campus events include Founders Day, Columbus Day Carnival, and Homecoming.

Sports: There are 12 intercollegiate sports for men and 8 for women, and 5 intramural sports for men and 2 for women. Athletic and recreation facilities include an all-weather football-soccer field, gymnasium, Nautilus fitness center, baseball field, saunas, track, and swimming pool. The campus stadium seats 1200 and the indoor gymnasium, 3000.

Disabled Students: 80% of the campus is accessible to disabled students. The following facilities are available: wheelchair ramps, elevators, special parking, specially equipped rest rooms, special class scheduling, lowered drinking fountains, and lowered telephones. All classes are held on the first floor.

Services: In addition to many counseling and information services, tutoring is available in some subjects, including mathematics, statistics, computer science, English composition, history, Spanish, scientific and technological literacy, accounting, business, and management science. There is a reader service for the blind, and remedial math, reading, and writing.

Campus Safety and Security: Campus safety and security measures include 24-hour foot and vehicle patrol, shuttle buses, informal discussions, and pamphlets/posters/films. In addition, there are lighted pathways/sidewalks.

Programs of Study: Iona confers B.A., B.S., B.B.A., and B.P.S. degrees. Associate and master's degrees are also awarded. Bachelor's degrees are awarded in BIOLOGICAL SCIENCE (biology/biological science and ecology), BUSINESS (accounting, banking and finance, business administration and management, business economics, business law, management information systems, management science, and marketing/retailing/merchandising), COMMUNICATIONS AND THE ARTS (advertising, communications, dramatic arts, English, film arts, French, Italian, journalism, and Spanish), COMPUTER AND PHYSICAL SCIENCE (computer science, information sciences and systems, mathematics, and physics), EDUCATION (elementary, foreign languages, middle school, science, and secondary), HEALTH PROFESSIONS (health care administration, medical laboratory technology, predentistry, premedicine, prepharmacy, preveterinary science, and speech pathology/audiology), SOCIAL SCIENCE (criminal justice, economics, history, international relations, philosophy, political science/government, prelaw, psychology, religion, social science, social work, sociology, and urban studies). Accounting, computer science, and management information systems are the strongest academically. Communication arts, accounting, and management have the largest enrollments.

Required: The core curriculum includes 24 credits of humanities, 12 credits of natural and symbolic languages, and 6 credits each of communications, social science, and science and technology. Computer literacy is required. The total number of credits required in liberal arts is 120, with 39 to 46 in the major; the business program requires 126 credits, with 30 in the major. The minimum GPA is 2.0.

Special: There are cross-registration and co-op programs with Concordia College, Marymount College Tarrytown, and the College of New Rochelle. There are internships for upperclassmen. Study abroad is available in Ireland, Belgium, France, Spain, Italy, and Morocco. There is work-study in Iona offices and academic departments. Students may earn a combined B.A.-B.S. degree in economics, psychology, elementary education, early secondary education, and mathematics education. The college offers dual and student-designed majors, a general studies degree, and credit by examination and for life/military/work experience. There is a freshman honors program on campus, as well as 15 national honor societies.

Faculty/Classroom: 65% of faculty are male; 35%, female. 95% teach undergraduates. No introductory courses are taught by graduate students. The average class size in an introductory lecture is 27; in a laboratory, 20; and in a regular course offering, 20.

Admissions: 80% of the 1995–96 applicants were accepted. SAT I scores for the 1995–96 freshman class were as follows: Verbal—89% below 500, 10% between 500 and 599, and 1% between 600 and 700; Math—75% below 500, 18% between 500 and 599, and 7% between 600 and 700. 20% of the current freshmen were in the top fifth of their class; 44% were in the top two fifths.

Requirements: SAT I is required and the ACT is recommended. Iona requires applicants to be in the upper 60% of their class. A minimum GPA of 2.5 is required. Applicants must complete 16 academic credits including 4 units of English, 3 of mathematics, 2 of foreign language, and 1 each of history, science, and social studies. A GED is accepted. An essay and an interview are recommended. AP and CLEP credits are accepted. Important factors in the admissions decision are recommendations by school officials, extracurricular activities record, and leadership record.

Procedure: Freshmen are admitted fall and spring. Entrance exams should be taken in the spring of the senior year. There are early admissions and deferred admissions plans. Applications should be filed by March 15 for fall entry and January 1 for spring entry, along with an application fee of $25. Notification is sent on a rolling basis.

Transfer: 131 transfer students enrolled in 1995–96. Applicants must have a GPA of at least 2.5, and must submit high school transcripts if they have earned fewer than 30 college credits. An interview is recommended. 30 credits of 120 must be completed at Iona.

Visiting: There are regularly scheduled orientations for prospective students, including a meeting with an admissions counselor, a campus tour, and a variety of on-campus programs during the spring and summer. There are guides for informal visits, and visitors may sit in on classes. To schedule a visit, contact the Admissions Office at (914) 633-2502.

Financial Aid: In 1995–96, 92% of all freshmen and 84% of continuing students received some form of financial aid. 80% of freshmen and 55% of continuing students received need-based aid. The average freshman award was $8480. Of that total, scholarships or need-based grants averaged $3500 ($11,200 maximum); loans averaged $2780; state and federal entitlements averaged $600; and work contracts averaged $1600 ($3500 maximum). 19% of undergraduate students work part time. Average earnings from campus work for the school year was $1130. The average financial indebtedness of the 1994–95 graduate was $8410. Iona is a member of CSS. The FAF, the college's own financial statement, and the TAP (Tuition Assistance Program) documents are required. The application deadline for fall entry is April 15.

International Students: There are currently 89 international students enrolled. They must score 550 on the TOEFL and also take SAT I or the ACT.

Computers: The college provides computer facilities for student use. The mainframe is an IBM 9121 Model 210. More than 1000 microcomputers throughout the campus provide access to local area networks and mainframe facilities. All students may access the system. There is unlimited access to PC software (24 hours) and mainframe facilities. There are no time limits. The fees are $25 per semester.

Graduates: In 1994–95, 831 bachelor's degrees were awarded. The most popular majors among graduates were communication arts (14%), elementary education (8%), and accounting (7%). Within an average freshman class, 1% graduate in 3 years, 40% in 4 years, 14% in 5 years, and 4% in 6 years. 62 companies recruited on campus in 1994–95.

Admissions Contact: Kevin Derlin, Director of Admissions. A video of the campus is available.

ITHACA COLLEGE
Ithaca, NY 14850

C-3

(607) 274-3124
(800) 429-4274; FAX: (607) 274-1900

Full-time: 2548 men, 2860 women	Faculty: 441; IIB, +$
Part-time: 59 men, 92 women	Ph.D.s: 89%
Graduate: 70 men, 169 women	Student/Faculty: 12 to 1
Year: semesters, summer session	Tuition: $15,250
Application Deadline: March 1	Room & Board: $6594
Freshman Class: 7058 applied, 5318 accepted, 1625 enrolled	
SAT I or ACT: required	COMPETITIVE

Ithaca College, founded in 1892, is a private, coeducational college offering undergraduate and graduate programs in business, communications, health science and human performance, humanities and sciences, and music. There are 5 undergraduate schools and 1 graduate school. In addition to regional accreditation, Ithaca has baccalaureate program accreditation with APTA, NASM, and NRPA. The library contains 335,288 volumes, 198,575 microform items, and 21,752 audiovisual forms, and subscribes to 2541 periodicals. Computerized library sources and services include interlibrary loans and database searching. Special learning facilities include a learning resource center, art gallery, radio station, TV station, film and photography complex, multi-image and interactive video laboratories, and a center for trading analysis of financial instruments. The 600-acre campus is in a small town 250 miles northwest of New York City. Including residence halls, there are 60 buildings on campus.

Student Life: 52% of undergraduates are from out-of-state, mostly the Middle Atlantic. Students come from 46 states, 56 foreign countries, and Canada. 85% are from public schools; 15% from private. 91% are white. The average age of freshmen is 18; all undergraduates, 20. 6% do not continue beyond their first year; 72% remain to graduate.

Housing: 3723 students can be accommodated in college housing. College-sponsored living facilities include single-sex and coed dormitories and on-campus apartments. In addition, there are special interest houses, freshmen only, quiet dorms, and music honor fraternities. On-campus housing is guaranteed for all 4 years. 68% of students live on campus; of those, 95% remain on campus on weekends. All students may keep cars on campus.

Activities: There are no social fraternities or sororities on campus. There are 132 groups on campus, including art, chess, choir, chorale, chorus, computers, dance, drama, ethnic, film, gay, honors, international, jazz band, literary magazine, musical theater, newspaper, opera, orchestra, pep band, photography, political, professional, radio and TV, religious, social, social service, student government, and yearbook. Popular campus events include Winter Carnival, Roctoberfest, and a spring concert.

Sports: There are 11 intercollegiate sports for men and 12 for women, and 16 intramural sports for men and 16 for women. Athletic and recreation facilities include a gymnasium, a dance studio, a student union, indoor and outdoor pools, wrestling and weight rooms, a sand volleyball court, tennis courts, and baseball, football, lacrosse, field hockey, and soccer fields.

Disabled Students: The following facilities are available: wheelchair ramps, elevators, special parking, specially equipped rest rooms, special class scheduling, lowered drinking fountains, and lowered telephones.

Services: Nonremedial tutoring is available.

Campus Safety and Security: Campus safety and security measures include 24-hour foot and vehicle patrol, escort service, shuttle buses, and pamphlets/posters/films. In addition, there are emergency telephones, lighted pathways/sidewalks, and crime prevention programs.

Programs of Study: Ithaca confers B.A., B.S., B.F.A., B.M., and Mus.B. degrees. Master's degrees are also awarded. Bachelor's degrees are awarded in BIOLOGICAL SCIENCE (biochemistry and biology/biological science), BUSINESS (accounting, banking and finance, business administration and management, international business management, marketing/retailing/merchandising, personnel management, recreation and leisure services, and sports management), COMMUNICATIONS AND THE ARTS (art, art history and appreciation, broadcasting, communications, dramatic arts, English, film arts, fine arts, French, German, jazz, journalism, music, music performance, music theory and composition, photography, Spanish, speech/debate/rhetoric, telecommunications, and visual and performing arts), COMPUTER AND PHYSICAL SCIENCE (chemistry, computer programming, computer science, mathematics, and physics), EDUCATION (education of the deaf and hearing impaired, foreign languages, health, music, physical, science, and secondary), HEALTH PROFESSIONS (health care administration, medical records administration/services, physical therapy, predentistry, premedicine, and speech pathology/audiology), SOCIAL SCIENCE (anthropology, economics, history, parks and recreation management, philosophy, physical fitness/movement, political science/government, prelaw, psychology, religion, social studies, and sociology). Physical therapy, communications, and cinema and photography are the strongest academically. Business, communications, and psychology have the largest enrollments.

Required: Students must successfully complete a minimum of 120 credit hours. In addition, each student must meet the requirements of a core curriculum, which varies with each school within the college and includes courses in the liberal arts and professional courses outside the student's major.

Special: Cross-registration is available with Cornell University. Opportunities are also provided for internships, work-study programs, dual majors, accelerated degree programs, nondegree study, pass/fail options, student-designed majors, a 3–2 engineering degree with Cornell University, a B.A.-B.S. degree, credit for life experience, and study abroad in the college's London Center and in other foreign cities. There is a freshman honors program on campus, as well as 19 national honor societies. 15 departments have honors programs.

Faculty/Classroom: 59% of faculty are male; 41%, female. All teach undergraduates. No introductory courses are taught by graduate students. The average class size in an introductory lecture is 20; in a laboratory, 10; and in a regular course offering, 16.

Admissions: 75% of the 1995–96 applicants were accepted. The SAT I scores for the 1995–96 freshman class were as follows: Verbal—50% below 500, 37% between 500 and 599, 12% between 600 and 700, and 1% above 700; Math—26% below 500, 41% between 500 and 599, 29% between 600 and 700, and 4% above 700. 50% of the current freshmen were in the top fifth of their class; 77% were in the top two fifths. 25 freshmen graduated first in their class.

Requirements: The SAT I or ACT is required. In addition, applicants should be graduates of an accredited secondary school with a minimum of 16 Carnegie units, including 4 years of English, 3 each of mathematics, science, and social studies, 2 of foreign language, and other college-preparatory electives. The GED is accepted. An essay is required, as is an audition for music students. In some majors, a portfolio and an interview are recommended. AP and CLEP credits are accepted.

Procedure: Freshmen are admitted fall and spring. Entrance exams should be taken in spring of the junior year or fall of the senior year. There are early decision, early admissions, and deferred admissions plans. Early decision applications should be filed by November 1;

regular applications, by March 1 for fall entry and November 1 for spring entry, along with an application fee of $40. Notification of early decision is sent December 15; regular decision, on a rolling basis. 200 early decision candidates were accepted for the 1995–96 class. A waiting list is an active part of the admissions procedure.

Transfer: 176 transfer students enrolled in 1995–96. Transfer applicants must submit SAT I or ACT scores, a high school transcript, and transcripts from previously attended colleges. A college GPA of 2.6 is required. 30 credits of 120 must be completed at Ithaca.

Visiting: There are regularly scheduled orientations for prospective students, including a campus tour and an interview with an admissions counselor. There are guides for informal visits and visitors may sit in on classes and stay overnight at the school. To schedule a visit, contact the Director of Admissions.

Financial Aid: In 1995–96, 83% of all freshmen and 63% of continuing students received some form of financial aid. 68% of freshmen and 57% of continuing students received need-based aid. The average freshman award was $13,000. Of that total, scholarships or need-based grants averaged $9100 ($21,700 maximum); loans averaged $2900 ($7600 maximum); and work contracts averaged $1000 ($2800 maximum). 42% of undergraduate students work part-time. Average earnings from campus work for the school year are $1400. The FAFSA is required. The application deadline for fall entry is March 1.

International Students: There are currently 115 international students enrolled. The school actively recruits these students. They must take the TOEFL or the MELAB and achieve a minimum score on the TOEFL of 550. The student must also take the SAT I or the ACT.

Computers: The college provides computer facilities for student use. The mainframes are a DEC VAX 11/750 and a DEC VAX 11/785. There are more than 2000 microcomputers on 20 local area networks. Students may access the VAX mainframes from microcomputers located in residence halls, computer laboratories, and classrooms. All students may access the system 24 hours a day. There are no time limits and no fees.

Graduates: In 1994–95, 1325 bachelor's degrees were awarded. The most popular majors among graduates were TV and radio (9%), sociology (7%), and physical therapy (6%). Within an average freshman class, 1% graduate in 3 years, 61% in 4 years, 71% in 5 years, and 72% in 6 years. 74 companies recruited on campus in 1994–95. Of a recent graduating class, 22% were enrolled in graduate school within 6 months of graduation and 77% had found employment.

Admissions Contact: Paula Mitchell, Director of Admissions.

JEWISH THEOLOGICAL SEMINARY/LIST COLLEGE OF JEWISH STUDIES
D-5

New York, NY 10027-4649

(212) 678-8832
FAX: (212) 678-8947

Full-time: 49 men, 61 women	Faculty: 40
Part-time: 1 man, 1 woman	Ph.D.s: 98%
Graduate: 177 men, 225 women	Student/Faculty: 3 to 1
Year: semesters, summer session	Tuition: $7020
Application Deadline: February 15	Room & Board: $6000
Freshman Class: 91 applied, 68 accepted, 37 enrolled	
SAT I Verbal/Math: 570/630	HIGHLY COMPETITIVE

The Jewish Theological Seminary/List College of Jewish Studies, founded in 1886, is a private, coeducational institution affiliated with the Conservative branch of the Jewish faith. List College offers undergraduate and graduate programs in all aspects of Judaica, including Bible, rabbinics, literature, history, philosophy, education, and communal service. There is also a combined undergraduate program with Columbia University and Barnard College. There are 3 graduate schools. The 3 libraries contain 275,000 volumes and 3500 microform items, and subscribe to 750 periodicals. Computerized library sources and services include the card catalog, interlibrary loans, and database searching. Special learning facilities include a learning resource center, art gallery, and a music center, the Melton Research Center, and the Jewish Museum Archives Center. The 1-acre campus is in an urban area on the upper west side of Manhattan. Including residence halls, there are 6 buildings on campus.

Student Life: 65% of undergraduates are from out-of-state, mostly the Middle Atlantic. Students come from 28 states, 5 foreign countries, and Canada. 60% are from public schools; 40% from private. 97% are white. Most are Jewish. The average age of freshmen is 18; all undergraduates, 20. 96% of freshmen remain to graduate.

Housing: 212 students can be accommodated in college housing. College-sponsored living facilities include coed dormitories, on-campus apartments, off-campus apartments, and married-student housing. In addition there is kosher housing. On-campus housing is guaranteed for all 4 years. 93% of students live on campus; of those, 95% remain on campus on weekends. Alcohol is not permitted. All students may keep cars on campus.

Activities: 12% of men belong to fraternities; 4% of women belong to sororities. There are 20 groups on campus, including art, band, choir, chorus, computers, dance, drama, ethnic, film, gay, honors, international, literary magazine, musical theater, newspaper, photography, political, professional, radio and TV, religious, social, social service, student government, and yearbook. Popular campus events include Purim, Simchat Torah, and Orientation.

Sports: There are 3 intramural sports for men and 3 for women. Athletic and recreation facilities include a gymnasium. Students enrolled in the dual-degree program may also use the facilities at Columbia University.

Disabled Students: All of the campus is accessible to disabled students. The following facilities are available: wheelchair ramps, elevators, special parking, specially equipped rest rooms, lowered drinking fountains, lowered telephones, and elevators with braille panels.

Services: In addition to many counseling and information services, tutoring is available in most subjects.

Campus Safety and Security: Campus safety and security measures include 24-hour foot and vehicle patrol, escort service, informal discussions, and pamphlets/posters/films. There are emergency telephones and lighted pathways/sidewalks.

Programs of Study: List College confers the B.A. degree. Master's and doctoral degrees are also awarded. Bachelor's degrees are awarded in SOCIAL SCIENCE (religion). Religion is the strongest academically. Education has the largest enrollment.

Required: Students must take a Hebrew language requirement, 9 credits in literature, 24 in Jewish history, and 6 each in Bible, Jewish philosophy, and the Talmud. In addition, there are 60 required credits in liberal arts, including 18 credits in English, history, philosophy or social science, and mathematics or laboratory science to be completed at another college or university. A total of 156 credits (96 taken at List College) is required for graduation, with 21 in a major field.

Special: There is a joint liberal arts program with Columbia University and a double-degree program with Barnard College, which enables students to earn 2 B.A. degrees in 4 to 4 1/2 years. Study abroad is available in Israel, England, France, and Spain. Student-designed majors, credit by exam, and nondegree study are also offered. There is a freshman honors program on campus

Faculty/Classroom: 68% of faculty are male; 32%, female. All teach and do research. Graduate students teach 1% of introductory courses. The average class size in an introductory lecture is 30 and in a regular course offering, 10.

Admissions: 75% of the 1995–96 applicants were accepted. The SAT I scores for the 1995–96 freshman class were as follows: Verbal—22% below 500, 34% between 500 and 599, 41% between 600 and 700, and 3% above 700; Math—12% below 500, 28% between 500 and 599, 44% between 600 and 700, and 16% above 700. There were 2 National Merit finalists and 1 semifinalist in a recent year.

Requirements: The SAT I is required as is the EN or ES SAT II: Subject tests. Applicants must be graduates of an accredited secondary school or have the GED. An essay and 2 recommendations are required. AP credits are accepted. Important factors in the admissions decision are advanced placement or honor courses, extracurricular activities record, and personality/intangible qualities.

Procedure: Freshmen are admitted fall and spring. Entrance exams should be taken in the spring of the junior year. There are early decision, early admissions, and deferred admissions plans. Early decision applications should be filed by November 15; regular applications, by February 15 for fall entry and November 1 for spring entry, along with an application fee of $60. Notification of early decision is sent December 15; regular decision, April 1.

Transfer: 6 transfer students enrolled in a recent year. Applicants must submit SAT I or ACT scores, an essay, a high school transcript, a college transcript, and 2 academic recommendations. A minimum college GPA of 2.5 is required. An interview is recommended. 48 credits of 156 must be completed at List College.

Visiting: There are regularly scheduled orientations for prospective students, including a tour of the campus and of Columbia University, an interview with the dean, and an overnight stay in the dormitory. There are guides for informal visits and visitors may sit in on classes and stay overnight at the school. To schedule a visit, contact Marci Harris Blumenthal, Admissions Director.

Financial Aid: In a recent year, 40% of all freshmen and 60% of continuing students received some form of financial aid including need-based aid. The average freshman award that year was $12,000. Of that total, scholarships or need-based grants averaged $5500 ($12,700 maximum); and loans averaged $2500 ($2625 maximum). 15% of undergraduate students work part-time. List College is a member of CSS. The FAF, the college's own financial statement, and the and 1040 tax forms are required. The application deadline for fall entry is February 15.

International Students: There were 33 international students enrolled in a recent year. They must score 500 on the TOEFL, or take the college's own test or the American Language English Placement Test.

Computers: Students may use Columbia University facilities. There are no time limits on using the system and no fees.

Graduates: In a recent year, 27 bachelor's degrees were awarded. Within an average freshman class, 60% graduate in 4 years and 40% in 5 years.

Admissions Contact: Marci Harris Blumenthal, Director of Admissions. E-mail: mablumenthal@jtsa.edu.

JUILLIARD SCHOOL D-5
New York, NY 10023–6590

(212) 799–5000, ext. 223
FAX: (212) 724–0263

Full-time: 223 men, 261 women	Faculty: 48
Part-time: none	Ph.D.s: n/av
Graduate: 178 men, 170 women	Student/Faculty: 10 to 1
Year: semesters	Tuition: $13,600
Application Deadline: see profile	Room & Board: $6300
Freshman Class: 1173 applied, 135 accepted, 107 enrolled	
SAT I or ACT: not required	SPECIAL

The Juilliard School, founded in 1905, is a private college of dance, music, and drama. There is one graduate school. The 2 libraries contain 65,000 volumes, 1300 microform items, and 15,000 audiovisual forms, and subscribe to 175 periodicals. Computerized library sources and services include interlibrary loans. Special learning facilities include 200 practice rooms, 5 theaters, scenery and costume shops, and dance studios. The campus is in an urban area in New York City.

Student Life: Students come from 31 states, 50 foreign countries, and Canada. 60% are white; 31% Asian American. The average age of freshmen is 18; all undergraduates, 21.

Housing: 375 students can be accommodated in college housing. College-sponsored living facilities include single-sex and coed dormitories and off-campus apartments. There are no-smoking and no-practice (silent) floors, as well as floors for new students. On-campus housing is guaranteed for the freshman year only, is available on a first-come, first-served basis, and is available on a lottery system for upperclassmen. 52% of students commute. All students may keep cars on campus.

Activities: There are no fraternities or sororities. There are 20 groups on campus, including band, choir, chorale, chorus, dance, drama, ethnic, gay, international, jazz band, marching band, newspaper, opera, orchestra, professional, religious, social service, student government, symphony, and yearbook. Popular campus events include performances by the Juilliard orchestras at Lincoln Center, dance concerts, drama and opera productions, and interdisciplinary performances combining music, dance, and drama.

Sports: There are 2 intercollegiate sports for men and 1 for women, and 2 intramural sports for men and 1 for women. Athletic and recreation facilities include a health club in the residence hall.

Disabled Students: All of the campus is accessible to disabled students. The following facilities are available: wheelchair ramps, elevators, specially equipped rest rooms, lowered drinking fountains, and lowered telephones.

Services: In addition to many counseling and information services, tutoring is available in some subjects, including ear training and literature and materials of music.

Campus Safety and Security: Campus safety and security measures include 24-hour foot and vehicle patrol, self-defense education, informal discussions, and pamphlets/posters/films. In addition, there are emergency telephones, lighted pathways/sidewalks, 24-hour guards in residence hall and main building, videocameras, and turnstiles with ID-card access.

Programs of Study: Juilliard confers B.Mus. and B.F.A. degrees. Master's and doctoral degrees are also awarded. Bachelor's degrees are awarded in COMMUNICATIONS AND THE ARTS (dance, dramatic arts, music theory and composition, piano/organ, strings, and voice). Piano, voice, and violin have the largest enrollments.

Required: Each division has its own requirements for graduation.

Special: A joint program with Columbia University and Barnard College allows students to obtain a 5-year B.A.-B.Mus. degree. Internships are available with cultural organizations in New York City. There is study abroad in music academies in England, Israel, and Russia. Work-study programs, accelerated degrees and dual majors in music, a combined B.Mus.-M.Mus. degree, nondegree study, and pass/fail options are available.

Faculty/Classroom: 65% of faculty are male; 35%, female. All teach undergraduates. Graduate students teach 1% of introductory courses. The average class size in a regular course offering is 12.

Admissions: 12% of the 1995–96 applicants were accepted.

Requirements: A high school diploma or GED is required. Students are accepted primarily on the basis of personal auditions rather than tests. AP credits are accepted. Important factors in the admissions decision are evidence of special talent and personality/intangible qualities.

Procedure: Freshmen are admitted in the fall. Personal auditions should be completed in December for opera, February for drama and regionals in dance and music, March for dance and music, and May for dance and music departments that remain open. Application deadlines are January 7 for all drama applicants and for dance and drama applicants to meet March auditions; and March 15 for dance and music applicants to meet May auditions. There is an early admissions plan. Application fee is $60. A waiting list is an active part of the admissions procedure, with about 5% of all applicants on the list.

Transfer: Transfer applicants must audition in person.

Visiting: There are regularly scheduled orientations for prospective students, including guided tours and question-and-answer sessions, Monday to Friday at 2:30 P.M. Visitors may sit in on classes and stay overnight at the school. To schedule a visit, contact David Stull, Assistant Director of Admissions.

Financial Aid: 80% of undergraduate students work part-time. Average earnings from campus work for the school year are $1500. Juilliard is a member of CSS. The FAF and the college's own financial statement are required.

International Students: There are currently 255 international students enrolled. They must take the college's own test of English proficiency. All students must audition in person.

Graduates: In 1994–95, 104 bachelor's degrees were awarded.

Admissions Contact: Office of Admissions.

KEUKA COLLEGE B-3
Keuka Park, NY 14478

(315) 536–4411, ext. 254
(800) 33-KEUKA

Full-time: 216 men, 624 women	Faculty: 44; IIB, --$
Part-time: 8 men, 73 women	Ph.D.s: 58%
Graduate: none	Student/Faculty: 19 to 1
Year: 4-1-4, summer session	Tuition: $10,200
Application Deadline: open	Room & Board: $4780
Freshman Class: 655 applied, 550 accepted, 202 enrolled	
SAT I Verbal/Math: 476/498	COMPETITIVE

Keuka College, founded in 1890, is an independent, coeducational college affiliated with the American Baptist Churches, and offers instruction in the liberal arts. In addition to regional accreditation, Keuka has baccalaureate program accreditation with AHEA, CSWE, and NLN. The library contains 150,000 volumes, 4408 microform items, and 2009 audiovisual forms, and subscribes to 388 periodicals. Computerized library sources and services include the card catalog and interlibrary loans. Special learning facilities include a learning resource center and art gallery. The 173-acre campus is in a rural area 60 miles south of Rochester. Including residence halls, there are 19 buildings on campus.

Student Life: 93% of undergraduates are from New York. Students come from 10 states, 4 foreign countries, and Canada. 80% are from public schools; 20% from private. 89% are white. 30% are Protestant. The average age of freshmen is 18; all undergraduates, 23. 20% do not continue beyond their first year; 55% remain to graduate.

Housing: 800 students can be accommodated in college housing. College-sponsored living facilities include single-sex and coed dormitories. On-campus housing is guaranteed for all 4 years. 69% of students live on campus; of those, 75% remain on campus on weekends. Alcohol is not permitted. Upperclassmen may keep cars on campus.

Activities: There are no fraternities or sororities. There are 42 groups on campus, including art, cheerleading, choir, chorale, computers, dance, drama, ethnic, gay, honors, international, literary magazine, newspaper, political, professional, religious, social, social service, student government, and yearbook. Popular campus events include Spring Weekend, May Day, Fall Weekend, Freshman Stunt, and crew races.

Sports: Athletic and recreation facilities include an Olympic-size pool, a gymnasium, a fitness center, and a weight room.

Disabled Students: The following facilities are available: wheelchair ramps, elevators, special parking, specially equipped rest rooms, and special class scheduling.

Services: In addition to many counseling and information services, tutoring is available in most subjects. There is remedial math, reading, and writing.

Campus Safety and Security: Campus safety and security measures include escort service, informal discussions, pamphlets/posters/films, and lighted pathways/sidewalks.

Programs of Study: Keuka confers B.A. and B.S. degrees. Bachelor's degrees are awarded in BIOLOGICAL SCIENCE (biochemistry and biology/biological science), BUSINESS (accounting, business administration and management, hotel/motel and restaurant management, marketing/retailing/merchandising, and personnel management), COMMUNICATIONS AND THE ARTS (English), COMPUTER AND PHYSICAL SCIENCE (mathematics), EDUCATION (elementary, secondary, and special), HEALTH PROFESSIONS (medical laboratory technology, nursing, and occupational therapy), SOCIAL SCIENCE (history, political science/government, social work, and sociology). Occupational therapy, education, and nursing have the largest enrollments.

Required: Students must complete 1 field period combining academic study and professional experience for each year of enrollment. The core curriculum consists of 43 to 46 credits, including required courses in physical education, computer science, and integrative studies. A total of 120 credit hours is required for graduation with a minimum of 30 credits in the major and a GPA of 2.0.

Special: There are co-op programs with other members of the Rochester Area Colleges Consortium. The college offers internships, study abroad, a Washington semester, dual majors, student-designed majors, and a 3-2 engineering degree with Clarkson University. Credit is also given by exam and for work experience. There is a freshman honors program on campus, as well as 16 national honor societies, including Phi Beta Kappa.

Faculty/Classroom: 50% of faculty are male; 50%, female. All teach undergraduates. The average class size in an introductory lecture is 22; in a laboratory, 12; and in a regular course offering, 22.

Admissions: 84% of the 1995–96 applicants were accepted. SAT I scores for the 1995–96 freshman class were as follows: Verbal—67% below 500, 30% between 500 and 599, and 3% between 600 and 700; Math—55% below 500, 31% between 500 and 599, 13% between 600 and 700, and 1% above 700. 27% of the current freshmen were in the top fifth of their class; 76% were in the top two fifths. There was 1 National Merit semifinalist. 5 freshmen graduated first in their class.

Requirements: The SAT I or ACT is required. Keuka requires applicants to be in the upper 50% of their class. A minimum GPA of 2.8 is required. Students should graduate from an accredited secondary school with a minimum GPA of 2.8. The GED is accepted. A minimum of 15 Carnegie units is required, including 4 years of English, 3 of history, 2 to 3 of mathematics and science, 2 of foreign language, and 1 of social studies. An essay is required, and an interview is recommended. AP and CLEP credits are accepted. Important factors in the admissions decision are recommendations by school officials, extracurricular activities record, and leadership record.

Procedure: Freshmen are admitted fall and spring. Entrance exams should be taken in the spring of the junior year or the fall of the senior year. There are early decision, early admissions, and deferred admissions plans. Application deadlines are open for regular admission and December 1 for early decision. Application fee is $30. Notification of early decision is sent December 15; regular decision, on a rolling basis. 12 early decision candidates were accepted for the 1995–96 class.

Transfer: 148 transfer students enrolled in 1995–96. Applicants must take the SAT I or ACT and submit transcripts. An interview is recommended. A minimum of 2.5 GPA is required in college work. 30 credits of 120 must be completed at Keuka.

Visiting: There are regularly scheduled orientations for prospective students, including open houses held in October, November, and February, when students can speak with faculty, student affairs and financial aid representatives, and current students. There are guides for informal visits, and visitors may sit in on classes and stay overnight at the school. To schedule a visit, contact the Admissions Office.

Financial Aid: In 1995–96, 96% of all freshmen and 92% of continuing students received some form of financial aid. 90% of freshmen and 82% of continuing students received need-based aid. The average freshman award was $12,400. Of that total, scholarships or need-based grants averaged $3700 ($9960 maximum); loans averaged $2200 ($2625 maximum); and work contracts averaged $1300 ($1500 maximum). 75% of undergraduate students work part-time. Average earnings from campus work for the school year are $1100. The average financial indebtedness of the 1994–95 graduate was $15,200. Keuka is a member of CSS. The college's own financial statement, the FAFSA, and TAP application for New York State residents are required. The application deadline for fall entry is March 15.

International Students: There are currently 4 international students enrolled. They must score 550 on the TOEFL.

Computers: The college provides computer facilities for student use. The mainframe is a DEC 11/34A. 2 fully equipped microcomputer laboratories, with some access to the mainframe, provide students with word processing, graphics, spreadsheet, and other academic support functions. All students may access the system. There are no time limits and no fees.

Graduates: In 1994–95, 194 bachelor's degrees were awarded. The most popular majors among graduates were occupational therapy (48%), elementary/special education (32%), and nursing (13%). Within an average freshman class, 2% graduate in 3 years, 47% in 4 years, 11% in 5 years, and 3% in 6 years.

Admissions Contact: Robert J. Iannuzzo, Dean of Admissions and Financial Aid. A video of the campus is available.

LABORATORY INSTITUTE OF MERCHANDISING

D-5

New York, NY 10022-5268   (212) 752-1530; (800) 677-1323

Full-time: 5 men, 164 women	Faculty: 7
Part-time: 4 women	Ph.D.s: 3%
Graduate: none	Student/Faculty: 24 to 1
Year: 4-1-4, summer session	Tuition: $10,450
Application Deadline: open	Room & Board: n/app
Freshman Class: 113 applied, 93 accepted, 40 enrolled	
SAT I or ACT: required	SPECIAL

The Laboratory Institute of Merchandising, founded in 1939, is a private college offering programs in fashion merchandising and visual merchandising. The library contains 9660 volumes, 63 microform items, and 350 audiovisual forms, and subscribes to 110 periodicals. Computerized library sources and services include database searching. Special learning facilities include a learning resource center. The campus is in midtown Manhattan. There is one building on campus.

Student Life: 55% of undergraduates are from out-of-state, mostly the Middle Atlantic. Students come from 15 states, 7 foreign countries, and Canada. 65% are from public schools; 35% from private. 54% are white; 24% African American; 14% Hispanic. The average age of freshmen is 18; all undergraduates, 20. 85% of freshmen remain to graduate.

Housing: There are no residence halls. All students commute. Alcohol is not permitted.

Activities: There are no fraternities or sororities. There are some groups and organizations on campus, including ethnic, film, student government, and yearbook. Popular campus events include an annual fashion show and designer sample sales.

Sports: There is no sports program at LIM.

Disabled Students: Elevators are available for disabled students.

Services: In addition to many counseling and information services, tutoring is available in most subjects. There is remedial math, reading, and writing.

Campus Safety and Security: Campus safety and security measures include informal discussions and pamphlets/posters/films.

Programs of Study: LIM confers the B.P.S. degree. Associate degrees are also awarded. Bachelor's degrees are awarded in BUSINESS (apparel and accessories marketing and fashion merchandising).

Required: Students must complete 33 credits in the liberal arts and a minimum of 70 in fashion/business courses. Freshmen and sophomores must successfully complete a 3-credit work project each year. Seniors must complete a 13-credit, semester-long co-op program. A total of 128 credits and a GPA of 2.0 are required to graduate.

Special: There is cross-registration with Fordham University and Marymount College. Internships are required in the first, second, and fourth years. Study abroad is available in London and Paris. There are co-op programs as well as work-study programs with major department stores and specialty shops, manufacturers, showrooms, magazine publishers, and cosmetics companies.

Faculty/Classroom: 48% of faculty are male; 52%, female. The average class size in an introductory lecture is 25.

Admissions: 82% of the 1995–96 applicants were accepted.

Requirements: The SAT I or ACT is required. An essay and interview are required. Applicants should be high school graduates or hold the GED. AP and CLEP credits are accepted. Important factors in the admissions decision are personality/intangible qualities, leadership record, and extracurricular activities record.

Procedure: Freshmen are admitted fall and spring. Application deadlines are open. Application fee is $35. Notification is sent on a rolling basis.

Transfer: 21 transfer students enrolled in 1995–96. Applicants for the upper division (junior or senior year) must have a GPA of 2.5 in at least 60 college credits, submit 2 letters of recommendation (one educational and one professional), and have 2 interviews at the college (one with Admissions and one with Placement). 46 credits of 128 must be completed at LIM.

Visiting: There are regularly scheduled orientations for prospective students, consisting of the Student for a Day program, which includes classroom visits, a financial aid presentation, lunch, interviews, and a scholarship exam. There are guides for informal visits and visitors may sit in on classes. To schedule a visit, contact the Admissions Office.

Financial Aid: In 1995–96, 82% of all students received some form of financial aid. The average financial indebtedness of the 1994–95 graduate was $12,000. LIM is a member of CSS. The FAF and the college's own financial statement are required. The application deadline for fall entry is April 1.

International Students: In a recent year, 6 international students were enrolled. They must take the TOEFL and achieve a minimum score of 550.

Computers: The college provides computer facilities for student use. All students may access the system. There are no time limits and no fees.

Graduates: In a recent year, 38 bachelor's degrees were awarded. Within an average freshman class, 89% graduate in 4 years.

Admissions Contact: Andrew Ippolito, Director of Admissions. A campus video is available.

LE MOYNE COLLEGE
Syracuse, NY 13214

C-3

(315) 445-4300
(800) 333-4733; FAX: (315) 445-4540

Full-time: 720 men, 1010 women	Faculty: 121
Part-time: 169 men, 278 women	Ph.Ds: 92%
Graduate: 342 men, 274 women	Student/Faculty: 14 to 1
Year: semesters, summer session	Tuition: $12,060
Application Deadline: March 15	Room & Board: $5040
Freshman Class: 1719 applied, 1344 accepted, 403 enrolled	
SAT I or ACT: required	COMPETITIVE +

Le Moyne College, founded in 1946, is a coeducational liberal arts college in the Jesuit tradition. The library contains 215,395 volumes, 35,291 microform items, and 5921 audiovisual forms, and subscribes to 1787 periodicals. Computerized library sources and services include the card catalog, interlibrary loans, and database searching. Special learning facilities include a learning resource center, art gallery, and radio station. The 161-acre campus is in a suburban area of Syracuse. Including residence halls, there are 30 buildings on campus.

Student Life: 94% of undergraduates are from New York. Students come from 25 states, 8 foreign countries, and Canada. 65% are from public schools; 35% from private. 89% are white. 85% are Catholic; 14% Protestant. The average age of freshmen is 18; all undergraduates, 21. 11% do not continue beyond their first year; 73% remain to graduate.

Housing: 1356 students can be accommodated in college housing. College-sponsored living facilities include single-sex and coed dormitories and on-campus apartments. In addition there are special interest houses. On-campus housing is guaranteed for all 4 years. 74% of students live on campus; of those, 85% remain on campus on weekends. All students may keep cars on campus.

Activities: There are no fraternities or sororities. There are 70 groups on campus, including art, cheerleading, chess, chorus, computers, drama, ethnic, honors, international, literary magazine, newspaper, photography, political, professional, radio and TV, religious, social, social service, student government, and yearbook. Popular campus events include Winter/Spring Olympics, Winter Formal, concerts, films, and Spring Formal.

Sports: There are 8 intercollegiate sports for men and 8 for women, and 8 intramural sports for men and 7 for women. Athletic and recreation facilities include a 2500-seat gymnasium, indoor batting cages, team rooms, athletic training facilities, a 25-yard pool, a whirlpool, a fitness room, an elevated jogging track, 4 racquetball courts, and a large multipurpose gymnasium. Outdoor facilities include a baseball diamond, tennis courts, 2 softball fields, cross-country trails, intramural fields, and 2 soccer/lacrosse fields.

Disabled Students: 95% of the campus is accessible to disabled students. The following facilities are available: wheelchair ramps, elevators, special parking, specially equipped rest rooms, lowered drinking fountains, and lowered telephones.

Services: In addition to many counseling and information services, tutoring is available in every subject. There is remedial math and writing.

Campus Safety and Security: Campus safety and security measures include 24-hour foot and vehicle patrol, self-defense education, escort service, and informal discussions. In addition, there are pamphlets/posters/films, emergency telephones, lighted pathways/sidewalks, a campus watch program, and student security guards.

Programs of Study: Le Moyne confers B.A. and B.S. degrees. Master's degrees are also awarded. Bachelor's degrees are awarded in BIOLOGICAL SCIENCE (biology/biological science), BUSINESS (accounting, business administration and management, human resources, marketing/retailing/merchandising, and operations research), COMMUNICATIONS AND THE ARTS (communications, dramatic arts, English, and languages), COMPUTER AND PHYSICAL SCIENCE (actuarial science, chemistry, computer science, mathematics, physics, science, and statistics), EDUCATION (business, elementary, foreign languages, science, secondary, and special), ENGINEERING AND ENVIRONMENTAL DESIGN (preengineering), HEALTH PROFESSIONS (predentistry and premedicine), SOCIAL SCIENCE (criminal justice, economics, history, philosophy, political science/government, prelaw, psychology, religion, and sociology). Business, accounting, and psychology have the largest enrollments.

Required: A core curriculum of 14 courses in the humanities is required. Students must earn a GPA of 2.0, 30 hours in the major, and 120 credit hours to graduate.

Special: Internships are available with businesses, government offices, and social service agencies. A campus work-study program, study abroad in a variety of countries, dual majors, and a Washington semester are offered. A 3–2 engineering degree is available with Manhattan College, Clarkson University, and University of Detroit Mercy, and there are early assurance medical and dental programs. Some pass/fail options are offered. There is a freshman honors program on campus, as well as 13 national honor societies.

Faculty/Classroom: 62% of faculty are male; 38%, female. All teach and do research. No introductory courses are taught by graduate students. The average class size in an introductory lecture is 23; in a laboratory, 16; and in a regular course offering, 19.

Admissions: 78% of the 1995–96 applicants were accepted. SAT I scores for the 1995–96 freshman class were as follows: Verbal—64% below 500, 29% between 500 and 599, 6% between 600 and 700, and 1% above 700; Math—30% below 500, 47% between 500 and 599, 20% between 600 and 700, and 3% above 700. The ACT scores were 12% below 21, 26% between 21 and 23, 36% between 24 and 26, 12% between 27 and 28, and 14% above 28. 50% of the current freshmen were in the top fifth of their class; 80% were in the top two fifths. There were 50 National Merit semifinalists. One freshman graduated first in the class.

Requirements: The SAT I or ACT is required. Students should graduate from an accredited high school in the upper half of their class with an 80% average in academic subjects. A total of 16 academic units is required: 4 in English, 3 in foreign language, and 3 to 4 each in mathematics, science, and social studies. Applications are accepted on computer disk via College Link. AP and CLEP credits are accepted. Important factors in the admissions decision are recommendations by school officials, extracurricular activities record, and leadership record.

Procedure: Freshmen are admitted fall and spring. Entrance exams should be taken in the spring of the junior year or fall of the senior year. There are early decision, early admissions, and deferred admissions plans. Early decision applications should be filed by December 1; regular applications, by March 15 for fall entry and December 1 for spring entry, along with an application fee of $25. Notification of early decision is sent December 15; regular decision, on a rolling basis. 100 early decision candidates were accepted for the 1995–96 class.

Transfer: 170 transfer students enrolled in a recent year. A 2.6 GPA is usually required for admission. 30 credits of 120 must be completed at Le Moyne.

Visiting: There are regularly scheduled orientations for prospective students, including a campus tour and an interview with admissions counselors. Accepted students are invited to attend class and stay overnight in a dormitory. There are guides for informal visits, and visitors may sit in on classes and stay overnight at the school. To schedule a visit, contact the Admissions Office.

Financial Aid: In 1995–96, 95% of all freshmen and 90% of continuing students received some form of financial aid. 63% of freshmen and 65% of continuing students received need-based aid. The average freshman award was $11,000. Of that total, scholarships or need-based grants averaged $7500 ($16,740 maximum); loans averaged $2625 ($4625 maximum); and work contracts averaged $1000 (maximum). 90% of undergraduate students work part time. Average earnings from campus work for the school year are $1200. The average financial indebtedness of the 1994–95 graduate was $15,053. Le Moyne is a member of CSS. The CSS Profile Application financial statement and the FAFSA are required. The application deadline for fall entry is February 15.

International Students: There are currently 22 international students enrolled. The school actively recruits these students. They must score 550 on the the TOEFL and also take the SAT I or the ACT.

Computers: The college provides computer facilities for student use. The mainframe is a DEC VAX 3100-80. Approximately 35 terminals provide public access to the VAX. Dial-in lines and department terminals are also available. There are also approximately 125 microcomputers in public and departmental laboratories, most with connections to the VAX and the academic Novell server. Available applications include language compilers, statistical packages, curriculum-specific programs, local and wide-area E-mail, word processing, spreadsheet, database, and presentation programs. All students may access the system 24 hours a day. There are no time limits and no fees.

Graduates: In 1994–95, 476 bachelor's degrees were awarded. The most popular majors among graduates were accounting (17%), English (14%), and business (14%). Within an average freshman class, 72% graduate in 4 years, 76% in 5 years, and 78% in 6 years. 40 companies recruited on campus in 1994–95. Of the 1994 graduating class, 26% were enrolled in graduate school within 6 months of graduation and 59% had found employment.

Admissions Contact: Office of Admissions.

LONG ISLAND UNIVERSITY SYSTEM

The Long Island University, established in 1886, is a private system in New York. It is governed by a board of trustees, whose chief administrator is the president. The primary goal of the system is to provide Long Island's communities with high-quality higher education. The main priorities are teaching in the liberal arts and professions, extending higher education to underrepresented populations, and providing every student with opportunities for cooperative education placements in a field related to his or her major. The total enrollment in a recent of all 6 campuses was 22,865; there were 1253 faculty members. Altogether there are 142 baccalaureate, 148 master's, and 4 doctoral programs offered at Long Island University. Four-year campuses are located in Brooklyn, Brookville, and Southampton. Profiles of the 4-year campuses are included in this chapter.

LONG ISLAND UNIVERSITY
(See Brooklyn Campus of Long Island University)

LONG ISLAND UNIVERSITY/C.W. POST CAMPUS
D-5

Brookville, NY 11548–1300	(516) 299-2413; (800) LIU-PLAN
Full-time: 1541 men, 1918 women	Faculty: 296; IIA, +$
Part-time: 317 men, 671 women	Ph.D.s: 90%
Graduate: 1173 men, 2440 women	Student/Faculty: 12 to 1
Year: semesters, summer session	Tuition: $12,990
Application Deadline: open	Room & Board: $5880
Freshman Class: 3500 applied, 2964 accepted, 680 enrolled	
SAT I Verbal/Math: 458/505	LESS COMPETITIVE

Long Island University/C.W. Post Campus, founded in 1954 as part of the private Long Island University system, offers 82 undergraduate and 64 graduate majors in liberal arts and sciences, accounting, business, public service, health professions, visual and performing arts, education, and library information science. There are 5 undergraduate and 6 graduate schools. In addition to regional accreditation, C.W. Post has baccalaureate program accreditation with ADA, ASLA, CAHEA, and NLN. The library contains 2,169,157 volumes, 913,544 microform items, and 38,478 audiovisual forms, and subscribes to 8042 periodicals. Computerized library sources and services include the card catalog, interlibrary loans, and database searching. Special learning facilities include a learning resource center, art gallery, radio station, TV station, an art museum, a tax institute, a speech and hearing center, a center for business research, a federal depository, a center for the performing arts, a visual and performing arts computer center, a center for excellence in communications and learning, and an early childhood development center. The 305-acre campus is in a suburban area 25 miles east of New York City, on the former estate of Marjorie Merriweather Post. Including residence halls, there are 49 buildings on campus.

Student Life: 93% of undergraduates are from New York. Students come from 26 states, 40 foreign countries, and Canada. 71% are from public schools; 29% from private. 70% are white. The average age of freshmen is 18; all undergraduates, 21. 31% do not continue beyond their first year; 37% remain to graduate.

Housing: 2100 students can be accommodated in college housing. College-sponsored living facilities include single-sex and coed dormitories, on-campus apartments, and married-student housing. In addition there are quiet dormitories and all-female dormitories. On-campus housing is guaranteed for the freshman year only, is available on a first-come, first-served basis, and is available on a lottery system for upperclassmen. Priority is given to out-of-town students. 60% of students commute. All students may keep cars on campus.

Activities: 6% of men and about 1% of women belong to 1 local fraternity and 9 national fraternities; 4% of women belong to 1 local sorority and 9 national sororities. There are 104 groups on campus, including art, band, chamber singing, cheerleading, chess, choir, chorale, chorus, computers, dance, drama, drill team, equestrian, ethnic, film, gay, honors, international, jazz band, literary magazine, madrigal, musical theater, newspaper, orchestra, photography, political, professional, radio and TV, religious, Renaissance music, social, social service, student government, and yearbook. Popular campus events include Homecoming, Senior Week, Spring Week, Renaissance Fair, Science Expo, Greek Olympiad, International Student Dinner, Winter Week, and Senior Week.

Sports: There are 7 intercollegiate sports for men and 8 for women, and 4 intramural sports for men and 2 for women. Athletic and recreation facilities include a 6000-seat football stadium, a 700-seat indoor gymnasium, an equestrian center, tennis courts, a fitness center, and soccer, baseball, and softball fields.

Disabled Students: 75% of the campus is accessible to disabled students. The following facilities are available: wheelchair ramps, elevators, special parking, specially equipped rest rooms, lowered drinking fountains, and electric doors.

Services: In addition to many counseling and information services, tutoring is available in most subjects. There is a reader service for the blind, and remedial math, reading, and writing, and an academic resource center for learning disabled.

Campus Safety and Security: Campus safety and security measures include 24-hour foot and vehicle patrol, self-defense education, escort service, and shuttle buses. In addition, there are informal discussions, pamphlets/posters/films, emergency telephones, lighted pathways/sidewalks, restricted night access to campus, dormitory security staff, women and safety conferences, Alcohol Awareness Week, and Aids Awareness Day.

Programs of Study: C.W. Post confers B.A., B.S., B.S.Ed., B.F.A., and B.P.S. degrees. Associate, master's, and doctoral degrees are also awarded. Bachelor's degrees are awarded in AGRICULTURE (conservation and regulation), BIOLOGICAL SCIENCE (biology/biological science, molecular biology, and nutrition), BUSINESS (accounting, banking and finance, business administration and management, and marketing/retailing/merchandising), COMMUNICATIONS AND THE ARTS (arts administration/management, broadcasting, communications, dramatic arts, English, film arts, fine arts, French, German, Italian, journalism, music, photography, public relations, and Spanish), COMPUTER AND PHYSICAL SCIENCE (chemistry, computer science, geology, mathematics, physics, and radiological technology), EDUCATION (art, early childhood, elementary, English, foreign languages, health, music, science, and secondary), ENGINEERING AND ENVIRONMENTAL DESIGN (preengineering), HEALTH PROFESSIONS (art therapy, biomedical science, health care administration, medical laboratory technology, medical records administration/services, nursing, predentistry, premedicine, prepharmacy, and speech pathology/audiology), SOCIAL SCIENCE (criminal justice, economics, geography, history, international studies, philosophy, political science/government, prelaw, psychology, public administration, and social work). Accounting, radiologic technology, and biology are the strongest academically. Accounting, business, and education have the largest enrollments.

Required: Core requirements include 8 credits of laboratory science, 9 each of history and philosophy, 6 each of language and literature, arts, political science and economics, sociology, psychology, and geography or anthropology, and 3 of mathematics. A minimum of 128 credits is required to graduate. GPA requirements range from 2.0 to 2.5 in most departments, 3.0 in interdisciplinary studies. Students must demonstrate competency in writing, quantitative skills, computer skills, oral communications, and library use.

Special: There is cross-registration with several other Long Island colleges. C.W. Post offers co-op programs in all majors, internships, study abroad in 11 countries, work-study in most departments, accelerated degree programs, and a Washington semester for outstanding criminal justice students. Dual majors and student designed majors are available. There is a 3–2 engineering degree with Polytechnic University and Pratt Institute, and credit is available for life, military, and work experience. Nondegree study is available, as are pass/fail options. There is a freshman honors program on campus, as well as 19 national honor societies. 16 departments have honors programs.

Faculty/Classroom: 39% of faculty are male; 61%, female. No introductory courses are taught by graduate students. The average class size in an introductory lecture is 26; in a laboratory, 20; and in a regular course offering, 17.

Admissions: 85% of the 1995–96 applicants were accepted. The SAT I scores for the 1995–96 freshman class were as follows: Verbal—73% below 500, 22% between 500 and 599, and 5% between 600 and 700; Math—43% below 500, 39% between 500 and 599, 16% between 600 and 700, and 2% above 700. 20% of the current freshmen were in the top fifth of their class; 46% were in the top two fifths.

Requirements: The SAT I or ACT is required, with a minimum composite SAT I score of 900 or a minimum ACT score of 20. Applicants should be graduates of an accredited secondary school or have a GED. Preparatory work should include 4 years of English, 3 of social science, 2 of foreign language, 2 of college-preparatory mathematics, and 1 of laboratory science. A minimum average grade of 75% is required. AP and CLEP credits are accepted. Important factors in the admissions decision are advanced placement or honor courses, recommendations by school officials, and recommendations by alumni.

Procedure: Freshmen are admitted to all sessions. Entrance exams should be taken from May of the junior year through December of the senior year. There are early admissions and deferred admissions plans. Application deadlines are open. Application fee is $30. Notification is sent on a rolling basis.

Transfer: 675 transfer students enrolled in 1995–96. Applicants should have appropriate high school credentials and a minimum college GPA of 2.25. 32 credits of 128 must be completed at C.W. Post.

Visiting: There are regularly scheduled orientations for prospective students, including an admissions interview and a student-guided campus tour. There are guides for informal visits and visitors may sit in on classes. To schedule a visit, contact the Office of Admissions.

Financial Aid: In a recent year, 70% of all freshmen and 75% of continuing students received some form of financial aid. 55% of freshmen and 65% of continuing students received need-based aid. The average freshman award was $6500. Of that total, scholarships or need-based grants averaged $3000 ($12,315 maximum); loans averaged $2000 ($2625 maximum); and work contracts averaged $1500 ($2000 maximum). 31% of undergraduate students work part-time. Average earnings from campus work for the school year are $900. The average financial indebtedness of a recent graduate was $12,000. C.W. Post is a member of CSS. The FAFSA and the CSS Profile Application are required. The application deadline for fall entry is May 15.

International Students: There are currently 280 international students enrolled. The school actively recruits these students. They must take the TOEFL and achieve a minimum score of 500. SAT I or ACT scores are recommended to help evaluate students' admissions eligibility.

Computers: The college provides computer facilities for student use. The mainframes are a DEC VAX 6210, 7500, and 8600 in the academic computing center. There are advanced Omega and Macintosh computer laboratories in the School of Visual and Performing Arts. More than 200 IBM, Apple, and other microcomputers are available in various other campus locations, including dormitories and academic buildings. Dial-up capabilities allow students access from home, office, or dormitory. All dormitory rooms are equipped with phone, cable, and two communication outlets allowing each student to directly connect with the university's computer network. All students may access the system Monday to Thursday, 8 A.M. to 11 P.M., and Friday to Sunday, 9 A.M. to 10 P.M. Dial-up capability is available 24 hours a day. There are no time limits and no fees.

Graduates: In 1994–95, 887 bachelor's degrees were awarded. The most popular majors among graduates were business and accounting (38%), education (14%), and political science (9%). Within an average freshman class, 4% graduate in 3 years, 63% in 4 years, 31% in 5 years, and 3% in 6 years. 500 companies recruited on campus in 1994–95. Of the 1994 graduating class, 16% were enrolled in graduate school within 6 months of graduation and 84% had found employment.

Admissions Contact: Christine Natali, Director of Admissions. E-mail: admissions@collegehall.liunet.edu.

LONG ISLAND UNIVERSITY/ SOUTHAMPTON CAMPUS
(See Long Island University/Southampton College)

LONG ISLAND UNIVERSITY/SOUTHAMPTON COLLEGE   E-5
(Formerly Long Island University/Southampton Campus)
Southampton, NY 11968

	(516) 283-4000, ext. 200
	(800) LIU-PLAN; FAX: (516) 283-4081
Full-time: 402 men, 603 women	Faculty: 74; IIA, +$
Part-time: 50 men, 74 women	Ph.D.s: 86%
Graduate: 29 men, 117 women	Student/Faculty: 14 to 1
Year: semesters, summer session	Tuition: $13,030
Application Deadline: open	Room & Board: $6230
Freshman Class: 1050 applied, 878 accepted, 242 enrolled	
SAT I Verbal/Math: 518/519	ACT: 26 COMPETITIVE +

Long Island University/Southampton College, established in 1963, is a private liberal arts institution offering undergraduate and graduate programs in the arts and sciences, business, and education. There are 6 undergraduate and 2 graduate schools. The library contains 1 million volumes, 1000 microform items, and 500 audiovisual forms, and subscribes to 690 periodicals. Computerized library sources and services include the card catalog, interlibrary loans, and database searching. Special learning facilities include a learning resource center, art gallery, radio station, on-campus marine station, seawater laboratories, and research vessels. The 110-acre campus is in a rural area 90 miles east of New York City. Including residence halls, there are 33 buildings on campus.

Student Life: 60% of undergraduates are from New York. Students come from 20 states, 5 foreign countries, and Canada. 85% are from public schools; 15% from private. 82% are white. 65% are Catholic; 20% Protestant. The average age of freshmen is 18; all undergraduates, 21. 10% do not continue beyond their first year; 78% remain to graduate.

Housing: 710 students can be accommodated in college housing. College-sponsored living facilities include single-sex and coed dormitories. In addition there are honors houses, quiet-study dormitories, an all-women dormitory, and nonsmoking houses. On-campus housing is guaranteed for all 4 years. 80% of students live on campus; of those, 55% remain on campus on weekends. All students may keep cars on campus.

Activities: There are no fraternities or sororities. There are 50 groups on campus, including art, cheerleading, choir, drama, ethnic, film, gay, honors, jazz band, literary magazine, musical theater, newspaper, photography, political, professional, radio and TV, religious, social, social service, student government, and yearbook. Popular campus events include Spring Fest, Fall Fest, Night Club Night, and Senior Ball.

Sports: There are 5 intercollegiate sports for men and 5 for women, and 6 intramural sports for men and 5 for women. Athletic and recreation facilities include a gymnasium, a swimming pool, basketball and volleyball courts, a weight room, a fitness trail, and soccer, softball, and lacrosse fields.

Disabled Students: 15% of the campus is accessible to disabled students. The following facilities are available: wheelchair ramps, special parking, and specially equipped rest rooms.

Services: In addition to many counseling and information services, tutoring is available in most subjects. There is remedial math, reading, and writing.

Campus Safety and Security: Campus safety and security measures include 24-hour foot and vehicle patrol, self-defense education, shuttle buses, and informal discussions. In addition, there are pamphlets/posters/films, emergency telephones, and lighted pathways/sidewalks. The college also conducts an alcohol awareness week and date-rape seminars.

Programs of Study: Southampton College confers B.A., B.S., and B.F.A. degrees. Master's degrees are also awarded. Bachelor's degrees are awarded in BIOLOGICAL SCIENCE (biology/biological science and marine science), COMMUNICATIONS AND THE ARTS (communications, English, fine arts, and graphic design), COMPUTER AND PHYSICAL SCIENCE (chemistry), EDUCATION (art and elementary), SOCIAL SCIENCE (history, political science/government, prelaw, psychology, social science, and sociology). Marine science and fine arts are the strongest academically. Marine science, fine arts, and social science have the largest enrollments.

Required: In order to graduate, students must complete 128 credits with an overall 2.0 GPA and a 2.25 GPA in the major. Core courses consist of 3 required courses in English (including Introduction to Composition) and 2 each in humanities, social science, science/mathematics, and fine arts. 45 to 88 hours must be completed in the major.

Special: Cross-registration is permitted with the C.W. Post and Brooklyn campuses of Long Island University, and the Friends World Program. Opportunities are provided for internships in science research, legislative offices, and the Smithsonian Institution. Study abroad, work-study programs, B.A.-B.S. degrees, dual majors in psychology and biology, credit by examination, credit for life experience, nondegree study, and pass/fail options are also available. Students in the Friends World Program receive credit based on experiential education, fieldwork, and overseas travel. There is a freshman honors program on campus, as well as 2 national honor societies. 2 departments have honors programs.

Faculty/Classroom: 79% of faculty are male; 21%, female. All teach undergraduates and 86% do research. No introductory courses are taught by graduate students. The average class size in an introductory lecture is 20; in a laboratory, 15; and in a regular course offering, 15.

Admissions: 84% of the 1995–96 applicants were accepted. The SAT I scores for the 1995–96 freshman class were as follows: Verbal—40% below 500, 39% between 500 and 599, 20% between 600 and 700, and 1% above 700; Math—42% below 500, 36% between 500 and 599, 20% between 600 and 700, and 2% above 700. The ACT scores were 10% below 21, 31% between 21 and 23, 37% between 24 and 26, 20% between 27 and 28, and 2% above 28. 26% of the current freshmen were in the top fifth of their class; 46% were in the top two fifths. 10 freshmen graduated first in their class.

Requirements: The SAT I or ACT is required. A minimum grade average of 78% is required. A minimum composite score of 1000 (500 verbal and 500 math) is required on the SAT I and a score of 20 is required on the ACT. Graduation from an accredited secondary school is required; the GED will be accepted. The academic record should include 4 credits in English, 3 each in history and social studies, 2 each in mathematics and science, and 1 in art. An essay, portfolio, audition, or interview may be recommended. Applications are accepted on-line. AP and CLEP credits are accepted. Important factors in the admissions decision are advanced placement or honor courses, personality/intangible qualities, and evidence of special talent.

Procedure: Freshmen are admitted fall and spring. Entrance exams should be taken during the junior year. There are early admissions and deferred admissions. Application deadlines are open. Application fee is $30. Notification is sent on a rolling basis.

Transfer: 128 transfer students enrolled in 1995–96. Applicants must have a 2.0 GPA in previous college work. An interview is recommended. High school grades and SAT I scores are required if the transfer has fewer than 30 college credits. 32 credits of 128 must be completed at Southampton College.

Visiting: There are regularly scheduled orientations for prospective students, including an interview, a tour, and lunch or dinner. Students may also attend a class, meet with a coach, and attend a cooperative education meeting. There are guides for informal visits and visitors may sit in on classes and stay overnight at the school. To schedule a visit, contact the Admissions Office.

Financial Aid: 65% of undergraduate students work part-time. Average earnings from campus work for the school year are $1100. Southampton College is a member of CSS. The FAFSA and the college's own financial statement are required. The application deadline for fall entry is June 1.

International Students: 22 international students were enrolled in a recent year. They must take the TOEFL and achieve a minimum score of 500. The student must also take SAT I, ACT, or TOEFL.

Computers: The college provides computer facilities for student use. The mainframes are a DEC VAX 750, 8600, and 6210 and an IBM 520. The Long Island University Network is connected to Internet. There are 120 microcomputers located at 6 campus locations and there are in-room PC hookups. The student-to-computer ratio is 12 to 1. All students may access the system 24 hours a day. There are no time limits and no fees.

Graduates: In 1994–95, 211 bachelor's degrees were awarded. The most popular majors among graduates were science (28%), business (24%), and fine arts (18%). Within an average freshman class, 1% graduate in 3 years, 39% in 4 years, and 10% in 5 years. 30 companies recruited on campus in 1994–95. Of the 1994 graduating class, 14% were enrolled in graduate school within 6 months of graduation and 60% had found employment.

Admissions Contact: Carol Gilbert, Director of Admissions. A campus video is available.

MANHATTAN COLLEGE
Riverdale, NY 10471

D-5

(718) 920-0200
(800) MC2-XCEL; FAX: (718) 548-1008

Full-time: 1311 men, 1033 women	Faculty: 194; IIA, av$
Part-time: 160 men, 91 women	Ph.D.s: 89%
Graduate: 318 men, 208 women	Student/Faculty: 12 to 1
Year: semesters, summer session	Tuition: $14,500
Application Deadline: March 1	Room & Board: $7000
Freshman Class: 2584 applied, 2050 accepted, 581 enrolled	
SAT I Verbal/Math: 450/502	COMPETITIVE

Manhattan College, founded in 1853, is a private, coeducational institution affiliated with the Christian Brothers of the Catholic Church. It offers degree programs in the arts, science, education and human services, business, and engineering. There are 5 undergraduate and 3 graduate schools. In addition to regional accreditation, Manhattan has baccalaureate program accreditation with ABET, AHEA, and CAHEA. The 2 libraries contain 193,100 volumes, 383,480 microform items, and 3244 audiovisual forms, and subscribe to 1527 periodicals. Computerized library sources and services include the card catalog, interlibrary loans, and database searching. Special learning facilities include a learning resource center, radio station, nuclear reactor laboratory, and media center. The 47-acre campus is in an urban area 12 miles north of midtown Manhattan. Including residence halls, there are 28 buildings on campus.

Student Life: 86% of undergraduates are from New York. Students come from 27 states, 50 foreign countries, and Canada. 35% are from public schools; 65% from private. 69% are white; 18% Hispanic. The average age of freshmen is 17; all undergraduates, 20. 14% do not continue beyond their first year; 70% remain to graduate.

Housing: 1617 students can be accommodated in college housing. College-sponsored living facilities include coed dormitories and off-campus apartments. On-campus housing is guaranteed for all 4 years. 52% of students commute. Alcohol is not permitted. All students may keep cars on campus.

Activities: 2% of men belong to 3 local fraternities and 1 national fraternity; 1% of women belong to 4 local sororities. There are 70 groups on campus, including bagpipe band, cheerleading, choir, chorus, computers, drama, ethnic, honors, international, jazz band, literary magazine, musical theater, newspaper, pep band, political, professional, radio and TV, religious, social, social service, student government, and yearbook. Popular campus events include Annual Springfest, Special Olympics, and Jasper Jingle.

Sports: There are 9 intercollegiate sports for men and 9 for women, and 10 intramural sports for men and 10 for women. Athletic and recreation facilities include 5 full basketball courts, which can also be used for volleyball and tennis, an indoor track, a weight room, a swimming pool, and a Nautilus center.

Disabled Students: 95% of the campus is accessible to disabled students. The following facilities are available: wheelchair ramps, elevators, special parking, and specially equipped rest rooms.

Services: In addition to many counseling and information services, tutoring is available in every subject.

Campus Safety and Security: Campus safety and security measures include 24-hour foot and vehicle patrol, escort service, pamphlets/posters/films, and lighted pathways/sidewalks.

Programs of Study: Manhattan confers B.A. and B.S. degrees. Associate and master's degrees are also awarded. Bachelor's degrees are awarded in BIOLOGICAL SCIENCE (biochemistry and biology/biological science), BUSINESS (accounting, banking and finance, business economics, international business management, and marketing/retailing/merchandising), COMMUNICATIONS AND THE ARTS (communications, English, fine arts, French, and Spanish), COMPUTER AND PHYSICAL SCIENCE (chemistry, computer science, information sciences and systems, mathematics, and physics), EDUCATION (early childhood, elementary, foreign languages, health, middle school, physical, science, secondary, and special), ENGINEERING AND ENVIRONMENTAL DESIGN (chemical engineering, civil engineering, electrical/electronics engineering, environmental engineering, and mechanical engineering), HEALTH PROFESSIONS (predentistry, premedicine, and radiological science), SOCIAL SCIENCE (economics, history, international studies, peace studies, philosophy, political science/government, prelaw, psychology, religion, social science, social work, sociology, and urban studies). Engineering and business are the strongest academically. Arts, business, and education have the largest enrollments.

Required: All students must take courses in English composition and literature, religious studies, philosophy, humanities, social science, science, and mathematics. About 130 credit hours are required for graduation, with about 36 in the major. The minimum GPA is 2.0.

Special: Manhattan offers co-op programs in 11 majors, cross-registration with the college of Mount St. Vincent, and off-campus internships in business, industry, government, and social or cultural organizations. Students may study abroad in 10 countries and enter work-study programs with major U.S. corporations or health services or in the arts. A general studies degree, a 3–2 engineering degree, credit by examination, and nondegree study are also available. There is a freshman honors program on campus, as well as 22 national honor societies, including Phi Beta Kappa.

Faculty/Classroom: 77% of faculty are male; 23%, female. All teach undergraduates. No introductory courses are taught by graduate students. The average class size in an introductory lecture is 15 and in a regular course offering, 22.

Admissions: 79% of the 1995–96 applicants were accepted. 38% of the current freshmen were in the top fifth of their class; 63% were in the top two fifths. There were 3 National Merit semifinalists. 12 freshmen graduated first in their class.

Requirements: The SAT I is required. Applicants must graduate from an accredited secondary school with a minimum GPA of 2.8. The GED is accepted. 16 academic units are required, including 4 of English, 3 each of history, mathematics, and science, and 2 of foreign language. An essay is required and an interview is recommended. The college accepts applications on computer disk and on-line via Common App, ExPAN, CollegeView, and CollegeLink. AP and CLEP credits are accepted. Important factors in the admissions decision are advanced placement or honor courses, leadership record, and evidence of special talent.

Procedure: Freshmen are admitted fall and spring. Entrance exams should be taken in the spring of the junior year or the fall of the senior year. There are early decision and deferred admissions plans. Early decision applications should be filed by December 1; regular applications, by March 1 for fall entry and December 1 for spring entry, along with an application fee of $25. Notification of early decision is sent December 15; regular decision, on a rolling basis. 30 early decision candidates were accepted for the 1995–96 class. A waiting list is an active part of the admissions procedure, with about 4% of all applicants on the list.

Transfer: 245 transfer students enrolled in 1995–96. Applicants must have a GPA of 2.5 and meet subject course requirements according to their course of study. They must submit transcripts from colleges and high schools attended. An interview is recommended. 66 credits of 130 must be completed at Manhattan.

Visiting: There are regularly scheduled orientations for prospective students during 2 days in the summer, which include scheduling, parent workshops, loan seminars, and English and mathematics testing. There are guides for informal visits and visitors may sit in on classes and stay overnight at the school. To schedule a visit, contact the Admission Center.

Financial Aid: In 1995–96, 83% of all freshmen received some form of financial aid. 73% of freshmen and 85% of continuing students received need-based aid. The average freshman award was $16,095. Of that total, scholarships or need-based grants averaged $4084 ($20,185 maximum); loans averaged $1596 ($2625 maximum); and work contracts averaged $927 ($1500 maximum). 13% of undergraduate students work part-time. Average earnings from campus work for the school year are $1700. The average financial indebtedness of the 1994–95 graduate was $17,000. Manhattan is a member of CSS. The FAFSA and the college's own financial statement are required. The application deadline for fall entry is February 1.

International Students: There are currently 140 international students enrolled. The school actively recruits these students. They must take the TOEFL and achieve a minimum score of 520.

Computers: The college provides computer facilities for student use. The mainframe is a DEC VAX 8350. Terminals and microcomputers are located in the computer center and in engineering laboratories. All students may access the system 13 hours a day in the laboratories and 24 hours a day by modem. There are no time limits and no fees.

Graduates: In 1994–95, 584 bachelor's degrees were awarded. The most popular majors among graduates were arts and science (28%), business (28%), and engineering (27%). Within an average freshman class, 52% graduate in 4 years, 67% in 5 years, and 70% in 6 years. 229 companies recruited on campus in 1994–95. Of the 1994 graduating class, 26% were enrolled in graduate school within 6 months of graduation and 51% had found employment.

Admissions Contact: John Brennan, Dean of Admissions. E-mail: admit@mancol.edu. A campus video is available.

MANHATTAN SCHOOL OF MUSIC   D-5
New York, NY 10027-4678

(212) 749-2802, ext. 2
FAX: (212) 749-5471

Full-time: 200 men, 223 women	Faculty: 74
Part-time: 5 men, 11 women	Ph.D.s: 60%
Graduate: 179 men, 268 women	Student/Faculty: 6 to 1
Year: semesters, summer session	Tuition: $14,730
Application Deadline: April 1	Room & Board: $9000
Freshman Class: 460 applied, 232 accepted, 93 enrolled	
SAT I or ACT: recommended	**SPECIAL**

The Manhattan School of Music, founded in 1917, is a private institution offering undergraduate and graduate degrees in music performance and composition. There is one graduate school. The library contains 70,000 volumes and 21,000 audiovisual forms, and subscribes to 125 periodicals. Computerized library sources and services include interlibrary loans. Special learning facilities include 2 electronic music studios, and a recording studio. The 1-acre campus is in an urban area in New York City and consists of 1 building.

Student Life: 76% of undergraduates are from out-of-state, mostly the Northeast. Students come from 41 states, 40 foreign countries, and Canada. 81% are from public schools; 19% from private. 43% are white; 39% foreign nationals; 11% Asian American. The average age of freshmen is 19; all undergraduates, 21. 13% do not continue beyond their first year; 65% remain to graduate.

Housing: 120 students can be accommodated in coed off-campus apartments, which are available on a first-come, first-served basis and on a lottery system for upperclassmen. Priority is given to out-of-town students. 86% of students commute. Alcohol is not permitted. All students may keep cars on campus.

Activities: There are no fraternities or sororities. There are a number of groups on campus, including band, chess, choir, chorale, chorus, ethnic, gay, international, jazz band, opera, orchestra, student government, and symphony. Popular campus events include a Halloween party, Christmas/Chanukah party, and prom.

Sports: There is no sports program at Manhattan.

Disabled Students: 70% of the campus is accessible to disabled students. The following facilities are available: wheelchair ramps, elevators, specially equipped rest rooms, and special class scheduling.

Services: In addition to many counseling and information services, tutoring is available in most subjects. There is a reader service for the blind.

Campus Safety and Security: Campus safety and security measures include 24-hour foot and vehicle patrol, informal discussions, and lighted pathways/sidewalks.

Programs of Study: Manhattan confers the B.Mus. degree. Master's and doctoral degrees are also awarded. Bachelor's degrees are awarded in COMMUNICATIONS AND THE ARTS (jazz, music, music performance, music theory and composition, piano/organ, strings, and voice). Classical piano, classical voice, and jazz have the largest enrollments.

Required: All students must take a 4-course core curriculum in the humanities and 4 elective humanities courses, and perform a final, senior-year recital. Composition majors must complete an original symphonic work. To graduate, students must earn 120 to 130 credit hours, including 90 in the major, with a minimum GPA of 2.0.

Special: There is cross-registration with Barnard College. Credit by exam in theory and music history, and nondegree study are available.

Faculty/Classroom: 67% of faculty are male; 33%, female. All teach undergraduates. Graduate students teach 1% of introductory courses. The average class size in an introductory lecture is 30 and in a regular course offering, 10.

Admissions: 50% of the 1995–96 applicants were accepted.

Requirements: The SAT I or ACT is recommended. Applicants should graduate from an accredited high school with a minimum GPA of 2.0. The GED is accepted. Admission is based on a performance audition, evaluation of scholastic achievements, and available openings in the major field. AP and CLEP credits are accepted. Important factors in the admissions decision are evidence of special talent, personality/intangible qualities, and extracurricular activities record.

Procedure: Freshmen are admitted fall and spring. Applications should be filed by April 1 for fall entry, along with an application fee of $85. A waiting list is an active part of the admissions procedure, with about 3% of all applicants on the list.

Transfer: 70 transfer students enrolled in 1995–96. Applicants must audition and submit college transcripts. 60 to 70 credits of 120 to 130 must be completed at Manhattan.

Visiting: There are regularly scheduled orientations for prospective students. There are guides for informal visits and visitors may sit in on classes. To schedule a visit, contact the Admission Office.

Financial Aid: In 1995–96, 72% of all freshmen and 70% of continuing students received some form of financial aid. 55% of freshmen and 56% of continuing students received need-based aid. The average freshman award was $5767. Of that total, scholarships or need-based grants averaged $7800 ($14,200 maximum); loans averaged $2511 ($2625 maximum); SLS and PLUS averaged $9287 ($26,380 maximum); and work contracts averaged $1200 (maximum). 61% of undergraduate students work part-time. Average earnings from campus work for the school year are $1200. The average financial indebtedness of the 1994–95 graduate was $18,000. Manhattan is a member of CSS. The FAFSA, the college's own financial statement, and the CSS Profile application are required. The application deadline for fall entry is April 15.

International Students: There are currently 360 international students enrolled. The school actively recruits these students. They must take the TOEFL and achieve a minimum score of 500.

Graduates: In 1994–95, 73 bachelor's degrees were awarded. The most popular majors among graduates were piano (21%), voice (14%), and commercial jazz (13%). Within an average freshman class, 50% graduate in 4 years, 58% in 5 years, and 65% in 6 years.

Admissions Contact: Carolyn Disnew, Director of Admission.

MANHATTANVILLE COLLEGE   D-5
Purchase, NY 10577

(914) 323-5464; (800) 328-4553

Full-time: 231 men, 507 women	Faculty: 65; IIB, av$
Part-time: 54 men, 106 women	Ph.D.s: 85%
Graduate: 97 men, 671 women	Student/Faculty: 11 to 1
Year: semesters, summer session	Tuition: $16,120
Application Deadline: open	Room & Board: $7680
Freshman Class: n/av	
SAT I or ACT: required	**COMPETITIVE**

Manhattanville College, founded in 1841, is an independent, coeducational institution offering programs in liberal and fine arts, business, health science, and teacher preparation. There are 2 graduate schools. In addition to regional accreditation, M'ville has baccalaureate program accreditation with NASM. The library contains 260,000 volumes, 3500 microform items, and 4000 audiovisual forms, and subscribes to 1600 periodicals. Computerized library sources and services include the card catalog, interlibrary loans, and database searching. Special learning facilities include a learning resource center, art gallery, and radio station. The 100-acre campus is in a suburban area 25 miles north of New York City. Including residence halls, there are 21 buildings on campus.

Student Life: 53% of undergraduates are from New York. Students come from 20 states and 18 foreign countries. 54% are from public schools; 46% from private. 63% are Catholic; 22% Protestant. The average age of freshmen is 18; all undergraduates, 20. 7% do not continue beyond their first year; 75% remain to graduate.

Housing: 900 students can be accommodated in college housing. College-sponsored living facilities include single-sex and coed dormitories. In addition there are language houses, special interest houses, and an intercultural residence hall. On-campus housing is guaranteed for all 4 years. 83% of students live on campus; of those, 75% remain on campus on weekends. All students may keep cars on campus.

Activities: There are no fraternities or sororities. There are 60 groups on campus, including art, band, choir, chorale, chorus, computers, dance, drama, ethnic, film, gay, honors, international, jazz band, literary magazine, musical theater, newspaper, orchestra, photography, political, professional, radio and TV, religious, social, social service, student government, and yearbook. Popular campus events include Christmas Concert, International Dinner/Dance, and Spring Formal.

Sports: There are 6 intercollegiate sports for men and 7 for women, 5 intramural sports for men and 5 for women. Athletic and recreation facilities include a 1000-seat gymnasium, a 25-yard indoor pool,

6 deco-turf tennis courts, a healthworks-wellness center, and baseball, lacrosse, field hockey, and softball fields.

Disabled Students: All of the campus is accessible to disabled students. The following facilities are available: wheelchair ramps, elevators, special parking, specially equipped rest rooms, and special class scheduling.

Services: In addition to many counseling and information services, tutoring is available in every subject and a program for students with documented learning disabilities.

Campus Safety and Security: Campus safety and security measures include 24-hour foot and vehicle patrol, escort service, informal discussions, and pamphlets/posters/films. There are emergency telephones and lighted pathways/sidewalks.

Programs of Study: M'ville confers B.A., B.F., and B.Mus. degrees. Master's degrees are also awarded. Bachelor's degrees are awarded in BIOLOGICAL SCIENCE (biochemistry and biology/biological science), BUSINESS (management science), COMMUNICATIONS AND THE ARTS (art history and appreciation, dance, design, dramatic arts, English, fine arts, French, German, music, photography, and Spanish), COMPUTER AND PHYSICAL SCIENCE (chemistry, computer science, mathematics, and physics), EDUCATION (art, early childhood, elementary, middle school, music, science, secondary, and special), ENGINEERING AND ENVIRONMENTAL DESIGN (environmental science), HEALTH PROFESSIONS (predentistry and premedicine), SOCIAL SCIENCE (American studies, Asian/Oriental studies, economics, history, international relations, medieval studies, philosophy, political science/government, prelaw, psychology, religion, Russian and Slavic studies, and sociology). Art, art history, and education have the largest enrollments.

Required: Distribution requirements include 18 credits in social sciences and humanities, and either a major or minor in foreign language or 18 credits in Western and non-Western courses, 8 credits in mathematics and natural sciences, and 6 in the arts. A year-long freshman humanities course, courses in library skills, writing, and global perspective, and a preceptorial are required. A total of 120 credit hours and a minimum GPA of 2.0 are needed to graduate.

Special: Manhattanville offers cross-registration with SUNY Purchase, internships in all majors for credit, and study abroad in 10 countries. Dual, student-designed, and interdisciplinary majors, and pass/fail options are also available. Under the portfolio degree plan, students develop an individualized program combining both academic and nonacademic training. There is a freshman honors program on campus, as well as 3 national honor societies. 16 departments have honors programs.

Faculty/Classroom: 50% of faculty are male; 50%, female. 95% teach undergraduates. No introductory courses are taught by graduate students. The average class size in an introductory lecture is 20; in a laboratory, 12; and in a regular course offering, 14.

Admissions: The SAT I scores for a recent freshman class were as follows: Verbal—77% below 500, 18% between 500 and 599, and 5% between 600 and 700; Math—59% below 500, 32% between 500 and 599, 9% between 600 and 700, and 1% above 700. 31% of freshmen were in the top fifth of their class; 56% were in the top two fifths.

Requirements: The SAT I or ACT is required. A minimum 2.5 GPA is required. Applicants should graduate in the upper 50% of their class with 4 years of English, 3 each of history, mathematics, and science, including 2 of laboratory science, and 1/2 year each of art and music. The GED is accepted. Interviews are strongly encouraged. Art applicants must submit a portfolio; music applicants must audition. AP and CLEP credits are accepted. Important factors in the admissions decision are leadership record, recommendations by alumni, and recommendations by school officials.

Procedure: Freshmen are admitted fall and spring. Entrance exams should be taken in the spring of the junior or fall of the senior year. Application deadlines are open. Application fee is $40. Notification is sent on a rolling basis.

Transfer: Applicants must submit college transcripts. A minimum GPA of 2.5 and a statement of good standing are required. Applicants with fewer than 40 credits must submit all high school records and SAT I scores. 60 credits of 120 must be completed at M'ville.

Visiting: There are regularly scheduled orientations for prospective students. There are guides for informal visits and visitors may sit in on classes and stay overnight at the school. To schedule a visit, contact the Office of Admissions and Financial Aid.

Financial Aid: 31% of undergraduate students work part-time. Average earnings from campus work for the school year are $1700. M'ville is a member of CSS. The FAFSA and the college's own financial statement are required. The application deadline for fall entry is March 1.

International Students: There were 121 international students enrolled in a recent year. The school actively recruits these students. They must score 550 on the TOEFL.

Computers: The college provides computer facilities for student use. The mainframe is a DEC PDP 11/44 minicomputer. Students may access the mainframe through the computer centers on campus. All students may access the system for 65 to 70 hours throughout the week. There are no time limits and no fees.

Graduates: In a recent year, 230 bachelor's degrees were awarded. Within an average freshman class, 3% graduate in 3 years, 68% in 4 years, 85% in 5 years, and 95% in 6 years. 100 companies recruited on campus in a recent year.

Admissions Contact: Barry W. Ward, Vice President for Enrollment Management and Student Development. E-mail: jflores@m.ville.edu.

MANNES COLLEGE OF MUSIC
New York, NY 10024

D-5

(212) 580-0210
(800) 292-3040; FAX: (212) 580-1738

Full-time: 60 men, 69 women	Faculty: 15
Part-time: 1 man, 2 women	Ph.D.s: n/av
Graduate: 57 men, 75 women	Student/Faculty: 9 to 1
Year: semesters	Tuition: $13,850
Application Deadline: January 31	Room: $5600
Freshman Class: 312 applied, 67 accepted, 21 enrolled	
SAT I or ACT: not required	SPECIAL

Mannes College of Music, founded in 1916 and today part of the New School for Social Research, is a private institution offering instruction in music. There is 1 graduate school. The library contains 28,000 volumes and 2600 audiovisual forms, and subscribes to 50 periodicals. Special learning facilities include 2 concert/recital halls, a recording studio, and an electronic music studio. The campus is in an urban area in Manhattan. There is 1 building on campus.

Student Life: 40% of undergraduates are from New York. Students come from 27 foreign countries and Canada. 44% are foreign nationals; 41% white; 10% Asian American. The average age of freshmen is 19; all undergraduates, 21. 15% do not continue beyond their first year; 60% remain to graduate.

Housing: 30 students can be accommodated in college housing. College-sponsored living facilities include coed dormitories. On-campus housing is available on a first-come, first-served basis. Priority is given to out-of-town students. Alcohol is not permitted.

Activities: There are no fraternities or sororities. There are some groups and organizations on campus, including choir, chorus, jazz band, opera, orchestra, and symphony. Popular campus events include orchestra/chorus concerts, Christmas parties, recitals, seminars, and master classes.

Sports: There is no sports program at Mannes.

Disabled Students: All of the campus is accessible to disabled students. The following facilities are available: elevators.

Services: In addition to many counseling and information services, tutoring is available in most subjects.

Campus Safety and Security: There is a security guard 24 hours a day at the front entrance of the dormitory, and from 8 A.M. to 11 P.M. at the front desk of the college lobby.

Programs of Study: Mannes confers B.S. and B.Mus. degrees. Master's degrees are also awarded. Bachelor's degrees are awarded in COMMUNICATIONS AND THE ARTS (music, music performance, music theory and composition, and voice). Voice, piano, and violin have the largest enrollments.

Required: The required core curriculum includes in courses in English, Western civilization, art history, and literature. Students majoring in all instruments and voice must participate in various ensemble classes. Courses are also required in techniques and history of music. To graduate, performance majors must perform before a faculty jury, and composition majors must submit 5 original pieces for juried consideration.

Special: Mannes offers cross-registration with Hunter College, Marymount Manhattan, and the New School for Social Research. There are some dual majors by permission.

Faculty/Classroom: No introductory courses are taught by graduate students. The average class size in a regular course offering is 10.

Admissions: 21% of the 1995–96 applicants were accepted.

Requirements: Applicants must be graduates of an accredited secondary school or have a GED certificate. An audition, an interview, a letter of recommendation, and a written test in music theory and musicianship are required. Important factors in the admissions decision are evidence of special talent, personality/intangible qualities, and advanced placement or honor courses.

Procedure: Freshmen are admitted fall and spring. There are early admissions and deferred admissions plans. Applications should be filed by January 31 for fall entry and December 1 for spring entry, along with an application fee of $60. Notification is sent on a rolling basis.

Transfer: 23 transfer students enrolled in a recent year. Applicants must complete the same procedures as entering freshmen and submit transcripts from all secondary schools and colleges attended.

Visiting: There are guides for informal visits and visitors may sit in on classes. To schedule a visit, contact Marilyn Groves, Director of Admissions.

Financial Aid: In a recent year, 78% of all freshmen and 83% of continuing students received some form of financial aid. 50% of all students received need-based aid. Scholarships or need-based grants averaged $3014 ($11,850 maximum); loans averaged $2000 ($5000 maximum); and other federal loans/grants averaged $6000 ($15,000 maximum). 35% of undergraduate students work part-time. Average earnings from campus work for the school year are $1200. The average financial indebtedness of a recent year's graduate was $5600. Mannes is a member of CSS. The FAF and the college's own financial statement are required.

International Students: In a recent year, 108 international students were enrolled. They must take the TOEFL and achieve a minimum score of 500. The student must also take the college's own entrance exam.

Graduates: In a recent year, 19 bachelor's degrees were awarded. The most popular majors among graduates were voice (32%), composition (16%), and piano (16%).

Admissions Contact: Marilyn Groves, Director of Admissions.

MARIST COLLEGE

D-4

Poughkeepsie, NY 12601

(914) 575-3226

(800) 436-5483; FAX: (914) 575-3215

Full-time: 1496 men, 1680 women	Faculty: 158; IIA, -$
Part-time: 280 men, 298 women	Ph.D.s: 80%
Graduate: 270 men, 245 women	Student/Faculty: 20 to 1
Year: semesters, summer session	Tuition: $11,680
Application Deadline: March 1	Room & Board: $6200
Freshman Class: 4488 applied, 2828 accepted, 843 enrolled	
SAT I Verbal/Math: 503/518	ACT: 25 COMPETITIVE

Marist College, founded in 1946, is an independent liberal arts college with a Catholic tradition. There is one graduate school. The library contains 150,000 volumes, 53,154 microform items, and 21,750 audiovisual forms, and subscribes to 1500 periodicals. Computerized library sources and services include interlibrary loans and database searching. Special learning facilities include a learning resource center, art gallery, radio station, TV station, aquarium, estuarine and environment studies laboratory, and public opinion institute. The 150-acre campus is in a suburban area 75 miles north of New York City. Including residence halls, there are 21 buildings on campus.

Student Life: 52% of undergraduates are from out of state, mostly New England and the Middle Atlantic. Students come from 26 states, 12 foreign countries, and Canada. 70% are from public schools. 86% are white. 60% are Catholic; 20% Protestant; 13% claim no religious affiliation. The average age of freshmen is 18; all undergraduates, 20. 10% do not continue beyond their first year; 67% remain to graduate.

Housing: 2200 students can be accommodated in college housing. College-sponsored living facilities include coed dormitories, on-campus apartments, and off-campus apartments. In addition there are language houses. On-campus housing is guaranteed for the freshman year only and is available on a lottery system for upperclassmen. 65% of students live on campus; of those, 70% remain on campus on weekends. Alcohol is not permitted. Upperclassmen may keep cars on campus.

Activities: 6% of men belong to 1 national and 3 local fraternities; 9% of women belong to 1 local and 1 national sorority. There are 70 groups on campus, including art, band, cheerleading, chess, choir, chorale, chorus, computers, dance, drama, ethnic, film, gay, honors, international, jazz band, literary magazine, marching band, musical theater, newspaper, pep band, photography, political, radio and TV, religious, social, social service, student government, and yearbook. Popular campus events include President's Cup Regatta, Parents Weekend, Senior Week, Spring Weekend, Community Unity, Foxfest, Medieval Banquet, and formal dances.

Sports: There are 12 intercollegiate sports for men and 9 for women, and 9 intramural sports for men and 7 for women. Athletic and recreation facilities include 2 boat houses, a 4000-seat basketball arena, a 3000-seat stadium, 6 outdoor tennis courts, playing fields, a field house, a swimming pool, a diving tank, racquetball courts, a dance and aerobics studio, a weight room, rowing tanks, 3 intramural basketball courts, and an all-purpose space (volleyball, tennis, and so on).

Disabled Students: The entire campus is accessible to physically disabled students. The following facilities are available: wheelchair ramps, elevators, special parking, specially equipped rest rooms, special class scheduling, lowered drinking fountains, and lowered telephones.

Services: In addition to many counseling and information services, tutoring is available in every subject. There is a reader service for the blind, and remedial math, reading, and writing.

Campus Safety and Security: Campus safety and security measures include 24-hour foot and vehicle patrol, escort service, shuttle buses, and informal discussions. In addition, there are pamphlets/posters/films, emergency telephones, lighted pathways/sidewalks, and security personnel in residence halls.

Programs of Study: Marist confers B.A., B.S., and B.P.S. degrees. Master's degrees are also awarded. Bachelor's degrees are awarded in BIOLOGICAL SCIENCE (biochemistry and biology/biological science), BUSINESS (accounting, business administration and management, business economics, and fashion merchandising), COMMUNICATIONS AND THE ARTS (communications, English, film arts, fine arts, French, journalism, Russian, and Spanish), COMPUTER AND PHYSICAL SCIENCE (chemistry, computer science, information sciences and systems, and mathematics), EDUCATION (elementary, science, secondary, and special), ENGINEERING AND ENVIRONMENTAL DESIGN (environmental science), HEALTH PROFESSIONS (medical laboratory technology, predentistry, premedicine, and speech pathology/audiology), SOCIAL SCIENCE (American studies, criminal justice, economics, fashion design and technology, history, interdisciplinary studies, political science/government, prelaw, psychology, and social work). Computer science, computer information systems, and natural sciences are the strongest academically. Business administration and communications have the largest enrollments.

Required: To graduate, students must maintain a minimum GPA of 2.0 in the major while taking 120 credits. A 30-credit core curriculum and 30 to 36 credits in a major field are required. Distribution requirements include 6 credits each in natural sciences, social sciences, history, literature, and mathematics, 3 credits each in fine arts and philosophy/religious studies, and up to 12 credits in foreign language and culture. Specific course requirements include English writing skills and foundation courses.

Special: Marist offers cross-registration with schools in the mid-Hudson area. Study abroad in Europe, Africa, Latin America, and the Far East, and a 3–2 engineering degree with the University of Detroit are offered. A 3-year bachelor's degree, co-op programs in computer science and computer information systems, work-study programs, a B.A.-B.S. degree, dual and student-designed majors, a 5-year program in psychology, and nondegree study are also available. There are internships available with more than 250 organizations. There is a freshman honors program on campus, as well as 1 national honor society.

Faculty/Classroom: 65% of faculty are male; 35%, female. All teach undergraduates, and 20% also do research. No introductory courses are taught by graduate students. The average class size in an introductory lecture is 35; in a laboratory, 15; and in a regular course offering, 25.

Admissions: 63% of the 1995–96 applicants were accepted. The SAT I scores for the 1995–96 freshman class were as follows: Verbal—46% below 500, 48% between 500 and 599, 6% between 600 and 700, and 1% above 700; Math—43% below 500, 48% between 500 and 599, 7% between 600 and 700, and 2% above 700. 36% of the current freshmen were in the top fifth of their class; 76% were in the top two fifths. There were 3 National Merit finalists and 7 semifinalists. 6 freshmen graduated first in their class.

Requirements: The SAT I or ACT is required. Marist requires applicants to be in the upper 50% of their class. Applicants should have 18 academic credits, including a recommended 4 each in English, science, and social studies, 3 each in mathematics and history, and 1 each in art and music. An essay and interview are recommended. Applications are accepted on computer disk via ExPAN and are also accepted on-line. AP and CLEP credits are accepted. Important factors in the admissions decision are leadership record, advanced placement or honor courses, and recommendations by school officials.

Procedure: Freshmen are admitted fall and spring. Entrance exams should be taken during the fall of the senior year. There are early decision, early admissions, and deferred admissions plans. Early decision applications should be filed by December 1; regular applications, by March 1 for fall entry and December 1 for spring entry, along with an application fee of $35. Notification of early decision is sent December 15; regular decision, starting February 15. 501 early decision candidates were accepted for the 1995–96 class. A waiting list is an active part of the admissions procedure, with about 7% of all applicants on the list.

Transfer: 141 transfer students enrolled in 1995–96. Applicants must have at least a 2.0 GPA (depending on the college and major programs) in at least 30 college credits. Students with fewer than 25 credits will be treated as freshmen. Grades of C or better transfer. 30 credits of 120 must be completed at Marist.

Visiting: There are regularly scheduled orientations for prospective students. There are guides for informal visits, and visitors may sit in on classes and stay overnight at the school. To schedule a visit, contact Jane Elise Schaffner in the Admissions Office.

Financial Aid: In 1995–96, 78% of all freshmen and 68% of continuing students received some form of financial aid. 68% of freshmen and 62% of continuing students received need-based aid. The average freshman award was $10,600. Of that total, scholarships or need-based grants averaged $3800 ($4500 maximum) and federal or state awards and external scholarships averaged $3000 (maximum). 40% of undergraduate students work part-time. Average earnings from campus work for the school year are $1200. The average financial indebtedness of the 1994–95 graduate was $10,000. The FAFSA is required. The application deadline for fall entry is February 15.

International Students: There are currently 51 international students enrolled. The school actively recruits these students. They must take the TOEFL and achieve a minimum score of 550.

Computers: The college provides computer facilities for student use. The mainframe is an E.S. 9000–9121-Model 621. The campus center has a drop-in laboratory available to all students from 8 A.M. to midnight during the week and longer on weekends. All dormitory rooms are equipped with data jacks allowing students to hook up PCs with the mainframe and to access library files. There are 5 areas on campus providing more than 260 terminals for student use, as well as 185 microcomputers and numerous printers. All students may access the system. There are no time limits and no fees.

Graduates: In 1994–95, 825 bachelor's degrees were awarded. The most popular majors among graduates were communications (23%), business (18%), and psychology (10%). Within an average freshman class, 4% graduate in 3 years, 63% in 4 years, and 65% in 5 years. 136 companies recruited on campus in 1994–95. Of the 1994 graduating class, 20% were enrolled in graduate school within 6 months of graduation and 63% had found employment.

Admissions Contact: Sean Kaylor, Associate Director of Admissions. E-mail: admissions@marist.edu.

MARYMOUNT COLLEGE/TARRYTOWN   D-5
Tarrytown, NY 10591

	(914) 332-8295
	(800) 724-4312; FAX: (914) 332-4956
Full-time: 30 men, 652 women	Faculty: 56; IIB, -$
Part-time: 54 men, 269 women	Ph.D.s: 95%
Graduate: none	Student/Faculty: 12 to 1
Year: semesters, summer session	Tuition: $12,500
Application Deadline: May 1	Room & Board: $6750
Freshman Class: 337 applied, 278 accepted, 113 enrolled	
SAT I: required	COMPETITIVE

Marymount College/Tarrytown, founded in 1907, is an independent women's undergraduate institution in the Catholic tradition. The college offers programs in liberal arts and career preparation. In addition to regional accreditation, the college has baccalaureate program accreditation with CSWE. The library contains 119,006 volumes, 106,394 microform items, and 160 audiovisual forms, and subscribes to 971 periodicals. Computerized library sources and services include the card catalog and database searching. Special learning facilities include a learning resource center. The 25-acre campus is in a suburban area 30 miles north of New York City. Including residence halls, there are 12 buildings on campus.

Student Life: 77% of undergraduates are from New York. Students come from 19 states and 12 foreign countries. 71% are from public schools; 29% from private. 60% are white; 16% African American; 14% Hispanic. 55% are Catholic; 21% Protestant; 13% claim no religious affiliation; the remaining 10% are Eastern Orthodox, Quaker, and Muslim. The average age of freshmen is 18.5; all undergraduates, 22.5. 5% do not continue beyond their first year; 63% remain to graduate.

Housing: 638 students can be accommodated in college housing. College-sponsored living facilities include single-sex dormitories. On-campus housing is guaranteed for all 4 years. 85% of students live on campus. Alcohol is not permitted. All students may keep cars on campus.

Activities: There are no fraternities or sororities. There are 25 groups on campus, including art, chorale, computers, dance, drama, ethnic, honors, international, literary magazine, newspaper, photography, political, professional, social, social service, student government, and yearbook. Popular campus events include Talent Show, Fashion Show and Competition, Women's Day, Octoberfest, and Springfest.

Sports: There are 7 intercollegiate sports for women and 2 intramural sports for women. Athletic and recreation facilities include a swimming pool, dance studio, fitness center, bowling alley, 2 tennis courts, and an athletic field. The campus stadium seats 350, the indoor gymnasium 375.

Disabled Students: 85% of the campus is accessible to disabled students. The following facilities are available: wheelchair ramps, elevators, special parking, specially equipped rest rooms, special class scheduling, automatic door openers, and paid notetakers.

Services: In addition to many counseling and information services, tutoring is available in every subject. There is remedial math, reading, and writing. There are writing and mathematics laboratories.

Campus Safety and Security: Campus safety and security measures include 24-hour foot and vehicle patrol, self-defense education, informal discussions, and pamphlets/posters/films. In addition, there are emergency telephones and lighted pathways/sidewalks.

Programs of Study: The college confers B.A. and B.S. degrees. Associate degrees are also awarded. Bachelor's degrees are awarded in BIOLOGICAL SCIENCE (biology/biological science), BUSINESS (accounting, banking and finance, business administration and management, business economics, fashion merchandising, international business management, marketing/retailing/merchandising, and personnel management), COMMUNICATIONS AND THE ARTS (art history and appreciation, communications, dramatic arts, English, fine arts, French, journalism, and Spanish), COMPUTER AND PHYSICAL SCIENCE (chemistry, information sciences and systems, and mathematics), EDUCATION (art, elementary, foreign languages, home economics, middle school, science, secondary, and special), ENGINEERING AND ENVIRONMENTAL DESIGN (interior design), SOCIAL SCIENCE (American studies, economics, fashion design and technology, food science, history, home economics, interdisciplinary studies, international studies, liberal arts/general studies, philosophy, political science/government, psychology, social work, and sociology). Business, education, and psychology have the largest enrollments.

Required: All students must take 3 semesters of English composition, 2 of mathematics, 4 of physical education, and a computer course. 3 humanities courses are also required. Distribution requirements include 2 semesters each of natural science and foreign language, and 1 each of social science, fine arts, and religious studies. A total of 120 credits is required for graduation, as is a minimum GPA of 2.0.

Special: Juniors and seniors in all disciplines may receive up to 12 credits for on-site internships. The college offers study abroad in 7 countries, a Washington semester, work-study programs, dual and student-designed majors, credit by exam, nondegree study, and pass/fail options. There are 3–2 business and education programs with Fordham University and a 5-year joint program in physical therapy with New York Medical College. The Weekend College is available to working men and women. There is a freshman honors program on campus, as well as 3 national honor societies.

Faculty/Classroom: 48% of faculty are male; 52%, female. All teach undergraduates, and 60% also do research. The average class size in an introductory lecture is 20; in a laboratory, 16; and in a regular course offering, 15.

Admissions: 82% of the 1995–96 applicants were accepted. The SAT I scores for the 1995–96 freshman class were as follows: Verbal—80% below 500, 15% between 500 and 599, and 4% between 600 and 700; Math—86% below 500, 8% between 500 and 599, and 6% between 600 and 700. 23% of the current freshmen were in the top fifth of their class; 51% were in the top two fifths. 1 freshman graduated first in the class.

Requirements: The SAT I is required but ACT scores may be submitted instead. A minimum GPA of 2.5 is required. Applicants must complete 16 academic credits, including 4 years of English, and 3 years each of foreign language, mathematics, science, and history or social studies. The GED is accepted. An interview is recommended. AP and CLEP credits are accepted. Important factors in the admissions decision are recommendations by school officials, extracurricular activities record, and leadership record.

Procedure: Freshmen are admitted fall and spring. Entrance exams should be taken in the fall of the year preceding enrollment. There are early admissions and deferred admissions plans. Early decision applications should be filed by November 1; regular applications, by May 1 for fall entry and January 10 for spring entry, along with an application fee of $25. Notification of early decision is sent December 1; regular decision, on a rolling basis.

Transfer: 63 transfer students enrolled in 1995–96. Applicants with fewer than 24 college credits must submit SAT I scores and a high school transcript. A GPA of at least 2.2 is required. 45 credits of 120 must be completed at the college.

Visiting: There are regularly scheduled orientations for prospective students, including meeting with a counselor and touring the campus. There are guides for informal visits, and visitors may sit in on classes. To schedule a visit, contact Christine G. Richard, Dean of Admissions.

Financial Aid: In 1995–96, 87% of all freshmen and 80% of continuing students received some form of financial aid. 87% of freshmen and 78% of continuing students received need-based aid. The average freshman award was $13,400. Of that total, scholarships or need-based grants averaged $9500; loans averaged $2625; and work contracts averaged $1200. 70% of undergraduate students work part-time. Average earnings from campus work for the school year are $1000. The average financial indebtedness of the 1994–95 graduate was $18,925. the college is a member of CSS. The FAFSA is required. The application deadline for fall entry is May 1.

International Students: There are currently 40 international students enrolled. The school actively recruits these students. They must take the TOEFL and achieve a minimum score of 500.

Computers: The college provides computer facilities for student use. The mainframe is a DEC ALPHA. There are 65 microcomputers on a Novell Network available to students in classroom, graphics, and drop-in laboratories. Available software includes word processing, spreadsheets, database, statistical packages, graphics, programming languages, and Internet utilities. All students may access the system 7 days a week. There are no time limits and no fees.

Graduates: In 1994–95, 224 bachelor's degrees were awarded. The most popular majors among graduates were business (17%), education (16%), and psychology (11%). Within an average freshman class, 2% graduate in 3 years, 61% in 4 years, and 1% in 6 years. 54 companies recruited on campus in 1994–95. Of the 1994 graduating class, 37% were enrolled in graduate school within 11 months of graduation and 63% had found employment.

Admissions Contact: Christine G. Richard, Dean of Admissions. E-mail: admiss@mmc.marymt.edu. A campus video is available.

MARYMOUNT MANHATTAN COLLEGE   D-5

New York, NY 10021   (212) 517-0555; (800) MARYMOUNT

Full-time: 247 men, 843 women   Faculty: 62; IIB, -$
Part-time: 103 men, 703 women   Ph.D.s: 75%
Graduate: none   Student/Faculty: 18 to 1
Year: semesters, summer session   Tuition: $11,450
Application Deadline: open   Room & Board: $5000
Freshman Class: 914 applied, 813 accepted, 247 enrolled
SAT I or ACT: required   **LESS COMPETITIVE**

Marymount Manhattan College is an urban, independent coeducational liberal arts college, offering programs in the arts and sciences for all ages, as well as substantial preprofessional preparation. The library contains 75,000 volumes, 70 microform items, and 1643 audiovisual forms, and subscribes to 600 periodicals. Computerized library sources and services include the card catalog, interlibrary loans, and database searching. Special learning facilities include a learning resource center, art gallery, radio station, and TV station. The 1-acre campus is in an urban area in Manhattan. Including residence halls, there are 2 buildings on campus.

Student Life: 69% of undergraduates are from New York. Students come from 37 states, 55 foreign countries, and Canada. 50% are from public schools; 30% from private. 51% are white; 20% African American; 17% Hispanic. The average age of freshmen is 19; all undergraduates, 26. 27% do not continue beyond their first year; 65% remain to graduate.

Housing: 300 students can be accommodated in college housing. College-sponsored living facilities include single-sex and coed dormitories and off-campus apartments. On-campus housing is available on a first-come, first-served basis and is available on a lottery system for upperclassmen. Priority is given to out-of-town students. 85% of students commute. Alcohol is not permitted. All students may keep cars on campus.

Activities: 3% of women belong to 1 national sorority. There are no fraternities. There are 30 groups on campus, including art, choir, computers, dance, drama, ethnic, film, gay, honors, international, literary magazine, musical theater, newspaper, photography, political, professional, radio and TV, religious, social, social service, student government, and yearbook. Popular campus events include Octoberfest, Strawberry Festival, International Day, Holiday Soiree, and Homecoming Weekend.

Sports: There is no sports program at MMC. Athletic and recreation facilities include an Olympic-size pool and a 300-seat auditorium.

Disabled Students: The entire campus is accessible to physically disabled students. The following facilities are available: wheelchair ramps, elevators, specially equipped rest rooms, special class scheduling, and lowered drinking fountains.

Services: In addition to many counseling and information services, tutoring is available in every subject. There is remedial math, reading, and writing.

Campus Safety and Security: Campus safety and security measures include 24-hour foot and vehicle patrol, informal discussions, pamphlets/posters/films, and lighted pathways/sidewalks. In addition, there are security cameras and photo ID check-in.

Programs of Study: MMC confers B.A., B.S., and B.F.A. degrees. Bachelor's degrees are awarded in BIOLOGICAL SCIENCE (biology/biological science), BUSINESS (accounting, business administration and management, and international business management), COMMUNICATIONS AND THE ARTS (communications, dance, dramatic arts, English, and fine arts), EDUCATION (early childhood, elementary, secondary, and special), HEALTH PROFESSIONS (premedicine and speech pathology/audiology), SOCIAL SCIENCE (history, international studies, liberal arts/general studies, political science/government, psychology, and sociology). Premedicine, English, and liberal arts are the strongest academically. Theater, business, and psychology have the largest enrollments.

Required: To graduate, students must complete 120 credit hours, including 37 to 70 in the major, with a minimum GPA of 2.5. The core curriculum totals 43 credits in the areas of critical thinking, psychology and philosophy, quantitative reasoning and science, the modern world, communications/language, and the arts.

Special: MMC offers study abroad, interdisciplinary courses, pass/fail options, nondegree study, credit for life experience, and some 250 internships in industry, government, and the media. Cooperative programs in business and finance, dance, music, languages, nursing, and urban education are offered in conjunction with local colleges and institutes. There is a January mini-session. There is a freshman honors program on campus, as well as 2 national honor societies.

Faculty/Classroom: 50% of faculty are male; 50%, female. The average class size in an introductory lecture is 25; in a laboratory, 6; and in a regular course offering, 16.

Admissions: 89% of the 1995–96 applicants were accepted. The SAT I scores for a recent freshman class were as follows: Verbal—69% below 500, 20% between 500 and 599, 10% between 600 and 700, and 1% above 700; Math—60% below 500, 29% between 500 and 599, and 11% between 600 and 700. 45% of the current freshmen were in the top fifth of their class; 60% were in the top two fifths.

Requirements: The SAT I or ACT is required. A minimum GPA of 2.5 is required. Applicants should be graduates of an accredited secondary school or have a GED certificate. MMC recommends completion of 16 academic units, including 4 each in English and electives, and 3 each in language, mathematics, social science, and science. Recommendations are required, and an interview is strongly advised. Applicants to the dance and acting programs must audition. AP and CLEP credits are accepted. Important factors in the admissions decision are personality/intangible qualities, evidence of special talent, and leadership record.

Procedure: Freshmen are admitted to all sessions. Entrance exams should be taken as early as possible. There are early decision, early admissions, and deferred admissions plans. Application deadlines are open for regular decision; for early decision, November 1. Application fee is $30. Notification of early decision is sent December 15; regular decision, on a rolling basis.

Transfer: 99 transfer students enrolled in 1995–96. Applicants who have graduated from high school since 1989 must meet standard freshman requirements and must submit official transcripts from all colleges attended. 30 credits of 120 must be completed at MMC.

Visiting: There are regularly scheduled orientations for prospective students, including an interview with an admissions counselor, a tour of the school and dormitories, and a meeting with a financial aid adviser. There are guides for informal visits, and visitors may sit in on classes and stay overnight at the school. To schedule a visit, contact the Admissions Office.

Financial Aid: In 1995–96, 85% of all students received some form of financial aid. 75% of all students received need-based aid. The average freshman award was $18,500. Of that total, scholarships or need-based grants averaged $5100 ($11,200 maximum); loans averaged $2625 (maximum); work contracts averaged $1500 ($3000 maximum); and PLUS loans averaged $9275 ($20,000 maximum). 10% of undergraduate students work part-time. Average earnings from campus work for the school year are $2000. The average financial indebtedness of the 1994–95 graduate was $12,000. MMC is a member of CSS. The FAFSA is required. The application deadline for fall entry is February 25.

International Students: There are currently 130 international students enrolled. The school actively recruits these students. They must take the TOEFL and achieve a minimum score of 550.

Computers: The college provides computer facilities for student use. There are Apple IIe and IBM PC microcomputers in the computer laboratory, as well as a Commodore Amiga 2000 for graphics work. Internet connection is available in the library. All students may access the system. There are no time limits and no fees.

Graduates: The most popular majors among graduates were business (16%), theater (14%), and psychology (12%). Within an average freshman class, 65% graduate in 4 years.

Admissions Contact: Tom Friebel, Director of Admissions.

MEDAILLE COLLEGE   A-3

Buffalo, NY 14214   (716) 884-3281
(800) 292-1582; FAX: (716) 884-0291

Full-time: 177 men, 469 women   Faculty: 41; IIB, -$
Part-time: 44 men, 151 women   Ph.D.s: 83%
Graduate: none   Student/Faculty: 16 to 1
Year: semesters, summer session   Tuition: $9560
Application Deadline: August 15   Room & Board: $4400
Freshman Class: 302 applied, 182 accepted, 98 enrolled
SAT I Verbal/Math: 400/410   **LESS COMPETITIVE**

Medaille College, founded in 1875, is a private, nonsectarian institution offering undergraduate programs in liberal arts, education, business, and sciences to a primarily commuter student body. The library contains 52,861 volumes, 36,990 microform items, and 1017 audio-visual forms, and subscribes to 281 periodicals. Computerized library sources and services include the card catalog, interlibrary loans, and database searching. Special learning facilities include a learning resource center, radio station, and TV station. The 13-acre campus is in an urban area 3 miles from Buffalo. Including residence halls, there are 7 buildings on campus.

Student Life: 92% of undergraduates are from New York. Students come from 3 states, 2 foreign countries, and Canada. 75% are white; 14% African American; 10% other. The average age of freshmen is 20; all undergraduates, 28. 27% of freshmen remain to graduate.

Housing: 50 students can be accommodated in college housing. College-sponsored living facilities include single-sex and coed on-campus apartments and off-campus apartments. On-campus housing is guaranteed for all 4 years. 95% of students commute. All students may keep cars on campus.

Activities: There are no fraternities or sororities. There are 20 groups on campus, including chorus, computers, drama, ethnic, honors, international, literary magazine, musical theater, newspaper, photography, political, professional, radio and TV, social, social service, student government, and yearbook. Popular campus events include Founders Day, Silent Auction, Honors Convocation, Awards Banquet, and Athletic Banquet.

Sports: There are 3 intercollegiate sports for women, and 3 intramural sports for men and 3 for women. Athletic and recreation facilities include an NCAA regulation gymnasium located in the student center, a softball and soccer field.

Disabled Students: The following facilities are available: wheelchair ramps, elevators, special parking, specially equipped rest rooms, lowered drinking fountains, and lowered telephones.

Services: In addition to many counseling and information services, tutoring is available in most subjects. There is a reader service for the blind, and remedial math, reading, and writing.

Campus Safety and Security: Campus safety and security measures include escort service, shuttle buses, informal discussions, and pamphlets/posters/films. In addition, there are emergency telephones and lighted pathways/sidewalks.

Programs of Study: Medaille confers B.A., B.S., and B.S.Ed. degrees. Associate degrees are also awarded. Bachelor's degrees are awarded in BUSINESS (business administration and management and human resources), EDUCATION (elementary), SOCIAL SCIENCE (human services, humanities, liberal arts/general studies, and social science). Education and veterinary technology are the strongest academically. Education, veterinary technology, and business administration have the largest enrollments.

Required: The bachelor's degree requires successful completion of 120 to 128 credit hours. In addition to specific course requirements for each major, students must maintain a minimum GPA of 2.0. Five theme areas must be satisfied: Theme I-Self and others; Theme II-Global Perspectives; Theme III-Creative Expression; Theme IV-Science, Technology, and Environment; and Theme V-Communication. Students must also complete 3 credits each in mathematics and computers.

Special: Cross-registration is available with colleges in the Western New York Consortium. Most degree programs require internships. Opportunities are provided for student-designed majors, credit by examination, pass/fail options, and credit for work experience. The 2-year veterinary technology program combined with additional liberal arts and sciences courses leads to the B.S. in liberal studies degree. A modular program of evening courses, as well as Weekend College classes, enable students to maintain full-time status by attending classes either 2 nights a week or on weekends. There is 1 national honor society on campus.

Faculty/Classroom: 58% of faculty are male; 42%, female. All teach undergraduates. The average class size in an introductory lecture is 20; in a laboratory, 10; and in a regular course offering, 16.

Admissions: 60% of the 1995-96 applicants were accepted.

Requirements: The SAT or ACT is not required. Applicants must be graduates of an accredited secondary school or hold the GED. An essay and an interview are required. AP and CLEP credits are accepted. Important factors in the admissions decision are advanced placement or honor courses, personality/intangible qualities, and leadership record.

Procedure: Freshmen are admitted to all sessions. Entrance exams should be taken in May. There is a deferred admissions plan. Applications should be filed by August 15 for fall entry, January 15 for spring entry, and June 15 for summer entry, along with an application fee of $25. Notification is sent on a rolling basis.

Transfer: 188 transfer students enrolled in 1995-96. Transfer applicants must have a minimum GPA of 2.0 in their previous college work. An interview and recommendations are required. 30 credits of 120 must be completed at Medaille.

Visiting: There are regularly scheduled orientations for prospective students, including campus tours, academic program meetings, ice-breakers, and a review of policies and procedures. There are guides for informal visits and visitors may sit in on classes and stay overnight at the school. To schedule a visit, contact Jacqueline S. Matheny.

Financial Aid: In 1995-96, 70% of all freshmen and 66% of continuing students received some form of financial aid. 76% of freshmen and 75% of continuing students received need-based aid. The average freshman award was $10,183. Of that total, scholarships or need-based grants averaged $1226 ($2850 maximum); loans averaged $2000 ($6000 maximum); and work contracts averaged $1200 ($1500 maximum). 13% of undergraduate students work part-time. Average earnings from campus work for the school year are $1500. The average financial indebtedness of the 1994-95 graduate was $12,000. Medaille is a member of CSS. The FAF and FAFSA are required. The application deadline for fall entry is March 30.

International Students: They must take the TOEFL and achieve a minimum score of 550.

Computers: The college provides computer facilities for student use. There are 40 IBM and Apple microcomputers available for academic use. All students may access the system. There are no time limits and no fees.

Graduates: In a recent year, 158 bachelor's degrees were awarded.

Admissions Contact: Jacqueline S. Matheny, Director of Enrollment Management.

MERCY COLLEGE
D-5
Dobbs Ferry, NY 10522-1189
(914) 693-7600
(800) MERCY NY; FAX: (904) 693-9455

Full-time: 1563 men, 2997 women	Faculty: 160; IIB, +$
Part-time: 670 men, 1452 women	Ph.D.s: 63%
Graduate: 65 men, 223 women	Student/Faculty: 29 to 1
Year: semesters, summer session	Tuition: $6600
Application Deadline: open	Room & Board: $6600
Freshman Class: 1969 applied, 1757 accepted, 1109 enrolled	
SAT I or ACT: not required	LESS COMPETITIVE

Mercy College, founded in 1950, is an independent institution offering programs in liberal arts, fine arts, business, and health science. There are 5 graduate schools. In addition to regional accreditation, Mercy has baccalaureate program accreditation with CSWE and NLN. The 10 libraries contain 600,000 volumes, and subscribe to 1170 periodicals. Computerized library sources and services include the card catalog, interlibrary loans, and database searching. Special learning facilities include a learning resource center, art gallery, radio station, and TV station. The 40-acre campus is in a suburban area 12 miles north of New York City. Including residence halls, there are 12 buildings on campus.

Student Life: 97% of undergraduates are from New York. Students come from 14 states and 10 foreign countries. 95% are from public schools; 5% from private. 60% are white; 20% African American; 19% Hispanic. The average age of freshmen is 19; all undergraduates, 28. 25% do not continue beyond their first year; 60% remain to graduate.

Housing: 160 students can be accommodated in college housing. College-sponsored living facilities include dormitories. 99% of students commute. All students may keep cars on campus.

Activities: There are no fraternities or sororities. There are 26 groups on campus, including art, cheerleading, chess, choir, chorale, chorus, computers, dance, drama, ethnic, film, honors, international, jazz band, literary magazine, musical theater, newspaper, orchestra, political, professional, radio and TV, religious, social, social service, student government, and yearbook. Popular campus events include plays and special honors programs.

Sports: Athletic and recreation facilities include a 200-seat gymnasium, a soccer/baseball field, a swimming pool, tennis courts, and a track.

Disabled Students: 75% of the campus is accessible to disabled students. The following facilities are available: wheelchair ramps, elevators, special parking, specially equipped rest rooms, lowered drinking fountains, and lowered telephones.

Services: In addition to many counseling and information services, tutoring is available in every subject. There is a reader service for the blind, and remedial math, reading, and writing.

Programs of Study: Mercy confers B.A., B.S., and B.F.A. degrees. Associate and master's degrees are also awarded. Bachelor's degrees are awarded in AGRICULTURE (animal science), BIOLOGICAL SCIENCE (biology/biological science), BUSINESS (accounting, banking and finance, business administration and management, hotel/motel and restaurant management, and marketing/retailing/merchandising), COMMUNICATIONS AND THE ARTS (broadcasting, communications, English, French, graphic design, Italian, journalism, music, Spanish, and speech/debate/rhetoric), COMPUTER AND PHYSICAL SCIENCE (actuarial science, computer programming, computer science, information sciences and systems, and mathematics), EDUCATION (art, early childhood, education of the deaf and hearing impaired, elementary, foreign languages, middle school, music, science, secondary, special, and teaching English as a second/foreign language (TESOL/TEFOL)), HEALTH PROFESSIONS (chiropractic, medical laboratory technology, nursing, predentistry, premedicine, prepharmacy, speech pathology/audiology, and veterinary science), SOCIAL SCIENCE (behavioral science, criminal justice, history, interdisciplinary studies, political science/government, prelaw, psychology, social science, social work, sociology, and urban studies). The health professions programs is the strongest academically. Business has the largest enrollment.

Required: To graduate, students must complete 120 semester hours with a minimum GPA of 2.0 overall and in the major. Distribution requirements include 12 credits each of mathematics/natural science and philosophy/language/fine arts, 9 of social science, 6 each of English and history, and 3 of speech.

Special: Mercy offers internships in each major, work-study programs through the Westchester Employee Association, study abroad, dual majors and degrees, credit for life experience, nondegree study, and pass/fail options. There is a freshman honors program on campus, as well as 14 national honor societies, including Phi Beta Kappa. 14 departments have honors programs.

Faculty/Classroom: 98% teach undergraduates and 5% do research. No introductory courses are taught by graduate students. The average class size in an introductory lecture is 15; in a laboratory, 12; and in a regular course offering, 14.

Admissions: 89% of the 1995–96 applicants were accepted.

Requirements: Applicants must be graduates of an accredited secondary school or have a GED certificate. They should have completed at least 16 academic units. An interview is encouraged and a letter of recommendation from the high school counselor or principal is required. Art students must submit a portfolio; music students must audition. AP and CLEP credits are accepted.

Procedure: Entrance exams should be taken between October and January of the senior year. There are early admissions and deferred admissions plans. Application deadlines are open. Application fee is $35. Notification is sent on a rolling basis.

Transfer: Applicants must submit official transcripts from all colleges attended. Students with fewer than 15 college credits must also submit their high school transcript. An interview is encouraged. 30 credits of 120 must be completed at Mercy.

Visiting: There are regularly scheduled orientations for prospective students. Visitors may sit in on classes. To schedule a visit, contact the Admissions Office.

Financial Aid: Mercy is a member of CSS. The FAF is required. The application deadline for fall entry is February 1.

International Students: There were 125 international students enrolled in a recent year. They must take the college's own test.

Computers: The college provides computer facilities for student use. The mainframe is an IBM 4381. There are also 250 IBM and Apple microcomputers, as well as graphics workstations with IBM XTs and Vectrix graphics boards. All students may access the system. There are no time limits. The fees are $35.

Admissions Contact: Acting Director of Admissions.

MOLLOY COLLEGE

D-5

Rockville Centre, NY 11570 — (516) 678-5000, ext. 240 — (800) 229-1020

Full-time: 254 men, 1144 women	Faculty: 133; IIB, -$
Part-time: 103 men, 628 women	Ph.D.s: 26%
Graduate: 4 men, 185 women	Student/Faculty: 11 to 1
Year: 4-1-4, summer session	Tuition: $9700
Application Deadline: open	Room & Board: n/app
Freshman Class: 457 applied, 352 accepted, 160 enrolled	
SAT I Verbal/Math: 400/420	LESS COMPETITIVE

Molloy College, founded in 1955, is a private coeducational commuter college affiliated with the Catholic Church. It offers programs in art, business, health science, liberal arts, music, and teacher preparation. There is 1 graduate school. In addition to regional accreditation, Molloy has baccalaureate program accreditation with CSWE and NLN. The library contains 120,070 volumes and 2755 microform items, and subscribes to 1045 periodicals. Computerized library sources and services include the card catalog, interlibrary loans, and database searching. Special learning facilities include a learning resource center and TV station. The 25-acre campus is in a suburban area 20 miles east of New York City. There are 4 buildings on campus.

Student Life: Students come from New York and 14 foreign countries. 23% are from public schools; 77% from private. 78% are white; 16% African American. The average age of freshmen is 18; all undergraduates, 20. 12% do not continue beyond their first year; 80% remain to graduate.

Housing: There are no residence halls. All students commute.

Activities: There are no fraternities or sororities. There are 20 groups on campus, including art, cheerleading, choir, chorus, dance, drama, ethnic, honors, international, literary magazine, musical theater, newspaper, orchestra, political, radio, religious, social, student government, and yearbook. Popular campus events include Tree Trimming Party, Senior 55 Nights Party, Junior Ring Night, and Graduate Champagne Brunch.

Sports: There are 3 intercollegiate sports for men and 5 for women, and 1 intramural sport for men and 1 for women. Athletic and recreation facilities include a gymnasium, a dance studio, a weight room, sports fields, and basketball and tennis courts.

Disabled Students: The entire campus is accessible to disabled students with wheelchair ramps, elevators, special parking, specially equipped rest rooms, special class scheduling, and lowered drinking fountains.

Services: In addition to many counseling and information services, tutoring is available in every subject. There is remedial math, reading, and writing.

Campus Safety and Security: Campus safety and security measures include 24-hour foot and vehicle patrol and a Campus Concerns Committee.

Programs of Study: Molloy confers B.A. and B.S. degrees. Associate and master's degrees are also awarded. Bachelor's degrees are awarded in BIOLOGICAL SCIENCE (biology/biological science), BUSINESS (accounting and business administration and management), COMMUNICATIONS AND THE ARTS (communications, English, music, and speech/debate/rhetoric), COMPUTER AND PHYSICAL SCIENCE (computer science and mathematics), EDUCATION (art, elementary, foreign languages, secondary, and special), HEALTH PROFESSIONS (music therapy, nursing, predentistry, and premedicine), SOCIAL SCIENCE (history, interdisciplinary studies, philosophy, prelaw, psychology, religion, social work, and sociology). Nursing and cardiorespiratory science are the strongest academically. Nursing, business, psychology, and education have the largest enrollments.

Required: Core requirements consist of 9 credits of philosophy and theology, 6 each of English and modern language, 1 of physical education, and courses in art and music history, speech, history, political science, psychology, sociology, mathematics, and science. A total of 128 credit hours is required for graduation.

Special: Students may cross-register with 16 area colleges. The college offers internships, a Washington semester, and dual and student-designed majors. Credit by examination and for life, military, and work experience, nondegree study, and pass/fail options are available. There is a freshman honors program on campus as well as 16 national honor societies.

Faculty/Classroom: 24% of faculty are male; 76%, female. All teach undergraduates; 25% also do research. No introductory courses are taught by graduate students. The average class size in an introductory lecture is 30; in a laboratory, 18; and in a regular course offering, 30.

Admissions: 77% of the 1995–96 applicants were accepted. 16% of the current freshmen were in the top fifth of their class; 53% were in the top two fifths. 2 freshmen graduated first in their class.

Requirements: The SAT I is required, with a minimum composite score of 800. A minimum grade average of 75 is required. Applicants should be graduates of a secondary school or have a GED. Preparation should include 4 years of English, 3 each of mathematics and history, and 2 each of foreign language and science. An essay is required, and an interview is recommended. AP and CLEP credits are accepted. Important factors in the admissions decision are leadership record, recommendations by school officials, and evidence of special talent.

Procedure: Freshmen are admitted fall and spring. Entrance exams should be taken in the fall of the senior year. There are early decision, early admissions, and deferred admissions plans. Application deadlines are open. The fee is $25. Notification is sent on a rolling basis. 118 early decision candidates were accepted for the 1995–96 class.

Transfer: 441 transfer students enrolled in 1995–96. A minimum college GPA of 2.0 is required and an interview is recommended. 30 credits of 128 must be completed at Molloy.

Visiting: There are regularly scheduled orientations for prospective students, including 2 open houses each year. There are guides for informal visits and visitors may sit in on classes. To schedule a visit, contact the Admissions Office.

Financial Aid: In 1995–96, 90% of all freshmen and 85% of continuing students received some form of financial aid. 74% of freshmen and 80% of continuing students received need-based aid. The average freshman award was $3906. Of that total, scholarships or need-based grants averaged $4000 ($6700 maximum); loans averaged $1000 ($2600 maximum); and work contracts averaged $1440. All undergraduate students work part-time. The average financial indebtedness of the 1994–95 graduate was $10,000. Molloy is a member of CSS. The FAF, the FAFSA, and the college's own financial statement are required. The application deadline for fall entry is August 15.

International Students: There are currently 11 international students enrolled. They must take the TOEFL or the college's own test and achieve a minimum score on the TOEFL of 500.

Computers: The college provides computer facilities for student use. There are 88 microcomputers available to students in 4 campus laboratories. Additional microcomputers are available within individual departments. All students may access the system. There are no time limits and no fees.

Graduates: In 1994-95, 411 bachelor's degrees were awarded. Within an average freshman class, 50% graduate in 4 years, 60% in 5 years, and 62% in 6 years.

Admissions Contact: Wayne F. James, Director of Admissions. E-mail: jamwa@mol.edu. A campus video is available.

MOUNT SAINT MARY COLLEGE   D-4
Newburgh, NY 12550

	(914) 569-3248
	(800) 558-0942; FAX: (914) 562-6762
Full-time: 320 men, 796 women	Faculty: 51; IIB, av$
Part-time: 184 men, 296 women	Ph.D.s: 67%
Graduate: 65 men, 252 women	Student/Faculty: 22 to 1
Year: semesters, summer session	Tuition: $8930
Application Deadline: open	Room & Board: $5000
Freshman Class: 1063 applied, 702 accepted, 252 enrolled	
SAT I Verbal/Math: 450/460	ACT: 20 COMPETITIVE

Mount Saint Mary College, founded in 1960, is a private coeducational institution offering programs in the liberal arts. There are 3 graduate schools. In addition to regional accreditation, The Mount has baccalaureate program accreditation with NLN. The library contains 118,020 volumes, 33,000 microform items, and 8072 audiovisual forms, and subscribes to 1085 periodicals. Computerized library sources and services include interlibrary loans and database searching. Special learning facilities include a learning resource center, an elementary school, a TV production studio, and an herbarium field station. The 72-acre campus is in a suburban area 58 miles north of New York City. Including residence halls, there are 37 buildings on campus.

Student Life: 72% of undergraduates are from New York. Students come from 20 states and 6 foreign countries. 50% are from public schools; 50% from private. 85% are white. 62% are Catholic; 12% Protestant. The average age of freshmen is 18; all undergraduates, 24. 23% do not continue beyond their first year; 50% remain to graduate.

Housing: 800 students can be accommodated in college housing. College-sponsored living facilities include single-sex dormitories. In addition, there are on-campus town houses. On-campus housing is guaranteed for all 4 years. 73% of students live on campus; of those, 78% remain on campus on weekends. All students may keep cars on campus.

Activities: There are no fraternities or sororities. There are 30 groups on campus, including art, cheerleading, choir, computers, drama, ethnic, honors, literary magazine, musical theater, newspaper, photography, political, professional, radio and TV, religious, social, student government, and yearbook. Popular campus events include Octoberfest, Siblings Weekend, Holiday Formal, and Parents Weekend.

Sports: There are 5 intercollegiate sports for men and 6 for women, and 15 intramural sports for men and 15 for women. Athletic and recreation facilities include a gymnasium, a weight room, tennis and handball courts, an indoor running track, a swimming pool, a Nautilus room, a game room, and an aerobics/dance studio.

Disabled Students: All of the campus is accessible to disabled students. The following facilities are available: wheelchair ramps, elevators, special parking, specially equipped rest rooms, lowered telephones, and special equipment in the library and computer centers to accommodate students with low vision.

Services: In addition to many counseling and information services, tutoring is available in every subject. There is remedial math, reading, and writing.

Campus Safety and Security: Campus safety and security measures include 24-hour foot and vehicle patrol, self-defense education, escort service, and informal discussions. There are pamphlets/posters/films, emergency telephones, and lighted pathways/sidewalks.

Programs of Study: The Mount confers B.A., B.S., B.S.Ed., and B.S.N. degrees. Master's degrees are also awarded. Bachelor's degrees are awarded in BIOLOGICAL SCIENCE (biology/biological science), BUSINESS (accounting and business administration and management), COMMUNICATIONS AND THE ARTS (communications, dramatic arts, English, media arts, and public relations), COMPUTER AND PHYSICAL SCIENCE (chemistry, computer science, and mathematics), EDUCATION (elementary, secondary, and special), HEALTH PROFESSIONS (medical laboratory technology, nursing, predentistry, premedicine, and preveterinary science), SOCIAL SCI-

ENCE (Hispanic American studies, history, human services, interdisciplinary studies, international studies, political science/government, prelaw, psychology, social science, and sociology). Nursing, physical therapy, and preprofessional are the strongest academically. Business management and administration has the largest enrollment.

Required: The required core curriculum includes 39 credits in natural sciences, mathematics, computer science, philosophy and religion, arts and letters, and social sciences. A total of 120 credit hours is required for the B.A. or B.S., with 24 to 40 in the major and a minimum GPA of 2.0. Overall requirements are higher for nursing, medical technology, and education students. All students must achieve computer literacy before graduation.

Special: Co-op programs and internships are available in all majors. There is cross-registration with other mid-Hudson area colleges, as well as accelerated degree programs in business, accounting, nursing, computer science, and public relations. There is a 3-2 degree in physical therapy with New York Medical College. The college also offers study abroad in more than 22 countries, a Washington semester, work-study, and dual and student-designed majors. Credit by examination and for life, military, and work experience, nondegree study, and pass/fail options are available. There is a freshman honors program on campus, as well as 8 national honor societies, including Phi Beta Kappa. 6 departments have honors programs.

Faculty/Classroom: 47% of faculty are male; 53%, female. All teach undergraduates and 40% do research. No introductory courses are taught by graduate students. The average class size in an introductory lecture is 33; in a laboratory, 8; and in a regular course offering, 22.

Admissions: 66% of the 1995-96 applicants were accepted. The SAT I scores for the 1995-96 freshman class were as follows: Verbal—71% below 500, 29% between 500 and 599, and 1% between 600 and 700; Math—67% below 500, 32% between 500 and 599, and 1% between 600 and 700. The ACT scores were 54% below 21, 22% between 21 and 23, 23% between 24 and 26, and 1% between 27 and 28. 18% of the current freshmen were in the top fifth of their class; 49% were in the top two fifths. There were 3 National Merit semifinalists. 1 freshman graduated first in the class.

Requirements: The SAT I or ACT is required. The Mount requires applicants to be in the upper 80% of their class and have a 2.0 GPA. students should be graduates of an accredited secondary school. The GED is accepted. Applicants should prepare with 4 years each of English and history, and at least 3 each of mathematics and science and 2 of foreign language. An essay and an interview are recommended. AP and CLEP credits are accepted. Important factors in the admissions decision are advanced placement or honor courses, personality/intangible qualities, and recommendations by school officials.

Procedure: Freshmen are admitted to all sessions. Entrance exams should be taken as early as possible. There are early decision, early admissions, and deferred admissions plans. Early decision applications should be filed by December 1; deadlines for regular applications are open. The application fee is $20. Notification of early decision is sent immediately; regular decision, on a rolling basis. 10 early decision candidates were accepted for the 1995-96 class.

Transfer: 102 transfer students enrolled in 1995-96. Applicants must have a GPA of at least 2.0 in all college work. The SAT I or ACT, an associate degree, and an interview are recommended. 30 credits of 120 to 128 must be completed at The Mount.

Visiting: There are regularly scheduled orientations for prospective students, including 6 open houses per year, a 4-day fall orientation program, and a Spend a Day with a Current Student program in the spring. There are guides for informal visits and visitors may sit in on classes and stay overnight at the school. To schedule a visit, contact Admissions.

Financial Aid: 20% of undergraduate students work part-time. Average earnings from campus work for the school year are $900. The Mount is a member of CSS. The FAFSA is required. The application deadline for fall entry is March 15.

International Students: There are currently 6 international students enrolled. They must score 525 on the TOEFL and also take SAT I or the ACT.

Computers: The college provides computer facilities for student use. The mainframe is an Intel 310 Super-Microcomputer Network. The student-computer ratio is 14 to 1. Microcomputers are located in the main computer center, laboratories, some classrooms, and the library. All students may access the system weekdays from 10 A.M. to 11 P.M., and weekends from 10 A.M. to 5 P.M. There are no time limits and no fees.

Graduates: In 1994-95, 381 bachelor's degrees were awarded. The most popular majors among graduates were education (24%), business (17%), and nursing (9%). Within an average freshman class, 1% graduate in 3 years, 83% in 4 years, 12% in 5 years, and 4% in 6 years. 10 companies recruited on campus in 1994-95. Of the 1994 graduating class, 27% were enrolled in graduate school within 6 months of graduation and 80% had found employment.

Admissions Contact: J. Randall Ognibene, Director of Admissions. A campus video is available.

NAZARETH COLLEGE OF ROCHESTER   B-3
Rochester, NY 14618-3790   (716) 586-2525, ext. 265
                                            (800) 462-3944

Full-time: 361 men, 974 women	Faculty: 109; IIB, +$
Part-time: 55 men, 365 women	Ph.Ds: 94%
Graduate: 170 men, 877 women	Student/Faculty: 12 to 1
Year: semesters, summer session	Tuition: $11,580
Application Deadline: March 1	Room & Board: $5220
Freshman Class: 1174 applied, 904 accepted, 304 enrolled	
SAT I Verbal/Math: 491/519	COMPETITIVE

Nazareth College of Rochester, founded in 1924, is an independent coeducational institution offering programs in the liberal arts and sciences and preprofessional areas. There are 4 graduate schools. In addition to regional accreditation, Nazareth has baccalaureate program accreditation with CSWE, NASM, and NLN. The library contains 262,845 volumes, 324,476 microform items, and 15,816 audiovisual forms, and subscribes to 1609 periodicals. Computerized library sources and services include the card catalog, interlibrary loans, and database searching. Special learning facilities include a learning resource center, art gallery, and radio station. The 75-acre campus is in a suburban area 7 miles east of Rochester. Including residence halls, there are 13 buildings on campus.

Student Life: 98% of undergraduates are from New York. Students come from 25 states, 6 foreign countries, and Canada. 88% are from public schools; 12% from private. 95% are white. The average age of freshmen is 18; all undergraduates, 21. 18% do not continue beyond their first year; 57% remain to graduate.

Housing: 825 students can be accommodated in college housing. College-sponsored living facilities include single-sex and coed dormitories. In addition there are honors houses and language houses. On-campus housing is guaranteed for all 4 years. 62% of students live on campus; of those, 75% remain on campus on weekends. All students may keep cars on campus.

Activities: There are no fraternities or sororities. There are 30 groups on campus, including art, band, cheerleading, choir, computers, dance, drama, ethnic, gay, honors, jazz band, literary magazine, musical theater, newspaper, political, religious, student government, and yearbook. Popular campus events include Springfest, Fall Formal Dance, Parents Weekend, and Alumni Weekend.

Sports: There are 6 intercollegiate sports for men and 7 for women, and 20 intramural sports for men and 20 for women. Athletic and recreation facilities include a gymnasium, a swimming pool, soccer and lacrosse fields, tennis and racquetball courts, a fitness center, and a sauna.

Disabled Students: All of the campus is accessible to disabled students. The following facilities are available: wheelchair ramps, elevators, special parking, specially equipped rest rooms, and special class scheduling.

Services: In addition to many counseling and information services, tutoring is available in every subject.

Campus Safety and Security: Campus safety and security measures include 24-hour foot and vehicle patrol, escort service, informal discussions, and emergency telephones. In addition, there are lighted pathways/sidewalks.

Programs of Study: Nazareth confers B.A., B.S., and B.Mus. degrees. Master's degrees are also awarded. Bachelor's degrees are awarded in BIOLOGICAL SCIENCE (biochemistry and biology/biological science), BUSINESS (accounting and business administration and management), COMMUNICATIONS AND THE ARTS (English, fine arts, French, German, Italian, music, and Spanish), COMPUTER AND PHYSICAL SCIENCE (chemistry, computer science, and mathematics), EDUCATION (art, business, elementary, foreign languages, middle school, and music), HEALTH PROFESSIONS (nursing, physical therapy, and speech pathology/audiology), SOCIAL SCIENCE (anthropology, economics, history, international studies, philosophy, political science/government, psychology, religion, social science, social work, and sociology). English, psychology, and physical therapy are the strongest academically. Psychology, English, and speech pathology have the largest enrollments.

Required: All students must take courses in English, mathematics, laboratory science, philosophy, social science, history, and religious studies. Two semesters of physical education, a course in computer literacy, and a writing competency examination in the junior year are required. Other requirements vary according to the major, with a total of anywhere from 30 to 75 upper-division credits needed. A total of 120 credit hours is required to graduate. The minimum GPA is 2.0.

Special: There is cross-registration with members of the Rochester Area Colleges Consortium. Internships are available in political science, law, and all other majors. A Washington semester, college-sponsored study abroad in France and Spain, a 3–2 chemical engineering degree with Clarkson University, and nondegree study are

also available. There is a freshman honors program on campus, as well as 11 national honor societies. 10 departments have honors programs.

Faculty/Classroom: 52% of faculty are male; 48%, female. All teach undergraduates. No introductory courses are taught by graduate students. The average class size in an introductory lecture is 25; in a laboratory, 15; and in a regular course offering, 24.

Admissions: 77% of the 1995–96 applicants were accepted. The SAT I scores for the 1995–96 freshman class were as follows: Verbal—59% below 500, 33% between 500 and 599, 7% between 600 and 700, and 1% above 700; Math—38% below 500, 39% between 500 and 599, 21% between 600 and 700, and 3% above 700. There were 2 National Merit semifinalists. 6 freshmen graduated first in their class.

Requirements: The SAT I or ACT is required, with minimum scores of 500 verbal and 500 math on the SAT I and 21 on the ACT. Applicants should graduate from an accredited secondary school or have a GED. A total of 17 academic credits is required, including 4 years each of English and social studies and 3 each of foreign language, mathematics, and science. An essay is required, as are an audition for music students and a portfolio for art students. An interview is recommended. AP and CLEP credits are accepted. Important factors in the admissions decision are personality, intangible qualities, geographic diversity, and ability to finance college education.

Procedure: Freshmen are admitted fall and spring. Entrance exams should be taken by December of the senior year. There are early decision, early admissions, and deferred admissions plans. Early decision applications should be filed by December 1; regular applications, by March 1 for fall entry and December 15 for spring entry, along with an application fee of $30. Notification of early decision is sent December 15; regular decision, February 1. A waiting list is an active part of the admissions procedure.

Transfer: 139 transfer students enrolled in 1995–96. Applicants must have a college GPA of 2.5. Those with fewer than 30 credits must submit high school transcripts. 30 credits of 120 must be completed at Nazareth.

Visiting: There are regularly scheduled orientations for prospective students, including individual appointments, group sessions, open houses, and summer academic orientation. There are guides for informal visits and visitors may sit in on classes and stay overnight at the school. To schedule a visit, contact the Admissions Office.

Financial Aid: In 1995–96, 84% of all freshmen and 85% of continuing students received some form of financial aid. 70% of freshmen and 72% of continuing students received need-based aid. The average freshman award was $10,697. Of that total, scholarships or need-based grants averaged $7402 ($10,240 maximum); loans averaged $2095 ($4125 maximum); and work contracts averaged $1200 ($1400 maximum). 64% of undergraduate students work part-time. Average earnings from campus work for the school year are $1159. The average financial indebtedness of the 1994–95 graduate was $10,874. Nazareth is a member of CSS. The FAFSA and the CSS Profile Application are required. The application deadline for fall entry is February 15.

International Students: There were 8 international students enrolled in a recent year. The school actively recruits these students. They must take the TOEFL and achieve a minimum score of 550.

Computers: The college provides computer facilities for student use. The mainframe is a DEC System 5260 ULTRIX. There are 120 microcomputers available for academic use in 6 laboratories. One of these laboratories is open 24 hours a day. All students may access the system. There are no time limits and no fees.

Graduates: In 1994–95, 385 bachelor's degrees were awarded. The most popular majors among graduates were education (32%), business administration (15%), and psychology (12%). Within an average freshman class, 50% graduate in 4 years and 60% in 5 years. 15 companies recruited on campus in 1994–95. Of the 1994 graduating class, 38% were enrolled in graduate school within 6 months of graduation and 81% had found employment.

Admissions Contact: Thomas DaRin, Dean of Admissions. E-mail: tkdarin@naz.edu. A campus video is available.

NEW YORK INSTITUTE OF TECHNOLOGY/ OLD WESTBURY

D-5

Old Westbury, NY 11568-8000

(516) 686-7520
(800) 345-NYIT; FAX: (516) 686-7613

Full-time: 2693 men, 1219 women	Faculty: 185; IIA, av$
Part-time: 1354 men, 591 women	Ph.D.s: 83%
Graduate: 1975 men, 1548 women	Student/Faculty: 21 to 1
Year: semesters, summer session	Tuition: $9700
Application Deadline: open	Room & Board: $5900
Freshman Class: 2787 applied, 2108 accepted, 1250 enrolled	
SAT I or ACT: see profile	LESS COMPETITIVE

The New York Institute of Technology, founded in 1955, is a private institution offering programs in architecture, engineering, technology, management, hospitality management, culinary arts, and the arts and sciences. NYIT has additional campuses in Central Islip on Long Island, and in Manhattan. There are 6 undergraduate and 6 graduate schools. In addition to regional accreditation, NYIT has baccalaureate program accreditation with ABET, FIDER, and NAAB. The 5 libraries contain 199,086 volumes, 579,800 microform items, and 3067 audiovisual forms, and subscribe to 3189 periodicals. Computerized library sources and services include interlibrary loans and database searching. Special learning facilities include a learning resource center, radio station, and TV studios. The 1050-acre campus is in a suburban area 25 miles east of New York City. Including residence halls, there are 25 buildings on campus.

Student Life: 88% of undergraduates are from New York. Students come from 36 states, 56 foreign countries, and Canada. 57% are white; 14% foreign nationals; 14% African American. The average age of freshmen is 18; all undergraduates, 26. 35% do not continue beyond their first year; 45% remain to graduate.

Housing: College-sponsored living facilities include single-sex and coed dormitories. In addition there are facilities for international, graduate, and architecture students. On-campus housing is guaranteed for all 4 years. 93% of students commute. Alcohol is not permitted. All students may keep cars on campus.

Activities: 3% of men belong to 2 local and 6 national fraternities; 3% of women belong to 2 local and 2 national sororities. There are 110 groups on campus, including academic, chorale, computers, drama, honors, international, newspaper, professional, radio and TV, religious, social, special interest, student government, and yearbook. Popular campus events include Club Fair Day, Earth Day, May Fest, Black History Month, and Women's Month.

Sports: There are 6 intercollegiate sports for men and 5 for women, and 5 intramural sports for men and 6 for women. Athletic and recreation facilities include a gymnasium, soccer fields, a track, and courts for tennis, handball, and basketball.

Disabled Students: The following facilities are available: wheelchair ramps, elevators, special parking, and specially equipped rest rooms.

Services: In addition to many counseling and information services, tutoring is available in every subject. There is remedial math, reading, and writing.

Campus Safety and Security: Campus safety and security measures include 24-hour foot and vehicle patrol, escort service, shuttle buses, and informal discussions. In addition, there are pamphlets/posters/films, emergency telephones, and lighted pathways/sidewalks.

Programs of Study: NYIT confers B.A., B.S., B.Arch., B.F.A., B.P.S., and B.Tech. degrees. Associate and master's degrees are also awarded. Bachelor's degrees are awarded in BIOLOGICAL SCIENCE (biology/biological science), BUSINESS (accounting, banking and finance, business administration and management, hotel/motel and restaurant management, and marketing/retailing/merchandising), COMMUNICATIONS AND THE ARTS (advertising, communications, English, fine arts, journalism, and telecommunications), COMPUTER AND PHYSICAL SCIENCE (chemistry, computer science, and mathematics), EDUCATION (art, business, education, health, and secondary), ENGINEERING AND ENVIRONMENTAL DESIGN (aeronautical engineering, architecture, electrical/electronics engineering, engineering technology, environmental engineering technology, interior design, and mechanical engineering), HEALTH PROFESSIONS (medical laboratory technology), SOCIAL SCIENCE (behavioral science, interdisciplinary studies, political science/government, and sociology). Architecture is the strongest academically. Business and architecture have the largest enrollments.

Required: All students take a core curriculum, sequenced over 8 semesters, that includes 42 credits in English, speech, behavioral and natural science, social science, philosophy, economics, and 2 capstone courses in the major field. A total of 120 to 138 credits and a minimum GPA of 2.0, both overall and in the major, are required for graduation.

Special: NYIT offers cooperative programs, cross-registration with the C.W. Post campus of Long Island University, summer study abroad, internships, student-designed majors, a general studies degree, and nondegree study. There are 5 national honor societies on campus. 6 departments have honors programs.

Faculty/Classroom: 74% of faculty are male; 26%, female. 72% teach undergraduates. No introductory courses are taught by graduate students. The average class size in an introductory lecture is 20; in a laboratory, 15; and in a regular course offering, 17.

Admissions: 76% of the 1995–96 applicants were accepted.

Requirements: The SAT I is required for the engineering and architecture programs; it is recommended for all other programs. Engineering programs require a minimum SAT I composite score of 1000, with 520 in mathematics; students failing to meet these standards may enter preengineering and transfer later. Architecture programs require a 950 composite SAT I score. Applicants must be graduates of an accredited secondary school or have a GED certificate. Completion of 16 academic units is required, but the specific courses needed vary by degree program. AP and CLEP credits are accepted.

Procedure: Freshmen are admitted fall and spring. Application deadlines are open. The application fee is $30. Notification is sent on a rolling basis.

Transfer: 615 transfer students enrolled in 1995–96. Applicants must submit official transcripts from all colleges attended. Engineering applicants must have a 2.3 GPA in mathematics, physics, and engineering courses. 30 credits of 120 to 138 must be completed at NYIT.

Visiting: There are regularly scheduled orientations for prospective students, including open houses in fall and spring, with campus tours, a president's address, financial aid seminars, and sessions with faculty advisers. There are guides for informal visits and visitors may sit in on classes. To schedule a visit, contact the Admissions Office.

Financial Aid: In 1995–96, 73% of all freshmen and 75% of continuing students received some form of financial aid. 69% of freshmen and 73% of continuing students received need-based aid. The average freshman award was $5125. Of that total, scholarships or need-based grants averaged $1500 ($2000 maximum); loans averaged $2625 (maximum); and work contracts averaged $1000 ($1500 maximum). 10% of undergraduate students work part-time. Average earnings from campus work for the school year are $1000. The average financial indebtedness of the 1994–95 graduate was $10,000. NYIT is a member of CSS. The FAFSA is required.

International Students: There are currently 1272 international students enrolled. The school actively recruits these students. They must take the TOEFL and achieve a minimum score of 550.

Computers: The college provides computer facilities for student use. The mainframes are a DEC VAX 8700 and 11/780 models. There are also 12 rooms equipped with Zenith, Commodore PC-40, Apple, IBM, and DEC microcomputers, and a laboratory with equipment for computer-aided design. All students may access the system. There are no time limits and no fees. It is recommended that engineering and technology majors have personal computers.

Graduates: In 1994–95, 1214 bachelor's degrees were awarded. The most popular majors among graduates were architectural technology (15%), communication arts (10%), and interdisciplinary studies (9%).

Admissions Contact: Beverly Tota, Director, Undergraduate Admissions.

NEW YORK UNIVERSITY

D-5

New York, NY 10011

(212) 998-4500; FAX: (212) 995-4902

Full-time: 13,558 men and women	Faculty: 2230; I, +$
Part-time: 2838 men and women	Ph.D.s: 94%
Graduate: 15,487 men and women	Student/Faculty: 6 to 1
Year: semesters, summer session	Tuition: $19,748
Application Deadline: January 15	Room & Board: $7552
Freshman Class: 16,491 applied, 7619 accepted, 2901 enrolled	
SAT I or ACT: required	VERY COMPETITIVE

New York University, founded in 1831, is a private liberal arts institution offering programs in arts and sciences, business, education, health, nursing, and social work. There are 7 undergraduate and 7 graduate schools. In addition to regional accreditation, NYU has baccalaureate program accreditation with AACSB, ABET, ADA, APTA, CSWE, FIDER, NAAB, NASAD, NASM, NCATE, and NLN. The 6 libraries contain 3.6 million volumes and 20,000 audiovisual forms, and subscribe to 15,936 periodicals. Computerized library sources and services include the card catalog, interlibrary loans, and database searching. Special learning facilities include a learning resource center, art gallery, radio station, TV station, and audiology laboratory. The 28-acre campus is in an urban area in New York City's Greenwich Village. Including residence halls, there are 109 buildings on campus.

Student Life: 60% of undergraduates are from New York. Students come from 50 states, 120 foreign countries, and Canada. 70% are from public schools; 26% from private. 51% are white; 18% Asian American. 12% do not continue beyond their first year; 71% remain to graduate.

Housing: 4500 students can be accommodated in college housing. College-sponsored living facilities include coed dormitories, on-campus apartments, and fraternity houses. In addition, there are special interest houses. On-campus housing is guaranteed for all 4 years. 60% of students live on campus. All students may keep cars on campus.

Activities: 7% of men and 6% of women belong to 11 national fraternities; 5% of women belong to 7 local and 3 national sororities. There are 250 groups on campus, including art, bagpipe band, band, cheerleading, chess, choir, chorale, chorus, computers, dance, drama, ethnic, film, gay, honors, international, jazz band, literary magazine, marching band, musical theater, newspaper, orchestra, pep band, photography, political, professional, radio and TV, religious, social, social service, student government, symphony, and yearbook. Popular campus events include Spring Strawberry Festival, Greek Olympics, Annual Club Fair, and Winter Festival.

Sports: There are 11 intercollegiate sports for men and 8 for women, and 19 intramural sports for men and 16 for women. Athletic and recreation facilities include a sports and recreation center that includes a pool, tennis courts, a track, a dance studio, an exercise prescription facility, a weight room, handball, racquetball, and squash courts, a fencing area, and multipurpose courts.

Disabled Students: 95% of the campus is accessible to disabled students. The following facilities are available: wheelchair ramps, elevators, special parking, specially equipped rest rooms, lowered drinking fountains, and lowered telephones.

Services: In addition to many counseling and information services, tutoring is available in every subject. There is a reader service for the blind.

Campus Safety and Security: Campus safety and security measures include self-defense education, escort service, shuttle buses, and informal discussions. In addition, there are pamphlets/posters/films, emergency telephones, lighted pathways/sidewalks, and vehicle patrol, 24-hour security in residence halls, and a neighborhood-merchant emergency help service.

Programs of Study: NYU confers B.A., B.S., B.B.A., and B.F.A. degrees. Associate, master's, and doctoral degrees are also awarded. Bachelor's degrees are awarded in BIOLOGICAL SCIENCE (biochemistry, biology/biological science, and neurosciences), BUSINESS (accounting, banking and finance, business administration and management, business economics, hotel/motel and restaurant management, and marketing/retailing/merchandising), COMMUNICATIONS AND THE ARTS (art history and appreciation, audio technology, broadcasting, classics, communications, comparative literature, creative writing, dance, dramatic arts, English, film arts, fine arts, French, German, Greek, Greek (classical), Hebrew, Italian, journalism, languages, Latin, linguistics, music, music business management, music performance, music theory and composition, musical theater, photography, Portuguese, radio/television technology, romance languages, Russian, Spanish, speech/debate/rhetoric, studio art, and theater design), COMPUTER AND PHYSICAL SCIENCE (actuarial science, chemistry, computer science, mathematics, physics, and statistics), EDUCATION (art, dance, early childhood, elementary, English, foreign languages, mathematics, music, science, secondary, social studies, and special), ENGINEERING AND ENVIRONMENTAL DESIGN (chemical engineering, civil engineering, electrical/electronics engineering, engineering physics, engineering technology, environmental engineering, graphic arts technology, materials engineering, and mechanical engineering), HEALTH PROFESSIONS (nursing, physical therapy, predentistry, premedicine, and speech pathology/audiology), SOCIAL SCIENCE (African studies, anthropology, dietetics, East Asian studies, economics, European studies, history, international relations, Judaic studies, Luso-Brazilian studies, medieval studies, Near Eastern studies, philosophy, political science/government, prelaw, psychology, public administration, religion, social science, social work, sociology, urban studies, and women's studies). Business, biology, and psychology have the largest enrollments.

Required: All students must complete a minimum of 128 credit hours and maintain a minimum GPA of 2.0. A course in expository writing is required. Students must complete a core liberal arts curriculum in addition to major and elective credit.

Special: A 3–2 engineering degree is available with the Stevens Institute of Technology in New Jersey. Opportunities are provided for internships, study abroad in more than 20 countries, a B.A.-B.S. degree, accelerated degrees, dual and student-designed majors, credit by examination, and pass/fail options. A Washington semester is available to political science majors. There is a freshman honors program on campus, as well as Phi Beta Kappa.

Faculty/Classroom: The average class size in an introductory lecture is 50; in a laboratory, 20; and in a regular course offering, 30.

Admissions: 46% of the 1995–96 applicants were accepted. There were 60 National Merit finalists.

Requirements: The SAT I or ACT is required. Applicants must graduate from an accredited secondary school. The GED is accepted. Students must present at least 16 Carnegie units, including 4 in English.

Some majors require an essay, an audition, submission of a creative portfolio, or an interview. Students may apply on computer disk. AP and CLEP credits are accepted. Important factors in the admissions decision are high school record, advanced placement or honor courses, and personality/intangible qualities.

Procedure: Freshmen are admitted to all sessions. Entrance exams should be taken by November of the senior year. There are early decision, early admissions, and deferred admissions plans. Early decision applications should be filed by November 15; regular applications, by January 15 for fall entry, December 1 for spring entry, and May 1 for summer entry, along with an application fee of $45. Notification of early decision is sent beginning December 15; regular decision, April 1. 535 early decision candidates were accepted for the 1995–96 class. A waiting list is an active part of the admissions procedure.

Transfer: 1076 transfer students enrolled in 1995–96. Students must submit official college transcripts from all postsecondary institutions attended and a final high school transcript. 32 credits of 128 must be completed at NYU.

Visiting: There are regularly scheduled orientations for prospective students, including campus tours and weekday information sessions by appointment. There are guides for informal visits and visitors may sit in on classes. To schedule a visit, contact the Admissions Office at (212) 998–4524.

Financial Aid: In 1995–96, 70% of all freshmen and 66% of continuing students received some form of financial aid. The average freshman award was $13,500. Average earnings from campus work for the school year are $3000. NYU is a member of CSS. The FAFSA is required. The application deadline for fall entry is February 15.

International Students: There are currently 956 international students enrolled. The school actively recruits these students. They must take the TOEFL or the college's own test. The student must also take the SAT I, ACT, or the college's own entrance exam.

Computers: The college provides computer facilities for student use. The mainframes are a CDC CYBER 180/830a; an IBM 4381; DEC VAX Models 11/785, 11/750, 8350/2, 8600, and 8650; and a SUN 4/280s. There are also IBM PS/2, IBM PC, and Apple Macintosh Plus microcomputers available in the academic computing center and in several departments and divisions. Those with course requirements to use the system may access the system 24 hours a day, 7 days a week in some cases. The fee is $2 per hour.

Graduates: In 1994–95, 3026 bachelor's degrees were awarded. The most popular majors among graduates were arts and humanities (35%), business (21%), and social sciences (17%). Within an average freshman class, 71% graduate in 5 years. 400 companies recruited on campus in 1994–95. Of the 1994 graduating class, over 70% had found employment within 6 months of graduation.

Admissions Contact: Office of Undergraduate Admissions. A campus video is available.

NIAGARA UNIVERSITY
Niagara University, NY 14109

A-3

(716) 286-8700, 8721
(800) 462-2111; FAX: (716) 286-8710

Full-time: 730 men, 1186 women	**Faculty:** 117; IIA, -$
Part-time: 85 men, 219 women	**Ph.D.s:** 83%
Graduate: 240 men, 405 women	**Student/Faculty:** 16 to 1
Year: semesters, summer session	**Tuition:** $11,560
Application Deadline: August 15	**Room & Board:** $5084
Freshman Class: 1990 applied, 1645 accepted, 423 enrolled	
SAT I Verbal/Math: 440/490	**ACT:** 22 COMPETITIVE

Niagara University, founded in 1856 by the Vincentian fathers and brothers, is today a private, nonsectarian institution rooted in a Roman Catholic tradition. Programs offered include those in liberal arts, business, education, nursing, and travel, hotel, and restaurant administration. There are 5 undergraduate and 3 graduate schools. In addition to regional accreditation, Niagara has baccalaureate program accreditation with ACCE, CSWE, NCATE, and NLN. The library contains 296,081 volumes, 76,427 microform items, and 772 audiovisual forms, and subscribes to 1319 periodicals. Computerized library sources and services include the card catalog, interlibrary loans, and database searching. Special learning facilities include a learning resource center, art gallery, radio station, TV station, 2 theaters, and a greenhouse. The 160-acre campus is in a suburban area 4 miles north of Niagara Falls, overlooking the Niagara River gorge, 20 miles north of Buffalo. Including residence halls, there are 25 buildings on campus.

Student Life: 88% of undergraduates are from New York. Students come from 26 states, 20 foreign countries, and Canada. 75% are from public schools; 25% from private. 88% are white. Most are Catholic. The average age of freshmen is 18; all undergraduates, 20. 25% do not continue beyond their first year; 58% remain to graduate.

Housing: 1314 students can be accommodated in college housing. College-sponsored living facilities include single-sex and coed dormitories. In addition, there is honors, international, and special interest housing. On-campus housing is guaranteed for all 4 years. 57% of students live on campus; of those, 75% remain on campus on weekends. Alcohol is not permitted. All students may keep cars on campus.

Activities: 2% of men belong to 2 national fraternities. There are no sororities. There are 78 groups on campus, including art, cheerleading, choir, chorale, computers, drama, drill team, ethnic, film, honors, international, musical theater, newspaper, pep band, political, professional, radio and TV, religious, social, social service, student government, and yearbook. Popular campus events include University Ball, Alumni Weekend, university theater productions, and art museum events.

Sports: There are 7 intercollegiate sports for men and 6 for women, and 25 intramural sports for men and 25 for women. Athletic and recreation facilities include a 3400-seat gymnasium, a 6-lane swimming and diving pool, exercise and weight rooms, saunas and dance areas, outdoor tennis courts, baseball and soccer fields, basketball and racquetball courts, and multipurpose courts with indoor track. Hiking and biking trails are nearby.

Disabled Students: 75% of the campus is accessible to disabled students. The following facilities are available: wheelchair ramps, elevators, special parking, specially equipped rest rooms, special class scheduling, and campus accommodation for the vision-impaired.

Services: In addition to many counseling and information services, tutoring is available in most subjects. There is a reader service for the blind, and remedial math, reading, and writing. Study skills development, note taking, and escort-assistance services are available, as are educational assistant services for the vision-impaired, educational/classroom services and machines for the hearing-impaired, and services for the learning-disabled.

Campus Safety and Security: Campus safety and security measures include 24-hour foot and vehicle patrol, self-defense education, escort service, and informal discussions. There are pamphlets/posters/films, emergency telephones, lighted pathways/sidewalks, and a campus security advisory board.

Programs of Study: Niagara confers B.A., B.S., B.B.A., and B.F.A. degrees. Associate and master's degrees are also awarded. Bachelor's degrees are awarded in BIOLOGICAL SCIENCE (biochemistry, biology/biological science, and life science), BUSINESS (accounting, business administration and management, business economics, hotel/motel and restaurant management, human resources, marketing/retailing/merchandising, tourism, and transportation management), COMMUNICATIONS AND THE ARTS (communications, dramatic arts, English, French, and Spanish), COMPUTER AND PHYSICAL SCIENCE (chemistry, computer science, information sciences and systems, and mathematics), EDUCATION (elementary, English, foreign languages, mathematics, science, secondary, and social studies), ENGINEERING AND ENVIRONMENTAL DESIGN (preengineering), HEALTH PROFESSIONS (nursing, predentistry, and premedicine), SOCIAL SCIENCE (criminal justice, history, international studies, philosophy, political science/government, prelaw, psychology, religion, social science, social work, and sociology). Business, social sciences, and education are the strongest academically. Business administration, travel and tourism, and social services have the largest enrollments.

Required: To graduate, students must earn 120 to 126 credit hours and a GPA of at least 2.0; 60 to 66 such hours are required in the major, 20 in specific disciplines, and 20 in liberal arts classes.

Special: Niagara offers a Washington semester, a semester at the state capitol in Albany, on-campus work-study, internships in most majors with such companies as the Big 6 accounting firms and Walt Disney World, and co-op programs in all areas except nursing, education, and social work. Students may study abroad in 4 countries and cross-register through the Western New York Consortium. Accelerated degree programs in business and nursing, B.A.-B.S. degrees, dual majors, a 2-3 engineering program with the University of Detroit, nondegree study, credit for life, military, and work experience, pass/fail options, and research are also available. There is also an academic exploration program for undeclared majors. There is a freshman honors program on campus, as well as 14 national honor societies.

Faculty/Classroom: 64% of faculty are male; 36%, female. All teach undergraduates. No introductory courses are taught by graduate students. The average class size in an introductory lecture is 25 and in a regular course offering, 20.

Admissions: 83% of the 1995-96 applicants were accepted. The SAT I scores for the 1995-96 freshman class were as follows: Verbal—72% below 500, 20% between 500 and 599, 7% between 600 and 700, and 1% above 700; Math—50% below 500, 28% between 500 and 599, 18% between 600 and 700, and 4% above 700. The ACT scores were 22% below 21, 38% between 21 and 23, 22% between 24 and 26, 12% between 27 and 28, and 5% above 28. 35% of the current freshmen were in the top fifth of their class; 62% were in the top two fifths.

Requirements: The SAT I or ACT is required. A minimum grade average of 80% is required. Applicants should be graduates of an accredited high school, but the GED is accepted. The high school program should include 16 academic credits, with 4 in English and 2 each in foreign language, history, mathematics, science, social studies, as well as academic electives. Science, mathematics, and computer majors should have 3 credits each in mathematics and science. The university accepts applications on-line via ExPAN. AP and CLEP credits are accepted. Important factors in the admissions decision are advanced placement or honor courses, parents or siblings attending the school, and recommendations by school officials.

Procedure: Freshmen are admitted to all sessions. Entrance exams should be taken in the junior year or fall of the senior year. There are early decision, early admissions, and deferred admissions plans. Early decision applications should be filed by August 15; regular applications, by August 15 for fall entry and January 10 for spring entry, along with an application fee of $25. Notification is sent on a rolling basis.

Transfer: 137 transfer students enrolled in 1995-96. Applicants must have a minimum GPA of 2.0 in travel, hotel, and restaurant administration, arts and sciences, and academic exploration (except for 2.25 in business and 2.5 for nursing and education majors) and submit all high school and college transcripts. The SAT I or ACT is recommended. 30 credits of 120 to 126 must be completed at Niagara.

Visiting: There are regularly scheduled orientations for prospective students, including individual interviews and campus tours. Other arrangements can be made individually, such as to attend a class, eat in the student cafeteria, and/or speak with a faculty member. There are guides for informal visits and visitors may sit in on classes and stay overnight at the school. To schedule a visit, contact the Admissions Office appointment desk at (716) 286-8700 or (800) 462-2111.

Financial Aid: In 1995-96, 94% of all students received some form of financial aid; 76% received need-based aid. The average freshman award was $12,964. Of that total, scholarships or need-based grants averaged $8889 ($16,700 maximum); loans averaged $3836 ($5100 maximum); and work contracts averaged $1600 ($2100 maximum). 27% of undergraduate students work part-time. Average earnings from campus work for the school year are $1408. The average financial indebtedness of the 1994-95 graduate was $11,577. Niagara is a member of CSS. The FAFSA and the college's own financial statement are required. The application deadline for fall entry is February 15.

International Students: There were 71 international students enrolled in a recent year. The school actively recruits these students. They must take the TOEFL and achieve a minimum score of 500.

Computers: The college provides computer facilities for student use. The mainframe is a DEC MicroVAX 3800. There are 150 terminals/PCs available to students in several academic computing laboratories and in the academic computing center. All dormitories are networked, and some rooms are tied in so students can access the system. All students may access the system 9 A.M. to 11 P.M. Monday to Thursday, 9 A.M. to 5 P.M. Friday, noon to 5 P.M. Saturday, and 3 P.M. to 10 P.M. Sunday. There are no time limits and no fees.

Graduates: In 1994-95, 481 bachelor's degrees were awarded. The most popular majors among graduates were commerce and accounting (23%), nursing (16%), and travel and tourism/and hotel and restaurant management (14%). Within an average freshman class, 47% graduate in 4 years, 56% in 5 years, and 60% in 6 years. 139 companies recruited on campus in 1994-95. Of the 1994 graduating class, 15% were enrolled in graduate school within 6 months of graduation and 64% had found employment.

Admissions Contact: George C. Pachter, Dean of Admissions and Records. E-mail: admissions@niagara.edu. A campus video is available.

NYACK COLLEGE

D-5

Nyack, NY 10960

(914) 358-1710
(800) 336-9225; FAX: (914) 358-3047

Full-time: 408 men, 448 women	**Faculty:** 53
Part-time: 20 men, 31 women	**Ph.Ds:** 50%
Graduate: 188 men, 97 women	**Student/Faculty:** 16 to 1
Year: semesters, summer session	**Tuition:** $9450
Application Deadline: open	**Room & Board:** $4130
Freshman Class: 464 applied, 293 accepted, 145 enrolled	
SAT I Verbal/Math: 420/430	**ACT:** 20 COMPETITIVE

Nyack College, founded in 1882, is a private, coeducational liberal arts institution affiliated with the Christian and Missionary Alliance. There are 2 undergraduate schools and 1 graduate school. In addition to regional accreditation, Nyack has baccalaureate program accreditation with NASM. The 2 libraries contain 76,000 volumes and 420 microform items, and subscribe to 614 periodicals. Computerized library sources and services include the card catalog, interlibrary loans, and database searching. Special learning facilities include a learning resource center and radio station. The 63-acre campus is in a suburban area 20 miles north of New York City. Including residence halls, there are 6 buildings on campus.

Student Life: 56% of undergraduates are from New York. Students come from 20 states and 23 foreign countries. 53% are white; 17% Hispanic; 15% Asian American; 14% African American. Most are Protestant. The average age of freshmen is 18.4; all undergraduates, 21.2. 22% do not continue beyond their first year; 31% remain to graduate.

Housing: 610 students can be accommodated in college housing. College-sponsored living facilities include single-sex dormitories and married-student housing. On-campus housing is guaranteed for all 4 years. Alcohol is not permitted. All students may keep cars on campus.

Activities: There are no fraternities or sororities. There are 17 groups on campus, including band, cheerleading, chorale, drama, ethnic, literary magazine, newspaper, orchestra, radio and TV, religious, student government, and yearbook. Popular campus events include music festivals and the Cultural Events Series.

Sports: There are 3 intercollegiate sports for men and 3 for women, and 2 intramural sports for men and 2 for women. Athletic and recreation facilities include a gym, soccer field, weight room, training room, softball field, tennis courts, and outdoor ball courts.

Disabled Students: 70% of the campus is accessible to disabled students. The following facilities are available: elevators and special parking.

Services: In addition to many counseling and information services, tutoring is available in every subject. There is a reader service for the blind.

Campus Safety and Security: Campus safety and security measures include 24-hour foot and vehicle patrol.

Programs of Study: Nyack confers B.A., B.S., B.Mus., and S.M.B. degrees. Associate degrees are also awarded. Bachelor's degrees are awarded in BUSINESS (business administration and management), COMMUNICATIONS AND THE ARTS (communications, English, music, music theory and composition, piano/organ, and voice), EDUCATION (early childhood, elementary, and secondary), SOCIAL SCIENCE (biblical studies, crosscultural studies, history, interdisciplinary studies, ministries, missions, pastoral studies, philosophy, psychology, religion, religious education, religious music, social science, and sociology). Psychology has the largest enrollment.

Required: To graduate, students must complete 128 to 148 credits with a minimum GPA of 2.0, or 2.3 for education majors. General education and major requirements vary by degree program. Students must adhere to the college's standards of Christian living and behavior.

Special: Nyack offers internships, cooperative programs with other schools, study abroad, a semester in Hollywood for communications majors, dual and student-designed majors, independent study, nondegree study, and pass/fail options.

Faculty/Classroom: 54% of faculty are male; 46%, female. All teach undergraduates. The average class size in an introductory lecture is 22; in a laboratory, 15; and in a regular course offering, 25.

Admissions: 63% of the 1995–96 applicants were accepted. The SAT I scores for the 1995–96 freshman class were as follows: Verbal—77% below 500, 17% between 500 and 599, and 6% between 600 and 700; Math—65% below 500, 24% between 500 and 599, and 11% between 600 and 700. The ACT scores were 50% below 21, 20% between 21 and 23, 15% between 24 and 26, and 15% between 27 and 28. 20% of the current freshmen were in the top fifth of their class; 50% were in the top two fifths.

Requirements: The SAT I or ACT is required. Nyack requires applicants to be in the upper 50% of their class. A minimum GPA of 2.5 is required. Applicants must be graduates of an accredited secondary school or have the GED. Completion of 16 academic credits is required and should include 4 units of English, 3 of history or social science, 3 of any combination of mathematics and science, 2 of a foreign language, and 4 of electives. Students must demonstrate sound Christian character through personal testimony and recommendations. An interview may be required. AP and CLEP credits are accepted.

Procedure: Freshmen are admitted to all sessions. Application deadlines are open. Application fee is $15. Notification is sent on a rolling basis.

Transfer: 75 transfer students enrolled in 1995–96. 30 credits of 128 must be completed at Nyack.

Visiting: There are regularly scheduled orientations for prospective students. There are guides for informal visits and visitors may sit in on classes and stay overnight at the school. To schedule a visit, contact the Office of Admissions.

Financial Aid: In a recent year, 87% of all freshmen received some form of financial aid. The FAF, the college's own financial statement, and parent and student tax returns are required. The application deadline for fall entry is May 1.

Computers: The college provides computer facilities for student use. All students may access the system. There are no time limits and no fees.

Graduates: In 1994–95, 246 bachelor's degrees were awarded.

Admissions Contact: Miguel Sanchez, Director of Admissions.

PACE UNIVERSITY
New York, NY 10038

D-5
(212) 346-1225
(800) 874-PACE; FAX: (212) 346-1040

Full-time: 2241 men, 3486 women	**Faculty:** 339; I, +$
Part-time: 712 men, 1430 women	**Ph.D.s:** 87%
Graduate: 1846 men, 1923 women	**Student/Faculty:** 17 to 1
Year: semesters, summer session	**Tuition:** $12,120
Application Deadline: July 15	**Room & Board:** $5240
Freshman Class: 4530 applied, 3747 accepted, 1175 enrolled	
SAT I Verbal/Math: 430/520	**COMPETITIVE**

Pace University, founded in 1906, is a private institution offering programs in arts and sciences, business, nursing, education, and computer and information science on 2 campuses, 1 in New York City and 1 in Pleasantville. There are 5 undergraduate and 6 graduate schools. In addition to regional accreditation, Pace has baccalaureate program accreditation with NLN. The 3 libraries contain 825,000 volumes, 655,000 microform items, and 5900 audiovisual forms, and subscribe to 7300 periodicals. Computerized library sources and services include the card catalog, interlibrary loans, and database searching. Special learning facilities include a learning resource center, radio station, TV station, 2 art galleries, a performing arts center, biological research laboratories, and an environmental center. The New York City campus occupies 1 city block in an urban area; the Pleasantville/Briarcliff campus is located on 200 acres in a small town. Including residence halls, there are 41 buildings on the campuses.

Student Life: 87% of undergraduates are from New York. Students come from 24 states, 61 foreign countries, and Canada. 47% are from public schools; 53% from private. 61% are white; 15% African American; 13% Asian American; 11% Hispanic. 40% are Catholic; 30% Protestant. The average age of freshmen is 18; all undergraduates, 22. 20% do not continue beyond their first year; 55% remain to graduate.

Housing: 2281 students can be accommodated in college housing. College-sponsored living facilities include coed dormitories. On-campus housing is guaranteed for all 4 years. 60% of students commute. Alcohol is not permitted. All students may keep cars on campus.

Activities: 10% of men belong to 2 local and 6 national fraternities; 10% of women belong to 10 local and 2 national sororities. There are 100 groups on campus, including art, cheerleading, chorus, computers, dance, drama, ethnic, film, gay, honors, international, literary magazine, musical theater, newspaper, photography, political, professional, radio and TV, religious, social, social service, student government, and yearbook. Popular campus events include Homecoming, talent shows, concerts, and Picnic.

Sports: There are 7 intercollegiate sports for men and 6 for women, and 6 intramural sports for men and 5 for women. Athletic and recreation facilities include the Civic Center Gym in New York City and gymnasiums, tennis courts, and playing fields at the Pleasantville campus.

Disabled Students: 70% of the campus is accessible to disabled students. The following facilities are available: wheelchair ramps, elevators, special parking, specially equipped rest rooms, special class scheduling, lowered drinking fountains, and lowered telephones.

Services: In addition to many counseling and information services, tutoring is available in every subject. There is remedial math, reading, and writing. All services are provided in the university's center for academic excellence.

Campus Safety and Security: Campus safety and security measures include 24-hour foot and vehicle patrol, escort service, shuttle buses, and informal discussions. In addition, there are pamphlets/posters/films, emergency telephones, and lighted pathways/sidewalks.

Programs of Study: Pace confers B.A., B.S., B.B.A., B.F.A., and B.S.N. degrees. Associate, master's, and doctoral degrees are also awarded. Bachelor's degrees are awarded in BIOLOGICAL SCIENCE (biology/biological science), BUSINESS (accounting, banking and finance, business administration and management, business economics, international business management, and marketing/retailing/merchandising), COMMUNICATIONS AND THE ARTS (communications, dramatic arts, English, fine arts, French, journalism, Spanish, and theater design), COMPUTER AND PHYSICAL SCIENCE (chemistry, computer science, information sciences and systems, mathematics, and physics), EDUCATION (business, early childhood, elementary, and secondary), ENGINEERING AND ENVIRONMENTAL DESIGN (chemical engineering, electrical/electronics engineering, and industrial administration/management),

HEALTH PROFESSIONS (medical laboratory technology, nursing, predentistry, premedicine, and speech pathology/audiology), SOCIAL SCIENCE (anthropology, criminal justice, economics, history, political science/government, psychology, social science, and sociology). Accounting is the strongest academically. Business administration has the largest enrollment.

Required: To graduate, students must complete at least 128 credit hours, including 32 to 50 in the major, with a minimum GPA of 2.0. A core curriculum of 60 credits and an introductory computer science course are required.

Special: Internships, study abroad, a Washington semester, and a cooperative education program in all majors are available. Pace also offers accelerated degree programs, B.A.-B.S. degrees, dual majors, general studies degrees, and 3–2 engineering degrees with Manhattan College and Rensselaer Polytechnic Institute. Credit for life, military, and work experience, nondegree study, and pass/fail options are available. There is a freshman honors program on campus, as well as 15 national honor societies. There is a universitywide honors program.

Faculty/Classroom: 59% of faculty are male; 41%, female. 84% teach undergraduates. No introductory courses are taught by graduate students. The average class size in an introductory lecture is 35; in a laboratory, 10; and in a regular course offering, 23.

Admissions: 83% of the 1995–96 applicants were accepted. The SAT I scores for the 1995–96 freshman class were as follows: Verbal—76% below 500, 19% between 500 and 599, 4% between 600 and 700, and 1% above 700; Math—41% below 500, 40% between 500 and 599, 17% between 600 and 700, and 2% above 700. 50% of the current freshmen were in the top fifth of their class; 50% were in the top two fifths. 10 freshmen graduated first in their class.

Requirements: The SAT I or ACT is required. Pace requires applicants to be in the upper 50% of their class. A minimum high school average of 80% is required. Applicants should be graduates of an accredited secondary school, with 16 to 18 academic credits, including 4 in English, 3 to 4 each in mathematics, science, and history, and 2 to 3 in foreign language. The GED is accepted. An essay and an interview are recommended. Applications are accepted on computer disk. AP and CLEP credits are accepted. Important factors in the admissions decision are advanced placement or honor courses, recommendations by school officials, and leadership record.

Procedure: Freshmen are admitted fall and spring. There are early admissions and deferred admissions plans. Early decision applications should be filed by November 1; regular applications, by July 15 for fall entry and November 15 for spring entry, along with an application fee of $35. Notification of early decision is sent December 15; regular decision, on a rolling basis.

Transfer: 635 transfer students enrolled in 1995–96. Applicants are admitted in the fall or spring. A college GPA of 2.5 is required. Grades of C or better transfer for credit. A maximum of 68 credits will be accepted from a 2-year school. 32 credits of 128 must be completed at Pace.

Visiting: There are regularly scheduled orientations, with invitations extended to prospective students. There are guides for informal visits and visitors may sit in on classes and stay overnight at the school. To schedule a visit, contact the Office of Undergraduate Admission at (212) 346-1225 (New York City campus) or (914) 773-3746 (Pleasantville).

Financial Aid: In 1995–96, 67% of all freshmen and 61% of continuing students received some form of financial aid. 64% of freshmen and 60% of continuing students received need-based aid. The average freshman award was $4260. Of that total, scholarships or need-based grants averaged $4156 ($11,400 maximum); loans averaged $4741; and work contracts averaged $2447 ($2500 maximum). 95% of undergraduate students work part-time. Average earnings from campus work for the school year are $3600. The average financial indebtedness of the 1994–95 graduate was $10,000. The FAFSA is required. The application deadline for fall entry is February 8.

International Students: There are currently 390 international students enrolled. The school actively recruits these students. They must score 550 on the TOEFL or take the college's own test.

Computers: The college provides computer facilities for student use. The mainframe is an IBM 4381/P13. There are about 850 terminals on both campuses and at the midtown center. All students may access the system 24 hours a day. There are no time limits and no fees.

Graduates: In 1994–95, 1798 bachelor's degrees were awarded. The most popular majors among graduates were business and management (55%), social science (13%), and nursing (8%). Within an average freshman class, 37% graduate in 4 years, 21% in 5 years, and 4% in 6 years. 450 companies recruited on campus in 1994–95.

Admissions Contact: Richard P. Alvarez (NYC) or Gina Shalhoub (Pleasantville). A campus video is available.

PARSONS SCHOOL OF DESIGN D-5

New York, NY 10011   (212) 229-8910; (800) 252-0852

Full-time: 528 men, 1185 women	**Faculty:** 33
Part-time: 29 men, 68 women	**Ph.D.s:** 6%
Graduate: 40 men, 83 women	**Student/Faculty:** 52 to 1
Year: semesters, summer session	**Tuition:** $16,220
Application Deadline: open	**Room & Board:** $8132

Freshman Class: 1564 applied, 801 accepted, 387 enrolled
SAT I or ACT: required   **SPECIAL**

Parsons School of Design, founded in 1896, is a private, coeducational professional art school and is part of the New School for Social Research. There is 1 graduate school. In addition to regional accreditation, Parsons has baccalaureate program accreditation with NASAD. The 2 libraries contain 177,000 volumes and 5000 audiovisual forms, and subscribe to 230 periodicals. Computerized library sources and services include the card catalog and database searching. Special learning facilities include an art gallery. The 2-acre campus is in an urban area in Manhattan's Greenwich Village. Including residence halls, there are 8 buildings on campus.

Student Life: 52% of undergraduates are from New York. Students come from 39 states, 39 foreign countries, and Canada. 80% are from public schools; 20% from private. 35% are white; 31% foreign nationals; 15% Asian American. The average age of freshmen is 18; all undergraduates, 20. 20% do not continue beyond their first year; 68% remain to graduate.

Housing: 700 students can be accommodated in college housing. College-sponsored living facilities include coed dormitories and off-campus apartments. On-campus housing is available on a first-come, first-served basis and is available on a lottery system for upperclassmen. Priority is given to out-of-town students. Alcohol is not permitted. All students may keep cars on campus.

Activities: There are no fraternities or sororities. There are some groups and organizations on campus, including ethnic, gay, international, literary magazine, political, religious, social, and student government. Popular campus events include the Fashion Critics Award Show and annual senior shows.

Sports: There is no sports program at Parsons.

Disabled Students: The entire campus is accessible to disabled students. The following facilities are available: wheelchair ramps, elevators, and specially equipped rest rooms.

Services: In addition to many counseling and information services, tutoring is available in some subjects, including English and art history.

Campus Safety and Security: Campus safety and security measures include informal discussions and pamphlets/posters/films.

Programs of Study: Parsons confers B.A.-B.F.A., B.B.A., and B.F.A. degrees. Associate and master's degrees are also awarded. Bachelor's degrees are awarded in BUSINESS (business administration and management), COMMUNICATIONS AND THE ARTS (advertising, design, fine arts, graphic design, illustration, photography, and studio art), ENGINEERING AND ENVIRONMENTAL DESIGN (environmental design and interior design), SOCIAL SCIENCE (fashion design and technology). Communication design, illustration, and fashion design have the largest enrollments.

Required: To graduate, students must complete 134 credit hours, including 97 in the major, with a minimum GPA of 2.0. Parsons requires a minimum of 30 credits in liberal arts and 12 in art history.

Special: Students may cross-register at the New School for Social Research, Cooper Union, and Pratt Institute. Internships are required for some majors. Students may study abroad at the Parsons campus in Paris or in 4 other countries. The 5-year combined B.A.-B.F.A. degree requires 180 credits for graduation. A mobility semester or year at any AICAD school is available, and interdisciplinary majors, including architecture and environmental design and design marketing, are possible. All departments have honors programs.

Faculty/Classroom: 55% of faculty are male; 45%, female. 89% teach undergraduates. No introductory courses are taught by graduate students. The average class size in an introductory lecture is 30 and in a regular course offering, 17.

Admissions: 51% of the 1995–96 applicants were accepted.

Requirements: The SAT I or ACT is required. A minimum GPA of 2.0 is required. Applicants must be graduates of an accredited secondary school. The GED is accepted. Applicants should have completed 4 years each of art, English, history, and social studies. A portfolio and home examination are required, and an interview is recommended. AP credits are accepted. Important factors in the admissions decision are evidence of special talent, advanced placement or honor courses, and personality/intangible qualities.

Procedure: Freshmen are admitted fall and spring. Entrance exams should be taken by spring of the junior year. There is an early admissions plan. Application deadlines are open. The fee is $30. Notification is sent on a rolling basis. A waiting list is an active part of the admissions procedure, with about 15% of all applicants on the list.

Transfer: 280 transfer students enrolled in a recent year. Applicants will receive credit for grade C work or better in college courses that are similar in content, purpose, and standards to the courses offered at Parsons. A high school transcript is required for undergraduates, and the SAT I or ACT is recommended. All students must present a portfolio and home examination. Transfers are admitted in the fall or spring. 67 credits of 134 must be completed at Parsons.

Visiting: There are guides for informal visits. To schedule a visit, contact the Office of Admissions.

Financial Aid: In 1995–96, 69% of all freshmen and 71% of continuing students received some form of financial need-based aid. The average freshman award was $12,125. Of that total, scholarships or need-based grants averaged $6500 ($12,500 maximum); loans averaged $2625 ($4625 maximum); and work contracts averaged $2000 ($2500 maximum). 15% of undergraduate students work part-time. Average earnings from campus work for the school year are $1210. The average financial indebtedness of the 1994–95 graduate was $13,125. Parsons is a member of CSS. The FAFSA, the college's own financial statement, and the CSS Profile Application are required. The application deadline for fall entry is April 1.

International Students: There are currently 575 international students enrolled. The school actively recruits these students. They must take the TOEFL and achieve a minimum score of 550.

Computers: The college provides computer facilities for student use. More than 160 PowerMacs are available, as well as graphical software, E-mail and Internet access, and AutoCad and fashion-design laboratories, as well as other advanced computing facilities. All students may access the system. There are no time limits and no fees.

Graduates: In 1994–95, 349 bachelor's degrees were awarded. The most popular majors among graduates were fashion design (21%), communication design (21%), and illustration (14%). Within an average freshman class, 2% graduate in 3 years, 36% in 4 years, 8% in 5 years, and 3% in 6 years. 100 companies recruited on campus in 1994–95.

Admissions Contact: Nadine M. Bourgeois, Director of Admissions.

POLYTECHNIC UNIVERSITY/BROOKLYN   D-5
Brooklyn, NY 11201-2999   (718) 260-3100
                                (800) POLYTEC; FAX: (718) 260-3136

Full-time: 853 men, 155 women	Faculty: 151
Part-time: 128 men, 28 women	Ph.D.s: 95%
Graduate: 911 men, 164 women	Student/Faculty: 7 to 1
Year: semesters, summer session	Tuition: $17,575
Application Deadline: open	Room & Board: $4700
Freshman Class: 702 applied, 522 accepted, 253 enrolled	
SAT I Verbal/Math: 430/610	**VERY COMPETITIVE**

Polytechnic University, founded in 1854, is a private, multicampus university offering undergraduate and graduate programs through the divisions of arts and sciences, engineering, and management. There are 2 undergraduate and 3 graduate schools. In addition to regional accreditation, Brooklyn Poly has baccalaureate program accreditation with ABET. The library contains 197,302 volumes and 56,628 microform items, and subscribes to 821 periodicals. Computerized library sources and services include the card catalog, interlibrary loans, and database searching. Special learning facilities include a learning resource center. The 3-acre campus is in an urban area 5 minutes from downtown Manhattan. Including residence halls, there are 4 buildings on campus.

Student Life: 92% of undergraduates are from New York. Students come from 19 states, 19 foreign countries, and Canada. 73% are from public schools; 27% from private. 43% are white; 28% Asian American; 11% African American; 10% Hispanic. The average age of freshmen is 18; all undergraduates, 21. 22% do not continue beyond their first year; 66% remain to graduate.

Housing: 80 students can be accommodated in college housing. College-sponsored living facilities include coed dormitories and fraternity houses. In addition, there are special interest houses. On-campus housing is available on a first-come, first-served basis. Priority is given to out-of-town students. 95% of students commute. Alcohol is not permitted.

Activities: 12% of men and about 3% of women belong to 2 local and 2 national fraternities. There are no sororities. There are 60 groups on campus, including chess, computers, drama, ethnic, film, honors, international, newspaper, photography, professional, religious, social, social service, student government, and yearbook. Popular campus events include Chinese New Year, International Food Fair, Indian-Pakistan dinner, and Comedy Night.

Sports: There are 7 intercollegiate sports for men and 3 for women, and 13 intramural sports for men and 10 for women. Athletic and recreation facilities include soccer, lacrosse, and baseball fields, a gymnasium, and 2 student centers.

Disabled Students: 70% of the campus is accessible to disabled students. The following facilities are available: wheelchair ramps, elevators, special parking, specially equipped rest rooms, lowered drinking fountains, and lowered telephones.

Services: In addition to many counseling and information services, tutoring is available in every subject. There is remedial writing.

Campus Safety and Security: Campus safety and security measures include 24-hour foot and vehicle patrol, informal discussions, pamphlets/posters/films, and emergency telephones. In addition, there are lighted pathways/sidewalks.

Programs of Study: Brooklyn Poly confers the B.S. degree. Master's and doctoral degrees are also awarded. Bachelor's degrees are awarded in COMMUNICATIONS AND THE ARTS (journalism and technical and business writing), COMPUTER AND PHYSICAL SCIENCE (chemistry, computer science, information sciences and systems, mathematics, and physics), ENGINEERING AND ENVIRONMENTAL DESIGN (aeronautical engineering, aerospace studies, chemical engineering, civil engineering, computer engineering, electrical/electronics engineering, environmental engineering, environmental science, and mechanical engineering), SOCIAL SCIENCE (humanities and social science). Engineering, management, and arts and sciences are the strongest academically. Electrical engineering, computer engineering, and civil engineering have the largest enrollments.

Required: Students must complete all university and departmental course requirements, including 24 credits in humanities/social science, 14 in mathematics, 10 in physics, 6 in chemistry, and 3 in computers with Pascal. A total of 126 to 136 credits must be earned, and a 2.0 GPA is required to graduate. A senior design project is also required.

Special: Cooperative programs are available in all majors. Opportunities are provided for internships, work-study programs, study abroad, accelerated degree programs in engineering and computer science, dual majors, student-designed majors, and nondegree study. There is a freshman honors program on campus, as well as 8 national honor societies. 3 departments have honors programs.

Faculty/Classroom: 84% of faculty are male; 16%, female. All teach undergraduates and 40% do research. No introductory courses are taught by graduate students. The average class size in an introductory lecture is 30; in a laboratory, 15; and in a regular course offering, 25.

Admissions: 74% of the 1995–96 applicants were accepted. The SAT I scores for the 1995–96 freshman class were as follows: Verbal—72% below 500, 21% between 500 and 599, and 7% between 600 and 700; Math—6% below 500, 32% between 500 and 599, 49% between 600 and 700, and 13% above 700. 83% of the current freshmen were in the top fifth of their class; 94% were in the top two fifths.

Requirements: The SAT I or ACT is required. In addition, graduation from an accredited secondary school is required; a GED will be accepted. Applicants must submit a minimum of 16 credit hours, including 4 each in English, mathematics, and science, and 1 each in foreign language, art, music, and social studies. SAT II: Subject tests in writing, mathematics I or II, and chemistry or physics are recommended. An essay and an interview are recommended. Applications are accepted on computer disk in a readable format such as Word, WordPerfect, or ASCII. AP credits are accepted. Important factors in the admissions decision are advanced placement or honor courses, leadership record, and evidence of special talent.

Procedure: Freshmen are admitted fall, spring, and summer. Entrance exams should be taken by November of the senior year. There is a deferred admissions plan. Application deadlines are open. Application fee is $40. Notification is sent on a rolling basis.

Transfer: 110 transfer students enrolled in 1995–96. Applicants must have a 2.75 cumulative GPA. Students with fewer than 30 credits must submit SAT I scores and secondary school transcripts in addition to official college-level transcripts. 36 credits of 126 to 136 must be completed at Brooklyn Poly.

Visiting: There are regularly scheduled orientations for prospective students, including a keynote speaker, major presentations, financial aid and scholarship sessions, and student life and career services sessions. There are guides for informal visits and visitors may stay overnight at the school. To schedule a visit, contact the Dean of Admissions.

Financial Aid: In 1995–96, 99% of all freshmen and 95% of continuing students received some form of financial aid. 85% of all students received need-based aid. The average freshman award was $6758. Of that total, scholarships or need-based grants averaged $7041 ($17,335 maximum); loans averaged $3411 ($4625 maximum); and work contracts averaged $1689 ($2000 maximum). 16% of undergraduate students work part-time. Average earnings from campus work for the school year are $1500. The average financial indebtedness of the 1994–95 graduate was $10,835. Brooklyn Poly is a member of CSS. The FAFSA and the college's own financial statement are required. The application deadline for fall entry is March 1.

International Students: There are currently 59 international students enrolled. The school actively recruits these students. They must take the TOEFL and achieve a minimum score of 500. The student must also take the SAT I or the ACT.

Computers: The college provides computer facilities for student use. There are also 150 DOS/Windows microcomputers, 100 X Windows terminals, and 100 Sun workstations available for student use, located primarily in 2 main computer laboratories. All students may access the system, and 24-hour dial-up service is available. Computer laboratories are open 13 hours a day. There are no time limits and no fees.

Graduates: In 1994–95, 249 bachelor's degrees were awarded. The most popular majors among graduates were electrical engineering (33%), mechanical engineering (17%), and computer science (13%). Within an average freshman class, 30% graduate in 4 years, 48% in 5 years, and 51% in 6 years. 60 companies recruited on campus in 1994–95. Of the 1994 graduating class, 16% were enrolled in graduate school within 6 months of graduation and 86% had found employment.

Admissions Contact: Peter Jordan, Dean of Admissions. E-mail: admitme@poly.edu.

POLYTECHNIC UNIVERSITY/FARMINGDALE   D-5
Farmingdale, NY 11735   (516) 755-4200
           (800) POLYTEC; FAX: (516) 755-4404

Full-time: 293 men, 40 women	**Faculty:** 150
Part-time: 26 men, 2 women	**Ph.D.s:** 90%
Graduate: 273 men, 38 women	**Student/Faculty:** 2 to 1
Year: semesters, summer session	**Tuition:** $17,575
Application Deadline: see profile	**Room & Board:** $4700
Freshman Class: 246 applied, 209 accepted, 92 enrolled	
SAT I Verbal/Math: 500/620	**VERY COMPETITIVE**

Polytechnic University, founded in 1854, is a private, coeducational university offering undergraduate and graduate programs through the divisions of arts and sciences, engineering, and management. There are 2 undergraduate and 3 graduate schools. In addition to regional accreditation, Polytechnic University/Farmingdale has baccalaureate program accreditation with ABET. The library contains 35,000 volumes and 100 audiovisual forms, and subscribes to 110 periodicals. Computerized library sources and services include the card catalog, interlibrary loans, and database searching. Special learning facilities include a learning resource center. The 25-acre campus is in a suburban area in the center of Long Island. Including residence halls, there are 6 buildings on campus.

Student Life: 95% of undergraduates are from New York. Students come from 8 states and 7 foreign countries. 70% are from public schools; 30% from private. 66% are white; 20% Asian American. The average age of freshmen is 18; all undergraduates, 21. 20% do not continue beyond their first year; 66% remain to graduate.

Housing: 100 students can be accommodated in college housing. College-sponsored living facilities include coed dormitories and fraternity houses. On-campus housing is available on a first-come, first-served basis. Priority is given to out-of-town students. 80% of students commute. Alcohol is not permitted. All students may keep cars on campus.

Activities: 12% of men and about 3% of women belong to 2 local and 2 national fraternities. There are no sororities. There are 52 groups on campus, including chess, computers, ethnic, honors, international, jazz band, newspaper, photography, professional, religious, social, social service, student government, and yearbook. Popular campus events include International Food Fair, barbecues, Comedy Night, and ski trips.

Sports: There are 6 intercollegiate sports for men and 1 for women, and 13 intramural sports for men and 10 for women. Athletic and recreation facilities include soccer, lacrosse, and baseball fields, a gymnasium, and 2 student centers.

Disabled Students: 70% of the campus is accessible to disabled students. The following facilities are available: wheelchair ramps, elevators, special parking, specially equipped rest rooms, lowered drinking fountains, and lowered telephones.

Services: In addition to many counseling and information services, tutoring is available in every subject. There is remedial writing.

Campus Safety and Security: Campus safety and security measures include 24-hour foot and vehicle patrol, informal discussions, pamphlets/posters/films, and emergency telephones. In addition, there are lighted pathways/sidewalks.

Programs of Study: Polytechnic University/Farmingdale confers the B.S. degree. Master's and doctoral degrees are also awarded. Bachelor's degrees are awarded in COMMUNICATIONS AND THE ARTS (journalism and technical and business writing), COMPUTER AND PHYSICAL SCIENCE (chemistry, computer science, information sciences and systems, mathematics, and physics), ENGINEERING AND ENVIRONMENTAL DESIGN (aeronautical engineering, chemical engineering, civil engineering, computer engineering, electrical/electronics engineering, engineering, environmental engineering,

mechanical engineering, and metallurgical engineering), SOCIAL SCIENCE (social science). Engineering, management, and arts and sciences are the strongest academically. Electrical, computer, and aerospace engineering have the largest enrollments.

Required: Students must complete all university and departmental course requirements, earn 126 to 136 credits, and maintain a minimum GPA of 2.0 in order to graduate.

Special: Cross-registration is permitted through a consortium of Long Island colleges. Opportunities are provided for internships, work-study programs, study abroad, accelerated degree programs in computer science and computer or electrical engineering, dual majors, student-designed majors, and nondegree study. There is a freshman honors program on campus, as well as 5 national honor societies. 3 departments have honors programs.

Faculty/Classroom: 91% of faculty are male; 9%, female. 75% teach undergraduates, 40% do research, and 25% do both. No introductory courses are taught by graduate students. The average class size in an introductory lecture is 30; in a laboratory, 15; and in a regular course offering, 20.

Admissions: 85% of the 1995–96 applicants were accepted. The SAT I scores for the 1995–96 freshman class were as follows: Verbal—49% below 500, 40% between 500 and 599, and 11% between 600 and 700; Math—3% below 500, 34% between 500 and 599, 48% between 600 and 700, and 15% above 700. 83% of the current freshmen were in the top fifth of their class; 94% were in the top two fifths.

Requirements: The SAT I or ACT is required. A minimum ACT score of 24 may be substituted for SAT I results. Graduation from an accredited secondary school is required; a GED will be accepted. Applicants must submit a minimum of 16 credit hours, including 4 each in English, mathematics, and science, and 1 each in foreign language, art, music, and social studies. The SAT II: Writing test, mathematics I or II, and chemistry or physics are recommended. An essay and an interview are also recommended. AP credits are accepted. Important factors in the admissions decision are advanced placement or honor courses, evidence of special talent, and leadership record.

Procedure: Freshmen are admitted to all sessions. Entrance exams should be taken by November of the senior year. There are early decision, early admissions, and deferred admissions plans. Early decision applications should be filed by November 1, along with an application fee of $40; regular application deadlines are open, but those received by February 1 (fall entry) or December 1 (spring entry) are given preference. Notification of early decision is sent December 1; regular decision, on a rolling basis within 2 weeks of completing the application. 12 early decision candidates were accepted for a recent class.

Transfer: 27 transfer students were enrolled in a recent year. Transfer applicants must have a 2.75 cumulative GPA. 36 credits of 126 to 136 must be completed at Polytechnic University/Farmingdale.

Visiting: There are regularly scheduled orientations for prospective students, including a keynote speaker, major presentations, financial aid and scholarship sessions, and student life and career services sessions. There are guides for informal visits and visitors may sit in on classes and stay overnight at the school. To schedule a visit, contact the Director of Admissions.

Financial Aid: In 1995–96, 88% of all freshmen and 85% of continuing students received some form of financial aid. 85% of all students received need-based aid. The average freshman award was $6758. Of that total, scholarships or need-based grants averaged $9865 ($17,335 maximum); loans averaged $4474 ($4625 maximum); and work contracts averaged $1000 ($2000 maximum). 16% of undergraduate students work part-time. Average earnings from campus work for the school year are $1500. The average financial indebtedness of the 1994–95 graduate was $10,835. Polytechnic University/Farmingdale is a member of CSS. The FAF and the college's own financial statement are required. The application deadline for fall entry is February 1.

International Students: There are currently 59 international students enrolled. The school actively recruits these students. They must score 500 on the TOEFL and also take the TSE, SAT I or the ACT.

Computers: The college provides computer facilities for student use. 40 DOS/Windows, 2 Sun workstations, 25 XWindows, and additional facilities are available as part of the Engineering 101 laboratory. All students may access the system 15 hours a day. There are no time limits and no fees.

Graduates: In 1994–95, 60 bachelor's degrees were awarded. The most popular majors among graduates were mechanical engineering (27%), civil engineering (20%), and electrical engineering (18%). Within an average freshman class, 30% graduate in 4 years, 48% in 5 years, and 51% in 6 years. 60 companies recruited on campus in 1994–95. Of the 1994 graduating class, 16% were enrolled in graduate school within 6 months of graduation and 98% had found employment.

Admissions Contact: Peter Jordan, Dean of Admissions. E-mail: admitme@poly.edu.

PRATT INSTITUTE

Brooklyn, NY 11205

D-5

(718) 636-3669; (800) 331-0834

Full-time: 1053 men, 730 women	Faculty: 84
Part-time: 109 men, 76 women	Ph.D.s: 51%
Graduate: 545 men, 827 women	Student/Faculty: 21 to 1
Year: semesters, summer session	Tuition: $15,564
Application Deadline: February 1	Room & Board: $7200
Freshman Class: 1618 applied, 1195 accepted, 446 enrolled	
SAT I Verbal/Math: 430/490	**COMPETITIVE**

Pratt Institute, founded in 1887, is a private, coeducational institution offering undergraduate and graduate programs in architecture, art and design education, art history, industrial interior and communication design, fine arts, and professional studies. There are 3 undergraduate and 2 graduate schools. In addition to regional accreditation, Pratt has baccalaureate program accreditation with FIDER, NAAB, and NASAD. The library contains 208,000 volumes, 50,000 microform items, and 1500 audiovisual forms, and subscribes to 500 periodicals. Computerized library sources and services include the card catalog and database searching. Special learning facilities include a learning resource center, art gallery, radio station, bronze foundry, and metal forge. The 25-acre campus is in an urban area 25 miles east of downtown Manhattan. Including residence halls, there are 23 buildings on campus.

Student Life: 50% of undergraduates are from New York. Students come from 43 states, 57 foreign countries, and Canada. 81% are from public schools; 19% from private. 55% are white; 13% Asian American; 10% African American. The average age of freshmen is 19; all undergraduates, 23. 10% do not continue beyond their first year; 65% remain to graduate.

Housing: 1088 students can be accommodated in college housing. College-sponsored living facilities include single-sex and coed dormitories, on-campus apartments, and married-student housing. In addition, there are honors houses. On-campus housing is available on a first-come, first-served basis and is available on a lottery system for upperclassmen. 55% of students live on campus; of those, 80% remain on campus on weekends. All students may keep cars on campus.

Activities: 3% of men belong to 1 local and 1 national fraternity; 1% of women belong to 1 local sorority. There are 60 groups on campus, including art, chess, drama, ethnic, film, gay, honors, international, literary magazine, musical theater, newspaper, professional, radio and TV, religious, social, student government, and yearbook. Popular campus events include Springfest, International Food Fair, Holiday Ball, Thursday Night Comedy, and President's Lecture Series.

Sports: There are 6 intercollegiate sports for men and 4 for women, and 3 intramural sports for men and 1 for women. Athletic and recreation facilities include an activities resource center containing a 325-by-130-foot clear span area with 5 indoor tennis courts, a 200-meter indoor track, volleyball and basketball courts, a weight room, and 2 dance studios.

Disabled Students: 75% of the campus is accessible to disabled students. The following facilities are available: wheelchair ramps, elevators, special parking, specially equipped rest rooms, lowered drinking fountains, and specially equipped residence hall spaces.

Services: In addition to many counseling and information services, tutoring is available in some subjects, including mathematics, English, science, social science, and art history. There is a reader service for the blind. Individual tutoring and testing services are also available.

Campus Safety and Security: Campus safety and security measures include 24-hour foot and vehicle patrol, escort service, shuttle buses, and informal discussions. In addition, there are pamphlets/posters/films, emergency telephones, lighted pathways/sidewalks, and trained security officers.

Programs of Study: Pratt confers B.Arch., B.F.A., B.I.D., and B.P.S. degrees. Associate and master's degrees are also awarded. Bachelor's degrees are awarded in BUSINESS (fashion merchandising), COMMUNICATIONS AND THE ARTS (art history and appreciation, communications, film arts, fine arts, industrial design, and photography), EDUCATION (art), ENGINEERING AND ENVIRONMENTAL DESIGN (architecture, computer graphics, construction management, and interior design), SOCIAL SCIENCE (fashion design and technology). Fine arts, industrial design, communications design, and architecture are the strongest academically. Architecture and communications design have the largest enrollments.

Required: The number of credits needed for graduation varies with the major, but a minimum of 132 is required, one quarter of which must be in liberal arts. Undergraduates must maintain a GPA of 2.0. All students must take 13 credits (15 for architecture majors) of liberal arts electives, 6 credits each of social sciences or philosophy, English, and cultural history, and 3 credits of science.

Special: Pratt offers co-op programs with the East Coast Consortium (art and design schools) and cross-registration with St. John's College and Queen's College. Internships, study abroad in 4 countries, accelerated degree programs, work-study programs, dual majors, credit for work experience, nondegree study, and pass/fail options are available. There are 4 national honor societies on campus.

Faculty/Classroom: 65% of faculty are male; 35%, female. 92% teach undergraduates and 1% do research. No introductory courses are taught by graduate students. The average class size in an introductory lecture is 22; in a laboratory, 20; and in a regular course offering, 15.

Admissions: 74% of the 1995–96 applicants were accepted. The SAT I scores for the 1995–96 freshman class were as follows: Verbal—70% below 500, 22% between 500 and 599, 7% between 600 and 700, and 1% above 700; Math—57% below 500, 27% between 500 and 599, 15% between 600 and 700, and 2% above 700. 40% of the current freshmen were in the top fifth of their class; 93% were in the top two fifths.

Requirements: The SAT I or ACT is required. SAT II: Subject tests in writing and (for architecture applicants) mathematics level I or II are recommended. Applicants must be graduates of an accredited secondary school. The GED is accepted. Students should have completed 4 years of English, 3 of mathematics, and 2 each of science, social studies, and history. A portfolio is required, as is an interview for all applicants who live within 100 miles of Pratt. Applications are accepted on computer disk and on-line. AP and CLEP credits are accepted. Important factors in the admissions decision are evidence of special talent, extracurricular activities record, and advanced placement or honor courses.

Procedure: Freshmen are admitted to all sessions. Entrance exams should be taken by November of the senior year. There is an early decision plan. Early decision applications should be filed by November 1; regular applications, by February 1 for fall entry and November 1 for spring entry, along with an application fee of $35. Notification of early decision is sent December 1; regular decision, on a rolling basis. A waiting list is an active part of the admissions procedure, with about 5% of all applicants on the list.

Transfer: 232 transfer students enrolled in 1995–96. Applicants should present college transcripts and recommendations. Students with fewer than 30 college credits must submit SAT I or ACT scores. All transfer applicants without an associate degree must submit high school transcripts as well. A portfolio is required for architecture and art and design students. An interview is recommended. 48 credits of 132 must be completed at Pratt.

Visiting: There are regularly scheduled orientations for prospective students, including a campus tour, schoolwide presentations, departmental presentations, and financial aid workshops. There are guides for informal visits and visitors may sit in on classes and stay overnight at the school. To schedule a visit, contact the Office of Admissions.

Financial Aid: In 1995–96, 74% of all freshmen and 75% of continuing students received some form of financial aid. 67% of freshmen and 66% of continuing students received need-based aid. The average freshman award was $13,715. Of that total, scholarships or need-based grants averaged $7840 ($14,000 maximum); loans averaged $3625 (maximum); and work contracts averaged $2250 (maximum). 40% of undergraduate students work part-time. Average earnings from campus work for the school year are $2250. Pratt is a member of CSS. The FAF, the FAFSA, the college's own financial statement, and parent and student tax returns are required. The application deadline for fall entry is February 1.

International Students: There are currently 775 international students enrolled. They must take the TOEFL and achieve a minimum score on the TOEFL of 500, or the college's own test. If the latter is not passed, the student must take an intensive English course.

Computers: The college provides computer facilities for student use. The mainframe is a DEC VAX 6210. The mainframe may be reached via 12 VT340 terminals in the engineering laboratory or by dial-up modem. All students may access the system 24 hours a day, 7 days a week. There are no time limits and no fees.

Graduates: In 1994–95, 345 bachelor's degrees were awarded. The most popular majors among graduates were architecture (41%), communications design (20%), and fine arts (9%). Within an average freshman class, 45% graduate in 4 years, 53% in 5 years, and 58% in 6 years. 23 companies recruited on campus in 1994–95. Of the 1994 graduating class, 3% were enrolled in graduate school within 6 months of graduation and 95% had found employment.

Admissions Contact: Judith Aaron, Dean of Admissions.

RENSSELAER POLYTECHNIC INSTITUTE   D-3
Troy, NY 12180–3590   (518) 276-6216
(800) 448-6562; FAX: (518) 276-4072

Full-time: 3328 men, 1018 women	Faculty: 349; I, +$
Part-time: 6 men, 8 women	Ph.D.s: 99%
Graduate: 1596 men, 444 women	Student/Faculty: 12 to 1
Year: semesters, summer session	Tuition: $18,555
Application Deadline: January 1	Room & Board: $6155
Freshman Class: 4543 applied, 3849 accepted, 863 enrolled	
SAT I Verbal/Math: 546/664	ACT: 30 HIGHLY COMPETITIVE

Rensselaer Polytechnic Institute, founded in 1824, is a private, coeducational institution that emphasizes science and engineering technology but also offers programs in architecture, management, the humanities, and social sciences. There are 5 undergraduate and 5 graduate schools. In addition to regional accreditation, RPI has baccalaureate program accreditation with AACSB and ABET. The 2 libraries contain 430,000 volumes, 588,000 microform items, and 4900 audiovisual forms, and subscribe to 3875 periodicals. Computerized library sources and services include the card catalog, interlibrary loans, and database searching. Special learning facilities include a learning resource center, art gallery, radio station, and observatory. The 262-acre campus is in an urban area 10 miles north of Albany. Including residence halls, there are 185 buildings on campus.

Student Life: 59% of undergraduates are from out-of-state, mostly the Northeast. Students come from 50 states, 53 foreign countries, and Canada. 71% are white; 14% Asian American. The average age of freshmen is 18; all undergraduates, 21. 10% do not continue beyond their first year; 77% remain to graduate.

Housing: 2923 students can be accommodated in college housing. College-sponsored living facilities include single-sex and coed dormitories, on-campus apartments, married-student housing, fraternity houses, and sorority houses. In addition, there are special interest houses and a black cultural center. On-campus housing is guaranteed for the freshman year only, is available on a first-come, first-served basis, and is available on a lottery system for upperclassmen. 54% of students live on campus; of those, 98% remain on campus on weekends. All students may keep cars on campus.

Activities: 37% of men and about 1% of women belong to 1 local fraternity and 29 national fraternities; 26% of women belong to 1 local sorority and 4 national sororities. There are 125 groups on campus, including art, band, cheerleading, chess, chorale, chorus, computers, dance, drama, drill team, ethnic, gay, honors, international, jazz band, literary magazine, musical theater, newspaper, orchestra, pep band, photography, political, professional, radio and TV, religious, social, social service, student government, symphony, and yearbook. Popular campus events include Grand Marshal Week, International Festival, Activities Fair, Career-athalon, Black History Month, Black Awareness Week, Big Red Freakout, and Spring Carnival.

Sports: There are 12 intercollegiate sports for men and 11 for women, and 21 intramural sports for men and 8 for women. Athletic and recreation facilities include a field house, 2 pools, a stadium, 2 gymnasiums, a sports and recreation center, several playing fields, 2 weight rooms, 6 tennis courts, an artificial turf field, and an ice hockey rink.

Disabled Students: 55% of the campus is accessible to disabled students. The following facilities are available: wheelchair ramps, elevators, special parking, specially equipped rest rooms, special class scheduling, lowered drinking fountains, and lowered telephones.

Services: In addition to many counseling and information services, tutoring is available in every subject. There is a writing center.

Campus Safety and Security: Campus safety and security measures include 24-hour foot and vehicle patrol, self-defense education, escort service, and shuttle buses. In addition, there are informal discussions, pamphlets/posters/films, emergency telephones, lighted pathways/sidewalks, locked residence halls, an on-campus bicycle patrol, and a student volunteer program.

Programs of Study: RPI confers B.S. and B.Arch. degrees. Master's and doctoral degrees are also awarded. Bachelor's degrees are awarded in BIOLOGICAL SCIENCE (biology/biological science), BUSINESS (management information systems and management science), COMMUNICATIONS AND THE ARTS (communications), COMPUTER AND PHYSICAL SCIENCE (chemistry, computer science, geology, hydrology, mathematics, physics, and science technology), ENGINEERING AND ENVIRONMENTAL DESIGN (aeronautical engineering, architecture, biomedical engineering, chemical engineering, civil engineering, computer engineering, electrical/electronics engineering, engineering, engineering physics, environmental engineering, industrial engineering, materials science, mechanical engineering, and nuclear engineering), HEALTH PROFESSIONS (predentistry and premedicine), SOCIAL SCIENCE (economics, interdisciplinary studies, philosophy, prelaw, and psychology). Mechanical engineering, electrical engineering, and computer and systems engineering are the strongest academically and have the largest enrollments.

Required: For graduation, students must earn at least 124 credits for the B.S. degree and 168 credits for the B.Arch., including 24 credits in physical, life, and engineering sciences and 24 credits in humanities and social sciences. Students must maintain a minimum GPA of 1.8 and must pass a writing assessment or take a writing course, and complete a computing requirement of 1 course.

Special: RPI offers an exchange program with Williams and Harvey Mudd colleges and cross-registration with the Hudson Mohawk Association of Colleges and Universities. Co-op programs, internships, study abroad in several countries, and pass/fail options are available. Students may pursue dual and student-designed majors, an accelerated 4-year B.S.-M.S. degree in engineering, and a 3-2 engineering degree. Continuing education programs are broadcast via TV satellite to various industrial locations. There are 14 national honor societies on campus. 3 departments have honors programs.

Faculty/Classroom: 88% of faculty are male; 12%, female. All both teach and do research. No introductory courses are taught by graduate students. The average class size in an introductory lecture is 350; in a laboratory, 25; and in a regular course offering, 24.

Admissions: 85% of the 1995–96 applicants were accepted. The SAT I scores for the 1995–96 freshman class were as follows: Verbal—32% below 500, 43% between 500 and 599, 24% between 600 and 700, and 1% above 700; Math—2% below 500, 16% between 500 and 599, 51% between 600 and 700, and 31% above 700. 80% of the current freshmen were in the top fifth of their class; 96% were in the top two fifths. There were 10 National Merit finalists and 40 semifinalists. 62 freshmen graduated first in their class.

Requirements: The SAT I or ACT is required. In addition, SAT II: Subject tests in writing, mathematics (level I, IC, II, or IIC), and chemistry or physics are recommended (required for accelerated programs applicants). Applicants must be graduates of an accredited secondary school. High school preparation should include 4 years each of English and mathematics and 3 years each of science and social studies. An essay is required, and an interview is recommended. Architecture applicants must submit a portfolio. RPI offers its application for use on PC systems, and an electronic application can be found on the College View Network. AP credits are accepted. Important factors in the admissions decision are advanced placement or honor courses, recommendations by school officials, and leadership record.

Procedure: Freshmen are admitted fall and spring. Entrance exams should be taken in the junior and/or senior year. There are early decision, early admissions, and deferred admissions plans. Early decision applications should be filed by December 1; regular applications, by January 1 for fall entry and December 1 for spring entry, along with an application fee of $45. Notification of early decision is sent 3 weeks after the application is received; regular decision, March 15. 125 early decision candidates were accepted for the 1995–96 class.

Transfer: 157 transfer students enrolled in 1995–96. The SAT I or ACT is required for applicants with fewer than 3 semesters of college. All students are encouraged to have an interview and must present faculty recommendations. Grades of C or better transfer for credit. 30 credits of 124 for the B.S. (30 of 168 for the B.Arch.) must be completed at RPI.

Visiting: There are regularly scheduled orientations for prospective students. There are guides for informal visits and visitors may sit in on classes and stay overnight at the school. To schedule a visit, contact the Admissions Office.

Financial Aid: In 1995–96, 89% of all freshmen and 84% of continuing students received some form of financial aid. 72% of freshmen and 84% of continuing students received need-based aid. The average freshman award was $16,272. Of that total, scholarships or need-based grants averaged $12,759; loans averaged $4469; and work contracts averaged $1475 (maximum). 23% of undergraduate students work part-time. Average earnings from campus work for the school year are $790. The average financial indebtedness of the 1994–95 graduate was $18,600. RPI is a member of CSS. The FAFSA is required. The application deadline for fall entry is February 15.

International Students: There were 137 international students enrolled in a recent year. The school actively recruits these students. They must take the TOEFL and achieve a minimum score of 550. The student must also take the SAT I or the ACT.

Computers: The college provides computer facilities for student use. The mainframe is an IBM ES/9000. There are several microcomputer laboratories on campus as well as sites in the dormitories. Students use more than 500 networked UNIX workstations. All students may access the system. There are no time limits and no fees. Students in the laptop pilot project must have a PC-compatible AT&T laptop.

Graduates: In 1994–95, 970 bachelor's degrees were awarded. The most popular majors among graduates were electrical engineering (14%), mechanical engineering (14%), and computer and systems engineering (7%). Within an average freshman class, 43% graduate in 4 years, 65% in 5 years, and 68% in 6 years.

Admissions Contact: Teresa C. Duffy, Dean of Admissions. E-mail: admissions@rpi.edu. A campus video is available.

ROBERTS WESLEYAN COLLEGE   B-3
Rochester, NY 14624–1997   (716) 594-6400
(800) 777-4RWC; FAX: (716) 594-6371

Full-time: 372 men, 642 women	Faculty: 56
Part-time: 33 men, 98 women	Ph.D.s: 47%
Graduate: 29 men, 93 women	Student/Faculty: 18 to 1
Year: semesters, summer session	Tuition: $11,042
Application Deadline: August 1	Room & Board: $3744
Freshman Class: 456 applied, 410 accepted, 207 enrolled	
SAT I Verbal/Math: 470/520	ACT: 23 COMPETITIVE

Roberts Wesleyan College, founded in 1866, is a private, coeducational institution affiliated with the Free Methodist Church. The curriculum offers a liberal arts education in the Christian tradition. In addition to regional accreditation, Roberts has baccalaureate program accreditation with CSWE, NASAD, NASM, and NLN. The library contains 100,750 volumes, 102,393 microform items, and 2978 audiovisual forms, and subscribes to 738 periodicals. Computerized library sources and services include interlibrary loans and database searching. Special learning facilities include a learning resource center and art gallery. The 75-acre campus is in a suburban area 8 miles southwest of Rochester. Including residence halls, there are 31 buildings on campus.

Student Life: 85% of undergraduates are from New York. Students come from 23 states, 16 foreign countries, and Canada. 80% are white. 76% are Protestant; 12% claim no religious affiliation; 12% Catholic. The average age of freshmen is 19; all undergraduates, 22. 19% do not continue beyond their first year; 50% remain to graduate.

Housing: 675 students can be accommodated in college housing. College-sponsored living facilities include single-sex dormitories, on-campus apartments, and off-campus apartments. On-campus housing is guaranteed for all 4 years. 67% of students live on campus; of those, 50% remain on campus on weekends. Alcohol is not permitted. All students may keep cars on campus.

Activities: There are no fraternities or sororities. There are many groups and organizations on campus, including band, cheerleading, choir, chorale, drama, ethnic, international, musical theater, newspaper, orchestra, pep band, religious, social, social service, student government, and yearbook. Popular campus events include Winter Weekend, Junior-Senior Banquet, Parents and Friends Weekend, and musical stage performances.

Sports: There are 4 intercollegiate sports for men and 5 for women, and 20 intramural sports for men and 21 for women. Athletic and recreation facilities include a fitness center with facilities for basketball, volleyball, tennis, badminton, track, soccer, weight lifting, walleyball, racquetball, swimming, and diving.

Disabled Students: 75% of the campus is accessible to disabled students. The following facilities are available: wheelchair ramps, elevators, special parking, specially equipped rest rooms, special class scheduling, lowered drinking fountains, and lowered telephones.

Services: In addition to many counseling and information services, tutoring is available in every subject. There is a reader service for the blind, and remedial math, reading, and writing.

Campus Safety and Security: Campus safety and security measures include 24-hour foot and vehicle patrol, self-defense education, escort service, and informal discussions. In addition, there are pamphlets/posters/films, emergency telephones, lighted pathways/sidewalks, and personal-safety education programs.

Programs of Study: Roberts confers B.A. and B.S. degrees. Associate and master's degrees are also awarded. Bachelor's degrees are awarded in BIOLOGICAL SCIENCE (biochemistry and biology/biological science), BUSINESS (accounting, business administration and management, and personnel management), COMMUNICATIONS AND THE ARTS (communications, English, fine arts, and music), COMPUTER AND PHYSICAL SCIENCE (chemistry, computer science, mathematics, and physics), EDUCATION (art, elementary, and music), HEALTH PROFESSIONS (nursing, premedicine, prepharmacy, and preveterinary science), SOCIAL SCIENCE (criminal justice, history, prelaw, psychology, social work, and sociology). Nursing and engineering are the strongest academically. Elementary education and organizational management have the largest enrollments.

Required: To graduate, students must complete 124 to 126 credit hours, with a minimum of 30 hours in the major and a GPA of 2.0. Required courses include freshman seminar, physical education, modern technology, world issues, speech, writing, history, and philosophy.

Special: Students may cross-register with members of the Rochester Area Colleges consortium. Internships, study abroad in 5 countries, a Washington semester, co-op programs, a B.A.-B.S. degree in natural science and mathematics, dual majors, and 3–2 engineering degrees with Clarkson University, Rensselaer Polytechnic Institute, and Rochester Institute of Technology are available. Nondegree study,

pass/fail options, and credit for life, military, and work experience are also offered. The organizational management program, geared to adults, consists of 4-hour weekly sessions with reliance on out-of-class work. There is a freshman honors program on campus.

Faculty/Classroom: 53% of faculty are male; 47%, female. 93% teach undergraduates. No introductory courses are taught by graduate students. The average class size in an introductory lecture is 38; in a laboratory, 15; and in a regular course offering, 23.

Admissions: 90% of the 1995–96 applicants were accepted. The SAT I scores for the 1995–96 freshman class were as follows: Verbal—71% below 500, 23% between 500 and 599, 5% between 600 and 700, and 1% above 700; Math—59% below 500, 22% between 500 and 599, 18% between 600 and 700, and 1% above 700. The ACT scores were 39% below 21, 26% between 21 and 23, 16% between 24 and 26, 11% between 27 and 28, and 8% above 28. 36% of the current freshmen were in the top fifth of their class; 63% were in the top two fifths. 4 freshmen graduated first in their class.

Requirements: The SAT I or ACT is required. Roberts requires applicants to be in the upper 50% of their class. A minimum GPA of 2.0 is required. In addition, applicants must be graduates of an accredited secondary school. The GED is accepted. At least 12 academic credits are required, including 4 years of English and 2 years each of mathematics and science. A foreign language and 3 years of social studies are recommended. The chosen major may modify requirements. An essay is required and an interview is recommended. AP and CLEP credits are accepted. Important factors in the admissions decision are advanced placement or honor courses, personality/intangible qualities, and extracurricular activities record.

Procedure: Freshmen are admitted to all sessions. There are early admissions and deferred admissions plans. Applications should be filed by August 1 for fall entry and December 1 for spring entry, along with an application fee of $35. Notification is sent on a rolling basis.

Transfer: 93 transfer students enrolled in 1995–96. Applicants must submit transcripts from all previous institutions attended. Credit is usually accepted for courses with grade C or better. 30 credits of 124 to 126 must be completed at Roberts.

Visiting: There are regularly scheduled orientations for prospective students including a campus tour, class visits, admissions and departmental interviews, and a financial aid presentation. Visitors may sit in on classes and stay overnight at the school. To schedule a visit, contact the Admissions Office.

Financial Aid: In 1995–96, 88% of all freshmen and 91% of continuing students received some form of financial aid. 87% of all students received need-based aid. The average freshman award was $7885. Of that total, scholarships or need-based grants averaged $4000; loans averaged $3734; work contracts averaged $1031 ($1500 maximum); and state/federal grants averaged $3989 ($6500 maximum). 35% of undergraduate students work part-time. Average earnings from campus work for the school year are $974. The FAFSA and the college's own financial statement, as well as the TAP for New York residents only are required. The application deadline for fall entry is April 15.

International Students: There are currently 29 international students enrolled. They must score 550 on the TOEFL and also take the Nelson-Denny.

Computers: The college provides computer facilities for student use. Apple Macintosh, Apple IIe, and IBM-compatible microcomputers are available to students for academic or personal use in the science center for about 90 hours per week and in the library learning center for about 48 hours per week. All students may access the system. There are no time limits and no fees.

Graduates: In 1994–95, 292 bachelor's degrees were awarded. The most popular majors among graduates were organizational management (45%), nursing (7%), and elementary education (7%). Within an average freshman class, 46% graduate in 4 years, 50% in 5 years, and 52% in 6 years. 120 companies recruited on campus in 1994–95. Of the 1994 graduating class, 8% were enrolled in graduate school within 6 months of graduation and 96% had found employment.

Admissions Contact: Linda Kurtz, Director of Admissions. A campus video is available.

ROCHESTER INSTITUTE OF TECHNOLOGY   B-3
Rochester, NY 14623   (716) 475-6631; FAX: (716) 475-7424

Full-time: 5370 men, 2529 women	Faculty: 665; IIA, av$
Part-time: 1630 men, 1023 women	Ph.D.s: 76%
Graduate: 1238 men, 810 women	Student/Faculty: 12 to 1
Year: quarters, summer session	Tuition: $14,937
Application Deadline: open	Room & Board: $5898
Freshman Class: 5635 applied, 4294 accepted, 1647 enrolled	
SAT I or ACT: required	VERY COMPETITIVE

Rochester Institute of Technology, a private coeducational institution founded in 1829, offers programs in science, computer science, allied health, engineering, fine arts, business, hotel management, graphic arts, and photography, as well as liberal arts, and includes the National Technical Institute for the Deaf. Most programs include a cooperative education component, which provides full-time work experience to complement classroom studies. There are 12 undergraduate and 11 graduate schools. In addition to regional accreditation, RIT has baccalaureate program accreditation with AACSB, ABET, ADA, CAHEA, CSAB, CSWE, and NASAD. The library contains 355,000 volumes, 392,000 microform items, and 9340 audiovisual forms, and subscribes to 6400 periodicals. Computerized library sources and services include the card catalog, interlibrary loans, and database searching. Special learning facilities include a learning resource center, art gallery, radio station, TV station, computer chip manufacturing facility, student-operated restaurant, electronic prepress laboratory, and imaging science facility. The 1300-acre campus is in a suburban area 5 miles south of Rochester. Including residence halls, there are 70 buildings on campus.

Student Life: 65% of undergraduates are from New York. Students come from 50 states, 80 foreign countries, and Canada. 90% are from public schools; 10% from private. 81% are white. The average age of freshmen is 18; all undergraduates, 21. 14% do not continue beyond their first year; 62% remain to graduate.

Housing: 6500 students can be accommodated in college housing. College-sponsored living facilities include single-sex and coed dormitories, on-campus apartments, married-student housing, fraternity houses, and sorority houses. In addition there are special interest houses. On-campus housing is guaranteed for all 4 years. 65% of students live on campus; of those, 90% remain on campus on weekends. All students may keep cars on campus.

Activities: 8% of men belong to 15 national fraternities; 5% of women belong to 1 local and 8 national sororities. There are 75 groups on campus, including art, band, cheerleading, choir, chorale, chorus, computers, dance, drama, ethnic, film, gay, gospel choir, honors, international, jazz band, literary magazine, newspaper, orchestra, pep band, photography, political, professional, radio and TV, religious, social, social service, student government, and yearbook. Popular campus events include Fall, Spring, and Winter Weekends and Martin Luther King, Jr. celebration.

Sports: There are 11 intercollegiate sports for men and 9 for women, and 22 intramural sports for men and 15 for women. Athletic and recreation facilities include 3 gymnasiums, 1 with seating for 2300, an ice rink, a swimming pool, 12 tennis courts, a fitness trail, many athletic fields, and a student life center with 8 racquetball courts, dance facilities, weight training facilities, and an indoor track.

Disabled Students: 90% of the campus is accessible to disabled students. The following facilities are available: wheelchair ramps, elevators, special parking, specially equipped rest rooms, special class scheduling, lowered drinking fountains, lowered telephones, and special fire alarm systems to accommodate the needs of deaf students.

Services: In addition to many counseling and information services, tutoring is available in most subjects. There is a reader service for the blind, remedial math, reading, and writing, and comprehensive support services for students with physical or learning disabilities and for first-generation college students.

Campus Safety and Security: Campus safety and security measures include 24-hour foot and vehicle patrol, self-defense education, escort service, and shuttle buses. In addition, there are informal discussions, pamphlets/posters/films, emergency telephones, and lighted pathways/sidewalks.

Programs of Study: RIT confers B.S., B.F.A., and B.Tech. degrees. Associate, master's, and doctoral degrees are also awarded. Bachelor's degrees are awarded in BIOLOGICAL SCIENCE (biology/biological science and biotechnology), BUSINESS (accounting, banking and finance, business administration and management, hotel/motel and restaurant management, international business management, management information systems, management science, marketing management, and tourism), COMMUNICATIONS AND THE ARTS (communications, crafts, design, film arts, fine arts, graphic design, illustration, industrial design, photography, printmaking, and telecommunications), COMPUTER AND PHYSICAL SCIENCE (chemistry, computer science, information sciences and systems, mathematics, physics, polymer science, and statistics), ENGINEERING AND ENVIRONMENTAL DESIGN (aerospace studies, civil engineering technology, computer engineering, computer technology, electrical/electronics engineering, electrical/electronics engineering technology, engineering technology, environmental engineering technology, environmental science, graphic and printing production, industrial administration/management, industrial engineering, interior design, manufacturing technology, materials science, mechanical engineering, mechanical engineering technology, printing technology, and woodworking), HEALTH PROFESSIONS (medical laboratory technology, nuclear medical technology, physician's assistant, and ultrasound technology), SOCIAL SCIENCE (criminal justice, dietetics, economics, food production/management/services, and social work). Engineering, computer science, and photography are the strongest

academically. Engineering, business, and art and design have the largest enrollments.

Required: Students must have a GPA of 2.0 and have completed 180 quarter credit hours to graduate. Distribution requirements include English, social sciences, science and mathematics, and humanities; specific courses include English composition, senior seminar, and physical education. B.S. programs also require a minimum of 20 quarter credit hours in science and mathematics. There are no general science or mathematics requirements for the B.F.A. programs in art, design, or photography.

Special: RIT offers internships in social work, criminal justice, and allied health, and work-study programs with IBM, Xerox, Kodak, Marriott, and 1300 co-op employers. Cooperative education is required or recommended in most programs and provides full-time paid work experience. Cross-registration with Rochester-area colleges is available. There are accelerated degree programs in science, engineering, mathematics, computer science, and business. The school grants credit for military and work experience. Students may study abroad in England or Japan, and student-designed majors are permitted in applied arts and sciences. There are 6 national honor societies on campus.

Faculty/Classroom: 85% of faculty are male; 15%, female. All teach undergraduates. No introductory courses are taught by graduate students. The average class size in an introductory lecture is 30; in a laboratory, 16; and in a regular course offering, 19.

Admissions: 76% of the 1995–96 applicants were accepted. The SAT I scores for the 1995–96 freshman class were as follows: Verbal—49% below 500, 37% between 500 and 599, 13% between 600 and 700, and 1% above 700; Math—19% below 500, 34% between 500 and 599, 35% between 600 and 700, and 12% above 700. The ACT scores were 11% below 21, 26% between 21 and 23, 24% between 24 and 26, 20% between 27 and 28, and 19% above 28. 50% of the current freshmen were in the top fifth of their class; 79% were in the top two fifths. 35 freshmen graduated first in their class.

Requirements: The SAT I or ACT is required. RIT requires applicants to be in the upper 50% of their class. A minimum GPA of 2.5 is required. Applicants must be high school graduates or show a GED certificate. Applicants are required to submit an essay, and an interview is recommended. The School of Art and Design emphasizes a required portfolio of artwork. Required high school mathematics and science credits vary by program, with 3 years in each area generally acceptable. Applications are accepted on-line via ExPAN or the electronic Common Application. AP and CLEP credits are accepted. Important factors in the admissions decision are advanced placement or honor courses, recommendations by school officials, and extracurricular activities record.

Procedure: Freshmen are admitted to all sessions. Entrance exams should be taken during the junior or senior year. There are early decision, early admissions, and deferred admissions plans. Application deadlines are open for regular decision; early decision applications should be filed by December 15. Application fee is $40. Notification of early decision is sent January 15; regular decision, on a rolling basis. 300 early decision candidates were accepted for the 1995–96 class.

Transfer: 1050 transfer students enrolled in 1995–96. Transfer students must have a GPA of 2.5 for admission to most programs; those with fewer than 30 college credits must supply a high school transcript. Other requirements vary by program. 45 quarter credits of 180 must be completed at RIT.

Visiting: There are regularly scheduled orientations for prospective students, including academic advising and information on housing and student services. There are guides for informal visits and visitors may sit in on classes and stay overnight at the school. To schedule a visit, contact Mary Menard at (716) 475-6736.

Financial Aid: In 1995–96, 75% of all freshmen and 68% of continuing students received some form of financial aid. 70% of freshmen and 65% of continuing students received need-based aid. The average freshman award was $13,700. Of that total, scholarships or need-based grants averaged $6500 ($14,000 maximum); loans averaged $3700 ($7375 maximum); work contracts averaged $1600 ($2200 maximum) and federal and state grants averaged $1900 ($5750 maximum). 70% of undergraduate students work part-time. Average earnings from campus work for the school year are $1400. The FAFSA is required. The application deadline for fall entry is March 15.

International Students: There are currently 550 international students enrolled. The school actively recruits these students. They must take the TOEFL and achieve a minimum score of 525.

Computers: The college provides computer facilities for student use. The mainframes are a VMS cluster of 5 DEC VAX Models 6000–620, 6000–430, and 6000–520, and 4 Digital VAXstation 4000–90 models. RIT has 15 computer centers and computer laboratories on campus for student use. There are more than 300 mainframe terminals available, as well as hundreds of microcomputers. Students may link their terminals or personal computers to the mainframe system from

individual dormitory rooms or from off-campus locations, and access to the Internet is available. All students may access the system 7 days per week, from 8 A.M. to 1 A.M. There are no time limits and no fees.
Graduates: In 1994–95, 1607 bachelor's degrees were awarded. The most popular majors among graduates were engineering technology (15%), engineering (14%), and business administration (12%). Within an average freshman class, 62% graduate in 6 years. Of the 1994 graduating class, 8% were enrolled in graduate school within 6 months of graduation and 90% had found employment.
Admissions Contact: Daniel Shelley, Director of Admissions. E-mail: admissions@rit.edu. A campus video is available.

RUSSELL SAGE COLLEGE D-3
Troy, NY 12180 (518) 270-2217
(800) 999–3RSC; FAX: (518) 270-6880

Full-time: 974 women	Faculty: 83; IIA, --$
Part-time: 141 women	Ph.D.s: 82%
Graduate: none	Student/Faculty: 12 to 1
Year: semesters, summer session	Tuition: $13,270
Application Deadline: August 1	Room & Board: $5566
Freshman Class: 494 applied, 436 accepted, 151 enrolled	
SAT I Verbal/Math: 448/485	ACT: 23 COMPETITIVE

Russell Sage College, founded in 1916 to give women access to the professions, is a private college offering baccalaureate degrees in the liberal arts, sciences, business, health science, and teacher preparation. In addition to regional accreditation, Russell Sage has baccalaureate program accreditation with APTA and NLN. The library contains 253,000 volumes, 22,000 microform items, and 20,000 audiovisual forms, and subscribes to 1600 periodicals. Computerized library sources and services include the card catalog, interlibrary loans, and database searching. Special learning facilities include a learning resource center, art gallery, the New York State Theatre Institute, and a human performance laboratory. The 8-acre campus is in an urban area 10 miles from Albany. Including residence halls, there are 38 buildings on campus.
Student Life: 85% of undergraduates are from New York. Students come from 21 states, 1 foreign country, and Canada. 86% are white. The average age of freshmen is 18; all undergraduates, 23. 11% do not continue beyond their first year; 62% remain to graduate.
Housing: 750 students can be accommodated in college housing. College-sponsored living facilities include dormitories. In addition, there are language and special interest houses; 24-hour quiet and substance-free/wellness housing is also available. On-campus housing is guaranteed for all 4 years. 70% of students live on campus. Upperclassmen may keep cars on campus.
Activities: There are no sororities. There are 40 groups on campus, including art, chorus, computers, dance, drama, ethnic, gay, honors, international, literary magazine, newspaper, political, professional, religious, social, social service, student government, and yearbook. Popular campus events include Rally Day, Sage Fest, interdorm sing, and class dinners.
Sports: Athletic and recreation facilities include athletic and weight-training rooms, a sports medicine facility, a human performance laboratory, a dance studio, an Olympic swimming pool, tennis courts, bowling lanes, a practice field, a 1200-seat auditorium, 2 gymnasiums, and a large multipurpose room for indoor recreation.
Disabled Students: 20% of the campus is accessible to disabled students. The following facilities are available: wheelchair ramps, elevators, special parking, specially equipped rest rooms, and special class scheduling.
Services: In addition to many counseling and information services, tutoring is available in every subject. There is remedial math, reading, and writing. Special services are available for those with learning disabilities.
Campus Safety and Security: Campus safety and security measures include self-defense education, escort service, shuttle buses, and informal discussions. There are pamphlets/posters/films, emergency telephones, and lighted pathways/sidewalks.
Programs of Study: Russell Sage confers B.A. and B.S. degrees. Master's degrees are also awarded. Bachelor's degrees are awarded in BIOLOGICAL SCIENCE (biochemistry, biology/biological science, and nutrition), BUSINESS (accounting and business administration and management), COMMUNICATIONS AND THE ARTS (arts administration/management, communications, dramatic arts, English, French, and Spanish), COMPUTER AND PHYSICAL SCIENCE (chemistry, computer science, information sciences and systems, and mathematics), EDUCATION (athletic training, elementary, and secondary), HEALTH PROFESSIONS (art therapy, medical technology, nursing, occupational therapy, and physical therapy), SOCIAL SCIENCE (criminal justice, economics, history, interdisciplinary studies, international studies, political science/government, psychology, and sociology). Physical therapy, biology, nursing, and psychology are the strongest academically. Physical therapy, nursing, and psychology have the largest enrollments.

Required: To graduate, students must complete 120 credits with a 2.0 GPA overall and at least 30 credits and a 2.2 GPA in the major. B.A. candidates must earn a minimum of 90 credits in the arts and sciences and B.S. candidates must earn a minimum of 60. A general education requirement of 39 credits focuses on understanding diversity, computer literacy, and the development of personal values. Students must also complete 6 credits in a single language or show proficiency.
Special: Students may cross-register with the 14 area schools of the Hudson-Mohawk Association of Colleges. Study abroad, internships, cooperative education, and work-study programs are available. There are several accelerated 5-year programs, a 6-year program with Albany Law School, and a 3–2 engineering degree with nearby Rensselaer Polytechnic Institute. 9 centers for interdisciplinary inquiry draw students from across majors. The college confers credit for life, military, or work experience. Nondegree study, student-designed majors, and pass/fail options are also available. There is a freshman honors program on campus, as well as 7 national honor societies. 15 departments have honors programs.
Faculty/Classroom: 37% of faculty are male; 63%, female. 68% both teach and do research. The average class size in an introductory lecture is 25; in a laboratory, 12; and in a regular course offering, 17.
Admissions: 88% of the 1995–96 applicants were accepted. The SAT I scores for the 1995–96 freshman class were as follows: Verbal—70% below 500, 25% between 500 and 599, and 5% between 600 and 700; Math—49% below 500, 29% between 500 and 599, 20% between 600 and 700, and 2% above 700. The ACT scores were 44% below 21, 33% between 21 and 23, 13% between 24 and 26, 6% between 27 and 28, and 4% above 28. 40% of the current freshmen were in the top fifth of their class; 63% were in the top two fifths. 3 freshmen graduated first in their class.
Requirements: The SAT I or ACT is required. Applicants must have graduated from an accredited secondary school, with a 2.0 GPA, or have a GED. 16 academic units are required, including courses in English, social sciences, natural sciences, and foreign languages. An essay is required and an interview is recommended for all applicants. Applications are accepted on-line. AP and CLEP credits are accepted. Important factors in the admissions decision are advanced placement or honor courses, recommendations by school officials, and leadership record.
Procedure: Freshmen are admitted to all sessions. Entrance exams should be taken during spring of the junior year or fall of the senior year. There are early decision, early admissions, and deferred admissions plans. Early decision applications should be filed by November 1; regular applications, by August 1 for fall entry and December 15 for spring entry, along with an application fee of $20. Notification of early decision is sent November 15; regular decision, on a rolling basis. 30 early decision candidates were accepted for the 1995–96 class.
Transfer: 120 transfer students enrolled in 1995–96. Applicants must have a minimum GPA of 2.5. Interviews are strongly encouraged and may be required in some instances. 45 credits of a minimum 120 must be completed at Russell Sage.
Visiting: There are regularly scheduled orientations for prospective students, including meetings with faculty, a campus tour, and a financial aid session, in addition to an admissions interview. There are guides for informal visits and visitors may sit in on classes and stay overnight at the school. To schedule a visit, contact the Office of Admission.
Financial Aid: In 1995–96, 90% of all students received some form of financial aid. 83% of freshmen and 88% of continuing students received need-based aid. The average freshman award was $11,200. Of that total, scholarships or need-based grants averaged $7300 ($8000 maximum); loans averaged $2900 ($6625 maximum); and work contracts averaged $1000 ($1200 maximum). 30% of undergraduate students work part-time. Average earnings from campus work for the school year are $1000. The average financial indebtedness of the 1994–95 graduate was $15,000. The FAFSA is required. The application deadline for fall entry is March 1.
International Students: There are currently 3 international students enrolled. The school actively recruits these students. They must score 550 on the TOEFL and also take SAT I or the ACT if English is their native language.
Computers: The college provides computer facilities for student use. A campuswide network (SageNet) provides hard-wired and dial-up access to E-mail and the Internet for all students. Laboratories for student use are equipped with 47 PCs, using both Intel and Macintosh technology. Word processing, spreadsheet, statistical analysis, graphics, and course-specific software are available. The mathematics and computer science department maintains a 17-station Macintosh laboratory/classroom hard-wired for SageNet. Small 2- to 3-workstation laboratories are maintained by various other departments. All students may access the system. The public computer laboratories are open 14 hours per day, 7 days a week; dial-in access is

available 24 hours a day. If students are waiting, users are asked to yield their stations after 1 hour. There are no fees.

Graduates: In 1994–95, 328 bachelor's degrees were awarded. The most popular majors among graduates were physical therapy (24%), nursing (21%), and psychology (13%). Within an average freshman class, 55% graduate in 4 years, 60% in 5 years, and 62% in 6 years. 79 companies recruited on campus in 1994–95.

Admissions Contact: Michael Sposili, Director of Admission. E-mail: rscadmin@sage.edu. A campus video is available.

SAINT BONAVENTURE UNIVERSITY A-3
St. Bonaventure, NY 14778–2284

(716) 375-2400
(800) 462-5050

Full-time: 884 men, 911 women	Faculty: 115; IIA, --$
Part-time: 39 men, 59 women	Ph.D.s: 91%
Graduate: 303 men, 395 women	Student/Faculty: 16 to 1
Year: semesters, summer session	Tuition: $11,604
Application Deadline: April 15	Room & Board: $4927
Freshman Class: 1561 applied, 1434 accepted, 548 enrolled	
SAT I Verbal/Math: 461/515	ACT: 23 COMPETITIVE

Saint Bonaventure University, founded in 1858, is a private, coeducational Roman Catholic institution in the Franciscan tradition, offering programs in the arts and sciences, education, business, and journalism and mass communication. There are 4 undergraduate schools and 1 graduate school. The library contains 241,000 volumes, 97,000 microform items, and 7000 audiovisual forms, and subscribes to 1500 periodicals. Computerized library sources and services include the card catalog, interlibrary loans, and database searching. Special learning facilities include a learning resource center, art gallery, radio station, and observatory. The 600-acre campus is in a small town 70 miles southeast of Buffalo. Including residence halls, there are 22 buildings on campus.

Student Life: 75% of undergraduates are from New York. Students come from 29 states, 17 foreign countries, and Canada. 60% are from public schools; 40% from private. 93% are white. The average age of freshmen is 18; all undergraduates, 20. 15% do not continue beyond their first year; 72% remain to graduate.

Housing: 1450 students can be accommodated in college housing. College-sponsored living facilities include single-sex and coed dormitories and on-campus apartments. On-campus housing is guaranteed for all 4 years. 75% of students live on campus; of those, 90% remain on campus on weekends. All students may keep cars on campus.

Activities: There are no fraternities or sororities. There are 73 groups on campus, including academic, art, band, cheerleading, chess, choir, chorale, chorus, computers, drama, ethnic, honors, international, jazz band, literary magazine, newspaper, orchestra, pep band, photography, political, professional, radio and TV, religious, social, social service, student government, and yearbook. Popular campus events include Family Weekend, Spring and Winter Weekends, and varsity basketball games.

Sports: There are 7 intercollegiate sports for men and 7 for women, and 10 intramural sports for men and 9 for women. Athletic and recreation facilities include a 6000-seat gymnasium with basketball and volleyball courts, an indoor swimming pool, a 9-hole golf course, weight facilities and free weights, and a fitness center with racquetball courts, Nautilus equipment, and an aerobics room. There is also a 77-acre area on campus with soccer, baseball, softball, rugby, and intramural fields.

Disabled Students: 90% of the campus is accessible to disabled students. The following facilities are available: wheelchair ramps, elevators, special parking, specially equipped rest rooms, a counseling center staffed by 2 professionals, and a teaching and learning center with a coordinator for disabled services.

Services: In addition to many counseling and information services, tutoring is available in some subjects. There is remedial math, reading, and writing.

Campus Safety and Security: Campus safety and security measures include 24-hour foot and vehicle patrol, self-defense education, escort service, and shuttle buses. In addition, there are informal discussions, pamphlets/posters/films, emergency telephones, and lighted pathways/sidewalks.

Programs of Study: SBU confers B.A., B.S., B.B.A., and B.S.Ed. degrees. Master's degrees are also awarded. Bachelor's degrees are awarded in BIOLOGICAL SCIENCE (biochemistry, biology/biological science, and biophysics), BUSINESS (accounting, banking and finance, management science, and marketing/retailing/merchandising), COMMUNICATIONS AND THE ARTS (classical languages, English, French, journalism, Spanish, and visual and performing arts), COMPUTER AND PHYSICAL SCIENCE (chemistry, computer science, mathematics, and physics), EDUCATION (elementary, physical, and secondary), ENGINEERING AND ENVIRONMENTAL DESIGN (engineering physics and environmental science), HEALTH PROFESSIONS (medical laboratory technology and premedicine), SOCIAL SCIENCE (history, philosophy, political science/

government, prelaw, psychology, social science, social work, and sociology). Psychology, accounting, and biology are the strongest academically. Mass communication, biology, and elementary education have the largest enrollments.

Required: To graduate, students must complete 129 credit hours, 30 of them in the major, with a minimum GPA of 2.0. The school requires 12 hours each in culture and civilization, mathematics and natural sciences, and social and behavioral sciences, and 9 credits each in theology and philosophy. Students must also demonstrate writing competency through testing or course work.

Special: Cross-registration can be arranged almost anywhere in the United States through the Visiting Student Program. Internships are available in business, mass communication, political science, psychology, and social science. Study abroad in 18 countries, B.A.-B.S. degrees, accelerated joint bachelor's/master's degree programs, dual and student-designed majors, a Washington semester with American University, and pass/fail options are offered. Students may complete a 2–2 or 2–3 engineering degree with the University of Detroit or a 2–3 engineering degree with Clarkson University. There is a freshman honors program on campus, as well as 10 national honor societies. All departments have honors programs.

Faculty/Classroom: 80% of faculty are male; 20%, female. 92% teach undergraduates. Graduate students teach 1% of introductory courses. The average class size in an introductory lecture is 35; in a laboratory, 20; and in a regular course offering, 30.

Admissions: 92% of the 1995–96 applicants were accepted. The SAT I scores for a recent freshman class were as follows: Verbal—63% below 500, 28% between 500 and 599, and 9% between 600 and 700; Math—35% below 500, 44% between 500 and 599, 21% between 600 and 700, and 2% above 700. The ACT scores were 23% below 21, 31% between 21 and 23, 26% between 24 and 26, 10% between 27 and 28, and 10% above 28. 38% of the current freshmen were in the top fifth of their class; 70% were in the top two fifths. 7 freshmen graduated first in their class.

Requirements: The SAT I or ACT is required, with a minimum composite score of 1000 on the SAT I (500 verbal, 500 mathematics) or 24 on the ACT. SBU requires applicants to be in the upper 60% of their class. A minimum average of 83% is required. Applicants must be graduates of an accredited secondary school or have a GED. 16 academic credits are required, including 4 years each of English and social studies, 3 each of mathematics and science, and 2 of a foreign language. An essay and an interview are recommended. AP and CLEP credits are accepted. Important factors in the admissions decision are recommendations by school officials, advanced placement or honor courses, and extracurricular activities record.

Procedure: Freshmen are admitted to all sessions. Entrance exams should be taken during the spring of the junior year or the fall of the senior year. There are early admissions and deferred admissions plans. Applications should be filed by April 15 for fall entry and December 1 for spring entry, along with an application fee of $30. Notification is sent on a rolling basis.

Transfer: 78 transfer students enrolled in a recent year. Applicants must have a minimum 2.5 GPA. Grades of D or better transfer for credit except in the major. 36 credits of 129 must be completed at SBU.

Visiting: There are regularly scheduled orientations for prospective students, including interviews, tours, class visits, and meetings with professors. There are guides for informal visits and visitors may sit in on classes. To schedule a visit, contact the Admissions Office.

Financial Aid: In 1995–96, 93% of all freshmen and 75% of continuing students received some form of financial aid. 71% of freshmen and 66% of continuing students received need-based aid. The average freshman award was $9624. Of that total, scholarships or need-based grants averaged $6589 ($8000 maximum); loans averaged $2182 ($4825 maximum); and work contracts averaged $432 ($1200 maximum); and $421 from outside private aid. 38% of undergraduate students work part-time. Average earnings from campus work for the school year are $700. The average financial indebtedness of the 1994–95 graduate was $9500. SBU is a member of CSS. The FAFSA is required. The application deadline for fall entry is February 1.

International Students: There are currently 30 international students enrolled. They must score 500 on the TOEFL.

Computers: The college provides computer facilities for student use. SBU has 5 PC and 2 Apple Macintosh laboratories, housing more than 100 IBM-compatible and 20 Apple Macintosh microcomputers connected to a campuswide network. The computer science laboratory is equipped with 5 Sun workstations and provides a UNIX environment used to support upper-division courses in computer science. Students have full Internet access. All students may access the system 24 hours per day via residence hall rooms or at designated laboratory hours. There are no time limits and no fees.

Graduates: In 1994–95, 433 bachelor's degrees were awarded. The most popular majors among graduates were elementary education (14%), psychology (12%), and journalism/mass communication

(11%). Within an average freshman class, 70% graduate in 4 years and 73% in 5 years. 40 companies recruited on campus in 1994–95.
Admissions Contact: Alexander P. Nazemetz.

SAINT FRANCIS COLLEGE
D-5
Brooklyn, NY 11201

(718) 522–2300, ext. 200
FAX: (718) 522–1274

Full-time: 664 men, 893 women	Faculty: 60; IIB, +$
Part-time: 185 men, 353 women	Ph.D.s: 70%
Graduate: none	Student/Faculty: 26 to 1
Year: semesters, summer session	Tuition: $7350
Application Deadline: open	Room & Board: n/app
Freshman Class: 900 applied, 794 accepted, 304 enrolled	
SAT I: required	**LESS COMPETITIVE**

Saint Francis College, chartered in 1884 by the Franciscan Brothers, is an independent commuter institution conferring degrees in the arts, sciences, business, and health sciences. The library contains 170,439 volumes, 19,152 microform items, and 2021 audiovisual forms, and subscribes to 571 periodicals. Computerized library sources and services include interlibrary loans and database searching. Special learning facilities include a learning resource center and a greenhouse. The 1-acre campus is in an urban area. There are 5 buildings on campus.

Student Life: 99% of undergraduates are from New York. Students come from 1 state, 42 foreign countries, and Canada. 40% are from public schools; 60% from private. 53% are white; 24% African American; 16% Hispanic. The average age of freshmen is 18; all undergraduates, 21. 24% do not continue beyond their first year; 40% remain to graduate.

Housing: There are no residence halls. All students commute.

Activities: 5% of men belong to 2 local fraternities; 5% of women belong to 1 local sorority. There are 28 groups on campus, including art, cheerleading, chess, chorus, computers, drama, ethnic, gay, international, literary magazine, newspaper, political, professional, radio and TV, religious, social, social service, student government, and yearbook. Popular campus events include Charter Day, Brooklyn Accents, and personal issues and public interest lecture series.

Sports: There are 9 intercollegiate sports for men and 8 for women, and 6 intramural sports for men and 6 for women. Athletic and recreation facilities include a 1100-seat gymnasium, an Olympic-size swimming pool, a weight-training room, and a roof recreation area.

Disabled Students: 85% of the campus is accessible to disabled students. The following facilities are available: wheelchair ramps, elevators, specially equipped rest rooms, lowered drinking fountains, and lowered telephones.

Services: In addition to many counseling and information services, tutoring is available in most subjects, including accounting, mathematics, economics, English, history, and the sciences. There is a reader service for the blind, and remedial math, reading, and writing. There are workshops in academic skills such as note- and test-taking techniques and study skills.

Campus Safety and Security: Campus safety and security measures include self-defense education, informal discussions, and pamphlets/posters/films.

Programs of Study: The college confers B.A. and B.S. degrees. Associate degrees are also awarded. Bachelor's degrees are awarded in BIOLOGICAL SCIENCE (biology/biological science), BUSINESS (accounting), COMMUNICATIONS AND THE ARTS (communications and English), COMPUTER AND PHYSICAL SCIENCE (mathematics), EDUCATION (elementary, middle school, physical, and secondary), ENGINEERING AND ENVIRONMENTAL DESIGN (aviation administration/management), HEALTH PROFESSIONS (biomedical science, health care administration, health science, medical laboratory technology, and premedicine), SOCIAL SCIENCE (economics, history, political science/government, psychology, social studies, and sociology). Management, accounting, and psychology have the largest enrollments.

Required: The core curriculum varies according to the major, but all baccalaureate degree programs require courses in communications, English, fine arts, physical education, history, philosophy, sociology, and science or mathematics. A minimum 2.0 GPA and 128 credit hours are required to graduate.

Special: There is an FAA co-op program for aviation students. A variety of internships are available in such areas as industrial and public accounting, and with the NYC Transit Authority, Public Interest Research, the NYS Assembly, and the Urban Fellow Program. Work-study with Methodist Hospital or the borough president's office is possible. Study abroad, dual majors, pass/fail options, and credit for life experience are possible. There is a freshman honors program on campus, as well as 15 national honor societies.

Faculty/Classroom: 62% of faculty are male; 38%, female. All teach undergraduates, and 25% also do research. The average class size in an introductory lecture is 23; in a laboratory, 19; and in a regular course offering, 23.

Admissions: 88% of the 1995–96 applicants were accepted. There was 1 National Merit semifinalist. 1 freshman graduated first in the class.

Requirements: The SAT I is required. A minimum average of 80% is required. Applicants should graduate from an accredited secondary school or have a GED. An entrance essay is required. AP and CLEP credits are accepted. Important factors in the admissions decision are recommendations by school officials, leadership record, and evidence of special talent.

Procedure: Freshmen are admitted to all sessions. Application deadlines are open. The application fee is $20. Notification is sent on a rolling basis.

Transfer: 124 transfer students enrolled in 1995–96. A minimum 2.0 GPA is required. 30 credits of 128 must be completed at the college.

Visiting: There are regularly scheduled orientations for prospective students, including meetings with faculty if desired. There are guides for informal visits and visitors may sit in on classes. To schedule a visit, contact the Office of Admissions.

Financial Aid: In 1995–96, 75% of all freshmen and 70% of continuing students received some form of financial aid. 68% of freshmen and 65% of continuing students received need-based aid. The average freshman award was $4850. Of that total, scholarships or need-based grants averaged $4500 ($6910 maximum); loans averaged $1250 ($2625 maximum); and college work-study averaged $875 ($1500 maximum). 5% of undergraduate students work part-time. Average earnings from campus work for the school year are $1350. The average financial indebtedness of the 1994–95 graduate was $6400. The FAFSA, the college's own financial statement, and the TAP (New York State) are required. The application deadline for fall entry is February 15.

International Students: There were 105 international students enrolled in a recent year. The school actively recruits these students. They must score 500 on the TOEFL.

Computers: The college provides computer facilities for student use. A microcomputer center is available to students. It has 40 microcomputers that are connected to a local area network. All students may access the system. There are no time limits. The fees are $35 per course, included in tuition.

Graduates: In 1994–95, 304 bachelor's degrees were awarded. The most popular majors among graduates were management (20%), special studies (17%), and accounting (9%). Within an average freshman class, 1% graduate in 3 years, 18% in 4 years, 33% in 5 years, and 40% in 6 years. 51 companies recruited on campus in 1994–95.
Admissions Contact: Brother George Larkin, O.S.F., Dean Of Admissions.

SAINT JOHN FISHER COLLEGE
B-3
Rochester, NY 14618

(716) 385-8064
(800) 444-4640; FAX: (716) 385-8129

Full-time: 674 men, 834 women	Faculty: 104; IIB, +$
Part-time: 152 men, 349 women	Ph.D.s: 90%
Graduate: 96 men, 220 women	Student/Faculty: 15 to 1
Year: semesters, summer session	Tuition: $11,540
Application Deadline: open	Room & Board: $5490
Freshman Class: 1225 applied, 963 accepted, 308 enrolled	
SAT I Verbal/Math: 460/510 (means)	ACT: 22 **COMPETITIVE**

St. John Fisher College, established in 1948, is a private institution affiliated with the Roman Catholic Church. It offers degrees through its divisions of liberal arts, business/accounting, education, and nursing. There are 2 graduate schools. In addition to regional accreditation, Fisher has baccalaureate program accreditation with NLN. The library contains 185,000 volumes, 130,000 microform items, and 30,000 audiovisual forms, and subscribes to 1052 periodicals. Computerized library sources and services include the card catalog, interlibrary loans, and database searching. Special learning facilities include a learning resource center, radio station, TV station, multimedia center, greenhouse, and language and science laboratories. The 125-acre campus is in a suburban area 12 miles southeast of Rochester. Including residence halls, there are 16 buildings on campus.

Student Life: 96% of undergraduates are from New York. Students come from 14 states, 6 foreign countries, and Canada. 65% are from public schools; 35% from private. 85% are white. 65% are Catholic; 30% Protestant. The average age of freshmen is 18; all undergraduates, 21. 20% do not continue beyond their first year; 63% remain to graduate.

Housing: 894 students can be accommodated in college housing. College-sponsored living facilities include single-sex and coed dormitories. Living facilities include residence halls providing a year-long freshman wellness program. On-campus housing is guaranteed for all 4 years. 55% of students live on campus; of those, 85% remain on campus on weekends. All students may keep cars on campus.

Activities: There are no fraternities or sororities. There are 52 groups on campus, including cheerleading, chess, choir, computers, drama, ethnic, honors, international, literary magazine, musical theater, newspaper, pep band, photography, political, professional, radio and TV, religious, social, social service, student government, and yearbook. Popular campus events include Winter Olympics, Winter Snow Ball, and Senior Week.

Sports: There are 7 intercollegiate sports for men and 7 for women, and 8 intramural sports for men and 7 for women. Athletic and recreation facilities include football, soccer, and softball fields, indoor and outdoor tracks, a 9-hole golf course, a weight/exercise room, a sauna, a game room, indoor and outdoor tennis courts, racquetball and volleyball courts, and 2 gymnasiums for basketball.

Disabled Students: 75% of the campus is accessible to disabled students. The following facilities are available: wheelchair ramps, elevators, special parking, specially equipped rest rooms, special class scheduling, lowered drinking fountains, and lowered telephones.

Services: In addition to many counseling and information services, tutoring is available in most subjects; the accounting department offers student tutors. There is also remedial math and writing. Mathematics and writing centers provide help to students at all levels.

Campus Safety and Security: Campus safety and security measures include 24-hour foot and vehicle patrol, self-defense education, escort service, and informal discussions. In addition, there are pamphlets/posters/films, emergency telephones, and lighted pathways/sidewalks.

Programs of Study: Fisher confers B.A., B.S., B.B.A., and B.S.N. degrees. Master's degrees are also awarded. Bachelor's degrees are awarded in BIOLOGICAL SCIENCE (biology/biological science), BUSINESS (accounting, business administration and management, and marketing/retailing/merchandising), COMMUNICATIONS AND THE ARTS (communications, English, French, German, Italian, journalism, and Spanish), COMPUTER AND PHYSICAL SCIENCE (chemistry, computer science, mathematics, optics, and physics), EDUCATION (elementary, science, and secondary), ENGINEERING AND ENVIRONMENTAL DESIGN (preengineering), HEALTH PROFESSIONS (nursing, predentistry, premedicine, and prepharmacy), SOCIAL SCIENCE (African American studies, anthropology, economics, history, interdisciplinary studies, international studies, philosophy, political science/government, prelaw, psychology, religion, and sociology). Accounting, biology, and management are the strongest academically. Management, accounting, and communications/journalism have the largest enrollments.

Required: To graduate, students must complete at least 120 credit hours, including at least 30 in the major, and maintain a 2.0 minimum GPA. Required core curriculum courses include 4 each in literature/language, social science, and religious studies/philosophy, and 3 in mathematics/natural science.

Special: College credit may be earned in selected Rochester high schools through the Step Ahead Program. The college has cooperative programs with the University of Rochester in public policy and with the Pennsylvania College of Optometry. Students may cross-register with 8 Rochester area colleges. Study abroad may be pursued in many countries. The college offers internships in 15 majors, independent research in 16 majors, Washington semesters, dual and student-designed majors, and degrees in interdisciplinary studies or liberal studies. A 3-2 engineering degree is offered in conjunction with the State University of New York at Buffalo, the University of Rochester, Rensselaer Polytechnic Institute, Clarkson University, and Manhattan College, a 2-2 engineering program with the University of Detroit, and a 4-2 program with Columbia University. Credit for life, military, and work experience, nondegree study, and pass/fail options are possible. There is a grant for collaborative research between physics and chemistry students and faculty and scientists at NASA's Goddard Space Center and Marshal Space Center. There is a freshman honors program on campus, as well as 9 national honor societies. 7 departments have honors programs.

Faculty/Classroom: 63% of faculty are male; 37%, female. All teach undergraduates and 65% do research. No introductory courses are taught by graduate students. The average class size in an introductory lecture is 35; in a laboratory, 14; and in a regular course offering, 28.

Admissions: 79% of the 1995-96 applicants were accepted. The SAT I scores for the 1995-96 freshman class were as follows: Verbal—72% below 500, 19% between 500 and 599, and 9% between 600 and 700; Math—45% below 500, 37% between 500 and 599, 15% between 600 and 700, and 3% above 700. The ACT scores were 37% below 21, 33% between 21 and 23, 19% between 24 and 26, 5% between 27 and 28, and 6% above 28. 33% of the current freshmen were in the top fifth of their class; 71% were in the top two fifths. 5 freshmen graduated first in their class.

Requirements: The SAT I or ACT is required. Applicants must be graduates of an accredited secondary school. 16 academic credits are required, including 4 years each in English, history, and social studies, 3 years each in mathematics and science, and 2 years in a foreign language. Essays are required and interviews recommended. Fisher requires a minimum high school average of 80%. Applications are accepted through ExPAN. AP and CLEP credits are accepted. Important factors in the admissions decision are advanced placement or honor courses, leadership record, and evidence of special talent.

Procedure: Freshmen are admitted to all sessions. Entrance exams should be taken in the spring of the junior year or fall of the senior year. There are early decision, early admissions, and deferred admissions plans. Early decision applications should be filed by November 15; regular applications, by open for fall entry, along with an application fee of $25. Notification of early decision is sent November ; regular decision, on a rolling basis. 15 early decision candidates were accepted for the 1995-96 class.

Transfer: 237 transfer students enrolled in 1995-96. Applicants must have a minimum GPA of 2.0 to be considered (mean GPA is 2.8). A high school transcript is required for students with fewer than 12 college credits. Interviews are recommended. 30 credits of 120 must be completed at Fisher.

Visiting: There are regularly scheduled orientations for prospective students, including a tour, an interview, and meetings with faculty and coaches. There are guides for informal visits and visitors may sit in on classes and stay overnight at the school. To schedule a visit, contact the Admissions Office.

Financial Aid: In 1995-96, 99% of all freshmen and 96% of continuing students received some form of financial aid. 86% of freshmen and 67% of continuing students received need-based aid. The average freshman award was $10,005. Of that total, scholarships or need-based grants averaged $5480 ($11,150 maximum); loans averaged $3425 ($5625 maximum); and work contracts averaged $1100 ($1500 maximum). 23% of undergraduate students work part-time. Average earnings from campus work for the school year are $767. The average financial indebtedness of the 1994-95 graduate was $10,000. The FAFSA and TAP Application for New York State residents are required. The application deadline for fall entry is March 1.

International Students: There are currently 13 international students enrolled. They must take the TOEFL or the MELAB and achieve a minimum score on the TOEFL of 500.

Computers: The college provides computer facilities for student use. The mainframes are a DEC Station 5000/260 and a DEC ALPHA 2000-4/233. A variety of programming languages are utilized by the DEC system, including BASIC, COBOL, Pascal, and FORTRAN. Facilities include Apple Macintosh, SUN computer, and 2 PC laboratories in the academic computing center. There is a 35-station PC laboratory in the library. The DEC Station can be accessed from terminals in 2 laboratories and from all computers in the academic computing center. All students may access the system 24 hours daily. There are no time limits. The fee is $90.

Graduates: In 1994-95, 468 bachelor's degrees were awarded. The most popular majors among graduates were business and management (19%), psychology (11%), and communications/journalism (11%). Within an average freshman class, 58% graduate in 4 years, 62% in 5 years, and 63% in 6 years. Of the 1994 graduating class, 12% were enrolled in graduate school within 6 months of graduation and 81% had found employment.

Admissions Contact: Peter E. Lindsey, Dean of Admissions. E-mail: admissions@fisher.sjfc.edu. World Wide Web home page: http://www.sjf.edu. A campus video is available.

SAINT JOHN'S UNIVERSITY

D-5

Jamaica, NY 11439   (718) 990-6114; (800) 232-4-SJU

Full-time: 5043 men, 5786 women	Faculty: 597
Part-time: 694 men, 872 women	Ph.D.s: 80%
Graduate: 2261 men, 2766 women	Student/Faculty: 18 to 1
Year: early semesters, summer session	Tuition: $10,550
	Room & Board: n/app

Application Deadline: see profile
Freshman Class: 7256 applied, 2293 enrolled
SAT I Verbal/Math: 440/510   **COMPETITIVE**

Saint John's University, founded in 1870 by the Vincentian Fathers, is a private, coeducational Roman Catholic institution offering programs in the arts and sciences, education, business, theology, pharmacy and allied health professions, and other preprofessional training to a commuter student body. The main campus is in the borough of Queens; a branch campus is on Staten Island. There are 6 undergraduate and 5 graduate schools. In addition to regional accreditation, St. John's has baccalaureate program accreditation with AACSB and ACPE. The 3 libraries contain 1.3 million volumes, 1.8 million microform items, and 43,271 audiovisual forms, and subscribe to 6753 periodicals. Computerized library sources and services include the card catalog, interlibrary loans, and database searching. Special learning facilities include a learning resource center, art gallery, radio station, TV station, health education resource center, model pharmacy, speech and hearing clinic, psychological services center, and instructional materials center. The 100-acre campus is in a suburban area of New York City. There are 17 buildings on campus.

Student Life: 95% of undergraduates are from New York. Students come from 24 states, 114 foreign countries, and Canada. 61% are white; 12% Hispanic; 12% African American; 11% Asian American. 59% are Catholic; 18% claim no religious affiliation. The average age of freshmen is 18; all undergraduates, 21. 18% do not continue beyond their first year; 66% remain to graduate.

Housing: There are no residence halls. All students commute.

Activities: 8% of men belong to 9 local and 11 national fraternities; 6% of women belong to 12 local and 6 national sororities. There are 140 groups on campus, including art, cheerleading, choir, chorus, computers, dance, drama, ethnic, film, honors, international, jazz band, literary magazine, musical theater, newspaper, pep band, photography, political, professional, radio and TV, religious, social, social service, student government, and yearbook. Popular campus events include Harmony Week, Culture Week, Spring Fling, Midnight Madness, Winter Carnival, Greek Week, organization and recognition banquets, and annual outdoor festivals.

Sports: There are 15 intercollegiate sports for men and 10 for women, and 15 intramural sports for men and 11 for women. Athletic and recreation facilities include gymnasiums, a swimming pool, squash and tennis courts, weight and exercise rooms, baseball and softball diamonds, and fields for football, lacrosse, and soccer.

Disabled Students: The entire campus is accessible to disabled students. The following facilities are available: wheelchair ramps, elevators, special parking, specially equipped rest rooms, special class scheduling, lowered drinking fountains, and lowered telephones.

Services: There is remedial math, reading, and writing.

Campus Safety and Security: Campus safety and security measures include 24-hour foot and vehicle patrol, escort service, informal discussions, and pamphlets/posters/films. In addition, there are emergency telephones and lighted pathways/sidewalks.

Programs of Study: St. John's confers B.A., B.S., B.F.A., B.S.Ed., B.S.Med.Tech., and B.S.Pharm. degrees. Associate, master's, and doctoral degrees are also awarded. Bachelor's degrees are awarded in BIOLOGICAL SCIENCE (biology/biological science and toxicology), BUSINESS (accounting, business administration and management, business economics, management science, and transportation management), COMMUNICATIONS AND THE ARTS (communications, English, fine arts, French, German, Italian, journalism, photography, Spanish, and speech/debate/rhetoric), COMPUTER AND PHYSICAL SCIENCE (chemistry, computer science, mathematics, physical sciences, and physics), EDUCATION (art, early childhood, education of the deaf and hearing impaired, elementary, foreign languages, middle school, science, secondary, and special), ENGINEERING AND ENVIRONMENTAL DESIGN (environmental science and preengineering), HEALTH PROFESSIONS (health care administration, medical technology, pharmacy, physician's assistant, predentistry, premedicine, and speech pathology/audiology), SOCIAL SCIENCE (American studies, anthropology, criminal justice, economics, history, human services, paralegal studies, philosophy, political science/government, prelaw, psychology, public administration, social science, and sociology). Pharmacy is the strongest academically. Pharmacy, accounting, and government and politics/political science have the largest enrollments.

Required: To graduate, students must complete at least 126 credit hours, including core courses in liberal arts, with a minimum GPA of 2.0 overall and in the major. Other requirements vary by program.

Special: St. John's offers internships, study-abroad in Europe and Japan, an accelerated degree program in many majors, B.A.-B.S. degrees, dual majors and combined degree programs, pass/fail options, and some credit for life, military, and work experience. There are cooperative programs in nursing with Niagara University, in dentistry with Columbia University, in engineering with Manhattan College, in photography with the International Center of Photography, and in funeral service administration with the McAllister Institute. There are 25 national honor societies on campus.

Faculty/Classroom: 69% of faculty are male; 31%, female. 99% teach undergraduates, and all do research. No introductory courses are taught by graduate students. The average class size in an introductory lecture is 28.

Admissions: The SAT I scores for the 1995-96 freshman class were as follows: Verbal—73% below 500, 21% between 500 and 599, and 5% between 600 and 700; Math—45% below 500, 31% between 500 and 599, 21% between 600 and 700, and 3% above 700.

Requirements: The SAT I or ACT is required. A minimum GPA of 3.0 is required. Admissions decisions are made by committee and are based on several criteria, including standardized test scores, academic curriculum, and high school average. AP and CLEP credits are accepted. Other important factors in the admissions decision are advanced placement or honor courses, extracurricular activities record and evidence of special talent.

Procedure: Freshmen are admitted to all sessions. Entrance exams should be taken late in the junior year or early in the senior year. There are early admissions and deferred admissions plans. The application fee is $30. Notification is sent on a rolling basis. A waiting list

is an active part of the admissions procedure for pharmacy majors only, with about 6% of all applicants on the list.

Transfer: 732 transfer students enrolled in 1995-96. Applicants must present official transcripts of high school and college work, as well as a list of courses in progress. If the student has been out of school a semester or more, a letter of explanation is also required. Admissions requirements for transfer students to the pharmacy program are stricter, and few places are available. 30 credits of 126 must be completed at St. John's.

Visiting: There are regularly scheduled orientations for prospective students. There are guides for informal visits and visitors may sit in on classes. To schedule a visit, contact Jeanne Umland, Associate Vice President, Admissions.

Financial Aid: In 1995-96, 82% of all freshmen and 75% of continuing students received some form of financial aid. The average freshman award was $7756. Of that total, scholarships or need-based grants averaged $5756 ($10,050 maximum); and loans averaged $2000 ($4125 maximum). 80% of undergraduate students work part-time. Average earnings from campus work for the school year are $5304. The average financial indebtedness of the 1994-95 graduate was $10,189. The FAFSA is required. The application deadline for fall entry is March 1.

International Students: There were 792 international students enrolled in a recent year. The school actively recruits these students. They must score 500 on the TOEFL or take the college's own test and also take SAT I or ACT (this requirement may be waived for international students educated outside of the United States.) and score 1000 on the SAT I.

Computers: The college provides computer facilities for student use. The mainframe is an IBM 4381 Model 22. Also available are hundreds of Apple Macintosh microcomputers, including Power PCs and Apple Macintosh IIcx machines, and IBM PS/2 models, including 486 DX and Pentium machines. All students may access the system. There are no time limits. A fee is charged for enrollment and system use for computer courses.

Graduates: In 1994-95, 2458 bachelor's degrees were awarded. The most popular majors among graduates were pharmacy (15%), criminal justice (9%), and accounting (8%). Within an average freshman class, 2% graduate in 3 years, 64% in 4 years, 3% in 5 years, and 1% in 6 years. 122 companies recruited on campus in 1994-95. Of the 1994 graduating class, 10% were enrolled in graduate school within 6 months of graduation and 69% had found employment.

Admissions Contact: Jeanne Umland, Associate Vice President and Executive Director of Admissions.

SAINT JOSEPH'S COLLEGE, NEW YORK   D-5

Brooklyn, NY 11205	(718) 636-6868; FAX: (718) 398-4936
Full-time: 104 men, 394 women	Faculty: 44; IIB, av$
Part-time: 219 men, 602 women	Ph.D.s: 51%
Graduate: none	Student/Faculty: 11 to 1
Year: semesters, summer session	Tuition: $7817
Application Deadline: August 1	Room & Board: n/app
Freshman Class: 302 applied, 191 accepted, 84 enrolled	
SAT I Verbal/Math: 454/481	COMPETITIVE

Saint Joseph's College, established in 1916, is a private, independent, multicampus, commuter institution offering undergraduate degrees in arts and sciences, child study, business, accounting, health professions, and nursing. There is a branch campus in Patchogue, Long Island. In addition to regional accreditation, Saint Joseph's has baccalaureate program accreditation with NLN. The library contains 120,203 volumes, 3283 microform items, and 3157 audiovisual forms, and subscribes to 435 periodicals. Computerized library sources and services include interlibrary loans and database searching. Special learning facilities include an on-campus laboratory preschool. The 3-acre Brooklyn campus is in an urban area 1 mile east of Manhattan. There are 5 buildings on campus.

Student Life: 99% of undergraduates are from New York. Students come from 2 states and 2 foreign countries. 20% are from public schools; 80% from private. 50% are white; 38% African American. The average age of freshmen is 18; all undergraduates, 32. 11% do not continue beyond their first year; 75% remain to graduate.

Housing: There are no residence halls. All students commute. Alcohol is not permitted. All students may keep cars on campus.

Activities: 6% of men belong to 1 local fraternity; 5% of women belong to 1 local sorority. There are 22 groups on campus, including art, cheerleading, chorus, computers, dance, drama, ethnic, honors, literary magazine, newspaper, political, professional, religious, social, social service, student government, and yearbook. Popular campus events include the Christmas party, costume party, and Theater Night.

Sports: There is 1 intercollegiate sport for men and 3 for women, and 4 intramural sports for men and 4 for women. Athletic and recreation facilities include a gymnasium, a handball court, an outdoor mall, recreation rooms, and an exercise/weight room.

Disabled Students: 20% of the campus is accessible to disabled students. The following facilities are available: wheelchair ramps, elevators, and specially equipped rest rooms.

Services: In addition to many counseling and information services, tutoring is available in most subjects. There is remedial writing.

Campus Safety and Security: Campus safety and security measures include self-defense education, escort service, informal discussions, and pamphlets/posters/films. There are lighted pathways/sidewalks.

Programs of Study: Saint Joseph's confers B.A. and B.S. degrees. Bachelor's degrees are awarded in BIOLOGICAL SCIENCE (biology/biological science), BUSINESS (accounting and business administration and management), COMMUNICATIONS AND THE ARTS (English, French, Spanish, and speech/debate/rhetoric), COMPUTER AND PHYSICAL SCIENCE (chemistry and mathematics), EDUCATION (early childhood, elementary, secondary, and special), HEALTH PROFESSIONS (community health work, health care administration, and nursing), SOCIAL SCIENCE (history, psychology, and social science). Child study, biology, and psychology have the largest enrollments.

Required: To graduate, students must complete a 51-credit core curriculum requirement consisting of 8 courses in humanities, 3 in social science and mathematics/science, and 1 English composition course. The minimum GPA is 2.0. Students must earn 128 credits, with 30 to 36 credits in the major. All students are required to take an English composition class. Most majors require a thesis.

Special: The college offers internship programs in history, political science, social work, speech and business/accounting, and an interdisciplinary major in human relations. Adult students may pursue a general studies degree in which the college allows credit for life, military, and work experience. There is a freshman honors program on campus, as well as 4 national honor societies.

Faculty/Classroom: 38% of faculty are male; 62%, female. All teach and 10% also do research. The average class size in an introductory lecture is 15; in a laboratory, 15; and in a regular course offering, 12.

Admissions: 63% of the 1995–96 applicants were accepted. The SAT I scores for the 1995–96 freshman class were as follows: Verbal—76% below 500, 18% between 500 and 599, and 6% between 600 and 700; Math—61% below 500, 30% between 500 and 599, 8% between 600 and 700, and 1% above 700. 44% of the current freshmen were in the top fifth of their class; 70% were in the top two fifths. 1 freshman graduated first in his class.

Requirements: The SAT I is required, with a minimum required composite score of 900. Applicants must graduate from an accredited secondary school with a 3.0 GPA or earn a GED. 16 Carnegie units are required, including 4 units of English and social studies, 2 of languages and science, 3 of mathematics, and 3 elective units. Interviews are recommended. AP and CLEP credits are accepted. Important factors in the admissions decision are advanced placement or honor courses, leadership record, and extracurricular activities record.

Procedure: Freshmen are admitted fall and spring. There are early decision, early admissions, and deferred admissions plans. Applications should be filed by August 1 for fall entry and January 1 for spring entry, along with an application fee of $25. Notification is sent on a rolling basis.

Transfer: 59 transfer students enrolled in 1995–96. Applicants must have a minimum GPA of 2.0. If fewer than 30 credits have been earned, an SAT I is required with a minimum composite score of 900. 48 credits of 128 must be completed at Saint Joseph's.

Visiting: There are regularly scheduled orientations for prospective students, including meetings with faculty advisers and student-to-student sessions. There are guides for informal visits and visitors may sit in on classes. To schedule a visit, contact the Admissions Office.

Financial Aid: In 1995–96, 90% of all freshmen and 85% of continuing students received some form of financial aid. 60% of freshmen and 65% of continuing students received need-based aid. The average freshman award was $6500. Of that total, scholarships or need-based grants averaged $3500 ($8000 maximum); loans averaged $1500 ($2625 maximum); and work contracts averaged $1500 ($2500 maximum). 4% of undergraduate students work part-time. Average earnings from campus work for the school year are $1000. The average financial indebtedness of the 1994–95 graduate was $6000. The FAFSA and the college's own financial statement are required. The application deadline for fall entry is February 25.

International Students: There are currently 2 international students enrolled. They must score 550 on the TOEFL and take SAT I.

Computers: The college provides computer facilities for student use. The mainframe is an IBM AS400/System 36. Microcomputers are available to students in the 2 computer labs, in department offices, and in the library. All students may access the system. There are no time limits and no fees.

Graduates: In 1994–95, 238 bachelor's degrees were awarded. Within an average freshman class, 1% graduate in 3 years, 72% in 4 years, 75% in 5 years, and 75% in 6 years. 23 companies recruited on campus in 1994–95. Of the 1994 graduating class, 42% were enrolled in graduate school within 6 months of graduation and 88% had found employment.

Admissions Contact: Geraldine Foudy, Director of Admissions. A campus video is available.

SAINT LAWRENCE UNIVERSITY   C-2

Canton, NY 13617	(315) 379–5261; (800) 285–1856
Full-time: 983 men, 993 women	Faculty: 153; IIB, +$
Part-time: 13 men, 17 women	Ph.Ds: 93%
Graduate: 34 men, 66 women	Student/Faculty: 13 to 1
Year: semesters, summer session	Tuition: $19,790
Application Deadline: February 15	Room & Board: $5885
Freshman Class: 2833 applied, 1711 accepted, 572 enrolled	
SAT I Verbal/Math: 580/570	VERY COMPETITIVE +

Saint Lawrence University, established in 1856, is a private, coeducational, liberal arts institution. There is 1 graduate school. The 2 libraries contain 428,345 volumes and 380,000 microform items, and subscribe to 2371 periodicals. Computerized library sources and services include the card catalog, interlibrary loans, and database searching. Special learning facilities include a learning resource center, art gallery, and radio station. The 1000-acre campus is in a rural area 80 miles south of Ottawa, Canada. Including residence halls, there are 30 buildings on campus.

Student Life: 51% of undergraduates are from out-of-state, mostly the Northeast. Students come from 42 states, 20 foreign countries, and Canada. 66% are from public schools; 34% from private. 90% are white. The average age of freshmen is 18; all undergraduates, 19. 15% do not continue beyond their first year; 82% remain to graduate.

Housing: 1480 students can be accommodated in college housing. College-sponsored living facilities include coed dormitories, fraternity houses, and sorority houses. In addition there are language houses, special interest houses, and theme cottages, such as Habitat for Humanity. On-campus housing is guaranteed for all 4 years. 96% of students live on campus; of those, 90% remain on campus on weekends. All students may keep cars on campus.

Activities: 23% of men belong to 7 national fraternities; 30% of women belong to 1 local and 3 national sororities. There are 75 groups on campus, including art, cheerleading, chess, choir, chorus, dance, drama, ethnic, gay, honors, international, literary magazine, musical theater, newspaper, orchestra, outdoor, pep band, photography, political, professional, radio and TV, religious, social service, student government, and yearbook. Popular campus events include St. Lawrence Festival of the Arts, Black History Week, Holiday Candlelight Service, Festival of Nations, and Moving Up Day.

Sports: There are 13 intercollegiate sports for men and 12 for women, and 12 intramural sports for men and 9 for women. Athletic and recreation facilities include basketball, squash, and tennis courts, a swimming pool, and weight, Nautilus, and exercise rooms. There is also a field house, an arena, an artificial ice rink, an 18-hole golf course, riding stables, and jogging and cross-country ski trails.

Disabled Students: 75% of the campus is accessible to disabled students. The following facilities are available: wheelchair ramps, elevators, special parking, specially equipped rest rooms, special class scheduling, and visual fire alarms.

Services: In addition to many counseling and information services, tutoring is available in every subject. In addition, there is a reader service for the blind, a writing center, and science and technology counseling.

Campus Safety and Security: Campus safety and security measures include 24-hour foot and vehicle patrol, self-defense education, escort service, and shuttle buses. In addition, there are informal discussions, pamphlets/posters/films, emergency telephones, lighted pathways/sidewalks, and student patrols.

Programs of Study: Saint Lawrence confers B.A. and B.S. degrees. Master's degrees are also awarded. Bachelor's degrees are awarded in BIOLOGICAL SCIENCE (biology/biological science), BUSINESS (recreation and leisure services), COMMUNICATIONS AND THE ARTS (English, fine arts, French, German, music, and Spanish), COMPUTER AND PHYSICAL SCIENCE (chemistry, computer science, geology, mathematics, and physics), ENGINEERING AND ENVIRONMENTAL DESIGN (environmental science), SOCIAL SCIENCE (anthropology, Asian/Oriental studies, Canadian studies, economics, history, philosophy, political science/government, psychology, religion, and sociology). Environmental studies, government, and economics are the strongest academically. Economics, government, and English have the largest enrollments.

Required: To graduate, students must maintain a minimum GPA of 2.0 and complete 34 course units, with 8 to 12 units in the major. Freshmen must take a first-year program, a 2-semester team-taught course. Distribution requirements must be fulfilled in natural science, social science, and humanities. Students must also complete 1 course in non-Western or Third World topics and 1 course each from 2 of the following areas: mathematics or symbolic logic, arts or forms of expression, and foreign languages, as well as 1 year of physical education.

Special: Students may cross-register with the Associated Colleges of the St. Lawrence Valley. Internships are available through the sociology, psychology, and English departments. Study abroad in 11 countries, a Washington semester, and a semester at sea are offered. Dual majors and student-designed majors can be arranged. Students may earn 3–2 engineering degrees in conjunction with 7 engineering schools. A 3–2 nursing degree program is available with the University of Rochester. Nondegree study and pass/fail options are available. There are 19 national honor societies on campus, including Phi Beta Kappa. 17 departments have honors programs.

Faculty/Classroom: 65% of faculty are male; 35%, female. 99% teach undergraduates and all do research. No introductory courses are taught by graduate students. The average class size in an introductory lecture is 30; in a laboratory, 20; and in a regular course offering, 15.

Admissions: 60% of the 1995–96 applicants were accepted. The SAT I scores for the 1995–96 freshman class were as follows: Verbal—17% below 500, 42% between 500 and 599, 33% between 600 and 700, and 8% above 700; Math—17% below 500, 43% between 500 and 599, 38% between 600 and 700, and 3% above 700. 54% of the current freshmen were in the top fifth of their class; 77% were in the top two fifths. There were 5 National Merit finalists. 16 freshmen graduated first in their class.

Requirements: The SAT I is required. The SAT II: Writing test is also required, and 2 other subject tests are recommended. Applicants must be graduates of an accredited high school. 16 or more academic credits are required, including 4 years of English and 3 years each of foreign languages, mathematics, science, and social studies. Essays are required and interviews are recommended for all applicants. AP and CLEP credits are accepted. Important factors in the admissions decision are advanced placement or honor courses, extracurricular activities record, and recommendations by school officials.

Procedure: Freshmen are admitted fall, spring, and summer. Entrance exams should be taken during the spring of the junior year or the fall of the senior year. There are early decision and deferred admissions plans. Applications should be filed by February 15 for fall entry and December 1 for spring entry, along with an application fee of $40. Notification is sent March 15. 144 early decision candidates were accepted for the 1995–96 class. A waiting list is an active part of the admissions procedure.

Transfer: 40 transfer students enrolled in a recent year. Applicants must have a 3.0 GPA, and a minimum of 4 courses must have been completed. The high school transcript and SAT I scores will be evaluated, but college work is more important. Interviews and high school and college recommendations are required. 16 course units of 34 must be completed at Saint Lawrence.

Visiting: There are guides for informal visits and visitors may sit in on classes and stay overnight at the school. To schedule a visit, contact the Admissions Office.

Financial Aid: In 1995–96, 76% of all freshmen and 72% of continuing students received some form of financial aid. 69% of freshmen and 68% of continuing students received need-based aid. The average freshman award was $17,921. Of that total, scholarships or need-based grants averaged $11,879 ($26,140 maximum); loans averaged $2796 ($5600 maximum); and work contracts averaged $1313 ($1700 maximum). 37% of undergraduate students work part-time. Average earnings from campus work for the school year are $1000. The average financial indebtedness of the 1994–95 graduate was $10,000. Saint Lawrence is a member of CSS. The FAFSA is required. The application deadline for fall entry is February 15.

International Students: There are currently 72 international students enrolled. The school actively recruits these students.

Computers: The college provides computer facilities for student use. The mainframe is an IBM 4381 Model 13. 600 personal computers are linked to the mainframe and card catalog. Word processing and spreadsheet software, and E-mail, calendars, bulletin boards, and Internet and World Wide Web access are available. Computer laboratories are located in all residence halls and most academic buildings. All students may access the system 24 hours per day. There are no time limits and no fees.

Graduates: In 1994–95, 382 bachelor's degrees were awarded. The most popular majors among graduates were government (13%), English (13%), and psychology (10%). Within an average freshman class, 75% graduate in 4 years, 80% in 5 years, and 82% in 6 years. 40 companies recruited on campus in 1994–95. Of the 1994 graduating class, 20% were enrolled in graduate school within 6 months of graduation and 74% had found employment.

Admissions Contact: Joel R. Wincowski.

SAINT THOMAS AQUINAS COLLEGE   D-5
Sparkill, NY 10976   (914) 398–4100
(800) 999-STAC; FAX: (914) 359–8136

Full-time: 700 men, 900 women	Faculty: 65; IIB, av$
Part-time: 125 men, 375 women	Ph.D.s: 75%
Graduate: 45 men, 85 women	Student/Faculty: 25 to 1
Year: 4–1–4, summer session	Tuition: $10,050
Application Deadline: open	Room & Board: $6050
Freshman Class: 982 applied, 786 accepted, 295 enrolled	
SAT I Verbal/Math: 420/450	ACT: 21 COMPETITIVE

Saint Thomas Aquinas College, founded in 1952, is an independent, coeducational, liberal arts institution. There is 1 graduate school. The library contains 102,943 volumes and 45,900 microform items, and subscribes to 108 periodicals. Computerized library sources and services include the card catalog, interlibrary loans, and database searching. Special learning facilities include a learning resource center, radio station, and TV station. The 42-acre campus is in a suburban area 13 miles north of New York City. Including residence halls, there are 12 buildings on campus.

Student Life: 75% of undergraduates are from New York. Students come from 6 states, 8 foreign countries, and Canada. 80% are from public schools; 20% from private. 84% are white. 62% are Catholic; 23% Protestant. The average age of freshmen is 18; all undergraduates, 22. 6% do not continue beyond their first year; 86% remain to graduate.

Housing: 450 students can be accommodated in college housing. College-sponsored living facilities include single-sex dormitories and on-campus apartments. On-campus housing is guaranteed for all 4 years. 75% of students commute. Alcohol is not permitted. All students may keep cars on campus.

Activities: There are no fraternities or sororities. There are 10 groups on campus, including chorus, drama, honors, literary magazine, newspaper, professional, radio and TV, social service, student government, and yearbook. Popular campus events include trips to Broadway shows and Halloween and Christmas mixers.

Sports: There are 4 intercollegiate sports for men and 4 for women, and 3 intramural sports for men and 3 for women. Athletic and recreation facilities include an auditorium, a 750-seat gymnasium, a weight room, and basketball and tennis courts.

Disabled Students: 90% of the campus is accessible to disabled students. The following facilities are available: wheelchair ramps, elevators, special parking, specially equipped rest rooms, special class scheduling, and lowered telephones.

Services: In addition to many counseling and information services, tutoring is available in most subjects. There is remedial math and writing.

Campus Safety and Security: Campus safety and security measures include 24-hour foot and vehicle patrol, escort service, pamphlets/posters/films, and emergency telephones. In addition, there are lighted pathways/sidewalks.

Programs of Study: The college confers B.A., B.S., and B.S.E. degrees. Master's degrees are also awarded. Bachelor's degrees are awarded in BUSINESS (accounting, banking and finance, business administration and management, marketing/retailing/merchandising, and recreation and leisure services), COMMUNICATIONS AND THE ARTS (communications, English, fine arts, romance languages, and Spanish), EDUCATION (art, bilingual/bicultural, early childhood, elementary, foreign languages, middle school, science, secondary, and special), ENGINEERING AND ENVIRONMENTAL DESIGN (commercial art), HEALTH PROFESSIONS (medical laboratory technology and premedicine), SOCIAL SCIENCE (criminal justice, history, philosophy, prelaw, psychology, religion, and social science). Education is the strongest academically. Business administration has the largest enrollment.

Required: To graduate, all students must complete a total of 120 credit hours, with 36 to 54 in the major and a minimum GPA of 2.0. A core curriculum of 51 credits in liberal arts courses is required.

Special: The college offers internships in business, criminal justice, commercial design, recreation and leisure, and communications. Study abroad in England, a 3–2 engineering degree with George Washington University and Manhattan College, and work-study programs are available. Nondegree study and pass/fail options are possible. There is a freshman honors program on campus, as well as 7 national honor societies.

Faculty/Classroom: 55% of faculty are male; 45%, female. All teach undergraduates. No introductory courses are taught by graduate students. The average class size in an introductory lecture is 35; in a laboratory, 15; and in a regular course offering, 25.

Admissions: 80% of the 1995–96 applicants were accepted. The SAT I scores for the 1995–96 freshman class were as follows: Verbal—43% below 500, 53% between 500 and 599, and 4% between 600 and 700; Math—40% below 500, 56% between 500 and 599, and 4% between 600 and 700. 30% of the current freshmen were in the top fifth of their class; 70% were in the top two fifths. 2 freshmen graduated first in their class in a recent year.

Requirements: The SAT I is required. The college requires applicants to be in the upper 75% of their class. A minimum GPA of 2.0 is required. Applicants must be graduates of an accredited secondary school or have a GED certificate. 16 Carnegie units are required, including 4 years of English, 2 each of mathematics and science, and 1 each of foreign language and history. An interview is recommended. AP and CLEP credits are accepted. Important factors in the admissions decision are leadership record, extracurricular activities record, and advanced placement or honor courses.

Procedure: Freshmen are admitted in the fall and spring. Entrance exams should be taken by the spring of the junior year. There are early admissions and deferred admissions plans. Application deadlines are open. Application fee is $25. Notification is sent on a rolling basis.

Transfer: 204 transfer students enrolled in a recent year. Applicants must have a 2.0 GPA from the previous school. 30 credits of 120 must be completed at the college.

Visiting: There are guides for informal visits and visitors may sit in on classes. To schedule a visit, contact the Admissions Office at (914) 398-4100 or (800) 999-STAC (out-of-state).

Financial Aid: In a recent year, 75% of all freshmen and 60% of continuing students received some form of financial aid. The average recent freshman award was $6300. Of that total, scholarships or need-based grants averaged $1500 ($6600 maximum); loans averaged $2000 ($2625 maximum); and work contracts averaged $1120 ($1500 maximum). 85% of undergraduate students work part-time. Average earnings from campus work for the school year are $1200. The average financial indebtedness of a recent graduate was $10,000. The college is a member of CSS. The FAF and the college's own financial statement are required. The application deadline for fall entry is April.

International Students: There were 18 international students enrolled in a recent year. They must take the TOEFL and achieve a minimum score of 450 in writing and mathematics.

Computers: The college provides computer facilities for student use. The mainframe is an HP 3000. There are also 50 IBM, Zenith, Apple, and HP microcomputers available throughout campus. Those enrolled in programming courses may access the system from 8:30 A.M. to 5 P.M. Monday through Thursday and 4 hours on Friday, Saturday, and Sunday. Students may access the system 1 hour per session per half day. The fees are $35.

Admissions Contact: Joseph L. Chillo, Director of Admissions.

SARAH LAWRENCE COLLEGE
Bronxville, NY 10708
D-5

(914) 395-2510
(800) 888-2858; FAX: (914) 395-2668

Full-time: 243 men, 705 women	Faculty: 165; IIB, + +$
Part-time: 5 men, 82 women	Ph.D.s: 92%
Graduate: 32 men, 212 women	Student/Faculty: 6 to 1
Year: semesters	Tuition: $20,708
Application Deadline: February 1	Room & Board: $6838
Freshman Class: 1284 applied, 755 accepted, 234 enrolled	
SAT I Verbal/Math: 590/570	ACT: 26 HIGHLY COMPETITIVE

Sarah Lawrence College, established in 1926, is an independent, coeducational institution conferring liberal arts degrees. The academic structure is based on the British don system. Students meet biweekly with professors in tutorials and are enrolled in small seminars. There are no formal majors. The 3 libraries contain 217,907 volumes, 16,737 microform items, and 17,202 audiovisual forms, and subscribe to 1111 periodicals. Computerized library sources and services include the card catalog, interlibrary loans, and database searching. Special learning facilities include an environmental theater, an early childhood center, an electronic music studio, and a slide library with 75,000 slides of art and architecture. The 40-acre campus is in a suburban area 15 miles north of New York City. Including residence halls, there are 50 buildings on campus.

Student Life: 76% of undergraduates are from out-of-state, mostly the Northeast. Students come from 45 states, 24 foreign countries, and Canada. 58% are from public schools; 42% from private. 81% are white. The average age of freshmen is 18; all undergraduates, 21. 10% do not continue beyond their first year; 80% remain to graduate.

Housing: 732 students can be accommodated in college housing. College-sponsored living facilities include single-sex and coed dormitories and on-campus apartments. On-campus housing is guaranteed for all 4 years. 90% of students live on campus; of those, 85% remain on campus on weekends. Upperclassmen may keep cars on campus.

Activities: There are no fraternities or sororities. There are 40 groups on campus, including art, band, chess, choir, chorale, chorus, computers, dance, drama, ethnic, film, gay, international, jazz band, literary magazine, musical theater, newspaper, orchestra, photography, political, religious, social, social service, student government, and yearbook. Popular campus events include Octoberfest, Mayfair, Winter Wonder Week, Dance-a-thon, and a student scholarship fundraising auction.

Sports: There are 3 intercollegiate sports for men and 4 for women, and 5 intramural sports for men and 5 for women. Athletic and recreation facilities include a fitness center, a weight room, billiards tables, tennis courts, and a number of open fields and lawns. Off campus, the college has the use of a boat house, stables, and a swimming pool.

Disabled Students: 50% of the campus is accessible to disabled students. The following facilities are available: wheelchair ramps, elevators, special parking, specially equipped rest rooms, special class scheduling, lowered drinking fountains, and lowered telephones.

Services: In addition to many counseling and information services, tutoring is available in some subjects, including writing. There is a reader service for the blind.

Campus Safety and Security: Campus safety and security measures include 24-hour foot and vehicle patrol, self-defense education, escort service, and shuttle buses. In addition, there are informal discussions, pamphlets/posters/films, emergency telephones, and lighted pathways/sidewalks.

Programs of Study: Sarah Lawrence confers the B.A. degree. Master's degrees are also awarded. Bachelor's degrees are awarded in BIOLOGICAL SCIENCE (biology/biological science), COMMUNICATIONS AND THE ARTS (creative writing, dance, English, film arts, fine arts, French, German, Greek, Italian, Latin, literature, music, photography, Russian, Spanish, and visual and performing arts), COMPUTER AND PHYSICAL SCIENCE (chemistry, computer science, earth science, geology, mathematics, physics, and statistics), EDUCATION (early childhood), HEALTH PROFESSIONS (premedicine), SOCIAL SCIENCE (anthropology, Asian/Oriental studies, economics, history, international relations, philosophy, political science/government, prelaw, psychology, religion, Russian and Slavic studies, sociology, urban studies, and women's studies). Literature, history, and creative writing have the largest enrollments.

Required: To graduate, students must meet distribution requirements in 3 of 4 academic areas, including history and social sciences, creative and performing arts, natural science and mathematics, and humanities, and they must complete 120 credit hours. Students must fulfill a first-year studies requirement in 1 of 18 areas, and meet a physical education requirement. Students must also take 2 lecture courses, where the average class size is 40.

Special: Internships are available in a variety of fields, with close proximity to New York City art galleries and agencies. Study abroad in 4 countries, work-study programs, and a general degree may be pursued. All concentrations are self-designed and can be combined.

Faculty/Classroom: 50% of faculty are male; 50%, female. All teach undergraduates. No introductory courses are taught by graduate students. The average class size in a regular course offering is 11.

Admissions: 59% of the 1995-96 applicants were accepted. The SAT I scores for the 1995-96 freshman class were as follows: Verbal—20% below 500, 41% between 500 and 599, 30% between 600 and 700, and 9% above 700; Math—25% below 500, 43% between 500 and 599, 27% between 600 and 700, and 5% above 700. The ACT scores were 4% below 21, 27% between 21 and 23, 20% between 24 and 26, 27% between 27 and 28, and 22% above 28. 57% of the current freshmen were in the top fifth of their class; 89% were in the top two fifths.

Requirements: The SAT I, ACT, or 3 SAT II: Subject tests are required. Applicants must graduate from an accredited secondary school or have a GED. The number of academic credits required depends on the high school attended. The college recommends completion of 4 years of English, 3 each of mathematics, science, social studies, and a foreign language, 2 to 3 of history, and 1 each of art and music. 3 essays are required. An interview is recommended. AP credits are accepted. Important factors in the admissions decision are essays, advanced placement or honor courses, and personality/intangible qualities.

Procedure: Freshmen are admitted fall and spring. There are early decision, early admissions, and deferred admissions plans. Early decision applications should be filed by November 15 or January 1; regular applications, by February 1 for fall entry and December 1 for spring entry, along with an application fee of $45. Notification of early decision is sent December 15; regular decision, April 1. 46 early decision candidates were accepted for the 1995-96 class. A waiting list is an active part of the admissions procedure, with about 11% of all applicants on the list.

Transfer: 35 transfer students enrolled in 1995-96. Transfer applicants must submit the Application for Admission (Form A); there is a supplement required for those using the common application. Applicants must also submit the College Report form, high school and college transcripts, 2 teacher evaluations, and a dean's report. A GPA of 3.0 is recommended. Students must have completed 1 full year of college. An interview is highly recommended. 60 credits of 120 must be completed at Sarah Lawrence.

Visiting: There are regularly scheduled orientations for prospective students, consisting of a full day of faculty and student panels, lectures, tours, and discussion with admissions officers, offered twice per year during the fall. There are guides for informal visits and visitors may sit in on classes and stay overnight at the school. To schedule a visit, contact Linda Bloom, Receptionist, Admissions Office, Monday through Thursday.

Financial Aid: In 1995–96, 63% of all freshmen and 50% of continuing students received some form of financial aid. 59% of freshmen and 47% of continuing students received need-based aid. The average freshman award was $18,674. Of that total, scholarships or need-based grants averaged $13,390 ($25,500 maximum); loans averaged $2625 (maximum); and work contracts averaged $1500 (maximum). 70% of undergraduate students work part-time. Average earnings from campus work for the school year are $1500. Sarah Lawrence is a member of CSS. The FAFSA, CSS Profile Application, and divorced/separated parents form are required. The application deadline for fall entry is February 1.

International Students: There are currently 42 international students enrolled. The school actively recruits these students. They must take the TOEFL and achieve a minimum score of 550. The student must also take the SAT I or the ACT.

Computers: The college provides computer facilities for student use. There are 40 stand-alone PCs, Macintosh microcomputers, and laser printers located in the student computer center, available 24 hours. All students may access the system. There are no time limits and no fees.

Graduates: In 1994–95, 230 bachelor's degrees were awarded. The most popular majors among graduates were literature/writing (35%), visual and performing arts (28%), and psychology (17%). Within an average freshman class, 70% graduate in 4 years, 75% in 5 years, and 80% in 6 years. 167 companies recruited on campus in 1994–95. Of the 1994 graduating class, 35% were enrolled in graduate school within 6 months of graduation.

Admissions Contact: Robert M. Kinnally, Dean of Admissions. E-mail: slcadmit@mail.slc.edu.

SCHOOL OF VISUAL ARTS   D-5
New York, NY 10010–3994

(212) 592–2100
(800) 436–4204; FAX: (212) 725–3584

Full-time: 1492 men, 997 women	Faculty: 90
Part-time: 1010 men, 1284 women	Ph.D.s: 36%
Graduate: 135 men, 172 women	Student/Faculty: 28 to 1
Year: semesters, summer session	Tuition: $12,600
Application Deadline: March 15	Room & Board: $7400
Freshman Class: 2015 applied, 1681 accepted, 709 enrolled	
SAT I Verbal/Math: 435/445	SPECIAL

The School of Visual Arts, established in 1947, is a private coeducational institution conferring the bachelor of fine arts degree. SVA has a branch campus in Savannah, Georgia. There are 8 undergraduate and 4 graduate schools. In addition to regional accreditation, SVA has baccalaureate program accreditation with NASAD. The library contains 66,000 volumes, 875 microform items, 1600 audiovisual forms, 128,000 slides, and subscribes to 265 periodicals. Computerized library sources and services include database searching. Special learning facilities include a learning resource center, art gallery, radio station, 5 student galleries, 3 media arts workshops, 3 film and 2 video studios, numerous editing facilities, an animation studio with 3 pencil test facilities, digital audio room, tape transfer room, and multimedia facility with digital printing and editing systems. The campus is in an urban area in the middle of Manhattan. Including residence halls, there are 8 buildings on campus.

Student Life: 70% of undergraduates are from New York. Students come from 40 states, 58 foreign countries, and Canada. 68% are white; 12% foreign nationals. The average age of freshmen is 18; all undergraduates, 26. 16% do not continue beyond their first year; 48% remain to graduate.

Housing: 566 students can be accommodated in college housing. College-sponsored living facilities include single-sex and coed dormitories and off-campus apartments. On-campus housing is available on a first-come, first-served basis. 82% of students commute. Alcohol is not permitted. All students may keep cars on campus.

Activities: There are no fraternities or sororities. There are many groups and organizations on campus, including art, computers, drama, ethnic, film, gay, honors, international, literary magazine, newspaper, photography, political, professional, radio and TV, religious, social, social service, student government, and yearbook. Popular campus events include 4 annual illustration, 3 advertising, 86 fine art and photography, 2 art therapy, and 2 art education exhibitions.

Sports: There is an intramural sports program.

Disabled Students: The entire campus is accessible to disabled students. The following facilities are available: wheelchair ramps, elevators, specially equipped rest rooms, special class scheduling, and lowered telephones.

Services: There is remedial reading and writing.

Campus Safety and Security: Campus safety and security measures include 24-hour foot and vehicle patrol, informal discussions, pamphlets/posters/films, and emergency telephones. In addition, there are lighted pathways/sidewalks.

Programs of Study: SVA confers the B.F.A. degree. Master's degrees are also awarded. Bachelor's degrees are awarded in COMMUNICATIONS AND THE ARTS (advertising, film arts, fine arts, graphic design, illustration, photography, and video), EDUCATION (art), ENGINEERING AND ENVIRONMENTAL DESIGN (computer graphics and interior design). Graphic design, advertising, and illustration have the largest enrollments.

Required: To graduate, students must complete 128 credits, including at least 70 in the major, with a minimum GPA of 2.0. Distribution requirements include 1 upper-level course each in history, social sciences, literature, and science.

Special: SVA offers study abroad in 9 countries and internships with media-related, design/advertising, and interior design firms in New York City. A summer internship with Walt Disney Studios is possible for illustration/cartooning majors. A certificate in art education or art therapy is offered in combination with fine arts.

Faculty/Classroom: 63% of faculty are male; 37%, female. 86% teach undergraduates. No introductory courses are taught by graduate students.

Admissions: 83% of the 1995–96 applicants were accepted. The SAT I scores for the 1995–96 freshman class were as follows: Verbal—70% below 500, 22% between 500 and 599, 6% between 600 and 700, and 2% above 700; Math—63% below 500, 32% between 500 and 599, 4% between 600 and 700, and 1% above 700.

Requirements: The SAT I or ACT is required. Applicants must graduate from an accredited secondary school with a 2.0 GPA or have a GED. A personal interview is required of all students living within a 250-mile radius of the school. An essay is required. A portfolio is also required, except for film applicants. AP credits are accepted. Important factors in the admissions decision are evidence of special talent, personality/intangible qualities, and leadership record.

Procedure: Freshmen are admitted to all sessions. There are early decision and deferred admissions plans. Early decision applications should be filed by December 15; regular applications, by March 15 for fall entry and December 15 for spring entry (for film, video, animation, and computer art applicants only). The application fee is $30. Notification of early decision is sent January 12; regular decision, on a rolling basis.

Transfer: 312 transfer students enrolled in 1995–96. 64 credits of 128 must be completed at SVA.

Visiting: There are regularly scheduled orientations for prospective students, including 6 Saturday Open House receptions and weekly tours. There are guides for informal visits. To schedule a visit, contact the Office of Admissions.

Financial Aid: In 1995–96, 74% of all freshmen and 72% of continuing students received some form of financial aid. 72% of freshmen and 71% of continuing students received need-based aid. The average freshman award was $5661. Of that total, scholarships or need-based grants averaged $3701 ($12,400 maximum); loans averaged $3205 ($3625 maximum); and work contracts averaged $1000 ($3000 maximum). 7% of undergraduate students work part-time. Average earnings from campus work for the school year are $5000. The average financial indebtedness of the 1994–95 graduate was $14,000. SVA is a member of CSS. The FAFSA and the college's own financial statement are required.

International Students: There are currently 586 international students enrolled. The school actively recruits these students. They must take the TOEFL and achieve a minimum score of 550.

Computers: The college provides computer facilities for student use. The mainframe is an IBM RS6000. There are 370 microcomputers available in the computer art department, media workshop, writing resource center, and library. All students may access the system during normal operating hours of the library and the writing resource center; use in other buildings varies by major. There are no time limits and no fees. It is recommended that students have a Macintosh personal computer.

Graduates: In 1994–95, 411 bachelor's degrees were awarded. The most popular majors among graduates were graphic design/advertising (29%), illistration/cartooning (28%), and fine arts (18%). Within an average freshman class, 37% graduate in 4 years, 40% in 5 years, and 42% in 6 years. More than 50 companies recruited on campus in 1994–95.

Admissions Contact: Lawrence Wilson, Director of Admissions.

SIENA COLLEGE
Loudonville, NY 12211-1462   **D-3**

(518) 783-2423; (800) 45 SIENA

Full-time: 1152 men, 1377 women	Faculty: 162; IIB, +$
Part-time: 363 men, 378 women	Ph.D.s: 81%
Graduate: 9 men, 9 women	Student/Faculty: 16 to 1
Year: semesters, summer session	Tuition: $11,340
Application Deadline: March 1	Room & Board: $5270

Freshman Class: 2447 applied, 1788 accepted, 593 enrolled

SAT I Verbal/Math: 470/540   **VERY COMPETITIVE**

Siena College, established in 1937, is an independent, coeducational liberal arts college operating within the Franciscan tradition. The college confers undergraduate degrees in liberal arts, business, and science, and provides continuing education programs for the surrounding community. There is 1 graduate school. In addition to regional accreditation, Siena has baccalaureate program accreditation with CSWE. The library contains 257,617 volumes, 30,341 microform items, and 4298 audiovisual forms, and subscribes to 1658 periodicals. Computerized library sources and services include the card catalog, interlibrary loans, and database searching. Special learning facilities include a radio station. The 155-acre campus is in a suburban area 2 miles north of Albany. Including residence halls, there are 24 buildings on campus.

Student Life: 82% of undergraduates are from New York. Students come from 27 states, 5 foreign countries, and Canada. 70% are from public schools; 30% from private. 93% are white. The average age of freshmen is 18; all undergraduates, 20. 10% do not continue beyond their first year; 80% remain to graduate.

Housing: 1974 students can be accommodated in college housing. College-sponsored living facilities include coed dormitories and on-campus apartments. On-campus housing is guaranteed for all 4 years. 57% of students live on campus; of those, 90% remain on campus on weekends. Upperclassmen may keep cars on campus.

Activities: There are no fraternities or sororities. There are 60 groups on campus, including art, cheerleading, choir, chorus, computers, drama, ethnic, gay, honors, international, literary magazine, musical theater, newspaper, pep band, political, professional, radio and TV, religious, social, social service, student government, and yearbook. Popular campus events include Spring Weekend, Junior/Senior Formal, and Family, Winter, and Sibling weekends.

Sports: There are 8 intercollegiate sports for men and 9 for women, and 8 intramural sports for men and 8 for women. Athletic and recreation facilities include an athletic complex, with free weights, a training facility, an indoor track, an 8-lane, 25-meter pool, fitness equipment, life cycles, 4 multipurpose courts, 6 outdoor tennis courts, 5 outdoor fields, 2 squash courts, and 2 racquetball courts.

Disabled Students: The following facilities are available: wheelchair ramps, elevators, special parking, specially equipped rest rooms, and special class scheduling.

Services: In addition to many counseling and information services, tutoring is available in most subjects. There is a reader service for the blind and remedial math and writing.

Campus Safety and Security: Campus safety and security measures include 24-hour foot and vehicle patrol, escort service, informal discussions, and pamphlets/posters/films. In addition, there are emergency telephones and lighted pathways/sidewalks.

Programs of Study: Siena confers B.A., B.S., and B.B.A. degrees. Master's degrees are also awarded. Bachelor's degrees are awarded in BIOLOGICAL SCIENCE (biology/biological science), BUSINESS (accounting, banking and finance, business economics, and marketing management), COMMUNICATIONS AND THE ARTS (classical languages, English, French, and Spanish), COMPUTER AND PHYSICAL SCIENCE (chemistry, computer science, mathematics, and physics), SOCIAL SCIENCE (American studies, economics, history, philosophy, political science/government, psychology, religion, social work, and sociology). Biology, premedical programs, and political science are the strongest academically. Accounting, marketing/management, and biology have the largest enrollments.

Required: To graduate, students must earn 120 credits, including 30 to 39 in the major, with a 2.0 GPA. The required core curriculum of 39 credits must include 2 courses each in English, history, social science, philosophy, religious studies, and mathematics/science, and 1 course in creative arts.

Special: The college offers a cooperative 4–1 business program with Clarkson University and a cooperative 2–2 program in environmental science and forestry with Syracuse University. Cross-registration with the Hudson-Mohawk Association and a Washington semester with American University are possible. Domestic and international internships, dual majors, B.A.-B.S. degrees, study abroad in 15 countries, and pass/fail options are available. Students may earn 3–2 engineering degrees with Clarkson and Catholic universities, Manhattan College, Western New England College, SUNY at Binghamton, and Rensselaer Polytechnic Institute. Siena also offers a 4–4 early assurance program with the Columbia University School of Dental and

Oral Surgery and SUNY College of Optometry, a 3–4 program with Boston University, School of Graduate Dentistry, and a 4–4 medical program with Albany Medical College. There is a freshman honors program on campus, as well as 7 national honor societies. 2 departments have honors programs.

Faculty/Classroom: 71% of faculty are male; 29%, female. All teach undergraduates. No introductory courses are taught by graduate students. The average class size in an introductory lecture is 30; in a laboratory, 20; and in a regular course offering, 22.

Admissions: 73% of the 1995–96 applicants were accepted. The SAT I scores for the 1995–96 freshman class were as follows: Verbal—65% below 500, 30% between 500 and 599, and 5% between 600 and 700; Math—32% below 500, 40% between 500 and 599, 26% between 600 and 700, and 2% above 700. The ACT scores were 24% below 21, 30% between 21 and 23, 24% between 24 and 26, 17% between 27 and 28, and 5% above 28. 38% of the current freshmen were in the top fifth of their class; 77% were in the top two fifths.

Requirements: The SAT I or ACT is required. Applicants must be graduates of an accredited secondary school or have a GED. 16 academic credits are required, including 4 years each of English and history, 3 to 4 years each of mathematics and science, and a recommended 3 years of foreign language study. All applicants must submit an essay; an interview is recommended. AP and CLEP credits are accepted. Important factors in the admissions decision are advanced placement or honor courses, recommendations by school officials, and extracurricular activities record.

Procedure: Freshmen are admitted fall and spring. Entrance exams should be taken during May of the junior year or November of the senior year. There are early decision, early admissions, and deferred admissions plans. Early decision applications should be filed by December 1; regular applications, by March 1 for fall entry, December 1 for spring entry, and January 1 for summer entry, along with an application fee of $40. Notification of early decision is sent January 15; regular decision, March 15. 50 early decision candidates were accepted for the 1995–96 class. A waiting list is an active part of the admissions procedure, with about 3% of all applicants on the list.

Transfer: 165 transfer students enrolled in 1995–96. Applicants must have a minimum 2.5 GPA. An interview is recommended. 30 credits of 120 must be completed at Siena.

Visiting: There are regularly scheduled orientations for prospective students, including an interview with an admissions counselor. There are guides for informal visits and visitors may sit in on classes and stay overnight at the school. To schedule a visit, contact the Admissions Office.

Financial Aid: In 1995–96, 82% of all freshmen and 86% of continuing students received some form of financial aid. 73% of freshmen and 72% of continuing students received need-based aid. The average freshman award was $6955. Of that total, scholarships or need-based grants averaged $7937 ($17,700 maximum); and loans averaged $2921 ($5625 maximum). 60% of undergraduate students work part-time. Average earnings from campus work for the school year are $800. The average financial indebtedness of the 1994–95 graduate was $9500. Siena is a member of CSS. The FAFSA, the college's own financial statement, and the TAP application are required. The application deadline for fall entry is February 1.

International Students: There are currently 5 international students enrolled. The school actively recruits these students. They must take the TOEFL and achieve a minimum score of 500.

Computers: The college provides computer facilities for student use. The mainframes are a VAX 6610, a VAX 6410, a Unisys V6000/75, and a Unisys system 80/20. Students obtain a student access number from the computer center to use terminals available at various locations throughout the campus. IBM-compatible and Apple Macintosh workstations are also available. All students may access the system 24 hours per day. There are no time limits and no fees.

Graduates: In 1994–95, 752 bachelor's degrees were awarded. The most popular majors among graduates were accounting (19%), marketing/management (16%), and biology (11%). Within an average freshman class, 75% graduate in 4 years, 80% in 5 years, and 80% in 6 years. 144 companies recruited on campus in 1994–95. Of the 1994 graduating class, 27% were enrolled in graduate school within 6 months of graduation and 71% had found employment.

Admissions Contact: Dean of Admissions.

SKIDMORE COLLEGE
Saratoga Springs, NY 12866-1632

D-3

(518) 581-7400, ext. 2213

Full-time: 830 men, 1270 women	Faculty: 195; IIB, +$
Part-time: 25 men and women	Ph.D.s: 95%
Graduate: 20 men and women	Student/Faculty: 11 to 1
Year: semesters, summer session	Tuition: $19,725
Application Deadline: February 1	Room & Board: $5890
Freshman Class: n/av	
SAT I or ACT: required	**VERY COMPETITIVE**

Skidmore College, established in 1903, is an independent, coeducational institution offering undergraduate programs in liberal arts and sciences, as well as business, social work, education, studio art, dance, and theater. Figures given in the above capsule are approximate. There is 1 graduate school. In addition to regional accreditation, Skidmore has baccalaureate program accreditation with CSWE and NASAD. The library contains 400,000 volumes, 245,000 microform items, and 9800 audiovisual forms, and subscribes to 1700 periodicals. Computerized library sources and services include the card catalog and database searching. Special learning facilities include a learning resource center, art gallery, radio station, TV station, electronic music studio, music and art studios, theater teaching facility, anthropology laboratory, and special biological habitats on campus. The 850-acre campus is in a small town 30 miles north of Albany. Including residence halls, there are 49 buildings on campus.

Student Life: 65% of undergraduates are from out-of-state, mostly the Northeast. Students come from 48 states, 20 foreign countries, and Canada. 61% are from public schools; 39% from private. 84% are white. 33% claim no religious affiliation; 22% Catholic; 18% Protestant; 17% Jewish. The average age of freshmen is 18; all undergraduates, 20. 9% do not continue beyond their first year; 81% remain to graduate.

Housing: 1800 students can be accommodated in college housing. College-sponsored living facilities include coed dormitories and on-campus apartments. In addition there are language houses and special interest houses. On-campus housing is guaranteed for all 4 years. 82% of students live on campus; of those, 90% remain on campus on weekends. All students may keep cars on campus.

Activities: There are no fraternities or sororities. There are 80 groups on campus, including art, chorale, chorus, computers, dance, drama, ethnic, film, gay, honors, international, jazz band, literary magazine, musical theater, newspaper, orchestra, photography, political, professional, radio and TV, religious, social, social service, student government, and yearbook. Popular campus events include Martin Luther King Week, Oktoberfest, Spring Fling, Parents Weekend, Winter Carnival, Homecoming, Women's Festival, and Senior Art Show.

Sports: There are 10 intercollegiate sports each for men and women, and 15 intramural sports for men and 13 for women. Athletic and recreation facilities include a fitness center, an indoor swimming and diving pool, 2 gymnasiums with 4 basketball courts, an indoor jogging track, a weight room, fields for baseball and other sports, dance studios, cross-country ski trails, a riding center, courts for tennis, handball, racquetball, and squash, and an outdoor facility with a synthetic surface soccer/lacrosse field, an all-weather 400-meter track, lights, and permanent stands.

Disabled Students: 75% of the campus is accessible to disabled students. The following facilities are available: wheelchair ramps, elevators, special parking, specially equipped rest rooms, and lowered drinking fountains.

Services: In addition to many counseling and information services, tutoring is available in most subjects. There is a reader service for the blind. Diagnostic services, note takers, and books on tape are also offered.

Campus Safety and Security: Campus safety and security measures include 24-hour foot and vehicle patrol, escort service, shuttle buses, and informal discussions. In addition, there are pamphlets/posters/films, emergency telephones, lighted pathways/sidewalks, and a special security alert system, rigorous fire response procedures, and a lock system on dormitory entrances after 8 P.M.

Programs of Study: Skidmore confers B.A. and B.S. degrees. Master's degrees are also awarded. Bachelor's degrees are awarded in BIOLOGICAL SCIENCE (biochemistry and biology/biological science), BUSINESS (business administration and management and business economics), COMMUNICATIONS AND THE ARTS (art history and appreciation, classics, dance, dramatic arts, English, fine arts, French, German, music, and Spanish), COMPUTER AND PHYSICAL SCIENCE (chemistry, computer science, geology, mathematics, and physics), EDUCATION (art, elementary, and physical), SOCIAL SCIENCE (American studies, anthropology, economics, history, liberal arts/general studies, philosophy, political science/government, psychology, social work, and sociology). English, business, psychology, government, and art have the largest enrollments.

Required: To graduate, students must complete 120 credits, including at least 24 of 300-level courses, with a minimum GPA of 2.0 overall and in the major. They must fulfill foundation requirements in writing and quantitative reasoning; meet a liberal studies requirement that includes 1 course each in the human experience, cultural traditions and social change, artistic forms and critical concepts, and science and human values; and complete distribution requirements in laboratory science, foreign language, non-Western culture, and creative expression in the arts.

Special: Skidmore offers cross-registration with the Hudson-Mohawk Consortium, individually designed internships, various study-abroad programs, a Washington semester in conjunction with American University, dual and student-designed majors, credit for life and experience, and pass/fail options, as well as a nondegree study program for senior citizens. There are cooperative programs in engineering with Dartmouth College and Clarkson University, in business with Clarkson and Rensselaer Polytechnic Institute, in education with Union College, and in law with the Benjamin Cardozo Law School. There is a 6-week internship period available at the end of the spring term. There are 9 national honor societies on campus, including Phi Beta Kappa.

Faculty/Classroom: 69% of faculty are male; 31%, female. 10% teach undergraduates and 90% both teach and do research. No introductory courses are taught by graduate students. The average class size in a laboratory is 16 and in a regular course offering, 19.

Admissions: The SAT I scores for a recent freshman class were as follows: Verbal—29% below 500, 46% between 500 and 599, 24% between 600 and 700, and 2% above 700; Math—10% below 500, 40% between 500 and 599, 40% between 600 and 700, and 8% above 700. 59% of recent freshmen were in the top fifth of their class; 88% were in the top two fifths.

Requirements: The SAT I or ACT is required. Skidmore recommends SAT II: Subject tests in writing, a foreign language, and 1 other subject. Applicants must be graduates of an accredited secondary school or have the GED. They must complete 16 academic units, including 4 years of English, 2 or more of laboratory science, and 3 each of mathematics, social science, and a foreign language. An essay is required and interviews are recommended. Applicants to creative arts programs may want to submit representations of their work. AP and CLEP credits are accepted. Important factors in the admissions decision are advanced placement or honor courses, recommendations by school officials, and evidence of special talent.

Procedure: Freshmen are admitted fall and spring. Entrance exams should be taken by December of the senior year. There are early decision and deferred admissions plans. Early decision applications should be filed by December 1; regular applications, by February 1 for fall entry and November 15 for spring entry, along with an application fee of $45. Notification of early decision is sent January 15; regular decision, April 1. A waiting list is an active part of the admissions procedure, with about 8% of all applicants on the list.

Transfer: 30 transfer students enrolled in 1995–96. Applicants must submit SAT I or ACT scores, a high school transcript, and official transcripts from all colleges attended. A dean's report and 2 recommendations by professors are also required. 60 credits of 120 must be completed at Skidmore.

Visiting: There are regularly scheduled orientations for prospective students, including full open-house day programs. There are guides for informal visits and visitors may sit in on classes and stay overnight at the school. To schedule a visit, contact the Admissions Office Overnight Host Coordinator at (518) 581–7400, ext 2721.

Financial Aid: In a recent year, 50% of all students received some form of financial aid. 35% of freshmen and 37% of continuing students received need-based aid. The average freshman award was $16,900. Of that total, scholarships or need-based grants averaged $13,100 ($20,500 maximum); loans averaged $2600; and work contracts averaged $1200. 47% of undergraduate students work part-time. Average earnings from campus work for the school year are $850. The average financial indebtedness of a recent graduate was $12,500. Skidmore is a member of CSS. The FAFSA and CSS Profile Application are required. The application deadline for fall entry is February 1.

International Students: In a recent year, 57 international students were enrolled. The school actively recruits these students. They must take the TOEFL and achieve a minimum score of 570. The student must also take the SAT I or the ACT.

Computers: The college provides computer facilities for student use. The mainframe is a DEC VAX 11/780. There are 200 microcomputers available in 3 major computing clusters, with networking capabilities throughout campus and through Internet and Bitnet. A computer graphics laboratory and teaching facility is available. A cluster of 9 Sun computers provides the backbone for time-shared computing, providing access to E-mail, electronic bulletin boards, and compilers. Statistical analysis software, free services, and technical support are provided. Students may connect to central computing facilities through personal computers via modem capabilities in each dormitory room. All students may access the system 24 hours per day. There are no time limits and no fees.

Graduates: In a recent year, 531 bachelor's degrees were awarded. The most popular majors among graduates were business (15%), English (14%), and government (12%). Within an average freshman class, 75% graduate in 4 years, 80% in 5 years, and 81% in 6 years. 65 companies recruited on campus in a recent year.

Admissions Contact: Mary Lou Bates, Director of Admissions.

STATE UNIVERSITY OF NEW YORK

The State University of New York, established in 1948, is one of two public university systems in New York State. Governed by a board of trustees, whose chief administrative officer is the chancellor, the university's broad mission focuses on improving the lives of New York citizens and on bolstering the state's economy through teaching, research, and public service. Its 64 campuses, located in urban and rural communities across the state, offer prospective students a variety of educational choices to meet their individual needs, including associate, baccalaureate, and doctoral degrees, as well as short-term vocational/technical courses, certificate programs, and post-doctoral studies. Because of its large community-college enrollment (more than 190,000 students annually), the university has enacted numerous programs to facilitate the transfer of students from its 2-year campuses to its senior institutions. Total enrollment is currently more than 380,000 students, taught by a full-time faculty that exceeds 15,000 members. Degrees are offered in 1587 associate, 1504 baccalaureate, 956 master's, 313 doctoral, and 16 advanced professional programs. Profiles of the 4-year institutions follow.

STATE UNIVERSITY OF NEW YORK AT ALBANY
D-3

Albany, NY 12222

Full-time: 5111 men, 4631 women	Faculty: 694; I, av$
Part-time: 609 men, 602 women	Ph.D.s: 96%
Graduate: 2069 men, 3021 women	Student/Faculty: 14 to 1
Year: semesters, summer session	Tuition: $3956 ($8856)
Application Deadline: February 15	Room & Board: $4836

(518) 442-5435; (800) 293-SUNY

Freshman Class: 14,967 applied, 9341 accepted, 1900 enrolled
SAT I Verbal/Math: 500/580   **VERY COMPETITIVE**

The State University of New York at Albany, established in 1844, is a public institution conferring undergraduate degrees in humanities and fine arts, science and mathematics, social and behavioral sciences, business, and social welfare. There are 5 undergraduate and 8 graduate schools. In addition to regional accreditation, University at Albany has baccalaureate program accreditation with AACSB and CSWE. The 2 libraries contain 1.8 million volumes, 2.7 million microform items, and 6800 audiovisual forms, and subscribe to 5500 periodicals. Computerized library sources and services include the card catalog, interlibrary loans, and database searching. Special learning facilities include a learning resource center, art gallery, radio station, and a linear accelerator, a sophisticated weather data system, a national lightning detection system, an interactive media center, and extensive art studios. The 560-acre campus is in a suburban area about 5 miles west of downtown Albany. Including residence halls, there are 90 buildings on campus.

Student Life: 97% of undergraduates are from New York. Students come from 20 states, 30 foreign countries, and Canada. 69% are white. The average age of freshmen is 18.1; all undergraduates, 21.5. 10% do not continue beyond their first year; 73% remain to graduate.

Housing: 6373 students can be accommodated in college housing. College-sponsored living facilities include single-sex and coed dormitories and on-campus apartments. In addition, there are honors houses and special interest houses. On-campus housing is guaranteed for the freshman year only, is available on a first-come, first-served basis, and is available on a lottery system for upperclassmen. Priority is given to out-of-town students. 64% of students live on campus. Alcohol is not permitted. Upperclassmen may keep cars on campus.

Activities: 22% of men and about 12% of women belong to 6 local and 23 national fraternities; 12% of women belong to 6 local and 13 national sororities. There are 190 groups on campus, including band, cheerleading, chess, chorale, computers, dance, drama, ethnic, honors, international, literary magazine, newspaper, orchestra, photography, political, professional, radio and TV, religious, social, social service, student government, and yearbook. Popular campus events include the week-long Rites of Spring and outdoor concerts.

Sports: There are 8 intercollegiate sports for men and 11 for women, and 13 intramural sports for men and 9 for women. Athletic and recreation facilities include a gymnasium with an Olympic-sized pool; an ancillary gymnasium with a quarter-mile track; football, softball, soccer, and practice fields; and a 5000-seat recreation and convocation center.

Disabled Students: The entire campus is accessible to persons with physical disabilities. The following facilities are available: wheelchair ramps, elevators, special parking, specially equipped rest rooms, lowered drinking fountains, and lowered telephones.

Services: In addition to many counseling and information services, tutoring is available in every subject. There is also remedial math, reading, and writing.

Campus Safety and Security: Campus safety and security measures include 24-hour foot and vehicle patrol, self-defense education, escort service, and shuttle buses. In addition, there are pamphlets/posters/films, emergency telephones, and lighted pathways/sidewalks.

Programs of Study: University at Albany confers B.A. and B.S. degrees. Master's and doctoral degrees are also awarded. Bachelor's degrees are awarded in BIOLOGICAL SCIENCE (biochemistry, biology/biological science, and molecular biology), BUSINESS (accounting and business administration and management), COMMUNICATIONS AND THE ARTS (art history and appreciation, Chinese, communications, English, fine arts, French, German, Hebrew, Italian, Latin, linguistics, music, Portuguese, Russian, and Spanish), COMPUTER AND PHYSICAL SCIENCE (applied mathematics, chemistry, computer science, geology, information sciences and systems, mathematics, and physics), EDUCATION (foreign languages, middle school, music, science, secondary, special, and teaching English as a second/foreign language (TESOL/TEFOL)), HEALTH PROFESSIONS (medical laboratory technology, predentistry, and premedicine), SOCIAL SCIENCE (African American studies, African studies, anthropology, Asian/Oriental studies, Caribbean studies, classical/ancient civilization, criminal justice, Eastern European studies, economics, geography, history, Latin American studies, medieval studies, philosophy, political science/government, prelaw, psychology, religion, Russian and Slavic studies, social work, sociology, and women's studies). Business and accounting, political science, and criminal justice are the strongest academically. Psychology, English, and political science have the largest enrollments.

Required: To graduate, students must complete a total of 120 credits with a 2.0 GPA, including 30 to 36 credits required in the major for a B.A. degree and 30 to 42 credits for a B.S. degree. B.A. degree candidates must complete 90 credits in liberal arts courses and B.S. candidates must complete 60. All students must complete a writing requirement and a general education core consisting of a minimum of 24 credits in natural sciences, social sciences, humanities, and the arts, 3 credits in an approved course in cultural and historical perspectives, and 3 credits of an approved course in human diversity.

Special: Cross-registration is available with Rensselaer Polytechnic Institute, Albany Law School, and Union, Siena, and Russell Sage colleges. Internships may be arranged with state government agencies and private organizations. Study abroad in many countries, work-study programs, B.A.-B.S. degrees in biology, mathematics, and economics, and 3-2 engineering degrees with Rensselaer Polytechnic Institute and Clarkson University are offered. Dual and student-designed majors, nondegree study, and pass/fail grading options are available. There is a freshman honors program on campus, as well as 14 national honor societies, including Phi Beta Kappa. 20 departments have honors programs.

Faculty/Classroom: 76% of faculty are male; 24%, female. All teach undergraduates; 75% also do research. Graduate students teach 10% of introductory courses. The average class size in an introductory lecture is 34; in a laboratory, 14; and in a regular course offering, 22.

Admissions: 62% of the 1995–96 applicants were accepted. The SAT I scores for the 1995–96 freshman class were as follows: Verbal—50% below 500, 39% between 500 and 599, 10% between 600 and 700, and 1% above 700; Math—14% below 500, 42% between 500 and 599, 37% between 600 and 700, and 7% above 700. 43% of the current freshmen were in the top fifth of their class; 85% were in the top two fifths. 3 freshmen graduated first in their class.

Requirements: The SAT I or ACT is required. Applicants must be graduates of an accredited secondary school or have a GED. Eighteen academic credits are required, including 2 to 3 units of mathematics and 2 units of laboratory sciences. Foreign language study is also recommended. AP credits are accepted. Important factors in the admissions decision are advanced placement or honor courses, evidence of special talent, and recommendations by school officials.

Procedure: Freshmen are admitted to all sessions. Entrance exams should be taken by November of the senior year. There are early decision, early admissions, and deferred admissions plans. Early decision applications should be filed by April 15; regular applications, by February 15 for fall entry, November 15 for spring entry, and February 15 for summer entry, along with an application fee of $25. Notification of early decision is sent December 15; regular decision, on a rolling basis. 65 early decision candidates were accepted for the 1995–96 class. A waiting list is an active part of the admissions procedure, with about 3% of all applicants on the list.

Transfer: Applicants must have a minimum GPA of C. Students will be admitted to programs according to availability of space and degree of competitiveness. SAT I or ACT requirements will be determined upon application. 30 credits of 120 must be completed at University at Albany.

Visiting: There are regularly scheduled orientations for prospective students, including a campus tour coupled with a group information session. There are guides for informal visits and visitors may sit in on classes. To schedule a visit, contact the Undergraduate Admissions Office.

Financial Aid: In 1995–96, 68% of all freshmen and 72% of continuing students received some form of financial aid. The average freshman award was $6018. Of that total, scholarships or need-based grants averaged $1994; and loans averaged $3905. 16% of undergraduate students work part-time. Average earnings from campus work for the school year are $1400. University at Albany is a member of CSS. The FAFSA is required. The application deadline for fall entry is March 15.

International Students: There are currently 384 international students enrolled. The school actively recruits these students. They must take the TOEFL and achieve a minimum score of 550.

Computers: The college provides computer facilities for student use. The mainframes are an IBM 3081 and VAX and UNIX systems. The computing services center networks provide electronic mail facilities and contact with computers throughout the world. Computer access rooms, terminals in residence halls, and phone hookups provide 24-hour access to mainframe computing facilities. All students may access the system. There are no time limits and no fees.

Graduates: The most popular majors among graduates were English (12%), psychology (12%), and political science (9%). Within an average freshman class, 1% graduate in 3 years, 60% in 4 years, 71% in 5 years, and 73% in 6 years. 100 companies recruited on campus in 1994–95. Of the 1994 graduating class, 48% were enrolled in graduate school within 6 months of graduation and 68% had found employment.

Admissions Contact: Dr. Micheleen Tredwell, Director of Admissions. E-mail: ugadmit@safnet.albany.edu.

STATE UNIVERSITY OF NEW YORK AT BINGHAMTON   C-4
Binghamton, NY 13902–6000

(607) 777-2171
FAX: (607) 777-6515

Full-time: 4100 men, 4706 women	Faculty: 448; I, -$
Part-time: 205 men, 262 women	Ph.Ds: 89%
Graduate: 1383 men, 1296 women	Student/Faculty: 20 to 1
Year: semesters, summer session	Tuition: $3910 ($8810)
Application Deadline: February 15	Room & Board: $4654
Freshman Class: 16,348 applied, 6507 accepted, 1790 enrolled	
SAT I Verbal/Math: 530/630	ACT: 26 HIGHLY COMPETITIVE

The State University of New York at Binghamton, founded in 1946, is part of the State University of New York System. The public coeducational institution offers programs through the Harpur College of Arts and Sciences and the schools of education and human development, nursing, management, and engineering and applied science. There are 5 undergraduate and 5 graduate schools. In addition to regional accreditation, Binghamton University has baccalaureate program accreditation with AACSB, ABET, CSAB, NASM, and NLN. The 6 libraries contain 1,548,040 volumes, 1,476,548 microform items, and 113,768 audiovisual forms, and subscribe to 9248 periodicals. Computerized library sources and services include the card catalog, interlibrary loans, and database searching. Special learning facilities include a learning resource center, art gallery, radio station, TV station, nature preserve, and 4-climate greenhouse. The 606-acre campus is in a suburban area 1 mile west of Binghamton. Including residence halls, there are 62 buildings on campus.

Student Life: 93% of undergraduates are from New York. Students come from 33 states, 48 foreign countries, and Canada. 87% are from public schools; 13% from private. 75% are white; 13% Asian American. 36% are Catholic; 28% Jewish; 21% Protestant. The average age of freshmen is 18; all undergraduates, 21. 7% do not continue beyond their first year; 80% remain to graduate.

Housing: 5087 students can be accommodated in college housing. College-sponsored living facilities include coed dormitories, on-campus apartments, off-campus apartments, and married-student housing. In addition there are language houses and special interest houses. On-campus housing is guaranteed for all 4 years. 57% of students live on campus; of those, 95% remain on campus on weekends. Upperclassmen may keep cars on campus.

Activities: 15% of men belong to 4 local and 17 national fraternities; 15% of women belong to 3 local and 11 national sororities. There are more than 150 groups on campus, including art, band, cheerleading, chess, choir, chorale, chorus, computers, dance, drama, ethnic, film, gay, honors, international, jazz band, literary magazine, musical thea-

ter, newspaper, orchestra, pep band, photography, political, professional, radio and TV, religious, social, social service, student government, symphony, and yearbook. Popular campus events include Martin Luther King, Jr. Day, Spring Carnival, Fall Fest, theater productions, and concerts.

Sports: There are 10 intercollegiate sports for men and 9 for women, and 20 intramural sports for men and 18 for women. Athletic and recreation facilities include 2 gymnasiums with swimming pools, an indoor track, dance and karate studios, basketball, volleyball, squash, racquetball, and tennis courts, a weight room, batting and driving cages, a fitness trail, a cross-country course, a fitness center, a 400-meter track and soccer complex, plus many playing fields. The larger gymnasium seats 2600.

Disabled Students: 90% of the campus is accessible to disabled students. The following facilities are available: wheelchair ramps, elevators, special parking, specially equipped rest rooms, special class scheduling, lowered drinking fountains, and lowered telephones.

Services: In addition to many counseling and information services, tutoring is available in most subjects. There is a reader service for the blind, peer tutoring, and some computer-assisted instruction, particularly in languages.

Campus Safety and Security: Campus safety and security measures include 24-hour foot and vehicle patrol, self-defense education, escort service, and shuttle buses. In addition, there are informal discussions, pamphlets/posters/films, emergency telephones, lighted pathways/sidewalks, public safety officers, monitored entrance to campus with proper identification between midnight and 6 A.M., and keycard entry to residence halls.

Programs of Study: Binghamton University confers B.A., B.S., B.F.A., and B.Mus. degrees. Master's and doctoral degrees are also awarded. Bachelor's degrees are awarded in BIOLOGICAL SCIENCE (biochemistry and biology/biological science), BUSINESS (accounting and business administration and management), COMMUNICATIONS AND THE ARTS (Arabic, art, art history and appreciation, classics, comparative literature, dramatic arts, English, film arts, fine arts, French, German, Hebrew, Italian, linguistics, music, Spanish, and studio art), COMPUTER AND PHYSICAL SCIENCE (chemistry, computer science, geology, geophysics and seismology, mathematics, and physics), ENGINEERING AND ENVIRONMENTAL DESIGN (electrical/electronics engineering and mechanical engineering), HEALTH PROFESSIONS (nursing), SOCIAL SCIENCE (African American studies, anthropology, Caribbean studies, classical/ancient civilization, economics, geography, history, human ecology, Judaic studies, Latin American studies, medieval studies, philosophy, political science/government, psychobiology, psychology, social science, and sociology). Accounting, anthropology, and applied social science are the strongest academically. Psychology, English, and management have the largest enrollments.

Required: In order to graduate, all students must complete 124 to 132 credit hours, with 36 to 72 in the major, and a minimum GPA of 2.0. General education requirements over the first 2 years include courses in language and communication, global vision, science and mathematics, aesthetic perspective, physical activity/wellness, and identity. Other requirements vary by school.

Special: The university offers cross-registration with Broome Community and Empire State colleges, internships with nonprofit agencies in Albany and in Washington, D.C. through the political science department, study abroad in 100 countries, on- and off-campus work-study programs, B.A.-B.S. degrees in 28 departments in arts and sciences and in the professional schools, dual and interdisciplinary majors such as philosophy, politics, and law, student-designed majors, pass/fail options, and independent study. The 3–2 engineering degree is possible with SUNY at Buffalo, SUNY at Stony Brook, Columbia University, Rochester Institute of Technology, University of Rochester, and Clarkson University. There is a freshman honors program in the School of Management, as well as 16 national honor societies, including Phi Beta Kappa. 32 departments have honors programs.

Faculty/Classroom: 75% of faculty are male; 25%, female. All teach undergraduates; 80% do research. Graduate students teach 27% of introductory courses. The average class size in an introductory lecture is 49; in a laboratory, 30; and in a regular course offering, 24.

Admissions: 40% of the 1995–96 applicants were accepted. The SAT I scores for the 1995–96 freshman class were as follows: Verbal—35% below 500, 46% between 500 and 599, 17% between 600 and 700, and 2% above 700; Math—6% below 500, 30% between 500 and 599, 49% between 600 and 700, and 15% above 700. The ACT scores were 10% between 18 and 21, 33% between 22 and 25, 42% between 26 and 29, and 15% above 30. 89% of the current freshmen were in the top fifth of their class; 99% were in the top two fifths. 12 freshmen graduated first in their class.

Requirements: The SAT I or ACT is required. Applicants must be graduates of an accredited secondary school, or have a GED certificate, and complete 16 academic credits. These include 4 units of English, 2.5 of mathematics, 2 each of science and social studies, and 3 units of 1 foreign language or 2 units each of 2 foreign languages.

Students may submit slides of artwork, request an audition for music, prepare a videotape for dance or theater, or share athletic achievements. An essay is required. AP and CLEP credits are accepted. Important factors in the admissions decision are advanced placement or honor courses, extracurricular activities record, and evidence of special talent.

Procedure: Freshmen are admitted fall and spring. Entrance exams should be taken in the spring of the junior year or the fall of the senior year. There are early decision, early admissions, and deferred admissions plans. Early decision applications should be filed by November 1; regular applications, by February 15 for fall entry and November 15 for spring entry, along with an application fee of $30. Notification of early decision is sent December 31; regular decision, March 15. 257 early decision candidates were accepted for the 1995–96 class. A waiting list is an active part of the admissions procedure.

Transfer: 771 transfer students enrolled in 1995–96. Applicants must submit college transcripts; students who wish to transfer after their first year of college must also submit their high school transcripts. An associate degree or equivalent is required for some programs. The SAT I and an interview are recommended, but not required. 30 credits of 124 to 132 must be completed at Binghamton University.

Visiting: There are regularly scheduled orientations for prospective students. An information session and a tour of campus may be scheduled a week in advance of a visit. Visitors may sit in on classes. To schedule a visit, contact the Office of Undergraduate Admissions.

Financial Aid: In 1995–96, 92% of all freshmen and 56% of continuing students received some form of financial aid. 53% of freshmen and 48% of continuing students received need-based aid. The average freshman award was $4860. Of that total, scholarships or need-based grants averaged $3802 ($7105 maximum); loans averaged $2010 ($10,700 maximum); and work contracts averaged $900 ($1000 maximum). 10% of undergraduate students work part-time. Average earnings from campus work for the school year are $850. The FAFSA is required. The application deadline for fall entry is March 1.

International Students: There are currently 424 international students enrolled. The school actively recruits these students. The TOEFL (minimum score 550) replaces the SAT I or ACT for non-native speakers of English.

Computers: The college provides computer facilities for student use. The mainframes are 2 IBM 9000 series, 1 DEC VAX 6440, and a cluster of 5 Sun Servers. Each student is given a computer account. Terminals and microcomputers are available in libraries, some academic areas, and some residential halls. All students may access the system 24 hours per day. Time limits vary by course. There are no fees.

Graduates: In 1994–95, 2251 bachelor's degrees were awarded. The most popular majors among graduates were management/accounting (14%), English (10%), and psychology (7%). Within an average freshman class, 67% graduate in 4 years and 80% in 5 years. More than 175 companies recruited on campus in 1994–95.

Admissions Contact: Geoffrey D. Gould, Director of Undergraduate Admissions. A campus video is available.

STATE UNIVERSITY OF NEW YORK AT BUFFALO
A-3

Buffalo, NY 14260

(716) 645–6900; FAX: (716) 645–6498

Full-time: 7588 men, 5938 women	Faculty: 1057; IIA, av$
Part-time: 1276 men, 1348 women	Ph.D.s: 97%
Graduate: 4298 men, 4045 women	Student/Faculty: 13 to 1
Year: semesters, summer session	Tuition: $4060 ($8960)
Application Deadline: see profile	Room & Board: $5256
Freshman Class: 15,461 applied, 10,624 accepted, 2685 enrolled	
SAT I or ACT: required	VERY COMPETITIVE

The State University of New York at Buffalo, established in 1846, is a public institution offering undergraduate degrees in liberal arts and sciences, architecture and planning, engineering, health-related professions, medicine, and management. There are 11 undergraduate and 16 graduate schools. In addition to regional accreditation, UB has baccalaureate program accreditation with AACSB, ABET, ACPE, ADA, APTA, ASLA, CAHEA, CSWE, NAAB, NASAD, NASM, and NLN. The 7 libraries contain 2,937,786 volumes, 4,565,039 microform items, and 119,000 audiovisual forms, and subscribe to 21,818 periodicals. Computerized library sources and services include the card catalog, interlibrary loans, and database searching. Special learning facilities include a learning resource center, art gallery, radio station, anthropology research museum, observatory, concert hall, theater, nature preserve, and nuclear reactor. The 1350-acre campus is in a suburban area 3 miles north of Buffalo. Including residence halls, there are 153 buildings on campus.

Student Life: 96% of undergraduates are from New York. Students come from 34 states, 61 foreign countries, and Canada. 75% are white; 12% Asian American. The average age of freshmen is 18; all

undergraduates, 22. 10% do not continue beyond their first year; 58% remain to graduate.

Housing: 5400 students can be accommodated in college housing. College-sponsored living facilities include coed dormitories. In addition there are honors houses, special interest houses, and freshman-only and transfer-only residence halls. On-campus housing is guaranteed for all 4 years. All students may keep cars on campus.

Activities: Less than 1% of all men belong to 4 local and 11 national fraternities; less than 1% of all women belong to 6 local and 7 national sororities. There are 428 groups on campus, including art, band, cheerleading, chess, choir, chorale, chorus, computers, dance, drama, ethnic, film, gay, honors, international, jazz band, literary magazine, musical theater, newspaper, opera, orchestra, pep band, photography, political, professional, radio and TV, religious, social, social service, student government, symphony, and yearbook. Popular campus events include International Fiesta, Senior Celebration, January Jumpstart, Festival of Traditions, and Midnight Madness.

Sports: There are 9 intercollegiate sports for men and 8 for women, and 16 intramural sports for men and 16 for women. Athletic and recreation facilities include racquetball, squash, tennis, basketball, volleyball, badminton, and handball courts; baseball, soccer, hockey, and multipurpose fields; a football, track, and field stadium; an indoor jogging track; an Olympic-size pool and diving well; a triple gymnasium; weight-training and wrestling rooms; a gymnastics arena; and dance studios.

Disabled Students: 95% of the campus is accessible to disabled students. The following facilities are available: wheelchair ramps, elevators, special parking, specially equipped rest rooms, lowered drinking fountains, and lowered telephones. Additional services include pool accessibility, wheelchair vans for transport, and specially equipped rooms in residence halls.

Services: In addition to many counseling and information services, tutoring is available in most subjects. There is also a reader service for the blind, and remedial math, reading, and writing.

Campus Safety and Security: Campus safety and security measures include 24-hour foot and vehicle patrol, self-defense education, escort service, and shuttle buses. There are informal discussions, pamphlets/posters/films, emergency telephones, and lighted pathways/sidewalks.

Programs of Study: UB confers B.A., B.S., B.F.A., B.P.S., B.S.Pharm., and Mus.B. degrees. Master's and doctoral degrees are also awarded. Bachelor's degrees are awarded in BIOLOGICAL SCIENCE (biochemistry, biology/biological science, and biophysics), BUSINESS (accounting and business administration and management), COMMUNICATIONS AND THE ARTS (art history and appreciation, communications, dramatic arts, English, fine arts, French, German, Italian, linguistics, media arts, music, music performance, Spanish, and studio art), COMPUTER AND PHYSICAL SCIENCE (chemistry, computer science, geology, mathematics, physics, and statistics), EDUCATION (foreign languages, music, and science), ENGINEERING AND ENVIRONMENTAL DESIGN (aeronautical engineering, architectural engineering, chemical engineering, civil engineering, electrical/electronics engineering, engineering physics, environmental design, industrial engineering, and mechanical engineering), HEALTH PROFESSIONS (medical laboratory technology, nuclear medical technology, nursing, occupational therapy, pharmacy, physical therapy, and speech pathology/audiology), SOCIAL SCIENCE (African American studies, anthropology, community services, economics, geography, history, philosophy, physical fitness/movement, political science/government, psychology, social science, sociology, and women's studies). Business administration, engineering, and psychology have the largest enrollments.

Required: In order to graduate, students must complete 120 semester hours with a minimum GPA of 2.0. General education requirements include writing and library skills, mathematics or computer science, and courses in world civilization, American pluralism, scientific literacy, and intermediate language proficiency.

Special: Students may cross-register with the Western New York Consortium. Internships are available, and students may study abroad in 13 countries. UB offers a Washington semester; B.A.-B.S. degrees; dual, student-designed, and interdisciplinary majors, including biochemical pharmacology and medicinal chemistry; nondegree study; and credit for military experience. A 3–2 engineering degree can be pursued. Students may choose a successful/unsuccessful (S/U) grading option for selected courses. There is an early assurance of admission program to medical school for students who have completed 3 semesters with a GPA of 3.5. There is a freshman honors program on campus, as well as 17 national honor societies, including Phi Beta Kappa.

Faculty/Classroom: 71% of faculty are male; 29%, female. All teach undergraduates and 73% both teach and do research. The average class size in a laboratory is 15 and in a regular course offering, 22.

Admissions: 69% of the 1995–96 applicants were accepted. SAT I scores for the 1995–96 freshman class were as follows: Verbal—59% below 500, 31% between 500 and 599, 9% between 600 and 700, and 1% above 700; Math—16% below 500, 39% between 500 and 599, 36% between 600 and 700, and 9% above 700. 51% of the current freshmen were in the top fifth of their class; 91% were in the top two fifths. There were 14 National Merit finalists.

Requirements: The SAT I or ACT is required. Applicants must be graduates of an accredited secondary school or have a GED. Art applicants must submit a portfolio; music applicants must audition. Applications may be submitted on disk and forwarded to the Application Processing Center by calling (800) 342-3811. AP and CLEP credits are accepted. Important factors in the admissions decision are advanced placement or honor courses, recommendations by school officials, and evidence of special talent.

Procedure: Freshmen are admitted fall and spring. Entrance exams should be taken during the spring of the junior year or the fall of the senior year. There are early decision and early admissions plans. Early decision applications should be filed by November 1, and regular decision applications should be filed as early as possible the preceding fall, along with an application fee of $30. Notification of early decision is sent December 15; regular decision, on a rolling basis beginning late December.

Transfer: 1656 transfer students enrolled in 1995–96. Applicants must have a minimum GPA of 2.0 with 24 semester hours completed at time of application. Students with fewer than 24 semester hours will be evaluated according to both college and high school work, and SAT I or ACT scores. 32 credits of 120 must be completed at UB.

Visiting: There are regularly scheduled orientations for prospective students, consisting of information sessions and tours. Visitors may sit in on classes. To schedule a visit, contact the Office of Admissions.

Financial Aid: In 1995–96, 56% of all freshmen and 49% of continuing students received some form of financial aid. 46% of freshmen and 42% of continuing students received need-based aid. The average freshman award was $3091. Of that total, scholarships or need-based grants averaged $1357 ($4998 maximum); and loans averaged $2625 (maximum). Average earnings from campus work for the school year are $1000. The average financial indebtedness of the 1994–95 graduate was $12,000. The FAFSA is required. The application deadline for fall entry is March 1.

International Students: There are currently 1110 international students enrolled. They must score 550 on the TOEFL and also take SAT I or the ACT.

Computers: The college provides computer facilities for student use. The mainframes are an IBM 3090/300J, a DEC 7100, and a DEC 6520. Students have access through 300 public terminals and 450 microcomputers and workstations. Dial-up access is also available. Numerous CD-ROMs are available at individual libraries, including student access to the World Wide Web. All students may access the system anytime. There are no time limits. The fees are $120.

Graduates: In 1994–95, 3079 bachelor's degrees were awarded. The most popular majors among graduates were business administration (14%), psychology (10%), and social science (9%). Within an average freshman class, 28% graduate in 4 years, 54% in 5 years, and 58% in 6 years. 442 companies recruited on campus in 1994–95. Of the 1994 graduating class, 30% were enrolled in graduate school within 6 months of graduation and 63% had found employment.

Admissions Contact: Kevin Durkin, Director of Admissions. E-mail: ub-admissions@acsu.buffalo.edu.

STATE UNIVERSITY OF NEW YORK AT STONY BROOK   E-5

Stony Brook, NY 11794	(516) 632-6868; FAX: (516) 632-9027
Full-time: 4983 men, 5096 women	Faculty: 1295; I, av$
Part-time: 615 men, 792 women	Ph.D.s: 95%
Graduate: 2833 men, 3339 women	Student/Faculty: 8 to 1
Year: semesters, summer session	Tuition: $3759 ($8659)
Application Deadline: July 10	Room & Board: $5166
Freshman Class: 13,741 applied, 7391 accepted, 1735 enrolled	
SAT I Verbal/Math: 465/557	**VERY COMPETITIVE**

The State University of New York at Stony Brook, founded in 1957, offers undergraduate and graduate degrees in arts and sciences, engineering and applied sciences, management and policy, nursing, health technology and management, and social welfare. There are 6 undergraduate and 9 graduate schools. In addition to regional accreditation, Stony Brook has baccalaureate program accreditation with ABET, APTA, CAHEA, CSWE, and NLN. The 7 libraries contain 1,891,079 volumes, 3,296,892 microform items, and 29,846 audiovisual forms, and subscribe to 14,024 periodicals. Computerized library sources and services include the card catalog, interlibrary loans, and database searching. Special learning facilities include a learning resource center, art gallery, radio station, the Museum of Long Island Natural Sciences, and the Fine Arts Center, which includes a 1100-seat main theater, a 400-seat recital hall, and 3 experimental theaters. The 1100-acre campus is in a suburban area on Long Island, 60 miles from New York City. Including residence halls, there are 113 buildings on campus.

Student Life: 96% of undergraduates are from New York. Students come from 30 states, 90 foreign countries, and Canada. 85% are from public schools; 15% from private. 49% are white; 17% Asian American; 10% African American. 41% are Catholic; 19% Protestant; 18% claim no religious affiliation; 15% Buddhist, Islamic, Mormon, and Eastern Orthodox. The average age of freshmen is 18; all undergraduates, 21. 17% do not continue beyond their first year; 56% remain to graduate.

Housing: 7430 students can be accommodated in college housing. College-sponsored living facilities include coed dormitories, on-campus apartments, and married-student housing. In addition, there are honors houses, special interest houses, and 6 living/learning centers that integrate academic experience with living environments. On-campus housing is guaranteed for all 4 years. 53% of students commute. Alcohol is not permitted. Upperclassmen may keep cars on campus.

Activities: There are 4 local and 9 national fraternities and 3 local and 8 national sororities. There are 140 groups on campus, including band, cheerleading, choir, chorale, dance, drama, ethnic, film, gay, honors, international, literary magazine, musical theater, newspaper, orchestra, photography, political, professional, radio and TV, religious, social, student government, and yearbook. Popular campus events include Fall Fest, Homecoming Weekend, Opening Week Activities, and Caribbean Weekend.

Sports: There are 11 intercollegiate sports for men and 9 for women, and 50 intramural sports for men and 50 for women. Athletic and recreation facilities include a gymnasium complex housing a swimming pool, 4 squash and 4 racquetball courts, a dance studio, and exercise and Universal gym rooms. There are also 18 tennis courts, a 400-meter track, 2 sand volleyball courts, 2 outdoor basketball courts, and separate fields for baseball, soccer, football, lacrosse, and intramural football. An additional facility contains a 5000-seat arena, an indoor track, and a squash court. The stadium seats 3000, and the indoor gymnasium seats 1900.

Disabled Students: 75% of the campus is accessible to disabled students. The following facilities are available: wheelchair ramps, elevators, special parking, specially equipped rest rooms, special class scheduling, lowered drinking fountains, lowered telephones, automatic door openers, and specially equipped living accommodations.

Services: There is a reader service for the blind and remedial math and writing.

Campus Safety and Security: Campus safety and security measures include 24-hour foot and vehicle patrol, self-defense education, escort service, and shuttle buses. In addition, there are informal discussions, pamphlets/posters/films, emergency telephones, lighted pathways/sidewalks, and a campus Crime Stoppers program.

Programs of Study: Stony Brook confers B.A., B.S., and B.E. degrees. Master's and doctoral degrees are also awarded. Bachelor's degrees are awarded in BIOLOGICAL SCIENCE (biochemistry and biology/biological science), BUSINESS (business administration and management), COMMUNICATIONS AND THE ARTS (art history and appreciation, comparative literature, English, French, German, Italian, linguistics, music, performing arts, Russian, Spanish, and studio art), COMPUTER AND PHYSICAL SCIENCE (applied mathematics, astronomy, atmospheric sciences and meteorology, chemistry, computer science, earth science, geology, information sciences and systems, mathematics, physics, and planetary and space science), ENGINEERING AND ENVIRONMENTAL DESIGN (chemical engineering, electrical/electronics engineering, engineering and applied science, and mechanical engineering), HEALTH PROFESSIONS (cytotechnology, medical technology, nursing, physical therapy, physician's assistant, and respiratory therapy), SOCIAL SCIENCE (African studies, anthropology, economics, history, humanities, interdisciplinary studies, philosophy, political science/government, psychology, religion, social science, social work, and sociology). Applied mathematics and statistics, biochemistry, and biology are the strongest academically. Psychology, biology, and social sciences have the largest enrollments.

Required: To graduate, students must have a minimum 2.0 GPA. B.A. and B.S. degree candidates need a total of 120 credit hours, B.E. degree candidates, 128. The required number of hours in the major varies. At least 39 credits must be earned in upper-division courses. Students must take 13 courses to satisfy the 11 general education requirements. These cover writing and quantitative reasoning skills, literary and philosophic analysis, exposure to the arts, disciplinary diversity, the interrelationship of science and society, and 3 culminating multicultural requirements. Arts and sciences majors must fulfill a foreign language requirement, unless they completed the requirement through advanced high-school study. Other requirements vary by school.

Special: Cross-registration may be arranged through the Long Island Regional Advisory Council for Higher Education. The college offers a Washington semester and internships with a variety of government, legal, and social agencies, with hospitals and clinics, and in business and industry. Study abroad in 7 countries, B.A.-B.S. degrees in chemistry, earth and space science, and psychology, and pass/fail options are available. The Federated Learning Communities enables students to concentrate on a major issue each year, and the URECA Program allows undergraduates to work with faculty on research and creative projects. An accelerated degree program in nursing, dual majors, student-designed majors, and a national student exchange program are offered. There is a freshman honors program on campus, as well as 4 national honor societies, including Phi Beta Kappa. 22 departments have honors programs.

Faculty/Classroom: 72% of faculty are male; 28%, female. 80% teach undergraduates, 90% do research, and 70% do both. Graduate students teach 37% of introductory courses. The average class size in an introductory lecture is 84; in a laboratory, 25; and in a regular course offering, 38.

Admissions: 54% of the 1995–96 applicants were accepted. The SAT I scores for the 1995–96 freshman class were as follows: Verbal—66% below 500, 28% between 500 and 599, and 6% between 600 and 700; Math—27% below 500, 38% between 500 and 599, 29% between 600 and 700, and 6% above 700. 56% of the current freshmen were in the top fifth of their class; 89% were in the top two fifths.

Requirements: The SAT I is required. A minimum grade average of 85% is required. Applicants must be graduates of an accredited secondary school or have a GED certificate. 16 or 17 academic credits are required, including 4 years of English, 3 or 4 years of mathematics, 3 years each of science and social studies, and 2 years of a foreign language. SAT II: Subject tests, an essay, and an interview are recommended. Stony Brook participates in the SUNY system common application form, available on diskette and through ExPAN. AP and CLEP credits are accepted. Important factors in the admissions decision are advanced placement or honor courses, extracurricular activities record, and evidence of special talent.

Procedure: Freshmen are admitted to all sessions. Entrance exams should be taken in the junior year of high school or fall of their senior year. There are early admissions and deferred admissions plans. Applications should be filed by July 10 for fall entry and December 20 for spring entry, along with an application fee of $30. Notification is sent on a rolling basis beginning January 15.

Transfer: 1374 transfer students enrolled in 1995–96. Transfer applicants must have a minimum 2.5 GPA. An associate degree and an interview are recommended. Other requirements vary by program. After the fifty-seventh credit, at least 36 credits must be earned at Stony Brook.

Visiting: There are regularly scheduled orientations for prospective students, consisting of 1-, 2-, or 3-day programs during which students may confer with faculty, register for classes, and take placement exams for English and mathematics. There are guides for informal visits and visitors may sit in on classes and stay overnight at the school. To schedule a visit, contact the Admissions Office.

Financial Aid: In 1995–96, 70% of all students received some form of financial aid. 53% of freshmen received need-based aid. The average freshman award was $5500. Of that total, scholarships or need-based grants averaged $2000 ($3000 maximum); loans averaged $3000 ($4000 maximum); and work contracts averaged $1200. 10% of undergraduate students work part-time. Average earnings from campus work for the school year are $1350. Stony Brook is a member of CSS. The FAFSA financial statement is required. The application deadline for fall entry is March 1.

International Students: There are currently 1148 international students enrolled. They must take the TOEFL and achieve a minimum score of 550.

Computers: The college provides computer facilities for student use. The mainframes are an IBM 3090 180E and a DEC ALPHA 2100/200. There are IBM and Apple microcomputers throughout the campus. There are also large HP UNIX and Sun SPARC workstation networks for student use. All students may access the system 24 hours per day. There are no time limits and no fees.

Graduates: In 1994–95, 2338 bachelor's degrees were awarded. The most popular majors among graduates were psychology (16%), social sciences (8%), and biology (6%). Within an average freshman class, 56% graduate in 6 years. Of the 1994 graduating class, 47% were enrolled in graduate school within 6 months of graduation and 22% had found employment.

Admissions Contact: Gigi Lamens, Dean of Admissions and Enrollment Services. E-mail: admiss@mail.vpsa.sunysb.edu. A campus video is available.

STATE UNIVERSITY OF NEW YORK COLLEGE OF ENVIRONMENTAL SCIENCE AND FORESTRY
C-3

Syracuse, NY 13210-2779

(315) 470-6600
(800) 7777-ESF; FAX: (315) 470-6933

Full-time: 719 men, 356 women	Faculty: 106; IIA, +$
Part-time: 52 men, 34 women	Ph.D.s: 90%
Graduate: 381 men, 204 women	Student/Faculty: 10 to 1
Year: semesters	Tuition: $3687 ($8587)
Application Deadline: open	Room & Board: $6780
Freshman Class: 820 applied, 135 accepted, 76 enrolled	
SAT I Verbal/Math: 523/602	HIGHLY COMPETITIVE +

The College of Environmental Science and Forestry, founded in 1911 and located adjacent to the campus of Syracuse University, is one of the colleges of the State University of New York. The public coeducational institution specializes in undergraduate and graduate degrees in agricultural, biological, environmental, health, and physical sciences, landscape architecture, and engineering. Students have access to the academic, cultural, and social life at Syracuse University. There is one graduate school. In addition to regional accreditation, ESF has baccalaureate program accreditation with ABET, ASLA, and SAF. The library contains 94,000 volumes. Computerized library sources and services include the card catalog, interlibrary loans, and database searching. Special learning facilities include a learning resource center, art gallery, radio station, and TV station. The 12-acre campus is in an urban area in Syracuse. Including residence halls, there are 7 buildings on campus.

Student Life: 90% of undergraduates are from New York. Students come from 11 states and 3 foreign countries. 89% are from public schools; 11% from private. 89% are white. The average age of freshmen is 18; all undergraduates, 22. 3% do not continue beyond their first year; 90% remain to graduate.

Housing: 9000 students can be accommodated in college housing. College-sponsored living facilities include single-sex and coed dormitories, on-campus apartments, married-student housing, fraternity houses, and sorority houses. In addition there are special interest houses and substance-free floors, quiet lifestyle floors, and a global living center. On-campus housing is guaranteed for the freshman year only, is available on a first-come, first-served basis, and is available on a lottery system for upperclassmen. 60% of students live on campus; of those, 90% remain on campus on weekends. Alcohol is not permitted. Upperclassmen may keep cars on campus.

Activities: 5% of men belong to 1 local fraternity and 27 national fraternities; 5% of women belong to 1 local sorority and 21 national sororities. There are many groups and organizations on campus, including art, band, cheerleading, choir, chorale, chorus, computers, dance, drama, drum and bugle corps, ethnic, film, honors, international, jazz band, marching band, musical theater, newspaper, orchestra, pep band, photography, professional, radio and TV, religious, student government, symphony, and yearbook. Popular campus events include Charter Day (Homecoming), Activities Fair, December Soiree, Winter Weekend, Earth Day, and Awards Banquet.

Sports: There are 21 intercollegiate sports for men and 21 for women, and 30 intramural sports for men and 30 for women. Athletic and recreational facilities are contracted through Syracuse University.

Disabled Students: 90% of the campus is accessible to disabled students. The following facilities are available: wheelchair ramps, elevators, special parking, specially equipped rest rooms, lowered drinking fountains, and lowered telephones.

Services: There is a reader service for the blind and remedial math.

Campus Safety and Security: Campus safety and security measures include 24-hour foot and vehicle patrol, shuttle buses, informal discussions, and pamphlets/posters/films. In addition, there are emergency telephones and lighted pathways/sidewalks.

Programs of Study: ESF confers B.S. and B.L.A. degrees. Associate, master's, and doctoral degrees are also awarded. Bachelor's degrees are awarded in AGRICULTURE (animal science, forest engineering, forestry and related sciences, natural resource management, plant science, and soil science), BIOLOGICAL SCIENCE (biology/biological science, botany, ecology, entomology, environmental biology, microbiology, molecular biology, plant genetics, and plant physiology), COMPUTER AND PHYSICAL SCIENCE (chemistry and polymer science), EDUCATION (environmental and science), ENGINEERING AND ENVIRONMENTAL DESIGN (chemical engineering, construction management, environmental design, environmental engineering, environmental science, landscape architecture/design, paper and pulp science, paper engineering, and survey and mapping technology), HEALTH PROFESSIONS (predentistry, premedicine, and prepharmacy), SOCIAL SCIENCE (prelaw). Engineering, chemistry, and biology are the strongest academically. Environmental and forest biology and environmental studies have the largest enrollments.

Required: Students must complete 125 to 130 credit hours for the B.S. (160 for the B.L.A.), including 60 in the major, with a minimum 2.0 GPA. Courses in chemistry, English, mathematics, and botany are required.

Special: Cross-registration is offered with Syracuse University. Co-op programs, accelerated degrees in biology and landscape architecture, and dual options in biology and forestry are available. There is 1 national honor society on campus.

Faculty/Classroom: 85% of faculty are male; 15%, female. All both teach and do research. No introductory courses are taught by graduate students. The average class size in an introductory lecture is 25; in a laboratory, 12; and in a regular course offering, 25.

Admissions: 16% of the 1995–96 applicants were accepted. The SAT I scores for the 1995–96 freshman class were as follows: Verbal—32% below 500, 47% between 500 and 599, 20% between 600 and 700, and 1% above 700; Math—8% below 500, 26% between 500 and 599, 56% between 600 and 700, and 10% above 700.

Requirements: The SAT I or ACT is required. ESF requires applicants to be in the upper 30% of their class. A minimum grade average of 86 is required. Applicants are required to have a minimum of 4 years of mathematics and science, including chemistry, in a college preparatory curriculum. An essay is required and an interview, letters of recommendation, and a personal portfolio or resume are recommended. AP and CLEP credits are accepted. Important factors in the admissions decision are advanced placement or honor courses, leadership record, and extracurricular activities record.

Procedure: Freshmen are admitted in the fall. There are early decision and deferred admissions plans. Early decision applications should be filed by November 15; regular application deadlines are open. The application fee is $25. Notification of early decision is sent December 15; regular decision, on a rolling basis. 13 early decision candidates were accepted for the 1995–96 class. A waiting list is an active part of the admissions procedure.

Transfer: 328 transfer students enrolled in 1995–96. Transfer requirements vary by major. Students must successfully complete prerequisite course work and should have a 2.5 or higher GPA. At least 24 of the last 30 credits of a total of 125 to 160 must be completed at ESF.

Visiting: There are regularly scheduled orientations for prospective students, including a fall open house, which provides campus tours, faculty sessions, an activities fair, and student affairs presentations. There are guides for informal visits and visitors may sit in on classes. To schedule a visit, contact the Admissions Office.

Financial Aid: In 1995–96, 80% of all freshmen and 85% of continuing students received some form of financial aid. 80% of all students received need-based aid. The average freshman award was $4000. Of that total, scholarships or need-based grants averaged $600; loans averaged $2600; and work contracts averaged $800. 45% of undergraduate students work part-time. Average earnings from campus work for the school year are $1200. The average financial indebtedness of the 1994–95 graduate was $3450. ESF is a member of CSS. The FAFSA and the college's own financial statement are required. The application deadline for fall entry is March 1.

International Students: There are currently 99 international students enrolled. They must take the TOEFL and achieve a minimum score of 550.

Computers: The college provides computer facilities for student use. Apple Macintosh and IBM microcomputers are available. There are several computer laboratories at ESF and Syracuse University. All students may access the system. There are no time limits and no fees.

Graduates: In 1994–95, 298 bachelor's degrees were awarded. The most popular majors among graduates were environmental and forest biology (31%), environmental studies (20%), and landscape architecture (14%). Within an average freshman class, 60% graduate in 4 years, 80% in 5 years, and 2% in 6 years. 28 companies recruited on campus in 1994–95.

Admissions Contact: Dennis O. Stratton, Director of Admissions and Inter-Institutional Relations. E-mail: esfinfo@mailbox.syr.edu. A campus video is available.

STATE UNIVERSITY OF NEW YORK COLLEGE OF TECHNOLOGY AT FARMINGDALE   E-5

Farmingdale, NY 11735	(516) 420-2200; FAX: (516) 420-2633
Full-time: 1978 men, 1367 women	Faculty: 200; III, ++$
Part-time: 1450 men, 1414 women	Ph.Ds: 37%
Graduate: none	Student/Faculty: 17 to 1
Year: semesters, summer session	Tuition: $3821 ($8721)
Application Deadline: open	Room & Board: $5491
Freshman Class: 6076 applied, 3631 accepted, 2477 enrolled	
SAT I or ACT: not required	COMPETITIVE

The State University of New York/College of Technology at Farmingdale, founded in 1912, is a public coeducational institution offering bachelor's degrees in the applied sciences and technology. There are 4 undergraduate schools. In addition to regional accreditation, State University of New York College of Technology at Farmingdale has baccalaureate program accreditation with ABET. The library contains 125,000 volumes, 60,000 microform items, and 3000 audiovisual forms, and subscribes to 1000 periodicals. Computerized library sources and services include the card catalog, interlibrary loans, and database searching. Special learning facilities include a learning resource center, art gallery, radio station, dental hygiene clinic, CAD/CAM and CIM laboratories, fleet of single-engine and twin-engine airplanes, and greenhouse complex. The 380-acre campus is in a suburban area on Long Island, about 35 miles east of New York City. Including residence halls, there are 40 buildings on campus.

Student Life: 99% of undergraduates are from New York. Students come from 5 states. 92% are from public schools; 8% from private. 73% are white; 11% African American. The average age of freshmen is 18; all undergraduates, 21. 19% do not continue beyond their first year; 38% remain to graduate.

Housing: 660 students can be accommodated in college housing. College-sponsored living facilities include coed dormitories. In addition there are honors houses, special interest houses, and residences for students 23 and older. On-campus housing is available on a first-come, first-served basis and is available on a lottery system for upperclassmen. Priority is given to out-of-town students. 92% of students commute. Alcohol is not permitted. All students may keep cars on campus.

Activities: There are no fraternities or sororities. There are 32 groups on campus, including academic, art, cheerleading, computers, dance, drama, ethnic, gay, gospel choir, honors, literary magazine, musical theater, newspaper, professional, radio, religious, social, social service, student government, and yearbook. Popular campus events include World Food Day, Homecoming, Holocaust Remembrance, and Black, Hispanic, and Women's History months.

Sports: There are 9 intercollegiate sports for men and 7 for women, and 11 intramural sports for men and 11 for women. Athletic and recreation facilities include basketball, badminton, volleyball, racquetball, handball, squash, and tennis courts, a swimming pool, a wrestling room, bowling alleys, weight training rooms, indoor and outdoor tracks, a golf driving range and 3-hole golf layout, and baseball, softball, soccer/lacrosse, and multipurpose fields.

Disabled Students: The entire campus is accessible to disabled students. The following facilities are available: wheelchair ramps, elevators, special parking, specially equipped rest rooms, lowered drinking fountains, and lowered telephones.

Services: In addition to many counseling and information services, tutoring is available in most subjects. In addition, there is remedial math, reading, and writing and a learning disabilities specialist counselor.

Campus Safety and Security: Campus safety and security measures include 24-hour foot and vehicle patrol, escort service, informal discussions, and pamphlets/posters/films. In addition, there are emergency telephones and lighted pathways/sidewalks.

Programs of Study: State University of New York College of Technology at Farmingdale confers B.S. and B.Tech. degrees. Associate degrees are also awarded. Bachelor's degrees are awarded in COMMUNICATIONS AND THE ARTS (communications technology), ENGINEERING AND ENVIRONMENTAL DESIGN (aeronautical science, aviation administration/management, electrical/electronics engineering technology, industrial engineering technology, and manufacturing technology). Electrical engineering technology is the strongest academically. Industrial technology and electrical engineering technology have the largest enrollments.

Required: To graduate, students must complete 124 to 141 credits with a minimum GPA of 2.0. The core curriculum includes 4 courses each in social science, mathematics/science, and English/humanities, including English composition.

Special: There are 3 national honor societies on campus. One department has an honors program.

Faculty/Classroom: 65% of faculty are male; 35%, female. All teach undergraduates. The average class size in an introductory lecture is 28; in a laboratory, 15; and in a regular course offering, 21.

Admissions: 60% of the 1995–96 applicants were accepted. 12% of the current freshmen were in the top fifth of their class; 37% were in the top two fifths.

Requirements: A minimum GPA of 2.0 is required. Applicants must be graduates of an accredited secondary school or have earned a GED. Specific entrance requirements vary by program, but recommended preparation includes 4 units of English and 3 each of mathematics, science, and social science. Art programs require a portfolio and interview. AP and CLEP credits are accepted.

Procedure: Freshmen are admitted fall and spring. There are early admissions and deferred admissions plans. Application deadlines are open. Application fee is $30. Notification is sent on a rolling basis.

Transfer: 471 transfer students enrolled in 1995–96. Applicants must have a minimum GPA of 2.0 and be eligible to return to their previous college. 30 credits out of 124 to 141 must be completed at State University of New York College of Technology at Farmingdale.

Visiting: There are regularly scheduled orientations for prospective students, including a tour of the campus and general information about the college, admissions, financial aid, and residence life. To schedule a visit, contact the Admissions Office.

Financial Aid: In 1995–96, 63% of all freshmen and 58% of continuing students received some form of financial aid. 60% of freshmen and 55% of continuing students received need-based aid. 3% of undergraduate students work part-time. Average earnings from campus work for the school year are $837. The FAFSA, the college's own financial statement, and a state aid form are required. Financial aid applications should be filed as early as possible.

International Students: There are currently 8 international students enrolled. They must take the TOEFL and achieve a minimum score of 500.

Computers: The college provides computer facilities for student use. The mainframe is a DEC VAX/AXP cluster. More than 250 microcomputers, both networked and stand-alone, are located in student laboratories in several classroom buildings and residence halls. All students may access the system during laboratory hours, Monday through Friday, 8 A.M. to 10 P.M., and Saturday, 9 A.M. to 2 P.M., or through dial-in access. There are no time limits and no fees.

Graduates: In 1994–95, 54 bachelor's degrees were awarded. The most popular majors among graduates were electrical engineering technology (30%), manufacturing engineering technology (28%), and industrial technology (26%). 72 companies recruited on campus in 1994–95.

Admissions Contact: Jeffrey Stein, Director of Admissions. E-mail: steinja@snyfarva. A campus video is available.

STATE UNIVERSITY OF NEW YORK EMPIRE STATE COLLEGE
Saratoga Springs, NY 12866–4390
D-3

(518) 587-2100
(800) 847-3000

Full-time: 584 men, 991 women	Faculty: 136, IIB, +$
Part-time: 2391 men, 2813 women	Ph.D.s: 85%
Graduate: 181 men, 209 women	Student/Faculty: 1:1
Year: see profile	Tuition: $3545 ($8445)
Application Deadline: open	Room & Board: n/app
Freshman Class: n/av	
SAT I or ACT: not required	SPECIAL

Empire State College, founded in 1971 as part of the State University of New York, offers degree programs in the arts and sciences through its statewide network of more than 40 regional centers and units. Students study on their own, with guidance from faculty advisers, or mentors, with whom they develop learning contracts. The college maintains year-round operation, and students study on flexible schedules. The college's headquarters as well as a regional center is in Saratoga Springs; other regional centers are in Buffalo, Rochester, Albany, Hartsdale in Westchester County, Old Westbury on Long Island, and in New York City along with the college's School of Labor Studies. Students gain access through the regional center to other schools, as well as businesses, government agencies, and other organizations. There is 1 graduate school. Computerized library sources and services include the card catalog and interlibrary loans. Special learning facilities include a learning resource center.

Student Life: 98% of undergraduates are from New York. Students come from 15 states, 14 foreign countries, and Canada. 81% are white; 11% African American. The average age of all undergraduates is 37.

Housing: There are no residence halls. All students commute to campus. Alcohol is not permitted.

Activities: There are no fraternities or sororities. There are 17 groups on campus, including student government. Regional centers sponsor events and outside speakers throughout the year.

Sports: There is no sports program at Empire State College.

Services: In addition to many counseling and information services, tutoring is available in most subjects.

Programs of Study: Empire State College confers B.A., B.S., and B.P.S. degrees. Associate and master's degrees are also awarded. Bachelor's degrees are awarded in BUSINESS (business administration and management and management science), COMPUTER AND PHYSICAL SCIENCE (mathematics and science), EDUCATION (education), SOCIAL SCIENCE (community services, economics, history, human development, humanities and social science, interdisciplinary studies, liberal arts/general studies, and sociology). Business, management, and economics have the largest enrollments.

Required: Students must earn 128 credits to graduate.

Special: Empire State uses a range of teaching methods, including learning contracts, study groups, and residencies, as well as distance learning in which students confer with faculty by mail and telephone. Students can cross-register with any SUNY or CUNY school and some private institutions, and may study abroad in England, Denmark, Cyprus, and Israel. Accelerated degree programs, internships through the Albany semester program, student-designed majors, nondegree study, and credit for life, military, and work experience are possible.

Faculty/Classroom: 57% of faculty are male; 43%, female.

Requirements: Applicants must be high school graduates, have a GED, or show ability to succeed at the college level. Empire State also considers the ability of a learning location to meet individual needs. AP and CLEP credits are accepted.

Procedure: There is an early admissions plan. Application deadlines are open. Application fee is $50. The college accepts all applicants. Notification is sent on a rolling basis.

Transfer: Empire State offers maximum flexibility to transfer applicants, who must provide official transcripts from previous colleges attended. 32 credits of 128 must be completed at Empire State College.

Visiting: There are regularly scheduled orientations for prospective students. There are guides for informal visits. To schedule a visit, contact the deans of the individual regional center.

Financial Aid: In 1995–96, 40% of continuing students received need-based financial aid. 1% of undergraduate students work part-time. Average earnings from campus work for the school year are $3000. The college's own financial statement and the FAFSA are required. The application deadline for priority financial aid fall entry is April 1.

International Students: There are currently 6 international students enrolled.

Computers: The college provides computer facilities for student use. The mainframe is a DEC VAX 11/750. There are also 400 microcomputers, primarily IBM and IBM-compatible models, distributed among the college's branches. Those with assigned IDs may access the system 24 hours a day. There are no time limits and no fees.

Graduates: In 1994–95, 1287 bachelor's degrees were awarded. The most popular majors among graduates were business, management, and economics (30%), community and human services (24%), and interdisciplinary studies (10%).

Admissions Contact: Martin N. Thorsland, Director of Admissions and Educational Assessment.

STATE UNIVERSITY OF NEW YORK/COLLEGE AT BROCKPORT
B-3

Brockport, NY 14420–2915 (716) 395-2751; **FAX:** (716) 395-5397

Full-time: 2720 men, 3110 women	Faculty: 231; IIA, +$
Part-time: 536 men, 804 women	Ph.D.s: 81%
Graduate: 708 men, 1169 women	Student/Faculty: 25 to 1
Year: semesters, summer session	Tuition: $3795 ($8725)
Application Deadline: February 1	Room & Board: $4660
Freshman Class: 3428 applied, 1714 accepted, 1102 enrolled	
SAT I or ACT: recommended	COMPETITIVE

The State University of New York/College at Brockport, established in 1867, is a public coeducational institution offering undergraduate programs in liberal arts, sciences, business, and teacher preparation. There are 4 undergraduate schools and 1 graduate school. In addition to regional accreditation, Brockport has baccalaureate program accreditation with CSWE, NLN, and NRPA. The library contains 535,000 volumes, 1.9 million microform items, and 9000 audiovisual forms, and subscribes to 2300 periodicals. Computerized library sources and services include the card catalog, interlibrary loans, and database searching. Special learning facilities include a learning resource center, art gallery, planetarium, radio station, and TV station. The 597-acre campus is in a small town 16 miles west of Rochester. Including residence halls, there are 37 buildings on campus.

Student Life: 99% of undergraduates are from New York. Students come from 22 states, 16 foreign countries, and Canada. 94% are from public schools; 6% from private. 91% are white. 46% are Catholic; 27% Protestant; 18% claim no religious affiliation. The average age of freshmen is 18; all undergraduates, 24. 23% do not continue beyond their first year; 43% remain to graduate.

Housing: 2540 students can be accommodated in college housing. College-sponsored living facilities include single-sex and coed dormitories. In addition, there are special interest houses, special living facilities for transfer and first-year students, and facilities offering wellness programs and international living/year-round housing. On-campus housing is guaranteed for all 4 years. All students may keep cars on campus.

Activities: 3% of men belong to 8 national fraternities; 5% of women belong to 7 national sororities. There are 75 groups on campus, including art, cheerleading, choir, chorus, computers, dance, drama, ethnic, film, gay, honors, international, literary magazine, newspaper, pep band, political, professional, radio and TV, religious, social, social service, student government, symphony, and yearbook. Popular campus events include Midnite Merry Madness, Kwanzaa, Scholar's Day, and Greek Olympics.

Sports: There are 10 intercollegiate sports for men and 12 for women, and 30 intramural sports for men and 30 for women. Athletic and recreation facilities include field hockey and softball fields, a swimming pool, 6 gymnasiums, a gymnastics area, wrestling and weight rooms, handball, squash, and racquetball courts, and a special Olympics stadium with an 8-lane, all-weather track.

Disabled Students: 90% of the campus is accessible to disabled students. The following facilities are available: wheelchair ramps, elevators, special parking, specially equipped rest rooms, special class scheduling, lowered drinking fountains, lowered telephones, and special classroom accommodations.

Services: In addition to many counseling and information services, tutoring is available in some subjects, which vary from semester to semester. There is remedial math and writing, as well as study skills support.

Campus Safety and Security: Campus safety and security measures include 24-hour foot and vehicle patrol, self-defense education, escort service, and shuttle buses. There are informal discussions, pamphlets/posters/films, emergency telephones, lighted pathways/sidewalks, a community policing program, and a crime prevention team.

Programs of Study: Brockport confers B.A., B.S., B.F.A., and B.S.N. degrees. Master's degrees are also awarded. Bachelor's degrees are awarded in BIOLOGICAL SCIENCE (biology/biological science), BUSINESS (accounting, business administration and management, international business management, and recreation and leisure services), COMMUNICATIONS AND THE ARTS (communications, dance, dramatic arts, English, fine arts, French, Spanish, speech/debate/rhetoric, and studio art), COMPUTER AND PHYSICAL SCIENCE (atmospheric sciences and meteorology, chemistry, computer science, earth science, geology, mathematics, and physics), EDUCATION (physical and secondary), HEALTH PROFESSIONS (health science, medical technology, and nursing), SOCIAL SCIENCE (African American studies, African studies, anthropology, criminal justice, history, international studies, philosophy, political science/government, psychology, social work, sociology, and water resources). English, political science, and international business are the strongest academically. Business administration, psychology, and physical education and sports have the largest enrollments.

Required: To graduate, students must complete a total of 120 credits, including 30 to 38 in the major, with a minimum 2.0 GPA. The core curriculum must include 6 credits each in fine arts, humanities, social science, and natural science and mathematics. All students must take courses in computer literacy, contemporary issues, perspectives on women, comparative culture, quantitative skills, and composition. An academic planning seminar is also required of entering freshmen.

Special: Co-op programs are offered in the sciences, business, communications, criminal justice, and computer science. Internships in most majors and work-study programs in education are available. Brockport offers cross-registration with Rochester area colleges, a Washington semester, study abroad in 11 countries, accelerated degree programs, student-designed majors, and an interdisciplinary major in arts for children, emphasizing art, dance, music, and theater. A 3-2 engineering degree is offered with SUNY-Binghamton, SUNY-Buffalo, and Clarkson, Case Western Reserve, and Syracuse universities. Credit for life, military, and work experience, nondegree study, and pass/fail grading options are available. An interdisciplinary program emphasizes global issues and provides opportunities for work or study in other countries, as well as locally, regionally, and nationally. There is a freshman honors program on campus, as well as 11 national honor societies. 3 departments have honors programs.

Faculty/Classroom: 67% of faculty are male; 33%, female. 95% teach undergraduates, 70% do research, and 68% do both. Graduate students teach fewer than 1% of introductory courses. The average class size in an introductory lecture is 35; in a laboratory, 15; and in a regular course offering, 25.

Admissions: 50% of the 1995–96 applicants were accepted. There were 7 National Merit semifinalists. 12 freshmen graduated first in their class.

Requirements: The SAT I or ACT is recommended for placement, with scores of at least 920 on the SAT I and 18 on the ACT preferred. A minimum grade average of C+ is required. Applicants must be graduates of an accredited secondary school or have a GED. Requirements include 17 Carnegie units or academic credits, including 4 years each in English and history and 2 years each in mathematics and science. Portfolios and auditions are recommended when appropriate. AP and CLEP credits are accepted. Important factors in the admissions decision are recommendations by school officials, advanced placement or honor courses, and leadership record.

Procedure: Freshmen are admitted fall and spring. Entrance exams should be taken during the fall of the senior year. There are early decision, early admissions, and deferred admissions plans. Early decision applications should be filed by November 15; regular applications, by February 1 for fall entry and December 15 for spring entry, along with an application fee of $30. Notification of early decision is sent December 15; regular decision, on a rolling basis beginning January 15. 22 early decision candidates were accepted for the 1995–96 class.

Transfer: 1131 transfer students enrolled in 1995–96. The applicant must have a minimum GPA of 2.25. Many departments specify prerequisite courses and a higher GPA. Brockport recommends that applicants have an associate degree or 54 credit hours. Preference is given to holders of associate degrees. 24 credits of 120 must be completed at Brockport.

Visiting: There are regularly scheduled orientations for prospective students, including weekly admissions information presentations and daily campus tours. Visits may be arranged on selected Saturdays and holidays. There are guides for informal visits and visitors may sit in on classes and stay overnight at the school. To schedule a visit, contact the Thompson Conference Center at (716) 395–2275.

Financial Aid: In 1995–96, 77% of all freshmen and 64% of continuing students received some form of financial aid. 61% of freshmen and 55% of continuing students received need-based aid. The average freshman award was $5425. Of that total, scholarships or need-based grants averaged $1343 ($3085 maximum); loans averaged $2454 ($6625 maximum); and work contracts averaged $1222 ($1500 maximum). 80% of undergraduate students work part-time. Average earnings from campus work for the school year are $600. The average financial indebtedness of the 1994–95 graduate was $5063. The FAFSA and the college's own financial statement are required. Transfer students must also provide a financial aid transcript. The application deadline for fall entry is March 15.

International Students: In a recent year, there were 47 international students enrolled. They must score 530 on the TOEFL or take the MELAB.

Computers: The college provides computer facilities for student use. The mainframes are a Prime 6650 and an IBM 9221 Model 150. There are more than 50 terminals available in central labs for student class projects. There are also 425 PCs available. All students may access the system 24 hours per day. There are no time limits and no fees.

Graduates: In 1994–95, 1602 bachelor's degrees were awarded. The most popular majors among graduates were business administration (16%), psychology (10%), and criminal justice (10%). Within an average freshman class, 2% graduate in 3 years, 24% in 4 years, 41% in 5 years, and 42% in 6 years. 271 companies recruited on campus in 1994–95. Of the 1994 graduating class, 12% were enrolled in graduate school within 6 months of graduation and 89% had found employment. A campus video is available.

Admissions Contact: James R. Cook, Director of Admissions.

STATE UNIVERSITY OF NEW YORK/COLLEGE AT BUFFALO
A-3

Buffalo, NY 14222   (716) 878–4017

Full-time: 3184 men, 4231 women	**Faculty:** 368; IIA, av$
Part-time: 1118 men, 1021 women	**Ph.D.s:** 90%
Graduate: 463 men, 1332 women	**Student/Faculty:** 20 to 1
Year: semesters, summer session	**Tuition:** $3640 ($8540)
Application Deadline: January 15	**Room & Board:** $4220
Freshman Class: 6904 applied, 3725 accepted, 1283 enrolled	
SAT I or ACT: not required	**COMPETITIVE**

The State University of New York/College at Buffalo, established in 1867, is a public institution conferring undergraduate liberal arts degrees. There is 1 graduate school. In addition to regional accreditation, Buffalo State has baccalaureate program accreditation with ABET, ADA, CSWE, and NCATE. The library contains 578,377 volumes, 726,811 microform items, and 9274 audiovisual forms, and subscribes to 2087 periodicals. Computerized library sources and services include the card catalog, interlibrary loans, and database searching. Special learning facilities include a learning resource center, an art gallery, a planetarium, a radio station, a speech, language, and hearing clinic, and a center for performing arts. The 115-acre campus is in an urban area in Buffalo. Including residence halls, there are 36 buildings on campus.

Student Life: 99% of undergraduates are from New York. Students come from 17 states, 36 foreign countries, and Canada. 82% are white; 11% African American. The average age of freshmen is 19; all undergraduates, 24. 29% do not continue beyond their first year; 36% remain to graduate.

Housing: 2086 students can be accommodated in college housing. College-sponsored living facilities include coed dormitories. In addition, there is an international student dormitory. On-campus housing is available on a first-come, first-served basis. 83% of students commute. Alcohol is not permitted. All students may keep cars on campus.

Activities: There is 1 local fraternity and 9 national fraternities and 3 local and 7 national sororities. There are 75 groups on campus, including art, cheerleading, chess, choir, chorus, computers, dance, drama, ethnic, gay, honors, international, jazz band, literary magazine, musical theater, newspaper, orchestra, political, professional, radio and TV, religious, social, social service, student government, and yearbook. Popular campus events include Homecoming, Commuter Daze, and The Gathering.

Sports: There are 8 intercollegiate sports for men and 10 for women, and 5 intramural sports for men and 3 for women. Athletic and recreation facilities include a gymnasium, a natatorium, and an arena.

Disabled Students: 90% of the campus is accessible to disabled students. The following facilities are available: wheelchair ramps, elevators, special parking, specially equipped rest rooms, special class scheduling, lowered drinking fountains, lowered telephones, and special dormitory accommodations.

Services: In addition to many counseling and information services, tutoring is available in every subject. There is a reader service for the blind, and remedial math, reading, and writing. Tutors for visually impaired and hearing-impaired students are also available.

Campus Safety and Security: Campus safety and security measures include escort service, shuttle buses, informal discussions, and pamphlets/posters/films. In addition, there are emergency telephones and lighted pathways/sidewalks.

Programs of Study: Buffalo State confers B.A., B.S., B.F.A., B.S.Ed., and B.T. degrees. Master's degrees are also awarded. Bachelor's degrees are awarded in BIOLOGICAL SCIENCE (biology/biological science), BUSINESS (business administration and management), COMMUNICATIONS AND THE ARTS (art, art history and appreciation, broadcasting, communications, design, dramatic arts, English, fine arts, French, Italian, journalism, music, photography, printmaking, sculpture, and Spanish), COMPUTER AND PHYSICAL SCIENCE (chemistry, earth science, geology, information sciences and systems, mathematics, and physics), EDUCATION (art, business, elementary, foreign languages, industrial arts, science, secondary, and special), ENGINEERING AND ENVIRONMENTAL DESIGN (electrical/electronics engineering technology and industrial engineering technology), HEALTH PROFESSIONS (speech pathology/audiology), SOCIAL SCIENCE (anthropology, child psychology/development, criminal justice, dietetics, economics, family/consumer studies, food production/management/services, geography, history, humanities, philosophy, political science/government, psychology, social work, sociology, and urban studies). Elementary education, psychology, and design have the largest enrollments.

Required: To graduate, students must complete a 60-hour general education requirement consisting of 42 core credits in applied science and education, arts, humanities, mathematics and science, and social science, and 18 hours of electives. Students must earn 123 credits with a minimum GPA of 2.0. The number of hours in the major varies. All students are required to complete 2 hours of physical education.

Special: Students may cross-register with the Western New York Consortium and the National Student Exchange. Internships, a Washington semester, study abroad in 5 countries, dual majors, and a general studies degree are offered. Students may earn 3–2 engineering degrees in association with the State University of New York centers at Buffalo and Binghamton, and Clarkson University. Credit for life, military, and work experience, nondegree study, and pass/fail grading options are available. There is a freshman honors program on campus. 13 departments have honors programs.

Faculty/Classroom: 73% of faculty are male; 27%, female. 95% teach undergraduates. No introductory courses are taught by graduate students.

Admissions: 54% of the 1995–96 applicants were accepted. The SAT I scores for the 1995–96 freshman class were as follows: Verbal—85% below 500, 13% between 500 and 599, and 2% between 600 and 700; Math—70% below 500, 23% between 500 and 599, and 7% between 600 and 700. 17% of the current freshmen were in the top fifth of their class; 55% were in the top two fifths.

Requirements: A minimum grade average of 85% is required. Students must graduate from an accredited secondary school or have a GED. They must complete 4 years of English, 3 each of mathematics, science, and social studies, and 2 of a foreign language. A portfolio is required for fine arts applicants. AP and CLEP credits are accepted. Important factors in the admissions decision are advanced placement or honor courses, evidence of special talent, and recommendations by school officials.

Procedure: Freshmen are admitted to all sessions. Entrance exams should be taken during the junior or senior years. There are early decision, early admissions, and deferred admissions plans. Early decision applications should be filed by November 15; the priority deadline for regular applications for fall entry is January 15. The application fee is $30. Notification of early decision is sent December 15; regular decision, on a rolling basis. A waiting list is an active part of the admissions procedure, with about 10% of all applicants on the list.

Transfer: 1927 transfer students enrolled in 1995–96. Transfer applicants must have a minimum GPA of 2.0. An associate degree is recommended, and a minimum of 15 credit hours must have been earned. 32 credits of 123 must be completed at Buffalo State.

Visiting: There are regularly scheduled orientations for prospective students. There are guides for informal visits and visitors may sit in on classes. To schedule a visit, contact the Admissions Office.

Financial Aid: In 1995–96, 66% of all freshmen and 60% of continuing students received some form of financial and need-based aid. The average freshman award was $5533. Of that total, scholarships or need-based grants averaged $3257 ($7425 maximum); loans averaged $2364 ($2625 maximum); and work contracts averaged $1760 ($1920 maximum). Average earnings from campus work for the school year are $1760. Buffalo State is a member of CSS. The FAFSA or FFS and TAP are required. The application deadline for fall entry is March 1.

International Students: There are currently 164 international students enrolled. The school actively recruits these students. They must take the TOEFL and achieve a minimum score of 500.

Computers: The college provides computer facilities for student use. The mainframe is an AXP-7600. Access to the mainframe is through the campus local area network. Approximately 350 terminals and microcomputers are available at various campus sites, including the library, classrooms, Computing Services' remote computing facilities, and departmental micro/terminal laboratories. All students may access the system during site hours. Dial-in access is available 24 hours per day. There are no time limits and no fees.

Graduates: In 1994–95, 1823 bachelor's degrees were awarded. The most popular majors among graduates were elementary education (9%), business studies (9%), and exceptional education (5%). Within an average freshman class, 1% graduate in 3 years, 17% in 4 years, 38% in 5 years, and 42% in 6 years. 47 companies recruited on campus in 1994–95.

Admissions Contact: Paul T. Collyer, Associate Director of Admissions.

STATE UNIVERSITY OF NEW YORK/COLLEGE AT CORTLAND

C-5

Cortland, NY 13045   **(607) 753-4711**

Full-time: 2190 men, 2726 women	Faculty: 241; IIA, -$
Part-time: 156 men, 206 women	Ph.D.s: 78%
Graduate: 416 men, 867 women	Student/Faculty: 20 to 1
Year: semesters, summer session	Tuition: $3842 ($8742)
Application Deadline: February 1	Room & Board: $5020
Freshman Class: 7937 applied, 3716 accepted, 1017 enrolled	
SAT I Verbal/Math: 441/508	ACT: 22 COMPETITIVE +

The State University of New York College at Cortland, founded in 1868, is a public, coeducational institution offering programs in liberal arts and professional studies. There are 2 undergraduate schools and one graduate school. In addition to regional accreditation, Cortland College has baccalaureate program accreditation with CAHEA and NRPA. The library contains 375,000 volumes, 533,060 microform items, and 9527 audiovisual forms, and subscribes to 1507 periodicals. Computerized library sources and services include the card catalog, interlibrary loans, and database searching. Special learning facilities include a learning resource center, art gallery, natural history museum, planetarium, radio station, TV station, and a natural science museum, a center for speech and hearing disorders, and many specialized laboratories to support program offerings. The 191-acre campus is in a small town 18 miles north of Ithaca. Including residence halls, there are 34 buildings on campus.

Student Life: 97% of undergraduates are from New York. Students come from 13 states, 11 foreign countries, and Canada. 91% are from public schools; 9% from private. 93% are white. The average age of freshmen is 18; all undergraduates, 20. 26% do not continue beyond their first year; 51% remain to graduate.

Housing: 2780 students can be accommodated in college housing. College-sponsored living facilities include coed dormitories, off-campus apartments, fraternity houses, and sorority houses. In addition, there are special interest houses and a wellness floor in a residence hall, computer residence hall, quiet residence halls, and a residence for Americans majoring in international studies and/or studying abroad. On-campus housing is guaranteed for all 4 years. Upperclassmen may keep cars on campus.

Activities: 10% of men belong to 1 local and 5 national fraternities; 10% of women belong to 1 local and 2 national sororities. There are 100 groups on campus, including art, band, cheerleading, choir, chorale, chorus, computers, dance, drama, ethnic, gay, honors, international, jazz band, literary magazine, musical theater, newspaper, orchestra, political, professional, radio and TV, religious, social, social service, student government, symphony, and yearbook. Popular campus events include the annual Cortland-Ithaca College football game, Winterfest, and Siblings Weekend.

Sports: There are 11 intercollegiate sports for men and 12 for women, and 30 intramural sports for men and 30 for women. Athletic and recreation facilities include an Olympic-sized pool, 3600-seat gymnasium, ice arena, gymnastics arena, wrestling and weight rooms, dance studio, handball/racquetball courts, squash courts, athletic training facility, fully equipped fitness centers, free-swimming pool, track, baseball field, football/lacrosse/track field seating 4000, lighted soccer field, field house, and 50 acres of athletic fields.

Disabled Students: The entire campus is accessible to persons with physical disabilities. The following facilities are available: wheelchair ramps, elevators, special parking, specially equipped rest rooms, special class scheduling, lowered drinking fountains, and lowered telephones.

Services: In addition to many counseling and information services, tutoring is available in some subjects. There is a fully staffed Academic Support and Achievement Program for writing, mathematics, study skills, and learning strategies. Also, specific course tutoring is avaialble with peer tutors. There is a reader service for the blind.

Campus Safety and Security: Campus safety and security measures include 24-hour foot and vehicle patrol, self-defense education, escort service, and shuttle buses. In addition, there are informal discussions, pamphlets/posters/films, emergency telephones, and lighted pathways/sidewalks.

Programs of Study: Cortland College confers B.A., B.S., and B.S.E. degrees. Master's degrees are also awarded. Bachelor's degrees are awarded in BIOLOGICAL SCIENCE (biology/biological science), BUSINESS (management science), COMMUNICATIONS AND THE ARTS (art, communications, dramatic arts, English, languages, and music), COMPUTER AND PHYSICAL SCIENCE (chemistry, geochemistry, geology, mathematics, and physics), EDUCATION (elementary, foreign languages, health, middle school, and secondary), HEALTH PROFESSIONS (recreation therapy and speech pathology/audiology), SOCIAL SCIENCE (anthropology, economics, geography, history, international studies, parks and recreation management, philosophy, political science/government, psychology, public administration, social science, and sociology). Biology, political science, sociology, and psychology are the strongest academically. Elementary education, physical education, communications, and management science have the largest enrollments.

Required: To graduate, students must complete specific course work in academic writing, quantitative skills, and foreign language. A general education requirement includes courses in American state and society, prejudice and discrimination, contrasting cultures, fine arts, history and history of ideas, literature, natural sciences, and science, technology and man. Students must maintain a 2.0 GPA and must complete 124 to 128 credits, with 36 to 45 in the major.

Special: Cortland has cooperative programs with the State University of New York College of Environmental Science and Forestry, centers at Binghamton and Buffalo, and Cornell and Case Western Reserve universities. Students may study abroad in 14 countries, and they may enroll in a Washington semester. Work-study programs are available. The college confers an individualized studies degree and dual majors. Student-designed majors can be arranged. Students may pursue a 3–2 engineering degree in conjunction with Alfred, Case Western Reserve, and Clarkson universities, and the State University of New York Centers at Binghamton, Buffalo, and Stony Brook. Credit may be granted for military and work experience. Cortland offers nondegree study programs. There is a freshman honors program on campus, as well as 15 national honor societies. 4 departments have honors programs.

Faculty/Classroom: 58% of faculty are male; 42%, female. All teach undergraduates. No introductory courses are taught by graduate students. The average class size in an introductory lecture is 40 and in a regular course offering, 25.

Admissions: 47% of the 1995–96 applicants were accepted. The SAT I scores for the 1995–96 freshman class were as follows: Verbal—86% below 500, 13% between 500 and 599, and 1% between 600 and 700; Math—51% below 500, 41% between 500 and 599, 7% between 600 and 700, and 1% above 700. The ACT scores were 35% below 21, 37% between 21 and 23, 23% between 24 and 26, 4% between 27 and 28, and 1% above 28. 22% of the current freshmen were in the top fifth of their class; 63% were in the top two fifths. There were 2 National Merit finalists.

Requirements: The SAT I or ACT is required. A minimum grade average of 80% is required. Applicants must graduate from an accredited secondary school or have a GED. They must have earned 16 Carnegie units and 16 to 20 academic credits, including 4 units each in English and history or social studies and 2 (3 units preferred) each in mathematics and science; the other 4 units must be taken in areas listed above or in a foreign language. Essays and recommendations are required, and in some cases auditions as well. Interviews are strongly

recommeded. AP and CLEP credits are accepted. Important factors in the admissions decision are advanced placement or honor courses, extracurricular activities record, and recommendations by school officials.

Procedure: Freshmen are admitted fall and spring. Entrance exams should be taken during the spring or fall. There are early decision, early admissions, and deferred admissions plans. Early decision applications should be filed by November 15; regular applications, by February 1 for fall entry and December 1 for spring entry, along with an application fee of $25. Notification of early decision is sent December 15; regular decision, February 15. 52 early decision candidates were accepted for the 1995–96 class. A waiting list is an active part of the admissions procedure, with about 8% of all applicants on the list.

Transfer: 783 transfer students enrolled in 1995–96. Transfer applicants must have a minimum GPA of 2.5. Essays and recommendations are required. Interviews are strongly encouraged. 45 credits of 124 to 128 must be completed at Cortland College.

Visiting: There are regularly scheduled orientations for prospective students, consisting of Autumn Preview Days for prospective students as well as Spring Open House for accepted students. There are guides for informal visits and visitors may sit in on classes. To schedule a visit, contact the Admission Appointment Secretary.

Financial Aid: In 1995–96, 75% of all freshmen and 79% of continuing students received some form of financial aid. 73% of freshmen and 74% of continuing students received need-based aid. The average freshman award was $3200. Of that total, loans averaged $2625 ($4125 maximum) and work contracts averaged $1300 (maximum). 75% of undergraduate students work part-time. Average earnings from campus work for the school year are $1500. The average financial indebtedness of the 1994–95 graduate was $15,000. Cortland College is a member of CSS. The FAFSA and the college's own financial statement are required. The application deadline for fall entry is February 15.

International Students: There are currently 16 international students enrolled. They must take the TOEFL and achieve a minimum score of 550.

Computers: The college provides computer facilities for student use. The mainframes are an ALPHA AXT 2100 and a Unisys A14. There are also 470 IBM, Apple, and IBM-compatible microcomputers available throughout the campus in 33 student-use laboratories. All students may access the system 24 hours per day in some laboratories connected to the campus network. There are no time limits and no fees.

Graduates: In 1994–95, 1101 bachelor's degrees were awarded. The most popular majors among graduates were physical education (21%), elementary education (16%), and sociology (6%). Within an average freshman class, 1% graduate in 3 years, 42% in 4 years, and 9% in 5 years. 80 to 85 companies recruited on campus in 1994–95. Of the 1994 graduating class, 52% were enrolled in graduate school within 6 months of graduation and 61% had found employment.

Admissions Contact: Gradin Avery, Director of Admission.

STATE UNIVERSITY OF NEW YORK/COLLEGE A-4 AT FREDONIA
Fredonia, NY 14063

(716) 673-3251
(800) 252-1212; FAX: (716) 673-3249

Full-time: 1799 men, 2262 women	Faculty: 220; IIA, av$
Part-time: 131 men, 182 women	Ph.D.s: 90%
Graduate: 83 men, 264 women	Student/Faculty: 18 to 1
Year: semesters, summer session	Tuition: $3919 ($8819)
Application Deadline: open	Room & Board: $4670
Freshman Class: 4903 applied, 2754 accepted, 898 enrolled	
SAT I Verbal/Math: 475/527	ACT: 23 COMPETITIVE

The State University of New York at Fredonia, established in 1826, is a public institution offering undergraduate programs in the arts and sciences, business and professional curricula, teacher preparation, and the fine and performing arts. There is 1 graduate school. In addition to regional accreditation, Fredonia has baccalaureate program accreditation with NASAD and NASM. The library contains 382,405 volumes, 932,635 microform items, and 18,225 audiovisual forms, and subscribes to 1936 periodicals. Computerized library sources and services include the card catalog, interlibrary loans, and database searching. Special learning facilities include a learning resource center, art gallery, planetarium, radio station, TV station, greenhouse, day care center, speech clinic, and arts center. The 266-acre campus is in a small town 50 miles south of Buffalo. Including residence halls, there are 24 buildings on campus.

Student Life: 98% of undergraduates are from New York. Students come from 23 states, 9 foreign countries, and Canada. 65% are from public schools; 35% from private. 95% are white. The average age of freshmen is 18. 16% do not continue beyond their first year; 69% remain to graduate.

Housing: 2621 students can be accommodated in college housing. College-sponsored living facilities include single-sex and coed dormitories and on-campus apartments. In addition, there are special interest houses. Living space for fraternities and sororities is available in residence halls. There are special interest houses for computer and athletics students and quiet-hour centers. On-campus housing is guaranteed for all 4 years. 55% of students live on campus; of those, 80% remain on campus on weekends. All students may keep cars on campus.

Activities: 5% of men belong to 3 national fraternities; 3% of women belong to 2 national sororities. There are 160 groups on campus, including art, band, cheerleading, choir, chorale, chorus, computers, dance, drama, drill team, ethnic, gay, honors, international, jazz band, literary magazine, musical theater, newspaper, opera, orchestra, pep band, photography, political, professional, radio and TV, religious, social, social service, student government, symphony, and yearbook. Popular campus events include various Art Center presentations, Homecoming, Spring Fest, Parents Weekend, Little Siblings Weekend, Superdance for MDA, Fashion Show, and various cultural celebrations.

Sports: There are 7 intercollegiate sports for men and 7 for women, and 6 intramural sports for men and 6 for women. Athletic and recreation facilities include a basketball arena, an ice rink, a swimming pool, a gymnasium, a weight room, dance studios, soccer fields, indoor and outdoor tracks, and racquetball, tennis, and volleyball courts.

Disabled Students: 50% of the campus is accessible to disabled students. The following facilities are available: wheelchair ramps, elevators, special parking, specially equipped rest rooms, lowered drinking fountains, and lowered telephones.

Services: In addition to many counseling and information services, tutoring is available in most subjects. There is a reader service for the blind.

Campus Safety and Security: Campus safety and security measures include 24-hour foot and vehicle patrol, escort service, shuttle buses, and informal discussions. In addition, there are pamphlets/posters/films, emergency telephones, and lighted pathways/sidewalks.

Programs of Study: Fredonia confers B.A., B.S., B.A.S.S., B.F.A., B.S.Ed., B.S.S.S., and Mus.B. degrees. Master's degrees are also awarded. Bachelor's degrees are awarded in BIOLOGICAL SCIENCE (biology/biological science), BUSINESS (accounting, business administration and management, and business economics), COMMUNICATIONS AND THE ARTS (communications, design, dramatic arts, English, fine arts, French, German, music, and Spanish), COMPUTER AND PHYSICAL SCIENCE (chemistry, computer science, earth science, geology, mathematics, and physics), EDUCATION (early childhood, elementary, foreign languages, middle school, music, science, and secondary), HEALTH PROFESSIONS (medical laboratory technology, predentistry, premedicine, and speech pathology/audiology), SOCIAL SCIENCE (interdisciplinary studies, philosophy, political science/government, psychology, and sociology). Business, education, and music have the largest enrollments.

Required: To graduate, students must complete 120 hours, including 33 to 45 or more in the major, with a 2.0 GPA. Students must take specific courses in English and mathematics and complete 36 hours of general education courses, including writing, statistical/quantitative abilities, oral communication, natural and social sciences, humanities, and arts.

Special: Cooperative programs are available with many other institutions. Students may cross-register with colleges in the Western New York Consortium. Fredonia offers a variety of internships, study-abroad programs in more than 90 countries, and a Washington semester. Accelerated degrees, a general studies degree, dual and student-designed majors, a 3–2 engineering degree program, nondegree study, and pass/fail grading options are available. There is a freshman honors program on campus, as well as 17 national honor societies. 17 departments have honors programs.

Faculty/Classroom: 67% of faculty are male; 33%, female. All teach undergraduates. No introductory courses are taught by graduate students. The average class size in an introductory lecture is 70; in a laboratory, 15; and in a regular course offering, 23.

Admissions: 56% of the 1995–96 applicants were accepted. The SAT I scores for the 1995–96 freshman class were as follows: Verbal—65% below 500, 28% between 500 and 599, and 7% between 600 and 700; Math—36% below 500, 45% between 500 and 599, 17% between 600 and 700, and 2% above 700. The ACT scores were 21% below 21, 38% between 21 and 23, 27% between 24 and 26, 9% between 27 and 28, and 5% above 28. 38% of the current freshmen were in the top fifth of their class; 80% were in the top two fifths. 10 freshmen graduated first in their class.

Requirements: The SAT I or ACT is required, with a minimum composite score of 900 on the SAT I or 18 on the ACT. Fredonia requires applicants to be in the upper 50% of their class. A minimum GPA of 2.5 is required. Applicants must possess a high school diploma or

have a GED. 16 academic credits are recommended, including 4 credits each in English and social studies, and 3 each in mathematics, science, and a foreign language. 4 years of mathematics and science are encouraged. Essays and interviews are recommended, and, where applicable, an audition or a portfolio is required. Electronic applications are available through the Albany Application Processing Center. AP and CLEP credits are accepted. Important factors in the admissions decision are advanced placement or honor courses, evidence of special talent, and recommendations by school officials.

Procedure: Freshmen are admitted fall and spring. Entrance exams should be taken during the spring of the junior year or fall of the senior year. There are early admissions and deferred admissions plans. Application deadlines are open. Application fee is $30. Notification is sent on a rolling basis beginning December 1. A waiting list is an active part of the admissions procedure, with about 1% of all applicants on the list.

Transfer: 531 transfer students enrolled in 1995–96. Applicants should have a minimum GPA of 2.0, and appropriate academic course work to be considered. An interview is recommended. 45 credits of 120 must be completed at Fredonia.

Visiting: There are regularly scheduled orientations for prospective students, including various open house programs. Visitors may sit in on classes and stay overnight at the school. To schedule a visit, contact the Office of Admissions.

Financial Aid: In 1995–96, 70% of all freshmen and 62% of continuing students received some form of financial aid. 64% of freshmen and 59% of continuing students received need-based aid. The average freshman award was $4786. Of that total, scholarships or need-based grants averaged $2272 ($5225 maximum); loans averaged $2857 ($3625 maximum); and work contracts averaged $1000. 20% of undergraduate students work part-time. Average earnings from campus work for the school year are $950. The average financial indebtedness of the 1994–95 graduate was $9500. Fredonia is a member of CSS. The FAFSA and TAP are required. Early applications are encouraged.

International Students: There are currently 29 international students enrolled. The school actively recruits these students. They must take the TOEFL and achieve a minimum score of 500.

Computers: The college provides computer facilities for student use. The mainframe is a Unisys A18 Enterprise Server. Other computer facilities include a Sun 4/470 server, student laboratories, more than 500 student workstations and terminals, and dial-up capabilities. All students may access the system. There are no time limits and no fees.

Graduates: In 1994–95, 949 bachelor's degrees were awarded. The most popular majors among graduates were elementary education (18%), business administration (13%), and English (7%). Within an average freshman class, 47% graduate in 4 years, 64% in 5 years, and 65% in 6 years. 70 companies recruited on campus in 1994–95. Of the 1994 graduating class, 26% were enrolled in graduate school within 6 months of graduation and 78% had found employment.

Admissions Contact: J. Denis Bolton, Director of Admissions. E-mail: admissionsinq@fredonia.edu. A campus video is available.

STATE UNIVERSITY OF NEW YORK/COLLEGE AT GENESEO
B-3

Geneseo, NY 14454

(716) 245-5571; FAX: (716) 245-5005

Full-time: 1880 men, 3312 women	Faculty: 251; IIA, --$
Part-time: 49 men, 84 women	Ph.D.s: 85%
Graduate: 83 men, 297 women	Student/Faculty: 21 to 1
Year: semesters, summer session	Tuition: $3859 ($8759)
Application Deadline: January 15	Room & Board: $4500
Freshman Class: 8934 applied, 4868 accepted, 1210 enrolled	
SAT I Verbal/Math: 540/608	ACT: 26 HIGHLY COMPETITIVE

The State University of New York/College at Geneseo, founded in 1867 and opened to students in 1871, offers liberal arts, business and accounting programs, teaching certification, and training in communicative disorders and sciences. In addition to regional accreditation, Geneseo has baccalaureate program accreditation with ASLA. The library contains 521,558 volumes, 837,812 microform items, and 3813 audiovisual forms, and subscribes to 3156 periodicals. Computerized library sources and services include the card catalog, interlibrary loans, and database searching. Special learning facilities include a learning resource center, art gallery, planetarium, radio station, TV station, and 3 theaters. The 220-acre campus is in a small town 30 miles south of Rochester. Including residence halls, there are 38 buildings on campus.

Student Life: 98% of undergraduates are from New York. Students come from 10 states, 5 foreign countries, and Canada. 83% are from public schools; 17% from private. 86% are white. 52% are Catholic; 25% Protestant. The average age of freshmen is 18; all undergraduates, 20. 8% do not continue beyond their first year; 78% remain to graduate.

Housing: 3100 students can be accommodated in college housing. College-sponsored living facilities include coed dormitories. In addition, there are special interest houses, including science and mathematics houses. On-campus housing is guaranteed for all 4 years. 58% of students live on campus. Alcohol is not permitted. All students may keep cars on campus.

Activities: 19% of men belong to 5 local and 4 national fraternities; 13% of women belong to 8 local and 3 national sororities. There are 155 groups on campus, including art, band, cheerleading, choir, chorale, chorus, computers, dance, drama, ethnic, gay, honors, international, jazz band, literary magazine, musical theater, newspaper, orchestra, political, professional, radio and TV, religious, social, social service, student government, symphony, and yearbook. Popular campus events include Homecoming, Siblings Weekend, Parents Weekend, and Spring Weekend.

Sports: There are 8 intercollegiate sports for men and 10 for women, and 24 intramural sports for men and 24 for women. Athletic and recreation facilities include an ice arena, 2 swimming pools, 3 gymnasiums, 8 squash and 8 tennis courts, an outdoor track and field stadium, bowling alleys, Nautilus and weight rooms, and a sauna. The stadium, indoor gymnasium, and largest auditorium/arena each seat 3000.

Disabled Students: 90% of the campus is accessible to disabled students. The following facilities are available: wheelchair ramps, elevators, special parking, specially equipped rest rooms, special class scheduling, lowered drinking fountains, lowered telephones, and fire alarms for hearing-impaired students.

Services: In addition to many counseling and information services, tutoring is available in every subject. There is a reader service for the blind and remedial math and writing.

Campus Safety and Security: Campus safety and security measures include 24-hour foot and vehicle patrol, escort service, informal discussions, and pamphlets/posters/films. In addition, there are emergency telephones and lighted pathways/sidewalks.

Programs of Study: Geneseo confers B.A., B.S., and B.S.Ed. degrees. Master's degrees are also awarded. Bachelor's degrees are awarded in BIOLOGICAL SCIENCE (biochemistry, biology/biological science, and biophysics), BUSINESS (accounting, business administration and management, and management science), COMMUNICATIONS AND THE ARTS (art history and appreciation, communications, comparative literature, dramatic arts, English, fine arts, French, music, Spanish, and studio art), COMPUTER AND PHYSICAL SCIENCE (applied physics, chemistry, computer science, geochemistry, geology, geophysics and seismology, mathematics, natural sciences, and physics), EDUCATION (elementary and special), HEALTH PROFESSIONS (medical laboratory technology and speech pathology/audiology), SOCIAL SCIENCE (African American studies, American studies, anthropology, economics, geography, history, philosophy, political science/government, psychology, and sociology). Biology, management, and accounting have the largest enrollments.

Required: To graduate, students must complete 120 credit hours with a minimum 2.0 GPA. The total number of hours in the major varies. The required core curriculum includes 2 courses each in humanities, fine arts, social sciences, natural sciences, and critical reasoning.

Special: The college offers a cooperative 3-2 engineering degree with Alfred, Case Western Reserve, Clarkson, Columbia, and Syracuse universities, SUNY at Binghamton and Buffalo, and the University of Rochester, as well as a 3-3 degree with Rochester Institute of Technology. Cross-registration is available with the Rochester Area Colleges Consortium. Geneseo offers internships in all majors, study abroad through more than 95 programs, a Washington semester, dual majors including theater/English, credit for military experience, and pass/fail options. There is a freshman honors program on campus, as well as 14 national honor societies. 5 departments have honors programs.

Faculty/Classroom: 66% of faculty are male; 34%, female. All teach undergraduates. No introductory courses are taught by graduate students. The average class size in an introductory lecture is 40; in a laboratory, 24; and in a regular course offering, 24.

Admissions: 54% of the 1995-96 applicants were accepted. SAT I scores for the 1995-96 freshman class were as follows: Verbal—25% below 500, 53% between 500 and 599, 20% between 600 and 700, and 2% above 700; Math—5% below 500, 35% between 500 and 599, 51% between 600 and 700, and 9% above 700. The ACT scores were 4% below 21, 5% between 21 and 23, 30% between 24 and 26, 48% between 27 and 28, and 13% above 28. 82% of the current freshmen were in the top fifth of their class; 98% were in the top two fifths. 35 freshmen graduated first in their class.

Requirements: The SAT I or ACT is required. Geneseo requires applicants to be in the upper 50% of their class. Applicants must be graduates of an accredited secondary school or have a GED certificate. The academic program must have included 4 years each of English, mathematics, science, and social studies, and 3 years of a foreign language. An essay is required. A portfolio or audition for certain programs and an interview are recommended. AP and CLEP credits are accepted. Important factors in the admissions decision are advanced placement or honor courses, recommendations by school officials, and evidence of special talent.

Procedure: Freshmen are admitted fall and spring. Entrance exams should be taken during the spring of the junior year. There are early decision, early admissions, and deferred admissions plans. Early decision applications should be filed by November 15; regular applications, by January 15 for fall entry and September 15 for spring entry, along with an application fee of $30. Notification of early decision is sent December 15; regular decision, on a rolling basis beginning February 15. 158 early decision candidates were accepted for the 1995-96 class. A waiting list is an active part of the admissions procedure, with about 10% of all applicants on the list.

Transfer: 334 transfer students enrolled in 1995-96. Applicants must provide transcripts from all previously attended colleges. A minimum 2.0 GPA is required. Students with fewer than 24 credit hours must submit SAT I or ACT scores. An essay is required and an interview is recommended. 32 credits of 120 must be completed at Geneseo.

Visiting: There are regularly scheduled orientations for prospective students, including a day-and-a-half summer program consisting of academic advisement, registration, and adjustment to college activities. There are guides for informal visits, and visitors may sit in on classes and stay overnight at the school. To schedule a visit, contact the Office of Admissions.

Financial Aid: In a recent year, 70% of all freshmen and 75% of continuing students received some form of financial aid. 65% of freshmen and 70% of continuing students received need-based aid. The average freshman award was $2830. Of that total, scholarships or need-based grants averaged $2000 ($6900 maximum); loans averaged $2135 ($4000 maximum); and work contracts averaged $1005 ($3500 maximum). 68% of undergraduate students work part-time. Geneseo is a member of CSS. The FAFSA is required. The application deadline for fall entry is February 15.

International Students: In a recent year, 9 international students enrolled were enrolled. They must take the TOEFL and achieve a minimum score of 530.

Computers: The college provides computer facilities for student use. The mainframes are a DEC VAX 6000-510 and an 8530. A variety of PCs are located throughout the campus. All students may access the system. There are no time limits. The fees are $50.

Graduates: In 1994-95, 1240 bachelor's degrees were awarded. The most popular majors among graduates were education (14%), psychology (12%), and business (9%). Within an average freshman class, 1% graduate in 3 years, 68% in 4 years, and 9% in 5 years. 31 companies recruited on campus in 1994-95. Of the 1994 graduating class, 35% were enrolled in graduate school within 6 months of graduation and 56% had found employment.

Admissions Contact: Jill Conlon, Director of Admissions. A video of the campus is available.

STATE UNIVERSITY OF NEW YORK/COLLEGE AT NEW PALTZ   D-4
New Paltz, NY 12561-2499

(914) 257-3200
FAX: (914) 257-3209

Full-time: 1976 men, 2751 women	Faculty: 280; IIA, av$
Part-time: 498 men, 862 women	Ph.D.s: 84%
Graduate: 394 men, 1169 women	Student/Faculty: 17 to 1
Year: semesters, summer session	Tuition: $3575 ($8475)
Application Deadline: May 1	Room & Board: $4868
Freshman Class: 8768 applied, 3820 accepted, 815 enrolled	
SAT I Verbal/Math: 479/537	VERY COMPETITIVE

State University of New York/College at New Paltz, founded in 1828, is a state-supported liberal arts college offering undergraduate and graduate programs in the arts and sciences, business, education, engineering, and the health professions. In addition to regional accreditation, SUNY New Paltz has baccalaureate program accreditation with ABET, ASLA, CSAB, NASM, and NLN. The library contains 410,000 volumes and 930,000 microform items, and subscribes to 1385 periodicals. Computerized library sources and services include the card catalog, interlibrary loans, and database searching. Special learning facilities include a learning resource center, art gallery, planetarium, radio station, TV station, greenhouse, robotics laboratory, electron microscope facility, speech and hearing clinic, music therapy training facility, observatory, and Fournier transform mass spectrometer. The 216-acre campus is in a rural area 100 miles north of New York City and 65 miles south of Albany. Including residence halls, there are 55 buildings on campus.

Student Life: 98% of undergraduates are from New York. Students come from 20 states and 42 foreign countries. 90% are from public schools; 10% from private. 73% are white; 10% African American. The average age of freshmen is 18; all undergraduates, 22. 22% do not continue beyond their first year; 51% remain to graduate.

Housing: 2400 students can be accommodated in college housing. College-sponsored living facilities include coed dormitories. On-campus housing is guaranteed for all 4 years. 51% of students live on campus; of those, 90% remain on campus on weekends. All students may keep cars on campus.

Activities: 3% of men belong to 8 local and 7 national fraternities; 3% of women belong to 8 local and 6 national sororities. There are 140 groups on campus, including art, band, cheerleading, choir, chorale, chorus, computers, dance, drama, ethnic, gay, honors, international, jazz band, literary magazine, musical theater, newspaper, orchestra, photography, political, professional, radio and TV, religious, social, social service, student government, and yearbook. Popular campus events include Spirit Weekend, Family Weekend, Black Weekend, Springfest, Greek Weekend, Welcome Week, New Paltz Summer Repertory Theatre, the Music in the Mountains summer concert series, Homecoming, International Weekend, and Latin Weekend.

Sports: There are 8 intercollegiate sports for men and 7 for women, and 20 intramural sports for men and 15 for women. Athletic and recreation facilities include a gymnasium, numerous playing fields, and a 35,000-square-foot air-supported structure for tennis, jogging, volleyball, and basketball.

Disabled Students: 90% of the campus is accessible to disabled students. The following facilities are available: wheelchair ramps, elevators, special parking, specially equipped rest rooms, special class scheduling, lowered drinking fountains, lowered telephones, and some specially equipped residence halls.

Services: In addition to many counseling and information services, tutoring is available in most subjects. There is a reader service for the blind, and remedial math, reading, and writing.

Campus Safety and Security: Campus safety and security measures include 24-hour foot and vehicle patrol, escort service, informal discussions, and pamphlets/posters/films. In addition, there are emergency telephones, lighted pathways/sidewalks, a bicycle patrol, locked residence halls, and a campus 911 system.

Programs of Study: SUNY New Paltz confers B.A., B.S., B.F.A., B.S.E.E., and B.S.N. degrees. Master's degrees are also awarded. Bachelor's degrees are awarded in BIOLOGICAL SCIENCE (biology/biological science), BUSINESS (accounting, banking and finance, business administration and management, and marketing/retailing/merchandising), COMMUNICATIONS AND THE ARTS (broadcasting, communications, design, dramatic arts, English, fine arts, French, German, journalism, music, photography, Spanish, and speech/debate/rhetoric), COMPUTER AND PHYSICAL SCIENCE (chemistry, computer science, geology, mathematics, and physics), EDUCATION (art, early childhood, elementary, foreign languages, middle school, science, and secondary), ENGINEERING AND ENVIRONMENTAL DESIGN (computer engineering and electrical/electronics engineering), HEALTH PROFESSIONS (premedicine and speech pathology/audiology), SOCIAL SCIENCE (anthropology, economics, geography, history, international relations, philosophy, political science/government, psychology, social science, and sociology). Business administration, communications, education, and psychology have the largest enrollments.

Required: To graduate, students must complete 120 credits with a 2.0 GPA. The number of credits required in the major varies. Other requirements include 45 credits in liberal arts and sciences, including courses in English, analytical skills, history, and physical education, and 60 credits in upper-division courses.

Special: There is cross-registration with the mid-Hudson Consortium of Colleges. The college offers co-op programs in most majors, internships with local companies and in Albany and New York City, work-study programs on campus and at the Childrens Center of New Paltz, student-designed and dual majors, and B.A.-B.S. degrees. Students may study abroad in 11 countries. A 3-2 degree in geological engineering is offered with the New Mexico Institute of Mining and Technology. There is a freshman honors program on campus.

Faculty/Classroom: 63% of faculty are male; 37%, female. The average class size in an introductory lecture is 25; in a laboratory, 10; and in a regular course offering, 25.

Admissions: 44% of the 1995-96 applicants were accepted. The SAT I scores for the 1995-96 freshman class were as follows: Verbal—62% below 500, 30% between 500 and 599, 7% between 600 and 700, and 1% above 700; Math—34% below 500, 42% between 500 and 599, 21% between 600 and 700, and 3% above 700. 40% of the current freshmen were in the top fifth of their class; 84% were in the top two fifths. 2 freshmen graduated first in their class.

Requirements: The SAT I or ACT is required, with a recommended minimum composite score of 950 on the SAT I or 22 on the ACT. SUNY New Paltz requires applicants to be in the upper 50% of their class. A minimum grade average of B is required. Graduation from an accredited secondary school is required; a GED will be accepted. The applicant's academic record must include 4 years each of English and social studies and 3 years each of a foreign language, mathematics, and science. Where required, a portfolio and an audition are

used for placement purposes only. AP and CLEP credits are accepted. Important factors in the admissions decision are advanced placement or honor courses, extracurricular activities record, and evidence of special talent.

Procedure: Freshmen are admitted fall and spring. There are early decision, early admissions, and deferred admissions plans. Early decision applications should be filed by November 1; regular applications, by May 1 for fall entry and December 1 for spring entry, along with an application fee of $30. Notification of early decision is sent December 15; regular decision, on a rolling basis. 15 early decision candidates were accepted for the 1995-96 class. A waiting list is an active part of the admissions procedure.

Transfer: 933 transfer students enrolled in 1995-96. To be considered, applicants must have maintained a minimum GPA of 2.5 in colleges previously attended. Some programs require a 3.0 GPA. 30 credits of 120 must be completed at SUNY New Paltz.

Visiting: There are regularly scheduled orientations for prospective students, including 4 to 5 sessions scheduled by appointment on Mondays, Wednesdays, and Fridays during the summer. An open house and Saturday sessions are conducted during the fall. Visitors may sit in on classes. To schedule a visit, contact the Office of Undergraduate Admissions.

Financial Aid: In 1995-96, 68% of all freshmen and 75% of continuing students received some form of financial and need-based aid. The average freshman award was $5000. Of that total, scholarships or need-based grants averaged $1000 ($5900 maximum); loans averaged $2500 ($3300 maximum); and work contracts averaged $800 ($1200 maximum). 35% of undergraduate students work part-time. Average earnings from campus work for the school year are $800. The average financial indebtedness of the 1994-95 graduate was $10,000. The college's own financial statement is required. The application deadline for fall entry is April 1.

International Students: There are currently 210 international students enrolled. The school actively recruits these students. They must take the TOEFL and achieve a minimum score of 550. The SAT I or ACT is required if the TOEFL has not been taken. Conditional acceptance is available; the applicant must take ESL courses until required proficiency is achieved.

Computers: The college provides computer facilities for student use. The mainframe is an IBM ES9000 9121-210. Students have access to mainframe terminals in the residence halls, the humanities building, the administration building, and the library. In addition, there are some 200 PCs in general access areas, departmental areas, and laboratories. All students may access the system during those hours that the buildings are open; residence hall terminals and personal PCs, 24 hours. There are no time limits and no fees.

Graduates: In 1994-95, 1295 bachelor's degrees were awarded. The most popular majors among graduates were psychology (10%), business administration (10%), and elementary education (7%). Within an average freshman class, 23% graduate in 4 years, 23% in 5 years, and 5% in 6 years. 419 companies recruited on campus in 1994-95. Of the 1994 graduating class, 10% were enrolled in graduate school within 6 months of graduation and 75% had found employment.

Admissions Contact: L. David Eaton, Dean of Admissions. E-mail: http://www.newpaltz.edu. A campus video is available.

STATE UNIVERSITY OF NEW YORK/COLLEGE AT OLD WESTBURY
D-5

Westbury, NY 11568-0210   (516) 876-3073; FAX: (516) 876-3307

Full-time: 1267 men, 1754 women	Faculty: 120; IIB, +$
Part-time: 453 men, 639 women	Ph.Ds: 75%
Graduate: none	Student/Faculty: 25 to 1
Year: semesters, summer session	Tuition: $3678 ($8578)
Application Deadline: March 15	Room & Board: $4616
Freshman Class: 2057 applied, 1710 accepted, 495 enrolled	
SAT I: recommended	COMPETITIVE

SUNY/College at Old Westbury, founded in 1965, is a public institution offering degree programs in the arts and sciences, business, education, fine arts, and health science. The library contains 243,511 volumes, 187,834 microform items, and 3893 audiovisual forms, and subscribes to 1146 periodicals. Computerized library sources and services include interlibrary loans and database searching. Special learning facilities include a learning resource center, art gallery, and radio station. The 605-acre campus is in a suburban area 20 miles east of New York City. Including residence halls, there are 14 buildings on campus.

Student Life: 98% of undergraduates are from New York. Students come from 7 states, 19 foreign countries, and Canada. 43% are white; 29% African American; 14% Hispanic. The average age of freshmen is 19; all undergraduates, 26. 38% do not continue beyond their first year; 30% remain to graduate.

Housing: 792 students can be accommodated in college housing. College-sponsored living facilities include coed dormitories. On-campus housing is available on a first-come, first-served basis. Priority is given to out-of-town students. 80% of students commute. Alcohol is not permitted. All students may keep cars on campus.

Activities: There are 9 national fraternities and 9 national sororities. There are 53 groups on campus, including art, cheerleading, choir, computers, dance, drama, ethnic, gay, international, jazz band, newspaper, political, professional, radio and TV, religious, social, social service, student government, and yearbook. Popular campus events include Welcome Back Festival, Spring Fling, May Festival, and Christmas Ball.

Sports: There are 5 intercollegiate sports for men and 5 for women, and 7 intramural sports for men and 7 for women. Athletic and recreation facilities include a 3000-seat gymnasium, an auxiliary gymnasium, playing fields, a swimming pool, a fitness center, a weight room, jogging trails, and courts for tennis, paddleball, handball, racquetball, and squash.

Disabled Students: All of the campus is accessible to disabled students. The following facilities are available: wheelchair ramps, elevators, special parking, specially equipped rest rooms, lowered drinking fountains, lowered telephones, and limited volunteer transportation.

Services: In addition to many counseling and information services, tutoring is available in most subjects. There is a reader service for the blind, and remedial math, reading, and writing.

Campus Safety and Security: Campus safety and security measures include 24-hour foot and vehicle patrol, escort service, shuttle buses, and informal discussions. In addition, there are pamphlets/posters/films, emergency telephones, and lighted pathways/sidewalks.

Programs of Study: SUNY Old Westbury confers B.A., B.S., and B.P.S. degrees. Bachelor's degrees are awarded in BIOLOGICAL SCIENCE (biology/biological science), BUSINESS (accounting, banking and finance, business administration and management, management information systems, and marketing/retailing/merchandising), COMMUNICATIONS AND THE ARTS (media arts, musical theater, Spanish, and visual and performing arts), COMPUTER AND PHYSICAL SCIENCE (chemistry, computer science, and mathematics), EDUCATION (bilingual/bicultural, elementary, foreign languages, mathematics, science, secondary, and special), HEALTH PROFESSIONS (community health work), SOCIAL SCIENCE (American studies, criminology, economics, humanities, international studies, philosophy, political science/government, psychology, and sociology). Teacher education is the strongest academically. Business has the largest enrollment.

Required: To graduate, students must maintain a GPA of 2.0 in 120 semester credits; accounting and special education majors require 128 credits. General education requirements include courses in writing and reasoning skills, creative arts, ideas and ideology, cross-cultural perspectives, U.S. society and history, physical or life science, and foreign language.

Special: SUNY Old Westbury offers cross-registration with SUNY Empire State, Lirache, and colleges in Nassau and Suffolk counties, internships in teacher education, study abroad, a B.A.-B.S. in biological science, dual majors, and a 3–2 engineering degree with SUNY at Stony Brook and SUNY Maritime College. Credit for military and life experience, nondegree study, and pass/fail options are available.

Faculty/Classroom: 51% of faculty are male; 49%, female. All teach undergraduates. The average class size in an introductory lecture is 35; in a laboratory, 13; and in a regular course offering, 23.

Admissions: 83% of the 1995–96 applicants were accepted. 13% of the current freshmen were in the top fifth of their class; 36% were in the top two fifths. 5 freshmen graduated first in their class.

Requirements: The SAT I is recommended. A minimum grade average of 80% is required. Applicants must be graduates of an accredited secondary school or have the GED. An essay, portfolio, and interview also are recommended. Students are evaluated according to qualifying categories of academic achievement, special knowledge and creative ability, paid work experience, and social or personal experience. AP and CLEP credits are accepted. Important factors in the admissions decision are leadership record, recommendations by school officials, and evidence of special talent.

Procedure: Freshmen are admitted fall and spring. There is a deferred admissions plan. Applications should be filed by March 15 for fall entry and December 1 for spring entry, along with an application fee of $25. Notification is sent on a rolling basis.

Transfer: 653 transfer students enrolled in 1995–96. Applicants must submit official transcripts from all colleges attended. Those students with fewer than 24 college credits must also submit a high school transcript. 48 credits of 120 or 128 must be completed at SUNY Old Westbury.

Visiting: There are regularly scheduled orientations for prospective students. There are guides for informal visits. To schedule a visit, contact the Admissions Office.

Financial Aid: 70% of undergraduate students work part-time. SUNY Old Westbury is a member of CSS. The FAF, the college's own financial statement, and the Singlefile Form are required. The application deadline for fall entry is April.

International Students: There are currently 60 international students enrolled. The school actively recruits these students. They must take the TOEFL and achieve a minimum score of 500.

Computers: The college provides computer facilities for student use. The mainframe is a DEC VAX 6610. The Educational Technology Center houses 3 laboratories with 35 Apple Macintosh Plus, 16 Apple IIe, and 25 Zenith 150 microcomputers. All students may access the system daily. There are no time limits and no fees.

Graduates: In 1994–95, 667 bachelor's degrees were awarded. The most popular majors among graduates were teacher education (17%), business management (14%), and accounting (13%). Within an average freshman class, 8% graduate in 4 years, 20% in 5 years, and 30% in 6 years. 38 companies recruited on campus in 1994–95.

Admissions Contact: Olga Dunning, Admissions Officer. A campus video is available.

STATE UNIVERSITY OF NEW YORK/COLLEGE AT ONEONTA   D-3

Oneonta, NY 13820   (607) 436-2524

Full-time: 1908 men, 2788 women	**Faculty:** 240; IIA, av$
Part-time: 133 men, 279 women	**Ph.D.s:** 70%
Graduate: 113 men, 347 women	**Student/Faculty:** 20 to 1
Year: semesters, summer session	**Tuition:** $3733 ($8633)
Application Deadline: April 1	**Room & Board:** $5458
Freshman Class: 6743 applied, 5217 accepted, 1090 enrolled	
SAT I Verbal/Math: 463/509	**ACT:** 22 **COMPETITIVE**

The State University of New York/College at Oneonta, founded in 1889, is a state-supported institution offering undergraduate and graduate programs in the arts and sciences. There is 1 graduate school. In addition to regional accreditation, Oneonta has baccalaureate program accreditation with ADA and AHEA. The library contains 534,779 volumes, 763,576 microform items, and 13,354 audiovisual forms, and subscribes to 2446 periodicals. Computerized library sources and services include the card catalog, interlibrary loans, and database searching. Special learning facilities include a learning resource center, natural history museum, planetarium, radio station, observatory, science discovery center, college camp, and off-campus biological field station. The 250-acre campus is in a rural area 75 miles southwest of Albany and 55 miles northeast of Binghamton. Including residence halls, there are 40 buildings on campus.

Student Life: 98% of undergraduates are from New York. Students come from 14 states and 13 foreign countries. 93% are white. The average age of all undergraduates is 20. 20% do not continue beyond their first year; 57% remain to graduate.

Housing: 2700 students can be accommodated in college housing. College-sponsored living facilities include single-sex and coed dormitories. In addition, there is a mathematics and science wing, an international wing, all-freshman housing, and other special interest groupings within residence halls. On-campus housing is available on a first-come, first-served basis and is available on a lottery system for upperclassmen. 53% of students live on campus; of those, 53% remain on campus on weekends. Alcohol is not permitted. Upperclassmen may keep cars on campus.

Activities: There are 7 local and 6 national fraternities and 3 local and 5 national sororities. There are 29 groups on campus, including art, band, cheerleading, choir, chorale, chorus, computers, dance, drama, ethnic, film, gay, honors, international, jazz band, musical theater, newspaper, orchestra, pep band, photography, political, professional, radio, religious, social, social service, student government, volunteer, and yearbook.

Sports: There are 7 intercollegiate sports for men and 9 for women, and 17 intramural sports for men and 17 for women. Athletic and recreation facilities include a field house, a dance studio, and weight rooms.

Disabled Students: The following facilities are available: wheelchair ramps, elevators, special parking, specially equipped rest rooms, special class scheduling, and lowered drinking fountains. All academic buildings are accessible, and some residence halls.

Services: In addition to many counseling and information services, tutoring is available in most subjects. There is a reader service for the blind, and remedial math, reading, and writing.

Campus Safety and Security: Campus safety and security measures include self-defense education, escort service, shuttle buses, and informal discussions. In addition, there are pamphlets/posters/films, emergency telephones, lighted pathways/sidewalks, 24-hour vehicle patrol, and formal workshops.

Programs of Study: Oneonta confers B.A. and B.S. degrees. Master's degrees are also awarded. Bachelor's degrees are awarded in BIOLOGICAL SCIENCE (biology/biological science), BUSINESS (accounting, business economics, and fashion merchandising), COMMUNICATIONS AND THE ARTS (dramatic arts, English, fine arts, French, music, Spanish, and speech/debate/rhetoric), COMPUTER AND PHYSICAL SCIENCE (chemistry, computer science, earth science, geology, mathematics, physics, and statistics), EDUCATION (art, business, elementary, foreign languages, home economics, middle school, science, and secondary), ENGINEERING AND ENVIRONMENTAL DESIGN (environmental science), HEALTH PROFESSIONS (predentistry and premedicine), SOCIAL SCIENCE (anthropology, child care/child and family studies, dietetics, economics, geography, gerontology, history, home economics, international studies, philosophy, political science/government, prelaw, psychology, and sociology). Business economics, home economics, and physical and natural sciences are the strongest academically. Business economics, education, and psychology have the largest enrollments.

Required: Students must complete 122 semester hours, with at least 48 hours in upper-division courses and 30 to 36 hours in the major. A minimum GPA of 2.0 (2.5 for education majors) must be maintained. In addition, students must complete core curriculum requirements in the fine arts, social and behavioral sciences, natural and mathematical sciences, and foreign language, as well as pass writing and speech proficiency examinations.

Special: Oneonta offers limited cross-registration with Hartwick College, internships in many fields, study abroad in 13 countries, a Washington semester, work-study programs, and dual majors. A 3–2 engineering degree is offered with Alfred, Clarkson, and Syracuse universities, SUNY at Buffalo and Binghamton, Georgia Institute of Technology, and Polytechnic University. Other cooperative programs include a 3–4 in optometry, a 3–2 in management, a 3–1 in fashion, and a 2–2 in physical therapy, medical technology, respiratory care, cytotechnology, or forestry. Credit for life experience, nondegree study, and pass/fail options are available. There is a chapter of Phi Beta Kappa on campus.

Faculty/Classroom: All faculty teach undergraduates. No introductory courses are taught by graduate students.

Admissions: 77% of the 1995–96 applicants were accepted. The SAT I scores for the 1995–96 freshman class were as follows: Verbal—86% below 500, 12% between 500 and 599, and 2% between 600 and 700; Math—66% below 500, 26% between 500 and 599, and 7% between 600 and 700.

Requirements: The SAT I or ACT is required. Oneonta requires applicants to be in the upper 50% of their class. Applicants should be graduates of an accredited secondary school and have 16 academic credits, including 4 years each of English and history, and 8 years combined of foreign language, mathematics, and science, with at least 2 years in each of these 3 broad areas. The GED is accepted. AP and CLEP credits are accepted. Important factors in the admissions decision are evidence of special talent, advanced placement or honor courses, and leadership record.

Procedure: Freshmen are admitted fall and spring. Entrance exams should be taken in the spring of the junior year or the fall of the senior year. There are early admissions and deferred admissions plans. Applications should be filed by April 1 for fall entry and November 15 for spring entry, along with an application fee of $25. Notification is sent on a rolling basis.

Transfer: 601 transfer students enrolled in 1995–96. Official transcripts of all previous college work must be submitted. A minimum of 15 semester hours of transferable credit and a minimum GPA of 2.5 are required. 45 credits of 122 must be completed at Oneonta.

Visiting: There are regularly scheduled orientations for prospective students, including 2 fall open houses, individual appointments, and group information sessions. There are guides for informal visits and visitors may sit in on classes. To schedule a visit, contact the Admissions Office.

Financial Aid: In 1995–96, 82% of all freshmen and 87% of continuing students received some form of financial and need-based aid. The average freshman award was $2200. Of that total, scholarships or need-based grants averaged $2169 ($9336 maximum); loans averaged $2952 ($7500 maximum); and work contracts averaged $181 ($1500 maximum). 40% of undergraduate students work part-time. Average earnings from campus work for the school year are $1200. Oneonta is a member of CSS. The FAFSA is required. The application deadline for fall entry is April 15.

International Students: There were 60 international students enrolled in a recent year. The school actively recruits these students. They must take the TOEFL and achieve a minimum score of 500.

Computers: The college provides computer facilities for student use. The mainframe is a DEC VAX. More than 200 microcomputers and terminals are available on campus. Students have access to E-mail on Bitnet and the Internet and to multimedia, graphics, and other specialized laboratories within departments. There is also a token ring network for education and service training courses. All students may access the system. There are no time limits and no fees.

Graduates: In 1994–95, 1033 bachelor's degrees were awarded. The most popular majors among graduates were business economics (20%), elementary education (16%), and psychology (11%). Within an average freshman class, 1% graduate in 3 years, 45% in 4 years, 55% in 5 years, and 57% in 6 years.

Admissions Contact: Steven R. Perry, Acting Director of Admissions.

STATE UNIVERSITY OF NEW YORK/COLLEGE AT OSWEGO
C-3

Oswego, NY 13126	(315) 341-2250; FAX: (315) 341-3260
Full-time: 3000 men, 3600 women	Faculty: 326; IIA, -$
Part-time: 468 men, 537 women	Ph.D.s: 72%
Graduate: 351 men, 778 women	Student/Faculty: 20 to 1
Year: semesters, summer session	Tuition: $3746 ($8762)
Application Deadline: January 15	Room & Board: $4990
Freshman Class: 7578 applied, 4006 accepted, 1350 enrolled	
SAT I Verbal/Math: 475/535	ACT: 23 COMPETITIVE

State University of New York/College at Oswego, founded in 1861, is a comprehensive institution with regional centers for vocational technical education in Albany and Syracuse. There is 1 graduate school. In addition to regional accreditation, Oswego has baccalaureate program accreditation with NASM. The library contains 427,000 volumes, 1,755,000 microform items, and 53,400 audiovisual forms, and subscribes to 1569 periodicals. Computerized library sources and services include the card catalog, interlibrary loans, and database searching. Special learning facilities include a learning resource center, art gallery, planetarium, radio station, TV station, and biological field station. The 696-acre campus is in a small town on the southeast shore of Lake Ontario, 35 miles north of Syracuse. Including residence halls, there are 45 buildings on campus.

Student Life: 98% of undergraduates are from New York. Students come from 13 states, 30 foreign countries, and Canada. 90% are from public schools; 10% from private. 89% are white. 42% are Catholic; 41% Protestant; 14% Jewish. The average age of freshmen is 18; all undergraduates, 21. 10% do not continue beyond their first year; 56% remain to graduate.

Housing: 3900 students can be accommodated in college housing. College-sponsored living facilities include coed dormitories. In addition, there are honors houses, language houses, and special interest houses. On-campus housing is guaranteed for all 4 years. All students may keep cars on campus.

Activities: 15% of men belong to 9 local and 9 national fraternities; 15% of women belong to 8 local and 6 national sororities. There are 95 groups on campus, including art, band, cheerleading, choir, chorale, chorus, computers, dance, drama, ethnic, gay, honors, international, jazz band, literary magazine, musical theater, newspaper, opera, orchestra, photography, political, professional, radio and TV, religious, social, social service, student government, and yearbook. Popular campus events include Honors Convocations and Quest, Alumni and Parents weekends, and College Open House.

Sports: There are 9 intercollegiate sports for men and 9 for women, and 14 intramural sports for men and 20 for women. Athletic and recreation facilities include an ice hockey rink, a field house with an artificial-grass practice area, 23 tennis courts, an outdoor track, 3 soccer and 3 lacrosse fields, baseball and softball fields, numerous basketball courts, handball, racquetball, and squash courts, 2 indoor pools, and a diving well. The gymnasium seats 3500. There are also 2 fitness centers, weight rooms, and a cross-country ski lodge.

Disabled Students: The entire campus is accessible to disabled students. The following facilities are available: elevators, special parking, specially equipped rest rooms, lowered drinking fountains, and a student support group.

Services: In addition to many counseling and information services, tutoring is available in every subject. There is a reader service for the blind, and remedial math, reading, and writing. The Office of Learning Support Services provides general foundation support.

Campus Safety and Security: Campus safety and security measures include 24-hour foot and vehicle patrol, escort service, shuttle buses, and informal discussions. In addition, there are emergency telephones, lighted pathways/sidewalks, a campus police force, and programs on safety issues and alcohol education.

Programs of Study: Oswego confers B.A., B.S., and B.F.A. degrees. Master's degrees are also awarded. Bachelor's degrees are awarded in BIOLOGICAL SCIENCE (biology/biological science and zoology), BUSINESS (accounting, business administration and management, human resources, and marketing/retailing/merchandising), COMMUNICATIONS AND THE ARTS (broadcasting, communications, dramatic arts, English, fine arts, French, German, linguistics, music, and Spanish), COMPUTER AND PHYSICAL SCIENCE (atmospheric sciences and meteorology, chemistry, computer science, earth science, geochemistry, geology, information sciences and systems, mathematics, and physics), EDUCATION (business, elementary, foreign languages, industrial arts, secondary, and vocational)

HEALTH PROFESSIONS (predentistry and premedicine), SOCIAL SCIENCE (American studies, anthropology, economics, history, human services, philosophy, political science/government, prelaw, psychology, and sociology). Chemistry, accounting, and English are the strongest academically. Elementary/secondary education, business administration, and accounting have the largest enrollments.

Required: To graduate, all students must complete 42 to 48 general education credits, including 9 credits each in social/behavioral sciences, natural sciences, and humanities and fine arts, 6 credits each in expository writing and mathematics, and a 6-credit human diversity sequence. Students must have a minimum 2.0 GPA and complete 122 total credit hours (126 hours for technology education and vocational education students). The total number of hours in the major varies from 30 to 78.

Special: Oswego offers cross-registration with ACUSNY-Visiting Student Program. More than 600 internships are available with business, social, cultural, and government agencies. The college also offers a Washington semester, study abroad in more than 80 programs, accelerated degree programs, dual majors, B.A.-B.S. degrees, a general studies degree, credit for military experience, nondegree study, and pass/fail options. A 3–2 engineering degree is offered with Clarkson University, SUNY at Binghamton, and Case Western Reserve University. There is a freshman honors program on campus, as well as 21 national honor societies. 9 departments have honors programs.

Faculty/Classroom: 70% of faculty are male; 30%, female. 97% teach undergraduates, and 91% also do research. No introductory courses are taught by graduate students. The average class size in an introductory lecture is 80; in a laboratory, 13; and in a regular course offering, 24.

Admissions: 53% of the 1995–96 applicants were accepted. The SAT I scores for the 1995–96 freshman class were as follows: Verbal—69% below 500, 27% between 500 and 599, and 4% between 600 and 700; Math—32% below 500, 50% between 500 and 599, 17% between 600 and 700, and 1% above 700. The ACT scores were 16% below 21, 41% between 21 and 23, 30% between 24 and 26, 8% between 27 and 28, and 5% above 28. 46% of the current freshmen were in the top fifth of their class; 72% were in the top two fifths. 10 freshmen graduated first in their class.

Requirements: The SAT I or ACT is required. Applicants must be graduates of an accredited secondary school or have a GED certificate. 18 academic credits are required, including 4 years each of English and social studies, 3 each of mathematics and science, and 2 of a foreign language. An essay and interview are recommended. AP and CLEP credits are accepted. Important factors in the admissions decision are advanced placement or honor courses, extracurricular activities record, and evidence of special talent.

Procedure: Freshmen are admitted fall and spring. Entrance exams should be taken during the spring of the junior year or fall of the senior year. There are early decision and deferred admissions plans. Early decision applications should be filed by November 15; regular applications, by January 15 for fall entry and November 1 for spring entry, along with an application fee of $30. Notification of early decision is sent December 15; regular decision, on a rolling basis. 85 early decision candidates were accepted for the 1995–96 class.

Transfer: 850 transfer students enrolled in 1995–96. Applicants must submit official transcripts from previously attended colleges. Students with a minimum GPA of 2.4 are encouraged to apply. SUNY associate degree holders are given preference. Secondary school records may be required for 1-year transfers. 30 credits of 122 to 126 must be completed at Oswego.

Visiting: There are regularly scheduled orientations for prospective students, usually including a campus tour and a meeting with a counselor. There are guides for informal visits and visitors may sit in on classes and stay overnight at the school. To schedule a visit, contact the Office of Admissions.

Financial Aid: In 1995–96, 81% of all freshmen and 86% of continuing students received some form of financial aid. 68% of freshmen and 61% of continuing students received need-based aid. The average freshman award was $3567. Of that total, scholarships or need-based grants averaged $1402 ($5240 maximum); loans averaged $1298 ($4125 maximum); and work contracts averaged $867 ($1200 maximum). 30% of undergraduate students work part-time. Average earnings from campus work for the school year are $1000. The average financial indebtedness of the 1994–95 graduate was $7089. The FAFSA is required. The application deadline for fall entry is March 1.

International Students: There are currently 95 international students enrolled. The school actively recruits these students. They must take the TOEFL and achieve a minimum score of 550.

Computers: The college provides computer facilities for student use. The mainframes are a DEC VAX 6000–520 and 6000–320, a Sun 4/280, 2 SPARC servers, 15 Sun or 4 VAX Station 4000 Pathworks file servers. There are more than 250 personal computers available for student access. Microcomputer laboratories are located throughout the campus for general access and in support of departmental pro-

grams. There is an instructional computing center that provides a 24-hour help line. All students may access the system. There are no time limits and no fees.

Graduates: In 1994–95, 1551 bachelor's degrees were awarded. The most popular majors among graduates were elementary education (10%), business administration (10%), and communications (7%). Within an average freshman class, 1% graduate in 3 years, 40% in 4 years, 56% in 5 years, and 59% in 6 years. 60 companies recruited on campus in 1994–95. Of the 1994 graduating class, 19% were enrolled in graduate school within 6 months of graduation and 69% had found employment.

Admissions Contact: Joseph F. Grant, Jr., Dean of Admissions. A campus video is available.

STATE UNIVERSITY OF NEW YORK/COLLEGE AT PLATTSBURGH   D-2

Plattsburgh, NY 12901   (518) 564-2040; FAX: (518) 564-2045

Full-time: 2106 men, 2699 women	Faculty: 244; IIA, -$
Part-time: 161 men, 327 women	Ph.D.s: 97%
Graduate: 204 men, 470 women	Student/Faculty: 20 to 1
Year: semesters, summer session	Tuition: $3883 ($8783)
Application Deadline: March 15	Room & Board: $4370
Freshman Class: 4562 applied, 3535 accepted, 942 enrolled	
SAT I Verbal/Math: 460/520	ACT: 22 **COMPETITIVE**

The State University of New York/College at Plattsburgh, founded in 1889, is a public institution offering degree programs in the liberal arts and professional programs. There is 1 graduate school. In addition to regional accreditation, SUNY Plattsburgh has baccalaureate program accreditation with ADA and NLN. The library contains 360,391 volumes, 840,466 microform items, and 22,910 audiovisual forms, and subscribes to 1447 periodicals. Computerized library sources and services include the card catalog, interlibrary loans, and database searching. Special learning facilities include a learning resource center, art gallery, planetarium, radio station, and TV station. The 300-acre campus is in a suburban area 150 miles north of Albany, 25 miles west of Burlington, Vermont and 65 miles south of Montreal, Canada. Including residence halls, there are 35 buildings on campus.

Student Life: 97% of undergraduates are from New York. Students come from 26 states, 14 foreign countries, and Canada. 98% are from public schools; 2% from private. 88% are white. The average age of freshmen is 19; all undergraduates, 22. 26% do not continue beyond their first year; 60% remain to graduate.

Housing: 2900 students can be accommodated in college housing. College-sponsored living facilities include coed dormitories. In addition, there are special interest houses and adult student halls/floors. On-campus housing is available on a first-come, first-served basis and is available on a lottery system for upperclassmen. Upperclassmen may keep cars on campus.

Activities: 7% of men belong to 4 local and 5 national fraternities; 7% of women belong to 6 local and 3 national sororities. There are 90 groups on campus, including art, band, cheerleading, choir, chorale, chorus, computers, drama, ethnic, film, gay, honors, international, jazz band, literary magazine, musical theater, newspaper, orchestra, photography, political, professional, radio and TV, religious, social, social service, student government, symphony, and yearbook. Popular campus events include Family Weekend, Arts and Crafts Fair, and the Showcase student/faculty research presentation.

Sports: There are 7 intercollegiate sports for men and 8 for women, and 13 intramural sports for men and 12 for women. Athletic and recreation facilities include a 3500-seat ice arena, a 1500-seat gymnasium, an indoor track, soccer and volleyball areas, an indoor swimming pool, bowling lanes, exercise and weight rooms, racquetball, lighted tennis courts, and a fitness center.

Disabled Students: 50% of the campus is accessible to disabled students. The following facilities are available: wheelchair ramps, elevators, special parking, specially equipped rest rooms, special class scheduling, lowered drinking fountains, and lowered telephones.

Services: In addition to many counseling and information services, tutoring is available in every subject. There is a reader service for the blind, and remedial math, reading, and writing.

Campus Safety and Security: Campus safety and security measures include 24-hour foot and vehicle patrol, escort service, shuttle buses, and informal discussions. In addition, there are pamphlets/posters/films, emergency telephones, lighted pathways/sidewalks, bicycle patrols, combination locks on student rooms, a computerized keyless entry system for residence hall access, door viewers, and basement and ground-level security windows in residence halls.

Programs of Study: SUNY Plattsburgh confers B.A., B.S., and B.S.Ed. degrees. Master's degrees are also awarded. Bachelor's degrees are awarded in BIOLOGICAL SCIENCE (biochemistry, biology/biological science, and cell biology), BUSINESS (accounting, business economics, and hotel/motel and restaurant management), COMMUNICATIONS AND THE ARTS (art history and appreciation, communications, dramatic arts, English, French, Spanish, and speech/debate/rhetoric), COMPUTER AND PHYSICAL SCIENCE (chemistry, computer science, geology, mathematics, and physics), EDUCATION (education of the deaf and hearing impaired, elementary, English, foreign languages, mathematics, science, secondary, social studies, and special), ENGINEERING AND ENVIRONMENTAL DESIGN (environmental science), HEALTH PROFESSIONS (medical laboratory technology, nursing, and speech pathology/audiology), SOCIAL SCIENCE (anthropology, Canadian studies, community services, criminal justice, dietetics, economics, family and community services, food science, geography, history, human services, Latin American studies, philosophy, political science/government, psychology, social science, social work, and sociology). Biochemistry, nursing, and business are the strongest academically. Psychology, nursing, and accounting have the largest enrollments.

Required: To graduate, students must have a 2.0 GPA and complete 125 to 128 semester hours. General education courses total 41 to 42 credits, including 7 or 8 credits in natural science, 6 in social science, 3 or 4 in mathematics, 3 each in English literature or philosophy, history, fine arts, foreign culture and language, and critical thinking/reading/speaking, and 1 in library skills, as well as 6 in upper-division, liberal arts courses. All students must demonstrate proficiency in writing by examination or course work.

Special: The college offers cross-registration with Clinton Community College, internships, study abroad in 6 countries, cooperative programs with a variety of employers, B.A.-B.S. degrees, dual and student-designed majors, and an accelerated degree program in any major except nursing. A 3-2 engineering degree is offered with Clarkson University, SUNY Stony Brook and Binghamton, Syracuse and McGill universities, and the University of Vermont. Credit for military experience, nondegree study if space is available, and limited pass/fail options are possible. There is a freshman honors program on campus, as well as 18 national honor societies. 15 departments have honors programs.

Faculty/Classroom: 70% of faculty are male; 30%, female. All both teach and do research. No introductory courses are taught by graduate students. The average class size in an introductory lecture is 24; in a laboratory, 17; and in a regular course offering, 22.

Admissions: 77% of the 1995–96 applicants were accepted. The SAT I scores for the 1995–96 freshman class were as follows: Verbal—73% below 500, 23% between 500 and 599, and 4% between 600 and 700; Math—39% below 500, 46% between 500 and 599, 14% between 600 and 700, and 1% above 700. The ACT scores were 33% below 21, 38% between 21 and 23, 20% between 24 and 26, 4% between 27 and 28, and 5% above 28. 22% of the current freshmen were in the top fifth of their class; 63% were in the top two fifths. 5 freshmen graduated first in their class.

Requirements: The SAT I or ACT is required. SUNY Plattsburgh requires applicants to be in the upper 50% of their class with an 80% grade average. Applicants must have at least 12 academic credits, including 4 years of English, 5 combined years of mathematics and science, and 3 years of social studies. An essay, portfolio, audition, and interview may be recommended in some programs. The GED is accepted. Applications are accepted on computer disk. AP and CLEP credits are accepted. Important factors in the admissions decision are advanced placement or honor courses, recommendations by school officials, and leadership record.

Procedure: Freshmen are admitted fall and spring. Entrance exams should be taken during the second half of the junior year or the beginning of the senior year. There are early decision, early admissions, and deferred admissions plans. Early decision applications should be filed by November 1; regular applications, by March 15 for fall entry and November 1 for spring entry, along with an application fee of $30. Notification of early decision is sent December 15; regular decision, on a rolling basis beginning January 15. 45 early decision candidates were accepted for the 1995–96 class.

Transfer: 805 transfer students enrolled in 1995–96. Applicants must have a minimum 2.0 GPA. Most academic programs require a 2.5 GPA or better. 36 credits of 125 to 128 must be completed at SUNY Plattsburgh.

Visiting: There are regularly scheduled orientations for prospective students, including a group, student-led tour and either a group or individual interview. Special overnight events for accepted freshman include meals with students and faculty, classroom visits, discussions with faculty, and special workshops. There are guides for informal visits and visitors may sit in on classes and stay overnight at the school. To schedule a visit, contact the Admissions Office.

Financial Aid: In 1995–96, 60% of all freshmen and 75% of continuing students received some form of financial aid. 50% of freshmen and 69% of continuing students received need-based aid. The average freshman award was $4502. Of that total, scholarships or need-based grants averaged $1760 ($3085 maximum); loans averaged $1742 ($2625 maximum); and work contracts averaged $1000 (maximum). 37% of undergraduate students work part-time. Average earn-

ings from campus work for the school year are $1000. The average financial indebtedness of the 1994–95 graduate was $10,000. The FAFSA is required, and in-state students must also file the TAP application. The application deadline for fall entry is April 15.

International Students: There are currently 52 international students enrolled. They must take the TOEFL and achieve a minimum score of 500.

Computers: The college provides computer facilities for student use. The mainframes are a DEC VAX 6610 and a DEC VAX 6430. There are also 219 student access PCs, including 22 DEC 486/66 MHzs, 20 Macintosh Performa 636CDs, 12 Macintosh LC IIs, 10 Power Macintosh 6100s, 30 DEC VT terminals, and 3 DEC Ultrix UNIX Workstations. Various other microcomputers are located in lecture hall and instructional laboratories. All students may access the system. There are no time limits and no fees.

Graduates: In 1994–95, 1257 bachelor's degrees were awarded. The most popular majors among graduates were psychology (13%), business (12%), and elementary education (9%). Within an average freshman class, 1% graduate in 3 years, 50% in 4 years, 58% in 5 years, and 61% in 6 years. 120 companies recruited on campus in 1994–95. Of the 1994 graduating class, 35% were enrolled in graduate school within 6 months of graduation and 87% had found employment.

Admissions Contact: Richard Higgins, Director of Admissions. E-mail: higginrj@splavb.cc.plattsburgh.edu. A campus video is available.

STATE UNIVERSITY OF NEW YORK/COLLEGE AT POTSDAM   C-2
(Formerly State University of New York/Potsdam College)
Potsdam, NY 13676

(315) 267-2180
(800) 433-3154; FAX: (315) 267-2163

Full-time: 3367 men and women	**Faculty:** 205; IIA, -$
Part-time: 217 men and women	**Ph.D.s:** 68%
Graduate: 518 men and women	**Student/Faculty:** 16 to 1
Year: semesters, summer session	**Tuition:** $3740 ($8640)
Application Deadline: April 1	**Room & Board:** $4670
Freshman Class: 3102 applied, 2314 accepted, 678 enrolled	
SAT I Verbal/Math: 450/525	**COMPETITIVE**

The State University of New York/College at Potsdam, founded in 1816 by early settlers of New York State's North Country, joined the state university system in 1948. The public coeducational institution offers liberal arts and teachers programs, and includes the Crane School of Music. There are 3 undergraduate schools and 1 graduate school. In addition to regional accreditation, SUNY Potsdam has baccalaureate program accreditation with NASM. The 2 libraries contain 1,030,000 volumes, 604,000 microform items, and 24,000 audiovisual forms, and subscribe to 1300 periodicals. Computerized library sources and services include the card catalog, interlibrary loans, and database searching. Special learning facilities include a learning resource center, art gallery, natural history museum, planetarium, radio station, electronic music and recording studios, and seismographic laboratory. The 240-acre campus is in a rural area 140 miles northeast of Syracuse. Including residence halls, there are 31 buildings on campus.

Student Life: 97% of undergraduates are from New York. Students come from 20 states, 11 foreign countries, and Canada. 98% are from public schools; 2% from private. 87% are white. The average age of freshmen is 18; all undergraduates, 22. 13% do not continue beyond their first year; 50% remain to graduate.

Housing: 2555 students can be accommodated in college housing. College-sponsored living facilities include single-sex and coed dormitories and on-campus apartments. In addition, there are language houses, special interest houses, a wellness house, an international house, and first-year experience housing. On-campus housing is guaranteed for all 4 years. 60% of students live on campus; of those, 85% remain on campus on weekends. Alcohol is not permitted. All students may keep cars on campus.

Activities: 10% of men belong to 4 local and 2 national fraternities; 15% of women belong to 7 local sororities and 1 national sorority. There are 88 groups on campus, including art, band, cheerleading, chess, choir, chorale, chorus, computers, dance, drama, environmental awareness, ethnic, gay, honors, international, jazz band, literary magazine, musical theater, newspaper, opera, orchestra, pep band, photography, political, professional, radio and TV, religious, social, social service, student government, symphony, and yearbook. Popular campus events include Potsdam Pride Day, Harvest Ball, Ice Carnival, and campus picnic.

Sports: There are 5 intercollegiate sports for men and 7 for women, and 8 intramural sports for men and 5 for women. Athletic and recreation facilities include a 2400-seat ice arena, an Olympic-size pool, a 3000-seat gymnasium, a field house, indoor and outdoor tracks, tennis, squash, handball, and basketball courts, a weight room, a wrestling room, and a dance studio. Potsdam's Star Lake Campus provides a recreational setting amidst the Adirondack Mountains wilderness.

Disabled Students: 85% of the campus is accessible to disabled students. The following facilities are available: wheelchair ramps, elevators, special parking, specially equipped rest rooms, special class scheduling, lowered drinking fountains, and lowered telephones.

Services: In addition to many counseling and information services, tutoring is available in some subjects. There is a reader service for the blind. mathematics laboratory, writing center, language laboratory, reading clinic, and the Educational Opportunity Summer Program.

Campus Safety and Security: Campus safety and security measures include 24-hour foot and vehicle patrol, self-defense education, escort service, and shuttle buses. There are informal discussions, pamphlets/posters/films, emergency telephones, and lighted pathways/sidewalks.

Programs of Study: SUNY Potsdam confers B.A., B.S., and B.M. degrees. Master's degrees are also awarded. Bachelor's degrees are awarded in BIOLOGICAL SCIENCE (biology/biological science), COMMUNICATIONS AND THE ARTS (art history and appreciation, dance, dramatic arts, English, fine arts, French, music, music performance, music theory and composition, Spanish, speech/debate/rhetoric, and studio art), COMPUTER AND PHYSICAL SCIENCE (chemistry, computer science, geology, mathematics, and physics), EDUCATION (art, elementary, foreign languages, middle school, music, science, and secondary), SOCIAL SCIENCE (anthropology, economics, history, industrial and organizational psychology, interdisciplinary studies, philosophy, political science/government, psychology, and sociology). Mathematics, education, and music education are the strongest academically. Music education, elementary education, and psychology have the largest enrollments.

Required: To graduate, students must earn 120 to 124 credit hours, with 30 to 33 in the major, and a minimum GPA of 2.0. General education requirements include 10 to 11 semester hours of freshman course work in verbal and quantitative skills, 21 of Modes of Inquiry in liberal arts, and 4 of physical education, as well as 1 course each in written and oral communication above the freshman level and demonstrated foreign language proficiency.

Special: Cross-registration is offered with Clarkson University, St. Lawrence University, and Canton College of Technology. Political science internships in Albany, as well as others, or an art apprenticeship in New York City are possible. SUNY Potsdam also offers work-study opportunities, co-op programs in premedicine, prelaw, and optometry, a 3–2 engineering degree with Clarkson University, study abroad in more than 40 countries, accelerated degree programs in mathematics, English, and education, 3–2 management and accounting degrees, student-designed majors, dual majors in interdisciplinary natural science, nondegree study, and pass/fail options. There is a freshman honors program on campus, as well as 20 national honor societies. 17 departments have honors programs.

Faculty/Classroom: 62% of faculty are male; 38%, female. All teach undergraduates. No introductory courses are taught by graduate students. The average class size in an introductory lecture is 40; in a laboratory, 18; and in a regular course offering, 29.

Admissions: 75% of the 1995–96 applicants were accepted. The SAT I scores for a recent freshman class were as follows: Verbal—68% below 500, 28% between 500 and 599, and 4% between 600 and 700; Math—35% below 500, 51% between 500 and 599, 12% between 600 and 700, and 2% above 700. 32% of the current freshmen were in the top fifth of their class; 70% were in the top two fifths.

Requirements: The SAT I or ACT is required. SUNY Potsdam requires applicants to be in the upper 50% of their class with a grade average of 80%. In addition, applicants must be high school graduates in a college preparatory program or hold a GED. Students should have earned 16 academic credits, preferably from 4 years of English, 3 each of mathematics, social sciences, and foreign language, 2 of science, and 1 of art or music. An interview is recommended; an audition, when appropriate, is required. AP and CLEP credits are accepted. Important factors in the admissions decision are advanced placement or honor courses, evidence of special talent, and leadership record.

Procedure: Freshmen are admitted fall and spring. Entrance exams should be taken in the junior year or early senior year. There are early decision, early admissions, and deferred admissions plans. Applications should be filed by April 1 for fall entry and December 1 for spring entry, along with an application fee of $30. Notification is sent on a rolling basis beginning January 15.

Transfer: 401 transfer students enrolled in 1995–96. Applicants must have earned 12 hours of college credit. Transfers with fewer than 24 credit hours must submit a high school transcript showing a minimum 2.0 GPA. An interview is recommended, as are supplemental recommendations. 30 credits of 120 to 124 must be completed at SUNY Potsdam.

Visiting: There are regularly scheduled orientations for prospective students, including open houses, off-campus interviews by faculty, and alumni receptions. There are guides for informal visits and visitors may sit in on classes and stay overnight at the school. To schedule a visit, contact the Admissions Office.

Financial Aid: The FAFSA is required. The application deadline for fall entry is March 1.

International Students: There were 44 international students enrolled in a recent year. The school actively recruits these students. They must take the TOEFL and achieve a minimum score of 500.

Computers: The college provides computer facilities for student use. The mainframes are 2 DEC ALPHA boxes. There are about 280 Apple Macintosh and MS-DOS microcomputers networked and connected to all campus buildings and residence hall computer laboratories. About 40 terminals are networked to a DEC VAX minicomputer. All students may access the system 7 days a week; schedules are flexible. There are no time limits. The fees are $50 per semester for full-time students. The college also has a microcomputer purchase plan for students, with Macintosh and MS-DOS models available.

Graduates: In 1994–95, 772 bachelor's degrees were awarded. The most popular majors among graduates were psychology (19%), English (12%), and music and music education (11%). Within an average freshman class, fewer than 1% graduate in 3 years, 30% in 4 years, 56% in 5 years, and 58% in 6 years.

Admissions Contact: Karen O'Brien, Director of Admissions and Financial Aid. E-mail: admissions@potsdam.edu. A campus video is available.

STATE UNIVERSITY OF NEW YORK/COLLEGE AT PURCHASE   D-5

Purchase, NY 10577-1400   (914) 251-6300; FAX: (914) 251-6314

Full-time: 1046 men, 1306 women	**Faculty:** 127; IIB, +$
Part-time: 473 men, 857 women	**Ph.D.s:** 100%
Graduate: 40 men, 29 women	**Student/Faculty:** 19 to 1
Year: semesters, summer session	**Tuition:** $3765 ($8665)
Application Deadline: August 1	**Room & Board:** $4872
Freshman Class: 2359 applied, 1326 accepted, 431 enrolled	
SAT I Verbal/Math: 480/480	**COMPETITIVE**

State University of New York/College at Purchase, founded in 1967, is a public, coeducational institution that offers programs in visual arts, music, acting, dance, film, theater/stage design technology, natural science, social science, and humanities. There are 2 undergraduate and 3 graduate schools. The library contains 253,600 volumes, 231,211 microform items, and 12,457 audiovisual forms, and subscribes to 1168 periodicals. Computerized library sources and services include the card catalog and interlibrary loans. Special learning facilities include a learning resource center, an art gallery, a listening and viewing center, science and photography laboratories, music practice rooms and instruments, multitrack synthesizers, an experimental stage, typesetting and computer graphics laboratories, a performing arts complex, and an electron microscope. The 500-acre campus is in a suburban area 35 miles north of midtown Manhattan. Including residence halls, there are 40 buildings on campus.

Student Life: 85% of undergraduates are from New York. Students come from 35 states, 20 foreign countries, and Canada. 73% are white; 10% African American. The average age of freshmen is 18.4; all undergraduates, 23.5. 30% do not continue beyond their first year; 35% remain to graduate.

Housing: 1498 students can be accommodated in college housing. College-sponsored living facilities include single-sex and coed dormitories, on-campus apartments, and married-student housing. In addition there are units for nonsmokers, freshmen, those interested in health and exercise, and other special interests. On-campus housing is guaranteed for all 4 years. 58% of students live on campus; of those, 60% remain on campus on weekends. Alcohol is not permitted. All students may keep cars on campus.

Activities: There are no fraternities or sororities. There are 40 groups on campus, including art, band, book publication, cheerleading, choir, chorale, chorus, computers, dance, drama, ethnic, film, gay, international, jazz band, literary magazine, newspaper, opera, orchestra, photography, political, professional, religious, social, social service, student government, symphony, and typesetting. Popular campus events include Family Day, Alcohol Awareness Week, film programs, art exhibits, and music, theater, and dance performances.

Sports: There are 5 intercollegiate sports for men and 3 for women, and 15 intramural sports for men and 14 for women. Athletic and recreation facilities include a gymnasium, weight and exercise rooms, basketball, racquetball, squash, and tennis courts, an Olympic swimming pool and diving area, and playing fields.

Disabled Students: All of the campus is accessible to disabled students. The following facilities are available: wheelchair ramps, elevators, special parking, and specially equipped rest rooms.

Services: In addition to many counseling and information services, tutoring is available in every subject. There is a reader service for the blind, and remedial math, reading, and writing.

Campus Safety and Security: Campus safety and security measures include 24-hour foot and vehicle patrol, escort service, informal discussions, and pamphlets/posters/films. In addition, there are emergency telephones and lighted pathways/sidewalks.

Programs of Study: SUNY Purchase confers B.A., B.S., B.A.L.A., and B.F.A. degrees. Master's degrees are also awarded. Bachelor's degrees are awarded in BIOLOGICAL SCIENCE (biology/biological science), COMMUNICATIONS AND THE ARTS (art history and appreciation, dance, dramatic arts, film arts, French, literature, music, music performance, music theory and composition, painting, photography, sculpture, Spanish, theater design, and visual and performing arts), COMPUTER AND PHYSICAL SCIENCE (chemistry and mathematics), ENGINEERING AND ENVIRONMENTAL DESIGN (environmental science), SOCIAL SCIENCE (anthropology, economics, history, liberal arts/general studies, philosophy, political science/government, psychology, and sociology). Literature, environmental and natural sciences, and psychology are the strongest academically. Visual arts, literature, and liberal arts have the largest enrollments.

Required: To graduate, students must prove proficiency in writing, mathematics, and language. A minimum 2.0 GPA is required in 120 total credit hours. Arts majors need 90 hours in the major and 30 hours in liberal arts. Letters and science majors need a minimum of 30 hours in the major. Students in the College of Letters and Science must complete the freshman seminar and the core curriculum, which includes 1 course each in origins of Western culture, structure of the Modern World, social and behavioral analysis, literature and literary analysis, quantitative or symbolic analysis, physical or biological science, visual or performing art, non-Western culture, and focus on race and gender, plus 2 credits of physical education. A senior thesis is required of all students.

Special: SUNY Purchase offers cross-registration with Manhattanville and Empire State colleges, internships with corporations, newspapers, and local agencies, and student-designed majors, dual majors, study abroad, work-study, nondegree study, and pass/fail options. There are also professional conservatory training programs in music, dance, visual arts, acting, film, and design technology.

Faculty/Classroom: 59% of faculty are male; 41%, female. All teach undergraduates. The average class size in an introductory lecture is 25; in a laboratory, 20; and in a regular course offering, 20.

Admissions: 56% of the 1995–96 applicants were accepted. The SAT I scores for the 1995–96 freshman class were as follows: Verbal—56% below 500, 29% between 500 and 599, 13% between 600 and 700, and 2% above 700; Math—56% below 500, 31% between 500 and 599, 12% between 600 and 700, and 1% above 700. 25% of the current freshmen were in the top fifth of their class; 54% were in the top two fifths. There were 2 National Merit semifinalists. 9 freshmen graduated first in their class.

Requirements: The SAT I or ACT is required. Minimum composite scores are 1000 on the SAT I or 19 on the ACT. Applicants must be graduates of an accredited secondary school and have completed 16 academic credits and 16 Carnegie units. The GED is accepted. Visual arts students must submit an essay and portfolio and have an interview. Film students need an essay and an interview. Design technology students need a portfolio and an interview. Performing arts students must audition. AP and CLEP credits are accepted. Important factors in the admissions decision are evidence of special talent, recommendations by school officials, and personality/intangible qualities.

Procedure: Freshmen are admitted fall and spring. Entrance exams should be taken no later than the fall of the senior year. There is a deferred admissions plan. Applications should be filed by August 1 for fall entry and December 1 for spring entry, along with an application fee of $25. Notification is sent on a rolling basis. A waiting list is an active part of the admissions procedure, with about 5% of all applicants on the list.

Transfer: 357 transfer students enrolled in 1995–96. Students transferring to the School of Arts with 60 earned credits may transfer only those courses with a minimum 2.0 GPA. Students with fewer than 30 earned credits need a minimum 2.5 GPA and must submit a high school transcript. To transfer into the visual or performing arts, students must pass an audition or portfolio review. The SAT I or ACT, with minimum composite scores of 1000 or 19, respectively, and a minimum 30 credit hours earned are required. 30 credits of 120 must be completed at SUNY Purchase.

Visiting: There are regularly scheduled orientations for prospective students. There are guides for informal visits and visitors may sit in on classes and stay overnight at the school. To schedule a visit, contact the Office of Campus and Residence Life or Campus Center North.

Financial Aid: In 1995–96, 75% of all freshmen and 65% of continuing students received some form of financial aid. 65% of freshmen and 60% of continuing students received need-based aid. The average freshman award was $4420. Of that total, scholarships or need-

based grants averaged $1730 ($5500 maximum); loans averaged $3020 ($6625 maximum); and work contracts averaged $970 ($1400 maximum). 15% of undergraduate students work part-time. Average earnings from campus work for the school year are $1000. The average financial indebtedness of the 1994–95 graduate was $8000. The FAFSA, the college's own financial statement, and the student and parent federal tax returns are required. The application deadline for fall entry is February 15.

International Students: There are currently 71 international students enrolled. The school actively recruits these students. They must take the TOEFL and achieve a minimum score of 550. The student must also take the SAT I or the ACT and score 1000 on the SAT I or 19 on the ACT.

Computers: The college provides computer facilities for student use. The mainframe is an IBM RISC/6000. IBM PCs are available in the computer center in the social sciences building. The natural sciences building houses PCs as well. All students may access the system when the computer center is open. There are no time limits and no fees.

Graduates: In 1994–95, 523 bachelor's degrees were awarded. The most popular majors among graduates were liberal arts (20%), visual arts (17%), and literature (10%). Within an average freshman class, 27% graduate in 4 years, 32% in 5 years, and 35% in 6 years. 50 companies recruited on campus in 1994–95.

Admissions Contact: Betsy Immergut, Director of Admissions. E-mail: immergut@brick.purchase.edu.

STATE UNIVERSITY OF NEW YORK/COLLEGE   D-3
OF AGRICULTURE AND TECHNOLOGY AT
COBLESKILL
Cobleskill, NY 12043

(518) 234-5525
(800) 295-8988; FAX: (518) 234-5333

Full-time: 1187 men, 1043 women	**Faculty:** 135; III, av$
Part-time: 66 men, 114 women	**Ph.Ds:** 16%
Graduate: none	**Student/Faculty:** 17 to 1
Year: semesters	**Tuition:** $3550 ($4500)
Application Deadline: open	**Room & Board:** $3700
Freshman Class: 3980 applied, 3450 accepted, 1040 enrolled	
SAT I or ACT: recommended	**LESS COMPETITIVE**

The State University of New York/College of Agriculture and Technology at Cobleskill, established in 1916, is a public institution conferring the Bachelor of Technology in Agriculture degree. The library contains 86,000 volumes and 55,000 audiovisual forms, and subscribes to 1000 periodicals. Computerized library sources and services include the card catalog, interlibrary loans, and database searching. Special learning facilities include a learning resource center, art gallery, radio station, arboretum, greenhouses, and plant nursery. The 750-acre campus is in a rural area 35 miles south of Albany. Including residence halls, there are 53 buildings on campus.

Student Life: 93% of undergraduates are from New York. Students come from 14 states and 5 foreign countries. 98% are from public schools; 2% from private. 92% are white. The average age of freshmen is 18; all undergraduates, 19.5. 20% do not continue beyond their first year; 50% remain to graduate.

Housing: College-sponsored living facilities include single-sex and coed dormitories. In addition, there are special interest floors in residence halls. On-campus housing is guaranteed for the freshman year only and is available on a lottery system for upperclassmen. 80% of students live on campus; of those, 90% remain on campus on weekends. Alcohol is not permitted. All students may keep cars on campus.

Activities: There are no fraternities or sororities. There are 50 groups on campus, including cheerleading, choir, chorus, computers, departmental, ethnic, honors, jazz band, musical theater, newspaper, professional, religious, social service, student government, and yearbook. Popular campus events include Parents Weekend and Alumni Weekend.

Sports: There are 10 intercollegiate sports for men and 9 for women, and 11 intramural sports for men and 10 for women. Athletic and recreation facilities include indoor and outdoor basketball and tennis courts, playing fields, a gymnasium, an exercise room, a swimming pool, bowling lanes, a field house, badminton, volleyball, and handball courts, archery and golf driving areas, a quarter-mile track, a ski center, and a fitness trail.

Disabled Students: 20% of the campus is accessible to disabled students. The following facilities are available: wheelchair ramps, elevators, special parking, specially equipped rest rooms, lowered drinking fountains, and lowered telephones.

Services: In addition to many counseling and information services, tutoring is available in some subjects, including biology, intermediate algebra, and chemistry. There is a reader service for the blind, and remedial math, reading, and writing. There is also an academic skills center.

Campus Safety and Security: Campus safety and security measures include 24-hour foot and vehicle patrol, informal discussions, pamphlets/posters/films, and emergency telephones. In addition, there are lighted pathways/sidewalks.

Programs of Study: SUNY Cobleskill confers the B.T. in Agriculture degree. Associate degrees are also awarded. Bachelor's degrees are awarded in AGRICULTURE (agricultural business management, agricultural mechanics, animal science, and plant science).

Required: Degree requirements include completion of 126 credit hours, with 30 to 32 upper-division credits in the major, 11 credits of technical electives, 7 to 15 credits in other electives, and a 15-credit internship. Students must maintain a minimum 2.0 GPA.

Special: The college sponsors internship programs. Students may study abroad at Thomas Danby and South Fields colleges in England. There is a freshman honors program on campus, as well as 1 national honor society. 1 department has an honors program.

Faculty/Classroom: 70% of faculty are male; 30%, female. All teach undergraduates and 40% both teach and do research. The average class size in an introductory lecture is 33; in a laboratory, 15; and in a regular course offering, 30.

Admissions: 87% of the 1995–96 applicants were accepted. 12% of the current freshmen were in the top fifth of their class; 48% were in the top two fifths.

Requirements: The SAT I or ACT is recommended. A minimum grade average of 70% is required. Applicants must have graduated from an accredited secondary school or earned a GED, and are encouraged to have completed college-preparatory courses. Students planning to enter the agricultural program should also take vocational agricultural courses. Applicants are required to visit the campus. AP and CLEP credits are accepted. Important factors in the admissions decision are evidence of special talent, advanced placement or honor courses, and leadership record.

Procedure: Freshmen are admitted fall and spring. There are early admissions and deferred admissions plans. Application deadlines are open. Application fee is $25. Notification is sent after November 1 if the application is complete, and on a rolling basis thereafter.

Transfer: 167 transfer students enrolled in a recent year. Applicants must have a minimum GPA of 2.0. 30 credits of 126 must be completed at SUNY Cobleskill.

Visiting: There are regularly scheduled orientations for prospective students. To schedule a visit, contact the Office of Admissions.

Financial Aid: 15% of undergraduate students work part-time. SUNY Cobleskill is a member of CSS. The college's own financial statement is required. The application deadline for fall entry is March 15.

International Students: There are currently 4 international students enrolled. The school actively recruits these students. They must take the TOEFL and achieve a minimum score of 500.

Computers: The college provides computer facilities for student use. The mainframe is a DEC. There are 3 computer laboratories, as well as network access in all residence halls. All students may access the system during computer center hours. There are no time limits and no fees.

Graduates: In 1994–95, 50 bachelor's degrees were awarded. Within an average freshman class, 54% graduate in 3 years and 60% in 4 years. 77 companies recruited on campus in 1994–95.

Admissions Contact: Dr. Carol Eaton, Director of Admissions. E-mail: eatoncw@scobua.cobleskill.edu. A campus video is available.

STATE UNIVERSITY OF NEW YORK/ MARITIME COLLEGE

D-5

Throgs Neck, NY 10465   (718) 409-7220
(800) 642-1874 (Northeast only); FAX: (718) 409-7465

Full-time: 605 men, 63 women	Faculty: 65; IIB, +$
Part-time: none	Ph.D.s: 49%
Graduate: 172 men, 21 women	Student/Faculty: 10 to 1
Year: semesters, summer session	Tuition: $3881 ($8781)
Application Deadline: open	Room & Board: $5000
Freshman Class: 697 applied, 460 accepted, 210 enrolled	
SAT I Verbal/Math: 460/520	COMPETITIVE

The Maritime College of the State University of New York, founded in 1874, is a public coeducational institution that prepares students for the U.S. Merchant Marine officers' license and for bachelor's degrees in engineering, naval architecture, marine environmental science, and marine transportation/business administration. The college curriculum includes 3 summer semesters at sea aboard the training ship Empire State VI. There is one graduate school. In addition to regional accreditation, New York Maritime has baccalaureate program accreditation with ABET. The library contains 76,854 volumes, 48,126 microform items, and 3025 audiovisual forms, and subscribes to 354 periodicals. Computerized library sources and services include interlibrary loans and database searching. Special learning facilities include a learning resource center, planetarium, a 17,000-ton training

ship, a tug, a barge, and a new training tanker center for marine operations and simulation. The 55-acre campus is in a suburban area on the peninsula where Long Island Sound meets the East River. Including residence halls, there are 27 buildings on campus.

Student Life: 75% of undergraduates are from New York. Students come from 17 states and 22 foreign countries. 53% are from public schools; 47% from private. 76% are white. The average age of freshmen is 18; all undergraduates, 20. 12% do not continue beyond their first year; 69% remain to graduate.

Housing: 800 students can be accommodated in college housing. College-sponsored living facilities include single-sex and coed dormitories. On-campus housing is guaranteed for all 4 years. 97% of students live on campus; of those, 65% remain on campus on weekends. Alcohol is not permitted. Upperclassmen may keep cars on campus.

Activities: There are no fraternities or sororities. There are 38 groups on campus, including bagpipe band, band, cheerleading, chess, chorus, computers, drill team, ethnic, honors, international, jazz band, marching band, newspaper, political, professional, religious, social, social service, student government, and yearbook. Popular campus events include spring formal, Friday night mixers, regattas, and Admiral's Ball.

Sports: There are 11 intercollegiate sports for men and 7 for women, and 11 intramural sports for men and 6 for women. Athletic and recreation facilities include an athletic center containing a 2000-seat gymnasium, swimming pools, exercise and weight rooms, a rifle and pistol range, and 4 handball/racquetball and squash courts; a sailing center; and baseball, lacrosse, and soccer fields.

Disabled Students: 90% of the campus is accessible to disabled students. The following facilities are available: wheelchair ramps, elevators, special parking, and specially equipped rest rooms.

Services: In addition to many counseling and information services, tutoring is available in every subject.

Campus Safety and Security: Campus safety and security measures include 24-hour foot and vehicle patrol, informal discussions, emergency telephones, and lighted pathways/sidewalks.

Programs of Study: New York Maritime confers B.S. and B.E. degrees. Master's degrees are also awarded. Bachelor's degrees are awarded in BIOLOGICAL SCIENCE (marine science), BUSINESS (transportation management), COMPUTER AND PHYSICAL SCIENCE (atmospheric sciences and meteorology), ENGINEERING AND ENVIRONMENTAL DESIGN (engineering, marine engineering, and naval architecture and marine engineering), SOCIAL SCIENCE (humanities). Engineering, naval architecture, and marine transportation/business administration are the strongest academically. Marine transportation/business administration has the largest enrollment.

Required: To graduate, students must complete the U.S. Merchant Marine officers' license program. Students must earn 160 credit hours, with a GPA of 2.0. Distribution requirements and the number of hours required in the major varies. All students must spend 3 summer semesters at sea acquiring hands-on experience aboard the college's training vessel.

Special: The college offers co-op programs in engineering, an accelerated degree program in marine transportation/transportation management, and internships as cadet observers aboard commercial ships. There are 2 national honor societies on campus. 2 departments have honors programs.

Faculty/Classroom: All faculty teach undergraduates and 12% also do research. No introductory courses are taught by graduate students. The average class size in an introductory lecture is 25; in a laboratory, 15; and in a regular course offering, 20.

Admissions: 66% of the 1995–96 applicants were accepted. The SAT I scores for the 1995–96 freshman class were as follows: Verbal—62% below 500, 28% between 500 and 599, and 10% between 600 and 700; Math—42% below 500, 37% between 500 and 599, 16% between 600 and 700, and 5% above 700. 29% of the current freshmen were in the top fifth of their class; 59% were in the top two fifths. There were 12 National Merit semifinalists.

Requirements: The SAT I is required. A minimum grade average of 80 is required. Applicants must be high school graduates or hold a GED. Sixteen Carnegie units are required, including 4 years of English, 3 of mathematics (4 are preferred), and 1 of physics or chemistry. An essay is required and an interview is recommended. Students may apply on computer disk by entering admissions data on blank preformatted disks available from the Admissions Office. AP and CLEP credits are accepted. Important factors in the admissions decision are advanced placement or honor courses, extracurricular activities record, and leadership record.

Procedure: Freshmen are admitted in the fall. Entrance exams should be taken during the junior or senior year. There are early decision, early admissions, and deferred admissions plans. Early decision applications should be filed by November 1; regular application deadlines are open. The application fee is $25. Notification of early decision is sent December 15; regular decision, February 1. 22 early decision candidates were accepted for the 1995–96 class.

Transfer: 28 transfer students enrolled in 1995–96. Transfer students must have a 2.5 GPA. Students having fewer than 30 credits must supply SAT I or ACT scores. All applicants must complete the Indoctrination Program and fulfill degree and license requirements at New York Maritime.

Visiting: There are regularly scheduled orientations for prospective students, including a tour of the campus and facilities, and meetings with faculty and students. There are guides for informal visits and visitors may sit in on classes and stay overnight at the school. To schedule a visit, contact the Admissions Office.

Financial Aid: In 1995–96, 85% of all freshmen and 78% of continuing students received some form of financial aid. 60% of all students received need-based aid. The average freshman award was $4625. Of that total, scholarships or need-based grants averaged $1050 ($5000 maximum); loans averaged $2625 ($5625 maximum); and work contracts averaged $500 ($1500 maximum). 92% of undergraduate students work part-time. Average earnings from campus work for the school year are $750. The average financial indebtedness of the 1994–95 graduate was $13,725. The FAFSA and student and parent federal income tax returns are required. The application deadline for fall entry is May 1.

International Students: There are currently 47 international students enrolled. The school actively recruits these students. They must take the TOEFL and achieve a minimum score of 500. The student must also take the SAT I or the ACT.

Computers: The college provides computer facilities for student use. The mainframe is a Prime 4050. There are 27 terminals, 8 CAD stations, and 58 microcomputers. All students may access the system from 8:30 A.M. to 11 P.M. The computer center stays open after 11 P.M. when there is sufficient demand. There are no time limits and no fees.

Graduates: In 1994–95, 139 bachelor's degrees were awarded. The most popular majors among graduates were marine transportation (40%), engineering (38%), and meteorology/oceanography (16%). 50 companies recruited on campus in 1994–95.

Admissions Contact: Peter Cooney, Director of Admissions and Financial Aid. E-mail: edmaritime@aol.com. A campus video is available.

STATE UNIVERSITY OF NEW YORK/ POTSDAM COLLEGE
(See State University of New York/College at Potsdam)

SYRACUSE UNIVERSITY
C-3

Syracuse, NY 13244
(315) 443-3611

Full-time: 4954 men, 5143 women	**Faculty:** 850; I, -$
Part-time: 95 men and women	**Ph.D.s:** 83%
Graduate: 4539 men and women	**Student/Faculty:** 12 to 1
Year: semesters, summer session	**Tuition:** $16,280
Application Deadline: February 1	**Room & Board:** $7150
Freshman Class: 10,150 applied, 6670 accepted, 2409 enrolled	
SAT I or ACT: required	**HIGHLY COMPETITIVE**

Syracuse University, founded in 1870, is a private, coeducational institution offering undergraduate programs in liberal arts and sciences, architecture, public communications, education, management, human development, information studies, nursing, social work, visual and performing arts, engineering, and computer science. There are 11 undergraduate and 13 graduate schools. In addition to regional accreditation, Syracuse has baccalaureate program accreditation with AACSB, ABET, ACEJMC, ADA, ASLA, CAHEA, CSWE, FIDER, NAAB, NASAD, NASM, NCATE, and NLN. The 5 libraries contain 2.3 million volumes, 4.3 million microform items, and 26,000 audiovisual forms, and subscribe to 16,559 periodicals. Computerized library sources and services include the card catalog, interlibrary loans, and database searching. Special learning facilities include a learning resource center, art gallery, radio station, TV station, gerontology center, speech and hearing clinic, audio archives, and a high-technology facility that provides hookups to international media events. The 200-acre campus is in an urban area 270 miles northwest of New York City. Including residence halls, there are 170 buildings on campus.

Student Life: 56% of undergraduates are from out-of-state, mostly the Northeast. Students come from 49 states, 98 foreign countries, and Canada. 75% are from public schools; 25% from private. 77% are white. The average age of freshmen is 18; all undergraduates, 20. 12% do not continue beyond their first year; 70% remain to graduate.

Housing: 6500 students can be accommodated in college housing. College-sponsored living facilities include single-sex and coed dormitories, on-campus apartments, married-student housing, fraternity houses and sorority houses. In addition, there are honors houses and special interest houses, including theme and language units in Shaw Living/Learning Center. On-campus housing is guaranteed for all 4 years. 75% of students live on campus; of those, 85% remain on campus on weekends. Alcohol is not permitted. Upperclassmen may keep cars on campus.

Activities: 20% of men belong to 1 local and 29 national fraternities; 25% of women belong to 2 local and 20 national sororities. There are 250 groups on campus, including art, band, cheerleading, chess, choir, chorale, computers, dance, drama, ethnic, film, gay, honors, international, jazz band, literary magazine, marching band, musical theater, newspaper, pep band, photography, political, professional, radio and TV, religious, social, social service, student government, and yearbook. Popular campus events include Homecoming and Parents Weekend.

Sports: There are 11 intercollegiate sports for men and 9 for women, and 22 intramural sports for men and 22 for women. Athletic and recreation facilities include 3 gymnasiums, 2 swimming pools, weight rooms, exercise rooms, a dance studio, courts for racquet sports, an indoor track, and playing fields. The multipurpose domed stadium seats 50,000 for football and 30,000 for basketball.

Disabled Students: Most of the campus is accessible to disabled students. The following facilities are available: wheelchair ramps, elevators, special parking, specially equipped rest rooms, special class scheduling, lowered drinking fountains, and lowered telephones.

Services: In addition to many counseling and information services, tutoring is available in most subjects. There is a reader service for the blind, and remedial math, reading, and writing. There are also special supportive services for the learning disabled.

Campus Safety and Security: Campus safety and security measures include 24-hour foot and vehicle patrol, self-defense education, escort service, and shuttle buses. In addition, there are informal discussions, pamphlets/posters/films, and lighted pathways/sidewalks. Other services include a blue-light security system that enables students to have an immediate link to security throughout the campus in case of an emergency, and a card-key access system in university residence halls.

Programs of Study: Syracuse confers A.B., B.S., B.Arch., B.F.A., B.I.D., and B.Mus. degrees. Master's and doctoral degrees are also awarded. Bachelor's degrees are awarded in BIOLOGICAL SCIENCE (biology/biological science, biophysics, and nutrition), BUSINESS (accounting, banking and finance, business administration and management, business law, human resources, management information systems, management science, marketing management, marketing/retailing/merchandising, retailing, and transportation management), COMMUNICATIONS AND THE ARTS (advertising, art history and appreciation, broadcasting, ceramic art and design, classics, communications technology, comparative literature, design, dramatic arts, English, English literature, fiber/textiles/weaving, film arts, fine arts, French, German, graphic design, illustration, industrial design, Italian, journalism, languages, linguistics, media arts, metal/jewelry, music, music business management, music performance, music theory and composition, musical theater, painting, photography, printmaking, public relations, publishing, Russian, sculpture, Spanish, speech/debate/rhetoric, theater design, and video), COMPUTER AND PHYSICAL SCIENCE (chemistry, computer science, geology, information sciences and systems, mathematics, physics, and statistics), EDUCATION (art, early childhood, elementary, health, mathematics, middle school, music, physical, science, secondary, social studies, and special), ENGINEERING AND ENVIRONMENTAL DESIGN (aerospace studies, architecture, bioengineering, chemical engineering, civil engineering, computer engineering, computer graphics, electrical/electronics engineering, environmental design, environmental engineering, industrial administration/management, interior design, and mechanical engineering), HEALTH PROFESSIONS (nursing, predentistry, premedicine, preveterinary science, and speech pathology/audiology), SOCIAL SCIENCE (African American studies, American studies, anthropology, child care/child and family studies, classical/ancient civilization, dietetics, economics, ethics/politics/social policy, family/consumer studies, fashion design and technology, food production/management/services, geography, history, international relations, Latin American studies, medieval studies, peace studies, philosophy, political science/government, prelaw, psychology, public affairs, religion, social science, social work, sociology, textiles and clothing, and women's studies). Communications, engineering, and biology/chemistry are the strongest academically. Psychology, nursing, and broadcast journalism have the largest enrollments.

Required: A minimum of 120 credits with a minimum GPA of 2.0 is required in order to graduate. All students must take a freshman writing seminar and fulfill core requirements in writing and literature, sciences and mathematics, social sciences, and humanities. Additional requirements vary by college and major.

Special: The Community Internship Program places students in off-campus field positions related to their major. Cooperative education programs are available in engineering, retailing, and information studies. Cross-registration is offered with SUNY College of Environmental Science and Forestry. Study abroad is available in 5 university-operated centers and through other special programs, and a Washington semester is offered through the International Relations Program. Syracuse also offers B.A.-B.S. degrees, dual and student-designed majors, work-study programs, a general studies degree, pass/fail options, and nondegree study. There is a freshman honors program on campus, as well as 14 national honor societies, including Phi Beta Kappa. All 11 colleges have honors programs.

Faculty/Classroom: 74% of faculty are male; 26%, female. 99% teach undergraduates and 1% do research. The average class size in an introductory lecture is 37; in a laboratory, 15; and in a regular course offering, 20.

Admissions: 66% of the 1995–96 applicants were accepted. The SAT I scores for the 1995–96 freshman class were as follows: Verbal—29% below 500, 53% between 500 and 599, 16% between 600 and 700, and 2% above 700; Math—9% below 500, 52% between 500 and 599, 30% between 600 and 700, and 9% above 700. 65% of the current freshmen were in the top fifth of their class; 93% were in the top two fifths. 22 freshmen graduated first in their class.

Requirements: The SAT I or ACT is required; the SAT I is preferred. Applicants should have a strong college preparatory record from an accredited secondary school or have a GED equivalent. An essay is required. A portfolio is required for art and architecture majors, and an audition for music and drama majors. AP and CLEP credits are accepted. Important factors in the admissions decision are advanced placement or honor courses, evidence of special talent, and recommendations by school officials.

Procedure: Freshmen are admitted in the fall and spring. Entrance exams should be taken prior to February 1 of the senior year. There are early decision, early admissions, and deferred admissions plans. Early decision applications should be filed by November 15; regular applications, by February 1 for fall entry, along with an application fee of $40. Notification is sent March 15. 356 early decision candidates were accepted for the 1995–96 class.

Transfer: 387 transfer students enrolled in a recent year. Requirements vary by college. SAT I or ACT scores and secondary school and college transcripts are required for applicants with fewer than 24 credit hours. A portfolio is required for art and architecture majors, and an audition for music and drama majors. 30 credits of 120 must be completed at Syracuse.

Visiting: There are regularly scheduled orientations for prospective students, including information programs, a campus tour, and personal interviews. There are guides for informal visits and visitors may sit in on classes and stay overnight at the school. To schedule a visit, contact the Admissions Office.

Financial Aid: In 1995–96, 73% of all freshmen and 65% of continuing students received some form of financial aid. 65% of freshmen and 58% of continuing students received need-based aid. The average freshman award was $13,800. Of that total, scholarships or need-based grants averaged $7840 (full-tuition maximum); loans averaged $3300 ($4625 maximum); and work contracts averaged $1900 ($2000 maximum). 45% of undergraduate students work part-time. Average earnings from campus work for the school year are $1500. The average financial indebtedness of the 1994–95 graduate was $14,500. FAFSA is required. The application deadline for fall entry is March 1.

International Students: There are currently 400 international students enrolled. The school actively recruits these students. They must take the TOEFL and achieve a minimum score of 550. The student must also take the SAT I or the ACT.

Computers: The university provides computer facilities for student use. Syracuse has a networked client/server computing environment which gives students access to almost 1000 IBM, IBM-compatible, and Apple Macintosh microcomputers and UNIX workstations located throughout the campus. High-speed connections are available in many residence halls. All students may access the system 24 hours per day. There are no time limits and no fees.

Graduates: In 1994–95, 2450 bachelor's degrees were awarded. The most popular majors among graduates were management (17%), social sciences (16%), and communications (14%). Within an average freshman class, 68% graduate in 5 years and 70% in 6 years. 300 companies recruited on campus in 1994–95.

Admissions Contact: David C. Smith, Dean of Admissions. E-mail: orange@suadmin.syr.edu. A campus video is available.

TOURO COLLEGE

	D-5
New York, NY 10010	(212) 463–0400, ext. 400
Full-time: 2920 men, 5030 women	Faculty: 160
Part-time: 170 men, 250 women	Ph.D.s: 65%
Graduate: 670 men, 510 women	Student/Faculty: 50 to 1
Year: semesters, summer session	Tuition: $7500
Application Deadline: open	Room & Board: $5000
Freshman Class: n/av	
SAT I or ACT: recommended	LESS COMPETITIVE

Touro College, founded in 1971, is a private coeducational institution offering undergraduate programs through the College of Liberal Arts and Sciences and the schools of General Studies and Health Sciences. Campuses are in midtown Manhattan and in Brooklyn. There are 3 undergraduate and 2 graduate schools. Figures given in the above capsules are approximate. In addition to regional accreditation, Touro has baccalaureate program accreditation with APTA and CAHEA. The library contains 140,000 volumes and subscribes to 750 periodicals. The campus is in an urban area.

Student Life: 65% of undergraduates are from New York.

Housing: College-sponsored living facilities include single-sex dormitories. Alcohol is not permitted. All students may keep cars on campus.

Activities: There are no fraternities or sororities. There are some groups and organizations on campus, including literary magazine, newspaper, student government, and yearbook. Popular campus events include a student-sponsored lecture series and student-faculty social events.

Sports: There are 2 intramural sports for men and 2 for women.

Disabled Students: Some facilities, including elevators, are available for physically disabled persons.

Services: In addition to many counseling and information services, tutoring is available in some subjects, including accounting, mathematics, and English.

Programs of Study: Touro confers B.A. and B.S. degrees. Associate and master's degrees are also awarded. Bachelor's degrees are awarded in BIOLOGICAL SCIENCE (biology/biological science), BUSINESS (accounting, business administration and management, and marketing/retailing/merchandising), COMPUTER AND PHYSICAL SCIENCE (chemistry, computer science, mathematics, and physics), EDUCATION (elementary), HEALTH PROFESSIONS (occupational therapy, physical therapy, predentistry, and premedicine), SOCIAL SCIENCE (economics, history, political science/government, prelaw, psychology, social science, and sociology).

Required: To graduate, all students must complete at least 120 credit hours, with 30 to 67 in the major. A 2.0 GPA is required.

Special: The college offers cross-registration, internships, study abroad in Israel, work-study programs, credit for life, military, and work experience, and pass/fail options. There is a freshman honors program on campus

Faculty/Classroom: 60% of faculty are male; 40%, female. No introductory courses are taught by graduate students.

Requirements: The SAT I, with scores of 500 verbal and 500 math, or the ACT is recommended for some programs. Applicants must be graduates of an accredited secondary school or have a GED certificate. AP and CLEP credits are accepted. Important factors in the admissions decision are leadership record, advanced placement or honor courses, and extracurricular activities record.

Procedure: Freshmen are admitted to all sessions. There are early admissions and deferred admissions plans. Application deadlines are open. Check with the school for current application fee. Notification is sent on a rolling basis.

Transfer: A 2.5 GPA is required. 30 credits of 120 must be completed at Touro.

Visiting: There are regularly scheduled orientations for prospective students. There are guides for informal visits and visitors may sit in on classes and stay overnight at the school. To schedule a visit, contact Admissions.

Financial Aid: Touro is a member of CSS. The FAF is required. Check with the school for current deadlines.

International Students: They must score 525 on the TOEFL.

Computers: The college provides computer facilities for student use. The mainframe is an IBM System/36. Microcomputers are also available in the Manhattan computing center. Students in computer clubs may access the system. There are no time limits, but fees are charged.

Admissions Contact: Jack Abramowitz, Director of Admissions.

UNION COLLEGE

	D-3
Schenectady, NY 12308–2311	(518) 388–6112
	FAX: (518) 388–6986
Full-time: 1082 men, 951 women	Faculty: 184; IIA, +$
Part-time: 64 men, 23 women	Ph.D.s: 95%
Graduate: 266 men, 125 women	Student/Faculty: 11 to 1
Year: trimesters, summer session	Tuition: $19,972
Application Deadline: February 1	Room & Board: $6234
Freshman Class: 3550 applied, 1845 accepted, 515 enrolled	
SAT I Verbal/Math: 538/642 (mean)	HIGHLY COMPETITIVE

Union College, founded in 1795, is an independent, coeducational liberal arts and engineering college. There is 1 graduate school. In addition to regional accreditation, Union has baccalaureate program accreditation with ABET. The library contains 502,115 volumes, 618,670 microform items, and 5037 audiovisual forms, and subscribes to 1970 periodicals. Computerized library sources and services include the card catalog, interlibrary loans, and database searching. Special learning facilities include a radio station, writing center, and theater. The 100-acre campus is in a small town 15 miles west of Albany. Including residence halls, there are 65 buildings on campus.

Student Life: 51% of undergraduates are from New York. Students come from 34 states, 13 foreign countries, and Canada. 73% are from public schools; 27% from private. 85% are white. The average age of freshmen is 18. 5% do not continue beyond their first year; 86% remain to graduate.

Housing: 1390 students can be accommodated in college housing. College-sponsored living facilities include single-sex and coed dormitories, fraternity houses, and sorority houses. In addition there are special interest houses and 5 theme houses, including an international house. There are also 2 substance-free living areas and a 24-hour quiet house. On-campus housing is available on a lottery system for upperclassmen. 80% of students live on campus. Upperclassmen may keep cars on campus.

Activities: 37% of men belong to fraternities; 30% of women belong to 4 national sororities. There are 82 groups on campus, including band, cheerleading, choir, computers, dance, drama, ethnic, gay, international, jazz band, literary magazine, newspaper, orchestra, photography, political, radio and TV, religious, social service, student government, and yearbook. Popular campus events include Homecoming Weekend, Parents Weekend, Women's Week, Black History Month, and Asian Awareness Week.

Sports: There are 10 intercollegiate sports for men and 10 for women, and 17 intramural sports for men and 17 for women. Athletic and recreation facilities include a field house for volleyball, basketball, and track, fields for soccer, football, lacrosse, and field hockey, an ice rink, a gymnasium, a swimming pool, weight rooms, and racquetball/squash courts.

Disabled Students: 60% of the campus is accessible to disabled students. The following facilities are available: wheelchair ramps, elevators, special parking, specially equipped rest rooms, and lowered drinking fountains.

Services: In addition to many counseling and information services, tutoring is available on a fee basis in most subjects. There is a writing center.

Campus Safety and Security: Campus safety and security measures include 24-hour foot and vehicle patrol, escort service, informal discussions, and pamphlets/posters/films. In addition, there are emergency telephones, lighted pathways/sidewalks, 24-hour locked residence halls, and desk attendants in most residence halls from late evening to early morning.

Programs of Study: Union confers B.A., B.S., B.S.C.E., B.S.E.E., and B.S.M.E. degrees. Master's and doctoral degrees are also awarded. Bachelor's degrees are awarded in BIOLOGICAL SCIENCE (biology/biological science), COMMUNICATIONS AND THE ARTS (classics, English, fine arts, modern language, and visual and performing arts), COMPUTER AND PHYSICAL SCIENCE (chemistry, computer science, geology, mathematics, physics, quantitative methods, and science), ENGINEERING AND ENVIRONMENTAL DESIGN (civil engineering, electrical/electronics engineering, engineering and applied science, and mechanical engineering), SOCIAL SCIENCE (American studies, anthropology, economics, history, humanities, interdisciplinary studies, philosophy, political science/government, psychology, social science, sociology, and women's studies). Mathematics, chemistry, and psychology are the strongest academically. Biology, political science, and psychology have the largest enrollments.

Required: Students must complete a minimum of 36 courses and must maintain a minimum GPA of 1.8 overall and 2.0 in the major. Students must also meet the requirements of the freshman preceptorial and the general education program, which includes courses distributed in 4 areas: history, literature, and civilization; social or behavioral science; mathematics and natural science; and foreign languages and non-Western studies.

Special: Cross-registration is permitted with the Hudson Mohawk Consortium. Opportunities are provided for legislative internships in Albany and Washington, D.C. Union also offers pass/fail options, B.A.-B.S. degrees, dual and student-designed majors, a Washington semester, accelerated degree programs in law and medicine, and study abroad in 22 countries. There are 12 national honor societies on campus, including Phi Beta Kappa. 11 departments have honors programs.

Faculty/Classroom: 73% of faculty are male; 27%, female. 97% both teach and do research. No introductory courses are taught by graduate students. The average class size in an introductory lecture is 43; in a regular course offering, 25; and in a laboratory, 15.

Admissions: 52% of the 1995-96 applicants were accepted. 75% of the current freshmen were in the top fifth of their class; 97% were in the top two fifths. There was 1 National Merit finalist.

Requirements: While SAT I is optional, the ACT or 3 SAT II: Subject tests, including writing are required. Graduation from an accredited secondary school is required. Applicants must submit a minimum of 16 full-year credits, distributed as follows: 4 years of English, 2 of a foreign language, 2 1/2 to 3 1/2 years of mathematics, 2 years each of science and social studies, and the remainder in college-preparatory courses. Engineering and mathematics majors are expected to have completed additional mathematics and science courses beyond the minimum requirements. An essay is also required, and an interview is recommended. Applications prepared on the computer are accepted. Union subscribes to CollegeLink and MacApply. AP credits are accepted. Important factors in the admissions decision are advanced placement or honor courses, recommendations by school officials, and extracurricular activities record.

Procedure: Freshmen are admitted in the fall. Entrance exams should be taken before February 1. There are early decision, early admissions, and deferred admissions plans. Early decision and regular applications for fall entry should be filed by February 1, along with an application fee of $50. Notification is sent April 1. 159 early decision candidates were accepted for the 1995-96 class. A waiting list is an active part of the admissions procedure, with about 12% of all applicants on the list.

Transfer: 30 transfer students enrolled in 1995-96. A 3.0 GPA and 1 full year of college academic work are required. Transfer students must study at Union for at least 2 years. The SAT I is optional. 18 courses of 36 must be completed at Union.

Visiting: There are regularly scheduled orientations for prospective students, including interviews and a tour of the campus. There are guides for informal visits, and visitors may sit in on classes and stay overnight at the school. To schedule a visit, contact the Admissions Office.

Financial Aid: In 1995-96, 60% of all freshmen and 55% of continuing students received need-based aid. The average freshman award was $17,500. Of that total, scholarships or need-based grants averaged $13,000 ($22,000 maximum); loans averaged $3300; and work contracts averaged $1200. 41% of undergraduate students work part-time. Average earnings from campus work for the school year are $952. The average financial indebtedness of the 1994-95 graduate was $13,000. Union is a member of CSS. The CSS Profile Application financial statement and the FAFSA are required. The application deadline for fall entry is February 1.

International Students: There are currently 70 international students enrolled. The school actively recruits these students. They must take the TOEFL and achieve a minimum score of 550 and must usually take the ACT or 3 SAT II: Subject tests (Writing and 2 others).

Computers: The college provides computer facilities for student use. Union's computer center houses a distributed network that provides access to varied computer resources, including a DEC ALPHA server running Open VMS and a DEC system 5000/200 running UNIX. There are more than 700 personal computers (and workstations) and 100 terminals on campus. All college-owned dormitory rooms are connected to the network. All students may access the system 24 hours per day, 7 days a week. There are no time limits and no fees.

Graduates: In 1994-95, 473 bachelor's degrees were awarded. The most popular majors among graduates were psychology (12%), political science (10%), and economics (8%). Within an average freshman class, 78% graduate in 4 years, 85% in 5 years, and 86% in 6 years. 65 companies recruited on campus in 1994-95. Of the 1994 graduating class, 37% were enrolled in graduate or professional school within a year of graduation and 60% had found employment.

Admissions Contact: Daniel Lundquist, Vice President of Admissions and Financial Aid. E-mail: admissions@union.edu. A campus video is available.

UNITED STATES MERCHANT MARINE ACADEMY

D-5

Kings Point, NY 11024-1699　　　　　　　　**(516) 773-5391**
(800) 732-6267; FAX: (516) 773-5390

Full-time: 855 men, 95 women	Faculty: 80
Part-time: none	Ph.D.s: 90%
Graduate: none	Student/Faculty: 12 to 1
Year: quarters	Tuition: see profile
Application Deadline: March 1	Room & Board: n/app
Freshman Class: 850 applied, 254 enrolled	
SAT I Math/Verbal: 539/598	**HIGHLY COMPETITIVE**

The United States Merchant Marine Academy, founded in 1943, is a publicly supported institution offering maritime, military, and engineering programs for the purpose of training officers for the U.S. merchant marine and the maritime industry. Students make no conventional tuition and board payments. Earnings at sea cover basic expenses at the academy. Cash deposits/fees required are $4800. In addition to regional accreditation, Kings Point has baccalaureate program accreditation with ABET. The library contains 225,000 volumes, 110,000 microform items, and 2000 audiovisual forms, and subscribes to 1000 periodicals. Computerized library sources and services include database searching. Special learning facilities include a maritime museum. The 80-acre campus is in a suburban area 19 miles east of New York City. Including residence halls, there are 28 buildings on campus.

Student Life: 86% of undergraduates are from out-of-state, mostly the Middle Atlantic. Students come from 48 states and 6 foreign countries. 92% are white. The average age of freshmen is 17; all undergraduates, 20. 20% do not continue beyond their first year; 65% remain to graduate.

Housing: 732 students can be accommodated in college housing. College-sponsored living facilities include coed dormitories. On-campus housing is guaranteed for all 4 years. All students live on campus; of those, 75% remain on campus on weekends. Alcohol is not permitted. Upperclassmen may keep cars on campus.

Activities: There are no fraternities or sororities. There are 45 groups on campus, including band, cheerleading, choir, computers, drill team, drum and bugle corps, ethnic, jazz band, marching band, newspaper, photography, professional, radio and TV, religious, social, student government, and yearbook. Popular campus events include Parents Weekend, Christmas Ball, and Graduation Ball.

Sports: There are 17 intercollegiate sports for men and 7 for women, and 4 intramural sports for men and 2 for women. Athletic and recreation facilities include a 4000-seat stadium, a 1000-seat gymnasium, athletic fields, and extensive sailing facilities.

Services: In addition to many counseling and information services, tutoring is available in most subjects, including calculus, chemistry, and physics.

Campus Safety and Security: Campus safety and security measures include 24-hour foot and vehicle patrol and lighted pathways/sidewalks.

Programs of Study: Kings Point confers the B.S. degree. Bachelor's degrees are awarded in BUSINESS (transportation management), ENGINEERING AND ENVIRONMENTAL DESIGN (engineering and marine engineering). Marine engineering systems is the strongest academically. Marine engineering has the largest enrollment.

Required: To graduate, students must complete 160 credit hours with a 2.0 minimum GPA. The required core curriculum includes courses in mathematics, science, English, humanities and history, naval science, physical education and ship's medicine, and computer science. Students must spend 5 months during their junior and senior years at sea on U.S. flagships. All students must pass resident and sea project courses, the U.S. Coast Guard licensing examination and all required certificates, and the academy physical fitness test. Students must apply for and accept, if offered, a commission in the U.S. Naval Reserve.

Special: The college offers internships in the maritime industry and work-study programs with U.S. shipping companies.

Faculty/Classroom: 91% of faculty are male; 9%, female. All teach undergraduates. The average class size in an introductory lecture is 25 and in a laboratory, 15.

Admissions: The SAT I scores for the 1995–96 freshman class were as follows: Verbal—36% below 500, 36% between 500 and 599, 20% between 600 and 700, and 8% above 700; Math—50% between 500 and 599, 48% between 600 and 700, and 2% above 700. 40% of the current freshmen were in the top fifth of their class; 90% were in the top two fifths.

Requirements: The SAT I or ACT is required, with minimum ACT scores of 21 verbal and 25 math. Kings Point requires applicants to be in the upper 50% of their class. A minimum GPA of 3.0 is required. SAT II: Subject tests are recommended. Candidates for admission to the academy must be nominated by a member of the U.S. Congress. They must be between the ages of 17 and 25, U.S. citizens (except by special arrangement), and in excellent physical condition. Applicants should be graduates of an accredited secondary school or have a GED equivalent. Sixteen academic credits are required, including 4 credits in English, 3 in mathematics, 1 credit in physics or chemistry with a laboratory, and 8 credits in electives. An essay is required. Important factors in the admissions decision are advanced placement or honor courses, leadership record, and extracurricular activities record.

Procedure: Freshmen are admitted in the spring. Entrance exams should be taken by the first test date of the year of requested admission. There is an early decision plan. Applications should be filed by March 1 for fall entry. Notification is sent on a rolling basis. A waiting list is an active part of the admissions procedure, with about 50% of all applicants on the list.

Transfer: All students must spend 4 years at the academy.

Visiting: There are guides for informal visits and visitors may sit in on classes and stay overnight at the school. To schedule a visit, contact the Admissions Office.

Financial Aid: In a recent year, 28% of all freshmen and 17% of continuing students received some form of financial aid. The average freshman award was $3339. Of that total, scholarships or need-based grants averaged $3339. 1% of undergraduate students work part-time. Kings Point is a member of CSS. The FAFSA is required.

International Students: In a recent year, 33 international students enrolled. They must score 500 on the TOEFL and also take SAT I or the ACT.

Computers: The college provides computer facilities for student use. The mainframes are a DEC VAX 8600, an IBM 4381, and a Honeywell GPS. There are also 1200 IBM-compatible and Apple Macintosh microcomputers available in dormitories and laboratories. All students may access the system 24 hours per day. There are no time limits and no fees.

Graduates: In a recent year, 203 bachelor's degrees were awarded. The most popular majors among graduates were marine transportation (32%), marine engineering systems (32%), and marine engineering (24%). Within an average freshman class, 65% graduate in 4 years, 71% in 5 years, and 72% in 6 years. 20 companies recruited on campus in a recent year.

Admissions Contact: Captain James Skinner, Director of Admission.

UNITED STATES MILITARY ACADEMY　D-4
West Point, NY 10996–1797　　　　　　　(914) 938-4041
　　　　　　　　　　　　　　(800) 822-ARMY; FAX: (914) 938-3021

Full-time: 3523 men, 484 women	**Faculty:** 529
Part-time: none	**Ph.D.s:** 34%
Graduate: none	**Student/Faculty:** 8 to 1
Year: semesters, summer session	**Tuition:** see profile
Application Deadline: see profile	**Room & Board:** see profile
Freshman Class: 12,429 applied, 1634 accepted, 1187 enrolled	
SAT I Verbal/Math: 554/655	**ACT:** 28　　**MOST COMPETITIVE**

The United States Military Academy, founded in 1802, offers military, engineering, and comprehensive arts and sciences programs leading to a bachelor's degree and a commission as a second lieutenant in the U.S. Army, with a 6-year active duty service obligation. All students receive free tuition and room and board as well as an annual salary of more than $6700. An initial deposit of $1800 is required. In addition to regional accreditation, West Point has baccalaureate program accreditation with ABET. The library contains 429,580 volumes, 732,661 microform items, and 11,070 audiovisual forms, and subscribes to 2400 periodicals. Computerized library sources and services include the card catalog, interlibrary loans, and database searching. Special learning facilities include a learning resource center, art gallery, radio station, TV station, and military museum. Cadets may conduct research in conjunction with the academic departments through the Operations Research Center, the Photonics Research Center, the Mechanical Engineering Research Center, and the Office of Artificial Intelligence, Analysis, and Evaluation. The 16,080-acre campus is in a small town 56 miles north of New York City. Including residence halls, there are 902 buildings on campus.

Student Life: 91% of undergraduates are from out-of-state, mostly the Northeast. Students come from 50 states and 20 foreign countries. 85% are from public schools; 15% from private. 83% are white. 46% are Protestant; 35% Catholic; 14% claim no religious affiliation. The average age of freshmen is 18; all undergraduates, 20. 8% do not continue beyond their first year; 82% remain to graduate.

Housing: 4500 students can be accommodated in college housing. College-sponsored housing is coed. All cadets live in cadet barracks. On-campus housing is guaranteed for all 4 years. Seniors may keep cars on campus.

Activities: There are no fraternities or sororities. There are 104 groups on campus, including bagpipe band, cheerleading, chess, choir, chorale, chorus, computers, drama, drill team, drum and bugle corps, ethnic, honors, international, literary magazine, musical theater, pep band, photography, professional, radio and TV, religious, social, social service, student government, and yearbook. Popular campus events include Ring Weekend and 100th Night for Seniors, 500th Night for Juniors, and Plebe-Parent Weekend for Freshmen.

Sports: There are 18 intercollegiate sports for men and 9 for women, and 16 intramural sports for men and 12 for women. Athletic and recreation facilities include a 40,000-seat football stadium, baseball fields, a 2500-seat gymnasium, a 2500-seat ice rink, a 5000-seat basketball arena, courts for squash, handball, tennis, and racquetball, 3 swimming pools, workout areas, indoor/outdoor tracks, a golf course and a ski slope, and hunting, fishing, and boating facilities.

Disabled Students: Because cadets must meet physical and medical prerequisites, the campus is not designed for physically disabled students. The following facilities are available, however: wheelchair ramps, elevators, special parking, specially equipped rest rooms, lowered drinking fountains, and lowered telephones.

Services: In addition to many counseling and information services, tutoring is available in every subject.

Campus Safety and Security: Campus safety and security measures include 24-hour foot and vehicle patrol, self-defense education, shuttle buses, and lighted pathways/sidewalks.

Programs of Study: West Point confers the B.S. degree. Bachelor's degrees are awarded in BIOLOGICAL SCIENCE (life science), BUSINESS (management science and operations research), COMMUNICATIONS AND THE ARTS (languages and literature), COMPUTER AND PHYSICAL SCIENCE (chemistry, computer science, mathematics, and physics), ENGINEERING AND ENVIRONMENTAL DESIGN (chemical engineering, civil engineering, computer engineering, electrical/electronics engineering, engineering management, engineering physics, environmental engineering, environmental science, mechanical engineering, military science, nuclear engineering, and systems engineering), SOCIAL SCIENCE (American studies, behavioral science, economics, geography, history, international studies, law, philosophy, and political science/government). Physical sciences are the strongest academically. Engineering, geography, and history have the largest enrollments.

Required: All cadets must complete a core of 31 courses and 9 academic electives pertinent to their field of study. The major requires an additional 1 to 3 electives in the field. In addition, all cadets must complete 4 courses each in physical education and military science. A total of 140 credits, including 127 academic, 6 military, and 7 physical, with at least a C average, is required to graduate.

Special: There is a freshman honors program on campus, as well as 7 national honor societies, including Phi Beta Kappa. 5 departments have honors programs.

Faculty/Classroom: 89% of faculty are male; 11%, female. All teach undergraduates and 1% also do research. The average class size in an introductory lecture is 15; in a laboratory, 15; and in a regular course offering, 15.

Admissions: 13% of the 1995–96 applicants were accepted. The SAT I scores for the 1995–96 freshman class were as follows: Verbal—21% below 500, 49% between 500 and 599, 27% between 600 and 700, and 3% above 700; Math—16% between 500 and 599, 60% between 600 and 700, and 24% above 700. The ACT scores were 1% below 21, 7% between 21 and 23, 24% between 24 and 26, 22% between 27 and 28, and 46% above 28. 79% of the current freshmen were in the top fifth of their class; 96% were in the top two fifths. There were 26 National Merit finalists and 22 semifinalists. 82 freshmen graduated first in their class.

Requirements: The SAT I or ACT is required. Applicants must be qualified academically, physically, and medically and must be nominated for admission by members of the U.S. Congress or executive sources. West Point recommends that applicants have 4 years each of English and mathematics, 2 each of foreign language and laboratory science, such as chemistry and physics, and 1 of U.S. history. Courses in geography, government, and economics are also suggested. An essay is required, and an interview is recommended. The GED is accepted. Applicants must be 17 to 22 years old, a U.S. citizen at the time of enrollment (except by agreement with another country), unmarried, and not pregnant or legally obligated to support children. AP credits are accepted. Important factors in the admissions decision are leadership record, extracurricular activities record, and recommendations by school officials.

Procedure: Freshmen are admitted in the summer. Entrance exams should be taken in the spring of the junior year and not later than the fall of the senior year. There are early decision and early admissions plans. Early decision applications should be filed by October 25; regular applications, by March 1 for summer entry. Notification of early decision is sent beginning January 15; regular decision, on a rolling basis, beginning in June. 548 early decision candidates were accepted for the 1995–96 class. A waiting list is an active part of the admissions procedure, with about 5% of all applicants on the list.

Transfer: All applicants must enter as freshmen. 140 credits of 140 must be completed at West Point.

Visiting: There are regularly scheduled orientations for prospective students. Candidates will be escorted by a cadet, will attend class, have lunch with the Corps of Cadets, and talk with cadets about all phases of West Point life. There are guides for informal visits and visitors may sit in on classes and stay overnight at the school. To schedule a visit, contact the Admissions Office.

International Students: There were 36 international students enrolled in a recent year. They must take the TOEFL. The student must also take the SAT I or the ACT.

Computers: The college provides computer facilities for student use. The mainframe is a Unisys 2200/425. Each cadet purchases a personal computer that is connected to all other users and the campus mainframe through a state-of-the-art local area network. All students may access the system 24 hours daily. There are no time limits and no fees.

Graduates: In 1994–95, 1005 bachelor's degrees were awarded. The most popular majors among graduates were engineering (33%), mathematics and science (11%), and geography (9%). Within an average freshman class, 99% graduate in 4 years and 1% in 5 years.

Admissions Contact: Michael C. Jones, Director of Admissions. E-mail: ts5642@trotter.usma.edu. A campus video is available.

UNIVERSITY OF ROCHESTER B-3
Rochester, NY 14627–0251   (716) 275-3221
FAX: (716) 461-4595/(716) 273-1086

Full-time: 2587 men, 2426 women	Faculty: 505; I, +$
Part-time: 51 men, 118 women	Ph.D.s: 99%
Graduate: 1643 men, 1295 women	Student/Faculty: 10 to 1
Year: semesters, summer session	Tuition: $18,260
Application Deadline: January 15	Room & Board: $6583
Freshman Class: 9195 applied, 5608 accepted, 1227 enrolled	
SAT I Verbal/Math: 550/640	ACT: 27 HIGHLY COMPETITIVE

The University of Rochester, founded in 1850, is a private, coeducational institution offering programs in the arts and sciences, engineering and applied science, nursing, medicine and dentistry, business administration, music, and education. There are 4 undergraduate and 7 graduate schools. In addition to regional accreditation, the university has baccalaureate program accreditation with AACSB, ABET, ACPE, NASM, and NLN. The 7 libraries contain 2,843,283 volumes, 4,060,725 microform items, and 63,917 audiovisual forms, and subscribe to 10,284 periodicals. Computerized library sources and services include the card catalog, interlibrary loans, and database searching. Special learning facilities include a learning resource center, art gallery, radio station, laboratories for nuclear structure research and laser energetics, center for visual science, the Strong Memorial Hospital, art center, observatory, and the Institute of Optics. The 600-acre campus is in a suburban area 2 miles south of downtown Rochester. Including residence halls, there are 152 buildings on campus.

Student Life: 54% of undergraduates are from out-of-state, mostly the Middle Atlantic. Students come from 52 states, 75 foreign countries, and Canada. 68% are white; 10% foreign nationals; 10% Asian American. 31% are Catholic; 26% Protestant; 16% claim no religious affiliation; 16% Jewish. 7% do not continue beyond their first year; 78% remain to graduate.

Housing: 3443 students can be accommodated in college housing. College-sponsored living facilities include single-sex and coed dormitories, on-campus apartments, married-student housing, and fraternity houses. In addition, there are language houses, special interest houses, drama and medieval houses, and faculty-in-residence housing. On-campus housing is guaranteed for freshmen and sophomores and is available on a lottery system for upperclassmen. 75% of students live on campus; of those, 90% remain on campus on weekends. All students may keep cars on campus.

Activities: 25% of men belong to 16 national fraternities; 20% of women belong to 9 national sororities. There are 150 groups on campus, including art, band, cheerleading, chess, choir, chorale, chorus, computers, dance, drama, drill team, ethnic, film, gay, honors, international, jazz band, literary magazine, musical theater, newspaper, opera, orchestra, pep band, photography, political, professional, radio and TV, religious, social, social service, student government, symphony, and yearbook. Popular campus events include Dandelion Day.

Sports: There are 11 intercollegiate sports for men and 10 for women, and 14 intramural sports for men and 13 for women. Athletic and recreation facilities include a sports center, a 5000-seat stadium, a 3000-seat gymnasium, a field house, an ice rink, courts for handball, racquetball, squash, and tennis, an indoor track, a fitness center and weight room, and a jogging path.

Disabled Students: 63% of the campus is accessible to disabled students. The following facilities are available: wheelchair ramps, elevators, special parking, specially equipped rest rooms, special class scheduling, lowered drinking fountains, lowered telephones, and pushers for wheelchairs.

Services: In addition to many counseling and information services, tutoring is available in every subject. There is also a reader service for the blind.

Campus Safety and Security: Campus safety and security measures include 24-hour foot and vehicle patrol, self-defense education, escort service, and shuttle buses. In addition, there are informal discussions, pamphlets/posters/films, emergency telephones, and lighted pathways/sidewalks.

Programs of Study: The university confers B.A., B.S., and B.M. degrees. Master's and doctoral degrees are also awarded. Bachelor's degrees are awarded in BIOLOGICAL SCIENCE (biochemistry, biology/biological science, cell biology, ecology, microbiology, and neurosciences), COMMUNICATIONS AND THE ARTS (art history and appreciation, Chinese, classics, comparative literature, English, film arts, fine arts, French, German, Japanese, linguistics, music, Russian, Spanish, and studio art), COMPUTER AND PHYSICAL SCIENCE (applied mathematics, chemistry, computer science, geology, mathematics, optics, physics, and statistics), ENGINEERING AND ENVIRONMENTAL DESIGN (chemical engineering, electrical/electronics engineering, engineering and applied science, geological engineering, and mechanical engineering), HEALTH PROFES-

SIONS (nursing), SOCIAL SCIENCE (anthropology, cognitive science, economics, history, philosophy, political science/government, psychology, religion, and women's studies). Psychology, political science, and economics have the largest enrollments.

Required: Students focus on the humanities, social sciences, and natural sciences; 1 of the 3 areas includes their major, and they select a 3-course cluster in each of the other 2. A total of 128 credit hours, with a minimum GPA of 2.0, is required to graduate.

Special: Cross-registration is offered with other Rochester area colleges. Internships, a Washington semester, B.A.-B.S. degrees, dual and student-designed majors, nondegree study, and pass/fail options are available. Study abroad is possible in Australia, China, Japan, Egypt, Israel, the former Soviet Union, and in several European countries. Other options include a fifth year of courses tuition-free, courses designed to teach first-year students about how to learn and how to make learning a lifetime habit, a management studies certificate, and music lessons for credit at the Eastman School of music. Qualified freshmen may obtain early assurance of admission to the university's medical school through the Rochester Early Medical Scholars program. There are 5 national honor societies on campus, including Phi Beta Kappa. 13 departments have honors programs.

Faculty/Classroom: 78% of faculty are male; 22%, female. Graduate students teach 7% of introductory courses. The average class size in an introductory lecture is 75; in a laboratory, 20; and in a regular course offering, 35.

Admissions: 61% of the 1995–96 applicants were accepted. The SAT I scores for the 1995–96 freshman class were as follows: Verbal—29% below 500, 41% between 500 and 599, 27% between 600 and 700, and 3% above 700; Math—9% below 500, 27% between 500 and 599, 43% between 600 and 700, and 21% above 700. The ACT scores were 6% below 21, 20% between 21 and 23, 24% between 24 and 26, 20% between 27 and 28, and 30% above 28. 78% of the current freshmen were in the top fifth of their class; 94% were in the top two fifths. There were 13 National Merit finalists. 86 freshmen graduated first in their class.

Requirements: The SAT I is required. SAT II: Subject tests are recommended. Applicants should be graduates of an accredited secondary school or have a GED equivalent. An essay is required and an interview is recommended. An audition is required for music majors. The school accepts the Common Application on computer disk and on-line via ExPAN. AP credits are accepted. Important factors in the admissions decision are advanced placement or honor courses, recommendations by school officials, and leadership record.

Procedure: Freshmen are admitted fall and spring. Entrance exams should be taken by February of the senior year. There are early decision, early admissions, and deferred admissions plans. Early decision applications should be filed by November 15; regular applications, by January 15 for fall entry and November 15 for spring entry, along with an application fee of $50. Notification of early decision is sent December 15 and regular decision between late March and early April for fall entry. 167 early decision candidates were accepted for a recent class. A waiting list is an active part of the admissions procedure, with about 8% of all applicants on the list.

Transfer: 208 transfer students enrolled in 1995–96. The most important criterion is an applicant's college record. Transfers are accepted on a rolling admissions basis. 32 credits of 128 must be completed at the university.

Visiting: There are regularly scheduled orientations for prospective students. There are guides for informal visits and visitors may sit in on classes and stay overnight at the school. To schedule a visit, contact the Admissions Office.

Financial Aid: In 1995–96, 89% of all freshmen and 91% of continuing students received some form of financial aid. 65% of freshmen and 62% of continuing students received need-based aid. The average freshman award was $21,145. Of that total, scholarships or need-based grants averaged $12,966 ($17,950 maximum); loans averaged $3391 ($4625 maximum); external grants averaged $3100; and work contracts averaged $1688 ($2000 maximum). 55% of undergraduate students work part-time. Average earnings from campus work for the school year are $1400. The average regular indebtedness of the 1994–95 graduate was $17,075. The university is a member of CSS. The FAF or FFS and the college's own financial statement are required. The application deadline for fall entry is January 31.

International Students: There are currently 386 international students enrolled. The school actively recruits these students. The student must take the SAT I or the ACT. The university strongly recommends that if English is not the student's first language, the TOEFL be taken.

Computers: The college provides computer facilities for student use. The mainframes are an IBM 4381, DEC VAX systems, SUN systems, and a Solbourne computer. Students have access to hundreds of PCs, workstations, printers, and terminals in the libraries, classrooms, laboratories, and resource centers on campus. Most residence hall rooms have lines accessing the mainframe computers. All students may access the system 24 hours daily. There are no time limits and no fees.

Graduates: In 1994–95, 1253 bachelor's degrees were awarded. The most popular majors among graduates were psychology (14%), political science (11%), and economics (9%). Within an average freshman class, 65% graduate in 4 years, 75% in 5 years, and 78% in 6 years. 87 companies recruited on campus in 1994–95. Of the 1994 graduating class, 36% were enrolled in graduate school within 6 months of graduation and 45% had found employment.

Admissions Contact: Wayne A. Locust, Director of Admissions. E-mail: admit@macmail.cc.rochester.edu.

UNIVERSITY OF THE STATE OF NEW YORK REGENTS COLLEGE DEGREES D-3

Albany, NY 12203–5159   **(518) 464-8500; FAX: (518) 464-8777**

Full-time: none	Faculty: n/app
Part-time: 19,443 men and women	Ph.D.s: n/app
Graduate: none	Student/Faculty: n/app
Year: see profile	Tuition: $565
Application Deadline: open	Room & Board: n/app
Freshman Class: 11,034 enrolled	
SAT I or ACT: not required	SPECIAL

Regents College, founded in 1971, is an external degree, noninstructional institution that is part of the state-affiliated University of the State of New York. Students earn undergraduate degrees without attending classes. Credit is given through proficiency examinations, course credit from accredited colleges, military training, and on-the-job training. There are 4 undergraduate schools. In addition to regional accreditation, Regents College has baccalaureate program accreditation with NLN. The 1-building campus is in Albany.

Student Life: 85% of undergraduates are from out-of-state. Students come from 50 states, 30 foreign countries, and Canada. 75% are white; 14% African American. The average age of all undergraduates is 39.

Housing: There are no residence halls.

Activities: There are no fraternities or sororities.

Sports: There is no sports program at Regents College.

Disabled Students: The entire campus is accessible to disabled students. The following facilities are available: wheelchair ramps, elevators, special parking, specially equipped rest rooms, lowered drinking fountains, and lowered telephones.

Campus Safety and Security: Campus safety and security measures include lighted pathways/sidewalks.

Programs of Study: Regents College confers B.A. and B.S. degrees. Associate degrees are also awarded. Bachelor's degrees are awarded in BUSINESS (accounting, banking and finance, business administration and management, human resources, international business management, management information systems, and marketing/retailing/merchandising), COMPUTER AND PHYSICAL SCIENCE (information sciences and systems and nuclear technology), ENGINEERING AND ENVIRONMENTAL DESIGN (computer technology, electrical/electronics engineering technology, and technological management), HEALTH PROFESSIONS (nursing), SOCIAL SCIENCE (liberal arts/general studies). Nursing has the largest enrollment.

Required: To graduate, students must complete 120 credits with a minimum 2.0 GPA. At least 50% of course work must be in the arts and sciences. The required core courses must include 6 to 12 credits each in humanities, mathematics/science, and social science/history. The nursing program requires a different set of core courses as well as the nursing performance examinations. All students must fulfill a written English requirement.

Special: B.A. or B.S. candidates may major in liberal studies or in most traditional academic disciplines. Faculty consultants design curricula, approve sources of credit, create examinations, and assess student learning. They do not offer instruction. Students receive academic advising by telephone, letter, computer, or in person. The flexibility of this alternate program enables adults to pursue an undergraduate degree independently. Examinations are available. Pass/fail options are possible.

Faculty/Classroom: 30% of faculty are male; 70%, female.

Requirements: There are no admissions requirements except for nursing students. Applicants need not be residents of New York State. Students without a high school diploma or equivalent are admitted as special students. Nursing enrollment is available only to students with certain health-care backgrounds. AP and CLEP credits are accepted.

Procedure: Application deadlines are open. The college accepts all applicants. Notification is sent on a rolling basis.

Financial Aid: The college's own financial statement is required. The application deadline for fall entry is July 1.

International Students: There are currently 531 international students enrolled.

Computers: The mainframe is a DEC Ultrix 5700. Students are encouraged to access a database of more than 7000 examinations and courses available at a distance.

Graduates: In 1994–95, 2130 bachelor's degrees were awarded. The most popular majors among graduates were liberal arts (77%), business (9%), and nursing (8%). Within an average freshman class, 58% graduate in 6 years.

UTICA COLLEGE OF SYRACUSE UNIVERSITY C-3

Utica, NY 13502-4892	(315) 792-3006; (800) 782-8884
Full-time: 530 men, 882 women	Faculty: 105; IIB, av$
Part-time: 99 men, 251 women	Ph.D.s: 91%
Graduate: none	Student/Faculty: 13 to 1
Year: semesters, summer session	Tuition: $13,406
Application Deadline: open	Room & Board: $5122
Freshman Class: 1139 applied, 932 accepted, 263 enrolled	
SAT I Verbal/Math: 440/490	ACT: 22 COMPETITIVE

Utica College of Syracuse University, a private liberal arts institution founded in 1946, is one of the academic divisions of Syracuse University. In addition to regional accreditation, UC has baccalaureate program accreditation with NLN. The library contains 165,624 volumes, 60,985 microform items, and 8032 audiovisual forms, and subscribes to 1038 periodicals. Computerized library sources and services include the card catalog, interlibrary loans, and database searching. Special learning facilities include an art gallery, radio station, and early childhood education laboratory. The 185-acre campus is in a suburban area 50 miles east of Syracuse. Including residence halls, there are 12 buildings on campus.
Student Life: 86% of undergraduates are from New York. Students come from 25 states and 9 foreign countries. 80% are from public schools; 20% from private. 88% are white. The average age of freshmen is 18; all undergraduates, 22. 29% do not continue beyond their first year; 50% remain to graduate.
Housing: 860 students can be accommodated in college housing. College-sponsored living facilities include single-sex and coed dormitories and on-campus apartments. On-campus housing is guaranteed for all 4 years. All students may keep cars on campus.
Activities: 3% of men belong to 1 local fraternity; 3% of women belong to 2 local and 4 national sororities. There are 79 groups on campus, including art, band, cheerleading, choir, chorus, computers, drama, ethnic, film, gay, honors, international, jazz band, literary magazine, musical theater, newspaper, pep band, photography, political, professional, radio and TV, religious, social, social service, student government, and yearbook. Popular campus events include outdoor concerts, mock elections, air and band competitions, Winter Weekend, and Family Weekend.
Sports: There are 7 intercollegiate sports for men and 7 for women, and 20 intramural sports for men and 20 for women. Athletic and recreation facilities include a 2200-seat gymnasium, a competition-size swimming pool, tennis, racquetball, handball and squash courts, a sauna, Nautilus and weight rooms, dance and aerobic rooms, and playing fields.
Disabled Students: 80% of the campus is accessible to disabled students. The following facilities are available: wheelchair ramps, elevators, special parking, specially equipped rest rooms, and lowered drinking fountains.
Services: In addition to many counseling and information services, tutoring is available in most subjects. There is a reader service for the blind, and remedial math, reading, and writing.
Campus Safety and Security: Campus safety and security measures include 24-hour foot and vehicle patrol, escort service, informal discussions, and pamphlets/posters/films. In addition, there are lighted pathways/sidewalks.
Programs of Study: UC confers B.A. and B.S. degrees. Bachelor's degrees are awarded in BIOLOGICAL SCIENCE (biology/biological science), BUSINESS (accounting, business administration and management, and business economics), COMMUNICATIONS AND THE ARTS (communications, dramatic arts, English, fine arts, journalism, public relations, and speech/debate/rhetoric), COMPUTER AND PHYSICAL SCIENCE (actuarial science, chemistry, computer science, mathematics, and physics), ENGINEERING AND ENVIRONMENTAL DESIGN (construction management), HEALTH PROFESSIONS (nursing, occupational therapy, physical therapy, predentistry, premedicine, and recreation therapy), SOCIAL SCIENCE (anthropology, child psychology/development, criminal justice, economics, history, international studies, philosophy, political science/government, prelaw, psychology, social studies, and sociology). Occupational therapy, criminal justice, and journalism are the strongest academically. Health sciences has the largest enrollment.
Required: To graduate, students must complete a total of 120 to 128 hours with a minimum 2.0 GPA. They must complete a general education requirement, including basic skills, distribution requirements, and a writing portfolio.
Special: UC offers co-op programs, internships, and work-study programs in all majors, and cross-registration with Hamilton College. Study abroad may be arranged in 7 countries. There is a 2–2 engineering degree with Syracuse University. There is a freshman honors

program on campus, as well as 5 national honor societies. All departments have honors programs.
Faculty/Classroom: 61% of faculty are male; 39%, female. All both teach and do research. The average class size in an introductory lecture is 23; in a laboratory, 10; and in a regular course offering, 18.
Admissions: 82% of the 1995–96 applicants were accepted. 28% of the current freshmen were in the top fifth of their class; 56% were in the top two fifths. 3 freshmen graduated first in their class.
Requirements: The SAT I or ACT is not required but either is accepted. Graduation from an accredited secondary school or satisfactory scores on the GED are required. Recommended high school courses include 4 years of English, 3 years each of mathematics and social studies, and 2 years each of foreign language and science. An essay and an interview are also recommended. AP and CLEP credits are accepted. Important factors in the admissions decision are advanced placement or honor courses, extracurricular activities record, and leadership record.
Procedure: Freshmen are admitted fall and spring. Entrance exams, if submitted, should be taken during the junior year. There are early decision, early admissions, and deferred admissions plans. Early decision applications should be filed by December 1, along with an application fee of $25. Notification of early decision is sent December 15; regular decision, on a rolling basis.
Transfer: 230 transfer students enrolled in 1995–96. Applicants must have a minimum GPA of 2.3. 30 credits of 120 to 128 must be completed at UC.
Visiting: There are regularly scheduled orientations for prospective students, including an interview, financial aid information, and a tour of the campus. There are guides for informal visits, and visitors may sit in on classes and stay overnight at the school. To schedule a visit, contact the Admissions Office.
Financial Aid: In 1995–96, 78% of all students received some form of financial aid. 74% of freshmen and 70% of continuing students received need-based aid. The average freshman award was $13,721. Of that total, scholarships or need-based grants averaged $2942 ($4500 maximum); loans averaged $5080 ($8625 maximum); and work contracts averaged $1250 ($1300 maximum). 43% of undergraduate students work part-time. Average earnings from campus work for the school year are $981. The average financial indebtedness of the 1994–95 graduate was $12,500. UC is a member of CSS. The college's own financial statement and the FAFSA are required. The application deadline for fall entry is March 15.
International Students: There are currently 20 international students enrolled. The school actively recruits these students. They must take the TOEFL and achieve a minimum score of 500.
Computers: The college provides computer facilities for student use. The mainframe is a Prime 5370. There are also 85 IBM and Macintosh microcomputers available in 4 laboratories. All students may access the system during posted hours. Time limits are imposed only during peak hours. There are no fees.
Graduates: In 1994–95, 419 bachelor's degrees were awarded. The most popular majors among graduates were occupational therapy (17%), criminal justice (11%), and business administration (11%). Within an average freshman class, 52% graduate in 6 years. 500 companies recruited on campus in 1994–95. Of the 1994 graduating class, 7% were enrolled in graduate school within 6 months of graduation and 90% had found employment.
Admissions Contact: Leslie North, Director of Admissions.

VASSAR COLLEGE D-4

Poughkeepsie, NY 12601	(914) 437-7300
Full-time: 849 men, 1404 women	Faculty: 202; IIB, ++$
Part-time: 24 men, 67 women	Ph.D.s: 90%
Graduate: 1 man, 1 woman	Student/Faculty: 11 to 1
Year: semesters	Tuition: $20,120
Application Deadline: January 1	Room & Board: $6150
Freshman Class: n/av	
SAT I Verbal/Math: 620/660	ACT: 28 HIGHLY COMPETITIVE +

Vassar College, founded in 1861, is a private, independent liberal arts college offering programs in the arts, sciences, education, and multicultural studies. The 2 libraries contain 716,921 volumes, 350,000 microform items, and 27,000 audiovisual forms, and subscribe to 3900 periodicals. Computerized library sources and services include the card catalog, interlibrary loans, and database searching. Special learning facilities include a learning resource center, art gallery, radio station, geological museum, satellite hook-up to receive television from Russia, observatory, 3 theaters, environmental field station, and intercultural center. The 1000-acre campus is in a suburban area 75 miles north of New York City. Including residence halls, there are 100 buildings on campus.
Student Life: 68% of undergraduates are from out of state, mostly the Middle Atlantic. Students come from 45 states, 36 foreign countries, and Canada. 60% are from public schools; 30% from private. 75% are white. The average age of freshmen is 18; all undergradu-

ates, 20. 2% do not continue beyond their first year; 88% remain to graduate.

Housing: 2250 students can be accommodated in college housing. College-sponsored living facilities include single-sex and coed dormitories, on-campus apartments, off-campus apartments, and married-student housing. In addition there is 1 all-women residence hall and 1 cooperative living unit. On-campus housing is guaranteed for all 4 years. 98% of students live on campus; of those, 90% remain on campus on weekends. All students may keep cars on campus.

Activities: There are no fraternities or sororities. There are 85 groups on campus, including art, band, chess, choir, chorale, chorus, computers, dance, drama, ethnic, film, gay, jazz band, literary magazine, newspaper, opera, orchestra, radio and TV, religious, social service, student government, and yearbook. Popular campus events include Founders Day, fall and spring convocations, serenading, spring and fall formals, All Parents Weekend, and Freshman Parents Weekend.

Sports: There are 10 intercollegiate sports for men and 10 for women, and 11 intramural sports for men and 10 for women. Athletic and recreation facilities include a field house with a swimming pool, 5 indoor tennis courts, a weight and conditioning room, a gymnasium with squash and racquetball courts and basketball facilities, a 9-hole golf course, 13 outdoor tennis courts, an all-weather track, 2 soccer fields, a baseball diamond, a rugby field, and various club and intramural fields.

Disabled Students: 30% of the campus is accessible to disabled students. The following facilities are available: wheelchair ramps, elevators, special parking, specially equipped rest rooms, and lowered drinking fountains.

Services: In addition to many counseling and information services, tutoring is available in most subjects. There is a reader service for the blind, and remedial math, reading, and writing.

Campus Safety and Security: Campus safety and security measures include 24-hour foot and vehicle patrol, escort service, informal discussions, and emergency telephones. In addition, there are lighted pathways/sidewalks.

Programs of Study: Vassar confers the A.B. degree. Master's degrees are also awarded. Bachelor's degrees are awarded in BIOLOGICAL SCIENCE (biochemistry and biology/biological science), COMMUNICATIONS AND THE ARTS (art, dramatic arts, English, film arts, fine arts, languages, and music), COMPUTER AND PHYSICAL SCIENCE (chemistry, computer science, geology, mathematics, and physics), EDUCATION (foreign languages), ENGINEERING AND ENVIRONMENTAL DESIGN (engineering and environmental science), HEALTH PROFESSIONS (premedicine), SOCIAL SCIENCE (African studies, American studies, anthropology, Asian/Oriental studies, economics, geography, history, international studies, philosophy, political science/government, prelaw, psychobiology, psychology, religion, social studies, sociology, urban studies, and women's studies). English, political science, and psychology have the largest enrollments.

Required: To graduate, students must have a total of 34 units equivalent to 120 credit hours, with a minimum GPA of 2.0. Of this total, no more than 17 units may be in a single field of concentration and 8 1/2 units must be outside the major field. Entering freshmen must take the freshman course. All students must meet the foreign language proficiency requirement, and must take a quantitative skills course before their third year.

Special: The school offers field work in social agencies and schools, a Washington semester, dual majors, independent majors, cross-registration with the 12-College Consortium, and pass/fail options. Study abroad programs may be arranged in 4 countries. A 3–2 engineering degree with Dartmouth College is offered. There is a chapter of Phi Beta Kappa on campus.

Faculty/Classroom: 60% of faculty are male; 40%, female. All both teach and do research. The average class size in an introductory lecture is 50; in a laboratory, 7; and in a regular course offering, 20.

Admissions: The SAT I scores for a recent year's freshman class were as follows: Verbal—9% below 500, 40% between 500 and 599, 47% between 600 and 700, and 4% above 700; Math—7% below 500, 31% between 500 and 599, 51% between 600 and 700, and 11% above 700. 79% of the current freshmen were in the top fifth of their class; 97% were in the top two fifths. There was 1 National Merit finalist and 22 semifinalists. 18 freshmen graduated first in their class.

Requirements: The SAT I is required and 3 SAT II: Subject tests (1 preferably in Writing), or the ACT is required. In addition, graduation from an accredited secondary school or satisfactory scores on the GED are required for admission. The high school program should typically include 4 years of English, 3 or more years of a foreign language, 3 or 4 years of social studies, 3 years of mathematics, and 2 or 3 years of science. An essay and a writing sample are required. AP and CLEP credits are accepted. Important factors in the admissions decision are advanced placement or honor courses, leadership record, and recommendations by school officials.

Procedure: Freshmen are admitted in the fall. Entrance exams should be taken as early as possible, but no later than December of the senior year. There are early decision, early admissions, and deferred admissions plans. Early decision applications should be filed by December 1; regular applications, by January 1 for fall entry, along with an application fee of $60. Notification is sent in early April. 177 early decision candidates were accepted for the 1995–96 class. A waiting list is an active part of the admissions procedure.

Transfer: 29 transfer students enrolled in a recent year. Transfer students must have at least 1 year of liberal arts course work with a minimum GPA of 3.0. 17 credits of 34 (120 credit hours) must be completed at Vassar.

Visiting: There are regularly scheduled orientations for prospective students, including a campus tour, an information session, and a class visit. There are guides for informal visits and visitors may sit in on classes and stay overnight at the school. To schedule a visit, contact the Admissions Office.

Financial Aid: In a recent year, 53% of all freshmen and 58% of continuing students received some form of financial aid. 52% of freshmen and 51% of continuing students received need-based aid. The average freshman award was $17,233. Of that total, scholarships or need-based grants averaged $13,948 ($21,016 maximum); loans averaged $2185 ($2625 maximum); and work contracts averaged $1100 ($1150 maximum). 60% of undergraduate students work part-time. Average earnings from campus work for the school year are $800. The average financial indebtedness of a recent year's graduate was $12,250. Vassar is a member of CSS. The FAF and the college's own financial statement are required. The application deadline for fall entry is January 15.

International Students: There were 92 international students enrolled in a recent year. The school actively recruits these students. They must take the TOEFL and achieve a minimum score of 600 and also take SAT I or SAT II: Subject tests.

Computers: The college provides computer facilities for student use. The mainframes are a DEC VAX 6200, an 11/780, an 11/750, and a MicroVAX II. There are also 350 Apple Macintosh and IBM microcomputers available throughout the campus. All students may access the system 24 hours per day. There are no time limits and no fees.

Graduates: In a recent year, 583 bachelor's degrees were awarded. The most popular majors among graduates were English (16%), political science (8%), and psychology (7%). Within an average freshman class, 1% graduate in 3 years, 78% in 4 years, 86% in 5 years, and 87% in 6 years. 14 companies recruited on campus in a recent year.

Admissions Contact: Richard Moll, Director of Admissions.

WAGNER COLLEGE
D-5
Staten Island, NY 10301   (718) 390-3411
(800) 221-1010; FAX: (718) 390-3105

Full-time: 595 men, 825 women	Faculty: 78; IIB, -$
Part-time: 33 men, 96 women	Ph.D.s: 85%
Graduate: 104 men, 243 women	Student/Faculty: 18 to 1
Year: semesters, summer session	Tuition: $14,450
Application Deadline: February 15	Room & Board: $5800
Freshman Class: 1494 applied, 1060 accepted, 371 enrolled	
SAT I Verbal/Math: 490/520	COMPETITIVE

Wagner College, founded in 1883, is a private liberal arts institution. There is 1 graduate school. In addition to regional accreditation, Wagner has baccalaureate program accreditation with NLN. The library contains 300,000 volumes and 225,000 microform items, and subscribes to 1000 periodicals. Computerized library sources and services include interlibrary loans and database searching. Special learning facilities include an art gallery, planetarium, and radio station. The 105-acre campus is in an urban area 10 miles from Manhattan. Including residence halls, there are 18 buildings on campus.

Student Life: 72% of undergraduates are from New York. Students come from 27 states, 27 foreign countries, and Canada. 61% are from public schools; 39% from private. 87% are white. 76% claim no religious affiliation; 17% Catholic. The average age of freshmen is 18; all undergraduates, 20. 17% do not continue beyond their first year; 68% remain to graduate.

Housing: 1315 students can be accommodated in college housing. College-sponsored living facilities include coed dormitories. In addition, there are fraternity/sorority floors in dormitories and quiet floors. On-campus housing is guaranteed for all 4 years. 65% of students live on campus; of those, 75% remain on campus on weekends. Alcohol is not permitted. Upperclassmen may keep cars on campus.

Activities: 30% of men belong to 4 local and 4 national fraternities; 20% of women belong to 1 local and 2 national sororities. There are 71 groups on campus, including art, band, cheerleading, chess, choir, chorale, computers, dance, drama, ethnic, gay, honors, international, jazz band, musical theater, newspaper, opera, pep band, political, professional, radio and TV, religious, social service, student government, symphony, and yearbook. Popular campus events include Songfest, Homecoming, and Community Chest.

Sports: There are 7 intercollegiate sports for men and 8 for women, and 4 intramural sports for men and 3 for women. Athletic and recreation facilities include a football stadium, a gymnasium, a fitness center, a track, and a basketball stadium.

Disabled Students: 25% of the campus is accessible to disabled students. The following facilities are available: wheelchair ramps, elevators, special parking, specially equipped rest rooms, and special class scheduling.

Services: In addition to many counseling and information services, tutoring is available in every subject. There is a reader service for the blind, and remedial math, reading, and writing.

Campus Safety and Security: Campus safety and security measures include 24-hour foot and vehicle patrol, escort service, shuttle buses, and informal discussions. There are emergency telephones, lighted pathways/sidewalks, and ID card access into residence halls.

Programs of Study: Wagner confers B.A. and B.S. degrees. Master's degrees are also awarded. Bachelor's degrees are awarded in BIOLOGICAL SCIENCE (biology/biological science and microbiology), BUSINESS (accounting, banking and finance, business administration and management, business economics, and marketing/retailing/merchandising), COMMUNICATIONS AND THE ARTS (arts administration/management, dramatic arts, English, fine arts, music, and speech/debate/rhetoric), COMPUTER AND PHYSICAL SCIENCE (chemistry, computer science, mathematics, and physics), EDUCATION (elementary, middle school, and secondary), HEALTH PROFESSIONS (medical laboratory technology, nursing, physician's assistant, predentistry, and premedicine), SOCIAL SCIENCE (anthropology, gerontology, history, philosophy, political science/government, prelaw, psychology, public administration, religion, social science, social work, and sociology). Natural sciences is the strongest academically. Business has the largest enrollment.

Required: To graduate, students must complete 128 credit hours with a 2.0 GPA. 60 hours are required in the major. All students must take courses in English, mathematics, and multidisciplinary studies. In addition, students must fulfill distribution requirements in physical science, life science, mathematics and computers, history, literature, philosophy and religion, foreign culture, aesthetics, and human behavior.

Special: Internships are required for business and English majors and recommended for all majors. Students may earn B.A.-B.S. degrees in mathematics, physics, and psychology. Student-designed and dual majors, credit for life experience, a Washington semester, nondegree study, and pass/fail options are available. Study abroad in 14 countries is possible. There is a freshman honors program on campus, as well as 9 national honor societies. All departments have honors programs.

Faculty/Classroom: 49% of faculty are male; 51%, female. All teach undergraduates. No introductory courses are taught by graduate students. The average class size in an introductory lecture is 23; in a laboratory, 13; and in a regular course offering, 20.

Admissions: 71% of the 1995–96 applicants were accepted. The SAT I scores for the 1995–96 freshman class were as follows: Verbal—48% below 500, 43% between 500 and 599, 9% between 600 and 700, and 1% above 700; Math—32% below 500, 52% between 500 and 599, 14% between 600 and 700, and 2% above 700. 28% of the current freshmen were in the top fifth of their class; 62% were in the top two fifths.

Requirements: The SAT I or ACT is required. For the SAT I, the required recentered scores are 510 for the verbal section and 480 for the mathematics. A composite score of 21 is required on the ACT. Graduation from an accredited secondary school is required for admission. 18 academic credits or Carnegie units are required, including 4 years of English, 3 each of history and mathematics, 2 each of foreign language, science, and social studies, and 1 each of art and music. An essay is required, and an interview is recommended. Auditions are required for music and theater applicants. A grade average of 80% is required. AP and CLEP credits are accepted. Important factors in the admissions decision are advanced placement or honor courses, recommendations by school officials, and extracurricular activities record.

Procedure: Freshmen are admitted in the fall and spring. Entrance exams should be taken by December of the senior year. There are early decision, early admissions, and deferred admissions plans. Early decision applications should be filed by December 15; regular applications, by February 15 for fall entry and December 1 for spring entry, along with an application fee of $40. Notification of early decision is sent January 15; regular decision, on a rolling basis. 26 early decision candidates were accepted for the 1995–96 class. A waiting list is an active part of the admissions procedure, with about 4% of all applicants on the list.

Transfer: 121 transfer students enrolled in 1995–96. Transfer students should have a minimum of 30 credit hours earned with a minimum GPA of 2.5. Applicants must submit all college and high school transcripts, a letter of recommendation, and a personal statement. An interview is recommended. SAT I or ACT scores taken within the last

5 years may be submitted. 30 credits of 128 must be completed at Wagner.

Visiting: There are regularly scheduled orientations for prospective students, including a presentation by the Admissions Office, a tour of the campus, and meetings with faculty and staff. There are guides for informal visits and visitors may sit in on classes and stay overnight at the school. To schedule a visit, contact the Admissions Office.

Financial Aid: In 1995–96, 87% of all freshmen and 88% of continuing students received some form of financial aid. 78% of freshmen and 70% of continuing students received need-based aid. The average freshman award was $9285. Of that total, scholarships or need-based grants averaged $4480 ($7300 maximum); loans averaged $2625; and work contracts averaged $900 ($1200 maximum). 25% of undergraduate students work part time. Average earnings from campus work for the school year are $800. The average financial indebtedness of the 1994–95 graduate was $6295. Wagner is a member of CSS. The FAFSA and the college's own financial statement are required. The application deadline for fall entry is April 1.

International Students: There are currently 62 international students enrolled. The school actively recruits these students. They must take the TOEFL or the college's own test and achieve a minimum score on the TOEFL of 550.

Computers: The college provides computer facilities for student use. The mainframe is a DEC VAX. There are 75 IBM microcomputers in the computer center that are connected to the mainframe. There are an additional 52 IBM microcomputers available for student use. Printers include 4 HP LaserJet, 2 Epson LQ dot-matrix, and 1 HP PaintJet. All students may access the system Monday through Thursday, 9 A.M. to 10 P.M.; Friday, 9 A.M. to 6 P.M.; and Saturday and Sunday, 11 A.M. to 5 P.M. There are no time limits and no fees.

Graduates: In a recent year, 283 bachelor's degrees were awarded. The most popular majors among graduates were education (17%), business adminstration (16%), and biological sciences (10%). Within an average freshman class, 60% graduate in 4 years and 7% in 5 years. 43 companies recruited on campus in a recent year.

Admissions Contact: Angelo Araimo, Director of Admissions. E-mail: adm@wagner.edu. A campus video is available.

WEBB INSTITUTE D-5
(Formerly Webb Institute of Naval Architecture)

Glen Cove, NY 11542	(516) 671-2213; FAX: (516) 674-9838
Full-time: 67 men, 12 women	Faculty: 9
Part-time: none	Ph.Ds: 44%
Graduate: none	Student/Faculty: 9 to 1
Year: semesters	Tuition: none
Application Deadline: February 15	Room & Board: $5500
Freshman Class: 87 applied, 32 accepted, 24 enrolled	
SAT I Verbal/Math: 620/710	MOST COMPETITIVE

Webb Institute, founded in 1889, is a private, primarily men's engineering school devoted to professional knowledge of ship construction, design, and motive power. In addition to regional accreditation, Webb has baccalaureate program accreditation with ABET. The library contains 49,839 volumes, 311 microform items, and 1167 audiovisual forms, and subscribes to 255 periodicals. Computerized library sources and services include interlibrary loans. Special learning facilities include a marine engineering laboratory and a ship model testing/towing tank. The 26-acre campus is in a suburban area 24 miles east of New York City. Including residence halls, there are 11 buildings on campus.

Student Life: 77% of undergraduates are from out-of-state, mostly the Middle Atlantic. Students come from 21 states. 75% are from public schools; 25% from private. 97% are white. The average age of freshmen is 18; all undergraduates, 20. 8% do not continue beyond their first year; 68% remain to graduate.

Housing: 90 students can be accommodated in college housing. College-sponsored living facilities include single-sex dormitories. On-campus housing is guaranteed for all 4 years. All students live on campus; of those, 80% remain on campus on weekends. All students may keep cars on campus.

Activities: There are no fraternities or sororities. There are some groups and organizations on campus, including marching band, orchestra, professional, social, student government, and yearbook. Popular campus events include Homecoming, Parents Day, and Webbstock.

Sports: There are 5 intercollegiate sports for men and 5 for women, and 2 intramural sports for men and 2 for women. Athletic and recreation facilities include a 60-seat gymnasium, tennis courts, an athletic field, a boat house, and a beach-front dock.

Disabled Students: 90% of the campus is accessible to disabled students. The following facilities are available: elevators and special parking.

Services: In addition to many counseling and information services, tutoring is available in some subjects.

Campus Safety and Security: Campus safety and security measures include informal discussions, pamphlets/posters/films, and student and professional security services.

Programs of Study: Webb confers the B.S. degree. Bachelor's degrees are awarded in ENGINEERING AND ENVIRONMENTAL DESIGN (naval architecture and marine engineering).

Required: The curriculum is prescribed, with all students taking the same courses in each of the 4 years. The Webb program has 4 practical 8-week paid work periods: freshman year, a helper mechanic in a shipyard; sophomore year, a cadet in the engine room of a ship; and junior and senior years, a draftsman or junior engineer in a design office. All students must complete a senior seminar, thesis, and technical reports, as well as make engineering inspection visits. A total of 147 credits with a minimum passing grade of 70% is required in order to graduate.

Special: All students are employed 2 months each year through co-op programs.

Faculty/Classroom: 86% of faculty are male; 14%, female. All teach undergraduates and 40% both teach and do research. The average class size in an introductory lecture is 25; in a laboratory, 9; and in a regular course offering, 25.

Admissions: 37% of the 1995–96 applicants were accepted. The SAT I scores for the 1995–96 freshman class were Verbal—42% between 500 and 599, 50% between 600 and 700, and 8% above 700; Math—42% between 600 and 700 and 58% above 700. 96% of the current freshmen were in the top fifth of their class; all were in the top two fifths. There was 1 National Merit finalist. 1 freshman graduated first in his class.

Requirements: The SAT I is required, with SAT I scores of 500 verbal and 660 mathematics. Webb requires applicants to be in the upper 20% of their class and have a 3.2 GPA. Applicants should be graduates of an accredited secondary school with 16 academic credits completed, including 4 each in English and mathematics, 2 each in history and science, 1 in foreign language, and 3 in electives. 3 SAT II: Subject tests in writing, mathematics level I or II, and physics or chemistry are required, as is an interview. Candidates must be U.S. citizens. Important factors in the admissions decision are advanced placement or honor courses, evidence of special talent, and personality/intangible qualities.

Procedure: Freshmen are admitted in the fall. Entrance exams should be taken by January of the senior year. There is an early decision plan. Early decision applications should be filed by October 15; regular applications, by February 15 for fall entry, along with an application fee of $15. Notification of early decision is sent December 10; regular decision, April 15. 1 early decision candidate was accepted for the 1995–96 class.

Transfer: 1 transfer student enrolled in 1995–96. Transfers must enter as freshmen. A 3.2 GPA is required. SAT I scores and an interview are required. All 147 credits must be completed at Webb.

Visiting: There are regularly scheduled orientations for prospective students, including an open house 1 weekend each October. There are guides for informal visits and visitors may sit in on classes and stay overnight at the school. To schedule a visit, contact the Director of Admissions.

Financial Aid: In 1995–96, 25% of all freshmen and 33% of continuing students received some form of financial aid. 12% of freshmen and 27% of continuing students received need-based aid. The average freshman award was $3400. Of that total, scholarships or need-based grants averaged $2600 ($4000 maximum); and loans averaged $3750 ($6000 maximum). The average financial indebtedness of the 1994–95 graduate was $3000. All students receive 4-year full tuition scholarships. Aid reported is to assist with room and board and is from external sources. Webb is a member of CSS. The FAF and the college's own financial statement are required. The application deadline for fall entry is July 1.

International Students: All applicants must be U.S. citizens.

Computers: The college provides computer facilities for student use. There are 28 microcomputers available on campus. All students may access the system 24 hours per day. There are no time limits and no fees.

Graduates: In 1994–95, 14 bachelor's degrees were awarded. Within an average freshman class, 68% graduate in 4 years. 4 companies recruited on campus in 1994–95. Of the 1994 graduating class, 17% were enrolled in graduate school within 6 months of graduation and 83% had found employment.

Admissions Contact: William G. Murray, Director of Admissions. A campus video is available.

WEBB INSTITUTE OF NAVAL ARCHITECTURE
(See Webb Institute)

WELLS COLLEGE
C-3
Aurora, NY 13026

(315) 364-3264
(800) 952-9355; FAX: (315) 364-3227

Full-time: 425 women	Faculty: 49; IIB, av$
Part-time: 16 women	Ph.D.s: 98%
Graduate: none	Student/Faculty: 9 to 1
Year: semesters	Tuition: $16,800
Application Deadline: March 1	Room & Board: $5800
Freshman Class: 305 applied, 272 accepted, 100 enrolled	
SAT I Verbal/Math: 540/540	ACT: 24 COMPETITIVE +

Wells College, founded in 1868, is a private liberal arts college for women offering programs in the humanities, social sciences, natural sciences, arts, and preprofessional areas. The library contains 230,000 volumes, 8000 microform items, and 920 audiovisual forms, and subscribes to 644 periodicals. Computerized library sources and services include interlibrary loans and database searching. Special learning facilities include a learning resource center and art gallery. The 360-acre campus is in a small town 25 miles north of Ithaca and 40 miles southeast of Syracuse on Cayuga Lake. Including residence halls, there are 22 buildings on campus.

Student Life: 60% of undergraduates are from New York. Students come from 38 states and 4 foreign countries. 85% are from public schools; 15% from private. 81% are white. The average age of freshmen is 18; all undergraduates, 20.3. 15% do not continue beyond their first year; 75% remain to graduate.

Housing: 500 students can be accommodated in college housing. College-sponsored living facilities include dormitories, off-campus apartments, and married-student housing. In addition, there is and nontraditional-age housing. On-campus housing is guaranteed for all 4 years. 93% of students live on campus; of those, 80% remain on campus on weekends. All students may keep cars on campus.

Activities: There are no fraternities. There are 30 groups on campus, including choir, chorale, dance, drama, ethnic, gay, international, jazz band, literary magazine, musical theater, newspaper, orchestra, photography, political, professional, religious, social, social service, student government, and yearbook. Popular campus events include the Odd-Even Basketball Game and Spring Weekend.

Sports: Athletic and recreation facilities include a competition-sized swimming pool, a gymnasium, a weight room, indoor tennis courts/practice space, a 9-hole golf course, 4 all-weather tennis courts, a boathouse and dock with canoes and sailboats, hiking trails, and a jogging path along the lake.

Disabled Students: 6% of the campus is accessible to disabled students. The following facilities are available: wheelchair ramps, elevators, special parking, specially equipped rest rooms, special class scheduling, and lowered drinking fountains.

Services: In addition to many counseling and information services, tutoring is available in every subject. There is a reader service for the blind. Assistance is provided on an individual, as-needed basis.

Campus Safety and Security: Campus safety and security measures include 24-hour foot and vehicle patrol, self-defense education, escort service, and shuttle buses. There are informal discussions, pamphlets/posters/films, emergency telephones, and lighted pathways/sidewalks.

Programs of Study: Wells confers the B.A. degree. Bachelor's degrees are awarded in BIOLOGICAL SCIENCE (biochemistry and biology/biological science), COMMUNICATIONS AND THE ARTS (dance, dramatic arts, English, fine arts, French, German, Italian, music, Russian, and Spanish), COMPUTER AND PHYSICAL SCIENCE (chemistry, computer science, and mathematics), EDUCATION (art, elementary, foreign languages, music, science, and secondary), ENGINEERING AND ENVIRONMENTAL DESIGN (environmental science), HEALTH PROFESSIONS (predentistry, premedicine, and preveterinary science), SOCIAL SCIENCE (American studies, economics, ethics, politics, and social policy, history, international studies, philosophy, political science/government, prelaw, psychology, public affairs, religion, sociology, and women's studies). Biology, chemistry, and premedicine are the strongest academically. Psychology, sociology, and English have the largest enrollments.

Required: To graduate, students must complete a total of 120 credit hours (36 courses) with a minimum GPA of 2.0. A range of 33 to 63 credit hours, depending on the major, and a minimum GPA of 2.0 in the major are required. All students must complete CORE I and II and courses in formal reasoning and a modern foreign language. In addition, all students must take 4 courses in physical education including wellness and swimming. A comprehensive examination and a thesis or project must be completed.

Special: Wells offers cross-registration with Cornell University and a Washington semester with American University. Internships are available with companies such as American Express, Dunn & Bradstreet, and Working Woman. Study abroad in 12 countries is permitted. A 3–2 engineering degree is available with Washington University in St. Louis and Columbia, Clarkson, Texas Argricultural and Mechanical and Cornell universities. Students may also earn 3–2 degrees in business and community health. Student-designed majors and pass-fail options are available. There is 1 national honor society on campus, Phi Beta Kappa.

Faculty/Classroom: 50% of faculty are male; 50%, female. All teach undergraduates. The average class size in an introductory lecture is 15; in a laboratory, 15; and in a regular course offering, 12.

Admissions: 89% of the 1995–96 applicants were accepted. The SAT I scores for the 1995–96 freshman class were as follows: Verbal—33% below 500, 38% between 500 and 599, 28% between 600 and 700, and 1% above 700; Math—33% below 500, 46% between 500 and 599, 20% between 600 and 700, and 1% above 700. 55% of the current freshmen were in the top fifth of their class; 79% were in the top two fifths. In a recent year, there were 7 National Merit semifinalists. 3 freshmen graduated first in their class.

Requirements: The SAT I or ACT is required. Applicants must be in the upper 50% of their class with a 2.0 GPA. Graduation from an accredited secondary school should include 16 academic credits or Carnegie units. High school courses must include 4 years each of English and history or social studies, 3 each of a foreign language and mathematics, and 2 of science. An essay is required and an interview is strongly recommended. AP and CLEP credits are accepted. Important factors in the admissions decision are advanced placement or honor courses, personality/intangible qualities, and evidence of special talent.

Procedure: Freshmen are admitted in the fall. Entrance exams should be taken prior to application. There are early decision, early admissions, and deferred admissions plans. Early decision applications should be filed by December 15; regular applications, by March 1 for fall entry, along with an application fee of $40. Notification of early decision is sent January 15; regular decision, April 1. 40 early decision candidates were accepted for the 1995–96 class.

Transfer: 27 transfer students enrolled in 1995–96. Applicants must be in good standing at the institution last attended. A minimum GPA of 2.5 is required. The school recommends composite scores of 1000 on the SAT I and 24 on the ACT. There is a 2-year residency requirement. 60 credits of 120 must be completed at Wells.

Visiting: There are regularly scheduled orientations for prospective students, including tours, interviews, and presentations, an overnight hostess program, and class attendance. There are guides for informal visits and visitors may sit in on classes and stay overnight at the school. To schedule a visit, contact the Admissions Office.

Financial Aid: In 1995–96, 95% of all freshmen and 93% of continuing students received some form of financial aid. 79% of freshmen and 82% of continuing students received need-based aid. The average freshman award was $8853. Of that total, scholarships or need-based grants averaged $8852 ($12,750 maximum); loans averaged $2000 ($2625 maximum); and work contracts averaged $1000 ($1500 maximum). 90% of undergraduate students work part-time. Average earnings from campus work for the school year are $1000. The average financial indebtedness of the 1994–95 graduate was $10,500. Wells is a member of CSS. The FAF or FFS is required. The application deadline for fall entry is February 15.

International Students: There are currently 8 international students enrolled. The school actively recruits these students. They must score 550 on the TOEFL.

Computers: The college provides computer facilities for student use. The mainframe is an IBM System/36. Apple and IBM microcomputers are available in academic buildings. The computer-to-student ratio is 9 to 1. All students may access the system. There are no time limits and no fees.

Graduates: In 1994–95, 93 bachelor's degrees were awarded. The most popular majors among graduates were English (15%), psychology (15%), and political science (9%). Within an average freshman class, 75% graduate in 4 years and 78% in 5 years.

Admissions Contact: Susan Sloan, Director of Admissions. E-mail: admissions@wells.edu. A campus video is available.

YESHIVA UNIVERSITY
New York, NY 10033–3201

D-5

(212) 960-5277
FAX: (212) 960-0086

Full-time: 1030 men, 920 women	**Faculty:** 120
Part-time: 20 men, 20 women	**Ph.D.s:** 79%
Graduate: 1370 men, 1620 women	**Student/Faculty:** 16 to 1
Year: semesters	**Tuition:** $13,000
Application Deadline: see profile	**Room & Board:** $6000
Freshman Class: n/av	
SAT I or ACT: required	**COMPETITIVE**

Yeshiva University, founded in 1886, is an independent liberal arts institution offering undergraduate programs through Yeshiva College, its undergraduate college for men; Stern College for Women; and Sy Syms School of Business. There are 3 undergraduate and 7 graduate schools. Figures given in the above capsule are approximate. In addition to regional accreditation, YU has baccalaureate program accreditation with CSWE. The 7 libraries contain 900,000 volumes, 759,000 microform items, and 980 audiovisual forms, and subscribe to 7790 periodicals. Computerized library sources and services include the card catalog, interlibrary loans, and database searching. Special learning facilities include an art gallery, radio station, and museum. The 26-acre campus is in an urban area in New York City.

Student Life: 48% of undergraduates are from New York. Students come from 31 states, 16 foreign countries, and Canada. 14% are from public schools; 86% from private. The average age of freshmen is 17; all undergraduates, 19. 8% do not continue beyond their first year; 90% remain to graduate.

Housing: 1600 students can be accommodated in college housing. College-sponsored living facilities include single-sex dormitories and off-campus apartments. On-campus housing is guaranteed for all 4 years. 85% of students live on campus. Alcohol is not permitted. All students may keep cars on campus.

Activities: There are no fraternities or sororities. There are 70 groups on campus, including art, choir, computers, drama, honors, international, jazz band, literary magazine, musical theater, newspaper, political, professional, religious, social service, student government, and yearbook. Popular campus events include holiday and dramatic presentations and Parents Day.

Sports: There are 8 intercollegiate sports for men and 2 for women, and 5 intramural sports for men and 4 for women. The athletic center at Yeshiva College houses a variety of facilities, including a 1000-seat gymnasium.

Disabled Students: 95% of the campus is accessible to disabled students. Wheelchair ramps and elevators are available.

Services: In addition to counseling and information services, there is remedial reading and writing. There is also a writing center, which helps students with composition and verbal skills.

Campus Safety and Security: Campus safety and security measures include 24-hour foot and vehicle patrol, escort service, shuttle buses, and informal discussions. There are pamphlets/posters/films, lighted pathways/sidewalks, ID cards, vulnerability surveys, fire drills, alarm systems, emergency telephone numbers, and transportation for routine and special events.

Programs of Study: YU confers B.A. and B.S. degrees. Associate degrees are also awarded. Bachelor's degrees are awarded in BIOLOGICAL SCIENCE (biology/biological science), BUSINESS (accounting, business administration and management, and marketing/retailing/merchandising), COMMUNICATIONS AND THE ARTS (classical languages, communications, English, French, Hebrew, music, and speech/debate/rhetoric), COMPUTER AND PHYSICAL SCIENCE (chemistry, computer science, and mathematics), ENGINEERING AND ENVIRONMENTAL DESIGN (preengineering), HEALTH PROFESSIONS (health science), SOCIAL SCIENCE (economics, history, philosophy, political science/government, psychology, religion, and sociology). The dual program of liberal arts and Jewish studies is the strongest academically. Accounting, psychology, and economics have the largest enrollments.

Required: To graduate, students must complete a total of 128 credit hours. Under the Dual Program, students pursue a liberal arts or business curriculum together with courses in Hebrew language, literature, and culture. Courses in Jewish learning are geared to the student's level of preparation.

Special: YU offers a 3–2 degree in occupational therapy with Columbia and New York Universities, a 3–4 degree in podiatry with the New York College of Podiatric Medicine, and a 3–2 or 4–2 degree in engineering with Columbia University. Stern College students may take courses in advertising, photography, and design at the Fashion Institute of Technology. Study-abroad programs may be arranged in Israel. The school offers independent study options and an optional pass/no credit system. There are 9 national honor societies on campus. 20 departments have honors programs.

Faculty/Classroom: 73% of faculty are male; 27%, female. 58% teach undergraduates, 60% do research, and 28% do both. No introductory courses are taught by graduate students. The average class size in an introductory lecture is 38; in a laboratory, 15; and in a regular course offering, 18.

Admissions: In a recent year, 84% of the applicants were accepted. The SAT I scores for a recent freshman class were as follows: Verbal—35% below 500, 39% between 500 and 599, 19% between 600 and 700, and 7% above 700; Math—18% below 500, 37% between 500 and 599, 31% between 600 and 700, and 14% above 700. There were 3 National Merit finalists.

Requirements: The SAT I or ACT is required. Graduation from an accredited secondary school with a 3.3 GPA and with 16 academic credits is required for admission. The GED is accepted under limited and specific circumstances. The SAT II: Hebrew test is recommended for placement purposes. An interview and an essay are required. AP and CLEP credits are accepted. Important factors in the admissions decision are extracurricular activities record, personality/intangible qualities, and evidence of special talent.

Procedure: Freshmen are admitted to all sessions. There are early admissions and deferred admissions plans. Check with the school for application deadlines and fee. Notification is sent on a rolling basis. A waiting list is an active part of the admissions procedure, with about 25% of all applicants on the list.

Transfer: 95 credits of 128 must be completed at YU.

Visiting: There are regularly scheduled orientations for prospective students, including open houses for high school students. There are guides for informal visits and visitors may sit in on classes and stay overnight at the school. To schedule a visit, contact the Office of Admissions.

Financial Aid: YU is a member of CSS. The FAF and the college's own financial statement are required. Check with the school for current deadlines.

International Students: In a recent year, there were 110 international students enrolled. The school actively recruits these students. They must score 500 on the TOEFL and also take SAT I or the ACT.

Computers: The college provides computer facilities for student use. The mainframe is an IBM RS6000. There are more than 200 networked and stand-alone IBM-compatible microcomputers and workstations at 4 academic centers; there are additional facilities at university libraries. All students may access the system 24 hours per day via modem or when buildings are open. There are no time limits. Fees are charged per course and for specific uses per semester; otherwise there is no charge for general, non-course-related use.

Admissions Contact: Michael Kranzler, Associate Director of Admissions.

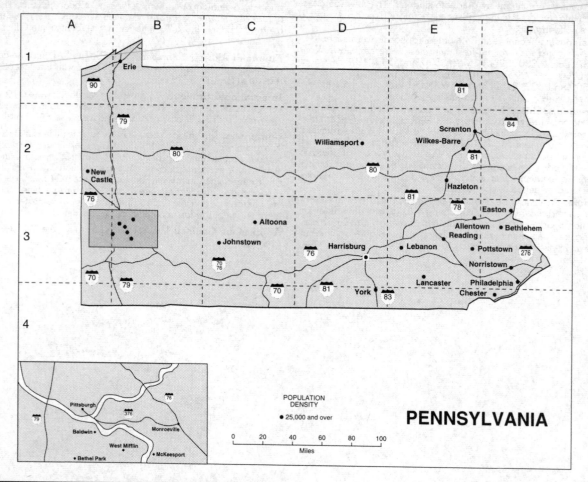

PENNSYLVANIA

POPULATION DENSITY
● 25,000 and over

0 20 40 60 80 100
Miles

ACADEMY OF THE NEW CHURCH COLLEGE F-3

Bryn Athyn, PA 19009 (215) 938-2503; FAX: (215) 938-2658

Full-time: 58 men, 52 women	Faculty: 27; IIB, -$
Part-time: 5 men, 4 women	Ph.D.s: 50%
Graduate: none	Student/Faculty: 4 to 1
Year: trimesters	Tuition: $4440
Application Deadline: March 1	Room & Board: $3729

Freshman Class: 53 applied, 53 accepted, 47 enrolled
SAT I Verbal/Math: 425/515 **NONCOMPETITIVE**

Academy of the New Church, founded in 1877, is an independent, coeducational liberal arts institution affiliated with the General Church of the New Jerusalem. There is 1 graduate school. The 2 libraries contain 95,000 volumes, 1400 microform items, and 493 audiovisual forms, and subscribe to 270 periodicals. Special learning facilities include the Glencairn Museum. The 170-acre campus is in a suburban area 15 miles north of Philadelphia. Including residence halls, there are 12 buildings on campus.

Student Life: 51% of undergraduates are from out-of-state, mostly the Midwest. Students come from 8 states, 12 foreign countries, and Canada. 25% are from public schools; 75% from private. 28% are foreign nationals. Most students have been baptized into the Church of the New Jerusalem. The average age of freshmen is 18; all undergraduates, 21. 5% do not continue beyond their first year.

Housing: 103 students can be accommodated in college housing. College-sponsored living facilities include single-sex dormitories and off-campus apartments. On-campus housing is guaranteed for all 4 years. Priority is given to out-of-town students. 70% of students live on campus; of those, all remain on campus on weekends. Alcohol is not permitted. All students may keep cars on campus.

Activities: There are no fraternities or sororities. There are 9 groups on campus, including chorale, dance, drama, political, religious, social, social service, student government, and yearbook. Popular campus events include Charter Day (Homecoming) and the annual college trip.

Sports: There are 3 intercollegiate sports for men and 4 for women, and 6 intramural sports for men and 6 for women. Athletic and recreation facilities include a field house, a 500-seat gymnasium, an outdoor skating rink, soccer and field hockey fields, and tennis courts.

Disabled Students: 75% of the campus is accessible to disabled students. The following facilities are available: wheelchair ramps and special parking.

Services: In addition to many counseling and information services, tutoring is available in some subjects, including in English and mathematics.

Campus Safety and Security: Campus safety and security measures include emergency telephones, lighted pathways/sidewalks, and an 18-hour foot and vehicle patrol.

Programs of Study: ANCC confers B.A. and B.S. degrees. Associate and master's degrees are also awarded. Bachelor's degrees are awarded in EDUCATION (education), SOCIAL SCIENCE (interdisciplinary studies and religion).

Required: To graduate, students must complete a total of 136 credit hours with a minimum GPA of 1.9. All students must take required courses in religion, English composition, introduction to literature, and philosophy.

Special: Cross-registration is available with Holy Family College. Also available are co-op interdisciplinary programs, a general studies degree, student-designed majors, nondegree study, and study abroad in Scotland and England in association with Beaver College.

Faculty/Classroom: 80% of faculty are male; 20%, female. All teach undergraduates. The average class size in an introductory lecture is 20 and in a laboratory, 15.

Admissions: All of the 1995-96 applicants were accepted. The SAT I scores for the 1995-96 freshman class were as follows: Verbal—69% below 500, 23% between 500 and 599, and 8% between 600 and 700; Math—38% below 500, 34% between 500 and 599, 23% between 600 and 700, and 5% above 700. There was 1 National Merit finalist in a recent year. 2 freshmen graduated first in a recent class.

Requirements: The SAT I is required. Applicants must be graduates of an accredited secondary school with a 2.2 GPA or achieve satisfactory scores on the GED. An interview is recommended. AP and

CLEP credits are accepted. Important factors in the admissions decision are personality/intangible qualities, advanced placement or honor courses, and evidence of special talent.

Procedure: Freshmen are admitted to all sessions. Applications should be filed by March 1 for fall entry, October 15 for winter entry, and February 1 for spring entry, along with an application fee of $30. The college accepts all applicants. Notification is sent on a rolling basis.

Transfer: 4 transfer students enrolled in a recent year. Each transfer student is reviewed on a case-by-case basis. An interview is recommended. 30 credits of 136 must be completed at ANCC.

Visiting: There are regularly scheduled orientations for prospective students. There are guides for informal visits and visitors may sit in on classes and stay overnight at the school. To schedule a visit, contact Brian D. Henderson at (215) 938–2511.

Financial Aid: In a recent year, 43% of all freshmen and 44% of continuing students received some form of financial aid including need-based aid. The average freshman award was $3611. Of that total, scholarships or need-based grants averaged $1600 ($5200 maximum); loans averaged $2000 ($5200 maximum); and work contracts averaged $600 ($1200 maximum). 30% of undergraduate students work part-time. Average earnings from campus work for the school year are $560. The average financial indebtedness of a recent graduate was $2370. The college's own financial statement is required. The application deadline for fall entry is April 1.

International Students: There were 40 international students enrolled in a recent year. They must take the TOEFL.

Computers: The college provides computer facilities for student use. The school provides 25 microcomputers for academic use in the computer laboratory. All students may access the system 8 A.M. to 1 A.M. There are no time limits and no fees.

Admissions Contact: Dan A. Synnestredt, Director of Admissions.

ALBRIGHT COLLEGE
Reading, PA 19612-5234

E-3
(610) 921-7512
(800) 252-1856; FAX: (610) 921-7530

Full-time: 490 men, 519 women	Faculty: 61; IIB, av$
Part-time: 143 men, 153 women	Ph.Ds: 92%
Graduate: none	Student/Faculty: 17 to 1
Year: 4-1-4, summer session	Tuition: $16,575
Application Deadline: February 15	Room & Board: $4820
Freshman Class: 1140 applied, 1010 accepted, 323 enrolled	
SAT I: required	COMPETITIVE

Albright College, founded in 1856, is a private, coeducational liberal arts institution affiliated with the United Methodist Church. The 2 libraries contain 175,000 volumes, 9000 microform items, and 6800 audiovisual forms, and subscribe to 750 periodicals. Computerized library sources and services include the card catalog, interlibrary loans, and database searching. Special learning facilities include an art gallery, radio station, a multicultural center, and centers for women and child development. The 100-acre campus is in a suburban area 55 miles west of Philadelphia. Including residence halls, there are 36 buildings on campus.

Student Life: 60% of undergraduates are from Pennsylvania. Students come from 23 states and 19 foreign countries. 77% are from public schools; 23% from private. 85% are white. 34% are Catholic; 32% Protestant; 27% claim no religious affiliation. The average age of freshmen is 18; all undergraduates, 20. 17% do not continue beyond their first year; 72% remain to graduate.

Housing: 1085 students can be accommodated in college housing. College-sponsored living facilities include single-sex and coed dormitories and on-campus apartments. In addition there are honors houses and special interest houses. On-campus housing is guaranteed for all 4 years. 80% of students live on campus; of those, 95% remain on campus on weekends. Upperclassmen may keep cars on campus.

Activities: 28% of men belong to 4 national fraternities; 28% of women belong to 3 national sororities. There are 70 groups on campus, including band, cheerleading, chess, choir, chorus, computers, drama, ethnic, film, gay, honors, international, jazz band, literary magazine, musical theater, newspaper, photography, political, professional, radio and TV, religious, social, social service, student government, and yearbook. Popular campus events include MDA Dance Marathon, Greek Weekend, Homecoming, Spring Fever Weekend, and Alumni Weekend.

Sports: There are 11 intercollegiate sports for men and 11 for women, and 3 intramural sports for men and 4 for women. Athletic and recreation facilities include a 6000-seat stadium, baseball and soccer fields, indoor and outdoor tracks, a bowling alley, a swimming pool, and racquetball courts.

Disabled Students: 75% of the campus is accessible to disabled students. The following facilities are available: wheelchair ramps, elevators, special parking, specially equipped rest rooms, and special class scheduling.

Services: In addition to many counseling and information services, tutoring is available in every subject. There is a reader service for the blind.

Campus Safety and Security: Campus safety and security measures include 24-hour foot and vehicle patrol, escort service, shuttle buses, and informal discussions. In addition, there are pamphlets/posters/films and lighted pathways/sidewalks.

Programs of Study: Albright confers B.A. and B.S. degrees. Bachelor's degrees are awarded in BIOLOGICAL SCIENCE (biochemistry and biology/biological science), BUSINESS (accounting, apparel and accessories marketing, and business administration and management), COMMUNICATIONS AND THE ARTS (English, French, and Spanish), COMPUTER AND PHYSICAL SCIENCE (chemistry, computer science, and mathematics), EDUCATION (elementary and secondary), ENGINEERING AND ENVIRONMENTAL DESIGN (environmental science), HEALTH PROFESSIONS (medical laboratory technology), SOCIAL SCIENCE (American studies, child care/child and family studies, criminal justice, economics, history, philosophy, political science/government, psychobiology, psychology, religion, and textiles and clothing). Biology, psychology, and business have the largest enrollments.

Required: To graduate, students must complete 32 courses, including 13 to 14 in the major, with a minimum GPA of 2.0. All students take 1 interdisciplinary course, and they must fulfill the cultural experience requirement. General studies requirements include 11 to 15 courses in English, literature, a foreign language, philosophy/religion, natural science, history, social science, and the arts.

Special: Co-op programs are available in forestry, environmental studies, and natural resources with Duke University and the University of Michigan. The school offers internships, a Washington semester, work-study programs, dual majors, student-designed majors, nondegree study, and pass/fail options. Study abroad may be arranged in any country. There is a freshman honors program on campus, as well as 11 national honor societies. All departments have honors programs.

Faculty/Classroom: 60% of faculty are male; 40%, female. All teach undergraduates. The average class size in an introductory lecture is 25; in a laboratory, 15; and in a regular course offering, 18.

Admissions: 89% of the 1995–96 applicants were accepted. 51% of the current freshmen were in the top fifth of their class; 80% were in the top two fifths. 6 freshmen graduated first in their class.

Requirements: The SAT I is required. SAT II: Subject tests in writing, mathematics, and a foreign language are recommended for placement purposes. Graduation from an accredited secondary school or satisfactory scores on the GED are required for admission. Students must have a total of 15 Carnegie units, including 4 years of English, 2 years each of a foreign language, mathematics, science, and social studies, and 3 electives in college preparatory subjects. An essay is required, and an interview highly recommended. The school accepts applications on computer disk. AP and CLEP credits are accepted. Important factors in the admissions decision are advanced placement or honor courses, evidence of special talent, and leadership record.

Procedure: Freshmen are admitted fall and spring. Entrance exams should be taken during the spring of the junior year or the fall of the senior year. There are early admissions and deferred admissions plans. Applications should be filed by February 15 for fall entry and December 15 for spring entry, along with an application fee of $25. Notification is sent on a rolling basis.

Transfer: 33 transfer students enrolled in 1995–96. Transfer students must have a minimum GPA of 2.5 and be in good standing. 16 courses of 32 must be completed at Albright.

Visiting: There are regularly scheduled orientations for prospective students, including an interview with a counselor and a tour of the campus with a currently enrolled student. There are guides for informal visits and visitors may sit in on classes and stay overnight at the school. To schedule a visit, contact the Admissions Office.

Financial Aid: In 1995–96, 95% of all freshmen and 89% of continuing students received some form of financial aid. 84% of freshmen and 71% of continuing students received need-based aid. The average freshman award was $11,800. Of that total, scholarships or need-based grants averaged $8300 ($10,000 maximum); loans averaged $3515 ($5625 maximum); and work contracts averaged $911 ($713 maximum). 67% of undergraduate students work part-time. Average earnings from campus work for the school year are $985. The average financial indebtedness of the 1994–95 graduate was $11,000. Albright is a member of CSS. The FAFSA and the CSS Profile Application are required. The application deadline for fall entry is March 1.

International Students: 48 international students were enrolled in a recent year. The school actively recruits these students. They must take the TOEFL and achieve a minimum score of 550.

Computers: The college provides computer facilities for student use. The mainframe is a DEC MicroVAX II. The Center for Computing and Mathematics houses IBM-compatible and Macintosh microcomputers in 5 laboratories and 75 workstations, as well as 2 Sun workstations. All terminals are networked. All students may access the system 24 hours per day. There are no time limits and no fees.

Graduates: In 1994–95, 217 bachelor's degrees were awarded. The most popular majors among graduates were biology/biochemistry (10%), business administration (10%), and psychology/psychobiology (9%). Within an average freshman class, 1% graduate in 3 years, 64% in 4 years, 71% in 5 years, and 74% in 6 years. 60 companies recruited on campus in 1994–95.

Admissions Contact: Dr. William J. Stahler, Vice President for Enrollment. E-mail: albright@joe.alb.edu.

ALLEGHENY COLLEGE
B-1
Meadville, PA 16335

(814) 332-4351
(800) 521-5293; FAX: (814) 337-0431

Full-time: 868 men, 930 women	Faculty: 153; IIB, av$
Part-time: 9 men, 31 women	Ph.D.s: 94%
Graduate: none	Student/Faculty: 12 to 1
Year: semesters	Tuition: $18,020
Application Deadline: February 15	Room & Board: $4550
Freshman Class: 2811 applied, 2083 accepted, 565 enrolled	
SAT I Verbal/Math: 520/590	ACT: 25 HIGHLY COMPETITIVE

Allegheny College, founded in 1815, is an independent, coeducational liberal arts institution affiliated with the United Methodist Church. The library contains 621,233 volumes, 215,521 microform items, and 3650 audiovisual forms, and subscribes to 1194 periodicals. Computerized library sources and services include the card catalog, interlibrary loans, and database searching. Special learning facilities include a learning resource center, art gallery, planetarium, radio station, TV studio, observatory, and a 283-acre experimental forest. The 254-acre campus is in a small town 90 miles north of Pittsburgh. Including residence halls, there are 38 buildings on campus.

Student Life: 58% of undergraduates are from Pennsylvania. Students come from 39 states, 16 foreign countries, and Canada. 80% are from public schools; 20% from private. 92% are white. 41% are Catholic; 37% Protestant; 10% claim no religious affiliation. The average age of freshmen is 18.6; all undergraduates, 20.2. 13% do not continue beyond their first year; 74% remain to graduate.

Housing: 1399 students can be accommodated in college housing. College-sponsored living facilities include single-sex and coed dormitories, on-campus apartments, off-campus apartments, and fraternity houses. In addition there are language houses, special interest houses, and a black cultural residence. On-campus housing is guaranteed for all 4 years. 76% of students live on campus; of those, 90% remain on campus on weekends. All students may keep cars on campus.

Activities: 30% of men belong to 5 national fraternities; 35% of women belong to 5 national sororities. There are 112 groups on campus, including art, band, cheerleading, chess, choir, chorale, chorus, computers, dance, drama, environmental, ethnic, film, gay, honors, international, jazz band, literary magazine, musical theater, newspaper, opera, orchestra, pep band, photography, political, professional, radio and TV, religious, social, social service, student government, symphony, women's issues, and yearbook. Popular campus events include Winter Carnival, Black History Month, and Latin Culture Week.

Sports: There are 10 intercollegiate sports for men and 10 for women, and 21 intramural sports for men and 20 for women. Athletic and recreation facilities include a 1700-seat gymnasium and field house, a natatorium, and a field complex with a stadium and 8 fields. In addition, there are 102 wooded acres for cross-country skiing.

Disabled Students: 75% of the campus is accessible to disabled students. The following facilities are available: wheelchair ramps, elevators, special parking, specially equipped rest rooms, special class scheduling, lowered drinking fountains, and lowered telephones.

Services: In addition to many counseling and information services, tutoring is available in most subjects. There is a reader service for the blind, and remedial math, reading, and writing.

Campus Safety and Security: Campus safety and security measures include 24-hour foot and vehicle patrol, self-defense education, escort service, and informal discussions. In addition, there are pamphlets/posters/films, emergency telephones, and lighted pathways/sidewalks.

Programs of Study: Allegheny confers B.A. and B.S. degrees. Bachelor's degrees are awarded in BIOLOGICAL SCIENCE (biology/biological science), COMMUNICATIONS AND THE ARTS (art history and appreciation, classical languages, classics, communications, dramatic arts, English, French, German, Greek (classical), Latin, music, Russian, Spanish, speech/debate/rhetoric, and studio art), COMPUTER AND PHYSICAL SCIENCE (chemistry, computer science, geology, mathematics, and physics), ENGINEERING AND ENVIRONMENTAL DESIGN (environmental science), HEALTH PROFESSIONS (predentistry, premedicine, and preveterinary science), SOCIAL SCIENCE (economics, history, international studies, philosophy, political science/government, prelaw, psychology, religion, sociology, and women's studies). Physical and biological sciences, En-

glish, and premedicine are the strongest academically. Economics, psychology, and political science have the largest enrollments.

Required: To graduate, students must complete a total of 128 credit hours with a minimum GPA of 2.0. Between 32 and 48 hours are required in the major, including the junior seminar and senior project. All students must fulfill liberal studies requirements of 2 courses each in arts and humanities, natural sciences, and social sciences. The liberal studies program extends through all 4 years and promotes breadth at both introductory and advanced levels of study. Additional required courses include the freshman seminar, a sophomore writing course, and a minor in an area outside the major. The school also requires 4 noncredit units in physical education.

Special: Allegheny offers cross-registration with Chatham College, a Washington semester, internships, dual majors, student-designed majors, study abroad in 30 countries, nondegree study, and pass/fail options. A 3–2 engineering degree is available with Case Western Reserve, Columbia, Duke, Pittsburgh, and Washington universities. There also are 3–2 forestry and environmental management programs available with Duke. Other cooperative arrangements are available in allied health fields, nursing, and physical therapy. There are 8 national honor societies on campus, including Phi Beta Kappa. All departments have honors programs.

Faculty/Classroom: 68% of faculty are male; 32%, female. All both teach and do research. The average class size in an introductory lecture is 21; in a laboratory, 18; and in a regular course offering, 16.

Admissions: 74% of the 1995–96 applicants were accepted. The SAT I scores for the 1995–96 freshman class were as follows: Verbal—33% below 500, 49% between 500 and 599, 16% between 600 and 700, and 2% above 700; Math—13% below 500, 40% between 500 and 599, 37% between 600 and 700, and 10% above 700. The ACT scores were 8% below 21, 29% between 21 and 23, 29% between 24 and 26, 18% between 27 and 28, and 17% above 28. 74% of the current freshmen were in the top fifth of their class; 94% were in the top two fifths. There were 6 National Merit semifinalists. 20 freshmen graduated first in their class.

Requirements: The SAT I or ACT is required. SAT II: Subject tests are recommended in Writing and in the student's expected major. Graduation from an accredited secondary school is required for admission. Students must have 16 Carnegie units, including 4 years of English, 3 years each of mathematics, science, and social studies, and 2 years of a foreign language. An essay is required, and an interview is recommended. Applications are accepted on computer disk and on-line, but hard copy is preferred. AP and CLEP credits are accepted. Important factors in the admissions decision are advanced placement or honor courses, personality/intangible qualities, and leadership record.

Procedure: Freshmen are admitted fall and winter. Entrance exams should be taken by December of the senior year. There are early decision, early admissions, and deferred admissions plans. Early decision applications should be filed by November 30; regular applications, by February 15 for fall entry and November 1 for winter entry, along with an application fee of $30. Notification of early decision is sent December 15; regular decision, April 1. 148 early decision candidates were accepted for the 1995–96 class. A waiting list is an active part of the admissions procedure, with about 4% of all applicants on the list.

Transfer: 19 transfer students enrolled in 1995–96. Transfer applicants must submit a transcript of all college courses and a letter describing reasons for transfer, and have a minimum GPA of 2.0, with 3.0 recommended. 64 credits of 128 must be completed at Allegheny.

Visiting: There are regularly scheduled orientations for prospective students, consisting of tours, panels, and presentations on academic programs, student life, admissions, and financial aid. There are guides for informal visits and visitors may sit in on classes and stay overnight at the school. To schedule a visit, contact the Office of Admissions.

Financial Aid: In 1995–96, 94% of all students received some form of financial aid. 85% of freshmen and 80% of continuing students received need-based aid. The average freshman award was $14,497. Of that total, scholarships or need-based grants averaged $10,564 ($23,400 maximum); loans averaged $3612 ($5625 maximum); and work contracts averaged $1324 ($1500 maximum). 55% of undergraduate students work part-time. Average earnings from campus work for the school year are $1345. The average financial indebtedness of the 1994–95 graduate was $13,071. The FAFSA and IRS 1040 for verification are required. The application deadline for fall entry is February 15.

International Students: There are currently 28 international students enrolled. The school actively recruits these students. They must take the TOEFL and achieve a minimum score of 550. The student must also take the SAT I or the ACT.

Computers: The college provides computer facilities for student use. More than 300 UNIX workstations are networked and available to students in the library and all academic buildings. All students may access the system 24 hours per day. There are no time limits and no fees.

Graduates: In 1994–95, 409 bachelor's degrees were awarded. The most popular majors among graduates were psychology (16%), English (14%), and political science (12%). Within an average freshman class, 67% graduate in 4 years, 73% in 5 years, and 74% in 6 years. 15 companies recruited on campus in 1994–95. Of the 1994 graduating class, 32% were enrolled in graduate school within 6 months of graduation and 52% had found employment.

Admissions Contact: Gayle W. Pollock, Director of Admissions. E-mail: admiss@admin.alleg.edu World Wide Web: http://www.alleg.edu. A campus video is available.

ALLENTOWN COLLEGE OF SAINT FRANCIS DE SALES   E-3

Center Valley, PA 18034–9568	(610) 282–1100; (800) 228–5114
Full-time: 477 men, 567 women	Faculty: 68; IIB, -$
Part-time: 308 men, 465 women	Ph.D.s: 79%
Graduate: 173 men, 230 women	Student/Faculty: 15 to 1
Year: semesters, summer session	Tuition: $10,440
Application Deadline: August 1	Room & Board: $5050
Freshman Class: 1100 applied, 886 accepted, 270 enrolled	
SAT I Verbal/Math: 446/477	**COMPETITIVE**

Allentown College of Saint Francis de Sales, founded in 1964, is a private, coeducational, liberal arts institution affiliated with the Roman Catholic Church. In addition to regional accreditation, Allentown has baccalaureate program accreditation with NLN. The library contains 150,000 volumes, 185,000 microform items, and 4000 audiovisual forms, and subscribes to 1400 periodicals. Computerized library sources and services include the card catalog, interlibrary loans, and database searching. Special learning facilities include a learning resource center and radio station. The 300-acre campus is in a rural area 50 miles north of Philadelphia. Including residence halls, there are 18 buildings on campus.

Student Life: 79% of undergraduates are from Pennsylvania. Students come from 14 states and 9 foreign countries. 39% are from public schools; 61% from private. 95% are white. 85% are Catholic; 14% Protestant. The average age of freshmen is 19; all undergraduates, 23. 13% do not continue beyond their first year; 62% remain to graduate.

Housing: 775 students can be accommodated in college housing. College-sponsored living facilities include single-sex dormitories and on-campus apartments. In addition there are special interest houses. On-campus housing is guaranteed for all 4 years. 80% of students live on campus; of those, 68% remain on campus on weekends. All students may keep cars on campus.

Activities: 8% of women belong to 1 local sorority. There are no fraternities. There are 38 groups on campus, including cheerleading, chorale, dance, drama, honors, international, literary magazine, musical theater, newspaper, orchestra, political, professional, radio and TV, religious, social, social service, student government, and yearbook. Popular campus events include lecture series, plays, Founders Day, and a dance recital.

Sports: There are 8 intercollegiate sports for men and 7 for women, and 9 intramural sports for men and 8 for women. Athletic and recreation facilities include a fitness center and facilities for soccer, baseball, softball, tennis, basketball, and volleyball.

Disabled Students: 80% of the campus is accessible to disabled students. The following facilities are available: wheelchair ramps, elevators, special parking, and specially equipped rest rooms.

Services: In addition to many counseling and information services, tutoring is available in every subject.

Campus Safety and Security: Campus safety and security measures include 24-hour foot and vehicle patrol, escort service, and lighted pathways/sidewalks.

Programs of Study: Allentown College confers B.A., B.S., and B.S.N. degrees. Master's degrees are also awarded. Bachelor's degrees are awarded in BIOLOGICAL SCIENCE (biology/biological science), BUSINESS (accounting, banking and finance, business administration and management, marketing/retailing/merchandising, and sports management), COMMUNICATIONS AND THE ARTS (dance, dramatic arts, English, French, Spanish, and technical and business writing), COMPUTER AND PHYSICAL SCIENCE (chemistry, computer science, and mathematics), ENGINEERING AND ENVIRONMENTAL DESIGN (environmental science), HEALTH PROFESSIONS (nursing), SOCIAL SCIENCE (criminal justice, human ecology, liberal arts/general studies, political science/government, psychology, and theological studies). Business, theater, and dance are the strongest academically. Business, theater, and criminal justice have the largest enrollments.

Required: For graduation, students must complete a minimum of 120 credit hours, including a maximum of 48 in the major, with a minimum GPA of 2.0. Liberal arts distribution requirements consist of 12

to 16 courses including cultural literacy, modes of thinking, and Christian values and theology, as well as 3 units in physical education. Internships are required for degrees in business communications and sports administration.

Special: Students may cross-register with schools in the Lehigh Valley Association of Independent Colleges. Internships are strongly encouraged in all majors. Study abroad in many countries and a Washington semester are available. Dual majors, pass/fail options, and credit for life, military, and work experience are offered. There is a freshman honors program on campus, as well as 9 national honor societies.

Faculty/Classroom: 64% of faculty are male; 36%, female. 98% teach undergraduates. No introductory courses are taught by graduate students. The average class size in an introductory lecture is 21; in a laboratory, 16; and in a regular course offering, 18.

Admissions: 81% of the 1995–96 applicants were accepted. The SAT I scores for the 1995–96 freshman class were as follows: Verbal—74% below 500, 18% between 500 and 599, and 8% between 600 and 700; Math—59% below 500, 31% between 500 and 599, 8% between 600 and 700, and 2% above 700. 30% of the current freshmen were in the top fifth of their class; 55% were in the top two fifths. 1 freshman graduated first in the class.

Requirements: The SAT I or ACT is required. Allentown College requires applicants to be in the upper 50% of their class. A minimum GPA of 2.5 is required. Applicants must be graduates of an accredited secondary school. The GED is accepted. Applicants should have completed 17 college preparatory courses, including 4 years each of English, history, and mathematics, 3 years of science, and 2 years of foreign language. The school will accept an essay but strongly recommends an interview. For theater students, a performance appraisal is required. For dance students, an audition is required. AP credits are accepted. Important factors in the admissions decision are advanced placement or honor courses, leadership record, and evidence of special talent.

Procedure: Freshmen are admitted fall and spring. Entrance exams should be taken during the junior or senior year. There are early admissions and deferred admissions plans. Applications should be filed by August 1 for fall entry and December 1 for spring entry, along with an application fee of $25. Notification is sent on a rolling basis. A waiting list is an active part of the admissions procedure, with about 15% of all applicants on the list.

Transfer: 62 transfer students enrolled in 1995–96. Applicants for transfer must have completed a minimum of 12 college credit hours with a GPA of 2.5. An interview is recommended. 60 credits of 120 must be completed at Allentown College.

Visiting: There are regularly scheduled orientations for prospective students that include meetings with faculty advisers, social activities, and completion of a writing sample. There are guides for informal visits and visitors may sit in on classes and stay overnight at the school. To schedule a visit, contact the Admissions Office at (610) 282–1100, ext. 1277 or (800) 228–5114.

Financial Aid: In 1995–96, 90% of all students received some form of financial aid. 70% of all students received need-based aid. The average freshman award was $5400. Of that total, scholarships or need-based grants averaged $5400 ($10,340 maximum); loans averaged $1400 ($2625 maximum); and work contracts averaged $750 ($1200 maximum). 55% of undergraduate students work part-time. Average earnings from campus work for the school year are $750. The average financial indebtedness of the 1994–95 graduate was $12,000. Allentown College is a member of CSS. The FAFSA and the college's own financial statement are required. The application deadline for fall entry is March 15.

International Students: There were 10 international students enrolled in a recent year. They must score 500 on the TOEFL and also take SAT I or the ACT.

Computers: The college provides computer facilities for student use. The mainframe is a DEC VAX 11. There are also 60 IBM and Apple Macintosh microcomputers available for students in the academic building and the library. All students may access the system from 8 A.M. to 11 P.M. Use of the system is limited to 1 hour when others are waiting. The fees are $25.

Graduates: In 1994–95, 345 bachelor's degrees were awarded. The most popular majors among graduates were nursing (12%), theater (11%), and accounting (11%). Within an average freshman class, 60% graduate in 4 years, 7% in 5 years, and 1% in 6 years. 20 companies recruited on campus in 1994–95. Of the 1994 graduating class, 9% were enrolled in graduate school within 6 months of graduation and 95% had found employment.

Admissions Contact: James R. McCarthy, Director of Admissions. E-mail: kelly@accnov.allencol.edu.

ALVERNIA COLLEGE
E-3

Reading, PA 19607   (610) 796-8220; FAX: (610) 796-8336

Full-time: 305 men, 477 women	Faculty: 62; IIB, --$
Part-time: n/av	Ph.D.s: 35%
Graduate: none	Student/Faculty: 13 to 1
Year: semesters, summer session	Tuition: $9850
Application Deadline: open	Room & Board: $4400
Freshman Class: 502 applied, 424 accepted, 175 enrolled	
SAT I Verbal/Math: 390/400	**LESS COMPETITIVE**

Alvernia College, established in 1958, is a Roman Catholic liberal arts institution. In addition to regional accreditation, Alvernia has baccalaureate program accreditation with AACSB and NLN. The library contains 66,000 volumes and 15,400 microform items, and subscribes to 1500 periodicals. Special learning facilities include a radio station. The 85-acre campus is in a suburban area 3 miles outside of Reading. Including residence halls, there are 8 buildings on campus.

Student Life: 90% of undergraduates are from Pennsylvania. 75% are from public schools. Most are Catholic. 10% do not continue beyond their first year; 87% remain to graduate.

Housing: College-sponsored living facilities include coed dormitories and on-campus apartments. On-campus housing is guaranteed for the freshman year only and is available on a lottery system for upperclassmen. All students may keep cars on campus.

Activities: There are no fraternities or sororities. There are 15 groups on campus, including chorale, drama, honors, international, literary magazine, musical theater, newspaper, professional, religious, and student government. Popular campus events include Charter Week, Harvest Weekend, and Parents Weekend.

Sports: There are 3 intercollegiate sports for men and 5 for women, and 6 intramural sports for men and 7 for women. Athletic and recreation facilities include a gymnasium, a physical fitness and recreation center, playing fields, and outdoor tennis, basketball, and volleyball courts.

Disabled Students: The following facilities are available: elevators, special parking, and specially equipped rest rooms.

Services: In addition to many counseling and information services, tutoring is available in every subject. Facilities include a writing center and a mathematics tutorial laboratory.

Campus Safety and Security: Campus safety and security measures include Photo ID cards that must be worn by students.

Programs of Study: Alvernia confers B.A. and B.S. degrees. Associate degrees are also awarded. Bachelor's degrees are awarded in BIOLOGICAL SCIENCE (biochemistry and biology/biological science), BUSINESS (accounting, banking and finance, and business administration and management), COMMUNICATIONS AND THE ARTS (communications, English, and Spanish), COMPUTER AND PHYSICAL SCIENCE (chemistry, information sciences and systems, mathematics, and science), EDUCATION (elementary and secondary), HEALTH PROFESSIONS (medical laboratory technology, nursing, predentistry, premedicine, and preveterinary science), SOCIAL SCIENCE (addiction studies, criminal justice, history, liberal arts/general studies, philosophy, political science/government, prelaw, psychology, social studies, social work, and theological studies). Biology, chemistry, and computer science are the strongest academically. Accounting, banking and finance, and addiction studies have the largest enrollments.

Required: To graduate, all students must complete at least 123 credit hours with a minimum GPA of 2.0 overall and in the major (2.5 for elementary education and nursing majors). Requirements include 40 credits in a liberal arts core, consisting of 15 credits of theology and philosophy, 6 each of fine arts, foreign language, and social science, and 3 each of communications, composition and research, contemporary American culture, human wellness, literature, mathematics, and science. All students also must perform 40 clock hours of service to others before graduation, complete course work in college success skills and in human diversity, and demonstrate computer proficiency.

Special: The college offers internships, study abroad, a Washington semester, dual majors, campus work-study, a general studies degree, nondegree study, and B.A.-B.S. degrees in biology, psychology, and chemistry.

Faculty/Classroom: 46% of faculty are male; 54%, female. All teach undergraduates.

Admissions: 84% of the 1995-96 applicants were accepted. The SAT I scores for the 1995-96 freshman class were as follows: Verbal—93% below 500, 6% between 500 and 599, and 1% between 600 and 700; Math—87% below 500, 8% between 500 and 599, and 5% between 600 and 700.

Requirements: The SAT I or ACT is required. All applicants must be graduates of an accredited secondary school with a 2.0 GPA or have a GED certificate. They should have completed at least 16 academic units, including 4 in English and electives, and 2 each in mathematics, foreign language, science, and social studies. An interview is required for physical therapist assistant and nursing applicants and

strongly recommended for all others. Nursing candidates also must submit results of the NLN prenursing test, and physical therapist assistant candidates must meet specific program requirements. AP and CLEP credits are accepted. Important factors in the admissions decision are advanced placement or honor courses, recommendations by school officials, and extracurricular activities record.

Procedure: Freshmen are admitted fall and spring. There are early admissions and deferred admissions plans. Application deadlines are open. Application fee is $25. Notification is sent on a rolling basis.

Transfer: Applicants must have a college GPA of 2.0 or better. 30 credits of 123 must be completed at Alvernia.

Visiting: There are guides for informal visits and visitors may sit in on classes and stay overnight at the school. To schedule a visit, contact the Admissions Office.

Financial Aid: Alvernia is a member of CSS. The FAF and Pennsylvania state grant application are required. The application deadline for fall entry is July 1.

International Students: They must take the TOEFL.

Computers: The college provides computer facilities for student use. The mainframe is an IBM System/38. DEC MicroVAX, Apple Macintosh, and IBM microcomputers are available to students in the science and mathematics building. Computer science students may access the system. The fees are $37 per semester.

Admissions Contact: Karin Allmendinger, Director of Admissions.

BEAVER COLLEGE
F-3

Glenside, PA 19038   (215) 572-2910

(800) 776-BEAVER (2328); FAX: (215) 572-4046

Full-time: 357 men, 726 women	Faculty: 77; IIA, --$
Part-time: 132 men, 309 women	Ph.D.s: 85%
Graduate: 271 men, 758 women	Student/Faculty: 14 to 1
Year: semesters, summer session	Tuition: $13,970
Application Deadline: open	Room & Board: $5750
Freshman Class: 1118 applied, 884 accepted, 255 enrolled	
SAT I Verbal/Math: 480/520	**COMPETITIVE**

Beaver College, founded in 1853, is a private institution affiliated with the Presbyterian Church (U.S.A.) offering undergraduate and graduate programs in the fine arts, the sciences, business, education, and preprofessional fields. There is 1 graduate school. In addition to regional accreditation, Beaver has baccalaureate program accreditation with APTA and NASAD. The library contains 143,469 volumes, 109,790 microform items, and 2421 audiovisual forms, and subscribes to 699 periodicals. Special learning facilities include a learning resource center, art gallery, radio station, an observatory, a theater, and computer graphics and communication laboratories. The 55-acre campus is in a suburban area 10 miles north of Philadelphia. Including residence halls, there are 14 buildings on campus.

Student Life: 78% of undergraduates are from Pennsylvania. Students come from 21 states and 11 foreign countries. 70% are from public schools; 30% from private. 86% are white. 35% are Catholic; 29% Protestant; 23% claim no religious affiliation. The average age of freshmen is 19; all undergraduates, 23. 15% do not continue beyond their first year; 71% remain to graduate.

Housing: 522 students can be accommodated in college housing. College-sponsored living facilities include single-sex and coed dormitories. On-campus housing is guaranteed for all 4 years. 75% of students live on campus; of those, 75% remain on campus on weekends. Upperclassmen may keep cars on campus.

Activities: There are no fraternities or sororities. There are 48 groups on campus, including art, cheerleading, choir, chorale, chorus, computers, dance, drama, ethnic, gay, honors, international, literary magazine, musical theater, newspaper, photography, political, professional, radio and TV, religious, social, social service, student government, and yearbook. Popular campus events include Woodstock Weekend, Parents Weekend, Black and White Formal, and International Festival.

Sports: There are 7 intercollegiate sports for men and 10 for women, and 6 intramural sports for men and 5 for women. Athletic and recreation facilities include a softball field, outdoor tennis and basketball courts, field hockey and soccer/lacrosse fields, and an atheletic and recreation center that includes a 1500-seat gymnasium for basketball and volleyball, an indoor track, an indoor NCAA regulation swimming pool, an aerobics and dance studio, and fitness and training rooms.

Disabled Students: 60% of the campus is accessible to disabled students. The following facilities are available: wheelchair ramps, elevators, special parking, specially equipped rest rooms, special class scheduling, and lowered telephones.

Services: In addition to many counseling and information services, tutoring is available in every subject. There is a reader service for the blind, and remedial math, reading, and writing.

Campus Safety and Security: Campus safety and security measures include 24-hour foot and vehicle patrol, escort service, informal discussions, and pamphlets/posters/films. There are emergency telephones, lighted pathways/sidewalks, doors with alarms, and night receptionists.

Programs of Study: Beaver confers B.A., B.S., and B.F.A. degrees. Associate and master's degrees are also awarded. Bachelor's degrees are awarded in BIOLOGICAL SCIENCE (biology/biological science), BUSINESS (accounting, banking and finance, business administration and management, marketing/retailing/merchandising, and personnel management), COMMUNICATIONS AND THE ARTS (communications, design, dramatic arts, English, fine arts, graphic design, and photography), COMPUTER AND PHYSICAL SCIENCE (chemistry, computer science, mathematics, and science), EDUCATION (art, early childhood, elementary, secondary, and special), ENGINEERING AND ENVIRONMENTAL DESIGN (interior design), HEALTH PROFESSIONS (art therapy, health care administration, predentistry, and premedicine), SOCIAL SCIENCE (history, liberal arts/general studies, philosophy, political science/government, prelaw, psychobiology, psychology, and sociology). Education, psychology, and chemistry are the strongest academically. Fine arts, business, and biology have the largest enrollments.

Required: Students must take English composition, mathematics, 1 semester of computer science, and 2 semesters each of a laboratory science, a foreign language, and physical education. They must also fulfill 24 credits of distribution requirements in the arts, humanities, and social sciences; core courses in American pluralism and non-Western cultures; and a final project or thesis. To graduate, completion of 128 credit hours is required, including 40 or more in the major with a 2.0 GPA.

Special: Internships are encouraged in all majors. There are study-abroad programs in 11 countries and co-op programs in business, computer science, chemistry, actuarial science, and accounting. There is a 3–2 engineering program with Columbia University, a 3–4 optometry program with the Pennsylvania College of Optometry, and a 4–2 physical therapy program. Beaver also offers a Washington semester, work-study, student-designed majors, a dual major in chemistry and business, interdisciplinary majors in artificial intelligence and science illustration, credit by exam and for life/military/work experience, and nondegree study. There is a freshman honors program on campus, as well as 1 national honor society, Phi Beta Kappa.

Faculty/Classroom: 51% of faculty are male; 49%, female. 72% teach undergraduates. No introductory courses are taught by graduate students. The average class size in an introductory lecture is 28; in a laboratory, 20; and in a regular course offering, 16.

Admissions: 79% of the 1995–96 applicants were accepted. The SAT I scores for the 1995–96 freshman class were Verbal—65% below 500, 32% between 500 and 599, 2% between 600 and 700, and 1% above 700; Math—38% below 500, 45% between 500 and 599, and 17% between 600 and 700. 44% of the current freshmen were in the top fifth of their class; 70% were in the top two fifths.

Requirements: The SAT I or the ACT is required. Applicants must be graduates of an accredited secondary school or have a GED. A total of 16 academic credits is required, including 4 years of English, 3 each of mathematics and social studies, and 2 each of a foreign language and science. An essay is required. Science illustration majors must submit a portfolio. AP and CLEP credits are accepted. Important factors in the admissions decision are advanced placement or honor courses, recommendations by school officials, and leadership record.

Procedure: Freshmen are admitted fall and spring. There are early decision, early admissions, and deferred admissions plans. Early decision applications should be filed by November 1; for regular applications, there is no deadline. The application fee is $30. Notification of early decision is sent December 1; regular decision, on a rolling basis. 16 early decision candidates were accepted for the 1995–96 class.

Transfer: 123 transfer students enrolled in a recent year. Applicants must have a GPA of 2.5. Art majors must submit a portfolio. The SAT I or ACT is required if the student has earned less than 1 year of college credit. An interview is encouraged. 32 credits of 128 must be completed at Beaver.

Visiting: There are regularly scheduled orientations for prospective students, including personal interviews Monday through Saturday, open houses, and opportunities to dine on campus and to meet with faculty, financial aid officers, and current students. There are guides for informal visits and visitors may sit in on classes and stay overnight at the school. To schedule a visit, contact the Office of Admissions.

Financial Aid: In a recent year, 73% of all freshmen and 64% of continuing students received some form of financial aid. 69% of freshmen and 58% of continuing students received need-based aid. The average freshman award was $11,042. Of that total, scholarships or need-based grants averaged $6748 ($9000 maximum); loans averaged $2625; and work contracts averaged $800 ($1000 maximum). 33% of undergraduate students work part-time. Average earnings from campus work for the school year are $920. The average financial indebtedness of a recent year's graduate was $13,250. Beaver is a member of CSS. The FAFSA, the college's own financial statement,

the PHEAA, and parent and student tax returns are required. The application deadline for fall entry is March 15.

International Students: There were 27 international students enrolled in a recent year. The school actively recruits these students. They must take the TOEFL and achieve a minimum score of 500.

Computers: The college provides computer facilities for student use. The mainframes are a DEC VAX 8250 and a DEC VAX 4000/500 Series. There are also IBM, Zenith, and Apple IIg microcomputers available in the library and in academic buildings linking with Novell network and the Internet. All students may access the system. There are no time limits and no fees.

Graduates: In a recent year, 215 bachelor's degrees were awarded. The most popular majors among graduates were education (17%), business administration (17%), and fine arts (13%). Within an average freshman class, 1% graduate in 3 years, 67% in 4 years, 2% in 5 years, and 1% in 6 years. 25 companies recruited on campus in a recent year.

Admissions Contact: Dennis L. Nostrand, Vice President for Enrollment Management. E-mail: admiss@beaver.edu. A campus video is available.

BLOOMSBURG UNIVERSITY OF PENNSYLVANIA   E-2
Bloomsburg, PA 17815   (717) 389-4316

Full-time: 2177 men, 3576 women	Faculty: 369; IIA, +$
Part-time: 302 men, 566 women	Ph.D.s: 64%
Graduate: 197 men, 494 women	Student/Faculty: 16 to 1
Year: semesters, summer session	Tuition: $3866 ($8840)
Application Deadline: open	Room & Board: $2984
Freshman Class: 6446 applied, 2995 accepted, 991 enrolled	
SAT I Verbal/Math: 462/525	ACT: 22 COMPETITIVE +

Bloomsburg University of Pennsylvania, founded in 1839, is a public, coeducational institution offering undergraduate programs in the liberal arts and sciences, business, and teacher education. There are 5 undergraduate schools and one graduate school. In addition to regional accreditation, BU has baccalaureate program accreditation with CSWE, NCATE, and NLN. The library contains 341,402 volumes, 1,751,790 microform items, and 6836 audiovisual forms, and subscribes to 1745 periodicals. Computerized library sources and services include the card catalog, interlibrary loans, and database searching. Special learning facilities include a learning resource center, art gallery, radio station, and TV station. The 192-acre campus is in a small town 80 miles northeast of Harrisburg. Including residence halls, there are 54 buildings on campus.

Student Life: 90% of undergraduates are from Pennsylvania. Students come from 26 states and 16 foreign countries. 86% are from public schools; 14% from private. 93% are white. 20% are Catholic; 17% Protestant. The average age of freshmen is 18.5; all undergraduates, 22.1. 16% do not continue beyond their first year; 66% remain to graduate.

Housing: 2698 students can be accommodated in college housing. College-sponsored living facilities include single-sex and coed dormitories and on-campus apartments. On-campus housing is guaranteed for all 4 years. Alcohol is not permitted. Upperclassmen may keep cars on campus.

Activities: 12% of men belong to 3 local and 7 national fraternities; 15% of women belong to 5 local and 5 national sororities. There are 124 groups on campus, including art, band, cheerleading, chess, choir, chorale, chorus, computers, drama, drill team, ethnic, film, gay, honors, international, literary magazine, marching band, musical theater, newspaper, orchestra, pep band, political, professional, radio and TV, religious, social, social service, student government, and yearbook. Popular campus events include Parents Weekend, Renaissance Jamboree, and Siblings and Childrens Weekend.

Sports: There are 9 intercollegiate sports for men and 9 for women, and 18 intramural sports for men and 12 for women. Athletic and recreation facilities include a 5000-seat stadium, 2 gymnasiums, an athletic field, an indoor track, a 6-lane swimming pool, 9 practice fields, and 18 Grasstex tennis courts.

Disabled Students: 70% of the campus is accessible to disabled students. The following facilities are available: wheelchair ramps, elevators, special parking, specially equipped rest rooms, special class scheduling, lowered drinking fountains, and lowered telephones.

Services: In addition to many counseling and information services, tutoring is available in some subjects. There is a reader service for the blind, and remedial math, reading, and writing.

Campus Safety and Security: Campus safety and security measures include 24-hour foot and vehicle patrol, escort service, shuttle buses, and emergency telephones. In addition, there are lighted pathways/sidewalks, monitored surveillance cameras, and strict residence hall security.

Programs of Study: BU confers B.A., B.S., B.S.Ed., B.S.N., and B.S.O.A. degrees. Associate and master's degrees are also awarded. Bachelor's degrees are awarded in BIOLOGICAL SCIENCE (biology/biological science), BUSINESS (accounting, business administration and management, business economics, and office supervision and management), COMMUNICATIONS AND THE ARTS (art history and appreciation, communications, dramatic arts, English, French, German, music, Spanish, speech/debate/rhetoric, and studio art), COMPUTER AND PHYSICAL SCIENCE (chemistry, computer science, earth science, geology, mathematics, natural sciences, physics, and radiological technology), EDUCATION (business, early childhood, elementary, science, secondary, social studies, and special), HEALTH PROFESSIONS (health, medical laboratory technology, nursing, and speech pathology/audiology), SOCIAL SCIENCE (anthropology, economics, ethics, politics, and social policy, geography, history, humanities, interpreter for the deaf, philosophy, political science/government, psychology, social science, social work, and sociology). Business and education have the largest enrollments.

Required: To graduate, students must complete 128 credit hours with a minimum GPA of 2.0. BU requires 12 semester hours each in humanities, social sciences, natural sciences, and mathematics. There are specific course requirements in communication, quantitative/analytical reasoning, values, ethics, responsible decision making, and survival, fitness, and recreational skills.

Special: Internships for upperclassmen, study abroad in more than 11 countries, work-study programs, and dual majors are available. BU offers a 3–2 engineering degree with Pennsylvania State and Wilkes universities. There is nondegree study, pass/fail options, and credit for life, military, and work experience. The school utilizes telecourses and interactive video. There is a freshman honors program on campus, as well as 9 national honor societies.

Faculty/Classroom: 65% of faculty are male; 35%, female. All teach undergraduates. No introductory courses are taught by graduate students. The average class size in a regular course offering is 28.

Admissions: 46% of the 1995–96 applicants were accepted. The SAT I scores for the 1995–96 freshman class were as follows: Verbal—65% below 500, 31% between 500 and 599, and 4% between 600 and 700; Math—32% below 500, 53% between 500 and 599, and 15% between 600 and 700. 40% of the current freshmen were in the top fifth of their class; 85% were in the top two fifths. 5 freshmen graduated first in their class.

Requirements: The SAT I is required, with a minimum composite score of 850. Applicants must be graduates of an accredited secondary school. To be competitive, a student should also rank in the top 30% of the high school class with a B average. The GED is accepted. Applicants should complete 4 years each of English and social studies, 3 years each of mathematics and science, and 2 years of a foreign language. An interview is recommended. AP and CLEP credits are accepted.

Procedure: Freshmen are admitted to all sessions. Entrance exams should be taken during the junior year. There is an early admissions plan. Application deadlines are open. Application fee is $25. Notification is sent on a rolling basis. A waiting list is an active part of the admissions procedure.

Transfer: 420 transfer students enrolled in 1995–96. Either the SAT or ACT is required from applicants who have completed fewer than 24 semester hours of college credits. An official secondary school transcript or a GED and official transcripts from any post-secondary schools attended are also required. Applicants must have a minimum GPA of 2.0, and be in good standing at the college last attended. Those who have completed 30 semester hours must select a major upon entering BU. 32 credits of 128 must be completed at BU.

Visiting: There are regularly scheduled orientations for prospective students, consisting of a general meeting with admissions staff, a question-and-answer session, a campus tour, lunch, and meetings with academic faculty. There are guides for informal visits and visitors may sit in on classes. To schedule a visit, contact the Admissions Office.

Financial Aid: In a recent year, 80% of all students received some form of financial aid. 28% of undergraduate students work part-time. Average earnings from campus work for the school year are $2500. BU is a member of CSS. The FAFSA and PHEAA Aid Information Request (PAIR) are required. The application deadline for fall entry is March 15.

International Students: In a recent year, 27 international students were enrolled. They must take the TOEFL and achieve a minimum score of 500.

Computers: The college provides computer facilities for student use. The mainframes are a Unisys 2200/402 and a Unisys U6000 UNIX System. Terminal direct attachment to the mainframe system is provided in several campus laboratories for use in instruction and research. Students can access the system through a modem over Ethernet lines on a selected-service basis. There are no time limits and no fees.

Graduates: In a recent year, 1347 bachelor's degrees were awarded. The most popular majors among graduates were business administration (17%), elementary education (14%), and accounting (8%). Within an average freshman class, 43% graduate in 4 years, 64% in 5 years, and 66% in 6 years. 154 companies recruited on campus in an earlier year.

Admissions Contact: Christopher Keller, Director of Admissions. A campus video is available.

BRYN MAWR COLLEGE   F-3
Bryn Mawr, PA 19010–2899
(610) 526-5152
(800) 262-1885; FAX: (610) 526-7471

Full-time: 1113 women	**Faculty:** 137; IIA, +$
Part-time: 86 women	**Ph.D.s:** 99%
Graduate: 542 men and women	**Student/Faculty:** 8 to 1
Year: semesters, summer session	**Tuition:** $19,810
Application Deadline: January 15	**Room & Board:** $7085
Freshman Class: 1719 applied, 977 accepted, 344 enrolled	
SAT I Verbal/Math: 620/630	**MOST COMPETITIVE**

Bryn Mawr College, founded in 1885, is an independent liberal arts institution, primarily for women. There are 2 graduate schools. The 3 libraries contain 926,464 volumes and 108,724 microform items, and subscribe to 1958 periodicals. Computerized library sources and services include the card catalog, interlibrary loans, and database searching. Special learning facilities include a radio station, an archeological museum, and a language learning center with audio, video, and computer technology. The 135-acre campus is in a suburban area 10 miles west of Philadelphia. Including residence halls, there are 57 buildings on campus.

Student Life: 89% of undergraduates are from out-of-state, mostly the Middle Atlantic. Students come from 50 states, 44 foreign countries, and Canada. 73% are from public schools; 27% from private. 68% are white; 15% Asian American; 11% foreign nationals. The average age of freshmen is 18; all undergraduates, 20. 3% do not continue beyond their first year; 86% remain to graduate.

Housing: 1180 students can be accommodated in college housing. College-sponsored living facilities include single-sex and coed dormitories and off-campus apartments. In addition there are language houses, special interest houses, and an African American culture center that houses several students. On-campus housing is guaranteed for all 4 years. 95% of students live on campus; of those, 80% remain on campus on weekends. Alcohol is not permitted. Upperclassmen may keep cars on campus.

Activities: There are no fraternities or sororities. There are 100 groups on campus, including art, chess, choir, chorale, chorus, computers, dance, drama, ethnic, gay, honors, international, jazz band, literary magazine, musical theater, newspaper, orchestra, photography, political, professional, radio and TV, religious, social, social service, student government, and yearbook. Popular campus events include May Day, Lantern Night, and Fall Frolic.

Sports: Athletic and recreation facilities include a gymnasium with an Olympic-size pool and diving well, basketball, badminton, and volleyball courts, a gymnastics room and dance floor, and a weight-training room; a 1000-seat auditorium; and a student center.

Disabled Students: 60% of the campus is accessible to disabled students. The following facilities are available: wheelchair ramps, elevators, special parking, specially equipped rest rooms, special class scheduling, and lowered telephones.

Services: In addition to many counseling and information services, tutoring is available in most subjects. There is a reader service for the blind and remedial math.

Campus Safety and Security: Campus safety and security measures include 24-hour foot and vehicle patrol, self-defense education, escort service, and shuttle buses. In addition, there are informal discussions, pamphlets/posters/films, emergency telephones, and lighted pathways/sidewalks.

Programs of Study: Bryn Mawr confers the A.B. degree. Master's and doctoral degrees are also awarded. Bachelor's degrees are awarded in BIOLOGICAL SCIENCE (biochemistry, biology/biological science, and neurosciences), BUSINESS (international economics), COMMUNICATIONS AND THE ARTS (art history and appreciation, classical languages, comparative literature, English, fine arts, French, German, Greek, Italian, Latin, music, romance languages, Russian, and Spanish), COMPUTER AND PHYSICAL SCIENCE (astronomy, chemistry, computer science, geology, mathematics, and physics), SOCIAL SCIENCE (African studies, anthropology, archeology, East Asian studies, economics, history, history of philosophy, peace studies, philosophy, political science/government, psychology, sociology, and urban studies). English, anthropology, and political science have the largest enrollments.

Required: To graduate, students must complete 32 semester courses, including 8 to 12 in the major. There are distribution requirements in social sciences, humanities, and laboratory sciences. Students must take foreign language, mathematics, and English composition.

Special: Students may cross-register with Haverford and Swarthmore colleges and the University of Pennsylvania. Bryn Mawr offers study abroad, student-designed and dual majors, pass/fail options, work-study, and a 3–2 engineering degree with the University of Pennsylvania.

Faculty/Classroom: 46% of faculty are male; 54%, female. 94% teach undergraduates. No introductory courses are taught by graduate students. The average class size in an introductory lecture is 80; in a laboratory, 15; and in a regular course offering, 20.

Admissions: 57% of the 1995–96 applicants were accepted. 88% of the current freshmen were in the top fifth of their class. 34 freshmen graduated first in their class.

Requirements: The SAT I is required, but the ACT may be substituted. SAT II: Subject tests in Writing and 2 other areas are required. Applicants must be graduates of an accredited secondary school. The GED is accepted. Applicants should complete 4 years of English, at least 3 years of foreign language, 3 years of mathematics, and 1 year each of science, social studies, and history. An essay is required. An interview is strongly recommended. AP credits are accepted. Important factors in the admissions decision are advanced placement or honor courses, evidence of special academic talent, and extracurricular activities record.

Procedure: Freshmen are admitted in the fall. Entrance exams should be taken in the spring of the junior year or fall of the senior year. There are early decision, early admissions, and deferred admissions plans. Early decision applications should be filed by November 15; regular applications, by January 15 for fall entry, along with an application fee of $50. Notification of early decision is sent December 15; regular decision, April 10. 93 early decision candidates were accepted for the 1995–96 class. A waiting list is an active part of the admissions procedure, with about 10% of all applicants on the list.

Transfer: 22 transfer students enrolled in 1995–96. Applicants must have a minimum college GPA of 3.0. The SAT I and recommendations from both college and high school are required. 16 semester courses of 32 must be completed at Bryn Mawr.

Visiting: There are regularly scheduled orientations for prospective students. Student-guided campus tours and interviews can be arranged. There are guides for informal visits and visitors may sit in on classes and stay overnight at the school. To schedule a visit, contact the Office of Admissions.

Financial Aid: In 1995–96, 53% of all freshmen and 51% of continuing students received some form of financial aid. 53% of freshmen and 51% of continuing students received need-based aid. Scholarships or need-based grants averaged $12,945 ($23,000 maximum); loans averaged $2800 ($3000 maximum); and work contracts averaged $1200 (maximum). 75% of undergraduate students work part-time. Average earnings from campus work for the school year are $1200. The average financial indebtedness of the 1994–95 graduate was $9000. Bryn Mawr is a member of CSS. The FAFSA and the college's own financial statement are required. The application deadline for fall entry is January 15.

International Students: In a recent year, 120 international students were enrolled. The school actively recruits these students. They must take the TOEFL and achieve a minimum score of 600. The student must also take the SAT I.

Computers: The college provides computer facilities for student use. The mainframe is an HP9000. The computing center, libraries, and some classrooms are equipped with terminals and/or microcomputers, including more than 100 IBM, Apple Macintosh, and other models. All students may access the system every day in 2-hour blocks which can be renewed. There are no fees.

Graduates: In a recent year, 295 bachelor's degrees were awarded. The most popular majors among graduates were English (15%), political science (9%), and biology (8%). Within an average freshman class, 85% graduate in 5 years and 86% in 6 years. 50 companies recruited on campus in a recent year. Of the 1994 graduating class, 40% were enrolled in graduate school within 6 months of graduation.

Admissions Contact: Nancy Monnich, Director of Admissions and Financial Aid.

BUCKNELL UNIVERSITY D-2

Lewisburg, PA 17837 (717) 524-1101

Full-time: 1704 men, 1637 women	Faculty: 254; IIA, +$
Part-time: 22 men, 49 women	Ph.Ds: 97%
Graduate: 101 men, 113 women	Student/Faculty: 13 to 1
Year: semesters, summer session	Tuition: $19,470
Application Deadline: January 1	Room & Board: $4925
Freshman Class: 6597 applied, 3641 accepted, 910 enrolled	
SAT I or ACT: required	**HIGHLY COMPETITIVE**

Bucknell University, established in 1846, is an independent, coeducational institution offering undergraduate and graduate programs in arts, music, education, humanities, management, engineering, sciences, and social sciences. There are 2 undergraduate schools and one graduate school. In addition to regional accreditation, Bucknell University has baccalaureate program accreditation with ABET, CSAB, and NASM. The library contains 563,800 volumes, 636,900 microform items, and 2275 audiovisual forms, and subscribes to 4694 periodicals. Computerized library sources and services include the card catalog, interlibrary loans, and database searching. Special learning facilities include an art gallery, radio station, outdoor natural area, greenhouse, primate facility, observatory, photography laboratory, art galllery, craft center, women's resource center, library resources training laboratory, multicultural center, writing center, poetry center, electronic classroom, and multimedia laboratory. The 320-acre campus is in a small town 60 miles north of Harrisburg. Including residence halls, there are 71 buildings on campus.

Student Life: 68% of undergraduates are from out-of-state, mostly the Middle Atlantic. Students come from 43 states, 39 foreign countries, and Canada. 72% are from public schools; 28% from private. 90% are white. 35% are Protestant; 32% Catholic; 26% claim no religious affiliation. The average age of freshmen is 18; all undergraduates, 20. 6% do not continue beyond their first year; 88% remain to graduate.

Housing: 2600 students can be accommodated in college housing. College-sponsored living facilities include single-sex and coed dormitories, on-campus apartments, and fraternity houses. In addition there are special interest houses and 5 residential colleges for the first year (arts, environmental, humanities, international, and social justice). On-campus housing is guaranteed for all 4 years. 81% of students live on campus; of those, 85% remain on campus on weekends. Upperclassmen may keep cars on campus.

Activities: 39% of men belong to 12 national fraternities; 43% of women belong to 1 local sorority and 7 national sororities. There are 86 groups on campus, including art, band, cheerleading, chess, choir, chorale, chorus, computers, dance, drama, drill team, ethnic, gay, honors, international, jazz band, literary magazine, musical theater, newspaper, opera, orchestra, pep band, photography, political, professional, radio and TV, religious, social, social service, student government, symphony, and yearbook. Popular campus events include Homecoming, Spring Weekend, Greek Weekend, Special Olympics, Christmas Candlelight Service, Kwaanza, Poetry Symposium, and Celebration for the Arts.

Sports: There are 14 intercollegiate sports for men and 12 for women, and 30 intramural sports for men and 25 for women. Athletic and recreation facilities include a field house with a 6-lane track, weight and wrestling rooms, a basketball arena, a dance studio, a gymnasium with a 6-lane pool, a 14,000-seat stadium, a golf course, a jogging course, tennis courts, soccer and lacrosse fields, and handball, racquetball, and squash courts.

Disabled Students: 85% of the campus is accessible to disabled students. The following facilities are available: wheelchair ramps, elevators, special parking, specially equipped rest rooms, lowered drinking fountains, and lowered telephones. Individual arrangements may be made with faculty for students with disabilities.

Services: In addition to many counseling and information services, tutoring is available in most subjects, including writing, computer, and library skills.

Campus Safety and Security: Campus safety and security measures include 24-hour foot and vehicle patrol, self-defense education, escort service, and informal discussions. In addition, there are pamphlets/posters/films, emergency telephones, and lighted pathways/sidewalks.

Programs of Study: Bucknell University confers B.A., B.S., B.Mus., B.S.B.A., B.S.C.E., B.S.CH.E., B.S.Ed., B.S.E.E., and B.S.M.E. degrees. Master's degrees are also awarded. Bachelor's degrees are awarded in BIOLOGICAL SCIENCE (biochemistry, biology/biological science, and cell biology), BUSINESS (accounting and business administration and management), COMMUNICATIONS AND THE ARTS (art, Chinese, classics, dramatic arts, English, fine arts, French, German, Greek, Japanese, Latin, music, Russian, and Spanish), COMPUTER AND PHYSICAL SCIENCE (chemistry, computer science, geology, mathematics, and physics), EDUCATION (early childhood, educational statistics and research, elementary, music, and secondary), ENGINEERING AND ENVIRONMENTAL DESIGN (chemical engineering, civil engineering, computer engineering, electrical/electronics engineering, engineering, environmental science, and mechanical engineering), SOCIAL SCIENCE (anthropology, East Asian studies, economics, geography, history, international relations, Latin American studies, philosophy, political science/government, psychology, religion, sociology, and women's studies). Engineering, natural science, and psychology are the strongest academically. Economics, management, and political science/international relations have the largest enrollments.

Required: All students enrolled in the College of Arts and Sciences must complete a foundation seminar during the first semester; distribution selections include 4 humanities courses, 2 social science courses, and 3 courses in natural science and mathematics; 2 courses in broadened perspectives for the 21st Century addressing issues of the natural and fabricated worlds and issues in human diversity; departmental, college, or interdepartmental majors; and a capstone seminar or experience during the senior year. In addition, Bucknell requires a minimum writing competency for graduation. All students enrolled in the College of Engineering have a common first semester and must complete Exploring Engineering (EG 100). A total of 128 credits or 32 courses (34 courses for engineering) and a minimum GPA of 2.0 are required to graduate.

Special: The university offers internships, study abroad in 15 countries, a Washington semester, a 5-year B.A.-B.S. degree in arts and engineering, and dual and student-designed majors. An interdisciplinary major in animal behavior is offered through the biology and psychology departments. Nondegree study is possible and a pass/fail grading option is offered in some courses. The Residential College program offers opportunities for an academic-residential mix and faculty-student collaborative learning. Undergraduate research opportunities are available in the humanities/social sciences and the sciences and engineering. There is a freshman honors program on campus, as well as 21 national honor societies, including Phi Beta Kappa. 36 departments have honors programs.

Faculty/Classroom: 72% of faculty are male; 28%, female. All both teach and do research. No introductory courses are taught by graduate students. The average class size in an introductory lecture is 55; in a laboratory, 21; and in a regular course offering, 20.

Admissions: 55% of the 1995–96 applicants were accepted. The SAT I scores for the 1995–96 freshman class were as follows: Verbal—27% below 500, 51% between 500 and 599, 19% between 600 and 700, and 2% above 700; Math—4% below 500, 22% between 500 and 599, 56% between 600 and 700, and 17% above 700. 78% of the current freshmen were in the top fifth of their class; 96% were in the top two fifths. 40 freshmen graduated first in their class.

Requirements: The SAT I or ACT is required. Applicants must graduate from an accredited secondary school or have a GED. Sixteen Carnegie units must be earned, including 4 courses in English, 3 in mathematics, and 2 each in history, science, social studies, and a foreign language. An essay is required, and an interview is recommended. Music applicants are required to audition. A portfolio is recommended for art applicants. AP credits are accepted. Important factors in the admissions decision are advanced placement or honor courses, recommendations by school officials, and evidence of special talent.

Procedure: Freshmen are admitted in the fall. Entrance exams should be taken before January 1. There are early decision, early admissions, and deferred admissions plans. Early decision applications should be filed by December 1; regular applications, by January 1 for fall entry and December 1 for spring entry, along with an application fee of $35. Notification of early decision is sent December 20; regular decision, by April 1. 284 early decision candidates were accepted for the 1995–96 class. A waiting list is an active part of the admissions procedure, with about 16% of all applicants on the list.

Transfer: 46 transfer students enrolled in a recent year. Transfer students must have a minimum GPA of 2.5 in courses comparable to those offered at Bucknell. The SAT I or ACT is required. A minimum of 16 credit hours must have been earned; 32 is recommended. Students are accepted on a space-available basis. An interview is recommended. 48 credits of 128 must be completed at Bucknell University.

Visiting: There are regularly scheduled orientations for prospective students. There are guides for informal visits and visitors may sit in on classes and stay overnight at the school. To schedule a visit, contact the Office of Admissions.

Financial Aid: In 1995–96, 54% of all freshmen and 60% of continuing students received some form of financial aid. 49% of freshmen and 48% of continuing students received need-based aid. The average freshman award was $14,534. Of that total, scholarships or need-based grants averaged $10,141 ($26,700 maximum); loans averaged $3382 ($4125 maximum); and work contracts averaged $1011 ($1500 maximum). 43% of undergraduate students work part-time. Average earnings from campus work for the school year are $1500. The average financial indebtedness of the 1994–95 graduate was $15,000. Bucknell University is a member of CSS. The FAF is required. The application deadline for fall entry is January 1.

International Students: In a recent year, 90 international students were enrolled. The school actively recruits these students. They must take the TOEFL and achieve a minimum score of 550.

Computers: The college provides computer facilities for student use. The mainframe is a DEC System 5000 Model 240. There are more than 450 microcomputers available in 15 student access sites, as well as more than 400 microcomputers on student and faculty desks. Access to the mainframe is through terminals, microcomputers, and dial-up from residence hall room phones using a modem. There are 50 Sun engineering work stations and numerous computers in laboratories. All students may access the system 24 hours per day, 7 days per week. There are no time limits and no fees.

Graduates: In 1994–95, 841 bachelor's degrees were awarded. The most popular majors among graduates were economics (13%), biology (12%), and business administration (10%). Within an average

freshman class, 86% graduate in 4 years and 88% in 5 years. 145 companies recruited on campus in 1994–95. Of the 1994 graduating class, 27% were enrolled in graduate school within 6 months of graduation and 68% had found employment.

Admissions Contact: Mark D. Davies, Director of Admissions. A campus video is available.

CABRINI COLLEGE
Radnor, PA 19087-3698

F-4

(610) 902-8552
(800) 848-1003; FAX: (610) 902-8309

Full-time: 349 men, 751 women	**Faculty:** 42; IIB, av$
Part-time: 151 men, 352 women	**Ph.D.s:** 73%
Graduate: 122 men, 298 women	**Student/Faculty:** 26 to 1
Year: semesters, summer session	**Tuition:** $11,600
Application Deadline: August 15	**Room & Board:** $6500
Freshman Class: 739 applied, 618 accepted, 220 enrolled	
SAT I Verbal/Math: 423/435	**COMPETITIVE**

Cabrini College, founded in 1957, is a private, coeducational, liberal arts college affiliated with the Roman Catholic Church and founded by the Missionary Sisters of the Sacred Heart. The library contains 122,701 volumes and subscribes to 528 periodicals. Computerized library sources and services include interlibrary loans and database searching. Special learning facilities include a learning resource center, art gallery, radio station, TV station, and a communications laboratory. The 110-acre campus is in a suburban area 20 miles west of Philadelphia. Including residence halls, there are 18 buildings on campus.

Student Life: 77% of undergraduates are from Pennsylvania. Students come from 10 states, 43 foreign countries, and Canada. 48% are from public schools; 52% from private. 88% are white. 73% are Catholic; 22% claim no religious affiliation; 11% Protestant. The average age of freshmen is 18; all undergraduates, 29. 17% do not continue beyond their first year; 65% remain to graduate.

Housing: 490 students can be accommodated in college housing. College-sponsored living facilities include single-sex and coed dormitories. In addition there are honors houses, language houses, and special-interest houses. On-campus housing is guaranteed for all 4 years. 54% of students live on campus; of those, 60% remain on campus on weekends. All students may keep cars on campus.

Activities: There are no fraternities or sororities. There are 37 groups on campus, including cheerleading, chess, chorus, computers, dance, drama, ethnic, honors, international, literary magazine, newspaper, photography, political, professional, radio and TV, religious, social, social service, student government, and yearbook. Popular campus events include Mother Cabrini Feast Day, Yule Log, Superthon, fall and spring concerts, and drama presentations.

Sports: There are 7 intercollegiate sports for men and 8 for women, and 2 intramural sports for men and 2 for women. Athletic and recreation facilities include a weight room, athletic fields, a game room, a 700-seat gymnasium, and tennis courts.

Disabled Students: 95% of the campus is accessible to disabled students. The following facilities are available: wheelchair ramps, elevators, special parking, specially equipped rest rooms, and special class scheduling.

Services: In addition to many counseling and information services, tutoring is available in most subjects. Students may enroll in a study skills course or participate in individual counseling to acquire learning skills.

Campus Safety and Security: Campus safety and security measures include 24-hour foot and vehicle patrol, self-defense education, escort service, and informal discussions. In addition, there are pamphlets/posters/films, emergency telephones, and lighted pathways/sidewalks.

Programs of Study: Cabrini confers B.A., B.S., B.S.W., and B.S.Ed. degrees. Master's degrees are also awarded. Bachelor's degrees are awarded in BIOLOGICAL SCIENCE (biology/biological science), BUSINESS (accounting, banking and finance, business administration and management, human resources, and marketing/retailing/merchandising), COMMUNICATIONS AND THE ARTS (arts administration/management, communications, English, French, graphic design, Spanish, and visual and performing arts), COMPUTER AND PHYSICAL SCIENCE (chemistry, information sciences and systems, and mathematics), EDUCATION (early childhood, education, elementary, and special), HEALTH PROFESSIONS (medical laboratory technology and sports medicine), SOCIAL SCIENCE (American studies, history, liberal arts/general studies, philosophy, political science/government, psychology, religion, social work, and sociology). Education and English/communications are the strongest academically. Business, education, and English/communications have the largest enrollments.

Required: Students must complete a minimum of 123 credits to graduate, with an average of 45 in the major, and a minimum GPA of 2.0. All students must complete a core curriculum, which includes English, mathematics, foreign language, computers, physical education, an interdisiplinary seminar in self-understanding, and a junior seminar exploring the common good. Distribution requirements cover science, heritage, cultural diversity, values, the individual and society, contemporary issues, creativity, and religion. A thesis is required in some majors, and a volunteer project is part of the junior seminar.

Special: Cabrini offers cooperative programs, internships, study abroad, work-study programs, and cross-registration with Eastern and Rosemont colleges and Villanova University. B.A.-B.S. degrees, dual majors, a general studies degree, and student-designed majors are available, as well as accelerated interdisciplinary degree program in organizational management and professional communications. Credit by examination, credit for life/military/work experience, nondegree study, and pass/fail options are also offered. There is a freshman honors program on campus, as well as 10 national honor societies. 10 departments have honors programs.

Faculty/Classroom: 45% of faculty are male; 55%, female. All teach undergraduates, and 49% both teach and do research. No introductory courses are taught by graduate students. The average class size in an introductory lecture is 20; in a laboratory, 16; and in a regular course offering, 19.

Admissions: 84% of the 1995–96 applicants were accepted. The SAT I scores for the 1995–96 freshman class were as follows: Verbal—83% below 500, 15% between 500 and 599, and 2% between 600 and 700; Math—79% below 500, 18% between 500 and 599, 34% between 600 and 700, and 1% above 700. 21% of the current freshmen were in the top fifth of their class; 49% were in the top two fifths.

Requirements: The SAT I or ACT is required. The SAT I with a minimum score of 500 each on the verbal and math or a total score of 1000 is recommended, or the ACT is required. Cabrini prefers applicants to be in the upper 50% of their class. A minimum GPA of 2.5 is preferred. All students must be graduates of an accredited secondary school or hold a GED certificate. A minimum of 17 Carnegie units are required, consisting of 4 in English, 3 each in mathematics, science, and social studies, 2 in a foreign language, and the rest in electives. A letter of recommendation from a guidance counselor or academic subject teacher and an essay are required. An interview is recommended. Applications are accepted on computer disk. AP and CLEP credits are accepted. Important factors in the admissions decision are recommendations by school officials, advanced placement or honor courses, and evidence of special talent.

Procedure: Freshmen are admitted fall, spring, and summer. Entrance exams should be taken before December of the senior year. There are early admissions and deferred admissions plans. Applications should be filed by August 15 for fall entry, December 15 for spring entry, and May 15 for summer entry, along with an application fee of $25. Notification is sent on a rolling basis. A waiting list is an active part of the admissions procedure, with about 5% of all applicants on the list.

Transfer: 155 transfer students enrolled in 1995–96. A mimimum of 15 credit hours with a minimum GPA of 2.2 is required. A 2.5 GPA is preferred. Some programs may have higher requirements. 45 credits of 123 must be completed at Cabrini.

Visiting: There are regularly scheduled orientations for prospective students. There are guides for informal visits, and visitors may sit in on classes and stay overnight at the school. To schedule a visit, contact the Admissions Office.

Financial Aid: In 1995–96, 71% of all freshmen and 70% of continuing students received some form of financial aid. 72% of freshmen and 70% of continuing students received need-based aid. The average freshman award was $8617. Of that total, scholarships or need-based grants averaged $3500 ($11,100 maximum); loans averaged $3225 ($4125 maximum); work contracts averaged $1000 ($1500 maximum); and Cabrini work grants averaged $1100. 85% of undergraduate students work part-time. Average earnings from campus work for the school year are $1000. The average financial indebtedness of the 1994–95 graduate was $15,500. The college's own financial statement, the FAFSA, and income tax forms are required. The application deadline for fall entry is February 15.

International Students: There are currently 47 international students enrolled. The school actively recruits these students. They must take the TOEFL and achieve a minimum score of 550. They must also take the SAT I or ACT, but it is optional for students whose native language is not English.

Computers: The college provides computer facilities for student use. There are 35 networked IBM microcomputers and a 12-unit Apple educational laboratory. All students may access the system more than 80 hours a week. There are no time limits and no fees.

Graduates: In 1994–95, 368 bachelor's degrees were awarded. The most popular majors among graduates were education (41%), business administration (30%), and communications (8%). Within an average freshman class, 1% graduate in 3 years, 54% in 4 years, 60% in 5 years, and 62% in 6 years. 35 companies recruited on campus in 1994–95. Of the 1994 graduating class, 17% were enrolled in graduate school within 6 months of graduation and 97% had found employ-

ment.

Admissions Contact: Nancy Gardner, Executive Director of Admissions and Financial Aid. A campus video is available.

CALIFORNIA UNIVERSITY OF PENNSYLVANIA B-3

California, PA 15419–1394   (412) 938–4404; FAX: (412) 938–4564

Full-time: 2209 men, 2236 women	Faculty: 315; IIA, +$
Part-time: 233 men, 428 women	Ph.Ds: 62%
Graduate: 320 men, 593 women	Student/Faculty: 14 to 1
Year: semesters, summer session	Tuition: $4136 ($9110)
Application Deadline: open	Room & Board: $3890
Freshman Class: 2622 applied, 2000 accepted, 917 enrolled	
SAT I Verbal/Math: 420/450	LESS COMPETITIVE

California University of Pennsylvania, founded in 1852, is a state-supported institution offering degree programs in the arts and sciences, engineering, and education. There are 3 undergraduate schools and 1 graduate school. In addition to regional accreditation, the university has baccalaureate program accreditation with CSWE, NCATE, and NLN. The library contains 330,728 volumes, 408,677 microform items, and 11,814 audiovisual forms, and subscribes to 1492 periodicals. Computerized library sources and services include the card catalog, interlibrary loans, and database searching. Special learning facilities include a learning resource center, art gallery, radio station, and TV station. The 148-acre campus is in a small town 35 miles south of Pittsburgh. Including residence halls, there are 38 buildings on campus.

Student Life: 94% of undergraduates are from Pennsylvania. Students come from 38 states, 25 foreign countries, and Canada. 94% are white. The average age of freshmen is 19; all undergraduates, 23. 20% do not continue beyond their first year; 50% remain to graduate.

Housing: 1500 students can be accommodated in college housing. College-sponsored living facilities include single-sex and coed dormitories. On-campus housing is available on a first-come, first-served basis. Alcohol is not permitted. All students may keep cars on campus.

Activities: There are 19 groups on campus, including band, cheerleading, chess, choir, chorale, chorus, computers, drama, drill team, ethnic, honors, international, marching band, newspaper, pep band, professional, radio and TV, student government, and yearbook.

Sports: Athletic and recreation facilities include tennis and basketball courts, an all-weather track, a swimming pool, and a 4500-seat stadium.

Disabled Students: The following facilities are available: wheelchair ramps, elevators, special parking, specially equipped rest rooms, special class scheduling, and lowered drinking fountains.

Services: In addition to many counseling and information services, tutoring is available in most subjects. There is a reader service for the blind, and remedial math, reading, and writing.

Programs of Study: The university confers B.A., B.S., and B.S.Ed. degrees. Associate and master's degrees are also awarded. Bachelor's degrees are awarded in BIOLOGICAL SCIENCE (biology/biological science), BUSINESS (business administration and management and business economics), COMMUNICATIONS AND THE ARTS (broadcasting, communications, dramatic arts, English, fine arts, French, German, Spanish, and speech/debate/rhetoric), COMPUTER AND PHYSICAL SCIENCE (chemistry, computer science, earth science, geology, mathematics, natural sciences, and physics), EDUCATION (early childhood, education of the mentally handicapped, education of the physically handicapped, elementary, English, foreign languages, industrial arts, mathematics, science, secondary, social science, special, and technical), ENGINEERING AND ENVIRONMENTAL DESIGN (electrical/electronics engineering technology, environmental science, graphic arts technology, manufacturing technology, and mining and petroleum technology), HEALTH PROFESSIONS (medical laboratory technology, nursing, predentistry, premedicine, and speech pathology/audiology), SOCIAL SCIENCE (anthropology, economics, geography, gerontology, history, parks and recreation management, philosophy, physical fitness/movement, political science/government, psychology, social science, social work, sociology, and urban studies).

Required: Students must complete a minimum of 128 semester credits and must maintain a minimum GPA of 2.5 in teacher education curricula, 2.3 in the student's area of concentration, and 2.0 overall.

Special: Cooperative programs are available with Pennsylvania State University and the University of Pittsburgh. Opportunities are provided for internships, study abroad, work-study programs, a B.A.-B.S. degree, a general studies degree, a 3–2 engineering degree, credit by examination, nondegree study, and pass/fail options. There is a freshman honors program on campus.

Faculty/Classroom: 75% of faculty are male; 25%, female. All teach undergraduates.

Admissions: 76% of the 1995–96 applicants were accepted. The SAT I scores for the 1995–96 freshman class were as follows: Verbal—92% below 500, 7% between 500 and 599, and 1% between 600 and 700; Math—83% below 500, 14% between 500 and 599, and 3% between 600 and 700. 15% of the current freshmen were in the top fifth of their class; 41% were in the top two fifths. In a recent year, 18 freshmen graduated first in their class.

Requirements: The SAT I is required, with a minimum composite score of 800 (400 verbal, 400 mathematics); the ACT may be substituted, with a minimum score of 20. The university requires applicants to be in the upper 60% of their class. Graduation from an accredited secondary school is required; a GED will be accepted. Applicants should submit an academic record that includes 4 credits each in English and history, 3 each in mathematics and academic electives, 2 in science, and 1 each in social studies and a foreign language. An essay and an interview are recommended. AP and CLEP credits are accepted. Important factors in the admissions decision are advanced placement or honor courses, evidence of special talent, and leadership record.

Procedure: Freshmen are admitted to all sessions. Entrance exams should be taken during the senior year. There are early decision, early admissions, and deferred admissions plans. Application deadlines are open. Application fee is $25. Notification is sent on a rolling basis. 35 early decision candidates were accepted for the 1995–96 class.

Transfer: 477 transfer students enrolled in a recent year. Applicants must submit official transcripts from all previous colleges attended. If fewer than 30 transferable credits are submitted, applicants must also include a high school transcript and standardized test score. Grades of D are not transferable. 38 credits of 128 must be completed at the university.

Visiting: There are regularly scheduled orientations for prospective students. There are guides for informal visits and visitors may sit in on classes and stay overnight at the school. To schedule a visit, contact the Admissions Office.

Financial Aid: The Pennsylvania State Grant and Federal Financial Aid Application financial statement is required. The application deadline for fall entry is April 1.

International Students: In a recent year, 97 international students were enrolled. The school actively recruits these students. They must take the TOEFL and achieve a minimum score of 450.

Computers: The college provides computer facilities for student use. The mainframe is a DEC VAX 11/780. 350 access points (terminal/PCs) are available for the mainframe. In addition, there are 700 IBM, IBM-compatible, and Apple PCs on campus in various laboratories and offices. All students may access the system. There are no time limits and no fees.

Graduates: In a recent year, 976 bachelor's degrees were awarded. The most popular majors among graduates were early childhood education (12%), elementary education (9%), and accounting (4%). Within an average freshman class, 30% graduate in 4 years, 40% in 5 years, and 30% in 6 years.

Admissions Contact: Norman G. Hasbrouck, Dean for Enrollment Management and Academic Services.

CARLOW COLLEGE
B-3
Pittsburgh, PA 15213
(412) 578-6059; (800) 333-CARLOW

Full-time: 71 men, 870 women	Faculty: 65; IIB, -$
Part-time: 105 men, 1131 women	Ph.D.s: 69%
Graduate: 143 women	Student/Faculty: 14 to 1
Year: semesters, summer session	Tuition: $10,588
Application Deadline: open	Room & Board: $4512
Freshman Class: 475 applied, 377 accepted, 180 enrolled	
SAT I or ACT: required	LESS COMPETITIVE

Carlow College, founded in 1929, is a private, primarily women's college, affiliated with the Roman Catholic Church, offering programs in liberal and fine arts, business, health science, professional training, and teacher preparation. In addition to regional accreditation, Carlow has baccalaureate program accreditation with NLN. The library contains 113,213 volumes, 11,233 microform items, and 6487 audiovisual forms, and subscribes to 451 periodicals. Computerized library sources and services include the card catalog, interlibrary loans, and database searching. Special learning facilities include a learning resource center. The 13-acre campus is in an urban area in the Oakland section of Pittsburgh. Including residence halls, there are 11 buildings on campus.

Student Life: 96% of undergraduates are from Pennsylvania. Students come from 11 states, 27 foreign countries, and Canada. 87% are white; 10% African American. 26% are Catholic; 11% Protestant. The average age of freshmen is 18; all undergraduates, 31. 24% do not continue beyond their first year; 47% remain to graduate.

Housing: 293 students can be accommodated in college housing. College-sponsored living facilities include single-sex dormitories. On-campus housing is guaranteed for all 4 years. 67% of students commute. Alcohol is not permitted. Resident students may keep cars on campus with special permission.

Activities: There are no fraternities or sororities. There are 29 groups on campus, including choir, drama, ethnic, honors, international, newspaper, professional, religious, social, social service, and student

government. Popular campus events include Christmas Concert, Saint Patrick's Day Parade, International Festival, and drama productions.

Sports: There are 3 intercollegiate sports for women and 2 intramural sports for women. Athletic and recreation facilities include a gymnasium, a pool, a weight room, fitness center, and dance room.

Disabled Students: Almsot all the campus is accessible to physically disabled students. The following facilities are available: wheelchair ramps, elevators, special parking, specially equipped rest rooms, special class scheduling, lowered drinking fountains, and lowered telephones.

Services: In addition to many counseling and information services, tutoring is available in writing, study skills, mathematics, and sciences. There is a reader service for the blind, and remedial math, reading, and writing.

Campus Safety and Security: Campus safety and security measures include 24-hour foot and vehicle patrol, self-defense education, escort service, and informal discussions. In addition, there are pamphlets/posters/films, emergency telephones, and lighted pathways/sidewalks.

Programs of Study: Carlow confers B.A., B.S., and B.S.N. degrees. Master's degrees are also awarded. Bachelor's degrees are awarded in BIOLOGICAL SCIENCE (biology/biological science), BUSINESS (accounting and business administration and management), COMMUNICATIONS AND THE ARTS (art, art history and appreciation, communications, creative writing, and English), COMPUTER AND PHYSICAL SCIENCE (computer mathematics, information sciences and systems, and mathematics), EDUCATION (art, early childhood, elementary, and special), HEALTH PROFESSIONS (health science and nursing), SOCIAL SCIENCE (history, liberal arts/general studies, philosophy, psychology, social studies, social work, sociology, and theological studies). Nursing and biology are the strongest academically. Nursing and business management have the largest enrollments.

Required: A total of 120 credit hours (125 for nursing students), including 27 to 44 in the major, and a 2.0 GPA are required to graduate. Credits must be earned in history, literature, art, music or drama, mathematics or logic, philosophy, anthropology, psychology or sociology, biology, chemistry or physics, and women's studies.

Special: Carlow offers cross-registration, internships, study abroad, work-study programs, accelerated degree programs, dual majors, interdisciplinary majors, including communication/business management, English/business management, medical marketing, and sociology and anthropology, student-designed majors, a weekend college, and nondegree study. Students may elect pass/fail options and receive credit for life, military, or work experience. There is a freshman honors program on campus, as well as 3 national honor societies.

Faculty/Classroom: 28% of faculty are male; 72%, female. No introductory courses are taught by graduate students. The average class size in an introductory lecture is 20; in a laboratory, 20; and in a regular course offering, 15.

Admissions: 79% of the 1995–96 applicants were accepted.

Requirements: The SAT I or ACT is required; minimum scores depend on the major selected. Carlow requires applicants to be in the upper 40% of their class. Candidates must be graduates of an accredited secondary school. 18 Carnegie units are required, including 4 each in English and arts/humanities, 3 each in mathematics and science, and 4 in electives. Applicants for nursing must have completed 4 units in English, 3 in social studies, and 2 each in mathematics (including algebra) and a laboratory science, as required by the State Board of Nursing. The GED is accepted. An essay is required and an interview is recommended. Art majors must have a portfolio. AP and CLEP credits are accepted. Important factors in the admissions decision are advanced placement or honor courses, leadership record, and personality/intangible qualities.

Procedure: Freshmen are admitted fall and spring. Entrance exams should be taken early in the senior year. There are early admissions and deferred admissions plans. Application deadlines are open. Application fee is $20. Notification is on a rolling basis.

Transfer: 430 transfer students enrolled in 1995–96. Applicants must have a minimum GPA of 2.0 and submit high school and college transcripts. Minimum SAT I and ACT scores depend on the major. The minimum credit hours required are 3, but 12 are recommended for scholarship consideration. An interview is also recommended. 32 credits of 120 must be completed at Carlow.

Visiting: There are regularly scheduled orientations for prospective students. There are guides for informal visits and visitors may sit in on classes and stay overnight at the school. To schedule a visit, contact the Admissions Office.

Financial Aid: In 1995–96, 85% of all freshmen and 89% of continuing students received some form of financial aid. 74% of freshmen and 78% of continuing students received need-based aid. The average freshman award was $9570. Of that total, scholarships or need-based grants averaged $6100 ($10,268 maximum); loans averaged $3000 ($6625 maximum); work contracts averaged $710 ($800 maximum); and tuition discounts and benefits averaged $3522 ($9540 maximum). 30% of undergraduate students work part-time. Average earnings from campus work for the school year are $630. Carlow is a member of CSS. The FAFSA, the college's own financial statement, tax returns, and financial aid transcripts are required. The application deadline for fall entry is May 1.

International Students: There are currently 28 international students enrolled. The school actively recruits these students. They must take the TOEFL and achieve a minimum score of 500.

Computers: The college provides computer facilities for student use. There are 40 computer terminals/PCs available on campus for student use in computer laboratories in the library and the residence halls. All students may access the system There are no time limits. The fee is $50.

Graduates: In 1994–95, 301 bachelor's degrees were awarded. The most popular majors among graduates were nursing (49%), business management (10%), and communication/business management (9%). Within an average freshman class, 36% graduate in 4 years, 37% in 5 years, and 40% in 6 years. 5 companies recruited on campus in 1994–95.

Admissions Contact: Carol Descak, Director of Admissions.

CARNEGIE MELLON UNIVERSITY   B-3

Pittsburgh, PA 15213   (412) 268–2082; FAX: (412) 268–7838

Full-time: 3049 men, 1417 women	Faculty: 547; I, +$
Part-time: 72 men, 34 women	Ph.D.s: 96%
Graduate: 1837 men, 774 women	Student/Faculty: 8 to 1
Year: semesters, summer session	Tuition: $18,700
Application Deadline: February 1	Room & Board: $5890
Freshman Class: 10,291 applied, 5608 accepted, 1237 enrolled	
SAT I: required	HIGHLY COMPETITIVE +

Carnegie Mellon University, established in 1900, is a private, coeducational nonsectarian institution offering undergraduate programs in liberal arts and science and professional technology. There are 6 undergraduate and 8 graduate schools. In addition to regional accreditation, Carnegie Mellon has baccalaureate program accreditation with AACSB, ABET, NAAB, NASAD, and NASM. The 3 libraries contain 852,241 volumes, 756,985 microform items, and 21,340 audiovisual forms, and subscribe to 3889 periodicals. Computerized library sources and services include the card catalog, interlibrary loans, and database searching. Special learning facilities include a learning resource center, art gallery, and radio station. The 103-acre campus is in a suburban area 4 miles from Pittsburgh. Including residence halls, there are 59 buildings on campus.

Student Life: 74% of undergraduates are from out-of-state, mostly the Middle Atlantic. Students come from 50 states, 45 foreign countries, and Canada. 70% are from public schools; 30% from private. 50% are white; 15% Asian American. The average age of freshmen is 18; all undergraduates, 20. 10% do not continue beyond their first year; 71% remain to graduate.

Housing: 3367 students can be accommodated in college housing. College-sponsored living facilities include single-sex and coed dormitories, on-campus apartments, off-campus apartments, fraternity houses, and sorority houses. In addition there are honors houses, language houses, and special interest houses. On-campus housing is guaranteed for all 4 years. 70% of students live on campus; of those, 90% remain on campus on weekends. Alcohol is not permitted. All students may keep cars on campus.

Activities: 25% of men belong to 14 national fraternities; 14% of women belong to 5 national sororities. There are more than 120 groups on campus, including art, bagpipe band, band, cheerleading, chess, choir, chorale, chorus, computers, drama, ethnic, gay, honors, international, jazz band, literary magazine, marching band, musical theater, newspaper, orchestra, pep band, political, professional, radio and TV, religious, social, social service, student government, symphony, and yearbook. Popular campus events include Spring Carnival, Homecoming, and International Festival.

Sports: There are 9 intercollegiate sports for men and 8 for women, and 22 intramural sports for men and 16 for women. Athletic and recreation facilities include a gymnasium, a stadium, athletic fields, tennis courts, and a pool.

Disabled Students: 98% of the campus is accessible to disabled students. The following facilities are available: wheelchair ramps, elevators, special parking, specially equipped rest rooms, special class scheduling, lowered drinking fountains, and lowered telephones.

Services: In addition to many counseling and information services, tutoring is available in most subjects. There is a reader service for the blind.

Campus Safety and Security: Campus safety and security measures include 24-hour foot and vehicle patrol, escort service, shuttle buses, and informal discussions. In addition, there are pamphlets/posters/films, emergency telephones, lighted pathways/sidewalks, and a SafeWalk Program.

Programs of Study: Carnegie Mellon confers B.A., B.S., B.A.H., B.Arch., and B.F.A. degrees. Master's and doctoral degrees are also awarded. Bachelor's degrees are awarded in BIOLOGICAL SCIENCE (biology/biological science), BUSINESS (business administration and management, business economics, and marketing/retailing/merchandising), COMMUNICATIONS AND THE ARTS (communications, design, dramatic arts, English, fine arts, French, German, journalism, languages, music, and Spanish), COMPUTER AND PHYSICAL SCIENCE (chemistry, computer programming, computer science, information sciences and systems, mathematics, physics, and statistics), EDUCATION (music), ENGINEERING AND ENVIRONMENTAL DESIGN (chemical engineering, civil engineering, computer engineering, electrical/electronics engineering, engineering, and mechanical engineering), SOCIAL SCIENCE (economics, history, philosophy, political science/government, psychology, public administration, social science, and urban studies). Electrical and computer engineering are the strongest programs academically and have the largest enrollments.

Required: To graduate, students must complete requirements in English, history, and computing skills, and they must have a GPA of 2.0. Distribution requirements, the number of credits needed to graduate, and the number of credits required in the major vary by college.

Special: Students may cross-register with other Pittsburgh Council of Higher Education institutions. Also available are internships, work-study programs, study abroad in Switzerland and Japan, a Washington semester, accelerated degrees, B.A.-B.S. degrees, co-op programs in metallurgical engineering and materials science, dual majors in biomedical engineering/engineering and public policy and in European study/foreign languages, and limited student-designed majors. There is a freshman honors program on campus, as well as 10 national honor societies.

Faculty/Classroom: 84% of faculty are male; 16%, female. All both teach and do research. Graduate students teach 34% of introductory courses. The average class size in an introductory lecture is 80; in a laboratory, 19; and in a regular course offering, 21.

Admissions: 54% of the 1995–96 applicants were accepted. 78% of the current freshmen were in the top fifth of their class; 95% were in the top two fifths.

Requirements: The SAT I is required. SAT II: Subject tests in writing and mathematics are required for all applicants. Engineering applicants must take the chemistry or physics test. Science applicants may take either of these or the biology test. Business and liberal arts applicants must take a third test of their choice. Applicants must graduate from an accredited secondary school or have a GED. They must earn 16 Carnegie units. All applicants must have completed 4 years of English. Applicants to the Carnegie Institute of Technology and the Mellon College of Science must take 4 years of mathematics and 1 year each of biology, chemistry, and physics. Essays are required, and interviews are recommended. Art and design applicants must submit a portfolio. Drama and music applicants must audition. AP credits are accepted. Important factors in the admissions decision are advanced placement or honor courses, leadership record, and evidence of special talent.

Procedure: Freshmen are admitted in the fall. Entrance exams should be taken by February 1. There are early decision, early admissions, and deferred admissions plans. Early decision applications should be filed by December 1; regular applications, by February 1 for fall entry, along with an application fee of $50. Notification of early decision is sent January 15; regular decision, April 15. 181 early decision candidates were accepted for a recent class. A waiting list is an active part of the admissions procedure, with about 10% of all applicants on the list.

Transfer: 69 transfer students enrolled in 1995–96. Applicants must have a minimum GPA of 3.3 in all previous college-level work. One academic year must be completed at Carnegie Mellon.

Visiting: There are regularly scheduled orientations for prospective students, including Saturday group sessions in September, October, November, and April. There are guides for informal visits and visitors may sit in on classes and stay overnight at the school. To schedule a visit, contact the Admissions Office.

Financial Aid: In 1995–96, 74% of all freshmen and 73% of continuing students received some form of financial aid. 59% of freshmen and 56% of continuing students received need-based aid. Scholarships or need-based grants averaged $11,260; loans averaged $5298; and work contracts averaged $1400. 70% of undergraduate students work part-time. Average earnings from campus work for the school year are $1450. The average financial indebtedness of the 1994–95 graduate was $14,000. Carnegie Mellon is a member of CSS. The FAF or FAFSA, the college's own financial statement and the parent and student federal tax returns and W-2 forms are required. The application deadline for fall entry is February 15.

International Students: In a recent year, 416 international students were enrolled. The school actively recruits these students. They must take the TOEFL or the MELAB and achieve a minimum score on the TOEFL of 600. The student must also take the SAT I or the ACT. Students must take SAT II Subject Tests in writing and mathematics level I or II..

Computers: The college provides computer facilities for student use. The mainframes are a DEC VAX 6320, 6330, and 11/780 models and a Sun 3280. The campuswide computer network extends to every office and dormitory room, connecting hundreds of personal computers and advanced workstations. All students may access the system 24 hours per day. There are no time limits and no fees.

Graduates: In 1994–95, 956 bachelor's degrees were awarded. The most popular majors among graduates were electrical and computer engineering (13%), industrial management (12%), and computer science (9%). Within an average freshman class, 56% graduate in 4 years, 70% in 5 years, and 71% in 6 years.

Admissions Contact: Michael Steidel, Director of Admissions. E-mail: undergraduate-admissions+@andrew.cmu.edu. A campus video is available.

CEDAR CREST COLLEGE

E-3

Allentown, PA 18104-6196	(610) 740-3780; (800) 360-1222
Full-time: 21 men, 814 women	Faculty: 65; IIB, -$
Part-time: 75 men, 693 women	Ph.D.s: 76%
Graduate: none	Student/Faculty: 13 to 1
Year: semesters, summer session	Tuition: $14,770
Application Deadline: open	Room & Board: $5365
Freshman Class: 788 applied, 692 accepted, 170 enrolled	
SAT I Verbal/Math: 490/500	COMPETITIVE

Cedar Crest College, founded in 1867, is a private, primarily women's liberal arts college affiliated with the United Church of Christ. In addition to regional accreditation, Cedar Crest has baccalaureate program accreditation with CAHEA, CSWE, and NLN. The library contains 124,331 volumes, 9503 microform items, and 13,386 audiovisual forms, and subscribes to 507 periodicals. Computerized library sources and services include the card catalog, interlibrary loans, and database searching. Special learning facilities include a learning resource center, art gallery, an arboretum, and a theater. The 84-acre campus is in a suburban area 55 miles north of Philadelphia and 90 miles west of New York City. Including residence halls, there are 15 buildings on campus.

Student Life: 83% of undergraduates are from Pennsylvania. Students come from 23 states, 20 foreign countries, and Canada. 88% are from public schools; 12% from private. 93% are white. 62% claim no religious affiliation; 16% Catholic. The average age of freshmen is 18; all undergraduates, 24. 18% do not continue beyond their first year; 63% remain to graduate.

Housing: 500 students can be accommodated in college housing. College-sponsored living facilities include single-sex dormitories. On-campus housing is available on a first-come, first-served basis and is available on a lottery system for upperclassmen. Priority is given to out-of-town students. 85% of students live on campus; of those, 70% remain on campus on weekends. All students may keep cars on campus.

Activities: There are no fraternities or sororities. There are 46 groups on campus, including art, choir, chorus, computers, dance, drama, ethnic, honors, international, literary magazine, musical theater, newspaper, political, professional, religious, social, social service, student government, and yearbook. Popular campus events include Song Contest, Junior Ring Ceremony, Student Faculty Frolic, and Midnight Breakfast.

Sports: There are 6 intercollegiate sports for women and 6 intramural sports for women. Athletic and recreation facilities include 5 tennis courts, field hockey and lacrosse fields, a cross-country course, a gymnasium with basketball, volleyball, and badminton courts, dance and aerobics studios, and weight and training rooms.

Disabled Students: 35% of the campus is accessible to disabled students. The following facilities are available: wheelchair ramps, elevators, special parking, specially equipped rest rooms, special class scheduling, and lowered telephones.

Services: In addition to many counseling and information services, tutoring is available in every subject. The Academic Support Center is available to all students and coordinates individual and group tutoring. There is remedial math and writing and a skills program for underprepared students.

Campus Safety and Security: Campus safety and security measures include 24-hour foot and vehicle patrol, self-defense education, escort service, and informal discussions. In addition, there are pamphlets/posters/films, emergency telephones, and lighted pathways/sidewalks. Residence halls are equipped with fire/intrusion alarms, which are monitored 24 hours a day. A keyless access system is in place; exterior doors are locked 24 hours a day.

Programs of Study: Cedar Crest confers B.A. and B.S degrees. Bachelor's degrees are awarded in BIOLOGICAL SCIENCE (biochemistry, biology/biological science, and genetics), BUSINESS (accounting and business administration and management), COMMUNICATIONS AND THE ARTS (art, communications, comparative

literature, dramatic arts, English, fine arts, French, languages, music, and Spanish), COMPUTER AND PHYSICAL SCIENCE (chemistry, computer science, and mathematics), EDUCATION (elementary, science, and secondary), ENGINEERING AND ENVIRONMENTAL DESIGN (bioengineering), HEALTH PROFESSIONS (medical laboratory technology, nuclear medical technology, and nursing), SOCIAL SCIENCE (history, international studies, philosophy, political science/government, psychology, social work, and sociology). Genetic engineering, nursing, psychology, and sciences are the strongest academically. Sciences, nursing, psychology, and business have the largest enrollments.

Required: To graduate, students must complete 120 credit hours (125 for nursing) with a minimum GPA of 2.0 (some majors have higher requirements). Distribution requirements include 53 credits in 8 departments, including English composition, junior seminar, foreign language, science literacy, humanities, aesthetic views and appreciation, historical and societal perspectives, and quantitative reasoning.

Special: Cross-registration is available with Lehigh Valley Association of Independent Colleges. Also available are internships, a Washington semester with American University, work-study programs, and B.A.-B.S. degrees in mathematics, biology, and psychology. Dual majors, student-designed majors, 3–2 engineering degrees with Georgia Institute of Technology and Lehigh University, pass/fail options, and credit for life, military, and work experience are offered. There is a freshman honors program on campus, as well as 13 national honor societies. 2 departments have honors programs.

Faculty/Classroom: 41% of faculty are male; 59%, female. All teach undergraduates. The average class size in an introductory lecture is 42; in a laboratory, 16; and in a regular course offering, 16.

Admissions: 88% of the 1995–96 applicants were accepted. The SAT I scores for the 1995–96 freshman class were as follows: Verbal—58% below 500, 23% between 500 and 599, 17% between 600 and 700, and 2% above 700; Math—50% below 500, 30% between 500 and 599, 18% between 600 and 700, and 2% above 700. 40% of the current freshmen were in the top fifth of their class; 70% were in the top two fifths. One freshman graduated first in their class.

Requirements: The SAT I or ACT is required. Cedar Crest requires that applicants are in the upper 50% of their class and carry a minimum GPA of 2.0. Applicants must be graduates of an accredited secondary school, but the GED is accepted. Students should have completed 16 high school academic credits, including 4 years of English, 3 of mathematics, 2 each of science, history, and foreign language, and 1 each of art, music, and social studies. An essay and an interview are required. A portfolio is recommended for art students and an audition for music students. AP and CLEP credits are accepted. Important factors in the admissions decision are advanced placement or honor courses, leadership record, and evidence of special talent.

Procedure: Freshmen are admitted fall and spring. Entrance exams should be taken in the junior year or early senior year. There are early admissions and deferred admissions plans. Application deadlines are open. Application fee is $30. Notification is sent on a rolling basis.

Transfer: 69 transfer students enrolled in 1995–96. Applicants for transfer should have a minimum GPA of 2.0. An interview is required. 30 credits of 120 must be completed at Cedar Crest.

Visiting: There are regularly scheduled orientations for prospective students. There are guides for informal visits and visitors may sit in on classes and stay overnight at the school. To schedule a visit, contact the Admissions Office.

Financial Aid: In 1995–96, 94% of all freshmen and 93% of continuing students received some form of financial aid. 92% of freshmen and 89% of continuing students received need-based aid. The average freshman award was $13,255. Of that total, scholarships or need-based grants averaged $8709 ($15,500 maximum); loans averaged $3246 ($5125 maximum); and work contracts averaged $1300 (maximum). 50% of undergraduate students work part-time. Average earnings from campus work for the school year are $1100. The average financial indebtedness of the 1994–95 graduate was $12,851. Cedar Crest is a member of CSS. The FAF or FAFSA and the college's own financial statement are required.

International Students: There are currently 34 international students enrolled. The school actively recruits these students. They must take the TOEFL and achieve a minimum score of 500. The student must also take the SAT I or the ACT.

Computers: The college provides computer facilities for student use. A total of 100 microcomputers are available in 5 computer laboratories and 4 residence hall laboratories. The network provides a variety of word processing, spreadsheet, and database applications, and high-speed, full Internet access. Stand-alone computers are also provided, and remote, dial-up access to the network is available. All students may access the system. There are no time limits and no fees.

Graduates: In 1994–95, 208 bachelor's degrees were awarded. The most popular majors among graduates were nursing (29%), psychology (14%), and business administration (12%). Within an average freshman class, 1% graduate in 3 years and 63% in 4 years. 12 companies recruited on campus in 1994–95.

Admissions Contact: Judith Neyhart, Director of Admissions and Financial Aid. A campus video is available.

CHATHAM COLLEGE

B-3

Pittsburgh, PA 15232	(412) 365-1290; (800) 837-1290
Full-time: 467 women	Faculty: 45; IIB, -$
Part-time: 76 women	Ph.Ds: 93%
Graduate: 38 men, 144 women	Student/Faculty: 10 to 1
Year: 4-1-4, summer session	Tuition: $14,196
Application Deadline: open	Room & Board: $5440
Freshman Class: 320 applied, 258 accepted, 110 enrolled	
SAT I Verbal/Math: 470/470	ACT: 25 COMPETITIVE

Chatham College, founded in 1869, is a private women's college offering undergraduate degree programs in more than 30 liberal arts and preprofessional majors. Graduate degree programs in health sciences and education are coeducational. The library contains 130,000 volumes, 500 microform items, and 4300 audiovisual forms, and subscribes to 600 periodicals. Computerized library sources and services include interlibrary loans and database searching. Special learning facilities include a learning resource center, art gallery, radio station, 285-seat theater, and a media center. The 34-acre campus is in an urban area 8 miles east of downtown Pittsburgh. Including residence halls, there are 30 buildings on campus.

Student Life: 83% of undergraduates are from Pennsylvania. Students come from 19 states and 5 foreign countries. 82% are from public schools; 18% from private. 84% are white; 10% African American. The average age of freshmen is 18; all undergraduates, 21. 27% do not continue beyond their first year; 51% remain to graduate.

Housing: 340 students can be accommodated in college housing. College-sponsored living facilities include dormitories and on-campus apartments. In addition there are special interest houses, a residence hall for adult students, and an intercultural residence hall. On-campus housing is guaranteed for all 4 years. 85% of students live on campus; of those, 75% remain on campus on weekends. Alcohol is not permitted. Upperclassmen may keep cars on campus.

Activities: There are no fraternities or sororities. There are 32 groups on campus, including choir, computers, dance, drama, ethnic, film, gay, honors, international, literary magazine, musical theater, newspaper, photography, political, professional, radio and TV, religious, social service, student government, and yearbook. Popular campus events include Fall Festival, Spring Fling, Candlelight Holiday Concert, and Senior Faculty Dinner.

Sports: There are 5 intercollegiate sports and 11 intramural sports for women. Athletic and recreation facilities include a swimming pool, tennis and platform tennis courts, a gymnasium, a dance studio, an athletic field, bowling alleys, free weights, a cardiovascular room, and a Cybex system.

Disabled Students: 75% of the campus is accessible to disabled students. The following facilities are available: wheelchair ramps, elevators, special parking, specially equipped rest rooms, and special class scheduling.

Services: In addition to many counseling and information services, there is student peer tutoring and organized study groups.

Campus Safety and Security: Campus safety and security measures include 24-hour foot and vehicle patrol, self-defense education, escort service, and shuttle buses. In addition, there are informal discussions, pamphlets/posters/films, emergency telephones, and lighted pathways/sidewalks.

Programs of Study: Chatham confers B.A. and B.S. degrees. Master's degrees are also awarded. Bachelor's degrees are awarded in BIOLOGICAL SCIENCE (biochemistry and biology/biological science), BUSINESS (accounting, international business management, and management science), COMMUNICATIONS AND THE ARTS (art history and appreciation, arts administration/management, communications, English, French, media arts, music, Spanish, and visual and performing arts), COMPUTER AND PHYSICAL SCIENCE (chemistry and mathematics), ENGINEERING AND ENVIRONMENTAL DESIGN (environmental science), SOCIAL SCIENCE (cognitive science, criminal justice, economics, European studies, history, human services, international studies, philosophy, political science/government, psychobiology, psychology, religion, and women's studies). Economics, management, English, information science, psychology, and communications are the strongest academically. Communications, education, psychology, economics, and management have the largest enrollments.

Required: For graduation, students must complete 120 credit hours, including a general education curriculum of 7 courses and a senior tutorial. A minimum GPA of 2.0 is required for graduation. Writing and language skills, mathematical skills, computer literacy, and reading and vocabulary skills are required proficiencies.

Special: Chatham offers a study-abroad program in 3 countries for juniors, cross-registration with other Pittsburgh Council on Higher Education institutions, internships in the public and private sectors, and a Washington semester in conjunction with American University and the Public Leadership Education Network. Accelerated degree programs, work-study, combined B.A.-B.S. degrees, a multidisciplinary major in global policy studies, and dual and student-designed majors are possible. Chatham students may complete a 3-2 engineering program with one of 3 partner institutions, gain early admission to the Medical College of Pennsylvania, or combine teacher certification with a master's degree from Carnegie Mellon University. There are 3 national honor societies on campus, including Phi Beta Kappa.

Faculty/Classroom: 41% of faculty are male; 59%, female. All both teach and do research. No introductory courses are taught by graduate students. The average class size in an introductory lecture is 15; in a laboratory, 18; and in a regular course offering, 14.

Admissions: 81% of the 1995-96 applicants were accepted. The SAT I scores for the 1995-96 freshman class were as follows: Verbal—61% below 500, 27% between 500 and 599, and 12% between 600 and 700; Math—60% below 500, 27% between 500 and 599, and 13% between 600 and 700. The ACT scores were 18% below 21, 14% between 21 and 23, 45% between 24 and 26, 13% between 27 and 28, and 10% above 28. 40% of the current freshmen were in the top fifth of their class; 70% were in the top two fifths.

Requirements: The SAT I or ACT is recommended. Chatham requires applicants to be in the upper 50% of their class. A minimum GPA of 2.5 is required. Applicants must be graduates of an accredited secondary school or have earned the GED. Students should have completed 4 years of high school English and 2 years each of mathematics, science, and social studies. A foreign language, an essay, and an interview are recommended. Applications are accepted on computer disk and on-line through CollegeLink. AP and CLEP credits are accepted. Important factors in the admissions decision are leadership record, advanced placement or honor courses, and extracurricular activities record.

Procedure: Freshmen are admitted fall, winter, and spring. Entrance exams should be taken by fall of the senior year. There are early admissions and deferred admissions plans. Application deadlines are open. Application fee is $25. Notification is sent on a rolling basis.

Transfer: 45 transfer students enrolled in 1995-96. Applicants must present high school and college transcripts and 3 recommendations. The SAT I or ACT and an interview are required. 45 credits of 120 must be completed at Chatham.

Visiting: There are regularly scheduled orientations for prospective students. There are guides for informal visits and visitors may sit in on classes and stay overnight at the school. To schedule a visit, contact the Admissions Office.

Financial Aid: In 1995-96, 96% of all freshmen and 80% of continuing students received some form of financial aid. 86% of freshmen and 69% of continuing students received need-based aid. The average freshman award was $13,822. Of that total, scholarships or need-based grants averaged $9033 ($15,772 maximum); loans averaged $3410 ($7125 maximum); and work contracts averaged $1791 ($1800 maximum). 65% of undergraduate students work part-time. Average earnings from campus work for the school year are $1800. The average financial indebtedness of the 1994-95 graduate was $18,940. Chatham is a member of CSS. The FAFSA and the college's own financial statement are required. The application deadline for fall entry is May 1.

International Students: There are currently 23 international students enrolled. The school actively recruits these students. They must take the TOEFL or the MELAB and achieve a minimum score on the TOEFL of 450.

Computers: The college provides computer facilities for student use. The mainframe is a DEC VAX Model 3100/80 minicomputer. There are also 40 IBM PC and 30 Apple Macintosh microcomputers available in the student computer cluster, communication department cluster, and service clusters. The PCs are connected to the campuswide Microsoft NT based network. The campus network also reaches all campus residence hall rooms. All students may access the system 24 hours via modem or residential network connects or 85 hours per week during normal operating hours of the main student computer cluster. There are no time limits and no fees.

Graduates: In 1994-95, 110 bachelor's degrees were awarded. The most popular majors among graduates were psychology (23%), English (17%), and communications (12%). Within an average freshman class, 46% graduate in 4 years, 51% in 5 years, and 53% in 6 years. 10 companies recruited on campus in 1994-95.

Admissions Contact: Suellen Ofe, Dean of Admissions and Financial Aid.

CHESTNUT HILL COLLEGE

F-3

Philadelphia, PA 19118-2695   (215) 248-7001; (800) 248-0052

Full-time: 421 women	Faculty: 66; IIB, --$
Part-time: 19 men, 225 women	Ph.D.s: 68%
Graduate: 81 men, 451 women	Student/Faculty: 6 to 1
Year: semesters, summer session	Tuition: $11,825
Application Deadline: March 15	Room & Board: $5445
Freshman Class: 244 applied, 182 accepted, 77 enrolled	
SAT I Verbal/Math: 477/465	**COMPETITIVE**

Chestnut Hill College, founded in 1924, is a private, liberal arts, primarily women's institution, affiliated with the Roman Catholic Church. Men may matriculate through the accelerated evening and weekend undergraduate program and the graduate division. There is one undergraduate and one graduate school. The library contains 139,484 volumes, 111,258 microform items, and 2113 audiovisual forms, and subscribes to 538 periodicals. Computerized library sources and services include the card catalog, interlibrary loans, and database searching. Special learning facilities include a learning resource center, planetarium, a rotating observatory, and a technology center. The 45-acre campus is in a suburban area 25 miles northwest of downtown Philadelphia. Including residence halls, there are 13 buildings on campus.

Student Life: 80% of undergraduates are from Pennsylvania. Students come from 16 states and 8 foreign countries. 47% are from public schools; 53% from private. 73% are white; 13% African American. 59% are Catholic; 26% claim no religious affiliation; 11% Protestant. The average age of freshmen is 18; all undergraduates, 20. 17% do not continue beyond their first year; 61% remain to graduate.

Housing: 400 students can be accommodated in college housing. College-sponsored living facilities include single-sex dormitories. On-campus housing is guaranteed for all 4 years. 66% of students live on campus; of those, 60% remain on campus on weekends. Alcohol is not permitted. All students may keep cars on campus.

Activities: There are no sororities. There are 34 groups on campus, including art, chorale, chorus, drama, ethnic, honors, international, jazz band, literary magazine, newspaper, opera, orchestra, political, professional, religious, social, social service, student government, and yearbook. Popular campus events include Opening and Honors convocations, International Gourmet Day, Road Rally, and Christmas Formal.

Sports: There are 6 intercollegiate sports and 6 intramural sports. Athletic and recreation facilities include a gymnasium, 8 tennis courts, an indoor pool, neighboring stables and golf course, an archery range, a weight and fitness center, and softball, lacrosse, and hockey fields.

Disabled Students: 90% of the campus is accessible to disabled students. The following facilities are available: wheelchair ramps, elevators, special parking, specially equipped rest rooms, and a shower area in residence halls.

Services: In addition to many counseling and information services, tutoring is available in most subjects. There is remedial math and writing.

Campus Safety and Security: Campus safety and security measures include 24-hour foot and vehicle patrol, self-defense education, informal discussions, and pamphlets/posters/films. There are lighted pathways/sidewalks. Doors are locked after 6 P.M. and on weekends and are monitored by cameras. Escorted shuttle carts to parking lots are available in the evenings.

Programs of Study: The college confers B.A. and B.S. degrees. Associate and master's degrees are also awarded. Bachelor's degrees are awarded in BIOLOGICAL SCIENCE (biochemistry, biology/biological science, and molecular biology), BUSINESS (accounting, business administration and management, management science, and marketing/retailing/merchandising), COMMUNICATIONS AND THE ARTS (art history and appreciation, communications technology, English, French, German, music, Spanish, and studio art), COMPUTER AND PHYSICAL SCIENCE (chemistry, computer science, and mathematics), EDUCATION (early childhood, elementary, and music), ENGINEERING AND ENVIRONMENTAL DESIGN (environmental science), SOCIAL SCIENCE (economics, history, political science/government, psychology, and sociology). Biological/computer/physical sciences, humanities, and social sciences are the strongest academically. Education, biological sciences, and psychology have the largest enrollments.

Required: To graduate, students must complete 120 credit hours, including 30 to 45 in the major, with a GPA of 2.0 overall and in the major. Among the course requirements are 21 hours in the humanities, 11 in the natural and laboratory sciences, 9 in social sciences, 6 in religious studies, 6 beyond elementary level in foreign language, 3 in writing, and a senior seminar. All students must complete a senior research paper prepared on a computer and defend it orally. Physical education and a first-year college experience seminar are required. All students must pass a swimming test.

Special: Cross-registration is available with LaSalle University and at the 10 colleges in the Sisters of St. Joseph College Consortium Student Exchange Program. The college offers internships, study abroad in England, Spain, Italy, and Austria, work-study programs, accelerated degree programs, interdisciplinary majors, including communications and technology and fine arts and technology, and dual and student-designed majors. Up to 6 credits may be given for life experience. Nondegree study and pass/fail options are available. The school offers unique career preparation programs in communications, international studies, and women in management. There is a freshman honors program on campus, as well as 4 national honor societies. All departments have honors programs.

Faculty/Classroom: 24% of faculty are male; 76%, female. All teach undergraduates and 8% both teach and do research. No introductory courses are taught by graduate students. The average class size in an introductory lecture is 15; in a laboratory, 17; and in a regular course offering, 11.

Admissions: 75% of the 1995-96 applicants were accepted. The SAT I scores for the 1995-96 freshman class were as follows: Verbal—59% below 500, 31% between 500 and 599, 8% between 600 and 700, and 2% above 700; Math—58% below 500, 25% between 500 and 599, 16% between 600 and 700, and 1% above 700. 44% of the current freshmen were in the top fifth of their class; 78% were in the top two fifths. One freshman graduated first in her class.

Requirements: The SAT I or ACT is required, with a score on the SAT I of 900 to 1000 (recentered). Applicants must be graduates of an accredited secondary school with a 2.5 GPA and have been in the upper 40% of their class. 16 Carnegie units are required, with a recommended 4 units each of English, mathematics, science, and social studies, and 3 of foreign language. An interview is recommended for all students, an audition is required for music students, and a portfolio is recommended for art studio majors. An essay is required. AP and CLEP credits are accepted. Important factors in the admissions decision are personality/intangible qualities, recommendations by alumni, and evidence of special talent.

Procedure: Freshmen are admitted fall and spring. Entrance exams should be taken early in the senior year. There are early admissions and deferred admissions plans. Applications should be filed by March 15 for fall entry, along with an application fee of $35. Notification is sent on a rolling basis.

Transfer: 18 transfer students enrolled in 1995-96. Applicants must have a minimum GPA of 2.0; a 2.5 is recommended. 60 credits of 120 must be completed at the college.

Visiting: There are regularly scheduled orientations for prospective students, including faculty presentations and workshops on specific issues. There are guides for informal visits and visitors may sit in on classes and stay overnight at the school. To schedule a visit, contact the Director of Admissions.

Financial Aid: In a recent year, 65% of all freshmen and 68% of continuing students received some form of financial aid. 65% of freshmen and 68% of continuing students received need-based aid. The average freshman award was $4000. Of that total, scholarships or need-based grants averaged $2100; college grants averaged $100 ($400 maximum); loans averaged $1250 ($2625 maximum); and work contracts averaged $700. 25% of undergraduate students work part-time. Average earnings from campus work for the school year are $700. The average financial indebtedness of a recent graduate was $6000. The college is a member of CSS. The college's own financial statement and PHEAA are required. The application deadline for fall entry is March 15.

International Students: There are currently 13 international students enrolled. The school actively recruits these students. They must score 550 on the TOEFL.

Computers: The college provides computer facilities for student use. Students use Apple, Macintosh, and IBM PCs in the multimedia technology center, other computer laboratories, and dormitories. All students may access the system. Published schedules of operating times regulate reservations. There are no fees.

Graduates: In 1994-95, 123 bachelor's degrees were awarded. The most popular majors among graduates were early childhood education (16%), biology (11%), and elementary education (11%). Within an average freshman class, 56% graduate in 4 years, 61% in 5 years, and 64% in 6 years. 40 companies recruited on campus in 1994-95. Of the 1994 graduating class, 15% were enrolled in graduate school within 6 months of graduation and 30% had found employment.

Admissions Contact: Sr. Margaret Anne Birtwistle, SSJ, Director of Admissions. A campus video is available.

CHEYNEY UNIVERSITY OF PENNSYLVANIA   F-4

Cheyney, PA 19319   (610) 399-2275
(800) 223-3608; FAX: (610) 399-2099

Full-time: 526 men, 509 women	Faculty: 88; IIA, +$
Part-time: 19 men, 34 women	Ph.D.s: 69%
Graduate: 111 men, 187 women	Student/Faculty: 12 to 1
Year: semesters, summer session	Tuition: $3729 ($8683)
Application Deadline: May 30	Room & Board: $4040
Freshman Class: 1039 applied, 732 accepted, 258 enrolled	
SAT I or ACT: required	COMPETITIVE

Cheyney University of Pennsylvania, founded in 1837, is a public, co-educational liberal arts institution offering programs in art, business, engineering, music, and teacher preparation. There are 2 undergraduate schools and 1 graduate school. In addition to regional accreditation, Cheyney has baccalaureate program accreditation with NCATE. The library contains 237,780 volumes, 517,955 microform items, and 3573 audiovisual forms, and subscribes to 655 periodicals. Computerized library sources and services include the card catalog. Special learning facilities include a planetarium, radio station, TV station, weather station, world cultures center, and theater arts center. The 275-acre campus is in a suburban area 24 miles west of Philadelphia. Including residence halls, there are 33 buildings on campus.

Student Life: 79% of undergraduates are from Pennsylvania. Students come from 17 states and 7 foreign countries. 85% are from public schools; 15% from private. 97% are African American. The average age of freshmen is 20; all undergraduates, 21.

Housing: 1300 students can be accommodated in college housing. College-sponsored living facilities include single-sex dormitories. On-campus housing is available on a first-come, first-served basis. 65% of students live on campus. Alcohol is not permitted. All students may keep cars on campus.

Activities: 6% of men belong to 4 national fraternities; 6% of women belong to 4 national sororities. There are 47 groups on campus, including art, cheerleading, chess, choir, computers, drama, ethnic, honors, international, newspaper, political, professional, radio and TV, religious, social, social service, student government, and yearbook. Popular campus events include Founders Day Ball, Wade Wilson Football Classic, and Black College Convention.

Sports: There are 7 intercollegiate sports for men and 5 for women, and 10 intramural sports for men and 10 for women. Athletic and recreation facilities include a track, tennis courts, outdoor and indoor basketball courts, a pool, a men's gymnasium, a women's gymnasium, a weight room, and a field house.

Disabled Students: 86% of the campus is accessible to disabled students. The following facilities are available: wheelchair ramps, elevators, special parking, specially equipped rest rooms, lowered drinking fountains, and lowered telephones.

Services: In addition to many counseling and information services, tutoring is available in most subjects. There is remedial math, reading, and writing. Both peers and professionals serve as tutors.

Campus Safety and Security: Campus safety and security measures include 24-hour foot and vehicle patrol, shuttle buses, informal discussions, and pamphlets/posters/films. In addition, there are lighted pathways/sidewalks.

Programs of Study: Cheyney confers B.A., B.S., and B.S.Ed. degrees. Master's degrees are also awarded. Bachelor's degrees are awarded in BIOLOGICAL SCIENCE (biology/biological science), BUSINESS (business administration and management and hotel/motel and restaurant management), COMMUNICATIONS AND THE ARTS (communications, dramatic arts, English, fine arts, music, and telecommunications), COMPUTER AND PHYSICAL SCIENCE (chemistry, computer science, mathematics, and science), EDUCATION (early childhood, elementary, home economics, secondary, and special), ENGINEERING AND ENVIRONMENTAL DESIGN (industrial administration/management and industrial engineering technology), HEALTH PROFESSIONS (medical laboratory technology), SOCIAL SCIENCE (clothing and textiles management/production/services, dietetics, economics, geography, history, parks and recreation management, political science/government, psychology, and social science). Psychology, political science, and social relations are the strongest academically. Business administration and social relations have the largest enrollments.

Required: To graduate, students must complete at least 128 credit hours, with 30 in the major and a minimum GPA of 2.0. Distribution requirements include 6 credits each in communications, humanities, science, and social science, 4 credits in health and physical education, and 3 credits in mathematics.

Special: Students may participate in a co-op program and cross-register with West Chester University of Pennsylvania. Internships, study abroad, work-study programs, a chemistry-biology dual degree, nondegree study, pass/fail options, and credit for life, military, and work experience are available. There is a freshman honors program on campus, as well as 9 national honor societies.

Faculty/Classroom: 60% of faculty are male; 40%, female. 91% teach undergraduates and 7% both teach and do research. No introductory courses are taught by graduate students. The average class size in an introductory lecture is 25; in a laboratory, 16; and in a regular course offering, 20.

Admissions: 70% of the 1995-96 applicants were accepted.

Requirements: The SAT I or ACT is required. Applicants must be graduates of an accredited secondary school or hold a GED. An interview is recommended. CLEP credit is accepted. Important factors in the admissions decision are ability to finance college education, extracurricular activities record, and geographic diversity.

Procedure: Freshmen are admitted fall and spring. Entrance exams should be taken during the junior or senior year. There are early decision and early admissions plans. Early decision applications should be filed by November 30; regular applications, by May 30 for fall entry and November 15 for spring entry, along with an application fee of $20. Notification is sent on a rolling basis. A waiting list is an active part of the admissions procedure, with about 10% of all applicants on the list.

Transfer: 58 transfer students enrolled in a recent year. Applicants must have a C average from an accredited postsecondary institution; others may be admitted on probation. Students with fewer than 30 credits must submit a high school transcript. 30 credits of 128 must be completed at Cheyney.

Visiting: There are regularly scheduled orientations for prospective students. There are guides for informal visits and visitors may sit in on classes. To schedule a visit, contact the Office of Admissions.

Financial Aid: In a recent year, 85% of all freshmen and 88% of continuing students received some form of financial aid. 81% of freshmen and 84% of continuing students received need-based aid. The average freshman award was $5600. Of that total, scholarships or need-based grants averaged $4000 ($4960 maximum); loans averaged $2625; and work contracts averaged $1000. 35% of undergraduate students work part-time. Average earnings from campus work for the school year are $967. The average financial indebtedness of the 1994-95 graduate was $14,500. Cheyney is a member of CSS. The FAFSA and the combined Application for PA State Grant and Federal Student Aid are required are required. The application deadline for fall entry is April 15.

International Students: In a recent year, 50 international students were enrolled. The school actively recruits these students. They must take the TOEFL.

Computers: The college provides computer facilities for student use. The mainframe is a Unisys A-5. 150 Apple, Macintosh, and IBM microcomputers are available in the library and departmental offices. Authorized terminal operators may access the system 24 hours a day. There are no time limits and no fees.

Graduates: In a recent year, 151 bachelor's degrees were awarded. The most popular majors among graduates were business administration (25%), elementary education (13%), and social relations (13%). 25 companies recently recruited on campus.

Admissions Contact: Sharon Cannon, Director of Admissions.

CLARION UNIVERSITY OF PENNSYLVANIA   B-2

Clarion, PA 16214   (814) 226-2306; (800) 672-7171

Full-time: 1892 men, 2886 women	Faculty: 341; IIA, +$
Part-time: 159 men, 453 women	Ph.D.s: n/av
Graduate: 141 men, 329 women	Student/Faculty: 14 to 1
Year: semesters, summer session	Tuition: $4054 ($9028)
Application Deadline: open	Room & Board: $2976
Freshman Class: 3265 applied, 1776 accepted, 1573 enrolled	
SAT I Verbal/Math: 425/459	COMPETITIVE

Clarion University of Pennsylvania, founded in 1867, is a public co-educational institution. There are 5 undergraduate and 5 graduate schools. In addition to regional accreditation, Clarion University has baccalaureate program accreditation with NCATE and NLN. The library contains 376,879 volumes, 1,372,772 microform items, and 5326 audiovisual forms, and subscribes to 1736 periodicals. Computerized library sources and services include the card catalog, interlibrary loans, and database searching. Special learning facilities include a learning resource center, art gallery, planetarium, radio station, and TV station. The 99-acre campus is in a small town 85 miles northeast of Pittsburgh. Including residence halls, there are 43 buildings on campus.

Student Life: 96% of undergraduates are from Pennsylvania. Students come from 28 states, 22 foreign countries, and Canada. 95% are white. The average age of all undergraduates is 23.

Housing: 2039 students can be accommodated in college housing. College-sponsored living facilities include single-sex and coed dormitories with special interest floors, nonsmoking floors, older student floors, and quiet floors. On-campus housing is guaranteed for all 4 years. Alcohol is not permitted. All students may keep cars on campus.

Activities: 18% of men belong to 10 national fraternities; 15% of women belong to 10 national sororities. There are 125 groups on campus, including art, band, cheerleading, chess, choir, chorus, computers, dance, drama, ethnic, honors, international, jazz band, literary magazine, marching band, musical theater, newspaper, orchestra, pep band, political, professional, radio and TV, religious, social, social service, student government, symphony, and yearbook. Popular campus events include Autumn Leaf Festival, Family Weekend, Activities Day, Black Heritage Week, and Greek Week.

Sports: There are 8 intercollegiate sports for men and 7 for women, and 20 intramural sports for men and 20 for women. Athletic and recreation facilities include a 5000-seat stadium, a gymnasium with physical fitness center and recreational swimming, and a natatorium.

Disabled Students: 85% of the campus is accessible to disabled students. The following facilities are available: wheelchair ramps, elevators, special parking, specially equipped rest rooms, special class scheduling, lowered drinking fountains, lowered telephones, and priority registration.

Services: In addition to many counseling and information services, tutoring is available in most subjects. There is a reader service for the blind, computer-assisted instruction, a learning skills laboratory, and remedial math, reading, and writing.

Campus Safety and Security: Campus safety and security measures include 24-hour foot and vehicle patrol, self-defense education, escort service, and informal discussions. In addition, there are pamphlets/posters/films, emergency telephones, lighted pathways/sidewalks, video surveillance cameras on campus, a bicycle patrol program, and a rape/aggressive defense program.

Programs of Study: Clarion University confers B.A., B.S., B.F.A., B.Mus., B.S.B.A., and B.S.E. degrees. Associate and master's degrees are also awarded. Bachelor's degrees are awarded in BIOLOGICAL SCIENCE (biology/biological science and molecular biology), BUSINESS (accounting, banking and finance, business economics, marketing/retailing/merchandising, and real estate), COMMUNICATIONS AND THE ARTS (communications, dramatic arts, English, fine arts, French, music, Spanish, and speech/debate/rhetoric), COMPUTER AND PHYSICAL SCIENCE (chemistry, computer management, computer science, earth science, geology, information sciences and systems, mathematics, natural sciences, and physics), EDUCATION (early childhood, elementary, foreign languages, library science, music, secondary, and special), ENGINEERING AND ENVIRONMENTAL DESIGN (industrial administration/management), HEALTH PROFESSIONS (medical laboratory technology, nursing, rehabilitation therapy, and speech pathology/audiology), SOCIAL SCIENCE (anthropology, economics, geography, history, humanities, liberal arts/general studies, philosophy, political science/government, psychology, social psychology, social science, and sociology). Sciences, business, and communication are the strongest academically. Education, communication, and biological sciences have the largest enrollments.

Required: To graduate, students must complete at least 128 credits, with a minimum GPA of 2.0 (2.5 for the College of Education and Human Services). Degree requirements include 18 credits in writing, mathematics, and communication; 9 credits each in physical and biological sciences, social and behavioral sciences, and arts and humanities; and 4 credits in health education, wellness, and creative and leisure activities.

Special: Clarion University has co-op programs in engineering with the University of Pittsburgh and Case Western Reserve University, in polymer science with the University of Akron, and in speech pathology and audiology with Gallaudet University. Internships, study abroad, a Washington semester, work-study programs, and dual majors are also available. There is a freshman honors program on campus, as well as 18 national honor societies.

Faculty/Classroom: All faculty teach undergraduates. No introductory courses are taught by graduate students. The average class size in an introductory lecture is 30; in a laboratory, 12; and in a regular course offering, 25.

Admissions: 54% of the 1995–96 applicants were accepted. The SAT I scores for the 1995–96 freshman class were as follows: Verbal—84% below 500, 14% between 500 and 599, and 2% between 600 and 700; Math—69% below 500, 24% between 500 and 599, 7% between 600 and 700, and 1% above 700. 26% of the current freshmen were in the top fifth of their class; 64% were in the top two fifths.

Requirements: The SAT I or ACT is required, with recommended minimum composite scores of 850 on the SAT I (at least 400 verbal and 400 mathematics) and 19 on the ACT. A minimum GPA of 2.0 is required. Applicants must be graduates of an accredited secondary school. The GED is accepted. Students should have completed 4 years each of English and social studies, and 2 years each of mathematics, science, and foreign language. An essay and interview are recommended. AP and CLEP credits are accepted. Important factors in the admissions decision are advanced placement or honor courses, evidence of special talent, and leadership record.

Procedure: Freshmen are admitted fall and spring. Entrance exams should be taken in the spring of the junior year or early fall of the senior year. There are early decision, early admissions, and deferred admissions plans. Application deadlines are open. Application fee is $25. Notification of early decision is sent October 1; regular decision, on a rolling basis beginning November 1.

Transfer: 281 transfer students enrolled in 1995–96. Applicants for transfer should have completed at least 12 college credit hours with a GPA of 2.75 for speech pathology and audiology majors, 2.5 for business and education majors, and 2.0 for other programs. An audition is required for music majors, and an interview and national test are required for nursing students. 45 credits of 128 must be completed at Clarion University.

Visiting: There are regularly scheduled orientations for prospective students, including a 1 1/2-day summer program for committed students. There are guides for informal visits and visitors may sit in on classes. To schedule a visit, contact the Admissions Office.

Financial Aid: In 1995–96, 85% of all freshmen and 76% of continuing students received some form of financial aid. 79% of freshmen and 68% of continuing students received need-based aid. The average freshman award was $4607. Of that total, scholarships or need-based grants averaged $1912 ($9028 maximum); loans averaged $2397 ($2625 maximum); and work contracts averaged $1174 ($1265 maximum). 34% of undergraduate students work part-time. Average earnings from campus work for the school year are $1040. The average financial indebtedness of the 1994–95 graduate was $12,600. The FAFSA is required. The application deadline for fall entry is May 1.

International Students: There are currently 52 international students enrolled. The school actively recruits these students. They must take the TOEFL and achieve a minimum score of 550.

Computers: The college provides computer facilities for student use. The mainframe is a DEC VAX 8810. There are also more than 200 IBM and Apple IIe microcomputers available in student laboratories. All students may access the system. There are no time limits and no fees.

Graduates: In 1994–95, 858 bachelor's degrees were awarded. The most popular majors among graduates were education (18%), communication (10%), and psychology (8%). Within an average freshman class, 38% graduate in 4 years and 55% in 5 years. 117 companies recruited on campus in 1994–95.

Admissions Contact: John Shropshire, Dean of Enrollment Management and Academic Records. A campus video is available.

COLLEGE MISERICORDIA   B-2

Dallas, PA 18612   (717) 674-6460; (800) 852-7675

Full-time: 313 men, 904 women	Faculty: 93; IIB, av$
Part-time: 81 men, 324 women	Ph.Ds: 50%
Graduate: 34 men, 123 women	Student/Faculty: 13 to 1
Year: semesters	Tuition: $12,190
Application Deadline: open	Room & Board: $5990
Freshman Class: 1378 applied, 846 accepted, 294 enrolled	
SAT I or ACT: required	COMPETITIVE

College Misericordia, established in 1924 and sponsored by the Religious Sisters of Mercy, is a coeducational liberal arts institution affiliated with the Roman Catholic Church and offering professional programs in health-related fields. In addition to regional accreditation, College Misericordia has baccalaureate program accreditation with CAHEA, CSWE, and NLN. The library contains 72,459 volumes, 5018 microform items, and 11,445 audiovisual forms, and subscribes to 804 periodicals. Computerized library sources and services include interlibrary loans and database searching. Special learning facilities include a learning resource center and art gallery. The 100-acre campus is in a small town 9 miles north of Wilkes-Barre. Including residence halls, there are 16 buildings on campus.

Student Life: 70% of undergraduates are from Pennsylvania. Students come from 10 states and 3 foreign countries. 45% are from public schools; 55% from private. 95% are white. 65% are Catholic; 32% Protestant. The average age of freshmen is 18; all undergraduates, 21.

Housing: 650 students can be accommodated in college housing. College-sponsored living facilities include single-sex and coed dormitories and on-campus apartments. In addition there are special interest houses. On-campus housing is guaranteed for all 4 years. 50% of students live on campus; of those, 70% remain on campus on weekends. Upperclassmen may keep cars on campus.

Activities: 10% of men and about 2% of women belong to 2 local fraternities. There are no sororities. There are 25 groups on campus, including cheerleading, choir, chorus, computers, drama, ethnic, honors, international, literary magazine, musical theater, newspaper, political, professional, religious, social service, student government, and yearbook. Popular campus events include Spring Fling, Winter Weekend, and Junior Ring Day.

Sports: There are 6 intercollegiate sports for men and 8 for women, and 10 intramural sports for men and 10 for women. Athletic and recreation facilities include a sports-health center and athletic fields.

Disabled Students: 95% of the campus is accessible to disabled students. The following facilities are available: wheelchair ramps, elevators, special parking, specially equipped rest rooms, and special class scheduling.

Services: In addition to many counseling and information services, tutoring is available in every subject. There is remedial math and reading.

Campus Safety and Security: Campus safety and security measures include 24-hour foot and vehicle patrol, informal discussions, pamphlets/posters/films, and lighted pathways/sidewalks.

Programs of Study: College Misericordia confers B.A., B.S., B.S.N., and B.S.W. degrees. Master's degrees are also awarded. Bachelor's degrees are awarded in BIOLOGICAL SCIENCE (biology/biological science), BUSINESS (accounting, business administration and management, and marketing/retailing/merchandising), COMMUNICATIONS AND THE ARTS (English), COMPUTER AND PHYSICAL SCIENCE (chemistry, computer science, information sciences and systems, and mathematics), EDUCATION (early childhood, elementary, secondary, and special), HEALTH PROFESSIONS (medical laboratory technology, nursing, occupational therapy, physical therapy, predentistry, premedicine, and radiograph medical technology), SOCIAL SCIENCE (history, liberal arts/general studies, prelaw, and social work). Occupational therapy and physical therapy are the strongest programs academically and have the largest enrollments.

Required: To graduate, students must earn a minimum of 120 credits, with at least 60 credits in the major. The required 54-credit core curriculum includes courses in anthropology, English composition and literature, fine arts, history, mathematics, philosophy, political science, psychology, religious studies, and science. A minimum GPA of 2.0 is required.

Special: Students may cross-register with King's College. The college offers co-op programs, internships in social work and psychology, work-study programs, study abroad in England, an accelerated degree program in business and nursing for adult students, student-designed majors, and dual majors in elementary and early childhood education, elementary and special education, and mathematics and computer science. Physical therapy and occupational therapy are 5-year programs leading to a master's degree in the major. Credit may be granted for life, military, and work experience. Nondegree study is also available. The college offers an alternative learner's project, which accepts a limited number of learning disabled students each year. There is a freshman honors program on campus, as well as 1 national honor society.

Faculty/Classroom: 49% of faculty are male; 51%, female. All teach undergraduates. 45% both teach and do research. No introductory courses are taught by graduate students. The average class size in an introductory lecture is 30; in a laboratory, 20; and in a regular course offering, 25.

Admissions: 61% of the 1995–96 applicants were accepted. The SAT I scores for a recent freshman class were Verbal—23% below 500, 67% between 500 and 599, and 10% between 600 and 700; Math—20% below 500, 65% between 500 and 599, and 15% between 600 and 700. 39% of the current freshmen were in the top fifth of their class; 61% were in the top two fifths. 4 freshmen graduated first in their class.

Requirements: The SAT I or ACT is required. Applicants must graduate from an accredited secondary school with a 2.0 GPA or have a GED. 16 Carnegie units must be earned, and students must complete 3 years each in English, mathematics, history, and science, and 2 to 3 years in social studies. Radiography applicants must take physics. Physical therapy students must take calculus. AP and CLEP credits are accepted. Important factors in the admissions decision are advanced placement or honor courses, personality/intangible qualities, and leadership record.

Procedure: Freshmen are admitted fall and spring. Entrance exams should be taken during junior year. There are early decision, early admissions, and deferred admissions plans. Application deadlines are open. Application fee is $15. Notification is sent on a rolling basis. 2 early decision candidates were accepted for the 1995–96 class. A waiting list is an active part of the admissions procedure, with about 5% of all applicants on the list.

Transfer: 97 transfer students enrolled in 1995–96. Applicants must have a minimum GPA of 2.0. Requirements may be higher for selected majors. 30 credits of a minimum of 120 must be completed at College Misericordia.

Visiting: There are regularly scheduled orientations for prospective students, including meetings with admission and financial aid counselors, and a tour of the campus. There are guides for informal visits and visitors may sit in on classes and stay overnight at the school. To schedule a visit, contact the Admissions Office.

Financial Aid: In 1995–96, more than 90% of all students received some form of financial aid. 80% of all students received need-based aid. The average freshman award was $8000. Of that total, scholarships or need-based grants averaged $3000 ($7000 maximum); loans averaged $2500 ($5000 maximum); and work contracts averaged $700 ($900 maximum). 93% of undergraduate students work part-time. Average earnings from campus work for the school year are $900. The average financial indebtedness of the 1994–95 graduate was $13,000. College Misericordia is a member of CSS. The FAF and PHEAA are required. The application deadline for fall entry is March 1.

International Students: There are currently 6 international students enrolled. They must take the TOEFL and achieve a minimum score of 500.

Computers: The college provides computer facilities for student use. The mainframe is an IBM AS/400. Microcomputers are available. All students may access the system. There are no time limits and no fees.

Graduates: In 1994–95, 302 bachelor's degrees were awarded. The most popular majors among graduates were occupational therapy (18%), physical therapy (16%), and nursing (11%). Within an average freshman class, 67% graduate in 4 years and 5% in 5 years. 40 companies recruited on campus in 1994–95.

Admissions Contact: Jane F. Dessoye, Executive Director of Admissions and Financial Aid.

CURTIS INSTITUTE OF MUSIC   F-3
Philadelphia, PA 19103–6187   (215) 893-5262

Full-time: 40 men, 80 women	**Faculty:** 87
Part-time: none	**Ph.D.s:** n/av
Graduate: 10 men, 10 women	**Student/Faculty:** n/av
Year: semesters	**Tuition:** see profile
Application Deadline: see profile	**Room & Board:** n/app
Freshman Class: n/av	
SAT I: required	**SPECIAL**

Curtis Institute of Music, founded in 1924, is a private coeducational conservatory offering undergraduate, graduate, and professional programs in music. The institution serves an entirely commuter student body. All applicants are accepted on full-tuition scholarships. However, they must pay $700 in fees and provide all their living expenses. Figures given in the above capsule are approximate. There are 2 graduate schools. In addition to regional accreditation, Curtis has baccalaureate program accreditation with NASM. The library contains 60,000 volumes, 100 microform items, and 10,000 audiovisual forms, and subscribes to 40 periodicals. Special learning facilities include the Leonard Stolowski Collection. The campus is in an urban area. There are 3 buildings on campus.

Student Life: 92% of undergraduates are from out-of-state, mostly the Northeast. Students come from 30 states, 21 foreign countries, and Canada. 90% are from public schools; 10% from private. 62% are white. The average age of freshmen is 18; all undergraduates, 18. 2% do not continue beyond their first year; 98% remain to graduate.

Housing: There are no residence halls. Alcohol is not permitted.

Activities: There are no fraternities or sororities. There are some groups and organizations on campus, including student government.

Sports: There is no sports program at Curtis.

Disabled Students: Elevators and specially equipped rest rooms are available.

Services: In addition to counseling and information services, tutoring is provided on an individual basis in every subject.

Campus Safety and Security: Campus safety and security measures include informal discussions, 24-hour security guards in the main building, and buzzer entry to other buildings.

Programs of Study: Curtis confers the B.M. degree. Master's degrees are also awarded. Bachelor's degrees are awarded in COMMUNICATIONS AND THE ARTS (music).

Required: To graduate, students must complete 131 semester hours, including 48 in applied music, with a minimum GPA of 2.0. General music requirements include courses in applied music, theory, solfege, techniques of 20th century music, music history, and elements of conducting. Academic requirements include courses in English composition, literature, and history of Western civilization.

Special: Curtis maintains a co-op program with the University of Pennsylvania and offers pass/fail options.

Faculty/Classroom: 70% of faculty are male; 30%, female. The average class size in an introductory lecture is 15 and in a regular course offering, 10.

Requirements: The SAT I is required. Applicant must be a graduate of an accredited secondary school or have earned a GED. Confidential letters of recommendation from 2 qualified musicians are required. Admission is based primarily on evidence of the applicant's special talent. An audition is required. AP and CLEP credits are accepted.

Procedure: Freshmen are admitted in the fall. Entrance exams should be taken by March of the senior year. Notification is sent by April 15. Check with the school for current application deadlines and fee.

Transfer: 97 credits of 131 must be completed at Curtis.

Financial Aid: Curtis is a member of CSS. The FAF and the college's own financial statement are required. Check with the school for current deadlines.

International Students: There were 60 international students enrolled in a recent year. Students must score 500 on the TOEFL, or take the SAT I.

Computers: The college provides computer facilities for student use. All students may access the system.

Admissions Contact: Judi L. Gattone, Director of Admissions.

DELAWARE VALLEY COLLEGE F-3
Doylestown, PA 18901-2697 (215) 345-1500, ext. 2211
(800) 233-5825

Full-time: 739 men, 648 women	Faculty: 74
Part-time: 345 men, 410 women	Ph.D.s: 57%
Graduate: none	Student/Faculty: 19 to 1
Year: semesters, summer session	Tuition: $13,340
Application Deadline: open	Room & Board: $5260
Freshman Class: 1410 applied, 1025 accepted, 390 enrolled	
SAT I Verbal/Math: 445/476	COMPETITIVE

Delaware Valley College, founded in 1896, is a private coeducational institution offering undergraduate programs in specialized fields of agriculture, business administration, English, the sciences, mathematics, criminal justice administration, and secondary education. The library contains 73,110 volumes, 50,554 microform items, and 950 audiovisual forms, and subscribes to 630 periodicals. Computerized library sources and services include interlibrary loans and database searching. Special learning facilities include a learning resource center, radio station, dairy science center, livestock farm, horse facilities, apiary, small animal laboratory, tissue culture laboratory, arboretum and greenhouses. The 600-acre campus is in a suburban area 20 miles north of Philadelphia. Including residence halls, there are 36 buildings on campus.

Student Life: 67% of undergraduates are from Pennsylvania. Students come from 21 states, 7 foreign countries, and Canada. 84% are from public schools; 16% from private. 96% are white. 37% are Catholic; 29% Protestant; 21% claim no religious affiliation. The average age of freshmen is 18.8; all undergraduates, 20. 23% do not continue beyond their first year; 62% remain to graduate.

Housing: 875 students can be accommodated in college housing. College-sponsored living facilities include single-sex and coed dormitories. In addition there are honors houses. On-campus housing is guaranteed for all 4 years. 70% of students live on campus; of those, 50% remain on campus on weekends. All students may keep cars on campus.

Activities: There are no fraternities or sororities. There are 40 groups on campus, including art, band, cheerleading, chess, choir, chorale, chorus, computers, dance, drama, ethnic, honors, international, literary magazine, newspaper, pep band, photography, professional, radio and TV, religious, social, social service, student government, and yearbook. Popular campus events include A-Day, Homecoming, and Parents Day.

Sports: There are 8 intercollegiate sports for men and 7 for women, and 9 intramural sports for men and 9 for women. Athletic and recreation facilities include 2 gymnasiums, tennis courts, outdoor playing courts and fields, a football stadium, a running track, a small lake, a video game room, picnic areas, nature walks, riding trails, and indoor and outdoor equine facilities.

Disabled Students: 65% of the campus is accessible to disabled students. The following facilities are available: wheelchair ramps, elevators, special parking, specially equipped rest rooms, special class scheduling, and lowered drinking fountains.

Services: In addition to many counseling and information services, tutoring is available in most subjects. There is a reader service for the blind, and remedial math, reading, and writing.

Campus Safety and Security: Campus safety and security measures include 24-hour foot and vehicle patrol, self-defense education, escort service, and shuttle buses. There are informal discussions, pamphlets/posters/films, emergency telephones, and lighted pathways/sidewalks.

Programs of Study: DVC confers B.A. and B.S. degrees. Associate degrees are also awarded. Bachelor's degrees are awarded in AGRICULTURE (agriculture, animal science, dairy science, and horticulture), BIOLOGICAL SCIENCE (biology/biological science), BUSINESS (accounting, business administration and management, and marketing/retailing/merchandising), COMMUNICATIONS AND THE ARTS (English), COMPUTER AND PHYSICAL SCIENCE (chemistry, computer science, and mathematics), EDUCATION (secondary), ENGINEERING AND ENVIRONMENTAL DESIGN (food services technology), SOCIAL SCIENCE (criminal justice, food production/

management/services, and food science). Science is the strongest academically. Business administration and animal science have the largest enrollments.

Required: The bachelor's degree requires completion of at least 128 credits, including 48 in the major, with a minimum GPA of 2.0. The core curriculum consists of 48 credits of liberal arts courses, including cultural enrichment, physical education, and an introduction to computers. Students must also fulfill employment program requirements.

Special: DVC offers a specialized methods and techniques program that enables students to learn laboratory techniques and gain experience in the practical aspects of their majors. There are co-op programs in biology and animal science, internships, and work-study programs in a wide variety of employment and research settings. Nondegree study and pass/fail options are available. There is a freshman honors program on campus, as well as 3 national honor societies.

Faculty/Classroom: 72% of faculty are male; 28%, female. All teach undergraduates. The average class size in an introductory lecture is 40; in a laboratory, 20; and in a regular course offering, 22.

Admissions: 73% of the 1995-96 applicants were accepted. The SAT I scores for the 1995-96 freshman class were as follows: Verbal—67% below 500, 27% between 500 and 599, 5% between 600 and 700, and 1% above 700; Math—57% below 500, 33% between 500 and 599, 9% between 600 and 700, and 1% above 700. 31% of the current freshmen were in the top fifth of their class; 60% were in the top two fifths. There were 8 National Merit semifinalists. 11 freshmen graduated first in their class.

Requirements: The SAT I is required. Applicants must be graduates of accredited secondary schools or have earned a GED. The college requires 15 academic units, including 6 in electives, 3 in English, and 2 each in mathematics, science, and social studies. An interview is recommended. AP and CLEP credits are accepted. Important factors in the admissions decision are leadership record, personality/intangible qualities, and extracurricular activities record.

Procedure: Freshmen are admitted fall and spring. Entrance exams should be taken in the junior or senior year. There are early decision and early admissions plans. Application deadlines are open. Application fee is $35. Notification is sent on a rolling basis.

Transfer: 100 transfer students enrolled in 1995-96. Applicants must have a minimum GPA of 2.0 and must submit SAT I scores. An interview is recommened. 48 credits of 128 must be completed at DVC.

Visiting: There are regularly scheduled orientations for prospective students, consisting of a student panel, meetings with department chairs, and general information sessions. There are guides for informal visits and visitors may sit in on classes and stay overnight at the school. To schedule a visit, contact the Admissions Department.

Financial Aid: In 1995-96, 87% of all freshmen and 75% of continuing students received some form of financial aid. 71% of freshmen and 69% of continuing students received need-based aid. The average freshman award was $9100. Of that total, scholarships or need-based grants averaged $4800; loans averaged $2750 ($3600 maximum); and work contracts averaged $1500 ($2000 maximum). 25% of undergraduate students work part-time. Average earnings from campus work for the school year are $1500. The average financial indebtedness of the 1994-95 graduate was $7950. DVC is a member of CSS. The Pennsylvania State Grant, and the Federal Grant Application financial statement is required. The application deadline for fall entry is May 1.

International Students: There are currently 6 international students enrolled. They must take the TOEFL and achieve a minimum score of 500.

Computers: The college provides computer facilities for student use. The mainframe is a Motorola 8125. There are also 52 microcomputers on system in the computer center, library, and tutoring center. Those students who are computer majors or in work-study programs may access the system. There are no time limits and no fees.

Graduates: In 1994-95, 254 bachelor's degrees were awarded. The most popular majors among graduates were business administration (26%), animal science (25%), and ornamental horticulture (14%). Within an average freshman class, 48% graduate in 4 years, 55% in 5 years, and 66% in 6 years. 120 companies recruited on campus in 1994-95. Of the 1994 graduating class, 10% were enrolled in graduate school within 6 months of graduation and 94% had found employment.

Admissions Contact: Stephen W. Zenko, Director of Admissions. A campus video is available.

DICKINSON COLLEGE

D-3

Carlisle, PA 17013   (717) 245-1231; FAX: (717) 245-1442

Full-time: 778 men, 1000 women	Faculty: 171; IIB, +$
Part-time: 19 men, 43 women	Ph.D.s: 99%
Graduate: none	Student/Faculty: 10 to 1
Year: semesters, summer session	Tuition: $19,750
Application Deadline: February 15	Room & Board: $5270
Freshman Class: 2920 applied, 2448 accepted, 529 enrolled	
SAT I or ACT: required	**VERY COMPETITIVE**

Dickinson College, founded in 1773, is a coeducational, private institution offering a liberal arts curriculum including international education and science. The library contains 421,710 volumes, 163,998 microform items, and 11,469 audiovisual forms, and subscribes to 1735 periodicals. Computerized library sources and services include the card catalog, interlibrary loans, and database searching. Special learning facilities include an art gallery, planetarium, radio station, fiber optic and satellite telecommunications networks, telescope observatory, and an archival collection. The 87-acre campus is in a suburban area about 20 miles west of Harrisburg and 2 hours from Washington DC. Including residence halls, there are 108 buildings on campus.

Student Life: 58% of undergraduates are from out-of-state, mostly the Middle Atlantic. Students come from 44 states and 31 foreign countries. 62% are from public schools; 38% from private. 91% are white. 42% are Catholic; 35% Protestant; 16% claim no religious affiliation. The average age of freshmen is 18; all undergraduates, 20. 8% do not continue beyond their first year; 86% remain to graduate.

Housing: 1679 students can be accommodated in college housing. College-sponsored living facilities include single-sex and coed dormitories, on-campus apartments, fraternity houses, and sorority houses. In addition there are language houses, special interest houses, including arts, Asian, environmental, equality, Hillel, and multicultural. On-campus housing is guaranteed for all 4 years. 90% of students live on campus; of those, 85% remain on campus on weekends. All students may keep cars on campus.

Activities: 35% of men belong to 1 local and 8 national fraternities; 35% of women belong to 1 local and 4 national sororities. There are 122 groups on campus, including art, band, cheerleading, chess, choir, chorale, chorus, computers, dance, drama, ethnic, film, gay, honors, international, jazz band, literary magazine, musical theater, newspaper, orchestra, photography, political, professional, radio, religious, social, social service, student government, symphony, and yearbook. Popular college events include Black Arts Festival, Fall Fest, Multicultural Fair, and Parents and Siblings weekends.

Sports: There are 11 intercollegiate sports for men and 11 for women, and 51 intramural sports for men and 38 for women. Athletic and recreation facilities include an indoor 86000-square-foot sports facility, including a basketball court, swimming pool, indoor track, and squash, racquetball, and handball courts. There are also tennis courts, a varsity football field plus 4 other fields, an outdoor track, and a 19-acre recreational park with a jogging trail.

Disabled Students: 75% of the campus is accessible to disabled students. The following facilities are available: wheelchair ramps, elevators, special parking, specially equipped rest rooms, special class scheduling, lowered drinking fountains, lowered telephones, and telephone access.

Services: In addition to many counseling and information services, tutoring is available in every subject. Services are provided as necessary on a case-by-case basis. There is a reader service for the blind. There also is a writing center.

Campus Safety and Security: Campus safety and security measures include 24-hour foot and vehicle patrol, self-defense education, escort service, and informal discussions. In addition, there are pamphlets/posters/films, emergency telephones, lighted pathways/sidewalks, and electronic access to residence halls.

Programs of Study: Dickinson confers B.A. and B.S. degrees. Bachelor's degrees are awarded in BIOLOGICAL SCIENCE (biology/biological science), COMMUNICATIONS AND THE ARTS (dramatic arts, English, fine arts, French, German, Greek, Latin, music, Russian, and Spanish), COMPUTER AND PHYSICAL SCIENCE (chemistry, computer science, geology, mathematics, and physics), ENGINEERING AND ENVIRONMENTAL DESIGN (environmental science), SOCIAL SCIENCE (American studies, anthropology, East Asian studies, economics, history, international studies, Italian studies, Judaic studies, philosophy, political science/government, psychology, public affairs, religion, Russian and Slavic studies, and sociology). International education/foreign languages, natural sciences, and preprofessional programs are the strongest academically. Biology, economics, English, and foreign languages have the largest enrollments.

Required: To graduate, students must complete 34 courses with a 2.0 GPA. The school requires 3 courses each in humanities, social sciences, and natural and mathematical sciences. Also required are

a freshman seminar, 1 to 4 courses of crosscultural studies (including foreign language), physical education, and the completion of a major.

Special: Students may cross-register with Central Pennsylvania Consortium Colleges. Also available are internships, study abroad in 9 countries, a Washington semester, work-study programs, accelerated degree programs, dual majors, student-designed majors, nondegree study, and pass/fail options. There are 3–2 engineering degrees offered with Case Western Reserve University, Rensselaer Polytechnic Institute, and University of Pennsylvania. Instruction in 12 languages is available. There are certification programs in Latin American studies, secondary education, and women's studies. Linkage programs are available with 7 graduate programs in business, accounting, and public administration at various institutions. There are 12 national honor societies on campus, including Phi Beta Kappa. 33 departments have honors programs.

Faculty/Classroom: 65% of faculty are male; 35%, female. All both teach and do research. The average class size in an introductory lecture is 23; in a laboratory, 19; and in a regular course offering, 15.

Admissions: 84% of the 1995–96 applicants were accepted. The SAT I scores for the 1995–96 freshman class were as follows: Verbal—48% below 500, 39% between 500 and 599, 12% between 600 and 700, and 2% above 700; Math—30% below 500, 38% between 500 and 599, 27% between 600 and 700, and 5% above 700. 56% of the current freshmen were in the top fifth of their class; 85% were in the top two fifths.

Requirements: The SAT I or ACT is required. SAT II: Subject tests are optional submissions. The GED is accepted. Applicants should have completed 16 academic credits, including 4 years of English, 3 each of mathematics and science, 2 (preferably 3) of foreign language, and 2 of social studies, and 2 additional courses drawn from the above areas. An essay is required and an interview is recommended. Applications are accepted on computer disk and on-line via Common App, CollegeView, CollegeLink, and others. AP credits are accepted. Important factors in the admissions decision are advanced placement or honor courses, extracurricular activities record, and recommendations by school officials.

Procedure: Freshmen are admitted in the fall. Entrance exams should be taken in the spring of the junior year or the fall of the senior year. There are early decision, early admissions, and deferred admissions plans. Early decision applications should be filed by February 1; regular applications, by February 15 for fall entry, along with an application fee of $35. Notification of early decision is sent on a rolling basis November 15 to February 15; regular decision, mid-March. 109 early decision candidates were accepted for the 1995–96 class. A waiting list is an active part of the admissions procedure, with about 7% of all applicants on the list.

Transfer: 38 transfer students enrolled in 1995–96. Applicants will normally have at least a 3.0 cumulative GPA and must submit secondary school and college transcripts and a dean's report form in addition to the standard application for admission. 17 courses of 34 must be completed at Dickinson.

Visiting: There are regularly scheduled orientations for prospective students, including campus tours, individual interviews, group information sessions, class visits, overnight stays in residence halls, and open houses. There are guides for informal visits and visitors may sit in on classes and stay overnight at the school. To schedule a visit, contact the Admissions Office.

Financial Aid: In 1995–96, 67% of all freshmen and 63% of continuing students received some form of financial aid. 65% of freshmen and 61% of continuing students received need-based aid. The average freshman award was $16,065. Of that total, scholarships or need-based grants averaged $12,102 ($18,540 maximum); loans averaged $3263 ($8625 maximum); and work contracts averaged $1171 ($1300 maximum). 63% of undergraduate students work part-time. Average earnings from campus work for the school year are $816. The average financial indebtedness of the 1994–95 graduate was $15,050. Dickinson is a member of CSS. The FAFSA and CSS Profile Application are required. The application deadline for fall entry is February 15.

International Students: There are currently 60 international students enrolled. The school actively recruits these students. They must take the TOEFL and achieve a minimum score of 600.

Computers: The college provides computer facilities for student use. The mainframe is a DEC 3600 ALPHA AXP. A fiber optics network enables students to have private personal computer hook-up to the mainframe from their residence hall rooms. All students are assigned ALPHA accounts for E-mail and Internet communications. There are more than 235 microcomputers and 48 terminals located in the library, student union, and classroom buildings. All students may access the system. There are no time limits and no fees.

Graduates: In 1994–95, 479 bachelor's degrees were awarded. The most popular majors among graduates were foreign languages (14%), political science (12%), and history (9%). Within an average freshman class, 83% graduate in 4 years, 84% in 5 years, and 86% in 6 years. 33 companies recruited on campus in 1994–95. Of the

1994 graduating class, 31% were enrolled in graduate school within 6 months of graduation and 97% had found employment.

Admissions Contact: R. Russell Shunk, Dean of Admissions. E-mail: admit@dickinson.edu World Wide Web address: http://www.dickinson.edu/. A campus video is available.

DREXEL UNIVERSITY   F-3

Philadelphia, PA 19104	(215) 895-2400; (800) 2-DREXEL
Full-time: 3114 men, 1551 women	Faculty: 393; I, av$
Part-time: 1204 men, 507 women	Ph.D.s: 97%
Graduate: 1730 men, 1052 women	Student/Faculty: 12 to 1
Year: quarters, summer session	Tuition: $13,844
Application Deadline: March 1	Room & Board: $6646
Freshman Class: 3513 applied, 2819 accepted, 949 enrolled	
SAT I: verbal/math: 460/560	LESS COMPETITIVE

Drexel University, established in 1891, is a private, nonsectarian coeducational institution, with undergraduate programs in business and administration, engineering, information studies, design arts, and arts and sciences. There are 6 undergraduate and 5 graduate schools. In addition to regional accreditation, Drexel has baccalaureate program accreditation with AACSB, ABET, ADA, and NAAB. The library contains 500,000 volumes and 740,000 microform items, and subscribes to 4800 periodicals. Computerized library sources and services include the card catalog, interlibrary loans, and database searching. Special learning facilities include a learning resource center, art gallery, radio station, and TV station. The 38-acre campus is in an urban area near the center of Philadelphia. Including residence halls, there are 34 buildings on campus.

Student Life: 66% of undergraduates are from Pennsylvania. Students come from 41 states, 75 foreign countries, and Canada. 71% are white; 11% Asian American. The average age of freshmen is 18.4; all undergraduates, 23. 25% do not continue beyond their first year; 59% remain to graduate.

Housing: 1600 students can be accommodated in college housing. College-sponsored living facilities include coed dormitories. In addition, there is an international house. On-campus housing is guaranteed for the freshman year only, is available on a first-come, first-served basis, and is available on a lottery system for upperclassmen. Priority is given to out-of-town students. All students may keep cars on campus.

Activities: 23% of men belong to 13 national fraternities; 22% of women belong to 5 national sororities. There are 78 groups on campus, including art, band, cheerleading, chess, choir, chorus, computers, dance, drama, ethnic, film, gay, honors, international, jazz band, literary magazine, musical theater, newspaper, orchestra, pep band, photography, political, professional, radio and TV, religious, social, social service, student government, and yearbook. Popular campus events include Annual Greek Block Party and an ongoing program of musical, cultural, and art events.

Sports: There are 12 intercollegiate sports for men and 9 for women, and 10 intramural sports for men and 10 for women. Athletic and recreation facilities include a physical education center with 3 gymnasiums, 6 squash courts, swimming pool, diving well, wrestling room, dance studio, fencing room, Nautilus weight training rooms, and special exercise rooms; a field house; a bowling alley and game room with billiards, table tennis, and arcade games; volleyball courts; and a 22-acre lodge outside of the city.

Disabled Students: The following facilities are available: wheelchair ramps, elevators, special parking, specially equipped rest rooms, special class scheduling, lowered drinking fountains, and lowered telephones.

Services: In addition to many counseling and information services, tutoring is available in most subjects. There is remedial math, reading, and writing and a resident tutor program.

Campus Safety and Security: Campus safety and security measures include 24-hour foot and vehicle patrol, escort service, shuttle buses, and pamphlets/posters/films. There are emergency telephones and lighted pathways/sidewalks.

Programs of Study: Drexel confers B.S. and B.Arch. degrees. Master's and doctoral degrees are also awarded. Bachelor's degrees are awarded in BIOLOGICAL SCIENCE (biology/biological science and nutrition), BUSINESS (accounting, banking and finance, business administration and management, business economics, fashion merchandising, hotel/motel and restaurant management, human resources, international business management, and marketing/retailing/merchandising), COMMUNICATIONS AND THE ARTS (communications, design, literature, music, and photography), COMPUTER AND PHYSICAL SCIENCE (chemistry, computer science, mathematics, physics, and science), EDUCATION (education), ENGINEERING AND ENVIRONMENTAL DESIGN (architecture, chemical engineering, civil engineering, computer engineering, electrical/electronics engineering, materials engineering, and mechanical engineering), HEALTH PROFESSIONS (predentistry and premedicine), SOCIAL SCIENCE (dietetics, fashion design and technology, history,

humanities, international studies, political science/government, pre-law, and sociology). Engineering, business, and design arts are the strongest academically. Electrical and computer engineering, business, and architecture have the largest enrollments.

Required: To graduate, students must complete 180 to 192 term credits with a minimum GPA of 2.0. There are requirements in mathematics, English, laboratory science, social science, history, and physical education.

Special: The Drexel Plan of Cooperative Education enables students to alternate periods of full-time classroom studies and full-time employment with university-approved employers. The student's participation in cooperative education is mandatory, except for a small percentage of students in the business and administration program. Cross-registration is available with Eastern Mennonite College, Indiana University of Pennsylvania, and Lincoln University. Drexel also offers study abroad, a general studies degree, 3–3 engineering degrees, nondegree study, credit/no credit options, and a Sea Education Association semester. There is a freshman honors program on campus.

Faculty/Classroom: 80% of faculty are male; 20%, female. 87% teach undergraduates. The average class size in a laboratory is 30 and in a regular course offering, 37.

Admissions: 80% of the 1995–96 applicants were accepted. 40% of the current freshmen were in the top fifth of their class; 72% were in the top two fifths. There were 26 National Merit finalists. 15 freshmen graduated first in their class.

Requirements: The SAT I or ACT is required. Applicants must be graduates of an accredited secondary school. The GED is accepted. An essay is required and an interview is recommended. AP and CLEP credits are accepted. Important factors in the admissions decision are advanced placement or honor courses, evidence of special talent, and recommendations by school officials.

Procedure: Freshmen are admitted in the fall. Entrance exams should be taken by January 15 of the senior year. There are early decision, early admissions, and deferred admissions plans. Early decision applications should be filed by November 15; regular applications, by March 1 for fall entry, along with an application fee of $35. Notification of early decision is sent December 15; regular decision, on a rolling basis. 145 early decision candidates were accepted for the 1995–96 class. A waiting list is an active part of the admissions procedure, with about 1% of all applicants on the list.

Transfer: 256 transfer students enrolled in a recent year. Applicants must have a minimum GPA of 2.5. Other requirements vary among the individual colleges within the university. 45 term credits of 180 to 192 must be completed at Drexel.

Visiting: There are regularly scheduled orientations for prospective students, consisting of a 2-day program for new freshmen and their parents in late July. There are guides for informal visits and visitors may sit in on classes and stay overnight at the school. To schedule a visit, contact the Admissions Office at (215) 895-6727.

Financial Aid: In a recent year, 80% of all freshmen and 75% of continuing students received some form of financial aid. 67% of freshmen and 64% of continuing students received need-based aid. The average freshman award was $8651. Of that total, scholarships or need-based grants averaged $5026; loans averaged $1744 ($2625 maximum); and work contracts averaged $600. In sophomore and later years, co-op earnings add an average income of over $10,000 per year. 11% of undergraduate students work part-time. Average earnings from campus work for the school year are $600. The average financial indebtedness of a recent year's graduate was $13,400. Drexel is a member of CSS. The PHEAA financial statement is required. The application deadline for fall entry is May 1.

International Students: There were 296 international students enrolled in a recent year. The school actively recruits these students. They must take the TOEFL and achieve a minimum score of 510. Freshman applicants must also take the SAT I or ACT.

Computers: The college provides computer facilities for student use. The mainframes are an IBM 9121–320 and a Sun Server 670. Students may access the mainframes, the library, and the Internet through Apple Macintosh microcomputers in dormitories or residences. There are also 150 networked public computers available. All students may access the system 24 hours a day. There are no time limits and no fees. It is recommended that students in all programs have personal computers. An Apple Macintosh is recommended.

Graduates: In 1994–95, 1246 bachelor's degrees were awarded. The most popular majors among graduates were accounting (11%), electrical and computer engineering (11%), and finance and banking (8%). Within an average freshman class, 5% graduate in 3 years, 15% in 4 years, 47% in 5 years, and 53% in 6 years. 265 companies recruited on campus in 1994–95. Of the 1994 graduating class, 82% had found employment within 6 months of graduation.

Admissions Contact: Donald Dickason, Vice Provost, Enrollment Management.

DUQUESNE UNIVERSITY
B-3

Pittsburgh, PA 15282-0201

(412) 396-6020

(800) 456-0590; FAX: (412) 396-5644

Full-time: 2069 men, 2708 women	Faculty: 358; IIA, av$
Part-time: 395 men, 546 women	Ph.D.s: 94%
Graduate: 1548 men, 2009 women	Student/Faculty: 13 to 1
Year: semesters, summer session	Tuition: $12,578
Application Deadline: July 1	Room & Board: $5580
Freshman Class: 4125 applied, 3380 accepted, 1413 enrolled	
SAT I or ACT: required	**VERY COMPETITIVE**

Duquesne University, founded in 1878, is a private institution affiliated with the Roman Catholic Church, offering programs in liberal arts, natural and environmental sciences, nursing, health sciences, pharmacy, business, music, teacher preparation, preprofessional training, and law. There are 8 undergraduate and 9 graduate schools. In addition to regional accreditation, Duquesne has baccalaureate program accreditation with AACSB, ACPE, APTA, CAHEA, NASM, NCATE, and NLN. The 3 libraries contain 496,168 volumes, 152,289 microform items, and 13,738 audiovisual forms, and subscribe to 2223 periodicals. Computerized library sources and services include the card catalog, interlibrary loans, and database searching. Special learning facilities include a learning resource center, art gallery, radio station, TV station, and 28 multimedia classrooms. The 40-acre campus is in an urban area on a private, self-contained campus in the center of Pittsburgh. Including residence halls, there are 25 buildings on campus.

Student Life: 80% of undergraduates are from Pennsylvania. Students come from 50 states, 80 foreign countries, and Canada. 86% are white. 65% are Catholic; 15% Protestant; 10% claim no religious affiliation. The average age of freshmen is 18; all undergraduates, 22. 10% do not continue beyond their first year; 71% remain to graduate.

Housing: 2540 students can be accommodated in college housing. College-sponsored living facilities include single-sex dormitories. On-campus housing is guaranteed for the freshman year only and is available on a lottery system for upperclassmen. 52% of students live on campus; of those, 65% remain on campus on weekends. All students may keep cars on campus.

Activities: 14% of men belong to 3 local and 6 national fraternities; 14% of women belong to 2 local and 7 national sororities. There are 127 groups on campus, including art, band, cheerleading, choir, chorale, chorus, computers, dance, drama, ethnic, film, honors, international, jazz band, literary magazine, marching band, musical theater, newspaper, opera, orchestra, pep band, photography, political, professional, radio and TV, religious, social, social service, student government, symphony, and yearbook. Popular campus events include Carnival, Valentine Ball, Dance Marathon, and Halloween Ball.

Sports: There are 14 intercollegiate sports for men and 11 for women, and 9 intramural sports for men and 9 for women. Athletic and recreation facilities include an athletic center, a student union, a football and soccer field, a baseball field, weight room and exercise facilities, volleyball courts, bowling alleys, a squash court, and racquetball courts.

Disabled Students: The entire campus is accessible to persons with physical disabilities. The following facilities are available: wheelchair ramps, elevators, special parking, specially equipped rest rooms, special class scheduling, lowered drinking fountains, and lowered telephones.

Services: In addition to many counseling and information services, tutoring is available in every subject. There is also a reader service for the blind, and remedial math, reading, and writing.

Campus Safety and Security: Campus safety and security measures include 24-hour foot and vehicle patrol, self-defense education, escort service, and shuttle buses. In addition, there are informal discussions, pamphlets/posters/films, emergency telephones, and lighted pathways/sidewalks. There are security cameras, and all resident buildings have 24 hour coverage with ID swipes and video cameras.

Programs of Study: Duquesne confers B.A., B.S., B.S.Ed., B.S.M., B.S.M.E., and B.S.N. degrees. Master's and doctoral degrees are also awarded. Bachelor's degrees are awarded in BIOLOGICAL SCIENCE (biochemistry, biology/biological science, and microbiology), BUSINESS (accounting, banking and finance, business administration and management, business economics, business law, human resources, international business management, and marketing/retailing/merchandising), COMMUNICATIONS AND THE ARTS (advertising, art history and appreciation, broadcasting, classical languages, communications, English, Greek, journalism, Latin, music, music performance, music theory and composition, Spanish, speech/debate/rhetoric, and studio art), COMPUTER AND PHYSICAL SCIENCE (chemistry, computer science, information sciences and systems, mathematics, and physics), EDUCATION (athletic training, early childhood, elementary, foreign languages, music, science, secondary, and special), HEALTH PROFESSIONS (health science, medical technology, music therapy, nursing, occupational therapy,

pharmacy, physical therapy, physician's assistant, predentistry, and premedicine), SOCIAL SCIENCE (criminal justice, economics, gerontology, history, international relations, philosophy, political science/government, prelaw, psychology, religion, social science, and sociology). Chemistry, biology, environmental science, and physical therapy/occupational therapy are the strongest academically. Communications, business, pharmacy, and liberal arts have the largest enrollments.

Required: Students are required to complete at least 120 credit hours, including at least 27 in the major, with a minimum 2.0 GPA. General requirements vary by department, but there is a 27-credit liberal arts core curriculum.

Special: The university offers co-op programs in business, communications, pharmacy, nursing, and health sciences, cross-registration through the Pittsburgh Council on Higher Education, internships, study abroad in 12 to 13 countries, work-study programs at 100 sites, and a Washington semester. Also available are B.A.-B.S. degrees, Saturday College, a general studies degree, an accelerated degree program, dual and student-designed majors, a 3–2 engineering program with Case Western Reserve University, pass/fail options, and credit for life, military, and work experience. There is a freshman honors program on campus, as well as 4 national honor societies. All departments have honors programs.

Faculty/Classroom: 68% of faculty are male; 32%, female. 94% both teach and do research. Graduate students teach 8% of introductory courses. The average class size in an introductory lecture is 26; in a laboratory, 20; and in a regular course offering, 22.

Admissions: 82% of the 1995–96 applicants were accepted. The SAT I scores for the 1995–96 freshman class were as follows: Verbal—32% below 500, 57% between 500 and 599, 9% between 600 and 700, and 2% above 700; Math—30% below 500, 50% between 500 and 599, 17% between 600 and 700, and 3% above 700. The ACT scores were 17% below 21, 35% between 21 and 23, 25% between 24 and 26, 13% between 27 and 28, and 9% above 28. 58% of the current freshmen were in the top fifth of their class; 88% were in the top two fifths. 58 freshmen graduated first in their class.

Requirements: The SAT I or ACT is required. Students should have either a high school diploma with a 2.8 GPA or the GED. Applicants are required to have 16 academic credits, including 4 each in English and academic electives, and 8 combined in social studies, language, mathematics, and/or science. An audition is required for music majors. An essay and interview are recommended. AP and CLEP credits are accepted. Important factors in the admissions decision are advanced placement or honor courses, geographic diversity, and ability to finance college education.

Procedure: Freshmen are admitted to all sessions. There are early decision, early admissions, and deferred admissions plans. Early decision applications should be filed by November 15; regular applications, by July 1 for fall entry, December 15 for spring entry, and April 1 for summer entry, along with an application fee of $45. Notification of early decision is sent December 1; regular decision, on a rolling basis. 358 early decision candidates were accepted for the 1995–96 class. A waiting list is an active part of the admissions procedure, with about 8% of all applicants on the list.

Transfer: 301 transfer students enrolled in 1995–96. Applicants must submit complete high school and college transcripts. Students should have a minimum GPA of 2.5 for the university, but some schools require a higher average. A minimum of 12 credits earned is required and an interview is recommended. 30 credits of 120 must be completed at Duquesne.

Visiting: There are regularly scheduled orientations for prospective students. There are guides for informal visits and visitors may sit in on classes and stay overnight at the school. To schedule a visit, contact the Student Admissions Advisors at (412) 396-6222.

Financial Aid: In 1995–96, 80% of all freshmen and 78% of continuing students received some form of financial aid. 65% of freshmen received need-based aid. The average freshman award was $9083. Of that total, scholarships or need-based grants averaged $5471 ($11,662 maximum); loans averaged $2472 ($4125 maximum); outside grants and loans averaged $200 ($5000 maximum); and work contracts averaged $950. 6% of undergraduate students work part-time. Average earnings from campus work for the school year are $1900. The average financial indebtedness of the 1994–95 graduate was $16,000. Duquesne is a member of CSS. The FAFSA and PHEAA are required. The application deadline for fall entry is May 1.

International Students: There are currently 496 international students enrolled. The school actively recruits these students. Any student who does not take the TOEFL must take the MELAB upon arriving on campus.

Computers: The college provides computer facilities for student use. The mainframes are a DEC VAX 6420 and 6210, DEC 5810, 5500, 5000–240, and clustered unit workstations. There are also microcomputers available in laboratories throughout the campus. All students can use the entire system 24 hours from residence halls, campus, and home. There are 28 multimedia sites. All students may access the system. There are no time limits. The fee is $25.

Graduates: In 1994–95, 947 bachelor's degrees were awarded. The most popular majors among graduates were education (18%), pharmacy (16%), and accounting (7%). Within an average freshman class, 66% graduate in 4 years, 71% in 5 years, and 72% in 6 years. 159 companies recruited on campus in 1994–95. Of the 1994 graduating class, 17% were enrolled in graduate school within 6 months of graduation and 69% had found employment.

Admissions Contact: Dean Thomas Schaefer, C.S.Sp., Office of Admissions. E-mail: admissions@duq2.cc.duq.edu. A campus video is available.

EAST STROUDSBURG UNIVERSITY
(See East Stroudsburg University of Pennsylvania)

EAST STROUDSBURG UNIVERSITY OF PENNSYLVANIA
(Formerly East Stroudsburg University)
East Stroudsburg, PA 18301

F-2

	(717) 422-3542
	FAX: (717) 422-3933
Full-time: 1719 men, 2202 women	Faculty: 235; IIA, +$
Part-time: 302 men, 345 women	Ph.D.s: 76%
Graduate: 262 men, 539 women	Student/Faculty: 17 to 1
Year: semesters, summer session	Tuition: $4017 ($8991)
Application Deadline: March 1	Room & Board: $3448
Freshman Class: 4232 applied, 2472 accepted, 854 enrolled	
SAT I Verbal/Math: 428/469	COMPETITIVE

East Stroudsburg University of Pennsylvania, founded in 1893, is a part of the Pennsylvania State System of Higher Education and offers programs in arts and science, health sciences and human performance, and professional studies. There are 3 undergraduate schools and one graduate school. In addition to regional accreditation, East Stroudsburg has baccalaureate program accreditation with NLN. The library contains 416,000 volumes, 1,176,000 microform items, and 7650 audiovisual forms, and subscribes to 2200 periodicals. Computerized library sources and services include the card catalog, interlibrary loans, and database searching. Special learning facilities include a learning resource center, art gallery, radio station, and a wildlife museum. The 183-acre campus is in a small town 75 miles west of New York City. Including residence halls, there are 39 buildings on campus.

Student Life: 84% of undergraduates are from Pennsylvania. Students come from 22 states, 21 foreign countries, and Canada. 94% are white. The average age of freshmen is 18; all undergraduates, 23. 17% do not continue beyond their first year; 60% remain to graduate.

Housing: 2140 students can be accommodated in college housing. College-sponsored living facilities include single-sex and coed dormitories and on-campus apartments. In addition there are honors floors. On-campus housing is guaranteed for all 4 years. 53% of students commute. Alcohol is not permitted. Upperclassmen may keep cars on campus.

Activities: 12% of men belong to 8 national fraternities; 15% of women belong to 2 local and 6 national sororities. There are 76 groups on campus, including art, band, cheerleading, chess, choir, computers, dance, drama, ethnic, gay, honors, international, jazz band, literary magazine, musical theater, newspaper, pep band, political, professional, radio and TV, religious, social, social service, student government, and yearbook. Popular campus events include concerts, Spring Music Festival, and International Celebrations.

Sports: There are 9 intercollegiate sports for men and 9 for women, and 11 intramural sports for men and 11 for women. Athletic and recreation facilities include a 5000-seat stadium, a 2600-seat gymnasium, another gymnasium, 8 athletic fields, 12 outdoor tennis courts, 1 indoor tennis court, a swimming pool, indoor and outdoor tracks, and weight rooms.

Disabled Students: 98% of the campus is accessible to disabled students. The following facilities are available: wheelchair ramps, elevators, special parking, specially equipped rest rooms, special class scheduling, lowered drinking fountains, lowered telephones, and visual fire alarms for hearing impaired persons.

Services: In addition to many counseling and information services, tutoring is available in every subject. There is remedial math, reading, and writing.

Campus Safety and Security: Campus safety and security measures include 24-hour foot and vehicle patrol, self-defense education, escort service, and informal discussions. In addition, there are pamphlets/posters/films, emergency telephones, lighted pathways/sidewalks, and a police bicycle patrol.

Programs of Study: East Stroudsburg confers B.A. and B.S. degrees. Master's degrees are also awarded. Bachelor's degrees are awarded in BIOLOGICAL SCIENCE (biochemistry, biology/

biological science, and marine science), BUSINESS (business administration and management and hotel/motel and restaurant management), COMMUNICATIONS AND THE ARTS (communications, communications technology, dramatic arts, English, fine arts, French, German, media arts, Spanish, and speech/debate/rhetoric), COMPUTER AND PHYSICAL SCIENCE (chemistry, computer science, earth science, mathematics, physical sciences, and science), EDUCATION (early childhood, elementary, foreign languages, physical, science, secondary, and special), ENGINEERING AND ENVIRONMENTAL DESIGN (engineering), HEALTH PROFESSIONS (allied health, medical laboratory technology, nursing, premedicine, public health, rehabilitation therapy, and speech pathology/audiology), SOCIAL SCIENCE (anthropology, economics, geography, history, parks and recreation management, philosophy, political science/government, psychology, social science, and sociology). Computer science, nursing, mathematics and chemistry are the strongest academically. Education, hospitality management, physical education, and management have the largest enrollments.

Required: All students must maintain a GPA of at least 2.0 while taking 128 semester hours, including 27 to 83 hours in the major. General education courses total 60 credits, with English composition and physical education required courses. Distribution requirements include 15 hours in arts and letters, science, and social science.

Special: Internships in most programs, B.A.-B.S. degrees, dual majors for most fields, 3–2 engineering degrees with Pennsylvania State University or the University of Pittsburgh, nondegree study, study abroad, and cross-registration through the National Student Exchange are available. There is a freshman honors program on campus, as well as 16 national honor societies.

Faculty/Classroom: 62% of faculty are male; 38%, female. All teach undergraduates. No introductory courses are taught by graduate students. The average class size in an introductory lecture is 40; in a laboratory, 25; and in a regular course offering, 25.

Admissions: 58% of the 1995–96 applicants were accepted. The SAT I scores for the 1995–96 freshman class were as follows: Verbal—87% below 500, 12% between 500 and 599, and 1% between 600 and 700; Math—69% below 500, 23% between 500 and 599, 7% between 600 and 700, and 1% above 700. 19% of the current freshmen were in the top fifth of their class; 56% were in the top two fifths. One freshman graduated first in their class.

Requirements: The SAT I or ACT is required, but the SAT I is preferred. Applicants must be graduates of an accredited secondary school. The GED is accepted. AP and CLEP credits are accepted. Important factors in the admissions decision are advanced placement or honor courses, evidence of special talent, and leadership record.

Procedure: Freshmen are admitted in the fall. Entrance exams should be taken during the fall of the senior year. Applications should be filed by March 1 for fall entry, along with an application fee of $25. Notification is sent March 1.

Transfer: 412 transfer students enrolled in 1995–96. Transfer students must have a 2.3 GPA earned over at least 24 credit hours. 32 credits of 128 must be completed at East Stroudsburg.

Visiting: There are regularly scheduled orientations for prospective students. There are guides for visits, and visitors may sit in on classes. To schedule a visit, contact the Admissions Office.

Financial Aid: In a recent year, 79% of all freshmen and 75% of continuing students received some form of financial aid. 79% of freshmen and 75% of continuing students received need-based aid. East Stroudsburg is a member of CSS. The FAFSA is required. The application deadline for fall entry is March 15.

International Students: There are currently 34 international students enrolled. They must take the TOEFL and achieve a minimum score of 500.

Computers: The college provides computer facilities for student use. The mainframe is a Unisys A-11. There is a DEC file server with 75 DEC workstations, and 150 PCs comprising an academic network. All students may access the system. Most computers are available 7 A.M. to 10 P.M., some are available on a 24-hour basis. There are no time limits and no fees.

Graduates: In a recent class, 864 bachelor's degrees were awarded. The most popular majors among graduates were elementary education (16%), physical education (12%), and management (9%). Within an average freshman class, 1% graduate in 3 years, 25% in 4 years, 45% in 5 years, and 50% in 6 years. 75 companies recruited on campus in a recent year.

Admissions Contact: Alan T. Chesterton, Director of Admissions. E-mail: atc@po-box.esu.edu.

EASTERN COLLEGE

F-3

St. Davids, PA 19087-3696   (610) 341-5967; FAX: (610) 341-1723

Full-time: 431 men, 757 women	Faculty: 57; IIA, --$
Part-time: 65 men, 255 women	Ph.D.s: 74%
Graduate: 259 men, 388 women	Student/Faculty: 21 to 1
Year: semesters, summer session	Tuition: $11,780
Application Deadline: open	Room & Board: $5036
Freshman Class: 608 applied, 481 accepted, 229 enrolled	
SAT I Verbal/Math: 461/489	ACT: 21 COMPETITIVE

Eastern College, founded in 1932, is a private, coeducational liberal arts institution affiliated with the American Baptist Church. There is 1 graduate school. In addition to regional accreditation, Eastern has baccalaureate program accreditation with CSWE and NLN. The 2 libraries contain 123,096 volumes, 700,000 microform items, and 1827 audiovisual forms, and subscribe to 1178 periodicals. Computerized library sources and services include interlibrary loans and database searching. Special learning facilities include a planetarium and radio station. The 107-acre campus is in a small town 20 miles northwest of Philadelphia. Including residence halls, there are 20 buildings on campus.

Student Life: 66% of undergraduates are from Pennsylvania. Students come from 36 states, 18 foreign countries, and Canada. 84% are white; 10% African American. 28% claim no religious affiliation; 22% Assembly of God, Christian, Evangelical, Mennonite, Pentecostal,; 16% Catholic. The average age of freshmen is 20; all undergraduates, 28. 28% do not continue beyond their first year; 50% remain to graduate.

Housing: 550 students can be accommodated in college housing. College-sponsored living facilities include coed dormitories and on-campus apartments. In addition there are honors houses. On-campus housing is guaranteed for the freshman year only, is available on a first-come, first-served basis, and is available on a lottery system for upperclassmen. Priority is given to out-of-town students. 57% of students commute. Alcohol is not permitted. All students may keep cars on campus.

Activities: There are no fraternities or sororities. There are more than 40 groups on campus, including band, cheerleading, choir, chorale, chorus, computers, dance, drama, ethnic, honors, international, literary magazine, musical theater, newspaper, photography, political, professional, radio and TV, religious, social service, student government, and yearbook. Popular campus events include Black History Week, Homecoming, Christmas Celebration, dances, coffee houses, chapel, spring banquet, and pizza harvest party.

Sports: There are 6 intercollegiate sports for men and 8 for women, and 11 intramural sports for men and 11 for women. Athletic and recreation facilities include a gymnasium, a game room, a soccer pitch, a baseball/field hockey field, a weight room, an outdoor track, 4 tennis courts, a health fitness trail, and an outdoor pool.

Disabled Students: 90% of the campus is accessible to disabled students. The following facilities are available: wheelchair ramps, elevators, special parking, specially equipped rest rooms, special class scheduling, lowered drinking fountains, lowered telephones, and special residence hall spaces.

Services: In addition to many counseling and information services, tutoring is available in every subject. There is a reader service for the blind, remedial math, reading, and writing, and a summer skills workshop.

Campus Safety and Security: Campus safety and security measures include 24-hour foot and vehicle patrol, escort service, shuttle buses, and informal discussions. In addition, there are pamphlets/posters/films, emergency telephones, and lighted pathways/sidewalks.

Programs of Study: Eastern confers B.A., B.S., B.S.N., and B.S.W. degrees. Associate and master's degrees are also awarded. Bachelor's degrees are awarded in BIOLOGICAL SCIENCE (biology/biological science), BUSINESS (business administration and management and management science), COMMUNICATIONS AND THE ARTS (art history and appreciation, communications, creative writing, English literature, French, music, Spanish, and studio art), COMPUTER AND PHYSICAL SCIENCE (astronomy, chemistry, and mathematics), EDUCATION (elementary, English, health, physical, and secondary), ENGINEERING AND ENVIRONMENTAL DESIGN (environmental science), HEALTH PROFESSIONS (medical laboratory technology and nursing), SOCIAL SCIENCE (biblical studies, history, philosophy, political science/government, psychology, social work, sociology, theological studies, urban studies, and youth ministry). Biology, elementary education, and pychology are the strongest academically. Elementary education, health and physical education, and social work have the largest enrollments.

Required: To graduate, all students must complete at least 127 credit hours with a minimum 2.0 GPA. The required hours in the major vary. Students must take courses in the Old and New Testament, humanities, social sciences, non-Western heritage, and capstone.

Special: The college offers cross-registration with Cabrini and Rosemont Colleges, cooperative programs with Roxborough Memorial Hospital School of Nursing and Bryn Mawr Hospital, dual majors, internships, a Washington semester in American studies through the Christian College Coalition, and student-designed majors. Also available are an accelerated degree program in organizational management, credit for experience, nondegree study, and pass/fail options. Eastern also has an interim winter session and a different calendar for the organizational management program. There is a freshman honors program on campus, as well as 10 national honor societies. There is a collegewide honors program.

Faculty/Classroom: 54% of faculty are male; 46%, female. 88% teach undergraduates. No introductory courses are taught by graduate students. The average class size in an introductory lecture is 45; in a laboratory, 14; and in a regular course offering, 14.

Admissions: 79% of the 1995–96 applicants were accepted. The SAT I scores for the 1995–96 freshman class were as follows: Verbal—67% below 500, 26% between 500 and 599, 7% between 600 and 700, and 1% above 700; Math—52% below 500, 33% between 500 and 599, 12% between 600 and 700, and 2% above 700. The ACT scores were 38% below 21, 25% between 21 and 23, and 38% between 24 and 26. 36% of the current freshmen were in the top fifth of their class; 69% were in the top two fifths. 4 freshmen graduated first in their class.

Requirements: The SAT I is required. A minimum GPA of 2.0 is required. Eastern admits students after analyzing SAT I and class rank. However, other factors within the application are evaluated to determine motivation to succeed. AP and CLEP credits are accepted. Important factors in the admissions decision are advanced placement or honor courses, leadership record, and parents or siblings attending the school.

Procedure: Freshmen are admitted to all sessions. Entrance exams should be taken as early as possible. There are early decision, early admissions, and deferred admissions plans. Application deadlines are open. Application fee is $25. Notification is sent on a rolling basis.

Transfer: 76 transfer students enrolled in 1995–96. Applicants should have a 2.0 GPA with more than 24 credits, and a 2.5 GPA with under 24 credits. Candidates must be in good standing at their previous institution. 30 credits of 127 must be completed at Eastern.

Visiting: There are regularly scheduled orientations for prospective students, including 2 orientations in the fall and 1 in the spring. There are guides for informal visits and visitors may sit in on classes and stay overnight at the school. To schedule a visit, contact the Admissions Office.

Financial Aid: In 1995–96, 92% of all freshmen and 86% of continuing students received some form of financial aid. 85% of freshmen received need-based aid. The average freshman award was $13,647. Of that total, scholarships or need-based grants averaged $500 ($5000 maximum); loans averaged $500 ($4000 maximum); and work contracts averaged $200 ($1200 maximum). 15% of undergraduate students work part-time. Average earnings from campus work for the school year are $1200. Eastern is a member of CSS. The FAFSA, the college's own financial statement, and income tax forms are required. The priority date for fall entry is July 1.

International Students: There are currently 26 international students enrolled. The school actively recruits these students. They must take the TOEFL, and achieve a minimum score of 550, or the Comprehensive English Language Test. The student must also take the SAT I or the ACT.

Computers: The college provides computer facilities for student use. Microcomputers are available for all students. All students may access the system. There are no time limits and no fees.

Graduates: In 1994–95, 457 bachelor's degrees were awarded. The most popular majors among graduates were organizational management (52%), elementary education (7%), and nursing (4%). Within an average freshman class, 50% graduate in 5 years. Of the 1994 graduating class, 16% were enrolled in graduate school within 6 months of graduation and 76% had found employment.

Admissions Contact: Mark Seymour, Director of Enrollment Management. A campus video is available.

EDINBORO UNIVERSITY OF PENNSYLVANIA

B-1

Edinboro, PA 16444   (814) 732-2761

(800) 626-2203; FAX: (814) 732-2420

Full-time: 2588 men, 3447 women	Faculty: 362; IIA, +$
Part-time: 264 men, 463 women	Ph.D.s: 62%
Graduate: 183 men, 532 women	Student/Faculty: 17 to 1
Year: semesters, summer session	Tuition: $3924 ($8898)
Application Deadline: open	Room & Board: $3578
Freshman Class: 3795 applied, 2926 accepted, 1361 enrolled	
SAT I or ACT: required	LESS COMPETITIVE

Edinboro University of Pennsylvania, founded in 1857, is a public coeducational institution and a member of the Pennsylvania State System of Higher Education. The university offers programs in fine and liberal arts, business, engineering, health science, and teacher preparation. There are 4 undergraduate schools and one graduate school. In addition to regional accreditation, the university has baccalaureate program accreditation with ADA, CSWE, NASM, and NLN. The 2 libraries contain 431,935 volumes, 1,268,478 microform items, and 13,140 audiovisual forms, and subscribe to 1878 periodicals. Computerized library sources and services include the card catalog, interlibrary loans, and database searching. Special learning facilities include an art gallery, planetarium, radio station, and a TV studio. The 585-acre campus is in a small town 20 miles south of Erie. Including residence halls, there are 42 buildings on campus.

Student Life: 92% of undergraduates are from Pennsylvania. Students come from 25 states, 29 foreign countries, and Canada. 92% are white. The average age of freshmen is 19; all undergraduates, 23. 30% do not continue beyond their first year; 50% remain to graduate.

Housing: 2604 students can be accommodated in college housing. College-sponsored living facilities include single-sex and coed dormitories. In addition there are honors houses. On-campus housing is guaranteed for the freshman year only and is available on a first-come, first-served basis. Alcohol is not permitted. All students may keep cars on campus.

Activities: 10% of men belong to 7 national fraternities; 15% of women belong to 5 national sororities. There are 100 groups on campus, including art, bagpipe band, band, cheerleading, chess, choir, chorale, chorus, commuter, computers, dance, drama, drill team, ethnic, film, gay, honors, international, jazz band, literary magazine, marching band, newspaper, opera, orchestra, pep band, photography, political, professional, radio and TV, religious, social, social service, student government, symphony, and yearbook. Popular campus events include Academic Festival, Friday Night Film Series, and a miniconcert series.

Sports: There are 9 intercollegiate sports for men and 8 for women, and 15 intramural sports for men and 15 for women. Athletic and recreation facilities include a field house, a stadium, a gymnasium, a swimming pool, racquetball courts, an aerobics room, an indoor track, a fitness center, saunas and whirlpools, and a weight room.

Disabled Students: 95% of the campus is accessible to disabled students. The following facilities are available: wheelchair ramps, elevators, special parking, specially equipped rest rooms, special class scheduling, lowered drinking fountains, and lowered telephones. The university also offers special residence halls, computer facilities, and transportation services for the physically challenged and learning disabled.

Services: In addition to many counseling and information services, tutoring is available in every subject. There is a reader service for the blind, and remedial math, reading, and writing.

Campus Safety and Security: Campus safety and security measures include 24-hour foot and vehicle patrol, informal discussions, pamphlets/posters/films, and emergency telephones. In addition, there are lighted pathways/sidewalks and a commissioned police force.

Programs of Study: The university confers B.A., B.S., B.S.Ed., B.F.A., and B.S.N. degrees. Associate and master's degrees are also awarded. Bachelor's degrees are awarded in BIOLOGICAL SCIENCE (biochemistry, biology/biological science, and nutrition), BUSINESS (accounting, business administration and management, and marketing management), COMMUNICATIONS AND THE ARTS (applied art, art, art history and appreciation, dramatic arts, English, fine arts, French, German, media arts, music, Russian, Spanish, and speech/debate/rhetoric), COMPUTER AND PHYSICAL SCIENCE (chemistry, computer science, earth science, geology, mathematics, natural sciences, and physics), EDUCATION (art, early childhood, elementary, English, foreign languages, health, mathematics, music, physical, science, secondary, social studies, and special), ENGINEERING AND ENVIRONMENTAL DESIGN (environmental science and industrial administration/management), HEALTH PROFESSIONS (medical technology, nuclear medical technology, nursing, predentistry, premedicine, prepharmacy, preveterinary science, and speech pathology/audiology), SOCIAL SCIENCE (African American studies, anthropology, criminal justice, economics, geography, history, human ecology, humanities, liberal arts/general studies, philosophy, political science/government, prelaw, psychology, social science, social work, and sociology). Elementary education, business, and psychology have the largest enrollments.

Required: To graduate, students must complete a total of 128 semester hours with a minimum GPA of 2.0. General education requirements include a 21-semester-hour core with 3 hours each in artistic expression, world civilizations, American civilizations, human behavior, cultural diversity and social pluralism, ethics, and science and technology; an 18-hour distribution with 6 hours each in humanities and fine arts, social and behavioral sciences, and science and mathematics; an additional 9 semester hours of general education electives; and 3 hours of health and physical education.

Special: The university offers cross-registration with Mercyhurst College and Gannon University, a Harrisburg semester, internships in many majors, a general studies program, student-designed majors, a 3-2 engineering degree, study abroad in 8 countries, and nondegree study. Students may select pass/fail options and receive credit for life, military, and work experience. There is a freshman honors program on campus, as well as 11 national honor societies.

Faculty/Classroom: 63% of faculty are male; 37%, female. All teach undergraduates. No introductory courses are taught by graduate students. The average class size in a regular course offering is 25.

Admissions: 77% of the 1995-96 applicants were accepted.

Requirements: The SAT I or ACT is required. Candidates for admission should be graduates of an accredited secondary school. The GED is accepted. A portfolio is recommended for art students and an audition is required for music students. An interview is recommended for all. Admissions decisions are based upon high school curriculum, grades, GPA, class rank, SAT I or ACT scores, and leadership and extracurricular activities record. AP and CLEP credits are accepted.

Procedure: Freshmen are admitted fall, spring, and summer. Entrance exams should be taken in the junior year or early in the senior year. There are early admissions and deferred admissions plans. Application deadlines are open. Application fee is $25. Notification is sent on a rolling basis. A waiting list is an active part of the admissions procedure, with about 5% of all applicants on the list.

Transfer: 654 transfer students enrolled in 1995-96. Applicants must have a 2.0 GPA and must submit transcripts from high school and all previous colleges. An interview is recommended. 32 credits of 128 must be completed at the university.

Visiting: There are regularly scheduled orientations for prospective students, including admissions, financial aid, and academic affairs presentations followed by campus tours. There are guides for informal visits and visitors may sit in on classes. To schedule a visit, contact the Admissions Office.

Financial Aid: In 1995-96, 80% of all students received some form of financial aid and need-based aid. The average freshman award was $4963. Of that total, scholarships or need-based grants averaged $1787 ($5940 maximum); loans averaged $3027 ($7750 maximum); and work contracts averaged $1200 ($1750 maximum). 50% of undergraduate students work part-time. Average earnings from campus work for the school year are $1200. The average financial indebtedness of the 1994-95 graduate was $15,000. The university is a member of CSS. The FAFSA is required. The application deadline for fall entry is May 1.

International Students: There are currently 115 international students enrolled. The school actively recruits these students. They must take the TOEFL or the MELAB and achieve a minimum score on the TOEFL of 450.

Computers: The college provides computer facilities for student use. The mainframe is a DEC VAX. More than 200 IBM, Apple Macintosh, Zenith, Tandy, and other microcomputers are available to students in locations across campus. All students may access the system. There are no time limits and no fees.

Graduates: In 1994-95, 1191 bachelor's degrees were awarded. The most popular majors among graduates were elementary education (10%), criminal justice (7%), and psychology (6%). 150 companies recruited on campus in 1994-95.

Admissions Contact: Terrence Carlin, Assistant Vice President for Admissions.

ELIZABETHTOWN COLLEGE   D-3

Elizabethtown, PA 17022   (717) 361-1400; FAX: (717) 361-1365

Full-time: 536 men, 994 women	**Faculty:** 104; IIB, +$
Part-time: 79 men, 144 women	**Ph.D.s:** 70%
Graduate: none	**Student/Faculty:** 15 to 1
Year: semesters, summer session	**Tuition:** $15,490
Application Deadline: see profile	**Room & Board:** $4550
Freshman Class: 2441 applied, 1818 accepted, 453 enrolled	
SAT I Verbal/Math: 490/550	**ACT: 22** **VERY COMPETITIVE**

Elizabethtown College, founded in 1899, is a private coeducational institution affiliated with the Church of the Brethren and offers undergraduate degrees in liberal arts, sciences, and preprofessional programs. In addition to regional accreditation, E-town has baccalaureate program accreditation with CSWE and NASM. The library contains 185,127 volumes, 117,221 microform items, and 9700 audiovisual forms, and subscribes to 1100 periodicals. Computerized library sources and services include the card catalog, interlibrary loans, and database searching. Special learning facilities include a learning resource center, art gallery, radio station, TV station, and a meeting house for the study of Anabaptist and Pietist groups. The 180-acre campus is in a small town 20 miles southeast of Harrisburg. Including residence halls, there are 28 buildings on campus.

Student Life: 62% of undergraduates are from Pennsylvania. Students come from 22 states and 21 foreign countries. 96% are white. 46% are Protestant; 33% Catholic. The average age of freshmen is

18; all undergraduates, 20. 18% do not continue beyond their first year; 66% remain to graduate.

Housing: 1307 students can be accommodated in college housing. College-sponsored living facilities include single-sex and coed dormitories and on-campus apartments. In addition, there are special interest houses. On-campus housing is guaranteed for all 4 years. 87% of students live on campus; of those, 80% remain on campus on weekends. All students may keep cars on campus.

Activities: There are no fraternities or sororities. There are 50 groups on campus, including art, band, cheerleading, choir, chorale, chorus, computers, drama, ethnic, gay, honors, international, jazz band, literary magazine, musical theater, newspaper, orchestra, photography, political, professional, radio and TV, religious, social, social service, student government, and yearbook. Popular campus events include Parents Weekend, theme weekends, and Spring Arts Festival.

Sports: There are 8 intercollegiate sports for men and 8 for women, and 9 intramural sports for men and 9 for women. Athletic and recreation facilities include a swimming pool, weight training rooms, a 2200-seat soccer complex, a 2400-seat gymnasium, racquetball and tennis courts, basketball courts, sand volleyball courts, aerobics classes, a fitness center, and baseball, softball, and hockey fields.

Disabled Students: 85% of the campus is accessible to disabled students. The following facilities are available: wheelchair ramps, elevators, special parking, specially equipped rest rooms, special class scheduling, lowered drinking fountains, and lowered telephones.

Services: In addition to many counseling and information services, tutoring is available in most subjects. There is also remedial math and writing. Workshops and individual help with study skills are also available.

Campus Safety and Security: Campus safety and security measures include 24-hour foot and vehicle patrol, self-defense education, escort service, and informal discussions. In addition, there are pamphlets/posters/films, emergency telephones, lighted pathways/sidewalks, a student patrol, and a crime prevention program.

Programs of Study: E-town confers B.A. and B.S. degrees. Bachelor's degrees are awarded in BIOLOGICAL SCIENCE (biochemistry and biology/biological science), BUSINESS (accounting, business administration and management, and international business management), COMMUNICATIONS AND THE ARTS (communications, English, French, German, music, and Spanish), COMPUTER AND PHYSICAL SCIENCE (chemistry, computer science, mathematics, physical chemistry, physics, and science), EDUCATION (early childhood, elementary, music, and secondary), ENGINEERING AND ENVIRONMENTAL DESIGN (computer engineering, engineering, environmental science, and industrial engineering), HEALTH PROFESSIONS (medical laboratory technology, music therapy, and occupational therapy), SOCIAL SCIENCE (economics, ethics, politics, and social policy, history, philosophy, political science/government, psychology, religion, social studies, social work, and sociology). Sciences, occupational therapy, and international business are the strongest academically. Business administration, communications, and elementary and early childhood education have the largest enrollments.

Required: The core curriculum includes a freshman seminar, a junior/senior colloquium, and courses in foreign cultures and international studies, mathematics analysis, the power of language, creative expression, cultural heritage, physical well-being, the natural and social worlds, and values and choice. Distribution requirements include 37 to 39 hours in 9 areas of understanding. Students must complete 125 credit hours, with at least 30 in the major, and maintain a GPA of 2.0 overall and in the major.

Special: Work-study programs, internships, study abroad in 9 countries, a Washington semester, accelerated degrees, and dual majors, including sociology/anthropology, are available. A 3–2 engineering degree is offered with Pennsylvania State University; a 2–2 allied health degree and a 2–3 physical therapy degree, with Thomas Jefferson University; and a 3–2 forestry or environmental management degree with Duke Univesity. There are 13 national honor societies on campus.

Faculty/Classroom: 72% of faculty are male; 28%, female. All teach; 33% both teach and do research. The average class size in an introductory lecture is 23; in a laboratory, 18; and in a regular course offering, 20.

Admissions: 74% of the 1995–96 applicants were accepted. The SAT I scores for the 1995–96 freshman class were as follows: Verbal—51% below 500, 38% between 500 and 599, 10% between 600 and 700, and 1% above 700; Math—27% below 500, 43% between 500 and 599, 27% between 600 and 700, and 3% above 700. The ACT scores were 18% below 21, 26% between 21 and 23, 21% between 24 and 26, 26% between 27 and 28, and 8% above 28. 62% of the current freshmen were in the top fifth of their class; 85% were in the top two fifths. 6 freshmen graduated first in their class.

Requirements: The SAT I or ACT is required. Recommended comtposite scores for the SAT I range from 950 to 1130; for the ACT, 23 to 27. Applicants must be graduates of an accredited secondary

school or have earned a GED. The college encourages completion of 18 academic credits based on 4 years of English, 3 of mathematics, 2 each of laboratory science, social studies, and consecutive foreign language, and 5 additional college preparatory units. An audition is required for music majors and an interview is required for occupational therapy majors. Applications are accepted on computer disk accompanied by hard copy. AP and CLEP credits are accepted. Important factors in the admissions decision are advanced placement or honor courses, recommendations by school officials, and extracurricular activities record.

Procedure: Freshmen are admitted to all sessions. Entrance exams should be taken in spring of the junior year or fall of the senior year. There are early admissions and deferred admissions plans. Application deadlines are December 15 for occupational therapy majors and March 15 for international business majors; for all others, deadlines are open. Application fee is $20. Notification is sent on a rolling basis.

Transfer: 24 transfer students enrolled in 1995–96. Applicants should present a minimum GPA of 3.0 in at least 15 credit hours earned from a community college, or 2.5 from a 4-year institution. 30 credits of 125 must be completed at E-town.

Visiting: There are regularly scheduled orientations for prospective students, including 6 open houses and weekday appointments throughout the year, with Saturday interviews available during the academic year. There are guides for informal visits and visitors may sit in on classes and stay overnight at the school. To schedule a visit, contact the Admissions Office.

Financial Aid: In 1995–96, 93% of all freshmen and 89% of continuing students received some form of financial aid. 82% of freshmen and 78% of continuing students received need-based aid. The average freshman award was $13,189. Of that total, scholarships or need-based grants averaged $9091 ($15,000 maximum); loans averaged $3625 (maximum); and work contracts averaged $1325 ($1500 maximum). 67% of undergraduate students work part-time. Average earnings from campus work for the school year are $797. The average financial indebtedness of the 1994–95 graduate was $15,000. The FAFSA, the college's own financial statement, and the CSS Profile Application are required. The application deadline for fall entry is April 1.

International Students: In a recent year, 34 international students were enrolled. The school actively recruits these students. They must take the TOEFL and achieve a minimum score of 525.

Computers: The college provides computer facilities for student use. The mainframe is a DEC MicroVAX 3100. A 24-hour terminal room allows student access to the mainframe. Several laboratories house a total of 40 Apple Macintosh and 43 IBM and IBM-compatible microcomputers, all of which are networked to the mainframe and provide access to the Internet system. All students may access the system almost 100 hours per week. There are no time limits and no fees. It is recommended that students in communications have Macintosh or IBM-compatible PCs.

Graduates: In 1994–95, 287 bachelor's degrees were awarded. The most popular majors among graduates were business (24%), education (17%), and communications (14%). Within an average freshman class, 60% graduate in 4 years, 65% in 5 years, and 66% in 6 years. Of the 1994 graduating class, 15% were enrolled in graduate school within 6 months of graduation and 83% had found employment.

Admissions Contact: Ronald Potier, Director of Admissions. E-mail: admissions@vax.etown.edu.

FRANKLIN AND MARSHALL COLLEGE　　E-3
Lancaster, PA 17604-3003　　(717) 291-3951; FAX: (717) 291-4389

Full-time: 975 men, 838 women	Faculty: 147; IIB, +$
Part-time: 27 men, 26 women	Ph.D.s: 95%
Graduate: none	Student/Faculty: 12 to 1
Year: semesters, summer session	Tuition,
Application Deadline: February 1	Room & Board: $ 25,630
Freshman Class: 3430 applied, 2366 accepted, 500 enrolled	
SAT I: required	HIGHLY COMPETITIVE

Franklin and Marshall College, founded in 1787, is a private, coeducational liberal arts institution. There is a comprehensive charge covering tuition, fees, and room and board. The 2 libraries contain 345,000 volumes, 250,000 microform items, and 8500 audiovisual forms, and subscribe to 1703 periodicals. Computerized library sources and services include the card catalog, interlibrary loans, and database searching. Special learning facilities include a learning resource center, art gallery, natural history museum, planetarium, radio station, TV station, instructional media services, and an advanced language laboratory. The 125-acre campus is in a suburban area 60 miles west of Philadelphia. Including residence halls, there are 44 buildings on campus.

Student Life: 65% of undergraduates are from out-of-state, mostly the Middle Atlantic. Students come from 40 states, 33 foreign countries, and Canada. 58% are from public schools; 42% from private. 78% are white. 30% are Orthodox Christian, Greek Catholic, Buddhist, Hindu, Moslem, and so on; 30% Catholic; 28% Protestant; 12% Jewish. The average age of freshmen is 18; all undergraduates, 19.5. 4% do not continue beyond their first year; 85% remain to graduate.

Housing: 1320 students can be accommodated in college housing. College-sponsored living facilities include coed dormitories and off-campus apartments. In addition, there are language houses, special interest houses, an arts house, a co-op house, and an international living center. On-campus housing is guaranteed for the freshman year only and is available on a lottery system for upperclassmen. 70% of students live on campus; of those, 85% remain on campus on weekends. All students may keep cars on campus.

Activities: 40% of men belong to independent, off-campus fraternities; 30% of women belong to independent sororities. There are 110 groups on campus, including art, band, cheerleading, chess, choir, chorale, chorus, computers, dance, drama, ethnic, film, gay, honors, international, jazz band, literary magazine, musical theater, newspaper, opera, orchestra, pep band, photography, political, professional, radio and TV, religious, social, social service, student government, symphony, and yearbook. Popular campus events include Spring and Fall Arts Weekends.

Sports: There are 13 intercollegiate sports each for men and women, and 12 intramural sports each for men and women. Athletic and recreation facilities include a 3000-seat gymnasium, a steam room, a swimming pool, 4 squash courts, a wrestling room, 54 acres of playing fields, a 400-meter all-weather track, a wellness/aerobic center, a strength training center, and tennis courts. A new sport center features a fitness center, 5 multipurpose courts, 2 jogging tracks, and an Olympic-size pool.

Disabled Students: 70% of the campus is accessible to disabled students. The following facilities are available: wheelchair ramps, elevators, special parking, specially equipped rest rooms, special class scheduling, lowered drinking fountains, and lowered telephones.

Services: In addition to many counseling and information services, tutoring is available in every subject.

Campus Safety and Security: Campus safety and security measures include 24-hour foot and vehicle patrol, self-defense education, escort service, and informal discussions. In addition, there are pamphlets/posters/films, emergency telephones, lighted pathways/sidewalks, and regular fire safety drills held in residence halls and academic buildings.

Programs of Study: F & M confers the B.A. degree. Bachelor's degrees are awarded in BIOLOGICAL SCIENCE (biology/biological science), BUSINESS (accounting and business administration and management), COMMUNICATIONS AND THE ARTS (classics, dramatic arts, English, fine arts, French, German, Greek, Latin, music, and Spanish), COMPUTER AND PHYSICAL SCIENCE (chemistry, geology, mathematics, and physics), SOCIAL SCIENCE (American studies, anthropology, biopsychology, economics, history, philosophy, political science/government, psychology, religion, and sociology). Biological and physical science and social sciences are the strongest academically. Government, business administration, and English have the largest enrollments.

Required: Students must complete 11 to 13 college studies courses from 8 areas of study, including scientific inquiry, social analysis, arts, foreign cultures, historical studies, literature, systems of knowledge and belief, and language studies. They must also demonstrate writing proficiency. The bachelor's degree requires completion of at least 32 courses, including a minimum of 8 in the major, with a minimum GPA of 2.0.

Special: There is a 3–2 degree program in forestry and environmental studies with Duke University, as well as 3–2 degree programs in engineering with the University of Pennsylvania, Columbia University, Rensselaer Polytechnic Institute, Case Western Reserve, Georgia Institute of Technology, and Washington University at St. Louis. Cross-registration with the Central Pennsylvania Consortium allows students to study at nearby Dickinson College or Gettysburg College. Students may also study architecture and urban planning at Columbia University, studio art at the School of Visual Arts in New York City, theater in Connecticut, oceanography in Massachusetts, and American studies at American University. There are study abroad programs in England, Greece, Italy, Denmark, India, the Orient, and other locations. F & M also offers internships, an accelerated degree program, dual majors, student-designed majors, independent study, interdisciplinary studies, optional freshman seminars, pass/fail options, and nondegree study. There are 12 national honor societies on campus, including Phi Beta Kappa.

Faculty/Classroom: 70% of faculty are male; 30%, female. All both teach and do research. The average class size in an introductory lecture is 23; in a laboratory, 18; and in a regular course offering, 18.

Admissions: 69% of the 1995–96 applicants were accepted. The SAT I scores for the 1995–96 freshman class were as follows: Verbal—21% below 500, 44% between 500 and 599, 30% between 600 and 700, and 5% above 700; Math—5% below 500, 22% between 500 and 599, 54% between 600 and 700, and 19% above 700. 71% of the current freshmen were in the top fifth of their class;

93% were in the top two fifths. There were 8 National Merit semifinalists. 39 freshmen graduated first in their class.

Requirements: The SAT I is required. Standardized tests are optional for students in the top 10% of their class. The SAT II: Subject test in writing is required. Applicants must be graduates of accredited secondary schools. Recommended college preparatory study includes 4 years each of English and mathematics, 3 or 4 of foreign language, 3 each of laboratory science and history/social studies, and 1 or 2 courses in art or music. All students must also submit their high school transcripts, recommendations from a teacher and a counselor, and a personal essay. An interview is recommended. AP and CLEP credits are accepted. Important factors in the admissions decision are advanced placement or honor courses, recommendations by school officials, and extracurricular activities record.

Procedure: Freshmen are admitted in the fall. Entrance exams should be taken by December of the senior year. There are early decision, early admissions, and deferred admissions plans. Early decision applications should be filed by January 15; regular applications, by February 1 for fall entry, along with an application fee of $35. Notification for early decision is sent within 1 month after receipt of application and supporting documentation. Notification for regular decision is sent on or before April 1. 117 early decision candidates were accepted for the 1995–96 class. A waiting list is an active part of the admissions procedure, with about 20% of all applicants on the list.

Transfer: 18 transfer students enrolled in 1995–96. Applicants must present a minimum GPA of 3.0 in course work completed at an accredited college. An interview, SAT I or ACT scores, college and secondary school transcripts, a dean's form, recommendations from 2 professors, and a letter explaining the reason for transfer are also required. An associate degree is recommended. 16 courses of a total of 32 must be completed at F & M.

Visiting: There are regularly scheduled orientations for prospective students, including a campus tour, interview, class visit, and overnight stay. There are guides for informal visits and visitors may sit in on classes and stay overnight at the school. To schedule a visit, contact the Admissions Office.

Financial Aid: 50% of freshmen and 46% of continuing students received need-based aid. The average freshman award was $16,350. Of that total, scholarships or need-based grants averaged $13,570 ($24,925 maximum); loans averaged $2625 ($3650 maximum); and work contracts averaged $1350 (maximum). 50% of undergraduate students work part-time. Average earnings from campus work for the school year are $1350. The average financial indebtedness of the 1994–95 graduate was $16,125. F & M is a member of CSS. The FAF or FAFSA are required. If applicable, the Business/Farm Supplement and Divorced/Separated Parents Statement must also be submitted. The application deadline for fall entry is February 1.

International Students: In a recent year, 106 international students enrolled. The school actively recruits these students. They must take the TOEFL and achieve a minimum score of 600. The student must also take the SAT I or the ACT.

Computers: The college provides computer facilities for student use. The mainframe is a DEC MicroVAX 3800. A computer workroom houses 32 Apple Macintoshes, 6 Apple LaserWriter printers, 1 Color Apple printer, and 1 HP laser printer which is directly connected to the mainframe. All of the Apple Macintoshes are on the campuswide network for access to file servers and the academic VAX. A team of 25 student computing consultants is available for computing support and problem-solving assistance. All students may access the system 16 hours on weekdays and 13 hours on weekends. There are no time limits and no fees.

Graduates: In a recent year, 400 bachelor's degrees were awarded. The most popular majors among graduates were government (18%), business (13%), and English (8%). Within an average freshman class, 75% graduate in 4 years, 83% in 5 years, and 84% in 6 years. 190 companies recruited on campus in a recent year.

Admissions Contact: Peter Van Buskirk, Dean of Admissions.

GANNON UNIVERSITY

B-1

Erie, PA 16541

(814) 871-7240

(800) GANNON U; FAX: (814) 871-5803

Full-time: 1127 men, 1406 women	Faculty: 189; IIA, --$
Part-time: 181 men, 277 women	Ph.D.s: 53%
Graduate: 212 men, 325 women	Student/Faculty: 13 to 1
Year: semesters, summer session	Tuition: $10,870-$11,114
Application Deadline: open	Room & Board: $4520
Freshman Class: 2673 applied, 2066 accepted, 596 enrolled	
SAT I Verbal/Math: 460/530	ACT: 23 COMPETITIVE

Gannon University, founded in 1925, is a private, coeducational, liberal arts and teacher preparation university affiliated with the Roman Catholic Church. There are 2 undergraduate schools and one graduate school. In addition to regional accreditation, Gannon has baccalaureate program accreditation with ABET, ADA, CAHEA, CSWE, and NLN. The library contains 248,938 volumes, 402,228 microform items, and 2300 audiovisual forms, and subscribes to 1245 periodicals. Computerized library sources and services include the card catalog, interlibrary loans, and database searching. Special learning facilities include a learning resource center, art gallery, and radio station. The 13-acre campus is in an urban area 135 miles north of Pittsburgh. Including residence halls, there are 29 buildings on campus.

Student Life: 80% of undergraduates are from Pennsylvania. Students come from 29 states, 12 foreign countries, and Canada. 80% are from public schools. 92% are white. 57% are Catholic; and 26% Protestant. The average age of freshmen is 19.3; all undergraduates, 21.4. 14% do not continue beyond their first year; 61% remain to graduate.

Housing: 1100 students can be accommodated in college housing. College-sponsored living facilities include single-sex and coed dormitories, on-campus apartments, fraternity houses, and sorority houses. On-campus housing is available on a lottery system for upperclassmen. 59% of students live on campus; of those, 85% remain on campus on weekends. Alcohol is not permitted. Upperclassmen may keep cars on campus.

Activities: 7% of men belong to 7 national fraternities; 6% of women belong to 5 national sororities. There are 70 groups on campus, including cheerleading, computers, drama, ethnic, honors, international, literary magazine, newspaper, orchestra, pep band, political, professional, religious, social, social service, and student government. Popular campus events include the MDA Dance Marathon, Family Weekend, and Earth Day.

Sports: There are 9 intercollegiate sports for men and 8 for women, and 18 intramural sports for men and 9 for women. Athletic and recreation facilities include a pool, a gymnasium, a track, a weight room, racquetball courts, an outdoor recreation field, outdoor tennis courts, and a 3000-seat basketball and volleyball venue.

Disabled Students: 85% of the campus is accessible to disabled students. The following facilities are available: wheelchair ramps, elevators, specially equipped rest rooms, special class scheduling, lowered drinking fountains, lowered telephones, and special drop-off points.

Services: In addition to many counseling and information services, tutoring is available in some subjects. There is also remedial math and writing. There are mathematics, writing, and advising centers.

Campus Safety and Security: Campus safety and security measures include 24-hour foot and vehicle patrol, escort service, informal discussions, and pamphlets/posters/films. In addition, there are emergency telephones, lighted pathways/sidewalks, and security cameras in most buildings.

Programs of Study: Gannon confers B.A., B.S., B.E.E., B.E.T., B.M.E., and B.S.N. degrees. Associate and master's degrees are also awarded. Bachelor's degrees are awarded in BIOLOGICAL SCIENCE (biology/biological science), BUSINESS (accounting, banking and finance, business administration and management, business economics, international business management, and marketing/retailing/merchandising), COMMUNICATIONS AND THE ARTS (communications and English), COMPUTER AND PHYSICAL SCIENCE (chemistry, computer science, earth science, mathematics, and physics), EDUCATION (early childhood, elementary, secondary, and special), ENGINEERING AND ENVIRONMENTAL DESIGN (electrical/electronics engineering, engineering technology, industrial administration/management, and industrial engineering technology), HEALTH PROFESSIONS (medical laboratory technology, mental health/human services, nursing, occupational therapy, physician's assistant, predentistry, premedicine, prepharmacy, preveterinary science, recreation therapy, and respiratory therapy), SOCIAL SCIENCE (anthropology, criminal justice, dietetics, history, international studies, paralegal studies, philosophy, political science/government, prelaw, psychology, social science, social work, and sociology). Engineering, preprofessional, and nursing are the strongest academically. Nursing, biology, criminal justice, and physician's assistant have the largest enrollments.

Required: Students must complete at least 128 hours of academic work. Each academic program has specific course requirements. Students must have a cumulative GPA of at least 2.0 overall and in the area of concentration. Three writing-intensive courses must be completed after the freshman year; 1 must be taken in the senior year.

Special: The university offers study abroad in more than 5 countries, co-op programs, summer internships, cross-registration with Mercyhurst College, pass/fail options, work-study programs, a general studies program, an accelerated degree program, a combined B.A.-B.S. degree, a 3-2 engineering degree with the universities of Akron, Pittsburgh, and Detroit, and nondegree study. The B.S. in mortuary science program consists of 2 or 3 years of study at Gannon with degree completion at a school of mortuary science. Gannon also offers a medical degree program in conjunction with Hahnemann University. There is a freshman honors program on campus, as well as 11 national honor societies. There is also a universitywide honors program.

Faculty/Classroom: 59% of faculty are male; 41%, female. 91% teach undergraduates and 6% do research. No introductory courses are taught by graduate students. The average class size in an introductory lecture is 30; in a laboratory, 20; and in a regular course offering, 17.

Admissions: 77% of the 1995–96 applicants were accepted. The SAT I scores for the 1995–96 freshman class were as follows: Verbal—19% below 500, 55% between 500 and 599, 23% between 600 and 700, and 3% above 700; Math—17% below 500, 60% between 500 and 599, 22% between 600 and 700, and 2% above 700. The ACT scores were 16% below 21, 41% between 21 and 23, 26% between 24 and 26, 11% between 27 and 28, and 7% above 28. 49% of the current freshmen were in the top fifth of their class; 79% were in the top two fifths. 12 freshmen graduated first in their class.

Requirements: The SAT I or ACT is required. Gannon requires applicants to be in the upper 50% of their class and have a 2.5 GPA. Candidates should have completed 16 academic units including 4 in English and 12 in social sciences, foreign languages, mathematics, and science, depending on the degree sought. Specific courses in mathematics and science are required for some majors in health sciences and engineering. AP and CLEP credits are accepted. Important factors in the admissions decision are advanced placement or honor courses, leadership record, and recommendations by school officials.

Procedure: Freshmen are admitted to all sessions. Entrance exams should be taken at the end of junior year or the beginning of senior year. There are early admissions and deferred admissions plans. Application deadlines are open. Application fee is $25. Notification is sent on a rolling basis. A waiting list is an active part of the admissions procedure.

Transfer: 102 transfer students enrolled in 1995–96. Applicants should be in good standing at their previous institution with at least a 2.0 GPA. They must submit all transcripts and a college clearance from the college most recently attended. A high school transcript is required from transfer students with fewer than 60 credits. Several health science programs are not designed to accomodate transfers. 30 credits of 128 must be completed at Gannon.

Visiting: There are regularly scheduled orientations for prospective students, consisting of open houses for prospective students in the fall and spring. Students may meet with faculty, tour the campus, and attend a variety of presentations. There are guides for informal visits and visitors may sit in on classes and stay overnight at the school. To schedule a visit, contact the Admissions Office.

Financial Aid: In 1995–96, 91% of all freshmen and 84% of continuing students received some form of financial aid. 76% of freshmen and 71% of continuing students received need-based aid. The average freshman award was $9593. Of that total, scholarships or need-based grants averaged $4131 ($11,764 maximum); loans averaged $2500 ($2625 maximum); and work contracts averaged $1200. 82% of undergraduate students work part-time. Average earnings from campus work for the school year are $1200. The average financial indebtedness of the 1994–95 graduate was $17,500. Gannon is a member of CSS. The FAFSA and the college's own financial statement are required. The application deadline for fall entry is March 1.

International Students: There are currently 46 international students enrolled. The school actively recruits these students. They must take the TOEFL and achieve a minimum score of 500.

Computers: The college provides computer facilities for student use. The mainframes are a DEC VAX 6000–410 cluster, 2 DEC VAX 6410 clusters, and a Sun 2000. There is 1 mainframe laboratory and 2 personal computer laboratories with about 30 personal computers in each laboratory. The departments of business, engineering, and education maintain special computer laboratories. All students may access the system Monday through Friday 9 A.M. to midnight, Saturday noon to 6 P.M., and Sunday noon to midnight. There are no time limits. The fees are $150 per year.

Graduates: In 1994–95, 487 bachelor's degrees were awarded. The most popular majors among graduates were biology (12%), nursing (10%), and criminal justice (6%). Within an average freshman class, 1% graduate in 3 years, 43% in 4 years, 15% in 5 years, and 1% in 6 years. 5 companies recruited on campus in 1994–95. Of the 1994 graduating class, 22% were enrolled in graduate school within 6 months of graduation and 54% had found employment.

Admissions Contact: Joyce Scheid-Gilman, Director of Freshman Admissions. E-mail: admissions@cluster.gannon.edu. World Wide Web home page: http://www.gannon.edu.

GENEVA COLLEGE
Beaver Falls, PA 15010

A-3

(412) 847-6500
(800) 847-8255; FAX: (412) 847-6776

Full-time: 1102 men and women	Faculty: 52; IIB, -$
Part-time: 104 men and women	Ph.D.s: 71%
Graduate: 108 men and women	Student/Faculty: 21 to 1
Year: semesters, summer session	Tuition: $10,084
Application Deadline: open	Room & Board: $4400
Freshman Class: 708 applied, 567 accepted, 266 enrolled	
SAT I Verbal/Math: 470/520	ACT: 22	COMPETITIVE

Geneva College, founded in 1848, is a private coeducational institution affiliated with the Reformed Presbyterian Church of North America. The college offers undergraduate programs in the arts and sciences, business, education, health science, biblical and religious studies, engineering, and preprofessional training. There are 2 graduate schools. In addition to regional accreditation, Geneva has baccalaureate program accreditation with ABET. The library contains 151,481 volumes, 80,434 microform items, and 22,229 audiovisual forms, and subscribes to 751 periodicals. Computerized library sources and services include the card catalog, interlibrary loans, and database searching. Special learning facilities include a radio station and TV station. The 50-acre campus is in a small town 35 miles northwest of Pittsburgh. Including residence halls, there are 30 buildings on campus.

Student Life: 78% of undergraduates are from Pennsylvania. Students come from 32 states, 17 foreign countries, and Canada. 87% are from public schools; 13% from private. 87% are white; 10% African American. 75% are Protestant; 16% Catholic. The average age of freshmen is 19; all undergraduates, 23. 21% do not continue beyond their first year; 48% remain to graduate.

Housing: 822 students can be accommodated in college housing. College-sponsored living facilities include single-sex dormitories and on-campus apartments. In addition there is Discipleship House for those interested in structural growth opportunities. On-campus housing is guaranteed for all 4 years. 52% of students live on campus. Alcohol is not permitted. All students may keep cars on campus.

Activities: There are no fraternities or sororities. There are 50 groups on campus, including band, cheerleading, choir, chorus, computers, drama, drill team, ethnic, honors, international, jazz band, literary magazine, marching band, musical theater, newspaper, pep band, photography, radio and TV, religious, social, social service, student government, and yearbook. Popular campus events include Parents Weekend and Homecoming.

Sports: There are 7 intercollegiate sports for men and 7 for women, and 4 intramural sports for men and 3 for women. Athletic and recreation facilities include a 5600-seat stadium, a field house, a 3200-seat gymnasium, a practice gymnasium, track, athletic fields, racquetball and tennis courts, and weight training rooms.

Disabled Students: The following facilities are available: wheelchair ramps, elevators, special parking, specially equipped rest rooms, and special class scheduling.

Services: In addition to many counseling and information services, tutoring is available in most subjects. There is remedial math, reading, and writing.

Campus Safety and Security: Campus safety and security measures include self-defense education, escort service, and informal discussions.

Programs of Study: Geneva confers B.A., B.S., B.S.B.A., B.S.Ed., and B.S.E. degrees. Associate and master's degrees are also awarded. Bachelor's degrees are awarded in BIOLOGICAL SCIENCE (biology/biological science), BUSINESS (accounting, business administration and management, and human resources), COMMUNICATIONS AND THE ARTS (applied music, broadcasting, communications, English, music, music business management, music performance, Spanish, speech/debate/rhetoric, and technical and business writing), COMPUTER AND PHYSICAL SCIENCE (applied mathematics, chemistry, computer science, physics, and science), EDUCATION (business, elementary, mathematics, and music), ENGINEERING AND ENVIRONMENTAL DESIGN (aviation administration/management, chemical engineering, civil engineering, electrical/electronics engineering, engineering, and mechanical engineering), HEALTH PROFESSIONS (medical technology, nursing, premedicine, and speech pathology/audiology), SOCIAL SCIENCE (biblical studies, counseling psychology, history, ministries, philosophy, political science/government, prelaw, psychology, and sociology). Engineering and business administration are the strongest academically. Elementary education, business administration, and psychology have the largest enrollments.

Required: The core curriculum includes 12 hours of humanities, 9 each of biblical studies and social science, 8 to 10 of natural science, 6 of communications, 2 of physical education, and the 1-hour Freshman Experience course. Students must also fulfill 1 chapel credit per semester or summer session. To graduate, students must complete

126 to 138 semester hours, including those required for a major, with a minimum GPA of 2.0.

Special: Cross-registration is offered in conjunction with Pennsylvania State University/Beaver Campus and Community College of Beaver County. There are 2-2 and 3-2 degree programs in nursing with the University of Rochester, a 3-1 degree program in cardiovascular technology, and an accelerated degree program in human resource management. Off-campus study includes programs at Philadelphia center for urban biblical studies, a Washington semester, a summer program at AuSable Trails Institute of Environmental Studies in Michigan, art studies in Pittsburgh, film studies in Los Angeles, and study abroad in Costa Rica, Russia, and the Middle East. Geneva also offers internships, independent study, and credit by proficiency exam. Non-degree study is available through adult education programs. There is a freshman honors program on campus, as well as 1 national honor society.

Faculty/Classroom: 85% of faculty are male; 15%, female. All teach undergraduates. No introductory courses are taught by graduate students.

Admissions: 80% of the 1995-96 applicants were accepted. The SAT I scores for the 1995-96 freshman class were as follows: Verbal—62% below 500, 28% between 500 and 599, and 10% between 600 and 700; Math—44% below 500, 32% between 500 and 599, 22% between 600 and 700, and 2% above 700. The ACT scores were 32% below 21, 37% between 21 and 23, 13% between 24 and 26, 13% between 27 and 28, and 5% above 28. 32% of the current freshmen were in the top fifth of their class; 61% were in the top two fifths. There were 2 National Merit semifinalists. 13 freshmen graduated first in their class.

Requirements: The SAT I or ACT is required. Geneva requires applicants to be in the upper 50% of their class and have a minimum GPA of 2.0. Applicants must be graduates of an accredited secondary school or have earned a GED. Geneva requires 16 academic units, based on 3 of social studies, 2 each of mathematics and foreign language, and 4 each of English and electives, and 1 of science. An essay is required, and an interview is recommended. AP and CLEP credits are accepted. Important factors in the admissions decision are recommendations by school officials, advanced placement or honor courses, and leadership record.

Procedure: Freshmen are admitted to all sessions. Entrance exams should be taken during the junior or senior year. There is an early admissions plan. Application deadlines are open. Application fee is $15. Notification is sent on a rolling basis within 2 weeks of receipt of the completed application.

Transfer: 116 transfer students enrolled in 1995-96. 48 credits of a minimum 126 must be completed at Geneva.

Visiting: There are regularly scheduled orientations for prospective students, including class visits, a campus tour, and meetings with faculty and admissions, and financial aid conselors. There are guides for informal visits and visitors may sit in on classes and stay overnight at the school. To schedule a visit, contact Jerryn Carson, Campus Visit Coordinator.

Financial Aid: In 1995-96, 93% of all freshmen and 90% of continuing students received some form of financial aid. 73% of freshmen and 65% of continuing students received need-based aid. The average freshman award was $6568. Of that total, scholarships or need-based grants averaged $4224 ($5000 maximum); and loans averaged $2234 ($2625 maximum). 65% of undergraduate students work part-time. Geneva is a member of CSS. The FAFSA is required. The application deadline for fall entry is March 1.

International Students: There are currently 25 international students enrolled. The school actively recruits these students. They must take the TOEFL and achieve a minimum score of 500.

Computers: The college provides computer facilities for student use. The mainframes are a DEC VAX 11/780 and an IBM AS/400. A DEC VAX 12 is used for classroom work. The computer center houses 2 microcomputer laboratories, as well as specialized computer resources for individual subjects. Computer science students may access the system during supervised laboratory hours. There are no time limits and no fees.

Graduates: In 1994-95, 495 bachelor's degrees were awarded. The most popular majors among graduates were education (20%), business (16%), and biology (10%). Within an average freshman class, 1% graduate in 3 years, 42% in 4 years, 54% in 5 years, and 58% in 6 years. 30 companies recruited on campus in 1994-95.

Admissions Contact: David Layton, Director of Admissions. A campus video is available.

GETTYSBURG COLLEGE
D-4

Gettysburg, PA 17325-1484

(717) 337-6100

(800) 431-0803; FAX: (717) 337-6145

Full-time: 975 men, 975 women	Faculty: 154; IIB, +$
Part-time: 10 men, 25 women	Ph.D.s: 95%
Graduate: none	Student/Faculty: 13 to 1
Year: semesters	Tuition: $20,744
Application Deadline: February 15	Room & Board: $4522
Freshman Class: 3910 applied, 2495 accepted, 605 enrolled	
SAT I or ACT: required	**HIGHLY COMPETITIVE**

Gettysburg College, founded in 1832, is an independent college affiliated with the Lutheran Church. It offers programs in the liberal arts. The library contains 350,000 volumes, 2900 microform items, and 30,000 audiovisual forms, and subscribes to 1500 periodicals. Computerized library sources and services include the card catalog, interlibrary loans, and database searching. Special learning facilities include a learning resource center, art gallery, planetarium, radio station, fine arts facilities, a greenhouse, an observatory, and 2 electron microscopes. The 225-acre campus is in a small town 30 miles south of Harrisburg. Including residence halls, there are 60 buildings.

Student Life: 75% of undergraduates are from out-of-state, mostly the Middle Atlantic. Students come from 40 states, 35 foreign countries, and Canada. 75% are from public schools; 25% from private. 89% are white. 38% are Protestant; 33% Catholic. The average age of freshmen is 18; all undergraduates, 20. 10% do not continue beyond their first year; 80% remain to graduate.

Housing: 1750 students can be accommodated in college housing. College-sponsored living facilities include single-sex and coed dormitories, on-campus apartments, off-campus apartments, and fraternity houses. In addition, there are language houses and special interest houses. On-campus housing is guaranteed for all 4 years. 90% of students live on campus; of those, 90% remain on campus on weekends. All students may keep cars on campus.

Activities: 55% of men belong to 11 national fraternities; 45% of women belong to 5 national sororities. There are 65 groups on campus, including art, band, cheerleading, chess, choir, chorale, chorus, computers, dance, drama, drill team, ethnic, gay, honors, international, jazz band, literary magazine, marching band, musical theater, newspaper, opera, orchestra, pep band, photography, political, professional, radio and TV, religious, social, social service, student government, symphony, and yearbook. Popular campus events include International Festival, Parents Weekend, and Get Acquainted Day.

Sports: There are 12 intercollegiate sports for men and 12 for women, and 15 intramural sports for men and 15 for women. Athletic and recreation facilities include 7 basketball courts, indoor and outdoor tennis courts, a pool, and several tracks and fields.

Disabled Students: 90% of the campus is accessible to disabled students. The following facilities are available: wheelchair ramps, elevators, special parking, specially equipped rest rooms, and special class scheduling.

Services: In addition to many counseling and information services, tutoring is available in most subjects.

Campus Safety and Security: Campus safety and security measures include 24-hour foot and vehicle patrol, self-defense education, escort service, and informal discussions. There are pamphlets/posters/films, emergency telephones, and lighted pathways/sidewalks.

Programs of Study: Gettysburg confers B.A., B.S., and B.S.M.E. degrees. Bachelor's degrees are awarded in BIOLOGICAL SCIENCE (biochemistry and biology/biological science), BUSINESS (business administration and management), COMMUNICATIONS AND THE ARTS (art history and appreciation, classics, dramatic arts, English, French, German, Greek, Latin, music, Spanish, and studio art), COMPUTER AND PHYSICAL SCIENCE (chemistry, computer science, mathematics, and physics), EDUCATION (elementary, foreign languages, music, science, and secondary), ENGINEERING AND ENVIRONMENTAL DESIGN (environmental science), HEALTH PROFESSIONS (health science, predentistry, and premedicine), SOCIAL SCIENCE (anthropology, economics, history, international relations, philosophy, political science/government, prelaw, psychology, religion, sociology, and women's studies). Management, political science, and psychology are the strongest academically and have the largest enrollments.

Required: All students must take a freshman colloquy, demonstrate proficiency in written English, take 3 courses in physical education, and fulfill distribution requirements consisting of 2 natural science courses, 1 to 4 foreign language courses, and 1 course each in the arts, history/philosophy, literature, social science, religion, and non-Western culture. A total of 35 courses is required, with 8 to 12 in the major. The minimum GPA is 2.0.

Special: The college offers study abroad and has special centers in 8 countries. There are summer internships and a Washington semester with American University. Cross-registration is possible with members of the Central Pennsylvania Consortium. There is a United Nations semester at Drew University, and a 3-2 engineering program with Columbia University, Rensselaer Polytechnic, and Washington University in St. Louis. There are also joint programs in optometry with the Pennsylvania College of Optometry, and forestry and environmental studies with Duke University. The college also offers dual majors, student-designed majors, and B.A.-B.S. degrees in biology, mathematics, chemistry, physics, and biochemistry. There are 16 national honor societies on campus, including Phi Beta Kappa.

Faculty/Classroom: 65% of faculty are male; 35%, female. All both teach undergraduates and do research. The average class size in an introductory lecture is 25; in a laboratory, 15; and in a regular course offering, 20.

Admissions: 64% of the 1995-96 applicants were accepted. The SAT I scores for the 1995-96 freshman class were as follows: Verbal—25% below 500, 52% between 500 and 599, 21% between 600 and 700, and 2% above 700; Math—10% below 500, 39% between 500 and 599, 43% between 600 and 700, and 9% above 700. The ACT scores were 20% between 21 and 23, 25% between 24 and 26, 34% between 27 and 28, and 21% above 28. 75% of the current freshmen were in the top fifth of their class; 99% were in the top two fifths. 15 freshmen graduated first in their class.

Requirements: The SAT I or ACT is required. Applicants must be in the upper 40% of their class and have a 2.0 GPA. The GED is accepted. An essay is required. Art students must submit a portfolio, and music students must audition. An interview and SAT II: Subject tests are recommended. Students may apply on computer disk via the Common App. AP credits are accepted. Important factors in the admissions decision are advanced placement or honor courses, recommendations by school officials, and evidence of special talent.

Procedure: Freshmen are admitted in the fall and spring. Entrance exams should be taken by the January testing date of the senior year. There are early decision, early admissions, and deferred admissions plans. Early decision applications should be filed by February 1; regular applications, by February 15 for fall entry and December 1 for spring entry, along with an application fee of $35. Notification of early decision is sent at the beginning of December; regular decision, by early April. 137 early decision candidates were accepted for the 1995-96 class. A waiting list is an active part of the admissions procedure, with about 5% of all applicants on the list.

Transfer: 35 transfer students enrolled in 1995-96. Transfer applicants must have a GPA of at least 2.0. An interview is required. The high school record and test scores are also considered. 9 courses of 35 must be completed at Gettysburg.

Visiting: There are regularly scheduled orientations for prospective students, including interviews, tours, and special programs. There are guides for informal visits and visitors may sit in on classes and stay overnight at the school. To schedule a visit, contact the Admissions Office.

Financial Aid: In 1995-96, 57% of all freshmen and 50% of continuing students received some form of financial aid. 53% of freshmen and 52% of continuing students received need-based aid. The average freshman award was $16,900. Of that total, scholarships or need-based grants averaged $13,000 ($20,500 maximum); loans averaged $2500 ($3000 maximum); and work contracts averaged $1290 ($1400 maximum). 38% of undergraduate students work part-time. Average earnings from campus work for the school year are $1300. The average financial indebtedness of the 1994-95 graduate was $10,300. Gettysburg is a member of CSS. The FAF and FAFSA are required. The application deadline for fall entry is February 1.

International Students: There are currently 39 international students enrolled. The school actively recruits these students. They must take the TOEFL and achieve a minimum score of 550. The student must also take the SAT I or the ACT.

Computers: The college provides computer facilities for student use. The mainframes are a 4 100+ mips multiprocessor Sun servers, 2 VAX/VMS computers, a MicroVAX II, and a VAX II/750. A campus-wide network has connections to Internet and Bitnet. Microcomputers are available in laboratories and other locations throughout the campus. All students may access the system 24 hours a day. There are no time limits and no fees.

Graduates: In 1994-95, 478 bachelor's degrees were awarded. The most popular majors among graduates were management (18%), political science (17%), and psychology (10%). Within an average freshman class, 1% graduate in 3 years, 75% in 4 years, 80% in 5 years, and 81% in 6 years. 91 companies recruited on campus in 1994-95. Of the 1994 graduating class, 35% were enrolled in graduate school within 6 months of graduation and 62% had found employment.

Admissions Contact: Delwin Gustafson, Dean of Admissions. E-mail: admissions@gettysburg.edu.

GRATZ COLLEGE

Melrose Park, PA 19027

F-3

(215) 635-7300
(800) 475-4635; FAX: (215) 635-7302

Full-time: 6 men, 11 women	Faculty: 8
Part-time: 70 men and women	Ph.D.s: All
Graduate: 104 men and women	Student/Faculty: 2 to 1
Year: semesters, summer session	Tuition: $6450
Application Deadline: open	Room & Board: n/app
Freshman Class: n/av	
SAT I or ACT: not required	NONCOMPETITIVE

Gratz College, founded in 1895, is an independent, nonsectarian college offering undergraduate and graduate programs in Jewish, Hebraic, and Middle Eastern studies and in Jewish education. There is 1 graduate school. The library contains 100,000 volumes, 250 microform items, and 2500 audiovisual forms, and subscribes to 145 periodicals. Computerized library sources and services include the card catalog, interlibrary loans, and database searching. Special learning facilities include a Holocaust oral history archive, and a music library. The 28-acre campus is in a suburban area 4 miles north of Philadelphia. There are 6 buildings on campus.

Student Life: 80% of undergraduates are from Pennsylvania. Students come from 3 states, 3 foreign countries, and Canada. 93% are white. Most are Jewish.

Housing: There are no residence halls. All students commute. All students may keep cars on campus.

Activities: There are no fraternities or sororities. There are 5 groups on campus, including chorus, dance, professional, religious, and student government.

Sports: There is no sports program at Gratz.

Disabled Students: All of the campus is accessible to disabled students. The following facilities are available: wheelchair ramps, elevators, special parking, and specially equipped rest rooms.

Services: In addition to many counseling and information services, tutoring is available in most subjects.

Campus Safety and Security: Campus safety and security measures include 24-hour foot and vehicle patrol and lighted pathways/sidewalks.

Programs of Study: Gratz confers the B.A.J.S. degree. Master's degrees are also awarded. Bachelor's degrees are awarded in SOCIAL SCIENCE (Judaic studies and religion). Jewish studies is the strongest academically and has the largest enrollment.

Required: All students must complete 120 semester hours including 78 in the major. Distribution requirements include biblical studies, history, Jewish literature, music and the arts, rabbinics, Jewish social science, Jewish thought, and electives. In addition, 15 hours are needed in the Hebrew language.

Special: Study abroad in Israel is available. A B.A.-B.S. degree in Jewish studies, dual majors, nondegree study, and pass/fail options for transfer students also are possible.

Faculty/Classroom: 50% of faculty are male; 50%, female. All teach undergraduates. No introductory courses are taught by graduate students. The average class size in an introductory lecture is 13 and in a regular course offering, 13.

Requirements: Gratz follows an open admissions policy for all applicants who are graduates of an accredited high school or Jewish secondary day school. An essay is required for admission. The GED is accepted and students may take a series of proficiency examinations for credit. AP credits are accepted. Important factors in the admissions decision are personality/intangible qualities, extracurricular activities record, and evidence of special talent.

Procedure: Freshmen are admitted fall and winter. There is a deferred admissions plan. Application deadlines are open. The application fee is $50. The college accepts all applicants. Notification is sent on a rolling basis.

Transfer: 39 credits of 120 must be completed at Gratz.

Visiting: There are guides for informal visits and visitors may sit in on classes. To schedule a visit, contact the Office of Enrollment Management.

Financial Aid: Scholarships or need-based grants averaged $875 ($1200 maximum) in a recent year. 10% of undergraduate students work part-time. The college's own financial statement is required. The application deadline for fall entry is September 11.

International Students: In a recent year, 13 international students were enrolled. They must take the TOEFL.

Graduates: In a recent year, 6 bachelor's degrees were awarded. The most popular major among graduates was Jewish studies (100%).

Admissions Contact: Evelyn Klein, Director of Admissions. E-mail: gratzgen@hslc.org.

GROVE CITY COLLEGE

Grove City, PA 16127-2104

B-2

(412) 458-2100
FAX: (412) 458-3395

Full-time: 1145 men, 1117 women	Faculty: 105
Part-time: 20 men, 20 women	Ph.D.s: 68%
Graduate: 12 men, 10 women	Student/Faculty: 22 to 1
Year: semesters	Tuition: $6174
Application Deadline: February 15	Room & Board: $3474
Freshman Class: 2570 applied, 1227 accepted, 625 enrolled	
SAT I Verbal/Math: 549/622	ACT: 26 HIGHLY COMPETITIVE

Grove City College, founded in 1876, is a private, coeducational, liberal arts college affiliated with the United Presbyterian Church (U.S.A.). There is 1 undergraduate school. In addition to regional accreditation, Grove City has baccalaureate program accreditation with ABET. The library contains 170,000 volumes, 260,000 microform items, and 520 audiovisual forms, and subscribes to 1200 periodicals. Computerized library sources and services include the card catalog, interlibrary loans, and database searching. Special learning facilities include a learning resource center, art gallery, and radio station. The 150-acre campus is in a small town 60 miles north of Pittsburgh. Including residence halls, there are 27 buildings on campus.

Student Life: 62% of undergraduates are from Pennsylvania. Students come from 39 states, 19 foreign countries, and Canada. 90% are from public schools; 10% from private. 97% are white. 75% are Protestant; 15% Catholic. The average age of freshmen is 17; all undergraduates, 20. 10% do not continue beyond their first year; 78% remain to graduate.

Housing: 2028 students can be accommodated in college housing. College-sponsored living facilities include single-sex dormitories. On-campus housing is guaranteed for all 4 years. 91% of students live on campus; of those, 90% remain on campus on weekends. Alcohol is not permitted. Upperclassmen may keep cars on campus.

Activities: 30% of men belong to 5 local fraternities; 50% of women belong to 8 local sororities. There are more than 100 groups on campus, including art, band, cheerleading, choir, chorale, chorus, computers, dance, drama, drill team, ethnic, film, honors, international, jazz band, literary magazine, marching band, musical theater, newspaper, orchestra, pep band, photography, political, professional, radio and TV, religious, social, social service, student government, symphony, and yearbook. Popular campus events include Christmas Candlelight Service, talent shows, and Faculty Follies.

Sports: There are 9 intercollegiate sports for men and 9 for women, and 4 intramural sports for men and 11 for women. Athletic and recreation facilities include a field house, a recreation building that includes 2 indoor pools, an indoor running track, 4 basketball, volleyball, or tennis courts, 8 racquetball courts, bowling lanes, and a weight room, 10 outdoor tennis courts, a football stadium with a track, baseball, soccer, and softball fields; and a basketball arena.

Disabled Students: The entire campus is accessible to physically disabled persons. The following facilities are available: wheelchair ramps, elevators, special parking, specially equipped rest rooms, special class scheduling, lowered drinking fountains, and lowered telephones. The college's hillside location presents some difficulty for the seriously handicapped.

Services: In addition to many counseling and information services, tutoring is available in most subjects. A student tutoring program is available for a small fee.

Campus Safety and Security: Campus safety and security measures include 24-hour foot and vehicle patrol, escort service, pamphlets/posters/films, and emergency telephones. There are lighted pathways/sidewalks.

Programs of Study: Grove City confers B.A., B.S., B.Mus., B.S.E.E., and B.S.M.E. degrees. Master's degrees are also awarded. Bachelor's degrees are awarded in BIOLOGICAL SCIENCE (biochemistry and biology/biological science), BUSINESS (accounting, banking and finance, business administration and management, international business management, management information systems, and marketing/retailing/merchandising), COMMUNICATIONS AND THE ARTS (communications, English, French, music, music business management, music performance, and Spanish), COMPUTER AND PHYSICAL SCIENCE (chemistry, computer science, mathematics, and physics), EDUCATION (elementary, music, science, and secondary), ENGINEERING AND ENVIRONMENTAL DESIGN (electrical/electronics engineering, industrial administration/management, and mechanical engineering), HEALTH PROFESSIONS (predentistry and premedicine), SOCIAL SCIENCE (economics, history, philosophy, political science/government, prelaw, psychology, religion, and religious music). Business, engineering, and education are the strongest academically and have the largest enrollments.

Required: Students are required to complete a minimum of 128 credit hours (136 for engineering students). All students must complete the 38 semester-hour general education curriculum, which includes 18 hours of humanities, 8 of natural science, and 6 each of social science and quantitative and logical reasoning, 2 hours in physical education, 4 chapel credits, and 2 years of foreign language. A minimum GPA of 2.0 is required.

Special: The college offers study abroad, summer internships, 3 accelerated degree programs, student-designed interdisciplinary majors, nondegree study for special students, and a Washington semester. There are 9 national honor societies on campus. 16 departments have honors programs.

Faculty/Classroom: 75% of faculty are male; 25%, female. 99% teach undergraduates and 25% both teach and do research. No introductory courses are taught by graduate students. The average class size in an introductory lecture is 41; in a laboratory, 25; and in a regular course offering, 32.

Admissions: 48% of the 1995–96 applicants were accepted. The SAT I scores for the 1995–96 freshman class were as follows: Verbal—22% below 500, 53% between 500 and 599, 23% between 600 and 700, and 2% above 700; Math—5% below 500, 30% between 500 and 599, 51% between 600 and 700, and 14% above 700. 82% of the current freshmen were in the top fifth of their class; 96% were in the top two fifths. There were 3 National Merit finalists. 59 freshmen graduated first in their class.

Requirements: The SAT I or ACT is required. The academic or college preparatory course is highly recommended, including 4 units each of English, history, mathematics, science, and a foreign language. An essay is required of all applicants, and an audition is required of music students. An interview is highly recommended. AP and CLEP credits are accepted. Important factors in the admissions decision are advanced placement or honor courses, leadership record, and extracurricular activities record.

Procedure: Freshmen are admitted fall and spring. Entrance exams should be taken in the spring of the junior year or the fall of the senior year. There are early decision, early admissions, and deferred admissions plans. Early decision applications should be filed by November 15; regular applications, by February 15 for fall entry and January 1 for spring entry, along with an application fee of $25. Notification of early decision is sent December 10; regular decision, March 15. 359 early decision candidates were accepted for the 1995–96 class. A waiting list is an active part of the admissions procedure, with about 36% of all applicants on the list.

Transfer: 16 transfer students enrolled in 1995–96. Applicants should have a minimum of 17 credit hours earned with a 2.0 minimum GPA. Either the SAT I or the ACT is recommended, as is an interview. 32 credits of 128 must be completed at Grove City.

Visiting: There are regularly scheduled orientations for prospective students, consisting of daily interviews and tours, 2 high school visitation days in the fall, and a career day in the spring. There is a science and engineering open house in the fall. There are guides for informal visits and visitors may sit in on classes and stay overnight at the school. To schedule a visit, contact the Admissions Office.

Financial Aid: In 1995–96, 58% of all freshmen and 51% of continuing students received some form of financial aid. 39% of freshmen and 36% of continuing students received need-based aid. The average freshman award was $4906. Of that total, scholarships or need-based grants averaged $2565 ($11,625 maximum); and loans averaged $3966 ($10,080 maximum). 37% of undergraduate students work part-time. Average earnings from campus work for the school year are $604. The average financial indebtedness of the 1994–95 graduate was $10,580. Grove City is a member of CSS. The college's own financial statement is required. The application deadline for fall entry is April 15.

International Students: There are currently 19 international students enrolled. The school actively recruits these students. They must take the TOEFL and achieve a minimum score of 550. If the TOEFL is not available, either the SAT I or the ACT is required.

Computers: The college provides computer facilities for student use. The mainframe is a DEC VAX 6250. The technological learning center houses 120 microcomputers and terminal stations. All students may access the system from 8:00 A.M. to 11 P.M., Monday through Friday; 8:00 A.M. to 5 P.M., Saturday; and 2 P.M. to 11 P.M., Sunday. There are no time limits and no fees. All freshman receive a Compaq Contura 410 notebook computer and printer. This cost is included in the total 4 year tuition.

Graduates: In 1994–95, 530 bachelor's degrees were awarded. The most popular majors among graduates were business administration (19%), engineering (12%), and elementary education (8%). Within an average freshman class, 69% graduate in 4 years, 75% in 5 years, and 75% in 6 years. 88 companies recruited on campus in 1994–95. Of the 1994 graduating class, 20% were enrolled in graduate school within 6 months of graduation and 67% had found employment.

Admissions Contact: Jeffrey C. Mincey, Director of Admissions.

GWYNEDD-MERCY COLLEGE   F-4
Gwynedd Valley, PA 19437   (215) 641-5510
(800) DIAL-GMC; FAX: (215) 641-5556

Full-time: 117 men, 552 women	Faculty: 88; IIB, --$
Part-time: 208 men, 780 women	Ph.D.s: 36%
Graduate: 8 men, 199 women	Student/Faculty: 8 to 1
Year: semesters, summer session	Tuition: $11,450
Application Deadline: open	Room & Board: $5800
Freshman Class: 217 applied, 204 accepted, 50 enrolled	
SAT I Verbal/Math: 450/490	COMPETITIVE

Gwynedd-Mercy College, founded in 1948, is a private coeducational institution affiliated with the Roman Catholic Church and offering degree programs in the arts and sciences, business, education, and health fields. There are 9 undergraduate and 2 graduate schools. In addition to regional accreditation, Gwynedd-Mercy has baccalaureate program accreditation with NLN. The library contains 91,000 volumes, 84 microform items, and 5918 audiovisual forms, and subscribes to 798 periodicals. Computerized library sources and services include the card catalog and database searching. Special learning facilities include a center for creative studies and a laboratory school for education majors. The 170-acre campus is in a suburban area 20 miles northwest of Philadelphia. Including residence halls, there are 15 buildings on campus.

Student Life: 94% of undergraduates are from Pennsylvania. Students come from 5 states, 23 foreign countries, and Canada. 45% are from public schools; 55% from private. 86% are white. 57% are Catholic; 21% Protestant. The average age of freshmen is 29; all undergraduates, 31. 6% do not continue beyond their first year; 90% remain to graduate.

Housing: 144 students can be accommodated in college housing. College-sponsored living facilities include a coed dormitory. On-campus housing is available on a first-come, first-served basis. 92% of students commute. Alcohol is not permitted. All students may keep cars on campus.

Activities: There are no fraternities or sororities. There are 21 groups on campus, including choir, chorus, drama, ethnic, honors, international, literary magazine, newspaper, professional, religious, social, social service, student government, and yearbook. Popular campus events include Family Day, Carol Night, and International Night.

Sports: There are 4 intercollegiate sports for men and 6 for women, and 2 intramural sports for men and 2 for women. Athletic and recreation facilities include a wellness recreation center/gymnasium, including a racquetball court, a weight room, an aerobics room, an outdoor pool, and a jogging trail.

Disabled Students: The entire campus is accessible to physically disabled persons. Wheelchair ramps, elevators, special parking, specially equipped rest rooms, and special class scheduling are available.

Services: In addition to many counseling and information services, tutoring is available in some subjects, including sciences. There is remedial math, reading, and writing. Tutoring is made available in conjunction with student needs.

Campus Safety and Security: Campus safety and security measures include 24-hour foot and vehicle patrol, escort service, informal discussions, and emergency telephones. There are lighted pathways/sidewalks.

Programs of Study: Gwynedd-Mercy confers B.A., B.S., and B.H.S. degrees. Associate and master's degrees are also awarded. Bachelor's degrees are awarded in BIOLOGICAL SCIENCE (biology/biological science), BUSINESS (accounting and business administration and management), COMMUNICATIONS AND THE ARTS (English), COMPUTER AND PHYSICAL SCIENCE (computer mathematics, information sciences and systems, and mathematics), EDUCATION (business, early childhood, elementary, English, mathematics, science, secondary, social studies, and special), HEALTH PROFESSIONS (health science, medical laboratory technology, nursing, and premedicine), SOCIAL SCIENCE (gerontology, history, psychology, and sociology). Nursing, biology, and medical technology are the strongest academically. Nursing, business, and education have the largest enrollments.

Required: All students must complete at least 125 credit hours, including 60 in the major, with a minimum GPA of 2.0. General education courses cover language, literature and fine arts, behavioral and social sciences, humanities, and natural science. Specific courses in English composition, literature, philosophy, and religious studies are required.

Special: The college offers a co-op program in computer science, internships, dual majors, B.A.-B.S. degrees, and pass/fail options. All programs require or have the option for hands-on experiences. There is a 3-1 program in medical technology available wherein the last year is a hospital rotation. There is a freshman honors program on campus, as well as 4 national honor societies. 3 departments have honors programs.

Faculty/Classroom: 72% of faculty are female. 97% teach undergraduates. The average class size in an introductory lecture is 25; in a laboratory, 15; and in a regular course offering, 25.

Admissions: 94% of the 1995–96 applicants were accepted. The SAT I scores for the 1995–96 freshman class were as follows: Verbal—70% below 500, 24% between 500 and 599, 6% between 600 and 700, and 1% above 700. 44% of the current freshmen were in the top fifth of their class; 81% were in the top two fifths.

Requirements: The SAT I or ACT is required, and applicants must be in the upper 50% of their class. Candidates for admission must be graduates of an accredited secondary school with a 2.0 GPA and have completed 16 academic credits/Carnegie units, including 4 credits in English, 3 each in mathematics, science, and college preparatory electives, 2 in a foreign language, and 1 in history. The GED is accepted. An interview is recommended for all candidates and required for some programs. AP and CLEP credits are accepted. Important factors in the admissions decision are advanced placement or honor courses, parents or siblings attending the school, and recommendations by school officials.

Procedure: Freshmen are admitted fall and spring. Entrance exams should be taken in the spring of the junior year or the fall of the senior year. There is a deferred admissions plan. Application deadlines are open. Application fee is $25. Notification is sent on a rolling basis.

Transfer: 211 transfer students enrolled in 1995–96. Neither the SAT I nor the ACT is required for transfer students out of high school for 2 or more years. A minimum GPA of 2.0 is necessary; some programs require a higher GPA. An interview is recommended. 60 credits of 125 must be completed at Gwynedd-Mercy.

Visiting: There are regularly scheduled orientations for prospective students, consisting of open houses with formal presentations and campus tours, and class days with class visitations and campus tours. There are guides for informal visits and visitors may sit in on classes and stay overnight at the school. To schedule a visit, contact the Admissions Office.

Financial Aid: In 1995–96, 89% of all freshmen and 95% of continuing students received some form of financial aid. 85% of freshmen and 91% of continuing students received need-based aid. The average freshman award was $11,476. Of that total, scholarships or need-based grants averaged $7058 ($15,000 maximum); loans averaged $2528 ($5125 maximum); and work contracts averaged $1054 ($1500 maximum). All undergraduate students work part-time. Average earnings from campus work for the school year are $503. The average financial indebtedness of the 1994–95 graduate was $11,382. Gwynedd-Mercy is a member of CSS. The college's own financial statement and federal income tax returns are required. The application deadline for fall entry is March 15.

International Students: There were 52 international students enrolled in a recent year. They must take the TOEFL or the MELAB and achieve a minimum score on the TOEFL of 500.

Computers: The college provides computer facilities for student use. There are 34 Compaq multimedia PCs in a Novell Network connected to the campus network and the Internet, with additional desktop packages available. All students may access the system 65 hours a week. There are no time limits and no fees for general usage, but $20 is charged for computer science classes with light usage and $40 for those requiring heavy usage.

Graduates: In 1994–95, 223 bachelor's degrees were awarded. The most popular majors among graduates were nursing (39%), elementary education (18%), and business administration (11%). Within an average freshman class, 60% graduate in 3 years, 68% in 4 years, and 80% in 5 years. 50 companies recruited on campus in a recent year.

Admissions Contact: Jacqueline Williams, Director of Admissions.

HAVERFORD COLLEGE   E-4

Haverford, PA 19041–1392   (610) 896-1350; FAX: (610) 896-1338
Full-time: 556 men, 559 women   Faculty: 98; IIB, + +$
Part-time: none   Ph.D.s: 97%
Graduate: none   Student/Faculty: 11 to 1
Year: semesters   Tuition: $20,075
Application Deadline: January 15   Room & Board: $6550
Freshman Class: 2622 applied, 975 accepted, 306 enrolled
SAT I: required   **MOST COMPETITIVE**

Haverford College, founded in 1833, is a private, coeducational liberal arts college. The 5 libraries contain 460,000 volumes, 76,100 microform items, and 8500 audiovisual forms, and subscribe to 1286 periodicals. Computerized library sources and services include the card catalog, interlibrary loans, and database searching. Special learning facilities include an art gallery, radio station, observatory, and arboretum. The 216-acre campus is in a suburban area 10 miles west of Philadelphia. Including residence halls, there are 70 buildings on campus.

Student Life: 86% of undergraduates are from out-of-state, mostly the Middle Atlantic. Students come from 43 states, 27 foreign countries, and Canada. 61% are from public schools; 39% from private.

83% are white. The average age of freshmen is 18; all undergraduates, 19. 2% do not continue beyond their first year; 90% remain to graduate.

Housing: 1100 students can be accommodated in college housing. College-sponsored living facilities include single-sex and coed dormitories and on-campus apartments. In addition there are language houses, and special interest houses. Haverford students may live at Bryn Mawr College through a dormitory exchange program. On-campus housing is guaranteed for all 4 years. 96% of students live on campus; of those, 90% remain on campus on weekends. Upperclassmen may keep cars on campus.

Activities: There are no fraternities or sororities. There are 75 groups on campus, including chorale, dance, drama, ethnic, gay, international, jazz band, literary magazine, musical theater, newspaper, orchestra, political, radio and TV, religious, social service, student government, and yearbook. Popular campus events include Haverfest, Snowball, and Swarthmore athletic competitions.

Sports: There are 11 intercollegiate sports for men and 11 for women and 6 intramural sports for men and women. Athletic and recreation facilities include a field house with an indoor track, tennis, squash, and basketball courts, extensive outdoor fields, and a new 400-meter, 8-lane, all-weather track.

Disabled Students: 50% of the campus is accessible to disabled students. The following facilities are available: wheelchair ramps, elevators, special parking, specially equipped rest rooms, special class scheduling, lowered drinking fountains, lowered telephones, and reasonable accommodation.

Services: In addition to many counseling and information services, tutoring is available in every subject. There is a reader service for the blind.

Campus Safety and Security: Campus safety and security measures include 24-hour foot and vehicle patrol, escort service, shuttle buses, and informal discussions. There are pamphlets/posters/films, emergency telephones, lighted pathways/sidewalks, and a fire safety program.

Programs of Study: Haverford confers B.A. and B.S. degrees. Bachelor's degrees are awarded in BIOLOGICAL SCIENCE (biology/biological science), COMMUNICATIONS AND THE ARTS (art history and appreciation, classics, comparative literature, English, fine arts, French, German, Italian, music, romance languages, Russian, and Spanish), COMPUTER AND PHYSICAL SCIENCE (astronomy, chemistry, geology, mathematics, and physics), SOCIAL SCIENCE (anthropology, archeology, East Asian studies, economics, history, philosophy, political science/government, psychology, religion, sociology, and urban studies). Natural and physical sciences, English, and history are the strongest academically. English, biology, and history have the largest enrollments.

Required: All students must take a minimum of 32 course credits, including freshman writing and 3 courses each in social science, natural science, and the humanities. One of the distribution courses must be quantitative and 1 must meet the social justice requirement. Students must also take 3 semesters of physical education and demonstrate proficiency in a foreign language. Students must take a minimum of 6 courses in the major and 6 in related fields. Each major includes a capstone experience (a comprehensive examination, thesis, or advanced project, a specially-designed course, or some combination), which varies by department.

Special: Haverford offers internship programs, cross-registration with Bryn Mawr College, Swarthmore College, and the University of Pennsylvania, study abroad in 33 countries, dual majors, student-designed majors, and a 3–2 engineering degree with the University of Pennsylvania. Pass/fail options are limited to 4 in 4 years. There is a chapter of Phi Beta Kappa on campus. 28 departments have honors programs.

Faculty/Classroom: 58% of faculty are male; 42%, female. All teach undergraduates and most do research. The average class size in an introductory lecture is 35; in a laboratory, 16; and in a regular course offering, 18.

Admissions: 37% of the 1995–96 applicants were accepted. The SAT I scores for the 1995–96 freshman class were as follows: Verbal—4% below 500, 26% between 500 and 599, 56% between 600 and 700, and 14% above 700; Math—2% below 500, 9% between 500 and 599, 46% between 600 and 700, and 43% above 700. 91% of the current freshmen were in the top fifth of their class; 99% were in the top two fifths.

Requirements: The SAT I is required along with the SAT II: Writing test, plus 2 others. Candidates for admission must be graduates of an accredited secondary school and have taken 4 courses in English, 3 each in a foreign language and mathematics, and 1 each in science and history. The GED is accepted. An essay is required and an interview is recommended. Haverford accepts the Common App on computer disk. AP credits are accepted. Important factors in the admissions decision are advanced placement or honor courses, leadership record, and recommendations by school officials.

Procedure: Freshmen are admitted in the fall. Entrance exams should be taken before January 15. There are early decision, early admissions, and deferred admissions plans. Early decision applications should be filed by November 15; regular applications, by January 15 for fall entry, along with an application fee of $45. Notification of early decision is sent December 15; regular decision, by April 15. 70 early decision candidates were accepted for the 1995–96 class. A waiting list is an active part of the admissions procedure.

Transfer: 6 transfer students enrolled in 1995–96. Applicants must be able to enter the sophomore or junior class. Admission depends mainly on the strength of college grades. A minimum GPA of 3.0 is necessary and the SAT I is recommended. Thirty minimum credit hours or the equivalent of 1 year of courses must have been earned. A liberal arts curriculum is also recommended. 16 credits of 32 must be completed at Haverford.

Visiting: There are guides for informal visits and visitors may sit in on classes and stay overnight at the school. To schedule a visit, contact the Admissions Office.

Financial Aid: 45% of all students receive some form of financial aid. 40% of all students receive need-based aid. The average freshman award was $18,254. Of that total, scholarships or need-based grants averaged $13,266; other scholarships and grants averaged $1392; loans averaged $2176; and work contracts averaged $1420. Haverford is a member of CSS. The CSS Profile Application financial statement is required. The application deadline for fall entry is January 31.

International Students: There were 28 international students enrolled in a recent year. The school actively recruits these students. They must take the TOEFL and achieve a minimum score of 600. The student must also take the SAT I.

Computers: The college provides computer facilities for student use. The mainframes are multiple Sun SPARCstations as distributed servers. There are approximately 80 publicly accessible Macintosh and IBM-compatible PCs available in 3 computer laboratories and in the library. There are special-purpose computing laboratories available to students in the physical sciences, biology, psychology, and mathematics/computer science, which has an additional 90 machines. Every student has a Unix account which allows use of the Unix systems on campus and the Internet. All publicly accessible computers are networked, as are all major dormitories. All students may access the system. There are no time limits and no fees.

Graduates: In 1994–95, 274 bachelor's degrees were awarded. The most popular majors among graduates were English (12%), history (11%), and biology (11%). Within an average freshman class, 83% graduate in 4 years, 89% in 5 years, and 90% in 6 years. 45 companies recruited on campus in 1994–95. Of the 1994 graduating class, 21% were enrolled in graduate school within 6 months of graduation and 66% had found employment.

Admissions Contact: Delsie Z. Phillips, Director of Admissions. E-mail: admitme@haverford.edu.

HOLY FAMILY COLLEGE

F-3

Philadelphia, PA 19114   (215) 637-3050

Full-time: 259 men, 816 women	**Faculty:** 86; IIB, -$
Part-time: 318 men, 979 women	**Ph.D.s:** 51%
Graduate: 82 men, 355 women	**Student/Faculty:** 13 to 1
Year: semesters, summer session	**Tuition:** $9500
Application Deadline: July 1	**Room & Board:** n/app
Freshman Class: 515 applied, 339 accepted, 144 enrolled	
SAT I or ACT: required	**LESS COMPETITIVE**

Holy Family College, established in 1954 and affiliated with the Roman Catholic Church, is a private, nonresidential institution with a liberal arts core. There is 1 graduate school. In addition to regional accreditation, Holy Family has baccalaureate program accreditation with AACSB, CSWE, and NLN. The library contains 101,309 volumes, 7054 microform items, and 2621 audiovisual forms, and subscribes to 683 periodicals. Computerized library sources and services include the card catalog, interlibrary loans, and database searching. The 46-acre campus is in a suburban area. There are 8 buildings on campus.

Student Life: 92% of undergraduates are from Pennsylvania. Students come from 4 states, 30 foreign countries, and Canada. 21% are from public schools; 79% from private. 94% are white. Most are Catholic. The average age of freshmen is 19; all undergraduates, 21. 15% do not continue beyond their first year; 60% remain to graduate.

Housing: There are no residence halls. All students commute. Alcohol is not permitted. All students may keep cars on campus.

Activities: There are no fraternities or sororities. There are many groups and organizations on campus, including cheerleading, choir, drama, honors, international, literary magazine, newspaper, professional, religious, social service, student government, and yearbook. Popular campus events include Buddy Day, Christmas Rose, and Senior Citizen Day.

Sports: There are 3 intercollegiate sports for men and 3 for women, and 3 intramural sports for men and 3 for women. Athletic and recreation facilities include a gymnasium, a weight room, and racquetball courts.

Disabled Students: The entire campus is accessible to physically disabled persons. The following facilities are available: wheelchair ramps, elevators, special parking, specially equipped rest rooms, lowered drinking fountains, and lowered telephones.

Services: In addition to many counseling and information services, tutoring is available in some subjects. There is remedial math and writing.

Campus Safety and Security: Campus safety and security measures include 24-hour foot and vehicle patrol, escort service, emergency telephones, and lighted pathways/sidewalks.

Programs of Study: Holy Family confers B.A., B.S., and B.S.N. degrees. Associate and master's degrees are also awarded. Bachelor's degrees are awarded in BIOLOGICAL SCIENCE (biochemistry and biology/biological science), BUSINESS (accounting, business administration and management, international business management, and marketing/retailing/merchandising), COMMUNICATIONS AND THE ARTS (communications, English, fine arts, French, and Spanish), COMPUTER AND PHYSICAL SCIENCE (chemistry, information sciences and systems, and mathematics), EDUCATION (early childhood, elementary, foreign languages, science, secondary, and special), HEALTH PROFESSIONS (medical laboratory technology, nursing, predentistry, and premedicine), SOCIAL SCIENCE (criminal justice, economics, history, humanities, prelaw, psychology, religion, social science, social work, and sociology). Nursing, elementary education, and accounting are the strongest academically. Nursing, education, and business have the largest enrollments.

Required: Students must complete 120 to 130 semester hours, including at least 30 in the major, with a minimum GPA of 2.0. Nursing, medical technology, and education majors must maintain a GPA of 2.5. Specific discipline requirements include English, science, mathematics, and philosophy. A core curriculum of communication, quantification, philosophy, humanities, and social science must be fulfilled. All majors require satisfactory performance on a comprehensive examination.

Special: Opportunities are provided for internships in English and social sciences, study abroad, co-op programs in 23 majors with many companies, a B.A.-B.S. degree, an accelerated degree program, independent study, credit by examination, nondegree study, and pass/fail options. Students may pursue dual majors in business and French or Spanish, international business and French or Spanish, and elementary and special education. There is a freshman honors program on campus, as well as 10 national honor societies. 2 departments have honors programs.

Faculty/Classroom: 33% of faculty are male; 67%, female. All teach undergraduates. 33% also do research. No introductory courses are taught by graduate students. The average class size in an introductory lecture is 20; in a laboratory, 17; and in a regular course offering, 21.

Admissions: 66% of the 1995–96 applicants were accepted.

Requirements: The SAT I or ACT is required. Graduation from an accredited secondary school is required; a GED will be accepted. Applicants must submit 16 academic credits, including 4 courses in English, 3 each in history and mathematics, 2 each in foreign language and science, 1 in social studies, and the remainder in other academic electives. AP and CLEP credits are accepted. Important factors in the admissions decision are recommendations by school officials, recommendations by alumni, and personality/intangible qualities.

Procedure: Freshmen are admitted to all sessions. Entrance exams should be taken by October or November of the senior year. There are early decision, early admissions, and deferred admissions plans. Early decision applications should be filed by December 1; regular applications, by July 1 for fall entry and January 2 for spring entry, along with an application fee of $25. Notification of early decision is sent January 7; regular decision, on a rolling basis. 12 early decision candidates were accepted for the 1995–96 class.

Transfer: 139 transfer students enrolled in 1995–96. Applicants must submit official transcripts from all previous colleges. Grades of D are not transferable. A maximum of 75 credits will be accepted for transfer. 45 credits of 120 must be completed at Holy Family.

Visiting: There are regularly scheduled orientations for prospective students, consisting of an interview and a tour. There are guides for informal visits and visitors may sit in on classes. To schedule a visit, contact the Office of Admissions.

Financial Aid: In 1995–96, 83% of all freshmen and 84% of continuing students received some need-based aid. The average freshman award was $17,000. Of that total, scholarships or need-based grants averaged $500 ($4000 maximum); loans averaged $2625 ($10,500 maximum); and work contracts averaged $200 ($1000 maximum). All undergraduate students work part-time. Average earnings from campus work for the school year are $200. The average financial indebtedness of the 1994–95 graduate was $17,000. Holy Family is a member of CSS. The FAFSA is required. The application deadline for fall entry is May 1.

International Students: There are currently 9 international students enrolled. They must take the TOEFL and achieve a minimum score of 530.

Computers: The college provides computer facilities for student use. There are 60 microcomputers networked in 3 laboratories available for student use; an additional 20 PCs are available in another laboratory. All students may access the networked PCs 7 days a week. There are no time limits and no fees.

Graduates: In 1994–95, 375 bachelor's degrees were awarded. The most popular majors among graduates were nursing (34%), elementary education (15%), and management (6%). Within an average freshman class, 4% graduate in 3 years, 46% in 4 years, 58% in 5 years, and 60% in 6 years. 92 companies recruited on campus in 1994–95.

Admissions Contact: Dr. Mott R. Linn, Director of Admissions.

IMMACULATA COLLEGE
Immaculata, PA 19345   E-4

	(610) 647-4400, ext. 3015
	FAX: (610) 251-1668
Full-time: 4 men, 383 women	Faculty: 62; IIA, --$
Part-time: 145 men, 875 women	Ph.Ds: 66%
Graduate: 102 men, 540 women	Student/Faculty: 6 to 1
Year: semesters, summer session	Tuition: $10,880
Application Deadline: May 1	Room & Board: $5678
Freshman Class: 287 applied, 256 accepted, 101 enrolled	
SAT I Verbal/Math: 428/436	**LESS COMPETITIVE**

Immaculata College, founded in 1920, is a private, primarily women's liberal arts and teacher preparation college affiliated with the Roman Catholic Church. There is 1 undergraduate school. In addition to regional accreditation, Immaculata has baccalaureate program accreditation with ADA, AHEA, NASM, and NLN. The library contains 160,000 volumes, 6500 microform items, and 3100 audiovisual forms, and subscribes to 650 periodicals. Computerized library sources and services include the card catalog, interlibrary loans, and database searching. Special learning facilities include computer and language laboratories. The 400-acre campus is in a suburban area 20 miles west of Philadelphia. Including residence halls, there are 13 buildings on campus.

Student Life: 81% of undergraduates are from Pennsylvania. Students come from 15 states, 25 foreign countries, and Canada. 75% are from public schools; 25% from private. 93% are white. 77% are Catholic; 15% Protestant. The average age of freshmen is 18; all undergraduates, 26. 12% do not continue beyond their first year; 72% remain to graduate.

Housing: 400 students can be accommodated in college housing. College-sponsored living facilities include single-sex dormitories. On-campus housing is guaranteed for all 4 years. 79% of students commute. Alcohol is not permitted. All students may keep cars on campus.

Activities: There are no fraternities or sororities. There are 30 groups on campus, including art, choir, chorale, chorus, computers, dance, drama, ethnic, honors, international, literary magazine, musical theater, newspaper, orchestra, photography, political, professional, religious, social, social service, student government, and yearbook. Popular campus events include Friday's Pub, Variety Show, Christmas Dance, and Carol Night.

Sports: There are 5 intercollegiate sports and 10 intramural sports. Athletic and recreation facilities include tennis courts, a full gymnasium, a handball gymnasium, an Olympic-size swimming pool, hockey and softball fields, and a weight room.

Disabled Students: 95% of the campus is accessible to disabled students. The following facilities are available: wheelchair ramps, elevators, special parking, specially equipped rest rooms, special class scheduling, lowered drinking fountains, and lowered telephones.

Services: In addition to many counseling and information services, tutoring is available in most subjects. There is a reader service for the blind, and remedial math, reading, and writing.

Campus Safety and Security: Campus safety and security measures include 24-hour foot and vehicle patrol, self-defense education, informal discussions, and pamphlets/posters/films. There are lighted pathways/sidewalks.

Programs of Study: Immaculata confers B.A., B.S., B.Mus., and B.S.N. degrees. Associate, master's, and doctoral degrees are also awarded. Bachelor's degrees are awarded in BIOLOGICAL SCIENCE (biochemistry and biology/biological science), BUSINESS (accounting, business administration and management, and fashion merchandising), COMMUNICATIONS AND THE ARTS (English, French, German, music, and Spanish), COMPUTER AND PHYSICAL SCIENCE (chemistry, information sciences and systems, and mathematics), EDUCATION (early childhood, elementary, foreign languages, home economics, middle school, music, science, and secondary), HEALTH PROFESSIONS (music therapy, nursing, and premedicine),

SOCIAL SCIENCE (dietetics, economics, food science, history, international relations, prelaw, psychology, social science, and sociology). Premedicine and education are the strongest academically. Education, business, and music therapy have the largest enrollments.

Required: To graduate, all students must complete 54 credits in liberal arts including distribution requirements in humanities, social sciences, and sciences. Students must take a minimum of 126 credits including 36 to 52 in the major. Four credits of physical education are also required. The college requires a minimum GPA of 2.0. A thesis, which is the outcome of a required senior seminar, is also required. Internships are required for dietetics, music therapy, and education.

Special: All majors offer opportunities for internships; most require them. Students may study abroad in 6 countries. The college offers dual-major combinations, student-designed majors, an accelerated degree program in organization dynamics, nondegree study, and pass/fail options. There is a freshman honors program on campus as well as 14 national honor societies. 12 departments have honors programs.

Faculty/Classroom: 29% of faculty are male; 71%, female. 91% teach undergraduates and 4% both teach and do research. No introductory courses are taught by graduate students. The average class size in an introductory lecture is 20; in a laboratory, 12; and in a regular course offering, 14.

Admissions: 89% of the 1995–96 applicants were accepted. 28% of the current freshmen were in the top fifth of their class; 48% were in the top two fifths. 19 freshmen graduated first in their class.

Requirements: The SAT I is required, with recentered score of 800, 400 verbal and 400 mathematics. Candidates for admission should be graduates of an accredited secondary school with an 2.3 GPA and with a minimum of 16 academic credits including 4 in English, 2 each in a foreign language, 2 in mathematics, science, and social studies, 1 in history, and 3 more in college preparatory courses. The GED is accepted. An audition is required for music students and an essay and an interview are recommended for all. AP and CLEP credits are accepted. Important factors in the admissions decision are advanced placement or honor courses, recommendations by school officials, and extracurricular activities record.

Procedure: Freshmen are admitted fall and spring. Entrance exams should be taken in the spring of the junior year. There are early decision, early admissions, and deferred admissions plans. Early decision applications should be filed by November 1; regular applications, by May 1 for fall entry and November 1 for spring entry, along with an application fee of $25. Notification of early decision is sent December 1; regular decision, on a rolling basis. 40 early decision candidates were accepted for the 1995–96 class.

Transfer: 19 transfer students enrolled in 1995–96. In addition to high school credentials, applicants must present college transcripts. Courses in which the student has achieved a C or better are accepted if they are comparable to Immaculata's courses. A score of 800 in the SAT I is required, as is an interview. Students must have a minimum GPA of 2.0. 36 credits of 126 must be completed at Immaculata.

Visiting: There are regularly scheduled orientations for prospective students, including an open house and class visitation. There are guides for informal visits and visitors may sit in on classes and stay overnight at the school. To schedule a visit, contact the Office of Admissions.

Financial Aid: In 1995–96, 94% of all freshmen and 83% of continuing students received some form of financial aid. 83% of freshmen and 75% of continuing students received need-based aid. The average freshman award was $4100. Of that total, scholarships or need-based grants averaged $3000 ($7500 maximum); loans averaged $2500 ($3400 maximum); and work contracts averaged $1000 ($1500 maximum). All undergraduate students work part-time. Average earnings from campus work for the school year are $600. The average financial indebtedness of the 1994–95 graduate was $9500. Immaculata is a member of CSS. The application deadline for fall entry is March 1.

International Students: There were 81 international students enrolled in a recent year. The school actively recruits these students. They must score 550 on the TOEFL.

Computers: The college provides computer facilities for student use. Students may use the networked computer terminals in the administrative offices, computer center, and library.

Graduates: In 1994–95, 191 bachelor's degrees were awarded. The most popular majors among graduates were psychology (14%), nursing (13%), and economics/business (12%). Within an average freshman class, 1% graduate in 3 years, 71% in 4 years, 3% in 5 years, and 4% in 6 years. 23 companies recruited on campus in 1994–95.

Admissions Contact: Ken Rasp, Dean of Enrollment Services. A campus video is available.

INDIANA UNIVERSITY OF PENNSYLVANIA B-3
Indiana, PA 15705 (412) 357-2230; (800) 442-6830

Full-time: 5008 men, 6156 women	Faculty: 700; IIA, +$
Part-time: 458 men, 579 women	Ph.D.s: 80%
Graduate: 668 men, 1010 women	Student/Faculty: 16 to 1
Year: semesters, summer session	Tuition: $3891 ($8865)
Application Deadline: December 31	Room & Board: $3138
Freshman Class: 8024 applied, 4637 accepted, 1914 enrolled	
SAT I Verbal/Math: 459/497	COMPETITIVE

Indiana University of Pennsylvania, founded in 1875, is a public, co-educational member of the Pennsylvania State System of Higher Education offering programs in liberal and fine arts, business, preengineering, health science, military science, teacher preparation, basic and applied science, social science and humanities, criminology, and safety science. There are 6 undergraduate schools and one graduate school. In addition to regional accreditation, IUP has baccalaureate program accreditation with AHEA, CAHEA, NASM, NCATE, NLN, and SAF. The library contains 754,796 volumes and 1,567,913 microform items, and subscribes to 4320 periodicals. Computerized library sources and services include the card catalog, interlibrary loans, and database searching. Special learning facilities include a learning resource center, art gallery, planetarium, radio station, and TV station. The 342-acre campus is in a small town 50 miles northeast of Pittsburgh. Including residence halls, there are 70 buildings on campus.

Student Life: 94% of undergraduates are from Pennsylvania. Students come from 51 states, 69 foreign countries, and Canada. 91% are from public schools. 90% are white. The average age of freshmen is 18; all undergraduates, 20. 23% do not continue beyond their first year; 63% remain to graduate.

Housing: 4130 students can be accommodated in college housing. College-sponsored living facilities include single-sex and coed dormitories and on-campus apartments. In addition there are honors houses and 24-hour intensified study floors, substance-free housing, academic specialty housing, and an international house. On-campus housing is guaranteed for the freshman year only and is available on a lottery system for upperclassmen. 67% of students commute. Alcohol is not permitted.

Activities: 20% of men belong to 5 local and 17 national fraternities; 15% of women belong to 3 local and 13 national sororities. There are 180 groups on campus, including band, cheerleading, choir, chorale, chorus, computers, dance, drama, ethnic, film, gay, honors, international, jazz band, marching band, musical theater, newspaper, orchestra, pep band, political, professional, radio and TV, religious, social, social service, student government, symphony, and yearbook. Popular campus events include Artist Series, Diversity Day, and Holiday Light-Up Night.

Sports: There are 9 intercollegiate sports for men and 9 for women, and 25 intramural sports for men and 20 for women. Athletic and recreation facilities include a 7600-seat stadium, swimming pools, a fitness trail, softball fields, and courts for tennis, badminton, handball/racquetball, basketball, and volleyball.

Disabled Students: The following facilities are available: wheelchair ramps, elevators, special parking, specially equipped rest rooms, special class scheduling, and lowered drinking fountains.

Services: In addition to many counseling and information services, tutoring is available in most subjects. There is a reader service for the blind, and remedial math, reading, and writing.

Campus Safety and Security: Campus safety and security measures include 24-hour foot and vehicle patrol, escort service, informal discussions, and pamphlets/posters/films. There are emergency telephones and lighted pathways/sidewalks.

Programs of Study: IUP confers B.A., B.S., B.F.A., and B.S.Ed. degrees. Associate, master's, and doctoral degrees are also awarded. Bachelor's degrees are awarded in BIOLOGICAL SCIENCE (biology/biological science), BUSINESS (hotel/motel and restaurant management and marketing/retailing/merchandising), COMMUNICATIONS AND THE ARTS (communications, dramatic arts, English, fine arts, French, German, journalism, music, and Spanish), COMPUTER AND PHYSICAL SCIENCE (chemistry, computer science, earth science, geology, geoscience, mathematics, and physics), EDUCATION (art, business, early childhood, education, elementary, health, home economics, marketing and distribution, mathematics, music, nutrition, science, secondary, social science, and special), HEALTH PROFESSIONS (medical technology, nursing, premedicine, preveterinary science, and respiratory therapy), SOCIAL SCIENCE (anthropology, criminal justice, economics, food science, geography, history, philosophy, political science/government, prelaw, psychology, religion, social science, and sociology). Elementary education, criminology, and accounting have the largest enrollments.

Required: All candidates for graduation must have completed approximately 124 credits, including 53 credits in the liberal studies core. The total number of hours and the minimum GPA vary with the major.

Special: The university offers various co-op programs, cross-registration through the National Student Exchange Consortium, a 3-2 engineering degree with the University of Pittsburgh and Drexel University, and a B.A.-B.S. degree. Internships and dual and student-designed majors are available. Students may study abroad in 30 countries. Also available are work-study programs, a Washington semester, an accelerated degree program, and credit for military experience. There is a freshman honors program on campus, as well as 15 national honor societies. All departments have honors programs.

Faculty/Classroom: 63% of faculty are male; 37%, female. No introductory courses are taught by graduate students. The average class size in a laboratory is 16 and in a regular course offering, 25.

Admissions: 58% of the 1995-96 applicants were accepted. 40% of the current freshmen were in the top fifth of their class; 73% were in the top two fifths.

Requirements: The SAT I is required. Candidates for admission should be graduates of an accredited secondary school. There are no specific course requirements. Art majors must have a portfolio and music majors must audition. AP and CLEP credits are accepted. Important factors in the admissions decision are advanced placement or honor courses, recommendations by school officials, and extracurricular activities record.

Procedure: Freshmen are admitted fall and spring. Entrance exams should be taken by December of the preceding year. There are early decision, early admissions, and deferred admissions plans. Early decision applications should be filed by October 15; regular applications, by December 31 for fall entry and November 1 for spring entry, along with an application fee of $30. Notification of early decision is sent November 30; regular decision, on a rolling basis. A waiting list is an active part of the admissions procedure for nursing students.

Transfer: 622 transfer students enrolled in 1995-96. Applicants must have a minimum GPA of 2.0 for all subjects (2.5 for education students). 45 credits of 124 must be completed at IUP.

Visiting: There are regularly scheduled orientations for prospective students. There are guides for informal visits and visitors may sit in on classes. To schedule a visit, contact the Admissions Office.

Financial Aid: In a recent year, 85% of all students received some form of financial aid. 85% of freshmen received need-based aid. Scholarships or need-based grants averaged $6613; and loans averaged $2930. 20% of undergraduate students work part-time. The average financial indebtedness of a recent graduate was $8800. IUP is a member of CSS. The The university requires the Pennsylvania State Grant and Federal Student Aid Application forms. The PHEAA financial statement is required. The application deadline for fall entry is May 1.

International Students: There are currently 302 international students enrolled. They must take the TOEFL and achieve a minimum score of 500.

Computers: The college provides computer facilities for student use. The mainframe is a DEC VAX cluster. There are also 500 IBM, Zenith, Apple, and Macintosh microcomputers available throughout the campus for student use in teaching facilities. There are more than 3000 microcomputers on campus. All students may access the system 8 A.M. to 4 A.M., Monday through Thursday; 9 A.M. to midnight, Friday and Saturday; noon to 4 A.M., Sunday; and 24 hours a day from external modems. There are no time limits and no fees.

Graduates: In 1994-95, 2175 bachelor's degrees were awarded. The most popular majors among graduates were elementary education (8%), accounting (5%), and criminology (3%). Within an average freshman class, 56% graduate in 5 years. 88 companies recruited on campus in 1994-95. Of the 1994 graduating class, 12% were enrolled in graduate school within 6 months of graduation and 75% had found employment.

Admissions Contact: William Nunn, Dean of Admissions. E-mail: admissions-inquiry@grove.iup.edu. A campus video is available.

JUNIATA COLLEGE C-3
Huntingdon, PA 16652 (814) 641-3420
(800) 526-1970; FAX: (814) 641-3100

Full-time: 455 men, 569 women	Faculty: 75; IIB, +$
Part-time: 41 men and women	Ph.D.s: 92%
Graduate: none	Student/Faculty: 14 to 1
Year: semesters, summer session	Tuition: $15,740
Application Deadline: March 1	Room & Board: $4620
Freshman Class: 1004 applied, 854 accepted, 277 enrolled	
SAT I Verbal/Math: 582/567	VERY COMPETITIVE +

Juniata College, founded in 1876, is an independent, coeducational liberal arts college affiliated with the Church of the Brethren. In addition to regional accreditation, Juniata has baccalaureate program accreditation with CSWE. The library contains 129,809 volumes, 9435 microform items, and 650 audiovisual forms, and subscribes to 950 periodicals. Computerized library sources and services include the card catalog, interlibrary loans, and database searching. Special learning facilities include an art gallery, radio station, and observatory. The 100-acre campus is in a small town 31 miles south of State College, in the heart of rural Pennsylvania. Including residence halls, there are 32 buildings on campus.

Student Life: 79% of undergraduates are from Pennsylvania. Students come from 25 states and 12 foreign countries. 85% are from public schools; 15% from private. 93% are white. 65% are Protestant; 30% Catholic. The average age of freshmen is 18; all undergraduates, 20. 15% do not continue beyond their first year; 70% remain to graduate.

Housing: 1041 students can be accommodated in college housing. College-sponsored living facilities include single-sex and coed dormitories, on-campus apartments, and off-campus apartments. On-campus housing is guaranteed for all 4 years. 92% of students live on campus; of those, 80% remain on campus on weekends. All students may keep cars on campus.

Activities: There are no fraternities or sororities. There are 50 groups on campus, including band, cheerleading, choir, chorale, chorus, computers, dance, ethnic, gay, honors, international, jazz band, literary magazine, musical theater, newspaper, orchestra, pep band, photography, political, professional, radio and TV, religious, social, social service, student government, and yearbook. Popular campus events include Mountain Day, Madrigal Dinner, Spring Fest, All Class Night, Homecoming, Parents Weekend, Presidential Ball, and International Week.

Sports: There are 6 intercollegiate sports for men and 9 for women, and 9 intramural sports for men and 8 for women. Athletic and recreation facilities include 2 gymnasiums, a swimming pool, 3 weight rooms, a wrestling room, 4 racquetball courts, a multipurpose room, a sauna, a varsity football field and stadium, baseball, soccer, and hockey fields, an outdoor running track, 7 tennis courts, and 1 outdoor basketball court.

Disabled Students: 80% of the campus is accessible to disabled students. The following facilities are available: wheelchair ramps, elevators, special parking, specially equipped rest rooms, lowered drinking fountains, and wide doors.

Services: In addition to many counseling and information services, tutoring is available in most subjects. There is a reader service for the blind. Juniata also offers courses and workshops in study, reading, and writing skills.

Campus Safety and Security: Campus safety and security measures include 24-hour foot and vehicle patrol, escort service, pamphlets/posters/films, and emergency telephones. In addition, there are lighted pathways/sidewalks.

Programs of Study: Juniata confers B.A. and B.S. degrees. Bachelor's degrees are awarded in BIOLOGICAL SCIENCE (biochemistry, biology/biological science, ecology, life science, and molecular biology), BUSINESS (accounting, banking and finance, business administration and management, business economics, and personnel management), COMMUNICATIONS AND THE ARTS (art, communications, English, fine arts, French, German, Russian, and Spanish), COMPUTER AND PHYSICAL SCIENCE (chemistry, computer science, earth science, geology, mathematics, and physics), EDUCATION (early childhood, elementary, English, foreign languages, science, secondary, and social studies), ENGINEERING AND ENVIRONMENTAL DESIGN (environmental science and preengineering), HEALTH PROFESSIONS (allied health, medical technology, predentistry, premedicine, and preveterinary science), SOCIAL SCIENCE (anthropology, economics, Hispanic American studies, history, international studies, peace studies, philosophy, political science/government, prelaw, psychology, social work, and sociology). Preprofessional programs, chemistry, and biology are the strongest academically. Biology, business, and education have the largest enrollments.

Required: Students are required to complete a minimum of 120 credit hours, including courses in the 5 areas of fine arts, international studies, social sciences, humanities, and natural sciences, as well as freshman English, a 200-level general education course, a senior value studies course, and a computer literacy course. The total number of hours required for the major varies from 45 to 60. Students must have a minimum GPA of 2.0.

Special: Juniata offers cooperative programs in forestry, marine science, cytotechnology, nursing, medical technology, diagnostic imaging, and occupational and physical therapy. Internships, study abroad in 9 countries, Washington and Philadelphia semesters, and nondegree study are also offered. There are 3-2 engineering degrees with Columbia, Clarkson, Washington, and Pennsylvania State universities, and various preprofessional programs, including optometry, pharmacy, and podiatry. With the assistance of 2 faculty advisers, all students design their own majors to meet their individual goals. There are 2 national honor societies on campus.

Faculty/Classroom: 69% of faculty are male; 31%, female. All teach undergraduates and 65% also do research. The average class size in an introductory lecture is 30; in a laboratory, 16; and in a regular course offering, 22.

Admissions: 85% of the 1995–96 applicants were accepted. The SAT I scores for the 1995–96 freshman class were as follows: Verbal—13% below 500, 45% between 500 and 599, 33% between 600 and 700, and 9% above 700; Math—13% below 500, 47% between 500 and 599, 38% between 600 and 700, and 3% above 700. 57% of the current freshmen were in the top fifth of their class; 70% were in the top two fifths. There were 3 National Merit finalists. 8 freshmen graduated first in their class.

Requirements: The SAT I is required. Juniata requires applicants to be in the upper 20% of their class. Candidates for admission should be graduates of an accredited secondary school and have completed 16 academic credits, including 4 in English, 2 in a foreign language, and a combination of 10 in mathematics, social studies, and laboratory science. The GED is accepted, and home schoolers are encouraged to apply. An essay is required, and an interview is recommended. Applications are accepted on-line via the Private School Consortium's Common App. AP credits are accepted. Important factors in the admissions decision are advanced placement or honor courses, leadership record, and recommendations by school officials.

Procedure: Freshmen are admitted fall and spring. Entrance exams should be taken in the junior or senior year. There are early decision, early admissions, and deferred admissions plans. Early decision applications should be filed by November 15; regular applications, by March 1 for fall entry and December 1 for spring entry, along with an application fee of $30. Notification of early decision is sent November 30; regular decision, on a rolling basis. 54 early decision candidates were accepted for the 1995–96 class.

Transfer: 32 transfer students enrolled in 1995–96. A GPA of 2.0 and SAT I scores are required. 30 credits of 120 must be completed at Juniata.

Visiting: There are regularly scheduled orientations for prospective students, including campus tours and interviews. There are guides for informal visits and visitors may sit in on classes and stay overnight at the school. To schedule a visit, contact Nancy Erisman, Campus Visit Coordinator.

Financial Aid: In 1995–96, 91% of all freshmen and 86% of continuing students received some form of financial aid. 80% of freshmen and 78% of continuing students received need-based aid. The average freshman award was $15,370. Of that total, scholarships or need-based grants averaged $10,011 ($15,740 maximum); loans averaged $2741 ($4125 maximum); parent loans and government-funded awards averaged $1477 ($10,000 maximum); and work contracts averaged $1138 ($1200 maximum). 55% of undergraduate students work part-time. Average earnings from campus work for the school year are $700. The average financial indebtedness of the 1994–95 graduate was $15,000. The FAFSA and the PHEAA grant application are required. The application deadline for fall entry is March 1.

International Students: There were 32 international students enrolled in a recent year. The school actively recruits these students. They must take the TOEFL and achieve a minimum score of 550.

Computers: The college provides computer facilities for student use. The mainframes are a DEC VAX 11/80 and an HP 9000. There are numerous maintenance terminals, PCs, and Apple Macintoshes located throughout the campus. Students have access to all locations and are provided with a personal account. All students may access the system 80 hours per week, usually 7 A.M. to 1:30 A.M. There are no time limits and no fees.

Graduates: In 1994–95, 230 bachelor's degrees were awarded. The most popular majors among graduates were education (21%), biology (18%), and business management (11%). 35 companies recruited on campus in 1994–95.

Admissions Contact: David Hawsey, Dean of Enrollment. E-mail: info@juncol.juniata.edu.

KING'S COLLEGE
E-2
Wilkes Barre, PA 18711

(717) 826–5858
(800) 955–5777; FAX: (717) 825–9049

Full-time: 968 men, 847 women	Faculty: 98; IIB, av$
Part-time: 172 men, 274 women	Ph.D.s: 80%
Graduate: 44 men, 53 women	Student/Faculty: 19 to 1
Year: semesters, summer session	Tuition: $12,260
Application Deadline: August 1	Room & Board: $5500
Freshman Class: 1537 applied, 1193 accepted, 428 enrolled	
SAT I or ACT: required	**COMPETITIVE**

King's College, founded in 1946, is a private, coeducational institution affiliated with the Roman Catholic Church. The college offers undergraduate programs in humanities, natural and social sciences, specialized programs in business and other professions, and graduate programs in reading, business, and health care administration.

The library contains 155,582 volumes, 468,792 microform items, and 5947 audiovisual forms, and subscribes to 960 periodicals. Computerized library sources and services include the card catalog and database searching. Special learning facilities include a learning resource center, art gallery, radio station, and TV station. The 48-acre campus is in an urban area in northeastern Pennsylvania 19 miles south of Scranton. Including residence halls, there are 18 buildings on campus.

Student Life: 71% of undergraduates are from Pennsylvania. Students come from 18 states, 17 foreign countries, and Canada. 67% are from public schools; 33% from private. 94% are white. 73% are Catholic; 15% Protestant; 11% unknown. The average age of freshmen is 18.5; all undergraduates, 20.5. 16% do not continue beyond their first year; 70% remain to graduate.

Housing: 748 students can be accommodated in college housing. College-sponsored living facilities include single-sex dormitories and on-campus apartments. On-campus housing is guaranteed for all 4 years. 62% of students commute. Alcohol is not permitted. All students may keep cars on campus.

Activities: There are no fraternities or sororities. There are 48 groups on campus, including art, cheerleading, choir, chorale, chorus, computers, dance, drama, ethnic, film, honors, international, jazz band, literary magazine, musical theater, newspaper, photography, political, professional, radio and TV, religious, social, social service, student government, and yearbook. Popular campus events include Spring Fling, All-College Ball, Student Activities Fair, and Christmas Fair.

Sports: There are 10 intercollegiate sports for men and 9 for women, and 9 intramural sports for men and 10 for women. Athletic and recreation facilities include a physical education center, outdoor basketball courts, a fitness center, a wrestling room, racquetball courts, a swimming pool, a multipurpose area, a 3200-seat gymnasium, a free weight-lifting area, an outdoor athletic complex with a field house, a field hockey field, a football stadium, and baseball, softball, and soccer fields.

Disabled Students: Nearly all of the campus is accessible to disabled students. The following facilities are available: wheelchair ramps, elevators, special parking, specially equipped rest rooms, special class scheduling, lowered drinking fountains, and lowered telephones.

Services: In addition to many counseling and information services, tutoring is available in every subject. The academic skills center provides a writing center, learning skills workshops, a tutoring program, and learning disability services.

Campus Safety and Security: Campus safety and security measures include 24-hour foot and vehicle patrol, self-defense education, escort service, and informal discussions. There are pamphlets/posters/films, emergency telephones, and lighted pathways/sidewalks.

Programs of Study: King's confers B.A. and B.S. degrees. Associate and master's degrees are also awarded. Bachelor's degrees are awarded in BIOLOGICAL SCIENCE (biology/biological science), BUSINESS (accounting, banking and finance, business administration and management, business economics, international business management, marketing/retailing/merchandising, and personnel management), COMMUNICATIONS AND THE ARTS (communications, dramatic arts, English, French, languages, and Spanish), COMPUTER AND PHYSICAL SCIENCE (chemistry, computer programming, computer science, information sciences and systems, mathematics, physics, and science), EDUCATION (elementary, foreign languages, middle school, science, and secondary), HEALTH PROFESSIONS (health care administration, medical laboratory technology, physician's assistant, predentistry, and premedicine), SOCIAL SCIENCE (criminal justice, economics, gerontology, history, philosophy, political science/government, prelaw, psychology, sociology, and theological studies). Accounting, English, and biology are the strongest academically. Accounting, business administration, and education have the largest enrollments.

Required: All students must earn a minimum of 120 credits and maintain a minimum GPA of 2.0. The core requirements represent 51 credits. The major comprises a maximum of 60 credits, of which a maximum of 40 credits can be specified in the major department with the balance designated for related fields.

Special: Co-op programs in early childhood and special education and cross-registration with Wilkes University and College Misericordia are offered. Experiential Learning Program provides internship opportunities in all majors with a variety of employers. King's also offers study abroad in 10 countries, a Washington semester, work-study programs, an accelerated degree program in business administration, B.A.-B.S. degrees, dual and student-designed majors, credit for life experience, and pass/fail options. There is a freshman honors program on campus, as well as 11 national honor societies.

Faculty/Classroom: 78% of faculty are male; 22%, female. All teach undergraduates. No introductory courses are taught by graduate students. The average class size in an introductory lecture is 24; in a laboratory, 18; and in a regular course offering, 20.

Admissions: 78% of the 1995–96 applicants were accepted. 36% of the current freshmen were in the top fifth of their class; 69% were in the top two fifths. There was 1 National Merit finalist and 3 semifinalists. 7 freshmen graduated first in their class.

Requirements: The SAT I or ACT is required. King's requires 15 academic credits, including 4 in English, 3 each in mathematics, science, and history, 2 in foreign language, and 1 in social studies. Applications are accepted on computer disk and on-line. King's has a home page on the World Wide Web at: http://www.kings.edu. AP and CLEP credits are accepted. Important factors in the admissions decision are advanced placement or honor courses, extracurricular activities record, and leadership record.

Procedure: Freshmen are admitted fall, spring, and summer. Entrance exams should be taken before December of the senior year. There are early decision, early admissions, and deferred admissions plans. Applications should be filed by August 1 for fall entry, December 1 for spring entry, and May 1 for summer entry, along with an application fee of $30. Notification is sent on a rolling basis. 4 early decision candidates were accepted for the 1995–96 class. A waiting list is an active part of the admissions procedure, with about 10% of all applicants on the list.

Transfer: 131 transfer students enrolled in 1995–96. Applicants planning to major in the sciences or business must present a minimum GPA of 2.5; all others must present a 2.0. Students must have earned at least 3 credit hours at another college. An interview is recommended. 60 credits of a minimum 120 must be completed at King's.

Visiting: There are regularly scheduled orientations for prospective students, consisting of classroom and financial aid presentations, faculty one-on-one meetings, admissions interviews, and campus tours. There are guides for informal visits and visitors may sit in on classes and stay overnight at the school. To schedule a visit, contact the Admissions Office.

Financial Aid: In 1995–96, 93% of all freshmen and 85% of continuing students received some form of financial aid. 84% of all students received need-based aid. The average freshman award was $10,070. Of that total, scholarships or need-based grants averaged $6110 ($13,422 maximum); loans averaged $3049 ($4625 maximum); and work contracts averaged $1000 ($1100 maximum). 60% of undergraduate students work part-time. Average earnings from campus work for the school year are $1100. The average financial indebtedness of the 1994–95 graduate was $12,700. King's is a member of CSS. The FAFSA and the college's own financial statement are required. The application deadline for fall entry is March 1.

International Students: There are currently 32 international students enrolled. The school actively recruits these students. They must take the TOEFL and achieve a minimum score of 525.

Computers: The college provides computer facilities for student use. The mainframes are an IBM AS/400 F45 and an IBM RS/6000 570. Programming courses, statistical research, and course work in SAS and SPSS utilize the mainframe computer with access provided through dial-in lines and 100 networked IBM PS/2 computers. Two networked Macintosh laboratories containing 62 Macs and a computer science/graphics laboratory containing 40 MS-DOS computers are available for student use. All students may access the system. A small 24-hour networked laboratory exists; other laboratories are available a total of 95 hours per week. There are no time limits and no fees.

Graduates: In 1994–95, 442 bachelor's degrees were awarded. The most popular majors among graduates were accounting (13%), elementary education (12%), and business administration (10%). Within an average freshman class, 67% graduate in 4 years, 71% in 5 years, and 72% in 6 years. 64 companies recruited on campus in 1994–95. Of the 1994 graduating class, 12% were enrolled in graduate school within 6 months of graduation and 82% had found employment.

Admissions Contact: Daniel Conry, Dean of Admissions. E-mail: sasocash@rs02.kings.edu. A campus video is available.

KUTZTOWN UNIVERSITY

E-3

Kutztown, PA 19530   (215) 683–4060

Full-time: 2630 men, 3308 women	**Faculty:** IIA, +$
Part-time: 286 men, 612 women	**Ph.D.s:** n/av
Graduate: 240 men, 735 women	**Student/Faculty:** n/av
Year: semesters, summer session	**Tuition:** $3940 ($8914)
Application Deadline: open	**Room & Board:** $3010
Freshman Class: 4945 applied, 3503 accepted, 1232 enrolled	
SAT I or ACT: required	**COMPETITIVE**

Kutztown University, founded in 1866, is a public, coeducational institution within the Pennsylvania State System of Higher Education. The university offers undergraduate programs in the arts and sciences, business, education, and visual and performing arts. There are 4 undergraduate schools and one graduate school. In addition to regional accreditation, KU has baccalaureate program accreditation with NCATE and NLN. The library contains 406,094 volumes, 1,177,981 microform items, and 11,012 audiovisual forms, and subscribes to

1926 periodicals. Computerized library sources and services include the card catalog, interlibrary loans, and database searching. Special learning facilities include a learning resource center, art gallery, planetarium, radio station, TV station, a women's center, a cartography laboratory, and a German cultural heritage center. The 325-acre campus is in a rural area 90 miles north of Philadelphia. Including residence halls, there are 42 buildings on campus.

Student Life: 91% of undergraduates are from Pennsylvania. Students come from 18 states, 30 foreign countries, and Canada. 94% are from public schools. 93% are white. The average age of freshmen is 18; all undergraduates, 21. 26% do not continue beyond their first year; 50% remain to graduate.

Housing: 2848 students can be accommodated in college housing. College-sponsored living facilities include single-sex and coed dormitories and on-campus apartments. In addition there are special interest houses. On-campus housing is available on a first-come, first-served basis. 60% of students commute. Alcohol is not permitted. Upperclassmen may keep cars on campus.

Activities: 4% of men belong to 6 national fraternities; 4% of women belong to 1 local and 5 national sororities. There are 120 groups on campus, including art, band, choir, chorus, computers, dance, drama, ethnic, honors, international, jazz band, literary magazine, marching band, musical theater, newspaper, orchestra, political, professional, radio and TV, religious, social, social service, student government, and yearbook. Popular campus events include Homecoming, International Animated Film Festival, and Family Day.

Sports: There are 10 intercollegiate sports for men and 10 for women, and 22 intramural sports for men and 19 for women. Athletic and recreation facilities include a 7500-seat stadium and track, a field house and indoor track, a swimming pool, tennis courts, a 4000-seat arena, athletic fields, and a rifle range.

Disabled Students: 70% of the campus is accessible to disabled students. The following facilities are available: wheelchair ramps, elevators, special parking, specially equipped rest rooms, and special class scheduling. All programs can be made accessible to physically disabled persons.

Services: In addition to many counseling and information services, tutoring is available in some subjects. There is a reader service for the blind and remedial math and reading.

Campus Safety and Security: Campus safety and security measures include 24-hour foot and vehicle patrol, self-defense education, escort service, and informal discussions. In addition, there are pamphlets/posters/films, emergency telephones, and lighted pathways/sidewalks.

Programs of Study: KU confers B.A., B.S., B.F.A., B.S.B.A., B.S.Ed., and B.S.N. degrees. Master's degrees are also awarded. Bachelor's degrees are awarded in BIOLOGICAL SCIENCE (biology/biological science and marine science), BUSINESS (accounting, business administration and management, business economics, international business management, marketing/retailing/merchandising, and personnel management), COMMUNICATIONS AND THE ARTS (communications, crafts, design, dramatic arts, English, fine arts, French, German, music, Russian, Spanish, speech/debate/rhetoric, and telecommunications), COMPUTER AND PHYSICAL SCIENCE (chemistry, geology, mathematics, and physics), EDUCATION (art, early childhood, elementary, library science, secondary, and special), ENGINEERING AND ENVIRONMENTAL DESIGN (environmental science), HEALTH PROFESSIONS (medical laboratory technology, nursing, and speech pathology/audiology), SOCIAL SCIENCE (American studies, anthropology, criminal justice, economics, geography, history, philosophy, political science/government, psychology, public administration, social work, and sociology). Communication design is the strongest academically. Education, business, and telecommunications have the largest enrollments.

Required: General education requirements vary by program, but all students must take physical education, speech 10, English composition, or introduction to dance. Distribution requirements also include courses in humanities, social sciences, natural sciences, and mathematics. To graduate, students must complete at least 128 semester hours, including 33 to 80 in a major field, with a minimum GPA of 2.0. Students in the College of Liberal Arts and Sciences must take a comprehensive examination.

Special: Students may study abroad in 7 countries. There is a 3–2 engineering degree program with Pennsylvania State University and an accelerated degree program in nursing. KU also offers internships, student-designed majors, and a general studies degree. Nondegree study is possible. There is a freshman honors program on campus, as well as 14 national honor societies. 13 departments have honors programs.

Admissions: 71% of the 1995–96 applicants were accepted. 17% of the current freshmen were in the top fifth of their class; 51% were in the top two fifths. 13 freshmen graduated first in their class.

Requirements: The SAT I or ACT is required. KU requires applicants to be in the upper 50% of their class. A minimum GPA of 2.0 is required. Applicants must be graduates of accredited secondary schools or have earned a GED. Admission to a special curriculum may require additional proof of ability. Students may apply on-line via ExPAN. The World Wide Web page also includes an application; the URL is http://www.kutztown.edu. AP and CLEP credits are accepted. Important factors in the admissions decision are advanced placement or honor courses, evidence of special talent, and leadership record.

Procedure: Freshmen are admitted fall and spring. Entrance exams should be taken in the fall of the senior year. There is a deferred admissions plan. Application deadlines are open. Application fee is $25. Notification is sent on a rolling basis. A waiting list is an active part of the admissions procedure, with about 5% of all applicants on the list.

Transfer: 490 transfer students enrolled in 1995–96. Applicants must present a GPA of 2.0 and official transcripts from all colleges and secondary schools previously attended. Students transferring fewer than 30 credit hours must also submit SAT I or ACT scores. 33 credits of 128 must be completed at KU.

Visiting: There are regularly scheduled orientations for prospective students, including 2 fall preview days, and 4 spring visitations. There are guides for informal visits. To schedule a visit, contact the Admissions Office.

Financial Aid: In 1995–96, 75% of all freshmen and 80% of continuing students received some form of financial aid. 50% of freshmen and 60% of continuing students received need-based aid. The average freshman award was $4000. Of that total, scholarships or need-based grants averaged $575 ($1000 maximum); loans averaged $2625; and work contracts averaged $900 ($3000 maximum). 40% of undergraduate students work part-time. Average earnings from campus work for the school year are $1600. The average financial indebtedness of the 1994–95 graduate was $13,000. The FAFSA is required. The application deadline for fall entry is March 15.

International Students: There are currently 149 international students enrolled. They must take the TOEFL and achieve a minimum score of 500.

Computers: The college provides computer facilities for student use. The mainframes are a Unisys A-11, 2200, and U6000. The Unisys U6000/70 is a parallel processor, UNIX-based system used exclusively by students and faculty. Students also have access to two Sun SPARCserver 1000s for various compilers and Internet connections. Approximately 150 terminals or microcomputers are available to students. There are also 32 dial-up lines available. The Unisys 2200 supports library automation. Students and faculty can access this at the library, over the network, or dial-ups. All students may access the system. There are no time limits and no fees.

Graduates: In 1994–95, 1153 bachelor's degrees were awarded. The most popular majors among graduates were elementary education (14%), psychology (8%), and special education (7%). Within an average freshman class, 25% graduate in 4 years, 50% in 5 years, and 52% in 6 years. 35 companies recruited on campus in 1994–95.

Admissions Contact: George McKinley, Director of Admissions. E-mail: admissions@kutztown.edu.

LA ROCHE COLLEGE
B-3
Pittsburgh, PA 15237   (412) 367-9241; FAX: (412) 367-9268

Full-time: 279 men, 411 women	Faculty: 44; IIB, -$
Part-time: 146 men, 473 women	Ph.D.s: n/av
Graduate: 63 men, 258 women	Student/Faculty: 16 to 1
Year: semesters, summer session	Tuition: $9426
Application Deadline: open	Room & Board: $5022
Freshman Class: 342 applied, 320 accepted, 148 enrolled	
SAT I Verbal/Math: 400/400	ACT: 20 LESS COMPETITIVE

La Roche College, founded in 1963, is a private, coeducational Catholic institution offering undergraduate programs in arts and sciences, business, graphic art and design, health science, upper-level nursing, professional training, and religious studies. There are 6 undergraduate and 3 graduate schools. In addition to regional accreditation, La Roche has baccalaureate program accreditation with FIDER, NASAD, and NLN. The library contains 66,000 volumes, 125 microform items, and 973 audiovisual forms, and subscribes to 700 periodicals. Computerized library sources and services include interlibrary loans and database searching. Special learning facilities include a learning resource center, art gallery, and interior and graphic design studios. The 100-acre campus is in a suburban area 10 miles north of Pittsburgh. Including residence halls, there are 11 buildings on campus.

Student Life: 93% of undergraduates are from Pennsylvania. Students come from 17 states and 7 foreign countries. 93% are white. 56% are Catholic; 27% Protestant. The average age of freshmen is 19; all undergraduates, 29. 23% do not continue beyond their first year; 40% remain to graduate.

Housing: 300 students can be accommodated in college housing. College-sponsored living facilities include coed dormitories, on-campus apartments, and off-campus apartments. On-campus housing is guaranteed for all 4 years. 54% of students commute. All students may keep cars on campus.

Activities: 10% of women belong to 1 local sorority. There are no fraternities. There are 25 groups on campus, including art, cheerleading, chorus, computers, drama, ethnic, honors, international, literary magazine, newspaper, pep band, photography, political, professional, religious, social, social service, student government, and yearbook. Popular campus events include Campus Picnic, Martin Luther King Day, Thanksgiving Interfaith Forum, Parents Day, Fall Semiformal Dinner Dance, Spring Semiformal River Cruise, Alumni Weekend, Spring Carnival, Battle of the Bands, Madrigal Dinner, and Day and Night at La Roche.

Sports: There are 3 intercollegiate sports each for men and women, and 10 intramural sports each for men and women. Athletic and recreation facilities include soccer and baseball fields, a gymnasium, hiking trails, a fitness/sports center that houses a gymnasium, racquetball courts, indoor track, an aerobics room, and a weight room, and a nearby county park with tennis courts and a swimming pool.

Disabled Students: 80% of the campus is accessible to disabled students. The following facilities are available: wheelchair ramps, elevators, special parking, specially equipped rest rooms, lowered drinking fountains, and lowered telephones.

Services: In addition to many counseling and information services, tutoring is available in every subject. There is remedial math, reading, and writing.

Campus Safety and Security: Campus safety and security measures include 24-hour foot and vehicle patrol, escort service, informal discussions, and pamphlets/posters/films. In addition, there are emergency telephones, lighted pathways/sidewalks, an intercom security system, and residence halls locked 24 hours a day.

Programs of Study: La Roche confers B.A., B.S., and B.S.N. degrees. Master's degrees are also awarded. Bachelor's degrees are awarded in BIOLOGICAL SCIENCE (biology/biological science), BUSINESS (accounting, banking and finance, business administration and management, international business management, and sports management), COMMUNICATIONS AND THE ARTS (communications, English, and graphic design), COMPUTER AND PHYSICAL SCIENCE (chemistry, computer programming, and natural sciences), EDUCATION (science), ENGINEERING AND ENVIRONMENTAL DESIGN (interior design), HEALTH PROFESSIONS (medical laboratory technology, medical technology, nursing, radiograph medical technology, and respiratory therapy), SOCIAL SCIENCE (history, human services, psychobiology, psychology, religion, religious education, and sociology). Graphic design, interior design, and professional writing are the strongest academically. Administration and management, design areas, and nursing have the largest enrollments.

Required: Students are required to complete 18 credits in basic skill areas, including writing, mathematics, computer applications, communication, and critical thinking, and 24 credits in the following liberal arts areas: ethical and spiritual values, aesthetics, imaginative literature, wellness, natural world, social systems, historical perspective, and global awareness. A minimum of 120 credit hours and a GPA of 2.0 are requirements for graduation, as is a senior seminar in most majors.

Special: There is cross-registration with members of the Pittsburgh Council of Higher Education. Internships for which students may receive up to 6 credits are available for juniors and seniors with numerous employers in the Pittsburgh area. La Roche also offers study abroad, a Washington semester, dual majors, credit for life experience, directed research, honors programs, independent study, and pass/fail options.

Faculty/Classroom: 50% of faculty are male; 50%, female. All teach undergraduates and 40% also do research. No introductory courses are taught by graduate students. The average class size in an introductory lecture is 30; in a laboratory, 15; and in a regular course offering, 20.

Admissions: 94% of the 1995–96 applicants were accepted. The SAT I scores for the 1995–96 freshman class were as follows: Verbal—89% below 500, 10% between 500 and 599, and 1% between 600 and 700; Math—81% below 500, 16% between 500 and 599, 2% between 600 and 700, and 1% above 700. The ACT scores were 58% below 21, 14% between 21 and 23, 15% between 24 and 26, and 13% above 28.

Requirements: The SAT I or ACT is required. In addition, applicants must be graduates of accredited secondary schools or have earned a GED. An interview is recommended for all applicants. AP and CLEP credits are accepted. Important factors in the admissions decision are advanced placement or honor courses, recommendations by school officials, and evidence of special talent.

Procedure: Freshmen are admitted to all sessions. Entrance exams should be taken by the fall of the senior year. There is an early admissions plan. Application deadlines are open. Application fee is $25. Notification is sent on a rolling basis.

Transfer: 102 transfer students enrolled in a recent year. Transfer design students may be required to submit a portfolio and must have a 2.0 GPA. 30 credits of 120 must be completed at La Roche.

Visiting: There are regularly scheduled orientations for prospective students, including an overnight stay, information sessions and interactive sessions, class attendance, and meeting with faculty. There are also 1-day visits on Saturday. There are guides for informal visits and visitors may sit in on classes and stay overnight at the school. To schedule a visit, contact the Admissions Office.

Financial Aid: In a recent year, 76% of all freshmen and 72% of continuing students received some form of financial aid. 75% of freshmen and 71% of continuing students received need-based aid. The average freshman award was $10,000. Of that total, scholarships or need-based grants averaged $6000 ($7000 maximum); loans averaged $2800 ($3625 maximum); and work contracts averaged $1200. 24% of undergraduate students work part-time. Average earnings from campus work for the school year are $1200. The average financial indebtedness of a recent year's graduate was $7500. La Roche is a member of CSS. The FAFSA is required. The application deadline for fall entry is May 1.

International Students: In a recent year, 30 international students were enrolled. The school actively recruits these students. They must take the TOEFL and achieve a minimum score of 550. The TOEFL is waived if the student takes the SAT I in writing and receives a score of 400 or better on the verbal section. Students must take SAT II: Subject test for college placement.

Computers: The college provides computer facilities for student use. Students have access to 40 microcomputers, including IBM, IBM-compatible, Apple and Apple Macintosh, which are part of a local area network. Students may access Dialog. The Macintosh computer laboratory offers software for illustration, Postscript, animation, dimensional design, and desktop publishing. All students may access the system. Student access time to the PCs varies by course, as does the fee for computer use, which ranges from $5 to $35.

Graduates: In a recent year, 278 bachelor's degrees were awarded. The most popular majors among graduates were administration and management (23%), nursing (12%), and graphic design (10%). Within an average freshman class, 60% graduate in 4 years and 90% in 5 years.

Admissions Contact: Lee-Ann Hilf, Acting Director of Admissions. E-mail: hilfl1@marie.laroche.edu.

LA SALLE UNIVERSITY
Philadelphia, PA 19141-1199

F-3
(215) 951-1500
(800) 328-1910; FAX: (215) 951-1656

Full-time: 1287 men, 1509 women	Faculty: 192; IIA, av$
Part-time: 348 men, 929 women	Ph.D.s: 87%
Graduate: 619 men, 757 women	Student/Faculty: 15 to 1
Year: semesters, summer session	Tuition: $13,160
Application Deadline: April 15	Room & Board: $6000
Freshman Class: 2742 applied, 2075 accepted, 742 enrolled	
ACT: 25	COMPETITIVE

La Salle University, founded in 1863, is a private coeducational institution conducted under the auspices of the Christian Brothers of the Roman Catholic Church. The university offers undergraduate programs in the arts and sciences, business, education, fine arts, religious studies, and nursing. There are 4 undergraduate and 3 graduate schools. In addition to regional accreditation, La Salle has baccalaureate program accreditation with AACSB, CSWE, and NLN. The library contains 330,000 volumes, 320,000 microform items, and 5200 audiovisual forms, and subscribes to 1600 periodicals. Computerized library sources and services include the card catalog, interlibrary loans, and database searching. Special learning facilities include a learning resource center, art gallery, radio station, TV station, and Japanese tea ceremony house. The 100-acre campus is in an urban area 8 miles northwest of the center of Philadelphia. Including residence halls, there are 56 buildings on campus.

Student Life: 68% of undergraduates are from Pennsylvania. Students come from 30 states, 8 foreign countries, and Canada. 47% are from public schools; 53% from private. 87% are white. 80% are Catholic; 12% Protestant. The average age of freshmen is 18; all undergraduates, 20. 12% do not continue beyond their first year; 73% remain to graduate.

Housing: 1810 students can be accommodated in college housing. College-sponsored living facilities include single-sex and coed dormitories and on-campus apartments. In addition there are honors houses and special interest houses, for which student groups may submit proposals for use. Townhouses and apartments are available to juniors and seniors. On-campus housing is guaranteed for all 4 years. 58% of students live on campus; of those, 65% remain on campus on weekends. All students may keep cars on campus.

Activities: 13% of men belong to 1 local fraternity and 7 national fraternities; 12% of women belong to 1 local sorority and 6 national sororities. There are 106 groups on campus, including band, cheerleading, choir, chorale, chorus, computers, dance, drama, drill team, ethnic, film, honors, international, jazz band, literary magazine, newspaper, orchestra, pep band, political, professional, radio and TV, religious, social, social service, student government, and yearbook. Popular campus events include concert and lecture series, Spring Fling, Oktoberfest, First Tuesday, Comedy Hour, Parents Weekend, Carnifall, Midnight Madness, and Charter Week.

Sports: There are 11 intercollegiate sports for men and 12 for women, and 14 intramural sports for men and 14 for women. Athletic and recreation facilities include a 7000-seat stadium, a 1200-seat gymnasium, a 500-seat auditorium, 4 playing fields, 6 tennis courts, a fully equipped athletic and exercise facility, wrestling rooms, a sauna, racquetball and squash courts, indoor and outdoor tracks, basketball and volleyball courts, and an indoor swimming pool.

Disabled Students: 95% of the campus is accessible to disabled students. The following facilities are available: wheelchair ramps, elevators, special parking, specially equipped rest rooms, special class scheduling, and lowered drinking fountains.

Services: In addition to many counseling and information services, tutoring is available in some subjects, including English, mathematics, and accounting. A writing center is also available.

Campus Safety and Security: Campus safety and security measures include 24-hour foot and vehicle patrol, escort service, shuttle buses, and emergency telephones. In addition, there are lighted pathways/sidewalks.

Programs of Study: La Salle confers B.A., B.S., B.S.N., and B.S.W. degrees. Associate and master's degrees are also awarded. Bachelor's degrees are awarded in BIOLOGICAL SCIENCE (biochemistry and biology/biological science), BUSINESS (accounting, banking and finance, business administration and management, management information systems, marketing/retailing/merchandising, organizational behavior, and personnel management), COMMUNICATIONS AND THE ARTS (classics, communications, English, fine arts, French, German, Italian, music, Russian, and Spanish), COMPUTER AND PHYSICAL SCIENCE (chemistry, computer science, geology, mathematics, physics, and quantitative methods), EDUCATION (elementary, foreign languages, science, secondary, social studies, and special), ENGINEERING AND ENVIRONMENTAL DESIGN (environmental science), HEALTH PROFESSIONS (nursing, predentistry, and premedicine), SOCIAL SCIENCE (criminal justice, economics, history, philosophy, political science/government, prelaw, psychology, public administration, religion, social work, and sociology). Chemistry, English, and accounting are the strongest academically. Accounting, education, and communication have the largest enrollments.

Required: Students must first complete 7 to 9 foundation courses in writing, literature, philosophy, religion, social science, history, science, and computer science, and then complete 8 core courses, including 3 in religion and philosophy and 5 in selected subjects. To graduate, students must complete at least 120 credit hours, including 45 in a major field, with a minimum GPA of 2.0; 38 of the courses must be 3 credits in value.

Special: Students may study abroad in Switzerland and Spain. Cross-registration is offered in conjunction with Chestnut Hill College, and there is a 2–2 program in allied health with Thomas Jefferson University. La Salle also offers co-op programs in all majors, work-study programs, internships for communication, business, and computer science majors, accelerated degree programs, dual and student-designed majors, B.A.-B.S. degrees, and pass/fail options. There is a freshman honors program on campus, as well as 13 national honor societies.

Faculty/Classroom: 68% of faculty are male; 32%, female. All teach undergraduates and 45% also do research. No introductory courses are taught by graduate students. The average class size in an introductory lecture is 20; in a laboratory, 14; and in a regular course offering, 19.

Admissions: 76% of the 1995–96 applicants were accepted. The SAT I scores for the 1995–96 freshman class were as follows: Verbal—46% below 500, 44% between 500 and 599, 9% between 600 and 700, and 1% above 700; Math—28% below 500, 42% between 500 and 599, 26% between 600 and 700, and 4% above 700. The ACT scores were all between 24 and 26. 45% of the current freshmen were in the top fifth of their class; 80% were in the top two fifths. 28 freshmen graduated first in a recent class.

Requirements: The SAT I or ACT is required. La Salle requires applicants to be in the upper 50% of their class. SAT II: Subject tests in writing and mathematics are recommended. Applicants must be graduates of accredited secondary schools or have earned a GED. La Salle requires 16 academic units, based on 4 years of English, 3 of mathematics, 2 of foreign language, and 1 of history, with the remaining 5 units in academic electives; science and mathematics majors must have an additional one-half unit of mathematics. An essay is required, and an interview is recommended. AP and CLEP credits are accepted. Important factors in the admissions decision are advanced placement or honor courses, leadership record, and recommendations by school officials.

Procedure: Freshmen are admitted fall and spring. Entrance exams should be taken before February of the senior year. There are early admissions and deferred admissions plans. Applications should be filed by April 15 for fall entry and December 15 for spring entry, along with an application fee of $30. Notification is sent on a rolling basis.

Transfer: 158 transfer students enrolled in 1995–96. Transfer applicants should have a minimum GPA of 2.25, with 2.5 preferred. 50 credits of 120 must be completed at La Salle.

Visiting: There are guides for informal visits and visitors may sit in on classes and stay overnight at the school. To schedule a visit, contact the Admissions Office.

Financial Aid: In 1995–96, 85% of all students received some form of financial aid. 80% of all students received need-based aid. The average freshman award was $12,619. Of that total, scholarships or need-based grants averaged $7000 ($13,360 maximum); loans averaged $3500 ($4000 maximum); and work contracts averaged $1800 (maximum). 52% of undergraduate students work part-time. Average earnings from campus work for the school year are $1600. The average financial indebtedness of the 1994–95 graduate was $12,000. La Salle is a member of CSS. The FAFSA is required. The application deadline for fall entry is February 15.

International Students: There were 82 international students enrolled in a recent year. The school actively recruits these students. They must take the TOEFL and achieve a minimum score of 500.

Computers: The college provides computer facilities for student use. The mainframe is an HP 9000/Model 8355E. The university provides 320 IBM and IBM-compatible microcomputers. A LAN is available for student use. The mainframe is used for computer science majors. All students may access the system from 7 A.M. to 11 P.M. There are no time limits and no fees.

Graduates: In 1994–95, 986 bachelor's degrees were awarded. The most popular majors among graduates were business and management (45%), health sciences (10%), and social sciences (8%). Within an average freshman class, 2% graduate in 3 years, 61% in 4 years, 69% in 5 years, and 73% in 6 years. 150 companies recruited on campus in 1994–95.

Admissions Contact: Christopher Lydon, Director of Admissions and Financial Aid. A campus video is available.

LAFAYETTE COLLEGE

Easton, PA 18042

F-3
(215) 250-5100

Full-time: 1104 men, 923 women	Faculty: 180; IIB, +$
Part-time: 142 men, 50 women	Ph.D.s: 100%
Graduate: none	Student/Faculty: 11 to 1
Year: semesters, summer session	Tuition: $19,546
Application Deadline: January 15	Room & Board: $6000
Freshman Class: 2401 accepted, 588 enrolled	
SAT I: required	VERY COMPETITIVE

Lafayette College, founded in 1826 and affiliated with the Presbyterian Church (U.S.A.) is a coeducational, private, undergraduate, liberal arts institution emphasizing the liberal arts and engineering. In addition to regional accreditation, Lafayette has baccalaureate program accreditation with ABET. The 2 libraries contain 438,911 volumes and 105,949 microform items, and subscribe to 1807 periodicals. Computerized library sources and services include the card catalog, interlibrary loans, and database searching. Special learning facilities include a learning resource center, art gallery, radio station, geological museum, foreign languages laboratory, and calculus laboratory. The 112-acre campus is in a residential area 70 miles west of New York City. Including residence halls, there are 64 buildings on campus.

Student Life: 75% of undergraduates are from out-of-state, mostly the Middle Atlantic. Students come from 39 states, 45 foreign countries, and Canada. 70% are from public schools; 30% from private. 84% are white. 38% are Catholic; 30% Protestant; 15% claim no religious affiliation; 10% Jewish. The average age of freshmen is 18; all undergraduates, 20. 6% do not continue beyond their first year; 92% remain to graduate.

Housing: 1965 students can be accommodated in college housing. College-sponsored living facilities include single-sex and coed dormitories, on-campus apartments, off-campus apartments, fraternity houses, and sorority houses. In addition there are honors houses, special interest houses, diversity-oriented houses, arts houses, a black cultural center, and language and special interest floors. On-campus housing is guaranteed for all 4 years. 98% of students live on campus; of those, 95% remain on campus on weekends. Upperclassmen may keep cars on campus.

Activities: 50% of men belong to 12 national fraternities; 70% of women belong to 6 national sororities. There are 100 groups on campus, including AIDS awareness, art, band, cheerleading, choir, chorale, chorus, computers, dance, drama, ethnic, film, gay, honors, international, jazz band, literary magazine, musical theater, newspaper, orchestra, pep band, photography, political, professional, radio and TV, religious, social, social service, student government, and yearbook. Popular campus events include All College Day, International Extravaganza, and Winterfest.

Sports: There are 11 intercollegiate sports for men and 11 for women, and 22 intramural sports for men and 22 for women. Athletic and recreation facilities include a 13,000-seat stadium, a 3500-seat gymnasium, a field house, a varsity house, a natatorium, a weight training room, an outdoor track, an indoor track, 9 tennis courts, and an 80-acre field complex for lacrosse, field hockey, soccer, and baseball.

Disabled Students: 90% of the campus is accessible to disabled students. The following facilities are available: wheelchair ramps, elevators, special parking, specially equipped rest rooms, special class scheduling, lowered drinking fountains, and lowered telephones.

Services: In addition to many counseling and information services, tutoring is available in most subjects, including most 100-level and many 200-level classes. Assistance is available for students in the use of textbooks for the blind.

Campus Safety and Security: Campus safety and security measures include 24-hour foot and vehicle patrol, self-defense education, escort service, and informal discussions. There are pamphlets/posters/films, emergency telephones, lighted pathways/sidewalks, and resident advisers in all residence halls. Residence halls are locked from 8 P.M. to 7 A.M. and are accessible by residents' room keys and outside telephones.

Programs of Study: Lafayette confers A.B., B.S., and B.S.Eng. degrees. Bachelor's degrees are awarded in BIOLOGICAL SCIENCE (biochemistry and biology/biological science), BUSINESS (business economics), COMMUNICATIONS AND THE ARTS (English, fine arts, French, German, music history and appreciation, music theory and composition, and Spanish), COMPUTER AND PHYSICAL SCIENCE (chemistry, computer science, geology, mathematics, and physics), ENGINEERING AND ENVIRONMENTAL DESIGN (chemical engineering, civil engineering, electrical/electronics engineering, and mechanical engineering), HEALTH PROFESSIONS (predentistry), SOCIAL SCIENCE (American studies, anthropology, economics, history, interdisciplinary studies, international relations, philosophy, political science/government, prelaw, psychology, religion, Russian and Slavic studies, and sociology). Engineering, government and law, psychology, English, biology, and economics and business are the strongest academically. Economics and business, engineering, biology, and psychology have the largest enrollments.

Required: All students must maintain a GPA of 1.8 and must complete a 120 semester hours. The common course of study, designed to build a background in the liberal arts and sciences in the first 2 years, includes interdisciplinary seminars, 4 courses in liberal arts and 4 in mathematics/science, as well as knowledge of foreign culture.

Special: Cross-registration through the Lehigh Valley Association of Independent Colleges, internships in all academic departments, study abroad in 3 countries, as well as through other individually arranged plans, a Washington semester at American University, and work-study programs with area employers are possible. An accelerated degree plan in all majors, dual and student-designed majors, and pass/fail options in any nonmajor subject also are available. Five-year, 2-degree programs are also offered. There are 12 national honor societies on campus, including Phi Beta Kappa. 24 departments have honors programs.

Faculty/Classroom: 74% of faculty are male; 26%, female. All both teach and do research. The average class size in a laboratory is 15 and in a regular course offering, 19.

Admissions: The SAT I scores for the 1995–96 freshman class were as follows: Verbal—24% below 500, 50% between 500 and 599, 24% between 600 and 700, and 2% above 700; Math—5% below 500, 26% between 500 and 599, 48% between 600 and 700, and 21% above 700. 59% of the current freshmen were in the top fifth of their class; 94% were in the top two fifths.

Requirements: The SAT I is required. Applicants need 4 years of English, 3 of mathematics (4 for science or engineering majors), 2 each of foreign language and science (with physics and chemistry for science or engineering students), and an additional 5 to 8 units. An essay is required and an interview recommended. The GED is accepted. AP credits are accepted. Important factors in the admissions decision are advanced placement or honor courses, evidence of special talent, and personality/intangible qualities.

Procedure: Freshmen are admitted in the fall. Entrance exams should be taken by January of the senior year. There are early decision, early admissions, and deferred admissions plans. Early decision applications should be filed by January 15; regular applications, by January 15 for fall entry, along with an application fee of $40. Notification of early decision is sent within 30 days; regular decision, mid-March. 138 early decision candidates were accepted for a recent class. A waiting list is an active part of the admissions procedure.

Transfer: 17 transfer students enrolled in 1995–96. Acceptance of transfer students usually depends on college-level performance and achievements. An interview is required if the student lives within 200 miles of the college. No minimum GPA is required, and neither the SAT I nor ACT is needed. The number of credit hours required varies with the program, but usually enough for freshman status with advanced standing is needed. 60 credits of 120 must be completed at Lafayette.

Visiting: There are regularly scheduled orientations for prospective students, including student/faculty panel discussions, tours, and departmental open houses. There are guides for informal visits and visitors may sit in on classes and stay overnight at the school. To schedule a visit, contact the Admissions Office.

Financial Aid: In a recent year, 60% of all freshmen and 66% of continuing students received some form of financial aid. 50% of freshmen and 48% of continuing students received need-based aid. The average freshman award was $15,697. Of that total, scholarships or need-based grants averaged $11,833 ($24,338 maximum); external grants averaged $2649 ($9000 maximum); loans averaged $3158 ($6625 maximum); and work contracts averaged $1232 ($2000 maximum). 54% of undergraduate students work part-time. Average earnings from campus work for the school year are $850. The average financial indebtedness of a recent graduate was $10,676. Lafayette is a member of CSS. The FAF, the college's own financial statement, the Business/Farm supplement, and the Divorce/Separation parent statement (if applicable) are required. The application deadline for fall entry is February 15.

International Students: There were 140 international students enrolled in a recent year. The school actively recruits these students. They must take the TOEFL and achieve a minimum score of 550. The student must also take the SAT I.

Computers: The college provides computer facilities for student use. The mainframes are a DEC VAX 6310, an ARIX, and an IBM 9375. Students have unlimited 24-hour access to the campus network, PCs, and multiuser systems. More than 200 computers are available for student use; all residence hall rooms are connected to the campus network. There are no time limits and no fees.

Graduates: In 1994–95, 481 bachelor's degrees were awarded. The most popular majors among graduates were economics and business (14%), government and law (10%), and English (8%). Within an average freshman class, 1% graduate in 3 years, 87% in 4 years, and 4% in 5 years. 100 companies recruited on campus in 1994–95.

Admissions Contact: Dr. G. Gary Ripple, Director of Admissions.

LEBANON VALLEY COLLEGE OF PENNSYLVANIA
Annville, PA 17003

E-3

(717) 867-6180
(800) 445-6181; FAX: (717) 867-6026

Full-time: 542 men, 621 women	Faculty: 72; IIB, av$
Part-time: 150 men, 337 women	Ph.D.s: 80%
Graduate: 131 men, 81 women	Student/Faculty: 16 to 1
Year: semesters, summer session	Tuition: $14,785
Application Deadline: open	Room & Board: $4755
Freshman Class: 1492 applied, 1136 accepted, 354 enrolled	
SAT I Verbal/Math: 470/535	COMPETITIVE

Lebanon Valley College of Pennsylvania, founded in 1866, is a private coeducational institution affiliated with the United Methodist Church. The college offers undergraduate programs in the arts and sciences, business, health science, professional training, and religious studies. In addition to regional accreditation, LVC has baccalaureate program accreditation with NASM. The library contains 140,426 volumes, 16,749 microform items, and 5767 audiovisual forms, and subscribes to 730 periodicals. Computerized library sources and services include the card catalog, interlibrary loans, and database searching. Special learning facilities include a learning resource center, art gallery, and radio station. The 200-acre campus is in a rural area 7 miles east of Hershey. Including residence halls, there are 26 buildings on campus.

Student Life: 82% of undergraduates are from Pennsylvania. Students come from 14 states and 18 foreign countries. 94% are from public schools; 6% from private. 94% are white. 60% are Protestant; 21% Catholic; 19% claim no religious affiliation. The average age of freshmen is 18; all undergraduates, 20. 14% do not continue beyond their first year; 68% remain to graduate.

Housing: 832 students can be accommodated in college housing. College-sponsored living facilities include single-sex and coed dormitories and on-campus apartments. In addition there are special interest houses. On-campus housing is guaranteed for all 4 years. 78% of students live on campus; of those, 70% remain on campus on weekends. All students may keep cars on campus.

Activities: 25% of men belong to 3 local and 2 national fraternities; 23% of women belong to 2 local and 1 national sororities. There are 48 groups on campus, including band, cheerleading, choir, chorus, computers, drama, drill team, ethnic, gay, honors, jazz band, literary magazine, marching band, musical theater, newspaper, orchestra, photography, political, professional, radio and TV, religious, social,

social service, student government, and yearbook. Popular campus events include Parents Weekend, Christmas at the Valley, and Spring Arts Festival.

Sports: There are 9 intercollegiate sports for men and 7 for women, and 10 intramural sports for men and 7 for women. Athletic and recreation facilities include a 3000-seat stadium, a sports center, athletic fields, indoor and outdoor tracks, a gymnasium, and playing courts for basketball, handball, squash, and tennis.

Disabled Students: 65% of the campus is accessible to disabled students. The following facilities are available: wheelchair ramps, elevators, special parking, specially equipped rest rooms, and special class scheduling.

Services: In addition to many counseling and information services, tutoring is available in every subject.

Campus Safety and Security: Campus safety and security measures include 24-hour foot and vehicle patrol, pamphlets/posters/films, and lighted pathways/sidewalks.

Programs of Study: LVC confers B.A., B.S., B.M., B.S.Ch., B.S.Med.Tech., and B.S.Ed. degrees. Associate and master's degrees are also awarded. Bachelor's degrees are awarded in BIOLOGICAL SCIENCE (biochemistry and biology/biological science), BUSINESS (accounting, hotel/motel and restaurant management, and international business management), COMMUNICATIONS AND THE ARTS (audio technology, English, French, German, music, music performance, and Spanish), COMPUTER AND PHYSICAL SCIENCE (actuarial science, chemistry, computer programming, computer science, mathematics, and physics), EDUCATION (elementary, music, and secondary), ENGINEERING AND ENVIRONMENTAL DESIGN (engineering), HEALTH PROFESSIONS (medical laboratory technology, nursing, occupational therapy, physical therapy, predentistry, premedicine, prepharmacy, and preveterinary science), SOCIAL SCIENCE (American studies, economics, history, philosophy, political science/government, prelaw, psychobiology, psychology, religion, and sociology). Actuarial science, natural sciences, and education are the strongest academically. Education, management, and natural sciences have the largest enrollments.

Required: The general education program consists of course work in four areas: communications, liberal studies, foreign studies, and disciplinary perspectives. Students are required to complete three writing-intensive courses and be proficient in computer applications and modes of information access and retrieval. To graduate, students must complete at least 120 credit hours, 2 units of physical education, and the requirements for the major with a minimum GPA of 2.0.

Special: The Freshman Experience Program assigns each entering freshman to a faculty member to facilitate student adjustment to college. Study abroad is available in 25 countries through the college's affiliation with the International Student Exchange Program and the LVC College in Cologne Program. LVC is also affiliated with several colleges and universities in England, France, and Spain, and with the Athens Centre in Greece. There are 3-2 degree programs in engineering with the University of Pennsylvnia and Case Western Reserve and Widener universities, in forestry with Duke University, and in medical technology with Hahnemann University. There is also a 2-2 degree program in allied health sciences with Thomas Jefferson University. LVC also offers internships in business, government, and nonprofit organizations, a Washington semester, work-study programs, an accelerated degree program, B.A.-B.S. degrees, student-designed majors, and nondegree study. Students can earn up to 12 credit hours for life experience and may select pass/fail options in 6 courses. There is a freshman honors program on campus, as well as 6 national honor societies. 11 departments have honors programs.

Faculty/Classroom: 76% of faculty are male; 24%, female. All teach undergraduates. No introductory courses are taught by graduate students. The average class size in an introductory lecture is 20; in a laboratory, 18; and in a regular course offering, 16.

Admissions: 76% of the 1995-96 applicants were accepted. The SAT I scores for the 1995-96 freshman class were as follows: Verbal—66% below 500, 26% between 500 and 599, and 7% between 600 and 700; Math—41% below 500, 36% between 500 and 599, 17% between 600 and 700, and 5% above 700. 54% of the current freshmen were in the top fifth of their class; 79% were in the top two fifths. There were 5 National Merit finalists. 10 freshmen graduated first in their class.

Requirements: The SAT I is required. Applicants must be graduates of accredited secondary schools or have earned a GED. LVC requires 16 academic units or 16 Carnegie units, including 4 in English, 2 each in mathematics and foreign language, and 1 each in science and social studies. An interview is recommended. Students applying as music majors must also audition. Applications are accepted on-line. AP and CLEP credits are accepted. Important factors in the admissions decision are leadership record, advanced placement or honor courses, and evidence of special talent.

Procedure: Freshmen are admitted fall and spring. Entrance exams should be taken in the spring of the junior year. There are early decision, early admissions, and deferred admissions plans. Application

deadlines are open. Application fee is $25. Notification is sent on a rolling basis.

Transfer: 46 transfer students enrolled in 1995-96. Requirements for applicants include a minimum GPA of 2.0, SAT I scores, and an interview. An associate degree is recommended. 30 credits of 120 must be completed at LVC.

Visiting: There are regularly scheduled orientations for prospective students, including tours, interviews, and meetings with professors. There are guides for informal visits and visitors may sit in on classes and stay overnight at the school. To schedule a visit, contact Mark Breztski, Assistant Director, Admissions at (717) 867-6181 or (800) 445-6181.

Financial Aid: In 1995-96, 83% of all students received some form of financial aid. 78% of freshmen and 72% of continuing students received need-based aid. The average freshman award was $9715. Of that total, scholarships or need-based grants averaged $6512 ($10,235 maximum); academic scholarships averaged $5836 ($7195 maximum); loans averaged $3903 ($4125 maximum); and work contracts averaged $1183. 50% of undergraduate students work part-time. Average earnings from campus work for the school year are $758. The average financial indebtedness of the 1994-95 graduate was $7720. LVC is a member of CSS. The college's own financial statement is required. The application deadline for fall entry is March 1.

International Students: There are currently 31 international students enrolled. The school actively recruits these students. They must take the TOEFL and achieve a minimum score of 550. The student must also take the SAT I or the ACT.

Computers: The college provides computer facilities for student use. The mainframes are a DEC VAX 8200 and a DEC System 5810. The mainframe can be accessed through 30 workstations and 40 networked microcomputers. The mainframe can also be accessed via 16 modems. All students may access the system. There are no time limits and no fees.

Graduates: More than 128 companies recruited on campus in 1994-95. Of the 1994 graduating class, 9% were enrolled in graduate school within 6 months of graduation and 82% had found employment.

Admissions Contact: William J. Brown, Jr., Dean of Admission and Financial Aid. E-mail: w-brown@lvc.edu.

LEHIGH UNIVERSITY
F-3

Bethlehem, PA 18015	**(610) 758-3100; FAX: (610) 758-4361**
Full-time: 2630 men, 1576 women	Faculty: 396; I, +$
Part-time: 114 men, 77 women	Ph.D.s: 99%
Graduate: 1069 men, 829 women	Student/Faculty: 11 to 1
Year: semesters, summer session	Tuition: $19,650
Application Deadline: February 15	Room & Board: $5810
Freshman Class: 6483 applied, 3870 accepted, 1046 enrolled	
SAT I or ACT: required	**HIGHLY COMPETITIVE**

Lehigh University, founded in 1865, is a private, coeducational university offering programs in liberal arts, and science, engineering, and business. There are 3 undergraduate and 2 graduate schools. In addition to regional accreditation, Lehigh has baccalaureate program accreditation with AACSB, ABET, and NCATE. The 3 libraries contain 1,101,513 volumes and 1.9 million microform items, and subscribe to 10,010 periodicals. Computerized library sources and services include the card catalog, interlibrary loans, and database searching. Special learning facilities include a learning resource center, art gallery, and radio station. The 1600-acre campus is in a suburban area 60 miles north of Philadelphia and 80 miles southwest of New York City. Including residence halls, there are 131 buildings on campus.

Student Life: 64% of undergraduates are from out-of-state, mostly the Middle Atlantic. Students come from 41 states, 43 foreign countries, and Canada. 70% are from public schools; 30% from private. 89% are white. The average age of freshmen is 18; all undergraduates, 20. 8% do not continue beyond their first year; 88% remain to graduate.

Housing: 3410 students can be accommodated in college housing. College-sponsored living facilities include single-sex and coed dormitories, on-campus apartments, married-student housing, fraternity houses, and sorority houses. In addition there are language houses, special interest houses, a community service volunteer house, a students-of-color house, an international house, and a creative arts house. On-campus housing is guaranteed for the freshman year only and is available on a lottery system for upperclassmen. 75% of students live on campus; of those, 75% remain on campus on weekends. Upperclassmen may keep cars on campus.

Activities: 35% of men belong to 28 national fraternities; 31% of women belong to 8 national sororities. There are 200 groups on campus, including art, band, cheerleading, chess, choir, chorale, chorus, computers, dance, drama, ethnic, gay, honors, international, jazz band, literary magazine, marching band, musical theater, newspaper, orchestra, photography, political, professional, radio and TV, religious, social, social service, student government, and yearbook. Popular campus events include Spring Fest, Bach Festival, Christmas Vespers, and Annual Pops Concert.

Sports: There are 12 intercollegiate sports for men and 11 for women, and 23 intramural sports for men and 22 for women. Athletic and recreation facilities include a 17,000-seat stadium, a 6500-seat arena, a gymnasium, a champion cross-country course, a field house with basketball and tennis courts, swimming pools, a track, indoor squash courts, playing fields for field hockey, football, lacrosse, and soccer, weight rooms, and a fitness center.

Disabled Students: The following facilities are available: wheelchair ramps, elevators, special parking, specially equipped rest rooms, special class scheduling, lowered drinking fountains, and lowered telephones.

Services: In addition to many counseling and information services, tutoring is available in most subjects, including calculus, physics, and English. Tutoring in other subjects is available on request.

Campus Safety and Security: Campus safety and security measures include 24-hour foot and vehicle patrol, self-defense education, escort service, and shuttle buses. There are informal discussions, pamphlets/posters/films, emergency telephones, and lighted pathways/sidewalks.

Programs of Study: Lehigh confers B.A., B.S., B.S.B.A., and B.S.E. degrees. Master's and doctoral degrees are also awarded. Bachelor's degrees are awarded in BIOLOGICAL SCIENCE (biochemistry, biology/biological science, and molecular biology), BUSINESS (accounting, banking and finance, business economics, management science, and marketing/retailing/merchandising), COMMUNICATIONS AND THE ARTS (classics, dramatic arts, English, fine arts, French, German, journalism, music, and Spanish), COMPUTER AND PHYSICAL SCIENCE (actuarial science, chemistry, computer science, earth science, geology, geophysics and seismology, mathematics, and physics), ENGINEERING AND ENVIRONMENTAL DESIGN (architectural engineering, architecture, chemical engineering, civil engineering, computer engineering, electrical/electronics engineering, engineering mechanics, engineering physics, environmental science, industrial engineering, materials engineering, and mechanical engineering), HEALTH PROFESSIONS (predentistry and premedicine), SOCIAL SCIENCE (American studies, anthropology, behavioral science, cognitive science, East Asian studies, economics, history, international relations, philosophy, political science/government, prelaw, psychology, religion, Russian and Slavic studies, social science, sociology, and urban studies). Architecture, accounting, and mechanical engineering have the largest enrollments.

Required: Graduation requirements vary by degree sought, but all students must complete 2 semesters of English, at least 30 credits in the chosen major, and a minimum of 121 credit hours. Students must also maintain a minimum GPA of 2.0.

Special: The university offers co-op programs through the Colleges of Engineering and Applied Science and Business and Economics, cross-registration with the Lehigh Valley Association of Independent Colleges, study abroad in 50 countries, internships, a Washington semester, several work-study programs, accelerated degree programs in medicine, dentistry and optometry, student-designed majors, many combinations of dual majors, a B.A.-B.S. degree, a 3–2 engineering degree, and pass/fail options. A 6-year B.A.-M.D. degree with the Medical College of Pennsylvania and a 7-year B.A.-D.D.S. degree with Pennsylvania State University are possible. There is a freshman honors program on campus, as well as 16 national honor societies, including Phi Beta Kappa. 60 departments have honors programs.

Faculty/Classroom: 82% of faculty are male; 18%, female. All both teach and do research. No introductory courses are taught by graduate students. The average class size in an introductory lecture is 150 and in a regular course offering, 29.

Admissions: 60% of the 1995–96 applicants were accepted. The SAT I scores for a recent freshman class were as follows: Verbal—37% below 500, 47% between 500 and 599, 15% between 600 and 700, and 1% above 700; Math—5% below 500, 29% between 500 and 599, 53% between 600 and 700, and 13% above 700. 67% of recent freshmen were in the top fifth of their class; 90% were in the top two fifths. There were 7 National Merit finalists and 7 semifinalists in a recent freshman class.

Requirements: The SAT I or ACT is required. Candidates for admission should have completed 4 years of English, 2 each of a foreign language, history, mathematics, science, and social science, and at least 1 each of art and music. Most students present 4 years each of science, mathematics, and English. A graded writing sample is required. An on-campus interview is recommended. Applications are accepted on-line and on computer disk via Common App. AP credits are accepted. Important factors in the admissions decision are advanced placement or honor courses, evidence of special talent, and leadership record.

Procedure: Freshmen are admitted in the fall and spring. Entrance exams should be taken by the January test date. There is an early decision plan. Early decision applications should be filed by December 1 and January 15; regular applications, by February 15 for fall entry and November 15 for spring entry, along with an application fee of $40. Notification of early decision is sent December 15 and February 1; regular decision, by April 1. 244 early decision candidates were accepted for the 1995–96 class. A waiting list is an active part of the admissions procedure, with about 20% of all applicants on the list.

Transfer: 100 transfer students enrolled in a recent year. Transfer candidates should have a minimum GPA of 2.8. An interview is recommended. 30 credits of 121 must be completed at Lehigh.

Visiting: There are regularly scheduled orientations for prospective students, consisting of interviews scheduled Monday through Friday, 9 A.M. to 3:30 P.M.; tours scheduled Monday through Friday, 10:15 A.M., 11:15 A.M., 1 P.M., 2 P.M., and 3 P.M., and interviews and tours also available on some Saturdays. There are guides for informal visits and visitors may sit in on classes and stay overnight at the school. To schedule a visit, contact the Office of Admissions.

Financial Aid: In 1995–96, 56% of all freshmen and 60% of continuing students received some form of financial aid. 53% of all students received need-based aid. The average freshman award was $17,645. Of that total, scholarships or need-based grants averaged $11,955 ($24,000 maximum); loans averaged $4590 ($6500 maximum); and work contracts averaged $1100 ($1500 maximum). 24% of undergraduate students work part time. Average earnings from campus work for the school year are $774. The average financial indebtedness of the 1994–95 graduate was $13,842. Lehigh is a member of CSS. The FAFSA, the college's own financial statement (for upperclassmen only), and the CSS Profile Application are required. The application deadline for fall entry is February 7.

International Students: There are currently 156 international students enrolled. The school actively recruits these students. They must take the TOEFL and achieve a minimum score of 550. The student must also take the SAT I or the ACT.

Computers: The college provides computer facilities for student use. There are clusters of high-speed IBM RS/6000 computers, with more than 115 workstations in public sites. There are also more than 400 microcomputers available for student use in libraries, academic buildings, and computer centers. There are computer ports in all classrooms, dormitories, and offices. Many LANs and a high-speed fiberoptic network are available. All students may access the system 24 hours per day, 7 days per week. There are no time limits and no fees.

Graduates: In 1994–95, 1042 bachelor's degrees were awarded. The most popular majors among graduates were accounting (10%), civil engineering (8%), and government (4%). Within an average freshman class, 75% graduate in 4 years and 88% in 5 years. 313 companies recruited on campus in 1994–95. Of the 1994 graduating class, 23% were enrolled in graduate school within 6 months of graduation and 60% had found employment.

Admissions Contact: Patricia G. Boig, Director of Admissions. E-mail: inado@lehigh.edu.

LINCOLN UNIVERSITY
Lincoln University, PA 19352

E-4

(610) 932-8300, ext. 3206
(800) 790-0191; FAX: (610) 932-1209

Full-time: 500 men, 700 women	**Faculty:** 90; IIB, av$
Part-time: 20 men, 40 women	**Ph.D.s:** 71%
Graduate: 50 men, 140 women	**Student/Faculty:** 13 to 1
Year: semesters	**Tuition:** n/av
Application Deadline: see profile	**Room & Board:** n/av
Freshman Class: n/av	
SAT I or ACT: required	**LESS COMPETITIVE**

Lincoln University, founded in 1854, is a public, coeducational institution offering programs in liberal arts and teacher preparation. Figures given in the above capsule are approximate. There is 1 graduate school. The library contains 167,438 volumes, 196,600 microform items, and 1419 audiovisual forms, and subscribes to 752 periodicals. Special learning facilities include an art gallery and radio station. The 422-acre campus is in a rural area 45 miles southwest of Philadelphia. Including residence halls, there are 28 buildings on campus.

Student Life: 53% of undergraduates are from out-of-state, mostly the Middle Atlantic. Students come from 26 states and 14 foreign countries. 95% are from public schools; 5% from private. 89% are African American. 50% are Protestant. The average age of freshmen is 18; all undergraduates, 19. 30% do not continue beyond their first year; 36% remain to graduate.

Housing: 1300 students can be accommodated in college housing. College-sponsored living facilities include single-sex and coed dormitories. In addition, there are honors houses and language houses. On-campus housing is guaranteed for the freshman year only and is available on a first-come, first-served basis. 89% of students live on campus; of those, 90% remain on campus on weekends. Alcohol is not permitted. Upperclassmen may keep cars on campus.

Activities: 10% of men belong to 4 national fraternities; 20% of women belong to 3 national sororities. There are 60 groups on campus, including art, band, cheerleading, choir, chorale, computers, dance, drama, honors, international, jazz band, newspaper, pep band, political, radio and TV, religious, social, social service, student government, and yearbook. Popular campus events include Homecoming, recitals, and convocations.

Sports: There are 9 intercollegiate sports for men and 6 for women, and 11 intramural sports for men and 11 for women. Athletic and recreation facilities include a 2000-seat gymnasium, tennis courts, softball and track fields, a fitness trail, a swimming pool, and a bowling alley.

Disabled Students: All of the campus is accessible to disabled students. The following facilities are available: wheelchair ramps, elevators, special parking, and specially equipped rest rooms.

Services: In addition to many counseling and information services, tutoring is available in every subject. There is also remedial math, reading, and writing.

Campus Safety and Security: Campus safety and security measures include 24-hour foot and vehicle patrol, self-defense education, escort service, and shuttle buses. There are informal discussions, pamphlets/posters/films, emergency telephones, and lighted pathways/sidewalks.

Programs of Study: Lincoln confers B.A. and B.S. degrees. Master's degrees are also awarded. Bachelor's degrees are awarded in BIOLOGICAL SCIENCE (biology/biological science), BUSINESS (accounting, banking and finance, and business administration and management), COMMUNICATIONS AND THE ARTS (Arabic, art, Chinese, communications, English, French, German, Japanese, journalism, music, Russian, and Spanish), COMPUTER AND PHYSICAL SCIENCE (actuarial science, applied mathematics, chemistry, computer science, mathematics, and physics), EDUCATION (early childhood, elementary, mathematics, music, physical, and secondary), ENGINEERING AND ENVIRONMENTAL DESIGN (preengineering), HEALTH PROFESSIONS (health science and recreation therapy), SOCIAL SCIENCE (anthropology, criminal justice, economics, history, human services, industrial and organizational psychology, international relations, philosophy, psychobiology, psychology, public affairs, religion, and sociology). Physics, chemistry, and biology are the strongest academically. Business administration has the largest enrollment.

Required: Required courses include 9 to 12 hours of social science, 2 courses each of speech, writing, and critical thinking, a freshman seminar, world literature, music, art, philosophy, and religion. All students must take Integrative Themes in the Liberal Arts. Students must pass a writing proficiency and a comprehensive exam. A total of 120 to 128 semester hours is required, along with a GPA of 2.0.

Special: Lincoln offers co-op programs, internships, study abroad in 9 countries, work-study, and pass/fail options. There are 3–2 engineering degrees offered with Drexel and Pennsylvania State universities, Lafayette College, and New Jersey Institute of Technology. There is a freshman honors program on campus, as well as 4 national honor societies. 1 department has an honors program.

Faculty/Classroom: 61% of faculty are male; 39%, female. 84% teach undergraduates. No introductory courses are taught by graduate students. The average class size in an introductory lecture is 15; in a laboratory, 15; and in a regular course offering, 15.

Admissions: 21% of recent freshmen were in the top fifth of their class; 27% were in the top two fifths.

Requirements: The SAT I or ACT is required. Lincoln requires applicants to be in the upper 50% of their class with a 2.0 GPA. Applicants should complete 21 credit hours, including 4 credits in English, 3 each in mathematics, science, and social studies, 2 in art, and 1 in physical education. A GED is accepted. An essay and an interview are required. Important factors in the admissions decision are advanced placement or honor courses, evidence of special talent, and leadership record.

Procedure: Freshmen are admitted to all sessions. Entrance exams should be taken prior to admission. Notification is sent on a rolling basis. A waiting list is an active part of the admissions procedure. Check with the school for current application deadlines and fee.

Transfer: Transfer applicants must be in good standing at all previously attended institutions and must submit official transcripts. They must have completed at least 12 semester hours. 60 credits of 120 to 128 must be completed at Lincoln.

Visiting: There are regularly scheduled orientations for prospective students. There are guides for informal visits and visitors may sit in on classes and stay overnight at the school. To schedule a visit, contact Jimmy Arrington, Director of Admissions.

Financial Aid: Lincoln is a member of CSS. The FAF and PHEAA are required. Check with the school for current deadlines.

International Students: There were 14 international students enrolled in a recent year. The school actively recruits these students. Students must take the TOEFL.

Computers: The college provides computer facilities for student use. The mainframe is a DEC VAX 11/750. There are also 180 IBM, Apple, and Apple Macintosh microcomputers available for student use in the library and in computer laboratories. All students may access the system. There are no time limits and no fees.

Admissions Contact: Jimmy Arrington, Director of Admissions.

LOCK HAVEN UNIVERSITY OF PENNSYLVANIA
D-2

Lock Haven, PA 17745   (717) 893-2027
(800) 233-8978; FAX: (717) 893-2201

Full-time: 1374 men, 1631 women	Faculty: 203; IIB, +$
Part-time: 94 men, 131 women	Ph.Ds: 54%
Graduate: 3 men, 11 women	Student/Faculty: 15 to 1
Year: semesters, summer session	Tuition: $3822 ($8796)
Application Deadline: June 1	Room & Board: $3856
Freshman Class: 3275 applied, 1956 accepted, 565 enrolled	
SAT I Verbal/Math: 520/530	COMPETITIVE +

Lock Haven University, established in 1870, is an independent coeducational institution offering undergraduate degrees in arts and sciences, education, and human services. The university maintains a branch campus in Clearfield. There are 2 undergraduate schools. In addition to regional accreditation, Lock Haven has baccalaureate program accreditation with CSWE, NCATE, and NLN. The library contains 344,716 volumes, 13,574 microform items, and 508,122 audiovisual forms, and subscribes to 1598 periodicals. Computerized library sources and services include the card catalog and interlibrary loans. Special learning facilities include a learning resource center, art gallery, planetarium, radio station, TV station, primate and human performance laboratories, and cadaver dissection laboratory. The 135-acre campus is in a rural area 30 miles west of Williamsport. Including residence halls, there are 28 buildings on campus.

Student Life: 90% of undergraduates are from Pennsylvania. Students come from 35 states, 30 foreign countries, and Canada. 95% are white. The average age of freshmen is 18; all undergraduates, 21. 15% do not continue beyond their first year; 60% remain to graduate.

Housing: 1630 students can be accommodated in college housing. College-sponsored living facilities include single-sex and coed dormitories. In addition, there are international student houses. On-campus housing is guaranteed for all 4 years. 54% of students live on campus; of those, 95% remain on campus on weekends. Alcohol is not permitted. Upperclassmen may keep cars on campus.

Activities: 11% of men belong to 7 national fraternities; 10% of women belong to 4 national sororities. There are 69 groups on campus, including art, band, cheerleading, choir, chorale, chorus, computers, dance, drama, ethnic, gay, honors, international, jazz band, literary magazine, marching band, musical theater, newspaper, orchestra, pep band, photography, political, professional, radio and TV, religious, social, social service, student government, and symphony. Popular campus events include Homecoming, Parents Weekend, and Alcohol Awareness Week.

Sports: There are 7 intercollegiate sports for men and 9 for women, and 19 intramural sports for men and 18 for women. Athletic and recreation facilities include a 5000-seat stadium containing a football field and an all-weather track, a 2500-seat field house with a wrestling room, a gymnasium used for intramurals and weight training, and a gymnasium that houses a swimming pool.

Disabled Students: The entire campus is accessible to disabled to students. The following facilities are available: wheelchair ramps, elevators, special parking, specially equipped rest rooms, special class scheduling, lowered drinking fountains, and lowered telephones.

Services: In addition to many counseling and information services, tutoring is available in most subjects. Reader services for the blind can be arranged. There are also writing and mathematics centers.

Campus Safety and Security: Campus safety and security measures include 24-hour foot and vehicle patrol, informal discussions, pamphlets/posters/films, and emergency telephones. There are lighted pathways/sidewalks.

Programs of Study: Lock Haven confers B.A., B.S., B.F.A., and B.S.Ed. degrees. Associate and master's degrees are also awarded. Bachelor's degrees are awarded in BIOLOGICAL SCIENCE (biology/biological science and environmental biology), BUSINESS (business administration and management), COMMUNICATIONS AND THE ARTS (communications, English, fine arts, French, German, journalism, music, Spanish, and speech/debate/rhetoric), COMPUTER AND PHYSICAL SCIENCE (chemistry, computer science, earth science, geology, information sciences and systems, mathematics, and physics), EDUCATION (early childhood, elementary, foreign languages, library science, physical, science, secondary, and special), HEALTH PROFESSIONS (health science and medical laboratory technology), SOCIAL SCIENCE (economics, geography, history, humanities and social science, international studies, Latin American studies, liberal arts/general studies, philosophy, political science/government, psychology, social science, social work, and sociology).

Health science is the strongest academically. Education, health science, and business management science have the largest enrollments.

Required: To graduate, students must complete 60 hours of general education, including 18 in humanities, 12 in social and behavioral sciences, 9 in mathematics and science, 3 in physical education, and the rest in electives. A total of 128 credit hours is required, including 61 to 68 in the major, with a minimum GPA of 2.0.

Special: There are cooperative programs in music education and engineering, including a 3–2 engineering degree with Pennsylvania State University. Lock Haven also offers study aboard programs in more than 18 countries, work-study options, an accelerated degree program for honor students, a general studies major, and internships, which are required in some majors. Pass/fail grading options are limited to 1 course outside the major per semester, not to exceed 12 credit hours. There is a freshman honors program on campus, as well as 9 national honor societies. 6 departments have honors programs.

Faculty/Classroom: All teach undergraduates and many also do research. No introductory courses are taught by graduate students. The average class size in an introductory lecture is 75; in a laboratory, 15; and in a regular course offering, 26.

Admissions: 60% of the 1995–96 applicants were accepted. The SAT I scores for a recent freshman class were as follows: Verbal—72% below 500, 26% between 500 and 599, and 2% between 600 and 700; Math—41% below 500, 45% between 500 and 599, 13% between 600 and 700, and 1% above 700. 20% of the current freshmen were in the top fifth of their class; 83% were in the top two fifths.

Requirements: The SAT I or ACT is required. Lock Haven requires applicants to be in the upper 60% of their class. Applicants must graduate from an accredited secondary school with a 2.3 GPA or have a GED. 16 academic credits are required, and a college preparatory course is recommended. Students may apply on-line via CollegeView. AP and CLEP credits are accepted. Important factors in the admissions decision are leadership record, advanced placement or honor courses, and evidence of special talent.

Procedure: Freshmen are admitted to all sessions. Entrance exams should be taken during the spring of the junior year and the fall of the senior year. There are early decision, early admissions, and deferred admissions plans. Applications should be filed by June 1 for fall entry, along with an application fee of $25. Notification is sent on a rolling basis. 2 early decision candidates were accepted for the 1995–96 class.

Transfer: 183 transfer students enrolled in 1995–96. Priority is given to applicants who have completed 24 or more transferable credits. A minimum GPA of 2.0 is required, and a composite SAT I score of 970 is recommended. 32 credits of 128 must be completed at Lock Haven.

Visiting: There are regularly scheduled orientations for prospective students, consisting of an introduction to the administration, sessions with faculty, and an information arena/departmental showcase; small group visits are also scheduled. There are guides for informal visits and visitors may sit in on classes. To schedule a visit, contact the Admissions Office.

Financial Aid: Lock Haven is a member of CSS. The FAFSA and PHEAA are required. The application deadline for fall entry is April 1.

International Students: There are currently 67 international students enrolled. The school actively recruits these students. They must take the TOEFL and achieve a minimum score of 550. The student must also take the SAT I or the ACT.

Computers: The college provides computer facilities for student use. The mainframe is an IBM 4381. All Internet services are accessible from the more than 225 microcomputers available in computer laboratories and residence halls. The library's card catalog is also accessible from all on-campus computers hooked up to the mainframe. All students may access the system. There are no time limits and no fees.

Graduates: In 1994–95, 682 bachelor's degrees were awarded. The most popular majors among graduates were education (27%), health sciences (12%), and business management science (9%). Within an average freshman class, 29% graduate in 4 years, 54% in 5 years, and 57% in 6 years. Of the 1994 graduating class, 11% were enrolled in graduate school within 6 months of graduation and 84% had found employment.

Admissions Contact: Joseph Coldren, Director of Admissions. E-mail: admissions@eagle.lhup.edu.

LYCOMING COLLEGE
D-2
Williamsport, PA 17701-5192

(800) 345-3920

FAX: (717) 321-4337

Full-time: 601 men, 773 women	Faculty: 94; IIB, av$
Part-time: 23 men, 72 women	Ph.D.s: 87%
Graduate: none	Student/Faculty: 15 to 1
Year: 4–4–1, summer session	Tuition: $14,700
Application Deadline: April 1	Room & Board: $4400
Freshman Class: 1442 applied, 1128 accepted, 373 enrolled	
SAT I Verbal/Math: 474/529	COMPETITIVE

Lycoming College, established in 1812, is a private, nonprofit, coeducational liberal arts institution affiliated with the Methodist Church. The library contains 160,000 volumes, and subscribes to 1069 periodicals. Computerized library sources and services include the card catalog, interlibrary loans, and database searching. Special learning facilities include a learning resource center, art gallery, planetarium, radio station, TV station, and a nursing skills laboratory. The 34-acre campus is in a small town 94 miles north of Harrisburg. Including residence halls, there are 23 buildings on campus.

Student Life: 72% of undergraduates are from Pennsylvania. Students come from 18 states, 14 foreign countries, and Canada. 75% are from public schools; 25% from private. 94% are white. 65% are Protestant; 32% Catholic. The average age of freshmen is 18.3; all undergraduates, 21.6. 20% do not continue beyond their first year; 63% remain to graduate.

Housing: 1110 students can be accommodated in college housing. College-sponsored living facilities include single-sex and coed dormitories and on-campus apartments. In addition there are special interest, nonsmoking, and contract study floors. On-campus housing is guaranteed for all 4 years. 75% of students live on campus; of those, 65% remain on campus on weekends. All students may keep cars on campus.

Activities: 31% of men belong to 5 national fraternities; 27% of women belong to 3 local and 1 national sororities. There are 52 groups on campus, including art, band, cheerleading, choir, chorus, computers, drama, ethnic, film, gay, honors, international, literary magazine, musical theater, newspaper, photography, political, professional, radio and TV, religious, social, social service, student government, and yearbook. Popular campus events include Campus Carnival, Christmas Party, and Parents Weekend.

Sports: There are 10 intercollegiate sports for men and 9 for women, and 6 intramural sports for men and 6 for women. Athletic and recreation facilities include an outdoor softball, football, soccer, and field hockey complex, indoor basketball courts, intramural fields, and tennis courts.

Disabled Students: 85% of the campus is accessible to disabled students. The following facilities are available: wheelchair ramps, elevators, special parking, specially equipped rest rooms, special class scheduling, lowered drinking fountains, lowered telephones, and specially designed residence hall rooms.

Services: In addition to many counseling and information services, tutoring is available in most subjects, including mathematics, languages, sciences, and accounting. There is remedial math, reading, and writing.

Campus Safety and Security: Campus safety and security measures include 24-hour foot and vehicle patrol, escort service, informal discussions, and pamphlets/posters/films. In addition, there are emergency telephones and lighted pathways/sidewalks.

Programs of Study: Lycoming confers B.A., B.F.A., and B.S.N. degrees. Bachelor's degrees are awarded in BIOLOGICAL SCIENCE (biology/biological science), BUSINESS (accounting and business administration and management), COMMUNICATIONS AND THE ARTS (art history and appreciation, communications, dramatic arts, English, French, German, literature, music, sculpture, Spanish, and studio art), COMPUTER AND PHYSICAL SCIENCE (astronomy, chemistry, computer science, mathematics, and physics), HEALTH PROFESSIONS (medical laboratory technology and nursing), SOCIAL SCIENCE (anthropology, archeology, criminal justice, economics, history, international relations, philosophy, political science/government, psychology, religion, and sociology). Business, psychology, nursing, and biology have the largest enrollments.

Required: To graduate, students must complete distribution requirements in English, foreign language, mathematics, religion or philosophy, fine arts, natural science, and history and social science. A total of 128 credits, with a minimum GPA of 2.0 is required. The number of hours required in the major varies. Students must also complete 4 semesters of physical education, community service, or wellness.

Special: Cooperative programs are available with the Ohio and Pennsylvania Colleges of Podiatric Medicine, Johnson Atelier Technical Institute of Sculpture, Pennsylvania College of Optometry, and Pennsylvania State and Duke universities. Cross-registration is available with the Pennsylvania College of Technology. More than 200 internships, including teacher programs, study abroad in 5 countries, and a Washington semester at American University are available. Lycoming offers work-study programs, dual and student-designed majors, and an accelerated degree program in conjunction with the college's Scholar Program in optometry, podiatric medicine, and dentistry. There is a 3–2 engineering degree program with Pennsylvania State and Washington universities. Nondegree study and pass/fail grading options are available. There is a freshman honors program on campus, as well as 12 national honor societies. 11 departments have honors programs.

Faculty/Classroom: 71% of faculty are male; 29%, female. All teach undergraduates. The average class size in an introductory lecture is 30; in a laboratory, 15; and in a regular course offering, 18.

Admissions: 78% of the 1995–96 applicants were accepted. The SAT I scores for the 1995–96 freshman class were as follows: Verbal—66% below 500, 25% between 500 and 599, 7% between 600 and 700, and 2% above 700; Math—43% below 500, 36% between 500 and 599, 18% between 600 and 700, and 3% above 700. 35% of the current freshmen were in the top fifth of their class; 70% were in the top two fifths. There was 1 National Merit finalist and 1 semifinalist. 12 freshmen graduated first in their class.

Requirements: The SAT I is required, with a minimum score of 800 (recentered), 400 on each section. Applicants must graduate from an accredited secondary school or have a GED. They must have earned 16 academic or Carnegie units, and completed 4 years in English, 3 each in history, mathematics, and social studies, and 2 each in science and a foreign language. An essay is optional, and an interview is recommended. Portfolios and auditions may be required for students seeking scholarships. AP and CLEP credits are accepted. Important factors in the admissions decision are advanced placement or honor courses, leadership record, and evidence of special talent.

Procedure: Freshmen are admitted fall and spring. Entrance exams should be taken during the junior or senior year. There are early admissions and deferred admissions plans. Applications should be filed by April 1 for fall entry and December 1 for spring entry, along with an application fee of $25. Notification is sent on a rolling basis.

Transfer: 55 transfer students enrolled in 1995–96. Applicants must submit appropriate transcripts, and have a minimum GPA of 2.0 in transferable courses. Students who have completed 30 transferable semester hours are not required to submit SAT I or ACT results. 32 credits of 128 must be completed at Lycoming.

Visiting: There are regularly scheduled orientations for prospective students. There are guides for informal visits and visitors may sit in on classes and stay overnight at the school. To schedule a visit, contact the Admissions House.

Financial Aid: In 1995–96, 84% of all students received some form of financial aid. 78% of freshmen and 77% of continuing students received need-based aid. The average freshman award was $13,080. Of that total, scholarships or need-based grants averaged $6895 ($15,000 maximum); loans averaged $3268 ($4025 maximum); and work contracts averaged $600 ($1500 maximum). 41% of undergraduate students work part-time. Average earnings from campus work for the school year are $535. The average financial indebtedness of the 1994–95 graduate was $13,543. Lycoming is a member of CSS. The college's own financial statement is required. The application deadline for fall entry is April 15.

International Students: There are currently 22 international students enrolled. They must take the TOEFL and achieve a minimum score of 500. The student must also take the SAT I or ACT. This requirement may be waived, however.

Computers: The college provides computer facilities for student use. The mainframes are a DEC MicroVAX 3600, an HP Model 8275, and a Prime-Exl 316. Students may access the mainframe through various computer laboratories. There are also 150 terminals and microcomputers available to students. All students may access the system 8 A.M. to 12 midnight. There are no time limits and no fees.

Graduates: In 1994–95, 256 bachelor's degrees were awarded. The most popular majors among graduates were biology (14%), psychology (14%), and business (12%). Within an average freshman class, 1% graduate in 3 years, 49% in 4 years, and 59% in 5 years. 25 companies recruited on campus in 1994–95. Of the 1994 graduating class, 15% were enrolled in graduate school within 6 months of graduation and 80% had found employment.

Admissions Contact: James Spencer, Dean of Admissions and Financial Aid. E-mail: admissions@lycoming.edu.

MANSFIELD UNIVERSITY D-1
Mansfield, PA 16933

(717) 662-4243
(800) 577-6826; FAX: (717) 662-4121

Full-time: 1062 men, 1390 women	Faculty: 180; IIB, ++$
Part-time: 66 men, 151 women	Ph.Ds: 47%
Graduate: 62 men, 223 women	Student/Faculty: 14 to 1
Year: semesters, summer session	Tuition: $4074 ($9048)
Application Deadline: July 1	Room & Board: $3438
Freshman Class: 2869 applied, 1976 accepted, 874 enrolled	
SAT I Verbal/Math: 444/490	COMPETITIVE

Mansfield University, founded in 1857, is a public university that is part of the Pennsylvania State System of Higher Education. It offers programs in professional studies and the arts and sciences. There is one graduate school. In addition to regional accreditation, Mansfield has baccalaureate program accreditation with CAHEA, CSWE, NASM, and NCATE. The 3 libraries contain 210,662 volumes, 994,649 microform items, and 16,993 audiovisual forms, and subscribe to 1952 periodicals. Computerized library sources and services include the card catalog, interlibrary loans, and database searching. Special learning facilities include a learning resource center, art gallery, natural history museum, planetarium, radio station, TV station, and a high-tech lecture laboratory. The 175-acre campus is in a rural area 28 miles south of Corning/Elmira, New York, and 58 miles north of Williamsport. Including residence halls, there are 38 buildings on campus.

Student Life: 87% of undergraduates are from Pennsylvania. Students come from 20 states, 18 foreign countries, and Canada. 93% are white. The average age of freshmen is 19; all undergraduates, 22. 22% do not continue beyond their first year; 50% remain to graduate.

Housing: 1864 students can be accommodated in college housing. College-sponsored living facilities include single-sex and coed dormitories and sorority houses. On-campus housing is guaranteed for all 4 years. 67% of students live on campus. Alcohol is not permitted. All students may keep cars on campus.

Activities: 22% of men belong to 6 national fraternities; 16% of women belong to 4 national sororities. There are 80 groups on campus, including band, cheerleading, choir, chorus, computers, drama, ethnic, honors, international, jazz band, literary magazine, marching band, musical theater, newspaper, orchestra, photography, political, professional, radio and TV, religious, social, social service, student government, symphony, and yearbook. Popular campus events include Parents Weekend, Fabulous 1890s Weekend, and Northern Appalachian Story Telling Festival.

Sports: There are 6 intercollegiate sports for men and 6 for women, and 13 intramural sports for men and 13 for women. Athletic and recreation facilities include football, baseball, and hockey fields, a gymnasium, a track, a recreation center, a 4000-seat stadium, a 2500-seat indoor gymnasium, and a 2500-seat auditorium.

Disabled Students: 80% of the campus is accessible to disabled students. The following facilities are available: wheelchair ramps, elevators, special parking, specially equipped rest rooms, special class scheduling, lowered drinking fountains, lowered telephones, and a wheelchair lift.

Services: In addition to many counseling and information services, tutoring is available in most subjects. There is remedial math, reading, and writing.

Campus Safety and Security: Campus safety and security measures include 24-hour foot and vehicle patrol, escort service, shuttle buses, and emergency telephones. In addition, there are lighted pathways/sidewalks.

Programs of Study: Mansfield confers B.A., B.S., B.M., B.M.E., B.S.Ed., B.S.N., and B.S.W. degrees. Associate and master's degrees are also awarded. Bachelor's degrees are awarded in AGRICULTURE (fishing and fisheries), BIOLOGICAL SCIENCE (biology/biological science), BUSINESS (accounting, business administration and management, business economics, marketing/retailing/merchandising, personnel management, and tourism), COMMUNICATIONS AND THE ARTS (art history and appreciation, broadcasting, dramatic arts, English, French, German, journalism, music, music business management, public relations, Spanish, and studio art), COMPUTER AND PHYSICAL SCIENCE (actuarial science, chemistry, computer science, geology, information sciences and systems, mathematics, and physics), EDUCATION (art, early childhood, elementary, English, foreign languages, mathematics, music, science, secondary, social studies, and special), ENGINEERING AND ENVIRONMENTAL DESIGN (city/community/regional planning, environmental science, and preengineering), HEALTH PROFESSIONS (medical laboratory technology, music therapy, nursing, and respiratory therapy), SOCIAL SCIENCE (anthropology, criminal justice, economics, geography, history, international studies, liberal arts/general studies, philosophy, political science/government, psychology, social science, social work, and sociology). Music, physical sciences, social sciences, and education are the strongest academically. Education, music, and social sciences have the largest enrollments.

Required: To graduate, students must complete 128 credit hours with a 2.0 GPA in core courses, distribution requirements, general education electives, and major requirements.

Special: There is study abroad in England, Spain, and Germany. There is a 3–2 engineering program with Pennsylvania State, George Washington University, the Georgia Institute of Technology, the University of Pittsburgh, and the University of Rochester. The university offers work-study, dual majors, a general studies degree, credit by examination, credit for military experience, nondegree study, and pass/fail options. There is a freshman honors program on campus.

Faculty/Classroom: 62% of faculty are male; 38%, female. 98% teach undergraduates and 2% do research. No introductory courses are taught by graduate students. The average class size in an introductory lecture is 35; in a laboratory, 20; and in a regular course offering, 25.

Admissions: 69% of the 1995–96 applicants were accepted. The SAT I scores for a recent freshman class were as follows: Verbal—83% below 500, 16% between 500 and 599, and 1% between 600 and 700; Math—66% below 500, 26% between 500 and 599, 7% between 600 and 700, and 1% above 700. 30% of the current freshmen were in the top fifth of their class; 69% were in the top two fifths. 2 freshmen graduated first in their class.

Requirements: The SAT I or ACT is required, with a composite SAT I score of 800 (recentered), or an ACT score of 19. Mansfield requires applicants to be in the upper 60% of their class. A minimum GPA of 2.5 is required. A GED is accepted. Applicants should prepare with 4 credits of English, 3 each of history, mathematics, science, and social studies, 2 of foreign language, and 6 of additional academic electives. Art students must submit a portfolio; music students must audition. AP and CLEP credits are accepted.

Procedure: Freshmen are admitted fall and spring. Entrance exams should be taken by the junior or senior year of high school. There are early decision, early admissions, and deferred admissions plans. Early decision applications should be filed by July 1; regular applications, by July 1 for fall entry and December 15 for spring entry, along with an application fee of $25. 2 early decision candidates were accepted for the 1995–96 class. A waiting list is an active part of the admissions procedure.

Transfer: 190 transfer students enrolled in 1995–96. Applicants must have a GPA of at least 2.0. 32 credits of 128 must be completed at Mansfield.

Visiting: There are regularly scheduled orientations for prospective students. There are guides for informal visits and visitors may sit in on classes. To schedule a visit, contact the Admissions Office.

Financial Aid: In a recent year, 75% of all students received some form of financial aid. 35% of all students received need-based aid. The average freshman award was $3100. Of that total, scholarships or need-based grants averaged $1000 ($7352 maximum); other grants averaged $900 ($4500 maximum); loans averaged $2500 ($5500 maximum); and work contracts averaged $900 ($1400 maximum). The average financial indebtedness of the 1994–95 graduate was $5000. Mansfield is a member of CSS. The PHEAA financial statement is required. The application deadline for fall entry is April 15.

International Students: There were 37 international students enrolled in a recent year. The school actively recruits these students. They must take the TOEFL and achieve a minimum score of 550. The student must also take the SAT I or the ACT.

Computers: The college provides computer facilities for student use. The mainframe is an IBM 4381 Model 23. There are also 70 Apple IIe and IIgs and IBM AT and PC microcomputers available. All students may access the system. There are no time limits and no fees.

Graduates: In 1994–95, 550 bachelor's degrees were awarded. Within an average freshman class, 55% graduate in 4 years.

Admissions Contact: Brian D. Barden, Interim Director of Admissions. E-mail: admissns@mnsfld.edu.

MARYWOOD COLLEGE
E-2

Scranton, PA 18509

Full-time: 314 men, 1120 women	(717) 348-6234; (800) 346-5024
Part-time: 110 men, 236 women	Faculty: 100; IIA, --$
Graduate: 297 men, 881 women	Ph.Ds: 87%
Year: semesters, summer session	Student/Faculty: 14 to 1
Application Deadline: open	Tuition: $12,240
Freshman Class: 970 applied, 746 accepted, 296 enrolled	Room & Board: $4800
SAT I Verbal/Math: 430/450	**COMPETITIVE**

Marywood College, established in 1915, is a private, coeducational nonprofit institution affiliated with the Roman Catholic Church, offering undergraduate degrees in the arts, business, professional training, liberal arts, religious studies, and teacher preparation. There are 2 graduate schools. In addition to regional accreditation, Marywood has baccalaureate program accreditation with ADA, CSWE, NASAD,

NASM, NCATE, and NLN. The library contains 205,293 volumes, 250,038 microform items, and 42,038 audiovisual forms, and subscribes to 1168 periodicals. Computerized library sources and services include the card catalog, interlibrary loans, and database searching. Special learning facilities include a learning resource center, art gallery, radio station, TV station, and a communication disorders clinic, an on-campus preschool and day care center, a psychology/education research laboratory, a science multimedia laboratory, and a language laboratory. The 115-acre campus is in a suburban area 120 miles west of New York City and 115 miles north of Philadelphia. Including residence halls, there are 24 buildings on campus.

Student Life: 78% of undergraduates are from Pennsylvania. Students come from 23 states, 13 foreign countries, and Canada. 82% are from public schools; 18% from private. 95% are white. 72% are Catholic; 12% Protestant. The average age of freshmen is 19; all undergraduates, 24. 19% do not continue beyond their first year; 62% remain to graduate.

Housing: 551 students can be accommodated in college housing. College-sponsored living facilities include single-sex dormitories and on-campus apartments. In addition, there are honors houses and and a separate study-oriented residence. On-campus housing is guaranteed for all 4 years. 73% of students commute. Alcohol is not permitted. All students may keep cars on campus.

Activities: There are no fraternities or sororities. There are 60 groups on campus, including art, cheerleading, choir, chorus, drama, ethnic, film, honors, international, jazz band, literary magazine, musical theater, newspaper, orchestra, photography, professional, radio and TV, religious, social, social service, student government, symphony, and yearbook. Popular campus events include Family Weekend, Halloween Haunted House, and Christmas Tree Lighting and Dinner.

Sports: There are 4 intercollegiate sports for men and 5 for women, and 25 intramural sports for men and 25 for women. Athletic and recreation facilities include an Olympic-sized pool, a human performance laboratory, a gymnasium, athletic training rooms, an athletic field, outdoor tennis courts, racquetball courts, an aerobic center, a game room, a hockey field, a sauna, and weight rooms.

Disabled Students: 75% of the campus is accessible to disabled students. The following facilities are available: wheelchair ramps, elevators, special parking, specially equipped rest rooms, lowered drinking fountains, and lowered telephones.

Services: In addition to many counseling and information services, tutoring is available in every subject. There is a reader service for the blind, and remedial math, reading, writing, and study skills. Oral tests, note taking, tutors, and tape recorders are available for physically challenged students.

Campus Safety and Security: Campus safety and security measures include 24-hour foot and vehicle patrol, self-defense education, escort service, and informal discussions. In addition, there are pamphlets/posters/films and lighted pathways/sidewalks.

Programs of Study: Marywood confers B.A., B.S., B.M., B.S.W., B.S.N., and B.F.A. degrees. Master's and doctoral degrees are also awarded. Bachelor's degrees are awarded in BIOLOGICAL SCIENCE (biology/biological science), BUSINESS (accounting, business administration and management, fashion merchandising, hotel/motel and restaurant management, and international business management), COMMUNICATIONS AND THE ARTS (advertising, arts administration/management, communications, design, English, French, music, performing arts, Spanish, studio art, and telecommunications), COMPUTER AND PHYSICAL SCIENCE (information sciences and systems and mathematics), EDUCATION (art, elementary, home economics, music, physical, science, secondary, and special), ENGINEERING AND ENVIRONMENTAL DESIGN (environmental science), HEALTH PROFESSIONS (medical laboratory technology, music therapy, nursing, and speech pathology/audiology), SOCIAL SCIENCE (clinical psychology, dietetics, paralegal studies, psychology, religion, religious music, social science, and social work). Communication disorders, art, and education are the strongest academically. Business administration, design, and psychology have the largest enrollments.

Required: To graduate, students must complete a liberal arts requirement consisting of religious studies, philosophy, mathematics, science, psychology, history, social science, world literature, foreign language, and fine arts. Additional course requirements include speech, writing, and physical education. Students must have a GPA of 2.0, with a 2.5 in the major. A minimum of 126 credits must be earned, with the number of credits required in the major varying.

Special: Marywood offers student-designed and dual majors. Internships, student teaching and study abroad, and study at other institutions in the United States are available. There are accelerated degree programs in dietetics and social work and opportunities for semester experience at a fashion institute. Credit for life, military, and work experience, an off-campus degree program, nondegree study, and a pass/fail grading option are also available. There is a freshman honors program on campus, as well as 17 national honor societies. All departments have honors programs.

Faculty/Classroom: 45% of faculty are male; 55%, female. 70% teach undergraduates and 100% do research. No introductory courses are taught by graduate students. The average class size in an introductory lecture is 25; in a laboratory, 14; and in a regular course offering, 16.

Admissions: 77% of the 1995–96 applicants were accepted. The SAT I scores for the 1995–96 freshman class were as follows: Verbal—78% below 500, 17% between 500 and 599, 4% between 600 and 700, and 1% above 700; Math—70% below 500, 20% between 500 and 599, 9% between 600 and 700, and 1% above 700. 26% of the current freshmen were in the top fifth of their class; 59% were in the top two fifths. 2 freshmen graduated first in their class.

Requirements: The SAT I or ACT is required, along with a 2.5 GPA. Marywood requires applicants to be in the upper 50% of their class. Applicants must be graduates of an accredited secondary school or have the GED. A minimum of 16 academic credits is required, including 4 in English, 3 in social studies, 2 in mathematics, and a science course. A letter of support is required. In selected majors, a portfolio or an audition is also required. A personal interview is strongly recommended. Marywood accepts applications on computer disk via CollegeLink and ExPAN. AP and CLEP credits are accepted. Important factors in the admissions decision are advanced placement or honor courses, recommendations by school officials, and extracurricular activities record.

Procedure: Freshmen are admitted to all sessions. Entrance exams should be taken by May 1. There are early admissions and deferred admissions plans. Application deadlines are open. Application fee is $20. Notification is sent on a rolling basis.

Transfer: 84 transfer students enrolled in 1995–96. SAT I or ACT scores are required of transfer applicants who have earned fewer than 12 credits; both secondary school and college transcripts are required. Transfer students are required to have earned a minimum GPA of 2.5 at their most recent college. A grade of C is the minimum requirement for transfer of academic credit. 60 credits of 126 must be completed at Marywood.

Visiting: There are regularly scheduled orientations for prospective students, including a campus tour, individual visits with admissions counselors, an appointment with a professor, and a financial aid appointment. There are guides for informal visits and visitors may sit in on classes and stay overnight at the school. To schedule a visit, contact the Admissions Office.

Financial Aid: In 1995–96, 90% of all freshmen and 80% of continuing students received some form of financial aid. 71% of freshmen and 70% of continuing students received need-based aid. The average freshman award was $9145. Of that total, scholarships or need-based grants averaged $5000 ($11,100 maximum); loans averaged $2625 ($3500 maximum); and work contracts averaged $800 ($1000 maximum). 31% of undergraduate students work part-time. Average earnings from campus work for the school year were $900. The average financial indebtedness of the 1994–95 graduate was $9100. Marywood is a member of CSS. The FAFSA and the college's own financial statement are required. The application deadline for fall entry is February 15.

International Students: There are currently 34 international students enrolled. The school actively recruits these students. They must take the TOEFL and achieve a minimum score of 500. The student must also take the SAT I or ACT, if available.

Computers: The college provides computer facilities for student use. The mainframes are a DEC VAX cluster with 3 mainframes: a DEC 5000 for the on-line library, a DEC MicroVAX 9100 for the academic network, and a DEC VAX 4000 for research. The computer facilities consist of an art laboratory, a psychology laboratory, 2 access laboratories with Macintoshes, a science laboratory with interactive video, 3 IBM-compatible laboratories, a CAD laboratory with IBM-compatible computers, a communication arts laboratory with Macintosh computers, and a DEC laboratory with 20 DEC terminals. More than 300 computers are available for student use in class laboratories, drop-in facilities, and dorms. Students may access the campus network in their dormitory rooms. All students may access the system 24 hours per day. There are no time limits and no fees.

Graduates: In 1994–95, 341 bachelor's degrees were awarded. The most popular majors among graduates were elementary educationion (14%), design and visual communications (9%), and business administration (8%). Within an average freshman class, 45% graduate in 4 years, 60% in 5 years, and 63% in 6 years. 66 companies recruited on campus in 1994–95.

Admissions Contact: Fred Brooks, Admissions Officer. E-mail: aadm01.mis.

MERCYHURST COLLEGE
B-1

Erie, PA 16546	(814) 824–2241; (800) 825–1926
Full-time: 1005 men, 1104 women	Faculty: 101; IIB, -$
Part-time: 180 men, 269 women	Ph.D.s: 55%
Graduate: 20 men, 26 women	Student/Faculty: 21 to 1
Year: trimesters, summer session	Tuition: $11,010
Application Deadline: open	Room & Board: $4251
Freshman Class: 1602 applied, 1194 accepted, 390 enrolled	
SAT I Verbal/Math: 460/510	ACT: 22 COMPETITIVE

Mercyhurst College, established in 1926, is a private, coeducational, nonprofit institution affiliated with the Roman Catholic Church and offers undergraduate degrees in the arts, business, health science, liberal arts, religious studies, and teacher preparation. The college also offers a degree-directed program for the learning disabled. In addition to regional accreditation, Mercyhurst has baccalaureate program accreditation with ADA and CSWE. The library contains 136,436 volumes, 9500 microform items, and 1645 audiovisual forms, and subscribes to 807 periodicals. Computerized library sources and services include interlibrary loans and database searching. Special learning facilities include an art gallery, planetarium, radio station, TV station, northwestern Pennsylvania historical archives, and an archeological institute. The 88-acre campus is in a suburban area within Erie. Including residence halls, there are 25 buildings on campus.

Student Life: 64% of undergraduates are from Pennsylvania. Students come from 37 states, 17 foreign countries, and Canada. 78% are from public schools; 22% from private. 88% are white. 61% are Catholic; 23% Protestant. The average age of freshmen is 18; all undergraduates, 24. 24% do not continue beyond their first year; 56% remain to graduate.

Housing: 1268 students can be accommodated in college housing. College-sponsored living facilities include single-sex and coed dormitories and on-campus apartments. On-campus housing is guaranteed for all 4 years. 56% of students live on campus; of those, 90% remain on campus on weekends. Alcohol is not permitted. All students may keep cars on campus.

Activities: There are no fraternities or sororities. There are 47 groups on campus, including art, band, cheerleading, choir, chorus, computers, dance, drama, ethnic, film, honors, international, jazz band, literary magazine, musical theater, newspaper, opera, orchestra, pep band, photography, political, professional, radio and TV, religious, social, social service, student government, and yearbook. Popular campus events include Activities Day, Parents Weekend, Homecoming, winter and spring formals, Academic Celebration, and D'Angelo Young Artist Competition.

Sports: There are 11 intercollegiate sports for men and 8 for women, and 3 intramural sports for men and 3 for women. Athletic and recreation facilities include indoor crew tanks, football and soccer fields, an ice hockey rink/arena, Nautilus facilities, a free weight room, a baseball/softball complex, and a training room.

Disabled Students: 90% of the campus is accessible to disabled students. The following facilities are available: wheelchair ramps, elevators, special parking, and lowered drinking fountains.

Services: In addition to many counseling and information services, tutoring is available in every subject. There is remedial math, reading, and writing.

Campus Safety and Security: Campus safety and security measures include 24-hour foot and vehicle patrol, self-defense education, shuttle buses, and informal discussions. In addition, there are emergency telephones, lighted pathways/sidewalks, and a 24-hour security camera surveillance system.

Programs of Study: Mercyhurst confers B.A., B.S., and B.M. degrees. Associate and master's degrees are also awarded. Bachelor's degrees are awarded in BIOLOGICAL SCIENCE (biology/biological science), BUSINESS (accounting, banking and finance, business administration and management, fashion merchandising, hotel/motel and restaurant management, insurance and risk management, management information systems, and marketing/retailing/merchandising), COMMUNICATIONS AND THE ARTS (broadcasting, communications, dance, English, graphic design, journalism, music, and studio art), COMPUTER AND PHYSICAL SCIENCE (chemistry, earth science, geology, and mathematics), EDUCATION (art, business, early childhood, elementary, home economics, mathematics, music, science, secondary, social science, and special), ENGINEERING AND ENVIRONMENTAL DESIGN (environmental science and interior design), HEALTH PROFESSIONS (art therapy, medical laboratory technology, predentistry, premedicine, prepharmacy, and preveterinary science), SOCIAL SCIENCE (anthropology, archeology, criminal justice, dietetics, family/consumer studies, history, political science/government, prelaw, psychology, religious education, social work, and sociology). Education, sciences, and business are the strongest academically. Business, education, and sports medicine have the largest enrollments.

Required: To graduate, students must take specified courses in English, mathematics, science, religion, philosophy, history, microcomputer systems, art, and music. They must complete 17 general education courses, 15 courses in the major, and 8 electives. A minimum GPA of 2.0 is required, with a 2.5 in the major, and a total minimum number of 120 credit hours. The number of credit hours in the major varies, with a minimum of 45. A thesis is necessary for history and English majors.

Special: Mercyhurst offers cross-registration with Gannon University. Internships are available in all majors through the co-op office and students may study abroad in London and Dublin. Dual and student-designed majors, credit for life, military, or work experience, nondegree study, work-study, a pass/fail grading option, and a 3–2 engineering degree with Penn State and the University of Pennsylvania are also available. There is a freshman honors program on campus, as well as 7 national honor societies. 4 departments have honors programs.

Faculty/Classroom: 62% of faculty are male; 38%, female. All teach undergraduates; 15% do research. No introductory courses are taught by graduate students. The average class size in an introductory lecture is 40; in a laboratory, 15; and in a regular course offering, 30.

Admissions: 75% of the 1995–96 applicants were accepted. The ACT scores for the 1995–96 freshman class were as follows: 31% below 21, 33% between 21 and 23, 29% between 24 and 26, 6% between 27 and 28, and 1% above 28. 34% of the current freshmen were in the top fifth of their class; 69% were in the top two fifths. 9 freshmen graduated first in their class.

Requirements: The SAT I or ACT is required, with a recommended minimum composite score of 800 on the SAT I, 400 on each section, or 18 on the ACT. Applicants must graduate from an accredited secondary school or have a GED. Sixteen academic credits are required, including 4 years of English, 3 years each of mathematics and social studies, and 2 years each of history, science, and a foreign language. Interviews are recommended. Art applicants must submit portfolios; auditions are required of music applicants. AP and CLEP credits are accepted. Important factors in the admissions decision are leadership record, evidence of special talent, and personality/intangible qualities.

Procedure: Freshmen are admitted to all sessions. Entrance exams should be taken during the spring of the junior year. There are early admissions and deferred admissions plans. Application deadlines are open. Application fee is $25. Notification is sent on a rolling basis after January 15.

Transfer: 129 transfer students enrolled in 1995–96. A minimum GPA of 2.0 on previous college work is required. 45 credits of 120 must be completed at Mercyhurst.

Visiting: There are regularly scheduled orientations for prospective students, including tours, class visits, faculty meetings, and interviews with financial aid and admissions counselors. There are guides for informal visits and visitors may sit in on classes and stay overnight at the school. To schedule a visit, contact the Admissions Office at (814) 824–2202.

Financial Aid: In 1995–96, 91% of all freshmen and 85% of continuing students received some form of financial aid. 83% of freshmen and 73% of continuing students received need-based aid. The average freshman award was $6500. Of that total, scholarships or need-based grants averaged $2650 ($8265 maximum); loans averaged $2100 ($4000 maximum); and work contracts averaged $750 ($1000 maximum). 88% of undergraduate students work part-time. Average earnings from campus work for the school year are $650. The average financial indebtedness of the 1994–95 graduate was $8000. Mercyhurst is a member of CSS. The FAFSA and the college's own financial statement are required. The application deadline for fall entry is May 1.

International Students: In a recent year, 72 international students were enrolled. The school actively recruits these students. They must take the TOEFL and achieve a minimum score of 550. The student must also take the SAT I or the ACT.

Computers: The college provides computer facilities for student use. The mainframe is an HP 3000/Series 70. Students may access the mainframe through more than 100 terminals in various buildings. In addition, there is a personal computer laboratory for students with more than 40 terminals, plus another 125 terminals and personal computers in academic departments for student use. All students may access the system during laboratory hours. There are no time limits and no fees.

Graduates: In a recent year, 281 bachelor's degrees were awarded. The most popular majors among graduates were business (13%), education (9%), and hotel/restaurant management (8%). Within an average freshman class, 2% graduate in 3 years, 56% in 4 years, 58% in 5 years, and 62% in 6 years. 137 companies recruited on campus in a recent year.

Admissions Contact: Andrew Roth, Dean of Enrollment. A campus video is available.

MESSIAH COLLEGE
Grantham, PA 17027

D-3
(717) 691–6000
(800) 233–4220; FAX: (717) 691–6025

Full-time: 973 men, 1455 women	**Faculty:** 128; IIB, av$
Part-time: 22 men, 31 women	**Ph.D.s:** 69%
Graduate: none	**Student/Faculty:** 19 to 1
Year: 4-1-4, summer session	**Tuition:** $10,954
Application Deadline: April 1	**Room & Board:** $5240
Freshman Class: 1876 applied, 1608 accepted, 671 enrolled	
SAT I Verbal/Math: 511/555	**ACT:** 25 **VERY COMPETITIVE**

Messiah College, founded in 1909, is a coeducational Christian liberal arts college affiliated with the Brethren in Christ Church. In addition to regional accreditation, Messiah has baccalaureate program accreditation with ABET, ADA, CSWE, NASM, and NLN. The library contains 200,000 volumes, 5000 microform items, and 5500 audiovisual forms, and subscribes to 1500 periodicals. Computerized library sources and services include the card catalog, interlibrary loans, and database searching. Special learning facilities include a learning resource center, art gallery, radio station, and a natural science museum. The 360-acre campus is in a suburban area 10 miles south of Harrisburg. Including residence halls, there are 24 buildings on campus.

Student Life: 55% of undergraduates are from out-of-state, mostly the Middle Atlantic. Students come from 34 states, 26 foreign countries, and Canada. 74% are from public schools; 26% from private. 90% are white. Most are Protestant. The average age of freshmen is 18; all undergraduates, 20. 14% do not continue beyond their first year; 70% remain to graduate.

Housing: 2110 students can be accommodated in college housing. College-sponsored living facilities include single-sex dormitories and on-campus apartments. In addition there are special interest houses. On-campus housing is guaranteed for all 4 years. 94% of students live on campus; of those, 65% remain on campus on weekends. Alcohol is not permitted. All students may keep cars on campus.

Activities: There are no fraternities or sororities. There are 50 groups on campus, including art, band, cheerleading, chess, choir, chorale, chorus, computers, dance, drama, ethnic, film, honors, international, jazz band, literary magazine, musical theater, newspaper, orchestra, pep band, photography, political, professional, radio and TV, religious, social, social service, student government, symphony, and yearbook. Popular campus events include a speaker series, Christian rock concerts, and Family Weekend.

Sports: There are 7 intercollegiate sports for men and 7 for women, and 10 intramural sports for men and 8 for women. Athletic and recreation facilities include indoor and outdoor tracks, a pool with separate diving well, wrestling and gymnastics areas, a weight room, numerous playing fields, and courts for racquetball, basketball, and tennis. The campus center provides additional recreational facilities.

Disabled Students: 95% of the campus is accessible to disabled students. The following facilities are available: wheelchair ramps, elevators, special parking, specially equipped rest rooms, and special class scheduling.

Services: There is a reader service for the blind and remedial reading. Tutoring can be arranged through the Student Life Office.

Campus Safety and Security: Campus safety and security measures include 24-hour foot and vehicle patrol, escort service, informal discussions, and pamphlets/posters/films. There are emergency telephones and lighted pathways/sidewalks.

Programs of Study: Messiah confers B.A. and B.S. degrees. Bachelor's degrees are awarded in BIOLOGICAL SCIENCE (biochemistry and biology/biological science), BUSINESS (accounting, business administration and management, international business management, marketing/retailing/merchandising, and personnel management), COMMUNICATIONS AND THE ARTS (applied music, art history and appreciation, communications, dramatic arts, English, fine arts, French, German, journalism, music, and Spanish), COMPUTER AND PHYSICAL SCIENCE (chemistry, computer science, mathematics, natural sciences, and physics), EDUCATION (art, early childhood, elementary, health, home economics, mathematics, music, physical, science, secondary, and social studies), ENGINEERING AND ENVIRONMENTAL DESIGN (civil engineering, electrical/electronics engineering, and mechanical engineering), HEALTH PROFESSIONS (medical laboratory technology, nursing, predentistry, premedicine, prepharmacy, preveterinary science, recreation therapy, and sports medicine), SOCIAL SCIENCE (behavioral science, biblical studies, dietetics, economics, family/consumer studies, history, home economics, humanities, ministries, philosophy, political science/government, prelaw, psychology, religion, religious education, social work, and sociology). Science, English, and mathematics are the strongest academically. Business, mathematics, and education have the largest enrollments.

Required: All students must complete at least 128 credits with a GPA of 2.0. The last 30 credits must be taken at Messiah College and 12 credits must be from the major. Proficiency in English must be demonstrated by examination. For general education requirements, students must take 9 credits each in mathematics/natural sciences, humanitites/arts, languages/cultures, and Christian faith, 6 credits in social sciences and history, and 3 credits each in freshman seminar, oral communications, ethics, non-Western studies, and world views/pluralism.

Special: Students may cross-register at Temple University in Philadelphia. Off-campus study is available in Washington, D.C., Costa Rica, and Jerusalem, and at any member colleges of the Christian College Consortium. Students may spend a semester or a year in any of 12 countries. Numerous internships, practical, and ministry opportunities are available. Individualized interdisciplinary majors and combined B.S.-B.A. degree programs are possible. There are some pass/fail options. There is a freshman honors program on campus, as well as 1 national honor society. 4 departments have honors programs.

Faculty/Classroom: 63% of faculty are male; 37%, female. All teach undergraduates. The average class size in an introductory lecture is 25; in a laboratory, 18; and in a regular course offering, 30.

Admissions: 86% of the 1995-96 applicants were accepted. The SAT I scores for the 1995-96 freshman class were as follows: Verbal—46% below 500, 36% between 500 and 599, 16% between 600 and 700, and 2% above 700; Math—27% below 500, 37% between 500 and 599, 30% between 600 and 700, and 6% above 700. The ACT scores were 20% below 21, 24% between 21 and 23, 24% between 24 and 26, 12% between 27 and 28, and 20% above 28. 53% of the current freshmen were in the top fifth of their class; 81% were in the top two fifths. There were 3 National Merit finalists and 2 semifinalists. 31 freshmen graduated first in their class.

Requirements: The SAT I or ACT is required. Messiah requires applicants to be in the upper 50% of their class. A minimum GPA of 2.5 is required. Minimum composite scores of 970 on the SAT I and 19 on the ACT are recommended. Applicants must have graduated from an accredited high school or the equivalent. Secondary preparation should include at least 4 units in English, and 2 each in mathematics, natural science, social studies, and a foreign language. An interview is strongly recommended. Potential music majors must audition. Applications are accepted on-line via World Wide Web: http:11www.messiah.edu. AP and CLEP credits are accepted. Important factors in the admissions decision are advanced placement or honor courses, recommendations by school officials, and leadership record.

Procedure: Entrance exams should be taken in the spring of the junior year. There are early admissions and deferred admissions plans. Applications should be filed by April 1 for fall entry, December 1 for spring entry, and May 1 for summer entry, along with an application fee of $20. Notification is sent on a rolling basis. A waiting list is an active part of the admissions procedure, with about 10% of all applicants on the list.

Transfer: 97 transfer students enrolled in 1995-96. Applicants should have earned a 2.5 GPA in at least 30 college credits. The college recommends that applicants also have composite SAT I scores of at least 900 or composite ACT scores of at least 20, and that they seek a personal interview. 60 credits of 128 must be completed at Messiah.

Visiting: There are regularly scheduled orientations for prospective students, including a campus tour, academic and career advising, and a financial aid information session. There are guides for informal visits and visitors may sit in on classes and stay overnight at the school. To schedule a visit, contact the Admissions Office.

Financial Aid: In 1995-96, 93% of all freshmen and 94% of continuing students received some form of financial aid. 62% of freshmen and 56% of continuing students received need-based aid. The average freshman award was $8086. Of that total, scholarships or need-based grants averaged $1500 ($16,810 maximum); loans averaged $3000 ($3635 maximum); and work contracts averaged $1450 ($1500 maximum). 64% of undergraduate students work part-time. Average earnings from campus work for the school year are $1250. The average financial indebtedness of the 1994-95 graduate was $11,467. Messiah is a member of CSS. The application deadline for fall entry is April 1.

International Students: There are currently 31 international students enrolled. They must take the TOEFL and achieve a minimum score of 550.

Computers: The college provides computer facilities for student use. The mainframes are an HP3000 models, some with multiple processors. There are 7 computer laboratories from which students can access the campus network and Internet resources. Dormitory access will be completed within a year. All students may access the system 24 hours a day. There are no time limits and no fees.

Graduates: In 1994-95, 490 bachelor's degrees were awarded. The most popular majors among graduates were business (16%), behavioral science (14%), and education (13%). Within an average freshman class, 1% graduate in 3 years, 65% in 4 years, 70% in 5 years, and 72% in 6 years. 327 companies recruited on campus in 1994-95. Of the 1994 graduating class, 8% were enrolled in graduate school within 6 months of graduation and 85% had found employment.

Admissions Contact: William G. Strausbaugh, Vice President for Enrollment Management. E-mail: strausba@mcis.messiah.edu.

MILLERSVILLE UNIVERSITY OF PENNSYLVANIA

E-4

Millersville, PA 17551-0302   (717) 872-3371

Full-time: 2239 men, 3245 women	Faculty: 322; IIA, +$
Part-time: 479 men, 852 women	Ph.D.s: 77%
Graduate: 162 men, 533 women	Student/Faculty: 17 to 1
Year: 4-1-4, summer session	Tuition: $4100 ($9074)
Application Deadline: open	Room & Board: $4038
Freshman Class: 6001 applied, 4183 accepted, 1163 enrolled	
SAT I Verbal/Math: 460/520	COMPETITIVE

Millersville University, founded as Lancaster County Normal School in 1855, is a public coeducational institution offering undergraduate and graduate programs in liberal arts and sciences and education. There are 3 undergraduate schools and 1 graduate school. In addition to regional accreditation, Millersville has baccalaureate program accreditation with ACBSP, CAHEA, CSWE, NASM, NCATE, and NLN. The library contains 479,999 volumes, 461,024 microform items, and 6449 audiovisual forms, and subscribes to 2775 periodicals. Computerized library sources and services include the card catalog, interlibrary loans, and database searching. Special learning facilities include a learning resource center, art gallery, radio station, TV station, early childhood center, and foreign language laboratory. The 250-acre campus is in a small town 5 miles west of Lancaster. Including residence halls, there are 85 buildings on campus.

Student Life: 94% of undergraduates are from Pennsylvania. Students come from 29 states, 36 foreign countries, and Canada. 90% are white. The average age of freshmen is 18; all undergraduates, 21. 17% do not continue beyond their first year; 65% remain to graduate.

Housing: 2440 students can be accommodated in college housing. College-sponsored living facilities include single-sex and coed dormitories and off-campus apartments. In addition there are honors houses, language houses, and special interest houses. On-campus housing is guaranteed for the freshman year only and is available on a first-come, first-served basis. 56% of students commute. Alcohol is not permitted. Upperclassmen may keep cars on campus.

Activities: 12% of men belong to 1 local fraternity and 10 national fraternities; 10% of women belong to 3 local and 8 national sororities. There are 148 groups on campus, including art, band, cheerleading, choir, chorale, chorus, dance, drama, ethnic, honors, international, jazz band, literary magazine, marching band, musical theater, newspaper, orchestra, pep band, political, professional, radio and TV, religious, social, social service, student government, symphony, and yearbook. Popular campus events include Homecoming, Parents Day, Wellness Week, International Week, Black History Celebration, and Latino Celebration.

Sports: There are 7 intercollegiate sports for men and 9 for women, and 20 intramural sports for men and 19 for women. Athletic and recreation facilities include a football stadium, 2 pools, 2 gymnasiums, a fitness center, a paracourse, an archery range, wrestling and weight rooms, basketball, volleyball, tennis, and badminton courts, and various playing fields.

Disabled Students: 80% of the campus is accessible to disabled students. The following facilities are available: wheelchair ramps, elevators, special parking, specially equipped rest rooms, special class scheduling, lowered drinking fountains, lowered telephones, and transportation assistance within campus.

Services: In addition to many counseling and information services, tutoring is available in most subjects. There is a reader service for the blind, and remedial math, reading, and writing. Every effort is made to tailor a tutoring program to individual needs. Note takers, interpreters, and some physical aids and other specialized equipment are provided, as available.

Campus Safety and Security: Campus safety and security measures include 24-hour foot and vehicle patrol, escort service, informal discussions, and pamphlets/posters/films. In addition, there are lighted pathways/sidewalks and monthly crime awareness programs.

Programs of Study: Millersville confers B.A., B.S., B.F.A., B.S.Ed., and B.S.N. degrees. Associate and master's degrees are also awarded. Bachelor's degrees are awarded in BIOLOGICAL SCIENCE (biochemistry, biology/biological science, biotechnology, environmental biology, marine biology, and molecular biology), BUSINESS (accounting, banking and finance, business administration and management, and marketing/retailing/merchandising), COMMUNICA-

TIONS AND THE ARTS (art, broadcasting, communications, comparative literature, English, French, German, Greek, journalism, Latin, linguistics, music, public relations, Russian, Spanish, and speech/debate/rhetoric), COMPUTER AND PHYSICAL SCIENCE (atmospheric sciences and meteorology, chemistry, computer science, earth science, geology, mathematics, oceanography, and physics), EDUCATION (art, early childhood, elementary, music, social studies, special, and teaching English as a second/foreign language (TESOL/TEFOL)), ENGINEERING AND ENVIRONMENTAL DESIGN (commercial art, computer engineering, industrial engineering technology, and occupational safety and health), HEALTH PROFESSIONS (medical laboratory technology, nuclear medical technology, nursing, and respiratory therapy), SOCIAL SCIENCE (anthropology, economics, geography, history, human services, industrial and organizational psychology, international studies, philosophy, political science/government, psychology, social work, and sociology). Physical sciences and teacher education are the strongest academically. Business administration, elementary education, and biology have the largest enrollments.

Required: All students must complete at least 120 hours, including 30 in the major, with a minimum 2.0 GPA. Courses are required in humanities, science and mathematics, social sciences, and perspectives as part of a core curriculum. Specific courses are required in writing, speech, and physical education.

Special: Numerous co-op and internship programs, including student teaching opportunities, are available. Millersville has exchange agreements with Franklin and Marshall College and Lancaster Theological Seminary, and 3–2 engineering programs with Pennsylvania State University and the University of Pennsylvania for chemistry and physics majors. Study abroad is offered in Germany, England, Japan, and Scotland and at teachers' colleges in Taiwan. Dual majors are possible in most disciplines, and accelerated degrees and B.A.-B.S. degrees are available in many. Nondegree study is offered, and there are limited pass/fail options. There is a freshman honors program on campus, as well as 9 national honor societies. 2 departments have honors programs.

Faculty/Classroom: 63% of faculty are male; 37%, female. 96% teach undergraduates. No introductory courses are taught by graduate students. The average class size in an introductory lecture is 35; in a laboratory, 24; and in a regular course offering, 25.

Admissions: 70% of the 1995–96 applicants were accepted. The SAT I scores for the 1995–96 freshman class were as follows: Verbal—66% below 500, 28% between 500 and 599, 5% between 600 and 700, and 1% above 700; Math—33% below 500, 49% between 500 and 599, 16% between 600 and 700, and 2% above 700. 42% of the current freshmen were in the top fifth of their class; 84% were in the top two fifths. 11 freshmen graduated first in their class.

Requirements: The SAT I or ACT is required, with minimum composite scores of 930 or 23, respectively. Millersville requires applicants to be in the upper 35% of their class. A minimum GPA of 2.0 is required. Applicants must be graduates of approved secondary schools or hold a GED. Secondary preparation should include 4 credits each in English and social studies, 3 credits in mathematics, and 2 credits in science. Music program applicants must audition. An interview is recommended for all applicants. AP and CLEP credits are accepted. Important factors in the admissions decision are advanced placement or honor courses, evidence of special talent, and recommendations by school officials.

Procedure: Freshmen are admitted to all sessions. Entrance exams should be taken in the spring of the junior year. There are early admissions and deferred admissions plans. Application deadlines are open. Application fee is $25. Notification is sent on a rolling basis.

Transfer: 375 transfer students enrolled in 1995–96. Applicants with fewer than 18 college credits must submit high school as well as college transcripts. Graduates of state community colleges are given preference over applicants with fewer than 2 and more than 5 semesters of study at other colleges. Applicants must have at least a 2.5 GPA. A personal interview is recommended. 30 credits of 120 must be completed at Millersville.

Visiting: There are regularly scheduled orientations for prospective students, including a president's welcome and admissions, financial aid, student organization, and department conferences. There are guides for informal visits and visitors may sit in on classes. To schedule a visit, contact the Admissions Office at (717) 872–3371 or (800) MU-ADMIT.

Financial Aid: In 1995–96, 68% of all freshmen and 70% of continuing students received some form of financial aid. 50% of freshmen and 44% of continuing students received need-based aid. The average freshman award was $3929. Of that total, scholarships or need-based grants averaged $2690 ($4100 maximum); loans averaged $2256 ($6625 maximum); and work contracts averaged $965 ($2400 maximum). 50% of undergraduate students work part-time. Average earnings from campus work for the school year are $965. Millersville is a member of CSS. The FAFSA, the college's own financial statement and the PHEAA state grant are required. The application deadline for fall entry is May 1.

International Students: There are currently 90 international students enrolled. The school actively recruits these students. They must take the TOEFL and achieve a minimum score of 500. The student must also take the SAT I (minimum score 930) or ACT (minimum score 23).

Computers: The college provides computer facilities for student use. The mainframes are an IBM 4381 and a DEC VAX 4000. Approved students are entitled to computer accounts to access the mainframes for E-mail, the Internet, and course work. There are 15 general-purpose computer laboratories on campus, housing IBM and Apple Macintosh microcomputers and Sun workstations. Most microcomputers are local area networked and some laboratories are connected to a campuswide network and the Internet. All students may access the system. There are no time limits and no fees.

Graduates: In 1994–95, 1215 bachelor's degrees were awarded. The most popular majors among graduates were elementary education (17%), business administration (10%), and biology (8%). Within an average freshman class, 1% graduate in 3 years, 37% in 4 years, 61% in 5 years, and 65% in 6 years. 44 companies recruited on campus in 1994–95. Of the 1994 graduating class, 20% were enrolled in graduate school within 6 months of graduation and 69% had found employment.

Admissions Contact: Darrell Davis, Director of Admissions.

MOORE COLLEGE OF ART AND DESIGN   F-3
Philadelphia, PA 19103   (215) 568–4515
(800) 523–2025, ext. 1105; FAX: (215) 568–3547

Full-time: 355 women	Faculty: 40
Part-time: 10 women	Ph.D.s: 10%
Graduate: none	Student/Faculty: 9 to 1
Year: semesters	Tuition: $14,522
Application Deadline: open	Room & Board: $5337
Freshman Class: 324 applied, 278 accepted, 164 enrolled	
SAT I Verbal/Math: 520/470	ACT: 21 SPECIAL

Moore College of Art and Design, founded in 1844, is the oldest professional and fine arts college for women in the country. In addition to regional accreditation, Moore has baccalaureate program accreditation with FIDER and NASAD. The library contains 34,000 volumes, and subscribes to 250 periodicals. Special learning facilities include 2 art galleries. The 4-acre campus is in an urban area in Philadelphia. Including residence halls, there are 3 buildings on campus.

Student Life: 60% of undergraduates are from Pennsylvania. Students come from 20 states, 8 foreign countries, and Canada. 60% are from public schools; 40% from private. 85% are white. The average age of freshmen is 18; all undergraduates, 20.

Housing: 200 students can be accommodated in college housing. College-sponsored living facilities include dormitories and on-campus apartments. On-campus housing is guaranteed for all 4 years. 50% of students live on campus; of those, 75% remain on campus on weekends. Alcohol is not permitted. All students may keep cars on campus.

Activities: There are 10 groups on campus, including computers, ethnic, film, gay, international, newspaper, professional, religious, social service, student government, and yearbook. Popular campus events include Family Day, Spring Fling, Convocation, student art shows, and openings at the college gallery.

Sports: There is no sports program at Moore. Athletic and recreation facilities include a fitness center with a weight room.

Disabled Students: All of the campus is accessible to disabled students. The following facilities are available: wheelchair ramps, elevators, special parking, and lowered telephones.

Services: In addition to many counseling and information services, tutoring is available in most subjects.

Campus Safety and Security: Campus safety and security measures include 24-hour foot and vehicle patrol, self-defense education, escort service, and informal discussions. In addition, there are pamphlets/posters/films and lighted pathways/sidewalks.

Programs of Study: Moore confers the B.F.A. degree. Bachelor's degrees are awarded in COMMUNICATIONS AND THE ARTS (drawing, fine arts, graphic design, illustration, metal/jewelry, painting, printmaking, and sculpture), EDUCATION (art), ENGINEERING AND ENVIRONMENTAL DESIGN (interior design), SOCIAL SCIENCE (fashion design and technology and textiles and clothing). Interior design is the strongest academically. Graphic design has the largest enrollment.

Required: All students take 31 credits in basic arts, including design, drawing, color, and art history, and a liberal arts core in history, humanities, and social science. A total of 124 to 127 credits, with a 2.0 minimum GPA, is required for graduation.

Special: Moore has long-established cooperative relationships with various employers who provide training to supplement academic studies in all majors. Dual majors, an individualized interdisciplinary major, nondegree study, and continuing education programs are offered.

Faculty/Classroom: 50% of faculty are male; 50%, female. All teach undergraduates. The average class size in an introductory lecture is 20 and in a regular course offering, 10.

Admissions: 86% of the 1995–96 applicants were accepted. The SAT I scores for the 1995–96 freshman class were as follows: Verbal—52% below 500, 45% between 500 and 599, and 5% between 600 and 700. 15% of the current freshmen were in the top fifth of their class; 85% were in the top two fifths. There were 2 National Merit finalists in a recent year.

Requirements: The SAT I or ACT is required. A minimum GPA of 2.0 is required. Applicants should be graduates of accredited high schools or the equivalent, having taken 4 years of English and 2 years each of social studies, science, and mathematics. At least 2 years of art study are also recommended. The most important part of the application is the portfolio of 8 to 12 original pieces, 6 of which should be drawings from observation. In addition, Moore strongly recommends a personal interview. AP and CLEP credits are accepted. Important factors in the admissions decision are evidence of special talent, personality/intangible qualities, and extracurricular activities record.

Procedure: Freshmen are admitted in the fall. There are early decision, early admissions, and deferred admissions plans. Application deadlines are open. Application fee is $35. Notification is sent on a rolling basis. 35 early decision candidates were accepted for the 1995–96 class.

Transfer: 35 transfer students enrolled in a recent year. Applicants from non-art programs must meet freshman admission requirements. Others must submit a portfolio for review. Applicants should have at least a 2.0 GPA in previous college work, and submit composite SAT I scores of at least 800. A personal interview is required. 62 credits of 124 to 127 must be completed at Moore.

Visiting: There are regularly scheduled orientations for prospective students, including an open house in November. There are guides for informal visits and visitors may sit in on classes and stay overnight at the school. To schedule a visit, contact the Admissions Office.

Financial Aid: In a recent year, 80% of all students received some form of financial aid. 70% of all students received need-based aid. Scholarships or need-based grants averaged $2827 ($5000 maximum); loans averaged $2731; and work contracts averaged $400 ($600 maximum). 40% of undergraduate students work part-time. Average earnings from campus work for the school year are $500. The average financial indebtedness of a recent year's graduate was $10,000. Moore is a member of CSS. The FAF and the college's own financial statement are required. The application deadline for fall entry is April 1.

International Students: In a recent year, 40 international students were enrolled. The school actively recruits these students. They must take the TOEFL and achieve a minimum score of 500.

Computers: The college provides computer facilities for student use. Apple IIe, Commodore Amiga, and Apple Macintosh PCs are available in the computer graphics laboratory. There are no time limits and no fees.

Graduates: In a recent year, 140 bachelor's degrees were awarded. The most popular majors among graduates were graphic design (17%), interior design (12%), and 2D fine arts (11%). Within an average freshman class, 80% graduate in 4 years. 20 companies recruited on campus in a recent year.

Admissions Contact: Karina Dayich, Director of Admissions.

MORAVIAN COLLEGE
Bethlehem, PA 18018

Full-time: 588 men, 635 women	(610) 861-1320; **FAX:** (610) 861-3956
Part-time: 13 men, 11 women	**Faculty:** 86; IIB, av$
Graduate: 91 men, 49 women	**Ph.D.s:** 91%
Year: semesters, summer session	**Student/Faculty:** 14 to 1
Application Deadline: March 1	**Tuition:** $15,900
Freshman Class: 1212 applied, 933 accepted, 320 enrolled	**Room & Board:** $5110
SAT I or ACT: required	**VERY COMPETITIVE**

F-3

Moravian College, established in 1742, is a private, coeducational liberal arts institution affiliated with the Moravian Church. In addition to regional accreditation, Moravian has baccalaureate program accreditation with CAHEA and NASM. The library contains 232,648 volumes, 7171 microform items, and 446 audiovisual forms, and subscribes to 1378 periodicals. Computerized library sources and services include the card catalog, interlibrary loans, and database searching. Special learning facilities include a learning resource center, art gallery, and radio station. The 70-acre campus is in a suburban area 60 miles north of Philadelphia. Including residence halls, there are 55 buildings on campus.

Student Life: 53% of undergraduates are from Pennsylvania. Students come from 25 states and 16 foreign countries. 75% are from public schools; 25% from private. 92% are white. 44% are Catholic; 31% Protestant; 19% claim no religious affiliation. The average age of

freshmen is 18; all undergraduates, 20. 10% do not continue beyond their first year; 78% remain to graduate.

Housing: 940 students can be accommodated in college housing. College-sponsored living facilities include single-sex and coed dormitories, on-campus apartments, off-campus apartments, fraternity houses, and sorority houses. In addition there are special interest houses. On-campus housing is guaranteed for all 4 years. 90% of students live on campus; of those, 75% remain on campus on weekends. Upperclassmen may keep cars on campus.

Activities: 10% of men belong to 2 local and 1 national fraternity; 18% of women belong to 4 local sororities. There are 65 groups on campus, including art, band, cheerleading, choir, chorus, computers, dance, drama, ethnic, gay, honors, international, jazz band, literary magazine, newspaper, orchestra, pep band, political, professional, religious, social, social service, student government, radio, and yearbook. Popular campus events include arts and lecture series, Christmas vesper services, foreign film series, and Homecoming.

Sports: There are 9 intercollegiate sports for men and 8 for women, and 14 intramural sports for men and 14 for women. Athletic and recreation facilities include a 1600-seat gymnasium, football and soccer fields, baseball and softball diamonds, indoor and all-weather tracks, tennis courts, a field house, a fitness room, an aerobics and dance studio, and 4 multipurpose courts.

Disabled Students: 30% of the campus is accessible to disabled students. The following facilities are available: wheelchair ramps, elevators, special parking, specially equipped rest rooms, special class scheduling, and lowered drinking fountains.

Services: In addition to many counseling and information services, tutoring is available in most subjects. There is a reader service for the blind.

Campus Safety and Security: Campus safety and security measures include 24-hour foot and vehicle patrol, escort service, shuttle buses, and informal discussions. In addition, there are pamphlets/posters/films, emergency telephones, lighted pathways/sidewalks, and ongoing crime prevention programming supervised by a crime prevention officer.

Programs of Study: Moravian confers B.A., B.S., and B.Mus. degrees. Master's degrees are also awarded. Bachelor's degrees are awarded in BIOLOGICAL SCIENCE (biology/biological science), BUSINESS (accounting, business economics, international business management, and management science), COMMUNICATIONS AND THE ARTS (art history and appreciation, dramatic arts, English, French, German, graphic design, Greek, journalism, Latin, music, Spanish, and studio art), COMPUTER AND PHYSICAL SCIENCE (chemistry, computer science, information sciences and systems, mathematics, and physics), EDUCATION (elementary, music, and secondary), SOCIAL SCIENCE (counseling psychology, criminal justice, developmental psychology, economics, experimental psychology, history, industrial and organizational psychology, philosophy, political science/government, prelaw, psychology, religion, social science, and sociology). Education, biology, and music are the strongest academically. Business, biology, and education have the largest enrollments.

Required: To graduate, students must complete distribution requirements in natural sciences, English, a foreign language, mathematics, social sciences, humanities, and physical education. They must maintain a minimum GPA of 2.0 and complete 32 courses equivalent to 128 credits. The number of courses required in the major varies.

Special: The college offers 3–2 engineering degrees in conjunction with Lafayette College, the University of Pennsylvania, and Washington University. Moravian also offers cooperative programs in allied health, natural resource management, and geology with Lehigh, Duke, and Thomas Jefferson universities. Cross-registration is available with Lehigh University and Lafayette, Muhlenberg, Cedar Crest, and Allentown colleges. Internships, study abroad in 4 countries, a Washington semester, dual majors, and student-designed majors may be pursued. Students have a pass/fail grading option. They may also enroll in a core program comprised of 7 courses that offer an integrated introduction to college study. There are 10 national honor societies on campus. 16 departments have honors programs.

Faculty/Classroom: 69% of faculty are male; 31%, female. All teach undergraduates. No introductory courses are taught by graduate students. The average class size in an introductory lecture is 30; in a laboratory, 15; and in a regular course offering, 22.

Admissions: 77% of the 1995–96 applicants were accepted. The SAT I scores for the 1995–96 freshman class were as follows: Verbal—55% below 500, 34% between 500 and 599, 9% between 600 and 700, and 2% above 700; Math—31% below 500, 45% between 500 and 599, 21% between 600 and 700, and 3% above 700. The ACT scores were 8% below 21, 45% between 21 and 23, 45% between 24 and 26, 1% between 27 and 28, and 1% above 28. 50% of the current freshmen were in the top fifth of their class; 82% were in the top two fifths. 3 freshmen graduated first in their class.

Requirements: The SAT I or ACT is required. Applicants must graduate from an accredited secondary school or have a GED. Moravian requires 16 Carnegie units, based on 4 years each of English and social science, 3 to 4 of mathematics, and 2 each of laboratory science, foreign language, and electives. Essays are required and interviews are recommended. For music students, auditions are required; for art students, portfolios are recommended. Applications are accepted on computer disk via Apply, CollegeLink, and Common App. AP and CLEP credits are accepted. Important factors in the admissions decision are advanced placement or honor courses, evidence of special talent, and personality/intangible qualities.

Procedure: Freshmen are admitted fall and spring. Entrance exams should be taken prior to January of the senior year. There are early decision, early admissions, and deferred admissions plans. Early decision applications should be filed by December 15; regular applications, by March 1 for fall entry and December 1 for spring entry, along with an application fee of $30. Notification of early decision is sent January 15; regular decision, March 15. 55 early decision candidates were accepted for the 1995–96 class. A waiting list is an active part of the admissions procedure, with about 15% of all applicants on the list.

Transfer: 65 transfer students enrolled in 1995–96. Applicants must have a minimum GPA of 2.5 and are required to submit recommendations. 32 credits of 128 must be completed at Moravian.

Visiting: There are regularly scheduled orientations for prospective students, including tours and meetings with admissions staff. There are guides for informal visits and visitors may sit in on classes and stay overnight at the school. To schedule a visit, contact the Office of Admissions.

Financial Aid: In 1995–96, 87% of all freshmen and 85% of continuing students received some form of financial aid. 78% of freshmen and 76% of continuing students received need-based aid. The average freshman award was $11,725. Of that total, scholarships or need-based grants averaged $8391; loans averaged $3101 ($5625 maximum); and work contracts averaged $1212 ($1300 maximum). 51% of undergraduate students work part-time. Average earnings from campus work for the school year are $771. The average financial indebtedness of the 1994–95 graduate was $11,535. Moravian is a member of CSS. The FAFSA, CSS Profile Application, and state grant applications are required. The application deadline for fall entry is March 15.

International Students: There were 20 international students enrolled in a recent year. The school actively recruits these students. They must take the TOEFL and achieve a minimum score of 550. The student must also take the SAT I if instruction has been in English.

Computers: The college provides computer facilities for student use. The mainframes are a Sun 3, a Sun 4, and an HP 9000. A high-speed campus network includes public access laboratories with 16 Sun workstations, 32 IBM-compatible microcomputers, and more than 15 Apple Macintosh PCs, all of which are accessible from the dormitories. All students may access the system 24 hours per day. There are no time limits and no fees.

Graduates: In 1994–95, 305 bachelor's degrees were awarded. The most popular majors among graduates were sociology (15%), psychology (14%), and art (9%). Within an average freshman class, 73% graduate in 4 years, 77% in 5 years, and 78% in 6 years. 25 companies recruited on campus in 1994–95. Of the 1994 graduating class, 14% were enrolled in graduate school within 6 months of graduation and 70% had found employment.

Admissions Contact: Bernard J. Story, Dean of Admissions and Financial Aid. E-mail: admissions@moravian.edu. A campus video is available.

MUHLENBERG COLLEGE E-3

Allentown, PA 18104 (610) 821-3200; FAX: (610) 821-3234

Full-time: 808 men, 927 women	Faculty: 131; IIB, +$
Part-time: 217 men, 256 women	Ph.D.s: 86%
Graduate: none	Student/Faculty: 13 to 1
Year: semesters, summer session	Tuition: $17,550
Application Deadline: February 15	Room & Board: $4720
Freshman Class: 2586 applied, 1919 accepted, 487 enrolled	
SAT I Verbal/Math: 506/568	VERY COMPETITIVE

Muhlenberg College, established in 1848, is a private, coeducational liberal arts institution affiliated with the Lutheran Church. The library contains 198,800 volumes, 160,000 microform items, and 4340 audiovisual forms, and subscribes to 690 periodicals. Computerized library sources and services include the card catalog, interlibrary loans, and database searching. Special learning facilities include a learning resource center, art gallery, natural history museum, radio station, and two 40-acre environmental field stations. The 75-acre campus is in a suburban area 50 miles north of Philadelphia and 90 miles west of New York City. Including residence halls, there are 30 buildings on campus.

Student Life: 67% of undergraduates are from out-of-state, mostly the Northeast. Students come from 31 states, 14 foreign countries, and Canada. 69% are from public schools; 31% from private. 91% are white. 40% are Protestant; 30% Catholic; 20% Jewish; 10% claim no religious affiliation. The average age of freshmen is 18; all undergraduates, 20. 8% do not continue beyond their first year; 80% remain to graduate.

Housing: 1585 students can be accommodated in college housing. College-sponsored living facilities include single-sex and coed dormitories, on-campus apartments, fraternity houses, and sorority houses. In addition there are language houses, special interest houses, and independent living experience houses. On-campus housing is guaranteed for all 4 years. 96% of students live on campus; of those, 80% remain on campus on weekends. Upperclassmen may keep cars on campus.

Activities: 38% of men belong to 4 national fraternities; 36% of women belong to 4 national sororities. There are 90 groups on campus, including art, band, cheerleading, chess, choir, chorale, chorus, computers, dance, drama, ethnic, gay, honors, human rights, international, jazz band, literary magazine, musical theater, newspaper, opera, orchestra, pep band, photography, political, professional, radio and TV, religious, social, social service, student government, and yearbook. Popular campus events include Spring Fling Weekend, Homecoming, Valentine Birthday Party, Community Service Weekend, Candlelight Holiday Concert, and Senior Week.

Sports: There are 9 intercollegiate sports for men and 9 for women, and 15 intramural sports for men and 14 for women. Athletic and recreation facilities include a sports center, which contains a 6-lane swimming pool, racquetball and squash courts, wrestling and weight training rooms, and a multipurpose field house with indoor tennis courts, a running track, a fitness loft, and outdoor volleyball courts, athletic fields, tennis courts, and a football stadium.

Disabled Students: 90% of the campus is accessible to disabled students. The following facilities are available: wheelchair ramps, elevators, special parking, specially equipped rest rooms, special class scheduling, lowered drinking fountains, lowered telephones, extra time on tests, tutors, and books on tape.

Services: In addition to many counseling and information services, tutoring is available in every subject. There is a reader service for the blind, and a writing center.

Campus Safety and Security: Campus safety and security measures include 24-hour foot and vehicle patrol, escort service, informal discussions, and pamphlets/posters/films. In addition, there are emergency telephones and lighted pathways/sidewalks.

Programs of Study: Muhlenberg confers B.A. and B.S. degrees. Bachelor's degrees are awarded in BIOLOGICAL SCIENCE (biology/biological science), BUSINESS (accounting and business administration and management), COMMUNICATIONS AND THE ARTS (communications, dramatic arts, English, fine arts, French, German, Greek, Latin, music, and Spanish), COMPUTER AND PHYSICAL SCIENCE (chemistry, computer science, information sciences and systems, mathematics, and physics), SOCIAL SCIENCE (economics, history, philosophy, political science/government, psychology, religion, social science, social work, and sociology). Sciences, drama, and English are the strongest academically. Physical sciences, business administration, and English have the largest enrollments.

Required: To graduate, students must complete requirements in literature and the arts, religion or philosophy, human behavior and social institutions, historical studies, physical and life sciences, and other cultures. They must have a minimum GPA of 2.0 in a total of 34 course units, with 9 to 14 units in the major. All students must take 4 quarters of physical education, including 2 wellness courses, as well as freshman and senior seminars.

Special: Students may cross-register with Lehigh, Lafayette, Cedar Crest, Moravian, and Allentown colleges. Internships, work-study programs, study-abroad in Asia, Latin America, Russia, and Europe, and a Washington semester are available. Dual majors and student-designed majors may be pursued. A 3–2 engineering degree is available in cooperation with Columbia and Washington universities, and a 3–2 forestry degree is offered in cooperation with Duke University. Nondegree study and a pass/fail grading option are also offered. There is a freshman honors program on campus, as well as 12 national honor societies, including Phi Beta Kappa. 9 departments have honors programs.

Faculty/Classroom: 69% of faculty are male; 31%, female. All teach undergraduates. The average class size in an introductory lecture is 25; in a laboratory, 20; and in a regular course offering, 23.

Admissions: 74% of the 1995–96 applicants were accepted. The SAT I scores for the 1995–96 freshman class were as follows: Verbal—45% below 500, 41% between 500 and 599, 13% between 600 and 700, and 1% above 700; Math—20% below 500, 42% between 500 and 599, 30% between 600 and 700, and 8% above 700. 52% of the current freshmen were in the top fifth of their class; 81% were in the top two fifths. There were 6 National Merit semifinalists. 7 freshmen graduated first in their class.

Requirements: The SAT I or ACT is required. Applicants must graduate from an accredited secondary school or have a GED. Sixteen Carnegie units are required, and students must complete 4 courses in English, 3 in mathematics, and 2 each in history, science, and a foreign language. All students must submit essays. Interviews are recommended. AP and CLEP credits are accepted. Important factors in the admissions decision are advanced placement or honor courses, leadership record, and evidence of special talent.

Procedure: Freshmen are admitted fall and spring. Entrance exams should be taken during the spring of the junior year or the fall of the senior year. There are early decision, early admissions, and deferred admissions plans. Early decision applications should be filed by January 15; regular applications, by February 15 for fall entry, along with an application fee of $30. Notification of early decision is sent February 1; regular decision, March 15. 152 early decision candidates were accepted for the 1995–96 class. A waiting list is an active part of the admissions procedure, with about 10% of all applicants on the list.

Transfer: 18 transfer students enrolled in 1995–96. A minimum GPA of 2.5 and an interview are required. 17 course units of 34 must be completed at Muhlenberg.

Visiting: There are regularly scheduled orientations for prospective students, consisting of a tour of the campus and a personal interview. There are 2 open houses in the fall, and 1 in the spring. There are guides for informal visits and visitors may sit in on classes and stay overnight at the school. To schedule a visit, contact Melissa Abramson or Beth Adderly in Admissions.

Financial Aid: In 1995–96, 70% of all freshmen and 62% of continuing students received some form of financial aid. 60% of freshmen and 52% of continuing students received need-based aid. The average freshman award was $12,676. Of that total, scholarships or need-based grants averaged $9190 ($14,250 maximum); loans averaged $2476 ($3625 maximum); and work contracts averaged $1000 (maximum). 38% of undergraduate students work part-time. Average earnings from campus work for the school year are $1000. The average financial indebtedness of the 1994–95 graduate was $8950. Muhlenberg is a member of CSS. The FAFSA, the college's own financial statement, and the CSS Profile Application are required. The application deadline for fall entry is February 15.

International Students: There are currently 25 international students enrolled. The school actively recruits these students. They must take the TOEFL and achieve a minimum score of 550.

Computers: The college provides computer facilities for student use. The mainframe is an HP 3000/Series 70. Students may access the mainframe from the computer laboratories. There are more than 100 personal computers available to students in laboratories and computer lounges throughout the campus. Residence halls are wired to provide Internet and campus network access. All students may access the system from 9 A.M. to midnight Monday through Thursday, 9 A.M. to 5 P.M. Friday, 1 P.M. to 5 P.M. Saturday, and 1 P.M. to midnight Sunday. There are no time limits and no fees.

Graduates: In a recent year, 433 bachelor's degrees were awarded. The most popular majors among graduates were biology (12%), business (12%), and psychology (11%). Within an average freshman class, 80% graduate in 4 years and 81% in 5 years. 42 companies recruited on campus in a recent year.

Admissions Contact: Christopher Hooker-Haring, Dean of Admissions.

NEUMANN COLLEGE
Aston, PA 19014

E-4

(215) 558-5616

Full-time: 112 men, 334 women	Faculty: 46; IIB, --$
Part-time: 134 men, 547 women	Ph.D.s: 43%
Graduate: 20 men, 67 women	Student/Faculty: 10 to 1
Year: semesters, summer session	Tuition: $11,090
Application Deadline: open	Room & Board: n/app
Freshman Class: n/av	
SAT I or ACT: required	**COMPETITIVE**

Neumann College, founded in 1965 by the Sisters of St. Francis, is a private, coeducational, nonresidential liberal arts institution affiliated with the Roman Catholic Church. There are 4 graduate schools. In addition to regional accreditation, Neumann has baccalaureate program accreditation with CAHEA and NLN. The library contains 88,000 volumes and 11,970 audiovisual forms, and subscribes to 600 periodicals. Computerized library sources and services include interlibrary loans and database searching. Special learning facilities include a learning resource center and a learning assistance center. The 14-acre campus is in a small town 12 miles southwest of Philadelphia. There are 4 buildings on campus.

Student Life: 78% of undergraduates are from Pennsylvania. Students come from 3 states and 2 foreign countries. 89% are white. 70% are Catholic; 16% Protestant. The average age of freshmen is 18; all undergraduates, 29. 10% do not continue beyond their first year.

Housing: There are no residence halls. All students commute. Alcohol is not permitted.

Activities: There are no fraternities or sororities. There are 18 groups on campus, including cheerleading, drama, honors, newspaper, political, student government, and yearbook. Popular campus events include dinner dances, Spring Fling, and charity fundraising.

Sports: Athletic and recreation facilities include a 350-seat gymnasium, weight and fitness rooms, tennis courts, baseball and softball fields, video games, and a theater.

Disabled Students: All of the campus is accessible to disabled students. The following facilities are available: wheelchair ramps, elevators, special parking, specially equipped rest rooms, and special class scheduling.

Services: In addition to many counseling and information services, tutoring is available in most subjects. There is remedial math, reading, and writing.

Campus Safety and Security: Campus safety and security measures include 24-hour foot and vehicle patrol, escort service, emergency telephones, and lighted pathways/sidewalks.

Programs of Study: Neumann confers B.A. and B.S. degrees. Associate and master's degrees are also awarded. Bachelor's degrees are awarded in BIOLOGICAL SCIENCE (biology/biological science), BUSINESS (accounting and business administration and management), COMMUNICATIONS AND THE ARTS (communications and English), COMPUTER AND PHYSICAL SCIENCE (computer science and information sciences and systems), EDUCATION (early childhood and elementary), HEALTH PROFESSIONS (clinical science and nursing), SOCIAL SCIENCE (political science/government, prelaw, psychology, and religion). Nursing is the strongest academically. Nursing and education have the largest enrollments.

Required: To graduate, all students must complete 121 to 130 credits, depending on the major. A minimum 2.0 GPA is required.

Special: The college offers co-op programs in all majors, internships, work-study programs, dual majors, and general studies degrees. Credit for life, work, and military experience, nondegree study, and pass/fail options are available. There is a freshman honors program on campus.

Faculty/Classroom: 41% of faculty are male; 59%, female. All teach undergraduates. No introductory courses are taught by graduate students.

Admissions: The SAT I scores for a recent freshman class were as follows: Verbal—86% below 500, 12% between 500 and 599, and 2% between 600 and 700; Math—75% below 500, 20% between 500 and 599, and 5% between 600 and 700. 27% of a recent freshman class were in the top fifth of their class; 54% were in the top two fifths.

Requirements: The SAT I or ACT is required. Neumann requires applicants to be in the upper 60% of their class with a 2.0 GPA. Applicants must be graduates of an accredited secondary school or have a GED. High school courses must include 4 years of English and 2 years each of a foreign language, history, and science. An interview is recommended. CLEP credit is accepted. Important factors in the admissions decision are recommendations by school officials, extracurricular activities record, and leadership record.

Procedure: Freshmen are admitted fall and spring. Entrance exams should be taken by December of the senior year. There is an early admissions plan. Application deadlines are open. Application fee is $25. Notification is sent on a rolling basis.

Transfer: 92 transfer students enrolled in a recent year. 30 credits of 121 to 130 must be completed at Neumann.

Visiting: There are regularly scheduled orientations for prospective students, including class visits and informal meetings with faculty. There are guides for informal visits and visitors may sit in on classes. To schedule a visit, contact the Admissions Office.

Financial Aid: In a recent year, 85% of all freshmen and 65% of continuing students received some form of financial aid. 70% of freshmen and 65% of continuing students received need-based aid. The average freshman award was $2300. Of that total, loans averaged $2625; the Neumannn College Scholarship averaged $808 ($1200 maximum); and work contracts averaged $550 ($600 maximum). 4% of undergraduate students work part-time. Average earnings from campus work for the school year are $600. The average financial indebtedness of the 1994–95 graduate was $10,300. The FAFSA and the college's own financial statement are required. The application deadline for fall entry is March 15.

International Students: They must score 500 on the TOEFL.

Computers: The college provides computer facilities for student use. About 50 IBM-compatible and Macintosh microcomputers and terminals are available in the computer laboratory and in the library. All students may access the system. There are no time limits and no fees.

Graduates: In a recent year, 173 bachelor's degrees were awarded. The most popular majors among graduates were nursing (29%), liberal studies (29%), and business administration (12%). 55 companies recruited on campus in a recent year.

Admissions Contact: Mark Osborn, Director of Admissions.

PENN STATE UNIVERSITY AT ERIE/BEHREND COLLEGE B-1

Erie, PA 16563   (814) 898-6100; FAX: (814) 898-6461

Full-time: 1412 men, 1157 women	Faculty: 143
Part-time: 340 men, 151 women	Ph.D.s: 90%
Graduate: 91 men, 57 women	Student/Faculty: 18 to 1
Year: semesters, summer session	Tuition: $5258 ($11,310)
Application Deadline: open	Room & Board: $4300
Freshman Class: 3244 applied, 2259 accepted, 614 enrolled	
SAT I Verbal/Math: 450/520	**VERY COMPETITIVE**

Penn State University at Erie/Behrend College, founded in 1948, offers 25 baccalaureate programs as well as the first 2 years of most Penn State University Park baccalaureate programs. It offers courses in business, humanities, social sciences, science, engineering technology, and engineering. There are 4 undergraduate schools and one graduate school. In addition to regional accreditation, Behrend has baccalaureate program accreditation with ABET. The library contains 82,517 volumes, 75,190 microform items, and 351 audiovisual forms, and subscribes to 950 periodicals. Computerized library sources and services include the card catalog, interlibrary loans, and database searching. Special learning facilities include a learning resource center, radio station, and an engineering workstation laboratory. The 700-acre campus is in a suburban area 5 miles east of Erie. Including residence halls, there are 39 buildings on campus.

Student Life: 93% of undergraduates are from Pennsylvania. Students come from 27 states, 5 foreign countries, and Canada. 92% are white. The average age of freshmen is 18; all undergraduates, 22. 9% do not continue beyond their first year; 61% remain to graduate.

Housing: 1186 students can be accommodated in college housing. College-sponsored living facilities include single-sex dormitories and on-campus apartments. In addition there are honors houses, special interest houses, and a substance-free interest house. On-campus housing is available on a first-come, first-served basis. 62% of students commute. Alcohol is not permitted. All students may keep cars on campus.

Activities: 12% of men belong to 1 local and 5 national fraternities; 16% of women belong to 1 local and 3 national sororities. There are 70 groups on campus, including cheerleading, chess, choir, computers, drama, ethnic, gay, honors, literary magazine, newspaper, pep band, political, professional, radio and TV, religious, social service, student government, and yearbook. Popular campus events include winter carnival, concert series, and Homecoming.

Sports: There are 6 intercollegiate sports for men and 6 for women, and 18 intramural sports for men and 18 for women. Athletic and recreation facilities include a 265-seat arena, tennis courts, a weight room, a fitness trail, basketball courts, and baseball, softball, and soccer playing fields.

Disabled Students: 90% of the campus is accessible to disabled students. The following facilities are available: wheelchair ramps, elevators, special parking, specially equipped rest rooms, special class scheduling, lowered drinking fountains, and lowered telephones.

Services: In addition to many counseling and information services, tutoring is available in most subjects. There is a reader service for the blind, and remedial math, reading, and writing.

Campus Safety and Security: Campus safety and security measures include 24-hour foot and vehicle patrol, self-defense education, escort service, and informal discussions. In addition, there are pamphlets/posters/films, emergency telephones, and lighted pathways/sidewalks.

Programs of Study: Behrend confers B.A. and B.S. degrees. Associate and master's degrees are also awarded. Bachelor's degrees are awarded in BIOLOGICAL SCIENCE (biology/biological science), BUSINESS (accounting, business administration and management, business economics, and management information systems), COMMUNICATIONS AND THE ARTS (communications and English), COMPUTER AND PHYSICAL SCIENCE (chemistry, mathematics, physics, and science), ENGINEERING AND ENVIRONMENTAL DESIGN (engineering, engineering technology, mechanical engineering technology, and plastics technology), SOCIAL SCIENCE (economics, history, political science/government, and psychology). Management information systems, psychology, and mathematics are the strongest academically. Engineering, business, and psychology have the largest enrollments.

Required: All baccalaureate degree candidates must take 46 general education credits, including 15 in quantification and communication skills, including a writing intensive course, 4 in health and physical education, and 27 in arts, humanities, natural science, and social and behavioral sciences, including a cultural diversity course. All students must complete a minimum of 120 credit hours with a minimum GPA of 2.0. Further requirements vary by degree program.

Special: Internships, study abroad in 14 countries, and work-study programs are available. In addition, B.A.-B.S. degrees in communications, history, and psychology, dual majors, a general studies degree,

and student-designed majors in business and behavioral sciences are offered. Nondegree study and up to 12 credits of pass/fail options are possible. There is a freshman honors program on campus, as well as 3 national honor societies.

Faculty/Classroom: 74% of faculty are male; 26%, female. All teach undergraduates. No introductory courses are taught by graduate students. The average class size in an introductory lecture is 35; in a laboratory, 18; and in a regular course offering, 29.

Admissions: 70% of the 1995–96 applicants were accepted. The SAT I scores for a recent freshman class were Verbal—76% below 500, 21% between 500 and 599, and 3% between 600 and 700; Math—43% below 500, 38% between 500 and 599, 18% between 600 and 700, and 1% above 700. 60% of the current freshmen were in the top fifth of their class; 85% were in the top two fifths.

Requirements: The SAT I or ACT is required. Candidates for admission must have 15 academic credits or 15 Carnegie units, including 4 years in English, 3 each in mathematics and science, 5 in social studies, and 2 in foreign language (for some majors). The GED is accepted. Students may apply on computer disk via the World Wide Web. AP and CLEP credits are accepted.

Procedure: Freshmen are admitted to all sessions. Entrance exams should be taken during the junior year. There is an early admissions plan. Application deadlines are open. Application fee is $40. Notification is sent on a rolling basis.

Transfer: 80 transfer students enrolled in 1995–96. Candidates need a minimum GPA of 2.0, good academic standing, and 18 or more credits from a regionally accredited institution at the college level. 36 credits of 120 must be completed at Behrend.

Visiting: There are regularly scheduled orientations for prospective students, including meetings with a counselor and faculty, a campus tour, and a class visit. There are guides for informal visits and visitors may sit in on classes and stay overnight at the school. To schedule a visit, contact the Admissions Office.

Financial Aid: In 1995–96, 70% of all freshmen and 75% of continuing students received some form of financial aid. The average freshman award was $5524. Of that total, scholarships or need-based grants averaged $1062; other grants averaged $2595; loans averaged $3980; and work contracts averaged $1200. Average earnings from campus work for the school year are $1200. The FAF is required. The application deadline for fall entry is February 15.

International Students: There are currently 4 international students enrolled. They must take the TOEFL and achieve a minimum score of 550.

Computers: The college provides computer facilities for student use. The mainframe is an IBM ES/3090–600S. 220 computers are available in the computer center, laboratories in the library, and in engineering buildings. All students may access the system at posted hours or anytime by modem. There are no time limits and no fees.

Graduates: In a recent year, 385 bachelor's degrees were awarded. The most popular majors among graduates were management (15%), accounting (12%), and engineering (11%). 30 companies recruited on campus in 1994–95.

Admissions Contact: Mary-Ellen Madigan, Director of Admissions. E-mail: mea1@oas.psu.edu.

PENN STATE UNIVERSITY/UNIVERSITY PARK CAMPUS C-3

University Park, PA 16802   (814) 865-5471; FAX: (814) 863-7590

Full-time: 18,362 men, 14,428 women	Faculty: 4,200; I, -$
Part-time: n/av	Ph.D.s: n/av
Graduate: 6856 men and women	Student/Faculty: 8 to 1
Year: semesters, summer session	Tuition: $5258 ($11,310)
Application Deadline: see profile	Room & Board: $4040
Freshman Class: 22,361 applied, 11,404 accepted, 4,310 enrolled	
SAT I or ACT: required	**VERY COMPETITIVE**

Penn State University/University Park Campus, founded in 1855, is the oldest and largest of the 22 campuses in the Penn State system, offering undergraduate and graduate degrees in agricultural science, arts and architecture, business administration, earth and mineral sciences, education, engineering, health and human development, liberal arts, science, and communications. Figures given in the above capsule are approximate. There are 10 undergraduate schools and 1 graduate school. In addition to regional accreditation, Penn State has baccalaureate program accreditation with AACSB, ABET, ACEJMC, ADA, ASLA, CSWE, NAAB, NASAD, NASM, NCATE, NLN, NRPA, and SAF. The 10 libraries contain 2,452,370 volumes, 1,917,033 microform items, and 38,931 audiovisual forms, and subscribe to 26,157 periodicals. Computerized library sources and services include the card catalog, interlibrary loans, and database searching. Special learning facilities include a learning resource center, art gallery, radio station, TV station, museums of art, anthropology, and earth and mineral sciences, an observatory, and a nuclear reactor. The 5013-acre campus is in a suburban area 90 miles west of

Harrisburg. Including residence halls, there are 358 buildings on campus.

Student Life: 82% of undergraduates are from Pennsylvania. Students come from 53 states and Canada. 86% are white. The average age of freshmen is 18; all undergraduates, 21. 16% do not continue beyond their first year; 61% remain to graduate.

Housing: 12,854 students can be accommodated in college housing. College-sponsored living facilities include single-sex dormitories, on-campus apartments, and married-student housing. In addition, there are honors houses, language houses, and special interest houses. On-campus housing is guaranteed for the freshman year only and is available on a lottery system for upperclassmen. 60% of students commute. Alcohol is not permitted. All students may keep cars on campus.

Activities: 15% of men belong to 55 national fraternities; 17% of women belong to 25 national sororities. There are 400 groups on campus, including art, band, cheerleading, chess, choir, chorale, chorus, computers, dance, drama, drill team, ethnic, film, gay, honors, international, jazz band, literary magazine, marching band, musical theater, newspaper, orchestra, pep band, photography, political, professional, radio and TV, religious, social, social service, student government, symphony, and yearbook. Popular campus events include Penn State Artists' Series, Central Pennsylvania Festival of the Arts, and several film series.

Sports: There are 15 intercollegiate sports for men and 13 for women, and 17 intramural sports for men and 17 for women. Athletic and recreation facilities include 6 gymnasiums, 5 swimming pools, indoor and outdoor tracks, 2 golf courses, a jogging course, a rink, 2 rifle ranges, 32 acres of practice fields, and numerous courts for tennis, handball, squash, and paddleball.

Disabled Students: 90% of the campus is accessible to disabled students. The following facilities are available: wheelchair ramps, elevators, special parking, specially equipped rest rooms, special class scheduling, lowered drinking fountains, and lowered telephones.

Services: In addition to many counseling and information services, tutoring is available in most subjects. There is also a reader service for the blind, and remedial math, reading, and writing.

Campus Safety and Security: Campus safety and security measures include 24-hour foot and vehicle patrol, self-defense education, escort service, and shuttle buses. There are informal discussions, pamphlets/posters/films, emergency telephones, and lighted pathways/sidewalks.

Programs of Study: Penn State confers B.A., B.S., B.Arch., B.Arch.Eng., B.F.A., B.M., B.Mus.Arts, and B.Ph. degrees. Associate, master's, and doctoral degrees are also awarded. Bachelor's degrees are awarded in AGRICULTURE (agricultural business management, agriculture, agronomy, animal science, dairy science, fishing and fisheries, forestry and related sciences, forestry production and processing, horticulture, natural resource management, plant science, poultry science, and soil science), BIOLOGICAL SCIENCE (biochemistry, biology/biological science, ecology, microbiology, molecular biology, nutrition, and wildlife biology), BUSINESS (accounting, banking and finance, business administration and management, hotel/motel and restaurant management, insurance, international business management, labor studies, management information systems, management science, marketing/retailing/merchandising, real estate, and transportation management), COMMUNICATIONS AND THE ARTS (advertising, art, art history and appreciation, broadcasting, classics, communications, comparative literature, dramatic arts, English, film arts, fine arts, French, German, Italian, journalism, music, Russian, Spanish, and speech/debate/rhetoric), COMPUTER AND PHYSICAL SCIENCE (actuarial science, astronomy, atmospheric sciences and meteorology, chemistry, computer science, earth science, geoscience, mathematics, physics, science, and statistics), EDUCATION (agricultural, art, elementary, health, industrial arts, music, secondary, and special), ENGINEERING AND ENVIRONMENTAL DESIGN (aeronautical engineering, agricultural engineering, architectural engineering, architecture, chemical engineering, civil engineering, computer engineering, electrical/electronics engineering, energy management technology, engineering, environmental engineering, industrial administration/management, industrial engineering, landscape architecture/design, materials science, mechanical engineering, mining and mineral engineering, nuclear engineering, and petroleum/natural gas engineering), HEALTH PROFESSIONS (health care administration, nursing, premedicine, public health, rehabilitation therapy, and speech pathology/audiology), SOCIAL SCIENCE (African American studies, American studies, anthropology, criminal justice, East Asian studies, economics, food science, geography, history, human development, international relations, Latin American studies, liberal arts/general studies, medieval studies, parks and recreation management, philosophy, physical fitness/movement, political science/government, prelaw, psychology, public administration, religion, sociology, and women's studies). Agriculture, architecture, and meteorology are the strongest academically. Electrical engineering, education, and accounting have the largest enrollments.

Required: All bachelor's degree candidates must take 46 general education credits, including 15 in quantitative and communication skills, 9 in natural sciences, 6 each in arts, humanities, and social and behavioral sciences, and 4 in health sciences and physical education. Further requirements vary by degree program.

Special: Intercollegiate programs in marine sciences and military studies, as well as the B.Ph. program, are offered by faculty from several university colleges. There are internships available in many disciplines. Study abroad is possible through more than 30 programs in 14 countries. Dual and student-designed majors, a general studies degree in arts and sciences, and dual degrees in liberal arts and either earth/natural sciences or engineering are offered with 26 other institutions, as well as a 3–2 engineering program. Co-op programs are available in most engineering majors. There are limited pass/fail options, and nondegree study is possible. There is a freshman honors program on campus, as well as 45 national honor societies, including Phi Beta Kappa. 10 departments have honors programs.

Faculty/Classroom: 74% of faculty are male; 26%, female. All both teach and do research. The average class size in a regular course offering is 26.

Admissions: 93% of current freshmen were in the top quarter of their class; 97% were in the top half.

Requirements: The SAT I or ACT is required; the SAT I is preferred. Applicants should be graduates of accredited high schools or have earned the GED. Required secondary preparation varies by the college or other academic unit applied to. Generally, all applicants should have 5 years in arts, humanities, and social studies, 4 of English, and 3 each of science and mathematics. 2 years of the same foreign language are required for the College of Liberal Arts and School of Communications, and recommended for all other programs. AP and CLEP credits are accepted. Important factors in the admissions decision are advanced placement or honor courses and evidence of special talent.

Procedure: Freshmen are admitted to all sessions. Entrance exams should be taken in the junior year. November 30 is the recommended filing date. Notification is sent on a rolling basis. Application fee is $40.

Transfer: 383 transfer students enrolled in a recent year. Transfer applicants need a minimum GPA of 2.0, good academic standing, and 18 or more credits from any regionally accredited college or institution at the college level. 36 credits of 120 must be completed at Penn State.

Visiting: There are regularly scheduled orientations for prospective students. There are guides for informal visits and visitors may sit in on classes and stay overnight at the school. To schedule a visit, contact the Undergraduate Admissions Office.

Financial Aid: In a recent year, 57% of all freshmen and 76% of continuing students received some form of financial aid. The average freshman award was $4548. Of that total, scholarships or need-based grants averaged $1000; other grants averaged $1364; loans averaged $2001; and work contracts averaged $183. Average earnings from campus work for the school year are $1119. The FAFSA is required; Pennsylvania residents must also complete the PHEAA form. Check with the school for current deadlines.

International Students: There were 1429 international students enrolled in a recent year. Students must score 550 on the TOEFL and students whose native language is English must submit SAT I or ACT scores.

Computers: The college provides computer facilities for student use. The mainframe is an IBM ES/3090–600s. The Center for Academic Computing is connected to a wide variety of academic facilities, the library, other Penn State campuses, the National Science Foundation network, Bitnet/CREN, and more than 1,000 other organizations worldwide. Microcomputer classrooms and laboratories are available throughout the campus, and special facilities for graphics applications and desktop publishing are available. All students may access the system 24 hours a day, every day. There are no time limits and no fees.

Graduates: In a recent year, 8307 bachelor's degrees were awarded. The most popular majors among graduates were elementary education (6%), accounting (4%), and administration of justice (3%). Within an average freshman class, 33% graduate in 4 years, 58% in 5 years, and 61% in 6 years. 106 companies recruited on campus in a recent year.

Admissions Contact: Geoffrey Harford, Director of Admissions. E-mail: admissions@psu.edu.

PENNSYLVANIA COLLEGE OF TECHNOLOGY D-2
Williamsport, PA 17701 (717) 327-4761
(800) 367-9222; FAX: (717) 321-5536

Full-time: 2226 men, 1348 women	Faculty: 222; III, +$
Part-time: 466 men, 689 women	Ph.D.s: 7%
Graduate: none	Student/Faculty: 16 to 1
Year: semesters, summer session	Tuition: $6200 ($7200)
Application Deadline: open	Room & Board: n/app
Freshman Class: 1977 applied, 1506 accepted, 985 enrolled	
SAT I: required	**LESS COMPETITIVE**

Pennsylvania College of Technology, founded in 1989, is a public, coeducational technical college affiliated with Pennsylvania State University. The 2 libraries contain 65,000 volumes, 462 microform items, and 3750 audiovisual forms, and subscribe to 941 periodicals. Computerized library sources and services include the card catalog, interlibrary loans, and database searching. Special learning facilities include a learning resource center, radio station, a restaurant open to the public, and a dental hygiene clinic open to the public. The 54-acre campus is in a small town 80 miles west of Wilkes Barre. There are 17 buildings on campus.

Student Life: 97% of undergraduates are from Pennsylvania. Students come from 12 states, 12 foreign countries, and Canada. 95% are white. 62% are Protestant; 18% Catholic; 14% claim no religious affiliation. The average age of freshmen is 21.2; all undergraduates, 25. 35% do not continue beyond their first year; 43% remain to graduate.

Housing: There are no residence halls. All students commute. Alcohol is not permitted. All students may keep cars on campus.

Activities: There are no fraternities or sororities. There are 25 groups on campus, including art, computers, drama, ethnic, international, newspaper, professional, religious, social, social service, and student government. Popular campus events include a cultural series, Spring Fling Week, and Penn Environment Week.

Sports: There are 5 intercollegiate sports for men and 5 for women, and 25 intramural sports for men and 23 for women. Athletic and recreation facilities include a fitness center, gymnasium, soccer field, softball complex, 5 tennis courts, and a sand volleyball court.

Disabled Students: All of the campus is accessible to disabled students. The following facilities are available: wheelchair ramps, elevators, special parking, specially equipped rest rooms, lowered drinking fountains, and lowered telephones.

Services: In addition to many counseling and information services, tutoring is available in every subject, if tutors are available and request has been made. There is a reader service for the blind, and remedial math, reading, and writing. Services for hearing-impaired students, adaptive equipment, and note-takers are available.

Campus Safety and Security: Campus safety and security measures include 24-hour foot and vehicle patrol, self-defense education, informal discussions, and pamphlets/posters/films. There are lighted pathways/sidewalks.

Programs of Study: Penn College confers B.S. and B.S.N. degrees. Associate degrees are also awarded. Bachelor's degrees are awarded in BUSINESS (business administration and management), COMMUNICATIONS AND THE ARTS (communications and graphic design), COMPUTER AND PHYSICAL SCIENCE (information sciences and systems and polymer science), ENGINEERING AND ENVIRONMENTAL DESIGN (aeronautical technology, automotive technology, computer engineering, construction management, electrical/electronics engineering technology, manufacturing technology, plastics engineering, technological management, and welding engineering), HEALTH PROFESSIONS (dental hygiene, nursing, and physician's assistant), SOCIAL SCIENCE (human services and paralegal studies). Electronics engineering technology, general studies, and business management have the largest enrollments.

Required: To graduate, students must complete a minimum of 120 credits with a GPA of 2.0 for all program courses, including the major.

Special: Penn College offers cooperative and internship programs, cross-registration with Lycoming College, dual majors, and credit by examination and for work and/or life experience.

Faculty/Classroom: 74% of faculty are male; 26%, female. The average class size in a regular course offering is 18.

Admissions: 76% of the 1995–96 applicants were accepted.

Requirements: The SAT I is required. Applicants must have a high school diploma and must take the college's placement examinations. Other admissions criteria vary by program. An admissions application is offered via the World Wide Web at http://www.pct.edu. AP and CLEP credits are accepted. Important factors in the admissions decision are ability to finance college education, advanced placement or honor courses, and recommendations by school officials.

Procedure: Freshmen are admitted to all sessions. Entrance exams should be taken prior to scheduling classes. There are early decision, early admissions, and deferred admissions plans. Application deadlines are open. Application fee is $35. Notification is sent on a rolling basis. 2 early decision candidates were accepted for the 1995–96 class. A waiting list is an active part of the admissions procedure, with about 10% of all applicants on the list.

Transfer: 283 transfer students enrolled in 1995–96. Transfer procedures vary with each degree program. Courses are evaluated for transfer equivalency. At least 120 credits must be completed at Penn College.

Visiting: There are regularly scheduled orientations for prospective students, include registration, a multimedia presentation, admission and financial aid sessions, a question-and-answer period, a tour of campus facilities, and a reception. Visitors may sit in on classes. To schedule a visit, contact the Office of Admissions.

Financial Aid: In 1995–96, 80% of all freshmen received some form of financial aid. The average freshman award was $5000. Average earnings from campus work for the school year are $2220. The application deadline for fall entry is April 1.

International Students: There are currently 39 international students enrolled. The school actively recruits these students. They must score 500 on the TOEFL.

Computers: The college provides computer facilities for student use. The mainframe is an IBM AS/400 F50. Approximately 1000 computers are available for student use in 25 labs. All students may access the system. There are no time limits and no fees.

Graduates: In 1994–95, 34 bachelor's degrees were awarded. The most popular majors among graduates were electronics technology (6%), business management (3%), and general studies (2%). Of the 1994 graduating class, 80% had found employment within 6 months of graduation.

Admissions Contact: Chester D. Schuman, Director of Admissions. E-mail: cschuman@pct.edu. A campus video is available.

PENNSYLVANIA STATE SYSTEM OF HIGHER EDUCATION

The Pennsylvania State System of Higher Education, established in 1983, is a public system. It is governed by a board of governors, whose chief administrator is the chancellor. The primary goal of the system is to provide high-quality, liberal arts education at an affordable cost, with a central mission of teaching and service. The main priorities are capital facilities, matters of maintenance and funding, social equity, and tuition stabilization through appropriate funding. The total enrollment of all 14 campuses is about 99,000, with more than 5200 faculty members. Altogether, there are 217 baccalaureate, 107 master's, and 6 doctoral programs offered in the system. Four-year campuses are located in Bloomsburg, California, Cheyney, Clarion, East Stroudsberg, Edinboro, Indiana, Kutztown, Lock Haven, Mansfield, Millersville, Shippensburg, Slippery Rock, and West Chester. Profiles of the 4-year campuses are included in this chapter.

PHILADELPHIA COLLEGE OF BIBLE F-3
Langhorne, PA 19047–2990 (215) 752-5800
(800) 366-0049; FAX: (215) 702-4248

Full-time: 355 men, 368 women	Faculty: 35
Part-time: 89 men, 52 women	Ph.D.s: 31%
Graduate: 124 men, 136 women	Student/Faculty: 21 to 1
Year: semesters, summer session	Tuition: $8060
Application Deadline: open	Room & Board: $4444
Freshman Class: 776 applied, 488 accepted, 324 enrolled	
SAT I Verbal/Math: 440/470	ACT: 22 **COMPETITIVE**

Philadelphia College of Bible, founded in 1913, is a private coeducational institution offering instruction in the Scriptures and liberal arts and professional theory. Other campuses include the Wisconsin Wilderness Campus and the New Jersey Campus. In addition to regional accreditation, PCB has baccalaureate program accreditation with CSWE and NASM. The library contains 117,000 volumes, 18,405 microform items, and 5461 audiovisual forms, and subscribes to 499 periodicals. Computerized library sources and services include the card catalog and database searching. Special learning facilities include a learning resource center. The 105-acre campus is in a suburban area 30 miles north of Philadelphia. Including residence halls, there are 11 buildings on campus.

Student Life: 51% of undergraduates are from Pennsylvania. Students come from 33 states, 26 foreign countries, and Canada. 73% are from public schools; 25% from private. 72% are white; 15% African American. Most are Protestant. The average age of freshmen is 18; all undergraduates, 20. 30% do not continue beyond their first year; 37% remain to graduate.

Housing: 372 students can be accommodated in college housing. College-sponsored living facilities include single-sex dormitories and married-student housing. On-campus housing is guaranteed for all 4 years. 56% of students live on campus. Alcohol is not permitted. All students may keep cars on campus.

Activities: There are no fraternities or sororities. There are many groups and organizations on campus, including art, band, cheerleading, choir, chorale, chorus, computers, drama, ethnic, international, newspaper, orchestra, pep band, professional, religious, social, student government, symphony, and yearbook. Popular campus events include Late Skates, Christmas and Valentine socials, and Spring Formal.

Sports: There are 4 intercollegiate sports for men and 4 for women, and 4 intramural sports for men and 4 for women. Athletic and recreation facilities include a gymnasium, baseball diamond, soccer field, hockey field, and sand volleyball court.

Disabled Students: The entire campus is accessible to disabled students. Wheelchair ramps, elevators, special parking, specially equipped rest rooms, and lowered drinking fountains are available.

Services: The AIMS Program provides academic support for freshmen who need it.

Campus Safety and Security: Campus safety and security measures include 24-hour foot and vehicle patrol, shuttle buses, informal discussions, and pamphlets/posters/films. There are emergency telephones and lighted pathways/sidewalks.

Programs of Study: PCB confers B.S., B.Mus., B.S.Ed., and B.S.W. degrees. Associate and master's degrees are also awarded. Bachelor's degrees are awarded in COMMUNICATIONS AND THE ARTS (music), EDUCATION (education), SOCIAL SCIENCE (biblical studies and social work). Bible is the strongest academically. Teacher education and Bible have the largest enrollments.

Required: Students must complete 51 credits in Bible, 48 in general education, and 27 in professional studies. A total of 126 credits, with a minimum GPA of 2.0, is required. 3 credits in physical education must be taken. The number of hours in the major varies: 57 in Bible, 80 in music, 43 in social work, and 47 in education.

Special: PCB offers co-op programs in accounting, business administration, computer science, and office administration; cross-registration with Bucks County Community College; various church ministries, education, social work, and music internships; and study abroad in Israel. There are dual majors in social work, music, and education, and a B.A.-B.S. degree in Bible. Student-designed interdisciplinary majors are possible.

Faculty/Classroom: 72% of faculty are male; 28%, female. 90% teach undergraduates. The average class size in an introductory lecture is 35.

Admissions: 63% of the 1995–96 applicants were accepted. The SAT I scores for the 1995–96 freshman class were as follows: Verbal—35% below 500, 25% between 500 and 599, 32% between 600 and 700, and 7% above 700; Math—50% below 500, 29% between 500 and 599, 19% between 600 and 700, and 2% above 700. The ACT scores were 40% below 21, 20% between 21 and 25, 24% between 26 and 29, and 16% 29 and above. 26% of the current freshmen were in the top fifth of their class; 55% were in the top two fifths.

Requirements: The SAT I or ACT is required, with minimum composite scores of 800 and 19, respectively. Applicants should be in the upper 50% of their class with a 2.0 GPA. A high school diploma or the GED is needed. An essay and a pastor's reference are required. Applications are accepted on computer disk. AP and CLEP credits are accepted. Important factors in the admissions decision are advanced placement or honor courses, personality/intangible qualities, and leadership record.

Procedure: Freshmen are admitted to all sessions. Entrance exams should be taken in the junior or senior year of high school. There are early admissions and deferred admissions plans. Application deadlines are open. Application fee is $15. Notification is sent on a rolling basis.

Transfer: 174 transfer students enrolled in 1995–96. Applicants must submit an application, a pastor's reference, college transcripts, and a health form. SAT I and high school transcripts are required if the student has less than 60 college credit hours. 60 credits of 126 must be completed at PCB.

Visiting: There are regularly scheduled orientations for prospective students, including chapel, class visits, a meal in the dining room, and an interview with a counselor. There are guides for informal visits and visitors may sit in on classes and stay overnight at the school. To schedule a visit, contact the Admissions Department.

Financial Aid: In 1995–96, 92% of all freshmen and 75% of continuing students received some form of financial aid. 40% of freshmen and 44% of continuing students received need-based aid. The average freshman award was $6286. Of that total, scholarships or need-based grants averaged $3586 ($10,800 maximum); loans averaged $2200 ($2625 maximum); and work contracts averaged $500 ($1500 maximum). 33% of undergraduate students work part-time. Average earnings from campus work for the school year are $800. The average financial indebtedness of the 1994–95 graduate was $9500. PCB is a member of CSS. The FAFSA is required.

International Students: There were 64 international students enrolled in a recent year. The school actively recruits these students. They must take the TOEFL and achieve a minimum score of 550.

Computers: The college provides computer facilities for student use. Some 40 PCs are located in computer laboratories. All students may access the system. There are no time limits and no fees.

Graduates: In 1994–95, 147 bachelor's degrees were awarded. The most popular majors among graduates were Bible (100%), and, in double-degree programs, education (18%), and music (12%). Within an average freshman class, 42% graduate in 5 years. 50 companies recruited on campus in 1994–95.

Admissions Contact: Mrs. Fran Emmons, Director of Admissions and Financial Aid. A campus video is available.

PHILADELPHIA COLLEGE OF PHARMACY AND SCIENCE

F-3

Philadelphia, PA 19104–4495

(215) 596–8810
FAX: (215) 895–1100

Full-time: 717 men, 1180 women	**Faculty:** 158; IIB, av$
Part-time: 9 men, 14 women	**Ph.D.s:** 64%
Graduate: 57 men, 96 women	**Student/Faculty:** 12 to 1
Year: semesters, summer session	**Tuition:** $11,950
Application Deadline: open	**Room & Board:** $4500
Freshman Class: n/av	
SAT I Verbal/Math: 470/570	**ACT:** 24 **VERY COMPETITIVE**

Philadelphia College of Pharmacy and Science, founded in 1821 and coeducational since 1876, is a private institution offering 10 undergraduate and graduate programs in the health and basic sciences. There is 1 graduate school. In addition to regional accreditation, PCPS has baccalaureate program accreditation with ACPE and APTA. The library contains 73,571 volumes, 420 microform items, and 150 audiovisual forms, and subscribes to 809 periodicals. Computerized library sources and services include the card catalog, interlibrary loans, and database searching. Special learning facilities include a learning resource center, a model pharmacy, and a center for the history of pharmacy. The 20-acre campus is in an urban area in the University City section of Philadelphia. Including residence halls, there are 16 buildings on campus.

Student Life: 73% of undergraduates are from Pennsylvania. Students come from 12 states, 8 foreign countries, and Canada. 72% are from public schools; 28% from private. 78% are white; 17% Asian American. The average age of freshmen is 18; all undergraduates, 21. 9% do not continue beyond their first year; 82% remain to graduate.

Housing: 680 students can be accommodated in college housing. College-sponsored living facilities include coed dormitories and fraternity houses. In addition, there are honors houses. On-campus housing is guaranteed for the freshman year only, is available on a first-come, first-served basis, and is available on a lottery system for upperclassmen. Priority is given to out-of-town students. Alcohol is not permitted. Upperclassmen may keep cars on campus.

Activities: 20% of men belong to 2 local and 9 national fraternities; 17% of women belong to 1 national sorority. There are 28 groups on campus, including cheerleading, chess, chorus, computers, drama, ethnic, honors, international, literary magazine, musical theater, newspaper, professional, religious, social, social service, student government, and yearbook. Popular campus events include Greek Week and Student Appreciation Days.

Sports: There are 7 intercollegiate sports for men and 8 for women, and 19 intramural sports for men and 19 for women. Athletic and recreation facilities include a gymnasium, a rifle range, and recreational areas in the residence halls.

Disabled Students: 90% of the campus is accessible to disabled students. The following facilities are available: wheelchair ramps, elevators, special parking, and specially equipped rest rooms.

Services: In addition to many counseling and information services, tutoring is available in every subject. There is also remedial math and writing.

Campus Safety and Security: Campus safety and security measures include 24-hour foot and vehicle patrol, self-defense education, escort service, and shuttle buses. In addition, there are informal discussions, pamphlets/posters/films, emergency telephones, and lighted pathways/sidewalks.

Programs of Study: PCPS confers the B.S. degree. Master's and doctoral degrees are also awarded. Bachelor's degrees are awarded in BIOLOGICAL SCIENCE (biochemistry, biology/biological science, microbiology, and toxicology), COMPUTER AND PHYSICAL SCIENCE (chemical technology and chemistry), HEALTH PROFESSIONS (medical laboratory technology, pharmacy, and physical therapy). Pharmacy, physical therapy, and biology are the strongest academically and have the largest enrollments.

Required: Requirements vary by major program. However, all students must take 3 English courses, introductory courses in psychology and sociology, a computer course, and physical education. They must pass a writing proficiency examination. In all programs, the first-year courses are required. Total credits required range from 98 to 187, depending on the major. A 2.0 GPA is required for graduation.

Special: PCPS offers a 6-year advanced degree in pharmacy and a 5-year integrated professional program in physical therapy. Internships are required in all disciplines. An open major is offered, as is a program of curriculum and advisement to prepare students to enter medical school. Students may elect a minor in communications, economics, psychology, or sociology. There are 4 national honor societies on campus.

Faculty/Classroom: All teach undergraduates, 20% do research, and 20% do both. No introductory courses are taught by graduate students. The average class size in an introductory lecture is 200; in a laboratory, 20; and in a regular course offering, 25.

Admissions: The SAT I scores for the 1995–96 freshman class were as follows: Verbal—61% below 500, 32% between 500 and 599, 6% between 600 and 700, and 1% above 700; Math—19% below 500, 51% between 500 and 599, 27% between 600 and 700, and 3% above 700. The ACT scores were 5% below 21, 20% between 21 and 23, 60% between 24 and 26, 10% between 27 and 28, and 5% above 28. 64% of the current freshmen were in the top fifth of their class; 93% were in the top two fifths. 15 freshmen graduated first in their class.

Requirements: The SAT I is required. PCPS requires applicants to be in the upper 50% of their class and have a 3.0 GPA. A composite score of 1100 (recentered) on the SAT I is recommended. Applicants must be high school graduates or hold the GED. Minimum academic requirements include 4 credits in English, 1 each in American history and social science, and 4 in academic electives. Mathematics requirements include 2 years of algebra and 1 year of plane geometry. The college strongly recommends an additional year of higher-level mathematics, such as calculus. 3 science credits are required; also recommended are 1 credit each in biology, chemistry, and physics. All applicants must submit a personal essay. Applicants to the 5-year physical therapy program must present evidence of at least 20 hours of experience in a clinical setting and participate in an interview with the faculty. AP and CLEP credits are accepted. Important factors in the admissions decision are advanced placement or honor courses, personality/intangible qualities, and geographic diversity.

Procedure: Freshmen are admitted in the fall. Entrance exams should be taken end of the junior year or fall of the senior year. There are early admissions and deferred admissions plans. Application deadlines are open. Application fee is $25. Notification is sent on a rolling basis. A waiting list is an active part of the admissions procedure for physical therapy majors, with about 10% of applicants on the list.

Transfer: 46 transfer students enrolled in a recent year. Pharmacy and physical therapy applicants must present a minimum GPA of 3.0. All other majors must have at least a 2.7 GPA. All applicants must meet high school requirements as well. 90 credits of 98 to 187 must be completed at PCPS.

Visiting: There are regularly scheduled orientations for prospective students, consisting of On Campus Days for juniors and seniors in the spring, open house for seniors and transfers in the fall, and summer group orientation. There are guides for informal visits and visitors may sit in on classes and stay overnight at the school. To schedule a visit, contact the Student Affairs Office at (215) 596–8536.

Financial Aid: In 1995–96, 90% of all freshmen and 70% of continuing students received some form of financial aid. 80% of freshmen and 50% of continuing students received need-based aid. The average freshman award was $3000. All undergraduate students work part-time. Average earnings from campus work for the school year are $1000. The average financial indebtedness of the 1994–95 graduate was $31,000. The FAFSA and the college's own financial statement are required. The application deadline for fall entry is March 15.

International Students: In a recent year, 45 international students were enrolled. They must take the TOEFL and achieve a minimum score of 550. The student must also take the SAT I.

Computers: The college provides computer facilities for student use. There are 34 IBM and Apple microcomputers available in the computer center. All students may access the system. There are no time limits and no fees.

Graduates: In 1994–95, 252 bachelor's degrees were awarded. Within an average freshman class, 10% graduate in 4 years, 80% in 5 years, and 10% in 6 years. Of the 1994 graduating class, 75% were enrolled in graduate school within 6 months of graduation and 98% had found employment.

Admissions Contact: Louis L. Hegyes, Director of Admissions. E-mail: pcpsadmit@shrsys.hslc.org.

PHILADELPHIA COLLEGE OF TEXTILES AND SCIENCE F-3
Philadelphia, PA 19144–5497

(215) 951-2800
(800) 951-7287; FAX: (215) 951-2907

Full-time: 721 men, 1135 women	**Faculty:** 89; IIB, av$
Part-time: 291 men, 622 women	**Ph.D.s:** 63%
Graduate: 322 men, 295 women	**Student/Faculty:** 21 to 1
Year: semesters, summer session	**Tuition:** $12,240
Application Deadline: open	**Room & Board:** $5676
Freshman Class: 2512 applied, 1938 accepted, 730 enrolled	
SAT I Verbal/Math: 450/510	**COMPETITIVE**

Philadelphia College of Textiles and Science, founded in 1884, is a private, coeducational institution offering preprofessional programs in architecture, design, business, the sciences, premedicine, prelaw, textiles, and engineering. There are 4 undergraduate and 3 graduate schools. In addition to regional accreditation, Philadelphia College of Textiles and Science has baccalaureate program accreditation with FIDER. The library contains 85,000 volumes, 5000 microform items, and 800 audiovisual forms, and subscribes to 1800 periodicals. Computerized library sources and services include the card catalog, interlibrary loans, and database searching. Special learning facilities include a learning resource center, art gallery, radio station, and a design center. The 100-acre campus is in a suburban area 10 minutes west of metropolitan Philadelphia. Including residence halls, there are 56 buildings on campus.

Student Life: 60% of undergraduates are from Pennsylvania. Students come from 40 states, 46 foreign countries, and Canada. 65% are from public schools; 35% from private. 77% are white; 10% African American. The average age of freshmen is 18; all undergraduates, 20. 24% do not continue beyond their first year; 60% remain to graduate.

Housing: 900 students can be accommodated in college housing. College-sponsored living facilities include single-sex and coed dormitories, on-campus apartments, and off-campus apartments. On-campus housing is guaranteed for all 4 years. 60% of students live on campus; of those, 60% remain on campus on weekends. Alcohol is not permitted. All students may keep cars on campus.

Activities: 8% of men belong to 1 local and 3 national fraternities; 4% of women belong to 2 national sororities. There are 45 groups on campus, including cheerleading, choir, computers, dance, drama, ethnic, gay, honors, international, literary magazine, newspaper, photography, professional, radio and TV, religious, social, social service, student government, and yearbook. Popular campus events include an annual fashion show and design competition, Welcome Week, and Spring Fling.

Sports: There are 5 intercollegiate sports for men and 6 for women, and 6 intramural sports for men and 6 for women. Athletic and recreation facilities include 2 gymnasiums, a fitness center and exercise facility, tennis courts, athletic fields, and a student center recreation room.

Disabled Students: 90% of the campus is accessible to disabled students. The following facilities are available: wheelchair ramps, elevators, special parking, specially equipped rest rooms, special class scheduling, and lowered telephones.

Services: In addition to many counseling and information services, tutoring is available in every subject. There is a reader service for the blind, and remedial math, reading, and writing.

Campus Safety and Security: Campus safety and security measures include 24-hour foot and vehicle patrol, self-defense education, escort service, and shuttle buses. In addition, there are informal discussions, pamphlets/posters/films, emergency telephones, and lighted pathways/sidewalks.

Programs of Study: Philadelphia College of Textiles and Science confers B.S. and B.Arch. degrees. Associate and master's degrees are also awarded. Bachelor's degrees are awarded in BIOLOGICAL SCIENCE (biochemistry and biology/biological science), BUSINESS (accounting, banking and finance, fashion merchandising, international business management, management science, marketing/retailing/merchandising, and retailing), COMMUNICATIONS AND THE ARTS (graphic design), COMPUTER AND PHYSICAL SCIENCE (applied mathematics, chemistry, computer science, information sciences and systems, and polymer science), ENGINEERING AND ENVIRONMENTAL DESIGN (architecture, environmental science, interior design, textile engineering, and textile technology), HEALTH PROFESSIONS (premedicine), SOCIAL SCIENCE (fashion design and technology, prelaw, psychology, and textiles and clothing). Interior design, accounting, and fashion apparel management are the strongest academically. Fashion merchandising, marketing, and architecture have the largest enrollments.

Required: All students are required to complete a 60-credit residency with courses in mathematics, science, social science, and the humanities, 2 semesters of physical education, and a professional studies core curriculum, which differs by major program. A number of requirements may be satisfied and elective credits earned by proficiency examination. A total of 121 to 146 credits is required with a 2.5 overall GPA.

Special: Textile offers special B.S. degree programs for registered nurses and allied health professionals. Work-study programs are available locally and in New York, Boston, Washington D.C., and London, England. Students may undertake independent study in 1 discipline for 1 semester. Cooperative programs in all academic majors, study abroad, summer internships, a dual major in international business, an accelerated business administration degree program, and an integrated major in business and science are available. There is a freshman honors program on campus.

Faculty/Classroom: 67% of faculty are male; 33%, female. All teach undergraduates. No introductory courses are taught by graduate students. The average class size in an introductory lecture is 30; in a laboratory, 18; and in a regular course offering, 25.

Admissions: 77% of the 1995–96 applicants were accepted. The SAT I scores for the 1995–96 freshman class were as follows: Verbal—69% below 500, 28% between 500 and 599, and 3% between 600 and 700; Math—50% below 500, 34% between 500 and 599, 13% between 600 and 700, and 3% above 700. 39% of the current freshmen were in the top fifth of their class; 72% were in the top two fifths.

Requirements: The SAT I or ACT is required. A minimum GPA of 2.0 is required. Applicants should be high school graduates or have earned the GED. Recommended secondary preparation includes 4 years each of English and history, 3 years of mathematics, and 2 years of science. Potential science majors are strongly urged to take 4 years of mathematics. AP and CLEP credits are accepted. Important factors in the admissions decision are evidence of special talent, advanced placement or honor courses, and personality/intangible qualities.

Procedure: Freshmen are admitted fall and spring. There is a deferred admissions plan. Application deadlines are open. Application fee is $35. Notification is sent on a rolling basis.

Transfer: 165 transfer students enrolled in 1995–96. Applicants usually need a 2.5 GPA. 60 credits of 121 to 146 must be completed at Philadelphia College of Textiles and Science.

Visiting: There are regularly scheduled orientations for prospective students, during the summer. There are guides for informal visits and visitors may sit in on classes and stay overnight at the school. To schedule a visit, contact the Admissions Office.

Financial Aid: In 1995–96, 90% of all freshmen and 70% of continuing students received some form of financial aid. 69% of freshmen and 62% of continuing students received need-based aid. The average freshman award was $11,613. Of that total, scholarships or need-based grants averaged $6540 ($17,915 maximum); loans averaged $3221 ($3425 maximum); and work contracts averaged $1451 ($1500 maximum). 28% of undergraduate students work part-time. Average earnings from campus work for the school year are $765. The average financial indebtedness of the 1994–95 graduate was $11,000. Philadelphia College of Textiles and Science is a member of CSS. The FAFSA is required. The application deadline for fall entry is April 15.

International Students: There are currently 230 international students enrolled. The school actively recruits these students. They must score 500 on the TOEFL and also take an English placement test.

Computers: The college provides computer facilities for student use. The mainframes are a DEC VAX 11/780, 6410, and 8250. There are also 50 IBM, Zenith, and Apple Macintosh microcomputers available in the computer center and design laboratories (with CAD and plotter facilities). All students may access the system 7 days a week. There are no time limits and no fees.

Graduates: In 1994–95, 291 bachelor's degrees were awarded. The most popular majors among graduates were fashion merchandising (15%), marketing (14%), and fashion design (13%). Within an average freshman class, 40% graduate in 4 years. 106 companies recruited on campus in 1994–95. Of the 1994 graduating class, 5% were enrolled in graduate school within 6 months of graduation and 92% had found employment.

Admissions Contact: Guy Brignola, Director of Admissions. E-mail: admissions@laurel.texsci.edu.

POINT PARK COLLEGE
Pittsburgh, PA 15222

B-3

Full-time: 446 men, 635 women	Faculty: 78; IIB, –$
Part-time: 656 men, 490 women	Ph.D.s: 44%
Graduate: 35 men, 36 women	Student/Faculty: 14 to 1
Year: semesters, summer session	Tuition: $10,552
Application Deadline: open	Room & Board: $5072
Freshman Class: 727 applied, 636 accepted, 197 enrolled	
SAT I Verbal/Math: 427/435	LESS COMPETITIVE

(412) 392–3430; (800) 321–0129

Point Park College, founded in 1960, is an independent coeducational institution offering programs in liberal arts, fine arts, business, engineering, health science, professional training, and teacher prepara-

tion. There are 2 graduate schools. In addition to regional accreditation, Point Park College has baccalaureate program accreditation with ABET. The library contains 124,371 volumes, 27,734 microform items, and 2432 audiovisual forms, and subscribes to 571 periodicals. Computerized library sources and services include the card catalog, interlibrary loans, and database searching. Special learning facilities include a radio station, TV station, theaters, and dance studios. The campus is in an urban area in downtown Pittsburgh. Including residence halls, there are 5 buildings on campus.

Student Life: 88% of undergraduates are from Pennsylvania. Students come from 16 states, 32 foreign countries, and Canada. 84% are white; 10% African American. 42% are Catholic; 34% Protestant; 13% claim no religious affiliation. The average age of freshmen is 18; all undergraduates, 28. 28% do not continue beyond their first year; 55% remain to graduate.

Housing: 650 students can be accommodated in college housing. College-sponsored living facilities include single-sex and coed dormitories. On-campus housing is guaranteed for all 4 years. 69% of students commute.

Activities: 8% of men belong to 2 local fraternities; 7% of women belong to 2 local sororities. There are 25 groups on campus, including cheerleading, choir, computers, dance, drama, ethnic, film, honors, international, literary magazine, musical theater, newspaper, photography, political, professional, radio and TV, religious, social, social service, student government, and yearbook. Popular campus events include Snowball Dance, Spring Fling, and dance and theater productions.

Sports: There are 3 intercollegiate sports for men and 3 for women, and 7 intramural sports for men and 7 for women. Athletic and recreation facilities include a recreation center and a 130-seat auditorium.

Disabled Students: 98% of the campus is accessible to disabled students. The following facilities are available: wheelchair ramps, elevators, specially equipped rest rooms, special class scheduling, lowered drinking fountains, and lowered telephones.

Services: In addition to many counseling and information services, tutoring is available in most subjects. Learning-disabled services are available, but they are handled on a case-by-case basis. There is a reader service for the blind, and remedial math, reading, and writing.

Campus Safety and Security: Campus safety and security measures include 24-hour foot and vehicle patrol, informal discussions, pamphlets/posters/films, and emergency telephones. There are lighted pathways/sidewalks.

Programs of Study: Point Park College confers B.A., B.S., and B.F.A. degrees. Associate and master's degrees are also awarded. Bachelor's degrees are awarded in BIOLOGICAL SCIENCE (biology/biological science), BUSINESS (accounting, business administration and management, human resources, and management science), COMMUNICATIONS AND THE ARTS (applied art, arts administration/management, communications, dance, dramatic arts, English, and journalism), COMPUTER AND PHYSICAL SCIENCE (computer science and mathematics), EDUCATION (drama, early childhood, elementary, and secondary), ENGINEERING AND ENVIRONMENTAL DESIGN (civil engineering technology, electrical/electronics engineering technology, environmental science, and mechanical engineering technology), HEALTH PROFESSIONS (health care administration), SOCIAL SCIENCE (behavioral science, history, international studies, liberal arts/general studies, paralegal studies, political science/government, psychology, and public administration). Education, history, and journalism and communications are the strongest academically. Electrical engineering technology, business management, and performing arts have the largest enrollments.

Required: All majors leading to a baccalaureate degree require a minimum of 120 credits. The basic distribution requirement is 30 or more credits in the liberal arts and sciences, with a minimum of 12 credits in English and humanities and 6 credits each in human, natural, and social sciences. A minimum GPA of 2.0 is required.

Special: There is cross-registration through the Pittsburgh Council of Higher Education, and cooperative programs with the Art Institute of Pittsburgh. Internships exist in journalism and communications, legal studies, and business management. The college offers a Washington semester, work-study, dual and student-designed majors, credit by examination and for life/military/work experience, nondegree study, and pass/fail options. Capstone programs are available for students with associate degrees in legal studies, management services, applied arts, international studies, general studies, human resources management, health services, and specialized professional studies-funeral service. An accelerated degree program in business with Saturday-only classes is also offered. There are 2 national honor societies on campus.

Faculty/Classroom: 64% of faculty are male; 36%, female. All teach undergraduates. The average class size in an introductory lecture is 40; in a laboratory, 12; and in a regular course offering, 25.

Admissions: 87% of the 1995–96 applicants were accepted. The SAT I scores for the 1995–96 freshman class were as follows: Verbal—75% below 500, 21% between 500 and 599, and 4% between

600 and 700; Math—70% below 500, 25% between 500 and 599, 4% between 600 and 700, and 1% above 700. 28% of the current freshmen were in the top fifth of their class; 50% were in the top two fifths.

Requirements: The SAT I or ACT is required. Students should have a 2.0 GPA and have completed 12 academic credits or 16 Carnegie units consisting of 4 in English and history, 3 in science, and 2 in mathematics. The GED is accepted. Theater and dance students must audition, and an interview is requested for all candidates. AP and CLEP credits are accepted. Important factors in the admissions decision are personality/intangible qualities, leadership record, and extracurricular activities record.

Procedure: Freshmen are admitted to all sessions. Entrance exams should be taken in the junior or senior year. There are early admissions and deferred admissions plans. Application deadlines are open. Application fee is $20. Notification is sent on a rolling basis.

Transfer: 184 transfer students enrolled in a recent year. Transfer applicants must have completed 12 credit hours with at least a 2.0 GPA. The SAT I or ACT, an associate degree, and an interview are recommended. 30 credits of 120 must be completed at Point Park College.

Visiting: There are regularly scheduled orientations for prospective students. There are guides for informal visits and visitors may sit in on classes and stay overnight at the school. To schedule a visit, contact the Office of Admissions at (412) 392-3439.

Financial Aid: In 1995–96, 94% of all freshmen received some form of financial aid. 88% of freshmen received need-based aid. The average freshman award was $10,183. Of that total, scholarships or need-based grants averaged $3944 ($10,552 maximum); Pell Grant averaged $1715 ($2340 maximum); loans averaged $2021 ($3625 maximum); and work contracts averaged $919 ($1600 maximum). 25% of undergraduate students work part-time. Average earnings from campus work for the school year are $1200. Point Park College is a member of CSS. The college's own financial statement and PHEAA are required.

International Students: There were 130 international students enrolled in a recent year. The school actively recruits these students. They must take the TOEFL and achieve a minimum score of 500.

Computers: The college provides computer facilities for student use. The mainframe is an HP 9000/825. There are 82 PCs and terminals for student use. Access to the mainframe is limited to computer science and engineering technology majors. PC laboratories are available to all students, with special facilities open to journalism students only. Laboratory hours vary by facility. Students may access the system according to the time available on the sign-up sheet. The fees are $60.

Graduates: In a recent year, 433 bachelor's degrees were awarded. The most popular majors among graduates were business management (11%), electrical engineering technology (11%), and journalism and communications (10%). Within an average freshman class, 2% graduate in 3 years and 55% in 6 years. 12 companies recruited on campus in a recent year.

Admissions Contact: Terrence R. Kizina, Director of Admissions.

ROBERT MORRIS COLLEGE
B-3
Coraopolis, PA 15108 (412) 262-8265
(800) 762-0097; FAX: (412) 262-8619

Full-time: 1424 men, 1142 women	Faculty: 137; II, +$
Part-time: 665 men, 1061 women	Ph.D.s: 55%
Graduate: 542 men, 387 women	Student/Faculty: 19 to 1
Year: semesters, summer session	Tuition: $7350
Application Deadline: open	Room & Board: $4554
Freshman Class: 1192 applied, 1146 accepted, 495 enrolled	
SAT I Verbal/Math: 390/430	LESS COMPETITIVE

Robert Morris College, founded in 1921, is an independent, coeducational, nonprofit institution offering programs in business administration, English, and communications. There is also a campus in Pittsburgh. There are 3 undergraduate and 3 graduate schools. In addition to regional accreditation, the college has baccalaureate program accreditation with CAHEA. The 2 libraries contain 124,789 volumes, 306,977 microform items, and 11,200 audiovisual forms, and subscribe to 856 periodicals. Computerized library sources and services include the card catalog and database searching. Special learning facilities include a TV station. The 230-acre campus is in a suburban area 17 miles northwest of Pittsburgh. Including residence halls, there are 24 buildings on campus.

Student Life: 91% of undergraduates are from Pennsylvania. Students come from 27 states, 23 foreign countries, and Canada. 91% are white. The average age of freshmen is 18; all undergraduates, 26. 20% do not continue beyond their first year; 55% remain to graduate.

Housing: 883 students can be accommodated in college housing. College-sponsored living facilities include single-sex dormitories. On-campus housing is guaranteed for all 4 years. 80% of students commute. All students may keep cars on campus.

Activities: 15% of men belong to 5 national fraternities; 5% of women belong to 3 national sororities. There are 38 groups on campus, including band, cheerleading, chorale, computers, dance, drama, drill team, ethnic, film, honors, international, literary magazine, marching band, musical theater, newspaper, pep band, photography, professional, religious, social, social service, student government, TV, and yearbook. Popular campus events include Spring Carnival, Snow Ball, ski trips, and Air Band Competition.

Sports: There are 7 intercollegiate sports for men and 7 for women, and 10 intramural sports for men and 10 for women. Athletic and recreation facilities include a student union, a weight room, an outdoor swimming pool, a 700-seat gymnasium, and a 300-seat arena.

Disabled Students: 35% of the campus is accessible to disabled students. The following facilities are available: wheelchair ramps, elevators, special parking, specially equipped rest rooms, and special class scheduling.

Services: In addition to many counseling and information services, tutoring is available in most subjects. There is also a reader service for the blind, and remedial math, reading, and writing.

Campus Safety and Security: Campus safety and security measures include 24-hour foot and vehicle patrol, escort service, shuttle buses, and informal discussions. There are pamphlets/posters/films, emergency telephones, and lighted pathways/sidewalks.

Programs of Study: The college confers B.A., B.S., and B.S.B.A. degrees. Associate and master's degrees are also awarded. Bachelor's degrees are awarded in BUSINESS (accounting, banking and finance, business administration and management, hospitality management services, human resources, management science, marketing/retailing/merchandising, office supervision and management, sports management, and transportation management), COMMUNICATIONS AND THE ARTS (communications and English), COMPUTER AND PHYSICAL SCIENCE (information sciences and systems), EDUCATION (business), ENGINEERING AND ENVIRONMENTAL DESIGN (aviation administration/management), HEALTH PROFESSIONS (health care administration), SOCIAL SCIENCE (economics). Accounting and computer information systems are the strongest academically. Accounting, management, and computer information systems have the largest enrollments.

Required: All candidates must complete 120 to 124 credit hours, including 18 to 39 in the major, with a 2.0 GPA overall and 2.5 in the major. There is a core curriculum that varies with each major, consisting of liberal arts or business components. All students must have 2 credits in physical education and demonstrate competency in computer software applications.

Special: The college offers cooperative programs in all majors, cross-registration with the 9 schools of the Pittsburgh Council of Higher Education, internships in 2 majors, work-study programs, dual majors, and nondegree study. Credit by exam and pass/fail options are available. There is a B.A.-B.S. degree in business administration and study abroad in Australia for sports management majors. There are 2 national honor societies on campus.

Faculty/Classroom: 74% of faculty are male; 26%, female. All teach undergraduates. No introductory courses are taught by graduate students. The average class size in an introductory lecture is 50 and in a regular course offering, 25.

Admissions: 96% of the 1995–96 applicants were accepted. The SAT I scores for the 1995–96 freshman class were as follows: Verbal—88% below 500, 11% between 500 and 599, and 1% between 600 and 700; Math—67% below 500, 25% between 500 and 599, 7% between 600 and 700, and 1% above 700. 21% of the current freshmen were in the top fifth of their class; 45% were in the top two fifths.

Requirements: The SAT I or ACT is recommended. The college requires applicants to be in the upper 60% of their class with a 2.0 GPA. Candidates should be graduates of an accredited secondary school or hold a GED diploma. They must have completed 16 Carnegie units, including 4 in English, 3 each in mathematics and social studies, 2 in science, and 1 in history. An interview is required for some and recommended for all others. AP and CLEP credits are accepted. Important factors in the admissions decision are advanced placement or honor courses, leadership record, and personality/intangible qualities.

Procedure: Freshmen are admitted to all sessions. Entrance exams should be taken by fall or late winter of the senior year. There are early admissions and deferred admissions plans. Application deadlines are open. Application fee is $20. Notification is sent on a rolling basis.

Transfer: 484 transfer students enrolled in 1995–96. Students must have a minimum 2.0 GPA in nondevelopmental academic courses. Those with fewer than 30 earned credits must also submit an official high school transcript and test results of the SAT I or ACT. An interview is recommended. 30 credits of 120 must be completed at the college.

Visiting: There are regularly scheduled orientations for prospective students. There are guides for informal visits and visitors may sit in on classes and stay overnight at the school. To schedule a visit, contact the Office of Admissions at (412) 262–8206 or (800) 762–0097.

Financial Aid: In 1995–96, 84% of all freshmen and 80% of continuing students received some form of financial aid. 73% of freshmen and 67% of continuing students received need-based aid. The average freshman award was $6141. Of that total, scholarships or need-based grants averaged $2958 ($6900 maximum); other grants averaged $900 ($6000 maxiumum); and loans averaged $2283 ($8200 maximum). 8% of undergraduate students work part-time. Average earnings from campus work for the school year are $1040. The college is a member of CSS. The college's own financial statement and PHEAA are required. The application deadline for fall entry is May 1.

International Students: There are currently 82 international students enrolled. They must take the TOEFL and achieve a minimum score of 500.

Computers: The college provides computer facilities for student use. The mainframes are a Prime 5370, an IBM 9370/90, and an IBM 9370/25. Students have access to 350 microcomputers at computer laboratories at each campus and 4 computerized classrooms. Students can also access mainframe systems with dial-up facilities. All students may access the system from 8 A.M. to 12 midnight Monday through Thursday, 8 A.M. to 9 P.M. Friday, 9 A.M. to 4 P.M. Saturday, and 9 A.M. to 11 P.M. Sunday. There are no time limits and no fees.

Graduates: In 1994–95, 792 bachelor's degrees were awarded. The most popular majors among graduates were accounting (22%), management (17%), and marketing (14%). Within an average freshman class, 32% graduate in 4 years, 19% in 5 years, and 4% in 6 years. 73 companies recruited on campus in 1994–95.

Admissions Contact: Jim Welsh, Dean of Admissions. E-mail: welsh@robert-morris.edu. A campus video is available.

ROSEMONT COLLEGE
F-4

Rosemont, PA 19010–1699   (610) 526–2966; (800) 331–0708

Full-time: 386 women	Faculty: 42; IIB, -$
Part-time: 20 men, 119 women	Ph.D.s: 80%
Graduate: 15 men, 49 women	Student/Faculty: 9 to 1
Year: semesters, summer session	Tuition: $12,375
Application Deadline: open	Room & Board: $6100
Freshman Class: 237 applied, 191 accepted, 81 enrolled	
SAT I Verbal/Math: 507/501	COMPETITIVE

Rosemont College, founded in 1921, is a private women's college, affiliated with the Roman Catholic Church, offering programs in liberal and fine arts, and business. An accelerated degree program is open to men. There is one graduate school. The library contains 154,776 volumes, 24,677 microform items, and 9879 audiovisual forms, and subscribes to 550 periodicals. Computerized library sources and services include the card catalog, interlibrary loans, and database searching. Special learning facilities include a learning resource center and art gallery. The 56-acre campus is in a suburban area 11 miles west of Philadelphia. Including residence halls, there are 15 buildings on campus.

Student Life: 50% of undergraduates are from out-of-state, mostly the Middle Atlantic. Students come from 18 states and 15 foreign countries. 40% are from public schools; 60% from private. 83% are white. 60% are Catholic; 17% Protestant; 15% Muslim. The average age of freshmen is 18; all undergraduates, 22. 15% do not continue beyond their first year; 70% remain to graduate.

Housing: 410 students can be accommodated in college housing. College-sponsored living facilities include dormitories. On-campus housing is guaranteed for all 4 years. 85% of students live on campus; of those, 50% remain on campus on weekends. All students may keep cars on campus.

Activities: There are no fraternities. There are 25 groups on campus, including art, chorus, drama, ethnic, international, literary magazine, newspaper, photography, political, religious, social service, student government, and yearbook. Popular campus events include Oktoberfest, 100 Days Party, Winter Luncheon, and Spring Luncheon.

Sports: Athletic and recreation facilities include facilities for indoor basketball, badminton, volleyball, hockey and softball fields, tennis courts, and a 500-seat auditorium.

Disabled Students: The following facilities are available: wheelchair ramps, elevators, special parking, special class scheduling, and lowered telephones.

Services: In addition to many counseling and information services, tutoring is available in every subject. There is a writing laboratory and learning resource center.

Campus Safety and Security: Campus safety and security measures include 24-hour foot and vehicle patrol, informal discussions, emergency telephones, and lighted pathways/sidewalks. In addition, there are electronically operated dormitory entrances activated by security cards.

Programs of Study: Rosemont confers B.A., B.S., and B.F.A. degrees. Master's degrees are also awarded. Bachelor's degrees are awarded in BIOLOGICAL SCIENCE (biochemistry and biology/biological science), BUSINESS (accounting and business administration and management), COMMUNICATIONS AND THE ARTS (English, fine arts, French, German, and Spanish), COMPUTER AND PHYSICAL SCIENCE (chemistry and mathematics), EDUCATION (art, elementary, foreign languages, and secondary), HEALTH PROFESSIONS (predentistry and premedicine), SOCIAL SCIENCE (American studies, economics, history, Italian studies, liberal arts/general studies, philosophy, political science/government, prelaw, psychology, religion, social science, and sociology). Psychology and English have the largest enrollments.

Required: All students take classes in rhetoric, literature, religious studies, foreign language, philosophy, history, calculus or natural science, social science, and physical education. A total of 120 credits is required for graduation, with 33 to 36 in the major, and a minimum GPA of 2.0.

Special: There is cross-registration with Villanova, Cabrini College, and the Eastern Art Institute, and a joint admission program with Medical College of Pennsylvania and Hahnemann University School of Medicine. Dual and student-designed majors are available, as well as various internships, a Washington semester, and study abroad. There is a freshman honors program on campus, as well as 4 national honor societies. 7 departments have honors programs.

Faculty/Classroom: 43% of faculty are male; 57%, female. All teach undergraduates and 70% both teach and do research. No introductory courses are taught by graduate students. The average class size in an introductory lecture is 22; in a laboratory, 15; and in a regular course offering, 12.

Admissions: 81% of the 1995–96 applicants were accepted. 30% of the current freshmen were in the top fifth of their class; 65% were in the top two fifths.

Requirements: The SAT I is required. A minimum GPA of 2.5 is required. The GED is accepted. Applicants must complete 16 academic credits, including 4 in English and 2 each in foreign language, history, mathematics, and science. An interview is recommended. AP and CLEP credits are accepted. Important factors in the admissions decision are leadership record, extracurricular activities record, and evidence of special talent.

Procedure: Freshmen are admitted fall and spring. There are early admissions and deferred admissions plans. Application deadlines are open. Application fee is $35. Notification is sent on a rolling basis.

Transfer: 35 transfer students enrolled in a recent year. Transfer applicants should submit transcripts from each college attended, a letter of good standing from the dean at the last college attended, and catalogs from the colleges from which the student wishes to transfer credits. Students with fewer than 30 credits are required to submit high school transcripts and SAT I scores. The minimum GPA is 2.0. An associate degree and interview are recommended. 60 credits of 120 must be completed at Rosemont.

Visiting: There are regularly scheduled orientations for prospective students, including campus visit days, overnight visits, and Class Visitations. There are guides for informal visits and visitors may sit in on classes and stay overnight at the school. To schedule a visit, contact Karin Pollin, Admissions.

Financial Aid: In 1995–96, 85% of all freshmen and 70% of continuing students received some form of financial aid. 75% of freshmen and 63% of continuing students received need-based aid. The average freshman award was $9050. Of that total, scholarships or need-based grants averaged $7888 ($16,952 maximum); loans averaged $2250 ($6625 maximum); and work contracts averaged $800 ($1500 maximum). 30% of undergraduate students work part-time. Average earnings from campus work for the school year are $600. The average financial indebtedness of the 1994–95 graduate was $8560. The FAF or FAFSA are required, and Pennsylvania residents must submit the PHEAA. The application deadline for fall entry is February 15.

International Students: There were recently 16 international students enrolled. The school actively recruits these students. They must take the TOEFL and achieve a minimum score of 500.

Computers: The college provides computer facilities for student use. The mainframe is an IBM 36. There are 75 Apple and IBM microcomputers available to all students in the library and the continuing education laboratory. All students may access the system during posted hours. There are no time limits and no fees.

Admissions Contact: Mary G. Van Arsdale, Director of Admissions. A campus video is available.

SAINT FRANCIS COLLEGE

Loretto, PA 15940

C-3

(814) 472-3100
(800) 342-5732; FAX: (814) 472-3335

Full-time: 578 men, 643 women
Part-time: 126 men, 233 women
Graduate: 164 men, 210 women
Year: semesters, summer session
Application Deadline: see profile
Freshman Class: 1215 applied, 1022 accepted, 334 enrolled
SAT I or ACT: required

Faculty: 76; IIB, -$
Ph.D.s: 72%
Student/Faculty: 16 to 1
Tuition: $12,590
Room & Board: $5350

COMPETITIVE

Saint Francis College, founded in 1847, is a private, coeducational, Franciscan institution affiliated with the Roman Catholic Church. It offers programs in business, education, humanities, sciences, social science, and preprofessional programs. There is 1 graduate school. In addition to regional accreditation, Saint Francis has baccalaureate program accreditation with CAHEA, CSWE, and NLN. The library contains 179,017 volumes, 48 microform items, and 108 audiovisual forms, and subscribes to 616 periodicals. Computerized library sources and services include the card catalog, interlibrary loans, and database searching. Special learning facilities include a learning resource center, art gallery, radio station, classroom satellite hookup, TV studio, and art studio. The 600-acre campus is in a rural area 85 miles east of Pittsburgh. Including residence halls, there are 23 buildings.

Student Life: 84% of undergraduates are from Pennsylvania. Students come from 33 states, 6 foreign countries, and Canada. 66% are from public schools; 34% from private. 95% are white. The average age of freshmen is 18.8; all undergraduates, 22.1. 18% do not continue beyond their first year; 70% remain to graduate.

Housing: 833 students can be accommodated in college housing. College-sponsored living facilities include single-sex dormitories, on-campus apartments, off-campus apartments, and married-student housing. In addition, there are intensive study floors. On-campus housing is guaranteed for all 4 years. 63% of students live on campus; of those, 80% remain on campus on weekends. Alcohol is not permitted. Upperclassmen may keep cars on campus.

Activities: 10% of men belong to 2 national fraternities; 17% of women belong to 1 local and 2 national sororities. There are 63 groups on campus, including art, cheerleading, choir, computers, drama, ethnic, honors, international, literary magazine, newspaper, pep band, photography, political, professional, radio and TV, religious, social, social service, student government, and yearbook. Popular campus events include a weekend movie program, soft rock cafe, and Springfest.

Sports: There are 8 intercollegiate sports for men and 8 for women, and 12 intramural sports for men and 12 for women. Athletic and recreation facilities include a physical education building with a pool for competition, racquetball courts, a suspended running track, a weight room, a 4000-seat gymnasium, and a multipurpose gymnasium for intramurals. Outdoor facilities include tennis and basketball courts, soccer, softball, and football facilities, a 9-hole golf course, a lake, and volleyball pits.

Disabled Students: 20% of the campus is accessible to disabled students. The following facilities are available: wheelchair ramps, elevators, special parking, and lowered telephones.

Services: In addition to many counseling and information services, tutoring is available in most subjects. There is remedial math, reading, and writing.

Campus Safety and Security: Campus safety and security measures include 24-hour foot and vehicle patrol, escort service, informal discussions, and pamphlets/posters/films. There are emergency telephones and lighted pathways/sidewalks.

Programs of Study: Saint Francis confers B.A., B.S., B.S.N., and B.S.W. degrees. Master's degrees are also awarded. Bachelor's degrees are awarded in BIOLOGICAL SCIENCE (biology/biological science), BUSINESS (accounting, human resources, management information systems, management science, and organizational behavior), COMMUNICATIONS AND THE ARTS (communications, English, French, modern language, and Spanish), COMPUTER AND PHYSICAL SCIENCE (chemistry, computer science, and mathematics), EDUCATION (elementary and secondary), ENGINEERING AND ENVIRONMENTAL DESIGN (engineering), HEALTH PROFESSIONS (medical laboratory technology, nursing, physical therapy, and physician's assistant), SOCIAL SCIENCE (American studies, anthropology, criminal justice, economics, history, international studies, philosophy, political science/government, psychology, public administration, religion, social work, and sociology). Business, allied health, sciences, and education have the largest enrollments.

Required: Students must complete 128 credits, with at least 36 in the major, while maintaining a 2.0 GPA. The core curriculum, totaling 58 credits, includes writing, public speaking, fine arts, foreign language, history, philosophy, religious studies (with required service component), psychology, sociology, political science, and economics. A word processing and research workshop is required in the freshman year.

Special: The college offers internships, co-op programs, study abroad, a Washington semester, work-study programs, and nondegree study. Student-designed majors and 3-2 engineering degrees with Penn State and Clarkson universities and the University of Pittsburgh are available. There is a dual major available in international business/modern languages. Credit by exam and pass/fail options are also offered. There is a freshman honors program on campus, as well as 8 national honor societies.

Faculty/Classroom: 68% of faculty are male; 32%, female. All teach undergraduates. The average class size in an introductory lecture is 25; in a laboratory, 20; and in a regular course offering, 16.

Admissions: 84% of the 1995-96 applicants were accepted. The SAT I scores for the 1995-96 freshman class were as follows: Verbal—80% below 500, 18% between 500 and 599, and 2% between 600 and 700; Math—46% below 500, 38% between 500 and 599, 15% between 600 and 700, and 1% above 700. The ACT scores were 32% below 21, 32% between 21 and 23, 23% between 24 and 26, 9% between 27 and 28, and 5% above 28. 39% of the current freshmen were in the top fifth of their class; 71% were in the top two fifths. 5 freshmen graduated first in their class.

Requirements: The SAT I or ACT is required. Applicants must have be graduated with a 2.0 GPA from an accredited secondary school or have earned a GED certificate. All applicants must have completed 16 Carnegie units, consisting of 4 years of English, 2 each of mathematics and social science, 1 laboratory science, and 7 academic electives. Applicants to biology and allied health majors need an additonal unit of science. Chemistry, computer science, engineering, and mathematics applicants need 4 mathematics units and 2 science units. Physical therapy applicants must have 4 units of mathematics and 4 of science. AP and CLEP credits are accepted. Important factors in the admissions decision are advanced placement or honor courses, recommendations by school officials, and extracurricular activities record.

Procedure: Freshmen are admitted to all sessions. Entrance exams should be taken spring of the junior year and fall of the senior year. There are early admissions and deferred admissions plans. Application deadlines are January 19 for physician's assistant and physical therapy majors; all other deadlines are open. The application fee is $30. Notification is sent on a rolling basis.

Transfer: 97 transfer students enrolled in a recent year. Applicants must have a minimum GPA of 2.0, 2.5 for nursing majors, and 2.75 for physician's assistant majors. 64 credits of 128 must be completed at Saint Francis.

Visiting: There are regularly scheduled orientations for prospective students, consisting of a campus tour, an admission interview, a financial aid interview, and class attendance. There are guides for informal visits and visitors may stay overnight at the school. To schedule a visit, contact the Admissions Office.

Financial Aid: In a recent year, 90% of all freshmen and 84% of continuing students received some form of financial aid. 83% of freshmen and 78% of continuing students received need-based aid. The average freshman award was $11,678. Of that total, scholarships or need-based grants averaged $8068 ($15,150 maximum); loans averaged $2620 ($3625 maximum); and work contracts averaged $990 ($1000 maximum). 51% of undergraduate students work part-time. Average earnings from campus work for the school year are $1010. Saint Francis is a member of CSS. The FAFSA and the college's own financial statement are required. The application deadline for fall entry is May 1.

International Students: In a recent year, 4 international students were enrolled. They must score 500 on the TOEFL and also take SAT I or the ACT.

Computers: The college provides computer facilities for student use. The mainframe is a DEC VAX 4000. Mainframe access is limited to computer science majors, who may gain access through only one of 3 computer laboratories. The microcomputer network of about 46 IBM PC, XT, AT, and compatible PCs is available to all students. There are no time limits and no fees.

Graduates: In a recent year, 192 bachelor's degrees were awarded. The most popular majors among graduates were management (23%), accounting (16%), and elementary education (9%). Within an average freshman class, 13% graduate in 3 years, 44% in 4 years, 11% in 5 years, and 2% in 6 years.

Admissions Contact: Gerard J. Rooney, Dean of Enrollment Management. E-mail: admissions@sfcpa.edu.

SAINT JOSEPH'S UNIVERSITY
Philadelphia, PA 19131

F-3

(610) 660-1300

Full-time: 1316 men, 1458 women	Faculty: 168; IIA, av$
Part-time: 530 men, 698 women	Ph.D.s: 94%
Graduate: 1354 men, 1588 women	Student/Faculty: 17 to 1
Year: semesters; summer session	Tuition: $13,950
Application Deadline: open	Room & Board: $6250
Freshman Class: 2791 applied, 2042 accepted, 804 enrolled	
SAT I Verbal/Math: 513/564	**VERY COMPETITIVE**

Saint Joseph's University, founded in 1851, is a Catholic, private, coeducational college affiliated with the Jesuit order. It offers undergraduate programs in arts and sciences and business administration. There are 3 undergraduate and 2 graduate schools. In addition to regional accreditation, Saint Joseph's has baccalaureate program accreditation with NCATE. The 2 libraries contain 324,000 volumes, 727,000 microform items, and 2000 audiovisual forms, and subscribe to 2000 periodicals. Computerized library sources and services include the card catalog, interlibrary loans, and database searching. Special learning facilities include a learning resource center, art gallery, radio station, instructional media center, and foreign language laboratories. The 60-acre campus is in a suburban area on the western edge of Philadelphia. Including residence halls, there are 48 buildings on campus.

Student Life: 60% of undergraduates are from Pennsylvania. Students come from 31 states, 26 foreign countries, and Canada. 34% are from public schools; 57% from private. 88% are white. Most are Catholic. The average age of freshmen is 18; all undergraduates, 20. 15% do not continue beyond their first year; 78% remain to graduate.

Housing: 1518 students can be accommodated in college housing. College-sponsored living facilities include single-sex and coed dormitories, on-campus apartments, and off-campus apartments. In addition there are honors houses and special interest houses. On-campus housing is guaranteed for all 4 years. 54% of students live on campus; of those, 65% remain on campus on weekends. Upperclassmen may keep cars on campus.

Activities: 19% of men belong to 4 national fraternities; 13% of women belong to 3 national sororities. There are 73 groups on campus, including art, cheerleading, choir, chorus, computers, dance, drama, ethnic, film, honors, international, jazz band, literary magazine, musical theater, newspaper, pep band, photography, political, professional, radio and TV, religious, social, social service, student government, and yearbook. Popular campus events include Hawktoberfest, Parents Weekend, Black Cultural Week, Thanksgiving Dinner Dance, Spring Fling, St. Joseph's Day, and Midnight Madness.

Sports: There are 10 intercollegiate sports for men and 9 for women, and 17 intramural sports for men and 14 for women. Athletic and recreation facilities include a gymnasium, fields, 4 multipurpose courts, an indoor and an outdoor track, 4 racquetball courts, a pool, Nautilus equipment, and tennis courts.

Disabled Students: 90% of the campus is accessible to disabled students. The following facilities are available: wheelchair ramps, elevators, special parking, specially equipped rest rooms, special class scheduling, lowered drinking fountains, lowered telephones, and automatic eye doors.

Services: In addition to many counseling and information services, tutoring is available in most subjects. There are also services for people with learning disabilities.

Campus Safety and Security: Campus safety and security measures include 24-hour foot and vehicle patrol, self-defense education, escort service, and shuttle buses. In addition, there are informal discussions, pamphlets/posters/films, emergency telephones, lighted pathways/sidewalks, and a bicycle patrol.

Programs of Study: Saint Joseph's confers B.A. and B.S. degrees. Associate and master's degrees are also awarded. Bachelor's degrees are awarded in BIOLOGICAL SCIENCE (biology/biological science), BUSINESS (accounting, banking and finance, business administration and management, labor studies, management science, and marketing/retailing/merchandising), COMMUNICATIONS AND THE ARTS (English, fine arts, French, German, and Spanish), COMPUTER AND PHYSICAL SCIENCE (chemistry, computer science, information sciences and systems, mathematics, and physics), EDUCATION (elementary and secondary), HEALTH PROFESSIONS (health care administration), SOCIAL SCIENCE (criminal justice, economics, food production/management/services, history, human services, humanities, industrial and organizational psychology, international relations, philosophy, political science/government, psychology, public administration, religion, social studies, and sociology). Social sciences, natural sciences, and English are the strongest academically. Biology, psychology, and English have the largest enrollments.

Required: All students must take general education common courses in language, theology, philosophy, and history. Distribution requirements include 3 courses each in social/behavioral sciences and theology, 2 courses of foreign language at the intermediate level, 2 courses each of mathematics and natural sciences, and a philosophy course. A total of 120 credit hours is required for graduation, with 21 to 54 in the major. A GPA of 2.0 is required.

Special: There is an exchange with a Japanese university and study abroad in 7 countries. The college offers internships, a Washington semester, dual majors, minor concentrations, and special programs in American, Latin American, European, Russian, gender, and medieval studies. There is a co-op program for food marketing majors and an interdisciplinary major in pharmaceutical marketing. There is a freshman honors program on campus, as well as 15 national honor societies. All departments have honors programs.

Faculty/Classroom: 72% of faculty are male; 28%, female. 98% teach undergraduates and 85% also do research. No introductory courses are taught by graduate students. The average class size in an introductory lecture is 29; in a laboratory, 20; and in a regular course offering, 22.

Admissions: 73% of the 1995-96 applicants were accepted. The SAT I scores for the 1995-96 freshman class were as follows: Verbal—50% below 500, 37% between 500 and 599, 12% between 600 and 700, and 1% above 700; Math—30% below 500, 44% between 500 and 599, 23% between 600 and 700, and 3% above 700. 57% of the current freshmen were in the top fifth of their class; 87% were in the top two fifths. 7 freshmen graduated first in their class.

Requirements: The SAT I or ACT is required. Saint Joseph's requires applicants to be in the upper 40% of their class. A minimum GPA of 2.75 is required. The SAT II: Subject test in writing is also recommended. Applicants must graduate from an accredited secondary school and prepare with 4 years of English, 3 of mathematics, 2 each of foreign language and science, and 1 each of history and social studies. Preference is given to students with 3 to 4 years of foreign language and natural science and 4 years of mathematics. An interview is recommended. Applications are accepted on computer disk via CollegeLink. AP and CLEP credits are accepted. Important factors in the admissions decision are advanced placement or honor courses, extracurricular activities record, and parents or siblings attending the school.

Procedure: Freshmen are admitted fall and spring. Entrance exams should be taken in the spring of the junior year or the fall of the senior year. There are early admissions and deferred admissions plans. Application deadlines are open. Application fee is $40. Notification is sent on a rolling basis.

Transfer: 85 transfer students enrolled in 1995-96. Transfer applicants must have a GPA of at least 2.5 and submit former test scores and high school and college transcripts. An interview is recommended. 60 credits of 120 must be completed at Saint Joseph's.

Visiting: There are regularly scheduled orientations for prospective students, including formal interviews, tours, and faculty visits. There are guides for informal visits and visitors may sit in on classes and stay overnight at the school. To schedule a visit, contact the Admissions Office.

Financial Aid: In 1995-96, 82% of all freshmen and 79% of continuing students received some form of financial aid. 77% of freshmen and 75% of continuing students received need-based aid. The average freshman award was $9532. Of that total, scholarships or need-based grants averaged $6407 ($13,990 maximum); loans averaged $2850 ($3625 maximum); and work contracts averaged $903 ($1000 maximum). 50% of undergraduate students work part-time. Average earnings from campus work for the school year are $1000. The average financial indebtedness of the 1994-95 graduate was $13,079. Saint Joseph's is a member of CSS. The FAFSA and the PHEAA financial statement are required. The application deadline for fall entry is May 1.

International Students: There were 224 international students enrolled in a recent year. The school actively recruits these students. They must take the TOEFL and achieve a minimum score of 500. The student must also take the SAT I or the ACT.

Computers: The college provides computer facilities for student use. The mainframes are minicomputers and servers. Campuswide access is provided by 6 computer laboratories and 3 PC classrooms (140 systems); in addition, residence facilities are networked (150 students). Dial-up access is also available. All students may access the system whenever the laboratory is open (about 90 hours per week) or any time if they are connected in their dormitory rooms. There are no time limits and no fees.

Graduates: In 1994-95, 617 bachelor's degrees were awarded. The most popular majors among graduates were food marketing (11%), accounting (11%), and psychology (10%). Within an average freshman class, 67% graduate in 4 years, 74% in 5 years, and 76% in 6 years. 96 companies recruited on campus in 1994-95. Of the 1994 graduating class, 14% were enrolled in graduate school within 6 months of graduation.

Admissions Contact: John M. Sullivan, Director of Admissions.

SAINT VINCENT COLLEGE
Latrobe, PA 15650

	B-2
	(412) 537-4540; FAX: (412) 537-4554
Full-time: 527 men, 516 women	Faculty: 79; IIB, -$
Part-time: 61 men, 78 women	Ph.D.s: 72%
Graduate: none	Student/Faculty: 13 to 1
Year: semesters	Tuition: $11,625
Application Deadline: May 1	Room & Board: $4200
Freshman Class: 684 applied, 582 accepted, 261 enrolled	
SAT I or ACT: required	COMPETITIVE

Saint Vincent College, founded in 1846, is a coeducational Catholic college of liberal arts and sciences sponsored by Benedictine monks. There is 1 graduate school. In addition to regional accreditation, Saint Vincent has baccalaureate program accreditation with AACSB. The library contains 251,498 volumes, 98,671 microform items, and 1287 audiovisual forms, and subscribes to 825 periodicals. Computerized library sources and services include the card catalog, interlibrary loans, and database searching. Special learning facilities include a learning resource center, art gallery, planetarium, radio station, TV station, an observatory, radio telescope, and a small business development center. The 100-acre campus is in a small town 35 miles east of Pittsburgh. Including residence halls, there are 21 buildings on campus.

Student Life: 88% of undergraduates are from Pennsylvania. Students come from 26 states and 10 foreign countries. 71% are from public schools; 29% from private. 95% are white. 74% are Catholic; 17% Protestant. The average age of freshmen is 18; all undergraduates, 20. 9% do not continue beyond their first year; 70% remain to graduate.

Housing: 835 students can be accommodated in college housing. College-sponsored living facilities include coed dormitories. In addition there is a 24-hour quiet, private study dormitory. On-campus housing is guaranteed for all 4 years. 78% of students live on campus; of those, 80% remain on campus on weekends. Alcohol is not permitted. All students may keep cars on campus.

Activities: There are no fraternities or sororities. There are 25 groups on campus, including art, campus ministry/service organization, choir, chorale, chorus, computers, dance, drama, ethnic, honors, international, jazz band, literary magazine, musical theater, newspaper, orchestra, political, professional, radio and TV, religious, social, social service, student government, symphony, and yearbook. Popular campus events include the indoor beach party, Challenge Program, and Sports Friendship Day.

Sports: There are 6 intercollegiate sports for men and 5 for women, and 4 intramural sports for men and 4 for women. Athletic and recreation facilities include a 2400-seat gymnasium, basketball and volleyball facilities, a weight and exercise room, indoor pool, tennis courts, baseball, soccer, and football fields, a mini movie theater, mini bowling alley, a 999-seat auditorium/arena, and a student union and game room area.

Disabled Students: 90% of the campus is accessible to disabled students. The following facilities are available: wheelchair ramps, elevators, special parking, specially equipped rest rooms, special class scheduling, lowered drinking fountains, and lowered telephones.

Services: In addition to many counseling and information services, tutoring is available in every subject. There is remedial math, reading, and writing. The Opportunity office provides individual counseling and a freshman study skills class.

Campus Safety and Security: Campus safety and security measures include 24-hour foot and vehicle patrol, informal discussions, pamphlets/posters/films, and lighted pathways/sidewalks.

Programs of Study: Saint Vincent confers B.A., B.S., and B.F.A. degrees. Master's degrees are also awarded. Bachelor's degrees are awarded in BIOLOGICAL SCIENCE (biochemistry and biology/biological science), BUSINESS (accounting, banking and finance, business administration and management, marketing/retailing/merchandising, and retailing), COMMUNICATIONS AND THE ARTS (art, communications, design, dramatic arts, English, fine arts, French, graphic design, music, music performance, Spanish, studio art, and visual and performing arts), COMPUTER AND PHYSICAL SCIENCE (chemistry, computer science, information sciences and systems, mathematics, and physics), EDUCATION (art, foreign languages, home economics, and music), ENGINEERING AND ENVIRONMENTAL DESIGN (environmental science and interior design), HEALTH PROFESSIONS (art therapy, medical laboratory technology, predentistry, premedicine, prepharmacy, and preveterinary science), SOCIAL SCIENCE (child care/child and family studies, dietetics, economics, history, philosophy, political science/government, prelaw, psychology, religion, social work, and sociology). Biology, accounting, and chemistry are the strongest academically. Accounting, biology, and management have the largest enrollments.

Required: All students are required to take Language and Rhetoric, Exploring Religious Meaning, and Philosophy I. The core curriculum includes 12 credits of social science, 9 each of English, history, philos-

ophy and religion, 8 of natural sciences, 6 of a foreign language, and 3 of mathematics. Some majors require comprehensive exams, and all majors except English and business require a thesis. Students must complete 124 credits and achieve a minimum GPA of 2.0.

Special: There is cross-registration with Seton Hill College, co-op programs, internships, study abroad in Europe and Asia, a Washington semester, a work-study program, dual majors, a general studies degree, credit by exam and for life/military/work experience, nondegree study and pass/fail options. There is an accelerated degree engineering program, and a 3–2 engineering option with Boston University and Pennsylvania State University, and the University of Pittsburgh. The college offers teacher certificate programs in early childhood, elementary, and secondary education. There is a freshman honors program on campus, as well as 4 national honor societies, including Phi Beta Kappa.

Faculty/Classroom: 80% of faculty are male; 20%, female. All both teach and do research. The average class size in an introductory lecture is 24; in a laboratory, 15; and in a regular course offering, 20.

Admissions: 85% of the 1995–96 applicants were accepted. The SAT I scores for the 1995–96 freshman class were as follows: Verbal—61% below 500, 29% between 500 and 599, 9% between 600 and 700, and 1% above 700; Math—43% below 500, 31% between 500 and 599, 22% between 600 and 700, and 4% above 700. 48% of the current freshmen were in the top fifth of their class; 77% were in the top two fifths. 7 freshmen graduated first in their class.

Requirements: The SAT I or ACT is required. Applicants must complete 15 academic credits, including 4 of English, 3 of social studies, 2 each of foreign language and mathematics, and 1 of a laboratory science. Art students must submit a portfolio, and music and theater students must audition. An essay is required. A GED is accepted. AP and CLEP credits are accepted. Important factors in the admissions decision are advanced placement or honor courses, evidence of special talent, and recommendations by school officials.

Procedure: Freshmen are admitted fall and spring. Entrance exams should be taken at the end of the junior year or beginning of the senior year. There are early admissions and deferred admissions plans. Applications should be filed by May 1 for fall entry and January 1 for spring entry, along with an application fee of $25. Notification is sent on a rolling basis.

Transfer: 36 transfer students enrolled in 1995–96. Applicants must submit transcripts from post-secondary schools attended and a catalog describing courses taken. 34 credits of 124 must be completed at Saint Vincent.

Visiting: There are regularly scheduled orientations for prospective students, consisting of a general information session, an informal meeting with faculty, and campus tours. There are guides for informal visits and visitors may sit in on classes and stay overnight at the school. To schedule a visit, contact the Admissions and Financial Aid Office.

Financial Aid: In 1995–96, 97% of all freshmen and 85% of continuing students received some form of financial aid. 81% of freshmen and 80% of continuing students received need-based aid. The average freshman award was $9894. Of that total, scholarships or need-based grants averaged $4880 ($11,625 maximum); loans averaged $2567 ($3950 maximum); and work contracts averaged $1200 ($2104 maximum). 44% of undergraduate students work part-time. Average earnings from campus work for the school year are $1066. The average financial indebtedness of the 1994–95 graduate was $16,400. Saint Vincent is a member of CSS. The FAFSA is required. The application deadline for fall entry is May 1.

International Students: There are currently 12 international students enrolled. They must take the TOEFL and achieve a minimum score of 525.

Computers: The college provides computer facilities for student use. The mainframe is an HP 9000/Series 800 G50. Two large computer terminal centers on campus can accommodate between 25 to 40 students each. In addition, there are 3 smaller computer centers located in various areas throughout the campus, 5 DOS PC laboratories and 2 Macintosh laboratories. All students may access the system during computer laboratory hours. The time limit is 30 minutes if someone is waiting. There are no fees.

Graduates: In 1994–95, 247 bachelor's degrees were awarded. The most popular majors among graduates were psychology (12%), liberal arts (9%), and accounting (9%). Within an average freshman class, 1% graduate in 3 years, 56% in 4 years, 10% in 5 years, and 2% in 6 years. 60 companies recruited on campus in 1994–95. Of the 1994 graduating class, 20% were enrolled in graduate school within 6 months of graduation and 73% had found employment.

Admissions Contact: Admission and Financial Aid Office. A campus video is available.

SETON HILL COLLEGE
Greensburg, PA 15601-1599

B-4

(412) 838-4255
(800) 826-6234; FAX: (412) 830-4611

Full-time: 36 men, 592 women	Faculty: 45; IIB, -$
Part-time: 45 men, 207 women	Ph.Ds: 67%
Graduate: 1 man, 11 women	Student/Faculty: 14 to 1
Year: semesters, summer session	Tuition: $11,775
Application Deadline: open	Room & Board: $4435
Freshman Class: 255 applied, 241 accepted, 114 enrolled	
SAT I Verbal/Math: 450/460	COMPETITIVE

Seton Hill College, founded in 1883, is a private, primarily women's college affiliated with the Catholic Church and offering programs in liberal arts. There is 1 graduate school. In addition to regional accreditation, Seton Hill has baccalaureate program accreditation with ADA and NASM. The library contains 105,000 volumes, 5500 microform items, and 4555 audiovisual forms, and subscribes to 465 periodicals. Computerized library sources and services include the card catalog, interlibrary loans, and database searching. Special learning facilities include an art gallery, TV station, a nursery school and kindergarten that function as laboratory schools for education students, performance hall, and 2 theaters. The 200-acre campus is in a small town 35 miles east of Pittsburgh. Including residence halls, there are 17 buildings on campus.

Student Life: 80% of undergraduates are from Pennsylvania. Students come from 15 states and 6 foreign countries. 80% are from public schools; 20% from private. 88% are white. The average age of freshmen is 18; all undergraduates, 21. 22% do not continue beyond their first year; 58% remain to graduate.

Housing: 550 students can be accommodated in college housing. College-sponsored living facilities include single-sex dormitories. On-campus housing is guaranteed for all 4 years. 70% of students live on campus. Alcohol is not permitted. All students may keep cars on campus.

Activities: There are no fraternities or sororities. There are 30 groups on campus, including animal rights, cheerleading, choir, chorale, chorus, drama, environment, ethnic, film, honors, international, literary magazine, newspaper, orchestra, political, professional, radio and TV, religious, social, social service, student government, symphony, and yearbook. Popular campus events include Christmas on the Hill, Senior Dinner Dance, and President's Reception.

Sports: There are 7 intercollegiate sports and a variety of intramural sports. Athletic and recreation facilities include a gymnasium, a swimming pool, tennis courts, softball and soccer fields, a weight room, a jacuzzi, a sauna, and a fitness trail. The indoor gymnasium seats 650, the largest auditorium/arena 300.

Disabled Students: 95% of the campus is accessible to disabled students. The following facilities are available: wheelchair ramps, elevators, special parking, specially equipped rest rooms, special class scheduling, lowered drinking fountains, and lowered telephones.

Services: In addition to many counseling and information services, tutoring is available in most subjects. There is a reader service for the blind and remedial math and writing.

Campus Safety and Security: Campus safety and security measures include 24-hour foot and vehicle patrol, self-defense education, escort service, and shuttle buses. In addition, there are informal discussions, pamphlets/posters/films, emergency telephones, and lighted pathways/sidewalks.

Programs of Study: Seton Hill confers B.A., B.S., B.F.A., B.Mus., B.S.Med.Tech., and B.S.W. degrees. Master's degrees are also awarded. Bachelor's degrees are awarded in BIOLOGICAL SCIENCE (biochemistry and biology/biological science), BUSINESS (accounting, banking and finance, business administration and management, business economics, fashion merchandising, international business management, marketing/retailing/merchandising, and personnel management), COMMUNICATIONS AND THE ARTS (communications, design, dramatic arts, English, fine arts, French, journalism, music, musical theater, performing arts, Spanish, and studio art), COMPUTER AND PHYSICAL SCIENCE (actuarial science, chemistry, computer science, mathematics, and physics), EDUCATION (art, early childhood, elementary, home economics, music, and secondary), HEALTH PROFESSIONS (art therapy, medical laboratory technology, nursing, occupational therapy, physical therapy, predentistry, premedicine, and preveterinary science), SOCIAL SCIENCE (dietetics, economics, family/consumer studies, food production/management/services, history, philosophy, political science/government, prelaw, psychology, religion, religious music, social work, and sociology). Psychology, biology, and art have the largest enrollments.

Required: The core curriculum requires 8 credits in Western cultural traditions, 7 in freshman seminar, 6 each in theology and philosophy/senior seminar, 4 each in mathematics and science, 3 each in intermediate-level foreign language, American studies, world cultures, and artistic expression, and 2 in self-awareness courses. A total

of 128 credit hours with a minimum GPA of 2.0 is required for graduation.

Special: There are cooperative programs in all majors and cross-registration with St. Vincent College, the University of Pittsburgh at Greensburg, and Westmoreland County Community College. Internships are encouraged. Seton Hill offers study abroad, a Washington semester, work-study, dual and student-designed majors, a 3–2 engineering program with Pennsylvania State University and Georgia Institute of Technology, a 2–2 nursing program with Catholic University of America, a 3–2 or 3–1 medical technology program with area hospitals, credit by examination and for life/military/work experience, nondegree study, and pass/fail options. There is a freshman honors program on campus, as well as 5 national honor societies.

Faculty/Classroom: 44% of faculty are male; 56%, female. All teach undergraduates. 60% also do research. The average class size in an introductory lecture is 25; in a laboratory, 16; and in a regular course offering, 18.

Admissions: 95% of the 1995–96 applicants were accepted. The SAT I scores for the 1995–96 freshman class were as follows: Verbal—20% between 500 and 599, 5% between 600 and 700, and 1% above 700; Math—25% between 500 and 599 and 7% between 600 and 700. 75% of the current freshmen were in the top two fifths of their class. 2 freshmen graduated first in their class.

Requirements: The SAT I or ACT is required. A 2.5 GPA and 15 Carnegie units are required, including 4 each of English and electives, 2 each of mathematics, social studies, and foreign language, and 1 of a laboratory science. Art students must submit a portfolio; music and theater students must audition. An interview is recommended. The GED is accepted with supporting recommendations. AP and CLEP credits are accepted. Important factors in the admissions decision are advanced placement or honor courses, evidence of special talent, and leadership record.

Procedure: Freshmen are admitted fall and spring. Entrance exams should be taken in spring of the junior year or fall of the senior year. There are early admissions and deferred admissions plans. Application deadlines are open. Application fee is $30. Notification is sent on a rolling basis.

Transfer: 55 transfer students enrolled in 1995–96. Applicants must submit college transcripts and have a GPA of at least 2.0. An interview is recommended, as are supporting letters. 48 credits of 128 must be completed at Seton Hill.

Visiting: There are regularly scheduled orientations for prospective students, consisting of an introduction, an address by the president or dean, an open reception with faculty, a financial aid session, a student panel, a campus tour, and an overnight visit followed by class attendance, if desired. There are guides for informal visits and visitors may sit in on classes and stay overnight at the school. To schedule a visit, contact the Director of Admissions.

Financial Aid: In 1995–96, 98% of all freshmen and 92% of continuing students received some form of financial aid. 90% of freshmen and 80% of continuing students received need-based aid. The average freshman award was $9805. Of that total, scholarships or need-based grants averaged $4500 ($11,775 maximum); loans averaged $2700 ($4125 maximum); and work contracts averaged $750 ($1148 maximum). 47% of undergraduate students work part-time. Average earnings from campus work for the school year are $900. The average financial indebtedness of the 1994–95 graduate was $10,865. Seton Hill is a member of CSS. The FAF or FAFSA, and the college's own financial statement are required. The PHEAA form may be used in place of the FAF. The application deadline for fall entry is July 1.

International Students: There are currently 15 international students enrolled. The school actively recruits these students. They must take the TOEFL and achieve a minimum score of 500.

Computers: The college provides computer facilities for student use. The mainframe is a DEC VAX. Students have access to 80 microcomputers on campus, including IBM and Apple units. All students may access the system. There are no time limits and no fees.

Graduates: In 1994–95, 174 bachelor's degrees were awarded. The most popular majors among graduates were management (13%), psychology (12%), and art (12%). Within an average freshman class, 50% graduate in 4 years, 55% in 5 years, and 58% in 6 years. 20 companies recruited on campus in 1994–95. Of the 1994 graduating class, 25% were enrolled in graduate school within 6 months of graduation and 91% had found employment.

Admissions Contact: Director of Admissions.

SHIPPENSBURG UNIVERSITY OF PENNSYLVANIA

C-4

Shippensburg, PA 17257-2299   (717) 532-1231
(800) 822-8028; FAX: (717) 530-4016

Full-time: 2457 men, 2830 women	Faculty: 299; IIA, + +$
Part-time: 136 men, 153 women	Ph.D.s: 80%
Graduate: 426 men, 599 women	Student/Faculty: 18 to 1
Year: semesters; summer session	Tuition: $4010 ($8984)
Application Deadline: open	Room & Board: $3600
Freshman Class: 5506 applied, 3597 accepted, 1281 enrolled	
SAT I Verbal/Math: 457/518	**COMPETITIVE**

Shippensburg University, founded in 1871, is a public university that is part of the Pennsylvania State System of Higher Education offering bachelor's and master's degree programs in the College of Arts and Sciences, College of Business, and College of Education and Human Services. There are 3 undergraduate schools and one graduate school. In addition to regional accreditation, Ship has baccalaureate program accreditation with AACSB, CSWE, and NCATE. The library contains 432,666 volumes, 1,605,704 microform items, and 10,771 audiovisual forms, and subscribes to 1783 periodicals. Computerized library sources and services include the card catalog, interlibrary loans, and database searching. Special learning facilities include a learning resource center, art gallery, planetarium, radio station, TV station, closed-circuit television, a fashion archives center, a vertebrate museum, and a women's center. The 200-acre campus is in a rural area 40 miles southwest of Harrisburg. Including residence halls, there are 35 buildings on campus.

Student Life: 92% of undergraduates are from Pennsylvania. Students come from 22 states, 40 foreign countries, and Canada. 93% are white. The average age of freshmen is 18; all undergraduates, 20. 17% do not continue beyond their first year; 66% remain to graduate.

Housing: 2366 students can be accommodated in college housing. College-sponsored living facilities include single-sex and coed dormitories and on-campus apartments. In addition there is a designated 'quiet' hall. On-campus housing is guaranteed for all 4 years. 57% of students commute. Alcohol is not permitted. All students may keep cars on campus.

Activities: 15% of men belong to 1 local and 12 national fraternities; 15% of women belong to 3 local and 8 national sororities. There are more than 100 groups on campus, including art, band, cheerleading, choir, chorale, chorus, computers, dance, drama, ethnic, gay, honors, international, jazz band, literary magazine, marching band, musical theater, newspaper, orchestra, political, professional, radio and TV, religious, social, social service, student government, and yearbook. Popular campus events include planetarium shows, Senior Olympics, and Summer Music Festival.

Sports: There are 8 intercollegiate sports for men and 10 for women, and 14 intramural sports for men and 9 for women. Athletic and recreation facilities include athletic fields, practice areas, an 8000-seat stadium, a gymnasium, a field house, 2 swimming pools, squash courts, a rehabilitation center, and a fitness center.

Disabled Students: 90% of the campus is accessible to disabled students. The following facilities are available: wheelchair ramps, elevators, special parking, specially equipped rest rooms, special class scheduling, lowered drinking fountains, lowered telephones, and facilities for hearing-impaired, visually impaired, and speech and communication disorders.

Services: In addition to many counseling and information services, tutoring is available in most subjects. There is a reader service for the blind, and remedial math, reading, and writing.

Campus Safety and Security: Campus safety and security measures include 24-hour foot and vehicle patrol, escort service, informal discussions, and pamphlets/posters/films. In addition, there are emergency telephones and lighted pathways/sidewalks.

Programs of Study: Ship confers B.A., B.S., B.S.B.A., and B.S.Ed. degrees. Master's degrees are also awarded. Bachelor's degrees are awarded in BIOLOGICAL SCIENCE (biology/biological science), BUSINESS (accounting, banking and finance, management science, marketing/retailing/merchandising, office supervision and management, and real estate), COMMUNICATIONS AND THE ARTS (art, English, French, German, journalism, media arts, Spanish, and speech/debate/rhetoric), COMPUTER AND PHYSICAL SCIENCE (applied physics, chemistry, computer science, earth science, information sciences and systems, mathematics, and physics), EDUCATION (business and elementary), ENGINEERING AND ENVIRONMENTAL DESIGN (environmental science), HEALTH PROFESSIONS (medical laboratory technology), SOCIAL SCIENCE (criminal justice, economics, geography, history, interdisciplinary studies, political science/government, psychology, public administration, social studies, social work, sociology, and urban studies). Elementary education, accounting, and criminal justice have the largest enrollments.

Required: General education courses include English composition, mathematics, and history, as well as courses in language and numbers for rational thinking; literary, artistic, and cultural traditions; laboratory science; biological and physical science; political, economic, and geographic sciences; and social and behavioral sciences. The core curriculum varies for degree programs. Most degree programs require 120 credit hours, with 22 to 30 hours in the major, and a 2.0 minimum GPA for graduation.

Special: The university offers internships, study abroad in Great Britain, Germany, Austria, France, and Spain, and a 3–2 engineering degree with Pennsylvania State University and the University of Maryland. There is a cooperative art program with design schools in Pennsylvania and 6 other states as well as a cooperative program in the health sciences. There is a freshman honors program on campus, as well as 21 national honor societies. One department has an honors program.

Faculty/Classroom: 66% of faculty are male; 34%, female. 95% teach undergraduates, 33% do research, and 33% do both. No introductory courses are taught by graduate students. The average class size in an introductory lecture is 30; in a laboratory, 18; and in a regular course offering, 18.

Admissions: 65% of the 1995–96 applicants were accepted. The SAT I scores for the 1995–96 freshman class were as follows: Verbal—73% below 500, 24% between 500 and 599, and 3% between 600 and 700; Math—41% below 500, 44% between 500 and 599, 14% between 600 and 700, and 1% above 700. 34% of the current freshmen were in the top fifth of their class; 72% were in the top two fifths.

Requirements: The SAT I is required. Applicants are urged to pursue a typical college preparatory program, which should include 4 years of English, 3 years each of social sciences, sequential mathematics, and laboratory science, and 2 years of 1 foreign language. A GED is accepted. AP and CLEP credits are accepted. Important factors in the admissions decision are advanced placement or honor courses, recommendations by school officials, and evidence of special talent.

Procedure: Freshmen are admitted fall and spring. Entrance exams should be taken in the junior year and no later than fall of the senior year. There are early admissions and deferred admissions plans. Application deadlines are open. Application fee is $25. Notification is sent on a rolling basis.

Transfer: 408 transfer students enrolled in a recent year. Candidates should have completed 30 semester hours of college-level work. 45 credits of 120 must be completed at Ship.

Visiting: There are regularly scheduled orientations for prospective students, including academic department group meetings, book discussion, workshops on study skills, time management, reading textbooks, and a campus tour. There are guides for informal visits and visitors may sit in on classes. To schedule a visit, contact the Admissions Office.

Financial Aid: In 1995–96, 65% of all freshmen and 62% of continuing students received some form of financial aid. 49% of freshmen and 42% of continuing students received need-based aid. The average freshman award was $4777. Of that total, scholarships or need-based grants averaged $4273 ($12,800 maximum); loans averaged $3470 ($13,927 maximum); and work contracts averaged $1116 ($3000 maximum). 25% of undergraduate students work part-time. Average earnings from campus work for the school year are $1200. Ship is a member of CSS. The FAF and PHEAA are required. The application deadline for fall entry is May 1.

International Students: There are currently 81 international students enrolled. They must take the TOEFL and achieve a minimum score of 550. The student must also take the SAT I or ACT if native language is English.

Computers: The college provides computer facilities for student use. The mainframe is a Unisys 2200/501. Terminals are located throughout the campus, and dial-in telephone lines give access to the mainframe. Student instruction and faculty research is also supported on a DEC AlphaServer. Access to the SAS statistical package, Internet, and instruction in the use of the ORACLE relational database are via this system. Shippen, Library, and Horton Hall microlaboratories contain 60 PCs and 60 Macintosh computers. Various departmental laboratories are also available. All students may access the system. There are no time limits and no fees. It is recommended that students in computer science and accounting have personal computers.

Graduates: In 1994–95, 1114 bachelor's degrees were awarded. The most popular majors among graduates were teacher education (21%), criminal justice (9%), and management (7%). Within an average freshman class, 41% graduate in 4 years, 62% in 5 years, and 65% in 6 years. More than 150 companies recruited on campus in 1994–95.

Admissions Contact: Joseph G. Cretella, Dean of Admissions. E-mail: admissions@ark.ship.edu. A campus video is available.

SLIPPERY ROCK UNIVERSITY

B-2

Slippery Rock, PA 16057
Full-time: 2666 men, 3202 women
Part-time: 288 men, 601 women
Graduate: 232 men, 504 women
Year: semesters, summer session
Application Deadline: April 1
Freshman Class: 3130 applied, 2688 accepted, 1239 enrolled
SAT I Verbal/Math: 410/450

(412) 738-2015; (800) 662-1102
Faculty: 376; IIA, +$
Ph.D.s: 66%
Student/Faculty: 16 to 1
Tuition: $4014 ($8988)
Room & Board: $3478 ($3478)

COMPETITIVE

Slippery Rock University, founded in 1889, is a public institution that is part of the Pennsylvania State System of Higher Education. It offers programs in the arts and sciences, education, health and human services, and information science and business administration. There are 4 undergraduate schools and one graduate school. In addition to regional accreditation, The Rock has baccalaureate program accreditation with APTA, CSWE, NCATE, and NLN. The library contains 767,220 volumes, 1,100,000 microform items, and 16,000 audiovisual forms, and subscribes to 1649 periodicals. Computerized library sources and services include the card catalog, interlibrary loans, and database searching. Special learning facilities include a learning resource center, art gallery, natural history museum, planetarium, radio station, TV station, and a wellness center. The 600-acre campus is in a small town 50 miles north of Pittsburgh. Including residence halls, there are 60 buildings on campus.

Student Life: 90% of undergraduates are from Pennsylvania. Students come from 43 states, 61 foreign countries, and Canada. 70% are from public schools; 30% from private. 92% are white. The average age of freshmen is 19; all undergraduates, 21. 22% do not continue beyond their first year; 54% remain to graduate.

Housing: 2800 students can be accommodated in college housing. College-sponsored living facilities include single-sex and coed dormitories. In addition there are honors houses and special interest houses. On-campus housing is guaranteed for all 4 years. 56% of students live on campus; of those, 75% remain on campus on weekends. Alcohol is not permitted. All students may keep cars on campus.

Activities: 10% of men belong to 10 national fraternities; 10% of women belong to 8 national sororities. There are 120 groups on campus, including art, band, cheerleading, chess, choir, chorale, chorus, computers, dance, drama, ethnic, film, gay, honors, international, jazz band, literary magazine, marching band, musical theater, newspaper, orchestra, pep band, photography, political, professional, radio and TV, religious, social, social service, student government, symphony, and yearbook. Popular campus events include Homecoming and Spring Weekend.

Sports: There are 12 intercollegiate sports for men and 12 for women, and 7 intramural sports for men and 7 for women. Athletic and recreation facilities include a field house, gymnasium, and fitness center. The campus stadium seats 10,000, the indoor gymnasium seats 3000, and the largest auditorium/arena seats 7500.

Disabled Students: 98% of the campus is accessible to disabled students. The following facilities are available: wheelchair ramps, elevators, special parking, specially equipped rest rooms, special class scheduling, lowered drinking fountains, and lowered telephones.

Services: In addition to many counseling and information services, tutoring is available in some subjects, including about 60 introductory-level general liberal studies courses. There is a reader service for the blind and remedial math and writing.

Campus Safety and Security: Campus safety and security measures include 24-hour foot and vehicle patrol, escort service, shuttle buses, and informal discussions. In addition, there are pamphlets/posters/films, and lighted pathways/sidewalks. The university maintains its own police department, with officers having the same powers as municipal police.

Programs of Study: The Rock confers B.A., B.S., B.B.A., B.F.A., B.Mus., B.Mus.Ed., B.S. Ed., and B.S.N. degrees. Master's and doctoral degrees are also awarded. Bachelor's degrees are awarded in BIOLOGICAL SCIENCE (biology/biological science), BUSINESS (accounting, business administration and management, international business management, and marketing/retailing/merchandising), COMMUNICATIONS AND THE ARTS (communications, dance, English, fine arts, French, German, music, and Spanish), COMPUTER AND PHYSICAL SCIENCE (chemistry, computer science, earth science, geology, information sciences and systems, mathematics, and physics), EDUCATION (early childhood, elementary, foreign languages, health, music, science, secondary, and special), HEALTH PROFESSIONS (community health work, medical laboratory technology, and nursing), SOCIAL SCIENCE (anthropology, economics, geography, history, parks and recreation management, philosophy, political science/government, psychology, public administration, social science, social work, and sociology). Business, education, and health science have the largest enrollments.

Required: B.A. students must demonstrate proficiency in a foreign language, and all must complete 42 to 53 credits in a 7-part liberal studies program, including basic competencies, arts, cultural diversity/global perspective, human institutions, science and mathematics, natural experience, and modern age. Specific requirements include public speaking, college writing, algebra, and physical education. A minimum of 128 credit hours, with at least 30 in the major, is required for graduation.

Special: Study abroad is available in 15 countries. Internships are offered in all majors, and international internships are available in Scotland and England. There is a 3-2 engineering program with Pennsylvania State University. The dual major is an option, and credit is given for military experience. Pass/fail options also are available. There is a freshman honors program on campus, as well as 26 national honor societies. 33 departments have honors programs.

Faculty/Classroom: 54% of faculty are male; 46%, female. All teach undergraduates. No introductory courses are taught by graduate students. The average class size in an introductory lecture is 35; in a laboratory, 15; and in a regular course offering, 25.

Admissions: 86% of the 1995-96 applicants were accepted. The SAT I scores for the 1995-96 freshman class were as follows: Verbal—87% below 500, 12% between 500 and 599, and 2% between 600 and 700; Math—70% below 500, 23% between 500 and 599, 6% between 600 and 700, and 1% above 700. 21% of the current freshmen were in the top fifth of their class; 50% were in the top two fifths.

Requirements: The SAT I or ACT is recommended. The Rock requires applicants to be in the upper 60% of their class. Students should graduate from an accredited secondary school with a 2.5 or have a GED. A total of 16 academic credits is required. The recommended college preparatory program includes 4 years of English and social studies, 3 each of science and mathematics, and 2 of a foreign language. An interview is recommended. AP and CLEP credits are accepted. Important factors in the admissions decision are advanced placement or honor courses, geographic diversity, and evidence of special talent.

Procedure: Freshmen are admitted to all sessions. Entrance exams should be taken in the junior year or fall of the senior year. There are early admissions and deferred admissions plans. Applications should be filed by April 1 for fall entry, November 1 for spring entry, and April 1 for summer entry. Notification is sent on a rolling basis.

Transfer: 566 transfer students enrolled in 1995-96. Applicants should have completed at least 24 credit hours with a GPA of 2.5. The SAT I or ACT, as well as an interview, is recommended. 36 credits of 128 must be completed at The Rock.

Visiting: There are regularly scheduled orientations for prospective students, including a meeting with faculty, an information fair, and a campus tour. There are guides for informal visits and visitors may sit in on classes and stay overnight at the school. To schedule a visit, contact the Admissions Office.

Financial Aid: In 1995-96, 78% of all freshmen and 81% of continuing students received some form of financial aid. 70% of freshmen and 73% of continuing students received need-based aid. The average freshman award was $3000. Of that total, scholarships or need-based grants averaged $1300 ($4900 maximum); loans averaged $2000 ($2625 maximum); and work contracts averaged $800 ($2720 maximum). 15% of undergraduate students work part-time. Average earnings from campus work for the school year are $800. The average financial indebtedness of the 1994-95 graduate was $9000. The Rock is a member of CSS. The application deadline for fall entry is May 1.

International Students: There are currently 211 international students enrolled. The school actively recruits these students. They must take the TOEFL and achieve a minimum score of 500.

Computers: The college provides computer facilities for student use. The mainframe is an IBM ES 9000. About 100 public-use terminals are available for students and faculty, along with 200 microcomputers in 8 public areas. Networked microcomputers also have access to the mainframe and its gateway to Bitnet and Internet. All students may access the system. The mainframe system is accessible 24 hours a day. Campus terminal and microcomputer laboratories are generally open about 90 hours per week. There are no time limits and no fees.

Graduates: In 1994-95, 1195 bachelor's degrees were awarded. The most popular majors among graduates were elementary education (18%), physical education (10%), and communications (8%). Within an average freshman class, 27% graduate in 4 years, 46% in 5 years, and 50% in 6 years. 400 companies recruited on campus in 1994-95.

Admissions Contact: Duncan Sargent, Director of Admissions.

SUSQUEHANNA UNIVERSITY

D-3

Selinsgrove, PA 17870–1001 (717) 372-4260; (800) 326-9672

Full-time: 747 men, 821 women	Faculty: 103; IIB, av$
Part-time: 5 men, 8 women	Ph.D.s: 88%
Graduate: none	Student/Faculty: 15 to 1
Year: semesters, summer session	Tuition: $17,080
Application Deadline: March 1	Room & Board: $4900
Freshman Class: 2081 applied, 1524 accepted, 449 enrolled	
SAT I: required	**VERY COMPETITIVE**

Susquehanna University, founded in 1858, is an independent, selective, undergraduate, coeducational residential institution affiliated with the Lutheran Church. It offers programs through schools of arts and sciences, fine arts and communications, and business. There are 3 undergraduate schools. In addition to regional accreditation, S.U. has baccalaureate program accreditation with AACSB and NASM. The library contains 229,000 volumes, 97,200 microform items, and 10,700 audiovisual forms, and subscribes to 1400 periodicals. Computerized library sources and services include the card catalog, interlibrary loans, and database searching. Special learning facilities include a learning resource center; an art gallery; a radio station; a campuswide voice and data telecommunications network, including residence hall connections, satellite dishes, and a distribution system for foreign language broadcasts; an interactive video conferencing facility; a special multimedia classroom; an ecological field station; a 28-inch reflecting telescope and an observatory; a greenhouse; a child development center; and a 450-seat theater. The 210-acre campus is in a small town 50 miles north of Harrisburg. Including residence halls, there are 52 buildings on campus.

Student Life: 58% of undergraduates are from Pennsylvania. Students come from 24 states and 8 foreign countries. 82% are from public schools; 18% from private. 84% are white. 55% are Protestant; 36% Catholic. The average age of freshmen is 18; all undergraduates, 20. 16% do not continue beyond their first year; 73% remain to graduate.

Housing: 1200 students can be accommodated in college housing. College-sponsored living facilities include single-sex and coed dormitories, on-campus apartments, fraternity houses, and sorority houses. In addition there are honors houses, special interest houses, and multicultural and international houses. Volunteer project groups may reside in former private homes adjacent to the university with suite-type accommodations. On-campus housing is guaranteed for all 4 years. 80% of students live on campus; of those, 85% remain on campus on weekends. All students may keep cars on campus.

Activities: 30% of men belong to 4 national fraternities; 30% of women belong to 4 national sororities. There are 100 groups on campus, including art, band, cheerleading, chess, choir, chorale, chorus, computers, drama, ethnic, film, gay, honors, international, jazz band, literary magazine, musical theater, newspaper, opera, pep band, photography, political, professional, radio and TV, religious, social, social service, student government, and yearbook. Popular campus events include Spring Weekend, Candlelight Christmas Service, tubing on the Susquehanna River, and Fall Frenzy Weekend.

Sports: There are 10 intercollegiate sports for men and 11 for women, and 14 intramural sports for men and 7 for women. Athletic and recreation facilities include football, soccer, baseball, and hockey fields, basketball courts, tennis courts, a swimming pool, an all-weather track, paddleball courts, a weight training room, and a sauna. The campus stadium seats 4600, and the indoor gymnasium 1800. The nearby Susquehanna River supports crew.

Disabled Students: 90% of the campus is accessible to disabled students. The following facilities are available: wheelchair ramps, elevators, special parking, specially equipped rest rooms, special class scheduling, lowered drinking fountains, and lowered telephones.

Services: In addition to many counseling and information services, tutoring is available in some subjects, including writing, mathematics, foreign languages, and reading. Academic departments also provide tutoring.

Campus Safety and Security: Campus safety and security measures include 24-hour foot and vehicle patrol, self-defense education, escort service, and informal discussions. There are pamphlets/posters/films and lighted pathways/sidewalks.

Programs of Study: S.U. confers B.A., B.S., and B.Mu. degrees. Associate degrees are also awarded. Bachelor's degrees are awarded in BIOLOGICAL SCIENCE (biochemistry and biology/biological science), BUSINESS (accounting, business administration and management, and business economics), COMMUNICATIONS AND THE ARTS (art, art history and appreciation, communications, English, French, German, Greek, Latin, music, music performance, and Spanish), COMPUTER AND PHYSICAL SCIENCE (chemistry, computer science, information sciences and systems, mathematics, and physics), EDUCATION (early childhood, elementary, music, and secondary), ENGINEERING AND ENVIRONMENTAL DESIGN (environmental science), HEALTH PROFESSIONS (predentistry, premedicine,

and preveterinary science), SOCIAL SCIENCE (economics, history, international studies, philosophy, political science/government, pre-law, psychology, religion, religious music, and sociology). Natural sciences, business administration, and psychology are the strongest academically. Business administration, communications and theater arts, and psychology have the largest enrollments.

Required: All students must complete a 3-part core curriculum of about 40 semester hours, including academic requirements in history, fine arts, literature, science, and social science, as well as philosophy or religion; skills in computers, mathematics/logic, and foreign language; and personal-development courses in academic skills, library research, wellness/fitness, and career development. An additional 36 to 44 hours are required in the major, and the remainder of a 130-hour required total in electives or a minor. A minimum GPA of 2.0 is also required to graduate.

Special: There is cross-registration with Bucknell University. Extensive programs include internships in almost all majors and study abroad in many countries. There is a Washington semester at American University and the Washington Center, a United Nations semester through Drew, and an Appalachian semester in Kentucky. The college offers dual and student-designed majors, work-study programs, credit by examination, nondegree study, and pass/fail options. The B.A.-B.S. degree is available in several majors, and there are 3–2 engineering programs with the University of Pennsylvania and Pennsylvania State University, a 3–2 program in forestry with Duke University, and a 2–2 program in allied health with Thomas Jefferson University. Susquehanna participates in the Philadelphia Center Program sponsored by the Great Lakes Colleges Association. The School of Business offers a fall semester in London for junior business majors. Highly motivated students have the option of earning their baccalaureate degree in 3 years. There is a freshman honors program on campus, as well as 17 national honor societies. 13 departments have honors programs.

Faculty/Classroom: 60% of faculty are male; 40%, female. All teach undergraduates and 50% also do research. The average class size in an introductory lecture is 25; in a laboratory, 15; and in a regular course offering, 20.

Admissions: 73% of the 1995–96 applicants were accepted. The SAT I scores for the 1995–96 freshman class were as follows: Verbal—56% below 500, 32% between 500 and 599, 11% between 600 and 700, and 1% above 700; Math—26% below 500, 41% between 500 and 599, 29% between 600 and 700, and 4% above 700. 56% of the current freshmen were in the top fifth of their class; 84% were in the top two fifths. There were 2 National Merit finalists and 5 semifinalists. 10 freshmen graduated first in their class.

Requirements: The SAT I is required, except for students with a cumulative class rank in the top 20% in a strong college preparatory program. Such students have the option of submitting either SAT I or 2 graded writing samples. Students need to graduate from an accredited high school. Preparation should include 4 years of English and mathematics, 3 to 4 of science, and 2 to 3 each of social studies and foreign language. In addition, 1 unit of art or music is recommended. 3 SAT II: Subject tests are recommended, including writing and mathematics. An essay is required, as are, for relevant fields, an art portfolio or music audition. An interview is strongly recommended. Applications are accepted on-line and on computer disk. AP and CLEP credits are accepted. Important factors in the admissions decision are advanced placement or honor courses, evidence of special talent, and recommendations by school officials.

Procedure: Freshmen are admitted fall and spring. Entrance exams should be taken by January of the senior year. There are early decision, early admissions, and deferred admissions plans. Early decision applications should be filed by December 15; regular applications, by March 1 for fall entry and December 1 for spring entry, along with an application fee of $30. Notification of early decision is sent by January 15; regular decision, on a rolling basis beginning January 15. 88 early decision candidates were accepted for the 1995–96 class. A waiting list is an active part of the admissions procedure, with about 5% of all applicants on the list.

Transfer: 32 transfer students enrolled in 1995–96. Transfer applicants must submit high school and college transcripts, test scores, and a recommendation from a dean. An interview is strongly recommended. 65 credits of 130 must be completed at S.U.

Visiting: There are regularly scheduled orientations for prospective students, including special visiting days for prospective students and their parents held in the spring and fall, which consist of sessions with faculty and admissions, financial aid, and placement staff and tours of the campus. There are guides for informal visits and visitors may sit in on classes and stay overnight at the school. To schedule a visit, contact the Office of Admissions.

Financial Aid: In 1995–96, 85% of all freshmen and 80% of continuing students received some form of financial aid. 72% of freshmen and 65% of continuing students received need-based aid. The average freshman award was $13,500. Of that total, scholarships or need-based grants averaged $9440 ($21,600 maximum); loans averaged

$2625 ($4125 maximum); and work contracts averaged $1435 ($1500 maximum). 69% of undergraduate students work part-time. Average earnings from campus work for the school year are $800. The average financial indebtedness of the 1994–95 graduate was $10,900. S.U. is a member of CSS. The FAFSA, the CSS Profile Application, and the federal tax return are required. The application deadline for fall entry is May 1 (March 1 priority).

International Students: There are currently 18 international students enrolled. The school actively recruits these students. They must score 550 on the TOEFL and also take SAT I.

Computers: The college provides computer facilities for student use. The mainframe is an HP 3000 series 947. Students may use 106 microcomputers in 4 computer laboratories. A wide variety of applications software is available. Students have worldwide access through the Internet as well as access to E-mail both on and off campus. All students may access the system 24 hours a day from multiple locations on campus, including all residence halls. There are no time limits and no fees. The college recommends students have IBM-compatible PCs or Zenith notebooks.

Graduates: In 1994–95, 275 bachelor's degrees were awarded. The most popular majors among graduates were business administration (17%), communications and theater arts (14%), and biology (7%). Within an average freshman class, 68% graduate in 4 years, 73% in 5 years, and 75% in 6 years. 38 companies recruited on campus in 1994–95. Of the 1994 graduating class, 20% were enrolled in graduate school within 6 months of graduation and 73% had found employment.

Admissions Contact: J. Richard Ziegler, Director of Admissions. E-mail: suadmiss@susqu.edu. A campus video is available.

SWARTHMORE COLLEGE
Swarthmore, PA 19081–1397

F-4

(610) 328-8300

Full-time: 645 men, 708 women	Faculty: 157; IIB, + +$
Part-time: none	Ph.D.s: 93%
Graduate: none	Student/Faculty: 9 to 1
Year: semesters	Tuition: $20,186
Application Deadline: January 1	Room & Board: $6880
Freshman Class: 3521 applied, 1200 accepted, 354 enrolled	
SAT I Verbal/Math: 650/700	MOST COMPETITIVE

Swarthmore College, established in 1864, is a private, nonprofit institution offering undergraduate courses in engineering and liberal arts. In addition to regional accreditation, Swarthmore has baccalaureate program accreditation with ABET. The 5 libraries contain 1 million volumes, 190,000 microform items, and 22,500 audiovisual forms, and subscribe to 5335 periodicals. Computerized library sources and services include the card catalog, interlibrary loans, and database searching. Special learning facilities include an art gallery, a radio station, an observatory, a performing arts center, a solar energy laboratory, an arboretum, and a collection of documents of the peace movement. The 330-acre campus is in a suburban area 10 miles southwest of Philadelphia. Including residence halls, there are 42 buildings on campus.

Student Life: 88% of undergraduates are from out-of-state, mostly the Middle Atlantic. Students come from 50 states, 42 foreign countries, and Canada. 65% are from public schools; 30% from private. 73% are white; 11% Asian American. 2% do not continue beyond their first year; 97% remain to graduate.

Housing: 1250 students can be accommodated in college housing. College-sponsored living facilities include single-sex and coed dormitories. In addition, there are substance-free dormitory wings. On-campus housing is guaranteed for the freshman year only and is available on a lottery system for upperclassmen. 91% of students live on campus. Upperclassmen may keep cars on campus.

Activities: 5% of men belong to 1 local and 1 national fraternity. There are no sororities. There are 150 groups on campus, including art, band, cheerleading, chess, choir, chorus, computers, dance, drama, ethnic, film, gay, honors, international, jazz band, literary magazine, musical theater, newspaper, orchestra, pep band, photography, political, radio and TV, religious, social, social service, student government, and yearbook. Popular campus events include fall and spring formals, a regatta, an all-day music festival, and a multicultural festival.

Sports: There are 11 intercollegiate sports for men and 11 for women, and 7 intramural sports for men and 7 for women. Athletic and recreation facilities include a field house with a 500-seat auditorium, an indoor track, and several multipurpose courts for basketball, volleyball, and tennis. There are 6 squash courts, an Olympic-size indoor pool, a 3,000-seat stadium, an all-weather track, and 12 newly surfaced tennis courts. Grass-surface playing fields are also available.

Disabled Students: 75% of the campus is accessible to disabled students. The following facilities are available: wheelchair ramps, elevators, special parking, specially equipped rest rooms, special class scheduling, and lowered drinking fountains.

Services: In addition to many counseling and information services, tutoring is available in most subjects. There is a reader service for the blind and computing support.

Campus Safety and Security: Campus safety and security measures include 24-hour foot and vehicle patrol, self-defense education, escort service, and shuttle buses. There are informal discussions, pamphlets/posters/films, emergency telephones, and lighted pathways/sidewalks.

Programs of Study: Swarthmore confers B.A. and B.S. degrees. Bachelor's degrees are awarded in BIOLOGICAL SCIENCE (biology/biological science), COMMUNICATIONS AND THE ARTS (art, art history and appreciation, classics, dramatic arts, English literature, French, German, Greek, Latin, linguistics, literature, music, Russian, and Spanish), COMPUTER AND PHYSICAL SCIENCE (chemistry, computer science, mathematics, and physics), EDUCATION (education), ENGINEERING AND ENVIRONMENTAL DESIGN (engineering), SOCIAL SCIENCE (Asian/Oriental studies, classical/ancient civilization, economics, history, medieval studies, philosophy, political science/government, psychology, religion, and sociology). English literature, biology, and economics have the largest enrollments.

Required: To graduate, students must complete 3 courses in each of 3 divisions consisting of humanities, natural sciences and engineering, and social sciences. They must have completed 32 courses or the equivalent, with a minimum of 20 credits earned outside the major. They must have a GPA of 2.0. Students must demonstrate foreign language competency and fulfill a physical education requirement including a swimming test.

Special: Students may cross-register with Haverford and Bryn Mawr colleges and the University of Pennsylvania. They may study abroad in their country of choice. Dual majors in physics and astronomy and in sociology and anthropology, student-designed majors, and a 4-year program leading to a B.A.-B.S. degree in engineering and liberal arts are available. Swarthmore offers a unique honors program whose features are student independence and responsibility and collegial relationship with faculty; students are evaluated by external examiners. There are 2 national honor societies on campus, including Phi Beta Kappa.

Faculty/Classroom: 62% of faculty are male; 38%, female. All teach undergraduates. The average class size in an introductory lecture is 21; in a laboratory, 15; and in a regular course offering, 14.

Admissions: 34% of the 1995–96 applicants were accepted. The SAT I scores for the 1995–96 freshman class were as follows: Verbal—4% below 500, 18% between 500 and 599, 50% between 600 and 700, and 28% above 700; Math—1% below 500, 5% between 500 and 599, 41% between 600 and 700, and 53% above 700. 97% of the current freshmen were in the top fifth of their class; all were in the top two fifths.

Requirements: The SAT I or ACT is required. SAT II: Subject tests in writing and 2 other areas of choice are required. Applicants must graduate from an accredited secondary school. Swarthmore does not require a specific high school curriculum. It does, however, recommend the inclusion of English, mathematics, 1 or 2 foreign languages, history and social studies, literature, art, and music, and the sciences. Interviews are strongly recommended. An essay, 2 teacher recommendations, and a counselor recommendation are required. AP credits are accepted. Important factors in the admissions decision are advanced placement or honor courses, extracurricular activities record, and recommendations by school officials.

Procedure: Freshmen are admitted in the fall. Entrance exams should be taken in the spring of the junior year or fall of the senior year. There are early decision and deferred admissions plans. Early decision applications should be filed by November 15; regular applications, by January 1 for fall entry, along with an application fee of $50. Notification of early decision is sent December 15; regular decision, April 10. 90 early decision candidates were accepted for the 1995–96 class. A waiting list is an active part of the admissions procedure.

Transfer: 11 transfer students enrolled in 1995–96. Students considered for transfer must have a GPA of 3.0. The SAT I is required if not taken previously. An essay is required. 16 courses of 32 must be completed at Swarthmore.

Visiting: There are guides for informal visits and visitors may sit in on classes and stay overnight at the school. To schedule a visit, contact the Admissions Receptionist.

Financial Aid: In 1995–96, 60% of all students received some form of financial aid. 50% of all students received need-based aid. The average freshman award was $19,400. Of that total, scholarships or need-based grants averaged $15,700 ($28,000 maximum); loans averaged $2500; and work contracts averaged $1200. 82% of undergraduate students work part-time. Average earnings from campus work for the school year are $1200. The average financial indebtedness of the 1994–95 graduate was $10,000. Swarthmore is a member of CSS. The FAF, the college's own financial statement, and the tax return are required. The application deadline for fall entry is February 1.

International Students: There are currently 132 international students enrolled. The school actively recruits these students. The student must take SAT I or the ACT. Students must take SAT II: Subject tests in writing and 2 other subjects.

Computers: The college provides computer facilities for student use. There are more than 100 networked microcomputers available throughout the campus in public areas for student use. Residence halls are fully hooked up to the network. Several Digital Alpha AXP servers run Digital UNIX. All students may access the system. There are no time limits and no fees.

Graduates: In 1994–95, 328 bachelor's degrees were awarded. The most popular majors among graduates were English (16%), biology (14%), and political science (11%). Within an average freshman class, 4% graduate in 3 years, 86% in 4 years, 97% in 5 years, and 97% in 6 years. 65 companies recruited on campus in 1994–95.

Admissions Contact: Susan Untereker, Director of Admissions. E-mail: admissio@swarthmore.edu.

TEMPLE UNIVERSITY F-3
Philadelphia, PA 19122–1803 (215) 204–7200

Full-time: 17,248 men and women	Faculty: 1732; I, +$
Part-time: 6700 men and women	Ph.D.s: 86%
Graduate: 10,000 men and women	Student/Faculty: 10 to 1
Year: semesters, summer session	Tuition: $5514 ($10,096)
Application Deadline: June 15	Room & Board: $5436
Freshman Class: 9000 applied, 6247 accepted, 2493 enrolled	
SAT I Verbal/Math: 470/508	COMPETITIVE

Temple University, founded in 1884, is part of the Commonwealth System of Higher Education in Pennsylvania. It offers programs in arts and sciences; allied health professions; education; engineering, computer sciences, and architecture; health, physical education, recreation, and dance; art; business and management; communications and theater; landscape architecture and horticulture; music; pharmacy; and social administration. Temple has 6 other campuses, including one in Rome and one in Tokyo. There are 11 undergraduate schools. In addition to regional accreditation, Temple has baccalaureate program accreditation with AACSB, ABET, ACEJMC, ACPE, ADA, APTA, CAHEA, CSWE, NAAB, NASAD, NASM, NCATE, NLN, and NRPA. The libraries contain more than 2 million volumes, and subscribe to 15,000 periodicals. Computerized library sources and services include the card catalog, interlibrary loans, and database searching. Special learning facilities include an art gallery, radio station, and dance laboratory theater, media learning center for the study of critical languages, and multimedia laboratory for teacher education in music. The 82-acre campus is in an urban area 1 mile north of center city Philadelphia. Including residence halls, there are 100 buildings on campus.

Student Life: 77% of undergraduates are from Pennsylvania. Students come from 50 states, 60 foreign countries, and Canada. 63% are white; 22% African American; 10% Asian American.

Housing: 3000 students can be accommodated in college housing. College-sponsored living facilities include single-sex and coed dormitories, on-campus apartments, off-campus apartments, fraternity houses, and sorority houses. On-campus housing is guaranteed for all 4 years. 80% of students commute. Alcohol is not permitted. All students may keep cars on campus.

Activities: 10% of men belong to 12 local fraternities; 10% of women belong to 11 local sororities. There are 125 groups on campus, including art, band, cheerleading, chess, choir, chorus, computers, dance, drama, drill team, ethnic, film, honors, international, jazz band, literary magazine, marching band, musical theater, newspaper, orchestra, pep band, photography, political, professional, radio and TV, religious, social, social service, student government, and yearbook. Popular campus events include Spring Fling.

Sports: There are 13 intercollegiate sports for men and 13 for women, and 15 intramural sports for men and 12 for women. Athletic and recreation facilities include 2 Olympic-size swimming pools, a diving well, several gymnasiums, weight-training rooms, 10 bowling lanes, racquetball courts, an 8-lane 400-meter track, and playing fields. The campus stadium seats 65,000, the indoor gymnasium 2000, and the largest auditorium/arena 600.

Disabled Students: The entire campus is accessible to physically disabled persons. The following facilities are available: wheelchair ramps, elevators, special parking, specially equipped rest rooms, special class scheduling, lowered drinking fountains, and lowered telephones. Additional services may be arranged through the Disabled Student Services Office.

Services: In addition to many counseling and information services, tutoring is available in most subjects. There is a reader service for the blind, and remedial math, reading, and writing.

Campus Safety and Security: Campus safety and security measures include 24-hour foot and vehicle patrol, escort service, shuttle buses, and informal discussions. In addition, there are pamphlets/posters/films, emergency telephones, lighted pathways/sidewalks, and 24-hour access-controlled security in residence halls.

Programs of Study: Temple confers B.A., B.S., B.Ar., B.B.A., B.F.A., B.M., B.S.Ar., B.S.E., B.S.Ed., B.S.E.E., B.S.N., and B.S.W. degrees. Associate, master's, and doctoral degrees are also awarded. Bachelor's degrees are awarded in AGRICULTURE (horticulture), BIOLOGICAL SCIENCE (biochemistry and biology/biological science), BUSINESS (accounting, banking and finance, business administration and management, business economics, business law, human resources, international business management, management science, marketing/retailing/merchandising, personnel management, real estate, and sports management), COMMUNICATIONS AND THE ARTS (art, art history and appreciation, broadcasting, Chinese, classics, communications, dance, English, film arts, fine arts, French, Germanic languages and literature, Greek, guitar, Hebrew, Italian, jazz, journalism, Latin, linguistics, music, music history and appreciation, music performance, music theory and composition, percussion, performing arts, photography, piano/organ, Portuguese, Russian, Spanish, speech/debate/rhetoric, strings, telecommunications, voice, and winds), COMPUTER AND PHYSICAL SCIENCE (actuarial science, chemistry, computer science, geology, mathematics, physics, and statistics), EDUCATION (art, business, early childhood, education, elementary, English, foreign languages, health, home economics, industrial arts, marketing and distribution, mathematics, middle school, music, physical, science, secondary, and social studies), ENGINEERING AND ENVIRONMENTAL DESIGN (architectural engineering, architecture, biomedical engineering, civil engineering, electrical/electronics engineering, electrical/electronics engineering technology, engineering, engineering technology, environmental engineering technology, landscape architecture/design, mechanical engineering, and mechanical engineering technology), HEALTH PROFESSIONS (health care administration, music therapy, nursing, occupational therapy, pharmacy, physical therapy, predentistry, and premedicine), SOCIAL SCIENCE (African American studies, American studies, anthropology, Asian/Oriental studies, community services, criminal justice, economics, geography, history, international relations, parks and recreation management, philosophy, political science/government, prelaw, psychology, public administration, religion, social science, social work, sociology, urban studies, and women's studies).

Required: The required core curriculum includes English composition, intellectual heritage, American culture, the arts, the individual and society, foreign language/international studies, mathematics/statistics/logic, and science and technology. A minimum 2.0 GPA and a total of 128 credit hours are required for graduation, including 24 credits in the major.

Special: The university offers study abroad, work-study programs, and up to 30 credits for life/military/work experience. There is a 5-year accelerated engineering technology program. There is a freshman honors program on campus

Faculty/Classroom: The average class size in a regular course offering is 24.

Admissions: 69% of the 1995–96 applicants were accepted. 34% of the current freshmen were in the top fifth of their class; 63% were in the top two fifths.

Requirements: The SAT I or ACT is required. Temple requires applicants to be in the upper 50% of their class. A minimum GPA of 2.0 is required. In addition, applicants should complete 16 academic credits/Carnegie units, including 4 years of English, 2 each of mathematics and a foreign language, and 1 each of history and a laboratory science. A GED is accepted. A portfolio and audition are required in relevant fields. AP and CLEP credits are accepted. Important factors in the admissions decision are advanced placement or honor courses, recommendations by school officials, and parents or siblings attending the school.

Procedure: Freshmen are admitted fall and spring. Entrance exams should be taken by March of the junior year or April of the senior year. Applications should be filed by June 15 for fall entry and November 15 for spring entry, along with an application fee of $30. Notification is sent on a rolling basis.

Transfer: 2308 transfer students enrolled in a recent year. Applicants must have earned at least 15 college credit hours with at least a 2.0 GPA and must submit official high school and college transcripts. 30 credits of 128 must be completed at Temple.

Visiting: There are regularly scheduled orientations for prospective students. There are guides for informal visits and visitors may sit in on classes. To schedule a visit, contact the Office of Undergraduate Admissions.

Financial Aid: Temple is a member of CSS. The FAFSA, the college's own financial statement, and the PHEAA (Pennsylvania residents) are required. The application deadline for fall entry is March 31.

International Students: The school actively recruits these students. They must take the TOEFL and achieve a minimum score of 500.

Computers: The college provides computer facilities for student use. The mainframes are a CDC Cyber 860 and 2 IBM 4381 VM/CMS. Students may access computer facilities through workstations distributed throughout the campus. Networked microcomputer laboratories and software libraries are available for student use. All students may access the system 24 hours per day. There are no time limits and no fees.

Admissions Contact: Admissions Counselor.

THIEL COLLEGE
A-2

Greenville, PA 16125   (412) 589-2345

(800) 24-THIEL; FAX: (412) 589-2013

Full-time: 380 men, 468 women	Faculty: 59; IIB, -$
Part-time: 48 men, 160 women	Ph.D.s: 71%
Graduate: none	Student/Faculty: 14 to 1
Year: semesters, 2 summer terms	Tuition: $11,972
Application Deadline: open	Room & Board: $4958
Freshman Class: 1273 applied, 1077 accepted, 247 enrolled	
SAT I Verbal/Math: 414/464	ACT: 20 LESS COMPETITIVE

Thiel College, founded in 1866, is an independent, coeducational college affiliated with the Lutheran Church. It offers programs in liberal arts, business, engineering, nursing, religion, teacher preparation, and professional programs. In addition to regional accreditation, Thiel has baccalaureate program accreditation with NLN. The library contains 152,403 volumes and 87,682 microform items, and subscribes to 700 periodicals. Computerized library sources and services include the card catalog, interlibrary loans, and database searching. Special learning facilities include a learning resource center, art gallery, radio station, and wildlife sanctuary. The 135-acre campus is in a rural area 75 miles north of Pittsburgh and 75 miles southeast of Cleveland, Ohio. Including residence halls, there are 21 buildings on campus.

Student Life: 84% of undergraduates are from Pennsylvania. Students come from 15 states and 9 foreign countries. 90% are from public schools; 10% from private. 91% are white. 38% are Protestant; 28% Catholic; 11% claim no religious affiliation. The average age of freshmen is 18; all undergraduates, 20. 22% do not continue beyond their first year; 50% remain to graduate.

Housing: 1076 students can be accommodated in college housing. College-sponsored living facilities include single-sex and coed dormitories, fraternity houses, and an honors residence hall. On-campus housing is guaranteed for all 4 years. 80% of students live on campus; of those, 60% remain on campus on weekends. Alcohol is not permitted. All students may keep cars on campus.

Activities: 20% of men belong to 1 local fraternity and 2 national fraternities; 30% of women belong to 5 national sororities. There are 35 groups on campus, including band, cheerleading, choir, chorus, computers, dance, drama, ethnic, honors, international, literary magazine, musical theater, newspaper, pep band, political, professional, radio, religious, social, student government, symphony, and yearbook. Popular campus events include Spring Weekend, Greek Week, and theatrical productions.

Sports: There are 8 intercollegiate sports for men and 6 for women, and 5 intramural sports for men and 5 for women. Athletic and recreation facilities include a 1200-seat gymnasium, basketball and handball courts, a swimming pool, and playing fields.

Disabled Students: 75% of the campus is accessible to disabled students. The following facilities are available: wheelchair ramps, elevators, special parking, specially equipped rest rooms, and special class scheduling.

Services: In addition to many counseling and information services, tutoring is available in every subject. There is remedial math, reading, and writing.

Campus Safety and Security: Campus safety and security measures include 24-hour foot and vehicle patrol, escort service, pamphlets/posters/films, and emergency telephones. There are lighted pathways/sidewalks.

Programs of Study: Thiel confers B.A. and B.S.N. degrees. Associate degrees are also awarded. Bachelor's degrees are awarded in BIOLOGICAL SCIENCE (biology/biological science), BUSINESS (accounting, business administration and management, international business management, and management information systems), COMMUNICATIONS AND THE ARTS (art, communications, English, French, Spanish, and technical and business writing), COMPUTER AND PHYSICAL SCIENCE (actuarial science, chemistry, computer science, geology, mathematics, and physics), EDUCATION (elementary and secondary), ENGINEERING AND ENVIRONMENTAL DESIGN (environmental science and preengineering), HEALTH PROFESSIONS (cytotechnology, medical laboratory technology, nursing, physical therapy, predentistry, premedicine, prepharmacy, preveterinary science, respiratory therapy, and speech pathology/audiology), SOCIAL SCIENCE (history, philosophy, political science/

government, prelaw, psychology, religion, religious education, and sociology). Nursing and engineering are the strongest academically. Accounting, business administration, and nursing have the largest enrollments.

Required: To graduate, students must complete a total of 124 credit hours, with 35 to 55 in the major and a minimum GPA of 2.0. Distribution requirements, for all except nursing students, include 14 to 15 hours of Western humanities, 9 of Christianity, 6 to 8 of science, 3 to 10 of cultural studies, and 4 of health.

Special: Students may spend a semester at Argonne National Laboratories, the Art Institute of Pittsburgh, or Drew University. Special programs include a UN semester, a Washington semester, an Appalachian semester, study at Pittsburgh Institute of Mortuary Science, and a forestry and environmental management semester at Duke University. There is a 3–2 engineering program with Case Western Reserve and the University of Pittsburgh. Internships, study abroad, work-study, dual majors, nondegree study, credit by examination, and credit for life, military, and work experience are also available. There is a freshman honors program on campus, as well as 11 national honor societies.

Faculty/Classroom: 67% of faculty are male; 33%, female. All teach undergraduates. The average class size in an introductory lecture is 25; in a laboratory, 15; and in a regular course offering, 12.

Admissions: 85% of the 1995–96 applicants were accepted. 24% of the current freshmen were in the top fifth of their class; 51% were in the top two fifths.

Requirements: The SAT I or ACT is required. Applicants should be high school graduates who have completed 16 academic units, including 4 years of English, 3 of social science, and 2 each of foreign language, mathematics, and science. The GED is accepted. An essay and an interview are recommended. AP and CLEP credits are accepted. Important factors in the admissions decision are advanced placement or honor courses, evidence of special talent, and leadership record.

Procedure: Freshmen are admitted to all sessions. There are early decision and deferred admissions plans. Application deadlines are open. Application fee is $25. Notification of early decision is sent October 15; regular decision, on a rolling basis.

Transfer: 57 transfer students enrolled in 1995–96. Applicants should meet the same criteria as entering freshmen and should submit official transcripts and statements of good standing from all previous colleges attended. Students must have a 2.0 GPA to transfer and must complete financial aid transcripts and transfer forms from all schools previously attended. 30 credits of 124 must be completed at Thiel.

Visiting: There are regularly scheduled orientations for prospective students, including orientation sessions for students enrolling in the fall and monthly sessions beginning in February. There are guides for informal visits and visitors may sit in on classes and stay overnight at the school. To schedule a visit, contact Robin Poklar in the Admissions Office.

Financial Aid: In 1995–96, 96% of all students received some form of financial aid. 93% of freshmen and 92% of continuing students received need-based aid. The average freshman award was $11,950. Of that total, scholarships or need-based grants averaged $6884 ($15,000 maximum); outside gift aid averaged $1200 ($2500 maximum); loans averaged $3300 ($4600 maximum); and work contracts averaged $1224. 46% of undergraduate students work part-time. Average earnings from campus work for the school year are $1224. Thiel is a member of CSS. The FAF, FAFSA, FFS, or SFS is required; the FAFSA is preferred.

International Students: There are currently 32 international students enrolled. The school actively recruits these students. They must score 500 on the TOEFL or take the MELAB.

Computers: The college provides computer facilities for student use. The mainframe is a DEC PDP 11/44. There are a number of computer systems in operation on campus, serving both administrative and academic applications. They are accessible to student workers and to other students for completing course assignments. There are no time limits and no fees.

Graduates: In 1994–95, 155 bachelor's degrees were awarded. The most popular majors among graduates were business (20%), nursing (18%), and psychology (9%). Within an average freshman class, 2% graduate in 3 years, 42% in 4 years, 47% in 5 years, and 51% in 6 years. 40 companies recruited on campus in 1994–95.

Admissions Contact: Nancy Christopher, Associate Director of Admissions. E-mail: thieladmis@shrys.hslc.org.

UNIVERSITY OF PENNSYLVANIA F-3

Philadelphia, PA 19104 (215) 898-7507; (215) 898-9876

Full-time: 5034 men, 4420 women	Faculty: 2239; I, + +$
Part-time: 702 men, 910 women	Ph.D.s: 99%
Graduate: 5427 men, 4730 women	Student/Faculty: 4 to 1
Year: semesters, summer session	Tuition: $19,898
Application Deadline: January 1	Room & Board: $7500
Freshman Class: 15,074 applied, 4981 accepted, 2384 enrolled	
SAT I Verbal/Math: 597/686	ACT: 28 MOST COMPETITIVE

University of Pennsylvania, founded in 1740, is a private institution offering undergraduate and graduate degrees in arts and sciences, business, engineering and applied science, and nursing. There are 4 undergraduate and 12 graduate schools. In addition to regional accreditation, Penn has baccalaureate program accreditation with AACSB, ABET, NAAB, NCATE, and NLN. The 14 libraries contain 4,324,225 volumes, 2,911,876 microform items, and 45,157 audiovisual forms, and subscribe to 33,558 periodicals. Special learning facilities include an art gallery, natural history museum, planetarium, radio station, TV station, arboretum, animal and primate research centers, language laboratory, center for performing arts, institute for contemporary art, wind tunnel, and electron microscope. The 260-acre campus is in an urban area in Philadelphia. Including residence halls, there are 119 buildings on campus.

Student Life: 79% of undergraduates are from out of state, mostly the Middle Atlantic. Students come from 50 states, 100 foreign countries, and Canada. 62% are from public schools; 38% from private. 66% are white; 22% Asian American; 11% Hispanic. The average age of freshmen is 18; all undergraduates, 20. 5% do not continue beyond their first year; 87% remain to graduate.

Housing: 6750 students can be accommodated in college housing. College-sponsored living facilities include coed dormitories, on-campus apartments, married-student housing, fraternity houses, and sorority houses. In addition there are honors houses, language houses, and special interest houses. On-campus housing is guaranteed for the freshman year only, is available on a first-come, first-served basis, and is available on a lottery system for upperclassmen. 57% of students live on campus; of those, 90% remain on campus on weekends. Alcohol is not permitted. All students may keep cars on campus.

Activities: 33% of men belong to 29 national fraternities; 32% of women belong to 14 national sororities. There are 250 groups on campus, including art, band, cheerleading, chess, choir, chorale, chorus, computers, dance, drama, ethnic, gay, honors, international, jazz band, literary magazine, marching band, musical theater, newspaper, opera, orchestra, political, professional, radio and TV, religious, social, social service, student government, symphony, and yearbook. Popular campus events include Spring Fling, Mask and Wig Show, and Franklin's Birthday.

Sports: There are 16 intercollegiate sports for men and 14 for women, and 15 intramural sports for men and 14 for women. Athletic and recreation facilities include 3 gymnasiums, a tennis pavilion, 2 swimming pools, squash courts, indoor/outdoor tennis courts, playing fields, an indoor ice rink, rowing tanks, saunas, and a weight room.

Disabled Students: 80% of the campus is accessible to disabled students. The following facilities are available: wheelchair ramps, elevators, special parking, specially equipped rest rooms, special class scheduling, lowered drinking fountains, lowered telephones, TDD, accessible housing, and an accessible van shuttle.

Services: In addition to many counseling and information services, tutoring is available in every subject. There is a reader service for the blind.

Campus Safety and Security: Campus safety and security measures include 24-hour foot and vehicle patrol, self-defense education, escort service, and shuttle buses. There are informal discussions, pamphlets/posters/films, emergency telephones, lighted pathways/sidewalks, 100 commissioned police officers, victim support/special services, and Student Walking Escort.

Programs of Study: Penn confers B.A., B.S., B.Applied Sc., B.S. in Econ., B.S.E., and B.S.N. degrees. Associate, master's, and doctoral degrees are also awarded. Bachelor's degrees are awarded in BIOLOGICAL SCIENCE (biochemistry, biology/biological science, and biophysics), BUSINESS (accounting, banking and finance, business administration and management, international business management, marketing/retailing/merchandising, organizational behavior, real estate, small business management, and transportation management), COMMUNICATIONS AND THE ARTS (art history and appreciation, communications, dramatic arts, English, German, languages, linguistics, music, romance languages, and Slavic languages), COMPUTER AND PHYSICAL SCIENCE (actuarial science, astronomy, chemistry, computer science, geology, mathematics, and physics), EDUCATION (education and elementary), ENGINEERING AND ENVIRONMENTAL DESIGN (bioengineering, chemical engineering, civil engineering, electrical/electronics engineering, engineering, environmental design, environmental science, materials engineering, and mechanical engineering), HEALTH PROFESSIONS (hospital administration and nursing), SOCIAL SCIENCE (American studies, anthropology, area studies, behavioral science, economics, history, humanities, international relations, law, liberal arts/general studies, philosophy, political science/government, psychology, public affairs, religion, social science, sociology, urban studies, and women's studies).

Required: The bachelor's degree requires completion of 32 to 40 course units, depending on the student's major, with 12 to 18 of these units in the major and a minimum GPA of 2.0. Students must also complete 10 courses from 6 areas of study in the humanities, science, and mathematics.

Special: Cross-registration is permitted with Haverford, Swarthmore, and Bryn Mawr colleges. Opportunities are provided for internships, a Washington semester, accelerated degree programs, B.A.-B.S. degrees, dual and student-designed majors, a 3-2 engineering degree, credit by examination, nondegree study, limited pass/fail options, and study abroad in 14 countries. Through the 'one university' concept, students in 1 undergraduate school may study in any of the other 3. There is a freshman honors program on campus, as well as 10 national honor societies, including Phi Beta Kappa. 27 departments have honors programs.

Faculty/Classroom: 76% of faculty are male; 24%, female. The average class size in lecture is 27; in a laboratory, 16; and in a regular course offering, 22.

Admissions: 33% of the 1995-96 applicants were accepted. The SAT I scores for the 1995-96 freshman class were as follows: Verbal—10% below 500, 36% between 500 and 599, 45% between 600 and 699, and 9% 699 and above; Math—9% between 500 and 599, 40% between 600 and 699, and 51% 699 and above. 95% of the current freshmen were in the top fifth of their class; 99% were in the top two fifths. 159 freshmen graduated first in their class.

Requirements: The SAT I or ACT is required. Graduation from an accredited secondary school is not required. Recommended preparation includes 4 years of high school English, 3 or 4 each of a foreign language and mathematics, and 3 each of history and science. An essay is required. A portfolio and an audition are recommended for prospective art and music majors, respectively. AP credits are accepted. Important factors in the admissions decision are advanced placement or honor courses, leadership record, and recommendations by school officials.

Procedure: Freshmen are admitted in the fall. Entrance exams should be taken by January of the senior year. There are early decision, early admissions, and deferred admissions plans. Early decision applications should be filed by November 1; regular applications, by January 1 for fall entry, along with an application fee of $55. Notification of early decision is sent December 15; regular decision, April 1. 922 early decision candidates were accepted for the 1995-96 class. A waiting list is an active part of the admissions procedure, with about 5% of all applicants on the list.

Transfer: 254 transfer students enrolled in 1995-96. Applicants must provide college and high school transcripts, essays, and 2 recommendations. They must pass a standardized test and meet the course credit requirements of the admitting school. A minimum 3.0 GPA is recommended. 20 courses units of 32 to 40 must be completed at Penn.

Visiting: There are regularly scheduled orientations for prospective students, including an information session by the admissions office and a tour of the campus led by current students. There are guides for informal visits and visitors may sit in on classes and stay overnight at the school. To schedule a visit, contact the Admissions Office.

Financial Aid: In 1995-96, 46% of all freshmen and 44% of continuing students received need-based aid. The average freshman award was $19,160. Of that total, scholarships or need-based grants averaged $13,679 ($22,500 maximum); loans averaged $3832 ($7125 maximum); and work contracts averaged $1649 ($7025 maximum). 47% of undergraduate students work part-time. Average earnings from campus work for the school year are $1310. The average financial indebtedness of the 1994-95 graduate was $17,621. Penn is a member of CSS. The FAF and the college's own financial statement are required. The application deadline for fall entry is February 15.

International Students: There are currently 907 international students enrolled. The school actively recruits these students. They must score 550 on the TOEFL and take SAT I or the ACT. Students must also take 3 SAT II: Subject tests, including writing and mathematics (for business and engineering).

Computers: The college provides computer facilities for student use. The mainframe is an IBM 3090. Students may use the 500 networked microcomputers to access information sources, including the on-line library catalog, a campuswide information system, and the Internet. All students may access the system. There are no time limits and no fees.

Graduates: In 1994-95, 2468 bachelor's degrees were awarded. The most popular majors among graduates were banking and finance (11%), history (6%), and psychology (5%). Within an average freshman class, 2% graduate in 3 years, 82% in 4 years, 90% in 5 years, and 90% in 6 years. 475 companies recruited on campus in 1994–95. Of the 1994 graduating class, 25% were enrolled in graduate school within 6 months of graduation and 67% had found employment.

Admissions Contact: Willis Stetson, Jr., Dean of Admissions. E-mail: info@admissions.ugao.upenn.edu. A campus video is available.

UNIVERSITY OF PITTSBURGH SYSTEM

The University of Pittsburgh, established in 1787, is a public resarch university system in Pennsylvania. It is governed by the board of trustees of the University of Pittsburgh, whose chief administrator is the president. The primary goal of the system is enhancing educational opportunities for the citizens of Pennsylvania and contributing to the state's social, intellectual, and economic development. The main priorities are to engage in research, artistic, and scholarly activities; to provide high-quality undergraduate, graduate, and professional programs; and, to offer expertise and educational services to meet the needs of the region and state. The total enrollment of all 5 campuses is about 33,000 with more than 3500 faculty members. There are 183 baccalaureate, 120 master's, 84 doctoral, and 4 first-professional degree programs offered through the system. Profiles of the 4-year campsues, located in Pittsburgh, Bradford, Greensburg, and Johnstown, are included in this chapter.

UNIVERSITY OF PITTSBURGH
B-3

Pittsburgh, PA 15260	(412) 624-PITT; FAX: (412) 624-5400
Full-time: 6267 men, 6666 women	Faculty: 2849; I, -$
Part-time: 1697 men, 1817 women	Ph.D.s: 90%
Graduate: 4803 men, 4833 women	Student/Faculty: 5 to 1
Year: semesters, summer session	Tuition: $5638 ($11,724)
Application Deadline: open	Room & Board: $4834
Freshman Class: 7709 applied, 5271 accepted, 2016 enrolled	
SAT I Verbal/Math: 480/540	**VERY COMPETITIVE**

The University of Pittsburgh, founded in 1787, is a state-related, coeducational, research university with programs in liberal arts and sciences, education, engineering, social work, business, and health fields. There are 12 undergraduate and 14 graduate schools. In addition to regional accreditation, Pitt has baccalaureate program accreditation with AACSB, ABET, ACPE, ADA, CAHEA, CSWE, and NLN. The 27 libraries contain 3,296,893 volumes and 3,312,645 microform items, and subscribe to 23,290 periodicals. Computerized library sources and services include the card catalog, interlibrary loans, and database searching. Special learning facilities include a learning resource center, art gallery, natural history museum, radio station, art museum, music hall, observatory, and international classrooms located in the 42-story Cathedral of Learning. The 132-acre campus is in an urban area 3 miles east of downtown Pittsburgh. Including residence halls, there are 90 buildings on campus.

Student Life: 88% of undergraduates are from Pennsylvania. Students come from 47 states, 53 foreign countries, and Canada. 85% are white. The average age of all undergraduates is 23. 14% do not continue beyond their first year; 64% remain to graduate.

Housing: 5000 students can be accommodated in college housing. College-sponsored living facilities include single-sex and coed dormitories, off-campus apartments, and fraternity houses. In addition, there are is a no-alcohol residence hall occupied by sorority members. On-campus housing is guaranteed for the freshman year only, is available on a first-come, first-served basis, and is available on a lottery system for upperclassmen. All students may keep cars on campus.

Activities: 14% of men belong to 21 national fraternities; 11% of women belong to 15 national sororities. There are 352 groups on campus, including art, band, cheerleading, chess, chorus, dance, drama, ethnic, gay, honors, international, jazz band, literary magazine, marching band, newspaper, political, professional, radio, religious, social, social service, student government, and yearbook. Popular campus events include Jazz Seminar, Black Week, and Greek Week.

Sports: There are 9 intercollegiate sports for men and 9 for women, and 11 intramural sports for men and 9 for women. Athletic and recreation facilities include a 56,500-seat stadium for football and track, a 6750-seat field house for basketball and track, a sports center that converts from a regulation football field to 9 tennis courts, and a hall for pool and racquetball. There are also billiard tables, table tennis, video games, and televisions in the student union.

Disabled Students: 90% of the campus is accessible to disabled students. The following facilities are available: wheelchair ramps, elevators, special parking, specially equipped rest rooms, special class scheduling, lowered drinking fountains, lowered telephones, and transportation.

Services: In addition to many counseling and information services, tutoring is available in some subjects, including many lower-level undergraduate science and humanities courses. There is a reader service for the blind, and remedial math, reading, and writing.

Campus Safety and Security: Campus safety and security measures include 24-hour foot and vehicle patrol, self-defense education, escort service, and shuttle buses. There are informal discussions, pamphlets/posters/films, emergency telephones, lighted pathways/sidewalks, taxi service, and crime alerts.

Programs of Study: Pitt confers B.A., B.S., B.A.S.W., B.Phil., B.S.B.A., B.S.E., B.S.N., and B.S.Phr. degrees. Master's and doctoral degrees are also awarded. Bachelor's degrees are awarded in BIOLOGICAL SCIENCE (biology/biological science, microbiology, molecular biology, neurosciences, and nutrition), BUSINESS (accounting), COMMUNICATIONS AND THE ARTS (Chinese, classics, communications, creative writing, English literature, film arts, fine arts, French, German, Italian, Japanese, linguistics, music, Russian, Spanish, speech/debate/rhetoric, and studio art), COMPUTER AND PHYSICAL SCIENCE (astronomy, chemistry, computer science, geology, information sciences and systems, mathematics, natural sciences, physics, and statistics), EDUCATION (vocational), ENGINEERING AND ENVIRONMENTAL DESIGN (architecture, chemical engineering, civil engineering, electrical/electronics engineering, engineering physics, industrial engineering, materials engineering, materials science, mechanical engineering, and metallurgical engineering), HEALTH PROFESSIONS (medical laboratory technology, medical records administration/services, nursing, occupational therapy, and pharmacy), SOCIAL SCIENCE (African American studies, anthropology, child psychology/development, economics, history, humanities, liberal arts/general studies, paralegal studies, philosophy, political science/government, psychology, public administration, religion, social work, sociology, and urban studies). Philosophy, history and philosophy of science, and anthropology are the strongest academically. Engineering, psychology, and communications have the largest enrollments.

Required: All students in the College of Arts and Sciences must take a minimum of 120 credits, including at least 1 course in first-level literature, first-level music or art, creative expression, philosophy, social science, history, public policy, natural sciences, foreign culture, and non-Western culture. A minimum of 24 credits in the major and a 2.0 GPA are required. Requirements for other schools may vary.

Special: Students may cross-register with 10 member colleges and universities of the Pittsburgh Council on Higher Education Consortium. Internships, study abroad, a semester at sea, a Washington semester, work-study programs, a dual major in business and any other subject in arts and sciences, and student-designed majors are available. There are freshman seminars and a 5-year joint degree in liberal arts/engineering. Nondegree study is available in a wide range of subjects. There is a freshman honors program on campus, as well as 27 national honor societies, including Phi Beta Kappa.

Faculty/Classroom: 68% of faculty are male; 32%, female.

Admissions: 68% of the 1995–96 applicants were accepted. The SAT I scores for the 1995–96 freshman class were as follows: Verbal—58% below 500, 32% between 500 and 599, 9% between 600 and 700, and 1% above 700; Math—27% below 500, 46% between 500 and 599, 22% between 600 and 700, and 5% above 700. 50% of the current freshmen were in the top fifth of their class; 83% were in the top two fifths.

Requirements: The SAT I or ACT is required. Applicants for admission to the College of Arts and Sciences must be graduates of an accredited secondary school. The GED is accepted. Students must have 15 high school academic credits, including 4 units of English, 3 each of mathematics and laboratory science, and 1 of social studies, plus 4 units in academic electives. Pitt recommends that the student have 3 or more years of a single foreign language. An essay is recommended if the student is seeking scholarship consideration, and music students must have an audition. Requirements for other colleges or schools may vary. AP and CLEP credits are accepted. Important factors in the admissions decision are advanced placement or honor courses, evidence of special talent, and extracurricular activities record.

Procedure: Freshmen are admitted to all sessions. There are early admissions and deferred admissions plans. Application deadlines are open. Application fee is $35. Notification is sent on a rolling basis.

Transfer: 623 transfer students enrolled in 1995–96. Applicants to the College of Arts and Sciences must supply transcripts of all secondary school and college course work and have a minimum GPA of 2.5. An interview is recommended. Grades of C or better transfer for credit. Application deadlines vary by school. 30 credits of 120 must be completed at Pitt.

Visiting: There are regularly scheduled orientations for prospective students. There are guides for informal visits and visitors may sit in on classes and stay overnight at the school. To schedule a visit, contact the Office of Admissions and Financial Aid.

Financial Aid: In 1995–96, 70% of all freshmen and 60% of continuing students received some form of financial aid. 68% of freshmen and 58% of continuing students received need-based aid. The average freshman award was $5000. Of that total, scholarships or need-based grants averaged $2500 ($15,000 maximum); loans averaged

$2000 ($8000 maximum); and work contracts averaged $1000 ($1500 maximum). 40% of undergraduate students work part-time. Average earnings from campus work for the school year are $900. The average financial indebtedness of the 1994–95 graduate was $9000. Pitt is a member of CSS. The FAFSA and the college's own financial statement are required. The priority application deadline for fall entry is March 1.

International Students: There are currently 261 international students enrolled. They must score 500 on the TOEFL and also take SAT I or the ACT.

Computers: The college provides computer facilities for student use. The mainframe is an IBM 3090/400J with UNIX and VMS timesharing service. 7 public computing laboratories, with more than 600 personal computers and workstations, provide access to a variety of software, printers, and graphic plotters. All students may access the system. There are no time limits. The fees are $220 per year.

Graduates: In 1994–95, 3159 bachelor's degrees were awarded. The most popular majors among graduates were engineering (11%), psychology (8%), and communications (7%). Within an average freshman class, 38% graduate in 4 years, 60% in 5 years, and 64% in 6 years. 300 companies recruited on campus in 1994–95.

Admissions Contact: Dr. Betsy A. Porter, Director, Office of Admissions and Financial Aid. A campus video is available.

UNIVERSITY OF PITTSBURGH AT BRADFORD   C-2
Bradford, PA 16701-2898   (814) 362-7555
                              (800) 872-1787; FAX: (814) 362-7578

Full-time: 383 men, 487 women	**Faculty:** 64; IIB, -$
Part-time: 128 men, 202 women	**Ph.D.s:** 80%
Graduate: none	**Student/Faculty:** 14 to 1
Year: semesters, summer session	**Tuition:** $5594 ($10,672)
Application Deadline: July 1	**Room & Board:** $4150
Freshman Class: 850 applied, 732 accepted, 285 enrolled	
SAT I Verbal/Math: 452/505	**COMPETITIVE**

The University of Pittsburgh at Bradford, established in 1963, is a private, state-related, coeducational liberal arts institution. In addition to regional accreditation, Pitt-Bradford has baccalaureate program accreditation with NLN. The library contains 126,000 volumes, 40,000 microform items, and 1700 audiovisual forms, and subscribes to 715 periodicals. Computerized library sources and services include the card catalog, interlibrary loans, and database searching. Special learning facilities include a learning resource center, art gallery, radio station, TV station, and sports medicine and rehabilitative therapy clinic. The 165-acre campus is in a small town 160 miles northeast of Pittsburgh and 80 miles south of Buffalo, New York. Including residence halls, there are 26 buildings on campus.

Student Life: 86% of undergraduates are from Pennsylvania. Students come from 13 states, 5 foreign countries, and Canada. 85% are white; 10% African American. The average age of freshmen is 19. 20% do not continue beyond their first year; 72% remain to graduate.

Housing: 579 students can be accommodated in college housing. College-sponsored living facilities include single-sex and coed on-campus apartments. On-campus housing is guaranteed for all 4 years. 56% of students live on campus; of those, 70% remain on campus on weekends. All students may keep cars on campus.

Activities: 8% of men belong to 4 local and 1 national fraternities; 10% of women belong to 3 local sororities. There are 44 groups on campus, including art, band, cheerleading, chess, choir, chorus, computers, drama, ethnic, film, gay, international, jazz band, literary magazine, newspaper, photography, political, professional, radio and TV, religious, social, social service, student government, and yearbook. Popular campus events include Winter Weekend, Spring Fling, and Alumni Weekend.

Sports: There are 4 intercollegiate sports for men and 5 for women, and 16 intramural sports for men and 16 for women. Athletic and recreation facilities include a sports complex with a 1500-seat gymnasium, a weight/fitness center, and men's and women's locker rooms, a soccer field, baseball and softball fields, intramural fields, outdoor basketball and tennis courts, a sand volleyball court, and saunas.

Disabled Students: The following facilities are available: wheelchair ramps when needed, elevators, special parking, specially equipped rest rooms, lowered drinking fountains, lowered telephones, and specially equipped dormitory space.

Services: In addition to many counseling and information services, tutoring is available in most subjects. There is a writing laboratory.

Campus Safety and Security: Campus safety and security measures include 24-hour foot and vehicle patrol, escort service, informal discussions, and pamphlets/posters/films. There are lighted pathways/sidewalks.

Programs of Study: Pitt-Bradford confers B.A., B.S., and B.S.N. degrees. Associate degrees are also awarded. Bachelor's degrees are awarded in BIOLOGICAL SCIENCE (biology/biological science), BUSINESS (business administration and management and sports management), COMMUNICATIONS AND THE ARTS (broadcasting, communications, English, and public relations), COMPUTER AND PHYSICAL SCIENCE (chemistry, computer programming, computer science, geology, and mathematics), EDUCATION (athletic training, elementary, and secondary), ENGINEERING AND ENVIRONMENTAL DESIGN (environmental science), HEALTH PROFESSIONS (predentistry and premedicine), SOCIAL SCIENCE (American studies, criminal justice, economics, history, political science/government, prelaw, psychology, social science, and sociology). Computer science, premedical, and engineering are the strongest academically. Business administration, prehealth-related, and psychology have the largest enrollments.

Required: To graduate, students must complete 120 credits, with 24 to 45 in the major, and maintain a minimum GPA of 2.0. Distribution requirements include 16 credits in humanities, up to 12 in natural sciences and 12 in social sciences, plus 7 in English composition, 3 each in mathematics and computer science, and 1 in physical education. Students also complete a senior seminar and a capstone course in their major.

Special: Students may cross-register with colleges in the University of Pittsburgh system. Internships are required or strongly recommended for all majors. The school offers study abroad, a Washington semester, cooperative programs in engineering, dual majors, B.A.-B.S. degrees, nondegree study, and accelerated degree programs in most majors. Interdisciplinary majors are offered in human relations, combining anthropology, psychology, and sociology, and in journalism and creative, technical, and business writing. There are 4 national honor societies on campus.

Faculty/Classroom: 62% of faculty are male; 38%, female. All teach undergraduates. The average class size in an introductory lecture is 25; in a laboratory, 15; and in a regular course offering, 18.

Admissions: 86% of the 1995–96 applicants were accepted. 33% of the current freshmen were in the top fifth of their class; 64% were in the top two fifths. There were 6 National Merit semifinalists. 9 freshmen graduated first in their class.

Requirements: The SAT I or ACT is required, with a minimum score of 800 (400 verbal and 400 mathematics) on SAT I or 19 on the ACT. Applicants must be in the upper 60% of their class with a 2.5 GPA. Students must be graduates of an accredited secondary school with 16 Carnegie units, including 4 each in English and social studies and 3 each in science and mathematics. The GED is accepted. An essay is recommended, as is an interview. AP and CLEP credits are accepted. Important factors in the admissions decision are advanced placement or honor courses, extracurricular activities record, and leadership record.

Procedure: Freshmen are admitted fall and spring. Entrance exams should be taken during the junior year or the fall of the senior year. There are early decision, early admissions, and deferred admissions plans. Applications should be filed by July 1 for fall entry, December 1 for spring entry, and May 1 for summer entry, along with an application fee of $35. Notification is sent on a rolling basis beginning in late November.

Transfer: 63 transfer students enrolled in 1995–96. A GPA of 2.25 or higher is required. The last 30 credits of 120 must be completed at Pitt-Bradford.

Visiting: There are regularly scheduled orientations for prospective students, consisting of a meeting with admissions and financial aid counselors, a tour of the campus, a meal in the dining hall, and a visit with a faculty member. There are guides for informal visits and visitors may sit in on classes and stay overnight at the school. To schedule a visit, contact the Admissions Office.

Financial Aid: In 1995–96, 73% of all freshmen and 78% of continuing students received some form of financial aid. 66% of freshmen received need-based aid. The average freshman award was $6534. Of that total, scholarships or need-based grants averaged $2507; loans averaged $2827; and work contracts averaged $1200. 25% of undergraduate students work part-time. Average earnings from campus work for the school year are $1200. Pitt-Bradford is a member of CSS. The application deadline for fall entry is March 1.

International Students: There are currently 12 international students enrolled. They must score 500 on the TOEFL.

Computers: The college provides computer facilities for student use. The mainframes are a DEC VAX 11/780 and a DEC VAX 8350. The campus features 100 computer stations, with 75 linked to the mainframe. All students may access the system. There are no time limits and no fees.

Graduates: In 1994–95, 190 bachelor's degrees were awarded. The most popular majors among graduates were business (20%), human relations (16%), and psychology (10%). Within an average freshman class, 1% graduate in 3 years, 50% in 4 years, and 9% in 5 years. 31 companies recruited on campus in 1994–95. Of the 1994 graduating class, 19% were enrolled in graduate school within 6 months of graduation and 92% had found employment.

Admissions Contact: Merrilyn Murnyack, Assistant Director of Admissions.

UNIVERSITY OF PITTSBURGH AT GREENSBURG

B-3

Greensburg, PA 15601-5898

(412) 836-9880
FAX: (412) 836-7160

Full-time: 500 men, 540 women	Faculty: 56; IIB, -$
Part-time: 139 men, 208 women	Ph.D.s: 77%
Graduate: none	Student/Faculty: 19 to 1
Year: semesters, summer session	Tuition: $5600 ($10,678)
Application Deadline: open	Room & Board: $3830
Freshman Class: 1001 applied, 869 accepted, 307 enrolled	
SAT I or ACT: required	LESS COMPETITIVE

The University of Pittsburgh at Greensburg, established in 1963, is a public, state-related, coeducational institution, offering undergraduate majors that can be completed at Pitt-Greensburg, as well as relocation programs that are begun at Greensburg and completed at another Pitt campus. The library contains 69,103 volumes, 7693 microform items, and 1247 audiovisual forms, and subscribes to 401 periodicals. Computerized library sources and services include the card catalog, interlibrary loans, and database searching. The 165-acre campus is in a suburban area 33 miles southeast of Pittsburgh. Including residence halls, there are 11 buildings on campus.

Student Life: 99% of undergraduates are from Pennsylvania. Students come from 7 states. 93% are from public schools; 7% from private. 98% are white. 50% are Catholic; 34% Protestant; 10% claim no religious affiliation. The average age of freshmen is 18; all undergraduates, 28. 26% do not continue beyond their first year; 55% remain to graduate.

Housing: 350 students can be accommodated in college housing. College-sponsored living facilities include coed dormitories and on-campus apartments. On-campus housing is guaranteed for all 4 years. 65% of students commute. Alcohol is not permitted. All students may keep cars on campus.

Activities: There are no fraternities or sororities. There are 21 groups on campus, including academic, chess, drama, ethnic, honors, literary magazine, newspaper, political, religious, social, social service, and student government. Popular campus events include Humanities Day.

Sports: There are 3 intercollegiate sports for men and 3 for women, and 8 intramural sports for men and 2 for women. Athletic and recreation facilities include a gymnasium, a weight room, playing fields, and tennis and racquetball courts.

Disabled Students: 95% of the campus is accessible to disabled students. The following facilities are available: wheelchair ramps, elevators, special parking, specially equipped rest rooms, special class scheduling, lowered drinking fountains, and lowered telephones.

Services: In addition to many counseling and information services, tutoring is available in some subjects, including mathematics, computer science, and English. There is remedial math, reading, and writing.

Campus Safety and Security: Campus safety and security measures include 24-hour foot and vehicle patrol, escort service, informal discussions, and pamphlets/posters/films. There are emergency telephones and lighted pathways/sidewalks.

Programs of Study: Pitt-Greensburg confers B.A. and B.S. degrees. Bachelor's degrees are awarded in BIOLOGICAL SCIENCE (biology/biological science), BUSINESS (accounting and management science), COMMUNICATIONS AND THE ARTS (communications, creative writing, and English literature), COMPUTER AND PHYSICAL SCIENCE (applied mathematics, information sciences and systems, and natural sciences), ENGINEERING AND ENVIRONMENTAL DESIGN (environmental science), SOCIAL SCIENCE (anthropology, criminal justice, humanities, political science/government, psychology, and social science). Management and psychology are the strongest academically. Management has the largest enrollment.

Required: To graduate, students must complete 120 to 126 hours, with 24 to 36 in the major, and maintain a minimum GPA of 2.0. General education requirements include 15 credits each in humanities, social sciences, and natural sciences, 6 to 15 in writing courses, 3 each in speech and critical reasoning, and 2 to 3 in mathematics.

Special: Pitt-Greensburg offers cross-registration with the Pittsburgh and Johnstown campuses of the university system and with Seton Hill College. Internships are available in all majors and required for English writing and criminology. Double majors, student-designed majors, a Washington semester, nondegree study, and pass/fail options are available. There are 2 national honor societies on campus.

Faculty/Classroom: 56% of faculty are male; 44%, female. All teach undergraduates and 50% also do research. The average class size in an introductory lecture is 30; in a laboratory, 15; and in a regular course offering, 25.

Admissions: 87% of the 1995-96 applicants were accepted. The SAT I scores for a recent freshman class were as follows: Verbal—72% below 500, 26% between 500 and 599, and 2% between 600 and 700; Math—59% below 500, 29% between 500 and 599, 10% between 600 and 700, and 2% above 700. 25% of freshmen in

a recent year were in the top fifth of their class; 53% were in the top two fifths. 1 freshman graduated first in the class.

Requirements: The SAT I or ACT is required. Pitt-Greensburg requires applicants to be in the upper 60% of their class with a 2.0 GPA. Students must be graduates of an accredited secondary school; the GED is accepted. Students must complete 15 high school units, including 4 each of English and academic electives, 3 of a single foreign language, 2 of mathematics, and 1 each of history and a laboratory science; additional units in all but English are recommended. An essay is optional; an interview is recommended. AP and CLEP credits are accepted. Important factors in the admissions decision are advanced placement or honor courses, recommendations by school officials, and leadership record.

Procedure: Freshmen are admitted fall and spring. Entrance exams should be taken by December of the senior year. There are early decision, early admissions, and deferred admissions plans. Application deadlines are open. Application fee is $35. Notification is sent on a rolling basis. 30 early decision candidates were accepted for the 1995-96 class.

Transfer: 105 transfer students enrolled in 1995-96. Applicants must have a minimum GPA of 2.0. The SAT I, at least 15 college credits, and an interview are recommended. Grades of C in comparable courses transfer for credit. 30 credits of 120 to 126 must be completed at Pitt-Greensburg.

Visiting: There are guides for informal visits and visitors may sit in on classes. To schedule a visit, contact the Admissions Office.

Financial Aid: In 1995-96, 65% of all freshmen and 55% of continuing students received some form of financial and need-based aid. The average freshman award was $5190. Of that total, scholarships or need-based grants averaged $550 ($1500 maximum); loans averaged $1600 ($2250 maximum); and work contracts averaged $1300. 56% of undergraduate students work part-time. Average earnings from campus work for the school year are $1300. The average financial indebtedness of the 1994-95 graduate was $11,000. The FAFSA and the college's own financial statement are required. The application deadline for fall entry is April 1.

International Students: There are currently 3 international students enrolled. They must score 550 on the TOEFL.

Computers: The college provides computer facilities for student use. The mainframes are a DEC VAX 9000 in a VAX cluster, a VAX 8800, and a DEC System 5000. All computers are networked locally and through wide-area networks to VMS and UNIX mainframe services. There are 30 DOS, 15 UNIX, and Apple Macintosh computers in the computer center. All students may access the system. There are no time limits and no fees.

Graduates: In 1994-95, 240 bachelor's degrees were awarded. The most popular majors among graduates were management (23%), psychology (21%), and accounting (15%). Within an average freshman class, 46% graduate in 4 years, 52% in 5 years, and 2% in 6 years.

Admissions Contact: John R. Sparks, Director of Admissions and Financial Aid.

UNIVERSITY OF PITTSBURGH AT JOHNSTOWN

C-3

Johnstown, PA 15904

(814) 269-7050
(800) 765-4875; FAX: (814) 269-7044

Full-time: 1282 men, 1358 women	Faculty: 145; IIB, av$
Part-time: 173 men, 338 women	Ph.D.s: 58%
Graduate: none	Student/Faculty: 18 to 1
Year: semesters, summer session	Tuition: $5656 ($11,742)
Application Deadline: open	Room & Board: $4100
Freshman Class: 1806 applied, 1447 accepted, 701 enrolled	
SAT I or ACT: required	COMPETITIVE

The University of Pittsburgh at Johnstown is a 4-year, coeducational institution offering programs in arts and sciences, education, and engineering technology. In addition to regional accreditation, UPJ has baccalaureate program accreditation with ABET. The library contains 130,173 volumes, 16,249 microform items, and 5710 audiovisual forms, and subscribes to 638 periodicals. Computerized library sources and services include the card catalog, interlibrary loans, and database searching. Special learning facilities include a learning resource center, art gallery, and radio station. The 650-acre campus is in a suburban area 70 miles east of Pittsburgh. Including residence halls, there are 28 buildings on campus.

Student Life: 98% of undergraduates are from Pennsylvania. Students come from 12 states. 89% are from public schools; 11% from private. 95% are white. 48% are Protestant; 47% Catholic. The average age of freshmen is 18; all undergraduates, 19. 9% do not continue beyond their first year; 70% remain to graduate.

Housing: 1400 students can be accommodated in college housing. College-sponsored living facilities include single-sex dormitories, on-campus apartments, off-campus apartments, fraternity houses, and sorority houses. In addition there are special interest houses and fraternities, sororities, clubs, and organizations. On-campus housing is guaranteed for all 4 years. 62% of students live on campus; of those, 70% remain on campus on weekends. All students may keep cars on campus.

Activities: 15% of men belong to 1 local and 4 national fraternities; 16% of women belong to 1 local and 4 national sororities. There are 70 groups on campus, including band, cheerleading, chess, choir, chorus, computers, dance, drama, ethnic, honors, literary magazine, musical theater, newspaper, pep band, political, professional, radio and TV, religious, social, social service, student government, symphony, and yearbook. Popular campus events include Ethnic Festival, Engineers' Week, and Winter Carnival.

Sports: There are 4 intercollegiate sports each for men and women, and 32 intramural sports for men and 21 for women. Athletic and recreation facilities include a 2300-seat gymnasium, a pool, a dance studio, a weight room, a sauna, a cross-country track, tennis and basketball courts, and a nature area.

Disabled Students: 80% of the campus is accessible to disabled students. The following facilities are available: elevators, special parking, specially equipped rest rooms, and special class scheduling.

Services: In addition to many counseling and information services, tutoring is available in most subjects.

Campus Safety and Security: Campus safety and security measures include 24-hour foot and vehicle patrol, informal discussions, and lighted pathways/sidewalks.

Programs of Study: UPJ confers B.A. and B.S. degrees. Associate degrees are also awarded. Bachelor's degrees are awarded in BIOLOGICAL SCIENCE (biology/biological science), BUSINESS (accounting, banking and finance, business administration and management, and business economics), COMMUNICATIONS AND THE ARTS (communications, creative writing, dramatic arts, English, and journalism), COMPUTER AND PHYSICAL SCIENCE (chemistry, computer science, geology, and mathematics), EDUCATION (elementary, English, mathematics, science, and secondary), ENGINEERING AND ENVIRONMENTAL DESIGN (civil engineering technology, electrical/electronics engineering technology, and mechanical engineering technology), HEALTH PROFESSIONS (medical laboratory technology, predentistry, and premedicine), SOCIAL SCIENCE (economics, geography, history, political science/government, prelaw, psychology, social science, and sociology). Business economics, biology, and education have the largest enrollments.

Required: For graduation, students must complete 120 to 139 credits, with 30 to 36 credits in the major and a minimum GPA of 2.0. The school requires 12 credits each in humanities, natural sciences, and social sciences.

Special: Students may cross-register with schools in the Pittsburgh Council for Higher Education. Internships are available both on and off campus for credit, pay, or both. The school offers study abroad, a Washington semester, work-study programs, accelerated degree programs, dual majors, student-designed majors, nondegree study, and pass/fail options. There are 6 national honor societies on campus.

Faculty/Classroom: 75% of faculty are male; 25%, female. 93% teach undergraduates and 70% do research. The average class size in an introductory lecture is 30; in a laboratory, 18; and in a regular course offering, 25.

Admissions: 80% of the 1995–96 applicants were accepted. The SAT I scores for the 1995–96 freshman class were as follows: Verbal—72% below 500, 23% between 500 and 599, and 5% between 600 and 700; Math—47% below 500, 36% between 500 and 599, 16% between 600 and 700, and 1% above 700. 48% of the current freshmen were in the top fifth of their class; 74% were in the top two fifths. 9 freshmen graduated first in their class in a recent year.

Requirements: The SAT I or ACT is required. Applicants must be graduates of an accredited secondary school with a 2.0 GPA. The GED is accepted. For admission to freshman standing, 15 academic credits are required, including 4 each of English and history, 3 each of social studies and mathematics (2 of algebra, 1 of geometry preferred), 2 of foreign language, and 1 to 2 of laboratory science. Engineering students must have completed chemistry, physics, and trigonometry. An interview is recommended and an essay is required. AP credits are accepted. Important factors in the admissions decision are advanced placement or honor courses, leadership record, and recommendations by school officials.

Procedure: Freshmen are admitted to all sessions. Entrance exams should be taken between April and June of the junior year or by November of the senior year. There are early admissions and deferred admissions plans. Application deadlines are open. The application fee is $35. Notification is sent on a rolling basis.

Transfer: 213 transfer students enrolled in a recent year. Applicants must have at a minimum GPA of 2.5 and at least 15 credit hours earned. The SAT I or ACT is required. Grades of C or better transfer for credit. 30 credits of 120 must be completed at UPJ.

Visiting: There are regularly scheduled orientations for prospective students, including 2 programs held on Saturdays in the fall. There are guides for informal visits and visitors may sit in on classes. To schedule a visit, contact the Office of Admissions.

Financial Aid: In a recent year, 84% of all freshmen and 86% of continuing students received some form of financial aid. 80% of freshmen and 81% of continuing students received need-based aid. The average freshman award was $3145. Of that total, scholarships or need-based grants averaged $1547 ($5300 maximum); loans averaged $2328 ($3425 maximum); and work contracts averaged $1210 ($1275 maximum). 10% of undergraduate students work part-time. Average earnings from campus work for the school year are $1275. The average financial indebtedness of a recent year's graduate was $13,250. The FAFSA, PHEAA, and State Grant application are required. The application deadline for fall entry is April 1.

International Students: In a recent year, 1 international student was enrolled. Applicants must score 525 on the TOEFL. The SAT I may be required for some students.

Computers: The college provides computer facilities for student use. The mainframe is a DEC VAX cluster. In addition, 130 Macintosh, IBM, and AT&T microcomputers are available for student use. Some laboratories have restricted use for education, engineering technology, or computer science majors. Others are open to all students. All students may access the system. There are no time limits. The fees are $110 per semester.

Graduates: Within an average freshman class, 70% graduate in 4 years.

Admissions Contact: James F. Gyure, Director of Admissions. E-mail: jgyure@upj.pitt.edu.

UNIVERSITY OF SCRANTON
E-2

Scranton, PA 18510–4699   (717) 941-7540; FAX: (717) 941-6369

Full-time: 1636 men, 2025 women	Faculty: 242; IIA, av$
Part-time: 210 men, 292 women	Ph.D.s: 83%
Graduate: 291 men, 477 women	Student/Faculty: 15 to 1
Year: 4-1-4, summer session	Tuition: $13,900
Application Deadline: March 1	Room & Board: $6074
Freshman Class: 4783 applied, 3068 accepted, 927 enrolled	
SAT I Verbal/Math: 481/539	COMPETITIVE

The University of Scranton, founded in 1888, is a private, coeducational institution operated by the Jesuit order of the Roman Catholic Church. It offers programs in business, behavioral sciences, education, health science, humanities, mathematics, science, and social science. There are 4 undergraduate schools and 1 graduate school. In addition to regional accreditation, the university has baccalaureate program accreditation with APTA, NCATE, and NLN. The library contains 340,630 volumes, 307,500 microform items, and 9820 audiovisual forms, and subscribes to 2052 periodicals. Computerized library sources and services include the card catalog, interlibrary loans, and database searching. Special learning facilities include a learning resource center, art gallery, radio station, TV station, satellite dish for telecommunication reception, music center, language laboratory, and greenhouse. The 50-acre campus is in an urban area 125 miles north of Philadelphia. Including residence halls, there are 60 buildings on campus.

Student Life: 53% of undergraduates are from out-of-state, mostly the Middle Atlantic. Students come from 26 states, 19 foreign countries, and Canada. 51% are from public schools; 49% from private. 94% are white. 84% are Catholic; 10% Protestant. The average age of freshmen is 18; all undergraduates, 20.

Housing: 1875 students can be accommodated in college housing. College-sponsored living facilities include single-sex and coed dormitories and on-campus apartments. In addition, there are language houses, special interest houses, an international house, a residential college, a Spanish house, a French house, a performing arts house, an education house, a volunteer/service house, and wellness dormitories. On-campus housing is guaranteed for all 4 years. 80% of students live on campus; of those, 75% remain on campus on weekends. Alcohol is not permitted. Upperclassmen may keep cars on campus.

Activities: There are no fraternities or sororities. There are 80 groups on campus, including art, band, cheerleading, chess, choir, chorale, chorus, computers, drama, drill team, ethnic, film, honors, international, jazz band, literary magazine, musical theater, newspaper, orchestra, pep band, photography, political, professional, radio and TV, religious, social, social service, student government, and yearbook. Popular campus events include Fall Review, Noel Night, Parents Day, and Hand-in-Hand Carnival.

Sports: There are 10 intercollegiate sports for men and 8 for women, and 11 intramural sports for men and 8 for women. Athletic and recreation facilities include a 3000-seat gymnasium, basketball courts, wrestling and weight rooms, handball/racquetball and tennis courts, a sand volleyball court, a soccer/lacrosse field, a softball field, a swimming pool, a golf course, a physical therapy room, and a sauna.

Disabled Students: All of the campus is accessible to disabled students. The following facilities are available: wheelchair ramps, elevators, special parking, specially equipped rest rooms, special class scheduling, lowered drinking fountains, and lowered telephones.

Services: In addition to many counseling and information services, tutoring is available in most subjects. There is a reader service for the blind, and computing and study skills seminars.

Campus Safety and Security: Campus safety and security measures include 24-hour foot and vehicle patrol, self-defense education, escort service, and informal discussions. In addition, there are pamphlets/posters/films, emergency telephones, and lighted pathways/sidewalks.

Programs of Study: The university confers B.A. and B.S. degrees. Associate and master's degrees are also awarded. Bachelor's degrees are awarded in BIOLOGICAL SCIENCE (biochemistry, biology/biological science, biophysics, and neurosciences), BUSINESS (accounting, banking and finance, business administration and management, business economics, international business management, marketing/retailing/merchandising, and operations research), COMMUNICATIONS AND THE ARTS (advertising, communications, English, French, German, Greek, Latin, and Spanish), COMPUTER AND PHYSICAL SCIENCE (chemistry, computer management, computer science, mathematics, and physics), EDUCATION (early childhood, elementary, science, and secondary), ENGINEERING AND ENVIRONMENTAL DESIGN (electrical/electronics engineering, environmental science, and preengineering), HEALTH PROFESSIONS (health care administration, medical laboratory technology, nursing, occupational therapy, physical therapy, predentistry, and premedicine), SOCIAL SCIENCE (criminal justice, economics, gerontology, history, human services, international relations, philosophy, political science/government, prelaw, psychology, public administration, sociology, and theological studies). Chemistry, biology, and physical therapy are the strongest academically. Biology, accounting, and communication have the largest enrollments.

Required: Students take distribution requirements according to their general area of study. All are required to take philosophy/theology, physical education, English composition, and speech. A total of 127 to 150 credit hours is required for graduation, with 36 in the major. The minimum GPA is 2.0.

Special: There are cooperative programs with the University of Detroit/Mercy and Widener University, and cross-registration with 27 other Jesuit colleges. Internships are available in all career-oriented majors, and foreign study is offered in many countries. There is a Washington semester for history and political science majors. Students may earn a B.A.-B.S. degree in economics and accelerated degrees in history, chemistry, and biochemistry. The university also offers dual, student-designed, and interdisciplinary majors, including chemistry-business, chemistry-computers, electronics-business, and international language-business, credit by examination and for life/military/work experience, nondegree study, and pass/fail options. There is also a special Jesuit-oriented general education program. There is a freshman honors program on campus, as well as 26 national honor societies. 2 departments have honors programs.

Faculty/Classroom: 71% of faculty are male; 29%, female. 97% teach undergraduates, 80% do research, and 77% do both. No introductory courses are taught by graduate students. The average class size in an introductory lecture is 24; in a laboratory, 14; and in a regular course offering, 23.

Admissions: 64% of the 1995–96 applicants were accepted. The SAT I scores for the 1995–96 freshman class were as follows: Verbal—63% below 500, 28% between 500 and 599, 8% between 600 and 700, and 1% above 700; Math—32% below 500, 40% between 500 and 599, 25% between 600 and 700, and 3% above 700. 46% of the current freshmen were in the top fifth of their class; 74% were in the top two fifths. There were 7 National Merit finalists and 7 semifinalists. 15 freshmen graduated first in their class.

Requirements: The SAT I or ACT is required. In addition, applicants should be graduates of an accredited secondary school, though in some cases a GED may be accepted. They should complete 18 academic or Carnegie units, including 4 years of high school English, 3 each of mathematics, science, history, and social studies, and 2 of foreign language. Two letters of reference/recommendation are required. Essays are not required, but for some students the additional information can be of assistance. Interviews are recommended but are not a factor in admissions. AP and CLEP credits are accepted. Important factors in the admissions decision are leadership record, advanced placement or honor courses, and extracurricular activities record.

Procedure: Freshmen are admitted fall and spring. Entrance exams should be taken by fall of the senior year. There are early decision, early admissions, and deferred admissions plans. Applications should be filed by March 1 for fall entry, December 15 for spring entry, and May 1 for summer entry, along with an application fee of $30. Notification of early decision is sent December 1; regular decision, on a

rolling basis. 240 early decision candidates were accepted for the 1995–96 class.

Transfer: 113 transfer students enrolled in a recent year. Applicants should have earned at least 15 credit hours with a GPA of at least 2.5. 63 credits of 127 to 150 must be completed at the university.

Visiting: There are regularly scheduled orientations for prospective students, including private interviews conducted Monday through Friday throughout the school year. Group information sessions are offered on Saturdays and holidays in the fall and spring and during the week in the summer. There are guides for informal visits and visitors may sit in on classes and stay overnight at the school. To schedule a visit, contact the Office of Admissions.

Financial Aid: In 1995–96, 80% of all students received some form of financial aid. 73% of freshmen and 72% of continuing students received need-based aid. The average freshman award was $10,700. Of that total, scholarships or need-based grants averaged $7270 ($13,650 maximum); loans averaged $2800 ($3825 maximum); and work contracts averaged $1200 ($1500 maximum). 16% of undergraduate students work part-time. Average earnings from campus work for the school year are $800. The average financial indebtedness of the 1994–95 graduate was $13,000. The FAFSA and the college's own financial statement are required. The application deadline for fall entry is February 15.

International Students: There are currently 141 international students enrolled. They must take the TOEFL and achieve a minimum score of 525.

Computers: The college provides computer facilities for student use. The mainframe is a DEC ALPHA 2100. There are more than 300 PCs and terminals on campus available for student use in the library, academic buildings, and residence halls. The campus is completely networked. All students may access the system 24 hours a day. There are no time limits and no fees.

Graduates: In 1994–95, 867 bachelor's degrees were awarded. The most popular majors among graduates were biology (9%), accounting (8%), and communication (7%). Within an average freshman class, 70% graduate in 4 years and 10% in 5 years. 100 companies recruited on campus in 1994–95. Of the 1994 graduating class, 20% were enrolled in graduate school within 6 months of graduation and 73% had found employment.

Admissions Contact: Rev. Bernard R. McIlhenny, S.J. E-mail: admissions@uofs.edu. A campus video is available.

UNIVERSITY OF THE ARTS   F-3
Philadelphia, PA 19102   (215) 732-4832
(800) 616–2787; FAX: (215) 875-5458

Full-time: 587 men, 601 women	Faculty: 91; IIB, --$
Part-time: 4 men, 10 women	Ph.D.s: 48%
Graduate: 36 men, 76 women	Student/Faculty: 13 to 1
Year: semesters, summer session	Tuition: $13,670
Application Deadline: open	Room & Board: $3860
Freshman Class: 926 applied, 785 accepted, 377 enrolled	
SAT I Verbal/Math: 454/459	SPECIAL

University of the Arts, founded in 1870, is a private, nonprofit institution offering education and professional training in visual and performing arts, with an emphasis on the humanities and interdisciplinary exploration. There are 2 undergraduate and 2 graduate schools. In addition to regional accreditation, UArts has baccalaureate program accreditation with NASAD and NASM. The 3 libraries contain 100,674 volumes, 788 microform items, and 12,396 audiovisual forms, and subscribe to 267 periodicals. Computerized library sources and services include the card catalog, interlibrary loans, and database searching. Special learning facilities include an art gallery, several theaters, and music, animation, and recording studios. The campus is in an urban area in Philadelphia. Including residence halls, there are 8 buildings on campus.

Student Life: 56% of undergraduates are from out-of-state, mostly the Middle Atlantic. Students come from 37 states, 24 foreign countries, and Canada. 70% are from public schools. 79% are white. 38% claim no religious affiliation; 27% Protestant; 22% Catholic. The average age of freshmen is 18; all undergraduates, 21. 23% do not continue beyond their first year; 47% remain to graduate.

Housing: 262 students can be accommodated in college housing. College-sponsored living facilities include coed on-campus apartments. On-campus housing is guaranteed for the freshman year only and is available on a first-come, first-served basis. Priority is given to out-of-town students. 79% of students commute. Alcohol is not permitted.

Activities: There are no fraternities or sororities. There are 20 groups on campus, including band, choir, chorale, chorus, dance, drama, ethnic, film, gay, international, jazz band, musical theater, newspaper, opera, orchestra, photography, professional, religious, student government, and symphony. Popular campus events include exhibitions, performances, and International Visual and Performing Arts seminars.

Sports: There is 1 intramural sport for men and 1 for women. Athletic facilities are available at the YM/YWHA adjacent to the campus, for which the university provides free membership.

Disabled Students: The entire campus is accessible to disabled students. The following facilities are available: wheelchair ramps, elevators, specially equipped rest rooms, lowered drinking fountains, and lowered telephones.

Services: In addition to many counseling and information services, tutoring is available in every subject. There is remedial math, reading, and writing, and assistance with study skills.

Campus Safety and Security: Campus safety and security measures include 24-hour foot and vehicle patrol, self-defense education, escort service, and informal discussions. In addition, there are pamphlets/posters/films and lighted pathways/sidewalks.

Programs of Study: UArts confers B.S., B.F.A., B.F.A. in Dance Education, and B.M. degrees. Associate and master's degrees are also awarded. Bachelor's degrees are awarded in COMMUNICATIONS AND THE ARTS (ceramic art and design, dance, fiber/textiles/ weaving, film arts, graphic design, illustration, industrial design, jazz, media arts, metal/jewelry, music performance, music theory and composition, painting, performing arts, photography, printmaking, and sculpture). Dance, music performance, and illustration have the largest enrollments.

Required: All students must complete a core program consisting of humanities courses in language and expression, literature, arts history and social studies, philosophy and science, and related arts. A GPA of 2.0 overall for 123 to 143 credits, with 21 to 45 in the major, depending on the curriculum, must be achieved for graduation.

Special: UArts offers cross-registration with the 10-member Consortium East Coast Art Schools as well as with the Pennsylvania Academy of Fine Arts and Philadelphia College of Textiles and Sciences. Internships may be arranged, and there are extensive summer programs and opportunities to study abroad.

Faculty/Classroom: 60% of faculty are male; 40%, female. All both teach and do research. No introductory courses are taught by graduate students. The average class size in an introductory lecture is 25 and in a regular course offering, 30.

Admissions: 85% of the 1995–96 applicants were accepted. The SAT I scores for the 1995–96 freshman class were as follows: Verbal—56% below 500, 34% between 500 and 599, 8% between 600 and 700, and 2% above 700; Math—66% below 500, 25% between 500 and 599, 8% between 600 and 700, and 1% above 700. 42% of the current freshmen were in the top fifth of their class; 60% were in the top two fifths.

Requirements: The SAT I or ACT is recommended. Students must have graduated from an accredited secondary school with a 2.0 GPA or hold a GED certificate. A minimum of 16 academic credits consisting of 4 each in English and mathematics, and 2 each in music or art and history are recommended. An essay and either a portfolio or an audition are required of all applicants. An interview is recommended. Applications are accepted on computer disk via CollegeLink. AP and CLEP credits are accepted. Important factors in the admissions decision are evidence of special talent, advanced placement or honor courses, and personality/intangible qualities.

Procedure: Freshmen are admitted fall and spring. Entrance exams should be taken late in the junior year or early in the senior year. There are early admissions and deferred admissions plans. Application deadlines are open. Application fee is $30. Notification is sent on a rolling basis.

Transfer: 117 transfer students enrolled in a recent year. Candidates must have a minimum 2.0 GPA overall. An interview is recommended, as well as test scores for either the SAT I or ACT if English composition has not been completed. 48 credits of 123 to 143 must be completed at UArts.

Visiting: There are regularly scheduled orientations for prospective students, including a spring and fall open house. There are guides for informal visits and visitors may sit in on classes and stay overnight at the school. To schedule a visit, contact the Office of Admissions.

Financial Aid: 28% of undergraduate students work part-time. Presidential Merit Scholarships are available. Average earnings from campus work for the school year are $1500. UArts is a member of CSS. The FAFSA is required. The application deadline for fall entry is February 15.

International Students: There were 80 international students enrolled in a recent year. The school actively recruits these students. They must take the TOEFL and achieve a minimum score of 500. The student must also take the SAT I or the ACT.

Computers: The mainframe is a DEC PDP 11. Students have access to 82 nonnetworked personal computers located in residence halls, student services, electronic media centers, and departmental laboratories. There are no fees.

Graduates: Within an average freshman class, 47% graduate in 4 years, 52% in 5 years, and 53% in 6 years.

Admissions Contact: Barbara Elliott, Director of Admissions.

URSINUS COLLEGE

E-3

Collegeville, PA 19426   (610) 409-3200; FAX: (610) 489-0627

Full-time: 587 men, 643 women	Faculty: 95; IIB, +$
Part-time: 6 men, 9 women	Ph.D.s: 81%
Graduate: none	Student/Faculty: 13 to 1
Year: semesters, summer session	Tuition: $15,840
Application Deadline: February 15	Room & Board: $5330
Freshman Class: 1486 applied, 1206 accepted, 317 enrolled	
SAT I or ACT: required	VERY COMPETITIVE

Ursinus College, founded in 1869, is a private college affiliated with the United Church of Christ. It offers programs in the liberal arts. The library contains 185,000 volumes, 155,000 microform items, and 17,500 audiovisual forms, and subscribes to 900 periodicals. Computerized library sources and services include the card catalog, interlibrary loans, and database searching. Special learning facilities include an art gallery, radio station, and TV station. The 140-acre campus is in a suburban area 30 miles west of Philadelphia. Including residence halls, there are 48 buildings on campus.

Student Life: 67% of undergraduates are from Pennsylvania. Students come from 20 states and 15 foreign countries. 75% are from public schools; 25% from private. 87% are white. 40% are Catholic; 21% claim no religious affiliation. The average age of freshmen is 18; all undergraduates, 20. 8% do not continue beyond their first year; 76% remain to graduate.

Housing: 1100 students can be accommodated in college housing. College-sponsored living facilities include single-sex and coed dormitories and on-campus apartments. In addition there are honors houses, language houses, special interest houses, and a cultural house. On-campus housing is guaranteed for all 4 years. 90% of students live on campus; of those, 80% remain on campus on weekends. All students may keep cars on campus.

Activities: 50% of men belong to 8 local fraternities and 1 national fraternity; 45% of women belong to 5 local sororities. There are 41 groups on campus, including art, band, cheerleading, chess, choir, chorale, chorus, computers, dance, drama, ethnic, film, gay, honors, international, jazz band, literary magazine, musical theater, newspaper, orchestra, pep band, political, professional, radio and TV, religious, social, social service, student government, and yearbook. Popular campus events include Homecoming, Parents Day, Founders Day, and Air Band competition.

Sports: There are 10 intercollegiate sports for men and 10 for women, and 14 intramural sports for men and 12 for women. Athletic and recreation facilities include a gymnasium, racquetball and squash courts, a weight room, dance rooms, tennis courts, and all types of playing fields.

Disabled Students: 95% of the campus is accessible to disabled students. The following facilities are available: wheelchair ramps, elevators, special parking, specially equipped rest rooms, special class scheduling, lowered drinking fountains, and lowered telephones.

Services: In addition to many counseling and information services, tutoring is available in every subject.

Campus Safety and Security: Campus safety and security measures include 24-hour foot and vehicle patrol, escort service, pamphlets/posters/films, and lighted pathways/sidewalks.

Programs of Study: Ursinus confers B.A. and B.S degrees. Bachelor's degrees are awarded in BIOLOGICAL SCIENCE (biology/ biological science), BUSINESS (accounting, business administration and management, and business economics), COMMUNICATIONS AND THE ARTS (communications, English, French, German, music, and Spanish), COMPUTER AND PHYSICAL SCIENCE (chemistry, computer science, mathematics, and physics), EDUCATION (secondary), HEALTH PROFESSIONS (premedicine), SOCIAL SCIENCE (anthropology, economics, history, international relations, political science/government, prelaw, psychology, religion, and sociology). Sciences, English, and foreign language are the strongest academically. Economics, business administration, sciences, and psychology have the largest enrollments.

Required: All students must fulfill requirements in English composition, mathematics or logic, foreign language, humanities, and natural and social science. A total of 128 semester hours, with 32 to 40 in the major, is required, as is a GPA of 2.0.

Special: The college offers study abroad, student-designed majors, internships, a Washington semester, a Harrisburg and Philadelphia semester, dual majors, and a 3–2 engineering degree. There are 14 national honor societies on campus, including Phi Beta Kappa. All departments have honors programs.

Faculty/Classroom: 60% of faculty are male; 40%, female. All both teach and do research. The average class size in a regular course offering is 18.

Admissions: 81% of the 1995–96 applicants were accepted. The SAT I scores for the 1995–96 freshman class were as follows: Verbal—44% below 500, 41% between 500 and 599, 14% between 600 and 700, and 1% above 700; Math—17% below 500, 41% between 500 and 599, 35% between 600 and 700, and 8% above 700. 63% of the current freshmen were in the top fifth of their class; 86% were in the top two fifths.

Requirements: The SAT I or ACT is required. SAT II: Subject tests are recommended. A GED is accepted. Applicants should prepare with 16 academic credits, including 4 years of English, 3 of mathematics, 2 of foreign language, and 1 each of science and social studies. An interview is recommended. Applications are accepted on computer disk and on-line. AP and CLEP credits are accepted. Important factors in the admissions decision are advanced placement or honor courses, recommendations by school officials, and leadership record.

Procedure: Freshmen are admitted fall and spring. Entrance exams should be taken in the junior or senior year. There are early decision, early admissions, and deferred admissions plans. Early decision applications should be filed by December 15; regular applications, by February 15 for fall entry and December 1 for spring entry, along with an application fee of $30. Notification of early decision is sent January 1; regular decision, April 1. 51 early decision candidates were accepted for the 1995–96 class. A waiting list is an active part of the admissions procedure, with about 5% of all applicants on the list.

Transfer: 15 transfer students enrolled in a recent year. Transfer applicants must submit transcripts from all institutions attended. A dean's letter is recommended, as is a listing of courses taken. 64 credits of 128 must be completed at Ursinus.

Visiting: There are regularly scheduled orientations for prospective students, including a campus interview and a tour. There are guides for informal visits and visitors may sit in on classes and stay overnight at the school. To schedule a visit, contact the Admissions Office.

Financial Aid: In 1995–96, 88% of all freshmen and 74% of continuing students received some form of financial aid. 76% of freshmen and 65% of continuing students received need-based aid. The average freshman award was $13,300. Of that total, scholarships or need-based grants averaged $9300 ($15,600 maximum); loans averaged $3000 ($4125 maximum); and work contracts averaged $1000 ($1500 maximum). 50% of undergraduate students work part-time. Average earnings from campus work for the school year are $1000. The average financial indebtedness of the 1994–95 graduate was $12,000. Ursinus is a member of CSS. The FAFSA and CSS Profile Application are required. The application deadline for fall entry is February 15.

International Students: There are currently 19 international students enrolled. The school actively recruits these students. They must take the TOEFL and achieve a minimum score of 550. The student must also take the SAT I.

Computers: The college provides computer facilities for student use. The mainframe is a DEC VAX. There are 150 IBM-compatible and 50 Macintosh microcomputers available for student use; all are linked to the VAX. All students may access the system during library hours, a total of 102 hours per week. There are no time limits and no fees.

Graduates: In a recent year, 323 bachelor's degrees were awarded. The most popular majors among graduates were social sciences (17%), economics (15%), and biological sciences (12%). Within an average freshman class, 76% graduate in 4 years and 78% in 5 years. Of the 1994 graduating class, 30% were enrolled in graduate school within 6 months of graduation and 62% had found employment.

Admissions Contact: Richard G. DiFeliciantonio, Vice President for Enrollment. E-mail: admissions@ursinus.edu.

VILLANOVA UNIVERSITY   F-4
Villanova, PA 19085–1672

	(610) 519-4000
	(800) 338-7927; FAX: (610) 519-6450
Full-time: 3050 men, 3100 women	Faculty: 463; IIA, +$
Part-time: 745 men, 745 women	Ph.D.s: 90%
Graduate: 1280 men, 1210 women	Student/Faculty: 14 to 1
Year: semesters, summer session	Tuition: $16,960
Application Deadline: January 15	Room & Board: $7200
Freshman Class: 7972 applied, 5864 accepted, 1669 enrolled	
SAT I or ACT: required	**HIGHLY COMPETITIVE**

Villanova University, founded in 1842, is a coeducational college affiliated with the Catholic Church. It offers undergraduate programs in arts and sciences, commerce and finance, engineering, and nursing. There are 4 undergraduate and 5 graduate schools. In addition to regional accreditation, Villanova has baccalaureate program accreditation with AACSB, ABET, and NLN. The library contains 650,000 volumes, 106,400 microform items, and 29,000 audiovisual forms, and subscribes to 2850 periodicals. Computerized library sources and services include the card catalog, interlibrary loans, and database searching. Special learning facilities include an art gallery, planetarium, radio station, and 2 observatories. The 222-acre campus is in a suburban area 12 miles west of Philadelphia. Including residence halls, there are 55 buildings on campus.

Student Life: 68% of undergraduates are from out-of-state, mostly the Middle Atlantic. Students come from 48 states, 52 foreign countries, and Canada. 50% are from public schools; 50% from private. 91% are white. Most are Catholic. The average age of freshmen is 18; all undergraduates, 20. 7% do not continue beyond their first year; 85% remain to graduate.

Housing: 4008 students can be accommodated in college housing. College-sponsored living facilities include single-sex and coed dormitories and on-campus apartments. On-campus housing is available on a lottery system for upperclassmen. 65% of students live on campus; of those, 90% remain on campus on weekends. Alcohol is not permitted. Upperclassmen may keep cars on campus.

Activities: 29% of men belong to 1 local fraternity and 13 national fraternities; 48% of women belong to 8 national sororities. There are 150 groups on campus, including art, band, cheerleading, choir, chorale, chorus, computers, dance, drama, drill team, ethnic, honors, international, jazz band, literary magazine, marching band, musical theater, newspaper, pep band, photography, political, professional, radio and TV, religious, social, social service, student government, and yearbook. Popular campus events include Spring Fever Week, Sibling Weekend, Fall Festival, and Special Olympics.

Sports: There are 13 intercollegiate sports for men and 11 for women, and 11 intramural sports for men and 11 for women. Athletic and recreation facilities include a 200-meter indoor track, 2 swimming pools, basketball, volleyball, and tennis courts, weight rooms, and a field house. The football stadium seats 11800; the gymnasium, 6500.

Disabled Students: 75% of the campus is accessible to disabled students. The following facilities are available: wheelchair ramps, elevators, special parking, specially equipped rest rooms, special class scheduling, lowered drinking fountains, lowered telephones, and a specially equipped van for campus transportation and proximity card readers for several buildings with automatic doors.

Services: In addition to many counseling and information services, tutoring is available in most subjects. There is a reader service for the blind, and remedial math, reading, and writing. Tutoring services are administered through each department on an individual basis.

Campus Safety and Security: Campus safety and security measures include 24-hour foot and vehicle patrol, escort service, shuttle buses, and informal discussions. There are pamphlets/posters/films, emergency telephones, and lighted pathways/sidewalks. Public Safety officers are on duty all night in women's residence halls and there is a card access system to all residence halls.

Programs of Study: Villanova confers B.A. and B.S. degrees. Associate, master's, and doctoral degrees are also awarded. Bachelor's degrees are awarded in BIOLOGICAL SCIENCE (biology/biological science), BUSINESS (accounting, banking and finance, business administration and management, business economics, and marketing/retailing/merchandising), COMMUNICATIONS AND THE ARTS (classics, communications, English, French, German, and Spanish), COMPUTER AND PHYSICAL SCIENCE (astronomy, astrophysics, chemistry, computer science, mathematics, and physics), EDUCATION (elementary, secondary, and special), ENGINEERING AND ENVIRONMENTAL DESIGN (chemical engineering, civil engineering, electrical/electronics engineering, and mechanical engineering), HEALTH PROFESSIONS (nursing, physical therapy, and premedicine), SOCIAL SCIENCE (economics, geography, history, human services, international studies, philosophy, political science/government, psychology, religion, and sociology). Sciences, business, and liberal arts are the strongest academically. Liberal arts, commerce, and finance have the largest enrollments.

Required: All students are required to take core courses in English, history, religious studies, sciences, philosophy, and mathematics. Students must complete a total of 122 credit hours with a 2.0 overall GPA and a 2.2 GPA in the major.

Special: There is a co-op program in elementary education with Rosemont College and one in special education with Cabrini College. Internships are available for each college in the Philadelphia area as well as in New York City and Washington. Students may study abroad in the British Isles, the Pacific Rim, East Africa, the former Soviet Union, and the Caribbean. Villanova offers a Washington semester, dual majors, a general studies degree, and credit by examination. There is a freshman honors program on campus, as well as 31 national honor societies, including Phi Beta Kappa. 1 department has an honors program.

Faculty/Classroom: 74% of faculty are male; 26%, female. All teach undergraduates and 8% both teach and do research. No introductory courses are taught by graduate students. The average class size in an introductory lecture is 24; in a laboratory, 17; and in a regular course offering, 24.

Admissions: 74% of the 1995–96 applicants were accepted. The SAT I scores for the 1995–96 freshman class were as follows: Verbal—38% below 500, 47% between 500 and 599, 14% between 600 and 700, and 1% above 700; Math—8% below 500, 45% between 500 and 599, 37% between 600 and 700, and 10% above

700. 57% of the current freshmen were in the top fifth of their class; 89% were in the top two fifths. There were 17 National Merit finalists. 22 freshmen graduated first in their class.

Requirements: The SAT I or ACT is required. Applicants must be graduates of an accredited secondary school and should have completed 16 academic units. The specific courses required vary according to the college. A GED is accepted. Applicants to the College of Arts and Sciences must also take SAT II: Subject test in foreign language. An essay is required. Students may apply on-line through Ex-PAN. AP and CLEP credits are accepted. Important factors in the admissions decision are advanced placement or honor courses, recommendations by school officials, and leadership record.

Procedure: Freshmen are admitted in the fall. Entrance exams should be taken by December of the senior year. There are early action, early admissions, and deferred admissions plans. Early decision applications should be filed by December 15; regular applications, by January 15 for fall entry, along with an application fee of $40. Notification of early action is sent January 15; regular decision, April 1. 137 early action candidates were accepted for the 1995–96 class. A waiting list is an active part of the admissions procedure, with about 10% of all applicants on the list.

Transfer: 90 transfer students enrolled in 1995–96. Applicants must be sophomores or upperclassmen who have completed at least 30 credit hours and have a GPA of at least 3.0 for the College of Arts and Sciences, and 2.5 for the colleges of Nursing, Engineering, and Commerce and Finance. 60 credits of 122 must be completed at Villanova.

Visiting: There are regularly scheduled orientations for prospective students, including campus tours and information sessions conducted several times daily and on selected Saturdays throughout the academic year. There are guides for informal visits and visitors may sit in on classes. To schedule a visit, contact the Office of Undergraduate Admission.

Financial Aid: In 1995–96, 67% of all freshmen and 58% of continuing students received some form of financial aid. 55% of freshmen and 49% of continuing students received need-based aid. The average freshman award was $13,170. Of that total, scholarships or need-based grants averaged $8275 ($10,000 maximum); loans averaged $4154 ($20,965 maximum); ROTC and employee remission plan aid averaged $13,354 ($21,989 maximum); and work contracts averaged $1800 ($2000 maximum). 22% of undergraduate students work part-time. Average earnings from campus work for the school year are $1500. The average financial indebtedness of the 1994–95 graduate was $10,000. The FAFSA, the college's own financial statement, and the parent and student federal income tax returns are required. The application deadline for fall entry is February 15.

International Students: There are currently 135 international students enrolled. The school actively recruits these students. They must score 550 on the TOEFL and also take SAT I or the ACT.

Computers: The college provides computer facilities for student use. The mainframes are a 2 clustered Data General Avion 9500, VAX cluster. More than 1000 IBM PC-compatibles in laboratories and classroom, plus 200 Apple Macintoshes. Network connectivity is available from all residence halls. All students may access the system. There are no time limits and no fees.

Graduates: In 1994–95, 1691 bachelor's degrees were awarded. The most popular majors among graduates were business administration (18%), accounting (12%), and political science (8%). Within an average freshman class, 81% graduate in 4 years, 84% in 5 years, and 85% in 6 years. 236 companies recruited on campus in 1994–95. Of the 1994 graduating class, 21% were enrolled in graduate school within 6 months of graduation and 61% had found employment.

Admissions Contact: Stephen R. Merritt, Director of Undergraduate Admission. E-mail: gotovu@ucis.vill.edu. A campus video is available.

WASHINGTON AND JEFFERSON COLLEGE · A-3

Washington, PA 15301	(412) 223-6025; FAX: (412) 223-5271
Full-time: 627 men, 488 women	**Faculty:** 88; IIB, +$
Part-time: 10 men, 3 women	**Ph.D.s:** 92%
Graduate: none	**Student/Faculty:** 13 to 1
Year: 4-1-4, summer session	**Tuition:** $16,840
Application Deadline: March 1	**Room & Board:** $4205
Freshman Class: 1140 applied, 1000 accepted, 281 enrolled	
SAT I Verbal/Math: 500/560	**VERY COMPETITIVE**

Washington and Jefferson College, founded in 1781, is a private, co-educational institution offering instruction in liberal arts. The library contains 195,000 volumes, 5400 microform items, and 2950 audiovisual forms, and subscribes to 715 periodicals. Computerized library sources and services include the card catalog, interlibrary loans, and database searching. Special learning facilities include an art gallery, radio station, and a biological field station. The 40-acre campus is in a small town 25 miles south of Pittsburgh. Including residence halls, there are 36 buildings on campus.

Student Life: 65% of undergraduates are from Pennsylvania. Students come from 30 states and 5 foreign countries. 70% are from public schools; 30% from private. 92% are white. 55% are Catholic; 30% Protestant. The average age of freshmen is 18; all undergraduates, 20. 7% do not continue beyond their first year; 84% remain to graduate.

Housing: 950 students can be accommodated in college housing. College-sponsored living facilities include single-sex and coed dormitories and fraternity houses. On-campus housing is guaranteed for all 4 years. 85% of students live on campus; of those, 90% remain on campus on weekends. Alcohol is not permitted. All students may keep cars on campus.

Activities: 55% of men belong to 10 national fraternities; 65% of women belong to 4 national sororities. There are 77 groups on campus, including art, cheerleading, choir, chorale, chorus, computers, drama, ethnic, jazz band, literary magazine, newspaper, orchestra, pep band, photography, political, professional, radio and TV, religious, social, social service, student government, and yearbook. Popular campus events include Homecoming, Carnival, and Greek Week.

Sports: There are 10 intercollegiate sports for men and 6 for women, and 8 intramural sports for men and 7 for women. Athletic and recreation facilities include swimming and diving pools, a track, a weight room, football, baseball, and soccer fields, and basketball, volleyball, squash, and racquetball courts. The stadium seats 4000, the largest auditorium/arena, 3500.

Disabled Students: Special class scheduling is available.

Services: In addition to many counseling and information services, tutoring is available in most subjects. There is a reader service for the blind, and remedial math, reading, and writing.

Campus Safety and Security: Campus safety and security measures include 24-hour foot and vehicle patrol, escort service, informal discussions, and pamphlets/posters/films. There are emergency telephones and lighted pathways/sidewalks.

Programs of Study: Washington and Jefferson confers the B.A. degree. Bachelor's degrees are awarded in BIOLOGICAL SCIENCE (biology/biological science), BUSINESS (accounting and business administration and management), COMMUNICATIONS AND THE ARTS (English, French, German, and Spanish), COMPUTER AND PHYSICAL SCIENCE (chemistry, computer science, mathematics, and physics), EDUCATION (art, foreign languages, and secondary), HEALTH PROFESSIONS (medical laboratory technology, predentistry, and premedicine), SOCIAL SCIENCE (economics, history, philosophy, political science/government, prelaw, psychology, and sociology). Prelaw and premedicine are the strongest academically. Business, English, and psychology have the largest enrollments.

Required: Students are required to take a core of 14 courses (56 credit hours) in history/philosophy/religion, art/music, language, literature, science/mathematics, economics/business, political science, and biology. Other requirements include physical education, freshman English, and freshman forum. A total of 36 courses (144 credit hours), with 8 to 10 courses in the major, is required for graduation, as is a 2.0 GPA.

Special: The college offers study abroad, internships in all majors, a Washington semester with American University, dual and student-designed majors, credit by examination, and pass/fail options. There is a 3–2 engineering program with Case Western Reserve University and Washington University in St. Louis. The college offers special human resources management and entrepreneurial studies programs. There is also a 3–4 podiatry program with Pennsylvania College of Podiatry and a 3–4 optometry program with Pennsylvania College of Optometry. There are 11 national honor societies on campus, including Phi Beta Kappa. 12 departments have honors programs.

Faculty/Classroom: 75% of faculty are male; 25%, female. All teach undergraduates. The average class size in an introductory lecture is 30; in a laboratory, 16; and in a regular course offering, 24.

Admissions: 88% of the 1995–96 applicants were accepted. The SAT I scores for a recent freshman class were as follows: Verbal—44% below 500, 47% between 500 and 599, 7% between 600 and 700, and 2% above 700; Math—35% below 500, 43% between 500 and 599, 18% between 600 and 700, and 4% above 700. 56% of the current freshmen were in the top fifth of their class; 90% were in the top two fifths. There were 3 National Merit semifinalists. 32 freshmen graduated first in their class.

Requirements: The SAT I, and SAT II: Subject test in writing and 2 other subjects or the ACT is required. Washington and Jefferson requires applicants to be in the upper 40% of their class. A GED is accepted. Applicants must complete 15 academic credits or Carnegie units, including 3 credits of English and mathematics, 2 of foreign language, and 1 of science. An essay and interview are recommended. Applications are accepted on computer disk and on-line. AP and CLEP credits are accepted. Important factors in the admissions decision are advanced placement or honor courses, recommendations by school officials, and personality/intangible qualities.

Procedure: Freshmen are admitted to all sessions. Entrance exams should be taken in the junior or senior year. There are early decision, early admissions, and deferred admissions plans. Early decision applications should be filed by November 1; regular applications, by March 1 for fall entry, January 1 for winter entry, February 1 for spring entry, and June 1 for summer entry, along with an application fee of $25. Notification of early decision is sent November 15; regular decision, February 1. 42 early decision candidates were accepted for the 1995–96 class. A waiting list is an active part of the admissions procedure, with about 7% of all applicants on the list.

Transfer: 47 transfer students enrolled in 1995–96. Transfer applicants must have a 2.5 GPA and must take the SAT I or ACT. 72 credits of 144 must be completed at Washington and Jefferson.

Visiting: There are regularly scheduled orientations for prospective students, including a general session, departmental meetings, preprofessional meetings, and a financial aid meeting. There are guides for informal visits and visitors may sit in on classes and stay overnight at the school. To schedule a visit, contact the Admission Office.

Financial Aid: In 1995–96, 75% of all students received some form of financial aid, including need-based aid. The average freshman award was $13,000. Of that total, scholarships or need-based grants averaged $8259; pell grants averaged $1518 and state grants averaged $2388; loans averaged $2625 ($4125 maximum); and work contracts averaged $1000. 15% of undergraduate students work part-time. Average earnings from campus work for the school year are $1000. The average financial indebtedness of the 1994–95 graduate was $13,900. Washington and Jefferson is a member of CSS. The FAFSA and state scholarship application are required. The application deadline for fall entry is March 15.

International Students: There were 7 international students enrolled in a recent year. They must take the TOEFL and achieve a minimum score of 500.

Computers: The college provides computer facilities for student use. The mainframes are a DEC VAX 3800 and a PDP 11/44. Some 200 terminals and microcomputers, including IBM PS/2, IBM-compatible, Apple II, and Macintosh, are located in the computer center and classrooms. All students may access the system as needed. There are no time limits and no fees.

Graduates: In 1994–95, 216 bachelor's degrees were awarded. The most popular majors among graduates were business administration (23%), accounting (13%), and English (12%). Within an average freshman class, 76% graduate in 4 years and 84% in 5 years. 45 companies recruited on campus in 1994–95. Of the 1994 graduating class, 45% were enrolled in graduate school within 6 months of graduation and 55% had found employment.

Admissions Contact: Thomas O'Connor, Director of Admission. E-mail: toconnor@washjeff.edu.

WAYNESBURG COLLEGE
Waynesburg, PA 15370-9930

B-4
(412) 852-3248
(800) 225-7393; **FAX:** (412) 627-6416

Full-time: 581 men, 640 women	Faculty: 67; IIB, --$
Part-time: 17 men, 29 women	Ph.D.s: n/av
Graduate: 17 men, 8 women	Student/Faculty: 18 to 1
Year: semesters, summer session	Tuition: $9600
Application Deadline: open	Room & Board: $3892
Freshman Class: 1420 applied, 1191 accepted, 364 enrolled	
SAT I Verbal/Math: 410/480	**COMPETITIVE**

Waynesburg College, founded in 1849, is a private, coeducational liberal arts institution affiliated with the Presbyterian Church (U.S.A.). In addition to regional accreditation, Waynesburg has baccalaureate program accreditation with NLN. The library contains 100,000 volumes, 65 microform items, and 263 audiovisual forms, and subscribes to 532 periodicals. Computerized library sources and services include the card catalog, interlibrary loans, and database searching. Special learning facilities include a learning resource center, natural history museum, radio station, and TV station. The 30-acre campus is in a small town 50 miles south of Pittsburgh. Including residence halls, there are 15 buildings on campus.

Student Life: 88% of undergraduates are from Pennsylvania. Students come from 17 states and 7 foreign countries. 94% are from public schools; 6% from private. 94% are white. 56% are Protestant; 30% Catholic; 14% claim no religious affiliation. The average age of freshmen is 18; all undergraduates, 21.

Housing: 600 students can be accommodated in college housing. College-sponsored living facilities include single-sex and coed dormitories. In addition there are special interest houses and a community service house. On-campus housing is guaranteed for all 4 years. Alcohol is not permitted. Upperclassmen may keep cars on campus.

Activities: 9% of men belong to 3 national fraternities; 11% of women belong to 3 national sororities. There are 25 groups on campus, including band, cheerleading, chorale, dance, drama, drill team, ethnic, film, honors, international, jazz band, literary magazine, marching band, musical theater, newspaper, orchestra, pep band, photogra-

phy, professional, radio and TV, religious, social, social service, student government, and yearbook. Popular campus events include Greek Week, Fine Arts Services, GNP-Alumni Concert, and Poetry Festival.

Sports: There are 7 intercollegiate sports for men and 7 for women, and 15 intramural sports for men and 12 for women. Athletic and recreation facilities include table tennis, billiards, fitness center, basketball courts, wrestling room, weight room, racquetball courts, golf driving net, and a gymnasium. The campus stadium seats 1500, the indoor gymnasium 1500, and the largest auditorium/arena 250.

Disabled Students: 85% of the campus is accessible to disabled students. The following facilities are available: wheelchair ramps, elevators, special parking, specially equipped rest rooms, special class scheduling, and lowered drinking fountains.

Services: In addition to many counseling and information services, tutoring is available in every subject. There is remedial math and writing.

Campus Safety and Security: Campus safety and security measures include 24-hour foot and vehicle patrol, self-defense education, escort service, and informal discussions. There are pamphlets/posters/films, lighted pathways/sidewalks, and 24-hour security access.

Programs of Study: Waynesburg confers B.A., B.S., B.S.B.A., and B.S.N. degrees. Associate and master's degrees are also awarded. Bachelor's degrees are awarded in BIOLOGICAL SCIENCE (biology/biological science), BUSINESS (accounting, banking and finance, management, marketing/retailing/merchandising, and small business management), COMMUNICATIONS AND THE ARTS (art and English), COMPUTER AND PHYSICAL SCIENCE (chemistry, computer science, and mathematics), EDUCATION (elementary and secondary), ENGINEERING AND ENVIRONMENTAL DESIGN (commercial art and environmental science), HEALTH PROFESSIONS (health care administration, medical laboratory technology, nursing, physical therapy, predentistry, premedicine, and sports medicine), SOCIAL SCIENCE (criminal justice, economics, history, political science/government, prelaw, psychology, public administration, social science, and sociology). Nursing, business, and education are the strongest academically and have the largest enrollments.

Required: To graduate, students must complete a minimum of 124 semester hours, with at least 30 hours in the major. A minimum 2.0 GPA and courses in life skills, computer sciences, and service learning are required. Other requirements include 9 credits of English/communications, 3 of mathematics, 8 of natural and physical sciences, 6 of literature and the arts, and 15 of humanities and social and behavioral sciences. Students must also pass an English usage and written competency test as well as a mathematics test.

Special: The college offers internships, dual majors, credit for experience, nondegree study, and pass/fail options. There is a 3–2 engineering degree program with Case Western Reserve, Washington, and Pennsylvania State Universities. There is a freshman honors program on campus, as well as 16 national honor societies. 13 departments have honors programs.

Faculty/Classroom: 55% of faculty are male; 45%, female. All teach undergraduates. No introductory courses are taught by graduate students. The average class size in an introductory lecture is 30; in a laboratory, 10; and in a regular course offering, 18.

Admissions: 84% of the 1995–96 applicants were accepted. The SAT I scores for the 1995–96 freshman class were as follows: Verbal—84% below 500, 15% between 500 and 599, and 1% between 600 and 700; Math—56% below 500, 35% between 500 and 599, and 10% between 600 and 700. 21% of the current freshmen were in the top fifth of their class; 53% were in the top two fifths. One freshman graduated first in the class.

Requirements: The SAT I or ACT is recommended. Some applicants may be required to submit scores to further validate academic potential. Waynesburg requires applicants to be in the upper 40% of their class with a 2.5 GPA. In addition, applicants must be graduates of an accredited secondary school or have a GED certificate and have completed 16 academic credits, including 4 in English and 2 each in mathematics, sciences, and history or social studies. An essay, interview, or enrollment in the summer Step Ahead Program may be required. Applications are accepted via the World Wide Web at http://waynesburg.edu/. AP and CLEP credits are accepted. Important factors in the admissions decision are advanced placement or honor courses, recommendations by school officials, and extracurricular activities record.

Procedure: Freshmen are admitted to all sessions. Entrance exams should be taken in April of the junior year or December of the senior year. There is an early admissions plan. Application deadlines are open. Application fee is $15. Notification is sent on a rolling basis.

Transfer: 73 transfer students enrolled in 1995–96. Students must submit a high school transcript and complete transcripts from all colleges previously attended. 45 credits of 124 must be completed at Waynesburg.

Visiting: There are regularly scheduled orientations for prospective students, including visits with faculty, students, administrators, and financial aid officers, and a tour of the campus. There are guides for informal visits and visitors may sit in on classes and stay overnight at the school. To schedule a visit, contact Robin L. Moore, Admissions Office.

Financial Aid: In 1995–96, 91% of all freshmen and 94% of continuing students received some form of financial aid. 86% of freshmen and 87% of continuing students received need-based aid. The average freshman award was $10,098. Of that total, scholarships or need-based grants averaged $6649 ($13,492 maximum); loans averaged $3205 ($6625 maximum); and work contracts averaged $531 ($1200 maximum). 18% of undergraduate students work part-time. Average earnings from campus work for the school year are $550. The average financial indebtedness of the 1994–95 graduate was $10,000. Waynesburg is a member of CSS. The college's own financial statement is required. The application deadline for fall entry is March 15.

International Students: There were 8 international students enrolled in a recent year. The school actively recruits these students. They must take the TOEFL and achieve a minimum score of 550.

Computers: The college provides computer facilities for student use. Five fully equipped computer laboratoires with microcomputers, including IBM, Macintosh, Apple II, and Amiga, are available for student use. All students may access the system. There are no time limits and no fees.

Graduates: In a recent year, 247 bachelor's degrees were awarded. The most popular majors among graduates were business (25%), nursing (23%), and education (15%). Within an average freshman class, 4% graduate in 3 years, 44% in 4 years, 54% in 5 years, and 54% in 6 years. 30 companies recruited on campus in a recent year.

Admissions Contact: Robin L. Moore, Director of Admissions.

WEST CHESTER UNIVERSITY OF PENNSYLVANIA
F-4

West Chester, PA 19383   (610) 436–3411; FAX: (610) 436–2907

Full-time: 3011 men, 4470 women	Faculty: 548; IIA, +$
Part-time: 764 men, 1029 women	Ph.D.s: 67%
Graduate: 1083 men, 2119 women	Student/Faculty: 14 to 1
Year: semesters, summer session	Tuition: $3544 ($8846)
Application Deadline: open	Room & Board: $5448
Freshman Class: 6157 applied, 3720 accepted, 1393 enrolled	
SAT I Verbal/Math: 450/500	**COMPETITIVE**

West Chester University, founded in 1871, is a public institution that is part of the Pennsylvania State System of Higher Education. It offers programs through the College of Arts and Sciences, and Schools of Business and Public Affairs, Education, Health Sciences, and Music. The Exton Center campus offers credit and noncredit classes geared to nontraditional populations. There are 5 undergraduate and 5 graduate schools. In addition to regional accreditation, the university has baccalaureate program accreditation with CSWE, NASM, NCATE, and NLN. The 2 libraries contain 521,724 volumes, 350,000 microform items, and 39,162 audiovisual forms, and subscribe to 3046 periodicals. Computerized library sources and services include the card catalog, interlibrary loans, and database searching. Special learning facilities include a learning resource center, art gallery, planetarium, radio station, an herbarium, a speech and hearing clinic, a center for government and community affairs, and a natural area for environmental studies. The 547-acre campus is in a small town 25 miles west of Philadelphia. Including residence halls, there are 61 buildings on campus.

Student Life: 87% of undergraduates are from Pennsylvania. Students come from 32 states, 53 foreign countries, and Canada. 79% are from public schools; 21% from private. 88% are white. 46% are Catholic; 34% Protestant; 11% claim no religious affiliation. The average age of freshmen is 18.1; all undergraduates, 23. 16% do not continue beyond their first year; 51% remain to graduate.

Housing: 3500 students can be accommodated in college housing. College-sponsored living facilities include single-sex and coed dormitories and on-campus apartments. Honors and international student sections are available. On-campus housing is guaranteed for all 4 years. 56% of students commute. Alcohol is not permitted. Upperclassmen may keep cars on campus.

Activities: 10% of men belong to 15 national fraternities; 7% of women belong to 10 national sororities. There are 184 groups on campus, including art, band, cheerleading, chess, choir, chorale, chorus, computers, dance, drama, drill team, drum and bugle corps, ethnic, film, gay, honors, international, jazz band, literary magazine, marching band, musical theater, newspaper, orchestra, photography, political, professional, radio and TV, religious, social, social service, student government, symphony, and yearbook. Popular campus events include International Day, Spring Weekend, and El Milagro (Latino Heritage) Week.

Sports: There are 11 intercollegiate sports for men and 12 for women, and 11 intramural sports for men and 7 for women. Athletic and recreation facilities include a field house, practice fields, a stadium, indoor and outdoor tracks, swimming pools, a training room, and tennis and basketball courts. The campus stadium seats 8000, the indoor gymnasium 2000, and the largest auditorium/arena 1800.

Disabled Students: 90% of the campus is accessible to disabled students. The following facilities are available: wheelchair ramps, elevators, special parking, specially equipped rest rooms, special class scheduling, lowered drinking fountains, and lowered telephones.

Services: In addition to many counseling and information services, tutoring is available in every subject. There is remedial math, reading, and writing.

Campus Safety and Security: Campus safety and security measures include 24-hour foot and vehicle patrol, self-defense education, escort service, and shuttle buses. There are informal discussions, pamphlets/posters/films, emergency telephones, and lighted pathways/sidewalks.

Programs of Study: The university confers B.A., B.S., B.F.A., B.Mu., B.S.Ed., and B.S.N. degrees. Associate and master's degrees are also awarded. Bachelor's degrees are awarded in BIOLOGICAL SCIENCE (biochemistry, biology/biological science, and microbiology), BUSINESS (accounting, business administration and management, business economics, and marketing/retailing/merchandising), COMMUNICATIONS AND THE ARTS (communications, dramatic arts, English, fine arts, French, German, Latin, music, Russian, Spanish, and speech/debate/rhetoric), COMPUTER AND PHYSICAL SCIENCE (chemistry, computer science, earth science, geology, mathematics, and physics), EDUCATION (early childhood, elementary, foreign languages, health, music, physical, secondary, and special), HEALTH PROFESSIONS (health, nursing, predentistry, premedicine, public health, and speech pathology/audiology), SOCIAL SCIENCE (anthropology, criminal justice, economics, geography, history, philosophy, political science/government, prelaw, psychology, public administration, religion, social work, and sociology). Premedical is the strongest academically. Physical education, elementary/early childhood education, business management, and psychology have the largest enrollments.

Required: All students must satisfy requirements in English composition, mathematics, interdisciplinary study, and physical education. Distribution requirements include 9 hours each of science, behavioral and social science, and humanities, and 3 hours in the arts. A total of 128 credit hours and a 2.0 GPA are required.

Special: There is cross-registration with Cheyney University and a 3–2 engineering program with Pennsylvania State University. The university offers internships in most majors, study abroad in France, Austria, and Wales, a Washington semester, work-study, some student-designed majors, credit by examination and for life, military, and work experience, and pass/fail options. There is a freshman honors program on campus, as well as 23 national honor societies. 10 departments have honors programs.

Faculty/Classroom: 60% of faculty are male; 40%, female. All teach undergraduates and 48% both teach and do research. No introductory courses are taught by graduate students. The average class size in an introductory lecture is 35; in a laboratory, 24; and in a regular course offering, 30.

Admissions: 60% of the 1995–96 applicants were accepted. The SAT I scores for the 1995–96 freshman class were as follows: Verbal—72% below 500, 25% between 500 and 599, and 3% between 600 and 700; Math—47% below 500, 40% between 500 and 599, 12% between 600 and 700, and 1% above 700. 30% of the current freshmen were in the top fifth of their class; 70% were in the top two fifths.

Requirements: The SAT I is required, with a recommended recentered score of 1000. The university requires applicants to be in the upper 50% of their class with a 2.5 GPA. In addition, applicants should graduate from an accredited secondary school or have a GED. A total of 16 academic credits is required, including 4 years of English, 3 each of history, mathematics, and social studies, and 2 of science. An essay is required; music students need to audition. AP and CLEP credits are accepted. Important factors in the admissions decision are advanced placement or honor courses, recommendations by school officials, and evidence of special talent.

Procedure: Freshmen are admitted fall and spring. Entrance exams should be taken in spring of the junior year or fall of the senior year. There are early admissions and deferred admissions plans. Application deadlines are open. Application fee is $25. Notification is sent on a rolling basis. A waiting list is an active part of the admissions procedure, with about 5% of all applicants on the list.

Transfer: 980 transfer students enrolled in 1995–96. Transfer applicants should have earned at least 30 credits and must have a recommended GPA of at least 2.5. Some departments require a higher GPA and specific course requirements. Transfers who have earned fewer than 30 credits must submit a high school transcript and standardized test scores. 30 credits of 128 must be completed at the university.

Visiting: There are regularly scheduled orientations for prospective students, including academic advising, scheduling, and social events over a 2-day period. There are guides for informal visits and visitors may sit in on classes and stay overnight at the school. To schedule a visit, contact the Office of Admissions.

Financial Aid: In 1995–96, 46% of all students received some form of financial aid, including need-based aid. The average freshman award was $4414. Of that total, scholarships or need-based grants averaged $1378 ($8196 maximum); loans averaged $2724 ($8625 maximum); and work contracts averaged $312 ($2137 maximum). 7% of undergraduate students work part-time. Average earnings from campus work for the school year are $1520. The average financial indebtedness of the 1994–95 graduate was $12,000. the university is a member of CSS. The FAFSA is required. The application deadline for fall entry is March 15.

International Students: There are currently 153 international students enrolled. They must take the TOEFL and achieve a minimum score of 550.

Computers: The college provides computer facilities for student use. The mainframe is an IBM 4381. More than 250 microcomputers are available in computer laboratories, classrooms, and residence halls. All students may access the system. There are no time limits and no fees.

Graduates: In a recent year, 1718 bachelor's degrees were awarded. The most popular majors among graduates were elementary education (15%), physical education (7%), and criminal justice (7%). Within an average freshman class, 25% graduate in 4 years, 46% in 5 years, and 51% in 6 years. 30 companies recruited on campus in a recent year.

Admissions Contact: Director of Admissions. E-mail: ugadmiss@wcupa.edu.

WESTMINSTER COLLEGE
New Wilmington, PA 16172

A-2

(412) 946-7100
(800) 942-8033 (in-state)

Full-time: 587 men, 824 women	Faculty: 96; IIB, av$
Part-time: 79 men and women	Ph.Ds: 77%
Graduate: 120 men and women	Student/Faculty: 15 to 1
Year: 4–1-4, summer session	Tuition: $13,515
Application Deadline: open	Room & Board: $3980
Freshman Class: n/av	
SAT I or ACT: required	**COMPETITIVE**

Westminster College, founded in 1852, is a private, coeducational liberal arts institution related to the Presbyterian Church (USA). In addition to regional accreditation, Westminster has baccalaureate program accreditation with NASM. The 2 libraries contain 220,000 volumes and subscribe to 1000 periodicals. Computerized library sources and services include interlibrary loans. Special learning facilities include a learning resource center, art gallery, planetarium, radio station, TV station, and electron microscope laboratories in the science center. The 300-acre campus is in a rural area 60 miles north of Pittsburgh. Including residence halls, there are 22 buildings on campus.

Student Life: 76% of undergraduates are from Pennsylvania. Students come from 23 states and 1 foreign country. 90% are from public schools; 10% from private. 97% are white. 56% are Protestant; 34% Catholic; 10% claim no religious affiliation. The average age of freshmen is 18; all undergraduates, 20. 1% do not continue beyond their first year; 78% remain to graduate.

Housing: 1120 students can be accommodated in college housing. College-sponsored living facilities include single-sex dormitories and fraternity houses. Some residence hall floors have 24-hour weekend visitation. On-campus housing is guaranteed for all 4 years. 90% of students live on campus. Alcohol is not permitted. All students may keep cars on campus.

Activities: 29% of men belong to 5 national fraternities; 30% of women belong to 5 national sororities. There are 85 groups on campus, including band, cheerleading, choir, chorus, dance, drama, drill team, ethnic, honors, jazz band, literary magazine, marching band, newspaper, orchestra, pep band, political, radio and TV, religious, social, social service, student government, and yearbook. Popular campus events include mock conventions, liberal arts forum, dances, and films.

Sports: There are 9 intercollegiate sports for men and 8 for women, and 7 intramural sports for men and 6 for women. Athletic and recreation facilities include a natatorium, racquetball, tennis, and basketball courts, a track, and weight and aerobics rooms.

Disabled Students: The following facilities are available: wheelchair ramps, elevators, special parking, specially equipped rest rooms, and special class scheduling.

Services: In addition to many counseling and information services, tutoring is available in most subjects through the learning center. There is remedial reading and writing.

Campus Safety and Security: Campus safety and security measures include 24-hour foot and vehicle patrol, escort service, informal discussions, and pamphlets/posters/films. In addition, there are emergency telephones and lighted pathways/sidewalks.

Programs of Study: Westminster confers B.A., B.S., and B.M. degrees. Master's degrees are also awarded. Bachelor's degrees are awarded in BIOLOGICAL SCIENCE (biology/biological science and molecular biology), BUSINESS (accounting, banking and finance, business administration and management, international business management, and marketing/retailing/merchandising), COMMUNICATIONS AND THE ARTS (art, broadcasting, communications, English, fine arts, French, German, Latin, music, music performance, music theory and composition, and Spanish), COMPUTER AND PHYSICAL SCIENCE (chemistry, computer science, mathematics, and physics), EDUCATION (Christian education, elementary, guidance, music, and secondary), HEALTH PROFESSIONS (predentistry and premedicine), SOCIAL SCIENCE (criminal justice, economics, history, international relations, philosophy, political science/government, prelaw, psychology, religion, social science, and sociology). Sciences, business, and education are the strongest academically and have the largest enrollments.

Required: To graduate, all students must complete 36 courses and 4 terms of physical education, with 9 to 15 courses in the major, for a total of 126 credit hours. Distribution requirements include 2 to 4 courses in a foreign language; 2 each in social science, natural science and mathematics, and humanities; and 1 each in writing, religion, literature, communications, computer science, and fine arts. A minimum GPA of 2.0 is required.

Special: The college offers internships, study abroad in many countries, a Washington semester, various dual and student-designed majors, nondegree study, and a 3–2 engineering degree with Case Western Reserve, Pennsylvania State, and Washington universities. There is a freshman honors program on campus, as well as 12 national honor societies.

Faculty/Classroom: 73% of faculty are male; 22%, female. All teach undergraduates. No introductory courses are taught by graduate students. The average class size in a regular course offering is 25.

Requirements: The SAT I or ACT is required, with a minimum recommended composite score of 900 on the SAT I or 20 on the ACT. Westminster requires applicants to be in the upper 50% of their class. A minimum GPA of 2.5 is required. Applicants must be graduates of an accredited secondary school and have a minimum of 16 academic credits, including 4 units in English, 3 in mathematics, and 2 each in foreign language, science, and social studies. The GED will be considered with a minimum composite score of 270. A portfolio, audition, and interview are recommended. An essay is required. AP and CLEP credits are accepted. Important factors in the admissions decision are advanced placement or honor courses, leadership record, and recommendations by school officials.

Procedure: Freshmen are admitted fall, winter, and spring. Entrance exams should be taken during the junior year. There is a deferred admissions plan. Application deadlines are open. Application fee is $20. Notification is sent on a rolling basis.

Transfer: Transfer students must have a college GPA of 2.0 or better.

Visiting: There are regularly scheduled orientations for prospective students, consisting of an introduction, a student panel, a financial aid workshop, a campus tour, a faculty fair, and lunch. Optional activities include a tour of residence halls and radio and TV stations and a football game. There are 2 visitation days in the fall and 2 in the spring. There are guides for informal visits and visitors may sit in on classes and stay overnight at the school. To schedule a visit, contact the Office of Admissions.

Financial Aid: In a recent year, 75% of all freshmen and 74% of continuing students received some form of financial aid. 72% of all students received need-based aid. The average freshman award was $8618. Of that total, scholarships or need-based grants averaged $5618 ($6000 maximum); loans averaged $3500; and work contracts averaged $1300. 26% of undergraduate students work part-time. Average earnings from campus work for the school year are $1300. The average financial indebtedness of a recent graduate was $13,500. Westminster is a member of CSS. The FAF and the college's own financial statement are required. The application deadline for fall entry is March 15.

International Students: In a recent year, there was 1 international student enrolled. Students must take the TOEFL or the MELAB and achieve a minimum score on the TOEFL of 550. The student must also take the SAT I, scoring a minimum composite of 900, or the ACT.

Computers: The college provides computer facilities for student use. The mainframe is a DEC VAX 11/85. Microcomputers are available throughout the campus. All students may access the system. There are no time limits and no fees.

Graduates: In a recent class, 335 bachelor's degrees were awarded. The most popular majors among graduates were business (21%), elementary education (14%), and history (7%). Within an average freshman class, 74% graduate in 4 years, 75% in 5 years, and 76% in 6 years. 50 companies recruited on campus in a recent year.

Admissions Contact: Richard Dana Paul, Director of Admissions.

WIDENER UNIVERSITY   F-4

Chester, PA 19013	(610) 499-4126; FAX: (610) 876-9751
Full-time: 1160 men, 1100 women	Faculty: 190; IIA, +$
Part-time: 80 men, 75 women	Ph.D.s: 92%
Graduate: none	Student/Faculty: 12 to 1
Year: semesters, summer session	Tuition: $12,950
Application Deadline: open	Room & Board: $5650
Freshman Class: 2246 applied, 561 enrolled	
SAT I Verbal/Math: 440/450	COMPETITIVE

Widener University, founded in 1821, is a private, coeducational liberal arts institution offering undergraduate programs in the arts and sciences, business management, engineering, nursing, and hotel and restaurant management. Other campuses are in Harrisburg and Wilmington, Delaware. There are 7 undergraduate and 5 graduate schools. In addition to regional accreditation, Widener has baccalaureate program accreditation with ABET, ACCE, CSWE, NCATE, and NLN. The library contains 211,237 volumes, 106,791 microform items, and 7998 audiovisual forms, and subscribes to 2310 periodicals. Computerized library sources and services include the card catalog, interlibrary loans, and database searching. Special learning facilities include a learning resource center, art gallery, radio station, and a child development center. The 105-acre campus is in a suburban area 15 miles south of Philadelphia. Including residence halls, there are 72 buildings on campus.

Student Life: 51% of undergraduates are from out-of-state, mostly the Middle Atlantic. Students come from 32 states, 42 foreign countries, and Canada. 51% are from public schools; 49% from private. 79% are white; 11% African American. 45% are Catholic; 44% Protestant. The average age of freshmen is 18; all undergraduates, 21. 9% do not continue beyond their first year; 56% remain to graduate.

Housing: 1400 students can be accommodated in college housing. College-sponsored living facilities include single-sex and coed dormitories, on-campus apartments, fraternity houses, and sorority houses. In addition there are special interest houses, a music house, and an international house. On-campus housing is guaranteed for all 4 years. 60% of students live on campus; of those, 75% remain on campus on weekends. All students may keep cars on campus.

Activities: 28% of men belong to 8 national fraternities; 18% of women belong to 4 national sororities. There are 92 groups on campus, including art, band, cheerleading, chess, chorale, chorus, computers, drama, ethnic, film, honors, international, jazz band, literary magazine, musical theater, newspaper, pep band, photography, political, professional, radio and TV, religious, social, social service, student government, and yearbook. Popular campus events include Greek Week, Hundredth Night, and Honors Week.

Sports: There are 12 intercollegiate sports for men and 10 for women, and 5 intramural sports for men and 2 for women. Athletic and recreation facilities include a 4000-seat stadium, an 1800-seat basketball gymnasium, a field house, a championship pool, a weight training room, an exercise room, squash and tennis courts, outdoor game and practice fields, and an 8-lane, all-weather championship track.

Disabled Students: 95% of the campus is accessible to disabled students. The following facilities are available: wheelchair ramps, elevators, special parking, specially equipped rest rooms, special class scheduling, lowered drinking fountains, and lowered telephones.

Services: In addition to many counseling and information services, tutoring is available in most subjects. There is a reader service for the blind, and remedial math, reading, and writing.

Campus Safety and Security: Campus safety and security measures include 24-hour foot and vehicle patrol, self-defense education, escort service, and informal discussions. There are pamphlets/posters/films, lighted pathways/sidewalks, and residence hall briefings on personal safety, housing security, and enforcement procedures.

Programs of Study: Widener confers B.A., B.S., B.S.B.A., B.S.C.E., B.S.Ch.E., B.S.E.E., B.S. in H.R.M., B.S.M.E., B.S.N., and B.S.W. degrees. Master's and doctoral degrees are also awarded. Bachelor's degrees are awarded in BIOLOGICAL SCIENCE (biochemistry and biology/biological science), BUSINESS (accounting, banking and finance, business administration and management, business economics, hotel/motel and restaurant management, and international business management), COMMUNICATIONS AND THE ARTS (communications, English, and modern language), COMPUTER AND PHYSICAL SCIENCE (chemistry, computer science, information sciences and systems, mathematics, and physics), EDUCATION (early childhood, elementary, foreign languages, science, and secondary), ENGINEERING AND ENVIRONMENTAL DESIGN (chemical engineering, civil engineering, electrical/electronics engineering, environmental science, and mechanical engineering), HEALTH PROFESSIONS (nursing, predentistry, and premedicine), SOCIAL SCIENCE (behavioral science, criminal justice, economics, history, humanities, international relations, political science/government, prelaw, psychology, social science, social work, and sociology). Engineering, chemistry, and management are the strongest academically. Nursing, engineering, and business have the largest enrollments.

Required: All students must complete 12 credits each in humanities, social sciences, and science/mathematics, and 1 credit in physical education. For graduation, students must have 121 credit hours and a GPA of 2.0. Hours in the major vary by program.

Special: Widener offers internships, study abroad in 6 countries, a Washington semester, accelerated degree programs, dual, student-designed, and interdisciplinary majors, including chemistry management, nondegree study, and pass/fail options. Cooperative education programs are available in management, engineering, and computer science and are required in hotel/restaurant management. There is also cross-registration with Swarthmore College and American University, a 3–2 engineering degree, and B.A.-B.S. degrees. There is a freshman honors program on campus, as well as 12 national honor societies. 8 departments have honors programs.

Faculty/Classroom: 56% of faculty are male; 44%, female. 66% teach undergraduates, 60% do research, and 65% do both. The average class size in an introductory lecture is 32; in a laboratory, 16; and in a regular course offering, 22.

Admissions: 46% of the current freshmen were in the top fifth of their class; 92% were in the top two fifths. There were 11 National Merit semifinalists in a recent year. 36 freshmen graduated first in a recent class.

Requirements: The SAT I is required with a score of 1000 (recentered). Applicants must be graduates of an accredited secondary school with a 2.0 GPA and have completed 4 units each of English and social studies, 3 units each of mathematics and science, and 1 unit each of art, history, and music. The GED is accepted under limited circumstances. An interview is recommended. AP and CLEP credits are accepted. Important factors in the admissions decision are advanced placement or honor courses, recommendations by school officials, and leadership record.

Procedure: Freshmen are admitted fall and spring. Entrance exams should be taken in the junior year and November or December of the senior year. There are early decision, early admissions, and deferred admissions plans. Application deadlines are open. Application fee is $25. Notification is sent on a rolling basis. 70 early decision candidates were accepted for the 1995–96 class.

Transfer: Applicants must have at least 12 college credits with a minimum GPA of 2.2. An associate's degree and an interview are recommended. 45 credits of 121 must be completed at Widener.

Visiting: There are regularly scheduled orientations for prospective students. There are guides for informal visits and visitors may sit in on classes and stay overnight at the school. To schedule a visit, contact the Admissions Office.

Financial Aid: In a recent year, 76% of all freshmen and 64% of continuing students received some form of financial aid. 73% of freshmen and 61% of continuing students received need-based aid. The average freshman award was $5200. Of that total, scholarships or need-based grants averaged $5000 ($7000 maximum); other need-based grants averaged $3980 ($4800 maximum); loans averaged $3443 ($3625 maximum); and work contracts averaged $1200. 35% of undergraduate students work part-time. Average earnings from campus work for the school year are $750. Widener is a member of CSS. The FAFSA and the college's own financial statement are required. The application deadline for fall entry is March 1.

International Students: There were 96 international students enrolled in a recent year. The school actively recruits these students. They must score 500 on the TOEFL and also take SAT I or the ACT. SAT I is preferred.

Computers: The college provides computer facilities for student use. The mainframes are a CYBER 932 and CDC 4680. The mainframes are accessed through IBM PS/2 computer laboratories throughout the university or from remote dial-in sites. There are 187 terminals on campus. All students may access the system 8 A.M. to midnight; longer during examination periods. There are no time limits and no fees.

Graduates: In a recent year, 690 bachelor's degrees were awarded. The most popular majors among graduates were nursing (18%), management (16%), and hotel/restaurant management (15%). Within an average freshman class, 1% graduate in 3 years, 4% in 4 years, 55% in 5 years, and 56% in 6 years. 65 companies recruited on campus in a recent year.

Admissions Contact: Dr. Michael L. Mahoney, Vice President for Admissions.

WILKES UNIVERSITY
Wilkes Barre, PA 18766

E-2

(717) 831-4400
(800) WILKESU (945-5378)

Full-time: 980 men, 820 women
Part-time: 250 men, 350 women
Graduate: 310 men, 550 women
Year: semesters, summer session
Application Deadline: open
Freshman Class: n/av
SAT I or ACT: required

Faculty: 137; IIA, -$
Ph.D.s: 85%
Student/Faculty: 13 to 1
Tuition: $12,600
Room & Board: $5500

LESS COMPETITIVE

Wilkes University, founded in 1933, is an independent, comprehensive university offering undergraduate programs in 36 fields, including the arts and sciences, business, and engineering. Figures given in the above capsule are approximate. There are 3 undergraduate schools and 1 graduate school. In addition to regional accreditation, Wilkes has baccalaureate program accreditation with ABET and NLN. The library contains 200,000 volumes, 620,000 microform items, and 2500 audiovisual forms, and subscribes to 1150 periodicals. Computerized library sources and services include the card catalog, interlibrary loans, and database searching. Special learning facilities include a learning resource center, art gallery, radio station, and TV station. The 25-acre campus is in an urban area 120 miles west of New York City. Including residence halls, there are 50 buildings on campus.

Student Life: 70% of undergraduates are from Pennsylvania. Students come from 17 states, 13 foreign countries, and Canada. 80% are from public schools; 20% from private. 96% are white. 54% are Catholic; 30% Protestant; 12% claim no religious affiliation. The average age of freshmen is 18; all undergraduates, 21. 18% do not continue beyond their first year; 63% remain to graduate.

Housing: 800 students can be accommodated in college housing. College-sponsored living facilities include single-sex and coed dormitories. On-campus housing is guaranteed for all 4 years. Alcohol is not permitted. All students may keep cars on campus.

Activities: There are no fraternities or sororities. There are 65 groups on campus, including art, band, cheerleading, choir, chorus, computers, drama, ethnic, gay, honors, international, jazz band, literary magazine, musical theater, newspaper, orchestra, pep band, political, professional, radio and TV, religious, social, social service, student government, and yearbook. Popular campus events include Casino Night, Cherry Blossom Festival, and Community Service Day.

Sports: There are 8 intercollegiate sports for men and 6 for women, and 10 intramural sports for men and 6 for women. Athletic and recreation facilities include tennis courts, a 5000-seat stadium, a 3500-seat gymnasium, a game room, and weight and exercise rooms.

Disabled Students: All of the campus is accessible to disabled students. The following facilities are available: wheelchair ramps, elevators, special parking, specially equipped rest rooms, special class scheduling, lowered drinking fountains, and lowered telephones.

Services: In addition to many counseling and information services, tutoring is available in every subject. There is also remedial math, reading, and writing. The Learning Center also provides individual tutoring, group study sessions, and small-group supplemental instruction seminars.

Campus Safety and Security: Campus safety and security measures include 24-hour foot and vehicle patrol, escort service, informal discussions, and pamphlets/posters/films. There are lighted pathways/sidewalks and Operation Alert, which provides personal alarm devices for students who wish to carry one, and Operation Identification, which allows students to engrave belongings with identifying information.

Programs of Study: Wilkes confers B.A., B.S., B.B.A., B.F.A., and B.M. degrees. Master's and doctoral degrees are also awarded. Bachelor's degrees are awarded in BIOLOGICAL SCIENCE (biochemistry and biology/biological science), BUSINESS (accounting and business administration and management), COMMUNICATIONS AND THE ARTS (art, communications, dramatic arts, English, French, German, music, and Spanish), COMPUTER AND PHYSICAL SCIENCE (chemistry, computer science, earth science, information sciences and systems, mathematics, and physics), EDUCATION (art, early childhood, elementary, and music), ENGINEERING AND ENVIRONMENTAL DESIGN (electrical/electronics engineering, engineering and applied science, engineering management, environmental engineering, materials engineering, and mechanical engineering), HEALTH PROFESSIONS (allied health, medical records administration/services, medical technology, nursing, predentistry, premedicine, prepharmacy, prepodiatry, and preveterinary science), SOCIAL SCIENCE (economics, history, international studies, liberal arts/general studies, philosophy, political science/government, prelaw, psychology, and sociology). Engineering and biology are the strongest academically. Business administration, psychology, and communication have the largest enrollments.

Required: To graduate, all students must complete at least 120 credit hours, with a minimum of 30 in the major, and a cumulative GPA of at least 2.0 overall and in the major. Students must demonstrate competency in written expression, computer literacy, oral expression, and mathematics, and complete 2 semesters of physical education. General education requirements consist of 12 to 15 credits in humanities, 9 to 12 in sciences, 6 to 9 in social sciences, and 3 in fine arts.

Special: Wilkes offers many opportunities for cooperative education and internships, and study abroad in more than 50 countries. Dual majors in all disciplines, credit for military experience, and nondegree study are also offered. There is a freshman honors program on campus, as well as 9 national honor societies. 5 departments have honors programs.

Faculty/Classroom: 66% of faculty are male; 34%, female. 99% teach undergraduates. No introductory courses are taught by graduate students. The average class size in an introductory lecture is 26; in a laboratory, 13; and in a regular course offering, 20.

Admissions: The SAT I scores for a recent freshman class were as follows: Verbal—77% below 500, 16% between 500 and 599, and 6% between 600 and 700; Math—59% below 500, 26% between 500 and 599, 11% between 600 and 700, and 3% above 700. 29% of recent freshmen were in the top fifth of their class; 50% were in the top two fifths. 11 freshmen graduated first in their class in a recent year.

Requirements: The SAT I or ACT is required. Applicants must be graduates of an accredited secondary school in the top 60% of their class or have the GED. Secondary-school preparation should include 4 years of English, 3 each of mathematics and social studies and 2 of science. Art majors must submit a portfolio and music majors and theater arts majors must audition. An interview is recommended. AP and CLEP credits are accepted. Important factors in the admissions decision are recommendations by school officials, advanced placement or honor courses, and leadership record.

Procedure: Freshmen are admitted to all sessions. There are early admissions and deferred admissions plans. Application deadlines are open. Notification is sent on a rolling basis. A waiting list is an active part of the admissions procedure. Check with the school for current application fee.

Transfer: 180 transfer students enrolled in a recent year. Transfer applicants must have a minimum college GPA of 2.0 and at least 30 earned credits. A GPA of 2.5 is required for engineering majors. Students with fewer than 30 credits must submit official high school transcripts and SAT I or ACT scores. An interview is recommended. 60 credits of 120 must be completed at Wilkes.

Visiting: There are regularly scheduled orientations for prospective students, including a general orientation session, a tour of the campus, and a meeting with faculty from the department of the student's intended major. There are guides for informal visits and visitors may sit in on classes and stay overnight at the school. To schedule a visit, contact the Admissions Office.

Financial Aid: In a recent year, 80% of all freshmen received some form of financial aid. 77% of all freshmen received need-based aid. The average freshman award was $9050. Of that total, scholarships or need-based grants averaged $4900 ($10,900 maximum); loans averaged $3200 ($5125 maximum); and work contracts averaged $950 ($2000 maximum). 25% of undergraduate students work part-time. Average earnings from campus work for the school year are $700. The average financial indebtedness of a recent graduate was $6636. Wilkes is a member of CSS. The PHEAA financial statement is required. Check with the school for current deadlines.

International Students: There were 35 international students enrolled in a recent year. The school actively recruits these students. Students must score 500 on the TOEFL and also take the SAT I or the ACT.

Computers: The college provides computer facilities for student use. The mainframes are a DEC VAX 6310 and a DEC VAX 3500. There are also 120 IBM, 20 Apple, and 100 Apple Macintosh microcomputers available throughout the campus. All students may access the system 24 hours daily. There are no time limits and no fees.

Graduates: In a recent year, 544 bachelor's degrees were awarded. The most popular majors among graduates were business administration (23%), psychology (10%), and accounting (8%). Within an average freshman class, 40% graduate in 4 years, 55% in 5 years, and 63% in 6 years. 120 companies recruited on campus in a recent year.

Admissions Contact: Emory P. Guffrovich, Jr., Dean of Admissions.

WILSON COLLEGE

D-4

Chambersburg, PA 17201-1285

(717) 262-2002

(800) 421-8402; FAX: (717) 264-1578

Full-time: 205 women	Faculty: 32; IIB, --$
Part-time: 33 women	Ph.D.s: 77%
Graduate: none	Student/Faculty: 6 to 1
Year: 4-1-4, summer session	Tuition: $12,117
Application Deadline: August 1	Room & Board: $5338
Freshman Class: 246 applied, 223 accepted, 95 enrolled	
SAT I Verbal/Math: 465/478	**COMPETITIVE**

Wilson College, founded in 1869, is a private liberal arts institution for women that is affiliated with the Presbyterian Church. The library contains 164,351 volumes, 10,505 microform items, and 1554 audiovisual forms, and subscribes to 385 periodicals. Computerized library sources and services include interlibrary loans and database searching. Special learning facilities include a learning resource center, art gallery, natural history museum, radio station, a veterinary technology suite, an electron microscope, and a classics collection. The 260-acre campus is in a small town 50 miles west of Harrisburg. Including residence halls, there are 34 buildings on campus.

Student Life: 55% of undergraduates are from out-of-state, mostly the Northeast. Students come from 14 states and 8 foreign countries. 84% are from public schools; 16% from private. 88% are white. 40% are Protestant; 31% Catholic. The average age of freshmen is 18; all undergraduates, 20. 10% do not continue beyond their first year; 70% remain to graduate.

Housing: 500 students can be accommodated in college housing. College-sponsored living facilities include dormitories. On-campus housing is guaranteed for all 4 years. 65% of students live on campus; of those, 50% remain on campus on weekends. All students may keep cars on campus.

Activities: There are 23 groups on campus, including art, choir, chorale, dance, drama, ethnic, gay, international, literary magazine, newspaper, photography, political, professional, radio and TV, religious, social, social service, student government, and yearbook. Popular campus events include May Weekend and Thanksgiving, Christmas, and Muhibbah dinners.

Sports: Athletic and recreation facilities include a 400-seat gymnasium, a field house, pool, gymnastics area, weight room, archery range, hockey field, tennis courts, 2-lane bowling alley, and equestrian center (indoor and outdoor arena).

Disabled Students: 35% of the campus is accessible to disabled students. The following facilities are available: wheelchair ramps, elevators, special parking, specially equipped rest rooms, and special class scheduling.

Services: In addition to many counseling and information services, tutoring is available in every subject. There is remedial math, reading, and writing.

Campus Safety and Security: Campus safety and security measures include 24-hour foot and vehicle patrol, shuttle buses, informal discussions, and pamphlets/posters/films. In addition, there are emergency telephones and lighted pathways/sidewalks.

Programs of Study: Wilson confers B.A. and B.S. degrees. Associate degrees are also awarded. Bachelor's degrees are awarded in AGRICULTURE (equine science), BIOLOGICAL SCIENCE (biology/biological science), BUSINESS (business economics), COMMUNICATIONS AND THE ARTS (communications, English, fine arts, and languages), COMPUTER AND PHYSICAL SCIENCE (chemistry and mathematics), EDUCATION (elementary), ENGINEERING AND ENVIRONMENTAL DESIGN (environmental science), HEALTH PROFESSIONS (veterinary science), SOCIAL SCIENCE (behavioral science, history, international studies, philosophy, political science/government, and psychobiology). Business and economics, equestrian studies, and veterinary medical technology have the largest enrollments.

Required: To graduate, students must complete a minimum of 36 courses, with a minimum GPA of 2.0. At least 18 of the 36 courses must be outside any single discipline.

Special: Cross-registration is available with Shippenburg University and Gettysburg College. Wilson offers internships, a Washington semester, student-designed majors, credit by examination, pass/fail options, and credit for noncollegiate learning. Students may participate in study-abroad programs sponsored by other colleges.

Faculty/Classroom: 31% of faculty are male; 69%, female. 97% teach undergraduates. The average class size in a regular course offering is 8.

Admissions: 91% of the 1995–96 applicants were accepted. The SAT I scores for the 1995–96 freshman class were as follows: Verbal—69% below 500, 20% between 500 and 599, and 11% between 600 and 700; Math—55% below 500, 36% between 500 and 599, and 9% between 600 and 700. The ACT scores were 58% below 21, 25% between 21 and 23, and 17% between 27 and 28. 39% of the current freshmen were in the top fifth of their class; 64% were in the top two fifths.

Requirements: The SAT I or ACT is required, with a recommended recentered score of 900 on SAT I or 21 on the ACT. Wilson requires applicants to be in the upper 50% of their class with a 2.5 GPA. In addition, applicants should prepare with 4 years each of English and social studies/history, 3 years of mathematics, and 2 of science and a foreign language. An essay is required, and an interview is recommended. AP and CLEP credits are accepted. Important factors in the admissions decision are advanced placement or honor courses, personality/intangible qualities, and leadership record.

Procedure: Freshmen are admitted fall and spring. Entrance exams should be taken in the spring of the junior year. There are early admissions and deferred admissions plans. Applications should be filed by August 1 for fall entry and January 1 for spring entry, along with an application fee of $20. Notification is sent on a rolling basis.

Transfer: 17 transfer students enrolled in 1995–96. Applicants must have a college GPA of at least 2.0. The SAT I or ACT is recommended, with a minimum composite score of 900 (recentered) or 21, respectively. 14 courses of 36 must be completed at Wilson.

Visiting: There are regularly scheduled orientations for prospective students, consisting of a campus tour and meetings with various faculty members or administration, if requested. There are guides for informal visits and visitors may sit in on classes and stay overnight at the school. To schedule a visit, contact the Office of Admissions.

Financial Aid: In 1995–96, 84% of all freshmen and 81% of continuing students received some form of financial aid. 74% of all students received need-based aid. The average freshman award was $10,179. Of that total, scholarships or need-based grants averaged $6107 ($14,490 maximum); loans averaged $2967 ($4475 maximum); and work contracts averaged $1105 (maximum). 48% of undergraduate students work part-time. Average earnings from campus work for the school year are $852. The average financial indebtedness of the 1994–95 graduate was $13,298. Wilson is a member of CSS. The college's own financial statement is required. The application deadline for fall entry is April 30.

International Students: There are currently 11 international students enrolled. The school actively recruits these students. They must take the TOEFL and achieve a minimum score of 550. The student must also take the SAT I or the ACT.

Computers: The college provides computer facilities for student use. IBM-compatible computers are available for student use throughout the campus. All students may access the system. There are no time limits and no fees.

Graduates: In 1994–95, 45 bachelor's degrees were awarded. The most popular majors among graduates were equestrian studies (27%), veterinary medical (20%), and behavioral sciences (13%). Within an average freshman class, 60% graduate in 4 years. Of the 1994 graduating class, 21% were enrolled in graduate school within 6 months of graduation and 70% had found employment.

Admissions Contact: Karen Jewell, Director of Admissions.

YORK COLLEGE OF PENNSYLVANIA

D-4

York, PA 17405-7199

(717) 849-1600

Full-time: 1398 men, 1916 women	Faculty: 130; IIB, +$
Part-time: 586 men, 1011 women	Ph.D.s: 75%
Graduate: 88 men, 55 women	Student/Faculty: 25 to 1
Year: semesters, summer session	Tuition: $5490
Application Deadline: open	Room & Board: $3810
Freshman Class: 2960 applied, 2099 accepted, 853 enrolled	
SAT I Verbal/Math: 470/523	**VERY COMPETITIVE**

York College of Pennsylvania, founded in 1787, is a private, coeducational institution offering undergraduate programs in the liberal arts and sciences, as well as professional programs. There are 9 undergraduate schools and one graduate school. In addition to regional accreditation, YCP has baccalaureate program accreditation with NLN. The library contains 300,000 volumes, 500,000 microform items, and 50,000 audiovisual forms, and subscribes to 1500 periodicals. Computerized library sources and services include interlibrary loans and database searching. Special learning facilities include a learning resource center, art gallery, radio station, TV station, and a telecommunications center. The 80-acre campus is in a suburban area 45 miles north of Baltimore, Maryland. Including residence halls, there are 28 buildings on campus.

Student Life: 58% of undergraduates are from Pennsylvania. Students come from 30 states, 19 foreign countries, and Canada. 83% are from public schools; 17% from private. 95% are white. 41% are Protestant; 40% Catholic. The average age of freshmen is 19; all undergraduates, 25. 20% do not continue beyond their first year; 78% remain to graduate.

Housing: 1450 students can be accommodated in college housing. College-sponsored living facilities include single-sex and coed dormitories, on-campus apartments, fraternity houses, and sorority houses. On-campus housing is guaranteed for the freshman year only and is available on a first-come, first-served basis. Alcohol is not permitted. All students may keep cars on campus.

Activities: 25% of men belong to 5 local and 5 national fraternities; 20% of women belong to 4 local and 4 national sororities. There are 70 groups on campus, including band, cheerleading, chess, choir, chorale, chorus, computers, drama, ethnic, film, honors, international, jazz band, literary magazine, musical theater, newspaper, orchestra, photography, political, professional, radio and TV, religious, social, social service, student government, symphony, and yearbook. Popular campus events include Parents Weekend, Spring Weekend Festival, and weekly movies.

Sports: There are 9 intercollegiate sports for men and 9 for women, and 10 intramural sports for men and 10 for women. Athletic and recreation facilities include 2 gymnasiums, a track, a swimming pool, a game room, weight training rooms, tennis courts, and soccer, hockey, baseball, softball, and intramural fields.

Disabled Students: 60% of the campus is accessible to disabled students. The following facilities are available: wheelchair ramps, elevators, special parking, specially equipped rest rooms, special class scheduling, lowered drinking fountains, and lowered telephones.

Services: In addition to many counseling and information services, tutoring is available in most subjects. In addition, there is remedial math and writing.

Campus Safety and Security: Campus safety and security measures include self-defense education, escort service, informal discussions, and pamphlets/posters/films. In addition, there are emergency telephones, lighted pathways/sidewalks, a 24-hour foot patrol, safety seminars, crime prevention speakers, a desk monitor in residence halls, and a personal property engraving program.

Programs of Study: YCP confers B.A. and B.S. degrees. Associate and master's degrees are also awarded. Bachelor's degrees are awarded in BIOLOGICAL SCIENCE (biology/biological science), BUSINESS (accounting, banking and finance, business administration and management, international business management, management science, marketing/retailing/merchandising, and office supervision and management), COMMUNICATIONS AND THE ARTS (broadcasting, communications, English, fine arts, music, and speech/debate/rhetoric), COMPUTER AND PHYSICAL SCIENCE (chemistry, computer programming, information sciences and systems, mathematics, and physical sciences), EDUCATION (business, elementary, science, and secondary), ENGINEERING AND ENVIRONMENTAL DESIGN (engineering management and mechanical engineering), HEALTH PROFESSIONS (health care administration, medical laboratory technology, medical records administration/services, nuclear medical technology, nursing, premedicine, and respiratory therapy), SOCIAL SCIENCE (behavioral science, criminal justice, history, humanities, Latin American studies, parks and recreation management, political science/government, prelaw, psychology, and sociology). Business, health professions, education, and social sciences are the strongest academically and have the largest enrollments.

Required: To graduate, all students must complete at least 124 credit hours, with 60 to 80 in the major. The required core curriculum includes 12 credits in foreign language and culture, 12 in social and behavioral science, 9 in English and speech, 9 in humanities and fine arts, 6 each in mathematics and laboratory science, 4 in physical education, and 3 in American civilization. A minimum GPA of 2.0 is required.

Special: YCP offers internships for upper-division students, an exchange program with the College of Ripon and York St. John in York, England, Regents College in London, England, and the American University in Rome, Italy, dual majors in any combination, a 3–2 engineering degree with Columbia University, nondegree study, and pass/fail options. There are 2 national honor societies on campus.

Faculty/Classroom: 63% of faculty are male; 37%, female. All teach undergraduates. No introductory courses are taught by graduate students. The average class size in an introductory lecture is 40; in a laboratory, 20; and in a regular course offering, 30.

Admissions: 71% of the 1995–96 applicants were accepted. The SAT I scores for the 1995–96 freshman class were as follows: Verbal—46% below 500, 40% between 500 and 599, 13% between 600 and 700, and 1% above 700; Math—25% below 500, 56% between 500 and 599, 17% between 600 and 700, and 2% above 700. 39% of the current freshmen were in the top fifth of their class; 76% were in the top two fifths. 4 freshmen graduated first in their class.

Requirements: The SAT I or ACT is required. YCP requires applicants to be in the upper 60% of their class. A minimum GPA of 2.5 is also required. In addition, applicants must be graduates of an accredited secondary school or have a GED certificate. 15 academic credits are required, including 4 units in English, 3 or 4 in mathematics, 2 or 3 in science, 2 in history, and 1 in social studies. Music students must audition. AP and CLEP credits are accepted. Important factors in the admissions decision are advanced placement or honor courses, leadership record, and extracurricular activities record.

Procedure: Freshmen are admitted fall and spring. Entrance exams should be taken in the spring of the junior year or the fall of the senior year. There is a deferred admissions plan. Application deadlines are open. Application fee is $20. Notification is sent on a rolling basis. A waiting list is an active part of the admissions procedure.

Transfer: 179 transfer students enrolled in a recent year. Applicants must have a minimum GPA of 2.0 from a regionally accredited institution. Students with fewer than 30 credit hours must submit a high school transcript. An interview is recommended. 30 credits of 124 must be completed at YCP.

Visiting: There are regularly scheduled orientations for prospective students, including 2 open houses in October/November and 2 spring orientation programs in April/May, featuring a general orientation, academic and support services sessions, and campus tours. There are guides for informal visits and visitors may sit in on classes. To schedule a visit, contact the Admissions Office.

Financial Aid: In 1995–96, 69% of all students received some form of financial aid. 43% of freshmen and 51% of continuing students received need-based aid. The average freshman award was $4500. Of that total, scholarships or need-based grants averaged $2894 ($8000 maximum); loans averaged $2670 ($6625 maximum); and work contracts averaged $1500 ($2000 maximum). 53% of undergraduate students work part-time. Average earnings from campus work for the school year are $1500. The average financial indebtedness of the 1994–95 graduate was $10,000. YCP is a member of CSS. The FAF, the college's own financial statement, and the PHEAA are required. The application deadline for fall entry is April 15.

International Students: In a recent year, 29 international students were enrolled. They must take the TOEFL and achieve a minimum score of 500. The student must also take the SAT I or the ACT.

Computers: The college provides computer facilities for student use. The mainframes are a DEC VAX 6000–310 and a DEC VAX 4000–4400. Mainframe terminals and Apple IIe, IBM-compatible, and Apple Macintosh microcomputers plus English composition facilities and numerous software packages are available to students 120 hours a week in the academic computer center. All students may access the system. There are no time limits and no fees.

Graduates: In 1994–95, 744 bachelor's degrees were awarded. The most popular majors among graduates were nursing (15%), elementary education (11%), and management (8%). Within an average freshman class, 15% graduate in 3 years, 62% in 4 years, 72% in 5 years, and 78% in 6 years. 33 companies recruited on campus in 1994–95. Of the 1994 graduating class, 26% were enrolled in graduate school within 6 months of graduation and 91% had found employment.

Admissions Contact: Director of Admissions. A campus video is available.

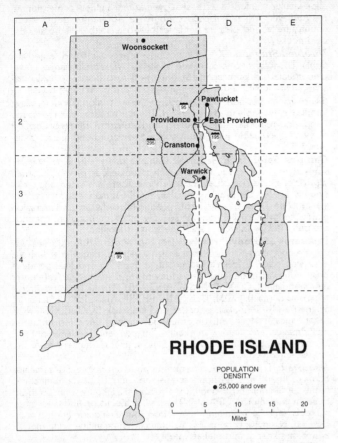

RHODE ISLAND

POPULATION
DENSITY

● 25,000 and over

0   5   10   15   20
Miles

BROWN UNIVERSITY

C-2

Providence, RI 02912   (401) 863-2378; FAX: (401) 863-9300

Full-time: 2643 men, 2916 women	Faculty: 541; I, +$
Part-time: 161 men, 222 women	Ph.D.s: 98%
Graduate: 926 men, 773 women	Student/Faculty: 10 to 1
Year: semesters, summer session	Tuition: $21,277
Application Deadline: January 1	Room & Board: $6212
Freshman Class: 13,904 applied, 2952 accepted, 1418 enrolled	
SAT I Verbal/Math: 630/700	ACT: 29 **MOST COMPETITIVE**

Brown University, founded in 1764, is a coeducational liberal arts institution and one of the Ivy League schools. There is one graduate school. In addition to regional accreditation, Brown has baccalaureate program accreditation with ABET. The 6 libraries contain 2,500,000 volumes, 1,000,000 microform items, and 26,342 audiovisual forms, and subscribe to 15,090 periodicals. Computerized library sources and services include the card catalog, interlibrary loans, and database searching. Special learning facilities include a learning resource center, art gallery, planetarium, radio station, TV station, and anthropology museum. The 140-acre campus is in an urban area 45 miles south of Boston. Including residence halls, there are 243 buildings on campus.

Student Life: 97% of undergraduates are from out-of-state, mostly the Middle Atlantic. Students come from 50 states, 63 foreign countries, and Canada. 80% are from public schools; 20% from private. 67% are white; 14% Asian American. The average age of freshmen is 18; all undergraduates, 20. 4% do not continue beyond their first year; 96% remain to graduate.

Housing: 4331 students can be accommodated in college housing. College-sponsored living facilities include single-sex and coed dormitories, on-campus apartments, off-campus apartments, fraternity houses, and sorority houses. In addition there are language houses and special interest houses. On-campus housing is guaranteed for all 4 years. 85% of students live on campus; of those, 90% remain on campus on weekends. Upperclassmen may keep cars on campus.

Activities: 12% of men belong to 11 national fraternities; 2% of women belong to 2 national sororities. There are 240 groups on campus, including band, cheerleading, chess, choir, chorale, chorus, computers, dance, drama, ethnic, film, gay, honors, international, jazz band, literary magazine, marching band, musical theater, newspaper, orchestra, photography, political, professional, radio and TV, religious, social, social service, student government, and yearbook. Pop-

ular campus events include Commencement, Spring Weekend, and Parents Weekend.

Sports: There are 17 intercollegiate sports each for men and women, and 15 intramural sports each for men and women. Athletic and recreation facilities include a 25,000-seat stadium, an Olympic-size pool, a 200-meter, 6-lane track, a hockey rink, playing fields, weight-training rooms, facilities for wrestling, and courts for squash, handball, racquetball, tennis, basketball, and volleyball.

Disabled Students: The following facilities are available: wheelchair ramps, elevators, and special parking.

Services: In addition to many counseling and information services, tutoring is available in most subjects. There is a reader service for the blind. Other services include class note taking, books on tape, diagnostic testing service, oral tests, tutors, and untimed tests.

Campus Safety and Security: Campus safety and security measures include 24-hour foot and vehicle patrol, self-defense education, escort service, and shuttle buses. There are informal discussions, pamphlets/posters/films, emergency telephones, lighted pathways/sidewalks, and the Safe Walk program.

Programs of Study: Brown confers A.B. and Sc.B. degrees. Master's and doctoral degrees are also awarded. Bachelor's degrees are awarded in BIOLOGICAL SCIENCE (biochemistry, biology/biological science, biophysics, and neurosciences), BUSINESS (organizational behavior), COMMUNICATIONS AND THE ARTS (American literature, art history and appreciation, classics, comparative literature, English, French, German, Italian, linguistics, music, performing arts, and Slavic languages), COMPUTER AND PHYSICAL SCIENCE (applied mathematics, chemistry, computer science, geology, mathematics, and physics), EDUCATION (education), ENGINEERING AND ENVIRONMENTAL DESIGN (architectural technology, engineering, and environmental science), HEALTH PROFESSIONS (biomedical science), SOCIAL SCIENCE (African American studies, anthropology, cognitive science, East Asian studies, economics, Hispanic American studies, history, international relations, Judaic studies, Latin American studies, medieval studies, philosophy, political science/government, psychology, Russian and Slavic studies, sociology, South Asian studies, urban studies, and women's studies). Biological sciences, history, and engineering have the largest enrollments.

Required: Students must pass 30 of 32 courses in order to graduate. There are no distribution requirements or specific required courses.

Special: Students may cross-register with Rhode Island School of Design, or study abroad in any of 21 programs in 18 countries. A combined B.A.-B.S. degree is possible in any major field with 5 years of study. Dual and student-designed majors, community internships, and pass/fail options are available. Students may pursue 5-year programs in the arts or sciences, or the 8-year program in liberal medical education continuum. There is a freshman honors program on campus, as well as a chapter of Phi Beta Kappa. 10 departments have honors programs.

Faculty/Classroom: All teach undergraduates and do research. Graduate students teach 13% of introductory courses. The average class size in an introductory lecture is 40; in a laboratory, 20; and in a regular course offering, 45.

Admissions: 21% of the 1995–96 applicants were accepted. The SAT I scores for the 1995–96 freshman class were as follows: Verbal—9% below 500, 24% between 500 and 599, 48% between 600 and 700, and 19% above 700; Math—1% below 500, 13% between 500 and 599, 39% between 600 and 700, and 47% above 700. The ACT scores were 9% between 21 and 23, 11% between 24 and 26, 39% between 27 and 28, and 41% above 28. 96% of the current freshmen were in the top fifth of their class; 99% were in the top two fifths. In a recent year, there were 150 National Merit finalists and 75 semifinalists.

Requirements: The SAT I or ACT is required, along with any 3 SAT II: Subject tests. Applicants must be graduates of accredited high schools. Secondary preparation is expected to include courses in English, foreign language, mathematics, science, and history. A personal essay is required. The high school transcript is a most important criterion for admission. AP credits are accepted. Important factors in the admissions decision are advanced placement or honor courses, evidence of special talent, and leadership record.

Procedure: Freshmen are admitted fall and spring. Entrance exams should be taken in the junior or senior year. There are early decision, early admissions, and deferred admissions plans. Early decision applications should be filed by November 1; regular applications, by January 1 for fall entry, along with an application fee of $55. Notification of early decision is sent December 15; regular decision, April 1. 544 early decision candidates were accepted for the 1995–96 class. A waiting list is an active part of the admissions procedure, with about 3% of all applicants on the list.

Transfer: 124 transfer students enrolled in a recent year. Applicants must submit high school and college transcripts, 2 recommendations from college professors, scores on the SAT I and 3 SAT II: Subject tests, a letter of good standing, and a personal essay. 15 courses of 30 must be completed at Brown.

Visiting: There are regularly scheduled orientations for prospective students, Monday through Friday at 2 P.M. and at 10 A.M. from mid-April through November, at 2 P.M. from December to April, and on Saturday mornings from mid-September to mid-November. There are guides for informal visits and visitors may sit in on classes and stay overnight at the school. To schedule a visit, contact the Admission Office receptionist.

Financial Aid: In a recent year, 32% of all freshmen received some form of financial aid. 40% of freshmen and 39% of continuing students received need-based aid. The average freshman award was $14,025. Of that total, scholarships or need-based grants averaged $10,000; loans averaged $2795; work contracts averaged $1215; and outside or state grants averaged $1100. Average earnings from campus work for the school year are $1360. The average financial indebtedness of a recent year's graduate was $12,000. Brown is a member of CSS. The FAF, the college's own financial statement, and some state forms are required. The application deadline for fall entry is January 1.

International Students: There are currently 415 international students enrolled. The school actively recruits these students. They must score 600 on the TOEFL and also take the SAT I or the ACT. Students must take SAT II Subject Tests in any 3 subjects.

Computers: The college provides computer facilities for student use. There are more than 300 workstations in several campus locations equipped with Macintosh and IBM microcomputers. Students may also access the mainframe from dormitory rooms. The main computer center is open 18 hours a day and around the clock during examination periods. All students may access the system. There are no time limits and no fees.

Graduates: In a recent year, 1422 bachelor's degrees were awarded. The most popular majors among graduates were biological sciences (10%), history (8%), and engineering (7%). Within an average freshman class, 80% graduate in 4 years, 92% in 5 years, and 94% in 6 years. 300 companies recruited on campus in a recent year.

Admissions Contact: Michael Goldberger, Director of Admission and Financial Aid. E-mail: admission-undergraduate@brown.edu.

BRYANT COLLEGE

C-2

Smithfield, RI 02917-1284

(401) 232-6100
(800) 622-7001; FAX: (401) 232-6741

Full-time: 1335 men, 954 women	Faculty: 132; IIB, + +$
Part-time: 268 men, 404 women	Ph.D.s: 89%
Graduate: 383 men, 271 women	Student/Faculty: 17 to 1
Year: semesters, summer session	Tuition: $13,100
Application Deadline: open	Room & Board: $6500
Freshman Class: 2159 applied, 1634 accepted, 577 enrolled	
SAT I Verbal/Math: 440/540	ACT: 23 COMPETITIVE

Bryant College, founded in 1863, is a private, coeducational, primarily residential institution that offers degrees in business and liberal arts. There is 1 graduate school. In addition to regional accreditation, Bryant has baccalaureate program accreditation with AACSB. The library contains 115,000 volumes, 11,806 microform items, 1300 CD-ROMS, and 700 audiovisual forms, and subscribes to 1295 periodicals. Computerized library sources and services include the card catalog, interlibrary loans, and database searching. Special learning facilities include a learning resource center, a radio station, the Koffler Technology Center, and a language laboratory. The 397-acre campus is in a suburban area 12 miles northwest of Providence. Including residence halls, there are 42 buildings on campus.

Student Life: 71% of undergraduates are from out-of-state, mostly the Northeast. Students come from 32 states and 38 foreign countries. 77% are from public schools; 23% from private. 89% are white. 60% are Catholic; 18% Protestant; 12% claim no religious affiliation. The average age of freshmen is 18; all undergraduates, 20. 16% do not continue beyond their first year; 73% remain to graduate.

Housing: 2484 students can be accommodated in college housing. College-sponsored living facilities include single-sex and coed dormitories and on-campus apartments. In addition, there are special interest houses, and individual fraternities and sororities may live as a group within a residence hall. On-campus housing is guaranteed for all 4 years. 85% of students live on campus; of those, 75% remain on campus on weekends. All students may keep cars on campus.

Activities: 16% of men belong to 8 national fraternities; 16% of women belong to 5 national sororities. There are 60 groups on campus, including cheerleading, chess, chorus, computers, dance, drama, ethnic, honors, international, jazz band, newspaper, political, professional, radio and TV, religious, social, student government, and yearbook. Popular campus events include Special Olympics Weekend, Spring Weekend, and Winter Festival.

Sports: There are 7 intercollegiate sports for men and 7 for women, and 8 intramural sports for men and 8 for women. Athletic and recreation facilities include a 2700-seat gymnasium, a fitness center, tennis, racquetball, and multipurpose courts, a 400-meter track, cross-country trails, and playing fields for baseball, softball, lacrosse, and field hockey.

Disabled Students: 90% of the campus is accessible to disabled students. The following facilities are available: wheelchair ramps, elevators, special parking, specially equipped rest rooms, special class scheduling, lowered drinking fountains, and lowered telephones.

Services: In addition to many counseling and information services, tutoring is available in every subject. There is a reader service for the blind, and remedial math, reading, and writing. A range of support services is available for the physically challenged and learning disabled.

Campus Safety and Security: Campus safety and security measures include 24-hour foot and vehicle patrol, escort service, informal discussions, and pamphlets/posters/films. There are emergency telephones, lighted pathways/sidewalks, a 24-hour manned-entry control station, one point of entry/exit, parking-lot cameras, and intrusion alarms sounded at the campus security office. In addition, grounds are patrolled on bicycle during the warmer months.

Programs of Study: Bryant confers B.A. and B.S.B.A. degrees. Associate and master's degrees are also awarded. Bachelor's degrees are awarded in BUSINESS (accounting, banking and finance, business administration and management, and marketing/retailing/merchandising), COMMUNICATIONS AND THE ARTS (communications and English), COMPUTER AND PHYSICAL SCIENCE (actuarial science and information sciences and systems), SOCIAL SCIENCE (economics, history, and international studies). Applied actuarial mathematics, accounting, marketing, finance, and management are the strongest academically. Accounting and management have the largest enrollments.

Required: To graduate, all students must complete 55 semester hours of liberal arts, 54 hours of business, and 12 hours of electives (none for accounting majors), for a total of 121 hours, with 18 to 30 hours in the major. A GPA of 2.0 overall, in the major, and in all other subjects, must be maintained. Required courses include English composition, business, economics, mathematics, humanities, computer, finance, marketing, and management.

Special: Bryant offers internships, study abroad in 21 countries, on-campus work-study programs, accelerated business programs, B.A.-B.S. degrees, dual and student-designed majors, credit for military experience, and nondegree study. There is a freshman honors program on campus, as well as 1 national honor society. 11 departments have honors programs.

Faculty/Classroom: 73% of faculty are male; 27%, female. All teach undergraduates and 75% also do research. No introductory courses are taught by graduate students. The average class size in an introductory lecture is 30; in a laboratory, 22; and in a regular course offering, 30.

Admissions: 76% of the 1995–96 applicants were accepted. The SAT I scores for the 1995–96 freshman class were as follows: Verbal—77% below 500, 20% between 500 and 599, and 3% between 600 and 700; Math—32% below 500, 42% between 500 and 599, 22% between 600 and 700, and 4% above 700. The ACT scores were 22% below 21, 32% between 21 and 23, 24% between 24 and 26, 8% between 27 and 28, and 14% above 28. 35% of the current freshmen were in the top fifth of their class; 71% were in the top two fifths. 3 freshmen graduated first in their class.

Requirements: The SAT I or ACT is required. Applicants must be graduates of an accredited secondary school with a 3.0 GPA or have a GED certificate. A total of 16 Carnegie units is required, including 4 years of English, 2 years each of mathematics (minimum algebra I and II) and social studies, and 1 year of laboratory science. An essay is required. An interview is highly recommended. Applicants may apply on-line via College Link if it is available in their high schools. AP and CLEP credits are accepted. Important factors in the admissions decision are advanced placement or honor courses, recommendations by school officials, and leadership record.

Procedure: Freshmen are admitted fall and spring. Entrance exams should be taken before January of the senior year. There is a deferred admissions plan. Application deadlines are open. Application fee is $30. Notification is sent beginning November 15.

Transfer: 131 transfer students enrolled in 1995–96. Applicants must have a minimum GPA of 2.0, although a 3.0 is recommended, as is an interview. 30 credits of 121 must be completed at Bryant.

Visiting: There are regularly scheduled orientations for prospective students, including campus tours, a financial aid presentation, a student activities overview, and an academic program overview. There are guides for informal visits and visitors may sit in on classes and stay overnight at the school. To schedule a visit, contact the Admission Office.

Financial Aid: In 1995–96, 82% of all freshmen and 80% of continuing students received some form of financial aid. 61% of all students received need-based aid. The average freshman award was $11,645. Of that total, scholarships or need-based grants averaged $6120 ($8000 maximum); loans averaged $4125 (maximum); and work contracts averaged $1400. 46% of undergraduate students work part-time. Average earnings from campus work for the school year are $1400. The average financial indebtedness of the 1994–95 graduate was $17,000. Bryant is a member of CSS. The FAF or FAFSA and the college's own financial statement are required. The application deadline for fall entry is February 15.

International Students: There are currently 137 international students enrolled. The school actively recruits these students. They must score 550 on the TOEFL and also take SAT I or the ACT.

Computers: The college provides computer facilities for student use. The mainframe is a DEC Station 5000 Model 240. There are 60 text terminals in 2 campus locations, directly connected to the central systems for E-mail and instructional support. In addition, more than 45 microcomputers provide graphical access to the World Wide Web. There are also more than 120 microcomputers on local area networks in the technology center and more than 150 in various classrooms. All students may access the system when the technology center is open and when dial-in lines are available. There are no time limits and no fees.

Graduates: In 1994–95, 651 bachelor's degrees were awarded. The most popular majors among graduates were accounting (24%), marketing (22%), and finance (20%). Within an average freshman class, 71% graduate in 4 years, 72% in 5 years, and 73% in 6 years. 188 companies recruited on campus in 1994–95. Of the 1994 graduating class, 3% were enrolled in graduate school within 6 months of graduation and 90% had found employment.

Admissions Contact: Margaret L. Drugovich, Dean of Admission. E-mail: admissions@bryant.edu. A campus video is available.

JOHNSON AND WALES UNIVERSITY   C-2
Providence, RI 02903

(401) 598-4664
(800) DIAL-JWU; FAX: (401) 598-4641

Full-time: 3415 men, 2801 women	Faculty: 216
Part-time: 556 men, 642 women	Ph.D.s: 20%
Graduate: 254 men, 256 women	Student/Faculty: 29 to 1
Year: quarters, summer session	Tuition: $10,884
Application Deadline: August 1	Room & Board: $5058
Freshman Class: 14,154 applied, 12,368 accepted, 2419 enrolled	
SAT I or ACT: not required	LESS COMPETITIVE

Johnson and Wales University, founded in 1914, is a private coeducational institution offering degree programs in business, food services, hospitality, and related technology. There are 4 undergraduate schools and one graduate school. The 2 libraries contain 70,000 volumes, 170,000 microform items, and 2800 audiovisual forms, and subscribe to 1230 periodicals. Computerized library sources and services include the card catalog, interlibrary loans, and database searching. Special learning facilities include a learning resource center and a culinary archives and museum. The 80-acre campus is in an urban area in Providence, with facilities in Warwick, Cranston, and Seekonk, as well as campuses in Charleston, South Carolina; Norfolk, Virginia; North Miami, Florida; and Vail, Colorado. Including residence halls, there are 32 buildings on campus.

Student Life: 78% of undergraduates are from out-of-state, mostly the Northeast. Students come from 50 states, 75 foreign countries, and Canada. 88% are from public schools; 12% from private. 75% are white; 11% African American. The average age of freshmen is 18; all undergraduates, 21. 21% do not continue beyond their first year; 71% remain to graduate.

Housing: 3239 students can be accommodated in college housing. College-sponsored living facilities include single-sex and coed dormitories, on-campus apartments, and married-student housing. In addition there are special interest houses and international housing, national student organization housing, honors floors, and wellness housing. On-campus housing is guaranteed for all 4 years. 51% of students live on campus; of those, 75% remain on campus on weekends. Alcohol is not permitted. All students may keep cars on campus.

Activities: 15% of men belong to 3 local and 12 national fraternities; 15% of women belong to 2 local and 10 national sororities. There are 75 groups on campus, including cheerleading, chess, choir, chorale, computers, dance, drama, ethnic, gay, honors, international, literary magazine, musical theater, newspaper, political, professional, religious, social, social service, student government, yearbook, and national student organizations. Popular campus events include Spring Weekend, Family Weekend, and SnoBall Dance.

Sports: There are 7 intercollegiate sports for men and 6 for women, and 7 intramural sports for men and 7 for women. Athletic and recreation facilities include 2 gymnasiums, 2 weight rooms, 2 fitness centers, and a swimming pool.

Disabled Students: 60% of the campus is accessible to disabled students. The following facilities are available: wheelchair ramps, elevators, special parking, specially equipped rest rooms, special class scheduling, lowered drinking fountains, lowered telephones, lowered fire alarms, emergency lighting, audiovisual fire alarms in public bathrooms, and a lowering chair for the swimming pool.

Services: In addition to many counseling and information services, tutoring is available in every subject. There is a reader service for the blind and remedial math and writing. Workshops in stress and time management, wellness, and learning strategies are offered. Special scheduling of courses and examinations and taping are available to accomodate special needs.

Campus Safety and Security: Campus safety and security measures include 24-hour foot and vehicle patrol, self-defense education, escort service, and shuttle buses. In addition, there are informal discussions, pamphlets/posters/films, emergency telephones, lighted pathways/sidewalks, 24-hour dormitory coverage, a phone hotline for campus emergencies, and crime alerts in student weekly newspaper.

Programs of Study: The university confers the B.S. degree. Associate and master's degrees are also awarded. Bachelor's degrees are awarded in AGRICULTURE (equine science), BUSINESS (accounting, business administration and management, court reporting, entrepreneurial studies, fashion merchandising, hospitality management services, hotel/motel and restaurant management, institutional management, international business management, investments and securities, management information systems, management science, marketing and distribution, marketing management, marketing/retailing/merchandising, office supervision and management, recreation and leisure services, recreational facilities management, retailing, secretarial studies/office management, small business management, sports management, tourism, and transportation and travel marketing), COMMUNICATIONS AND THE ARTS (advertising and communications), COMPUTER AND PHYSICAL SCIENCE (computer management, computer science, information sciences and systems, and systems analysis), EDUCATION (marketing and distribution), ENGINEERING AND ENVIRONMENTAL DESIGN (electrical/electronics engineering and food services technology), HEALTH PROFESSIONS (health care administration), SOCIAL SCIENCE (clothing and textiles management/production/services, criminal justice, food production/management/services, paralegal studies, parks and recreation management, and systems science). Culinary arts, hotel/restaurant management, and marketing are the strongest academically. Culinary arts, hotel/restaurant management, and accounting have the largest enrollments.

Required: To graduate, students must complete 180 quarter credit hours, including at least 36 in the major, with a minimum GPA of 2.0. Required courses include English, mathematics, history, psychology, sociology, and professional development.

Special: The university offers co-op programs, accelerated degree programs, dual majors, study abroad, and worldwide work-study opportunities in business, hospitality, and culinary arts. There are required 11-week internships in culinary arts, hotel/restaurant management, travel/tourism management, and retail merchandising management. There is a freshman honors program on campus, as well as 1 national honor society. 5 departments have honors programs.

Faculty/Classroom: 63% of faculty are male; 37%, female. All teach undergraduates. No introductory courses are taught by graduate students. The average class size in an introductory lecture is 30; in a laboratory, 18; and in a regular course offering, 30.

Admissions: 87% of the 1995–96 applicants were accepted. 11% of the current freshmen were in the top fifth of their class; 33% were in the top two fifths. 2 freshmen graduated first in their class.

Requirements: The university requires applicants to be in the upper 70% of their class. A minimum GPA of 2.0 is required. For honors program consideration, SAT I and SAT II: Subject tests must be taken. Graduation from high school or an equivalent credential is required. AP and CLEP credits are accepted. Important factors in the admissions decision are advanced placement or honor courses, recommendations by school officials, and extracurricular activities record.

Procedure: Freshmen are admitted to all sessions. There are early admissions and deferred admissions plans. Applications should be filed by August 1 for fall entry, November 1 for winter entry, February 1 for spring entry, and May 1 for summer entry. Notification is sent on a rolling basis.

Transfer: 458 transfer students enrolled in 1995–96. Applicants are required to submit official high school and college transcripts and must have earned a minimum college GPA of 2.0. 45 quarter hours of 180 must be completed at the university.

Visiting: There are regularly scheduled orientations for prospective students, including parent/student orientation, financial services, student testing, academic orientation, preparation for September registration, and parent-to-parent orientation. There are guides for informal visits and visitors may sit in on classes and stay overnight at the school. To schedule a visit, contact the Admissions Office.

Financial Aid: In 1995–96, 76% of all freshmen and 78% of continuing students received some form of financial aid. 70% of freshmen and 66% of continuing students received need-based aid. The average freshman award was $8026. Of that total, scholarships or need-based grants averaged $2115 ($10,554 maximum); loans averaged $2316 ($5500 maximum); and work contracts averaged $1784 ($1800 maximum). 55% of undergraduate students work part-time. Average earnings from campus work for the school year are $528. The average financial indebtedness of the 1994–95 graduate was $7675. The FAFSA and the college's own financial statement are required. The application deadline for fall entry is August 1.

International Students: There are currently 696 international students enrolled. The school actively recruits these students. They must take the TOEFL and achieve a minimum score of 550.

Computers: The college provides computer facilities for student use. The mainframe is a Wang VS 7380A. There are 400 personal computers dedicated to student use, including 60 networked workstations for hospitality students. All students may access the system daily, a total of 82 hours per week. There are no time limits and no fees.

Graduates: In 1994–95, 1051 bachelor's degrees were awarded. The most popular majors among graduates were food service management (26%), hospitality management (20%), and hotel/restaurant management (12%). Within an average freshman class, 24% graduate in 3 years, 75% in 4 years, and 1% in 5 years. 219 companies recruited on campus in a recent year.

Admissions Contact: Mark Burke, Director of Enrollment Management. E-mail: webmaster@jwu.edu. A campus video is available.

PROVIDENCE COLLEGE

C-2

Providence, RI 02918

(401) 865–2535
(800) 721–6444; FAX: (401) 865–2826

Full-time: 1400 men, 2100 women	Faculty: 257; IIA, +$
Part-time: 1200 men and women	Ph.D.s: 82%
Graduate: 793 men and women	Student/Faculty: 14 to 1
Year: semesters, summer session	Tuition: $15,500
Application Deadline: January 15	Room & Board: $6475
Freshman Class: 3836 applied, 2871 accepted, 962 enrolled	
SAT I Verbal/Math: 486/546	**VERY COMPETITIVE**

Providence College, founded in 1917, is a liberal arts and sciences institution operated by the Dominican order of the Catholic Church. There is 1 graduate school. In addition to regional accreditation, Providence has baccalaureate program accreditation with AACSB, CSWE, and NCATE. The library contains 270,000 volumes, 25,709 microform items, and 1113 audiovisual forms, and subscribes to more than 2000 periodicals. Computerized library sources and services include interlibrary loans and database searching. Special learning facilities include a learning resource center, art gallery, radio station, and Blackfriars Theatre. The 105-acre campus is in a suburban area 50 miles south of Boston. Including residence halls, there are 40 buildings on campus.

Student Life: 84% of undergraduates are from out-of-state, mostly the Northeast. Students come from 39 states, 12 foreign countries, and Canada. 61% are from public schools; 39% from private. 92% are white. Most are Catholic. The average age of freshmen is 18; all undergraduates, 20. 4% do not continue beyond their first year; 92% remain to graduate.

Housing: 2610 students can be accommodated in college housing. College-sponsored living facilities include single-sex and coed dormitories and on-campus apartments. In addition, there are honors floors, living and learning floors, and international floors. On-campus housing is available on a first-come, first-served basis and is available on a lottery system for upperclassmen. Priority is given to out-of-town students. 71% of students live on campus; of those, 80% remain on campus on weekends. All students may keep cars on campus.

Activities: There are no fraternities or sororities. There are 85 groups on campus, including art, band, cheerleading, choir, chorale, computers, dance, drama, ethnic, honors, international, jazz band, literary magazine, musical theater, newspaper, pep band, photography, political, professional, radio and TV, religious, social, social service, student government, and yearbook. Popular campus events include Supersports Competition, Harvest Fest, Blind Date Balls, and Midnight Madness.

Sports: There are 10 intercollegiate sports for men and 10 for women, and 30 intramural sports for men and 27 for women. Athletic and recreation facilities include an ice arena, indoor and outdoor tracks, courts for tennis, racquetball, handball, squash, basketball, and volleyball, a pool, a Nautilus program, facilities for weightlifting, aerobics, and ballet, a soccer field, and a baseball field.

Disabled Students: 70% of the campus is accessible to disabled students. The following facilities are available: wheelchair ramps, elevators, special parking, specially equipped rest rooms, special class

scheduling, lowered drinking fountains, lowered telephones, and specially equipped dormitory rooms for full-time day students.

Services: In addition to many counseling and information services, tutoring is available in most subjects. There is a reader service for the blind and academic support services, including evaluation of learning-disabled students.

Campus Safety and Security: Campus safety and security measures include 24-hour foot and vehicle patrol, self-defense education, escort service, and shuttle buses. There are informal discussions, pamphlets/posters/films, emergency telephones, lighted pathways/sidewalks, and a campuswide computerized card access system for entry into all dormitories and apartment buildings.

Programs of Study: Providence confers B.A. and B.S. degrees. Master's and doctoral degrees are also awarded. Bachelor's degrees are awarded in BIOLOGICAL SCIENCE (biology/biological science), BUSINESS (accounting, banking and finance, business administration and management, business economics, and marketing/retailing/merchandising), COMMUNICATIONS AND THE ARTS (art history and appreciation, dramatic arts, English, fine arts, French, Italian, music, and Spanish), COMPUTER AND PHYSICAL SCIENCE (chemistry, computer science, mathematics, and quantitative methods), EDUCATION (elementary, secondary, and special), ENGINEERING AND ENVIRONMENTAL DESIGN (engineering), HEALTH PROFESSIONS (health care administration), SOCIAL SCIENCE (American studies, community services, economics, history, humanities, Latin American studies, philosophy, political science/government, psychology, religion, social science, social work, sociology, systems science, and theological studies). Biology, chemistry, and business are the strongest academically. Business, political science, and English have the largest enrollments.

Required: To graduate, all students must complete at least 116 credit hours, with 24 upper-division hours in the major, and maintain a GPA of 2.0. Students must also meet an English proficiency requirement, complete 20 credits in Western civilization, and fulfill the 30-credit core curriculum, including 6 credits each in natural science, social science, philosophy, and religion, and 3 each in mathematics and fine arts.

Special: Providence offers cross-registration with Rhode Island School of Design, internships in politics, broadcasting, journalism, and business, and study abroad in Europe and Japan and through the New England-Quebec Exchange Program. Also available are B.A.-B.S. degrees in science majors, dual and student-designed majors, a 3–2 engineering degree with Columbia University or Washington University in St. Louis, nondegree study, and pass/fail options. There is a freshman honors program on campus, as well as 14 national honor societies.

Faculty/Classroom: 72% of faculty are male; 28%, female. No introductory courses are taught by graduate students. The average class size in an introductory lecture is 30; in a laboratory, 7; and in a regular course offering, 25.

Admissions: 75% of the 1995–96 applicants were accepted. The SAT I scores for the 1995–96 freshman class were as follows: Verbal—47% below 500, 43% between 500 and 599, 9% between 600 and 700, and 1% above 700; Math—25% below 500, 42% between 500 and 599, 28% between 600 and 700, and 5% above 700. 52% of the current freshmen were in the top fifth of their class; 85% were in the top two fifths. There were 36 National Merit finalists and 32 semifinalists. 17 freshmen graduated first in their class.

Requirements: The SAT I or ACT is required. SAT II: Subject tests in writing and 2 others of the applicant's choice are recommended. Applicants must be graduates of an accredited secondary school with a 3.0 GPA or have a GED certificate. High school preparation should include 4 years of English, 3 each of foreign language and mathematics, and 2 each of history, science, and social studies. 2 essays are required. Students may file applications on-line via CollegeLink. AP and CLEP credits are accepted. Important factors in the admissions decision are advanced placement or honor courses, leadership record, and extracurricular activities record.

Procedure: Freshmen are admitted fall and spring. Entrance exams should be taken in the junior or senior year. There are early decision, early admissions, and deferred admissions plans. Early decision applications should be filed by November 15; regular applications, by January 15 for fall entry and November 1 for spring entry, along with an application fee of $40. Notification of early decision is sent January 1; regular decision, April 1. 224 early decision candidates were accepted for the 1995–96 class. A waiting list is an active part of the admissions procedure, with about 7% of all applicants on the list.

Transfer: 88 transfer students enrolled in 1995–96. Applicants should have a minimum college GPA of 3.0 in a strong liberal arts program with a recommended 24 credit hours. The SAT I or ACT is required, and an interview is recommended. 60 credits of 116 must be completed at Providence.

Visiting: There are regularly scheduled orientations for prospective students, including campus tours and group information sessions. There are guides for informal visits and visitors may sit in on classes and stay overnight at the school. To schedule a visit, contact the Admissions Office.

Financial Aid: In 1995–96, 81% of all freshmen and 67% of continuing students received some form of financial aid. 64% of freshmen and 62% of continuing students received need-based aid. The average freshman award was $12,130. Of that total, scholarships or need-based grants averaged $6530 ($15,250 maximum); loans averaged $4000; and work contracts averaged $1600 ($2000 maximum). 66% of undergraduate students work part-time. Average earnings from campus work for the school year are $1525. The average financial indebtedness of the 1994–95 graduate was $19,000. Providence is a member of CSS. The CSS Profile Application financial statement is required. The application deadline for fall entry is February 1.

International Students: There are currently 35 international students enrolled. The school actively recruits these students. They must score 550 on the TOEFL and must also take the SAT I or the ACT. SAT II: Subject tests are strongly encouraged.

Computers: The college provides computer facilities for student use. The mainframe is a Wang VS 8000. There are 8 computer laboratories equipped with IBM, Apple, AT&T, and Compupro computers. Also, students have access to the information superhighway via the Internet. There are 100 IBM-compatible PCs and 20 Macintosh computers. All students may access the system. There are no time limits and no fees.

Graduates: In a recent year, 1012 bachelor's degrees were awarded. The most popular majors among graduates were business (32%), English (10%), and history (8%). Within an average freshman class, 96% graduate in 4 years. 136 companies recruited on campus in a recent year. Of the 1994 graduating class, 96% had found employment within 6 months of graduation.

Admissions Contact: William DiBrienza, Dean of Admissions and Financial Aid.

RHODE ISLAND COLLEGE
C-2
Providence, RI 02908 (401) 456-8234

Full-time: 4701 men and women	Faculty: 363; IIA, av$
Part-time: 2705 men and women	Ph.Ds: 70%
Graduate: 1818 men and women	Student/Faculty: 13 to 1
Year: semesters, summer session	Tuition: $2969 ($7489)
Application Deadline: May 1	Room & Board: $5100–5600
Freshman Class: n/av	
SAT I: required	LESS COMPETITIVE

Rhode Island College, founded in 1854, is a state-supported liberal arts institution offering undergraduate and graduate programs in the liberal arts and sciences, social work, education, and human development. There are 3 undergraduate schools and 1 graduate school. In addition to regional accreditation, the college has baccalaureate program accreditation with NASAD, NASM, NCATE, and NLN. The library contains 373,000 volumes and subscribes to 1500 periodicals. Special learning facilities include an art gallery and radio station. The 125-acre campus is in a suburban area 50 miles southwest of Boston. Including residence halls, there are 26 buildings on campus.

Student Life: 90% of undergraduates are from Rhode Island. 91% are white. 68% are Catholic; 16% Protestant. The average age of freshmen is 18; all undergraduates, 21.

Housing: 830 students can be accommodated in college housing. College-sponsored living facilities include single-sex and coed dormitories. In addition, there are honors houses. On-campus housing is available on a first-come, first-served basis. Priority is given to out-of-town students. 80% of students commute. Alcohol is not permitted. All students may keep cars on campus.

Activities: There is 1 national fraternity and 3 national sororities. There are 64 groups on campus, including art, band, cheerleading, chess, chorale, chorus, dance, drama, ethnic, gay, honors, international, literary magazine, musical theater, newspaper, orchestra, political, professional, radio and TV, religious, social, social service, student government, symphony, and yearbook. Popular campus events include a fine and performing arts calendar, chess tournaments, and campus center activities.

Sports: Athletic and recreation facilities include playing fields, an athletic center, and a recreation center.

Disabled Students: All of the campus is accessible to disabled students. The following facilities are available: wheelchair ramps, elevators, special parking, specially equipped rest rooms, and special class scheduling. A peer adviser is available to assist disabled students.

Services: In addition to many counseling and information services, tutoring is available in most subjects. There is a reader service for the blind, remedial math, reading, and writing, and services for learning-disabled students and any student needing academic assistance.

Campus Safety and Security: Campus safety and security measures include 24-hour foot and vehicle patrol, self-defense education, escort service, and informal discussions. In addition, there are pamphlets/posters/films, emergency telephones, and lighted pathways/sidewalks.

Programs of Study: The college confers B.A., B.S., B.F.A., B.M., B.S.N., and B.S.W. degrees. Master's degrees are also awarded. Bachelor's degrees are awarded in BIOLOGICAL SCIENCE (biology/biological science), BUSINESS (accounting, business administration and management, business economics, marketing/retailing/merchandising, and personnel management), COMMUNICATIONS AND THE ARTS (communications, dramatic arts, English, film arts, fine arts, French, music, photography, and Spanish), COMPUTER AND PHYSICAL SCIENCE (chemistry, computer programming, computer science, information sciences and systems, mathematics, and physics), EDUCATION (art, early childhood, elementary, foreign languages, health, industrial arts, middle school, music, science, secondary, and special), ENGINEERING AND ENVIRONMENTAL DESIGN (industrial engineering technology), HEALTH PROFESSIONS (medical laboratory technology and nursing), SOCIAL SCIENCE (anthropology, economics, geography, history, philosophy, political science/government, prelaw, psychology, public administration, social science, social work, sociology, and urban studies). Education, management, and psychology have the largest enrollments.

Required: To graduate, students must complete 120 credits and maintain a minimum GPA of 2.0. All students must complete courses in Western civilization and literature and fulfill 9 distribution requirements.

Special: Cross-registration is available with other Rhode Island schools. The college offers internships, a general studies degree, dual and student-designed majors, credit by examination, credit for prior learning, and pass/fail options. There is a freshman honors program on campus, as well as 6 national honor societies. 21 departments have honors programs.

Faculty/Classroom: 56% of faculty are male; 44%, female. 98% both teach and do research. The average class size in an introductory lecture is 30; in a laboratory, 14; and in a regular course offering, 30.

Admissions: The SAT I scores for a recent freshman class were as follows: Verbal—83% below 500, 12% between 500 and 599, and 5% between 600 and 700; Math—72% below 500, 23% between 500 and 599, and 5% between 600 and 700. 29% of the freshmen were in the top fifth of their class; 62% were in the top two fifths.

Requirements: The SAT I is required. ACT scores will be accepted. Applicants should be graduates of an accredited secondary school with 18 academic credits, including 4 in English, 3 in mathematics, 2 each in foreign languages, science, and social studies, one-half credit in either art or music, one-half credit in computer literacy, and the remainder in academic electives. The GED is accepted. An essay is required, along with a portfolio for art students and an audition for music students. AP and CLEP credits are accepted. Important factors in the admissions decision are advanced placement or honor courses, evidence of special talent, and leadership record.

Procedure: Freshmen are admitted fall and spring. Entrance exams should be taken by December of the senior year. There are early admissions and deferred admissions plans. Applications should be filed by May 1 for fall entry and November 15 for spring entry, along with an application fee of $25. Notification is sent on a rolling basis.

Transfer: Applicants must submit at least 30 college credits and a minimum GPA of 2.0. 30 credits of 120 must be completed at The college.

Visiting: There are regularly scheduled orientations for prospective students, information sessions and a campus tour. There are guides for informal visits who may sit in on classes and stay overnight at the school. To schedule a visit, contact the Admissions Office.

Financial Aid: 88% of undergraduate applicants receive financial aid. The average award is $4900 per year. The college is a member of CSS. The FAFSA and the CSS Profile Application are required. The application deadline for fall entry is March 1.

International Students: International students must take the TOEFL and achieve a minimum score of 550.

Computers: The college provides computer facilities for student use. The mainframe is a DEC VAX 11/780. Apple Macintosh and IBM computer laboratories are available for student use. All students may access the system. There are no time limits and no fees.

Admissions Contact: William H. Hurry, Jr., Dean of Admissions and Financial Aid.

RHODE ISLAND SCHOOL OF DESIGN
C-2
Providence, RI 02903 (401) 454-6300
(800) 364-7473; FAX: (401) 454-6309

Full-time: 811 men, 1005 women	Faculty: 122; IIB, +$
Part-time: none	Ph.Ds: 71%
Graduate: 69 men, 101 women	Student/Faculty: 15 to 1
Year: 4-1-4	Tuition: $17,780
Application Deadline: February 15	Room & Board: $6618
Freshman Class: 1496 applied, 863 accepted, 378 enrolled	
SAT I: required	SPECIAL

Rhode Island School of Design, founded in 1877, is a private coeducational institution offering degree programs in fine arts, design, and architecture. In addition to regional accreditation, RISD has baccalaureate program accreditation with ASLA, NAAB, and NASAD. The library contains 80,000 volumes and 780 audiovisual forms, and subscribes to 360 periodicals. Computerized library sources and services include the card catalog, interlibrary loans, and database searching. Special learning facilities include an art gallery, an art museum, and a nature laboratory. The 13-acre campus is in an urban area 50 miles south of Boston, Massachusetts. Including residence halls, there are 40 buildings on campus.

Student Life: 92% of undergraduates are from out-of-state, mostly the Northeast. Students come from 50 states, 48 foreign countries, and Canada. 60% are from public schools; 40% from private. 65% are white; 19% foreign nationals. The average age of freshmen is 18; all undergraduates, 23. 7% do not continue beyond their first year; 85% remain to graduate.

Housing: 700 students can be accommodated in college housing. College-sponsored living facilities include coed dormitories and on-campus apartments. In addition, there is choice housing for freshmen participating in health-related programs within a chemical-free living space. On-campus housing is guaranteed for all 4 years. 65% of students commute. Alcohol is not permitted.

Activities: There are no fraternities or sororities. There are 60 groups on campus, including art, computers, dance, drama, ethnic, film, gay, international, literary magazine, newspaper, photography, political, professional, religious, social, social service, student government, and yearbook. Popular campus events include Artists Ball, student film festival, and Collection showcase of student-designed apparel.

Sports: There is an intramural sports program. Athletic and recreation facilities include a student center with dance, aerobics, weightlifting, and Nautilus and other exercise equipment, and Tillinghast Farm, a retreat on Narragansett Bay, 15 minutes from campus. Students may also use Brown University's athletic complex and enroll in activity classes.

Disabled Students: The following facilities are available: wheelchair ramps, elevators, special parking, specially equipped rest rooms, and special class scheduling.

Services: A writing program for learning-disabled students, access to taped lectures/note takers, and alternative test-taking procedures are available.

Campus Safety and Security: Campus safety and security measures include 24-hour foot and vehicle patrol, escort service, shuttle buses, and informal discussions. There are pamphlets/posters/films, emergency telephones, lighted pathways/sidewalks, evening studio monitors, and studio access keys.

Programs of Study: RISD confers B.Arch., B.F.A., B.G.D., B.I.D., B.Int.Arch., and B.Land.Arch. degrees. Master's degrees are also awarded. Bachelor's degrees are awarded in COMMUNICATIONS AND THE ARTS (ceramic art and design, design, film arts, glass, graphic design, illustration, industrial design, metal/jewelry, painting, photography, printmaking, and sculpture), ENGINEERING AND ENVIRONMENTAL DESIGN (architecture, furniture design, interior design, and landscape architecture/design), SOCIAL SCIENCE (textiles and clothing). Illustration, graphic design, and architecture have the largest enrollments.

Required: To graduate, all students must complete at least 126 credit hours, including 54 in the major, 42 in liberal arts, 18 in the freshman foundation program, and 12 in nonmajor electives. Liberal arts credits must include 12 each in art/architectural history and electives and 9 each in English and history/philosophy/social science. Core courses include 2 semesters each of foundation drawing, 2-dimensional design, and 3-dimensional design. A minimum GPA of 2.0 and completion of the final-year project are required.

Special: RISD offers cross-registration with Brown University and the Art Schools Mobility Consortium, 6-week internships during the midyear winter session, study abroad through the senior-year European Honors Program in Rome, and various 3- to 6-week travel courses.

Faculty/Classroom: 60% of faculty are male; 40%, female. All teach undergraduates. The average class size in an introductory lecture is 20 and in a laboratory, 17.

Admissions: 58% of the 1995–96 applicants were accepted. The SAT I scores for the 1995–96 freshman class were as follows: Verbal—50% below 500, 33% between 500 and 599, and 17% between 600 and 700; Math—27% below 500, 37% between 500 and 599, 28% between 600 and 700, and 8% above 700. 34% of the current freshmen were in the top fifth of their class; 67% were in the top two fifths.

Requirements: The SAT I is required. Applicants must be graduates of an accredited secondary school or have a GED. An essay, assigned drawings, and a portfolio (optional for architecture majors) are also required. AP credits are accepted. Important factors in the admissions decision are evidence of special talent, advanced placement or honor courses, and personality/intangible qualities.

Procedure: Freshmen are admitted fall and spring. Entrance exams should be taken at least 6 weeks before the application deadline. There are early admissions and deferred admissions plans. Applica-

tions should be filed by February 15 for fall entry and November 25 for spring entry, along with an application fee of $35. Notification is sent by April 1. A waiting list is an active part of the admissions procedure.

Transfer: 135 transfer students enrolled in 1995–96. Applicants must have at least 27 college credits and should submit an essay along with academic transcripts from the previous 3 years. The SAT I or ACT is required for architecture applicants; others must submit a portfolio. Letters of recommendation are encouraged. 2 years' residency and 66 credits of 126 must be completed at RISD.

Visiting: There are regularly scheduled orientations for prospective students, including a presentation by the admissions staff and a campus tour. Visitors may sit in on classes. To schedule a visit, contact the Admissions Office.

Financial Aid: In 1995–96, 57% of all freshmen and 63% of continuing students received some form of financial aid. 56% of freshmen and 61% of continuing students received need-based aid. The average freshman award was $11,937. Of that total, scholarships or need-based grants averaged $8494 ($19,000 maximum); loans averaged $2625 ($7375 maximum); and work contracts averaged $1100 (maximum). 57% of undergraduate students work part-time. Average earnings from campus work for the school year are $1100. The average financial indebtedness of the 1994–95 graduate was $17,500. RISD is a member of CSS. The FAFSA and CSS Profile Application are required. The application deadline for fall entry is February 15.

International Students: There are currently 309 international students enrolled. They must score 550 on the TOEFL and must also take SAT I or the ACT.

Computers: The college provides computer facilities for student use. There are 220 Apple Macintosh, IBM, IBM-compatible, and Amiga PCs located in the computer center and various departments. All students may access the system. There are no time limits and no fees.

Graduates: In a recent year, 500 bachelor's degrees were awarded. The most popular majors among graduates were architecture (25%), illustration (15%), and graphic design (12%). Within an average freshman class, 85% graduate in 5 years. 25 companies recruited on campus in a recent year.

Admissions Contact: Edward Newhall, Director of Admissions. E-mail: admissions@risd.edu.

ROGER WILLIAMS UNIVERSITY D-3
Bristol, RI 02809–2921

Full-time: 1241 men, 989 women	(401) 254–3500; (800) 458–7144
Part-time: 801 men, 650 women	**Faculty:** 113; IIB, +$
Graduate: 287 men, 183 women	**Ph.D.s:** 65%
Year: 4–1–4, summer session	**Student/Faculty:** 20 to 1
Application Deadline: see profile	**Tuition:** $13,980
Freshman Class: 3073 applied, 2490 accepted, 653 enrolled	**Room & Board:** $6660
SAT I Verbal/Math: 440/483	**COMPETITIVE**

Roger Williams University, founded in 1956, is a liberal arts institution that offers programs in the arts and sciences, professional studies, architecture, and law. There are 4 undergraduate schools and 1 graduate school. In addition to regional accreditation, RWU has baccalaureate program accreditation with NAAB and NCATE. The 3 libraries contain 302,680 volumes, 27,135 microform items, and 3179 audiovisual forms, and subscribe to 1037 periodicals. Computerized library sources and services include interlibrary loans and database searching. Special learning facilities include a learning resource center, art gallery, and radio station. The 120-acre campus is in a small town 18 miles southeast of Providence. Including residence halls, there are 22 buildings on campus.

Student Life: 85% of undergraduates are from out-of-state, mostly the Northeast. Students come from 32 states, 48 foreign countries, and Canada. 75% are from public schools; 25% from private. 92% are white. 65% are Catholic; 20% Protestant; 15% Jewish. The average age of freshmen is 18; all undergraduates, 20. 20% do not continue beyond their first year; 60% remain to graduate.

Housing: 1700 students can be accommodated in college housing. College-sponsored living facilities include single-sex and coed dormitories and on-campus apartments. In addition, there are honors houses and special interest houses. On-campus housing is guaranteed for all freshmen. 65% of students live on campus; of those, 60% remain on campus on weekends. Upperclassmen may keep cars on campus.

Activities: There are no fraternities or sororities. There are 28 groups on campus, including art, band, cheerleading, chess, choir, chorus, computers, dance, drama, ethnic, film, gay, honors, international, jazz band, literary magazine, musical theater, newspaper, orchestra, photography, political, professional, radio and TV, religious, social service, student government, and yearbook. Popular campus events include Spring Weekend, International Dinner, and Campus Entertainment Network (concerts and comedians).

Sports: There are 12 intercollegiate sports for men and 9 for women, and 12 intramural sports for men and 12 for women. Athletic and recreation facilities include a 2500-seat gymnasium, exercise and weight rooms, jogging facilities, and tennis, volleyball, and basketball courts.

Disabled Students: 80% of the campus is accessible to disabled students. The following facilities are available: wheelchair ramps, elevators, special parking, specially equipped rest rooms, and special class scheduling.

Services: In addition to many counseling and information services, tutoring is available in every subject. There is a reader service for the blind, and remedial math, reading, and writing.

Campus Safety and Security: Campus safety and security measures include 24-hour foot and vehicle patrol, escort service, shuttle buses, and pamphlets/posters/films. There are lighted pathways/sidewalks.

Programs of Study: RWU confers B.A., B.S., B.Arch., and B.F.A. degrees. Master's degrees are also awarded. Bachelor's degrees are awarded in BIOLOGICAL SCIENCE (biology/biological science and marine biology), BUSINESS (accounting, business administration and management, management science, and marketing/retailing/merchandising), COMMUNICATIONS AND THE ARTS (communications, creative writing, dance, dramatic arts, English, fine arts, and historic preservation), COMPUTER AND PHYSICAL SCIENCE (chemistry, computer programming, computer science, and mathematics), ENGINEERING AND ENVIRONMENTAL DESIGN (architecture and engineering), SOCIAL SCIENCE (history, paralegal studies, philosophy, political science/government, prelaw, and psychology). Architecture, sciences, engineering, and law are the strongest academically. Business has the largest enrollment.

Required: To graduate, all students must complete 3 skills courses, 5 courses in interdisciplinary studies, 5 courses within a specific concentration, and an integrative senior seminar. A minimum of 120 credit hours, with 30 to 66 hours in the major and a GPA of 2.0, is required.

Special: RWU offers co-op programs, internships, study abroad in London and Europe, student-designed majors, and credit for life, military, and work experience. There is a freshman honors program on campus, as well as 1 national honor society.

Faculty/Classroom: 82% of faculty are male; 18%, female. The average class size in an introductory lecture is 20; in a laboratory, 12; and in a regular course offering, 28.

Admissions: 81% of the 1995–96 applicants were accepted. 25% of the current freshmen were in the top fifth of their class; 60% were in the top two fifths.

Requirements: The SAT I or ACT is required. Applicants should be graduates of an accredited secondary school with a 2.0 GPA. The GED is accepted. Students should have 4 years of English, 3 of mathematics, 2 each of social and natural sciences, and 4 to 6 electives, for a total of 16 Carnegie units. Art and architecture students must submit portfolios. An essay and an interview are recommended. AP and CLEP credits are accepted. Important factors in the admissions decision are advanced placement or honor courses, leadership record, and evidence of special talent.

Procedure: Freshmen are admitted fall and spring. Entrance exams should be taken in November or December of the senior year. There are early decision, early admissions, and deferred admissions plans. Early decision applications should be filed by December 1; regular deadlines are February 1 for architecture majors and open for others. The application fee is $35. Notification of early decision is sent December 15; regular decision, on a rolling basis.

Transfer: 144 transfer students enrolled in 1995–96. Transfer applicants need a minimum college GPA of 2.0. The SAT I is recommended. 30 credits of 120 must be completed at RWU.

Visiting: There are regularly scheduled orientations for prospective students. There are guides for informal visits and visitors may sit in on classes. To schedule a visit, contact the Office of Admissions.

Financial Aid: In 1995–96, 80% of all freshmen and 54% of continuing students received some form of financial aid. The average freshman award was $4900. Of that total, scholarships or need-based grants averaged $3000 ($10,000 maximum); loans averaged $2500 ($6000 maximum); and work contracts averaged $1000 ($1800 maximum). 27% of undergraduate students work part-time. Average earnings from campus work for the school year are $1000. The average financial indebtedness of the 1994–95 graduate was $14,000. RWU is a member of CSS. The FAFSA and the college's own financial statement are required. The application deadline for fall entry is March 1.

International Students: There are currently 140 international students enrolled. The school actively recruits these students. They must take the MELAB or the college's own test.

Computers: The college provides computer facilities for student use. The mainframe is a UNIX-based network. 3 academic computer centers with a wide variety of application software are available to students more than 100 hours per week. There are no time limits and no fees.

Admissions Contact: William B. Galloway, Dean of Admissions. A campus video is available.

SALVE REGINA UNIVERSITY D-4
Newport, RI 02840–4192

(401) 847-6650, ext. 2908
(800) 321-7124; FAX: (401) 848-2823

Full-time: 440 men, 884 women	Faculty: 97; IIA, --$
Part-time: 67 men, 114 women	Ph.D.s: 72%
Graduate: 264 men, 325 women	Student/Faculty: 14 to 1
Year: semesters, summer session	Tuition: $14,650
Application Deadline: August 8	Room & Board: $6700
Freshman Class: 1487 applied, 1325 accepted, 374 enrolled	
SAT I Verbal/Math: 394/418	LESS COMPETITIVE

Salve Regina University, founded in 1947 and sponsored by the Sisters of Mercy, is an independent, coeducational institution affiliated with the Roman Catholic Church. The university offers programs in liberal arts, business, health science, and professional training. There is 1 graduate school. In addition to regional accreditation, Salve has baccalaureate program accreditation with CSWE, NASAD, and NLN. The library contains 94,829 volumes, 20,599 microform items, and 17,333 audiovisual forms, and subscribes to 946 periodicals. Computerized library sources and services include the card catalog, interlibrary loans, and database searching. Special learning facilities include a learning resource center, art gallery, and information systems and computer science laboratories. The 70-acre campus is in a suburban area on Newport's waterfront, 60 miles south of Boston. Including residence halls, there are 36 buildings on campus.

Student Life: 70% of undergraduates are from out-of-state, mostly the Northeast. Students come from 30 states, 4 foreign countries, and Canada. 64% are from public schools; 36% from private. 94% are white. The average age of freshmen is 18; all undergraduates, 21. 25% do not continue beyond their first year; 64% remain to graduate.

Housing: 720 students can be accommodated in college housing. College-sponsored living facilities include single-sex dormitories, on-campus apartments, and off-campus apartments. On-campus housing is guaranteed for all 4 years. 55% of students commute. Alcohol is not permitted. Upperclassmen may keep cars on campus.

Activities: There are no fraternities or sororities. There are 43 groups on campus, including art, band, cheerleading, choir, chorale, chorus, computers, dance, drama, ethnic, honors, international, jazz band, literary magazine, musical theater, newspaper, orchestra, pep band, photography, political, professional, religious, social, social service, student government, and yearbook. Popular campus events include Octoberfest Weekend, New Year's Eve Ball, Christmas in Newport, Cotillion, and Alumni Weekend.

Sports: There are 9 intercollegiate sports for men and 8 for women, and 7 intramural sports for men and 7 for women. Athletic and recreation facilities include soccer, baseball, and softball fields, tennis courts, outdoor basketball courts, an indoor track, a yacht club, a weight room, and a fitness center.

Disabled Students: 66% of the campus is accessible to disabled students. The following facilities are available: wheelchair ramps, elevators, special parking, specially equipped rest rooms, lowered drinking fountains, and lowered telephones.

Services: In addition to many counseling and information services, tutoring is available in most subjects. There is remedial math, reading, and writing.

Campus Safety and Security: Campus safety and security measures include 24-hour foot and vehicle patrol, self-defense education, shuttle buses, and informal discussions. In addition, there are pamphlets/posters/films, emergency telephones, and lighted pathways/sidewalks.

Programs of Study: Salve confers B.A., B.S., and B.A.S. degrees. Associate, master's, and doctoral degrees are also awarded. Bachelor's degrees are awarded in BIOLOGICAL SCIENCE (biology/biological science), BUSINESS (accounting and management science), COMMUNICATIONS AND THE ARTS (dramatic arts, English, French, music, Spanish, and studio art), COMPUTER AND PHYSICAL SCIENCE (chemistry, information sciences and systems, and mathematics), EDUCATION (early childhood, elementary, secondary, and special), HEALTH PROFESSIONS (cytotechnology, medical laboratory technology, and nursing), SOCIAL SCIENCE (American studies, criminal justice, economics, history, philosophy, political science/government, psychology, religion, social work, and sociology). Accounting, psychology, politics, chemistry, English, administration of justice, nursing, and medical technology are the strongest academically. Management, administration of justice, elementary education, and nursing have the largest enrollments.

Required: To graduate, students must have 128 credit hours, consisting of about 36 in the major, 44 in electives, and 48 in general distribution requirements. Required credits include 9 in religious studies, 6 each in English, science, and foreign language, and 3 each in logic, mathematics, philosophy, fine arts, social science, economics or geography, and history or politics. Computer literacy is also required. Students must maintain a minimum GPA of 2.0.

Special: Salve offers internships in most academic disciplines as well as work-study programs on campus. Study abroad, B.A.-B.S. degrees in chemistry, mathematics, biology, and economics, dual majors in all programs, and accelerated degree programs in administration of justice, health services administration, business, and international relations are available. A liberal studies degree, 5-year bachelor's and master's programs, credit for life, military, and work experience, nondegree study, and pass/fail options are also offered. There are 8 national honor societies on campus. 6 departments have honors programs.

Faculty/Classroom: 52% of faculty are male; 48%, female. 87% teach undergraduates and 5% both teach and do research. No introductory courses are taught by graduate students. The average class size in an introductory lecture is 24; in a laboratory, 20; and in a regular course offering, 19.

Admissions: 89% of the 1995–96 applicants were accepted. The SAT I scores for the 1995–96 freshman class were as follows: Verbal—92% below 500, 7% between 500 and 599, and 1% between 600 and 700; Math—80% below 500, 16% between 500 and 599, 3% between 600 and 700, and 1% above 700. 11% of the current freshmen were in the top fifth of their class; 28% were in the top two fifths.

Requirements: The SAT I or ACT is recommended. Applicants must be high school graduates or hold a GED. Students should have 16 Carnegie units, consisting of 4 in English, 3 in mathematics, including algebra and geometry, 2 each in science and foreign language, 1 in history, and 4 in electives. An essay is required; an interview is recommended. AP and CLEP credits are accepted. Important factors in the admissions decision are advanced placement or honor courses, leadership record, and extracurricular activities record.

Procedure: Freshmen are admitted in the fall and spring. Entrance exams should be taken as early as possible. There are early decision, early admissions, and deferred admissions plans. Early decision applications should be filed by November 1; regular applications, by August 8 for fall entry and January 1 for spring entry, along with an application fee of $25. Notification of early decision is sent December 10; regular decision, on a rolling basis. 10 early decision candidates were accepted for the 1995–96 class.

Transfer: 73 transfer students enrolled in 1995–96. Applicants must have a college GPA of 2.5. An interview is recommended. 36 credits of 128 must be completed at Salve.

Visiting: There are regularly scheduled orientations for prospective students, including an introduction to the academic experience, history and visions for the university, a library orientation, student life expectations, social activities, residence hall orientation, preregistration for courses, a cookout, and meetings with faculty, advisers, and administrators. There are guides for informal visits and visitors may sit in on classes. To schedule a visit, contact the Admissions Office at (401) 847–6650 or (800) 321–7124 (out-of-state).

Financial Aid: In 1995–96, 75% of all freshmen and 59% of continuing students received some form of financial aid. 70% of freshmen and 58% of continuing students received need-based aid. The average freshman award was $12,500. Of that total, scholarships or need-based grants averaged $6700 ($10,000 maximum); loans averaged $4300 ($5225 maximum); and work contracts averaged $1300 ($2000 maximum). 31% of undergraduate students work part-time. Average earnings from campus work for the school year are $1200. The average financial indebtedness of the 1994–95 graduate was $18,000. Salve is a member of CSS. The FAFSA, the college's own financial statement, the CSS Profile Application, and tax forms are required. The application deadline for fall entry is March 1.

International Students: There are currently 31 international students enrolled. They must score 500 on the TOEFL.

Computers: The college provides computer facilities for student use. The mainframes are an IBM 4381 and an IBM AS/400. There are 108 IBM PS/2, Apple Macintosh, and DEC microcomputers available in computer and science laboratories for undergraduate use. An additional 150 IBM PS/2 microcomputers are assigned to faculty and academic departments, as well as computer networks using Novell NetWare, color printers, and Internet services. All students may access the system 16 hours per day in laboratories and 24 hours per day by dial-in access to the Internet. There are no time limits and no fees.

Graduates: In 1994–95, 357 bachelor's degrees were awarded. The most popular majors among graduates were administration of justice (21%), management (15%), and elementary education (12%). Within an average freshman class, 63% graduate in 4 years, 1% in 5 years, and 1% in 6 years. 105 companies recruited on campus in 1994–95.

Admissions Contact: Laura E. McPhie, Dean of Enrollment Services. A campus video is available.

UNIVERSITY OF RHODE ISLAND
C-4

Kingston, RI 02881   (401) 874-9800; FAX: (401) 874-5523

Full-time: 3862 men, 4471 women	Faculty: 600; I, av$
Part-time: 902 men, 1296 women	Ph.D.s: 88%
Graduate: 1452 men, 1715 women	Student/Faculty: 14 to 1
Year: semesters, summer session	Tuition: $4404 ($12,096)
Application Deadline: March 1	Room & Board: $5750
Freshman Class: 8836 applied, 6887 accepted, 1978 enrolled	
SAT I Verbal/Math: 462/525	ACT: 24 COMPETITIVE

The University of Rhode Island, founded in 1892, is a coeducational land-grant, sea-grant, and urban-grant institution offering programs in liberal arts, business, engineering, human services, nursing, and pharmacy. Located near the ocean and the bay, the university has strong marine and environmental programs. There are satellite campuses in Providence, West Greenwich, and Narragansett. There are 8 undergraduate and 3 graduate schools. In addition to regional accreditation, URI has baccalaureate program accreditation with AACSB, ABET, ACPE, ADA, NASM, NCATE, and NLN. The 3 libraries contain 1,060,000 volumes, 1,430,000 microform items, and 6000 audiovisual forms, and subscribe to 8713 periodicals. Computerized library sources and services include the card catalog, interlibrary loans, and database searching. Special learning facilities include a learning resource center, art gallery, planetarium, radio station, TV station, historic textile collection, and early childhood education center. The 1248-acre campus is in a small town 30 miles south of Providence. Including residence halls, there are 314 buildings on campus.

Student Life: 63% of undergraduates are from Rhode Island. Students come from 50 states, 74 foreign countries, and Canada. 85% are from public schools; 15% from private. 79% are white. The average age of freshmen is 18; all undergraduates, 19.5. 15% do not continue beyond their first year; 65% remain to graduate.

Housing: 4100 students can be accommodated in college housing. College-sponsored living facilities include single-sex and coed dormitories and married-student housing. In addition there are language houses, special interest houses, a freshman dormitory, and a wellness dormitory. On-campus housing is guaranteed for all 4 years. 53% of students live on campus; of those, 75% remain on campus on weekends. Alcohol is not permitted. All students may keep cars on campus.

Activities: 20% of men belong to 18 national fraternities; 20% of women belong to 1 local and 8 national sororities. There are 90 groups on campus, including band, cheerleading, chess, choir, chorale, chorus, dance, drama, ethnic, gay, honors, international, jazz band, literary magazine, marching band, musical theater, newspaper, orchestra, pep band, photography, political, professional, radio and TV, religious, social, social service, student government, and yearbook. Popular campus events include Winterfest, International Week, and Spring Fest.

Sports: There are 10 intercollegiate sports for men and 11 for women, and 18 intramural sports for men and 18 for women. Athletic and recreation facilities include a 4000-seat area, a 10000-seat stadium, 3 pools, and a multipurpose field house with an indoor track, a gymnastics center, 3 fitness rooms, and courts for basketball, tennis, and volleyball. There are also outdoor tennis courts, an all-weather track, 2 beach volleyball courts, and varsity and practice fields.

Disabled Students: The following facilities are available: wheelchair ramps, elevators, special parking, specially equipped rest rooms, special class scheduling, lowered drinking fountains, lowered telephones, and special transportation around campus.

Services: In addition to many counseling and information services, tutoring is available in some subjects, including ESL and popular freshman courses. There is a reader service for the blind, and remedial math, reading, and writing.

Campus Safety and Security: Campus safety and security measures include 24-hour foot and vehicle patrol, self-defense education, escort service, and shuttle buses. In addition, there are informal discussions, pamphlets/posters/films, emergency telephones, and lighted pathways/sidewalks.

Programs of Study: URI confers B.A., B.S., B.F.A., B.G.S., B.L.A., and B.M. degrees. Master's and doctoral degrees are also awarded. Bachelor's degrees are awarded in AGRICULTURE (animal science, fishing and fisheries, horticulture, and wildlife management), BIOLOGICAL SCIENCE (biology/biological science, marine science, microbiology, and zoology), BUSINESS (accounting, banking and finance, business administration and management, fashion merchandising, management information systems, and marketing/retailing/merchandising), COMMUNICATIONS AND THE ARTS (art, classics, communications, comparative literature, dramatic arts, English, fine arts, French, German, Italian, journalism, literature, music, Spanish, and speech/debate/rhetoric), COMPUTER AND PHYSICAL SCIENCE (chemistry, computer science, geology, mathematics, oceanography, physics, and statistics), EDUCATION (elementary, music, physical, and secondary), ENGINEERING AND ENVIRON-

MENTAL DESIGN (chemical engineering, civil engineering, computer engineering, electrical/electronics engineering, environmental science, industrial engineering, landscape architecture/design, and mechanical engineering), HEALTH PROFESSIONS (clinical science, dental hygiene, medical laboratory technology, nursing, and pharmacy), SOCIAL SCIENCE (anthropology, dietetics, economics, food science, geography, history, human development, human services, Latin American studies, philosophy, political science/government, psychology, sociology, textiles and clothing, water resources, and women's studies). Pharmacy, engineering, and biology are the strongest academically. Psychology, pharmacy, and human development and family studies have the largest enrollments.

Required: To graduate, the student must earn 120 to 150 credit hours, at least 30 in the major, with a GPA of 2.0. Distribution requirements include 6 credits each in English communication, fine arts and literature, foreign language or culture, letters, natural sciences, and social sciences, as well as 3 credits in mathematics.

Special: Cross-registration is available with Rhode Island College and Community College of Rhode Island. URI also offers a Washington semester as well as semester-long internships with businesses and state agencies, study abroad in 6 countries, a B.A.-B.S. degree in German and engineering and in languages and business, a general studies degree, dual majors, pass/fail options, and credit for life, military, and work experience. The College of Engineering offers co-op programs, an international internship, and 5-year advanced business degree option. There is a freshman honors program on campus, as well as 30 national honor societies, including Phi Beta Kappa.

Faculty/Classroom: 70% of faculty are male; 30%, female. All both teach and do research. Graduate students teach 6% of introductory courses. The average class size in an introductory lecture is 28; in a laboratory, 12; and in a regular course offering, 19.

Admissions: 78% of the 1995–96 applicants were accepted. The SAT I scores for the 1995–96 freshman class were as follows: Verbal—70% below 500, 26% between 500 and 599, 3% between 600 and 700, and 1% above 700; Math—37% below 500, 43% between 500 and 599, 18% between 600 and 700, and 2% above 700. 39% of the current freshmen were in the top fifth of their class; 67% were in the top two fifths. 30 freshmen graduated first in their class.

Requirements: The SAT I or ACT is required. URI requires applicants to be in the upper 30% of their class. In addition, applicants should be high school graduates, having completed 18 courses, including 4 of English, 3 to 4 of mathematics, and 2 each of science (chemistry and physics for engineering majors), foreign language, and history or social studies. Remaining units should be college preparatory. Music majors must audition. AP and CLEP credits are accepted. Important factors in the admissions decision are advanced

placement or honor courses, evidence of special talent, and recommendations by school officials.

Procedure: Freshmen are admitted fall and spring. Entrance exams should be taken during the spring of the junior year or fall of the senior year. There are early action plans. Early action applications should be filed by December 15; regular applications, by March 1 for fall entry and November 1 for spring entry, along with an application fee of $30 ($45 for out-of-state applicants). Notification of early action is sent January 15; regular decision, on a rolling basis.

Transfer: 584 transfer students enrolled in 1995–96. Applicants must submit transcripts from high school and all colleges or universities attended. A minimum GPA of 2.4 is required; many programs require higher. 24 credits of 120 to 150 must be completed at URI.

Visiting: There are regularly scheduled orientations for prospective students, including open house programs in October and campus tours. There are guides for informal visits and visitors may sit in on classes. To schedule a visit, contact the Admissions Office.

Financial Aid: In a recent year, 66% of all freshmen and 63% of continuing students received some form of financial aid. 60% of freshmen and 58% of continuing students received need-based aid. The average freshman award was $4200. Of that total, scholarships or need-based grants averaged $2000 ($10,500 maximum); loans averaged $1400 ($3500 maximum); and work contracts averaged $1000. 20% of undergraduate students work part-time. Average earnings from campus work for the school year are $1200. URI is a member of CSS. The FAFSA is required. The application deadline for fall entry is March 1.

International Students: There are currently 344 international students enrolled. The school actively recruits these students. They must take the TOEFL, and achieve a minimum score of 550; or the English proficiency test administered by the American consulate. The student must also take the SAT I or the ACT.

Computers: The college provides computer facilities for student use. The mainframes are an IBM ES/9000–210VF and a Prime 6350. Students may access the mainframes through more than 200 on-site and remote terminals. There are also 350 IBM-compatible and Apple Macintosh microcomputers available at various locations. All students may access the system 24 hours per day. There are no time limits and no fees.

Graduates: In a recent year, 2156 bachelor's degrees were awarded. The most popular majors among graduates were psychology (7%), political science (5%), and speech communications (5%). Within an average freshman class, 46% graduate in 4 years and 60% in 5 years. 156 companies recruited on campus in 1994–95.

Admissions Contact: David Taggart, Dean of Admissions. E-mail: uriadmit@uriacc.uri.edu.

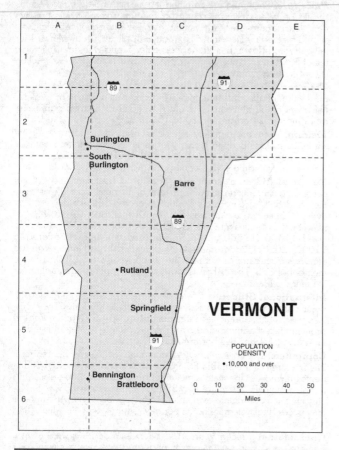

POPULATION DENSITY

• 10,000 and over

0   10   20   30   40   50
Miles

VERMONT

BENNINGTON COLLEGE
Bennington, VT 05201

A-6

(802) 442–6349
(800) 833–6845; FAX: (802) 442–6164

Full-time: 101 men, 184 women	Faculty: 41
Part-time: none	Ph.D.s: 42%
Graduate: 31 men, 71 women	Student/Faculty: 7 to 1
Year: 4–1–4	Tuition
Application Deadline: February 1	Room & Board: $25,800
Freshman Class: 376 applied, 241 accepted, 78 enrolled	
SAT I Verbal/Math: 579/553	ACT: 28 **VERY COMPETITIVE +**

Bennington College, founded in 1932, is a private, coeducational liberal arts school where students design their own programs in consultation with faculty. There are 4 graduate schools. The 3 libraries contain 118,000 volumes, 6342 microform items, and 1015 audiovisual forms, and subscribe to 580 periodicals. Computerized library sources and services include the card catalog, interlibrary loans, and database searching. Special learning facilities include an art gallery, radio station, dance archives, script library, photography darkrooms, observatory, music practice rooms, greenhouse, and a pond for biological studies. The 550-acre campus is in a small town 45 miles east of Albany, New York. Including residence halls, there are 59 buildings on campus.

Student Life: 94% of undergraduates are from out-of-state, mostly the Northeast. Students come from 39 states, 15 foreign countries, and Canada. 85% are white; 10% foreign nationals. The average age of freshmen is 17; all undergraduates, 20. 15% do not continue beyond their first year; 62% remain to graduate.

Housing: 600 students can be accommodated in college housing. College-sponsored living facilities include coed dormitories and off-campus apartments. In addition, there are quiet study houses. On-campus housing is guaranteed for all 4 years. 98% of students live on campus; of those, 95% remain on campus on weekends. All students may keep cars on campus.

Activities: There are no fraternities or sororities. There are 20 groups on campus, including art, band, choir, chorus, dance, drama, ethnic, film, gay, international, jazz band, literary magazine, musical theater, newspaper, opera, orchestra, photography, political, radio, social, social service, student government, and symphony. Popular campus events include Sunfest, faculty concerts, Swing into Spring, dance concerts, and theater productions.

Sports: There are 4 intramural sports for men and 4 for women. Athletic and recreation facilities include soccer and other playing fields, outdoor clay tennis courts, a basketball court, a karate studio, a weight room, hiking and biking areas, rock climbing, white-water rafting, yoga, and tai chi.

Disabled Students: The following facilities are available: wheelchair ramps, special parking, special fire alarms in houses, and amplifiers on phones.

Services: Remedial writing is available. Tutoring for learning disabilities is available in the town of Bennington at a cost to the student.

Campus Safety and Security: Campus safety and security measures include 24-hour foot and vehicle patrol, self-defense education, escort service, and informal discussions. In addition, there are pamphlets/posters/films, emergency telephones, and lighted pathways/sidewalks.

Programs of Study: Bennington confers the B.A. degree. Master's degrees are also awarded. Bachelor's degrees are awarded in BIOLOGICAL SCIENCE (biology/biological science), COMMUNICATIONS AND THE ARTS (Chinese, creative writing, dance, dramatic arts, English, fine arts, French, German, languages, literature, music, photography, and Spanish), COMPUTER AND PHYSICAL SCIENCE (chemistry, computer science, mathematics, and physics), EDUCATION (early childhood), ENGINEERING AND ENVIRONMENTAL DESIGN (architecture), SOCIAL SCIENCE (anthropology, history, philosophy, political science/government, and psychology). Literature and languages, visual arts, and drama have the largest enrollments.

Required: A minimum of 128 credit hours is required to graduate. By the end of their second year, all students must have taken courses from 4 of 7 disciplines in addition to classes beyond the introductory level in 2 fields outside their major. Before the end of the second year, students also must write a tentative academic plan. A thesis or final project is required of all majors, and 3 fieldwork terms must be successfully completed.

Special: Eight-week work/internships are required all four years (during January and February). Cross-registration with Southern Vermont and Williams colleges is possible. A cooperative program with the Bank Street College of Education in New York City offers a joint advanced degree in education. In addition, study abroad in England, Germany, and other countries, an individually arranged Washington semester, and dual and student-designed majors are offered. Grading is pass/fail with extensive written evaluation.

Faculty/Classroom: 60% of faculty are male; 40%, female. All both teach and do research. Graduate students teach 1% of introductory courses. The average class size in an introductory lecture is 12; in a laboratory, 8; and in a regular course offering, 9.

Admissions: 64% of the 1995–96 applicants were accepted. The SAT I scores for the 1995–96 freshman class were as follows: Verbal—23% below 500, 49% between 500 and 599, 24% between 600 and 700, and 4% above 700; Math—20% below 500, 33% between 500 and 599, 36% between 600 and 700, and 11% above 700. 47% of the current freshmen were in the top fifth of their class; 85% were in the top two fifths. There were 4 National Merit finalists and 7 semifinalists. In a recent year, 4 freshmen graduated first in their class.

Requirements: The SAT I or ACT is required. Applicants should have 16 credits, including 4 units in English, 3 each in mathematics, science, and social studies, 2 or 3 in foreign language, and 2 in history. Art and music courses are highly recommended. An essay and interview are required, and a portfolio is recommended for certain majors. The GED is accepted. Applications may be submitted on-line. Important factors in the admissions decision are evidence of special talent, parents or siblings attending the school, and personality/intangible qualities.

Procedure: Freshmen are admitted fall and spring. Entrance exams should be taken during the spring of the junior year or the fall of the senior year. There are early decision, early admissions, and deferred admissions plans. Early decision applications should be filed by December 1; regular applications, by February 1 for fall entry and January 1 for spring entry, along with an application fee of $45. Notification of early decision is sent January 1; regular decision, April 1. 3 early decision candidates were accepted for the 1995–96 class. A waiting list is an active part of the admissions procedure.

Transfer: 17 transfer students enrolled in 1995–96. Two-year transfers must have a faculty interview. All candidates must submit secondary school reports, college transcripts, and 2 recommendations from 2 faculty members. They must also submit SAT I or ACT scores and interview with a member of the admissions staff. 64 credits of 128 must be completed at Bennington.

Visiting: There are regularly scheduled orientations for prospective students, including faculty student panels, dinner and socializing, class visitation, and interviews. There are guides for informal visits and visitors may stay overnight at the school. To schedule a visit, contact the Admissions Office at (802) 442–5401, ext. 255 or (800) 833–6845.

Financial Aid: In 1995–96, 90% of all freshmen and 83% of continuing students received some form of financial aid. 93% of freshmen and 82% of continuing students received need-based aid. The average freshman award was $20,660. Of that total, scholarships or need-based grants averaged $17,560; loans averaged $2570 ($2625 maximum); and work contracts averaged $1100 ($1205 maximum). Average earnings from campus work for the school year are $1200. The average financial indebtedness of the 1994–95 graduate was $14,500. Bennington is a member of CSS. The FAFSA and the college's own financial statement are required. The application deadline for fall entry is March 1.

International Students: In a recent year, 37 international students were enrolled. The school actively recruits these students. They must take the TOEFL and achieve a minimum score of 550. The student must also take the SAT I or the ACT.

Computers: The college provides computer facilities for student use. Microcomputers are available in the media and language and culture centers. All students may access the system. There are no time limits and no fees. Bennington requires that every student has a Macintosh computer.

Graduates: In 1994–95, 130 bachelor's degrees were awarded. The most popular majors among graduates were interdisciplinary (24%), literature and languages (22%), and visual arts (13%). Within an average freshman class, 65% graduate in 5 years.

Admissions Contact: Elena Ruocco Bachrach, Dean of Admissions and the Freshman Year. E-mail: admissions@bennington.edu. A campus video is available.

BURLINGTON COLLEGE
A-2

Burlington, VT 05401   (802) 862–9616

Full-time: 20 men, 40 women	**Faculty:** n/av
Part-time: 30 men, 50 women	**Ph.D.s:** 20%
Graduate: none	**Student/Faculty:** 2 to 1
Year: semesters, summer session	**Tuition:** $6200
Application Deadline: see profile	**Room & Board:** n/app
Freshman Class: n/av	
ACT: required	**NONCOMPETITIVE**

Burlington College, founded in 1972, is a private, coeducational institution offering a small, flexible liberal arts program, residential and nonresidential, geared toward the adult learner. Figures given in the above capsule are approximate. The library contains 45,000 volumes, and subscribes to 350 periodicals. Computerized library sources and services include interlibrary loans and database searching. Special learning facilities include a learning resource center and art gallery. The 1-acre campus is in an urban area in Burlington. There is 1 building on campus.

Student Life: 90% of undergraduates are from Vermont. Students come from 8 states, 4 foreign countries, and Canada. 95% are from public schools; 5% from private. 87% are white. The average age of freshmen is 30; all undergraduates, 34.

Housing: There are no residence halls. All students commute. Alcohol is not permitted. All students may keep cars on campus.

Activities: There are no fraternities or sororities. There are some groups and organizations on campus, including newspaper and student government. Popular campus events include coffeehouses, Christmas party, an evening video series, and the archetype series.

Sports: There is no sports program at Burlington College.

Disabled Students: 60% of the campus is accessible to disabled students. The following facilities are available: wheelchair ramps, special parking, specially equipped rest rooms, special class scheduling, lowered drinking fountains, and lowered telephones.

Services: In addition to many counseling and information services, tutoring is available in every subject. There is remedial math, reading, and writing.

Programs of Study: Burlington College confers the B.A. degree. Associate degrees are also awarded. Bachelor's degrees are awarded in COMMUNICATIONS AND THE ARTS (fine arts), SOCIAL SCIENCE (human services, humanities, psychology, and women's studies). Psychology, transpersonal psychology, and individualized (self-designed) programs have the largest enrollments.

Required: All students are required to satisfactorily complete at least 120 semester credits, including 36 upper level credits in their major. Distribution requirements include 9 credits each in the following divisions: personal vision, human community, and natural environment. Specific course requirements include 3 credits each in writing and mathematics. Students are also required to take a 3-credit practicum within their areas of concentration.

Special: Cross-registration is available with the University of Vermont, St. Michael's Trinity College, Champlain College, and the Community College of Vermont; internships through various organizations and work-study programs with nonprofit organizations are also available. The college offers dual majors, interdisciplinary majors, including transpersonal psychology, individualized majors, independent study, a non-residential degree program, credit for life experience, and pass/fail options.

Faculty/Classroom: 48% of faculty are male; 52%, female. All teach undergraduates. The average class size in a regular course offering is 8.

Requirements: The ACT is required. Burlington also requires a high school diploma or the GED, and a successful interview with the Director of Admissions. CLEP credit is accepted. Personality/intangible qualities is an important factor in the admission decision.

Procedure: Freshmen are admitted to all sessions. There are early admissions and deferred admissions plans. Check with the school for current deadlines and fee. The college accepts all applicants. Notification is sent on a rolling basis.

Transfer: 30 credits of 120 must be completed at Burlington College.

Visiting: There are guides for informal visits and visitors may sit in on classes. To schedule a visit, contact the Admissions Office.

Financial Aid: 72% of undergraduate students work part-time. Average earnings from campus work for the school year are $1500. Burlington College is a member of CSS. The FAF and the college's own financial statement are required. Check with the school for current deadlines.

International Students: There were recently 4 international students enrolled. Foreign students should score 550 on the TOEFL.

Computers: The college provides computer facilities for student use. There are 10 stand-alone PCs and 1 Macintosh available for student use, all in the student computer room. All students may access the system 80 hours per week. There are no time limits and no fees.

Graduates: About 30 bachelor's degrees are awarded in a typical year.

Admissions Contact: Nancy Wilson, Director of Admissions.

CASTLETON STATE COLLEGE
B-4

Castleton, VT 05735   (802) 468–5611, ext. 213
(800) 639–8521; FAX: (802) 468–5237

Full-time: 685 men, 793 women	**Faculty:** 88; IIB, -$
Part-time: 265 men and women	**Ph.D.s:** 80%
Graduate: 66 men, 154 women	**Student/Faculty:** 17 to 1
Year: semesters, summer session	**Tuition:** $3882 ($8226)
Application Deadline: open	**Room & Board:** $4690
Freshman Class: 1143 applied, 894 accepted, 309 enrolled	
SAT I Verbal/Math: 415/449	**LESS COMPETITIVE**

Castleton State College, founded in 1787, is the oldest institution of higher learning in Vermont. As part of the Vermont State Colleges system, it offers a state-supported undergraduate and graduate program that includes liberal arts, teacher preparation, and professional programs. There is 1 graduate school. In addition to regional accreditation, Castleton has baccalaureate program accreditation with CSWE and NLN. The library contains 110,000 volumes, 400,000 microform items, and 1750 audiovisual forms, and subscribes to 657 periodicals. Computerized library sources and services include the card catalog, interlibrary loans, and database searching. Special learning facilities include a learning resource center, art gallery, radio station, TV studio, observatory, and theater. The 130-acre campus is in a rural area 11 miles west of Rutland. Including residence halls, there are 24 buildings on campus.

Student Life: 65% of undergraduates are from Vermont. Students come from 28 states, 4 foreign countries, and Canada. 80% are from public schools; 20% from private. 98% are white. The average age of freshmen is 18. 26% do not continue beyond their first year; 53% remain to graduate.

Housing: 734 students can be accommodated in college housing. College-sponsored living facilities include single-sex and coed dormitories. In addition there are honors houses. On-campus housing is guaranteed for the freshman year only and is available on a lottery system for upperclassmen. 50% of students live on campus; of those, 85% remain on campus on weekends. All students may keep cars on campus.

Activities: There are no fraternities or sororities. There are 48 groups on campus, including art, band, cheerleading, choir, chorale, chorus, computers, dance, drama, film, honors, international, jazz band, literary magazine, musical theater, newspaper, photography, political, professional, radio and TV, religious, social, social service, student government, and yearbook. Popular campus events include Spring and Winter Weekends, Alumni Weekend, and Martin Luther King Week.

Sports: There are 6 intercollegiate sports for men and 6 for women, and 4 intramural sports for men and 4 for women. Athletic and recreation facilities include a 6-lane swimming pool, 2 racquetball courts, a recreation gymnasium, and the nearby 2000-acre Pond Hill Ranch with more than 70 miles of trails, swimming, sailing, fishing, and golf facilities.

Disabled Students: 90% of the campus is accessible to disabled students. The following facilities are available: wheelchair ramps, elevators, special parking, specially equipped rest rooms, special class scheduling, lowered drinking fountains, and lowered telephones.

Services: In addition to many counseling and information services, tutoring is available in most subjects. There is remedial math, reading, and writing.

Campus Safety and Security: Campus safety and security measures include 24-hour foot and vehicle patrol, self-defense education, escort service, and shuttle buses. In addition, there are informal discussions, pamphlets/posters/films, emergency telephones, and lighted pathways/sidewalks.

Programs of Study: Castleton confers B.A., B.S., and B.S.W. degrees. Associate and master's degrees are also awarded. Bachelor's degrees are awarded in BUSINESS (business administration and management), COMMUNICATIONS AND THE ARTS (communications, dramatic arts, fine arts, languages, literature, music, and Spanish), COMPUTER AND PHYSICAL SCIENCE (information sciences and systems, mathematics, and natural sciences), EDUCATION (business, elementary, foreign languages, mathematics, physical, science, and secondary), SOCIAL SCIENCE (criminal justice, history, psychology, social science, social work, and sociology). Nursing, athletic training, and science are the strongest academically. Business and education have the largest enrollments.

Required: All students must maintain a GPA of 2.0 while taking 128 semester hours, including 30 to 84 in their major. Distribution requirements include 1 course each in foreign cultures, history, philosophy and psychology, and social analysis, 3 in literature and the arts, and 2 each in mathematics and natural sciences. Specific courses include computers, communication, and an introduction to liberal arts.

Special: Cooperative programs with Clarkson University, internships, study abroad in 14 countries, and many work-study programs are available. In addition, B.A.-B.S. degrees, dual majors, student-designed majors in business and secondary and elementary education, a 3–2 engineering degree with Clarkson University, a 2–3 pharmacy degree with Albany College of Pharmacy, credit for life experience, nondegree study, and pass/fail options are offered. There are 2 national honor societies on campus. 4 departments have honors programs.

Faculty/Classroom: 66% of faculty are male; 34%, female. All teach undergraduates. No introductory courses are taught by graduate students. The average class size in an introductory lecture is 18; in a laboratory, 15; and in a regular course offering, 18.

Admissions: 78% of the 1995–96 applicants were accepted. 18% of the current freshmen were in the top fifth of their class; 41% were in the top two fifths. 4 freshmen graduated first in their class.

Requirements: The SAT I or ACT is required. The college recommends that candidates have 4 years of English, 3 years each of mathematics, social studies, or history, 2 each of foreign language and science, and 2 to 4 of electives. An essay is required and an interview is recommended. The GED is accepted. AP and CLEP credits are accepted. Important factors in the admissions decision are advanced placement or honor courses, leadership record, and recommendations by school officials.

Procedure: Freshmen are admitted fall and spring. Entrance exams should be taken during spring of the junior year or fall of the senior year. There are early admissions and deferred admissions plans. Application deadlines are open. Application fee is $40. Notification is sent on a rolling basis. A waiting list is an active part of the admissions procedure, with about 10% of all applicants on the list.

Transfer: 144 transfer students enrolled in 1995–96. Applicants must have a 2.0 GPA. An associate degree, 15 credit hours, and an interview are recommended. 30 credits of 128 must be completed at Castleton.

Visiting: There are regularly scheduled orientations for prospective students, including meetings with admissions counselors, faculty, and coaches as well as a campus tour. Visitors may sit in on classes and stay overnight at the school. To schedule a visit, contact the Admissions Office.

Financial Aid: In a recent year, 75% of all students received some form of financial aid. 25% of undergraduate students work part-time. Castleton is a member of CSS. The FAFSA is required. The application deadline for fall entry is March 15.

International Students: There were 6 international students enrolled in a recent year. They must take the TOEFL and achieve a minimum score of 500.

Computers: The college provides computer facilities for student use. The mainframes are a DEC VAX 11/750 and 11/785. More than 180 terminals and microcomputers are available for student use at the academic computing center, the business department, and the education department, as well as several smaller areas. All students may access the system. There are no time limits and no fees.

Admissions Contact: Patricia A. Tencza, Director of Admissions. E-mail: tenczap@cscacs.csc.ysc.edu. A campus video is available.

CHAMPLAIN COLLEGE
Burlington, VT 05402–0670

A-2

(802) 860-2727
(800) 570-5858; FAX: (802) 860-2775

Full-time: 509 men, 743 women	**Faculty:** 61; III, -$
Part-time: 330 men, 503 women	**Ph.D.s:** 12%
Graduate: none	**Student/Faculty:** 21 to 1
Year: semesters, summer session	**Tuition:** $8770
Application Deadline: open	**Room & Board:** $6285
Freshman Class: 1273 accepted, 727 enrolled	
SAT I Verbal/Math: 369/404	**ACT:** 21 **LESS COMPETITIVE**

Champlain College, founded in 1878, is a private coeducational institution offering '2 plus 2' bachelor's degree programs in accounting and in business management through the Walter Cerf School of Business. In addition to regional accreditation, Champlain has baccalaureate program accreditation with ABET. The library contains 36,500 volumes, 1100 microform items, and 1350 audiovisual forms, and subscribes to 1300 periodicals. Computerized library sources and services include the card catalog, interlibrary loans, and database searching. Special learning facilities include a learning resource center, video production studio, and child-care center. The 18-acre campus is in a suburban area in the Hill Section of Burlington. Including residence halls, there are 31 buildings on campus.

Student Life: 75% of undergraduates are from Vermont. Students come from 19 states, 23 foreign countries, and Canada. 96% are white. The average age of freshmen is 19; all undergraduates, 22.5. 30% do not continue beyond their first year; 67% remain to graduate.

Housing: 525 students can be accommodated in college housing. College-sponsored living facilities include single-sex and coed dormitories. In addition, there is an international dormitory. On-campus housing is available on a first-come, first-served basis. 64% of students commute. Alcohol is not permitted.

Activities: There are no fraternities or sororities. There are 10 groups on campus, including cheerleading, computers, drama, international, photography, social service, student government, and yearbook. Popular campus events include Family Day, Senior Week, basketball tournaments, skiing trips, outing club trips, and seasonal dances.

Sports: There are 4 intercollegiate sports for men and 4 for women, and 8 intramural sports for men and 8 for women. Athletic and recreation facilities are offered through the community YMCA and a local tennis club, park, and ski resort.

Disabled Students: 50% of the campus is accessible to disabled students. The following facilities are available: wheelchair ramps, elevators, special parking, specially equipped rest rooms, special class scheduling, lowered drinking fountains, and lowered telephones.

Services: In addition to many counseling and information services, peer tutoring is available in most subjects. Other support services include supplementary classes, a writing assistance laboratory, a mathematics laboratory, foreign language (ESL) tutors, and note-taking services.

Campus Safety and Security: Campus safety and security measures include 24-hour foot and vehicle patrol, self-defense education, escort service, and shuttle buses. In addition, there are informal discussions, pamphlets/posters/films, emergency telephones, and lighted pathways/sidewalks.

Programs of Study: Champlain confers the B.S. degree. Associate degrees are also awarded. Bachelor's degrees are awarded in BUSINESS (accounting and business administration and management).

Required: A GPA of 2.0 and 120 credits are required for the B.S. degree. The core curriculum is career oriented, with a focus on the major.

Special: Co-op programs and internships are available. There is cross-registration with Trinity College. Dual majors are possible. There is a professional studies program.

Faculty/Classroom: 49% of faculty are male; 51%, female. All teach undergraduates. The average class size in an introductory lecture is 35; in a laboratory, 15; and in a regular course offering, 25.

Admissions: 21% of the current freshmen were in the top fifth of their class; 45% were in the top two fifths.

Requirements: The SAT I or ACT is recommended. A minimum GPA of 2.0 is required. Applicants should be graduates of an accredited high school or the equivalent. AP and CLEP credits are accepted. Important factors in the admissions decision are advanced placement or honor courses, recommendations by school officials, and leadership record.

Procedure: Freshmen are admitted fall and spring. There are early decision, early admissions, and deferred admissions plans. Application deadlines are open. Application fee is $25. Notification is sent on a rolling basis. 5 early decision candidates were accepted for the

1995–96 class. A waiting list is an active part of the admissions procedure.

Transfer: 229 transfer students enrolled in 1995–96. High school and college transcripts are required. 60 credits of 120 must be completed at Champlain.

Visiting: There are regularly scheduled orientations for prospective students, including an open house, a guided campus tour, and a personal interview. There are guides for informal visits and visitors may sit in on classes. To schedule a visit, contact the Admissions Office.

Financial Aid: In 1995–96, 68% of all freshmen and 65% of continuing students received some form of financial aid. 89% of freshmen and 70% of continuing students received need-based aid. The average freshman award was $8550. Of that total, scholarships or need-based grants averaged $3600 ($7550 maximum); loans averaged $3200 ($6625 maximum); and work contracts averaged $1750 ($2000 maximum). 14% of undergraduate students work part-time. Average earnings from campus work for the school year are $1800. The average financial indebtedness of the 1994–95 graduate was $5900. Champlain is a member of CSS. The FAFSA and the college's own financial statement are required. The application deadline for fall entry is May 1.

International Students: There are currently 60 international students enrolled. The school actively recruits these students. They must take the TOEFL and achieve a minimum score of 500.

Computers: The college provides computer facilities for student use. The mainframe is an IBM AS/400. Champlain provides more than 150 IBM personal computers, with 4 supervised computer laboratories open 7 days a week. All students may access the system. There are no time limits and no fees. It is recommended that all students have IBM-compatible personal computers.

Graduates: In 1994–95, 59 bachelor's degrees were awarded. 60 companies recruited on campus in 1994–95.

Admissions Contact: Josephine Churchill, Director of Admissions. E-mail: admission@champlain.edu. A campus video is available.

COLLEGE OF SAINT JOSEPH
Rutland, VT 05701–3899
B-4
(802) 773-5905; FAX: (802) 773-5900

Full-time: 71 men, 111 women	Faculty: 14
Part-time: 52 men, 109 women	Ph.D.s: 65%
Graduate: 29 men, 119 women	Student/Faculty: 13 to 1
Year: semesters, summer session	Tuition: $9070
Application Deadline: open	Room & Board: $5100
Freshman Class: 165 applied, 136 accepted, 75 enrolled	
SAT I Verbal/Math: required	ACT: 21 COMPETITIVE

The College of St. Joseph, founded in 1950, is a private, coeducational Catholic institution offering undergraduate programs in the arts and sciences, business, education, and human services. The college serves a primarily commuter student body. There are 2 graduate schools. The library contains 45,000 volumes, 60,000 microform items, and 6000 audiovisual forms, and subscribes to 225 periodicals. Computerized library sources and services include interlibrary loans and database searching. Special learning facilities include a learning resource center. The 99-acre campus is in a rural area 1 mile west of Rutland. Including residence halls, there are 4 buildings on campus.

Student Life: 81% of undergraduates are from Vermont. Students come from 10 states and 3 foreign countries. 95% are white. 32% do not continue beyond their first year; 52% remain to graduate.

Housing: 160 students can be accommodated in college housing. College-sponsored living facilities include single-sex dormitories. On-campus housing is guaranteed for all 4 years. 75% of students commute. Alcohol is not permitted. All students may keep cars on campus.

Activities: There are no fraternities or sororities. There are 13 groups on campus, including chorus, drama, honors, literary magazine, newspaper, professional, social, social service, student government, and yearbook. Popular campus events include Spring Fling, Fright Night, Parents Weekend, Annual Sno-Ball, and Choral Christmas Concert.

Sports: There are 2 intercollegiate sports for men and 3 for women, and 1 intramural sport for men and 1 for women. Athletic and recreation facilities include a 200-seat gymnasium, a weight room, a cross-country skiing/running trail, a softball diamond, and a soccer field.

Disabled Students: All of the campus is accessible to disabled students. The following facilities are available: wheelchair ramps, special parking, specially equipped rest rooms, special class scheduling, lowered drinking fountains, and lowered telephones.

Services: In addition to many counseling and information services, tutoring is available in every subject. There is remedial math, reading, and writing, personal growth counseling, and spiritual counseling.

Campus Safety and Security: Campus safety and security measures include shuttle buses, informal discussions, pamphlets/posters/films, and emergency telephones. There are lighted pathways/sidewalks.

Programs of Study: St. Joseph's confers B.A. and B.S. degrees. Associate and master's degrees are also awarded. Bachelor's degrees are awarded in BUSINESS (accounting and business administration and management), COMMUNICATIONS AND THE ARTS (broadcasting, English, and journalism), COMPUTER AND PHYSICAL SCIENCE (computer science), EDUCATION (early childhood, elementary, secondary, and special), SOCIAL SCIENCE (American studies, history, human services, liberal arts/general studies, political science/government, prelaw, psychology, and social science). Education is the strongest academically. Arts and sciences have the largest enrollments.

Required: To graduate, students must complete 127 credit hours with a minimum GPA of 2.0, including 15 credits in English/speech, 12 in social/behavioral sciences, 9 each in mathematics/computer and philosophy/religious studies, 6 in natural sciences, and 3 in fine arts. Human services majors must complete 2 internships.

Special: The college offers internships in Rutland County businesses, human service agencies, and elementary and secondary schools. In addition, the B.A.-B.S. degree, dual majors, and independent and directed study options are available. There are 2 national honor societies on campus. 1 department has an honors program.

Faculty/Classroom: 58% of faculty are male; 42%, female. All teach undergraduates. No introductory courses are taught by graduate students. The average class size in an introductory lecture is 20 and in a regular course offering, 14.

Admissions: 82% of the 1995–96 applicants were accepted. The SAT I scores for the 1995–96 freshman class were as follows: Verbal—70% below 500, 26% between 500 and 599, and 4% between 600 and 700; Math—76% below 500, 21% between 500 and 599, and 3% between 600 and 700. The ACT scores were 71% below 21, 20% between 21 and 23, 8% between 24 and 26, and 1% between 27 and 28. 10% of the current freshmen were in the top fifth of their class; 55% were in the top two fifths.

Requirements: The SAT I or ACT is required. Applicants should be in the upper 70% of their class, with a 2.0 GPA. In addition, they should be graduates of accredited secondary schools or have earned a GED. College preparatory study must include 4 years of English, 3 of mathematics, 2 each of science and social studies, and 5 other academic electives. An essay is required and an interview is recommended. AP and CLEP credits are accepted. Important factors in the admissions decision are advanced placement or honor courses, leadership record, and extracurricular activities record.

Procedure: Freshmen are admitted to all sessions. Entrance exams should be taken by December of the senior year. There is an early decision plan. Application deadlines are open. The application fee is $25. Notification is sent on a rolling basis.

Transfer: 15 transfer students enrolled in 1995–96. Transfers must present a 2.0 GPA. 30 credits of 127 must be completed at St. Joseph's.

Visiting: There are regularly scheduled orientations for prospective students, including a campus tour, admissions interview, and visits to classes. There are guides for informal visits and visitors may sit in on classes and stay overnight at the school. To schedule a visit, contact the Admissions Office.

Financial Aid: In a recent year 79% of all freshmen and 80% of continuing students received some form of financial aid. The average freshman award was $5077. Of that total, scholarships or need-based grants averaged $3345 ($5000 maximum); loans averaged $3243 ($5500 maximum); athletic assistance averaged $426 ($4000 maximum); and work contracts averaged $225 ($1200 maximum). 13% of undergraduate students work part-time. Average earnings from campus work for the school year are $850. The average financial indebtedness of the recent graduate was $11,017. St. Joseph's is a member of CSS. The FAFSA and VSAC Incentive Grant application are required. The application deadline for fall entry is March 1.

International Students: In a recent year 4 international students were enrolled. They must score 550 on the TOEFL.

Computers: The college provides computer facilities for student use. The mainframe is a DEC PDP 11/84. A network of 14 microcomputers is also available for academic use. All students may access the system. There are no time limits and no fees.

Graduates: In a recent year, 50 bachelor's degrees were awarded. The most popular majors among graduates were business (40%), liberal studies (31%), and education (27%). Within an average freshman class, 52% graduate in 4 years.

Admissions Contact: Walt Crutchfield, Dean of Admissions.

GODDARD COLLEGE

C-2

Plainfield, VT 05667

(802) 454-8311

(800) 468-4888; FAX: (802) 454-8017

Full-time: 100 men, 146 women	Faculty: 14
Part-time: none	Ph.D.s: 71%
Graduate: 68 men, 152 women	Student/Faculty: 18 to 1
Year: semesters	Tuition: $15,056
Application Deadline: open	Room & Board: $4936
Freshman Class: 136 applied, 98 accepted, 58 enrolled	
SAT I Verbal/Math: 515/499	COMPETITIVE

Goddard College, founded in 1938, is a private coeducational college that stresses progressive, individualized education for personal and community transformation, based on John Dewey's learning-by-involvement theory. There is one graduate school. The library contains 7000 volumes, 5500 microform items, and 1100 audiovisual forms, and subscribes to 280 periodicals. Computerized library sources and services include interlibrary loans and database searching. Special learning facilities include a learning resource center, radio station, holograph laboratory, and video/photo studio. The 200-acre campus is in a rural area 10 miles from Montpelier. Including residence halls, there are 26 buildings on campus.

Student Life: 82% of undergraduates are from out-of-state, mostly the Northeast. Students come from 33 states, 6 foreign countries, and Canada. 90% are from public schools; 10% from private. 90% are white. The average age of freshmen is 19; all undergraduates, 22. 3% do not continue beyond their first year; 60% remain to graduate.

Housing: 225 students can be accommodated in college housing. College-sponsored living facilities include single-sex and coed dormitories and married-student housing. In addition there are special interest houses and single-parent houses. On-campus housing is guaranteed for all 4 years. 85% of students live on campus; of those, 75% remain on campus on weekends. Alcohol is not permitted. All students may keep cars on campus.

Activities: There are no fraternities or sororities. There are 8 groups on campus, including art, drama, gay, jazz band, literary magazine, newspaper, radio and TV, and student government.

Sports: There is no sports program at Goddard. Athletic and recreation facilities include tennis and volleyball courts, and hiking and cross-country ski trails.

Disabled Students: The following facilities are available: wheelchair ramps, elevators, special parking, and specially equipped rest rooms.

Services: In addition to many counseling and information services, tutoring is available in every subject. A faculty adviser system requires a 1-hour weekly meeting.

Campus Safety and Security: Campus safety and security measures include informal discussions, lighted pathways/sidewalks, and evening security guard.

Programs of Study: Goddard confers the B.A. degree. Master's degrees are also awarded. Bachelor's degrees are awarded in COMMUNICATIONS AND THE ARTS (creative writing, media arts, and visual and performing arts), EDUCATION (education), ENGINEERING AND ENVIRONMENTAL DESIGN (environmental science), SOCIAL SCIENCE (counseling psychology, crosscultural studies, human ecology, interdisciplinary studies, social science, and women's studies).

Required: All degree programs are full-time only, provide individual faculty advisers for every semester (except study leaves), and require written study plans and narrative evaluations. Individual programs of study are student designed, although the program in general is course based. There are no declared majors, but in the last semester of enrollment, all students must complete an in-depth senior study or project that may be cross- or multi-disciplinary, and requires foundation work comparable to a major. A total of 120 credits is required to graduate.

Special: Students and faculty design all curriculum; there are no prescribed courses. Learning takes the form of group or independent studies, workshops, action projects, research, field trips, seminars, and performances. There are a number of away-from-campus study options, including a field semester involving an internship, apprenticeship, or study-travel and a semester-abroad program offered in 20 countries.

Faculty/Classroom: 64% of faculty are male; 36%, female. No introductory courses are taught by graduate students. The average class size in an introductory lecture is 8 and in a regular course offering, 10.

Admissions: 72% of the 1995–96 applicants were accepted.

Requirements: The SAT I or ACT is not required, but scores, when submitted, are considered. Goddard admits students who can contribute to its learning community and who will thrive in a self-directed study program. The admission decision is based on the student's application, which includes several essays, letters of recommendation and transcripts, and samples of the student's work. A personal interview is also considered. AP and CLEP credits are accepted. Important factors in the admissions decision are personality/intangible qualities, advanced placement or honor courses, and evidence of special talent.

Procedure: Freshmen are admitted to all sessions. There are early admissions and deferred admissions plans. Application deadlines are open. Application fee is $35. Notification is sent on a rolling basis.

Transfer: 42 transfer students enrolled in 1995–96. College transcripts must be submitted. 30 credits of 120 must be completed at Goddard.

Visiting: There are regularly scheduled orientations for prospective students, including Discover Goddard Days held in fall and spring and individual tours and interviews. There are guides for informal visits and visitors may sit in on classes and stay overnight at the school. To schedule a visit, contact the Admissions Office.

Financial Aid: In 1995–96, all freshmen and 72% of continuing students received some form of financial aid. 96% of freshmen and 72% of continuing students received need-based aid. The average freshman award was $12,456. Of that total, scholarships or need-based grants averaged $7690 ($12,500 maximum); loans averaged $3964 ($4625 maximum); and work contracts averaged $1000 ($1500 maximum). All undergraduate students work part-time. Average earnings from campus work for the school year are $900. The average financial indebtedness of the 1994–95 graduate was $14,900. The FAF or FFS is required.

International Students: In a recent year, there was 1 international student enrolled. International students must take the TOEFL and achieve a minimum score of 550.

Computers: The college provides computer facilities for student use. The mainframes are an IBM 5/34 and an AS/400. Many types of microcomputers are available for student use in the computer center, and dormitories have computer network access. All students may access the system. There are no time limits and no fees.

Graduates: In 1994–95, 71 bachelor's degrees were awarded.

Admissions Contact: Peter S. Burns, Director of Admissions. E-mail: peterb@earth.goddard.edu. A campus video is available.

GREEN MOUNTAIN COLLEGE

A-4

Poultney, VT 05764

(802) 287-8208

(800) 776-6675; FAX: (802) 287-8099

Full-time: 242 men, 251 women	Faculty: 37
Part-time: 10 men, 5 women	Ph.D.s: 78%
Graduate: none	Student/Faculty: 13 to 1
Year: semesters	Tuition: $13,480
Application Deadline: open	Room & Board: $2920
Freshman Class: 671 applied, 563 accepted, 167 enrolled	
ACT: 21	COMPETITIVE

Green Mountain College, established in 1834, is a private, nonprofit, liberal arts institution. The library contains 60,000 volumes, 10,000 microform items, and 2000 audiovisual forms, and subscribes to 300 periodicals. Computerized library sources and services include database searching. Special learning facilities include a writing clinic and a skills advancement center. The 155-acre campus is in a small town 20 miles southwest of Rutland. Including residence halls, there are 26 buildings on campus.

Student Life: 90% of undergraduates are from out-of-state, mostly the Northeast. Students come from 26 states and 13 foreign countries. 70% are from public schools; 30% from private. 97% are white. The average age of freshmen is 18; all undergraduates, 21. 15% do not continue beyond their first year; 70% remain to graduate.

Housing: 600 students can be accommodated in college housing. College-sponsored living facilities include coed dormitories. On-campus housing is guaranteed for all 4 years. 95% of students live on campus; of those, 80% remain on campus on weekends. All students may keep cars on campus.

Activities: There are no fraternities or sororities. There are 30 groups on campus, including art, cheerleading, chorus, dance, drama, international, newspaper, professional, social, social service, student government, and yearbook. Popular campus events include fall and spring formals, Winter Carnival, and Honors Banquet.

Sports: There are 4 intercollegiate sports for men and 5 for women, and 8 intramural sports for men and 7 for women. Athletic and recreation facilities include a gymnasium with an indoor pool, a dance studio, a weight room, playing fields, tennis courts, a par course, and a fitness trail.

Disabled Students: 70% of the campus is accessible to disabled students. The following facilities are available: wheelchair ramps, elevators, special parking, specially equipped rest rooms, special class scheduling, and lowered drinking fountains.

Services: In addition to many counseling and information services, tutoring is available in every subject. There is remedial math, reading, and writing.

Campus Safety and Security: Campus safety and security measures include 24-hour foot and vehicle patrol and lighted pathways/sidewalks.

Programs of Study: GMC confers B.A., B.S., and B.F.A. degrees. Bachelor's degrees are awarded in BUSINESS (business administration and management, recreation and leisure services, and recreational facilities management), COMMUNICATIONS AND THE ARTS (English and fine arts), EDUCATION (elementary and special), HEALTH PROFESSIONS (recreation therapy), SOCIAL SCIENCE (behavioral science and liberal arts/general studies). Elementary education and recreation are the strongest academically. Elementary education, special education, and fine arts have the largest enrollments.

Required: To graduate, students must complete 39 semester hours in general education, including 2 courses each in human culture and language and expression, and 3 courses each in scientific endeavor, individual and social worlds, and health and well-being. A minimum GPA of 2.0 is required. Students must complete 120 to 130 hours, with 80 to 90 credits in the major. Some programs require prescribed computer science course work.

Special: Semester-long internships are required in all majors. Students may study abroad in England, Spain, Japan, France, and Italy. Work-study programs are available. Students may opt for a dual major in education or a general studies degree, which may be pursued alone or in conjunction with a concentrated area of study. There are 2 national honor societies on campus, including Phi Beta Kappa.

Faculty/Classroom: 63% of faculty are male; 37%, female. All teach undergraduates. The average class size in an introductory lecture is 14; in a laboratory, 14; and in a regular course offering, 14.

Admissions: 84% of the 1995–96 applicants were accepted. The SAT I scores for the 1995–96 freshman class were as follows: Verbal—92% below 500, 7% between 500 and 599, and 1% between 600 and 700; Math—77% below 500, 18% between 500 and 599, and 5% between 600 and 700. The ACT scores were 47% below 21, 42% between 21 and 23, 5% between 24 and 26, and 5% between 27 and 28.

Requirements: The SAT I or ACT is required. Applicants must graduate from an accredited secondary school or have a GED. 16 academic credits are required. Students must complete 4 years in English, 3 years in mathematics, 2 to 3 years in science, and 2 years each in history and social studies. An essay is required. Interviews are recommended, along with portfolios where appropriate. AP and CLEP credits are accepted. Important factors in the admissions decision are personality/intangible qualities, advanced placement or honor courses, and evidence of special talent.

Procedure: Freshmen are admitted to all sessions. Entrance exams should be taken in the fall of the senior year of high school. There are early decision, early admissions, and deferred admissions plans. Early decision applications should be filed by November 1; regular applications, open for fall entry, along with an application fee of $20. Notification of early decision is sent December 1; regular decision, on a rolling basis.

Transfer: 25 transfer students enrolled in a recent year. Transfer students need a GPA of 2.0. They must have earned a minimum of 12 credits and are required to submit an essay. The SAT I or ACT is required. 30 credits of 120 to 130 must be completed at GMC.

Visiting: There are regularly scheduled orientations for prospective students. There are guides for informal visits and visitors may sit in on classes and stay overnight at the school. To schedule a visit, contact Lori Patten, Campus Visit Coordinator.

Financial Aid: In a recent year, 48% of all freshmen and 52% of continuing students received some form of financial aid. 43% of freshmen and 41% of continuing students received need-based aid. The average freshman award was $7500. Of that total, scholarships or need-based grants averaged $4000 ($13,900 maximum); loans averaged $2625 ($4225 maximum); and work contracts averaged $1000 ($2500 maximum). 40% of undergraduate students work part-time. Average earnings from campus work for the school year are $1000. GMC is a member of CSS. The FFS is required. The application deadline for fall entry is February 15.

International Students: There were 28 international students enrolled in a recent year. The school actively recruits these students. They must score 450 on the TOEFL.

Computers: The college provides computer facilities for student use. Personal computers are available for student use in the computer center. All students may access the system. There are no time limits and no fees.

Graduates: In a recent year, 98 bachelor's degrees were awarded. The most popular majors among graduates were elementary education (22%), business management (21%), and recreation (16%). 50 companies recruited on campus in a recent year.

Admissions Contact: Peter L. Freyberg, Vice President for Enrollment Services. E-mail: admiss@greenmtn.edu.

JOHNSON STATE COLLEGE C-2
Johnson, VT 05656 (802) 635-1219
(800) 635-2356; FAX: (802) 635-2145

Full-time: 585 men, 509 women	**Faculty:** 64; IIB, --$
Part-time: 400 men and women	**Ph.D.s:** 80%
Graduate: 124 men and women	**Student/Faculty:** 17 to 1
Year: semesters, summer session	**Tuition:** $4040 ($8552)
Application Deadline: open	**Room & Board:** $4794
Freshman Class: 811 applied, 604 accepted, 249 enrolled	
SAT I Verbal/Math: 403/432 (mean)	**LESS COMPETITIVE**

Johnson State College, founded in 1828, is a public coeducational liberal arts and teacher preparation college. There is 1 undergraduate and 1 graduate school. The library contains 89,323 volumes, 128,480 microform items, and 6589 audiovisual forms, and subscribes to 531 periodicals. Computerized library sources and services include the card catalog, interlibrary loans, and database searching. Special learning facilities include a learning resource center, art gallery, and radio station. The 350-acre campus is in a rural area 45 miles northeast of Burlington. Including residence halls, there are 16 buildings on campus.

Student Life: 71% of undergraduates are from Vermont. Students come from 18 states, 8 foreign countries, and Canada. 94% are white. 41% do not continue beyond their first year; 39% remain to graduate.

Housing: 600 students can be accommodated in college housing. College-sponsored living facilities include single-sex and coed dormitories, on-campus apartments, and married-student housing. In addition, there are special interest houses, an alcohol-free residence hall, and an international house. On-campus housing is available on a first-come, first-served basis and is available on a lottery system for upperclassmen. 50% of students live on campus. All students may keep cars on campus.

Activities: There are no fraternities or sororities. There are 30 groups on campus, including art, band, chorus, dance, drama, film, gay, honors, international, jazz band, literary magazine, musical theater, newspaper, orchestra, photography, political, radio and TV, religious, social, social service, student government, and yearbook. Popular campus events include Spring and Winter Weekends, Parents Weekends, and alumni athletic competitions.

Sports: There are 6 intercollegiate sports each for men and women, and 22 intramural sports each for men and women. Athletic and recreation facilities include a gymnasium, 3 athletic fields, 4 tennis courts, a swimming pool, racquetball and basketball courts, weight training, a fitness center, and a climbing wall.

Disabled Students: 60% of the campus is accessible to disabled students. The following facilities are available: wheelchair ramps, elevators, special parking, specially equipped rest rooms, special class scheduling, lowered drinking fountains, and swimming pool access.

Services: In addition to many counseling and information services, tutoring is available in most subjects. There is a reader service for the blind, and remedial math, reading, and writing. Other services include provisions for the learning-disabled, casework, and academic and personal growth workshops.

Campus Safety and Security: Campus safety and security measures include 24-hour foot and vehicle patrol, self-defense education, informal discussions, and pamphlets/posters/films. In addition, there are lighted pathways/sidewalks.

Programs of Study: The college confers B.A., B.S., and B.F.A. degrees. Associate and master's degrees are also awarded. Bachelor's degrees are awarded in BIOLOGICAL SCIENCE (biology/biological science), BUSINESS (business administration and management and hospitality management services), COMMUNICATIONS AND THE ARTS (art, English, fine arts, literature, music, performing arts, and studio art), COMPUTER AND PHYSICAL SCIENCE (mathematics), EDUCATION (elementary and middle school), ENGINEERING AND ENVIRONMENTAL DESIGN (environmental science), HEALTH PROFESSIONS (health science), SOCIAL SCIENCE (anthropology, history, political science/government, and psychology). Teaching certification programs and hotel/hospitality management are the strongest academically. Environmental science, sports medicine, and business management have the largest enrollments.

Required: Candidates for the bachelor's degree must complete at least 120 semester credits, including 40 in upper-level courses. Requirements for the major vary. Students must earn a certification of writing competency. General education requirements include 12 interdisciplinary credits and 13 disciplinary credits in arts/humanities, science, and social science, and 6 credits each in writing and mathematics. Students should achieve a minimum GPA of 2.0.

Special: The college offers nondegree study, a semester in London or at a Quebec university, cooperative programs, a B.A.-B.S degree, pass/fail options, a general studies degree, internships, student-designed majors, dual majors, and work-study programs.

Faculty/Classroom: 38% of faculty are male; 42%, female. No introductory courses are taught by graduate students. The average class size in an introductory lecture is 28; in a laboratory, 16; and in a regular course offering, 15.

Admissions: 74% of the 1995–96 applicants were accepted. The SAT I scores for a recent freshman class were as follows: Verbal—89% below 500, 10% between 500 and 599, and 1% between 600 and 700; Math—77% below 500, 21% between 500 and 599, and 2% between 600 and 700. 6% of a recent year's current freshmen were in the top fifth of their class; 25% were in the top two fifths.

Requirements: The SAT I or ACT is required. Students should have completed a college preparatory program including 4 years of English, at least 3 of mathematics including algebra, and 2 of science. Students should have at least a C average. AP and CLEP credits are accepted. Important factors in the admissions decision are advanced placement or honor courses, extracurricular activities record, and recommendations by school officials.

Procedure: Freshmen are admitted fall and spring. There is a deferred admissions plan. Application deadlines are open. Application fee is $40. Notification is sent on a rolling basis.

Transfer: 104 transfer students enrolled in 1995–96. Applicants should submit transcripts from each institution previously attended and a recommendation from their academic adviser. A GPA of at least 2.0 is required. 30 credits of 120 must be completed at the college.

Visiting: There are regularly scheduled orientations for prospective students, including a campus video, a campus tour, and an admission interview. There are guides for informal visits and visitors may sit in on classes and stay overnight at the school. To schedule a visit, contact the Admissions Office.

Financial Aid: In a recent year, 67% of all freshmen received some form of financial aid. Average earnings from campus work for the school year are $1300. The college is a member of CSS. The FAFSA is required. The application deadline for fall entry is March 1.

International Students: There are currently 13 international students enrolled. The school actively recruits these students. They must take the TOEFL, and achieve a minimum score of 475, and diagnostic tests for placement.

Computers: The college provides computer facilities for student use. The mainframe is a DEC VAX 11/780. There are also 200 IBM-compatible microcomputers available in 6 laboratories. All students may access the system. There are no time limits and no fees.

Graduates: Within an average freshman class, 39% graduate in 5 years. 5 companies recruited on campus in a recent year.

Admissions Contact: Jonathan H. Henry, Director of Admissions. E-mail: jscappy@vscacs.vsc.edu.

LYNDON STATE COLLEGE
Lyndonville, VT 05851

D-2

(802) 626-6413
(800) 225-1998; FAX: (802) 626-9770

Full-time: 547 men, 446 women	Faculty: 62; IIB, -$
Part-time: 44 men, 78 women	Ph.D.s: 90%
Graduate: 7 men, 23 women	Student/Faculty: 16 to 1
Year: semesters, summer session	Tuition: $4036 ($8548)
Application Deadline: see profile	Room & Board: $4854
Freshman Class: 939 applied, 848 accepted, 407 enrolled	
SAT I: required	LESS COMPETITIVE

Lyndon State College, founded in 1911 as a teachers' college, became a liberal arts school in 1962, offering undergraduate and graduate courses. There is 1 graduate school. In addition to regional accreditation, LSC has baccalaureate program accreditation with NRPA. The library contains 80,000 volumes, 10,000 microform items, and 1483 audiovisual forms, and subscribes to 500 periodicals. Computerized library sources and services include the card catalog, interlibrary loans, and database searching. Special learning facilities include a learning resource center, art gallery, radio station, TV station, founder's museum, and meteorology laboratory. The 175-acre campus is in a small town 184 miles north of Boston. Including residence halls, there are 17 buildings on campus.

Student Life: 57% of undergraduates are from Vermont. Students come from 19 states, 5 foreign countries, and Canada. 99% are white. The average age of freshmen is 18; all undergraduates, 20. 30% do not continue beyond their first year; 47% remain to graduate.

Housing: 500 students can be accommodated in college housing. College-sponsored living facilities include coed dormitories. On-campus housing is guaranteed for all 4 years. 50% of students live on campus; of those, 75% remain on campus on weekends. All students may keep cars on campus.

Activities: There are no fraternities or sororities. There are 22 groups on campus, including cheerleading, choir, chorale, chorus, drama, film, honors, international, jazz band, literary magazine, newspaper, photography, political, professional, radio and TV, social, social service, student government, and yearbook. Popular campus events include Family Weekend, Alumni Weekend, Winter and Spring Weekends, and a concert series.

Sports: There are 5 intercollegiate sports each for men and women, and 12 intramural sports each for men and women. Athletic and recreation facilities include a gymnasium complex with a weight room, squash, handball, and racquetball courts, an auxiliary gymnasium, and an Olympic-size pool; outdoor tennis courts; fields for hockey, softball, and soccer; cross-country ski trails and running trails; and access to an ice rink, nearby mountains, and a ski resort.

Disabled Students: 70% of the campus is accessible to disabled students. The following facilities are available: wheelchair ramps, elevators, special parking, specially equipped rest rooms, and lowered drinking fountains.

Services: In addition to many counseling and information services, tutoring is available in every subject. There is remedial math, reading, and writing. A mathematics laboratory and a writing center are available for student use.

Campus Safety and Security: Campus safety and security measures include 24-hour foot and vehicle patrol, escort service, lighted pathways/sidewalks, and and a security and safety service on campus as well as a 24-hour emergency rescue squad.

Programs of Study: LSC confers B.A. and B.S. degrees. Associate and master's degrees are also awarded. Bachelor's degrees are awarded in BUSINESS (accounting, business administration and management, recreation and leisure services, and sports management), COMMUNICATIONS AND THE ARTS (communications, English, and journalism), COMPUTER AND PHYSICAL SCIENCE (atmospheric sciences and meteorology, computer science, mathematics, and natural sciences), EDUCATION (early childhood, elementary, English, physical, recreation, and science), HEALTH PROFESSIONS (sports medicine), SOCIAL SCIENCE (human services, interdisciplinary studies, psychology, and social science). Meteorology, natural science, mathematics, and computer science are the strongest academically. Education, communications, and business have the largest enrollments.

Required: All students must maintain a minimum GPA of 2.0 while taking 122 semester hours. Distribution requirements include 12 credits in arts and humanities, 7 credits in mathematics and science, and 6 in social and behavioral sciences. Required courses include freshman English, composition and literature, and elementary functions in mathematics.

Special: Cooperative programs in a variety of businesses, including local ski areas, social agencies, and radio and TV stations, internships in recreation programs and communications, and study abroad in Nova Scotia and England are available. B.A.-B.S. degrees, work-study, a general studies degree, dual and student-designed majors, a 3–2 engineering degree with Norwich University, credit for life experience, nondegree study, and pass/fail options also are offered. There is 1 national honor society on campus. 2 departments have honors programs.

Faculty/Classroom: 69% of faculty are male; 31%, female. All teach undergraduates. No introductory courses are taught by graduate students. The average class size in an introductory lecture is 25; in a laboratory, 16; and in a regular course offering, 16.

Admissions: 90% of the 1995–96 applicants were accepted. 4 freshmen graduated first in their class.

Requirements: The SAT I is required. LSC recommends that applicants have 4 years of English and 2 each of mathematics, foreign language, history, and science. An essay is required, as is a recommendation from the high school principal or guidance counselor. An interview is recommended. The GED is accepted. AP and CLEP credits are accepted. Important factors in the admissions decision are advanced placement or honor courses, recommendations by school officials, and leadership record.

Procedure: Freshmen are admitted in the fall and spring. There are early decision, early admissions, and deferred admissions plans. Early decision applications should be filed by November 1; regular application deadlines are open. Application fee is $30. Notification of early decision is sent December 1; regular decision, on a rolling basis.

Transfer: Interviews are recommended for transfer students. An official transcript from each college attended is required. 30 credits of 122 must be completed at LSC.

Visiting: There are regularly scheduled orientations for prospective students, including a tour, information session, and faculty presentations. There are guides for informal visits and visitors may sit in on classes and stay overnight at the school. To schedule a visit, contact the Admissions Office.

Financial Aid: In 1995–96, 60% of all students received some form of financial aid. Scholarships or need-based grants averaged $1200 ($4500 maximum); loans averaged $1500 ($8875 maximum); and work contracts averaged $1200 ($4000 maximum). The average financial indebtedness of the 1994–95 graduate was $5000. LSC is a member of CSS. The FAF or FFS and parents and student income tax forms. are required. The application deadline for fall entry is March 15.

International Students: There were 10 international students enrolled in a recent year. They must take the TOEFL and achieve a minimum score of 500.

Computers: The college provides computer facilities for student use. The mainframe is a DEC VAX 11/785. There are also PCs and Apple Macintosh microcomputers available, as well as 7 computer laboratories on campus. All students may access the system. There are no time limits. There is a $10 laboratory fee.

Admissions Contact: R. Joseph Bellavance, Jr., Director of College Recruitment.

MARLBORO COLLEGE B-6

Marlboro, VT 05344　　　　　(802) 257-4333; (800) 343-0049

Full-time: 130 men, 126 women	Faculty: 34
Part-time: 5 men, 1 woman	Ph.D.s: 60%
Graduate: none	Student/Faculty: 8 to 1
Year: semesters, summer session	Tuition: $18,841
Application Deadline: August 1	Room & Board: $6140
Freshman Class: 275 applied, 192 accepted	
SAT I Verbal/Math: 550/510	**VERY COMPETITIVE**

Marlboro College, established in 1946, is a private institution offering degrees in the liberal and fine arts and humanities, and employing self-designed programs of study that include one-on-one tutorials and oral examinations. The library contains 60,000 volumes and 6555 microform items, and subscribes to 189 periodicals. Computerized library sources and services include interlibrary loans and database searching. Special learning facilities include a learning resource center, art gallery, and planetarium. The 350-acre campus is in a rural area 9 miles west of Brattleboro. Including residence halls, there are 34 buildings on campus.

Student Life: 83% of undergraduates are from out-of-state, mostly the Northeast. Students come from 22 states, 6 foreign countries, and Canada. 70% are from public schools; 30% from private. 92% are white. The average age of freshmen is 19. 17% do not continue beyond their first year; 55% remain to graduate.

Housing: 210 students can be accommodated in college housing. College-sponsored living facilities include single-sex and coed dormitories, on-campus apartments, and married-student housing. In addition, there are alcohol-free and smoke-free dormitories. On-campus housing is guaranteed for the freshman year only and is available on a first-come, first-served basis. 79% of students live on campus; of those, 90% remain on campus on weekends. All students may keep cars on campus.

Activities: There are no fraternities or sororities. There are 19 groups on campus, including art, chess, choir, chorale, chorus, computers, dance, drama, film, gay, jazz band, literary magazine, musical theater, newspaper, photography, political, social, social service, and student government. Popular campus events include Green-up Day, Cabaret, and Fall and Spring Rites.

Sports: Athletic and recreation facilities include a soccer field, a volleyball field, cross-country trails, basketball court, a weight room, a climbing wall, and field trips for canoeing, white-water rafting, skiing, and skydiving.

Disabled Students: 95% of the campus is accessible to disabled students. The following facilities are available: wheelchair ramps, special parking, and specially equipped rest rooms.

Services: In addition to many counseling and information services, tutoring is available in some subjects, including writing and languages.

Campus Safety and Security: Campus safety and security measures include self-defense education, informal discussions, pamphlets/posters/films, and lighted pathways/sidewalks. In addition, there is a buddy system.

Programs of Study: Marlboro confers B.A., B.S., and B.A. in World Studies degrees. Master's degrees are also awarded. Bachelor's degrees are awarded in BIOLOGICAL SCIENCE (biochemistry, biology/biological science, botany, and microbiology), COMMUNICATIONS AND THE ARTS (creative writing, dance, dramatic arts, English, fine arts, French, German, Greek, Italian, Latin, linguistics, music, Russian, and Spanish), COMPUTER AND PHYSICAL SCIENCE (chemistry, computer science, mathematics, physics, and statistics), HEALTH PROFESSIONS (premedicine), SOCIAL SCIENCE (anthropology, economics, history, interdisciplinary studies, international studies, philosophy, political science/government, prelaw, psychology, social science, and sociology). Sciences, humanities, and world studies are the strongest academically. Humanities has the largest enrollment.

Required: To graduate, students must complete a core curriculum and a writing requirement. A minimum GPA of 2.0 is required. Students must earn 120 credits, with 50 credits in the major, and complete a thesis and an oral examination.

Special: Marlboro offers cross-registration with the School for International Training, a variety of internships, and study abroad in many countries. The World Studies Program combines liberal arts with international studies, including 6 months of internship work in another culture. Accelerated and B.A.-B.S. degree programs are available. Students may pursue dual majors. Majors reflect an integrated course of study designed by students and their faculty advisers during the junior year.

Faculty/Classroom: 71% of faculty are male; 29%, female. All teach undergraduates. The average class size in an introductory lecture is 10; in a laboratory, 8; and in a regular course offering, 8.

Admissions: 70% of the 1995–96 applicants were accepted. The SAT I scores for the 1995–96 freshman class were as follows: Verbal—26% below 500, 47% between 500 and 599, 25% between 600 and 700, and 2% above 700; Math—51% below 500, 29% between 500 and 599, 17% between 600 and 700, and 3% above 700. 50% of the current freshmen were in the top fifth of their class; 60% were in the top two fifths.

Requirements: The SAT I is required. Applicants must graduate from an accredited secondary school or have a GED. They must earn 16 Carnegie units and complete 4 years of English and 3 years each of mathematics, science, history, and a foreign language. SAT II: Subject tests are recommended. Essays and interviews are required. Auditions and portfolios are recommended in appropriate cases. AP and CLEP credits are accepted. Important factors in the admissions decision are advanced placement or honor courses, evidence of special talent, and leadership record.

Procedure: Freshmen are admitted in the fall and spring. Entrance exams should be taken by October before entry. There are early decision, early admissions, and deferred admissions plans. Early decision applications should be filed by December 1; regular applications, by August 1 for fall entry and January 1 for spring entry, along with an application fee of $30. Notification of early decision is sent December 15; regular decision, on a rolling basis.

Transfer: 17 transfer students enrolled in a recent year. Transfers must have a minimum GPA of 2.0. 30 credits of 120 must be completed at Marlboro.

Visiting: There are regularly scheduled orientations for prospective students, including camping trips and testing. There are guides for informal visits and visitors may sit in on classes and stay overnight at the school. To schedule a visit, contact Dora Poulos at (800) 343-0049.

Financial Aid: In a recent year, 65% of all freshmen and 60% of continuing students received some form of financial aid. All students received need-based aid. The average freshman award was $12,000. Of that total, scholarships or need-based grants averaged $8000 ($14,000 maximum); loans averaged $3000 ($5500 maximum); and work contracts averaged $1400. 65% of undergraduate students work part-time. Average earnings from campus work for the school year are $2600. The average financial indebtedness of a recent graduate was $12,000. Marlboro is a member of CSS. The FAF and the college's own financial statement are required. The application deadline for fall entry is April 1.

International Students: There were 18 international students enrolled in a recent year. The school actively recruits these students. They must take the TOEFL and achieve a minimum score of 550. The student must also take the SAT I.

Computers: The college provides computer facilities for student use. Apple Macintoshes are available in a computer laboratory. All students may access the system 24 hours a day. There are no time limits and no fees.

Admissions Contact: Wayne R. Wood, Director of Admissions.

MIDDLEBURY COLLEGE A-3

Middlebury, VT 05753　　　　　(802) 388-3711, ext. 5153

Full-time: 1020 men, 1021 women	Faculty: 182; IIB, + +$
Part-time: none	Ph.D.s: 80%
Graduate: none	Student/Faculty: 11 to 1
Year: 4-1-4	Tuition: $27,190
Application Deadline: December 15	Room & Board: see profile
Freshman Class: 3818 applied, 1367 accepted, 585 enrolled	
SAT I or ACT: see profile	**MOST COMPETITIVE**

Middlebury College, founded in 1800, is a small, independent, coeducational liberal arts institution offering degree programs in languages, humanities, and social and natural sciences. The $27,190 comprehensive fee includes room and board. There are 2 graduate schools. The 3 libraries contain 751,161 holdings, 26,157 microform items, and 23,244 audiovisual forms, and subscribe to 1894 periodicals. Computerized library sources and services include the card catalog, interlibrary loans, and database searching. Special learning facilities include a learning resource center, art gallery, and radio station. The 350-acre campus is in a small town 35 miles south of Burlington. Including residence halls, there are 61 buildings on campus.

Student Life: 96% of undergraduates are from out-of-state, mostly the Northeast. Students come from 49 states, 64 foreign countries, and Canada. 55% are from public schools; 45% from private. 74% are white. The average age of freshmen is 18; all undergraduates, 20. 3% do not continue beyond their first year; 93% remain to graduate.

Housing: 1960 students can be accommodated in college housing. College-sponsored living facilities include single-sex and coed dormitories. In addition, there are language houses, special interest houses, and coed social houses. On-campus housing is guaranteed for all 4 years. 98% of students live on campus; of those, 90% remain on campus on weekends. All students may keep cars on campus.

Activities: There are no fraternities or sororities. There are 96 groups on campus, including art, band, chess, choir, chorus, computers, dance, drama, ethnic, film, gay, honors, international, jazz band, literary magazine, newspaper, orchestra, pep band, photography, political, professional, radio and TV, religious, social, social service, student government, symphony, and yearbook. Popular campus events include Winter Carnival, May Day, and Martin Luther King weekend.

Sports: There are 13 intercollegiate sports for men and 13 for women, and 16 intramural sports for men and 16 for women. Athletic and recreation facilities include 2 field houses, gymnasiums, a swimming pool, a fitness center, tennis courts, playing fields, an 18-hole golf course, alpine and nordic ski areas, a 3000-seat campus stadium, and an 8-lane 400-meter outdoor track.

Disabled Students: The following facilities are available: wheelchair ramps, elevators, special parking, specially equipped rest rooms, special class scheduling, and lowered drinking fountains.

Services: In addition to many counseling and information services, tutoring is available in every subject. There is a reader service for the blind, and remedial math, reading, and writing.

Campus Safety and Security: Campus safety and security measures include 24-hour foot or vehicle patrol, self-defense education, escort service, and informal discussions. There are pamphlets/posters/films, emergency telephones, lighted pathways/sidewalks, a paid student patrol, and a ski patrol at the Snow Bowl.

Programs of Study: Middlebury confers the A.B. degree. Master's and doctoral degrees are also awarded. Bachelor's degrees are awarded in BIOLOGICAL SCIENCE (biochemistry, biology/biological science, and molecular biology), BUSINESS (international economics), COMMUNICATIONS AND THE ARTS (American literature, art, Chinese, classics, dance, dramatic arts, English, film arts, French, German, Italian, Japanese, literature, music, Russian, and Spanish), COMPUTER AND PHYSICAL SCIENCE (chemistry, computer science, geology, mathematics, and physics), ENGINEERING AND ENVIRONMENTAL DESIGN (environmental science), SOCIAL SCIENCE (American studies, anthropology, classical/ancient civilization, East Asian studies, economics, geography, history, international relations, philosophy, political science/government, psychology, religion, Russian and Slavic studies, sociology, and women's studies). Foreign languages, international relations, and science are the strongest academically. English, political science, and history have the largest enrollments.

Required: Students must complete 36 courses, including winter-term courses. Freshmen must take a freshman seminar and a writing course, and all students must take physical education. A major normally requires 12 courses, and most students can fulfill the distribution requirement and the cultures and civilization requirement by taking 6 to 8 courses outside of their major. Students may also elect to complete a minor.

Special: Off-campus opportunities include an international major program at one of the Middlebury College schools abroad; exchange programs with Berea, St. Mary's, and Swarthmore; a junior year abroad; study through the American Collegiate Consortium for East-West Cultural and Academic Exchange; a 1-year program at Lincoln and Worcester Colleges, Oxford; a Washington semester; and a maritime studies program with Williams College at Mystic Seaport. Middlebury also offers an independent scholar program, joint and double majors, various professional programs, dual degrees in business management, forestry/environmental studies, engineering, and nursing, and an early assurance premed program with Dartmouth, Rochester, Tufts, and the Medical College of Pennsylvania, which ensures medical school acceptance by the end of the sophomore year. There is a chapter of Phi Beta Kappa on campus. All departments have honors programs.

Faculty/Classroom: 70% of faculty are male; 30%, female. All teach undergraduates. The average class size in a regular course offering is 15.

Admissions: 36% of the 1995–96 applicants were accepted. The SAT I scores for the 1995–96 freshman class were Verbal—11% below 500, 25% between 500 and 599, 53% between 600 and 700, and 11% above 700; Math—4% below 500, 16% between 500 and 599, 53% between 600 and 700, and 28% above 700. 85% of the current freshmen were in the top fifth of their class; 97% were in the top two fifths.

Requirements: Students should submit 3 test scores as follows: SAT II: Subject tests; AP tests; IB Subsidiary tests; or any combination thereof that includes 1 English or writing and 1 quantitative test; the ACT is also accepted. Secondary school preparation should include 4 years each of English, mathematics and/or computer science, and 1 foreign language, 3 or more years of laboratory science and history

and social science, and some study of music, art, and/or drama. Middlebury accepts applications on-line via ExPAN. AP credits are accepted. Important factors in the admissions decision are advanced placement or honor courses, recommendations by school officials, and evidence of special talent.

Procedure: Freshmen are admitted fall and spring. Entrance exams should be taken by December of the senior year. There are early decision and deferred admissions plans. Early decision I applications should be filed by November 15; early decision II applications, by December 15; regular applications, by December 15 for both fall and spring entry, along with an application fee of $50. Notification of early decision is sent December 15; regular decision, by April 5. 185 early decision candidates were accepted for the 1995–96 class. A waiting list is an active part of the admissions procedure, with about 12% of all applicants on the list.

Transfer: 17 transfer students enrolled in 1995–96. Transfer students must have the strongest academic record possible through high school and a minimum 3.0 average in college. 18 courses of 36 must be completed at Middlebury.

Visiting: There are regularly scheduled orientations for prospective students, including campus tours and a group or individual interview. There are guides for informal visits and visitors may sit in on classes and stay overnight at the school.

Financial Aid: In 1995–96, 39% of all freshmen received some form of financial aid. 60% of undergraduate students work part time. Average earnings from campus work for the school year are $650. The FAF, the college's own financial statement, and the federal tax form are required. The application deadline for fall entry is January 15.

International Students: There were 173 international students enrolled in a recent year. The school actively recruits these students. They must take the TOEFL. The student must also fulfill the same standardized test requirements as freshman applicants.

Computers: The college provides computer facilities for student use. The main computers are an IBM F70 AS400 and 6 IBM RS/6000s. Individual student rooms are wired to the network. More than half of the students have their own personal computers, and there are more than 150 public microcomputers easily available in 7 buildings on campus. There are connections to the Internet and to Bitnet, and a variety of software is available. All students may access the system 24 hours a day. There are no time limits and no fees.

Admissions Contact: John E. Hanson, Director of Admissions.

NORWICH UNIVERSITY
Northfield, VT 05663

C-3

(802) 485-2001

(800) 468-6679; FAX: (802) 485-2032

Full-time: 1260 men, 600 women	Faculty: 110; IIA, --$
Part-time: 80 men, 300 women	Ph.D.s: 85%
Graduate: 140 men, 305 women	Student/Faculty: 17 to 1
Year: semesters, summer session	Tuition: $14,134
Application Deadline: open	Room & Board: $5270
Freshman Class: 1678 applied, 1549 accepted, 527 enrolled	
SAT I or ACT: required	COMPETITIVE

Norwich University, founded in 1819, is a private coeducational institution offering programs in arts and sciences, engineering, and education, and in the military, health science, and business professions. In addition to regional accreditation, Norwich has baccalaureate program accreditation with ABET, ACBSP, and NLN. The library contains 230,000 volumes, 75,000 microform items, and 4487 audiovisual forms, and subscribes to 1364 periodicals. Computerized library sources and services include the card catalog, interlibrary loans, and database searching. Special learning facilities include a learning resource center, art gallery, radio station, and greenhouse. The 1125-acre campus is in a rural area 11 miles south of Montpelier. Including residence halls, there are 34 buildings on campus.

Student Life: 80% of undergraduates are from out-of-state, mostly the Northeast. Students come from 48 states, 29 foreign countries, and Canada. 75% are from public schools; 25% from private. 94% are white. The average age of freshmen is 18; all undergraduates, 20. 15% do not continue beyond their first year; 65% remain to graduate.

Housing: 1725 students can be accommodated in college housing. College-sponsored living facilities include single-sex and coed dormitories. On-campus housing is guaranteed for the freshman year only and is available on a lottery system for upperclassmen. Priority is given to out-of-town students. 82% of students live on campus; of those, 65% remain on campus on weekends. Alcohol is not permitted. Upperclassmen may keep cars on campus.

Activities: There are no fraternities or sororities. There are 75 groups on campus, including band, cheerleading, chess, choir, chorus, computers, drama, drill team, ethnic, honors, international, jazz band, literary magazine, marching band, musical theater, newspaper, orchestra, pep band, photography, political, professional, radio and TV, religious, social service, student government, and yearbook. Popular campus events include Regimental Ball, Winter Carnival, Junior

Weekend, Homecoming/Alumni Weekend, and Parents and Family Weekend.

Sports: There are 15 intercollegiate sports for men and 10 for women, and 17 intramural sports for men and 12 for women. Athletic and recreation facilities include an ice hockey arena, a field house with an indoor track, an indoor swimming pool, an aerobics room, weight and wrestling rooms, playing fields, an outdoor track, a 1200-seat basketball arena, and a 1000-seat stadium.

Disabled Students: The following facilities are available: wheelchair ramps, elevators, special parking, specially equipped rest rooms, and lowered drinking fountains.

Services: In addition to many counseling and information services, tutoring is available in most subjects. There is remedial math, reading, and writing.

Campus Safety and Security: Campus safety and security measures include 24-hour foot and vehicle patrol and lighted pathways/sidewalks.

Programs of Study: Norwich confers B.A., B.S., and B.Arch. degrees. Associate degrees are also awarded. Bachelor's degrees are awarded in BIOLOGICAL SCIENCE (biology/biological science), BUSINESS (accounting, business administration and management, and business economics), COMMUNICATIONS AND THE ARTS (communications and English), COMPUTER AND PHYSICAL SCIENCE (chemistry, computer science, geology, information sciences and systems, mathematics, and physics), EDUCATION (physical and secondary), ENGINEERING AND ENVIRONMENTAL DESIGN (architecture, civil engineering, electrical/electronics engineering, environmental science, mechanical engineering, and military science), HEALTH PROFESSIONS (medical laboratory technology, nursing, and sports medicine), SOCIAL SCIENCE (criminal justice, history, international studies, peace studies, political science/government, and psychology). Engineering and architecture are the strongest academically. Criminal justice and nursing have the largest enrollments.

Required: Total number of required credits and courses vary by program. All students are required to complete 3 credit hours in history, English 101 and 102, and 2 semesters in physical education. A 2.0 GPA is required to graduate.

Special: Many internships are available. Study abroad through other schools and through the Vermont Overseas Studies Program is accepted. The B.A.-B.S. degree, a general studies degree, pass/fail options, and student-designed majors are possible. Co-op programs in business and criminal justice, a Washington semester, on- and off-campus work-study programs for service organizations and in criminal justice, plus a special Adult Degree Program are offered. The Russian School offers a special intensive summer session. There are 5 national honor societies on campus, including Phi Beta Kappa. 5 departments have honors programs.

Faculty/Classroom: All teach undergraduates. No introductory courses are taught by graduate students. The average class size in an introductory lecture is 25; in a laboratory, 15; and in a regular course offering, 20.

Admissions: 92% of the 1995–96 applicants were accepted. The SAT I scores for a recent freshman class were as follows: Verbal—73% below 500, 20% between 500 and 599, 6% between 600 and 700, and 1% above 700; Math—53% below 500, 36% between 500 and 599, 10% between 600 and 700, and 1% above 700. 25% of a recent freshmen class were in the top fifth of their class; 70% were in the top two fifths. In a recent year, 10 freshmen graduated first in their class.

Requirements: The SAT I or ACT is required. Norwich requires applicants to be in the upper 50% of their class. A minimum GPA of 2.5 is required. Applicants should graduate from an accredited secondary school with 18 academic credits or achieve the GED equivalent. Applications are accepted on IBM/Windows formatted computer disks, and on-line through the World Wide Web. AP and CLEP credits are accepted. Important factors in the admissions decision are leadership record, extracurricular activities record, and evidence of special talent.

Procedure: Freshmen are admitted fall and spring. Entrance exams should be taken starting with spring of the junior year. There are early decision and deferred admissions plans. Early decision applications should be filed by November 15; application deadlines for regular decision are open. Application fee is $25. Notification of early decision is sent December 30; regular decision, on a rolling basis. 60 early decision candidates were accepted for the 1995–96 class.

Transfer: 30 transfer students enrolled in 1995–96. Candidates should present a 2.0 GPA and meet all standards for entering freshmen. 60 credits of 114 must be completed at Norwich.

Visiting: There are regularly scheduled orientations for prospective students, including meetings with representatives from admissions, financial aid, academic offices, Dean of Students or Commandant's Office, and athletics (if desired), and a campus tour. There are guides for informal visits and visitors may sit in on classes and stay overnight at the school. To schedule a visit, contact Admissions, Main Office.

Financial Aid: In 1995–96, 92% of all freshmen and 80% of continuing students received some form of financial aid. 80% of all students received need-based aid. Norwich is a member of CSS. The FAFSA and CSS Profile Application are required.

International Students: In a recent year, there were 32 international students enrolled. The school actively recruits these students. They must take the TOEFL and achieve a minimum score of 500.

Computers: The college provides computer facilities for student use. The mainframes are a DEC VAX 11/780 and a DEC VAX 11/785. There are laboratories in the business department, computer center, and architecture department, and computers are also available in the library. All students may access the system 20 hours per day. There are no time limits and no fees.

Graduates: In 1994–95, 225 bachelor's degrees were awarded. Within an average freshman class, 65% graduate in 4 years. 25 companies recruited on campus in 1994–95.

Admissions Contact: Frank E. Griffis, Dean of Admissions. E-mail: nuadm@norwich.edu. A campus video is available.

SAINT MICHAEL'S COLLEGE

A-2
Colchester, VT 05439 (802) 654-3000
(800) 762-8000; FAX: (802) 654-2591

Full-time: 799 men, 921 women	**Faculty:** 122; IIB, av$
Part-time: 32 men, 44 women	**Ph.D.s:** 80%
Graduate: 232 men, 446 women	**Student/Faculty:** 14 to 1
Year: semesters, summer session	**Tuition:** $13,950
Application Deadline: February 15	**Room & Board:** $6010
Freshman Class: 2270 applied, 1544 accepted, 539 enrolled	
SAT I Verbal/Math: 476/533	COMPETITIVE

St. Michael's College, established in 1904, is a nonprofit liberal arts and sciences institution affiliated with the Roman Catholic Church. There are 5 graduate schools. The library contains 170,000 volumes, 25,000 microform items, and 3000 audiovisual forms, and subscribes to 1400 periodicals. Computerized library sources and services include the card catalog, interlibrary loans, and database searching. Special learning facilities include a radio station and an observatory. The 400-acre campus is in a suburban area 2 miles east of Burlington. Including residence halls, there are 56 buildings on campus.

Student Life: 77% of undergraduates are from out-of-state, mostly the Northeast. Students come from 28 states, 25 foreign countries, and Canada. 69% are from public schools; 31% from private. 94% are white. 85% are Catholic; 10% Protestant. The average age of freshmen is 18; all undergraduates, 20. 11% do not continue beyond their first year; 78% remain to graduate.

Housing: 1500 students can be accommodated in college housing. College-sponsored living facilities include single-sex and coed dormitories and on-campus apartments. In addition, there are small homes on the campus periphery accommodating many special interests and themes, including substance-free housing. On-campus housing is guaranteed for all 4 years. 87% of students live on campus; of those, 95% remain on campus on weekends. All students may keep cars on campus after their first semester freshman year.

Activities: There are no fraternities or sororities. There are 45 groups on campus, including band, cheerleading, choir, chorale, dance, drama, ethnic, gay, honors, international, jazz band, literary magazine, musical theater, newspaper, photography, political, professional, radio and TV, religious, social, social service, student government, and yearbook. Popular campus events include Dorm Daze, Homecoming, Winter Weekend, Spring Weekend, Parents Weekend, Academic Convocation, and a variety of seminars and symposia.

Sports: There are 10 intercollegiate sports each for men and women, and 9 intramural sports each for men and women and 3 coed. Athletic and recreation facilities include a 2100-seat gymnasium with basketball, volleyball, badminton, and tennis courts, a 6-lane swimming pool, weight, exercise, and training rooms, soccer, field hockey, lacrosse, baseball, and softball fields, and outdoor tennis courts.

Disabled Students: 75% of the campus is accessible to disabled students. The following facilities are available: wheelchair ramps, elevators, special parking, specially equipped rest rooms, special class scheduling, lowered drinking fountains, lowered telephones, and specially equipped residential space.

Services: In addition to many counseling and information services, tutoring is available in every subject. There is a writing center and departmental help sessions are available.

Campus Safety and Security: Campus safety and security measures include 24-hour foot and vehicle patrol, shuttle buses, informal discussions, and pamphlets/posters/films. In addition, there are emergency telephones, lighted pathways/sidewalks, and a campus fire and rescue squad.

Programs of Study: St. Michael's confers B.A. and B.S. degrees. Master's degrees are also awarded. Bachelor's degrees are awarded in BIOLOGICAL SCIENCE (biochemistry and biology/biological science), BUSINESS (accounting and business administration and management), COMMUNICATIONS AND THE ARTS (dramatic arts, English, fine arts, French, journalism, music, and Spanish), COMPUTER AND PHYSICAL SCIENCE (chemistry, computer science, mathematics, and physics), EDUCATION (art, elementary, foreign languages, science, and secondary), ENGINEERING AND ENVIRONMENTAL DESIGN (environmental science and preengineering), HEALTH PROFESSIONS (predentistry and premedicine), SOCIAL SCIENCE (American studies, anthropology, economics, history, philosophy, political science/government, prelaw, psychology, religion, and sociology). Business administration, psychology, and English literature have the largest enrollments.

Required: To graduate, students must complete 9 to 12 credits in humanities and social science and organizational skills, 6 to 8 each in religious studies, philosophy, science, and mathematics; 2 to 4 in fine arts; and a foreign language and writing proficiency. They must have a GPA of 2.0. The college requires a minimum of 124 credits, including 34 different courses, for graduation. A maximum of 52 credits may be taken in the major.

Special: Students may cross-register with Trinity College or Xavier University of Louisiana. A variety of internships are available. There is a Washington semester with American University and study abroad in 20 countries. Student-designed majors may be pursued. The college offers a 3–2 engineering degree program in cooperation with Clarkson University and the University of Vermont, and a 4+1 graduate business program with Clarkson University. Nondegree study and pass/fail grading options are offered on a limited basis. There is a freshman honors program on campus, as well as 1 national honor society. 1 department has an honors program.

Faculty/Classroom: 69% of faculty are male; 31%, female. All both teach and do research. The average class size in an introductory lecture is 30; in a laboratory, 15; and in a regular course offering, 20.

Admissions: 68% of the 1995–96 applicants were accepted. The SAT I scores for the 1995–96 freshman class were as follows: Verbal—64% below 500, 28% between 500 and 599, and 7% between 600 and 700; Math—32% below 500, 45% between 500 and 599, 19% between 600 and 700, and 3% above 700. 42% of the current freshmen were in the top fifth of their class; 78% were in the top two fifths. 8 freshmen graduated first in their class.

Requirements: The SAT I or ACT is required. St. Michael's requires applicants to be in the upper 50% of their class. Applicants must graduate from an accredited secondary school or have a GED. They must complete 16 Carnegie units, including 4 credits in English, 3 to 4 in mathematics, 2 to 4 in science, and 2 to 3 each in history, social studies, and a foreign language. An essay is required and an interview is recommended. St. Michael's accepts on-line applications through ExPAN and applications on computer disk only through approved vendors. AP and CLEP credits are accepted. Important factors in the admissions decision are advanced placement or honor courses, evidence of special talent, and recommendations by school officials.

Procedure: Freshmen are admitted in the fall and spring. Entrance exams should be taken in the fall of the senior year. There are early decision and deferred admissions plans. Early decision applications should be filed by November 15; regular applications, by February 15 for fall entry and November 1 for spring entry, along with an application fee of $35. Notification of early decision is sent January 1; regular decision, April 1. 256 early decision candidates were accepted for the 1995–96 class. A waiting list is an active part of the admissions procedure, with about 4% of all applicants on the list.

Transfer: 46 transfer students enrolled in 1995–96. Applicants must have a minimum GPA of 2.5; generally, those admitted have a GPA of at least 3.3. The SAT I is required. An interview is recommended. 30 credits of 124 must be completed at St. Michael's.

Visiting: There are regularly scheduled orientations for prospective students, including a group information session, video about the school, campus tour, and admissions criteria review with a staff member. There are guides for informal visits and visitors may sit in on classes. To schedule a visit, contact the Admissions Office.

Financial Aid: In 1995–96, 79% of all freshmen and 78% of continuing students received some form of financial aid. 70% of freshmen and 64% of continuing students received need-based aid. The average freshman award was $12,718. Of that total, scholarships or need-based grants averaged $6904 ($10,500 maximum); loans averaged $3712 ($4625 maximum); and work contracts averaged $982 ($2000 maximum). 40% of undergraduate students work part-time. Average earnings from campus work for the school year are $1084. The average financial indebtedness of the 1994–95 graduate was $12,800. St. Michael's is a member of CSS. The FAFSA and federal tax forms from both student and parents including W-2 forms are required. The application deadline for fall entry is March 15.

International Students: There were 65 international students enrolled in a recent year. The school actively recruits these students. They must take the TOEFL, and achieve a minimum score of 550, or the college's own test. The student must also take the SAT I or ACT if possible, or St. Michael's will consider the TOEFL in place of the SAT I.

Computers: The college provides computer facilities for student use. The mainframes are 2 DEC VAX 3400s, 2 DEC VAX 4000s, and 2 DEC ALPHA 2100 Systems. There are 10 microcomputer laboratories available for student use, 8 of them connected to the campus network (Mikenet), plus 2 Apple Macintosh laboratories also connected to Mikenet. Over 175 computers are available for student use. All students may access the system. There are no time limits and no fees. It is recommended that all students have personal computers.

Graduates: In 1994–95, 440 bachelor's degrees were awarded. The most popular majors among graduates were English literature (17%), psychology (17%), and business administration (14%). Within an average freshman class, 75% graduate in 4 years, 78% in 5 years, and 79% in 6 years. 40 companies recruited on campus in 1994–95. Of the 1994 graduating class, 17% were enrolled in graduate school within 6 months of graduation and 75% had found employment.

Admissions Contact: Jerry E. Flanagan, Vice President for Admission and Enrollment Management. E-mail: admission@smcvax.smcvt.edu. A campus video is available.

SOUTHERN VERMONT COLLEGE

A-6

Bennington, VT 05201   (802) 442-5427
             (800) 378-2782; FAX: (802) 442-5529

Full-time: 202 men, 209 women	**Faculty:** 27
Part-time: 60 men, 157 women	**Ph.D.s:** 13%
Graduate: none	**Student/Faculty:** 15 to 1
Year: semesters, summer session	**Tuition:** $10,160
Application Deadline: open	**Room & Board:** $4650
Freshman Class: 360 applied, 310 accepted, 145 enrolled	
SAT I or ACT: not required	**LESS COMPETITIVE**

Southern Vermont College, established in 1926, is a private institution offering undergraduate degrees in liberal arts, professional training, and business, and through a weekend program that accommodates adult students. The library contains 25,000 volumes, and subscribes to 270 periodicals. Computerized library sources and services include interlibrary loans and database searching. Special learning facilities include a learning resource center and art gallery. The 371-acre campus is in a small town 40 miles east of Albany, New York. Including residence halls, there are 10 buildings on campus.

Student Life: 58% of undergraduates are from out-of-state, mostly the Northeast. Students come from 26 states, 5 foreign countries, and Canada. 85% are from public schools. 95% are white. The average age of freshmen is 19; all undergraduates, 20. 21% do not continue beyond their first year; 79% remain to graduate.

Housing: 250 students can be accommodated in college housing. College-sponsored living facilities include coed dormitories. College-sponsored off-campus housing, and quiet, nonsmoking, and fitness residence halls are available. On-campus housing is guaranteed for all 4 years. 65% of students commute. Alcohol is not permitted. All students may keep cars on campus.

Activities: There are no fraternities or sororities. There are 28 groups on campus, including criminal justice, drama, environmental, ethnic, gay, honors, international, literary magazine, newspaper, photography, professional, radio and TV, social, social service, student government, and yearbook. Popular campus events include Octoberfest, Spree Day, Superstars Weekend, and Family Weekend.

Sports: There are 4 intercollegiate sports for men and 4 for women, and 8 intramural sports for men and 8 for women. Athletic and recreation facilities include a multipurpose field for softball, baseball, and soccer, a gymnasium and health education facility, putting greens, and a 9-hole par 3 golf course.

Disabled Students: 50% of the campus is accessible to disabled students. The following facilities are available: wheelchair ramps and special parking.

Services: In addition to many counseling and information services, tutoring is available in every subject. There is remedial math, reading, and writing. Skills workshops, a freshman seminar, and a program to assist students with basic college skills are also available.

Campus Safety and Security: Campus safety and security measures include 24-hour foot and vehicle patrol, escort service, shuttle buses, and informal discussions. In addition, there are pamphlets/posters/films, emergency telephones, lighted pathways/sidewalks, 2-way radios, fire drills, and safe rides on weekends from places that alcohol is served.

Programs of Study: SVC confers B.A., B.S., and B.S.N. degrees. Associate degrees are also awarded. Bachelor's degrees are awarded in BUSINESS (accounting, business administration and management, and hotel/motel and restaurant management), COMMUNICATIONS AND THE ARTS (communications and English), ENGINEERING AND ENVIRONMENTAL DESIGN (environmental science), HEALTH PROFESSIONS (nursing), SOCIAL SCIENCE (child psychology/development, criminal justice, gerontology, human services, liberal arts/general studies, psychology, safety and security technology, and social work). English, environmental studies, and accounting are the strongest academically. Business, criminal justice, liberal arts, and environmental studies have the largest enrollments.

Required: To graduate, students must complete a 48-credit core requirement consisting of course work in economics, English, environmental studies, government, history, cultural arts, mathematics (including computer science), natural sciences, philosophy, psychology, and sociology. Management students must take courses in accounting, writing, management, organizational behavior, marketing, supervision, and management ethics, and they must take management decision making or complete an internship. Students who do not pursue the management program must complete a minor in addition to the major. A minimum GPA of 2.0 is required. Students must earn a minimum of 120 credits.

Special: There are cooperative programs in criminal justice and environmental studies, cross-registration with Bennington College, and internships and work-study programs. Students may study abroad in Oxford, England or spend a semester at sea. The college offers a liberal arts degree, individualized degree programs, dual majors, an accelerated degree program, and credit for life, military, and work experience. Nondegree study and a pass/fail grading option are also available. There is a freshman honors program on campus.

Faculty/Classroom: 46% of faculty are male; 54%, female. All teach undergraduates. The average class size in an introductory lecture is 25 and in a regular course offering, 18.

Admissions: 86% of the 1995–96 applicants were accepted. 20% of the current freshmen were in the top fifth of their class; 40% were in the top two fifths.

Requirements: A minimum GPA of 2.0 is required. Applicants must graduate from an accredited secondary school or have a GED. The college requires 3 years of English and 2 years of mathematics. Applications are accepted on computer disk or on-line via CollegeLink or E-mail. AP and CLEP credits are accepted. Important factors in the admissions decision are leadership record, extracurricular activities record, and recommendations by school officials.

Procedure: Freshmen are admitted in the fall, spring, and summer. There are early decision, early admissions, and deferred admissions plans. Application deadlines are open. Application fee is $25. Notification is sent on a rolling basis. 4 early decision candidates were accepted for the 1995–96 class.

Transfer: Transfer applicants must have a GPA of 2.0 and be in good standing. Interviews are recommended. 30 credits of 120 must be completed at SVC.

Visiting: There are regularly scheduled orientations for prospective students. There are guides for informal visits and visitors may sit in on classes and stay overnight at the school. To schedule a visit, contact Admissions at (802) 442–5427, ext. 150.

Financial Aid: In a recent year, 92% of all freshmen and 65% of continuing students received some form of financial aid. 89% of freshmen and 65% of continuing students received need-based aid. The average freshman award was $5825. Of that total, scholarships or need-based grants averaged $3545 ($12,500 maximum); loans averaged $3154 ($5500 maximum); and work contracts averaged $1500. 20% of undergraduate students work part-time. Average earnings from campus work for the school year are $1500. The average financial indebtedness of a recent graduate was $13,250. SVC is a member of CSS. The FAFSA is required. The application deadline for fall entry is May 1.

International Students: There were 5 international students enrolled in a recent year. They must take the TOEFL and achieve a minimum score of 500.

Computers: The college provides computer facilities for student use, including word processors for academic use. All students may access the system. There are no time limits and no fees.

Graduates: In 1994–95, 70 bachelor's degrees were awarded. The most popular majors among graduates were business and management (47%), environmental studies (31%), and letters/literature (9%). Within an average freshman class, 22% graduate in 4 years and 40% in 5 years. 39 companies recruited on campus in 1994–95.

Admissions Contact: Todd M. Crandall, Director of Admissions.

TRINITY COLLEGE OF VERMONT

A-2

Burlington, VT 05401   (802) 658–0337
                          (800) 639–8885; FAX: (802) 658–5446

Full-time: 28 men, 474 women	Faculty: 47; IIB, --$
Part-time: 102 men, 318 women	Ph.D.s: 78%
Graduate: 162 men and women	Student/Faculty: 11 to 1
Year: semesters, summer session	Tuition: $12,050
Application Deadline: open	Room & Board: $5704
Freshman Class: 257 applied, 225 accepted, 107 enrolled	
SAT I Verbal/Math: 420/430	**LESS COMPETITIVE**

Trinity College of Vermont, established in 1925, is a nonprofit, private, primarily women's liberal arts institution operated by the Sisters of Mercy of the Roman Catholic Church. Its traditional admissions program accepts qualified women students who have been gradu-

ates from high school for less than 4 years. Trinity's nontraditional program provides motivated adults, both women and men, an opportunity to begin or resume college careers. There is 1 graduate school. In addition to regional accreditation, Trinity has baccalaureate program accreditation with CSWE. The library contains 62,000 volumes, 43,000 microform items, and 1200 audiovisual forms, and subscribes to 420 periodicals. Computerized library sources and services include the card catalog, interlibrary loans, and database searching. Special learning facilities include a learning resource center. The 20-acre campus is in a small town near downtown Burlington. Including residence halls, there are 14 buildings on campus.

Student Life: 86% of undergraduates are from Vermont. Students come from 10 states, 3 foreign countries, and Canada. 89% are from public schools; 11% from private. 96% are white. 50% are Catholic. The average age of freshmen is 18; all undergraduates, 29. 30% do not continue beyond their first year; 51% remain to graduate.

Housing: 315 students can be accommodated in college housing. College-sponsored living facilities include single-sex dormitories. On-campus housing is guaranteed for all 4 years. 69% of students live on campus; of those, 65% remain on campus on weekends. All students may keep cars on campus.

Activities: There are no fraternities or sororities. There are 13 groups on campus, including choir, chorale, drama, honors, international, musical theater, newspaper, political, religious, social service, student government, and yearbook. Popular campus events include Family Weekend, Silver Bells Dinner, and Women's History Month.

Sports: There are 2 intercollegiate sports for women and 3 intramural sports for women. Athletic and recreation facilities include a fitness center and an agreement with St. Michael's College in nearby Colchester that permits use of its facilities.

Disabled Students: 92% of the campus is accessible to disabled students. The following facilities are available: wheelchair ramps, elevators, special parking, specially equipped rest rooms, and lowered drinking fountains.

Services: In addition to many counseling and information services, tutoring is available in most subjects. There is remedial math and writing.

Campus Safety and Security: Campus safety and security measures include 24-hour foot and vehicle patrol, self-defense education, escort service, and informal discussions. In addition, there are pamphlets/posters/films and lighted pathways/sidewalks.

Programs of Study: Trinity confers B.A. and B.S. degrees. Associate and master's degrees are also awarded. Bachelor's degrees are awarded in BIOLOGICAL SCIENCE (biology/biological science), BUSINESS (accounting and business administration and management), COMMUNICATIONS AND THE ARTS (communications, crafts, English, French, modern language, and Spanish), COMPUTER AND PHYSICAL SCIENCE (chemistry and mathematics), EDUCATION (business, early childhood, elementary, science, secondary, and special), ENGINEERING AND ENVIRONMENTAL DESIGN (environmental science), HEALTH PROFESSIONS (clinical science), SOCIAL SCIENCE (criminal justice, crosscultural studies, economics, history, human services, interdisciplinary studies, philosophy, psychology, social work, and sociology). Education, business, and social work are the strongest academically. Business, psychology, and education have the largest enrollments.

Required: Students must complete 120 credits, with from 30 to 45 in the major, and maintain a minimum GPA of 2.0. The general education program includes 39 credits, with 6 credits required in each of humanities, social sciences, and natural sciences/mathematics. Writing, speaking, quantitative, and computing competencies must be completed as well. A first-year advising seminar is also required.

Special: Special academic programs include on-campus work-study, internships, and study abroad in England, Korea, and Belgium. There is cross-registration with St. Michael's College. Dual majors are offered, and interdisciplinary degree programs include those in communication, comparative cultural studies, computer programming, and business. Student-designed majors are an option, as is nondegree study. There are 3 national honor societies on campus.

Faculty/Classroom: 43% of faculty are male; 57%, female. All teach undergraduates. No introductory courses are taught by graduate students. The average class size in an introductory lecture is 25; in a laboratory, 15; in a regular course offering, 10.

Admissions: 88% of the 1995–96 applicants were accepted. The SAT I scores for the 1995–96 freshman class were as follows: Verbal—79% below 500, 17% between 500 and 599, and 4% between 600 and 700; Math—74% below 500, 20% between 500 and 599, and 6% between 600 and 700. 39% of the current freshmen were in the top fifth of their class; 61% were in the top two fifths.

Requirements: The SAT I is required, along with a minimum GPA of 2.0. Other admissions requirements include graduation from an accredited secondary school with 16 Carnegie units. Strongly recommended are 4 years of English, 2 each of a foreign language, mathematics, science, social studies, and history, and 1 of a laboratory science. An essay must be submitted, and an interview is advised.

The GED is also accepted. AP and CLEP credits are accepted. Important factors in the admissions decision are advanced placement or honor courses, recommendations by school officials, and leadership record.

Procedure: Freshmen are admitted to all sessions. Entrance exams should be taken by fall of the senior year. There are early admissions and deferred admissions plans. Application deadlines are open. Application fee is $40. Notification is sent on a rolling basis.

Transfer: 18 transfer students enrolled in 1995–96. The criteria for transfer students are the same as for freshmen if they have earned fewer than 12 credits. Otherwise, applicants should have a minimum GPA of 2.0 and schedule an interview; each student is reviewed individually, taking into account the previous academic record. 30 of the last 45 credits of 120 must be completed at Trinity.

Visiting: There are regularly scheduled orientations for prospective students, including campus tours, visits to classes, and panel discussions. There are guides for informal visits and visitors may sit in on classes and stay overnight at the school. To schedule a visit, contact the Admissions Office.

Financial Aid: In 1995–96, 95% of all freshmen and 88% of continuing students received some form of financial aid. 94% of freshmen and 85% of continuing students received need-based aid. The average freshman award was $13,530. Of that total, scholarships or need-based grants averaged $6908 ($11,000 maximum); loans averaged $2978 ($3125 maximum); and work contracts averaged $747 ($1000 maximum). 47% of undergraduate students work part-time. Average earnings from campus work for the school year are $1150. The average financial indebtedness of the 1994–95 graduate was $15,970. Trinity is a member of CSS. The FAFSA, FFS, and the college's own financial statement are required. The application deadline for fall entry is May 1.

International Students: There are currently 7 international students enrolled. The school actively recruits these students. They must take the TOEFL and achieve a minimum score of 500.

Computers: The college provides computer facilities for student use. The mainframe is an IBM AS 400. IBM microcomputers are available in the computer laboratory. All students may access the system. There are no time limits and no fees.

Graduates: In 1994–95, 205 bachelor's degrees were awarded. The most popular majors among graduates were business (22%), psychology (14%), and elementary education (12%). Of the 1994 graduating class, 8% were enrolled in graduate school within 6 months of graduation and 91% had found employment.

Admissions Contact: Pamela Chisholm, Director of Admissions and Financial Aid.

UNIVERSITY OF VERMONT
A-2

Burlington, VT 05405   (802) 656-3370; FAX: (802) 656-8611

Full-time: 3210 men, 3808 women	Faculty: 866; I, --$
Part-time: 249 men, 272 women	Ph.D.s: 86%
Graduate: 517 men, 678 women	Student/Faculty: 8 to 1
Year: semesters, summer session	Tuition: $6909 ($16,605)
Application Deadline: February 1	Room & Board: $4632
Freshman Class: 7966 applied, 6475 accepted, 1975 enrolled	
SAT I Verbal/Math: 480/540	COMPETITIVE

The University of Vermont, established in 1791, is a public, land-grant, comprehensive coeducational institution. Its undergraduate and graduate programs stress the liberal arts, business administration, engineering, mathematics, natural resources, agricultural studies, fine arts, professional training, teacher preparation, social services, environmental studies, and health science, including nursing. There are 8 undergraduate schools and 1 graduate school. In addition to regional accreditation, UVM has baccalaureate program accreditation with AACSB, ABET, ADA, APTA, ASLA, CAHEA, CSWE, NASM, NCATE, NLN, and SAF. The 5 libraries contain 1.3 million volumes, 1.2 million microform items, and 18,000 audiovisual forms, and subscribe to 10,000 periodicals. Computerized library sources and services include database searching. Special learning facilities include a learning resource center, art gallery, and radio station. In addition, the Medical Center Hospital of Vermont, the largest research hospital in the state, is located on the campus. The 425-acre campus is in a small town 90 miles south of Montreal, and 200 miles north of Boston. Including residence halls, there are 90 buildings on campus.

Student Life: 58% of undergraduates are from out-of-state, mostly the Northeast. Students come from 45 states, 40 foreign countries, and Canada. 95% are white. The average age of freshmen is 18; all undergraduates, 21. 17% do not continue beyond their first year; 76% remain to graduate.

Housing: 3800 students can be accommodated in college housing. College-sponsored living facilities include coed dormitories, on-campus apartments, off-campus apartments, married-student housing, fraternity houses, and sorority houses. In addition, there are environmental halls and language and special interest suites/floors. On-campus housing is available on a lottery system for upperclassmen. 55% of students commute. Upperclassmen may keep cars on campus.

Activities: 8% of men belong to 14 national fraternities; 10% of women belong to 6 national sororities. There are 100 groups on campus, including art, band, cheerleading, choir, chorus, computers, dance, drama, ethnic, gay, international, jazz band, literary magazine, musical theater, newspaper, orchestra, pep band, photography, political, professional, religious, social service, student government, TV, and yearbook. Popular campus events include Octoberfest, Ebonyfest (Black History Month), and Women's History Month.

Sports: There are 12 intercollegiate sports for men and 12 for women, and 30 intramural sports for men and 30 for women. Athletic and recreation facilities include a 3228-seat gymnasium, a 4000-seat stadium, a field house, and Centennial Field.

Disabled Students: 87% of the campus is accessible to disabled students. The following facilities are available: wheelchair ramps, elevators, special parking, specially equipped rest rooms, special class scheduling, and lowered drinking fountains.

Services: In addition to many counseling and information services, tutoring is available in most subjects. There is a reader service for the blind, supplemental instruction, note-taking and test-taking seminars, and writing tutors, as well as support for ESL students.

Campus Safety and Security: Campus safety and security measures include 24-hour foot and vehicle patrol, self-defense education, escort service, and shuttle buses. In addition, there are informal discussions, pamphlets/posters/films, emergency telephones, and lighted pathways/sidewalks.

Programs of Study: UVM confers B.A., B.S., and B.M. degrees. Associate, master's, and doctoral degrees are also awarded. Bachelor's degrees are awarded in AGRICULTURE (animal science), BIOLOGICAL SCIENCE (biochemistry, biology/biological science, botany, microbiology, and zoology), BUSINESS (business administration and management and marketing/retailing/merchandising), COMMUNICATIONS AND THE ARTS (classics, dramatic arts, English, French, German, Greek, Latin, music, Russian, and Spanish), COMPUTER AND PHYSICAL SCIENCE (chemistry, computer science, geology, mathematics, physics, and statistics), EDUCATION (art, early childhood, elementary, foreign languages, health, music, secondary, and special), ENGINEERING AND ENVIRONMENTAL DESIGN (civil engineering, electrical/electronics engineering, engineering management, environmental science, and mechanical engineering), HEALTH PROFESSIONS (medical laboratory technology, nursing, and physical therapy), SOCIAL SCIENCE (anthropology, dietetics, economics, food science, geography, history, parks and recreation management, philosophy, political science/government, psychology, religion, social work, and sociology). Physical therapy, chemistry, and environmental studies are the strongest academically. Political science and psychology have the largest enrollments.

Required: Degree requirements vary among the individual colleges, but all require at least a 2.0 GPA and 2 semesters of physical education. For a B.A., the College of Arts and Sciences requires a minimum of 122 semester hours, completion of general requirements, including a foreign language, mathematics, and non-European cultures, and distribution requirements comprised of fine arts, literature, humanities, social sciences, and natural sciences.

Special: UVM offers internships, study abroad, a Washington semester, work-study, cooperative programs in business and engineering, dual and student-designed majors, a 3–4 veterinary medicine degree with Tufts University, nondegree study, and pass/fail options. A special feature of the school is the Living/Learning Center, an integrated academic and student-support unit with a 588-student residence; it sponsors 30 to 35 year-long programs, each including course work, independent study, seminars, and field trips that support a particular theme. There are 17 national honor societies on campus, including Phi Beta Kappa. 10 departments have honors programs.

Faculty/Classroom: 69% of faculty are male; 31%, female. Graduate students teach 5% of introductory courses. The average class size in a regular course offering is 23.

Admissions: 81% of the 1995–96 applicants were accepted. The SAT I scores for the 1995–96 freshman class were as follows: Verbal—58% below 500, 33% between 500 and 599, 8% between 600 and 700, and 1% above 700; Math—30% below 500, 41% between 500 and 599, 26% between 600 and 700, and 4% above 700. 36% of the current freshmen were in the top fifth of their class; 78% were in the top two fifths.

Requirements: The SAT I is required. Other admissions requirements include graduation from an accredited secondary school with 16 Carnegie units, including 4 years of English, 3 of mathematics (algebra I and II and geometry), and 2 each of a foreign language, science, and social studies. An essay must be submitted. The GED is also accepted. AP and CLEP credits are accepted. Important factors in the admissions decision are leadership record, recommendations by school officials, and advanced placement or honor courses.

Procedure: Freshmen are admitted fall and spring. Entrance exams should be taken by November of the senior year. There are early decision, early admissions, and deferred admissions plans. Early decision applications should be filed by November 1; regular applications, by February 1 for fall entry and November 1 for spring entry, along with an application fee of $45. Notification of early decision is sent December 15; regular decision, March 16. A waiting list is an active part of the admissions procedure.

Transfer: 358 transfer students enrolled in 1995–96. Candidates must have a minimum GPA of 2.5 in credited courses and meet the same criteria as freshmen. Considerations include the college and high school records, the major indicated, SAT I or ACT scores, and availability of space at UVM. 30 credits of 122 must be completed at UVM.

Visiting: There are regularly scheduled orientations for prospective students. There are guides for informal visits and visitors may sit in on classes and stay overnight at the school. To schedule a visit, contact the Admissions Office.

Financial Aid: In 1995–96, 53% of all freshmen and 51% of continuing students received some form of financial aid, including need-based aid. The average freshman award was $10,011. Of that total, scholarships or need-based grants averaged $4027 ($7812 maximum); loans averaged $4867 ($6625 maximum); and work contracts averaged $1117 ($2400 maximum). 25% of undergraduate students work part-time. The average financial indebtedness of the 1994–95 graduate was $20,050. UVM is a member of CSS. The FAFSA is required. The application deadline for fall entry is March 1.

International Students: There are currently 143 international students enrolled. The school actively recruits these students. They must take the TOEFL and achieve a minimum score of 550. The student must also take the SAT I or the ACT.

Computers: The college provides computer facilities for student use. The mainframes are an IBM 4381 and a DEC VAX 8600. There are also microcomputers located in laboratories throughout the campus. All students may access the system. There are no time limits and no fees. It is recommended that students in all business and engineering majors have personal computers.

Graduates: In 1994–95, 1559 bachelor's degrees were awarded. The most popular majors among graduates were business (9%), political science (8%), and psychology (7%). Within an average freshman class, 56% graduate in 4 years, 73% in 5 years, and 76% in 6 years. 200 companies recruited on campus in 1994–95. Of the 1994 graduating class, 20% were enrolled in graduate school within 6 months of graduation and 74% had found employment.

Admissions Contact: Barbara O'Reilly, Director of Admissions. E-mail: admadm@sis-em.uvm.edu. A campus video is available.

VERMONT STATE COLLEGES

The Vermont State Colleges, established in 1962, is a public system. It is governed by a board of trustees, whose chief administrator is the chancellor. The primary goal of the system is teaching. The main priorities are to ensure that Vermonters and others have access to higher education, to provide educational programs that permit individuals to lead more productive and responsible lives, and to maintain a high quality of cultural, social, and economic life in Vermont. The total enrollment of all 4 campuses is about 9000 with some 250 faculty members. Altogether there are 60 baccalaureate and 5 master's programs offered in Vermont State Colleges. Profiles of the 4-year campuses are included in this chapter.

INDEX